PRICEWATERHOUSECOOPERS

Student's Manual of Accounting

The Guide to UK Accounting Law and Practice

PRICEWATERHOUSECOOPERS

Student's Manual of Accounting

The Guide to UK Accounting Law and Practice

The Accounting Technical Department
of PricewaterhouseCoopers, Chartered Accountants

Legal consultant editor
Hon Mrs Justice Arden DBE

INTERNATIONAL THOMSON BUSINESS PRESS
I(T)P® An International Thomson Publishing Company

Student's Manual of Accounting

I(T)P® A division of International Thomson Publishing Inc.
The ITP logo is a trademark under licence

British Library Cataloguing-in-Publication Data
A catalogue record for this book is available from the British Library

First published in 1999 by International Thomson Business Press, a division of International Thomson Publishing Inc. The Student's Manual of Accounting is the student's edition of The PricewaterhouseCoopers' Manual of Accounting, published by Gee Publishing Limited.

Printed in the UK by Clays Ltd, St. Ives plc

ISBN 1–86152–506–0

International Thomson Business Press
Berkshire House
168–173 High Holborn
London WC1V 7AA
UK

http://www.itbp.com

Authors

PricewaterhouseCoopers' Manual of Accounting is written by the Accounting Technical Department at PricewaterhouseCoopers.

Writing team led by

Barry Johnson
Peter Holgate

Principal authors

Jyoti Ghosh
Eddie Hodgson (and technical reviewer)
Peter Holgate
Barry Johnson
Helen McCann
Margaret Morris-Marsham
Hans Nailor

Other contributors

Nigel Dealy
Elizabeth Harper
Peter Hogarth
Mitchell Hogg
Orla Horgan
Hugh Morgan
Chris Nobes
Craig Stafford
George Stylianides
John Williamson

Foreword

By Sir Bryan Carsberg
Secretary-General
International Accounting Standards Committee

Many people feel today that we have too many rules and regulations. Politicians try from time to time to have 'bonfires of red tape' and journalists cheer us with their exposure of cases where regulations have gone to ridiculous lengths. People praise the qualities of individual judgement and self-reliance. This is a healthy emphasis. Regulations have a cost: there is a cost in developing them, a cost in understanding and implementing them and, perhaps insidiously because the effect is hidden, a cost in deterring people from worthwhile enterprise because of regulatory obstacles and uncertainties. Regulations also have benefits; but we must make sure that we stop regulating at the point where the costs outweigh the benefits.

The impartial observer of the accounting scene might feel that the deregulatory message has not been heard in accounting. The rules which govern financial reporting grow steadily. More accounting standards are issued each year and they become more detailed. The requirements have to be related to the requirements of Company Law, including those which are needed to implement the directives of the European Commission. Companies with multi-national operations have a particular challenge in implementing and making sense of requirements which differ from country to country. That is one reason why the work of the International Accounting Standards Committee in seeking international harmonisation is so important.

To some extent, the increasing complexity of accounting regulations is the result of increasing complexity in the transactions undertaken in modern business, as new contractual arrangements are developed to enable risks to be shared or reduced. Furthermore, the costs of the regulations can be reduced by sharing the expertise of those who have extensive experience of their application. That is why works like this are so important. It is comprehensive, clear and authoritative. I feel confident in recommending it.

Bryan Carsberg

Preface

PricewaterhouseCoopers' Manual of Accounting is a practical guide to UK accounting law and practice. It encompasses: the accounting provisions of the Companies Act 1985; the requirements of accounting standards; Urgent Issues Task Force Abstracts; the accounting requirements of the London Stock Exchange's Listing Rules; and other Generally Accepted Accounting Principles. The manual includes practical advice based on our work in the Accounting Technical department of PricewaterhouseCoopers in advising the firm's clients, partners and staff.

Accounting principles and rules are dealt with in the Manual's first four chapters. The chapters that follow then cover the profit and loss account and the balance sheet and deal with diverse areas of accounting, from disclosure of directors' remuneration including the implications of Greenbury Report, to accounting for taxation. The rules that apply to preparing consolidated financial statements are then considered; followed by commentaries on the other statements that appear in annual reports such as cash flow statements, the directors' report and the operating and financial review. The Manual also has chapters dealing with current reporting requirements under the Combined Code and interim reporting practice as well as chapters on the concessions given to smaller companies and oversea companies. An example set of company financial statements and an example set of consolidated financial statements are includes as appendices. Also included as appendices are the EC 4th Directive and the EC 7th Directive.

Even in a work of this size it is not possible to cover every aspect of company reporting. For example, the manual does not cover the specific accounting requirements in Schedule 9 and 9A of the Act that apply to banking and insurance companies, although much of the advice given in the text will assist them.

We hope that finance directors, accountants, legal practitioners, company administrators, financial advisers and auditors will find this manual useful.

On behalf of the whole writing team we thank the Hon Mrs Justice Arden, DBE (our legal consultant) for reviewing legal content in the manual. Barbara Willis has performed an invaluable role in editing the text and project managing the whole process. Our special thanks also to Barbara Willis, Margaret Cooke and Amber Rollinson for their great contribution in desk-top publishing the text.

Barry Johnson and Peter Holgate
PricewaterhouseCoopers
London
November 1998

P010

Contents

Page

Other reports and statements

Directors' and related party disclosures

Concessions, interims and secretarial

VIII – Emerging Issues

Appendices

Abbreviations and terms used

AAPA	=	Association of Authorised Public Accountants
AC	=	Appeal Cases, law reports
accounts	=	financial statements
the Act/the 1985 Act/ the Companies Act	=	the Companies Act 1985 (as amended by the Companies Act 1989)
the 1989 Act	=	the Companies Act 1989
ACCA	=	Association of Chartered Certified Accountants
ACT	=	advance corporation tax
AGM	=	Annual General Meeting
AIM	=	Alternative Investment Market
AIMR	=	Alternative Investment Market Rules
AITC	=	Association of Investment Trust Companies
All ER	=	All England Law Reports
AMPS	=	Auction market preferred shares
APB	=	Auditing Practices Board
APC	=	Auditing Practices Committee
App	=	Application note of a Financial Reporting Standard
app	=	appendix
ASB	=	Accounting Standards Board
ASC	=	Accounting Standards Committee
BBA	=	British Bankers' Association
BCLC	=	Butterworths Company Law Cases
BES	=	Business expansion scheme
BNA 1985	=	Business Names Act 1985
CCA	=	Current cost accounting
CCAB	=	Consultative Committee of Accountancy Bodies Limited
CC	=	The Combined Code – Principles of good governance and code of best practice proposed by the Committee on Corporate Governance chaired by Sir Ronald Hampel
CC(CP)	=	Companies Consolidation (Consequential Provisions) Act 1985
CEO	=	chief executive officer
Ch	=	Chancery Division, law reports
chp	=	chapter
chapter (1)	=	'PricewaterhouseCoopers Manual of accounting' – chapter (1)
CIF	=	Cost, insurance, freight
CIMA	=	Chartered Institute of Management Accountants
CIPFA	=	Chartered Institute of Public Finance and Accountancy
CISCO	=	The City Group for Smaller Companies
Cmnd	=	Command Paper
COSO	=	Committee of Sponsoring Organisations of the Treadway Commission

CPP	=	Current purchasing power
CR	=	Report of the committee on The Financial Aspects of Corporate Governance (the 'Cadbury Report')
DG XV	=	Directorate General XV
DP	=	discussion paper
DRC	=	Depreciated replacement cost
DSP	=	ASB draft Statement of principles
DTR	=	Double taxation relief
EC	=	European Community
ECU	=	European currency unit
ED	=	exposure draft
EGM	=	Extraordinary general meeting
EPS	=	Earnings per share
ESOP	=	Employee Share Ownership Plan
ESOT	=	Employee Share Ownership Trust
EU	=	European Union
FASB	=	Financial Accounting Standards Board
financial statements	=	accounts
the 7th Directive	=	EC 7th Directive on Company Law
FIFO	=	First-in, first-out
FLA	=	Finance and Leasing Association
FM	=	Facilities management
FOB	=	Free on board
FRAG	=	Financial Reporting and Auditing Group of the ICAEW
FRED	=	Financial Reporting Exposure Draft
FRC	=	Financial Reporting Council
FRRP	=	Financial Reporting Review Panel
FRS	=	Financial Reporting Standard
FRSSE	=	Financial Reporting Standard for Smaller Entities
GAAP	=	Generally accepted accounting principles (and practices)
GCFR	=	Going Concern and Financial Reporting published by the joint working group of the Hundred Group of finance directors, ICAEW and ICAS
HP	=	Hire purchase
IAS	=	International Accounting Standard
IASC	=	International Accounting Standards Committee
IBF	=	Irish Bankers' Federation
IBNR	=	Incurred but not reported
ICAEW	=	Institute of Chartered Accountants in England and Wales
ICAI	=	Institute of Chartered Accountants in Ireland
ICAS	=	Institute of Chartered Accountants of Scotland

ICFR	=	Internal Control and Financial Reporting published by the joint working group of the Hundred Group of finance directors, ICAEW and ICAS
ICR	=	Industrial Cases Reports
IFAC	=	International Federation of Accountants
IGU	=	Income generating unit
IIMR	=	Institute of Investment Management and Research
IOSCO	=	International Organisation of Securities Commissions
IR	=	Statement of Interim reporting issued by ASB
ISDA	=	International Swap Dealers Association
LIBOR	=	London inter-bank offered rate
LIFO	=	Last-in, first-out
LR	=	The London Stock Exchange's Listing Rules
MBO	=	Management buy-out
MR	=	Master of the Rolls
NASDAQ	=	National Association of Securities Dealers & Quotations
NCU	=	National currency unit
OFR	=	Operating and Financial Review statement issued by ASB
OIAC	=	Oil Industry Accounting Committee
PA	=	Preliminary announcement
para(s)	=	paragraph(s) of Schedules to the Companies Acts, or FRSs, or SSAPs, or FREDs, or EDs, or DPs, or text
PFI	=	Private Finance Initiative
PRAG	=	Pensions Research Accountants Group
PS	=	Practice statements
QC	=	Queen's Counsel
RDG	=	Regional development grant
Reg	=	Regulation of a statutory instrument (eg SI 1995/2092 Reg 5 = regulation 5 of The Companies (Summary Financial Statements) Regulations 1995)
RICS	=	Royal Institution of Chartered Surveyors
SAS	=	Statement of Auditing Standards
SC	=	Session Cases
Sch	=	Schedule to the Companies Act 1985 (eg 4A Sch 85 = Schedule 4A, paragraph 85)
SEC	=	Securities and Exchange Commission
Sec(s)	=	Section(s) of the 1985 Act
SERPS	=	State earnings related pension scheme
SFAS	=	Statement of Financial Accounting Standards issued in the US
SI	=	Statutory Instrument

SIC	=	Standing Interpretation Committee of the IASC
SMEs	=	Small and medium-sized entities
SOI	=	Statement of Intent
SORP	=	Statement of Recommended Practice
SPV	=	Special purpose vehicle
SSAP	=	Statement of Standard Accounting Practice
Stock Exchange	=	The London Stock Exchange
STRGL	=	Statement of total recognised gains and losses
TR	=	Technical Release of the ICAEW
UITF	=	Urgent Issues Task Force
UK	=	United Kingdom
US	=	United States of America
VAT	=	value added tax
WACC	=	weighted average cost of capital
WLR	=	Weekly Law Reports
Yellow book	=	The London Stock Exchange's Listing Rules

Chapter 1

Introduction

Page

Chapter 1

Introduction

UK accounting

1.1 The PricewaterhouseCoopers 'Manual of Accounting' is a work of truly staggering proportions and it is worth considering why this is so. UK generally accepted accounting principles (GAAP) has grown to such an extent in recent years – largely as a result of the work of the Accounting Standards Board – that it takes a Manual of well over 3,000 pages to do it justice. Not only is GAAP in the UK now very extensive, but it is also constantly being reformed, so much so that this Manual is kept up to date through regular updates.

The volume of regulation

1.2 The compendium 'Accounting Standards 1998/99', an annual publication which includes all Statements of Standard Accounting Practice (SSAPs), Financial Reporting Standards (FRSs), Urgent Issues Task Force (UITF) Abstracts, exposure drafts, discussion papers and other similar material, is now 1,743 pages long. This length is worrying. However, a relatively small proportion of each FRS comprises rules: the rest is explanation, legal background and so on. Moreover, with discussion papers, if the ASB's views are to be taken seriously both here and overseas, they have to be seen to be fully explored and rationalised. But even allowing for these points, it seems to us that the extent of regulation of UK accounting has become out of proportion. Solutions are being developed whereby the problem either does not need to be solved or needs to be solved in a simpler way, a way that is less prescriptive and leaves more room for judgement.

1.3 Too much regulation has, in our view, many undesirable consequences. It is tempting, in the light of poor practice, to set further rules. But as is evident from the highly regulated US accounting environment, there is no end to this process. Regulations are now developed dealing with arcane areas of practice, but this merely leads to two things: it encourages those who look for loopholes to look elsewhere; and it can implant in accountants in both industry and practice a mentality of compliance, of expecting to be told what to do and of feeling incapable of forming an independent professional opinion.

1.4 Such a trend is clearly undesirable. We accept that there is a need for accounting to be regulated and for accounting standards to be complied with – largely because of the importance of improving comparability of financial statements – but we firmly believe that regulation should be confined to dealing with principles only and not stray unduly into detailed implementation. We take this view because:

- The overriding requirement for financial statements is that they should give a true and fair view. This is a judgemental matter.

- As professional accountants, we make a valuable contribution by exercising independent judgement and skill. This comment applies as much to accountants in industry as to those in professional firms.

- It is no exaggeration to say that the future of the profession depends on this issue. If accounting becomes excessively rule-based, there is a great danger that the next generation of accountants will become men and women who have learned the rules and know how to use a good index or a database word-search, but who do not know how to think through an accounting issue based on analysis, judgement and commercial and financial experience.

1.5 But we should not catalogue and complain about the volume of regulation without understanding its origin. It is fair to acknowledge that, at the end of the 1980s, although there was much good quality accounting and auditing going on, some bad practices had developed. Standards of the type we had at the time did not seem effective in the business environment of the day. There were too many examples of cavalier attitudes being adopted and the overriding true and fair requirement seemed to be increasingly overlooked. There was, in this environment, widespread agreement that serious reform was needed and, following the Dearing report in 1988, the Accounting Standards Board, the Urgent Issues Task Force and the Financial Reporting Review Panel were brought into operation in 1990. This new regime, and the ASB in particular, is at least partly responsible for the volume of regulation to which we refer. Whilst this volume and the rate of change now seem excessive when viewed in total, we do accept that many of the reforms the new regime has brought have been both necessary and good.

The need to earn concessions

1.6 Moreover, it is idle simply to assert that there should be fewer rules. It is not realistic to expect them to be repealed overnight; it is more a case of seeking to curtail their growth, perhaps of seeking to cross out two or three unnecessary rules for every new rule introduced. But more fundamentally, a lighter hand of regulation would have to be *earned* – both by companies and auditors. To deserve fewer rules, companies would have to agree to abide by the spirit and intention of accounting standards. They would have to take seriously, perhaps more seriously than some do at present, the need for financial statements to give a true and fair view. They would have to understand that looking for ways around rules and taking the *"where does it say that I can't do* *that?"* approach will ultimately lead merely to more and more rules – and in those circumstances it would be hard to say that their imposition was unfair.

1.7 A lighter hand of regulation would have to be earned by auditors too. In order to have a realistic claim for fewer rules, auditors would have to be, and be seen to be, tougher and more independent than perhaps some have been in the past. They would have to be prepared to say to companies: *"that isn't right and I can't put our name to it; and no, there is no specific rule that stops you, it's merely that, in my view, doing that doesn't give a true and fair view"*. Auditors do say this kind of thing, perhaps far more often than is widely appreciated, but more of it is needed. Those who need the crutch of a detailed rule book are not helping the case.

1.8 It may seem anomalous that we argue for fewer rules, but at the same time publish a manual of this proportion. In fact there is no contradiction. We wish there were fewer standards, or shorter standards, to write about. We believe that standards should set out the principles that apply to major issues, but we believe that there is an important role for practical guidance and judgement. Hence although we inevitably describe the Companies Act and the accounting standards in some detail, much of this book consists of interpretation and guidance drawn from years of experience in advising companies on accounting.

Principles and rules

1.9 A key aspect of the debate about the volume of regulation has been the question of the relative roles of principles and detailed rules. An emphasis on principles tends to mean two different things. First, it means standards on specific subjects – but short ones, that set out the general principles of (say) accounting for depreciation or accounting for leases, rather than a raft of detailed implementation rules. And, secondly, underpinning those standards, a 'Statement of principles'.

1.10 In the debate that led to formation of the ASB, there were strong calls for it to base its work on a set of coherent underlying principles. This, it was believed, would result in individual standards being consistent with each other, rather than being developed in a pragmatic, but unconnected manner. The ASB has embraced this idea and has devoted part of its time to such a Statement of principles. Although from 1991 to 1994 the board published seven chapters in the form of discussion drafts, it was not until November 1995 that the Statement of principles appeared as a single document, albeit still in draft form. Some of its proposals and implications are discussed in this Manual, in particular in chapter 2.

1.11 We support the development of a Statement of principles. But, despite this, we have concerns about the ASB's approach and the document's specific proposals. It seems churlish to say this, but even the Statement of principles, at 132 pages, seems unnecessarily long and complex. Many of the so-called principles seem to fall short of such a lofty description. Yet the Statement of principles seems virtually to ignore some key concepts. Consistency and substance over form are well represented, but going concern, prudence and accruals receive little, if any, attention. Equally important concepts like the true and fair view and the central notion of realised profits are given a brief mention, but far less than they merit.

1.12 So it is clear that a statement of principles may be useful, but is not a panacea. If its content can be improved, and if it can be shortened so that it deals only with genuine, enduring principles, then it will be helpful. We, therefore, welcome the ASB's July 1996 announcement that, in the light of extensive criticism of the draft Statement of principles, it plans to re-expose a revised and shorter version before finalising it.

What accounting information do users want?

1.13 As outlined above, financial statements have gradually become longer and longer. Skilled financial analysts, investment managers and bankers use the information they receive. But what use are current financial statements to most lay users of financial statements? Realistically, we must acknowledge that many shareholders, on receipt of the annual report, look at the pictures, read the chairman's statement and *"file it in the round file"*. The profit and loss accounts, balance sheets and notes are complex and off-putting. By contrast, interim reports and preliminary announcements, already very influential in terms of market reaction, are gaining ground. Companies are putting more emphasis on them, knowing that they appeal to users: to professionals in terms of timing and to amateurs in terms of level of detail.

1.14 Against this background, it is perhaps not surprising that the ASB has devoted some time recently to interims and prelims. The ASB has developed 'statements' – that is, non-mandatory guidance – on interims and on prelims. This guidance, which is discussed in chapter 39, may improve practice in these areas to some degree, but what is striking is that practice has in the past three or so years moved so far ahead of what is required by the Stock Exchange that the ASB guidance is in many ways simply reflecting current best practice.

1.15 But this guidance may be a precursor to a more fundamental reform. It may take a change in the law to achieve it, but what may happen is that the emphasis as between prelims and full statutory financial statements changes around. Prelims could be circulated promptly to analysts, institutional investors and private shareholders alike. The full statutory financial statements would follow and would be available on request to any shareholder. We assume that only a small proportion would request them. The statutories would be filed at Companies House and would be, as it were, the small print, the document of record.

1.16 Such a reform would give various groups of shareholders something closer to what they want, but would of course not in any way diminish the work that companies have to do at the year end. Indeed there is the possibility that it could open the way for the ASB to press ahead with further disclosures and complex rulings, citing the fact that their introduction would not further complicate the reports received by non-specialist readers.

1.17 These thoughts relate to financial reports printed on paper. But for how much longer will that be the framework of debate? Some companies already put their annual reports – and interims and prelims – on the internet, and more are sure to follow. Analysts receive information on screens and it is only a matter of time before sufficient private individuals are hooked up to either the internet or a screen-based equivalent source of company information that companies stop printing and distributing their financial statements and take to merely releasing them through electronic means. In that setting, there is scope for financial information to be 'layered' – in other words to be issued in full detail but to be accessible in two or three (or 10) levels of detail, at the touch of a mouse. Level one would be the earnings per share figure and a photo of the chairman; level four would be roughly like the existing prelim; and so on. If we think in these terms, it is easy to see that many of the disclosure and presentation issues with which we struggle could change fundamentally.

Smooth earnings or volatility?

1.18 Another key issue in accounting today is the measurement of earnings that companies report and the pattern of those figures over time. It has for some time been an unwritten virtue for companies to publish profits that followed a relatively even trend - preferably upwards. But a number of recent and current accounting reforms point very much in the direction of volatility. This is a world-wide phenomenon: similar issues are arising in the US and at the IASC. For example, changes to the rules on provisions now specify when companies should provide for liabilities and thus will make it harder for companies to make provisions on a discretionary basis.

1.19 Perhaps the most extreme example is derivatives and other financial instruments. The UK, US and IASC have introduced standards on disclosures. But the big debate is about measurement and the main contender is fair value. Thus swings in fair values would in some way affect total recognised gains and losses. The prospect of this in the US led 20 senior business leaders to write to the chairman of the FASB asking him to stop or delay the project. The chief accountant of the SEC came to the defence with words that are worth quoting, for they sum up the whole issue:

> *"... reporting that volatility however is not the same as reporting artificial volatility. Rather it is capturing, in the financial statements, real economic events which often are not reported today."*

1.20 Put another way: do we want smoothed results that give a warm feeling of contentment; or do we want to know what happened in the year in terms of the effect of outside economic events on the company? It is a very fundamental issue. Its various ramifications will encounter opposition from directors who would rather be able to control the financial information about their companies. Opposition may also come from institutional investors who may become unlikely bedfellows sharing a wish for predictability and stability.

International harmonisation

1.21 Comparability of financial information is a key issue in the international environment and it is here that significant changes are taking place, changes that are already having major implications for UK GAAP.

1.22 National accounting rules have been developed in many countries, based on local factors: the need for financial statements to measure performance; the need to assist in the collection of taxation; the desire to be prudent; or the desire to reflect, or in some cases avoid reflecting, valuations. The information produced by these different systems may suit local needs, but is not comparable. Indeed, it is a major indictment of accounting that a company's performance can be reported in so many different ways, according to which GAAP is applied.

1.23 Despite the original reasons for different local rules, there is now a powerful argument for not just harmonisation, but also uniformity. The point is not just that applying different systems and producing different results is an embarrassment – though that is true. It is that business and capital markets are global. Investors need to have confidence in accounting information produced in different countries. And it is in the interests of companies in all locations to produce financial statements that can be understood by investors and other users worldwide. These are among the forces that have led to the increased role and standing of the International Accounting Standards Committee (IASC).

1.24 We support the work of the IASC, for various reasons:

- It seems to be the best option for genuinely international harmonisation. In this regard it is better placed than systems based on (say) the EC directives or US GAAP.

- The standards that the IASC produces are generally of high quality, especially since the recent 'improvements' project eliminated a number of options in IASs. They are quality standards not least because, being stateless, they are unconstrained by any local or regional legal framework. Thus the IASC is able to address itself solely to what it considers to be good accounting.

1.25 Given that IASs are now being used increasingly – by multinationals for group reporting and for foreign listings and in countries that lack good quality local standards – the question is where this movement will lead. The implications seem to us very far-reaching. The IASC is currently in a period of frenetic activity as it seeks to meet the target that it has agreed with the International Organisation of Securities Commissions (IOSCO). Under this agreement, IASC will improve its standards by the end of 1998, in the hope that IOSCO will agree that IASs are of sufficiently high standard that they can be recommended for use by companies for secondary listings on any stock market. In particular, this would mean that a UK company (or a French company, etc) could secure a listing on the US markets reporting under IAS rather than US GAAP. It is too early to say whether the US SEC will decide to accept, from foreign registrants, financial statements drawn up under IAS for US filings. But if they do, then a number of consequences seem likely to follow:

- Companies that have more than one listing for their shares will be more likely to report under IAS. These will tend to be large multi-nationals.
- As this trend builds up, groups in many locations, including groups that are not seeking overseas listings or even local listings, may well wish to join the movement.
- As the use of IASs becomes more common, so there will be greater pressure than at present for national standard setters in many countries either to adopt IAS rather than invent or expand different, national rules, or at least to make their national standards very similar indeed to IASs.

1.26 As a result of these factors, in some countries, questions are already being asked about why national standards should continue to be developed. The UK is very visibly moving in that direction. On subjects such as deferred tax, pension costs, and segmental reporting, the central issue in the current UK discussions is: should we develop what seems best in a UK context or should we adopt the IASC's approach in the interests of harmonisation?

1.27 That is a very difficult question. We support the ASB's view that international harmonisation based around IASs is a good thing, but that there are limits to it. This is not the meaningless *"we support harmonisation so long as that means everyone else doing what we do"*. The ASB has put forward a number of changes to assist harmonisation, which have been supported by the UK accounting and business community. But there are also issues on which UK opinion has until now been firmly against the international approach. The two most important current examples of this are accounting for deferred tax and accounting for pension costs.

1.28 It is easy to gain the impression that the UK is only on the receiving end of pressures for harmonisation. In fact, the traffic is by no means all one way. The ASB is active in the international accounting arena and there are examples of it seeking to export its own accounting proposals and have them accepted by the IASC and the US FASB. Examples are: the Statement of total recognised gains and losses from FRS 3; and the idea in FRS 10 that goodwill and intangibles need not always be amortised. Furthermore, there are examples that are neither import nor export, but simply co-operation. The UK, the US, Canada and Australia work together with the IASC on some subjects with a view to securing agreement at the development stage of a project. Current examples are derivatives and lease accounting. But whatever direction the flow of ideas and influence, the principle is clear, namely that accounting and standard-setting can no longer be regarded as purely national issues. They are firmly placed in the international arena and that focus is likely to become more important still over the next few months and years.

The approach in this Manual

1.29 We believe that a trend towards compliance with IASs, such as that outlined above, is likely to occur in the medium-term. But, for the moment, there are many aspects of UK GAAP that demand analysis and interpretation and the remainder of this work seeks to provide helpful guidance in that regard. We discuss in detail the requirements of company law, accounting standards, UITF abstracts and the Listing Rules. But we also give our views on what is good accounting in the many areas in which there are no rules or guidance. As part of that approach, this Manual contains hundreds of examples and extracts from financial statements. This Manual also has a strong company law bias: we are aware from practical experience that many of the questions that arise in practice cannot be answered based solely on accounting principles, but that many of them have to be answered at the interface of accounting and company law. Many of the chapters that follow reflect this.

Chapter 2

Accounting principles and rules

Page

Chapter 2

Accounting principles and rules

Introduction

2.1 As discussed in chapter 1, the accounting framework in the UK is becoming subject to increasing, and increasingly, complicated rules. The sources of UK accounting principles and rules range from legislation and accounting standards to customs practised by professionals over many years. In addition, accounting in the UK is becoming more influenced by practice overseas, for example, in the US and the IASC.

2.2 This chapter explores the framework and sources of authority for the generally accepted accounting principles in the UK and how the Act and accounting standards impact on the overriding requirement for financial statements to give a true and fair view.

2.3 This chapter also introduces the concepts underlying accounting practices that are discussed in greater detail throughout this manual as they relate to particular accounting issues and problems. The ASB is working on formalising these concepts. The draft Statement of principles and its sources in the US and the IASC are also discussed.

2.4 Lastly, in view of the increasing importance to companies of IAS, this chapter discusses their relevance in the UK and outlines where UK practice diverges from compliance with International Standards.

UK GAAP

The meaning and composition of UK GAAP

2.5 Generally Accepted Accounting Principles in the United Kingdom (UK GAAP) is a much-used, but undefined term. The components of UK GAAP vary according to the type of company or entity in question. However, in general terms, UK GAAP can be described as follows. The components are divided into elements that are mandatory (in law or in practice) and elements that are not mandatory. The core *mandatory* elements are:

- The Companies Act 1985.

- Accounting standards. That is:
  - Statements of standard accounting practice (SSAP s) developed originally by the Accounting Standards Committee (ASC) and adopted in 1990 by the Accounting Standards Board (ASB).
  - Financial reporting standards (FRSs) issued by the ASB since 1990.
- Abstracts issued by the ASB's Urgent Issues Task Force (UITF).
- For listed companies, the Stock Exchange's Listing Rules.

2.6 Other elements of UK GAAP are authoritative to varying degrees but non-mandatory. These include:

- The ASB's draft Statement of principles. The Statement of principles is still under development by the ASB, but it is likely that, even when it is finalised, it will be non-mandatory. Nevertheless, it will be authoritative in two senses. First, the main purpose of the final Statement of principles is to guide the ASB in its development of standards. Therefore, it should be helpful in guiding companies and auditors as to the meaning and intention of individual accounting standards, if they are not clear. Secondly, the Statement should be a valuable source of reference in connection with the accounting treatment of transactions for which there is no specific GAAP.
- Other statements issued by the ASB. A leading example is the Operating and Financial Review (OFR). This was published as a non-mandatory document, but compliance with it was encouraged. The OFR is discussed in detail in chapter 33. As a further example, the ASB's guidance on interim reporting and preliminary announcements have both been issued as non-mandatory statements (see chapter 39).
- Other statements issued by the ASC. An example of such a statement is 'Accounting for the effects of changing prices: a handbook' issued by the ASC as a guide for those companies wishing to produce financial statements on a current cost basis.
- Statements and recommendations from the professional bodies. Examples are ICAEW Technical Releases (recently called 'FRAGs') such as TR 481 and TR 482 on realised and distributable profits (see chapter 19) and ICAEW accounting recommendations such as the members' handbook statements on materiality and 'Accounting for goods sold subject to reservation of title'.

- Established practice. Quite literally, practices that are generally accepted, even though not codified in official literature, can be regarded as part of UK GAAP. Much of this practice is set out in the guidance from leading accounting firms, such as in this Manual.

[The next page is 2003.]

2.7 A key question is whether the output of the Financial Reporting Review Panel (FRRP) constitutes part of UK GAAP. The practical answer to the question is that it does. As discussed from paragraph 2.81, the FRRP does not issue rules, but announces its findings in relation to individual companies. In general, the companies in question have changed their accounting practices or given additional disclosure, following discussion with the Panel. The Panel generally issues formal statements only where it has concluded that companies have deviated from existing requirements of the Act or accounting standards. However, in some cases, the Panel's views have added to, or modified, the previous understanding of UK GAAP. For example, the Review Panel's press release on the financial statements of Trafalgar House led to the UITF issuing an Abstract on accounting for transfers from current assets to fixed assets. Consequently, companies and auditors should pay particular heed to the announcements from the Panel.

2.8 In addition, there are elements of UK GAAP that relate to specific sectors. Examples are the accounting requirements contained in legislation for banks, housing associations, and charities. Some sector-specific guidance is non-mandatory, and much of this appears in the form of Statements of recommended practice (SORPs), which are discussed from paragraph 2.71.

2.9 The Act does not define the term 'generally accepted accounting principles', but references are included in section 262(3) (definition of realised profits and realised losses), in Schedule 4A paragraph 2(1) (consolidation adjustments) and paragraph 10(d) (adoption of the merger method of accounting). In addition, the Companies Act 1989 introduced a new requirement for companies to state whether the financial statements have been prepared in accordance with applicable Accounting standards and to give particulars of any departures and the reasons for it (see also from para 2.37). [4 Sch 36A].

The development of UK GAAP

2.10 In recent years, the financial statements of UK companies have changed considerably, reflecting the development of UK GAAP.

2.11 Prior to 1970, the regulatory framework was modest. The Companies Acts 1948 and 1967 contained general requirements relating to the need to prepare, distribute and file financial statements for companies and groups. However, there was very little detail in the Act – the detail was left to the practices of accountants. This began to change in 1970 with the formation of the ASC. The SSAPs issued by the ASC between 1970 and 1990 gradually changed practice – mostly for the better – and the standards were in general complied with even though the six Institutes that comprise the CCAB and which sponsored the ASC had no authority over companies as such. Their authority, such as it was, was over their members, both as preparers and auditors of financial statements. This authority was undermined around 1980 as a result of widespread objections to, and eventually non-acceptance of, the ASC's standard SSAP 16 on current cost accounting. Following the withdrawal of SSAP 16, the ASC continued to issue standards until 1990, but its authority had been injured by the SSAP 16 débâcle.

2.12 During the late 1980s the inadequacy in the ASC's authority was recognised and this led to the appointment of the Dearing Committee in 1987. The Dearing report, 'The making of accounting standards' was published in 1988. It recommended that the ASC be replaced by a structure headed by an independent Financial Reporting Council (FRC). The structure that was put in place with effect from 1990 is very closely based on the Dearing proposals. Indeed, Sir Ron Dearing was appointed the first chairman of the FRC, a post he held until 1993. The FRC structure is discussed in more detail from paragraph 2.47.

2.13 The ASC's programme of accounting standards added to the regulatory framework gradually during the 1970s and 1980s, but a major impact was also made by new legislation. The Companies Act 1981 introduced major reforms to UK accounting. Its main function was to implement in the UK the provisions of the EC 4th company law directive.

2.14 The 4th directive is a major element of the EC's harmonisation programme. It sought to harmonise the accounting practice of companies within the EC and did so by making rules about:

- Format of accounts.
- Accounting principles.
- Valuation rules.
- Disclosures.

2.15 In doing so, the directive achieved a degree of harmonisation. However, the process can only be regarded as a partial success. The directive did not deal with all accounting issues. For example, it is silent on foreign currency translation, pension costs and leasing. In addition, there is flexibility in the directive. There are choices in the formats and choices as to measurement basis. The benchmark treatment is historical cost, but valuations can be introduced on a voluntary basis. Furthermore, Member States have not in all cases interpreted the directive in the same way. For example, there are different views as to how the requirement for prudence should be put into practice.

2.16 The implementation of the 4th directive through the 1981 Act was a major upheaval at the time. Following its introduction, changes were necessary to some standards. For example, SSAP 9's provisions relating to work in progress were incompatible with the 1981 Act's requirement that stock should be stated at purchase price or production cost (that is, it was not permissible to include a profit element in the figure for stock and work in progress). Also, SSAP 4's treatment of capital grants had to be changed, as the Act does not allow a grant to the deducted from the cost of an asset.

2.17 More generally, the 1981 Act restricted considerably the possible treatments that could be adopted. The formats were regarded as something of a straitjacket, and the very fact that many accounting issues were set out in legislation resulted in the ASC and the ASB having less scope than perhaps they would like to develop accounting rules. A current example is that the ASB's ability to introduce 'marking to market' as a method of accounting for current asset investments is restricted by the Act's rules.

2.18 The EC 7th directive has a similar role to the 4th, but in connection with consolidated accounts. Its objective again was to harmonise practice within the Community, but its effect on the UK was less dramatic than had been the case with the 4th directive. This is because the basis of the 7th directive was, to a large extent, the Anglo-Saxon model of consolidation, whereas the 4th directive had been based more on continental practices.

2.19 Nevertheless, the 7th directive, which was implemented in the UK through the Companies Act 1989, had the following effects:

- Compared with the previous position, there were more rules regarding consolidations enshrined in legislation. For example, most of Schedule 4A to the 1985 Act (the 1989 Act introduced changes to the 1985 Act) is derived from the 7th directive.
- Although the overall model of consolidation is broadly in line with previous practice, there were major changes affecting the composition of groups for the purposes of consolidated financial statements. These changes rendered SSAP 14 inconsistent with the Act and so led to the replacement of SSAP 14 on group accounts with a new standard, FRS 2.
- The 7th directive was aimed at larger groups, whereas previous UK legislation had required all groups, however small, to prepare group accounts. The 1989 Act introduced exemptions for small and medium-sized groups, as explained in detail in chapter 36.

2.20 There is now considerable overlap between the accounting requirements of the Act and the requirements of accounting standards. This applies to both the accounting principles and the disclosure requirements.

The Companies Act

2.21 Although many detailed accounting rules have been added to companies legislation in recent years, its most important accounting requirements are, perhaps unsurprisingly, those that have been there longest (although not in exactly the same words), namely the requirement for companies to prepare financial statements and the true and fair requirement.

The requirement to prepare financial statements

2.22 Directors are required to prepare a balance sheet as at the last day of the financial year and a profit and loss account for each financial year of the company. [Sec 226(1)]. In addition, if, at the end of the financial year, the company is a parent company, the directors must also prepare a consolidated balance sheet and profit and loss account that deal with the state of affairs and the profit and loss of the parent and its subsidiary undertakings. These consolidated financial statements must give a true and fair view of the state of affairs at the end of the financial year and of the profit or loss for the financial year of the undertakings included in the consolidation as a whole, so far as concerns the parent company's members. [Sec 227(1)(2)]. The exemptions from the requirement to prepare consolidated financial statements provided in the Act are discussed in chapter 21.

The true and fair requirement

2.23 In relation to individual accounts, in addition to requiring companies to prepare accounts, section 226 requires that:

- *"The balance sheet shall give a true and fair view of the state of affairs of the company as at the end of the financial year; and the profit and loss account shall give a true and fair view of the profit or loss of the company for the financial year."* [Sec 226(2)].
- *"A company's individual accounts shall comply with the provisions of Schedule 4 as to the form and content of the balance sheet and profit and loss account and additional information to be provided by way of notes to the accounts."* [Sec 226(3)].

2.24 In most cases, companies are able to comply with both of these sub-sections at the same time. That is, compliance with the detailed rules of Schedule 4, together with compliance with accounting standards, will result in the accounts giving a true and fair view.

2.25 However, this will not always be the case. The Act makes clear that the true and fair requirement is overriding, and sets this out in the following way:

- Section 226(4) provides that:

> *"Where compliance with the provisions of [Schedule 4] and the other provisions of this Act as to the matters to be included in a company's individual accounts or in notes to those accounts, would not be sufficient to give a true and fair view, the necessary additional information shall be given in the accounts or in a note to them."*

- Section 226(5) adds that:

> *"If in special circumstances compliance with any of those provisions is inconsistent with the requirement to give a true and fair view, the directors shall depart from that provision to the extent necessary to give a true and fair view. Particulars of any such departure, the reasons for it and its effect shall be given in a note to the accounts."*

2.26 The true and fair requirement, as set out in these sub-sections, is a very important element of the Act and of UK GAAP. Questions are sometimes asked about the interplay between sections 226(4) and 226(5). In a previous version of the Act, it was more explicit that they were sequential. That is, if following Schedule 4 did not result in a true and fair view, the first requirement was to add more information. If the financial statements then gave a true and fair view, compliance with the Act was achieved and resort to section 226(5) did not arise. Only if a true and fair view was still not obtained, even after the addition of more information, was a company required to resort to section 226(5).

2.27 The wording is now not so explicitly sequential. However, the practical effect is much the same as before, in that additional information satisfies the requirement in some cases, but not others. Section 226(4) can be seen as saying merely that the specific requirements of Schedule 4 and other parts of the Act are the minimum requirement. There may be a number of situations in which additional information has to be given, for example, to explain a somewhat unusual transaction. Without that explanation, the accounts could not be said to give a true and fair view; but with the explanation added they do. Adding the information is the obvious solution and there is no need to consider departing from the specific rules. An example might be that, in order to give a true and fair view, it might be necessary to give information about a transaction with a related party.

2.28 Section 226(5), on the other hand, comes into operation when, owing to 'special circumstances', the accounting treatment otherwise required by the Act does not give a true and fair view, that is, if the treatment otherwise required by the Act is inconsistent with a true and fair view. Such treatment cannot become true and fair even if extensive additional information is given.

2.29 Sub-sections 226(4) and 226(5) can, therefore, be seen not so much as sequential provisions, but as alternative provisions to assist in achieving a true and fair view. Each has a role in its own circumstances: sub-section 226(4) comes into play where there is *insufficient* information; sub-section 226(5) comes into play where there is the *wrong kind* of accounting treatment.

2.30 Although the notion of departing from the otherwise specific rules in order to give a true and fair view is a powerful and important one, that does not mean it is something that should be done frequently or cavalierly. Indeed, it is a treatment to be adopted sparingly. As sub-section 226(5) makes clear, it is only to be used 'in special circumstances'. This means that it is not intended to be used as a route through which all companies can disregard a specific rule of the Act.

2.31 With few exceptions, such as SSAP 19 (where companies are required to value investment properties rather than depreciate them, which is what the Act requires), the general understanding is that the override should only be used in the special circumstances of an individual company that has a different situation from most other companies. In practice, this can be extended to a class of companies, for example, in an particular industry, which have considerations that differ from the generality of companies. An example here is that it is regarded as acceptable for companies in the securities industry to use the override to 'mark to market' their current asset investments and take the resultant gains to the profit and loss account rather than, as the Act requires, to the revaluation reserve. The reason it is acceptable for these type of companies is that, because of the nature of their businesses, this treatment gives a true and fair view of their performance whereas the Act's treatment would not generally do so. However, other types of companies that adopt this practice must demonstrate that they have special circumstances of their own.

2.32 The final sentence of sub-section 226(5) requires certain disclosures to be given when the override is used. These disclosures are detailed in paragraph 2.34.

2.33 As discussed above, consolidated financial statements are also required to give a true and fair view. [Section 227(3)]. Sub-sections 227(5) and 227(6) contain identical provisions with respect to consolidated financial statements as sub-sections 226(4) and 226(5) respectively. Therefore, the discussion above applies equally to consolidated financial statements.

True and fair override disclosures

2.34 Where a company departs from any of the Act's accounting provisions in order to give a true and fair view, the Act requires that *"...particulars of any such departure, the reasons for it and its effect shall be given in a note to the accounts"*. [Sec 226(5)].

2.35 The UITF issued an interpretation of this disclosure requirement in UITF Abstract 7, as follows:

- The 'particulars' means a statement of the treatment the Act would normally require in the circumstances and a description of the treatment actually adopted.
- The 'reasons' means a statement as to why the treatment prescribed by the Act would not give a true and fair view.
- The 'effect' means a description of how the position shown in the accounts is different as a result of the departure, normally with quantification of the difference (except where quantification is self-evident or cannot reasonably be made, in which case the circumstances should be explained).

[UITF 7 para 4].

2.36 The disclosures referred to in the previous paragraph should be given considerable prominence. They should either be included in the note that discloses compliance with accounting standards (see para 2.37), or that note should include a cross reference to where such disclosures can be found. [UITF 7 para 7]. An example is given in Table 2.1.

Table 2.1 – Land Securities PLC – Report and Financial Statements – 31 March 1998

1 ACCOUNTING POLICIES (extract)

The financial statements have been prepared under the historical cost convention modified by the revaluation of properties and in accordance with applicable accounting standards. Compliance with SSAP 19 "Accounting for Investment Properties" requires a departure from the requirements of the Companies Act 1985 relating to depreciation and amortisation and an explanation of this departure is given in (e) below.

(e) DEPRECIATION AND AMORTISATION

In accordance with SSAP 19, no depreciation or amortisation is provided in respect of freehold or leasehold properties held on leases having more than 20 years unexpired. This departure from the requirements of the Companies Act 1985, for all properties to be depreciated, is, in the opinion of the Directors, necessary for the financial statements to give a true and fair view in accordance with applicable accounting standards, as properties are included in the financial statements at their open market value.

The effect of depreciation and amortisation on value is already reflected annually in the valuation of properties, and the amount attributed to this factor by the valuers cannot reasonably be separately identified or quantified. Had the provisions of the Act been followed, net assets would not have been affected but revenue profits would have been reduced for this and earlier years.

Paragraph 36A statements

2.37 There is a general presumption that compliance with accounting standards is required to meet the true and fair requirement. The legal opinion supporting this presumption is discussed from paragraph 2.74. In addition, paragraph 36A of Schedule 4 to the Act requires companies to state in their financial statements whether they have been prepared in accordance with applicable accounting standards and to give the particulars and reasons for any material departures from those standards. Table 2.2 contains an example of a paragraph 36A statement.

Table 2.2 – Marks and Spencer p.l.c. – Annual Report and Financial Statements – 31 March 1995

Accounting policies (extract)

The financial statements are prepared in accordance with applicable accounting standards in the United Kingdom. A summary of the more important Group accounting policies, which are applied consistently, is given below.

2.38 Companies that qualify as small or medium-sized in accordance with section 247 are exempt from this requirement. [Section 246(1)(a)].

2.39 While compliance with applicable accounting standards is usually required in order for financial statements to give a true and fair view, in exceptional circumstances a departure from an applicable accounting standard may be necessary to meet the true and fair requirement. In these circumstances, the Foreword to accounting standards states that:

> "*Particulars of any material departure from an accounting standard, the reasons for it and its financial effects should be disclosed in the financial statements. The disclosure made should be equivalent to that given in respect of departures from specific accounting provisions of companies legislation.*" [Foreword para 19].

2.40 Therefore, all companies must give particulars of any departure from applicable accounting standards, the reasons for it and describe how the position set out in the financial statements is different from that which would be expected if the accounting standard had been followed. The differences should be quantified unless it is impractical to do so. This disclosure is identical to that required where there is a departure from a specific accounting provision of the Act. This is discussed in detail from paragraph 2.34.

The UK financial reporting structure

The Dearing Report proposals

2.41 In November 1987, the Consultative Committee of Accountancy Bodies (the CCAB) appointed a Review Committee under the chairmanship of Sir Ron Dearing to review and make recommendations on the standard-setting process. The terms of reference were to consider, *inter alia*, the status of accounting standards in relation to company law and the procedures for monitoring compliance with standards and their enforcement.

2.42 In discharge of that remit, the Review Committee in their report (the Dearing Report) submitted to the CCAB in September 1988 stated that accounting standards should remain, as far as possible, the responsibility of auditors, preparers and users of financial statements and there should not be a general move towards incorporating them into law. But the report recommended the government should introduce legislation along the following lines:

- For all large companies, directors should be required to state in the notes to the financial statements whether they are drawn up in accordance with applicable accounting standards and to draw attention to any material departures, explaining the reasons for the departures.
- There should be a new statutory power under civil law for certain authorised bodies or the secretary of state to apply to the courts for an order requiring the revision of financial statements that do not give a true and fair view.
- A small levy should be added to the fees paid by all companies to the Companies Registration Office to assist meeting the cost of setting and monitoring standards.

2.43 In addition, the Committee recommended that the task of devising accounting standards should be discharged by a newly constituted, expert Accounting Standards Board that would issue standards on its own authority. A Financial Reporting Council should be created that would provide guidance to the Accounting Standards Board on priorities for its work programme and on issues of public interest and would act as an instrument for promoting good practice in relation to accounting standards. In securing compliance with accounting standards in support of the 'true and fair' requirement, the Committee recommended establishing a Review Panel to examine contentious departures from accounting standards by large companies.

The Companies Act 1989 requirements

2.44 The legislative changes necessary to bring the above recommendations of the Review Committee into effect were implemented by the Companies Act 1989. Paragraph 36A of Schedule 4 to the Companies Act 1985 (as amended by the Companies Act 1989) requires all companies to state whether the financial statements have been prepared in accordance with applicable accounting standards as discussed in paragraph 2.37 above.

2.45 In providing a framework for the implementation of the Dearing Committee proposals for an independent Accounting Standards Board overseen by a Financial Reporting Council and backed up by a Review Panel, the Act gave the secretary of state power to make grants to such bodies concerning:

- Issuing accounting standards.
- Overseeing and directing the issue of such standards.
- Investigating departures from such standards or from the Act's accounting requirements and taking steps to secure compliance with them.

[Sec 256(3)].

2.46 In addition, the Companies Act 1989 introduced new procedures enabling directors voluntarily to revise financial statements that are discovered to be defective. [Sec 245]. Further enabling provisions permit the Secretary of State to improve the enforcement of accounting provisions by requiring an explanation from directors of apparent failures to prepare financial statements that comply with the Act. [Sec 245A(1)]. If a satisfactory explanation is not received, the Secretary of State may apply to the court for a declaration that a company's financial statements do not comply with the Act and to order them to be revised. [Sec 245A(3)]. The Act's provisions relating to the revision of defective financial statements are dealt with in chapter 38.

The FRC

2.47 The Financial Reporting Council Limited and its two subsidiaries, the Accounting Standards Board Limited and the Financial Reporting Review Panel Limited were established in 1990 as companies limited by guarantee. The purpose of these bodies is to provide an institutional framework to underpin financial reporting in the UK and to implement the proposals of the Dearing Report. The accountancy profession, the City and the government share equally in the funding of these bodies.

2.48 The FRC supports the work of the ASB and the FRRP and encourages high standards of financial reporting generally through its Council whose function is to determine policy. The 30 members and observers of the Council are drawn at senior level and include a wide and balanced representation from preparers, auditors, users and others with an interest in financial statements. The Chairman and three Deputy Chairmen of the Council, who are appointed by the Secretary of State for Trade and Industry and the Governor of the Bank of England, act as the FRC's directors and deal with its business affairs.

2.49 The Council views its role as:

- Promoting good financial reporting, and in that context from time to time making public its views on reporting standards; and making representations to government on current legislation when appropriate.

- Providing guidance to the ASB on work programmes and on broad policy issues.

- Verifying that the arrangements under the Council's umbrella are conducted with efficiency and economy and that they are adequately funded.

[FRC Annual Review 1994].

The ASB

2.50 The ASB is the authority that has been prescribed by statutory instrument as the standard making body for the purposes of section 256(1) of the Companies Act 1985. The accounting standards (designated FRSs) that it issues, amends and withdraws are 'accounting standards' for the purpose of the Act's accounting requirements. This is in contrast to the accounting standards that were set by the ASC that were designated as SSAPs. Previously neither the ASC nor its SSAPs were given statutory recognition. At its inception, the ASB adopted the SSAPs extant at that time so that, until they are withdrawn by the ASB, they now have the same authority and statutory backing as FRSs.

2.51 Unlike the ASC, the ASB is totally independent and needs no outside approval for its actions either from the Council, from government, or from any other source. The ASC had been criticised as being slow in setting standards since agreement for a new standard was required from all its sponsoring bodies. These sponsoring bodies were the six accountancy bodies making up the CCAB. The ASB has a full-time chairman and full-time technical director and is supported by greater staff resources than the ASC. However, the Board has fewer members than the ASC. In addition, other part-time Board members are drawn from industry and commerce, investor institutions and others with an interest in financial reporting as well as the accountancy profession. Membership of the ASB is limited to ten and since a majority of seven is needed for any decision to adopt, revise or withdraw an accounting standard, the standard setting process is designed be more streamlined.

2.52 However, the ASB has stated that it wishes to ensure wide consultation and to be as open as possible in its dealings. As well as issuing exposure drafts of proposed FRSs (FREDs), it publishes discussion papers on topics as they reach an appropriate stage of development and, in exceptional circumstances, it may hold public hearings about a particular problem. The ASB held the first such public hearings, on accounting for goodwill, in September and October 1995.

2.53 The ASB has published a 'Statement of aims' which sets out its approach to the task of setting standards and lists the guidelines it will follow in conducting its affairs. The ASB intends to achieve its aims by:

- Developing principles to guide it in establishing standards and to provide a framework within which others can exercise judgement in resolving accounting issues.

- Issuing new accounting standards, or amending existing ones, in response to evolving business practices, new economic developments and deficiencies being identified in current practice.

- Addressing urgent issues promptly.

[Statement of aims].

2.54 The seven draft chapters of the ASB's Statement of principles were the first stage in the development of a framework within which standards can be developed and revised on a consistent basis and within which preparers and auditors can address issues where an accounting standard is not available. The draft Statement of principles was reissued as an omnibus exposure draft late in 1995 to allow commentators to express views on the complete statement. The development of the Statement of principles and its current contents are discussed from paragraph 2.175.

2.55 In order to improve the timeliness of its response to issues, a committee of the ASB, the Urgent Issues Task Force, was set up to assist the Board in areas where an accounting standard or Companies Act provision exists, but where unsatisfactory or conflicting interpretations have developed or seem likely to develop. The UITF is considered further from paragraph 2.77.

2.56 When the ASB first took responsibility for accounting standards in 1990, it set about fundamentally reforming those aspects of financial reporting practices where there were significant perceived shortcomings. A significant part of the ASB's early work programme consisted of projects where the ASC had issued exposure drafts. In its first four years, the ASB issued seven new FRSs. This completed its first major phase of reforms. In the process, it changed the appearance of the profit and loss account and balance sheet and introduced new primary statements; a cash flow statement and a statement of total recognised gains and losses.

2.57 This phase of eliminating perceived abuses seems to be passing. Current ASB projects concentrate on reviewing and amending standards taken over from the ASC, addressing emerging areas not covered by existing standards (most notably derivatives) and, increasingly, harmonising its agenda with that of the IASC and other national standard setters.

2.58 The continuing project to put in place a Statement of principles on which new standards, and revisions of existing standards, can be based is another important aspect of the ASB's work. The effort to create such a framework places much more emphasis on the underlying concepts. The Statement of principles also supports the ASB's expectation that the spirit and reasoning of accounting standards should be followed, not merely the rules contained within them.

2.59 International accounting developments also influence the ASB's work. Some parts of the ASB's agenda seem to be quite strongly influenced by US accounting. FRS 4 'Capital instruments', for example, although bound by the Act's formats, appears to be influenced by North American practice in clearly identifying financial instruments as debt or equity. With regard to International Accounting Standards (IASs), the ASB has always said that it takes international developments into account in developing its own domestic rules. All FRSs contain a statement of compliance with IASs. However, the ASB is prepared to adopt a different approach if it considers that there are good reasons for doing so. Nevertheless, the FRC's own financial statements state that, while they have been prepared in accordance with applicable accounting standards, they also comply in all material respects with IASs. As IASs develop further and as links between the ASB and the IASC strengthen, it will remain to be seen whether UK standards harmonise with IAS.

2.60 In addition to issuing accounting standards, the ASB may, from time to time, issue other forms of guidance on best practice. For example, the 'Operating and financial review', published in July 1993, is not mandatory, but offers directors a framework within which they can discuss the performance of their company in an open and objective manner. As well as assisting directors in developing commentary, the FRC stated in its preface to the OFR that it considers that the statement has an important role in encouraging other major companies to emulate the achievements of the best. The ASB is attempting to create a virtuous circle where companies are encouraged to provide more informative financial statements. A similar statement may also be issued on interim reporting. Such guidance is unlikely to be mandatory, but would encourage companies to provide more information in their interim reports.

FRSs and SSAPs

2.61 FRSs and SSAPs are applicable to all financial statements of an entity that are intended to give a true and fair view. These accounting standards also apply to consolidated financial statements, including amounts relating to overseas entities that are included in the consolidation.

2.62 However, accounting standards need not be applied to immaterial items. Accounting standards also do not override exemptions from disclosure given by law to certain types of entity. For example, groups that are exempt by virtue of their size from the Companies Act requirements to prepare consolidated financial statements, are not expected to comply with accounting standards dealing with consolidated financial statements.

2.63 In addition, accounting standards themselves may exclude certain entities from their scope. For example, the requirements of SSAP 25, 'Segmental reporting', that are additional to the statutory segmental disclosure requirements and certain disclosure requirements of SSAP 13, 'Accounting for research and development', do not apply to private limited companies unless they exceed the criteria, multiplied in each case by 10, for defining a medium-sized company under section 248 of the Act.

2.64 A working party of CCAB was set up at the request of the ASB to consider whether smaller entities should be exempt from all or parts of accounting standards on a standard-by-standard basis on the grounds of their smaller size and relative lack of public interest in their financial statements. The initial conclusion was that companies that met the Act's definition of a small company should be exempt from most standards.

2.65 However, the issue – the 'big GAAP, little GAAP' debate – has proved controversial. Many smaller companies already do not have to comply with certain standards: they might be exempt from preparing consolidated financial statements due to their size; and they may not enter into some of the complex transactions that are the subject of accounting standards. However, if smaller companies enter into complex transactions then, arguably, they must account for them in accordance with accounting standards in order for their financial statements to give a true and fair view. A new approach has emerged, that small companies should comply with a single simplified accounting standard designed specifically for them. The ASB published an exposure draft 'Financial reporting standard for smaller entities' in December 1996 (see chapter 36).

2.66 The Foreword to accounting standards states that the prescription of accounting requirements for the public sector in the UK is a matter for government. The government's requirements with regard to public sector bodies that prepare financial statements may or may not refer to accounting standards. Therefore public sector bodies are not specifically required to comply with accounting standards although there is an expectation that they should do so if their financial statements are required to give a true and fair view, unless the government considers it inappropriate.

2.67 The ASB has stated that, in general, when a new accounting standard is issued, it should be applied to all material transactions regardless of the date they were entered into. This would prevent similar transactions being accounted for in different ways in the same financial statements depending on when they occurred. It would also aid comparability between the financial statements of different entities.

2.68 However, the ASB accepts that in a few instances the application of a new accounting standard to past transactions would involve considerable work and may result in information that would be difficult for users to interpret. In these instances, the ASB may exclude transactions that took place before the standard came into force from its scope. FRS 6 and FRS 7, for example, apply in respect of business combinations first accounted for in financial statements relating to accounting periods on or after 23 December 1994. Therefore, the accounting treatment of acquisitions and mergers that were first accounted for before these standards came into effect is not changed.

2.69 The ASB states in the Foreword that until an exposure draft (or discussion paper) is converted into a standard, the requirements of any existing standard that would be affected by the proposals remain in force. Exposure drafts are subject to amendment and even more amendment can be expected to proposals contained in discussion papers. Companies wishing to incorporate new proposals into their financial statements may do so as long as the new proposal does not conflict with an existing accounting standard. Alternatively, additional information could be provided in a supplementary form such as in pro forma financial statements. [Foreword paras 31,32].

2.70 The ASB has stated that it will initiate a process of formal post-issue review of accounting standards. The business environment changes over time and standards may need to be changed to ensure that they reflect economic reality. In addition, while the ASB intends to be receptive to comments on accounting standards, it also wants to ensure that standards are given an appropriate period to become established before they are subject to review. This review process began with FRS 1, a revised standard being published five years after the original standard.

SORPs

2.71 The ASB has reviewed its policy toward the development of Statements of Recommended Practice (SORPs). Specific industry groups develop SORPs to set out current best practice and narrow the areas of difference and the variety of accounting treatments in the matters they address. Previously, SORPs were issued under the authority of the ASC or the industry group concerned after approval and franking by the ASC. The ASB does not frank SORPs. Rather, in respect of SORPs developed in accordance with ASB guidelines by bodies recognised by the ASB for that purpose, the ASB will give a negative assurance statement confirming that the SORP does not appear to contain any fundamental points of principle that are unacceptable in the context of current accounting practice or conflict with existing accounting standards.

2.72 The following SORP-making bodies have been recognised by the ASC or the ASB:

- Pensions Research Accountants Group.
- Oil Industry Accounting Committee
- Investment Management Regulatory Organisation
- British Bankers' Association/Irish Bankers' Federation
- Committee of Vice-Chancellors and Principals of Universities of the United Kingdom
- Chartered Institute of Public Finance and Accountancy
- Charity Commission
- Association of Investment Trust Companies
- Association of British Insurers
- Finance & Leasing Association
- National Federation of Housing Associations

2.73 Although SORPs are themselves non-mandatory, another authority may nonetheless encourage compliance. For example, the Occupational Pension Schemes (Requirement to obtain Audited Accounts and a Statement from the Auditor) Regulations 1996 require pension schemes to which the regulations apply to state whether the financial statements have been prepared in accordance with the relevant SORP and to disclose any material departures.

Counsel's opinion on true and fair view and role of accounting standards

2.74 As discussed from paragraph 2.23 above, the Act's overriding requirement is that financial statements must give a true and fair view of the entity's state of affairs at the balance sheet date and its profit and loss for the financial period ending on that date. The question then arises as to what is meant by a 'true and fair view'. In particular, there is the question of whether the requirement that all financial statements should give a true and fair view includes compliance with the relevant accounting standards. True and fair is a legal concept that can only be interpreted by the courts.

2.75 In light of the changes to the Companies Act detailed in paragraph 2.44 above, the ASB obtained a revised opinion from Mary Arden QC on the relationship between compliance with accounting standards and the requirement that all financial statements should give a true and fair view.

2.76 To obtain a full understanding of Counsel's arguments, the opinion should be read in its entirety. It is reproduced as an annex to this chapter. However, the opinion makes the following important points.

- Although the question of whether financial statements satisfy the true and fair requirement is a matter of law, the court cannot interpret the requirement without evidence as to the practices and views of accountants. The more authoritative these practices and views are, the more ready the court will be to follow them.

- Accounting standards initially identify proper accounting practice for the benefit of preparers and auditors of financial statements. However, because financial statements commonly comply with accounting standards, the effect of the standards is to create a common understanding between users and preparers about how particular items are dealt with and to create an expectation that financial statements will comply with applicable accounting standards, unless there is a good reason not to comply.

- The Companies Act 1989 gives statutory recognition to the existence of accounting standards. The court will infer from section 256 that statutory policy favours both the issue of accounting standards (by a body prescribed by regulation) and compliance with them. The court will also infer from paragraph 36A of Schedule 4 that, since there is a requirement to disclose particulars of non-compliance, financial statements that meet the true and fair requirement will generally follow rather than depart from accounting standards. Therefore, the likelihood is increased that the courts will hold that, in general, compliance with applicable accounting standards is necessary to meet the true and fair requirement.

- As a result of implementing the Dearing Report recommendations, the court is bound to give even further weight to the opinions of the ASB than to ASC. If a standard was not generally accepted in practice, it does not follow that the court would conclude that compliance with the standard was not necessary to meet the true and fair requirement.

- Paragraph 36A of the Act envisages the possibility of a departure from applicable accounting standards, provided that particulars of the departure and the reasons for it are disclosed in the financial statements. However, the departure must be appropriate in the particular circumstances of the company. If the court is satisfied that an accounting standard should have been followed to meet the true and fair requirement, then non-compliance, even with the necessary disclosure, will result in a breach of the true and fair requirement.

The Urgent Issues Task Force

2.77 Although not envisaged by the revisions to the Act, the ASB also issues UITF Abstracts that set out the consensus reached by its committee, the Urgent Issues Task Force. The main role of the UITF is not to write new accounting standards, but to assist in areas where an accounting standard or Companies Act provision exists, but where unsatisfactory or conflicting interpretations have developed or seem likely to develop. In addition, the ASB may seek the UITF's view on significant accounting developments in areas where there is no extant legal provision or accounting standard.

2.78 The UITF seeks to reach a consensus among its fifteen voting members who are drawn from the accounting profession and the wider business community. Eleven voting members constitute a quorum at meetings and a consensus is achieved if not more than two of the voting members present at a meeting dissent. Although the UITF exposes draft Abstracts, the time for comment is generally much shorter than for accounting standards. Therefore, the UITF should be able to respond more quickly to emerging issues than the ASB. However, since the consultation time is reduced, the ASB ensures that matters on the UITF's agenda and other information about its activities are published.

2.79 The ASB regards UITF Abstracts as generally accepted accounting practice in the areas they address and as part of the body of accounting pronouncements that must be followed in order for financial statements to give a true and fair view. The ASB expects to adopt a UITF consensus, unless it conflicts with law, accounting standards or the ASB's policy or future plans. To date, the ASB has not rejected any Abstracts prepared by the UITF. However, one Abstract, UITF 10, 'Disclosure of directors' share options', was issued in non-mandatory form since the ASB received legal advice that disclosures proposed by the Abstract went beyond what is required by the Companies Act, and so did not fall within the powers delegated to the UITF. However, the subsequent adoption of this UITF by the Greenbury committee has effectively made it mandatory.

2.80 The status of UITF Abstracts is considered in the ASB's legal opinion that is included as an annex to this chapter. This opinion sets out the process of creating UITF Abstracts and their consideration and publishing by the ASB. It then argues that since the CCAB, the ASB and the profession expect UITF Abstracts to be followed and this expectation has been borne out in practice, there will be a readiness on the part of the court to accept that compliance with UITF Abstracts is also necessary to meet the true and fair requirement.

Financial Reporting Review Panel

2.81 The role of the Financial Reporting Review Panel (FRRP) is to examine material departures from the Act's accounting requirements, including departures from the requirements of applicable accounting standards. The Secretary of State for Trade and Industry authorised the FRRP to discuss such departures with the company's directors and, if necessary, seek an order from the court to remedy them under section 245B of the Act as discussed in paragraph 2.46 above. By agreement with the DTI, the FRRP considers the financial statements of public and large private companies, with the DTI dealing with all other companies. Therefore, the following types of companies fall within the FRRP's authority:

- Public limited companies, unless they are subsidiaries in small or medium-sized groups.

- Companies within a group headed by a public limited company.
- Any company that does not qualify as small or medium-sized as defined by section 247 of the Act.
- Any company within a group that does not qualify as small or medium-sized as defined by section 249 of the Act.

[FRC, Annual Review 1994].

The FRRP does not routinely examine all the financial statements of the companies falling within its authority. Rather, it acts on matters drawn to its attention either directly or indirectly.

2.82 The formal procedures that the FRRP follows in considering financial statements were revised in September 1993 in order to reduce the time taken to reach decisions. No outside approval, either from the FRC or from the company's directors, is required for the FRRP's actions. Members of the FRRP are selected by the appointments committee of the FRC which attempts to ensure that its membership is drawn from the wider business community. Generally, a group of five or more members, drawn from its membership of 20, is assembled to investigate individual cases.

2.83 The FRRP normally attempt to seek a voluntary agreement with the company's directors about any necessary revisions to the financial statements in question. This allows the directors to follow the rules regarding the voluntary revision of defective financial statements rather than those for revision by court order (see chapter 38). However, if the FRRP cannot reach an agreement with the company's directors, it has authority from the Secretary of State for Trade and Industry to use the Act's powers to compel the revision of financial statements if the court finds that they are defective. It also has £2 million available to it to fund any legal proceedings. To date, all cases examined by the FRRP have been resolved without involving adjudication by the courts.

Companies Act and SSAP 2 – accounting principles and concepts

2.84 Despite the ASB's quest to create a Statement of principles, certain basic accounting principles and concepts have been contained in accounting standards since 1971 and in the Act since 1981. Indeed, in many respects, the ASB's project builds on these requirements.

2.85 Many of the accounting principles and rules that are included in accounting standards appear also in Part II of Schedule 4 to the Act and Schedule 4A.

2.86 Part II of Schedule 4 is divided into three sections:

- Accounting principles. This section covers the fundamental accounting concepts that are discussed in the remainder of this section.

- Historical cost accounting rules. This section covers accounting bases, specific accounting rules, depreciation and amounts necessary to write down cost to a lower net realisable value. These are discussed in chapter 5.

- Alternative accounting rules. This section deals with the accounting treatment of items where the accounting rules applied are designed to take account, in some way, of either inflation or other fluctuations in value (such as, the change in a property's value). These are also discussed in chapter 5.

2.87 Schedule 4A deals exclusively with the provisions concerning consolidated financial statements. The Schedule covers, *inter alia*: the elimination of intra-group transactions; acquisition and merger accounting; the treatment of minority interests; interests of subsidiary undertakings excluded from consolidation; and the consolidation of joint ventures and associated companies.

2.88 SSAP 2 sets out the four fundamental accounting concepts that underlie the preparation of financial statements. These are: the going concern concept; the consistency concept; the prudence concept; and the accruals concept. These, together with a fifth concept that requires assets and liabilities to be valued separately, are reproduced in the Act as the 'accounting principles'. Increasingly, however, and in particular since the publication of FRS 5, the economic substance of transactions needs to be recognised, rather than their legal form, in order to give a true and fair view. The concept of 'Substance over form' is considered from paragraph 2.126 below.

2.89 A company's directors are permitted to depart from any of the accounting concepts where there are special reasons to do so. If they do so, however, the notes to the financial statements must give particulars of the departure, the directors' reasons for it, and its effect (see para 2.34 above). [4 Sch 15]. Special reasons would include circumstances in which the directors conclude that the company is not a going concern.

Going concern

2.90 One of the accounting principles contained in the Act is that "*the company shall be presumed to be carrying on business as a going concern*". [4 Sch 10]. Of course, this is merely a presumption and as such it can be rebutted. It would have to be rebutted, for example, if the company were on the brink of being wound up.

2.91 While the term 'going concern' is not defined in the Act, SSAP 2 defines it and states that:

> *"The enterprise will continue in operational existence for the foreseeable future. This means in particular that the profit and loss account and balance sheet assume no intention or necessity to liquidate or curtail significantly the scale of operation."*
> [SSAP 2 para 14].

SSAP 2 also requires that, where financial statements are prepared on a basis of assumptions that differ from those set out in the SSAP, this should be explained in the financial statements.

2.92 The importance of the going concern concept relates to the bases a company uses to arrive at the amounts at which it states items in the balance sheet. For example, the amount at which fixed assets are stated takes into account how useful they are to the business as a going concern. If, however, the business is not a going concern, the fixed assets should be valued at their 'break-up' value.

2.93 The following example illustrates this:

Example

A company that manufactures a particular children's toy has the following fixed assets:

	Cost £000	Depreciation £000	Net book value £000	Break-up value £000
Factory buildings	500	25	475	350
Plant and machinery	150	75	75	10
	650	100	550	360

The net book value of the fixed assets is £550,000 whereas their break-up value is £360,000. This difference results from two facts. First, in order to adapt the factory from its present use to a different use, it would need to be altered considerably. Secondly, the plant and machinery would have only a scrap value if the company ceased to manufacture the toy.

So long as the company is a going concern, the financial statements will properly reflect the fixed assets at their net book value of £550,000 (assuming their recoverable amount exceeds this figure). If, however, the company ran into severe financial difficulty (so that it could no longer be regarded as a going concern), the fixed assets would have to be written down to their break-up value of £360,000. Therefore, in order to reflect the fact that the company could no longer be regarded as a going concern, there would need to be a provision of £190,000 to reduce the amount at which the fixed assets were stated in the balance sheet.

2.94 With most companies, if the company changed the presumption that it is a going concern, it would have a considerable effect. In addition to having to make possible provisions against the book value of fixed and current assets, the company would need to make provision for other costs such as redundancy payments, dilapidations and guarantees. Also, changes may be needed to the amounts and the dates of maturity of liabilities and the classification of fixed assets and long-term liabilities. Such assets and liabilities would need to be reclassified as current assets and liabilities.

2.95 In a few situations, the effect of ceasing to regard the business as a going concern may be negligible. The question then arises as to whether the financial statements need to disclose that the company is no longer carrying on business as a going concern. Unless there is a statement to the contrary, the Act allows a reader to *presume* that the company is carrying on business as a going concern. Consequently, where necessary, the company should state that it has prepared its financial statements on a break-up basis, even if the effect of doing so has not been significant.

2.96 In some situations, while it may be reasonable to prepare financial statements on a going concern basis, significant doubt may exist about whether the company will in fact be able to continue in operational existence for the foreseeable future. As discussed above, these uncertainties may need to be explained in order for the financial statements to give a true and fair view. This requirement of the Act has been reinforced by recent guidance given to directors and auditors.

2.97 According to SAS 600, 'Auditors reports on financial statements', where there is a fundamental uncertainty for instance about the validity of the going concern basis, auditors are required to draw attention, by means of an explanatory note, to the note to the financial statements that explains the uncertainty. SAS 130, 'The going concern basis in financial statements', a more specific auditing standard, dealing with going concern, contains a list of factors that may need to be disclosed in relation to such an uncertainty.

2.98 SAS 130 was issued by the APB in November 1994. SAS 130 acknowledges that SSAP 2 did not define the term 'foreseeable future' and that it would be impossible to specify a minimum length for the future period the directors should consider particularly in assessing going concern. The appropriate period of time that the directors should consider will depend on many factors such as the company's reporting and budgeting systems and the nature of the business and industry in which it operates.

2.99 However, the auditing standard considers that, where the directors have paid particular attention to a period less than one year from the date of approval of the financial statements in assessing going concern, they will need to consider whether additional disclosure is needed in the financial statements in order to explain the assumptions underlying adopting the going concern basis. In addition, the standard requires that, where the directors have paid particular attention to a period less than one year from the date of approval of the financial statements and have not disclosed this fact, then the auditors should disclose this in their report. Although the mention of this in the audit report does not in itself amount to a qualified audit opinion, directors may well feel compelled to ensure that the financial statements adequately explain why, in their opinion, the going concern basis is appropriate in these circumstances.

2.100 The requirement in the Cadbury Code for directors to confirm that the going concern basis is appropriate has, in effect, changed it from a presumption to an explicit statement for listed companies. Paragraph 4.6 of the Code says that directors should state in their report and accounts "*that the business is a going concern, with supporting assumptions or qualifications as necessary*". The guidance that directors should use to interpret this requirement, 'Going concern and financial reporting: Guidance for directors of listed companies' was issued in November 1994. This guidance recommends that directors should include their statement on going concern in the OFR. However, it also notes that if there are doubts as to the appropriateness of the going concern presumption, then the financial statements may need to reflect any relevant factors in greater detail if they are to show a true and fair view. [Going concern and financial reporting: Guidance for directors of listed companies, para 45]. The Cadbury Code requirements are discussed in detail in chapter 32.

Consistency

2.101 In preparing its financial statements, a company must apply accounting policies consistently within the same financial statements and from one financial year to the next. [4 Sch 11]. Without this rule, it would be difficult to ensure comparability from year to year, or to prevent companies manipulating their results. This is because it is possible for a company to increase or decrease its profit merely by changing its accounting policies. This rule does not prevent a company from changing its accounting policies where there are good reasons for doing so.

2.102 Consistency is also a fundamental accounting concept set out in SSAP 2. This concept provides that "*there is consistency of accounting treatment of like items within each accounting period and from one period to the next*". [SSAP 2 para 14].

2.103 The ASB's draft Statement of principles also identifies comparability as a qualitative characteristic of financial statements. Sensible comparisons can only be made between the results and position of different years for the same entity or between different entities, if the financial statements are prepared on a consistent basis and the accounting policies, including changes to accounting policies, are adequately disclosed.

2.104 However, whilst consistency is a fundamental principle so far as an individual company's financial statements is concerned, since some accounting standards contain alternative treatments that are each permissible (such as the different treatments of goodwill permitted by SSAP 22), it can be difficult to ensure consistency between different companies.

Accounting policies

2.105 The notes to the financial statements must set out the accounting policies the company has adopted in determining the amounts to be included in the financial statements. [4 Sch 36].

2.106 Legal advice obtained by the FRRP confirmed that this requirement is separate from, and in addition to, the requirement in paragraph 36A to state in the financial statements whether they have been prepared in accordance with applicable accounting standards and to give the particulars and reasons for any material departures from these standards (see para 2.37). Therefore, in addition to the paragraph 36A requirement, there must be stated in the financial statements both the accounting policies adopted as the result of applying accounting standards and those, not covered by standards, that a company chooses to adopt.

2.107 Accounting policies are defined in SSAP 2 as *"...the specific accounting bases selected and consistently followed by a business enterprise as being, in the opinion of the management, appropriate to its circumstances and best suited to present fairly its results and financial position"*. [SSAP 2 para 16]. The consistent application of accounting policy is also required by the Act. Paragraph 11 of Schedule 4 states "*Accounting policies shall be applied consistently within the same accounts and from one financial year to the next*".

2.108 The standard requires companies to disclose by way of a note to their financial statements the accounting policies they judge to be either material or critical in determining the profit or loss for the year and also in stating the financial position at the end of the year. The explanations should be clear, fair, and as brief as possible. [SSAP 2 para 18]. However, the explanation of accounting treatments must be adequate to ensure users understand their effect. This requirement was highlighted in the Review Panel's press release concerning Williamson Tea Holdings plc in 1992. The company was criticised for providing inadequate explanations of certain of its accounting policies and subsequently agreed to provide further explanations in its financial statements for the next financial year.

2.109 The standard gives some examples of matters for which different accounting bases are recognised and that may have a material effect both on reported results and on the financial position. These matters include:

- Depreciation of fixed assets.
- Treatment and amortisation of intangibles, such as, research and development expenditure, patents and trademarks.
- Stocks.
- Long-term contracts.
- Deferred taxation.
- Hire purchase or instalment transactions.
- Leasing and rental transactions.
- Conversion of foreign currencies.
- Repairs and renewals.
- Consolidation policies.
- Property development transactions.
- Warranties for products or services.

This list is not exhaustive and it will vary according to the nature of the company's operations. [SSAP 2 para 13]. In particular, the Act requires disclosure of the method of determining the provision for both depreciation and for diminution in value of assets and the method of translating foreign currency amounts into sterling. [4 Sch 36, 58(1)]. Also, certain accounting standards, for example SSAP 24, 'Accounting for pension costs', require disclosure of the policy adopted.

2.110 Once set, accounting policies should be applied consistently from transaction to transaction and from year to year. There are, of course, circumstances where a change of accounting policy is justified. For example, consider a company that has formerly written off both research and development expenditure at the time the expenditure was incurred. If the company determined to embark on a large-scale programme of research and development, it may decide to change its policy to one of capitalising development expenditure that meets the criteria set out in SSAP 13. In these circumstances, a change in accounting policy would be permitted by the Act. Companies should change an accounting policy only if it can be justified on the grounds that the new policy is preferable to the one it replaces because it will give a fairer presentation of the results and of the financial position of the business. The disclosure required when there is a change in accounting policy is considered in more detail in chapter 7.

Prudence

2.111 A company must use a prudent basis in determining the amount of any item that it includes in its financial statements. [4 Sch 12]. The Act specifies two particular rules in relation to this. The first is that the profit and loss account may include only those profits that have been realised at the balance sheet date. [4 Sch 12(a)]. This means that profits may not be anticipated and so they should be included only when they are earned. For this purpose, realised profits are defined as:

> *"Such profits ... of the company as fall to be treated as realised in accordance with principles generally accepted, at the time when the accounts are prepared, with respect to the determination for accounting purposes of realised profits ..."* [Sec 262(3)].

2.112 This definition may at first sight appear to be rather too general to be useful. However, a company must determine whether a profit or a loss is realised or unrealised in the light of generally accepted accounting practice at the time. Under SSAP 2, 'realised' effectively means realised in the form either of cash or of other assets, whose ultimate cash realisation can be assessed with reasonable certainty. The concepts of 'realised' and 'distributable' profits are considered further in chapters 3 and 19.

2.113 The second rule that the Act specifies in connection with the prudence concept relates to liabilities and losses. A company must take account of all liabilities and losses that either have already arisen, or are likely to arise, in respect of either the financial year in question or a previous financial year. Moreover, they must be included even when they become apparent only in the period between the balance sheet date and the date on which the directors sign the financial statements. [4 Sch 12(b)]. This means, for example, that if a major debtor becomes insolvent after the balance sheet date, and if the directors have not already signed the financial statements in accordance with section 233 of the Act, the resulting loss must be reflected in the financial statements. However, this requirement deals with losses and liabilities relating to the financial year in question, or a previous financial year and does not extend to anticipating losses and liabilities relating to future years.

2.114 The ASB's draft Statement of principles identifies reliability as a primary quality of financial statements. Reliable information needs to be unbiased and neutral. In this context, prudence is the exercise of a degree of caution in making judgements that determine the amount at which items are stated in the financial statements. Prudence requires stronger evidence for the recognition of gains than for the recognition of losses or liabilities. However, in terms of the draft Statement of principles, prudence does not extend to recognising liabilities or losses that do not represent obligations or commitments resulting from past transactions or events. Neither does it justify understating asset values by making excessive write-downs.

2.115 Recent accounting standards have set rules about when companies should make provision for losses and liabilities that are likely to occur in the future as a result of management decisions in certain areas. FRS 3 deals with provisions in the context of the decision to sell or terminate an operation. Provision for the direct costs of the sale or termination and for future operating losses should not be made until there is a demonstrable commitment to the sale or termination. [FRS 3 para 18]. FRS 7 prevents provisions for future losses or reorganisation costs from being included in the fair value exercise as liabilities acquired since it argues that they are not liabilities of the acquired undertaking at the date of the acquisition. [FRS 7 para 7]. The ASB has a project underway that deals with all aspects of provisioning.

2.116 Application of the draft Statement of principles may also result in companies recognising certain anticipated costs and losses later than they might have done if prudence were the only consideration. Provisions would only be recognised when the company is committed to the course of action which results in the loss or liability. This would prevent directors from setting up large provisions in respect of decisions they have taken, but to which they have not committed the company, for example, by making a public announcement.

2.117 In October 1994, the FASB published a research study, 'Future events: A conceptual study of their significance for recognition and measurement' which was produced by an international working group comprising representatives from the US, UK, Australia, Canada and the IASC. The study examines the question of whether and when financial statements should reflect future events. The concept of prudence is, therefore, under review as part of the framework of financial reporting. There is likely to be a trend towards greater neutrality in financial reporting, although greater evidence will still be required for the recognition of gains than losses.

Accruals

2.118 The financial statements must reflect all income and expenditure that relate to the financial year in question. This applies irrespective of the dates on which amounts fall due to be received or paid. [4 Sch 13]. The resulting difference between cash transactions and amounts recognised under the accruals basis must be shown as either an accrual or a prepayment.

2.119 This concept is expanded in SSAP 2 which considers that revenue and expenses should also be "...matched with one another so far as their relationship can be established or justifiably assumed, and dealt with in the profit and loss account of the period to which they relate". [SSAP 2 para 14]. However, this 'matching concept' is distinguishable from the accruals concept. Income and its related expenditure can be matched together in the profit and loss account, but this will only produce the correct result if the income and expense are recognised in the period in which the related transaction or event occurs.

2.120 The Act is silent as to what happens where the accruals concept is inconsistent with the prudence concept, such as where significant uncertainties exist about whether an item should be recognised, as can occur with revenue recognition. SSAP 2, however, makes it quite clear that, in that circumstance, the prudence concept prevails. Revenue recognition issues are discussed in detail in chapter 3.

Separate valuation

2.121 When a company is determining the aggregate amount of any item, it must determine separately the amount of each individual asset or liability that makes up that item. [4 Sch 14]. Although this rule is not described in SSAP 2 as a fundamental accounting concept, it has long been regarded as good accounting practice.

2.122 The treatment of investments is a good example of the separate valuation principle, although the general principle applies equally to other items, such as stocks. Those investments that are treated as fixed assets will normally be accounted for at cost, less write-downs for any permanent decrease in value. Before the implementation of the separate valuation rules in the Companies Act 1981, investments (and particularly parents' investments in subsidiaries) were sometimes considered as a whole. If one investment had a market value that was less than book value, and all the other investments had an excess of market value over book value that more than compensated, it was argued that the investments as a whole were not overstated at book value and, therefore, no provision against the one overstated investment was necessary.

2.123 However, under the 1985 Act, investments have to be considered individually. By law, a provision must be made against an investment if there is a permanent decrease in value below cost. This applies irrespective of the value and the quality of the other investments.

2.124 The only statutory exception to the separate valuation rule is that tangible assets and raw materials and consumables may, in certain circumstances, be included in the financial statements at a fixed quantity and value (see chapter 5). [4 Sch 25(1)].

2.125 Where there is a legal right of set-off, assets and liabilities should, in some circumstances, be netted because they do not constitute separate assets and liabilities. The rules concerning the set off of assets and liabilities have been reinforced by FRS 5. This is considered in detail in chapter 4.

Substance over form

2.126 Accounting for transactions according to their substance rather than their legal form was first explicitly adopted in 1984 in SSAP 21 'Accounting for leases and hire purchase contracts'. This standard requires companies to capitalise assets held under finance leases rather than just charging lease payments when made to the profit and loss account. Since then the significance of substance over form for the true and fair view has been recognised more fully. The rapid innovation in financial markets during the

1980s led to arrangements for financing a company's operations which, if they were accounted for in accordance with their legal form, would result in the finance not appearing on the company's balance sheet.

2.127 FRS 5, 'Reporting the substance of transactions', was the eventual result of the debate in the profession on the issue of substance over form. The intention of this standard is not to change the accounting treatment of the majority of transactions. However, for more complex transactions, their true commercial substance may not be adequately expressed by their legal form and in these situations it would not be sufficient to account for them by recording that legal form. Therefore, the need to account for a transaction in accordance with its substance is a consequence of the concept of 'true and fair'.

2.128 In the terms of the draft Statement of principles, in order for financial statements to be reliable, they must faithfully represent the transactions that the entity has entered into, the resources at the entity's disposal and how these resources were financed. Thus, an emphasis on substance over legal form is now established as an important accounting concept.

Accounting conventions

2.129 All accounting systems depend on the capital maintenance concept adopted, the basis used to value assets and the unit of measurement used. The different options available for each of these components are considered briefly in this section.

Capital maintenance concepts

2.130 Capital maintenance is linked with the measurement of accounting profit. Disregarding additions to capital or repayments of capital and distributions, accounting profit is the difference between a company's capital at the start of the period and at the end of the period. A company can only be considered to have made a profit if it has increased its net assets, which are represented by its capital, over and above that necessary to maintain its opening capital. Thus profit can be measured only once a definition has been established as to what capital is to be maintained.

2.131 There are at least two different concepts of capital maintenance: operating capital maintenance and financial capital maintenance. Operating capital maintenance, although it can be measured in a variety of different ways, generally seeks to ensure that the business' physical operating capacity is preserved. Financial capital maintenance attempts to conserve the value of the funds that shareholders have invested in the business. Financial capital maintained can either be the monetary value of capital attributable to shareholders or a value adjusted by a general purchasing power index to maintain capital as a fund of real purchasing power. Consider the following example.

Example

A sole trader starts a business buying and selling second-hand cars. In his first year of trading he buys one car for £1,000 and sells it for £2,000. At the time he sells the car, the cost of buying an equivalent car is £1,200 and general inflation between the dates of buying and selling is 10%. Under monetary capital maintenance, maintenance of the general purchasing power of financial capital and operating capital maintenance the trader's profit and loss account would be as follows:

Capital maintenance concepts	Financial capital maintenance		Operating
	Monetary capital	General purchasing power	capital maintenance
	£	£	£
Sales	2,000	2,000	2,000
Cost of sales	(1,000)	(1,000)	(1,200)
Operating profit	1,000	1,000	800
Inflation adjustment to opening capital	–	(100)	–
Total gain	1,000	900	800

Monetary financial capital maintenance, which is the basis most commonly used in accounting, takes no account of the effects of inflation. The profit of £1,000 is the amount in excess of the original capital of the business. In the second column the inflation adjustment shows the effect of the general increase in prices on the opening financial capital of £1,000 and seeks to ensure that profit is only measured after preserving the opening capital in the business in terms of its general purchasing power. The profit of £900 leaves capital of £1,100 in the business to maintain its purchasing power. Operating capital maintenance, on the other hand, is concerned with preserving the productive capacity of the business. In this example, this is the trader's ability to replace the item of stock sold. Under operating capital maintenance, the trader has a profit of £800 and capital in the business of £1,200 which is sufficient to purchase a car to begin the next period's trade.

Valuation bases

2.132 The measurement of profit is also affected by the valuation basis chosen. Assets can either be valued at their historical cost or their current cost. In both instances, assets are stated at this cost less depreciation or provision for permanent diminution in value. Current cost is the value of the asset to the business. However, valuing assets at current cost does not result in a balance sheet that reflects the total worth of the business. Valuation bases are considered further in chapter 5.

Units of measurement

2.133 The unit of measurement chosen affects how profit is determined. Companies can choose between reporting in nominal pounds (or other currency) or in units of constant purchasing power. Financial statements for two different years may be denominated in pounds, but because of inflation, the purchasing power of these pounds is not the same. The use of a unit of constant purchasing power eliminates these difficulties in comparability. One method is the unit of *current* purchasing power. All non-monetary assets and liabilities relating to dates prior to the reporting date are restated by reference to movements in a general price index, such as the retail price index, into the value of pounds at the reporting date. During the 1970s an attempt was made to establish a method of accounting for inflation that involved companies restating their financial statements into units of current purchasing power. The result was a short-lived accounting standard, 'Provisional SSAP 7', which is discussed in chapter 5.

Conventions

2.134 Capital maintenance concepts, asset valuation bases, and the units of measurement used can be combined in different ways to create different accounting conventions. Theoretically the options outlined above would result in many different accounting conventions, but not all the combinations are sensible. The more common conventions are summarised below and considered in more detail in chapter 5.

Historical cost convention

2.135 The most common accounting convention is the historical cost convention. This convention values assets at their historical cost, operates financial capital maintenance and uses the nominal pound as its unit of measurement. Although this convention is familiar to all accountants, when prices are rising, historical cost accounting may distort reported profits and balance sheet values. Historical cost accounting, being simple and relatively well understood, is useful for preparing stewardship accounts. It is perhaps less useful for making investment decisions or decisions about amounts to distribute. In the example in paragraph 2.131 above, if the trader had taken the profit of £1,000 for his own use, there would not be sufficient funds in the business for it to continue to trade at the same level.

Modified historical cost convention

2.136 Sometimes the historical cost convention is modified by the revaluation of certain fixed assets. Modified historical cost accounting operates financial capital maintenance and uses the pound as its unit of measurement, but certain fixed assets, usually land and buildings, are included at a valuation above historical cost. This gives some indication of the value to the business of some of the assets employed. The unrealised gains as a result of revaluing assets are generally not recognised in the profit and loss account. This suggests that the gain is an element of the capital of the business that must be retained in order to maintain the business' operating capacity, although no formalised attempt is made to employ operating capital maintenance. In addition, not all companies revalue their assets and not all companies that revalue their assets do so on a regular basis. Therefore, comparability between different companies is reduced and, if valuations are allowed to become out of date, their usefulness as an indication of the value of the assets to the business diminishes. The ASB is considering these problems as part of its project on valuations which is discussed in chapter 5.

Current purchasing power

2.137 The current purchasing power (CPP) convention also values assets at their historical cost and operates financial capital maintenance. CPP, however, uses a unit of constant purchasing power rather than the nominal pound for measurement. Therefore, all non-monetary items in the financial statements, including capital, are restated by reference to a general price index. While this maintains capital in terms of what shareholders can do with their funds in the economy as a whole, the general price index used may not move the same way as the input prices specific to the company. Therefore, the resulting asset values may bear no relationship to their current value to the business; moreover, the capital maintained may be either too much or too little to maintain the operating capacity of the business. In the example in paragraph 2.131 above, the increase in the general price index was less than the increase specific to second hand cars. As a result, if the trader had taken all the CPP profit out of the business, he would not have had sufficient capital to replace his stock.

2.138 The principal current example of the use of CPP accounting is in the countries that experience hyper-inflation. IAS 29, 'Financial reporting in hyper-inflationary economies', gives guidance in this area (see also chapter 29).

Current cost accounting

2.139 Current cost accounting conventions value assets at their current value to the business. Although this is often combined with operating capital maintenance and measurement in pounds it can also be combined with financial capital maintenance and units of constant purchasing power. Since combining current costs with nominal pounds usually results in useful information, the additional complexity introduced by using units of constant purchasing power is often not warranted except in trend information. Current cost operating profit shows the current trading margin achieved by the business since it charges the costs incurred at the prices applying when the sales were made. Put another way, it takes inflationary 'holding gains' out of the measurement of income. It gives an indication of the companies' ability to generate profits from its current operations and also maintains its current operating capacity. In the operating capital maintenance example in paragraph 2.131, the operating profit is lower than under financial capital maintenance. This allows sufficient capital to be retained to replace stock and continue trading and may also give a more forward-looking perspective on future profits.

Frameworks for setting accounting standards

Background to the frameworks

2.140 The tradition in many countries, such as most of continental Europe, is that accounting rules should be made by parliaments or committees under government control. Given that accounting is closely related to the collection of tax, the distribution of profits and the protection of creditors, there are clear arguments for this control of accounting by the state in the public interest. This tradition can be seen at work in the EU, which uses governmental processes which lead to harmonising laws on accounting, such as the Companies Acts 1981 and 1989.

2.141 By contrast, the tradition in the English-speaking world is to see accounting as a technical tool designed to be commercially useful. If the capital market needs extensive audited accounting information, it will be in the interests of the relevant companies to provide it. Consequently, such rules as are necessary should be created to enable, rather than to control, accounting.

2.142 Of course, even in this tradition, governments may feel obliged to intervene in accounting, in order to protect the public interest, such as creditors or the customers of banks. The intervention usually follows a crisis. For example, compulsory audit of banks was introduced in Britain soon after the collapse of the City of Glasgow Bank in 1878. Most spectacularly, the Securities and Exchange Commission in the US was created in order to protect investors after the Wall Street crash of 1929.

2.143 Despite many such interventions, the creation of accounting rules (though not necessarily the enforcement of them) is still largely in the hands of accountants rather than governments throughout the English-speaking world. At first, the 'rules' were unpromulgated 'best practice', but gradually the accountancy profession wrote the rules down; for example, as 'Accounting research bulletins' from the 1930s in the US or as 'Recommendations' from the 1940s in the UK.

2.144 However, this system gradually came to be criticised on the grounds that the interests of the professional rule makers (mostly representatives of large audit firms and large companies) are different from the public interest, in particular the preparers and users of financial statements. The criticisms reached a crescendo in the US in the early

1970s. This led to two investigations set up by the profession: the Wheat Committee and the Trueblood Committee.

2.145 Wheat recommended that standard setting should be taken away from the profession and given to an independent body. Trueblood recommended that a vital philosophical support for an independent standard setter should be a 'conceptual framework'. It was argued that, in the absence of democratic election, the authority of standard setters needs to rest on independence backed up by due process, openness of procedure and an overt statement of objectives and fundamental principles.

2.146 These recommendations led to the setting up of the Financial Accounting Standards Board (FASB) in 1973 and to its major project which led to the 'Statements of financial accounting concepts'. Parts of a conceptual framework had been published by the FASB's predecessor, the Accounting Principles Board, in the 1960s, but a full framework was not published until the 1980s.

2.147 Meanwhile, in the UK, the ASC had been established in 1969, with no overt conceptual framework. The ASC was often criticised for standards which were not coherent or consistent. As the authority of the ASC came increasingly into question in the 1980s, some attention was given to conceptual frameworks. Indeed, in 1989, the ASC acknowledged the existence of the IASC's 'Framework for the preparation and presentation of financial statements' which had been published in that year. The IASC's framework clearly derives from that of the FASB, to some extent *via* the Australian version.

2.148 The criticisms of standard setting in the UK in the late 1980s were similar to those in the US in the early 1970s, and the solutions were similar also. Consequently, when the ASB was set up in the UK in 1990, it was no surprise that it immediately began to work on a draft of a 'Statement of principles' which is very close to the documents mentioned above.

The FASB's framework

2.149 The FASB's definition of a conceptual framework is *"a constitution, a coherent system of interrelated objectives and fundamentals that can lead to consistent standards and that prescribes the nature, function, and limits of financial accounting and financial statements"*. Two of the main purposes of the framework would be to guide the FASB when setting standards and to help preparers in the absence of specific rules.

2.150 By the mid-1980s, the FASB had constructed its framework of four statements of financial accounting concepts:

- SFAC 1, 'Objectives of financial reporting'.
- SFAC 2, 'Qualitative characteristics of accounting information'.
- SFAC 3 (replaced by SFAC 6), 'Elements of financial statements'.
- SFAC 5, 'Recognition and measurement'.

There is also an SFAC 4 which relates to objectives for financial statements of non-business enterprises.

2.151 SFAC 1 concentrates on the use of financial statements by investors and creditors for the purpose of making financial decisions. Consequently, financial statements should help users to assess 'the amounts, timing, and uncertainty of prospective net cash inflows'. This is a clear statement that financial reporting is mainly about decision making, which is forward looking, rather than being about stewardship, which is backward looking. The implications of this are fundamental. For example, current values would seem more suitable than historical costs.

2.152 SFAC 2 concludes that decision usefulness rests on the relevance and reliability of financial information. Comparability and consistency will help this. Various qualitative characteristics are also implied:

Relevance requires:

- Predictive value.
- Feedback value.
- Timeliness.

Reliability requires:

- Verifiability.
- Neutrality.
- Representational faithfulness.

2.153 SFAC 6 (replacing SFAC 3) defines ten elements of financial statements:

(i)	Assets.
(ii)	Liabilities.
(iii)	Equity, which is (i) – (ii).
(iv & v)	Investments by owners and distributions to owners.
(vi)	Comprehensive income, which comprises.
(vii to x)	Revenues and gains less expenses and losses.

2.154 The definitions from (iii) to (x) rest on the definitions of assets and liabilities. Assets are *"...probable future economic benefits obtained or controlled by a particular entity as a result of past transactions or events"*. Liabilities are

"...probable future sacrifices of economic benefits arising from present obligations of a particular entity to transfer assets or provide services to other entities in the future as a result of past transactions or events". Equity is defined effectively in terms of net assets; revenues in terms of increases in assets or reductions in liabilities; and so on.

2.155 SFAC 5 concerns recognition and measurement. This should be the point at which the really difficult conclusions and the practical implications become clear. However, SFAC 5 is indecisive, for example, between fair values and historical costs. The danger of coming to clear conclusions in SFAC 5 would have been that revolutionary changes to current practices would have seemed necessary. The FASB obviously prefers modest evolutionary steps.

IASC's framework

2.156 As mentioned earlier, the IASC's framework of 1989 owes a considerable debt to the FASB's. The purposes, coverage and conclusions of the two frameworks are broadly similar. The main headings of the IASC's framework are:

- Preface, including a decision usefulness stance.
- Introduction, including comments on the purpose of the framework and the needs of users (who are assumed to be investors or those with similar needs to investors).
- Objectives of financial statements, including a concentration on assessment of future cash flows.
- Underlying assumptions, including the accrual basis and the going concern convention.
- Qualitative characteristics, including understandability, relevance, reliability, comparability and fairness.
- Elements of financial statements, including financial position (assets, liabilities and equity) and performance (income and expenses).
- Recognition of elements, including probability of future benefit, reliability of measurement, and recognition of assets, liabilities, income and expenses.
- Measurement of elements, including an inconclusive discussion on historical cost and its alternatives.

- Concepts of capital and its maintenance, including a further inconclusive discussion on financial as opposed to physical capital maintenance.

2.157 It will be useful here to examine in some more detail the three longer sections of the framework, that is those on qualitative characteristics, elements, and recognition.

Qualitative characteristics

2.158 The four main characteristics are understandability, relevance, reliability and comparability. Understandability allows for reasonable expertise on the part of the users. Relevance suggests the ability to influence users' economic decisions by helping or confirming the evaluation of events of the past, present or future. A subsidiary concept here is materiality which provides a *"threshold or cut-off point"* for relevance.

2.159 Reliability is required before information can be useful. This, in turn, requires information to be *"free from material error and bias"*. It is also necessary for the information to give a faithful representation of the transactions or other events it purports to represent. This requires presentation in accordance with substance not legal form. The freedom from bias (or neutrality) may have to be tempered by prudence because of uncertainties. However, prudence does not allow *"hidden reserves or excess provisions, the deliberate understatement of assets or income, or the deliberate overstatement of liabilities or expenses"*. Finally, reliability requires completeness, restrained by considerations of materiality and cost.

2.160 The fourth characteristic is comparability, over time and from one company to another. This clearly requires consistency and the disclosure of accounting policies and any changes in them. It also requires disclosure of corresponding figures for previous periods.

2.161 A constraint on reliability is timeliness. A constraint on standard setters and preparers is a consideration of costs compared to benefits. It may also be necessary to trade off the loss of a degree of one characteristic with a gain of a degree of another. This requires professional judgement. If all this is done properly, it will generally lead to a true and fair view or a fair presentation.

Elements of financial statements

2.162 Like the FASB's framework, all the other definitions rest on those for assets and liabilities. An asset is *"...a resource controlled by the enterprise as a result of past events and from which future economic benefits are expected to flow"*.

2.163 This definition may be compared with that of the FASB outlined earlier. The IASC's definition seems neater because the asset is, presumably, not the benefits but the thing from which the benefits flow. In practice, there seems to be no difference, and the FASB's SFAC 6 does say that 'resources' and 'assets' are much the same thing.

2.164 The future economic benefits may come from assisting in production or in the direct increase of cash. The framework stresses economic substance over legal form and reminds us that not all assets and liabilities will meet the criteria for recognition (discussed in para 2.170 below).

2.165 The IASC's definition of liability is *"a present obligation ... arising from past events, the settlement of which is expected to result in an outflow ... of resources embodying economic benefits"*.

2.166 Again, this definition seems to run more smoothly than the FASB's by being based on the obligation rather than the sacrifice of benefits. Obligations do not have to be legally binding, but they do not include future commitments. Liabilities include those provisions which require estimation.

2.167 Equity is a residual item; that is, net assets. However, it can be sub-classified into various types of capital and reserves. These can reflect legal restrictions or differing rights of various owners.

2.168 The income and expense elements of performance are also measured in terms of assets and liabilities. Income is measured by increases in assets or decreases in liabilities other than those relating to equity participants. Expenses are the reverse.

2.169 Sub-components of income are:

- Revenue from the ordinary activities of the enterprise.
- Gains such as the disposal of fixed assets which may be ordinary or otherwise.

Income also includes unrealised gains, although of course these may not be recognised. Similarly, expenses include realised and unrealised losses.

Recognition

2.170 The IASC's framework calls for recognition of elements when:

- it is probable that any future economic benefit associated with the item will flow to or from the enterprise; and
- the item has a cost or value that can be measured with reliability.

2.171 Some uncertainty surrounds the meaning of 'probable'. Some see it as including 51 per cent likelihood, others feel that a higher threshold is required for asset or income recognition. Unrecognised elements may often need to be disclosed in the notes.

2.172 The greatest detail in the recognition section is given to the discussion of expenses. Matching is considered an important process here, but it should not be allowed to lead to the recognition of assets or liabilities which do not meet the definitions of those elements. Another point is that expenses may need to be allocated in a systematic and rational way if the flow of related benefits is unclear.

2.173 Also, expenses should be recognised immediately when costs do not lead to future benefits which qualify as assets or when liabilities are incurred without a related asset.

Presentation of financial statements

2.174 To some extent the above ideas have been taken further by the IASC with its 'presentation' project, for which a draft statement of principles was published in 1995. The draft was finalised in August 1997 and issued as IAS 1 (revised), 'Presentation of financial statements'. The statement becomes effective for accounting periods beginning on or after 1 July 1998 and will significantly improve the quality and comparability of financial statements prepared in compliance with IASs. IAS 1 is discussed further in chapter 6.

The ASB's draft Statement of principles

2.175 The ASB's draft Statement of principles acknowledges the previous work of other standard setters, including the FASB. As a deliberate policy, the ASB decided to use the words of the IASC framework wherever possible.

2.176 There are seven chapters in the ASB's statement. These were issued in draft from 1991 onwards. A complete exposure draft of the statement was issued in November 1995. Some parts of the exposure draft present a fairly radical agenda for the future direction of financial reporting. However, the ASB promises that changes will be evolutionary rather than revolutionary. The Statement of principles will not be an accounting standard and will not override the requirements of any accounting standard or the law. In fact, there are some significant conflicts between the principles as set out in the exposure draft and companies legislation in the UK. The seven chapters are:

- Objective of financial statements.
- Qualitative characteristics of financial information.
- Elements of financial statements.
- Recognition in financial statements.
- Measurement in financial statements.
- Presentation of financial information.
- The reporting entity.

[The next page is 2043.]

Objective

2.177 Here the ASB is closely in line with the IASC, in identifying present and potential investors as the target (or the proxy for other targets) of financial statements. The ASB has included in the objective the role of financial statements for assessing the stewardship of management as well as their usefulness for making economic decisions. The ASB specifically identifies information on 'financial adaptability' as being useful for economic decisions. Financial adaptability is described as the ability of an enterprise to alter its cash flows so that it can respond to unexpected events and opportunities.

Qualitative characteristics

2.178 Like the FASB, the ASB identifies relevance and reliability as the primary characteristics relating to the content of financial information. Relevance has predictive and confirmatory aspects. Reliability requires faithful representation (which requires an emphasis on substance), neutrality (that is, freedom from bias), prudence and completeness.

2.179 Primary characteristics relating to how information is presented in financial statements, which follow from the above two, are comparability (which includes consistency and disclosure of policies and changes in them) and understandability. Taking these four characteristics together, the package is very much the same as the IASC's four characteristics.

2.180 Again, like the IASC, the ASB recognises the need to trade relevance off against reliability, partly by considering timeliness and cost/benefit. Nevertheless, the importance of relevance seems to imply a move towards current values rather than historical costs.

2.181 The ASB has omitted the IASC's discussion of the accruals and going concern conventions on the grounds that these are measurement conventions which arise from *applying* the qualitative characteristics.

Materiality

2.182 Materiality sets the threshold for determining whether an item is relevant. The draft Statement of principles explains materiality as follows:

> *"Information is material if it could influence users' decisions taken on the basis of the financial statements. If that information is misstated or if certain information is omitted the materiality of the misstatement or omission depends on the size and nature of the item in question judged in the particular circumstances of the case."* [DSP chp 2 para 7].

2.183 An item that is not material is not relevant; it cannot influence the decisions of a user and need not be reported in financial statements. Indeed, if immaterial items are reported in financial statements, they can interfere with decision making because they may obscure the relevant information amid excessive detail. However, determining what is material is a matter of professional judgement and it would be inappropriate to set fixed monetary limits or rules.

2.184 In view of the increasing emphasis on materiality due to the draft Statement of principles and the public interest in materiality as a result of certain FRRP decisions, the Financial Reporting Committee of the ICAEW issued a statement in December 1996 which replaced the existing guidance on materiality in the ICAEW Members' Handbook. The statement, TECH 32/96, contains guidance to help those preparing financial statements decide what information is material, in the context of the principle that an item is material if it could influence users' economic decisions.

2.185 The statement stresses that any guidelines on determining what is material cannot substitute for careful consideration by preparers of how information could influence users' economic decisions such as whether to hold or sell investments or whether to reappoint or replace management. Judgements should be based on the needs of knowledgeable and diligent investors who are reasonable in their use of financial information.

2.186 The statement considers that there are three aspects to consider when deciding whether an item is material and then discusses each aspect in turn. These aspects are:

- Size. Whilst the monetary value of items needs to be taken into account, materiality can never be judged purely on the basis of absolute size, and no specific rule of thumb tests are recommended. In some cases size may in fact be irrelevant, for example, where the quality of management stewardship or corporate governance are at issue.

- Nature. Consideration needs to be given to the events or transactions giving rise to the item as well as their legality, sensitivity, normality and potential consequences. In addition, the identity of the parties involved in the events or transactions and the accounts captions and disclosure affected may also impact on users' decisions.

- Circumstances. When preparers consider the potential impact of information on users, they should not take a narrow view of the financial statements for a single period. They will often need to modify their views on the materiality of an item in the light of comparative figures, expected future trends, the financial statements of comparable entities and other information relating to the economic and industry background.

2.187 The statement emphasises management's responsibility by encouraging companies to develop internal guidelines on assessing materiality. These would provide relatively objective rebuttable presumptions against which subsequent judgements about particular situations can be gauged. The statement suggests guidelines can be developed by addressing the following questions:

- Who are the relevant users?
- What are their decision-making needs?
- For a given item, what is the appropriate context for assessing its materiality?
- In what range of values do items become critical in terms of materiality?
- How should particular items in these critical ranges be decided and reported?

2.188 Some practical examples are given of situations where preparers should be particularly sensitive in their judgements because critical thresholds are reached. These are where trends reverse, profits become losses, technical insolvency occurs, compliance with debt covenants is in doubt or where it is known that individuals are deciding whether or not to buy or sell shares.

Elements

2.189 The ASB identifies seven elements: assets; liabilities; ownership interest; gains; losses; contributions from owners; and distributions to owners. This is much the same as the IASC's five elements, because the ASB's last two are subsumed within the IASC's equity heading. Once more, all the other definitions depend on those of asset and liability which are:

> *"Assets are rights or other access to future economic benefits controlled by an entity as a result of past transactions or events."* [DSP chp 3 para 5].

> *"Liabilities are obligations of an entity to transfer economic benefits as a result of past transactions or events."* [DSP chp 3 para 21].

2.190 These are not exactly the same words as those of the FASB or the IASC, but it is hard to see any difference in effect. They are also repeated in FRS 5, which is considered in chapter 4. Ownership interest is the residual net assets.

2.191 'Gains' is the equivalent of the IASC's 'income' (which includes 'revenues' and 'gains') and of the FASB's 'revenues' and 'gains'. Somewhat similarly, 'losses' are the equivalent of the IASC's 'expenses' (which include losses) and of the FASB's 'expenses' and 'losses'. The ASB's wording is rather ungainly as it is unusual to talk, for example, of wages being a loss.

2.192 Leaving aside transfers to and from owners in their capacity as owners (for example, dividends), gains and losses can be defined as increases or decreases in ownership interest.

2.193 The definitions still leave room for interpretation and may in due course lead to changes in specific accounting standards. For example, it is not altogether clear what sort of element is the deferred income which is shown as a credit balance as a result of a government grant.

Recognition

2.194 An element (as defined above) should be recognised when there is sufficient evidence (for example, as a result of a transaction or a contract) that there has been a change in assets or liabilities which can be measured with sufficient reliability. [DSP chp 4 para 6]. As with the previous chapters of the statement of principles, there are implicit challenges to existing practices. For example, are SSAP 21's operating leases recognisable assets and liabilities? They appear to fit the definitions of the elements and to meet the 'evidence' threshold for recognition. Indeed, the draft Statement of principles acknowledges this and states that the lessee should recognise an asset (the rights to use the leased property) and a liability (the obligation to pay the rentals) at the time of delivery of any leased property.

2.195 Chapter 4 of the draft Statement of principles also deals with de-recognition, (which should occur when any of the criteria for recognition no longer apply) and subsequent remeasurement (which should occur when changes in assets and liabilities can be measured reliably). This seems to imply a move towards greater use of current values. Uncertainty is to be dealt with by prudent application of the recognition criteria. There are lengthy explanations of these criteria.

Measurement

2.196 Chapter 5 describes the pros and cons of historical cost versus current value accounting. The ASB declares its hand by stating that practice should develop by evolving in the direction of greater use of current values, which it believes are more relevant than historical costs for depicting a company's resources, subject to reliability and cost-benefit considerations.

Presentation

2.197 Chapter 6 examines considerations that should guide the presentation of financial statements: aggregation; classification; structure; articulation; disclosure of policies; notes; and supplementary information. The major financial statements are analysed as to purpose and resulting implications.

2.198 Controversially, the exposure draft seeks to redefine the roles of the profit and loss account and the SORG. The previous discussion draft contained a useful discussion of the meaning of 'realised' profits for identifying gains that should be included in the profit and loss account. In the exposure draft the ASB has abandoned the distinction between realised and unrealised gains as a basis for presenting profits in the primary statements and suggests that this can be dealt with adequately in the note of historical cost profits and losses. The suggestion is that:

- Gains and losses on assets and liabilities that are held on a continuing basis, primarily in order to enable the trading operations to be carried out, should be reported in the SORG and not in the profit and loss account. (As an example, all profits and losses on disposals of fixed assets, as well as revaluation gains and losses, would be reported in the SORG.)
- All other gains and losses should be reported in the profit and loss account. (An example would be gains resulting from marking to market current asset investments that are readily marketable.)

2.199 The ASB's vision is that the profit and loss account should be primarily an operating statement. All gains and losses relating to capital items should be shown in the SORG.

2.200 There is no direct equivalent to this chapter in the IASC or FASB frameworks.

The reporting entity

2.201 The last chapter also has no equivalent in the IASC or FASB frameworks. It explains the rationale behind consolidated accounts, equity accounting and proportional consolidation.

2.202 An issue here is the boundary of the reporting entity, particularly when that entity is a group. The main criterion for inclusion within the boundary is control, whether of assets or entities, which requires both *"(a) the ability to deploy the economic resources, or direct the entities; and (b) the ability to ensure that any resulting benefits accrue to itself (with corresponding exposure to losses), and to restrict the access of others to those benefits."* [DSP chp 7 para 10].

2.203 The greatest difficulty in applying these ideas occurs with associates and joint ventures, where there is something less than full control. The ASB argues that equity accounting, rather than proportional consolidation, is appropriate for most associates and joint ventures. Proportional consolidation would be used only where an investor has a direct interest in assets, liabilities and cash flows of a joint venture, rather than a share in the joint venture itself as an entity.

IASC standard setting

2.204 In Sydney in 1972, a world congress of accountants was held, at which discussions leading to the IASC's formation were conducted. The late Sir Henry (later Lord) Benson played a leading role in this, and he became IASC's first chairman. The IASC began work in 1973. Its aims are: *"to formulate and publish in the public interest accounting standards to be observed in the presentation of financial statements and to promote their worldwide acceptance and observance, and to work generally for the improvement and harmonisation of regulations, accounting standards and procedures relating to the presentation of financial statements"*. [IASC preface 1982].

2.205 The members of the IASC are professional bodies throughout the world (more than 120 of them from more than 90 countries). They promise to *"use their best endeavours"* to persuade national standard setters to publish statements in accord with IASs and to work for acceptance of IASs by companies, auditors and exchange regulators.

2.206 The IASC is independent from other bodies, but from 1983 a close relationship with the International Federation of Accountants (IFAC) was forged, whereby the two bodies work together, but in different fields. For example, IFAC deals with auditing standards. The member bodies of IFAC and IASC are identical, and part of the funding of IASC comes through IFAC. The founder members of IASC were professional accountancy bodies from:

- Australia.
- Canada.
- France.
- Germany (Federal Republic).
- Japan.
- Mexico.
- The Netherlands.
- UK and Ireland.
- USA.

2.207 In 1998, all of these are Board members, although Ireland is not now officially part of the UK membership. The remaining seven current Board members are:

- India (with Sri Lanka).
- Malaysia.

- Nordic Federation of Public Accountants.
- South Africa (with Zimbabwe).
- International Co-ordinating Committee of Financial Analysts' Associations.
- Federation of Swiss Industrial Holding Companies.
- International Association of Financial Executives Institutes.

2.208 The Board generally meets for about one week, three times per year. Usually this meeting includes a day with an eclectic Consultative Group, including the International Organization of Securities Commissions (IOSCO), the UN, the OECD and the EU. A two-thirds majority of the Board is necessary to issue an exposure draft and a three-quarters majority for a standard.

2.209 In order to make progress, the Board often had to retain some widely used options in its standards so that sufficient Board votes could be obtained and so that companies in many countries could follow IASs without too great a difficulty.

2.210 In order to advance the IASC's work, it was decided in the late 1980s to begin a programme of reviewing major standards in order to improve them, particularly by removing as many options as possible, so that IASs constituted a tighter set of standards. This was called the comparability or improvements project. One objective was to persuade securities regulators, particularly IOSCO and its US member the SEC, to accept financial statements drawn up in accordance with IASs for multinational listings. Such statements are already accepted on several exchanges (for example, London), but not on others (for example, New York).

2.211 The IASC published its comparability exposure draft (E32) in 1989. This led to the release of many exposure drafts and standards in the subsequent years. The process was completed at the end of 1993 with the issue of ten revised standards. A new feature of the revised standards (and subsequent standards) is that any remaining options are specifically pointed out and divided between 'benchmark treatments' and 'allowed alternatives'. Companies must disclose their accounting policies, although in most cases numerical reconciliation to the benchmark is not required. An exception to this is that those adopting the 'last in, first out' (LIFO) allowed alternative for inventory valuation under IAS 2 must disclose the numerical effect of this.

2.212 IOSCO responded in 1994 to the IASC's completion of its improvements project by recommending its members to accept IAS 7 (cash flow statements) and by giving the IASC a list of further topics and amendments to be completed before the full package of IASs could be recommended. The SEC also now accepts IAS 7 statements and recognises elements of some other IASs (for example, the goodwill treatment in IAS 22).

2.213 At an IOSCO meeting in Paris in July 1995, a joint press release was issued by IOSCO and the IASC. IOSCO accepted that IASC's work programme (with a target date for completion in 1998) will lead to a comprehensive core set of standards, which should allow IOSCO to recommend endorsement of them for cross-border listing purposes world wide. This process is now almost complete, with the issue of IAS 37 and IAS 38 in September 1998. The last remaining topic is financial instruments, on which an exposure draft was issued in April 1998 and a standard is planned for December 1998. Whether IOSCO will endorse this resulting package of standards is still unclear.

Annex – Counsel's opinions on 'true and fair'

The Accounting Standards Committee – Joint Opinion

1 The Accounting Standards Committee ("ASC") from time to time issues Statements of Standard Accounting Practice ("SSAPs"). These are declared in the Explanatory Foreword to be "methods of accounting approved . . . for application to all financial accounts intended to give a true and fair view of financial position and profit or loss." They are not intended to be "a comprehensive code of rigid rules" but departures from them should be disclosed and explained. The Committee also noted in its Explanatory Foreword that "methods of financial accounting evolve and alter in response to changing business and economic needs. From time to time new accounting standards will be drawn at progressive levels, and established standards will be reviewed with the object of improvement in the light of new needs and developments."

2 The ASC has recently undertaken a review of the standard setting process and decided that future standards will "deal only with those matters which are of major and fundamental importance and affect the generality of companies" but that, as in the past, the standards will apply "to all accounts which are intended to show a true and fair view of financial position and profit or loss". A SSAP is therefore a declaration by the ASC, on behalf of its constituent professional bodies, that save in exceptional circumstances, accounts which do not comply with the standard will not give a true and fair view.

3 But the preparation of accounts which give a true and fair view is not merely a matter of compliance with professional standards. In many important cases it is a requirement of law. Since 1947 all accounts prepared for the purpose of compliance with the Companies Acts have been required to "give a true and fair view": s 13(1) of the Companies Act 1947, re-enacted as s 149(1) of the Companies Act 1948. In 1978 the concept of a true and fair view was adopted by the EEC Council in its Fourth Directive "on the annual accounts of certain types of companies". The Directive combined the requirement of giving a true and fair view with extremely detailed provisions about the form and contents of the accounts but the obligation to give a true and fair view was declared to be overriding. Accounts must not comply with the detailed requirements if this would prevent them from giving a true and fair view. Parliament gave effect to the Directive, by passing the Companies Act 1981. This substitutes a new s 149(2) in the 1948 Act *[that is now Section 226(2) of the Companies Act 1985]*, reproducing the old s 149(1) in substantially similar words. The detailed requirements of the Directive appear as a new Eighth Schedule to the 1948 Act *[now Schedule 4 to the Companies Act 1985]*. The old s 149(1) (now renumbered

149A(1)) and the old Eighth Schedule (now Sch 8A) are retained for the accounts of banking, insurance [and shipping] companies. *[These are now Section 255(1) of, and Schedule 9 to, the Companies Act 1985.]* So far as the requirement to give a true and fair view is concerned, a difference between 149(2) and 149A(1) is that the former has come into the law via Brussels, whereas the latter has no EEC pedigree.

4 "True and fair view" is thus a legal concept and the question of whether company accounts comply with s 149(2) (or s 149A(l)) can be authoritatively decided only by a court. This gives rise to a number of questions about the relationship between the legal requirement and the SSAPs issued by the ASC, which also claim to be authoritative statements on what is a true and fair view. What happens if there is a conflict between the professional standards demanded by the ASC and the decisions of the courts on the requirements of the Companies Acts? Furthermore, the ASC issues new SSAPs "at progressive levels" and reviews established ones. How is this consistent with a statutory requirement of a true and fair view which has been embodied in the law in the same language since 1947? Can the issue of a new SSAP make it unlawful to prepare accounts in a form which would previously have been lawful? How can the ASC have power to legislate in this way?

5 To answer these questions it is necessary first to examine the nature of the "true and fair view" concept as used in the Companies Act. It is an abstraction or philosophical concept expressed in simple English. The law uses many similar concepts, of which "reasonable care" is perhaps the most familiar example. It is a common feature of such concepts that there is seldom any difficulty in understanding what they mean but frequent controversy over their application to particular facts. One reason for this phenomenon is that because such concepts represent a very high level of abstraction which has to be applied to an infinite variety of concrete facts, there can never be a sharply defined line between, for example, what is reasonable care and what is not. There will always be a penumbral area in which views may reasonably differ.

6 The courts have never attempted to define "true and fair" in the sense of offering a paraphrase in other languages and in our opinion have been wise not to do so. When a concept can be expressed in ordinary English words, we do not think that it illuminates their meaning to attempt to frame a definition. We doubt, for example, whether the man on the Clapham omnibus has really contributed very much to the understanding of "reasonable care" or that accountants have found it helpful to ask themselves how this imaginary passenger would have prepared a set of accounts. It is much more useful to illustrate the concept in action, for example, to explain why certain accounts do or do not give a true and fair view.

7 It is however important to observe that the application of the concept involves judgment in questions of degree. The information contained in accounts must be accurate and comprehensive (to mention two of the most obvious elements which contribute to a true and fair view) to within acceptable limits. What is acceptable and how is this to be achieved? Reasonable businessmen and accountants may differ over the degree of accuracy or comprehensiveness which in particular cases the accounts should attain. Equally, there may sometimes be room for differences over the method to adopt in order to give a true and fair view, cases in which there may be more than one "true and fair view" of the same financial position. Again, because "true and fair view" involves questions of degree, we think that cost-effectiveness must play a part in deciding the amount of information which is sufficient to make accounts true and fair.

8 In the end, as we have said, the question of whether accounts give a true and fair view in compliance with the Companies Act must be decided by a judge. But the courts look for guidance on this question to the ordinary practices of professional accountants. This is not merely because accounts are expressed in a language which judges find difficult to understand. This may sometimes be true but it is a minor reason for the importance which the courts attach to evidence of accountancy practice. The important reason is inherent in the nature of the "true and fair" concept. Accounts will not be true and fair unless the information they contain is sufficient in quantity and quality to satisfy the reasonable expectations of the readers to whom they are addressed. On this question, accountants can express an informed professional opinion on what, in current circumstances, it is thought that accounts should reasonably contain. But they can do more than that. The readership of accounts will consist of businessmen, investors, bankers and so forth, as well as professional accountants. But the expectations of the readers will have been moulded by the practices of accountants because by and large they will expect to get what they ordinarily get and that in turn will depend upon the normal practices of accountants.

9 For these reasons, the courts will treat compliance with accepted accounting principles as *prima facie* evidence that the accounts are true and fair. Equally, deviation from accepted principles will be *prima facie* evidence that they are not. We have not been able to find reported cases on the specific question of whether accounts are true and fair, although the question has been adverted to in the course of judgments on other matters; see for example *Willingale v. International Commercial Bank Ltd* [1978] A.C.834. There are however some cases on the analogous question arising in income tax cases of whether profit or loss has been calculated in accordance with "the correct principles of commercial accountancy" and there is a helpful statement of principle (approved in subsequent cases in the Court of Appeal) by Pennycuick V-C in Odeon Associated Theatres Ltd v. Jones *(Inspector of Taxes)* [1971] 1 W.L.R. 442 at 454:

> "In order to ascertain what are the correct principles [the court] has recourse to the evidence of accountants. That evidence is conclusive on the practice of accountants in the sense of the principles on which accountants act in practice. That is a question of pure fact, but the court itself has to make a final decision as to whether that practice corresponds to the correct principles of commercial accountancy. No

> doubt in the vast proportion of cases the court will agree with the accountants but it will not necessarily do so. Again, there may be a divergency of views between the accountants, or there may be alternative principles, none of which can be said to be incorrect, or of course there may be no accountancy evidence at all . . . At the end of the day the court must determine what is the correct principle of commercial accountancy to be applied."

10 This is also in our opinion the relationship between generally accepted accounting principles and the legal concept of "true and fair". The function of the ASC is to formulate what it considers should be generally accepted accounting principles. Thus the value of a SSAP to a court which has to decide whether accounts are true and fair is two-fold. First, it represents an important statement of professional opinion about the standards which readers may reasonably expect in accounts which are intended to be true and fair. The SSAP is intended to crystallise professional opinion and reduce penumbral areas in which divergent practices exist and can each have claim to being "true and fair". Secondly, because accountants are professionally obliged to comply with a SSAP, it creates in the readers an expectation that the accounts will be in conformity with the prescribed standards. This is in itself a reason why accounts which depart from the standard without adequate justification or explanation may be held not to be true and fair. The importance of expectations was emphasised by the Court of Appeal in what may be regarded as a converse case, *Re Press Caps* [1949] Ch.434. An ordinary historic cost balance sheet was said to be "true and fair" notwithstanding that it gave no information about the current value of freehold properties because, it was said, no one familiar with accounting conventions would expect it to include such information.

11 A SSAP therefore has no direct legal effect. It is simply a rule of professional conduct for accountants. But in our opinion it is likely to have an indirect effect on the content which the courts will give to the "true and fair" concept. The effect of a SSAP may therefore be to make it likely that accounts which would previously have been considered true and fair will no longer satisfy the law. Perhaps the most dramatic example arises out of the recent statement by the ASC in connection with its review of SSAP 16 "Current Cost Accounting". The Statement puts forward for discussion the proposition that "where a company is materially affected by changing prices, pure HC accounts do not give a true and fair view". If this proposition were embodied in a new SSAP and accepted by the courts, the legal requirements of a true and fair view will have undergone a revolutionary change.

12 There is no inconsistency between such a change brought about by changing professional opinion and the rule that words in a statute must be construed in accordance with the meaning which they bore when the statute was passed. The *meaning* of true and fair remains what it was in 1947. It is the *content* given to the concept which has changed. This is something which constantly happens to such concepts. For example, the Bill of Rights 1688 prohibited "cruel and unusual punishments". There has been no change in the meaning of "cruel" since 1688. The definition in Dr Johnson's Dictionary of 1755 ("pleased with hurting others, inhuman, hard-hearted, without pity, barbarous") is much the same as in a modern dictionary. But changes in society mean that a judge in 1983 would unquestionably characterise punishments as "cruel" which his predecessor of 1688 would not have thought to come within this description. The meaning of the concept remains the same; the facts to which it is applied have changed.

13 The possibility of changing accounting standards has been recognised both by the courts and the legislature. In *Associated Portland Cement Manufacturers Ltd v. Price Commission* [1975] I.C.R.27, esp. at 45-6, the court recognised changes since 1945 in the permissible methods of calculating depreciation. Similarly para 90 of the new Eighth Schedule to the Companies Act 1948 refers to "principles generally accepted . . . at the time when those accounts are prepared".

14 We therefore see no conflict between the functions of the ASC in formulating standards which it declares to be essential to true and fair accounts and the function of the courts in deciding whether the accounts satisfy the law. The courts are of course not bound by a SSAP. A court may say that accounts which ignore them are nevertheless true and fair. But the immediate effect of a SSAP is to strengthen the likelihood that a court will hold that compliance with the prescribed standard is necessary for the accounts to give a true and fair view. In the absence of a SSAP, a court is unlikely to reject accounts drawn up in accordance with principles which command some respectable professional support. The issue of a SSAP has the effect, for the two reasons which we have given in para 10, of creating a *prima facie* presumption that accounts which do not comply are not true and fair. This presumption is then strengthened or weakened by the extent to which the SSAP is actually accepted and applied. Universal acceptance means that it is highly unlikely that a court would accept accounts drawn up according to different principles. On the other hand, if there remains a strong body of professional opinion which consistently opts out of applying the SSAP, giving reasons which the ASC may consider inadequate, the *prima facie* presumption against such accounts is weakened.

15 We therefore do not think that the ASC should be concerned by the possibility that a court may hold that compliance with one of its SSAPs is not necessary for the purposes of the Companies Acts. This possibility is inherent in the fact that the courts are not bound by professional opinion. The function of the ASC is to express their professional judgment on the standards which in their opinion are required.

16 There are two further points to be considered. The first is the relationship between the "true and fair" requirement and the detailed provisions of the new Eighth Schedule. The Act is quite explicit on this point: the true and fair view is overriding. Nevertheless it may be said that the detailed requirements offer some guidance as to the principles which Parliament considered would give a true and fair view. In particular, the Schedule plainly regards historic cost accounting as the norm and current cost accounting as an optional alternative. In these circumstances, is a court likely to follow a SSAP which declares that for certain companies, historic cost accounts *cannot* give a true and fair view? In our opinion, whatever reasons there may be for taking one view or the other, the provisions of the Eighth Schedule are no obstacle to accepting such a SSAP. As we have already pointed out, the provisions of the Schedule are static whereas the concept of a true and fair view is dynamic. If the latter is overriding, it is not impossible that the effect in time will be to render obsolete some of the provisions of the Schedule. But we think that this is what must have been intended when overriding force was given to a concept with a changing content.

17 Lastly, there is the effect of the adoption of "true and fair view" by the EEC. Because s 149(2) of the 1948 Act now gives effect to a Directive, it must (unlike s 149A(1)) be construed in accordance with any decision of the European Court on the meaning of Article 2.3 of the Directive. In practice we do not think that this is likely to affect the evolution of the concept in England. Just as the concept may have a different content at different times, so it may have a different content in different countries. Although the European Court may seek to achieve some uniformity by laying down minimum standards for the accounts of all EEC countries, it seems to us that they are unlikely to disapprove of higher standards being required by the professional bodies of individual states and in consequence, higher legal criteria for what is a true and fair view being adopted in the national courts of some member states.

18 So for example Article 33 of the Directive gives member states the right to "permit or require" companies to use current cost accounting instead of historic cost principles. In the UK, as we have said, current cost accounts are permitted by the Eighth Schedule but the only circumstances in which they may be required is if a court should decide, on the basis of prevailing principles, that they were necessary to give a true and fair view. In Germany, on the other hand, the equivalent of the Eighth Schedule does not even permit current cost accounts. In Germany therefore, the only way they could be permitted would be if the German court applied "true and fair view" as an overriding requirement. For the reasons given in para 16, we do not regard it as illogical or impossible that even a German court may take this view. But having regard to the Directive, we think it is very unlikely that the European Court would decide as a matter of community law that there are circumstances in which historic cost accounts do not give a true and fair view. Developments of this kind are more likely to be left to national courts to make in the light of local professional opinion.

Leonard Hoffman
M. H. Arden

Lincoln's Inn
13 September 1983

The Joint Opinion that follows was given in relation to the Statement of Intent issued by the ASC on the proposed revision of SSAP 16. However, this Opinion has a more general application to the relationship between SSAPs and the 'true and fair' concept. In particular, it discusses the question of cost-effectiveness and whether a SSAP should apply to all companies.

The Accounting Standards Committee - Supplementary Joint Opinion

1 This Opinion is intended to be supplementary to our Joint Opinion dated 13 September 1983. We do not propose to repeat the contents of that Opinion more than is necessary in order to make this one intelligible. The two Opinions should therefore be read together.

2 The ASC proposed to issue a Statement of Intent concerning the future of SSAP 16 "Current Cost Accounting". In summary, the proposal is that all public limited companies ("PLCs") other than insurance companies, property companies and investment-based companies ("value-based companies") should show the effects of changing prices when these effects are material, but this should be indicated in a note and not in separate current cost accounts. The present position is that SSAP 16 applies only to large and quoted companies (as therein defined) and does not apply to value-based companies, whatever their size. The ASC is not satisfied that a method has yet been developed for producing useful information about the effects of changing prices on the businesses of private companies and value-based companies at a cost that can be justified. It is therefore commissioning further work on the application of current cost accounting to these companies. However, the ASC draws attention to the principal factors which have led them to their conclusion that significant benefits result from the disclosure of current cost information by PLCs, including the large number and wide range of users of their accounts and in many cases the sophistication of those users. These factors generally do not apply to private companies. The benefits of providing information about the effects of changing prices on the businesses of private companies are therefore likely to be significantly less than in the case of PLCs.

3 The Statement of Intent therefore recognises that while in principle and subject to cost-effectiveness, all accounts should, in order to give a true and a fair view, show the effects of changing prices when such effects are material, there are practical difficulties about devising cost-effective methods for implementing this principle in the case of certain companies.

4 This practical approach has been criticised on the ground that if a footnote about the effects of changing prices is regarded as necessary for accounts to give a true and fair view, this requirement should apply to all sets of accounts. Questions of cost and expediency are said to be irrelevant to whether or not the accounts give a true and fair view and it is argued that there can be no justification for the ASC distinguishing between different kinds of companies.

5 We think that this criticism is misconceived. In the first place, questions of cost-effectiveness are in our opinion relevant to whether accounts give a true and fair view or not. "True and fair view" is not an absolute and unique concept. If that was what the legislature had meant, it would no doubt have said "the true and fair view". More than one view may be true and fair and whether a particular set of accounts satisfies this test or not involves questions of degree and a consideration of many factors relating both to the affairs of the particular business and the reasonable expectations of the people likely to use the accounts. In paragraph 7 of our Joint Opinion we said:

> "Again, because 'true and fair view' involves questions of degree, we think that cost-effectiveness must play a part in deciding the amount of information which is sufficient to make accounts true and fair."

Some elaboration of this statement may be useful. The information contained in accounts may vary in its comprehensiveness, usefulness and degree of precision. These are all factors which bear upon the question of whether the accounts are "true and fair". The accounts must satisfy criteria of acceptability in regard to each of these and other matters. But the question of whether it is necessary for particular kinds of information to be included must take into account the cost and difficulty of providing such information. There is in our opinion nothing illogical in saying: "This information would be useful to (say) investors in assessing the condition of the business. If it could be provided relatively easily, we think that fairness to investors demands that it should be included. *Prima facie* therefore, accounts which do not include such information would not be true and fair. On the other hand, if the information could be provided only with great expense and difficulty, we do not think that it would be reasonable to insist upon it. Therefore we would accept accounts without such information as still being true and fair."1

6 In our earlier Opinion we mentioned for another purpose the analogy of the legal concept of reasonable care. On this point too, we think that reasonable care provides a useful comparison. The question of whether a person has taken reasonable care to guard against some danger depends upon weighing a number of factors, including the likelihood that the risk may materialise, the seriousness of the loss or injury which may be caused if the risk does materialise, the importance of the activity giving rise to the risk, and the cost of taking various kinds of precautions. As Lord Wilberforce put it, more succinctly than we have done:

> "What is reasonable depends on the nature and degree of the danger. It also depends upon the difficulty and expense of guarding against it."[2]

This process of weighing risks against the difficulty and expense of guarding against them would apply equally to the question of whether an accountant had taken reasonable care in the preparation of a set of accounts. And although the question of whether reasonable care has been taken in the preparation of accounts is not the same as whether they are true and fair, we think that the questions of "reasonableness" and "fairness" have enough in common to make the analogy a valid one.

7 At this point the critic may say: "Well, I can see that questions of cost - effectiveness may enter into the decision on whether accounts are true and fair and that information about the effects of price changes may have to be given in the accounts of some companies but not others. But the SSAP should still be capable of expression in general terms. How can one justify an arbitrary dividing line which requires such information in the accounts of one company which happens to be a PLC and does not require it in the accounts of a private company of the same size and carrying on a substantially similar business?"

8 This criticism in our opinion misses the true function of SSAPs, which is to reduce the level of abstraction at which rules of good accounting practice are expressed. The more abstract the rule, the more pure and universally applicable it is, but the less useful it is to the practitioner seeking to apply it to the facts of a particular case. If universality were all that one wanted, the proposition that accounts should be true and fair would be sufficient. The point of a SSAP is to concretise that proposition, while recognising that every case must depend upon its own facts and that any rules expressed at a lower level of abstraction must to a greater or lesser extent be "rules of thumb". This point is made with great clarity in the Explanatory Foreword. We therefore see nothing illogical in a SSAP which gives guidance to the profession by taking a (necessarily) arbitrary but practical dividing line and saying that for PLCs which are not value-based companies it will ordinarily be assumed that the public benefit from the provision of information about the effects of changing prices will be sufficient to justify the cost of providing such information, whereas this will not be assumed, or will not yet be assumed, in the case of private or value-based companies.

9 We said in our earlier opinion that "true and fair" was a dynamic concept and that its detailed content could change by degrees over time. We also said that one of the functions of the ASC was to initiate and promote such changes. A SSAP in accordance with the draft Statement of Intent seems to us to give effect to that function.

Leonard Hoffman
M. H. Arden

Lincoln's Inn
20 March 1984

1 In saying this we have in mind expense and difficulty applicable to any company of that kind. We are not saying that it would be right to take into account the difficulty which a particular company might have in providing certain information, e.g. because its records had been badly maintained. There is again an analogy here with "reasonable care" (see paragraph 6) in which difficulties or handicaps peculiar to an individual are usually disregarded on the ground that a person suffering from such a difficulty or handicap should not have undertaken the activity which gave rise to the risk.

2 *Herrington v. British Railways Board* [1972] A.C.877,920.

The two preceding opinions are reproduced with the kind permission of Accountancy, The Accounting Standards Committee, Leonard Hoffman and Mary H. Arden.

The Institute of Chartered Accountants of Scotland - Opinion

I have been asked to consider the meaning of the term 'true and fair view' from the Scottish point of view, in the light of the Joint Opinion given by English leading Counsel to the Accounting Standards Committee dated 13th September 1983.

In their Opinion English Counsel examine the nature of the 'true and fair' view concept as used in the Companies Acts in some detail. They draw attention to the fact that the Courts have never attempted to define this term, in the sense of offering a paraphrase of it, and go on to say that the application of the concept involves judgment in questions of degree. Turning to the relationship between the legal concept of 'true and fair' on the one hand and generally accepted accounting principles on the other, they say that the Courts will treat compliance with accepted accounting principles as *prima facie* evidence that the accounts are true and fair, and that equally deviation from accepted principles will be *prima facie* evidence that they are not. This leads them to consider the problem of the effect upon the 'true and fair view' concept of a new Statement of Standard Accounting Practice. ['SSAP']. Their answer to it is to say that there is no inconsistency between a change in the legal requirements for a true and fair view resulting from a new SSAP and the rule that words in a statute must be construed in accordance with the meaning which they bore when the statute was passed. As they put it, 'The *meaning* of true and fair remains what it was in 1947. It is the *content* given to the concept which has changed.' Thus the concept of the 'true and fair view' is, they say, dynamic, with a changing content as accounting practices are revised and developed with time. The importance of this conclusion is revealed when they recognise, in paragraph 16 of their Opinion, that since the 'true and fair' view requirement in section 149(2) of the Companies Act 1948 *[now Section 226(6) of the Companies Act 1985]* as amended overrides the provisions of the new Schedule 8 *[now Schedule 4]* to the Act, it may have the effect in time of rendering obsolete some of the detailed provisions of the Schedule.

Had I been approaching the matter afresh I would have reached the same conclusions as English Counsel have done, for substantially the same reasons. While the various authorities to which they refer in the course of their discussion are cases decided in the English Courts, the principles upon which their opinion is based are all familiar to a Scottish lawyer, and the statutes are of course applicable with equal force in both countries. It is equally true of Scotland to say that the Courts have not attempted to provide a definition of the term 'true and fair view', although there have been a number of recent cases where the sufficiency of a company's accounts in that regard have come under consideration. In each case the question whether or not they present a 'true and fair view' is a question of fact, which the Court will decide in the light of the evidence including evidence of current accounting practice. As in England, the Court is likely to pay close attention to the evidence of accountants without feeling bound by that evidence: cf. Lord Advocate v. Ruffle, 1979 SC 351. The statement of principle by Pennycuick V-C in Odeon Associated Theatres v. Jones (1971) 1 WLR 442 at p. 454, which English Counsel quote in paragraph 9 of their Opinion, as explained by Lord Denning MR. in Heather v. P.E. Consulting Group Limited (1973) Ch. 189, is familiar in this country, and has been referred to in the Scottish Court on a number of occasions particularly in tax cases.

The distinction which English Counsel draw between the meaning of the term 'true and fair' on the one hand and its content on the other is entirely sound in my opinion. This is because the answer to the question whether a true and fair view is given by the accounts inevitably involves questions of fact and degree, which must always be decided by reference to the state of affairs generally at the time when the accounts were prepared. An analogy can be drawn with other concepts used by the law, such as 'reasonable care' and 'reasonably practicable'. The latter expression, for instance, is used in a variety of provisions to be found in the Factories Act 1961 and its subordinate legislation. The meaning of the phrase, no doubt, must be taken to have remained the same since the date of the enactment, but it is well established in Scotland as well as in England that when it comes to considering whether in any particular case measures which might have been taken so as to avoid the accident were or were not reasonably practicable regard must be had to the state of current knowledge and invention. In my opinion an argument to the effect that the question whether a particular set of accounts gave a true and fair view had to be decided with reference to principles of accounting which, while current in 1947 or 1948, had become obsolete by the time the accounts were prepared only has to be stated to be seen to be unacceptable. I agree with English Counsel that it is reasonable to think that the reason why overriding force was given by the Companies Act 1981 to the concept of the 'true and fair view' is that it was recognised that this was a dynamic concept with a changing content, capable of rendering obsolete any particular provision in the Schedule which had become inconsistent with current practice.

For these reasons I am of opinion that the guidance which English Counsel have given to the Accounting Standards Committee can be accepted as being in accordance with the Scottish approach.

J. A. D. Hope
Edinburgh, 22 December 1983

This legal opinion is reproduced with the kind permission of The Institute of Chartered Accountants of Scotland and J. A. D. Hope.

Chapter 3

Revenue recognition

Page

Chapter 3

Revenue recognition

Introduction

3.1 This chapter deals mainly with the issues relating to the recognition of income in the profit and loss account. It considers:

- What types of income, commonly referred to as 'revenue', may be included in the profit and loss account.
- How to measure the amount of revenue included in the profit and loss account.
- When to recognise revenue.
- Presentation and disclosure issues concerning turnover, other operating income and government grants.

3.2 This chapter also considers how sources of revenue are presented in the profit and loss account. Some types of revenue and expenditure are generally presented gross. That is, similar types of transactions are aggregated and included in the profit and loss account under the income or expenditure heading to which they relate. For example, all the income derived from the principal activities of a company will be combined together under the category of 'turnover' and the expenditure directly relating to this income may be included under the category of 'cost of sales.' Other types of revenue or expenditure are usually presented net. These types may be considered so significant that they need to be shown separately in the profit and loss account under their own descriptive category. This is the principle that requires, for example, the profit or loss on the sale of a fixed asset to be shown after the operating profit in accordance with FRS 3.

Definition of 'revenue'

3.3 The term 'revenue' is not defined either in the Act or in any current accounting standard.

3.4 The ASB's draft Statement of principles defines gains and losses in broad terms as all increases or decreases in ownership interests other than those relating to contributions from or distributions to owners. It mentions briefly that gains arising in the ordinary course of business are sometimes referred to as revenue.

3.5 IAS 18 (revised 1993), 'Revenue recognition', paragraph 7 defines revenue as *"...the gross inflow of economic benefits during the period arising in the course of the ordinary activities of an enterprise when those inflows result in increases in equity, other than increases relating to contributions from equity participants"*.

Companies Act requirements

3.6 In the UK, the types of revenue that can legally be included in the profit and loss account are restricted by paragraph 12(a) of Schedule 4 to the Act which states that *"...only profits realised at the balance sheet date shall be included in the profit and loss account"*. For the purpose of defining realised profits, reference should be made to *"...principles generally accepted, at the time when the accounts are prepared, with respect to the determination for accounting purposes of realised profits or losses"*. [Sec 262(3)].

3.7 The term 'principles generally accepted' for the determination of realised profits is not elaborated on further in the Act. However, it has been given a judicial interpretation, as being *"...principles which are generally regarded as permissible or legitimate by the accountancy profession. That is sufficient even though only one company actually applies it in practice"*. [*Lord Denning, MR, in Associated Portland Cement Manufacturers Ltd v Price Commission.* [1975] ICR 27]. Thus an accounting treatment does not necessarily have to be very common as long as it is thought to be acceptable by accountants. Further implications of the Act's definition of realised profits are discussed in chapter 19.

SSAP 2 requirements

3.8 The only direct references to revenue recognition in UK accounting standards are contained in the definition section of SSAP 2. According to SSAP 2, under the accruals concept:

> *"...revenue and costs are accrued (that is, recognised as they are earned or incurred, not as money is received or paid), matched with one another so far as their relationship can be established or justifiably assumed, and dealt with in the profit and loss account of the period to which they relate; provided that where the accruals concept is inconsistent with the 'prudence' concept ... the latter prevails."* [SSAP 2 para 14].

3.9 SSAP 2 defines the prudence concept as:

> *"...revenue and profits are not anticipated, but are recognised by inclusion in the profit and loss account only when realised in the form either of cash or of other assets the ultimate cash realisation*

of which can be assessed with reasonable certainty; provision is made for all known liabilities (expenses and losses) whether the amount of these is known with certainty or is a best estimate in the light of the information available."
[SSAP 2 para 14].

Prudence, therefore, modifies the accruals concept so that revenue is not only matched with its related costs, but also only recognised when its realisation is reasonably assured.

ASB's draft Statement of principles

3.10 The original discussion drafts of the ASB's Statement of principles proposed criteria under which revenue should be both earned and realised before it qualified for recognition in the profit and loss account. The exposure draft of the Statement of principles is unhelpful in this respect because the ASB now proposes to abandon the distinction between realised and unrealised gains as a basis for presenting gains in the profit and loss account.

[The next paragraph is 3.19.]

Revenue and capital distinction

3.19 The profit and loss account should not only exclude unrealised profits, but also should exclude certain capital items. Both IAS 18 and the draft Statement of principles exclude changes in shareholders' funds which relate to contributions from or distributions to owners from their definitions of gains.

Capital contributions

3.20 Contributions from owners are defined in the draft Statement of principles as "*...increases in ownership interest resulting from investments made by owners in their capacity as owners*". [DSP chp 3 para 49]. Such contributions are usually in the form of cash, but may also occur when other forms of property are transferred into the business or when equity is accepted in satisfaction of a liability. One of the application notes in FRS 4 also deals with the accounting treatment of capital contributions. Such gifts of a capital amount are often made by parent companies to their subsidiaries. What constitutes a capital contribution might be difficult to determine in practice. A genuine gift without condition from a third party unconnected with the receiving company, and therefore not in the capacity of an owner, should generally be treated as a gift and reported as a profit in the year of receipt. In addition, a receipt by a company might not be a capital contribution where it is repaid shortly thereafter other than by way of distribution and this was envisaged at the time the contribution was made. Such a payment would be a loan, if in effect there is an obligation to transfer economic benefits as the contribution is made on the basis that it will be repaid. On the other hand, a contribution that is made without conditions, but is subsequently repaid by a distribution at the discretion of the receiving company, would be a capital contribution rather than a loan.

3.21 There has in the past been considerable controversy over how to account for capital contributions, not least because of their taxation implications. If, for example, such a contribution were to be recognised in the profit and loss account it may become taxable. Capital contributions are attractive in that they enable the receiving company to avoid issuing debt or shares which may have some adverse tax consequences. Furthermore, there is no servicing cost to the receiving company. Therefore, in accordance with FRS 4, as there is no obligation on the part of the receiving company to transfer economic benefits to the company making the contribution, the capital contribution should be reported within shareholders' funds.

3.22 In the year the contribution is received, FRS 4 also requires that the capital contribution should be credited to reserves by the receiving company and reported in its reconciliation of movements in shareholders' funds. Therefore, there is no longer a question as to whether such a contribution should be recorded in the receiving company's profit and loss account or total gains statement. Nevertheless,

[The next page is 3007.]

it appears that where the amount is received in cash it is legally a realised profit and as such can be taken into account in determining whether a company has sufficient distributable reserves to pay a dividend. Where, however, a contribution is in the form of an asset (for example, shares in a subsidiary) that is not either cash or readily convertible into cash the contribution is not a realised profit and may not, therefore, be taken into account in determining distributable profits. It is best recorded in a separate reserve to distinguish it from other reserves, because of its difference in nature.

3.23 It seems logical that in the paying company (in a group of companies) the opposite accounting treatment should be adopted. Therefore, the contribution should not be recorded as an expense in the profit and loss account, but should be added to the cost of the investment in the subsidiary. Only if there is a permanent diminution in the underlying value of the investment in the subsidiary would the investing company need to make a provision against its carrying value.

Other gifts

3.24 Gifts in the form of grants may also be given to a company to help finance a particular asset or specific profit and loss account expenditure. When these grants are given by government, including inter-governmental agencies and EU bodies, guidance on the accounting treatment is contained in SSAP 4 (revised) which differentiates between the treatment for revenue and capital based grants. The treatment of revenue grants is discussed in paragraph 3.92. The treatment of capital grants is discussed in chapter 14. Payments given to companies from sources other than government should be subject to similar analysis since SSAP 4 is indicative of best practice for accounting for grants and assistance from other sources. Thus, for example, a non-refundable payment by a third party franchiser to assist the franchisee with the purchase of specific assets would be more in the nature of a grant than a capital contribution.

Measurement of revenue

3.25 The draft Statement of principles requires that items must be able to be reliably measured before they can be included in financial statements. Reliability means that, for the same basis of measurement, different people would calculate amounts that are not materially different. Measurement would be relatively straightforward in the circumstance of an arm's length transaction for a monetary amount, although future cash flows may require discounting. If a transaction is not at arm's length, then this lack of independence could mean that it is not at fair value. In this situation, further information may need to be provided about the transaction or it may need to be presented differently from the more usual arm's length transactions in order for users to understand the transaction. These issues are discussed in detail in chapter 35, which deals with related party transactions. Non-monetary transactions, perhaps involving barter, are also more difficult to measure, but where there are frequent monetary transactions of similar items or where the item traded can be readily converted to a monetary item, these difficulties may be reduced.

3.26 In the absence of a UK standard on revenue recognition, guidance on measurement issues can be obtained from IAS 18. IAS 18 states that revenue should be measured at the fair value of the consideration received or receivable. [IAS 18 para 9]. In a straightforward transaction involving the sale of an asset or the provision of a service, this fair value is generally determined by agreement between the buyer and the seller and equates to the consideration receivable on the transaction (after taking into account any trade discounts or volume rebates allowed). In the case of services provided by an agent or a broker, the measurement would not be based on the gross value of the transaction, but on the commission or margin to which he becomes entitled as a result of the transaction. Measurement of revenue becomes more difficult if some or all of the cash consideration is deferred and settled in the future. In this situation, the fair value of the consideration may be less than the actual cash receivable at the future date.

Discounting deferred consideration

3.27 The fair value of the consideration may be less than the actual amount receivable in cash if, for example, a company grants a significant period of interest free credit to the customer or accepts a note receivable bearing a below market rate in order to make the sale. When such an agreement amounts to a financing transaction, IAS 18 states that the fair value of the consideration is determined by discounting all the future receipts using an imputed rate of interest. This interest rate is the more clearly determinable of either:

- the prevailing rate of interest for a similar instrument of an issuer with a similar credit rating; or

- a rate of interest that discounts the nominal amount of the instrument to the current cash sales price.

[IAS 18 para 11].

The revenue from the sale would initially be recorded at a discounted amount and the difference between this amount and the actual consideration receivable would be recognised as interest on a time basis over the credit period.

Example

A company sells a large item of industrial plant. The terms of the sale allow an interest free period of credit of five years in exchange for the customer paying a deposit of £5m and a further £45m in five years. The current cash sales price of the plant is £35m.

The sale should be recorded at the amount of the initial payment of £5m plus the present value of the further £45m. Interest can then be credited to the profit and loss account as interest receivable over the credit period so that at the end of five years there is a debtor of £45m on the balance sheet as follows:

	Sale	Interest	Debtor
	£m	£m	£m
Year 0			
Initial deposit	5.0		
Present value of future receivable	30.0		30.0
Year 1		2.5	32.5
Year 2		2.8	35.3
Year 3		3.0	38.3
Year 4		3.2	41.5
Year 5		3.5	45.0
Payment			(45.0)
	35.0	15.0	–

3.28 There are three principal variables in applying discounting techniques. These are:

- The amount of the future cash flows.
- The timing of those future cash flows.
- The interest rate to be used to discount the cash flows.

Where two of these are known it is possible to calculate the value for the third. For instance, where a deep discounted bond has been issued, the proceeds are known and the future cash outflows will be stipulated in the contract. Thus the issuer can calculate the rate of interest, which, when used to discount future cash flows, will equal the proceeds. This basis applies equally to receivables; where a company acquires a deep discounted bond such as zero coupon loan stock, the discount is effectively the interest it will receive on the loan. Although this 'interest' is not received until the stock is redeemed, the company should treat it as interest receivable on an annual basis and credit it to the profit and loss account each year until it is redeemed. The amount of the income can be precisely measured. The cash realisation of the 'interest' may not be for many years, but, provided that the creditworthiness of the issuer is not in doubt, there is a reasonable certainty that the income will be realised so the income can be recognised. An accounting policy for all types of discounts and premiums on debt securities held as investments is illustrated in Table 3.1.

Table 3.1 – The Royal Bank of Scotland Group plc – Report & Accounts – 30 September 1994

Accounting policies (extract)

10 Debt securities and equity shares

Debt securities and equity shares intended for use on a continuing basis in the Group's activities are classified as investment securities and are stated at cost less provision for any permanent diminution in value. The cost of dated investment securities is adjusted for the amortisation of premiums or discounts over periods to redemption and any such amortisation is included in interest receivable. Debt securities held for the purpose of hedging are carried at a value which reflects the accounting treatment of the items hedged. Debt securities and equity shares held for dealing purposes are included in the consolidated balance sheet at market value.

Barter and transactions involving exchanges of assets

3.29 In some situations, consideration may not take the form of cash or cash equivalents at all. Transactions may involve the exchange of either similar or different assets. Transactions may even involve the exchange of an asset for a service. An example of a commercial reason for swapping similar assets would be in the oil industry where two companies may exchange quantities of oil which are held in different locations in order to be able to meet demand. IAS 18 does not regard transactions involving exchanges of similar assets as generating revenue although it does regard exchanges of dissimilar assets as transactions which generate revenue. SSAP 2 takes a stricter view of the concept of realisation, requiring the receipt of cash or of other assets that can be expected with reasonable certainty to be converted into cash.

Example

A port operator swapped its wharf for a different wharf owned by a local council. There was a revaluation reserve of £1m relating to the wharf that was traded. The value of the wharf received in exchange was equal to the value of the wharf given up, according to independent valuations. How should the revaluation reserve be treated?

The consideration received for the wharf given up does not meet the criteria in SSAP 2 for the recognition of a profit, because it is not realised in the form of cash or other assets whose ultimate cash realisation can be assessed with reasonable certainty. Therefore this exchange cannot turn an unrealised revaluation reserve into a realised profit. The £1m should continue to be treated as an unrealised reserve.

3.30 According to IAS 18, in the case of exchanging dissimilar assets or services, the revenue generated should be measured at the fair value of the items received or at the fair value of the items given in exchange, if the fair value of the items received cannot be reliably measured. For example, where a property is exchanged for shares, the fair value of the shares would be their current market value, provided there is a ready market and the quantity of shares to be sold would not distort the market price.

Example

A company supplies goods to an overseas customer and receives oil paintings in exchange. The paintings have been independently valued. The company intends to sell the paintings as soon as possible.

The amount of revenue which could be recognised on this transaction should be based on the reliably measured value of the oil paintings. This value may need to be measured in different ways in different circumstances. Whether this value is the independent valuation would depend on whether there was a ready market for such paintings or if a lower value would need to be placed on them in order to get a quick sale. If there is significant uncertainty about the realisable value of the paintings, then it would be prudent to delay revenue recognition until the paintings are sold and their ultimate realisable value accurately determined. Alternatively, the company could base the amount of revenue recognised on the value of the goods supplied, perhaps recognising a normal profit margin on the goods if they are confident that the valuation of the paintings exceeds the normal selling price of the goods, but are otherwise uncertain as to their value.

Since the company intends to sell the paintings, it will be able to generate a realised profit as long as the measurement issues can be resolved. If the company intended to keep the paintings as a fixed asset, perhaps adorning the office walls, then the question arises of whether the profit, although able to be measured and recognised (because of the exchange of dissimilar assets), would be a realised profit. It seems that it should not be regarded as a realised profit. One argument for not regarding it as a realised profit is that, whilst the asset received in exchange can be valued at the present time, in this instance the asset will be held for the long term during which it would fluctuate in value. This uncertainty inherent in the value of this type of asset prevents it from being regarded as a realised profit.

Another view is that the value of the stock must be at least equal to the value of the painting, otherwise the company would not have been willing to enter into the swap. The company could have revalued the stock before the exchange took place and this revaluation would have been taken to the revaluation reserve and not to the profit and loss account. Therefore, the excess of the value of the painting over the book value of the stock could be taken to the revaluation reserve since it represents an unrealised profit. It is because the company intends to sell the painting immediately, in effect generating a cash equivalent, that it could recognise a realised profit.

3.31 Verson International Group plc received assets in consideration for the settlement of certain claims. Where the assets were professionally valued, had a use in the business and would generate future income streams, or were sold, Verson included their value in the profit and loss account as detailed in Table 3.2. However, if the assets received had no use in the business and were, therefore, not going to generate future income, Verson delayed recognition until they were sold. Like the paintings in the example above, the realisation of these assets cannot be assured until their sale. Presumably, in the absence of a use in the business that will generate income, they cannot be sufficiently reliably measured.

Table 3.2 – Verson International Group plc – Annual Report – 31 January 1994

Notes to the Accounts (extract)

4. Other operating income:

Other operating income comprises:	**1994** **£000**	1993 £000
Exceptional royalty and commission income	**3,201**	3,682
Exceptional service fee income	**746**	1,892
Realised currency gains	**270**	899
Profit on disposal of fixed assets	**41**	–
	4,258	6,473

Exceptional royalty and commission income in 1994 arose principally from the settlement of claims against a former licensee of Hitachi Zosen, the rights to which were transferred to the group under the arrangements entered into with Hitachi Zosen in the prior year (note 19e). The settlement comprised £2,055,000 in cash, and machine tools professionally valued on an open market basis by Gray Machinery Company, member of the Association of Machinery and Equipment Appraisers, at £1,067,000, which have been retained and put into production in one of the group's US factories.

Service fee income relates to assets received in the prior year as a result of the arrangements entered into with Hitachi Zosen, referred to above, which have now been sold (£323,000) or put into productive operations (£423,000) in the US. The group still has certain assets with an estimated value of some £750,000, which it is free to dispose of and which will not be retained or used in the business. As the realisation of these assets is uncertain as to timing and value, no income will be recognised on these items until they are sold to a third party.

Timing of revenue recognition in financial statements

3.32 The timing of the revenue recognition in the financial statements is possibly the most difficult factor in accounting for revenue and one which can have a significant impact on a company's reported results. The draft Statement of principles provides a broad framework underlying specific recognition criteria.

Gains can only be included in financial statements if there is both sufficient evidence that a change in assets or liabilities has occurred and that the item can be reliably measured. An arm's length transaction provides the best evidence that there has been a change in assets or liabilities. The negotiation of a contract to supply goods or services cannot generally provide sufficient evidence that revenue has been earned even if it creates a firm commitment between the parties. There is likely to be a significant act or event outstanding at the time a contract is signed, such as the actual delivery of the goods, so that the revenue should not be recognised.

3.33 Detailed guidance on the area of revenue recognition is often obtained from IAS 18. IAS 18 starts with the premise that revenue is recognised when it is probable that future economic benefits will flow to the enterprise and that these benefits can be measured reliably. The standard identifies when these criteria will be met for:

- Selling goods.
- Rendering services.
- The use by others of an enterprise's assets yielding interest, royalties and dividends.

[IAS 18 para 1].

Sale of goods

3.34 IAS 18 states that revenue from a transaction involving the sale of goods should be recognised when the following conditions are satisfied:

- The enterprise has transferred to the buyer the significant risks and rewards of ownership of the goods.
- The seller retains neither continuing managerial involvement to a degree usually associated with ownership nor effective control over the goods sold.
- The amount of revenue can be measured reliably.
- It is probable that the economic benefits associated with the transaction will flow to the enterprise.
- The costs incurred or to be incurred in respect of the transaction can be measured reliably.

[IAS 18 para 14].

3.35 IAS 18 recognises that in many instances it will be clear when the significant risks and rewards of ownership pass and this will often coincide with the transfer of legal title or the passing of possession to the buyer. For example, in a retail sale where a refund is offered if the customer is not satisfied with the merchandise, the customer pays for goods whether by cash or credit card and then takes them out of the shop. The significant risks and rewards of ownership have passed to the customer and, provided that the seller can reliably estimate future returns, it should record a sale. Similarly, in conventional sale or return contracts, revenue is usually recognised when the goods are in the possession of the purchaser, provided that a reliable estimate of future returns can be made.

3.36 Another example is a credit sale where the seller retains legal title to the goods only to protect himself in the event of the debt not being paid. In substance, significant risks and rewards have been transferred to the seller, hence the legal form does not affect the recognition of the sale. Further advice on this issue can be found in the ICAEW guidance statement, 'Accounting for goods sold subject to reservation of title'. This statement differentiates between transactions where the reservation of title is regarded by both parties as having no practical relevance, other than on the insolvency of the purchaser, and those where the intention is to create consignment stocks. The guidance confirms that these transactions should be accounted for according to the intention of the parties. FRS 5 contains an application note which covers treatments of consignment stock; this is considered in detail in chapter 17.

3.37 In other situations the transfer of risks and rewards will not coincide with the transfer of either legal title or possession. IAS 18 gives the following examples of situations where the enterprise may retain the significant risks and rewards of ownership:

- The enterprise retains an obligation for unsatisfactory performance not covered by normal warranty provisions.
- The receipt of revenue from a particular sale is contingent on deriving revenue by the buyer from its sale of goods.
- The goods are shipped subject to installation and the installation is a significant part of the contract, which has not yet been completed by the enterprise.
- The buyer has the right to rescind the purchase for a reason specified in the sales contract and the enterprise is uncertain about the probability of return.

[IAS 18 para 16].

3.38 Although FRS 5 deals primarily with identifying and recording assets and liabilities, it gives some guidance on when a sale should be recognised in respect of a transaction involving a previously recognised asset. A transaction results in a sale when it transfers to others:

- All significant rights or other access to benefits relating to the asset.

- All significant exposure to the risks inherent in those benefits.

[FRS 5 para 22].

3.39 FRS 5 also deals with situations where not all the significant risks and rewards relating to assets are transferred or where they are not transferred for the entire life of the asset. The rules concerning these 'partial derecognition' situations are considered in chapter 4.

Sale of property

3.40 Transactions involving the sale of property often straddle a financial year end. For example, a contract may be exchanged before the year end and completed after the year end. The legal documentation surrounding the sale should clarify when rights to the property are transferred and legal advice may be necessary in specific cases. In general, however, where an unconditional and irrevocable contract has been entered into for the sale of a property, the profit arising on the sale can be recognised at the time when the contract is exchanged (see Table 3.3).

Table 3.3 – Associated British Ports Holdings PLC – Annual report and accounts – 31 December 1997

NOTES ON THE ACCOUNTS (extract)

RECOGNITION OF PROFIT ON PROPERTY DEVELOPMENTS

Profits or losses arising on the sale of sites or completed developments are recognised when contracts for sale have been exchanged and have become unconditional.

3.41 It is appropriate to recognise the income when an unconditional and irrevocable contract has been entered into, because the equitable and the beneficial interests already vest in the purchaser, who has a legal commitment for the outstanding purchase consideration. The situation is, therefore, no different from goods sold on credit. If, however, the contract is conditional, recognition should be delayed until the last material condition is satisfied. It is only when all the material conditions have been satisfied that the gain can be considered to be earned.

Example

A company sold land to a Housing Association. At the company's year end the contracts had been exchanged and were unconditional and irrevocable. This is the company's usual policy for the recognition of revenue. However, completion is in two stages, with part of the consideration payable six months after the year end and part payable twelve months after the year end. The delay in payment is possibly linked to the development of a block of flats on the land and the housing association receiving the necessary funding to complete the project, although this is not specifically mentioned in the contract.

In this situation, although the receipt of funding is not a condition of the contract, there would appear to be significant doubt that the housing association would be able to pay for the land at the time of the exchange of contracts. Therefore recognition should be delayed until the uncertainty is resolved. The accounting treatment is no different to that which would be required if the contract were in fact conditional on the housing association receiving funding; recognition should be delayed until the condition was satisfied or until completion if it were only then the situation could be resolved with sufficient certainty.

If, however, there were no uncertainty about whether the Housing Association would receive the necessary funding, then all the risks and rewards of the land have been transferred at the year end, so under FRS 5 and IAS 18 credit should in principle be taken for the sale.

If at some later stage after the sale has been properly recognised, doubt arises about whether the Housing Association will be able to meet the payment schedule, provision against the debt would have to be made. This should not, however, prevent the original profit being recognised in the absence of uncertainty.

3.42 Property is often sold subject to planning consent being obtained. In these situations, the vendor may be involved in obtaining the required planning consent and may incur costs in submitting planning applications and attending planning hearings. Obtaining the required planning permission is a material condition of the contract. Therefore, even if the vendor has performed all the tasks necessary to obtain consent before the year end, the sale cannot be recognised until the condition is satisfied and the consent has been granted. If such consent is received after the year end, then the sale should be recognised the following year when the material condition is fulfilled. Significant costs incurred in obtaining consent may be carried forward to be matched with the sale where it is reasonable to assume that planning permission will be obtained and the sale will take place.

3.43 Many companies do not take credit for sales, commonly of private houses, until legal completion has taken place, as is illustrated in Table 3.4. This policy is, therefore, more conservative than recognising revenue on the exchange of unconditional contracts. The property industry has historically taken a more prudent approach to the sale of homes to individual buyers. However, the choice of either of these methods will usually depend on the circumstances of the sale.

Table 3.4 – Tarmac PLC – Annual Report – 31 December 1994

Principal Accounting Policies (extract)

Turnover

Turnover represents the net amount receivable, excluding value added tax, for goods and services supplied to external customers and, in respect of long term contracting activities, the value of work executed during the year. Sales of newly constructed private houses are included in turnover on legal completion.

3.44 Therefore, revenue should only be recognised on sales of property in a year if a binding and unconditional contract has been entered into before the year end or if the last material condition on a conditional contract has been satisfied before the year end. If the contract is entered into after the year end or if a condition is only fulfilled after the year end, then that sale represents the next year's revenue since it is only in the following year that it has been earned.

3.45 Some property companies enter into transactions in which they build developments for particular customers rather than building speculative developments. The properties built may be effectively pre-sold so that the contract has been entered into before construction begins and all the terms and conditions of the sale are known. In such situations, the transaction may effectively be a long-term contract which should be accounted for in accordance with SSAP 9 with profit being recognised according to the percentage of completion of the development, provided that the outcome can be assessed with reasonable certainty (see para 3.57). The accounting policy of Slough Estates plc in Table 3.5 is an example of pre-sold properties being accounted for as long-term contracts.

Table 3.5 – Slough Estates plc – Annual Report – 31 December 1993

ACCOUNTING POLICIES (extract)

Trading properties

Unless pre-sold, properties are held at the lower of cost, including finance costs, and market value. Pre-sold properties are stated at cost plus attributable profits less losses, where the outcome can be assessed with reasonable certainty, less progress payments receivable. Attributable profit consists of the relevant proportion of the total estimated profit appropriate to the progress made in construction and letting. Cost includes direct expenditure and interest, less any relevant income.

Payments in advance

3.46 In other industries it can be no less difficult to determine whether the enterprise has transferred to the buyer the significant risks and rewards of ownership and retains no further involvement or control of the goods. Payments received in advance of performance do not represent revenue, because they have not been earned. Until the selling entity performs, the increase in cash is matched by an increase in liabilities, such as an obligation to supply goods or services or to make a refund. This principle is recognised in the ASB's draft Statement of principles.

Example 1

A company manufactures and supplies reproduction furniture. Since the choice of the final colouring and polishing of the furniture is left to the customer, the company takes a large non-refundable deposit from the customer at the time of the initial order. In some situations the piece ordered is in stock and only needs finishing before it can be shipped to the customer, in other cases the item needs to be completely manufactured.

There are obviously many points along the production process at which revenue could be recognised: at the initial order and deposit regardless of whether the furniture is in stock, when the deposit is received provided the item only needs to be polished, or only when the goods have been shipped to the customer and the invoice has been raised. However, the Appendix to IAS 18 specifically states that revenue must not be recognised when there is simply an intention to acquire or manufacture the goods in time for delivery. In this case it is not enough to have received payment: it cannot be considered to be earned until the manufacturing process is complete, including the finishing since this is a significant part of the manufacturing technique. Recognition may need to be delayed until the acceptance of the goods by the customer if the conditions of sale allow the customer to return furniture if the final colour and polish are unsatisfactory and the incidence of such returns cannot be assessed and provided for. If acceptance is unlikely to cause difficulty, then revenue can be recognised on despatch of the completed items.

Example 2

A distiller has obtained a contract to supply whisky at a later date for which the purchaser has made part payment at the time the contract was signed. The contract is for the sale of 600,000 gallons, but the distiller only has a stock of 200,000 gallons. The contract contains specific instructions with regard to the timing and location of the delivery.

For the 400,000 gallons which are not in stock there can be no recognition of a sale; revenue cannot be recognised when there is merely an intention to acquire goods in time for delivery. The 200,000 gallons which are in stock may fall under the provisions of the Appendix to IAS 18 with regard to 'bill and hold' sales, in which delivery is delayed at the buyer's request, but the buyer takes title and accepts billing. Revenue can be recognised on 'bill and hold' sales when the buyer takes title provided that:

- it is probable that delivery will be made;

- the item is on hand, identified and ready for delivery at the time the sale is recognised;
- the buyer specifically acknowledges the deferred delivery instructions; and
- the usual payment terms apply.

The transaction must genuinely be one in which the risks and rewards have passed to the purchaser, but the goods are physically stored with the seller for the purchaser's convenience. In this situation, it is possible that there is a 'bill and hold' sale of the 200,000 gallons in stock, but the terms would need to be examined carefully to ensure that: the buyer actually has title to those 200,000 gallons of whisky; the payment terms do not affect the transfer of risks and rewards; and the stock cannot be applied to satisfy other orders. For example, the existence of a holding fee might indicate that the stock is dedicated to that specific customer.

3.47 The concept that revenue must be earned before it can be recognised in the profit and loss account is also relevant to other types of sales, where payment is received in advance of supply, such as subscriptions. If the subscription consists of the provision of items of a similar value over its duration, such as a typical magazine subscription, then the income should be recognised over the life of the subscription on a straight line basis so as to match the cost of providing the items. If the items provided vary in value, such as a wine of the month club, then the income should be recognised on the basis of the sales value despatched in relation to the total estimated sales value of all the items covered by the subscription. Table 3.6 illustrates an accounting policy where subscription income is recognised on a straight line basis. Such a policy would be similar in the UK.

Table 3.6 – Sotheby's Holdings Inc – Annual Report – 31 December 1992

Note B – Summary of significant accounting policies (extract)

Revenue Recognition Auction commission income is generally recognized at the date of the related sale. Financial Services interest income is recognized using the interest method. Commissions on real estate transactions are recognized at the closing date. Catalogue subscription income is recognized over the twelve-month period of the subscription from the date of receipt of the proceeds. Other income is recognized at the time service is rendered by the Company.

3.48 When an event is held at a particular time, income and costs may be received and incurred in advance. For example, exhibitions and conferences or courses may involve delegates paying in advance of attending and certain of the costs, such as advertising, may also be incurred in advance. Since revenue is not earned until the exhibition is held or the course is given, the payments in advance represent deferred income, which can be released to the profit and loss account when the event takes place. A stringent review of the costs incurred before the event is necessary since prudence would require that such costs should only be carried forward if it is reasonably certain that the future related income will be sufficient to ensure their recovery. Table 3.7 gives an example of such an accounting policy for exhibition income and expenditure.

Table 3.7 – EMAP plc – Annual Report – 2 April 1994

Accounting Policies (extract)

Exhibition Income and Costs

Income and direct costs arising in the year relating to future events are deferred until those events have taken place, but only to the extent that the costs are expected to be recoverable.

Sale or return

3.49 Consignment sales or items shipped on a sale or return basis are also covered by the principle of ensuring that risks and rewards of ownership pass before recognising revenue. These are included as specific examples in the Appendix to IAS 18. If the purchaser of goods on consignment has undertaken to sell the items on behalf of the seller, then revenue should not be recognised until the purchaser has sold the goods to a third party. This recognition point is the same for goods sold on a sale or return basis or sales to distributors or dealers where the purchaser is merely acting as an agent for the seller.

Example 1

A company imports sports clothing and has a number of distributors in the UK. It gives its distributors an extended credit deal whereby it supplies new fashion items worth £10,000 to each distributor which can be sold on to third parties in order to encourage a market in these new items. The distributor does not have to pay for the goods until he has received the payment from the third party to whom they are sold. If they are not sold within six months of receipt, the distributor can either return them to the company or pay for them and keep them.

In this situation, revenue should not be recognised by the company until the earlier of the distributor receiving payment for his sale of the goods to a third party or six months after the distributor receives them, provided that they are not returned. It is only at this point that the company can determine whether the risks and rewards of ownership have passed to the distributor, because until then the goods may be returned to the company. Until it is known whether the goods have been sold, the goods should continue to be treated as the company's stocks.

Example 2

The facts are the same as in example 1, except that each distributor does not have to pay for the goods ever, unless he ceases to act as distributor. The purpose is to encourage new distributors into the market.

The company should again not treat this supply of the goods as a sale. The initial double entry would be to credit stock and debit a long-term asset. There would be no profit recorded. It is then necessary to consider whether the asset is recoverable. It would not be recoverable for so long as the distributor acted for the company and, therefore, it would be prudent to write the amount off to the profit and loss account.

Dealing with uncertainty

3.50 Revenue should not be recognised until it is probable that the economic benefits associated with the transaction will flow to the enterprise. For example, if there is doubt that a foreign government will grant permission for the consideration from a sale to a customer in a foreign country to be remitted, then the revenue cannot be recognised until the permission has been granted and the uncertainty is removed. However, if uncertainty arises about the collectibility of an amount already recorded as revenue, any provision necessary for bad debts should be recorded as an expense rather than as a deduction from revenue. [IAS 18 para 18].

Example 1

A company sold a property with a book value of £250,000 for £450,000 before the year end. Since the year end the purchaser has run into financial difficulties and cannot pay. The company has, however, received a £75,000 deposit and has a first charge over the property to secure the debt. It is difficult to assess the current value of the property, but it is possibly worth about £400,000. How should the transaction be accounted for?

Since the sale has actually taken place, it should be recorded as revenue in the financial statements. However, there will need to be a provision against the debtor. If the charge can be enforced, the debtor should be written down to original cost of £250,000, or to £325,000 (that is £250,000 plus £75,000) if the deposit received is not refundable. Account should not be taken of the current value of £400,000 as no new buyer at that figure has yet been found.

Example 2

A car hire business only rents cars to people who have been in a car accident which is not their fault. Customers rent cars while their own cars are being repaired and they are not charged for the hire period. Invoices are sent to the insurance company of the driver who was at fault in the accident. Negotiations then ensue between the car hire business and the insurance company which eventually result in the invoice being paid either in full or in part depending on the specific circumstances of each case.

Revenue should only be recognised when the service has been performed, the amount of revenue can be measured reliably and significant risks of collection do not exist. In this case only the service has been performed at the time the invoice is raised. The invoice is merely the starting point for negotiations which establish the amount of the revenue, if any. Until the insurance company agrees a price, the fee for the rental service and indeed whether this can be collected is not known. Since there is significant doubt about the probability of economic benefit flowing to the car hire company, revenue recognition must be delayed until the final fee is agreed by both parties.

3.51 The process of matching revenue with expenses means that revenue and costs are recognised at the same time. In most cases, expenses, such as warranties and other costs, which may be incurred after the shipment of goods, can be reliably measured when the other recognition criteria are met. However, if the expenses cannot be measured reliably then the revenue cannot be recognised. If this is the case then any consideration received for the sale of goods is treated as a liability until the criteria for recognition can be met. [IAS 18 para 19].

Services

3.52 Where a transaction involves rendering services, IAS 18 states that when the outcome of the transaction can be estimated reliably the revenue associated with the transaction should be recognised by reference to the stage of completion of the transaction at the balance sheet date. The outcome of a transaction will be able to be estimated reliably when all of the following conditions are satisfied:

- The amount of revenue can be measured reliably.
- It is probable that the economic benefits associated with the transaction will flow to the enterprise.
- The stage of completion of the transaction at the balance sheet date can be measured reliably.
- The costs incurred for the transaction and the costs to complete the transaction can be measured reliably.

[IAS 18 para 20].

3.53 The first two conditions are identical to conditions for the recognition of revenue on the sale of goods. Reasonable certainty must exist about the amount of revenue and about the probability that the company will in fact benefit from having provided a service.

Example

A fund manager earns a basic fee and a performance fee. The performance fee is based on a percentage of the amount by which the managed funds exceed the performance of the 'all share index' during a three year period. The fund manager can receive part of the performance fee in years one and two based on the performance in those years, but in year three the whole of the fee received to date may be clawed back if the fund underperforms in the third year. The costs of managing the funds tend to accrue evenly over the three year management period.

The most prudent approach to revenue recognition would be to recognise the performance fee only in year three when the actual amount of the fee due, if any, is known and it is certain that the growth of the managed funds is such that the fee is earned. This may be considered to be too prudent if there is a high level of confidence that some performance fee will be earned and the costs incurred in providing the service during the period are also reasonably certain. For example, there might be a history of always earning performance fees. A possible approach, provided that it is sensible to assume that some performance fee will be earned, would be to look at past performance and make a reasonable and prudent assessment of how much is usually earned in such fees. Then one third of the estimate could be recognised in years one and two with an adjustment to the actual fee earned in the final year. This would also allow the costs incurred in managing the fund to be matched with a reasonable estimate of the related income.

3.54 The fee for providing a service must also relate to the work performed; it must be earned. Sometimes the circumstances surrounding the transaction need to be examined closely in order to determine whether income has been earned or whether the substance of the transaction is capital in nature.

Example

Company A led a consortium including other parties B and C, which makes a successful bid. B and C pay company A a fee for letting them join the consortium. What is the nature of the fee?

If it is a genuine fee equivalent to a finders' fee then it could be considered to be income earned for acting as the leader and locating a suitable target and recognised in the profit and loss account immediately. If it is a reimbursement by B and C of an agreed proportion of A's expenses then it might be revenue or a reduction of the costs which A has incurred. However, if it is a larger fee unconnected with either finding the target or costs incurred in the deal, then the view could be taken that the 'fee' represents a reduction in the cost of A's investment in the target rather than revenue and should not be included in the profit and loss account.

Advertising agency commissions

3.55 The appendix to IAS 18 specifically discusses advertising and insurance agency commissions. Revenue should only be recognised on these transactions when the service is completed. The income of advertising agencies may consist of media commissions, which relate to the advert appearing before the public, and production commissions, which relate to production of the advert. Recognition should occur for media commissions when the advert appears before the public and for production commissions when the project is completed, for example as in Table 3.8.

Table 3.8 – Cordiant Communications Group plc – report and accounts – 31 December 1997

Principal accounting policies (extract)

Turnover

Turnover comprises amounts billed to clients, excluding sales taxes and intragroup transactions. Billings are usually rendered upon presentation date for media advertising and upon the completion of radio, television and print production.

Insurance agency commissions

3.56 According to IAS 18, insurance agency commissions should be recognised on the effective date of commencement or renewal dates of the policies. The amount recognised should be on a prudent basis so that if the commissions are adjusted depending on the claims experience of the policies written by the agent, then the amount recognised may need to be adjusted in line with the expected claims. If the policy will need additional servicing during its life, the commission, or a relevant part of it, may be recognised over the life of the policy to match with the expected costs; or provision may be made for any expected future costs. In practice, a more prudent policy may be adopted that delays recognition of the commission until the later of the effective date of commencement of the policy or the receipt of the insurance premium. This is illustrated in Table 3.9.

Table 3.9 – Steel Burrill Jones Group plc – Report and Accounts – 31 December 1997

Accounting policies (extract)

Turnover

Net retained brokerage and fees are generally credited when the client is debited, or at the inception date of the policy, whichever is the later. Where premiums are due in instalments, brokerage is deferred to the due date of such instalments. In relation to business where the group has an obligation to service future claims, provision has been made for the cost of such activity.

Commissions for the provision of advice on pensions, other employee benefits and personal financial planning services are credited when received. Consultancy fees for such advice are credited on the accruals basis.

Stage of completion

3.57 With regard to recognising revenue based on the stage of completion of a service IAS 18 is not dissimilar from the requirements in SSAP 9. Under SSAP 9 where the outcome of long-term contracts can be assessed with reasonable certainty before their conclusion, then the prudently calculated attributable profit should be recognised in the profit and loss account. Turnover should be ascertained in a manner appropriate to the stage of completion of the contract, the business and the industry in which it operates. [SSAP 9 para 28-29].

3.58 According to IAS 18, the stage of completion may be determined by a variety of methods depending on the nature of the service being provided. If the service consists of an indeterminate number of acts over a specified period of time, for example, the provision of a maintenance contract, then the revenue should be recognised on a straight line basis over the duration of the contract, unless there is evidence that another basis more accurately reflects the stage of completion. If one particular act in the performance of the contract has a much greater significance than any of the other acts, then the recognition of the revenue should be postponed until the significant act is completed.

3.59 In general, the methods to determine the stage of completion would include:

- Surveys of work performed.
- Services performed to date as a percentage of total services to be performed.
- The proportion that costs incurred to date bear to the estimated total costs of the transaction. Only costs that reflect services performed to date are

included in the costs to date. Only costs that reflect services performed or to be performed are included in the estimated total costs of the transaction. [IAS 18 paras 24-25].

Example 1

A company has entered into fixed rate contracts with local authorities to inspect and report on local property values. Valuation reports were completed and sent out before the year end, but due to administrative problems, invoicing was delayed until after the year end.

Since the work has been completed as evidenced by the submission of the valuation reports and since the contracts are fixed rate, it is acceptable to recognise the revenue and profits on the work performed before the year end.

Example 2

The facts are the same as in example 1 except that the valuation reports were not completed until after the year end.

If the valuation project was sufficiently material to the activity of the year that not to record any turnover for it would distort the financial statements (provided that a consistent policy is followed from year to year), it would fall to be classified as a long-term contract under SSAP 9, even if the duration of the contract did not exceed a year. If writing the reports does not form the majority of the work involved, then an appropriate percentage of the total contract price or of the costs to date against the total costs should be taken to turnover with a reasonable margin recognised, provided the outcome can be assessed with reasonable certainty.

On the other hand, if writing and submitting the reports formed the majority of the work required to complete the contracts or if the contracts were not long-term contracts under SSAP 9, then it would be appropriate to delay recognition until the reports were completed.

3.60 Until the outcome of the transaction can be estimated reliably, revenue should only be recognised to the extent of the costs incurred that are expected to be recoverable. If it is not probable that the costs can be recovered, then they should be expensed immediately. [IAS 18 paras 27-28]

3.61 In other situations, determining the stage of completion may be more a matter of industry practice and applying the accruals and prudence concepts than an application of long-term contract accounting. For example, in the shipping industry, ships may be engaged in journeys to more than one port which are not completed at the year end. In these circumstances, revenue is often recognised by reference to the last leg of the journey completed before the year end, as long as there is no doubt that payment will be received (see Table 3.20 on page 44). Similarly, a tour operator may have a package tour that departs before the year end, but which does not return until after the year end. An argument could be made for recognising revenue when the package tour has been completed since it is only then that the service has been provided. However, in practice tour operators recognise revenue on departure provided that all the costs of the package are known and have been accrued. For example, in Table 3.10 Airtours recognises income and expenditure on departure.

Table 3.10 – Airtours plc – Report and accounts – 30 September 1997

Accounting policies (extract)

3) Income recognition Turnover represents the aggregate amount of revenue receivable from inclusive tours (net of agents' commissions), travel agency commissions received and other services supplied to customers in the ordinary course of business. Revenues and expenses relating to inclusive tours are taken to the profit and loss account on holiday departure.

Sale of software

3.62 In the software industry, revenue recognition poses a number of problems which combine elements of sale of goods and sale of services. Software houses normally earn their revenue from three principal sources:

- Sale of off-the-shelf or ready made software where the licensing arrangement gives the customer the right to use the software for a specified period.
- Sale of customised software developed for specific application by the customer.
- Sale of software support services related to either own software or customised software.

3.63 Selling software is different from selling a tangible product since what is being sold is the right to use a piece of intellectual property rather than the actual computer disk or other media on which the programme is held. The actual delivery of the product in the form of the computer disk may, therefore, appear to be less important than it is where other types of goods are sold. On the other hand, if there is any risk that the customer may reject the software and the product is sold subject to customer satisfaction, then recognition may need to be delayed until after delivery and acceptance by the customer. For example, an off-the-shelf package may require tailoring to meet the customer's specifications. In this situation, if the supply does not qualify as a long-term contract, revenue may not be earned until after delivery, set up and the subsequent testing of the software by the customer.

3.64 The sale of a completely standard package such as a word processor package or spreadsheet may, therefore, need to be treated differently from software that needs to be individually tailored for each customer. Companies that sell standard off-the-shelf packages generally treat their sales no differently than the sale of a physical product and recognise revenue on delivery. For example, Micro Focus Group's accounting policy adopts this approach (see Table 3.11).

Table 3.11 – Micro Focus Group Plc – Annual Report – 31 January 1994

NOTES TO CONSOLIDATED FINANCIAL STATEMENTS (extract)

Revenue recognition

Revenue represents the amounts derived from the provision of goods and services which fall within Micro Focus' ordinary activities, stated net of applicable sales taxes.

Revenue from sales of software packaged products to end users and resellers is recognised when the product is delivered.

Revenue from sales to original equipment manufacturers ("OEMs") under non-cancellable licence agreements generally provide for development fees and initial licence fees, which are recognised at the latter of (a) the date product is delivered to the OEM and (b) the date payment becomes due within twelve months and (c) the date of receipt of monies if collection cannot be assessed with reasonable assurance. When sales by the OEM exceed the initial licence fee commitment, revenue is recognised as unit shipments are required by the OEM.

Revenue from maintenance agreements is recognised pro-rata over the life of the agreement corresponding to notional delivery of the service.

3.65 Where a product is sold subject to continuing obligations under the agreement or the provision of updates free of charge, full provision should be made for any further costs that are likely to be incurred in connection with the sale. In addition, if customer acceptance is in doubt then recognition should be delayed until this is assured.

Example

A company sells software packages which may be modified to meet the customer's exact requirements. The sequence of the transaction is: order; invoice and delivery; and acceptance by the customer. The order, invoice and delivery may be before the year end, but the acceptance may be after the year end.

The Appendix to IAS 18 covers the issue of the buyer accepting delivery subject to installation and inspection. If the installation process is simple in nature – the example given is that of installing a factory tested television receiver which only needs to be unpacked and connected – then it is acceptable to recognise revenue immediately upon the buyer's acceptance of delivery. In general, though, recognition should be delayed until the installation and inspection processes are complete. For many types of software packages it is acceptable to recognise revenue when delivery has taken place by the year end. However, when there is a risk that the customer may not accept the package, sufficient evidence must be obtained of the acceptance before revenue can be recognised. There may be no need to wait for acceptance to occur before the year end, provided that all sales invoiced are delivered at the year end and have been subsequently accepted by the date the financial statements are signed. Provision should be made for any costs incurred after the year end that are necessary to obtain acceptance. Unlike television receivers, software bears more risk of customer rejection and, therefore, acceptance before financial statements are signed is required to give the necessary assurance of a completed sale if there is doubt.

3.66 The creation of software specifically developed for use by a customer normally requires executing a number of separate acts over a period of time. The product has to be designed and developed according to the customer's specification, adequately tested and finally installed on the customer's hardware. Where a contractual obligation is performed by an indeterminate number of acts over a period of time, revenue should normally be recognised in accordance with the principles outlined in SSAP 9. Consequently, the software house should recognise revenue in a manner appropriate to the stage of completion of the contract, provided that the outcome can be assessed with reasonable certainty. The requirements of SSAP 9 are discussed in detail in chapter 17.

3.67 The procedure to recognise profit is to include an appropriate proportion of total contract value as turnover in the profit and loss account as the contract activity progresses. The costs incurred in reaching that stage of completion should be matched with this turnover, resulting in the reporting of results that can be attributed to the proportion of work completed. Where, however, the outcome cannot be assessed with reasonable certainty before the conclusion of the contract, or where the contract is of a relatively short duration, the completed contracts method should be applied and, accordingly, revenue should be recognised when final completion takes place. Tables 3.12 and 3.13 give examples of accounting policies in this area.

Table 3.12 – MISYS plc – Report and Accounts – 31 May 1994

Accounting Policies (extract)

e) INCOME RECOGNITION

Turnover represents amounts invoiced to customers (net of value added tax) for goods and services. Revenue from sales of hardware and packaged software products is recognised when the product is despatched. Bespoke contracts are taken to profit when the project has reached the point of practical completion. Contracted income invoiced in advance for fixed periods is taken to income in equal monthly instalments over the period of the contract. Contractual retentions are recognised upon receipt of cash.

Commissions on insurance business are credited to income upon the relevant policy coming into force, with a provision for expected future lapses of those policies.

Table 3.13 – Logica plc – Annual Report – 30 June 1994

Report of the directors (extract)

Principal activities

Logica companies throughout the year were in the business of providing information technology services, concentrating on:

- the marketing, design, production, integration and maintenance of custom built software and associated hardware systems
- consultancy and project management in the field of information technology
- the design, development, implementation and marketing of software products and the re-usable elements of applications software, called system kernels.

Accounting policies (extract)

3 Recognition of Profits

Profit on contracts for the supply of professional services at pre-determined rates is taken as and when the work is billed irrespective of the duration of the contract.

Profit is taken on fixed price contracts whilst the contract is in progress, having regard to the proportion of the total contract which has been completed at the balance sheet date. Provision is made for all foreseeable future losses.

3.68 When the project involves the provision of hardware as well as software, the contract will need to be carefully reviewed to ensure that income is not recognised before it is earned.

Example

A company is developing a computer system for a customer. It has sold the hardware to the customer for a profit and this has been installed on the site where it will be eventually used, but the company is still working on developing the necessary software. The customer has the right to return the hardware if the software does not work. The company does not anticipate any problems with the software development which should take about 12 months.

It seems that there is one contract for the supply of both hardware and software. If this is the case then the treatment in SSAP 9 should be followed so that, if it is not a long-term contract, then no profit is taken until the contract is complete. This would ensure that income is not recognised until all the costs of developing the software to the customer's satisfaction are known. If the contract is a long-term contract under SSAP 9 then profit would be required to be taken before its conclusion, provided that the outcome can be assessed with reasonable certainty. The attributable profit should be accounted for on a prudent basis and included in the profit and loss account. The extent of profit recognition will depend on the degree of certainty over the contract's outcome and the degree of prudence built into the forecast of the contract's overall performance rather than the margin on the hardware in isolation. If the outcome of the project cannot be assessed with reasonable certainty then no profit should be reflected in the profit and loss account. If the costs of creating software of the required standard cannot be assessed with reasonable certainty it is appropriate to delay recognition of the sale.

Even if the contract for the supply of the hardware could be separated from the supply of the software there would still be an argument for delaying recognition of the sale of the hardware. The Appendix to IAS 18 states that if there is uncertainty about the possibility of return, revenue should only be recognised when the goods have been formally accepted by the customer or the goods have been delivered and the time allowed for their possible rejection has passed. Therefore, until the software has been installed and tested to the customer's satisfaction, revenue should not be recognised and any payments received for the hardware should be included in the financial statements as deferred income.

3.69 Where the software house provides an after sales support service (for example, product enhancement) through a separate maintenance contract, the question arises as to whether the maintenance income is capable of being regarded as earned 'up front' or whether the income should be deferred and recognised on a straight line basis over the period of the contract. It can be argued that if the cost of maintenance is negligible, the maintenance contract effectively provides the company with income with no material costs of earning that income. In this situation, it might be acceptable to recognise the income when it becomes due, that is, usually all at the start of the maintenance period. However, it would be necessary to accrue any related maintenance costs. Alternatively, if the cost of maintenance is material, the likelihood is that such costs will be incurred over the period of the agreement. In such a situation, the more prudent approach should be adopted of spreading the income over the period to which it relates, that is, the period of the maintenance agreement. This approach is illustrated in Table 3.14.

Table 3.14 – Total Systems plc – Annual Report and Accounts – 31 March 1994

Accounting Policies (extract)

(d) *Software maintenance*

For software covered by maintenance contracts, income is credited to the profit and loss account over the period to which the contract relates. Costs associated with these contracts are expensed as incurred.

Franchise fees

3.70 Franchise agreements may provide for the supply of initial services such as training and assistance to help the franchisee set up and operate the franchise operation, subsequent services and the supply of equipment, stocks and other tangible assets and know-how. Therefore, these agreements may generate different types of revenue such as initial franchise fees, profits and losses from the sale of fixed assets and royalties as illustrated in Table 3.15.

Table 3.15 – Grand Metropolitan Public Limited Company – Annual Report – 30 September 1994

ACCOUNTING POLICIES (extract)

FRANCHISING

Franchising generates initial franchise fees, as well as profits or losses arising from the franchising of developed or purchased outlets previously operated by the group, and ongoing royalty revenues based on sales made by franchisees. Income from franchising is included in operating profit, apart from any property element which is treated as a sale of fixed assets.

The appendix to IAS 18 deals with franchise fees. In general, such fees should be recognised on a basis that reflects the purpose for which they were charged.

3.71 The appendix to IAS 18 states that, in general, revenue from the supplies of assets should be recognised when the items are delivered or title passes. Fees charged for the use of continuing rights granted by a franchise agreement or for other continuing services provided during the period of the agreement should be recognised as the service is provided or the rights are used.

3.72 However the appendix to IAS 18 goes on to require, where the franchise agreement provides for the franchiser to supply equipment, stocks or other assets at a price lower than that charged to others, or at a price that does not allow the franchiser to make a reasonable profit on the supplies, that part of the initial fee should be deferred. The amount of the initial fee deferred should be sufficient to cover the estimated costs in excess of the price charged to the franchisee for any assets and to allow the franchiser to make a reasonable profit on these sales. This deferred income can then be recognised over the period the goods are likely to be provided. The balance of the initial fee should be recognised when the initial services have been substantially accomplished.

3.73 Similarly, if there is no separate fee for the supply of continuing services after the initial fee or if the separate fee is not sufficient to cover the cost of providing any subsequent services together with a reasonable profit, then part of the initial fee should also be deferred and recognised as the subsequent services are provided.

The use by others of an enterprise's resources

3.74 IAS 18 states that revenues arising from others using an enterprise's resources, which yield interest, royalties and dividends should only be recognised when it is probable that the economic benefits associated with the transaction will flow to the enterprise and the amount of the revenue can be measured reliably. These revenues are recognised on the following bases:

- Interest.

  On a time proportion basis taking account of the effective yield on the asset.

- Royalties.

  On an accruals basis in accordance with the substance of the relevant agreement.

- Dividends.

  When the shareholder's right to receive payment is established.

[IAS 18 para 29].

Interest

3.75 In many situations, the actual rate of interest charged by a lender will be the same as the effective rate (that is, the rate required to discount the expected future income streams over the life of the loan to its initial carrying amount). Discounting is discussed above from paragraph 3.27. Other transactions may include elements both of interest and of other financial service fees. For these transactions it is necessary to differentiate between fees that are part of the effective yield of the transaction and fees that are earned for performing a certain act. For example, Table 3.16 gives National Westminster Bank's accounting policy for fees receivable.

Table 3.16 – National Westminster Bank Plc – Annual Report and Accounts – 31 December 1997

Principal accounting policies (extract)

(iv) Fees receivable

Fees receivable that represent a return for services provided are brought into profit when the related service is performed. Certain front-end fees relating to loans and advances are, subject to yield criteria, taken to profit over the period of the loan.

3.76 The appendix to IAS 18 gives guidance on accounting for the different types of financial service fees. Reviewing the borrower's credit rating or registering charges, for example, are necessary and integral parts of the lending process. Fees for performing such services should be deferred and recognised as an adjustment to the effective yield. Commitment fees that are charged by the lender when it is probable that a specific transaction will take place should similarly be included in the effective yield, but if the commitment expires without the transaction taking place, then the fee may be recognised as revenue on expiration.

3.77 Other types of financial service fees are earned as the service is provided. For example, commitment fees that are charged by a lender when it is unlikely that a lending arrangement will be entered into should be recognised on a time apportioned basis over the commitment period. Fees for servicing a loan should also be recognised as the service is provided.

3.78 A third type of financial service fee relates to performing a particular, significant act. Commissions received on the allotment of shares or placement fees for arranging a loan between a borrower and an investor are examples of such significant acts. Revenue should be recognised when the act has been performed, for example when the shares have been allotted or the loan arranged. However, fees earned for the completion of a significant act must be distinguished from fees that relate to future performance or to any risk retained. A loan syndication fee, for example, may be earned when the transaction takes place, if the enterprise that arranges the loan either has no further involvement or retains part of the loan package at the same effective yield for comparable risk as the other participants. If the enterprise has a lower effective yield for comparable risk than other participants, then some of the syndication fee should be deferred and recognised as revenue as an adjustment to the effective yield of the loan. If the effective yield is higher than the other participants, then part of the yield that relates to the syndication fee should be recognised when the syndicate is complete. [IAS 18 appendix]. The purpose of such adjustments is to ensure that the effective yield of the loan, for comparable risk, is the same for all participants to the syndicate so that the syndication fee earned relates only to setting up the syndicate.

Royalties

3.79 Royalties include other fees for the use of assets such as trademarks, patents, software, copyright, record masters, films and TV programmes. The terms of an agreement will normally indicate when the revenue has been earned. In general, revenue may be recognised on a straight line basis over the life of the agreement or another systematic basis such as in relation to sales to which the royalty relates (Table 3.17).

Table 3.17 – Chrysalis Group PLC – Annual Report and Accounts – 31 August 1994

notes to the accounts (extract)

1. Accounting policies (extracts)

Record royalties (excluding record producer services and music publishing royalties)(extract)

Royalty income is included on a receivable basis calculated on sales of records arising during each accounting period as reported by licensees, any unrecouped advances being included in the period in which the licence agreement expires.

Record producer services and music publishing royalties

Royalties are dealt with on a received/paid basis except that:

(i) provision is made for royalties payable at the end of each accounting period in respect of royalties received during each accounting period; and

(ii) music publishing royalty advances are carried forward and recognised as an asset where such advances relate to proven artists or songwriters and where it is estimated that sufficient future royalties will be earned for recoupment of these advances.

Film licensing and distribution income

Income from productions for cinema and television exhibition is recognised in the profit and loss account from the date of release for distribution or telecasting.

Television production costs
Turnover and attributable profits are recognised on contracts which are incomplete at the end of the year in the proportion that costs incurred to date bear to estimated ultimate costs after making provision for anticipated losses.

3.80 In general, revenue should not be recognised under licensing agreements until the critical event has occurred and it has been earned.

Example 1

A film distributor grants a licence to a cinema operator. The licence entitles the theatre to show the film once for consideration of the higher of a non-refundable guarantee or a percentage of the box office receipts.

The film distributor should recognise the revenue on the date the film is shown. It is usual industry practice for the recognition of both the guaranteed minimum amount and any percentage of box office receipts to be delayed until the exhibition of the film. It is only when the film is shown that the revenue has been earned.

Example 2

A computer games software house grants two different licences to arcade games machine manufacturers to use the software for a certain game. The annual licence, which has a fee of £100,000, allows the software to be used for one year and can be renewed annually. The perpetual licence, which has a fee of £400,000, allows the software to be used indefinitely with the licensee entitled to upgrades free of charge, although the software house is under no obligation to upgrade the software and does not expect to incur significant costs in performing any upgrades.

Under the perpetual licence there may be a commercial or at least a moral obligation to upgrade the software and there is some cost in doing so. This is also supported by the fact that the perpetual licence costs more than the annual licence. In this situation, there is a strong argument for spreading the licence fee over the expected life of the game in order to match it with the costs of providing the upgrades. The annual licence fee, on the other hand, does not carry any further obligations on the part of the software house and may, therefore, be recognised immediately.

3.81 In some situations, a licensing agreement may be recognised as an outright sale. For example, if a non-refundable one-off fee has been received for the foreign exhibition rights to a film that allow the licensee to use the rights at any time in certain countries without restriction, then it may be appropriate to recognise the income when the fee is received. Since the licensor has no control over any further use or distribution of the product and has no further action to perform under the contract he has effectively sold the rights detailed in the licensing agreement.

Dividends

3.82 Dividend income should be recognised when the shareholder's right to receive payment is established. For shares held as trade investments, the right to receive payment is likely to be established at the ex-dividend date or when the dividend is declared if there is no ex-dividend date. Dividends are usually recommended by the directors and then declared by the shareholders who cannot declare a dividend which exceeds the amount recommended. It is rare for the amount of the dividend to be subsequently reduced by the shareholders or for the dividend not to be approved. Therefore, for holdings in listed companies, recognition need not be delayed until the approval by the shareholders or even until payment, as long as there is no reason to believe that the amount of the dividend will be reduced by the shareholders. If the right to the dividend cannot be established until the income is received, then recognition should be delayed until then.

3.83 The situation for parent companies' investments in subsidiaries is different from that where the shareholding is held as a trade investment. Groups usually prepare financial statements to the same year end. Parent companies recognise their subsidiaries' dividends in the year to which they relate, rather than in the following period when they are declared and paid. This is in accordance with SSAP 17, 'Accounting for post balance sheet events'. This standard includes dividends receivable from subsidiary and associated undertakings as examples of adjusting events that are reflected in financial statements because of customary accounting practice. However, chapter 20 contains information on developments in this area (the 'Tomberger' case).

3.84 A related issue concerning some dividends is whether the credit should be regarded as a revenue or capital item. One example of this is the treatment of dividends paid by a subsidiary to its parent. This treatment is discussed in detail in chapter 22. Before the Companies Act 1948 was amended by the Companies Act 1981, when a subsidiary paid a dividend out of pre-acquisition profits to its parent, the parent was required to reduce the carrying value of its investment in the subsidiary by this amount. The parent could not treat this amount as realised and could not distribute it; the dividend received was therefore a capital item rather than revenue. Following the 1981 Act, when a dividend is paid out of pre-acquisition profits by a subsidiary it need not be applied in reducing the value of the investment in the subsidiary in the parent's books. It can be taken to the profit and loss account. Only if the underlying value of the subsidiary does not support the carrying value of the parent's investment in it following the dividend, does the parent have to make a provision against its investment if that diminution in value is expected to be permanent.

3.85 Bonus issues of shares by a subsidiary to its parent do not transfer any value from the subsidiary to the parent. There are more shares in issue, but there is no economic significance to the transaction. Therefore, a bonus issue does not give the parent a reason to recognise a gain, realised or unrealised, by increasing the carrying value of its investment in the subsidiary.

3.86 Many listed companies choose to make arrangements for ordinary shareholders to elect to receive their dividends in the form of additional shares rather than in cash. The share equivalent is sometimes referred to as a scrip dividend or a stock dividend and consists of shares fully paid up out of the company's reserves. The advantages of issuing scrip dividends are that, in the short term, the company's cash position is improved. Secondly, no ACT is payable in respect of those dividends taken in the form of shares.

3.87 The treatment of scrip dividends from companies held as trade investments rather than as subsidiaries is analogous to that of bonus issues by subsidiaries. If the investment is a current asset investment and the company marks to market, then the benefit of the dividend will come through in the profit and loss account when the investment is revalued. If, however, the company does not mark to market then the investment could be revalued under the alternative accounting rules with a corresponding increase in the revaluation reserve rather than recording a gain in the profit and loss account (see chapters 5 and 16).

3.88 Generally, most recipient companies merely record normal scrip dividends (and enhanced dividends that are discussed below) as an increase in the number of shares that they have in the company making the scrip. In this situation, no adjustment would be made to the carrying value of the investment nor would any amount be credited to the profit and loss account. However, some companies, for example investment trust companies, account for a scrip alternative as income in their profit and loss account. Shareholders who would normally get the benefit of a cash dividend taken to revenue might be prejudiced if the scrip is merely recorded as an increase in the shareholding in the investment.

3.89 The Association of Investment Trust Companies (AITC) published a draft SORP for investment trust companies in April 1995. The guidance in the draft SORP is that the receipt of scrip dividends is in substance the receipt of cash dividends with a simultaneous reinvestment of the proceeds in the issue of new shares. Therefore, the accounting treatment for investment trusts should be to debit the carrying value of the investment and credit income with an amount equivalent to the cash dividend.

3.90 Scrip dividends can be of significant benefit to the issuing company where ACT payable in respect of a cash dividend would otherwise be irrecoverable, so much so that in recent years enhanced scrip dividends have been offered by companies. Enhanced scrip dividends give the shareholder an incentive to elect to take the shares rather than the cash dividend. For example, the cash dividend might be worth £100 to an individual investor, but the shares issued as an alternative might be worth £150. This means that a rational shareholder will invariably opt for the share alternative rather than the cash. In addition, a number of third party financial institutions may, in conjunction with the paying company, offer placing facilities to shareholders taking the scrip, such that if a shareholder opts to take (say) £150 of shares they will immediately be placed for cash of (say) £140. This makes it virtually certain that the shareholder will elect to take the shares rather than the dividend alternative.

3.91 Enhanced scrip dividends further complicate the revenue recognition issue for investment trusts since it could be argued that only part of the enhanced scrip dividend (the amount equivalent to the cash dividend) is of a revenue nature. Following this argument part of the scrip dividend would be recognised as revenue and part would be treated as capital. The guidance in the draft SORP regards the enhanced element as in substance a bonus issue of shares. Therefore only the amount of the cash dividend alternative should be regarded as revenue and treated in the same way as a normal scrip dividend. The enhanced element should be treated as capital in the same manner as a bonus issue of shares. Other specialist investment entities may wish to follow the SORP when it is finalised. However, for most companies, such dividends should be accounted for as outlined in paragraph 3.88 above.

Example

A pension scheme has received an enhanced scrip dividend. The shares received have been retained.

A pension scheme has a choice between showing the dividend in the revenue account or showing it as part of the change in market value of investments in the reconciliation of net assets. The former treatment would show a higher level of income than if the cash alternative had been taken. The latter treatment would distort the revenue account as it would appear that no income had been received. Therefore, in the absence of other guidance, a pension scheme should take the equivalent of the cash dividend to the revenue account and the enhanced element to the reconciliation of net assets as this will retain comparability with previous years when cash dividends were received. If material, the treatment should be explained in the accounting policies.

Revenue grants

3.92 The recognition of government grants is covered by SSAP 4 (revised), 'Accounting for government grants'. This standard starts from the premise that the basic concepts that should be applied in recognising grants in the profit and loss account are those of 'accruals' and 'prudence'. The 'accruals' concept implies that government grants should be recognised in the profit and loss account to match them with the expenditure towards which they are intended to contribute. The relationship between the grant and the related expenditure is, therefore, of paramount importance in establishing the accounting treatment to be adopted. Grants made as contributions to revenue expenditure should be credited to the profit and loss account of the period in which the related expenditure is incurred. For example, see Westland Group plc's accounting policy in Table 3.18.

Table 3.18 – Westland Group plc – Annual Report – 1 October 1993

Accounting policies (extract)

8 Research, development, launching costs and launch aid

To the extent that design, development and learning costs are not recoverable under specific contracts, including risk sharing contracts, they are written off as incurred, net of any launch aid recovered under the Civil Aviation Act 1982. Learning costs are the estimated excess cost of manufacturing initial production batches.

Launch aid from H.M. Government is credited in full against the initial research, development and learning costs in the year in which it is receivable. Additional research, development and learning costs required under launch aid agreements in excess of launch aid receivable are charged against revenue as incurred.

3.93 It is fundamental to the 'prudence' concept that government grants should not be recognised until the conditions for their receipt have been complied with and there is reasonable assurance that the grant will be received. In the event that a grant appears likely to have to be repaid, provision should be made for the estimated liability.

3.94 Difficulties of matching may arise where the terms of the grant do not specify precisely the expenditure towards which it is intended to contribute. For example, grants may be awarded to defray project costs comprising both revenue and capital expenditure. Project grants are normally awarded on this basis and may be related to the project's capital expenditure costs and the number of jobs created or safeguarded. In such circumstances, the expenditure eligible for grant aid may be all the costs incurred that are directly attributable to the project. The terms of the grant itself often need to be carefully examined to establish whether the intent is to defray costs or to establish a condition relating to the entire amount of the grant.

Example

A company obtains a grant from an Industrial Development agency for an investment project in Scotland. The project is a building to house a manufacturing plant. The principal terms are that the grant payments relate to the level of capital expenditure and the intention of the grant is to help ensure that imports of the product can be replaced with UK sourced products and to safeguard 500 jobs. The grant will have to be repaid if there is an underspend on capital or if the jobs are not safeguarded until 18 months after the date of the last fixed asset purchase.

This grant is related to capital expenditure. The employment condition should be seen as an additional condition to prevent replacement of labour by capital, rather than as the reason for the grant. If the grant was revenue it would be related to revenue expenditure such as a percentage of the payroll cost or a fixed amount per job safeguarded.

3.95 SSAP 4 states that where the terms of the grant do not specify precisely the expenditure it is intended to meet, the most appropriate matching may be achieved by assuming that the grant is contributing towards the expenditure that forms the basis for its payment, that is, the expenditure included on the claim form. It will then be possible to account for the grant according to the different types of expenditure towards which it is intended to contribute. If the grant is paid when evidence is produced that certain expenditure has been incurred, then the grant should be matched with that expenditure.

3.96 In certain circumstances, however, the actual expenditure the grant is intended to contribute towards may differ from the expenditure that forms the basis of its payment. For example, the grant may relate to a total project expenditure that may include, in addition to capital expenditure, working capital costs, training costs and removal costs. However, the grant may become payable in instalments on incurring specific amounts of capital expenditure as the project progresses. In this situation, it would be wrong to match the grant with the capital expenditure alone. The most appropriate treatment, therefore, would be to match the grant received rateably with the expenditure towards which the grant is assisting, that is, the grant would have to be spread rateably over the constituent parts of the project expenditure. This treatment is in accordance with the SSAP 4 which provides that where such evidence exists and is sufficiently persuasive, then it is appropriate to match grants received with identified expenditure and this approach should always be preferred.

3.97 Sometimes grants may be payable on a different basis, for example on the achievement of a non-financial objective. In such situations, the grant should be matched with the identifiable costs of achieving that objective. Such costs must be identified or estimated on a reasonable basis. For example, if a grant is given on condition that jobs are created and maintained for a minimum period, the grant should be matched with the cost of providing the jobs for that period. As a result, a greater proportion of the grant may fall to be recognised in the early stages of the project because of higher non-productive and set-up costs.

3.98 In certain circumstances, government grants may be awarded unconditionally without regard to the enterprise's future actions, or requirement to incur further costs. Such grants may be given for the immediate financial support, or assistance of an enterprise, or for the reimbursement of costs previously incurred. They may also be given to finance the general activities of an enterprise over a specified period, or to compensate for a loss of income. In some instances, the extent of these grants may constitute a major source of revenue for the enterprise.

Where grants are awarded on such a basis, they should be recognised in the profit and loss account of the period in respect of which they are paid, or, if they are not stated to be paid in respect of a particular period, in the profit and loss account of the period in which they are receivable. The presentation and disclosure requirements of SSAP 4 are detailed from paragraph 3.112.

Insurance recoveries

3.99 Amounts receivable from insurance recoveries may represent a significant source of income to a company, especially when disaster strikes. For example, in the event of a factory being destroyed by fire, a company may be insured for the replacement cost of the fixed assets and stock, which may be higher than the carrying value of the assets, as well as for any consequential loss of profits. Compensation received for loss of profits should be credited in arriving at the operating profit for the period to which it relates and be shown as an exceptional item if material.

3.100 Insurance proceeds relating to fixed assets and stocks should also be credited to the profit and loss account. The assets lost would be written off and, hence, the net gain or loss, that is, the difference between the insurance proceeds and the carrying value of the assets written off, would be recognised as a profit. In order to comply with FRS 3, the gain or loss relating to the fixed assets would be shown as an exceptional item after operating profit, under the caption of profits or losses on the disposal of fixed assets. The gain or loss relating to the stocks destroyed would be included in operating profit, disclosed as an exceptional item, if material.

3.101 When the destroyed assets are replaced, they should be included at their actual replacement cost. Generally, there is no basis for deferring recognition of the insurance proceeds to reduce the cost of the replacement assets.

Presentation and disclosure

3.102 The Act requires the profit and loss account of a company or a group to comply with one of four formats. FRS 3 also affects the disclosure requirements of the profit and loss account. These requirements and the format requirements are set out in detail in chapter 6. The remainder of this chapter will deal with the different types of income that may be included in the turnover and other operating income lines of the profit and loss account and the disclosure requirements relating to grants.

Turnover

3.103 The Act specifies the amount a company must include in its profit and loss account under the heading of 'Turnover.' This comprises the amounts a company derives from providing goods and services that fall within its ordinary activities, after deducting trade discounts, VAT and any other taxes based on the amounts it so derives. [Sec 262(1)]. The definition accords with the requirement in SSAP 5 that turnover should exclude VAT on taxable outputs. However, SSAP 5 goes further: it says that, if a company intends to show also its gross turnover, it should show the VAT relevant to that turnover as a deduction in arriving at the turnover exclusive of VAT. Although this treatment is not common, it is practised by companies that may wish to emphasise the amount of VAT and duty that is included in their gross turnover. An example of a company that gives gross and net turnover is given in Table 3.19.

Table 3.19 – Rothmans International p.l.c. – Annual Report and Accounts – 31 March 1994

Accounting policy (extract)

GROSS SALES REVENUE AND TURNOVER Gross sales revenue is the amount receivable by the Companies and their subsidiary undertakings from sales to third parties, inclusive of value added taxes, tobacco duties and all other sales taxes. It is stated after deducting trade discounts. Turnover represents gross sales revenue less value added taxes, tobacco duties and all other sales taxes.

Combined profit and loss account (extract)

	Notes	1994 £m	1993 £m
Gross sales revenue		**6,697.2**	6,583.6
Less: duty, excise and sales taxes		**(4,212.1)**	(4,171.0)
Turnover	1	**2,485.1**	2,412.6

Trading activities

3.104 Since the income created by the ordinary trading activities of a company is by definition its turnover, the nature of the company's business will dictate what is included in turnover rather than the nature of the income. For most companies, other types of income or gains such as the profit on disposal of a subsidiary or interest receivable which is ancillary to the company's main business activities would be reported in the profit and loss account, but not in the turnover line. Other gains, such as those relating to holding non-trading assets such as buildings which have increased in value may be reported as revaluation movements in the statement of total recognised gains and losses or may not be acknowledged in the financial statements at all depending on the accounting convention chosen. Groups with diverse activities have turnover from different sources that may be subject to different recognition criteria, for example see Table 3.20.

Table 3.20 – Trafalgar House Public Limited Company – Report and Accounts – 30 September 1994

Principal accounting policies (extract)

Turnover, which excludes inter-company trading, represents the following:

Engineering and Construction	sales value of work done
Residential property	property sales
Commercial property	property sale and gross rental income
Hotels	gross receipts
Shipping	receipts to the last voyage leg completed at the year end

Long-term contracts

3.105 For a company that engages in long-term contracts, SSAP 9 requires that "*...turnover is ascertained in a manner appropriate to the stage of completion of the contract, the business and the industry in which it operates*". [SSAP 9 para 28]. Therefore, provided that the outcome of each contract, on a project by project basis, can be assessed with reasonable certainty and all losses are provided for in full, the sales value of the work performed during the period should represent turnover. The amounts recorded as turnover may not correspond to the amounts invoiced to customers since invoicing may be ahead of or behind the actual progress on the contract. Amounts receivable from customers in excess of the amounts recorded as turnover should be included in creditors as payments on account. Amounts recorded as turnover in excess of amounts receivable from customers should be included in debtors as amounts recoverable on contracts. The accounting policies of George Wimpey provide an example of accounting for long-term contracts (Table 3.21) and the accounting treatment is discussed in greater detail in chapter 17.

Table 3.21 – George Wimpey PLC – Annual Report – 31 December 1994

Accounting Policies (extracts)

Turnover

Contracting turnover comprises the value of work executed during the year including the settlement of claims arising from previous years, amounts received on management fee contracts funded by the client and the Group's share of unincorporated joint venture turnover. Other turnover is based on the invoiced value of goods and services supplied during the year and includes house and land sales completed, trading and investment property sales completed and rental income. Turnover excludes value added tax and intra-group turnover.

Profit

Operating profit comprises the results of contracting, the provision of goods and services, private housing development, land sales, property development and investment. It includes the results attributable to contracts completed and long-term contracts in progress where a profitable outcome can prudently be foreseen, after deducting amounts recognised in previous years and after making provision for foreseeable losses. Claims receivable are recognised as income when received or if certified for payment. Estate development profit is taken on the number of houses of an estate in respect of which legal completions have taken place.

Long-term contracts

The amount of long-term contracts, at costs incurred, net of amounts transferred to cost of sales, after deducting foreseeable losses and payments on account not matched with turnover, is included in work in progress and stock as long-term contract balances. The amount by which recorded turnover is in excess of payments on account is included in debtors as amounts recoverable on long-term contracts. Payments in excess of recorded turnover and long-term contract balances are included in creditors as payments received on account on long-term contracts. The amount by which provisions or accruals for foreseeable losses exceed costs incurred, after transfers to cost of sales, is included within either provisions for liabilities and charges or creditors, as appropriate.

Commissions and agency fees

3.106 Where a company acts as an agent or broker, such as a travel agent or stock broker, it should not include the gross value of the contracts in its turnover, but only the commission or margin that it charges on each deal. The inclusion of such net amounts in turnover is consistent with IAS 18 which excludes amounts collected on behalf of third parties from its definition of revenue. An estate agent, for example, should only recognise the commission that is earned on each property sold. This is illustrated in Table 3.22.

Table 3.22 – Debenham Tewson & Chinnocks Holdings plc – Report & Accounts – 30 April 1994

Notes to the accounts (extract)

1. Accounting policies (extract)

Turnover	Turnover comprises commissions and fees receivable exclusive of sales related taxes. Agency commissions are recognised on completion of the transaction.

Sale of goods CIF

3.107 Where a company sells certain items either FOB (free on board) or CIF (cost, insurance, freight), it may wish to reduce the CIF items to FOB by deducting these expenses from turnover. If there is no profit element in the insurance and freight being charged to the customer, then it could be argued that these charges are merely reimbursement of expenses, and not income and, therefore, should be used to reduce the carriage costs included in the profit and loss account. However, where there is a profit element in the CIF charges, because there is no right of set-off of expenditure against income under the Act, the amount for turnover should include the full CIF selling price. This is illustrated in Table 3.23. If, however, the amount of these charges is significant in comparison to the selling price of the product and if there is no cost of sales relating to the charges (because such carriage charges are included in distribution costs, for example) it may be acceptable to take the element of reimbursement to reduce the costs and the element of profit to other operating income. In this situation, the reimbursement of the costs without any element of profit would not be considered to be income.

Table 3.23 – The RTZ Corporation PLC – Annual Report and Accounts – 31 December 1993

Notes to the 1993 Accounts (extract)

1 TURNOVER (extract)

This comprises sales to third parties at invoiced amounts which vary between ex works and c.i.f price depending on contract terms.

Other operating income

3.108 'Other operating income' will include income that is associated with a company's normal activities, but that falls outside the definition of turnover. An item would not be put into 'Other operating income' just because it was small. For example, the revenue of the company's smallest division would nevertheless be included in turnover. Amounts shown in 'Other operating income' are typically both incidental to the main activities of the company and are different in nature from amounts included in turnover.

3.109 For example, a manufacturing company which receives a small amount of royalty income may wish to include it in 'Other operating income' rather than in turnover since to add it to turnover may overstate the company's margin if the royalty has no associated cost of sales.

3.110 In certain circumstances, commissions may also fall to be treated as 'Other operating income'. This analysis is illustrated in the following example.

Example

A retail business sells National Lottery tickets in addition to confectionery, tobacco and newspapers. Customers say which numbers they want and the retailer obtains them via the computer provided by the National Lottery. Then the customers pay for their tickets and the retailer pays this amount less a commission to the National Lottery.

Since turnover as defined in the Act is amounts derived from the provision of goods and services falling within the company's ordinary activities (para 3.103), this commission could be seen as more of an incidental activity. If this is the case it may be more appropriate to include the commission under 'other operating income' rather than as turnover. This would prevent the fact that there is no cost of sales attributable to the income from distorting the gross margins, especially if these commissions are not disclosed as a separate segment in the segmental analysis of turnover and profit. On the other hand, the distribution of lottery tickets could be seen as a service to customers in which case it may be appropriate to include the commission in turnover. The category into which the commission falls should be determined based on how significant the provision of lottery tickets is to the activities of the business.

Rent

3.111 In addition, 'other operating income' could include rents from land, unless the company involved were a property company that derived income from the renting of property. However, the notes to the profit and loss account must disclose the amount of rents from land, after deducting ground rents, rates and other outgoings. This requirement applies only if a substantial part of the company's revenue for the financial year consists of such rents. [4 Sch 53(1)(5)].

Government grants

3.112 The Act specifically does not allow income to be set off against expenditure [4 Sch 5]. In general, therefore, income that is received in compensation for expenditure incurred should not be netted off against the related expenditure. For example, a government grant that is received for employing a certain number of people for a certain length of time should be recognised on a basis that matches the costs of employing the people, but should not be used to reduce those employment costs. Such a grant is not turnover, so therefore should be included in other operating income.

3.113 Where an enterprise receives government grants, the disclosures required by SSAP 4 are as follows:

- The accounting policy adopted for government grants.

- The effects of government grants on the results and/or the financial position of the enterprise.

- Where an enterprise is in receipt of government assistance other than grants that have a material effect on its results, the nature of the assistance and, where possible, an estimate of the financial effects.

- Where applicable, the potential liabilities to repay grants.

[SSAP 4 para 28].

The accounting policy note should include the period or periods over which grants are credited to the profit and loss account. Where an enterprise is in receipt of various types of grants, it will normally be sufficient to give a broad indication of the period or periods over which they will be credited to the profit and loss account.

3.114 Where an enterprise is in receipt of a government grant that has a material effect on its results for the period and any future periods, the most practical way of identifying the effect of the grant on reported earnings may be to disclose the total amount credited in the profit and loss as an exceptional item.

3.115 Any unamortised deferred income relating to the grant will be included under the heading 'Accruals and deferred income'. Where the amount of unamortised deferred income is material, it may also be appropriate to identify this amount separately in a note to the balance sheet. It will provide readers of the financial statements with an indication of the extent to which future results may be expected to benefit from grants already received. Another way of showing the effect could be to include a statement of the changes during the period in the amount of the deferred income carried forward, showing: grants received; grants credited to the profit and loss account; and grants repaid, if any. For example, see Table 3.24.

Table 3.24 – Pilkington plc – Directors' Report and Accounts – 31 March 1994

Notes to the financial statements (extract)

	1994		1993	
26 Deferred Income	**Group £m**	**Company £m**	Group £m	Company £m
At beginning of year	**15.7**	**30.8**	23.7	-
Investment grants receivable	**-**	**-**	2.7	-
Other deferred income receivable	**-**	**-**	0.3	30.8
Exchange rate adjustments	**(0.1)**	**-**	2.2	-
Changes in composition of the Group	**(0.4)**	**-**	-	-
	15.2	**30.8**	28.9	30.8
Release to profit and loss account in the year:				
Investment grants	**(2.9)**	**-**	(11.5)	-
Other deferred income	**(0.4)**	**(3.1)**	(1.7)	-
At end of year	**11.9**	**27.7**	15.7	30.8

3.116 Where government assistance is given in a form other than grants, SSAP 4 requires that the nature and, where measurable, the effects of the assistance should be disclosed. Similar disclosures should be given for significant assistance received from a source other than the government as discussed in paragraphs 3.24 and 3.92.

3.117 Once a grant is recognised, any related contingency, such as the requirement to repay the grant under certain circumstances, should be treated in accordance with SSAP 18, 'Accounting for contingencies'. These requirements are detailed in chapter 20.

Annex – Text of TR 481 and TR 482

Technical Release 481, The Determination of Realised Profits and Disclosure of Distributable Profits in the Context of the Companies Acts 1948 to 1981, and Technical Release 482, The Determination of Distributable Profits in the Context of the Companies Acts 1948 to 1981, were issued in September 1982 by the Consultative Committee of Accountancy Bodies (CCAB), whose members are as follows: The Institute of Chartered Accountants in England and Wales; The Institute of Chartered Accountants in Ireland; The Chartered Association of Certified Accountants' The Institute of Cost and Management Accountants; and The Chartered Institute of Public Finance and Accountancy.

Set out below is the complete text of Technical Release 481 and Technical Release 482. These Technical Releases refer to the Companies Act 1985 that correspond to those references to the previous Acts that were included in the text are as follows:

Reference to previous Act			**Reference to Companies Act 1985**	
Companies Act 1948	s 56		Sec 130	
	s 57		(Repealed by Companies Act 1980)	
	s 58		(Repealed by Companies Act 1981)	
	s 149		Sec 226	
	s 152		Sec 227	
	new Schedule 8 para	12	Sch 4 para:	12
		13		13
		15		15
		19		19
		20		20
		34		34
		61 to 66	Sch 4A	
		87	Sch 4 para: 88	
		88	89	
		90	Sec 262 (3)	
	Schedule 8A		Sch 9	
Companies Act 1967,	s 14		Sec 235	
Companies Act 1976,	s 1		Sec 241 and 242	

Companies Act Part III	Part VIII	
	s 39	Sec 263 and 275
	s 40	Sec 264
	s 41	Sec 265 to 267
	s 42	Sec 268
	s 42A	Sec 269
	s 43	Sec 270 to 275
	s 43A	Sec 276
	s 45	Sec 263 and 280
	s 87	Sec 264
Companies Act 1981	s 53	Sec 170
	s 60	Sec 274

Technical Release 481

Explanatory note

The Consultative Committee of Accountancy Bodies wishes to draw readers' attention to the fact that the attached (*sic*) guidance statement does not deal with the special problems arising in connection with the determination of realised profits in the context of foreign currency translation. It is intended that these problems should be dealt with in the future by the issue of an accounting standard on foreign currency translation. (*Such a standard has since been issued as SSAP 20.*)

The following statement of guidance on the determination of realised profits and disclosure of distributable profits in the context of the Companies Act 1948 to 1981 is issued by the Councils of the member bodies of the Consultative Committee of Accountancy Bodies. The guidance given in this statement may need to be amended as the law is interpreted in particular cases, or as existing Accounting Standards are revised and new Standards are issued.

The statement and its appendix have been considered and approved by Counsel. They are, however, not definitive. Interpretation of the law rests ultimately with the courts.

References to the '1948 Act', the '1980 Act' and the '1981 Act' are to the Companies Acts 1948, 1980 and 1981 respectively.

References to the 'new Schedule 8' are to Schedule 8 to the 1948 Act as inserted by Section 1(2) of the 1981 Act, and as set out in Schedule 1 to the 1981 Act.

Realised profits: The statutory framework

1 The term 'realised profits' was introduced into UK company law statutes as a result of the implementation of the 2nd and 4th EEC directives on company law in the Companies Act 1980 (Part III) and the Companies Act 1981 (Part I) respectively:

(a) Part III of the 1980 Act imposes statutory restrictions on the distribution of profits and assets by companies. These restrictions include a prohibitions on the distribution of unrealised profits.*

(b) Paragraph 12(a) of the new Schedule 8 requires that 'Only profits realised at the balance sheet date shall be included in the profit and loss account'. Paragraph 34(4) contains a similar requirement applicable to transfers from the revaluation reserve to the profit and loss account. These requirements are extended to consolidated accounts by paragraphs 61 to 66 of the new Schedule 8. They do not apply to accounts prepared under Schedule 8A to the 1948 Act.

*There is an exception to this rule where distributions are made in kind (see Section 43A of the 1980 Act, as inserted by Section 85 of the 1981 Act).

2 The new Schedule 8 states that 'references to realised profits . . . are references to such profits . . . as fall to be treated as realised profits . . . in accordance with principles generally accepted with respect to the determination for accounting purposes of realised profits at the time when those accounts are prepared' (new Schedule 8, para. 90, extended to the 1980 Act by reason of Section 21(1) of the 1981 Act). The term 'principles generally accepted' for the determination of realised profits is not defined in the Act.

3 This statement gives guidance as to the interpretation of 'principles generally accepted' for the determination of realised profits in the context of these statutory requirements. Both the statutory requirements and the following guidance must throughout be viewed in the context of Section 149 of the 1948 Act, as amended by Section 1 of the 1981 Act, which states that the requirement for company accounts to give a true and fair view overrides all other provisions of the Companies Act 1948 to 1981 as to the matters to be included in a company's accounts. Section 152 of the 1948 Act, as amended by Section 2 of the 1981 Act, imposes a corresponding requirement for group accounts.

'Principles generally accepted' for realised profits

4 'Principles generally accepted' for the determination of realised profits should be considered in conjunction with, inter alia, the legal principles laid down in the new Schedule 8, statements of standard accounting practice ('SSAPs'), and in particular the fundamental accounting concepts referred to in SSAP 2 'Disclosure of accounting policies'. As stated in the Explanatory Foreword to Accounting Standards, SSAPs describe methods of accounting for all accounts intended to give a true and fair view. They must therefore, where applicable, be considered to be highly persuasive in the interpretation of 'principles generally accepted' for the determination of realised profits.

5 Accordingly thought and practice develop over time. This is recognised in the statutory requirement that realised profits should be determined 'in accordance with principles generally accepted . . .at the time when those accounts are prepared'. Because of this, the guidance set out in this statement is itself liable to amendment from time to time.

6 In determining whether a profit is realised, particular regard should be has to the statutory accounting principles at paragraphs 12 and 13 of the new schedule 8, and to the parallel fundamental accounting concepts of 'prudence' and 'accruals' as set out in SSAP 2.

7 Paragraph 12 of the new Schedule 8 requires that 'The amount of any item shall be determined on a prudent basis' and, in particular, as already noted, that 'only profits realised at the balance sheet date shall be included in the profit and loss account'. SSAP 2 amplifies the prudence concept as follows:

> 'revenues and profits are not anticipated but are recognised by inclusion in the profit and loss account only when realised in the form either of cash or of other assets the ultimate cash realisation of which can be assessed with reasonable certainty'.

In the light of the new statutory requirements, it should be borne in mind that the phrases 'ultimate cash realisation' and 'assessed with reasonable certainty' are intended to clarify the extent to which a profit can be said to be 'realised' under the prudence concept in circumstances other than where the profit has already been realised in the form of cash 'Reasonable certainty' is the limiting factor.

8 This approach is consistent with paragraph 13 of the new Schedule 8 which requires that:

> 'All income and charges relating to the financial year to which the accounts relate shall be taken into account, without regard to the date of receipt or payment'

The statutory requirement corresponds with the accruals concept as explained at paragraph 14(b) of SSAP2 2. This states that:

> 'revenue and costs are accrued (that is, recognised as they are earned or incurred, not as money is received or paid), matched with one another so far as their relationship can be established or justifiably assumed, and dealt with in the profit and loss account of the period to which they relate'.

9 In determining realised profits, it is also necessary to comply with paragraph 12(b) of the new Schedule 8, which states that:

> 'all liabilities and losses which have arisen or are likely to arise in respect of the financial year to which the accounts relate or a previous financial year shall be taken into account, including those which only become apparent between the balance sheet date and the date on which it is signed on behalf of the board of directors . . .'.

This statutory requirement corresponds with the prudence concept as explained at paragraph 14(d) of SSAP 2. This states that:

'provision is made for all known liabilities (expenses and losses) whether the amount of these is known with certainty or is a best estimate in the light of the information available'.

Realised profits: Summary of guidance

10 A profit which is required by statements of standard accounting practice to be recognised in the profit and loss account should normally be treated as a realised profit, unless the SSAP specifically indicates that it should be treated as unrealised. *See Appendix.*

11 A profit may be recognised in the profit and loss account in accordance with an accounting policy which is not the subject of a SSAP, or, exceptionally, which is contrary to a SSAP. Such a profit will normally be realised profit if the accounting policy adopted is consistent with paragraphs 12 and 13 of the new Schedule 8 and with the accruals and prudence concepts as set out in SSAP 2.

12 Where, in special circumstances, a true and fair view could not be given, even if additional information were provided, without including in the profit and loss account an unrealised profit, the effect of Section 149(3) of the 1948 Act (as amended) is to require inclusion of that unrealised profit notwithstanding paragraph 12(a) of the new Schedule 8. Moreover, paragraph 15 of the new Schedule 8 allows the directors to include an unrealised profit in the profit and loss account where there are special reasons for doing so. Where unrealised profits are thus recognised in the profit and loss account, particulars of this departure from the statutory accounting principle, the reasons for it and its effect are required to be given in a note to the accounts.

Distributable profits

13 The definition of realised profits contained in the new Schedule 8 is extended by Section 21(1) of the 1981 Act to apply to any of the Companies Acts. It therefore applies to the provisions of Part III of the 1980 Act, dealing with distributions. In that context this guidance should be read in conjunction with the statutory rules as to what constitute distributable profits and losses in particular circumstances for the purposes of that part in the Act.

14 It is essential that all companies should keep sufficient records to enable them to distinguish between those reserves which are distributable and those which are not. While most realised profits will be passed on through the profit and loss account, there may be some realised profits which will originally have been brought into the accounts as unrealised profits by way of direct credit to reserves. Similarly, while most unrealised profits will be credited direct to reserves, there may be some unrealised profits passed through the profit and loss account (see paragraph 12 above). Subsequently, when such profits are realised either in whole or in part, a reclassification needs to be made between unrealised and realised profits.

15 There is no legal requirement for a company to distinguish in its balance sheet between distributable and non-distributable reserves as such. However, where material non-distributable profits are included in the profit and loss account or in other reserves which might reasonably be assumed to be distributable, it may be necessary for this to be disclosed and quantified in a note to the accounts in order for them to give a true and fair view.

16 Distributions are made by companies and not by groups. It follows that the profits of a group are only distributable to members of the group's profits. The concept of distributable profit is not, therefore, strictly applicable to groups. However, it is reasonable to assume that the distributable retained profits. The concept of distributable profit is not, therefore, strictly applicable to groups. However, it is reasonable to assume that the distributable retained profits of subsidiaries can be distributed to the holding company. Where this is not the case, the requirements of paragraph 36 of SSAP14 'Group accounts' should be complied with. This states:

> 'If there are significant restrictions on the ability of the holding company to distribute the retained profits of the group (other than those shown as non-distributable) because of statutory, contractual or exchange control restrictions the extent of the restrictions should be indicated.'

Appendix to TR 481

Accounting standards and realised profits: Examples

1 As statements of standard accounting practice are revised and as new standards are issued, it is expected that they will deal with any matters relevant to the determination of realised profits.

2 This has already been done in the case of SSAP 1 'Accounting for Associated Companies', revised in April 1982. This provides an example of the way in which the true and fair view requirements should be satisfied by giving additional information rather than by including unrealised profits in profit and loss account (see paragraph 12 above). As far as an investing company is concerned, the profits of its associated companies are not realised until they are passed on as dividends; the true and fair view, however, requires that they should be reflected in the investing company's financial statements. There is no problem where group accounts are prepared because specific provision is made for this situation in paragraph 65(1) of the new Schedule 8. Where, however, the investing company does not prepare group accounts, the revised SSAP 1 states that it should show the information required as to its share of the associated company's profit by preparing a separate profit and loss account or by adding the information to its own profit and loss account in supplementary form in such a way that its share of the profits of the associated company is not treated as realised.

3 An example of the principle that profit recognised in accordance with an Accounting Standard should normally be treated as realised (see paragraph 10 above) is provided by SSAP 9 'Stocks and work in progress'. This requires that long-term contract work in progress should be stated in periodic financial statements at cost plus any attributable profit, less any foreseeable losses and progress payments received and receivable. There was initially some concern as to whether profit thus recognised on long-term contract work in progress would be constructed as realised profit within the provisions of the Companies Acts. However, the relevant principles of recognising profits in SSAP 9 are based on the concept of 'reasonable certainty' as to the eventual outcome and are not in conflict with the statutory accounting principles. Such profits should be treated as realised profits. The Department of Trade does not dissent from this view.

Technical Release 482

Guidance statement issued in September 1982 on behalf of the Councils of the constituent members of the Consultative Committee of Accountancy Bodies, on the determination of distributable profits. This statement gives guidance on the interpretation of Part III of the Companies Act 1980 and on the determination of the maximum amount of profit which can be legally distributed under that Act.

It should be emphasised that it does not seek to deal with the many commercial factors which need to be taken into account before a company decides on the amount of a distribution to be recommended to its shareholders. It should also be borne in mind that its guidance relates solely to the determination of profits legally available for distribution and that it does not give guidance on the recognition of profit in the accounts.

This statement should be read in conjunction with the guidance statement issued by the Councils of the constituent members of the CCAB on 'The determination of realised profits and disclosure of distributable profits in the context of the Companies Act 1948 to 1981', issued in September 1982.

This statement has been considered and approved by Counsel. However, it is not definitive. Interpretation of the law rests ultimately with the courts.

References to the '1948 Act', the '1967 Act', the '1980 Act' and the '1981 Act' are to the Companies Act 1948, 1967, 1980 and 1981 respectively. Section references without ascription refer to the 1980 Act.

References to the 'new Schedule 8' are to Schedule 8 to the 1948 Act as inserted by S 1(2) of the 1981 Act, and as set out in Schedule 1 to the 1981 Act.

Introduction

1 The 1980 Act restricts distributions of both public and private companies. Previously the determination of legally distributable reserves and profits was governed only by a company's articles of association. Sections 56 to 58 of the 1948 Act, and a significant body of case law. After the commencement of the provisions of the 1980 Act, a company must restrict its distributions to those permitted by the 1980 Act, subject to any further restrictions imposed under its memorandum or articles of association.

2 In general, companies are only able to make distributions out of realised profits less realised losses, but further restrictions are imposed on public companies (see paragraph 6 below). The 1980 Act also includes special provisions for certain investment companies and insurance companies (ss 41 and 42): these are not discussed in this guidance statement.

Provision of the Companies Act 1980 (as amended)

Distribution

3 A 'distribution' is defined (s 45(2)) as 'every description of distribution of a company's assets to members of the company, whether in cash or otherwise, except distributions made by way of:

(a) an issue of shares as fully or partly paid bonus shares;

(b) redemption or purchase of any of the company's own shares our of capital (including a new issue of shares) or out of unrealised profits;

(c) reduction of share capital; and

(d) a distribution of assets to members of the company on its winding-up.

Profits available for distribution

4 A company may only make a distribution out of profits available for that purpose (s 39(1)). A company's profits available for distribution are stated to be its accumulated, realised profits (so far as not previously distributed or capitalised) less its accumulated, realised losses (so far as not previously written off in a reduction or reorganisation of its share capital) (s 39(2)). Realised losses may not be offset against unrealised profits. Public companies are subject to a further restriction (see paragraph 6 below).

5 A company may only distribute an unrealised profit when the distribution is in kind and the unrealised profit arises from the writing up of the asset being distributed (s 43A, as inserted by s 85 of the 1981 Act).

Public companies

6 A further restriction is placed on distributions by public companies (s 40). A public company may only make a distribution if, after giving effect to such distribution, the amount of its net assets (as defined in s 87(4)(c)) is not less than the aggregate of its called up share capital and undistributable reserves. This means that a public company must deduct any net unrealised losses from net realised profits before making a distribution, whereas a private company need not make such a deduction (see also paragraphs 29 to 31 below).

7 Under section 40(2) the following are undistributable reserves:

(a) share premium account (see also s 56 of the 1948 Act as amended by the 1981 Act);

(b) capital redemption reserve (see also s 53 of the 1981 Act);

(c) the excess of accumulated, unrealised profits, over the accumulated, unrealised losses so far as not previously written off in a reduction or reorganisation of its share capital;

(d) any other reserve which the company is prohibited from distributing by any enactment, or by its memorandum or articles of association (or equivalent).

Section 40 only applies to public companies. However, because of the effect of Section 39(2) of the 1980 Act, Section 56 of the 1948 Act, and Section 53 of the 1981 Act, none of the above mentioned reserves is distributable by private companies. (The restrictions which are placed upon public companies which have distributed or utilised unrealised profits prior to the commencement of the Act are discussed at paragraph 30 below).

Relevant accounts

8 Whether or not a distribution may be made within the terms of the 1980 Act is determined by reference to 'relevant items' as stated in the 'relevant accounts'. A 'relevant item' is defined by s 43(8) as profits losses, assets, liabilities, provisions, share capital and reserves. Thus, valuations or contingencies included in notes to the financial statements, but not incorporated in the accounts themselves, have no effect on the amount of distributable profit. There is no requirement that distributions can only be made out of distributable profits described as such in the accounts.

9 The 'relevant accounts' (annual, interim or initial) are defined in Section 43(2) and, except for the initial or interim accounts of private companies, must be properly prepared in accordance with Section 43(8).

10 Annual accounts must be accompanied by an audit report complying with Section 14 of the 1967 Act, and must have been laid before the company in general meeting in accordance with Section 1 of the 1976 Act (s 43(3)). Interim and initial accounts of public companies (there is no such requirement for private companies) must have been delivered to the Registrar of Companies (s 43(5)(b) and s 43(6)(d)). Initial accounts of public companies must be accompanied by a report by the auditor stating whether in his opinion the accounts have been properly prepared (s 43(6)(b)). The interim accounts need not be accompanied by an audit report.

11 There are no requirements in Section 43(3)(c) and Section 43(6)(c), where an auditor has issued a qualified report on either annual or initial accounts as appropriate, that before a distribution may be made in reliance on those accounts the auditor must issue an additional statement. In this statement he must express an opinion on whether the subject of his qualification is material for the purposes of determining whether the proposed distribution complies with the requirements of the Act.

Adjustments to relevant accounts

12 Adjustments to distributable profits calculated from the relevant accounts are required where one or more distributions have already been made 'in pursuance of determination made by reference to those accounts (s 43(7)). Adjustments are also required where a company has, since those accounts were prepared, provided financial assistance for the purchase of its own shares which depletes its net assets or made certain payments in respect of or in connection with the purchase of its own shares (s 60(1) of the 1981 Act).

Basis for calculating profits available for distribution

13 The starting point in determining profits available for distribution, the 'accumulated, realised profits . . . less accumulated, realised losses' will be the profit or loss recognised in the relevant accounts. That is the accumulated balance on the profit and loss account. This figure may require adjustment to take into account any items which are required to be excluded in the determination of distributable profits (e.g. see paragraph 21 below). The amount so arrived at will require further adjustment for any items taken to reserve accounts which may properly be included in the determination of distributable profits. For example, an unrealised profit or an asset revaluation will originally be credited direct to a revaluation reserve. On a subsequent disposal of the asset part or all of the profit is clearly realised notwithstanding the fact that it may not have been passed through the profit and loss account.

14 If an item has not been recognised in the relevant accounts, it cannot be taken into account in determining the profits or net assets available for distribution.

Aspects requiring special consideration

Realised losses

15 Section 39(4) as amended states that certain provisions are to be treated as a realised loss. These are provisions of any kind mentioned in paragraphs 87(1) and 88 of the new Schedule 8, namely:

> '... any amount written off by way of providing for depreciation or diminution in value of assets' and '... any amount retained as reasonably necessary for the

purpose of providing for any liability or loss which is likely to be incurred, or certain to be incurred but uncertain as to amount or as to the date on which it will arise.'

16 Section 39(4) as amended makes one specific exception to the rule that any provision of any kind mentioned in these paragraphs is to be treated as a realised loss, namely a provision arising on a revaluation of a fixed asset when all the fixed assets, or all fixed assets other than goodwill, have been revalued (see paragraph 19 below.)

17 In view of the requirement of s 39(4), any loss recognised in the profit and loss account will normally be a realised loss. (An exception to this rule at s 39(5) is discussed at paragraph 21 below.)

Revaluation of assets

18 A surplus over original cost recognised on revaluation of any asset is unrealised. There is no statutory requirement specifying whether the balance, if any, of the surplus that represents the writing back of past depreciation or of provisions for diminution in value should be regarded as realised or unrealised. Moreover, there is at present no unanimity of opinion as to whether such a surplus, to the extent that it represents the writing back of a realised loss, particularly where the realised loss arises from past depreciation, constitutes a realised profit. In view of the division of opinion on this matter, and in the absence of any statutory rule or clearly decisive precedent case law, it is considered inappropriate to offer guidance on the question in this statement. Where reliance is placed on such a profit being realised in order to make a distribution, it may be appropriate for the directors of the company to seek legal advice. To the extent that the surplus represents the writing beck of an unrealised loss, it should be treated as an unrealised profit.

19 A deficit on the revaluation of an asset (unless offsetting a previous unrealised surplus on the same asset) gives rise to a provision and is required to be treated as a realised loss. A realised loss thus created cannot be reduced by being offset wholly or partially against revaluation surpluses on other assets, whether or not of the same class. However, there is an exception to the general rule where a provision for diminution in value of a fixed asset arises on a revaluation of all the fixed assets (other than goodwill) (s 39(4) as amended). Although not explicitly stated, the Act implies that such a provision may be treated as unrealised, and therefore that it does not reduce the profits available for distribution.

20 For the purpose of s 39(4) a 'revaluation' of all the fixed assets may comprise actual revaluations of some of the fixed assets combined with consideration by the directors of the value of the remaining fixed assets. However, if an actual revaluation of all the fixed assets has not occurred the directors must be satisfied that the aggregate value of all fixed assets 'considered' but not actually revalued is not less then the aggregate amount at which they are for the time being stated in the company's accounts (s 39(4A): see paragraph 45(2) of Schedule 3 to the 1981 Act). If the accounts include 'revalued' fixed assets which have been 'considered', but which have not been subject to an actual revaluation, certain additional information is required to be disclosed for the 'revaluation' to be valid (s 43(7A): see paragraph 47 (c) of Schedule 3 to the 1981 Act).

Revalued fixed assets and depreciation

21 Provisions for depreciation of revalued fixed assets require special treatment to the extent that these provisions exceed the amounts which would have been provided if an unrealised profit had not been made on revaluation (s 39(5)). For the purpose of calculating the amount of profit which is legally available for distribution, s 39(5) requires an amount equivalent to this excess depreciation to 'be treated . . . as a realised profit;, thereby reducing the provision of this purpose of that relating to the original cost of the asset. As a result, while the depreciation of a surplus on a fixed asset revaluation will affect the published profits, it will not normally effect the amount of a company's distributable profits, provided of course that this revaluation surplus has not been capitalised ('capitalisation' in this context is defined at s 45(3)).

Disposal of revalued assets

22 On the disposal of a revalued asset any surplus over cost immediately becomes realised. Any loss which has been treated as unrealised (see paragraph 20 above) should on disposal of the asset be redesignated as a realised loss.

Development costs

23 Development costs carried forward in accordance with SSAP 13 'Accounting for research and development' will not normally affect distributable profits. Although Section 42A(1) (inserted by s 84 of the 1981 Act) requires that development costs shown as an asset should be treated as a realised loss, this requirement does not apply (s 42A(3)) if the directors justify the costs carried forward not being treated as a realised loss. This they will normally be able to do if the costs are carried forward in accordance with SSAP 13. Such justification must be included in the note on capitalised development costs required by paragraph 20(2) of the new Schedule 8.

Holding company

24 It should be noted that although the whole of the distributable profits of a subsidiary are (subject to the interests of minority shareholders and a tax on distributions) available to the holding company, the latter cannot distribute these profits to its own shareholders until such time as they are recognised in the accounts of the holding company.

25 It is not normal practice to take credit for dividends from investments unless the amounts are declared prior to the investing company's year-end. However, dividends receivable from subsidiaries and associates in respect of accounting periods ending on or before that of the holding company are normally accrued in the holding company's accounts even if declared after the holding company's year-end. Such dividends should be treated as realised by the holding company whether they are paid or passed through a current account, provided that, in the latter case, an appropriate reassessment of the realisable value of the current account balance is made.

26 Exchange control or other restrictions may affect the ability of overseas subsidiaries to remit dividends to the UK. In accordance with the prudence concept such dividends receivable should be treated as realised only when their eventual receipt can be assessed with reasonable certainty.

27 Whilst there is no legal requirements for a holding company to take into accounts its share of the net losses (if any) of its subsidiaries in determining its distributable profits, the holding company may need to make a provision against a permanent diminution in the value of its investment in any such subsidiary (paragraph 19(2) of the new Schedule 8).

Current cost accounts

28 It will normally make no difference to a company's legally distributable profit whether its relevant accounts are drawn up under the historical or the current cost convention. Where net assets under the current cost convention exceed net assets under the historical cost convention, the difference consists of net unrealised profits which form part of the current cost reserve. The remainder of the current cost reserve consists of an amount equal to the cumulative current cost adjustments charged in the profit and loss account each year. According to SSAP 16 this amount is regarded as realised (in the case of the depreciation adjustments in the 1980 Act specifically requires it to be so treated). This part of the current cost reserve, being realised, is legally distributable even though there would be a reduction in the operating capability of the business as a result of making such a distribution, which might, therefore, be commercially inadvisable.

Transitional provisions

Determination of distributable profits at the commencement date

29 Where the directors of a company are, after making all reasonable enquiries, unable to determine whether a particular profit or loss made before the commencement date of the 1980 Act is realised or unrealised, they may treat such a profit as realised and such a loss as unrealised (s39(7)). Such a position will occur when there are no records of the original cost of an asset or the original amount of a liability.

30 Where a public company has distributed or utilised (otherwise than by captialisation) unrealised profits prior to the commencement date of the 1980 Act and such profits have not subsequently been realised, an amount equal to the unrealised profits so distributed or utilised falls to be included as part of the undistributable reserves (s 40(2) and s 45(4)). This prevents a public company which has so distributed or utilised unrealised profits in the past from making any further distribution until the shortfall has been made good.

31 If, prior to the commencement of the 1980 Act, a company has realised losses (insofar as they have not been previously written off in either a reduction or a reorganisation of capital), such losses must be made good before making any distribution (s 39(2)).

32 The part of the 1980 Act dealing with distributable profits came into operation as follows (s 45(6)):

New public companies	On their registration under Part I of the 1980 Act.
Existing public companies	On their re-registration as a public limited company under Part I of the 1980 Act, or on 22 June 1982 (18 months after the appointed day), whichever is the earlier.
Private companies	22 June 1982.

Chapter 4

Reporting the substance of transactions

Chapter 4

Reporting the substance of transactions

Background

4.1 One of the big issues of principle in financial reporting in recent years has been that of substance versus form. Where the economic substance of a transaction differs from its legal form, which one should govern the accounting treatment? As the title of this chapter makes clear, the view has been established that substance should be followed. Following substance rather than form was first adopted in SSAP 21, 'Leases and hire purchase contracts', in 1981, but the principle was not applied more widely until the 1990s. From the mid 1980s, the ASC and, in due course, the ASB began to develop proposals to establish substance over form more widely. For a number of years the debate was characterised as being an attack on off balance sheet finance and indeed that has remained an important component. But by the time the proposals reached fruition in 1994 as FRS 5, 'Reporting the substance of transactions', they changed their focus away from being just anti-avoidance rules to being a broadly-based requirement to reflect the substance of transactions. While FRS 5 often results in assets and liabilities coming back on balance sheet, that is not always its effect. Aspects of the standard, such as partial de-recognition and linked presentation (both described later), have the effect, in special circumstances, of not showing the gross asset and gross liability on the balance sheet. The ASB would regard that as the intended outcome, being the presentation that best reflects the substance of the transaction in question.

4.2 Over the last decade, off balance sheet finance has been widely regarded as an accounting abuse. During that time, some companies have chosen methods of financing that allow them to increase their borrowings and risks without the substance of those transactions being reflected in their financial statements. This has been criticised because the ability to 'hide' assets and, more importantly, liabilities from the balance sheet arguably produces misleading financial statements that do not faithfully record the economic reality of resources controlled by an enterprise or a group, nor the obligations that finance them. As the debate progressed over the years and as each successive paper was issued the proposed rules became more widely accepted as best practice and some off balance sheet finance schemes came back on balance sheet.

4.3 The accountancy profession and other interested parties have long debated how to account effectively for off balance sheet finance transactions in order to present them in an appropriate way to meet the legal requirement for a balance sheet to give a true and fair view of a company's financial position. In addition, over that period of debate corporate collapses led to criticism that the methods of accounting for some financing techniques produced the impression that borrowings were less than they really were. One company that had significant off balance sheet arrangements in 1985 was Burnett & Hallamshire Holdings plc. Many of that company's problems related to transactions that were not accounted for on balance sheet, but were merely mentioned briefly in its financial statements in the contingent liabilities note.

4.4 The ASB, and the ASC before it, tackled this problem by seeking to gain acceptance for the principle that financial statements should reflect the substance of transactions and not merely their legal form, which can be open to manipulation. FRS 5, 'Reporting the substance of transactions', states that its objective is to ensure that the substance of an entity's transactions is reported in its financial statements. Accounting for transactions in accordance with their commercial substance is now central to the concept of the true and fair view.

TR 603 – Off balance sheet finance and window dressing

4.5 The first venture into the area of off balance sheet finance was in December 1985 when the Technical Committee of the ICAEW issued TR 603. This statement recommended that in order to give a 'true and fair view' the economic substance of transactions should be considered rather than their mere legal form when determining their nature and, as a consequence, their accounting treatment. It suggested that the company's balance sheet should be adjusted to reflect the transaction's substance.

4.6 The technical release was issued as a discussion document to members of the ICAEW by its Technical Committee and, as such, was not mandatory. It was, however, intended to be persuasive in considering whether a company's financial statements gave a true and fair view.

Overriding requirement of true and fair

4.7 The Companies Act 1985 requirement that a company's and a group's financial statements must give a 'true and fair view' is fundamental. It overrides the detailed rules on the form and content of company, and group, financial statements and the Act's other requirements concerning matters to be included in the financial statements. The Act requires that, if necessary, either additional disclosure should be made or, in special circumstances, the financial statements should depart from the detailed rules.

4.8 Where the 'true and fair override' is used to depart from the Act's other provisions the financial statements must disclose, in accordance with sections 226 and 227, particulars of the departure, the reasons for it, and its effect. TR 603 suggested that recognising the substance of a transaction in the balance sheet was necessary in order to give a true and fair view. Consequently, to ensure compliance with the Act's disclosure requirements, TR 603 stated that the legal form of the transactions would need to be disclosed in the notes to the financial statements. Now, however, following further debate it is generally accepted that it is necessary to reflect a transaction's substance in a company's financial statements in order to give a true and fair view and that this can be achieved without recourse to the Act's true and fair override provisions. As a consequence under FRS 5, the transaction's legal form is not generally required to be disclosed in the notes to the financial statements, although there is a general disclosure requirement which requires the financial statements to disclose enough information for users to understand the transaction's commercial effect.

Law Society response to TR 603

4.9 The Law Society wrote to the Technical Committee concerning TR 603 in June 1986. Although the Law Society was sympathetic to the concerns that led to the technical release, it believed that it went too far in its recommendations. The Law Society agreed with the technical release's objective, but not with the proposed solution. They argued that applying substance over form would introduce unacceptable subjectivity, lead to accounting treatments that conflict with the law and make legal analysis of financial statements impossible. The Law Society argued that disclosure would be adequate for a true and fair view and that departure from the rules would be unnecessary. In contrast, the ASB now believes that accounting for a transaction's substance is a basic concept that is embedded in a 'true and fair view' and that disclosure alone is inadequate; and this is the line pursued in FRS 5.

ED 42 – Accounting for special purpose transactions

4.10 The Technical Committee passed its work to the ASC and the ASC issued ED 42 in March 1988. It was written in very broad terms and attempted to establish the concept that a transaction's accounting treatment should fairly reflect its economic substance and commercial effect. Its issue opened up a conceptual debate in the UK about financial reporting.

4.11 The exposure draft concentrated on identifying and dealing with the commercial effect of what it termed 'special purpose transactions'. It argued that by analysing a transaction's commercial effect it was possible to ascertain the benefits and obligations that flowed from it. The substance of a transaction would become clear when those benefits and obligations were considered.

4.12 Instead of trying to identify and prescribe detailed accounting rules for types of transactions that might be termed 'off balance sheet' or 'window dressing', which would inevitably lead to an immediate search for loopholes by an army of professional advisers, the ASC chose to set out general concepts that could be applied to a variety of situations. It adopted wide descriptions of assets and liabilities. Assets were described in terms of the control of future economic benefits. Liabilities were described in terms of present obligations entailing a probable future sacrifice of benefits involving the transfer of assets or provision of services to another party. Both of these descriptions flow through substantially unchanged as definitions in FRS 5.

4.13 ED 42 proposed that the benefits and obligations arising from special purpose transactions, having particular regard to their commercial effect, should be considered against the characteristics of assets and liabilities as defined. Companies then needed to determine whether they would represent assets and liabilities that should be included on balance sheet. The exposure draft gave some guidance on how the general principles should be applied to a number of different transactions. These included controlled non-subsidiaries, factoring, consignment stock, sale and leaseback, securitised receivables and sub-participations.

4.14 The exposure draft received considerable support. However, some commentators were concerned that the proposed standard was too general in its approach and would be capable of wide and varying interpretations. Companies and their professional advisers found that applying it to actual situations was fraught with difficult judgements and involved considerable subjectivity. It could lead to differing interpretations and inconsistency. This had to be balanced with the view that a more prescriptive standard containing detailed rules about particular types of scheme would never keep abreast of newly emerging financial arrangements and the search for avoidance.

4.15 In addition, parties interested in mortgage securitisation schemes complained that the requirements were, for them, unduly restrictive and warranted further consideration.

Companies Act 1989

4.16 The Companies Act 1989 had an important effect on off balance sheet finance by redefining subsidiaries for consolidation purposes. It extended the scope of consolidations by including all undertakings within the revised definitions and not just companies. Consequently, partnerships and other unincorporated entities could become subsidiaries of a group and require consolidation. The major change affecting off balance sheet finance schemes was the change in emphasis in the definitions of subsidiaries from looking at the legal ownership of shares to focussing on the control over the undertaking. This was achieved in a number of ways. The Act changed the main criterion used to determine a subsidiary from considering who had more than 50 per cent of the equity share capital of a company to looking at who controlled the voting rights of the undertaking.

4.17 In addition, the notion of dominant influence was introduced, which can exist by way of a contract (known as a control contract) or, more importantly, which might arise in conjunction with a company having a 'participating interest' in another undertaking. A 'participating interest' is presumed to exist where a company owns more than 20 per cent of the shares of another undertaking, but can exist where the holding is below that level. In this situation, even where dominant influence is not found, but the undertaking is 'managed on a unified basis', the undertaking is a subsidiary. The terms 'dominant influence' and 'managed on a unified basis' were later defined in FRS 2, 'Accounting for subsidiary undertakings', published in July 1992. Hence the changes to definitions in the Companies Act 1989 brought back on balance sheet many off balance sheet vehicles and represented a large step forward along the path towards accounting on the basis of substance over form.

4.18 The 1989 Act's requirements and those of FRS 2 are considered in chapter 21.

ED 49 – Reflecting the substance of transactions in assets and liabilities

4.19 ED 49, the successor to ED 42, was published on 31 May 1990. Importantly, the general guidance on recognising items in financial statements by analysing their commercial substance was reinforced by a series of detailed application notes addressing a number of arrangements that had caused difficulty in practice. These were:

- Consignment stock.
- Sale and repurchase agreements.
- Factoring of debts.
- Securitised mortgages.
- Loan transfers.

The proposal was that the application notes should be regarded as standard accounting practice for the arrangements they described. Similar application notes now appear in FRS 5. The proposals concerning securitised mortgages in ED 42 that were heavily criticised were revised, and in ED 49 the ASC proposed that companies should show the net investment in such schemes rather than the gross amounts.

4.20 The ASC believed that ED 49 achieved the right mixture of general concepts and detailed guidance on application that satisfied those who argued that an over-conceptual approach was too subjective and those who believed too many rules lead to literal interpretation and to scope for avoidance. ED 49 still retained provisions concerning quasi-subsidiaries (previously referred to in ED 42 as 'controlled non-subsidiaries'), even though the changes brought about by the Companies Act 1989 effectively dealt with many off balance sheet schemes set up using special purpose vehicles, which would have been classified as controlled non-subsidiaries under ED 42.

Statement of principles

4.21 In July 1991, the ASB issued a chapter of its draft statement of principles entitled 'The objective of financial statements and the qualitative characteristics of financial information'. In that statement substance over form is identified as one of the principles that should be followed in order to help make financial information reliable. It states that if information is to represent faithfully the transactions and other events that it purports to represent, it is necessary that they are accounted for and presented in accordance with their substance and economic reality and not merely their legal form.

4.22 The ASB has followed a similar approach to that adopted by the International Accounting Standards Committee's (IASC) in its Framework for the preparation of financial statements, published in July 1989. The Framework identifies four qualitative characteristics, one of which is reliability. To be reliable the IASC considers that it is necessary for transactions to be accounted for and presented in the financial statements in accordance with their substance and economic reality and not merely their legal form.

Bulletin No. 15 – Accounting for securitisation

4.23 The demise of the ASC left off balance sheet finance to be tackled by its successor body the ASB. The ASB agreed with and pursued the general approach of substance over form, but initially took the view that the ASC's proposals on securitisation in ED 49 were too weak. Hence the ASB issued some stronger proposals in November 1991 in Bulletin No. 15. In that paper, it commented that its views largely corresponded with those of the ASC and that accordingly no further exposure draft was planned. However, it did propose to depart from the approach used in ED 49 in one important respect concerning securitisations. This was primarily because commentators on ED 49 had pointed out that, despite similarities in the substance, there was inconsistency between the application note on debt factoring, which generally required such arrangements to be accounted for on balance sheet, and securitisation schemes, which would more often than not be off balance sheet.

4.24 The ASB believed that there were two separate key issues to be addressed:

- Whether the transfer of assets from the originator to the issuer constituted a sale.
- Whether the relationship between the issuer and the originator was such that the issuer ought to be consolidated in the originator's consolidated financial statements.

4.25 The effect of Bulletin 15 would have been to require most securitisation schemes to be accounted for on balance sheet. There was considerable objection to this proposal by the banking industry who made representations that because the transfer of risk in a securitisation scheme was significant, it was not appropriate for the whole of the finance to appear on the originator's balance sheet, particularly where the finance raised was non-recourse to other assets of the company. Furthermore, the Bank of England's treatment of securitised assets and their related finance for risk asset ratio purposes differed from the rules proposed in the bulletin.

4.26 Because of the furore surrounding securitisation, it was not possible for the ASB to continue with its plan to produce a standard based principally on ED 49. The ASB had to find a satisfactory way of dealing with securitisation schemes, which not only complied with the proposed standard's principles, but also reflected the true reduction in risk to the originator of such schemes.

FRED 4 – Reporting the substance of transactions

4.27 After much debate the ASB issued yet another exposure draft on the subject in February 1993, with the stated objective that its proposals were to ensure that the substance of an entity's transactions was reported in its financial statements. They dealt with the securitisation problem by introducing a new concept known as the 'linked presentation'.

4.28 The proposal was that, for certain non-recourse finance arrangements, related assets and liabilities would be shown on the face of the balance sheet, but linked in such a way that the finance was deducted from the related asset to show a net figure. The Act does not allow netting of assets and liabilities, but it was argued that the 'net asset' was the true asset identified for recognition under the proposed rules and that the original asset and related finance were not assets and liabilities as defined, but were merely shown on the face of the balance sheet as additional information. The situations where the presentation could be used were to be strictly controlled by a number of detailed tests, all of which had to be satisfied. The proposals meant that for many securitisation schemes a net presentation could be achieved, where the finance was clearly non-recourse to the company's other assets and where the other conditions were met.

4.29 In most respects, these proposals dealt with the objections raised by the banking industry to the rules proposed in Bulletin 15. Furthermore, the linked presentation could be used for other transactions, such as debt factoring, where non-recourse finance was involved. The new basis met with mixed reactions, but has been preserved in FRS 5 substantially unchanged.

4.30 Another area of controversy in FRED 4 was the derecognition rule. Under the proposed rule, apart from a straightforward sale, it would have been very difficult to take an asset off a company's balance sheet ('derecognise' it) once it had been recognised on that balance sheet. Respondents to the FRED thought that the conditions imposed for derecognition were too onerous when compared to the rules requiring a previously unrecognised asset to be recorded on the balance sheet. The ASB also proposed in FRED 4 to amend the offset rules concerning when an asset and liability could be shown net on the balance sheet. They proposed not to allow assets and liabilities to be offset where they were denominated in different currencies, even where there was a legal right of set-off. Again this change was criticised by respondents to the FRED as unnecessary. Both these areas were subsequently amended in FRS 5.

4.31 FRED 4 also included definitions of assets and liabilities that followed the definitions of these terms given in the ASB's draft Statement of Principles. Previously in ED 49 a description of the essential characteristics of assets and liabilities was given. Many of the other proposals in FRED 4 followed those in ED 49 including the provision of detailed guidance notes.

FRS 5 – Reporting the substance of transactions

4.32 Another year went by before the ASB published its final standard on reporting the substance of transactions, FRS 5. At nearly 140 pages it reflects the considerable amount of work and debate on the subject that had taken place over the eight years since the first discussion in TR 603. The volume also gives an idea of the complexity of the subject, even though the standard's basic principles cover only ten pages.

4.33 Many of FRED 4's proposals remain in FRS 5 and the objective is stated in similar terms. There were just two main changes from the proposals in FRED 4. The first, and more controversial, concerned the derecognition rule. FRED 4 took the position that an item either remained on, or was taken off, balance sheet in its entirety according to whether an asset or liability was, or was not, present and the recognition criteria were met. FRS 5 introduced a new category which recognised that in special cases the original asset can be derecognised and replaced by a different asset. This new category is referred to in this chapter as 'partial derecognition'.

4.34 Partial derecognition was introduced because the proposals in FRED 4 had the effect that, once an item was on balance sheet, the criteria that had to be satisfied in order for it to be taken off balance sheet were very difficult to satisfy in practice. Partial derecognition basically says that where there is a significant change in the entity's rights to benefits *and* exposure to risks, but the entity has not disposed of all significant rights and all significant exposure to risks, then the original asset should be derecognised and in its place there should be shown a new asset and corresponding liability reflecting the benefits and risks retained by the entity after the transaction.

4.35 The second change from FRED 4 concerns the offset rule. Under FRS 5 it is still possible to offset assets and liabilities denominated in different currencies where there is a legal right of set-off and the conditions in the FRS are met.

Future debate

4.36 FRS 5's publication has not seen an end to the debate on off balance sheet finance as its provisions are very difficult to implement in practice, because of their complexity and subjectivity. In addition, the partial derecognition rules are still controversial. The ASB recognised this at the outset and stated in its press release accompanying the publication of the FRS that it is determined to see that the spirit and reasoning of FRS 5 are applied. The ASB's Chairman Sir David Tweedie also said that *"the standard has been deliberately constructed on general principles rather than as a series of detailed rules so that it will be applicable to new schemes as they develop"*. It is the ASB's intention that, if new schemes are developed to circumvent its provisions, it will refer them to the UITF, or if necessary revise the standard itself. To date only two issues have been dealt with in this way. The UITF issued Abstract 13, 'Employee share ownership plans', in June 1995 and this abstract is considered from paragraph 4.198. The ASB published an application note to FRS 5 in September 1998 dealing with how to account for transactions undertaken as part of the Government's Private Finance Initiative (PFI). Prior to the publication of the ASB's application note, the Treasury issued accounting guidance which dealt only with the accounting treatment from the perspective of the public sector body. The Treasury is preparing new guidance effective from 1 January 1999 that will apply the FRS 5 application note principles in a way that will ensure consistency and cost-effective compliance throughout the public sector. PFI is considered from paragraph 4.179.1.

Scope and basic principles

4.37 This section examines FRS 5's scope and sets out the standard's basic principles. FRS 5's provisions applied to accounting periods ending on or after 22 September 1994 but, as with other recent standards, the ASB encouraged early adoption. There were no transitional provisions in the standard and, therefore, its provisions applied to all transactions that existed when the standard came into force or when it was first applied, including those that affected the prior year figures.

Scope

4.38 FRS 5 applies to all transactions of a company; it also applies to transactions undertaken by other unincorporated entities, such as partnerships, where their financial statements are required to give a true and fair view. However, the ASB has stated that the accounting treatment and disclosure of most transactions will remain unchanged, as FRS 5's provisions only result in a different accounting treatment for a relatively small number of the more complex transactions, where the economic substance and the legal form of the transaction differ. In addition, many of those transactions have in recent years been reported in accordance with their substance as the accounting rules have been developed. By 'transaction' the FRS means both single transactions and also arrangements that cover a series of transactions that are designed to have an overall commercial effect. [FRS 5 para 11].

4.39 No exemptions for particular types of undertaking are given in the FRS, although subsequent to its issue both insurance brokers and insurance companies have been exempted from FRS 5's requirements in relation to specific transactions (see further from para 4.225). The FRS does, however, exclude certain specific transactions from its scope, which are:

- Forward contracts.
- Futures contracts.
- Foreign exchange.
- Interest rate swaps.
- Expenditure commitments.
- Orders.
- Contracts for differences.
- Employment contracts.

[FRS 5 para 12].

4.40 All of the transactions listed above are contracts for future performance and have been removed by the ASB from the scope of FRS 5 except in situations where they form part of a transaction (or series of transactions) that falls within the standard's scope. The standard cites as an example an interest rate swap forming part of a securitisation. In this case the swap is an integral component of the overall securitisation transaction which needs to be considered under the standard's rules (see further para 4.156), whereas a swap that is merely part of a company's treasury management does not come within the standard's scope.

4.41 Expenditure commitments and orders fall outside the scope until they are either delivered or paid for, whichever happens first. Contracts for differences, which are contracts where a net amount will be paid or received based on the movement in a price or an index, also fall outside the standard's scope.

4.42 Employment contracts are sometimes termed 'executory contracts' and generally involve agreements where performance by both parties lies in the future. Unless a person's salary is paid in advance, no asset is recognised in the employer's balance sheet in respect of the future benefit of the employee's service. Similarly, no liability is recognised in respect of the future payment that the employer has contracted to make. There is a remote contingent liability in relation to the person's employment, but this will only crystallise into a liability, for example, when the decision is taken to make the person redundant and would only be provided for where necessary in accordance with the requirements of SSAP 18, 'Accounting for contingencies'.

Interaction with the Act and accounting standards

4.43 Where transactions fall within FRS 5's scope and also directly within the scope of other accounting standards or legislation (for example, leasing) the FRS states that the standard or legislation that contains the more specific provisions should be applied. [FRS 5 para 13]. But there is a subtle implication here because the provisions of that more specific standard or legislation have to be applied to the *transaction's substance* and not to its legal form and for that purpose the general provisions of FRS 5 apply. [FRS 5 para 43].

4.44 There are two areas where these provisions become particularly important. The first is with pension schemes where clearly SSAP 24 has specific provisions that deal with how companies should account for pension obligations. Although SSAP 24 does not deal specifically with the consolidation of pension schemes into the employing company's financial statements, the ASB contends that such schemes should not be consolidated as quasi-subsidiaries (see further para 4.100). [FRS 5 para 44]. FRS 5 does, however, apply to certain pension scheme transactions, for example, where a scheme enters into a sale and leaseback arrangement for the employing company's properties.

4.45 The second area where there is considerable interaction is leasing. Generally for stand-alone leases the more specific provisions will be contained in SSAP 21. But it is now even clearer that the classification of such leases as either finance or operating should be made according to their substance. This should have been the case under SSAP 21, but in practice there has tended to be undue reliance on arithmetical analysis and insufficient attention to the substance. That is, FRS 5 confirms that it is not acceptable to look only to the 90 per cent test, but that all other aspects of the transaction must also be considered to determine the transaction's substance. The term 'stand-alone' refers to simple leasing arrangements, which are not complicated by options and buy-back clauses. However, for some leases, an example being sale and leaseback arrangements where there is also an option for the lessee to repurchase the asset, FRS 5's provisions are more specific. Generally, more complex leasing arrangements where there are a number of elements will fall within FRS 5's scope. [FRS 5 para 45]. Indeed this was confirmed by an FRRP ruling issued in February 1997 in respect of the accounting treatment of a sale and leaseback transaction undertaken by Associated Nursing Services plc (see further para 4.128.1). Table 4.1 below illustrates a situation where a group has brought leasing transactions back on balance sheet where the Group retains the risks and rewards of ownership.

Table 4.1 – Inchcape plc – Annual Report & Accounts – 31 December 1994

accounting policies (extract)

b Basis of Group accounts (extract)

Following the adoption of Financial Reporting Standard 5 (FRS 5) Reporting the Substance of Transactions comparative figures in the balance sheet, cash flow statement and relevant notes to the financial statements have been adjusted but there was no material effect on reported profit. The Group has taken advantage of the modification of FRS 5 in respect of certain insurance broking transactions which continue to be offset in the Group's accounts.

notes to the accounts (extract)

14 **Fixed assets – tangible assets (extract)**	Freehold and leasehold land and buildings **£m**	Plant, machinery and equipment **£m**	Total **£m**
Cost or valuation at 1st January 1994	**422.0**	**451.1**	**873.1**
FRS 5 adjustment	–	**40.3**	**40.3**
Cost or valuation at 1st January 1994 – restated	**422.0**	**491.4**	**913.4**
Exchange adjustments	**(2.6)**	**0.8**	**(1.8)**
Assets of subsidiaries acquired	**22.1**	**32.1**	**54.2**
Assets of subsidiaries sold	**(26.8)**	**(43.0)**	**(69.8)**
Additions	**18.1**	**81.0**	**99.1**
Disposals	**(9.1)**	**(72.4)**	**(81.5)**
Transfers (including assets held for resale)	**(10.4)**	**8.8**	**(1.6)**
Cost or valuation at 31st December 1994	**413.3**	**498.7**	**912.0**

The book value of plant, machinery and equipment includes £36.5m (1993 – £22.8m) in respect of assets held under finance leases, and £Nil (1993 – £27.2m) of assets relating to contract hire operations. The FRS 5 adjustment relates to motor vehicles leased to customers where the Group retains the risk and rewards of ownership, and includes £34.0m in respect of KCVR UK which was sold in December 1994.

4.46 This means that, for the time being, straightforward operating leases will remain off the lessee's balance sheet. There is, however, a conflict between the partial derecognition rules included in the standard (see further para 4.67) and SSAP 21. For example, if the partial derecognition rules were applied to operating leases, the effect would be that the lessor would derecognise the whole asset, but would recognise new assets representing the entitlement to a stream of receivables and a residual asset. This conflict will remain unless SSAP 21 is revised to fall in line with FRS 5. In the meantime, the provisions of SSAP 21 are generally more specific for a straightforward lease. For an example of how the interaction between FRS 5 and SSAP 21 applies see examples 1 and 2 in paragraph 4.78.

Principles of FRS 5

Objective

4.47 The standard's overriding objective is to ensure that the substance of an entity's transactions is reported in its financial statements. That means that the commercial effect of the undertaking's transactions and any resulting assets, liabilities, gains or losses should be faithfully represented in its financial statements. [FRS 5 para 1].

[The next page is 4013.]

4.48 The objective is simply stated and the standard's provisions are simple to apply where the transaction is itself simple in nature. However, determining how to account in practice for more complex transactions in accordance with their substance is fraught with difficulties. The nature of the accounting decisions made will inevitably be subjective and the resulting accounting treatment will differ depending upon the perception of the transaction's substance and its effect in practice. The answer to whether an item is on or off balance sheet under the standard will not necessarily be clear even after analysing the transaction in detail following the standard's guidance. The standard places particular emphasis on the transaction's *commercial effect in practice*. It is not adequate to review the transaction from a theoretical standpoint; it is what is likely to happen in practice and what actually happens in practice that is important.

4.49 The commercial effect in practice of a complex transaction might change from year to year as the actual or likely economic outcome becomes clearer. At the outset, the transaction has to be analysed and the likely outcome in practice determined in accordance with the facts and best estimates where future factors of the transaction are uncertain. After the transaction is initially recorded in accordance with its substance, the actual or likely outcome will have to be monitored in future accounting periods to determine whether the transaction's substance changes in practice. Where there is a subsequent change in the transaction's substance, that change will have to be accounted for when it becomes apparent.

4.50 The basic principles concerning reporting the substance of transactions can be summarised under five heads:

- Identifying and recognising assets and liabilities.
- Transactions in previously recognised assets.
- Linked presentation for non-recourse transactions.
- Offset rules.
- Accounting for quasi-subsidiaries.

Each of these is explained in the paragraphs below.

Identifying and recognising assets and liabilities

4.51 FRS 5's identification and recognition principles can be illustrated in a flow diagram (see diagram 1). As can be seen from the diagram, the steps to recognise an asset or liability are relatively straightforward in principle. It is simply a matter of analysing the relevant transactions to ascertain whether they give rise to new assets or liabilities that need to be recognised on the balance sheet or give rise to changes in existing assets and liabilities. Once an asset or liability has been identified and there is sufficient evidence that it exists *and* it can be measured sufficiently reliably, it should be recognised in the financial statements. [FRS 5 para 20]. These steps are considered in more detail below.

Diagram 1 – Recognising the substance of transactions

The numbers in square brackets refer to paragraphs of the standard.

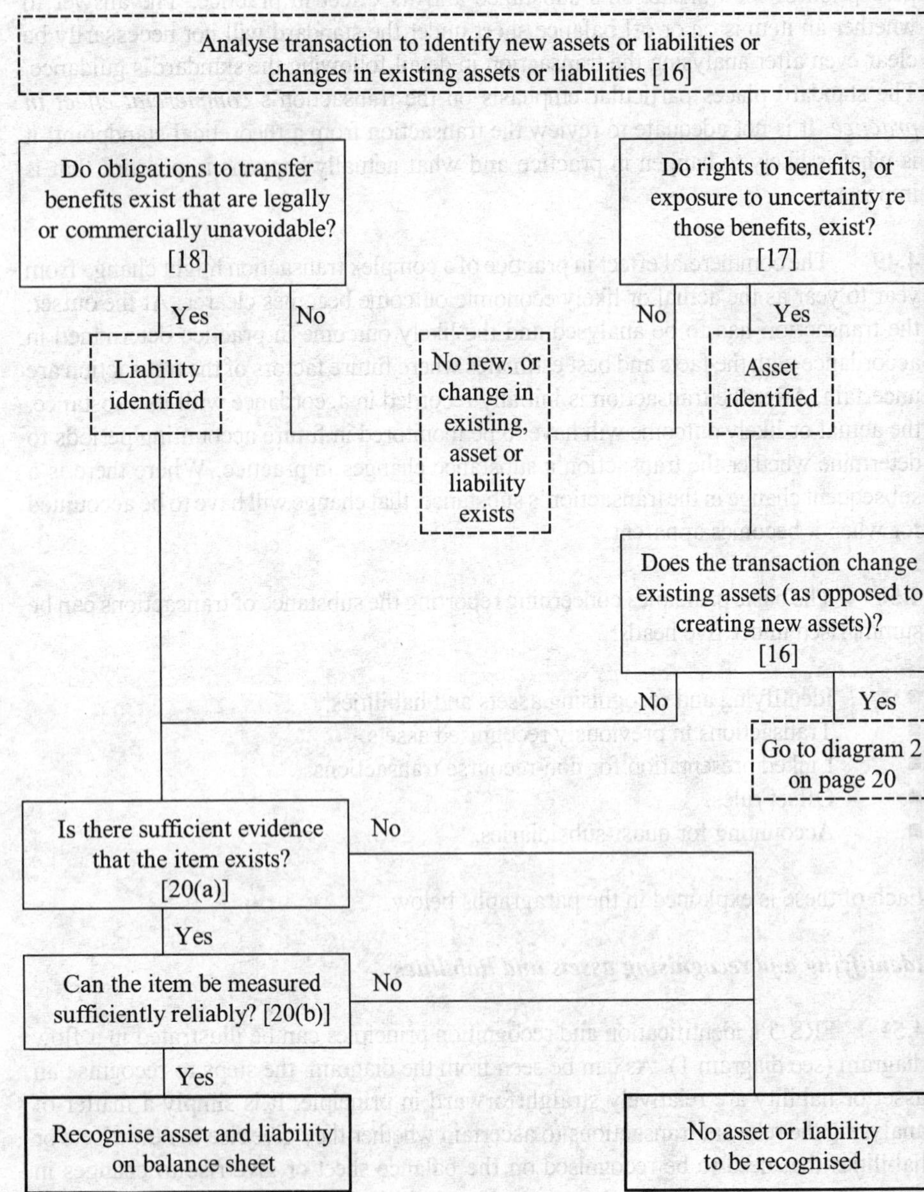

Analysing complex transactions

4.52 The first step in the process outlined above is to analyse the transaction. The most important aspect of analysing complex transactions is to consider carefully the reasons why each of the parties has entered into the transaction. What is the true commercial effect of the transaction? Is the transaction being entered into for tax reasons? Is one of the parties intending to acquire or dispose of an asset or is it intending to raise finance? What is the role of the other party? Once the commercial reason for the arrangement has been ascertained it may become obvious whether one of the parties to the transaction is merely receiving a lender's return. If this is so, then the transaction will almost certainly be a financing arrangement. More complex transactions often include the severance of legal title from the transaction's benefits and risks, some form of linkage with other transactions and put or call options.

Severance of legal title

4.53 Although the legal title to an asset may pass from a company because it enters into a particular transaction, the benefits and obligations associated with the asset often remain with the company. An example of such a transaction is a sale and repurchase of stock, where the seller agrees to repurchase stock at a price based on the original sales price. The title to the stocks passes, but the mark up in the buy-back price in substance represents a finance charge. Therefore, to accord with the standard's principles, such a transaction should remain on the seller's balance sheet with the receipt recorded as a liability. The mark up would be charged to the profit and loss account as a finance cost over the term of the transaction. Similarly, goods sold under reservation of title enable the selling company to have a lien on the goods until the purchaser has paid for them, although the benefits and risks in the goods have been transferred to the purchaser. It is common practice for the purchaser to account for the arrangement's substance and recognise such stocks in its balance sheet, although the supplier retains legal title to the goods. The supplier will treat the transaction as a sale. Conversely, with a finance lease, the lessor retains the legal title, but the transaction's substance is such that the asset and related obligation are recorded in the lessee's books.

Linkage with other transactions

4.54 A transaction is often linked with other transactions so that the commercial effect cannot be understood without considering the transactions as a whole. A simple example would be a transaction where a company sells an asset, but enters into a separate agreement to repurchase the asset at some time in the future. The commitment to repurchase is clearly linked to the sale and, therefore, the commercial outcome of the transaction should be considered as if they were a single transaction. This might, depending on the repurchase conditions, result in the transactions being accounted for as a financing arrangement rather than a sale of the asset with a separate repurchase.

Options and conditions

4.55 Simple options, such as an option to purchase shares, generally represent assets in their own right. A share option of this nature represents the right to purchase the shares at a future date and does not represent the actual shares that will be acquired on exercising the option. But with more complex transactions, options are often used in conjunction with the transaction's other aspects to give one party access to the future benefits associated with an asset, although that party might not have legal ownership of the asset.

4.56 Often options or conditions are included in the terms of a transaction which, by their nature, are almost certain to be fulfilled. In such transactions it is common for the company entering into the agreement to suffer an economic penalty if the option or condition is not fulfilled (or to receive an economic benefit if it is fulfilled). This economic penalty or benefit may be so great that the option or condition will inevitably be taken up by the entity. In determining the outcome of options in practice, greater weight should be given to those aspects and implications that are *more likely to have a commercial effect in practice*. The option's likely outcome has to be considered carefully, for example:

- Where there is no genuine commercial possibility that the option *will* be exercised, it should be ignored.

- Where there is no genuine commercial possibility that the option *will not* be exercised, its future exercise should be assumed.

[FRS 5 para 61].

4.57 In between these two extremes it will be a matter of judgement and the overall transaction's true commercial effect, including the option's likely impact, will have to be considered very carefully. As a consequence, the standard states that where a transaction incorporates one or more options, guarantees or conditional provisions, their commercial effect should be assessed in the context of all aspects and implications of the transaction in practice in order to determine what assets and liabilities exist. [FRS 5 para 19]. This does not mean, however, that the effect of an option should be judged on its probable outcome. In certain situations it might be assessed that the party's obligations and access to benefits are genuinely optional or conditional, in which case the option can be ignored. [FRS 5 para 61]. In other circumstances, the operation of options might indicate that one party has obligations (liabilities) or access to benefits (assets) that require to be recognised in its financial statements. The standard also points out that it should be assumed in the transaction's analysis that each of the parties will act in accordance with its economic interests. [FRS 5 para 62].

4.58 The following examples illustrate the application of these rules:

- Where the cost of exercising an option is expected to be lower than the benefits obtained by its exercise, it will generally be exercised and so in analysing the transaction the option's exercise should be assumed.
- If the cost of exercising an option is expected to be higher than the benefits obtained then generally it can be assumed that it will not be exercised and it can be ignored when analysing the transaction.
- Where the seller of an asset retains a call option over the asset and the buyer retains a put option, then it is almost certain that either the seller will call back the asset or the buyer will put it back to the seller. If for example, the asset is sold for £100,000 and the options are both priced at £110,000, then if the value of the asset decreases to (say) £90,000, the buyer will put it back to the seller at £110,000. Conversely, if the value moves up to £115,000, the seller will call back the asset for £110,000. In this case the asset should remain on the seller's balance sheet as a financing arrangement as the seller continues to bear the risks and rewards of ownership.
- Where the seller of an asset retains a call option over the asset and the buyer does not have an option to put the asset back to the seller the intentions of the seller and the rationale for including the option will have to be considered very carefully. As in the first two examples, the price of the option might indicate whether or not it will be exercised.

Identifying assets and liabilities

4.59 Once the transaction's commercial purpose has been ascertained it is then necessary to determine whether the transaction gives rise to new assets or liabilities or changes the entity's existing assets or liabilities.

Assets

4.60 Assets are defined in the standard as:

> *"Rights or other access to future economic benefits controlled by an entity as a result of past transactions or events."* [FRS 5 para 2].

4.61 Control over the rights to economic benefits means the ability to obtain the future economic benefits relating to an asset and the ability to restrict the access of others to those benefits. [FRS 5 para 3]. Control can be contrasted with management, which is the ability to direct the use of the item that generates the benefits. An example is a unit trust manager, who has day-to-day management of the trust's portfolio of investments, but it is the unit holders who gain the economic benefits from those assets, not the manager.

4.62 There will often be uncertainty regarding the amount of benefit flowing from an asset and this is the risk associated with the benefit. [FRS 5 para 5]. The standard uses the word 'benefit' to encompass also the risks that the benefit will be greater or smaller than expected and to cover the risks associated with the timing of the benefit's receipt. Risk is also defined in terms of the uncertainty of the amount of the benefits, including both the potential for gain and the exposure to loss. [FRS 5 para 5]. However, generally people understand and refer to benefits and risks (or risks and rewards) rather than using the term benefits to cover both. The party who has access to the benefits of an asset will also generally be subject to the risk that they will turn out to be different from expected. Therefore, evidence of whether an entity is exposed to risks associated with an asset (that is, whether it is exposed to a loss) is evidence that the entity has access to the asset's future economic benefits.

Liabilities

4.63 Liabilities are defined as:

> *"An entity's obligations to transfer economic benefits as a result of past transactions or events."* [FRS 5 para 4].

An entity, therefore, has a liability if it has an obligation which will result in an outflow of funds. Such an obligation will exist if the entity is unable to avoid either legally or commercially an outflow of benefits. [FRS 5 para 18].

4.64 Where an entity's obligation is contingent on the outcome of one or more future events which are uncertain, a liability should not necessarily be recognised. Such an obligation should be accounted for in accordance with SSAP 18 and will only give rise to recognising a liability where it is probable that a future event will confirm a loss which can be estimated with reasonable accuracy at the date the financial statements are approved for publication. [FRS 5 para 58; SSAP 18 para 14, 15]. As a consequence, generally guarantees will not give rise to liabilities that require to be recognised in the financial statements unless a loss is foreseen (but they may prevent derecognition of previously recognised assets – see further para 4.67 onwards). But the commercial effects of guarantees do need to be considered very carefully as part of the overall transaction. Furthermore, some guarantees might operate in a similar way to options. Where this is so, they will need to be considered in the context of the overall transaction (see para 4.55).

Recognition of assets and liabilities

4.65 Once an asset or liability has been identified it should be recognised in the entity's balance sheet if both of the following conditions are satisfied:

- There is sufficient evidence of the item's existence.
- The item can be measured at a monetary amount with sufficient reliability.

4.66 Recognition is defined in the standard as the "*process of incorporating an item into the primary financial statements under the appropriate heading. It involves depiction of the item in words and by a monetary amount and inclusion of that amount in the statement totals*". [FRS 5 para 6].

Transactions in previously recognised assets

4.67 FRS 5, following representations made on FRED 4, includes rules concerning when a previously recognised asset can be taken off balance sheet (discontinued recognition, or derecognition). Before a previously recognised asset can be derecognised there must be an effective sale or disposal of the particular asset. That is, *all significant* benefits and risks relating to the asset must be transferred to another party. On the other hand, if after a transaction has been entered into by the company there has been no significant change in the entity's benefits or risks associated with a previously recognised asset, there has been no sale and the relevant asset should remain on the balance sheet.

4.68 In between these two extremes, the ASB has introduced new rules to deal with the middle ground. These new rules (called in this chapter 'partial derecognition') deal with situations where:

- Part of an asset has been transferred to another party.
- All of the asset has been transferred, but for only part of its life.
- All of the asset has been transferred for all of its life, but where some significant benefits and risks are retained.

4.69 The new rules mean that where there is a significant change in the entity's rights to benefits *and* exposure to risks, but the entity has not got rid of all significant rights and/or significant exposure to risks, then the original asset should be derecognised. But in its place there should be shown a new asset and corresponding liability reflecting the benefits and risks retained by the entity after the transaction. This can be contrasted with the use of the linked presentation (see para 4.83); the linked presentation typically applies in situations where significant benefits and risks are retained which are associated with the performance of the *gross* asset in question (see further para 4.84). The situations that can arise are shown in diagram 2 and are explained in more detail below.

Diagram 2 – Transactions in previously recognised assets

The numbers in square brackets refer to paragraphs of the standard.

Continued recognition of the asset on balance sheet [18]	
Rewards retained	**Risks retained**
All significant	All significant
All significant	Some or none
Some or none	All significant
Ceasing to recognise the asset in its entirety – derecognition [22]	
Rewards retained	**Risks retained**
No significant	No significant
Special cases – partial derecognition [23]	
Rewards retained	**Risks retained**
Some	Some
No significant	Some
Some	No significant

4.70 The term 'significant' is not included in the list of the standard's definitions, but in respect of these rules it should be judged in relation to the benefits and risks that are likely to occur in practice and not in relation to the total possible benefits and risks. [FRS 5 para 25]. This again emphasises the importance of the transaction's commercial effect in practice. The problem in practice will be deciding what benefits and risks are significant and this will be a matter of judgement. The standard illustrates the principle using an example: an entity sells debts of £100m and bad debts are expected to be £2m. There is recourse to the seller for the first £5m of bad debts. In this case, the seller has retained all significant risks of non-payment.

Continued recognition

4.71 As can be seen from diagram 2, an asset should remain on balance sheet where there is no significant change to the entity's rights or benefits relating to the asset. Similarly, unless there is also a significant change in the risks associated with the asset, the entity's asset still has to be retained on balance sheet. [FRS 5 para 21]. Therefore if the entity retains all significant benefits *or* all significant risks (or both) the asset should remain on balance sheet.

4.72 The standard cites a debt factoring arrangement where the entity selling the debts retains the bad debt risk and slow payment risk as an example of a transaction where the debts clearly cannot be derecognised. In that example, the entity retains the significant risks associated with the transaction and the factor is merely supplying finance and receiving a lender's return, even though the legal title to the debts may have passed. Furthermore, the example illustrates that derecognition is not allowed where the transaction finances the entity's existing assets, even where the finance is non-recourse. With such an arrangement the entity is left with the same benefits and risks relating to the asset that existed before the financing, but in addition the transaction creates an obligation (a liability) to repay the finance, which must be recognised on the balance sheet. The only exception to this rule is where the transaction is a financing arrangement and the conditions for the linked presentation are met (see further para 4.83).

Full derecognition

4.73 A previously recognised asset can only be derecognised in its entirety (without being replaced by another asset – see para 4.74) where all significant benefits *and* all significant risks relating to the asset have been transferred. This situation will arise where an asset is sold for a single non-returnable cash payment where there is no recourse by the buyer to the entity's other assets and no further entitlements to rights on the part of the seller (for example, in a sale of a subsidiary where part of the consideration is deferred).

Partial derecognition

4.74 The standard indicates that partial derecognition only applies where there is a significant change in the entity's rights to benefits *and* exposure to risks. It should be borne in mind that the type of situations where partial derecognition applies are few in number; generally previously recognised assets will either have to be retained on the balance sheet or, if they meet the criteria, derecognised in their entirety. Partial derecognition might arise where the transaction takes the form of a transfer of:

- Part of the asset.
- All of the asset for part of its life.
- All of the asset for all its life, but where the entity retains significant benefits or risks.

4.75 The principles can be illustrated as follows:

- Transfer of part of the asset – proportionate share

  A loan transfer might involve the transfer of a proportionate share of a loan (including rights to interest and principal) such that cash flows and profits and losses are shared by the transferee and transferor in fixed proportions. In this case, the proportionate share transferred should be derecognised.

- Transfer of part of the asset – splitting benefit streams.

  The interest benefit stream is stripped from a loan being held as an asset such that one party has the benefits and risks associated with the interest stream and the other has the benefits and risks associated with the principal. In this case, the party retaining the investment in the principal should derecognise the original asset and in its place recognise a new asset namely an investment in the non-interest bearing principal. The original carrying amount would have to be allocated to the principal and the interest stream. If the element of cost allocated to the interest stream equals the proceeds, then no profit or loss arises and the remainder is allocated to the principal. However, in principle the principal is recognised at a different amount than its original carrying value. The amount at which the principal is recorded would then earn interest, which would be added to the principal each year and credited to the profit and loss account, until the loan is redeemed at its full amount. For example, if an interest strip is made on a loan, and the amount received is £50,000, the amount of the original carrying value of the principal allocated to the interest may also be £50,000 (and would probably be arrived at by discounting the interest receivable). Therefore, no gain or loss arises on the transaction. The discount of £50,000 would be deducted from the balance of the loan and credited to the profit and loss account over the remaining term of the loan, thereby building up the loan to its redemption amount at the end of its term.

- Transfer of asset for part of its life.

  An entity sells a car, but agrees to repurchase it towards the end of its life at a value that fairly reflects the usage and depreciation over the period to repurchase. The entity now only has an interest in the residual, and also has a liability, which is its obligation to repurchase the item. Any profit or loss on sale will be the difference between the proceeds and the old book value. Whether accounting for a residual asset and liability is actually appropriate depends on the likely commercial outcome. If repurchase is intended or likely, the residual asset and liability should be recognised; and if a loss is likely on repurchase, that would be accounted for at the start by recording a residual liability in excess of a residual asset (that is, by making a provision against the asset to reduce it to its recoverable amount). But if, as for example with some manufacturer's buy-back guarantees, the manufacturer agrees to buy back an asset after say five years, but does so only at a low price such that it is much more likely that the customer will retain the asset or sell it to a third party, it would not be appropriate to record a residual asset or liability. All that is necessary in such situations is for the manufacturer to make provision for any loss that might arise on the (relatively few) units that are expected to be returned.

- Transfer of asset for all of its life where some benefit or risk is retained.

  A subsidiary might be sold with an earn-out (that is, an amount of deferred performance-related consideration), in which case the original asset (the subsidiary) would be derecognised and something else would appear in its place, namely a debtor, being a prudent estimate of the amount of further proceeds under the earn-out, discounted if appropriate.

  Another example is where an asset has been sold subject to a warranty agreement. The party selling the asset has disposed of the benefits and risks associated with the asset and can derecognise it, but has retained a liability which is the obligation under the warranty agreement. Whether this liability will be recognised will depend on the circumstances and where necessary an adequate provision should be made in accordance with the requirements of SSAP 18 'Accounting for contingencies'. If a provision is necessary, a corresponding loss is recognised in the profit and loss account.

4.76 Under the partial derecognition rules, where there is a significant change in the entity's rights to benefits and exposure to risks, the original asset should be derecognised in its entirety and a different asset recognised in its place, together with a liability representing any obligations assumed. If there is no new asset, then it is necessary to provide for any liability for loss if an obligation is likely to arise.

4.77 In this type of situation, where an asset has been derecognised in its entirety a profit or loss will arise and this should be recognised on a prudent basis. For example, where the resulting profit or loss is uncertain, the standard requires that full provision should be made for any probable loss and, to the extent that any gain is in doubt, it should be deferred. [FRS 5 para 24].

4.78 The examples that follow illustrate situations where the partial derecognition rules apply and also show how the standard's provisions interact with those of SSAP 21.

Example 1

A vehicle contract hire company buys cars and enters into three-year operating leases with lessees. Economically, what was a single asset (a car) has become two assets: (a) a stream of receivables over three years; and (b) a risk on the residual value at year three. The lessor then sells the stream of rentals to a bank (with the bank taking the bad debt risk); the lessor is left with the residual position.

Under FRED 4's tough derecognition rules (see para 4.30), the transaction would arguably have led to the lessor retaining the whole of the car on the balance sheet on the grounds that it still retained the risks and rewards relating to it. Following FRS 5's partial derecognition rules, the asset would be split in two (as above), the receivables would be regarded as having been sold and there would remain a different asset, namely a three-year residual, on the balance sheet. This assumes that the lessor would hold the asset at that time or would buy it back at a pre-agreed price. In these circumstances there would be an equivalent liability for the funding of the residual or the repurchase obligation.

Example 2

A slightly different example to that above is where a lessor enters into arrangements with a third party such that the lessor does not buy back the car, but merely guarantees to make good a shortfall if the market value at year three was not as great as the expected amount and, similarly, benefits from any increase in the market value above the guaranteed amount. In this circumstance, the asset would be the extent (if any) to which the market value might exceed the guaranteed amount (this would probably be booked as nil initially on prudence grounds). The obligation would be the provision (if any) that the lessor needs to make in respect of the loss that is likely to occur, which would be recognised and taken to the profit and loss account in accordance with the requirements of SSAP 18.

4.79 Thus there seems to be a difference, under the new partial de-recognition approach, between cases where the lessor actually holds the asset or will (or may) buy it back (that is, a new asset, the residual, is shown on the balance sheet) and cases where the lessor merely guarantees the residual value (that is, no asset is likely to arise on the balance sheet, but a provision will be required for any expected loss). Previously, before the introduction of the new partial derecognition rules, many would have argued that the economic exposure in the two examples was very similar and that they should be accounted for in the same way.

4.80 Where there is an overlap with the provisions of FRS 5 and SSAP 21, the standard states that the statement that contains the more specific provisions should be applied. In the examples above, the provisions of FRS 5 are more specific than those of SSAP 21 and hence should be applied in the way indicated.

4.81 In Table 4.2, J Bibby & Sons have brought back on balance sheet following the introduction of FRS 5, repurchase obligations to re-acquire certain equipment at the end of its primary lease period.

Table 4.2 – J. Bibby & Sons PLC – Annual Report and Accounts 24 September 1994

Financial Review (extract)

FRS 5

The implementation of FRS 5 (Reporting the Substance of Transactions), which applies to accounting periods ending after 22nd September 1994, has resulted in bills and leases discounted with recourse and repurchase obligations for equipment sold being included on the balance sheet. All the transactions which gave rise to these items were entered into entirely within the normal course of business and have been included in debtors or stocks on the one hand and creditors on the other hand. The amounts are as follows:

	1994			1993		
	Total	Recourse commitments	Repurchase obligations	Total	Recourse commitments	Repurchase obligations
	£000's	£000's	£000's	£000's	£000's	£000's
Under one year	25,477	21,241	4,236	27,195	25,296	1,899
Over one year	12,593	508	12,085	6,989	1,253	5,736
	38,070	21,749	16,321	34,184	26,549	7,635

The repurchase obligations enable our Capital Equipment and Materials Handling Divisions to re-acquire equipment, which has usually been maintained by themselves, at the end of primary periods thus providing opportunities in the used equipment market.

Insurance

4.82 It is often wrongly thought that insuring against the risks associated with a particular transaction might enable the company concerned to derecognise the related assets on the basis that it has transferred significant risks associated with the asset. This is a misconception because the risks associated with the asset (for example, bad debt risk) remain with the company and the company has a counter claim against its insurer should that risk arise (for example, when a debt is bad). In practice, this counter claim may or may not be met by the insurance company depending on whether the company has complied with its insurance conditions. It is only possible to derecognise an asset if the significant risks and benefits have been sold to another party and the risks and rewards have been transferred to that same party. However, if that other party itself insures against the same risks that the company would have insured against, then it may be possible for the transaction to be derecognised, because the company has successfully transferred its significant risks.

Linked presentation

General rules

4.83 Following representations made to the ASB by the banking industry and others, the ASB developed the 'linked presentation' for certain specialised transactions such as securitisations where non-recourse finance is involved. The only recourse allowed to the provider of the finance in such a transaction is to the specific assets being financed and not to the entity's other assets. The specific assets are, therefore, 'ring-fenced'. There must be *no recourse whatsoever* to other assets of the entity. The linked presentation represents a compromise which allows certain assets and their related finance to be 'linked' on the face of the balance sheet, whereby the finance is deducted from the asset. The presentation is said not to offend the Act's offset rules because, under the standard's principles, the asset that is being recognised on the face of the balance sheet is the net item and not the gross amount. Furthermore, as the amount of finance received is non-refundable, it does not meet the standard's definition of a liability. The gross asset and liability are being disclosed on the face of the balance sheet merely as additional information to enable the user to appreciate the full extent of the transaction.

4.84 An important condition of using this presentation is that the provider of the finance must only be repaid from the benefits generated by the assets or from the realisation of the assets themselves. The entity can retain rights to any surplus benefits that remain after repayment of the finance, but it must not have any right or obligation to keep the assets or to repay the finance from its own resources. Often in such transactions, the entity will be exposed to certain benefits and risks that will have a commercial effect in practice. This might arise, for example, because the future outcome measured in both terms of profits and cash flows will often be dependent on the performance of the gross assets transferred to the other party (for example, in the case of receivables, the performance will be affected by the amount of bad debts and the timing of payment). The ASB contends that it is the retention of these *significant* benefits or risks associated with the gross asset that distinguish this type of non-recourse financing from transactions that can be partially derecognised; where there is a transfer of the whole asset for part of its life or a transfer of part of the asset for all of its life (see para 4.74). This is an important distinction, as without it all transactions eligible for linked presentation might alternatively be partially derecognised. Where significant benefits or risks are retained and the transaction is in the nature of a financing arrangement it is still only eligible for the linked presentation if the strict conditions set out in paragraph 4.89 below can be satisfied.

4.85 The following example illustrates these points.

Example

If a company has debtors of £10m it might factor these and in return receive non-returnable proceeds of £9m. As the debtors are collected it will recover the balance of £1m less the factor's fees, but it is still subject to credit risk (that is, bad debt risk) up to a maximum of £1m on the full amount of the debt of £10m. If the bad debt risk is expected to be £0.5m it is likely to receive only a further £0.5m from the factor. In addition, the factor will charge a financing fee for providing the £9m of funds to the company which varies depending on the speed of collection (late payment risk). Consequently, the company still retains the significant risks associated with the debts (the bad debt risk and the late payment risk), albeit it has transferred the risk of catastrophe (which is negligible) to the factor. The factor's risk of loss would arise only if the bad debts exceeded £1m, which is highly unlikely. Therefore, the company has retained significant risks relating to the whole of the assets and, as a consequence, they cannot be partially derecognised, but (because the £9m is non-returnable and assuming the other criteria are met) the assets are eligible for the linked presentation. The transaction is precluded from being partially derecognised, because the company still bears the risk associated with the *gross* amount of the portfolio of debts and in practice bears the same bad debt risk before and after the transaction (albeit after the sale, it has transferred the risk of catastrophe). If, for example, the company had sold 90% of *each* debt then its risks have changed significantly and its bad debt risk on the portfolio will be very different before and after the sale. In this latter circumstance, the transaction might be eligible for the partial derecognition rules and if so it could be appropriate to derecognise the part of the debt that has been sold (that is, 90% of each debt) and retain on balance sheet the balance (that is, 10% of each debt).

If the transaction complies with the conditions for the linked presentation it would be disclosed on the face of the balance sheet in the following way:

Balance sheet (extract)	£m	£m
Current assets		
Debtors		
Trade debtors		50.0
Trade debtors subject to financing arrangements	9.5	
Less: non-returnable amounts received	9.0	0.5
Total trade debtors		50.5

The trade debtors of £9.5m is made up of the total debtors of £10m less the expected bad debt provision of £0.5m. The required disclosure clearly shows the asset of £0.5m to which the entity is exposed separately from other debtors, there being no other recourse from the providers of the finance to other assets of the entity.

If subsequently, one of the debtors that owes £3m goes into liquidation and the debt is bad, it will be necessary to reduce the gross trade debtors by this amount. However, because part of this debt is covered by non-returnable funds received from the factor it is possible to reduce the liability to the factor by £2m. Of the difference of £1m, 0.5m would be charged to the profit and loss account and the balance of 0.5m used to reduce the provision. In effect, the net presentation is carried through to the profit and loss account, the loss that falls to the company is only £0.5m: of the remainder of the loss, £2m is borne by the factor as a result of the £9m being non-returnable and £0.5m has already been provided for. Therefore, at this stage, the company has provided in full for the risks relating to the debtors of £1m that are not covered by non-recourse finance (that is, £0.5m initial bad debt provision and an additional provision of £0.5m). The linked presentation would then show gross debtors of £7m (£10m less £3m) less a gross liability of the same amount (£9m less £2m) coming to a net balance of nil. Even though the net balance is nil, the linked presentation disclosing the gross figures still has to be shown on the face of the balance sheet.

4.86 The amount of funding received may not always equate exactly to the non-returnable amount as happened in the example above. This is illustrated in the example in paragraph 4.91.

4.87 Another important restriction is that the linked presentation cannot be used where the finance relates to a business unit or to assets that are used in conjunction with other assets of the entity to generate the funds to repay the finance. Therefore, for example, a company cannot use the linked presentation for the debt it might raise to finance the company's operating properties. However, it will be a matter of judgement as to how far this rule should be taken. For example, can a property investment company use the linked presentation for an investment property that it has financed ring-fenced? The answer is probably no, because even if the company is funding the repayment of the finance from the asset's rental income, if it has the right to retain the asset at the end of its life it falls foul of one of the linked presentation conditions mentioned below.

Conditions in detail

4.88 Under the rules in the standard the linked presentation can only be used where a transaction involving a previously recognised asset is in substance a financing, but the company 'ring-fences' the asset such that:

- The finance will be repaid only from proceeds generated by the specific item it finances (or by transfer of the item itself) and there is *no possibility whatsoever* of a claim on the entity being established other than against funds generated by that item (or against the item itself).

- There is *no* provision whereby the entity may either keep the item on repayment of the finance or re-acquire it at any time.

[FRS 5 para 26].

4.89 Following these initial requirements the standard then sets down detailed conditions that must be met before the linked presentation can be used:

- The finance must relate to a specific item (or portfolio of similar items) and, in the case of a loan, must be secured on that item, but not on any other assets of the entity. [FRS 5 para 27(a)].

  The linked presentation cannot be used where the finance relates to two or more assets that are not part of a portfolio or to a portfolio covering assets that would otherwise be shown under different balance sheet captions.

- The provider of the finance must have no recourse whatsoever, either explicit or implicit, to the other assets of the entity for losses and the entity must have no obligation whatsoever to repay the provider of the finance. [FRS 5 para 27(b)].

  This means that there must be no obligation whatsoever (not even a moral one) to fund losses on the assets being financed. For example, a moral obligation on an originator in a mortgage securitisation might arise if the originator were to fund a mortgage interest rate increase which could not be borne by the mortgagors (the borrowers).

- The entity's directors must state explicitly in each set of financial statements where a linked presentation is used that the entity is not obliged to support any losses, nor does it intend to do so (see for example Table 4.3 on page 32). [FRS 5 para 27(c)].

- The provider of the finance must agree in writing (in the finance documentation or otherwise) that it will seek repayment of the finance, as to both principal and interest, only to the extent that sufficient funds are generated by the specific item it has financed and that it will not seek recourse in any other form, and such agreement is noted in each set of financial statements where a linked presentation is used (see also Table 4.3 on page 32). [FRS 5 para 27(d)].

- If the funds generated by the item are insufficient to pay off the provider of the finance, this must not constitute an event of default for the entity. [FRS 5 para 27(e)].

  This means, for example, that where an originator in a securitisation transaction has other funds lent to it by the provider of the finance, if there are insufficient funds from the securitisation transaction to repay the finance for that deal, the provider of the finance should not be able to regard that as constituting a default on the other funds lent to the originator and, as a consequence, require their repayment. The provision would also extend to a different lender where there is a cross-default clause linked to all the company's borrowings including the securitisation.

- There must be no provision whatsoever, either in the financing arrangement or otherwise, whereby the entity has a right or an obligation either to keep the item upon repayment of the finance or (where title to the item has been transferred) to re-acquire it at any time. Accordingly:

  - where the item is one (such as a monetary receivable) that directly generates cash, the provider of the finance must be repaid out of the resulting cash receipts (to the extent these are sufficient); or

  - where the item is one (such as a physical asset) that does not directly generate cash, there is a definite point at which either the item must be sold to a third party and the provider of the finance repaid from the proceeds (to the extent these are sufficient) or the item must be transferred to the provider of the finance in full and final settlement.

  [FRS 5 para 27(f)].

  Even where there is merely an understanding between the parties that the seller will re-acquire the asset at some time in the future, this fact is enough for this condition to be breached. This clearly illustrates that all of the aspects of the transaction need to be considered including the intentions of the parties even where these are not evidenced in writing. Put and call options are commonly used to effect a repurchase and where these exist in a transaction, the linked presentation should not be used.

4.90 It is necessary to analyse a transaction very carefully to establish whether there are any recourse provisions, because recourse can come in different forms, such as:

- Substitution clauses whereby good debts are substituted for non-performing debts (see further para 4.161).
- Guarantees for performance, proceeds or other support.
- Put options to transfer assets back to the originating entity.
- Swap arrangements (see para 4.156).
- Penalty arrangements.

Warranties in relation to the condition of the assets when the arrangement is being entered into (for example, the seller has good title or has delivered the asset or warrants that the assets are in good condition) do not preclude use of the linked presentation, but warranties relating to the future condition or performance (for example, payment or speed of payment) of the assets do preclude use of the linked presentation. [FRS 5 para 83].

Linking part of the finance

4.91 If the conditions hold for only part of the finance, then the linked presentation is still used for that part of the finance for which all the conditions are met.

Example

A company sells its debtors of £10m to a third party and receives in return an amount of £9m. Of the £9m, £7.5m is non-returnable, but £1.5m of the finance is returnable depending on the performance of the debtors. The bad debts are expected on past experience to be £0.5m. In effect, the company retains the risks associated with the first £2.5m of losses and as £1.5m is potentially returnable it cannot be included in the linked presentation and must be shown as a liability. The transaction would be disclosed in the balance sheet in the following way.

Balance sheet (extract)	£m	£m
Current assets		
Debtors		
Trade debtors		50.0
Trade debtors subject to financing arrangements	9.5	
Less: non-returnable amounts received	7.5	2.0
Total trade debtors		52.0
Creditors		
Financing of trade debtors		1.5

It would be necessary for the notes to the financial statements to explain fully the implications of the transaction and in particular to indicate that certain of the finance related to it is returnable and is included in creditors.

4.92 An example of a company that has non-recourse finance for part of its debts is given in Table 4.3.

Table 4.3 – WPP Group plc – Annual Report and Accounts – 31 December 1997

Consolidated balance sheet (extract)
As at 31 December 1997

Notes		1997 £m	1996 £m
	Current assets		
15	Stocks and work in progress	**99.7**	94.1
16	Debtors	**827.6**	765.0
17	Debtors within working capital facility:		
	Gross debts	**335.2**	264.1
	Non-returnable proceeds	**(211.7)**	(175.0)
		123.5	89.1

Notes to the consolidated balance sheet

17 **Debtors within working capital facility**

The following are included in debtors within the Group's working capital facilities:	1997 £m	1996 £m
Gross debts	**335.2**	264.1
Non-returnable proceeds	**(211.7)**	(175.0)
	123.5	89.1

Within the Group's overall working capital facilities, certain trade debts have been assigned as security against the advance of cash. This security is represented by the assignment of a pool of trade debts, held by one of the Group's subsidiaries, to a trust for the benefit of the providers of this working capital facility. The financing provided against this pool takes into account, *inter alia*, the risks that may be attached to individual debtors and the expected collection period.

The Group is not obliged (and does not intend) to support any credit-related losses arising from the assigned debts against which cash has been advanced. The providers of the finance have confirmed in writing that, in the event of default in payment by a debtor, they will only seek repayment of cash advanced from the remainder of the pool of debts in which they hold an interest, and that repayment will not be sought from the Group in any other way.

Profit recognition

4.93 Much of FRS 5 is aimed at the balance sheet and how assets and liabilities should be recognised there, but for linked presentations there is also some guidance on when profits and losses should be recognised. At the inception of the transaction a gain will only arise to the extent that the non-returnable proceeds received exceed the asset's previous carrying value. [FRS 5 para 28]. During the transaction's life, a profit or loss will arise to the extent that the income from the asset is different from the amount due to the financier. Finally, if the transaction is such that the asset is eventually sold at the end of the transaction a further profit or loss may arise, but this amount can only be recognised in the period that the onward sale takes place. Furthermore, where for example the asset generates income and there is a cost of finance in a period, it will be the net amount of profit or loss that is generally recognised in the profit and loss account (as these amounts should also be linked in a similar way to the balance sheet items from which they are generated). The gross components should be given in a note to the financial statements, unless in order to give a true and fair view it is necessary to show the gross amounts linked on the face of the profit and loss account. This latter situation might arise where the transaction is of such significance to the company's trading results that the net presentation alone does not give the transaction sufficient prominence.

4.94 What the standard does not discuss is where to show such profits and losses in the profit and loss account. On the inception of the transaction, although it is a financing arrangement, there will be a one off gain or loss that arises in effect on the transfer of benefits and risks to the other party, which is akin to a sale of an asset. For example, if debtors of £10,000 are sold for £9,000, which is non-returnable and further amounts receivable are prudently estimated at nil, a loss of £1,000 should be charged to the profit and loss account and included in the format item 'interest payable and similar charges', because it is in substance a finance charge.

4.95 During the life of a simple financing arrangement, it would seem sensible to show any net losses in an accounting period as part of the company's cost of finance and record it in the profit and loss account as interest payable and similar charges. Where the transaction generates a net profit this is similarly a finance item and should also be included within 'other interest receivable and similar income' in the profit and loss account.

4.96 If on the eventual outcome of the transaction there is a sale of the linked assets then the profit or loss arising on this part of the transaction should be accounted for in accordance with the normal rules for such profits or losses on the sale of fixed or current assets (see further chapters 4 and 7).

Offset rules

4.97 In the past, assets and liabilities have only been allowed to be offset against one another in the financial statements where there was a legally enforceable right of set-off between the balances. This stems from the requirement in paragraph 5 of Schedule 4 to the Act, which states that amounts in respect of items representing assets or income may not be set off against amounts in respect of items representing liabilities or expenditure, or *vice versa*. The proposal in FRED 4 was to restrict substantially the ability to offset debit and credit balances, particularly where the monetary amounts were denominated in different currencies. An effect of the proposed rules would have been to force certain industries such as money brokers and insurance brokers to change their accounting practices significantly. These industries have in the past netted balances with counterparties even where there is no legal right of offset (see further paras 4.225 and 4.232).

4.98 Following representations made on FRED 4, the ASB relaxed the wording. FRS 5, therefore, allows offset where amounts are denominated in different currencies, but only where the standard's conditions are met. Now the standard's rules only allow offset where the balances do not constitute separate assets and liabilities and where the following conditions are met:

- The company and the other party owe each other determinable monetary amounts denominated either in the same currency, or in different but freely convertible currencies.

  A freely convertible currency is one for which quoted exchange rates are available in an active market that can rapidly absorb the amount to be offset without significantly affecting the exchange rate. This condition is necessary in order to get as close as possible to the situation where the obligation associated with the credit balance eliminates access to the benefits associated with the debit balance, which would not be the case were the currencies not freely convertible.

- The company has the ability to insist on net settlement.

  Any such right to insist on net settlement should only be taken into account if the company is able to enforce net settlement in all situations of default by the other party. This would obviously include the other party's liquidation, but also includes all other situations that might arise during the term of the transactions. In the past companies have often considered the position on liquidation, but may not have considered adequately what happens at other times. For example, FRED 4 illustrated this provision by considering the situation where a bank has the right to enforce net settlement of a particular deposit and loan, but only in the event that the customer breaches certain covenants. In this example, the bank cannot insist on net settlement all of the time, so the deposit and loan could not be offset in the bank's financial statements in the absence of a breach. Therefore, generally in a normal trading company, if it has debit and credit balances with a bank and the bank can insist on net settlement, but the company cannot, then the company will not be able to offset these balances in its financial statements.

- The company's ability to insist on net settlement is assured beyond reasonable doubt and would survive the insolvency of the other party. A contractual agreement for set-off will not survive insolvency unless it complies also with the statutory rules for set-off in a winding up included in regulation 4.90 of the Insolvency Rules 1986.

- The debit balance matures no later than the credit balance.

  This condition will be met if the company can ensure that result by accelerating the maturity of the deposit with the other party or deferring the maturity of the credit balance with that party.

[FRS 5 para 29].

4.99 Extreme care needs to be taken in consolidated financial statements, where it is not generally possible for an amount that one group company owes to another party (such as a bank) to be offset against the amount of a deposit that another member of the group has lodged with that party. Equally, the liability of one member of a group to a bank cannot be reduced or extinguished because the company that made the deposit has guaranteed the liability of the debtor company. However, where a bank funds members of a group of companies this situation would be different if both of the following conditions applied:

- Each individual depositing company in the group has a joint and several liability to pay the same debts as the borrowing companies (that is, each is deemed to be a principal debtor for the same debts).

- The bank has a liability to each individual depositing company in respect of its deposit.

In these circumstances such assets and liabilities may be offset against each other if all the criteria are met.

Accounting for quasi-subsidiaries

4.100 The notion of quasi-subsidiaries is not new, because they were first identified in TR 603, but at that time were referred to as 'non-subsidiary dependent companies' and were later termed 'controlled non-subsidiaries' in ED 42. A quasi-subsidiary is now defined in FRS 5 as:

> "*...a company, trust, partnership or other vehicle that, though not fulfilling the definition of a subsidiary, is directly or indirectly controlled by the reporting entity and gives rise to benefits for that entity that are in substance no different from those that would arise were the vehicle a subsidiary.*" [FRS 5 para 7].

In this context, control of another entity means the ability to direct the financial and operating policies of that entity with a view to gaining economic benefit from its activities. [FRS 5 para 8]. BICC appears to have this type of influence over certain property development associated undertakings as explained in Table 4.4.

Table 4.4 – BICC plc – Annual Report and Accounts – 31 December 1994

Principal accounting policies (extract)

1 Basis of accounting (extract)

In accordance with FRS 5 certain property development associated undertakings have been consolidated as quasi-subsidiaries and other commitments have been treated as borrowings of the Group. Comparative figures have been restated with the effect that Group capital employed and net borrowings at 31 December 1993 have been increased by £103 million and related finance costs in 1993 of £7 million have been included within net interest rather than operating profit.

There has been no effect on profit for the year to 31 December 1993 resulting from these restatements.

4.101 As mentioned in paragraph 4.16, a change in the legal definition of subsidiaries came about because of the amendments made to the Companies Act 1985 by the Companies Act 1989, which implemented the provisions of the EC 7th Directive into UK law. The amendments moved the definitions of subsidiaries away from concentrating on the legal ownership of companies to looking at who controls an undertaking's activities. The effect was to include in a group's consolidated financial statements other undertakings some of which (albeit a minority) had previously been designed specifically to maintain their legal ownership outside the group so as to avoid consolidation. Although these vehicles were designed to avoid legal ownership, they were also designed to retain control over the vehicle's activities and the benefits arising from those activities. In addition, prior to the Companies Act 1989's changes, it was relatively easy to set up a company that was a subsidiary for tax purposes, but was not a subsidiary for Companies Act purposes. This was because the definition of subsidiary in the Corporation Taxes Act differed fundamentally from that in the Companies Act. The fundamental difference was removed by the changes to the definitions of subsidiaries in the Companies Act 1989, but the definitions do still differ.

4.102 As a consequence of the changes in the Companies Act 1989, many off balance sheet vehicles came back on balance sheet. Furthermore, the scope of consolidation was extended to include not only companies that fell within the definitions of subsidiaries, but also other undertakings (such as, partnerships and other unincorporated associations). (See further chapter 21.)

4.103 Although the Companies Act 1989 did much to restrict the use of vehicles to take assets and liabilities off balance sheet, the ASB has retained the notion of quasi-subsidiaries to close any remaining loopholes. For example, it is not clear under the Act whether trusts come within the definitions of subsidiaries, although it can be argued that they do. However, it is quite clear that even if they did fall outside the scope of the Act's definitions, they are covered by FRS 5's definition of quasi-subsidiary. In addition, many securitisation schemes are set up using vehicles which now fall within the definition of quasi-subsidiaries.

4.104 The definition focuses on the control over the entity whether that control is direct or indirect and looks at the benefits that the control gives rise to. Where the benefits are no different from those that would arise if the entity were a subsidiary, a quasi-subsidiary exists. The benefits that are of concern are those that arise from the vehicle's net assets, as with any normal subsidiary, and similarly any exposure to risks will relate again to the benefits associated with the vehicle's net assets.

4.105 In determining whether the company controls a vehicle, regard should be had to who in practice directs the vehicle's financial and operating policies. The rules here are the same as those in FRS 2 where control is defined in terms of the ability of a company to direct the entity's financial and operating policies. The ability to prevent others from enjoying the benefits arising from the vehicle's net assets is also evidence of control. However, a company will not control another entity where there is another party that has the ability to determine all major issues of policy. Consequently, if it is obvious that another party controls the entity, then it cannot be a quasi-subsidiary.

4.106 Another situation where an entity should be accounted for as a quasi-subsidiary is where the company gains the benefits arising from a vehicle's net assets, because the vehicle's financial and operating policies are predetermined (contractually or otherwise). [FRS 5 para 34]. In this type of circumstance, neither party to the contract might seem to have day-to-day control of the vehicle's financial and operating policies, but the contract might specify and determine who gains the benefits and who is exposed to the risks related to the vehicle. This is typically the case with the special purpose vehicles (SPVs) used in securitisation schemes. It will, therefore, be necessary to look at the detail of the contract very carefully to determine which party has control. The party that gains the benefits and is exposed to the risks arising from the vehicle's net assets will be the party that has control.

4.106.1 An FRRP ruling in February 1997 concerned joint ventures which were determined to be quasi-subsidiaries. Associated Nursing Services plc had entered into joint ventures with two partners and had treated the joint ventures as associated undertakings. In one case, which involved a joint venture with a bank, the board of the joint venture company in question was 'deadlocked'. In the FRRP's view, however, the financial and operating policies of that company were substantially predetermined by underlying agreements; and through its interest in the joint venture Associated Nursing Services plc gained benefits arising from the company's net assets such that it had control. This suggests that its share of benefits and risk did not equate to its participation in the venture.

4.106.2 In the other case a venture capital arrangement with five venture capital funds had been set up through an intermediary. In the FRRP's view that company's financial and operating policies were again substantially predetermined by underlying agreements. Although in this case Associated Nursing Services plc held only a minority of the ordinary share capital, the investors' interests were effectively limited and the FRRP took the view that Associated Nursing Services plc gained benefits arising from the net assets of the company such that it had control.

4.106.3 In the FRRP's view the substance of the arrangements was such that the companies were quasi-subsidiaries as defined by FRS 5 and should not have been accounted for by the equity method, but should have been treated as though they were subsidiaries. Consequently, where a company enters into a joint venture with a financier who takes an equity stake, it is important to assess the substance of the arrangement. If the other party has a cap on its investment return, then this indicates that the structure may be a financing one, in which case it might be necessary to treat the entity as a quasi-subsidiary.

[The next paragraph is 4.107.]

Conflict with the law?

4.107 If an entity is a quasi-subsidiary it cannot be a legal subsidiary (and *vice versa*). As the Act only requires subsidiaries to be consolidated the question arises as to whether consolidation of a quasi-subsidiary as required by FRS 5 is a departure from the Act. The ASB contends that consolidation of quasi-subsidiaries represents the provision of additional information in accordance with section 227(5) of the Act, without which the consolidated financial statements would not give a true and fair view. Therefore, accepting ASB's reasoning, consolidation of a quasi-subsidiary is not regarded as a departure from the Act's provisions in order to give a true and fair view (section 227(6)). As a consequence, consolidation of quasi-subsidiaries does not constitute a true and fair override and, therefore, the resulting disclosures required by the Act and UITF Abstract 7 do not have to be made.

Accounting treatment

4.108 Quasi-subsidiaries should be consolidated into the group's financial statements in the same way as for other subsidiaries and the same types of consolidation adjustments should be made (for example, the elimination of intra-group trading and profits). Therefore, the consolidated financial statements should include the quasi-subsidiary's assets, liabilities, profits, losses and cash flows in the same way as if it was a subsidiary. [FRS 5 para 35].

4.109 If a company does not have any legal subsidiaries and, therefore, does not prepare consolidated financial statements, it should provide, along with its individual financial statements, consolidated financial statements including the quasi-subsidiary. Those consolidated financial statements should be presented with equal prominence to the company's individual financial statements. [FRS 5 para 35]

4.110 An intermediate holding company does not have to prepare consolidated financial statements in certain situations where, for example, it is wholly-owned by another company incorporated in the EU that prepares its financial statements in accordance with the 7th Directive [see chapter 21). It might be inferred from the wording in paragraph 36 of the standard that, because such an intermediate holding company does not need to deal in its individual financial statements with its subsidiaries (other than by giving the normal disclosures concerning such investments) that it would similarly not need to deal with its quasi-subsidiaries in those financial statements. This, however, does not appear to be so, because as explained in the application note on securitisation (Application Note D), such an intermediate holding company will have to determine whether it has assets and liabilities, including those in the quasi-subsidiary, that need to be recognised in its own financial statements. There are three possible ways of dealing with the assets and liabilities of the quasi-subsidiary:

- The individual company need not recognise any of the quasi-subsidiary's assets and liabilities in its financial statements, because they can be regarded as completely derecognised by the company.

- The individual company should adopt the linked presentation in its financial statements, where the conditions for its use are met (see para 4.113).

[The next page is 4039.]

- The individual company should record its interest in the assets and liabilities of the quasi-subsidiary gross.

4.111 The accounting treatment of a quasi-subsidiary's transactions in the individual company's financial statements, the group's financial statement and in the quasi-subsidiary's financial statements is considered in more detail from paragraph 4.143.

4.112 The rules concerning exclusions of a quasi-subsidiary from consolidation work in the same way as for normal subsidiaries. Quasi-subsidiaries need not be consolidated if they are immaterial or where the quasi-subsidiary is held exclusively with a view to subsequent resale and has not been previously consolidated. Where there are severe long-term restrictions that substantially hinder the exercise of the company's rights over the assets or the management of the other entity, this indicates that the company does not have the requisite control over that other entity for it to be a quasi-subsidiary. The other exceptions from consolidation given in the Companies Act, that is disproportionate expense and undue delay and where there are significant differences between the activities of the quasi-subsidiary and the rest of the group, cannot be used under the standard to justify the non-consolidation of a quasi-subsidiary, just as they cannot be used under FRS 2 (see further chapter 21).

Linked presentation of quasi-subsidiaries

4.113 In certain circumstances, a quasi-subsidiary's assets and liabilities can be consolidated into the group's consolidated financial statements using the linked presentation. The circumstances where the linked presentation can be used are where a company (the originator) puts some of its assets into a vehicle to be financed and where the vehicle is a quasi-subsidiary and effectively 'ring-fences' the transaction. If there is no recourse whatsoever to the group's other assets and the other conditions for linked presentation (set out in para 4.89 above) are met from the group's point of view, the group may account for the quasi-subsidiary in its consolidated financial statements using the linked presentation. The noteholders in the quasi-subsidiary may well have recourse to the quasi-subsidiary's other assets and this will often preclude the use of the linked presentation in its financial statements. However, the important issue from the group's point of view is that, for it to be eligible to use the linked presentation in its consolidated financial statements, there must be no recourse to the group's assets other than those within the securitised vehicle itself.

4.114 This presentation has been designed specifically for securitisation schemes, but may also apply to other schemes. In a securitisation, assets such as mortgages or credit card receivables are in effect sold to a thinly capitalised vehicle. The vehicle raises debt finance to pay for the mortgages or receivables. This debt may come in more than one form. For example, the majority may be raised from third parties on a non-recourse basis (that is, debt is secured solely on the vehicle's assets). In addition, to provide greater security to the third parties and thereby to reduce the cost of that third party debt, the originator may lend to the vehicle, for example investing in a zero coupon bond issued by the vehicle. In this situation the originator's loan will typically be subordinated to the third party debt; thus the originator will bear the first tranche of losses. Moreover, the originator will participate in any residual profits earned by the vehicle. That is, the originator will still have the benefits and risks associated with the vehicle and as a result the vehicle will be a quasi-subsidiary of the originator. Despite its being a quasi-subsidiary, where the conditions for the linked presentation can be met by the group (that is, the quasi-subsidiary is ring-fenced from the group's point of view), it does not have an asset equal to the gross amount of the vehicle's assets, nor does it have a liability for the full amount of the finance. The vehicle is a quasi-subsidiary and, in accordance with FRS 5, additional information concerning the quasi-subsidiary has to be given in the consolidated financial statements in order to give a true and fair view. In this case, the additional information is that required by the linked presentation and not that required by full consolidation.

Subordinated debt and credit enhancement

4.115 The originator may enhance the credit rating of quasi-subsidiaries (and hence the debt that the quasi-subsidiary issues to the public) by using a number of techniques varying from participation via subordinated debt or zero coupon loans to insurance against bad debts. If the originator participates via subordinated debt or a zero coupon loan, such debt will be eliminated in the group's consolidated financial statements. This will have the effect that, where the linked presentation is used, the group will recognise in its consolidated financial statements an amount of securitised assets greater than the amount of linked finance. The resulting asset is in effect financed by the company's subordinated debt or zero coupon loan and is the amount on which the group is at risk. A participation by an originator of this nature does not preclude the use of the linked presentation in the group's consolidated financial statements.

4.116 Another form of credit enhancement that is often used is 'over-collateralisation', which basically means financing a pool of assets by a smaller amount of external debt. For example, the pool of securitised assets might be worth £1m, but loan notes of only £900,000 are issued to finance the assets. The difference of £100,000 provides a cushion against bad debts and also may cover the costs of the SPV.

Securitising in a legal subsidiary

4.117 If a similar securitisation scheme to that using a SPV is entered into, but using a legal subsidiary instead of a quasi-subsidiary, the same rationale and treatment as described above does *not* necessarily apply. This is because the entity is a legal subsidiary and is required to be consolidated in full by the Act. It will also not generally be possible in a subsidiary to link the finance with the securitised assets in a way that satisfies the standard's conditions, because the providers of the finance will often have recourse to other assets of the subsidiary (see further para 4.143). The only situation where the same result would be achieved is where the subsidiary meets the conditions for linked presentation in its own financial statements. Then on consolidation the linked presentation used by the subsidiary will be retained in the group's financial statements.

Accounting treatment in the parent's financial statements

4.118 Where a company has put some of its assets into a quasi-subsidiary under a securitisation and a linked presentation applies on consolidation, the accounting treatment adopted in that company's individual financial statements will have to be considered carefully. In contrast to a subsidiary where the parent's financial statements merely record the investment in the subsidiary, with a quasi-subsidiary three different presentations might apply (as explained in para 4.110) and it will be necessary to determine which presentation should be adopted. These presentations are considered in more detail in paragraph 4.143 onwards.

Disclosure

4.119 Where one or more quasi-subsidiaries are included in the consolidated financial statements it is necessary to disclose that fact in the financial statements and to give a summary of the financial statements of each quasi-subsidiary in the notes (quasi-subsidiaries of a similar nature may be combined). The summarised financial statements must show separately each main heading in the balance sheet, profit and loss account, statement of total recognised gains and losses and cash flow statement for which there is a material item, together with comparative figures. This disclosure seems to be too extensive and many would argue unnecessarily burdensome. An example of the type of disclosure required is shown in Table 4.5. This example is unusual in that it consolidates fixed assets and non-recourse finance held in a quasi-subsidiary using the linked presentation, whereas the linked presentation is more generally used for debt factoring arrangements (see chapter 17) or securitisations (see Table 4.9 on page 59 and Table 4.10 on page 60).

Table 4.5 – NFC plc – ANNUAL REPORT & ACCOUNTS – 1 October 1994

Accounting Policies (extract)

a **Accounting Convention (extract)**

Under FRS 5 "Reporting the Substance of Transactions" the accounts of two companies, previously accounted for as associated undertakings, are now consolidated as quasi-subsidiaries using the linked presentation provided for in FRS 5.

Group Balance Sheet (extract)

at 1 October 1994

	Note	1.10.94		2.10.93	
				As restated	
		£m	**£m**	£m	£m
Fixed assets					
Tangible assets	*12*		**587.6**		542.0
Tangible assets subject to financing arrangements	*13*	**43.5**		27.6	
Non-recourse debt		**(36.5)**		(26.6)	
			7.0		1.0
Investments	*14*		**28.5**		26.5
			623.1		569.5

Notes to the Accounts (extract)

13 Tangible fixed assets subject to financing arrangements

As noted under accounting policy *a*, under FRS 5 two companies previously accounted for as associated companies become quasi-subsidiaries. They are consolidated using a linked presentation and the comparative figures have been restated accordingly, with no effects on the prior year's profit or shareholders' funds.

The tangible assets subject to financing arrangements are revenue earning vehicles on hire to third parties. The principal quasi-subsidiary is NFC Finance 1991 (S) Limited, the shares in which are owned equally by NFC plc and Ebbgate Investments Limited, a subsidiary of Barclays PLC. The other quasi-subsidiary is NFC Contracts Limited which is a wholly-owned subsidiary of NFC Finance 1991 (S) Limited. The group has entered into interest rate cap agreements on normal commercial terms to limit the interest rate exposure of these companies.

The directors confirm that there is no obligation on any part of the group to support any losses that may be incurred, in respect of the assets being financed, in excess of the net amount shown in the balance sheet and they do not intend to support any such losses in the unlikely event that they were to be incurred. The providers of the finance have agreed in writing that they will seek repayment of principal and interest only to the extent that sufficient funds are generated by the assets being financed and they will not seek recourse in any other form.

The summarised combined accounts of the quasi-subsidiaries are as follows:

Profit and loss account	**1994 £m**	1993 £m
Turnover	**23.2**	9.8
Operating profit after management charges	**3.8**	1.2
Interest	**(3.8)**	(1.2)
Profit on ordinary activities before taxation	–	–
Taxation	–	–
Profit for the financial year	–	–

There are no recognised gains and losses other than the profit for the financial year.

	1994		1993	
Cash flow statement	**£m**	**£m**	£m	£m
Net cash inflow from operating activities		**16.7**		3.9
Interest paid		**(3.8)**		(1.2)
Net cash inflow before investing and financing		**12.9**		2.7
Investing activities				
Purchases of tangible fixed assets	**(39.5)**		(37.0)	
Disposals of tangible fixed assets	**7.5**		3.5	
Net cash outflow from investing activities	**–**	**(32.0)**		(33.5)
Net cash outflow before financing		**(19.1)**		(30.8)
Financing				
Allotment of shares	**0.5**		–	
New loans	**40.5**		37.0	
Repayment of loans	**(14.5)**		(3.0)	
Net cash inflow from financing		**26.5**		34.0
Increase in cash and cash equivalents		**7.4**		3.2

Balance sheet		**1.10.94**	2.10.93
		£m	£m
Tangible fixed assets		**43.5**	27.6
Cash at bank and in hand		**10.6**	3.2
Debtors:	Amounts due from NFC group companies	**6.8**	3.5
Creditors:	Amounts falling due within one year	**(22.4)**	(12.3)
	Amounts due to NFC group companies	**(6.5)**	(1.0)
	Other amounts falling due after more than one year	**(31.5)**	(21.0)
		0.5	–
Share capital		**0.5**	–
Reserves		**–**	–
Shareholders' funds		**0.5**	–

Application notes

4.120 FRS 5's principles have to be applied to the recognition and presentation in financial statements of all transactions although, as noted earlier, FRS 5 will tend to make a difference only to the accounting for complex transactions, including those where the substance and form differ. This section considers the transactions covered by the application notes in FRS 5. Brief descriptions are given below and in chapter 17, but reference should be made to the application notes themselves for a full appreciation of the analysis. The application notes are included within FRS 5 and cover:

A Consignment stock.
B Sale and repurchase agreements.
C Debt factoring.

D Securitised assets.
E Loan transfers.

4.120.1 An application note is being developed by the ASB to explain how FRS 5 applies to transactions undertaken under the Government's Private Finance Initiative. These issues are considered in this section together with interim guidance on the subject published by the Treasury.

[The next paragraph is 4.121.]

4.121 Each of the application notes in the standard includes a table that summarises how the FRS's principles should be applied in the analysis of the transactions. These tables are reproduced below or in chapter 17 for consignment stock and debt factoring in each of the sections that deal with the particular application notes.

Consignment stock

4.122 Arrangements where goods are supplied from a manufacturer to a dealer on a consignment basis are common in certain industries, particularly in the motor vehicle trade. Application Note A to FRS 5 shows how the principles of recognising assets and liabilities should be applied to these arrangements and these matters are fully considered in chapter 17.

Sale and repurchase agreements

4.123 The standard's Application Note B covers sale and repurchase agreements. These are arrangements where one party sells assets to another on terms that permit, or commit, it to repurchase those assets at some future date, for example, through the use of put and/or call options. Although in some sale and repurchase agreements, the initial transaction should be accounted for as a sale, equally such agreements have been developed quite widely as methods of raising finance for assets such as properties and development land banks. Sale and repurchase arrangements also cover bed and breakfast deals (see further para 4.243). The seller often remains in control of the use or disposal of the asset, because it may continue to be used in the seller's business during the period of the agreement.

Principal sources of benefits and risks

4.124 The principles involved in analysing these transactions are relatively straightforward. The objective is to determine whether the transaction's commercial effect is that of a sale or that of a secured loan. Under the standard's provisions the main features of such transactions need to be analysed and greater weight given to those aspects that are more likely to have a commercial effect in practice. The application note identifies the main features that need to be considered in this type of transaction as:

- The sale price.
- The nature of the repurchase provision.
- The repurchase price.
- Other relevant provisions (for example, the seller's continued use of the asset).

[FRS 5 App B para B2].

4.125 he principal sources of benefits and risks arising from the main features listed above are considered in detail in the application note and the principles stemming from that discussion are then summarised in a table. The summary table is reproduced below, but with the principal features added as headings; also references are included to the paragraphs of the application note that give the narrative explanation:

Indicates sale of original asset (seller may retain a different asset)	Indicates no sale of original asset (secured loan)
Sale price [App B para B].	
	Sale price does not equal market value at date of sale.
Nature of repurchase provision	
No commitment for seller to repurchase asset, for example: – call option where there is a real possibility the option will fail to be exercised. [App B para B12].	Commitment for seller to repurchase asset, for example: – put and call option with the same exercise price [App B para B12]; – either a put or a call option with no genuine commercial possibility that the option will fail to be exercised [App B para B12]; or – seller requires asset back to use in its business, or asset is in effect the only source of seller's future sales. [App B para B11].

Repurchase price [App B para B13].	
Risk of changes in asset value borne by buyer such that buyer does not receive solely a lender's return, for example: – both sale and repurchase price equal market value at date of sale/repurchase.	Risk of changes in asset value borne by seller such that buyer receives solely a lender's return, for example: – repurchase price equals sale price plus costs plus interest; – original purchase price adjusted retrospectively to pass variations in the value of the asset to the seller; – seller provides residual value guarantee to buyer or subordinated debt to protect buyer from falls in the value of the asset.
Other relevant provisions	
Nature of the asset is such that it will be used over the life of the agreement, and seller has no rights to determine its use. Seller has no rights to determine asset's development or future sale. [App B para B15].	Seller retains right to determine asset's use, development or sale, or rights to profits therefrom. [App B paras B15, B17].

4.126 Important points of guidance drawn from the application note are summarised as follows:

- It is necessary to consider all the features of the agreement (particularly the terms of options and any guarantees) that are likely to have a commercial effect in practice, in order to understand them individually and how they interact.

- Determining which party is exposed to, or protected from, a fall in the value of the assets transferred is normally central to the analysis of whether there is really a sale of an asset or whether it is in substance a refinancing.

- A transaction structured so that in practice the purchaser secures just a lender's return on the purchase price without genuine exposure to, or benefit from, changes in value of the underlying assets should be treated as a financing arrangement.

4.127 Following the analysis summarised above, the true commercial effect of a transaction is a sale if the seller genuinely relinquishes control of significant benefits and transfers the exposure to significant risks associated with the asset to the buyer. In a sale, the exposure to changes in the market value of the underlying asset will in practice be passed to the buyer.

4.128 If the repurchase price in an option to repurchase is the market value at the date of exercise, it is probable that the buyer acquires both the opportunity to benefit from any increase in the value of the asset and the risk of loss due to an adverse change in its value. In terms of FRS 5's asset recognition tests, the asset has been transferred to the buyer. If, however, the repurchase price is predetermined so that, however it is formulated, it assures the buyer of a return of the original price together with the cost of holding and financing the asset, the agreement is likely to be in substance a secured borrowing. That is because the principal benefits and risks associated with holding the asset remain with the seller. The buyer (probably a financial institution) is not taking any significantly greater risk than if it made a loan secured on the asset concerned.

4.128.1 An FRRP ruling issued in February 1997 concerned a sale and leaseback undertaken by Associated Nursing Services plc. The complex sale and leaseback arrangement involved a 25-year lease, renewable for a further 25 years, with a call option held by Associated Nursing Services plc. The FRRP's view was that the nature of the transaction was such that not all the significant rights and not all the significant exposure to the risk relating to the asset had been transferred to the purchaser. Therefore, in accordance with FRS 5, an asset should have remained on the balance sheet and the sale proceeds should have been included in borrowings. As outlined above, indicators that a substance of a sale and leaseback is a financing arrangement include an initial sale not at market value and/or an option to repurchase based on a pre-determined price (rather than market price at the date of repurchase).

[The next paragraph is 4.129.]

4.129 One aspect of the guidance that differs from that given in FRED 4 is that the application note now recognises that, in more complex situations, it may be determined that a sale and repurchase agreement is not in substance a financing transaction and that the seller only retains access to some of the benefits of the original asset. In this circumstance, the partial derecognition rules in paragraph 23 of the standard might apply (see para 4.74). [FRS 5 App B para B14]. If, for example, the buyer receives more than merely a lender's return, as other benefits and risks associated with the asset have been transferred to the buyer, the seller will *not* have retained the original asset. In this situation, the original asset should be derecognised and the analysis should determine whether another asset should be recognised in its place. For example, the seller might have an interest in the asset's residual value at the end of its life, in which case this asset and/or liability should be recognised in the seller's balance sheet.

Accounting treatment

4.130 Where the analysis of the particular sale and repurchase transaction shows that it is in substance a secured loan, the original asset should continue to be recognised and the proceeds received from the buyer should be shown as a liability (often under a separate heading), but if the amount were considered material separate disclosure might be appropriate. No profit or loss should be recognised on the transaction's sale as, in substance, no sale has been made. Interest on the liability should be accrued and the finance cost of the liability might, for example, represent the difference between the proceeds received and the repurchase price of the asset. Therefore, the liability would be built up over its life to equal the amount at which the liability will be repaid (which is, in legal form, the repurchase of the asset). The asset's value should be reviewed for diminution in value in the normal way and, if it is a depreciable asset, it should be depreciated. Sale and finance leasebacks would also be accounted for in this manner as explained in paragraphs 153 to 155 of the guidance notes to SSAP 21 (see Tables 4.6 and 4.7).

Table 4.6 – Ladbroke Group PLC – Report and Accounts – 31 December 1994

Financial review (extract)

Financial Reporting Standard 5

Under Financial Reporting Standard 5 (FRS 5), a change is required in the reporting of certain sale and leaseback transactions entered into by the group in prior years. The leases of five hotels and one property, previously accounted for as operating leases, are now included in the accounts with the properties shown as assets and the sale proceeds as borrowings in the balance sheet; rental charges are now shown as interest in the profit and loss account, calculated at the effective rate over the period of the leases. The effect of these presentational changes on the balance sheet is the recognition of £233 million of future lease rental obligations as liabilities at 31st December 1994 and an increase of £172 million in assets, with appropriate changes to the revaluation reserve and retained earnings. In the profit and loss account, operating profits for the year have been increased by £11.8 million (1993: £12.2 million), representing the amount of lease payments, and the interest charge has increased by £23.1 million (1993: £22.9 million). Comparative figures have been restated accordingly and the financial commentary in these financial statements is based upon the restated figures.

Table 4.7 – Arjo Wiggins Appleton p.l.c. – Directors' Report and Financial Statements – 31 December 1994

Notes to the financial statements (extract)

1. Change in presentation of the financial statements

Hitherto, obligations under finance leases have been included in 'Other creditors' in the balance sheet. Following the sale and lease-back arrangement explained in notes 13 and 17, the directors consider that it is more appropriate to treat all finance lease obligations as a form of borrowing and, consequently, these liabilities are now included within 'Short-term borrowings' and 'Medium-term and long-term borrowings', as appropriate, in the balance sheet, with a corresponding change in the presentation of prior year comparative figures. The related security deposit is deducted in arriving at the Group's net debt figure shown in note 26.

[The next page is 4049.]

13. Security deposit

In December, 1994, the Group entered into a sale and lease-back arrangement in relation to the No. 7 paper machine situated at Locks mill and operated by Appleton Papers. This has been accounted for as a finance lease in accordance with Statement of Standard Accounting Practice (SSAP) 21. The lease has a primary period of 28 years, but can be terminated at any time by the Group. The lease obligation recorded at 31 December, 1994 resulting from this transaction amounted to £65.8 million.

The Group was able to secure lower lease-financing costs by providing a deposit as security for the lease obligations. This deposit, which bears interest at LIBOR minus 3/16% must be maintained at a minimum of 92.5% of the obligations under the lease in order to retain the benefit of the lower finance charges. These obligations have, in addition, been guaranteed by the Company as set out in note 28.

17 Borrowings (extract)

The finance lease obligations include an amount of £65.8 million (1993: nil) in respect of the lease of the No. 7 paper machine situated at Locks mill and operated by Appleton Papers. A deposit of £62.5 million (1993: nil) by a subsidiary and a guarantee by the Company have been provided as security (see notes 13 and 28).

4.131 The notes to the financial statements should include the following information concerning all sale and repurchase transactions:

- The transaction's principal features. [FRS 5 App B para B19].

- The asset's status. [FRS 5 App B para B19].

  For example, this requirement presumably means disclosure that an asset has been legally sold to another party, but has been retained on balance sheet.

- The relationship between the asset and the liability. [FRS 5 App B para B19].

  Again, where an asset has been legally sold, but has been retained on balance sheet because the transaction is considered to be a financing arrangement, the notes should explain how the finance is connected with the asset (for example, whether it is non-recourse).

4.132 In some cases a sale and repurchase transaction might entitle the seller to repurchase certain rights associated with the asset rather than the entire the asset. In this type of situation, where the seller has derecognised an asset, but has in its place recognised another asset or liability, because it has retained some benefits or risks as explained in paragraph 4.129, it should deal with the liability on a prudent basis, following the provisions of SSAP 18. This means, for example, that where there is some remaining obligation it should be determined whether it should be provided for in accordance with SSAP 18. In addition, where there are any doubts about the amount of profit or loss that might arise from derecognising the original asset, adequate provision should be made for any expected loss. If there is an entitlement to a residual profit, that should be recognised as an asset, but in practice, it is very likely that it should be recognised at a value of nil on prudence grounds. Also, the notes to the financial statements should give the similar information to that outlined in paragraph 4.130, noting also the terms of any provisions for repurchase or any guarantees. [FRS 5 App B para B21].

Examples of required analysis

4.133 The application note provides examples of arrangements where a property developer finances its land bank by a straightforward sale and repurchase arrangement and by a similar arrangement that makes use of a special purpose vehicle.

4.134 The following example, which is not one included in the application note, illustrates the type of analysis under FRS 5 that needs to be applied to many BES arrangements.

Example

A BES scheme was set up two years ago, whereby the BES company acquired a number of properties from a property development company and raised £20m of BES finance to make the purchase. The property company sold sufficient properties (at a discount of 10% to their market value at the time of the sale) to the BES company to utilise the amount raised from shareholders. The properties were let by the BES company on assured tenancies. An independent firm of property managers was appointed to be responsible for the day to day letting and management of the properties.

After four years the BES company will start to sell the properties with a view to selling them all by shortly after the end of the fifth year. The BES company will then be put into members' voluntary liquidation and the net assets distributed in cash to investors to provide a guaranteed return. Any surpluses over the guaranteed return will also be distributed to investors. If the properties have not been sold by the distribution date at a price sufficient to provide the guaranteed return, the BES company will put the properties back to the property development company at a price that guarantees the required return to the BES company investors.

The principal benefits and risks of the transaction can be analysed as follows from the point of view of the property company:

	Off B/sheet	On B/sheet
Sale price Sold to BES company at 10% below market price.		✓
Nature of repurchase provision The company must re-acquire the properties should their value be below the amount necessary to provide the guaranteed return to the BES investors.		✓
Repurchase price Risk of fall in the asset's value is borne by the seller as it provides a residual value guarantee.		✓
Benefit in increase in asset's value accrues to investors.	✓	
Other relevant provisions Properties are not managed and are not occupied by the property development company	✓	

In determining the presentation it is not merely a matter of looking at how many ticks are in the left-hand column and how many are in the right-hand column. It is necessary to consider which of the parties bears the benefits and risks of ownership. In this example, the property development company has retained risks in the form of the residual guarantee. Whether it will be called upon to fulfil its obligation under the guarantee will depend on how the property market performs over the five years and how optimistically the guarantee price is set. Certainly over the past few years it has been difficult to determine how property prices will move and, hence, it cannot be assumed in the present market that such a guarantee will not be called.

It seems relatively clear from the analysis that the transaction's substance is that of a deferred sale (that is, the property should remain on the property development company's balance sheet until there is no further obligation under the guarantee). This is because there has been no significant change in the property development company's exposure to risks because of the existence of the guarantee. Therefore, partial derecognition cannot be justified in this case.

Furthermore, if the properties cost £80m and they were sold to the BES company at £90m being 10% less than their market value of £100m at the date of sale, then the potential profit on sale to the property company would be £10m. However, this profit cannot be recognised, because in substance no sale has taken place. Therefore, the entries in the property development company's books would be as follows:

	£m	£m
Dr Cash	90	
Cr Liabilities		90
To record the financing of the properties.		

The properties would be retained at their cost of £80m. If the guaranteed repurchase price is £120m, then the difference between the £90m and the £120m would represent a finance cost on the obligation of £90m. Hence this finance cost should be charged as interest to the profit and loss account at a constant rate on the outstanding amount of the obligation (as required by FRS 4) and credited to increase the obligation to £120m over the term of the scheme. If this line or argument is followed, then, if the guarantee is called, the obligation will be fully provided for and be settled at £120m and the properties retained at a cost of £80m until they are sold. If the guarantee is not called, the sale of the properties is in substance complete and a profit of £40m can be recognised, which is the difference between the outstanding obligation of £120m and the cost of the properties of £80m. This might seem a curious result, because in the latter situation, the finance cost is being charged to the profit and loss account over the five years and a substantial profit on sale is recognised at the end of year five. However, it can be rationalised as follows. The property company did not sell the properties in substance until year five. It received cash in advance at year one. Economically, such an advance payment earns interest, which matches the finance cost on the obligation. Moreover, the value of the properties at year five was clearly at least £120m, so it is right that a profit based on selling at that value should be recognised given that the sale occurred in substance at year five.

4.135 n illustration of the accounting treatment of a BES schemes is given in Table 4.8.

Table 4.8 – Persimmon plc – Report & Accounts – 31 December 1997

NOTES TO THE FINANCIAL STATEMENTS
for the year ended 31 December 1997 (extract)

26 Contingent liabilities (extract)
The company has guaranteed the return to investors in the companies formed under the Business Expansion Scheme and has indemnified the company's bankers who have provided guarantees of up to £40,500,000 in support of these obligations.

27 Properties in Business Expansion Scheme (BES) companies
The group sold properties into BES companies set up under BES assured tenancy schemes from 1989 to 1993.
Persimmon plc has guaranteed the return to investors in the companies formed under the BES (see note 26). Because the company has guaranteed that the BES companies will have sufficient cash resources at scheme maturity to pay the guaranteed return to investors, the proceeds received for the properties are treated as loans under BES advances on the balance sheet. The finance cost implicit in the BES arrangements, calculated by reference to the difference between the sales proceeds received and the guaranteed distribution to investors, is being charged in the profit and loss account over the appropriate term. In addition, the net rental income arising in the BES companies is recognised in the profit and loss account in the appropriate period.

Turnover does not include properties sold to BES companies until the schemes mature, the properties being held at cost on the balance sheet as BES assets until the sale is recognised.

At 31 December 1997 only two schemes now remain, all obligations under the previous schemes having been fulfilled. The maturity dates of the two remaining schemes are 5 March 1998 and 24 January 1999. The company acts on behalf of the BES companies in the sale of the properties prior to the scheme maturity date in accordance with the original scheme rules. The company has the right to exercise its option to repurchase any properties that remain unsold at maturity date in fulfilling its obligations under the guarantees.

Debt factoring

4.136 Debt factoring is considered in Application Note C and encompasses also invoice discounting. Factoring arrangements come with many different features; at their simplest they might, for example, feature a clean sale of debts at a fixed price without recourse. More complex arrangements might feature a sale of debts on terms where there is both recourse to the seller in respect of non-payment (bad debt or credit risk) and the price received for the debts varies according to the actual period the debts remain unpaid (slow payment risk). In the former case, the seller has no further interest in the debts so they can be removed from the balance sheet by crediting them with the proceeds from the factor. In the latter case, the seller clearly retains a significant economic interest in the underlying debts and the arrangement should be accounted for as a financing with the debts remaining on balance sheet. In addition, there is now a middle ground where significant benefits and risks have been transferred to the factor. In such a transaction the company might be eligible to use the linked presentation where the conditions discussed in paragraph 4.88 and 4.89 are met. Partial derecognition is *not* an option for such transactions, because they are financing arrangements. These matters are fully explored in chapter 17.

Securitised assets

4.137 Securitisation of assets is dealt with in the standard in Application Note D. It is a method, first used by originators of mortgage loans, to package assets together to sell as a block or pool to a thinly capitalised vehicle (known as a special purpose vehicle (SPV)). The SPV finances its purchase by issuing loan notes or other marketable debt instruments to outside investors that are secured solely on the assets securitised. In recent years other pools of debts, such as credit card receivables, hire purchase loans and trade debtors, have also been securitised in a similar way to mortgages (for example see the example concerning debt factoring in chapter 17).

4.138 The originator of the securitised assets may or may not hold an equity investment in the issuing vehicle. The loan notes issued by the SPV are attractive to investors because, by covering any risks associated with the scheme with some form of credit enhancement, the asset-backed debt provides a very high level of security. The credit enhancement used (covering most risks associated with the assets apart from catastrophe), varies in form from insurance for bad debts to the originator investing in a deep discounted bond or in subordinated debt, whose repayment at the end of the scheme depends on the liquidity of the SPV (see further para 4.115). Many of these schemes hinge on Standard & Poors (a US rating entity) giving the loan notes AAA rating, a higher credit rating than would be available for a debt issued by the originator. Consequently, the note holders' instrument can be given a lower rate of interest because of the debt's high security.

4.139 The SPVs are often companies that are owned by a charitable trust. The charitable purpose of the trust is normally 'obscure', as it is not generally the intention of such schemes that the charitable trust would benefit greatly from the business of its subsidiary. It is merely a convenient way of structuring the scheme. The trust exists to own legally the SPV in order to assist in 'ring-fencing' the transaction.

4.140 The commercial reasons for companies securitising their assets are varied. Securitisation is a means of both tapping alternative markets for funds at very competitive funding rates and permitting the institutions to take on more business by removing their risk exposure for regulatory purposes on substantial tranches of long-term receivables. The sums of money involved in securitisation schemes (particularly mortgage securitisations) are substantial. Consequently, the commercial impact of the accounting treatment is very significant.

4.141 Developing an acceptable accounting treatment has been difficult, because the original lender normally retains some economic interest in the gross assets transferred and also in the issuing vehicle. For example, the originator in a mortgage securitisation may continue to administer the mortgages and take the majority of the vehicle's profit, although the vehicle may be structured so that the originator does not control it.

4.142 The ASB developed the linked presentation specifically to apply to securitisation schemes where the originator retains significant benefits and risks associated with the assets securitised, but where the downside exposure to risk is capped. The linked presentation also lends itself to other complex transactions, such as factoring (see chapter 17).

4.143 Because securitisations make use of SPVs it is necessary to consider the accounting treatment in three sets of financial statements: the originator's individual financial statements; the SPV's financial statements; and the originator group's consolidated financial statements. The SPV's financial statements are probably the simplest to deal with as separate presentation of the transaction is normally appropriate. This is because the SPV often has access to all of the future benefits and risks related to the securitised assets and the noteholders usually have recourse to all of the vehicle's assets (which would include assets other than the pool of assets being securitised, such as cash balances). In the originator's individual financial statements and its group's financial statements there are three possible accounting treatments:

- Derecognition – where *no* significant benefits *or* risks are retained.

- Linked presentation – where significant benefits and/or risks are retained, but the downside exposure to loss is limited to a fixed amount and the other conditions for use of the linked presentation are met.

- Separate presentation – where significant benefits and/or risks are retained and the conditions for the linked presentation cannot be met.

Originator's financial statements

4.144 The benefits and risks associated with securitisations are considered in detail in the application note and the principles stemming from that discussion are then summarised in a table. The summary table is reproduced below, but split in two. The first section of the table below considers the analysis necessary to determine the accounting treatment in the originator's financial statements and includes references to the paragraphs of the application note that give the narrative explanation:

Indicates derecognition	**Indicates linked presentation**	**Indicates separate presentation**
Transaction price is arm's length price for an outright sale. [App D para D8].	Transaction price is not arm's length price for an outright sale.	Transaction price is not arm's length price for an outright sale.
Transfer is for a single, non-returnable fixed sum. [App D para D8].	Some non-returnable proceeds received, but originator has rights to further sums from the issuer, the amount of which depends on the performance of the securitised assets. [App D para D9].	Proceeds received are returnable, or there is a provision whereby the originator may keep the securitised asset on repayment of the loan notes or re-acquire them. [App D para D14].
There is no recourse to the originator for losses. [App D para D8].	There is either no recourse for losses, or such recourse has a fixed monetary ceiling. [App D para D10].	There is or may be full recourse to the originator for losses, for example: – originator's directors are unable or unwilling to state that it is not obliged to fund any losses; – noteholders have not agreed in writing that they will seek repayment only from funds generated by the securitised assets. [App D para D14].

4.145 In order for securitised assets to be derecognised in the originator's individual financial statements, the originator must not retain any significant benefits or risks associated with those assets. Derecognition is, therefore, only appropriate where all of the following apply:

- The transaction takes place at an arm's length price for an outright sale.

- The transaction is for a fixed amount of consideration and there is no recourse (other than to the securitised assets) either implicit or explicit.

  Warranties given in respect of the asset's condition (for example, to good title or to the completeness/correctness of the documentation relating to the asset) at the time of transfer are allowed, but warranties concerning the condition of the assets in the future, or their future performance (for example, payment or speed of payment), are not allowed.

- The originator will not benefit or suffer if the assets perform better or worse than expected.

[FRS 5 App D para D8].

4.146 Derecognition cannot be used in the originator's financial statements where the originator retains significant benefits or risks, but in such a situation the linked presentation might apply. Again, as with factoring, 'significant' is judged in relation to those benefits and risks that are likely to occur in practice and not in relation to the total possible benefits and risks. It is common in securitisation schemes for the originator to retain some benefits related to the securitised assets, for example, *via* involvement in management of the securitised assets or *via* a residual interest in the SPV. Furthermore, as explained in paragraph 4.115, the linked presentation can still be used where the originator has an interest in the SPV by way of a subordinated loan or a zero coupon loan. The important point is that the linked presentation is only appropriate where the downside exposure to risk is limited to a fixed monetary amount and where the conditions for the linked presentation are met (see para 4.88).

4.147 The linked presentation should not, however, be used where the assets that have been securitised cannot be separately identified. There must generally be no provision for the originator to repurchase the securitised assets. Where there is such a provision, but for only part of the securitised assets, the maximum payment that could result should be excluded from the amount of finance deducted from the securitised assets on the face of the balance sheet and this amount should be shown separately as a liability.

Disclosure requirements

4.148 Where the originator derecognises the securitised assets, they will no longer be recognised in the balance sheet and a profit or loss will arise on their sale, which will equal the difference between their carrying amount and the proceeds of sale. Where separate gross presentation is deemed to be necessary, no profit or loss should be recognised when the securitisation transaction is entered into, unless there is a need to reassess the carrying value of the assets securitised. The notes to the financial statements should disclose the gross amount of the assets securitised at the balance sheet date.

4.149 Where the conditions for the linked presentation are satisfied, the proceeds of the note issue should be deducted from the securitised assets on the face of the balance sheet. In addition, the following disclosures should be given:

- A description of the asset securitised. [FRS 5 App D para D22(a)].

- The amount of any income or expense recognised in the period, analysed as appropriate. [FRS 5 App D para D22(b)].

- The terms of any options for the originator to repurchase assets or to transfer additional assets to the issuer. [FRS 5 App D para D22(c)].

  Where the originator can repurchase the assets, this would invalidate the use of the linked presentation and, therefore, this would seem to make the first disclosure of this requirement redundant, because the linked presentation would be precluded.

- The terms of any interest rate swap or interest rate cap agreements between the issuer and the originator that meet the conditions set out in paragraph 4.157 below. [FRS 5 App D para D22(d)].

- A description of the priority and amount of claims on the proceeds generated by the assets, including any rights of the originator to proceeds from the assets in addition to the non-recourse amounts already received. [FRS 5 App D para D22(e)].

- The ownership of the issuer. [FRS 5 App D para D22(f)].

- A statement by the directors that the company is not obliged and does not intend to support any losses beyond the recourse to the specific assets linked under the scheme. [FRS 5 para 27(c)].

- A note explaining that the noteholders have subscribed to a prospectus or offering circular that clearly stated that the originator will not support any losses of either the issuer or the noteholders. [FRS 5 App D para D10].

4.150 The standard only allows aggregation on the face of the balance sheet and in the notes where a company enters into more than one securitisation which relates to a single type of asset. Where securitisation schemes relate to different types of asset, the balance sheet disclosures and those outlined above should not be aggregated.

Group's financial statements

4.151 The table below is taken from the table given in the application note and considers the analysis necessary to determine the accounting treatment in the group's financial statements and includes references to the paragraphs of the application note that give the narrative explanation:

Indicates derecognition	Indicates linked presentation	Indicates separate presentation
Issuer is owned by an independent third party that made a substantial capital investment, has control of the issuer, and has the benefits and risks of its net assets. [App D para D19].	Issuer is a quasi-subsidiary of the originator, but the conditions for a linked presentation are met from the point of view of the group. [App D para D20].	Issuer is a subsidiary of the originator. [App D para D17].

4.152 Where the special purpose vehicle meets the definition of a subsidiary under the Act and FRS 2, it should be consolidated in the group's financial statements in the normal way (that is, separate presentation, unless the linked presentation is possible in the subsidiary – see para 4.117). Generally, SPVs used in securitisation schemes will fall within the definition of a quasi-subsidiary given in paragraph 4.100. This will also be so even where the vehicle's financial and operating policies are predetermined as explained in paragraph 4.106.

4.153 Furthermore, it should be presumed that a vehicle, which is not a legal subsidiary, is a quasi-subsidiary where either of the following apply:

- The originator has rights to the benefits generated by the securitised assets that remain after meeting the claims of noteholders and other expenses of the issue.
- The originator has the risks inherent in those benefits. That is, where the benefits are greater or less than expected, the originator gains or suffers.

[FRS 5 App D para D18].

Disclosure requirements

4.154 Where the undertaking is a quasi-subsidiary and the conditions for the linked presentation (see para 4.88) are met at the group level, that presentation should be used in the consolidated financial statements. Where the linked presentation is used in the consolidated financial statements, then the same disclosures as outlined in paragraph 4.149 should be given. Where the conditions are not met at the group level, then the quasi-subsidiary should be accounted for in the same way as a legal subsidiary, that is, by full consolidation (see para 4.108).

4.155 An illustration of a company that has used the linked presentation for a mortgage securitisation scheme is given below in Table 4.9 and an example of a group using the linked presentation for securitising rent receivables is given in Table 4.10.

Table 4.9 – Legal & General Group plc – Annual Reports & Accounts – 31 December 1994

Consolidated Balance Sheet (extract)
on 31 December 1994

	1994 £m	1993 £m	Notes
ASSETS			
Investments	29,204	29,110	11a
Mortgage lending and related assets	416	338	11b
other assets	982	951	11c
	30,602	30,400	
Securitised mortgages and related assets	149	228	20
Non-recourse borrowings	(149)	(228)	20

Notes to Financial Statements (extract)

20. SECURITISED MORTGAGES AND RELATED ASSETS

During 1989 and 1991 Legal & General Mortgage Services Limited (LGMSL) sold £298m of mortgages, via Temple Court Originations Limited (TCO) to Temple Court Mortgages (No.1) Plc and Temple Court Mortgages (No.2) Plc (TCM 1&2). TCM2 redeemed all of its securities during 1994. These companies issued debt to purchase the mortgages, the written terms of which provide no recourse to LGMSL. Neither LGMSL nor any other member of the Group is obliged, or intends, to support any losses in respect of the sold mortgages. Mortgage payments (interest and principal) in respect of the portfolio are used to pay the capital and interest due on borrowings and other administration expenses. Any residue is payable as deferred consideration to LGMSL. During 1994 this amounted to £3.9m (1993, £5.3m) and is reported within the mortgage lending result under Other Operations. TCO and TCM1&2 are quasi subsidiaries of the Group and their summarised financial statements at 31 December, which form the basis of the linked presentation in the consolidated balance sheet are:

	Assets 1994 £m	Liabilities 1994 £m	Assets 1993 £m	Liabilities 1993 £m
Securitised mortgages	152	–	234	–
Other related assets	7	–	10	–
Non-recourse borrowings	–	(159)	–	(244)
Share capital and reserves	–	0	–	0
Amount reported by quasi subsidiaries	159	(159)	244	(244)
Mortgage backed securities purchased by LGMSL*	(10)	–	16	–
Borrowings for mortgage lending*	–	10	–	16
Amounts shown in linked presentation	149	(149)	228	(228)

The quasi subsidiaries had gross financial income and expenses of approximately £16m (1993, £22.3m). At 31 December 1994 LGMSL held as investments £10m of notes issued by TCM1.

* These investments have been included as mortgage lending and related assets and the related borrowings have been included in borrowings for financing mortgage lending.

Table 4.10 – Zeneca Group PLC – Annual Report and Accounts – 31 December 1994

Notes relating to the accounts (extract)

2 BASIS OF PRESENTATION OF FINANCIAL INFORMATION (extract)

In accordance with the provisions of FRS 5 "Reporting the Substance of Transactions", the financial statements include the securitisation of rent receivables from a property which had been effected by Stauffer Chemical Company in 1984, prior to its acquisition by the Group in 1987 (see Note 15). The net effect of these transactions was recorded in the accounts as part of the acquisition accounting in 1987. The adoption of FRS 5 also resulted in recognition of an insurance liability and its related reinsurance recovery, with separate recording in debtors and creditors.

Balance sheets (extract)

As at 31 December	*Notes*		*Group* *1994* *£m*		*Group* **1993* *£m*	*Company* *1994* *£m*	*Company* *1993* *£m*
Current assets							
Stocks	14		776		776	–	–
Debtors	15		1,396		1,483	1,765	1,483
Securitised rent receivables	15	56		58		–	–
Less: Non-recourse Secured Notes	15	(54)	2	(57)	1	–	–
Short-term investments	16		594		925	–	401
Cash	16		141		124	–	–
			2,909		3,309	1,765	1,884

15 DEBTORS (extract)

Included in debtors are amounts totalling £177m (1993 £145m) in respect of the Group's insurance subsidiaries relating to reinsurance contracts.

Rent receivables in respect of a property were securitised under an arrangement established by Stauffer Chemical Company (SCC) in 1984. The receivables were securitised under a Trust Indenture in connection with the issue of $245m of non-recourse Zero Coupon Secured Notes due 1994-2018 on behalf of SCC. SCC's interest in the receivables and its obligations under the Trust Indenture were vested in Zeneca Holdings Inc. (ZHI) by way of an assignment and assumption agreement. Neither SCC as the issuer of the notes nor ZHI as assignee of SCC's interest is obliged to support any losses of the assets pledged under the trust indenture, nor does either intend to do so. Repayment of the finance is solely secured by rent receivables from the property, payment of which is further secured by an irrecoverable letter of credit drawn on a first class bank. The net present value of these arrangements amounts to a net asset of £6m – this asset was recorded in the accounts as part of the acquisition accounting of Stauffer since 1987. Under FRS 5 this is now reported as an asset of £56m and a liability of £54m, using a linked presentation, with £4m included in cash and short-term investments. The net income recorded in the Group accounts amounted to £1m (1993 £1m). A summary of the financial statements of Stauffer Chemical Company Trust is set out below.

Stauffer Chemical Company Trust	*1994* *£m*	*1993* *£m*
Income and Expenditure account		
Surplus for the financial year	1	1
Trust distributions	(1)	–
Surplus retained for the year	–	1
Balance sheet		
Debtors	56	58
Cash and short–term investments	4	5
Total assets	60	63
Creditors	(54)	(57)
Net assets	6	6
Cash flow		
Increase in cash and cash equivalents	–	–

Interest rate swaps

4.156 Often securitisation schemes originated by banks make use of interest rate swaps between the originator and the issuer. The British Bankers Association (BBA) made representations to the ASB to deal specifically with interest rate swaps in the standard, because it was concerned that under the proposals in FRED 4 the linked presentation could not be used for many securitisations undertaken by banks. Swaps have a number of benefits in securitisation schemes as, from the point of view of the issuer, they provide a way in which noteholders can receive an interest stream in a form that accommodates their needs (for example, payment at a rate based on LIBOR, rather than a bank's mortgage rate). In addition, a swap can help the originator to manage its own interest rate position. For example, a bank might have a portfolio of mortgages on which it is receiving a fixed rate. A bank would normally hedge this interest rate exposure. Hence when it sells the mortgages to the securitisation vehicle, without further action the bank's interest rate position becomes unmatched. If the bank arranges a swap with the issuer, such that it receives a fixed rate and pays a rate based on LIBOR, the bank's interest rate position is restored. The issuer will then receive fixed rate interest on the mortgages which it will pay to the bank and receive in return a rate based on LIBOR, which will cover its liability to its noteholders. This type of arrangement provides a cost-effective way of protecting a bank's position. Therefore, in such circumstances, it can be argued that the interest rate swap does not expose the bank to additional risk.

4.157 As a result of its discussions with the BBA and others, the ASB confirmed that the conditions for the linked presentation can be regarded as being met notwithstanding the existence of an interest rate swap, provided all of the following conditions are met:

- The swap is on arm's length market-related terms and the obligations of the issuer under the swap are not subordinated to any of its obligations under the loan notes.

  The words 'arm's length market-related terms' have been used rather than just merely 'arm's length' to allow originator banks to provide the interest rate swap instrument for their own securitisation schemes. If this wording was not included, originator banks would have to look to outside third parties to provide swap instruments.

- The variable interest rates that are swapped are determined by reference to publicly quoted rates that are not under the originator's control.

  Again, this condition has been made to ensure that if an originator bank provides the interest swap it does so at arm's length prices.

- At the time of transfer of the assets to the issuer, the originator had hedged exposures relating to these assets (either individually or as part of a larger portfolio) and entering into the swap effectively restores the hedge position left open by their transfer. Thereafter, where the hedging of the originator's exposure under the swap requires continuing management, any necessary adjustments to the hedging position are made on an ongoing basis.

[FRS 5 App D para D11].

4.158 In some securitisations interest rate cap agreements have been used instead of interest swaps to achieve a similar result. The ASB has given interim relief to such agreements, so that where there is an interest rate cap agreement between the originator and the issuer, the linked presentation can also be used if the conditions in paragraph 4.157 are met and the securitisation was entered into before 22 September 1994.

Revolving assets

4.159 There have been few credit card securitisations in the UK (for the reasons explained below), but there are many examples of such schemes in the US. Because of the fluctuating nature of credit card balances, a special structure is used in the US to effect the securitisation. A trust is set up which acquires the rights to the credit card balances from the originator (usually a bank). The balances are then split in two: the first element is a fixed amount; and the second element is the balance of the credit card receivables, which fluctuates. A SPV issues loan notes to investors and finances the fixed amount of the credit card receivables, the fluctuating balance is financed by the originator as illustrated in the graph below. Some form of credit enhancement will also be used. The originator's staff normally administer the receivables.

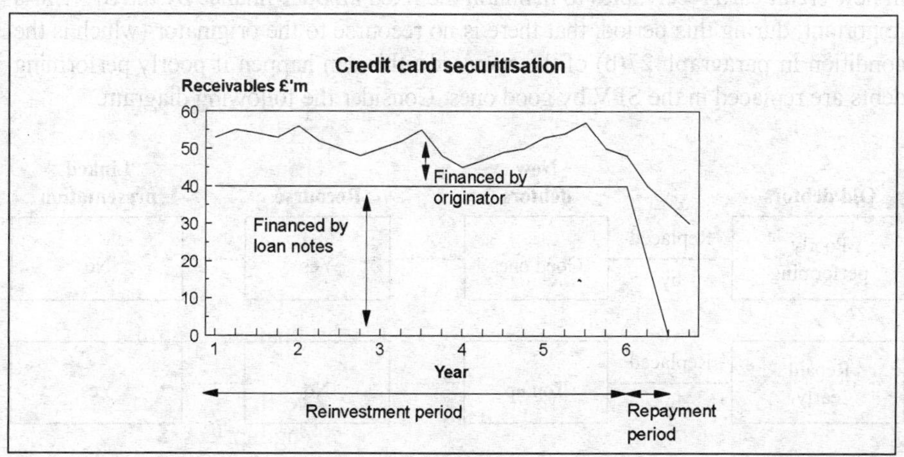

4.160 Generally, in the US, the monies collected, being the repayment of principal and interest, are applied in proportion to the outstanding fixed and fluctuating balances. The proportion of interest collected allocated to the fixed amount is used by the SPV to pay interest on its loan notes. The interest differential between that charged on the receivables and that paid on the loan notes is considerable and the excess is used to finance expenses of the SPV and its bad debts. The amount of principal collected is initially, during the reinvestment period, invested in new receivables such that the balance securitised remains constant. After a set period (typically five years) the amount of principal received stops being used to reinvest in new receivables and is instead used to repay the loan notes during the repayment period.

4.161 In the UK the requirements of FRS 5, have precluded the use of the linked presentation for US-style credit card securitisations, because it has proved difficult for companies to satisfy two of the linked presentation conditions. The two problematical conditions are: condition (b) in paragraph 27, which requires the provider of the finance to have no recourse (implicit or explicit) and the originator no obligation to repay the finance; and condition (f) in paragraph 27, which seeks to ensure that the originator has no obligation or right to re-acquire the securitised assets. These conditions need to be considered carefully.

Reinvestment period

4.162 During the reinvestment period the proceeds from old balances are reinvested in new credit card receivables to maintain the fixed amount finance by the SPV. It is important, during this period, that there is no recourse to the originator (which is the condition in paragraph 27(b) of the standard); this can happen if poorly performing debts are replaced in the SPV by good ones. Consider the following diagram:

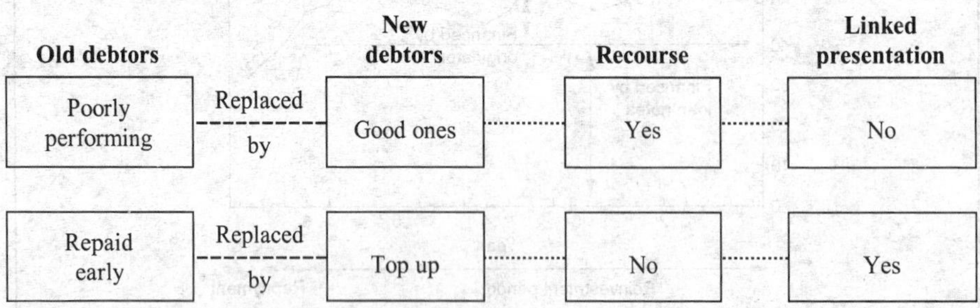

Where, in the pool of debtors securitised, old poorly performing debtors are replaced by sound ones, there is recourse as the originator in effect re-acquires some of the old debts. As a consequence, the linked presentation cannot be used. However, where the old debtors are repaid early then it is acceptable to top up the pool of debtors with new debtors and the linked presentation can be used provided the other conditions for its use are met. [FRS 5 App D para D13]. It is important, therefore, in a credit card securitisation that the SPV is allocated its share of bad debts and that these do not fall solely to the originator.

Repayment period

4.163 As mentioned above, in a credit card securitisation the loan notes are usually repaid from proceeds received during the repayment period. The monies collected during that period arise from balances existing at the beginning of the repayment period and new balances arising subsequently that continue to be financed by the originator. In the US schemes, the proceeds from the repayment of principal relating both to old and to new balances are allocated in proportion to the fixed amount and to the fluctuating balance of the receivables that arises at the beginning of the repayment period. However, in practice, this proportion will change significantly during the repayment period as the old balances financed by the SPV are repaid. For example, if the proportion of fixed to fluctuating debt is 80:20 at the beginning of the repayment period, it can soon become (say) 40:60. If the SPV is still being allocated 80% (and in some US schemes they allocate an arbitrary 99%) of the cash balances received, when it should only be receiving 40%, the effect is that the noteholders are being repaid out of proceeds of the new balances as well as the old ones that existed at the beginning of the repayment period. Therefore, because of this apportionment, the noteholders are being repaid partly out of assets belonging to the originator and only partly out of the assets they were financing at the beginning of the repayment period. As a consequence, the condition in paragraph 27(f) is not met, because the noteholders are not being repaid solely out of the cash receipts generated by the balances that existed at the start of the repayment period.

4.164 In order for conditions (b) and (f) to be satisfied, only the cash collected from the old balances can be used to repay the loan notes during the repayment period. This is necessary to ensure that the issuer is allocated its proper share of losses on those old balances so they do not fall to the originator. [FRS 5 App D para D12]. Therefore, in order for such a scheme to work in the UK it is necessary to analyse the amounts collected during the repayment period on an actual basis such that the SPV only receives its proportion based on the original balances and hence bears its share of losses arising on those balances.

4.165 The type of situation that can arise is illustrated by the following example:

Example

An originator sells the rights to a pool of £600,000 credit card receivables to a SPV, of which £400,000 is funded by noteholders and the balance £200,000 by a loan from the originator. The rights to all new receivables generated during a reinvestment period will be offered for sale to and purchased by the SPV. Increases in the balances of rights to receivables bought by the SPV are to be funded by the originator. The funding by noteholders remains constant. Initially the securitisation covers the rights to a portfolio of 400 debtors and soon after the initial securitisation a number of the card holders have increased their balances as follows:

Pool debtors	**On securitisation**	**Shortly thereafter**
	£	£
1	100	450
2	500	500
3	1,200	1,200
4	750	750
5	240	280
6 – 400	597,210	696,820
	600,000	700,000
Funded by:		
Originator	200,000	300,000
Noteholders	400,000	400,000
	600,000	700,000
Originator's interest in debtor 3 (for example)		
On securitisation		
$1{,}200 \times \frac{200{,}000}{600{,}000}$	400	
Shortly thereafter		
$1{,}200 \times \frac{300{,}000}{700{,}000}$		514

If the debtor of £1,200 went bad, then the originator would bear £400 of the loss initially, but after the increase in the pool would bear a loss of £514. The example shows that the originator is exposed to a bigger loss on the original asset, which breaches paragraphs 27(f) as it seems that in effect it has re-acquired part of its interest in the debtor of £1,200. This outcome might seem to indicate that it would not be possible under that standard to securitise credit card receivables in this way. However, it can be argued in this case, that this is purely an arithmetic result rather than a matter of principle and in reality the originator's participation will move up and down over the life of the credit card scheme and so fluctuations of this nature can be ignored. This is a pragmatic argument and one that would probably be accepted in practice. What is important is that new credit card balances introduced to the scheme in this period are only used to top up the scheme and not to replace bad debts. Furthermore, in the repayment period, where there is a desire to unwind the scheme and repay the loan notes as fast as possible, it is necessary to ensure that sufficient cash is generated from those balances that existed at the beginning of the repayment period, to make the relevant repayments to the noteholders; or that, if there is not, the relevant part of any loss falls to the noteholders.

Multi-originator programmes

4.166 In certain securitisation schemes, the SPV might serve a number of originators. Such arrangements are often structured so that the originator's benefits and risks are based on the performance of a defined pool of assets (that is, those that it has transferred to the SPV). Where this is so, and the originator is shielded from the benefits and risks on the other assets held by the SPV, the originator should include as an asset in its financial statements the pool of mortgages from which its benefits and risks arise. The related finance can be linked on the face of the balance sheet provided the conditions for that presentation are met, otherwise it should be recorded separately as a liability. [FRS 5 App D para D15].

Example of required analysis

4.167 Application note D unfortunately provides no examples of securitisation transactions to illustrate its provision. The example below illustrates the principles as they apply to a credit card securitisation:

Example

Company A owns credit card receivables that it wishes to securitise. A third party company, company B, acquires the rights from company A to the credit card receivables. Company C is a SPV owned by a charitable trust. The rights sold to company B entitle it to all present and future credit card receivables on those accounts. The legal ownership remains with company A. The transaction is illustrated in the diagram below.

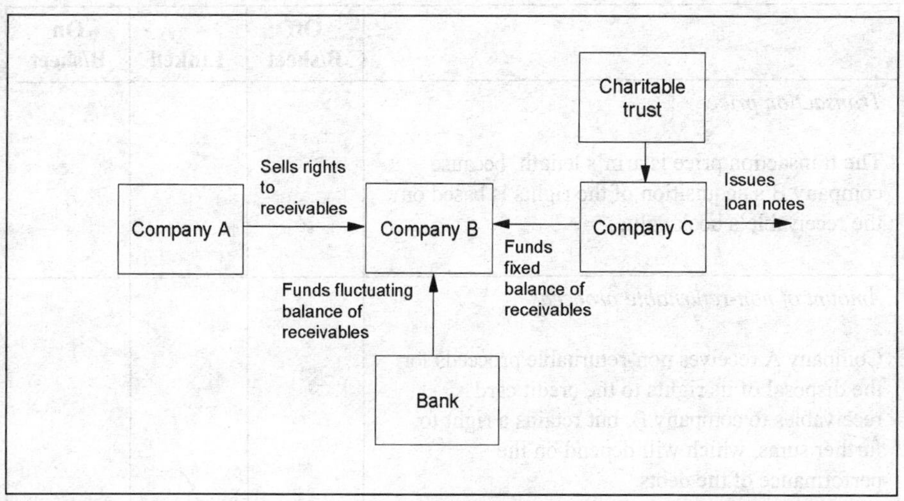

Company A services the accounts and charges company B a fee for doing so and is also entitled to a share of the profits of company B during the first five years of the scheme. The acquisition of the rights to the credit card balances by company B is funded partly by company B issuing loan notes to company C and partly by company B raising money from a third party bank. The total amount funded equals the book value of the debts whose rights are transferred. Company B's loan notes held by company C entitle company C to a share of the cash flows generated by the receivables. Company C's share is a fixed amount which does not fluctuate with the change of the amounts due on the credit card receivables. Company C funds its acquisition of the loan notes in company B by issuing loan notes to third party investors. The amount of the bank's share of the receivables varies and is the difference between company C's share and the total of the receivables.

During the scheme's first five years, repayments in respect of principal are reinvested in new credit card receivables. The level of funding provided by company C remains constant, any variations being funded by the bank. After year five the repayment period starts and company C's loan to company B is repaid from its proportionate share of the principal of the receivables collected. The bank's funding will reduce, but at a slower rate than that of company A, so that eventually the bank will fund whatever receivables are left in company B, which will continue to fall.

In analysing the transaction it is necessary to consider how the transaction should be accounted for in company A's financial statements and in company A's group consolidated financial statements. In company A's financial statements, there are three possible treatments: derecognition of the credit card receivables in their entirety; linked presentation where the conditions for its use are satisfied; and full gross presentation on the balance sheet. Using the principles of Application Note D, the benefits and risks of the transaction can be analysed as follows:

	Off B/sheet	Linked	On B/sheet
Transaction price The transaction price is arm's length, because company B's acquisition of the rights is based on the receivable's book value.	✓		
Amount of non-returnable proceeds Company A receives non-returnable proceeds for the disposal of its rights to the credit card receivables to company B, but retains a right to further sums, which will depend on the performance of the debts.		✓	
Recourse to the originator for losses There is recourse to company A for losses to the extent that there is a variation in the profits of company B that it shares in, however, the recourse is limited to that share.		✓	

The initial analysis indicates that the linked presentation might be available for this transaction, but before it can be used it is necessary to check that the conditions for its use can be met. In this regard, the condition in paragraph 27(a) is met as the finance for the transaction relates to a specific portfolio of items (the credit card receivables). The condition in paragraph 27(c) can be easily met, because this merely requires the directors of company A to confirm that they have no obligation to support losses of company B and company C in their financial statements. The provider of the finance, company B, is required in the condition in paragraph 27(d) to agree in writing (and for that agreement to be noted in the financial statements) that it will seek repayment of the finance only to the extent that sufficient funds are generated by the assets it has financed and that it will not seek recourse in any other form. The condition in paragraph 27(e) is met as long as the bank cannot regard company A as being in default on any other loans it might have from the bank if there are insufficient funds generated in company B to repay the bank's finance.

The problematical conditions with regard to credit card securitisations are those in paragraphs 27(b) and 27(f) as explained in paragraph 4.161. In typical credit card securitisations in the US, there is recourse to the originator, and the originator in effect re-acquires a proportion of bad balances, because the allocation of proceeds from the repayment of the principal might include a share of the losses on the balances that are outstanding at the beginning of the repayment period. This is because the originator generally finances the fluctuating balance of the receivables. However, in this example, the bank takes that risk and, as a consequence, there is no recourse to the originator. In conclusion, therefore, it appears that company A can present this securitisation using the linked presentation in its individual financial statements. It would show the finance provided by company B deducted from the credit card receivables on the face of its balance sheet (that is, all of it, not just that from company C's loan notes).

With regard to the presentation in the group's consolidated financial statements, it seems that company B and company C may be quasi-subsidiaries of company A. However, following the arguments above, the conditions for the linked presentation can also be justified at the group level. In the consolidated financial statements, the same presentation would be given as in company A's individual financial statements, except that the description of the finance would change and the loan from company B would be replaced by a loan from the bank and the loan notes issued to third parties.

Loan transfers

4.168 Application Note E deals with other types of loan transfers that do not involve the use of SPVs. The principles involved in analysing these transactions closely follow those applicable to securitisation schemes and factoring. The application note refers to three methods under which the benefits and risks associated with loans can be transferred to a third party:

- Novation – where with the consent of the parties a new contract is substituted for an existing one, generally, in this context, having the effect of changing the party who is the lender.

- Assignment – where rights to interest and repayment of principal (but not obligations) are transferred to a third party (assignee – sub-participant). There are two types of assignment. First, a statutory assignment which must relate to the whole loan and comply with certain conditions before it will be a valid statutory assignment. For instance, the assignment must take the form of an out and out transfer which deprives the assignor of all further interest in the loan. In addition, notice in writing must be given to the borrower and guarantors. Secondly, an equitable assignment (which may only relate to part of the loan and does not require all the legal formalities of a statutory assignment). No particular form is required to constitute a valid equitable assignment.

- Sub-participation – where the lender enters into an agreement with a third party (sub-participant) for that party to deposit an amount equal to the whole or part of the loan with the lender on a non-recourse basis. The sub-participant receives an interest in the cash flows arising on the loan, but the loan itself is not transferred. The sub-participant, therefore, assumes a risk exposure to the original borrower, because it only receives its share of the interest and principal if the borrower performs on the loan. The sub-participant is also exposed to the original lender, because the cash flows are often routed through the lender.

4.169 As with securitisation schemes, there are three possible treatments in the lender's financial statements:

- Derecognition – where the loan or part of it is removed from the balance sheet and no liability is shown in respect of the amounts received from the transferee.

- Linked presentation – where the liability in respect of the amounts received from the transferee is deducted from the amount of the loan on the face of the balance sheet.

- Separate presentation – where the loan continues to be shown as an asset and the amount received from the transferee is shown as a liability.

4.170 The benefits to the lender associated with such loan transfers remain the cash flows of interest and principal received from the borrower, although these will eventually be paid to the transferee. The risks associated with such transactions are:

- Credit risk – risk of bad debts.

- Slow payment risk.

- Interest rate risk – risk that the interest rate received from the borrower will not match the rate paid to the transferee.
- Reinvestment/early redemption risk – risk that interest earned on amounts received and reinvested by the lender, before repayment to the transferee, are lower than those payable to the transferee.
- Moral risk – risk that the lender is morally obliged to fund any losses on the loans, because of its association with them.

[FRS 5 App E para E6].

4.171 These main benefits and risks are considered in detail in the application note and the principles stemming from that discussion are then summarised in a table. The summary table is reproduced below; also included are references to the paragraphs of the application note that give the narrative explanation:

Indicates derecognition [App E para E15].	**Indicates linked presentation** [App E para E17].	**Indicates separate presentation** [App E para E18].
Transfer is for a single, non-returnable fixed sum.	Some non-returnable proceeds received, but lender has rights to further sums whose amount depends on whether or when the borrowers pay.	The proceeds received are returnable in the event of losses occurring on the loans.
There is no recourse to the lender for losses from any cause.	There is either no recourse for losses, or such recourse has a fixed monetary ceiling.	There is full recourse to the lender for losses.
Transferee is paid all amounts received from the loans (and no more), as and when received. Lender has no rights to further sums from the loans or the transferee.	Transferee is paid only out of amounts received from the loans, and lender has no right or obligation to repurchase them.	Lender is required to repay amounts received from the transferee on or before a set date, regardless of the timing or amount of payments by the borrowers.

4.172 In order for loans to be derecognised in the lender's financial statements, the lender must not retain any significant benefits *or* risks associated with the loan. Derecognition is, therefore, only appropriate where all of the following apply:

- The transaction takes place at an arm's length price for an outright sale.

- The transaction is for a fixed amount of consideration and there is no recourse (other than to the loan itself) either implicit or explicit.

  Warranties given in respect of the loan's condition (for example, that the loan is not in arrears) at the time of transfer are allowed, but warranties concerning the loan's condition in the future or its future performance (for example, the loan will not move into arrears) are not allowed.

- The lender will not benefit or suffer if the loans perform better or worse than expected.

[FRS 5 App E para E15].

4.173 Generally, whether or not the lender continues to administer the loans will be of no consequence unless, for example, its servicing fee is not priced at arm's length. This might indicate that the lender has retained significant benefits and risks.

4.174 Normally, in novation agreements all the significant benefits and risks are transferred and the loan can be derecognised (subject to any side agreements). Also in assignments, all significant benefits and risks might be transferred as long as there are no outstanding obligations (for example, to supply additional funds if the loan is restructured), no side agreements and doubts concerning intervening equitable rights can be satisfied. [FRS 5 App E para E14].

4.175 With sub-participations, derecognition might be appropriate, but only where the lender's obligation to pay amounts to the transferee eliminates its access to benefits from the loans, but extends only to those benefits. There must be no possibility that the lender could be required to pay amounts to the sub-participant, where it has not received equivalent amounts from the borrower. If the lender has an obligation to agree to rescheduling the loan without a similar undertaking by the sub-participant, derecognition is not appropriate. [FRS App E para E14].

4.176 Where derecognition is inappropriate the linked presentation may be used, but only if there is absolutely no doubt that the lender's downside exposure to loss is limited to a fixed monetary amount and the linked presentation conditions can be met. If these conditions are not met then the lender will have to adopt separate presentation.

4.177 In some loan transfers only part of the loan is transferred to the sub-participant. In this circumstance, part of the loan might be able to be derecognised or linked with the related finance, but only where the principles of the standard apply. Such arrangements are considered in detail in paragraphs E19 and E20 of Application Note D.

Disclosure requirements

4.178 Where the conditions for the linked presentation are met and that presentation is given on the face of the balance sheet, the notes to the financial statements should also disclose:

- The arrangement's main terms. [FRS 5 App E para E23].

- The gross amount of the loans transferred and outstanding at the balance sheet date. [FRS 5 App E para E23].

  This information will normally already be given on the face of the balance sheet as part of the linked presentation, unless there are any provisions against the loan to cover irrecoverability.

- Any profit or loss recognised in the period, analysed as appropriate. [FRS 5 App E para E23].

- A statement by the directors that the company is not obliged and does not intend to support any losses beyond the recourse to the specific loans linked under the scheme. [FRS 5 para 27(c)].

- A note that the sub-participant has agreed in writing that it will seek recourse to both principal and interest only to the extent that sufficient funds are generated by the specific loans it has financed. [FRS 5 para 27(d)].

4.179 Where the conditions for the linked presentation cannot be met and derecognition is not appropriate, separate presentation should be adopted and the gross loans should be shown on the face of the balance sheet (but not linked). The notes to the financial statements should also disclose the amount of the loans subject to transfer agreements that are outstanding at the balance sheet date. [FRS 5 App E para E24].

Private Finance Initiative

4.179.1 The Private Finance Initiative (PFI) was developed to allow the public sector to procure the provision of services from the private sector. Good PFI is all about giving the public sector a value for money service. If this is done in an effective way, the public sector is not buying the assets associated with delivering the service and, as a consequence, the finance needed to construct the asset is not on the public sector's balance sheet; and is excluded from the Public Sector Borrowing Requirement. The accounting issue is whether or not sufficient risks and rewards relating to the assets included within the contract are retained by the service provider to ensure that the assets are kept off the public sector's balance sheet. The most specific accounting standard that applies to PFI transactions is FRS 5, but SSAP 21 is also relevant.

4.179.2 On 10 September 1998, the ASB published a further application note 'F' to FRS 5 entitled 'Private finance initiative and similar contracts'. The application note applies for accounting periods ending on or after 10 September 1998 to all PFI and similar transactions. In addition, the HM Treasury interim guidance on accounting for PFI, which was published in September 1997 before the ASB's own guidance, formed best practice for public sector bodies and for some public sector entities for their 31 March 1998 year ends. These rules are considered further from paragraph 4.179.46. The Treasury is preparing new guidance effective from 1 January 1999 that will apply the FRS 5 application note principles in a way that will ensure consistency and cost effective compliance throughout the public sector. Until then, the existing Treasury guidance applies for expenditure scoring purposes.

4.179.3 FRS 5's objective is to ensure that the substance of an entity's transactions is reported in its financial statements. This is done by considering the risks and rewards associated with a transaction to determine whether assets and liabilities arise which need to be reflected in the entity's financial statements. For good PFI it is essential that the public sector is provided with a value for money service for which it pays a unitary amount (that is, the single payment made for both the use of the asset and any facilities management (FM) services); its constituent parts should be of no real concern to the public sector. In all PFI contracts, the unitary payment covers both the cost of the asset and the cost of the other ancillary services being provided.

4.179.4 As mentioned above, the key question in accounting for PFI is who should include on their balance sheet the assets used to fulfil the contract. In essence, the application note requires that, unless the contract contains a stand-alone lease (in which case SSAP 21 should apply), this question should be answered by looking at the extent to which each party bears variations in profits and losses. The problem is which payments and variations should be taken into account and whether the contract should be separated into different elements or regarded as a whole.

4.179.5 The main difference between the ASB's standard (set out in application note F) and the Treasury's guidance concerns which risks and variations should be taken into account in the monetary analysis. The analysis is necessary to determine whether the purchaser or the operator bears the risks and rewards of ownership of the assets used in the provision of the service. Under the ASB rules any fluctuations in the unitary payment that are caused by service failures unrelated to the asset should be excluded from the analysis. This is a significant change from the Treasury's interim guidance and might have the effect that many of the PFI schemes signed before the publication of the ASB's application note would under the new rules be judged to be on the public sector's balance sheet.

4.179.6 It is also important to note that the ASB's application note applies also to contracts that are similar to PFI transactions, such as, capital intensive outsourcing/franchising arrangements.

4.179.7 There are a number of stages that have to be considered in establishing on whose balance sheet the PFI assets will reside and these are considered in the paragraphs that follow.

Contract separability

4.179.8 In many schemes it is possible to see clearly how the unitary payment is made up because, for example, the asset element is indexed by a different factor to the ancillary service element. Where such an analysis can be made, the rules in SSAP 21 are easily applied to the asset element and an evaluation of these payments will often result in the conclusion that the transaction is a full pay-out finance lease, which should be on the public sector's balance sheet.

4.179.9 Where it is possible to see through the unitary payment and identify the element that relates to the property and the element that relates to the provision of the facilities management (FM) service, the property element should be analysed using SSAP 21 principles (as it represents a stand-alone lease) and the service element should be ignored. [FRS 5 App F paras F11, F12].The discount rate to be applied in the SSAP 21 net present value test should not be the return from the entire PFI contract, but should be estimated by reference to the rate that would be expected on a similar lease. [FRS 5 App F para F16]. The minimum lease payments to be taken into account include the expected PFI payments for the property, less any amounts for which there is a genuine possibility of non-payment. [FRS 5 App F para F17]. (See chapter 15 for further explanation concerning lease evaluation under SSAP 21.) The application note lists three examples of situations where a contract may be separable as explained in the paragraphs that follow.

4.179.10 The standard says the contract will be separable where an element of the payment stream varies according to the availability of the property and another element varies according to the usage or performance of services. [FRS 5 App F para F10(a)]. However, as explained above, the underlying intention in most PFI schemes is that individual elements of the unitary payment should not be related to the delivery of specific inputs and should not contain an element designed to cover the debt service costs of the operator with no variation for performance.

4.179.11 Another example of separability is where different parts of the contract run for different periods or can be terminated separately, which might arise where a particular service element can be terminated independently.[FRS 5 App F para F10(b)]. An example is where a property contract running for 20 years includes provision of IT services, but this element of the service can be renegotiated at the end of 10 years. However, changes to the service requirements during the contract term that result in the entire unitary payment being renegotiated would not indicate separability.

4.179.12 A further example of separability is where different parts of the contract can be renegotiated separately. This covers market testing and would apply where a service element is market tested and *some or all* of the cost increases or reductions are passed on to the purchaser in such a way that the part of the unitary payment that relates specifically to that service can be identified. [FRS 5 App F para F10(c)]. Clearly, such testing will only result in separability if the part of the payment by the purchaser that relates specifically to the market tested service can be identified. Where the purchaser is allowed to market test certain aspects of the service and the unitary payment is adjusted accordingly, this is clear evidence of separability. However, where the operator is required to market test part of the service and passes some or all of its cost savings to the purchaser, with the adjustment being made to the total unitary payment rather than to a separate service element, the contract would be judged not to be separable.

4.179.13 For other contracts where there are some non-separable service elements, the provisions of FRS 5 and application note F should be applied.

How to apply FRS 5

4.179.14 PFI is all about delivering outputs to a definable standard for the payment of a unitary amount. If the payment mechanism is effective there should be sufficient risk transfer to ensure that the asset remains off the public sector balance sheet. The key is to ensure that the unitary payment varies depending on a number of measurable deliverables. For example, if the demand for the service (demand risk) is greater or less than predicted or expected, this must reduce the unitary payment. If the service is not being performed to a high enough standard (performance risk) then this must also have an impact on the unitary payment. Similarly, if the service is not available (availability risk) this must also bite into the amount paid by the public sector purchaser. The key is in designing realistic performance and availability criteria that do have an impact in practice, but which are not related purely to services (see further para 4.179.5 above). The criteria should not be set at such a high level that they never affect the amount paid by the public sector purchaser. If the contract is truly the provision of an integrated service then it is right that it should not be paid for, or there should be a reduction in the payment, if that integrated service is not provided or it is not up to the specified standard. So, there is no reason in principle under PFI why a service provider should not be in the business of providing, for example, heat and light to definable standards or providing serviced office accommodation, subject to the demand, availability and performance criteria being set realistically.

4.179.15 From an accounting view point, FRS 5 is concerned with what actually happens in practice. So it is not sufficient just to set realistic levels of performance and availability; rather the targets must be measurable and this measurement must take place in practice. There is growing expertise in this area and very sophisticated measurement techniques are now being applied effectively.

4.179.16 The party that should recognise the asset on its balance sheet is the one that has access to the asset's benefits and exposure to its risks. In this analysis it is necessary to look at the potential variations in property profits (or losses) that each party bears. Any profit variations that relate purely to service should be ignored. For example, penalties arising from the inadequacy in the training of prison security staff or from the standard of food used in catering facilities should not be taken into account even if those penalties affect the whole of the unitary payment. [FRS 5 App F para F20].

4.179.17 After excluding variations related to service, there may still be a significant number of property factors that need to be considered. In this analysis, greater weight should be given to those factors that are more likely to have a commercial effect in practice. [FRS 5 App F para F21]. It is not appropriate to focus on one feature in isolation, rather the combined effect of all relevant factors should be considered for a range of reasonable possible scenarios. [FRS 5 App F para F49]. It is necessary to consider both the probability of any future profit variation arising from a property factor and its likely financial effect. For example, if it is cheaper to correct a problem rather than to incur a much larger penalty, the relevant variation to consider is the rectification cost. [FRS 5 App F para F21].

4.179.18 Furthermore, a financing transaction will be indicated where, in the event that the contract is terminated early, the bank financing it will be paid in full by the purchaser under all events of default. [FRS 5 App F para F50].

4.179.19 Hence it is clear from the above that to establish on whose balance sheet the assets associated with the PFI contract should lie, the analysis should focus on the variations in property profits and losses that each of the parties to the contract bear. The application note gives no guidance on how this should be done in practice, but the variations that seem to be the key in this analysis are the costs borne by the operator, as these together with a profit margin are what are passed onto the purchaser *via* the unitary payment. Consequently, it is necessary to consider how the variations in the costs of providing the property element of the service are passed onto the purchaser. Where the balance (that is, more than 50 per cent) of these risks and rewards remain with the operator, then the assets should remain as fixed assets on the operator's balance sheet. The purchaser would in this case merely record the unitary payment. Where in contrast the balance of the risks and rewards associated with the property lie with the purchaser, the purchaser would record the assets in its balance sheet (based on the fair value of the asset) and an equivalent obligation. The operator in this situation would record a receivable (similar to a finance lease receivable) representing the present value of the property element of the minimum unitary payments it would receive over the term of the contract, which should equate to the market value of the property.

4.179.20 The analysis, therefore, will concentrate on the variation in profits and losses that arise from the property related risks and rewards. These risks and rewards are considered in the paragraphs that follow.

Property factors to be considered

Demand risk

4.179.21 Demand risk is the risk that the demand for the property will be greater or less than predicted or expected. [FRS 5 App F para F24]. Where demand risk is insignificant little weight should be given to it in the analysis. Longer term contracts create greater demand risk, because of the uncertainties concerning demand in the future. Demand risk might be insignificant even, where there is uncertainty over demand for a particular type of property in the long-term, if the purchaser would fill the PFI property in preference to non-PFI properties. [FRS 5 App F para F27].

4.179.22 Demand risk is significant and borne by the *operator,* for example, where the payments between the operator and the purchaser vary proportionately to reflect usage of the property over all reasonably likely levels of demand – the purchaser will not have to pay the operator for the property to the extent it is not used. Another indication would be where the operator gains if future demand is greater than expected. [FRS 5 App F para F28].

4.179.23 It should be relatively obvious who bears the demand risk from the contract terms and how this impacts on the analysis. For example, where the operator bears the demand risk the unitary payment will vary with demand, but the operator's cost base may stay substantially the same or vary in a non-proportionate way, such that operator bears these variations in profits and losses. Where the purchaser bears demand risk, the operator's revenue is protected and the operator can pass on variations in its costs to the purchaser.

4.179.24 Certain types of PFI transaction have significantly less demand risk, for example with a prison contract or a contract for a hospital the variation in demand may not be very great. In these circumstances, the assets associated with such contracts might be judged to be on the public sector's balance sheet, unless there are significant variations in the profits and losses stemming from the property which arise from the other risks associated with the transaction, which are considered below.

Third party revenues

4.179.25 An indication that a property is an asset of the operator is if there are extensive third party revenues, which are necessary for the operator to cover its costs. Significant restrictions on third party usage might on the other hand indicate that the asset is the property of the purchaser. In addition, where there is a guarantee of the operator's property income this indicates that the asset should be on the purchaser's balance sheet. [FRS 5 App F para F32-F34].

4.179.26 Third party revenues which can be taken into the analysis are those that are expected to cover the operator's property costs and flow from features of the property. This might include, for example, income from a car park provided for hospital patients.

Who determines the nature of the property

4.179.27 If the purchaser determines the key features of how the property is to be built and how it will be operated, then this is an indication that it should be on the purchaser's balance sheet as it bears the design risk. For example, a road contract might specify that the road should revert to the purchaser in a predefined state after a short operating period. This might indicate that the operator has no discretion over the standard of road built and how it will be maintained. [FRS 5 App F paras F35-F37].

4.179.28 Although design risk is a key indicator, it is the costs flowing from the design that will impact the analysis. For example, even where the property is designed by the purchaser, if the design is faulty then this will have an impact on running costs. It will then be the party that bears these cost variations which will have an impact on the analysis. If the costs incurred through faulty design can be passed straight onto the purchaser, then the purchaser clearly has this risk. However, if no matter who specifies the design, costs associated with faulty design are borne by the operator, then this indicates that the assets should remain on the operator's balance sheet.

4.179.29 Construction risk refers to who bears the financial implications of cost and time overruns during the construction period and are generally not relevant in the analysis, because such risk has no impact during the property's operational life. But where the purchaser bears construction risk and the property is claimed to be that of the operator it is necessary to consider carefully whether the property is actually the purchaser's asset. [FRS 5 App F para F37].

4.179.30 Where, however, a delay in completing the property means that the unitary payment will not start on the expected date, this variation in the operator's revenue should be taken into account in the analysis.

Penalties for under-performance or non-availability

4.179.31 Only those penalties for under-performance or non-availability that are significant and have a reasonable possibility of occurring should be taken into the analysis. For example, significant penalties on the operator arising from lane closures for more than a minimal period in a road contract should be taken into account and are an indication that the property is an asset of the operator. [FRS 5 App F para F38, F39].

4.179.32 Clearly, where it is more cost effective for the operator to rectify a problem rather than incur a significant penalty, the cost of the rectification should come into the analysis rather than the penalty. [FRS 5 App F para F21]. This in based on the FRS 5 principle that only those matters that are likely to have an impact in practice should be taken into account.

Changes in relevant costs

4.179.33 Where significant increases in future costs are passed onto the purchaser this is an indication that the asset should be on its balance sheet. For example, this would be the case where the PFI payments vary with specific indices to reflect the operator's increased costs, but this would not be so where the payments vary with a general price index, such as the RPI. [FRS 5 App F paras F40,F41].

4.179.34 It is also necessary to determine which costs should be taken into the analysis. Clearly the costs should be those that relate to the property, but the distinction between the costs associated with the asset and those related to the service might not be obvious. The costs will include capital expenditure to be incurred in replacing the asset over the term of the contract, which would include those costs associated with the buildings, equipment and furniture and fittings. Furthermore, operating costs associated with repairing the fixed assets would also be included. As explained in paragraph 4.179.28 above, the costs associated with rectifying design faults will need to be taken into account, but other costs associated with design might also be relevant. For example, if the design of serviced accommodation specified single-glazed windows, then variations in heating costs and who bears those variations are relevant to the analysis as they stem from a feature of the property.

4.179.35 Other costs that are totally independent of the property, for example, the costs of the raw materials and consumables in a catering facility which is part of a hospital contract, should be excluded from the analysis where they relate purely to services.

Obsolescence and changes in technology

4.179.36 Where the potential for obsolescence or changes in technology are significant who bears the costs and gains any associated benefits will be an indication of who should recognise the asset. [FRS 5 App F para F42]. Although separately identified in the standard, this is just another cost variation that needs to be taken into account in the analysis together with the other cost variations mentioned above.

Contract termination and residual value risk

4.179.37 Another problem with PFI contracts is that they are generally for the long term. Primary terms of 25 to 30 years are typical. Such long periods might indicate that the arrangement is a full payout one for the asset and this is another reason why it is necessary to get the variability of the unitary payment risk transfer right. There is also a problem with what happens to the asset at the end of the term. Often the asset reverts back to the public sector for nil or a nominal sum. Some argue that the residual should not matter over such a long term, because its discounted value will be minimal. However, reversion back to the public sector for a nominal amount could equally be viewed as further evidence that the public sector is buying an asset over the contract term.

4.179.38 Residual value risk is explained in the standard as the risk that the actual residual value of the property at the end of the contract will be different from that expected. The risk is obviously more significant the shorter the contract term. Where residual value risk is significant the purchaser will bear it if it has agreed to purchase the property for a substantially fixed or nominal amount; or if the asset is transferred to a new operator selected by the purchaser for a substantially fixed or nominal amount; or if payments over the contract term are sufficiently large for the operator not to rely on an uncertain residual value. The practical effect of options for the purchaser to acquire the asset or for the operator to 'walk' from the contract need to be considered carefully. [FRS 5 para F44-F48].

4.179.39 The simple solution to ensure that residual value risk does not have a significant impact on the analysis is, where practicable, for any options, for the public sector to acquire the asset during the term of the contract or at the end of the contract, to be based on a market value payment for the asset. Alternatively, there could be arrangements whereby the public sector body can re-negotiate an extension of the service term. Sometimes, there are clauses that allow other service providers to re-compete for a subsequent term of the contract. Again it is necessary to ensure that any transfer of assets to the new service provider is made at market value in order to ensure the risks associated with assets do not reside with the public sector.

Summary of risks to consider

4.179.40 The principles stemming from the above discussion are summarised inapplication note F in a table. The summary table is reproduced below; also included are references to the paragraphs of the application note that include the narrative explanation.

Variations in profits/losses for the property, in transactions falling directly within FRS 5 rather than SSAP 21

Three principles govern the assessment of the indications set out below:

- Only variations in property profits/losses are relevant.
- The overall effect of all of the factors taken together must be considered.
- Greater weight should be given to those factors that are more likely to have a commercial effect in practice.

Indications that the property is an asset of the purchaser	**Indications that the property is an asset of the operator**
Demand risk is significant and borne by the purchaser, for example: ■ The payments between the operator and the purchaser will not reflect usage of the property so that the purchaser, will have to pay the operator for the property whether or not it is used . [App F para F28(a)]. ■ The purchaser gains where future demand is greater than expected. [App F para F28(b)].	Demand risk is significant and borne by the operator, for example: ■ The payments between the operator and the purchaser will vary proportionately to reflect usage of the property over all reasonably likely levels of demand so that the purchaser will not have to pay the operator for the property to the extent it is not used. [App F para F28(a)]. ■ The operator gains where future demand is greater than expected. [App F para F28(b)].
There is genuine scope for significant third-party use of the property but the purchaser significantly restricts such use. [App F para F33].	The property can be used, and paid for, to a significant extent by third parties and such revenues are necessary for the operator to cover its costs. [App F para F32]. The purchaser does not guarantee the operator's property income. [App F para F33].
The purchaser determines the key features of the property and how it will be operated. [App F para F35].	The operator has significant ongoing discretion over what property is to be built and how it will be replaced. [App F para F36].
Potential penalties for under-performance or non-availability of the property are either not significant or are unlikely to occur. [App F para F38].	Potential penalties for under-performance or non-availability of the property are significant and have a reasonable possibility of occurring. [App F para F39].
Relevant costs are both significant and highly uncertain and all potential material cost variations will be passed on to the purchaser. [App F para F40].	Relevant costs are both significant and highly uncertain and all potential material cost variations will be borne by the operator. [App F para F41].
Obsolescence or changes in technology are significant and the purchaser will bear the costs and any associated benefits. [App F para F43].	Obsolescence or changes in technology are significant and the operator will bear the costs and any associated benefits. [App F para F43].
Residual value risk is significant (the term of the PFI contract is materially less than the useful economic life of the property) and borne by the purchaser. [App F para F44-48].	Residual value risk is significant (the term of the PFI contract is materially less than the useful economic life of the property) and borne by the operator. [App F para F44-48].

The position of the parties to the transaction is consistent with the property being an asset of the purchaser, for example:	The position of the parties to the transaction is consistent with the property being an asset of the operator, for example:
■ The operator's debt funding is such that it implies the contract is in effect a financing arrangement. [App F para F50].	■ The operator's funding includes a significant amount of equity. [App F para F50].
■ The bank financing would be fully paid out by the purchaser if the contract is terminated under all events of default including operator default. [App F para F50].	■ The bank financing would be fully paid out by the purchaser only in the event of purchaser default or limited force majeure circumstances. [App F para F50].

Accounting treatment

4.179.41 Where the analysis indicates that the asset should be recognised by the purchaser, it should be recognised in its balance sheet when it is brought into use at its fair value and a liability recognised for an equivalent obligation. The asset should be depreciated over its useful economic life. The unitary payment should be split between a repayment of the obligation and a related finance charge (based on a property specific rate), the balance being recorded as an operating cost. [FRS 5 para F51]. There may be practical problems with this treatment where, for instance, there is a significant variation in the unitary payment due to a service related issue.

Example

Under a small PFI contract the normal monthly unitary payment is £1,000, which having been allocated splits between a finance cost of £100, a repayment of capital of £700 and the balance attributable to the provision of the integrated service of £200. During, this particular month there is a complete breakdown in the service provision, which has a significant impact on the unitary payment. Instead of £1,000, only £600 is payable for the month. The question then arises as to how to allocate the reduced payment. If £700 is treated as a capital repayment and £100 the finance cost, a credit of £200 would have to be recorded in the profit and loss account for the service element. This might be the appropriate treatment over the term of the contract if the credit represents a claw-back of the element of the unitary payment that relates to service. It will, however, in practice be necessary to determine whether or not the reduced payment has an impact on the value of the asset. It might indicate, for example, that there is an impairment and that it is necessary to provide against the asset's carrying value. If the impairment is likely to impact further unitary payments, it might be appropriate to reduce both the asset and the corresponding liability.

4.179.42 Where the asset is recognised by the purchaser, the operator will have a finance receivable similar to a finance lease receivable rather than a fixed asset. The unitary payment it receives will similarly have to be split between a repayment of capital, interest income and an element to cover service costs. The advantage of this outcome to an operator that has constructed the assets used within the contract is that it will be possible to recognise its construction profit on the effective sale of the property to the public sector body. The finance receivable being recorded at the asset's market value. The normal rules in SSAP 21 for leasing by manufacturers would apply. [SSAP 21 Guidance notes Part III C].

4.179.43 Where the analysis indicates that the asset should be recognised by the operator, the purchaser may need to recognise other assets and liabilities, particularly where it has contributed assets under the scheme. If the asset is recognised by the operator it should be capitalised and amortised in the normal way. [FRS 5 App F para F59]. But in such a situation a manufacturer operator cannot recognise its manufacturing profit and the assets must, accordingly, be recorded at their cost. The purchaser would record the unitary payment as an expense on the accruals basis.

4.179.44 Contributions by the purchaser of an existing property or other assets to the operator may result in lower payments, in which case the carrying amount of the assets should be reclassified as a prepayment and charged as an operating cost over the period of reduced payments. If the contribution does not give rise to a future benefit for the purchaser it should be expensed. [FRS 5 App F para F54].

4.179.45 If the contract specifies a sum to be paid by the purchaser on transfer of the asset at the end of the contract, then the difference between that amount and the expected fair value of the residual (estimated at the start of the contract) should be built up over the contract's life out of the unitary payment. [FRS 5 App F para F56].

Treasury guidance

4.179.46 Following the Government's review of PFI in the summer of 1997, it recommended that the Treasury should issue guidance on accounting for PFI transactions. The Private Finance Panel had been working on accounting guidance for some time and passed its work on to the ASB's Public Sector and Not-for-profit Committee with a view in due course to ASB turning it into an application note to be appended to FRS 5. As mentioned above, the ASB published its guidance in an application note to FRS 5 in September 1998. The Treasury's paper preceded the publication of the ASB's exposure draft of that application note and was published on 29 September 1997. The ASB's proposals differ from the Treasury guidance in some important respects and these are considered in paragraph 4.179.5 above. The paragraphs that follow summarise the Treasury's paper, which deals only with the accounting treatment from the perspective of the public sector body (known as the 'procurer' in the Treasury guidance and the 'purchaser' in the FRS 5 application note) prior to the publication of the application note to FRS 5. The guidance is applicable for PFI transactions accounted for by the public sector in financial years ending on 31 March 1998 and, until the Treasury issues its new guidance on how FRS 5's application note should be implemented, will continue to apply for expenditure scoring purposes. The guidance considers four key stages in analysing PFI transactions as outlined below.

Stage one

4.179.47 Stage one provides a series of tests to isolate the transaction's components to which the remainder of the guidance should be applied. If the underlying assets can be separated into those that provide services exclusively to the purchaser and those that provide services exclusively for third parties, the latter should be ignored in the analysis that follows.

4.179.48 Contracts should be considered as a whole and not broken down into separate components, unless the cost of the different elements of the service or the underlying asset can be identified and the contract is separable in substance (for example, separate elements are run for different periods or can be terminated or renegotiated without affecting the other parts of the contract).

4.179.49 If the capital cost of the underlying asset is less than 10 per cent of the NPV of the expected unitary payments, then the purchaser should not recognise the asset and any further analysis in unnecessary, unless the underlying asset is material to the purchaser. If the capital cost of the underlying asset is more than 90 per cent of the NPV of the expected unitary payments, the transaction is a lease and should be evaluated under SSAP 21 and no further analysis is necessary using these rules.

Stage two

4.179.50 Where the capital cost of the underlying asset is between 10 per cent and 90 per cent of the NPV of the expected unitary payment payments, it is necessary to consider the substance of the transaction further. In stage two, the key risks of such transactions need to be evaluated to determine the extent to which they are expected to have a commercial effect in practice. The purchaser should not recognise the underlying asset if the key risks expose the operator's equity shareholders to real commercial risk. The key risks to be assessed are as follows:

- Demand risk
  - Volume risk – the unitary payment may vary depending on the volume of the service consumed by the purchaser, in which case the commercial risk might be transferred to the operator. The analysis must take account of the extent and likelihood in practice of volume variability.
  - Third party revenue – if the service is being used by third parties to a significant extent then the operator is likely to receive variable

revenues, but this can be rebutted where, for example, the contract period varies in order to achieve a fixed total revenue.

- Availability and performance risk – some of the unitary payment may be linked to availability or performance, but to be effective these performance criteria must have an impact in practice. The more challenging the performance criteria the greater expectation that the operator's revenue will vary.
- Price risk – if the unitary payment varies in relation to an inflation index such as the RPI, then the operator bears the pricing risk that its costs will move differently, but this will not be the case where each component of the unitary payment is indexed using different bases.
- Residual value risk – if the underlying asset reverts to the purchaser at a fixed value the purchaser bears the residual risk. If the underlying asset reverts at nil consideration the purchaser has a bargain purchase, unless the residual risk is transferred to the operator by the asset being returned in a defined condition. If the purchaser has the option to acquire the underlying asset at the end of the term at market value the operator bears the risk.
- Operating cost risk – the greater the scope for variability in operating costs the more significant will be the impact on the operator's return. Uncertainty over future maintenance costs represents one of the most significant operating cost risks.
- Design risk – it is a key feature of PFI that the operator can make investment decisions concerning design and development to improve operating efficiency of the underlying assets.

4.179.51 Construction risk derives from construction cost and time overruns, which are no different from those borne by a contractor under a traditional fixed price contract and the Treasury's guidance says these should be excluded from the risk analysis.

4.179.52 The following table is included in the Treasury guidance and provides some examples of how these risks can, in practice, provide evidence of commercial risk being taken by the operator.

Risk categories	Indicates on balance sheet of the purchaser	Indicates off balance sheet for the purchaser
Demand risk – Volume – Third party revenue	The service payment does not vary with volume. There is no third party revenue to the operator.	All payments are volume related. There is significant third party revenue to the operator.
Availability and performance risk	The service payment is fixed and not subject to availability of the service or achievement of performance criteria	The service payment is entirely dependent on the availability of the service and/or the achievement of challenging performance criteria.
Pricing risk	The service payment varies with the underlying cost base.	The service payment is inflated by a pre-agreed factor, for example RPI – 1%.
Residual value risk	The underlying asset reverts to the purchaser at the end of the contract at nil consideration or a fixed value.	The underlying asset remains with the operator or the purchaser has an option to acquire the asset at market value at the end of the contract.
Operating cost risk	The operator passes back to the purchaser the impact of significant changes in its operating cost base.	The operator is responsible for all operating costs and must absorb all variations.
Design risk	The operator provides services from a design provided by the purchaser which guarantees that the underlying asset will be fit for purpose.	The operator bears full responsibility for ensuring the underlying asset is fit for purpose.

4.179.53 Once the key risks that have real commercial effect on the operator have been identified, the financial impact on the operator's equity shareholders' return needs to be evaluated numerically. This involves assessing the financial impact over a range of scenarios from best case, to most likely outcome, to worst case. Where the proportion of equity to debt is below ten per cent, it is necessary to consider the levels of commercial risk relative to the size of the project rather than the return to equity shareholders. Real commercial risk will be demonstrated where the operator's equity shareholders are exposed to the potential for significant variation in their return and some risk that their actual return will fall below the lender's return. This is illustrated in the following diagram included in the Treasury guidance.

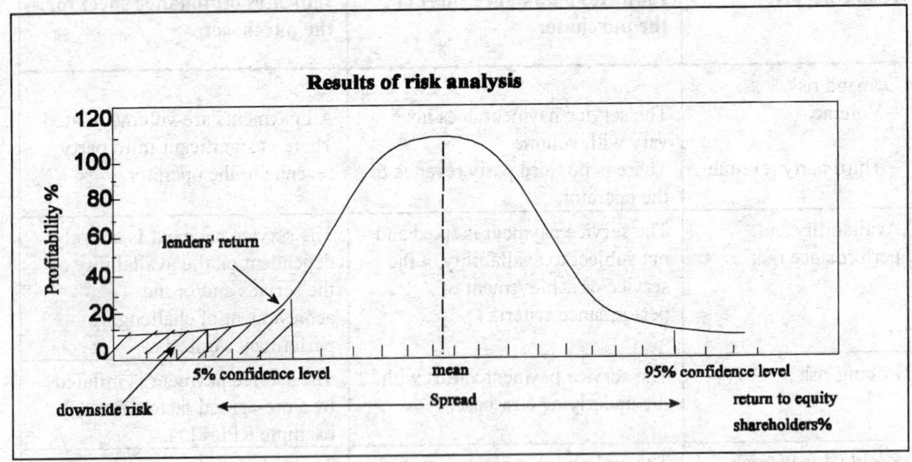

Stage three

4.179.54 To determine the transaction's substance factors such as the intentions of the parties should be considered to determine whether they are consistent with the results from the risk analysis in stage two. The type of factors to be considered are listed below together with a table taken from the Treasury guidance which includes examples that indicate whether the transaction is on or off balance sheet.

- Purchaser's intention.
- Operator's intention and substance.
- Nature of the funding.
- Control of the purchaser.
- Change control.
- Termination and events of default.

Feature	Indicates asset on balance sheet for thepurchaser	Indicates off balance sheet for the purchaser
Intention of purchaser	Purchaser is seeking alternative financing for the underlying asset.	Purchaser has no interest in managing the underlying asset.
Intention and substance of operator	The operator is a constructor whose principal interest is the construction subcontract. A shell company commissions subcontractors to manage the facilities.	The operator is recognised as a provider of similar services with a dedicated staff and management to carry out the functions and holds a separate competition to subcontract the construction element.

Nature and funding	The funding is similar to a financing arrangement. For example 95% senior debt, 5% subordinated debt and pinpoint equity.	The funding structure is not similar to a financing arrangement. For example 80% senior debt, 10% subordinated debt and 10% equity.
Control by the purchaser	The purchaser specifies the circumstances in which the underlying asset will be used, including placing restrictions on the operator making it available for third parties.	The purchaser places no restrictions on the underlying asset beyond the specification of the services (outputs) it wishes to receive
Change control	All changes to the method of operation which have a cost implication to the operator are recharged to the purchaser.	All cost implications arising from changes to the method of operation (inputs) are borne by the operator.
Termination and events of default	The bank financing and equity will be fully paid out if the contract is terminated under all events of default, including operator default.	In the event of termination of the contract, equity is only paid out under procuring entity default or limited force majeure circumstances.

Stage four

4.179.55 Stage four considers the accounting treatment following the above analysis and also the accounting treatment of any assets contributed to the transaction and any reversionary interests. The Treasury's guidance states that the decision regarding how to account for the transaction should be determined at the transaction's inception and should not be subsequently changed unless there is a fundamental change in the transaction's circumstances.

4.179.56 If on completion of stages two and three the purchaser concludes that it should recognise an underlying asset, it should treat the transaction like a finance lease.

4.179.57 The accounting treatment for up front cash payments or donation of existing assets is dependant on the existence of any rights to future benefits attaching to the contribution. For example, if a property is contributed to a transaction and this results in a lower unitary payment, the property's market value should be treated as a prepayment.

4.179.58 Where the analysis indicates that the purchaser should not recognise the underlying asset, but it retains significant residual risk in the transaction, then a different asset may be recognised by the operator representing the reversionary interest if there is sufficient evidence of its existence and it can be measured reliably.

[The next paragraph is 4.180.]

Practical issues

4.180 The implications of FRS 5's provisions are very wide; potentially they can have an effect on *any* transaction. A considerable amount of thought and work was undertaken by the ASB and others in developing the guidance concerning six complex transactions included in the application notes, that is: consignment stock; sale and repurchase agreements; debt factoring; securitised assets; loan transfers and transactions arising from PFI. These transactions are considered from paragraph 4.120. As accountants have considered the standard's implications it has become clearer what other transactions are affected by it. A number of these types of transactions are considered in the paragraphs that follow and might cause some surprises; for example, few would have thought that discounted bills of exchange would come back on balance sheet under the standard's requirements (see para 4.197). This section also considers the implications of the standard for a number of particular industries.

Partial derecognition

4.181 One of the main differences between FRS 5's provisions and those of FRED 4 is that, in certain special situations, an asset can be derecognised and in its place another asset recorded. A simple example is where a company sells an asset, but retains an interest in its residual. This might mean that the asset is derecognised and in its place is recognised another asset – its interest in the residual. This aspect of the standard allows certain transactions that would have been on balance sheet under FRED 4's provisions to be removed from the balance sheet. These rules are explained in more detail in paragraph 4.67 onwards and the example that follows illustrates how the standard's revised rules might apply in practice:

Example

Company A has a property that cost £75m whose market value is £90m. It is sold at £90m to a joint venture company which is party financed by company A and partly by company B. Company B, as a consequence, acquires some significant benefits and risks associated with the asset. The idea is that the joint venture will sell the asset in five years and that there is a sharing of risks and rewards. The likely range of outcomes as to the value in year five is (say) £70m to £120m (that is, any reduction in value below £70m is considered remote).

The agreement is that if the value in year five:

- Is above £90m, company A benefits from 60% of the excess and company B from 40%.
- Falls between £80m to £90m, company A and company B share the loss.
- Is worth less than £80m, company B will bear the loss.

Company A's position is that it gains 60% of any excess above £90m and suffers 50% of the loss in the range £80m to £90m. Company B gains 40% of the excess above £90m, bears 50%

of the loss in the range £80m to £90m and bears 100% of the loss below £80m (but a value below £70m is considered remote).

In analysing the above transaction it has to be established whether the joint venture is a quasi-subsidiary of company A, but if company A does not have the requisite control over the joint venture then it will be an associate. In the transaction some, but not all, significant benefits and risks have been transferred from company A to company B. Therefore, it appears that it is acceptable under FRS 5's rules for company A to derecognise the asset and to recognise another one in its place. However, the question then arises as to what type of asset and liability should be recognised on the balance sheet in its place. If partial

[The next page is 4075.]

derecognition is considered in isolation, then because there is sufficient uncertainty concerning the risks and rewards to company A, it can be argued that the new asset is a contingent one and that it should be prudently measured at nil. Therefore, only when profits arise in the joint venture should they be taken into account by company A. Furthermore, if subsequently the directors of company A believe that the property is worth only (say) £80m, they should make a provision for the 50% of the loss, that is £5m. But the partial derecognition rules cannot be considered in isolation in this circumstance, because the properties are held by an associate which should be equity accounted in company A's consolidated financial statements. In that case, company A will recognise, through equity accounting, its share of any subsequent profits or losses of the joint venture. Consequently, where in this type or arrangement the entity holding the assets and related finance is an associate of the group, its treatment under equity accounting arrives at the same result as required under the partial derecognition rules.

With regard to the profit to be recognised on the disposal of the properties to the joint venture, if initially the property is worth £90m on transfer, the company would recognise a profit on the disposal which represents the proportion acquired by the other party to the joint venture, that is, 50% of the total profit of £15, but less if it is thought it likely to be worth say £80m.

In conclusion, the result under FRS 5 is that, albeit certain risks and rewards are retained, the asset and liability will be taken off balance sheet, except to the extent that there is a need to make provision for subsequent diminution in value. If, however, it were company A's intention to re-acquire the asset, then the answer would be different and the standard's Application Note B (on sale and repurchase transactions) would apply. Also another factor that might have an impact on the accounting treatment would be if company A continued to occupy the property. In that situation, it would be harder to justify removing the property from the balance sheet.

4.182 It is also important to remember that partial derecognition cannot be used where the transaction is of a financing nature. For example, it cannot be used for securitisation transactions or factoring arrangements (see para 4.137 and 4.136). This is why the tables at the end of Application Notes C and D do not include columns for partial derecognition.

Trade loans

4.183 Trade loans are often given by brewers to their tied houses and in consideration for the loan the tied house will agree to take a certain quantity of beer from the brewer. Such arrangements can be financed in a variety of ways and these issues are considered further in chapter 17.

Insubstance debt defeasance

4.184 In the US, FAS 76, 'Extinguishment of debt', details two circumstances where a debt obligation can be extinguished on a company's balance sheet. The second of these is where a company irrevocably places cash or other essentially risk-free monetary assets in a trust solely for satisfying the debt and the possibility that the company concerned will be required to make further payments is remote. This is known as 'insubstance defeasance of debt'. The essence of insubstance debt defeasance is that the assets put into trust are ring-fenced such that they can only be used to repay the loan in due course. However, typically the creditor is not aware of the arrangement.

4.185 Although a debt obligation can be derecognised in such circumstances in the US, following the publication of FRS 5, it is not possible to adopt a similar treatment in the UK. This is because such arrangements do not meet FRS 5's offset rules as the company cannot insist on net settlement. In addition, it is not possible to use the linked presentation for such arrangements unless the conditions for the linked presentation are met, which is unlikely because, for one reason, the creditor will usually have recourse to the company's other assets.

Example

A company has a fixed interest sterling Eurobond in issue and has invested in fixed interest gilts to match exactly the repayment of interest and principal on the Eurobond. The company wishes to offset these two balances and considers that this should be acceptable because as the asset is a gilt, and a sterling one, there is no settlement risk attached to the transaction. In addition, there is no interest rate risk because both interest rates are fixed and matched.

Although these transactions appear to be perfectly matched, it is not possible to offset the balances under FRS 5 because the company cannot insist on net settlement. In addition, the Eurobond holders on liquidation of the company would have recourse to the company's other assets. Therefore, also the linked presentation is denied in such an arrangement. In fact it is unlikely that it would ever be possible to link a Eurobond with an asset it finances, because it would be difficult to get the Eurobond holders' consent in writing that they would seek repayment of the finance only to the extent that sufficient funds are generated by the specific assets it has financed.

Convertible bonds

4.186 The main focus of FRS 5 is, perhaps not surprisingly, directed towards specific types of off balance sheet financing. However, as its name suggests, it has applications beyond the problems of off balance sheet finance. Its objective is clear that: *"the substance of an entity's transactions is reported in its financial statements"*. One problem area that has been identified in recent years is how to recognise and present in the balance sheet certain types of hybrid capital instruments that are issued as debt, but convert into equity shares. Although the legal form of the issue is debt until conversion into equity occurs, the terms of the issue and the options surrounding conversion may lead to a different interpretation of the instrument's substance. Therefore, following FRS 5's substance arguments this might lead to the conclusion that such an instrument should be shown near or within shareholders' funds in the issuing company's balance sheet, although the contrary argument was that this treatment unduly anticipated the occurrence of an uncertain future event.

4.187 The provisions of some convertible capital bonds can be complex and they are often issued by offshore subsidiaries. The conversion process may be complicated because the bonds may first be converted into preference shares in the subsidiary. The preference shares are then exchanged for equity shares in the parent company. The bonds themselves may never be redeemed in cash, except in the case of default, because the exercise of a redemption option by the bondholders may also be effected through the conversion into preference shares in the subsidiary.

4.188 However, although the substance of such instruments is arguably nearer equity than debt, their treatment is now specified in FRS 4, 'Capital instruments'. Whatever its substance, convertible debt is now required under FRS 4 to be shown as a liability and separately stated from other liabilities on the face of the balance sheet. [FRS 4 para 25]. Therefore, the presentation adopted by certain companies in the past, whereby they recorded convertible debt below shareholders' funds (in accordance with its substance) is no longer permitted. This is because FRS 5 states that, where the substance of a transaction falls within the scope of FRS 5 and another FRS, the standard that contains the more specific provisions should be applied. In this case, the provisions of FRS 4 are more specific and are fully explained in chapter 18.

Preference shares in a subsidiary

4.189 Another capital raising technique where the concept of accounting for substance is relevant is where a subsidiary company issues preference shares to a third party. These are issued in different forms. For example, one variant is that the preference shares are subject to mandatory redemption and carry a dividend rate that is comparable with the rate of interest charged on equivalent loan finance. Again, as with convertible debt, this is an area that is covered by FRS 4, but unlike convertible debt, FRS 4 requires in certain circumstances that preference shares issued by subsidiaries to persons outside the group that are akin to debt should be treated in accordance with their substance as a loan, rather than as minority interests.

4.190 The circumstances where such a share should be accounted for in this way are where the group (taken as a whole) has an obligation to transfer economic benefits in connection with those shares. In this situation, the shares are required by FRS 4 to be accounted for in the consolidated financial statements not as minority interests, but as a liability [FRS 4 para 49]. This is one of only a few situations in FRS 4 where the substance of the transaction prevails over its legal form.

4.191 The rationale for this treatment is that the group is a single reporting entity and may have an obligation in respect of shares of certain subsidiaries held outside the group and that obligation is not abated even where the subsidiary itself has insufficient resources to meet it. For example, a member of the group might give a guarantee to pay amounts in respect of those shares such as dividends or amounts due on their redemption or another group member might undertake to purchase the shares in the event that the subsidiary issuing them fails to make the expected payments. Where this is so, the outside shareholders will look to the guarantor if the subsidiary has defaulted. Consequently, in such a situation the group as a whole is unable to avoid the transfer of economic benefits. Accordingly, FRS 4 states that it would be incorrect for the shares to be shown as part of minority interests and they should instead be shown as liabilities. This will also be the case where there is a similar guarantee and the shares are issued by a subsidiary incorporated in a country whose laws, unlike those of the UK, do not require that dividend payments or redemption amounts are financed primarily out of distributable profits. [FRS 4 para 89].

4.192 The treatment of preference shares of a subsidiary issued to persons outside the group is considered in more detail in chapter 18.

[The next paragraph is 4.197.]

Bills of exchange

4.197 Even with a relatively simple transaction such as a bill of exchange the accounting treatment following FRS 5 changed and this issue is discussed in chapter 17.

ESOPs

4.198 Employee share ownership plans (ESOPs) are designed to assist employees to purchase shares in their employing company. The structures of ESOPs vary, but typically they are arrangements whereby a trust is set up by a sponsoring company to acquire shares in that company for the benefit of its employees, who generally acquire them at a later stage through share option schemes, profit sharing arrangements or other share incentive schemes. The commercial reasons for establishing an ESOP include the following:

- It allows a share scheme to be extended to new participants without diluting existing shareholders' interests, because it can operate by acquiring and distributing shares that are already in issue rather than by requiring new shares to be issued.

- It can provide a private company with a market in its shares in order to operate an employee share scheme, by buying shares from departing employees and other shareholders, warehousing them and then distributing them to new and continuing employees.

- It can facilitate employee participation in connection with a management buyout, privatisation or flotation of a private company.

- A company can hedge its obligations in respect of options issued under executive share option schemes by avoiding exposure to the cost of increases in the market value of shares between the dates of granting the options and the dates of exercising those options.

ESOPs have to comply with a number of regulations including those of the Act, the Financial Services Act and, where the company is listed, the Stock Exchange.

4.199 The vehicle used to hold the shares in an ESOP is a discretionary employee benefit trust set up by the sponsoring company for the benefit of all, or most, of its employees. For capital gains tax purposes, the trustee will normally be resident outside the UK and, for FSA reasons, a subsidiary of the company will often act as a corporate trustee. The trust buys shares with funds provided by way of cash or loans from the company or by a loan from a third party (which will be guaranteed by the company). The shares held by the trust are typically distributed to employees through an employee share scheme. The trust's beneficiaries can only include the company's or group's employees or former employees and certain of their close relations. Generally the sponsoring company will have no beneficial interest in the trust's residual assets.

4.200 The detailed structures of individual ESOPs are many and varied. However, the main features are often as follows:

- The trust provides a warehouse for the sponsoring company's shares, for example, by acquiring and holding shares that are to be sold or transferred to employees in the future. The trust will normally purchase the shares with finance provided by the sponsoring company (by way of cash contributions or loans), or by a third party bank loan, or by a combination of the two. Loans from the company are usually interest free.

- Where the trust borrows from a third party, the sponsoring company will often guarantee the loan, that is, it will be responsible for any shortfall if the trust's assets are insufficient to meet its debt repayment obligations. The company will also generally make regular contributions to the trust to enable the trust to meet its interest payments (that is, to make good the shortfall between the dividend income of the trust and the interest payable). As part of this arrangement, the trustees sometimes waive their right to dividends on the shares the trust holds.

[The next page is 4081.]

- Shares held by the trust are distributed to employees through an employee share scheme. There are many different arrangements, which include: the purchase of shares by employees when exercising their share options under an executive share option scheme; the purchase of shares by the trustees of an approved profit sharing scheme for allocation to employees under the scheme's rules; or the transfer of shares to employees under an incentive scheme.

An example of structure of an ESOP trust is given in Table 4.11.

Table 4.11 – SmithKline Beecham plc – Annual Report and Accounts – 31 December 1994

NOTES TO THE FINANCIAL STATEMENTS (extract)

33 SHARE OPTION PLANS (extract)

Employee Share Ownership Trust.

An Employee Share Ownership Trust (ESOT) was established on 9 March 1992. The ESOT has purchased the Company's A Shares in the open market, which are held on trust for employees participating in the 1991 share option plan. The ESOT has purchased 15.7 million A Shares at a cost of £86 million. The ESOT has borrowed £83 million from third party banks which is guaranteed by the Company and the Company has also lent £3 million to the ESOT. The Company gifts payments to the ESOT to pay the interest on the loans. These payments to third parties amounted to £4.7 million (1993 £1.5 million) and the Company also incurred further interest charges of £3.4 million in 1993. The ESOT has waived its rights to dividends. The external borrowings of the ESOT are now included on the balance sheet (see accounting policies page 48).

4.201 n the sponsoring company's individual financial statements, there are two possible accounting treatments for ESOPs:

- Show the shares held by the trust as an asset of the company (as an investment in own shares) in place of any loan from the company to the trust and to show any debt issued by the trust to third parties as a liability of the company. That is, treating the trust as on balance sheet.

- To show any amount owed from the trust as an asset of the company (that is, as a loan to the trust). Any borrowings by the trust from third parties that are guaranteed by the company would be disclosed and accounted for as contingent liabilities in accordance with SSAP 18. Hence, the assets held by the trust are treated as off balance sheet.

4.202 As there has been varying treatment of ESOPs in companies' financial statements with some companies bringing them fully on balance sheet and others keeping them off, the issue was taken up by the UITF. UITF Abstract 13, 'Employee share ownership plans' was published in June 1995 to deal with this issue and applies to accounting periods ending on or after 22 June 1995, but earlier adoption is encouraged. [UITF 13 para 10].

4.203 The UITF pointed out that although the trustees of an ESOP trust must act under the trust at all times in accordance with the beneficiaries' interests, most ESOP trusts (particularly those set up to remunerate employees) are specifically designed to serve the sponsoring company's purposes and to ensure that there will be minimal risk of any conflict arising between the trustees' duties and the company's interest. Where this type of arrangement exists, the UITF considers that the sponsoring company has *de facto* control of the ESOP and, as a consequence, certain of the ESOP's assets and liabilities should be brought back onto the sponsoring company's balance sheet to accord with the transaction's substance. This is on the basis that, for all practical purposes, the sponsoring company is in the same position as if it had purchased the shares directly and, therefore, should account for them in a similar way.

Analysing the risks and rewards

4.204 In the type of arrangement described above, the sponsoring company generally bears the risks and obtains many of the benefits of the shares until they vest unconditionally with the employees (for example, by gift or by the exercise of options). Where the ESOP has unallocated shares, the benefit of increases in value are said to accrue to the sponsoring company because, for example, the company can pass increased benefits to its employees without using the company's other resources. The company's risk is that the shares will fall in value and that, as a consequence, it will have to use the company's other resources to make good the benefits given to its employees. [UITF 13 app 1].

4.205 If the shares are under option, the employees' asset is the options rather than the shares themselves and the risks associated with any fall in value below the option price remains with the sponsoring company. [UITF 13 app 1].

4.206 When shares are conditionally gifted to the employees, they do not cease to be the sponsoring company's assets, because the benefits and risks associated with the shares remain with the sponsoring company until the conditions are fulfilled. [UITF 13 app 1]. However in this case, it is likely that a provision against the shares will be required (see para 4.210 below).

4.207 In many ESOPs, dividends on the shares held by the trust are waived until they vest with employees. In other trusts dividends continue to be paid and these will accrue to the trust thereby benefiting the sponsoring company by either defraying the trust's costs or by reducing the cost of future employee incentive arrangements, which are ultimately borne by the sponsoring company. [UITF 13 app 1].

4.208 The Abstract argues out that the substance of an ESOP trust is different from that of a pension scheme as pension schemes have longer time-frames and are wider in scope with the result that the obligations imposed by trust law and statute have a much greater commercial effect in practice. [UITF 13 app 1]. Furthermore, FRS 5 states that for pension obligations SSAP 24 contains the more specific accounting provisions. SSAP 24 does not require consolidation by a sponsoring company of its pension fund and for the purposes of FRS 5 such funds should not be regarded as quasi-subsidiaries. [FRS 5 para 44].

UITF consensus

4.209 The consensus reached in UITF Abstract 13 is that FRS 5's principles require an ESOP trust's sponsoring company to recognise certain of the trust's assets and liabilities as its own where the sponsoring company has *de facto* control of the shares held by the ESOP trust and reaps their benefits or bears their risks. This will generally be the case where the trust is established to hold shares for an employee remuneration scheme. Where this type of trust exists, the shares held by the ESOP trust should be recognised as the sponsoring company's assets until they vest unconditionally with the employees. [UITF 13 para 8(a)]. The sponsoring company should also recognise as its own liability any of the ESOP trust's borrowings that it formally, or informally, guarantees. [UITF 13 para 8(e)].

4.210 Where the shares are to be recognised by the sponsoring company in its financial statements, they should be classified as 'own shares'. [UITF 13 para 8(b)]. The balance sheet formats set out in Schedule 4 to the Act include sub-headings for 'own shares' in both fixed and current assets. The Abstract requires that where the shares are held for the continuing benefit of the sponsoring company's business they should be classified as fixed assets; otherwise they should be classified as current assets. [UITF 13 para 8(b)]. It is difficult to envisage when such shares would not be held for the continuing benefit of the sponsoring company, consequently, we believe that generally such shares will be classified as fixed assets. The shares should be carried at cost (unless the alternative accounting rules are applied) less, where necessary, provisions for any permanent diminution in the shares' value, which should be recognised through the profit and loss account immediately such a diminution arises.

4.211 When the ESOP shares have been gifted unconditionally to the company's employees, they should no longer be recognised as the sponsoring company's assets, even where they are still held by the trust. [UITF 13 para 8(a)]. On the other hand, where the shares are conditionally gifted or put under option to employees at below their book value the difference between the shares' book value and their residual value should be charged to the profit and loss account as an operating (normally a staff) cost. This charge should be spread over the employees' period of service in respect of which the gifts or options have been granted. [UITF 13 para 8(d)]. This means writing down the shares to their residual value (nil where they have been gifted or to the option price where they are under option) over a period ending on the earlier of:

- the end of the employee's period of service to which the gift or discount relates; or
- the first date the gift becomes unconditional or the option can be exercised.

[UITF 13 para 6(b)].

4.212 Finance costs and administrative expenses should be charged as they become due and not as funding payments are made to the ESOP trust. [UITF 13 para 8(f)]. Interest costs incurred on external funding should be shown as interest paid in the company's financial statements and not as staff costs.

4.213 Any dividend income arising on shares held by the ESOP trust and included in the balance sheet of the sponsor should be excluded in arriving at profit before tax and deducted from the aggregate of dividends paid and proposed. The deduction should be disclosed on the face of the profit and loss account if material, or in a note. Until such time as the shares vest unconditionally in employees, the shares should also be excluded from earnings per share calculation under FRS 14. [UITF Abstract13 paras 7, 8(g) as amended by FRS 14]. (The calculation of earnings per share is considered in detail in chapter 8.)

4.213.1 A more recent development is the increasing use of share awards where shares are awarded to employees at nominal value or at nil cost (for instance, where an ESOP subscribes for shares at nominal value). There was concern that this would enable a company to avoid a charge in its profit and loss account. The UITF has addressed this issue with the publication of UITF Abstract 17, 'Employee share schemes' in May 1997. This abstract requires a charge in the profit and loss account based on the fair value of the shares at the date an award is granted. If the award is in the form of share options then UITF Abstract 17 requires that the intrinsic value of share options granted (that is, any difference between the exercise price and the market value at date of grant) should, as a minimum, be charged to the profit and loss account on a basis similar to that required for other share awards. [UITF 17 para 15]. This is covered in chapter 10.

[The next paragraph is 4.214].

Disclosure requirements

4.214 The Abstract requires the following information to be disclosed concerning the ESOP trust:

- A description of the ESOP trust's main features, including the arrangements for distributing the shares.

- The manner in which the costs are dealt with in the profit and loss account.

- The number and market value of shares held by the ESOP trust and whether dividends on those shares have been waived.

- The extent to which the shares are under option to employees or have been conditionally gifted to them.

[UITF 13 para 9].

[The next page is 4085.]

4.215 The object of the disclosures in paragraph 4.214 is to enable the readers of the financial statements to understand the significance of the ESOP trust in the context of the sponsoring company. Where this is not achieved by disclosing the above information, the sponsoring company should give additional information to achieve this objective. [UITF 13 para 9].

Benefit to employees

4.216 Apart from the disclosure required by UITF Abstract 13 set out above, it is also important to consider what additional disclosure is required in particular for directors, but also for employees. The benefit that employees derive from such a scheme should be included in staff costs. With regard to directors the disclosure is more complex and is influenced by the Act, UITF Abstract 10, 'Disclosure of directors' share options', and the Greenbury Code. These matters are fully considered in chapter 11.

Illustrative examples

4.217 The examples that follow illustrate the Abstract's principles and include the examples reproduced in appendix II to the Abstract.

Example 1

The ESOP trust holds unallocated shares costing £100,000, funded by a bank loan. The sponsoring company undertakes to make contributions to the trust whenever the loan-to-value ratio falls below a set figure. At the reporting date the market value is at least £100,000 and the shares are held for the sponsoring company's continuing benefit.

The company should record the shares in fixed assets at a cost of £100,000. The loan is effectively guaranteed by the company and should also be recorded on its own balance sheet. Interest expense should be accrued in the usual way.

Example 2

The facts are the same as in example 1, except that the market value of the shares falls to £80,000 by the company's year end.

Provision should be made if, and to the extent that, the diminution in value is considered to be permanent. All the facts and circumstances will need to be considered.

Example 3

The facts are the same as in example 1, but options are granted over the shares at £80,000 (the market value is at least £100,000).

The shares should be written down to their residual value of £80,000. The resulting charge of £20,000 should be recognised immediately in the profit and loss account if it is considered to relate to past service of the employees or over the relevant period of future service, if that is considered more appropriate.

Example 4

The facts are the same as in example 3, except subsequent to granting the options the market value of the shares falls to £50,000 and the diminution in value is considered to be permanent.

The shares should be written down to £50,000 with the provision taken directly to the profit and loss account. If the expense that arose on granting the options was being amortised, the unamortised balance should now be written off.

Example 5

An annual profit share of £100,000 is paid to a profit-sharing share trust in order that it may buy and hold shares for specified employees for a tax efficient period. Dividends are passed through to the employees.

If the shares have vested unconditionally in the employees, there is no asset to record since the shares are in substance those of the employees. Nor is there a liability since the purchase has been fully funded by the company (and should be charged in the year to which the profit share relates). This is likely to be so even if some or all of the dividends are retained by the trust to cover administrative costs, since the main risk (that is, price risk) has been transferred. If the entitlement lapses in the event that the employees do not remain with the company for a specified period, the shares do not yet belong to the employees, but the residual value of the shares should be taken as nil.

Example 6

The facts are the same as in example 5 above, except that the shares do not vest in the employees until the earlier of a period of three years or the date on which they leave the company.

The shares do not vest unconditionally with the employees until the three-year period expires or the employees leave the company's employment. Therefore, the shares do not yet belong to the employees, but the residual value of the shares should be taken as nil. The resulting charge should be recognised immediately rather than being spread over the period to vesting, since the bonus is a share of profit for the year and allocations under a profit-sharing scheme generally happen periodically; an employee who receives an allocation in one year will often expect to receive a further allocation in the next.

Example 7

The facts are the same as in example 6 above, except that in addition to the shares given in lieu of a cash bonus, if the employee stays for the period of three years he is given an equivalent amount of additional shares. These additional shares are bought and given to the trust in the current year.

The additional shares do not vest unconditionally with the employees until the three-year period expires and if they leave the company they lose this additional entitlement. Again as in example 6 above, the additional shares do not yet belong to the employees and their residual value should be taken as nil. The resulting charge should probably be recognised immediately since the additional bonus shares can be said to relate to the employees' profit sharing scheme and as such should be charged in the profit and loss account in the current year.

Example 8

The facts are the same as in example 7 above, except that as part of the bonus scheme the company also gives its employees an additional loyalty bonus in the form of further shares. The number of shares allocated to each employee depends upon the company's performance over the subsequent three years and are given to the employees at the end of year three.

These further shares do not vest unconditionally with the employees until the three-year period has expired and similarly if they leave the company's employment they lose their entitlement. As in example 6 and 7, the residual value of the shares is nil, but unlike those two examples this further entitlement should be spread over the period of the entitlement, as it does not relate specifically to any one year and awards depend on future performance. Therefore, the company would record these further shares initially as an asset and amortise this amount over the three year period until they vest unconditionally with employees.

Example 9

In connection with a flotation it is considered desirable to 'lock in' key employees for a number of years. On flotation, the ESOP trust purchases or subscribes for shares worth £100,000, funded by a gift from the company. The shares are allocated to the specific employees, but the entitlements will not vest unless they remain with the company for three years.

As in example 5 above, the residual value of the shares should be taken as nil. However, in this case the transaction is a one-off designed to secure the benefit of the employees' service for the next three years. Accordingly, the expense should be recognised over that period.

Example 10

A company is a co-operative, owned by its employees. All of its shares are held in a trust for the employees' benefit collectively and the trust receives dividends from the company which are distributed to employees in accordance with the trust deed's provisions. The shares never vest in individual employees. The company does not have *de facto* control of the trust's shares.

The trust's shares are not assets of the company since it neither controls them nor bears their benefits or risks. The company should not record them in its balance sheet.

Example 11

The facts are the same as in example 5, except that the dividends are waived by the ESOP trust and the shares vest with employees three months after the year end.

As in example 5, there is no asset to record, because the shares have a nil residual value and as a consequence their cost to the company should be written off to the profit and loss account in the current period. A strict reading of the Abstract would then require the company to exclude these shares from the earnings per share figure, because the dividends on them have been waived. This would have the effect of boosting earnings per share. We consider that where an ESOP holds the shares for such a short period of time, they should not be excluded from the earnings per share calculation even where dividends for the period they are retained by the trust are waived (see further chapter 8). In the majority of situations, such an adjustment is likely to be immaterial anyway.

4.218 Table 4.12 below illustrates a company which has provided fully against the shares held by its ESOP trust.

Table 4.12 – Tiphook plc – Annual Report and Accounts – 30 April 1994

Notes to the Financial Statements

14 EMPLOYEE BENEFITS (extract)

b) The Employee Share Ownership Plan

In December 1990 the Company established the Tiphook plc Employee Share Ownership Plan Trust (the "ESOP"). The trustee of the ESOP is Barclays Private Bank Trust (Isle of Man) Limited (the "Trustee") which is an independent professional trust company resident in the Isle of Man. The ESOP is a discretionary trust for the benefit of employees (including Directors and officers) and former employees of the Group. The ESOP provides for the issue of options and the payment of bonuses to the Group's employees (including Executive Directors and Officers) at the discretion of the Trustee acting upon the recommendation of a committee of one executive and two non-executive Directors.

The assets, liabilities, income and costs of the ESOP are incorporated into the financial statements.

At 30 April 1994 the Trustee owned 5,970,489 Ordinary shares which represented 5.39% of the issued share capital of the Company. In light of the fall in the price of the Company's shares during the year and the current financial pressures, the Board has reconsidered the value at which the ESOP's investment in the Company's shares should be stated in the balance sheet. In arriving at its view the Board has taken account, inter alia, of the inherent uncertainty as to the future prospects of the Company and the potential volatility of the ESOP investment and has concluded that it is prudent to write this investment down to £nil. See note 2(v).

Funding for the share purchases by the ESOP was originally provided by a bank loan of £25.0 million. During the year the ESOP has repaid £26.1 million of capital and rolled up interest (£22.4 million prior to the half year). The loan has been refinanced over an extended period to August 1998, is guaranteed by the Company and secured on shares owned by the ESOP except for shares in respect of which options have been granted prior to 2 August 1993. Interest in the loan is paid quarterly by the ESOP and funded by the Company as necessary. At 30 April 1994 the principal amount of the loan was £3.6 million (1993: £29.1 million).

The total ESOP costs charged to the Profit and Loss Account for the year ended 30 April 1994 were £21.6 million (1993: £2.0 million) of which the exceptional writedown in the value of the ESOP's investment in the shares of the Company was £21.4 million (1993: £nil) and the net interest expense was £0.2 million (1993: £2.0 million).

16 INVESTMENTS (extract)

	ESOP Investment in the Ordinary Shares £m	Listed Investments £m	Unlisted Investments £m	Total £m
Fixed asset investments				
At 1 May 1993	16.6	4.1	4.3	25.0
Additions	0.8	0.1	–	0.9
Disposals	–	(4.2)	–	(4.2)
Provisions (see note 2(v) and 2(x))	(17.4)	–	(4.3)	(21.7)
	–	–	–	–
Current asset investments				
At 1 May 1993	4.0	–	–	4.0
Provisions (see note 2(v))	(4.0)	–	–	(4.0)
	–	–	–	–

The market value of the investment of the Tiphook plc Employee Share Ownership Plan in the Ordinary shares at 30 April 1994 was £1.9 million (1993: £13.0 million). Following the fall in the price of the Company's shares and the current financial circumstances and remaining uncertainties, the Board has concluded that it is prudent to write this investment down to £nil.

The Company holds 10% of the ordinary shares of Thos. Storey (Engineers) Limited, an unlisted company registered in England and Wales, and an investment in all of its preference shares of £2.5 million. The Directors have carefully considered the carrying value of this investment and for the sake of prudence have decided to provide in full (see note 2(x)).

Repurchase agreements – Repos

4.219 Repo agreements are transactions involving the sale of a security with a simultaneous agreement to repurchase the same or a substantially identical security at a specified future date. The main accounting issue, therefore, is whether the repo should be accounted for as a sale or a financing transaction. Whilst a repo transfers legal title to the securities from the seller to the buyer, the accounting treatment depends on whether the risks and rewards of ownership have in substance been transferred.

4.220 Such transactions clearly fall within the scope of FRS 5's Application Note B (see para 4.123). They are also dealt with in the BBA SORP, 'Securities' and the treatment required by the SORP is consistent with the requirements of FRS 5, which in effect has superseded the SORP in this respect. The standard's application note states that in a straightforward situation, the substance of a sale and repurchase agreement will be that of a secured loan. It goes on to say that the seller in such a transaction should account for the arrangement by showing the original asset on its balance sheet together with a liability for the amounts received from the buyer. Some repo transactions are complex and the guidance in the application note is useful in determining whether the instrument's buyer is merely receiving a lender's return. If it is, then, in substance, no sale has been made and the asset and related finance should be retained on the seller's balance sheet.

4.221 Even in repo transactions where different securities are returned to the seller, if they are substantially similar, such that the risks and rewards are unchanged, the substance of the transaction will still be that of a financing. Therefore, generally the securities subject to a repo should be retained on the seller's balance sheet and valued in accordance with the company's normal accounting policy for its legally owned securities (which would normally be market value). The cash advanced by the buyer would be recorded as a liability and termed, for example, 'securities sold under agreements to repurchase'. Where material the liability should be disclosed separately on the face of the balance sheet. The interest expense (in whatever legal form) should then be charged to the profit and loss account over the life of the agreement.

4.222 From the buyer's point of view, in substance it has not bought an asset, therefore, it will not record the security in its balance sheet or recognise any profits or losses arising from changes in its market value. The cash it has advanced to the seller should be shown as an asset and termed, for example, 'securities purchased under agreements to resell'. The interest income (in whatever legal form) should be accrued over the life of the instrument. The notes to the financial statements and accounting policies of both the seller and the buyer would have to explain the treatment they have adopted.

4.223 It is also necessary to consider the accounting treatment of any additional collateral that passes between the seller and the buyer as a result of changes in the market value of the securities underlying the repo. Collateral takes one of two forms: cash or securities. To the extent that cash collateral is used, this should be treated as a separate asset or liability unless the relevant conditions for offset can be met (see para 4.98) in which case it should be offset against the amount of the repo. If additional securities are used, then these should be treated consistently with those of the original repo.

4.224 For some more complex repo arrangements it is possible that the criteria for derecognition could be met, that is where the seller transfers all significant benefits and all significant risks of ownership to the buyer. This might arise, for example, if the agreement incorporates terms whereby the buyer assumes price risk or in the case of repos to maturity where the repo's maturity date coincides with that of the underlying securities. In such circumstances, the transaction should be treated as a sale. However, if material the nature of the repurchase commitment should still be disclosed in the financial statements.

Insurance brokers

4.225 The standard's revised rules on offset (see para 4.97) have a significant impact on insurance brokers, as they are no longer allowed to net certain of their balances. For example, an insurance broker's client might place separate motor and fire business through the same broker. At the broker's year end, the client owes £1,000 for the motor premium and has submitted a claim for £5,000 on the fire policy that has been agreed, but not collected. These items cannot legally be offset and under FRS 5 are separate assets and liabilities. However, until FRS 5 was issued the practice for virtually all brokers was to show a net creditor of £4,000 in the circumstances described. The argument for this accounting practice was that it reflected the way that settlement actually occurred in the market. In practice, there is considerable netting of items on settlement and in the example above the broker would often send a cheque to the client for £4,000 only.

4.226 The accounting treatment before FRS 5 was dealt with in TR 625 on Accounting by Insurance Brokers. The technical release considered the issues outlined above and indicated that the net disclosure on the balance sheet was acceptable if it was accompanied by an accounting policy note to disclose the treatment adopted. This guidance has now been superseded and many of the balances previously netted by insurance brokers have to be disclosed gross in their financial statements in order to comply with FRS 5. This is a significant change for the industry and has involved some brokers in considerable amounts of work to determine the balances to be disclosed, because many did not have the systems in place to give them the required information.

4.227 The insurance broking industry took its concerns to the ASB and it accepted that there was a real practical problem with insurance brokers' accounting systems as they could not at the time generate the necessary information to make it possible for them to comply fully with FRS 5's requirements within the timescale for the standard's implementation (which was accounting periods ending on or after 22 September 1994). As a consequence, the ASB issued an amendment to FRS 5 in December 1994, which allows insurance brokers to offset balances from insurance broking transactions for a further two years. This is to allow them time to set up the necessary accounting systems to generate the gross balances essential to fulfil FRS 5's requirements. A similar exemption has been afforded to insurers (including Lloyd's syndicates) to allow them to offset their insurance transactions placed through insurance brokers. These exemptions, however, cease for accounting periods ending on or after 22 September 1996, from which time such entities will be required to comply fully with FRS 5.

Contract purchase arrangements

4.228 In a typical hire purchase contract, the substance of the transaction is a sale of an asset where the price is paid over a period of time, with interest charged on the outstanding balance. However, the legal form is that of a hire of the asset to the purchaser with the rentals being equivalent to the purchase price plus interest on the outstanding balance. The title to the goods remains with the vendor and the purchaser is given an option to acquire the asset for a nominal amount (normally for £1) at the end of the hire term and it is at this stage that the title to the asset passes. It is clear, however, in a hire purchase agreement that the risks and rewards of ownership rest with the purchaser and the asset is consequently reflected in its financial statements, with its obligation to the vendor shown as a liability.

4.229 In a contract *hire* arrangement, the hirer does not take title to the goods at the end of the contract term, but the goods are returned to the lessor and are either relet by him or more commonly sold to another party. Such arrangements are clearly operating leases under SSAP 21 as the residual risk remains with the lessor. The hired assets will, therefore, remain on the lessor's balance sheet. In a contract *purchase* transaction there is generally a balloon rental at the end of the lease term (as illustrated in the graph on page 93) and a nominal sum is paid to acquire the title to the asset (in a similar way to a hire purchase agreement). In addition, the lessee has a put option to sell the vehicle on to another party for a pre-agreed price, which is often a subsidiary of the lessor. Therefore, the transaction is a full pay-out lease, but it can be argued that as the option mechanism puts the residual risk back to the lessor the asset should not be recognised on the hirer's balance sheet.

4.230 If the lessee exercises his put option, and puts the asset back to the subsidiary of the lessor, the commercial effect of the balloon payment and the option taken together is similar in cash flow terms to a contract hire arrangement, in that the residual risks are in practice being taken by the lessor's group. However, the lessee's liability to the lessor is for the full amount of the asset purchased and the related finance costs – often the contract will be non-cancellable – and the title will pass at the end of the lease term. The right to sell the asset to a subsidiary of the lessor in the future does not remove or limit the obligation in any way. Therefore, a liability exits in FRS 5 terms and should be recognised in the lessee's financial statements.

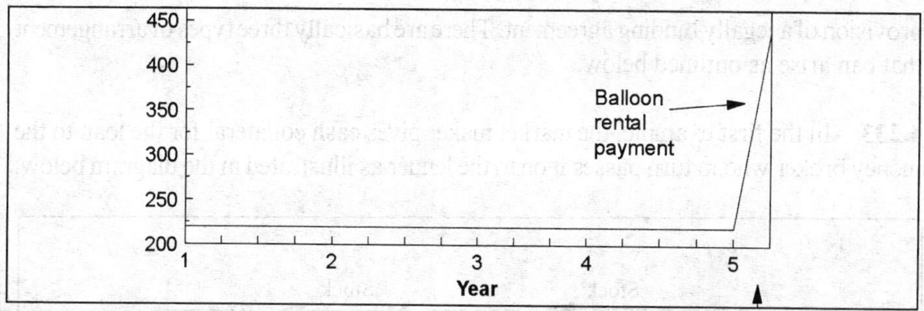

4.231 Consequently, also in accordance with SSAP 21, the asset and liability should appear on the lessee's balance sheet and the transaction should be treated as a finance lease. The partial derecognition rules of FRS 5 may also be relevant to such transactions. These rules state that, in special cases, an asset can be derecognised and another recognised in its place where significant risks and rewards relating to the original asset have been transferred to another party. It could be argued that because of the option's existence, the lessee has in substance transferred significant risks and rewards with regard to the residual to the other party. However, generally in such transactions this will not be so, because the sale will be contingent until it takes place. Normally there are important conditions that the lessee will have to comply with before the option can be exercised and these will often affect the price. Therefore, it is unlikely that the partial derecognition rules can be applied to contract purchase arrangements, because the risks and rewards of ownership reside with the lessee until the conditions to exercise the option have been complied with.

Stock lending

4.232 Another type of arrangement that can be affected by FRS 5 is stock lending. Stock lending is a growing activity within the investment management industry, affecting the assets of insurance companies, investment and unit trusts and the pension fund sector. Stock lending involves three parties: the lender (such as pension funds, insurance companies or building societies); a money broker (who acts as an intermediary); and a market maker (the borrower). Stock lending is a method used to help the liquidity of the stock market, by allowing a market maker who is short of a particular stock to borrow that stock from another party (the lender). Such arrangements are, therefore, generally only entered into for a short period of time. The borrowing is made through a money broker in order to ensure that the identity of the borrower and lender remain confidential. On receipt of the stock the market maker provides collateral to the money broker for the loan. If dividends are paid during the lending period on the stock transferred, the holder of the stock receives the dividends and the market maker pays an equivalent amount to the lender with relevant tax deducted and accounted for by the market maker as manufactured dividends. Although the process is called stock lending, the title to the stock actually passes to the market maker. Most of the business risks associated with stock lending can be managed by the provision of a legally binding agreement. There are basically three types of arrangement that can arise as outlined below.

4.233 In the first example, the market maker gives cash collateral for the loan to the money broker who in turn passes it on to the lender as illustrated in the diagram below:

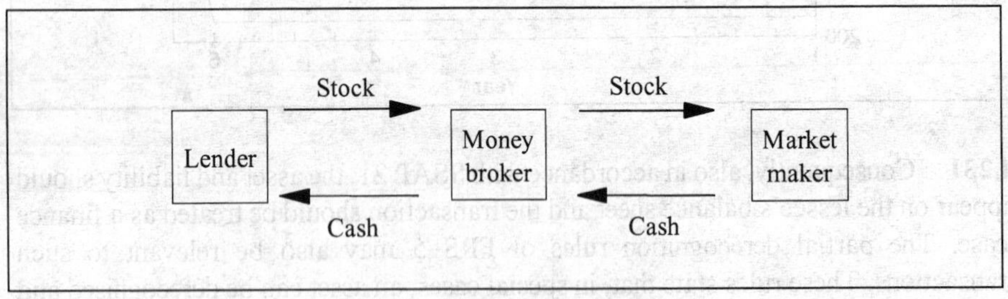

Although this is the simplest example of stock lending it is not the most frequent method used. In the situation described, the market maker deposits the cash collateral with the money broker and the money broker passes it on to the stock lender. Interest earned on the cash is passed to the market maker, but after the money broker and lender have deducted their fee.

4.234 In the next example illustrated below, the market maker borrows back the cash given to the money broker as collateral and deposits gilts with the money broker, who in turn passes these on to the lender.

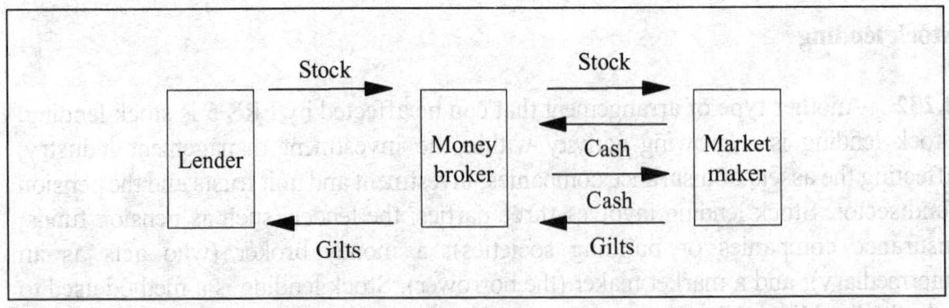

The market maker will pay a higher rate of interest on the cash it borrows back from the money broker than the rate it receives on the initial cash deposit. The difference is partly kept by the money broker and partly paid to the lender as his fee under the arrangement. If an interest payment is due on the gilts during the term of the loan, the market maker has to take the gilts back (and receive the income), but also has to substitute equivalent collateral for the gilts returned. This is the most common form of stock lending.

4.235 In some situations, the market maker will not borrow back the cash and the money broker will invest it in short-term paper (for example, certificates of deposit) and this investment is then passed to the lender as collateral. The interest earned on the collateral is passed to the market maker after deducting the lender and money broker's fees.

4.236 The position of the entity lending the stock is relatively simple in that it is exposed to normal market risks on the price of the stock and receives the equivalent of dividends on the stocks lent. Therefore, under FRS 5 the lender should retain the investment on its balance sheet and this was the practice adopted prior to FRS 5. In the event of default there is a legal right of offset of the amounts owed to and by the lender and the borrower. The practical effect of this for the lender is that he should show on his balance sheet the original securities lent, but should not show the collateral as an asset received or a as creditor in respect of collateral received. Therefore, stock lending transactions have no accounting effect, other than that the lending company receives a stock lending fee, which it recognises as income.

4.237 The market maker's position is also relatively simple because, although it is the legal owner of the stock (until it is sold to another party), it is not exposed to the risk of changes in the stock's market value. In addition, any dividends received on the stock are paid to the lender. Therefore, under FRS 5 the market maker does not retain any of the risks or rewards of ownership and hence should not recognise the stock on its balance sheet, but will reflect any cash collateral deposited with the money broker as a debtor in its balance sheet.

4.238 Both the lender and the market maker should disclose the arrangements and any contingencies or commitments in their financial statements. This might include the aggregate value of the securities on loan (or borrowed) at the balance sheet date, together with the value of collateral held (or given) in respect of those securities. The 'margin' should be accounted for separately and noted where material in the financial statements.

4.239 The money broker is not exposed to price risk on the stock or the collateral and does not have any rights to dividends or interest other than the fee charged for managing the deal. But, legally, the money broker acts as principal in both sides of the transaction and is at risk, because it can be called upon by either party to return stock or collateral, should the other party default on the transaction. The broker is, therefore, exposed to credit risk on the transaction. In the examples in paragraphs 4.233 and 4.234 the money broker potentially has the following assets and liabilities:

- Right to receive stock from the borrower.
- Obligation to give stock to the lender.
- Right to receive stock collateral from the lender.
- Obligation to give stock collateral to the borrower.

4.240 Some might argue that under FRS 5's requirements the money broker should recognise the rights and obligations as assets and liabilities in its financial statements. However, it can also be argued that in substance the conditions for offset are met and, as a consequence, the rights and obligations should remain off balance sheet. One of the offset conditions is that the company and the other party must owe each other determinable monetary amounts. For this condition, it can be argued that the amounts owed are determinable, because the money brokers attribute values to stock loans and associated collateral on a daily basis to ensure that the stock loans are adequately collateralised. The collateral is revalued each day and, if insufficient, additional collateral is obtained from the borrower. Furthermore, under many stock lending agreements, the broker has the right to settle net at any time if it is not satisfied that the other party can deliver the stock or the collateral. Whether the argument for netting can be sustained in practice depends on the particular stock lending agreement and care needs to be taken in analysing its terms in accordance with the standard, but certainly it appears that an argument can be made to justify not including them on the balance sheet.

4.241 Even where no assets or liabilities are recognised in the money broker's financial statements, FRS 5 requires that there should be sufficient disclosure in the financial statements to enable the user to understand the commercial effect of the transaction. Furthermore, any contingent obligations under the transaction should be disclosed, because of the general requirement in SSAP 18 to disclosure all financial commitments and contingencies which are relevant to assessing the company's state of affairs.

4.242 An example of a group that has taken stock lending assets and liabilities off balance sheet following FRS 5 is given in Table 4.13.

Table 4.13 – B.A.T Industries p.l.c. – Directors' Report and Accounts – 31 December 1994

Directors' Report (extract)

Accounting policies (extract)

The group has adopted three new accounting standards. FRS 5 'Reporting the Substance of Transactions', FRS 6 'Mergers and Acquisitions' and FRS 7 'Fair Values in Acquisition Accounting'.

> **FRS5** has required reclassification of certain comparative figures, although there is no effect on the Group's equity or profit.....
> ...Thirdly, stock lending arrangements with financial institutions, previously shown as separate assets and liabilities on the balance sheet, are now deemed not to result in the creation of an additional asset or liability. As a result, the comparative figures for life business 'other assets' and 'other liabilities' have each been reduced by £113 million.

Bed and breakfast transactions

4.243 Bed and breakfast transactions are examples of sale and repurchase transactions to which the provisions of Application Note B apply. In such transactions, a company agrees to sell certain assets (such as securities) to a third party (normally a broker) and arranges to repurchase them, or identical assets, shortly thereafter, usually over night, for the same price. The essence of the agreement is that the entity takes no risk of loss, other than the extremely remote risk that the counterparty will default and similarly has no reward apart from any tax effect and potentially an effect on realised profits. Normally such transactions are undertaken to crystallise a capital gain or a capital loss for taxation purposes. Also transactions of this nature are sometimes used in an attempt to turn unrealised revaluation gains on investments into realised gains so that they can be used for distribution by way of dividends to shareholders.

4.244 Under FRS 5, it is necessary to determine whether an actual sale has taken place in a bed and breakfast transaction. Although the legal title to the asset may have passed, generally the benefits and risks associated with it will not have. Normally, a transaction of this nature should be treated as a financing arrangement rather than a sale, leaving the asset and a corresponding liability on the balance sheet of the original owner. Furthermore, any profit or loss would not be reflected in the company's financial statements. The information required by Application Note B would also have to be given in the notes to the financial statements (see para 4.130).

4.245 There may be a few situations in practice where the substance of the transaction is a disposal of the asset and a reacquisition, which should be accounted for as such. In such transactions a realised profit may arise. In general in order to recognise a realised gain on such a transaction it is necessary to show that the risks and rewards of ownership have passed to the party buying the asset. However, there are also a number of other issues which are discussed below in the context of transactions in current asset investments and transactions in fixed asset investments.

[The next paragraph is 4.247.]

4.247 Marking to market of current asset investments is at present generally regarded as giving rise to realised profits, albeit that a true and fair override is required to take such profits to the profit and loss account, as the Act requires valuation increases to be taken to the revaluation reserve (see further chapter 5). Therefore, for current asset investments, it seems unnecessary to bed and breakfast them to generate a realised profit as it is generally considered that marking to market creates realised profits as well as realised losses (there may, however, be a need to do so for tax purposes). Generally, therefore, bed and breakfast transactions involving current asset investments are unnecessary to generate a realised profit, but irrespective of that, the investment should remain on the balance sheet because the entity does not relinquish the risks and rewards of ownership.

[The next paragraph is 4.249.]

4.249 In practice, a bed and breakfast transaction involves contracting to sell to a broker with no express contract to buy back the following day. However, it is clearly understood that the shares will be repurchased at an agreed price. If the seller does not repurchase, the broker will be unlikely to deal for him again. Thus there is a moral contract. Consequently, it can be strongly argued that the sale and repurchase are linked and that the transaction is not 'arm's length', because there is an obligation, moral if not legal, for the sale to be reversed the next day. It seems reasonable to conclude that if the substance is not to dispose of the asset, but merely to change the tax base then no sale has occurred in substance and, in addition, no gain should be recognised. This conclusion is further reinforced by the probability that, because the sale and repurchase are generally between the same parties, no cash will actually pass.

Purchase commitments

4.250 One of the types of transaction that falls outside the scope of FRS 5 is a purchase commitment. In certain transactions it might not be as straightforward as it seems to spot a purchase commitment, for example:

Example

A vehicle manufacturer sells a vehicle to a dealer (an outright sale). At the same time a subsidiary of the manufacturer grants the dealer an option to sell the vehicle to the subsidiary after three years for 40% of the original sales price charged by the manufacturer (40% is the estimated residual value). In the subsidiary's financial statements the residual value and corresponding liability would not be recorded unless and until the dealer exercises his option and delivery takes place. This is because, even if the subsidiary were committed from day one to purchase the residual, it would not record the asset and liability until delivery takes place. In the manufacturer's consolidated financial statements, it would be necessary to determine whether or not it was likely that the option would be exercised. If it was likely then the sale of the vehicle would still be recognised, but the residual value and corresponding liability might need to be recorded in the consolidated financial statements under the partial derecognition provisions of FRS 5 (see further para 4.74). This would mean that any probable loss if the residual value is expected to be less than 40% should be provided for and a similar provision would be required in the subsidiary company.

Linked presentation and the cash flow statement

4.251 There is no guidance in FRS 5 concerning how to account for transactions in the cash flow statement where the linked presentation is used for the balance sheet and profit and loss account. For example, where a company uses the linked presentation for a factoring arrangement where the conditions in FRS 5 are met (see para 4.88), there are two possible ways that the arrangement can be reflected in the cash flow statement: either treat the movement in the net debtors as an operating cash flow; or treat the proceeds from factoring as a source of finance under 'financing'. FRS 5 states that a scheme that qualifies for the linked presentation is in substance a financing, but the non-returnable proceeds are not a liability, nor is the original gross amount of the debtor an asset. These two statements may seem contradictory, but since the net amount is regarded as the asset, it is logical to show the non-returnable proceeds in the cash flow statement as an operating cash flow, that is, to treat the non-returnable proceeds as a partial collection of the debtors.

Take-or-pay contracts

4.252 In 'take-or-pay' contracts an entity enters into a long-term contract with a supplier at a predetermined price for the supply of either goods or services and undertakes to pay for a minimum quantity whether or not the quantity is actually required. The advantage for the purchaser is that he is guaranteed delivery of a certain quantity of goods and will be able to negotiate a competitive price. Throughput contracts are very similar in nature to take-or-pay contracts. They are common in the oil industry, where more than one company might share, for example, an oil pipe line. The parties to the contract enter into an agreement to share the use of the facility and each party will pay a certain amount that will not necessarily depend on the amount of their oil that they transport through the pipe line.

4.253 Take-or-pay contracts and throughput contracts have not been specifically dealt with in FRS 5, although they were mentioned in ED 42 and under that exposure draft were exempted from its provisions. They are not, however, dealt with specifically under FRS 5, but an argument can be made that they fall under the heading of expenditure commitments and as such are exempted from the standard's provisions. Essentially under such a contract the purchaser has a contractual commitment to pay a minimum amount to the supplier. The purchaser may or may not receive goods or services to the value of the amount committed, but he has the right to.

4.254 The guidance notes on SSAP 21 refer to take or pay contracts in a discussion of whether certain arrangements should, in exceptional cases, be treated as being in substance leases, although different terms might be used to describe them. They give the example of a company (company A) that builds a plant on the basis that company B is obliged to buy sufficient of the plant's output in order to give company A a full payout on the cost of the assets involved, together with a normal profit margin. They state that such arrangements will in many cases be in substance more in the nature of long-term purchase and supply contracts than contracts which are in substance leases of assets.

4.255 Therefore, if such a contract is a lease it will have to be accounted for in accordance with the requirements of SSAP 21 and, if it is a finance lease, recorded on the lessee's balance sheet. Alternatively, such an arrangement might purely be a long-term purchase or supply contract that is exempted form the requirements of

FRS 5 because its is an expenditure commitment, in which case the purchaser has a contingent obligation which should be treated in accordance with the provisions of SSAP 18. [FRS 5 para 58; SSAP 18 para 14, 15]. If it is necessary to make a provision for the purchase commitment in accordance with SSAP 18, then this should be charged to the profit and loss account rather than recognised as an asset. Where it is determined that no provision should be made for the contract after considering SSAP 18, the notes to the financial statements still have to give particulars of the financial commitment to comply with the Act.

4.256 Table 4.14 below illustrates the treatment and disclosure of a typical take-or-pay contract.

Table 4.14 – Imperial Chemical Industries PLC – Annual report and accounts – 31 December 1997

Notes relating to the accounts

41 Commitments and contingent liabilities (extract)

Significant take-or-pay contracts entered into by subsidiaries are as follows:

(i) the purchase of electric power which commenced April 1993 for 15 years. The present value of the remaining commitment is estimated at £688m.

(ii) the purchase of electric power, which will commence in the second quarter of 1998, for 15 years. The present value of this commitment is estimated at £141m.

Chapter 5

Valuation bases

Chapter 5

Valuation bases

Introduction

5.1 There has long been controversy about the basis on which financial statements are drawn up in the UK and much of this has surrounded the valuation issue. The question of whether a balance sheet should present costs or values is a very fundamental one and the present position is an unhappy compromise between these two approaches. However, the point at issue is not restricted to the balance sheet, but also fundamentally affects the measurement of income.

5.2 Chapter 5 of the ASB's draft statement of principles, 'Measurement in financial statements', discusses in detail the 'larger' questions surrounding the basis on which financial statements may be prepared. The statement of principles discusses the various bases of valuation used and the capital maintenance concepts that may be applied in preparing financial statements. The statement of principles is discussed in detail in chapter 2.

5.3 The UK accounting model is based on historical cost. The Act, based on the EC 4th Directive, sets out the 'historical cost accounting rules' as the principal framework, but also includes the 'alternative accounting rules', which are optional under the directive. The use of the alternative accounting rules is patchy. Many companies stick to historical cost accounting, but many also revalue at least some assets. The extent of this is very varied. Despite intense debate in the late 1970s and early 1980s about various forms of accounting for the effects of changing prices (see 'Current cost accounting rules' from para 5.246), very few companies now use a comprehensive system of inflation accounting. Much more common is to revalue assets selectively. It is quite common, for example, for companies to revalue properties held as fixed assets, but fairly uncommon to revalue plant and vehicles. Moreover, there is at present no requirement to keep asset values up to date (although FRED 17, referred to below, proposes such a requirement).

5.4 This mixture of approaches makes the balance sheets of many UK companies hard to interpret and, in particular, hard to compare with each other. The ASB has now developed FRED 17, 'Measurement of tangible fixed assets', which addresses some of the concerns relating to current revaluation practice. One of these concerns is that there is presently no requirement for valuations to be kept up-to-date. Another is that presently an entity can 'cherry-pick' those assets which it revalues, that is, it can revalue only some out of a class of fixed assets. FRED 17 proposes that where a tangible fixed asset is revalued, the whole of that class of asset should be revalued as well.

5.5 Additionally, the ASB published FRS 11, 'Impairment of fixed assets and goodwill', in July 1998. This new standard is considered partly in this chapter and partly in chapter 23. FRS 11 is effective for accounting periods ending on or after 23 December 1998.

5.6 In this chapter the Companies Act rules relating to determining cost and valuation are described, together with the provisions of FRS 11, where relevant, and the proposals contained in FRED 17.

General

5.7 Companies prepare their accounts in accordance with one of two basic conventions, or by using a combination. They may use:

- The historical cost convention, which complies with the historical cost accounting rules set out in the Act.
- The current cost convention, which values all items at their current rather than historical cost and which adopts the alternative accounting rules of the Act, whilst giving supplementary historical cost information.
- The modified historical cost convention, which complies with the historical cost rules for most items, but adopts the alternative accounting rules set out in the Act for other items (usually fixed asset properties) so that they are carried at valuation.

5.8 The rules for valuing items under each of these conventions are discussed in turn below.

Historical cost accounting rules

5.9 Paragraphs 16 to 28 of Schedule 4 to the Act set out the rules companies must apply in arriving at the amounts at which they must disclose items in their financial statements. These rules cover:

- Fixed assets.
- Current assets.
- Purchase price and production cost of assets.
- Other items.

In addition, UITF Abstract 5 sets out rules where current assets are transferred to fixed assets. Each of these is discussed in detail in the paragraphs that follow.

Fixed assets

5.10 The basic rule is that fixed assets are shown at either their purchase price or their production cost (see paras 5.92 to 5.134), less any provision for depreciation or diminution in value. [4 Sch 17]. For this purpose, a fixed asset is defined as any asset that is *"...intended for use on a continuing basis in the company's activities"*. [Sec 262(1)]. Fixed assets include intangible assets, tangible assets and fixed asset investments. Fixed assets are also dealt with in chapter 14.

Depreciation

5.11 Where a fixed asset has a limited useful economic life, a company must make provisions for depreciation so as to write off its purchase price or its production cost less its estimated residual value, if any, systematically over the period of that life. [4 Sch 18]. Although depreciation is not defined in the Act, it is defined in SSAP 12 as *"...the measure of the wearing out, consumption or other reduction in the useful economic life of a fixed asset whether arising from use, effluxion of time or obsolescence through technological or market changes"*. [SSAP 12 para 10]. The definition proposed in FRED 17 is very similar:

> *"The measure of the cost or revalued amount of the economic benefits of the tangible fixed asset that have been consumed during the period. Consumption includes the wearing out, using up or other reduction in the useful economic life of a tangible fixed asset whether arising from use, effluxion of time or obsolescence through either changes in technology or demand for the goods and services produced by the asset."* [FRED 17 para 2].

Depreciation is not necessarily intended to result in a company setting aside profits or funds to replace an asset at the end of its useful economic life, but, coincidentally, that may be the result.

5.12 In determining the amount to be written off each asset (other than goodwill) each year, the Act (and also SSAP 12) specifically requires companies to take account of the asset's estimated residual value at the end of its useful economic life. [4 Sch 18(b)]. 'Useful economic life' is defined in SSAP 12 as *"...the period over which the present owner will derive economic benefits from [the asset's] use"*. [SSAP 12 para 11]. The definition proposed in FRED 17 is again similar: *"...the period over which the entity expects to derive economic benefits from that asset"*. However, under FRED 17 reasonably expected technological changes should be taken into account in determining the useful economic life. [FRED 17 para 2].

5.13 'Residual value' is defined as *"...the realisable value of the asset at the end of its useful economic life, based on prices prevailing at the date of acquisition or revaluation, where this has taken place. Realisation costs should be deducted in arriving at the residual value"*. [SSAP 12 para 12]. Again, the definition in FRED 17 is similar, but with the additional factor that reasonably expected technological changes should be taken into account in determining residual value.

5.14 The effect of this definition is that future inflation should not be taken into account when calculating an asset's residual value. Strictly, therefore, the value of the asset in question should be considered at the end of its useful economic life, but expressed in pounds of the date of acquisition or revaluation.

Example 1

An asset is bought for £1,000. Its estimated useful economic life is 6 years and its estimated residual value, based on prices prevailing at the date of acquisition, is £100. However, if future inflation is taken into account, the estimated residual value would be £400. The rule in SSAP 12 (and FRED 17) would lead to a company making annual provisions for depreciation of £150 (assuming the straight-line method is used). At the end of the useful life, the asset would be written down to £100 and, if estimates proved correct, it would be sold for £400, resulting in a profit on sale of £300. Under the alternative (but not permissible) method – taking inflation into account – depreciation would have been charged at the rate of £100 a year and there would have been no profit or loss reported on sale.

The (presumably intentional) effect of the rule in the standard is that, in an inflationary environment, assets should be depreciated at a rate which is higher than the rate necessary to produce no profit or loss in the year of disposal. This effect may seem strange, although in support of the method required by the standard, it must be acknowledged that there is considerable difficulty in estimating future inflation and its effect on residual values. It can also be argued that the gain (or loss) on disposal is a holding gain (or loss) on a fixed asset that should not be recognised in historical cost accounts until it is realised.

Example 2

The facts are the same as in the above example. The asset is bought for £1,000 and its useful economic life is estimated at 6 years. The residual value is expected to be £100 based on prices prevailing at the date of acquisition, but if future inflation is taken into account the residual value is estimated to be £400. In this example, however, the asset is revalued in year 3. The written down value at that point is £700, and the revalued amount is £900. Based on prices prevailing at the time of the revaluation the residual value is expected to be £150. Accordingly, depreciation for year 3 will be based on the revalued amount of £900 less the revised residual value of £150 divided by the remaining useful life. Depreciation for the year would, therefore, be £187. The increase in the depreciation charge of £37 is the revaluation surplus of £200 less the increase in the residual value of £50 divided by the remaining life of 4 years, that is, £37 (rounded down). (For the purpose of the above it has been assumed that the company has a policy of revaluation but that there has been no significant change in the value in years 1 and 2. Depreciation has been charged after the revaluation.)

Methods of depreciation

5.15 SSAP 12 notes that there is a range of acceptable depreciation methods and that management should select the method regarded as most appropriate to the type of asset and its use in the business so as to allocate depreciation as fairly as possible to the periods expected to benefit from the asset's use. [SSAP 12 para 8]. The standard notes that, although the straight line method is the simplest to apply, it might not always be the most appropriate. FRED 17, whilst not specifying a preference, similarly states that the depreciation method used should reflect as fairly as possible the pattern in which the asset's economic benefits are consumed by the entity. [FRED 17 para 68]. This section describes some of the most common methods.

Straight line method

5.16 This is the most common method used in practice. The cost (or revalued amount – see 'Alternative accounting rules' from para 5.137 below) – less the estimated residual value is allocated over the useful economic life so as to charge each accounting period with the same amount.

Reducing balance method

5.17 This method is designed to charge higher amounts of depreciation in the earlier years of an asset's use, as follows:

Example

	£
Cost	125
Depreciation (20%)	25
Year 1	100
Depreciation (20% of 100)	20
Year 2	80
Depreciation (20% of 100)	16
Year 3	64
and so on	

5.18 Part of the rationale for this method is that charges for repairs and maintenance of assets are often higher in later years. Early years, therefore, bear a high depreciation charge and a low repair and maintenance charge; later years bear a low depreciation charge and a high repair and maintenance charge; the overall effect is to produce an approximately constant charge, taking the two costs together.

Sum of the digits (or 'rule of 78')

5.19 This method is similar in its effect to the reducing balance method although the mechanics are different. If an asset is expected to last, say, 12 periods (years, months, etc), the digits 1 to 12 are added (total 78); the first period is charged with 12/78, the next period with 11/78 and so on – hence the name 'rule of 78'.

Unit-of-production method

5.20 This method relates depreciation to the estimated production capability of an asset. The rate of depreciation per hour of usage or unit of production is given by dividing the depreciable amount by the estimated total service capability of the asset, measured in terms of hours or units. This method is sometimes employed when the usage of an asset varies considerably from period to period because, in these circumstances, it matches cost against revenue more satisfactorily. Examples of the types of asset that are often depreciated in this way are: for hourly rates – airline engines; and for unit of production – mineral resources.

Example 1

A machine cost £100,000 and its expected residual value is £10,000. The useful life of the machine is expected to be 500,000 hours. The depreciation rate per hour is, therefore, £0.18 (£100,000 – £10,000 divided by 500,000).

Example 2

Exploration costs amounting to £5,000,000 are incurred in finding mineral reserves. The reserves are expected to be 5 million tonnes. The rate of depreciation to be applied to the exploration costs is worked out as £1 per tonne. In the first year of production 200,000 tonnes are extracted and depreciation charged at £1 per tonne is £200,000.

Annuity method

5.21 This accounting method makes an adjustment for the cost of capital. The objective is to produce an approximately constant charge for the total depreciation and cost of capital. Depreciation is allocated so as to give a low charge in earlier years (when interest or other finance cost is relatively high) and a high charge in later years (when interest or other finance cost is relatively low). The method is not commonly used as it is generally considered that depreciation, being the measure of the wearing out, consumption or other reduction in the useful economic life of an asset, is independent of the manner in which an asset is financed.

Assets where components have different lives

5.22 FRED 17 proposes that where a tangible fixed asset comprises two or more major components with substantially different useful economic lives, each component should be accounted for as a separate asset and depreciated over its useful economic life. Examples of this that are given in FRED 17 are the lining of a blast furnace and the roof of a building. Where such components have been depreciated and are replaced the cost of the replacement should then be capitalised. [FRED 17 paras 32, 72].

Non-depreciation of certain assets

5.23 One issue that has caused debate and variations in practice over many years is whether, in some circumstances, it is appropriate to omit annual charges for depreciation in respect of certain fixed assets.

5.24 ED 37, the exposure draft that preceded the latest revision of SSAP 12 in 1987, proposed that:

> *"...in certain very restricted instances, it may not be appropriate to charge depreciation in respect of what would normally be a depreciable asset. This would arise only where an asset is maintained to such a standard that:*
>
> *(a) the estimated residual value is equal to or greater than its net book amount; or*
>
> *(b) its estimated useful economic life is either infinite or such that any depreciation charge would be insignificant."*

5.25 ED 37 noted that *"...for an asset to be treated in this way maintenance should be undertaken on a regular basis and the cost charged in the profit and loss account. In assessing whether any depreciation should be charged, regard should be had not only to the physical condition of the asset but also to the risk of obsolescence".*

5.26 The issue is generally discussed in the context of buildings. For example, some brewers do not depreciate their tied properties and the practice is also sometimes applied to other assets such as hotels and various retail and office premises.

5.27 SSAP 12 is silent on the question of non-depreciation. The reason is that commentators on ED 37 had made two principal criticisms of the proposal. First, they had argued that the treatment could be open to misinterpretation and abuse and companies might seek to use it beyond the circumstances for which it was intended. Second, there was concern that too much emphasis was placed on maintenance. As some commentators pointed out, expenditure on maintenance is only one of the factors that affect the value of an asset: a well-maintained asset may still be subject to depreciation through the results of obsolescence from technological and market changes. In the case of a building, its location may be at least as relevant as its state of repair. Although the proposal was not mentioned in the revised standard, the matter was referred to in the accompanying Technical Release. In that statement the ASC referred to the general principle of SSAP 12 – that where a fixed asset has a finite useful economic life, its cost (or revalued amount) less residual value should be depreciated over that life – and acknowledged that there might be circumstances where following the principle rendered any depreciation charge unnecessary.

Example

A property costing £1m is bought in 19X6. Its estimated useful economic life is 50 years. However, the company considers it likely that it will sell the property after 20 years. The estimated residual value in 20 years' time, based on 19X6 prices, is (a) £1,000,000, (b) £900,000. A residual value that is the same as or close to original cost is likely to be rare, as it assumes that in 20 years' time potential purchasers would pay, for a 20 year old property, an amount similar to what they would pay for a new property.

In case (a), the company considers that the residual value will equal the cost. There is, therefore, no depreciable amount and depreciation is correctly zero.

In case (b) the company considers that the residual value will be £900,000 and the depreciable amount is therefore £100,000. Annual depreciation (on a straight line basis) will be £5,000 (1,000,000 – 900,000\20). Depending on the context, the annual depreciation charge of £5,000 may be immaterial and it may, therefore, be acceptable not to provide for depreciation of the property on those grounds. It is, however, necessary to consider the materiality of the cumulative depreciation as well as the depreciation in the year.

5.28 This example demonstrates two points mentioned in paragraphs 5.12 and 5.13 above.

- The useful economic life is defined by SSAP 12 (para 11) in terms of the present owner; therefore, 20 years rather than 50 years is the relevant period.

- Residual value is defined by SSAP 12 (para 12) as being based on prices prevailing at the date of acquisition (or revaluation), that is, excluding the effects of future inflation.

5.29 In this example, maintaining the asset to a high standard is not assumed. Maintenance is of course one of the factors that determines the estimated residual value and in practice is almost invariably quoted as the reason why the residual value of particular assets is expected to be at least as high, in terms of prices prevailing at the date of acquisition or revaluation, as the present carrying value. It is also usually quoted as the reason why useful economic lives are expected to be infinite, an argument used frequently to justify non-depreciation of intangible assets, such as brands or publishing titles.

5.30 Examples of each of the situations where non-depreciation is justified by reference to the 'residual value' or 'infinite life' argument are illustrated in Tables 5.1 and 5.2.

Table 5.1 – Bass PLC – Report and Accounts – 30 September 1994

Accounting Policies (extract)

Fixed assets and depreciation (extract)

e) Hotels and UK public houses held as freehold or with a leasehold interest in excess of 50 years are maintained, as a matter of Group policy, by a programme of repair and refurbishment such that the residual values of these properties, based on prices prevailing at the time of acquisition or subsequent valuation, are at least equal to their book values. Having regard to this, it is the opinion of the directors that depreciation on any such property as required by the Companies Act 1985 and accounting standards would not be material.

Table 5.2 – Scottish Hydro-Electric plc – Annual Report and Accounts – 31 March 1997

Accounting Policies (extract)

7 Depreciation of Tangible Fixed Assets (extract)

The Group is obliged under the Reservoirs Act 1975 to maintain its dams. Such dams and associated hydro civil assets, specifically tunnels, roads and stone buildings, are considered to have an infinite life and are not depreciated as they are maintained in good repair.

5.31 Another example, where non-depreciation is justified by the maintenance argument, is shown in Table 5.3. Following discussions with the Financial Reporting Review Panel (FRRP), Forte amended the description of its policy in 1992 to make clear that the appraisal of residual values was based on prices prevailing at the time of acquisition or subsequent revaluation and that its policy was to make provision in the profit and loss account in the event of the occurrence of any permanent diminution in value. The FRRP, for its part, stated that it was satisfied with the explanation for the absence of depreciation and concluded that there was no cause for action in respect of the matter.

Table 5.3 – Forte Plc – Report and Accounts – 31 January 1994

Accounting Policies (extract)

5 Fixed assets (extract)

(b) Revaluation reserve: The difference between the resultant valuation and historic cost is recorded in the valuation reserve to the extent that the valuation exceeds historic cost on a property by property basis. Any permanent diminution in the value of fixed assets is charged to the profit and loss account as appropriate after making any associated adjustment to the revaluation reserve.

(d) Depreciation of properties: In accordance with normal practice in the UK hotel industry, no depreciation is provided on freehold properties or properties on leases with twenty years or more to run at the balance sheet date or on integral fixed plant. It is the Group's practice to maintain these assets in a continual state of sound repair and to extend and make improvements thereto from time to time. Accordingly the Directors consider that the lives of these assets and residual values (based on prices prevailing at the time of acquisition or subsequent valuation) are such that their depreciation is insignificant. All leasehold properties held for less than twenty years and amortised over the unexpired term.

5.32 Whilst the arguments for non-depreciation described in paragraphs 5.23 to 5.28 above may well be valid, they are not always capable of being verified by a reader of financial statements. Disclosure of annual maintenance charged on property that is not depreciated would go some way to meeting this drawback. One company that discloses maintenance charges, albeit in total only, is shown in Table 5.4.

5.33 Land is normally considered to be a non-depreciable asset, because it does not generally have a limited useful economic life. Mineral bearing land, however, comprises two elements: the mineral reserves and the land itself. Mineral reserves are depreciated as they are extracted, whilst the land itself is not depreciated.

Table 5.4 – Bass PLC – Annual Report – 30 September 1996

Notes to the Financial Statements (extract)

5 Costs and overheads, less other income	**1996 £m**	1995 £m
Raw materials and consumables	**1,678**	1,509
Staff costs (note 6)	**848**	807
Excise duty on own products	**600**	543
Depreciation of tangible fixed assets	**229**	206
Maintenance and repairs	**89**	84
Changes in stocks of finished goods and work in progress	**(16)**	(8)
Advertising costs	**54**	43
Other external charges	**875**	685
	4,357	3,869

5.34 In recent years, because of the decline in property values during the early 1990s, several companies have begun to depreciate properties which formerly they had not depreciated, because they expected that residual values would be so high or that useful lives would be so long as to render any depreciation immaterial. Some retail store groups have even commenced depreciation of land, on the grounds that the cost of the land which was bought at the height of the property boom of the eighties will not be recovered at the end of the useful economic life of the site. Whilst it might seem strange that land can, therefore, be seen to have a finite useful economic life, it is explained by the fact that economic life is measured, for the purpose of the standard, as the period that the present owner is intending to use the land. Where a retail company, for instance, bought an out of town site in the mid 1980s at a very high cost, it might understandably consider that it will not be able to recover that cost, in terms of prices prevailing at the date of purchase, even after, say, ten or twenty years being the period that the company expects to operate that particular site. An example of such a change is shown in Table 5.5.

5.35 Investment properties other than short leaseholds (20 years or less) are not depreciated. This is a requirement of SSAP 19, 'Accounting for investment properties', and is discussed further in chapter 14.

Table 5.5 – Tesco PLC – Annual Report and Accounts – 26 February 1994

Financial and Business Review (extract)

Accounting for Property We have reviewed our accounting treatment and asset values to align them more closely to the changed market conditions and the recent revisions to our store development programme. The new, more prudent, policies are in line with best practice and will enhance the quality of future reported earnings.

We have made the following changes:

Land We have reviewed the book value of the land at our superstores. We recognise that in many cases the prices we originally paid were higher than they would have been had the land not been used for food superstores and that Tesco therefore paid a premium for the right to operate on those sites. We believe that these premiums were, and still are, appropriate in that they helped to secure a large number of excellent stores with long-term profit flows. The premiums will therefore continue to be carried in our balance sheet.

However, we now consider it prudent to amortise the premiums over the estimated lives of the stores, which we assume to be 25 years. Accordingly, a proportion is charged each year on a straight-line basis against the resulting cash flows throughout the useful life of the investment. We have therefore altered our accounting policies to amortise the premiums, making an annual charge to profits. In 1993/94, this amounted to £32.1m.

An adjustment has also been made for the retrospective amortisation. This totals £59.4m, of which £22.9m relates to 1992/93.

> Having revised the number of stores we intend to open, we have also reviewed our current portfolio of land and our commitments over the next few years – these being at various stages in the planning cycle. We now recognise that a small proportion of the portfolio is surplus to requirements. In the interest of prudent accounting, we have therefore written down by £85m the book value of this land to its estimated net realisable value.
>
> ***Buildings*** We have also reviewed our depreciation policy on freehold and long leasehold properties. Having reassessed the estimated useful lives of our buildings, we have decided to provide depreciation on all freehold and long leasehold buildings at a rate of 2.5% of the cost, per annum, as from February 1993. This adjustment has reduced our 1993/94 profits by £36.4m.

5.36 In FRED 17 the ASB challenges the idea that non-depreciation can be justified on the grounds described in paragraphs 5.24 and 5.25 above. In respect of the residual value argument the FRED states *"...an entity should assume that the residual value of an asset will be materially different from its cost unless it intends to dispose of the asset shortly after purchasing it and it is reasonably expected that the asset can be disposed of within approximately one year of its date of acquisition"*. [FRED 17 para 78].

5.37 Whilst there is some opposition to the stance taken by the ASB in this matter and questioning of the logic of its position, it is fair to say that there has been a convergence of views on the issue. There is perhaps an increasing acceptance that certain assets, or components of assets, that previously have not been depreciated, should be depreciated in future. The standard that is produced from FRED 17 will show whether the ASB relaxes its position or makes clearer the logic behind it so that it can be applied sensibly in practice.

Change in estimate of asset life

5.38 SSAP 12 requires that the useful economic lives of assets should be reviewed regularly and, when necessary, revised. It also notes that, usually, there will be no material distortion of future results or financial position if the net book amount is written off over the revised remaining useful life. It provides, however, that where future results would be materially distorted, the adjustment to accumulated depreciation should be recognised in the accounts, in accordance with FRS 3, 'Reporting financial performance', as an exceptional item.

5.39 An example that illustrates both of these treatments is as follows:

Example

A company purchased an asset on 1 January 19X0 for £100,000, and the asset had an estimated useful life of ten years and a residual value of nil. The company has charged depreciation using the straight-line method at £10,000 per annum. On 1 January 1994 when the asset's net book value is £60,000, the directors review the estimated life and decide that the asset will probably be useful for a further four years and, therefore, the total life is revised to eight years. Where the adjustment does not have a material effect on future results, the company should amend the annual provision for depreciation to charge the unamortised cost (namely, £60,000) over the revised remaining life of four years. Consequently, it should charge depreciation for the next four years at £15,000 per annum.

5.40 Where, however, the future results would be materially distorted, as a result of increasing the annual provision for depreciation, an adjustment to accumulated depreciation should be made in accordance with FRS 3. Referring to the example above, the adjustment to accumulated depreciation that should be made for 19X4 is £10,000, which is calculated as follows:

	£
Cumulative depreciation to 1 January 19X4 (8 year life)	50,000
Cumulative depreciation to 1 January 19X4 (10 year life)	40,000
Adjustment to accumulated depreciation for 19X4	10,000
Current year's charge for 19X4	12,500

In 19X4 the profit and loss account is charged with both the adjustment of £10,000 (shown as an exceptional item) and a revised annual charge of £12,500. In the remaining three years, the depreciation charge in arriving at operating profit will be £12,500 each year.

5.41 The adjustment of £10,000 will be made in arriving at operating profit and will probably be shown, in accordance with FRS 3, as an exceptional item under the appropriate format heading.

5.42 An example of a company which has changed the useful lives of some of its assets and shown the effect as a current year exceptional item is Table 5.6.

Table 5.6 – Ford Motor Company Limited – Annual Report and Accounts – 31 December 1990

NOTES TO THE ACCOUNTS (extract)

3 Operating profit (extract)

The expected useful lives of plant and machinery were re-assessed during the year and were extended, to a maximum of 16 years. It is considered that a material distortion to future results would occur if this change were effected by writing down the present balances over the remaining useful lives. Therefore, under the provisions of Statement of Standard Accounting Practice 12, depreciation has been recalculated from the dates of acquisition of the plant and machinery using the re-assessed asset lives resulting in a credit, in the Company and the group, of £84 million to operating profit in the year.

5.43 An example of a company which has changed the useful lives and is amortising the balance of the assets over the remaining useful life is given in Table 5.7.

Table 5.7 – Cable & Wireless plc – Report and Accounts – 31 March 1993

Financial Overview (extract)

Depreciation

Our depreciation policies are reviewed on a regular basis against the background of rapidly changing technology and competitive developments. In recent years, there have been significant changes in submarine cable technology and markets. This is reflected in significantly lower unit costs and capacity availability. The Group has considerable investments in both analogue and digital cable systems which were being depreciated over a 25 year estimated useful economic life. In the case of analogue cables, revised lives have been established having regard to both known plans to lay digital cables over similar routings and the view that it would be prudent for all existing analogue cables to be fully depreciated by the year 2000. With regard to digital cables, depreciation will be based upon an estimated economic life of 15 years. This takes account of anticipated cost trends and the related cost benefit economics that will influence future cable replacement decisions.

14 Tangible fixed assets (extract)

During the year the Group revised the life of its cables and repeaters to take account of technological changes. The effect of this revision is an increase in the depreciation charge for the year of £11.6m.

5.44 Where asset lives are revised, by far the largest majority of companies choose to amortise the net book value of the assets over the remaining useful lives. It is questionable as to whether adjusting the cumulative effect in the profit and loss account of the year, where future profits would otherwise be distorted, is really the ideal solution to the problem, because such an adjustment invariably distorts the profits of the current year. It might be more appropriate in any revision of SSAP 12 if the prospective write off of net book value was made the only acceptable treatment. This treatment is required by FRS 10 in respect of intangible assets and goodwill. [FRS 10 para 33]. Indeed, this is the proposed treatment in FRED 17 which states that:

> *"The useful economic life of a tangible fixed asset should be reviewed annually and, if expectations are significantly different from previous estimates, the change should be accounted for prospectively over its remaining useful economic life."* [FRED 17 para 74].

The FRED proposes that changes in the estimated residual value of an asset should also be accounted for prospectively over the asset's remaining useful economic life. [FRED 17 para 79].

Change in method of providing depreciation

5.45 If there is a change from one *method* of providing depreciation to another, the unamortised cost of the asset should be written off over the remaining useful life on the new basis, commencing with the period in which the change is made. A change from one method of providing depreciation to another is permitted only if the new method will give a fairer presentation of the enterprise's results and financial position. A change of method does not constitute a change of accounting policy. [SSAP 12 para 21]. FRED 17's proposals are virtually identical to the SSAP 12 requirements. [FRED 17 para 71].

5.46 Consequently, in the example given above (but assuming that the life remains as ten years) the company may decide that, from 1 January 19X4, the sum-of-the-digits method of calculation would give a fairer presentation than the straight-line method. If so, the depreciation charge for 19X4 would be £17,143 (namely, £60,000 × 6/6+5+4+3+2+1), because the asset still has a remaining useful life of six years. SSAP 12 states that where the effect of the change is material, it should be disclosed in the year of change. Furthermore, the reasons for the change should also be disclosed. [SSAP 12 para 26]. Such an alteration is not considered a change in accounting policy and, therefore, a prior period adjustment is not permissible.

Impairments

5.47 The Companies Act requires that a company must make provision if *any* fixed asset (including a fixed asset investment) has diminished in value, and this reduction is expected to be *permanent*. In such a situation, the company must reduce the amount at which it discloses the asset in its financial statements by the amount of this diminution in value. This requirement applies whether or not the asset has a limited useful economic life. [4 Sch 19(2)]. This accords with the treatment required by paragraph 14 of FRS 11, 'Impairment of fixed assets and goodwill', which states:

> *"To the extent that the carrying amount exceeds the recoverable amount, the fixed asset or goodwill is impaired and should be written down."*

5.48 FRS 11 expresses the rule in terms of impairment rather than 'diminution in value'. 'Impairment' is defined as *"...a reduction in the recoverable amount of a fixed asset or goodwill below its carrying amount"*. [FRS 11 para 2]. 'Recoverable amount' is defined in FRS 11 as *"... the higher of net realisable value and value in use"* [FRS 11 para 2]. See also paragraph 5.161 below.

5.49 FRS 11 does not specifically use the term 'permanent diminution' or contrast this with a temporary diminution. This is because, in the case of fixed assets carried on the historical cost basis, the tests in the standard are designed to identify impairments that should be regarded as permanent. Where assets are carried at revaluation the impairment identified using the tests in the standard will still be permanent, but the presentation of the loss will vary according to whether the impairment arises from:

- A clear consumption of economic benefits; or
- Other impairments, for example impairments arising from general changes in prices.

5.50 FRS 11 also introduced the concept of the income-generating unit (IGU). This is defined as *"...a group of assets, liabilities and associated goodwill that generates income that is largely independent of the reporting entity's other income streams. The assets and liabilities include those directly involved in generating the income and an appropriate portion of those used to generate more than one income stream"*. [FRS 11 para 2].

5.51 The concept of an income-generating unit contrasts with the Act's requirements that *"...in determining the aggregate of any item the amount of each individual asset or liability that falls to be taken into account shall be determined separately"*. Whilst the Act, therefore, appears to require each asset or liability to be looked at separately, the standard permits assets and liabilities to be grouped together for the purpose of testing assets for impairment.

5.52 The standard, however, makes it clear that IGUs should be identified by dividing the total income of an entity into as many largely independent income steams as is reasonably practicable. Thus, it aims to ensure that the smallest possible grouping of income-earning assets and liabilities that is independent of the rest of the entity's income is chosen. This aims to come as close to the Act's requirements as is in practice possible, whilst at the same time being practical by recognising that assets that are inter-dependent can only be tested as one unit. Nonetheless, the standard emphasises that the value in use of a fixed asset should be estimated individually where reasonably practicable.

5.53 In addition, where a fixed asset *investment* has suffered a diminution in value that the directors consider to be only *temporary,* the Act permits the company to make provision in respect of that diminution in value. Accordingly, it permits it to reduce the amount at which the investment is disclosed in its financial statements. [4 Sch 19(1)]. It should be stressed that this provision is permissive not mandatory. The Act imposes no obligation on a company to make such provision, but it may do so if the directors think it prudent. There is no equivalent provision for a temporary diminution in value of a fixed asset other than an investment.

Impairment indicators

5.54 FRS 11 requires that a review for impairment of a fixed asset or goodwill should be carried out if events or changes in circumstances indicate that the carrying amount of the fixed asset or goodwill may not be recoverable. [FRS 11 para 8].

5.55 FRS 11 includes a list of circumstances which may indicate that there has been an impairment. These are:

- A current period operating loss in the business in which the fixed asset or goodwill is involved or net cash outflow from the operating activities of that business, combined with either past operating losses or net cash outflows from such operating activities or an expectation of continuing operating losses or net cash outflows from such operating activities.
- A significant decline in a fixed asset's market value during the period.
- Evidence of obsolescence or physical damage to the fixed asset.
- A significant adverse change in:
  - Either the business or the market in which the fixed asset or goodwill is involved, such as the entrance of a major competitor.
  - The statutory or other regulatory environment in which the business operates.
  - Any 'indicator of value' (for example, turnover) used to measure the fair value of a fixed asset on acquisition.
- A commitment by management to undertake a significant reorganisation.
- A major loss of key employees.
- A significant increase in market interest rates or other market rates of return that are likely to affect materially the fixed asset's recoverable amount. [FRS 11 para 10].

To these might be added other indicators, such as a significant devaluation of the currency in which the enterprise derives its cash flows.

5.56 The above indicators should normally trigger a review for impairment where they are relevant to the measurement of the fixed assets or goodwill. In some cases they may not be relevant, for example short-term market interest rates may increase without affecting the rate of return that the market would require on long-term assets. Such increases in short-term rates would not trigger an impairment review assuming that the asset is held for the long-term. Even if it is decided after the review that no impairment has occurred it may still be necessary to review the useful economic lives and residual values of the fixed assets.

5.57 If no such events are identified in relation to tangible fixed assets and there are no other factors that indicate impairment a review is not required (although the rules in FRS 10 relating to goodwill and intangible assets may nonetheless require a review – see chapter 23). However, this should not prevent a review being carried out if there are other factors which indicate an impairment to be present. The standard states that for tangible fixed assets impairments will be an infrequent addition to depreciation, which is reasonable provided that depreciation rates and useful economic lives of assets have been realistically determined.

The impairment review

5.58 FRS 11 includes detailed rules on how impairment tests should be carried out. The review for impairment should consist of comparing the carrying amount of the fixed asset with its recoverable amount. To the extent that the carrying amount exceeds the recoverable amount the fixed asset should be written down. Where fixed assets are reviewed for impairment as part of an IGU the review will take account of the carrying amount of all the assets and liabilities, together with purchased goodwill associated with that unit. The detailed rules for carrying out the impairment review in respect of IGUs are described in chapter 23.

5.59 The application of the detailed rules relating to individual tangible fixed assets that can be assessed individually, rather than as part of an IGU, are considered in the following paragraphs.

5.60 The basic rule is that the tangible fixed asset may not be carried at more than it is recoverable amount. The recoverable amount is the higher of net realisable value and value in use. Net realisable value is defined as *"...the amount at which an asset could be disposed of, less any direct selling cost"*. [FRS 11 para 2]. Value in use is defined as *"...the present value of the future cash flows obtainable as a result of an asset's continued use, including those resulting from its ultimate disposal"*. [FRS 11 para 2].

5.61 To calculate net realisable value reference may be made to market value, where there is an active market. Whilst an active market exists, for example, in second-hand cars and many types of property, it may not exist for large plant or specialised buildings. Where no active market exists and, therefore, net realisable value cannot be ascertained the recoverable amount is determined by reference to value in use alone. [FRS 11 para 16].

5.62 If net realisable value is found to be lower than the carrying amount of the asset, it should not automatically be written down to that value. This is because recoverable amount is the higher of net realisable value and value in use. Therefore, in this situation, it first has to be determined whether value in use is higher than net realisable value. If it is then the impairment write-down, if any, is calculated by reference to value in use.

5.63 In calculating net realisable value direct selling costs are deducted. Such costs include, for instance, legal costs and stamp duty or indeed costs of removing a sitting tenant before selling a building. However, they do not include costs associated with reducing or reorganising the business, such as costs of making staff redundant, before selling a factory building. [FRS 11 para 23].

5.64 To calculate value in use it is necessary to calculate the present value of the future cash flows obtainable as a result of the asset's continued use, including those resulting from its ultimate disposal. The FRS states that it is not normally possible to estimate the value in use of an individual fixed asset and that, therefore, value in use will usually have to be estimated in total for groups of assets and liabilities (income-generating units). As stated above these are dealt with in chapter 23, because often the income-generating unit will include goodwill, which must be reviewed for impairment as part of the overall review.

5.65 Where it is possible to estimate the value in use of an individual fixed asset (examples might include an hotel, or a motor vehicle, or indeed a chemical plant) the basic process is the same:

- The expected future cash flows are estimated, based on the most up-to-date budgets and plans that have been formally approved by management. Cash flows beyond the period covered by the formal budgets or plans should normally assume a steady or declining growth rate that does not exceed the long-term average growth rate for the country in which the business operates. Only in exceptional circumstances should:

  - the period before the steady or declining growth rate is assumed extend to more than five years; or

  - the steady or declining growth rate exceed the long-term average growth rate for the country or countries in which the business operates.

[FRS 11 para 36].

- The expected future cash flows should be discounted, using a discount rate which is an estimate of the rate the market would expect on an equally risky investment. The discount rate should exclude the effects of any risk for which the cash flows have been adjusted and should be calculated on a pre-tax basis. [FRS 11 para 41].

5.66 The exceptional circumstances referred to in the first bullet point above, which justify the use of a higher long-term growth rate might, for example, be where:

- the long-term growth rate for the relevant industry is expected to be higher than the relevant country growth rate; and
- the business under review is expected to grow as rapidly as the industry as a whole, taking into account the likelihood of new competitors entering such an industry.

[FRS 11 para 37].

5.67 The discount rate may alternatively be a risk-free rate (that is, a government-bond based rate), provided that the cash flows themselves are adjusted for risk. The important thing is to avoid adjusting both the cash flows and the discount rate for risk as only one of them should be adjusted. [FRS 11 para 45].

5.68 The use of pre-tax cash flows and a pre-tax discount rate means that any taxation is provided in the normal way and is not reflected in the carrying amount of the asset.

5.69 Future cash flows to be taken into account should be estimated for fixed assets in their current condition. They should not include future capital expenditure that will improve the assets in excess of their originally assessed standard of performance or the related future benefits of this future expenditure. [FRS 11 para 38(b)]. Nor should they include future cash outflows or related cost savings or benefits that are expected to arise from a future reorganisation for which provision has not yet been made. [FRS 11 para 38(a)].

Example 1

Calculating the pre-tax rate of return required if only the post-tax rate of return is known.

A fixed tangible asset is purchased at the end of year 1 for £1,000. The required post-tax rate of return is 14%. All the cash flows will be generated at the end of year 2.

The required pre-tax rate of return is the rate of return that will, after tax has been deducted, give the required post-tax rate of return. Because the tax consequences of different cash flows may be different (for example, where the result is a net tax benefit or the taxable cash flows are not proportionate to the pre and post-tax flows) the pre-tax rate of return is not always the post-tax rate of return grossed up by a standard rate of tax.

In this example, however, all the cash flows are taxable and the rate of tax is the same for all the cash flows and is assumed to be 30%. Therefore, the pre-tax rate of return is 20%, illustrated as follows:

Pre-tax cash flows		1,200
Tax at 30% of £1,200	(360)	
Tax relief on cost of asset at 30%	300	
Tax outflow		(60)
After-tax cash flows		£1,140

In this case the value of the asset would be £1,000 whether calculated by discounting the pre-tax cash flows by 20% or by discounting the post-tax cash flows by 14%.

Example 2

Illustration of impairment calculation

The facts are the same as in example 1, except that immediately after acquisition the asset is damaged, as a result of which the expected pre-tax cash flows are reduced from £1,200 to £800. In this example the taxable cash flows are such that a net deferred tax asset is created. As explained in the last example the result is that discounting the pre-tax cash flows by the pre-tax rate of return no longer produces the same result as discounting the post-tax cash flows by the post-tax rate of return.

Pre-tax cash flows (revised)		800
Tax at 30% of £800	(240)	
Tax relief on cost of asset at 30%	300	
Tax inflow		60
After-tax cash flows		£860

In this case £800 discounted at 20% gives £666 for the carrying value of the asset (£800 ÷ 1.20). On an after-tax basis the asset would be £860 ÷ 1.14 or £754. The difference represents deferred tax on the impairment. A deferred tax asset may then be calculated as follows:

£334 (£1,000 – £666) × 30% =	£100

If in the particular circumstances of the company SSAP 15 allows recognition of the deferred tax asset, the total amount recognised in relation to the asset will be:

Carrying value	666
Deferred tax asset	100
	£766

Nevertheless, the asset must be shown at the figure of £666 being the discounted pre-tax cash flows. The deferred tax asset, if recognised, is shown separately.

This does not give the same answer as discounting the after-tax cash flows of £860 by 14% – £754 as explained above. The reason for this is that the deferred tax asset has not been discounted, because discounting of deferred tax is not accepted in the UK. If the deferred tax asset was discounted at the after-tax rate of 14% the figures would be the same as that achieved by discounting the after-tax cash flows:

Carrying value	666
Deferred tax asset £100 ÷ 1.14	88
	£754

5.70 In the above example the impairment was caused by damage to the asset. However, other external factors might equally cause an impairment. If, for instance, the cash flows are receivable in a foreign currency, and there was a devaluation of the currency such that expected cash flows, whilst not reduced, were significantly less in value when translated into the reporting currency, this could give rise to a similar impairment.

5.71 Where the impairment review results in an impairment loss that should be recognised, the loss should be recognised within operating profit in the profit and loss account, where the fixed assets have been carried at historical cost. [FRS 11 para 67]. The loss should be included under the appropriate statutory format heading and disclosed as exceptional if appropriate.

5.72 Impairment losses on revalued assets may be treated differently, depending on whether they arise from a clear consumption of economic benefits or from other impairments such as impairments arising from general changes in prices. Accounting for impairment losses on revalued fixed assets is dealt with below from paragraph 5.184

Example

The following example illustrates how the provisions of FRS 11 may result in the earlier recognition of impairment losses than in the past.

A company carries a fixed asset at £100. The asset has a useful life of 5 years and no residual value. In year 3 major overhaul work will be required costing £20. After assessing future cash inflows and outflows the company determines that the recoverable amount of the fixed asset is £90. In the example discounting and tax are ignored.

On day one the asset is written down to its recoverable amount of £90. The remaining carrying value of £90 is depreciated over the useful life of 5 years, giving an annual depreciation charge of £18. The profit and loss account charges and the depreciation profile are as follows:

	Year 1	Year 2	Year 3	Year 4	Year 5
Fixed asset b/f	100	72	54	36	18
Impairment	(10)	–	–	–	–
	90	72	54	36	18
Depreciation	(18)	(18)	(18)	(18)	(18)
Fixed asset c/f	72	54	36	18	–
Repairs	–	–	(20)	–	–
Total p&l charge	28	18	38	18	18

This is the treatment required by FRS 11. The asset is reviewed for impairment on day one and if total future cash flows do not support the carrying value the asset is written down. Because the cash outflow of £20 for major repairs in year 3 is taken into account the effect on the first year's impairment review is greater than it would otherwise have been. In accordance with FRS 11, when the outflow occurs the asset is not written back up.

This may be contrasted with the situation, prior to FRS 11, where the costs of major overhaul may not have been taken into account in year 1. Had that not been done the asset profile over the five years might have been as follows:

	Year 1	Year 2	Year 3	Year 4	Year 5
Fixed asset b/f	100	80	60	40	20
Depreciation	(20)	(20)	(20)	(20)	(20)
Fixed asset c/f	80	60	40	20	–
Repairs	–	–	(20)	–	–
Total p&l charge	20	20	40	20	20

Contrasting the two approaches, although the total profit and loss charge is £120 in each case, under FRS 11 the charge in year 1 is higher, and in subsequent years it is lower. This emphasises the more prudent approach adopted in the standard.

5.73 Examples of impairments are given in Tables 5.8 and 5.9.

Table 5.8 – Tiphook plc – Annual Report and Accounts – 30 April 1994

Notes to the Financial Statements

2 Exceptional costs and write-offs (extract)

ii) Provisions for permanent diminution in value of operating assets £38.4 million (1993: £nil) Charges are included in respect of anticipated losses on disposal or provisions against the carrying value of certain of the Group's operating assets which are either targeted for early disposal, as a result of the financial circumstances described above, or have suffered a permanent diminution in value. Assets written down are principally those which have remained under-utilised despite the gradually improving economic climate and which although previously considered to be viable in the long-term are now expected to be unprofitable in the short-term due to the continued effects of recession in certain of the Group's markets. The assets have therefore been written down to values which it is estimated can be recovered from operations or disposal. These charges included a writedown totalling £6.1 million in respect of the Rail Division's specialist "Piggyback" intermodal equipment where plans for redeployment following the liquidation of Charterail have not been realised and the future earnings potential is sufficiently uncertain to merit a write down.

Table 5.9 – ASDA Group PLC – Report and Accounts – 30 April 1994

Financial Review (extract)

Exceptional Items

PROPERTY VALUES AND DEPRECIATION:
It is our practice to review regularly and value our store portfolio on a conservative basis, taking the realities of the industry into account. As we predicted, the continuing addition of superstore space, together with increased competition from the new discounters, has moved the market toward saturation. In this environment, ASDA will continue to upgrade its store portfolio and replace compromised stores wherever possible. We have therefore decided to reduce our property values so that older and compromised stores are written down to alternative use value. In consequence, an exceptional charge of £153.9 million has been made, which includes the cost of acquiring related freehold interests. This results in 20% of the store portfolio now being carried at an alternative use value, reflecting our commitment to upgrade the overall quality of our stores.
It is transparently obvious that superstores do not last forever. Therefore, from 1993 onwards, the stores which were not carried at an alternative use value have been depreciated over their estimated economic life. To reflect the lives of the stores the minimum depreciation rate is 2% per annum with 20 of the mostly older stores depreciated at 5% per annum. The resultant additional depreciation charge for the year was £18.4 million. We believe that our accounting treatment for stores is the most conservative in the sector.

Notes to the Accounts (extract)

4. EXCEPTIONAL ITEMS (extract)	1994 £m	1993 £m
Provision for losses and profits on disposal of fixed assets		
Property provision *(note 9)*	(116.3)	-
Provision to acquire freeholds *(note 20)*	(37.6)	-
Provision against investment in The Burwood House Group plc *(note 12)*	(30.0)	-
Profit on disposal of retail properties	5.0	25.9
Profit on disposal of investment in MFI Furniture Group plc	-	71.9
	(178.9)	97.8

9. TANGIBLE FIXED ASSETS (extract)

The Directors have performed a further review of the property portfolio in the current year, identifying an additional number of properties which have limited future economic life and do not form part of the long term trading strategy of the Group. In respect of these properties, the Directors' lower, alternative use valuation has resulted in a reduction in the carrying amount of the Group's properties by £138.4 million.
Of this amount, a permanent diminution in value adjustment of £116.3 million has been charged to the profit and loss account and £22.1 million charged against previous upward revaluations included in the revaluation reserve (note 22).

Reversals of impairments

5.74 The Companies Act requires that where a company has made provision for a diminution in value, but the factors that gave rise to it no longer apply to any extent, then the company must write back the provision to that extent. [4 Sch 19(3)].

5.75 The Act's requirement is expanded and amplified in FRS 11. The standard also requires that the reversal of an impairment loss in respect of a tangible fixed asset or investment should be recognised, but only where the recoverable amount increases because of a change in economic conditions or in the expected use of the asset. [FRS 11 para 56]. This rule is based on the premise that the original impairment is caused by the inability of the asset to generate sufficient returns to recover its carrying amount. Once there is a change in economic conditions or in the expected use of the asset that enables the asset to recover its former carrying amount, the reason for the impairment ceases to apply. Such changes include situations where the recoverable amount increases as a result of further capital investment or a reorganisation, the benefits of which had been excluded from the original measurement of value in use (see para 5.69). The criteria for reversing impairment losses on intangible assets and goodwill are stricter than for other assets (see chapters 14 and 23).

5.76 The standard explains that a change in economic circumstances or expected use giving rise to the reversal of an impairment does not include:

- The passage of time, that is the unwinding of discounted cash flows.

- The occurrence of forecast cash outflows, this is because once the forecast cash outflows have happened they are no longer part of the value in use calculation and the value in use, therefore, increases. [FRS 11 para 58].

5.77 The reason why the two events described in the previous paragraph do not give rise to the reversal of an impairment is because, whilst the value in use admittedly increases, the underlying reasons for the original impairment have not been removed. All that has happened is that time has passed and the expected cash flows have occurred.

5.78 Where an impairment loss has reversed and the fixed asset is held at historical cost, the reversal should be recognised in the current year's profit and loss account up to the amount that it would have been had the original impairment not occurred (that is, after taking account, of course, of normal depreciation). Reversals of impairment losses on revalued assets are dealt with from paragraph 5.207.

5.79 To illustrate these provisions, consider the following example:

Example

The history of a company's fixed assets is as follows:

	Investment in subsidiary £'000	Tangible fixed assets £'000
Cost at 1 January 19X3	10	6
Value at 31 December 19X3	8	5
Value at 31 December 19X4	* 5	* 3
Value at 31 December 19X5	9	4

* only these impairments in value are expected at the time to be permanent. All other diminutions in value have arisen from a general fall in prices.

Ignoring the normal depreciation rules for the purposes of this example, the Act and the standard apply as follows:

- At 31 December 19X3 both the investment and the fixed asset have fallen in value, but this is due solely to a general fall in prices. It is determined, following an impairment review that the recoverable amount of the investment and the fixed asset remain at £10,000 and £6,000 respectively. In these circumstances, the directors *could* (if they wish) write down the amount of the investment in subsidiary to £8,000. (However, they could not write down the value of the tangible fixed asset to £5,000 under the historical cost rules. This is because the Act allows tangible fixed assets to be written down in value only in circumstances where the diminution in value is expected to be *permanent*.) Also, in terms of FRS 11, there has been no impairment of the fixed asset.

- At 31 December 19X4 a change in economic circumstances has occurred which leads the directors to believe that the recoverable amounts of the investment and the fixed asset have fallen to £5,000 and £3,000 respectively. Accordingly, the directors must write down the amount of the investment in subsidiary to £5,000 (whether or not they wrote it down to £8,000 at 31 December 19X3). In addition, they *must* write down the value of the tangible fixed asset to £3,000. This is because the fall in value of each of them is expected to be *permanent*, and because, in terms of FRS 11 there has been an impairment loss.

- At 31 December 19X5, due to a further change in economic circumstances the recoverable amounts have been restored to £9,000 and £4,000 respectively and the reasons for the original impairment have disappeared. Therefore, the directors must write back £4,000 in respect of the investment in subsidiary and £1,000 in respect of the tangible fixed asset. This is because the reasons that gave rise to the provision for diminution in value/impairment loss on each of them have ceased to apply to that extent. Had the increase in the recoverable amount occurred only because of the passage of time (unwinding of discount) or because forecast cash outflows had occurred, the impairment losses could not be written back, because the reasons for the original impairment would not have ceased to apply.

Disclosure

5.80 The Companies Act requires that where a company has made any provision for diminution in value, or has written back any provision for diminution in value, it must disclose the amounts involved (either in the profit and loss account or in the notes to the financial statements). [4 Sch 19]. The amounts to be disclosed are:

- Provisions made in respect of the permanent diminution in value of fixed assets (see para 5.47). [4 Sch 19(2)].

- Provisions made in respect of the temporary diminution in value of fixed asset investments (see para 5.53). [4 Sch 19(1)].

- Amounts written back to the extent that the circumstances that gave rise to the provisions no longer apply (see para 5.74). [4 Sch 19(3)].

5.81 The amounts disclosed must be split between the three headings, but amounts that fall within the same heading may be aggregated. [4 Sch 19]. To illustrate this, consider the following example:

Example

In the financial year in question, the following events occurred:

- The company wrote down a building by £15,000 and a machine by £7,000, because they had both fallen in value and the fall was expected to be permanent.
- The company wrote down an investment in a subsidiary company and a long-term investment by £20,000 and £5,000 respectively, because they had temporarily fallen in value.
- The company wrote back to cost an overseas investment that it had previously written down by £3,000, because the circumstances that gave rise to the previous write-down had ceased to apply.

In such circumstances, the aggregate amounts the company must disclose are:

(a)	Provisions made in respect of a *permanent* fall in value of fixed assets	£22,000
(b)	Provisions made in respect of a *temporary* fall in value of fixed asset investments	£25,000
(c)	Write-back of provisions no longer required	£3,000

The amounts in (a) and (b) may not be aggregated together or reduced by the amount in (c).

5.82 Impairment losses (which normally will be the same as the Act's definition of permanent diminutions in value) that are recognised in the profit and loss account should be included within operating profit under the appropriate statutory format heading and disclosed as an exceptional item if appropriate. Disclosure of impairment losses on revalued assets is dealt with in paragraphs 5.204 and 5.205

5.83 Reversals of impairment losses should be disclosed in the same way as described in paragraphs 5.80 and 5.81 above. In addition, the reasons for the reversal should be disclosed, including any changes in the assumptions upon which calculation of recoverable amount is based. [FRS 11 para 70].

5.84 The discount rate applied to cash flows should be disclosed where the impairment loss is measured by reference to value in use. If a risk-free discount rate is used, some indication of the risk adjustments made to the cash flows should be given. [FRS 11 para 69].

5.85 For the five years following each impairment review, where recoverable amount has been based on value in use, the cash flows achieved should be compared with those forecast. If the cash flows achieved show that an impairment loss should have been recognised in previous periods, that loss should be recognised in the current period, unless it has already reversed. Where an impairment loss would have been recognised in a previous period had forecasts of future cash flows been more accurate, but the impairment has since reversed and the reversal is permitted to be recognised by FRS 11, the impairment now identified and its subsequent reversal should be disclosed. [FRS 11 para 71].

5.86 Where, in measuring value in use, the period before a steady or declining growth rate is assumed extends to more than five years, the financial statements should disclose the length of the longer period and the circumstances justifying it. [FRS 11 para 72].

5.87 Where, in the measurement of value in use, the long-term growth rate used has exceeded the long-term average growth rate for the country or countries in which the business operates, the financial statements should disclose the growth rate assumed and the circumstances justifying it. [FRS 11 para 73].

5.88 In the fixed assets note, impairment losses should be disclosed as follows:

- For assets held at historical cost, the impairment loss should be included within the cumulative depreciation. The cost of the asset should not be reduced.

- For revalued assets held at market value (that is, existing use value or open-market value) the impairment loss should be included within the revalued carrying amount and not shown within any cumulative depreciation.

- For revalued assets held at depreciated replacement cost, an impairment loss charged to the profit and loss account should be included within cumulative depreciation. The revalued carrying amount of the asset should not be reduced. An impairment loss charged to the statement of total recognised gains and losses should be deducted from the revalued carrying amount of the asset. [FRS 11 para 68].

5.89 Any impairment losses recognised when FRS 11 is implemented for the first time are not the result of a change in accounting policy and should be recognised in accordance with the requirements of the standard and should not be treated as prior period adjustments. [FRS 11 para 75].

Current assets

5.90 In general, current assets are to be shown at the lower of purchase price or production cost (see paras 5.92 to 5.105) and net realisable value. [4 Sch 22, 23(1)]. For example, debtors should be stated after any provision for bad and doubtful debts. For this purpose, current assets are defined as any assets that are not intended for use on a continuing basis in a company's activities. [Sec 262(1)].

5.91 Where a company has written down the value of a current asset to its net realisable value, but the circumstances that gave rise to the write-down cease to apply to any extent (that is, the net realisable value becomes greater than the amount to which the asset was written down), the company must write back the amount of the write-down to that extent. [4 Sch 23(2)]. This means that even where an asset regains only part of its value, the company must write it back to that extent.

Purchase price and production cost of assets

5.92 The Act contains a definition of purchase price, and states how the amount to be shown in the accounts in respect of an asset's purchase price or production cost is to be determined.

5.93 Purchase price, in relation to an asset of a company or any raw materials or consumables used in the production of such an asset, is defined as including any consideration (whether in cash or otherwise) given by the company in respect of that asset or those materials or consumables, as the case may be. [Sec 262(1)].

5.94 The purchase price of an asset (as so defined) is ascertained by adding to the actual price the company paid for the asset any expenses that were incidental to its acquisition. [4 Sch 26(1)]. These incidental expenses include, for example, the expenses that the company had to incur in order to get the asset to its present location and into its present condition.

5.95 The amount to be shown as the production cost of an asset is ascertained by adding the following amounts:

- The purchase price of the raw materials and consumables the company used in producing the asset.
- The direct costs of production the company incurred (excluding distribution costs in the case of current assets).
- Other costs may be included as follows:
    - A reasonable proportion of indirect overheads, to the extent that they relate to the period of production.
    - Interest on any capital the company borrowed in order to finance the production of that asset, to the extent that it relates to the period of production. Where such interest has been included in the production cost, the fact that it has been included and its amount must be stated in the notes to the financial statements.

[4 Sch 26(2)-(4)].

5.96 The Act states that *"...in the case of current assets distribution costs may not be included in production costs"*. [4 Sch 26(4)]. A company should not include external distribution costs such as those relating to the transfer of goods from a sales depot to an external customer. It may, however, include a proportion of the costs that a company incurs in distributing goods from its factory to its sales depot in the valuation. SSAP 9 requires that the costs the company incurs in bringing the goods to their present location and condition should be included in the stocks valuation. [SSAP 9 para 17].

5.97 When determining the purchase price or the production cost of their stocks and other fungible items, companies may apply special rules. These rules are considered in chapter 17.

5.98 FRED 17, 'Measurement of tangible fixed assets', whilst it has yet to become a standard, contains some useful further guidance on the types of cost that might be regarded as qualifying for capitalisation as 'incidental expenses'. These include:

- Acquisition costs (such as stamp duty).
- The cost of site preparation and clearance.
- Initial delivery and handling costs.
- Installation costs.
- Professional fees (such as legal, architects' and engineers' fees).

5.99 The FRED also identifies expenditure that should not be included. For example:

- Administrative and other general overheads, unless they can be reasonably attributed to the purchase of the asset or bringing it to its working condition (that is, such costs would be included only when they would have been avoided if there had been no expenditure on the asset).

- Abnormal costs arising from inefficiencies (such as costs relating to design errors, industrial disputes, idle capacity, wasted materials, labour or other resources and production delays).

5.100 Incremental borrowing costs arising from inefficiencies should be excluded from cost. Other costs such as operating losses that occur because a revenue activity has been suspended during the construction of a tangible fixed asset should also be excluded, because they are not directly attributable to bringing the asset into working condition for its intended use.

5.101 In addition, intra-group profits or losses should be excluded from cost in the consolidated financial statements.

5.102 The FRED states that costs associated with a start-up or commissioning period should be included in the cost of a tangible fixed asset only where the asset is available for use but incapable of operating at normal levels without such a start-up or commissioning period.

5.103 A distinction is drawn between a commissioning period for plant, where the plant cannot yet operate at normal levels, and a start-up period, where plant can operate at normal levels, but it is not doing so because demand has not yet built up. The costs of an essential commissioning period, as in the former case, are capitalised, whilst the machinery is run in and equipment is tested. In the latter case, where the asset is ready for use, but demand has not yet built up, costs should not be capitalised.

5.104 Another type of cost not specifically mentioned in the FRED, but sometimes put forward as a candidate for capitalisation, is the cost of training operatives for new machinery or computer equipment. Such costs should not be capitalised as operatives may leave at short notice and training costs are not part of the purchase price or production cost of an asset.

5.105 The FRED states that capitalisation of costs should take place only during the period in which the activities necessary to bring the asset into use are in progress. Thus, capitalisation should cease when the fixed asset is complete and starts to be used in, or is available for use in, commercial production. The example is given of development properties where the FRED states that capitalisation should cease with the end of the production period, even if the properties are not fully let.

Inclusion of interest in purchase price or production cost

5.106 Views differ on whether borrowing costs should be included in the production cost of an asset or whether they should be expensed as incurred. Some regard such costs as forming part of the cost of the particular asset with which they can be either directly or indirectly identified. Others regard them as essentially period costs that should be charged to income regardless of how the borrowing is applied. As mentioned in paragraph 5.95 above, the Act permits both treatments.

5.107 FRED 17 gives useful guidance on the issue and a description of the main features of the guidance is given below.

5.108 Borrowing costs are defined in FRED 17 as *"Interest and other finance costs incurred by an entity"*.

5.109 Whilst the FRED is silent on whether or not foreign currency exchange differences on funds borrowed to finance construction of a fixed asset are included in borrowing costs, the international accounting standard IAS 23, 'Borrowing costs', states that such exchange differences are included in borrowing costs to the extent that they are regarded as an adjustment to interest costs. In addition, SSAP 20, 'Foreign currency translation', suggests that exchange gains or losses from financing should be disclosed as part of interest payable and similar charges. Consequently, such borrowing costs may be capitalised if the other criteria for capitalisation are complied with.

Example

A property company is building a shopping centre. It finances the development by taking out a US dollar loan. There is an exchange loss at the year end. This amount can be capitalised as part of the cost of the building, but only to the extent that it is regarded as an adjustment to interest. However, care should be taken to ensure that capitalisation does not take the costs of construction above the asset's net realisable value.

5.110 The arguments for and against capitalisation of borrowing costs are set out in the 'The development of the FRED' section of FRED 17. The conclusion reached is that the arguments for and against are not conclusive and that enterprises should be permitted to choose whether or not to capitalise borrowing costs on fixed assets that take a substantial period of time to bring into service. Once a policy has been selected it should be applied consistently.

5.111 By contrast the benchmark treatment in IAS 23 requires that borrowing costs should be recognised as an expense in the period in which they are incurred. [IAS 23 para 7]. It permits as an alternative treatment that borrowing costs should be recognised as an expense in the period in which they are incurred except to the extent that they are capitalised in accordance with the standard. [IAS 23 para 10]. The standard, as part of the alternative treatment, states that borrowing costs that are directly attributable to the acquisition, construction or production of a qualifying asset should be capitalised as part of the cost of that asset. [IAS 23 para 11]. A qualifying asset is an asset that necessarily takes a substantial period of time to get ready for its intended use or sale. [IAS 23 para 4]. FRED 17 contains a similar requirement that borrowing costs must be directly attributable. [FRED 17 para 16].

5.112 FRED 17 deals with the question of when capitalisation of borrowing costs is to begin and when it should cease. It states:

> *"Where borrowing costs are capitalised, capitalisation should commence when:*
>
> *(a) borrowing costs are being incurred; and*
> *(b) expenditures for the asset are being incurred; and*
> *(c) activities that are necessary to get the asset ready for use are in progress."*
>
> [FRED 17 para 21].

> *Capitalisation of borrowing costs should cease when substantially all the activities necessary to get the asset ready for use are complete.*
> [FRED 17 para 25].
>
> *Capitalisation of borrowing costs should be suspended during extended periods in which active development is interrupted.*
> [FRED 17 para 23].
>
> *When construction of an asset is completed in parts and each part is capable of being used while construction continues on other parts, capitalisation of borrowing costs relating to a part should cease when substantially all the activities that are necessary to get that part ready for use are completed."*
> [FRED 17 para 25].

5.113 The proposals in FRED 17 are substantially the same as the requirements of IAS 23. The explanatory material also makes it clear that borrowing costs should not be capitalised while land acquired for building purposes is held without any development activity taking place. In addition, where the development activities necessary to get an asset ready for its use are interrupted, costs of holding partially completed assets do not qualify for capitalisation during the interruption.

5.114 Both IAS 23 and FRED 17 are consistent with the requirement in the Companies Act 1985 that *"...there may be included in the production cost of an asset ...interest on capital borrowed to finance the production of that asset, to the extent that it accrues in respect of the period of production"*. [4 Sch 26(3)].

5.115 SSAP 9 on stocks and long-term contracts states that in ascertaining the cost of long-term contracts it is not normally appropriate to include interest on borrowed money. However, where sums borrowed can be identified as financing specific long-term contracts, SSAP 9 states that it may be appropriate to include such related interest in cost, in which circumstances the inclusion of interest and the amount included should be disclosed in a note. [SSAP 9 Appendix 1 para 21].

5.116 FRED 17 gives guidance on how borrowing costs to be capitalised should be determined. If a particular borrowing can be specifically associated with expenditure on constructing or producing the asset, the borrowing costs capitalised should be determined on the basis of the actual borrowing costs incurred on that borrowing less any investment income on the temporary investment of those borrowings. Where funds are borrowed generally and used for financing the construction or production of the asset, the amount of borrowing costs eligible for capitalisation should be determined by applying a capitalisation rate to the expenditure on that asset. The capitalisation rate should be the weighted average of the borrowing costs applicable to the borrowings of the enterprise that are outstanding during the period other than borrowings made specifically for the purpose of constructing or producing an asset. The 'expenditure' on the asset is the weighted average carrying amount of the asset during the period including borrowing costs previously capitalised. The guidance in IAS 23 is similar. An example of disclosure of the accounting policy for capitalisation is given in Table 5.10.

Table 5.10 – MEPC plc – Report and Financial Statements – 30 September 1997

Notes to the accounts (extract)

Accounting policies (extract)

An amount equivalent to interest and other outgoings less rental income attributable to properties in course of development is transferred to the cost of properties. For this purpose the interest rate applied to funds provided for property development is arrived at by reference, where appropriate, to the actual rate payable on borrowings for development purposes and, in regard to that part of the development cost financed out of general funds, to the average rate paid on funding the assets employed by the Group.

5.117 A limit is placed by both FRED 17 and IAS 23 on the amount of borrowing costs that may be capitalised. The amount should not exceed the total amount of borrowing costs incurred by the enterprise in that period. In consolidated financial statements the limitation applied is the consolidated amount of borrowing costs because the Act requires consolidated financial statements to be prepared so far as possible as if they are the financial statements of a single company. The limitation on capitalisation of borrowing costs, described above, is sometimes objected to by companies, which have little borrowings, but which are using cash resources to finance the construction of fixed assets. The argument put forward is that cash being used to finance the construction could otherwise have been used to earn interest and it is therefore fair to attribute a notional borrowing cost representing the deprival cost of the cash employed in financing the construction of the asset. FRED 17 does not accept this argument and acknowledges in the 'Development of the FRED' section that the inability to capitalise notional interest was one of the reasons for not requiring compulsory capitalisation of interest. A further reason for rejecting the argument is that the Act refers to 'interest' and not to 'notional interest'. [4 Sch 26(3)(b)].

5.118 Some groups of companies with little or no borrowings have subsidiaries that are engaged in constructing assets. In such circumstances, it is possible for the subsidiary to capitalise interest in its own financial statements on finance provided by another group company, even though at the consolidated financial statements level such intra-group interest must be eliminated, because the group as a whole has not incurred interest on those borrowings.

5.119 IAS 23 does not deal with the question of whether interest should be capitalised gross or net of tax relief. In practice, each treatment has its supporters. The argument for capitalising net of tax relief is based on the matching concept which suggests that the tax relief should be treated in the same way as the interest. If this is not done, the profit and loss account reflects the benefit of the tax relief without at the same time suffering a charge for interest. The argument for gross capitalisation is that all other costs are capitalised gross, so there is no reason for interest capitalisation to be any different. The requirements of the Stock Exchange are that listed companies should disclose the amount of interest capitalised in the year together with an indication of the amount and treatment of the related tax relief. [LR 12.43(c)]. FRED 17 proposes that interest should be capitalised gross. [FRED 17 para 17]. An example of capitalisation gross of tax and the associated disclosures is given in Table 5.11.

Table 5.11 – Argyll Group PLC – Annual Report and Accounts – 2 April 1994

Statement of Accounting Policies (extract)

Interest costs relating to the financing of freehold and long leasehold developments are capitalised at the weighted average cost of the related borrowings up to the date of completion of the project.

5.0 **Net interest (payable)/receivable**	**1994 £m**	1993 £m
Interest payable:		
Loans repayable by instalments within five years	**(3.4)**	(4.1)
Bank overdrafts and loans repayable other than by instalments within five years	**(12.9)**	(22.9)
Loans not wholly repayable within five years	**(16.4)**	(5.4)
Convertible bonds	**-**	(3.2)
	(32.7)	(35.6)
Interest capitalised on freehold and long leasehold developments	**16.5**	16.8
	(16.2)	(18.8)
Interest receivable on money market investments and deposits	**12.9**	44.4
	(3.3)	25.6

The interest element of charges payable under finance leases amounted to £5.8 million (1993-£6.1 million).

Fixed assets (extract)

11.1.3 Interest capitalised on freehold and long leasehold developments included in additions during the year amounted to £16.5 million (1993-£16.8 million). The cumulative amount of interest capitalised in the total cost above amounts to £83.4 million (1993-£67.4 million).

8.0 **Tax on profit on ordinary activities (extract)**

The principal reasons for the lower than standard tax charge are tax relief for capital allowances on fixed assets exceeding related depreciation by £8.1 million (1993-£17.5 million) and tax relief for interest capitalised on freehold and long leasehold developments of £5.5 million (1993-£5.5 million).

5.120 FRED 17 proposes disclosure of the following in financial statements:

- The enterprise's policy concerning the capitalisation of borrowing costs on fixed assets.
- The amount of borrowing costs capitalised during the period.
- The amount of borrowing costs recognised in the profit and loss account during the period.
- The capitalisation rate used to determine the amount of capitalised borrowing costs.

[FRED 17 para 27].

5.121 The disclosure requirements in IAS 23 are substantially the same as those of FRED 17:

- The accounting policy adopted for borrowing costs.
- The amount of borrowing costs capitalised during the period.
- The capitalisation rate used to determine the amount of borrowing costs eligible for capitalisation.

5.122 Whilst the FRED 17 disclosures are not yet required in the UK, there are other limited disclosures that must be made. Where borrowing costs are capitalised the Act requires disclosure in the notes of the fact that interest is included in determining the production cost of particular assets and of the amount of interest so included. [4 Sch 26(3)]. In addition, as stated in paragraph 5.83 above, the Stock Exchange requires listed companies to disclose the amount of interest capitalised in the year together with an indication of the amount and treatment of the related tax relief. In practice, many companies also disclose their accounting policy where they capitalise interest.

Subsequent expenditure

5.123 FRED 17 proposes that, as a general rule, subsequent expenditure on a tangible fixed asset should be written off to the profit and loss account as incurred. Such expenditure is generally of a repairs and maintenance nature and does not improve the asset beyond the standard of performance originally expected of it.

5.124 There are two exceptions to this general rule. In each of the following circumstances subsequent expenditure should be capitalised:

- Where a component of a tangible asset that has been treated as a separate asset (see paragraph 5.22 above), and depreciated over its individual useful economic life, is replaced or restored.

- Where the subsequent expenditure provides an enhancement of economic benefits of the asset in excess of the originally assessed standard of performance.

5.125 Examples of components of an asset that might have different lives from the rest of an asset, and thus might be depreciated separately, are the roof of a building and the lining of a blast furnace. Decisions on whether or not to identify separate components of an asset in this way will depend on the degree of regularity in the replacement expenditure required and the materiality of the component.

5.126 Examples given in FRED 17 of subsequent expenditure that results in the enhancement of economic benefits include:

- Modification of an item of plant to extend its useful life or to increase its capacity.

- Upgrading machine parts to achieve a substantial improvement in the quality of output.

- Installation of new production processes enabling a substantial reduction in previously assessed operating costs.

5.127 The FRED makes clear that provisions for future maintenance should not be made in advance. The argument in the FRED revolves around the question of whether such future maintenance constitutes a liability of the entity. The FRED concludes that even where there is a legal or constructive obligation the appropriate accounting treatment is to recognise depreciation to take account of the actual consumption of the asset's economic benefits. Thus, for example, where a separate component of an asset wears out more quickly than the rest, it is depreciated over a shorter period and subsequent expenditure on restoring the component is then capitalised. This replaces the previous general practice of depreciating such components over the same period as the rest of the asset, but providing in advance for the maintenance/replacement of the component.

Unknown purchase price or production cost

5.128 In certain circumstances, an asset's purchase price or production cost is to be taken as the value the company ascribed to the asset in the earliest available record of its value that the company made on or after it either acquired or produced the asset. These circumstances are where there is no record of either of the following:

- The actual purchase price or the actual production cost.
- Any price, any expenses or any costs that are relevant for determining the purchase price or the production cost.

This exemption applies also where the relevant record is available, but it could be obtained only with unreasonable expense or delay. [4 Sch 28].

5.129 Where a company has determined, for the first time, an asset's purchase price or production cost according to its earliest known value, the company must disclose this fact in the notes to its financial statements. [4 Sch 51(1)].

Other items

Assets shown at fixed amounts

5.130 Where certain conditions are satisfied, tangible fixed assets and raw materials and consumables can be shown at a fixed quantity and at a fixed value. These conditions (all of which must be satisfied) are as follows:

- The assets must be assets of a kind that are constantly being replaced.
- Their overall value must not be material to the assessment of the company's state of affairs.
- Their quantity, value and composition must not be subject to material variation.

[4 Sch 25].

5.131 Where this provision applies, all subsequent purchases of the assets in question will be charged directly against profit. This provision enables companies to include (for example) loose tools in either tangible fixed assets or stocks, at a fixed quantity and at a fixed value. However, SSAP 9 says that when valuing stocks, a company must choose a method that produces the fairest practicable approximation to actual cost. It says that base stock, which is in effect what this approach is, would not usually bear such a relationship. [SSAP 9 appendix 1 para 12]. Consequently, although permitted by law in the circumstances described above, the base stock method of valuing stocks is not usually allowed by SSAP 9.

Excess of money owed over value received

5.132 Where the amount that a company owes a creditor exceeds the value of the consideration it received in the transaction that gave rise to the liability, the company *may* treat the amount of the difference as an asset. [4 Sch 24(1)]. If it does so, however, it must write off the amount it shows as an asset by reasonable amounts each year, and it must write off the asset fully before the date on which the debt becomes due for payment. [4 Sch 24(2)(a)].

5.133 Any amount the company includes under assets under this provision must be disclosed separately either on the face of the balance sheet or in the notes to the financial statements. [4 Sch 24(2)(b)].

5.134 Prior to the introduction of FRS 4, 'Capital Instruments', an example of the application of this provision was the accounting treatment of 'deep-discounted bonds', where the discount was sometimes treated as an asset, with the nominal value of the debt being shown as a creditor. This treatment is not now permitted by FRS 4 which requires debt to be shown initially at the amount of the net proceeds.

Transfers from current assets to fixed assets

5.135 During 1992, the issue of transfers from current assets to fixed assets was addressed by the UITF. In UITF Abstract 5, 'Transfers from current assets to fixed assets', the UITF took the view that any diminution in value of a current asset that had taken place before a transfer of that asset to fixed assets, should be charged in the profit and loss account. In other words the asset should be transferred at the lower of cost and net realisable value. The Abstract was effective for financial statements for accounting periods ending on or after 23 December 1992 with comparatives being adjusted where applicable.

5.136 There is at present no equivalent guidance regarding transfers from fixed assets to current assets. It would seem sensible, however, for fixed assets to be transferred to current assets at the lower of cost and net realisable value, as this is the normal basis for recording current assets. Any previous revaluation surpluses on the fixed assets would, therefore, have to be reversed through the statement of total recognised gains and losses on the transfer. In cases where the Act and accounting standards permit certain current assets, such as investments, to be carried at current cost, (see paras 5.140 and 5.145 below) the transfer could be made at current cost rather than the lower of cost and net realisable value.

Alternative accounting rules

5.137 Paragraphs 29 to 34 of Schedule 4 to the Act set out the rules companies may apply in arriving at the amounts (other than cost) at which they may measure items in their financial statements. These amounts may reflect changes in the value of the assets (for example, the increase in the value of property) that may arise as a result of general or specific price increases.

5.138 These provisions of Schedule 4 are purely permissive in character. That is to say, provided that companies comply with certain conditions, they may (but are not obliged to) adopt any of the alternative accounting rules set out in the Act.

5.139 Legally, companies may adopt all or any of these rules. So, for example, a company could include plant and machinery in its balance sheet at current cost and include every other item on an historical cost basis. However, although it might be reasonable for a company to include certain assets at a valuation, if it mixed the historical cost rules and the alternative accounting rules indiscriminately it might produce meaningless financial statements. Therefore, the overriding requirement for 'truth and fairness' precludes this approach.

5.140 The alternative accounting rules that the Act permits companies to follow when preparing their financial statements are as follows:

- Intangible fixed assets may be stated at their current cost. [4 Sch 31(1)]. This does not apply to goodwill, which can be shown only at the value of the consideration for which it was acquired (less any amounts by which it has been amortised or written down for impairment).

- Tangible fixed assets may be stated either at their market value on the date when they were last valued or at their current cost. [4 Sch 31(2)]. Where a policy of revaluing assets is adopted, however, accounting standards recommend that such valuations should be kept up to date. [SSAP 12 para 5]. For example, many companies state in their accounting policies that they revalue their properties on a revolving basis to cover all properties once in, say, five years. However, there is only mixed compliance with this recommendation and other companies do not revalue on a regular basis and instead carry their assets at valuations which are out of date. FRED 17, if converted to a standard, will require valuations to be kept up-to-date.

- Fixed asset investments may be shown either at their market value on the date on which they were last valued or at a value determined on a basis that the directors think appropriate in the light of the company's circumstances. However, if a company adopts the latter approach, it must state, in the notes to its financial statements, particulars of the method it has adopted, and the reasons for adopting it. [4 Sch 31(3)]. A value determined on a basis that the directors thought appropriate could, for example, include the valuation of unlisted investments on either a net asset basis or an earnings basis. However, it would not be sufficient for the notes merely to state that unlisted investments are included 'at the directors' valuation'.

- Current asset investments may be stated at their current cost. [4 Sch 31(4)].

  A practice normally adopted by dealing companies is to value readily marketable current asset investments at market value and any profit or loss arising on the valuation is taken to profit and loss account *(marking to market)*. Certain commodity stocks may also be 'marked to market'. Marking to market is discussed under 'Current Assets' from paragraph 5.221.

- Stocks may be stated at their current cost. [4 Sch 31(5)]. (SSAP 9 requires stocks to be included at the lower of cost and net realisable value in historical cost financial statements, but permits valuation at current cost in current cost financial statements).

5.141 FRED 17 proposes that a policy of revaluation for tangible fixed assets should remain optional. If a policy of revaluation is adopted, however, valuations must be kept up-to-date. For non-specialised properties, FRED 17 proposes that there should be either:

- a full valuation at least every five years with an interim valuation in year three and interim valuations in years one, two and four where there has been a material change in value; or

- a full valuation of the portfolio on a rolling basis over five year cycles and an interim valuation of the remaining four-fifths of the portfolio where there has been a material change in value. This approach is appropriate only where the portfolio either consists of a broadly similar range of properties, which are likely to be affected by the same market factors, or can be divided on a continuing basis into five groups of a broadly similar spread.

5.142 FRED 17 proposes that full valuations should be conducted either by an external valuer or by a qualified internal valuer with a review by an external valuer.

5.143 The exposure draft proposes that where a tangible fixed asset is revalued, all the fixed assets of the same class should be revalued.

5.144 The bases of valuation proposed in FRED 17 are the same as those described below under 'Bases of valuation' from paragraph 5.146 onwards. The FRED proposes that:

- Non-specialised properties should be valued on the existing use basis. Where the open-market value differs significantly from existing use basis valuation the open-market value and the reasons for the difference should be disclosed.

- Specialised properties should be valued on the depreciated replacement cost basis.

- Investment properties and properties surplus to an entity's requirements should be valued on the open-market value basis.

5.145 The Act does not define 'current cost'. Therefore, where a company chooses to show some assets at their current cost under the alternative accounting rules, their value should normally be determined, in the absence of any agreed financial reporting standard, by considering the guidance given in the ASC's handbook, 'Accounting for the effects of changing prices'. Current cost (or value to the business), as defined by the handbook, is the lower of the asset's current replacement cost and its recoverable amount. Recoverable amount is the higher of the asset's net realisable value and the amount recoverable from its future use. Recoverable amount is defined in paragraph 5.161 below and is discussed further in chapter 23. This is illustrated diagrammatically below. There may in certain circumstances, however, be good reasons for choosing some other method of valuation. For example, properties would generally be valued in accordance with The Royal Institution of Chartered Surveyors' Appraisal and Valuation Manual.

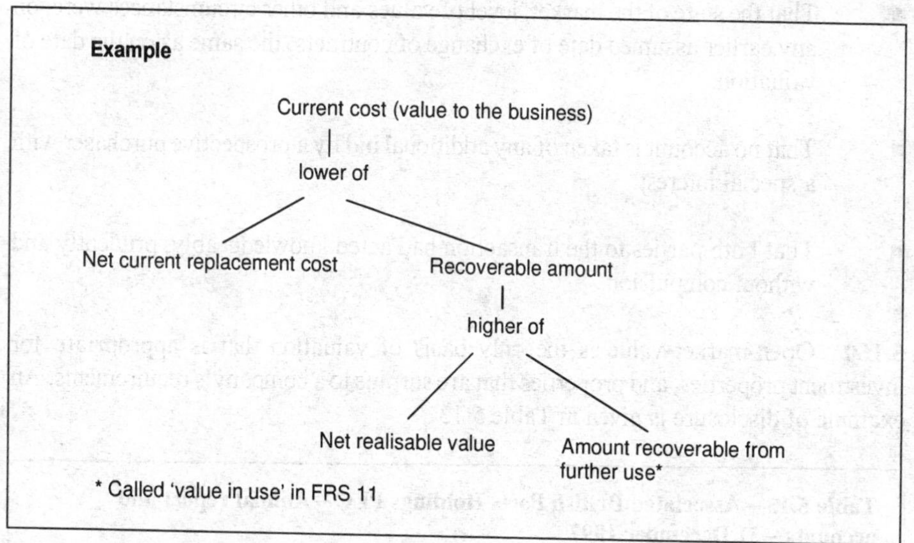

Bases of valuation

5.146 The Royal Institution of Chartered Surveyors publishes Practice Statements (PSs) and Guidance Notes that apply to valuations for incorporation in company financial statements and other financial statements which are subject to audit. [PS 1 and 12].

5.147 The PSs prescribe the bases of valuation that are appropriate for the types of asset normally found in company financial statements. These bases of valuation are briefly summarised below.

Open-market value

5.148 Open-market value, not qualified by any reference to existing use or alternative use, implies the value for *any* use to the extent to which that value is reflected in the price obtainable in the open market.

5.149 Open-market value means the best price at which the sale of an interest in property would have been completed unconditionally for cash at the valuation date assuming:

- A willing seller.
- A reasonable period, prior to the date of valuation, for the proper marketing of the interest, for agreement of price and terms and for the completion of the sale.
- That the state of the market, level of values and other circumstances were, on any earlier assumed date of exchange of contracts, the same as on the date of valuation.
- That no account is taken of any additional bid by a prospective purchaser with a special interest.
- That both parties to the transaction had acted knowledgeably, prudently and without compulsion.

5.150 Open-market value is the only basis of valuation that is appropriate for investment properties, and properties that are surplus to a company's requirements. An example of disclosure is given in Table 5.13.

Table 5.13 – Associated British Ports Holdings PLC – Annual report and accounts – 31 December 1997

Notes on the Accounts (extract)

Fixed assets – property (extract)

Investment properties, other than properties in the course of construction, and land at ports held for development and retention have been valued on the basis of open market value in accordance with the Appraisal and Valuation Manual issued by The Royal Institution of Chartered Surveyors. The valuations were carried out as at 31 December 1997 by external valuers Healey & Baker.

Existing use value

5.151 The existing use value reflects the use of the property for the same or similar purposes as hitherto. It ignores any alternative use for the property, any 'hope value' for an alternative use, any value attributable to goodwill and any other possible increase in value due to special transactions, such as a sale and leaseback. This basis should be used for all owner occupied properties. An example of disclosure is given in Table 5.14.

Table 5.14 – Cattles plc – Annual Report and Accounts – 31 December 1995

Notes on the Accounts (extract)

Tangible fixed assets (extract)

The freehold/feuhold and leasehold properties with 50 or more years unexpired owned and or occupied by Cattles plc and its subsidiary undertakings were valued by external valuers, G L Hearn & Partners, Chartered Surveyors as at 31st December 1995 on the basis of "existing use value", except those premises held as investment and surplus to requirements which were valued on the basis of "open market value" in accordance with the *Appraisal & Valuation Manual* of the Royal Institution of Chartered Surveyors.

The total value which includes freehold/feuhold/long leasehold occupied, part occupied and part tenanted, freehold/feuhold/long leasehold held as investment, and freehold/feuhold/long leasehold surplus to requirements was £5,371,750.

5.152 An example of the distinction between the open-market value (unqualified) basis and the existing use basis is where a company operates a factory on the outskirts of a town. The site on which it operates might have a considerably increased value if it were to be sold for redevelopment. In such a case, the financial statements of the company should reflect any valuation on an open-market value for existing use basis, because it is intending to continue to operate the site as a factory, and the additional value that could be obtained from closing the factory and selling the site for redevelopment should not be reflected in the valuation.

5.153 A variation of existing use value is for property *"equipped as an operational entity and to be valued having regard to trading potential"*. [PS 12.6]. This basis applies to land and buildings which invariably change hands in the open-market at prices based directly on trading potential for a strictly limited use.

5.154 Examples of such properties include hotels, private hospitals and nursing homes, public houses, cinemas, theatres, bingo clubs, gaming clubs, petrol filling stations, licensed betting offices and specialised leisure and sporting facilities.

5.155 This basis of valuation includes the value of the trading potential which runs with the property, but should not include any goodwill which has been created by the owner and which would not remain with the property should it be sold.

Open-market value for alternative use

5.156 This basis reflects the prospective use of a property for purposes other than its existing use and should be reported by a valuer where there is a significant difference between the value of a property on an existing use basis and its value on the alternative use basis. In the example above of the factory that would have a substantially higher value if sold for redevelopment, the alternative use value should also be reported by the valuer. This alternative use value does not, however, have to be disclosed in the company's financial statements under current accounting practice even though it would presumably be of considerable interest and relevance to the company's investors.

Depreciated replacement cost

5.157 The Depreciated Replacement Cost (DRC) basis of valuation is used for properties which, due to their specialised nature, are rarely if ever sold on the open-market for single owner occupation for a continuation of their existing use, except as part of a sale of the business. Such specialised properties might include oil refineries, chemical works, buildings which are no more than cladding for special plant and standard buildings of great size in isolated or unusual locations.

5.158 Where there is no means of ascertaining an existing use value of such properties depreciated replacement cost is calculated. For a property this involves estimating the value of land in its existing use and the gross replacement cost of buildings and other site works from which appropriate deductions are made to allow for age, condition and economic or functional obsolescence and other factors which might result in the existing property being worth less than a new replacement.

5.159 Because of the nature of DRC valuations a valuer will qualify all valuations on this basis as being subject to the adequate potential profitability of the business compared with the value of the total assets employed. However, for properties in public ownership, or not occupied primarily for profit, where the test of adequate potential profitability is not available, DRC is expressed as subject to the prospect and viability of the continuance of the occupation and use.

Net current replacement cost

5.160 Where plant and machinery is valued, the basis of valuation is normally value to the business. Value to the business (or value in use) is the lower of net current replacement cost and recoverable amount as dealt with below. Depreciated replacement cost (DRC) referred to above is one method of using net current replacement costs to arrive at the valuation of property where it is not practicable to use existing use value. For plant and machinery the process is similar. Net current replacement cost is calculated by establishing the gross current replacement cost and then depreciating it so as to arrive at a figure that reflects the value attributable to the asset's remaining useful life, taking account of age, condition, obsolescence and other relevant factors, including the expected residual value at the end of the asset's life.

5.161 Where there has been a permanent diminution in value (impairment) of the asset such that the net current replacement cost is above recoverable amount, the value to the business is the higher of the net realisable value and the recoverable amount.

Recoverable amount is defined in PS4 as the capitalised value attributable to the remaining use (if any) of the asset in the business of the company plus its net realisable value. Impairments are discussed further in paragraphs 5.189 to 5.207.

5.162 The above bases of valuation are those most commonly used in financial statements prepared under the modified historical cost convention. For financial statements prepared under the current cost convention the basic model used is value to the business or current cost, which, though used only selectively in the modified historical cost convention as illustrated above, is used comprehensively in current cost accounting. The principal bases used in current cost accounting are:

- Fixed asset properties – open-market value or depreciated replacement cost as appropriate – see paragraphs 5.148 to 5.159 above.
- Plant and machinery – net current replacement cost or recoverable amount (if lower) – see paragraphs 5.160 to 5.161 above.
- Stock – lower of current replacement cost and recoverable amount. In the case of stock, recoverable amount will be its net realisable value.
- Investments – fixed assets at market value and current assets at current replacement cost.

5.163 An example of disclosure of valuation bases used in current cost financial statements is given in Table 5.15.

Table 5.15 – British Gas plc – Annual Report and Accounts – 31 December 1995

Principal accounting policies (extract)

Tangible fixed assets (extract)
Tangible fixed assets are included in the balance sheets at their value to the business. The value to the business has been assessed on the following bases:

a) Current replacement cost
i) land and buildings – periodic valuation by chartered surveyors employed by the Group determined on the basis of open market value for existing use where occupied by the business and open market value where unoccupied by the business or likely to become unoccupied within the near future, excepting specialised properties for which depreciated replacement cost is used. Valuations take into account estimated non-statutory decontamination costs;
ii) distribution mains, services, meters and gas storage – application of calculated average unit replacement costs to the physical lengths or quantities in use;

iii) transmission system and transmission mains – based upon engineering assessments of replacing existing assets; and
iv) exploration and production tangible assets and other tangible fixed assets – indexation of historical costs using appropriate indices, or estimates of replacement cost provided to the Group by third parties.

The assessment of value to the business involves certain estimates being made which are subject to continuing revision.

Stocks
Stocks are valued at historical cost less provision for deterioration and obsolescence. The difference between current replacement cost and historical cost is immaterial.

Disclosure

5.164 The RICS Appraisal and Valuation annual (PS 7) sets out minimum disclosures that should be made when reference is made to a valuation in a company's financial statements. The disclosures include:

- The name and qualification of the valuer or the valuer's organisation and a description of its nature.
- A reference as to whether the valuer is internal, external or independent.
- The date and basis or bases of valuation.
- Confirmation that the valuation has been made in accordance with the RICS Appraisal and Valuation Manual or the extent of and reasons for departure therefrom.
- Where valuation figures are given, the valuation basis and, in full, any special assumptions adopted.
- Where a definition (as distinct from merely the basis or bases of valuation adopted) is included, the whole of the definition.
- Where statements attributed to the valuer, upon the prospect of future growth in rent and/or capital values are made, a statement to the effect that such growth may not occur and that values can fall as well as rise.
- Where the subject property has been valued as a fully equipped operational entity and with regard to its trading potential, a statement to that effect.

5.165 The Appraisal and Valuation Manual includes useful examples of disclosures in Appendix 7 to the Practice Statements. One example where the existing use basis has been used is as follows:

> *"The freehold and leasehold properties occupied by the company were valued by External Valuers, ABC Chartered Surveyors, as at 31 December 19xx, on the basis of Existing Use Value in accordance with the Appraisal and Valuation Manual of The Royal Institution of Chartered Surveyors".*

Actual examples of disclosure are given above in Tables 5.13 and 5.14.

5.166 The disclosure requirements proposed in FRED 17 broadly encompass and expand on those laid down by the RICS and those of the Act, but would be given for each class of revalued assets. The disclosures for each class are:

- The name and qualification of the valuer.
- The basis or bases of valuation.
- The date and amounts of the valuation.
- Where historical cost records are available, the net carrying amount that would have been shown under the historical cost.
- Whether the qualified valuer is internal or external.
- Where there has been no material change in value and, therefore, the valuation has not been updated by an interim valuation as specified in paragraph 5.141 above, a statement that there has been no material change in value.

5.167 In addition, for revalued non-specialised properties FRED 17 proposes that there should be disclosure as follows:

- Whether the valuations are interim valuations or full valuations.
- Where the valuation is an internal valuation, disclosure of the date and amount of the last full valuation.
- Where the rolling valuation method (see para 5.141 above) has been adopted, disclosure of the method.

- Where properties have been valued as fully equipped operational entities and having regard to their trading potential, the carrying value of the properties and a statement to that effect (see para 5.153 above).

5.168 The FRED also proposes that where an entity does not revalue properties as a matter of policy and there is a significant difference between the current value of the properties and their carrying value, this fact and the current value should be disclosed in the financial statements, if the directors think the difference is of such significance that members should be made aware of it. Whilst this merely repeats the existing requirement of Schedule 7 to the Act, which requires similar disclosure in the directors' report, the FRED proposes that the difference should be regarded as significant where:

- The market value of a property is significantly less than its carrying value.
- The property has a significantly more valuable alternative use.

The revaluation reserve

5.169 The Act specifies the following rules that relate to the creation and use of the revaluation reserve:

- Any difference between the amount of any item that a company has determined according to one of the alternative accounting rules, and the amount that the company would have disclosed if it had adhered to the historical cost convention, must be credited or debited (as applicable) to a 'revaluation reserve'. [4 Sch 34(1)].

  In determining the amount of this difference, a company should take account, where appropriate, of any provisions for depreciation or diminution in value that it made otherwise than by reference to the value it determined under the alternative accounting rules. It should also take account of any adjustments of any such provisions that it made in the light of that determination. [4 Sch 34(1)]. This wording seems simply to mean that the figures on the historical cost basis and the figures on the basis of the alternative accounting rules should be compared net of any depreciation. For example, if an asset shown under the historical cost rules at cost of £100 less depreciation of £40 (net carrying amount £60) were revalued to a gross figure of £150 less cumulative depreciation £60 (net revalued amount under the alternative accounting rules £90), the credit to the revaluation reserve should be £30 (that is, £90 – £60).

5.170 When a company values its assets in accordance with the alternative accounting rules, it must:

- Value each asset separately. (It must do this in order to comply with the separate valuation principle contained in paragraph 14 of Schedule 4.)

- Transfer the surplus or deficit that arises on the revaluation of each asset to the revaluation reserve (after allowing for provision for depreciation or diminutions in value made otherwise than by reference to the revalued amount and any adjustments of such provisions made in the light of the revaluation).

- The Act restricts the circumstances in which a company can transfer an amount from the revaluation reserve. It can do this only where one of the following circumstances exists.

  - An amount may be transferred to the profit and loss account if the amount in question was previously charged to that account or represents a realised profit. [4 Sch 34(3)(a)].

  - An amount may be transferred to capital on capitalisation. Capitalisation means applying the amount standing to the credit of the revaluation reserve wholly or partly to paying up unissued shares in the company to be allotted to the company's members as fully or partly paid shares, thereby allowing bonus and scrip issues to be made out of the revaluation reserve. [4 Sch 34(3)(a) as amended by SI 1996/189, 34(3A)].

  Furthermore, it is possible to transfer from the revaluation reserve an amount in respect of the taxation relating to any profit or loss credited or debited to that reserve. [4 Sch 34(3)(b) inserted by SI 1996/189]. This applies for example to the deferred tax arising on a revaluation.

5.171 In addition the revaluation reserve must be reduced to the extent that the amounts transferred to it are no longer necessary for the purpose of the valuation method that the company has adopted. [4 Sch 34(3)(b)]. An example of this would be where an asset with a previous revaluation surplus has been realised. On realisation the surplus should be transferred from the revaluation reserve to the profit and loss account reserve.

5.172 Schedule 4 paragraph 34(3B), which was introduced by the Companies Act 1989, states that the revaluation reserve shall not be reduced except as mentioned above. This means that it is no longer available, for example, to write off goodwill, which companies had sometimes done prior to the 1989 Act. This prohibition does not, however, affect goodwill write offs made before the introduction of the Companies Act 1989. However, for companies that became subsidiaries because of the changes in the definitions in the Companies Act 1989, the provisions of that Act apply and consolidated goodwill is prohibited from being written off to the revaluation reserve.

Following the introduction of FRS 10, which is effective for periods ending on or after 23 December 1998, it is no longer permissible to write goodwill off immediately to reserves.

5.173 The revaluation reserve must be shown on the face of the balance sheet as a separate amount, although it need not be shown under that name. [4 Sch 34(2)].

5.174 Where any amount has been either credited or debited to the revaluation reserve, its treatment for taxation purposes must be disclosed in a note to the financial statements. [4 Sch 34(4)].

5.175 The implications of these rules in practice are considered in more detail below. The question of whether a revaluation surplus or deficit is realised or unrealised is considered in chapter 19.

Depreciation

5.176 The rules relating to depreciation of fixed assets that have been valued under the alternative accounting rules are essentially the same as those described above under 'Historical cost accounting rules' with the revalued amount being substituted for historical cost. The application of the rules for revalued assets is described in the following paragraphs.

5.177 Where a company has determined an asset's value in accordance with one of the alternative accounting rules, that value (rather than the purchase price or the production cost) is to be (or else is to be the starting point for determining) the amount at which it discloses that asset in its financial statements. Where the asset in question has been subject to a previous valuation, its value according to the latest revaluation supersedes its previous value as the basis the company should use when including it in its financial statements. Accordingly, any references in the depreciation rules to purchase price or production cost must be substituted by a reference to the value determined by the alternative accounting rules the company applied. [4 Sch 32(1)]. This means that, in determining the amount to be written off systematically over a fixed asset's useful economic life, a company must have regard to the asset's value determined according to the latest application of the alternative accounting rules, rather than to its purchase price or its production cost. Even where a company revalues its assets at the end of the year, it is not exempt from charging depreciation against the profits of the year based on the opening cost or valuation and the cost of subsequent additions. This is because until the year end valuation "*the most recently determined value*" would be the valuation carried out at the last year end and if depreciation is deemed to accrue evenly over the life of an asset, depreciation should be charged on that opening value plus additions throughout the year until the next valuation at the year end. Note, however, that FRED 17 proposes that depreciation should be charged by reference to the closing valuation. [FRED 17 para 69].

5.178 The Act also says that where the value of any fixed asset has been determined according to the alternative accounting rules, the amount of any provision for depreciation to be charged in the profit and loss account may be either the amount based on the valuation of the asset, or the amount based on its historical cost. However, where the amount so charged is based on historical cost, the difference between that charge and the charge based on the asset's valuation must be disclosed separately. It must be so disclosed either on the face of the profit and loss account or in the notes. [4 Sch 32(2))(3)]. This would appear to allow a company to either debit or credit the difference (as appropriate) direct to the revaluation reserve. This is, however, prohibited by SSAP 12.

5.179 SSAP 12 echoes the Act's rules in most respects, but it requires that where a company revalues assets, and gives effect to the revaluation in its financial statements, it should base the charge for depreciation on the revalued amount. [SSAP 12 para 16]. If this results in a material increase in depreciation compared to previous years' depreciation charges, then the financial statements should disclose in the notes in the year of revaluation the depreciation charge split between that applicable to original cost and that applicable to the change in value on revaluation. [SSAP 12 para 27]. No depreciation previously charged should be written back to the profit and loss account on revaluation of an asset. [SSAP 12 para 22 as amended by FRS 11]. The standard states also that an increase in the value of an asset does not remove the necessity for a company to charge depreciation even where the market value of an asset is greater than its net book value. [SSAP 12 para 9].

5.180 Consequently, it is clear that SSAP 12 requires a company to charge depreciation on the carrying value of the revalued asset in the balance sheet, and to charge it in its entirety to the profit and loss account. The practice of 'split depreciation' where depreciation on the historical cost is charged to the profit and loss account, and depreciation on the revaluation is charged to the revaluation reserve, has been prohibited. [SSAP 12 para 16]. FRED 17, which will replace SSAP 12 in due course, will also prohibit split depreciation. [FRED 17, 'The development of the FRED' paras 30 to 32].

5.181 Whilst chapter 19 considers realised reserves and distributable profits in detail, it should be noted that section 275(2) of the Act has a bearing on the way in which companies should treat depreciation on revalued assets. This section says that if the revaluation of an asset produces an unrealised profit, then an amount equal to any excess depreciation charged as a result of the revaluation may be treated as a realised profit. This section is concerned only with the determination of distributable profits (and not with the accounting treatment of excess depreciation). Despite this, it means that where a company properly charges the whole of the depreciation based on the revalued assets to the profit and loss account, it may also transfer an amount equal to the excess depreciation from the revaluation reserve to the profit and loss account reserve.

5.182 Because the amount transferred from the revaluation reserve to the profit and loss account reserve represents a realised profit, this treatment would not contravene paragraph 34(3) of Schedule 4 (see para 5.170 above).

5.183 The transfer should be made between reserves in the notes. Where such an adjustment is made, the revaluation reserve is systematically reduced over the asset's life and, consequently, if the asset is sold any net profit on the sale that is credited to the profit and loss account reserve will ultimately be the same whether the asset has been revalued or not.

Impairments

FRS 11 approach and the Act's requirements

5.184 The Act's rules on impairments are framed in terms of 'permanent diminutions in value' and 'temporary diminutions in value'. There has often been difficulty in determining what is permanent and what is temporary. FRS 11 takes a different approach, abandoning the permanent/temporary distinction in favour of an approach that looks at whether an impairment is due to consumption of economic benefits or whether it is due to some other factor such as a general change in prices.

5.185 In the following paragraphs both the Act's rules and those of FRS 11 are described. Because FRS 11 does not apply to investment properties the first paragraphs dealing with the Act and SSAP 19 are particularly relevant for accounting for such assets, whilst FRS 11 is more relevant for other tangible fixed assets.

Investment properties – temporary diminutions in value

5.186 When a company applies the alternative accounting rules of the Act, it *must* debit to the revaluation reserve those deficits that arise from a *temporary diminution* in value of a fixed asset (other than a fixed asset investment, see para 5.53 above). This is because it would seem that the Act does not permit such revaluation deficits to be charged to the profit and loss account (see para 5.170 above). The deficit would instead be disclosed in the statement of total recognised gains and losses.

5.187 On a revaluation that gives rise to deficits which are *temporary* (for example, the situation when a diminution arises as part of an annual revaluation exercise and there are no indications that any of the deficit is permanent), it is possible for these deficits to be taken to the revaluation reserve and, in effect, netted off against surpluses on other assets. If the net of surpluses and deficits results in an overall deficit on the revaluation reserve it used to be the case that this overall deficit was charged in the profit and loss account on the grounds of prudence. This was consistent with the treatment prescribed in SSAP 19, 'Accounting for investment properties'.

5.188 In July 1994 the ASB amended SSAP 19 so as to require all changes in the market value of investment properties (including deficits) to be taken to the statement of total recognised gains and losses unless a deficit on an individual investment property was expected to be permanent, in which case it should be charged to the profit and loss account. The reason for the change was that the original SSAP 19 was considered to be inconsistent with FRS 3, 'Reporting financial performance' which had provided a second primary statement, the 'Statement of total recognised gains and losses', in which unrealised gains and losses were recognised.

Investment properties – permanent diminutions in value

5.189 The treatment of permanent diminutions in value of previously revalued assets is governed by paragraph 32 of Schedule 4 which, as described in paragraph 5.177 above, requires that the rules relating to permanent diminutions should be applied by substituting the revalued amount for the historical cost of the asset.

5.190 The effect of this is that the amount of the permanent diminution includes not only the diminution below cost, but also the diminution in value between cost and revalued amount. Thus, for example, if an asset costing £100 has subsequently been revalued to £150 and then suffers a permanent diminution to £70, the amount of the permanent diminution under paragraph 32 of Schedule 4 is £80 (that is, £150 – £70) and not £30.

5.191 One view which follows from this is that the whole of the permanent diminution in value should be charged to the profit and loss account. Any previous revaluation surplus relating to the asset would then be transferred through reserves from the revaluation reserve to the profit and loss account reserve up to the amount of the permanent diminution. Thus, in the above example, £80 would be charged to the profit and loss account and the previous revaluation surplus of £50 would be transferred from revaluation reserve to profit and loss account reserve.

5.192 There is an alternative treatment of provisions for permanent diminution in value of previously revalued assets. The effect is that only that element of the diminution that represents the loss below cost is charged to the profit and loss account. There are two different technical routes through which this alternative treatment can be rationalised.

5.193 One route is to argue that when a permanent diminution occurs, it can be seen as the result of a valuation process that is governed by the rules in Schedule 4. Under this interpretation, the diminution in value from the previous revalued amount down to cost is seen as the result of a valuation which, in accordance with paragraph 34(1) of

Schedule 4, should be taken to the revaluation reserve. Once this is done the asset is stated at cost, but there is still a permanent diminution in value which, under the historical cost accounting rules, must be taken to profit and loss account. [4 Sch 19(2)].

5.194 The second route is to argue as follows. The full amount of the permanent diminution in value is charged to the profit and loss account (that is, £80 in the example). [4 Sch 19(2)]. As noted above, paragraph 19(2) applies in the context of the historical cost rules, but it can be argued that it also applies in the context of the alternative accounting rules. However, when the alternative accounting rules are used, Schedule 4 also states that *"an amount may be transferred from the revaluation reserve ... to the profit and loss account if the amount was previously charged to that account or represents realised profits"*. [4 Sch 34(3)]. In the example, the £50 has been charged to the profit and loss account (as part of the £80) and so paragraph 34(3) allows the relevant amount of the revaluation (that is, £50) to be transferred to the profit and loss account.

5.195 Both of these ways of rationalising the alternative treatment have the same effect, namely that only the diminution below cost of £30 would be charged in the profit and loss account, with the diminution of £50 between original cost and the revalued carrying amount being debited to the revaluation reserve and shown in the statement of total recognised gains and losses.

5.196 We believe that this alternative treatment is acceptable. The first view (see para 5.191) has the disadvantage that the initial uplift in value is credited to reserves and shown in the statement of total recognised gains and losses, whilst the subsequent reversal of the uplift is charged to the profit and loss account. This asymmetrical treatment is avoided in the alternative treatment.

Other tangible fixed assets – impairments

5.197 FRS 11 does not apply to investment properties. For other properties and other tangible fixed assets FRS 11 introduces rules for recognition of impairment that are more conservative and prudent than the Act's requirements in respect of temporary diminutions in value.

5.198 Although FRS 11 does not use the term 'temporary diminutions in value' it distinguishes between impairments that arise from two different causes. These are impairments arising from:

- A clear consumption of economic benefits.
- Other impairments of revalued fixed assets, for example impairments resulting from a general slump in the property market. [FRS 11 paras 64 and 65].

5.199 The FRS requires that the former of these two types of impairment should be recognised in the profit and loss account in its entirety. No part of it should be taken to the statement of total recognised gains and losses. [FRS 11 para 63]. In this respect the accounting treatment is the same as that required by the Act for permanent diminutions in value under the interpretation of the Act's requirements that is described in paragraphs 5.190 and 5.191 above.

5.200 Other impairments, the latter of the two types described in paragraph 5.198 above, are accounted for by recognising them in the statement of total recognised gains and losses, until the carrying amount reaches depreciated historical cost. Thereafter, the balance of the impairment is recognised in the profit and loss account. [FRS 11 para 63]. This treatment is similar to the accounting treatment required by the Act for permanent diminutions under the alternative interpretation of the Act's requirements that is described in paragraphs 5.192 to 5.195 above. Note, however, that a valuation adjustment below recoverable amount, that arises only because the company follows a policy of revaluation, is not an impairment under FRS 11, but would be recognised in the statement of total recognised gains and losses as a temporary diminution in value – see paragraph 5.206 below.

5.201 The treatment of temporary diminutions (see paras 5.186 to 5.188 above) in value allowed by the Act, and applied to investment properties by SSAP 19, is not permitted by FRS 11 to be used for tangible fixed assets other than investment properties unless the diminution does not constitute an impairment – see paragraph 5.206 below.

5.202 All impairments that are charged to the profit and loss account under the rules of FRS 11 represent permanent diminutions in value under the Act and should be charged in arriving at operating profit, generally under the same statutory format headings as depreciation.

5.203 The FRS appears to acknowledge that a downward revaluation of a previously revalued asset may constitute partly an impairment due to consumption of economic benefits and partly an impairment due to general price changes. It may be difficult, in practice, to determine whether or not this is the case. The prudent approach taken by the standard, however, makes this less of an issue, because the standard requires all impairments of an asset below depreciated historical cost to be taken to the profit and loss account.

Disclosure

5.204 As explained in paragraph 5.88 above, impairment losses on assets stated at market value (that is, existing use value or open-market value) should be included in the revalued carrying amount and not within accumulated depreciation. However, where assets are included at depreciated replacement cost any impairment losses charged to the profit and loss account should be shown within cumulative depreciation and any impairment losses charged to the statement of total recognised gains and losses should be deducted from the revalued carrying amount of the asset.

5.205 Impairment losses recognised in the profit and loss account should be included in operating profit under the appropriate statutory heading and disclosed as exceptional if appropriate. Impairment losses recognised in the statement of total recognised gains and losses should be disclosed separately on the face of that statement. [FRS 11 para 67].

5.206 It should be noted that FRS 11 only requires a tangible fixed asset to be written down for impairment where its carrying value exceeds its recoverable amount. Recoverable amount is the higher of net realisable value and value in use. Where, therefore, the revaluation of a fixed asset results in a revalued amount that is below the previous carrying value and is below the value in use of that asset, FRS 11 only requires the asset to be written down, if necessary, to the value in use figure. The difference between the value in use figure and the (lower) revalued amount is simply a valuation adjustment which is then shown in the statement of total recognised gains and losses.

Example

A tangible fixed asset cost £100 and has been revalued to £150 in previous years, with the surplus of £50 being taken to the statement of total recognised gains and losses and the revaluation reserve.

In the current year the fixed asset is revalued and the revalued amount is £80 (in this example, for simplicity, depreciation has been ignored).

An impairment review is done on the asset and the recoverable amount (higher of net realisable value and value in use) is determined to be £90.

The following describes how the revaluation deficit of £70 (£150 – £80) should be accounted for.

(a) If the impairment of £60, that is the difference between carrying value of £150 and recoverable amount of £90, is considered to have arisen due to a clear consumption of economic benefits, it should be charged in its entirety to the profit and loss account, and shown under the appropriate statutory heading in arriving at operating profit (see paras 5.199 and 5.202 above).

The previous revaluation surplus of £50 in the revaluation reserve may then be transferred through reserves (but not through the statement of total recognised gains and losses) to profit and loss reserve.

(b) If the impairment of £60 is considered not to have arisen from a clear consumption of economic benefits, it should be charged as to £50 to the statement of total recognised gains and losses and £10 to the profit and loss account, again under the appropriate heading in arriving at operating profit. The charge of £50 to the statement of total recognised gains and losses should be shown on the face of that statement (see paras 5.200 and 5.205).

(c) In both cases, that is whether the impairment loss is due to a clear consumption of economic benefits or not, the remaining revaluation adjustment of £10 to reduce the asset from its recoverable amount of £90 to its revalued amount of £80 is shown in the statement of total recognised gains and losses. This is because it corresponds to a temporary diminution under the Companies Act rules, and such diminutions should be taken, via the statement of total recognised gains and losses, to the revaluation reserve.

Reversals of impairments

5.207 In those cases where the reasons for making a provision for impairment have ceased to apply, the provision should be written back to the extent that it is no longer necessary. Clearly, where this is required, the reversal of the provision should be consistent with the accounting treatment adopted when the provision was set up. It would not be acceptable to adopt one treatment for setting up the provision and a different one for reversing it. Thus, the reversal of an impairment loss should be recognised in the profit and loss account to the extent that the original impairment loss (adjusted for subsequent depreciation) was recognised in the profit and loss account. Any remaining balance of the reversal of an impairment loss should be recognised in the statement of total recognised gains and losses. [FRS 11 para 66].

Treatment of accumulated depreciation when assets are revalued

5.208 In the past, before the revision of SSAP 12 in January 1987, companies adopted one or other of two different ways of treating their existing accumulated depreciation when they revalued fixed assets.

5.209 The first method, which is now the only one allowed under SSAP 12, is the simple one of comparing the revalued amount with the net book value and taking the difference to the revaluation reserve. This method is illustrated by the following example:

Example

Details of a fixed asset before revaluation are as follows:	£
Fixed asset at cost	1,000
Accumulated depreciation	400
Net book value	600
The asset is revalued to	1,500

Details of the fixed asset after revaluation are as follows:	£
Fixed asset at cost	1,000
Surplus on revaluation	500
	1,500
Accumulated depreciation	400
Surplus on revaluation	(400)
	-

The amount transferred to the revaluation reserve is £900 (namely, £1,500 – £600). This includes £400 of accumulated depreciation.

5.210 The second approach, which is now prohibited, was to write back the accumulated depreciation of £400 to the profit and loss account and to transfer the difference between the revalued amount of the asset and its historical cost or previous valuation to the revaluation reserve.

5.211 The proponents of this approach argued that the depreciation charged to date in the light of the revaluation was unnecessary and that the retained profits should reflect the position which would have existed had no such depreciation been charged. This approach appears also to be permitted by paragraph 34(1) of Schedule 4, which says:

> *"With respect to any determination of the value of an asset of a company... [under the alternative accounting rules]..., the amount of any profit or loss arising from that determination (after allowing, where appropriate, for any provisions for depreciation or diminution in value made otherwise than by reference to the value so determined and any adjustments of any such provisions made in the light of that determination) shall be credited or (as the case may be) debited to a separate reserve ('the revaluation reserve')."*

5.212 However, the approach is not now allowed because SSAP 12, paragraph 22 (as amended by FRS 11 para 77) states that:

> *"Depreciation charged before the revaluation should not be written back to the profit and loss account."*

Accordingly, companies should not write back their existing accumulated depreciation when they revalue fixed assets.

5.213 Although the standard makes clear that the reversal of accumulated depreciation should be credited to the revaluation reserve, it is unclear as to whether or not the amount thus credited in respect of the depreciation represents a realised profit or not. In our view the amount should not be assumed to be a realised profit and if a company wished to treat it as such it should seek legal advice.

Sale of revalued assets

5.214 As noted in paragraph 5.171 above, the revaluation reserve must be reduced where it is no longer necessary for the purpose of the valuation method that the company has adopted. The most likely situation where this will happen is where the company sells an asset that it has previously revalued.

5.215 Paragraph 34(3) of Schedule 4 allows a company to make a transfer from the revaluation reserve to the profit and loss account where the amount transferred represents a realised profit. Consequently, when a company sells a revalued asset, the Act permits it to credit the profit on the sale (including the amount of the realised revaluation surplus) to the profit and loss account.

5.216 However this treatment is prohibited by FRS 3. This standard introduced a new primary statement, the statement of total recognised gains and losses, to which unrealised gains, such as revaluation surpluses, must be taken. Performance is then measured by reference to total recognised gains for the year, which includes the profit or loss for the year and the other gains and losses which have been taken direct to the statement of total recognised gains and losses.

5.217 It follows from the 'performance' measurement set out in FRS 3 that if a gain has been recognised when an asset was initially revalued, that gain should not be recognised a second time in either the profit and loss account or the statement of total recognised gains and losses, when the asset is sold.

5.218 FRS 3 therefore prescribes that:

> *"The profit or loss on disposal of an asset should be accounted for in the profit and loss account of the period in which the disposal occurs as the difference between the net sale proceeds and the net carrying amount, whether carried at historical cost (less any provisions made) or at a valuation."*
> [FRS 3 para 21].

5.219 Any revaluation surplus that is realised on sale should, therefore, be transferred direct to the profit and loss account reserve and not to the profit and loss account for the year. As mentioned above in paragraph 5.179 this is also consistent with the SSAP 12 treatment of depreciation on revalued assets.

5.220 FRED 17 proposes an entirely new method of accounting for profits and losses on disposal of fixed assets which would require an amendment to FRS 3 (see para 5.259 onwards). The new method would require a 'death bed' revaluation of fixed assets immediately prior to sale, thus removing any gains on sale from the profit and loss account. Judging from the opposition to this proposal from respondents to the FRED this proposal is unlikely to be reflected in a standard produced from the FRED.

Current assets

5.221 The alternative accounting rules are sometimes applied to current assets, principally by dealers. The following paragraphs describe the implications of marking to market readily marketable investments, but the discussion applies equally to readily marketable commodities held by commodity dealers.

5.222 In ED 55, 'Accounting for Investments', the legal implications of marking to market were considered. ED 55 stated *"Whilst the alternative accounting rules in Schedule 4 would permit this balance sheet treatment, they would require any movement in the market value to be treated as a revaluation surplus or deficit and taken to the revaluation reserve, rather than being accounted for in the profit and loss account as part of the realised profit or loss for the period, as under marking to market"*. [ED 55 para 1.17].

5.223 The question of whether or not profits arising under marking to market of readily marketable investments are realised or unrealised is not relevant to whether or not taking such profits to the profit and loss account would involve a departure from the Act's requirement that such profits should be taken to the revaluation reserve. In fact ED 55 concluded that such profits are realised. It states *"...where such investments are held as current assets it is appropriate to regard any increases in their value as realised and such investments should be marked to market"*. [ED 55 para 21].

5.224 ED 55 goes on to say that, because marking to market involves a departure from the Companies Act, it is necessary to invoke a true and fair override under section 226(5) in order to take the profits to the profit and loss account. It considers that this is justified in the case of dealing companies. However, the DTI suggested that it might not be appropriate in the case of other companies, because invoking the true and fair override is only possible where there are special circumstances. The DTI considered that the special circumstances that applied in this case were not narrowly enough defined and as a result the application of marking to market for all companies rather than just dealing companies or market makers could be unjustified. It is clear from the discussion in ED 55 that it is generally accepted for dealing companies and market makers to mark to market readily marketable securities and to take any resultant profits to the profit and loss account. However this treatment requires adoption of a true and fair override of the Act's requirement to take such profits to the revaluation reserve. An example of an appropriate wording for a note describing such an override would be:

Example

[Marketable securities]/[commodities]/[etc] held as current trading assets are stated at market value and profits and losses arising from this valuation are taken to the profit and loss account. This is not in accordance with Schedule 4 to the Companies Act 1985, which requires that such assets be stated at the lower of cost and net realisable value, or that if revalued any revaluation differences be taken to revaluation reserve. The directors consider that these requirements would fail to give a true and fair view of the profit for the year of the company since the marketability of the [securities] enables decisions to be taken continually about whether to hold or sell them and hence the economic measure of profit in any period is properly made by reference to market values.

THEN: EITHER

The effect of the departure on the accounts is to increase profits before taxation by £W (1993 – £X) and increase the value of current asset investments by £Y (1993 – £Z).

OR

It is not practicable to quantify the effect on the accounts of this departure, since information on original cost, being of no continuing relevance to the business, is not available.

5.225 The above note refers alternatively to commodities, because similar considerations apply to marking to market commodity stocks.

5.226 Where companies other than dealing companies or market makers wish to adopt marking to market it is less certain whether a true and fair override can be adopted to take profits to the profit and loss account. The UITF has a working party which has been considering this issue for some time. As an indication of its view, however, the UITF stated in March 1993:

"Marking current asset investments to market

A number of companies hold significant proportions of their current assets in the form of highly liquid and readily marketable investments, although the holding of such investments is only an incidental part of their trading activities. The question arises as to whether the practice of marking such investments to market, with any differences arising being taken through the profit and loss account, could or should be adopted by such companies. It is already an established industry practice for market makers and other dealers in investments. The Task Force agreed that the preferred accounting treatment would be that the practice be followed by all enterprises, including those that report under Schedule 4 to the Companies Act 1985, but noted that legal constraints had been cited as a barrier to any general requirement to account in this way. (This treatment had been proposed in ED 55 'Accounting for Investments' issued by the ASC in 1990 but the ED also referred to representations made as to the legal position.) The Task Force decided to examine these constraints in conjunction with its legal advisers. In the meantime, it noted that it was for any individual company to consider whether, in the light of its particular circumstances, the need to show a true and fair view required departure from the normal valuation rules and adoption of marking to market in respect of investments held as current assets for which there was an active market."
[UITF Information Sheet No 7].

5.227 We consider that an example of a situation where special circumstances justifying a true and fair override exists is where a company has a significant portfolio of readily marketable current asset investments which it manages separately from its principal business as part of its corporate treasury activities.

Disclosure of the revaluation reserve

5.228 As noted in paragraph 5.173 above, the Act requires that the revaluation reserve must be shown on the face of the balance sheet. However, it may be shown under another name. [4 Sch 34(2)]. This concession is necessary for several reasons, as discussed below.

5.229 Where a company prepares full current cost financial statements in accordance with the ASC's handbook, 'Accounting for the effects of changing prices', the current cost balance sheet includes a reserve that is referred to as the 'current cost reserve'.

5.230 The current cost reserve will include:

- Unrealised revaluation surpluses on fixed assets, stocks and investments.

- Realised amounts equal to the cumulative net total of the current cost adjustments made in accordance with the handbook, namely:
  - The depreciation adjustment (and any adjustments on the disposal of fixed assets).
  - The cost of sales adjustment.
  - The monetary working capital adjustment.
  - The gearing adjustment.

5.231 In effect, this current cost reserve is very similar to the revaluation reserve outlined in the Act. The main difference between the current cost reserve and the revaluation reserve is that the current cost reserve comprises two parts: an unrealised part that includes surpluses on revaluations, and a realised element that includes items (such as the cost of sales adjustment) that have been either debited or credited to the profit and loss account. The unrealised part of the current cost reserve corresponds to the revaluation reserve under the terms of the Act. To comply with the Act, it is necessary to present the item in the balance sheet, or in the notes to the balance sheet, as follows:

		£
Current cost reserve	– unrealised	X
	– realised	X
		X

5.232 The disclosure of the 'current cost reserve' is discussed in detail in the ASC's handbook appendices 3 and 9.

5.233 It should also be noted that sometimes a company's articles of association will govern the way in which the company operates its revaluation reserve and these articles may stipulate also the name of the reserve. Consequently, the company should use that name in its financial statements. Articles of this nature are commonly found in investment companies and pension funds.

Taxation implications

5.234 The Act requires the taxation implications of a revaluation to be noted in the financial statements. [4 Sch 34(4)].

5.235 This does not mean that there must be a statement of whether the amount is taxable or allowable under tax legislation. It means that there must be an explanation of the tax effect of the revaluation.

5.236 The tax effect will often be deferred until a later period. SSAP 15 says that the revaluation of an asset will give rise to a deferred tax timing difference, insofar as the profit or loss that would result from the asset's realisation at the revalued amount is taxable. But this will not apply if the disposal of the revalued asset and of any subsequent replacement assets would not result in a tax liability after taking account of any expected rollover relief. [SSAP 15 para 20].

5.237 The standard requires that tax deferred or accelerated by the effect of timing differences (including any deferred tax on a capital gain) should be accounted for to the extent that it is probable that a liability or asset will crystallise. [SSAP 15 para 25]. In addition to making this provision, a company should disclose, in a note to its financial statements, the total amount of deferred tax (including that on capital gains) that it has not provided for, analysed into its major components. [SSAP 15 para 40]. The standard goes on to say that where the potential amount of deferred tax on a revalued asset is not shown because the revaluation does not constitute a timing difference for the reason explained in paragraph 5.236 above, this fact should be stated. [SSAP 15 para 41].

5.238 Compliance with the disclosure requirements of SSAP 15 will ensure compliance with paragraph 34(4) of Schedule 4.

Additional disclosure required

5.239 Where a company has applied any of the alternative accounting rules, the Act requires it to disclose certain information in the notes to its financial statements. [4 Sch 33(1)].

5.240 First, the notes must state the items affected and the basis of valuation the company has adopted in respect of each such item. [4 Sch 33(2)]. Second, either the balance sheet or the notes must disclose, in respect of every item affected (except stocks), one or other of the following amounts:

- The comparable amounts determined according to the historical cost convention.

- The differences between those comparable amounts and the actual amounts shown in the balance sheet.

[4 Sch 33(3)].

5.241 For this purpose, 'comparable amounts' means the aggregate amount the company would have shown if it had applied the historical cost convention, and the aggregate amount of the cumulative provisions for depreciation or diminution in value that would have been permitted or required in determining those amounts according to that convention. [4 Sch 33(4)].

5.242 To illustrate this requirement, consider the following example:

Example

Details of a company's fixed assets are as follows:

	Cost	Valuation
	£	£
Fixed assets	10,000	15,000
Accumulated depreciation	6,000	4,000
	4,000	11,000

If the company states the fixed assets in the balance sheet at valuation, the effect of the Act's provisions is to require the balance sheet or the notes to the financial statements to state either the comparable amounts (namely, cost £10,000 and depreciation £6,000) or the difference between the comparable amounts and the amounts at which they are actually stated (namely, £5,000 and £2,000 respectively).

The historical cost net book amount (namely, £4,000) or the difference between the comparable net book amounts (namely, £7,000) is another interpretation of the amounts that are required to be disclosed. This latter disclosure is arguable because the Act refers to the amounts stated in the balance sheet and the amounts so stated will be the net book value of the assets.

5.243 As a result of this requirement, a company that has revalued its fixed assets has to maintain records of both the historical cost and the valuation of those fixed assets. In addition, the company has to calculate depreciation on the historical cost as well as on the valuation.

5.244 Table 5.19 shows how a company complies with these disclosure requirements.

Table 5.19 – Lonrho plc – Annual Report and Accounts – 30 September 1994

Notes to the Accounts (extract)

12. Tangible assets (extract)

Assets shown below at valuation were valued by independent professional valuers or by the Directors after advice from independent professional advisers in the year shown, on the basis of open market value for existing use or depreciated replacement cost where considered the most appropriate basis of valuation. Assets shown below at valuation and valued at depreciated replacement cost amounted to £202m.

	Land and buildings						
		Leasehold				Fixtures	
				Mining	Plant and	fittings and	
	Freehold	Long term	Short term	assets	machinery	equipment	Total
	£m	£m	£m	£m	£m	£m	£m
Up to 1990	59	12		119	7	1	198
1991							
1992	262						262
1993	147	80			6		233
1994	**3**	**2**					**5**
Valuation	471	94		119	13	1	698
Cost	83	58	24	528	226	281	1,200
	554	152	24	647	239	282	1,898
Capital work in progress							15
At 30 September 1994							**1,913**
Depreciation:							
Valuation	5	1		15	9	1	31
Cost	5	5	6	51	86	157	310
At 30 September 1994	**10**	**6**	**6**	**66**	**95**	**158**	**341**
Historical cost of revalued assets							
Cost	195	25		25	10	1	256
Depreciation	2			7	7	1	17
Net historical cost at 30 September 1994	**193**	**25**		**18**	**3**		**239**
Cost	109	27	5	27	16	11	195
Depreciation	2	1		7	9	5	24
Net historical cost at 30 September 1993	107	26	5	20	7	6	171

5.245 Where any fixed assets other than listed investments are included at a valuation the following information is required to be disclosed:

- The years (so far as they are known to the directors) in which the assets were valued and the values.

- Where assets have been valued during the year, the names of the persons who valued them or particulars of their qualifications for doing so and (whichever is stated) the bases of valuation used by them.

[4 Sch 43].

Current cost accounting rules

Background

5.246 In the 1970s, during a period of high inflation there was significant concern that the true performance of companies was masked by the effects of inflation. It was suggested, for instance, that dividend policy pursued by companies did not allow for sufficient retention of profits in real terms to maintain their capital base, with the results that borrowings had to be increased. This in turn led to companies becoming more vulnerable to adverse economic events.

Current purchasing power (CPP)

5.247 As a result of this concern it was proposed that a method of accounting for inflation should be applied that sought to have companies restate figures in terms of 'current purchasing power' (CPP). In 1974 an accounting standard 'Provisional SSAP 7' was published. This proposed that:

- Companies should continue to keep their records and present their basic financial statements in historical pounds, that is, in terms of the value of the pound at the time of each transaction or revaluation.
- All listed companies should, in addition, provide shareholders with a supplementary statement in terms of the value of the pound at the end of the accounting period.
- The conversion of the historical cost figures in the basic financial statements into the figures in the supplementary statement should be by means of a general index of the purchasing power of the pound.
- The directors should provide a note of the basis on which the supplementary statement was prepared and comment on the significance of the figures.

Provisional SSAP 7 was applied for only a short time and was not universally popular.

Sandilands

5.248 In September 1975 a report was presented to parliament by the Inflation Accounting Committee ('The Sandilands Report'). The terms of reference of the committee included, *inter alia*:

> *"To consider whether, and if so how, company accounts should allow for changes (including relative changes) in costs and prices,*

> *having regard to established accounting conventions based on historical costs, the proposal for current general purchasing power accounting put forward by the Accounting Standards Steering Committee, and other possible accounting methods for allowing for price changes, and to make recommendations."*

5.249 The Sandilands report reached three main conclusions:

- It was essential that financial statements should allow for changes in costs and prices.

- Existing accounting conventions did not do so adequately and tended to present the affairs of companies in a misleading way.

- Whilst acknowledging the valuable contribution made by SSAP 7 (see above) the committee considered that the most fruitful line of development in inflation accounting was a system based on the principles of value accounting, which would show the specific effect of inflation on individual companies. This system would be known as current cost accounting (CCA).

5.250 The criticism of the CPP accounting methods set out in Provisional SSAP 7 was that the provisional standard did not, and did not attempt to, provide a comprehensive statement of the value to the business of net assets. Also, the use of the Retail Price Index as a measure of the change in purchasing power of money gave a poor indication of the effects of inflation. The concept of profit adopted by CPP accounting was considered unlikely to be useful to the majority of users of company financial statements and such users might be seriously misled if they assumed that CPP profit, which included 'gains' on monetary items, was available for distribution in full.

SSAP 16 and beyond

5.251 The system of current cost accounting that the Sandilands report recommended was not, in fact, introduced in the form that Sandilands envisaged. Instead the Accounting Standards Committee (ASC) established an Inflation Accounting Steering Group which first produced ED 18, 'Current cost accounting'. The proposals in that exposure draft were not well received, and the ASC then published interim guidelines, known as the 'Hyde Guidelines'.

5.252 From ED 18 and the Hyde Guidelines the ASC then produced ED 24, 'Current cost accounting'. Subsequently ED 24 became SSAP 16, which was published in March 1980. SSAP 16 required that those companies that fell within its scope (principally listed companies and other large companies) should produce current cost accounts in addition to their historical cost accounts.

5.253 The principal provisions of the standard in relation to the profit and loss account were that the current cost operating profit should be derived by making the following main adjustments to the historical cost trading profit before interest, to allow for the impact of price changes in the funds needed to maintain operating assets:

- In relation to fixed assets, a depreciation adjustment, being the difference between the proportion of their value to the business consumed in the period and the depreciation calculated on the historical cost basis.
- In relation to working capital:
  - a cost of sales adjustment, being the difference between the value to the business and the historical cost of stock consumed in the period; and
  - an adjustment based on monetary working capital.

5.254 Where a proportion of the net operating assets was financed by net borrowing, a 'gearing adjustment' was also required in arriving at the current cost operating profit attributable to the shareholders. This was calculated by:

(a) expressing net borrowing as a proportion of the net operating assets using average figures for the year from the current cost balance sheets; and

(b) multiplying the total of the charges or credits made to allow for the impact of the price changes on the net operating assets of the business by the proportion determined at (a).

The gearing adjustment, normally a credit, could be a debit if prices fell.

5.255 The principal provisions of the standard in relation to the balance sheet were that the assets and liabilities should be included in the balance sheet at their value to the business. Value to the business is explained in paragraph 5.145 above. The principal bases of valuation used are detailed above in paragraph 5.162. Reserves in the current cost balance sheet should include revaluation surpluses and deficits and adjustments made to reflect the impact of price changes in arriving at the current cost profit attributable to shareholders. The contents of the current cost reserve are described in paragraph 5.230 above.

5.256 Although SSAP 16 achieved some success, particularly among nationalised industries, falling inflation, a general reluctance by companies to accept the principles of accounting for the effects of changing prices and the rather cumbersome calculations necessary to calculate current cost profit figures, meant that there was also widespread dissatisfaction and, in due course, non-compliance with the standard.

5.257 Accordingly, in order to simplify the requirements and reduce the burden on companies, the ASC issued ED 35 in 1984 which proposed that limited current cost information should be required, in note form, as part of main historical cost financial statements. The proposals of ED 35 were not widely accepted, however, and in early 1985 it was withdrawn.

5.258 Faced with continuing non-compliance with SSAP 16, the ASC first made it non-mandatory and then withdrew it. In its place the ASC issued 'Accounting for the effects of changing prices: a handbook' as a guide for those companies that wished to continue to produce financial statements on a current cost basis. The handbook remains the principal guidance for the presentation of current cost financial statements. It reflects closely the provisions of SSAP 16, described above.

The ASB's project on valuations and our views on future developments

FRED 17 on measurement of tangible fixed assets

5.259 In March 1993, the ASB issued a first discussion paper 'The role of valuation in financial reporting' which was superseded by a second discussion paper, issued in October 1996, entitled 'Measurement of tangible fixed assets'. The latter discussion paper contained proposals for initial measurement, valuation and depreciation of tangible fixed assets. Whilst there was not significant concern over the existing standards, SSAP 12 and SSAP 19, there was no standard dealing with the initial recognition of tangible fixed assets. The discussion paper, and now FRED 17, 'Measurement of tangible fixed assets' published in October 1997, aims to introduce rules to deal with this and with valuations of assets. FRED 17 also seeks to clarify certain aspects of SSAP 12. In particular, it deals with the issue of non-depreciation of assets, mostly properties, on the grounds that they are regularly maintained or refurbished.

Objective and scope

5.260 The objective of the proposals is to ensure that uniform principles are applied to the initial measurement of tangible fixed assets; that the valuation of investment properties and other tangible fixed assets (where an entity chooses to revalue those other assets) is performed on a consistent basis and is kept up to date; and that depreciation is calculated consistently and recognised as the economic benefits are consumed over the assets' useful economic lives.

5.261 The proposals apply to all financial statements intended to give a true and fair view. However, insurance companies and groups, pension funds and investment companies as defined in companies legislation, need not comply with the rules relating to reporting of gains and losses on revaluation.

Initial measurement

5.262 A tangible fixed asset should initially be measured at its cost. Only costs that are directly attributable to bringing the asset into working condition for its intended use should be included in its measurement.

5.263 The proposals permit capitalisation of costs incurred in an essential commissioning period to bring an asset up to its normal operating potential, but do not permit capitalisation of costs relating to other start-up periods where the asset is available for use but not yet operating at normal levels, for example because of lack of demand. An example of the latter is the start-up period of a new hotel where the hotel could operate at normal levels almost immediately, but where demand builds up slowly. Capitalisation of costs should cease once the asset is substantially complete and ready for use, even if it has not yet been brought into use. For example, capitalisation of costs of development properties should cease with the end of the construction period, even if the properties are not fully tenanted.

5.264 Companies may choose whether or not to adopt a policy of capitalisation of borrowing costs. Where such a policy is adopted, borrowing costs that are directly attributable to the construction of a tangible fixed asset should be capitalised on a gross basis, that is, before deduction of tax relief. The amount of borrowing costs capitalised in a period should not exceed the borrowing costs incurred in the period. Disclosure should be made of: the accounting policy adopted; the amount of borrowing costs capitalised in the period; the amount of borrowing costs charged in the profit and loss account in the period; and the capitalisation rate used to determine the amount of capitalised borrowing costs.

5.265 The amount recognised when a tangible fixed asset is acquired or constructed should not exceed its recoverable amount.

Subsequent expenditure

5.266 Subsequent expenditure to ensure that the asset maintains its originally assessed standard of performance should be recognised in the profit and loss account as it is incurred.

5.267 This type of expenditure includes repairs and maintenance and the FRED explains that in assessing the useful life of an asset it is assumed that such expenditure will be carried out. Without such expenditure the depreciation expense would be increased, because the useful life or residual value of the asset would be reduced.

5.268 Subsequent expenditure that results in either:

(a) the restoration or replacement of a component of an asset which has been treated as a separate asset and depreciated over its individual useful economic life; or

(b) the enhancement of economic benefits of an asset in excess of the originally assessed standard of performance,

should be capitalised as incurred and depreciated over the useful economic life of the resulting asset (or component).

5.269 The proposals include an argument as to why subsequent expenditure should not be provided for in advance, which is similar to that already contained in FRED 14.

Renewals accounting

5.270 An exception is made for infrastructure assets that meet certain conditions and which are accounted for using 'renewals' accounting. Where infrastructure assets meet certain conditions, the proposals are that the annual level of expenditure required to maintain the operating capacity of the infrastructure assets is treated as a depreciation provision and deducted from the carrying value of the asset. When the actual expenditure takes place it is capitalised to the carrying value of the asset.

5.271 This has the effect of deducting a provision for maintenance from the asset as if it were depreciation and then capitalising maintenance cost as it is incurred.

5.272 The conditions to be satisfied for renewals accounting are:

- The infrastructure asset must be a system or network that is intended to be maintained as a whole at a specified level of service potential by the continuing replacement and refurbishment of its components.

- The level of annual expenditure required is calculated from an asset management plan that is certified by a person who is appropriately qualified and independent.

- The system or network is in a mature or steady state.

- The cost of definable major components with finite lives that form part of the system or network are treated as separate assets and depreciated over their useful economic lives.

Valuation

5.273 Investment properties should be revalued annually. In the case of other tangible fixed assets an entity may choose either to adopt a policy of valuation or not. Where a policy of valuation is adopted the valuation must be kept up to date and all the assets of the same class must be revalued.

5.274 FRED 17 proposes that non-specialised properties should either be fully revalued every five years with an interim valuation in year three (and in years one, two and four where there has been a material change in value), or a full valuation should be carried out on a five-year rolling basis, that is one-fifth per year (with an interim valuation of the remaining four-fifths if there has been a material change in value).

5.275 The full valuations should be made by a qualified external valuer or by a qualified internal valuer so long as the valuation has been reviewed by a qualified external valuer. The interim valuations may be made either by a qualified external valuer or by a qualified internal valuer.

5.276 Investment properties should be revalued annually. The valuation should be by a qualified external valuer at least every five years and in the intervening years either by a qualified external valuer or by a qualified internal valuer.

5.277 The FRED also contains proposals for valuation of specialised properties and for tangible fixed assets other than properties. The bases to be used for properties are similar to those currently used, that is:

- Non-specialised properties – existing use.
- Specialised properties – depreciated replacement cost.
- Investment properties – open-market value.
- Surplus properties – open-market value.

Gains and losses on revaluation

5.278 Revaluation gains should be recognised in the statement of total recognised gains and losses (STRGL) unless they reverse revaluation losses that were previously recognised in the profit and loss account, in which case the gains should be recognised in the profit and loss account.

5.279 All revaluation losses that are clearly due to the consumption of economic benefits should be recognised in the profit and loss account. An example would be physical damage.

5.280 Other revaluation losses should be recognised:

- In the STRGL to the extent that they reverse revaluation gains that were previously recognised in the STRGL.
- Thereafter in the profit and loss account, unless it can be demonstrated that the value in use of the asset to the entity is greater than its replacement cost, in which case the loss may be recognised in the STRGL to the extent that the value in use is greater than its replacement cost.

Gains and losses on disposal

5.281 FRED 17 proposes that for all fixed assets, whether previously revalued or not, immediately prior to disposal the carrying value of the asset should be adjusted to the disposal proceeds. Any gain or loss (excluding those that result from marginal adjustments to depreciation) should be accounted for in accordance with the rules relating to revaluation gains and losses.

5.282 However, where under this rule losses are included in the profit and loss account they are charged in arriving at operating profit and not as a non-operating profit item. This is because the ASB regards such losses on disposal as a form of consumption similar to depreciation.

5.283 As a result of this new proposal, it is also proposed to amend FRS 3, 'Reporting financial performance', to remove the category of non-operating exceptional item 'Profits and losses on the disposal of fixed assets'.

Depreciation

5.284 Depreciation should be allocated on a systematic basis over a tangible asset's useful economic life. Where an asset comprises two or more major components with substantially different lives, each component should be accounted for separately and depreciated over its useful economic life.

5.285 Changes to the useful economic life or residual value of an asset should be accounted for prospectively over the asset's remaining useful life.

5.286 Where an entity incurs subsequent expenditure (such as repairs and maintenance) on a tangible fixed asset, that expenditure does not obviate the need to charge depreciation. The FRED states that an entity should assume that the residual value of an asset will be materially different from its cost unless it intends to dispose of the asset shortly after purchasing it and it is reasonably expected that an asset can be disposed of within a year. The proposal appears to be intended to discourage, if not completely rule out, the presently common argument that depreciation is immaterial on certain types of asset because maintenance is charged to profit and loss and is such that the residual value (based on prices at the date of acquisition or later revaluation) is always equal to or greater than the carrying value. Investment properties are exempt from the requirement to depreciate.

Our views on future developments

5.287 We agree with the conclusion in the ASB's two discussion papers and FRED 17 that the modified historical cost system represents the best way forward. However, we do not believe that the modified historical cost system should provide a single measure of performance to the exclusion of all others. In our view, the 'pure' historical cost system has significant virtues that should be preserved.

5.288 FRS 3 acknowledges that users are interested in historical cost performance, by requiring that a *"Note of historical cost profits and losses"* should be provided where the profit on an historical cost basis differs from that on a modified historical cost basis. The Companies Act also provides that where assets are recorded at valuation, the historical cost equivalents should be given by way of note. In our view the provision of historical cost information in financial statements loses its impact because of the fragmented and subordinate nature of its presentation. In order to acknowledge properly the needs of users who are interested in that information it should be presented with the same degree of prominence as information on the modified historical cost basis.

5.289 FRS 3 also provides that a statement of total recognised gains and losses should be presented as a primary statement. This statement includes unrealised revaluation surpluses created by the revaluation of assets. At present the statement has, in our view, limited relevance because it does not enable the performance of different companies to be compared. This is because there is no requirement for companies to revalue assets and if they do revalue assets there is no requirement for them to do so on a regular basis.

5.290 We agree with FRED 17 that revaluations, where a policy of revaluation is adopted, should be performed on a regular basis. However, we also believe that the statement of total recognised gains and losses will continue to be relevant only for comparing companies that have a policy of revaluing assets on a regular basis.

5.291 Our proposals for the profit and loss account would be that historical cost information and information on a modified historical cost basis could be given equal prominence. This could be simply achieved by using the note of historical cost profits as a link between the two.

Example

The present form of profit and loss account presentation and historical cost information under FRS 3 is as follows:

Profit and loss account	
	£'000
Continuing operations	
Turnover	237
Cost of sales	150
Gross profit	87
Distribution costs	(10)
Administration expenses	(20)
Operating profit	57
Profit on sale of properties	5
Profit before interest	62
Interest	(8)
Profit on ordinary activities before tax	54
Taxation	(20)
Profit for the financial year	34
Note of historical cost profits and losses	
Reported profit on ordinary activities before tax	54
Realisation of property revaluation gains of previous years	15
Difference between historical cost depreciation charge and the actual charge calculated on the revalued amount	3
Historical cost profit on ordinary activities before tax	72
Historical cost profit for the year retained after tax, minority items and dividends	52

The form of presentation that we would suggest would be:

Profit and loss account	Modified historical cost basis £'000	Adjustments £'000	Historical cost basis £'000
Continuing operations			
Turnover	237		237
Cost of sales	150		150
Gross profit	87		87
Distribution costs	(10)		(10)
Administration costs	(20)	3	(17)
Operating profit	57		60
Profit on sale of properties	5	15	20
Profit before interest	62		80
Interest	(8)		(8)
Profit on ordinary activities before tax	54		72
Taxation	(20)		(20)
Profit for the financial year	34		52

The adjustments would be explained in a note.

5.292 For the balance sheet we would propose that historical cost figures should similarly be given equal prominence with a reconciliation to the modified historical cost information. In order to avoid too much information on the face of the profit and loss account or the balance sheet such information would only be needed to be given on the face of the primary statements for the current financial year with comparative figures for historical cost given in the notes. The provision of historical cost financial information in this way might also enable cash flows to be reconciled more readily with figures in the balance sheet and the profit and loss account.

5.293 With the provision of historical cost information separate from, and with equal prominence to, information on a modified historical cost basis, the need for a statement of total recognised gains and losses would need to be reconsidered. As the total differences between historical cost figures and revalued figures would be disclosed in the balance sheet and notes for both the current and the prior years, the movement for the year would be ascertainable and could be shown in a summary of reserve movements; this would effectively be the same as the statement of total recognised gains and losses.

5.294 Our proposals for the presentation of financial statements also envisage that, whilst the historical cost information forms the 'bedrock' of the financial statements, the valuation information could be the subject of experimentation. This experimentation might take the form of applying different valuation techniques to particular assets, such as fixed assets or intangible assets, and extending the application of valuation techniques to items such as long-term liabilities, that have rarely been valued in the past.

5.295 In addition, we consider that it may be useful to users to provide a reconciliation between the balance sheet figures and the total market capitalisation of a company. This would indicate the amount of goodwill that is present in the market capitalisation. Clearly this would at first be an imperfect measure, as the difference could include, as well as goodwill, the value of unrecognised assets (or liabilities). However, it might provide a useful indication of a company's performance in very general terms by comparison with other companies in the same sector. The figure for market capitalisation might need to be averaged over a period if the market price fluctuates significantly. As the valuation techniques applied to the balance sheet evolve and become more refined the difference between the balance sheet value and the market capitalisation may be better understood and directors might be expected to analyse and comment on the difference.

5.296 The suggested approach in paragraph 5.295 above can be illustrated as follows:

Example

Statement of value

	£'m
Book amount of net assets per historical cost balance sheet	100
Revaluation surplus on properties	30
Revaluation surplus on other assets on balance sheet	20
Valuation of off balance sheet assets	
Brands	70
Other assets	40
Value of identifiable net assets	260
Total goodwill of the business	50
Average market capitalisation in the year	310

5.297 A statement such as the above would show the value of the total identifiable net assets and the value of the business as a whole. The difference would be goodwill – but the whole of the goodwill, rather than just the purchased goodwill that is sometimes seen in balance sheets. Clearly there would be specific factors affecting the share price and the value of goodwill that would need to be explained for each company, but such a statement could provide a useful means of comparing company performance within specific industry sectors and between sectors.

Comparison with IASs

5.298 Compared to the wide range of valuation methods allowed for fixed assets in the UK, the IASC rules (in IAS 16 as revised in 1993) are more restrictive. The benchmark treatment is historical cost and all assets should initially be measured at cost. [IAS 16 paras 15, 29]. However, there is an allowed alternative for measurement subsequent to initial recognition: depreciated fair value. [IAS 16 para 30]. For this purpose, 'fair value' is defined as the amount for which the asset could be exchanged at arm's length. [IAS 16 para 7]. Revaluation on this basis is not explicitly required every year, but *"...with sufficient regularity such that the carrying amount does not differ materially from that which would be determined using fair value"*. [IAS 16 para 30].

5.299 When the revaluation alternative is being used, the entire class to which the asset belongs must be revalued. [IAS 16 para 36]. A class is not precisely defined, but is a grouping of assets of similar nature and use, for example, land or land and buildings. [IAS 16 para 37].

5.300 Unlike the rules of the Companies Act 1985, IAS 16 does not distinguish between permanent and temporary diminutions in value. When recoverable amount falls below carrying amount (or when there are other reasons for a downward valuation), the reduction in carrying amount must be charged to income except to the extent that it is covered by related revaluation reserves. [IAS 16 paras 40, 56].

5.301 One issue that is dealt with in more detail by IASC rules than by UK rules is borrowing costs. As mentioned earlier, IAS 23 (also revised in 1993) has a benchmark treatment that borrowing costs should be expensed, but allows an alternative that directly attributable borrowing costs may be capitalised under certain conditions. [IAS 23 paras 7, 10].

5.302 Depreciation is covered by IAS 4, although most of the content related to tangible assets seems to be included in IAS 16 also. There seem to be few differences between UK and IASC rules for depreciation. Whereas, UK law allows previous depreciation to be credited to income on the reversal of a permanent diminution in value, SSAP 12 does not allow this and the IASC would probably not allow it either. [SSAP 12 para 22; IAS 16 para 35].

5.303 The IASC's rules on impairment (IAS 36, 'Impairment of assets') are similar to those in FRS 11. The principle is that impairment is measured by comparing an asset's carrying value with the higher of net selling price (equivalent to net realisable value) and value in use. The details of the impairment reviews are also similar. IAS 36 differs from FRS 11 in its treatment of impairments of previously revalued assets in that IAS 36 does not differentiate between impairments that are clearly caused by the consumption of economic benefits and other impairments: IAS 36 requires all impairments to be recognised in the profit and loss account *only* to the extent that the loss exceeds the balance of the related revaluation reserve.

5.304 Also relevant in this chapter are IAS 15, 'Information reflecting the effects of changing prices' and IAS 29, 'Financial reporting in hyperinflationary economies'. IAS 15 is unusual in not being mandatory. Furthermore, it is not clearly addressed to any particular enterprises, nor does it require any particular methods, nor does it specify whether price adjusted information should be primary or supplementary. IAS 15 largely restricts itself to a list of items to be presented in the financial statements:

- Adjusted depreciation.
- Adjusted cost of sales.
- Monetary items, where adjusted.
- Methods used.
- Where the current cost method is used, the current cost of tangible fixed assets and stocks.

[IAS 15 paras 23 to 26].

5.305 IAS 29 is a slightly more focussed document than IAS 15. It is mandatory for companies in a hyperinflationary economy, which is defined as involving such aspects as a cumulative inflation rate of 100 per cent or more over three years. [IAS 29 para 3].

5.306 IAS 29 allows either historical cost or current cost to be used, but does require financial statements to be stated in terms of the measuring unit current at the balance sheet date. This also applies to corresponding figures for previous years. [IAS 29 para 8]. Basically, this requires that items not already expressed in current terms should be re-stated using a general price index.

Chapter 6

Format of financial statements

Page

Chapter 6

Format of financial statements

Introduction

6.1 The general provisions that relate to the format and content of company financial statements are detailed in Schedule 4 to the Act. Schedule 4A deals with the format of consolidated financial statements. These provisions are supplemented by specific requirements of accounting standards. The formats set out in the Act apply both to the financial statements of those companies that are limited by either shares or guarantee and to the financial statements of unlimited companies. Special accounting and disclosure provisions apply to the financial statements of banks and insurance companies and are included in Schedule 9 and 9A respectively to the Act. These special provisions are not considered in this chapter.

6.2 Four primary statements are included within a company's financial statements:

- Balance sheet.
- Profit and loss account.
- Statement of total recognised gains and losses.
- Cash flow statement.

6.3 Schedule 4 sets out two alternative formats for the balance sheet and four alternative formats for the profit and loss account. It also lays down certain general guidelines to be followed. In addition, the Schedule requires companies to disclose considerable detail both in the notes to the balance sheet and in the notes to the profit and loss account. These formats, guidelines and notes are discussed in this chapter.

6.4 The Act does not require companies to include in their financial statements a statement of total recognised gains and losses or a cash flow statement. These primary statements are required by FRS 3 and FRS 1, respectively, for all reporting entities' financial statements that are intended to give a true and fair view. The only exceptions to these requirements are that a cash flow statement is not required for most small companies and for wholly owned subsidiaries of parents established in the EC that publish consolidated financial statements, including a consolidated cash flow statement.

6.5 The formats of consolidated financial statements are substantially similar to those of financial statements prepared by individual companies.

Consolidated financial statements have to comply as far as practicable with the provisions of Schedule 4 to the Act as if the undertakings included in the consolidation were a single company. [4A Sch 1(1)]. In addition, the consolidated financial statements have to comply with the provisions of Schedule 4A as to their form and content. [Sec 227(4)]. A group's consolidated financial statements will include the following:

- The consolidated balance sheet and related notes of the parent company and its subsidiary undertakings. [Sec 227(2)(a), (4)].
- The consolidated profit and loss account and related notes of the parent company and its subsidiary undertakings. [Sec 227(2)(b), (4)].
- The group's cash flow statement and related notes. [FRS 1 para 5].
- The group's statement of total recognised gains and losses. [FRS 3 para 27].
- A note of the group's historical cost profits and losses, appearing immediately after the profit and loss account or the statement of total recognised gains and losses. [FRS 3 para 26].
- A reconciliation of the group's movements in shareholders' funds. [FRS 3 para 28].
- The parent company's individual balance sheet and related notes. [Sec 226(1)(a)].

In addition, the parent company's individual profit and loss account should be published, unless advantage is taken of the exemption given by section 230 of the Act (see para 6.67 below). In practice, the exemption is usually taken and the parent's own profit and loss account is omitted from the financial statements.

6.6 The contents of the financial statements required by FRS 1 (cash flow) and FRS 3 (financial performance) are considered in chapters 30 and 7 respectively. The other statements mentioned above – balance sheet, profit and loss account and related notes – whose form and content is governed by the Act, are considered in this chapter, together with a summary of the rules that apply to the formats.

General rules

Choice of formats

6.7 Schedule 4 leaves the choice of particular formats to the company's directors. Once the directors have selected the particular formats that they are going to adopt for the balance sheet and the profit and loss account, they should not subsequently change them without good reason. [4 Sch 2(1)]. An example of such a reason might occur if a company changes both its operations and its accounting methods significantly and considers that, following the changes, its financial statements fit more naturally into a different format.

6.8 In most situations, however, few companies will have good reason to change their formats, and so they must select carefully the formats that they wish to adopt when they prepare their first set of financial statements after incorporation. If a company does eventually change its formats, it may incur a considerable amount of extra work, because it will have to restate the corresponding amounts for the previous year in accordance with the new formats. In addition, where the formats are changed, the notes to the financial statements must disclose:

- The fact that the company has adopted a different format.
- The directors' reasons for the change.

[4 Sch 2(2)].

6.9 Table 6.1 illustrates the disclosure relating to a change of profit and loss account format.

Table 6.1 – British Gas plc – Annual Report and Accounts – 31 December 1993

Notes to the accounts (extract)

2 Operating costs – continuing operations

The Group profit and loss account in the 1992 Annual Report and Accounts was prepared on the basis of Format 1 of the Companies Act 1985, under which non-exceptional operating costs were divided into cost of sales, distribution costs and administrative expenses. In the opinion of the Directors such a division has become increasingly less appropriate for the Group for the reasons set out below.

There has always been a substantial degree of subjectivity and discretion in the allocation and apportionment of costs over these categories. More recently the Group has diversified and grown in areas outside the traditional gas business, for which the cost structures are different and the division of operating costs under Format 1 is less appropriate. Further, the major restructuring of the UK Gas Business into five units will result in an organisation where, for the Transportation and Storage Unit, Format 1 would be inappropriate. Finally FRS 3 requires exceptional charges before operating profit to be allocated over the statutory format headings to which they relate. The allocation of such charges over cost of sales, distribution costs and administrative expenses (Format 1) would be subject to the same reservations as for the allocation and apportionment of operating costs for non-exceptional charges.

> Accordingly, at the same time as implementing the changes to the Group profit and loss account required by FRS 3, the Directors have decided that the Company should adopt for the Group profit and loss account another format, referred to in the Companies Act 1985 as Format 2, under which the operating costs are allocated according to type of expense. They consider that this will enable the operating costs, including the exceptional charges, to be divided in a less subjective and more helpful way and will enable readers of the Group's accounts to more easily compare and follow trends in particular operating costs.

Headings and sub-headings

6.10 The formats give a list of items either as main headings or as sub-headings. In the balance sheet, main headings are designated either by letters or by Roman numerals, and sub-headings are designated by Arabic numerals. The object of this notation is for identification purposes only, so that the Act can refer to items by their prefix. There is no requirement for financial statements, when they are prepared, actually to show these letters or numbers. [4 Sch 1(2)]. In the profit and loss account Formats 1 and 2, all items are designated by Arabic numerals.

6.11 Whichever of the balance sheet formats and profit and loss account formats a company chooses, the company must show the items in the fixed order and under the headings and the sub-headings set out in the formats it has adopted. [4 Sch 1(1)]. There are, however, certain exceptions to this rule, which are explained in paragraphs 6.12 to 6.16 below.

6.12 An item may be shown in greater detail than the prescribed formats require. [4 Sch 3(1)]. For example, most companies include motor vehicles under the sub-heading 'Fixtures, fittings, tools and equipment'. But where such motor vehicles are significant in value, additional details may be disclosed as follows:

Fixtures, fittings, tools and equipment:		
Motor vehicles	X	
Other	X	X

6.13 An item representing an asset or a liability, or an item of income or expenditure that is not covered in any of the prescribed formats may be shown separately. [4 Sch 3(2)]. An example is where a company holds stocks that do not fall easily within the sub-headings of raw materials and consumables, work in progress, finished goods and goods for resale, and payments on account. Tables 6.2 and 6.3 give two examples where companies have provided additional headings: Bellway p.l.c included showhouses and part exchange properties as a separate category of stocks; Carlton Communications Plc included programme and film rights as a separate category of current assets.

Table 6.2 – Bellway p.l.c. – Annual Report – 31 July 1997

NOTES TO THE ACCOUNTS (extract)

10 Stocks	**1997**	1996
	£000	£000
Group		
Work in progress and stocks	**317,440**	281,793
Grants	**(13,061)**	(13,231)
Payments on account	**(4,986)**	(3,129)
	299,393	265,433
Showhomes	**14,560**	14,926
Part exchange properties	**5,760**	7,569
	319,713	287,928

Table 6.3 – Carlton Communications Plc – Annual report and accounts – 30 September 1997

Consolidated balance sheet (extract)

	Notes	1997 £m	1996 £m
Current assets			
Stocks	14	**59.7**	55.8
Programme and film rights	15	**136.8**	114.4
Trade debtors		**390.1**	411.5
Other debtors	16	**179.2**	107.1
Investments	17	**12.4**	14.8
Cash and other liquid funds	18	**470.9**	339.6
		1,249.1	1,043.2

6.14 Items that are preceded by Arabic numerals in the Act may be combined in the company's financial statements where either of the following circumstances apply:

- Their individual amounts are not material in assessing the company's state of affairs or profit or loss. [4 Sch 3(4)(a)].
- The combination facilitates the assessment of the company's state of affairs or profit or loss (that is, it results in greater clarity). Where this applies, however, the detailed breakdown of the combined items must be given in the notes to the financial statements. [4 Sch 3(4)(b)].

6.15 A heading or a sub-heading need not be shown where there is no amount to be included for both the financial year in question and the immediately preceding financial year. [4 Sch 3(5), 4(3)].

6.16 The arrangement, the headings and the sub-headings of items set out in the formats and preceded by Arabic numerals must be adapted if the special nature of the company's business requires this. [4 Sch 3(3)]. Table 6.4 shows an example where a company has adapted the format prescribed by the Act.

Table 6.4 – British Telecommunications plc – Report and Accounts – 31 March 1994

Notes to the financial statements (extract)

2 Operating costs	**1994 £m**	1993 £m
Staff costs		
Wages and salaries	**3,486**	3,625
Social Security costs	**294**	276
Pension costs (note 23)	**272**	161
Total staff costs	**4,052**	4,062
Own work capitalised	**(465)**	(473)
Depreciation (note 12)	**2,156**	2,116
Payments to telecommunication operators	**1,174**	1,020
Redundancy charges (a)	**517**	1,034
Other operating costs	**3,279**	3,120
Other operating income	**(53)**	(73)
Total operating costs	**10,660**	10,806
Operating costs included the following:		
Research and development	**265**	233
Rental costs relating to operating leases, including plant and equipment hire £21m (1993 – £27m)	**277**	234
Costs relating to HM Government sale of BT shares under combined offers	**3**	-

(a) Redundancy charges for the year ended 31 March 1994 included £305m (1993 – £550m) being the cost of providing incremental pension benefits for employees taking early retirement in the year.

In prior years' accounts, the group's share of results of associated undertakings, which have been immaterial, was included within operating costs. In this year's accounts, these results are shown on the face of the group profit and loss account. Prior year comparative figures have been restated for this reclassification.

The directors believe that the nature of the group's business is such that the analysis of operating costs required by the Companies Act 1985 is not appropriate. As required by the Act, the directors have therefore adapted the prescribed format so that operating costs are disclosed in a manner appropriate to the group's principal activity.

6.17 The Act requires that companies should use the headings and sub-headings detailed in the formats [4 Sch 1(1)] and this was certainly the intention of the 4th Directive. Nevertheless, some companies in practice depart from this requirement, for example, describing 'land and buildings' as 'property', or 'stocks' as 'inventories' or 'turnover' as 'sales'. This practice is considered allowable, provided that the revised wording is not likely to mislead readers of the financial statements and provided that the item remains the same.

6.18 A company should consider the presentation of its financial statements in three stages.

- First, it should consider which of the formats are most suitable for its purposes.

- Secondly, if the special nature of its business requires it, it must adapt the arrangement and headings and sub-headings of any items designated by Arabic numerals in the selected formats as set out in Schedule 4.

- Thirdly, it should consider whether it needs to show any item listed in the formats in greater detail, and, if so, it may do so. (Unlike the adaptation of the formats, which is compulsory if the special nature of a company's business requires it, the reporting company has the option to include greater detail under any heading if it wishes to do so.)

6.19 After having considered the presentation of the financial statements, the company must next consider whether compliance with the requirements of Schedule 4 as regards the format of the financial statements, and compliance with other statutory requirements as to the information to be included in the notes to the financial statements, enable the financial statements to give a true and fair view of the state of the company's affairs as at the end of the financial year and of its profit or loss for the year. If the company decides that compliance with Schedule 4 would not give a true and fair view, it should examine whether the solution to this problem might be to provide additional information in the financial statements. If in special circumstances, compliance with the Act would be inconsistent with the requirement to give a true and fair view, the directors must depart from the Act's provisions. In such a situation, particulars of the departure, the reasons for it, and its effect must be given in the notes to the financial statements (see further chapter 2).

Corresponding amounts

6.20 Corresponding amounts for the year immediately preceding the year in question must be shown in respect of every item in a company's balance sheet or profit and loss account. [4 Sch 4(1)]. This applies even when no such item exists to be disclosed in respect of the current financial year. [4 Sch 4(3)].

6.21 Also, in general, the corresponding amounts for the previous financial year must be given in respect of each item shown in the notes to the financial statements. [4 Sch 58(2)]. The only exceptions to this relate to:

- Information required under Schedule 4A, paragraph 13 (information relating to acquisitions taking place in the financial year).
- Details concerning the identity and class of shares held in subsidiary undertakings required by paragraphs 2 and 16 of Schedule 5.
- Details concerning the identity and class of shares held in undertakings (and the proportion of nominal value represented by those shares) where the investment is ten per cent or more of any class of shares required by paragraphs 8(3), 24(3)(4) and 27(3)(4) of Schedule 5.
- The proportion of capital held in joint ventures required by paragraph 21(1)(d) of Schedule 5.
- The identity and proportion of each class of shares held in associated undertakings required by paragraph 22(4)(5) of Schedule 5.
- The information that must be disclosed in respect of loans and other dealings in favour of directors and others under Parts II and III of Schedule 6.
- Movements on fixed assets required by paragraph 42 of Schedule 4.
- Movements on reserves and provisions required by paragraph 46 of Schedule 4.

[4 Sch 58(3)].

6.22 Where the amount for the previous year is not comparable with the amount to be shown in respect of the current year, the previous year's amount must be adjusted. Where this applies, particulars of the adjustment and the reasons for it must be disclosed in the notes to the financial statements. This requirement applies in respect of every item in a company's balance sheet or profit and loss account and in respect of each item shown in the notes to the financial statements. [4 Sch 4(2),58(2)]. An example is shown in Table 6.5.

Table 6.5 – Royal Doulton plc – Annual Report – 31 December 1994

Notes to the financial statements (extract)

2 COMPARATIVE FIGURES

The comparative figures for the cost of sales, distribution costs and administrative expenses have been adjusted to reflect a reclassification between the administrative and distribution activities of the group. The effect is as follows:

	As previously reported *£000*	*Transfer* *£000*	*1993 (as restated)* *£000*
Cost of sales	129,218	(1,370)	127,848
Distribution costs	8,060	51,967	60,027
Administrative expenses – ordinary	73,315	(50,597)	22,718
	210,593	-	210,593

6.23 This provision accords with the treatment required by FRS 3 in respect of prior period adjustments. A prior period adjustment (that has arisen, for example, because there has been a change of accounting policy during the year) is accounted for by restating the previous year's figures in the primary statements and notes and, where it is affected, by adjusting the opening balance of reserves accordingly. Where practicable, the effect of the change on the results for the previous year should be disclosed. [FRS 3 para 29].

6.24 In addition, the Act requires that accounting policies should be applied consistently within the same financial statements and from one financial year to the next. [4 Sch 11]. It allows the directors to depart from this principle (that is, to change an accounting policy) if there are special reasons for doing so, but the particulars, reasons and effect of the departure from the principle of consistency should be disclosed. [4 Sch 15]. The accounting and disclosure implications of changes in accounting policies are considered in chapter 7.

Offsetting

6.25 Asset and liability items may not be set off against each other. Similarly, income and expenditure items may not be set off against each other. [4 Sch 5]. Consequently, companies cannot, for example, show hire-purchase liabilities as a deduction from the related asset. (They may, however, deduct from stock the payments they have received on account of orders.) [Note 8 on the balance sheet formats]. It should be noted that the offset rules do not preclude netting, for example, depreciation of fixed assets against their cost or provisions for bad debts against debtors – they are simply adjustments to asset values.

6.26 The rule against offsetting assets and liabilities is also covered in FRS 5. FRS 5 sets out conditions that must be met before debit and credit balances can be aggregated into a single net asset or liability, that is, where they do not constitute separate assets and liabilities. This is discussed in chapter 4.

The balance sheet

Individual company formats

6.27 The Act sets out alternative balance sheet formats.

Format 1

6.28 In Format 1, net assets can be shown as equal in total to the aggregate of share capital and reserves. This method of presentation probably represents UK companies' most common practice. The Act does not, however, prescribe the place where the totals should be struck. Consequently, in this format a company can equate total assets less current liabilities, on the one hand, with the aggregate of creditors falling due after more than one year, provisions for liabilities and charges, and capital and reserves, on the other hand. Format 1 is set out below and is also illustrated in Table 6.6 (where the company's balance sheet total is struck at the earlier position of total assets less current liabilities).

Balance sheet -- Format 1

A Called up share capital not paid

B Fixed assets

I Intangible assets
1 Development costs
2 Concessions, patents, licences, trade marks and similar rights and assets
3 Goodwill
4 Payments on account

II Tangible assets
1 Land and buildings
2 Plant and machinery
3 Fixtures, fittings, tools and equipment
4 Payments on account and assets in course of construction

III Investments
1 Shares in group undertakings
2 Loans to group undertakings
3 Participating interests
4 Loans to undertakings in which the company has a participating interest
5 Other investments other than loans
6 Other loans
7 Own shares

C Current assets

I Stocks
1 Raw materials and consumables
2 Work in progress
3 Finished goods and goods for resale
4 Payments on account

II Debtors
1 Trade debtors
2 Amounts owed by group undertakings
3 Amounts owed by undertakings in which the company has a participating interest
4 Other debtors
5 Called-up share capital not paid
6 Prepayments and accrued income

III Investments
1 Shares in group undertakings
2 Own shares
3 Other investments

IV Cash at bank and in hand

D Prepayments and accrued income

E Creditors: amounts falling due within one year
 1 Debenture loans
 2 Bank loans and overdrafts
 3 Payments received on account
 4 Trade creditors
 5 Bills of exchange payable
 6 Amounts owed to group undertakings
 7 Amounts owed to undertakings in which the company has a participating interest
 8 Other creditors including taxation and social security
 9 Accruals and deferred income

F Net current assets (liabilities)

G Total assets less current liabilities

H Creditors: amounts falling due after more than one year
 1 Debenture loans
 2 Bank loans and overdrafts
 3 Payments received on account
 4 Trade creditors
 5 Bills of exchange payable
 6 Amounts owed to group undertakings
 7 Amounts owed to undertakings in which the company has a participating interest
 8 Other creditors including taxation and social security
 9 Accruals and deferred income

I Provisions for liabilities and charges
 1 Pensions and similar obligations
 2 Taxation, including deferred taxation
 3 Other provisions

J Accruals and deferred income

K Capital and reserves
 I Called up share capital
 II Share premium account
 III Revaluation reserve
 IV Other reserves
 1 Capital redemption reserve
 2 Reserve for own shares
 3 Reserves provided for by the articles of association
 4 Other reserves
 V Profit and loss account

Table 6.6 – British Telecommunications plc – Report and Accounts – 31 March 1994

Balance sheet of the company

	Notes	1994 £m	1993 £m
Fixed assets			
Tangible assets	12	**13,603**	13,710
Investments	13	**3,518**	2,822
Total fixed assets		**17,121**	16,532
Current assets			
Stocks		**118**	139
Debtors	14	**2,908**	2,702
Investments	15	**2,311**	1,327
Cash at bank and in hand		**2**	1
Total current assets		**5,339**	4,169
Creditors: amounts falling due within one year			
Loans and other borrowings	16	**1,269**	637
Other creditors	17	**5,472**	4,335
Total creditors: amounts falling due within one year		**6,741**	4,972
Net current liabilities		**(1,402)**	(803)
Total assets less current liabilities		**15,719**	15,729
Creditors: amounts falling due after more than one year			
Loans and other borrowings	16	**3,173**	3,323
Provisions for liabilities and charges	18	**506**	929
Capital and reserves			
Called up share capital	19	**1,553**	1,546
Share premium account	20	**364**	314
Capital redemption reserve	20	**750**	750
Profit and loss account	20	**9,373**	8,867
Total capital and reserves	21	**12,040**	11,477
		15,719	15,729

Debtors include amounts receivable after more than one year of £297m (1993 – £354m).

Format 2

6.29 In Format 2, assets are shown as equal in total to liabilities (which include capital and reserves). Because the information disclosed in Format 2 is identical in all respects (apart from one) to the information disclosed in Format 1, Format 2 has not been reproduced here, but an example is given in Table 6.7. The only difference between Format 1 and Format 2 is that Format 2 aggregates, on the face of the balance sheet, creditors due within one year and those due after more than one year. However, in respect of each item included in creditors the split between the amount due within one year and the amount due after more than one year, together with the aggregate, must still be disclosed either on the face of the balance sheet or in the notes. [Note 13 on the balance sheet formats]. This method of presentation is more common in some other EC countries (for example, France and Germany) than in the UK.

Table 6.7 – The Peninsular and Oriental Steam Navigation Company – Annual report and accounts – 31 December 1994

Company balance sheet
at 31 December 1994

	Note	Company 1994 £m	Company 1993 £m
Assets			
Fixed assets			
Tangible assets	10	**264.1**	266.6
Ships	11	**0.7**	0.7
Properties	12	**8.9**	9.8
Other fixed assets			
Investments			
Subsidiaries	13	**3,143.9**	3,059.9
Other investments	14	**73.9**	74.0
		3,491.5	3,411.0
Current assets			
Development properties	15	**-**	-
Stocks	16	**1.6**	1.6
Debtors	17	**352.7**	294.1
Cash at bank and in hand		**4.2**	480.8
		358.5	776.5
		3,850.0	4,187.5

Liabilities			
Capital and reserves			
Called up share capital	18	**729.7**	724.1
Share premium account	19	**547.5**	534.8
Revaluation reserve	19	**0.5**	0.5
Other reserves	19	**-**	-
Profit and loss account	19	**568.1**	586.5
Equity stockholders' funds	19	**1,695.4**	1,695.4
Non-equity stockholders' funds		**150.4**	150.5
Stockholders' funds		**1,845.8**	1,845.9
Other liabilities			
Equity minority interests	20	**-**	-
Provisions for liabilities and charges	21	**33.3**	27.9
Loans: convertible	22	**191.0**	286.5
non-convertible	22	**603.0**	654.3
Other creditors	23	**1,176.9**	1,372.9
		2,004.2	2,341.6
		3,850.0	4,187.5

Rules concerning particular items

6.30 In determining the amount to be shown under 'Net current assets (liabilities)' in Format 1, a company must take into account any amount that is shown separately under the heading 'Prepayments and accrued income'. [Note 11 on the balance sheet formats]. This applies whether the amount in question is shown as a sub-heading of debtors (C.II.6) or as a main heading (D). But as the alternative positions of this heading within Format 1 both automatically fall within net current assets (liabilities), this seems to be a self-evident requirement. In practice, it is fairly rare for prepayments to be disclosed as a main heading.

6.31 Prepayments and accrued income are deemed by the Act to be current assets, even where the assets are not recoverable in the short term. The Act requires the amount falling due after more than one year to be shown separately for each item included under debtors. [Note 5 on the balance sheet formats]. In contrast, provisions and other long-term creditors fall outside the balance sheet total of net current assets (liabilities) in Format 1. UITF Abstract 4 (issued July 1992) addresses this anomaly, but does not advocate a general departure from the formats in the Act. The UITF concluded that, where necessary to prevent readers from misinterpreting the financial statements, the amount of debtors due after more than one year should be disclosed on the face of the balance sheet, but as part of the normal caption for such items within current assets. The footnote in Table 6.6 on page 6013 and the balance sheet caption of current assets in Table 6.12 on page 6041 illustrate alternative methods of disclosure. Where an individual company believes that it is necessary to depart from the format prescribed in the

Act, it would need to justify invoking a true and fair override (see further chapter 2).

6.32 Where a company discloses holdings in its own shares under the heading 'Investments', it must show separately the nominal value of the shares it holds. [Note 4 on the balance sheet formats]. A company will generally hold its own shares only where it has acquired them by forfeiture, or by surrender in lieu of forfeiture, or by way of a gift. [Sec 143]. In addition, shares held by certain employee share ownership plan (ESOP) trusts are required by UITF Abstract 13, Accounting for ESOP Trusts, to be included in the balance sheet of the sponsoring company under the 'own shares' heading, normally within fixed assets (see further chapter 4). Where a company either purchases or redeems its own shares, they are treated as cancelled (see chapter 40), but this does not apply to shares held by ESOP trusts. [Secs 160(4), 162(2)].

6.33 A company must show the amount for creditors in respect of taxation and social security separately from the amount of the other creditors. [Note 9 on the balance sheet formats]. This applies in respect both of creditors payable within one year and of those payable in more than one year (see further chapter 17).

6.34 In determining the split between creditors due within one year and those due after more than one year, a company should normally treat a creditor as being payable on the earliest date on which payment falls due (that is, the date on which the creditor can require payment) rather than on the earliest date on which it expects to make payment (see further chapter 18). This is consistent with the Act's interpretation of the date a loan is to be treated as falling due for repayment. [4 Sch 85].

6.35 The Act requires the amount of any convertible loans included in the caption of debenture loans to be shown separately. [Note 7 on the balance sheet formats]. In addition, FRS 4 requires convertible debt to be reported within liabilities and shown separately on the face of the balance sheet; however, where the convertible debt is not material, this analysis may be given in the notes provided that the relevant balance sheet caption indicates that it includes convertible debt. Conversion into shares should not be anticipated. [FRS 4 paras 25, 54]. FRS 4 is considered in detail in chapter 18.

6.36 Unless a company shows the payments it has received on account of orders as a deduction from stocks, it must show them under creditors. [Note 8 on the balance sheet formats].

6.37 The following items may be shown in alternative positions in the balance sheet:

- Called up share capital not paid (A and C.II.5).
- Prepayments and accrued income (C.II.6 and D).
- Accruals and deferred income (E.9, H.9 and J).

6.38 In addition, two other balance sheet items require further comment:

- 'Payments on account' relate, as appropriate, to payments that a company makes in respect of the acquisition of intangible assets, tangible assets or stocks (see chapters 14 and 17).

- 'Participating interest' means an interest held by an undertaking in the shares of another undertaking which it holds on a long-term basis for the purpose of securing a contribution to its activities by the exercise of control or influence arising from or related to that interest. [Sec 260(1)]. A holding of 20 per cent or more of the shares of an undertaking is presumed to be a participating interest unless the contrary is shown. [Sec 260(2)]. In this context, a participating interest does not include an interest in a subsidiary undertaking. [Sec 260(6)]. It will however include associated companies as defined in SSAP 1 (see further chapter 28).

6.39 FRS 4 requires the balance sheet total of shareholders' funds (that is, capital and reserves) to be analysed between the amounts attributable to equity and to non-equity interests. The standard requires this analysis to be disclosed on the balance sheet; however, where the non-equity interests are not material, this analysis may be given in the notes provided that the balance sheet caption indicates that it includes non-equity interests (see chapter 18). [FRS 4 paras 40, 54].

Consolidated formats

6.40 The Act requires consolidated financial statements to comply as far as practicable with the provisions of Schedule 4 to the Act as if the undertakings included in the consolidation were a single company. [4A Sch 1(1)]. In addition, the consolidated financial statements have to comply with the provisions of Schedule 4A as to their form and content. [Sec 227(4)].

6.41 Schedule 4A to the Act includes provisions that modify the formats detailed in Schedule 4, to include certain additional items that require disclosure in the consolidated balance sheet. [4A Sch 17(2), 21(2)]. Set out below is balance sheet format 1 amended to include those additional items (shown in bold). (For illustrative purposes, modifications have also been made to the numbering and lettering.)

6.42 The format chosen by the group's parent for its individual balance sheet would normally also be used to present the consolidated balance sheet. However, there is nothing in the legislation to prevent the parent from adopting a different format for its consolidated balance sheet, although this is unlikely to happen in practice, unless the group has banking or insurance activities and the parent does not.

Consolidated balance sheet – Format 1

A Called up share capital not paid

B Fixed assets

- I Intangible assets
  - 1 Development costs
  - 2 Concessions, patents, licences, trade marks and similar rights and assets
  - 3 Goodwill
  - 4 Payments on account
- II Tangible assets
  - 1 Land and buildings
  - 2 Plant and machinery
  - 3 Fixtures, fittings, tools and equipment
  - 4 Payments on account and assets in course of construction
- III Investments
  - 1 Shares in group undertakings
  - 2 Loans to group undertakings
  - **3 Interests in associated undertakings**
  - **4 Other participating interests**
  - 5 Loans to undertakings in which the company has a participating interest
  - 6 Other investments other than loans
  - 7 Other loans
  - 8 Own shares

C Current assets

- I Stocks
  - 1 Raw materials and consumables
  - 2 Work in progress
  - 3 Finished goods and goods for resale
  - 4 Payments on account
- II Debtors
  - 1 Trade debtors
  - 2 Amounts owed by group undertakings
  - 3 Amounts owed by undertakings in which the company has a participating interest
  - 4 Other debtors
  - 5 Called-up share capital not paid
  - 6 Prepayments and accrued income

III Investments
1 Shares in group undertakings
2 Own shares
3 Other investments

IV Cash at bank and in hand

D Prepayments and accrued income

E Creditors: amounts falling due within one year
1 Debenture loans
2 Bank loans and overdrafts
3 Payments received on account
4 Trade creditors
5 Bills of exchange payable
6 Amounts owed to group undertakings
7 Amounts owed to undertakings in which the company has a participating interest
8 Other creditors including taxation and social security
9 Accruals and deferred income

F Net current assets (liabilities)

G Total assets less current liabilities

H Creditors: amounts falling due after more than one year
1 Debenture loans
2 Bank loans and overdrafts
3 Payments received on account
4 Trade creditors
5 Bills of exchange payable
6 Amounts owed to group undertakings
7 Amounts owed to undertakings in which the company has a participating interest
8 Other creditors including taxation and social security
9 Accruals and deferred income

I Provisions for liabilities and charges
1 Pensions and similar obligations
2 Taxation, including deferred taxation
3 Other provisions

J Accruals and deferred income

K **Minority interests** (alternative position M)

L	Capital and reserves
	I Called up share capital
	II Share premium account
	III Revaluation reserve
	IV Other reserves
	1 Capital redemption reserve
	2 Reserve for own shares
	3 Reserves provided for by the articles of association
	4 Other reserves
	V Profit and loss account
M	**Minority interests** (alternative position K)

Rules concerning particular items in consolidated formats

6.43 The following items may be shown in the alternative positions in the formats.

- Called up share capital not paid (A and C.II.5).
- Prepayments and accrued income (C.II.6 and D).
- Accruals and deferred income (E.9, H.9 and J).
- Minority interests (K and M).

6.44 Where minority interests include non-equity shares issued by subsidiaries, FRS 4 requires a further analysis of minority interests between the aggregate amounts attributable to equity and to non-equity interests. This analysis should be shown on the balance sheet or it may, if the non-equity interests are immaterial, be given in the notes provided that the relevant balance sheet caption indicates that non-equity interests are included (see further chapter 18). [FRS 4 paras 50, 54].

6.45 An example of a Format 1 consolidated balance sheet is given in Table 6.8.

Table 6.8 – Glaxo Holdings p.l.c. – Annual Report and Accounts – 30 June 1994

Consolidated Balance Sheet

At 30th June	Notes	1994 £m	1993 £m
FIXED ASSETS			
Tangible assets	11	**3,184**	2,959
Investments	12	**55**	61
		3,239	3,020
CURRENT ASSETS			
Stocks	13	**575**	595
Debtors	14	**1,310**	1,346
Investments	15/17	**2,708**	2,434
Cash at bank	17	**55**	63
		4,648	4,438
CREDITORS: Amounts falling due within one year	16	**2,130**	2,200
NET CURRENT ASSETS		**2,518**	2,238
TOTAL ASSETS LESS CURRENT LIABILITIES		**5,757**	5,258
CREDITORS: Amounts falling due after more than one year	16	**169**	120
CONVERTIBLE BONDS	18	**129**	123
PROVISIONS FOR LIABILITIES AND CHARGES	19	**293**	358
NET ASSETS	4	**5,166**	4,657
CAPITAL AND RESERVES			
Called up share capital	22	**762**	758
Share premium account	23	**229**	151
Other reserves	23	**4,052**	3,637
EQUITY SHAREHOLDERS' FUNDS	24	**5,043**	4,546
MINORITY INTERESTS		**123**	111
CAPITAL EMPLOYED		**5,166**	4,657

6.46 As explained in paragraph 6.29, in Format 2 assets are shown as equal in total to liabilities. An example is given in Table 6.9. In Format 2 there is only one position for minority interests, between 'capital and reserves' and 'provisions for liabilities and charges'. [4A Sch 17(2)].

Table 6.9 – The Peninsular and Oriental Steam Navigation Company – Annual report and accounts – 31 December 1994

Group balance sheet
at 31 December 1994

	Note	Group 1994 £m	Group 1993 £m
Assets			
Fixed assets			
Tangible assets			
Ships	10	1,857.0	1,763.6
Properties	11	1,747.9	1,719.5
Other fixed assets	12	679.0	575.2
Investments			
Subsidiaries	13	-	-
Other investments	14	238.4	215.0
		4,522.3	4,273.3
Current assets			
Development properties	15	288.3	284.5
Stocks	16	462.2	453.5
Debtors	17	1,149.4	1,098.4
Cash at bank and in hand		115.8	596.0
		2,015.7	2,432.4
		6,538.0	6,705.7
Liabilities			
Capital and reserves			
Called up share capital	18	729.7	724.1
Share premium account	19	547.5	534.8
Revaluation reserve	19	100.1	61.8
Other reserves	19	358.2	402.7
Profit and loss account	19	918.4	911.4
Equity stockholders' funds		2,503.5	2,484.3
Non-equity stockholders' funds	19	150.4	150.5
Stockholders' funds		2,653.9	2,634.8
Other liabilities			
Equity minority interests	20	25.4	11.2
Provisions for liabilities and charges	21	182.8	167.7
Loans: convertible	22	191.0	286.5
non-convertible	22	1,645.9	1,945.4
Other creditors	23	1,839.0	1,660.1
		3,884.1	4,070.9
		6,538.0	6,705.7

Interests in and amounts due to and from group undertakings

6.47 The balance sheet format detailed above specifies the place where the aggregate amounts should be shown of any amounts owed to and from, and any interests in, group undertakings. In Format 1 these items can be summarised as follows:

B	Fixed assets
III	Investments
	1 Shares in group undertakings
	2 Loans to group undertakings
C	Current assets
II	Debtors
	2 Amounts owed by group undertakings
III	Investments
	1 Shares in group undertakings
E	Creditors: amounts falling due within one year
	6 Amounts owed to group undertakings
H	Creditors: amounts falling due after more than one year
	6 Amounts owed to group undertakings

[The next paragraph is 6.49.]

6.49 Because amounts owed by and to group undertakings have to be shown in specific positions in the formats, these balances should not be netted off into a single balance disclosed in the balance sheet as 'Investment in subsidiaries'. This applies even where a note to the financial statements gives additional information that explains the net balance. Although shares in and loans to subsidiaries may, if they qualify as fixed asset investments and 4 Sch 3(4) applies, be aggregated on the face of the balance sheet, the disclosure that follows is not permitted (because it is outside 4 Sch 3(4)).

Investment in subsidiaries – presentation *not* permitted

Shares in subsidiaries	X
Amounts owed by subsidiaries	X
Amounts owed to subsidiaries	(X)
	X

6.50 Moreover, the amounts owed and owing have to be ascertained on an undertaking by undertaking basis. [4 Sch 5]. Consequently, for accounting disclosure purposes in the parent's financial statements, amounts that one subsidiary owes to the parent cannot be offset against amounts the parent owes to another subsidiary. Set-off can be allowed only in circumstances where there is a legal right of set-off (see chapter 4).

6.51 Undertakings have to analyse 'amounts owed by (and to) group undertakings' between amounts that will fall due within one year and amounts that will fall due after more than one year. [Notes 5 and 13 on the balance sheet formats]. The results of this analysis will largely depend both on the way in which group undertakings are financed and on the terms of any formal or informal agreements between the undertakings.

The profit and loss account

Individual company formats

6.52 The Act permits companies to use any one of the four alternative formats of the profit and loss account and it leaves the choice between these formats to the company's directors.

6.53 Unlike the choice between the balance sheet formats, the choice between the profit and loss account formats is significant. A company can choose not only between a vertical presentation (Formats 1 and 2) and a presentation in which it shows charges separately from income (Formats 3 and 4), but also between classifying expenses by function or by type. Thus, depending on which format a company chooses, its financial statements will contain certain additional information, for example, own work capitalised, as well as certain different information.

Classification of expenses by function

6.54 In Formats 1 and 3, expenses are classified by function (for example, cost of sales, distribution costs, administrative expenses). These formats, both of which require identical information, have much in common with the management accounts that many UK companies prepare on a regular basis. It should be noted that there is no line item for 'operating profit' in the statutory profit and loss account formats – the disclosure of operating profit derives from FRS 3 (see para 6.65). Format 1, which is the vertical presentation, is set out below, and illustrated in Table 6.10.

Profit and loss account – Format 1

1	Turnover
2	Cost of sales
3	Gross profit or loss
4	Distribution costs
5	Administrative expenses
6	Other operating income
7	Income from shares in group undertakings
8	Income from participating interests
9	Income from other fixed asset investments
10	Other interest receivable and similar income
11	Amounts written off investments
12	Interest payable and similar charges
13	Tax on profit or loss on ordinary activities
14	Profit or loss on ordinary activities after taxation
15	Extraordinary income
16	Extraordinary charges
17	Extraordinary profit or loss
18	Tax on extraordinary profit or loss
19	Other taxes not shown under the above items
20	Profit or loss for the financial year

Classification of expenses by type

6.55 In Formats 2 and 4, expenses are classified by type (for example, raw materials and consumables, staff costs, and depreciation). Format 2, which is the vertical presentation, is set out below, and also illustrated in Table 6.11.

Profit and loss account – Format 2

1	Turnover
2	Change in stocks of finished goods and in work in progress
3	Own work capitalised
4	Other operating income
5	(a) Raw materials and consumables
	(b) Other external charges
6	Staff costs:
	(a) Wages and salaries
	(b) Social security costs
	(c) Other pension costs
7	(a) Depreciation and other amounts written off tangible and intangible fixed assets
	(b) Exceptional amounts written off current assets
8	Other operating charges
9	Income from shares in group undertakings
10	Income from participating interests
11	Income from other fixed asset investments
12	Other interest receivable and similar income
13	Amounts written off investments
14	Interest payable and similar charges
15	Tax on profit or loss on ordinary activities
16	Profit or loss on ordinary activities after taxation
17	Extraordinary income
18	Extraordinary charges
19	Extraordinary profit or loss
20	Tax on extraordinary profit or loss
21	Other taxes not shown under the above items
22	Profit or loss for the financial year

Consolidated formats

6.56 For a consolidated profit and loss account, Schedule 4A to the Act details the items that should be added to the formats prescribed in Schedule 4. [4A Sch 17(3)(4), 21(3)]. The formats illustrated below include the requirements of both Schedule 4 and 4A (the additional requirements of Schedule 4A are shown in bold and modifications to the numbering have also been made). Formats 3 and 4 are not given as they are rarely used and they replicate the information in Formats 1 and 2.

Consolidated profit and loss account – Format 1

1	Turnover
2	Cost of sales
3	Gross profit or loss
4	Distribution costs
5	Administrative expenses
6	Other operating income
7	Income from shares in group undertakings
8	**Income from interests in associated undertakings**
9	**Income from other participating interests**
10	Income from other fixed asset investments
11	Other interest receivable and similar income
12	Amounts written off investments
13	Interest payable and similar charges
14	Tax on profit or loss on ordinary activities
15	Profit or loss on ordinary activities after taxation
16	**Minority interests**
17	Extraordinary income
18	Extraordinary charges
19	Extraordinary profit or loss
20	Tax on extraordinary profit or loss
21	**Minority interests** (in extraordinary items)
22	Other taxes not shown under the above items
23	Profit or loss for the financial year

Consolidated profit and loss account – Format 2	
1	Turnover
2	Change in stocks of finished goods and in work in progress
3	Own work capitalised
4	Other operating income
5	(a) Raw materials and consumables
	(b) Other external charges
6	Staff costs:
	(a) Wages and salaries
	(b) Social security costs
	(c) Other pension costs
7	(a) Depreciation and other amounts written off tangible and intangible fixed assets
	(b) Exceptional amounts written off current assets
8	Other operating charges
9	Income from shares in group undertakings
10	**Income from interests in associated undertakings**
11	**Income from other participating interests**
12	Income from other fixed asset investments
13	Other interest receivable and similar income
14	Amounts written off investments
15	Interest payable and similar charges
16	Tax on profit or loss on ordinary activities
17	Profit or loss on ordinary activities after taxation
18	**Minority interests**
19	Extraordinary income
20	Extraordinary charges
21	Extraordinary profit or loss
22	Tax on extraordinary profit or loss
23	**Minority interests** (in extraordinary items)
24	Other taxes not shown under the above items
25	Profit or loss for the financial year

Rules concerning particular items

6.57 All items in the profit and loss account are preceded by an Arabic numeral and so they may be combined on the face of the profit and loss account and disclosed individually in the notes, if that treatment is considered to make a company's results more understandable. [4 Sch 3(4)]. Whichever format of profit and loss account a company adopts, the account must, however, show separately on its face the amount of the company's or group's profit or loss on ordinary activities before taxation. [4 Sch 3(6)].

6.58 Furthermore, whichever format of the profit and loss account a company adopts, the financial statements must show separately as additional items on the face:

- Any amount that has been set aside, or that it is proposed to set aside, to reserves.
- Any amount that has been withdrawn, or that it is proposed to withdraw, from reserves.
- The aggregate amount of any dividends that have been paid and that are proposed.

[4 Sch 3(7)].

6.59 Where dividends have been paid or proposed, or other appropriations made, in respect of non-equity shares, FRS 4 requires the amounts to be disclosed separately either on the face of the profit and loss account or in the notes and, in the latter case, the relevant caption in the profit and loss account should indicate their existence (see further chapter 18). [FRS 4 para 59].

6.60 The Act attaches to the formats certain notes and comments on specific profit and loss account items.

6.61 Where expenses are classified by function (Formats 1 and 3), the amounts to be shown under cost of sales, distribution costs and administrative expenses are to be stated after taking into account any necessary provisions for depreciation and for diminution in the value of assets. [Note 14 on the profit and loss account formats]. The amounts of the provisions for depreciation, or for the diminution in the value of tangible and intangible fixed assets, must be disclosed separately in the notes to the financial statements. [Note 17 on the profit and loss account formats].

6.62 Income or interest derived from group undertakings must be shown separately from income and interest derived from other sources. [Note 15 on the profit and loss account formats]. Similarly, any interest or similar charges payable to group undertakings must be shown separately. [Note 16 on the profit and loss account formats].

6.63 In the light of present practice in the UK, it is unlikely that any amount would fall to be disclosed under the heading 'Other taxes not shown under the above items'.

6.64 The two items for 'minority interests' in each of the consolidated formats are not alternatives, as the item on line 21 of Format 1 and on line 23 of Format 2 relate to the minority's share of extraordinary items. [4A Sch 17(4)]. FRS 4 requires the minority interests charge to be analysed between equity and non-equity minority interests (see further chapter 18). [FRS 4 para 60].

The effect of FRS 3 on the profit and loss account formats

6.65 FRS 3 contains supplementary provisions relating to the format of the profit and loss account. These do not alter the requirements of the Act, but include standards for minimum disclosure that should be given on the face of the profit and loss account, together with certain additional disclosures. The detailed requirements of FRS 3 are considered in chapter 7. The following requirements are relevant to the formats.

- The face of the profit and loss account should include, as a minimum, an analysis of turnover and operating profit showing separately amounts attributable to continuing operations, acquisitions as a component of continuing operations, and discontinued operations. (There is no format heading for 'operating profit' in the Act; FRS 3 defines it as being normally, for non-financial entities, the profit before 'income from shares in group undertakings'.)

- Exceptional items (apart from those items listed below) should be included under the statutory format headings to which they relate and should be disclosed on the face of the profit and loss account if that is necessary to give a true and fair view.

- The following items, including provisions in respect of such items, should be disclosed separately on the face of the profit and loss account after operating profit and before interest, classified under continuing or discontinued operations as appropriate:

  - Profits or losses on the sale or termination of an operation.

  - Costs of a fundamental reorganisation or restructuring having a material effect on the nature and focus of the reporting entity's operations.

  - Profits or losses on the disposal of fixed assets.

- A company's ordinary activities have been defined so broadly that extraordinary items have all but disappeared from the profit and loss accounts of UK companies. Consequently, the line items in the Act's formats for extraordinary income and charges, tax on and minority interests in extraordinary items, are practically redundant.

6.66 Tables 6.10 and 6.11 are examples of published profit and loss accounts that follow Formats 1 and 2 respectively.

Table 6.10 – BPB Industries plc – Annual Report – 31 March 1995

Group profit and loss account
Year to 31 March

	Note	1995 £m	1994 £m
Turnover	2	**1,328.3**	1,150.8
Cost of sales		**(853.1)**	(733.0)
Gross profit		**475.2**	417.8
Net operating expenses	2	**(315.1)**	(300.0)
Operating profit	2/6	**160.1**	117.8
Share of profits of associated companies		**8.2**	6.7
Exceptional items: continuing operations			
Disposals of fixed assets		**3.4**	2.5
Disposals of shareholdings		**-**	(1.3)
Profit on ordinary activities before interest		**171.7**	125.7
Net interest payable	5	**(8.4)**	(18.0)
Profit on ordinary activities before tax		**163.3**	107.7
Tax on profit on ordinary activities	3	**(48.5)**	(30.5)
Profit on ordinary activities after tax		**114.8**	77.2
Minority interests		**(4.9)**	(2.3)
Profit attributable to BPB Industries plc		**109.9**	74.9
Dividends	10	**(45.0)**	(40.4)
Retained profit for the year		**64.9**	34.5
Earnings per share	10	**22.0p**	15.0p

2 Operational information (extract)

	1995 £m	1994 £m
Net operating expenses		
Distribution costs	**190.2**	170.1
Administrative expenses	**92.8**	84.8
Other operating expenses		
Exceptional items: redundancy costs	**7.8**	9.9
paper and packaging re-organisation	**-**	5.3
Other expenses	**32.9**	36.8
Other operating income	**(8.6)**	(6.9)
	315.1	300.0

Research and development costs, which are included within administrative expenses, were £5.9 million *(1994 £4.8 million).*

Table 6.11 – English China Clays plc 1994 – Annual Report and Accounts – 31 December 1994

Group Profit and Loss Account (extract)

for the year ended 31st December 1994

	Note		1994 £M		1993 £M (Re-stated – see Accounting policies)
Turnover					
Continuing operations			**877.6**		766.0
Discontinued operations			**163.2**		364.7
	1(a)		**1,040.8**		1,130.7
Operating costs	2(a)		**(927.5)**		(1,025.5)
Operating profit					
Continuing operations		**109.6**		89.7	
Discontinued operations		**3.7**		15.5	
			113.3		105.2
Non operating items					
Continuing operations					
Profit on sale of properties			**-**		0.8
(Loss)/Profit on disposal of operations			**(1.6)**		0.1
Discontinued operations					
Profit on sale of properties			**-**		0.9
Costs of fundamental restructuring			**(4.4)**		(1.7)
Profit on ordinary activities before interest and taxation			**107.3**		105.3
Net interest expense	2(b)		**(14.3)**		(17.4)
Profit on ordinary activities before taxation	1(b)		**93.0**		87.9
Tax on profit on ordinary activities	3(a)		**(31.6)**		(27.3)
Profit on ordinary activities after taxation			**61.4**		60.6
Minority interests			**(0.4)**		(0.3)
Profit for the year			**61.0**		60.3
Dividends paid and proposed	4				
Equity shareholders					
– ordinary shares			**(49.7)**		(60.5)
– demerger			**(224.0)**		-
Non-equity shareholders			**-**		(1.6)
Retained deficit			**(212.7)**		(1.8)

Movements in reserves are set out in Note 16.

Notes to the Accounts (extract)

2 PROFIT AND LOSS ACCOUNT (extract)

	Continuing £M	Dis-continued £M	1994 Total £M	Continuing £M	Dis-continued £M	1993 Total £M
(a) Operating costs						
Change in stocks of finished goods and work in progress	**17.6**	**5.8**	**23.4**	24.5	1.0	25.5
Own work capitalised	**(1.8)**	**(0.2)**	**(2.0)**	(1.6)	(0.8)	(2.4)
Other operating income	**(10.3)**	**(0.7)**	**(11.0)**	(5.1)	(1.6)	(6.7)
Raw materials and consumables	**163.0**	**54.7**	**217.7**	139.9	116.6	256.5
Other external charges	**317.1**	**42.1**	**359.2**	275.8	100.5	376.3
Employment costs (Note 6(b))	**210.3**	**41.6**	**251.9**	175.1	95.1	270.2
Depreciation of tangible fixed assets	**50.0**	**6.3**	**56.3**	46.5	16.3	62.8
Net income from interests in associated undertakings	**(0.7)**	**(0.4)**	**(1.1)**	(0.6)	(0.5)	(1.1)
Income from loan to unlisted undertakings	**-**	**-**	**-**	-	(0.1)	(0.1)
Operating lease rentals – property	**3.6**	**0.6**	**4.2**	4.2	1.2	5.4
- plant and machinery	**8.4**	**3.4**	**11.8**	7.5	8.2	15.7
Hire of plant and machinery	**10.1**	**6.3**	**16.4**	9.3	13.1	22.4
Auditors' remuneration	**0.7**	**-**	**0.7**	0.8	0.2	1.0
	768.0	**159.5**	**927.5**	676.3	349.2	1,025.5

Parent's profit and loss account

6.67 When a parent company prepares consolidated financial statements in accordance with the Act, it is not required to include its own profit and loss account and related notes if the financial statements satisfy the following requirements:

- The notes to the parent company's individual balance sheet show the company's profit or loss for the financial year determined in accordance with the provisions of the Act. [Sec 230(1)(b)].

- The parent company's board of directors must approve the company's individual profit and loss account in accordance with the rules concerning approval of the company's financial statements. [Sec 230(3)].

- The notes to the financial statements disclose the fact that the parent company has taken advantage of this exemption. [Sec 230(4)].

6.68 Where the consolidated financial statements do not include the company's profit and loss account, it need not include certain supplementary information when presented to the Board for their approval. [Sec 230(2)]. The information that can be excluded is specified in paragraphs 52 to 57 of Schedule 4 to the Act, which includes the following:

- Certain items of income and expenditure including:
  - Interest and similar charges.
  - Amounts set aside for the redemption of shares and loans.
  - Income from listed investments.
  - Rents from land.
  - Hire of plant and machinery.

  [4 Sch 53].
- Detailed particulars concerning tax. [4 Sch 54].
- Disaggregated information concerning turnover. [4 Sch 55].
- Particulars of the average number of staff. [4 Sch 56].
- Certain miscellaneous matters including:
  - The effect of including any preceding year items in the current year's profit and loss account.
  - Particulars of extraordinary income or extraordinary charges.
  - The effect of any exceptional items.

  [4 Sch 57].

6.69 Suitable wording for a note to be included in the consolidated financial statements when the parent's profit and loss account is not reproduced would be:

Example

As permitted by section 230(3) of the Companies Act 1985, the parent company's profit and loss account has not been included in these financial statements. The parent company's profit for the financial year was £x (19XX: £y).

The notes to the balance sheet and the profit and loss account

General requirements of the Act

6.70 Schedule 4 to the Act requires companies to disclose considerable detail in the notes to their financial statements. The objects of the requirements are:

- To supplement the information given in the financial statements in respect of any particular items that are shown in either the balance sheet or the profit and loss account.

- To give details of anything else that is relevant, in the light of the information so given, to the assessment of the state of the company's affairs.

- To explain any particular circumstances that affect items shown in the profit and loss account.

[4 Sch 37, 52].

6.71 Any information that the Act requires to be shown by way of a note to the financial statements may, alternatively, be shown in the company's profit or loss account or balance sheet. [4 Sch 35]. However, the Act does not permit a company to use the directors' report as an alternative method of disclosure.

6.72 Schedule 5 to the Act requires companies to disclose considerable detail about their investments in subsidiaries and other related undertakings. The disclosures are grouped in the following categories:

- Subsidiaries included in consolidated financial statements (considered in chapter 22).
- Subsidiaries that are excluded from consolidation (considered in chapter 22).
- Disclosures about subsidiaries where the parent does not prepare consolidated financial statements (considered in chapter 16).
- Joint ventures, associated undertakings and other significant holdings (considered in chapter 28).

6.73 Schedule 5 also requires a subsidiary to name its ultimate holding company and indicate where that company was incorporated (or registered if incorporated in Great Britain). This is considered in chapter 22.

6.74 Schedule 6 to the Act sets out the disclosure requirements concerning directors' emoluments and transactions and other arrangements involving directors. These disclosures are considered in chapters 11 and 34.

6.75 The Act's disclosure requirements are supplemented by the requirements contained in individual accounting standards considered in the paragraphs that follow.

Additional statements required by FRS 3

6.76 FRS 3 requires two statements of a memorandum nature:

- A note of historical profits and losses should appear immediately after the profit and loss account or the statement of total recognised gains and losses. This note is required where assets have been revalued in the financial statements and there is a material difference between the results as disclosed in the profit and loss account and the results as they would have been reported on a pure historical cost basis. Where consolidated financial statements are presented this note need only deal with the consolidated results and not those of the parent company.

- A reconciliation of movements in shareholders' funds, providing a statement of all changes in shareholders' funds in the period, should be disclosed in a note or as a primary statement. This statement brings together the gains and losses for the period as reported in the primary financial statements, with other changes including dividends, new share capital issued and share capital redeemed.

These statements are considered in greater detail in chapter 7.

Compliance with accounting standards

6.77 The Act requires companies to state whether the financial statements have been prepared in accordance with applicable accounting standards. In addition, if there are any material departures from these standards, the particulars and the reasons for the departure must be given. [4 Sch 36A]. These requirements are dealt with in chapter 2.

6.78 These requirements do not, however, apply to a company that qualifies as a small or medium-sized company in relation to a financial year. [Sec 246(1)(a)].

True and fair override disclosures

6.79 Where a company departs from any of the accounting provisions of the Act in order to give a true and fair view, The Act requires that *"particulars of any such departure, the reasons for it and its effect shall be given in a note to the accounts"*. [Sec 226(5), 227(6)]. These disclosure requirements are dealt with in chapter 2.

Accounting policies

6.80 The notes to the financial statements must set out the accounting policies the company has adopted in determining the amounts to be included in the financial statements. [4 Sch 36]. In particular, they must include:

- The method of determining the provision both for depreciation and for diminution in the value of assets. [4 Sch 36].

- The method of translating foreign currency amounts into sterling. [4 Sch 58(1)].

The disclosure of accounting policies is considered in chapter 2.

6.81 Many companies disclose their accounting policies as a separate statement that they locate before the remainder of the notes. This is generally accepted accounting practice and it has the advantage that the accounting policies are given more prominence and are not lost within the individual notes to the financial statements. Where this treatment is adopted, to ensure that the accounting policies are shown in compliance with the Act, the page numbers that identify the financial statements for the purpose of the directors' adoption of the financial statements, and for the purpose of the auditors' opinion, should include the statement of accounting policies.

6.82 Where a company's financial statements have been drawn up under the alternative accounting rules the accounting convention used should be stated in those financial statements. The company should usually also refer to the specific policy for each item that it has accounted for under the alternative rules and this disclosure would normally be made as part of the company's accounting policies.

6.83 The accounting and disclosure requirements in respect of changes in accounting policies are dealt with in chapter 7.

Summary financial statements

6.84 The Act permits, in certain circumstances, summary financial statements to be sent to members of listed companies instead of the company's full financial statements. The conditions that must be complied with, together with the form and content of the statements, are considered in chapter 38.

Format for small companies

6.85 The Act exempts small companies from certain disclosure requirements of Schedule 4 that relate to the annual accounts and directors' report that are prepared for shareholders. The Act also permits abbreviated financial statements to be filed with the Registrar for small and medium-sized companies and exempts certain small and medium-sized groups from preparing group accounts. The form and content of small and medium-sized company financial statements are considered in chapter 36.

Half-yearly reports and preliminary results statements

6.86 The formats set out in the Act do not apply to half-yearly reports and preliminary profits statements made by listed companies, since they are *non-statutory* accounts. These reports and statements must, however, be presented in a form that includes the items that are disclosable under the Stock Exchange's Listing Rules. Chapter 39 considers current Stock Exchange requirements for interim reporting and preliminary announcements. The recommendations of the ASB's statement of best practice for interim reports and proposals contained in the ASB's draft statement on preliminary announcements are also discussed fully in chapter 39.

[The next paragraph is 6.89.]

[The next page is 6039.]

Listed companies' historical summaries

6.89 Although the Act does not require a company to include a historical summary of information in its financial statements, many companies do so. This practice arose because the chairman of the Stock Exchange wrote to all listed companies in 1964 recommending that they should include a ten-year historical summary in their annual financial statements. Disclosure of a historical summary has never become a Stock Exchange requirement, but it has become well established practice, although most companies give a historical summary for a shorter period such as five years.

6.90 There is no set format for historical summaries, but the type of information that listed companies normally give in them is as follows:

Balance sheet

- Tangible assets.
- Other assets.
- Net borrowings.
- Capital and reserves.
- Minority interests.

Profit and loss account

- Turnover.
- Operating profit.
- Interest.
- Profit on ordinary activities before taxation.
- Taxation.
- Profit after taxation.
- Minority interests and preference dividends.
- Ordinary dividends and retained earnings.

Statistical information

- Earnings per share.
- Dividends per ordinary share.
- Dividend cover.
- Return on capital employed.

6.91 The historical summary will normally show the actual figures that were reported for each year. However, in certain situations, the reported figures for earlier years may need to be adjusted. The circumstances where adjustments may be necessary are as follows:

- Where there is a change in accounting policy, FRS 3 requires the comparative figures for the preceding period to be restated if this is necessary to ensure that the reported figures for each year are stated on a consistent basis. In historical summaries, the figures for each year would usually be restated if it is practical to do so; it should also be made clear which figures have been restated. If the figures have not been restated, then this fact should be disclosed.

- Where the results of operations are shown separately as discontinued in a financial year, FRS 3 requires the comparative profit and loss account figures to be adjusted to show those discontinued operations separately. In historical summaries, the figures for each previous year would usually also be adjusted where it is practical to do so; thus the results attributable to continuing operations would relate to operations that are currently continuing.

- Where fundamental errors have been corrected by a prior year adjustment, then the historical summary should be changed and again it should be made clear which figures have been restated.

- Earnings per share figures that are reported should be amended to reflect any:

    - New equity shares that have been issued by capitalising reserves.

    - Equity shares that have been split into shares of a lower nominal value.

    - New equity shares that have been issued by way of rights issues.

  The earnings per share figures should be adjusted in the ways explained in chapter 8.

- Dividends per share should also be adjusted where there have been changes in the number of equity shares in issue due to capitalisation of reserves, a rights issue, or a split in the nominal value of shares in issue.

6.92 Because an historical summary is not a requirement of law or of accounting standards, and it is not required in order for the financial statements to show a true and fair view, the auditors do not need to report on it. They should, however, read such information and, if they identify any apparent misstatements or inconsistencies with the audited financial statements, should take appropriate action. [SAS 160, 'Other information in documents containing audited financial statements'].

Proforma financial statements

6.93 Some companies include, as additional information, proforma balance sheet or profit and loss information where this assists disclosure about the financial effect of certain significant post balance sheet events. Such events would be classified as non-adjusting events under SSAP 17, 'Accounting for post balance sheet events', that is, they do not result in changes to the amounts recognised in financial statements but they are so significant to the company that disclosure of their financial effect may be required. Examples include:

- Material business disposals occurring after the year end.
- Material acquisitions and mergers.
- Rights issues or other financings and financial reconstructions.
- Redemptions or purchases of own shares.

6.94 Formats vary where proformas are used. They are sometimes presented as additional columns (sometimes headed as unaudited proforma) on the face of the balance sheet or profit and loss account; in other cases proforma summarised balance sheets or profit and loss accounts are presented as part of the note to the financial statements disclosing the effect of a post balance sheet event.

6.95 Table 6.12 is an example of a proforma statement on the face of the balance sheet; Table 6.13 is an example of a proforma balance sheet included in a post balance sheet event note.

Table 6.12 – Babcock International Group PLC – Annual Report & Financial Statements – 31 March 1994

GROUP BALANCE SHEET

	Notes	Pro forma 1994 £'000	**1994 £'000**	1993 £'000
Fixed Assets				
Tangible assets	12	58,354	**58,354**	99,021
Investments	14	4,434	**4,434**	5,715
		62,788	**62,788**	104,736
Current Assets				
Stocks	15	27,968	**27,968**	36,054
Debtors - due within one year	16	185,343	**185,343**	158,324
- due after more than one year	16	39,248	**39,248**	54,114
Cash and bank balances	17	125,342	**88,047**	64,507
		377,901	**340,606**	312,999
Creditors: Amounts due within one year	18	(279,778)	**(321,083)**	(279,399)
Net current assets		98,123	**19,523**	33,600
Total assets less current liabilities		160,911	**82,311**	138,336
Creditors: Amounts due after more than one year	19	(10,292)	**(10,292)**	(14,018)
Provisions for liabilities and charges	21	(24,674)	**(24,674)**	(31,437)
Net assets	1	125,945	47,345	92,881
Capital and reserves				
Called up share capital	24	84,572	53,819	53,764
Share premium account	25	67,054	19,207	19,262
Profit and loss account	26	9,234	9,234	55,939
Goodwill	26	(38,446)	(38,446)	(38,204)
Shareholders' funds		122,414	43,814	90,761
Minority interests		3,531	3,531	2,120
		125,945	47,345	92,881

The pro forma balance sheet shows the effect on the 31 March 1994 group balance sheet of the rights issue announced on 21 April 1994 as if the net proceeds of the rights issue had been received on 31 March 1994. Of the proceeds, £41.3 million has been set off against borrowings and £37.3 million has been added to cash and bank balances.

Table 6.13 – Kingfisher plc – Annual Report & Accounts – 30 January 1993

Notes to the accounts (extract)

28 Post balance sheet event

Proposed merger with Darty and rights issue

On 18 February 1993 Kingfisher announced agreement on the terms of a merger with Financière Darty. Kingfisher has agreed to purchase up to the whole of the issued share capital of Financière Darty, which owns 95.3% of the share capital of Darty. The merger agreement has been entered into with shareholders representing over 95% of Financière Darty's issued share capital and Kingfisher has agreed to acquire the balance on the same terms upon the remaining shareholders agreeing to dispose of the shares. If 100% of Financière Darty is acquired the total consideration will comprise 68m Kingfisher shares and cash of FF 1,650m. After taking account of Financière Darty's term borrowings the total consideration for the whole of Financière Darty is approximately £1,139m. Following the merger and the related rights issue the vendors will hold approximately 11% of the Kingfisher's enlarged share capital.

The merger has been partly financed by a rights issue which will raise £313m net of expenses. The Company is issuing 71,286,966 stock units by way of rights. Qualifying holders are being offered the right to subscribe for stock units on the basis of one stock unit for every seven Kingfisher shares. The stock units are being issued at the price of 450p each payable in two instalments of 225p each. The first instalment, which is payable irrespective of whether the merger is completed, is due not later than 15 March 1993. The obligation to pay the second instalment is conditional on the merger being completed. If the merger is not completed every two partly paid stock units will automatically convert into one new Kingfisher share and the aggregate amount received net of expenses, totalling approximately £155m will be used to reduce Group borrowings. If the merger is completed each fully paid stock unit will convert into one new Kingfisher share. The new Kingfisher shares arising on conversion of the stock will be credited issued as fully paid and will rank pari passu in all respects with the Kingfisher shares currently in issue including the right to receive the final dividend in respect of the year ended 30 January 1993.

Proforma Statement of net assets of the enlarged Group

An illustrative proforma statement of the combined net assets of the enlarged Group taking into account the merger and the rights issue is set out below. This is based on the net assets of Kingfisher at 30 January 1993, extracted from the audited consolidated balance sheet, and of the Financière Darty Group at 31 August 1992, extracted from the accountant's report issued by Price Waterhouse dated 18 February 1993 and translated at an exchange rate of FF7.96 = £1. This proforma statement is prepared on the basis set out in the notes below.

28 Post balance sheet event continued

£millions	Kingfisher	Financière Darty	Adjustments	Proforma statement of combined net assets
Fixed assets				
Tangible assets	992.4	271.7	-	1,264.1
Investments	37.2	5.8	-	43.0
	1,029.6	277.5	-	1,307.1
Current assets				
Development work in progress	59.3	-	-	59.3
Stocks	571.7	131.0	-	702.7
Debtors	254.7	64.6	-	319.3
Investments	153.9	109.4	-	263.3
Cash at bank and in hand	161.7	19.4	-	230.8
	1,201.3	324.4	49.7	1,575.4
Creditors				
Amounts falling due within one year	(940.2)	(256.0)	-	(1,196.2)
Net current assets	261.1	68.4	49.7	379.2
Total assets less current liabilities	1,290.7	345.9	49.7	1,686.3
Creditors				
Amounts falling due after more than one year	(132.3)	(652.0)	-	(784.3)
Provisions for liabilities and charges	(0.6)	1.0	-	0.4
Net assets/(liabilities)	1,157.8	(305.1)	49.7	902.4

Notes

1 The adjustments comprise the net effect of:

Net cash proceeds of the 1 for 7 rights issue
Cash element of the consideration payable to the vendors of Financière Darty
Purchase of the 4.7% minority shareholding in Darty

2 No adjustment has been made for the fair value of the assets to be acquired

3 No adjustment has been made to take account of trading since the respective balance sheet dates

6.96 Proforma financial statements are not used exclusively in connection with post balance sheet events. Other reasons may include: presenting a continuous track record where a group reorganisation has occurred; presenting annualised figures where a company has changed its accounting reference period; and presenting financial statements that show the effect of eliminating from comparative figures the results and balance sheets of operations that have been demerged during the period. Table 6.14 shows extracts from the financial statements of Charter plc where the existing parent company was acquired by a newly incorporated parent company in a group reorganisation. Whilst the statutory consolidated financial statements only included the results of the group from the date of transfer to the new parent company, extensive use was made of proforma information to present results, balance sheets and cash flows of the group as if it had always been a single reporting entity.

Table 6.14 – Charter plc – Annual Report – 31 March 1994

Consolidated profit and loss account
Year ended 31 March 1994

Note		Proforma 1994 £m	Proforma 1993 £m	Statutory Period £m
2&3	**Turnover**			
	Continuing operations	**545.8**	537.7	301.7
	Discontinued operations	**-**	667.1	-
		545.8	1,204.8	301.7
2&3	**Operating profit**			
	Continuing operations	**33.8**	35.2	18.7
	Discontinued operations	**-**	24.9	-
		33.8	60.1	18.7
4	**Non-operating exceptional items**			
	Profit on sale of fixed assets in continuing operations	**2.4**	0.3	-
	Profits on losses on sale or termination of discontinued operations	**-**	217.2	-
		2.4	217.5	-
	Profit on ordinary activities before interest	**36.2**	277.6	18.7
5	Net interest	**13.9**	11.6	5.3
2	**Profit on ordinary activities before taxation**	**50.1**	289.2	24.0
	Tax on ordinary activities	**(16.3)**	(27.4)	(7.1)
	Profit on ordinary activities after taxation	**33.8**	261.8	16.9
	Minority interests – equity	**(3.5)**	(4.3)	(2.2)
	Profit for the financial year	**30.3**	257.5	14.7
10	Dividends – equity	**(15.4)**	(23.3)	(15.4)
	Prior year dividend waived by Minorco	**5.7**		-
25	Retained profit/(loss) for the financial year	**20.6**	234.2	(0.7)
11	**Earnings per share**	**36.4p**	242.9p	21.5p

The first statutory accounting reference period for Charter plc was from incorporation on 1 March 1993 to 31 March 1994. The company commenced operations on 23 August 1993.

OPERATING AND FINANCIAL REVIEW (extract)

Scheme of Arrangement and presentation of results

Charter plc acquired Charter Consolidated P.L.C. on 23 August 1993 through a Scheme of Arrangement. The figures for the year are presented on a proforma basis to provide an annual record of the group's operations, unbroken by the consequences of the Scheme of Arrangement. The proforma accounts have been prepared on the same basis as that adopted for the statutory accounts. The consolidated statutory accounts of Charter plc include only the results of the operations of the group from 23 August 1993 to 31 March 1994.

The proforma accounts are presented to provide all the disclosures that would have been given had they been a normal set of statutory accounts. In so doing these proforma accounts also provide, particularly in respect of the balance sheet, a significant number of the disclosures necessary for this year's actual statutory accounts. The remaining statutory disclosures are provided on a shaded background, either on the face of the relevant primary statements or in the separate section of the notes headed 'Additional notes to the accounts for statutory purposes'. The additional notes on pages 39 to 43 must be read in conjunction with the notes to the accounts on pages 22 to 38, as common disclosures have not been repeated in the additional notes.

The comparative figures have been taken from the accounts of Charter Consolidated P.L.C. for the year to 31 March 1993 as amended by the prior year adjustment detailed in note 14.

Comparison with IASs

6.97 In September 1997, the IASC published IAS 1 (Revised), 'Presentation of financial statements'. The revised standard prescribes the basis for the presentation of financial statements in order to improve their quality and make them comparable between periods and between enterprises. The revised standard is a very comprehensive document and covers the following matters:

- Contents of financial statements.
- Minimum requirements for items that should be presented on the face of the balance sheet, the profit and loss account, accounting policies and explanatory notes. Such presentations are loosely based on the EC 4th and 7th Directives.
- Criteria for the determination and presentation of additional line items, headings and sub-headings in the balance sheet and the profit and loss account.
- Accounting concepts and the selection and presentation of accounting policies.
- Fair presentation, materiality and aggregation considerations and rules for offsetting assets and liabilities and income and expense.

- Criteria for the classification and presentation of current and non-current assets and current and non-current liabilities.

- Departure from IASs and fairness override disclosures.

- Example of financial statement presentation in the Appendix that is likely to be adopted without significant modifications by the majority of commercial organisations.

6.98 The standard, therefore, replaces IAS 1, 'Disclosure of accounting policies', IAS 5, 'Information to be disclosed in financial statements', and IAS 13, 'Presentation of current assets and current liabilities'. It is effective for accounting periods beginning on or after 1 July 1998. However, because the requirements are consistent with those in existing standards, earlier adoption is strongly encouraged.

6.99 The first part of the standard deals with the underlying accounting concepts, thus providing a bridge between the concepts discussed in the Framework and the specific requirements in other standards. The guidance on fair presentation, aggregation of items, amendments to comparative information and materiality are consistent with those found under UK GAAP. In addition, the revised standard introduces for the first time an overriding provision which is similar to that found under the Act.

6.100 The content of the financial statements under IAS 1 is similar to UK GAAP. In particular, IASC imports the UK concept that performance should be measured more broadly than the 'profit' shown in the income statement. As a result the idea behind the statement of total recognised gains and losses required by FRS 3 has been adopted in IAS 1. The key difference is that under IAS 1 this new primary statement can be presented either as 'traditional' equity reconciliation in columnar form showing all the components of equity (but not distinguishing those that are a component of performance from those that are not), or as a separate statement of performance in its own right. Both types of presentation are included in the illustrative examples included in the standard.

6.101 Unlike UK GAAP, the revised standard does not prescribe the strict order or format in which items are to be presented in the financial statements. It simply provides a list of items that are so different in nature or function that they deserve separate presentation on the face of the balance sheet and the profit and loss account. However, the list is very similar to the format line items specified in the EC 4th and 7th Directives. As a result, the recommended format of the balance sheet provided in the illustrative example follows closely the Companies Act balance sheet Format 2 which equates assets with liabilities. Similarly, the recommended format for the income statement closely follows the Companies Act profit and loss account Format 1 which classifies expenses by function, and Format 2 which classifies expenses by type. An enterprise can choose either presentation appropriate to its circumstances.

6.102 Like UK GAAP, there is a basic principle that a fair presentation is achieved if financial statements are prepared in compliance with each applicable IAS (and each applicable interpretation by the IASC's Standard Interpretations Committee (SIC). An enterprise whose financial statements comply with IASs should disclose that fact. However, an enterprise is required to depart from the specific provisions of an IAS when management concludes that compliance with the specific requirement would be misleading and, therefore, that departure from the requirement is necessary to achieve a fair presentation. This will be the case only in those extremely rare circumstances when the treatment required by an IAS is clearly inappropriate and thus a fair presentation cannot be achieved either by applying the IAS or through additional disclosure alone. The existence of conflicting national requirements cannot, in itself, justify departure from an IAS in financial statements prepared in accordance with international standards. Departure is not appropriate simply because another treatment would also give a fair presentation.

6.103 In those extremely rare circumstances, an enterprise should disclose:

- That management has concluded that the financial statements fairly present the enterprise's financial position, financial performance and cash flows.
- That it has complied in all material respects with applicable IASs except that it has departed from a standard in order to achieve a fair presentation.
- The standard from which the enterprise has departed, the nature of the departure, including the treatment that the standard would require, the reason why that treatment would be misleading in the circumstances and the treatment adopted.
- The financial impact of the departure on the enterprise's net profit or loss, assets, liabilities, equity and cash flows for each period presented.

As can be seen from the above, the disclosure requirements are very similar to those required by the Act and UITF Abstract 7.

6.104 Enterprises are also encouraged to present, outside the financial statements, a financial review by management similar to the non-mandatory OFR required under UK GAAP.

Chapter 7

Reporting financial performance

Page

Chapter 7

Reporting financial performance

Introduction

7.1 FRS 3, 'Reporting financial performance', was published in October 1992. It superseded SSAP 6, 'Extraordinary items and prior year adjustments', which was first published in 1974 and revised in 1986.

7.2 The establishment of the ASB in August 1990 coincided with a general feeling of dissatisfaction with several of the accounting standards that were in force at the time, including SSAP 6. In particular, there was evidence that SSAP 6 was not effective, either because of non-compliance or because of a lack of clarity in its provisions, or both.

7.3 An objective of SSAP 6 had been to ensure that, with certain exceptions, all profits and losses were included in the profit and loss account. It divided such profits and losses between ordinary activities and extraordinary activities. The distinction between ordinary and extraordinary was critical, because one of the more widely used measures of performance, earnings per share, *included* profits on ordinary activities, but *excluded* extraordinary items.

7.4 Despite the standard setters' attempts to define 'ordinary activities' and 'extraordinary items' in such a way as to give clear guidance to preparers and users, the distinction between ordinary and extraordinary was frequently blurred. A particular example of this was reorganisation and restructuring costs. SSAP 6 had made it quite clear that the costs of reorganising a continuing business segment were part of ordinary activities. However, some companies, who had carried out what they termed a 'fundamental restructuring' took the view that such a restructuring was extraordinary in nature. In some instances this was because the restructuring involved closures of certain business segments as well as reorganisation of continuing segments and it was considered that it was not possible or meaningful to isolate the costs of the closures (extraordinary) from the other reorganisation (exceptional). As a result of the distinction between ordinary and extraordinary becoming blurred, inconsistencies developed between companies. Because earnings per share excluded extraordinary items, its value as a measure of performance also suffered.

7.5 Furthermore, the frequency with which extraordinary items appeared in companies' profit and loss accounts meant that in practice there was nothing rare or extraordinary about their occurrence. Disillusionment with SSAP 6 gradually increased and pressure grew for eliminating extraordinary items completely. The UITF made a limited attempt to patch up SSAP 6 by issuing UITF Abstract 2, 'Restructuring costs', in October 1991. The UITF's statement referred to preventing *"a perceived drift towards the inclusion of more and more items as extraordinary"*. However, this interim measure was short-lived since the ASB's project on reporting financial performance was already well underway.

7.6 A second important problem with SSAP 6 was that it dealt principally with the profit and loss account and required only that the note disclosing movements on reserves should either follow the profit and loss account or that a cross- reference should be made to where in the notes the reserves summary could be found. It became apparent as a result of several specific cases that items taken directly to reserves, for example, exchange losses on re-translation of opening net assets of overseas subsidiaries, were not always given the importance they merited by shareholders and analysts. This was possibly because the reserves note was often 'hidden' in the body of the financial statements.

7.7 FRS 3's principal purpose was to produce a more effective set of rules for presenting statements of financial performance. To do this the ASB adopted a twofold approach. First, it broadened the range of information that needs to be given both in terms of the amount of detail required and in terms of prominence given to the information. Secondly, it removed the emphasis placed on individual measures of performance by preparers and users by, in particular, reducing the importance of earnings per share. The main reforming measures in FRS 3 were as follows:

- Two primary statements of financial performance are required. These are the profit and loss account and the statement of total recognised gains and losses. These formats are intended to provide an 'information set' that captures all recognised changes in shareholders' funds arising from a company's activities, except for capital contributed by shareholders, distributions and capital repaid to shareholders and purchased goodwill eliminated on consolidation.

- The profit and loss account should disclose separately the results of a company's operations attributable to continuing operations, acquisitions as a component of continuing operations and discontinued operations.

- The definition of ordinary activities was drawn so widely that extraordinary items have all but disappeared from UK companies' profit and loss accounts.

- A framework for disclosing exceptional items was introduced, with rules to control their positioning in the profit and loss account formats.

- The emphasis on earnings per share as a single measure of performance was diminished. Since it is now based on a company's profit or loss for the year after all exceptional charges and credits, including those that would previously have been treated as extraordinary, it is a volatile measure and does not attempt to capture any underlying trends in a company's operating performance. However, alternative earnings per share figures may be disclosed provided that: the basic earnings per share required by the standard is given at least as much prominence as the alternative; a reconciliation between the two figures is given; and the reason for showing the alternative figure is explained. (Chapter 8 contains a guide to earnings per share.)

- The statement of total recognised gains and losses includes in one place all the gains and losses of the year, whether recognised in the profit and loss account or taken directly to reserves. Its purpose is to show the year's total financial performance. In addition to the profit for the financial year, the statement includes unrealised revaluation surpluses, exchange gains and losses on translation of net assets of overseas subsidiaries and other gains and losses recognised in the year.

7.8 Thus, FRS 3 requires statements of performance which, taken together, give an information set that depicts the major elements of a company's performance, including all gains and losses of the period whether accounted for in the profit and loss account or in reserves. The aim of this approach is to give analysts and other users sufficient information to enable them to make judgements about a company's past performance and to assist them in forming a basis for predicting future trends in performance.

Profit and loss account formats – an overview

7.9 FRS 3 requires that the profit and loss account should include all gains and losses recognised in the financial statements for the period, except those that are specifically permitted or required by the FRS or by other accounting standards to be taken directly to reserves, or (in the absence of a relevant accounting standard) specifically permitted or required by law to be taken directly to reserves. [FRS 3 para 13]. Gains and losses that go directly to reserves must be included in the statement of total recognised gains and losses, together with the profit or loss for the year.

Layered format

7.10 FRS 3 sets out a layered format for the profit and loss account that is designed to highlight a number of important components of financial performance. These are:

- Results of continuing operations, including separate disclosure of the results of acquisitions, where material.
- Results of discontinued operations.
- Certain types of income or expense that are required to be shown on the face of the profit and loss account after operating profit, but before interest. These include:
  - Profits or losses on the sale or termination of an operation.
  - Costs of a fundamental reorganisation or restructuring having a material effect on the nature and focus of the reporting entity's operations.
  - Profits or losses on the disposal of fixed assets.

  Provisions made in respect of these items should also be included.

7.11 Exceptional items, other than those that fall into the category of post-operating profit items listed above, should be shown under the statutory format headings to which they relate, either in the notes or on the face of the profit and loss account if this is necessary in order to give a true and fair view. [FRS 3 para 19].

7.12 FRS 3 supplements the Act's requirements as to the form and content of the profit and loss account. The Act provides a choice of four formats – of the two formats most commonly used by UK companies, Format 1 analyses operating expenses by function, Format 2 by type. These formats are fully described in chapter 6.

Operating profit

7.13 The standard requires that turnover and operating profit should be shown separately on the face of the profit and loss account split between: continuing operations; acquisitions as a component of continuing operations; and discontinued operations. [FRS 3 para 14]. As standards deal only with material items, the requirement to disclose results of acquisitions applies if those results are material in aggregate and the requirement to disclose results of discontinued operations similarly depends on those results being material in aggregate. FRS 6 added the requirement that the results of each material acquisition should be shown separately. [FRS 6 paras 23, 28].

7.14 Where operations that have been sold or terminated are classified as discontinued in the profit and loss account, the comparative profit and loss account figures are restated in order to show the previous year's results attributable to those operations as discontinued. Consequently, the results shown under the heading of continuing operations for both the current year and the previous year are attributable to the operations that are continuing at the end of the current year. This presents something of a track record of the operations that are currently continuing.

7.15 Analysis of other format headings between turnover and operating profit (under Format 1 these are: cost of sales; gross profit or loss; distribution costs; administrative expenses; and other operating income) should also be given, but this analysis may be by way of note, rather than on the face of the profit and loss account. [FRS 3 para 14].

7.16 The standard uses the term 'operating profit' as an important element of performance although there is no such heading in the statutory profit and loss account formats of Schedule 4 to the Act. The term is described, however, in the standard as being normally the profit before income from shares in group undertakings. In consolidated financial statements, this would mean profit before income from interests in associated undertakings, although the standard acknowledges that, in certain situations, income from associated undertakings or from other participating interests may be considered to be part of the operating profit. In fact, FRS 9, 'Associates and joint ventures', introduced a new requirement that the group's share of operating results of associates and joint ventures should be included immediately after the group's operating result (see further chapter 28). [FRS 9 paras 21, 27].

7.17 A comparison of the two formats is given below, down to the operating profit line.

	Format 1		Format 2
1	Turnover	1	Turnover
2	Cost of sales	2	Change in stocks of finished goods and in work in progress
3	Gross profit or loss	3	Own work capitalised
4	Distribution costs	4	Other operating income
5	Administrative expenses	5a	Raw materials and consumables
6	Other operating income	5b	Other external charges
7	Operating profit or loss	6	Staff costs (a) wages and salaries (b) social security costs (c) other pension costs
		7a	Depreciation and other amounts written off tangible and intangible fixed assets
		7b	Exceptional amounts written off current assets
		8	Other operating charges
		9	Operating profit or loss

As explained above 'Operating profit or loss' is not an item in either of the formats, but has been included to show where the requirement for analysis ends.

7.18 The illustrative examples in the FRS are prepared using Format 1, but the examples section explains that *equivalent information* should be shown if any of the other statutory formats are used. Turnover and operating profit or loss would, as for Format 1 companies, be analysed on the face of the profit and loss account, with the remainder of the analysis being permitted to be given in the notes.

7.19 Two basic styles of profit and loss account analysis are envisaged in the illustrative examples in FRS 3. A multi-column approach isolates figures relating to continuing operations, acquisitions and discontinued operations into separate columns. A single-column approach lists such figures in a vertical analysis, with sub-totals providing further analysis. Table 7.1 shows an example of a multi-column analysis; Table 7.2 shows a single-column analysis. The multi-column approach has also been used increasingly to isolate exceptional items included in operating results (see para 7.128 below).

Table 7.1 – Coats Viyella Plc – Annual report and accounts – 31 December 1994

CONSOLIDATED PROFIT AND LOSS ACCOUNT (extract)

For the year ended 31December 1994	Notes	Continuing operations 1994 £m	Acquisitions 1994 £m	Discontinued operations 1994 £m	Total 1994 £m	Total 1993 £m
Turnover	1&2	**2,154.2**	**29.7**	**404.6**	**2,588.5**	2,443.8
Cost of sales	1	**(1,464.0)**	**(22.2)**	**(323.3)**	**(1,809.5)**	(1,702.6)
Gross profit		**690.2**	**7.5**	**81.3**	**779.0**	741.2
Distribution costs	1	**(362.2)**	**(3.9)**	**(50.8)**	**(416.9)**	(398.0)
Administrative expenses	1	**(168.7)**	**(1.8)**	**(19.9)**	**(190.4)**	(179.8)
Other operating income	1&3	**8.2**	**-**	**0.2**	**8.4**	8.3
Operating profit	1,2&3	**167.5**	**1.8**	**10.8**	**180.1**	171.7
Profit on sale of fixed assets	1	**1.3**	**-**	**-**	**1.3**	14.8
Provision for loss on sale or termination of operations	1	**-**	**-**	**(51.0)**	**(51.0)**	-
Gains/(losses) on sale or termination of operations	1	**2.3**	**-**	**0.1**	**2.4**	6.4
Profit/(loss) on ordinary activities before interest	2	**171.10**	**1.80**	**(40.10)**	**132.8**	192.9
Share of profits of associated companies					**0.8**	1.3
Interest receivable and similar income	6				**15.6**	21.5
Interest payable and similar charges	7				**(44.1)**	(65.4)
Profit on ordinary activities before taxation					**105.1**	150.3

Table 7.2 – Pearson plc – Directors' Report and Accounts – 31 December 1994

Consolidated Profit and Loss Account (extract)
for the year ended 31 December 1994

		Notes	**1994 £m**	1993 £m
Sales turnover				
Continuing operations			**1,469.9**	1,319.6
Acquisitions			**80.2**	
Discontinued operations			**-**	550.5
		2	**1,550.1**	1,870.1
Cost of sales		3	**(775.8)**	(1,005.6)
Gross profit			**774.3**	864.5
Net operating expenses	- normal	3	**(533.2)**	(628.4)
	- exceptional	3	**31.3**	(20.0)
Operating profit				
Continuing operations			**265.1**	190.3
Acquisitions			**7.3**	
Discontinued operations			**-**	25.8
		2	**272.4**	216.1
Continuing operations				
Profit on sale of fixed assets		3	**26.4**	4.4
Discontinued operations				
Profit/(loss) on sale of businesses		3	**15.2**	(68.4)
Write back of provision on investment in BSkyB			**-**	71.4
Profit before interest			**314.0**	223.5
Net interest payable		4	**(16.2)**	(14.9)
Profit before taxation		7	**297.8**	208.6

Allocation of interest and taxation

7.20 The standard explains that the analysis of results is only required down to the operating profit line, because an analysis of the interest cost and taxation charge between continuing, discontinued and acquired operations would normally be too subjective to be reliable. However, analysis of interest and taxation may also be given provided that the method and assumptions used in making the analysis are disclosed. In practice, such further analysis is rarely given. One example is shown in Table 7.3.

Table 7.3 – Glynwed International plc – Report & Accounts – 31 December 1994

notes to the accounts (extract)

1. Accounting Policies (extract)

Discontinued activities

The principle used in allocating interest is that the interest cost or credit of discontinued activities is the additional interest cost or credit arising during the period as a result of retaining the discontinued activity up to the date of discontinuance. The taxation charge or credit on discontinued activities is that which directly arises as a result of their trading operations and discontinuance.

7.21 Some of the issues that arise in respect of the allocation of interest to discontinued operations and acquisitions are:

- Allocating group interest costs where operations acquired or discontinued are funded by intra-group borrowings rather than external borrowings. One method has been to allocate interest to intra-group funding at a rate of interest that represents an average cost of group borrowings.

- Allocating interest costs in respect of new borrowings raised to finance acquisitions. The issue is whether the incremental borrowing costs should be allocated to the group's continuing operations (excluding acquisitions) or to the results of acquisitions. Either method would probably be acceptable. Allocating to the group's continuing operations excluding acquisitions emphasises the *actual results* of the acquired operations, whilst allocating to the acquisitions column emphasises the *effect* of the acquisition.

Exceptional items

7.22 Exceptional items charged or credited in arriving at operating profit should be analysed between continuing or discontinued operations as appropriate. [FRS 3 para 19]. Furthermore, the three categories of exceptional items that are required to be presented after operating profit (disposals of operations, fundamental reorganisations and disposals of fixed assets) should also be attributed to continuing and discontinued operations. [FRS 3 para 20]. The latter analysis is illustrated in Tables 7.1 and 7.2 above.

7.23 The treatment of exceptional items is considered from para 7.79 below.

Discontinued operations

Definition

7.24 Discontinued operations are defined as those operations that satisfy all of the following conditions:

- The sale or termination is completed either in the period or before the earlier of three months after the commencement of the subsequent period and the date on which the financial statements are approved.

- If a termination, the former activities have ceased permanently.

- The sale or termination has a material effect on the nature and focus of the reporting entity's operations and represents a material reduction in its operating facilities resulting either from its withdrawal from a particular market (whether class of business or geographical) or from a material reduction in turnover in the reporting entity's continuing markets.

- The assets, liabilities, results of operations and activities are clearly distinguishable, physically, operationally and for financial reporting purposes.

[FRS 3 para 4].

Discontinued compared to discontinuing

7.25 The ASB deliberately chose the term 'discontinued' rather than 'discontinuing' because it considered that there must be a cut off point to avoid manipulation. If it had chosen 'discontinuing' it would have left the way open for a company to declare that it intended to discontinue a loss making activity in the future and thus to separate out the results of that activity. The company would thereby be able to focus attention on the remaining profitable activities.

7.26 The explanatory note to the standard emphasises that any income and costs relating to a sale or termination that has not been completed within the prescribed period after the financial year end should be included in the continuing category. However, it then states that it may be appropriate in some cases to disclose separately in a note to the profit and loss account the results of operations which, although not 'discontinued', are in the process of discontinuing. They should not be classed as discontinued, but might be a subdivision of continuing operations. Such analysis would enable a company to enhance the predictive value of its financial statements by giving additional disclosure of its results exclusive of those activities that are not expected to be there at the next year end. An example of such a note is given in Table 7.4.

Table 7.4 – BM Group PLC – Annual Report – 30 June 1993

Notes to the financial statements (extract)

2 Continuing operations

As detailed in the Financial Review and Note 28, the Group has disposed of various subsidiary undertakings after the year end. The requirements of Financial Reporting Standard No. 3 (FRS 3) only permit those companies disposed of prior to 30th September 1993 to be classified for the purposes of these financial statements as a discontinued operation. The analysis below provides additional information regarding those companies which have been sold prior to the approval of these financial statements but after 30th September 1993 or are proposed to be disposed of as part of the Group's reorganisation plan. Continuing operations can be further analysed as follows:

	Turnover		Trading profit	
	1993	1992	**1993**	1992
	£000	£000	**£000**	£000
Businesses to be retained	**153,959**	111,812	**11,703**	16,593
Businesses to be sold	**301,831**	293,246	**6,088**	23,134
	455,790	405,058	**17,791**	39,727

Businesses to be retained for the year to 30th June 1992 include four months turnover and trading profit in respect of Thomas Robinson Group companies.

Meaning of 'ceased permanently'

7.27 For an operation that is closed down to qualify as discontinued, its former activities must have 'ceased permanently' within the prescribed time limit. In many situations this is clear-cut because all sources of revenues and costs have been terminated and all assets disposed of. In other situations, it is less clear-cut whether activities have ceased permanently. For example, whilst all revenue earning activities may have ceased, there may be run-off costs still to be incurred and assets still to be sold or scrapped. In those situations it is necessary to consider the nature of the costs still to be incurred (and, if applicable, the credits still to be received) and to form a judgement as to whether they comprise an activity.

Example 1

A company carried out a pharmaceutical wholesaling business which it operated from several leasehold premises throughout the country. The business has been closed, all stocks have been disposed of and employees made redundant before the end of three months into the next financial year. At that time some debtors remain to be collected and costs will continue to be incurred in respect of the vacated premises until the leases are disposed of.

In this example the former activity of pharmaceutical wholesaling has ceased permanently. The outstanding future transactions do not constitute the continuation of the activity and, consequently, the operation has been discontinued.

Example 2

A group is closing its household insurance underwriting business. No new policies are being written. A few staff have been retained to handle claims made on the existing policies. Has the activity ceased permanently when the revenue earning activity ceased or will it be when the last claim is paid?

In our view the complete cessation of carrying on the revenue earning activity is the most meaningful criterion. This is notwithstanding the possibility that the financial effect of settling as yet unknown liabilities may be significant to the results of future periods.

Example 3

A group has announced it is closing an engineering contracting segment. Although no new contracts are being undertaken, all existing contracts will be completed and the business will be run down accordingly.

In our view the operation will have ceased permanently when the contracting activity has been completed, that is, at the end of the last contract. In the period during which existing contracts are completed, the group is continuing to carry out a revenue earning activity, albeit that the activity is being wound down.

Materiality and separability of activities

7.28 The standard's definition of discontinued operations (see para 7.24) requires business disposals and closures to satisfy a high threshold of materiality if they are to be classified as discontinued in the profit and loss account. In addition, the operations discontinued must be clearly separable from the rest of the reporting entity's operations.

7.29 However, this does not mean that the discontinued activity has to constitute a complete business segment for the purposes of SSAP 25, 'Segmental reporting'. This is because the definition of discontinued operations also includes a material reduction in operating facilities resulting from a material reduction in turnover in the entity's *continuing* markets. This means that, although the activity should be *separate* from the rest of the entity's operations, it does not necessarily have to be *different*.

Example

A group had three subsidiaries of equal size, all operating in the field of car leasing. The sale of one of the subsidiaries would not be the disposal of the whole car leasing segment as defined for the purposes of SSAP 25. However, it is likely that it would constitute a discontinued operation for the purposes of FRS 3, because it is a material reduction in operating facilities and causes a material reduction in turnover in the group's continuing markets. The disposal is, therefore, likely to have had a material effect on the nature and focus of the group's operations as a whole, particularly if the proceeds are to be used to refocus the group on new activities and markets. In addition, the assets, liabilities, results and activities can be distinguished physically, operationally and for financial reporting purposes. The nature of the operations is *not* different, but that is not a test that has to be satisfied under the standard in order for the disposal of the subsidiary to qualify as a discontinued operation.

7.30 The nature and focus of a reporting entity's operations refers to the positioning of its products or services in their markets including the aspects of both quality and location. The example of a material change in the nature and focus of operations given in the standard is a hotel group which disposes of all its hotels in the US and buys instead hotels in Europe. Another example relating to products rather than geographical markets might be a property company, involved in development and investment properties, that decided to withdraw from the development activity and to hold only investment properties.

7.31 The standard makes it clear that unless there is a material effect on the nature and focus of operations any disposals should be treated as continuing operations. For example, a sale or termination that is undertaken primarily to achieve productivity improvements or other cost savings is part of an entity's continuing operations. In the example in paragraph 7.29 of a company with three car leasing subsidiaries, the disposal of one subsidiary might be regarded as part of continuing operations if it were not sold, but instead was closed primarily to achieve cost savings to the group, with its business and markets being transferred to the other two subsidiaries.

7.32 The following example combines several elements of the treatment of discontinued operations.

Example

The facts in this example are:

(a) The company's year end is 31 December 19X1.

(b) The directors approve the accounts for the year to 31 December 19X1 in May 19X2.

(c) In the year to 31 December 19X1 the company sold subsidiary A and closed a surplus warehouse.

(d) The company achieved a reduction in its workforce of 5% through voluntary and compulsory redundancies.

(e) Before the year end the company decided to close subsidiary B and this was completed on 31 March 19X2. It also announced the decision to close subsidiary C, but this was not completed until April 19X2. It also announced, before the year end, a strategic withdrawal from one if its business segments that was to take place over the next two years.

(f) After the year end it decided to sell subsidiary D and found a buyer for a quick sale that was completed by February 19X2.

The various items would be treated under FRS 3 as follows:

- Sale of subsidiary A – assuming the disposal materially affected the nature and focus of the group's operations and represented a material reduction in its operating facilities, it should be shown as discontinued operations, because the sale was completed in the year.

- Closure of warehouse – if the assets, liabilities, results of operations and activities cannot be clearly distinguished, physically, operationally and for financial reporting purposes, then this would be classed as continuing operations. If they could be clearly distinguished, but the closure has neither a material effect on the nature and focus of the company's operations nor represents a material reduction in its operating facilities resulting from a withdrawal from a particular market or from a material reduction in turnover of continuing markets, then again it would be disclosed as continuing operations. It is most probable that as the warehouse was surplus it would not satisfy the latter condition and the costs would be shown as continuing operations.

- Reduction in workforce of 5% – assuming that no sale or closure was involved this would be shown as continuing, but exceptional if material.

- Closure of subsidiary B – assuming that this could be clearly distinguished and materially affected the nature and focus of operations and represented a material reduction in operating facilities, it should be classed as discontinued. This is, because it also satisfies the condition of having been completed by the earlier of three months after the year end or the date of approval of the financial statements.

- Closure of subsidiary C – whether or not this satisfies all the other conditions it does not satisfy the condition of being completed by the earlier of three months after the year end or the date of approval of the financial statements. Therefore, it should be classed as continuing. As the announcement of the closure was made before the year end a provision for loss on closure of C should be made. The provision would be disclosed as a non-operating exceptional item, under continuing operations.

- Strategic withdrawal – this must be classed as continuing, but FRS 3's requirements for disclosing any provisions should be followed, and the company could analyse continuing operations between continuing and discontinuing in a note.

- Sale of subsidiary D – this would be treated as discontinued (assuming the materiality conditions are satisfied), irrespective of the decision date, because the sale has been completed by the earlier of three months after the year end or the date of approval of the financial statements.

7.33 FRS 3 only requires the analysis of results down to the 'operating profit' level. One of the criteria for qualifying as a discontinued operation is that the operating results of the operation that has been sold or terminated must be clearly distinguishable for financial reporting purposes from the rest of the group's activities. This implies that its turnover and operating costs must be readily identifiable from the accounting records. Nevertheless, there are still allocation issues to be dealt with in practice, in particular, in respect of central overheads. For example, the parent company of a group may allocate its head office overheads to all its subsidiaries on some *pro-rata* basis. If an operation is disposed of, the relevant central overheads may not decrease, at least in the short term. In these circumstances, it seems logical to attribute the whole of the central overheads to continuing operations in the group's profit and loss account, because the costs are not being taken out of the group by the disposal.

Disposal of subsidiary with retained interest

7.34 A company may dispose of a controlling interest in a subsidiary and retain an interest that is treated either as a trade investment or as an associated company. The question arises as to whether the turnover and operating profit of the subsidiary up to the date of disposal should be included as continuing operations or discontinued operations in the consolidated profit and loss account (assuming the subsidiary is material to the group). Where the retained interest is accounted for as an associate the group's share of associate's results will in future be brought into the consolidated profit and loss account on an equity accounting basis, but the full amount of turnover and operating profit of the associate will not be shown in the group profit and loss account because it is no longer a subsidiary .

7.35 We consider that the results of the subsidiary should be classified as discontinued if the retained interest is not regarded as being subject to significant influence by the group. This would be if the retained interest is accounted for as a trade investment rather than as an associate.

7.36 If, however, the remaining interest qualifies as an associated company and is regarded as an integral part of the group's operations then we consider that it would be appropriate to show the subsidiary's results as continuing operations up to the date of disposal. The group's share of the associated company's operating results would then be included on the equity basis in the group's profit and loss account from the date it ceases to be a subsidiary. A note giving details of the subsidiary's results that are included in the profit and loss account in these circumstances would be appropriate. An example of such disclosure is given in Table 7.5.

Table 7.5 – Dobson Park Industries plc – Annual Report – 2 October 1993

Consolidated Profit and Loss Account (extract)

For the 52 weeks ended 2 October 1993	Note	Continuing operations 1993 £000	Acquisitions 1993 £000	Discontinued operations 1993 £000	Total 1993 £000
Turnover	2	98,628	9,359	15,451	123,438
Cost of sales		(62,265)	(4,765)	(10,790)	(77,820)
Gross profit		36,363	4,594	4,661	45,618
Distribution costs		(15,797)	(1,429)	(1,217)	(18,443)
Administration expenses		(14,664)	(2,410)	(3,526)	(20,600)
Operating profit		5,902	755	(82)	6,575
Share of profits of associated companies		2,945	-	-	2,945
Net operating income	2	8,847	755	(82)	9,520

Notes on the Accounts (extract)

1 Mining Equipment (extract)

With effect from 18 January 1993, Dobson Park's Mining Equipment Division was merged with Meco International Limited to form Longwall International Limited (LIL).

As a result of this transaction, the Company acquired a 50% interest in the ordinary share capital of LIL together with certain preference shares having a redemption value of £2m.

Prior to the formation of LIL, the turnover and trading results of the Mining Equipment Division have been included in the consolidated profit and loss account within continuing operations. After that date, Dobson Park's interest in LIL's trading results has also been included within continuing operations although LIL's turnover has been excluded from the consolidated profit and loss account thus adopting the accounting convention for associated companies.

In the 9 month period to 2 October 1993, LIL's turnover and pre-tax profits were £169.3m and £4.4m respectively. LIL's net assets at 2 October 1993 were £31.6m comprising fixed assets £28.3m, other net assets £35.1m and borrowings £31.8m.

The profit before tax of the Mining Equipment Division for the 52 weeks ended 2 October 1993 comprises:

	£000
Trading profits for the period to 18 January 1993	1,153
Share of profits of LIL for the period from 19 January to 2 October 1993	2,723
Other fees and rents, after depreciation, received from LIL	606
	4,482

Operations discontinued by sale

7.37 Where an operation that qualifies as discontinued is sold its results up to the date of sale should be disclosed as part of the normal profit and loss account captions under the heading 'discontinued operations'. The profit or loss on sale should be shown as an exceptional item after operating profit and before interest and should also be disclosed as 'discontinued operations'. Any reorganisation or restructuring of continuing operations resulting from the sale should be treated as part of continuing operations.

7.38 Where the operation is sold after the financial year end, that is by the earlier of three months after the year end and the date of approval of the financial statements, only the operating results up to the year end should be included in the profit and loss account for that year as discontinued operations. In the subsequent year when the operation is actually sold, the operating results up to the date of sale will be shown as discontinued operations in that year.

Example

A group sells a subsidiary which had turnover and operating profits of £30,000 and £6,000 respectively in the previous year. Up to the date of sale it had turnover and operating profit of £8,000 and £2,000 respectively. It is sold for £15,000. Goodwill previously written off directly to reserves on acquisition (prior to FRS 10) was £4,000. Net assets at the date of sale were £5,000. The borrowings of the subsidiary were £7,000 on which it paid interest of £700 in the previous year and £200 in the current year up to the date of sale. The tax rate is 30%.

The sale would be accounted for as follows:

Profit and loss account (extract)

		19X2	19X1
	£	£	£
Turnover			
Discontinued operations		8,000	30,000
Cost of sales (say)		(5,000)	(20,000)
Gross profit		3,000	10,000
Net operating expenses		(1,000)	(4,000)
Operating profit – discontinued operations		2,000	6,000
Profit on disposal of discontinued operations –			
surplus over net assets	10,000		
less: goodwill previously written off	(4,000)	6,000	-
Interest payable		200	(700)
Profit on ordinary activities before tax		7,800	5,300
Tax on profit on ordinary activities		(2,340)	(1,590)
Profit on ordinary activities after taxation		5,460	3,710

Note: the further analysis of net operating expenses and tax required by the standard would be given in a note.

Profits and losses on sale

7.39 In the above example, the re-classification of operating results as discontinued and the profit on disposal of the operation are recognised in the same period. Under FRS 2, 'Accounting for subsidiary undertakings', the date on which an undertaking ceases to be another undertaking's subsidiary is the date on which control passes (see further chapter 21). Where control is transferred by public offer the relevant date is usually when an offer becomes unconditional. Where it is transferred by private treaty the date is usually when an unconditional offer is accepted. Therefore, if the date on which the company ceases to be a subsidiary is after the year end, the operating results up to the disposal date and the profit on disposal would be recognised in the profit and loss account in the following year, classified as discontinued.

7.40 Where an operation in the process of being sold is trading profitably and is expected to be sold at a profit, those profits will be recognised as they arise. Where the operation is loss-making or a loss on sale is expected, the rules are somewhat different. Provision for such expected losses may sometimes be recognised earlier than they arise. FRS 3 introduced rules aimed at controlling the recognition of provisions for future losses.

Provisions for losses on sale of operations

7.41 Where a decision has been taken to dispose of an operation, whether by sale or closure, the standard requires provision to be made for expected future losses if, but not before, the company is *"demonstrably committed to the sale or termination"*. In the case of a sale, the standard requires evidence of the commitment by the existence of a *"binding sale agreement"* that obliges the company to complete the sale. [FRS 3 para 18].

7.42 For most practical purposes, the date of a binding agreement as envisaged in FRS 3 would be the same as the date on which control passes, as defined in FRS 2 (see para 7.39 above), when a subsidiary ceases to be consolidated.

7.43 FRS 3 states that any provision should cover the following:

- The direct costs of the sale.
- Any operating losses of the operation up to the date of the sale.

In both cases, the provision should take account of the aggregate profit, if any, to be recognised in the profit and loss account from the future profits of the operation or disposal of its assets. [FRS 3 para 18]. It should be noted that FRS 3 is amended by FRS 12 (effective for accounting periods ending on or after 23 March 1999) to preclude profits on disposals of assets from being taken into account in measuring such provisions.

7.44 The explanatory section of the standard deals with the situation where a decision to sell an operation has been made, but no legally binding sale agreement exists. In such circumstances, the standard says that no obligation has been entered into by the reporting entity and so provision for the direct costs of the decision to sell and for future operating losses should not be made.

7.45 Although it may not be appropriate to provide for a loss on sale, any impairments in asset values, including any capitalised goodwill, should be recognised regardless of whether a binding sale agreement has been entered into for the sale of the operation. Such impairments should be calculated in accordance with FRS 11 'Impairment of fixed assets and goodwill'. If the carrying values of the net assets and capitalised goodwill of a business for sale exceed in aggregate their recoverable amount (which would usually be based on the expected sale proceeds), the assets are impaired. FRS 11 requires that, unless specific assets can be identified as having been impaired, the impairment loss should be allocated first to any capitalised goodwill, thereafter to any capitalised intangible assets and finally to tangible assets on a *pro rata* or more appropriate basis. [FRS 11 para 48].

7.46 If, say, a subsidiary was acquired several years ago and goodwill was written off to reserves, it would also be appropriate, if the goodwill is now worth little or nothing, to make a provision in the profit and loss account in respect of that goodwill in advance of any binding agreement, as the goodwill would in any event have to be included in the loss on sale when the disposal is accounted for (see para 7.54 below).

Example

A parent company carries its investments in subsidiaries at net asset value in its individual financial statements. It has decided to sell a subsidiary, but has no legally binding agreement for sale. The price it expects is below the net asset value of the subsidiary.

The parent company should provide for the impairment of the investment in the subsidiary. In the consolidated profit and loss account, no provision for loss on sale is made per se. However, the subsidiary's assets are impaired, because the carrying value of its net assets exceeds their recoverable amount (which would be based on the subsidiary's expected selling price). The impairment loss should, in accordance with FRS 11, be allocated to write down the consolidated carrying values of the subsidiary's assets in the following order: first, any attributable goodwill; secondly, any capitalised intangible assets; and finally, other assets on a *pro rata* or more appropriate basis.

[The next paragraph is 7.48.]

7.48 FRS 3 also allows some degree of hindsight because it states that a binding contract entered into after the balance sheet date may provide additional evidence of asset values and commitments at the balance sheet date. [FRS 3 para 45].

7.49 The following example illustrates the accounting for the sale of an operation that takes place after the year end.

Example

A group decides before the year end to sell a subsidiary. The sale will take place after the year end and after the financial statements of the group are signed. The subsidiary's net assets at the year end are £300,000 and the book value of the attributable purchased goodwill is £100,000. The subsidiary makes a loss of £110,000 from the year end to the date the financial statements are signed. The group expects the company to make further losses up to the possible date of sale estimated to be £20,000. The group is negotiating the sale at the time of signing the financial statements and expects the proceeds on sale will be £150,000.

As mentioned above, where there is no binding sale agreement, no provision for loss on sale should be made, but the value of the subsidiary's net assets consolidated will still have to be considered to determine whether an impairment loss needs to be recognised. If no impairment losses were recognised in respect of the net assets and goodwill amounting to £400,000, the group would expect to incur losses of £250,000 in the subsequent year, comprising the subsidiary's expected future losses of £130,000 and an estimated loss on sale of £120,000, as illustrated below:

	£'000	£'000
Net assets		300
Goodwill		100
Assets to be reviewed for impairment		400
Loss up to date of sale	(110)	
	(20)	(130)
Estimated net assets at date of sale		270
Expected proceeds on sale		150
Estimated loss on sale		(120)

It is clear in this example that the subsidiary's net assets plus attributable goodwill are impaired, because their carrying value is not recoverable. The recoverable amount (being the higher of net realisable value and value in use) at the balance sheet date should be determined for the subsidiary in accordance with the methods specified in FRS 11. The calculation would be based on the present value of the estimated future cash flows of the subsidiary, including the net proceeds expected from its ultimate disposal. These cash flows would include the net cash outflows in respect of the expected future losses. The impairment loss would be calculated as the amount of the shortfall between the estimated recoverable amount and the carrying value of the subsidiary's net assets, and would be allocated first to write off the goodwill of £100,000 and secondly among the subsidiary's assets.

The impairment loss would be included in the results of the group's continuing operations; the loss would not be categorised as a discontinued operation because in the example the sale is not completed before the earlier of three months after the year end and the date on which the financial statements are approved.

7.50 The above example demonstrates that, whereas FRS 3 restricts the circumstances where provisions for losses on sale can be recognised, FRS 11 has increased the emphasis on recognising impairments of assets at an earlier point in time.

7.51 Paragraph 18 of FRS 3 specifies, and illustrates, how any future loss provisions set up in one year in advance of a sale of an operation should be disclosed in the next year when they are utilised, that is, when the sale is completed (but note that this does not apply to any impairment losses recognised before a disposal). The results of the operation in the subsequent period should be presented under the normal profit and loss account headings and should be described as 'discontinued operations' if they qualify as such. Any part of the preceding year's provision that related to trading losses should be credited and separately disclosed under the actual operating loss incurred. Although the standard actually states that the provision should be separately highlighted under the operating loss, the examples in the appendices show it as being deducted from the format heading 'net operating expenses'. Therefore, it seems reasonable to interpret the requirement as being to match the provision with the costs with which it is associated under the appropriate format heading, although either presentation is acceptable. The actual loss on sale should be disclosed after operating profit and before interest, again under the 'discontinued' heading if applicable. The balance of the provision relating to the loss on sale should be credited and separately disclosed under the actual loss on sale.

7.52 The standard could be interpreted as implying that the accounting described above is only required for operations that qualify as 'discontinued'. That is because paragraph 18 uses the words "*...when the operation does qualify as discontinued, the provisions should be used to offset the results of the operation in the discontinued category*". However, we consider that it was not intended to restrict the treatment only to discontinued operations and that such treatment should also be used where the results of operations sold in the subsequent year are shown as part of the group's continuing operations, because they do not meet all the conditions described in para 7.24 above.

7.53 An example showing loss provisions created in one year and utilised the next is given in Table 7.6.

Table 7.6 – The Davis Service Group Plc – Annual Report and Accounts – 31 December 1993

Consolidated profit and loss account (extract)

	Note	*1993* *£000*	*1992* *£000*
Turnover			
Continuing operations		**225,325**	213,291
Acquisition		**46,681**	
		272,006	
Discontinued operations		**7,987**	34,155
	2	**279,993**	247,446
Cost of sales	3	**177,597**	172,627
Gross profit		**102,396**	74,819
Other operating expenses		**(82,089)**	(55,404)
Other operating income		**2,483**	2,359
Operating profit			
Continuing operations		**19,050**	19,221
Acquisition		**3,740**	
		22,790	
Discontinued operations		**(611)**	2,553
Less utilisation of 1992 provision		**611**	
	2	**22,790**	21,774
(Loss)/profit on disposal of discontinued operations	4	**(889)**	72
Less utilisation of 1992 provision	4	**889**	
Provision for loss on operations to be discontinued	4	**-**	(1,500)
Profit on sale of properties in continuing operations	4	**50**	73
Profit on sale of properties in discontinued operations	4	**291**	-
Profit on ordinary activities before interest		**23,131**	20,419

Treatment of goodwill on disposals

7.54 The previous section referred to provisions for losses on operations being sold and to impairments in asset values. Where goodwill relating to a previously acquired operation has been capitalised (shown separately among intangible fixed assets) on the balance sheet, the goodwill is subject to the same impairment rules as apply to other fixed assets. When the operation is disposed of, the unamortised carrying value of attributable goodwill is eliminated from the balance sheet and forms part of the calculation of the profit or loss on disposal.

7.54.1 Where goodwill relating to a previously acquired operation remains eliminated against reserves, special rules apply to disposals. UITF Abstract 3 (superseded by FRS 10) requires any acquisition goodwill that has previously been eliminated against reserves and has not been charged in the profit and loss account to be credited in reserves and debited in the profit and loss account as part of the profit and loss on disposal. This requirement has the effect of treating purchased goodwill as an asset with continuing value, even though it is debited to reserves during the period of ownership of the acquired operation.

[The next paragraph is 7.55.]

7.55 Where provision is made in accordance with paragraph 18 of FRS 3 for a loss on disposal that occurs after the year end, the question arises whether a provision should be made for impairment of the attributable goodwill that has been eliminated against reserves. This question can be extended further to the situation where the write-off of such goodwill turns an expected profit on disposal into a loss – should provision be made for part of the goodwill that has been lost? Neither UITF 3 nor FRS 10 deal with the issue of whether provisions should be made in respect of purchased goodwill eliminated against reserves that has lost its value, that is, before the actual disposal occurs. In addition, FRS 11's rules for recognising and measuring impairments of fixed assets and goodwill do not apply to pre-FRS 10 goodwill that remains eliminated against reserves. [FRS 11 para 7]. We believe that in both situations the attributable goodwill should be written off. This also has the desirable effect that the whole of the write-down relating to the impending disposal is recognised in the same period.

7.56 The same principle could be applied where there is no binding contract at the date the financial statements are approved, but the directors consider that the value of attributable goodwill that remains eliminated against reserves has been lost. It has become common practice for the write-off to be recognised in such circumstances before the disposal occurs. Table 7.7 shows an example where a company has written off goodwill in anticipation of a loss on disposal.

Table 7.7 – Cable and Wireless plc – Report and accounts – 31 March 1995
Consolidated profit and loss account (extract)

for the year ended 31 March	Note	1995 £m	1994 £m
Operating profit	4	1,133.7	1,091.2
Other exceptional items			
Profits less losses on sale and termination of operations	9	(17.7)	-
Losses on disposal of fixed assets	9	(43.7)	-
Provision for goodwill charge on impending sale of a business	9	(178.0)	-
Profit on ordinary activities before associated undertakings and minorities		894.3	1,091.2

> **Note 9 Exceptional items (extract)**
> The exceptional charge of £178m relates to goodwill associated with the acquisition of Telephone Rentals plc (TR) in 1988. This acquisition was made in order to achieve rapid growth in Mercury's business customer base which continues to be reflected in the overall business. The Group has now decided to focus Mercury's activities on service provision and is seeking purchasers for the non-strategic elements of the former TR activities in the UK. The provision reflects the expected outcome of the disposal at the current time and is in accordance with accepted accounting practice required by Abstract 3 issued by the Urgent Issues Task Force of the Accounting Standards Board. There are no taxation or minority interest charges or credits applicable to this charge.

7.57 Where goodwill that has been eliminated against reserves is written off in the profit and loss account in the period before the disposal occurs, a further question is whether the profit and loss account of the next period in which the disposal occurs should show the actual loss on sale including the goodwill, with the utilisation of the provision set against it, or whether, once written off in the profit and loss account, the goodwill does not re-enter the calculation of the loss on sale (or the provision set against it). The net effect on profit is the same in both cases. We believe that either treatment is acceptable. The latter treatment would be automatic where the goodwill had been capitalised.

Operations discontinued by closure

7.58 Where an operation that qualifies as discontinued is closed, its results up to the date of closure should be shown as part of the normal profit and loss account captions, under the 'discontinued operations' heading. The profit or loss on closure should be shown as an exceptional item after operating profit and before interest and should also be described as 'discontinued operations'. Any reorganisation or restructuring of continuing operations resulting from the closure should be treated as part of continuing operations.

7.59 FRS 3 states that the profit or loss on termination should only include revenue and costs that are directly related to the termination. [FRS 3 para 20]. Whilst this is not explained in more detail in the standard, the exposure draft (FRED 1) stated that such items should be limited to redundancy costs and profits or losses arising from the disposal of fixed assets. Certainly these items may be included, but it may also be appropriate to include other items (see para 7.65 for examples). Trading losses and profits from the date of the decision should, however, not be included in the loss on closure. They should be included as stated above under the appropriate format headings under the discontinued heading.

Provisions for losses on termination

7.60 Where a closure of an operation is completed within an accounting period there will be no need to consider the question of provisioning for losses on closure at the year end. However, where a decision has been made by the year end to close, but the closure is not made until the following period, a provision will be necessary for future losses to be incurred if the company is committed to the closure at the balance sheet date.

7.61 In addition, where a business closure occurs after the year end, a provision for losses will also be necessary if the closure falls to be treated as an adjusting event, because it indicates that the application of the going concern concept to the whole or a material part of the company is not appropriate. This is a requirement of SSAP 17, 'Accounting for post balance sheet events'. [SSAP 17 para 22].

7.62 FRS 3 requires a provision to be made if, but only if, a decision to close has been made *and* the decision is evidenced by a detailed formal plan for termination from which the reporting entity cannot realistically withdraw. [FRS 3 para 18]. Where a business termination is contemplated but no demonstrable commitment has been made by the company, no obligation has been incurred and, therefore, there is no liability to be provided for. This rule applies in respect of all terminations and not just those that are so significant to the reporting entity that they will qualify as discontinued operations.

7.63 FRS 3 gives two examples of what might be regarded as sufficient evidence of a demonstrable commitment, that is, they would effectively oblige the company to complete the termination. These are:

- Public announcement of specific plans.
- Commencement of implementation.

[FRS 3 para 45].

In practice, the point at which a management decision to close an operation becomes a demonstrable commitment is less objectively determinable than where a sale is involved.

7.64 The provision required by the standard should include:

- Direct costs of the termination.
- Operating losses to be incurred by the operation between the year end and the date of termination.

In both cases, the provision should take into account the aggregate profit, if any, to be recognised in the profit and loss account from the future profits of the operation or disposal of its assets. [FRS 3 para 18]. It should be noted that FRS 3 is amended by

FRS 12 (effective for accounting periods ending on or after 23 March 1999) to preclude profits on disposals of assets from being taken into account in measuring such provisions.

7.65 The standard does not give details of the costs that are intended to be included as direct costs of the termination. It would appear reasonable for the following items to be included:

- Redundancy costs (net of government contributions).
- Costs of retaining key personnel during the run-down period.
- Profits or losses arising from the disposal of fixed assets and stocks.
- Ongoing costs relating to facilities being closed, such as rent, rates and security.
- Pension costs attributable to the termination.

[The next page is 7027.]

- Bad and doubtful debts arising from the decision to close.
- Any losses due to penalty clauses in contracts relating to early termination.

7.66 The provision for loss on closure should be included as an exceptional item in the profit and loss account after operating profit. This applies whether the operation to be closed falls to be treated as discontinued in the current period, in the following period when it is closed (although it could be described in the notes to the financial statements as 'discontinuing' within the category of continuing operations), or whether it remains within continuing operations because it does not satisfy the threshold to be categorised as a discontinued operation.

7.67 It should be noted that where the closure commitment is made in one financial year, but the closure is completed in the following year, the items that may be included in the provision for loss on closure are different from those that may be included in the actual loss on closure where the whole closure process is completed within one financial year. Where a closure is completed within a period the trading results *up to the date of closure* should be shown under each of the profit and loss account headings used in arriving at operating profit. This means that trading losses between the commitment date and the date of closure would *not* be included in the profit or loss on sale, nor would on-going normal costs, such as rent and rates. They would form part of the operating profits or losses included as discontinued, but under the normal format headings up to the date of closure. In contrast, trading losses included in a provision for a closure that spans the year end do not reduce operating profits, because the element of the provision for such losses charged in one period (a non-operating charge) is credited back in the next period as an operating item to offset the operating loss in that period.

7.68 The disclosure requirements relating to the utilisation in a subsequent year of provisions for operations to be terminated are the same as for provisions for losses on sales (see para 7.51 above). The treatment described applies irrespective of whether the operation being terminated qualifies as a 'discontinued operation' or whether its results are included under continuing operations (see para 7.52 above which applies to terminated operations as well as sales).

7.69 The following example illustrates the accounting for provisions for losses on termination.

Example

In 19X1 a company announced a decision to close a subsidiary. The announcement was made three months before the year end, but the closure is not expected to take place until six months into the following year. The subsidiary had turnover and operating losses of £15,000 and £4,000 respectively up to the date of the announcement and had turnover of £3,000 and operating losses of £2,000 between the date of the announcement and the year end. It is expected to have turnover of £6,000 and operating losses of £3,000 in the first six months of next year up to the date of disposal. In addition, there will be stock write downs of £2,000 and fixed asset write downs of £4,000 resulting from the decision to close.

Strictly speaking, under the standard a provision should be established at the date of the announcement. However, if the operating losses were provided from the date of the announcement to the year end, the financial statements to the year end would still have to show the subsidiary's turnover and operating profit up to the year end under the appropriate headings and the reversal of the provision alongside them, which would be pointless. It is, therefore, more appropriate to make the provision as at the year end. The provision will contain the expected operating loss from the year end to the subsidiary's date of closure together with the write downs of stocks and fixed assets amounting in total to £9,000. In this example it is assumed that there was no goodwill written off to reserves on the subsidiary's acquisition. If there had been, it would be included in the provision.

The relevant extract from the profit and loss account will be as follows:

Profit and loss account – Year 1	19X1 £
Turnover	
Continuing operations	18,000
Cost of sales (say)	(22,000)
Gross loss	(4,000)
Net operating expenses	(2,000)
Operating loss – continuing operations	(6,000)
Provision for loss on operations to be discontinued	(9,000)
Loss on ordinary activities before taxation	(15,000)

In the notes the analysis may be given of continuing operations between 'continuing' and 'discontinuing' as the standard permits this where an operation, although not qualifying as 'discontinued' is, nevertheless, 'discontinuing'.

In the following year the losses prove to have been underestimated and turnover and operating losses from the balance sheet date to the date of closure are £12,000 and £7,000 respectively. However, stock and plant write downs only amount to £5,000 in total. The figures in the profit and loss account in year two are:

Profit and loss account – year 2		19X2	19X1
	£	£	£
Turnover			
Discontinued operations		12,000	18,000
Cost of sales (say)		(15,000)	(22,000)
Gross loss		(3,000)	(4,000)
Net operating expenses		(4,000)	(2,000)
Less: release of provision made in 19X1		3,000	-
Operating loss			
Discontinued operations		(4,000)	(6,000)
Provision for loss on operations to be discontinued		-	(9,000)
Loss on disposal of discontinued operations	(5,000)		
Less: release of provision made in 19X1	6,000	1,000	-
Loss on ordinary activities before taxation		(3,000)	(15,000)

Although the provision is wholly included after operating profit in 19X1 it has to be allocated in 19X2 between operating profit and loss on disposal in 19X2. The total loss provided for in 19X1 was £9,000, but the actual loss incurred was £7,000 operating loss plus £5,000 loss on closure, which gives rise to the additional overall loss of £3,000 before taxation in 19X2. Note that 19X1 turnover and operating profit, which in the 19X1 financial statements were classified as continuing, are classified as discontinued in 19X2. Details of taxation on the loss on disposal would be given in the notes. In 19X2 the provision made for losses up to the date of termination of £3,000 has been released against net operating expenses as it is considered that this is the appropriate statutory format heading. Had the provision been in respect of increased cost of sales it would have been released against that heading. Alternatively, the provision could have been released against the total operating loss which would then be shown as an operating loss of £7,000 less provision released of £3,000.

Acquisitions

7.70 Acquisitions are defined in FRS 3 as those operations of the reporting entity that are acquired in the period. [FRS 3 para 3]. The results of acquisitions, excluding those that are also discontinued in the period, should, if material, be disclosed separately in aggregate as a component of continuing operations. As with the other continuing operations the minimum analysis given on the face of the profit and loss account should be turnover and operating profit. The analysis of each of the other profit and loss account headings between turnover and operating profit may be given in a note, instead of on the face of the profit and loss account. [FRS 3 para 14].

7.71 The standard recognises that sometimes it may not be possible to determine an operation's post-acquisition results to the end of the period. This might occur, for instance, where the business of an acquired subsidiary is transferred to another group company and merged with the existing business of that company shortly after the acquisition. If the results of the acquisition cannot be obtained, the standard requires an indication to be given of the acquisition's contribution to turnover and operating profit of the continuing operations in addition to the information required by the Act (see para 7.74 below). [FRS 3 para 16]. The indication might take the form of a general statement, such as that shown below:

Example

The effect of the acquisition is that the plastics division, into which it has been integrated, has been able to reduce costs relative to turnover. In addition, the acquisition has enabled the group to lift turnover in the division by 25 per cent and the division's operating profit has increased by 15 per cent.

7.72 Where an indication of the contribution of an acquisition cannot be given, that fact and the reason should be explained as illustrated below. [FRS 3 para 16].

Example

No indication can be given of the contribution to turnover and operating profit of XYZ Limited, which was acquired in the year. This is because the business and assets of XYZ Limited were divided up between and integrated into the group's existing subsidiaries immediately after acquisition and it is not now possible to identify the separate results or turnover of each of the separate parts of the business.

7.73 The requirements of FRS 3 concerning the reporting of the results of acquisitions are repeated in FRS 6. However, FRS 6 has added an important new interpretation of the requirements as summarised above. It requires the post-acquisition results of businesses acquired in the financial year to be disclosed separately for each material acquisition and for other acquisitions in aggregate. [FRS 6 para 23]. FRS 3 only requires such disclosures in aggregate. An example of the enhanced disclosure required by FRS 6 is given in Table 7.8.

Table 7.8 – GKN plc – Report and Accounts – 31 December 1994

CONSOLIDATED PROFIT AND LOSS ACCOUNT (extract)

FOR THE YEAR ENDED 31ST DECEMBER 1994

	Notes	WESTLAND £m	OTHER COMPANIES £m	**TOTAL CONTINUING OPERATIONS £m**	DISCONTINUED OPERATIONS £m	**1994 TOTAL £m**
Sales						
Subsidiaries		300.8	2139.2	**2440.0**	30.2	**2470.2**
Share of associated companies		59.8	559.6	**619.4**	-	**619.4**
	2	360.6	2698.8	**3059.4**	30.2	**3089.6**
Operating profit	3	18.9	166.5	**185.4**	(2.0)	**183.4**
Exceptional items: profits less losses on sale or closure of businesses		50.9	(44.8)	**6.1**	(31.5)	**(25.4)**
Share of net profit before taxation of associated companies:						
Before exceptional items		4.2	43.6	**47.8**	-	**47.8**
Exceptional items: profits less losses on sale or closure of businesses	4	4.0	(0.8)	**3.2**	-	**3.2**
Fundamental restructuring costs	4	-	-	**-**	-	**-**
Profit before interest and taxation		78.0	164.5	**242.5**	(33.5)	**209.0**

7.74 The Act requires certain disclosures in respect of the pre-acquisition results of companies acquired. They are intended to help in comparing post and pre-acquisition results of acquisitions. The requirements are to disclose the profit and loss of the undertaking or group acquired:

- For the period from the beginning of the financial year of the undertaking or, as the case may be, of the parent undertaking of the group up to the date of the acquisition

- For the previous financial year of that undertaking or parent undertaking [4A Sch 13(4)].

Also the date on which the financial year referred to in the first bullet point began should be disclosed. [4A Sch 13(4)].

7.75 FRS 6 incorporates and extends the disclosures required by the Act in respect of companies acquired. It also requires disclosures about post-acquisition performance that are intended to make the post-acquisition profit and loss account of a group that has made a substantial acquisition more transparent. These disclosures cover exceptional profits and losses that arise from acquisition accounting and, in particular, post-acquisition reorganisation and integration costs. Disclosures for acquisition accounting are considered fully in chapter 23.

7.76 The information required by FRS 3 and FRS 6 in respect of the post-acquisition operating results of acquisitions may be of limited practical use where the acquisition has taken place late in the financial year. That is, because the standards only require the results to be shown separately in the financial year in which the acquisition occurs. FRS 3 suggests that in some circumstances it would be useful for the company to disclose voluntarily in the notes the operating results for the first full financial year for which the acquisition is included. [FRS 3 para 38]. Such disclosure would provide a more useful track record of recent acquisitions and would complement the disclosure of pre-acquisition results required by FRS 6. Table 7.9 provides an example of such additional disclosure; in fact, the company has shown the results of acquisitions made in both the current year and the previous year on the face of the profit and loss account.

Table 7.9 – Arjo Wiggins Appleton p.l.c. – Directors' Report and Financial Statements – 31 December 1992

Consolidated profit and loss account (extract)

Note			1992		1991
		£m	**£m**	£m	£m
	Turnover				
	Continuing operations (excluding acquisitions in 1991 and 1992)	**2,476.4**		2,456.8	
	Acquisition in 1991	**79.1**		29.9	
	Acquisitions in 1992	**67.1**		-	
2			**2,622.6**		2,486.7
3	Operating expenses		**(2,429.6)**		(2,239.9)
	Operating profit				
	Continuing operations (excluding acquisitions in 1991 and 1992)	**196.8**		245.9	
	Acquisition in 1991	**(4.8)**		0.9	
	Acquisitions in 1992	**1.0**		-	
			193.0		246.8

Mergers

7.77 Where a business combination is accounted for as a merger in the consolidated financial statements of the parent company that heads the new group, those financial statements are prepared as if the acquiring group and the new subsidiary had been combined throughout the current period, the previous period and at the previous balance sheet date. The reporting entity is, therefore, restated as an enlarged group that includes the new subsidiary throughout. FRS 3 defines acquisitions as operations of the reporting entity that are acquired in the period. Under merger accounting principles there is deemed for reporting purposes to be no acquisition in the period. Consequently, the results of the combined operations of the enlarged group would be shown as continuing without any separate analysis of acquisitions relating to the results of the new subsidiary.

7.78 FRS 6 requires extensive analysis of the results of the enlarged group that is formed by a merger. These disclosures are considered in chapter 27.

Exceptional items

Definition

7.79 Exceptional items are defined in FRS 3 as:

> *"Material items which derive from events or transactions that fall within the ordinary activities of the reporting entity and which individually or, if of a similar type, in aggregate, need to be disclosed by virtue of their size or incidence if the financial statements are to give a true and fair view."* [FRS 3 para 5].

7.80 The definition is very similar to that previously given in SSAP 6, but it is FRS 3's definition of 'ordinary activities' that brings within the scope of exceptional items all those items that under SSAP 6 would have been extraordinary. This is because the definition of ordinary activities includes almost every conceivable activity or event that occurs in a company's life.

7.81 The definition of ordinary activities is:

> *"Any activities which are undertaken by a reporting entity as part of its business and such related activities in which the reporting entity engages in furtherance of, incidental to, or arising from, these activities. Ordinary activities include the effects on the reporting entity of any event in the various environments in which it operates, including the political, regulatory, economic and geographical environments, irrespective of the frequency or unusual nature of the events."* [FRS 3 para 2].

7.82 The last sentence of the definition appears to be all embracing and, therefore, even the effects of events such as a war (political environment), a natural disaster (geographical environment), a devaluation (economic environment) or a fundamental change in the basis of taxation (regulatory) would be exceptional items.

7.83 In relation to the last of these examples, a fundamental change in the basis of taxation, the standard specifically covers this situation and states that such a change should be included in the tax charge or credit for the period and separately disclosed on the face of the profit and loss account. [FRS 3 para 23]. Previously, SSAP 15 on deferred tax required such a change to be treated as extraordinary, but FRS 3 amended SSAP 15 in this respect.

Non-operating exceptional items

7.84 The standard sets down rules for presenting exceptional items. Three types of profit or loss must, where material, be shown on the face of the profit and loss account after operating profit and before interest and described as continuing or discontinued, as appropriate. These profits and losses will normally be exceptional items, but need not always be so, as they may not always meet the definition of exceptional items given in the standard. However, for convenience they are referred to as non-operating exceptional items in this text (they are sometimes also referred to as 'super-exceptional'). The three are:

- Profits or losses on the sale or termination of an operation.
- Costs of a fundamental reorganisation or restructuring having a material effect on the nature and focus of the reporting entity's operations.
- Profits or losses on the disposal of fixed assets.

Provisions in respect of such items should also be included and in calculating the profit or loss in respect of the items consideration should only be given to revenue and costs directly related to the items in question. [FRS 3 para 20].

7.85 The reason for requiring these items to be disclosed *after* operating profit is probably because they would distort the operating profit line if included above it. Disposals of operations and certain fixed assets are in a sense capital transactions that involve either dealing in the operations themselves or in the assets that support them. Often the figures involved are very material – all the more so as profits or losses on the disposal of operations have to take account of goodwill previously written off direct to reserves following UITF Abstract 3. Furthermore, the operations or assets may have been held for a long time. Consequently, such transactions can be distinguished from profits and losses generated by the underlying operating activities and so it is reasonable to exclude them from operating profit.

7.86 The rationale for including costs of a fundamental reorganisation or restructuring in the non-operating exceptional item category is less obvious. The treatment of fundamental restructurings, that is, where the line was to be drawn between exceptional and extraordinary, was a contentious issue under SSAP 6 and was also dealt with by the UITF in UITF Abstract 2 (since withdrawn). It is probable that they are given such prominence in FRS 3 because a fundamental restructuring should occur only very infrequently and the costs are so material that a separate classification is necessary to give a true and fair view.

7.87 Table 7.1 on page 7 and Table 7.2 on page 8 show extracts from published profit and loss accounts containing non-operating exceptional items.

[The next paragraph is 7.90.]

Profits or losses on the sale or termination of an operation

7.90 The accounting and presentation issues relating to the sale of an operation are considered from para 7.39 above; those relating to terminated operations are considered from para 7.58. The standard requires profits or losses on the sale or termination of an operation to be included under the appropriate heading of continuing or discontinued operations.

7.91 FRS 10 requires disclosure of the profit or loss on each material disposal of a previously acquired business or business segment. [FRS 10 para 54]. UITF Abstract 3 (incorporated within FRS 10), which applies to goodwill that has been eliminated against reserves, requires the amount of purchased goodwill attributable to an operation sold or terminated and included in the calculation of the profit or loss on disposal to be separately identified as a component of the profit or loss on disposal, either on the face of the profit and loss account or in the notes (see also para 7.54 above). [UITF 3 para 10]. An equivalent disclosure requirement is carried into FRS 10 in respect of goodwill on past acquisitions that remains eliminated against reserves under FRS 10's transitional arrangements. [FRS 10 para 71(c)]. Where goodwill attributable to the disposed operation has been capitalised, there is no requirement in FRS 10 to disclose the amount separately as part of the profit or loss on disposal (although the figures can be worked out in aggregate from the note reconciling the balance sheet movements, including disposals, of goodwill).

7.92 In December 1992, the ASB took the unusual step of issuing a statement emphasising that companies should be guided by the spirit and reasoning of UITF Abstracts. This statement was prompted by what the UITF considered "*the unsatisfactory application*" of UITF 3 by a small minority of companies. The statement cited two approaches regarding goodwill on disposals that the UITF had found unacceptable. These approaches, which had attempted to mitigate the presentational impact of charging goodwill in the profit and loss account, were as follows:

- Goodwill should not be debited in the profit and loss account separately from, rather than as part of, the profit or loss on disposal. For example, the goodwill should not be distanced from the profit or loss on disposal as a separate item. A caption such as 'loss on sale of subsidiary' should not be used to describe an item that does not take account of related goodwill.

- The corresponding release of goodwill from reserves should not be credited in arriving at the profit or loss for the year or in the statement of total recognised gains and losses. It should be shown as a credit adjustment in the reconciliation of movements in shareholders' funds.

[ASB Statement 'The Application of UITF Abstracts' Dec 1992].

7.93 Table 7.10 illustrates one method of disclosing a loss on disposal, including the goodwill write-off.

Table 7.10 – Dixons Group plc – Annual Report – 30 April 1994

Consolidated Profit and Loss Account (extract)
for the 52 weeks ended 30 April 1994

	Note	1993/94 Before exceptional charges £million	1993/94 Exceptional charges £million	1993/94 Total £million	1992/93 Total £million
Discontinued operations – exceptional charges (extract)					
(Loss)/surplus on disposal of operations		-	**(19.4)**	**(19.4)**	1.9
Goodwill previously written off to reserves		-	**(191.1)**	**(191.1)**	(2.9)
Net loss on disposal	*6*	-	**(210.5)**	**(210.5)**	(1.0)

Notes to the Financial Statements (extract)

	1993/4 £million	1992/93 £million
6 Disposal of operations		
Loss on disposal of Dixons US Holdings, Inc.	**(19.4)**	-
Surplus on disposal of Supasnaps Limited	-	1.9
Goodwill previously written off to reserves	**(191.1)**	(2.9)
	(210.5)	(1.0)

The sale of Dixons US Holdings, Inc., the parent company of Silo Holdings, Inc., to Fretter, Inc. in exchange for common and preferred stock in the enlarged Fretter group was completed on 3 December 1993. The loss on disposal represents the difference between the book value of assets disposed of and the directors' valuation of the investment in Fretter, Inc. at that date.

Fundamental reorganisation or restructuring

7.94 Apart from indicating that it should have "*a material effect on the nature and focus of the reporting entity's operations*", FRS 3 does not give any further guidance on how to identify a fundamental reorganisation. Some companies may feel under pressure to describe costs as part of a fundamental reorganisation in order to exclude them from operating profit.

7.95 From the dictionary definition of 'fundamental' it could be assumed that the ASB intends that to qualify as fundamental, a reorganisation must go to the root of the company's or group's operations and must involve a change in the basic operations. The 'nature and focus' test is discussed in FRS 3 in the context of discontinued operations. The standard states: "*the nature and focus of a reporting entity's operations refers to the positioning of its products or services in their markets* *including the aspects of both quality and location*". [FRS 3 para 42]. An example is given of a hotel company which traditionally served the lower end of the hotel market selling its existing chain and buying luxury hotels. While remaining in the business of managing hotels the group would be changing the nature and focus of its operations.

7.96 We consider that a fundamental reorganisation is likely to be restricted to one that satisfies the following conditions:

- The reorganisation costs must be material.
- The reorganisation should go to the root of and should encompass the whole or a substantial part of the company's or group's total operations (and not be a reorganisation of only one among many different operations).
- The reorganisation, to affect materially the nature and focus of operations, must achieve more than cost savings which leave the existing operations intact.
- The reorganisation must involve a material change in the nature and focus of the group's operations, resulting in the repositioning of its products or services.

[The next paragraph is 7.98.]

7.98 Tables 7.11 and 7.12 give two examples of disclosures relating to group reorganisations that have been treated as fundamental.

Table 7.11 – TSB Group plc – Report to Shareholders and Accounts – 31 October 1993

CONSOLIDATED PROFIT AND LOSS ACCOUNT (extract)

Note		**1993** **£m**	1992 restated (note 1) £m
	Operating profit	**366**	40
7	Reorganisation costs	**(70)**	2
	Profit before sale or termination of activities	**296**	42
8	Profit/(loss) on sale or termination of activities, including goodwill written off	**5**	(37)
4	Profit before taxation	**301**	5

Notes to the Accounts (extract)

Note 7

Reorganisation costs

Reorganisation costs of £70m (the major part being redundancy costs) relate to the implementation of the Group's announced policy of fundamentally reorganising TSB Retail Banking and Insurance and Hill Samuel Bank. In TSB the management, sales force and administration of TSB Retail Banking and TSB Insurance are being integrated to create a "bancassurance" business. Hill Samuel Bank has withdrawn from a number of areas of business, including branch banking, in order to focus on its merchant banking activities. This involves a reduction in its balance sheet and capital employed together with the consequent reduction in support operations.

In the year ended 31 October 1992, as a result of the decision to integrate the TSB Retail Banking and Insurance businesses, the value of long-term life assurance and pension businesses no longer required a provision for commission payable to TSB Retail Banking. As a result £30m (before taxation) was released to the profit and loss account and included as an offset against reorganisation costs (£28m).

Table 7.12 – Unigate PLC – Report and Accounts – 31 March 1995

Group Profit and Loss Account for the year ended 31 March (extract)

	1995		
	Before exceptional items £m	Exceptional items (note 7) £m	Total £m
Total operating profit	108.2	-	108.2
Income from associated undertakings	20.9	(2.5)	18.4
Continuing operations			
– Fundamental restructuring of dairy businesses	-	(55.1)	(55.1)
– Profit on sale of fixed assets	-	-	-
Discontinued operations			
– Loss on disposal of businesses	-	(0.7)	(0.7)
– Release of 1991 provision	-	-	-
Profit on ordinary activities before interest	129.1	(58.3)	70.8

Notes to the Financial Statements (extract)

7 Exceptional items (extract)

a The costs of the fundamental restructuring of the dairy-related businesses comprise

	Cash spend £m	Asset write-off £m	Total £m
Dairies	15.4	16.6	32.0
Fresh Foods	9.6	10.6	20.2
Wincanton	2.8	0.1	2.9
	27.8	27.3	55.1

The background to, and basis of, the fundamental restructuring costs are set out in the Financial Review on page 19.

Financial Review (extract)

Exceptional Items Exceptional items principally comprise a charge for the fundamental restructuring of the Group's dairy-related activities in response to the upheaval in milk procurement in the UK, and our share of the extraordinary items reflected in the accounts of our associate, Nutricia.

As discussed in the Chief Executive's Review on page 7, the change in milk procurement arrangements and resultant milk cost increases, together with the changing pattern of milk sales away from doorstep to supermarket customers, which has been exacerbated by the milk cost increases, has necessitated a radical review and restructuring of the Group's dairy-related activities. The cost of this restructuring is £55.1 million before tax (£40.1 million after tax), and is separately identified as an exceptional cost as required by FRS 3. The provision comprises £27.8 million of cash costs and £27.3 million of asset write-off allocated across the Group's businesses as shown in Note 7 to the financial statements.

The restructuring plans envisage a 40 per cent reduction in liquid milk bottling capacity over the next three years, as well as rationalisation of our dairy products' activities. Also included are the costs of restructuring Wincanton's milk haulage operations. The cash costs analysed by year of expected implementation and the planned benefits are as follows:

Year ended 31 March	Cash spend **£m**	Planned cost reductions (cumulative) **£m**
1995	**3.1**	-
1996	**14.5**	**7.9**
1997	**7.3**	**16.6**
1998	**2.9**	**24.7**
	27.8	

£18.6 million of the £24.7 million total planned cost reductions arise in the Group's liquid milk operations and will mitigate the impact on profitability of the switch from doorstep to wholesale and supermarket customers.

7.99 When a reorganisation is related to an acquisition, FRS 6 makes it clear that the reorganisation is not fundamental unless it is fundamental to the enlarged group. This issue is considered in chapter 23.

7.100 A problem that frequently arises in practice is that restructuring often involves asset disposals and closures of operations. Fixed asset disposals and disposals of operations are required to be shown after operating profit. However, the costs of reorganisations that are not fundamental are required to be included in operating profit. The fairest presentation then becomes a matter of judgement in individual cases.

Example

As part of a (non-fundamental) reorganisation involving significant redundancy costs, some properties are vacated and sold, giving rise to profits and losses on sale. Should such profits and losses be shown separately from the other reorganisation costs and after operating profit, because FRS 3 requires profits or losses on disposals of fixed assets to be shown after operating profit, or should they be included with the other reorganisation costs that are charged in arriving at operating profit?

This is a grey area in FRS 3. It is arguable that it is misleading to show redundancy costs incurred in closing a site in operating profit and the related profit or loss on sale of the site after operating profit. If the items are part of the same reorganisation, it is in general preferable to show them in one place. If the profits or losses on the property disposals were incidental to the reorganisation, they could be shown as part of the reorganisation costs, that is, as part of operating profit. However, if the profits or losses on the property disposals were very material and the redundancy costs were less significant in relation thereto, the reorganisation could be treated as an asset disposal, with the redundancy costs included in the profit or loss on disposal.

[The next paragraph is 7.103.]

Profits or losses on disposals of fixed assets

7.103 The third type of item that must be disclosed after operating profit is profits or losses on the disposal of fixed assets. This is intended to include profits or losses on sales of major assets, such as properties. It is not intended to include profits or losses on disposal that are in effect no more than normal adjustments to depreciation previously charged. Those adjustments would be included in operating profit as part of the normal depreciation charge.

7.104 The standard requires that the profit or loss on disposal of an asset should be accounted for in the profit and loss account for the period in which the disposal occurs as the difference between the net sale proceeds and the net carrying amount, whether carried at historical cost or at a valuation. [FRS 3 para 21].

7.105 This requirement was new in UK accounting because before FRS 3 it had been quite acceptable to calculate the profit or loss on a previously revalued asset *either* on the above basis *or* by reference to the asset's depreciated historical cost. The difference between the two bases is that under the latter basis the previous revaluation surplus is passed through the profit and loss account on disposal whereas under the former basis it is not.

7.106 It should be noted that the requirement introduced by FRS 3 applies to all assets and not just to fixed assets.

7.107 The reasoning behind the change stems from the ASB's new approach to the presentation of statements of financial performance. As described earlier, the ASB considers that performance should be viewed by reference to the profit and loss account *taken together with* the statement of total recognised gains and losses. A valuation surplus in one year is a recognised gain of that year and is part of the performance of that year. It is shown as an unrealised gain in the statement of total recognised gains and losses. When that gain is realised in a future year it makes no sense, under the ASB view of performance, to recognise it again in the profit and loss account, because it is not part of the performance of that year. It was part of the performance of earlier years.

7.108 The requirement was controversial because many people did not accept the ASB concept of 'performance' as measured by both principal statements referred to above. They considered that the profit and loss account was *the* primary statement which should include all gains *realised* in the year, whether or not they have previously been recognised as unrealised. To some extent this view stemmed from a more prudent view of performance, because it took no account of unrealised profits, but on the other hand it still allowed for the recognition of revaluation gains in the balance sheet before they were realised.

7.109 The ASB acknowledged the difference of view and, therefore, also required a note of historical cost profits or losses for the period to be presented immediately following the profit or loss account or the statement of total recognised gains and losses, where there is a material difference between the result as disclosed in the profit and loss account and the result on an unmodified historical cost basis.

[The next page is 7045.]

7.110 The following example illustrates the treatment of revaluation surpluses on the sale of an asset.

Example

A company has a property which cost £100,000. In year one it revalued it to £150,000. In year three it sells the property for £170,000. Taxation and depreciation are ignored.

In year one the asset is written up to £150,000 and the surplus of £50,000 is credited to revaluation reserve and appears in the statement of total recognised gains and losses. In year three the profit is calculated by reference to the carrying amount of £150,000 and is recorded as £20,000 in the profit and loss account (as an exceptional item after operating profit and before interest). Before FRS 3 the company could have calculated the profit by reference to historical cost of £100,000 and recorded a profit of £70,000 in the profit and loss account by transferring the revaluation reserve to profit and loss account. Under FRS 3, the previous revaluation surplus of £50,000 is taken to profit and loss account *reserve* and only the £20,000 is shown in the profit and loss account for the year.

In this example, if the taxation is calculated on the full surplus of £70,000 then the taxation attributable to the previous revaluation surplus of £50,000 would be charged in the statement of total recognised gains and losses.

7.111 The standard states that profits *and* losses are to be calculated by reference to carrying amount. Where fixed assets have been revalued downwards below cost, and the diminution in value is not considered to be an impairment (because, say, their value in use at the date of the revaluation is considered to be greater than their current market value), this could have the following effect:

Example

A company revalues all its fixed assets and there is a net surplus of £100,000 which is transferred to the revaluation reserve and shown in the statement of total recognised gains and losses. However, the net surplus is made up of a surplus of £150,000 above cost on one property and a diminution in value below cost on another property of £50,000. (If the diminution was an impairment it would have to be charged to profit and loss account.) There is no intention to sell the property with the diminution at the year end.

Three years later the company receives an offer for the second property and sells it for the revalued amount, that is, cost less the diminution of £50,000. As the profit or loss is calculated on the carrying value there is no profit or loss on sale. Thus the loss calculated by reference to historical cost never passes through the profit and loss account. Instead there is a transfer from the revaluation reserve to the profit and loss account *reserve* in the reserves note. This is consistent with the ASB's view of performance, as the loss was recognised in the year of revaluation in the statement of total recognised gains and losses. It emphasises the need, however, to make a clear distinction between diminutions that are impairments and diminutions that are downward revaluations.

A similar result would be obtained if, instead of the asset being sold in year three, the board decided that the asset was now impaired (that is, its recoverable amount had fallen to its carrying value). Under the law the impairment (as a permanent diminution in value) should be charged to the profit and loss account. However, as it has already been recognised (albeit as a downward revaluation) in one of the primary statements of performance (the STRGL), it is not shown in the profit and loss account for that year. Instead, under FRS 3 it would be charged to profit and loss account reserve by means of a reserve transfer in the reserves note.

7.112 A loss that arises on sale of a previously revalued asset must be recorded in the profit and loss account even if the loss arises wholly from the reversal of a previous revaluation surplus.

Example

A company revalues an asset costing £100,000 in year one to £150,000. The surplus of £50,000 is shown in the statement of total recognised gains and losses. The revaluation reserve is credited with £50,000 and the asset written up by that amount. In year five the asset is sold for £130,000. The loss on sale should be accounted for in the profit and loss account for the period as the difference between the net sale proceeds and the net carrying amount. This means that there will be a loss on sale of £20,000 recorded in the profit and loss account. The fact that the profit and loss account never recorded a *surplus* of £50,000 in the past is not relevant under the ASB approach, which looks at the profit and loss account and the statement of total recognised gains and losses *together* in assessing performance.

There will, of course, be a transfer from the revaluation reserve to profit and loss account reserve of £50,000 as the previous revaluation surplus is now realised. In the profit and loss account *reserve* the result will be a net gain of £30,000, but the profit and loss account will, in the year of disposal, record only the loss of £20,000, because the unrealised gain of £50,000 was recognised in the statement of total recognised gains and losses in year one.

[The next paragraph is 7.114.]

Impairments

7.114 FRS 3 requires losses on disposals of fixed assets or operations (including provisions in respect of them) to be charged after operating profit and before interest. [FRS 3 para 20]. FRS 11 requires impairment losses recognised in the profit and loss account to be charged in operating profit under the appropriate statutory heading. [FRS 11 para 67]. For example, Format 2 has a heading 'Depreciation and other amounts written off tangible and intangible fixed assets'. Impairment losses would be separately disclosed as exceptional items, if material. If FRS 11 was interpreted in isolation, most losses recognised in connection with asset disposals would be impairments (charged against operating profit) rather than losses on disposals (non-operating exceptional items). That is because in most cases any previously unidentified shortfall between an asset's carrying value and its recoverable amount that is identified as a result of a decision to sell or terminate would be an impairment, not a loss on disposal.

7.115 We consider that the requirements of FRS 3 and FRS 11 taken together should be interpreted as follows. Impairment losses in respect of fixed assets and businesses that are to be retained must be charged in arriving at operating profit. Impairment losses that, in FRS 3 terms, are provisions for losses on disposals (that is, they are recognised as a result of a decision to dispose of the assets or business concerned) should be shown under the relevant one of the three headings in paragraph 20 of FRS 3. In the latter case, if the disposal has not occurred before the balance sheet date, the company would be expected to be able to evidence that the asset or operation would not be retained. For example, the asset or business would probably be being actively marketed and it would be reasonable to expect that the disposal would be completed before the next interim accounts and in any event before the end of the next financial year.

7.116 This apparent inconsistency between FRS 3 and FRS 11 gives rise to some anomalies. If an asset is put up for sale and has not previously been reviewed for impairment, the loss on sale is presented in accordance with paragraph 20 of FRS 3. If, however, an impairment loss is identified earlier as a result of carrying out an impairment review in circumstances required by FRS 11, the loss would be presented as part of operating profit in accordance with FRS 11. An exception is for investment properties (which are outside the scope of FRS 11), where impairment losses recognised in the profit and loss account would usually be charged after operating profit under a caption that corresponds to 'amounts written off investments' in the Formats (that is, after operating profit and before interest payable).

7.117 The rule in FRS 3 relating to calculating profits or losses on disposals of assets is only one part of accounting for revalued assets. The accounting treatment of impairments of revalued assets is considered in chapter 5.

[The next paragraph is 7.121.]

Other exceptional items

7.121 All exceptional items, other than the three described above, should be shown under the statutory format headings to which they relate. In practice, this means that almost all other exceptional items (except any exceptional item relating to finance costs, investment income, amounts written off investments or the tax charge) would be shown in arriving at operating profit. The amount of each exceptional item, either individually or in aggregate (if they are of a similar type), should be disclosed separately by way of a note or on the face of the profit and loss account if that is necessary in order to give a true and fair view. [FRS 3 para 19].

7.122 The format 1 headings used in arriving at operating profit are:

- Turnover.
- Cost of sales.
- Gross profit.
- Distribution costs.
- Administrative expenses.
- Other operating income.

7.123 This is a relatively small number of headings to absorb every single type and description of exceptional item that may occur. Some types of exceptional items are relatively straightforward, for instance a provision for loss on a contract in a construction company might well be exceptional and would be shown under the cost of sales heading. The proceeds of an insurance claim for loss of profits could be accommodated under the 'Other operating income' heading. Provisions for redundancy and reorganisation costs might have to be allocated among several headings however. If, for instance, the reorganisation involved a relocation, the costs of that might be put under administrative costs, but any redundancy costs might have to be allocated to several headings (according to where the salary costs of those made redundant were charged). Costs of disposing of delivery vans and sub-contracting the distribution of goods to outside hauliers would be an exceptional distribution cost.

7.124 Some items may at first not appear to have an appropriate statutory format heading. One example would be the expropriation of assets by a foreign government. If this is the case, then it may well fit within one of the three categories of exceptional item that must be shown after operating profit. Because the expropriation results in a loss on disposal of assets, or of a business, it should be shown separately after operating profit.

7.125 One item that has come to be accepted as a non-operating exceptional item is the cost of defending a hostile takeover bid. Disclosure outside operating profit may reflect the fact that the cost relates to defending the independent ownership of the company and is nothing to do with the company's operations. In contrast, abortive bid costs incurred by a company that launched a (failed) takeover bid would be shown as exceptional administrative costs, that is, charged in arriving at operating profit, because they relate to the company's attempt to expand its operations by acquisition (see, for example, Table 7.14 on page 53). Listing costs or abortive listing costs are also shown as operating exceptionals under the appropriate format heading.

7.126 The following example illustrates the treatment of exceptional items.

Example

A group disposed of a subsidiary during the year making a profit on disposal (after goodwill) of £500,000. A leakage of toxic chemicals from one of its factories caused damage to nearby farmland which cost £1m to clean up. The group was fined £300,000. As part of a reorganisation programme 5% of the employees in the administrative function were made redundant at a cost of £250,000 and plant and machinery with a carrying value of £200,000 was scrapped. The group sold certain patents which were not reflected in its financial statements at a profit of £100,000 in order to raise working capital. The group also obtained a listing for its shares in Luxembourg and the costs of the listing were £150,000. The operating profit of the group prior to these items was £1m as follows:

	£'000
Turnover	8,000
Cost of sales	(5,000)
Gross profit	3,000
Net operating expenses	(2,000)
Operating profit	1,000

After accounting for the exceptional items the figures would be as follows:

	£'000	£'000
Turnover		8,000
Cost of sales	5,000	
Exceptional items:		
Plant write down	200	
Cost of environmental damage	1,300	(6,500)
Gross profit		1,500
Net operating expenses	2,000	
Exceptional operating expenses	300	2,300
Operating loss		(800)
Profit on sale of discontinued operations		500
Interest		-
Loss on ordinary activities before taxation		(300)

Clearly each company will have to decide which heading is appropriate for each exceptional item and the above is only a guide to illustrate how the disclosure might appear.

In the notes the net operating expenses and exceptional net operating expenses would be analysed to show the split between distribution costs and administrative expenses and other operating income.

The costs of listing would be administrative expenses, the profit on sale of patents would be other operating income, and the costs of redundancy of the employees in the administrative function would be under the administrative expenses heading.

All of the above exceptional items would be shown under the heading of continuing activities except for the profit on disposal of the subsidiary.

The exceptional item in respect of the costs of environmental damage would need to be shown on the face of the profit and loss account in order to give a true and fair view. Because the balance of the exceptional cost of sales has to be shown separately, it has also been described on the face of the profit and loss account, but it could be relegated to a note.

In practice, the total of exceptional items in respect of net operating expenses might not be shown on the face of the profit and loss account. Instead net operating expenses might be shown as £2,300,000 and the exceptional element would be analysed only in the notes. This is because it may not be considered necessary to the true and fair view to show the amount separately on the face of the profit and loss account.

The tax effect of the profit on disposal of the subsidiary would be shown in a note as required by the standard.

[The next paragraph is 7.128.]

7.128 Since FRS 3 was introduced, considerable experimentation has taken place with the presentation of operating exceptional items on the face of the profit and loss account. Various approaches have been adopted as some companies have sought to highlight operating profit before exceptional items as a key performance indicator and a measure of underlying operating performance excluding the distortive and volatile effect of significant one-off charges or credits. These approaches have been combined with disclosures of alternative measures of earnings per share, sometimes excluding the effect of certain exceptional items, as permitted by FRS 3. (Alternative earnings per share is dealt with in chapter 8.) The approaches include:

- Multi-column analysis to segregate operating exceptionals as well as discontinued operations (see example in Table 7.13).
- Single-column analysis with imaginative use of boxes or sub-totals to highlight operating profit before and after operating exceptionals (see example in Table 7.14).
- Separate column to segregate operating exceptionals, whilst all other continuing operations, acquisitions and discontinued operations are analysed under a single column (see example in Table 7.15).
- Straightforward disclosure of operating exceptionals under the statutory caption on the face of the profit and loss account, perhaps with additional commentary or analysis in the operating and financial review (see example in Table 7.16).

Table 7.13 – Manweb plc – Annual Report & Accounts – 31 March 1995

Consolidated Profit and Loss Account (extract)
FOR THE YEAR ENDED 31 MARCH 1995

		Continuing Businesses				
	Note	Before Exceptional Items 1995 £ million	Exceptional Items 1995 £ million	Total 1995 £ million	Discontinued Businesses 1995 £ million	1995 £ million
Turnover	1	**850.1**	-	**850.1**	**28.5**	**878.6**
Operating costs		**(719.9)**	-	**(719.9)**	**(30.8)**	**(750.7)**
Reorganisation and restructuring costs		-	**(26.9)**	**(26.9)**	-	**(26.9)**
Total operating costs		**(719.9)**	**(26.9)**	**(746.8)**	**(30.8)**	**(777.6)**
Operating profit	2	**130.2**	**(26.9)**	**103.3**	**(2.3)**	**101.0**

Table 7.14 – Anglo United plc – Annual Report – 31 March 1993

Consolidated Profit and Loss Account (extract)

For the year ended 31 March 1993

Notes		1993 £000	(Restated) 1992 £000
1	Turnover from continuing operations	544,742	555,959
	Cost of sales (including exceptional items) from continuing operations	(463,224)	(458,291)
	Gross profit	81,518	97,668
2	Net operating expenses (including exceptional items)	(80,009)	(63,943)
	Operating profit before exceptional items	20,313	34,345
3	Exceptional items	(18,804)	(620)
	Operating profit from continuing operations	1,509	33,725

Notes to the Accounts (extract)

3 Exceptional items

	Cost of Sales **£000**	Distribution Costs **£000**	Adminis-trative Expenses **£000**	**1993 Total £000**	1992 Total £000
Legal, professional and banking fees in respect of debt restructuring	-	-	**8,894**	**8,894**	-
Costs in connection with aborted disposals and acquisitions	-	-	**2,360**	**2,360**	-
Future discounted rents receivable	-	-	**(1,370)**	**(1,370)**	-
Reorganisation and restructuring costs of ongoing businesses	**1,450**	**720**	**4,853**	**7,023**	-
Write-off of loan to Employees' Share Ownership Plan Trust	-	-	**1,367**	**1,367**	-
Professional costs in respect of environmental matters	-	-	**530**	**530**	620
	1,450	**720**	**16,634**	**18,804**	620

The comparative cost for 1992 relates wholly to administrative expenses.

In order to assist in understanding the Group's results for the year, and in view of the unusual materiality of exceptional items to the current year's results, the directors believe that it is appropriate to show separately the operating profit of the Group before exceptional items on the face of the profit and loss account as additional information.

Table 7.15 – Booker plc – Annual Report and Financial Statements – 31 December 1994

Consolidated Profit and Loss Account (extract)

for the fifty-two weeks ended 31 December 1994

	note	Before exceptional items £m	Exceptional items (Note 3) £m	1994 £m
Turnover:				
Continuing operations		3,688.7		3,688.7
Acquisitions		10.5		10.5
		3,699.2		3,699.2
Discontinued operations		23.1		23.1
Total turnover		3,722.3	-	3,722.3
Operating costs	2	(3,620.1)	(20.8)	(3,640.9)
Operating profit				
Continuing operations		98.1	(18.3)	79.8
Acquisitions		1.6	(2.5)	(0.9)
		99.7	(20.8)	78.9
Discontinued operations		2.5		2.5
Total operating profit		102.2	(20.8)	81.4

Notes to the Financial Statements (extract)

2. **OPERATING COSTS (extract)**

	Continuing operations £m	Acquisitions £m	Discontinued operations £m	Pre-exceptional items £m	Exceptional items £m	Total 1994 £m
Cost of sales	3,459.0	7.4	18.9	3,485.3	14.8	3,500.1
Distribution costs	63.3	0.8	1.9	66.0	0.5	66.5
Administrative expenses	66.4	0.7	1.7	68.8	5.5	74.3
Total operating costs	3,588.7	8.9	22.5	3,620.1	20.8	3,640.9
Income from investments	-	-	-	-	-	-
Total operating costs *less* other income	3,588.7	8.9	22.5	3,620.1	20.8	3,640.9
Gross profit as defined by the Companies Act 1985	229.7	3.1	4.2	237.0	(14.8)	222.2

Table 7.16 – Cable and Wireless plc – Report and accounts – 31 March 1995

Consolidated profit and loss account (extract)

for the year ended 31 March	Note	**1995 £m**	1994 £m
Turnover	3,4	**5,132.8**	4,699.2
Operating costs before exceptional items	5	**(3,938.6)**	(3,608.0)
Exceptional items: charged against operating costs	5,9	**(60.5)**	-
Total operating costs		**(3,999.1)**	(3,608.0)
Operating profit	4	**1,133.7**	1,091.2

Note 5. Operating costs (extract)

	1995	**1995**	1994
	After Exceptional items	Exceptional items therein	
	£m	**£m**	£m
Outpayments to other telecommunications administrations and carriers	**1,564.6**	-	1,459.9
Employee costs	**799.2**	**30.3**	686.6
Pension costs (Note 8) – principal schemes	**51.1**	-	48.6
- other schemes	**8.9**	-	11.2
Rental of transmission facilities	**71.5**	-	58.9
Hire of plant and machinery	**19.9**	-	20.7
Other operating lease rentals	**23.0**	-	21.3
Other operating costs	**942.1**	**30.2**	833.6
Depreciation of owned tangible fixed assets	**510.9**	-	461.1
Depreciation of tangible fixed assets held under finance leases	**6.3**	-	4.5
Auditors' remuneration – for audit services	**1.6**	-	1.6
	3,999.1	**60.5**	3,608.0

Having regard to the special nature of the Group's business an analysis of operating costs in the manner prescribed by the Companies Act 1985 is not meaningful. In the circumstances therefore the Directors have, as required by paragraph 3(3) of schedule 4 to the Companies Act 1985, adapted the prescribed format to the requirements of the Group's business.

Note 9. Exceptional items (extract)

Exceptional items are as follows:	**1995 £m**	1994 £m
Mercury reorganisation costs		
Shown as:		
Charge to operating profit	**60.5**	-
Profit less losses on sale and termination of operations	**17.7**	-
Losses on disposal of fixed assets	**43.7**	-
	121.9	-

The exceptional pre-tax charge of £121.9m relates to the Mercury reorganisation announced in December 1994 to streamline its operations and strengthen its competitive position in the UK telecommunications market. Applicable to this exceptional charge is a tax credit of £13.2m relating to the operating cost element of the charge, and a minority interest share of £21.7m.

[The next paragraph is 7.130.]

7.130 There are different schools of thought on the emerging trend towards greater segregation of exceptional items in the profit and loss account.

7.131 One view is that such treatment is consistent with the 'information set' approach that FRS 3 promulgates, because each component of performance is presented fully in the way management believes is most useful for and understandable to shareholders. Investors are particularly interested in analysing the quality of maintainable underlying profits and, hence, growth and dividend prospects. Prominent disclosure of exceptional items is an essential part of the overall picture.

7.132 A different view is that excessive emphasis on underlying or maintainable earnings after stripping out unusual items is a flawed concept that reintroduces the problems caused by extraordinary items in the pre-FRS 3 regime. Focus on operating profit before exceptionals can lead to abuse of exceptional items and presenting them in a way that leads them to be discounted by the market.

7.133 We believe that such treatment remains within the spirit of the standard if the exceptionals warrant that degree of prominence and provided that the overall position, including relevant commentary, is presented in an unbiased way and is not misleading.

7.134 Although the above examples illustrate that there is considerable room for experimentation with formats, companies should take great care that they comply with the letter of the standard that requires exceptional items to be shown on the profit and loss account under the statutory format headings to whi5ch they relate. The FRRP published a statement on this issue in May 1994. Following an investigation by the FRRP of BET's financial statements for the year ended 27 March 1993, in which FRS 3 was adopted early, the company restated within its 1994 financial statements the presentation of the 1993 comparative exceptional items. The FRRP had concluded that the 1993 presentation *"did not fulfil the requirement of the standard that these items should be shown on the profit and loss account under the statutory format headings to which they relate"*.

7.135 Relevant extracts from the 1993 financial statements are shown in Table 7.17. The problem was that, although the operating exceptional items totalling £76 million were analysed between cost of sales, distribution costs and administrative expenses in the notes, they were not included in the totals shown under the format headings. The FRRP's quibble on this point seemed to many commentators to be rather pedantic, but showed that it was determined to enforce the new standards rigorously.

Table 7.17 – BET Public Limited Company – Annual Report – 27 March 1993

Consolidated profit and loss account (extract)

for the year ended 27th March 1993	Notes	Continuing Operations £m	Discontinued operations £m	1993 Total £m
TURNOVER	1	2,003.2	173.0	2,176.2
Cost of sales		(1,533.2)	(125.8)	(1,659.0)
Gross profit		470.0	47.2	517.2
Distribution costs		(187.5)	(32.2)	(219.7)
Administrative expenses		(231.0)	(20.9)	(251.9)
Other operating income		19.3	1.2	20.5
Income from interests in associated undertakings	4	8.1	-	8.1
OPERATING PROFIT/(LOSS) BEFORE EXCEPTIONAL ITEMS	1&2	78.9	(4.7)	74.2
Permanent diminution in asset values		(42.0)	-	(42.0)
Reorganisation costs		(34.0)	-	(34.0)
Deferred costs		-	-	-
OPERATING EXCEPTIONAL ITEMS	3	(76.0)	-	(76.0)
OPERATING PROFIT/(LOSS)		2.9	(4.7)	(1.8)

Note 3 Exceptional items (extract)

The operating exceptional items referred to above can be categorised as follows:

1993	Cost of sales £m	Distribution costs £m	Adminis-trative expenses £m	Total £m
Permanent diminution in asset values	35.7	-	6.3	42.0
Reorganisation costs	24.5	-	9.5	34.0
	60.2	-	15.8	76.0

7.136 Extracts from the restated comparatives in the 1994 financial statements are shown in Table 7.18.

Table 7.18 – BET Public Limited Company – Annual Report – 2 April 1994

Consolidated profit and loss account (extract)

For the year ended 2nd April 1994	Notes	Continuing Operations £m	Discontinued operations £m	1994 Total £m	1993 Restated (see page 36) £m
TURNOVER	1	**1,785.1**	**188.9**	**1,974.0**	2,176.2
Cost of sales		**(1,318.7)**	**(154.7)**	**(1,473.4)**	(1,719.2)
Gross profit		**466.4**	**34.2**	**500.6**	457.0
Distribution costs		**(170.1)**	**(14.5)**	**(184.6)**	(219.7)
Administrative expenses		**(202.6)**	**(23.2)**	**(225.8)**	(267.7)
Other operating income / (expense)		**(0.5)**	**1.1**	**0.6**	20.5
Income from interests in associated undertakings	4	**5.6**	**0.2**	**5.8**	8.1
OPERATING PROFIT/(LOSS)	1	**98.8**	**(2.2)**	**96.6**	(1.8)

Note 3 Exceptional items (extract)

The following operating exceptional items are included within the statutory format headings on the face of the profit and loss account. In 1993 they were disclosed as separate line items on the face of the profit and loss account.

	1994 £m	1993 £m
OPERATING EXCEPTIONAL ITEMS		
Permanent diminution in asset values	-	(42.0)
Reorganisation costs	-	(34.0)
	-	(76.0)

In the previous year a provision was made for reorganisation costs of £34.0 million. This has been fully utilised in the current year (see note 19). The £42.0 million operating exceptional item in 1993 provided for a permanent diminution in the value of land and buildings of £10.5 million, other fixed assets of £21.2 million and current assets of £10.3 million.

The operating exceptional items referred to above are categorised as follows:

	1994			1993		
	Cost of sales £m	**Administrative expenses £m**	**Total £m**	Cost of sales £m	Administrative expenses £m	Total £m
Permanent diminution in asset values	-	-	-	35.7	6.3	42.0
Reorganisation costs	-	-	-	24.5	9.5	34.0
	-	-	-	60.2	15.8	76.0

Tax attributable to exceptional items

7.137 The taxation relating to the three types of exceptional item that are required to be disclosed after operating profit must be shown in a note to the profit and loss account. [FRS 3 para 23]. The three items again are:

- Profits or losses on sale or termination of an operation.
- Costs of a fundamental reorganisation or restructuring having a material effect on the nature and focus of the reporting entity's operations.
- Profits or losses on the disposal of fixed assets.

Provisions in respect of such items should also be included.

7.138 The related tax is required to be shown only in aggregate and not for each individual item, unless the effect of the tax on each of the items differs, when further information should be given, where practicable.

7.139 There is no requirement to disclose taxation relating to other exceptional items.

7.140 The amount of tax attributable to exceptional items falling within any of the three categories set out above should be calculated by computing the tax on the profit or loss on ordinary activities as if the items did not exist and comparing this notional tax charge with the tax charge on the profit or loss for the period. Any additional tax charge or credit (including deferred tax) should be attributed to the items. [FRS 3 para 24].

7.141 If there were both exceptional items and extraordinary items in the same period, the tax on the items combined should be calculated and then apportioned between them in relation to their respective amounts, unless a more precise basis is available. If the latter basis is adopted the method of apportionment should be disclosed. [FRS 3 para 24]. In practice, this requirement is largely academic because extraordinary items have been virtually eliminated by FRS 3.

7.142 Although the FRS states that the tax attributable to the above types of exceptional item should be disclosed in a note, there could be no objection to disclosing the tax separately within the tax charge on the face of the profit and loss account, as the items are themselves disclosed there.

7.143 Further commentary is included in chapter 13.

Extraordinary items

7.144 As mentioned earlier, extraordinary items have all but disappeared from UK financial reporting. In our view there should be no extraordinary items under FRS 3, however unusual the transaction or event may be.

Statement of total recognised gains and losses

7.145 The statement of total recognised gains and losses (which has become to be known as the STRGL) was a major innovation in UK accounting and is fundamental to the concept of 'performance' embraced by the ASB in FRS 3.

7.146 As explained earlier in this chapter, the ASB's aim was to turn attention away from particular numbers and to encourage users to make their own judgements about a company's performance, based on an 'information set'. Part of that information set is the statement of total recognised gains and losses.

7.147 Several accounting standards permit amounts to be taken direct to reserves and the law requires certain amounts to be so treated. In the past a casual reader of financial statements could be forgiven for not being aware of such amounts, as they were often only disclosed in a reserves note that was not prominently displayed, but instead appeared only a long way into the financial statements. SSAP 6 required the reserves note either to be immediately following the profit and loss account or a cross-reference to be made to it on the face of the profit and loss account. In practice, the cross-reference often consisted only of a note number.

7.148 Because amounts taken directly to reserves are often important in assessing a company's performance, in FRS 3 the ASB required such amounts to be shown in a new primary statement 'The statement of total recognised gains and losses'. This statement, which should have equal prominence to the other primary statements includes the profit for the year (from the profit and loss account) and other amounts taken directly to reserves, including the following principal items:

- Exchange gains and losses on retranslation of opening net assets of overseas subsidiaries. (These would be offset by any exchange gains or losses on foreign currency borrowings that hedge those investments.)
- Revaluation surpluses and certain unrealised revaluation deficits. (Examples of how revaluation surpluses and deficits are to be treated in the statement are given from para 7.110 above.)

7.149 Other items that are sometimes recognised in the statement of total recognised gains and losses include:

- Gains arising from lapsed warrants. This treatment is a specific requirement of FRS 4. [FRS 4 para 47].
- Unrealised gains resulting from sales of assets to associated companies.
- Tax attributable to gains or losses recognised in the statement.

7.150 The 'total recognised gains and losses' are the gains and losses arising from a company's activities as distinct from capital introduced or withdrawn by shareholders. Consequently, they do not include payments to shareholders in respect of capital redeemed or inflows of new capital from shareholders, nor do they include dividends to shareholders. These items are not elements of a company's performance, and so instead are recorded in the reconciliation of movements in shareholders' funds.

7.151 One of the compelling reasons for bringing the effects of reserve accounting into greater prominence through this new statement was the case of Polly Peck. After the collapse of that company, considerable attention was focused on the very large exchange movements that had been shown in its reserves. Although these movements had been disclosed in the notes, their size and the circumstances at the time emphasised the importance of bringing such movements prominently to the attention of users of financial statements. This idea was, however, by no means a radical one, as it had long been argued by users and preparers of financial statements that the statement of reserves should be prominently displayed. Indeed, until SSAP 6 was revised in 1986 it had been a requirement of that standard that a statement of reserves should immediately follow the profit and loss account.

7.152 What *was* new in FRS 3 was the introduction of the figure of total gains and losses for the year, which was intended in due course to have as much importance to readers and analysts as the figure of profit for the financial year.

7.153 An example of a statement of total recognised gains and losses is given in Table 7.19.

Table 7.19 – Grand Metropolitan Public Limited Company – Annual Report - 30 September 1994

Statement of Total Recognised Gains and Losses
For the year ended 30th September 1994

	1994 £m	*1993 £m*
Profit for the financial year	450	*410*
Deficit on revaluation of properties in associate	(10)	*(80)*
Exchange adjustments	(47)	*(39)*
Total recognised gains and losses for the financial year	393	*291*
Prior year adjustment (note 1)	(21)	
Total gains and losses recognised since last annual report	372	

7.154 Where a reporting entity has no recognised gains and losses in a period, other than the profit or loss for the period, it should state this fact immediately below the profit and loss account. [FRS 3 para 57].

Purchased goodwill

7.155 Goodwill that is written off directly to reserves on acquisition before the adoption of FRS 10 should not be included in the STRGL in the year when it is written off. There is a footnote in FRS 3 to this effect. [FRS 3 para 27]. So far as goodwill that is capitalised and amortised through the profit and loss account is concerned, the annual amortisation (and any impairment write-off) *will* appear indirectly as part of the profit for the financial year figure that appears in the STRGL.

7.156 The rationale for this was first given in UITF Abstract 3, 'The treatment of goodwill on the disposal of a business'. The ASB included an opinion on the relationship between the Abstract and FRED 1 (the exposure draft that preceded FRS 3). This included the following:

> *"The Task Force considered that it would be helpful for the Board to clarify the inter-relationship of this consensus with the treatment of purchased goodwill in the context of FRED 1. In this respect, the Board confirms that it does not consider purchased goodwill eliminated against reserves on acquisition and, consequently, any reinstatement of such goodwill on disposal, to be a recognised loss or gain. This view is consistent with SSAP 22... Accordingly, the elimination and reinstatement of goodwill would not be included in the statement of total recognised gains and losses."*

7.157 This makes it clear that the immediate write off of goodwill to reserves is not a recognised gain or loss. When a business is disposed of or closed and there has been goodwill written off direct to reserves on acquisition of the business in the past, UITF 3 (incorporated within FRS 10) requires that the profit or loss on disposal should take account of that goodwill. Thus the goodwill *will*, on disposal, be part of the profit or loss for the financial year and in this way *will* be a recognised loss, but only when the business is disposed of or the goodwill is otherwise written off in the profit and loss account. The credit to reserves that results from reinstating the goodwill on disposal will *not* be a recognised gain, in the same way that the original write off was not a recognised loss (see also para 7.92 above).

7.158 The following example illustrates the treatment of goodwill on the disposal of a subsidiary where the goodwill remained eliminated against reserves.

Example

A company buys a subsidiary in year one and goodwill of £200m arises which is written off directly to reserves. The goodwill is not shown as a recognised loss in the statement of total recognised gains and losses. In year three the subsidiary is sold. The profit or loss on sale is calculated as the difference between the proceeds of sale and the net assets at the date of sale plus goodwill previously written off. The subsidiary is sold for net asset value and, therefore, a loss on sale of £200m is incurred. This loss on sale forms part of the profit or loss for the financial year, which is reported in the statement of total recognised gains and losses. In order to reinstate the goodwill there was a credit to reserves and a debit to profit and loss account. Whilst the debit forms part of the profit or loss on sale and is a recognised loss, the credit is not a recognised gain and does not appear in the statement of total recognised gains and losses.

7.159 A second example showing the treatment when goodwill is capitalised and amortised is as follows:

Example

A company buys a subsidiary in year one and goodwill arises of £200m which is capitalised and amortised over ten years. In years one to six a charge for amortisation of £20m per year is made in the profit and loss account and is thus a recognised loss in the statement of total recognised gains and losses (because it is included in the profit or loss for the financial year). In year six the subsidiary is sold. Only the *unamortised* goodwill of £80m is included in the calculation of the profit or loss on sale and this £80m is also recognised in the statement of total recognised gains and losses, as it forms part of the profit or loss for the financial year.

Movements in reserves

7.160 The statement of total recognised gains and losses does not include movements between reserves. These are shown in a reserves note which is required by Schedule 4 to the Act.

7.161 The Act's requirements in relation to reserves are that where any amounts are transferred to or from reserves that are required to be shown separately in the balance sheet the following information has to be given:

- The amount of the reserves at the beginning and end of the year.
- The amounts transferred to or from the reserves during the year.
- The source and application of any amounts so transferred.

[4 Sch 46].

7.162 This means, for example, that the reserves note is required to show movements between the revaluation reserve and the profit and loss account reserve in respect of previous revaluation surpluses realised in the year. Although the standard does not require the note to be given the same prominence as, for instance, the statement of total recognised gains and losses, it remains an important note to the financial statements.

7.163 Because the reserves note is required by law to show movements in each reserve and movements between reserves, it is not possible to substitute for such movements in the reserves note a figure, such as, the total recognised gains and losses figure for the year from the statement of total recognised gains and losses. That figure, which summarises several different types of reserve movements must be broken down into its component parts in the reserves note and transfers between reserves must also be shown in the note.

7.164 Many of the respondents to the exposure draft, FRED 1, considered that the statement of total recognised gains and losses should be extended to include other reserve movements and to provide a reconciliation between opening and closing shareholders' equity. The ASB did not amend its proposals, but instead introduced in FRS 3 the requirement for an additional statement or note reconciling movements in shareholders' funds (see para 7.183).

Usefulness of the statement

7.165 The objective of the statement of total recognised gains and losses was to gather all the gains and losses recorded as reserve movements and display them prominently just after the profit for the year, to give a total of gains and losses recognised in the year. This total was meant to be at least as important as profit for the year.

7.166 Our observation is that users of financial statements are not treating it as a primary statement containing important information. The statement is rarely mentioned in the financial press when companies' results are reported. One reason for this is that, with the current system of optional and irregular revaluations, the gains and losses reported in the statement are: arbitrary; often do not relate to the year under review; and lack comparability. These drawbacks would be eliminated only if companies had to revalue all assets every year, which we do not believe is a feasible approach.

7.167 Furthermore, the statement, by treating revaluation surpluses and deficits as part of total recognised gains, has in our view the unfortunate effect of giving revaluation gains – and the figure of total recognised gains and losses that includes them – a credibility that is ill-founded. For example, valuation bases presume a willing seller and willing buyer, yet directors often assert: there is no intention to sell, and thus no provision is made for deferred tax; the valuation surpluses recorded will not necessarily be realised in due course; and irregular valuations allow gains to be recognised at one time without subsequent falls in value being recognised, because no further formal valuations have been carried out.

7.168 We would prefer revaluations to be down-played and not represented as recognised gains in assessing performance. We would suggest the effective removal of the statement of total recognised gains and losses and its replacement with value information in the form of a supplementary statement. A statement of value might include, for example, revaluations of assets on the balance sheet; valuations of separable assets not on the balance sheet; and an estimate of total goodwill (purchased and internally generated), as indicated by the value of the business as a whole. Further details of this approach are given in chapters 5 and 33.

Note of historical cost profits and losses

7.169 FRS 3 requires that a note of historical cost profits and losses for the period should be presented immediately following the profit and loss account or the statement of total recognised gains and losses, in those instances where there is a material difference between the result as disclosed in the profit and loss account and the result on an unmodified historical cost basis.

7.170 The standard gives the reasons for requiring this note. First, it is argued that for so long as discretion exists on the scale and timing of revaluations included in financial statements, the unmodified historical cost basis will give the reported profits or losses of different enterprises on a more comparable basis. Secondly, certain users wish to assess the profit or loss on sale of fixed assets based on their historical cost rather than, as the standard requires, on their revalued carrying amount.

7.171 The lack of comparability referred to occurs, for instance, where two companies have similar assets costing £100,000 each. The second company revalues the asset to £150,000 and the gain is shown in the statement of total recognised gains and losses in year one. In year two the companies sell the assets for £150,000.

The first company will record a profit of £50,000 in the profit and loss account whilst the second will record neither gain nor loss.

7.172 Under the ASB's view of performance the gain occurs in year one and is recognised in the picture of performance given by the profit and loss account taken together with the statement of total recognised gains and losses. Nonetheless, the two companies' results in year one are not comparable because the first company has not revalued and, therefore, shows no gain. The same lack of comparability occurs in the second year, because the first company reports a profit and the second does not.

7.173 The note of historical cost profits remedies this. In the second company in year two adjustments are made in the note to show the profit on an unmodified historical cost basis and these results can then be fairly compared with those of the first company.

7.174 Clearly the ASB envisages introducing rules on the scale and frequency of valuations in the future and a project is underway. This reason for having a note of historical cost profits may, therefore, disappear in due course.

7.175 The second reason referred to is that some users prefer to see results based on unmodified historical cost. This is perhaps because such users are concerned to assess profits that have been *realised* by a company and which are, therefore, distributable, rather than base their judgements on a mixture of realised and unrealised profits.

7.176 What the ASB's rules on fixed assets obscure is the process of realisation of previously unrealised profits that happens on a sale of a revalued asset. The standard is based on the view that since such unrealised revaluation surpluses have been recognised in the past in the statement of total recognised gains and losses, they should not be recognised again when realised. Opponents of the view consider that profits are not really earned until they are realised. They focus on the profit and loss account, which may under the law contain only realised profits, as the measure of performance and argue that that account should contain *all* profits realised in the year, irrespective of whether or not they have previously been recognised as unrealised.

7.177 The note of historical cost profits and losses is the ASB's way of meeting the requirements of those who put more trust in realised and historical cost figures.

7.178 The note includes adjustments to the reported profit to remove depreciation charged on the revalued element of fixed assets and to restate profits and losses on sale of assets onto the historical cost basis.

7.179 Investment and dealing companies that mark to market their quoted investments and take the movements to the profit and loss account are not required by the standard to make adjustments in the note of historical cost profits and losses to eliminate gains taken to profit and loss account as a result of marking to market. This is because the standard's explanation section states that where marking to market is an established industry practice it is not considered to be a departure from the historical cost convention for the purposes of the note of historical cost profits and losses.

7.180 Companies holding investment properties, which are required by SSAP 19 to be revalued annually in the financial statements, generally do not include a depreciation adjustment in the note of historical profits and losses. That is because it is probable that either no depreciation would have been charged on a revalued or historical cost basis, so there is no difference to record or it is not possible to quantify depreciation on a revalued or historical cost basis.

7.181 Other companies that do not maintain records of historical costs may instead use the earliest available values. The standard specifically states that where full historical cost information cannot be obtained without unreasonable expense or delay, the earliest available values should be used.

7.182 An example of a note of historical cost profits and losses is given in Table 7.20.

Table 7.20 – Grand Metropolitan Public Limited Company – Annual Report – 30 September 1994

NOTE OF HISTORICAL COST PROFITS AND LOSSES
for the year ended 30th September 1994

	1994 £m	*1993 £m*
Profit on ordinary activities before taxation	654	*625*
Realisation of property revaluation gains of prior years	429	*6*
Difference between the historical cost depreciation charge and the actual depreciation charge for the year calculated on the revalued amount	1	*2*
Asset provisions created/(utilised) not required on an historical cost basis	26	*(7)*
Historical cost profit on ordinary activities before taxation	1,110	*626*
Historical cost profit for the year retained after taxation, minority interests and dividends	614	*142*

Reconciliation of movements in shareholders' funds

7.183 There was concern among commentators on FRED 1 that the statement of total recognised gains and losses did not completely achieve the desired effect of bringing into a primary statement all the important movements in shareholders' funds that have hitherto been included only in the notes to the financial statements.

7.184 The ASB's reaction to this concern was to keep the statement of total recognised gains and losses as a primary statement containing only gains and losses – that is, as a statement of performance – but to introduce a new note or primary statement that reconciles the opening and closing totals of shareholders' funds. The reconciliation is not a statement of performance, but just brings together all items that affect shareholders' funds as reported in the financial statements, that is:

- Profit for the year.
- Other recognised gains and losses relating to the year (included in the statement of total recognised gains and losses).
- Other items that are not part of performance such as: dividends; the net proceeds of new share issues; payments for the redemption or repurchase of shares; and purchased goodwill eliminated against reserves.

7.185 As the reconciliation may be either in the form of a note or in the form of a primary statement, considerable flexibility is given as to where the reconciliation appears in financial statements and thus to the prominence or lack of prominence given to it. If included as a primary statement, however, it must be shown separately from the statement of total recognised gains and losses.

7.186 The reconciliation should include the components of the total recognised gains and losses of the year. The example in the standard shows dividends deducted from profit for the financial year rather than from total recognised gains and losses. This must be correct as dividends cannot be paid out of unrealised profits. The reconciliation should also include goodwill written off and share capital subscribed or repaid. Other items could include amounts written off against the share premium account where permitted by law.

7.187 An example is shown in Table 7.21.

Table 7.21 – Grand Metropolitan Public Limited Company – Annual Report - 30 September 1994

Reconciliation of Movements in Shareholders' Funds
for the year ended 30th September 1994

	1994 £m	*1993 £m*
Profit for the financial year	450	*410*
Ordinary dividends	(292)	*(269)*
	158	*141*
Other recognised gains and losses relating to the year	(57)	*(119)*
New share capital issued	31	*33*
Adjustment in respect of share dividend	20	*10*
Goodwill written off during the year	(320)	*(146)*
Goodwill transferred to the profit and loss account in respect of disposals of businesses	34	*24*
Net movement in shareholders' funds	(134)	*(57)*
Shareholders' funds at 30th September 1993 (originally £3,715m, restated for prior year adjustment of £41m)	3,674	*3,731*
Shareholders' funds at 30th September 1994	3,540	*3,674*

Prior period adjustments

Introduction

7.188 FRS 3 requires that prior period adjustments should be accounted for by restating the corresponding primary statements and notes for the preceding period and adjusting the opening balance of reserves accordingly. In the statement of total recognised gains and losses the cumulative effect of the adjustments should also be noted at the foot of the current year column, as shown in Tables 7.19 on page 62 and Table 7.22 below. [FRS 3 para 29].

Table 7.22 – Trafalgar House Public Limited Company – Report and Accounts - 30 September 1994

Statement of total recognised gains and losses

for the year ended 30 September 1994

	1994 £m	1993 £m
		(restated)
Profit for the year	30.0	(366.6)
Surplus on revaluation	6.3	(38.9)
Exchange translation differences	(3.3)	(5.2)
Total recognised gains and losses relating to the year	33.0	(410.7)
Prior year adjustment (as explained in note 1)	(2.7)	
Total gains and losses recognised since last annual report	30.3	

Notes to the accounts (extract)

1 Changes in accounting policy and in presentation (extract)

(a) Changes in accounting policy

Comparative figures have been restated to reflect two changes of accounting policy:

(i) Trading results denominated in foreign currencies are translated into sterling at average rates of exchange. Previously trading results were translated at the rates of exchange ruling at the year end. The accounting policy has been changed because the directors consider the new policy gives a fairer presentation of the group's results and cash flows as they arise during the course of an accounting period.

(ii) Sales of UK residential property are recognised on legal completion. Previously, sales were recognised when contracts were exchanged. The accounting policy has been changed because the new policy is adopted by most other UK housebuilders.

As a result, comparative figures for the year ended 30 September 1993 have been adjusted as follows:

	Loss for the year after dividends £m	Net assets £m
As previously reported	(402.1)	290.2
Effect of the change from year end to average exchange rates	1.5	-
Effect of the change in the timing of recognition of UK residential property sales	(1.3)	(2.7)
As restated	(401.9)	(287.5)

Current year profit before tax is reduced by £0.9 million following the change in the foreign exchange policy and reduced by £0.6 million following the change in policy for the recognition of UK residential property sales.

7.189 Normally, items relating to prior periods arise from the corrections and adjustments that are the natural result of estimates inherent in accounting and in the periodic preparation of financial statements. Therefore, they should be dealt with in the profit and loss account of the period in which they are identified. The only types of prior period items that should be adjusted against opening reserves are those that arise from a change of accounting policy or from the correction of a fundamental error.

Changes in accounting policies

7.190 Changes of accounting policy result from a choice between two or more accounting bases. They do not arise from the adoption or modification of an accounting basis necessitated by transactions or events that are clearly different in substance from those previously occurring. A change from accounting for post-retirement benefits on a cash basis to an accruals basis *would* be a change of accounting policy. A change in accounting for rent payable from accruing a quarter's rent at each year end to not accruing *would not* be a change in policy if the basis of paying rent changed from a quarter in arrear to a quarter in advance (assuming no payment was made at the year end in either case).

7.191 The accounting bases are described in SSAP 2 as the methods developed for applying fundamental accounting concepts to financial transactions and items, for the purpose of financial statements, and in particular:

- For determining the accounting periods in which revenue and costs should be recognised in the profit and loss account.

- For determining the amounts at which material items should be stated in the balance sheet.

[SSAP 2 para 15].

7.192 Accounting policies are the specific accounting bases selected and consistently followed by a business enterprise as being, in the opinion of the management, appropriate to its circumstances and best suited to present fairly its results and financial position. [SSAP 2 para 16].

7.193 A significant proportion of accounting policy changes are brought about by the introduction of new accounting standards. Others are changes voluntarily adopted by the directors. In respect of the latter, it is important to note that FRS 3 specifically mentions that, owing to the fundamental concept of consistency, a change in accounting policy can only be justified if the new policy is preferable to the old policy because it will give a fairer presentation of the result and financial position of a reporting entity. [FRS 3 para 62].

7.194 The concept of consistency is also embodied in the Act, which requires a company to apply accounting policies consistently within the same financial statements and from one financial year to the next. [4 Sch 11]. It also permits a company to depart from the principle that accounting policies should be applied consistently only if there are special reasons. [4 Sch 15].

Disclosures

7.195 A change of policy must be adequately explained and justified in the financial statements. The Act requires that where there is a change of accounting policy (that is, a departure from the consistency principle) the financial statements must disclose "*particulars of the departure, the reasons for it and its effect*". [4 Sch 15].

7.196 Changes in accounting policies have interested the Financial Reporting Review Panel. Two of its published findings have referred to policy changes. In the first of these, Associated Nursing Services PLC, the Panel examined the adequacy of the explanation provided in respect of a change of policy. Although the Panel concluded that it was satisfied with the explanations provided, it stated that it "*welcomes the intention of the directors to ensure that future notes of changes in accounting policy will include reiteration of the former policy as well as a description of the new policy*".

7.197 In the second case, Ptarmigan Holdings PLC, the Panel investigated a change of policy in respect of purchased goodwill from immediate write-off to reserves to capitalisation and amortisation. The Panel concluded that, although it was satisfied that the company had special reasons for making the change, it considered the reasons for the change had not been adequately disclosed in the financial statements. The Panel noted that, although SSAP 22 permits the use of both methods for different acquisitions, changes from one method to another must nevertheless comply with the Act's requirements for a change of accounting policy.

7.198 The Act requires disclosure of the *effect* of a change of policy (see para 7.195 above). FRS 3 requires the effect of the change on the results for the preceding period to be disclosed where practicable. [FRS 3 para 29]. The FRS 3 requirement is satisfied by quantifying the adjustment to the comparative figures as a result of changing from the old policy to the new policy.

7.199 UITF Abstract 14, 'Disclosure of changes in accounting policy', issued in November 1995, confirmed that the Act's requirement to disclose the effect of a change of policy goes further than FRS 3, in that it relates to the current year, not the previous year. That is because the departure from the consistent application of accounting policies occurs in the current year. The effect of the departure is, therefore, the difference in the current year between applying the old policy and the new policy, and this difference also needs stating. The issue is relevant because users may be particularly interested to know how much more or less profit the company has made this year as a result of changing its accounting policies.

7.200 Before the UITF's interpretation of the Act, some accountants had taken the view that FRS 3's requirement to state the effect on the previous year was generally sufficient. UITF Abstract 14 explains that:

- Where the effect on the current year is immaterial or similar to the quantified effect on the previous year, a simple statement to that effect will suffice.

- Where it is not practicable to give the effect on the current year, that fact, together with the reasons, should be stated.

7.200.1 The law does not differentiate between changes brought about by new accounting standards and changes voluntarily adopted by the directors. Therefore, in general, the effect of all changes should be disclosed. However, it may be impracticable to give the effect of changes when certain new accounting standards are implemented. One example is FRS 7, 'Fair values in acquisition accounting', where the effect could only be quantified by performing a hypothetical fair value exercise using different fair valuing principles.

(The next paragraph is 7.201.)

7.201 Table 7.22 on page 70 above shows the financial statement disclosures in respect of two voluntary changes of accounting policy: a change from the closing rate method to the average rate method for translating the results of foreign subsidiaries; and a change relating to revenue recognition on property sales. This example discloses the effect of the change on both the current and previous year.

7.202 Table 7.23 shows the disclosures relating to a change in accounting policy stemming from a new accounting pronouncement, in this case a change from a cash basis to an accruals basis of accounting for post-retirement medical benefits. This example also shows the effect of adopting the new policy on the results of both years.

Table 7.23 – Imperial Chemical Industries PLC – Annual Report and Accounts – 31 December 1994

statement of group total recognised gains and losses

for the year ended 31 December 1994

	Notes	1994 £m	1993† £m
Net profit for the financial year		**188**	129
Currency translation differences on foreign currency net investments and related loans		**(96)**	(23)
Share of other reserve movements of associated undertakings and other items		**(7)**	-
Total recognised gains and losses relating to the year		**85**	106
Prior year adjustment	2	**(95)**	
Total gains and losses recognised since last annual report		**10**	

† restated (note 2)

notes relating to the accounts (extract)

2 Basis of presentation of financial information (extract)

The results reflect the initial adoption of the accounting requirements of pronouncement UITF 6 "Accounting for Post-retirement Benefits other than Pensions". The cumulative cost of the benefits relating to previous years has been recognised in the accounts as a prior year adjustment and comparative figures for 1993 have been restated. The effect on continuing operations of implementing this new accounting policy was to reduce trading profit for the year by £12m (1993 £10m), to reduce the tax charge by £4m (1993 £4m) and to reduce the value of Group reserves at 1 January 1994 by £95m (1993 £89m) (Company £3m, 1993 £3m).

23 Reserves (extract)

	Share premium account £m	Revaluation £m	Associated under-takings £m	Profit and loss account £m	1994 Total £m	1993 Total £m
GROUP						
Reserves attributable to parent company						
At beginning of year as previously stated						3,572
Prior year adjustment (note 2)						(89)
At beginning of year as restated	561	46	66	2,493	**3,166**	3,483

7.202.1 In the information sheet accompanying UITF Abstract 14, the UITF issued a clear message reminding companies and auditors of the following:

- Both the Act and FRS 3 require a company to have compelling reasons for making a change of accounting policy. (FRS 3 states that a change may be made only if the new policy is preferable to the one it replaces, because it will give a fairer presentation of the results and the financial position.)

- The reasons for any change of accounting policy should be fully disclosed.

7.202.2 Where accounting policy changes are brought about by new accounting standards, the reason is self-evident if the old policy is no longer permitted. Consequently, only a simple statement to this effect should normally be necessary. However, where a company voluntarily changes from one acceptable policy to another, the directors should be able to demonstrate that the new policy provides better information to users. In such circumstances, the reasons justifying the change need to be clearly and fully disclosed. The UITF has indicated that this would imply a statement as to why the continuation of the previous policy would not be appropriate. Opportunistic changes of accounting policy could be challenged.

[The next paragraph is 7.203.]

Fundamental errors

7.203 Fundamental errors are those that are of such significance as to destroy the true and fair view and hence the validity of financial statements. [FRS 3 para 63]. The correction of such errors should not be included in the current year's profit and loss account. Instead, they should be adjusted by restating previous years' results and adjusting the opening balance of retained profits.

7.204 In practice, this means that if the error had been known about at the time the previous year's financial statements were about to be approved, it would have been corrected prior to approval. Equally, if the error came to light between the approval of the prior year's financial statements and the date of preparation of the current year's financial statements, the directors could have withdrawn the previous financial statements and revised them voluntarily under the Act (but this does not mean that every such revision is necessarily a fundamental error).

7.205 The incidence of fundamental errors is extremely rare in practice.

Chapter 8

Earnings per share

Page

Chapter 8

Earnings per share

Introduction

8.1 Earnings per share (EPS) is a ratio that is widely used by financial analysts, investors and others to gauge the profitability of a company and to value its shares. Its purpose is to indicate how effective a company has been in using the resources provided by the equity shareholders. The allocation of earnings accruing to other providers of finance, such as non-equity shareholders (for example, preference shareholders) is a prior charge and is often fixed. Therefore, the income remaining after making allocations to those parties is attributable to equity shareholders. This amount, when presented on the face of the profit and loss account on a pence per share basis, assists the equity shareholders to gauge the company's current net earnings and changes in its net earnings from period to period. It can, therefore, be relevant as a measure of performance in evaluating management's effectiveness. Another reason for the popularity of EPS is that it forms the basis for calculating the 'price-earnings ratio', which is a standard stock market indicator. Price-earnings ratios relating to both past and prospective profits are widely used by investors and analysts in valuing shares.

8.2 EPS is simply a ratio of the numerator – *earnings measured in terms of profits available to equity shareholders* – to the denominator – *the number of equity shares.* Therefore, it is very simple in concept, but it is the determination of the numerator and in particular, the denominator that can make the calculation of this ratio rather complex in practice. Also if the ratio is to be meaningful it must be calculated on a similar basis for every entity so as to facilitate comparisons between different accounting periods for the same entity and between different entities in the same period. It is for this reason that the original standard, SSAP 3, 'Earnings per share', was issued in February 1972 with the objective of providing a minimum standard of measurement and disclosure of EPS in financial statements of listed companies. SSAP 3 was revised in August 1974 to take account of SSAP 8, 'The treatment of taxation under the imputation system in the accounts of companies', and further revised in October 1992 on the introduction of FRS 3, 'Reporting financial performance'.

8.3 The revision in October 1992 was quite significant. Prior to 1992, earnings for the period comprised the residual profit (after tax, minority interest and preference dividend) attributable to equity shareholders, but *before* taking into account the effects of any extraordinary items. Given this basis of calculation, the fact that management remuneration is often linked with EPS performance and its perceived importance in affecting share prices, there were pressures to report EPS in the most favourable light.

For example, there was a tendency to classify 'abnormal items' as exceptional when they were profits, but to treat them as 'extraordinary' when they were losses. The credibility of the reported EPS in faithfully representing the financial performance of the reporting entity was thus suspect. Views had also been expressed that, hitherto, too much importance had been given to the EPS figures. Many accountants maintained that an understanding of an entity's performance requires a more comprehensive analysis of all aspects of its activities than is provided by a single ratio, particularly when it is the only ratio required to be disclosed in financial statements.

8.4 Against this background, the ASB issued FRS 3 with the objective of shifting the emphasis from a single performance indicator and adopting an 'information set' approach that highlights a range of important components of performance. The ASB argued that it is up to users to identify particular components they consider of significance in varying circumstances and adapt any headline number to give the performance measure required. Paragraph 52 of FRS 3 states that:

> *"It is not possible to distil the performance of a complex organisation into a single measure. Undue significance, therefore, should not be placed on any one measure which may purport to achieve this aim."*

Whilst the ASB recognised that EPS will continue to be used in the assessment of a company's financial performance, it was its clear intention to make it less useful and, therefore, less used.

8.5 In doing so, the ASB amended the definition of EPS contained in SSAP 3 by requiring that an 'all inclusive' earnings figure should form the basis of the calculation. The amended definition, which is considered further in paragraph 8.16 below, requires EPS to be calculated on the profits after minority interest and preference dividends (as before), but also *after* extraordinary items, if any.

8.6 The use of an all inclusive earnings figure in the EPS calculation has the benefit of including the effects of all transactions reported in the profit and loss account, thus removing the possibility of any manipulation or smoothing of results over a period. As a consequence, the EPS figure becomes more volatile and its importance as an indicator of the trend of financial performance is considerably lessened – an objective that FRS 3 seeks to achieve as is evident from the above quotation.

International harmonisation in measuring EPS

8.7 SSAP 3 has been working reasonably well in the UK. On the international front, however, the IASC had been co-operating with the FASB in the US to develop a new international standard on earnings per share. The FASB was already working on a project to improve and simplify its existing guidance on earnings per share that had become unduly complicated. Early in 1996, the two standard setting bodies published exposure drafts on earnings per share which contained proposals that were considerably closer to the current UK requirement than to US GAAP. The ASB's support for international harmonisation of accounting standards and the recognition that EPS is a popular statistic that has international appeal, gave it the opportunity to bring the UK guidance in line with an internationally acceptable method for calculating and presenting earnings per share data.

8.8 In May 1996, the ASB issued a discussion paper that contained the full text of E52, 'Earnings per share', issued by the IASC. As international harmonisation was the primary motivation of the project, the ASB saw little merit in developing its own proposals at the time. Rather, it preferred to give the UK financial reporting community the opportunity to comment on the international proposals. While the majority of the UK respondents favoured the international approach to the computation of earnings per share, many were unhappy about the excessive disclosure requirements proposed. Comments on the discussion papers were communicated to the IASC. When the IASC issued IAS 33 in February 1997 at the same time as the FASB issued a substantially similar but more detailed standard (FAS 128) in the US, a number of changes had been made to the proposals put forward by E52, certain of which reflected the views of the UK respondents.

8.9 In June 1997, the ASB issued FRED 16 which adopted, with minimal exceptions, the requirements and to a large extent the text of IAS 33. Comments on the FRED, however, highlighted a need to customise the international requirements to minimise inconsistencies between UK law and other accounting standards. Several commentators also requested guidance on how some of the general principles of IAS 33 would apply, in practice, to a number of areas. As a result of these comments, the ASB issued a final standard FRS 14, 'Earnings per share', which includes specific guidance on some aspects, in particular contingently issuable shares, employee share schemes and special dividends, which were either not adequately dealt with or considered in IAS 33. These three issues were separately exposed for comments in a supplement to FRED 16 in March 1998 and were treated in a manner consistent with the more detailed requirements of FAS 128, except for the last item, which was not addressed in the US standard.

8.10 FRS 14 was issued on 1 October 1998 and applies to financial statements ending on or after 23 December 1998. It supersedes SSAP 3 and is significantly different from the original standard, both in the way it perceives earnings per share figures, particularly diluted earnings per share, and the way in which these figures are calculated.

Objectives and scope of FRS 14

Objectives

8.11 The FRS specifies the way in which earnings per share data should be calculated, presented and disclosed in the financial statements of entities. In doing so, it focuses primarily on determining the number of shares to be included in the denominator of the earnings per share calculation.

8.12 Although it is accepted that earnings per share data may have limitations because of the different accounting policies used for determining 'earnings', a consistently calculated denominator will improve the comparison of the performance of different entities in the same period and of the same entity in different accounting periods. Furthermore, a denominator calculated in accordance with international consensus will go a long way in enhancing global comparison of earnings per share data in spite of different national methods for determining 'earnings'.

Scope

8.13 The standard applies to entities whose ordinary shares or potential ordinary shares (for example, convertible debt, warrants etc) are publicly traded. [FRS 14 para 3]. Therefore, entities whose securities are listed on the London Stock Exchange or an overseas stock exchange (for example, NASDAQ) or traded on the AIM will have to calculate earnings per share data in accordance with the standard. Furthermore, entities that are in the process of issuing ordinary shares or potential ordinary shares in public securities markets (that is, not private placings) should also comply with the standard. [FRS 14 para 3].

8.14 Entities whose securities are not publicly traded are not required to disclose earnings per share data because, generally, they have few ordinary shareholders. However, where such entities choose to disclose earnings per share data they should comply with the provisions of the standard to maintain comparability in financial reporting. [FRS 14 para 6]. Such entities are likely to be those that intend to establish a track record before seeking entry to the public securities market at a future date.

8.15 As stated in paragraph 8.11 above, the focus of the standard is on the denominator of the EPS figure. Therefore, the principles in the standard can be applied to other per share data, such as net assets per share. Some listed entities disclose such information in their historical summaries (see para 8.128).

Basic earnings per share

Measurement

8.16 Basic EPS should be calculated by dividing the net profit or loss for the period attributable to ordinary shareholders by the weighted average number of ordinary shares outstanding during the period. [FRS 14 para 9].

8.17 In the above definition, the term 'ordinary shares' relates to those shares that are defined as equity in FRS 4, 'Capital instruments' (see chapter 18). Therefore, shares that are regarded as equity shares under the Companies Act but not under FRS 4 should be disregarded. This situation, however, is likely to arise very rarely.

8.18 The computation of the EPS figure requires a calculation of the earnings as the numerator and the relevant number of equity shares as the denominator. The computation is relatively easy where no adjustments are required to the numerator or the denominator. In that situation, the net profit or loss attributable to the equity shareholders and the relevant number of equity shares can be obtained easily from the financial statements and the figure computed. However, in practice some adjustments are usually necessary either to the numerator or to the denominator or both. The circumstances in which such adjustments should be made are considered in the paragraphs that follow.

Computation of earnings

8.19 Earnings for the purposes of calculating basic EPS are defined as the net profit or loss for the period attributable to ordinary or equity shareholders. The net profit or loss attributable to equity shareholders is the net profit or loss after tax, minority interest and extraordinary items and after deducting dividends and other appropriations in respect of non-equity shares. [FRS 14 paras 10, 11]. Given this definition, it is relatively simple to obtain the relevant components from the profit and loss account to calculate the earnings figure for EPS purposes. However, in practice, this calculated figure may require some further adjustments, particularly in respect of dividends and other appropriations in respect of non-equity shares. The ways in which such adjustments are likely to affect earnings for the purposes of calculating basic EPS are considered below.

Preference dividends

8.20 Where preference shares carry the right to a fixed dividend, then those dividends can either be cumulative or non-cumulative. If the preference dividends are cumulative, the dividend for the period should be taken into account, whether or not it has been declared. [FRS 14 para 12(b)]. Thus, in a year in which the company is unable to pay or declare a cumulative preference dividend, because of insufficient distributable profits (for example, the company has accumulated losses), the undeclared amount of the cumulative preference dividend should still be deducted in arriving at earnings for the purposes of the EPS calculation. Indeed, under FRS 4 such cumulative dividends would, in any event, fall to be shown as an appropriation in the profit and loss account rather than simply being noted as being in arrears, even in the absence of sufficient distributable profits. It follows that in the year in which these arrears of preference dividends are paid, they should be ignored in the calculation of EPS for that year. On the other hand, if the preference dividends are non-cumulative, only the amount of dividends paid and payable in the year and shown as an appropriation in the profit and loss account should be deducted in arriving at the profits attributable to equity shareholders. [FRS 14 para 12(a)(b)].

Participating dividends

8.21 Preference shares may be given the right to participate in the net profit with equity shares according to a predetermined formula, but with an upper limit or cap on the extent of participation by the preference shares. Such participation is usually in addition to a fixed dividend. Participating preference shares are treated as non-equity shares under FRS 4, which also requires separate disclosure of participating dividends payable as an appropriation in the profit and loss account. Consequently, the amount of earnings attributable to the non-equity shares would include both the participating and the fixed element and the total would be deducted from profit for the financial year to arrive at the earnings attributable to the equity shareholders. If there is no upper limit on the extent of the profit participation by the non-equity shareholders, the appropriate proportion of the earnings attributable to these shareholders should be calculated by reference to their dividend rights and other rights to participate in profits. This entire amount including the fixed element should then be deducted from earnings to arrive at the earnings attributable to the equity shareholders.

Other appropriations in respect of non-equity shares

8.22 Under FRS 4, the appropriations made in the profit and loss account in respect of preference shares will include not only the preference and/or participating dividends paid and proposed, but will also include other appropriations such as the amortisation of issue costs and accrual for any premium payable on redemption. It follows that these other appropriations should also be deducted from profit for the financial year to arrive at the earnings available to equity shareholders. In the year in which the preference shares are redeemed, any premium payable on redemption should be ignored in calculating EPS for that year to the extent that it has been accrued (and, therefore, already taken into account) in earlier years.

Different classes of equity shares

8.23 Where there is only one class of equity shares, all the earnings for the period should be attributed to that class. However, it is possible for a company to have more than one class of equity shares, for example shares with different rights to share in net profits, which would all qualify as equity under FRS 4. Where this is so, the earnings for the period should be apportioned over the different classes of equity shares in issue in accordance with either their dividend rights or their other rights to participate in profits. [FRS 14 para 13]. This means that a company could disclose a number of EPS figures, each attributable to a different class of equity shares.

Computation of number of equity shares

8.24 The denominator of the basic EPS should be calculated using the weighted average number of those equity shares that are *outstanding during the period* under review. [FRS 14 para 14]. This is a change from SSAP 3 where the shares used were those ranking for dividends (see further para 8.27). As explained in paragraph 8.122, the period under review may include the period between the balance sheet date and the date when the financial statements are approved by the board.

8.25 In a simple situation where there have been no changes in capital structure during the year, the relevant denominator is the number of equity shares outstanding at the year end. However, if additional equity shares have been issued during the year, it would not give a true and fair view to apportion the earnings for the whole of the year over the larger equity base. This is because the capital invested through the issue of the additional shares was available to the entity to increase its earnings only for part of the year. Therefore, in order to take this factor into account, as well as to permit comparison of EPS with the previous period when there may have been no such change in the issued equity capital, an average of the number of shares weighted by the number of days outstanding (a 'weighted average equity share capital') is considered to be necessary in the calculation of the denominator. The weighted average number, therefore, reflects the fact that the amount of equity capital may have been varied during the period as a result of a larger or smaller number of shares being outstanding at any time. The time-weighting factor should generally be the number of days that the specific shares are outstanding as a proportion of the total number of days, although, in practice, a reasonable approximation such as a fraction of a month should be adequate.

8.26 An example of how the weighted average number of shares should be calculated is given below. The example is derived from the example in the standard.

		Shares issued	Own shares acquired	Shares Outstanding
1 Jan 20X1	Balance at beginning of year	2,400		2,400
31 May 20X1	Issue of new shares for cash	800		3,200
1 Dec 20X1	Purchase of shares for cash	–	(200)	3,000
31 Dec 20X1	Balance at end of year	3,200	(200)	3,000

Computation of weighted average

(2,400 × 5/12) + (3,200 × 6/12) + (3,000 × 1/12) = 2,850 shares

or

(2,400 × 12/12) + (800 × 7/12) – (200 × 1/12) = 2,850 shares

8.27 The requirement to include in the weighted average calculation only those shares that are outstanding during the period is a significant change from SSAP 3. Under SSAP 3 only shares that ranked for dividends during the period were included in the basic EPS calculation. Those that did not were included in the diluted EPS calculation. The amendment to include all outstanding shares without reference to their dividend entitlements is sensible because they represent capital that has been used to generate income after the date of issue. Hence, it is proper that they should be brought into the EPS calculation on a weighted average basis.

8.28 Indeed, the general principle under FRS 14 is that shares should be included in the weighted average calculation from the date the consideration is receivable (which is generally the date of their issue). [FRS 14, para 17]. Therefore, shares issued for cash are brought into the calculation from the date the cash is receivable. Where shares are issued as consideration for the acquisition of an asset or a satisfaction of a liability, the shares are included in the averaging calculation from the date the asset is recognised or the liability is settled. In other situations, the date of inclusion should be determined from the terms and conditions attaching to the issue. The substance of any contract associated with the issue should also be considered. The standard provides a number of examples illustrating the timing of inclusion of ordinary shares in the weighted average calculation. These examples are listed below:

- Ordinary shares issued in exchange for cash are included when cash is receivable.
- Ordinary shares issued on the voluntary reinvestment of dividends on ordinary or preference shares are included at the dividend payment date.
- Ordinary shares issued as a result of the conversion of a debt instrument to ordinary shares are included as of the date when interest ceases accruing.

- Ordinary shares issued in place of interest or principal on other financial instruments are included as of the date when interest ceases accruing.

- Ordinary shares issued in exchange for the settlement of a liability of the entity are included as of the settlement date.

- Ordinary shares issued as consideration for the acquisition of an asset other than cash are included as of the date on which the acquisition is recognised.

[FRS 14 para 17].

8.29 The general rule that shares should be included in the basic EPS calculation from the date consideration is receivable does not apply to shares that are issued in partly paid form. Partly paid shares are treated as fractions of shares (payments received to date as a proportion of the total subscription price) and included in the averaging calculation only to the extent that they participate in dividends for the period. [FRS 14 para 19]. Partly paid shares that do not participate in dividends are excluded from the basic EPS calculation, but included in the diluted EPS (see further para 8.63).

Example

A company issues 100,000 ordinary shares of £1 each for a consideration of £2.50 per share. Calls amounting to £1.75 per share were received by the balance sheet date. The partly-paid shares are entitled to participate in dividends for the period in proportion to the amount paid. The number of ordinary share equivalents that would be included in the basic EPS calculation on a weighted basis is as follows:

$$100{,}000 \times \frac{£1.75}{£2.50} = 70{,}000 \text{ shares}$$

8.30 Whenever changes in equity shares occur during the accounting period, an amendment is necessary to the number of shares used in the EPS calculation. In some situations, the EPS in prior periods will also have to be adjusted. Some of the ways in which a company can change its equity capital and the consequential effect on the number of shares used in the EPS calculation are considered below.

Purchase of own shares

8.31 Where a company has purchased its own equity shares during the year, there will be a lesser number of equity shares in issue after the repurchase. In such circumstances, a weighted average number of shares in issue should be used in the basic EPS calculation, taking account of the number of shares purchased and the date of purchase. Any premium payable on the purchase of equity shares will be charged against distributable reserves and will not affect earnings for the year. The effect of the repurchase is likely to enhance EPS in the year of repurchase. No adjustments should be made to the prior year's EPS.

Own shares held

8.32 A company may sometimes hold its own shares. This situation may arise where it has acquired them by forfeiture, or by surrender in lieu of forfeiture, or by way of a gift. A public company that acquires shares by forfeiture must generally dispose of them within three years. Otherwise it must cancel them and effectively bring about a capital reduction. [Sec 146]. A not uncommon situation is where a subsidiary continues to hold the shares in the parent that were acquired before it became a group member. This is permitted by section 23(4), but the shares do not carry any voting or dividend rights. For the purpose of calculating EPS these outstanding shares should be treated as if they were cancelled and excluded from the calculation. [FRS 14 para 16].

8.33 Another common situation where a company holds its own shares arises where it operates an Employee Share Ownership Plan (ESOP) for the benefit of its employees. UITF Abstract 13, 'Accounting for ESOP trusts', stipulates that company's shares held by the ESOP trust should be classified as 'own shares' where the company has *de facto* control of those shares and bears their benefits and risks (see further chapter 4). For the purpose of calculating EPS these outstanding shares should also be treated as if they were cancelled and excluded from the calculation, until such time as they vest unconditionally in the employees. [FRS 14 para 16]. This is a significant change from the previous treatment in UITF Abstract 13 under which the exclusion of ESOP shares from the EPS calculation was dependent on the trust waiving its rights to dividends on those shares. UITF Abstract 13 is thus amended by FRS 14. The other aspect of this amendment addresses the situation where the trust has not waived its rights to dividends. In this situation, the dividend income arising on the ESOP shares is no longer included in arriving at profit before tax; hence no adjustment to earnings is necessary. Moreover, the amended UITF Abstract 13 requires that dividends on ESOP shares should be deducted from the aggregate of dividends paid and proposed (see further chapter 4).

8.34 An example where a company has ignored shares held in an ESOP trust for the purposes of determining the weighted average number of shares for calculating EPS is given in Table 8.1 below.

Table 8.1 – Reuters Holdings PLC – Annual Report – 31 December 1997

Notes on the Consolidated Profit and Loss Account continued (extract)

6. Earnings per ordinary share (extract)

The weighted average number of shares in issue may be reconciled to the number used in the earnings per ordinary share calculation as follows:

Weighted average number in millions	1997	1996	1995
Ordinary shares in issue	**1,692**	1,684	1,672
Reuters interest in ordinary shares held by:			
Telfer Investments (Australia) Pty Limited	**(55)**	(55)	(55)
Instinet Corporation	**(4)**	(4)	(4)
Shares owned by Employee Share Ownership Trust	**(11)**	(9)	(8)
	1,622	1,616	1,605

Bonus issue, share split and share consolidation

8.35 Where a company issues new shares by way of capitalisation of reserves (a bonus issue) during the period, the effect is to increase only the number of shares outstanding after the issue. There is no effect on earnings as there is no flow of funds as a result of the issue. Consequently, the shares should be treated as outstanding as if the issue had occurred at the beginning of the earliest period reported. This means that the earnings for the year should be apportioned over the number of shares after the capitalisation. The EPS figure disclosed for the previous year should be recalculated using the new number of shares in issue. [FRS 14 para 23].

8.36 Similar considerations apply where equity shares are split into shares of smaller nominal value (a share of £1 nominal value is divided into four shares of 25p each) or consolidated into shares of a higher nominal amount (four shares of 25p each are consolidated into one share of £1). In both these situations, the number of shares outstanding before the event is adjusted for the proportionate change in the number of shares outstanding after the event.

Example

On 31 December 19X7, the issued share capital of a company consisted of £1,000,000 in ordinary shares of 25p each and £500,000 in 10% cumulative preference shares of £1 each. On 1 October 19X8, the company issued 1,000,000 ordinary shares fully paid by way of capitalisation of reserves in the proportion of 1:4 for the year ended 31 December 19X8.

	19X8 £'000	19X7 £'000
Calculation of earnings		
Profit for the year	550	450
Less: preference dividend	(50)	(50)
Earnings	500	400
Number of ordinary shares		
Shares in issue for full year	4,000	4,000
Capitalisation issue at 1 October 19X8	1,000	1,000
Number of shares	5,000	5,000
Earnings per ordinary shares of 25p	10.0p	8.0p

The comparative earnings per share for 19X7 can also be calculated by adjusting the previously disclosed EPS in 19X7, in this example 10p, by the following factor:

$$\frac{\text{Number of shares before the bonus issue}}{\text{Number of shares after the bonus issue}}$$

Adjusted EPS for 19X7: $10\text{p} \times \frac{4{,}000}{5{,}000} = 8.0\text{p}$

The above ratio should also be used to restate previous years' EPS and other financial ratios (for example, dividend per share) disclosed in the historical summary.

Issue of shares at full market price

8.37 Where new equity shares are issued during the year for cash at full market price, the earnings should be apportioned over the average number of shares outstanding during the period weighted on a time basis.

Example

On 31 December 19X7, the issued share capital of a company consisted of £1,000,000 in ordinary shares of 25p each and £500,000 in 10% cumulative preference shares of £1 each. On 1 October 19X8, the company issued 1,000,000 ordinary shares at full market price in cash for the year ended 31 December 19X8.

	19X8 £'000	19X7 £'000
Calculation of earnings		
Profit for the year	550	450
Less: preference dividend	(50)	(50)
Earnings	500	400

Weighted average number of ordinary shares		
Shares in issue for full year	4,000	4,000
Issued on 1 October 19X8 (1,000,000 × 3/12)	250	–
Number of shares	4,250	4,000
Earnings per ordinary share of 25p	11.8p	10.0p

The calculation of earnings per share is based on earnings of £500,000 (19X7: £400,000) and on the weighted average of 4,250,000 ordinary shares in issue during the year (19X7: 4,000,000).

Issue of shares at less than full market price

8.38 Sometimes shares may be issued at a discount to the market price, such as for the acquisition of an asset or the cancellation of a liability. Although the standard does not specifically deal with this situation, it would be appropriate to include the shares in the EPS calculation for the period on a weighted basis without adjusting for any bonus element. Shares issued in exchange for shares in another company are considered in paragraphs 8.52 to 8.53 below.

Rights issue

8.39 Companies sometimes raise additional capital during the year by issuing shares to existing shareholders on a *pro rata* basis to their existing holdings in the form of a rights issue. The rights shares may either be offered at the current market price or at a price that is below the current market price. Where shares are issued at full market price, the weighting is carried out on a time basis and the calculation is relatively straight-forward as considered in paragraph 8.37 above. However, where equity shares are issued during the year by way of a rights issue at a discount to the market price, the weighting calculation is not so straight-forward. This is because the discount can be viewed as a bonus given to the shareholders in the form of shares for no consideration, which must be taken into account in calculating the weighted average number of shares. In fact, it can be demonstrated (see example below) that a rights issue is equivalent to a capitalisation issue of part of the shares for no consideration and an issue of the remainder of the shares at full market price. The notional capitalisation issue reflects the bonus element inherent in the rights issue and is measured by the following fraction:

$$\frac{\text{Fair value per share immediately before the exercise of rights}}{\text{Theoretical ex-rights price}}$$

8.40 Where the rights themselves are publicly traded separately from the shares themselves, as is the case in the UK, the fair value for the purpose of the above calculation is established at the close of the last day on which the shares are traded together with the rights. [FRS 14 para 24]. In other words, it is the *actual* closing mid-market price at which the shares are quoted on the last date inclusive of the right to subscribe for the new shares (that is, the market price immediately prior to the exercise of rights). This is often referred to as the 'cum-rights price', being the price on the last day of quotation cum-rights. The 'ex-rights price', on the other hand, is the *theoretical* price at which, in a perfect market and without any external influences, the shares would trade after the exercise of the rights.

8.41 The above factor should be used to adjust the number of shares in issue before the rights issue in order to correct for the bonus element in the rights issue. This correction should be made both for the current period prior to the rights issue and the previous period. The way in which EPS should be calculated following a rights issue and the adjustment that should be made to the comparative EPS figure are considered in the example below.

Example

At 31 December 19X7, the issued capital of a company consisted of 1.8m ordinary shares of 10p each, fully paid. The profit for the year ended 31 December 19X7 and 19X8 amounted to £630,000 and £875,000 respectively. On 31 March 19X8, the company made a rights issue on a 1 for 4 basis at 30p. The market price of the shares immediately before the rights issue was 60p

Calculation of theoretical ex rights price

	No		p
Initial holding	4	Market value	240
Rights taken up	1	Cost	30
New holding	5	Theoretical price	270

Theoretical ex rights price $\frac{270}{5}$ = 54p

The market price is the fair value of the shares immediately prior to the exercise of rights, that is, the actual cum-rights price.

Cost is the amount payable for each new share under the rights issue.

Calculation of bonus element

The bonus element of the rights issue is given by the fraction:

$$\frac{\text{Market price before rights issue}}{\text{Theoretical ex-rights price}} \quad \frac{60}{54} = \frac{10}{9}$$

This corresponds to a bonus issue of 1 for 9. The bonus ratio will usually be greater than 1, that is, the market price of the shares immediately prior to the exercise of rights is greater than the theoretical ex-rights price. If the ratio is less than 1 it may indicate that the market price has fallen significantly during the rights period which was not anticipated when the rights issue was announced. In this situation, the rights issue should be treated as an issue of shares for cash at full market price (see para 8.37 above).

As stated in paragraph 8.39 above, it can be demonstrated, using the figures in the example, that a rights issue of 1 for 4 at 30p is equivalent to a bonus issue of 1 for 9 combined with an issue of shares at full market price of 54p per share. Consider an individual shareholder holding 180 shares.

	No	Value	£
Original holding	180	Value at 60p per share	108.00
Rights shares (1:4)	45	Value at 30p per share	13.50
Holding after rights issue	225	Value at 54p per share	121.50

The additional 45 rights shares at 30p can be shown to be equivalent to a bonus issue of 1 for 9 on the original holding followed by an issue of 1: 8 at full market price of 54p following the bonus issue as follows:

Original holding	180	Value at 60p per share	108.00
Bonus issue of 1 for 9	20	Value nil	nil
	200	Value at 54p per share	108.00
Issue of 1 for 8 at full price	25	Value at 54p per share	13.50
Total holding	225	Value at 54p per share	121.50

The shareholder is therefore indifferent as to whether the company makes a rights issue of 1 for 4 at 30p per share or a combination of a bonus issue of 1 for 9 followed by a rights issue of 1 for 8 at full market price of 54p per share.

Having calculated the bonus ratio, the ratio should be applied to adjust the number of shares in issue before the rights issue both for the current year and for the previous year. Therefore, the weighted average number of shares in issue for the current and the previous period, adjusted for the bonus element would be:

Weighted average number of shares		
	19X8	19X7
Number of actual shares in issue before rights	1,800,000	1,800,000
Correction for bonus issue (1:9)	200,000	200,000
Deemed number of shares in issue before rights issue (1.8m × 10/9)	2,000,000	2,000,000

The number of shares after the rights issue would be:
1.8m × 5/4 = 2,250,000

Therefore, the weighted average number of shares would be:

2.0m for the whole year		2,000,000
2.0m × 3/12 (before rights issue)	500,000	–
2.25m × 9/12 (after rights issue)	1,687,500	–
Weighted average number	2,187,500	2,000,000

Calculation of EPS following a rights issue

	19X8	19X7 (as previously stated)
Basic EPS	£875,000	£630,000
	2,187,500	1,800,000
	40.0p	35.0p
Basic EPS for 19X7 (as restated)		£630,000
		2,000,000
		31.5p

The restated EPS for 19X7 can also be calculated by adjusting the earnings per share figure of the previous year by the *reciprocal* of the bonus element factor as shown below.

$$35p \times \frac{9}{10} = 31.5p$$

In practice, the EPS for the corresponding period should be adjusted directly by using the reciprocal of the bonus element factor above, because this is a much easier way of making the adjustment rather than using a restated number of shares.

8.42 A question arises as to whether the averaging calculation in a rights issue made during the year should be performed from the announcement date, or from the last date of acceptance of the subscription price, or from the share issue date following despatch of the share certificates. Depending on the circumstances of each case, there is often a delay of between 60 to 80 days between the date of announcement of the rights issue and the share issue date. Following the principle in the standard that shares should generally be included from the date consideration is receivable, it follows that the averaging calculation should be performed from the day following the last date of acceptance of the subscription price, which is also the date when the rights are legally exercised. This is because the company begins to generate income from all the proceeds received from that date, which is often midway between the announcement date and the share issue date. Therefore, the new shares should be included in the EPS calculation from the day following the last date on which proceeds are received and not from the announcement date or from the date when the new shares are actually issued.

Scrip dividends and enhanced scrip dividends

8.43 Where a company issues shares in lieu of scrip dividends or enhanced scrip dividends during the year, the shares allotted would increase the weighted average number of shares used in the EPS calculation. This is rather obvious, but the question arises as to how these new shares should be treated for the purposes of the EPS calculation.

8.44 Under FRS 14, paragraph 2, scrip dividends may be regarded as potential ordinary shares that may entitle the recipient to ordinary shares. These potential ordinary shares are converted into ordinary shares when the scrip shares are issued, which is after the balance sheet date. Since the general rule is that shares are normally receivable from the date consideration is receivable, ordinary shares issued on the voluntary reinvestment of dividends on ordinary or preference shares should be included on a weighted average basis at the dividend payment date. [FRS 14 para 17(b)].

8.45 Furthermore, under FRS 4 the cash dividend foregone by the shareholders electing to take a scrip dividend of shares is taken to be the consideration paid for those shares, which would normally be equivalent to the current market value of the shares. [FRS 4 paras 48, 99]. The rationale for this is based on the substance argument that the cash dividend foregone by the shareholders electing to take shares instead of cash is effectively reinvested in the company as fully paid up shares at market value. As a result, the earnings figure in the numerator already reflects the income generated by the additional cash retained from the dividend payment date. Consequently, for the purposes of the EPS calculation the issue of scrip shares should be treated as an issue at full market price and the relevant number of shares should be included in the denominator on a weighted basis from the dividend payment date as stated above. This treatment is often adopted by companies when accounting for the issue of scrip shares on the balance sheet. Under this method, the provision for dividends not taken up in cash is applied to paying up the nominal value of shares and share premium. The method is referred to as the 'reinvestment method'.

8.46 Another alternative method that is sometimes followed in practice is the bonus issue method. Under this method, the provision for the scrip dividend and enhanced scrip dividend not taken up in cash is written back to the profit and loss account reserve and the actual shares issued are treated as a bonus issue made out of reserves at nominal value. Where a company uses this method to account for the scrip dividend, it should, nevertheless, use the 'reinvestment method' for the purposes of calculating EPS under FRS 14.

Special dividend followed by share consolidation

8.47 In recent years, there has been an increasing trend for companies to return surplus cash to shareholders. This has normally been effected by means of a share repurchase, but a new development pioneered by East Midlands Electricity Plc is that of a synthetic share repurchase that is achieved by the payment of a special dividend to shareholders followed by a consolidation of share capital (for example, changing five 20p shares into four 25p shares). In this combined transaction, the amount of the special dividend and the reduction in the number of shares under the share consolidation are arranged in such a way as to achieve an economic effect, in terms of net assets, number of shares and shareholder wealth, similar to a repurchase of shares at fair value.

8.48 Prior to the issue of FRS 14, the effect of such a combined transaction on the EPS figure was not very clear. Some argued that where a special dividend payment is accompanied by a share consolidation, the subsequent share consolidation should be accounted for in the same way as any other share consolidation, that is, by adjusting the prior periods' earnings per share as if the event had occurred at the beginning of the earliest period reported. Others argued that it was anomalous to adjust prior years' EPS for a synthetic share repurchase but not for an actual share repurchase, when the economic effects of the arrangements was identical.

8.49 As a result of the above controversy, the ASB exposed this issue for comment in a special supplement to FRED 16, the exposure draft that preceded FRS 14. The supplement put forward three possible options in respect of the problem. The first, option 1, required adjustment to prior periods' earnings per share for the special dividend. Option 2 took the view that there should be no adjustment to period periods' earnings per share for the effects of a share consolidation that is combined with a special dividend to replicate the economic effect of a share repurchase. Option 3 required restatement of prior periods' earnings per share in respect of the share consolidation element of the transaction. A clear majority of the respondents supported option 2. Consequently, FRS 14 requires no adjustment to be made to the number of ordinary shares outstanding before the event when a share consolidation is combined with a special dividend and the overall commercial effect in terms of net assets earnings and number of shares is of a repurchase at fair value. [FRS 14 para 26].

Example

A company has in issue 10,000 shares with a nominal value of 10p each. At the beginning of 19X8, it decides either to launch a share repurchase of 1,000 shares at the current market price of £1 per share or pay a special dividend of 10p per share (net) followed by a share consolidation of 9 new shares for 10 old shares. The profit after tax for 19X8 and 19X7 is £2,000. Interest rates are 8% per annum and the company pays corporation tax at 31%.

	Balance sheet before transactions	Repurchase of 1,000 shares at £1 per share	Special dividend of 10p per share followed by share consolidation of 10:9
	£	£	£
Net assets	5,000	4,000	4,000
Share capital			
10,000 shares at 10p each	1,000		
9,000 shares at 10p each		900	
9,000 shares at 11.1p each			1,000
Capital Redemption Reserve		100	
Profit and loss account	4,000	3,000	3,000
	5,000	4,000	4,000
Net assets per share	£0.50	£0.44	£0.44

Effect on earnings per share – share repurchase

	19X8	19X7
	£	£
Profit for the year	2,000.00	2,000.00
Loss of interest on cash paid out (£1,000 × 0.08 × 0.69)	55.20	–
Earnings	1,944.80	2,000.00
Number of shares in issue	9,000	10,000
EPS	21.61p	20.00p

Effect on earnings per share – special dividend followed by share consolidation

The total nominal value of the shares remain unchanged, but whereas before there were 10,000 shares of 10p each there are now 9,000 shares of 11.1p each.

	19X8	19X7
	£	£
Profit for the year	2,000.00	2,000.00
Loss of interest on cash paid out (£1,000 × 0.08 × 0.69)	55.20	–
Earnings	1,944.48	2,000.00
Number of shares in issue (unadjusted)	9,000	10,000
EPS unadjusted	21.61p	20.00p
Number of shares in issue (adjusted for consolidation)	9,000	9,000
EPS adjusted	21.61p	22.22p

8.50 As can be seen from the above example, the economic effect, in terms of net asset per share, of an actual share repurchase is identical to a synthetic share repurchase that is achieved by the combination of a special dividend with a share consolidation. It follows that the earnings per share figures for the two transactions should also be identical. If an adjustment is made to the previous year's EPS for the share consolidation as shown above, there is an apparent dilution of 2.75 per cent ((22.22-21.61)/22.22) that would make the share repurchase look significantly more attractive than the special dividend route. But this would be misleading as the economic effect of the two transactions is identical. Therefore, no adjustment to prior year's EPS should be made for the share consolidation, which is but one part of a larger event, that is, the combination of the share consolidation with the special dividend. [FRS 14 para 26].

8.51 In the above example, it was assumed for simplicity that the combined transaction took place at the beginning of the year and so the new shares were treated as outstanding for a full year. In practice, the combined transaction is likely to take place part way through the year. In that situation, the weighted average number of ordinary shares outstanding for the period in which the combined transaction takes place should be adjusted for the reduction in the number of shares from the date the special dividend is paid, that is, when resources leave the entity. [FRS 14 para 26]. An example of a company that has treated the payment of an exceptional dividend and a share consolidation carried out at the same time as equivalent to a share buy-back is given in the Table 8.2 below.

Table 8.2 – Reckitt & Colman – Annual Report and Accounts – 31 December 1996

Notes to the accounts (extract)

7. Dividends (extract)

b) Exceptional dividend	1996 Pence per ordinary share	1996 £m	1995 Pence per ordinary share	1995 £m
Exceptional dividend	35.65	151.9	–	–

At the Extraordinary General Meeting held on 18 November 1996, the shareholders approved the payment of an exceptional dividend of 35.65p per share amounting to £151.9m and a consolidation of the share capital by the issue of 19 new ordinary shares of 10 10/19p each for every 20 existing ordinary shares of 10p each.

8. Earnings per ordinary share (extract)

As described in Note 7, during the year the company paid an exceptional dividend of £151.9m and at the same time carried out a consolidation of its share capital. These transactions were conditional on each other. They were specifically designed to achieve the same overall effect on the company's capital structure as a buy back of shares in a way in which all shareholders could participate. Accordingly, earnings per share is presented on the basis that in substance a share buy-back has occurred.

The transaction occurred in November and only marginally reduced the weighted average number of shares in issue.

Share exchange

8.52 Where equity shares are issued during the financial year in exchange for a majority interest in the equity of another company (that is, as non-cash consideration) and acquisition accounting is used for the business combination, the results of the new subsidiary are included in the consolidation from the date of acquisition. Therefore, the shares issued as consideration to obtain those earnings should be included in the EPS calculation on a weighted average basis from the same date. [FRS 14 para 18].

8.53 However, where the business combination is accounted for as a merger, the results of the acquired subsidiary are included in the consolidated profit and loss account as if the acquired subsidiary has always been part of the same group. This means that the acquired subsidiary's results for both the current and the previous year are included in full in the current and the corresponding amounts shown in the consolidated profit and loss account. It follows that, for the purposes of calculating EPS, the consideration shares should be treated as having been issued at the beginning of the previous year, even though they may have been issued part way through the current year. Therefore, the new shares should be included for a full year for the purposes of calculating the EPS of the current and the previous year. In other words, the aggregate of the weighted average number of shares of the combined entities, adjusted to equivalent shares of the entity whose shares are outstanding after the combination is included in basic EPS calculation for all periods presented. [FRS 14 para 18].

Diluted earnings per share

Measurement

8.54 As discussed above, the basic EPS is calculated on the number of shares outstanding in respect of the period. Sometimes companies may have 'potential ordinary shares' in issue. The standard defines a 'potential ordinary share' as a financial instrument or a right that may entitle its holder to ordinary shares. [FRS 14 para 2]. Typical examples are convertible debt, share options and share warrants that do not have the current right to participate fully in earnings, but may do so in the future by virtue of their conversion or option rights. In each of these situations, the effect of the conversion into ordinary shares may be to dilute future EPS. It should be noted that not all potential ordinary shares in issue will have a diluting effect (see further 8.69). Any potential dilution, however, is of considerable interest to existing equity shareholders, because it indicates the possible reduction in current earnings that may be distributed to them by way of dividends in the future and the possible increase in the number of shares over which the total market value of the company may be divided.

8.55 The standard, therefore, requires the disclosure of diluted EPS, in addition to the basic EPS, in all situations where dilutive potential ordinary shares are in issue. For the purpose of calculating diluted EPS, the net profit or loss for the period attributable to ordinary shareholders should be divided by the sum of the weighted average number of ordinary shares used in the basic EPS calculation and the weighted average number of shares that would be issued on the conversion of all the dilutive potential ordinary shares into ordinary shares. [FRS 14 paras 27, 29].

8.56 It should be noted that although existing equity shareholders are interested about future dilution, the diluted EPS figure calculated in accordance with the standard is not intended to be a predictor of dilution, or a forward-looking number. It is seen as an additional historical measure. All the three standard setting bodies – the IASC, the FASB and the ASB – concluded that as the objective of basic EPS is to measure performance over the reporting period, the objective of diluted EPS should be consistent with that objective while giving effect to all dilutive potential ordinary shares that were outstanding during the period. A past performance method of computing diluted EPS will aid comparison between diluted EPS of different periods. In addition, presenting diluted EPS with undiluted EPS that are calculated on a consistent basis will enable users to view the spread between the two figures as representing a reasonable estimate of the potential dilution that exits in the entity's capital structure.

Computation of earnings

8.57 For the purpose of calculating diluted EPS, the net profit or loss attributable to ordinary shareholders should be adjusted for the after-tax effect of:

- Dividends on dilutive potential ordinary shares that have been deducted in arriving at net profit attributable to ordinary shares, such as dividends on convertible dilutive preference shares.
- Interest recognised in the period on dilutive potential ordinary shares such as interest on dilutive convertible debt.
- Any other changes in income or expense that would result from the conversion of the dilutive potential ordinary shares.

[FRS 14 para 53].

8.58 Once potential ordinary shares are converted into ordinary shares during the period, the dividends, interest and other expense associated with those potential ordinary shares will no longer be incurred. The effect of the conversion, therefore, will be to increase net profit attributable to ordinary shareholders as well as the number of shares in issue. This is illustrated in paragraph 8.64 dealing with convertible securities. Adjustments to net profit or loss should also include any fees, discounts or premiums on potential ordinary shares that allocated to periods over their term on a constant rate in accordance with FRS 4. The adjustments should include not only the direct savings in debt servicing cost or dividends and other appropriations in respect of convertible non-equity shares, but also any other consequential changes in other income or expense arising as a result of the conversion. An example included in the standard is an increase in employee discretionary profit sharing plan as a result of the savings in after-tax interest cost following conversion of convertible debt. [FRS 14 para 55].

Computation of number of ordinary shares

8.59 Entities may have more than one type of potential ordinary share in issue at the reporting date. Whether all these potential ordinary shares actually will be converted into ordinary shares in the future is usually not determinable at the reporting date. However, it is possible to make certain assumptions to arrive at a reasonable estimate of what the earnings per share would have been had all the ordinary shares been issued for those securities. The standard, therefore, makes the assumption that potential ordinary shares should be deemed to have been converted into ordinary shares at the beginning of the period or, if not in existence at the beginning of the period, the date of the issue of the financial instrument or the granting of the rights by which they are generated. [FRS 14 para 29]. This is sometimes referred to as the 'if converted' method.

8.60 The conversion into ordinary shares should be determined from the terms of the financial instrument or the rights granted and this determination should assume the most advantageous conversion rate from the standpoint of the holder of the potential ordinary shares. [FRS 14 para 31]. The effect is to ensure that the diluted EPS is based on the maximum number of new shares that would be issuable under the terms of the instrument. In practice, it may be that not all conversion rights or warrants are exercised in which case the dilutive effect would be less than the diluted figure suggests.

8.61 Potential ordinary shares are included in the diluted EPS calculation on a weighted basis only for the period they were outstanding. Therefore, potential ordinary shares that are issued during the year are included on a weighted basis from the date of issue to the balance sheet date. Where potential ordinary shares that are outstanding at the beginning of the period are converted during the year, they are included on a weighted average basis from the beginning of the year to the date of conversion. This is illustrated in the examples in paragraph 8.64. The new ordinary shares that are issued on conversion are included from the date of conversion in both basic and diluted EPS on a weighted basis. The same principles apply where potential ordinary shares, instead of being converted, are cancelled or allowed to lapse during the reporting period. [FRS 14 para 62].

8.62 In computing diluted EPS, only potential ordinary shares that are dilutive are considered in the calculation. Potential ordinary shares should be treated as dilutive when, and only when, their conversion to ordinary shares would decrease net profit or increase net loss per share *from continuing operations*. [FRS 14 para 56]. Where a company has a number of different type of potential ordinary shares in issue, each one would need to be considered separately rather than in aggregate. The way in which this should be done is considered further from paragraph 8.69 below.

Partly paid shares

8.63 As stated in paragraph 8.29, partly paid shares are included in the computation of basic EPS to the extent that they rank for dividends during the period. Partly paid shares that do not rank for dividends during the period – for example, they do not rank until they are fully paid – are regarded as the equivalent of share options and warrants. [FRS 14 para 34]. That is the unpaid balance should be assumed to be the proceeds used to purchase shares under the treasury stock method (see further para 8.65). The number of shares that is included in the diluted EPS is the difference between the number of partly paid shares already in issue and the number of shares assumed to be purchased at fair value.

Convertible securities

8.64 Where a company has issued capital instruments in the form of debentures, loan stocks or preference shares that are convertible into equity shares of the company, the terms of the instrument will specify the dates, the number of shares and, in effect, the conversion price or prices at which the new shares will be issued. A convertible security is a particularly good example to illustrate the application of the principles discussed from paragraphs 8.57 to 8.62 above for the calculation of diluted EPS.

Example

No conversion during the year

At 30 June 19X1, the issued share capital of a company consisted of 1,500,000 ordinary shares of £1 each. On 1 October 19X1 the company issued £1,250,000 of 8% convertible loan stock for cash at par. Each £100 nominal of the loan stock may be converted at any time during the years ended 19X6/X9 into the number of ordinary shares set out below:

30 June 19X6	135 ordinary shares
30 June 19X7	130 ordinary shares
30 June 19X8	125 ordinary shares
30 June 19X9	120 ordinary shares

The profit before interest and taxation for the year ended 30 June 19X2 and 19X3 amounted to £825,000 and £895,000 respectively and relate wholly to continuing operations. Corporation tax for both periods is 33%.

	19X3	19X2
Trading results	£	£
Profit before interest and tax	895,000	825,000
Interest on 8% convertible loan stock (19X2: 9/12 x £100,000)	100,000	75,000
Profit before tax	795,000	750,000
Taxation @ 33%	262,350	247,500
Profit after tax	532,650	502,500
Number of equity shares outstanding	1,500,000	1,500,000
Calculation of basic EPS		
Basic EPS	£532,650	£502,500
	1,500,000	1,500,000
	35.5p	33.5p

Calculation of diluted EPS

Test whether convertibles are dilutive:
The saving in after-tax earnings resulting from not paying interest on £100 nominal of loan stock amounts to £100 × 8% × 67% = £5.36. There will then be 135 extra shares in issue. Therefore, the incremental earnings per share = 3.97p (that is, £5.36/135). This will have the effect of reducing the basic EPS of 35.5p. Hence the convertibles are dilutive (see further para 8.76).

	19X3	19X2
Adjusted earnings	£	£
Profit for basic EPS	532,650	502,500
Add: interest saved	100,000	75,000
Less: tax relief thereon	(33,000)	(24,750)
Adjusted earnings for equity	599,650	552,750

Adjusted number of shares
From the conversion terms, it is clear that the maximum number of shares issuable on conversion of £1,250,000 after the end of the financial year would be at the rate of 135 shares per £100 nominal, that is, 1,687,500 shares.

	19X3	19X2
Number of equity shares for basic EPS	1,500,000	1,500,000
Maximum conversion at date of issue 1,687,500 × 9/12	–	1,265,625
Maximum conversion after balance sheet date	1,687,500	–
Adjusted Capital	3,187,500	2,765,625
Diluted EPS	£599,650 / 3,187,500	£552,750 / 2,765,625
	18.8p	20.0p

Example

Partial conversion during the year

The facts are the same as set out in the previous example, but at 1 January 19X6, the holders of half the loan stock exercised their right of conversion.

Trading results	30/06/X6 £	30/06/X5 £
Profit before interest and tax	1,220,000	1,000,000
Interest on 8% convertible loan stock*	75,000	100,000
Profit before tax	1,145,000	900,000
Taxation @ 33%	377,850	297,000
Profit after tax	767,150	603,000

* Interest = £1,250,000 x 8% x ½ + £625,000 x 8% x ½ = £75,000

Computation of basic EPS		
Adjusted number of shares		
Number outstanding before conversion	1,500,000	1,500,000
Weighted average shares issued on conversion at 1 January 19X6 = 843,750/2	421,875	–
Adjusted number of shares	1,921,875	1,500,000
Basic EPS	£767,150	£603,000
	1,921,875	1,500,000
	39.9p	40.2p

Calculation of diluted EPS

Adjusted earnings	£	£
Profit for basic EPS	767,150	603,000
Add: interest saved	50,000	100,000
Less: tax relief thereon	(16,500)	(33,000)
Adjusted earnings	800,650	670,000
Adjusted number of shares		
Number of equity shares for basic EPS	1,921,875	1,500,000
Assumed conversion of £1,250,000 loan stock outstanding at the beginning of the year at the maximum rate of 135 shares per £100 of stock up to 1 January 19X6 (6 months)	843,750	–
Assumed conversion of £625,000 of remaining stock outstanding at 30 June 19X6 at the maximum rate of 130 shares per £100 of stock (6 months)	406,250	–
Maximum conversion after balance sheet date at the rate of 135 shares per £100 of stock	–	1,687,500
Adjusted number of shares	3,171,875	3,187,500

Diluted EPS	£800,650	£670,000
	3,171,875	3,187,500
	25.2p	21.0p

Example

Final conversion during the year

The facts are the same as set out in the previous example, but the holders of half of the loan stock had exercised their right of conversion on 1 January 19X6 at 135 shares per £100 stock and the remaining stock was converted on 30 June 19X7 at 130 shares per £100 stock.

Trading results	19X7	19X6
	£	£
Profit before interest and tax	1,450,000	1,220,000
Interest on 8% convertible loan stock*	50,000	75,000
Profit before tax	1,400,000	1,145,000
Taxation @ 33%	462,000	377,850
Profit after tax	938,000	767,150
* Interest = £625,000 x 8% = £50,000		
Number of equity shares outstanding	2,343,750	1,921,875
Basic EPS	£938,000	£767,150
	2,343,750	1.921,875
	40.0p	39.9p
Calculation of diluted EPS		
Adjusted earnings	£	£
Profit after tax for basic EPS	938,000	767,150
Add: interest saved	50,000	50,000
Less: tax thereon	(16,500)	(16,500)
Adjusted earnings	971,500	800,650
Adjusted number of shares		
Number of equity shares for basic EPS	2,343,750*	1,921,875
Assumed conversion of £1,250,000 loan stock outstanding at the beginning of the year at the maximum rate of 135 shares per £100 of stock up to 1 January 19X6 (6 months)	–	843,750

Assumed conversion of £625,000 of remaining stock outstanding at 30 June 19X6 at the maximum rate of 130 shares per £100 of stock (6 months)	–	406,250
Assumed conversion of £625,000 of stock outstanding at the maximum rate of 130 shares per £100 of stock†	812,500	–
Adjusted number of shares	3,140,625	3,171,875

*Actual number of shares outstanding = 1,500,000 + 843,750 = 2,343,750

†Deemed to be outstanding for the whole year because the remaining loan stock of £625,000 was redeemed on the last day of the financial year, that is, on 30 June 19X7.

Diluted EPS	£971,500	£800,650
	3,140,250	3,171,875
	30.9p	25.2p

Share warrants and options

8.65 Where a company has issued warrants to subscribe for shares at fixed prices on specified dates in the future or granted share options to directors and employees, the calculation of diluted EPS is based on a method which is significantly different from the previous SSAP 3 method. Under FRS 14, the expected proceeds of dilutive share warrants and options are not deemed to be invested in a Government bond for adjusting net profit for the purposes of calculating diluted EPS. Rather these proceeds are deemed to be used by the company in purchasing as many of its ordinary shares as possible in the open market, using an average price for the period. Since these shares are fairly priced and are neither dilutive or anti-dilutive, they are ignored in the diluted EPS calculation. They are, therefore, deducted from the number of shares to be issued under the options or warrants to give the number of shares deemed to be issued at no consideration. As these shares are dilutive, they are added to the number of ordinary shares outstanding in the computation of diluted EPS.

8.66 The method reflects more dilution as the value of options and warrants increases relative to the value of the underlying share. That is, as the average market price for the underlying share increases, the assumed proceeds from exercise will buy fewer shares, thus increasing the number of shares issued for nil consideration and, hence, the denominator. This method of accounting for share warrants and options and other share purchase agreements is often referred to as 'the treasury stock method'.

8.67 It should be noted that the fair value of share options and warrants under the treasury stock method should always be calculated on the basis of the average price of an ordinary share for the period rather than the period-end market price. Although use of a period end market price is likely to give a better indication of the potential future dilution than an average for the period, this would go against the past performance measure for diluted EPS adopted in the standard as discussed in paragraph 8.56 above. The standard does not stipulate how average price for the period should be calculated. However, FAS 128 indicates that a pragmatic basis of calculation, such as a simple average of weekly or monthly prices should be adequate. The method should be used consistently unless it becomes unrepresentative due to changed market conditions. [FAS 128, paras 47,48].

8.68 An example that illustrates the mechanics of calculating diluted EPS where a company has granted options under an employee share scheme is given below.

Example

At 31 December 19X7 and 19X8 the issued share capital of a company consisted of 4,000,000 ordinary shares of 25p each. Under an employee share option scheme, the company granted options that give holders the right to subscribe for ordinary shares between 20X2 and 20X3 at 70p per share. Options outstanding at 31 December 19X7 and 19X8 were 630,000 and 680,000 respectively. The profit after tax attributable to equity shareholders for the years ended 31 December 19X7 and 19X8 amounted to £500,000 and £600,000 respectively.

Average market price of share:
Year ended 31 December 19X7 = £1.20
Year ended 31 December 19X8 = £1.60

Calculation of basic EPS	19X8	19X7
Basic EPS	£600,000	£500,000
	4,000,000	4,000,000
	15.0p	12.5p
Calculation of diluted EPS		
Adjusted number of shares		
Number of shares under option:		
Issued at full market price:		
(630,000 × 0.70) ÷ 1.20		367,500
(680,000 × 0.70) ÷ 1.60	297,500	
Issued at nil consideration – dilutive	382,500	262,500
Total number of shares under option	680,000	630,000
Number of equity shares for basic EPS	4,000,000	4,000,000
Number of dilutive shares under option	382,500	262,500
Adjusted number of shares	4,382,500	4,262,500

Diluted EPS	£600,000	£500,000
	4,382,500	4,262,500
	13.6p	11.7p
Percentage dilution	9.33%	6.40%

Dilutive potential ordinary shares

8.69 As stated in paragraph 8.62 above, only potential ordinary shares that are dilutive are considered in the calculation of diluted EPS. Potential ordinary shares should be treated as dilutive when, and only when, their conversion to ordinary shares would decrease net profit or increase net loss per share from *continuing* operations. [FRS 14 para 56]. The net profit from continuing operations is the net profit from continuing operations after deducting interest, tax, preference dividends and other appropriations in respect of non-equity shares, but excluding items relating to discontinued operations and extraordinary items which would be included in normal earnings. [FRS 14 para 58]. This means that the company would need to calculate a basic earnings per share from continuing operations. A potential ordinary share would be dilutive if its assumed conversion results in reducing this earnings per share from continuing operations below the basic level. On the other hand, if the effect is to increase this earnings per share above the basic level, the security is not dilutive and should be excluded from the standard diluted EPS calculation.

8.70 It follows from the above that on no account should the dilution be tested by reference to whether the conversion of a potential ordinary share reduces the standard basic EPS. The reason for choosing, as a control number, the 'net profit from continuing ordinary operations' is because this level of profit, unaffected by discontinued operations, is likely to remain stable over time and reflect the earnings that will exist in the future when the dilution occurs. This is a sensible approach for the reason that if the net profit or loss attributable to ordinary shareholders is a loss because the net return from discontinued operations is a loss, the exercise of say an option will increase the denominator and result in a lower loss per share (that is, the figure becomes less negative). In that situation, the option is antidilutive at this level, but may well be dilutive at the continuing operations level.

8.71 However, the implications of the above requirement for companies can be problematic. At present, FRS 3 requires an analysis of continuing operations and acquisitions (as a component of continuing operations) and discontinued operations only to the level of profit before interest and expressly discourages allocation of interest between continuing and discontinued operations on the grounds that it is likely to involve a considerable degree of subjectivity that may confuse users. [FRS 3 para 40]. Notwithstanding this, companies need to make such an allocation in order to arrive at the control number for testing whether a security is dilutive or antidilutive. The standard envisages that many companies will have the necessary data to make a reasonable allocation of interest and tax, in particular, where it relates to non-operating exceptional items that are reported under paragraph 20 of FRS 3.

8.72 If a company is unable to make a reliable and reasonably accurate allocation of interest and tax in order to calculate net profit from continuing operations as defined in paragraph 8.69 above, the standard permits interest and tax to be allocated in the proportion of profit from continuing operations to total profit at the operating profit level. This allocation should generally be carried out after tax and interest has been specifically allocated where possible to non-operating exceptional items.

8.73 However any allocation will only be meaningful when both the numerator and the denominator of the above proportion are positive quantities indicating that the company records an operating profit from both continuing and discontinued operations. If a company records a loss from continuing operations, the allocation becomes redundant as the exercise or conversion of a potential ordinary share will lower loss per share and will be antidilutive. On the other hand, if the company makes a large operating loss from discontinued operations (for example, a loss of £120,000) which eliminates all the operating profit from continuing operations (a profit of £100,000), any allocation becomes meaningless as the ratio *profit* from continuing operation of £100,000 to total *operating loss* of £20,000 is itself meaningless. In this situation, it is likely that after interest and tax are taken into account, the company will report a net loss attributable to ordinary shareholders. Although a basic loss per share can be calculated on an undiluted basis, the company will be unable to calculate a diluted loss per share in the absence of a more reliable allocation method. In that situation, the company would need to make some reasonable approximation. For instance, it may be possible to identify the tax charge more specifically to continuing operations, but any allocation of interest may well involve a considerable degree of subjectivity.

8.74 An example where a company has made an allocation of interest and tax for the purposes of presenting earnings per share for continuing businesses and a loss per share for discontinued operations is given in Table 8.3 below.

Table 8.3 – Courtaulds Textiles plc – Report and & Accounts – 31 December 1993

Notes to the accounts (extract)

10. Earnings per share

The calculation of the 1993 earnings per share is based on the profit attributable to shareholders of £29.5m and on 101.2m shares, being the weighted average number of shares in issue during the year (1992 101.0m). Earnings per share on a nil basis are 28.8p (1992 20.0p).

In view of the degree of portfolio restructuring in recent years, the directors believe that it is appropriate to show an estimate of earnings per share for the continuing businesses. The basis of the calculation of this figure is set out in the following table and notes.

	CONTINUING BUSINESSES		DISCONTINUED BUSINESSES		TOTAL GROUP	
	1993	1992 restated	**1993**	1992 restated	**1993**	1992 restated
	£m	£m	**£m**	£m	**£m**	£m
Profit before interest	**41.9**	42.9	**1.1**	(2.0)	**43.0**	40.9
Interest	**(3.9)**	(1.0)	**(0.3)**	(0.8)	**(4.2)**	(1.8)
Taxation	**(9.6)**	(8.1)	**0.2**	(0.2)	**(9.4)**	(8.3)
Minority interests	**0.1**	(0.4)	**–**	–	**0.1**	(0.4)
Earnings	**28.5**	33.4	**1.0**	(3.0)	**29.5**	30.4
Average number or ordinary shares (millions)	**101.2**	101.0	**101.2**	101.0	**101.2**	101.0
Earnings per share (pence)	**28.2**	33.1	**1.0**	(3.0)	**29.2**	30.1

The purpose of allocating the actual interest and tax charge is to provide an estimate of the interest and tax charge that would have arisen in the continuing businesses if the discontinued businesses had not existed. The interest charge allocated to the discontinued businesses has been calculated by applying the group's effective interest rate to the average debt of the discontinued businesses. It is assumed that the group's net debt at 31 December 1993 relates entirely to the continuing businesses and the average debt for the discontinued businesses is then calculated retrospectively using the actual cash flow generated, so as to leave the discontinued businesses with no debt at 31 December 1993. The tax charge allocated to discontinued businesses is determined on a country specific basis by applying the marginal tax rate in each country to the profit before tax, after charging interest as calculated above.

8.75 There is no requirement in the standard to disclose the method of allocation and the underlying assumptions adopted where the only purpose is to test whether potential ordinary shares are dilutive. The disclosure should, nevertheless, be given in compliance with FRS 3 where a company voluntarily discloses results from continuing and discontinued operations after tax and interest as illustrated in Table 8.4 above. If no discontinued operations are reported in the period, the control number used for testing dilution is easily calculated from the figures reported in the profit and loss account.

8.76 In order to determine whether a particular convertible security, option or warrant will have a diluting effect, it is necessary to consider each of them separately rather than in aggregate. This consideration is complicated and involves the following steps:

- The company first calculates the net profit from continuing operations if this information is not already available.

- The company next calculates the earnings per incremental share for each type of potential ordinary share. The earnings per incremental share – or the incremental per share effect of any security that entitles its holder to ordinary shares – is the increase in net profit that would result from the exercise or conversion of the security divided by the weighted average increase in the number of ordinary shares that would result from the conversion.

- The company next ranks all potential ordinary shares from the most dilutive (lowest earnings per incremental share) to the least dilutive (highest earnings per incremental share).

- The company then calculates a basic EPS using net profit from continuing operations as the numerator.

- The most dilutive potential ordinary share with the lowest earnings per incremental share is then included and a new EPS as indicated above is calculated. If this new figure is lower than the previous one, the company recalculates EPS including the potential shares with the next lowest earnings per incremental share.

- The above process of including increasingly less dilutive shares continues until the resulting EPS figure increases or there are no more potential ordinary shares to consider.

- Any potential ordinary share that has the effect of increasing the cumulative EPS from continuing operations is considered to be antidilutive and is excluded from the diluted per share calculation.

- All other potential ordinary shares with higher rankings are considered to be dilutive potential ordinary shares and included in the diluted EPS calculation in the normal way.

The sequence of including each issue or series of potential ordinary shares from the most dilutive to the least dilutive guarantees that the final diluted EPS figure expresses maximum dilution of the basic earnings per share. A numerical example depicting the above steps is shown below:

Example

The issued share capital of Complex Plc at 31 December 19X7 and 19X8 comprises 2,000,000 ordinary shares of 10p each. The company granted options over 100,000 ordinary shares in 19X6 to directors and certain key employees. The options can be exercised between 19X9 and 20X1 at 60p per share. The average market price of Complex Plc's share during 19X8 was 75p.

In addition, Complex Plc has 800,000 8% £1 Convertible cumulative preference shares and £1,000,000 5% Convertible bonds in issue throughout 19X8. Each preference share and bond is convertible into 2 ordinary shares.

The company's results for the year ended 31 December 19X8 comprised operating profit from continuing operations of £150,000 and operating profit from discontinued operations of £100,000. Interest and tax at 30% amounted to £60,000 and £57,000 respectively. The net profit was £133,000.

The necessary steps to calculate Complex plc's diluted earnings per share for 19X8 are set out below. Comparative figures for 19X7 have not been included in this example.

1 Calculation of net profit from continuing operations

	Total £	Continuing Operations £	Discontinued Operations £
Operating profit from continuing operations	150,000	150,000	
Operating profit from discontinued operations	100,000		100,000
Profit before interest	250,000	150,000	100,000
Interest*	60,000	36,000	24,000
Profit after interest	190,000	114,000	76,000
Tax @ 30%*	57,000	34,200	22,800
Net profit	133,000	79,800	53,200

* In absence of a practical, more reliable basis of allocation, interest and tax has been allocated in the proportion of profit before interest of continuing operations (£150,000) to total profit at the operating profit level (£250,000). This is permitted by FRS 14 (see para 8.72). In practice a profit-based allocation method may be more suitable for taxation, which is levied on profits than for interest, which services debt capital.

2 Determine earnings per incremental share for each class of potential ordinary share and rank them from the most dilutive to least dilutive.

	Increase in earnings	Increase in number of ordinary shares	Earnings per incremental share (pence)	Rank (note)
Options				
Increase in earnings	nil			
Incremental shares issued for nil consideration 100,000 × (75-60)/75		20,000	nil	1
8% Convertible preference shares				
Increase in earnings 8% × £800,000	64,000			
Incremental shares 2 × 800,000		1,600,000	4.00	3
5% Convertible bonds				
Increase in net profit 1,000,000 × 5% × 70%	35,000			
Incremental shares 1,000,000 × 2		2,000,000	1.75	2

Note: Ranking is in ascending order of earnings per incremental share.

Since the options, convertible preference shares and convertible bonds have been in issue throughout 1998, the increase in number of ordinary shares is also their weighted average for the year. If options are granted during the year, they are brought into the averaging calculation from the date of grant.

If there were more than one series, say, of options these would have to be ranked by series.

3 Calculate the cumulative dilution effect on net profit per share from continuing operations

	Net profit from continuing operations £	Weighted average number of shares	Net profit from continuing operations per share (p)	
Net profit	79,800	2,000,000	3.99	
Options	—	20,000		
	79,800	2,020,000	3.95	Dilutive
5% Convertible bonds	35,000	2,000,000		
	114,800	4,020,000	2.86	Dilutive
8% Convertible preference shares	64,000	1,600,000		
	178,800	5,620,000	3.18	Anti-dilutive

Since diluted earnings per share from continuing operations is increased when taking the convertible preference shares into account (from 2.86 to 3.18), the convertible preference shares are antidilutive and are ignored in the calculation of diluted earnings per share.

4 Calculate diluted earnings per shares including only dilutive potential ordinary shares

	Earnings £	Weighted average number of shares	Earnings per share (p)
Net profit attributable to ordinary shareholders	133,000	2,000,000	6.65
Options		20,000	–
	133,000	2,020,000	–
5% Convertible bonds	35,000	2,000,000	–
Diluted earnings	168,000	4,020,000	4.18

The final diluted EPS is calculated by reference to net profit attributable to ordinary shareholders, but the dilution test is carried out by using the net profit from continuing operation as the control number as set out in step three above.

Securities of subsidiaries

8.77 The effect on consolidated EPS of options, warrants and convertible securities issued by a subsidiary depends on whether these potential ordinary shares enable their holders to obtain ordinary shares in the subsidiary undertaking or ordinary shares in the parent undertaking. In general, if the potential ordinary shares issued by the subsidiary enable their holders to obtain ordinary shares in the subsidiary, then those potential ordinary shares should be included in computing the subsidiary's EPS figures (if indeed the subsidiary is calculating an EPS figure). In any event, those earnings per share amounts would be included in the consolidated EPS based on the group's holdings of the subsidiary's securities. On the other hand, if the potential shares issued by the subsidiary enable their holders to obtain ordinary shares in the parent, then these potential ordinary shares should be considered along with the other potential ordinary shares issued by the parent in the computation of consolidated diluted EPS. [FRS 14 para 33].

8.78 The same considerations apply where potential ordinary shares issued by an associate or a joint venture are exchangeable into ordinary shares of the associate or joint venture, or into ordinary shares of the reporting entity. They should be included in the EPS computation of the reporting entity if they are considered to be dilutive. [FRS 14 para 33].

Employee share and incentive plans

8.79 Many companies have in place share options and other share award schemes to remunerate officers and other employees. Under some schemes, share options or share purchase rights are granted solely on the basis that the employees continue to render service for a specified period of time, that is, the award does not specify a performance condition for vesting. In other schemes, vesting of the shares depends on both the employee's rendering service to the employer for a specified period of time and the achievement of a specified performance target, for example, attaining a specified growth rate in return on assets or a specified earnings target.

8.80 Although share-based remuneration schemes give rise to potential ordinary shares, the way in which these potential shares are treated in the calculation of diluted EPS depends on whether or not the awards are based on performance criteria. Performance-based awards are treated as contingently issuable shares in accordance with the guidance included from paragraph 8.85 below, since their issue or exercise is contingent upon factors other than the passage of time. [FRS 14 para 40].

8.81 All other awards that do not specify a performance criteria should be regarded as options for the purposes of computing diluted EPS. They should be considered to be outstanding as of the grant date for purposes of computing diluted EPS even though their exercise may be contingent upon vesting. They are included in the diluted EPS computation even if the employee may not receive (or be able to sell) the stock until some future date. Accordingly, all shares to be issued should be included in computing diluted EPS if the effect is dilutive. The dilutive effect should be computed using the treasury stock method described in paragraph 8.65 above. If the share awards were granted during the period, the shares issuable must be weighted to reflect the portion of the period during which the awards were outstanding. [FRS 14 para 41].

8.82 In applying the treasury stock method described in paragraph 8.65 above, the assumed exercise price, for the purpose of determining the incremental number of shares issued for nil consideration, would comprise the amount, if any, the employee must pay upon exercise and the balance of any unamortised discount calculated under UITF 17, which has not yet been charged to the profit and loss account. [FRS 14 para 42]. The assumed proceeds should not include cost attributable to past service. Neither should any adjustments be made to the numerator in respect of the UITF 17 charge to the profit and loss account as the charge represents the cost of issuing potential ordinary shares that would not be saved on conversion. [FRS 14 para 43]. Example 5 in the standard illustrates how share option schemes not related to performance should be included in the diluted EPS computation and this example is reproduced below.

Example 5 - Share option scheme not related to performance

Company A has in place an employee share option scheme that awards share options to employees and their dependants on the basis of period of service with the company.

The provisions of the scheme are as follows at the 20X0 year-end.

Date of grant	1 January 20X0
Market price at grant date	£4.00
Exercise price of option	£2.50
Date of vesting	31 December 20X2
Number of shares under option	1 million

Applying UITF 17, the profit and loss account is charged with 50p per option in each of the three years 20X0-20X2.

Net profit for year 20X0	£1,200,000
Weighted average number of ordinary shares outstanding	5 million
Average fair value of an ordinary share during the year	£5.00
Assumed proceeds per option	£3.50 (exercise price of £2.50 and compensation cost attributable to future service, not yet recognised, of £1.00). Next year £3.00 (ie £2.50 plus 50p).

Computation of earnings per share

	per share	*earnings*	*shares*
Net profit for year 20X0		£1,200,000	
Weighted average shares outstanding for 20X0			5m
Basic earnings per share	24p		
Number of shares under option			1m
Number of shares that would have been issued at fair value: (1 million × £3.50) / £5.00			(0.7m)
Diluted earnings per share	22.6p	£1,200,000	5.3m

8.83 Where shares to be issued to satisfy the company's obligations under share award schemes have already been purchased by an ESOP trust and are held by the trust as pre-funding for options or other performance related shares, those non-vesting shares should be treated as cancelled and excluded from both basic and diluted EPS as discussed in paragraph 8.33 above. Instead, the calculation of diluted EPS should include non-performance related shares in the same way as options as set out from paragraph 8.81 above and performance related shares in the same way as contingently issuable shares as discussed from paragraph 8.85 below.

8.84 If share based awards are payable in ordinary shares or in cash at the election of either the entity or the employee, the determination of whether such awards are potential ordinary shares should be made in the same way as discussed in paragraph 8.98. [FRS 14 para 44].

Contingently issuable shares

8.85 It is not uncommon for acquisition agreements to include a clause under which the purchaser of an acquired entity is required to make an additional consideration payment in the form of equity shares in future. The value of such shares may either be known precisely at the time of the acquisition, or may be contingent upon the future performance or future evaluation of the acquired entity. In the first instance, the acquirer has an obligation to issue equity shares in future, but the obligation is simply deferred (deferred consideration). In the second instance an obligation may or may not arise depending on whether or not certain earnings conditions are met (contingent consideration). In any event, the need to issue equity shares in future could lead to dilution of EPS. The standard refers to these as 'contingently issuable shares'. In general, contingently issuable shares are financial instruments that give the holder the right to ordinary shares that are contingent upon the satisfaction of certain conditions resulting from contractual arrangements, such as the purchase of a business or other assets.

8.86 The way in which diluted EPS should be calculated to take account of contingently issuable shares is described below:

- Contingently issuable shares are included in the calculation of diluted EPS as if the conditions of the contingency are deemed to have been met, based on the information available, at the end of reporting period. In effect this means that the diluted EPS computation includes those shares that would be issued under the terms of the contingency, based on the current status of conditions, as if the end of the reporting period was the end of the contingency period. [FRS 14 para 46]. An example would be an estimate of the number of shares that would have been issued under an earn-out if that agreement had terminated at the balance sheet date (see further para 8.88). Ordinary shares issuable under such contingent share agreements are included in the diluted EPS calculation as of the beginning of the period or as of the date of the contingent share agreement, if later. [FRS 14 para 45]. Restatement is not permitted if the conditions are not met when the actual contingency period expires. [FRS 14 para 52].

- Where the conditions relating to the issue have been met (the events occurred) by the end of the period, the relevant shares are included in the computation of both basic and diluted EPS. In effect, this will be when issuing the shares is no longer contingent and when there is no circumstances under which the shares would not be issued. [FRS 14 para 20].

8.87 The criteria under which additional shares are issuable under contingent consideration agreements are many and varied, although in practice most involve either future levels of earnings or the future shares price of the issuing company or a mixture of both. It should be noted, however, that such contingently issuable shares should be included in the diluted EPS calculation only if the effect is dilutive.

8.88 Where the number of contingently issuable shares depends upon the level of earnings, the diluted EPS computation should include those shares to the extent that that they would be issuable under the agreement based on the current amount of earnings. However, earnings conditions in earn out agreements come in various forms. Sometimes the terms may specify that further shares will be issued if the average profit earned over a period is a specific amount. Sometimes the maintenance of current earnings level, or the attainment of specified increased level of earnings of the acquired entity for a specified number of years may be the condition. Other earnings conditions may specify the issue of shares when a minimum earnings target is reached, increasing rateably until the maximum earnings target is reached, with a cap on the maximum number of shares that could be issued.

8.89 Whatever the earnings criteria, the guiding principle is that the current level of earnings should be used to determine the number of shares that could be issued under the terms, assuming that the contingency period ended on the balance sheet date. They should be included in the diluted EPS calculation only if dilution results. If in the subsequent period, or until the end of the agreement, there is a decline in earnings such that the contingent shares no longer need to be issued, previous period's diluted EPS should not be restated. Hence, basic EPS should not include any contingently issuable shares, because all the necessary conditions have not been satisfied, but the shares would be included in the calculation of the diluted figure. The following examples illustrate the application of the above principle.

Example 1

Average earnings condition

On 1 January 19X7, company A acquired the whole of the issued share capital of company B. The total consideration payable in respect of the acquisition comprises initial consideration and deferred contingent consideration. Under the terms of the deferred contingent consideration, company A is required to issue 100,000 shares if the net profit of company B averages £100,000 over a three-year period. Any additional shares will be issued on 1 January

20X0 after the end of the three year contingency period. Company B's net profit for the year ended 31 December 19X7 amounted to £120,000.

Given that the terms stipulate the achievement of £100,000 of average profit for the three year period, it would appear at first sight that the contingency condition at the balance sheet date has been met as the profit for the year ended 31 December 19X7 exceeds £100,000. This is not the case as it assumes that the company will earn at least £120,000 for each of the next two years ended 31 December 19X9. Projecting future earnings level in this way is not permitted under the standard because as stated in paragraph 8.56 above, the standard takes a historical approach and not a predictive or forward-looking approach in measuring dilution. The provisions relating to contingently issuable shares in the standard are quite specific and do not allow an entity to consider the probability of a contingent issue occurring.

The correct analysis is to measure whether performance achieved in the current period is deemed to be that achieved over the whole of the contingency period as if the end of the reporting period was the end of the contingency period. On this basis, an average over a period has the same effect as if it were expressed as a cumulative amount over the period. So in this situation, the contingency condition should be expressed in terms of a cumulative target of £300,000 over the three year period. Since the profit for the year ended 31 December 19X7 is only £120,000, which is less than £300,000, the contingency condition is not met at the balance sheet and no additional shares would be brought into the diluted EPS computation.

Similarly, if the profit for the year ended 31 December 19X8 were to increase to £150,000 again the contingency condition is not met in that year, because the cumulative earnings to date amounts to £270,000. So no additional shares would be included in that year. In the final year ended 31 December 19X9 when the contingency period comes to an end, the company will know for certain whether the contingency conditions have been met or not. If the condition is met in that year, the company will include 100,000 shares in both basic and diluted EPS.

Example 2

Attainment of a specified increased level of earnings

The facts are the same as in the previous example except that the deferred consideration agreement provides for the issue of 1000 shares for each £1000 of total net profit in excess of £250,000 over the three years ending 19X9.

Using the above principles, the company did not earn £250,000 for the year ended 31 December 19X7. Again projecting future earnings level (£120,000 for 3 years = £360,000) and including 110,000 ((£360,000 – £250,000) ÷ £1,000 x 1,000) contingent shares in the diluted EPS calculation is not permitted by the standard.

For the year ended 31 December 19X8, the cumulative amount earned to that date is £270,000. As this amount exceeds £250,000, the contingency condition is met in that year and the company will include 20,000 contingently issuable shares in the diluted EPS calculation for that year. For the year ended 31 December 19X9, the cumulative amount earned to that date would be known and the actual number of shares issued would be included in both basic and diluted EPS. If the actual number of shares amounts to say 50,000 shares, prior year's diluted EPS, which was based on 20,000 contingent shares, should not be restated.

8.90 Similar considerations apply when computing diluted EPS for interim reports. If at 30 June 1998, the cumulative amount earned to that date was £245,000 (£120,000 to 31 December 19997 + £125,000 to 30 June 1998), the contingency provision is not met and no contingently issuable shares would be included in calculating the diluted EPS for the half year, even though at the time of preparing the interim report it is apparent that 20,000 shares will be included in the year end diluted EPS calculation.

8.91 Where the number of shares issuable in the future depends on the market price of the shares at the future date, the computation of diluted EPS should reflect the number of shares that would be issued based on the current market price at the end of the reporting period if the effect is dilutive. If the condition is based on an average of market prices over some period of time, the average for that period should be used. [FRS 14 para 47]. Because the market price may change in a future period, basic EPS should not include such contingently issuable shares, because all necessary conditions have not been satisfied.

8.92 In some deferred consideration agreements, the value of the deferred consideration is known, but the number of shares to be issued when the deferred consideration falls due is not known. In that situation, the number of shares to be included in the calculation should be based on the market price at the balance sheet date as if it were the end of the contingency period. [FRS 14 para 48].

8.93 If the contingency is based on a condition other than earnings or market price (for example, opening a certain number of retail stores), the contingent shares should be included in the computation of diluted EPS based on the assumption that the current status of the condition will remain unchanged until the end of the contingency period. So, if during the period only half the required number of new stores that would result in the issue of shares were opened, no contingently issuable shares are included in the diluted EPS computation. [FRS 14 para 49].

8.94 If, on the other hand, the contingency is based on a number of different conditions, the determination of the number of shares included in diluted EPS should be based on the status of all relevant conditions as they exist at the end of each reporting period. If one of the conditions is not met at the end of the reporting period, no contingently issuable shares should be included in diluted EPS. [FRS 14 para 50].

8.95 Sometimes the terms of a deferred consideration agreement may provide for the issue of convertible loan stock if certain conditions are met. Such contingently issuable potential ordinary shares, including share options, warrants and contracts that may be settled in shares or cash, should be included in diluted EPS on the following basis:

- It is first necessary to determine the number of potential ordinary shares that may be issued under the terms of the agreement in accordance with the contingently issuable share provisions discussed from paragraph 8.85.

- Depending on the type of those potential ordinary shares, they should be reflected in diluted EPS by following the provisions for convertible securities discussed from paragraph 8.64 , the provisions for share options and warrants discussed from paragraph 8.65 , and the provisions for contracts that may be settled in shares or cash discussed from paragraph 8.96.

However, exercise or conversion should not be assumed for purposes of computing diluted EPS unless exercise or conversion of similar outstanding potential ordinary shares that are not contingently issuable is also assumed. [FRS 14 para 51].

Contracts that may be settled in shares or cash

8.96 If an entity issues a contract that may be settled in shares or in cash at the election of either the entity or the holder, the determination of whether that contract should be reflected in the computation of diluted EPS should be made based on the facts available each period. [FRS 14 para 32]. An example of such a contract is a deferred or contingent consideration agreement where either the acquirer or the vendor has the option to take or settle the consideration in the form of shares or cash. Consequently, at the date of acquisition it may not be possible to determine how the deferred consideration will be settled. It should, therefore, be presumed that the contract will be settled in shares, the more dilutive method, and the resulting potential ordinary shares included in diluted EPS in accordance with the relevant provisions of the standard.

8.97 The above treatment is consistent with the treatment required under paragraph 83 of FRS 7 where the deferred or contingent consideration is reported as part of shareholders' funds in circumstances where the *acquiror* has the option to settle the consideration in shares or cash. However, where the *vendor* has the option to demand shares or cash, FRS 7 requires the consideration to be recorded as a liability. In that situation, the diluted EPS should nevertheless be calculated on the assumption that the consideration would be settled in shares. Since the deferred consideration is recorded as a liability for accounting purposes and may also result in an interest cost in the profit and loss account to take account of the time value of the deferral of the monetary consideration, the numerator of the EPS calculation should be adjusted for this interest, the related tax and other effects. This adjustment is similar to the adjustments required for a convertible debt as discussed in paragraph 8.64. The presumption that the contract will be settled in shares for EPS calculation purposes may be rebutted if past experience or a stated policy provides a reasonable basis to believe that the contract will be paid partially or wholly in cash. [FRS 14 para 32].

8.98 Another example is an incentive scheme where annual bonuses may be payable in either shares or cash at the election of either the entity or the employee. In those situations, past experience may provide a reasonable basis for concluding how the bonuses will be taken in the future – in cash or shares – and that basis should be followed in the EPS calculation. Where there is no stated policy and the entity has no past experience of settling such contracts, it should be presumed that the contract will be settled by the more dilutive method. [FRS 14 para 32].

Presentation and disclosure

Presentation of basic and diluted EPS

8.99 An entity should present both basic and diluted EPS on the face of the profit and loss account. The basic and diluted EPS should be presented with equal prominence for all periods presented. The five per cent materiality threshold for disclosure of dilution in SSAP 3 is therefore withdrawn. Where there is more than one class of equity shares in issue (for example, equity shares with different rights to share in the net profit), basic and diluted EPS figure must be calculated and disclosed for each class of equity shares. [FRS 14 para 69]. The way in which such calculations should be performed is considered in paragraph 8.23 above.

8.100 If a company incurs a loss or the amount it earns for the equity shareholders is a negative figure, basic and diluted EPS should be determined in the normal manner and should be shown as a loss per share. [FRS 14 para 70]. An example is given in Table 8.4 below.

Table 8.4 – Tarmac PLC – Annual Report – 31 December 1993

Notes to the accounts (extract)

10 Loss per Ordinary Share

This has been calculated by reference to the weighted average of 808.4 million (1992 – 735.5 million) ordinary shares in issue during the year and the group loss for the financial year of £61.8 million (1992 – £263.8 million) plus the redeemable preference share dividend, including in 1993, an after tax provision of £18.4 million for the settlement of interest rate swaps, which amounts to £29.7 million (1992 – £10.4 million), giving a loss of £91.5 million (1992 – £274.2 million). The weighted average number of shares for both 1992 and 1993 has been adjusted to reflect the bonus element inherent in the rights issue. Convertible capital bonds are at present anti-dilutive.

Additional disclosures

8.101 The following additional information should be given for both basic and diluted EPS:

- The amounts used as the numerators in calculating the basic and diluted EPS figures. These amounts should also be reconciled with the net profit or loss for the period. As the numerator used in the basic EPS will be the same as the net profit or loss for the period after preference dividend, the reconciliation will be relevant normally to the numerator used in the diluted EPS calculation for the reasons stated in paragraph 8.57 above.

- The weighted average number of ordinary shares used as the denominator in calculating the basic and diluted EPS figures. The denominators used in the basic and diluted EPS should also be reconciled to each other. This reconciliation should list all the dilutive potential ordinary shares from the most to the least dilutive that have affected the basic weighted average number.

[FRS 14 para 71].

8.102 An example of how a company can give the above information in a concise manner is shown in the table below.

	Year ended 31 December 19X8		
	Earnings	Number of shares	Per-share amount
Net profit for the year	6,525,000		
Less: preference dividends	75,000		
Basic EPS:			
Earnings available to ordinary shareholders	6,450,000	2,500,000	£2.58
Effect of dilutive securities:			
Options		45,000	
Convertible preferred stock	35,000	255,000	
6% convertible debentures	60,000	60,000	
Diluted EPS:			
Adjusted earnings	6,545,000	2,860,000	£2.29

8.103 A reconciliation of the numerator and denominator of basic and diluted EPS presumably will help users better understand the dilutive effect of certain securities included in the EPS calculation. It should be noted, however, that prior to the issue of FRS 14 there was no requirement to reconcile the weighted average number of ordinary shares used in the basic EPS calculation to the corresponding number used in the diluted EPS calculation. Companies simply disclosed both figures as shown in a number of examples included in this chapter. Companies with complex capital structures will be required to give a reasonably detailed computation of EPS and are likely to adopt the type of disclosure illustrated above or some other variation of it.

8.104 The standard also encourages companies to disclose the terms and conditions of financial instruments and the granting of rights that result in the issue of ordinary shares in the future whether or not disclosure is already required by FRS 4. Such disclosure may help users to understand the extent to which these instruments are dilutive and, if so, the effect they have on the disclosed diluted EPS data. Disclosure of the terms and conditions are particularly relevant for those antidilutive securities that are not included in the computation of diluted EPS. [FRS 14 para 72].

Volatility of published EPS

8.105 The EPS figure, which is based on the profits available to ordinary shareholders, is an 'all inclusive' figure and is inevitably volatile. This is because profits or losses of a period may be affected by certain non-operating exceptional items, such as: profits or losses on the sale or termination of an operation; costs incurred in connection with a fundamental reorganisation; and profits and losses on the disposal of fixed assets. As a result, the EPS figure from one period to another would be affected by their presence or absence. However, many companies prefer to report a normalised EPS unaffected by profits and losses of an unusual nature that do not relate to the trading activities of an enterprise. A normalised EPS is also very popular with analysts (see from para 8.113 below).

8.106 Nevertheless, the reporting of a volatile EPS is in keeping with the ASB's objective of taking the gloss off the reported EPS as a measure of financial performance so that other equally important components of financial performance are highlighted. This view is also consistent with IAS 33, which requires EPS to be calculated after extraordinary items.

Additional earnings per share

8.107 The ASB recognises that there may be instances where a company would wish to disclose an additional EPS calculated on another level of earnings. It, therefore, permits companies to disclose an additional EPS using a reported component of net profit other than net profit or loss for the period attributable to ordinary shareholders. Such EPS data should, however, be calculated using the weighted average number of ordinary shares determined in accordance with the standard. [FRS 14, para 73]. This means that the weighted average number used in the calculation of this additional EPS should generally be the same as the number used in the basic and diluted EPS required by the standard. In addition, all of the following conditions need to be satisfied:

- The additional EPS is presented on a consistent basis over time.
- It is reconciled to the EPS figure required by the standard. The reconciliation should list the items for which an adjustment is being made and disclose the effect of each such item on the calculation.
- The EPS required by the standard is displayed at least as prominently as the additional EPS.
- The reasons for calculating the additional EPS are explained.
- The reconciliation and the explanation appear adjacent to the EPS disclosure, or a reference given to where they may be found.

[FRS 14 para 74].

8.108 Where a company has disclosed an EPS that is additional to the one required by FRS 3, the requirements stated in paragraph 8.107 above should be followed. A good example where a company has followed the standard's requirements where an additional EPS is presented (as explained in para 8.107) is shown in Table 8.5 below.

Table 8.5 – The General Electric Company p.l.c. – Annual Report and Accounts – 31 March 1998

Consolidated Profit and Loss Account (extract)

	Notes	1998 £ million	1997 £ million
Earnings per share	8	**24.4p**	14.7p
Adjusted earnings per share	8	**24.7p**	23.6p

Notes to the Accounts (extract)

8 Earnings per share

Earnings per share are calculated by reference to a weighted average of 2,773,033,068 ordinary shares (1997 2,770,577,459 ordinary shares) in issue during the year.

Exceptional costs charged against operating profit and non-operating exceptional gains and loses do not relate to the profitability of the Group on an ongoing basis. Therefore and adjusted earnings per share is presented, as follows:

	1998		1997	
	Earnings £ million	**Earnings per share pence**	Earnings £ million	Earnings per share pence
Earnings per share	**677**	**24.4**	408	14.7
Exceptional items:				
Continuing operations	**45**	**1.6**	203	7.3
Gains less losses on disposals of subsidiaries and other fixed assets	**(20)**	**(0.7)**	100	3.6
Taxation arising on exceptional items (Note 5)	**(16)**	**(0.6)**	(55)	(2.0)
Minority interest share of exceptional items	**–**	**–**	(1)	–
Earnings excluding exceptional items and adjusted earnings per share	**686**	**24.7**	655	23.6

8.109 Some companies tend to disclose diluted EPS on an adjusted basis that takes into account the effect of exceptional items and potential dilution, whilst disclosing the basic EPS on an unadjusted basis. This is not strictly in accordance with the standard, which requires disclosure of diluted EPS on an unadjusted basis. The example in Table 8.6 below illustrates how the company has disclosed diluted EPS both on an adjusted and unadjusted basis.

Table 8.6– British Telecommunications plc – Annual report and accounts – 31 March 1998

***Group profit and loss account* (extract)**

	Notes	**1998 £m**	1997 £m	1996 £m
Earnings per share	*10*	**26.7p**	32.8p	31.6p
Earnings per share before exceptional items		**31.7p**	32.8p	31.6p
Fully diluted earnings per share		**26.3p**	32.2p	31.0p
Fully diluted earnings per share before exceptional items		**31.2p**	32.2p	31.0p
(a) Including MCI merger break up fee net of expenses		**238**	–	–
(b) Including redundancy charges		**206**	367	421

Notes to the financial statements (extract)

10. Earnings per share

Earnings per share are calculated by dividing the profit for the financial year ended 31 March 1998, amounting to £1,706m (1997 – £2,077m, 1996 – £1,986m), by 6,394 million shares, the weighted average number of shares in issue during the financial year (1997 – 6,336 million, 1996 – 6,283 million). The fully diluted earnings per share are based on share options outstanding.

The exceptional items in the calculation of the earnings per share before exceptional items in the year ended 31 March 1998 and the individual earnings per share effects are:

	Pence per share	£m
MCI merger break up fee received less expenses		238
Less tax charge attributable to the MCI merger break up fee		(50)
Net merger break up fee after tax	3.0	188
Windfall tax charge	(8.0)	(510)
Net charge	(5.0)	(322)

8.110 It should be noted that although the standard refers to the disclosure of an additional EPS, there is nothing to prevent a company from disclosing more than one additional EPS calculated at various levels of profits, in addition to that required by the standard, provided that the above conditions are met for each additional EPS given. Obviously comparative figures would also have to be given for each additional EPS figure. An example of a company disclosing multiple earnings per share figures is given in Table 8.8 on page 8055 below. Although disclosure of multiple earnings per share figures could be confusing to users, nevertheless, it would appear to serve the ASB's objective of diminishing the significance of any single level of earnings.

8.111 Directors should carefully consider what profit measure to choose when calculating additional EPS figures and what information they would wish those figures to convey. This is because whatever profit measure is chosen it must be used consistently. It is not possible to choose a profit measure to present a particular aspect of a company's performance in one year, because performance at that level is good, and then to ignore that measure in the following year when performance at that level is not so good.

8.112 Given that an entity can choose any profit level for calculating another version of EPS, it is not surprising that there is variety in the measures adopted in practice. Consequently, such additional EPS will not be comparable between entities, although they will be comparable between different accounting periods for the same entity. Any comparability between entities that may be achieved will probably be by accident rather than by design. There is, therefore, something to be said for adopting the 'headline' earnings figure devised by the Institute of Investment Management and Research (IIMR).

IIMR headline earnings

8.113 In September 1993, the IIMR issued Statement of Investment Practice No 1 concerning the calculation of the earnings of a company or group in response to the changes in published financial statements introduced by FRS 3. The aim of the statement is to define a factual 'headline' figure for historical earnings that can be a benchmark figure for assessing the trading performance for the year. In recommending a benchmark figure, the IIMR praised the ASB's efforts to disclose as much relevant information as possible on the face of the profit and loss account and, like the ASB, expressed the view that:

> *"...it is of the first importance to recognise that one consequence of the fact that a company's performance is reflected in a range of information, and not in a single number, is that to attempt to define a single earnings figure for all purposes is bound to fail."*

The statement goes on to state that there is evidence that investors take account of a wider information set than any particular published earnings figure, before going on to argue that *"there are several reasons why efforts should be made to delineate some clearly acceptable earnings figure (or figures)"*. One of these reasons is that *"there are a large number of users who do not have the time or the expertise to make the necessary detailed investigations which are distilled into the final market price. They should be provided with an understandable figure"*.

8.114 The IIMR has, therefore, defined a headline earnings figure for use in this context. The IIMR headline figure is simply a figure that is a measure of trading performance, factual and robust. It does not attempt to remove the effects of non-recurring or exceptional items and so does not purport to be a maintainable earnings figure. Rather, it focuses on the old distinction between capital and revenue and so, reflects the outcomes of all the trading operations (including interest, but excluding 'capital' items) for the year. It is obviously different from the FRS 14 figure and is intended as an additional and complementary figure that can be reconciled to the FRS 14 figure, rather than as a competing figure or a substitute for it.

8.115 There are 12 parts to the definition of IIMR headline earnings that are dealt with in considerable detail in the Statement. The key features of the headline earnings are summarised below:

- All trading profits and losses including any abnormal trading items should be included. Abnormal trading items relate to exceptional items included within operating profit and costs of a fundamental reorganisation or restructuring presented after operating profit. Significant abnormal items should be displayed in a note to the earnings figure.

- Profits and losses arising from operations discontinued during the year should be included in earnings, as should the contribution from acquisitions made during the year.

- All capital items should be excluded. Therefore, any impairment in value of fixed assets, profits and losses on the sale of fixed assets other than those acquired for resale, such as marketable securities, profits and losses on sale or termination of an operation or of businesses, should be excluded.

- Provisions made in respect of certain items (typically those mentioned in FRS 3 paragraph 20) should be reversed, so that the expenses are charged in the year in which they occur, rather than in the year in which the provisions were made. For example, provisions for losses on sale or termination of a business to be discontinued in a subsequent year should be added back. Similarly, such provisions made in prior years and now released should be excluded.

8.116 As can be seen from the above, the adjustments exclude the effect of capital items and certain provisions for future consequences of commitments made in the current year, so as not to distort the trading outcome for the year. This is in keeping with the objective of the headline figure to reflect only the trading as opposed to capital earnings obtained during the year. Companies seeking to disclose an additional EPS figure based on the IIMR headline earnings would, in practice, derive the figure from the FRS 14 earnings disclosed in the profit and loss account. In this way the derivation will form part of the additional disclosure required under FRS 14 whenever an alternative EPS figure is disclosed (see para 8.107). The various adjustments that should normally be made to the FRS 14 all inclusive earnings in order to arrive at the IIMR headline earnings figure are illustrated below.

FRS 14 earnings:	
Profit for the financial year per P&L account	a
Less: preference dividends, participating dividends and other appropriations in respect of non-equity shares	b
FRS 3 profits attributable to equity shareholders	x
IIMR adjustments:	
Exclusion of items included in operating profit:	
Release of provisions for operating losses made in prior year for businesses discontinued in the current year	c
Impairments in fixed assets	d
Profit or loss on sale of fixed assets	e
Goodwill amortisation	f
Exclusion of FRS 3 paragraph 20 non-operating exceptional items	
Provision for loss on sale or termination of an operation to be discontinued	g
Provision for loss on sale or disposal of fixed assets including permanent diminution in asset values	h
Profit or loss on sale or termination of an operation less provisions made in past years and now released.	i
Profit or loss on sale of fixed assets less provisions made in past years and now released.	j
Other	
Exclude profit and losses arising from the reorganisation or redemption of long-term debts (not treated as normal cost of debt finance)	k
Extraordinary items (if any) should be excluded	l
Total IIMR adjustments	y
IIMR 'headline' earnings	z

Note: The above adjustments should reflect the effects of tax and minority interest where applicable.

8.117 An example of a company that has disclosed the IIMR headline figure and has reconciled this figure to the one required by SSAP 3 is given in Table 8.7 below.

Table 8.7 – Stakis plc – Annual Report & Accounts – 28 September 1997

Group profit and loss account (extract)

	Notes	1997 £'000	1996 £'000
Profit for the financial year		**46,907**	27,965
Dividends paid and proposed	7	**(19,118)**	(10,418)
Retained profit for the year	22	**27,789**	17,547
Earnings per share	8	**6.58p**	5.44p
IIMR headline earnings per share	8	**6.56p**	5.74p
Dividends per share	7	**2.50p**	2.15p

The profit for the year on an unmodified historical cost basis is not significantly different from that shown above. Details of the movements in Group reserves are given in note 22 to the Accounts.

Notes to the accounts (extract)

8 Earnings per share

Earnings per share are calculated on the Group profit after taxation of £46.9m (1996 – £28.0m) divided by the weighted average number of shares in issue during the year, being 713m shares (1996 – 514m), after adjusting for the bonus element inherent in the rights issue during the year. The calculation of earnings per share has been restated for 1996 to take account of the bonus element of the rights issue resulting from shares being issued through the rights issue at a discount to market price.

Fully diluted earnings per share are not stated as the dilution would relate only to share options (see Legal Review), and would not be material. Earnings per share based on the Institute of Investment Management and Research definition of earnings per share (IIMR headline earnings per share) are also given, to assist year on year comparison, as it excludes certain exceptional items.

A reconciliation of earnings per share with IIMR headline earnings per share is as follows

	1997 £000	1997 pence per share	1996 £000	1996 pence per share
Earnings	**46,907**	**6.58**	27,965	5.44
Eliminate:				
Profit on sale of properties in continuing businesses	**(87)**	**(0.02)**	(8,335)	(1.62)
Interest swap termination premium	–	–	9,918	1.92
IIMR headline earnings	**42,820**	**6.56**	29,548	5.74

8.118 Some companies, in addition to disclosing the standard and IIMR EPS figures, also disclose a further adjusted EPS figure which, in the opinion of the directors, gives a better understanding of the group's performance. An example is given in Table 8.8 below.

Table 8.8 – Cordiant plc – Report and Accounts – 31 December 1996

Notes to the accounts (extract)

6 **Earnings (loss) per Ordinary share**

- The earnings (loss) per Ordinary share are based on the weighted average number of Ordinary shares in issue, during the year ended 31 December 1996, of 443,615,772 (1995: 292,441,558). The number of Ordinary shares in issue at 31 December 1996 was 443,672,881.
- The definition of IIMR headline earnings is given in the Statement of Investment Practice No.1 published by the Institute of Investment Management and Research (IIMR).

	Year ended 31 Dec 1996		Year ended 31 Dec 1995	
	£ million	*Per share*	*£ million*	*Per share*
Earnings (loss)	24.2	5.5p	(37.3)	(12.8)p
(Profit) loss on disposal of operations	(17.8)	(4.1p)	30.3	10.4p
IIMR headline earnings (loss)	6.4	1.4p	**(7.0)**	**(2.4)p**
Exceptional items (net of tax credit of £nil; 1995: (£2.1m)	16.5	3.8p	22.1	7.6p
Adjusted earnings	**22.9**	**5.2p**	**15.1**	**5.2p**

- In the opinion of the Directors the adjusted earnings per Ordinary share assists in understanding the underlying performance of the Group.
- Earnings per share on the nil distribution and fully diluted bases have not been disclosed as they are not materially different.

8.119 When the IIMR headline EPS was introduced in 1993, it was envisaged that many listed companies would adopt the figure as standard disclosure in their financial statements. However, this did not happen. Although there was initial excitement among listed companies to disclose headline EPS, there has been a significant fall in disclosure since 1995 and the trend appears to be continuing. Currently very few companies disclose IIMR headline EPS. The current trend is for companies to disclose their own definition of 'headline profits' which involves the removal of all exceptional expenses. Two such examples are given below in Tables 8.9 and 8.10. Indeed, this may be one of the main reasons why so many listed companies have dropped the IIMR figure. As stated in paragraph 8.114 IIMR figure eliminates all capital items, but not all exceptional items.

Table 8.9 – Thorn plc – Annual Report and Accounts – 31 March 1998

CONSOLIDATED PROFIT AND LOSS ACCOUNT (extract)

Note: Reconciliation of adjusted earnings		1998	1998	1997	1997
	Notes	Earnings £m	Earnings per share	Earnings £m	Earnings per share
Profit for the financial year		**32.9**	**8.6p**	41.4	9.7p
Dividends on B preference shares		**(0.2)**	**(0.1p)**	–	–
	9	**32.7**	**8.5p**	41.4	9.7p
Adjustments:					
Exceptional and non-recurring items		**48.6**	**12.7p**	68.1	15.9p
Attributable taxation		**(1.1)**	**(0.3p)**	1.7	0.4p
Adjusted earnings	9	**80.2**	**20.9p**	111.2	26.0p

The basic earnings per Ordinary share of 8.5p (1997:9.7p) is calculated upon the profit for the financial year adjusted for dividends paid on B preference shares of £0.2m (1997: nil). There is no material difference between the basic and fully diluted earnings per share.

Notes to the accounts (extract)

9 Earnings per share

	1998	1997
Basic	**8.5p**	9.7p
Adjusted basic	**20.9p**	26.0p

Reconciliation of adjusted earnings:

	1998	1998	1997	1997
	£m	Per share	£m	Per share
Profit for the financial year	**32.9**	**8.6p**	41.4	9.7p
Dividends on B preference shares	**(0.2)**	**(0.1p)**	–	–
	32.7	**8.5p**	41.4	9.7p
Adjustments:				
Operating exceptional items	**39.6**	**10.3p**	50.0	11.7p
Non-operating exceptional items	**9.0**	**2.4p**	8.6	2.0p
Non-recurring pre-demerger finance charges	–	–	9.5	2.2p
Attributable taxation	**(1.1)**	**(0.3p)**	1.7	0.4p
	80.2	**20.9p**	111.2	26.0p

Adjusted earnings per share is based on earnings before the impact of all exceptional items and non-recurring pre-demerger finance charges. It is included as it provides a better understanding of the underlying trading performance of the Group.

Weighted average number of shares:

	1998	1997
Basic	**384.1m**	428.3m

The weighted average number of shares is calculated excluding those held by the EBT on which the right to other than nominal dividends has been waived.

There is no material difference between the basic and fully diluted earnings per share.

Table 8.10 – United News & Media plc – Annual Report and Accounts – 31 December 1997

Notes to the financial statements (extract)

9. Earnings per share		**1997 pence**	**1996 pence**
Earnings per share before Channel 5 and exceptional items		**47.6**	40.0
Adjustment in respect of Channel 5 trading losses		**(3.8)**	–
Earnings per share before exceptional items		**43.8**	40.0
Adjustment in respect of exceptional items	– charged to operating profits	**2.0**	(19.6)
	– interests in associated undertakings	–	(12.8)
	– profit (loss) on sale and closure of businesses	**(1.3)**	28.2
	– merger expenses	–	(6.3)
	– profit on the disposal of fixed asset investments	**11.6**	1.6
Earnings per share		**56.1**	31.1

Basic earnings per share is calculated by reference to profit on ordinary activities after charging exception items, tax and minority interests of £277.1 million (1996 – £152.4 million) and to the weighted average of 493,888,661 ordinary shares (1996 – 489,941,000) in issue during the year. Earnings per share has also been calculated by reference to earnings before exceptional items and related tax of £216.6 million (1996 – £196.1 million) and, additionally, by reference to earnings before the share of Channel 5 trading losses and exceptional items and related tax of £234.9 million (1996–£196.1 million). The directors consider that these measures of earnings per share are key indicators of the underlying performance of the group.

8.120 It should be appreciated that it was never the intention of IIMR that the measure should be capable of wholesale adoption by companies. It was simply meant to be a robust and comparable figure that could be worked out from the figure required by the standard with very little subjectivity. Nevertheless, in spite of its loss of appeal among companies, it still continues to be used by the Financial Times for the basis of calculating its daily p/e ratios and by other statistical houses. It could regain its popularity, however, when companies begin to capitalise and amortise goodwill under FRS 10. The IIMR headline figure excludes goodwill amortisation and since goodwill amortisation cannot be an exceptional item, some companies will be keen to show earnings before and after goodwill amortisation and may adopt the IIMR figure as a way of presenting this information.

Restatement of EPS data

8.121 As stated in paragraph 8.49 above, the prior period's EPS should not be restated in respect of a share consolidation combined with a special dividend, where the overall effect is that of a share repurchase at fair value. Where this applies, that fact should be disclosed. [FRS 14 para 64]. Similarly, diluted EPS of any prior period presented should not be restated for changes in the assumptions used (such as for contingently issuable shares) or for the conversion of potential ordinary shares (such as convertible debt) outstanding at the end of the previous period. [FRS 14 para 65]. This is because these factors are already taken into account in calculating the basic and, where applicable, the diluted EPS for the current period. However, in some circumstances, prior period's EPS data should be restated and these circumstances are discussed below.

Post balance sheet changes in capital

8.122 As stated in paragraph 8.35, basic and diluted EPS for all periods presented should be restated for bonus issues, stock splits and similar events occurring during the period that change the number of shares in issue without a corresponding change in the resources of the entity. If these events occur after the balance sheet date, but before the date of approval of the financial statements, the EPS figures for the current, and those of any prior, periods should be based on the new number of shares issued. As a result, the number of shares used in the EPS calculation will not be consistent with that shown in the balance sheet. Therefore, disclosure should be made to that effect. [FRS 14 para 63].

8.123 A company should disclose details of all material ordinary share transactions or potential ordinary share transactions entered into after the balance sheet date, other than those described in the preceding paragraph. Such transactions include the issue and repurchase of shares for cash, conversion of convertible debt into ordinary shares or the issue of potential ordinary shares. These transactions would not have any effect on the disclosed EPS figures, because they do not affect the amount of capital used to produce the net profit or loss for the period. [FRS 14 para 66]. Most of these transactions would fall to be disclosed anyway as material non-adjusting post balance sheet events under SSAP 17. [FRS 14 para 66].

Prior period adjustments

8.124 The standard is silent on the restatement of prior period EPS data following a change in accounting policy or as a result of adopting a new FRS. In these situations, the general rule should be followed. That is, the EPS figure for the prior period should be restated as if the restated profit or loss had been reported originally in the prior period or periods. The effect of the restatement should be disclosed, if material.

8.125 Where a company adopts FRS 14 for the first time, it is possible that prior period diluted EPS may include the dilutive effect of outstanding share options calculated under the imputed interest method under SSAP 3. If those options are still outstanding in the current period, they would be included in diluted EPS under the treasury stock method. In those circumstances, prior period diluted EPS should be recalculated using the new method and restated, if the effect is considered to be material. Disclosure about the change in policy should also be made.

8.126 It is also possible that ordinary shares assumed to be issued upon exercise or conversion of potential ordinary shares were excluded from prior year's diluted EPS figure, because they were considered to be antidilutive. If those potential ordinary shares are outstanding at the end of the current period, the use of net income from continuing operations as the control number to test dilution may cause the potential ordinary shares originally determined as antidilutive to be dilutive. The reverse may also be true. In these circumstances, prior period EPS data should be calculated in accordance with FRS 14 and restated where material.

Business combination accounted for as a merger

8.127 As stated in paragraph 8.53 above, where a business combination is accounted for as a merger, the financial statements of the combined entity is presented as if the combined entity had always existed. Therefore, EPS computations should be based on the aggregate of the weighted average number of ordinary shares of the combined entity, adjusted to equivalent shares of the entity whose shares are outstanding after the combination for all period presented. [FRS 14 para 63].

Financial statistics in the historical summary

8.128 In order to present a fair comparison of EPS figures published in a five year summary, the basic EPS figure will need to be adjusted for subsequent changes in capital as set out below:

- Where a capitalisation issue or share split has taken place during the financial year, all previously published EPS figures should be adjusted by the bonus factor as explained in paragraph 8.35 above.

- Where a rights issue at less than full market has taken place during the financial year, all previously published EPS figures should be adjusted by the reciprocal of the bonus element inherent in the rights issue as explained from paragraph 8.39 above.

- Where a business combination has taken place during the financial year that has been accounted for as a merger, all previously published EPS figures should be adjusted as if the merged company has always been part of the group as explained in paragraph 8.53 above.

Where there is more than one capitalisation or rights issue during the year, both these factors will operate cumulatively. The cumulative effect of all the above events should be taken into account. The resultant figures should be described as restated EPS and should be set out separately from the other financial data which is not so adjusted. [FRS 14 para 76].

8.129 Where there has been a bonus or rights issue in the period covered by the summary, the equity dividend actually paid in those period should be set out in the form of pence per share and similarly adjusted by the same factors used in restating EPS. This adjustment is necessary to ensure that the equity dividends and EPS data are comparable. The adjusted dividend per share should be described as restated. In practice, the adjusted EPS and the adjusted dividend per share are normally presented next to each other. [FRS 14 para 77].

8.130 Sometimes companies also disclose a dividend cover which is the number of times dividend is covered by current earnings. Following the abolition of ACT from 6 April 1999, dividend cover will simply be stated by dividing EPS by actual dividend per share.

Chapter 9

Segmental reporting

Page

Chapter 9

Segmental reporting

Introduction

9.1 As the UK is heavily dependent on overseas trade, many of its foreign and trade policies are directed maintaining and expanding overseas markets. In order to be able to carry out these policies successfully, however, reasonable levels of access to foreign competitors must be allowed in the home markets. Consequently, over the past fifteen years or so, there has been a massive rationalisation of industrial practices within UK organisations as they have faced up to increased competition from goods produced abroad. UK companies have introduced new products, extended the range of their commercial activities and implemented measures intended to make their existing operations more efficient and competitive. In many instances, companies have achieved their objectives of exploiting new or existing markets and producing goods more efficiently for those markets by acquiring or setting up manufacturing operations abroad.

9.2 For companies that operate in a variety of classes of business or in a number of different geographical locations, the availability of segmental information (also called 'disaggregated information'), setting out meaningful analyses of turnover and profits, is essential for good management. Such information is essential if management is to be able to detect trends in performance and sales within its specific businesses and geographical regions. Armed with such information, management is better placed to devise strategies and focus actions towards countering adverse trends or exploiting opportunities in specific business lines or market places.

9.3 The form of segmental information that is of use in a business depends to a great extent on how the management of the business is organised. A business may be managed on a product basis, a geographical basis, or on a mixture of both. Where a business is managed on a geographical basis, the information that may be most useful is a geographical analysis of turnover and profits. An analysis by class of business may be difficult to obtain because, for instance, different classes of business within a geographical segment may be financed as one operation and may share resources. Where a business is managed on a product basis, an analysis of turnover and profits by product will be more important. The management structure of the majority of international companies, however, includes both geographical and product structures. Therefore, segmental information by product and by geographical region is relevant to most companies.

9.4 The value of segmental information is not limited to its application as an internal management tool. It also has an important role in external reporting, since by providing segmental information in financial statements, the management of a company can explain to investors and to the market in general many of the factors which have contributed to the result for the year. These factors might be developments instigated by management, such as the expansion of products or markets, or events outside management's control, such as political disturbances abroad.

Arguments against segmental reporting

9.5 There are critics of segmental reporting who oppose its general application on a number of grounds. These grounds include a belief that the costs of providing segmental information outweigh the real benefits, the possibility of commercial damage being occasioned by making public confidential information and the practical difficulties in identifying distinct and reportable business segments. Another concern is that readers of accounts are, or should be, interested in the reporting entity as a whole, rather than the underlying business segments. In spite of this opposition, however, it is generally recognised by parliament and standard setters that the benefits of segmental reporting, where applied in a constructive manner, far outweigh the potential disadvantages.

Arguments in favour of segmental reporting

9.6 The proponents of segmental reporting argue that shareholders and analysts need and welcome segmental information, because it indicates to them the spread of a company's activities and geographical markets. They consider that this information is essential to assessing the on-going risks and prospects of an enterprise. Indeed, segmental information is the analysis most frequently requested by users of financial statements. Armed with such information, users of financial statements are able to compare turnover and results between segments and from one year to another in a meaningful manner. Moreover, by applying their own knowledge of markets and products, they are able to appreciate more fully the risks and opportunities that may affect a company's performance in the future. Hence, their judgements are likely to be better informed and to be reflected in any investment advice they give or in their own investment strategies and decisions. These are, of course, matters which can have a direct influence upon the share price of the company.

9.7 A further justification given in support of segmental reporting is in the context of consolidated financial statements. These consolidated statements may include the results, assets and liabilities of businesses which are very different from those of the rest of the group (known as 'dissimilar' businesses or activities).

Segmental reporting can facilitate an understanding of the constituent parts of the group and an appreciation of the different activities of individual subsidiaries.

9.8 Proponents also argue that, although consolidated financial statements are useful in showing the aggregate of the parent company's interests, they have the disadvantage of concealing the underlying performance of individual business segments. Segmental information can help to remedy this deficiency, by enabling the reader to obtain a fuller understanding of the individual businesses that constitute the group.

9.9 For the reasons outlined above, even before the publication in 1990 of SSAP 25, 'Segmental reporting', many large UK-based companies provided voluntary segmental information in their financial statements. The range of these disclosures went beyond the limited disclosures already prescribed by law and required at that time by the Stock Exchange.

The regulatory framework

9.10 As users of financial statements began to recognise the shortcomings of statements that contained only aggregate information, interest in segmental reporting gradually developed in the UK. As a result, a regulatory framework was eventually established that comprised of legislation, Stock Exchange rules and accounting standards. The position of each of these elements in the regulatory framework is considered below.

Statutory requirements and exemptions

9.11 The Companies Act 1967 introduced the initial statutory requirements for segmental reporting by UK companies. This Act required the directors' report to disclose an analysis of turnover and profit before tax by class, where the directors considered that the company carried on two or more classes of business that differed substantially from each other. In addition, unless the Board of Trade agreed otherwise on the grounds of national interest, the directors' report was required to state the value of goods exported from the UK, unless annual turnover was less than £50,000.

9.12 These initial requirements have been extended by subsequent legislation. The Companies Act 1981 switched disclosures from the directors' report to the notes to the financial statements. In addition, it introduced a requirement to disclose turnover by export market and, in so doing, replaced the earlier requirement to state the total value of goods exported from the UK. At the same time the exemption from disclosure clause was extended in a way that empowered the directors to make the final decision. In effect, no disclosure was required where the directors considered the interests of the company would be seriously prejudiced by making such disclosures.

9.13 The Companies Act 1985 consolidated the existing legislative requirements. Thus, all companies must comply with the Act's requirements, in that the notes to the profit and loss account must include certain information analysed by both class of business and geographical market. The specific disclosures are considered in detail in paragraphs 9.75 to 9.81. However, the 1981 exemption remains, that is, disaggregated information need not be disclosed where the directors have determined that such disclosure would be seriously prejudicial to the company's interests. Where this exemption is utilised, however, the financial statements must state that disaggregated information has not been disclosed on the grounds that disclosure would be prejudicial. However, there is no requirement to give any further detail on why such disclosure would be prejudicial.

9.14 An example of the circumstances that might result in the directors deciding to utilise the exemption is where a company or a group supplies customers in two countries only. If these companies are politically opposed to each other, to publish a geographical split of turnover could be considered to be prejudicial to the interests of the company or the group. Provided that the notes to the profit and loss account disclose the fact that this analysis has not been given, no further information is required to be published. In practice, the prejudicial exemption is applied by surprisingly few reporting entities. Company Reporting's survey of 460 companies, as published in October 1994, indicated that only six per cent of companies reported that certain segmental disclosures would be seriously prejudicial. Further, where prejudice is claimed, it is frequently limited to specific segmental disclosures rather than the whole range.

9.15 The fact that the Act gives the directors the responsibility for determining whether segmental information should be reported is a matter of note. This is because they alone determine:

- Whether two or more classes of substantially different business have been carried out by the company.
- Whether turnover has been generated in two or more substantially different geographical markets.
- Whether non-disclosure on the grounds of seriously prejudicing the company's interests is appropriate.

However, it is implicit that, in making their decisions on reportable segments, the directors should act in good faith.

9.16 More recently, small companies (and groups headed by a small company) have been granted a specific exemption from the disclosure requirements of the Act. They need not give details of segmental information by market, as required by paragraph 55 of Schedule 4 to the Act, if they have taken advantage of the exemptions contained in Schedule 8 to the Act in drawing up their financial statements. However, if the company or group has supplied geographical markets outside the UK (turnover by destination), the notes must state the percentage of turnover (but not profit or loss) attributable to those markets. The analysis made for these purposes must still have regard to the manner in which the company's activities are organised. [8 Sch 49 inserted by SI 1997/220]. The disclosure requirements applicable to small companies are considered in detail in chapter 36.

The Stock Exchange requirements

9.17 In the past, the Continuing Obligations section of the Listing Rules of the Stock Exchange required member companies to disclose a geographical analysis of both net turnover and contribution to trading results in respect of those trading operations carried on by the company or group outside the UK. In this context, transactions within a group were excluded and it was acceptable to give a broad geographical analysis of net turnover by way of figures or percentages, analysed by market and not necessarily given country by country. Where 50 per cent of total overseas operations related to one continent, a further analysis, by country within that continent, needed to be given. 'Overseas operations' was defined so as to include direct exports and activities carried on other than in the country where the main place of business of the company (or group) was situated.

9.18 In effect, therefore, the Continuing Obligations' requirement for segmental disclosure by geographic region implied a mixture of the source and destination bases, because it included exports to a particular region as well as activities carried on within that region.

9.19 The Listing Rules of the Stock Exchange, as revised in 1994, no longer prescribe specific segmental disclosure requirements. Instead they note the Exchange's support for the aims of the Financial Reporting Council (see chapter 12). Accordingly, the Continuing Obligations require that the annual report and accounts of listed companies must be *"...prepared in accordance with the issuer's national law and, in all material respects, with United Kingdom Generally Accepted Accounting Principles, United States Generally Accepted Accounting Principles or International Accounting Standards..."*. [LR 12.42]. In effect, therefore, member companies are required to comply with the segmental disclosure requirements of the Act, SSAP 25 and other subsequent accounting standards insofar as they add to or amend the requirements of SSAP 25.

[The next paragraph is 9.21.]

SSAP 25

9.21 Although the original International Accounting Standard, IAS 14, 'Reporting financial information by segment', was published in August 1981, it was not until 1986 that work commenced in the UK on developing an accounting standard on the subject. In January 1987 a consultative paper was published and circulated to representatives of preparers and auditors of financial statements. However, the paper included a number of ambitious proposals, including presentation of segmental information in matrix format. As a result it failed to secure the necessary support levels. A less ambitious exposure draft, ED 45, 'Segmental reporting', was published in November 1988. The exposure draft contained proposals which were similar to the requirements of the original IAS 14. Subsequently, in July 1990, the current standard, SSAP 25, 'Segmental reporting', was issued. While this standard remains in force, the ASB has issued a number of subsequent standards that also have implications for segmental-type reporting. These are referred to later in this chapter.

Scope and exemptions

9.22 Insofar as they repeat the requirements of paragraph 55 of Schedule 4, the segmental disclosure requirements of SSAP 25 apply to all entities subject to the Companies Act 1985.

9.23 SSAP 25, however, sets out requirements that are additional to those contained in the Act and which apply to certain entities only. In effect, smaller companies are excluded from the standard's disclosure requirements, other than where those requirements are also prescribed by the Act. However, exempt entities can, and are encouraged to, adopt these additional disclosures on a voluntary basis.

9.24 The entities to which the additional disclosures apply on a mandatory basis are:

- All public companies or parent companies that have a public company as a subsidiary.
- Banking and insurance companies and groups.

- All other entities that exceed two of the three criteria for defining a medium-sized company under section 247 of the Act multiplied in each case by ten.

9.25 The three criteria referred to in the paragraph above and as multiplied by ten result in the following cut-off points:

- Turnover in excess of £112m.
- Balance sheet total in excess of £56m.
- Number of employees in excess of 2,500.

9.26 The three criteria for turnover, balance sheet total and number of employees are amended from time to time by statutory instrument. However, their impact is intended to ensure that larger companies present the full segmental disclosures required by the standard. Conversely, all companies below that size are left with the freedom to choose what, if any, additional segmental disclosures they might make beyond those required by the Act.

9.27 In addition to the exemption available to smaller companies, there is a further exemption from complying with the non-statutory aspects of the standard. This exemption is intended to be a practical one, in that it seeks to avoid the need for voluminous disclosures by subsidiaries, where the group financial statements provide full segmental disclosures in accordance with the standard. Accordingly, where a subsidiary undertaking is neither a public company, nor a banking or insurance company, it need not comply with the provisions of the standard provided that its parent provides segmental information in compliance with the standard.

9.28 It should be emphasised that, whether or not companies are exempt from the requirements of the standard, as a minimum, all companies still have to comply with the legal requirements contained in the Act. Thus, a subsidiary undertaking that takes advantage of the exemptions described in paragraph 9.27 will still be required to disclose the segmental information required by the Act, unless it can also takes advantage of the Act's exemptions not to disclose segmental information.

9.29 It is not totally clear why subsidiary undertakings engaged in banking and insurance activities have been selected for special treatment, particularly as FRS 2 indicates that there are very few instances where such undertakings would not be fully consolidated within the group's consolidated financial statements. Thus, in most circumstances, segmental information will have been provided at a group level, presumably with financial service operations disclosed as a separate segment or segments. Consequently, there seems little benefit in requiring fuller segmental information in the subsidiaries' financial statements unless it is undertaking a wide spread of financial activities. For insurance groups this situation is compounded by UK insurers being required to submit annual returns to the DTI. The returns set out detailed revenue account analyses by insurance class in a prescribed format. The information contained therein seems likely to be of far greater benefit to analysts, than the more limited segmental information disclosed within statutory financial statements.

9.30 There is a further limitation on the scope and application of the standard in that the standard repeats the exemption contained in paragraph 55(5) of Schedule 4 of the Act in the wider context of the standard. Thus where, in the opinion of the directors, the disclosure of any information required by the standard would be seriously prejudicial to the interests of the company, that information need not be disclosed. However, like the Act, the standard requires the fact that any such information has not been disclosed to be stated. [SSAP 25 para 6]. Asprey plc, a group that trades internationally and whose principal activities comprise goldsmiths, jewellers, silversmiths, watch retailers and antique dealers, is an example of a reporting entity that takes advantage of this exemption (see Table 9.1). A number of other entities provide some segmental information, but apply the prejudicial override clause to limit certain types of segmental disclosures. For example, the Weir Group, an engineering products and services group, provides segmental analyses of turnover and operating profit by class of business and geographical area of origin (and destination for turnover), but does not provide a segmental analysis of net assets by class of business or geographical area of origin on the grounds that to disclose such information would be seriously prejudicial to the group's interests (see Table 9.2).

Table 9.1 – Asprey plc – Annual Report and Accounts – 31 March 1993

Notes to the Accounts (extract)

---

2 TURNOVER

Turnover represents sales to third parties exclusive of V.A.T.

Segmental information has not been disclosed as in the opinion of the Directors it would be seriously prejudicial to the interests of the business.

Table 9.2 – The Weir Group PLC – Report & accounts – 27 December 1996

Auditors' Report

Notes to the Accounts

For the 52 weeks ended 27th December 1996

1 Turnover And Profit on Ordinary Activities Before Tax

Turnover represents the amount invoiced to third parties in respect of goods sold and services provided excluding value added tax. In the case of long term contracts, it represents the value of work done during the year.

Turnover and profit on ordinary activities before tax were contributed as follows:

		Group			
		1996		1995	
		Turnover £'000	**Profit £'000**	Turnover £'000	Profit £'000
Engineering Products:	Group	**492,715**	**33,491**	473,141	28,173
	Associates	**5**	**(5)**	7	(10)
		429,720	**33,486**	473,148	28,163
Engineering Services:	Group	**127,185**	**12,550**	119,490	11,624
	Associates	**98,260**	**5,166**	67,784	5,019
		225,445	**17,716**	187,274	16,643
Total:	Group	**619,900**	**46,041**	592,631	39,797
	Associates	**98,265**	**5,161**	67,791	5,009
	Unallocated costs	**–**	**(709)**	–	(378)
	Exchange adjustment – Group	**–**	**–**	29,375	2,674
		718,165	**50,493**	689,797	47,102
	Interest and other income	**–**	**(1,453)**	–	(1,598)
		718,165	**49,040**	689,797	45,504

***** *For comparative purposes 1995 figures have been restated at the 1996 closing exchange rates.*

The analyses of Group turnover and Group operating profit before unallocated costs and associates by geographical area of origin are as follows:

	Group			
	1996		1995	
	Turnover £'000	**Operating profit £'000**	Turnover £'000	Operating Profit £'000
United Kingdom	**346,950**	**22,023**	333,170	18,518
Rest of Europe	**34,643**	**3,933**	30,585	1,189
Americas	**182,715**	**16,710**	180,521	18,329
Africa	**20,695**	**2,137**	15,391	1,799
Asia	**4,456**	**(155)**	4,833	211
Australia	**30,441**	**1,393**	28,131	(249)
	619,900	**46,041**	592,631	39,797

1 Turnover And Profit On Ordinary Activities Before Tax

The analyses of Group turnover by geographical area of destination is as follows:

	Group	
	1996	1995
	£'000	£'000
United Kingdom	**186,523**	179,671
Rest of Europe	**60,843**	52,016
Americas	**177,784**	174,746
Africa	**32,704**	23,594
Asia	**125,454**	124,096
Australia	**36,592**	38,508
	619,900	592,631

An analysis of net assets by class of business and geographical area of origin has not been disclosed. The directors are of the opinion that to disclose such information would be seriously prejudicial to the interests of the group.

Truth and fairness implications

9.31 Where an entity takes advantage of the exemption referred to in paragraph 9.30 above not to make segmental disclosures on the grounds that they would be seriously prejudicial, the question arises as to the impact of such non-disclosure on the truth and fairness of the financial statements as a whole.

9.32 The standard allows non-disclosure where the information, if disclosed, would be seriously prejudicial to the company. As noted above, this is based on an equivalent provision in the Act. The standard implies that, in such a situation, segmental information is not essential to the true and fair view.

9.33 The Foreword to Accounting Standards is helpful in this regard. It indicates that the prescription of information to be contained with financial statements does *"...not override exemptions from disclosure given by law to, and utilised, by certain kinds of entity"*. [Foreword to Accounting Standards para 15].

9.34 Auditors have to decide whether failure to provide segmental information should result in qualifying their opinion on financial statements on the grounds that the truth and fairness of those financial statements is affected. Clearly, if such information is not disclosed, but there are no grounds on which disclosure could be considered to be seriously prejudicial, then the auditor should state that the financial statements have not been properly prepared in accordance with the Act. If the auditor considers that the non-disclosure is so material as to affect the truth and fairness of the financial statements, it will be necessary to qualify the opinion given on their truth and fairness.

9.35 However, if disclosure is not made and there is reason to believe that disclosure would be seriously prejudicial, then clearly the auditor could state that the financial statements had been properly prepared in accordance with the Act. The omission of the information would also be in accordance with the standard and, therefore, qualification of the audit opinion on the truth and fairness of the financial statements would not be appropriate.

9.36 A similar issue potentially arises in the situation where small companies take advantage of exemptions not to provide the same level of segmental information disclosures as are prescribed for large and public companies. In essence, if detailed segmental information is considered necessary for a true and fair view to be given by those types of entity, how can smaller entities be said to give a true and fair view, unless they mirror that level of segmental disclosure?

9.37 The matter of limited disclosure exemptions permitted to certain types of entity has been addressed in Counsel's opinion, reproduced in the Appendix to the Foreword to Accounting Standards. This indicates that, while it is a question of law as to whether financial statements give a true and fair view, the courts will look to the requirements of accounting standards in reaching their decision. It can be inferred from this that, if accounting standards permit exemptions to certain categories or sizes of company, the courts would not interpret these exemptions as detracting from the true and fair view.

[The next paragraph is 9.39.]

Other accounting standards

9.39 Subsequent to the publication of SSAP 25 in 1990, the ASB has published a number of financial reporting standards that have an impact on segmental disclosures. The disclosure implications of these standards, in terms of segmental reporting, are considered in paragraphs 9.114 to 9.144 below.

General guidance

9.40 Before examining in detail the specific segmental reporting disclosure requirements prescribed by law and accounting standards, it may be helpful to consider a number of difficult judgemental areas that directors face as they consider the most appropriate forms of segmental reporting for their individual companies. These problem areas are considered in detail below.

Determining segments

9.41 For financial statements that disclose segmental information to readers to have real value, a high level of consistency of approach across reporting entities is required.

This is particularly important in terms of how directors determine what constitutes a reportable segment, so that different companies apply similar principles in determining what should be reported. This should enable readers of financial statements to make better comparisons of performance and prospects across reporting entities.

9.42 Both the Act and the standard clearly view reportable segments in terms of either class of business segments or geographical segments and both conclude that the determination of a company's classes of business and geographical segments must depend on the judgement of the directors. Thus, it is the directors – and they alone – who decide whether the company operates in more than one class of business or geographical segment. However, as this could lead to inevitable inconsistencies across boards of companies, the standard sets out additional guidance on the matter.

9.43 The advice given by the standard emphasises how the directors should have regard to the overall purpose of presenting segmental information, in making their judgements about reportable segments. Of primary concern to the directors in their deliberations should be the question of whether the provision of segmental information is likely to be helpful and informative to users of financial statements.

9.44 The emphasis of the standard is that, for segmental reporting to be of real value to users of financial statements, the segmental information reported needs both to reflect the company's risk and reward profile and to inform users of the nature of that profile. This sentiment is reiterated in the explanatory note to the standard, which discusses the circumstances where the provision of segmental information may enhance a reader's understanding of the financial statements. Where an entity operates in more than one class of business or more than one geographical market, the circumstances described above arise where businesses:

- Earn a return on the investment that is out of line with the return earned by the remainder of the business.
- Are subject to different degrees of risk.
- Have experienced different degrees of growth.
- Have different potentials for future development.

[SSAP 25 para 8].

9.45 It follows from the above that in determining business or geographical segments, products or services (or a related group of products or services), with significantly differing risks, rewards and future prospects should not be combined together to create a reportable segment. Instead, they should be treated as separate segments and reported as such, provided that they are of sufficient materiality to justify separate disclosure.

9.46 The standard also emphasises the need for the directors to reconsider segment definitions periodically and re-define them where appropriate. [SSAP 25 para 10]. This means that the directors should reconsider the position on each occasion that financial statements are produced.

Classes of business

9.47 When the directors of a reporting entity consider the provision of segmental analysis in that entity's financial statements, they are inevitably faced with the question of whether the entity has distinct business segments and, if so, how these are to be identified.

9.48 In the past, a number of different approaches to defining business segments have been proposed. For instance, a number of approaches were considered by an IASC steering group in developing the revised international accounting standard, IAS 14 'Segment reporting'. The approaches include:

- Defining business segments by products or services grouped together on an industry basis according to a national or international industry or product classification system. Although this could enhance consistency across reporting entities in terms of segment identification, it is not generally considered an appropriate approach. This is because it could result in very broad segments and may not adequately consider differences in risks and rewards within an entity.

- Defining business segments as distinct components of an enterprise that are capable of sale or separation from the rest of the entity without affecting other business segments. A problem with this approach is that it does not necessarily reflect the risk and reward profile of the reporting entity.

- Defining business segments by way of a management approach, whereby financial reporting is based on the major operating units of the reporting entity. In effect, reportable segments constitute organisational units for which financial results are maintained and analysed by management as an integral part of their management and control procedures. This approach has been adopted by the national standard setting body in the US. However, where organisational groupings combine products and services with significantly different risk and reward profiles, this method of reporting fails to achieve the objective of segmental reporting, because the user of the financial statements is not provided with information on a risk and reward basis.

- Defining a business segment as a distinguishable component that provides a product or service, or a group of related products or services; where that distinguishable component is subject to different risks and rewards from other business segments of the entity. This risk and reward approach is the one underlying SSAP 25.

9.49 The UK accounting standard appears to acknowledge the last two approaches. Having defined 'class of business' in paragraph 30 of the standard, as *"...a distinguishable component of an enterprise that provides a separate product or service or a separate group of related products"*, it moves on to provide guidance on identification. In assessing whether the reporting entity has different classes of products or services, the standard suggests that directors should consider the following factors:

- The nature of the products or services.
- The nature of the production processes.
- The markets in which the products or services are sold.
- The distribution channels for the products.
- The manner in which the entity's activities are organised.
- Any separate legislative framework relating to part of the business, for example, a bank or an insurance company.

[SSAP 25 para 12].

9.50 Most of the criteria above are consistent with the risks and reward approach in that they look to the separability of products and services. However, the reference to the way in which activities are organised is more indicative of the management approach. In fact, for operating and management reporting purposes, directors often use the above criteria for organising corporate entities into divisions, branches or subsidiaries. In such situations, the management approach referred to in paragraph 9.48 also acknowledges risk and reward considerations. Consequently, in these instances class of business analysis based on risk and reward considerations will also reflect the organisation structure of the reporting entity.

9.51 Although the standard explains the criteria for identifying whether separate business segments exist, this explanation is merely guidance. The directors have to exercise their own judgement in this area based on the particular circumstances of their reporting entity. In effect, the standard recognises that no one set of characteristics can claim universal application, nor can any individual characteristic claim to be determinative in every situation. Consequently, although different boards might reach different decisions on identifiable and reportable segments, by providing guidance on types of segment and their characteristics, the standard should reduce the degree of difference, so long as boards act in good faith.

Geographical segments

9.52 When directors consider the reporting of segmental information, both the Act and the standard require them to give such information by geographical segments. As for business segments, judgement is required by the directors, who have responsibility for determining whether distinct geographical segments exist and for identifying them. In this context, it is important to understand the guidance available to directors.

9.53 The standard's definition of geographical segment indicates that it is *"...a geographical area comprising an individual country or group of countries in which an entity operates, or to which it supplies products or services"*. [SSAP 25 para 31]. This is helpful insofar as it clearly envisages aggregations of groups of countries to form one geographical segment for reporting purposes. In addition, it emphasises that geographical analysis needs to consider two distinct aspects:

[The next page is 9015.]

- Analysis by operating location (origin basis).
- Analysis by destination of sale or service (destination basis).

[SSAP 25 para 14].

9.54 The standard defines both origin of turnover and destination of turnover. The former term comprises *"...the geographical segment from which products or services are supplied to a third party or to another segment"*. [SSAP 25 para 32]. The latter term is identified as *"...the geographical segment to which products or services are supplied"*. [SSAP 25 para 33].

9.55 Beyond the above, the guidance given by the standard is very limited, insofar as criteria for determining the choice of geographical segments is concerned. In emphasising that the groupings selected should reflect the overriding purpose of presenting segmental information, the standard suggests that they should indicate to the reader the extent to which a company's operations are subject to factors such as:

- Expansionist or restrictive economic climates.
- Stable or unstable political regimes.
- Exchange control regulations.
- Exchange rate fluctuations.

[SSAP 25 para 15].

9.56 These suggestions indicate that the different risk environments in which a reporting entity operates are an important factor in determining segments. A multinational operation might take account of its geographical risk profiles, for example, by treating EC member states as a single geographical market, Eastern Europe as a second and the Far East as a third. On the other hand, an operation which trades out of, or sells into, four overseas countries only, may well treat each of those as a distinct geographical segments. This might be irrespective of whether all or the majority of them are, say, EC states, provided that each of them is significant to the results and future prospects of the reporting entity as a whole.

[The next paragraph is 9.58.]

9.58 A number of examples of segmental disclosures are set out below. GEC provides a wealth of geographical segmental analysis as Table 9.3 illustrates. Not only are turnover, profit and net assets analysed by territory of origin, but turnover is also analysed by territory of destination. The analysis provided enables the reader to understand that:

- The UK is the major originator of sales, but exports a significant proportion of its production. The company's UK-based operations are also responsible for approximately half of the group's worldwide profit.

- France is the other major European originator of sales and also exports a large proportion of its production. It appears to achieve this from a negative local asset base.

- While the rest of Europe represents a material element of GEC's business, no individual European country, other than the UK and France, is considered to constitute a segment in its own right. However, this geographical segment purchases more GEC products than it produces.

- The Americas constitutes another major originator of sales. However, in 1994, the segment was a net importer of GEC products and services, since total sales within the segment slightly exceeded the value of sales originated therein. This is a reversal of the position that was reported for 1993.

- Although three other segments are identified, namely Australasia, Asia and Africa, they are relative immaterial in terms of their local production, asset levels and impact on profit. However, when considered from a destination perspective, they are clearly important to GEC as notable importers of its products and services originating out of other geographical segments.

Table 9.3 – The General Electric Company p.l.c. – Annual Report and Accounts – 31 March 1994

Notes to the Accounts (Extract)

1 PRINCIPAL ACTIVITIES, PROFIT CONTRIBUTIONS, MARKETS AND NET ASSETS EMPLOYED (extract)

Analysis of turnover by classes of business

	To customers in the United Kingdom		To customers overseas	
	1994 £ million	1993 £ million	**1994 £ million**	1993 £ million
Electronic Systems	**930**	943	**1,819**	1,774
Power Systems	**535**	596	**2,568**	2,539
Telecommunications	**715**	759	**335**	253
Consumer Goods	**236**	233	**23**	20
Electronic Metrology	**139**	132	**350**	281
Office Equipment & Printing	**17**	16	**306**	287
Medical Equipment	**3**	–	**671**	568
Electronic Components	**94**	107	**197**	195
Industrial Apparatus	**207**	236	**126**	106
Distribution & Trading	**–**	–	**351**	290
Other	**59**	77	**13**	20
Intra-Activity sales	**(83)**	(93)	**(68)**	(41)
	2,852	3,006	**6,691**	6,292

Analysis of turnover by territory of destination

	1994 £ million	1993 £ million
United Kingdom	**2,852**	3,006
France	**1,122**	1,068
Rest of Europe	**1,618**	1,793
The Americas	**2,044**	1,886
Australasia	**341**	310
Asia	**1,353**	1,038
Africa	**213**	197
	9,543	9,298

Analysis of profit, turnover and net assets by territory of origin

					Net assets	
	1994 £ million	1993 £ million	**1994 £ million**	1993 £ million	**1994 £ million**	1993 £ million
United Kingdom	**344**	367	**4,425**	4,364	**650**	983
France	**93**	85	**1,846**	1,914	**(180)**	(104)
Rest of Europe	**82**	108	**976**	1,032	**143**	231
The Americas	**142**	116	**1,884**	1,620	**506**	473
Australasia	**12**	9	**273**	246	**65**	69
Asia	**6**	5	**115**	100	**7**	6
Africa	**5**	5	**24**	22	**20**	21
	684	695	**9,543**	9,298	**1,211**	1,679

9.59 The GEC extract is also notable for the analysis it provides of turnover by class of business. Where many companies provide such analysis on a total basis, GEC sub-analyses such turnover between:

- Sales to UK customers.
- Sales to overseas customers.

9.60 In Table 9.4, Coats Viyella Plc also provides geographical analysis on both location and destination bases. In so doing, it treats *"Rest of Europe"* as a distinct geographical segment, but, identifies *"North America"* and *"South America"* as two separate segments. It also has a further segment described as *"Africa, Asia, Australasia"*, rather than employing the term, *"Rest of World"* adopted by many companies. Whether these three continents can be said to have similar risk and reward characteristics is open to question. The merging together of miscellaneous, individually non-material, geographical territories into a 'catch all' segment is practical. However, drawing conclusions about such segments needs to be undertaken with particular caution.

Table 9.4 – Coats Viyella Plc – Annual report and accounts – 31 December 1993

NOTES TO THE ACCOUNTS (extract)

	Turnover		Operating profit		Net assets	
2 Analysis of turnover, operating profit and net assets continued	**1993** **£m**	1992 £m	**1993** **£m**	1992 £m	**1993** **£m**	1992 Restated £m
Geographical analysis by location:						
United Kingdom	**1,049.2**	1,008.5	**55.7**	60.0	**369.5**	334.9
Rest of Europe	**516.2**	462.3	**24.0**	31.7	**189.2**	202.3
North America	**440.2**	369.7	**51.1**	41.3	**248.1**	222.9
South America	**116.2**	106.9	**3.7**	(3.9)	**97.6**	96.9
Africa, Asia, Australasia	**322.0**	162.4	**37.2**	17.1	**193.7**	131.6
	2,443.8	2,109.8	**171.7**	146.2	**1,098.1**	988.6
Other items			**21.2**	9.7		
Profit before interest			**192.9**	155.9		
Associated companies					**3.9**	17.9
					1,102.0	1,006.5
Net borrowings					**(266.3)**	(404.8)
Other fixed and current asset investments					**24.6**	24.6

Net assets per consolidated balance sheet				**860.3**	626.3
Acquisitions in the year have been included in the following segments:					
United Kingdom	**0.7**		**–**	**(0.6)**	
Rest of Europe	**51.4**		**7.6**	**15.0**	
North America	**15.0**		**1.5**	**14.2**	
Africa, Asia, Australasia	**132.9**		**19.3**	**61.0**	
	200.0		**28.4**	**89.6**	
Geographical analysis of sales by destination:					
United Kingdom	**968.2**	913.5			
Rest of Europe	**551.4**	506.9			
North America	**459.7**	378.3			
South America	**118.2**	109.4			
Africa, Asia, Australasia	**346.3**	201.7			
	2,443.8	2,109.8			

Notes
Associated companies are principally Thread and Fabrics businesses based in Asia.

9.61 Although identifying geographical segments by risk and reward profile may be the preferred approach, multinationals that operate in a very large number of countries appear to find it either impractical to adopt or not their primary consideration. In practice, decisions may be influenced by the volume of disclosure that the basis chosen leads to. For example, consider a global entity that operates out of the majority of African countries. The directors will need to consider whether they should analyse these individually or in small risk groupings to reflect the different circumstances of each. Alternatively, they may decide that an aggregation as 'Africa' is the most sensible presentation. In any event, in making their judgements, the directors will need to take account of the significance of individual countries, aggregations of countries and the continent as a whole to the results and financial status of the reporting entity.

9.62 A further point of interest in this area is the way in which some companies redefine their chosen geographical segments for disclosing segmental information by origin, when they disclose turnover information on a destination basis. This is understandable where a reporting entity sells significant volumes of business into a geographical location where it has no production capacity or minimal physical representation, but this does not appear to be the only determining factor. Examples of this approach include Pilkington plc, which treats *"Europe (excluding United*

Kingdom)", as one segment in disclosing information by origin, but splits it into two segments, *"EEC"* and *"Non EEC"* for disclosure of turnover on a destination basis. Similarly, the *"Rest of the World"* segment on an origin basis becomes three segments for the destination basis: *"Australasia"*, *"South America"* and *"Rest of the World"* (see Table 9.5).

Table 9.5 – Pilkington plc – Directors' Report and Accounts – 31 March 1994

Notes on the Financial Statements (extract)

	1994			1993		
1 Segmental analysis of Continuing Operations	**Turnover £m**	**Operating profit/ (loss) £m**	**Net operating assets £m**	Turnover £m	Operating profit/ loss £m	Net operating assets £m
Flat and safety glass –						
Europe	**1,321.7**	**33.2**	**948.3**	1,196.7	42.8	975.6
North America	**691.6**	**26.8**	**372.1**	626.7	5.0	393.6
Rest of the World	**337.0**	**49.7**	**235.3**	304.6	39.0	227.2
Total	**2,350.3**	**109.7**	**1,555.7**	2,128.0	86.8	1,596.4
Other trading companies	**164.5**	**(0.5)**	**158.3**	171.4	(1.0)	153.4
Group technology management	**0.3**	**4.8**	**(16.3)**	1.1	7.0	9.0
Group operations	–	**(22.8)**	**(4.6)**	–	(16.3)	18.4
	2,515.1	**91.2**	**1,693.1**	2,300.5	76.5	1,777.2
United Kingdom	**453.8**	**17.4**	**293.3**	331.3	(1.7)	277.3
Europe (excluding United Kingdom)	**925.5**	**14.2**	**754.7**	936.1	37.8	791.2
North America	**780.3**	**25.1**	**427.7**	712.9	5.1	450.9
Rest of the World	**355.2**	**52.5**	**238.3**	319.1	44.6	230.4
Group operations /technology management	**0.3**	**(18.0)**	**(20.9)**	1.1	(9.3)	27.4
	2,515.1	**91.2**	**1,693.1**	2,300.5	76.5	1,777.2

Comparative figures have been restated in accordance with FRS 3 and to take account of the repositioning of Pilkington Aerospace from other trading companies to flat and safety glass, and float process/product development costs from flat and safety glass to Group technology management.

The Companies Act 1985 requires the analysis of profit before tax but the analysis of operating profit is considered by the directors to be more meaningful.

Turnover derived from intra-segmental transactions is not material

Net operating assets are analysed in note 4.

2 Segmental Analysis of Discontinued Operations	1994 **Turnover £m**	**Operating profit/ (loss) £m**	**Net operating assets £m**	1993 Turnover £m	Operating profit/ (loss) £m	Net operating assets £m
Flat and safety glass						
Europe	–	–	–	4.0	(3.6)	–
North America	–	–	–	–	–	–
Rest of the World	–	–	–	–	–	–
Total	–	–	–	4.0	(3.6)	–
Other trading companies	**222.3**	**13.0**	**56.1**	268.0	15.1	191.4
	222.3	**13.0**	**56.1**	272.0	11.5	191.4
United Kingdom	**95.1**	**0.5**	**57.0**	92.2	2.3	76.1
Europe (excluding United Kingdom)	**29.8**	**2.4**	**–**	47.7	0.3	27.2
North America	**67.8**	**5.3**	**(0.9)**	93.4	3.1	52.1
Rest of the World	**29.6**	**4.8**	**–**	38.7	5.8	36.0
	222.3	**13.0**	**56.1**	272.0	11.5	191.4

Net operating assets are analysed in note 4.

3 Geographical Analysis of Turnover by Markets	**1994** **Group £m**	%	1993 Group £m	%

This analysis of turnover shows the markets in which the Group's products are sold, whereas the regional analysis in notes 1 and 2 relate to the domicile of the Group undertakings making the sales.

Continuing Operations				
United Kingdom	**376.6**	**15**	268.0	12
Europe (excluding United Kingdom)				
– EEC	**768.9**	**31**	792.3	34
– Non EEC	**179.6**	**7**	165.0	7
North America	**770.2**	**31**	702.4	30
Australasia	**197.8**	**8**	180.4	8
South America	**156.7**	**6**	130.9	6
Rest of the World	**65.3**	**2**	61.5	3
	2,515.1	**100**	2,300.5	100
Discontinued Operations				
United Kingdom	**92.9**	**42**	87.9	32
Europe (excluding United Kingdom)				
– EEC	**27.5**	**12**	44.1	16
– Non EEC	**3.2**	**1**	6.5	2
North America	**67.9**	**31**	93.5	34
Australasia	**8.6**	**4**	11.1	4
South America	**6.1**	**3**	9.7	4
Rest of the World	**16.1**	**7**	19.2	8
	222.3	**100**	272.0	100

	Continuing Operations		Discontinued Operations	
4 Net Operating Assets	**1994 £m**	1993 £m	**1994 £m**	1993 £m
The net operating assets referred to in notes 1 and 2 comprise the following:				
Tangible assets	**1,618.4**	1,634.0	**44.8**	97.9
Stocks	**382.5**	391.3	**13.2**	86.9
Debtors	**435.7**	424.9	**16.8**	61.8
Creditors – falling due within one year	**(430.1)**	(370.4)	**(13.7)**	(52.3)
– falling due after more than one year	**(16.8)**	(11.7)	**(0.7)**	(2.9)
Provisions	**(296.6)**	(290.9)	**(4.3)**	
	1,693.1	1,777.2	56.1	191.4

Creditors exclude loans and overdrafts, taxation on profits, finance leases and dividends. Debtors exclude taxation recoverable. Provisions exclude deferred taxation.

9.63 Enterprise Oil's 1994 Report and Accounts provides a further illustration of this point, as Table 9.6 demonstrates. In terms of turnover, the analysis by production location reveals two significant geographical segments, the UK and Norway. A 'catch all' category, described as *"Rest of World"*, is introduced to produce an analysis of total entity turnover. However, this segment is responsible for generating less than two per cent of total turnover in the current or prior year. When the company analyses its turnover by geographical area of destination, it identifies its markets as *"UK"*, *"Europe, excluding UK"*, *"North America"* and *"Asia – Pacific"*. Unusually, the geographical destination disclosures are made on a percentage basis, rather than on a monetary value basis.

Table 9.6 – Enterprise Oil plc – Annual Report and Accounts – 31 December 1994

Notes to the financial statements (extract)
for the year ended 31 December 1994

1. TURNOVER AND GEOGRAPHICAL ANALYSIS

The group's activities predominantly comprise oil and gas exploration and production. The geographical analysis of the group's turnover (by location of production) and profit before tax and net assets is as follows:

	Turnover		Profit before tax		Net assets	
	1994 £m	1993 £m	**1994 £m**	1993 £m	**1994 £m**	1993 £m
UK	**528.0**	391.5	**180.4**	91.2	**1,058.0**	1,123.2
Norway	**118.5**	144.0	**32.8**	42.1	**121.6**	69.2
Rest of World	**4.8**	10.6	**(32.2)**	(43.5)	**93.1**	77.4
	651.3	546.1	**181.0**	89.8	**1,272.7**	1,269.8
Costs and expenses of the offer for LASMO plc			**(5.7)**	–	**–**	–
Equity in associated undertaking			**(19.6)**	2.1	**59.8**	74.3
Investment in LASMO plc			**(18.1)**	–	**141.9**	–
Net interest/net debt and loan to associate			**(43.7)**	7.9	**(538.1)**	(392.8)
			93.9	99.8	**936.3**	951.3

Analysis of turnover by geographical area of destination:	**1994 %**	1993 %
UK	36.1	62.8
Europe, excluding UK	46.0	28.4
North America	17.7	7.6
Asia-Pacific	0.2	1.2
	100.0	100.0

Significant business segments

9.64 The problems which can arise when a reporting entity operates out of, or sells into, a large number of different countries have been alluded to above. In a similar vein, when an entity is organised into a large number of relatively small business units or produces an extensive product range, the identification of reportable segments requires careful consideration and judgement. The challenge facing directors is to produce segmental information that is of value to the reader in understanding underlying business performance and the entity's risk profile for the future, without burying the reader in an avalanche of analysis. It is, in effect, a balancing act, between providing too little analysis and supplying so much that it obscures the reader's understanding. In effect, therefore, directors need to consider what guidance exists to assist them in determining whether a segment is of sufficient importance or materiality to merit separate disclosure.

9.65 The explanatory notes to the standard are of some assistance in this respect, in that they attempt to set out size criteria for determining whether a segment should be considered significant enough to justify separate identification and reporting. The standard suggests that a segment would normally be regarded as significant if:

- its third party turnover is ten per cent or more of the entity's total third party turnover; or
- its segment result, whether profit or loss, is ten per cent or more of the combined result of all segments in profit or of all segments in loss, whichever combined result is the greater; or
- its net assets are ten per cent or more of the entity's total net assets.

[SSAP 25 para 9].

9.66 The term 'net assets' is discussed later in this chapter in paragraphs 9.96 to 9.104. Although the second of the criteria set out above is tortuously worded, it means that, if a group makes an overall loss of £100, with some segments making losses amounting to £600 and others making profits amounting to £500, an individual segment that makes a profit or loss of £50 is not significant, whereas a segment that makes a profit or loss of £60 is significant.

[The next paragraph is 9.68.]

Allocation of costs

9.68 Reporting entities that provide detailed segmental information face further practical difficulties in dealing with cost allocation and attribution. How should they deal with costs that have been incurred on behalf of a number of reportable segments? Or that have been incurred on a segment's behalf by another party?

9.69 The golden rule is that segment costs should be determined by their nature rather than by the location where they are incurred. For example, where costs are incurred at enterprise or head office level solely on behalf of one specific business segment, it seems equitable in such circumstances to include them within that segment's results for segmental reporting purposes. As a result, this treatment will present a true picture of that segment's performance to the reader.

9.70 A similar situation arises where a head office or one segment incurs costs that relate to a number of segments. Such costs are normally referred to as common costs. The guidance given in the standard is that common costs should be treated in the way that the directors consider most appropriate. However, where these costs are apportioned across different segments for the purposes of internal reporting, it may be appropriate to apportion them in a like manner for external segmental reporting purposes. Conversely, the guidance acknowledges that some companies may not wish to apportion common costs, because any such apportionment would be done on an arbitrary basis and, therefore, could be misleading. Consequently in such circumstances, the common costs should be deducted from the total of the segment results.

9.71 In practical terms, the allocation of common costs is a particular area of difficulty, because the basis of allocation may significantly affect the reported segmental results. This is demonstrated by the following example:

Example

A company has three distinct business segments, A, B and C. Prior to the allocation of any common costs to these segments, the financial position of these segments is as follows:

	A £m	B £m	C £m
Net assets	2,000	300	800
Turnover	5,000	2,000	3,000
Profit before common costs	200	40	100

On the assumption that the common costs total £100m, the allocation of such costs on the basis of the turnover of each segment as a percentage of total turnover would lead to the following depiction of segment results:

	A £m	B £m	C £m
Profit before common costs	200	40	100
Allocation of common costs	50	20	30
Profit after common costs	150	20	70

This contrasts with the situation where common costs are allocated on the basis of the individual segment's proportion of total net assets. In this instance, the results would be as follows:

	A £m	B £m	C £m
Profit before common costs	200	40	100
Allocation of common costs	64	10	26
Profit after common costs	136	30	74

Thus, the basis of allocation chosen may have a material effect on the segment result that is reported. Despite this, the standard does not require disclosure of the basis of allocation, although voluntary disclosure is permissible.

9.72 If it is not possible to determine a reasonable basis for allocation, the standard allows common costs to be shown separately as a deduction from the total of segment results. [SSAP 25 para 23]. In practice it may be possible to allocate some of the common costs, but not others. For instance, if a group bears the costs of managing group properties centrally, it should be possible to allocate such costs reasonably fairly to each segment, on a basis that takes account of the type, age and value of properties used by each segment. Similarly, central administrative overheads in respect of personnel might be allocated on the basis of the number of employees in each segment. If more than one basis is appropriate for different types of common cost, it would be reasonable to apply each of these bases in allocating the respective costs. However, costs which cannot be allocated (except on an arbitrary basis), should be shown as a separate, unallocated, figure deducted from the total of segment results.

[The next paragraph is 9.74.]

Disclosure requirements

9.74 Having discussed the ways in which directors should identify class of business and geographical segments, it is necessary to consider the financial information that should be disclosed in financial statements in respect of such segments. The specific disclosure requirements of the Act, SSAP 25 and other financial reporting standards are considered in detail below. In addition, a summary of the requirements of the Act and SSAP 25 is set out in annex 1 to this chapter.

Legislative requirements

9.75 Although the Act's disclosure requirements in respect of segmental information are few in number, they apply to all reporting entities. Indeed, except for the very limited exemptions granted to small companies by Schedule 8 (as inserted by SI 1997/220), all companies must comply with the Act's disclosure requirements, subject only to the specific exemptions allowed by it. Thus, unless they adopt the prejudicial override clause, as referred to in paragraph 9.13, or take advantage of the exemptions available to small companies, the notes to the profit and loss account must include certain specified information, analysed by both class of business and geographical market.

9.76 Specifically, the Act requires that, where a company has carried on two or more classes of business during the financial year in question, and these, in the directors' opinion, differ substantially from each other, the notes to the financial statements must give:

- A description of each class of business.
- The amount of turnover that is attributable to each class of business.

[4 Sch 55(1) as amended by SI 1996/189].

9.77 'Turnover' comprises the amounts a company derives from providing goods and services that fall within its ordinary activities, after deducting trade discounts, VAT and any other taxes based on the amounts it so derives. In this context, turnover will include that of both continuing and discontinued operations, as defined by FRS 3.

9.78 The definition of turnover also has implications for inter-segment sales, since it seems that these are to be included within the segmental analyses of turnover. In this event, it seems fundamental that the reader should be able to differentiate between third party sales and inter-segment sales, as the latter are eliminated on consolidation, on the grounds that they are unrealised at an aggregated reporting level. However, the common interpretation, which the standard follows, is that this disclosure is only required in respect of turnover by origin. The matter is further discussed in paragraphs 9.88 to 9.91.

9.79 The Act states that, in determining the turnover attributable to each class, the directors must have regard to the way in which the company's activities are organised. [4 Sch 55(3) as amended by SI 1996/189]. Where classes of business do not, in the directors' opinion, differ substantially, they are to be treated as one class. Similarly, where the directors believe that markets do not differ substantially, those markets are to be treated as one market. [4 Sch 55(4)]. In interpreting these matters the directors should have regard to the practical issues discussed in paragraphs 9.40 to 9.72. They should also re-evaluate the position on each occasion that segmental information is published, to ensure that previous decisions on segmental determination remain valid.

9.80 Under the Act, where a company has supplied goods or services to two or more markets during the financial year in question, the turnover must also be disaggregated between markets. This is necessary, however, only if the directors believe that the markets differ substantially. For this purpose, 'market' means a market delimited by geographical bounds. [4 Sch 55(2)].

9.81 Details of the limited exemptions available to small companies, in respect of the Act's disclosure requirements, are set out in paragraph 9.16 above. In addition, details of exemptions available because segmental analysis would be prejudicial to the reporting entity, irrespective of its size, are set out in paragraph 9.13 above.

Additional disclosures required by the standard

9.82 SSAP 25 does not limit itself to a repetition of the requirements of the Act. Instead it imposes additional, mandatory, segmental disclosure requirements on public and large companies and all banking and insurance companies, unless they avoid disclosure by taking advantage of the prejudicial override exemption. Thus, while smaller companies are never required to make disclosures beyond those specified in the Act, public and large companies and all banking and insurance companies are required to provide the additional, wider disclosures specified by the standard.

9.83 Under the standard, where such companies have two or more classes of business, or operate in two or more geographical segments which differ substantially from each other, the following information should be disclosed in the financial statements in respect of each class of business or geographical segment:

- Turnover.
- Result, before accounting for taxation, minority interests and extraordinary items.
- Net assets.

[SSAP 25 para 34].

9.84 In practical terms, the directors of the entity are responsible for defining:

- Their identified classes of business.
- Their identified geographical segments.

[SSAP 25 para 34].

9.85 Furthermore, as indicated earlier, the standard requires the directors to *"...re-define the segments where appropriate"*. [SSAP 25 para 39]. Thus, as the classes of business or geographical segments of a reporting entity change over time, the financial statements are required to reflect those changes. In this event, the nature of and reason for the change(s) must be explained, as well as the effect of the change(s) being disclosed. Where this occurs, the standard states that the previous year's figures should be re-stated to reflect the change.

9.86 As an illustration of this in practice, in its 1994 financial statements, Lonrho re-defined certain of its classes of business, to reflect the changing circumstances of the group. The segmental analysis, as set out in Table 9.7, highlights this.

Table 9.7 – Lonrho Plc– Annual Report and Accounts – 30 September 1994

Notes to the accounts (extract)

2 Turnover

Turnover represents sales of goods and services outside the Group net of discounts, and allowances and value added taxation and includes commission earned.

Due to the reduction in significance of the contribution from financial services this activity is now included in general trade whereas it was previously separately disclosed.

Turnover by origin is analysed by activity below:–

	1994			1993		
	Group	**Associates**	**Total**	Group *Restated*	Associates *Restated*	Total *Restated*
	£m	**£m**	**£m**	£m	£m	£m
Motor and equipment distribution	**578**	**8**	**586**	526	7	533
Mining and refining	**281**	**92**	**373**	249	95	344
Manufacturing	**346**	**6**	**352**	410	5	415
Hotels	**237**	**16**	**253**	227	15	242
General trade	**240**	**9**	**249**	224	14	238
Agriculture	**142**	**9**	**151**	112	8	120
Discounted operations				258	572	830
	1,824	**140**	**1,964**	2,006	716	2,722

Turnover by origin is analysed by geographical area below:–

	1994			1993		
	Group	**Associates**	**Total**	Group *Restated*	Associates *Restated*	Total *Restated*
	£m	**£m**	**£m**	£m	£m	£m
United Kingdom	**781**	**2**	**783**	728	4	732
East, Central and West Africa	**346**	**112**	**458**	368	106	474
Southern Africa	**424**	**5**	**429**	406	15	421
The Americas	**160**	**16**	**176**	163	16	179
Europe and Other	**113**	**5**	**118**	83	3	86
Discontinued operations				258	572	830
	1,824	**140**	**1,964**	2,006	716	2,722

Turnover by destination is analysed below:–

	Group	**Associates**	**Total**	Group	Associates	Total
United Kingdom	**679**	**1**	**680**	626		626
East, Central and West Africa	**333**	**23**	**356**	361	26	387
Southern Africa	**320**	**3**	**323**	293	15	308
The Americas	**220**	**16**	**236**	210	16	226
Europe and Other	**272**	**97**	**369**	258	87	345
Discontinued operations				258	572	830
	1,824	**140**	**1,964**	2,006	716	2,722

9.87 In a similar vein, Pilkington plc, which provided segmental analysis under continuing and discontinued operation categorisations in its 1994 financial statements, indicated that it had undertaken restatements not merely to meet FRS 3 requirements, but also to take account of the segmental *"repositioning"* of certain of its activities (see Table 9.5).

Turnover and inter-segment sales

9.88 If the financial statements are to comply with the standard, they must distinguish between:

- Turnover derived from external customers.
- Turnover derived from other segments.

In providing this analysis, geographical turnover should be disclosed on both an origin and a destination basis, unless there is no material difference between the two bases. In effect, therefore, where no material difference between the two bases exists, disclosure by origin will be deemed to suffice. In making this distinction the standard recognises that the origin basis is generally considered to be more important than the destination basis of disclosure. This is logical, since disclosure of other segment information about results and net assets can often be provided only on the origin basis. Thus, as Table 9.5 indicates, Pilkington plc's 1994 financial statements provided geographical analyses on an origin basis for both continuing and discontinued businesses at turnover, operating profit and net operating assets levels. However, information on the geographical destination basis is given only for turnover.

9.89 By disclosing turnover on the origin basis, it is possible to assess turnover, results and net assets on a consistent basis and relate all three to the perceived risks and opportunities of the segments. Where turnover on the destination basis is not disclosed, because the amount is not materially different from turnover on an origin basis, the fact that there is no material difference must be stated. In this context, the probability of origin and destination bases not being materially different is likely to be substantially influenced by the nature of the entity's operating activities. As an example, Johnson Group Cleaners PLC (see Table 9.8) is principally engaged in dry cleaning services and workwear and towel rental, operating nationwide in the UK and US. Identified business segments are dry cleaning and rental; while geographical markets are the UK and the US. The services the members of the group offer are not by nature exportable, so geographical markets are serviced by local operating units. In effect, therefore, the UK business segment sells into the UK and the US segment services the US. Accordingly, the financial statements note that *"...there is no material difference between turnover by origin and destination"*. On the other hand, where a company is structured with operations in a limited number of different countries, but these are export bases for servicing a large number of other locations, the origin and destination basis will be materially different and disclosure under both bases will be required.

Table 9.8 – Johnson Group Cleaners PLC – Annual Report – 31 December 1993

SEGMENTAL INFORMATION RESULTS (EXTRACT)

	1993 TURNOVER £000	1993 PROFIT £000	1992 TURNOVER £000	1992 PROFIT £000
GEOGRAPHICAL REGION				
United Kingdom	99,542	16,076	96,457	14,971
United States	65,623	2,871	54,376	2,572
Group	165,165	18,947	150,833	17,543
CLASS OF BUSINESS				
Drycleaning	120,036	8,873	109,839	8,818
Rental	45,129	10,074	40,994	8,725
Group	165,165	18,947	150,833	17,543
Profit on sales of property		77		(76)
Deficit on a property valuation		–		(689)
Profit before interest		19,024		16,778
Net interest payable		814		1,663
PROFIT ON ORDINARY ACTIVITIES BEFORE TAXATION		18,210		15,115

There is no material difference between turnover by origin and by destination.

	1993 £000	1992 £000
NET ASSETS		
GEOGRAPHICAL REGION		
United Kingdom	69,199	66,561
United States	22,064	21,521
Group	91,263	88,082
CLASS OF BUSINESS		
Drycleaning	61,481	60,576
Rental	29,782	27,506
Group	91,263	88,082
Unallocated net liabilities	(23,315)	(25,170)
Group share of net assets of associated undertakings	482	438
Net assets	68,430	63,350

9.90 Inter-segmental turnover is only required to be shown in the segmental disclosure of turnover by origin. It is not required to be disclosed by destination. In practice, where inter-segmental sales are not material in the context of the reporting entity as a whole, companies state that fact and avoid the need to provide further analysis. Pilkington plc adopt this approach in their 1994 financial statements (see Table 9.5 on page 20).

9.91 Disclosure of segmental analysis of turnover need not be given where it is not required by law. An example of this is the turnover of a banking company attributable to banking. The fact that such turnover has not been disclosed should be stated.

Segment result

9.92 The standard requires the financial statements to analyse the result by class of business and geographical segment. In this context, the result is defined as being before taxation, minority interests and extraordinary items. Normally, it will also be before accounting for interest. However, this will depend on the nature of the business. In effect, where the nature of the business is such that interest income and expense are central to the business, the segment result should be shown after interest. In the majority of companies, however, segments will be financed by a mixture of debt and equity. In such situations, interest earned or incurred will be the result of the company's overall financial policy rather than reflecting the result of individual segments. For this reason, segment result should normally be disclosed before interest, with interest shown separately. [SSAP 25 para 34].

9.93 Pilkington plc, as noted above, discloses operating profit or loss before exceptional items and investment income and interest. (See Table 9.5 on page 20.) Similarly, in Table 9.4 on page 18, Coats Viyella analyses operating profit before *"other items"* and interest.

9.94 As Table 9.9 demonstrates, British Aerospace provides an interesting set of segmental disclosures in that it provides segmental analysis by class of business on the two following bases:

- Profit/(loss) before interest and exceptional items.
- Profit/(loss) before tax on ordinary activities.

Table 9.9 – British Aerospace Public Limited Company – Annual Report – 31 December 1993

2 Segmental Analysis (extract)

Following the implementation of FRS3, the comparative figures for 1992 have been restated to include exceptional items (note 7).

	Sales		Profit/(loss) before interest	
	1993	1992	1993	1992
	£m	£m	**£m**	£m
Continuing operations				
Defence	**3,963**	4,003	**345**	352
Commercial aircraft	**1,580**	1,485	**(162)**	(337)
Motor vehicles	**4,301**	3,684	**56**	(49)
Property development	**166**	88	**(17)**	(2)
Other businesses and headquarters	**347**	332	**(13)**	(38)
	10,357	9,592	**209**	(74)
Discontinued operations				
Construction	**947**	792	**28**	14
	11,304	10,384	**237**	(60)
Less: intra-group				
Continuing operations	**(211)**	(181)	**–**	–
Discontinued operations	**(333)**	(226)	**–**	–
Exceptional items	**–**	–	**(288)**	(1,015)
	10,760	9,977	**(51)**	(1,075)

Sales include rental income from operating leases of £46 million (1992 £93 million).

Included within loss before interest of Other businesses and headquarters in 1992 is a charge of £36 million in respect of full provision against the carrying value of the Group's investment in DAF NV. The Group disposed of all its investment in DAF NV during 1993.

	Profit and loss before tax on ordinary activities		Assets employed	
	1993	1992	1993	1992
	£m	£m	£m	£m
Continuing operations				
Defence	**513**	533	**1,731**	1,416
Commercial aircraft	**(224)**	(410)	**(248)**	(133)
Motor vehicles	**(9)**	(115)	**1,389**	1,444
Property development	**(31)**	(26)	**152**	130
Other businesses and headquarters	**(12)**	(40)	**282**	428
	237	(58)	**3,306**	3,285
Discontinued operations				
Construction	**31**	23	**–**	181
Exceptional items	**(308)**	(1,015)	**–**	–
Unallocated interest and borrowings	**(197)**	(151)	**(1,575)**	(1,448)
	(237)	(1,201)	**1,731**	2,018

7 Exceptional Items

The **exceptional recourse provision** of £250 million represents an additional provision at net present value for the expected level of financial exposure arising over the lifetime of aircraft finance arranged by the Group or by third parties in respect of turboprop aircraft. A deferred tax asset of £30 million has been established in respect of this provision.

The **exceptional loss on sale or termination of operations** of £38 million arises in respect of the disposal of the Group's interest in Ballast Nedam.

The Ballast Nedam group of construction companies was disposed of on 30th December, 1993 for a cash consideration equivalent to £175 million. The proceeds net of disposal costs approximated to the net assets of the Ballast Nedam construction companies at the date of disposal. The disposal therefore had no impact upon shareholders' funds, however inclusion of £38 million of goodwill previously written off against capital reserves on acquisition has resulted in an accounting loss of £38 million being disclosed in the profit and loss account. There was no tax charge or credit arising in respect of this disposal.

Corporate Jets was disposed of with effect from 6th August, 1993. Completion accounts remain under discussion; no profit or loss has been recognised in these accounts in respect of this disposal.

The disposal of the Group's communications business in 1992 gave rise to a loss of £15 million. There was no tax charge or credit arising in respect of this disposal.

The **exceptional reorganisation provision** of £1,000 million in 1992 was in respect of the Group's Regional Aircraft activities. The provision was dealt with in the 1992 accounts as £830 million within provisions for liabilities and charges and £170 million within stocks. A deferred tax asset of £250 million was established in respect of these costs. In view of the long term nature of these liabilities, the provision was calculated on a net present value basis, and accordingly, an **interest charge** of £20 million has been included in 1993.

9.95 The standard suggests that in most cases the disclosure of results by segment should be based on the areas from which products or services are supplied (that is, the origin basis). As was indicated in paragraph 9.88, this is a practical measure. Indeed, it is probable that many companies would claim that providing a geographical analysis of profit on a destination basis would be seriously prejudicial to their on-going interests, as well as being very difficult to obtain.

Segment net assets

9.96 Companies that have to comply with the segmental reporting disclosure requirements of the standard must disclose the net assets of each business segment and geographical segment. In this context, the standard explains that in most cases net assets will be the non-interest bearing operating assets less the non-interest bearing operating liabilities. This is consistent with the standard's general emphasis on looking at operational performance. However, where segment result has been disclosed after accounting for interest, because investment policy is a principal business activity of the segment and, therefore, a fair measure of the segment's performance, the corresponding interest bearing operating assets and liabilities should be included in net assets.[SSAP 25 para 24].

9.97 The standard provides further guidance on the allocation of assets and liabilities to segments. It indicates that a segment's assets and liabilities may include not only assets and liabilities relating exclusively to that segment, but also an allocated portion of assets and liabilities that are shared by it with other segments. The standard also states that assets and liabilities that are shared by segments should be allocated to those segments on a reasonable basis.[SSAP 25 para 25].

9.98 The words *"reasonable basis"* are not further explained in the standard. However, the guidance on the allocation of common costs, which was discussed in paragraphs 9.68 to ? above, would seem equally relevant to the allocation of shared assets and liabilities. Accordingly, if the entity apportions such assets and liabilities for the purpose of internal reporting, it may be reasonable for such assets and liabilities to be similarly apportioned for external reporting purposes. If apportionment of such assets and liabilities would be misleading, however, it would seem sensible not to apportion them, but, instead, to show them separately. It would, however, be rare for an entity to be unable to find some reasonable basis for allocating shared assets and liabilities, and a preferable method of avoiding any possibility of the allocation being misleading would be to quantify the amount of such assets and liabilities and disclose the basis of allocation.

9.99 The standard also indicates that assets and liabilities that are not used in the operations of any segment should not be allocated to any segment. [SSAP 25 para 25]. These would be shown as a separate figure in reconciling the total of net assets to the balance sheet. Furthermore, operating assets of a segment should not normally include loans or advances to, or investments in, another segment, unless interest on them has been included in arriving at the results of the first segment.

9.100 Pilkington plc's 1994 financial statements include segmental information structured on an operating basis. As was indicated earlier, they depart from the literal requirements of the Act in this regard. For consistency, however, the segmental disclosures of net assets is given on an equivalent operating basis to that used in disclosing operating result. This means that not all of the assets employed by the group are included therein, so a helpful summarisation of net operating assets is provided in a separate note (see Table 9.5 on page 20).

9.101 The Mersey Docks And Harbour Company's approach in its 1993 financial statements, as set out in Table 9.10, was to provide business segment information both gross and net of intra-segment sales. It also provided segmental analysis of profit on ordinary activities before interest and taxation, indicating by this treatment that interest could not be attributed on a fair basis to individual business segments. In disclosing segmental information on net assets, it excluded interest bearing assets and liabilities, which were then shown separately in the note, effectively reconciling the segmental net assets to the balance sheet.

Table 9.10 – The Mersey Docks and Harbour Company – Annual Report & Accounts – 31 December 1993

notes to the accounts
for the year ended 31st December 1993

2. SEGMENTAL ANALYSIS BY CLASS OF BUSINESS

The analysis by class of business of the Group's turnover, profit before taxation and net assets is set out below:

TURNOVER

	1993			1992		
	Total sales	**Inter-segment sales**	**External sales**	Total sales	Inter-segment sales	External sales
	£000	**£000**	**£000**	£000	£000	£000
Port operations	**71,716**	**(3,685)**	**68,031**	64,867	(2,574)	62,293
Irish Sea subsidiaries	**25,112**	**(1,630)**	**23,482**	18,378	(1,621)	16,757
Property and property development	**2,674**	**(460)**	**2,214**	2,605	(500)	2,105
Non-port activities	**5,673**	**(980)**	**4,693**	6,189	(982)	5,207
	105,175	**(6,755)**	**98,420**	92,039	(5,677)	86,362

PROFIT ON ORDINARY ACTIVITIES BEFORE TAXATION

	1993	1992 as re-stated
	£000	£000
Port operations	**18,054**	12,496
Irish Sea subsidiaries	**1,321**	1,243
Property and property development	**1,698**	1,583
Non-port activities	**590**	287
	21,663	15,609
Net interest	**(798)**	(449)
	20,865	15,160

NET ASSETS/(LIABILITIES)		
Port operations	**124,739**	102,690
Irish Sea subsidiaries	**1,272**	597
Property and property development	**20,005**	20,316
Non-port activities	**(693)**	(344)
	145,323	123,259
Interest-bearing assets	**14,930**	9,478
Interest-bearing liabilities	**(10,092)**	(8,656)
	150,161	124,081

Turnover and profit are predominantly derived from U.K. operations.

Turnover and profit before taxation for Liverpool Conservancy were £2,922,000 (1992 £2,837,000) **and £8,000** (1992: loss £188,000) **respectively.**

Turnover for Liverpool Pilotage services was £3,859,000 (1992: £4,173,000). **The aggregate expenditure incurred in providing Liverpool Pilotage services was £3,827,000** (1992: £3,753,000).

9.102 In both of the above examples, the amount of net assets attributed to the identified segments is less than the sum of the total net assets in the balance sheet. However, the items excluded can be separately identified to facilitate a full reconciliation to the financial statements. This contrasts with the disclosure approach adopted by British Aerospace (see Table 9.9 on page 34) and Johnson Group Cleaners PLC (see Table 9.8 on page 32) in their 1993 financial statements. These companies analyse total net assets between segments and then deduct unallocated net liabilities in total to reconcile back to the net assets stated in the balance sheet. This is less helpful to the reader in understanding the real level of net assets used in individual segments, but probably cannot be avoided.

9.103 In disclosing the net assets employed by individual segments, most reporting entities base the disclosures on the balance sheet at the accounting reference date. The standard is silent on this matter and it is possible to base disclosure on the average position for the year. This may be particularly appropriate in the context of evaluating the return on capital employed, in instances where the year end position is materially different from the average position. This may occur in an industry of a seasonal nature, where the balance sheet date may coincide with either a trading peak or trough and where stock, debtor and creditor levels are reflective of that situation. BTR plc is one company that has made disclosure on the basis of average net assets (see Table 9.11).

Table 9.11 – BTR plc – Annual Report and Accounts – 31 December 1997

Notes (extract)

1 Analysis of sales, profit before tax and average operating net assets (extract)

Average operating net assets represent, in the opinion of the Directors, the best estimate of net asset utilisation by the Business Groups, and exclude taxation, dividends, net debt and provisions for liabilities and charges.

9.104 The segmental analysis of net assets will usually be based on the areas from which goods are supplied. This is a practical application, for in many instances the provision of such information on a destination basis would be difficult to obtain and its value dubious.

Associates and joint ventures

9.105 SSAP 25 and FRS 9 set out the segmental information to be disclosed in respect of associates and joint ventures. These requirements apply unless publication of such information would be prejudicial to the business of the associate or joint venture. Where disclosure is not made for this reason, the reason for non-disclosure should be stated in the notes, together with a brief description of the omitted business or businesses. SSAP 25 also allowed segmental information concerning associates or joint ventures not to be given, because the associate or joint venture was not prepared to provide it. But following the publication of FRS 9 and the increased emphasis on associates and joint ventures being able to exercise in practice significant influence or joint control (respectively), where such a problem exists this calls into question whether or not the entity should be treated as an associate or a joint venture (see further chapter 28).

9.105.1 FRS 9 introduced the 'gross equity' method of accounting for joint ventures which entails investors disclosing additionally their share of joint ventures' turnover and gross assets and liabilities. In addition, the standard requires that the share of the joint ventures' turnover should be included in the segmental analysis and should be clearly distinguished from the turnover of the group itself. [FRS 9 para 21]. Furthermore, an investor can if it so wishes disclose its share of its associates' turnover as a memorandum item in the profit and loss account where it considers that this is helpful in giving an indication of the group's size. But where this voluntary disclosure is made, the segmental analysis of turnover should, in addition, clearly distinguish between that of the group and that of associates. [FRS 9 para 27].

[The next paragraph is 9.106]

9.106 SSAP 25 also requires additional segmental information of results and net assets for associates and joint ventures but only where they form a significant part of a reporting entity's results or assets. In this regard, it notes that associates (including joint ventures) undertakings are considered significant if, in total, they account for at least 20 per cent of the total result or 20 per cent of the total net assets of the reporting entity. There is nothing in SSAP 25 or FRS 9 which suggests this threshold should be applied separately for associates and joint ventures (although the additional disclosures in FRS 9 apply on this basis) and so it appears that it can be applied in aggregate. But it appears that the required disclosures should separate joint ventures from associates, following the general requirement to do so in FRS 9, which is also implied in paragraphs 21 and 27 of FRS 9.

9.107 The information required in respect of associates and joint ventures is a segmental analysis of both of the following:

- The reporting entity's share of profits or losses of associates and joint ventures before accounting for taxation, minority interests and extraordinary items.

- The reporting entity's share of the net assets of associates and joint ventures (including goodwill to the extent that it has not been written off) stated, where possible, after attributing fair values to the net assets at the date of acquisition of the interest in each associate or joint venture.

[SSAP 25 para 26].

9.108 Following the introduction of FRS 9, the share of associates' and joint ventures' operating results, interest, super-exceptional items and taxation is required to be disclosed for each of those line items. Consequently, if the reporting group analyses its segment result before charging interest, for the reasons discussed in paragraphs 9.92 and 9.93, it will, following the introduction of FRS 9, now be able to disclose segment information for its associates and joint ventures on an equivalent basis.

9.109 Lonrho provides segmental analysis of associates by both business and geographical segment, in respect of the turnover (see Table 9.7 on page 9030), as well as profit before taxation and net non-interest bearing operating assets (see Table 9.12 on page 9041).

9.110 GEC also provides segmental analysis of its interests in joint ventures, as Table 9.13 on page 9043 indicates. Again the analysis is provided on both a business and geographical segment basis.

Joint arrangements

9.111 FRS 9 introduced a third category of investment namely, joint arrangements. This is a contractual arrangement under which the participants engage in joint activities that do not create an entity, because it would not be carrying on a trade or business of its own. [FRS 9 para 4]. FRS 9 requires that such arrangements should not be accounted for following the equity method of accounting, but participants should account for their own assets, liabilities and cash flows, measured according to the terms of the agreement governing the arrangement. Although SSAP 25 does not cover this type of entity, it seems appropriate that the amounts of the arrangement accounted for under FRS 9 should also be included within the segmental analysis. Joint arrangements are considered in more detail in chapter 28.

Table 9.12 – Lonrho Plc – Annual Report and Accounts – 30 September 1994

Notes to the Accounts (extract)

3. Profit on ordinary activities before taxation (extract)

	1994					
	Group	**Associates**	**Total**	Group *Restated*	Associates *Restated*	Total *Restated*
	£m	**£m**	**£m**	£m	£m	£m
Motor and equipment distribution	**20**		**20**	9		9
Mining and refining	**55**	**35**	**90**	41	30	71
Manufacturing	**(6)**	**1**	**(5)**	3	1	4
Hotels	**27**	**1**	**28**	20	(1)	19
General trade	**21**		**21**	32	1	33
Agriculture	**32**	**2**	**34**	20	(2)	18
Discontinued operations				6	6	12
	149	**39**	**188**	131	35	166
Central costs	**(23)**		**(23)**	(25)		(25)
	126	**39**	**165**	106	35	141
Exceptional items (note 7)			**4**			96
Net interest payable			**(57)**			(72)
Profit before taxation			**112**			165
United Kingdom	**18**		**18**	11		11
East, Central and West Africa	**58**	**37**	**95**	58	31	89
Southern Africa	**56**	**1**	**57**	45	2	47
The Americas	**11**	**1**	**12**	5	(4)	1
Europe and Other	**6**		**6**	6		6
Discontinued operations				6	6	12
	149	**39**	**188**	131	35	166
Central costs	**(23)**		**(23)**	(25)		(25)
	126	**39**	**165**	106	35	141
Exceptional items (note 7)			**4**			96
Net interest payable			**(57)**			(72)
Profit before taxation			112			165

The 1993 comparative figures have been restated to reflect the changes of accounting policy as described on page 34 of the Report of the Directors.

26 Net non-interest bearing operating assets

An analysis of Group net non-interest bearing operating assets and of associates' net assets by activity and geographical area is given below:-

	1994			1993		
	Group	**Associates**	**Total**	Group *Restated*	Associates *Restated*	Total *Restated*
	£m	**£m**	**£m**	£m	£m	£m
Motor and equipment distribution	**128**	**2**	**130**	118	1	119
Mining and refining	**590**	**133**	**723**	617	104	721
Manufacturing	**91**	**1**	**92**	132	1	133
Hotels	**603**	**13**	**616**	616	12	628
General trade	**107**	**6**	**113**	98	8	106
Agriculture	**164**	**5**	**169**	171	7	178
Central finance	**49**		**49**	56		56
	1,732	**160**	**1,892**	1,808	133	1,941
Net interest bearing liabilities			**(467)**			(484)
Proposed dividend and ACT			**(41)**			(35)
Net total assets			**1,384**			1,422
United Kingdom	**402**		**402**	392		392
East, Central and West Africa	**272**	**136**	**408**	314	112	426
Southern Africa	**628**	**2**	**630**	658	1	659
The Americas	**301**	**21**	**322**	317	19	336
Europe and Other	**80**	**1**	**81**	71	1	72
Central finance	**49**		**49**	56		56
	1,732	**160**	**1,892**	1,808	133	1,941
Net interest bearing liabilities			**(467)**			(484)
Proposed dividend and ACT			**(41)**			(35)
Net total assets			**1,384**			1,422

The 1993 comparative figures have been restated to reflect the changes of accounting policy as described on page 34 of the Report of the Directors. The effect of the change is to increase 1994 net non-interest bearing operating assets by £53m (1993 – £51m).

The format of the above note has been changed in order to disclose separately central finance net non-interest bearing operating assets.

Due to the reduction in significance of the contribution from financial services this activity is now included in general trade whereas it was previously separately disclosed.

Table 9.13 – The General Electric Company p.l.c. – Annual Report and Accounts – 31 March 1994

Notes to the Accounts (extract)

10. FIXED ASSET INVESTMENTS – OTHER (extract)

Information in respect of the Group interest in joint venture associated companies included in note 1 is as follows:

	Profit		**Turnover**		Net assets at 31st March	
	1994 £ million	1993 £ million	**1994 £ million**	1993 £ million	**1994 £ million**	1993 £ million
By classes of business						
Electronic Systems	**17**	16	**306**	289	**(8)**	(9)
Power Systems	**159**	165	**3,030**	3,014	**(591)**	(85)
Telecommunications	**–**	–	**157**	130	**65**	65
Consumer Goods	**17**	16	**259**	253	**59**	57
	193	197	**3,752**	3,686	**(475)**	28
Interest bearing assets and liabilities	**72**	56			**1,410**	921
Unallocated net liabilities					**(71)**	(104)
	265	253	**3,752**	3,686	**864**	845
By territory of origin						
United Kingdom	**72**	76	**1,093**	971	**(190)**	75
France	**93**	83	**1,801**	1,867	**(194)**	(120)
Rest of Europe	**27**	32	**508**	548	**(159)**	(7)
The Americas		3	**286**	236	**51**	60
Australasia	**–**	1	**38**	39	**3**	4
Asia	**–**	–	**26**	25	**5**	7
Africa	**–**		**–**	–	**9**	9
	1	2				
	193	197	**3,752**	3,686	**(475)**	28

Reconciliation of figures

9.112 The standard requires the reporting entity to provide a reconciliation where the total of the amounts disclosed by segment does not agree with the related total in the financial statements. In this situation, the difference between the two figures should be identified and explained. [SSAP 25 para 28]. The issue of reconciling segmental net assets to total reported net assets has been discussed in paragraphs 9.96 to 9.104. Table 9.14 shows a helpful example of a company, namely The Rank Organisation, reconciling the major areas of segmental disclosures to the figures reported in its primary statements.

Table 9.14 – The Rank Organisation Plc – Directors' Report and Accounts – 31 October 1994

Notes to the Accounts (extract)

1 SEGMENTAL INFORMATION

Analysis by division

	Turnover		Profit before tax		Year end net assets		Net cash flow	
	1994 £m	1993 £m	**1994 £m**	1993 £m	**1994 £m**	1993 £m	**1994 £m**	1993 £m
Film and Television	**680.1**	571.7	**66.9**	49.4	**335.1**	357.1	**78.1**	29.2
Holidays	**459.9**	424.5	**57.0**	52.0	**485.6**	462.1	**39.5**	47.3
Recreation	**729.5**	692.1	**69.0**	64.0	**511.4**	493.5	**51.4**	54.7
Leisure	**281.7**	269.4	**47.7**	49.1	**334.7**	313.8	**3.5**	13.0
Other	**17.9**	17.1	**(10.8)**	(6.8)	**9.6**	8.6	**(13.2)**	(6.3)
Continuing operations	**2,169.1**	1,974.8	**229.8**	207.7	**1,676.4**	1,635.1	**159.3**	137.9
Discontinued operations	**30.3**	132.0	**(2.8)**	(7.3)	**31.7**	122.1	**58.8**	101.9
	2,199.4	2,106.8	**227.0**	200.4	**1,708.1**	1,757.2	**218.1**	239.8
Share of associated undertakings:								
Rank Xerox			**151.5**	151.2	**606.9**	586.5	**61.5**	72.1
Universal Studios Florida			**11.4**	13.0	**171.1**	199.9	**22.7**	24.4
Other			**(0.3)**	(1.5)	**31.8**	26.4	**(6.7)**	(19.7)
			162.6	162.7	**809.8**	812.8	**77.5**	76.8
			389.6	363.1	**2,517.9**	2,570.0	**295.6**	316.6
Non-operating items			**(30.6)**	2.0				
Interest			**(75.0)**	(88.5)			**(85.1)**	(57.3)
Profit before tax			**284.0**	276.6				
Tax and dividends					**(102.3)**	(17.0)	**(83.0)**	(135.1)
Other non-operating liabilities (net)					**(50.0)**	(64.9)		
Net borrowings					**(759.0)**	(955.3)		
					1,606.6	1,532.8	**127.5**	124.2

Comparative figures

9.113 The standard requires the provision of comparatives figures unless it is the first occasion on which an entity produces a segmental report. In that situation, if the necessary information to produce comparative figures is not readily available, then they need not be provided. [SSAP 25 para 29].

Other disclosure requirements

9.114 Since SSAP 25's publication in 1990, the intervening period has been marked by a notable increase in standard setting by the ASB. Although none of these standards and pronouncements relate specifically to segmental reporting, some of them have an impact upon the nature of segmental disclosures in financial statements. A number of these instances are considered below.

Cash flow statements

9.115 FRS 1, 'Cash flow statements', revised in 1996, encourages, but does not require, entities to provide segmental breakdown of cash flows. [FRS 1 para 8]. While segmental cash flow information might be useful to readers of financial statements, by helping them to understand the relationship between the cash flows of the reporting entity as a whole and those of its constituent segments, the FRS is silent on how segmental cash flow information might be given. This contrasts with the position in the earlier exposure draft, ED 54, 'Cash flow statements', which proposed that, as a minimum, an enterprise should give an analysis of the most important elements of operating cash flows between the major reportable segments. An example of a company giving a segmental breakdown of its operating cash flows is shown in chapter 30.

[The next paragraph is 9.118.]

9.118 The UK situation remains one of non-mandatory disclosure of segmental cash flow analysis. Furthermore, voluntary application by reporting entities may prove complex and expensive to them in terms of information gathering, on-going monitoring and determining appropriate allocation methods for such items as common costs and interest. Consequently, it is hardly surprising that most companies have shied away from the issue. It is unlikely, therefore, that there will be any notable increase in the number of reporting entities that present segmental cash flow information, unless it becomes mandatory. At present this does not seem likely.

9.119 However, the point was discussed in the ASB's 1993 statement, the 'Operating and financial review' (OFR). Best described as a statement of perceived best practice, directed primarily towards listed companies, the OFR does not have accounting standard status, nor is compliance with it mandatory. The ASB views it, however, as being an integral part of the annual report, despite its being outside of the financial statements and unaudited. The OFR recommends discussion of the reporting entity's cash flows, specifically commenting that:

> *"Although segmental analysis of profit may be indicative of the cash flow generated by each segment, this will not always be so – for example, because of fluctuations in capital expenditure. Where segmental cash flows are significantly out of line with segmental profits, this should be indicated and explained."*

9.120 There are few existing examples of reporting entities providing segmental analysis of cash flows. While Pearson discloses operating cash flows for each of its main business lines (newspapers, books, television and visitor attractions) in its OFR, it does not provide segmental cash flow analysis in the main body of the audited financial statements. Rank Organisation, which provides a segmental analysis of cash flow, appears to be the exception rather than the rule (see Table 9.14 on page 45).

9.121 One situation where segmental reporting of cash flows has been disclosed is where consolidated financial statements include subsidiary undertakings with a wide variety of activities. The extracts from B.A.T. Industries plc financial statements, set out in Table 9.15, provide an illustration of this.

Table 9.15 – B.A.T Industries p.l.c. – Directors' Report and Accounts – 31 December 1993

Accounting Policies

1 The Group accounts have been prepared in accordance with applicable accounting standards and combine the accounts of Group undertakings at 31 December. As permitted by the Companies Act 1985 the accounts formats have been adapted, as necessary, to give a true and fair view of the state of affairs and profit of the commercial activities of the Group and to present the insurance activities in accordance with the provisions of that Act applicable to insurance companies. The accounts are on an historical cost basis as modified to include certain insurance assets at market value.

The accounts formats have been developed to reflect more appropriately the operations of the Group. All the assets and liabilities of the Group's businesses are included in the consolidated balance sheet. To equity account for either tobacco or financial services would not give a true and fair view of the total Group. However, given the differences between the two main businesses of the Group and the constraints of the regulatory environment within which insurance companies operate, the assets and liabilities are shown separately under headings covering commercial and corporate activities, financial services general business and financial service life business. This approach has been reflected in preparing separate cash flow statements for the three businesses as the regulatory environment in insurance limits the availability of cash flows between businesses. The Directors are of the opinion that this approach, where it differs from the Companies Act 1985 and applicable accounting standards as described further in the Directors' Report on page 1, is necessary to present a true and fair view of the Group.

Group Cash Flow Statements
for the year ended 31 December

COMMERCIAL AND CORPORATE ACTIVITIES	NOTES		**1993 £m**	1992 £m
Net cash inflows from commercial operating activities	13		**977**	1,165
Dividends from – financial services subsidiary undertakings				
– general			**114**	137
– life			**119**	114
– associates			**59**	44
Net cash inflows from operating activities	13		**1,269**	1,460
Investment income		**113**		129
Interest paid		**(226)**		(239)
Dividends to B.A.T. Industries' shareholders		**(276)**		(528)
Dividends to minorities		**(46)**		(30)
Net cash outflows from returns on investments and servicing of finance			**(435)**	(668)
Taxation paid			**(288)**	(396)
Capital expenditure		**(338)**		(278)
Sale of fixed assets		**16**		26
Purchase of other investments	14	**(21)**		(8)
Sale of other investments	14	**42**		59
Subsidiary and associated undertakings				
– purchases	14	**(8)**		(42)
– sales	14			26
Investment in Farmers' insurance exchanges				(128)
Net cash outflows from investing activities			**(309)**	(345)
Other cash outflows with financial services activities	15		**(15)**	(342)
Net cash inflow/(outflow) before external financing (from above items)			**222**	(291)
Proceeds from issue of shares		**5**		5
Commercial paper		**(1,296)**		76
Bank and other loans		**(38)**		58
Medium term debt issues		**727**		286
Eurobond issues		**595**		
Net cash (outflows)/inflows financing activities	16		**(7)**	425
Increase in cash and cash equivalents	16		**215**	134

Certain comparative figures have been restated as explained in accounting policy 1 on page 8 and details of these changes are given in the individual notes to which they relate.

FINANCIAL SERVICES	Notes	GENERAL 1993 £m	GENERAL 1992 £m	LIFE 1993 £m	LIFE 1992 £m
Net cash inflows from operating activities excluding investment gains	17	**558**	330	**495**	337
Dividend to – Group companies		**(114)**	(137)	**(119)**	(114)
– minority shareholders		**(2)**	(2)		
Interest paid		**(49)**	(28)		
Net cash outflows from servicing of finance		**(165)**	(167)	**(119)**	(114)
Taxation paid		**(193)**	(56)		
Sale of investments		**2,886**	1,494	**667**	362
Less: purchase of investments		**(3,090)**	(1,884)	**(1,088)**	(567)
Sale proceeds less reinvestments	19	**(204)**	(390)	**(421)**	(205)
Capital expenditure		**(51)**	(42)	**(21)**	(21)
Sale of fixed assets		**7**	2	**9**	7
Proceeds on sale at subsidiary undertakings	18		119	**17**	
Investment in life fund					(102)
Investment in Farmers' insurance exchanges					(100)
Net cash outflows from investing activities		**(248)**	(311)	**(416)**	(421)
Other cash flows with the life funds			18		
Other cash flows between Group businesses	15	**(24)**	176	**39**	166
Other cash flows with commercial activities and financial services businesses		**(24)**	194	**39**	166
Net cash outflows before external financing (from above items)		**(72)**	(10)	**(1)**	(32)
Borrowings		**3**	59		
Issue of shares				**1**	4
Net cash inflows from financing activities	19	**3**	59	**1**	4
(Decrease)/increase in cash and cash equivalents	16,19	**(69)**	49		(28)

The life business cash flows above exclude flows of the Allied Dunbar and Eagle Star life funds.

9.122 Cash flow statements are considered in more detail in chapter 30.

Subsidiary undertakings

9.123 FRS 2, 'Accounting for subsidiary undertakings', issued in 1992, indicates that parent undertakings should consider how best to provide segmental information for their group. It suggests that the ensuing disclosures should indicate the different risks and rewards, growth and prospects of the different parts of the group. In this regard, the requirements of SSAP 25 should been seen as the minimum disclosure level, rather than as the maximum. [FRS 2 para 94].

9.124 Although FRS 2 recognises the importance of segmental reporting in consolidated financial statements, it does not introduce any specific new requirements. However, it does suggest two situations where segmental information could supplement consolidated financial statements, namely:

- In respect of subsidiary undertakings whose activities are so dissimilar to those of the rest of the group that full consolidation would be inappropriate.
- In respect of disclosures relating to minority interests.

[FRS 2 para 94].

9.125 In considering the preferred accounting treatment for subsidiary undertakings that have dissimilar activities from their group as a whole, FRS 2 emphasises the importance of the completeness of the information presented in the consolidated financial statements. It recognises that such subsidiary undertakings are controlled by the parent and contribute to the overall wealth and performance of the group. Accordingly, the exclusion from consolidation of such entities would not normally be justifiable, unless inclusion would be incompatible with the obligation to give a true and fair view. In this context, the standard specifically considers the contrast between Schedule 9 companies (banking and insurance companies and groups) and other companies and states that of itself this contrast is not sufficient to justify non-consolidation. The standard also states that the contrast between profit and not-for-profit undertakings is also insufficient to justify non-consolidation.

9.126 In view of the above, instances where full consolidation of a subsidiary undertaking would not be appropriate will be extremely rare. However, when they do occur, it seems that, by virtue of its being so dissimilar to the rest of its group, the unconsolidated subsidiary must constitute a separate, reportable segment, subject only to the question of its materiality. Furthermore, when full consolidation is inappropriate, the standard indicates that the equity method of accounting should be employed. In this situation, disclosure would be necessary to explain the treatment adopted and to indicate the key financial information of the segment in question. For example, the turnover, results and net assets of the subsidiary with such dissimilar activities from its group would need to be explained segmentally. [FRS 2 para 94(a)].

9.127 FRS 2 also suggests that users of consolidated financial statements may wish to assess the effect of the existence of minority interests in certain parts of the group, on the expected returns to investors in the parent. Consequently, it may be helpful to present information setting out the amounts attributable to the minority interest in different segments. To date, however, this has not proved to be an area where reporting groups have considered segmental disclosures to be of prime importance.

Acquisitions and discontinued operations

9.128 FRS 3, 'Reporting financial performance', issued in 1992, comments that an appreciation of the impact of changes on material components of the business is essential, if a reader is to obtain a thorough understanding of the results and financial position of a reporting entity. In this regard, the standard states that *"...if an acquisition, a sale or a termination has a material impact on a major business segment ... this impact should be disclosed and explained"*. [FRS 3 para 53]. To promote this understanding, FRS 3 requires reporting entities to analyse and disclose turnover, operating profit and exceptional items, as set out in the profit and loss account, between continuing and discontinued operations.

9.129 In making this distinction between continuing and discontinued operations, the standard requires that, for a component of a reporting entity's operations to be reported as discontinued, its *"...assets, liabilities, results of operations and activities of an operation must be clearly distinguishable, physically, operationally and for financial reporting purposes"*. In addition, *"...a sale or termination should have resulted from a strategic decision by the reporting entity either to withdraw from a particular market (whether class of business or geographical) or to curtail materially its presence in a continuing market (i.e. 'downsizing')"*. [FRS 3 paras 43, 44].

9.130 Since FRS 3 requires detailed analyses of aggregate financial information, it is important to understand its relationship with SSAP 25. In this regard, for a business to be analysed and disclosed as discontinued in accordance with FRS 3, it does not necessarily have to constitute a complete business segment for the purposes of SSAP 25. This is because the definition of discontinued operations also includes a material reduction in operating facilities resulting from a material reduction in turnover in the entity's continuing markets. In effect, therefore, what constitutes a discontinued operation for FRS 3 purposes may only be part of a segment for SSAP 25 reporting purposes.

9.131 An example of the above distinction between FRS 3 and SSAP 25 could be in the case of a group with three equally-sized subsidiaries, all operating in the field of car leasing, but in different geographical markets. The sale of one of the subsidiaries would not be the disposal of the whole car leasing segment as defined for the purposes of SSAP 25. However, it would constitute a discontinued operation for the purposes of FRS 3, because it is a material reduction in operating facilities and results from a material reduction in turnover in the group's continuing markets. In addition, the assets, liabilities, results and activities can be distinguished physically, operationally and for financial reporting purposes. The nature of the operations is not different, but that is not a test that has to be satisfied under FRS 3 in order for the disposal of the subsidiary to qualify as a discontinued operation.

9.132 In practice, some entities, that have transacted material sales or terminations, have disclosed the impact of these in their financial statements by analysing continuing and discontinued operations by segment. Pilkington plc adopts this approach, providing detailed business segment and geographical segment analysis for both categories. Even its additional note analysing net operating assets by balance sheet category is disclosed on a continuing and discontinued basis (see Table 9.5 on page 20).

9.133 Although some companies have disclosed discontinued operations for both business class and geographical segment, others have limited the disclosures made to business class. Grand Metropolitan provides segmental information on this basis. However, this may occur because, as the notes explain, the discontinued operations all relate to the UK (see Table 9.16).

Table 9.16 – Grand Metropolitan Public Limited Company – Annual Report – 30 September 1994

Notes (extract)

2 SEGMENT ANALYSIS

	1994			*1993*		
Class of business:	Turnover £m	Profit £m	Net assets £m	*Turnover £m*	*Profit £m*	*Net assets £m*
Continuing operations						
Food – branded	3,267	267	2,007	*3,066*	*227*	*2,226*
– retailing	1,104	230	1,353	*1,153*	*175*	*1,378*
Drinks	3,371	520	1,657	*3,418*	*563*	*1,856*
	7,742	1,017	5,017	*7,637*	*965*	*5,460*
Discontinued operations	38	6	–	*483*	*77*	*658*
	7,780		5,017	*8,120*		*6,118*
Operating profit before exceptional items		1,023			*1,042*	
Associates before exceptional items		45	729		*24*	*620*
Exceptional items		(291)			*(286)*	
Interest		(123)			*(155)*	
Profit before taxation		654			*625*	
Capital employed			5,746			*6,738*
Net borrowings			(2,159)			*(3,025)*
Net assets			3,587			*3,713*

Geographical area by country of operation

United Kingdom	815	101	339	*1,245*	*173*	*975*
Rest of Europe	1,613	180	627	*1,648*	*210*	*685*
United States of America	4,644	677	3,714	*4,499*	*582*	*4,140*
Rest of North America	173	26	116	*214*	*26*	*151*
Africa and Middle East	183	15	32	*182*	*15*	*31*
Rest of World	352	24	189	*332*	*36*	*136*
	7,780		5,017	*8,120*		*6,118*
Operating profit before exceptional items		1,023			*1,042*	
Associates before exceptional items		45	729		*24*	*620*
Exceptional items		(291)			*(286)*	
Interest		(123)			*(155)*	
Profit before taxation		654			*625*	
Capital employed			5,746			*6,738*
Net borrowings			(2,159)			*(3,025)*
Net assets			3,587			*3,713*

Profit before interest relates to the following activities and geographical areas: Food – branded £214m, Food – retailing £183m, Drinks £351m, and discounted businesses £29m (1993 – £184m, £85m, £560m, and £23m respectively, and a £50m charge in respect of a writedown of the group's UK properties); United Kingdom £71m, Rest of Europe £81m, United States of America £556m, Rest of World £69m (1993 – £117m, £136m, £458m and £91m respectively).

The group interest expense is arranged centrally and is not attributable to individual activities or geographical areas. The analysis of capital employed by activity and geographical area is calculated on net assets excluding associates, cash and borrowings.

Turnover between the above classes of business is not material.

Following the disposal of The Chef & Brewer Group, Burger King and Pearle are now disclosed as a separate segment of the Food sector and the loans to IEL are included in associates. Discontinued operations comprise The Chef & Brewer Group and, in the prior period, Express Foods; both businesses operated almost exclusively in the United Kingdom. On 19th September 1994, the group announced the sale, subject to regulatory approval, of ALPO Petfoods; the sale was not completed by 1st December 1994 and ALPO Petfoods has been classified as a continuing operation in these accounts.

The weighted average exchange rate used in translation of US dollar profit and loss accounts was £1 = $1.51 (1993 – £1 = $1.52). The exchange rate used to translate US dollar assets and liabilities at the balance sheet date was £1 = $1.58 (1993 – £1 = $1.50).

3 TURNOVER		1994				1993
	Continuing £m	Discontinued £m	Total £m	*Continuing £m*	*Discontinued £m*	*Total £m*
Geographical area by destination:						
United Kingdom	741	38	779	*724*	*483*	*1,207*
Rest of Europe	1,610	–	1,610	*1,641*	–	*1,641*
United States of America	4,546	–	4,546	*4,389*	–	*4,389*
Rest of North America	219	–	219	*239*	–	*239*
Africa and Middle East	210	–	210	*221*	–	*221*
Rest of World	416	–	416	*423*	–	*423*
	7,742	38	7,780	*7,637*	*483*	*8,120*

Exports from the United Kingdom were £297m (1993 – £298m).

9.134 Although FRS 3 does not define a business segment, best practice would seem to be to disclose the effect of acquisitions and discontinued activities on both a business class and geographical location basis by segment. In the case of the geographical disclosures, these would be made on both a source and a destination basis. Comparative information would also be provided.

9.135 FRS 3 also requires that the results of acquisitions, excluding those that are also discontinued in the period, should be disclosed separately in aggregate as a component of continuing operations. As with the other continuing operations the minimum analysis given on the face of the profit and loss account should be turnover and operating profit. The analysis of each of the other profit and loss account headings between turnover and operating profit may be given in a note, instead of on the face of the profit and loss account.

9.136 In practice, some companies have disclosed separate, detailed segmental information in respect of acquisitions. For example, Coats Viyella's 1993 financial statements provide analyses of the turnover, operating profit and net assets of its acquisitions, by both product category and geographical location (see Table 9.4 on page 18).

9.137 Other companies have disclosed the effect of acquisitions in such a way that the effect cannot be separately identified for each segment. In Table 9.17, Pilkington, for example, discloses the turnover and operating profit of acquisitions on the face of the profit and loss account, as well as more detailed analyses in notes 7 and 31. However, it does not analyse acquisitions within the segmental product and geographical analyses. Nonetheless, given the disclosure elsewhere in the financial statements, including the directors' report, the reader should be able to assimilate this information.

Table 9.17 – Pilkington plc – Directors' Report and Accounts – 31 March 1994

Notes to the accounts (extract)

7 Statutory Information	1994 Continuing £m	1994 Acquisitions £m	1994 Discontinued £m	1994 Total £m	1993 Continuing £m	1993 Discontinued £m	1993 Total £m
Turnover	**2344.40**	**170.70**	**222.30**	**2737.40**	2300.50	272.00	2572.50
Cost of sales	**(1814.40)**	**(161.70)**	**(169.50)**	**(2145.60)**	(1808.60)	(204.90)	(2013.50)
Gross profit	**530.00**	**9.00**	**52.80**	**591.80**	491.90	67.10	559.00
Net operating expenses							
Distribution costs	**(228.70)**	**(1.30)**	**(16.20)**	**(246.20)**	(219.50)	(20.50)	(240.00)
Administrative expenses	**(235.50)**	**(1.40)**	**(23.60)**	**(260.50)**	(213.40)	(35.10)	(248.50)
Trading profit	**65.80**	**6.30**	**13.00**	**85.10**	59.00	11.50	70.50
Group licensing income	**19.10**	–	–	**19.10**	17.50	–	17.50
Operating profit	**84.90**	**6.30**	**13.00**	**104.20**	76.50	11.50	88.00

31 Acquisitions and Disposals	Acquisitions 1994 £m	Acquisitions 1993 £m	Disposals 1994 £m	Disposals 1993 £m
Net assets of subsidiary undertakings comprised:				
Fixed tangible assets	**(30.0)**	(20.0)	**53.7**	2.5
Investments	**(0.6)**	–	**0.3**	1.4
Stocks	**(11.3)**	(11.3)	**74.6**	1.0
Debtors	**(38.8)**	(7.1)	**54.9**	3.8
Marketable investments	–	–	–	0.4
Loans and finance leases	**9.6**	17.2	**(8.0)**	–
Creditors and provisions	**39.1**	14.6	**(48.8)**	(4.9)
Minority interests	**2.1**	(3.7)	**7.3**	–
	(29.9)	(10.3)	**134.0**	4.2
Costs incurred on disposals	–	–	**5.7**	–
Provision for costs	–	–	**11.5**	–
Goodwill	**(67.9)**	(13.1)	**18.3**	–
Profit on disposal	–	–	**30.8**	5.2
	(97.80)	(23.40)	**200.30**	9.40
Satisfied by – cash	**(97.8)**	(22.7)	**200.3**	9.4
– transfer from other investments	–	(0.7)	–	–
	(97.80)	(23.40)	**200.30**	9.40

The principal acquisition was the United Kingdom glass processing and merchanting businesses of Heywood Williams Group PLC.

The principal disposal was the Sola spectacle lens business.

Exceptional items

9.138 FRS 3 also revised the guidance on exceptional and extraordinary items that had been in force since the publication of SSAP 6, 'Extraordinary items and prior year adjustments'. In so doing, it identified exceptional items as *"...material items which derive from events or transactions that fall within the ordinary activities of the reporting entity and which individually or, if of a similar type, in aggregate, need to be disclosed by virtue of their size or incidence if the financial statements are to give a true and fair view"*. Key to the revision was the re-definition of ordinary activities to the effect that they included all those activities or events that SSAP 6 would have determined to have been extraordinary. In view of this, the general consensus seems to be that the extraordinary item is now virtually extinct.

9.139 As a result of the above changes, a far greater number of exceptional items are being reported within financial statements than was previously the case. This increase reflects the need for reporting entities to explain the nature and financial effect of any material transactions of an infrequent nature which have affected the results. These exceptional items also need to be integrated within the segmental analysis sections of the financial statements.

9.140 FRS 3 does not give specific guidance on the effect of the *"exceptional"* items on segmental reporting, other than by stating that the effect of such items on segment results should be disclosed where material. We consider that the effect can be shown in one of several ways:

- Analyse 'profits after exceptional but before interest', and then disclose the effect of the exceptionals in narrative form.
- Analyse operating profit (that is before super-exceptionals) and then show these exceptionals as one figure in the reconciliation to profit before tax, again with narrative explanation of their effect on individual segments.
- Analyse operating profit by segment and then give a separate column analysing the super-exceptionals by segment.

9.141 The important point is that the segmental analyses published must provide sufficient disclosure to enable the reader to understand the impact of exceptional items on business and geographical segments.

9.142 Practical examples of companies providing segmental information in respect of exceptional items include Trafalgar House, which, in addition to a detailed analysis of exceptional items in the notes to the financial statements, sets out a business segment analysis of their effect on operating (loss)/profit (see Table 9.18).

Table 9.18 – Trafalgar House Public Limited Company – Report and Accounts – 30 September 1994

Notes to the Accounts

3 Analysis by geographical area and class of business

Exceptional items charged to operating (loss)/profit analysed by class of business:

	Rationalis-ation costs 1994 £m	Rationalis-ation costs* 1993 £m	**Asset write downs and other items 1994 £m**	Asset write downs 1993 £m	**Total 1994 £m**	Total restated 1993 £m
		(restated)		(restated)		(restated)
Engineering	**(21.8)**	(45.8)	**(15.2)**	(21.1)	**(37.0)**	(66.9)
Construction	**(1.5)**	(10.1)	–	(6.2)	**(1.5)**	(16.3)
Residential Property	**(0.4)**	(6.3)	**5.7**	(17.4)	**5.3**	(23.7)
Commercial Property	**(0.7)**	(2.9)	**(6.6)**	(129.2)	**(7.3)**	(132.1)
Hotels	–	–	**1.9**	(12.5)	**1.9**	(12.5)
Shipping	–	(1.5)	–	(15.5)	–	(17.0)
Other activities	–	–	–	(57.2)	–	(57.2)
	(24.4)	(66.6)	**(14.2)**	(259.1)	**(38.6)**	(325.7)

* 1993 rationalisation costs include directors' compensation of £1.3 million.

9.143 AMEC p.l.c. analyses profit or loss by business and geographical segment gross of exceptional items, showing the gross amount of exceptional items as an aggregate one-line deduction. However, in a note analysing exceptional items, it provides various analyses including by class of business and by geographical area (see Table 9.19).

Table 9.19 – AMEC p.l.c. – Annual Report and Accounts – 31 December 1993

Notes to the accounts (extract)

2 Analysis by class of business and geographical origin

	Turnover 1993 £million	Turnover 1992 £million	Profit (loss) 1993 £million	Profit (loss) 1992 £million	Assets employed 1993 £million	Assets employed 1992 £million
By class of business						
Building and civil engineering	704.8	674.7	9.6	22.7	30.4	11.0
Mechanical and electrical engineering	1,361.1	1,361.9	22.8	18.0	62.7	83.9
Housing and development	138.1	109.1	(7.6)	(17.1)	150.0	176.2
	2,204.0	2,145.7	24.8	23.6	243.1	271.1
Internal trading	(19.8)	(24.0)	–	–	–	–
Exceptional items (note 7)	–	–	–	(114.6)	–	–
Loss on disposals of operations	–	–	(2.2)	–	–	–
Net interest	–	–	(1.6)	2.8	–	
Unallocated net liabilities	–	–	–	–	(2.7)	(28.9)
	2,184.2	2,121.7	21.0	(88.2)	240.4	242.2
By geographical origin						
United Kingdom	1,751.4	1,838.4	28.0	37.3	196.0	220.8
Europe	201.4	106.0	3.7	3.2	24.2	17.8
Americas	132.0	117.6	(6.1)	(2.6)	21.6	31.3
Middle East Asia and Australasia	119.2	83.7	(0.8)	(14.3)	1.3	1.2
	2,204.0	2,145.7	24.8	23.6	243.1	271.1
Internal trading	(19.8)	(24.0)	–	–	–	–
Exceptional items (note 7)	–	–	–	(114.6)	–	–
Loss on disposal of operations	–	–	(2.2)	–	–	–
Net interest	–	–	(1.6)	2.8	–	–
Unallocated net liabilities	–	–	–	–	(2.7)	(28.9)
	2,184.2	2,121.7	21.0	(88.2)	240.4	242.2

FRS 3 has been adopted in preparing the consolidated profit and loss account.

Certain businesses have been disposed of or terminated during the year none of which falls within the materiality definition of discontinued operations.

The results of businesses acquired during the year have not had a significant impact on the profit for the year.

Accordingly information disclosed in the consolidated profit and loss account includes the results of business disposals and acquisitions during the year.

The analysis of turnover by geographical market is not materially different from that by geographical origin.

7 Exceptional items

There were no exceptional items in 1993

	1992 £million
Exceptional items in 1992 are made up as follows	
Housing and development – write down of value of land and work in progress	63.0
Construction – Trafalgar Place Brighton – contract loss	15.9
Losses relating to investment in Power Corporation Plc	18.0
Closure and reorganisation costs	17.7
	114.6
Analysis by statutory profit and loss account format heading	
Cost of sales	85.1
Administrative expenses	11.5
Share of results of associated undertakings	18.0
	114.6
Analysis by class of business	
Building and civil engineering	20.7
Mechanical and electrical engineering	12.7
Housing and development	81.2
	114.6
Analysis by geographical area	
United Kingdom	88.3
Rest of Europe	20.0
Americas	0.8
Middle East, Asia and Australasia	5.5
	114.6

9.144 Lucas Industries plc's 1994 financial statements provide an interesting illustration of disclosure in that the prejudicial override exemption is claimed and applied in respect of analysis of certain restructuring and claims provisions. This happens to be the most material exceptional item in the financial statements. It remains to be seen whether many companies will adopt a similar approach to segmental disclosure of exceptional provisions (see Table 9.20).

Table 9.20 – Lucas Industries plc – Annual Report and Accounts – 31 July 1994

Consolidated profit and loss account (extract)

For the year ended 31 July

	Notes	**Before exceptional items 1994 £million**	**Exceptional items 1994 £million**	**1994 £million**	1993 £million
Turnover	1	**2,487.9**	–	**2,487.9**	2,439.3
Cost of sales	3	**(2,357.3)**	–	**(2,357.3)**	(2,341.7)
Redundancy and reorganisation costs	4	**(7.6)**	**(6.0)**	**(13.6)**	(9.6)
Provision for restructuring and claims	4	–	**(87.6)**	**(87.6)**	–
Reappraisal of Aerospace stocks	4	–	**(16.4)**	**(16.4)**	–
		(2,364.9)	**(110.0)**	**(2,474.9)**	(2,351.3)
Surplus on trading		**123.0**	**(110.0)**	**13.0**	88.0
Share of profits less losses of associated undertakings		**3.6**	–	**3.6**	(2.6)
Group operating profit	1	**126.6**	**(110.0)**	**16.6**	85.4

Notes to the accounts (extract)

Note 1: Results of the business by activity

Turnover represents sales to third parties excluding both sales-related taxes and sales of discontinuing business segments.

Sales by origin to third parties and the group operating profit attributable to the continuing principal classes of business were as follows:

	1994 Sales £million	1993 Sales £million	1994 Group operating Profit £million	1993 Group operating Profit £million
By class of business:				
Automotive	**1,815.7**	1,627.4	**88.1**	44.5
Aerospace	**537.1**	633.6	**13.2**	30.3
Applied Technology	**237.7**	308.9	**2.9**	10.6
Provision for restructuring and claims	–	–	**(87.6)**	–
Total including share of associated undertakings' results	**2,590.5**	2,569.9	**16.6**	85.4
Less: Share of associated undertakings' sales	**102.6**	130.6		
Group sales to third parties	**2,487.9**	2,439.3		
By geographical region:				
United Kingdom subsidiary undertakings	**953.6**	935.7	**30.4**	37.9
Other European subsidiary undertakings	**879.5**	811.3	**54.8**	38.1
North American subsidiary undertakings	**436.0**	490.6	**(5.2)**	(6.4)
Other overseas subsidiary undertakings	**218.8**	201.7	**20.6**	18.4
Share of associated undertakings	**102.6**	130.6	**3.6**	(2.6)
Provision for restructuring and claims		–	**(87.6)**	–
	2,590.5	2,569.9	**16.6**	85.4

The provision for restructuring and claims has not been analysed by class of business, or by geographical region in order to protect the group's commercial and legal position.

Note 4: Exceptional items

The following exceptional items have been charged in arriving at the year's operating profits:

- Redundancy and reorganisation costs – £6.0 million. These are costs incurred during the year which are non-recurring and relate to factory closures and relocation of business activities. The ongoing redundancy and reorganisation costs totalled £7.6 million.

- Provision for restructuring and claims – £87.6 million. Provision has been made for the significant costs expected in rationalising the manufacturing facilities and the creation of more efficient production units in the Diesel Systems, Flight Control Systems and Electronics businesses. These programmes will lead to higher productivity and enhanced profitability.

  Provision has also been made for the anticipated costs of settling certain legal claims with the US Government. The settlement process is in the early stages and it is impossible to determine the eventual outcome. The directors have taken legal advice and have provided an amount which they believe to be appropriate.

- Reappraisal of Aerospace stock values – £16.4 million. Production volumes in the Aerospace market have been, and are forecast to remain, at levels substantially lower than before the recession. It has therefore been necessary to review the valuations of Aerospace stocks, and the provision now reduces valuations to a realistic level in line with future market expectations.

Voluntary segmental disclosures

Introduction

9.145 There are many other types of segmental disclosure given by companies in practice. A number of examples are given below. While none of them are required by the standard, all are potentially useful and informative for the reader and analyst.

Employees

9.146 The Act requires the average number of employees to be disclosed. This disclosure should be both in total and by category of employee, with the categories being determined by the directors, having regard to the manner in which the company's activities are organised. [4 Sch 56(5)]. Various types of disclosure have been adopted by companies, including by geographical region and by business segment. Lonrho, for example, adopts the geographical basis approach, with further analysis between employees of the group and employees of associates (see Table 9.21).

Table 9.21 – Lonrho Plc – Annual Report and Accounts – 30 September 1994

Notes to the Accounts (extract)

5 Staff Numbers

The average number of persons employed during the year was as follows:–

	1994			1993		
	Group	**Associates**	**Total**	Group	Associates	Total
United Kingdom	**7,815**		**7,815**	8,246		8,246
East, Central and West Africa	**59,203**	**25,283**	**84,486**	56,710	26,708	83,418
Southern Africa	**22,637**	**35**	**22,672**	23,160	14	23,174
The Americas	**4,796**	**969**	**5,765**	4,881	949	5,830
Europe and Other	**5,662**	**1,050**	**6,712**	5,822	979	6,801
Discontinued operations				490	2,085	2,575
	100,113	**27,337**	**127,450**	99,309	30,735	130,044

9.147 Grand Metropolitan, on the other hand, provides analysis by business segment. This analysis separates out full-time and part-time employees, distinguished between continuing and discontinued businesses (see Table 9.22).

Table 9.22 – Grand Metropolitan Public Limited Company – Annual Report – 30 September 1994

Notes (extract)

11 Employees

The average number of employees during the year was:			**1994**			*1993*
	Full time	**Part time**	**Total**	*Full time*	*Part time*	*Total*
Continuing operations						
Food –branded	**19,074**	**1,950**	**21,024**	20,293	2,047	22,340
–retailing	**11,554**	**18,498**	**30,052**	13,422	22,083	35,505
Drinks	**11,464**	**335**	**11,799**	11,612	342	11,954
	42,092	**20,783**	**62,875**	45,327	24,472	69,799
Discontinued operations	**595**	**830**	**1,425**	7,391	9,973	17,364
	42,687	**21,613**	**64,300**	52,718	34,445	87,163

9.148 In contrast to the two above examples, BOC provides segmental analysis on both a business and a territorial basis (see Table 9.23).

Table 9.23 – The BOC Group plc – Report and Accounts – 30 September 1994

Notes on Financial Statements (extract)

6 Employees

	1994		1993	
a) Number of employees by business	**Year end**	**Average**	Year end	Average
Gases & related products	**26,551**	**26,686**	27,615	26,037
Health Care	**5,754**	**6,002**	6,228	6,459
Vacuum Technology & Distribution Services	**6,880**	**6,470**	6,193	5,723
Corporate	**236**	**232**	230	215
	39,421	**39,390**	40,266	38,434

	1994		1993	
b) Number of employees by region	**Year end**	**Average**	Year end	Average
Europe	**13,849**	**13,601**	13,506	12,746
Africa	**8,427**	**7,944**	7,602	7,493
Americas	**8,858**	**9,201**	9,691	9,760
Asia/Pacific	**8,287**	**8,644**	9,467	8,435
	39,421	**39,390**	40,266	38,434

Fixed assets and capital expenditure

9.149 There is a view that segmental disclosure of expenditure on tangible fixed assets assists readers in assessing the growth potential and possible on-going capital needs of individual segments. While a number of reporting entities, including BOC, as Table 9.24 shows, provide analyses of capital expenditure by either or both of business segment and/or geographical segment, few companies have extended this analysis so as to provide detailed segmental analyses of their tangible fixed assets. BP is one of the exceptions, as it provides such an analysis by business segment (see Table 9.25).

Table 9.24 – The BOC Group plc – Report and Accounts – 30 September 1994

Notes on Financial Statements (extract)

b) Business analysis	Gases and Related Products £million	Health Care £million	Vacuum Technology and Distribution Services £million	Corporate £million	Total £million
1994					
Operating profit before exceptional items	**331.9**	**54.6**	**51.0**	**(2.1)**	**435.4**
Exceptional restructuring costs	**(25.0)**	**(60.0)**	**–**	**–**	**(85.0)**
Capital employed	**2,404.8**	**338.9**	**233.9**	**(12.1)**	**2,965.5**
Capital expenditure [4]	**341.6**	**22.3**	**49.9**	**1.8**	**415.6**

1993					
Operating profit	304.6	86.2	33.0	(3.0)	420.8
Capital employed	2,325.5	381.0	200.2	(0.5)	2,906.2
Capital expenditure [4]	331.0	48.9	28.8	2.2	410.9

c) Regional analysis	Europe £million	Africa £million	Americas £million	Asia/ Pacific £million	Total £million
1994					
Operating profit before exceptional items	**151.9**	**56.0**	**95.2**	**132.3**	**435.4**
Exceptional restructuring costs	**(48.4)**	**–**	**(26.7)**	**(9.9)**	**(85.0)**
Capital employed	**1,035.3**	**191.4**	**823.9**	**914.9**	**2,965.5**
Capital expenditure [4]	**135.6**	**27.7**	**105.8**	**146.5**	**415.6**
1993					
Operating profit	130.6	52.3	128.0	109.9	420.8
Capital employed	980.3	158.9	901.7	865.3	2,906.2
Capital expenditure [4]	149.8	30.0	94.1	137.0	410.9

[4] includes capital expenditure of related undertakings of £59.3 million (1993: £51.1 million) mainly in Gases and Related Products and Asia/Pacific region.

Table 9.25 – The British Petroleum Company p.l.c. – Annual Report and Accounts – 31 December 1994

15 Tangible assets – property, plant and equipment [extract]

£million

	Exploration and Production	Refining and Marketing	Chemicals	Other businesses and corporate	Total	of which: Assets under Construction
Cost						
At 1 January 1994	25,986	9,329	3,159	1,030	39,504	1,791
Exchange adjustments	(730)	124	–	6	(600)	(27)
Additions	1,157	655	110	32	1,954	1,409
Transfers	121	31	8	(38)	122	(801)
Deletions	(400)	(426)	(78)	(527)	(1,431)	(399)
At 31 December 1994	**26,134**	**9,713**	**3,199**	**503**	**39,549**	**1,973**
Depreciation						
At 1 January 1994	12,907	4,343	1,735	565	19,550	
Exchange adjustments	(421)	92	(4)	6	(327)	
Charge for the year	1,248	489	205	48	1,990	
Transfers	2	8	7	(15)	2	
Deletions	(341)	(262)	(61)	(395)	(1,059)	
At 31 December 1994	**13,395**	**4,670**	**1,882**	**209**	**20,156**	
Net book amount						
At 31 December 1994	**12,739**	**5,043**	**1,317**	**294**	**19,393**	**1,973**

At 31 December 1993	13,079	4,986	1,424	465	19,954	1,791
Principal rates of depreciation	*	2-25%	5-12%	3-25%		

*Mainly unit-of-production

Assets held under finance leases, capitalised interest and land at net book amount included above:	Leased assets			Capitalised interest		
	Cost	Depreciation	Net	Cost	Depreciation	Net
At 31 December 1994	**1,420**	**506**	**914**	**1,518**	**814**	**704**
At 31 December 1993	1,442	448	994	1,519	746	773

	Freehold land	Leasehold land	
		Over 50 years unexpired	Other
At 31 December 1994	**677**	**20**	**44**
At 31 December 1993	704	10	57

Depreciation

9.150 In addition to the segmental disclosure of capital expenditure referred to above, a number of companies also give segmental disclosures for depreciation. This enables readers to assess the impact of the employment of fixed assets during the period on the segment result and asset base. BP's full analysis of fixed assets by business segment *per se* means that it gives this segmental depreciation information.

Research and development

9.151 This is another category of expenditure where companies can provide useful segmental information to readers of financial statements. Readers could, thereby, better understand the levels of investment in research and development made by different business and geographical segments. Indeed, in industries such as the pharmaceutical industry, many fledgling companies are likely to have a substantial proportion of their total assets invested in research and development activities, generating from this relatively little turnover and, in many instances, operating losses. In such circumstances, the directors may form the view that research and development is actually a separate business segment. ML Laboratories PLC provides a practical example of this approach (see Table 9.26).

Table 9.26 – ML Laboratories PLC – Annual Report – 30 September 1995

DIRECTORS' REPORT (extract)
PRINCIPAL ACTIVITIES

The Group continues to research into, and develop, a small number of ethical pharmaceutical and other products, with a view to achieving sales on a worldwide basis and provides regulatory affairs consultancy and educational programmes for the pharmaceutical industry.

NOTES TO THE FINANCIAL STATEMENTS (extract)

1 SEGMENTAL ANALYSIS BY CLASS OF BUSINESS

The analysis by class of business of the Group's turnover, loss before taxation and net assets is set out below:

Classes of Business

	RESEARCH & DEVELOPMENT		TRAINING & CONSULTANCY		INSTRUMENT SALES	
	1995 £	1994 £	1995 £	1994 £	1995 £	1994 £
Turnover	–	–	526,680	551,032	224,103	191,196
Loss before taxation	(3,181,011)	(2,157,076)	(76,827)	2,734	(49,109)	(55,563)
Net assets/ (liabilities)	15,908,994	19,085,571	(306,549)	(223,721)	(254,228)	(205,119)

	PRODUCT SALES		MATERIALS ANALYSIS		GROUP	
	1995 £	1994 £	1995 £	1994 £	1995 £	1994 £
Turnover	348,015	63,554	40,184	4,760	1,138,982	810,542
Loss before taxation	–	–	(96,649)	(53,673)	(3,403,596)	(2,263,578)
Net assets/(liabilities)	–	–	(171,767)	(75,118)	15,176,450	18,581,613

It is impractical to isolate the loss before taxation and net assets/liabilities related to product sales. They have, therefore, been left in research and development.

Geographical Segments

	UNITED KINGDOM		NORTH AMERICA		EUROPE		GROUP	
	1995 £	1994 £	1995 £	1994 £	1995 £	1994 £	1995 £	1994 £
Turnover by destination	862,274	569,012	80,259	88,818	196,449*	152,712*	1,138,982	810,542
Turnover by origin	1,138,982	766,238	–	–	–	44,304	1,138,982	810,542
Loss before taxation	(3,400,191)	(2,245,680)	–	–	(3,405)	(17,898)	(3,403,596)	(2,263,578)
Net assets/ (liabilities)	15,276,314	18,678,071	–	–	(99,864)	(96,458)	15,176,450	18,581,613

*Includes sales to other countries of £5,149 (1994 £16,115).

Future revisions to SSAP 25

9.152 Since SSAP 25's publication in 1990, there has been a marked increase in the amount of segmental information disclosed in financial statements. Nonetheless, the range of these disclosures has varied significantly from entity to entity, even between entities operating in the same industries. At one end of the spectrum are those entities where the directors have applied the prejudicial override clause contained in both the standard and the Act, to the effect that the financial statements present either reduced segmental disclosure or none whatsoever. At the other end of the spectrum are those entities where the directors have not only adopted the disclosures sought by the standard, but have extended the range of segmental disclosure in the financial statements to areas such as employee information.

9.153 While the latitude allowed by the Act and the standard may be justifiable in commercial terms, it has an unfortunate consequence. In an age when there is greater external pressure for companies, not only to present fuller and more meaningful information to the readers of financial statements, but also for consistency in the format and content of financial statements across companies, the prejudicial override clause can be considered to be an anachronism. This will remain the position, for as long as the directors of the reporting entity remain empowered to decide whether the disclosure of disaggregated information would be seriously prejudicial to the reporting entity's interests. Thus, while it is understandable that the standard should have followed the Act, rather than have overridden it, perhaps it is now time for parliament to re-consider the subject of prejudicial override.

9.154 The rules on segmental reporting have not been exempt from the ASB's programme of improving financial reporting. The ASB has tested the need for change in this area by publishing a discussion paper on segmental reporting. Issued in May 1996, it is largely a response to the proposals in exposure drafts issued by the IASC and the US FASB. The ASB is seeking a consensus of views on this subject to determine whether SSAP 25 needs amending.

9.155 The two main areas the discussion paper deals with are the identification of segments and the disclosure of information to be given in each segment. In contrast to the risks and returns approach of SSAP 25, the new FASB accounting standard requires a management approach to identifying segments, so that the internal reporting system forms the basis of the segmental report. The management approach is also a feature of the IASC accounting standard, but risks and rewards analysis continues to play a significant role. Both standards also require more detailed disclosure than SSAP 25.

Comparison with IASs

Comparison with IASs

9.156 The current IASC rules are found in IAS 14 which came into force in 1983. This standard was revised in August 1997 and the new rules in IAS 14 (revised), 'Segment reporting', are applicable for accounting periods beginning on or after 1 July 1998.

9.157 IAS 14 (revised) applies to enterprises whose equity or debt securities are publicly traded, including enterprises in the process of issuing equity or debt securities in a public securities market. [IAS 14 (revised) para 3]. This is somewhat similar to SSAP 25, but less extensive than the Companies Act 1985. IAS 14 (revised) contains no 'seriously prejudicial' exemption as in the UK rules.

9.158 IAS 14 (revised) provides that one basis of segmentation is primary and the other is secondary, with considerably less information required to be disclosed for secondary segments. This differs from SSAP 25 which does not make such a distinction. The dominant source and nature of an enterprise's risks and returns should govern whether its primary segment will be business segments or geographical segments. [IAS 14 (revised) para 26]. Furthermore, geographical segments are based on either (a) the location of an enterprise's production or service facilities and other assets; or (b) the location of its markets and customers. [IAS 14 (revised) para 13].

9.159 The revised standard is based on management's approach to organising the business. An enterprise's internal organisational and management structure and its system of internal financial reporting to the board of directors and the chief executive officer should normally be the basis for determining which reporting format is primary and which is secondary. [IAS 14 (revised) para 27]. There are exceptions: if the enterprise's risks and rates of return are strongly affected by both products/services and geography; and if the internal reporting is not based on products/services or on geography. This management-based approach differs from the risk/returns approach of SSAP 25, although in practice the results may be similar.

9.160 The disclosure requirements of the revised standard are more extensive than in SSAP 25. For an enterprise's primary basis of segment reporting (business segments or geographical segments), IAS 14 (revised) requires disclosure of:

- Segment revenue, distinguishing between sales to external customers and segment revenue from transactions with other segments. [IAS 14 (revised) para 51].

- Segment result. [IAS 14 (revised) para 52].

- Segment assets. [IAS 14 (revised) para 55].
- Segment liabilities [IAS 14 (revised) para 56].
- Cost of property, plant, equipment, and intangible assets acquired during the period. [IAS 14 (revised) para 57].
- Depreciation and amortisation expense. [IAS 14 (revised) para 58].
- Non-cash expenses other than depreciation and amortisation. [IAS 14 (revised) para 61].
- For each reportable segment, the enterprise's share of the net profit or loss of associates, joint ventures, or other investments accounted for under the equity method if substantially all of the associates' operations are within that segment, and the amount of the related investment. [IAS 14 (revised) paras 64, 65].

9.161 For an enterprise's secondary basis of segment reporting IAS 14 (revised) requires disclosure of segment revenue, segment assets and the cost of property, plant, equipment, and intangible assets acquired during the period. [IAS 14 (revised) paras 69 to 72].

9.162 In measuring and reporting segment revenue from transactions with other segments, inter-segment transfers should be measured on the basis that the enterprise actually used to price those transfers. Disclosure is required of the basis of pricing inter-segment transfers. [IAS 14 (revised) para 75].

Annex – Comparison of segmental reporting requirements

	Companies Act 1985	SSAP 25
Description of segments	✓	✓
Turnover		
Origin basis		✓
Destination basis	✓	✓
Class of business	✓	✓
Inter-segment turnover		✓
Profit before tax		
Class of business		✓(1)
Geographic segment		✓(1)
Net assets/capital employed		
Class of business		✓(2)
Geographical segment		✓(2)
Associated company profit before tax		
Class of business		✓
Geographical segment		✓
Associated company net assets		
Class of business		✓
Geographical segment		✓

Notes:

(1) Before or after interest.

(2) Including or excluding interest bearing assets and liabilities dependent or whether or not profit before tax is analysed before or after interest.

Chapter 10

Other profit and loss account items

Chapter 10

Other profit and loss account items

Introduction

10.1 The profit and loss account is one of the primary statements that a company must include in its financial statements. The Act requires the profit and loss account to comply with one of four alternative formats: Formats 1 and 3 are vertical presentations; and Formats 2 and 4 show charges separately from income. These formats are set out and discussed in chapter 6. The format a company chooses can be significant because, depending on the format, some of the information the company discloses in its profit and loss account will be different. Some of the items that are discussed below may relate only to one pair of formats.

10.2 Chapter 3 deals with the measurement and disclosure of items included under the main revenue headings in the profit and loss account. This chapter considers other categories of income and expenditure that are recognised in the profit and loss account, insofar as they are not dealt with separately in other chapters, together with supplementary disclosure requirements.

10.3 Of the items included in the Act's formats, only 'turnover' (see chapter 3) and 'staff costs' (see para 10.15 below) are actually defined in the Act. The allocation to statutory captions of certain other items of income and expenditure included in companies' charts of accounts requires companies to reach internal definitions and interpretations in order to achieve reasonable and consistent classifications.

Cost of sales, distribution costs and administrative expenses

10.4 These headings from Formats 1 and 3, which require the classification of expenditure by its function, give rise to many questions concerning the allocation of costs and overheads. The following lists are intended to provide guidance as to the items that may be included under each heading.

10.5 *Cost of sales* will normally include:

- Opening (less closing) stocks.
- Direct materials.

- Other external charges (such as the hire of plant and machinery or the cost of casual labour used in the productive process).

- Direct labour.

- All direct production overheads, including depreciation, and indirect overheads that can reasonably be allocated to the production function.

- Product development expenditure.

- Cash discounts received on 'cost of sales' expenditure (this is not a set-off, but an effective reduction in the purchase price of an item).

- Stock provisions.

10.6 *Distribution costs* are generally interpreted more widely than the name suggests and often include selling and marketing costs. Items normally included in this caption comprise:

- Payroll costs of the sales, marketing and distribution functions.
- Advertising.
- Salesperson's travel and entertaining.
- Warehouse costs for finished goods.
- Transport costs concerning the distribution of finished goods.
- All costs of maintaining sales outlets.
- Agents' commission payable.

10.7 *Administrative expenses* will normally include:

- The costs of general management.
- All costs of maintaining the administration buildings.
- Bad debts.
- Professional costs.
- Cash discounts on sales.
- Research and development expenditure that is not allocated to cost of sales (sometimes this is shown as a separate item).

10.8 If Format 1 or 3 is adopted, charges for depreciation or the diminution in value of assets have to be analysed under the above headings. [Note 14 on the profit and loss account sheet formats]. The type of analysis will depend on the function of the related assets (see also para 10.29).

10.9 In some specific instances, the above analyses may not be appropriate. For example, in the context of a mail order company, agents' commission payable may be regarded as a cost of sale rather than as a distribution cost.

10.10 The way in which a company analyses its costs will depend very much on the nature of its business. Where a company incurs significant operating expenses that it considers do not fall under any one of the headings 'cost of sales', 'distribution costs' and 'administrative expenses', there is nothing to prevent the company including an additional item for these expenses in Formats 1 or 3. The overriding consideration is that a company should analyse its operating expenses consistently from year to year.

10.11 Some companies have adapted these items or shown additional items. However, these companies are in a minority. This is probably because the items are general enough to apply to most companies' expenditure. Examples of adaptations and additional items that companies have used in their financial statements are shown below.

Examples of adaptation of items:

- Selling and distribution costs.
- Marketing, selling and distribution costs.
- Distribution costs, including marketing.
- Administrative and selling expenses.
- Selling and general administration expenses.

Examples of additional items:

- Sales commission (shown in addition to distribution costs).
- Redundancy costs (although these are usually allocated to statutory headings).
- Research and development.
- Costs of unsuccessful bids and bid defence costs.

10.12 Table 10.1 shows an extract from the profit and loss account of Rolls-Royce plc, where the analysis of operating expenses has been adapted.

Table 10.1 – Rolls-Royce plc – Annual Report – 31 December 1994

Group Profit and Loss Account (extract)
for the year ended December 31, 1994

	Notes	1994 £m	1993 £m
Turnover	2	3,163	3,518
Cost of sales	3	(2,646)	(2,995)
Gross profit		517	523
Commercial, marketing and product support costs		(117)	(105)
General and administrative costs		(91)	(89)
Research and development (net)		(218)	(253)
Operating profit		91	76

Gross profit

10.13 The gross profit or loss has to be shown as a separate item in Format 1, and it can be readily ascertained from the items that are disclosed in Format 3. Formats 2 and 4 analyse expenditure in a different manner, that is, by its nature rather than its function and, as a result, gross profit is not disclosed.

Own work capitalised

10.14 Where a company has constructed some of its own tangible fixed assets, and it adopts either Format 2 or Format 4 for its profit and loss account, it should include the costs of direct materials, direct labour and overheads it has capitalised as a credit under the heading 'own work capitalised'. The costs of direct materials, direct labour and overheads are charged in the profit and loss account, by including these amounts under the relevant expenditure headings. The amount capitalised is then credited in the profit and loss account as own work capitalised and it is debited to tangible fixed assets. Thus, items such as raw material costs in the profit and loss account will include the costs connected with such work.

Staff costs and numbers

Employee costs

10.15 Staff costs are defined in paragraph 94 of Schedule 4 to the Act as being the costs a company incurs in respect of the persons it employs under contracts of service. A contract *of service* (or a contract of employment as it is also called) is an agreement under which the employer agrees to employ the employee for a wage or a salary in return for the employee's labour. This agreement must be made in writing. However, self-employed persons are not employed by the company, but merely have contracts to perform specific services for that company. The costs of self-employed people should normally be excluded from staff costs, because their contracts will be contracts *for services*. Examples of such persons are consultants and contractors. Their costs should normally be included under 'other external charges' in Formats 2 and 4, and under an appropriate functional expense heading in Formats 1 and 3.

10.16 The item 'staff costs' does not appear in the profit and loss account Formats 1 and 3. This is because expenses are classified in these formats by function, rather than by type. However, where a company prepares its profit and loss account in the style of either Format 1 or Format 3, it has to disclose, in the notes to the profit and loss account, the equivalent information to that given when Formats 2 and 4 are used.

10.17 In summary, either the profit and loss account format or the notes must disclose, in aggregate, each of the following amounts:

- The wages and salaries that were either paid to employees or are payable to them, in respect of the financial year in question.

- Social security costs that the company has incurred on behalf of its employees. For this purpose, social security costs are any contributions the company makes to any social security or pension scheme, or fund or arrangement that the State runs. These costs will include the employer's national insurance contributions.

- Other pension costs the company has incurred on behalf of employees. For this purpose, pension costs include:

  - Any costs incurred by a company in respect of any non-State occupational pension scheme that is established to provide pensions for employees or past employees.

  - Any sums the company has set aside for the future payment of pensions directly to current and former employees.

  - Any amounts the company has paid in respect of pensions, without those amounts having first been so set aside.

  Pension costs will, therefore, include the cost in respect of the company's participation in any pension scheme other than the State scheme. [4 Sch 56(4), 94 as amended by SI 1996/189].

10.18 An illustration of these disclosure requirements is given in Table 10.2.

Table 10.2 – Scottish & Newcastle plc – Annual Report and Accounts – 1 May 1994

Notes to the Accounts (extract)

5 STAFF COSTS, EMPLOYEES AND DIRECTORS' REMUNERATION (extract)

(i) Staff costs	**1994 £m**	1993 £m
Wages and salaries	**279.7**	227.1
Social security costs	**33.2**	29.8
Other pension costs	**10.1**	9.9
Employee profit sharing scheme	**4.0**	3.7
	327.0	270.5

(ii) Number of employees	**1994**	1993
The average numbers of employees during the year were:		
Retail	**21,656**	12,724
Beer	**4,827**	5,261
Leisure	**10,082**	9,961
Group central functions	**265**	334
	36,830	28,280

The 1994 Retail figure includes 9,414 relating to the Chef & Brewer estate.

10.19 The Act says that wages and salaries should be determined by reference to either the payments the company makes or the costs it incurs in respect of all persons it employs. [4 Sch 94(3)]. There is no definition in the Act of 'costs incurred'. Although it is likely that a strict interpretation of this term would include the money value of benefits in kind, as in the case of directors' remuneration under paragraph 1(4) of Schedule 6 to the Act (see further para 10.25 below), in practice, companies sometimes charge the cost of staff benefits to other items in the profit and loss account and not to staff costs.

10.20 Some companies have adopted profit sharing schemes for their employees. Amounts provided under such schemes are sometimes shown separately as additional items in the analysis of staff costs (see Table 10.2).

Average number of employees

10.21 In addition to requiring that the notes to the profit and loss account should disclose employee costs, the Act requires that those notes should include information in respect of the number of employees.

10.22 The two disclosures that the notes must contain in connection with the number of employees are:

- The average number of employees in the financial year. The number must be calculated by:

  - Ascertaining the number of persons employed under contract of service, whether full-time or part-time, for each month in the year.

  - Adding together all the monthly numbers.
  - Dividing the resulting total by the number of months in the financial year.

  The average number of employees includes persons who work wholly or mainly overseas, as well as persons who work in the UK.

- The average number of employees by category. This number must be calculated by applying the same method of calculation as outlined above to each category of employees. For this purpose, the categories of persons employed are to be such categories as the directors select, having regard to the way in which the company's activities are organised.

  Because the guidance on how to select categories is rather vague, directors of companies have chosen a variety of different categories. Methods have included splitting between part-time employees and full-time employees; between hourly-paid, weekly-paid and salaried staff; between production, sales and administration staff; and between staff employed in different geographical areas.

[4 Sch 56 as amended by SI 1996/189].

These disclosure requirements are illustrated in Table 10.2.

10.23 Consolidated financial statements in which the parent company has taken the exemption from publishing its own profit and loss account should include the information outlined above only for the group as a whole.

10.24 There is no exemption from disclosure where the number of employees is small, or (for example) where a company is a wholly-owned subsidiary.

Directors

10.25 Directors who have a contract of service with the company are to be regarded as employees. Therefore, their salaries, their social security costs and their other pension costs must be included in the required analysis under staff costs, even if a note is included stating that directors' emoluments are shown elsewhere. In addition, directors' emoluments have also to be disclosed separately in accordance with the requirements of Part I of Schedule 6 to the Act. In this situation, their emoluments will exclude those social security costs that the company bears, because such amounts are neither paid to the director nor paid in respect of a pension scheme. The disclosure of directors' aggregate emoluments, will, however, include the estimated money value of any benefits in kind.

10.26 In contrast to payments under a contract *of service* (where the director is employed), amounts paid to directors under contracts *for services* (equivalent to the director being self-employed) should not be disclosed under staff costs. But, under Part I of Schedule 6 to the Act, they must be disclosed as directors' emoluments in the notes to the financial statements. Whether a director's contract with the company is a contract *of service* or a contract *for services* is a question of fact in each circumstance. Usually, however, executive directors will have contracts *of service,* whereas non-executive directors will have contracts *for services.* Contracts for services might include, for example, consultancy arrangements. Directors' emoluments are dealt with further in chapter 11.

Practical problems relating to employee costs

10.27 In practice, there may be problems in deciding on the employees to include in staff costs and in identifying the average number of employees. One of the most frequent problems arises where employees clearly work for one company, but their contracts of service are with another company (for example, the holding company). Also, further complications arise when that other company pays the wages and salaries of these employees. If paragraph 56 of Schedule 4 to the Act was strictly interpreted in these situations, it could lead to the disclosure of misleading information in the financial statements. Accordingly, as well as giving the statutory disclosures, a company may need to give additional information to enable its financial statements to give a true and fair view.

10.28 Some of the more common problems that arise in this respect are considered in the examples that follow:

Example 1

Employees work full time for, and are paid by, a subsidiary company, but their contracts of service are with the parent company.

It would be misleading if there were no disclosure of staff costs or numbers in the subsidiary company's financial statements. Consequently, the wages and salaries the subsidiary company pays to those employees should be disclosed as 'staff costs' in its financial statements and those employees should be included in the calculation of the average number of staff employed.

The notes to the subsidiary company's financial statements should explain that those staff have contracts of service with another group company. They should also explain why their remuneration and average number are disclosed in the financial statements.

The parent company's consolidated financial statements normally will not be affected (unless the subsidiary is not included in the consolidated financial statements), because they will show the average number of employees and staff costs of the group as a whole, but not those of the parent company separately. Consequently, no additional disclosure should be necessary in the parent company's financial statements.

(However, if the contracts of service are with a fellow subsidiary company, then that fellow subsidiary company's financial statements should include those employees in the calculation of staff costs and average number of employees and explain that certain employees having service contracts with the company work for and are paid for wholly by a fellow subsidiary company.)

Example 2

Employees work full time for the subsidiary company, but they are not paid by the subsidiary company and they do not have service contracts with it. However, the subsidiary company bears a management charge for their services from the company that pays the employees and it can ascertain the proportion of the management charge that relates to staff costs.

Again, in this situation it could be misleading if the subsidiary company's financial statements disclosed no information about staff costs or numbers. Accordingly, the proportion of the management charge that relates to staff costs should be disclosed in the subsidiary company's financial statements as 'staff costs'. The employees concerned should be included in the calculation of the average number of employees. The notes to the financial statements should explain that the employees do not have contracts of service with the company, and they should also explain why their costs and average number are disclosed in the financial statements. For the reason outlined in example 1 above, the parent company's consolidated financial statements should not be affected.

(If the contracts of service are with, and the employees are paid by, a fellow subsidiary company then that fellow subsidiary's financial statements should disclose the staff costs and average number in respect of all its employees and give details regarding the staff costs that are recharged to the fellow subsidiary.)

Example 3

The facts are the same as in example 2 except that the subsidiary company is unable to break down the management charge and ascertain the part of it that relates to staff costs.

In this situation, for the same reason as explained in example 2, the parent company's consolidated financial statements will be unaffected. The notes to the subsidiary company's financial statements should explain that the employees' contracts of service are with the parent company and that their remuneration is included in the parent company's financial statements. The notes should also explain that the management charge that the parent company makes includes the cost of these employees, but that it is impossible to ascertain separately the element of the management charge that relates to staff costs.

(If the employees' contracts of service are with a fellow subsidiary, rather than with the parent company, and that fellow subsidiary also pays the employees, the fellow subsidiary's financial statements should disclose the employees' remuneration in its staff costs and should also include the employees in the calculation of average number employed. The notes should explain that these employees work for a fellow subsidiary company and that the company recharges the cost of their employment to that fellow subsidiary as part of a management charge.)

Example 4

The facts are the same as in example 2 above, except that no management charge is made for the employees' services. This will often apply where staff work either full-time or part-time for small companies.

In this situation, the notes to the subsidiary company's financial statements should explain that the company is not charged for the services provided by the employees that work for it. If appropriate, the notes should also indicate that the cost of these employees and their average number are included in the parent company's consolidated financial statements. For the same reason as given in example 1 above, however, the parent company's consolidated financial statements should not be affected.

(Once again, if it is a fellow subsidiary that employs and pays the employees, its financial statements should include the cost of these employees in its staff costs and should include these employees in the average number employed. If appropriate, the notes to the financial statements should explain that these employees work for a fellow subsidiary company, but that no management charge is made for their services to that company.)

Employee share schemes

Background

10.28.1 Many companies use share option schemes for the purpose of employee remuneration either as a management incentive or through Save As You Earn (SAYE) schemes that are available to all employees. A more recent development is the increasing use of share awards, either through annual bonuses or long-term incentive plans (LTIPs) as an alternative, or in addition, to share option plans. In such schemes the amount of the award is normally based on performance criteria; if these criteria are partially achieved, but not met in full, participants may be entitled to a proportion of the full award. Typically, the shares are awarded to employees at nominal value or at nil cost (for instance, where an employee share ownership plan (ESOP) subscribes for shares at nominal value) and there has been concern that this would enable a company to avoid a charge in its profit and loss account.

10.28.2 Where a company satisfies share awards to employees through the purchase of shares by an ESOP then the accounting treatment is addressed by UITF Abstract 13, 'Employee share ownership plans'. This is covered in detail in chapter 4. It requires that the shares purchased by the ESOP are carried as an asset on the sponsoring company's balance sheet and written down to recoverable amount over the period of service of the employees in respect of which the awards are granted. This means that if the ESOP trust purchases shares in the market at the date of grant of the award and subsequently gifts these to employees, then the purchase price of the shares will be charged in the sponsoring company's profit and loss account.

10.28.3 However, if the employee share scheme is set up so that shares are issued by the company rather than purchased in the market then, if the strict legal form is followed, any charge in the company's profit and loss account may be nil or significantly lower than the fair value at the date of grant of the award. No charge would arise, for instance, if the company issued shares to an employee at nominal value. The UITF has addressed this issue with the publication in May 1997 of UITF Abstract 17, 'Employee share schemes'. This abstract requires a charge in the profit and loss based on the fair value of the shares at the date an award is granted and applies to accounting periods ending on or after 22 June 1997, but earlier adoption is encouraged.

Scope of the abstract

10.28.4 UITF abstracts are applicable to financial statements of reporting entities that are intended to give a true and fair view and so apply to all companies. The abstract applies to all employee share schemes, including share option schemes, but there is an exemption for certain types of scheme as discussed below.

10.28.5 A majority of the UITF believed that the accounting for SAYE schemes should, in principle, be the same as that for other share schemes. However, the accounting for SAYE schemes has been established for many years and there was no consensus within the UITF for including such schemes within the abstract's scope. Consequently the UITF ruled that the abstract need not be applied to Inland Revenue approved SAYE and similar schemes. [UITF 17 para 12].

10.28.6 Although the UITF's intention seems clear, the wording used for the exemption in the consensus can be argued to be capable of broader interpretation. It states that *"this abstract need not be applied in accounting for an employees' share scheme under which participation is offered on similar terms to all or substantially* *all employees of the issuer and any of its subsidiary undertakings whose employees are eligible to participate in the scheme (providing that all or substantially all employees are not directors of the issuer)"*. [UITF 17 para 17].

10.28.7 Our view is that the exemption is intended to apply only to Inland Revenue-approved SAYE schemes and other similar savings-related schemes. Therefore, we consider that the exemption should not be regarded as applying to other employee share schemes such as profit-share schemes that are available to all employees.

10.28.8 Furthermore, whilst advantage may be taken of the above exemption, this does not prevent companies from applying the abstract to SAYE schemes if they wish to do this as a matter of policy.

10.28.9 The scope of the abstract covers all awards to employees that take the form of shares or rights to shares. This includes conditional awards and awards provided through convertible or other exchangeable instruments. [UITF 17 para 13(a)].

Requirements of the abstract

10.28.10 UITF Abstract 17 deals with the timing of recognition of the charge in the profit and loss account and with the quantification of the charge for share awards.

Timing of recognition of the charge

10.28.11 The amount recognised in the profit and loss account in respect of share awards should be charged over the period to which the employee's performance relates. This means:

- For annual bonuses - the year to which the bonus relates.
- For long-term incentive plans - the period to which the performance criteria relate.

[UITF 17 para 13(a)].

10.28.12 Where the scheme has an additional service condition requiring that the employee remains with the company for a specified period before becoming unconditionally entitled to the shares, the period over which the cost is recognised should not normally include that additional service period unless it is clear that the effect of the scheme is to reward services over the longer period. [UITF 17 para 13(d)].

10.28.13 Where there are no performance criteria and the award is clearly unrelated to past performance, the period over which the cost is recognised in the profit and loss account should be from the date of the award to the date the employee becomes unconditionally entitled to the shares. [UITF 17 para 14]. However, if the award is related to past service, for instance where it represents an annual bonus, then it should be charged to profit and loss account in the year to which it relates.

Quantification of the charge

10.28.14 The amount recognised should be based on the fair value of the shares at the date an award has been made to participants in the scheme. [UITF 17 para 13(b)]. The minimum amount recognised in respect of awards of shares or rights to shares should be:

- the fair value of the shares at the date an award is granted, reduced by any consideration payable by the employee for the shares; or
- where shares have been purchased by an ESOP trust at fair value, the difference between the book value of the shares (as recorded in the company's books under UITF Abstract 13) and any consideration payable by the employee.

[UITF 17 para 13(c)].

10.28.15 For LTIPs, the amount initially recognised should be based on a reasonable expectation of the extent that performance criteria will be met. This amount should be charged to the profit and loss account on a straight-line basis (or another basis that more fairly reflects the services received). [UITF 17 para 13(d)].

10.28.16 In subsequent periods, the charge to the profit and loss account will also include adjustments for changes in the estimate of shares to be issued (for example, changes in the probability of performance criteria being met or conditional awards lapsing if employees leave the company) or for purchases of shares at different prices to the fair value at the date of grant. [UITF 17 para 13(d)]. This is illustrated in the examples below.

10.28.17 The abstract does not require the profit and loss account charge to reflect subsequent increases in the value of the shares to which the participant would become entitled (that is, increases in value between the date of grant and the date of exercise). Similarly the amount would not be reduced if the share price falls, except to the extent that the company is able to take advantage of the fall by fulfilling its obligation with shares purchased at a lower price than that originally envisaged. [UITF 17 para 10].

10.28.18 Companies whose schemes provide for the award of shares often use ESOPs to facilitate this. The accounting for ESOPs is addressed in UITF Abstract 13 (see chapter 4) which is consistent with UITF Abstract 17. [UITF 17 para 3]. However, UITF Abstract 17 clarifies the accounting treatment where share options are involved and requires that the intrinsic value of share options granted (that is, any difference between the exercise price and the market value at date of grant) should, as a minimum, be charged to the profit and loss account on a basis similar to that required for other share awards. [UITF 17 para 15]. This is relevant, for instance, where the ESOP subscribes for shares rather than purchasing them at fair value.

Practical implications

Implementation

10.28.19 Where a company has employee share schemes in existence in previous years then implementation of the requirements of the abstract will represent a change of accounting policy and, if the amounts involved are material, this should be accounted for by means of a prior year adjustment in accordance with FRS 3. Comparative figures should be restated.

10.28.20 The legal share premium will normally be determined by the amount of cash subscribed for the shares by the employee (or the ESOP, as the case may be). In such cases, any difference between the subscription price and the fair value of the shares at the date of grant (being the amount to be charged in the profit and loss account) should be credited to a reserve within shareholders' funds, other than share premium account – for instance, other reserves or profit and loss reserve. However, as the commentary on the legal issues included in the abstract makes clear, this is a complicated area and companies may need to take legal advice.

10.28.21 Where new shares are to be issued under an employee share scheme the credit entry for the charge in the profit and loss account should be reported in the reconciliation of movements in shareholders' funds, reflecting the fact that it represents the proceeds of an equity instrument. It should not be reported in the statement of total recognised gains and losses. [UITF 17 para 16].

Changes in estimates

10.28.22 Under LTIPs the abstract requires that the amount initially recognised should be based on a reasonable expectation of the extent that performance criteria will be met. However, as the final amount received under an LTIP will depend upon the actual performance achieved, it is likely that the initial estimate will have to be revised during the performance period. The abstract requires that the charge to the profit and loss account in subsequent periods should include adjustments for changes in the estimate of shares to be issued. For example, this would include changes in the probability of performance criteria being met.

10.28.23 The best estimate of the liability is recalculated in subsequent reporting periods. This means that where a previous estimate is revised, the backlog adjustment relating to prior years is charged in full in the current year's profit and loss account. It is not spread over the remaining performance period. This is illustrated in example 1 in the appendix to the abstract as set out below.

Example 1 – changes in estimates

Scheme participants receive a conditional LTIP award of up to 1,000 shares (with a nominal value of 10p each) on 1 January 1997, when the market price of the shares is £5. The maximum number of shares will be transferred to participants after three years, provided various performance targets are fully met. A lesser number of shares will be transferred if the targets are only partially met. Participants make no contribution for any shares transferred to them.

When the accounts for the year ended 31 December 1997 are being finalised it is considered that 50 per cent of the maximum number of shares is likely to be awarded. This estimate was re-assessed at 80 per cent for the 1998 accounts. At the end of the three year period 75 per cent of the maximum number of shares was awarded and these were issued on 1 January 2000 when the share price was £8.

By 31 December 1997 the company would accrue one third of 1,000 × £5 × 50% = £833. By 31 December 1998 the company would accrue two-thirds of 1,000 × £5 × 80% = £2,667; that is a charge for the year of £1,834. By 31 December 1999 the company would accrue 750 × £5 = £3,750; that is a charge for the year of £1,093.

In the balance sheet the amount accrued would be included within shareholders' funds. On issue of the shares on 1 January 2000 the total amount accrued of £3,750 would be allocated between share capital (£75) and reserves other than share premium account (£3,675). As shares cannot be issued at a discount it is assumed that an ESOP has paid cash equal to the par value of the shares.

The market price of the shares at that date, whether higher or lower than £5, has no relevance for the purpose of the accounting required by the Abstract.

Other illustrative examples

10.28.24 The following examples are based on those in the appendix to the abstract and illustrate the effect on the charge in the profit and loss account if shares are purchased at various dates in order to satisfy the awards. The facts are similar to those in example 1.

Example 2 – purchase of shares by an ESOP at the date of grant

1,000 shares are acquired on 1 January 1997 and are held in an ESOP at a cost of £5,000 until 750 shares are transferred to participants on 1 January 2000. The remaining 250 shares continue to be held in the ESOP.

The accounting is as for Example 1 above, except that in the balance sheet the shares will be shown as 'own shares' within fixed assets in accordance with UITF Abstract 13, with the accrual reflecting a diminution in value of those shares.

The abstract does not deal with the subsequent treatment of the surplus 250 shares. These will be carried as an asset in the sponsoring company's balance sheet under UITF Abstract 13. If the shares are subsequently gifted to employees under new remuneration schemes, then the carrying value of the shares will be written down over that performance period (see example 4).

Alternatively, the ESOP may sell the shares in the market at a price in excess of cost, giving rise to a profit. A consequence of the UITF Abstract 13 approach is that gains as well as losses in the ESOP form part of the sponsoring company's results and so the profit on sale of the shares would be recognised in the company's profit and loss account. We consider that the profit on disposal of shares should be disclosed separately from the charge resulting from the write-down of shares gifted to employees if the figures are material. Where shares are acquired by the ESOP at below market price, it might not be appropriate to take any resulting gain on sale to the sponsoring company's profit and loss account.

Example 3 – purchase of shares by an ESOP subsequent to date of grant

1,000 shares are acquired on 30 June 1998 at a cost of £6,000 and are held in an ESOP until 750 shares are transferred to participants on 1 January 2000.

By 31 December 1997 the company would accrue £833 (as example 1). By 31 December 1998 the company would accrue two-thirds of £6,000 × 80% = £3,200; that is a charge for the year of £2,367. By 31 December 1999 the company would accrue 750 × £6 = £4,500; that is a charge for the year of £1,300.

The profit and loss account charge is higher than in example 1 because the shares were acquired at a cost higher than their value at the time of the initial award.

In the balance sheet at 31 December 1997, a creditor of £833 will be recognised as the terms of the arrangement are that the ESOP will purchase shares. At 31 December 1998, the shares will be shown as 'own shares' within fixed assets in accordance with UITF Abstract 13, with the accruals in 1998 and 1999 reflecting a diminution in value of those shares.

Example 4 – purchase of shares by an ESOP prior to date of grant

Shares already held in an ESOP at 1 January 1997 at a book value of £4,000. The accounting would be as example 2, but based on a cost of £4 each rather than £5.

In the balance sheet the shares will be shown as 'own shares' within fixed assets in accordance with UITF Abstract 13, with the accrual reflecting a diminution in value of those shares.

Example 5 – purchase of shares by ESOP at end of performance period

750 shares are acquired on 31 December 1999 at a cost of £5,250

The accounting for 1997 and 1998 would be as example 1 – that is:
By 31 December 1997 the company would accrue one third of 1,000 × £5 × 50% = £833.
By 31 December 1998 the company would accrue two-thirds of 1,000 × £5 × 80% = £2,667.

By 31 December 1999 the company would accrue £5,250.

10.28.25 The accounting for the charge in the profit and loss account is further complicated if the shares are purchased in tranches. The abstract does not deal with this, but this is illustrated in example 6 using similar facts to example 1.

Example 6 – purchase of shares by an ESOP in tranches

500 shares are acquired on 1 January 1997 and are held in an ESOP at a cost of £2,500. A further 500 shares are acquired on 30 June 1998 at a cost of £3,000 and are held in the ESOP until 750 shares are transferred to participants on 1 January 2000.

By 31 December 1997 the company would accrue one third of 1,000 × £5 × 50% = £833. This would be credited against the cost of the investment in own shares leaving a carrying value of £1,667 (£2,500 – £833).

By 31 December 1998 the company would accrue two-thirds of the total cost of £5,500 × 80% = £2,933; that is, a charge for the year of £2,100. This would be credited against the cost of the investment in own shares leaving a carrying value of £2,567 (£1,667 + £3,000 – £2,100).

By 31 December 1999 the company would accrue £5,500 × 75% = £4,125; that is a charge for the year of £1,192. This would be credited against the cost of the investment in own shares leaving a carrying value of £1,375 (£2,567 – £1,192) representing the cost of the remaining shares held by the ESOP (£5,500 × 25%).

10.28.26 It should be noted that the profit and loss account charge is not determined by spreading the cost of the shares purchased over the remaining period. The best estimate of the liability should be calculated at the end of each period. The resulting charge reduces the carrying value of any shares held on the reporting entity's balance sheet under UITF Abstract 13. If the charge exceeds the carrying value of the shares then the balance would be carried as a provision (for instance, if shares are to be purchased at a later date) or written back to reserves (to the extent that it represents the excess of market value at the date of grant over the proceeds on shares that are to be issued).

Directors' emoluments disclosure

10.28.27 UITF Abstract 17 does not deal with the disclosure of directors' emoluments. Disclosure requirements for long-term incentive schemes are contained in Schedule 6 of the Companies Act 1985 (as amended by SI 1997/570) and in the Stock Exchange Listing Rules. Details of these requirements are covered in chapter 11.

[The next paragraph is 10.29.]

Depreciation (including other amounts written off assets)

10.29 Where the company prepares its profit and loss account in accordance with either Format 1 or Format 3, expenses are classified by function. Consequently, any provisions for either depreciation or the diminution in value of tangible and intangible fixed assets will not be disclosed in the profit and loss account format. Accordingly, the Act requires that this information must be disclosed separately in the notes to the financial statements. [Note 17 on the profit and loss account formats].

10.30 In addition, the Act requires separate disclosure of the aggregate amount of:

[The next page is 10011.]

- Any provision against a fixed asset investment for diminution in value.
- Any provision against a fixed asset for permanent diminution in value.
- Any write back of such provisions which are no longer necessary.

[4 Sch 19(1) – (3)].

10.31 Accounting for depreciation and diminutions in value of fixed assets (under both the historical cost and alternative accounting rules) is considered fully in chapter 5.

Other operating charges (including other external charges)

10.32 The relevant formats (Formats 2 and 4) place 'other external charges' next to 'raw materials and consumables' under a single item number. Therefore, such charges are likely to include any production costs from external sources that are not included under other headings (for example, equipment rentals and the costs of subcontractors).

10.33 'Other operating charges' is a separate line item which tends to be a residual class of all charges relating to the trading activities of a business that do not fall into any other category. Losses on exchange may also be included under this heading (except for losses that are required by SSAP 20, 'Foreign currency translation', to be taken directly to reserves and as a result, are included in the statement of total recognised gains and losses).

10.34 In practice, the distinction between 'other external charges' and 'other operating charges' is blurred. Some companies do not attempt to make a distinction, and include only one heading to cover all residual operating costs. Table 10.3 gives an example in which a company discloses no 'other external charges', but analyses residual operating expenses under the heading 'other operating charges'.

Table 10.3 – British Gas plc – Annual Report and Accounts – 31 December 1994

Notes to the accounts (extract)

4 Operating costs (extract)

	1994			
	Continuing operations £m	Other Discontinued operations £m	Exceptional charges £m	Total £m
Other operating charges:				
Other exploration expenditure	88	–	–	88
Monetary working capital adjustment	24	–	–	24
Lease rentals:				
Plant, machinery and equipment	24	–	–	24
Other assets	38	–	–	38
Research and development	74	1	–	75
Environmental costs	–	–	90	90
Other expenses	1,550	31	105	1,686

Income from investments

10.35 Each of the four profit and loss account formats for individual companies contain the same four investment income captions.

- Income from shares in group undertakings.
- Income from participating interests.
- Income from other fixed asset investments.
- Other interest receivable and similar income.

10.36 The Act also requires the last two items referred to above, that is income from other fixed asset investments and other interest, to be split between that derived from group undertakings and that derived from other sources. [Note 15 on the profit and loss account formats].

10.37 SSAP 8 requires that dividends received from UK resident companies should be included in the profit and loss account at the amount of cash received or receivable, plus the related tax credit. The amount of the tax credit is then disclosed under UK corporation tax as 'tax attributable to franked investment income'.

10.38 Where a company pays a dividend as a 'foreign income dividend' (see further chapter 13), the company receiving the dividend should simply recognise the dividend in the profit and loss account at the amount of the dividend received. That is because a foreign income dividend does not carry a tax credit; nor is a corporate investor subject to tax in respect of the receipt of such a dividend. Consequently, there is little justification for grossing up the foreign income dividend received by a notional tax credit.

10.39 Dividends received and receivable from both subsidiary and fellow subsidiary companies will be included in 'income from shares in group undertakings'. Traditionally, dividends are included in the receiving company's financial statements in the year to which they relate, even though they may not be declared or paid by the paying company until the subsequent year. In a group's consolidated financial statements, this line will appear only if dividends are received or receivable from subsidiaries that have not been consolidated.

10.40 In an investing company's individual profit and loss account 'Income from participating interests' will include, for example, income from the following undertakings in which the investing company holds on a long-term basis 20 per cent or more of the shares in that undertaking.

- Income from bodies corporate (including dividends received from associated undertakings).
- Share of profits from partnerships.
- Share of profits from unincorporated associations carrying on a trade or business, with or without a profit.

10.41 Chapter 28 explains the meaning of participating interests and associated undertakings and describes the accounting treatment of income from interests in associated undertakings in consolidated financial statements.

Interest payable and similar charges

10.42 'Interest payable and similar charges' appears as a separate item in all the profit and loss account formats. Apart from interest, the caption may include other finance costs such as:

- Accrued discounts in respect of zero coupon and deep discount bonds.
- Accrual of the premium payable on the redemption of debt.
- Gains or losses arising on the repurchase or early settlement of debt.

10.43 The Act requires certain additional disclosures in respect of interest. Note 16 to the profit and loss account formats requires that interest payable to group undertakings must be disclosed separately. In addition, Schedule 4 requires the disclosure of the amount of the interest on or any similar charges in respect of:

- Bank loans and overdrafts.
- Loans of any other kind made to the company.

[4 Sch 53(2) as amended by SI 1996/189].

10.44 The requirement to give the above analyses does not apply to either interest or charges on loans from group undertakings. But it does apply to interest or charges on all other loans, whether or not these are made on the security of a debenture. [4 Sch 53(2)].

10.45 FRS 4 specifically requires gains or losses arising on the repurchase or early settlement of debt to be disclosed in the profit and loss account as separate items within or adjacent to 'interest payable and similar charges' (see further chapter 18). [FRS 4 para 64].

Dividends paid and payable

10.46 Dividends, proposed and paid, is not an item that is found in the detailed profit and loss account formats. However, paragraph 3(7)(b) of Schedule 4 to the Act requires that a company's profit and loss account shall show the aggregate amount of any dividends paid and proposed. Dividends cannot be relegated to the notes to the profit and loss account: they must be disclosed in aggregate on the face of it. Where, however, the aggregate amount of proposed dividends is not disclosed in the notes it must be shown separately from dividends paid on the face of the profit and loss account. [4 Sch 3(7)(c) inserted by SI 1996/189]. The amount of dividends paid and proposed that is disclosed should exclude any amount of related ACT. [SSAP 8 para 4].

10.47 Although there is no specified position for dividends in the profit and loss account, the formats in the Act and the form of reporting required by FRS 3 mean that dividends are usually deducted from the profit or loss for the financial year in arriving at the profit or loss retained for the year.

10.48 In order to pay a dividend, a company has to have sufficient distributable reserves. Distributable reserves are considered in detail in chapter 19.

10.49 FRS 4 introduced new rules for measuring the costs of servicing non-equity shares, including preference shares. Dividends are only one element of the overall finance cost. Consequently, dividends paid and payable in respect of each financial year do not necessarily equal the total cost shown in the profit and loss account. Under FRS 4 the amounts shown as appropriations of profit will also include, where applicable, items such as the accrual of redemption premiums and amortisation of issue costs. Such items should be disclosed separately from dividends. [FRS 4 para 59]. An example of such disclosure is given in Table 10.5. The accounting and disclosure implications of FRS 4 in respect of dividends and other appropriations are covered fully in chapter 18.

Table 10.5 – The Rank Organisation Plc – Directors' Report and Accounts – 31 October 1994

GROUP PROFIT & LOSS ACCOUNT (extract)

	Note	**1994 £m**	1993 £m
Profit for the financial year		**168.1**	168.2
Dividends and other appropriations			
Preference	7	**(20.9)**	(20.9)
Ordinary	7	**(110.0)**	(5.9)
Transfer to reserves	20	**37.2**	141.4

NOTES TO THE ACCOUNTS

7 DIVIDENDS (extract)

	Per share 1994	Per share 1993	**1994 £m**	1993 £m
Convertible redeemable preference shares				
Dividends payable for year			**18.8**	18.8
Provision for redemption premium			**2.1**	2.1
			20.9	20.9
Ordinary shares				
Interim paid	**4.25p**	–	**35.3**	–
Special interim dividend paid	–	12.16p	–	5.9
Final proposed	**9.00p**	–	**74.7**	–
	13.25p	12.16p	**110.0**	5.9
			130.9	26.8

10.50 In addition to the Act's requirements regarding dividends, the Stock Exchange's Listing Rules for listed companies require particulars to be disclosed of any arrangements under which a shareholder has either waived or agreed to waive any dividends. [LR 12.43(e)].

Shares in lieu of cash dividends (scrip dividends)

10.51 Many listed companies choose to make arrangements for ordinary shareholders to elect to receive their dividends in the form of additional ordinary shares rather than in cash. The share equivalent is sometimes referred to as a scrip dividend or a stock dividend and consists of shares fully paid up out of the company's profits. The advantages of issuing scrip dividends are that in the short term, the company's cash position would be improved. Secondly, no ACT is payable in respect of those dividends taken in the form of shares. FRS 4 requires scrip dividends to be shown as an appropriation at the value of the cash alternative. Accounting for scrip dividends is considered in chapter 18.

Other profit and loss disclosures

10.52 In addition to the items required to be disclosed by the formats, a number of supplementary disclosures relating to the profit and loss account are also required. The following paragraphs set out some significant ones.

Auditors' remuneration – audit work

10.53 The Act requires disclosure of the amount of the remuneration of the company's auditors in their capacity as auditors. This amount includes any expenses and the estimated money value of any benefits in kind (nature of any such benefits should also be disclosed). [Sec 390A, 4A Sch 1(1) as amended by SI 1996/189].

10.54 The Act requires disclosure of the remuneration of the company's auditors for the audit of the company. Furthermore, in group accounts paragraph 1 of Schedule 4A requires in addition disclosure of the aggregate remuneration of the auditors of all group companies and not merely that of the parent. The requirement is to aggregate all audit fees whether or not they are earned by different firms of auditors (and not merely to aggregate the fees attributable to the group's principal auditors).

Auditors' remuneration – non-audit work

10.55 Companies are also required to disclose the aggregate remuneration (including expenses and any benefits in kind) of their auditors (or the auditor's associates) for all non-audit services provided to the company and any UK subsidiary undertakings audited by the same auditor as the company (or by the same auditor's associates). [SI 1991/2128].

10.56 Non-audit fees include, for example, fees for accountancy or taxation services, investigations or other corporate finance work or management consultancy.

10.57 Disclosure is not required of remuneration for services rendered to subsidiaries not audited by the parent company's auditors or to subsidiaries incorporated outside the UK, although some companies voluntarily disclose such information.

10.58 There is no statutory requirement to disclose any information concerning the nature of non-audit services provided. Some companies do, however, provide an indication of the nature of the work in order to make the disclosure more meaningful. Others also disclose fees of a similar nature paid to other organisations.

10.59 Judgement may be required as to whether remuneration is paid to auditors in their capacity as auditors or otherwise (that is, audit or non-audit). All work that auditors necessarily undertake in forming and communicating their audit opinion is audit work.

10.60 The disclosure is required of remuneration 'in respect of work carried out in' the financial year. This may be based on amounts invoiced in the period adjusted for the estimated fees payable for work carried out, but not invoiced at the beginning and end of the period (that is on an accruals basis). Work relating to a period (such as, tax compliance work) that is carried out after the year end should be disclosed in the period in which the work is performed rather than in the period to which it relates.

10.61 The disclosure must include remuneration of all 'associates' of the auditors both in the UK and overseas. The definition is complex and the regulations require the auditors to provide directors with information to identify the auditors' associates.

10.62 Intermediate parent companies are not exempted from the requirement to include aggregate non-audit remuneration payable by both the company and its relevant subsidiaries, even though the intermediate parent company may be exempt from preparing consolidated financial statements.

10.63 The disclosure requirements do not apply to small and medium-sized companies, as defined by the Act, unless the company is:

- A public limited company.
- A banking, insurance or financial services company.
- Part of a group containing a public, banking, insurance or financial services company.
- Parent of a group which is neither small nor medium-sized.

Operating lease rentals and hire of plant and machinery

10.64 The total of operating lease rentals (including charges under a hire purchase agreement similar in nature to an operating lease) charged as an expense in the profit and loss account should be disclosed, analysed between amounts payable in respect of hire of plant and machinery and in respect of other operating leases (for example, for land and buildings). [SSAP 21 para 55].

10.65 The words 'plant and machinery' usually cover whatever items in the nature of fixed assets (other than land and buildings) are hired for use in the business (for example, vehicles, ships or other equipment).

Research and development

10.66 Other than for companies described below, the total amount of research and development expenditure charged in the profit and loss account should be disclosed, analysed between the current year's expenditure and amounts amortised from deferred expenditure (see also chapter 14). [SSAP 13 para 31].

10.67 A company is exempt from the above disclosure if it satisfies both the following conditions:

- It must not be a public limited company nor a banking or insurance company, nor be a holding company which has such a company as a subsidiary.

- It satisfies the Act's criteria, multiplied in each case by ten, for defining a medium-sized company (see chapter 36).

[SSAP 13 para 22].

Year 2000 issues – accounting and disclosures

10.68 The year 2000 will be the first century change ever faced by an automated society. As the year 2000 approaches, a critical issue has emerged regarding how existing computer application software programs can accommodate this date value. The vast majority of existing computer application software in the marketplace, as well as in-house developed systems, in use throughout the world today has date processing logic based on a two-digit year (for example, '96' is stored on the system and represents the year 1996). The assumption in the system logic is that later dates have higher numbers. When the year 2000 arrives, the two digit year becomes '00' and the logic will not function properly leading to processing inaccuracies and system failures. Therefore, it has become imperative for virtually every enterprise to consider the potential ramifications of the year 2000 issue and to take appropriate action on a timely basis. Industry experts estimate that companies worldwide could spend billions of pounds to correct their information systems. The issue is how to account for the external and internal costs specifically associated with modifying internal-use computer software to achieve year 2000 compliance.

10.69 The above issue was addressed by the UITF in Abstract 20, 'Year 2000 issues: accounting and disclosures', which is effective for accounting periods ending on or after 23 March 1998. The Abstract states that costs incurred in rendering existing software year 2000 compliant should be written off to the profit and loss account except in those cases where the entity already has a policy of capitalising software costs. In that situation, the costs should be capitalised and depreciated only if the expenditure clearly enhances the software service potential beyond that originally assessed, rather than merely ensuring the continued effectiveness of the faulty software for its originally assessed useful life. In practice, some costs are likely to be a combination of repair and upgrading and appropriate proportions should be charged as an expense or capitalised accordingly.

10.70 The second aspect of the Abstract is disclosures and these have turned out to be quite extensive. In this connection, the Abstract first notes that in some cases year 2000 software modification costs will need to be disclosed as exceptional in accordance with FRS 3. This is as regards expenditure in the year. It then moves on to commitments at the balance sheet and says that these costs (whether treated as capital and revenue) should be disclosed when they are considered to fall within the requirement of the Act to give particulars of financial commitments.

10.71 There are then some different disclosures which may be given in the directors' report or in the OFR or other statement included in the annual report published by the entity. These are as follows:

- The risks and uncertainties associated with the year 2000 problem. This would be a description of the problem as the company assesses it. But if the entity has not made an assessment of the problem or has not determined its materiality, that fact should be disclosed.

- The entity's general plans to address the year 2000 issues relating to its business and operations and, if material, its relationship with customers, suppliers and other relevant parties.

- Whether the total estimated costs of these plans – current and future – have been quantified and, where applicable, an indication of the total costs likely to be incurred, together with an explanation of the basis on which these figures are calculated (for example, the treatment of internal costs and replacement expenditure).

10.72 These three disclosures are quite extensive and obviously in their nature not very precise. Indeed, it is important for the entity not to create a perception of assurance that any rectification efforts will be successful. On this point the UITF information sheet number 27 announcing the publication of the abstract noted the following statement made by the US SEC:

> *"It is not, and will not, be possible for any single entity or collective enterprise to represent that it has achieved complete year 2000 compliance and thus to guarantee its remediation efforts. The*

problem is simply too complex for such a claim to have legitimacy. Efforts to solve year 2000 problems are best described as 'risk mitigation'. Success in the effort will have been achieved if the number and seriousness of any technical failures is minimised, and they are quickly identified and repaired if they do occur."

10.73 The SEC is one of the many regulators worldwide that have issued pronouncements on this topic and the disclosures that it requires are similar to those included in Abstract 20. Indeed, the London Stock Exchange encourages all listed companies to make disclosures equivalent to those required by the Abstract by 31 December 1998. This may mean including such disclosures in interim statements. Listed companies are also required to consider whether, under the general disclosure obligations set out in chapter 9 of the Listing Rules, announcements are required in respect of potential problems or uncertainties associated with the year 2000 issues.

10.74 In the light of the above observations, it is right that the disclosures required by paragraph 10.71 above should be outside the audited statutory accounts and companies will in general, therefore, include them in their directors' report or OFR rather than in the financial statements themselves. A number of major companies in the UK have already disclosed their plans to address this problem, including disclosure of significant estimated costs being and to be incurred. An example of a company that has given extensive disclosures in the directors' report and in the OFR is given below.

Table 10.6 – Reuters Holdings PLC – Annual Report – 31 December 1997

REPORT OF THE DIRECTORS (extract)

MILLENNIUM PROGRAMME In 1996 Reuters established a Millennium Compliance Programme to address the issues arising as a result of the millennium date. Many computer systems store or process date information by the last two digits of the year only, resulting in incorrect or unpredictable treatment of dates after the year 2000 in software applications.

The purpose of the programme is to determine which software components and systems have to be upgraded and which will need to be replaced. The process will also be used to confirm which products will be discontinued before the millennium. For further details see pages 37-38.

OPERATING AND FINANCIAL REVIEW (extract)

MILLENNIUM PROGRAMME In 1996 Reuters established a Millennium Compliance Programme to address the issues arising as a result of the millennium date. Many computer systems store or process date information by the last two digits of the year only, resulting in incorrect or unpredictable treatment of dates after the year 2000 is software applications. The Programme is led by an executive director of Reuters supported by and central group of technical staff and a full-time programme director.

The Programme will certify products, operations and internal processes for millennium compliance and establish safeguards and procedures in respect of third parties from whom Reuters obtains software or services. A key third-party dependency is the external global telecommunications infrastructure which Reuters uses to deliver its products.

Reuters has launched "Millennium Challenge", a global communications exercise for customers and other external audiences to explain the changes to the shape of the Reuters product line over the millennium period. Further information will be made available as the Programme progresses.

In order to underline the importance of the Programme, a series of milestones has been established, and the incentive remuneration of Reuters senior executives is based in part upon achievement of these milestones.

The purpose of the Programme is to determine which software components and systems have to be upgraded and which will need to be replaced. The process will also be used to confirm which products will be discontinued before the millennium.

Reuters is bearing the costs of its Millennium Programme. There may be some instances in which customers will choose upgrades at additional cost to higher product specifications than required for millennium compliance. There may also be cases where customers request high levels of out-of-hours work for which there will be an additional charge. These charges to customers are not expected to be significant and will be in accordance with existing agreements and practices.

The effort associated with the Programme falls into two main categories:

1. The diversion of existing internal resources. This includes development staff who would otherwise be deployed on other projects and operational staff involved in the implementation at customer sites.

2. Incremental external resources, largely contractors and consultants, who will not remain following the completion of the Programme.

Details of the effort incurred in 1997 and budgeted for 1998, together with estimated costs of incremental external resource, are set out below.

	MAN YEARS	INCREMENTAL COST (£m)
1997		
Internal effort		
Development	155	n/a
External effort		
Development	120	11
Total	275	11
1998		
Internal effort		
Development	325	n/a
Implementation	440	n/a
External effort		
Development	150	16
Implementation	230	15
Total	1,145	31

The implementation process is complex and reliant upon co-ordination with customers and suppliers. The effort and costs in 1999 will depend upon progress during 1998 and Reuters current assessment is that these will not exceed those incurred in 1998.

The above figures are based on the current status of the Programme and may be subject to change. They include estimates and allocations of time in those cases where Reuters staff have other responsibilities in addition to the Millennium Programme.

10.75 There is one further matter discussed in the Abstract. The explanation section deals with the question of whether companies can provide for the expected future costs to modify software for year 2000 problems. It notes that under the proposals in FRED 14, 'Provisions and contingencies', such costs cannot be provided in advance of the expenditure being incurred. This is because the FRED says that for a provision to be recognised the entity must have a legal obligation or constructive obligation to transfer economic benefits as a result of past events. As the year 2000 is yet to arrive, the mere intention or even necessity to undertake expenditure relating to the future would not create a constructive obligation under the FRED. Therefore, no provision would be made for estimated future software modification costs and such costs would be recognised in the accounting period in which the modification work is carried out. As a result, a provision set up for estimated future costs (before a standard prohibiting this became mandatory) may need to be reversed and the costs charged when the modification costs are incurred. These proposals have now been implemented in FRS 12, 'Provisions, contingent liabilities and contingent assets' and are effective for accounting periods ending on or after 23 March 1999. These new rules are summarised in chapter 17.

Chapter 11

Disclosure of directors' remuneration

Chapter 11

Disclosure of directors' remuneration

Introduction

11.1 Directors' remuneration is one of the most sensitive and closely regulated aspects of financial reporting. Generally, directors are well rewarded, and it is inevitable, given their stewardship role, that comparisons will be made by investors and others between the company's performance and the level of the directors' remuneration. The subject of directors' remuneration has even become a political issue in recent times, with the issue of the salaries of directors of privatised utilities being raised in parliament. One facet of this subject is the extent of the disclosure of remuneration in the financial statements. In 1995 a Study Group on Directors' remuneration was set up on the initiative of the CBI under the chairmanship of Sir Richard Greenbury. The Study Group published a report in July 1995 (The Greenbury Report). One of the recommendations of the Greenbury Report was that there should be substantially increased disclosure of directors' remuneration. Some of the recommended disclosures had the effect of codifying existing best practice. Others, particularly in the area of pensions, required further guidance and changes in the law. The principal developments since 1995 have been:

- Following publication of the Greenbury Report and further consultation the Stock Exchange introduced new requirements for disclosure of directors' emoluments by UK listed companies. These requirements were broadly based on the Greenbury Report recommendations.

- Major changes in the law relating to disclosure of directors' remuneration (including pensions) by amendment to the 1985 Act have also been introduced, which are effective for accounting periods ending on or after 31 March 1997.

- The Stock Exchange has introduced a new Listing Rule requiring disclosure of individual directors' pension entitlements, which is effective for accounting periods ending on or after 1 July 1997.

- In 1998 a Committee on Corporate Governance, chaired by Sir Ronald Hampel issued its final report (The Hampel Report). The report generally supported the requirements that had been introduced by the Greenbury Report and subsequently by the Stock Exchange. A summary of the Committee's conclusions in respect of directors' remuneration is given from paragraph 11.197 below.

- Following the publication of the Hampel report, the Committee on Corporate Governance published in June 1998 the 'Combined Code' which was a new code of corporate governance derived by the committee from its own report and from the Cadbury and Greenbury reports.

- Also in June 1998 the Stock Exchange published a new Listing Rule which requires listed companies to make a statement of compliance with the new Combined Code. The requirements of the new Listing Rule in respect of directors' emoluments disclosure remain substantially the same as before. The new Listing Rule is effective for accounting periods ending on or after 31 December 1998.

11.2 This chapter discusses the detailed rules relating to the disclosure of directors' remuneration that are contained in the Act, including the changes introduced in 1997 and sets out the requirements of the Stock Exchange Listing Rules for UK listed companies including the new Listing Rule on disclosure of pension entitlements also issued in 1997.

11.3 The new legal requirements are effective for accounting periods ending on or after 31 March 1997. Accordingly, all references to Schedule 6 are to the provisions of that Schedule as amended by The Company Accounts (Disclosure of Directors' Emoluments) Regulations 1997, (SI 1997/570). This chapter does not deal with the different disclosure requirements in respect of accounting periods ending before 31 March 1997, but a brief indication is given, where appropriate, of how the previous requirements have changed.

11.4 The rules relating to disclosure of directors' remuneration are contained in Part I of Schedule 6 to the Act. Whilst these rules are extensive they had not, until recently, kept pace with the demands of investors and others for fuller and clearer disclosure of directors' rewards, nor were the rules sufficiently wide or exact to bring clearly within their scope forms of remuneration that have become increasingly prevalent in recent years, such as share options or unfunded pension arrangements.

11.5 Partly because of this the Cadbury committee issued a report entitled 'The Financial Aspects of Corporate Governance' in December 1992. The report contained, *inter alia*, recommendations relating to the disclosure of directors' remuneration and stated:

> *"The overriding principle in respect of board remuneration is that of openness. Shareholders are entitled to a full and clear statement*

of directors' present and future benefits, and of how they have been determined."

11.6 The report went on to indicate in a 'Code of best practice' (the Code) the types of additional disclosures that it recommended. The recommended disclosures applied to listed companies registered in the UK. The Stock Exchange required such companies to state in their financial statements whether or not they had complied throughout the period with the recommendations of the Code or to specify any non-compliance and how long it continued, with reasons for the non-compliance. [LR 12.43(j)]. With effect for accounting periods beginning on or after 31 December 1995 the statement of compliance with the Code did not cover the paragraphs of the Code relating to directors' remuneration. Instead a UK listed company had to make a separate statement of compliance with Section A of the best practice provisions annexed to the Listing Rules and also state that, in framing its remuneration policy, the remuneration committee (or the board itself if there is no such committee) had given full consideration to Section B of the best practice provisions annexed to the Listing Rules. [LR 12.43(w) and 12.43(x)(ii)].

11.7 In June 1998 the Stock Exchange introduced a new Listing Rule 12.43A which requires, for accounting periods ending on or after 31 December 1998, a statement of compliance with a new Combined Code, based on Hampel, Cadbury and Greenbury. This new statement of compliance will replace the one described above. The Listing Rule retains the same disclosure requirements in respect of directors remuneration as before. See further paragraph 11.131 below.

11.8 The disclosure of directors' remuneration can be considered under a number of headings and sub-headings:

- Companies Act requirements – general rules.
- Aggregate emoluments and other benefits.
  - Aggregate emoluments.
  - Gains made on exercise of share options and amounts received or receivable under long-term incentive schemes.
  - Pension contributions.
  - Banding of emoluments (requirement removed for accounting periods ending on or after 31 March 1997).
  - Highest paid directors' emoluments and other benefits.
  - Excess retirement benefits of directors and past directors.
  - Compensation for loss of office.
  - Sums paid to third parties in respect of directors' services.
- Share options – disclosures under UITF 10.
- Stock Exchange Listing Rules.
  - Compliance rules.
  - Disclosure rules.

- Definitions and examples.
- Long-term incentive schemes.
- Deferred bonuses.
- Pension entitlements.
- Audit.
- Emoluments waived.

- Group situations.

Each of these is considered in turn below.

Companies Act requirements – general rules

Directors' and auditors' duties

11.9 A company's directors have a duty to give information about their remuneration (including pensions, compensation for loss of office and sums paid to third parties) to the company so that the information discussed below can be disclosed in the financial statements. This requirement applies also to a person who has been a director of the company within the preceding five years. If a director does not give notice of the required information to the company, he is liable to a fine. [Sec 232(3)(4)].

11.10 If the required information is not disclosed in the financial statements, the auditors have a duty to include the information (so far as they are reasonably able to do so) in their audit report. [Sec 237(4)]. Auditors also have a duty to report if certain information required by the Stock Exchange Listing Rules has not been disclosed (see para 11.169 below).

Payment for directors' services

11.11 The remuneration to be disclosed should include all amounts paid to a director for his services as a director of the company and any subsidiary, or for managing the company and its subsidiaries (see para 11.36 below). All payments should be included, whether those payments are made by the company, or by a subsidiary undertaking of the company or by any other person, unless the director has to account in turn to another group company, or to members under section 314 or section 315, for the receipt of the remuneration. [6 Sch 10(2)]. This also applies to payments by way of compensation for loss of office.

Example

Mr Smith spends part of his time as an executive director of company A and part of his time as an employee of company B, which is controlled by Mr Smith. Company B pays Mr Smith's salary, and it invoices company A for an amount to cover that part of the time that Mr Smith spends working for company A. Although Mr Smith is paid by company B (and not by company A of which he is a director), the amount that he receives from company B is partially in respect of his services as a director of company A. Consequently, he should disclose to company A, and company A should disclose in its financial statements as remuneration, the proportion of his salary that relates to his services as a director of company A. This figure may or may not be the same as the amount that company B has invoiced company A. This will depend on whether the invoiced amount is intended to cover an amount that is either more or less than the actual cost of the director's services to company A.

11.12 Overlooking this point can have serious consequences as illustrated by the findings of the Financial Reporting Review Panel (FRRP) on the financial statements of Foreign & Colonial Investment Trust plc (FCIT) for the year ended 31 December 1991. The FRRP found that the financial statements of FCIT reflected the emoluments receivable by the directors from the company and its subsidiaries. However, remuneration receivable by five directors from the company's investment manager, an associate of one of its subsidiaries, relating to services provided to FCIT and its subsidiaries had not been disclosed in FCIT's financial statements. Following discussions with the Panel, the directors agreed to provide, in the 1992 financial statements, additional information concerning that proportion of remuneration receivable by the directors from the company's investment manager, which related to

[The next page is 11005.]

services to FCIT and its subsidiary undertakings. Appropriate comparative figures for 1991 were also presented in the 1992 financial statements.

11.13 The disclosure in the 1992 financial statements is shown in Table 11.1.

Table 11.1 – Foreign & Colonial Investment Trust PLC – Report and Accounts – 31 December 1992

Directors' emoluments (extract)

Mr A.C. Barker, Mr O.N. Dawson, Mr E.C. Elstob, Mr M.J. Hart and The Hon. James Ogilvy receive emoluments from Foreign & Colonial Management Limited for their services to that company. The proportion of their emoluments which relates to the management of the affairs of the Company or any of its subsidiary undertakings amounts to approximately £227,000 (1991 – £195,000). This amount has been taken into account, together with the £106,000 (1991 – £100,000) paid directly by the Company to the non-executive directors, in providing the following disclosure:

Directors' emoluments (including payments by all subsidiary undertakings but excluding pensions contributions).

Comparatives for 1991 have been restated.

	1992	1991
Chairman	**£29,000**	£25,000
Highest paid director	**£138,000**	£114,000
£1 – £5,000	**1**	-
£10,001 – £15,000	**6**	7
£15,001 – £20,000	**1**	1
£25,001 – £30,000	**2**	2

11.14 There is also nothing in the Act to suggest that the director must receive payments personally in order that they should be subject to disclosure as remuneration. Amounts paid to or receivable by a director, including amounts paid in respect of compensation for loss of office, will include amounts paid to or receivable by a person connected with him, or a body corporate controlled by him (but such amounts should not be counted twice). [6 Sch 10(4)]. The definitions of connected persons and body corporate controlled by a director are in section 346 of the Act. Consequently, even where a director sets up another company specifically to receive his remuneration, that remuneration will be deemed to be remuneration received by him if that company is controlled by him.

11.15 Furthermore, if the company has nominated (either directly or indirectly) the director to be a director of another company, that other company is treated as if it were a subsidiary undertaking for the purposes of determining the amounts to be disclosed for directors' remuneration, compensation for loss of office and payments to third parties for directors' services. Accordingly, the director's remuneration and compensation for loss of office should include any amount he receives as a director of that other company (whether or not that other company is a subsidiary of the company). [6 Sch 13(2)(a)]. Any sums that the other company pays to third parties in respect of his services should be disclosed as sums paid to third parties.

Example

Company A has nominated one of its directors to the board of company B (company A and B are not connected). Company B pays £20,000 per year to the director in respect of his services. In this situation, the director must disclose to company A, as remuneration, the amount of £20,000 that he receives from company B. Company A will need to disclose, as directors' remuneration, the aggregate of the amount paid to the director in respect of his services as director of company A and the amount of £20,000 he receives from company B. If, on the other hand, the amount of £20,000 is paid to company A (that is, as a sum to be accounted for to the company, see para 11.11) and not to the director personally, then this amount need not be included as directors' emoluments in the financial statements of company A. However, company B will need to disclose the payment of £20,000 in its own financial statements as a sum paid to a third party in respect of the director's services (see para 11.113 below).

Disclosure in which year

11.16 A director's remuneration that should be disclosed in the financial statements for a particular year is the remuneration receivable by the director in respect of that year, regardless of when it is paid to the director. [6 Sch 11(1)]. For example, if a bonus is receivable by a director in respect of services performed in year one, but is not paid to the director until year two, it is disclosable as that director's emoluments in year one.

11.17 In the case of remuneration that is receivable by a director in respect of a period that extends beyond the financial year, for example, a long-term incentive scheme covering a period of three years, with no further conditions to be satisfied, it can be argued that the remuneration is still *"receivable in respect of a year"*, that is, the remuneration is receivable in respect of the third year of the scheme. In that case the remuneration for the whole three-year period would be disclosable in the third year.

11.18 The argument in paragraph 11.17 above seems to be supported by the rule that remuneration not receivable in respect of a period should be disclosed in the year it is paid. [6 Sch 11(1)]. Whilst not explicitly stated, the implication of this is that where remuneration is receivable in respect of a period, be that a period of one year or more that one year, it should be disclosed when due, that is in the year in which it becomes receivable.

11.19 Where remuneration is not receivable in respect of a period, whether of a single financial year or a period of over one financial year, it should be disclosed in the financial statements of the period in which it is paid. This might apply, for instance, when a single *ex gratia* payment is made to a director that is unrelated to a financial year or other period. An example might be a payment made as compensation for a reduction in the length of a director's service contract.

11.20 One problem that sometimes arises in respect of long-term incentive schemes is where the performance period lasts three years, but a director must then remain with the company for a further period, say six months, before he becomes entitled to receive any amounts under the scheme. The question that arises in such a case is whether the amounts due under the scheme are receivable in respect of the three-year performance period and are, therefore, disclosable in the third year of the scheme, or whether they are receivable only after a further six months, when the additional service period has been completed, in which case they would be disclosable in the fourth year.

11.21 The answer to the question may depend on the particular terms of the scheme and on when the remuneration becomes a firm entitlement. If, for instance, the additional service period has no real effect in practice, and the director would receive the remuneration whether or not he stayed for the extra six months, this would imply that the substance was that the remuneration was effectively a firm entitlement in respect of the three-year performance period and should be disclosed in the third year. If, however, the additional service period was of real significance, for instance if the director would get nothing if he were to leave the company within that additional period, then it is probable that the remuneration should be disclosed in the fourth year.

11.22 In practice, there is some variation on the way that companies apply the rules to the situation described in paragraphs 11.20 to 11.21 above, with some companies preferring to disclose when all performance conditions have been satisfied, even when there is a further service period. For listed companies, where the problem mainly arises, the Listing Rule requirements for disclosure of full details of long-term incentive schemes mean that, whichever approach is taken, there is still full disclosure of benefits arising, or which have arisen, under such schemes during the period for which they operate.

11.23 The above rules apply to emoluments generally and also extend to compensation for loss of office.

Other rules

11.24 If it is necessary to apportion remuneration and compensation for loss of office paid to a director between the matters in respect of which it has been paid or is receivable, the directors may apportion it in any way that they consider appropriate. [6 Sch 12].

11.25 In certain situations, directors' remuneration might not be included in the notes to the financial statements of a period because either the director is liable to account for it to another group company, or because it is considered to be an expense allowance not chargeable to UK income tax. Where this is so, and these reasons are subsequently found not to be justified, the remuneration must be disclosed in a note to the first financial statements in which it is practicable for this to be done, and the remuneration must be identified separately. This also applies to compensation for loss of office. [6 Sch 11(2)].

11.26 An example of disclosure is given in Table 11.2.

Table 11.2 – The Plessey Company plc – Report and Accounts – 1 April 1988

Directors and senior employees (extract)

The emoluments of the Chairman, who in 1988 was the highest paid director, amounted to £391,956. The emoluments of the highest paid director in 1987 amounted to £237,347.

The above amount of £391,956 includes an adjustment of £93,750 resulting from the reclassification of expenses in respect of the financial years 1979/80 to 1986/87 following a settlement agreed with the Inland Revenue.

11.27 Where information (other than the aggregate of gains made by the directors on the exercise of share options) required to be disclosed under the Act is readily ascertainable from the other information that is disclosed in the financial statements, this satisfies the Act's disclosure requirements. [6 Sch 1(6)(a),2(6),8(5)]. For instance, if all the details of individual directors' emoluments are disclosed in the Remuneration Committee report in accordance with the Stock Exchange Listing Rule requirements (together with other disclosures such as long-term incentive scheme benefits received and receivable, company contributions to money purchase pension schemes and disclosure of pension entitlements under defined benefit schemes) and it is evident from that disclosure which director is the highest paid (according to the Act's definition of highest paid director), then separate disclosure of the emoluments and other benefits of the highest paid director is not required.

11.28 Presumably the reason for excluding gains on the exercise of share options from this provision is to avoid readers having to multiply the number of options exercised by the market price and then deducting the amount payable on exercise by the director, on the basis that this does not constitute 'readily ascertainable'.

Companies Act requirements – detailed rules

Aggregate emoluments and other benefits

11.29 The Act requires the following information to be disclosed in the notes to the annual accounts:

- The aggregate amount of emoluments paid to or receivable by directors in respect of qualifying services. [6 Sch 1(1)(a)].

- The aggregate of the amount of gains made by directors on the exercise of share options. [6 Sch 1(1)(b)].

- The aggregate of the following:

  - the amount of money paid to or receivable by directors under long-term incentive schemes in respect of qualifying services; and

  - the net value of assets (other than money and share options) received or receivable by directors under such schemes in respect of such services.

  [6 Sch 1(1)(c)].

- The aggregate value of any company contributions paid, or treated as paid, to a pension scheme in respect of directors' qualifying services, being contributions by reference to which the rate or amount of any money purchase benefits that may become payable will be calculated. [6 Sch 1(1)(d)].

- In the case of each of the following:

  - money purchase schemes; and
  - defined benefit schemes

  the number of directors (if any) to whom retirement benefits are accruing under such schemes in respect of qualifying services. [6 Sch 1(1)(e)].

11.30 The above requirements relate to *listed* companies. 'Listed company' means a company whose securities have been admitted to the Official List of the Stock Exchange or whose securities are dealt in on an approved exchange, for example, companies dealt in on the Alternative Investment Market (AIM). [6 Sch 1(5)].

11.31 The above definition of listed differs from the Stock Exchange definition, which includes only companies whose securities have been admitted to the Official List.

AIM companies, therefore, whilst required to comply with the detailed requirements of the Act relating to directors' emoluments, do not have to comply with the additional disclosure requirements relating to directors' emoluments that are contained in the Listing Rules (see further para 11.139). In order to distinguish 'listed' as defined in the Act from 'listed' as defined by the Stock Exchange the former is referred to hereafter in this chapter as 'listed/AIM' and the latter as 'listed', when describing the disclosure rules. 'Unlisted' when used hereafter means neither listed on the Official List nor dealt in on AIM unless otherwise stated.

Unlisted companies

11.32 Unlisted companies also have to comply with the requirements set out above, but with two important exceptions. Firstly, unlisted companies do not have to disclose the amount of gains made by directors on the exercise of share options. Instead, they have merely to disclose the number of directors who exercised share options. Secondly, unlisted companies do not have to disclose the net value of any assets that comprise shares, which would otherwise be disclosed in respect of assets received under long-term incentive schemes. Instead, they have to disclose the number of directors in respect of whose qualifying services shares were received or receivable under long-term incentive schemes. [6 Sch 1(2)(a)(b)].

11.33 The reason for the modification in the requirements for unlisted companies is that, in the absence of a readily available market price for shares in unlisted companies, the information necessary for disclosure of gains made under share option schemes and the value of shares received under long-term incentive schemes would be difficult to obtain. Instead of requiring this information, therefore, the Act merely requires the notes to disclose the number of directors in each case who exercised options and by whom shares were received or receivable under long-term incentive schemes.

11.34 Each of the elements of the disclosure described above is discussed in turn in the following paragraphs.

Aggregate emoluments

All companies

11.35 All companies (that is, listed, AIM and unlisted) have to disclose aggregate emoluments paid to or receivable by directors in respect of qualifying services.

11.36 Qualifying services means:

- His services as a director of the company.

- His services as a director of any subsidiary undertaking of the company, during the time in which he is a director of the company.

- His services in connection with the management of the affairs of either the company or any subsidiary undertaking of the company, during the time in which he is a director of the company.

[6 Sch 1(5)].

11.37 If an undertaking is a subsidiary undertaking at the time the service is rendered by the directors, it should be included even where the undertaking is no longer a subsidiary at the reporting date. [6 Sch 13(2)(b)].

11.38 For this purpose, 'emoluments' paid to or receivable by a director include not only his salary, but also the following:

- Fees and bonuses.

- Any expense allowances (to the extent that they are chargeable to UK income tax).

- The estimated money value of any other benefits received otherwise than in cash (but see para 11.39 below).

- Emoluments in respect of a person accepting office as director.

[6 Sch 1(3),(6)(b)].

11.39 The term emoluments does not include the value of share options granted to or exercised by directors. It does not include any company pension contributions paid on behalf of directors (although it *does* include contributions that directors themselves pay by way of a compulsory deduction from salary) nor any benefits to which directors are entitled under any pension scheme. Also excluded from the definition are money or other assets paid to or receivable by directors under long-term incentive schemes.

11.40 The reason for excluding those elements from the disclosure of emoluments is, quite simply, that they are picked up by separate disclosure requirements which are discussed below.

11.41 The term 'paid to or receivable by' is discussed from paragraph 11.16 above.

11.42 Whether the director receives emoluments for services as a director of the company or in connection with the management of its affairs is a question of fact. It should be presumed that all payments made to a director, except for reimbursement of expenses, will generally fall within one of these categories, unless it can clearly be demonstrated otherwise. However, an exception could be where payments have been made to a director in a self-employed or professional capacity. Consider the following example:

Example

A director of a company is paid for technical services supplied on a 'self employed persons' basis. How should this be disclosed?

Provided that it can be clearly established that the fees are genuinely for technical services and that they are not connected with management services (which they might be if the director were a technical director), then the amounts paid need not be disclosed as emoluments. However, the transaction may need to be disclosed as one in which the director has a material interest (see further chapter 34) or as a related party transaction (see chapter 35). In practice, however, it is often difficult to make such a precise distinction and the remuneration for other services is often included with directors' remuneration.

11.43 When considering directors' emoluments, there is no need to distinguish between a director's service contract and a contract for services that a director has with the company. Remuneration received in either capacity will fall to be disclosed in the company's financial statements as directors' emoluments. However, a director's service contract makes him essentially an employee of the company and, therefore, such emoluments will have to be included in staff costs. On the other hand, a contract for services puts the director in essentially the same position as a third party hired to do a particular job. Amounts invoiced to the company should be charged to the profit and loss account, but should not be classified as 'staff costs'.

Rolling contracts

11.44 In recent years there has been some criticism of companies for granting three year rolling contracts to directors, thus often making it a very costly business for a company when it wishes to dispense with a director's services. As a result of this criticism some companies have reduced the term of contracts granted to directors and paid them compensation for the reduction. In our view such compensation falls within the definition of emoluments and should be included in directors' emoluments for the year. In Table 11.3 the compensation is so included and a note is also given to explain the unusual nature of the emoluments.

Table 11.3 – Meyer International PLC – Annual Report and Accounts – 31 March 1994

Directors' emoluments (extract)

During the year the Committee also decided to rationalise the benefits of the Executive Directors including a reduction in the period of their rolling service agreements from three to two years. As a consequence of these changes there were non-recurring payments totalling £75,000 and certain adjustments to their base salaries, both of which are included within current year Executive Directors' salaries as stated above.

Benefits in kind

11.45 The estimated money value of a benefit in kind that must be included in directors' emoluments should be taken as the market value of the facility that is provided for the director's private benefit, less any contribution the director pays. The amount used to assess the taxable benefit should be used only where it is an approximation of the market value of the benefit. However, in practice the value of the taxable benefit is often a good starting point for considering the value that should be placed on the amounts for accounting disclosure purposes.

11.46 Benefits in kind may include: provision of accommodation at below market rates; provision of a motor car or health benefits; and share options. The last of these has become particularly prevalent in recent years and has caused considerable controversy. Gains on exercise of share options are now dealt with separately (see para 11.49 below).

11.47 Whilst separate disclosure of expenses or benefits in kind is not required by the Act some companies do so. An example is in Table 11.4. For UK listed companies separate disclosure of benefits is now required (see para 11.131 onwards).

Table 11.4 – National Westminster Bank Plc – Annual Report and Accounts - 31 December 1993

Emoluments of directors (extract)

The total remuneration and benefits of the highest paid director in the UK, Mr R K Goeltz, were £554,238 (1992 £383,900), which comprised £230,564 basic salary and other emoluments (inclusive of director's fee), a performance related bonus of £72,739, expenses and disbursements amounting to £242,170 incurred by the Bank and Mr Goeltz in connection with his relocation from New York to London and £8,765 of benefits in kind. Mr Goeltz participates in the Bank's pension fund.

11.48 Emoluments in respect of a person accepting office as director (see the last point in para 11.38) was a category brought in by the Companies Act 1989. Its effect was to require disclosure of various incentive payments (so-called 'golden hellos') that are made by companies to attract people to join the board of directors.

Exercise of share options and long-term incentive schemes

Listed/AIM companies

11.49 For listed/AIM companies separate totals for the aggregate of gains made by directors on exercising share options and for the aggregate of amounts of money and the net value of other assets received or receivable under long-term incentive schemes must be disclosed. [6 Sch 1(1)(b)(c)]. An example of disclosure of gains made on the exercise of share options is given in Table 11.5.

Table 11.5 – Fine Art Developments p.l.c. – Annual Report & Accounts – 31 March 1997

Report of the Remuneration Committee (extract)

The eight executive directors are members of the defined benefit scheme and were so in the previous year. The accrued pension of the highest paid director under the defined benefit scheme at 31 March 1997 was £127,529 per annum. No director is a member of a money purchase scheme. In accordance with the recommendation of the actuaries, no company pension contributions were paid to the Fine Art Developments Group Pension Fund in either 1997 or 1996.

No share options were exercised by the directors in the year to 31 March 1997. In the previous year the seven executive directors on the board in that year exercised options granted under the savings related share option scheme. The aggregate of the gains made on these exercises, calculated on the difference between the option price and the mid-market price on the date of the option maturity, was £92,949, of which £14,676 related to the gain attributable to the highest paid director.

11.50 The amount of the gain on exercising share options (listed/AIM companies only) is the difference between market price of the shares on the day of exercise and the price actually paid for the shares. [6 Sch 1(5)].

11.51 Share options granted in respect of a person's accepting office as a director are to be treated as share options granted in respect of that person's services as a director. [6 Sch 1(6)(b)]. Accordingly the exercise of such options would require disclosure by listed/AIM companies of the amount of the gain made in accordance with the requirement in paragraph 11.49 above.

Unlisted companies

11.52 Unlisted companies are not required to include the amount of gains made by directors on the exercise of share options. Nor do they have to include the value of any shares received or receivable under long-term incentive schemes. Instead they should give the aggregate amount of money and net value of other assets (excluding shares) received and receivable under long-term incentive schemes and disclose separately:

- The number of directors who exercised share options.
- The number of directors in respect of whose qualifying services shares were received or receivable under long-term incentive schemes.

[6 Sch 1(2)].

Definitions

11.53 Share options are defined as the right to acquire shares. [6 Sch 1(5)]. We interpret this to include the right to acquire shares through subscription, by way of gift, by purchasing shares from an ESOP or indeed any other form of acquisition.

11.54 A long-term incentive scheme is defined as *"any agreement or arrangement under which money or other assets may become receivable by a director and which includes one or more qualifying conditions with respect to service or performance which cannot be fulfilled within a single financial year"*. [6 Sch 1(4)]. The definition specifically excludes:

- Bonuses the amount of which is determined by reference to service or performance within a single financial year.
- Compensation for loss of office, payments for breach of contract and other termination payments.
- Retirement benefits.

[6 Sch 1(4)].

11.55 The Act's definition of long-term incentive schemes is substantially the same as the definition contained in the Stock Exchange's Listing Rules (see para 11.142 below).

11.56 Amounts received or receivable means amounts that become due to directors during the financial year. For example, if a long-term incentive scheme runs for three years and amounts or other assets become due to the directors at the end of the third year, they are disclosable in that year, even if they are not actually paid over to or received by the directors until the following year (see from para 11.16 above).

11.57 Other assets received or receivable under long-term incentive schemes may include all sorts of non-cash items, for example, diamonds, gold, wine or works of art. Most commonly, however, such assets will be in the form of shares. Shares are defined as shares (whether allotted or not) in the company, or any undertaking which is a group undertaking in relation to the company and it includes share warrants. [6 Sch 1(5)]. A share warrant is a warrant that states that the bearer of the warrant is entitled to the shares specified in it. The phrase *"any undertaking which is a group undertaking in relation to the company"* would, we believe, include the parent undertaking and fellow subsidiary undertakings as well as subsidiary undertakings of the company. The 'value' of the shares received or receivable is the market price of the shares on the day the shares are received or receivable. [6 Sch 1(5)].

11.58 The net value of other assets received or receivable by a director under a long-term incentive scheme means the value after deducting any money paid or other value given by the director. [6 Sch 1(5)].

Pension contributions

11.59 Before the changes introduced in 1997 the aggregate of directors' emoluments to be disclosed included company contributions to both defined benefit and defined contribution (money purchase) schemes.

11.60 Following extensive consultation it is now generally accepted that, whilst contributions to money purchase schemes give a reasonable indication of the benefit to a director, contributions to defined benefit schemes may often not do so, particularly, for instance, if the scheme is in surplus and no contributions are required. The Stock Exchange Listing Rules have been amended to require listed companies to disclose directors' pension entitlements under defined benefit schemes, with effect for accounting periods ending on or after 1 July 1997 (see para 11.161 below). Because of this the Act now limits its disclosure requirements to the amount of company contributions paid or treated as paid to money purchase schemes, and the separate disclosure of the number of directors to whom retirement benefits are accruing under money purchase and under defined benefit schemes, respectively. [6 Sch 1(1)(d)(e)]. The only requirement that the Act makes in respect of pension entitlement under defined benefit schemes relates to the disclosure of the highest paid director's emoluments (see para 11.83 below).

11.61 Company pension contributions no longer form part of aggregate emoluments. Instead, the Act requires separate disclosure of the aggregate value of company contributions paid, or treated as paid, to a money purchase pension scheme in respect of directors' qualifying services by a person other than the director. Contributions mean those according to which the rate or amount of any money purchase benefits that may become payable will be calculated. [6 Sch 1(1)(d)].

11.62 In addition, a company must separately disclose the number of directors to whom retirement benefits are accruing under money purchase schemes and under defined benefit schemes in respect of qualifying services. [6 Sch 1(1)(e)]. An example of disclosure is Table 11.5 on page 11014).

11.63 This latter requirement for disclosure of the numbers of directors who are accruing benefits in each type of scheme may not seem to be particularly useful information. In the case of listed companies (but not AIM companies) the Listing Rules will ensure that extensive disclosure of entitlements under defined benefit schemes is made in the Remuneration Committee report. The disclosure of the numbers of directors in each type of scheme is, therefore, aimed more at unlisted and AIM companies where, although full disclosure of entitlements under defined benefit schemes would be unduly expensive and onerous to give, it was considered that disclosure of the numbers of participating directors would at least put members of the company on notice that such schemes existed. Members could then follow up this matter if they so wished by other means.

11.64 Pension schemes are defined as meaning the same as a retirement benefits scheme under section 611 of ICTA 1988. Section 611 defines a retirement benefits scheme as a scheme for the provision of benefits consisting of or including relevant benefits, but not including any national scheme providing such benefits. References to a scheme include references to a deed, agreement, series of agreements or other arrangements providing for relevant benefits notwithstanding that it relates or they relate only to:

- A small number of employees, or to a single employee.
- The payments of a pension starting immediately on the making of the arrangements.

11.65 The definition above is generally interpreted as extending to unfunded pension arrangements. Accordingly, where a company makes provisions in respect of unfunded pensions of a money purchase type, it should disclose the amounts provided as contributions to money purchase schemes. Where it makes provisions in respect of unfunded pensions of a defined benefit type it should take the related benefits provided to directors into account when determining the amounts to be disclosed in respect of directors' pension entitlements under defined benefit schemes.

11.66 Retirement benefits has the meaning assigned to 'relevant benefits' under section 612 of ICTA 1988. That is, any pension, lump sum, gratuity or other like benefit given or to be given:

- on retirement; or
- on death; or
- in anticipation of retirement; or

- in connection with past service, after retirement or death; or
- to be given on or in anticipation of or in connection with any change in the nature of the service of the employee in question;

except that it does not include any benefit which is to be afforded solely by reason of the disablement by accident of a person occurring during his service or of his death by accident so occurring and for no other reason.

11.67 'Money purchase benefits' for the purpose of the requirement set out in paragraph 11.61 above means retirement benefits payable under a pension scheme the rate or amount of which is calculated by reference to payments made, or treated as made, by the director or by any other person in respect of the director and which are not average salary benefits. [6 Sch 1(5)].

11.68 'Company contributions' do not have to be paid by the company itself as the definition states that the term means any payments (including insurance premiums) made, or treated as made to the scheme in respect of the director by a person other than the director. [6 Sch 1(5)]. Thus, for instance, contributions paid by the company's parent undertaking would qualify for disclosure as company contributions.

11.69 A 'money purchase scheme' for the purpose of the requirement set out in paragraph 11.62 above means a pension scheme under which all of the benefits that may become payable to or in respect of the director are money purchase benefits. A 'defined benefit scheme' is a pension scheme that is not a money purchase scheme. [6 Sch 1(5)].

11.70 Where a pension scheme is a hybrid scheme and provides that any benefits that become payable will be the greater of money purchase benefits as determined under the scheme and defined benefits as determined, then the company may elect to treat the scheme as a money purchase scheme or as a defined benefit scheme, whichever seems more likely at the end of the financial year. [6 Sch 1(7)]. (Hybrid schemes are currently very rare.)

11.71 The effect of the provision in the preceding paragraph is that where a pension scheme has both money purchase and defined benefit elements the company has an option as to how disclosure is made. It can either take advantage of the provision and classify the scheme as money purchase or defined benefit in its entirety according to the type of benefits which appear to be higher in respect of the director at the end of the year. If the scheme is classified as a money purchase arrangement, the relevant disclosures as described in paragraphs 11.60 to 11.62 above are made. If the scheme is classified as a defined benefit arrangement, the disclosure required by paragraph 11.62 is made.

11.72 Alternatively, the company can elect not to take advantage of the option and in that case make separate disclosure of information relating to the money purchase element of the scheme following the requirement in paragraph 11.61 above. If this is done then the scheme is counted as a defined benefit scheme for the purpose of the requirement in paragraph 11.62.

11.73 The choice between the two alternatives may also be influenced by the requirement (discussed below from para 11.83) to disclose the pension entitlement of the highest paid director under any defined benefit scheme.

Banding of emoluments

11.74 Prior to the changes in the Act introduced in 1997 and applicable to financial years ending on or after 31 March 1997, there was a requirement to show the number of directors whose emoluments fell within bands of £0 to £5,000 increasing by intervals of £5,000. Also required were details of the chairman's and highest paid director's emoluments. The only one of these disclosure requirements that has been retained is the requirement to disclose the highest paid director's emoluments and other benefits. This requirement has been amended and is discussed in the following paragraphs.

Highest paid director's emoluments and other benefits

11.75 The Act requires details of the highest paid director's emoluments and other benefits to be disclosed.

11.76 For listed companies, which have to give details of individual directors' emoluments and other benefits (see para 11.139 below) this requirement may seem superfluous. However, the Act does allow the information (other than the aggregate amount of gains made on the exercise of options) not to be given again where it can be readily ascertained from other disclosures (see para 11.27 above) so the requirement should not be unduly burdensome for listed companies. [6 Sch (6)(a), 2(b)].

11.77 For unlisted and AIM companies the requirement to disclose additional information on the highest paid director enables the reader of the financial statements at least to determine the maximum amounts received or receivable by any director and thus to assess and evaluate this against company performance or whichever other criteria the reader chooses.

Ascertaining the highest paid director

11.78 There is a *de minimis* level below which the highest paid director's emoluments and other benefits need not be disclosed. If the total of the following items shown for all directors exceeds or is equal to £200,000 the information on the highest paid director must be given. These items are:

- Aggregate emoluments paid to or receivable by directors in respect of qualifying services.

- Aggregate amount of gains made by directors on exercise of share options.

- Aggregate amount of (a) money paid to or receivable by directors under long-term incentive schemes in respect of qualifying services and (b) net value of assets (other than money and share options) received or receivable by directors under such schemes in respect of such services.

[6 Sch 2(1)].

11.79 The highest paid director is the director to whom is attributable the greatest part of the total calculated in paragraph 11.78 above. [6 Sch 2(5)]. Note that only the elements listed above are included in the calculation. Other items, for example compensation for loss of office, are not included in determining the highest paid director.

11.80 The total of these amounts (which does not include company pension contributions) is the figure to be taken into account in determining whether the £200,000 level is reached or exceeded.

11.80.1 The threshold figure of £200,000 is not increased or decreased when the financial year for which financial statements are prepared exceeds or is less than 12 months. This is because it is determined by reference to the actual figures disclosed (see para 11.78 above) which are those for the financial period, whether that period is 12 months or not.

[The next paragraph is 11.81.]

Unlisted companies

11.81 For unlisted companies the items described do not include the amounts of gains made on exercise of share options or the value of shares received under long-term incentive schemes, because these amounts do not have to be calculated or disclosed by unlisted companies (see para 11.32 above).

Disclosure – all companies

11.82 If the limit of £200,000 is reached or exceeded the following two amounts must be disclosed in respect of the highest paid director:

- The total of the aggregate amounts described in paragraph 11.78 above that is attributable to the director.

- The amount of any company contributions paid, or treated as paid to a money purchase pension scheme in respect of the director's qualifying services.

[6 Sch 2(1)].

11.83 If the highest paid director has also participated in a defined benefit pension scheme, in respect of his qualifying services during the year, then the following information must also be disclosed:

- The amount at the end of the year of his accrued pension.
- Where applicable, the amount at the end of the year of his accrued lump sum.

[6 Sch 2(2)].

[The next page is 11021.]

11.84 An example of disclosure of the highest paid director's accrued pension (which takes advantage of the transitional relief from giving comparative figures for the director's accrued pension – see para 11.92 below) is Table 11.5 on page 11014.

Disclosure – unlisted companies

11.85 Where a company is unlisted and, therefore, does not include details of gains on options exercised or the value of shares awarded under long-term incentive schemes, it must disclose:

- Whether the highest paid director exercised any share options.
- Whether any shares were received or receivable by that director in respect of qualifying services under a long-term incentive scheme.

[6 Sch 2(3)].

11.86 However, if the director has not been involved in any such transactions there is no need to state that fact. [6 Sch 2(4)].

11.87 The main disclosure that is new, particularly for unlisted companies, is the disclosure of the amount of accrued pension and the amount of the accrued lump sum at the end of the year.

Meaning of 'accrued pension' and 'accrued lump sum'

11.88 The terms 'accrued pension' and 'accrued lump sum' mean the amount of the annual pension and the amount of the lump sum that would be payable to the director when he reaches normal pension age if:

- He had left the company's service at the end of the financial year.
- There were no increase in the general level of prices during the period from the end of the year to the director's pension age.
- There was no question of there being any commutation of the pension or inverse commutation of the lump sum.
- Any amounts attributable to voluntary contributions (AVCs) paid by the director to the scheme, and any money purchase benefits payable under the scheme were disregarded.

[6 Sch 2(5)].

11.89 'Normal pension age' is the earliest date at which the director is entitled to receive a full pension on retirement of an amount determined without reduction to take account of its payment before a later age (but disregarding any entitlement to pension upon retirement in the event of illness, incapacity or redundancy). [6 Sch 2(5)]. This means that a pension is not a 'full pension' if the benefits are reduced to take account of early payment and that any entitlement in the event of illness, incapacity or redundancy is disregarded for these purposes.

11.90 The third bullet point in paragraph 11.88, which refers to commutation of the pension or inverse commutation of the lump sum, should be interpreted as follows. Disclosure of the amount of accrued lump sum should only be made where, under the pension scheme rules, the director will automatically receive a lump sum on retirement. No disclosure should be made of a lump sum when a lump sum may be payable by way of commutation (that is, reduction) of rights to an annual pension. In the same way, disclosure of the amount of accrued pension should not include any reverse commutation of a lump sum entitlement. In practice schemes that have both lump sums *and* pensions are extremely rare outside the public sector.

11.91 If, for example, a director was entitled at the end of the year to an accrued pension of £30,000, but could commute that into a pension of £20,000 per annum and a lump sum of £100,000, the only disclosure to be made would be the accrued pension of £30,000. If he was entitled to a pension of £30,000 and a lump sum of £50,000 (without any reduction in the pension), both figures would be disclosed. If he was entitled to a pension of £30,000 and a lump sum of £50,000, but could commute the lump sum such that he could instead take a pension of £35,000 and no lump sum, then the figures to be disclosed would be £30,000 and £50,000, that is ignoring the right to the reverse commutation of the lump sum.

Example 1

The highest paid director is 50 at the beginning of the year. He joined the company when he was 40 and is entitled to retire at 60. His salary in the previous year was £120,000 per annum. In the current year his salary is also £120,000. His maximum pension is 20/30 of his final salary after 20 years, but he has no entitlement to a lump sum (although he may commute part of his pension and take a lump sum in place of the amount commuted).

The pension accrual would be calculated as follows:

Accrued pension at the end of the previous year	10/30 × £120,000 = £40,000
Accrued pension at the end of the current year	11/30 × £120,000 = £44,000

The disclosure would, therefore, be:

Accrued pension of the highest paid director	£44,000 (previous year £40,000)

Example 2

The highest paid director is 50 at the beginning of the year. He joined the company at 20 and is entitled to retire at 60. His salary in the previous year was £150,000 and is £160,000 in the current year. His maximum pension is 40/80 of his final salary after 40 years and he is also entitled to a maximum lump sum of 120/80 of his final salary after 40 years. (He may commute the lump sum by taking an increased pension instead of all or part of the lump sum.)

The pension accrued and accrual of the lump sum entitlement would be as follows:

Accrued pension at the end of the previous year	30/80 × £150,000 = £56,250
Accrued pension at the end of the current year	31/80 × £160,000 = £62,000
Accrued lump sum at the end of the previous year	90/80 × £150,000 = £168,750
Accrued lump sum at the end of the current year	93/80 × £160,000 = £186,000

The disclosure would, therefore, be:

Accrued pension of highest paid director	£62,000 (previous year £56,250)
Accrued lump sum of highest paid director	£186,000 (previous year £168,750)

Example 3

An example of disclosure in respect of the highest paid director that incorporates all of the above elements would be as follows for a listed/AIM company:

Highest paid director	1998 £	1997 £
Aggregate emoluments, gains on share options exercised and benefits under long-term incentive schemes	200,000	180,000
Company pension contributions to money purchase scheme	2,000	2,000
Defined benefit scheme:		
Accrued pension at end of year	30,000	25,000
Accrued lump sum at end of year	60,000	50,000

For an unlisted company disclosure that incorporates all the above elements would be:

Highest paid director	1998	1997
	£	£
Aggregate emoluments and benefits (excluding gains on exercise of share options and value of shares received) under long-term incentive schemes	250,000	240,000
Company pension contributions to money purchase scheme	2,000	2,000
Defined benefit pension schemes:		
Accrued pension at end of year	60,000	53,000
Accrued lump sum at end of year	100,000	90,000

The highest paid director exercised share options during the year and received shares under the executive long-term incentive scheme.

Comparative figures

11.92 Comparative figures are required for the director's emoluments information in the normal way, except that there is an important transitional relief. This is that comparative figures for the information to be disclosed about the highest paid director's accrued pension and accrued lump sum is not required to be given in a company's accounts for financial years ending before 31 March 1998. [SI 1997/570, para 3(2)].

Excess retirement benefits of directors and past directors

11.93 If retirement benefits paid to or receivable by directors or past directors are in excess of the retirement benefits to which they were entitled at the time when the benefits first became payable or 31 March 1997 (whichever is the later) the notes must disclose the aggregate amount of:

- The amount of the excess benefits paid to or receivable by directors under pension schemes.

- The amount of the excess benefits paid to or receivable by past directors, again under pension schemes.

[6 Sch 7(1)].

11.94 The excess amounts referred to above do not include amounts paid or receivable if:

- The scheme's funding was such that the amounts were or could have been paid without recourse to additional contributions; and

- The amounts were paid to or receivable by all pensioner members of the scheme on the same basis ('pensioner members' being persons entitled to the present payment of retirement benefits under the scheme).

[6 Sch 7(2)].

11.95 The exception described above means that the excess retirement benefits disclosed do not include retirement benefits paid to all pensioners on the same basis out of an adequately funded pension scheme.

11.96 'Retirement benefits' for the purpose of the above includes benefits otherwise than in cash, and where benefits other than in cash are given the amount should be calculated as their estimated money value. The nature of any such benefit should also be disclosed. [6 Sch 7(3)].

Compensation for loss of office

11.97 Disclosure must be made of the aggregate amount of any compensation received or receivable by directors or past directors in respect of loss of office. [6 Sch 8(1)]. This disclosure should include amounts received or receivable in respect of the loss of office by the director of the reporting company. It should also include amounts received or receivable in respect of loss, while a director of the reporting company or in connection with ceasing to be a director of that company, of office as a director of any subsidiary undertaking or of any office that involved management of the affairs of the company or of any subsidiary undertaking. [6 Sch 8(2)].

11.98 Compensation for loss of office includes compensation for or in connection with a person's retirement from office. Where such retirement is caused by a breach of the person's contract with the company or with a subsidiary undertaking compensation includes payments made by way of damages for the breach or payments made in settlement or compromise of any claim in respect of the breach. [6 Sch 8(4)].

Pension scheme top ups

11.99 We consider that a payment made to top up a pension scheme for the benefit of a director on his retirement is disclosable as it is effectively a benefit in kind (see para 11.101 below). This would be so even if the top up were funded out of an existing scheme surplus [6 Sch 10(2)(c)], and in any event, the reduction in the surplus would involve the company in paying increased contributions to the scheme and the top up is, therefore, even in that case, indirectly a cost to the company.

11.100 An example of disclosure of a top up payment made by the company is given in Table 11.6.

Table 11.6 – North West Water Group PLC – Annual Report – 31 March 1994

Directors' emoluments (extract)

During the year, Mr R P Thian, the previous chief executive, left the company. Mr Thian had a service contract with the company terminable by the company on three years' notice. The company has agreed to pay Mr Thian as compensation for loss of office an amount approximately equivalent to one year's salary and other benefits. This amount was £398,400, which is subject to deduction of tax, and includes a sum of £60,000 in respect of Mr Thian's pension arrangements.

Following the termination of Mr Thian's employment with the company, the directors agreed to him retaining options to subscribe for 157,000 ordinary shares which had been granted to him in 1990 under the executive option scheme as follows:

Date of grant of option	Number of ordinary shares	Exercise price per share
30 January 1990	143,750	278.0p
30 December 1990	13,250	315.5p

Options to subscribe for ordinary shares granted subsequently under the executive option scheme and options granted under the employee sharesave scheme to Mr Thian lapsed on termination of his employment with the company.

11.100.1 Where a company is listed and provides a table setting out directors' pension entitlements (see para 11.161 onwards) the emerging practice appears to be to exclude the pensions augmentation from the pension entitlements table and disclose it separately. In a few cases the effect on the pension entitlement of 'pension augmentation' on retirement is included in the pensions entitlement table, but a note is given to state that this has been done and to indicate the effect. Whilst both approaches appear to be acceptable it is important to make clear by a relevant note what the effect of the pension augmentation has been. An example where the augmentation has been included in the entitlements table, but a separate note indicates the effect is given in Table 11.18.4 on page 11.60.2.

[The next paragraph is 11.101.]

Benefits in kind

11.101 In addition to any monetary payment, the term compensation for loss of office includes benefits received or receivable otherwise than in cash. The value of the benefit should be determined according to its estimated money value. [6 Sch 8(3)]. Where compensation is given in kind, the company's financial statements should disclose its nature. [6 Sch 8(3)]. For example, the compensation might be the gift to the director of a car that he had previously used, but that was owned by the company. In this situation, the money value of the car and the fact that the compensation is in the form of a car will have to be disclosed. Normally, the market value of the car at the time of transfer should be used for this purpose. If, however, compensation includes both cash and a car, only the nature and not the amount of the benefit relating to the car needs to be separately disclosed. The cash and the amount of the benefit may be shown as one figure.

Ex gratia payments

11.102 The statutory description of 'compensation to directors for loss of office' is widely drawn. In deciding whether compensation to a director or a former director is

[The next page is 11027.]

required to be disclosed, regard should be had to both the nature of the compensation and the circumstances in which it was made, rather than just to the description the company gives to it. For example, most *'ex gratia'* payments made on either a director's retirement or his removal from office could well be regarded not as gratuitous payments, but as payments in compensation for loss of office. As such, they should be disclosed.

Payments made on retirement

11.103 In some cases, directors may have terms in their service contracts which entitle them to continue to receive remuneration for a period after they cease to be directors, perhaps in their capacity as employees. In other cases, they may have more than one service contract with different companies in a group. In such cases, the company may be obliged to make payments for periods after the directors cease to act as directors of the parent company. Where such arrangements exist or where they are terminated by payment of an additional lump sum on retirement as director we consider that the amounts should be disclosed as part of the compensation for loss of office disclosure.

11.104 Additionally, on retirement a director might enter into a consultancy agreement with a company whereby he is paid an annual retainer for one or more years. Again we consider that such arrangements should be disclosed. In some cases, where genuine services are to be provided disclosure may be as a transaction in which a director is interested (see chapter 34). In others where no genuine services will be provided we consider that the amounts payable under the arrangement are, in substance, compensation for loss of office.

11.105 A further benefit sometimes allowed to directors on retirement is that they may retain share options previously granted to them where such options would normally lapse on their leaving the company. Alternatively, they may be able to keep the options as a result of the terms in their service contract. Again, where there is a benefit to the retiring director, disclosure should be made (see Table 11.6).

11.106 Further examples of disclosure of compensation which include the above features are Tables 11.7 to 11.10 below.

Table 11.7 – Glaxo Holdings p.l.c. – Annual Report and Accounts – 30 June 1994

Remuneration of directors (extract)

h) Mr A M Pappas resigned as a Director on 16th February 1994 and his contracts of employment with the Company and a Group subsidiary undertaking in the USA were terminated with effect from 31st March 1994. Under the terms of his contract with the Company, he has been paid £105,000 upon termination of that contract. Under the terms of his contract with the US subsidiary undertaking he is entitled, subject to certain conditions, to continue to receive his annual salary of US$635,000 and certain other incidental benefits for a period of up to three years from 31st March 1994; these salary payments have been fully provided for in these accounts and are disclosed as payments for termination of executive office when paid. He will retain his participation in the cycle of the long-term performance-related incentive plan ending on 30th June 1994, pro rata to the period during which he was an employee of the Group. Payments to him under this plan will be disclosed as payments to a former Director when paid. He retains his right to share options, numbering 93,217 at 31st March 1994, which lapse on dates up to 20th March 1997.

Table 11.8 – Guinness PLC – Report and Accounts – 31 December 1993

7. EMOLUMENTS OF THE DIRECTORS OF THE HOLDING COMPANY (extract)

Mr. C. H. L. Davis, a former Director of the Company and of United Distillers plc, resigned on 12 October 1993. He will continue to receive cash and non-cash benefits under the terms of his contract of employment dated 19 March 1990 for the two year period to 31 October 1995. As compensation for his loss of office as Managing Director of United Distillers plc, this contract was changed so that over the two year period he is free to undertake other employment, subject to certain non-compete conditions, and is to be available for consultation by the Company. The estimated money value of the benefit to Mr. C. H. L. Davis, being the estimated total cash and non-cash benefits, is £670,000.

Table 11.9 – Enterprise Oil plc – Annual Report and Accounts – 31 December 1992

Directors and employees (extract)

Following Mr P E Kingston's resignation as director on 6 July 1992, Peter Kingston and Associates, of which Mr Kingston is a partner, entered into a consultancy agreement with the company. The agreement has a term of two years from 1 August 1992. Under the provisions of the agreement, Peter Kingston and Associates will provide consultancy services as required by the company and receive remuneration comprising a day rate and payments at specified intervals. The agreement also provides for the partnership to receive a start-up loan of £50,000 free of interest but repayable by three instalments at specified dates in 1993 and 1994. The amount paid to the partnership for the services rendered in 1992 was £95,750. The amount payable in 1993 and 1994, provided the agreement is not terminated, will depend on the work undertaken but will include specified payments which may total a maximum of £145,000.

Table 11.10 – Storehouse PLC – Annual Report and Accounts – 2 April 1994

SUPPLEMENTARY PROFIT AND LOSS INFORMATION (extract)

The value of the compensation received by a former director for loss of office amounted to £100,000 (1993 – £1,162,536 relating to five directors). He also retained and has exercised options over 113,732 shares (granted under the executive share option scheme in May 1992), and 144,975 shares (granted in May 1993).

Disclosure to members of the company

11.107 A company must disclose details (including the amount) of any payment by way of compensation for loss of office, or as consideration for or in connection with retirement from office, to members of the company, and the proposal must be disclosed to members of the company and approved by the company. Otherwise the payment is unlawful. [Sec 312]. Similarly, particulars of any such payment to a director in connection with the transfer of any part of a company (for example, following a management buy-out) or property of a company must also be disclosed to members of the company and approved by the company. Otherwise again the payment is unlawful and, in this situation, section 313(2) provides that the amount received by the director is deemed to be received by him in trust for the company.

11.108 However, *bona fide* compensation or consideration paid to a director for damages for breach of contract or as a pension for past services does not require approval at a general meeting or disclosure to shareholders. [Sec 316(3)]. Approval may still, however, be required under section 320 (substantial property transactions involving directors). Whether or not the payment is made in respect of a breach of contract or as a pension for past services, it is still required to be disclosed in the company's financial statements as compensation for loss of office.

Disclosure in the financial statements

11.109 Amounts to be disclosed include all relevant sums paid by or receivable from the company, the company's subsidiary undertakings and any other person, unless the director has to account for the sums to the company, its subsidiaries or to members. [6 Sch 10(2)].

11.110 For this purpose, a subsidiary undertaking includes a company that was a subsidiary undertaking immediately before the date on which the director lost office. [6 Sch 13(2)(b)].

11.111 Compensation paid to a director for loss of office is a category of payment different from an 'emolument'. Consequently, it should not be included in the disclosure of that person's aggregate emoluments.

11.112 For UK listed companies the new Stock Exchange Listing Rules now require disclosure of compensation for loss of office by individual director, which contrasts with the Act's requirement for the total of all directors' compensation only. The Stock Exchange requirements also require disclosure of significant payments made to former directors during the period, which we consider should also be given by individual director (see from para 11.131).

Sums paid to third parties in respect of directors' services

11.113 Paragraph 9 of Schedule 6 (which was not affected by the 1997 revisions to Schedule 6) requires companies to disclose in their financial statements any consideration paid to or receivable by third parties for making available the services of any person:

- As a director of the company.
- While a director of the company, as director of any of its subsidiary undertakings, or otherwise in connection with the management of the affairs of the company or any of its subsidiary undertakings.

[6 Sch 9(1)].

11.114 In this context, third parties do not include:

- The director himself or a person connected with him or a body corporate controlled by him.
- The company or any of its subsidiary undertakings.

[6 Sch 9(3)].

11.115 For the purposes of this disclosure, the definition of consideration includes non-cash benefits. Where a benefit is given, its amount should be determined by reference to its estimated money value. The nature of the non-cash benefit must also be disclosed. [6 Sch 9(2)].

Example

Company A borrows money from a venture capital company. As part of the financing arrangement, a director of the venture capital company has been appointed to the board of directors of company A. Company A pays £10,000 per year to the venture capital company in respect of the director's services. The director is remunerated by the venture capital company and does not receive the money paid in respect of his services by company A personally. In this situation, the amount of £10,000 would be disclosed in the financial statements of the company as sums paid to third parties in respect of directors' services in accordance with paragraph 9 of Schedule 6.

11.116 A further example is given in Table 11.11.

Table 11.11 – ASDA Group PLC – Report and Accounts – 2 May 1992

EMOLUMENTS OF DIRECTORS (extract)

Kleinwort Benson Group plc, of which Mr KJ Morton was a director, were paid fees of £23,000 during the period for the release of Mr Morton's services during the illness of the then Chairman.

Examples of disclosure

Example 1

The following is an example of disclosure under the Act by a listed/AIM company.

Directors	1998 £	1997 £
Aggregate emoluments	650,000	580,000
Gains made on exercise of share options	50,000	-
Amounts receivable under long-term incentive schemes	400,000	350,000
Company pension contributions to money purchase schemes	50,000	50,000
Compensation for loss of office	-	100,000
Sums paid to third parties for directors' services	20,000	20,000
Excess retirement benefits – current directors	5,000	5,000
- past directors	10,000	10,000

Retirement benefits are accruing to two directors under the company's money purchase pension scheme and to one director under a defined benefit scheme.

(Note: details of highest paid director's emoluments must also be disclosed. An example of the disclosure is given following para 11.91. Listed companies must also continue to comply with the additional requirements of the Stock Exchange Listing Rules. See para 11.131 onwards.)

Example 2

The following is an example of disclosure under the Act by an unlisted company.

Directors	1998 £	1997 £
Aggregate emoluments	350,000	320,000
Amounts (excluding shares) receivable under long-term incentive schemes	50,000	40,000
Company pension contributions to money purchase schemes	5,000	5,000
Compensation for loss of office	100,000	-
Sums paid to third parties for directors' services	-	20,000
Excess retirement benefits – current directors	5,000	5,000
– past directors	10,000	10,000

Two directors exercised share options in the year and one director became entitled to receive shares under the long-term incentive scheme. Retirement benefits are accruing to two directors under the company's money purchase pension scheme and to one director under a defined benefit scheme.

(Note: details of the highest paid director's emoluments must also be disclosed. An example of disclosure is given following para 11.91.)

Share options – disclosures under UITF 10

11.117 Share options are generally granted to directors and employees as a reward for services or as part of a savings scheme. They are a tax efficient form of remuneration and increasingly are offered as medium to long-term performance-related remuneration.

11.118 It is clear that the grant of share options is, in principle, a benefit in kind and the value of that benefit should be included in emoluments. However, this has rarely been done in the past for several reasons. First there has been some doubt as to when the benefit actually arises. Legal opinion is that the benefit arises at the time of the grant of the option rather than at the date of exercise. Where options have been granted at or marginally below market value this was often taken to mean that the benefit was immaterial. However, this view stood uneasily alongside reports of directors making substantial profits from the exercise of options and prompted commentators to criticise companies for concealing the true measure of rewards given to directors.

11.119 Secondly, even where options are granted below market value it is claimed that there are no reliable methods of valuing the options. Reasons given are that the options are generally not transferable and often may be exercisable only on the fulfilment of conditions, such as satisfaction of a set period of service or performance criteria being met. Also, it is argued that the value accrues over time, the period from grant to exercise, and is not all present immediately after the grant.

11.120 Because of the public concern expressed about the disclosure of directors' remuneration in the early nineties and the particular significance of options in many companies' remuneration policies, the UITF decided to look at the issue. After unsuccessfully attempting to find a way of reliably valuing options, the UITF decided that a disclosure solution was best.

11.121 In September 1994 the UITF published Abstract 10, 'Disclosure of directors' share options'. This Abstract made recommendations for disclosure of directors' options which were designed to give shareholders and others full information about the number and value of options held by directors. Because some of the recommendations went beyond what was required by law the UITF was advised that it could not make the Abstract mandatory (but see para 11.129 below). It is nonetheless persuasive in that it quotes the Cadbury Report's belief that the overriding principle in respect of board remuneration is openness, and states that the disclosures recommended *"would be a practicable way of providing improved disclosures regarding directors' share options that would be consistent with the recommendations of the Cadbury Report"*.

11.122 The Abstract recommends that for each director the following information should be given:

- The number of shares under option at the end of the year and at the beginning of the year (or date of appointment if later).
- The number of options: granted; exercised; or lapsed unexercised in the year.
- The exercise prices.
- The dates from which the options may be exercised.
- The expiry dates.
- The cost of the options (if any).
- For any options exercised in the year, the market price of the shares at the date of exercise.
- A concise summary of any performance criteria conditional upon which the options are exercised.

11.123 Where directors have options exercisable at different prices and/or dates then separate figures for all but the last of the above would be given for each date/price combination.

11.124 The market price at the end of the year and the high and low prices for the year should also be given.

11.125 When the information would, for a particular company, be excessive in length a more concise disclosure can be given, for instance by using weighted average prices for each director. But if this is done there may need to be additional explanation to show separately, for instance, options that are 'out of the money', (that is, the exercise price is above the market price). Where a summarised approach is taken disclosure should be made of:

- Total shares under option at the beginning and end of the year for each director with appropriate weighted average exercise prices for shares under option at the year end.
- Full details of any movements during the year (covering options granted and lapsed during the year with disclosure of the exercise price and options exercised in the year with disclosure of the exercise price and the market price at the date of exercise).

11.126 When the summarised approach is adopted reference should be made to the fact that the company's register of directors' interests contains full details of directors' shareholdings and options to subscribe. The company must maintain this register under section 325 of the 1985 Act.

11.127 Although the Abstract does not mention disclosure of exercise dates in the summarised disclosure, these should also be given where that approach is adopted.

11.128 Following the issue of UITF Abstract 10, disclosures by companies have generally improved considerably. An example of disclosure that complies with the Abstract is given in Table 11.12.

Table 11.12 – Granada Group PLC – Annual Report and Accounts – 1 October 1994

Directors' emoluments (extract)

Shareholdings in Granada Group PLC beneficially owned – except where otherwise stated – by directors and their family interests and trusts of which their families are beneficiaries are shown in the following table.

	Ordinary shares		Ordinary share options							
	2 October 1993	1 October 1994	2 October 1993	Granted in the period	See notes below	Exer-cised in the period	1 October 1994	Exer-cise price (pence)	Market price at exercise (pence)	Exercise period (from/to)
Charles Allen	185,000	43,329	268,500				268,500	190		Jan 1995-Jan 2002
			59,000				59,000	336		Dec 1995-Dec 2002
				57,000	a(i)		57,000	494		Jun 1997-Jun 2004
				210,000	a(ii)		210,000	494		Jun 1999-Jun 2004
					b		4,369			Sept 1999-Feb 2000
John Ashworth	2,831	2,882	-	4,369			-	394.8		
Alex Bernstein	977,359	977,359	72,410	-			72,410			Aug 1989-Aug 1996
as a trustee*	1,513,500	1,513,500	43,446	-			43,446	263		Aug 1990-Aug 1997
			52,239	-			52,239	304		Jan 1993-Jan 2000
			130,500	-			130,500	322		Dec 1994-Dec 2001
Alan Clements	5,000	5,000	-	-			-	184		
Ian Martin	-	2,000	-	-			-			
Michael Orr	-	-	-	-			-			
Graham Parrott	3,822	25,890	12,930	-		12,930	-		534	
as a trustee*	2,062,020	1,423,909	8,275			8,275	-	304	534	
			16,034			16,034	-	280	534	
			35,500			35,500	-	322	534	
			46,000				46,000	144		Dec 1995-Dec 2002
					a(i)		39,000	336		Jun 1997-Jun 2004
				39,000	a(ii)		109,000	494		Jun 1999-Jun 2004
				109,000	b		4,369	494		Sept 1999-Feb 2000
Gerry Robinson	299,172	299,172	737,500	4,369			737,500			Dec 1994-Dec 2001
					a(i)		80,000	394.8		Jun 1997-Jun 2004
				80,000	a(ii)		364,000	184		Jun 1999-Jun 2004
Henry Staunton	10,000	10,000	184,000	364,000			184,000	494		Jun 1996-Jun 2003
					a(i)		16,000	494		Jun 1997-Jun 2004
				16,000	a(ii)		178,000	411		Jun 1999-Jun 2004
				178,000	b		4,369			Sept 1999-Feb 2000
Graham Wallace	746	758	10,344	4,369			10,344	494		Aug 1993-Aug 2000
			57,500				57,500	494		Jul 1994-Jul 2001
			100,000				100,000			Dec 1995-Dec 2002
					a(i)		96,000	394.8		Jun 1997-Jun 2004
				96,000	a(ii)		194,000	196		Jun 1999-Jun 2004
				194,000	b		4,369	140		Sept 1999-Feb 2000
				4,369				336		
								494		
								494		
								394.8		

* Non-beneficial interests

Between the end of the financial year and 22 November 1994 there were no changes in the directors' interests except for the following beneficial acquisitions of Ordinary Shares under the Share Dividend Scheme: Charles Allen 1,261, John Ashworth 19, Graham Parrott 27 and Graham Wallace 6.

No options granted to directors over Granada Ordinary Shares lapsed during the period.

The mid market price of Granada Ordinary Shares on 1 October 1993 and 30 September 1994 was 450.5p and 508.5p respectively. During the period the market price of Granada Ordinary Shares ranged between 444p and 596p.

Notes

a The Granada 1994 Executive Share Option Scheme (the "1994 Scheme"):

(i) Options granted under Part A of the 1994 Scheme may not be exercised for a period of three years from the date of grant and are subject to performance conditions set out in note 21 to the accounts.

(ii) Options granted under Part B of the 1994 Scheme may not be exercised for a period of five years from the date of grant and are subject to the performance conditions set out in note 21 to the accounts.

b Options granted under the Granada Savings-Related Share Option Scheme are linked to a monthly savings contract details of which are given in note 21 to the accounts.

c At 1 October 1994 options over Granada Ordinary Shares granted to directors, executives and staff were outstanding as follows:

Scheme	Option scheme notes	Option exercise dates	Exercise price	Number of shares
1984 Scheme	i	February 1988-July 2003	140p-411p	5,946,464
1987 Scheme	i	August 1990-July 2002	144p-352p	235,307
1994 Scheme	ii	June 1997-June 2004	494p	2,936,500
Sharesave Scheme	iii	September 1999-February 2000	394.8p	5,034,051

Notes to share schemes:

i) The Granada 1984 Executive Share Option Scheme and the Granada 1987 Overseas Executive Share Option Scheme: The normal exercise period for options granted under those Schemes is between the 3rd and 10th anniversaries of the date of the grant.

ii) The Granada 1994 Executive Share Option Scheme:

- Options granted under Part A of the Scheme are subject to the achievement of performance conditions before they can be exercised. The conditions are that over the period of three years prior to exercise the Company's Total Shareholder Return, representing the growth in the Company's share price plus the reinvestment of dividends shall;

a exceed the rate of inflation by at least 10% and,

b be not less than that of half the constituent companies of the FT-SE 100 Index over the same period of time.

- Options granted under Part B of the Scheme are subject to the condition that over a five year period prior to exercise the Total Shareholder Return shall equal or exceed that achieved by three quarters of the constituent companies of the FT-SE 100 Index over the same period of time.

d iii) The Granada Savings-Related Share Option Scheme:
Under the terms of the Scheme employees enter into a savings contract at amounts ranging between £10 and £250 per month and the normal exercise period for options granted under the Scheme is the six month period following the 5th anniversary of the date of the grant.

e At 1 October 1994 options at prices between 150p and 268p were outstanding over 27,439 Granada Ordinary Shares which had been converted from options over Electronic Rentals Group plc Ordinary Shares.

At 1 October 1994 options at a price of 259p were outstanding over 1,727 Granada Ordinary Shares which had been converted from options over DPCE Holdings plc Ordinary Shares.

11.129 The Stock Exchange Listing Rule (see para 11.131) has effectively given UITF Abstract 10 the status of a requirement for UK listed companies rather than a recommendation. The new Listing Rule specifically requires UK listed companies to give the information required by UITF 10 with such explanatory notes as are necessary.

11.130 In addition, the changes to Schedule 6, introduced for years ending on or after 31 March 1997, include a requirement for listed/AIM companies to disclose the aggregate gains made by directors on exercise of share options (see para 11.29 above). It is likely that such companies will, in fact, go further than this and disclose gains by individual director. If a company does so, it must still total the gains to comply with the Act's requirements to show the aggregate of gains.

Stock Exchange Listing Rules

11.131 In October 1995 the Stock Exchange published new Listing Rules which substantially implemented the Greenbury Report proposals. The rules applied to listed companies incorporated in the UK (with certain exceptions for companies with only debt securities listed). The Listing Rules were further extended in 1997 to implement a requirement for disclosure of individual directors' pension entitlements, effective for accounting periods ending on or after 1 July 1997.

11.131.1 In June 1998 the Stock Exchange introduced a new Listing Rule which retained substantially the same disclosure requirements in respect of directors emoluments as before, but required a statement of compliance with a new 'Combined Code' and removed the need to refer specifically to compliance with best practice provisions in respect of directors remuneration – see paragraphs 11.132 to 11.138.7 below.

[The next paragraph is 11.132.]

Compliance rules

11.132 The rules, which applied for accounting periods ending prior to 31 December 1998, were published together with two non-mandatory appendices: Section A which dealt with best practice in relation to remuneration committees; and Section B which dealt with best practice relating to remuneration policy, service contracts and compensation.

11.133 The compliance rules were of two types. First, there was a specific requirement to state whether the company had complied throughout the accounting period with Section A of the best practice provisions concerning the operation of the remuneration committee and, if not, to explain and justify any area of non-compliance. [LR 12.43(w)].

11.134 Secondly, a company had to state in its remuneration committee report that the committee (or the board itself, if there was no such committee) had given full consideration to Section B of the best practice provisions which concerned remuneration policy, service contracts and compensation. [LR 12.43(x)(ii)].

11.135 Both of the new requirements in paragraphs 11.133 and 11.134 were effective for accounting periods beginning on or after 31 December 1995, but are superseded by a new Listing Rule 12.43A for accounting periods ending on or after 31 December 1998, as explained below. Accordingly, Sections A and B of the best practice provisions are not further described in this chapter.

11.136 For accounting periods ending on or after 31 December 1998 the Stock Exchange has introduced a new Listing Rule, 12.43A. This rule replaces the requirements to state compliance with Section A of the best practice provisions [LR 12.43(w)] and to state that the remuneration committee or board has given full consideration to Section B of the best practice provisions. Instead companies are required to state compliance with the provisions of section 1 of a new 'Combined Code' which is defined as *"...the principles of good governance and code of best practice prepared by the Committee on Corporate Governance chaired by Sir Ronald Hampel published in June 1998 and appended to, but not forming part of, the Listing Rules"*.

11.137 Thus, for accounting periods ending on or after 31 December 1998 section A and section B of the best practice provisions annexed to the Listing Rules are no longer to be referred to by companies in their compliance statement. Instead the compliance statement is in respect of the Combined Code. Listing Rule 12.43A requires that a company provides:

- A narrative statement of how it has applied the principles set out in section 1 of the Combined Code, providing explanation that enables its shareholders to evaluate how the principles have been applied.

- A statement as to whether or not it has complied throughout the accounting period with the Code provisions set out in section 1 of the Combined Code. A company that has not complied with the Code provisions, or complied with only some of the Code provisions or (in the case of provisions whose requirements are of a continuing nature) complied for only part of an accounting period, must specify the Code provisions with which it has not complied, and (where relevant) for what part of the period such non-compliance continued, and give reasons for any non-compliance.

11.138 Section 1 of the Combined Code contains three principles relating to directors' remuneration. The principles and related best practice are described below.

The level and make-up of remuneration

11.138.1 The first principle concerning directors' remuneration requires that levels of remuneration should be sufficient to attract and retain the directors needed to run the company successfully. However, companies should avoid paying more than is necessary for this purpose. A proportion of executive directors' remuneration should be structured so as to link rewards to corporate and individual performance. [CC Sec 1B.1]

11.138.2 The code principle above is supplemented by best practice provisions concerning remuneration policy. The best practice provisions include the following requirements:

- The remuneration committee should provide the packages needed to attract, retain and motivate executive directors of the required quality, but should avoid paying more than is necessary.

- Remuneration committees should consider where to position their company relative to other companies. They should be aware what other comparable companies are paying and should take account of relative performance. They should however, use such comparisons with caution, in view of the risk that they can result in an upward ratchet of remuneration levels without a corresponding improvement in performance.

- Remuneration committees should be sensitive to the wider scene, which should include the pay and employment conditions elsewhere in the group, especially when determining annual salary increases.

- Performance-related elements of remuneration should form a significant proportion of the total remuneration package for executive directors and should be designed to align their interests with those of shareholders. In addition, they should give directors keen incentives to perform at the highest levels.

- Executive share options should not be offered at a discount except as permitted by paragraphs 13.30 and 13.31 of the Listing Rules.

- In designing performance related remuneration schemes, remuneration committees should follow the provisions in Schedule A to the Combined Code.

[CC Sec 2B.1.1 to B.1.6].

11.138.3 The best practice provision also include the following requirements relating to service contracts and compensation:

- There is a strong case for setting notice or contract periods at, or reducing them to, one year or less and boards should set this as an objective. However, boards should recognise that it may not be possible to achieve it immediately.

- It may be necessary to offer longer notice or contract periods to new directors recruited from outside and where this is so, such periods should reduce after the initial period.

- Remuneration committees should consider what compensation commitments (including pension contributions) their directors' contracts of service, if any, would entail in the event of early termination. Remuneration Committees should in particular consider the advantages of providing explicitly in the initial contract for such compensation commitments except in the case of removal for misconduct.

- Where the initial contract does not explicitly provide for compensation commitments, remuneration committees should, within legal constraints, tailor their approach in individual early termination cases to the wide variety of circumstances. The aim should be to avoid rewarding poor performance while dealing fairly with situations where departure is not due to poor performance and to take a robust line on reducing compensation to reflect departing directors' obligations to mitigate loss.

[CC Sec 2B.17 to B.1.10].

11.138.4 The second principle concerning directors' remuneration requires that companies should establish a formal and transparent procedure for developing policy on executive remuneration and for fixing the remuneration packages of individual directors. Furthermore, no director should be involved in deciding his or her own remuneration. [CC Sec 1B.2]. The best practice provisions include the following requirements:

- To avoid potential conflicts of interest, boards should set up remuneration committees of independent non-executive directors to make recommendations to the board, within agreed terms of reference, on the company's framework of executive remuneration and its cost. In addition, remuneration committees should determine on the board's behalf specific remuneration packages for each of the executive directors, including pension rights and any compensation payments.

- Remuneration committees should consist exclusively of non-executive directors who are independent of management and free from any business or other relationship that could materially interfere with the exercise of their independent judgement.

- The remuneration committee's members should be listed each year in the board's remuneration report to shareholders.

- The board itself or, where required by the company's Articles, the shareholders, should determine the non-executive directors' remuneration, including members of the remuneration committee, within the limits set in the company's Articles. Where permitted by the company's Articles, the board may, however, delegate this responsibility to a small sub-committee, which might include the CEO.

- Remuneration committees should consult the chairman and/or the CEO about their proposals relating to the remuneration of other executive directors and have access to professional advice inside and outside the company.

- The chairman should ensure that the company maintains contact as required with its principal shareholders about remuneration in the same way as for other matters.

[CC Sec 2 B.2].

Disclosure

11.138.5 The third principle with regard to directors' remuneration requires the company's annual report to contain a statement of remuneration policy and details of the remuneration of each director. [CC Sec 1B.3]. This is supported by the following best practice provisions:

- The board should report on remuneration to the shareholders each year. The report should form part of the company's annual report and accounts, or be annexed to it. It should be the main vehicle through which the company reports to shareholders on directors' remuneration. Each year the members of the remuneration committee should be listed in the remuneration report.

- The report should set out the company's policy on executive directors' remuneration and should draw attention to factors specific to the company.

- In preparing the remuneration report, the board should follow the provisions in Schedule B to the Combined Code.

- Shareholders should be invited to approve all new long-term incentive schemes (as defined in the Listing Rules) except for those circumstances permitted by paragraph 13.13A of the Listing Rules (see para 11.141 below).

- The board's annual remuneration report to shareholders need not be a standard item of agenda for annual general meetings. But the board should consider each year whether the circumstances are such that the annual general meeting should be invited to approve the policy set out in the report and should minute their conclusions.

[CC Sec 2 B.3].

11.138.6 Schedules A and B of the Combined Code, which are referred to above, concern the design of performance-related remuneration and what should be included in the remuneration report, respectively. Schedule A deals with the design of performance related remuneration and includes the following rules:

- Remuneration committees need to consider whether the directors should be eligible for annual bonuses. If so, performance conditions for annual bonuses should be relevant, stretching and designed to enhance the business and upper limits should always be considered. There may be a case for part of the bonuses to be paid in shares and for those shares to be held for a significant period.

- Remuneration committees need to consider whether the directors should be eligible for benefits under long-term incentive schemes. Traditional share option schemes should be compared to other kinds of long-term incentive scheme. Generally, shares granted or other forms of deferred remuneration should not vest, and options should not be exercisable, in under three years. Directors should be encouraged to hold their shares for a further period after they vest or are exercised, subject to the need to finance any costs of acquisition and associated tax liability.

- Any new long-term incentive schemes that are proposed should be approved by shareholders and should preferably replace existing schemes or at least form part of a well considered overall plan, which should incorporate existing schemes. Furthermore, the total rewards potentially available should not be excessive.

- Payouts or grants under all incentive schemes, including new grants under existing share option schemes, need to be subject to challenging performance criteria reflecting the company's objectives. Consideration needs to be given to criteria that reflect the company's performance relative to a group of comparator companies in some key variables, for example total shareholder return.

- Normally grants under executive share option and other long-term incentive schemes should be phased rather than awarded in one large block.

- Remuneration committees need to consider the pension consequences and associated costs to the company of basic salary increases and other changes in remuneration, especially for directors close to retirement.

- Generally, neither annual bonuses nor benefits in kind should be pensionable.

[CC Sch A].

11.138.7 Schedule B to the combined code considers the matters that should be included in the Remuneration Report and sets out the following rules:

- The report should include full details for each individual director by name of all elements in the remuneration package, such as basic salary, benefits in kind, annual bonuses and long-term incentive schemes including share options.

- Information on share options, including SAYE options, should be given for each director in accordance with the recommendations of UITF Abstract 10 and its successors.

- The report should explain and justify grants under executive share option or other long-term incentive schemes where these are awarded in one large block rather than being phased.

- Also included in the report should be pension entitlements earned by each individual director during the year, disclosed on one of the alternative bases recommended by the Faculty and Institute of Actuaries and included in the Stock Exchange Listing Rules. Companies may also wish to make clear that the transfer value represents a liability of the company, not a sum paid or due to the individual.

- The report should explain and justify annual bonuses or benefits in kind that are pensionable.

- The amounts received by, and commitments made to, each director under the first, second and fourth bullet points above should be subject to audit.

- Any service contracts that provide for, or imply, notice periods in excess of one year (or any provisions for predetermined compensation on termination which exceed one year's salary and benefits) should be disclosed and the reasons for the longer notice periods explained.

[CC App B].

[The next paragraph is 11.139.]

Disclosure rules

11.139 The disclosure rules contained in the new Listing Rule 12.43A are identical to those which apply prior to years ending on or after 31 December 1998 except that the requirement to disclose consideration of Section B of the best practice provisions has been deleted. The rules provide that the report and accounts of a UK listed company must include a report to the shareholders by the Board. The report must contain:

(a) A statement of the company's policy on executive directors' remuneration.

(b) The amount of each element in the remuneration package for the period under review of each director by name, including, but not restricted to, basic salary and fees, the estimated money value of benefits in kind, annual bonuses, deferred bonuses, compensation for loss of office and payments for breach of contract or other termination payments, together with the total for each director for the period under review and for the corresponding prior period, and any significant payments made to former directors during the period under review; such details to be presented in tabular form, unless inappropriate, together with explanatory notes as necessary.

(c) Information on share options, including SAYE options, for each director by name in accordance with the recommendations of UITF Abstract 10; such information to be presented in tabular form together with explanatory notes as necessary.

(d) Details of any long-term incentive schemes (see definition in para 11.142), other than share options details of which have been disclosed under (c) above, including:

[The next page is 11041.]

- The interests of each director by name in the long-term incentive schemes at the start of the period under review.

- Entitlements or awards granted and commitments made to each director under such schemes during the period, showing which crystallise either in the same year or subsequent years.

- The money value and number of shares, cash payments or other benefits received by each director under such schemes during the period.

- The interests of each director in the long-term incentive schemes at the end of the period.

(e) Explanation and justification of any element of remuneration, other than basic salary, which is pensionable.

(f) Details of any directors' service contract with a notice period in excess of one year or with provisions for pre-determined compensation on termination which exceeds one year's salary and benefits in kind, giving the reasons for such notice period.

(g) The unexpired term of any directors' service contract of a director proposed for election or re-election at the forthcoming annual general meeting and, if any director proposed for election or re-election does not have a directors' service contract, a statement to that effect.

(h) A statement of the company's policy on the granting of options or awards under its employees' share schemes and other long-term incentive schemes, explaining and justifying any departure from that policy in the period under review and any change in the policy from the preceding year.

(i) for defined benefit schemes (as in Part 1 of Schedule 6 to the Companies Act 1985):

(a) details of the amount of the increase during the period under review (excluding inflation) and of the accumulated total amount at the end of the period in respect of the accrued benefit to which each director would be entitled on leaving service or is entitled having left service during the period under review;

(b) and either:

(i) the transfer value (less director's contributions) of the relevant increase in accrued benefit (to be calculated in accordance with Actuarial Guidance Note GN11, but making no deduction for any underfunding) as at the end of the period; or

(ii) so much of the following information as is necessary to make a reasonable assessment of the transfer value in respect of each director:

(a) current age;
(b) normal retirement age;
(c) the amount of any contributions paid or payable by the director under the terms of the scheme during the period under review;
(d) details of spouse's and dependants' benefits;
(e) early retirement rights and options, expectations of pension increases after retirement (whether guaranteed or discretionary); and
(f) discretionary benefits for which allowance is made in transfer values on leaving and any other relevant information which will significantly affect the value of the benefits.

(Note that the Hampel Report (see para 11.197) recommends in addition that companies spell out that the transfer value represents a liability of the company, but not a sum paid or due to the individual; and that it cannot meaningfully be added to annual remuneration.)

Voluntary contributions and benefits should not be disclosed; and

(j) for money purchase schemes (as in Part 1 of Schedule 6 to the Companies Act 1985) details of the contribution or allowance payable or made by the company in respect of each director during the period under review.

The scope of the auditors' report on the financial statements must cover the disclosures made pursuant to paragraph (b), (c), (d), (i) and (j) above. The auditors must state in their report if in their opinion the company has not complied with any of the requirements of those paragraphs and, in such a case, must include in their report, so far as they are reasonably able to do so, a statement giving the required particulars. [LR 12.43A].

[The next paragraph is 11.141.]

11.141 In addition to the above requirements, the amendment to the Listing Rules issued in June 1996 introduced a requirement for disclosure in the report and accounts of details of certain long-term incentive schemes. The long-term incentive schemes in question are those where the only participant is a director (or a prospective director) and the arrangement is established specifically to facilitate, in unusual circumstances, the recruitment or retention of the relevant individual. The amendment to the Listing Rules introduced a requirement for other types of long-term incentive schemes to be approved by shareholders before their adoption, but exempted the type of scheme described above, provided that disclosure of details of that type of scheme is given in the first annual report and accounts published by the company following the date on which the individual becomes eligible to participate in the arrangement. The information required to be disclosed includes:

- The full text of the scheme or a description of its principal terms.
- Details of trusteeship in the scheme or interest in the trustees, if any, of directors of the company.
- A statement that the principal provisions of the scheme (set out in detail in rule 13.14c of the Listing Rules) cannot be altered to the advantage of the participant without shareholders' approval.
- A statement as to whether benefits under the scheme will be pensionable, and if so the reasons for this.
- The name of the sole participant.
- The date on which he or she first became eligible to participate in the arrangement.
- An explanation as to why the circumstances in which the arrangement was established were unusual.
- The conditions to be satisfied under the terms of the arrangement.
- The maximum award(s) under the terms of the arrangement, or, if there is no maximum, the basis on which the awards will be determined.

[LR 12.43(u), 13.13A(b), 13.14(a) to (d)].

This requirement became effective on 30 September 1996. An example of disclosure is Table 11.12.1.

Table 11.12.1 – First Leisure Corporation PLC – Annual report and financial statements – 31 October 1997

Report of the Remuneration Committee (extract)

(iv) Senior executive long term incentive scheme

The Remuneration Committee approved the introduction of the senior executive long term incentive scheme as from 1st November 1994. The total potential bonus for each executive was fixed at the beginning of the scheme which covers the four financial years up to and including 1997/98. The maximum bonus payable in respect of each of the four years covered by the scheme increases evenly from 22% to 28% of the total potential bonus payable.

The scheme provides executives with the opportunity of earning significant cash bonuses if sustained real earnings per share growth and share price appreciation are achieved. In order to qualify for the maximum bonus in any year, the real growth in the Group's earnings per share and share price must exceed 6% over a maximum three year rolling period. Where real growth is below 6% the maximum potential bonus is reduced on a sliding scale. Where real growth is below 1.2% no bonus is payable.

Each annual bonus is deferred for a minimum of two years, except for the final award which is deferred for a minimum of one year. Payment of the annual bonus is subject to the following further conditions:

- 25% of the annual bonus is contingent solely on the executive being in the Group's employment at the end of the minimum deferral period. This element of the bonus is accrued for in the year in which it is conditionally earned;
- the remaining 75% of the annual bonus is dependent upon an additional condition that there is a further increase in earnings per share over the deferral period. The maximum deferral period is unlimited. This element of the bonus is accrued for evenly over the minimum deferral period.

Currently, Mr Coles is the only scheme member. However, Mr Payne's service contract with the Company entitles him to receive bonuses equivalent to Mr Coles under the scheme, as though he was a scheme member.

For the annual awards in respect of the 1994/95 and 1995/96 financial years, the growth in earnings per share and share price were such that the maximum bonus in respect of these years will become payable if the further conditions relating to employment and further earnings per share growth are met. No annual award has been made in respect of the 1996/97 financial year since the required level of real growth in earnings per share and share price was not achieved. Accordingly, the total conditional interests of Mr Payne and Mr Coles, which relate to the 1994/95 and 1995/96 annual awards, are the same at the beginning and end of the year and amounted to £230,000 each.

> The maximum average annual award payable to Mr Payne and Mr Coles over the life of the scheme is £125,000 each.
>
> To date no amounts have been paid under the scheme to either Mr Coles or Mr Payne although the conditions attaching to the payment of the first 25% of 1994/95 have been satisfied and this amount is now payable. However, as regards the remaining 75% of the 1994/95 award, the required further increase in earnings per share was not achieved in 1996/97 and therefore this payment remains deferred.
>
> Senior executive long term incentive scheme (1997)
> The Remuneration Committee approved the introduction of the senior executive long term incentive scheme (1997) from 1st November 1997. Mr Grade is the sole participant. The terms and conditions to apply will reflect the advice received by the Remuneration Committee from independent remuneration consultants, and will be broadly the same as those described above except that the scheme will cover the four financial years from 1997/98 up to 2000/01 and the minimum real growth that must be achieved before an award can be made has been increased from 1.2% to 2%. The average maximum annual award payable under the scheme is £625,000.
>
> As permitted by paragraph 13.13A of the Listing Rules, the scheme was not approved by shareholders in advance, since in establishing the scheme the Remuneration Committee considered that exceptional circumstances existed in that these arrangements needed to be put in place at the earliest opportunity to attract, motivate and retain the services of a senior executive of Mr Grade's calibre. For similar reasons the Remuneration Committee approved the grant of options to Mr Grade under the 1994 executive share option scheme set out on page 28.

Definitions and examples

11.142 The amendment to the Listing Rules issued in June 1996 introduced new definitions for long-term incentive schemes, retirement benefit plans and deferred bonuses. These definitions will be of assistance in interpreting the disclosure requirements set out in paragraph 11.139 above. The definitions are:

- *Long-term incentive scheme* – any arrangement (other than a retirement benefit plan, a deferred bonus or any other arrangement specified by paragraph 12.43(x)(iii) (reproduced in para 11.139(c) above) as an element of a remuneration package) which may involve the receipt of any asset (including cash or any security) by a director or employee of the group: (a) which includes one or more conditions in respect of service and/or performance to be satisfied over more than one financial year; and (b) pursuant to which the group may incur (other than in relation to the establishment and administration of the arrangement) either cost or a liability, whether actual or contingent.

- *Retirement benefit plan* – an arrangement for the provision of 'relevant benefits' as defined in section 612 of the Income and Corporation Taxes Act 1988.

- *Deferred bonus* – any arrangement pursuant to the terms of which the participant(s) may receive an award of any asset (including cash or any security) in respect of service and/or performance in a period not exceeding the length of the relevant financial year notwithstanding that any such asset may, subject only to the participant(s) remaining a director or employee of the group, be receivable by the participant(s) after the end of the period to which the award relates.

Long-term incentive schemes

11.143 Long-term incentive schemes as defined above can take various forms and be described in different ways. 'Share appreciation rights', 'phantom share options' and 'restricted share schemes' are examples. The schemes may pay out in cash or in shares or a combination of both, but all impose some performance conditions that must be satisfied over a period exceeding one financial year before the awards can vest. There may also be other conditions of service that apply before awards can vest such as the condition in many schemes that, even after performance conditions over, say, a three year period have been satisfied, the participant in the scheme must remain with the company for a further period, usually in excess of a year, before the award can vest.

11.144 Because of the complexity of long-term incentive schemes it is not always easy to fit the disclosures required into the rather neat compartments which the requirement of the Listing Rule set out in paragraph 11.139(e) above suggests. An analysis of two typical schemes illustrates this.

11.145 In the first example, Table 11.13, covering a three year period, a notional allocation of shares based on a percentage of salary is made to each director at the start of the period. However, depending on performance over the three year period the director may receive between nil per cent and two hundred per cent or more of this notional allocation. In this case all that can really be disclosed at the end of year one of

[The next page is 11045.]

the scheme is a description of the scheme and the number of shares notionally allocated to each director. It is also useful, however, to indicate the amount accrued in respect of the scheme.

Table 11.13 – LASMO plc – annual report and accounts – 31 December 1995

Report of the Remuneration Committee (extract)

(ii) Equity Plan Executive directors and other senior executives may be granted a notional allocation of ordinary shares in the Company by the Trustee of the LASMO Equity Plan based on a percentage of salary and calculated by reference to share price. Participants may choose to commit to the Plan up to the same number of LASMO shares which will be matched by a further notional allocation of shares by the Trustee.

Subject to the achievement of two performance targets, the actual number of shares (if any) to be given to each participant will be determined after the third year or, if not met by then, after the fourth or fifth year. The shares, which will be provided from existing ordinary shares in issue acquired by the Trustee, will not normally be released to participants earlier than five years from the date of the award. The performance targets operate as follows: first, the number of shares notionally allocated to a participant will be adjusted so that, on a sliding scale, 100 per cent will become available if there is an increase in the LASMO share price of 2.5 per cent per annum over the Retail Price Index over the awarded period, with a further 100 per cent for each additional 5 per cent real increase. Secondly, the actual number of shares to be awarded will be determined by comparing the total shareholder return ("TSR") to LASMO ordinary shareholders against the Comparator Group. If LASMO's TSR is bottom, the participant will get none of the shares notionally allocated to him or to her. If LASMO's TSR ranks number 10, the participant will receive shares equal to 20 per cent of the adjusted notional allocation, increasing by incremental amounts of 20 per cent up to a maximum of 200 per cent if the LASMO TSR is in first place. An accrual totalling £966,000 has been included in the financial statements in respect of the cost of the Equity Plan for the year ended 31 December 1995.

Directors' interests in shares under the Equity Plan

The interests of the executive directors who held office at the year end in ordinary shares of the Company notionally allocated under the Equity Plan were as follows:

	31 December 1995 number	1 January 1995 number
J Darby	30,674	–
J A Hogan	23,926	–
T G King	23,926	–
R L Smernoff	24,540	–

The ordinary shares were notionally allocated effective 2 May 1995 at a price of 163p. The actual number of shares to which the directors may finally become entitled (if any) will depend upon the achievement of the performance targets under the Equity Plan.

There has been no change in the interests shown above between 31 December 1995 and 28 February 1996.

11.146 In the second example, Table 11.14, two schemes are described, one that is still in progress and one that has matured. No allocation of shares is made at the start of the period. Instead the reward is based on a percentage of the individual director's average annual salary over the three year performance period. The amount of the award depends on performance criteria being met and is determined only after the end of the performance period. It may be paid in cash or a combination of shares and cash depending on the terms of the scheme. In the case of the scheme that has not yet matured, it is probably not possible to determine accurately a figure for each director at the end of each year prior to the completion of the performance period. What can be given is a description of the scheme, an indication of whether the targets have been achieved for the intermediate years and the amount provided.

11.147 Additionally in the example in Table 11.14, there is disclosure of amounts paid or payable in respect of a scheme that has matured. The amount payable under the scheme is spread over the three years following the completion of the performance period and is disclosed in emoluments as it is due. This is in accordance with the Companies Act requirement (see para 11.16 above) that amounts receivable in respect of a period other than a financial year should be disclosed in directors' emoluments when due.

11.148 Whilst it might be argued that the Listing Rule referred to in paragraph 11.139, 11.139, 11.161(e) above would require the amount receivable in the year to be disclosed in a long-term incentive table separate from the individual directors' emoluments table required by the rule set out in paragraph 11.139, 11.139, 11.161(c) above, such additional disclosure would seem superfluous in this case as the amount is already disclosed in the latter table. Following the changes in the Companies Act disclosure requirements, however, which are effective for accounting periods ending on or after 31 March 1997, there would have to be separate disclosure of the totals for aggregate emoluments excluding mid/long-term incentives and for aggregate amounts receivable under mid/long-term incentive schemes (see para 11.29 above).

Table 11.14 – Cookson Group plc – Annual Report – 31 December 1995

Senior Remuneration and Succession Committee's report (extract)

Mid-Term Incentive

This is measured on cumulative headline earnings per share ("headline EPS") performance over the period 1995-1997 for executive Directors, other members of the Group Executive Committee and corporate staff. The headline EPS targets were set by the Committee at the start of the Programme. Operational managers are assessed partly against this objective and partly against divisional/subsidiary business profit measures.

Mid-term incentives are delivered in three equal instalments, 50% in cash and 50% in Company shares, in each of the three years following completion of the Programme, i.e. 1998, 1999 and 2000, subject to continuing employment with the Group. Awards are calculated as an average of individual annual base salaries paid in the Programme years of 1995, 1996 and 1997. Achievement of target performance would result in awards covering the Programme period ranging between 45% and 150%. Above target performance would result in maximum awards ranging between 75% and 250% respectively. These percentage sums are the total award for the 3 year period.

The attainment of headline EPS of 18.9p in 1995 exceeded the target set for the first year of the Programme. Awards for the period 1995-1997 will only be made after the results for the final year of the Programme, 1997, have been agreed.

For the period 1992-1994, assessment was by reference to an aggressive target based upon a compound increase of 50% in headline EPS of the Group and, on a comparable basis, the achievement was an increase of nearly 60%. Awards relating to the 1992-1994 period, payable in 1995, 1996 and 1997, are made in cash.

Directors' emoluments (extract)

In addition to the annual bonus scheme, the executive Directors participate in a mid-term incentive scheme, under which they receive a bonus based upon the Group's achievement of a certain target level of overall performance over a three year period, such bonus being payable in three equal annual instalments commencing in the year after the end of the period for which the bonus is being paid. Amounts due to each Director as part of this scheme are included as emoluments in the year in which they become entitled to receive payment. The first such mid-term incentive scheme was for the years 1992-1994. Assessment for this period was by reference to an aggressive target based upon a compound increase of 50% in headline EPS of the Group and, on a comparable basis, the achievement was an increase of nearly 60%. The first of the annual cash payments to be made under this scheme are included within the table below. These same sums will also be paid in the years 1996 and 1997. A similar scheme operates for the years 1995 to 1997. As at 31 December 1995, the total cumulative amount provided by the Group in respect of bonus payments anticipated to be paid to executive Directors under the 1995 to 1997 scheme amounted to £0.9 million.

For the executive Directors to achieve the maximum annual incentive payment for 1995 required the achievement of an increase of profit before tax and exceptional items over 1994 of 40%. The actual achievement was an increase of 50%. The profit objectives are adjusted to include the effect of acquisitions and disposals made during the year.

Further details of the Group's annual and mid-term incentive programmes are given on page 39.

	Basic salary[(1)] £	Other emoluments /non-executive Director's fees £	Annual incentive bonuses £	Mid-Term incentive bonuses £	1995 Total emoluments £	Total adjusted for exchange rates[(4)] £	1994 Total emoluments £
Chairman							
R Malpas[(5)]	220,000	11,376	-	-	231,376	226,836	226,836
Executive Directors							
I S Barr	187,000	10,803	140,250	92,164	430,217	294,920	294,920
D L Carcieri	369,427	27,910	295,541	241,750	934,628	674,860	688,007
R Grosso	-	-	-	-	-	245,297	225,505
S L Howard	337,580	119,898[(2)]	253,185	187,934	898,597	662,714	668,590
R M Oster	581,032	221,332[(2)]	544,717	384,504	1,731,585	1,320,301	1,354,026
R P Sharpe[(6)]	133,758	330,227[(3)]	100,318	50,668	614,971	-	-
Non-executive Directors							
I G Butler[(7)]	-	24,760	-	-	24,760	23,978	23,978
R Iley	-	-	-	-	-	24,146	24,146
J B McGrath	-	21,250	-	-	21,250	17,500	17,500
G T Parkos	-	21,250	-	-	21,250	20,608	20,608
M J Sindzingre	-	21,875	-	-	21,875	20,000	20,000
B A Walsh	-	-	-	-	-	9,613	9,613
Total Directors' remuneration	1,828,797	810,681	1,334,011	957,020	4,930,509	3,540,773	3,573,729
Pension contributions[(8)]					981,260	877,900	894,007
Total Directors' emoluments					5,911,769	4,418,673	4,467,736

Notes to the above table

(1) Executive Directors' base salary has been increased during the year to take into account only the domestic inflation rates, unless associated with an increase in responsibility. The base salary of Mr R M Oster in 1995 was $912,220 (1994: $890,142).

(2) The other emoluments of Mr S L Howard and Mr R M Oster relate mainly to housing allowances and other relocation expenses paid to them because they were required to relocate in order to perform their duties. Also included is the assessed benefit of the provision of a company car, medical insurance and life assurance.

(3) Other emoluments for Mr R P Sharpe include $479,520 (£305,427) in respect of compensation for the cancellation of entitlement to the third year of notice which was provided in his contract of employment immediately prior to him becoming a Director.

(4) Four out of the five executive Directors in office during 1995 receive base salaries and other benefits which are based on levels prevailing in the USA. Changes in currency translation rates from year to year can significantly affect the sterling equivalents disclosed and, therefore, comparative figures are shown which eliminate this effect.

(5) Mr R Malpas served as Chairman throughout the year. His salary has remained unchanged since March 1993. The Company made no pension contributions in respect of Mr Malpas in either 1994 or 1995. He does not participate in the Company's annual or mid-term incentive schemes, nor in a Group pension scheme.

(6) Emoluments given for Mr R P Sharpe relate to the period since 3 July 1995 when he was appointed a Director.

(7) Mr I G Butler received a pension of £93,518 (1994: £90,934) from the UK Group Pension Plan as a result of his service as an employee from 30 January 1956 to 30 September 1987.

(8) In addition to the above, ex gratia pensions of £15,562 (1994: £15,124) were paid to former Directors in 1995.

11.149 The examples above demonstrate the difficulties of fitting disclosures of long-term incentive schemes into the rather 'neat' tables required by the Listing Rules. However an example that does present the information in the form of a table and that additionally gives disclosure of amounts charged as a provision in the profit and loss account in respect of each director is Table 11.15.

Table 11.15 – Cattles plc – Annual Report and Accounts – 31 December 1995

Report of the Remuneration Committee (extract)

(b) Restricted Share Schemes

The Restricted Share Schemes were adopted in December 1994 to provide longer term incentives to executive directors and other key senior executives. Participation in these schemes is as follows:

	Scheme	No. of shares notionally awarded at 1.1.95	Awarded in the year	Vested in the year	Lapsed in the year	Potential interest in shares at 31.12.95	Share price at date of notional award	Amount charged against profits in the year £'000	Earliest vesting date
J. E. G. Cran	1	163,817	-	-	-	163,817	146.5p	120	12.12.97
	2	163,817	-	-	-	163,817	146.5p	80	06.04.98
G. Clappison	1	99,826	-	-	-	99,826	146.5p	73	12.12.97
	2	99,826	-	-	-	99,826	146.5p	49	06.04.98
G. R. Dunn	1	89,587	-	-	-	89,587	146.5p	65	12.12.97
	2	89,587	-	-	-	89,587	146.5p	44	06.04.98
Total – directors		706,460	-	-	-	706,460		431	
Other executives	2	143,340	-	-	58,018	85,322	146.5p	42	06.04.98
	2	-	38,860	-	-	38,860	193.0p	-	06.04.99
Total		849,800	38,860	-	58,018	830,642		473	

In accordance with the rules of the schemes, the vesting of the shares is contingent upon pre-determined performance criteria being attained over the periods of the schemes.

Deferred bonuses

11.150 Deferred bonuses are distinguished from long-term incentive schemes by the fact that any performance conditions are to be satisfied within the relevant financial year. However, there may be one condition that extends beyond the financial year. This condition is usually that the director must remain a director or employee of the group for a period of time following the end of the financial year before he becomes entitled to the bonus.

11.151 Unlike long-term incentive schemes the amount of any deferred bonus should be disclosed as emoluments under the Companies Act requirements in the year that it is earned (long-term incentives are generally not earned specifically in respect of a particular year end and so are disclosed as emoluments, under the Companies Act, when due).

11.152 Like long-term incentives, deferred bonuses come in many shapes and sizes. Two examples are considered below.

11.153 In the example in Table 11.16, directors may apply part or all of their annual bonus to the purchase of shares in the company. After three years these shares are released to the director together with an equal number of shares provided by the company.

11.154 In the example the total amount of directors' bonuses, including the amounts that they have elected to apply in purchasing the company's shares, are included in emoluments disclosed under the Companies Act and in the table of individual directors' emoluments. The extra shares, to which the directors become entitled if they remain with the company for three years, are shown in a separate table (with directors' interests in shares and debentures) and the value of those shares will be disclosed if and when they are received by the directors.

11.155 As can be seen the arrangement has been treated partly as a deferred bonus in respect of the benefit that has been earned and partly as a long-term incentive scheme where the value of the contingent benefit is only shown when it has been earned.

Table 11.16 – Imperial Chemical Industries PLC – Annual report and accounts – 31 December 1997

Remuneration report (extract)

The level of bonus (if any) under the Annual Performance Related Bonus Scheme is determined by the Remuneration Committee on the basis of criteria established at the beginning of the year to encourage performance in a manner which the Remuneration Committee considers will contribute most to increasing shareholder value for that year.

The maximum bonus available to Executive Directors for 1997 was 40%. The Remuneration Committee sets targets related to the achievement of specific levels of profit before tax which were not reached, and therefore no bonus was paid other than to Mr R J Margetts, for whom 10% out of the 40% bonus depended upon progress in the restructuring of the Industrial Chemicals Business. The National Starch bonus scheme in which Mr J A Kennedy participates is described below.

The details of the short-term benefits for individual Executive Directors are set out on page 38.

The medium-term benefit – is the Bonus Conversion Plan ('the Plan') designed to encourage the conversion of any annual bonus (as described above) into shares in the Company and the holding of those shares for a minimum of three years. Under the plan, if the Remuneration Committee so determines, the recipient of a bonus may elect in the following March to have shares purchased at market value in the Plan with part or all of his net bonus after tax. Shares purchased in the Plan are released at the end of a three year retention period and are then matched by an equal number of shares by the Company on which the participant is liable to income tax.

The details of each Executive Director's contingent interests in the matched shares are set out in the table on page 39.

J A Kennedy – Mr J A Kennedy, Chairman and Chief Executive of National Starch and Chemical Company, was appointed a Director on 23 July 1997 upon the acquisition of the Speciality Chemicals business from Unilever. The salary data for Mr Kennedy shown in the table on page 38 includes his salary as a Director of the Company, £50,000 per annum, and the balance represents his salary from National Starch. The amounts shown are those received by Mr Kennedy from the date of his appointment as a Director of the Company.

In 1997 Mr Kennedy participated in National Starch's annual performance related bonus scheme. The amount of bonus was based on targets related to the achievement of specific levels of trading profit of National Starch in 1997. This resulted in the payment of the maximum bonus of 50% of base salary.

Remuneration of Directors

	Salary		Benefits		Annual bonus		Total	
	1997	1996	**1997**	1996	**1997**	1996	**1997**	1996
	£000	£000	**£000**	£000	**£000**	£000	**£000**	£000
Emoluments of Executive Directors								
Sir Ronald Hampel	**200**	200	**10**	9			**210** *	209
C Miller Smith	**500**	500	**16**	16			**516** *	516
ME Brogden (retired 30 June 1997)	**187**	310	**25**	13			**212** †	323
J A Kennedy (appointed 23 July 1997)	**203**		**5**		**91**		**299**	
R J Margetts	**342**	325	**13**	10	**34**		**389** *	335
A G Spall	**325**	310	**10**	6			**335** *	316
	1,757	1,645	**79**	54	**125**		**1,961**	1,699
Fees to Non-Executive Directors (note 1)								
Sir Roger Hurn							**30**	30
H C Lee							**25**	21
Sir Antony Pilkington							**30**	30
Miss Ellen R Schneider-Lenné								25
Lord Simpson							**25**	25
Sir Alex Trotman (appointed 1 July 1997)							**13**	
							123	131
Total							**2,084**	1,830

† In addition, 14,818 ICI shares with a market value of £120,000 were released to Mr M E Brogden upon his retirement on 30 June 1997 by the Remuneration Committee under the Rules of the Bonus Conversion Plan. These shares are matched shares provided by the Company in respect of bonuses awarded to Mr Brogden in 1994 and 1995 and converted by him into ICI shares.

Upon the retirement of Mr Brogden, the Company entered into a consultancy agreement for his services relating to the integration of the Speciality Chemical businesses acquired from Unilever. Payments under this agreement in 1997 amounted to £75,000.

* See also notes 2 and 3 to Directors' interests in share options table on page 39.

(1) Non-Executive Directors receive an annual fee of £25,000. An additional £5,000 is paid to the Chairman of a Board Committee.

Pensions and commutations of pensions paid by the Company in respect of service of former Directors amounted to £194,000 (1996 £190,000).

Directors' interests in shares and debentures

The interests of Directors in shares and debentures of the Company and of its subsidiaries, including the interests of their families are shown below.

	1 January 1997 or on date of appointment	31 December 1997	Contingent interests in matched shares* 1 January 1997	31 December 1997
ICI £1 Ordinary Shares				
Sir Ronald Hampel	40,948	40,948	14,571	14,571
C Miller Smith	13,886	18,886	7,086	7,086
Sir Roger Hurn	500	500		
J A Kennedy		1,000		
H C Lee	500	500		
R J Margetts	49,011	61,944	16,213	16,213
Sir Anthony Pilkington – beneficial	8,400	8,400		
– non-beneficial	20,860	20,860		
Lord Simpson	5,000	5,000		
A G Spall	19,309	19,309	15,744	15,744
Sir Alex Trotman		500		

* Matched shares to be provided by the Company under the Bonus Conversion Plan in respect of 1994 and 1995 bonuses (see *The medium-term benefit* page 37).

11.155.1 In the example in Table 11.16A the scheme is similar, but here the cost to the company of purchasing the extra contingent shares is included in directors' emoluments for the year. Whilst the disclosures in Table 11.16 and 11.16A are thus different, each gives a clear description of the nature of the scheme and of the benefits.

[The next paragraph is 11.156.]

Table 11.16A – Zeneca Group PLC – Annual Report and Accounts – 31 December 1997

Report of the Remuneration and Nomination Committee (extract)

Annual performance incentive: an annual bonus is available to the Executive Directors, calculated on the performance of the Company as measured against targets agreed with the Committee for that particular year. For Directors, the annual bonus calculated on this basis is 20% of salary for 100% achievement of targets. This could increase (on a sliding scale) to a maximum of 40% where achievement is greater than 100% of target. The Committee may apply an individual multiplier of 0 to 1.5 to the bonus on a discretionary and exceptional basis to reward or reflect individual performance. 50% of the bonus must be taken in Ordinary Shares in the Company and the remainder in cash or shares at the option of the individual Director. Bonus taken in shares is normally matched by an equivalent contribution of shares by the Company. Shares are awarded through an employee benefit trust, by way of a conditional appropriation, and will be released to the Director upon satisfaction of the condition which, subject to exceptions, is that the Director must remain employed by the Company for four years after the appropriation. Shares are otherwise forfeited. No dividends are payable prior to release. Resolutions are being put to the Annual General Meeting to reduce the said four year period to three years and to increase the percentage multipliers used to determine the bonus. Under the proposed new percentages, for 100% achievement of targets a bonus of 25% of salary (rather than 20%) will be paid which could rise (on a sliding scale) to a maximum of 50% (rather than 40%) where achievement is greater than 100% of target. This is described more fully in the Chairman's letter to shareholders accompanying the Notice of Annual General Meeting.

Note 31 Emoluments of Directors (extract)

The total emoluments of the Directors of the Company for the year are set out below.

	Salary and fees £'000	Bonuses Cash £'000	Bonuses Shares* £'000	Taxable benefits £'000	Other+ £'000	Total 1997 £'000	Total 1996 £'000
Sir Sydney Lipworth	165			1		**166**	151
Sir David Barnes	590	15	30	10		**645**	852
P Doyle	325	8	16	13		**362**	468
J.C. Mayo	266	13		16	169	**464**	577
T.F.W. McKillop	335		84	11		**430**	487
A.I.H Pink	355	9	18	12		**394**	508
M.P. Pragnell	285		14	11		**310**	–
J.R. Symonds	79		8	3		**90**	–
Sir Peter Bonfield	27					**27**	24
Sir Richard Greenbury	32					**32**	28
F.LV. Meysman	27					**27**	5
Sir Jeremy Morse	27					**27**	24
Dame Bridget Ogilvie	27					**27**	–
T.H. Wyman	32					**32**	43
Former Directors							8
	2,572	45	170	77	169	**3,033**	3,175

Details of share options granted to, and exercised by, Directors and the aggregate of gains realised on exercised options in the year are given in Note 30.

* The figures stated above include the cost to the Company of providing the matching contribution of shares in respect of that part of the bonus which is to be taken in shares by each Director. All such shares are held in trust and will be released to each Director upon fulfilment of the conditions and under the terms of the plan described on page 36 as part of the Report of the Remuneration and Nomination Committee.

+ Payment related to the conversion of an unfunded pension promise with regard to earnings above the earnings cap into a funded unapproved retirement benefit (FURB).

Note 30 Directors' interests in shares and debentures (extract)

The interests at 31 December 1997 of the persons who on that date were Directors (including the interests of their families) in shares and debentures of the Company and its subsidiaries are shown below, all of which were beneficial.

	Interest in Ordinary Shares, including shares held in trust, at 1 January 1997 or appointment date	Shares held in trust at 1 January 1997 or appointment date	Net shares acquired	Interest in Ordinary Shares, including shares held in trust at 31 Dec 1997	Shares held in trust at 31 Dec 1997
Sir Sydney Lipworth	5,000			5,000	
Sir David Barnes	96,339	14,276	111,444	207,783	25,720
P Doyle	16,714	8,270	46,062	62,776	14,482
T.F.W. McKillop	18,842	11,996	38,196	57,038	23,644
A.I.H Pink	20,310	18,746	65,649	85,959	25,502
M.P. Pragnell	3,990	3,490	3,268	7,258	6,758
J.R. Symonds			2,950	2,950	
Sir Peter Bonfield	500			500	
Sir Richard Greenbury	500			500	
F.LV. Meysman	500			500	
Sir Jeremy Morse	2,387			2,387	
Dame Bridget Ogilvie	500			500	
T.H. Wyman	656			656	

Shares held in trust above are long-term incentive bonus shares appropriated under the Zeneca Executive Performance Bonus Plan which have not yet been released. During the period 1 January 1998 to 4 March 1998 there was no change in the interests of Directors shown in this note. In the event that Ordinary Shares are appropriated in 1998 to Directors pursuant to the Executive Performance Bonus Plan in respect of the year to 31 December 1997 the Directors would have an interest in such appropriated shares.

The interests of Directors in options to subscribe for Ordinary Shares of the Company, which include options granted under the Savings Related Share Option Scheme, together with options granted and exercised during the year are included in the table opposite.

11.156 The example in Table 11.17 is simpler in that no additional shares are awarded by the company at the end of the service period. The full amount of the deferred bonus is included in the emoluments for the year, because it is earned in respect of the year. The bonus, which is performance related, is payable in shares once the director has satisfied a further condition concerning continuing employment (which is usually two years).

[The next page is 11053.]

Table 11.17 – The Spring Ram Corporation PLC – Annual Report – 3 January 1998

Report of the Remuneration Committee of the Board (extract)

Annual Bonus Plan

In 1997 the Committee approved the introduction of a performance related annual deferred bonus plan under which, subject to achievement of an annual performance target which the Committee determines to be sufficiently challenging, key executives, including Directors, may be awarded a deferred bonus in the form of ordinary shares in the Company. These shares are gifted to the executive by the Trustees of the Company's Employee Share Trust after the executive has satisfied a further condition as to continuing employment (usually two years following the end of the relevant financial year).

The Trust is empowered to purchase shares in the market (at times at which Directors would be free to deal in the Company's shares) in order to meet any obligation to make awards. The Company may not issue any new shares to be used for the Annual Bonus Plan without shareholder approval.

The Committee determined a target for the 1997 financial year based on the kitchens and bathrooms and acrylics divisions achieving a profit after interest of £2.6 million. This target represented a turnaround of £3.0 million in comparison with the 1996 financial year, and the Committee are pleased to report that it has been met. Details of contingent awards which may consequently be made by the Trustees to Directors in respect of the 1997 financial year are included in the table on page 34. Bonuses under the plan do not form part of pensionable earnings.

Notes to the Accounts (extract)

Note 9 (extract)

The emoluments of the Executive Directors are determined on the advice of the Remuneration Committee. The emoluments of each of the Directors who served during the year are set out in the table below:

	Basic remuneration and fees		Deferred bonus*		Benefits		Sub total		Pension contributions		Total	
	1997 £000	1996 £000	**1997 £000**	1996 £000	**1997 £000**	1996 £000	**1997 £000**	1996 £000	**1997 £000**	1996 £000	**1997 £000**	1996 £000
Executive Directors												
B.R. Regan (Chairman)	**262**	238	–	–	**3**	11	**265**	249	–	–	**265**	249
M.G. Towers	**150**	150	**36**	–	**16**	15	**202**	165	**30**	–	**232**	165
S.J. Brown	**112**	112	**36**	–	**11**	10	**159**	122	–	–	**159**	122
R.H. Trotter	**112**	63	**36**	–	**9**	5	**157**	68	**17**	–	**174**	68
Non-Executive Directors												
R. Barber	–	18	–	–	–	–	–	18	–	–	–	18
D.E. Bucknall	**30**	–	–	–	–	–	**30**	–	–	–	**30**	–
R.C.G. Fortin	–	19	–	–	–	–	–	19	–	–	–	19
P.M. Hanscombe	**30**	30	–	–	–	–	**30**	30	–	–	**30**	30
T.Smith	**30**	–	–	–	–	–	**30**	–	–	–	**30**	–
	726	630	**108**	–	**39**	41	**873**	671	**47**	–	**920**	671

From 1 April 1997 the services of B.R. Regan have been provided to the Company under a contract with Cadismark Securities Limited. Prior to 1 April 1997 Mr Regan was employed by the Company. The change in arrangements does not give rise to an increase in the overall cost to the Company in obtaining his services.

***Deferred Bonus Plan**

The number of Ordinary Shares apportioned to Executive Directors under the 1997 bonus plan (see page 18) are:

Ordinary Shares	1997 No.	1997 Cost £000
B.R. Regan	–	–
M.G. Towers	250,000	36
S.J. Brown	250,000	36
R.H. Trotter	250,000	36

The plan provides for shares to vest at the expiry of 2 years from the end of the financial year in respect of which an award is made provided the individual remains an employee of the Company. The number of shares shown above will not vest before 31 December 1999. The shares are shown at their cost to the Company in 1997.

During the year the Company established a Funded Unapproved Retirement Benefits Scheme for M.G. Towers and for R.H. Trotter (see pages 18 to 20). The contributions paid into these schemes on their behalf are disclosed above.

Further pension contributions are payable into a defined benefit scheme, see pages 18 to 20.

R.H. Trotter was appointed as a Director on 10 June 1996. The emoluments in 1996 relate to the period subsequent to his appointment. R. Barber and R.C.G. Fortin resigned as Non-Executive Directors on 15 August 1996. D.E. Bucknall and T. Smith were appointed as Non-Executive Directors on 16 January 1997.

[The next paragraph is 11.160.]

11.160 The schemes described above are among the more straightforward of those that are in operation at present. There are much more complicated schemes which mix elements of deferred bonus and long-term incentive within single schemes. However, whilst it is not always possible to fit a scheme neatly within the disclosure tables required by the Listing Rules it is generally possible to give sufficient information in one form or another to meet the spirit of the rules.

Pension entitlements and company contributions to money purchase schemes

Entitlements

11.161 The Institute of Actuaries and Faculty of Actuaries issued a consultation paper in January 1996 inviting comments on five possible methods for calculating pension entitlements. Following analysis of the responses the Institute of Actuaries and Faculty of Actuaries issued recommendations on 30 April 1996 which were based on their analysis of the responses to the consultation process and which represented a reasonable reflection of the diverse and indeed opposing views expressed by providers and users of the information.

11.162 The Institute of Actuaries and Faculty of Actuaries recommended that disclosure should combine the benefits of two of the five methods that they had initially set out in their consultation paper. These two methods were the accrued benefit and transfer value methods. As a result the Institute and Faculty recommended disclosure of:

- The amount of the increase in the accrued pension to which the director would be entitled on leaving service over and above any general increase to compensate for inflation to which early leavers would be entitled.

- The transfer value at the reporting date of the increase in benefit so calculated.

11.163 As an alternative to the second part of the recommended disclosure it would be acceptable to disclose enough information about the director and his benefits to enable a reasonable assessment of the transfer value to be made by a user of the financial statements. Such information would include the director's normal retirement age, current age, details of spouse's and dependants' benefits, early retirement rights or options, expectations of pension increases after retirement and any other relevant information.

11.164 Following the issue of the recommendations by the Institute of Actuaries and Faculty of Actuaries and further consultation, the Stock Exchange issued a new Listing Rule in May 1997 which requires UK listed companies to make disclosures similar to those recommended by the actuaries. The new Listing Rule is effective for accounting periods ending on or after 1 July 1997.

11.165 The text of the new Listing Rules is set out in paragraph 11.139(j) above. In addition to the new rule, the Stock Exchange published examples of disclosure and of how the pension entitlement should be calculated. Details are set out below.

Example 1

This example is of disclosure of directors' pension entitlements including transfer values (the first alternative in paragraph 11.139(i)(b)(i) above). Note that comparatives are not required for the information by the Stock Exchange rule, but that the Act's requirement to disclose the accrued pension entitlement of the highest-paid director will require a comparative for that figure to be given in future (see paras 11.83 and 11.92 above).

Pension benefits earned by the directors.

Name of director	Increase in accrued pension during the year	Transfer value of increase	Accumulated total accrued pension at year end
J Smith	×	×	×

Notes: (i) The pension entitlement shown is the amount that would be paid each year on retirement based on service to the end of the current year.

(ii) The increase in accrued pension during the year excludes any increase for inflation.

(iii) The transfer value has been calculated on the basis of actuarial advice in accordance with Actuarial Guidance Note GN11, less director's contributions.

(iv) Members of the scheme have the option of paying Additional Voluntary Contributions. Neither the contributions nor the resulting benefits are included in the above table.

Example 2

This example is of disclosure of directors' pension entitlements excluding transfer values but giving sufficient information to enable a reasonable assessment to be made of the transfer value of the increase in accrued pension (the second alternative in paragraph 11.139(i)(b)(ii) above). Again comparatives are not required. Note that in this example directors' contributions under the terms of the scheme should be disclosed.

Pension benefits earned by the directors.

Name of director	Age at year end	Director's contributions in the year	Increase in accrued pension during the year	Accumulated total accrued pension at year end
J Smith	×	×	×	×

Notes: (i) The pension entitlement shown is the amount that would be paid each year on retirement based on service to the end of the current year.

(ii) The increase in accrued pension during the year excludes any increase for inflation.

(iii) Director's contributions are the contributions paid or payable in the year by the directors under the terms of the scheme.

(iv) Members of the scheme have the option of paying Additional Voluntary Contributions. Neither the contributions nor the resulting benefits are included in the above table.

(v) The following is additional information relating to directors' pensions:
(a) Normal retirement age: (give details)
(b) Dependants' pensions: (give details of spouse's and dependants' benefits)
(c) Early retirement rights: (give details of early retirement rights and options)
(d) Pension increases: (give details of expected pension increases after retirement indicating whether guaranteed or discretionary)
(e) Other discretionary benefits: (give details of discretionary benefits that are taken into account in calculating transfer values on leaving service and any other relevant information that will significantly affect the value of benefits)

Example 3

This example shows how the entitlement should be calculated for a director given the relevant facts as follows:

A director has ten years service at the beginning of the year and earns £120,000 per annum. He is entitled to a pension of one-sixtieth of final pensionable salary for each year of pensionable service. At the end of the year his salary was £130,000. The increase for the year and the accumulated total at the year end are calculated as follows:

Accumulated totals

At the beginning of the year: 10/60 × £120,000 = £20,000
At the end of the year: 11/60 × £130,000 = £23,833

Calculation of increase in the year (excluding inflation)

Increase: £23,833 less £20,000 = £3,833

Inflation is assumed to be 5%.
The increase due to inflation is: £20,000 × 5% = £1,000

The increase excluding inflation is, therefore, £2,833.

Note: The inflation rate used should be that published by the Secretary of State for Social Security each year (Schedule 3 of the Pension Schemes Act 1993).

11.166 Table 11.18 includes the disclosure of details of pension entitlements that shows compliance with the requirement described in example 1 of paragraph 11.165 above. The example includes slightly more information than the new rule requires, for instance where the transfer value is disclosed, no information on ages or length of service need be given, and the comparative is not required (except for the highest paid director – see paras 11.83 and 11.92 above).

11.166.1 Table 11.18 also illustrates a further point that where a director is appointed or retires during the year the figures disclosed for the increase in accrued pension during the year will be for the period of service only, that is from the date of appointment or to the date of retirement. Where a director retires in the year the figure for the total accrued pension will be as at the date of retirement.

Table 11.18 – First Leisure Corporation PLC – Annual report and financial statements – 31 October 1997

Report of the Remuneration Committee (extract)

7 Directors' pension information

The executive Directors are members of the Company's senior executive pension scheme, which is a defined benefits scheme. This entitles each of them to a pension at the date of retirement based on final salary (subject, where relevant, to Inland Revenue limits on approved pension benefits) and years of completed service. In accordance with the scheme rules, the annual performance-related bonuses, which form a significant element of senior management remuneration, are pensionable. However, benefits in kind and amounts payable under the senior executive long term incentive scheme are not pensionable. The normal retirement age for executive Directors is 62½ although early retirement may be permitted from age 50. Each member contributes 6% of pensionable pay in the year.

The amended Stock Exchange Listing Rules published in May 1997 (effective for accounting periods ending on or after 1st July 1997) state that for defined benefit schemes, companies should disclose the following details which are given in the table below.

- the amount of the increase during the year and of the accumulated total amount as at the reporting date in respect of the accrued pension to which each director would be entitled on leaving service, over and above any general increase to compensate for inflation to which early leavers would be entitled;
- the transfer value of the relevant increase in accrued pension or sufficient information in order to make a reasonable estimate of this value.

	Age	Years of service	Increase in transfer value in excess of inflation during the year ended 31st October 1997 £000	Additional pension earned in excess of inflation during the year ended 31st October 1997 £000	Accrued annual entitlement at 31st October (or date of appointment or resignation) 1997 £000	1996 £000
M I Grade	54	–	3	–	–	–
C G Coles	45	5	15	2	13	10
M K Payne	60	16	231	17	102	83
J O Conlan (resigned 2nd June 1997) (i)	55	17	115	10	154	142
N Tamblyn (resigned 6th June 1997) (i)	46	16	27	4	58	54

Notes

(i) Mr Conlan and Mr Tamblyn resigned as Directors on 2nd June 1997 and 6th June 1997 respectively and the 1997 figures above relate to benefits accrued between 31st October 1996 and that date.

(ii) The pension entitlement shown in the table is that which would be payable on retirement, based on service to 31st October 1997 (or date of resignation, if earlier).

(iii) The increase in transfer value, which is net of the member's contributions, has been based on actuarial advice in accordance with Actuarial Guidance Note GN11.

(iv) The increase in accrued pension during the year excludes any increase for inflation.

(v) The pension entitlement shown excludes any additional pension purchased by the member's Additional Voluntary Contributions.

All scheme benefits are subject to Inland Revenue limits. Where such limitation is due to the earnings 'cap', the Company's funded unapproved retirement and death benefits scheme, which is separate from the Company's senior executive pension scheme, is used to provide benefits above the level of the 'cap'. This is a defined contribution scheme from which the executives are entitled to a lump sum from the accumulated investment.

Mr Coles is a member of the Company's funded unapproved retirement and death benefits scheme. During the year contributions of £89,000 were paid into the scheme by the Company on his behalf covering the period 13th July 1992 (when Mr Coles joined the Company) to 5th October 1997. The level of the Company's contributions were determined upon actuarial advice. Mr Coles is subject to income tax on these contributions and pays no contributions himself.

Mr Grade's benefits under the Company's senior executive pension scheme are limited due to the earnings 'cap'. He is entitled to benefits above the level of the cap but the arrangement of benefits has yet to be finalised. The maximum amount of the Company's aggregate annual pension contributions in respect of Mr Grade is fixed at £150,000.

11.166.2 Table 11.18.1 includes the disclosure of pension entitlement that shows compliance with the requirement described in example 2 in paragraph 11.165 above. This example also illustrates the situation where a person has reached retirement age, but continues to be employed as a director. Where the person's present employment as a director no longer accrues entitlement under the pension scheme there is nothing to disclose in the pensions entitlement table. A note may be added, however, to explain the situation. Another example of such a note where the director is actually drawing a pension whilst remaining a director is Table 11.18.2 on page 11.60.1.

Table 11.18.1 – Associated British Ports Holdings PLC – Annual report and accounts – 31 December 1997

Notes on the accounts (extract)

6 Directors and employees (extract)
Pensions
The Executive Directors are eligible to join the ABP Group Pension Scheme, under which they are entitled to earn pension benefits, dependent on their length of service, as agreed by the Company. In some circumstances, the Inland Revenue will not permit the Scheme to meet an Executive Director's full pension entitlement, in which case the Company has promised to make good any shortfall by means of unfunded arrangements. Set out below are details of the pension benefits earned by directors over the year ended 31 December 1997.

	Additional pension earned during the year ended 31 December 1997 £000	Accrued pension entitlement at 31 December 1997 £000	Members' contributions in the year ended 31 December 1997 £000	Age at 31 December 1997
Sir Keith Stuart	15	201	26	57
R A Channing	2	63	4	54
C W Orange	12	86	15	55
J N Shaw	7	34	10	53
A W Smith	5	5	9	47

- The additional pension earned during the year excludes any increase for inflation.
- The accrued pension entitlement shown is that which would be paid annually on retirement based on service to the end of the year.
- On retirement at any age after age 50, A W Smith and J N Shaw would be paid a pension of one-thirtieth of pensionable salary for each year of Company service, subject to a maximum of two-thirds of pensionable salary, inclusive of retained benefits from former employments. Each of the other Executive Directors would be paid a pension equal to the maximum permitted by the Inland Revenue, subject to a maximum of two-thirds at age 60.
- Once in payment, pensions are guaranteed to increase in line with the Retail Price Index, limited in the cases of J N Shaw and A W Smith to a maximum of 5 per cent per annum.
- A spouse's pension, equal to half of the member's pension, is payable on the death of each Executive Director except A W Smith, where the spouse's pension would be two-thirds of his pension.
- No bonuses are paid to directors. In the case of A W Smith, pensionable salary does not include the taxable value of benefits in kind. For each of the other directors shown in the table above, the taxable value of benefits in kind (excluding any amounts which arise from rights in respect of shares) are pensionable.
- C S Bradley is a director of the Company but retired from the employment of Associated British Ports during 1996 and is no longer accruing pension benefits.
- R A Channing retired on 22 April 1997. The table shows the additional pension accrued during the part year to his retirement.

Table 11.18.2 – ARRIVA plc – Annual Report and Accounts – 31 December 1997

remuneration committee report (extract)

Directors' Pensions (extract)

Each of the executive Directors is provided with pension benefits under the ARRIVA Pension Scheme. Mr. Hodgson became entitled to a pension of two thirds of his final salary on attaining his sixtieth birthday; the payment of this pension commenced on 1 October 1996 following Mr. Hodgson's sixty-fifth birthday.

11.166.3 Another situation that may arise is where a director leaves a company defined benefit scheme and sets up a private scheme to which the company contributes. In such a case the entitlements are disclosed up to the date of leaving the scheme and thereafter the company's contribution to the personal pension scheme is disclosed in the same way as for a defined contribution scheme. Table 11.18.3 illustrates this situation.

Table 11.18.3 – BELLWAY p.l.c. – Annual Report – 31 July 1997

NOTES TO THE ACCOUNTS (extract)

(b) Directors' pension information

	Date of birth	Date service commenced	Accrued pension entitlement (pa) at age 60 as at 31 July 1997 (see note 1)	Accrued pension entitlement (pa) at age 60 as at 31 July 1996 (see note 1)	Increase in accrued pension entitlement for the year (see note 2)	Transfer value of the increase in entitlement for the year (see note 3)
			£	£	£	£
Executives						
H C Dawe	7 April 1944	20 August 1961	140,076	126,427	10,994	130,120
A G Robson (see note 4)	1 April 1937	3 October 1983	116,157	106,467	8,014	122,237
A K Bell	20 August 1957	10 December 1975	70,667	65,720	3,567	24,197
P J Stoker	23 May 1956	2 March 1981	55,429	50,537	3,831	26,607
J K Watson	21 March 1954	1 July 1978	34,466	27,246	6,240	48,770

Notes

1. The pension entitlement shown is that which would be paid annually on retirement based on service to the end of the year, but excluding any statutory increases which would be due after the year end.
2. The increase in accrued pension during the year excludes any increase for inflation. The inflation rate used is that published by the Secretary of State for Social Security in accordance with Schedule 3 of the Pension Schemes Act 1993. The inflation rate for the year to 31 July 1997 was 2.1%.
3. There are no contributions from the directors to the 1972 pension scheme, therefore there are no contributions to offset the transfer value shown. The transfer value shown has been calculated in accordance with Actuarial Guidance Note GN11. This value represents the cash equivalent of the increase in accrued benefit. For this purpose it is assumed that with the exception of Mr A G Robson whose membership ceased on 25 March 1997, the benefit entitlement is increased until the normal retirement date in accordance with the scheme rules.
4. The pension entitlement for Mr A G Robson has been calculated as at 25 March 1997, being the date he left the scheme. His accrued benefits at that date were transferred into a Self Invested Personal Pension Scheme (SIPPS). Since the transfer the Company has contributed £23,520 into Mr Robson's SIPPS.

11.166.4 Where a director leaves a company and receives a pension augmentation as part of his compensation for loss of office, the augmentation is sometimes disclosed separately from the pension entitlements table, and sometimes the value of the augmentation is included in the table (see para 11.100.1 above). Inclusion in the table is more common where there is no actual payment, but the entitlement to pension is augmented because the director is allowed to take early retirement. An example of disclosure where a payment for compensation has been made but has then been used to augment the pension entitlement is Table 11.18.4. In this example the payment has been disclosed in the main emoluments table with a note (only the note is reproduced below) and has also been included in the pension entitlements table, but the disclosure is such that it is quite clear as to how the amount has been treated.

Table 11.18.4 – English China Clays plc – Annual report and accounts – 31 December 1997

Report of the Remuneration Committee (extract)

Directors' remuneration (extract)

8) A severance payment of £227,032 was used to augment the early retirement benefits of T.T. Sharland, at the time of the termination of his service contract.

Directors' pension disclosures

Director	Total accrued pension as at 31 December 1996 £'000 pa (Note 1)	**Total accrued pension as at 31 December 1997 £'000 pa (Note 1)**	**Increase in accrued pension during 1997 £'000 pa (Note 2)**	**Transfer value of the increase in accrued pension during 1997 £'000 pa (Note 3)**
D.L. Rediker (Note 4)	28	**43**	**15**	**201**
P. Drayton (Note 5)	6	**7**	**1**	**3**
C.W. Gronow	94	**104**	**10**	**135**
T.T. Sharland (Note 6)	86	**86**	**n/a**	**256**

Notes

1) These pension entitlements are those which have been earned based on service and pensionable salary at the end of the year. The December 1996 figures include inflation-linked revaluation to 31st December, 1997.

2) These increases in accrued pension are net of any increase for inflation.

3) These transfer values have been calculated on the basis of actuarial advice in accordance with Actuarial Guidance Note GN11 and exclude the director's contributions paid during the year. This is a liability of the Company's pension arrangements and not a sum paid or due to the directors by the Company.

4) D.L. Rediker will receive benefits from the approved UK pension arrangement (described above), a non-tax approved UK pension arrangement for benefits in respect of earnings above the UK earnings cap and from US pension arrangements, since he is employed on a split UK/US contract basis. The combined value of the UK and US benefits is shown above. In addition, contributions totalling £1,745 were paid to a separate US defined contribution arrangement (401(k) plan).

5) For P. Drayton, the Company also paid contributions of £33,000 to a non-tax approved pension arrangement to provide benefits in respect of earnings above the earnings cap. These benefits are excluded from the table above but are included in the Directors' Remuneration table.

6) T.T. Sharland took early retirement on 30th June 1997. His accrued pension as at 31st December 1997 therefore represents the pension he was receiving at that date. His severance payment was used to augment his early retirement benefits, and this augmentation has been included in the December 1997 pension figure.

7) Members of the Company's approved UK pension arrangements have the option to pay Additional Voluntary Contributions; neither the contributions nor the resulting benefits are included in the table above.

[The next paragraph is 11.167.]

Company contributions to money purchase schemes

11.167 The Listing Rule amendment in May 1997 also introduced a requirement to disclose, by individual director, details of the contribution or allowance payable or made by the company for money purchase schemes. The text of the new rule is set out in paragraph 11.139(j) above.

11.168 The words *"contribution or allowance payable or made"* would include provisions for unfunded money purchase benefits as well as actual contributions paid or payable to a scheme (see para 11.65 above). In addition *"made by the company"* should presumably be interpreted as meaning the same as *"company contributions"* under the Companies Act rules, that is the term would include payments by other parties than the company in respect of the director (see para 11.68 above for Companies Act definitions).

11.168.1 An example of disclosure is Table 11.18.5.

Table 11.18.5 – DFS Furniture Company plc – Annual Report and Accounts – 2 August 1997

DIRECTORS AND EMPLOYEES (extract)

3.1 *DIRECTORS' EMOLUMENTS*

	Salary and fees	Performance related incentives	Benefits	Total	Total	Pension Contributions		Gains on share options	
				1997	1996	1997	1996	1997	1996
	£000	£000	£000	£000	£000	£000	£000	£000	£000
Executive									
G. Kirkham	200	–	31	231	245	50	50	–	–
J.H. Massey	81	40	10	131	123	10	10	241	–
I.F. Bowness	81	30	13	124	115	10	9	–	–
Non-executive									
K.T Morley	25	–	–	25	25	–	–	–	–
M.C. Walker	25	–	–	25	25	–	–	–	–
	412	70	54	536	533	70	69	241	–

All of the directors' pension contributions are to individual defined contribution pension schemes.

[The next paragraph is 11.169.]

Audit

11.169 The rules also provide that the auditors' report on the financial statements must cover the disclosures in paragraphs 11.139(c), (d), (e), (i) and (j) above. If the auditors consider that the company has not complied with any of the requirements of these paragraphs they must say so in their report and must then give the required information in their report, so far as they are reasonably able to do so.

11.170 The audit requirement mentioned in paragraph 11.169 gives considerable force to the new Listing Rules. It is extremely rare for auditors to have to comply in their statutory audit report with reporting requirements imposed other than by law. It is a measure of the importance placed on the new disclosure requirements by all the regulatory bodies that they will be policed by the auditors as an extension of the statutory audit. The APB issued a Bulletin 'Stock Exchange Listing Rules regarding disclosure of directors' remuneration' which gives guidance for auditors.

Differences from the Greenbury recommendations

11.171 Both the Greenbury Report and the Listing Rules require that a remuneration committee report should be included as part of the annual report and financial statements and the report should set out a statement of the company's policy on executive directors' remuneration. Whilst the Greenbury Report recommended that the members of the committee should be named in the report, the Listing Rules do not specifically require this, although it is a provision of the non-mandatory best practice provisions of Section A on remuneration committees (see para 11.136).

11.172 The Listing Rules do not specify the matters that should be covered in the statement of the company's policy on executive directors' remuneration. Companies may, therefore, turn to the detailed list of matters that are contained in the Greenbury Report.

11.173 Whilst the Greenbury Report recommended that the remuneration committee report should also say by whom the fees and other benefits of non-executive directors are determined, the Listing Rules include a provision in the non-mandatory best practice provisions of Section A on remuneration committees, to the effect that the Board or the shareholders should determine the remuneration of all non-executives. In practice companies may, therefore, cover this point through their statement of compliance with Section A, (see paras 11.133, 11.135 above), but some may also wish to include additional disclosure in the remuneration committee report. An example of disclosure is given in Table 11.19.

Table 11.19 – The Albert Fisher Group PLC – Annual Report and Financial Statements – 31 August 1995

Remuneration policy (extract)

9 Non-executive directors

The basic fees payable to the non-executive directors are set by the board as a whole and are currently £20,000 each per annum. The chairman of the audit committee and the chairman of the remuneration committee each receive an additional £5,000 per annum. A fee of £2,500 per annum is also payable to the other members of each of these committees.

The deputy chairman receives a further £10,000 in respect of additional responsibilities associated with this position.

The non-executive directors receive no other benefits from their office.

11.174 The items to be disclosed in the table of individual directors' remuneration (including overseas directors) are very similar in both the Greenbury Report recommendations and in the Listing Rules. In the Listing Rules, however, disclosure of long-term incentive schemes including share options is not included. This is because the Listing Rules now provide that an additional, separate, table should be presented, giving details of long-term incentive schemes. This form of presentation was hinted at in an appendix to the Greenbury Report, but has been translated into a requirement in the Listing Rules. The table should show entitlements at the beginning and end of the year, grants made and payments received in the year. Disclosure of long-term incentives is illustrated in Tables 11.13 to 11.15.

11.175 The Listing Rules also provide for significant payments made to former directors during the period to be included in the table of individual directors' remuneration. The Greenbury Report recommended that any payments and benefits not previously disclosed should be included. The listing rule provision is presumably intended to catch the type of payment or benefit that the Greenbury Report has identified, as well as any other benefit, but it is noticeable that the Listing Rules apply to any former directors and not just to those who have retired during the current or prior periods. Whilst the Listing Rule requirement to disclose significant payments to former directors does not specifically say so, we consider that it should be taken to mean that disclosure should be given by individual former director rather than as an aggregate figure.

[The next page is 11061.]

11.176 Both the Greenbury Report and the Listing Rules require disclosure if any elements of remuneration, other than basic salary, are pensionable, though the wording of the Listing Rules is more all-embracing. Greenbury referred to disclosure if annual bonuses or benefits were pensionable, whereas the Listing Rules require disclosure of any element of remuneration that is pensionable, other than basic salary. An example of disclosure is given in Table 11.20.

Table 11.20 – Smiths Industries Public Limited Company – Annual Reports and Accounts – 5 August 1995

Directors' Emoluments and Interests (extract)

The annual bonus and any gains under share option schemes are not pensionable. Company car and health insurance benefits are subject to income tax. The former, for which a cash alternative is available, is pensionable; the latter is not.

11.177 Greenbury proposed that the report should explain and justify, if grants under executive or other long-term incentive schemes are awarded in one large block rather than being phased). The Stock Exchange has included this point in the best practice provisions of Section B on remuneration policy, service contracts and compensation, which is covered by a compliance statement (see para 11.134), and by a specific requirement for the company's policy on the granting of options to be disclosed, effective for periods ending on or after 30 September 1996 (see para 11.139(i)).

11.178 The Listing Rules require the same details of service contracts of over one year as recommended by Greenbury together with details of the unexpired term of the service contract of a director proposed for election or re-election at the AGM, or if he or she has no contract, a statement to that effect. The latter requirement was an existing listing rule that has now been included in the rules relating to the remuneration committee report. An example of disclosure is given in Table 11.21.

Table 11.21 – Tate & Lyle Public Limited Company – Annual Report – 30 September 1995

Remuneration and Appointments Committee Report (extract)

Service Contracts All executive directors appointed since 1993 have service contracts terminable by the Company on not more than two years' notice (prior to 1993 notice periods were normally three years) and by the individual directors on up to six months' notice. These notice periods take into account the international nature of Tate & Lyle's business and the need to remain competitive. The Chairman's contract is for a two year fixed term expiring on 30th June 1996 and is renewable. It is terminable by the Chairman on six months' notice. P S Lewis's service contract terminates at his normal retirement date of 30th November 1996. The Committee considers individually any case of early termination of a service contract.

The unexpired terms of service contracts for executive directors proposed for re-election at the forthcoming AGM are shown below:

	Unexpired term as at 28th November 1995
Sir Neil Shaw	7 months
S Gifford	24 months
P J Mirsky	24 months
J H W Walker	24 months

L R Wilson, a non-executive director proposed for re-election at the forthcoming AGM, does not have a service contract.

Emoluments waived

11.179 Prior to the changes introduced in 1997 for 31 March 1997 year ends the Act required certain details of emoluments waived by directors to be disclosed. This requirement has been dropped. However, for listed companies the Stock Exchange requirements remain.

11.180 The Stock Exchange's Listing Rules require listed companies to disclose particulars of any arrangement under which a director has either waived or agreed to waive any future or current emoluments and details of such waivers. This applies in respect of emoluments from either the company or any of its subsidiaries. [LR 12.43(d)]. An example of disclosure of waivers is given in Table 11.22.

Table 11.22 – Saatchi & Saatchi Company PLC – Report and Accounts – 31 December 1993

Directors' and senior executives' emoluments (extract)

In addition to the emoluments shown above, certain Directors were entitled to the following amounts which were waived. These waivers were without prejudice to any existing entitlements to pension contributions and to entitlements of those Directors to emoluments in the future.

WAIVERS BY EXECUTIVE DIRECTORS	Year ended 31 Dec 1993 £	Year ended 31 Dec 1992 £
M. Saatchi (Chairman)	312,500	312,500
C. Saatchi	290,064	312,500
C.T. Scott	-	83,355
J.T. Sinclair	70,000	70,000
R.L.M. Louis-Dreyfus	53,420	230,473
	725,984	1,008,828

In addition, M. Saatchi and J.T. Sinclair have agreed to waive a portion of their emoluments, £312,500 and £70,000 respectively, for the year to 31st December 1994.

Group situations

11.181 Common problems arise with the disclosure of directors' emoluments in a group context. Consider the following examples where a director of a parent company has also been nominated to the board of one of its subsidiaries. In all the situations it is assumed that the director is remunerated by the parent company in connection with his services as director of the parent company. It is also assumed that all the relevant information concerning emoluments is available to the reporting company.

Example 1

Where the subsidiary pays the director directly in respect of his services as a director of the subsidiary.

In this situation the parent company will need to disclose, as directors' emoluments, the aggregate of the amount paid to the director in respect of his services as a director of the parent company and the amount he receives in respect of his services as a director of the subsidiary. [6 Sch 10(2)]. The subsidiary will also need to disclose the amount paid to the director by the subsidiary, as directors' emoluments, in its own financial statements.

Example 2

Where the subsidiary pays the director, but the director is liable to account to the parent company for the remuneration he receives in respect of his services as director of the subsidiary.

In this situation, the notes to the financial statements of the parent company need only disclose, as directors' emoluments, the amounts paid to the director in respect of his services as director of the parent company. The amount paid by the subsidiary needs to be disclosed, as directors' emoluments, in the subsidiary's financial statements. Where, however, the director is subsequently released from the obligation to account for the remuneration, the remuneration must be disclosed in a note to the first financial statements of the parent company in which it is practicable to show it, and the remuneration must be distinguished from other remuneration. [6 Sch 11(2)].

Example 3

Where the parent company pays the director directly and recharges the subsidiary for his services as a director of the subsidiary.

The aggregate amount that needs to be disclosed, as directors' emoluments, in the parent company's financial statements is the same as in example 1. The notes to the subsidiary's financial statements must disclose, as directors' emoluments, the amount receivable by the director for services to the subsidiary, that is, in this situation, the amount recharged by the parent company in respect of the director's services.

Example 4

Where the parent company pays the director directly, but no recharge is made to the subsidiary.

Again, the aggregate amount that needs to be disclosed, as directors' emoluments, in the parent company's financial statements is the same as in example 1. The notes to the financial statements of the subsidiary, however, must include details of the remuneration paid by the parent company in respect of the director's services to the subsidiary. An explanation to the effect that the charge for director's remuneration has been borne by the parent company may be useful, although there is no requirement in the Act to do so. If it is necessary for the parent company to apportion the director's remuneration, the directors may apportion it in any way they consider appropriate. [6 Sch 12].

11.182 Practical difficulties may arise in connection with disclosure of remuneration in a subsidiary's financial statements where a director of the subsidiary is also:

- A director or employee of the parent and is paid by the parent; or
- A director of another subsidiary and is paid by that other subsidiary.

11.183 In such cases, it is often difficult to ascertain the emoluments of the director that are paid to or receivable by him in respect of his services to the subsidiary in question. This difficulty may be aggravated if there is no charge made to the subsidiary by the payer of the emoluments. It may also sometimes be aggravated by a desire on the part of either the parent or the subsidiary to limit the amount of disclosure in the subsidiary's financial statements, if, for instance, the parent-appointed director is more highly rewarded than other directors.

11.184 Paragraph 14 of Schedule 6 states that the schedule requires information to be given regarding emoluments, pensions and compensation for loss of office only so far as it is contained in the company's books and papers or the company has the right to obtain it from the persons concerned. 'Books and papers' are defined in section 744 to include accounts, deeds, writings and documents.

11.185 As noted in paragraph 11.7 above, section 232 of the Companies Act 1985 states that *"...it is the duty of any director of a company, and any person who is or has at any time in the preceding five years been an officer of the company, to give notice to the company of such matters relating to himself as may be necessary for the purposes of Part 1 of Schedule 6"*.

11.186 Where, despite the requirements of section 232, there are difficulties in obtaining information one or more of the steps described below might be taken.

11.187 If the subsidiary is a party to the directors' service agreement, and that agreement stipulates what the director is paid in respect of his services to the subsidiary, then the information is contained in the subsidiary's books and papers and the subsidiary should disclose it.

11.188 If the subsidiary is not a party to the service agreement (possibly because the agreement is with the parent or a fellow subsidiary) the subsidiary or its directors should *"make reasonable efforts"* to obtain the information, for instance by asking the parent or fellow subsidiary for details of the terms of the service agreement, or by obtaining a detailed breakdown of any management charge.

11.189 If any fellow director of the subsidiary has obtained the necessary information in his capacity as a director of the subsidiary, he should disclose it to the board of the subsidiary. The information will then be under the subsidiary's control and it should disclose it.

11.190 If the information needed is not obtainable by any of the above means, companies often make an apportionment. This is relatively simple where a director is a director of both the subsidiary and the parent, but spends the vast majority of his time in an executive capacity on the subsidiary's affairs. It is less easy if the director is also a director of a large number of different subsidiaries. The Companies Act, Schedule 6 permits apportionment (see para 11.24 above). We suggest that where apportionment is relatively straightforward it may be the best way of determining the emoluments to be disclosed in the subsidiary.

11.191 The above steps may be summarised as follows:

- Inspect the subsidiary's relevant books and papers including service contracts to which it is party.
- Analyse any management charges for details of emoluments charged.
- Request information from other group companies that have service contracts with directors to which the company is not a party or from the director himself.
- Apportion where total emoluments are known and the apportionment can be made with a high degree of confidence and accuracy.

These steps should result in disclosure in the majority of cases.

11.192 If, in rare circumstances, the necessary information is not contained in the company's books and papers and the company does not have the right to obtain it from the director, the company is not required to disclose it, (see para 11.184 above). In addition, the auditors would not be able to give the information required in their report (see para 11.10 above).

11.193 Where this situation occurs it might be that the financial statements would not give a true and fair view if no disclosure were made of the facts. Hence in these circumstances, if the financial statements are to give a true and fair view, some narrative needs to be given. Table 11.23 is an example of such a note.

11.194 We suggest that appropriate notes for three situations that may arise where no information is available would be as follows:

Example 1

A recharge is made to the subsidiary by a parent company or fellow subsidiary, but the management charge includes other costs and the emoluments cannot be separately identified.

> *"The above details of directors' emoluments do not include the emoluments of Mr X, which are paid by the parent company (fellow subsidiary) and recharged to the company as part of a management charge. This management charge, which in 19XX amounted to £95,000 also includes a recharge of administration costs borne by the parent company (fellow subsidiary) on behalf of the company and it is not possible to identify separately the amount of Mr X's emoluments."*

11.195 It is envisaged that this situation would be very rare as normally a full breakdown of management charges should be possible.

Table 11.23 – The Telegraph plc – Annual Report and Accounts – 31 December 1994

Directors (extract)

During the year a charge of £871,192 was made by Hollinger Inc. under the services agreement referred to in note 26(c). It is not possible to identify whether any portion of the charge relates to services provided by any director of the company.

26(c) Services agreement

Under the terms of a services agreement with Hollinger Inc., for so long as Mr Black remains chairman of the board, The Telegraph will bear 66.7% of the cost of the office of the chairman incurred by Hollinger or such other proportion as may be agreed from time to time by the Audit Committee. Other services will be provided at cost and may include the arrangement of insurance, assistance in the arrangement of finance and assistance and advice on acquisitions, disposals and joint venture arrangements. Charges to the company in respect of Mr Black's office and these other services amounted to £871,192 in 1994 *(1993: £1,044,000)*.

32. Ultimate parent company

Hollinger Inc., incorporated in Canada and listed on the Toronto, Montreal and Vancouver stock exchanges, is regarded by the directors of the company as the company's ultimate parent company.

The largest group in which the results of the company are consolidated is that of which Hollinger Inc. is the parent company. The consolidated accounts of Hollinger Inc. may be obtained from Montreal Trust Company of Canada, 151 Front Street West, 8th Floor, Toronto, Ontario, Canada M5J 2N1.

The smallest such group is that of which DT Holdings Limited is the parent company, whose consolidated accounts may be obtained from 21 Wilson Street, London EC2M 2TQ. DT Holdings Limited is registered in England and Wales.

Example 2

The director is an executive of the parent and also a director of a large number of other subsidiaries for which he carries on work. He is paid by the parent company which makes no recharge to the subsidiaries. His role is chiefly that of non-executive director of the subsidiaries overseeing the subsidiaries' affairs on behalf of the parent.

> *"The emoluments of Mr X are paid by the parent company. Mr X's services to this company and to a number of fellow subsidiaries are of a non-executive nature and his emoluments are deemed to be wholly attributable to his services to the parent company. Accordingly, the above details include no emoluments in respect of Mr X."*

Example 3

The director is also a director of a number of other subsidiaries for which he carries on work. He is paid by the parent company which makes no recharge to the subsidiaries. His role is that of an executive director of each of the subsidiaries.

> *"The emoluments of Mr X are paid by the parent company which makes no recharge to the company. Mr X is a director of the parent company and a number of fellow subsidiaries and it is not possible to make an accurate apportionment of his emoluments in respect of each of the subsidiaries. Accordingly, the above details include no emoluments in respect of Mr X. His total emoluments are included in the aggregate of directors' emoluments disclosed in the financial statements of the parent company."*

11.196 It is suggested that where a similar situation applies, but the emoluments are paid by a fellow subsidiary, there should normally be a recharge. This is because the situation of a subsidiary paying emoluments of group directors normally only arises with a group services company and such a company would usually recharge for the services it performs. In such a case, the note would not be needed, because the appropriate amount to be disclosed should be ascertainable.

11.197 A committee on corporate governance, chaired by Sir Ronald Hampel ('The Hampel Committee'), issued its final report in January 1998. The committee had been set up to review the implementation of the findings of the earlier Cadbury and Greenbury Committees.

11.198 In respect of directors' remuneration the Hampel Committee generally found that the implementation of the Cadbury and Greenbury Committees' findings had been satisfactory. A summary of the conclusions of the committee in this area is set out below.

- The committee urged caution in using inter-company comparisons and remuneration surveys in setting levels of directors' remuneration.

- The committee did not recommend further refinement in the Greenbury code provisions relating to performance-related pay. Instead, it urged remuneration committees to use their judgement in devising schemes appropriate for the company's specific circumstances. Total rewards from such schemes should not be excessive.

- The committee saw no objection to paying a non-executive director's remuneration in the company's shares, but does not recommend this as universal practice.

- The committee considered that boards should set as their objective the reduction of directors' contract periods to one year or less, but recognised that this cannot be achieved immediately.

- The committee saw some advantage in dealing with a director's early departure by agreeing in advance on the payments to which he or she would be entitled in such circumstances.

- Boards should establish a remuneration committee, made up of independent non-executive directors, to develop policy on remuneration and devise remuneration packages for individual executive directors.

- Decisions on the remuneration packages of executive directors should be delegated to the remuneration committee; the broad framework and cost of executive remuneration should be a matter for the board on the advice of the remuneration committee. The board should itself devise remuneration packages for non-executive directors.

- The requirement on directors to include in the annual report a general statement on remuneration policy should be retained. The committee hoped that these statements will be made more informative.

- Disclosure of individual remuneration packages should be retained; but the committee considered that this has become too complicated. The committee welcomed recent simplification of the Companies Act rules; and it hoped that the authorities concerned would explore the scope for further simplification.

- The committee considered that the requirement to disclose details of individual remuneration should continue to apply to overseas-based directors of UK companies.

- The committee supported the requirement to disclose the pension implications of pay increases, included in the Stock Exchange Listing Rules. It suggested that companies should make clear that transfer values cannot meaningfully be aggregated with annual remuneration.

- The committee agreed that shareholder approval should be sought for new long-term incentive plans; but it did not favour obliging companies to seek shareholder approval for the remuneration report.

11.199 As explained in paragraph 11.136 the Stock Exchange has now introduced a new Listing Rule 12.43A which implements the recommendations of the Hampel committee with effect for financial years ending on or after 31 December 1998.

Chapter 12

Pension costs

Page

Chapter 12

Pension costs

Introduction

The nature of pension arrangements

12.1 Where an employer undertakes to contribute towards the provision of pensions for its employees after their retirement, the cost of the employer's commitment represents a form of deferred remuneration for the employees' services during their period of employment.

12.2 There are three basic types of pension arrangement in the UK, each of which involves a cost to the employer insofar as it is obligated to contribute towards the cost of the benefits receivable by its employees or their dependants. These are:

- The state scheme.
- Occupational pension schemes.
- Personal pension schemes.

State scheme

12.3 The state scheme consists of two elements, the basic pension and the earnings related pension. All employers and employees make contributions towards the state scheme through their national insurance payments. Those who are members of the State Earnings Related Pension Scheme (SERPS) make additional national insurance contributions. It is possible to 'contract out' of SERPS either through an occupational pension scheme or through a personal pension.

Occupational pension schemes

12.4 The Social Security Pensions Act 1975 defines an occupational pension scheme as follows:

> *"Occupational pension scheme means any scheme or arrangement which is comprised in one or more instruments or agreements and which has, or is capable of having, effect in relation to one or more descriptions or categories of employment so as to provide benefits, in the form of pensions or otherwise, payable on termination of service, or on death or retirement, to*

or in respect of earners with qualifying service in an employment of any such description or category."

12.5 In a contracted out occupational scheme, both employer and employee pay a lower rate of national insurance contributions. The occupational scheme is then used to provide employees with benefits which replace part of their state earnings related benefits. The broad intention is that the pension provided by a contracted out scheme is at least as good as the pension that would have been available from SERPS. On retirement, the employee receives a state basic pension and a pension from the occupational scheme.

12.6 Occupational pension schemes are not required to contract out of SERPS and many do not. Where a scheme is 'contracted in' to SERPS, employer and employee pay the full rate of national insurance contributions. The responsibility for payment of SERPS remains with the state. On retirement, the employee receives a state basic and earnings related pension, together with a pension from the occupational scheme.

Personal pension schemes

12.7 Personal pension schemes, which were introduced in their current form in 1988, are pension arrangements available to the self-employed, employees with no company scheme, employees with non-pensionable earnings and those who wish to contract out of SERPS or opt out of an occupational pension scheme. The aim of personal pension schemes is to make pension arrangements more portable and to encourage employees to contract out of SERPS.

Types of pension scheme

12.8 Accounting for the cost of providing pension benefits is particularly affected by the type of benefits that are promised by a scheme and by the way in which the employer's obligations in respect of such benefits are funded. The broad classifications used in pensions terminology are summarised in the following paragraphs.

Defined benefit schemes

12.9 Defined benefit schemes are pension schemes where the rules specify the benefits to be paid, typically by reference to final salary levels, and such schemes are financed accordingly. The majority of such schemes define benefits in relation to an employee's final salary (typically the pension will be based on 1/60th of final salary for each year of pensionable service, up to a maximum of 40 years). They are often referred to as final salary schemes. Another, less common, form of defined benefit scheme is the average salary scheme where the pension is calculated by reference to average pay over a defined period, such as the last three years' service.

Defined contribution schemes

12.10 Defined contribution schemes (often referred to as money purchase schemes) are pension schemes where the benefits are determined directly by the value of contributions paid in respect of each member and the investment performance achieved on those contributions. Normally, the rate of contribution to be paid by the employer company will be specified in the scheme's rules. If the investments have performed well the individual will obtain a higher pension than if the investments have performed badly. In such schemes the risk of poor investment performance lies with the individual. In defined benefit schemes it lies with the sponsoring company. Defined contribution schemes have become more popular with employers since the introduction of personal pension plans.

Funded schemes

12.11 Funded pension schemes are schemes where the future liabilities for pension benefits are provided for in advance by the accumulation of assets held externally to the employing company's business. The assets are usually placed under the control of trustees, who administer the scheme in accordance with the provisions of trust law and the terms of the trust deed governing the particular scheme. Employer and employee contributions paid to the trust are invested by the trustees; pensions are paid out of the accumulated funds of the trust.

12.12 Most funded schemes in the UK that are established under trusts enjoy considerable tax benefits through Inland Revenue recognition as exempt approved schemes. The main benefits are:

- Relief, as an expense, for the employer's contributions.

- Relief for employees from assessment to tax both as regards employer's contributions and employees' own contributions.

- Exemption from income or capital gains tax on investments held by the scheme.

12.13 The Finance Act 1989 introduced an upper limit on the amount of final salary that may be taken into account for pension purposes in determining the amount of the salary cap, which for the tax year 1995-96 is £78,600. Since the Finance Act 1989, employers have been able to establish unapproved schemes to run alongside existing exempt approved schemes. Unapproved schemes can provide unlimited benefits and are mainly used to provide 'top-up' pensions for higher paid employees whose pensionable earnings in the exempt approved scheme are capped. Unapproved arrangements, which may be funded or unfunded, do not enjoy the tax benefits that apply to exempt approved schemes.

Unfunded schemes

12.14 Unfunded pension schemes are schemes where pension benefits are paid directly by the employer. No assets are set aside in advance to provide for future liabilities; instead pension liabilities are met out of the employing company's own resources. Such schemes are not common in the UK, but are the normal method of pension provision in Germany. However, the incidence of unfunded arrangements in the UK has increased, particularly in respect of higher paid executives as a result of changes in the Finance Act 1989 relating to the capping of pensions that affect approved funded schemes.

The need for SSAP 24

12.15 SSAP 24, 'Accounting for pension costs', was issued in May 1988. The standard took many years to be developed and represented a fundamental change from previous practice. It introduced an 'accruals' basis for measuring the annual cost of providing pension benefits. Before SSAP 24 was implemented, the pension charge in a company's profit and loss account was normally based on the amount of cash contributions paid to a pension scheme during a financial year or, in the case of unfunded schemes, on the amount of pensions paid by the company.

12.16 SSAP 24 also introduced extensive disclosure standards regarding companies' pension schemes, that were intended to enable users to analyse the significance of companies' pension obligations. Before the standard's issue the Act contained only limited disclosure requirements concerning pension commitments, and it provided no guidance on the accounting treatment that should be adopted.

UITF 6

12.17 The accruals accounting principles of SSAP 24 were extended to cover all other types of post-retirement benefits offered by employers, including health care, when the UITF issued Abstract 6, 'Accounting for post-retirement benefits other than pensions', in November 1992. Previously, such benefits had often been accounted for on a cash basis. UITF 6 was issued primarily in response to accounting developments in the USA (FAS 106), where the provision of such benefits is more common than in the UK. UITF 6's disclosure requirements became mandatory from calendar year 1992 onwards and its accounting requirements from calendar year 1994.

Scope of SSAP 24

12.18 SSAP 24 applies to all reporting entities that have a legal, contractual or implied obligation to provide pensions to their employees. The standard deals with both the measurement of pension costs and the disclosure of pension information in reporting entities' financial statements.

12.19 Most pension schemes in the UK are funded. This means that the future liabilities for benefits are provided for by the accumulation of assets held independently from the employing company's own assets. The principles of SSAP 24 apply, however, whether a scheme is funded or unfunded. [SSAP 24 para 73].

12.20 The standard applies to both 'defined contribution' and 'defined benefit' schemes. [SSAP 24 para 74]. The main impact of the standard, however, is on those companies that provide defined benefit schemes. In those schemes, employers' obligations are not capable of being defined in an absolute sense, but actuarial expertise is required to determine an appropriate level of contributions to fund those obligations.

12.21 Some schemes cannot clearly be classified as either defined contribution or defined benefit schemes, because they contain features of both. For example, there are schemes that provide money purchase benefits, but with an underlying final salary guarantee. In these circumstances, it is necessary to determine the most suitable classification and to consider what are the appropriate accounting and disclosure requirements.

12.22 The standard does not apply to the national insurance contributions that employers make to the state scheme. These are simply expensed as they fall due. Neither does the standard apply to redundancy payments. [SSAP 24 para 76].

Accounting objective of SSAP 24

12.23 The following principle underlies the standard's accounting requirements. Because the cost of providing pensions is part of the remuneration of employees, the cost should be allocated as fairly as possible so as to match the benefit derived from the services of the employees. Hence the accounting objective in SSAP 24 is stated to be that *"...the employer should recognise the expected cost of providing pensions on a systematic and rational basis over the period during which he derives benefit from the employees' services"*. [SSAP 24 para 77].

12.24 Therefore, the root of the standard is little more than applying to pension costs the same basis as is applied to all other items in a company's profit and loss account, namely the accruals basis of accounting instead of the cash basis.

Table 12.1 shows a typical disclosure of a company's accounting policy in respect of pension costs.

Table 12.1 – The British Petroleum Company p.l.c. – Annual Report and Accounts – 31 December 1997

Accounting policies (extract)

Pensions and other post-retirement benefits

The cost of providing pensions and other post-retirement benefits is charged to income on a systematic basis, with pension surpluses and deficits amortised over the expected average remaining service lives of current employees. The difference between the amounts charged to income and the contributions made to pension plans is included within other provisions or debtors as appropriate. The amounts accrued for other post-retirement benefits and unfunded pension liabilities are included within other provisions.

12.25 SSAP 24's approach to the recognition of pension costs is sometimes described as an 'income approach'. This is because it seeks to account for the cost of providing pension benefits on a basis that matches the cost with the revenues derived from the services provided by the employees. For funded defined benefit schemes, amounts recognised in the balance sheet of the sponsoring company as assets and liabilities are generally no more than timing differences between pension costs accrued and charged in the profit and loss account and contributions made by the company to the scheme.

12.26 An alternative approach, that has not hitherto been favoured by standard setters in the UK, has been described as a 'balance sheet approach' to measuring pension cost. Under this approach, the pension cost for a period is derived from changes during that period in the market values of a scheme's assets and in the present value of the accumulated liabilities for benefits earned by employees. The balance sheet approach has hitherto been rejected in the UK, not least because short-term changes in stock market values and interest rates could cause significant fluctuations in the annual profit and loss account charge. Under the income approach, a long-term view of the pension cost is taken and such changes in values are effectively smoothed over many financial years.

ASB's review of SSAP 24

12.27 SSAP 24 was a significant move into relatively uncharted areas for accountants. Many complex issues emerged as practical experience was gained in introducing the standard's actuarial principles into financial statements. The ASB commissioned two independent reports on the working of SSAP 24 as part of its review of all existing SSAPs. These were prepared by the Financial Reporting and Auditing Group (FRAG) of ICAEW and the Pensions Research Accountants Group

(PRAG). Two main criticisms of SSAP 24 emerged: that it allowed too much flexibility in methods of valuing pension liabilities and in spreading surpluses and deficiencies; and that the disclosures were poorly focused and made analysis of pension costs difficult.

12.28 The ASB decided that SSAP 24 should be replaced and issued a discussion paper in June 1995 as the first stage of that process. The discussion paper explored, from first principles, two distinct approaches to accounting for pensions.

12.29 The first – referred to as the ASB's 'preferred approach', was to continue broadly with the SSAP 24 approach, but to narrow down the available measurement options and to make the disclosures more relevant.

12.30 The second – referred to as the 'alternative approach', would require assets and liabilities of a pension scheme to be valued by reference to current market values, rather than on the basis of long-term actuarial projections.

12.31 A further discussion paper in July 1998 endorses an approach based on market values, which has been embraced by international accounting standards. A summary of the ASB's proposals is given from paragraph 12.221.

Defined contribution schemes

Accounting

12.32 In a defined contribution scheme, the employer's obligation at any point in time is restricted to the amount of the contributions payable to date. Consequently, the company will meet the accounting objective by charging against profits the amount of contributions payable to the pension scheme in respect of the accounting period. [SSAP 24 para 78]. Accounting for the cost of such schemes under SSAP 24 is, therefore, straightforward.

12.33 Any changes in the level of employer contributions, for example an increased rate of contribution resulting from an improvement to a scheme, would, in accordance with the standard, also be expensed as the contributions fall due.

Disclosure

12.34 A company should disclose the following:

- The nature of the scheme (that is, defined contribution).
- The accounting policy.

- The pension cost charge for the period.
- Any outstanding or prepaid contributions at the balance sheet date.

[SSAP 24 para 87].

The appendix to the standard gives an example of disclosure in respect of a defined contribution scheme. The disclosure is illustrated in Table 12.2.

Table 12.2 – Dalgety PLC – Annual Report and Accounts – 30 June 1997

Notes to the Accounts (extract)

1 Accounting policies (extract)

l) Pensions

Contributions to pension schemes in respect of current and past services, ex gratia pensions, and cost of living adjustments to existing pensions are based on the advice of actuaries. Contributions are charged to the profit and loss account on a basis that spreads the expected cost of providing pensions over the employees' working lives with the Group.

23 Pensions (extract)

The Group operates a number of pension schemes throughout its businesses, of both the defined contribution and defined benefit type.

a) The pension cost for defined contribution schemes, which represents contributions payable by the Group, amounted to £2.7m (£3.5m). Included in creditors is £0.4m (£0.7m) in respect of contributions to the schemes.

Defined benefit schemes

Funding considerations

12.35 In a defined benefit scheme, the employing company participates in an agreement to supply a certain level of benefits to employees when they retire. For a funded scheme, the company is normally under an obligation to ensure that the accumulated funds of the scheme are sufficient to enable the promised pensions to be paid. Most schemes are designed so that the employer is responsible for meeting the balance of cost after taking account of employee contributions.

12.36 Companies, in conjunction with actuaries and trustees to the scheme, will normally design a funding plan for their schemes. Actuarial methods are used to determine a size of fund and contribution pattern that build up a pension scheme's assets in a manner that has regard both to the desired level of security in respect of the scheme members' pension rights and to the employer's cash flow objectives.

Typically schemes aim for a funding target based on accrued pensions with full allowance for projected future salary increases.

12.37 New legislation in the Pensions Act 1995 introduced minimum solvency requirements for most defined benefit schemes in order to protect the accrued rights of pension scheme members. For example, if a deficiency is identified, the trustee and employer would need to agree a schedule of contributions to achieve 100 per cent solvency within a set period. Furthermore, for pensions earned after 6 April 1997, all occupational schemes will be required to provide pension increases that match the rise in the retail price index, subject to a maximum of five per cent per annum. This is known as limited price indexation (LPI).

Actuarial considerations

12.38 In a defined benefit scheme, the members' benefits are not directly related to the value of contributions and the fund's investment performance, but are typically determined by a formula based on pensionable service and salary. The majority of schemes operated by larger companies are 'final salary' schemes, where an employee's retirement pension will be based on the level of his salary at, or near, retirement date. Actuarial techniques are required to value pension liabilities. There are several methods that an actuary can use to determine a contribution rate that will provide a scheme with sufficient assets to meet its liabilities to pay the promised benefits. Some methods will produce a different contribution level each year, others will provide a level rate of contribution for all future years.

12.39 Further, the actuary must make key assumptions about such factors as return on investments in a scheme, increases in wages and salaries and increases in pension payments. SSAP 24 does not specify any particular actuarial method and assumptions that should be used. The standard is deliberately flexible and leaves the choice of methods to be adopted to the company's actuary in consultation with his client. It does, however, require that the chosen valuation method and assumption used for accounting purposes should satisfy the accounting objective described in paragraph 12.23 above and should make full provision over the employees' service lives for the expected costs of their pensions.

12.40 Actuarial methods and assumptions are considered further from paragraph 12.162 below.

Regular cost and variations

Regular cost

12.41 Consistent with its objective, SSAP 24 requires that the method of providing for pension costs in respect of defined benefit schemes *"...should be such* *that the regular pension cost is a substantially level percentage of the current and expected future pensionable payroll in the light of the current actuarial assumptions".* [SSAP 24 para 79].

12.42 The 'regular cost' is the consistent ongoing cost that is recognised under the actuarial method used. It is a measure of the cost incurred by a company in each period in respect of current employees' accruing pension rights. SSAP 24 uses the amount of the payroll expense in each period as a basis for allocating the cost. The standard states that where a stable percentage contribution rate is determined, which makes full provision for the expected benefits over the expected service lives of employees, then this will normally be the appropriate amount to charge in the profit and loss account. [SSAP 24 para 20].

12.43 The pattern of contributions determined by a scheme's funding plan does not necessarily meet SSAP 24's accounting objective as a basis for matching pension costs with employees' services. Where the regular cost calculated for the purpose of the company's financial statements differs from the rate of contributions in the funding plan, a pension prepayment or provision will be recognised in the company's balance sheet.

12.44 If all actuarial assumptions were borne out in practice, then the regular cost charged in each period would be sufficient to provide for the pension benefits earned in respect of current and past service. But in practice, regular cost will normally be only one element of the pension cost under SSAP 24. It would be most unusual for actual experience to coincide with all the actuarial assumptions.

Variations

12.45 'Variations from regular cost' arise in the following circumstances:

- Experience surpluses or deficiencies arising from actuarial valuations (see para 12.46 below).
- Increases to pensions in payment or to deferred pensions for which provision has not previously been made (see para 12.102 below).
- Changes in actuarial methods or assumptions that affect the actuarial value of accrued benefits (see para 12.109 below).
- Improvements in benefits or changes in conditions for membership. These generally increase the cost of providing the pension benefits and have an element of past service cost which gives rise to a variation (see para 12.115 below).

[SSAP 24 para 21].

These sources of variations from regular cost are considered below.

Accounting for experience surpluses and deficiencies

12.46 Experience surpluses and deficiencies arise where actuarial assumptions made at the previous valuation have not been borne out in practice. As successive valuations are carried out, they bring to light the fact that actual events may not have coincided with those previously assumed. For example, elements of the financial scheme's performance such as the rate of return on investments, and demographic statistics such as the number of employees leaving service, may differ from those that were assumed. These differences will give rise to a surplus or a deficiency in the scheme.

12.47 The methods of accounting for experience surpluses under SSAP 24 assume that a scheme surplus is a source of future benefits to the employer company. In fact, the question of ownership of a pension fund surplus has remained unresolved, despite many legal cases involving claims by employers and employees to participate in such surpluses. Such cases have focused on the wording of individual schemes.

12.48 In cash terms, variations from regular cost that derive from a surplus or deficiency may be reflected in the form of one or more of the following sources of benefits or obligations:

- Contribution holidays.
- A period of reduced contributions.
- Cash refunds to employers (see para 12.94 below).
- Additional lump sum contributions or a period of increased contributions.

12.49 The general accounting rule in SSAP 24 is that variations from regular cost caused by surpluses or deficiencies should be spread forward over the expected remaining service lives of current employees in the scheme after making allowances for future withdrawals. SSAP 24 does not suggest a period, but says it will be determined by the actuary. The standard permits the use of the expected *average* remaining service lives of the current membership and in practice this is often adopted. [SSAP 24 paras 23, 80].

12.50 Such variations can be material to a company's results. The standard does not require disclosure in the financial statements of the period over which a surplus or deficiency is being spread for accounting purposes. Neither does it require disclosure of variations from regular cost that are included in the total pension cost. Some companies voluntarily provide such information, as it assists analysis of their results and of the future trend in pension costs. Examples where groups have analysed the components of the pension cost are given in Tables 12.14 on page 57 and 12.16 on page 64.

12.51 Unless the funding plan for eliminating a surplus or deficiency in a scheme provides a pattern of cash contributions that matches the pension cost obtained by spreading the surplus or deficiency for accounting purposes, a timing difference will arise which will result in an asset or liability being recognised in the company's balance sheet.

12.52 The standard does not specify how variations from regular cost should be spread and different methods can produce very different reported pension costs. Practice has settled on three main methods:

- Level percentage of current and future pensionable payroll.
- 'Straight line' method.
- 'Mortgage' method.

These methods are described in the following paragraphs and illustrated with worked examples.

12.53 The ASB has proposed in its discussion paper that an accounting standard that replaces SSAP 24 should require the use of a single specified method and has provisionally concluded that it prefers the straight-line method.

Level percentage method

12.54 Under this method, the adjustment to the regular cost in respect of the allocation of the surplus or deficiency is weighted so that the net pension cost is expected to be a stable percentage of pensionable payroll each year.

12.55 Consequently, the variation allocated to each financial year would increase in line with expected salary inflation.

Straight line method

12.56 Under this method, the surplus to be reduced, or deficiency to be funded, will be allocated on a straight-line basis, so that the annual pension cost would be calculated as follows:

$$\text{Regular cost} - \frac{\text{Surplus to be reduced}}{\text{Average remaining service life}}$$

$$\text{Regular cost} + \frac{\text{Deficiency to be funded}}{\text{Average remaining service life}}$$

12.57 The amount of the variation deducted or added is increased by interest on the balance of the surplus or deficiency that has not yet been allocated to the profit and loss account.

12.58 In this situation, the variation is calculated independently of the pensionable payroll. The variation allocated to each financial year would reduce as the amount of interest added decreases. Consequently, the annual pension cost, expressed as a percentage of total pensionable payroll, will tend to vary over the chosen number of years where the payroll cost varies owing to, for example, annual pay rises or changes in the number of employees. Because the variation credited or debited in each successive year decreases, the annual cost expressed as a percentage of payroll costs will rise over time where there is a scheme surplus and fall where there is a scheme deficiency.

Mortgage method

12.59 The variation is calculated as a fixed annual amount over the chosen period for allocating the surplus or deficiency. Like a repayment mortgage, the annual variation will be represented by a decreasing amount of interest and an increasing amount of capital in respect of the surplus or deficiency that has not yet been allocated to the profit and loss account.

12.60 As with the straight line method, the variation is calculated independently of the pensionable payroll. Because the annual variation including interest is a constant figure, salary inflation will cause the annual pension cost to rise as a percentage of payroll costs where there is a scheme surplus and to fall where there is a scheme deficiency.

Discounting

12.61 The preceding paragraphs have referred to the effect of interest on the calculation of variations from regular cost attributable to experience surpluses and deficiencies.

12.62 Notional interest arises because discounting is implicit in the methods used by actuaries to value pension funds. Any surpluses or deficits reported by the actuary are discounted amounts which increase with the passage of time. For example, where a surplus of (say) £200,000 is to be absorbed by a contribution holiday, the holiday might extend over a period to save (say) £230,000 in contributions. The amount of £30,000 represents notional interest. It arises because, if the surplus is not withdrawn from the scheme immediately, the underlying assets continue to earn interest. There is little guidance in SSAP 24 on how to account for a notional interest benefit or cost. The standard states that discounting in financial statements is a general issue and not unique to pensions. [SSAP 24 para 40].

12.63 In general, the interest effects arising from short-term timing differences between the payment of contributions and the recognition of cost are not likely to be material and can be ignored. [SSAP 24 para 40]. Where, however, the difference is long-term (for example, where a surplus giving rise to a contribution holiday is spread for accounting purposes over a much longer period), it would be correct, in principle, to account for any notional interest on balance sheet assets or liabilities arising.

12.64 The interest rate that should be applied will be the long-term rate inherent in the actuarial assumptions, because this rate is used by the actuary to project the unwinding of the surplus or deficit in the scheme. Consequently, the actuary should have information concerning notional interest that can be used to account each year for such interest as it arises.

Examples of spreading methods

12.65 The three methods of spreading a variation from regular cost are illustrated in the following example. It should be noted that this example illustrates the accounting that arises from a single actuarial valuation. As most pension schemes in the UK undergo actuarial valuations every three years, new variations are likely to arise each time a new valuation occurs. Accounting for the effects of subsequent actuarial valuations is considered from paragraph 12.120.

Example

The actuarial valuation at 31 December 19X4 of the pension scheme of a company showed a surplus of £50 million. The current annual pensionable payroll is £100 million and this is expected to grow by 8% per annum. The actuary has determined the long-term contribution rate (regular cost) to be 10% of payroll and the valuation rate of interest is 10%. The average remaining service life of employees in the scheme at 31 December 19X4 was 10 years. After consultation with its actuary, the company decided to eliminate the surplus by reducing its contributions to the scheme by £10 million per annum over a period of approximately 8 years.

Figure 1 shows the actuarial projections for the actual elimination of the surplus in the scheme over the period of reduced contributions). Figures 2 to 4 show the SSAP 24 calculations for spreading the surplus over the average remaining service life of employees under the three spreading methods referred to above.

Figure 1

Projected actual elimination of surplus

Year	Surplus B/Fwd £'m	Interest £'m	Reduction in Contributions £'m	Reduction of Surplus £'m
1	50.0	5.0	10.0	5.0
2	45.0	4.5	10.0	5.5
3	39.5	4.0	10.0	6.0
4	33.5	3.3	10.0	6.7
5	26.8	2.7	10.0	7.3
6	19.5	1.9	10.0	8.1
7	11.4	1.1	10.0	8.9
8	2.5	0.3	2.8	2.5
9	0	0	0	0
10	0	0	0	0
		22.8	72.8	50.0

Figure 2 calculates the variation under the 'level percentage' method, so that it increases by 8% per annum, in line with expected salary inflation. The variation is computed as a rate of 6% of pensionable payroll.

Figure 2

'Level percentage' calculation of variation

Year	Deferred Surplus B/Fwd £'m	Interest £'m	Amortisation of Surplus £'m	Variation £'m
1	50.0	5.0	1.0	6.0
2	49.0	4.9	1.5	6.4
3	47.5	4.7	2.2	6.9
4	45.3	4.5	3.0	7.5
5	42.3	4.2	3.9	8.1
6	38.4	3.8	4.9	8.7
7	33.5	3.3	6.1	9.4
8	27.4	2.7	7.5	10.2
9	19.9	2.0	9.1	11.1
10	10.8	1.1	10.8	11.9
		36.2	50.0	86.2

Figure 3 calculates the variation under the 'straight line' method as a fixed annual amount of £5 million, plus interest at 10% per annum on the declining balance of the unamortised surplus.

Figure 3

'Straight-line' calculation of variation

Year	Deferred surplus B/Fwd £'m	Interest £'m	Amortisation of Surplus £'m	Variation £'m
1	50.0	5.0	5.0	10.0
2	45.0	4.5	5.0	9.5
3	40.0	4.0	5.0	9.0
4	35.0	3.5	5.0	8.5
5	30.0	3.0	5.0	8.0
6	25.0	2.5	5.0	7.5
7	20.0	2.0	5.0	7.0
8	15.0	1.5	5.0	6.5
9	10.0	1.0	5.0	6.0
10	5.0	0.5	5.0	5.5
		27.5	50.0	77.5

Figure 4 calculates the variation under the 'mortgage' method as an annuity of £8.1 million over the 10 years amortisation period.

Figure 4

'Mortgage' calculation of variation

Year	Deferred surplus B/Fwd £'m	Interest £'m	Amortisation of Surplus £'m	Variation £'m
1	50.0	5.0	3.1	8.1
2	46.9	4.7	3.5	8.2
3	43.4	4.3	3.8	8.1
4	39.6	4.0	4.2	8.2
5	35.4	3.5	4.6	8.1
6	30.8	3.1	5.0	8.1
7	25.8	2.6	5.6	8.2
8	20.2	2.0	6.1	8.1
9	14.1	1.4	6.7	8.1
10	7.4	0.7	7.4	8.1
		31.3	50.0	81.3

The 'variation' columns in Figures 2, 3 and 4 provide acceptable calculations of the variation from regular cost under SSAP 24; they all amortise the surplus over the average service life of 10 years. This contrasts with the actual elimination of the surplus over 8 years in Figure 1. It should be noted that the present value of the variation in each case is £50 million, being the actuarial value of the initial surplus.

Figures 5 to 7 translate these profiles into the profit and loss account and balance sheet entries that would arise under each of the methods. The pension cost derives from a regular cost of £10 million in year 1 (10% of pensionable payroll), increasing at an assumed 8% per annum. The figures for contributions expected to be paid comprise the anticipated regular cost less the annual reduction in contributions of £10 million in years 1 to 7, falling to £2.8 million in year 8 and nil thereafter.

Figure 5 shows the level-percentage method of spreading the surplus. Under this method the variation, taken from Figure 2, is a constant percentage of estimated pensionable payroll and hence of regular cost. Net pension cost includes notional interest at the valuation rate (10%) on the balance sheet provision that arises and reverses due to the timing difference between payment of contributions and recognition of net pension cost.

Figure 5

Accounting –
'Level percentage' method of spreading surplus

Year	Regular cost £'m	Variation £'m	Notional Interest £'m	Net Pension Cost £'m	Contributions Paid £'m	Provision £'m
0						0
1	10.0	(6.0)	0	4.0	0	4.0
2	10.8	(6.4)	0.4	4.8	0.8	8.0
3	11.7	(6.9)	0.8	5.6	1.7	11.9
4	12.6	(7.5)	1.2	6.3	2.6	15.6
5	13.6	(8.1)	1.5	7.0	3.6	19.0
6	14.7	(8.7)	1.9	7.9	4.7	22.2
7	15.8	(9.4)	2.2	8.6	5.8	25.0
8	17.1	(10.2)	2.5	9.4	14.3	20.1
9	18.5	(11.1)	2.0	9.4	18.5	11.0
10	20.0	(11.9)	0.9	9.0	20.0	0
	144.8	(86.2)	13.4	72.0	72.0	

Figure 6 shows the straight-line method of spreading the surplus. Net pension cost comprises regular cost less the variation calculated in Figure 3, plus notional interest on the outstanding balance sheet provision.

Figure 6

Accounting – 'Straight-line' method of spreading surplus

Year	Regular cost £'m	Variation £'m	Notional Interest £'m	Net Pension Cost £'m	Contributions Paid £'m	Provision £'m
0						0
1	10.0	(10.0)	0	0	0	0
2	10.8	(9.5)	0	1.3	0.8	0.5
3	11.7	(9.0)	0.1	2.8	1.7	1.6
4	12.6	(8.5)	0.2	4.3	2.6	3.3
5	13.6	(8.0)	0.3	5.9	3.6	5.6
6	14.7	(7.5)	0.5	7.7	4.7	8.6
7	15.8	(7.0)	0.9	9.7	5.8	12.5
8	17.1	(6.5)	1.2	11.8	14.3	10.0
9	18.5	(6.0)	1.0	13.5	18.5	5.0
10	20.0	(5.5)	0.5	15.0	20.0	0
	144.8	(77.5)	4.7	72.0	72.0	

Figure 7 shows the mortgage method of spreading the surplus. Net pension cost comprises regular cost less the variation calculated in Figure 4, plus notional interest on the 'outstanding balance sheet provision.

Figure 7

Accounting – 'Mortgage' method of spreading surplus

Year	Regular cost £'m	Variation £'m	Notional Interest £'m	Net Pension Cost £'m	Contributions Paid £'m	Provision £'m
0						0
1	10.0	(8.1)	0	1.9	0	1.9
2	10.8	(8.2)	0.2	2.8	0.8	3.9
3	11.7	(8.1)	0.4	4.0	1.7	6.2
4	12.6	(8.2)	0.6	5.0	2.6	8.6
5	13.6	(8.1)	0.9	6.4	3.6	11.4
6	14.7	(8.1)	1.1	7.7	4.7	14.4
7	15.8	(8.2)	1.4	9.0	5.8	17.6
8	17.1	(8.1)	1.8	10.8	14.3	14.1
9	18.5	(8.1)	1.4	11.8	18.5	7.4
10	20.0	(8.1)	0.7	12.6	20.0	0
	144.8	(81.3)	8.5	72.0	72.0	

Figure 8 compares the projected pension cost obtained under each of the spreading methods. This is one area where SSAP 24 has been criticised for its flexibility. There is no logical reason why such different amortisation profiles should be available in a given set of circumstances. In each case, the total pension cost over the ten-year period is equal to the total contributions to be paid; the differences arise in the allocation of this total to each accounting period. It can be seen that the 'straight-line' method, which front loads the interest earned on the surplus, produces the greatest variation credit (and lowest pension cost) in the early years. Conversely, it produces the lowest variation credit (and highest pension cost) in the later years; consequently, there is less of an increase in the annual cost at the end of the spreading period, when the pension cost reverts to the regular cost.

Figure 8

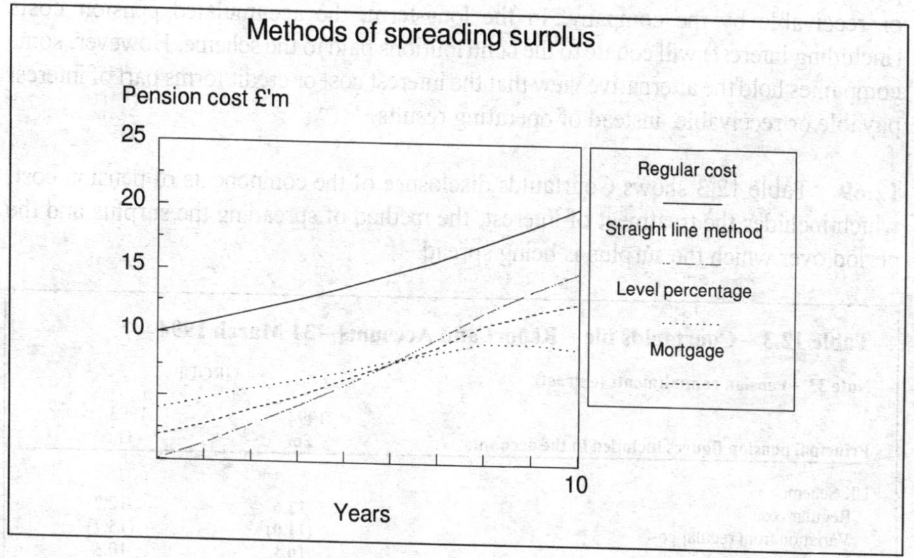

12.66 Figures 5 to 7 in paragraph 12.65 illustrate SSAP 24's 'income approach' to accounting for pension costs that focuses on the profit and loss charge. The balance sheet asset or liability is then derived as a consequence. Thus where the scheme is in surplus, a net pension provision will arise where the cumulative pension cost charged exceeds contributions paid. This will happen, as in the example above, where a company takes a contribution holiday or a reduction in contributions. A provision will accumulate each year that the allocated pension cost exceeds the contributions paid. The amount provided in this way will be reversed over the chosen period of employees' service lives as the regular contributions paid following the holiday exceed the annual profit and loss charge.

12.67 Conversely, where a scheme is in deficit, a net pension prepayment will arise where contributions paid over a limited period to fund the deficit exceed the cumulative annual charge to profit and loss account.

12.68 It is good practice to explain in the accounting policy or disclosure note how interest on balance sheet items has been taken into account. Another consideration is whether the interest component should be included with the pension cost charge (that is, as an operating cost), or with interest payable or receivable in the profit and loss account. The example above has adopted the former approach. This is a reasonable treatment, because the net pension cost is derived from discounting expected future pension liabilities and the interest component does not represent interest that is payable or receivable by the company. In the long-term, the accumulated pension costs (including interest) will equate to the contributions paid to the scheme. However, some companies hold the alternative view that the interest cost or credit forms part of interest payable or receivable, instead of operating results.

12.69 Table 12.3 shows Courtaulds disclosure of the components of pension cost, which includes the treatment of interest, the method of spreading the surplus and the period over which the surplus is being spread.

Table 12.3 – Courtaulds plc – Report and Accounts – 31 March 1994

Note 33 – Pension commitments (extract)

	GROUP	
Principal pension figures included in the accounts	**1994 £m**	1993 £m
UK Scheme		
Regular cost	**12.6**	12.7
Variation from regular cost	**(11.0)**	(15.7)
Other schemes	**10.5**	10.3
Charge to operating profit (note 4)	**12.1**	7.3
Credit to interest payable (note 6)	**(11.0)**	(18.3)
	1.1	(11.0)
Prepayment included in debtors being excess of pension credits to profit and loss account over amounts funded	**42.4**	33.4

For accounting purposes, the actuarial surplus including interest is spread as a level amount each year over the 12 year average remaining service life of the employees in the Scheme.

12.70 It may seem anomalous to some users that the financial statements of the sponsoring company can show a liability (pension provision) when the scheme is in surplus and an asset (pension prepayment) when the scheme is in deficit. However, on closer analysis it can be seen that the balance sheet figure is in reality a composite one made up of two long-term items – the surplus in the fund (excess of scheme assets over employer's liability) and the amount of surplus that has been deferred for accounting purposes, that is, awaiting recognition in the profit and loss account. With reference to the example in paragraph 12.65, the following example shows how the entries in the balance sheet can be reconciled to the underlying surplus in the pension scheme.

Example

Facts as in the example in paragraph 12.65. At the end of year 2, the projected surplus in the scheme is £39.5 million (see Figure 1). Figure 9 reconciles this surplus to the amounts shown in the balance sheet under each of the spreading methods in Figures 5, 6 and 7.

Figure 9

Balance sheet reconciliation

Method	**Provision - B/S** £'m	**Deferred Surplus** £'m	**Surplus in Scheme** £'m
Level percentage	(8.0)	47.5	39.5
Straight line	(0.5)	40.0	39.5
Mortgage	(3.9)	43.4	39.5

The first column shows the derived balances to be included in the balance sheet – in this example there is a provision in each case – from Figures 5, 6 and 7.

The second column shows the amount of surplus that has been deferred under each of the spreading methods as at the end of year 2; the figures are taken from Figures 2, 3 and 4. The deferred surplus represents the amounts available to be credited in the profit and loss account in future years. It differs from the surplus in the scheme, because whereas the original surplus of £50 million in the scheme has been reduced as a result of reduced employer contributions, it is being recognised more gradually and over a longer period in the company's profit and loss account.

In descending order of magnitude, the amounts of surplus deferred or unrecognised relate to the level percentage method, the mortgage method and the straight line method. This is to be expected, because the level percentage method produces the lowest variation credit in the early years, whereas the straight line method produces the highest.

12.71 A reconciliation of the pension balances in the balance sheet to the actual surplus or deficiency in the scheme would assist analysts to assess the impact of any deferred surplus or deficiency on the trend of future pension costs. This is one of the proposals in the ASB's discussion paper.

[The next paragraph is 12.80.]

Exceptions to the principle of spreading variations

12.80 Apart from the optional transitional treatment described above, there are three exceptions to the general rule of spreading surpluses and deficiencies as described above:

- Where a surplus or deficiency that causes a 'significant change' in the level of contributions has resulted from a significant reduction in the number of employees.
- Where a company takes a cash refund as part of a scheme to reduce a surplus in accordance with the provisions of the Finance Act 1986.
- Where prudence requires it, a material deficiency should be recognised over a shorter period.

Significant reduction in number of employees

12.81 The standard refers to situations where a surplus or deficiency in a pension scheme results from a significant reduction in the number of employees covered by a company's pension arrangements and where this leads to a significant change in the normal level of employer contributions to the scheme. In these circumstances, the surplus or deficiency should not be spread forward over the remaining service lives of the remaining workforce. Except where the reduction in the number of employees is related to the sale or termination of an operation (see para 12.87 below), the standard requires any reduction in contributions to be recognised in the profit and loss account as it occurs. [SSAP 24 para 81].

12.82 This treatment recognises the fact that a surplus arising from, say, a major redundancy programme falls outside the normal process of revising estimates of contribution levels. The surplus may arise because the pension benefits accrued and retained by employees when they leave a scheme earlier than expected are likely to be lower than the level of benefits previously accrued in the valuation of the scheme's liabilities, where a normal level of staff turnover would have been assumed. It would be inappropriate to spread forward this element of a surplus over the future service lives of employees who remain in the scheme. This different treatment is a requirement, not an option. What is 'significant' in this context may be open to debate, but the company's actuary needs to be involved in isolating the cause of a surplus and quantifying the effect on contribution levels of a significant reduction in the number of employees. A special actuarial valuation may be required if the event falls between normal valuations.

12.83 Although the standard does not permit such a surplus or deficiency to be spread forward, neither should a surplus be recognised immediately in the accounting period in which the related event, for example the restructuring giving rise to the redundancies, occurs. The standard requires that, in the case of a surplus, any refund, contributions holiday or reduction in contributions should not be anticipated, but should be recognised in the profit and loss account as it occurs. [SSAP 24 paras 26, 81]. Therefore, in effect, a cash basis of accounting is required.

12.84 In our view, the 'cash basis' of accounting that is required where the pension cost or credit is not related to the sale or termination of an operation is arbitrary and can cause unnecessary complications in practice. A scheme surplus or deficiency might be attributed to several sources, for example, the termination of an operation, a business reorganisation involving significant redundancies and a normal experience surplus or deficiency. Each of those causes requires different recognition criteria for the consequential pension costs or credits. The allocation of such costs may lead to accounting solutions that are difficult to interpret both from a profit and loss account and balance sheet perspective. It would, in our view, be a step forward if the bases for recognising variations in pension costs were narrowed to spreading and immediate recognition.

12.85 The proposals in the ASB's discussion paper for replacing SSAP 24 would have the effect of removing this anomaly in a future accounting standard. The discussion paper refers to 'curtailments' as a single category of events that includes a significant reduction in the number of employees arising from either a sale or termination of an operation or from a reduction in the workforce following an efficiency review. The discussion paper proposes that surpluses and deficiencies resulting from all such events should be recognised in full in the profit and loss account at the point when the employer company becomes demonstrably committed to the transaction.

Example

The facts are the same as in the example in paragraph 12.65, except that in year 3 the company decides to reorganise and downsize its operations. The pension effects of the reorganisation, which involve a significant number of redundancies, are as follows.

The reduction in the workforce results in an additional surplus in the pension scheme of £8 million, calculated as at the end of year 3. From year 4 onwards the estimated regular cost, which remains at 10% of pensionable earnings, is reduced by 20% as a result of the reduced membership (projected inflation in earnings remains at 8%). The company and trustees agree that the company should extend the annual reduction in contributions of £10 million until the increased surplus is eliminated. It is assumed there have been no other variations or changes in assumptions since the previous valuation.

Figure 11 shows the revised projection of movements in the surplus in the scheme, based on the original projections in Figure 1 on page 15. It shows that the period of reduced contributions is extended so that it will end in year 9 rather than year 8. The benefit to the company of the new surplus in nominal cash terms is £13.6 million, that is, the reduction in contributions has increased from £72.8 million in Figure 1 to £86.4 million in Figure 11. The reason for the increase of £13.6 million is that the surplus on termination of £8 million is expressed in present value terms at the end of year 3, whilst the cash benefit of that surplus is not realised until years 8 and 9.

Figure 11 – Projected actual elimination of surplus

Year	Surplus b/fwd	Surplus on termination	Interest	Reduction in contributions	Contributions payable	Surplus c/fwd
	£m	£m	£m	£m	£m	£m
1	50.0	-	5.0	10.0	0.0	45.0
2	45.0	-	4.5	10.0	0.8	39.5
3	39.5	8.0	4.0	10.0	1.7	41.5
4	41.5	-	4.2	10.0	0.2	35.7
5	35.7	-	3.6	10.0	1.0	29.3
6	29.3	-	2.9	10.0	1.9	22.2
7	22.2	-	2.2	10.0	2.9	14.4
8	14.4	-	1.4	10.0	3.9	5.8
9	5.8	-	0.6	6.4	5.0	0.0
10	0.0	-	0.0	0.0	16.2	0.0
			28.4	86.4	33.6	

Because the company is already enjoying an extended period of reduced contributions, the cash flow effect of the new surplus is to extend the period of reduced contributions further. It is not entirely clear how this new reduction should be accounted for. One possibility, a literal interpretation of paragraph 81 of SSAP 24, which states that *"the reduction of contributions should be recognised as it occurs"*, is shown in Figure 12. Figure 12 is based on the 'mortgage' method of calculating the variation shown in Figure 7 on page 18.

Figure 12 – Accounting for surplus on downsizing

Year	Regular cost	Variation	Reorganis-ation surplus	Notional Interest	Net pension cost	Contribution paid	Provision
	£m	£m	£m	£m	£m	£m	£m
1	10.0	(8.1)		0.0	1.9	0.0	1.9
2	10.8	(8.2)		0.2	2.8	0.8	3.9
3	11.7	(8.1)		0.4	4.0	1.7	6.2
4	10.2	(8.6)		0.6	2.2	0.2	8.2
5	11.0	(8.6)		0.8	3.2	1.0	10.4
6	11.9	(8.5)		1.0	4.4	1.9	12.9
7	12.9	(8.5)		1.3	5.7	2.9	15.7
8	13.9	(8.6)	(7.2)	1.6	(0.3)	3.9	11.5
9	15.0	(8.5)	(6.4)	1.1	1.2	5.0	7.7
10	16.2	(8.5)		0.8	8.5	16.2	0.0
		(84.2)	(13.6)	7.8	33.6	33.6	

[The next page is 12029.]

In this example, the reduction in contributions occurs in years 8 and 9. Consequently, £7.2 million and £6.4 million are credited to profit and loss account, as additional variations, in years 8 and 9 respectively.

The decrease in the regular cost in year 4 is due to a reduction in the pensionable payroll of 20% following the redundancies plus salary inflation of 8%.

The annual variation from regular cost from year 4 onwards has been recalculated as an annuity of £8.5 million over the remainder of the 10 years' amortisation period, in order to recognise the interest benefit that derives from realising, in cash terms, the surplus from the termination in years 8 and 9 rather than year 3.

In practice it is difficult to attribute specific contribution reductions to specific causes, and there is considerable leeway in choosing an accounting result. Furthermore, a different result would be obtained if the level of the annual contribution reduction were varied as a result of the additional surplus in the scheme. In addition, there will be further actuarial valuations at three-yearly intervals. If these introduce new experience surpluses or deficiencies, the accounting would become even more problematical.

Accounting for the surplus on downsizing in this way appears fairly meaningless, because it is not accounted for at the time the downsizing event occurs. There is, for example, no basis for matching the credit in the profit and loss account with the costs of making the employees redundant.

12.86 The standard does not specifically refer to increases in contributions resulting from a deficiency that stems from significant redundancies other than to preclude the usual method of spreading the deficit forward. A deficit might occur where employees made redundant are granted enhanced pension benefits in lieu of, or additional to, redundancy payments. Alternative treatments appear to be available. The additional pension cost could either be recognised as additional contributions become payable (mirroring the treatment of surpluses), or the deficiency could be charged immediately in the profit and loss account on grounds of prudence. The latter treatment is also consistent with the treatment of *ex gratia* pensions (see para 12.105 below) and has been adopted by British Telecommunications plc (see Table 12.6).

Table 12.6 – British Telecommunications plc – Report and Accounts 31 March 1995

Extract from accounting policies

XI Redundancy costs

Redundancy costs arising from periodic reviews of staff levels are charged against profit in the year in which employees leave the group.

When the most recent actuarial valuation of the group's pension scheme shows a deficit, the estimated cost of providing incremental pension benefits in respect of employees leaving the group is charged against profit in the year in which the employees leave the group, within redundancy charges.

XII Pension schemes

The cost of providing pensions is charged against profits over employees' working lives with the group using the projected unit method. Variations from this regular cost are allocated over the average remaining service lives of current employees to the extent that these variations do not relate to the estimated cost of providing incremental pension benefits in the circumstances described in XI above.

Notes to the financial statements (extract)

23 Pension costs (extract)

The pension cost for the year was based on the valuation of the BT Pension Scheme at 31 December 1993. The valuation, carried out by professionally qualified independent actuaries, used the projected unit method. The major assumptions used by the actuaries were that, over the long-term, the return on the existing assets of the scheme, relative to market values, would be 8.6% per annum and on future investments the return would be 9.7% per annum (allowing for real equity dividend growth of 0.5% per annum), the retail price index would increase at an average of 5.0%, and wages and salary rates would increase at an average of 6.8%. The assets of the scheme, which had a market value of £17,196m at the valuation date, were sufficient to cover 97% of the benefits that had accrued to members by 31 December 1993, after allowing for expected future increases in wages and salaries but not taking into account the cost of providing incremental pension benefits for employees taking early retirement under release schemes since that date. This cost, charged within redundancy costs, amounted to £483m in the year ended 31 March 1995 (1994 – £305m).

The group made a special contribution of £250m to the scheme in the year ended 31 March 1995 (1994 – £800m), in addition to regular contributions of £251m (1994 – £246m).

Sale or termination of operation

12.87 Where a significant reduction in the number of employees is caused directly by the sale or termination of an operation, the requirements of FRS 3 override the provisions outlined above. FRS 3 requires separate disclosure, as exceptional items after operating profit, of profits or losses on the sale or termination of operations. [FRS 3 para 20]. A pension cost or credit in respect of employees who leave the scheme as a result of the sale or termination will form part of the calculation of the profit or loss on disposal.

12.88 If the sale or termination of an operation results in a profit on disposal, such profit should be recognised in the period the sale or termination occurs. If a loss on disposal is expected, a provision for the loss should be recognised in the preceding period if the decision to dispose of the operation had been taken in that period and the company was demonstrably committed to the sale or termination. [FRS 3 para 18].

12.89 SSAP 24 states that where a significant reduction in the number of employees is related to the sale or termination of an operation, the associated pension cost or credit should be recognised immediately to the extent necessary to comply with FRS 3. [SSAP 24 para 81]. Such costs or credits should not be deferred until they become receivable or payable.

12.90 FRS 3 states that the amount of any provision for losses in respect of a sale or termination should take into account the aggregate profit, if any, to be recognised in the profit and loss account from the future profits of the operation or disposal of its assets. [FRS 3 paras 18]. Such profits would include any pension surplus arising from the disposal.

12.91 In practice, therefore, the individual elements of income and expenditure, including pension costs or credits, that derive from a sale or termination of an operation are aggregated, and they would normally be recognised in the profit and loss account in the same period as the profit or loss on disposal is booked. For example, if a company closes a business segment and makes a large number of employees redundant, then the effect of any attributable pension scheme surplus should be recognised immediately by its inclusion in arriving at the overall loss (or provision for loss) on termination. This applies even though the surplus may give rise to a contribution holiday or reduced contribution rate over a number of years in respect of the remaining membership of the scheme. The resulting pension credit would be reflected as an asset in the balance sheet, or as a reduction in any existing provision.

12.92 Where a sale or termination falls between normal valuations, a special actuarial valuation may be required in order to include the pension effect of the disposal in the profit and loss account.

Example

The facts as in the example in paragraph 12.84, except that the surplus of £8 million in year 3 arose from the company's decision to close a segment of its operations. A provision for loss on termination is included in the financial statements for year 3.

Figure 13 shows a suggested method of accounting for the increased surplus from year 3 onwards. It is also based on the 'mortgage' method of calculating the variation shown in Figure 7 on page 18.

Figure 13

Accounting for new surplus on termination

Year	Regular cost	Surplus on termination	Variation	Notional Interest	Net pension cost	Contributions paid	Provision
	£m	£m	£m	£m	£m	£m	£m
1	10.0		(8.1)	0.0	1.9	0.0	1.9
2	10.8		(8.2)	0.2	2.8	0.8	3.9
3	11.7	(8.0)	(8.1)	0.4	(4.0)	1.7	(1.8)
4	10.2		(8.6)	(0.2)	1.4	0.2	(0.6)
5	11.0		(8.6)	(0.1)	2.3	1.0	0.7
6	11.9		(8.6)	0.1	3.4	1.9	2.2
7	12.9		(8.5)	0.2	4.6	2.9	3.9
8	13.9		(8.6)	0.4	5.7	3.9	5.7
9	15.0		(8.5)	0.6	7.1	5.0	7.8
10	16.2		(8.6)	0.8	8.4	16.2	0.0
		(8.0)	(84.4)	2.4	33.6	33.6	

The surplus of £8 million arising from the termination is credited to the profit and loss account at the end of year 3. Thus the net pension cost for year 3 is a credit of £4.0 million. In accordance with paragraph 20 of FRS 3, the surplus of £8 million would be credited in arriving at the provision for loss on termination of the business that is shown as an exceptional item after operating profit, because it is a revenue that relates directly to the termination. This would leave a pension cost of £4 million included in operating costs.

The derived balance sheet figures now fluctuate between provisions and prepayments. The movement from a provision of £3.9 million at the end of year 2 to a prepayment of £1.8 million at the end of year 3 arises because the pension contributions in year 3 of £1.7 million exceed the net pension cost – in this case a pension credit of £4.0 million. Thereafter, the net pension cost exceeds the contributions paid until year 10 when the company reverts to a normal level of contributions. Assuming no other variations occur during the period of spreading the surplus, the balance sheet figures unwind by the end of the period.

12.93 Before FRS 3 was introduced, SSAP 24 dealt with the situation where a material surplus or deficiency was caused directly by an extraordinary event. FRS 3 effectively defined extraordinary items out of existence and included consequential amendments to SSAP 24 to replace the passages relating to extraordinary items with those relating to the sale or termination of an operation as described above.

Cash refunds

12.94 Where a company takes a refund of a surplus under the provisions of the Finance Act 1986 or equivalent legislation, then it *may* depart from the spreading principle and credit the refund to profit and loss account in the period in which it occurs. [SSAP 24 para 83].

12.95 Where this policy has been adopted in respect of any refund during the accounting period, the treatment should be disclosed in the financial statements. [SSAP 24 para 88(j)].

12.96 Alternatively, the company *may* defer recognition of the refund and spread the surplus over the average remaining service lives of current employees, that is, the normal treatment used for a contribution holiday.

12.97 It is unfortunate that the standard allows a choice of methods. A refund is in effect just a negative cash contribution. Under the principles of the standard the timing of contributions to a pension scheme does not affect the allocation of pension costs to accounting periods. There is no logical reason why a refund should be accounted for differently from a contribution holiday, which would mean crediting the refund to the balance sheet rather than the profit and loss account.

12.98 In some circumstances, the method of crediting the refund to the profit and loss account is in any case inappropriate. A company may already have recognised an asset on its balance sheet in respect of a pension scheme surplus. Examples include:

- A residual asset relating to a surplus that was recognised on balance sheet under the transitional provisions for implementing SSAP 24.
- A surplus of a newly acquired subsidiary that is required by FRS 7 to be recognised as an asset in the financial statements of the acquiring group at its fair value.
- A surplus that has already been credited to the profit and loss account as a result of the termination of a business.

12.99 Where the pension credit has already been recognised in the financial statements, a cash refund simply realises the asset held on the balance sheet and should be credited against it. In these circumstances, a credit to the profit and loss account would not, where material, give a true and fair view. The example in Table 12.7 illustrates this effect.

Table 12.7 – Molins PLC – Annual report and accounts – 31 December 1993

Notes to the accounts (extract)

14 Pension fund prepayment	1993 £000 Group	1992 £000 Group	1993 £000 Company	1992 £000 Company
Pension fund prepayment	**61,640**	69,420	**59,340**	67,450

UK pension schemes

In accordance with the Group's accounting policy under SSAP 24 the cumulative adjustment in respect of the pension funds' surpluses is included in the balance sheet and interest accruing on the pension funds' surpluses is taken into account in determining the net pension credit in the profit and loss account. As a result of the repayment to the Company in the year (see para iv below), the pension fund prepayment on the Company's balance sheet was reduced by £11.5m, being the repayment net of costs of £0.3m.

iv) Deployment of UK pension surpluses

Following a favourable response in April 1993 from members of the two UK pension schemes to the proposals for deploying the prescribed surpluses, the Company received on 2 September 1993 the sum of £11.8 million, net after tax, from these surpluses. The associated improvements in benefits to the members of the schemes were also implemented.

12.100 Refunds to employers are liable to corporation tax or income tax (as appropriate) at a flat rate of 40 per cent. The employer cannot reduce this charge by offsetting allowances and reliefs, although it can be avoided if he would otherwise be exempt from tax. This tax charge is intended to recover the tax relief previously given on the employer's contributions to the scheme. Where a refund is credited to the profit and loss account, the logical treatment of the refund and attributable tax is to credit the gross amount in arriving at profit before tax, with the tax shown as part of the tax charge. However, as the rate of taxation deducted from the refund is greater than the standard corporation tax rate, the basis of the tax charge may need to be explained in the notes if the charge is materially distorted.

Prudence – material deficiency

12.101 Where prudence requires it, a material deficiency should be recognised over a shorter period than the expected remaining service lives of current employees. This is expected to arise, however, only in very limited circumstances. SSAP 24 states that the deficiency must have been caused by a major event outside the normal scope of actuarial assumptions and must have resulted in significant additional contributions being paid into the scheme. One example given is where there has been a major mismanagement of pension scheme assets. In most situations where deficiencies give rise to additional 'top up' funding, the standard requires that the additional payments should be allocated over the expected average remaining service lives rather than written off when paid. [SSAP 24 paras 28, 82].

Increases to pensions in payment and deferred pensions

12.102 Increases to pensions in payment and deferred pensions were mentioned earlier as one source of variation from regular cost. Increases that are required to be given by law or by contract and increases that are on paper discretionary, but are in practice customarily granted as a measure of protection against inflation, are usually taken into account in the actuarial assumptions that form part of the calculation of the ongoing pension cost. Consequently, the cost of such increases is accrued in the regular pension cost over the service lives of the beneficiaries.

12.103 Where the granting of discretionary pension increases has not previously been taken into account in the pension cost of past accounting periods, an additional liability arises to provide pensions in respect of the past service of ex-employees.

12.104 Where such a liability is borne by the company's pension scheme, it may have the effect of either reducing an existing surplus or creating a scheme deficiency. If the cost (that is, capitalised present value) of additional benefits is covered by a surplus in the scheme, this will reduce the surplus to be recovered by the company in future years. The reduction in the surplus will be factored into the variation being spread forward, with the cost of the pension increase, therefore, also being spread forward. This will result in an increase in the annual net pension cost in the company's profit and loss account.

12.105 Where an increase in pensions or deferred pensions creates a scheme deficiency, the consequential cost that falls on the company cannot be matched with future services that provide value to the company. SSAP 24, therefore, requires an immediate write-off of the liability in the following circumstances:

- Where an employer grants a one-off *ex-gratia* increase that affects pensions paid in the current period, but that will not affect pensions paid in future periods, the cost should be charged against profits in the period in which the increase is granted.

- Where an employer grants an *ex-gratia* pension to an employee on retirement, that is outside the benefits provided by a scheme, the capital cost should be charged against profits in the period in which it is granted.
- Where an employer grants a single discretionary improvement to pensions in payment for the current and future periods, without creating an expectation of similar increases in the future, the capitalised value of the improvement should be charged against profits in the period in which it is granted.
- Where discretionary increases are granted periodically, and if no allowance has been made in the actuarial assumptions (see para 12.107 below), the capitalised value of each increase should be provided for in the period in which it is granted.

[SSAP 24 paras 33 to 38, 84 to 85].

12.106 The treatment described above also applies where the company, rather than the scheme, is responsible for paying the increased pensions, as may be the case where *ex-gratia* pensions are granted to certain employees in connection with their retirement.

12.107 The preferred treatment where discretionary increases are granted periodically is for such increases to be allowed for in the actuarial assumptions. This applies even though there is no contractual commitment to award future increases, but there is a reasonable expectation that they will be forthcoming on a regular basis. The cost would then be charged over the service lives of the employees. [SSAP 24 para 35].

12.108 Increases that are specified in the rules of a pension scheme or by law will be taken into account in the actuarial assumptions. Therefore, the cost of such increases will be charged over the service lives of the employees. [SSAP 24 para 34].

Changes in actuarial methods and assumptions

12.109 Where the actuarial assumptions made at the previous valuation have not been borne out in practice, an experience surplus or deficiency will arise. Similarly, where shifts occur in the long-term assumptions about the future financial performance of a scheme, or its demographic features, there will be corresponding changes in the estimated cost of providing pensions.

12.110 Any increase or decrease in the estimated cost of future service benefits resulting from changed assumptions would be accounted for by increasing the regular cost that is charged in future accounting periods.

12.111 Any change in the values of a scheme's assets, or of its liabilities in respect of past service, that result from changed assumptions used in their measurement will give rise to a surplus or deficiency at the date of the new valuation and a new variation from regular cost to be accounted for.

12.112 Similarly, a change in actuarial method may produce both a change in the estimated cost of future service (regular cost) and a change in the value of the accumulated assets and liabilities of the scheme, giving a new variation to be accounted for.

12.113 SSAP 24 requires variations from regular costs that are caused by changes in actuarial methods or assumptions to be spread forward according to the general rule for accounting for experience surpluses and deficiencies. [SSAP 24 para 30].

12.114 Table 12.7 shows an extract from the financial statements of Marks and Spencer p.l.c., where changes in the advance corporation tax rules have led to a reduction in the amount of imputed tax credits recoverable by the scheme in respect of dividends receivable on its investments, which gives rise to a consequential reduction to the scheme surplus recoverable by the group and an increase in the pension cost.

Table 12.8 – Marks & Spencer p.l.c. – Annual Report and Financial Statements – 31 March 1994

Notes to the financial statements (extract)

10 Employees (extract)

The latest actuarial valuation of the UK scheme was carried out at 1 April 1992. The assumptions which have the most significant effect on the results of the valuation are those relating to the rate of return on investments and the rates of increase in salaries and pensions. It has been assumed that the investment return is 2% higher per annum than future salary increases, with a further 2% differential between salaries and pension increases.

> At the date of the latest actuarial valuation, the market value of the assets of the UK scheme was £1,405.8m and the actuarial valuation of these assets represented 106% of the benefits that had accrued to members, after allowing for expected future increases in earnings. The surplus of the actuarial valuation of assets over the benefits accrued to members was £77.8m. At that time, it was decided that this should be spread over six years from 1 April 1992, being the remaining estimated service lives of the existing members, by a reduction in the annual contribution made to the scheme.
>
> Since this valuation, the Government has changed the rules concerning Advance Corporation Tax. As this has adversely affected the income of the UK scheme the directors have decided, on actuarial advice, that it would be prudent to suspend with effect from 1 April 1993, the reduction in annual contributions described above. This change has increased the UK pension cost by £16m this year.
>
> The next actuarial valuation will be carried out at 1 April 1995.

Improvements in pension benefits

12.115 Companies may grant improved pension benefits as part of employees' remuneration packages. If such improvements are made retroactive, they will result in an additional liability for employees' past service. Examples of benefit improvements include the following plan amendments:

- A reduction in the normal retirement date.
- An increase in the multiplier for each year of service in a final salary scheme.
- And an increase in spouses' benefits if they survive the retired employees.

12.116 Furthermore, benefit improvements are sometimes granted across the whole scheme membership, including pensioners and deferred pensioners.

12.117 Benefit improvements may produce both an increase in the estimated cost of future service (regular cost) and an increased liability for past service, giving a new variation to be accounted for.

12.118 SSAP 24 requires additional past service liabilities to be spread forward, that is written off over the remaining service lives of the current employees. [SSAP 24 para 31].

12.119 The standard does not permit either a prior period adjustment or an immediate write-off in respect of such liabilities in the period the benefit improvements are granted. One argument for the spreading forward treatment is that retroactive benefit improvements are nevertheless usually considered part of an enhanced remuneration package of current employees, the cost of which should be matched with the benefits to the employer of the future service to be rendered by the employees in return for the greater reward.

12.120 The standard makes no distinction between the additional past service costs of current employees and ex-employees, that is both should be written off over the remaining service lives of current employees. Thus the costs are treated differently from *ex-gratia* payments in respect of past service as described in paragraph 12.105 above. Many would argue that the costs of scheme benefit improvements that relate to the past service of ex-employees should be written off immediately, because there is no directly matching benefit.

12.121 Benefit improvements are sometimes granted when a scheme is in surplus, whereupon the scheme surplus is shared between the company and the employees (and sometimes ex-employees). The reduction in the scheme surplus amounts to a new variation to be accounted for, as illustrated in the following example.

Example

The facts are the same as in the example in paragraph 12.65, except that in year 4 the company decides to introduce a plan amendment to improve members' benefits in order to utilise part of the surplus in the scheme.

The present value of the past service cost of the plan amendment is £20 million as at the beginning of year 4. The future service cost increases the regular cost from 10% of pensionable pay to 10.2%. The company and trustees agree that the company should curtail the period of reduced contributions when the reduced surplus is eliminated. It is assumed there have been no other variations or changes in assumptions since the previous valuation.

Figure 14 shows the revised projection of movements in the surplus in the scheme, based on the original projections in Figure 1 on page 15. It shows that the period of reduced contributions is curtailed so that it will end in year 5 rather than year 8.

The contributions payable represent the regular cost shown in Figure 15 less the reduction in contributions shown in Figure 14.

Figure 14

Projected actual elimination of surplus

Year	Surplus b/fwd	Cost of benefit improvements	Interest	Reduction in contributions	Contributions payable	Surplus c/fwd
	£m	£m	£m	£m	£m	£m
1	50.0	-	5.0	10.0	0.0	45.0
2	45.0	-	4.5	10.0	0.8	39.5
3	39.5	(20.0)	4.0	10.0	1.7	13.5
4	13.5	-	1.4	10.0	2.9	4.9
5	4.9	-	0.5	5.4	8.5	0.0
6	0.0	-	0.0	0.0	15.0	0.0
7	0.0	-	0.0	0.0	16.2	0.0
8	0.0	-	0.0	0.0	17.5	0.0
9	0.0	-	0.0	0.0	18.9	0.0
10	0.0	-	0.0	0.0	20.4	0.0
			15.4	45.4	101.9	

Figure 15 is based on the 'mortgage' method of calculating the variation shown in Figure 7 on page 18. The regular cost is increased from year 4 onwards and the annual variation credit is reduced. The variation has been recalculated as an annuity of £4.1 million over the remainder of the 10 years' amortisation period.

The provision on the balance sheet reaches a peak in year 5 and reverses from year 6 when the company reverts to a full contribution rate.

Figure 15

Accounting for benefit improvement

Year	Regular cost	Variation	Notional Interest	Net pension cost	Contributions payable	Provision
	£m	£m	£m	£m	£m	£m
1	10.0	(8.1)	0.0	1.9	0.0	1.9
2	10.8	(8.2)	0.2	2.8	0.8	3.9
3	11.7	(8.1)	0.4	4.0	1.7	6.2
4	12.9	(4.0)	0.6	9.5	2.9	12.8
5	13.9	(4.0)	1.3	11.2	8.5	15.5
6	15.0	(4.1)	1.6	12.5	15.0	13.0
7	16.2	(4.1)	1.3	13.4	16.2	10.2
8	17.5	(4.1)	1.0	14.4	17.5	7.1
9	18.9	(4.1)	0.7	15.5	18.9	3.7
10	20.4	(4.1)	0.4	16.7	20.4	0.0
		(52.9)	7.5	101.9	101.9	

Subsequent actuarial valuations

12.122 In the UK most pension schemes undergo a formal actuarial valuation every three years. The examples considered thus far have shown long-term projections of pension costs, together with projected balance sheet provisions or prepayments that arise and unwind during employees' remaining service lives. These examples have related to the first valuation that identified a surplus or deficiency in the scheme, together with further variations caused by specific events, such as the termination of a business segment and the granting of enhanced benefits. In practice, new surpluses or deficiencies are likely to arise and will be identified each time a new actuarial valuation is undertaken.

12.123 Apart from the general principles of dealing with surpluses or deficiencies that are set out in the standard, the standard does not provide any guidance on how to account for the effects of each successive valuation where a further variation in pension cost has to be dealt with.

12.124 Alternative methods have been recognised in practice:

- Continuing to spread the initial surplus or deficiency according to the existing amortisation pattern and spreading the new surplus or deficiency separately over the period representing the average expected remaining service lives of the employees in the scheme at the date of the new valuation.

- Combining the new surplus or deficiency that has arisen since the last valuation with the part of the initial surplus or deficiency that has not yet been amortised to the profit and loss account and spreading the total over the average expected remaining service lives of the new membership (this is sometimes referred to as 're-spreading').

12.125 The two methods are illustrated in the following example. To keep the illustration simple, this example ignores the effects of discounting and inflation.

Example

A company's year end is 31 March. An actuarial valuation of the pension scheme at 31 March 19X2 showed a surplus of £200 million. The company decided to eliminate the surplus by suspending contributions to the scheme for the four years from 1 April 19X2 to 31 March 19X6. Thereafter, the contributions were expected to be equal to the regular cost of £50 million per annum. The surplus was being spread forward on a straight line basis over 10 years, being the average remaining service life of employees in the scheme at 31 March 19X2. The projected elimination of the surplus would be reflected in the financial statements of each of the 10 years ending 31 March as shown in Figure 16.

Figure 16

Elimination of surplus in financial statements

Year	Contributions Paid £'m	Regular cost £'m	Variation £'m	Pension cost £'m	Provision £'m
19X3	Nil	50	(20)	30	(30)
19X4	Nil	50	(20)	30	(60)
19X5	Nil	50	(20)	30	(90)
19X6	Nil	50	(20)	30	(120)
19X7	50	50	(20)	30	(100)
19X8	50	50	(20)	30	(80)
19X9	50	50	(20)	30	(60)
19Y0	50	50	(20)	30	(40)
19Y1	50	50	(20)	30	(20)
19Y2	50	50	(20)	30	Nil
	300	500	(200)	300	

The initial surplus of £200 million would, therefore, have been expected to be reduced in the first 3 years before the next valuation as shown in Figure 17. By 31 March 19X5 the surplus in the scheme was projected to have been reduced by £150 million to £50 million. The profit and loss account has been credited with a cumulative variation of £60 million, leaving £140 million to be credited over the remaining 7 years. The difference between the cash benefit of the contribution holiday taken to 31 March 19X5, £150 million, and the surplus credited in the financial statements, £60 million, is carried forward as a provision of £90 million.

Figure 17

Balance sheet reconciliation

Year	Actual Surplus in scheme £'m	Deferred surplus for accounts £'m	Provision £'m
19X2	200	200	Nil
19X3	150	180	(30)
19X4	100	160	(60)
19X5	50	140	(90)

The next valuation at 31 March 19X5 shows a surplus in the scheme of only £20 million. There has, therefore, been a deterioration since the last valuation, because the surplus is £30 million less than predicted. As a result, the contribution holiday is curtailed and a contribution of £30 million is to be made in the year to 31 March 19X6.

This shortfall of £30 million is a new variation, which must be spread forward in the profit and loss account. The average remaining service life of employees in the scheme at 31 March 19X5 is still 10 years.

The projected accounting treatment from the year ending 31 March 19X6 would be as shown in Figure 18, depending on which option is chosen.

Figure 18

Method of spreading subsequent variation

Year	Funded	Method 1 Charged	Method 1 Provision	Method 2 Charged	Method 2 Provision
	£'m	£'m	£'m	£'m	£'m
			(90)		(90)
19X6	30	33	(93)	39	(99)
19X7	50	33	(76)	39	(88)
19X8	50	33	(59)	39	(77)
19X9	50	33	(42)	39	(66)
19Y0	50	33	(25)	39	(55)
19Y1	50	33	(8)	39	(44)
19Y2	50	33	9	39	(33)
19Y3	50	53	6	39	(22)
19Y4	50	53	3	39	(11)
19Y5	50	53	-	39	-
19Y6	50	50	-	50	-

Method 1 spreads the deferred balance of the initial surplus of £140 million over the remaining 7 years of the original period (that is, a credit of £20 million per annum) separately from the new experience variation of £30 million which is written off over a new 10 year period (that is, a debit of £3 million per annum).

Thus the pension cost in years 19X6 to 19Y2 of £33 million comprises the regular cost of £50 million less a variation for the initial surplus of £20 million plus a variation for the reduced surplus of £3 million. By 19Y2, the benefit of the initial surplus is eliminated. For the next 3 years from 19Y3 to 19Y6, the projected pension cost increases to £53 million, comprising the regular cost of £50 million plus the variation of £3 million attributed to the subsequent valuation. This variation is fully written off by 19Y5.

It is interesting to note the balance sheet effect in this example. The provision reverses each year that the contributions exceed the net pension cost. A prepayment arises in 19Y2, which reverses in the three years to 19Y5 when the annual pension cost exceeds the contributions payable.

Method 2 recalculates the variation to be spread forward from the date of the new valuation. As a result of the valuation, the new balance of the deferred surplus is £110 million. That is calculated as the deferred surplus at 31 March 1995, £140 million (see Figure 17), less the shortfall of £30 million uncovered by the new valuation. Alternatively, the variation is calculated as the surplus in the scheme as at the date of the new valuation, £20 million, plus the provision in the balance sheet at that date of £90 million that relates to the spreading of the initial surplus.

The balance of £110 million is spread forward over a new 10 year period to give a revised variation credit of £11 million per annum. This gives a constant pension cost of £39 million for the next 10 years, being the regular cost of £50 million less the variation of £11 million.

12.126 The processes described in the previous example are repeated each time a new actuarial valuation reveals a further variation to be accounted for.

12.127 Some accountants would argue that the first method is theoretically more correct because it matches the spreading of each new surplus or deficiency with the average remaining service lives of employees in the scheme at the time. Thus, for example, the initial surplus is completely amortised over the initial fixed period, as it would be if no subsequent surpluses or deficiencies were identified. Under the second method, the deferred balance of the initial surplus is rolled up with the new surplus or deficiency and re-spread over a new period. Therefore, the period for spreading each identified surplus or deficiency may be continually extended as each successive valuation provides a new result.

12.128 In practical terms, the first method means that each triennial valuation may produce a further layer of surplus or deficiency which must be spread forward over a separately identified period. Notwithstanding possible theoretical arguments in favour of this method, it seems to suggest a degree of certainty and precision in actuarial valuations about future events that in practice does not exist. Apart from the obvious merit of simplicity, accounting for successive valuations on a rolling basis would in most cases provide at each valuation date the smoothest forecast of pension costs in the longer term.

Negative pension cost

12.129 Where a surplus is large, it is possible that the annual pension cost calculations will result in a net credit in some years. This is likely to be the case in the following circumstances or in a combination of such circumstances:

- The variation exceeds the regular cost under the chosen method for spreading the surplus, because the surplus is so large.

- A large balance sheet asset recognised under the transitional provisions of SSAP 24 or under the acquisition accounting rules of FRS 7 attracts an interest credit in excess of regular cost.

- A surplus arising in connection with the sale or termination of an operation is required by SSAP 24 to be credited immediately to the profit and loss account.

12.130 A surplus resulting from a sale or termination of an operation is dealt with separately by SSAP 24. The credit will usually be included as part of the profit or loss on disposal (see para 12.84).

12.131 A variation is more likely to exceed the regular cost under the 'straight-line' method of spreading a surplus, because that method produces a profile with the largest credit in the first year, followed by a systematically declining credit in subsequent years – see, for example, the illustration in Figure 8 on page 19.

12.132 There are two schools of thought as to whether it is appropriate to recognise negative pension costs. On the one hand, negative pension costs may, in appropriate situations, be considered a natural consequence of amortising a pension surplus over a fixed period under methods that use present valuing techniques. On the other hand, some accountants consider it imprudent; they also believe it to be anomalous that credits should be recognised in the profit and loss account in some years only to be overtaken by debits in later years in cases where, in the long-term, there is a positive cash cost to the employer. They would prefer to restrict the variation credit to an amount that fully offsets the regular cost, so that the net cost in the profit and loss account is, in fact, zero. Furthermore, financial analysts tend to regard pension credits as 'soft' profits.

12.133 Both views have emerged in practice. Table 12.9 shows an example of a company, Granada Group PLC, that has disclosed a negative pension cost in respect of a significant surplus. It has also disclosed a significant prepayment, which relates partly to a previous acquisition and partly to the cumulative excess of pension credits taken in the profit and loss account over contributions paid.

Table 12.9 – Granada Group PLC – Annual Report and Accounts – 1 October 1994

Notes to the accounts (extract)

	1994 £m	1993 £m
2 Staff costs		
Wages and salaries	**448.3**	347.1
Social security	**41.6**	31.6
Pension and other costs (see note 5)	**(7.0)**	(8.2)
	482.9	370.5

5 Pension scheme

The Group operates a number of pension schemes around the world. The major schemes are of the defined benefit type with assets held in separate trustee administered funds.

The Group's main UK scheme, which covers the majority of UK employees, was assessed by William M Mercer Limited, consulting actuaries, as at 1 October 1992 using the projected unit method.

The principal actuarial assumptions adopted were that, over the long term, the annual rate of return on investments would be 2% higher than the annual increase in total pensionable remuneration, 4.75% higher than the annual increase in present and future pensions in payment and 4% higher than the annual increase in dividends. Based on the 1 October 1992 assessment the actuarial value of the assets of the scheme was sufficient to cover 165% of the benefits that had accrued to members, after allowing for expected future increases in pensionable remuneration. On the recommendation of the actuaries no company contributions will be made to the scheme until at least the next actuarial valuation which is anticipated to be as at 1 October 1995. The market value of the scheme's assets as at 1 October 1992 was £436.3 million. The accounting treatment that has been adopted in accordance with SSAP 24 is as follows:

- an amount of £84.1 million was credited to goodwill in 1989 representing the element of the total surplus on the Granada scheme relating to the Electronic Rentals Group which was purchased in 1988.

- the remaining actuarial surplus on the Granada pension scheme is being spread over the average remaining service lives of current employees.

- the net credit for pensions and associated costs for the Group, which arises principally as a result of the actuarial surplus in the main UK scheme, is £7.0 million (1993: £8.2 million).

- a prepayment of £159.4 million (1993: £150.8 million) is included in debtors, amounts falling due after more than one year, representing the element of the surplus relating to the Electronic Rentals Group pension scheme and the excess of the net pensions credit to profit over the amounts funded since 1989.

12.134 Table 12.10 shows an example of a company, THORN EMI plc, that has a policy of not recognising negative costs in respect of a surplus that is being spread forward.

Table 12.10 – THORN EMI plc – Report and Accounts – 31 March 1995

Extract from Notes to the accounts

28 Pension arrangements (extract)

The latest actuarial valuation of the THORN EMI Pension Fund was made by a qualified actuary at 31 March 1994 using the projected unit method. At that date, the market value of the assets of the THORN EMI Pension Fund amounted to £1,410m. The actuarial value of the assets was sufficient to cover 121 per cent of the value of the benefits that had accrued to the members, after allowing for assumed increases in earnings and for improvements to the benefits of the Fund implemented with effect from 1 January 1995. Part of the surplus disclosed by the 1994 valuation was allocated towards the reduction of employer contributions below the long-term rate, the balance being carried forward as a reserve in the Fund.

With effect from 1 April 1988 employer expense in respect of the Fund has been calculated in accordance with SSAP 24 – Accounting for Pension Costs. On the basis of actuarial advice, it is calculated that employer expense would represent a credit to the profit and loss account on full application of SSAP 24 principles. However, for reasons of conservatism, such expense has been taken as nil for the years ended 31 March 1995 and 31 March 1994. The long-term annual growth rate assumptions used for calculating employer expense under SSAP 24 are shown below:

	Growth relative to investment return
Pay increases	(2.5)%
Pension increases	(5.0)%
Dividend increases	(4.5)%

12.135 In its original discussion paper containing proposals for revising SSAP 24, the ASB indicated that negative pension costs are in principle allowable, but any resulting asset should be subject to the test of recoverability.

Balance sheet

Sources of assets and liabilities

12.136 As SSAP 24 generally follows an 'income approach' to the recognition of pension costs, amounts recognised in the balance sheet of the sponsoring company are often no more than timing differences between pension costs charged in the profit and loss account and contributions paid by the company to the pension scheme.

12.137 Pension assets may arise from the following sources:

- The balance of any surplus recognised on the balance sheet under the transitional options of SSAP 24.
- A surplus in a scheme operated by a newly acquired subsidiary that is recognised in a fair value exercise.
- Where, under the normal principles for spreading a surplus, the cumulative pension cost is negative.
- Where, under the normal principles for spreading a deficiency, the contributions paid to fund the deficiency exceed the cumulative pension costs charged in the profit and loss account.
- A surplus arising in connection with the sale or termination of an operation that has been credited immediately to the profit and loss account.

12.138 Pension provisions may arise from the following sources:

- The balance of any deficiency recognised on the balance sheet under the transitional options of SSAP 24.
- A deficiency in a scheme operated by a newly acquired subsidiary that is recognised in a fair value exercise.
- Accrued pension costs in respect of unfunded obligations.
- Where, under the normal principles for spreading a surplus, the cumulative pension costs exceed the contributions paid (for example, where a company takes a contribution holiday).
- A deficiency arising in connection with the sale or termination of an operation, or in other circumstances that requires the deficiency to be charged immediately to the profit and loss account.

Presentation of assets and liabilities

12.139 SSAP 24 requires the following balance sheet presentation.

- Any excess of the cumulative pension cost over contributions paid or directly paid pensions should be shown as a net pension provision.

- Any excess of contributions paid or directly paid pensions over the cumulative pension cost should be shown as a prepayment.

[SSAP 24 para 86].

12.140 Prepayments fall within the total of current assets in the balance sheet formats in the Act, even where the assets are not recoverable in the short term. The Act requires the amount falling due after more than one year to be shown separately for each item included under debtors. [4 Sch format, note 6]. In contrast, provisions and other long-term creditors fall outside the balance sheet total of current liabilities. UITF Abstract 4 (issued July 1992) addresses this anomaly and cites a pension fund surplus (to the extent recognised on the balance sheet) as an example of a long-term debtor included in current assets. Some accountants had argued for a departure from the Act's format in special circumstances, for example by including a material pension asset that is not recoverable in the short term as a separate item outside both fixed and current assets.

12.141 UITF Abstract 4 does not advocate a general departure from the formats in the Act. The UITF concluded that, where necessary to prevent readers from misinterpreting the financial statements, the amount of debtors due after more than one year should be disclosed on the face of the balance sheet, but as part of the normal caption for such items within current assets. Table 12.11 gives an example of such disclosure.

Table 12.11 – Bowater PLC – Annual Report – 31 December 1994

EXTRACT FROM BALANCE SHEET

		Group	
	Notes	**1994** **£m**	1993 £m
CURRENT ASSETS			
Stocks	13	**268**	226
Debtors	14		
Receivable within one year		**410**	352
Receivable after more than one year		**105**	89
Properties surplus to requirements		**9**	8
Investments	15	**248**	69
Cash at bank and in hand		**131**	273
		1,171	1,017

NOTES TO THE ACCOUNTS (extract)

14 DEBTORS	Group	
	1994	1993
	£m	£m
Receivable within one year:		
Trade debtors	**350**	296
Subsidiary undertakings	**-**	-
Taxation recoverable	**3**	2
Other debtors	**57**	54
	410	352
Receivable after more than one year:		
Pension schemes	**70**	59
Accrued gains from gilts	**28**	18
Other debtors	**7**	12
	105	89

Recoverability of pension assets

12.142 Pension assets that derive from the spreading principles of SSAP 24 should usually unwind as the underlying surplus is completely amortised by the end of the chosen period representing the service lives of the employees. Similarly, assets recognised under the alternative transitional arrangements or under fair valuing principles are usually recovered by reductions in employer contributions or refunds.

12.143 However, there may be situations, such as the following, where the accounting surplus is not expected to be used up in the foreseeable future:

- Where the company uses different (less prudent) actuarial assumptions for determining pension cost from those used for funding purposes, such that the cumulative contributions permanently exceed the cumulative pension cost.

- Where, in extreme cases, a scheme is 'self-financing' because the return on its investments exceeds the regular cost, a refund is not possible and even a permanent cessation of contributions may not fully recover the surplus.

12.144 In the first situation, asset recognition is a natural consequence of using different accounting and funding assumptions. Accounting assumptions are required to be 'best estimates', whereas funding assumptions may be more conservative.

12.145 In the second situation, the refund of a pension fund surplus to the employer company may be forbidden by the rules of the scheme. Furthermore, the rules may not permit the trust deed to be altered to permit a refund. In such circumstances, a company may wish to take a prudent approach and restrict the amount of surplus recognised in the financial statements to an amount that can be expected to be recovered. Where such a surplus arises from an acquisition, FRS 7 places an important limitation on the amount of any surplus that should be recognised as an asset in the financial statements of the acquiring group. The acquiring group should take into account *"...the extent to which the surplus could be realised in cash terms, by way of reduction of future contributions or otherwise, and the timescale of such potential realisations"*. [FRS 7 para 71]. One approach would be to recognise a smaller surplus, for example the present value of a contribution holiday.

12.146 There are a number of other scenarios where pension assets may not be 'recovered' in the traditional sense, including the following:

- The company amends the plan to improve employees' pension benefits.
- A subsequent valuation shows an unexpected reduction in the surplus in the scheme.

12.147 In the first situation, the cost of the benefit improvement would usually be spread forward, that is written off over the remaining service lives of the current employees. To the extent that the cost of the benefit improvement reduces the recoverable amount of a surplus recognised as an asset, the SSAP 24 treatment is, therefore, to write the asset off gradually over the chosen period.

12.148 The second situation is illustrated by the following example.

Example

The facts are the same as in the example in paragraph 12.125 on page 41 except that the initial surplus of £200 million was in a scheme operated by a subsidiary that was acquired in 19X2; consequently, it had been recognised as an asset in the consolidated financial statements of the acquiring group. This example ignores the effects of discounting.

The employer had taken a contribution holiday and by 31 March 19X5 the surplus in the scheme was projected to have been reduced by £150 million to £50 million as shown in Figure 17 on page 42.

In the consolidated financial statements, the prepayment of £200 million was reduced in the 3 years to 31 March 19X5, as shown in Figure 19. The new valuation at 31 March 19X5 shows a surplus of only £20 million. The prepayment still in the financial statements is £50 million. How should the shortfall of £30 million be accounted for?

Figure 19

Movement in prepayment

Year	Prepayment	Contributions	Pension cost
	£'m	£'m	£'m
19X2	200		
19X3	150	Nil	50
19X4	100	Nil	50
19X5	50	Nil	50

In the example in paragraph 12.125 where the initial surplus was spread forward, the shortfall was sheltered because the majority of the surplus had not yet been credited in the company's financial statements by the time of the next valuation. In fact, there was a provision of £90 million still to be released to profit and loss.

In this example, only £20 million of the prepayment of £50 million is recoverable by the group by reduced contributions. SSAP 24 generally requires experience deficiencies to be spread forward over average remaining service lives. This suggests the shortfall of £30 million would be written off over 10 years, as shown in Figure 20.

Figure 20

Spreading forward new variation

Year	Prepayment B/fwd	Contributions paid	Regular cost	Variation	Pension cost
	£'m	£'m	£'m	£'m	£'m
19X6	50	30	50	3	53
19X7	27	50	50	3	53
19X8	24	50	50	3	53
19X9	21	50	50	3	53
19Y0	18	50	50	3	53
19Y1	15	50	50	3	53
19Y2	12	50	50	3	53
19Y3	9	50	50	3	53
19Y4	6	50	50	3	53
19Y5	3	50	50	3	53

However, this treatment might conflict with generally accepted accounting rules on the valuation of assets which suggest an immediate write off would be required, because the asset has suffered a permanent diminution in value of £30 million. The Act requires all current assets to be reduced to net realisable value where this is lower than their carrying value. [4 Sch 23]. If this approach is followed, the shortfall of £30 million would be charged to the profit and loss account as soon as it is identified.

12.149 Table 12.12 is an example of a company that has adopted this latter approach, and described the immediate write off of the prepayment as a departure from SSAP 24 that was necessary to give a true and fair view.

Table 12.12 – BM Group PLC – Annual Report – 30 June 1993

Notes to the financial statements (extract)

6. Exceptional items (extract)

A) Exceptional items within operating profit/(loss)

i) Write down of pension prepayment

As stated in Note 29, the Directors have re-assessed the assumptions used in evaluating the pension prepayment under Statement of Standard Accounting Practice No. 24 (SSAP 24). This change of assumptions resulted in a £13.1 million reduction in the prepayment carried on the Group's balance sheet. Under SSAP 24, this reduction should be spread forward over the expected remaining service lives of the current employees.

The Directors are of the view that if this was done the SSAP 24 prepayment would be overstated and in order to reflect a true and fair view, this reduction of £13.1 million should be charged to this year's profit and loss account and not spread forward. This treatment is contrary to the requirements of SSAP 24. If SSAP 24 was followed there would be no charge in the current year in relation to this reduction.

18. Pension prepayment (recoverable after more than one year)

	Note	**1993 £000**	1992 £000
As at 1st July		**41,589**	13,769
Acquisitions of subsidiary undertakings		-	25,800
Credit taken to profit and loss account	29	**3,459**	2,020
Exceptional write down	6A(i)	**(13,100)**	-
As at 30th June		**31,948**	41,589

29. Pension schemes

The Group operates two major schemes covering all UK based companies which are of the defined benefit type, with the assets held in a separate trustee-administered fund. There are also defined benefit schemes in Canada and Australia and defined contribution schemes in the USA.

> The last full actuarial assessment of the UK scheme was undertaken on 1st April 1991. The Directors have asked the actuaries to review the results of that assessment using assumptions that are both more commonly adopted and more conservative. The principal actuarial assumptions used for the purposes of this review were based upon an investment return of 9.5% per annum, pay growth of 7.5% and dividend growth of 5% per annum.
>
> The effect of revising these assumptions is to reduce the value of the prepayment and net excess funding previously held on the Group's balance sheet by £13.1 million to £31,948,000 (Note 18). This amount has been written off as an exceptional item in the current year (Note 6).
>
> During the year a credit of £3,459,000 has been taken to the profit and loss account. This represents a regular cost of £1,788,000 less a variation credit of £1,072,000 and a notional interest credit of £4,175,000.
>
> At the date of the latest actuarial review, which was completed using the projected unit method, the market value of the scheme assets was £93 million. The actuarial value of the assets is 115% of the value of accrued benefits, after allowing for expected future increases in earnings. The UK surplus is being spread over the expected service lives of current employees as a variation from the regular cost of pensions.

Unfunded schemes

12.150 An unfunded scheme is one where the future liabilities for benefits payable to employees or their dependants are not provided for by the accumulation of assets held externally to the employing company's business. Instead, pension liabilities are met out of the employing company's own resources. Unfunded schemes are more common in the public sector or with institutions such as research foundations or charities. They are also sometimes found overseas; in particular, they are common in Germany. They have become more popular in UK companies, particularly in respect of higher paid executives as a result of tax changes in the Finance Act 1989 relating to the capping of pensions that affected approved funded schemes.

12.151 The same accounting principles apply to unfunded as to funded schemes. The transitional provisions of SSAP 24 permitted any unprovided obligation that existed when the standard was first implemented to be recognised gradually by annual charges to the profit and loss account over the expected remaining service lives of current employees. In other respects, except for the requirements for spreading forward variations from regular cost, the balance sheet should reflect the full actuarial value (discounted to present value) of past service obligations.

12.152 The amount charged to the profit and loss account is based on the same principle whether the scheme is funded or unfunded. That is, the cost comprises an amount equivalent to contributions to a funded scheme, together with notional interest on the unfunded liability. The difference is that whilst in a funded scheme contributions are paid to the trustees who invest them in order to fund the future pension liabilities, with an unfunded scheme the resources are retained within the company.

12.153 Table 12.13 gives an example of the financial statement disclosure by a multinational group with significant unfunded pension obligations.

Table 12.13 – The British Petroleum Company p.l.c. – Annual Report and Accounts – 31 December 1997

Notes on accounts (extract)

24 Pensions (extract)

Most group companies have pension plans, the forms and benefits of which vary with conditions and practices in the countries concerned. The main plans provide benefits that are computed based on an employee's years of service and final pensionable salary. In most cases group companies make contributions to separately administered trusts, based on advice from independent actuaries using actuarial methods, the objective of which is to provide adequate funds to meet pension obligations as they fall due. In certain countries the plans are unfunded and the obligation for pension benefits is included within other provisions.

At 31 December 1997 the obligation for accrued benefits in respect of the principal unfunded schemes was £891 million (£982 million). Of this amount, £735 million (£799 million) has been provided in these accounts.

Disclosure of pension information

12.154 Company law contains very limited disclosure provisions in respect of pensions. The Act requires disclosure of:

- The pension costs charged.
- Any pension commitments included under any provision shown in the company's balance sheet.
- Any such commitments for which no provision has been made.

[4 Sch 50(4)].

12.155 The standard contains a general requirement for sufficient information to be disclosed to give the user a proper understanding of the impact of the pension arrangements on a company's financial statements. [SSAP 24 para 45].

12.156 More specifically, SSAP 24 prescribes extensive disclosure about defined benefit obligations, which is summarised below.

- The nature of the scheme (that is, defined benefit).

- Whether it is funded or unfunded.

- The accounting policy and, if different, the funding policy.

- A statement as to whether the pension cost is assessed in accordance with the advice of a professionally qualified actuary and, if so, the date of the most recent formal actuarial valuation. If the actuary is an employee or officer of the company or group, then this fact should be disclosed.

- The pension cost charge for the period together with explanations of significant changes in the charge compared to that in the previous accounting period.

- Any provisions or prepayments in the balance sheet resulting from a difference between the amounts recognised as cost and the amounts funded or paid directly.

- The amount of any deficiency on a current funding level basis, together with the action taken to rectify it. This is analogous to a discontinuance valuation. It is a measure of solvency that compares the assets of the scheme with the actuarial value of liabilities, in respect of benefits that would arise if all the members were to leave the scheme at the valuation date. There is no requirement to disclose a surplus on a current funding level basis.

- An outline of the results of the most recent actuarial valuation on an ongoing basis. An 'ongoing valuation' is defined as a valuation that assumes the scheme will continue in existence, new members will be admitted (if appropriate), and that allows for expected increases in earnings in valuing its liabilities. The actuarial information to be disclosed includes:

    - The actuarial method used and the main actuarial assumptions.

    - The market value of the scheme assets at the date of their valuation or review.

    - The level of funding expressed in percentage terms, and comments on any material surplus or deficit revealed by this.

- Any commitment to make additional payments over a limited number of years.

- The accounting treatment adopted in respect of a refund made under deduction of tax where a credit appears in the financial statements in relation to it.

- Details of the expected effects on future costs of any material changes in the group's and/or company's pension arrangements.

[SSAP 24 para 88].

12.157 Table 12.14 shows the pension cost disclosures in the financial statements of The BOC Group plc. The group has provided a greater analysis of its net pension cost than is required by the standard and also discloses the basis for spreading variations from regular cost.

Table 12.14 – The BOC Group plc – Report and Accounts – 30 September 1994

Accounting Policies (extract)

4. Retirement benefits

The regular cost of providing benefits is charged to operating profit over the employees' service lives on the basis of a constant percentage of earnings. Variations from regular cost, arising from periodic actuarial valuations, are allocated to operating profit over the expected remaining service lives of current employees on the basis of a constant percentage of current and estimated future earnings.

Notes to the financial statements (extract)

6. (extract)
e) Retirement benefits
i) Pensions

The Group operates a number of pension schemes throughout the world. The majority of the schemes are self-administered and the schemes' assets are held independently of the Group's finances. Pension costs are assessed in accordance with the advice of independent professionally qualified actuaries. The cost for the year was:

	1994 £ million	1993 £ million
Principal schemes		
Regular pension cost	33.2	30.4
Variations from regular cost	(29.7)	(30.8)
Interest	(1.4)	(1.5)
Other schemes	12.6	12.6
Net pension cost	14.7	10.7

ii) Principal schemes

The principal schemes are of the defined benefit type. In the UK and Australia they are based on final salary and in the US on annual salary. On the advice of respective actuaries, Group funding is suspended and is unlikely to be required during the next financial year. The results of the most recent valuations of the principal schemes were:

	UK	US	Australia
Date of last valuation or review	31 March 1993	1 January 1993	30 June 1992
Market value of investments (£ million)	653	262	102
Method used	Projected Unit	Projected Unit	Attained Age
Main assumptions			
Rate of price inflation	5.0%	6.0%	6.0%
Return on investments[1]	4.5%	3.0%	3.5%
Increase in earnings[1]	2.0%	-	1.5%
Level of funding[2]	119%	135%	174%

[1]Above price inflation.
[2]The actuarial value of assets expressed as a percentage of the accrued service liabilities.

12.158 Actuarial methods and assumptions are considered from paragraph 12.162.

12.159 The level of funding that must be disclosed for the most recent valuation is an actuarial measure of the extent to which the assets of the scheme are sufficient to cover its liabilities (as illustrated in Table 12.14). [SSAP 24 para 66]. It compares the actuarial obligations with the actuarial valuation of assets.

12.160 Where a company or group operates more than one pension scheme, SSAP 24 allows disclosure to be given on a combined basis. This is so unless disclosure of information about individual schemes is necessary for a proper understanding of the financial statements. [SSAP 24 para 89]. However, where one scheme produces a deficiency on a current funding level basis, disclosure of the deficiency should not be avoided by setting it off against a surplus in another scheme.

12.161 Although the disclosures required by SSAP 24 can be voluminous, analysts and other interested commentators have criticised them for missing information that is important for proper financial analysis. In its original discussion paper, the ASB considered the disclosure aspects as part of its review of SSAP 24 and proposed the following key requirements, some of which a number of companies have voluntarily provided.

- Analysis of the components of pension cost – regular cost, variations and interest (see para 12.50).

- Reconciliation of derived balance sheet figures to the pension scheme valuation (see para 12.70).

Actuarial issues

Actuarial methods

12.162 SSAP 24 defines two principal categories of valuation methods, namely 'accrued benefits methods' and 'prospective benefits methods'. Prior to SSAP 24, these methods were primarily used to determine patterns of funding defined benefit schemes. The choice of method would depend on factors such as the degree of security required for members' benefits and the desired level of contributions. Some methods lead to higher levels of funding than others. Since SSAP 24 was introduced, they have also been used to measure the accrual of pension costs for accounting purposes.

12.163 The explanatory note to the standard discusses the requirement for choosing a valuation method that is likely to provide a recommended level of contributions representing a stable percentage of payroll costs. The method adopted should take account of expected future increases in earnings, including merit increases, up to the date of expected retirement, withdrawal or death, and increases in pensions on the basis of the employer's express or implied commitments. [SSAP 24 para 18]. Methods that do not allow for future salary increases would usually fail SSAP 24's accounting objective because they are unlikely to produce a regular contribution rate that is a level percentage of payroll costs.

12.164 The standard is very flexible on the choice of valuation methods in the measurement of pension cost, a matter that has been frequently challenged by commentators. For example, reports submitted to the ASB from the ICAEW and PRAG both urged the ASB to consider imposing a single valuation method in any revised accounting standard.

Accrued benefits methods

12.165 As the name suggests, accrued benefits valuation methods measure the present value of pension benefits earned by employees and past employees to the date of the valuation. They also measure the present value of the benefits earned by employees for each period of service. Allowance may be made for future increases in earnings; this is required by SSAP 24 for accounting purposes.

12.166 Under these methods, the cost attributable to an individual employee increases each year as the employee gets older. This is because the present value of the benefits earned each year increases as retirement approaches and the date of payment of a pension draws nearer. This rising trend in cost is compounded for final salary schemes when inflation is taken into account. Consequently, in some situations these methods may not satisfy the accounting objective of SSAP 24, that the regular pension cost should be a substantially level percentage of pensionable payroll.

12.167 However, in a mature scheme where the composition of the workforce remains relatively stable over time in terms of age, average remuneration and pensionable service, as a result of employees leaving and joining, the annual regular cost for the scheme as a whole tends to have a relatively stable relationship as a percentage of annual aggregate remuneration. In such circumstances, the accounting objective of SSAP 24 would be met.

12.168 Surveys have shown that the 'projected unit method' has become by far the single most commonly used valuation method in practice. This is an accrued benefits method that produces a standard contribution rate in respect of the cost of the benefits accruing in the year following the valuation and a funding target in respect of the value of the benefits accrued to the date of the valuation (making allowance, where appropriate, for future earnings increases).

12.169 The ASB proposed in its original discussion paper that a future accounting standard on pension costs should require use of an accrued benefits method, in effect the projected unit method.

Prospective benefits methods

12.170 Prospective benefits valuation methods estimate the total cost of providing benefits earned and expected to be earned in the future by employees. The total cost is spread evenly over the service lives of the employees, usually as a level percentage of salaries. Consequently, such methods would normally meet SSAP 24's accounting objective.

12.171 The important difference from accrued benefits methods is that prospective benefits methods tend to smooth out changes in the annual regular cost that may arise under the former. For example, where there is an ageing workforce, the regular cost under an accrued benefits method will tend to rise as a percentage of salary; under a prospective benefits method, it should remain constant, because the rise has been anticipated in the cost allocated to the earlier years.

Actuarial assumptions

12.172 The measurement of pension cost depends on long-term valuation assumptions. These comprise demographic assumptions and financial assumptions.

12.173 Demographic assumptions are important in measuring the liabilities to pay pensions. They comprise assumptions about the present and future membership of the scheme such as:

- Mortality rates (before and after retirement).
- Rates of leaving service before retirement.
- Early retirement.
- Sex and marital status.
- Details of members' spouses and children.

12.174 Financial assumptions are important for valuing, on an actuarial basis, both the liabilities for future pensions and the assets of the scheme that are held to fund those pensions. They include the following:

- Rate of return on investments.
- Rate of growth of dividends.
- Price inflation.
- Rate of increases in pensionable earnings.
- Rate of increases in pensions.

12.175 SSAP 24 requires that the *"...actuarial assumptions and method, taken as a whole, should be compatible and should lead to the actuary's best estimate of the cost of providing the pension benefits promised"*. [SSAP 24 para 79].

12.176 For example, asset valuation methods should be consistent with the method and assumptions used to value the liabilities to pay future pensions. Thus, pension fund investments are normally valued on an actuarial basis, based on the discounted value of expected future dividend income, rather than on a market value basis. Consequently, short-term fluctuations in market values do not necessarily require changes to the long-term cost of providing pensions. (However, changes that affect dividend income, such as the changes in the rules concerning advance corporation tax in 1993, do affect the long-term cost.)

12.177 The choice of assumptions is a difficult area of judgement, because relatively small changes in certain key assumptions, such as the long-term rate of return on investments and the rate of growth in pensionable earnings, can have a material impact on the amount of pension scheme surplus or deficiency to be accounted for. Consequently, SSAP 24 requires key assumptions to be disclosed in the notes to the financial statements.

12.178 Different practices have emerged regarding disclosure of financial assumptions. Some companies disclose each assumption in absolute terms (see Tables 12.6 on page 64, 12.14 on page 57 and 12.15 below); others disclose certain assumptions relative to each other (see Table 12.9 on page 46).

12.179 Most commentators consider that the amount by which the assumed rate of return on investments exceeds the assumed rate of increase in pensionable earnings is the most important assumption, because the valuation result is very sensitive to relatively small changes in this assumption. A higher differential produces a more favourable valuation result. Surveys of pension cost disclosures in company financial statements have shown that this difference ranges between one per cent and four per cent, with the majority around two per cent.

12.180 Furthermore, it is not unusual for the assumptions that are made for a funding strategy to differ from an actuary's 'best estimates'. For example, there may be a deliberate policy of funding very conservatively, so that the members' benefits are given a high degree of security. Table 12.15 is an example of a company that has disclosed different funding and accounting assumptions.

Table 12.15 – Courtaulds plc – Report and Accounts – 31 March 1994

Note 33 Pension commitments (extract)

The main Courtaulds UK Pension Scheme, which makes benefits available to the majority of the Group's UK employees, was valued by independent actuaries as at 31 March 1993.

The valuation used the projected unit method and was carried out on two different bases, using a conservative set of actuarial assumptions for funding purposes and a 'best estimate' set for accounting purposes (as required by SSAP 24). After allowing for benefit improvements announced in December 1993 and future increases in pensionable remuneration, the actuarial value of the assets was sufficient to cover the benefits that had accrued to members by 114% on the funding basis and by 124% on the SSAP 24 basis. The market value of the Scheme assets at the date of the valuation was £883m.

The principal actuarial assumptions used in the valuation were:	Funding basis	SSAP 24 basis
Long-term annual rate of return on investment	9.5%	10.0%
Annual increase in dividends	5.0%	5.5%
Average annual increase in total pensionable remuneration	7.5%	7.5%
Average annual increase in present and future pension payments	5.0%	5.0%

A further valuation will be carried out as at 31 March 1995 and, on the recommendation of the actuaries, no further company contributions will be made to the scheme at least until the results of that valuation are known.

12.181 The Institute and Faculty of Actuaries has produced guidance for its members on the actuarial requirements of SSAP 24. Guidance Note GN 17, which is regarded as best practice, requires that the actuarial assumptions taken as a whole, in isolation from the method, should meet the requirement of providing a best estimate.

Other matters

European Court of Justice rulings

12.182 Decisions of the European Court of Justice in recent years have introduced changes to the rights of members of occupational pension schemes. Rulings that have required employers to provide equal pension benefits for men and women started with the landmark case of *Barber v Guardian Royal Exchange* [1990] 2 All ER. More recent rulings in September 1994 have meant that employers who have excluded female part-time employees from their pension schemes may have been discriminating illegally. Furthermore, the requirements for equal treatment have, to a degree, been made retrospective.

12.183 The Pensions Act 1995 contains provisions to ensure that occupational schemes provide equal treatment for men and women for periods of service after 17 May 1990 (the date of the Barber judgement).

12.184 The accounting implications of these rulings have provided an interesting practical application of SSAP 24. The potential financial effects, if any, need to be assessed individually by companies. Under SSAP 24 the effect of any changes required to an employer's pension arrangements may be twofold:

- Restructuring the cost of benefits accruing for future service will give rise to a change in the regular cost that is charged in future periods.
- Recognising an additional past service liability for any retrospective improvements to pension benefits may either reduce an existing surplus or create a deficiency in the scheme, resulting in a new variation to be accounted for.

12.185 An additional past service liability will normally be written off by spreading the cost forward over the current employees' remaining service lives, whether there is a reduced surplus or a deficiency. This will result in an immediate increase in the net pension cost in the profit and loss account.

12.186 There are possible exceptions to the spreading treatment where a deficiency is created. First, in extreme situations, where the deficiency is material and necessitates additional short-term funding through employer contributions, it could be written off over a shorter period on the grounds that the cause is abnormal (that is, in effect the result of a change in legislation), would not have been allowed for in earlier actuarial assumptions and it is prudent to do so. Secondly, where any deficiency results from a liability to provide increased pensions to pensioners and deferred pensioners, there is a strong argument that, by analogy with the treatment of *ex-gratia* pensions, this liability should not be spread forward, but should be written off immediately because it cannot be matched with services that provide future value to the company.

12.187 Where an additional past service liability reduces a surplus treated as an asset in a previous year under the alternative transitional arrangements of SSAP 24 or through fair value accounting for an acquisition, the asset may no longer be recoverable. The alternative approaches of gradual amortisation and immediate write-off of the shortfall are considered in paragraphs 12.142 to 12.149 above.

Foreign schemes

12.188 SSAP 24 offers a practical concession to companies and groups that operate foreign pension arrangements in respect of overseas operations. Although in principle, adjustments should be made to account for the costs of foreign schemes in accordance with the UK standard, SSAP 24 recognises that in some situations it may be impractical and costly to obtain the necessary actuarial information. In such circumstances, compliance is encouraged, but is not mandatory. The consolidated financial statements should disclose as a minimum the amount charged against profit in respect of the foreign scheme and the basis of that charge. [SSAP 24 para 91]. The appendix to the standard includes an example of how such disclosure might be incorporated into the notes.

12.189 Many groups in fact calculate pension costs for foreign operations on a measurement basis that is consistent with SSAP 24. An example of a company that has used the concessionary treatment is shown in Table 12.16.

Table 12.16 – Johnson Matthey Public Limited Company – Annual Report – 31 March 1994

Notes on the Accounts (extract)

12(c) Retirement benefits (extract)

(ii) Foreign schemes
Pension costs relating to foreign schemes are charged in accordance with local best practice using different accounting policies. The group's largest foreign scheme is in the US which is of the defined benefit type which requires contributions to be made to a separately administered fund. This scheme is accounted for using the applicable US accounting standard. The cost of obtaining actuarial valuations for the purpose of adjusting to the applicable UK accounting standard is considered to be out of proportion to the benefits to be gained.

(iv) Profit and loss account and balance sheet impact of providing retirement benefits (extract)
The effect of providing pensions and other retirement benefits on operating profit was as follows:

	1994 £ million	1993 £ million
United Kingdom		
Regular pension cost	(6.5)	(5.7)
Variation from regular cost	11.2	9.6
Interest on prepayment	2.5	1.7
	7.2	5.6
Overseas		
Cost of foreign pension schemes	(2.5)	(2.1)
Cost of post-retirement medical benefits	(0.9)	(0.7)
Total cost of retirement benefits	3.8	2.8

Group schemes

Accounting by subsidiaries

12.190 SSAP 24 includes only a brief reference to the accounting treatment that should be adopted by subsidiaries that participate in group defined benefit pension schemes. Where a common contribution rate, expressed as a percentage of payroll, is applied across the group as a whole, the standard permits the pension cost of each group company to be based on this rate. Therefore, differences that might arise between individual companies in the group if the pension cost were calculated independently for each company may be ignored. If this approach is adopted, the financial statements of a subsidiary should disclose this fact. [SSAP 24 paras 52, 90].

12.191 SSAP 24 does not address the allocation of a surplus or deficiency in a group scheme across the individual participating companies. Practice varies and is affected *inter alia* by the nature of a subsidiary's rights and obligations to participate in a surplus or deficiency and the extent to which the level of contributions paid by subsidiaries is adjusted as a result of changes in the level of funding in the scheme.

12.192 The accounting should reflect the arrangement between the parent company and its subsidiaries. Some groups do not allocate surpluses or deficiencies in group schemes to participating subsidiaries, but account for the surplus or deficiency at parent company level. If the subsidiaries continue to be charged with the regular cost for the group as a whole, their financial statements need also to reflect that cost. In other situations, the employer's contribution rate across the whole group may be varied as a result of a surplus or deficiency, in which case the net pension cost for each subsidiary should in principle reflect this variation by allocating it under a method that is appropriate to the circumstances that gave rise to the surplus or deficiency. It is important that subsidiaries' financial statements should adequately disclose the basis for recognising pension costs under a group scheme.

Disclosure by subsidiaries

12.193 A subsidiary that is a member of a group pension scheme and whose holding company is registered in the UK or the Republic of Ireland is exempted from disclosing most of the actuarial information required by the standard [SSAP 24 para 90]. Instead, it need in effect only disclose the nature of the group scheme to which it belongs, together with the name of the parent company in whose financial statements the actuarial particulars relating to the group are given, indicating where appropriate that the contributions are based on pension costs across the group as a whole. The remaining disclosure requirements of the standard are applicable to all group companies.

12.194 A suggested example of pension disclosure for a subsidiary company that is a member of a group scheme is given below.

Example

Accounting Policy

The company contributes to a group pension scheme operated by Parent Company plc. Contributions and pension costs are based on pension costs across the group as a whole. Pension costs are accounted for on the basis of charging the expected cost of providing pensions over the period during which the company benefits from the employees' services. The effects of variations from regular costs are spread over the expected remaining working lifetime of members of the scheme after making suitable allowances for future withdrawals.

Notes to the accounts

The company participates in a group pension scheme operated by Parent Company plc. The pension scheme is of the defined benefit type and its assets are held in a separate trustee administered fund. The fund is valued every three years by a professionally qualified independent actuary, the rates of contribution payable being determined by the actuary. In the intervening years the actuary reviews the continuing appropriateness of the rates. The latest actuarial assessment of the scheme was at 31 December 19X4. Particulars of the valuation are contained in the accounts of Parent Company plc.

The total pension cost for the company was £136,000 (19X4 £121,000).

A provision of £34,000 (19X4 £23,000) is included in provisions, this being the excess of the accumulated pension cost over the amount funded.

Multi-employer pension schemes

12.195 Some companies participate in industry-wide pension schemes, which provide centralised pension arrangements for identifiable groups of unrelated employers. Examples in the UK include the merchant navy pension funds for seafaring employees, the Electricity Supply Pension Scheme, the Retail Motor Industry Pension Plan and the Pensions Trust for Charities and Voluntary Organisations.

12.196 Where the arrangements are of the defined benefit type, the measurement and disclosure provisions of SSAP 24 should be followed. For example, where the assets and accrued pension liabilities in a multi-employer scheme are allocated to individual participating companies, there should be little problem in each company giving the full disclosures, including the actuarial information, required by SSAP 24. In other circumstances where such information is not available on an entity-specific basis, it may be necessary to modify the disclosures.

12.197 Table 12.17 shows the disclosures given by SEEBOARD in respect of the group's participation in the electricity supply pension scheme.

Table 12.17 – SEEBOARD plc – Annual Report and Accounts – 31 March 1995

Note 20 Pension costs

The Company's employees are entitled to join the Electricity Supply Pension Scheme which provides pension and other related benefits, based on final pensionable pay, to employees throughout the Electricity Supply Industry. The assets of the Scheme are held in a separate trustee administered fund. A full actuarial valuation of the Scheme is carried out on a triennial basis. These accounts incorporate the results of the latest valuation of the Scheme carried out as at 31 March 1992.

Pension costs charged to the profit and loss account for the year were £12.7m (1994 £4.6m as reduced by the release of a provision of £9.0m for the equalisation of pension rights no longer required). The latest full actuarial valuation of the Company's section of the Scheme was carried out by Bacon and Woodrow, consulting actuaries, as at 31 March 1992 and the results of this valuation have been used as the basis for assessing pension costs. The 'attained age' method was used for the valuation and the principal actuarial assumptions adopted were that the investment return would exceed salary increases by 2% per annum (exclusive of merit awards) and exceed future pension increases by 4% per annum.

> The actuarial value of the assets of the Company's section of the Scheme as at 31 March 1992 represented 104% of the actuarial value of the accrued benefits. After allowing for benefit improvements granted as a result of the valuation and the provision made from surplus to cover contingencies and anticipated short term early retirement costs, this reduces to 100%. The accrued benefits include all benefits for pensioners and other former members as well as benefits based on service completed to date for active members, allowing for future salary rises.
>
> The total market value of the assets of the Scheme as at 31 March 1992 was £9,492m of which £414m represented the section of the Scheme which relates to the members and beneficiaries of the Company. Contributions payable by the Company to the Scheme during the year (excluding provisions) were £12.2m (1994 £13.6m).

Deferred tax

12.198 Tax relief on employers' pension contributions is generally granted in the period in which they are paid rather than when they are expensed. In an unfunded scheme the tax relief is given when the pensions are paid after the employees have retired. Therefore, whenever pension costs recognised under SSAP 24 differ from actual contributions paid, the resulting pension provision or prepayment shown on the balance sheet potentially represents a timing difference for deferred tax purposes.

12.199 In most cases these timing differences will reverse, albeit over a relatively long time scale. For example, timing differences caused by a contribution holiday will generally reverse over the average remaining service lives of employees, when the pension surplus has been fully amortised in the financial statements. An initial surplus or deficiency that is recognised as an asset or liability under the alternative transitional provisions is a timing difference that reverses over the period of reduced or additional contributions until the surplus or deficiency is eliminated.

12.200 A problem that soon emerged after SSAP 24 was introduced was that SSAP 24 and SSAP 15 use different principles for recognising costs and assets and liabilities. SSAP 24 follows an 'income approach' and this leads to the recognition of long-term debtors and creditors. SSAP 15 follows a 'balance sheet approach', but on a 'partial provision' basis where deferred tax is only accounted for to the extent that it is probable that a liability or asset will crystallise. In particular, it does not permit deferred tax assets and liabilities to be recognised where they are expected to be replaced by new ones as the old ones are settled.

12.201 In many cases this caused no particular difficulty. However for SSAP 24 purposes, in assessing whether deferred tax assets or liabilities should be recognised in respect of these timing differences under SSAP 15, their long-term nature meant that a company needed to assess the pattern of overall timing differences arising and reversing over a much longer time scale than is usual.

12.202 The conflict was exacerbated in accounting for unfunded schemes, and in particular for unfunded post-retirement benefits other than pensions that are dealt with by UITF Abstract 6. SSAP 24 and UITF Abstract 6 require full provision to be made for such obligations over the employees' working lives. The provision represents a timing difference, because tax relief should be obtained when pensions or other benefits are paid. The individual timing differences will ultimately reverse, but the aggregate liability of an unfunded scheme may well continue to grow, because as pensions and benefits are paid to retired employees, new provisions are accrued in respect of existing employees. SSAP 15 would not allow a corresponding deferred tax asset to be recognised where the reversing provision is replaced by a new one. This was generally considered to be unfair.

12.203 The ASB addressed this anomaly in an amendment to SSAP 15, issued in December 1992. The amendment permitted companies to use the same recognition criteria for the deferred tax implications of pensions and other post-retirement benefits as in accounting for the obligations to provide those benefits. Accordingly, either the full provision basis or the partial provision basis may be used.

12.204 However, the amended SSAP 15 requires any recognised deferred tax asset relating to a pension provision to pass the normal recoverability test for assets. [SSAP 15 para 12B]. Consequently, before a deferred tax asset is recognised, consideration should be given as to whether there will be sufficient taxable profits in future periods to ensure that tax relief is obtained when the pensions, pension contributions or other benefits are paid.

12.205 Pension assets or liabilities are themselves discounted amounts. It follows that the related tax balances should be similarly calculated. In most cases this would be achieved by calculating the tax asset or liability as an appropriate percentage (that is, the corporation tax rate) of the pension asset or liability.

12.206 Although this amendment removed an inconsistency between SSAP 24 and SSAP 15, it introduced a major inconsistency into SSAP 15. Using a mixture of full and partial provision is likely to make analysis of deferred tax figures difficult. The ASB has acknowledged this as a pragmatic short-term solution to a particular problem, and it is unlikely to survive the ASB's review of SSAP 15.

12.207 An illustration of the adoption of the full provision basis is shown in Table 12.18.

Table 12.18 – TATE & LYLE Public Limited Company – Annual Report – 24 September 1994

Notes to the Financial Statements (extract)

1 Accounting Policies (extract)

Deferred taxation

Deferred taxation is recognised at the anticipated tax rate using the liability method on differences arising from the inclusion of income and expenditure in taxation computations in periods different from those in which they are included in the financial statements, to the extent that it is probable that a liability or asset will crystallise. Deferred tax on post-retirement benefits is recognised in full.

13 Debtors (extract)	1994 Group £ million	1993 Group £ million
Due after one year		
Deferred taxation	45.7	39.6
Owed by associated undertakings	0.4	0.6
Other debtors	36.8	39.8
	82.9	80.0

18 Provisions for Liabilities and Charges (extract)		
Analysis of Deferred Taxation		
Provided Liabilities		
UK - capital allowances	8.6	5.6
- other timing differences	0.3	10.6
Overseas – on fixed assets	32.1	17.8
– other timing differences	5.7	4.8
Assets		
UK - other timing differences	-	-
- Advance Corporation Tax recoverable	(10.1)	(11.0)
Overseas – post-retirement benefits	(41.3)	(36.9)
– other timing differences	(18.9)	(17.0)
	(23.6)	(26.1)
Assets included as debtors in note 13	45.7	39.6
Deferred taxation liabilities provided	22.1	13.5
Potential liabilities		
UK - capital allowances	35.4	31.2
- other timing differences	0.3	10.6
Overseas – on fixed assets	180.4	184.3
– other timing differences	5.7	6.1
Assets		
UK - other timing differences	(7.3)	(7.2)
- Advance Corporation Tax recoverable	(10.1)	(11.0)
Overseas – post-retirement benefits	(41.3)	(37.6)
– other timing differences	(66.4)	(32.7)
Potential full deferred taxation provision	96.7	143.7

Post-retirement benefits other than pensions

Introduction

12.208 The most common example of other post-retirement benefits is the provision of post-retirement private medical insurance. Whilst still relatively uncommon in the UK, it is widespread practice in the US for employers to provide such benefits to their employees after retirement. The accounting has a particular impact on groups with significant US subsidiaries.

12.209 These post-retirement obligations are usually unfunded, that is there is no external accumulation of assets to meet the future liabilities. The costs are borne by the employer company as payments fall due.

12.210 There was uncertainty regarding the accounting treatment of such obligations when SSAP 24 was introduced. SSAP 24 stated: *"Although this statement primarily addresses pensions, its principles may be equally applicable to the cost of providing other post-retirement benefits"*. [SSAP 24 para 75]. Subsequently, the ASC issued a Technical Release (TR 756) which stated that there was no obligation to apply the principles of SSAP 24 to such benefits, although companies might consider it appropriate to do so.

12.211 The accounting issues were addressed by the UITF following the introduction of an accounting standard in the US (FAS 106 'Employers' accounting for post-retirement benefits other than pensions') which required a change from a cash basis to an accruals basis of accounting.

Accounting treatment

12.212 UITF Abstract 6 established that the accruals principles of SSAP 24 should be applied to all forms of post-retirement benefits, that is they should be fully accrued over the service lives of the employees. Following a transitional period in which disclosure of such commitments was an option, UITF Abstract 6 became fully effective for accounting periods ending on or after 23 December 1994.

12.213 Where benefits are unfunded, the full liability in respect of employees' past service will (ultimately) be recognised on the employer company's balance sheet. Like SSAP 24 for pensions, UITF Abstract 6 offered a choice of transitional methods for implementing the accruals basis of accounting. The following options were available for recognising the initial unprovided liability.

- Recognise immediately in full on the balance sheet by making a prior period adjustment.

- Recognise gradually over the employees' expected remaining service lives.

12.214 Following the principles of SSAP 24 described in this chapter, the annual cost of unfunded post-retirement benefits comprises:

- Cost of benefits earned during the year (regular cost).
- Variations resulting from new valuations or other changes in benefit arrangements.
- Allocation of the transitional obligation (where the spreading option is adopted).
- Interest on the accumulated unfunded liability. (The interest rate will be equal to the discount rate assumed in present valuing the liabilities, see para 12.216 below.)

12.215 There is less experience of measuring the cost of other post-retirement benefits than of measuring pension costs. Also there are other important assumptions to factor into the calculations that are unique to the type of benefit being measured. Where a UK reporting entity has operations in the US that are governed by the requirements of FAS 106, UITF Abstract 6 permits the cost calculations made under FAS 106 to be used as a proxy for compliance with SSAP 24. This includes the transitional option in FAS 106, where a period of 20 years may be used in some cases to spread the initial liability, instead of the employees' average remaining service lives.

12.216 Consistent with pensions, the regular cost and past service liabilities relating to other post-retirement benefits are measured using actuarial assumptions and present value techniques. For post-retirement healthcare benefits, FAS 106 sets out some principal assumptions that are critical to the calculations. These include:

- Discount rates used for determining the present value of future cash outflows expected to be required to satisfy the obligations. (The discount rate is based on current rates of return on high quality fixed-income investments currently available whose cash flows match the timing and amount of expected benefit payments.)
- Factors affecting the amount and timing of future benefit payments, including:
  - claims cost experience according to age; and
  - future trends in the cost of healthcare.

- Demographic assumptions specific to the participants in any plan, together with eligible dependents.

12.217 The period over which the benefit costs are accrued may be shorter than the employees' service lives. That is because a plan may grant credit for service from a date after joining service, or it may grant eligibility for full benefits by a date before the employee retires. FAS 106 requires the cost to be accrued over the shorter period in which the benefits are earned.

12.218 Generally, tax relief is granted on unfunded post-retirement benefits when benefit payments are made. Consequently, there are significant deferred tax implications where unfunded liabilities are recognised on the balance sheet. The ASB issued an amendment to SSAP 15 in December 1992 which was primarily addressed at deferred tax on other post-retirement liabilities. The amendment permits either full or partial provision to be applied to timing differences attributable to such liabilities (see para 12.198 above). As a result of this amendment, a company may choose, as a matter of accounting policy, to recognise deferred tax assets related to the corresponding provisions for future benefits, assuming the company expects to obtain the tax relief when benefits are paid.

Disclosure

12.219 UITF 6 requires footnote disclosures about other post-retirement obligations that are equivalent to the SSAP 24 disclosures of pension obligations. In particular:

- Important assumptions that are specific to the measurement of such benefits should be disclosed.

- Material balance sheet provisions relating to such benefits should be distinguished from other provisions.

[UITF 6 para 9].

12.220 A disclosure example is given in Table 12.19.

Table 12.19 – Hanson PLC – Directors' Report & Accounts – 31 December 1997

Note 28 Pensions and other post retirement benefits (extract)

Hanson also provides post-retirement health care and life insurance benefits under plans mainly in the United States to certain groups of its retired and active employees. Hanson conforms with the provisions of the Urgent Issues Task Force Abstract 6 "Accounting for Post-Retirement Benefits other than Pensions", which requires accrual of these costs over the period during which employees become eligible for such benefits.

At December 31, 1997 the accumulated post-retirement benefit obligation excluding pensions, as assessed by independent qualified actuaries, for retirees and the obligation for prior service costs of currently active employees is approximately £150.6m (£698.0m). The 15 month 1997 expense has been accrued based upon actuarial calculations determined in accordance with required accounting standards. This resulted in the recognition of service costs for benefits earned during the 15 month period of approximately £2.5m (£10.0m), and interest cost on accumulated benefit obligations of approximately £5.2m (£46.0m). The actuarial assumptions used to estimate the obligations vary according to the claims experience and economic conditions relevant to each plan. It has been assumed that the annual per capita cost of benefits will increase 9½% depending on claims experience and economic conditions relevant to each plan. This rate is assumed to decrease½% a year to 5½%. The weighted average discount rates used in determining the accumulated post-retirement benefit obligation were 7% and 7½% at December 31, 1997 and October 1, 1996 respectively.

UITF 18

12.220.1 The Finance (No 2) Act 1997 no longer allows pension schemes to reclaim a tax credit on dividend income. This loss of tax credit may have the effect of reducing the scheme's surplus or increasing the scheme's deficit. The question arises as to how any deficiency should be recognised under the principles of SSAP 24.

12.220.2 As stated in paragraph 12.49 the general rule in SSAP 24 is that variations from regular cost caused by surpluses or deficiencies should be spread forward and recognised over the average remaining service lives of current employees in the scheme. Exceptions to the spreading principle are allowed only in limited specific circumstances, for example, where the circumstances set out in paragraph 82 of SSAP 24 are met (see para 12.101).

12.220.3 The above issue was addressed by the UITF in Abstract 18, 'Pension costs following the 1997 tax changes in respect of dividend income', which came into effect for accounting periods ending on or after 23 December 1997. The Abstract states that this change to tax legislation does not, of itself, fall outside the normal scope of the actuarial assumptions as set out in paragraph 82 of SSAP 24. It is simply a change in the expected return on assets, similar to those arising from changes in tax rates. Hence, the loss should be spread forward over the expected remaining service lives of current employees in the scheme whatever the financial position of the scheme and regardless of any additional contributions that are made. If the amount of the loss charged in the period is material, suitable explanations should be given.

[The next paragraph is 12.221.]

ASB's proposals

12.221 The ASB published a discussion paper reviewing SSAP 24 in June 1995. Two distinct approaches to pension cost accounting in respect of defined benefit schemes were explored from first principles. The ASB's 'preferred' approach was to continue with an actuarial approach based on SSAP 24's principles, but improved to standardise the measurement rules and to make the disclosures more relevant. The 'alternative' approach explored a balance sheet driven treatment that embraced the use of market, rather than actuarial, values.

12.222 The pensions project has since been overtaken by international developments. The IASC rejected the UK's practice of measuring pension assets and liabilities on a smoothed actuarial basis. IAS 19 (revised) 'Employee benefits', issued in March 1998, adopted a market value approach. It requires pension scheme assets to be measured at market values rather than actuarial values; and pension liabilities should be discounted at a risk-free rate rather than the rate of return on scheme assets under the actuarial approach. There is strong pressure for harmonisation with international standards and the ASB published a further discussion paper, 'Aspects of accounting for pension costs', in July 1998. The proposals in that discussion paper are consistent with much of IAS 19, although there are important differences.

12.223 The discussion paper focuses on four key issues:

- Valuation of pension scheme assets.
- The rate at which pension liabilities should be discounted.
- The treatment of actuarial gains and losses (surpluses and deficiencies).
- Past service costs arising from benefit improvements.

12.224 Pension scheme assets should be measured at market values. Actuarial values (based on discounted cash flow methodology) would no longer be permitted.

12.225 Pension liabilities should be measured by forecasting expected cash flows and using a discount rate on a (perfect) portfolio of assets that properly matches the liabilities. The ASB opposes the rate required by IAS 19 – a risk-free rate related to current market yields on high quality fixed-rate corporate bonds with a maturity period consistent with the estimated maturity of the pension liabilities. The ASB considers that a risk-free rate would overstate the pension liability and pension cost. An appropriate discount rate should include some element of equity return in respect of current employees with a promise of final salary pensions, but is not (except by coincidence) the rate of return on the actual assets in the scheme. The ASB is consulting the actuarial profession for guidance on determining appropriate discount rates for different classes of liability.

12.226 Actuarial gains or losses arise from changes in the market values of pension scheme assets or in the estimates of defined benefit liabilities. The discussion paper considers four possible methods of accounting for actuarial gains and losses:

- Amortisation over the employees' average remaining service lives (as presently required by SSAP 24).
- Crediting or charging the whole gain or loss immediately in the profit and loss account (as a separate exceptional item).
- Crediting or charging the whole gain or loss immediately in the statement of total recognised gains and losses (STRGL).
- Crediting or charging the whole gain or loss immediately in the STRGL, but amortising the gain or loss from there to the profit and loss account over the employees' average remaining service lives (this is referred to as 'recycling' the gain or loss).

12.227 Under the last three methods above, the pension asset or liability on the balance sheet is the current estimate of the surplus or deficit in the scheme. Using the STRGL to deal with actuarial gains and losses in the ways described above depends on the outcome of the review of FRS 3 that the ASB is currently undertaking as part of a wider project on reporting financial performance, which includes the future role of the STRGL. A single performance statement may evolve from this project.

12.228 Past service costs arise from benefit improvements awarded to current and former employees that are not provided for in the actuarial assumptions. The ASB's preferred view is that all past service costs should be charged immediately to the profit and loss account when the improved benefits are awarded. Two alternative approaches are also considered:

- Charging past service costs relating to former employees immediately, and spreading forward those relating to current employees.

- Offsetting past service costs against any surplus funding them and recognising as a cost only any excess amount.

Comparison with IASs

12.229 IAS 19 (revised 1998), 'Employee benefits', is effective for financial years commencing 1 January 1999. It replaces IAS 19 (revised 1993). IAS 19 (revised 1998) is much wider in scope than SSAP 24. It covers all employee benefits, including pensions and other post-retirement benefits, short-term and long-term employee benefits, and termination benefits. The rules of the old standard were broadly similar to those of SSAP 24. The new standard is similar in most respects to the US standard FAS 87.

12.230 The key features of IAS 19 (revised) in respect of defined benefit pension schemes are as follows:

- Pension fund assets should be measured at market values. Actuarial values are not permitted.

- The present value of pension liabilities should be measured using a risk-free discount rate related to market yields at the balance sheet date on high quality fixed-rate corporate bonds with a maturity period consistent with the estimated maturity of the pension liabilities. The expected rate of return on a fund's assets should *not* be used to measure the liability.

- The projected unit credit method must be used to measure the pension expense and pension obligation.

- Valuations of plan assets and pension liabilities should be carried out with sufficient regularity to ensure that the amounts recognised in the financial statements do not differ materially from the amounts that would be determined at the balance sheet date. Thus, the three-yearly valuations that are common in the UK would not be sufficient.

- Actuarial gains and losses (resulting from changes in the present value of the pension obligation or differences between the actual and expected return on fund assets) should be spread forward in the income statement over the participating employees' expected average remaining working lives to the extent that they exceed the greater of:

  - Ten per cent of the present value of the pension obligation.

  - Ten per cent of the market value of fund assets.

The standard also permits systematic methods of faster recognition of actuarial gains and losses to be used, such as a policy of recognising all actuarial gains and losses immediately, (including those that fall within the range specified above). However, such a policy should be applied consistently to both gains and losses and from period to period.

The ten per cent 'corridor' approach is borrowed from the US standard FAS 87; the reason given for such an approach is that annual valuations are very volatile and this is a practical way of dealing with frequent changes in estimates.

- Additional past service costs resulting from benefit improvements (former and current employees) should be expensed immediately to the extent that the benefits are already vested; otherwise they should be spread forward over the average period until the amended benefits become vested.

- A liability or asset will appear on the employer company's balance sheet comprising the present value of the pension obligation less the market value of the fund assets, together with any actuarial gains or losses deferred because they are inside the 'corridor' or are being spread forward.

- Gains or losses on the curtailment or settlement of a defined benefit plan should be recognised when the curtailment or settlement occurs.

12.231 The standard has transitional provisions that permit an entity to spread forward (over not more than five years) any increase in its defined benefit pension liability that arises on adopting the new standard. Any surplus arising, however, should be recognised immediately.

Chapter 13

Taxation

Chapter 13

Taxation

Introduction

13.1 Accounting for tax is based on the premise that tax is an expense incurred as a result of doing business. As tax is levied by national government, it is an expense that is quite different from all other expenses appearing in the financial statements. In the UK, companies pay corporation tax at a single rate on taxable profits, regardless of whether those profits are distributed to the shareholders or retained in the business. However, the amount of tax payable on the taxable profits of a particular period often bears little relationship to the amount of income and expenditure appearing in the financial statements. This is because the computation of accounting profit is governed by the application of generally accepted accounting principles and company law, whereas the computation of taxable profit is governed by the application of tax law. For example, certain items of income appearing in the financial statements may be tax free, whilst others may be taxable in a different period. Similarly, certain items of expenditure may be disallowable for tax, whilst others may fall to be tax deductible in a period different from that in which they were recognised in the financial statements.

13.2 If the profit and loss account tax charge were based simply on the amount of tax payable on taxable profits, it would be inconsistent with the accruals concept, the basis on which all other expenses are stated in the financial statements. Therefore, it is generally accepted that the tax charge in the profit and loss account should include not only the current tax charge based on taxable profit that takes into account the effects of tax free income and disallowable expenses, but also an amount that recognises the tax effects of transactions appearing in the financial statements in one period, but which fall to be taxed or tax deductible in a different period. This additional amount, comprising the tax effects of what are generally referred to as 'timing differences' resulting from the difference between fiscal and accounting rules, ensures that the correct tax expense is recognised in the financial statements in the same periods as the income and expenditure to which it relates. The recognition of this additional amount gives rise to deferred taxation either payable or recoverable in a subsequent accounting period. Therefore, the tax charge in the profit and the loss account comprises deferred tax as well as current tax. Deferred tax was conceived and developed as a means of recognising the tax effects of the difference between accounting and taxable profit.

13.3 Although the concept of deferred taxation can be explained in the context of matching income and expenditure with their tax effects, it can also be viewed from the perspective of accounting for a liability and indeed, as the debate on deferred tax has progressed, this has become a preferable way of understanding deferred tax. Given that a future liability would arise through the tax effects of timing differences, the principle of prudence would require that provision be made in full for this known liability. On the other hand, taxation deferred as a result of timing differences could be permanently deferred under a tax system that gives initially high tax reliefs, for example, where capital allowances claimed in a period always exceed the depreciation charged in that period. In that situation, the accepted principle of not accounting for remote contingencies becomes relevant.

13.4 Given that there are different, often conflicting ways, of looking at deferred taxation, a number of methods of accounting for deferred taxation, each having its own objectives, have evolved over the years. It is, therefore, not surprising that the development of the standard dealing with deferred taxation has had a checkered history in the UK. The ASC experimented with these methods during the 1970s, beginning with the first exposure draft ED 11 in May 1973, followed by SSAP 11 which was short-lived, until the current system of accounting for deferred tax was established with the publication of SSAP 15 in October 1978.

13.5 Because deferred taxation attempts to bridge the gap between accounting and tax rules, changes to the fiscal system also have a profound effect on the way in which deferred tax is measured. In fact, the tax system in the UK has changed significantly over the years since SSAP 15 was introduced with the result that some have begun to question whether the present method of accounting for deferred tax is still relevant in the current fiscal climate. The ASB is uncomfortable with the SSAP 15 approach and published a discussion document on 'Accounting for tax', in March 1995 as a first step towards replacing SSAP 15 with a new FRS (see further para 13.200). Most of the responses to the discussion document, however, favoured retaining the SSAP 15 approach. The international community, on the other hand, is at odds with the UK. The IASC issued a new standard IAS 12 (revised) in September 1996 which is significantly different from SSAP 15 (see further para 13.209). This has major implications for the UK and the ASB is now seeking to identify the best way forward.

13.6 The accounting for current tax in the UK is also not straightforward. The imputation system of company taxation, which was introduced in the UK in April 1973, raises accounting issues that are unique to UK companies. The accounting standard dealing with these issues is SSAP 8, 'The treatment of taxation under the imputation system in the accounts of companies'.

13.7 This chapter deals with accounting for current and deferred taxation in the light of the provisions contained in the Companies Act, SSAP 8 and SSAP 15. It also contains a section on future developments that deals with the ASB's current thinking on accounting for deferred taxation. There is also a further accounting standard SSAP 5, 'Accounting for value added tax', but as accounting for value added tax, although extremely complicated to administer in practice, poses few technical accounting problems, it is not dealt with in this chapter.

[The next page is 13003.]

Corporation tax

General principles

13.8 A UK resident company is, in general, chargeable to corporation tax on its profits wherever they arise, other than dividends received from other UK companies. Corporation tax is assessed on a company's profits, whether distributed or retained, at the end of each accounting period. The tax charge is calculated by applying the current basic rate of corporation tax to the taxable profit for the period. The general rate of corporation tax for the 1995 financial year to 31 March 1996 is 33 per cent. This basic rate is reduced for smaller companies to a small company rate, which is 25 per cent for the 1995 financial year. The taxable profit is arrived at by applying relevant tax laws and rules and is rarely the same as the accounting profit disclosed in the financial statements. As stated previously, differences between taxable and accounting profit form the basis of accounting for deferred taxation, which is considered later in this chapter.

13.9 Although the rate of corporation tax is set for a financial year, it should be noted that the assessments are made on the basis of the company's actual accounting period. If a company prepares financial statements for a year which straddles 31 March, and the rate of corporation tax is different for different financial years, an effective rate will have to be computed and disclosed.

Example

A company has an accounting period ending on 30 October 19X1 and the rates of corporation tax for the financial years 19X0 and 19X1 are 30% and 35% respectively. The effective rate of tax that should be disclosed in the financial statements is calculated as follows:

Period 1 November 19X0 to 31 March 19X1 (FY 19X1)	5/12 @ 30%	12.50%
Period 1 April 19X1 to 30 October 19X1 (FY 19X2)	7/12 @ 35%	20.42%
Effective rate of corporation tax		32.92%

Furthermore, the accounting period for corporation tax purposes can never exceed 12 months. If the financial statements cover a period longer than 12 months, the first 12 months constitute one accounting period and the remainder of the period constitutes the second accounting period for tax purposes.

13.10 As stated in paragraph 13.8 above, dividends received from other UK companies are not subject to corporation tax because the profits from which they have been paid will already have been subject to corporation tax in the company where they were earned, and a double tax charge is not intended. This is a consequence of the imputation system of corporation tax, which is considered below.

13.11 The imputation system also affects the timing of the payment of corporation tax. Normally, corporation tax is payable nine months after the end of the company's accounting period. This payment date applies only if the company has made no distributions during the accounting period. Although distributions do not in general affect the amount of tax that must be paid on the profits of an accounting period, they do affect the time at which the payments are made.

The imputation tax system

13.12 Under the imputation system, part of the corporation tax paid by a company on distributed profits is treated as a payment on account of the shareholders' income tax liability on his dividends. Thus, when a company makes a distribution to shareholders in an accounting period, it does not withhold income tax from the payment, but is required to make an advance payment of corporation tax to the Inland Revenue. This Advance Corporation Tax (ACT) was formerly paid at a rate that related to the current basic rate of personal income tax. For 1994/95 and subsequent years the ACT is paid at a rate that relates to the lower rate of income tax. For the 1995/96 tax year, ACT is paid at an amount equal to 25 per cent of the actual dividend paid (net), or 20 per cent of the gross dividend (net plus the related ACT). The ACT is paid within 14 days after the quarter days (31 March, 30 June, 30 September and 31 December) following the payment of the dividend. For example, if a dividend is paid on 17 July, the ACT becomes payable on 14 October.

13.13 The corporation tax 'imputed' to the shareholder is normally an amount equal to the ACT paid in respect of the dividend. The shareholder is then given a tax credit equal to the amount of the ACT paid by the company. This tax credit discharges the basic rate taxpayer's liability to income tax chargeable on the amount of the income equivalent to the dividend plus the imputed tax credit. For 1994/95 and subsequent years taxpayers chargeable at the basic rate on other income are chargeable only at the lower rate on dividend income. These taxpayers, therefore, do not have to pay any further tax in respect of UK dividend income after taking account of the tax credit given in respect of the dividends they receive. If the shareholder is chargeable to tax at a higher rate, then he will still have a tax liability at the higher rate and will be assessed on the amounts of dividend income declared in his tax return and the tax credit attributed to the dividend will be set against that liability. If the shareholder is exempt from tax he will be able to reclaim the amount of tax credit.

13.14 At the end of the company's accounting period, the corporation tax payable on profit is computed. ACT in respect of distributions made in that accounting period is set off against the company's total liability for corporation tax (subject to a current maximum of 20 per cent of that profit). The balance of the tax due is known as the mainstream corporation tax and is due nine months after the end of the accounting period. Therefore, the total tax charge for corporation tax comprises the mainstream corporation tax liability and the ACT paid.

13.15 ACT payment is, in essence, a cash flow item. It does not affect the amount of the liability for corporation tax, only the timing of the payment. The exception to this occurs when a company pays a dividend, and thus ACT, and then has such a low tax charge that it is unable to utilise the full amount of ACT paid to offset the tax liability arising. Thus irrecoverable ACT, the excess of ACT paid over that utilised, arises. This problem is considered further from paragraph 13.28 below.

13.16 The imputation system provides a link between the corporation tax and income tax regimes and has the effect of ensuring that:

- The double taxation of distributed profits (once in the hands of the company and once on shareholders on distributions) is partly eliminated.
- Tax is charged to basic rate tax paying shareholders at the appropriate (lower) rate on their dividend income.
- A large part of the tax (that is, tax at the lower rate) is collected in an efficient manner (from companies paying the dividends rather than from all the individual shareholders receiving the dividends).

SSAP 8

13.17 The imputation system raises a number of problems in accounting for taxation. These problems are addressed in SSAP 8 that was issued a year after the imputation system came into force from April 1973. However, it should be remembered that since the standard was originally issued there have been some significant changes to the taxation system in the UK that render parts of the standard obsolete. Reference has, therefore, been made in this chapter, where applicable, to TR 805, issued by the ICAEW in July 1990. The changes to SSAP 8 suggested in TR 805 do not formally amend SSAP 8, but the changes remain valid under the present tax system.

13.18 SSAP 8 identifies five main accounting problems arising from the imputation system. These are:

- The treatment in the profit and loss account of outgoing dividends and the related ACT.
- Determining the recoverability of ACT.

- The treatment of irrecoverable ACT and of unrelieved overseas tax arising from the payment or proposed payment of dividends.

- The treatment of franked investment income.

- The treatment in the balance sheet of taxation liabilities, recoverable ACT and dividends.

[SSAP 8 para 3].

Each of the above issues is discussed in the paragraphs that follow, except the last item, which is considered under the section dealing with disclosures.

Outgoing dividends and the related ACT

13.19 The issue is concerned with whether ACT on outgoing dividends should be treated as part of the cost of the dividend, or whether it should be treated as part of tax on the company's profits. The standard argues that as the concept of 'gross' dividends and the deduction of income tax at source is no longer relevant since the imputation system came into force, whatever dividend is declared (either as an amount payable per share or as a percentage), that is the amount which the company pays its members. The related ACT paid is, from the company's point of view, no more than a payment on account of corporation tax, because the dividend payment simply affects the timing and not the amount of tax paid by the company. The fact that the dividend carries a tax credit equal to the ACT paid and which is treated, in assessing the shareholder's liability to income tax, as if it had been paid by the shareholder, is a matter for the shareholder alone; it is not relevant to the accounting treatment that the company should adopt for the dividend paid. Accordingly, the standard takes the view that outgoing dividends should be shown in the profit and loss account at the amount paid or payable to the shareholder and that neither the related ACT nor the imputed tax credit should be included as part of the cost of the dividend. It follows that the charge for corporation tax in the profit and loss account should include the full amount of the tax and not merely the mainstream liability. [SSAP 8 para 4].

13.20 It should be noted that the inclusion of ACT on dividends as part of the tax charge and not as part of the cost of the dividend has the effect of understating the after tax rate of return to shareholders. For this reason, some companies argue that the current accounting treatment of ACT prescribed by SSAP 8 is misleading because of its failure to recognise that, in economic terms, ACT is a distribution to shareholders. These companies assert that the current treatment has the effect of discouraging potential investors in investing funds in UK companies and puts many UK companies at a disadvantage compared with similar overseas companies. In fact, the issue as to whether ACT paid by a company should be shown as part of the tax charge or as part of the cost of the dividend has recently resurfaced with the publication of the discussion paper by the ASB. The ASB has stated that it does not propose to change current practice, unless there is a consensus that such a change is desirable.

Recoverability of ACT

13.21 Given that ACT becomes payable within 14 days of the end of the relevant quarter following the payment of the dividend, it follows that whenever a company provides for a dividend it must also provide for the associated ACT payable. Such ACT payable is a current liability that is extinguished when the ACT is paid. As explained in paragraph 13.14 above, the ACT is primarily recoverable in due course by being set off against the corporation tax on the taxable profits of the year in which the related distribution is made.

13.22 Where a sufficient corporation tax liability is available for ACT offset, no problem arises. However, where there is insufficient or no corporation tax liability against which to set off ACT, it is necessary to consider whether any debit balance in respect of ACT recoverable can properly be regarded as an asset or whether it should instead be written off to the profit and loss account as irrecoverable ACT.

13.23 In considering this question it is necessary to distinguish between tax and accounting rules. Under current tax rules, ACT will always fall to be recoverable either by set off against the corporation tax on the taxable profits of the year under review, or to the extent unrelieved, carried back to accounting periods beginning in the six years preceding the accounting period in which the unrelieved ACT arose. Where there is still unrelieved ACT it can normally be carried forward indefinitely to be set against the mainstream liability of future years. In each year there is an overriding restriction on the use of ACT for set off by reference to the taxable profits of that year (currently restricted to 20 per cent of taxable profits).

13.24 Where the ACT has been relieved in the current year, or as a result of carry back, it is effectively recovered and no further problem arises. Although unrelieved ACT is, in principle, carried forward with a right of set-off against future tax liabilities for as long as the company is in existence, nevertheless, the ACT can only be recovered if there are sufficient taxable profits in future years. Therefore, for accounting purposes, prudence dictates that the ACT recoverable should be treated as an asset only if its recoverability is reasonably certain and foreseeable. Otherwise it should be written off to the profit and loss account. How long this future period should be depends on the circumstances of each case, but SSAP 8 states that it is prudent only to have regard to the immediate and foreseeable future and suggests that this should normally not extend beyond the next accounting period. [SSAP 8 para 6].

13.25 SSAP 8 defines recoverable ACT as the amount of ACT paid or payable on outgoing dividends paid and proposed that can either be:

- Set off against a corporation tax liability on the profits of the period under review or of previous periods.

- Properly set off against a credit balance on the deferred tax account.

- Expected to be recoverable taking into account expected profits and dividends – *normally* those of the next accounting period only.

[SSAP 8 para 20].

13.26 The requirement of the third point in the above paragraph may imply that, in certain circumstances, it is possible to depart from the strict one year timescale provided the company can foresee with reasonable certainty that its expected profits and dividends will enable the ACT to be relieved. To answer this question unambiguously, it is necessary to consider the provisions of SSAP 15, which also covers the treatment of carrying forward ACT on dividends paid and proposed as an asset where a deferred tax account is maintained. The rules in SSAP 15 are somewhat different from SSAP 8 and are discussed further from paragraph 13.86. Suffice it to say at this stage that ACT carried forward on the grounds that it will be relieved against future profits, when not set off against a credit balance on a deferred tax account as in point two above, should be shown as a deferred asset under the caption 'prepayments and accrued income'.

13.27 The rules for set-off of ACT are best illustrated by means of an example.

Example

A company prepares its financial statements to 31 December each year and pays mainstream corporation tax nine months after that date. In the year ended 31 December 19X4, it made a taxable profit of £1,000,000. The company paid an interim dividend of £300,000 on 15 July 19X4 and proposed a final dividend of £500,000 payable on 15 April 19X5. The final dividend for the previous financial year amounting to £400,000 was paid on 15 April 19X4. The mainstream corporation tax liability for 19X3 amounted to £95,000. The lower rate of income tax and corporation tax rate for both years is 20% and 33% respectively. It is assumed that all payments are made on the due dates.

The ACT relating to the previous year's final dividend is 25% of £400,000 = £100,000 and this amount will be included in the return of franked payments submitted by the company for the quarter ended 30 June 19X4. Similarly, the ACT relating to the interim dividend, being 25% of £300,000 = £75,000, will be included in the return of franked payments for the quarter ended 30 September 19X4. These amounts will have been paid on 14 July 19X4 and 14 October 19X4 respectively, being 14 days after the end of the quarter in which the relevant dividend was paid. The mainstream corporation tax liability payable on 30 September 19X5 is, therefore, calculated as follows:

	£'000	£'000
Corporation tax for the year ended 31 December 19X4, 33% of £1,000,000		330
Less: ACT on dividends paid in year ended 31 December 19X4*		
ACT on 19X3 proposed final dividend	100	
Act on 19X4 interim dividend	75	175
Mainstream corporation tax		155

* Maximum offset in year limited to 20% of £1,000,000 = £200,000

It should be noted that only the ACT on dividends paid during the year, whether in respect of the previous year or in respect of the current year, can be offset against the corporation tax liability of that year. There is also an overriding restriction on the use of ACT for set-off by reference to the taxable profits of that year (currently restricted to 20% of taxable profits).

The entries relating to taxation for the year ended 31 December 19X4, assuming no deferred tax account is maintained, are as follows:

Corporation tax payable

19X4		£'000	19X4		£'000
30 Sep	Cash	95	B/fwd	19X3 mainstream CT	95
31 Dec	ACT recoverable	175			
	Mainstream CT c/d	155	31 Dec	P&L account	330
		425			425
			19X5	Mainstream CT payable 30 September 19X5	155

ACT Payable

19X4		£'000	19X4		£'000
14 Jul	Cash	100	B/fwd	19X3 proposed final	100
14 Oct	Cash	75	15 Jul	19X4 interim	75
		175			175
			31 Dec	ACT recoverable re proposed final	125

ACT Recoverable

19X4		£'000	19X4		£'000
B/fwd	19X3 proposed final	100	31 Dec	Corporation tax payable	175
15 Jul	19X4 interim	75			
		175			175
31 Dec	ACT payable re proposed final	125			

The ACT relating to the final dividend for 19X4 cannot be set off against the corporation tax liability for the year ended 31 December 19X4. In the absence of a deferred tax account, it is carried forward as a deferred asset which would fall to be recoverable against the corporation tax liability for the year ended 31 December 19X5.

Irrecoverable ACT

13.28 Irrecoverable ACT is ACT paid or payable on outgoing dividends paid and proposed other than recoverable ACT. [SSAP 8 para 21]. Any irrecoverable ACT should be written off to the profit and loss account in the same period as the related dividend is shown. [SSAP 8 para 8]. If the ACT has previously been regarded as recoverable and has, therefore, been carried forward, it should be written off in the period that it is first considered to have become irrecoverable.

13.29 As with the presentation of ACT paid in the profit and loss account, there are two differing views on the presentation in the profit and loss account of irrecoverable ACT written off. SSAP 8 takes the view that irrecoverable ACT should be treated as part of the tax charge for the year, because unrelieved ACT constitutes tax upon the company or group, as opposed to tax on the shareholders and is not an appropriation of profits. SSAP 8, however, accepts that some readers or analysts may wish to treat irrecoverable ACT *"in some other manner"* and, therefore, requires separate disclosure of irrecoverable ACT. [SSAP 8 para 9]. In fact, the ASB's discussion paper indicates that some board members support the alternative view that irrecoverable ACT should be treated as part of the cost of the dividend. They argue that irrecoverable ACT is an incremental cost that arises directly as a result of paying a dividend, unlike recoverable ACT, the amount of which must be paid either as ACT or as mainstream corporation tax. The ASB has stated that it will consider whether this aspect of SSAP 8 should be amended in the light of comments received.

13.30 It should be noted that where unrelieved ACT has been written off in the profit and loss account, it still remains available for carry-forward for tax purposes. Such ACT may be recovered in a future period if the ACT on dividends paid in that period is less than the maximum offset permissible against profits arising in that period (currently 20 per cent of taxable profits). In that situation, the company may have a contingent asset. SSAP 18, paragraph 17, states that a material contingent gain should be disclosed in the financial statements only if it is probable that a gain will be realised. However, as stated in the above paragraph, SSAP 8 requires separate disclosure of irrecoverable ACT as part of the tax charge where the amount involved is material because some readers or analysts may wish to regard irrecoverable ACT as something other than tax on the company. It may, therefore, be appropriate to include a suitable note stating that ACT written off remains available for offset against future UK corporation tax liabilities. An example of such a note is given in Table 13.1 below.

13.31 Where unrelieved ACT has been written off, and is subsequently recovered in a later period, the ACT write back should be reported as a reduction of the current tax charge of that later period with suitable disclosure of the amounts involved. An example of such a write back is also given in Table 13.1 below.

Table 13.1 – Pilkington plc – Directors' Report and Accounts – 31 March 1995

Notes on the Financial Statements (extract)

12 Taxation	1995 £m	1994 £m
Profit and loss account		
The taxation charge in the Group profit and loss account comprises:		
United Kingdom corporation tax at 33% (1994 – 33%)	**4**	16
Less double taxation relief	**(4)**	(16)
	–	–
Overseas taxation	**23**	30
Deferred taxation	**(1)**	(3)
Advance corporation tax, previously written off, now written back	**(14)**	–
Irrecoverable advance corporation tax	**–**	2
	8	29
Under/(over) provision in respect of prior years	**20**	(3)
	28	26
Associated undertakings	**16**	6
....		
	44	32

United Kingdom corporation tax includes a taxation credit of £1 million in respect of exceptional items (1994 charge of £2 million) (note 7). The prior year's corporation tax charge arises from the shortfall of credits for overseas taxation.

	1995		1994 as restated	
	Group £m	**Company £m**	Group £m	Company £m
Balance sheets				
Assets (Notes 21 and 22)				
Debtors – amounts falling due within one year				
Advance corporation tax recoverable	**4**	**7**	–	–
Corporation tax recoverable	**4**	**–**	11	–
Overseas tax recoverable	**4**	**–**	1	1
	12	**7**	12	1
Debtors – amounts falling due after more than one year				
Advance corporation tax recoverable	**5**	**5**	–	–
Deferred taxation on post retirement healthcare	**57**	**–**	64	–
....				
	62	**5**	64	–
Liabilities (Note 24)				
United Kingdom corporation tax	**12**	**2**	1	–
United Kingdom advance corporation tax on dividends	**8**	**5**	2	–
Overseas taxation	**25**	**–**	27	–
....				
	45	**7**	30	–

No provision has been made for additional taxation which would arise on the distribution of profits retained by overseas subsidiary and associated undertakings.

At 31st March 1995 certain United Kingdom and overseas subsidiary undertakings had accumulated tax losses estimated at £348 million (1994 £331 million) which are available for offset against future taxable profits in those companies. Advance corporation tax written off to date amounts to £30 million (1994 £44 million) and is available for offset against future United Kingdom corporation tax liabilities. The future benefit of these losses and advance corporation tax has not been accounted for in the provision for deferred taxation (note 28).

The taxation charge on profits for deferred taxation calculated on a full liability basis would amount to £11 million (1994 £31 million).

Overseas taxation

13.32 A company resident in the UK is, in general, liable to corporation tax on all its profits, whether they arise in the UK or overseas. Because profits arising in overseas operations are normally subject to tax in the relevant overseas country, they may be subject to double taxation if they are also remitted to the UK company by way of dividends. Such dividends are neither franked investment income nor group income and, therefore, are also subject to corporation tax.

13.33 A UK resident company is usually able to obtain relief to mitigate the double tax charge. Relief for dividends from an overseas company is, in general, only available for foreign withholding tax levied directly on those dividends. In some situations, relief is also available for foreign 'underlying tax' (that is, tax on the company's profits out of which the dividends are paid). Often double tax agreements between the UK government and the overseas government provide that a UK resident company in receipt of foreign dividends is entitled to a tax credit for underlying tax if a specified percentage (usually ten per cent) of the voting control of the overseas company is held by the UK company. However, many treaties are silent on this point, in which case unilateral relief for underlying overseas tax is provided for in section 790 of the Taxes Act 1988. This is subject also to a requirement of ten per cent voting control of the paying company.

13.34 The double taxation relief is normally obtained by setting the overseas tax first against the gross corporation tax liability before ACT offset. It should be noted that when SSAP 8 was published, the reverse treatment applied; which meant that where the corporation tax (net of ACT) was less than foreign tax, the excess was lost since unused overseas tax cannot be carried forward. Therefore, the part of the standard dealing with overseas taxation is no longer relevant. Reference should, therefore, be made to TR 805.

13.35 In some circumstances, it is possible to obtain relief against UK corporation tax for the whole of the foreign tax payable. This arises where the rate of overseas tax is less than or at least equal to the rate of UK corporation tax. Where, however, the rate of overseas tax exceeds the rate of UK corporation tax, a proportion of the overseas tax can remained unrelieved. The amount of overseas tax unrelieved, unlike the irrecoverable ACT, cannot be carried forward and falls to be written off in the profit and loss account. This write off need not be disclosed separately as it is included within overseas taxation in the profit and loss account taxation charge. Consider the following example.

Example

A UK company has taxable profits of £1,000,000 generated in the UK and a further £450,000 generated overseas. The rate of overseas tax is 40%, whilst the rate of UK corporation tax is 33%.

The UK corporation tax payable on the whole of the company's profits is £478,500 (£1,450,000 @33%). The overseas tax payable is £180,000 (£450,000 @40%). As the UK corporation tax payable on overseas profits is £148,500 (£450,000 @33%) this is the maximum relief which is allowed against the overseas tax of £180,000. Therefore, the amount unrelieved is £31,500, which is £450,000 @7% and must be written off in the profit and loss account.

	£'000	£'000	£'000
	Total	UK	Foreign
Profits chargeable to UK corporation tax	1,450.0	1,000.0	450.0
Corporation tax @ 33%	478.5	330.0	148.5
Double tax relief	(148.5)	–	(148.5)
Corporation tax liability	330.0	330.0	–

The way in which this amount is effectively included as part of the tax charge for the year, following the presentation given in Appendix 1 to SSAP 8, is as follows:

	£
Corporation tax on profits at 33%	478,500
Less relief for overseas tax	(148,500)
	330,000
Overseas taxation	180,000
	510,000

The total tax charge of £510,000 is effectively made up of UK corporation tax payable on all the company's profits, that is, £478,500 plus the amount of unrelieved overseas tax of £31,500.

13.36 The fact that double taxation relief is normally obtained by setting the overseas tax first against the corporation tax liability may give rise to unrelieved ACT on dividends paid during the year. This is because there may be an inadequate corporation tax liability after double taxation relief to absorb the ACT paid. In practice, this situation is likely to arise in companies with significant overseas profits that have borne foreign tax at rates at least as high as the rate of UK corporation tax. Although ACT is set off by reference to amounts after double tax relief, the effective restriction to an amount equal to ACT on a distribution of the total profit must be calculated by reference to each source, that is, UK source and foreign source. This means that the amount of ACT which may be set off against the company's corporation tax liability in respect of foreign income from which double taxation relief has been deducted is limited to the lesser of:

- The ACT limit calculated as if that foreign income were the company's only income for the relevant accounting period. This means that currently only 20 per cent of the foreign income would qualify for set-off.

- The amount of corporation tax which, after deducting the foreign tax credit, the company is liable to pay in respect of that income. This is because the ACT set-off can never exceed the actual corporation tax paid.

[TR 805 para 2.9].

Consider the following example where surplus ACT arises as a result of the distribution of foreign income.

Example

A UK company earns profits of £700,000 overseas and a further £200,000 in the UK. The company pays a dividend of £500,000. The company paid overseas tax of £175,000 at the rate of 25%. The rate of UK corporation tax and ACT is 33% and 20% respectively.

The amount of ACT available for offset is calculated as follows:

	£'000 Total	£'000 UK	£'000 Foreign
Profits chargeable to UK corporation tax	900	200	700
Corporation tax @ 33%	297	66	231
Double tax relief	(175)	–	(175)
	122	66	56
(a) ACT available for offset: Distribution of £500,000 × 25% = £125,000			
(b) ACT set-off calculated: On UK profits: 20% × £200,000 = £40,000	(40)	(40)	
On Foreign income: 20% × £700,000 = £140,000, but restricted to corporation tax paid on foreign income after double tax relief = £56,000	(56)	–	(56)
Net corporation tax liability	26	26	Nil

Therefore, the ACT that can be set off against the corporation tax liability is £96,000. The balance of £29,000 (£125,000 – £96,000) is surplus ACT.

13.37 The above example demonstrates that companies with significant foreign income may have surplus ACT. Although this surplus ACT may be set off against either the corporation tax liability of the previous six years or the corporation tax liability of any future year, there is the possibility that the company cannot foresee recoverability of the surplus ACT in this way. This will happen in particular if the company is one that generates a significant amount of its profits overseas. In that situation, the surplus ACT falls to be written off as irrecoverable. Because many UK based multinationals depend on profits earned abroad to pay dividends to their shareholders, the Government introduced a Foreign Income Dividend (FID) scheme that is intended to relieve surplus ACT that arises as a result of the distribution of foreign income. FIDs are considered further from paragraph 13.192.

Franked investment income

13.38 If a company makes a qualifying distribution to another UK resident company, the company which receives the distribution is entitled to a tax credit, typically equal to the ACT accountable in respect of it. The distribution plus the tax credit in the hands of the recipient company is called franked investment income (FII). Where a UK group or consortium has elected to pay dividends within the group without ACT being paid, a dividend paid under the election is group income and it is not FII in the hands of the recipient company. Where the recipient company makes a qualifying distribution to its own shareholders, ACT is paid only on the excess of its franked payments over FII received in the same period.

13.39 SSAP 8 considers two methods of accounting for FII:

- to include in the profit and loss account the cash received or receivable (that is, the net income); or

- to include the total of the FII as income from investments and include an amount equal to the tax credit in the charge for taxation.

[SSAP 8 para 13].

13.40 The standard requires the second option on the basis that it allows recognition of the income both at the pre-tax stage and at the after-tax stage in a way which is consistent with other elements of profit. [SSAP 8 para 13].

Deferred tax

Introduction

13.41 In most countries, including the UK, profits disclosed in the company's financial statements form the basis for the computation of taxable profits on which the company's liability to tax is calculated. In practice, however, many governments introduce various incentives and disincentives in their fiscal policy for economic and social reasons. As a consequence, the taxable profits of a particular period often bear little relationship to the accounting profits disclosed in the financial statements. Deferred taxation was conceived and developed as a means of recognising the tax effects of the difference between accounting and taxable profit.

13.42 The differences between accounting and taxable profits can be analysed into two categories: permanent differences and timing differences. Permanent differences arise because certain types of income appearing in the financial statements are not taxable, whilst certain types of expenditure are not tax deductible. Timing differences, on the other hand, arise from items that are either taxable or tax deductible, but in periods different from those in which they are dealt with in the financial statements. Therefore, such items are included in the measurement of both accounting and taxable profits, but in different periods. These differences are said to 'originate' in one period and are capable of 'reversal' in one or more subsequent periods.

13.43 It follows from the nature of permanent and timing differences that, over time, cumulative taxable and accounting profits are the same, except for permanent differences. Because permanent differences are the inevitable result of the differences between accounting and tax rules and do not give rise to any accounting entries, they do not represent an accounting problem. They merely gives rise to effective tax charges that differ from the stated rate. However, the question arises as to whether and to what extent the tax effects of timing differences between accounting and taxable profits should be recognised in the financial statements.

13.44 Some take the view that as the obligation to pay tax arises when a company has taxable profits and not accounting profits and as the amount payable is usually unaffected by the accounting treatment of assets, liabilities, income and expenses, only the immediate liability to the tax authorities should be the amount recorded in the financial statements. This in effect involves no accounting for deferred tax and is called the flow-through method. Others believe that the liability recorded under the flow-through method is incomplete, because it fails to recognise all liabilities that are the consequences of accounting entries, and also because it fails to match tax expense with the profits giving rise to it. They argue that, under accrual accounting, it is necessary to recognise the tax effects of all taxable income and tax deductible expenses in the period in which those income and expenditure items are recognised themselves, and not in the period in which they form part of taxable profit. Such recognition gives rise to taxation that is deferred. Deferred taxation is, therefore, taxation which is attributable to timing differences.

13.45 Even if flow-through is rejected, there remain a number of ways in which the nature of deferred tax accounting can be seen. Some see it as a bridge between accounting and taxable profits, in other words that deferred tax is primarily a matter of allocating tax expense to periods (the profit and loss account view point). This leads to the deferral method. Others see deferred tax accounting as primarily a matter of ensuring that the resultant liability fits properly into the balance sheet framework (the balance sheet view point). The balance sheet approach, referred to as the 'liability method', is now accepted as being the conceptually sound basis for accounting for deferred tax.

13.46 There are two approaches to the liability method: full provision and partial provision. The deferral method and the two variations of the liability method are considered below. Before examining these methods, it is first necessary to consider in some detail the nature of timing differences.

Timing differences

13.47 Timing differences are defined in SSAP 15 as differences between profits or losses as computed for tax purposes and results as stated in financial statements, which arise from the inclusion of items of income and expenditure in tax computations in periods different from those in which they are included in the financial statements. Timing differences originate in one period and are capable of reversal in one or more subsequent periods. [SSAP 15 para 18].

13.48 It follows from the above definition that there are only two situations under which timing differences can arise, as illustrated below:

- An item of income or expenditure is included in accounting profit of the period, but recognised in taxable profit in later periods. For example, income receivable might be accrued in the financial statements in one year, but fall to be taxed in the subsequent year when received. Similarly, provisions might be made for restructuring costs in the financial statements in one period, but would qualify for tax deduction at some later period when the expenditure is incurred.

- An item of income or expenditure is included in taxable profit of the period, but recognised in accounting profit in later years. For example, income received in advance might be taxed in the period of receipt, but treated as earned in the financial statements in a later period. Similarly, development expenditure might be tax deductible in the year in which it is incurred, but capitalised and amortised over a period for financial reporting purposes.

13.49 A timing difference is said to 'originate' when a transaction is first reflected in the financial statements, but not yet in the tax computation (or vice versa). It is said to 'reverse' when in due course the transaction is reflected in the tax computation or the financial statements either wholly or partly as the case may be. It is not necessary for a timing difference to originate in the financial statements and reverse in the tax computation (or *vice versa*). A timing difference can also originate in the financial statements of one period and reverse in the financial statements of a subsequent period without ever having been reflected in the tax computations. An example is a general provision for bad debts made in one year, but written back as not required in the following year. Similarly, a transaction might be reflected in the tax computation of one period and reverse in the tax computation of a later period, without ever having been reflected in the financial statements, although such situations are rare.

13.50 Timing differences are sometimes categorised as short-term differences and other differences. A short-term timing difference is one that arises from the use of the receipts and payments basis for tax purposes and the accruals basis in financial statements. A short-term timing difference usually reverses in the accounting period following the one in which it originated (hence the name). A reversal of a short-term timing difference is often followed by replacement by a new, originating timing difference. A typical example of a short-term timing difference is interest payable which is accrued in the financial statements, but allowed for tax purposes when paid. The reversal of the accrued interest in the year of payment for tax purposes is often replaced by a new accrual in the financial statements. The appendix to SSAP 15 provides the following list of timing differences:

- Interest receivable accrued in the accounting period, but taxed when received.
- Dividends from foreign subsidiaries accrued in a period prior to that in which they arise for tax purposes.
- Intra-group profits in stock deferred upon consolidation until realisation to third parties.
- Interest or royalties payable accrued in the accounting period, but allowed when paid.
- Pension costs accrued in the financial statements, but allowed for tax purposes when paid or contributed at some later date.
- Provisions for repairs and maintenance made in the financial statements, but not allowed for tax purposes until the expenditure is incurred.
- Bad debt provisions not allowed for tax purposes unless and until they become 'specific'.
- Provisions for revenue losses on closing down plants or for costs of reorganisation upon which tax relief is not obtained until the costs or losses are incurred.
- Revenue expenditure deferred in the financial statements, such as development or advertising, if it is allowed for tax purposes as it is incurred.

[SSAP 15 app].

A number of the timing differences in the above list would be short-term timing differences depending upon the particular circumstances.

13.51 In addition to short-term timing differences, there are other timing differences which do not reverse within a year of their origination. These timing difference are quite specific and can relate to a number of different transactions that are recognised in the financial statements on a basis different from that on which they are treated for tax purposes. A classic example is the difference between the carrying value of an asset in the financial statements and its tax base for tax purposes. In the UK, tax relief in respect of capital expenditure on plant and machinery is given by means of capital allowances that are a form of standardised tax depreciation. Since capital allowances are deducted from accounting profit to arrive at taxable profit, the amount of depreciation charged in the financial statements is always disallowed in the tax computation. Although depreciation for taxation and accounting purposes will be the same over the life of the asset, they will differ from year to year, thus giving rise to timing differences. Usually the capital allowances depreciate the asset at a faster rate for tax purposes than the rate of depreciation charged in the financial statements, and the timing differences created are often referred to as 'accelerated capital allowances'. The following example illustrates the creation of the timing differences:

Example

A company purchases a machine in 19X1 for £100,000. The asset is expected to be sold at the end of its useful life of five years for £10,000. Depreciation is charged on a straight line basis for accounting purposes and amounts to £18,000 ((£100,000 – £10,000)/5) per annum. The rate of capital allowances is 25% per annum on a reducing balance basis.

The timing difference will arise as follows:

	19X1 £'000	19X2 £'000	19X3 £'000	19X4 £'000	19X5 £'000
Per Financial statements					
Carrying value of asset	100	82	64	46	28
Depreciation charge	18	18	18	18	18
Book written down value	82	64	46	28	10
Per tax computation					
Carrying value of asset	100	75	56	42	32
Capital allowance	25	19	14	10	8
Tax written down value	75	56	42	32	24
Timing difference					
Capital allowance allowed	25	19	14	10	8
Depreciation charged	18	18	18	18	18
Originating (reversing)	7	1	(4)	(8)	(10)
Cumulative	7	8	4	(4)	(14)

The table shows that a timing difference of £7,000 originates in the first year, but this gradually reverses from year three onwards. Over the useful life of the asset depreciation charged exceeds capital allowances by £14,000. For the first two years, capital allowances exceed depreciation and, hence, the tax assessed and provided in the profit and loss account as current tax payable is less than the tax that would eventually become payable on the profit reported in the financial statements. This early benefit of lower taxation gradually reverses from year three onwards when capital allowances have fallen below depreciation. In those years, the tax assessed and, hence, provided in the profit and loss account as current tax is higher than the amount due on the profit reported in the financial statements. The cumulative timing difference at the end of 19X5 of £14,000 will either gradually reverse from 19X6 onwards if the asset is included in the pool for capital allowance purposes, or it will give rise to a balancing allowance if the asset is sold in 19X6 for £10,000.

13.52 Timing differences can be viewed in two ways, either in terms of the differences arising in a particular year or on a cumulative basis. As can be seen from the above table, the individual timing difference (originating or reversing) arising in each year is the difference between the capital allowances claimed and the depreciation charged, whilst the cumulative timing difference at the end of each year is the difference between the asset's book written down value and its tax written down value.

13.53 In addition to accelerated capital allowances, there are also other timing differences that often arise in practice. Revaluation of assets is a good example. When an asset is revalued above cost and the revaluation is incorporated in the financial statements, a timing difference potentially arises in that, in the absence of rollover relief, tax on the chargeable gain may be payable if and when the asset is sold at the revalued amount. Accounting for some specific timing differences, including revaluation of fixed assets, is considered later in this chapter.

Method of computation

13.54 The calculation of timing differences is the first step towards the calculation of deferred taxation. As stated in paragraph 13.45 above, there are essentially two different methods of computing deferred taxation. The first method is the deferral method which takes a profit and loss account viewpoint. The other method is the liability method which takes the balance sheet view.

Deferral method

13.55 The deferral method, as the name implies, is based on the premise that the tax effects of originating timing differences are simply deferred and recognised as income or expense in the future period in which the timing differences reverse. Under this method, deferred tax on the timing differences originating in the period is provided using the current rate. The resulting deferred tax balance in the balance sheet represents a benefit in the form of temporary tax savings (deferred tax credit).

When the timing differences reverse, the 'cost' is merely the amount of the earlier benefit and, therefore, the amount taken out of the deferred tax account is measured using the tax rates applied when the timing differences originated. It follows that the deferred taxation account (representing tax on the originating timing differences at the rate in force for the year in which those differences arose) remains unchanged, despite subsequent changes in tax rates, and that reversals take place at that same original rate. Thus the tax charge or credit for the period relates solely to that period and is not distorted by any adjustments relating to prior periods. The deferral method, therefore, looks at deferred tax balances as deferred credits or charges and not as tax balances payable (deferred tax liability) or recoverable (deferred tax asset). At any point in time, the balance on the deferred tax account represents the sum of the tax savings that have been obtained on originating timing differences which have not been wholly reversed. The mechanics of the method are illustrated in the following example:

Example

A company prepares its financial statements to 31 December each year. The company makes an annual profit of £100,000 and incurs the following capital expenditure.

Machine purchased on 1 January 19X1: Cost £100,000, residual value £nil, life 5 years.
Machine purchased on 1 January 19X3: Cost £230,000, residual value £20,000, life 7 years.

Depreciation is charged on a straight line basis and amounts to £20,000 for the first machine and £30,000 for the second machine. The rate of capital allowances is 25% per annum on a reducing balance basis. The rate of corporation tax for 19X1 and 19X2 is 50% and falls to 30% in 19X3 and remains at that level.

The calculation of the deferred tax charge and the balances arising are shown in the table below.

	19X1	19X2	19X3	19X4	19X5
	£	£	£	£	£
Per financial statements					
Carrying value b/f	–	80,000	60,000	240,000	190,000
Addition	100,000	–	230,000	–	–
Depreciation	(20,000)	(20,000)	(50,000)	(50,000)	(50,000)
Carrying value c/f	80,000	60,000	240,000	190,000	140,000
Per tax computation					
Pool b/f	–	75,000	56,250	214,687	161,015
Addition	100,000	–	230,000	–	–
Capital allowances	(25,000)	(18,750)	(71,563)	(53,672)	(40,254)
Pool c/f	75,000	56,250	214,687	161,015	120,761

Timing differences					
Capital allowances allowed	25,000	18,750	71,563	53,672	40,254
Depreciation charged	(20,000)	(20,000)	(50,000)	(50,000)	(50,000)
Originating (reversing)	5,000	(1,250)	21,563	3,672	(9,746)
Cumulative	5,000	3,750	25,313	28,985	19,239
Accounting Profit	100,000	100,000	100,000	100,000	100,000
Taxable profit	95,000	101,250	78,437	96,328	109,746
Rate of corporation tax	50%	50%	30%	30%	30%
Tax charge in P&L account					
Current tax on taxable profit	47,500	50,625	23,531	28,898	32,924
Deferred tax on timing difference	2,500	(625)	6,469	1,102	(2,924)
Total tax charge	50,000	50,000	30,000	30,000	30,000
Deferred tax balances	2,500	1,875	8,344	9,446	6,522

It is evident from the above table that deferred tax has the effect of smoothing the tax charge for the year. Under the deferral method, deferred tax is provided on timing difference in each period using the tax rate ruling in that period. In 19X3 when the tax rate falls to 30%, deferred tax on timing differences that originate in the year is provided at the same rate. As a result, the deferred tax balance at the end of year three comprises the tax effects of timing differences calculated at 50% and 30%, that is, the deferred tax balance of £8,344 at the end of 19X3 is the aggregate of £1,875 (being £3,750 @ 50%) and £6,469 (being £21,563 @ 30%), The balance represents a total tax saving to date and has no meaning in terms of tax payable.

13.56 Supporters of the deferral method argue that it is the best method of accounting for deferred tax as it meets the objective of matching tax expense with the related income and expenses in the period in which the income and expenses are recognised in determining accounting profit. They argue that the deferred tax balance, which remains unaffected by changes in tax rates in the years between origination and reversal, is simply a consequence of matching and does not seek to quantify a liability or an asset that would eventually be payable or recoverable. The method can be viewed as 'tax equalisation' whose purpose is to preserve the relationship between pre- and post-tax profit by ensuring that reported profits are matched with the appropriate amount of tax expense as indicated in the above example.

Liability method

13.57 Notwithstanding its origin as a means of matching income and expenditure with their tax effects, critics of the deferral method argue that the method is deficient in that it produces balance sheet figures that are meaningless when tax rates change. They view deferred tax as an asset or a liability. In their view, a deferred tax liability relating to an asset represents an obligation to refund a temporary cash flow advantage obtained by claiming capital allowances on that asset. Therefore, the tax effects of accelerated capital allowances should be reported as liabilities for taxes. Similarly, a deferred tax asset relating to a liability, for example pension costs, represents tax relief that is expected to be received when the pension liability is settled, Therefore, the tax effects of timing differences relating to pension costs should be reported as assets representing future tax recoverable.

13.58 However, this traditional view of deferred tax is not universally shared. Some see deferred tax as a 'valuation adjustment', reflecting an enhancement or impairment to the value of the entity's other assets or liabilities arising from its tax position. In their view, for example, an asset which is not tax deductible is worth less than an identical one which is. This fact should be recognised by providing for the deferred tax liability, which would allow future profit after tax to be smoothed. Under this approach, tax is provided on all 'temporary differences', including timing differences and other temporary differences between future accounting and taxable profit. Examples of other temporary differences include, for example, amortisation of an asset that is not tax deductible, release of deferred income in respect of a non-taxable government grant, fair value adjustments and revaluation of an asset irrespective of whether it is to be sold, which under the traditional approach described in paragraph 13.57 are normally regarded as a permanent differences and not generally reflected in the deferred tax computation in the UK. This approach is similar to that followed in the US under FAS 109 and IAS 12 (revised) with some exceptions. It is also discussed in the ASB discussion paper and is favoured by some board members. Nevertheless, current practice in the UK is based on the liability view, on timing differences and not on temporary differences and the valuation adjustment view.

Liability method with full provisioning

13.59 The objective of the liability method is to recognise the expected tax effects of timing differences either as liabilities for taxes payable in the future or as assets recoverable in the future. Under this method, deferred tax on the timing differences originating in the period is provided using the rate of tax expected to apply when the asset is recovered or the liability is settled. Since the rate at which the timing difference will reverse is not normally known, the current rate of tax is taken as the best approximation to the rate that will apply in the future. This means that the deferred taxation account is always maintained at the current rate of tax and the movement in the balance sheet amounts is reflected as a deferred tax charge or credit in the profit and loss account. It follows that whenever there is a change in the rate of tax, the balance on the deferred taxation account is adjusted to that current rate with the result that the charge for deferred tax in the profit and loss account will include the effects of any such change in rate, which is applied to the opening balance of cumulative timing differences.

13.60 The way in which deferred taxation is calculated under the liability method and how it differs from the deferral method is illustrated below.

Example

Facts are the same as in the previous example

	19X1	19X2	19X3	19X4	19X5
Liability method					
Timing difference	£	£	£	£	£
Book written down value	80,000	60,000	240,000	190,000	140,000
Tax written down value	75,000	56,250	214,687	161,015	120,761
Cumulative originating (reversing)	5,000	3,750	25,313	28,985	19,239
Rate of corporation tax	50%	50%	30%	30%	30%
Deferred tax balances					
Tax on opening cumulative difference	–	2,500	1,875	7,594	8,696
Tax on closing cumulative difference	2,500	1,875	7,594	8,696	5,772
Tax provided (released)	2,500	(625)	5,719	1,102	(2,924)
Deferred tax charge					
Deferral method	2,500	(625)	6,469	1,102	(2,924)
Liability method	2,500	(625)	5,719	1,102	(2,924)
Adjustment for change in tax rates	–	–	(750)	–	–
Deferred tax balances					
Deferral method	2,500	1,875	8,344	9,446	6,522
Liability method	2,500	1,875	7,594	8,696	5,772
Adjustment for change in tax rates	–	–	750	750	750

In 19X1, the deferred tax charge is the same as that calculated under the deferral method. In 19X2, the deferred tax charge is arriving at by comparing the tax on the closing cumulative timing difference with the tax on the opening cumulative timing difference. This also is the same as the deferral method. However, in 19X3, when the tax rate changes from 50% to 30%, a further adjustment of £750 is necessary under the liability method. The adjustment is simply due to the effect of the change in rate on the opening balance of cumulative timing difference of £3,750 × (50% – 30%) = £750, which is reflected in the tax charge under the liability method, but ignored under the deferral method. The effect of this adjustment is to ensure that deferred tax liability or asset in the balance sheet is always maintained at the current rate as indicated in the table above.

13.61 It is also evident from the above table that the deferred tax liability at the end of 19X5 amounting to £5,772 comprises tax on the whole of the cumulative timing difference of £19,239 at 30 per cent that would crystallise when the timing difference reverses. This basis of providing in full for deferred tax on all timing differences is referred to as 'full provision' or 'comprehensive allocation'.

13.62 The profile of timing differences in the above example also indicates that in years 19X1, 19X3 and 19X4 originating timing differences exceed reversing timing differences, thus leading to an increase in the deferred tax liability for that year. It follows that whenever new timing differences originating in later periods more than offset the effect of timing differences reversing in those periods, the balance on the deferred tax account will keep on increasing. This may lead to the accumulation of large liabilities since their settlement is indefinitely postponed. This is particularly true in times of high inflation or under a tax system offering tax reliefs in the form of high capital investment allowances.

13.63 Critics of the full provision method argue that although the method is reasonably straightforward, it may lead to the creation of an excessively prudent provision for deferred tax liabilities where there is only a remote possibility of those liabilities ever crystallising. This could lead to an understatement of profits and capital employed. It could also affect the company's ability to raise finance, because of limitations on borrowing powers (where computed by reference to capital and reserves) due to the understatement of reserves and apparent high gearing.

Liability method with partial provisioning

13.64 The partial provision approach attempts to overcome the above concerns by requiring that the provision for deferred tax, whilst still on the liability method, should be made on the basis of the expected amount of the deferred tax liability that would actually become payable in the future. Under this approach, the full amount of the deferred tax liability, in terms of the total cumulative timing differences at a point in time, is first calculated as before, but only a proportion is provided to the extent that tax is likely to be actually paid or tax relief received. In order to determine the extent to which those timing differences will reverse, and a tax liability or asset will thus crystallise, it is necessary to forecast the likely future pattern of new originating timing differences. The practical effect is that any company that does not significantly reduce its scale of operations will have a proportion of timing differences that can be viewed as non-reversing ('hard core').

13.65 Although the individual timing differences making up the hard core at any time reverse, they are simultaneously replaced by new originating timing differences with the result that the deferred tax balance (considered as a whole) is not reduced. This 'hard core' of timing differences, therefore, has the effect of permanently deferring the payment of tax (or receipt of tax). On this basis, deferred tax is not provided on hard core timing differences, but only where it is probable that tax will become payable as a result of the reversal of timing differences. The essence of the partial provision method, therefore, is to provide for the tax effects of timing differences to the extent that is probable that a liability or asset will crystallise and not to provide to the extent that it is probable that a liability or asset will not crystallise.

13.66 The way in which deferred tax is calculated under the partial provision approach is illustrated in the following example.

Example

A company commences trading on 1 January 19X1. It incurs capital expenditure of £80,000 during its first financial year ended 31 December 19X1. The capital expenditures planned for the next three years are £100,000 in 19X2; £110,000 in 19X3 and £170,000 in 19X4. All assets are fully depreciated on a straight line basis over 5 years. Capital allowances of 25% are claimed every year. The rate of corporation tax is expected to remain constant at 33%.

A timing difference relating to accelerated capital allowances of £4,000 arises in 19X1. Therefore, on a full provision basis, deferred tax of £4,000 @ 33% = £1,320 would be provided. However, in order to assess the size of the deferred tax provision at 31 December 19X1, it is necessary to consider, based on future projections, the extent to which the originating timing difference of £4,000 will reverse. The timing differences arising in each of the next three years are given below.

	19X1	19X2	19X3	19X4
Per financial statements	£	£	£	£
Opening balance	–	64,000	128,000	180,000
Additions	80,000	100,000	110,000	170,000
Depreciation @ 20%	(16,000)	(36,000)	(58,000)	(92,000)
Closing balance	64,000	128,000	180,000	258,000
Per tax computation				
Opening balance	–	60,000	120,000	172,500
Additions	80,000	100,000	110,000	170,000
Capital allowances @ 25%	(20,000)	(40,000)	(57,500)	(85,625)
Closing balance	60,000	120,000	172,500	256,875
Timing difference				
Capital allowances	20,000	40,000	57,500	85,625
Depreciation	16,000	36,000	58,000	92,000
Originating (reversing)	4,000	4,000	(500)	(6,375)
Cumulative	4,000	8,000	7,500	1,125

It is evident from the above table that the originating timing difference of £4,000 falls to £1,125 in 19X4, indicating that during this period there is likely to be a net reversal of £4,000 – £1,250 = £2,750 based on future capital expenditure plans. Therefore, under the partial provision approach, the company would provide deferred tax on this amount, that is, £2,750 @ 33% = £908.

It should be noted that a net reversal arises when the cumulative timing differences in any year fall below the current level of £4,000. If the pattern of timing difference were such that the cumulative timing differences in any year are at a level higher than the current level then no deferred tax would be provided under the partial provision approach. If the pattern of cumulative timing differences in 19X5 and beyond falls to below zero, then the whole of the potential liability would be provided.

Standardisation of deferred tax accounting

13.67 The ASC made its first attempt at a standard method of accounting for deferred tax in the UK when it issued ED 11 in May 1973. ED 11 proposed that companies should account for deferred tax on all material timing differences using the deferral method. Many commentators objected to the use of the deferral method, so when the ensuing standard SSAP 11 was issued in 1975, it permitted companies to use either the deferral method or the liability method.

13.68 SSAP 11 came under heavy criticism because the requirement for comprehensive tax allocation was considered to be incompatible with the economic and fiscal climate at that time. In the 1970s, inflation in the UK was at a very high level. Capital allowances and stock appreciation reliefs were available which allowed companies to deduct for tax purposes the full cost of most plant, machinery and industrial buildings and the inflationary increases in the carrying amount of stock. The continuation of inflation coupled with high tax reliefs had the effect of establishing large deferred tax provisions in many companies. In some companies the deferred tax provisions exceeded shareholders' funds. Furthermore, the effect of these high deductions meant that companies could postpone payment of some or all of their deferred tax indefinitely and actually paid tax at well below the enacted rate (50-52 per cent), in some cases paying no tax apart from ACT on dividends.

13.69 The ASC responded to the criticism by publishing ED 19 in May 1977, which adopted a very different approach from SSAP 11. The method of comprehensive tax allocation requiring provision for deferred tax on all timing differences was replaced by a pragmatic system of partial tax allocation. The ASC recognised that not all timing differences would reverse in the foreseeable future, so it allowed companies not to provide for the tax effects of timing differences if the directors could demonstrate with reasonable probability that the tax effects of the timing differences would not reverse in the future.

13.70 SSAP 15, issued in October 1978 followed the ED 19 approach, but more specific criteria were laid down to justify the non-provision of deferred tax. In particular, a company had to be a going concern and the directors had to demonstrate, on the basis of reasonable evidence, that no liability was likely to arise as a result of reversal of timing differences for some considerable period (at least three years); and there was no indication that reversals were likely after that period. The standard required, however, that the full liability should be disclosed in the financial statements. The standard became effective for accounting periods beginning on or after 1 January 1979.

13.71 In 1982, the ASC set up a working party to review SSAP 15 so as to incorporate the new legal requirements of the Companies Act 1981 and to take account of the change in the basis of stock relief in the Finance Act 1981. The Finance Act 1981 prescribed a new method of calculating stock relief, which made the relief effectively permanent until it was finally abolished by the Finance Act 1984. The revision also took account of comments made as a result of experience with SSAP 15. In particular, it was recognised that the original standard had introduced an unwarranted bias in that a company that wished to leave some or all of the liability unprovided had to provide the necessary evidence, but a company that wished to provide the whole potential liability did not need to provide any justification. As a consequence, the revised standard stipulates that deferred tax should be provided to the extent that it is probable that a liability or asset will crystallise, but not to the extent that it is probable that a liability or asset will not crystallise. For this purpose, there is no longer a need to consider a period of three years for which positive evidence is required when considering any potential reversal of timing differences. Furthermore, all timing differences are to be considered jointly when considering the need to provide deferred tax, thus removing the distinction between short-term and other timing differences.

13.72 On the above basis, the ASC issued ED 33 in 1983. A revised version of SSAP 15 was finally issued in May 1985 which was similar to ED 33, but which clarified a number of other minor aspects that had caused difficulties in practice. The requirements of SSAP 15 (revised), which became effective in respect of accounting periods beginning on or after 1 April 1985, are discussed in detail below. References included in this chapter are to this revised version.

SSAP 15

General principles

13.73 The standard is particularly concerned with deferred corporation tax and income tax in the UK and in the Republic of Ireland and, insofar as the principles are similar, with overseas taxes on profits payable by UK and Irish enterprises or their subsidiaries. A number of other taxes, such as VAT, petroleum revenue tax and some overseas taxes, which are not assessed directly on profits for an accounting period, are not addressed specifically in the statement. For the taxes covered by the standard, enterprises should follow the general principles of SSAP 15, which are stated below:

- Deferred tax should be computed using the liability method. [SSAP 15 para 24].
- Tax deferred or accelerated by the effect of timing differences should be accounted for to the extent that it is probable that a liability or asset will crystallise. [SSAP 15 para 25].
- Tax deferred or accelerated by the effect of timing differences should not be accounted for to the extent that it is probable that a liability or asset will not crystallise. [SSAP 15 para 26].
- The combined effect of timing differences should be considered when attempting to assess whether a tax liability will crystallise, rather than looking at each timing difference separately. [SSAP 15 app para 4].
- The provision for deferred tax liabilities should be reduced by any deferred tax debit balances arising from separate categories of timing differences and any advance corporation tax which is available for offset against those liabilities. [SSAP 15 para 29].

13.74 The above principles are, therefore, consistent with the partial provision approach discussed in paragraphs 13.64 and 13.65 above. Under the partial provision approach, deferred tax should be accounted for in respect of the net amount by which it is probable that any payment of tax will be temporarily deferred or accelerated by the operation of timing differences which will reverse in the foreseeable future without being replaced. [SSAP 15 para 12].

13.75 The principles are also consistent with the requirement in SSAP 18, 'Accounting for contingencies', to accrue a material contingent loss where it is probable that a future event will confirm a loss which can be estimated with reasonable accuracy at the date on which the financial statements are approved by the board of directors. [SSAP 18 para 15]. This is based on legal advice obtained by the ASC to the effect that unprovided deferred tax is a contingent liability, except where the prospect of it becoming payable is so remote that it does not amount to a contingent liability at all. [SSAP 15 para 53]. It also accords with the requirements of Schedule 4 to account for any amount retained as reasonably necessary for the purpose of providing for any liability or loss which is either likely to be incurred, or certain to be incurred, but uncertain as to amount or as to date on which it will arise. [4 Sch 89].

Future projections

13.76 As explained in paragraph 13.64 above, the essence of the partial provision approach is to determine the extent to which timing differences at the balance sheet date will reverse in future and a tax liability or asset will thus crystallise. Clearly, a considerable degree of judgement is required in making this assessment. The standard, therefore, states that the assessment of whether deferred tax liabilities or assets will or will not crystallise should be based upon reasonable assumptions. [SSAP 15 para 27]. The assumptions should take into account all relevant information available up to the date on which the financial statements are approved by the board of directors and should also take into account the management's intentions. [SSAP 15 para 28].

13.77 Typically, evidence in support of the assumptions underlying the assessment will comprise future plans in the form of budgets or projections. The projections should be prepared in a sufficient degree of detail and cover a period of years necessary to establish a likely pattern of future tax liabilities (and hence enable the directors to determine the likely deferred tax liability). Although the original standard suggested a period of three years as a minimum period that should be covered by the projections, the revised standard rightly leaves that choice to the company in the light of its own particular circumstances. However, the appendix to the standard suggests a relatively short period of three to five years where the pattern of timing differences is expected to be regular. It may need to be longer for an enterprise with an irregular pattern of timing differences. [SSAP 15 app para 4]. Clearly the further an assessment goes into the future the more likely it is that the projections would be susceptible to a high degree of uncertainty. In practice, therefore, it is likely that projections will cover a period not exceeding three to five years. The important point to note is whether the projections reveal a pattern of originating or reversing timing differences arising from the overall expansion or contraction of the business and whether capital expenditure has a cyclical nature.

13.78 In assessing the reasonableness of assumptions underlying the deferred tax computations, the financial plans and other information on which they are based should be realistic and reliable. This is rather obvious and may require comparison of the future pattern of timing differences against the past pattern of timing differences and whether forecasts made in the past have proved to be reliable. It is also necessary for management to carry out a regular review and revision of financial plans in the light of any changed circumstances and the availability of new information. For example, in assessing whether timing differences in respect of accelerated capital allowances will reverse, it is necessary to consider such factors as revision of asset lives, provision for permanent diminutions in value of existing assets and whether assets will be surplus to requirements following a decision to close down a particular part of the business. It is also necessary to ensure that adequate resources are available to finance any planned expansion built into the projections. This may entail reviewing the plans against the latest cash flow projections.

Short-term timing differences

13.79 Before SSAP 15 was revised in May 1985, it required deferred tax to be provided on all short-term timing differences, such as interest accruals and short-term provisions. However, the revised standard recognised that not all short-term differences led to the crystallisation of a liability when they reversed. The revised standard now requires that all types of timing difference should be considered together when attempting to assess whether a tax liability will crystallise. [SSAP 15 para 6]. It is the overall pattern of timing differences that is important and, therefore, the distinction between short-term or long-term nature of individual components in isolation is irrelevant to the assessment.

Deferred tax debit balances

13.80 Under SSAP 15, the basic rule for recognising a deferred tax asset is no different from that relating to the recognition of a deferred tax liability. This is that a deferred tax asset should be recognised to the extent that it is probable that an asset will crystallise. [SSAP 15 para 26]. Crystallisation of an asset means that it should be capable of recovery *without replacement by equivalent debit balances*. In other words, there must be sufficient evidence that a future inflow of benefits will actually occur and not simply be rolled over. If replacement were to occur, the realisation of the tax benefit would be permanently deferred. The principle of non- recognition of an asset when there is a replacement is, therefore, complementary to the principle of non-provision for liabilities that never crystallise. Accordingly, deferred tax net debit balances should not be carried forward as assets, except to the extent that they are expected to be recoverable without replacement by equivalent debit balances. [SSAP 15 para 30].

13.81 Many items give rise to deferred tax debit balances. Typical among these are timing differences arising on provisions, tax losses and capitalisation of finance leases. These situations are considered in the paragraphs that follow.

Combining timing differences

13.82 A company is likely to have a mixture of timing differences, some giving rise to deferred tax liabilities and some giving rise to deferred tax assets. As stated in paragraph 13.79 above, it is necessary to look at timing differences in aggregate, rather than individually, when considering to what extent deferred tax on the net timing differences should be provided for. This means that it is permissible to net off timing differences giving rise to debit balances against those giving rise to credit balances and *vice versa*.

13.83 To the extent that deferred tax provisions exceed deferred tax assets, the standard states that the provision for deferred tax liabilities should be reduced by any deferred tax debit balances arising from separate categories of timing differences and any advance corporation tax which is available for offset against those liabilities. [SSAP 15 para 29]. Similarly, the standard permits net deferred tax assets to be carried forward subject to the rules discussed in paragraph 13.80 above. This is because deferred tax assets and liabilities are both elements of any aggregate deferred tax balance and are not separate items which cannot be offset under paragraph 5 of Schedule 4. [SSAP 15 para 51]. However, such offset should only apply where they are capable of offset for tax purposes. The following example demonstrates the effect of combining timing differences.

Example

A company is preparing its financial statements at the end of 19X1 and the projection of cumulative timing differences is as follows:

	19X1	19X2	19X3	19X4	19X5
	£'000	£'000	£'000	£'000	£'000
Accelerated capital allowances	800	720	680	630	700
Other timing differences	(300)	(340)	(380)	(400)	(400)
Net timing difference	500	380	300	230	300

It is evident from the above profile of timing differences that the net cumulative timing difference is lowest in year 19X4, indicating that the amount of net reversal of timing differences over this period since 19X1 is £270,000 (£500,000 – £230,000). Therefore, under the standard, the company would set up a deferred tax provision in 19X1 of £270,000 @ 33% = £89,100. If, say, the cumulative timing difference in year 19X4 falls below zero, the whole of the potential liability, that is, £500,000 @ 33% = £165,000 would be provided.

Similarly, where the net reversing timing difference leads to the creation of a net deferred tax asset then, as discussed in paragraph 13.80 above, the net deferred tax asset should be recognised if it falls to be recoverable without replacement by equivalent debit balances.

13.84 The above example demonstrates that it is appropriate to consider all timing differences in aggregate when attempting to assess whether a tax liability or asset will crystallise. However, if the profile of other timing differences in the example above is viewed in isolation, it appears that the deferred tax debit balance will not crystallise, because recovery of the tax is continually deferred. In that situation, the question arises as to whether it should be ignored and deferred tax provided only on accelerated capital allowances. The Accountants Digest No 174, 'A Guide to Accounting Standards – Deferred tax', takes the view that timing differences which give rise to debit balances may not be used to offset other timing differences if they are expected to be perpetuated. Paragraph 7.8 of the Digest states:

"It is important to note that, just as deferred tax liabilities should not be created unless it is probable that a liability will crystallise, so deferred tax liabilities should not be reduced by deferred tax debit balances which will not crystallise because recovery of the tax is continually deferred. For example, deferred tax liabilities should not be reduced by deferred tax debit balances arising from timing differences on recurring general bad debt provision."

13.85 The above view, albeit prudent and logical, appears to be at odds with the standard which requires that the combined effect of *all* timing differences should be considered when providing for deferred tax. In practice, most companies tend to follow the aggregation rule. An example where deferred tax liabilities have been offset against deferred tax assets is given in Table 13.12 on page 64. Obviously, the problem will disappear altogether if the ASB moves towards full provisioning for deferred tax.

ACT recoverable

13.86 The rules relating to the treatment of recoverable ACT under SSAP 8 are considered in paragraphs 13.21 to 13.26 above. SSAP 15 also contains rules relating to the treatment of recoverable ACT that is carried forward as an asset, but these rules are somewhat different from those dealt with in SSAP 8. Unlike SSAP 8, which deals with ACT on dividends paid and proposed on the same basis, the rules in SSAP 15 for ACT on dividends payable or proposed at the balance sheet date are different from those arising on dividends paid by the balance sheet date. These are:

Dividends payable or proposed at the balance sheet date

- Debit balances arising in respect of advance corporation tax on dividends payable or proposed at the balance sheet date should be carried forward to the extent that it is foreseen that sufficient corporation tax will be assessed on the profits or income of the succeeding accounting period, against which advance corporation tax is available for offset. [SSAP 15 para 31].

Dividends already paid by the balance sheet date

- Debit balances arising in respect of advance corporation tax other than on dividends payable or proposed at the balance sheet date should be written off unless their recovery is assured beyond reasonable doubt. Such recovery will normally be assured only where the debit balances are recoverable out of the corporation tax arising on the profits or income of the succeeding accounting period, *without replacement by equivalent debit balances*. [SSAP 15 para 32].

13.87 SSAP 8, on the other hand, states that where there is no deferred tax account, ACT on dividends paid or proposed can be carried forward as an asset if it is *"expected to be recoverable taking into account expected profits and dividends – normally those of the next accounting period only"*. It would, therefore, appear that when considering the recoverability of ACT on dividends paid by the balance sheet date, SSAP 8 does not rule out the possibility of taking a slightly longer view. On the other hand, it is clear from the SSAP 15 rule that in evaluating recoverability for financial reporting purposes, regard should be paid only to the succeeding accounting period, a point which is reinforced by the use of the key phrase *"without replacement by equivalent debit balances"*.

13.88 Although it is accepted that ACT is a prepayment of tax and not a timing difference, in our view if ACT on dividends paid in the period cannot be recovered out of the corporation tax liability of the next accounting period, it should be written off, as part of the tax charge for the year, as irrecoverable ACT on the grounds of prudence. The Accountants Digest also takes a similar view which is given below:

> *"If ACT cannot be recovered out of the current mainstream corporation tax liability because taxable profits are insufficient to absorb full ACT set off, then it will only be recoverable out of the future mainstream corporation tax if profits increase or if dividend policy becomes more modest. In general, it is not considered prudent to assume that things will get better in the future although it may be reasonable to assume that things will not get much worse. Accordingly where the recovery of ACT relies on a future improvement in fortunes, such an improvement should not be assumed and the ACT should be written off, in the tax charge for the year, as irrecoverable."*

13.89 Therefore, too much significance should not be attached to the word *"normally"* as used in SSAP 8. In this context, it should be noted that SSAP 8 was not revised at the same time as SSAP 15 and its provisions regarding ACT do not include the key phrase as stated above. However, appendix 3 to SSAP 8, which deals with the application of SSAP 8 in the Republic of Ireland and was revised in 1988, does contain a statement that the approach to be adopted to recoverable ACT should be consistent with SSAP 15 (revised), and quotes the two paragraphs set out in paragraph 13.86 above.

13.90 It should be noted that ACT relating to dividends payable or proposed at the balance sheet date is permitted to be carried forward even where it is to be replaced by equivalent debit balances. The less stringent rule for ACT on dividends payable and proposed is because the first possible set off is against the following year's tax liability as the related ACT will be paid in that year. In the event that the following year's tax liability is insufficient to absorb the ACT, then the more stringent conditions (for dividends paid) will be applied in the year subsequent to the following year when the ACT carry-forward is being considered. The way in which recoverable ACT that is carried forward as an asset should be presented in the financial statements is considered in paragraph 13.142.

Example

A company has paid a large dividend and cannot relieve ACT against corporation tax in the current accounting period. It, therefore, wishes to carry-forward the related ACT to the next accounting period as an asset. It is likely to recover the ACT by reducing the mainstream corporation tax liability of the next period. However, the ACT asset will be replaced by another as the present level of dividend payout is anticipated to continue.

As the ACT will be replaced next year by an equivalent amount, it should not be carried forward, but should be written off to the profit and loss account and included in the current year's tax charge. However, if the ACT had related to a dividend proposed at the balance sheet date, it would have been permissible to carry it forward as an asset to be set off against corporation tax profits of the next accounting period.

Accounting for some common timing differences

Accelerated capital allowances

13.91 Accelerated capital allowances are defined in the Appendix to SSAP 15 as *"...timing differences which arise from the availability of capital allowances in tax computations which are in excess of the related depreciation charges in financial statements. The reverse may also occur, whereby the depreciation charges in the financial statements exceed the capital allowances available in tax computations"*. [SSAP 15 app para 7].

13.92 Currently, capital allowances are available on qualifying plant and machinery at a rate of 25 per cent per annum on the reducing balance basis. Allowances are also available on qualifying industrial buildings. In most companies, the main component of timing differences arises from accelerated capital allowances and the decision to provide deferred tax will depend on whether future years' capital allowances will exceed the depreciation charge on the company's pool of assets. If the company is budgeting for an increased level of expenditure on qualifying fixed assets and the depreciation rate for those assets is less than capital allowances claimed, the company would not create a deferred tax provision, because it would be able to show that reversing timing differences will be replaced or indeed exceeded by further originating differences. Where this is not so, it is likely that timing differences will reverse and a liability will crystallise. In this situation, the company would need to create a provision calculated by applying the tax rates expected to apply to net reversing timing differences. An example that illustrates the way in which timing differences arising on accelerated capital allowances should be reflected in the deferred tax calculation under the partial provision approach is given in paragraph 13.66.

Provisions

13.93 Provisions, such as those made for refurbishment, or for plant closures following a reorganisation, or for those arising on pensions and unfunded retirement benefits give rise to timing differences in that tax relief is obtained when the expenditure is actually incurred and not when they are recognised in the financial statements. It follows that provisions will always give rise to a deferred tax asset, because taxable profits are higher than accounting profits in the year in which the provisions are made. The tax asset will be recovered in the year in which the actual expenditure is incurred, but for some provisions, like pensions and other post-retirement benefits, recoverability of the tax benefit may take very many years (see further para 13.97).

13.94 To the extent that deferred tax liabilities arise on other timing differences, the deferred tax asset in respect of the provision would be offset against those so that deferred tax is provided on the net position. It may be that the deferred tax asset arising in respect of say, a reorganisation provision is so large that a net deferred tax asset arises after deferred tax liabilities on other timing differences are deducted. In that situation, the rules considered in paragraph 13.80 should be followed in considering whether the net deferred tax asset should be recognised or written off. For deferred tax assets arising in respect of pensions and other post-retirement benefits, an alternative treatment is permitted (see further para 13.99).

Deferred revenue expenditure

13.95 Deferred revenue expenditure, on the other hand, gives rise to deferred tax liabilities. In this situation, tax relief is obtained on the full amount of the expenditure in the year in which it is incurred, but only a proportion is recognised in the financial statements, the balance being carried forward as an asset to be charged to income over a period of time. The difference between book and tax treatment gives rise to a deferred tax liability to reflect the fact that the company has obtained full tax benefit on an expenditure of which only a proportion has passed through the profit and loss account in the year.

13.96 Capitalisation of interest gives rise to similar tax considerations. The full interest incurred in the year is allowed for tax, but for accounting purposes the tax benefit is effectively recognised over the years in which the interest capitalised in the financial statements is charged through depreciation of the asset in the profit and account.

Pension costs

13.97 The accounting for pension costs and post-retirement benefits is another example which gives rise to a timing difference for deferred tax purposes. In the financial statements, pension costs and other post-retirement benefits are recognised on an accruals basis in accordance with the principles set out in SSAP 24 and UITF Abstract 6 respectively, but tax relief on pension contributions and post-retirement benefit payments is generally granted in the period in which they are paid, rather than when they are expensed. In most cases, these timing differences will reverse, albeit over a long time scale. This is particularly relevant for defined benefit pension schemes and unfunded pensions and post-retirement benefit schemes.

13.98 Under SSAP 24 and UITF Abstract 6 these long-term obligations are accounted for on a full provision basis, even though in many cases it is likely that they will continually roll over (that is, as one obligation is settled another will arise). If the tax consequences of these long-term liabilities were accounted for on the same basis, it would result in the recognition of a deferred tax asset where the reversing provision is replaced by a new one. This is contrary to the principles of SSAP 15 which requires recognition of deferred tax debit balances only where they are expected to be recoverable without replacement by equivalent debit balances.

13.99 However, many argued that the tax treatment of these provisions in accordance with SSAP 15 was not consistent with the treatment of the provision required by SSAP 24 and UITF Abstract 6. They maintained that it was unfair to set up a provision on a gross basis without recognising the related tax relief. In order to resolve this conflict, the ASB issued an amendment to SSAP 15 in December 1992 as a 'sweetener', which permitted the use of either the full provision basis or the partial provision basis in accounting for the deferred tax implications of pensions and other post-retirement benefits. Whichever policy a company adopts, it should be disclosed. [SSAP 15 para 32A]. An example of a company adopting the full provision approach for providing deferred tax on unfunded retirement benefits is given on Table 13.3 on page 49. The deferred tax treatment of pensions and other post-retirement benefits is considered further in chapter 12.

Trading losses

13.100 Where a company incurs a trading loss for tax purposes, that loss, which is determined after the deduction of any capital allowances given in that trade, may be set off against other profits (including chargeable gains) made in the same accounting period. To the extent that it cannot be used against the current period's profits, it can be carried back against profits arising in the previous 36 months. Any trading losses of a company which are not relieved by offset against current profits or profits of previous periods can be carried forward to be set off against the first available profits of the same trade for subsequent accounting periods.

13.101 Therefore, where a company has tax losses that can be relieved against a tax liability for a previous year, it is appropriate to recognise those losses as an asset because the tax relief is recoverable by refund of tax previously paid. This asset can be shown either separately in the financial statements as a debtor, or offset against an existing deferred tax balance.

13.102 Where tax losses can be relieved only by carry-forward against taxable profits of future periods, a timing difference arises. [SSAP 15 para 19]. In such circumstances, a deferred tax asset can be recognised in the financial statement only if there is strong evidence that it will be recoverable against future taxable profits. If the company is maintaining a deferred tax account that will result in future tax payable, then there is strong evidence that the tax relief on the losses will be recoverable by offset against taxable income that arises when those timing differences will reverse. Accordingly, losses carried forward can be set off against deferred tax liabilities carried in the balance sheet. This treatment is also explicit in paragraph 29 of SSAP 15 as discussed in paragraph 13.83 above. An example of such an offset is shown in Table 13.11 on page 63.

13.103 Where a net deferred tax asset arises from a surplus of losses, because they cannot be fully absorbed by set off against other deferred tax liabilities, recognition of the asset is permitted only if all of the following conditions are satisfied:

- The loss arises from an identifiable and non-recurring cause.
- The enterprise, or predecessor enterprise, has been consistently profitable over a considerable period, with any past losses being more than offset by income in subsequent periods.
- It is assured beyond reasonable doubt that future taxable profits will be sufficient to offset the current loss during the carry-forward period prescribed by tax legislation.

[SSAP 15 app para 14].

The purpose of these rules is to ensure that a deferred tax asset in respect of trading losses is created only when its recoverability is assured with a very high degree of certainty. This is borne out by the test of 'beyond reasonable doubt' in the third point, which is a stringent test to meet in its own right.

Capital losses

13.104 Whereas trading losses can be offset against chargeable gains, capital losses, on the other hand, cannot be offset against trading profits. Where a company makes capital losses in an accounting period, those losses can generally be set off only against chargeable gains which it makes in the same period. If those capital losses are greater than the chargeable gains, they may be set off against gains of a later accounting period.

13.105 A capital loss which is available to relieve against chargeable gains creates a timing difference. However, a deferred tax asset in respect of a capital loss cannot be offset against deferred tax liabilities arising from trading items, because of the offset rules in tax legislation. Consequently, a deferred tax asset in respect of a capital loss will be recognised only if there is strong evidence that it will be recoverable against any available chargeable gains. The appendix to SSAP 15 sets out a number of conditions that should be met for the recognition of a deferred tax asset in respect of a capital loss. These conditions, all of which should be satisfied, are as follows:

- A potential chargeable gain not expected to be covered by rollover relief is present in respect of assets which have not been revalued in the financial statements to reflect that gain and which are not essential to the enterprise's future operations.

- The enterprise has decided to dispose of these assets and thus realise the potential chargeable gain.

- The unrealised chargeable gain (after allowing for any possible loss in value before disposal) is sufficient to offset the loss in question, such that it is assured beyond any reasonable doubt that a tax liability on the relevant portion of the chargeable gain will not crystallise.

[SSAP 15 app para 15].

Revaluation of fixed assets

13.106 Many companies revalue their fixed assets. In the UK, revaluation of assets *per se* does not give rise to a timing difference because taxable profits are not affected and no future tax liability arises as a result of the revaluation. If, however, a revalued asset is subsequently sold at the revalued amount, a tax liability may well arise. Therefore, SSAP 15 states that revaluation of an asset (including an investment in an associated company or a subsidiary company) will create a timing difference when it is incorporated in the balance sheet, insofar as the profit or loss that would result from the realisation at the revalued amount is taxable, unless disposal of the revalued asset and of any subsequent replacement assets would not result in a tax liability, after taking account of any expected rollover relief. [SSAP 15 para 20].

13.107 However, the precise nature of the liability arising on the disposal of a revalued asset will depend on the taxation status of the asset. For tax purposes, assets that do not attract capital allowances, such as land and investments, give rise to chargeable gains or losses if they are sold above or below their tax indexed cost (original cost uplifted by an indexation allowance intended to exempt purely inflationary gains from taxation). For accounting purposes, such assets are sometimes revalued, but rarely depreciated. Depreciable assets, on the other hand, may or may not be revalued. If such an asset is revalued in excess of cost and sold at the revalued amount, then, in addition to any liability arising on the capital gain, a further tax liability may well arise if it was also eligible for capital allowances. This further liability, which arises by way of a balancing charge, is designed to claw back any capital allowances previously claimed in respect of the asset. SSAP 15 generally deals with the deferred tax consequences of revaluing assets which are not deductible for tax purposes, but is silent on the effects of revaluation on the deferred tax relating to accelerated capital allowances. These two situations are considered below.

Revaluations of assets not qualifying for capital allowances

13.108 Where a non-depreciable asset not qualifying for capital allowances, such as land or an investment is revalued upwards above tax indexed cost, a timing difference arises in that, in the absence of rollover relief (see para 13.121 below), a chargeable gain will arise if and when the asset is disposed of at the revalued amount. In this situation, SSAP 15 requires that provision for the tax payable should be made as soon as it is foreseen that a liability will arise. [SSAP 15 app para 9]. A liability may be foreseen at the time the company decides in principle to sell the asset. This may be at the time of the revaluation or at a later date.

13.109 Any provision for tax payable should be made out of the revaluation surplus, based on the value at which the fixed asset is carried in the balance sheet. [SSAP 15 app para 9]. This means that where tax is provided at the time of revaluation the amount transferred to the revaluation reserve should be net of tax. This treatment is also consistent with the Act's requirements in connection with the use of the revaluation reserve. [4 Sch 34(3)(b); SI 1996/189].

13.110 It should also be noted that FRS 3 requires the revaluation surplus arising in the year of revaluation to be reported in the statement of total recognised gains and losses. It follows that any deferred tax provision arising on the revaluation should similarly be reported in that statement. When FRS 3 was issued, this treatment was considered appropriate and the ASB's discussion paper confirms this by making it clear that the tax effects of items that are dealt with in the statement of total recognised gains and losses should also be reflected in that statement.

13.111 Where a company intends to dispose of a previously revalued asset, it may not actually do so for a number of years. In that situation, the deferred tax provision that was set up at the time the company intended to dispose of the asset may require adjustments to take account of any indexation allowance that may accrue in those years prior to sale. Any adjustments required should be included in the statement of total recognised gains and losses and the revaluation reserve.

13.112 Where the revaluation is downwards, a timing difference arises in that, a capital loss will arise if and when the asset is disposed of at the revalued amount. However, as the capital loss can only be utilised by offset against chargeable capital gains arising during or after the accounting period of disposal, a deferred tax asset should not be recorded on the grounds of prudence unless:

- It can be offset against deferred tax provided in respect of chargeable gains on other upward revaluations arising in the current or previous accounting periods, or.

- It can be demonstrated that a capital gain at least equivalent to the capital loss will occur in the current or next accounting period.

If the downward revaluation merely reverses a previous upward revaluation, any deferred tax provision set up in respect of the previous upward revaluation will simply be reversed.

Example

A company buys a property for £2,500,000 in 19X1. It is revalued to £3,000,000 in 19X2 and sold at the revalued amount in 19X3. The chargeable gain ignoring indexation allowance is £500,000 on which tax is payable @ 33%, that is, £165,000.

Ignoring depreciation to the date of disposal, the company would need to provide for the tax effect of the revaluation in 19X2, since there is an intention to dispose of the asset. As the tax payable of £165,000 should be provided out of the revaluation surplus, the amount transferred to the revaluation reserve and also recorded in the statement of total recognised gains and losses would be £335,000 (£500,000 – £165,000). The carrying value of the asset would be increased by the gross amount of the upward revaluation, namely £500,000 and the deferred tax liability will be recorded at £165,000.

In 19X3 when the asset is sold, no profit or loss is recorded in the profit and loss account, but there is a tax payable on the gain of £165,000. This amount should be charged to the provision of £165,000 that was set up by charging the statement of total recognised gains and loss in 19X2. The revaluation surplus would be transferred to the profit and loss account as a movement on reserves.

If the asset is sold for an amount in excess of the revalued amount, an accounting gain will be recorded. In that situation, a tax liability in excess of £165,000 referred to above would arise. This excess should be recorded in the profit and loss account as the surplus over revalued carrying amount will also be credited to profit and loss account in accordance with FRS 3.

13.113 The same principles as discussed above also apply to depreciable assets, such as an office building, that do not qualify for capital allowances. If such an asset is revalued in excess of tax indexed cost, the revaluation will represent a timing difference which will reverse:

- if and when the asset is sold at the revalued amount (in the absence of rollover relief); or
- if it is not sold, as it is subsequently depreciated (although the effect may be offset by further revaluations).

13.114 With respect to the first point above, the treatment is no different from the treatment for non-depreciable assets discussed in paragraphs 13.108 and 13.109 above, and deferred tax will be provided if it is probable that a liability will crystallise. Similarly, a downward revaluation will represent a timing difference to the extent that, if the asset were sold at its revalued amount, a capital loss would arise. The treatment is then identical to that considered in paragraph 13.112 above.

13.115 With respect to the second point above, no deferred tax would be provided under SSAP 15 because there is no commitment to sell the asset. In the absence of a commitment to sell, the revaluation gain, and its subsequent reversal through depreciation, is a permanent difference, because it does not enter into the determination of taxable profits. As no additional future tax payments will occur as a result of the revaluation, no additional deferred tax liability need be recognised. However, the standard requires disclosure of the fact that any potential deferred tax has not been quantified. (See further para 13.148.)

Revaluation of assets qualifying for capital allowances

13.116 The standard is silent on the deferred tax treatment of revaluing depreciable assets which attract capital allowances. However, some guidance is contained in the Accountants Digest No 174 (now out of print) and the discussion that follows is based on that guidance.

13.117 Where a depreciable asset that qualifies for capital allowances, such as plant and machinery or industrial buildings, is revalued upwards, the revaluation gives rise to a further originating timing difference, in addition to that which arises from accelerated capital allowances. As the revaluation represents a new originating timing difference, the view taken by the Digest is that deferred tax should be provided in the normal way if there are plans to dispose of the asset. Consider the following example:

Example

A company purchased specialised plant in 19X1 for £1,000,000, the cost being written off over its useful life of 10 years. At the end of 19X2, the plant was revalued to £1,200,000. The company intended to sell the plant and deferred tax was provided on the revalued amount. During 19X5, the plant was sold at its original cost. The tax rate is 33% per annum. The rate of capital allowances is 25% per annum. Indexation allowance is ignored. The timing differences arising and the deferred tax computation are shown below for the periods from acquisition to disposal.

	19X1	19X2	19X3	19X4	19X5
Per financial statements	£'000	£'000	£'000	£'000	£'000
Cost/valuation	1,000.0	900.0	1,200.0	1,050.0	900.0
Depreciation	(100.0)	(100.0)	(150.0)	(150.0)	–
	900.0	800.0	1,050.0	900.0	900.0
Revaluation/ (disposal)	–	400.0	–	–	(900.0)
Net book value	900.0	1,200.0	1,050.0	900.0	–
The gain arising on sale in 19X5 is £100,000 (£1,000,000 – £900,000).					
Per tax computation					
Cost/Pool	1,000.0	750.0	562.5	421.9	316.4
Capital allowances @ 25%	(250.0)	(187.5)	(140.6)	(105.5)	–
Tax written down value	750.0	562.5	421.9	316.4	316.4
Sales proceeds					1,000.0
Balancing charge					683.6
In 19X5, no chargeable gain or loss arises on the sale of the asset. There is, however, a claw back of allowances previously claimed.					
Timing difference					
CA (balancing charge)	250.0	187.5	140.6	105.5	(683.6)
Depreciation (profit on sale)	100.0	100.0	150.0	150.0	(100.0)
Originating (reversing)	150.0	87.5	(9.4)	(44.5)	(583.6)
Tax @ 33%	49.5	28.9	(3.1)	(14.7)	(192.6)

	19X1	19X2	19X3	19X4	19X5
Tax computation	£'000	£'000	£'000	£'000	£'000
Profit before depreciation	2,000.0	2,000.0	2,000.0	2,000.0	2,000.0
Capital allowance	(250.0)	(187.5)	(140.6)	(105.5)	683.6
Taxable profit	1,750.0	1,812.5	1,859.4	1,894.5	2,683.6
Tax @ 33%	577.5	598.1	613.6	625.2	885.6

Profit and loss account	19X1 £'000	19X2 £'000	19X3 £'000	19X4 £'000	19X5 £'000
Profit before depreciation	2,000.0	2,000.0	2,000.0	2,000.0	2,000.0
Depreciation	(100.0)	(100.0)	(150.0)	(150.0)	–
Operating profit	1,900.0	1,900.0	1,850.0	1,850.0	2,000.0
Profit on disposal of asset	–	–	–	–	100.0
Profit before tax	1,900.0	1,900.0	1,850.0	1,850.0	2,100.0
Taxation	627.0	627.0	610.5	610.5	693.0
Profit after tax	1,273.0	1,273.0	1,239.5	1,239.5	1,407.0
Effective tax rate (%)	33.0	33.0	33.0	33.0	33.0
Taxation	£'000	£'000	£'000	£'000	£'000
Current tax @ 33%	577.5	598.1	613.6	625.2	885.6
Deferred tax	49.5	28.9	(3.1)	(14.7)	(192.6)
P&L charge	627.0	627.0	610.5	610.5	693.0
Deferred tax					
Opening balance	–	49.5	210.4	207.3	192.6
P&L account	49.5	28.9	(3.1)	(14.7)	(192.6)
STRGL on revaluation	–	132.0	–	–	–
Closing balance	49.5	210.4	207.3	192.6	–

At the end of 19X2 when the asset is revalued by £400,000, deferred tax of £132,000 (£400,000 @ 33%) is provided through the statement of total recognised gains and losses. This liability of £132,000 is reduced in 19X3 and 19X4 by the amount of tax arising on the excess depreciation of £50,000 in each of those years, which reverses part of the original revaluation, the credit being taken to the tax charge in the profit and loss account. In 19X5, when the asset is sold, the balance on the deferred tax account is £192,6000, which is simply tax on the difference between the net book value of £900 and the tax written down value of £316,400 prior to sale. This amount must be released to the profit and loss account to match the tax of £225,600 arising on the balancing charge. The effect is that the profit and loss account bears tax of £33,000 arising on the profit on disposal.

13.118 Where a depreciable asset that attracts capital allowances is revalued downwards, the downward revaluation effectively represents the reversal of an originating timing difference resulting from accelerated capital allowances. Therefore, as long as this reversal was foreseen and a deferred tax provision set up, the downward revaluation may be accounted for as a reduction in the provision with the credit going to the STRGL along with the revaluation deficit. If a depreciable asset is revalued downwards such that its book value is lower than its tax value, then a potential deferred tax asset will arise. This may be recognised as long as there are foreseeable taxable profits in future years when capital allowances will arise. If revaluations are not recorded in the financial statements, but are only disclosed by way of note, the note should also disclose any tax effects of disposal at the revalued amount (see para 13.148).

13.119 A particular problem arises on utilities, such as water-supply companies, which do not depreciate their infra-structure assets yet are eligible to claim capital allowances. In that situation, it would appear that the difference between capital allowances and nil depreciation gives rise to a timing difference that is unlikely to reverse in the foreseeable future. Some of the originating difference may reverse if the infra-structure assets are written down or sold in excess of their written down value for tax purposes. But such events are unlikely in view of the large amounts that are spent in maintaining the operating capability of such assets. As a result, it is unlikely that any deferred tax would be provided. An example is included in Table 13.2 below.

Table 13.2 –Thames Water Plc – Annual Report and Accounts – 31 March 1997

Notes to the accounts (extract)

9 Deferred taxation

The Group's medium and long-term plans for capital investment together with the capital allowances available in respect of the asset base transferred from Thames Water Authority on vesting indicate that for the foreseeable future the amount of tax allowances in respect of eligible plant and machinery will exceed the depreciation on existing and new assets. Accordingly, no provision for deferred taxation is required in the Group accounts. If a provision for deferred tax had been made on the full liability method, there would have been a corporate tax charge of £121.9m (1996: £108.6m).

	Group	
	1997	1996
	£m	£m
An analysis of amounts unprovided is as follows:		
Accelerated capital allowances		
• Infrastructure assets	**302.5**	272.2
• Other assets	**354.2**	314.9
Other timing differences	**(3.9)**	(12.5)
Losses	**(0.5)**	(2.1)
Advance corporation tax	**(195.8)**	(141.6)
	456.5	430.9

Advance corporation tax includes £44.9m in respect of the purchase of shares which has been charged directly to Profit and Loss Reserves (see note 24.)

As infrastructure assets are not depreciated, deferred taxation will crystallise only in the event of any disposal of these assets at amounts in excess of their written down value for tax purposes. In the opinion of the Directors the likelihood of such a liability crystallising in the future is remote.

13.120 The discussion paper contains a detailed consideration of the deferred tax implications of revaluing assets. At present, there are two views among the ASB members as to whether deferred tax should be provided for on revaluations. Some board members regard deferred tax as an increment or decrement of future liabilities and take the view that deferred tax should be provided for on revaluations of assets only where there is a commitment to disposal. This view is consistent with the current treatment required by SSAP 15 as discussed above. Others regard deferred tax as a 'valuation adjustment' and take the view that deferred tax should be provided for on revaluation of assets which are deductible for tax purposes. For non-tax deductible assets where only capital gains would be relevant, deferred tax should be provided for only once there is a commitment to sell. Which view will ultimately prevail will depend on the chosen method for accounting for deferred tax.

Rollover relief

13.121 On the disposal of certain assets used for trading purposes, such as properties, it may be possible to defer immediate payment of the tax arising on the chargeable gain provided the proceeds of the sale are reinvested within certain time limits in other qualifying assets. This relief, known as 'rollover relief', reduces the 'base cost' of the replacement asset by the chargeable gain rolled over so that the tax becomes payable when the replacement asset is sold. It is also possible to claim rollover relief on the gain arising on the sale of the replacement asset such that payment of the tax is postponed indefinitely.

13.122 It is, therefore, important to take account of the possibility of obtaining rollover relief when assessing whether a tax liability will arise on the sale of an asset. This is because the relief has the effect of deferring the reversal of any timing differences arising on the revaluation of an asset beyond the sale date, or of creating a timing difference on the sale of an asset that has not been revalued, or a combination of the two. However, the guidance given in the appendix to the standard is rather confusing. The appendix states that where rollover relief has been obtained on the sale of an asset with a consequent reduction in the 'base cost' of the replacement asset, and the potential deferred tax has not been disclosed, the standard requires disclosure of the fact that the revaluation does not constitute a timing difference and that tax has, therefore, not been quantified, as it will not otherwise be evident from the financial statements (see para 13.148). [SSAP 15 app para 11].

13.123 The above guidance appears to mix up the sale of an asset on which deferred tax has not been provided, because rollover relief has been obtained with the timing difference arising on the revaluation. But these are two unrelated matters. In essence, if a revalued asset is sold at the revalued amount and gives rise to a tax liability, but rollover relief is expected to be available, then there is no need to provide for deferred tax on the revaluation. However, there is a need to disclose the potential liability as rollover relief merely postpones, but does not extinguish altogether, the liability. Even where an asset that has not been revalued is sold at a profit, there is no need to provide for the tax if the tax payable has been deferred by the operation of rollover relief, although again there is a need to disclose the potential liability. However, the guidance contained in the appendix to the standard would appear to imply that if rollover relief is available, a revaluation does not create a timing difference. This is confusing.

13.124 An alternative view, considered in the discussion paper, is that it is inappropriate to take account of the impact of rollover relief until the relief is actually claimed. A decision to take advantage of the relief is a future event, whose effect should be reflected in the period in which the relief is claimed and not anticipated in the current financial statements. Although it is hard to imagine that a company will not take advantage of rollover relief if it is available, the issue is much wider in scope and affects the way in which future events impact on the recognition and measurement of items appearing in the financial statements.

Disclosure of taxation in financial statements

General

13.125 It is generally accepted that, however they have been calculated, tax effects should be shown in the financial statements separately from the items or transactions to which they relate. [SSAP 15 para 16]. It is not surprising, therefore, that a considerable number of disclosure requirements in respect of taxation are contained both in the Act and the relevant accounting standards although there is significant overlap between the two. Most of the disclosure requirements apply to the financial statements of individual companies as well as to consolidated financial statements. However, small companies preparing annual financial statements under the modified formats are permitted to omit many of the statutory disclosure requirements relating to taxation (see further chapter 36). [8 Sch 6]. The paragraphs that follow deal with the disclosure requirements of corporation tax as well as deferred tax.

Accounting policies

13.126 Both the Act and SSAP 2 require that the accounting policies adopted in determining the amounts to be included in respect of all material items in the balance sheet and profit and loss account must be stated in a note to the financial statements. [4 Sch 36, SSAP 2 para 18]. SSAP 15 requires that deferred tax should be computed under the liability method. [SSAP 15 para 24]. Therefore, the basis on which deferred tax has been calculated will have to be stated as one of the company's accounting policies. In practice, the matters that are included in the accounting policy for taxation vary, but many companies are simply content in meeting the SSAP 15 requirement as indicated in Table 13.3 below.

Table 13.3 – Glaxo Holdings p.l.c. – Annual Report and Accounts – 30 June 1994

NOTES TO THE ACCOUNTS

***1 ACCOUNTING POLICIES AND DEFINITIONS* (extract)**

Deferred taxation: Deferred taxation, calculated using the liability method, is accounted for by each Group company for taxation deferred or accelerated by reason of timing differences. Deferred taxation relief is accounted for in full on long-term timing differences in respect of provisions for unfunded retirement benefits. Taxation deferred or accelerated by reason of short-term and other timing differences is accounted for to the extent that it is probable that a liability or asset will crystallise. Advance corporation tax is carried forward to the extent that it is expected to be recovered.

Others, however, go beyond the basic requirement and include such matters as deferred tax treatment of ACT, overseas profits and revaluations, although such matters generally fall to be included in the taxation note. An example of a company that has included such matters in the accounting policy note dealing with deferred taxation is illustrated in Table 13.4 below.

Table 13.4 – Bass PLC – Annual Report – 30 September 1997

Accounting Policies (extract)

Deferred taxation

Deferred taxation is provided using the liability method on all timing differences which are expected to reverse in the foreseeable future. Where this policy gives rise to a balance which will be offset against future taxation liabilities, this balance is carried forward as a debtor.

Advance corporation tax on dividends paid or proposed which is expected to be recovered after one year is included in deferred taxation.

No provision is made for UK deferred taxation in respect of UK industrial buildings allowances as the properties are expected to be used in the business for periods longer than that for which the allowances could be reclaimed on disposal. Similarly, no provision is made for taxation deferred by UK roll-over relief due to the level of continuing capital investment.

UK deferred taxation is provided in respect of liabilities expected to arise on the distribution of profits from overseas subsidiary undertakings to the extent such distributions are required, or expected, to be made.

Profit and loss account

Disclosures required by the Act

13.127 The Act's requirements in relation to the presentation of taxation in the profit and loss account are as follows:

- There must be disclosed separately 'tax on profit or loss on ordinary activities' and 'tax on extraordinary profit or loss'. The latter is unlikely to arise following publication of FRS 3. These are separate headings included in each of the four profit and loss account formats. In addition, all the profit and loss account formats include a further heading 'other taxes not shown under the above items'. As the Act does not indicate the type of information that must be included under this heading and as no such 'other taxes' are presently collected in the UK, this heading in the format appears to be superfluous for the time being.

- The taxation charge in the profit and loss account should be analysed, distinguishing between:

  - UK corporation tax, both before and after double tax relief.
  - UK income tax.
  - Overseas tax.

  [4 Sch 54(3)].

- Particulars are required of any special circumstances that affect the overall tax charge or credit for the period or that may affect those of future periods, whether in respect of profits, income or capital gains. [4 Sch 54(2)]. This requirement is also contained in FRS 3 which is discussed in paragraph 13.137.

Disclosure required by accounting standards

13.128 A considerable amount of information relating to both corporation tax and deferred tax falls to be disclosed in the profit and loss account under the provisions contained in SSAP 8, SSAP 15 and more recently FRS 3. These disclosure requirements have been grouped under appropriate headings for ease of reference and examples from published financial statements to illustrate the disclosure requirements of the Act and accounting standards are included where relevant.

General

13.129 There must be disclosed separately deferred tax relating to the ordinary activities as part of the 'tax on profit or loss on ordinary activities'. This separate disclosure of the deferred tax element should be made either on the face of the profit and loss account or in a note. [SSAP 15 para 33]. There is no equivalent provision in the Act requiring the disclosure of the deferred tax element of the profit and loss account tax charge. In practice, an analysis of the total tax charge in the profit and loss account between current and deferred elements is not generally given, although it can be readily computed from the available information given in the taxation note. An example of a company that has given this split is shown in Table 13.5.

Table 13.5 – Forte Plc – Report and Accounts – 31 January 1995

Notes to the Accounts

8 Taxation (extract)	1995 £ million	1994 £ million
UK corporation tax	19	6
Deferred taxation	4	–
Overseas taxation	7	7
Advance corporation tax written off	–	9
Taxation before exceptional items	**30**	**22**
Tax relating to the disposal of discontinued operations	–	5
	30	**27**
Comprising:		
Current taxation	26	27
Deferred taxation	4	–
	30	**27**

13.130 The amount of the UK corporation tax charge should specify:

- The charge for corporation tax on the income of the year (where such corporation tax includes transfers between the deferred taxation account and the profit and loss account, these should be separately disclosed where material). [SSAP 8 para 22(a)]. Although such a transfer is generally given in aggregate in the tax note, an example of a company that has further analysed the deferred tax element of the tax charge into its major components is given in Table 13.6 below.

Table 13.6 – British Gas plc – Annual Report and Accounts – 31 December 1994

8 Taxation	**1994 £m**	1993 (as restated (i)) £m
UK – corporation tax at 33% (1993 33%)	**292**	260
– deferred corporation tax:		
pension costs	**(49)**	(97)
restructuring costs	**91**	(377)
deferred petroleum revenue tax	**(39)**	(48)
capitalised interest	**14**	18
accelerated capital allowances and other timing differences	**20**	–
	37	(504)
	329	(244)
Deferred petroleum revenue tax at 50% (1993 50%)	**125**	144
Overseas taxation – current	**45**	47
– deferred	**–**	14
Associated undertakings	**5**	7
Taxation charge/(credit)	**504**	(32)

i) See note 1, pages 36 and 37 – Changes in accounting policy.

Based on the historical cost results before exceptional charges, the effective taxation rate for the year ended 31 December 1994 was 35.3% (31 December 1993 31.9% as restated). Taxation attributable to exceptional charges in 1994 was a credit of £5m (1993 a credit of £500m). Before exceptional charges, the taxation charge for the year ended 31 December 1994 was £509m (1993 £468m as restated) and the historical cost profit on ordinary activities before exceptional charges was £1 440m (1993 £1 468m as restated).

For 1994 the UK corporation tax charge before exceptional charges was reduced by approximately £65m (1993 £140m as restated) mainly in respect of accelerated capital allowances. UK deferred petroleum revenue tax has been included on the basis of actual volumes of production. Tax attributable to the profit on sale of tangible fixed assets and subsidiary undertakings is not material. The movement in the deferred corporation tax asset is disclosed in note 17, page 49.

- Tax attributable to franked investment income (see para 13.38). [SSAP 8 para 22(a)].
- Irrecoverable ACT (see para 13.28). [SSAP 8 para 22(a)].
- The relief for overseas taxation (see para 13.32). [SSAP 8 para 22(a)].
- The total overseas taxation, relieved and unrelieved (specifying that part of the unrelieved overseas taxation that arises from the payment or proposed payment of dividends). [SSAP 8 para 22(b)]. The additional requirement included in

parentheses is now redundant as explained in paragraph 13.34 above. Although there is no specific requirement to analyse the overseas tax charge further into its current and deferred elements, many companies consider it appropriate to give this analysis.

- If the rate of corporation tax is not known for all or part of the financial year, the latest known rate should be used and disclosed. [SSAP 8 para 23]. However, it is generally accepted accounting practice to disclose the rate.

- It is also standard practice that any material over or under provisions relating to the taxation charge in respect of previous years should be separately disclosed as an adjustment to an accounting estimate. Many companies disclose this adjustment in total; however, some prefer to give a detailed breakdown.

The above disclosure requirements, which reinforce the disclosures already required by the Act as discussed in paragraph 13.127 above, are illustrated in Table 13.7 below.

Table 13.7 – Coats Viyella Plc – Annual report and accounts – 31 December 1994

Notes to the Accounts (extract)

8 Tax on profit on ordinary activities			**1994 £m**		1993 £m
UK taxation based on profit for the year:					
Corporation tax at 33% (1993 – 33%)			**33.0**		35.2
Double taxation relief			**(19.3)**		(16.0)
Deferred taxation			**3.3**		(1.7)
Advance corporation tax			**(9.8)**		(12.2)
Prior year adjustments	– Corporation tax	**(4.5)**		(2.2)	
	Deferred taxation	–		(0.9)	
	Advance corporation tax	–		2.1	
			(4.5)		(1.0)
			2.7		4.3
Overseas taxation:					
Current taxation			**34.7**		40.9
Deferred taxation			**3.6**		4.0
			41.0		49.2
Associated companies taxation			**0.2**		0.3
			41.2		49.5

The enhanced share dividend has increased the advance corporation tax credit for the year by £7.6m (1993 – £8.2m together with a prior year adjustment of £3.5m).

In addition, the interim dividend was paid as a Foreign Income Dividend (FID) and the related advance corporation tax is therefore recoverable during 1995. If the interim dividend had been paid as conventional dividend, the advance corporation tax credit for the year would have been reduced by £6.1m.

	1994 £m	1993 £m
Excluding advance corporation tax movement, the UK charge for the year has been increased/(decreased) by:		
Losses forward and capital allowances not dealt with in the deferred tax provision	**1.6**	(2.6)
Profit on sale of fixed assets and shares in subsidiary company covered by reliefs	**(1.4)**	(1.9)
The overseas tax charge for the year has benefited from the utilisation of brought forward losses (1993 suffered as a result of unrelieved tax losses)	**(0.1)**	7.4
Tax attributable to the profits on sale of fixed assets amounts to	**0.1**	0.6
Tax relief attributable to the loss on sale or termination of operations amounts to	**(1.0)**	–

13.131 The amount of any unprovided deferred tax in respect of the period should be disclosed in a note, analysed into its major components. [SSAP 15 para 35]. Not all companies tend to give this information as they consider it sufficient to analyse the unprovided deferred tax balance into its major components as required by SSAP 15 (see further para 13.145). An example of a company that has given this information is illustrated in Table 13.8 below.

Table 13.8 – Smith & Nephew plc – Annual Report and Accounts – 31 December 1994

Notes to the accounts

9 Taxation	**1994 *£ million***	1993 *£ million*
United Kingdom taxation		
Corporation tax at 33% (1993 – 33%)	**45.1**	32.8
Double taxation relief	**(26.3)**	(19.6)
Deferred taxation	**0.1**	4.2
Advance corporation tax	**0.7**	1.8
Adjustments in respect of prior years	**–**	(1.8)
	19.6	17.4

	1994	1993
Overseas taxation		
Current taxation	**36.4**	34.8
Deferred taxation	**(4.7)**	5.3
Adjustments in respect of prior years	**(2.9)**	(1.3)
	28.8	38.8
Taxation charged	**48.4**	56.2

If full provision had been made for deferred tax, the tax charge would have decreased by £3.5m (1993 – £0.6m) as follows:

	1994	1993
	£ million	*£ million*
Fixed asset timing differences	**(0.3)**	(1.3)
Other timing differences	**3.1**	0.1
Advance corporation tax	**0.7**	1.8
	3.5	0.6

The tax charge is reduced by £6.8m as a consequence of the rationalisation programme and by £1.6m (1993 – increased by £3.2m) as a consequence of the exceptional loss/profit on disposal.

13.132 The effect of a fundamental change in the basis of taxation should be included in the tax charge for the period and separately disclosed on the face of the profit and loss account. [FRS 3 para 23]. In addition, adjustments to deferred tax arising from changes in the tax rates and tax allowances should normally be disclosed separately as part of the tax charge for the period. [SSAP 15 para 36].

Tax on non-operating exceptional items

13.133 The amount of tax attributable to the three non-operating exceptional items described in paragraph 20 of FRS 3 (sometimes referred to as 'super-exceptionals') should be disclosed in a note. The three items are: profits or losses on sale or termination of an operation; costs of a fundamental reorganisation or restructuring having a material effect on the nature and focus of the reporting entity's operations; and profits or losses on the disposal of fixed assets (and provisions in respect of each of these). The related tax is required to be shown only in aggregate and not for each individual item, unless the effect of the tax on each of the items differs, when further information should be given, where practicable. An example of the relevant disclosure required under FRS 3 is shown in Table 13.8 above. Although the FRS states that the tax attributable to the above types of exceptional item should be disclosed in a note, there could be no objection to disclosing the tax separately within the tax charge on the face of the profit and loss account, as the items are themselves disclosed there.

13.134 FRS 3 recognises that the above disclosure can be useful in understanding the period's charge or credit in respect of taxation. In support of this disclosure requirement, paragraph 50 of FRS 3 states:

> *"It is recognised that analysing an entity's total taxation charge between component parts of its result for a period can involve arbitrary allocations that tend to become less meaningful the more components there are. However, in respect of items such as disposal profits or losses the tax can often be identified with the exceptional item concerned and the relationship between the profit or loss and the attributable tax may be significantly different from that in respect of operating profits or losses. In such circumstances it is relevant to identify the tax charge or credit more specifically."*

13.135 FRS 3 then goes on to stipulate the way in which tax attributable to exceptional items falling within any of the three categories set out above should be calculated for accounting disclosure purposes. The amount of tax attributable to the exceptional items should be calculated by computing the tax on the profit or loss on ordinary activities as if the items did not exist and comparing this notional tax charge with the tax charge on the profit or loss for the year (after extraordinary items if any). Any additional tax charge or credit (including deferred tax) that arises should be attributable to the items. If there are both non-operating exceptional items and extraordinary items in the same period, the tax attributable to the items combined should be calculated and then apportioned between the two groups in relation to their respective amounts. If a more appropriate basis is adopted the method of apportionment must be disclosed. [FRS 3 para 24]. In practice, it is unlikely that under FRS 3 there will be extraordinary items and so the apportionment of tax between the two categories should not arise.

13.136 The following examples illustrate some of the difficulties that may arise in calculating the taxation that relates to the non-operating exceptional items described above:

Example 1

Apportionment of tax relating to exceptional profit on a business disposal

A group makes substantial losses on ordinary activities (excluding non-operating exceptionals) but makes a large exceptional profit on the disposal of a business, which is taxable. It is able to set its losses against the profit on disposal. After doing so there remains a taxable profit and it is able to relieve some ACT which it has written off in previous years.

In this case there would be a tax credit on the loss on ordinary activities *excluding* the exceptional item. There would be a corresponding charge shown in the notes in respect of the exceptional item, to the extent of the tax effect of the losses relieved against the exceptional profit. In addition, there would be a further charge on the balance of the exceptional profit not relieved by losses, but this would be reduced by the ACT recovered which should also be taken into account in determining the tax on the exceptional item. The reason for this is that the recovery of the ACT is a direct result of the exceptional item. This might work as follows:

Assuming that the exceptional profit exceeds the trading losses there may be a net tax charge on profit on ordinary activities before tax of say £25,000. Excluding the exceptional item there may be a tax credit of say £30,000. The difference of £55,000 would be attributed to the exceptional item which has been relieved by ACT now recovered of £5,000. Therefore, the total tax charge of £25,000 comprises a tax credit of £30,000 attributable to the trading losses and an exceptional tax charge of £55,000.

Example 2

Apportionment of tax relating to exceptional loss on a business disposal.

A group makes a profit on ordinary activities (excluding non-operating exceptionals), but there is a large exceptional loss on disposal of a business. As a result the overall tax charge is nil and the group is unable to relieve ACT paid in the year. This ACT is not recoverable without replacement in the following year and so has to be written off, with the result that there is no overall accounts profit or loss but there is a tax charge, being irrecoverable ACT.

In this case there will be a tax charge when tax is computed *excluding* the exceptional item. The tax on the exceptional item is shown in a note as a credit to correspond with the notional tax charge on profit on ordinary activities, but that credit should then be reduced by the ACT written off, because the write off is caused by the exceptional item.

This might work as follows:

The accounts show no profit or loss as the exceptional loss equals the operating profit less interest. However, there is a tax charge of £10,000 representing irrecoverable ACT. The tax charge on the profit excluding the exceptional item and ACT is £50,000. The tax attributable to the exceptional item is therefore a credit of £50,000 less a charge of £10,000 in respect of the ACT that has proved irrecoverable solely because of the exceptional item.

Example 3

Apportionment of tax where losses brought forward absorb a profit on ordinary activities

A group makes a profit on ordinary activities (excluding non-operating exceptionals) and there is an exceptional loss of the same amount. The group has sufficient tax losses brought forward which can be surrendered to relieve the tax charge on the profit on ordinary activities, or it can use the taxable loss arising from the exceptional item. It uses the former. The question arises as to whether or not the notes to the financial statements should assume a taxation charge on the profit on ordinary activities and show a taxation credit attributable to the exceptional item? The overall tax charge is nil.

In this situation, if the exceptional item were ignored, the tax charge on the profit on ordinary activities would still be nil, as the group would have used taxable losses to eliminate the tax charge. Therefore, the notes should not assume a tax charge on ordinary activities and should not show a tax credit on exceptional items. However, there will still be tax losses carried forward and the notes could disclose that part of the losses brought forward have been utilised to relieve the taxable profit of the group leaving other taxable losses attributable to the exceptional item to be carried forward.

Example 4

Apportionment of tax where goodwill previously written off is treated as non-operating exceptional item

A company makes a profit before non-operating exceptional items and then has an exceptional loss on disposal of a subsidiary. The exceptional loss arises wholly because of the inclusion, in the calculation of the loss, of goodwill previously written off to reserves on the acquisition of the subsidiary. After taking account of the exceptional loss the result before tax is neither a profit nor loss, but there is a substantial tax charge. This is wholly attributable to the profit excluding exceptional items and accordingly there is no taxation attributable to the exceptional item. In this case, however, there would need to be an explanation in the notes of the reasons for an apparently high tax charge relative to the profit on ordinary activities before tax.

Special circumstances affecting the tax charge

13.137 In addition to the requirement to disclose the tax effects of the non-operating exceptional items, FRS 3 expands the Act's requirement to disclose details of any special circumstances affecting the tax charge or credit as stated in paragraph 13.127 above by requiring quantification of the individual effects of any special circumstances. Such disclosures should include any special circumstances affecting the tax attributable to the exceptional items. [FRS 3 para 23]. 'Special circumstances' could also include, for example, the effect on the tax charge of losses either utilised or carried forward, or the surrender or claim of losses by way of group relief, or the surrender or claim of ACT. Other examples are tax free income or disallowables, including goodwill written off per UITF Abstract 3. Disclosure and quantification of individual matters affecting the tax charge or credit for the year should be restricted to those where the tax effect is considered to be significant.

13.138 A number of matters may have a significant effect on the tax charge for the period, but the ways in which explanation of the special circumstances are disclosed in practice varies. Some companies give a narrative description of the special matters with quantification of the amounts involved as illustrated in Table 13.7 on page 13053. Others find it more useful way to provide the explanation of special circumstances affecting the tax charge by way of a reconciliation between the expected tax charge (the profit before tax multiplied by the UK statutory tax rate) to the actual tax charge, as illustrated in Table 13.9 below.

Table 13.9 – Glaxo Wellcome plc – Annual Accounts – 30 June 1995

NOTES TO THE ACCOUNTS

10 Taxation

		18 months to 31.12.95	12 months to 30.6.94 (restated)
		£m	£m
Taxation charge based on profits for the period	UK corporation tax at 33 per cent:	**1,026**	321
	Less double taxation relief	**605**	52
		421	269
	Overseas taxation	**660**	311
	Deferred taxation	**(251)**	(56)
	Irrecoverable Advance Corporation Tax	**37**	–
		867	524
Attributable to	Holding company and subsidiary undertakings	**864**	524
	Associated undertakings	**3**	–
Reconciliation of the taxation charge:	Profit on ordinary activities before taxation at the UK statutory rate of 33 per cent	**788**	606
	Deferred taxation not provided on fixed assets	**(48)**	(58)
	Effect of special taxation status in Singapore		
	Net cost of different rates of taxation in overseas undertakings	**(112)**	(46)
	Taxation effect of disallowed integration costs	**34**	32
	Advance Corporation Tax written off	**134**	–
	Other differences	**37**	–
		34	(10)
	Taxation charge in the accounts	**867**	524

Included in the taxation charge is a credit of £230 million in respect of integration. Profits arising from manufacturing operations in Singapore are taxed at a reduced rate until 30th June 2002.

13.139 An alternative presentation, also followed in practice, is to provide a reconciliation between the effective tax rate (actual tax charge as a percentage of profit before tax) to the UK statutory tax rate. An example is given in Table 13.10 below. Whichever method of presentation is chosen, the reconciliation itself would assist in standardising the way in which companies tend to present information concerning special circumstances affecting the tax charge. Presentation of such a reconciliation as part of the taxation note is proposed by the ASB's discussion paper.

Table 13.10 – Hanson PLC – Annual Report – 30 September 1994

NOTES TO THE ACCOUNTS (extract)

7 Taxation

	1994 £ million	1993 £ million
UK		
Corporation tax at 33% (33%)	**5**	160
Advance corporation tax	**150**	53
Deferred	**(6)**	5
	149	218
Overseas		
Current taxation	**77**	61
Deferred	**47**	(1)
	124	60
Associated undertakings	**8**	4
	281	282
Reconciliation of effective tax rate	**%**	%
Statutory United Kingdom corporation tax rate	**33.0**	33.0
Non-deductible and non-taxable items	**(5.5)**	(9.4)
Tax rate differences	**0.5**	1.2
Exceptional items	**(7.3)**	(0.8)
Other	**0.2**	3.8
Effective tax rate	**20.9**	27.8

The tax charge in respect of disposals of fixed asset investments, costs of closures and discontinued operations was £13mn (£12mn credit).

Balance sheet

Disclosures required by the Act

13.140 The requirements of the Act which relate specifically to the presentation of taxation in the balance sheet are as follows:

- Liabilities, as opposed to provisions, for taxation must be included in the balance sheet heading 'other creditors including taxation and social security', with the liability for taxation and social security being shown separately from 'other creditors'. [Note 9 to the balance sheet formats]. 'Other creditors including taxation and social security', like other categories of creditors, has to be split between amounts that will fall due within one year and amounts that will fall due after more than one year. [Note 13 to the balance sheet formats]. However, as all companies pay corporation tax within nine months of the financial year end no corporation tax balances payable in over one year should arise.

- The provision for deferred taxation should be included under the balance sheet heading 'Provisions for liabilities and charges' as part of the provision for 'Taxation, including deferred taxation', and stated separately from any other provision for other taxation. [Balance sheet formats 1 and 2, 4 Sch 47].

- Where there has been a transfer to or from any provision in respect of tax other than a transfer from that provision for the purpose for which it was set up, the following information should be disclosed:

  - The aggregate amount of the provision at both the beginning and end of the financial year.

  - Any amounts transferred either to or from the provision during the financial year.

  - The source and the application of any amounts so transferred.

  [4 Sch 46(1)(2)].

- The tax treatment of amounts credited or debited to the revaluation reserve should be disclosed. [4 Sch 34(4)].

Disclosure required by accounting standards

13.141 The paragraphs that follow deal with various information that should be included in respect of taxation in the balance sheet (or notes thereto) in accordance with the disclosure requirements contained in SSAP 8 and SSAP 15. As with disclosures in the profit and loss account, examples from published financial statements are given to illustrate the disclosure requirements of the Act and the accounting standards.

ACT on proposed dividends

13.142 The ACT payable on proposed dividends (whether recoverable or irrecoverable) should be included as a current tax liability and, therefore, falls to be included under 'taxation and social security'. [SSAP 8 para 26].

13.143 If the ACT on proposed dividends is regarded as recoverable, it should be deducted from the deferred tax account if such an account is available for the purpose. In the absence of a deferred tax account, ACT recoverable should be shown as a deferred asset. [SSAP 8 para 27]. However, the amount of ACT that can be properly offset is currently limited to 20/33 of the total corporation tax liability for the year. It follows that it may be incorrect to offset ACT against a deferred tax balance to a greater extent than it is actually recoverable against that deferred tax liability when it becomes payable. SSAP 15 also takes a similar view. [SSAP 15 app para 17].

13.144 In practice, however, a number of different treatments are followed. Some companies follow the offset rules precisely, any excess balance being shown separately as an asset. In some situations, the excess may be written off as a matter of accounting policy. Some companies set the ACT recoverable against the deferred tax balance without regard to the limit, whilst others ignore the deferred tax balance and include it separately as a deferred tax asset. Although there is some merit in the last two approaches, in our view the offset of ACT should be limited to the amount that can properly be deductible against deferred tax as if it were a mainstream corporation tax liability. Indeed, the disparity of ACT treatment in this area has been acknowledged in the ASB's discussion paper and it is likely that a standard method will be specified in the forthcoming standard on deferred taxation.

Analysis of deferred tax balance

13.145 The deferred tax balance, and its major components, should be disclosed in the balance sheet or in the notes. [SSAP 15 para 37]. The total amount of any unprovided deferred tax should also be disclosed in a note, analysed into its major components. [SSAP 15 para 40]. In practice, this requirement is not always followed literally. In order to determine the total amount of unprovided deferred tax, it is necessary to calculate the full potential liability. Many companies, therefore, tend to disclose the full potential liability and the amount provided, analysed into major components.

13.146 There is considerable merit in disclosing the full potential liability as this provides useful information concerning the company's total liability arising from its tax position at the balance sheet date. However, it remains doubtful whether companies can simply avoid disclosing the unprovided deferred tax liability on the grounds that it can be readily computed from the available information. This is because the ASC obtained legal advice that unprovided deferred tax liability is a contingent liability, except where the prospect of it becoming payable is so remote that it does not amount to a contingent liability at all. [SSAP 15 para 53]. As paragraph 50(2) of Schedule 4 requires information to be given with respect to the amount or estimated amount of any contingent liability not provided for, its legal nature and any valuable security provided, non-disclosure of the unprovided element of deferred tax does not meet strictly the legal requirements. An example of a company that has followed the requirements of the standard is given in Table 13.11 below.

Table 13.11 – Bass PLC – Annual Report – 30 September 1994

Note to the Financial Statements (extract)

	Group				Company
	Reorganisation provisions	Acquisition provisions	Deferred taxation	Total	Deferred taxation
19 Provisions for liabilities and charges	£m	£m	£m	£m	£m
At 30th September 1993	40	35	10	85	–
Transfer from debtors (note 15)	–	–	–	–	(30)
Profit and loss account	–	(2)	11	9	(5)
Expenditure	(24)	(7)	–	(31)	–
Write-off of redundant assets	(3)	–	–	(3)	–
ACT transfers to corporation tax	–	–	36	36	36
ACT recoverable	–	–	(31)	(31)	(31)
Exchange and other adjustments	–	(2)	(1)	(3)	–
Transfer to debtors (note 15)	–	–	–	–	30
At 30 September 1994	**13**	**24**	**25**	**62**	**–**

Reorganisation provisions were created over a number of years in relation to a major programme of fundamental reorganisation which established the present divisional structure and led to rationalisation within the Pubs and Brewing divisions designed in part to reduce the operational costs bases and in part to improve efficiency. Acquisition provisions were created in connection with the purchase of the Holiday Inn Business in North America to reflect the costs of integrating this business into the Group.

Deferred taxation

Deferred taxation has been provided to the extent that the directors have concluded on the basis of reasonable assumptions that it is probable that the liability will crystallise in the foreseeable future.

	Group		Company	
	1994	1993	**1994**	1993
	£m	£m	**£m**	£m
Amounts provided				
Timing differences related to:				
short-term items	**22**	25	**1**	6
long-term items	**91**	81	**–**	–
Tax effect of losses carried forward	**(57)**	(60)	**–**	–
ACT recoverable	**(31)**	(36)	**(31)**	(36)
	25	10	**(30)**	(30)
Amounts not provided				
Excess of tax allowances over book depreciation of fixed assets	**265**	258	**1**	2
Other timing differences	**(4)**	(15)	**2**	(1)
	261	243	**3**	1

Disclosure of deferred tax asset

13.147 There is no heading in the balance sheet formats for taxation recoverable, although any material amount recoverable is likely to be shown as a separate line item within debtors, as the Act permits an item of asset or liability that is not covered by any of the prescribed formats to be shown separately. [4 Sch 3(2)]. However, this issue is clarified in the note on the legal requirements to SSAP 15 which states that any deferred tax carried forward as an asset should be included under the heading of 'Prepayments and accrued income' either within 'Current assets/debtors', if it is current, or separately under main heading 'Prepayments and accrued income' (Format heading D). In the former situation, any amounts falling due after more than one year should be shown separately (note 5 on balance sheet formats). [SSAP 15 para 50]. A net deferred tax balance should be analysed into its major components in a manner similar to provisions. An example is given in Table 13.12 below.

Table 13.12 – National Power PLC – Report and Accounts – 26 March 1995

Notes to the accounts

14 Debtors (extract)

	Group		**Company**	
	1995	1994	**1995**	1994
Amounts recoverable after more than one year:				
Deferred taxation (note 18)	**47**	28	**50**	30
Other debtors	**4**	2	**4**	2
Due from subsidiary undertakings	**–**	–	**117**	11
Pension fund prepayments (note 7)	**88**	83	**88**	83
Total amounts recoverable after more than one year	**139**	113	**259**	126

18 Deferred taxation

Deferred taxation accounted for in the consolidated balance sheet and the potential amounts of deferred taxation are:

	1995 £m	1994 £m
Deferred tax liabilities:		
Tangible fixed assets accelerated capital allowances	**679**	651
Other timing differences	**14**	26
Dividends of overseas subsidiaries	**9**	10
Total gross deferred tax liabilities	**702**	687
Less: deferred tax liabilities not provided	**(690)**	(677)
Deferred tax liabilities	**12**	10
Deferred tax assets:		
Provisions	**114**	135
Other timing differences	**7**	4
Advance Corporation Tax recoverable	**33**	28
Total gross deferred tax assets	**154**	167
Less: deferred tax assets not provided	**(95)**	(129)
Deferred tax asset	**59**	38
Net deferred tax asset	**47**	28

The net deferred tax asset at 26 March 1995 is net of a deferred tax liability held by a subsidiary undertaking of £3 million (1994 £2 million) arising from accelerated capital allowances.

Analysis of deferred tax not provided

The analysis of deferred tax not provided is as follows:

	Accelerated capital allowances £m	Provisions £m	Other timing differences £m	Total £m
As at 28 March 1994	(651)	129	(23)	(545)
Movement in respect of the year ended 26 March 1995	(25)	(41)	16	(50)
As at 26 March 1995	(676)	88	(7)	(595)

Deferred tax provided

The movement on deferred taxation is as follows:

	£m
At 28 March 1994	28
Credited to profit and loss	14
Transfer to corporation tax	(28)
Advance corporation tax on proposed dividends	33
At 26 March 1995	**47**

Overseas subsidiaries

Cumulative unremitted earnings of overseas subsidiaries were £38 million at 26 March 1995 and £32 million at 27 March 1994.

Other disclosures

13.148 The other disclosure requirements of SSAP 15 that are relevant in respect of deferred taxation are as follows:

- Transfers to and from deferred tax account should be disclosed in a note. [SSAP 15 para 38]. A similar requirement to disclose movements during the year on any provision for tax is also contained in the Act as stated in paragraph 13.140 above. An example of such a movement is given in the Table 13.11 on page 63.

- Where amounts of deferred tax arise which relate to movements on reserves (for example, resulting from the expected disposal of revalued assets) the amount transferred to or from the deferred tax account should be shown separately as part of such movements. [SSAP 15 para 39].

- Where an asset is revalued, but the revaluation does not constitute a timing difference, because its disposal would not result in a tax liability, the fact that it does not constitute a timing difference and that tax has, therefore, not been quantified should be stated (see also para 13.122). [SSAP 15 para 41]. An example of such a disclosure is given in Table 13.13 below.

Table 13.13 – Scottish & Newcastle plc – Annual Report & Accounts – 1 May 1994

NOTES TO THE ACCOUNTS

18 PROVISIONS FOR LIABILITIES AND CHARGES (extract)

The full provision for other timing differences, in both the Group and the Company, includes an advance corporation tax debtor of £15.0m (1993 – £13.5m). The potential tax liabilities which might arise in the event of the disposal of revalued properties or for capital gains deferred under the terms of S.152, Taxation of Chargeable Gains Act 1992, are not quantified as the Directors do not consider them to constitute timing differences, after taking account of expected rollover relief.

- Where the value of an asset is shown in a note (or in the directors' report) because it differs materially from its book amount, the note should also show, if material, the tax effects, if any, that would arise if the asset were realised at the balance sheet date at the noted value (see also para 13.115). [SSAP 15 para 42]. In this situation, the 'tax effect' means that the potential amount of tax should be disclosed.

- Where a company is a member of a group, any assumptions made as to the availability of group relief and payment therefor which are relevant to an understanding of the company's deferred tax position should be stated. [SSAP 15 para 43].

- Where a company is a member of a group, any contingent deferred tax liability on behalf of other members of the group has to be shown separately in the financial statements of any company which has undertaken the commitment, analysed between amounts in respect of any subsidiary and amounts in respect of any parent company or fellow subsidiary. [SSAP 15 para 54; 4 Sch 59A]. An example of a company that actually provides for the subsidiary's tax in its own financial statements is given below in Table 13.14.

- The extent to which deferred tax has been accounted for in respect of future remittances of the accumulated reserves of overseas subsidiary undertakings should be disclosed. Where deferred tax has not been provided in respect of all the accumulated reserves of overseas subsidiary undertakings, the reason for not fully providing should be disclosed in the notes (see further para 13.188 and Table 13.4 on page 49). [FRS 2 para 54].

Table 13.14 – THORN EMI plc – Report and accounts – 31 March 1995

Notes to the accounts

21. Taxation (extract)

The Company has undertaken to discharge the liability to corporation tax of the majority of its wholly-owned UK subsidiaries. Their deferred tax liabilities are therefore dealt with in the accounts of the Company.

Groups of companies

Group relief

13.149 Subject to meeting detailed provisions in the tax legislation, trading profits and losses arising in the same accounting period may be offset for tax purposes between companies in the same group by way of group relief. For example, a subsidiary that incurred a loss during an accounting period may surrender that loss to another group member that made a profit during the same accounting period. The tax rules allow the profitable subsidiary (the claimant company) to pay to the loss making subsidiary (the surrendering company) any amount up to the full amount of the loss surrendered by way of group relief, without giving rise to any tax impact in either company.

13.150 Whether payment should or should not be made is a matter for the group to decide and does not affect the granting of the relief. However, non-payment or underpayment for group relief received may be objectionable if there are minority interests in the company. The reason for this is that if a company that has minority shareholders surrenders its losses for group relief purposes without receiving an adequate compensation payment, the minority shareholders' interests will be impaired. Likewise, overpayment for group relief may be objectionable if there are minority interests in the receiving company. Therefore, it is advisable that a fair payment should be made where there are minority interests in either the surrendering company, or the receiving company.

13.151 Where a payment is made to the surrendering company, the payment may take one of the following forms:

- The payment may be of the amount of the corporation tax saving by reason of group relief. In this situation, the claimant company pays as group relief what it would have paid as corporation tax at the applicable rate in force and the surrendering company receives the benefit of losses relieved at the same time.

- The payment may be made of any other amount up to a maximum of the gross amount of the loss surrendered by way of group relief. For example, it could be for an amount that is less than the amount of tax savings, or it could be more than the amount of tax savings, but less than the gross amount of the losses surrendered.

- The payment may be equal to the gross loss, that is the loss that has been incurred and surrendered by way of group relief, but no more than that. Any part of a payment in excess of the tax relief on the loss surrendered by way of group relief (for example, to finance the balance of the underlying loss) is not a payment in respect of group relief and it should not be dealt with as such in the financial statements.

13.152 Different accounting considerations arise in the financial statements of the claimant company and the surrendering company depending on whether payment is made for group relief or not. For the purposes of illustrating the impact of group relief made with or without payment, the tax computations of two wholly-owned fellow subsidiary undertakings, company X and company Y, for the year ended 31 December 19X1 are given in the table below. The rate of corporation tax is 33 per cent and is expected to remain constant for the foreseeable future.

Tax computations	**Company X 31 Dec 19X1 £**	**Company Y 31 Dec 19X1 £**
Profit (loss) before tax	(90,000)	180,000
Timing differences	(10,000)	(30,000)
	(100,000)	150,000
Group relief	100,000	(100,000)
Taxable profit (loss) chargeable to tax	–	50,000
UK corporation tax @ 33%	–	16,500

No payments made for group relief

13.153 In the financial statements of company X, the surrendering company, losses surrendered without payment being received are of no value to the company and, therefore, no credit can be taken in the profit and loss account. However, part of the losses surrendered may relate to timing differences, as indicated in the example. In that situation, if it is probable that the timing difference is likely to reverse, a deferred tax liability should be set up with a corresponding debit to the profit and loss account tax charge even if there is no current corporation tax charge. This is because the surrendering company has lost the benefit of these losses which could have been utilised by way of recovery of tax previously paid or by carry-forward for offset against future trading profits. As a result, they cannot be included in the deferred tax calculation.

13.154 Where the surrendering company has been advised by its parent to surrender losses without receiving payment, the taxation note to the profit and loss account should disclose the fact and the financial impact. An appropriate note is included in the profit and loss account presentation below.

Company X – The surrendering company		31 Dec 19X1 £
Loss on ordinary activities before taxation		(90,000)
Taxation:		
UK corporation tax @ 33%	–	
Deferred tax	3,300	(3,300)
Loss for the financial year		(93,300)

Note on taxation:
The company has surrendered the benefit of tax losses amounting to £100,000 to a fellow subsidiary undertaking without receiving any payment. Accordingly, no tax losses are available for carry-forward and the company has provided deferred tax amounting to £3,300 in respect of timing differences of £10,000 included in the losses surrendered.

13.155 In the financial statements of the claimant company, different considerations apply. Group relief received without payment is effectively a gift as far as the claimant is concerned. As the relief is included in arriving at the taxable profit of the claimant, it will reduce, or sometimes completely eliminate, the claimant's liability to current corporation tax. As a result, there could be a significant difference between the actual effective tax rate (tax charge as a percentage of profit before tax) and the prevailing corporation tax rate. In that situation, the difference will have to be explained and quantified as *"special circumstances affecting the liability to taxation for the current year"* to comply with the requirements of the Act and FRS 3 (see para 13.137 above). The presentation in the profit and loss account of the claimant company will be as follows:

Company Y – The claimant company

		31 Dec 19X1
	£	£
Profit on ordinary activities before taxation		180,000
Taxation:		
UK corporation tax @ 33%	16,500	
Deferred tax	9,900	26,400
Profit on ordinary activities after taxation		153,600
Effective tax rate		14.67%

Note on taxation:
The corporation tax charge for the year has been reduced by £33,000 because of losses surrendered by a fellow subsidiary undertaking. No payment for this surrender is to be made by the company.

The explanation can also be provided by way of a reconciliation between the actual rate of 33% and the effective rate of 14.67% as follows:

Actual UK corporation tax rate	33.00%
Group relief received without payment	(18.33)%
Effective tax rate	14.67%

Workings:
Group relief received £33,000 ÷ £180,000 = 18.33%.

13.156 Although deferred tax on the timing difference has been provided in the above example because reversal is expected, SSAP 15 requires that a company that is a member of a group should take into account any group relief that it expects (on reasonable evidence) to be available and also any charge for that relief in determining the amount of deferred taxation to be provided. [SSAP 15 para 43]. The implication is that deferred tax need not be provided on the expected reversal of timing differences where sufficient losses are expected to be made available to the claimant without any cost being incurred by it, thus eliminating the need for any provision. This situation may arise where the group can foresee that a member will continue to have current tax liabilities because of expected reversal of originating timing differences, but other group members are expected to make losses for tax purposes because of higher capital expenditure or otherwise. In that situation, the group may take advantage of the group relief provisions by requiring the profitable company to utilise losses made available to it by other group members without payment being made, thus avoiding the need to provide any deferred tax. The standard requires that any assumptions the company has made in anticipation of either the receipt or the surrender of group relief should be noted. [SSAP 15 para 43].

Payments made for group relief

13.157 Where a payment passes between the companies concerned, the accounting treatment in the financial statements of the claimant and the surrendering company will depend upon the nature of the payment as illustrated in the various situations discussed below.

Payment represents the amount of tax saving

13.158 In the financial statements of the surrendering company, the payment received or receivable will be credited as part of the tax charge with a corresponding debit to cash or amounts receivable from group companies. The treatment is similar to the repayment of tax. In some situations, it may not be prudent to take credit until the group's tax affairs have been finalised and the appropriate group election has been made. An appropriate note should be included in the tax note as illustrated below.

Company X – The surrendering company

		31 Dec 19X1
	£	£
Loss on ordinary activities before taxation		(90,000)
Taxation:		
Amount receivable from a fellow subsidiary in respect of group relief	33,000	
Deferred taxation	(3,300)	29,700
Loss for the financial year		(60,300)

Note on Taxation:
The company has surrendered the benefit of tax losses to another group company for a consideration of £33,000 which will be receivable on 30 September 19X2. Accordingly, no tax losses are available for carry-forward and the company has provided deferred tax amounting to £3,300 in respect of timing differences of £10,000 included in the losses surrendered.

13.159 As far as the claimant company is concerned, no particular problem arises because payment of tax is being made to a group member, rather than to the Inland Revenue. Therefore, the payment made should be dealt with as part of the tax charge to bring this into proper relationship with the profits, but suitably described as payment made for group relief. The presentation in the profit and loss account for the claimant company will be as follows:

Company Y – The claimant company

		31 Dec 19X1
	£	£
Profit on ordinary activities before taxation		180,000
Taxation:		
UK corporation tax @ 33%	16,500	
Amount payable to a fellow subsidiary in respect of tax saved by group relief	33,000	
Deferred tax	9,900	59,400
Profit on ordinary activities after taxation		120,600

Note on taxation:
The corporation tax payable for the year has been reduced by £33,000 because of group relief received from a fellow subsidiary for which a payment of £33,000 will be made on 30 September 19X2.

Payment is less than the amount of tax savings

13.160 Where the group relief payment is for an amount that is less than the amount of the tax saving, the payment should be shown as part of the tax charge in the financial statements of the claimant company. Assuming that the claimant makes a payment of £20,000 in consideration for tax savings of £33,000, the disclosure in the financial statements of the claimant company would be as follows.

Company Y – The claimant company

	31 Dec 19X1	
	£	£
Profit on ordinary activities before taxation		180,000
Taxation:		
UK corporation tax @ 33%	16,500	
Amount payable to a fellow subsidiary in respect of tax saved by group relief	20,000	
Deferred tax	9,900	46,400
Profit on ordinary activities after taxation		133,600

Note on taxation:
The corporation tax charge for the year has been reduced by £13,000 because of group relief received from a fellow subsidiary for which no payment has been made.

A symmetrical treatment is followed in the financial statements of the surrendering company as indicated below:

Company X – The surrendering company

	31 Dec 19X1	
	£	£
Loss on ordinary activities before taxation		(90,000)
Taxation:		
UK corporation tax @ 33%	–	
Amount receivable from a fellow subsidiary in respect of group relief	20,000	
Deferred tax	(3,300)	16,700
Loss on ordinary activities after taxation		(73,300)

Note on taxation:
The company has surrendered the benefit of tax losses of £100,000 to another group company for a consideration of £20,000 which will be receivable on 30 September 19X2. Accordingly, no tax losses are available for carry-forward and the company has provided deferred tax amounting to £3,300 in respect of timing differences of £10,000 included in the losses surrendered.

Payment is less than the gross amount of the loss surrendered

13.161 Where the payment is of any amount greater than the tax saving, but less than the gross amount of the group relief, the consideration in respect of the group relief should be dealt with in arriving at the profit before taxation. Assuming that the claimant makes a contribution of £60,000 in consideration for financing only part of the surrendering company's tax loss of £100,000, the payment should be suitably described and the effect on the tax charge amplified by a note, as shown below. An alternative treatment would be to treat the payment for the amount of tax savings as part of the tax charge and any excess payment as part of operating profit. But this treatment would result in a higher tax charge and will not ensure a correct match between pre- and post-tax profits as indicated below.

Company Y – The claimant company

		31 Dec 19X1
	£	£
Operating profit		180,000
Contribution towards loss of a fellow subsidiary payable by way of group relief		(60,000)
Profit on ordinary activities before taxation		120,000
Taxation:		
UK corporation tax @ 33%	16,500	
Deferred tax	9,900	26,400
Profit on ordinary activities after taxation		93,600

Note on taxation:
The charge for taxation has been reduced by £13,200 (being, £40,000 @ 33%) by reason of group relief receivable in addition to that appropriate to the contribution towards the loss of a fellow subsidiary that is charged against operating profit.

Alternative treatment

		£
Operating profit		180,000
Contribution towards loss of a fellow subsidiary in excess of tax saved by way of group relief		(27,000)
Profit on ordinary activities before taxation		153,000
Taxation:		
UK corporation tax @ 33%	16,500	
Amount payable to a fellow subsidiary in respect of tax saved by way of group relief	33,000	
Deferred tax	9,900	59,400
Profit on ordinary activities after taxation		93,600

As can be seen, in this situation, the tax charge is 38.8% of profit before tax, which is not very easy to understand unless the view is taken that the £27,000 is made in respect of financing losses and, therefore, disallowed for tax.

Company X – The surrendering company

		31 Dec 19X1
	£	£
Operating loss		(90,000)
Contribution receivable from a fellow subsidiary		60,000
Loss on ordinary activities before taxation		(30,000)
Taxation:		
UK corporation tax @ 33%	–	
Deferred tax	3,300	3,300
Loss for the financial year		(33,300)

Note on Taxation:
The company has surrendered the benefit of tax losses of £100,000 to another group company for a consideration of £60,000 which will be receivable on 30 September 19X2. Accordingly, no tax losses are available for carry-forward and the company has provided deferred tax amounting to £3,300 in respect of timing differences of £10,000 included in the losses surrendered.

In the above example, it has been assumed that the claimant has paid £60,000 in consideration for receiving tax losses of a value amounting to £100,000. It is possible for the surrendering company to surrender only part of the loss, leaving the balance to absorb any deferred tax on timing differences that are likely to crystallise in the future.

An alternative treatment similar to the one illustrated above may also be adopted in the financial statements of the surrendering company, but the tax credit for the loss will be out of line with the pre-tax loss.

Payment represents the gross amount of the loss surrendered

13.162 Where the claimant company makes a payment equal to the whole of the loss surrendered, the effect would be to take out of charge to corporation tax an equivalent amount of profit for both financial reporting and tax purposes. Consequently, the payment would be dealt with in arriving at profit before taxation, and it should be disclosed as shown below.

Company Y – The claimant company

		31 Dec 19X1
	£	£
Operating profit		180,000
Amount payable to a fellow subsidiary in respect of group relief		(100,000)
Profit on ordinary activities before taxation		80,000
Taxation:		
UK corporation tax @ 33%	16,500	
Deferred tax	9,900	26,400
Profit for the financial year		53,600

An alternative treatment would be to split the payment of £100,000 between the actual tax relief of £33,000, which would be included within the tax charge in the profit and loss account and include the excess payment for £67,000 within operating profit as expenses incurred in financing the losses of the surrendering company.

13.163 A symmetrical treatment should also be adopted in the financial statements of the surrendering company. That is, the amount received or receivable should be credited in arriving at profit before taxation. However, in this situation, the surrendering company receives payment for the full amount of the timing differences included in the loss surrendered and this creates a book profit. Although no tax loss is available for carry-forward, a deferred tax charge is required in respect of the timing differences included in the surrendered loss if it is concluded that the timing differences are likely to reverse as illustrated below.

Company X – The surrendering company

		31 Dec 19X1
	£	£
Operating loss		(90,000)
Contribution receivable from a fellow subsidiary		100,000
Profit on ordinary activities before taxation		10,000
Taxation:		
UK corporation tax @ 33%	–	
Deferred tax	3,300	3,300
Profit for the financial year		6,700

Note on Taxation:
The company has surrendered the benefit of tax losses to another group company for a consideration of £100,000 which will be receivable on 30 September 19X2. Accordingly, no tax losses are available for carry-forward and the company has provided deferred tax amounting to £3,300 in respect of timing differences of £10,000 included in the losses surrendered.

Again the alternative presentation discussed in paragraph 13.161 may be adopted.

13.164 Where a payment for group relief is brought into account in a year subsequent to that to which it relates, because the group relief position and group election for the current year were not finalised by the time the financial statements were approved, it should be appropriately described (depending upon the nature of the payment) as set out in the examples above, with the addition of words indicating that it relates to previous years. If the tax relief relating to the payment is brought to account at the same time, that too should be described appropriately.

Surrender of ACT

13.165 ACT can also be surrendered from one group company to another for a payment of any amount up to the amount of the ACT surrendered. It should be noted that ACT can only be surrendered in this way by a parent company to any of its subsidiaries, which are owned, directly or indirectly, at least 51 per cent throughout the relevant period. A subsidiary cannot surrender ACT either to its parent company or to a fellow subsidiary. The ACT that can be surrendered in this way applies only to ACT paid in the accounting period and does not apply to ACT brought forward from an earlier period or carried back from a later period. The ability to surrender ACT in this way is particularly important to a parent company where it earns a significant part of its profits from group income on which no ACT has been paid.

13.166 Although SSAP 8 and SSAP 15 do not specifically deal with the accounting treatment of surrendered ACT, the rules specified in these standards in respect of recoverable and irrecoverable ACT remain applicable. A subsidiary receiving an ACT credit from its parent can treat it as though it had paid the ACT itself. Where the payment made by the subsidiary to its parent company is for an amount equal to the amount of the ACT surrendered, no problem arises. The subsidiary receiving the surrendered ACT can offset it against its current corporation tax liability. Where the payment is for an amount that is less than the ACT surrendered, then the difference should be credited to the tax charged in the subsidiary's profit and loss account. A note similar to those applying in group relief situations should explain the treatment adopted both in the financial statements of the parent and the subsidiary company. If all of the surrendered ACT cannot be offset, the balance is available for carry-forward so long as the subsidiary remains in the group. The accounting considerations in respect of surrendered ACT carried forward in this way are no different from ACT on normal dividends (see paras 13.86 to 13.90).

Practical issues

13.167 This section deals with a number of practical issues that are not specifically dealt with in SSAP 15. These matters are fairly complex and may cause difficulty in practice. Although they involve considerations that may be contentious, the treatments proposed are considered to be in keeping with the spirit of SSAP 15. Some of these matters may well be addressed by the ASB when the new standard on deferred taxation is finalised.

Deferred tax treatment of government grants

13.168 The accounting treatment of government grants and their treatment for tax purposes may give rise to timing differences. SSAP 4, 'Accounting for government grants', requires grants to be treated as deferred income and amortised either over the periods in which the related revenue expenditure is recognised or, if the grant is made as a contribution towards capital expenditure, over the expected useful life of the related asset. In the latter situation, an alternative treatment of deducting the grant from the capital cost of the asset is permitted for entities not preparing their financial statements in accordance with Schedule 4 to the Act (see further, chapter 14). Some grants, given as a contribution towards the cost of acquisition of an asset are non-taxable. Other grants, such as revenue-based grants, are usually taxable on a cash received basis, whilst most capital-based grants, such as Selective Financial Assistance grants, are taxed by reducing the cost of fixed assets for capital allowances purposes.

13.169 If the grant is not taxable, the amount of the grant represents a permanent difference between accounting and taxable profits. Non-taxable revenue-based grants do not have any deferred tax consequences, because the amortised credit to the profit and loss account is simply a permanent difference in arriving at taxable profits of each year. Similarly, receipts of non-taxable capital-based grants do not give rise to deferred tax adjustments, except that accelerated capital allowances will need to be calculated as the difference between the net book value of the asset (gross cost less accumulated depreciation calculated on the gross cost) and the tax written down value (gross cost less tax allowances claimed). This applies even if the asset is stated in the financial statements net of the grant since the balance sheet presentation permitted by SSAP 4 (revised) for entities that do not report under Schedule 4 to the Companies Act 1985 does not affect the deferred tax calculation.

13.170 If the grant is taxable, a timing difference will arise between the taxable profits and the accounting profits. Revenue-based grants that are taxed on receipt, but amortised over a period for financial reporting purposes give rise to a timing difference on which a deferred tax asset may need to be set up on the unamortised balance carried forward in the financial statements. The deferred tax asset will fall to be recoverable in subsequent accounting periods as the deferred credit unwinds through amortisation. Where a grant that has been taxed on receipt becomes repayable, the repayment will qualify for tax relief in the year in which the repayment is made. In that situation, any deferred tax asset previously carried forward should be immediately written off as part of the tax charge.

13.171 Where a taxable grant is made as a contribution towards expenditure on a fixed asset, the nature of the deferred tax adjustment will depend on how the grant is treated for tax and accounting purposes. If the grant is deducted from the cost of fixed assets both for financial reporting and tax purposes, the deferred tax calculation is relatively straightforward as accelerated capital allowances are calculated on a reduced cost. On the other hand, if the grant is treated as a deferred credit for financial reporting purposes, but deducted against the cost of the asset for capital allowances purposes, the deferred tax calculation will consist of two components. A deferred tax debit balance will arise on the unamortised grant, which will be netted off against the deferred tax credit balance arising on the accelerated capital allowances. In practice, the balance on the deferred income account is netted off against the book value of the asset for the purposes of calculating the timing difference. Consider the following example:

Example

A company purchases a fixed asset for £120,000. The asset qualifies for a grant of £20,000 which is treated in the financial statements as a deferred credit. The asset has a useful economic life of five years. The company claims capital allowances, but these are restricted by the amount of the grant. The timing differences for deferred tax purposes are calculated as follows:

	19X1	19X2	19X3	19X4	19X5
Per financial statements	£	£	£	£	£
Cost of asset	120,000	96,000	72,000	48,000	24,000
Depreciation	(24,000)	(24,000)	(24,000)	(24,000)	(24,000)
Net book value	96,000	72,000	48,000	24,000	–
Unamortised deferred income	16,000	12,000	8,000	4,000	–

Per tax computation	19X1 £	19X2 £	19X3 £	19X4 £	19X5 £
Cost of asset	120,000				
Less grant	(20,000)				
Cost net of grant/pool	100,000	75,000	56,250	42,187	31,640
Capital allowances @ 25%	(25,000)	(18,750)	(14,063)	(10,547)	(7,910)
Tax written down value	75,000	56,250	42,187	31,640	23,730
Timing difference					
Capital allowances	25,000	18,750	14,063	10,547	7,910
Depreciation	(24,000)	(24,000)	(24,000)	(24,000)	(24,000)
Accelerated capital allowances	1,000	(5,250)	(9,937)	(13,453)	(16,090)
Amortisation of grant	4,000	4,000	4,000	4,000	4,000
Net timing difference	5,000	(1,250)	(5,937)	(9,453)	(12,090)
Net book value of fixed asset	96,000	72,000	48,000	24,000	–
Unamortised grant	(16,000)	(12,000)	(8,000)	(4,000)	–
	80,000	60,000	40,000	20,000	–
Tax written down value	(75,000)	(56,250)	(42,187)	(31,640)	(23,730)
Cumulative timing difference	5,000	3,750	(2,187)	(11,640)	(23,730)

The timing difference profile will be the same if the grant is deducted directly from the cost of the asset and the net amount written off over the five year period.

Deferred tax treatment of leases

13.172 Many companies enter into lease and hire purchase contracts under which they obtain the right to use or purchase assets. In the UK there is normally no provision in a lease contract for legal title to the leased asset to pass to the lessee. A hire purchase contract has similar features to a lease, except that the hirer may acquire legal title by exercising an option to purchase the asset upon fulfilment of certain conditions (normally the payment of a specified number of instalments). Current tax legislation provides that capital allowances may be claimed by a lessor under a lease contract, but by a hirer under a hirer purchase contract.

13.173 Accordingly, assets acquired under leases and hire purchase contracts give rise to timing differences between the amounts recorded in the profit and loss account and the amounts recorded in the tax computations. Where the asset is purchased under a hire purchase agreement, the hirer will normally account for the acquisition of the fixed asset in question and will be able to claim the capital allowances. Therefore, no particular deferred tax problems arise. Similarly, no deferred tax problems arise in accounting for an operating lease. This is because the amount that is charged to rentals in the profit and loss account for financial reporting purposes will be the same as the amount charged in arriving at the taxable profit. The only exception to this will arise where there are accrued rentals that may give rise to a potential short-term timing difference.

13.174 A timing difference will arise in circumstances where the lessee enters into a finance lease which is accounted for under the provisions of SSAP 21. In that situation, the asset acquired under a finance lease will be recorded as a fixed asset with a corresponding liability for the obligation to pay future rentals. The asset is then depreciated over the lease term or the useful life of the asset, whichever is shorter. Rents payable are apportioned between the finance charge and a reduction of the outstanding obligation for future amounts payable. The total finance charge is allocated to accounting periods during the lease term so as to produce a constant periodic rate of charge on the remaining balance of the obligation for each accounting period. A reasonable approximation is permitted (see further chapter 15).

13.175 As the finance lessee does not qualify for capital allowances, but is able to obtain a tax deduction for the whole of each rental payment, a timing difference arises as a result of the differing treatment for accounting and tax purposes. In some situations, the Inland Revenue may accept the SSAP 21 treatment for tax purposes, in which case there are no deferred tax consequences. However, in principle, a timing difference arises and this is illustrated in the following example:

Example

A company leases a fixed asset under a finance lease over a five year period. The annual lease payments amount to £12,000 per annum. The asset is recorded at the present value of the minimum lease payments of £48,000 and is depreciated at £9,600 per annum.
The timing difference arising is calculated as follows:

	Year 1	Year 2	Year 3	Year 4	Year 5
	£	£	£	£	£
Rentals	12,000	12,000	12,000	12,000	12,000
Finance cost @ 7.93%	(3,806)	(3,158)	(2,455)	(1,699)	(882)
Capital repayment	8,194	8,842	9,545	10,301	11,118

Timing difference					
Tax computations: rentals	12,000	12,000	12,000	12,000	12,000
P&L account:					
Finance cost	3,806	3,158	2,455	1,699	882
Depreciation	9,600	9,600	9,600	9,600	9,600
	13,406	12,758	12,055	11,299	10,482
Timing difference	(1,406)	(758)	(55)	701	1,518
Net book value of fixed asset	38,400	28,800	19,200	9,600	–
Outstanding obligation (capital)	39,806	30,964	21,419	11,118	–
Cumulative timing difference	(1,406)	(2,164)	(2,219)	(1,518)	–

Finance leases capitalised under SSAP 21, therefore, tend to produce an originating negative timing difference (deferred tax asset) as greater finance charges are allocated to earlier years to reflect the reducing capital amount owed under the lease. This asset should be recognised if it results in a net deferred tax asset that can be carried forward without replacement by equivalent debit balances (see further paragraph 13.80).

Treatment of tax in consolidated financial statements

General principles

13.176 The treatment of taxation in the consolidated financial statements involves considerations that are different from those that apply to individual financial statements. In a group, the tax positions of the individual group members are unlikely to be similar. Some group members may be profitable, whilst others may be loss making, leading to different tax considerations. Some may operate in the same tax jurisdiction, whilst others may operate in different tax jurisdictions. Given that consolidated financial statements are prepared as if the parent company and its subsidiary undertakings were a single entity, it follows that the group's tax position has to be viewed as a whole.

13.177 In the context of deferred taxation, therefore, it will not be a simple matter of netting off deferred tax assets in some group companies against deferred tax provisions in others to arrive at the overall group deferred tax provision. Rather, it is necessary to look at the net reversal of timing differences from a group perspective in order to determine what, if any, provision for deferred taxation is needed in the consolidated financial statements. Consider the following example.

Example

Company H, which is the parent company of two subsidiaries S1 and S2, is preparing its consolidated financial statements for the year ended 31 December 19X1. The profile of cumulative timing differences for each company is given below. Each company pays tax at the current rate of 33%, which is expected to remain unchanged for the foreseeable future.

Cumulative timing differences (gross)

	19X1	19X2	19X3	19X4	19X5
	£'000	£'000	£'000	£'000	£'000
Company H	100	150	200	250	300
Company S1	500	380	150	150	200
Company S2	200	400	300	100	50
Group as a whole	800	930	650	500	550

Provision for deferred tax – 31 Dec 19X1

	£'000	**Basis of provision**
Company H	–	No reversal anticipated
Company S1	115.5	Net reversal of 500 – 150 = 350 @ 33%
Company S2	49.5	Net reversal of 200 – 50 = 150 @ 33%
Total	165.0	
Group	99.0	Net reversal of 800 – 500 = 300 @ 33%

The above example illustrates that if the deferred tax provisions of the individual companies were simply aggregated, a provision of £165,000 would be needed on a net reversal of £500,000. However, from a group perspective only a net reversal of £300,000 is foreseen resulting in a deferred tax provision of £99,000, which is significantly less than the aggregate amount.

13.178 Although the above treatment is theoretically correct, it is likely that, in practice, such a calculation would not be performed and the deferred tax provision on a group basis would be arrived at by simply aggregating the deferred tax liabilities of the individual companies.

13.179 Where group members become subject to different tax rates because they operate in different tax jurisdictions, the above calculation would not be valid, even if it was computed in tax terms. This is because originating timing differences in one jurisdiction would not fall to be set off against reversing timing differences in others. For this reason, it is likely that the deferred tax provision from a group perspective would be arrived at by aggregating the deferred tax provisions of the individual companies where they operate in different tax jurisdictions.

Consolidation adjustments

13.180 In preparing consolidated financial statements, consolidation adjustments are made for various reasons. It is a requirement of the Act and FRS 2 that a group should follow uniform accounting policies in preparing consolidated financial statements. This may result in appropriate adjustments being made at the consolidation level where a subsidiary has not followed uniform group policies in preparing its own financial statements because of local requirements. Adjustments are also required to eliminate various intra-group transactions for the group to be treated as a single entity.

13.181 The total tax liability of a group is determined by aggregating the actual tax liability assessed under local tax laws and borne by individual group members. Consolidation adjustments may have tax consequences. In order to avoid distorting the group's tax charge, the tax effect of consolidation adjustments should be reflected therein without affecting the group's total tax liability. This can only be achieved if those tax effects are recognised as part of the deferred tax account of the group. The effect is that consolidation adjustments are treated as giving rise to timing differences, even though they do not appear in the tax computations of any group members and, therefore, do not fall within the definition of timing differences under SSAP 15. Nevertheless, they do have the effect of deferring or accelerating tax when viewed from the perspective of treating the group as a single entity.

13.182 A typical example of a consolidation adjustment is the elimination of profits and losses on intra–group transfer of goods. Assuming that a subsidiary sells goods costing £60,000 to its parent company for £70,000 and these goods are still held in stock at the year end, a consolidation adjustment is required to eliminate the profit of £10,000 from the consolidated profit and loss account. The subsidiary would have provided tax of £3,300 (£10,000 @ 33%) as part of its current tax liability. If this tax is not eliminated on consolidation, it would distort the group's tax charge. Therefore, some consider it necessary to make the adjustment through the group's deferred tax account. Although this is a sensible treatment, as the tax should only be recognised at the consolidation level when the goods are sold to third parties, it is not in accordance with SSAP 15. In this situation, a deferred tax asset of £3,300 would be created and if this asset is replaced by an equivalent asset it would appear that it may not be carried forward. Views are divided as to whether deferred tax should be provided on consolidation adjustments. Notwithstanding this, in practice it has become customary to make such adjustments.

Fair value adjustments

13.183 Under acquisition accounting, the identifiable assets and liabilities of the companies acquired are included in the acquirer's consolidated balance sheet at their fair value at the date of acquisition. This principle is recognised both in FRS 6 and the Act. SSAP 15 does not deal with the deferred tax consequences of fair value adjustments, although its principles may still be relevant. The guidance given in FRS 7, 'Fair values in acquisition accounting', is hardly adequate in that it simply reconfirms present practice that deferred tax should be determined on a group basis and that the enlarged group's deferred tax provision should be calculated at a single amount based on assumptions applicable to the group as a whole.

13.184 Like normal consolidation adjustments, fair value adjustments made to identifiable assets and liabilities acquired do not give rise to timing differences as defined in SSAP 15. This is because fair value adjustments that feed through the consolidated profit and loss account in the post-acquisition period are never recognised in post-acquisition tax computations of any group member. Whereas it has become customary to provide deferred tax on consolidation adjustments, the position is not so clear in respect of fair value adjustments.

13.185 For example, if stocks are revalued above cost, the profit in the post-acquisition period in the acquired company's profit and loss account would be calculated on the difference between sales proceeds and historical cost, and current tax would be provided on that profit. In the consolidated profit and loss account, the profit would be calculated on the difference between sales proceeds and the revalued amount, which is cost to the group, but the current tax charge would be the same as that provided in the acquired company's financial statements. This higher tax charge in the consolidated financial statements would have the effect of distorting the group's tax charge. The only way this imbalance could be rectified would be for the group to provide deferred tax on the revalued amount at acquisition, which would be released to the consolidated profit and loss account when the stock is sold. Some ASB board members take the view that deferred tax is a 'valuation adjustment' and that the effect of acquiring stock that is not fully tax deductible should be recognised by providing for deferred tax. This view is, however, not shared by those who believe that deferred tax represents an increment or decrement of a future tax liability. On this basis, since the acquisition of the stock does not affect the future tax liability, no deferred tax should be provided. We consider that providing deferred tax on the fair value adjustment reflects a proper allocation of the tax charge between the pre- and post-acquisition performance of the acquired company.

13.186 In the context of the revaluation of properties, which is a common fair value adjustment, the position is also far from clear. It can be argued that although the purpose of fair value adjustments is to establish a historical cost to the acquiring group, nevertheless an adjustment to the value of a property is clearly a revaluation from the point of view of the acquired company that will pay tax if the property is sold at the revalued amount. Accordingly, where a property has been revalued at acquisition, deferred tax should be provided in accordance with the principles of SSAP 15 if the new owners have entered into a commitment to sell the property that will result in a tax liability. However, this treatment in SSAP 15 is at odds with the principles on which FRS 7 is built. Whereas the identification and measurement of deferred tax liabilities under SSAP 15 in consolidated financial statements are heavily influenced by the management's intention concerning the future plans of the group as a whole, under FRS 7 management's future intentions are not supposed to affect fair values attributed at the date of acquisition. This inconsistency has been recognised by the ASB.

13.187 The issues discussed above demonstrate that at present there is no consensus as to what should be the correct treatment, even among ASB board members. However, the ASB has acknowledged in its discussion paper that any new FRS on tax will specifically address acquisition accounting and prescribe a single treatment. The deferred tax treatment of fair value adjustments is further considered in chapter 23.

Overseas operations

Unremitted earnings of overseas subsidiaries

13.188 Earnings of an overseas subsidiary that are not remitted to the UK do not normally suffer UK corporation tax. However, if such profits are remitted by way of dividends, they may suffer foreign withholding tax and UK corporation tax to the extent that they are not covered by double tax relief. Because the potential UK corporation tax liability has been deferred until such time as overseas earnings are remitted by way of dividends, the retention of those earnings will create a timing difference, but only if:

- there is an intention or obligation to remit them; and
- remittance would result in a tax liability after taking account of any related double tax relief.

[SSAP 15 para 21].

13.189 Therefore, where there is no intention of the directors to remit overseas earnings to the UK, no timing difference is created as no UK corporation tax is payable. In this situation, SSAP 15 does not require quantification of the unprovided deferred tax, only a statement that deferred tax has not been provided on these earnings. [SSAP 15 para 44]. However, FRS 2 has amended this requirement by requiring that the reason for not fully providing deferred tax in respect of all the accumulated reserves of overseas subsidiary should be stated. [FRS 2 para 54]. A typical reason for not providing deferred tax is given in Table 13.4 on page 49.

13.190 Where there is an intention to remit overseas earnings a timing difference will arise, because the earnings are included in the consolidated financial statements, but are not fully taxed until remitted. In this situation, provision should be made for UK deferred tax and any overseas withholding tax after taking account of any double tax relief to the extent that it is probable that a liability will crystallise. In practice, it may be difficult to quantify the further tax payable as it would depend on a number of factors, such as: the tax laws and rates in force in the UK; the relevant overseas country at the time when the remittances are made; and the terms of any tax treaty that may exist between the two countries at that time. Nevertheless, an estimate should be made using the tax laws and rates that are in force at the balance sheet date. Disclosure of the amount is also required. [FRS 2 para 54].

Foreign exchange differences

13.191 Gains or losses arising on the translation of the financial statements of overseas subsidiaries and associated companies are not regarded as creating a timing difference. However, gains or losses arising on the translation of an enterprise's own overseas assets (including investments in subsidiaries and associated companies) and liabilities may give rise to timing differences depending on whether or not the gains or losses have a tax effect. [SSAP 15 app para 12].

Foreign income dividend scheme

General features

13.192 As stated in paragraph 13.37 above, the Government introduced a Foreign income dividend (FID) scheme in 1994 to relieve the surplus ACT that arises as a result of the distribution of foreign income. Under this scheme, a company can elect for dividends paid after 30 June 1994 to be FIDs. While the company may elect for some dividends to be paid as FIDs, it may choose to pay others as normal dividends. The main features of FIDs are:

- A FID does not carry a tax credit. Therefore, there is no repayment of tax to shareholders, such as exempt funds who are normally entitled to claim refunds in respect of tax credits. However, an individual UK shareholder who receives a FID is treated as receiving income that has borne tax at the lower rate – thus, a higher rate taxpayer pays tax at the higher rate on the grossed up amount of the dividend less the imputed lower rate.

- A company paying a FID (which must be paid in cash) has to account for ACT in the normal way.

- A company receiving a FID cannot use the FID to frank a normal dividend that it pays. If a company receiving FIDs during an accounting period also pays FIDs during that period, it has to pay ACT on the FIDs paid only to the extent that they exceeded the FIDs received.

- ACT attributable to the FID can be reclaimed from the Inland Revenue to the extent that, owing to foreign tax on profits, it is surplus. The rules for determining the amount of surplus ACT attributable to the FID that can be repaid are complex. The company must match the FID with foreign source profits (that is, profits on which the company was charged to corporation tax and was allowed a credit for double taxation relief) and calculate the repayable ACT as the lower of:

    - the company's total surplus ACT for the period; and

- the surplus ACT attributable to any FIDs paid in the period that could be treated as having been paid out of foreign source profits.

The foreign source profits can be those of the company or, in certain cases, those of a 51 per cent subsidiary.

Accounting treatment – paying company

13.193 Where a company pays a FID from foreign source dividends, the accounting treatment that should be followed is illustrated in the example below.

Example

A company that is liable to UK corporation tax at 33% has foreign source profits of £1,000,000 which have also borne foreign tax at a rate of 33%. The company intends to pay a dividend of £400,000.

The following table shows the profit and loss accounts in the cases of a normal dividend of £400,000, a FID of the same amount, and an 'enhanced' FID of £500,000:

	Normal dividend	FID	Enhanced FID
	£'000	£'000	£'000
Profit before tax	1,000	1,000	1,000
UK tax (33%)	330	330	330
less: DTR	(330)	(330)	(330)
UK mainstream	–	–	–
Overseas tax	330	330	330
Irrecoverable ACT	100	–	–
Total tax	430	330	330
Profit after tax	570	670	670
Dividend paid	(400)	(400)	(500)
Retained profit	170	270	170

Normal dividend

If the company pays a normal dividend of £400,000, it must pay ACT of £100,000 (that is, 25%). As shown in the table above, there is no mainstream UK corporation tax liability, because the UK liability is fully offset by the credit for double tax relief. The ACT is, therefore, surplus and, in accordance with SSAP 8, is deemed to be irrecoverable unless its recovery is reasonably certain and foreseeable, normally not looking beyond the next accounting period. Irrecoverable ACT is written off as part of the tax charge.

Foreign income dividend

If the company elects to pay the dividend as a FID, it can recover the ACT if the surplus ACT arises from foreign tax on its profits. Payment of a FID has the effect of increasing the profit after tax, retained profit and, hence, basic earnings per share by the amount of recoverable ACT that would otherwise have been written off. This effect is sometimes disclosed in the notes (see Table 13.7 on page 53).

'Enhanced' foreign income dividend

Unlike a normal dividend, a FID does not carry a tax credit. A FID is, therefore, less valuable than a normal dividend to non-taxpaying shareholders such as exempt funds, which are usually entitled to claim refunds in respect of tax credits. Consequently, it is likely that companies would wish to protect the position of those shareholders by increasing the amount of a dividend paid as a FID to compensate them for the loss of tax credit – this is shown as an 'enhanced FID' in the example above.

Where an enhanced FID is paid, the retained profit for the year would be the same as the retained profit after payment of a normal dividend plus surplus ACT related to that dividend and written off as irrecoverable. However, because surplus ACT written off is required to be treated as part of the tax charge on the company, the company paying a normal dividend with an ACT write-off would have a lower after-tax profit than a company paying a FID, although the after-dividend retained profit would be the same. Thus the earnings per share would be lower for a company paying a normal dividend.

Balance sheet

In the case of the FID, the ACT paid or payable of £100,000 is recoverable. It should be shown within debtors as falling due either within one year (if the FID was paid during the financial year) or after one year (if the FID was proposed at the year end and paid in the next financial year). If the FID is an enhanced FID, the ACT payable and recoverable is £125,000 (25% of the enhanced dividend of £500,000). It should be noted that any repayable surplus ACT would become repayable at the same time as mainstream corporation tax would become payable, that is, nine months after the end of the accounting period in which the FID is paid.

Effect of different foreign tax rates

13.194 If the foreign tax suffered on the company's profits was less than the current UK corporation tax rate of 33 per cent, not all of the ACT paid on the FID would be repaid. That is because there would be a UK tax liability after credit for double tax relief in respect of the foreign tax on foreign source profits. Consequently, the maximum recovery of ACT would be where foreign source profits have borne tax at rates equal to or higher than UK rates.

Example

Facts are the same as in the previous example except that the foreign source profits of £1,000,000 have borne foreign tax at a rate of 25%.

Profit and loss account

The following table shows the profit and loss accounts in the cases of a normal dividend of £400,000, a FID of the same amount, and an enhanced FID of £500,000:

	Normal dividend £'000	**FID** £'000	**Enhanced FID** £'000
Profit before tax	1,000	1,000	1,000
UK tax (33%)	330	330	330
less: DTR	(250)	(250)	(250)
UK mainstream	80	80	80
Overseas tax	250	250	250
Irrecoverable ACT	20	–	–
Total tax	350	330	330
Profit after tax	650	670	670
Dividend paid	(400)	(400)	(500)
Retained profit	250	270	170

In the above example, there is some ACT capacity in respect of the foreign source profits, that is, £80,000 for every £1,000,000 of profits (33% less 25%); thus where a normal dividend is paid there is surplus ACT of £20,000 (ACT payable of £100,000 less ACT recoverable of £80,000). If a normal dividend is paid, this surplus ACT may have to be written off as irrecoverable. Where a FID is paid, the surplus ACT of £20,000 could be recovered.

Where the dividend is paid as a FID rather than as a normal dividend, profit after tax and, hence, earnings per share are higher as a result of the irrecoverable ACT of £20,000 that results from the payment of a normal dividend.

If the foreign source profits had borne foreign tax at a rate of 16.25% or lower, there would be a UK mainstream tax liability of £167,500 or greater, which would be sufficient to cover any ACT paid on a distribution of those profits. For example, a maximum dividend of £670,000 would attract ACT of £167,500. Consequently, if in these circumstances a distribution were paid as a FID and treated as paid out of those profits, there would be no surplus ACT which could be repaid.

Balance sheet

In the above example, ACT recoverable amounts to £80,000, £100,000 and £125,000 in respect of the normal dividend, the FID and the enhanced FID respectively.

Accounting treatment – receiving entity

13.195 Under SSAP 8 a corporate shareholder receiving a normal franked dividend should include in profit before tax the dividend received grossed up by the amount of the tax credit. An amount equivalent to the tax credit is shown as part of the tax charge. However, where a FID is received it does not carry a tax credit; neither is a corporate investor subject to tax in respect of a FID. Accordingly, the dividend should be recognised in the profit and loss account at the amount of the dividend received; it should not be grossed up by a notional tax credit. Other tax exempt investors, such as exempt funds, should similarly record FIDs received as the actual dividends received, because there is no tax credit available. As noted above, it is probable that companies paying FIDs will set the FID at a level to compensate investors for the loss of tax credit.

13.196 It may seem anomalous that FIDs received should be treated differently from franked investment income, when neither are taxable income in the hands of companies. The difference arises from the 'grossing up' treatment of imputed tax credits required by SSAP 8 where franked investment income is received (see para 13.40).

Assessing the recoverability of ACT

13.197 When a claim for repayment of ACT in respect of a FID is made, the company must establish that the FID is matched with foreign source profits of the accounting period in which the FID is paid or the preceding accounting period (but not for any accounting period beginning before 1 July 1993).

13.198 When a company pays a FID, it would not necessarily know the amount of foreign source profits for the period, because that is established later. If, having elected to treat the dividend as a FID, the company discovers subsequently that it has insufficient foreign source profits, the ACT paid on the FIDs cannot be recovered from the Inland Revenue (although it may be carried forward and matched against foreign source profits of the next period).

13.199 The requirements of SSAP 8 and SSAP 15 regarding the treatment of recoverable ACT and irrecoverable ACT apply to ACT on FIDs in the same way as they apply to ACT on normal dividends. Therefore, where a FID is paid or proposed in the expectation that surplus ACT will be repaid to the company, it is necessary to be satisfied that the recovery of ACT is reasonably certain and foreseeable in order to recognise recoverable ACT as an asset. The treatment of ACT recoverable in respect of dividends paid during the period and those proposed at the year end are considered in detail from paragraph 13.86.

Income and expenses subject to non-standard rates of tax

13.199.1 It is necessary to distinguish income that is received after deduction of tax as discussed in paragraph 13.38 from income that is taxable at non-standard rates. It is not uncommon for companies to enter into transactions that give rise to income or expense that is not subject to the standard rate of corporation tax. Examples include some leasing transactions and advances and investments made by financial institutions. In some situations, the transaction may, after taking account of the financing cost, result in a pre-tax loss and a post-tax profit. Consider the following example:

Example

A financial institution borrows £10 million which bears interest at 9% per annum. The proceeds are immediately invested in an instrument that yields 8% per annum, but the income is taxable at 20 per cent. The standard rate of corporation tax is 33%. The company makes a pre-tax loss of £100,000, but the transaction is profitable after tax effects are taken into account as shown below:

Profit and loss account	£'000	£'000
Investment income @ 8%		800
Less: interest expense		(900)
Pre-tax loss		(100)
Taxation:		
On income @ 20%	(160)	
Tax relief on interest @ 33%	297	
Tax credit		137
Post-tax profit		37

13.199.2 Banks and other institutions enter into such transactions precisely because it is profitable on an after tax basis. However, they contend that the presentation shown above is misleading because it makes it difficult to interpret the profit and loss account and inhibits comparison between different companies, especially as pre-tax profits are seen as an important measure of performance. They advocate that income subject to the non-standard rate of tax should be presented on a grossed up basis as shown below to eliminate the distortion between pre and post-tax profits by reporting tax at the standard rate.

Profit and loss account (grossed-up)	£'000	£'000
Investment income (grossed up) : 640/(100%–33%)*		955
Less: interest expense		(900)
Pre-tax profit*		55
Tax charge @ 33%†		(18)
Post-tax profit		37
* Includes notional income of £155		
† Includes notional tax charge of £155		

13.199.3 However, many argue that grossing up, because it is notional, fails to report the true nature of the transaction. They believe that if a transaction results in a pre-tax loss and a tax benefit it is necessary that it be reported as such in order to achieve a faithful representation. Grossing up reports a false amount both as pre-tax profits and as the tax charge for the year. The tax treatment of the transaction should have no bearing on the way in which the transaction is reported for financial reporting purposes. If grossing up were allowed as a general rule then non-deductible expenditure could be presented on a grossed-up basis. This treatment would be inconsistent with general accepted practice in accounting for such items, where no adjustments are usually made.

13.199.4 The issue was referred to the UITF. On 13 February 1997, the UITF issued Abstract 16 which prohibits the practice of reporting transactions that are taxed at a non-standard rate with notional adjustments to show what the position would have been if a standard rate had applied. Therefore, income and expenses subject to non-standard rates of tax should be reported in the pre-tax results on the basis of the income or expenses actually receivable or payable. No adjustment should be made to reflect a notional amount of tax that would have been paid or relieved in respect of the transaction if it had been taxable, or allowable for tax purposes, on a different basis. [UITF Abstract 16].

13.199.5 Companies whose results are significantly affected by transactions that are subject to tax other than at a standard rate should disclose the full effects of such transactions in their financial statements. Indeed, both the Act and FRS 3 require disclosure of any special circumstances that affect the tax charge or credit during the period. These disclosure requirements are considered from paragraph 13.137.

[The next paragraph is 13.200.]

Future developments

ASB's discussion paper

13.200 The ASB issued a discussion paper, 'Accounting for tax', in March 1995. This Paper is the first stage in the project to develop a new FRS to replace SSAP 15 and some of the disclosure requirements of SSAP 8. When SSAP 15 was issued in 1978, it was generally agreed to be a pragmatic response to the UK tax system at that time. SSAP 15 was identified as requiring an urgent review and was, therefore, placed high on the ASB's list of existing standards to be reviewed. It was amended in 1992 as a temporary measure to remove an inconsistency with SSAP 24 and UITF 6, which is discussed in paragraph 13.99 above. For reasons stated in the discussion paper, the ASB believes that SSAP 15 is not capable of further amendment and what is required is a thorough review of accounting for tax in the UK. The discussion paper is a first stage in that process.

13.201 The paper explores accounting for tax from first principles and presents arguments for and against three methods: flow-through method, under which no provision is made for deferred tax (see para 13.44); the full provision method, under which deferred tax is provided in full (see para 13.59); and the partial provision method, under which deferred tax is provided for to the extent that a liability will crystallise, taking into account the tax effects of likely future transactions (see para 13.64).

13.202 The paper does not express support for the flow-through method, because it gives rise to too much volatility in earnings, results in misstating the tax liability and is not used internationally. So it is rightly discarded. The serious debate is between the partial and the full provision methods. But having reached the conclusion that the partial provision method cannot be further amended, the ASB recommends the adoption of the full provision as being consistent with its draft statement of principles and international practice. Although the ASB favours full provision, board members are divided between the traditional view, and the 'valuation adjustment' view, of deferred tax as described in paragraphs 13.57 and 13.58 above.

13.203 Comments on the discussion paper were due by the 16 June 1995. It would appear that the ASB's provisional conclusion is not widely shared. Too much play has been made of the fact that the full provision method is consistent both with the ASB's draft Statement of principles and with international practice and very little attention has been devoted to what the final answer means. Furthermore, the full provision method recommended by the board (the traditional approach) differs significantly from the full provision method (temporary difference approach) that is used in the US and that is (with some exceptions) proposed in IASC E49. Also some board members' view that deferred tax is a 'valuation adjustment' is considered by many in the UK as being largely academic.

13.204 The ASB acknowledged that the use of the full provision method may lead to the accumulation of large provisions, which will not reverse for many years. As a solution, it proposed that the overstatement problem could be overcome if discounting is applied to future timing differences. The idea of discounting is proposed as an attempt to 'sweeten the pill', a pragmatic approach to a serious problem, the very reason for which partial provision is criticised, rather than an argument of conviction.

13.205 The arguments for rejecting SSAP 15 have not yet been won and there is strong support in favour of retaining it in the UK, even by those who recommended its review in the first place. The fact that this basis requires the exercise of judgment, backed up by evidence in the form of forecasts, is considered by many as a poor reason for dismissing it. The paper also argues that because of its reliance on management projections, it is subjective and the amount of provision is 'manageable' depending on, for example, management's stated plans for capital expenditure. But there is no concrete evidence to suggest that the current standard is being abused to the extent that the financial statements are misleading, as was the case with fair value provisioning prior to the issue of FRS 7.

13.206 Another criticism is that the balances recognised under SSAP 15 are measured by reference to future events and management intentions which departs from the draft Statement of principles, in particular, the definition of liability. But the partial provision approach can be reconciled with the draft Statement of principles if it is viewed, not simply as a method of recognising a liability, but as an integral approach to recognising and measuring the liability. First, it is accepted that the current tax asset is a legal liability, which clearly should be provided. Therefore, the liability definition is met and the existence of the liability is recognised. Further amounts (deferred tax) can be regarded as contingent liabilities rather than actual ones. Under SSAP 18, material contingent losses should be accrued to the extent that it is probable that the loss will crystallise. As stated in paragraph 13.146 above, the ASC has obtained legal advice that unprovided deferred tax is a contingent liability, except where the prospect of it becoming payable is so remote that it does not amount to a contingent liability at all. In this second process, probable future events, such as future capital expenditure plans, can be taken into account in measuring the liability at the amount at which it will be paid. This is a sensible approach, because such events are taken into account in measuring other items in financial statements, such as pension costs based on future salary increases and tax loss assets based on future profits.

13.207 Whilst the aim of international harmonisation of accounting standards is to be commended, many in the UK would argue that lack of international comparability is not of itself a sufficiently good reason for rejecting a standard that has worked well in the UK and where there are valid reasons for such differences. In the case of deferred tax there are both differences between the tax regimes of the UK, the US and Europe and valid differences of view, in principle, on the methods of measuring deferred tax liabilities. The question is, therefore, whether these factors justify the UK taking a different line on deferred tax from international and US standards.

13.208 Judging by the wide range of differing views, both within the Board and outside it, it would appear that a consensus on what should replace SSAP 15 will be difficult to achieve. Indeed, most of the responses to the discussion paper favoured keeping the partial provision method of accounting for deferred tax. In September 1996, however, despite the ASB's vigorous arguments against it, the IASC issued a new standard on income taxes which will require deferred tax to be provided under the full provision method. It is now clear that the international community no longer regards partial provision as a credible method of accounting for deferred tax. This has major implications for the UK. Unless the ASB develops an alternative approach that might be recognised internationally as being more meaningful and conceptually valid than the IASC approach, the pressure will be on the UK to fall in line with the USA and the IASC. The ASB intends to publish a further discussion paper on the topic during the summer of 1997.

Presentation of dividend income

13.208.1 On 16 October 1997 the ASB published an exposure draft of an Amendment to SSAP 8 – presentation of dividend income. This follows changes to the treatment of tax credits in the 1997 budget. The current accounting treatment for UK dividends received, as explained in paragraph 13.38, is to gross up for the tax credit in pre-tax profit, then to include the amount of the tax credit in the tax line, and show the actual cash dividend received in the post-tax line. The 1977 budget changed the rules regarding reclaiming the tax credit and, as a consequence, the arguments for grossing up franked investment income by the amount of ACT seem weaker than before. The ASB's exposure draft proposes revising SSAP 8 to reflect only the cash dividend received in both the pre-tax and post-tax lines.

13.208.2 One of the effects of the budget change was to stop pension schemes from being able to recover tax credits on their dividend income. As a consequence, SSAP 8 would, without this change, require pension schemes to gross up the dividend received and report a tax charge in respect of its investment income in an entity that is exempt from tax.

[The next paragraph is 13.209.]

Comparison with IASs

13.209 In September 1996, the IASC issued IAS 12 (revised), 'Income Taxes', which replaces the original IAS 12, 'Accounting for Taxes on Income'. IAS 12 (revised) is significantly different from the original standard and is seriously inconsistent with SSAP 15. It becomes effective for accounting periods beginning on or after 1 January 1988.

13.210 IAS 12 (revised) is based on a new liability method that moves deferred tax calculation from the profit and loss account basis to a balance sheet basis. That is, instead of accounting for timing differences, the basis used in SSAP 15 and the original IAS 12, it uses a balance sheet concept of *temporary differences* – differences between the carrying amount of an asset or liability and its tax base (the amount attributed to it for tax purposes). Temporary difference is a broad concept and includes not only timing differences, but other differences between the accounting and tax bases of assets and liabilities that are not timing differences, for example, revaluation of assets for which no equivalent adjustment is made for tax purposes.

13.211 The revised standard requires an enterprise to recognise a deferred tax liability (or, subject to a recovery test, deferred tax assets) for all temporary differences with certain exceptions. This means that the partial provision approach, which was also permitted by the original IAS 12, is no longer allowed.

13.212 Providing deferred tax on temporary differences, which is also the basis adopted in the US, will lead to deferred tax provisions being created automatically in circumstances where the company does not necessarily have an obligation arising from past events. As a result, the revised standard provides three exceptions for temporary differences on which deferred tax should not be provided. These are

- Non-taxable goodwill (positive or negative).

- Certain items whose initial carrying amount differs from its initial tax base, for example, when an enterprise receives a non-taxable government grant.

- Investments in subsidiaries, branches and associates and interests in joint ventures in certain circumstances.

13.213 Except for the exceptions noted above, deferred tax should be provided on all other temporary differences. In particular, IAS 12 (revised) requires deferred tax to be provided on temporary differences arising from revaluation of assets and fair value adjustments arising on acquisitions. Under IAS 12 (revised), the difference between the carrying amount of a revalued asset and its tax base is a temporary difference and gives rise to a deferred tax liability or asset. Similarly, when the carrying amount of an asset is increased to fair value in a business combination that is an acquisition, but the tax base of the asset remains at cost to the previous owner, a taxable temporary difference arises which results in a deferred tax liability with a corresponding effect on goodwill.

13.214 All deferred tax assets and liabilities should be classified in the balance sheet as non-current. The disclosure requirements are also quite extensive. In particular, an explanation of the relationship between the tax expense (income) and the accounting profit should be provided by means of a numerical reconciliation either between the tax expense (income) and the accounting profit, or between the applicable tax rate and the average effective tax rate. An explanation should also be provided of the changes in the applicable tax rate.

Chapter 14

Tangible and intangible fixed assets

Page

Chapter 14

Tangible and intangible fixed assets

Introduction

14.1 This chapter considers the accounting requirements affecting tangible and intangible fixed assets, excluding finance leases and investments, which are considered in chapters 15 and 16 respectively. The chapter should also be read in conjunction with chapter 5, which deals in detail with the valuation rules, including:

- Historical cost, including determination of production cost and purchase price.
- The concept and methods of depreciation.
- Diminutions in value.
- The alternative accounting rules, including bases of valuation.

14.2 This chapter considers the accounting treatment and disclosure of: the standard categories of tangible fixed assets; capital grants; and investment properties. This chapter also considers the accounting for intangible assets covered by FRS 10 and the Act, research and development expenditure and computer software expenditure. Goodwill is not dealt with in this chapter, but is considered in detail in chapter 23.

Background

14.3 The key accounting issues relating to fixed assets are, first, what assets should be treated as fixed assets and, secondly, how should they be measured. The first question is largely answered by the legal definition, as set out in paragraph 14.7.

14.4 As regards the second issue – measurement – various options are available to companies. Companies can present financial statements which are:

- prepared under the historical cost convention; or
- prepared under the historical cost convention as modified by the revaluation of certain assets; or
- prepared under the current cost convention.

14.5 These alternative conventions are discussed in detail in chapter 5. The effect of these options is a wide degree of inconsistency from one reporting entity to another and, in some cases, within one entity from year to year. This is particularly pronounced where the modified historical cost convention is followed, since it results in a mixture of historical cost assets and revalued assets. This can mean that the individual components of, say, a property portfolio, as set out in financial statements, are stated at either cost or a revalued amount. Furthermore, the properties revalued may have been revalued over a period of years, rather than all at the same date. An example of such a presentation is set out in Table 14.5 on page 14012. With the publication of FRED 17 in October 1997, the ASB aims to ensure that valuations are kept up-to-date by proposing that, where a policy of revaluation is adopted, properties are revalued fully every five years with interim valuations in year three or more often if there has been a material change in value.

14.6 The issues that surround fixed asset accounting reflect the current uncertainty surrounding the purpose of statutory financial statements. The ASB's development of a Statement of principles may in due course clarify this issue. However, as the draft statement acknowledges, there is inevitably a trade-off between relevance of financial information and its reliability. In the context of fixed assets, cost-based methods represent reliability and valuation approaches lead to more relevant information. Neither one, alone, fully satisfies the needs of users of financial statements, yet both together may be regarded as a burden on the preparer and, in some cases, as an information overload on the user. There is no simple resolution to these issues.

Defining fixed assets

14.7 In terms of definition, the Act gives only limited assistance because its guidance is of a general nature. The Schedule 4 formats indicate that all assets are either fixed or current. The Act says that assets are fixed assets where they *"...are intended for use on a continuing basis in the company's activities"*. Consequently, current assets are *"...assets not intended for such use"*. [Sec 262(1)].

Categories of fixed asset under the Act

14.8 Schedule 4 to the Act provides further guidance, in that it sets out standard presentation formats. These formats are to be adopted, in respect of fixed assets, so far as is relevant to their individual circumstances, by reporting entities governed by the Act. The balance sheet formats identify the following sub-classifications of fixed assets and their constituent parts:

- Intangible assets:
  - Development costs.
  - Concessions, patents, licences, trademarks and similar rights and assets.

- Goodwill.
- Payments on account.

- Tangible assets:
  - Land and buildings.
  - Plant and machinery.
  - Fixtures, fittings, tools and equipment.
  - Payments on account and assets in course of construction.

- Investments:
  - Shares in group undertakings.
  - Loans to group undertakings.
  - Participating interests.
  - Loans to undertakings in which the company has a participating interest.
  - Other investments other than loans.
  - Other loans.
  - Own shares.

14.9 The Act requires companies to use the headings and sub-headings prescribed in the formats other than in certain instances where the special nature of the company's business requires their adaptation. Some companies have changed the headings used on the face of the balance sheet. This is particularly true in the context of intangible assets, where the term has been replaced by reference to the specific nature of the asset capitalised. Examples of this treatment are given in Tables 14.1 and 14.2.

Table 14.1 – Guinness PLC – Report and Accounts – 31 December 1994

Group balance sheet (extract)

At 31 December 1994	Notes	1994 £m	1994 £m	1993 £m	1993 £m
NET ASSETS					
Fixed assets					
Acquired brands at cost	13		**1,395**		1,395
Tangible assets	14		**1,784**		1,725
Investment in MH	15	**900**		-	
Investment in LVMH	16	-		1,282	
Other long term investments	17	**149**		157	
			1,049		1,439
			4,228		4,559

Accounting policies (extract)

Brands

The fair value of businesses acquired and of interests taken in associated undertakings includes brands, which are recognised where the brand has a value which is substantial and long-term. Acquired brands are only recognised where title is clear, brand earnings are separately identifiable, the brand could be sold separately from the rest of the business and where the brand achieves earnings in excess of those achieved by unbranded products.

Amortisation is not provided except where the end of the useful economic life of the acquired brand can be foreseen. The useful economic lives of brands and their carrying value are subject to annual review and any amortisation or provision for permanent impairment would be charged against profit for the period in which they arose.

Table 14.2 – THORN EMI plc – Report and Accounts – 31 March 1995

Balance sheets (extract)

		Group		Company	
		1995	1994	**1995**	1994
	Notes	**£m**	£m	**£m**	£m
Fixed assets					
Music publishing copyrights	10	**379.5**	400.6	**-**	-
Tangible fixed assets	11	**1,401.2**	1,158.8	**43.5**	44.5
Investments	12	**52.3**	131.8	**3,506.9**	2,942.1
		1,833.0	1,691.2	**3,550.4**	2,986.6

Accounting policies (extract)

Music publishing copyrights
Music publishing copyrights purchased prior to 1 April 1989 were written off against shareholders' funds on acquisition. Copyrights acquired as a result of the acquisitions on or after 1 April 1989 are treated as intangible assets in the Group balance sheet. The capitalised amount of such copyrights, being their purchase cost, is subject to amortisation only to the extent that royalty income generated by the total music publishing copyright portfolio is insufficient to support its book value. All costs attributable to copyrights obtained in the normal course of trade, and not as a result of the acquisition of a business, are written off as incurred.

FRED 17

14.10 Further guidance on what constitutes a tangible fixed asset is provided in FRED 17, 'Measurement of tangible fixed assets'. This was published in October 1997 by the ASB. FRED 17 defines tangible fixed assets as:

"Assets that have physical substance and are held for use in the production or supply of goods and services, for rental to others, or for administrative purposes on a continuing basis in the reporting entity's activities." [FRED 17 para 2].

[The next paragraph is 14.15]

Specifically excluded items

14.15 In addition to the guidance on asset recognition referred to in paragraphs 14.7 and 14.8 the Act specifically states that the following three items cannot be treated as assets – either fixed or current – in any company's balance sheet:

- Preliminary expenses.
- Expenses of, and commission on, any issue of shares or debentures.
- Costs of research.

[4 Sch 3(2)].

14.16 In view of the Act's prohibition, the above items should not be capitalised. Historically, they have been written off to the profit and loss account, except where a company had a share premium account, in which case, the first two items could be written off to that account. [Sec 130(2)]. However, this treatment has been

[The next page is 14007.]

amended by FRS 4, 'Capital instruments', insofar as issue costs connected with such instruments are concerned. This is considered further in chapter 18.

Tangible fixed assets

14.17 As indicated in paragraph 14.8, the Act sub-analyses tangible fixed assets into the following four categories:

- Land and buildings.
- Plant and machinery.
- Fixtures, fittings, tools and equipment.
- Payments on account and assets in course of construction.

However, many companies face practical problems when categorising their tangible assets into these four fairly restrictive headings. In particular, some companies find it difficult to decide whether certain assets should be described as 'plant and machinery' or 'fixtures, fittings, tools and equipment'. Some companies also have difficulty in deciding the category in which to include motor vehicles.

14.18 In practice, companies categorise their assets according to the nature of their particular business. As a general rule, companies treat major manufacturing assets (including motor vehicles involved in the manufacturing process – for example, fork-lift trucks and cranes) as plant and machinery. They include other assets not involved in the manufacturing process in 'fixtures, fittings, tools and equipment'.

14.19 Because the Act allows a company to show any item in greater detail than the format it adopts requires, a company may, for example, disclose the amount for motor vehicles as a subdivision of either plant and machinery or fixtures, fittings, tools and equipment. [4 Sch 3(1)]. However, where an asset does not fall under any of the headings given in the formats, paragraph 3(2) of Schedule 4 allows a company to include the amount of it under a separate heading. Consequently, motor vehicles could be included in the balance sheet as a separate item, a presentation format adopted by Stanley Leisure Organisation plc in Table 14.3.

Table 14.3 – Stanley Leisure Organisation plc – Report & Accounts – 1 May 1994

Notes to the accounts (extract)

	Properties			Leasehold	Fixtures,		
	Freehold £000	Long lease £000	Short lease £000	improve-ments £000	fittings and equipment £000	Motor vehicles £000	Total £000
Cost or valuation							
At 2 May 1993	53,511	18,599	47,818	3,463	18,729	995	143,115
Additions	926	-	422	370	2,845	261	4,824
Acquisitions	5,097	-	5,907	271	1,141	17	12,433
Disposals			-				
Translation adjustments	(110)	(17)		(102)	(33)	(182)	(444)
Reclassifications			(43)				
Adjustments to valuation	(21)	(17)		(7)	(8)	(1)	(97)
	1,373	25	(1,398)	-	-	-	-
	-	-	-		-	-	
				(93)			(93)
At 1 May 1994	**60,776**	**18,590**	**52,706**	**3,902**	**22,674**	**1,090**	**159,738**
At cost	7,264	-	8,750	3,902	22,674	1,090	43,680
Valuation 1993	53,512	18,590	43,956	-	-	-	116,058
	60,776	18,590	52,706	3,902	22,674	1,090	159,738

Payments on account and assets under construction

14.20 The category of payments on account and assets in course of construction is in effect a suspense categorisation, pending the transfer of the assets to one of the other three categories.

14.21 'Payments on account' represent payments a company has made in respect of tangible assets of which it has not yet taken delivery. As the assets are not yet being employed by the company, it would seem inappropriate in most circumstances to depreciate them until they are received and utilised. However, in exceptional circumstances where their value is perceived to have permanently diminished, prudence would require a provision to be made to reduce their carrying value. This situation could occur, for example, where a company has contracted for specialised machinery with a lead-time for delivery and where adverse changes in the company's circumstances or in technology during the lead-time means that the intended use either disappears or is seriously reduced.

14.22 'Assets in course of construction' represent the cost of purchasing, constructing and installing fixed assets ahead of their productive use. As a category of asset, it seems more prevalent in published financial reports than 'payments on account'. It is a category of a temporary nature, pending completion of the asset and its transfer to the appropriate and permanent category of tangible fixed assets. The timing of the transfer of an asset from this category to the appropriate heading will vary. Unless the exceptional circumstance described in paragraph 14.21 occurs, a company will not normally charge depreciation on an asset that is in the course of construction until it is completed and it is transferred to an asset heading that is appropriate. ED 51 also provided some guidance in respect of assets under construction, by indicating that:

- The capitalisation of costs should not commence until there is reasonable probability that the project will be undertaken, or has been undertaken, and is expected to be successfully completed.

- When the construction of a fixed asset is completed in parts and each part is capable of being used commercially whilst construction continues on the other parts, capitalisation of costs on each part should cease when it is completed.

- When costs are incurred in commissioning a fixed asset, capitalisation of costs should cease when the fixed asset starts to be used in, or is available for use in, commercial production.

[ED 51 para 69].

14.23 In Table 14.4, the BOC Group provides an illustration of a company with assets under construction and clearly sets out the nature of the assets reclassified during the reporting period. In addition, its accounting policies state that *"no depreciation is charged on ... construction in progress"*.

Table 14.4 – The BOC Group plc – Report and Accounts – 30 September 1994

Notes on Financial Statements (extract)

7. Fixed Assets – tangible assets (extract) a) Group summary	Land & buildings £ million	Plant machinery & vehicles £ million	Cylinders £ million	Construction in progress £ million	Total £ million
Gross book value					
At 1 October 1993	654.0	2 706.8	448.8	167.9	3 977.5
Exchange adjustment	7.9	(14.5)	9.5	(3.5)	(0.6)
Capital expenditure	27.1	184.3	27.5	117.4	356.3
Revaluation	2.1	-	-	-	2.1
Disposals	(26.2)	(77.4)	(7.7)	-	(111.3)
Transfers	15.7	57.0	11.8	(84.5)	-
Acquisitions & disposals of businesses	(6.9)	7.8	(9.8)	1.2	(7.7)
At 30 September 1994	673.70	2 864.0	480.10	198.50	4 216.3

Depreciation					
At 1 October 1993	137.7	1 373.1	171.2	-	1 682.0
Exchange adjustment	(0.9)	(8.1)	6.8	-	(2.2)
Provided during the year	26.8	196.2	22.1	-	245.1
Revaluation	0.7	-	-	-	0.7
Disposals	(10.6)	(51.6)	(5.9)	-	(68.1)
Transfers	1.8	(1.8)	-	-	-
Acquisitions & disposals of businesses	(1.8)	(8.3)	(5.4)	-	(15.5)
At 30 September 1994	153.70	1 499.5	188.80	-	1 842.0
Net book value at 30 September 1994					
Owned assets	482.4	1 355.6	283.8	198.5	2 320.3
Leased assets	37.6	8.9	7.5	-	54.0
	520.00	1 364.5	291.30	198.50	2 374.3

Disclosure requirements

14.24 In the absence of an accounting standard on tangible fixed assets, it is necessary to look to the Act for disclosure requirements.

Balance sheet and related notes

14.25 In respect of either the cost or the valuation (before any provisions for depreciation or diminution in value) of each category included within the general heading 'Fixed assets' (whether the item is shown on the face of the balance sheet or in the notes), the notes to the financial statements must disclose:

- The aggregate amount of that item at both the beginning and the end of the financial year in question.
- The effect of any application of the alternative accounting rules during that financial year.
- The amount of any acquisitions, and the amount of any disposals, during that financial year.
- The amount of any transfers of assets to, or from, that item during that financial year.

[4 Sch 42(1)(2)].

14.26 It should be noted that these requirements apply to all categories of fixed assets, including intangible assets and investments. Moreover, they require the information to be given in respect of each of the sub-classifications of fixed asset.

14.27 In addition, the Act requires details to be disclosed about any provisions made in respect of each fixed asset category. The need for, and the calculation of, provisions both for depreciation and for the diminution in value of assets are discussed in detail in chapter 5. Consequently, they are not discussed in detail here. In summary, however, the notes must disclose:

- The cumulative amounts of provisions for depreciation or diminution in value of assets at both the beginning and the end of the financial year in question.
- The amount of any such provisions that have been made during the financial year.
- The amount of any such provisions that have been eliminated during that financial year on the disposal of the fixed asset to which they related.
- The amount of any other adjustments made in respect of any such provisions during that financial year.

[4 Sch 42(3)].

14.28 Where a company has applied one of the alternative accounting rules to any fixed asset other than a listed investment, the notes must disclose the years in which the assets were separately valued (so far as the directors know these), the separate values and the bases of valuation. If any assets were valued during the financial year in question, the notes must also disclose:

- The valuers' names or the qualifications of the persons who acted as valuers.
- The bases of valuation that the valuers applied.

[4 Sch 43].

14.29 Where a company chooses to apply the alternative accounting rules to fixed assets, the Act does not require blanket application. Thus, many companies revalue only land and buildings, retaining other fixed assets at historical cost less depreciation. Furthermore, many companies may revalue only part of their holdings in land and buildings, or may revalue their properties on a rotation or even random basis. Although companies disclose the assets revalued and the years of revaluation, the mixture of revalued properties with different revaluation dates and properties at cost calls into question the value of the information presented. In this context, SSAP 12 does indicate that, where a policy of revaluing assets is adopted, the valuations should be kept up to date. [SSAP 12 para 5]. Moreover, the ASB has now published FRED 17, in October 1997, which will in due course require the whole of a class of assets to be carried at either historical cost or at an up-to-date valuation.

14.30 As Table 14.5 illustrates, Dobson Park Industries has a mixture of revalued and historical cost properties and different revaluation dates. It is not clear how helpful this mixed treatment is to users of financial statements.

Table 14.5 – Dobson Park Industries plc – Annual Report & Accounts – 1 October 1994

Notes on the Accounts (extract)

12. **Tangible Fixed Assets (extract)**

	Cost or Valuation		Depreciation		Net Book Value	
12.1 Summary	**1994 £000**	1993 £000	**1994 £000**	1993 £000	**1994 £000**	1993 £000
Freehold land and buildings	**12,748**	15,284	**440**	558	**12,308**	14,726
Leasehold land and buildings:						
Over 50 years	**672**	660	**15**	-	**657**	660
Under 50 years	**1,981**	2,140	**667**	1,817	**1,314**	323
Total land and buildings	**15,401**	18,084	**1,122**	2,375	**14,279**	15,709
Plant and equipment	**31,349**	32,468	**21,487**	22,949	**9,862**	9,519
Group total	**46,750**	50,552	**22,609**	25,324	**24,141**	25,228

Land and buildings include properties with a net book value of approximately £4m which are presently subject to short-term lease arrangements. These properties will be available for sale when the short-term leases expire.

The Group total includes plant and equipment having a net book value of £90,000 (1993: £84,000) carried in the books of the Company after depreciation of £328,000 (1993: £322,000)

12.3 Valuation of Land and Buildings

The total of land and buildings shown above at cost or valuation comprises:	**1994 £000**	1993 £000
Properties as valued at open market value on the basis of current existing use in:		
1980	-	184
1987	**1,000**	1,000
1990	**1,623**	3,278
1992	**1,928**	1,928
1993	**8,682**	8,682
Other properties at cost (including subsequent additions)	**2,168**	3,012
Total of land and buildings	**15,401**	18,084

	1994 £000	1993 £000
If land and buildings had not been revalued they would have been included at the following amounts:		
Cost	**13,596**	14,993
Aggregate depreciation	**4,810**	5,959

14.31 The Act also requires that disclosures in respect of land and buildings should include an analysis of freehold, long leasehold and short leasehold.

[4 Sch 44]. For this purpose, a lease includes an agreement for a lease. It will be a long lease if it still has 50 years or more to run at the end of the financial year in question. Otherwise, it will be a short lease. [4 Sch 83]. Table 14.5 also illustrates these disclosures.

14.32 Although the Act requires comparative figures to be provided for every item included in a note to the financial statements, this requirement does not apply in respect of the disclosures discussed in paragraphs 14.25 and 14.27.

Depreciation of tangible assets

14.33 A company will normally include those tangible fixed assets that have a limited useful economic life in its balance sheet at their purchase price or production cost less a provision for depreciation. [4 Sch 17, 18]. If a company adopts the alternative accounting rules, these assets may be shown in the balance sheet at market value or current cost. [4 Sch 31(2)].

14.34 The calculation of depreciation and rules that relate to depreciation that are contained both within the Act and in SSAP 12 are discussed in detail in chapter 5.

14.35 The provision for depreciation will be based on the difference between cost (or valuation) and residual value. In an extreme situation, if the residual value (which would need to be based on prices prevailing at the date of acquisition or subsequent valuation) is high, it is possible that very little depreciation will be required. Where a company fails to provide a small amount of depreciation because it is not material, the company can nevertheless regard itself as complying in principle with both the Act and SSAP 12 on accounting for depreciation. However, where a company has not charged any depreciation on its properties on the grounds that such depreciation would be immaterial, the FRRP has indicated that the treatment must be fully explained in the notes to the financial statements.

14.36 Where a company does not wish to depreciate a particular asset because it considers the charge for depreciation would not be material, it should first consider the following two matters:

- Although a depreciation charge may not be material in any one year, the cumulative depreciation can, within a few years, have a material effect on the financial statements. Consequently, materiality will need to be judged in connection with other key items (for example, retained profits and the book values of the relevant assets).

- Although a depreciation charge may not be significant in a particular year, a similar charge may have a significant effect on the financial statements of a following year. This can occur, for example, where a company's profit decreases.

14.37 The standard also states that the depreciation methods used should be those that are the most appropriate having regard to the types of assets and their uses in the business. [SSAP 12 para 8]. There is a range of acceptable depreciation methods that are used in practice and these are discussed in greater detail in chapter 5. Although the straight-line method is the simplest one to apply, it may not always be the most suitable.

14.38 In addition, the standard defines an asset's useful economic life as the period over which the present owner will derive economic benefits from using it. [SSAP 12 para 11]. Any useful economic life remaining at the end of the present owner's period of ownership should be taken into account in determining the residual value. The reason for this is that the residual value to be used in calculating depreciation should be the asset's estimated value at the end of this period. However, the estimated residual value should exclude the effects of inflation. [SSAP 12 para 12].

Intended disposal of fixed assets

14.39 Where a company intends to dispose of a fixed asset, the asset is no longer intended for use on a continuing basis in the company's activities. Consequently, it may be inferred that the asset no longer satisfies the criteria for classification as a fixed asset. Accordingly, in such circumstances, some companies consider that the asset needs to be reclassified as a current asset.

14.40 Where assets are transferred from fixed to current assets, it is not appropriate to include the asset in the balance sheet at an amount that exceeds cost, unless it is disclosed as a current asset investment. This is because the alternative accounting rules can only be adopted for stocks and current asset investments and not other current asset items. [4 Sch 31(4)(5)]. However, SSAP 9 does not allow stocks to be stated at current cost in either historical cost financial statements or financial statements modified to include the revaluation of only certain assets.

14.41 Not all companies that intend to dispose of fixed assets follow the transfer to current assets approach. As an alternative treatment, these companies consider it more appropriate to retain the asset within fixed assets under a new sub-heading 'assets held for resale'. However, in many situations assets that are disposed of quickly, rather than held for disposal for some time, are simply retired from the sub-heading in which they have been held during their life.

Transfers from current assets to fixed assets

14.42 Following an FRRP case, this area has been considered by the UITF. UITF Abstract 5 was published in 1992 and is discussed in chapter 17.

Capital grants

14.43 The accounting options available in respect of grants are dealt with in detail in discussing revenue recognition in chapter 3. This chapter, therefore, considers only grants awarded to companies because of their investment in fixed assets.

SSAP 4

14.44 Grants received against capital investment are dealt with in SSAP 4, 'Accounting for government grants'. The original version of the standard, as published in 1974, was developed following the introduction of Regional Development Grants by the Industry Act 1972. As such, however, its scope was relatively limited, with its main requirement being that companies should credit the grant received to revenue over the useful life of the related asset. In effect, this could be achieved in one of two ways:

- The grant could be deducted from the cost of the asset thereby reducing the depreciation charged to revenue.
- The grant could be treated as a deferred credit of which a proportion would be credited to revenue annually. In this situation, the amount of the deferred credit should be shown separately on the balance sheet if material.

SSAP 4 (revised)

14.45 SSAP 4 was revised in 1990, following the issue of ED 43 in 1988 whose proposals it broadly adopted. One of the main reasons for the revision was the proliferation of types of grant that had occurred since the standard's original publication. In particular, there had been a growth not only in the range of both capital and revenue grants, but also in hybrid varieties whereby a grant might be partly capital and partly revenue in nature. The revised standard, therefore, sought to provide broader guidance on the area of grant recognition and accounting.

14.46 When the ASC first published ED 43, it proposed to remove the option to account for capital grants by deducting them from the cost of the related asset. This was proposed partly to further the ASC's objective of narrowing the differences in accounting treatment and partly on an interpretation of company law.

14.47 Schedule 4 to the Act requires that (subject to any provision for depreciation or diminution in value) fixed assets should be stated, under the historical cost accounting rules, at their purchase price or production cost. The statutory definitions of purchase price or production cost make no provision for any deduction from that amount in respect of a grant or subvention from a third party. The references are to paragraphs 17 and 26 of Schedule 4 respectively. These requirements could be read as prohibiting the deduction of capital-based grants from the cost of fixed assets, a treatment previously permitted by SSAP 4. In addition, the general rule that amounts in respect of items representing assets or income may not be set off against amounts in respect of items representing liabilities or expenditure can be interpreted as specifically forbidding this practice.

14.48 The proposal in ED 43 had the DTI's support, which expressed the view that the deduction from the cost method is contrary to paragraph 17 of Schedule 4. The DTI also indicated that the 'true and fair override' could not be held to apply, since the deferred income method is capable of giving a true and fair view. In effect, the override could only be invoked in specific, exceptional circumstances where the deferred income method failed to give a true and fair view, rather than in a blanket fashion to circumvent a particular legal problem.

14.49 Reactions to ED 43 were generally unfavourable, with many commentators opposing the proposal to remove the option allowed in the original version of SSAP 4. Their rationale was that the deduction from cost method was both expedient and generally acceptable in practice, while the interpretation of company law was also considered to be questionable.

14.50 In the face of this opposition, the ASC decided that the proposal in ED 43 to remove the option in SSAP 4 should be withdrawn. Consequently, the existing provisions, whereby both the deferred income and deduction from cost methods were permitted, were retained. In adopting this stance, the ASC recognised that, from a practical perspective, not all reporting entities are governed by Schedule 4. Thus, there was no legal reason why those other entities should not retain the option. However, the ASC also recognised that most reporting entities are governed by Schedule 4 to the Act, so Counsel's opinion on the legality of the deduction from cost method was sought to clarify the position for such entities.

14.51 Counsel reiterated the DTI's opposition to the deduction from cost method and concluded that this treatment is not justifiable for companies that follow Schedule 4, even as a permitted option. Nor would the Act's requirements be satisfied by the disclosure in the notes to the financial statements of the gross cost of the related asset before deduction of the grant, together with the amount of the grant deducted.

14.52 As a result, the revised standard was issued in a way that continues to allow both treatments as being acceptable in practice and capable of giving a true and fair view. However, the standard also warns that Counsel's opinion is that the deduction from cost method is unlawful and cannot be used by enterprises to which Schedule 4 to the Act applies.

Disclosure requirements

14.53 Where an enterprise receives grants, SSAP 4 (revised) requires the following disclosures:

- The accounting policy adopted for government grants.
- The effect of government grants on the results and/or the enterprise's financial position.
- Where an enterprise is in receipt of government assistance other than grants that have a material effect on its results, the nature of the assistance and, where possible, an estimate of the financial effects.
- Where applicable, the potential liabilities to repay grants.

[SSAP 4 paras 28, 29].

14.54 In this context, 'government' is defined in the broader context to include government and inter-governmental agencies and similar bodies whether local, national or international. [SSAP 4 para 21]. Thus, the basic requirements of the standard are interpreted to encompass grants made by such organisations as the National Lottery, the Foundation for Sport and the Arts and the Football Trust.

Grants on non-depreciable fixed assets

14.55 While the general rule is that tangible fixed assets are depreciated over their estimated useful life to reduce them to their residual value, there are instances where assets are not depreciated on the grounds that they do not have a finite life. The commonest asset to which this applies is freehold land. However, the treatment is also commonly employed by entities that operate in the utilities industries, primarily in respect of their *infrastructure* assets.

14.56 The essential difficulty facing such companies is that, should they receive grants on such assets, it would not make sense to employ the deferred income method of accounting. This is because such assets have an infinite life and, therefore, there is no appropriate method for releasing the grant. In effect, it would never be released. The deferred income figure on the balance sheet would simply get bigger and bigger and would become meaningless. Faced with this situation, recipients of grants appear to have no alternative to employing the deduction from cost method of accounting. In so doing they are, in effect, invoking the true and fair override.

14.57 North West Water Group PLC is an example of such an entity, as Table 14.6 indicates.

Table 14.6 – North West Water Group PLC – Annual Report – 31 March 1994

Notes to the accounts (extracts)

1 Accounting policies (extracts)

(f) **Tangible fixed assets**
Tangible fixed assets comprise infrastructure assets (mains, sewers, impounding and pumped raw water storage reservoirs, dams, sludge pipelines and sea outfalls) and other assets (including properties, overground plant and equipment).

(i) Infrastructure assets
Infrastructure assets comprise a network of systems. Expenditure on infrastructure assets relating to increases in capacity or enhancements of the network is treated as additions, which are included at cost after deducting related grants and contributions.

Expenditure on maintaining the operating capability of the network in accordance with defined standards of service is charged as an operating cost. No depreciation is charged on infrastructure assets because the network of systems is required to be maintained in perpetuity and therefore has no finite economic life.

(g) **Grants and contributions**
Grants and contributions relating to infrastructure assets have been deducted from the cost of fixed assets. This is not in accordance with schedule 4 to the Act, which requires fixed assets to be shown at their purchase price or production cost and hence grants and contributions would be presented as deferred income. This departure from the requirements of the Act is, in the opinion of the directors, necessary for the accounts to give a true and fair view as no provision is made for depreciation and any grants and contributions relating to such assets would not be taken to the profit and loss account.

Grants receivable in respect of other tangible fixed assets are treated as deferred income, which is credited to the profit and loss account over the estimated economic lives of the related assets.

11 Tangible fixed assets

	Land and buildings £m	Infra-structure assets £m	Opera-tional structures £m	Fixtures, fittings, tools and equipment £m	Pre-1974 assets £m	Assets in course of con-struction £m	Total £m
Cost:							
At 1 April 1993	89.3	1,133.5	543.4	526.7	177.4	417.9	2,888.2
Additions	11.9	37.8	55.4	31.9	-	231.2	368.2
Grants and contributions	-	(5.2)	-	-	-	(0.6)	(5.8)
Transfers	27.6	77.8	114.0	50.7	-	(272.8)	(2.7)
Reclassifications	-	-	277.8	(277.8)	-	-	-
Disposals	(1.0)	-	(0.6)	(7.1)	-	(0.4)	(9.1)
At 31 March 1994	**127.8**	**1,243.9**	**990.0**	**324.4**	**177.4**	**375.3**	**3,238.8**
Depreciation:							
At 1 April 1993	14.6	-	54.3	151.4	105.6	-	325.9
Charge for the year	4.1	-	21.8	35.9	5.5	-	67.3
Transfers	(1.4)	-	-	(0.7)	-	-	(2.1)
Reclassifications	-	-	58.0	(58.0)	-	-	-
Disposals	(0.3)	-	(0.1)	(6.7)	-	-	(7.1)
At 31 March 1994	**17.0**	-	**134.0**	**121.9**	**111.1**	-	**384.0**
Net book value:							
At 31 March 1994	**110.8**	**1,243.9**	**856.0**	**202.5**	**66.3**	**375.3**	**2,854.8**
At 31 March 1993	74.7	1,133.5	489.1	375.3	71.8	417.9	2,562.3

Grants and contributions received relating to infrastructure assets have been deducted from the cost of fixed assets in order to show a true and fair view. As a consequence, the net book value of fixed assets is £59.7 million (1993 – £53.9 million) lower than it would have been had this treatment not been adopted.

Investment properties

14.58 The classification of certain properties as 'investment properties' for financial reporting purposes arose because of representations made by the property industry against the general principle that properties should be depreciated. Thus, although SSAP 12, 'Accounting for depreciation', stated that all assets with finite useful lives should be depreciated, it allowed an exemption insofar as investment properties were concerned. This exemption remained in force until SSAP 19, 'Accounting for investment properties', was published in 1981, with subsequent amendment to SSAP 12 to make it consistent with SSAP 19.

14.59 The underlying reason for the depreciation exemption allowed by SSAP 12 and formalised by SSAP 19 was a perception that investment properties were fundamentally investments and, as such, were not assets which were used and consumed by the reporting entity. Consequently, it was held that it would be misleading to depreciate investment properties, since it is the current value of such properties and changes to those values that are the key measures of performance.

SSAP 19

14.60 While the Act does not use the term 'investment property', SSAP 19 defines it as an interest in land and/or buildings, where:

- the construction work and development have been completed; and
- the interest is held for its investment potential, with any rental income being negotiated at arm's length.

[SSAP 19 para 7].

14.61 In addition to this definition, the standard indicates that the following properties should not be treated as investment properties:

- A property that is owned and occupied by a company for its own purposes.
- A property that is let to, and occupied by, another group company.

[SSAP 19 para 8].

14.62 On the other hand, the standard is relatively generous in terms of its scope, since it does not limit its application to companies such as investment trusts and property investment companies, whose main or sole activity is the holding of investments. Rather it also brings into its scope any investment properties held by companies whose main activity is other than investment holding and management. However, it specifically excludes investment properties owned by charities from its scope. [SSAP 19 para 9].

Accounting requirements

14.63 The key requirements of the standard are that:

- Investment properties should not be depreciated, but should be included in the balance sheet at their open market value. The exception to this occurs when the investment properties are held on leases that have less than twenty years to run. In such instances, they should be depreciated over the remaining term of the lease. [SSAP 19 paras 11, 12].

- The carrying value of investment properties and the investment valuation reserve should be displayed prominently in the financial statements. [SSAP 19 para 15].

- Changes in the value of investment properties should not be taken to the profit and loss account, but should be taken to the investment revaluation reserve. This is subject to an exception which is discussed from paragraph 14.71. [SSAP 19 para 13].

14.64 In Table 14.7, Hammerson's 1997 financial statements provide an illustration of investment property accounting in practice.

Table 14.7 – Hammerson plc – Annual Report – 31 December 1997

Notes to the Accounts (extract)

12 LAND AND BUILDINGS (extract)

	Book value		Cost	
	1997	1996	**1997**	1996
	£m	£m	**£m**	£m
Investment properties				
Fully developed properties	**1,840.5**	1,776.9	**1,401.5**	1,518.7
Properties held for or in the course of development	**94.6**	63.3	**94.6**	63.3
	1,935.1	1,840.2	**1,496.1**	1,582.0

Fully developed properties are stated at market value as at 31 December 1997, valued in each region by professionally qualified external valuers, Jones Lang Wootton, Chartered Surveyors. In the United Kingdom the valuation was performed jointly with Donaldsons, Chartered Surveyors, who also acted in the capacity of external valuers. The valuations have been prepared in accordance with the Appraisal and Valuation Manual of The Royal Institution of Chartered Surveyors.

As at 31 December 1997 the market value of properties held for development was £121.3m (1996: £66.6m). The total amount of interest included in development properties at 31 December 1997 was £3.6m (1996: £2.3m). Included within properties held for development is the group's 50% share in The Oracle Limited Partnership, a joint arrangement with Abu Dhabi Investment Authority for the development of The Oracle Shopping Centre, Reading.

Should the group's properties be sold at their market value a tax liability of approximately £83m (1996: £78m) would arise. No provision for this contingent liability has been made as it is not expected that any liability will arise in the foreseeable future.

A geographical analysis of the group's properties is provided on page 59.

	Freeholds	Long leaseholds	Short leaseholds	Total
	£m	£m	£m	£m
Movements in the year				
Balance 1 January 1997	1,084.4	750.9	4.9	1,840.2
Exchange adjustment	(41.2)	–	(0.2)	(41.4)
Additions at cost	63.7	38.7	–	102.4
Disposals at valuation	(87.6)	(24.8)	–	(112.4)
Development outgoings capitalised	1.9	0.5	–	2.4
Revaluation surplus	41.4	101.3	1.2	143.9
Balance 31 December 1997	**1,062.6**	**866.6**	**5.9**	**1,935.1**

20 RESERVES	Share premium account £m	Revaluation reserve £m	Other reserves £m	Profit and loss account £m
Balance 1 January 1997	524.2	212.0	1.5	292.3
Exchange adjustment	–	4.8	–	(10.4)
Premium on issue of shares	2.0	–	–	–
Adjustment in respect of scrip dividends	(0.3)	–	–	5.4
Surplus arising on revaluation of properties	–	140.0	–	–
Revaluation of properties in associated undertaking	–	(1.2)	–	–
Transfer to profit and loss account on disposal	–	35.5	–	(35.5)
Retained profit for the year	–	–	–	11.1
Balance 31 December 1997	**525.9**	**391.1**	**1.5**	**262.9**

14.65 The standard requires the names of the persons making the valuation, or particulars of their qualifications, to be disclosed, accompanied by an explanation of the bases of valuation applied. Moreover, where the valuer is an officer or employee of the company or group which owns the property, that fact should be disclosed. [SSAP 19 para 12]. Hence, whilst the standard does not require the valuation to be made by qualified or independent valuers, there is an underlying assumption that the persons responsible for making the valuation are sufficiently knowledgeable about property valuation principles to enable them to undertake the valuation in a competent manner. The explanatory note to the standard indicates that where investment properties represent a substantial proportion of the total assets of a major company (for example, a listed company), the valuation should normally be carried out:

- Annually by persons holding a recognised professional qualification and having recent post-qualification experience in the location and category of properties concerned.

- At least every five years by an external valuer.

[SSAP 19 para 6].

Balance sheet presentation

14.66 A further issue that arises with investment properties is whether they should be treated as tangible fixed assets or as fixed asset investments. While the description of such properties as 'investment' and their non-depreciation for that reason might suggest that they should be included within the investments' category, neither the Act nor SSAP 19 gives any clear guidance on this question. Consequently, both practices are adopted in practice. In Table 14.8, Trafalgar House, for example, includes its investment properties with fixed assets as part of its property portfolio, specifying also the net book value of investment properties, the basis of valuation and the names of the valuers.

Table 14.8 – Trafalgar House Public Limited Company – Report and Accounts – 30 September 1994

Notes to the Accounts (extract)

13 Properties	**Freehold**	**Leasehold**		**Total**
		Long	**Short**	
	£m	**£m**	**£m**	**£m**
Group				
Cost or valuation				
As at 1 October 1993	**192.4**	**35.0**	**19.9**	**247.3**
Exchange translation differences	**(0.3)**	**(0.2)**	**(0.5)**	**(1.0)**
Additions	**5.4**	**4.4**	**0.2**	**10.0**
Disposals	**(24.2)**	**(10.7)**	**(0.4)**	**(35.3)**
Surplus on revaluation	**8.9**	**0.6**	**-**	**9.5**
As at 30 September 1994	**182.2**	**29.1**	**19.2**	**230.5**
Aggregate depreciation				
As at 1 October 1993	**7.3**	**2.4**	**6.4**	**16.1**
Exchange translation differences	**(0.2)**	**(0.1)**	**(0.2)**	**(0.5)**
Provided for the year	**3.7**	**-**	**2.7**	**6.4**
Disposals	**-**	**-**	**(0.2)**	**(0.2)**
Revaluation adjustment	**(1.8)**	**-**	**-**	**(1.8)**
As at 30 September 1994	**9.0**	**2.3**	**8.7**	**20.0**
Book value 30 September 1994	**173.2**	**26.8**	**10.5**	**210.5**
Book value 30 September 1993	**185.1**	**32.6**	**13.5**	**231.2**
Historic cost equivalent:				
As at 30 September 1994	**124.7**	**26.2**	**10.3**	**161.2**
As at 30 September 1993	146.2	32.6	13.5	192.3

Summary of net book values of properties:	**1994**	1993
	£m	£m
Properties owned and occupied as business premises	**97.1**	115.1
Fixed asset developments	**22.2**	22.0
Investment properties	**17.3**	17.9
Hotels	**73.9**	76.2
	210.5	231.2

The properties owned and occupied as business premises are carried at their 30 September 1993 valuations. All major properties were valued as at 30 September 1993 by Jones Lang Wootton, Chartered Surveyors, on an open market existing use basis or, for specialised properties, on a depreciated replacement cost basis. Minor properties were valued as at 30 September 1993 on an open market existing use basis jointly with the group's Chartered Surveyors.

All fixed asset development and investment properties were valued as at 30 September 1994 by Jones Lang Wootton, Chartered Surveyors, on an open market basis.

Hotels were valued as at 30 September 1994 by Christie & Co. Surveyors, Valuers and Agents, on an open market existing use basis at £74,750,000. Included within the valuation is £850,000 classified within plant and equipment.

All of the above valuations were carried out in accordance with the Statements of Asset Valuation Practice and Guidance Notes published by the Royal Institution of Chartered Surveyors.

The net book value of leased assets included in freehold property above is £24.0 million (1993: £23.3 million).

14.67 A number of other companies account for such properties within investments. This seems to be the common practice of entities such as general insurers with large investment portfolios and relatively small levels of tangible fixed assets for consumption by the business.

True and fair override

14.68 Although non-depreciation of investment properties is required by SSAP 19, it may be a departure from the Act in certain circumstances. Such circumstances would include where the amount of depreciation would be material. UITF 7, 'True and fair override disclosures', issued in December 1992, provides guidance on disclosures necessary in financial statements where the true and fair override has been applied. These are fully discussed in chapter 2. The key disclosures are:

- A statement of the treatment which the Act would normally require in the circumstances and a description of the treatment actually adopted.
- A statement as to why the treatment prescribed would not give a true and fair view.
- A description of how the position shown in the financial statements is different as a result of the departure, normally with quantification, except:
    - where quantification is already evident in the financial statements themselves (an example of which might be a presentation rather

than a measurement matter, such as an adaptation of the headings in the Act's format requirements not covered by paragraph 3(3) of Schedule 4); or

- whenever the effect cannot reasonably be quantified, in which case the directors should explain the circumstances.

[UITF 7 para 4].

[The next paragraph is 14.70.]

14.70 In Table 14.9, Trafalgar House's 1994 financial statements provide a clear example of such a disclosure, including a statement that the effect of non-depreciation cannot be quantified.

Table 14.9 – Trafalgar House Public Limited Company – Report and Accounts – 30 September 1994

Principal accounting policies (extract)

d) Fixed assets (extract)

Investment properties
Investment properties are included in the balance sheet at their open market value at the balance sheet date on the basis of an annual professional valuation.

e) Depreciation (extract)

Depreciation is not provided on investment properties. This treatment, as regards certain of the company's investment properties, may be a departure from the requirements of the Companies Act concerning depreciation of fixed assets. However, these properties are not held for consumption but for investment and the directors consider that systematic annual depreciation would be inappropriate. The accounting policy adopted is therefore necessary for the accounts to give a true and fair view. Depreciation or amortisation is only one of the many factors reflected in the annual valuation and the amount which might otherwise have been shown cannot be separately identified or quantified.

Investment revaluation reserve

14.71 When the standard was first published in 1981, changes in the value of investment properties had to be disclosed as a movement on an investment revaluation reserve, unless the total of the investment revaluation reserve was insufficient to cover a deficit. In the latter case the amount by which the deficit exceeded the amount in the investment revaluation reserve was to be charged in the profit and loss account. [SSAP 19 para 14].

14.72 In July 1994, SSAP 19 was amended by the ASB, with the amendments regarded as standard in respect of financial statements relating to accounting periods ending on or after 22 September 1994. The amendments were made because it had been argued that certain of the standard's provisions were at variance with FRS 3, 'Reporting financial performance'. The standard, as revised, states that:

> *"Subject to paragraph 14 below, changes in the market value of investment properties should not be taken to the profit and loss account but should be taken to the statement of total recognised gains and losses (being a movement on an investment revaluation reserve), unless a deficit (or its reversal) on an individual investment property is expected to be permanent, in which case it should be charged (or credited) in the profit and loss account of the period. In the special circumstances of investment companies as defined in companies legislation (as mentioned in paragraphs 31 and 66 of FRS 3 'Reporting Financial Performance') and of property unit trusts it may not be appropriate to deal with such deficits in the profit and loss account. In such cases they should be shown only in the statement of total recognised gains and losses."* [SSAP 19 para 13].

14.73 Paragraph 14 of the revised standard confirms that:

> *"Paragraph 13 does not apply to the financial statements of:*
>
> *(a) insurance companies and groups (and consolidated financial statements incorporating such entities) where changes in the market value of investment properties (including those comprising assets of the long-term business) are included in the profit and loss account;*
>
> *(b) pension funds where changes in the market value of investment properties are dealt with in the relevant fund account."*

14.74 The revised standard also indicates that where an enterprise changes its presentation of revaluation deficits as a result of this amendment, the classification of reserves and comparative figures should be restated in accordance with FRS 3, 'Reporting financial performance'.

[The next paragraph is 14.76.]

Negative revaluation reserves

14.76 The amendment to SSAP 19 means that a net deficit on an investment revaluation reserve, provided that it is temporary, is now not charged to the profit and loss account, but instead is shown in the STRGL. The amendment is silent as to whether a net deficit should remain on the revaluation reserve or whether there should then be a transfer to the profit and loss reserve. The implication appears to be that temporary net deficits can remain on an investment revaluation reserve.

14.77 As far as revaluation reserves on other assets are concerned, in the past it has been normal practice to charge net debit balances to the profit and loss account on the grounds of prudence using the principles in SSAP 19. In view of the amendment to SSAP 19, more companies may begin to show negative revaluation reserves where these result from temporary deficits on other assets. As with investment properties, however, considerable care will be needed in determining whether a diminution is temporary or permanent as this is a judgemental area. Furthermore, any deficit carried forward as a negative reserve would have to be reassessed in subsequent years.

[The next paragraph is 14.79]

14.79 A further point of note is that, despite the standard referring specifically to the 'investment revaluation reserve', the term is rarely used in practice. In fact, the majority of companies refer simply to the 'revaluation reserve', although other terms are used such as 'property revaluation reserve' and 'unrealised capital account'. Furthermore, as the standard requires the investment revaluation reserve to be displayed prominently in the financial statements, this can be interpreted to mean that where companies with investment properties also revalue other properties, the standard requires the revaluation reserve to provide an analysis of the reserve between investment properties and other revalued assets. However, this is not done very often in practice and the ASB has suggested amending the standard to remove the requirement, on the grounds that the revaluation surplus relating to investment properties is no different from the other components of the revaluation reserve.

Owner-occupied properties

14.80 Although the standard indicates that a property that is used and occupied by a company for its own purposes is not an investment property, there may be instances where a property is only partially owner occupied. [SSAP 19 para 8]. In such circumstances, where a property is held for its investment potential, but is either partly occupied by the company or partly let to and occupied by another group company, it would normally be appropriate to apportion the property between an 'investment' element and a 'non-investment' element. This apportionment could, for example, be done on the basis of arm's length rentals. However, before a company apportions properties in this way, it should consider materiality. For example, if a company has a number of investment properties and one small 'split' property, all the properties could reasonably be treated as investment properties.

Intangible fixed assets

Introduction

14.81 Accounting for intangible fixed assets, and in particular brands, has been one of the major issues facing the accounting profession for many years. The issue was closely related to the problems of accounting for goodwill. This is because, for many people, brands and certain other intangibles, irrespective of whether purchased or generated internally, are merely a part of goodwill. For others, however, brands are distinct from goodwill and their value can be independently measured.

14.82 In many takeovers the consideration paid for a company far exceeds the fair value of the acquired company's recognised net assets, thus giving rise to large amounts of goodwill. Some acquiring companies found it difficult to absorb this goodwill by writing it off to reserves when that was the preferred method of accounting for goodwill (under SSAP 22). They had also been reluctant to capitalise and amortise the goodwill, which was the other method allowed by SSAP 22, partly because the effect of such amortisation was to reduce earnings per share.

14.83 In those circumstances, many companies questioned whether the large premiums that they paid for acquisitions were really goodwill. This led them to examine the nature of the goodwill and to divide it into elements such as brands, which they argued should be treated as separately identified intangible fixed assets. One accounting effect of identifying part of the premium paid on acquisition as intangible assets rather than goodwill was that such intangible assets were subject to the accounting rules that applied to fixed assets rather than to the rules that applied to goodwill.

14.84 Some companies argue, in respect of certain fixed assets, that the useful lives of those assets are extended indefinitely, or that their residual value is always kept equal to or greater than their carrying value. Their justification is that the ongoing maintenance of these assets, the cost of which is charged to the profit and loss account, is sufficient to have this effect. As a result, depreciation, if charged, would not be material. The maintenance argument is frequently applied to intangibles, and particularly to brands and publishing titles. In contrast, neither the Act nor SSAP 22 allowed goodwill to be carried permanently as an asset.

14.85 The issue of brands and intangibles came to the fore in the second half of the 1980s, when several major companies changed their accounting policies, so as either to incorporate the value of 'home grown' brands in the balance sheet, or to reflect the fair value of acquired brands in the balance sheet following an acquisition. Other companies have been including intangibles, such as newspaper and other publishing titles, in their balance sheets for many years. One reason for the increased popularity of intangible assets was that the directors believed this presented a more realistic picture of the company and the specific assets it had acquired or developed. Another reason was that this treatment allowed a stronger balance sheet to be presented without any adverse effect on earnings if the directors could justify charging no depreciation on such intangible assets.

14.86 The standard-setters produced several sets of proposals over the years, some of which took a very restrictive attitude towards recognising intangibles. The main issues were separability from goodwill, valuation and depreciation. Proposals that sought to curtail the recognition of intangibles, and brands in particular, were criticised as being unrealistic in the context of an economy in which intangibles were increasingly the foundations of business success.

14.87 The problem of accounting for intangibles was eventually settled with the publication of new rules on goodwill in FRS 10. The ASB found it convenient to deal with both goodwill and intangibles in a single standard, because they are so closely related. The ASB also decided the same accounting rules should apply to both in order to avoid the sort of accounting arbitrage described above that would otherwise arise from labelling similar items differently on the balance sheet.

Act's requirements

14.88 Recognition of intangible assets in company balance sheets is specifically permitted by Schedule 4 to the Act. The model formats for the balance sheet include a heading for 'Intangible assets'. Under that heading there are separate sub-headings for:

- Concessions, patents, licences, trademarks, and similar rights and assets.
- Development costs.
- Goodwill.
- Payments on account.

14.89 The balance sheet may include amounts for concessions, patents, licences, trademarks and other similar rights and assets only where either of the following conditions is satisfied:

- They were acquired for valuable consideration in circumstances that do not qualify them to be shown as goodwill.

- They were created by the company itself. (FRS 10, however, restricts the circumstances where costs of self-developed intangibles may be capitalised.)

[Note 2 to the balance sheet formats].

14.90 The Act also permits intangible assets, other than goodwill, to be included in financial statements at their current cost (but FRS 10 is much more restrictive). Goodwill on the other hand may not be revalued. [4 Sch 31(1)].

14.91 Where capitalised intangible assets (including brands) are acquired or internally generated, they must be amortised over their estimated useful economic lives. [4 Sch 18]. If the lives are finite, the assets should be depreciated to their residual values. There is, however, an important distinction between the rule that applies to the depreciation of assets generally, and as a consequence to intangible assets, and the specific rule that applies to the amortisation of goodwill. For assets generally, it is acceptable to estimate the asset's residual value and to amortise the asset's cost or valuation down to its residual value over its useful life. However, the equivalent rule for goodwill requires that it is reduced by provisions for depreciation calculated to write it off completely on a systematic basis over a period chosen by the company's directors, which cannot exceed its useful economic life. [4 Sch 21]. This legal distinction has had important consequences for the development of the amortisation and impairment rules in FRS 10. In effect it is easier to justify carrying certain intangible assets permanently on the balance sheet without amortisation than it is for goodwill.

14.92 The disclosure requirements for intangible fixed assets are governed by paragraph 42 of Schedule 4 to the Act. These requirements are identical to those for tangible fixed assets. The Act requires the information to be given in respect of each of the sub-headings that are preceded in the formats by Arabic numerals. FRS 10 requires detail of the movements to be disclosed for each class of intangible assets.

14.93 Where a company has applied one of the alternative accounting rules (see further chapter 5) to any intangible fixed asset, the notes must disclose the years in which the assets were separately valued (so far as the directors know these) and also the separate values. If any assets are valued during the financial year in question, the notes must also disclose the valuers' names or particulars of their qualifications and the basis of valuation used by them. [4 Sch 43]. (FRS 10, however, limits the circumstances where intangible assets may be revalued.)

Scope of FRS 10

14.94 In addition to goodwill, FRS 10 applies to all intangible assets except for oil and gas exploration and development costs, research and development costs (covered by SSAP 13) and any other intangible assets that are specifically addressed by another accounting standard.

14.95 The definition of intangible assets (see below) also scopes out items that are financial assets and items included as current assets (including prepaid expenditure).

14.96 FRS 10 deals with the following issues in respect of intangible assets:

- Recognition rules.
  - Intangible assets developed internally.
  - Intangible assets purchased separately.
  - Intangible assets acquired as part of the acquisition of a business.
- Valuation rules.
- Amortisation and impairment rules.
- Financial statement disclosures.

Definition of intangible assets

14.97 FRS 10 defines intangible assets as: *"non-financial fixed assets that do not have physical substance but are identifiable and are controlled by the entity through custody or legal rights"*. [FRS 10 para 2].

14.98 Application of the definition is important, first, to distinguish intangible from tangible assets and, secondly, to distinguish intangible assets from goodwill. These distinctions are important, because different accounting rules apply to each category. In particular, the rules for capitalising and revaluing intangible assets are much more conservative than those for tangible assets.

14.99 In some respects, it is arguable that the distinction between tangible and intangible assets, based on physical or non-physical substance, no longer has much relevance in the modern business world. For example, assets associated with electronic systems do not fit neatly into either category. FRS 10 recognises that software development costs present a problem within this framework and provides a convenient response. It explains that such costs should be treated as part of the cost of the related hardware (and, hence, as a tangible, rather than intangible, asset) where they are *"directly attributable to bringing a computer system or other computer-operated machinery into working condition for its intended use within the business"*. [FRS 10 para 2]. Costs that might fall to be treated as tangible assets in this way include the costs of developing electronic dealing systems and websites.

14.100 There are other examples in practice where the benefit of intangible rights, such as the right to operate a licensed trading activity from specific premises (such as casinos), is treated as an integral part of the physical property rather than as a separate intangible asset (see, for example, Stakis plc in Table 14.10).

Table 14.10 – Stakis plc – Annual Report and Accounts – 28 September 1997

Accounting policies (extract)

Fixed Assets and Valuations
A professional valuation of approximately one-third of the Group's freehold and leasehold properties, excluding health clubs, is carried out annually on a rolling basis and the valuations incorporated in the accounts. In the year of acquisition, properties acquired are included at cost or fair value. Valuation or cost includes the benefit of licences where applicable. All other fixed assets are stated at cost.

Depreciation (extract)
(iii) The element of the carrying value of casino properties attributable to the casino licence is written down only if the trend in maintainable casino profits indicates that such value has reduced.

Separability from goodwill

14.101 Separability is a key component of the definition of an identifiable asset. The Act includes the requirement for separability in the definition of identifiable assets and liabilities that relates to acquisition accounting. [4A Sch 9(2)]. FRS 10 basically repeats the legal position without adding much to clarify the longstanding issue of whether certain intangibles that have characteristics that make them similar to goodwill are separable or not. FRS 10 states:

> *"An identifiable asset is defined by companies legislation as one that can be disposed of separately without disposing of a business of the entity. If an asset can be disposed of only as part of the revenue-earning activity to which it contributes, it is regarded as indistinguishable from the goodwill relating to that activity and is accounted for as such."*[FRS 10 para 2].

14.102 Some intangibles are more clearly separable than others, but defining the cut remains subjective. The ASB considered that, because intangibles, such as brand names, are in any case very similar to goodwill whether they are separable or not, the most important consideration was that the accounting treatment should be the same. Separability is less of an issue under FRS 10 than it was before, because in general neither intangible assets nor goodwill may be capitalised if they have been developed internally, whereas both purchased intangible assets and purchased goodwill must be capitalised. But there are still differences between the rules for purchased intangible assets and purchased goodwill – for example, non-amortisation of goodwill requires a 'true and fair override' of the Act's specific requirement that goodwill should be amortised to zero over a period that does not exceed its useful economic life, whereas non-amortisation of separable intangible assets does not require a true and fair override.

14.103 Some would consider that many brands and publishing titles do not meet the separability criteria, because they cannot be disposed of without at least reducing the revenue-earning activity that they are part of. However, FRS 10 refers to brands and publishing titles as examples of intangible assets that are unique, and so there is an expectation that they are regarded as identifiable assets at least in some circumstances.

14.104 Many brand names are identified with single products that form only part of a company's business. For example, a particular detergent may have a well known brand name, but the name could be sold and the company would still carry on making the product, even though that product might generate lower profits, because it was no longer 'branded'. Guinness PLC and SmithKline Beecham plc provide examples where brands have been recognised separately from goodwill in acquisition accounting. Both refer to the fact that the recognised brands could be sold separately from the rest of the business acquired (see Tables 14.11 and 14.12 on page 14042).

Table 14.11 – Guinness PLC – Report and accounts – 31 December 1996

Accounting policies (extract)

Brands
The fair value of businesses acquired and of interests taken in associated undertakings includes brands, which are recognised where the brand has a value which is substantial and long term. Acquired brands are only recognised where title is clear, brand earnings are separately identifiable, the brand could be sold separately from the rest of the business and where the brand achieves earnings in excess of those achieved by unbranded products.

Amortisation is not provided except where the end of the useful economic life of the acquired brand can be foreseen. The useful economic lives of brands and their carrying value are subject to annual review and any amortisation or provision for permanent impairment would be charged against the profit for the period in which it arose.

14.105 Other brand names cover a range of products or services. Where a product brand name is the same as that of the company itself, it is much less likely that the name could be sold without disposing of a business. It is sometimes argued that names can be exploited by granting licences or franchises to third parties and, hence, that they are identifiable assets not goodwill. For example, a name associated with a particular type of footwear may be exploited by granting a licence for a third party manufacturer of sports clothes to use the name. Another example is where a fast food chain grants franchises to third parties to use the name for their restaurants. In these situations, however, it is difficult to see how the separability criteria are met, because licensing the use of the name does not necessarily imply that it can be disposed of separately from the business; indeed, licensing and franchising may not involve disposals at all.

Control

14.106 Another key component of the definition of intangible assets is control. More generally, FRS 5 defines control in the context of an asset as: *"the ability to obtain the future economic benefits relating to an asset and to restrict the access of others to those benefits"*. [FRS 5 para 3]. In the context of intangible assets, FRS 10 says control must be exercised through custody or legal rights.

14.107 In respect of items such as trademarks, patents, copyrights, licences and franchises, control is secured by legal rights that restrict the access of others. The standard also recognises that control could be evidenced without legal rights, but this would be more difficult – for example, the benefits of know-how could be controlled by secrecy.

14.108 According to FRS 10, a company's workforce and clients cannot be recognised as intangible assets. Although they may be extremely valuable to a business, the business does not control them and, hence, their value is part of its goodwill.

Readily ascertainable market value

14.109 FRS 10 identifies a special type of intangible assets – ones that have a readily ascertainable market value – where the accounting rules differ from the rules that apply to all other intangible assets.

14.110 FRS 10 defines readily ascertainable market value as a value that derives from:

- an asset belonging to a homogeneous population of assets that are equivalent in all material respects; and

- an active market in those assets, evidenced by frequent transactions.

[FRS 10 para 2].

14.111 Most intangible assets are unique to the business that controls them. In practice, hardly any intangible assets have a readily ascertainable market value. Possible examples given in the standard are certain operating licences, franchises and quotas. Many of these assets are in practice also unique. Intangible assets that may have a readily ascertainable market include milk quotas, taxi licences and airport landing rights.

14.112 The differences between the accounting rules are summarised in the table below. In effect, intangible assets with readily ascertainable market values are accounted for in the same way as tangible fixed assets, whereas more restrictions are placed on the recognition and valuation of unique intangible assets. The ASB's rationale for the distinction is twofold: first, it considers that many unique intangible assets are similar to goodwill and should be treated similarly; secondly, it considers that the valuation of unique intangible assets is too subjective to allow them to be recognised (other than where they have actually been purchased) or revalued.

	Intangibles with readily ascertainable market value	**Unique intangibles**
Initial recognition (cost or fair value)		
Internally generated	Yes	No
Purchased separately	Yes	Yes
Business acquisition	Yes	Yes, but only if it can be measured reliably and does not create or increase negative goodwill
Subsequent revaluation	Yes, to market value	No
Impairment loss allocation	Not written down below net realisable value	Written down fully before any tangible assets
Impairment loss reversal	Yes, if net realisable value increases above impaired carrying value	Yes, but only if an external event is reversed in a way that was not originally foreseen

Internally developed intangible assets

14.113 An internally developed intangible asset may be capitalised only if it has a readily ascertainable market value. [FRS 10 para 14]. In all other cases, the costs of developing intangible assets must (as for internally developed goodwill) be written off as incurred.

14.114 As noted above, in practice hardly any intangible assets have a readily ascertainable market value. Those that do are in any case unlikely to have been developed internally.

14.115 Capitalisation of internal costs of obtaining copyrights, patents, licences and similar rights is not, therefore, permitted even though they may satisfy the conditions of identifiability embodied in the definition of intangible assets. Here the ASB has taken a very restrictive approach and thus avoided addressing issues that would be associated with a more permissive approach, such as defining which costs should and should not be capitalised.

Purchased intangible assets

14.116 An intangible asset purchased separately from a business should be capitalised at its cost. [FRS 10 para 9].

14.117 One issue that is not altogether clear in the standard is whether external costs of patent applications and external costs of securing other legal rights in respect of products that a company has developed itself should be capitalised or expensed as incurred.

14.118 One view is that these are internally developed, not purchased, intangibles. The costs are incurred to secure legal protection for and, hence, control of intangible assets that the company has developed itself. Under this view, neither internal costs (for example, the salaries of in-house legal people involved in registering legal rights), nor external costs attributable to generating the intangible asset, would be capitalised.

14.119 However, FRS 10 can be interpreted as making a different cut, that is, between internal and external costs. The emphasis is on preventing internally created value from being recognised. Thus internally generated value and internal costs cannot be capitalised. But external costs of securing legal rights may be objectively determined and fall within the category of purchased intangible assets.

Acquisition accounting

14.120 An intangible asset acquired as part of the acquisition of a business should be capitalised separately from goodwill if its value can be measured reliably on initial recognition.[FRS 10 para 10].

14.121 The normal principles for fair valuing the identifiable assets in acquisition accounting (in FRS 7) apply to intangible as well as tangible assets. FRS 7 merely states that where an intangible asset is recognised, its fair value should be based on its replacement cost, which is normally its estimated market value. [FRS 7 para 10]. FRS 10 introduces a third criterion – reliable measurement – over and above the separability and control issues considered earlier.

14.122 The standard makes another accounting distinction between those rare types of intangible assets that have a readily ascertainable market value (see para 14.109) and those that are unique. Whereas the former should be included at their market value at the date of acquisition, the fair value of the latter should be limited to an amount that does not create or increase any negative goodwill arising on the acquisition (see chapter 23 for further discussion of the interaction between fair valued assets and negative goodwill).

14.123 During the development of FRS 10, the ASB has been sceptical about the reliability of valuations of unique intangible assets, such as brands and publishing titles, where there is no market value as such. FRS 10, however, accepts that certain entities that regularly buy and sell them have developed reliable valuation techniques that would allow them to be capitalised separately from purchased goodwill as a result of an acquisition. The price paid for the acquisition of a business as a whole in effect forms a ceiling on the value that may be ascribed to such intangible assets and goodwill in aggregate.

14.124 The wording in FRS 10 on the reliability of measurement issue implies a degree of flexibility as regards the separate recognition of intangibles in acquisition accounting. Those entities that are not in a position that they have developed valuation techniques from their regular involvement in the purchase and sale of unique intangibles may legitimately subsume the value of intangibles within goodwill. [FRS 10 para 13]. No accounting advantage is gained from doing so. The onus is on those entities that wish to capitalise intangibles separately from goodwill to demonstrate that they can measure them reliably.

Valuation methods

14.125 FRS 10 refers briefly to valuation techniques that may be used to estimate fair values of intangible assets at the date of acquisition. It mentions techniques based on 'indicators of value', such as multiples of turnover or present value of royalties that would be payable to license the asset from a third party. [FRS 10 para 12].

14.126 There are a number of methods commonly used by specialist valuers to value intangibles. These are not mutually exclusive – more than one method would normally be used in a valuation exercise and each would be used to cross-check the reasonableness of the valuation. Methods include:

- Relief from royalties.
- Premium profits.
- Capitalisation of earnings.
- Comparison with market transactions.

14.127 FRS 10 requires the method used to value intangible assets to be disclosed in the financial statements. [FRS 10 para 52]. The methods noted above are described briefly below.

Relief from royalties

14.128 Under the royalty method, an attempt is made to determine the value that could be obtained by licensing out the right to exploit the intangible asset to a third party or, alternatively, to determine the royalties that the owner of the intangible asset is relieved from paying by virtue of being the owner rather than the licensee.

14.129 A notional royalty rate is estimated as a percentage of revenue. This is applied to an estimate of the revenue to be generated by the intangible asset. This estimated royalty stream is capitalised, for example, by discounting at a risk-adjusted market rate, to arrive at an estimated market value.

14.130 The methodology is relatively simple, especially if the intangible asset is already subject to licensing agreements. Where this is not the case, the valuer may research licensing arrangements for comparable intangible assets or, where such information is not available, estimate a theoretical royalty rate that would give an acceptable return both to the owner and the licensee.

Premium profits

14.131 The premium profits approach attempts to determine a value that is based on capitalising the additional profits generated by the intangible asset (for example, a brand) over and above the profits achieved by similar businesses that do not benefit from the intangible asset (for example, similar unbranded products).

14.132 This approach is often used for brands. There are various methods of estimating the premium profits contributed by brands. These include calculating a margin differential, identifying the premium price compared with the price of generic equivalents and comparing the rate of return on capital employed of the business that owns the intangible asset with the normal rate of return of a comparable business that does not benefit from the asset.

14.133 The estimated premium profits attributable to the intangible asset are capitalised, for example, by discounting at a risk-adjusted market rate, to arrive at an estimated market value.

14.134 It is important that the premium profits identified are specifically attributable to the brand or other intangible asset and not some other factor, such as an efficient production facility or distribution network, that relates to the business as a whole.

14.135 In determining the value of a brand under this or similar methods, various specific factors may need to be taken into account, which include the following:

- The market sector.

  Brands that are established in a business sector that generates high sales, margins, or both, will clearly have a higher value than those in markets that are restricted in terms of total sales volume or profit margins. Expanding markets for a product will enhance the prospects for exploiting the brand name and will, therefore, increase its value.

- Durability.

  If a brand name has lasted for many years, it is likely to have considerable customer loyalty and will, therefore, support a higher valuation than a name that may be fashionable, but that is in a business sector where fashions change rapidly and brand names are less durable.

- Overseas markets.

  A brand name that is also known in overseas markets and which, therefore, has a larger potential customer base will usually be worth more than a brand that can be sold only in the domestic market.

- Market position.

  A brand that is a market leader will be worth more than one that is not recognised as a leader.

- Advertising support.

  This could be either a negative or a positive factor in valuing a brand. If a brand requires substantial advertising to maintain its place in the market, this could be a sign that the value of the brand is declining. If, however, advertising spend increases sales and/or margins significantly, so that the brand is better known, the value of the brand itself could be enhanced.

- Changes or prospective changes in legislation, or technological advances.

  Many brands are vulnerable to changes in legislation or environmental factors. However, if a brand name has survived such changes, the fact that it is able to adapt to new conditions may enhance its value.

- Competition.

  The introduction of alternatives to the branded product or indications that competitors are likely to increase spending on rival products could also affect the value of brands.

Capitalisation of earnings

14.136 The capitalised earnings method involves estimating the maintainable earnings that accrue to the intangible asset. A capitalisation factor, or earnings multiple, is then applied to the earnings. The multiple should take account of the expected risks and rewards, which include the prospects for future earnings growth and the risks involved.

14.137 This method is often used to value publishing titles and mastheads.

Comparison with market transactions

14.138 This approach considers actual market transactions in similar intangible assets. A multiple of turnover or earnings associated with an intangible asset would be derived from a market transaction and be applied to the asset being valued.

14.139 However, many intangible assets are unique and comparable market transactions may be infrequent. As a result, the scope for making direct comparisons with values actually achieved in the marketplace is limited. Nevertheless, acquisitions and disposals of businesses that include similar intangible assets can sometimes provide useful indicators of value that complement the other valuation methods.

Revaluation of intangible assets

14.140 With the following exception, no intangible assets may be revalued after their initial recognition at cost or fair value on acquisition. The exceptions are those rare intangible assets that have a readily ascertainable market value (see para 14.109 above). Such assets may be revalued to their market value, provided that all such intangible assets of the same class are revalued and that further revaluations are performed on a regular basis to ensure that the carrying value does not differ from the market value at the balance sheet date. [FRS 10 para 43].

14.141 It follows that for most recognised intangible assets, no value created after their acquisition may be recognised on the balance sheet. For example, if an ailing brand is purchased cheaply and relaunched by the new management, the carrying value must continue to be based on the historical cost or fair value. Furthermore, the brand development costs must be written off as incurred. This is consistent with the treatment of purchased goodwill.

Amortisation and impairment

14.142 FRS 10's objective, in relation to capitalised intangible assets, is to ensure that they are charged in the profit and loss account in the periods in which they are depleted. [FRS 10 para 1]. The same amortisation and impairment rules apply whether intangible assets have been purchased separately or have been recognised as a result of fair valuing an acquisition.

14.143 Intangible assets should be amortised quickly, slowly or not at all according to the circumstances:

- Where an intangible asset has a limited useful economic life, it should be amortised systematically over that life.

- There is a rebuttable presumption that the useful economic life does not exceed 20 years.

- A longer life than 20 years, or an indefinite life, may be chosen where the asset can be demonstrated to be more durable.

14.144 Amortisation over more than 20 years or non-amortisation must be supported by annual impairment reviews to ensure that the carrying value of the intangible asset does not exceed its recoverable amount. If the review identifies an impairment, the asset should be written down to its recoverable amount.

14.145 Intangible assets that are amortised over 20 years or less should be reviewed for impairment at the end of the first full financial year following their acquisition. In other years an impairment review is required only if adverse events indicate the amortised carrying value of the asset may not be recoverable and an impairment write-down should be made if the review confirms this.

Useful economic life

14.146 The useful economic life of an intangible asset is defined in FRS 10 as: *"the period over which the entity expects to derive economic benefits from that asset"*. [FRS 10 para 2].

14.147 A useful economic life of more than 20 years, or an indefinite life, may be chosen only if:

- the durability of the intangible asset for the longer (or indefinite) period can be demonstrated; and

- the intangible asset is capable of continued measurement (so that annual impairment reviews will be feasible).

[FRS 10 para 19].

14.148 One reason for having a presumed arbitrary upper limit on the useful economic life is that it would otherwise frequently be difficult to estimate it. A period of 20 years is a benchmark that has some significance internationally. However, the uncertainty involved in estimating useful economic life does not allow 20 years to be automatically used by default, nor does it allow intangibles to be written off over an unrealistically short period. [FRS 10 paras 21, 22].

14.149 FRS 10 states that the 20 year upper limit *may* be rebutted if the conditions (that is, evidence of durability and continued measurability) are met. The assumptions used in forecasting become more vulnerable the longer the estimated life is. For example, in many industries the pace of developments means that consumer patterns cannot be predicted with much certainty over very long periods. The emphasis in the FRS is, therefore, on being prudent when choosing asset lives, without being unrealistically prudent.

14.150 The second condition for rebutting the 20 year upper limit, that the intangible asset must be capable of continued measurement, is also important. The annual impairment reviews, which must be carried out in accordance with FRS 11 'Impairment of fixed assets and goodwill', have to be feasible. FRS 10 states that intangible assets will not be capable of continued measurement if the cost of such measurement is viewed as being unjustifiably high. This clearly invites directors to opt not to rebut the presumption of a 20 year life if they judge that the cost of carrying out annual impairment reviews outweighs the benefits. This may be so where, for example, an acquisition comprises a large number of publishing titles that individually are not material. [FRS 10 para 23].

[The next paragraph is 14.152.]

14.152 FRS 10 gives examples of factors that contribute to the durability of intangible assets and goodwill. These factors refer to the nature of the business, the stability of the industry, the effects of future competition, the typical lifespans of the products involved and (in respect of business acquisitions) the extent to which the acquisition overcomes market entry barriers that will continue to exist.

14.153 These factors often combine to present an overall picture of durability. A long life (20 years plus) will generally require a business, industry and products with a long track record of stability and achievement and having high barriers to market entry. Added to this, of course, is the commitment of the new management to continue to invest for the long term to extend the period over which the intangible asset is expected to continue to provide economic benefits. Long or indefinite lives may be justified for certain long established brands and publishing titles that have demonstrated their ability to survive changes in the economic environment. Lives much shorter than 20 years may be appropriate for other brands and publishing titles that are relatively new and operate in more volatile sectors, where they are more likely to be affected by changes in fashions or technology.

14.154 In addition to the economic factors outlined above, for certain intangible assets useful economic lives are also restricted by the period for which legal rights are held. For some intangible assets, the legal rights either remain in force indefinitely or can be continually renewed (for example, trademarks that secure brand names). For others, the legal rights that protect a product's position in the market expire after a fixed period (that is, they are non-renewable), when competitors can introduce similar products (for example, drug patents). In other situations, a licence may give an entity the right to carry out a business activity for a fixed period and, although the entity can apply for renewal, there is no guarantee that it will be renewed (for example, broadcasting licences).

14.155 FRS 10 states that where legal rights are granted for a finite period, the useful economic life of the related intangible asset cannot extend beyond that period unless *"the legal rights are renewable and renewal is assured"*. [FRS 10 para 24]. In other cases, the useful economic life is restricted by the expiry date of the existing legal right. The FRS also limits the circumstances in which the renewal of a legal right may be regarded as assured to those where:

- The value of the intangible asset does not reduce as the expiry date approaches (or reduces only by the cost of renewal).
- There is evidence that the legal rights will be renewed.
- There is no evidence that any conditions that have to be complied with in respect of renewal have been or will be breached.

[FRS 10 para 26].

14.156 If the capitalised cost of an intangible asset includes costs that will recur each time the legal right is renewed, the amortisation period for that element of the cost should not extend past the renewal date. [FRS 10 para 24].

Residual values

14.157 Before FRS 10, two arguments were sometimes advanced to demonstrate that, in certain circumstances, no amortisation was required. Some companies stated that the lives of brands and publishing titles were indefinite and, therefore, no amortisation charge was necessary. Others considered that expenditure on advertising and other brand support costs meant that the brand's or publishing title's residual value was always equal to or greater than its cost and this was put forward as an alternative reason for not amortising.

14.158 Under FRS 10, a residual value at the end of the asset's useful economic life may be assumed only if it can be measured reliably. [FRS 10 para 28]. In practice, an intangible asset is only likely to have a significant residual value that can be measured reliably where a company has a legal or contractual right to receive an amount of cash when its right to use the asset expires, or in those rare cases where there is a readily ascertainable market value for the residual asset. [FRS 10 para 29]. This means that in practice a low or nil amortisation charge must generally be justified in terms of a long or indefinite useful economic life rather than the maintenance of a high residual value, although in many respects they amount to the same thing.

Methods of amortising intangible assets

14.159 FRS 10 states that the method of amortising an intangible asset should reflect the expected pattern of its depletion. However, a straight-line method should be chosen, unless another method can be demonstrated to be more appropriate. [FRS 10 para 30]. An example of an alternative amortisation method is a unit of production method in respect of a licence to produce a fixed quantity of output. [FRS 10 para 31]. The FRS also requires disclosure of the methods used. [FRS 10 para 55]. Although arbitrary, specifying straight-line as a benchmark method is a practical means of dealing with the difficulty of measuring depletion and it does promote comparability. The FRS also explains that it is unlikely that methods that are less conservative than the straight-line method could be justified with sufficient evidence.

14.160 A company may conceivably wish to change its method of amortising intangible assets, say, to revert to the straight-line method from some other method. Where this occurs, FRS 10 requires the reason and the effect, if material, to be disclosed in the year of change. [FRS 10 para 57]. The effect of a change is the difference between the amortisation charge that results from applying the previous and the revised amortisation methods (that is, how much more or less profit a company records as a result of changing amortisation methods).

Impairment reviews

14.161 The requirements for impairment reviews on intangible assets are integrated with those for capitalised goodwill, which are explained in more detail in chapter 23. The details of impairment reviews for tangible and intangible fixed assets and goodwill are contained in a separate standard FRS 11 'Impairment of fixed assets and goodwill'. The requirements for impairment reviews differ according to whether an intangible asset is attributed a useful live of more or less than 20 years, as illustrated below.

Useful life 20 years or less	**Useful life more than 20 years**
End of first full year (simplified review)	Every year (detailed review)
Other years – high level check for impairment indicators detailed review only if impairment indicators are present	

14.162 Where intangible assets or goodwill are carried permanently as assets or amortised over very long periods, there is a greater risk of impairment in the future. Where they are written off over shorter periods, there is less risk of impairment, because their net book value in any case diminishes more quickly. A threshold of 20 years has been chosen, below which the impairment reviews are less onerous than for longer periods.

Useful life 20 years or less – first year review

14.163 Intangible assets should be reviewed for impairment at the end of the first full year after their acquisition. Most recognised intangible assets are acquired through business acquisitions and the timing of this review corresponds with the end of the investigation period in FRS 7, when the fair value exercise on the assets and liabilities of the acquired business should be completed.

14.164 The first year review has two stages. The first stage in effect requires management formally to consider whether the acquisition has lived up to expectations. This is done by comparing post-acquisition performance with the forecasts used in the acquisition appraisal and by considering whether there have been any other unexpected adverse events or changes in circumstances that throw doubt on the recoverability of the intangible asset or capitalised goodwill. If the acquisition passes this test, there is no need to go on to the second stage.

14.165 The second stage, which is a full impairment review, is only necessary if the first stage indicates that there may be an impairment problem. [FRS 10 para 40].

Useful life 20 years or less – reviews in other years

14.166 After the first full year, management has to consider whether events or changes in circumstances indicate that the amortised carrying value of intangible assets or goodwill may not be recoverable. If there are no such indicators, no further work is required. FRS 11 gives a list of examples of situations that indicate that fixed assets generally and goodwill may have been impaired. The list of impairment indicators is not intended to be exhaustive; management should consider the effect of any other material adverse changes to the business and the environment in which it operates. The main indicators to be considered are:

- Operating losses or net cash outflows incurred or expected.
- Adverse change in the business or market, such as the entrance of a major competitor.
- Adverse change in any 'indicator of value' used to measure the fair value of an intangible asset on acquisition (see methods described from para 14.125).
- Adverse change in the statutory or regulatory environment.
- Commitment to a significant reorganisation.

- Major loss of key employees.

- Significant increase in market interest rates or rates of return.

14.167 In the case of brands, for example, an impairment may be indicated by any one of a number of factors, which might include:

- A fall in the volume of sales or market share.
- A fall in the profit margins attainable from sales.
- The launch by a competitor of a generic alternative to the branded product.
- A withdrawal of a product from a market owing to safety concerns.
- The need for increased advertising costs to support the existing levels of sales and margins.

14.168 If there are factors that indicate that the carrying value of an intangible asset may not be recoverable, a full impairment review has to be carried out and, if impairment is confirmed, the carrying value should be written down to the recoverable amount.

Detailed impairment review

14.169 A detailed impairment review is required in the following situations:

- Where intangible assets or goodwill are amortised over more than 20 years or carried permanently without amortisation: at each year end automatically (including the end of the year in which the acquisition took place).

- Where intangible assets or goodwill are amortised over 20 years or less:

  - At the end of the first full year following the acquisition, *only* if there is an indicator of impairment or if the first year review indicates that the post-acquisition performance has failed to meet pre-acquisition expectations.

  - In other years, *only* if there is an indicator of impairment.

14.170 The details of the impairment review are contained in FRS 11. An impairment review is a recoverable amount check on individual assets or groups of assets that may comprise tangible and intangible assets and capitalised goodwill. It follows the long-established principle that an asset's balance sheet carrying value should not exceed its recoverable amount, which is measured by reference to the future cash flows that can be generated from its continued use (value in use) or disposal (net realisable value), whichever is higher. To the extent that an asset's carrying value exceeds its recoverable amount, it is impaired and should be written down to the higher of its net realisable value or value in use.

14.170.1 The net realisable value of an intangible asset (that is, the amount for which it could be sold, less direct selling costs) may be difficult to determine unless there is an active market from which a reliable market value can be derived. For example, FRS 10 states that it is not possible to determine a market value for unique intangible assets such as brands and publishing titles. Where a reliable net realisable value cannot be estimated directly, FRS 11 requires the recoverable amount to be determined by value in use alone. [FRS 11 para 16].

14.170.2 If the net realisable value of an intangible asset can be determined and is lower than its carrying value, it should not automatically be written down to that value. The asset's value in use also needs to be estimated in order to determine whether it is higher than its net realisable value. If it is, the impairment write-down, if any, is calculated by reference to value in use.

[The next paragraph is 14.171.]

14.171 Measuring the recoverable amount of most intangible assets (as well as goodwill and, indeed, many tangible fixed assets) by reference to value in use is not straightforward, because they do not generate cash flows by themselves. If assets cannot be reviewed for impairment individually, they should be reviewed in groups that generate income streams that are largely independent of each other. These are referred to as income-generating units (IGUs). Where an impairment review is required, because there is an indicator that the assets of a business might be impaired, the review is intended to cover all its tangible assets, intangible assets and attributable goodwill.

14.172 In summary, the steps in an impairment review are:

- Identifying separate income-generating units.
- Establishing balance sheets for each income-generating unit, comprising the net tangible and intangible assets plus allocated purchased goodwill.
- Forecasting the future cash flows of the income-generating unit and discounting them to their present value.
- Comparing the PV of the cash flows with the net assets of the income-generating unit and recognising any shortfall as an impairment loss.

- Allocating any impairment loss to write down the assets of the income-generating unit in the following order:
  - Purchased goodwill.
  - Capitalised intangibles.
  - Tangible assets, on a *pro rata* or more appropriate basis.

The above requirements for impairment reviews are considered in more detail in chapter 23.

14.173 Where an intangible asset has to be reviewed annually for impairment, but is not actually expected to be impaired, the reviews in subsequent years after the first annual review can often be performed by updating the calculations performed for the first review. FRS 10 notes that if there have been no adverse changes since the first review, it may be possible to ascertain immediately that there has been no impairment. [FRS 10 para 38].

Reversals of past losses

14.174 If an intangible asset is considered to have been amortised too quickly in the past, its useful economic life may be increased, but the carrying value should be amortised prospectively over the remaining revised useful economic life. FRS 10 does not allow past amortisation charges in respect of intangible assets or goodwill to be reversed and credited in the profit and loss account. [FRS 10 paras 33, 45].

14.175 Impairment losses in respect of intangible assets may be reversed (that is, credited back in the profit and loss account), but only in limited circumstances. These are where (a) an external event caused the original impairment loss, and (b) subsequent external events clearly and demonstrably reverse the effects of that event in a way that was not foreseen in the original impairment calculations. [FRS 10 para 44; FRS 11 para 60]. FRS 11 makes an exception to this rule for intangible assets with a readily ascertainable market value, where impairment losses may be reversed to the extent that the net realisable value (based on market value) subsequently increases to above the impaired carrying value. [FRS 11 para 60]. As mentioned earlier, however, there are very few intangible assets in that category.

14.176 These restricted conditions under which impairment losses on intangible assets can be reversed are the same as for purchased goodwill. For goodwill, the objective of restricting reversals of impairment losses is to prevent a goodwill write-off from being credited back to the profit and loss account if the credit were in effect attributable to the generation of new non-purchased goodwill. Consequently, situations that justify reversals are likely to be rare and in most cases amounts written off intangible assets or goodwill will stay written off.

14.177 An example of a situation that would meet the reversal criteria is as follows.

Example

A brand name had previously been written off because a product had been withdrawn from the market as a result of a health scare that raised concerns about its safety. The safety concerns subsequently prove to be unfounded and the health authorities approved the product's reintroduction. The company's management had assumed that the product's withdrawal would be permanent when they recognised the impairment loss.

In this example, the impairment loss was caused by an external event (the health scare). An external event (the removal of the safety concerns and the permission to reintroduce the product to the market) clearly and demonstrably has reversed the effects of the external event that caused the impairment loss in a way that was not foreseen in the original impairment calculations. Consequently, the impairment loss should be reversed to the extent that the brand's recoverable amount has increased above its current written down value (assuming that the brand regains some value after the health scare).

14.177.1 The amount that can be written back to reverse an impairment loss is restricted to an amount that increases the asset's carrying value to the carrying value that would have been recognised had the original impairment not occurred. [FRS 11 para 61].

14.177.2 FRS 11 requires that the reason for the reversal of impairment losses should be disclosed, together with any changes in the assumptions upon which the calculation of recoverable amount is based. [FRS 11 para 70].

[The next paragraph is 14.178.]

Disclosures

14.178 FRS 10 requires the following disclosures in respect of intangible assets:

- The method of valuation. [FRS 10 para 52]
- For each class of intangible asset:
  - The cost or revalued amount at the beginning and end of the period.
  - The cumulative provisions for amortisation or impairment at the beginning and end of the period.
  - A reconciliation of the movements, showing additions, disposals, revaluations, transfers, amortisation, impairment losses and reversals of past impairment losses.

- The net carrying amount at the balance sheet date. [FRS 10 para 53].

- The methods and periods of amortisation and the reasons for choosing those periods. [FRS 10 para 55].

- The reason for, and effect of, changing useful economic lives. [FRS 10 para 56]

- The reason for, and the effect of, changing amortisation methods. [FRS 10 para 57].

- Where an intangible asset is amortised over more than 20 years or is not amortised, the reasons for rebutting the 20 year presumption. (This should be a reasoned explanation based on the specific factors contributing to its durability). [FRS 10 para 58].

- The following details where a class of assets has been revalued:

  - The year in which the assets were valued, the values and the bases of valuation.

  - The original cost or fair value of the assets and the amount of any provision for amortisation that would have been recognised if the assets had been valued at their original cost or fair value. [FRS 10 para 61].

- The name and qualifications of the person who valued any intangible asset that has been revalued during the year. [FRS 10 para 62].

14.179 In respect of the last two bullet points above concerning revaluations, it should be noted that FRS 10 only permits revaluation (to their market value) of those intangible assets that have a readily ascertainable market value.

14.180 Two of the above disclosure points refer to a 'class of intangible assets'. The most commonly encountered will be the second bullet point, which requires the analysis and movements on intangible assets to be shown separately for each class. A class of intangible assets is defined in FRS 10 as: *"a category of intangible assets having a similar nature, function or use in the business of the entity"*. The explanatory paragraph to the definition indicates that items such as licences, quotas, patents, copyrights, franchises and trademarks may be treated as separate classes, as may intangible assets that are used within different business segments. Further sub-division may be appropriate where there are different types of licences, etc, which have different functions within the business. [FRS 10 para 2]. For entities that recognise several types of intangible assets, the analysis has, therefore, to be given under several headings.

Implementing FRS 10 – transitional arrangements

14.181 The transitional arrangements of FRS 10 (which must be complied with in accounting periods ending on or after 23 December 1998) relate both to intangible assets and goodwill and are considered in detail in chapter 23. The following issues should be considered in the context of companies' previous accounting policies for recognising and valuing intangible assets.

14.182 Any intangible assets that had already been capitalised before the adoption of FRS 10 would thereafter be subject to the recognition, amortisation and impairment rules of the FRS. Several issues arise:

- Previously capitalised intangibles may not meet FRS 10's recognition criteria.
- Previously capitalised intangibles that do not have a readily ascertainable market value may have been revalued since their acquisition and may, therefore, have to be written down.
- An impairment may be identified when the new procedures for carrying out impairment reviews are adopted.
- Companies may wish to modify their amortisation policy, for example to comply with FRS 10's rebuttable presumption of a maximum useful economic life of 20 years.

Intangibles not meeting FRS 10's recognition criteria

14.183 As FRS 10 does not permit internally developed intangibles to be capitalised (except for those intangibles that are excluded from the scope of the standard), any such items appearing on a company's balance sheet should be written off as a prior period adjustment.

14.184 Some intangibles recognised separately from goodwill when previous acquisitions were fair valued may not satisfy all the elements of FRS 10's definition of intangible assets. Customer lists and similar items may fall into this category. Such intangibles should also be eliminated as a prior period adjustment, that is, they should be subsumed within goodwill.

Previously revalued intangibles

14.185 Where any purchased intangibles have been revalued since their acquisition and are not of the rare type that has a readily ascertainable market value, FRS 10 does not permit them to be carried at valuations. The revaluations should, therefore, be reversed as a prior period adjustment, in order to restate the intangibles at cost (that is, fair value attributed on acquisition) less amortisation or impairment attributed to previous periods.

Impairment losses

14.186 FRS 10 specifically requires that any impairment loss relating to previously capitalised goodwill and intangible assets that is recognised when the FRS is first adopted (that is, when the specified impairment reviews are first applied) should be charged as an expense in the current period and not as a prior period adjustment. [FRS 10 para 74]. The reason is that any impairment is regarded as having resulted from a change of estimate of an asset's recoverable amount and not from a change of accounting policy.

Change of amortisation policy

14.187 A company may decide to adopt a more prudent amortisation policy for previously capitalised intangibles as a result of FRS 10. For example, a company may have previously not amortised certain intangibles, because their useful economic lives had been deemed to be indefinite. On implementing FRS 10, the company may consider they should be amortised over a period of 20 years from the date of acquisition in view of FRS 10's tougher rules for adopting a longer period. One reason is that the company may not be able or willing (owing to the unjustifiably high costs) to carry out the additional impairment review procedures that are required if a longer amortisation period is chosen. Therefore, the intangibles might not be capable of continued measurement in the context of FRS 10's requirements for determining useful economic lives and so FRS 10's presumed maximum life of 20 years would not be rebutted.

14.188 The question arises whether this is a change of accounting policy or a revision of the intangible asset's useful economic life. If it is a change of accounting policy, the intangible would be restated net of amortisation attributed to the period since its purchase; the 'backlog' amortisation would be treated as a prior year adjustment and would not affect current or future earnings. If it is a revision of the asset's useful economic life, the whole of the previous carrying value would be amortised prospectively against earnings over the remaining portion of the 20 year life (which could be a short period if the intangible was bought many years ago).

14.189 A prior year adjustment for a change of accounting policy would be justified if the company's amortisation policy was changed purely as a result of FRS 10's new rules for determining asset lives rather than because there had been a genuine revision of the asset's useful life in the context of the previous policy.

Intangible assets – other information

14.190 In practice, given the lack of authoritative guidance on intangibles before FRS 10, the range of intangibles in addition to brands and publishing titles capitalised in financial statements has been relatively extensive and includes:

- Copyrights.
- Know-how.
- Licences.
- Patents and trademarks.

Copyrights

14.191 Copyrights are designed to provide the holder with the exclusive right to produce copies of, and control over, an original musical, artistic or literary work. They are granted by law for a specified number of years, which in the UK was, until 1 January 1996, 50 years from the date of the author's or composer's death. A statutory instrument, the Duration of Copyright and Rights in Performances Regulations 1995 (SI 1995/3297), enacting an EC Directive to harmonise the term of protection of copyright and related rights, has altered the period of copyright. For literary (including compilations and computer programs), dramatic, musical and artistic works, copyright expires 70 years from the end of the calendar year in which the author died. Where such a work is computer generated, the period of copyright is 50 years from the end of the calendar year in which the work was made. Copyright in films will generally expire 70 years from the last to die of the director, authors of the screenplay and dialogue and composer of any specially created music. Copyright in sound recordings expires 50 years from the end of the calendar year in which it is made or is released.

14.192 There are complex transitional provisions of which the following is a very brief summary. The new provisions apply to new works and existing copyright works. However, the period of copyright existing before 1 January 1996 will continue to apply to an existing work if this period would expire later than the new period. The provisions may also apply to existing works in which copyright expired before 31 December 1995 where the authors died between 1925 and 1945. Consequently, some copyright which had expired may be revived under these provisions. As such, where companies acquire a copyright for exclusive rights to publish an author's or composer's work, it is done in the expectation of receiving future income streams. The copyright is an intangible asset which will result in potential financial benefits to a company over a considerable number of years.

14.193 In practice, a number of different accounting policies have been adopted, varying from those companies that amortise the asset over a few years, to those that do not amortise unless a permanent fall in value occurs.

Know-how

14.194 Know-how is, in effect, a technical aptitude or skill. As such, it may be people-reliant or process-reliant; it may be purchased by acquisition of, say, a specialist service unit; or it may be internally generated. Its nature and characteristics suggest that it is more nebulous than say a copyright and, therefore, more difficult to measure or prone to greater subjectivity in terms of both identification and valuation.

14.195 As an example, a company that acquires a specialist testing unit is likely to acquire few tangible assets and, therefore, the difference between the price it pays and the fair value of the tangible assets acquired could be significant. Many commentators would argue that what the company is buying is: the tangible assets; the know-how in terms of methodologies and personnel; and future trading opportunities. While the third of these equates to goodwill, the second does not. In effect, a prime element of the difference between the purchase price and the fair value of tangible fixed assets would be the bespoke testing procedures acquired and the specialist personnel taken on, or, put another way, know-how.

14.196 Under FRS 10, any value attributed to purchased know-how could not be recognised separately as an intangible asset, unless it is controlled through custody or legal rights. This is unlikely to be the case where, for example, the know-how is essentially related to specific people who have freedom of movement in the labour market, but it could be the case if the know-how relates to a secret process.

Licences

14.197 Licences are agreements that a reporting company enters into with a third party which enable it to carry out certain trading functions. Examples may be brewing concerns, which operate out of licensed premises, or bookmakers, who are required to obtain a gaming licence. Similarly, companies may purchase licences allowing them to use software and technology developed by third parties.

14.198 As with copyrights, licences are generally acquired to obtain access to benefits that may continue for many years. Under FRS 10, the cost of licences should be capitalised if they have been purchased separately from a business. If they have been acquired through the acquisition of a business, they should be capitalised separately from goodwill if their fair value can be measured reliably. They should generally be amortised over the life of the licences.

14.199 Some companies have included the benefit of licences within tangible fixed assets where they operate from licensed premises, that is, as part of the valuation of the properties that carry on the licensed activity (see para 14.100).

Patents and trademarks

14.200 A patent is in effect a document granted by the government assuring an inventor of the sole right to make, use and sell his invention for a determined period. Registering a trademark provides legal protection to the name or symbol used to differentiate the products supplied by a manufacturer or authorised distributor from those of competing manufacturers and dealers. Brands are likely to be secured by trademarks. Such protection is clearly of vital importance to entities that invest in product development (such as pharmaceutical companies), to ensure that their competitors do not merely copy their commercially successful inventions. The legal rights may be granted for long periods (17 or 18 years for drug patents) or may be renewable indefinitely (some trademarks).

14.201 Under FRS 10, the cost of patents and trademarks should be capitalised if they have been purchased separately from a business. If they have been acquired through the acquisition of a business, they should be capitalised separately from goodwill if their fair value can be measured reliably. They should generally be amortised over the period covered by the legal rights or the period for which the owner expects to derive economic benefits, if shorter.

Research and development

14.202 The Act permits development costs to be capitalised in certain circumstances. [4 Sch 20(1)]. In contrast, however, research costs, whether pure or applied, must be written off to the profit and loss account as they are incurred. [4 Sch 3(2)(c)].

SSAP 13

14.203 The Act does not define development. However, SSAP 13, 'Accounting for research and development', defines development as *"use of scientific or technical knowledge in order to produce new or substantially improved materials, devices, products or services, to install new processes or systems prior to the commencement of commercial production or commercial applications, or to improving substantially those already produced or installed"*. [SSAP 13 para 21]. Therefore, development is the work a company performs after it has planned or designed a new or substantially improved product or service until the time that this is ready either to be manufactured or to be put into operation commercially.

14.204 In making this definition of development, the standard distinguishes it from pure and applied research, which are defined as follows:

- Pure or basic research is *"experimental or theoretical work undertaken primarily to acquire new scientific or technical knowledge for its own sake rather than directed towards any specific aim or application"*.
- Applied research is *"original or critical investigation undertaken in order to gain new scientific or technical knowledge and directed towards a specific practical aim or objective"*.

[SSAP 13, para 21(a),(b)].

14.205 The standard also specifically indicates that where companies enter into firm contracts to carry out development work on behalf of third parties, on terms such that the related expenditure will be fully reimbursed, then expenditure that has not been reimbursed at any period end is contract work-in-progress and not development expenditure. A similar situation occurs where companies contract to develop and manufacture at an agreed price calculated to reimburse expenditure on development as well as on manufacture. [SSAP 13, para 17].

14.206 Racal Electronics' and Oxford Instruments' accounting policies provide examples of this, as Tables 14.14 and 14.15 indicate.

Table 14.14 – Racal Electronics Plc – Annual Report and Accounts - 31 March 1995

Statement of Accounting Policies (extract)

7 RESEARCH AND DEVELOPMENT
Private venture research and development expenditure is written off in the year in which it is incurred. Uninvoiced research and development fully funded by customers is carried forward as work in progress.

Table 14.15 – Oxford Instruments plc – Report and Accounts – 27 March 1994

Notes on the Financial Statements (extract)

1 Accounting policies (extract)

Research and development
Research and development expenditure, net of the relevant proportion of grants receivable, is charged to the profit and loss account in the year in which it is incurred, unless it is recoverable under a customer contract when it is carried forward as work in progress at the lower of cost and net realisable value.

14.207 SSAP 13 also provides examples of activities that would normally be *included* in research and development. The examples are:

- Experimental, theoretical or other work aimed at the discovery of new knowledge, or the advancement of existing knowledge.
- Searching for applications of that knowledge.
- Formulation and design of possible applications for such work.
- Testing in search for, or evaluation of, product, service or process alternatives.
- Design, construction and testing of pre-production prototypes and models and development batches.
- Design of products, services, processes or systems involving new technology or substantially improving those already produced or installed.
- Construction and operation of pilot plants.

[SSAP 13 para 6].

14.208 The standard also gives examples of activities typically *excluded* from research and development activities:

- Testing and analysis either of equipment or product for purposes of quality or quantity control.
- Periodic alterations to existing products, services or processes even though these may represent some improvement.
- Operational research not tied to a specific research and development activity.
- Cost of corrective action in connection with breakdowns during commercial production.
- Legal and administrative work in connection with patent applications, records and litigation and the sale or licensing of patents.
- Activity, including design and construction engineering, relating to the construction, relocation, rearrangement or start-up of facilities or equipment other than facilities or equipment whose sole use is for a particular research and development project.

- Market research.

[SSAP 13 para 7].

14.209 The original standard, prior to revision in 1989, specifically permitted market research to be capitalised, if it was incurred in order to determine whether a product under development was commercially viable in terms of market conditions, public opinion and consumer and environmental legislation. Its exclusion from expenditure that can be carried forward under the revised version, represents a tightening of the rules.

Development costs

14.210 The types of development costs that may be capitalised are not defined either in the Act or in the revised standard. However, IAS 9, 'Accounting for research and development', does give some guidance on the type of costs that may be capitalised. It indicates that development costs may include:

- Salaries, wages and related costs of personnel.
- The costs of materials and services consumed.
- The depreciation of equipment and facilities.
- A reasonable allocation of overhead costs.
- Other related costs, such as the amortisation of patents and licences.

[IAS 9 para 15].

Special circumstances

14.211 The Act permits development costs to be capitalised, but only in 'special circumstances'. However, as it does not define the term 'special circumstances', it is necessary to look to SSAP 13 for guidance. We interpret this to imply that, if all the conditions set out in paragraph 25 of SSAP 13 are met, special circumstances exist and so development costs may be capitalised. However, if any one of the conditions is not met, then development costs must be written off as they are incurred.

14.212 Paragraph 25 of SSAP 13 lays down the following conditions, all of which must all be satisfied if development expenditure is to be capitalised:

- There is a clearly defined project.

- The related expenditure is separately identifiable.

- The outcome of the project has been assessed with reasonable certainty as to both its technical feasibility and its ultimate commercial viability, considered in the light of factors such as likely market conditions (including competing products), public opinion, and consumer and environmental legislation.

- The aggregate of the deferred development costs, any further development costs, and related production, selling and administration costs, is reasonably expected to be exceeded by related future sales or other revenues.

- Adequate resources exist, or are reasonably expected to be available, to enable the project to be completed, and to provide any consequential increases in working capital.

14.213 Where these conditions are satisfied, a company can defer development expenditure, but only until commercial production begins. SSAP 13 requires a company to amortise the expenditure it has capitalised from the time that commercial production of the product or service begins. Where a company is developing a product, commercial production begins when the company is manufacturing the product with a view to selling it commercially. [SSAP 13 para 28].

Amortisation

14.214 Amortisation of development expenditure must be allocated to each accounting period on a systematic basis. This can be done by reference to the sales or the use of the product or the service, or by reference to the period over which the product or service is expected to be sold or used. However, the period of amortisation may be difficult to determine. In determining this period, the directors must establish a realistic and prudent number of years over which they expect the development expenditure to produce a benefit. They must decide also whether they expect the benefit to occur evenly over these years.

14.215 As an example, a cable television company might write its development expenditure off over a period that begins with the date when it first relays programmes and ends on the date that the franchise period ends. However, if, for example, only a small number of subscribers has signed up during the initial operation period, the company may calculate the amount of amortisation that it charges during that period differently from the amount it charges once the company reaches its projected number of subscribers. The company may, for instance, calculate the amount of amortisation it charges in this initial operation period by reference to the actual number of subscribers to the service, as compared to the estimate of the final number of subscribers. However, amortising on a straight-line basis is more prudent. A more prudent treatment still would be to expense such costs immediately and that approach may be more appropriate where there is significant competition or uncertainty.

Disclosure

14.216 SSAP 13 requires the following disclosures to be made in the financial statements where development costs are deferred and are shown as an asset in the balance sheet:

- The accounting policy should be stated, as required by SSAP 2, and explained.

- The total amount of research and development expenditure written off to the profit and loss account in the period should be disclosed, analysed between the current year's expenditure and amounts amortised from deferred expenditure.

- Movements on deferred development expenditure and the amount carried forward at the beginning and the end of the period should be disclosed. Deferred development expenditure should be disclosed under the heading of 'intangible assets' in the balance sheet.

[SSAP 13, paras 30-32].

14.217 In addition, the Act requires that further disclosure should also be made of the period over which the amount of those costs that were originally capitalised is being, or is to be, written off, together with the reasons for capitalising the development costs in question. [4 Sch 20(2)].

14.218 Capitalising development cost is an option and, in practice, many companies write off all research and development expenditure as it is incurred, rather than attempt to justify capitalising development expenditure under the SSAP 13 rules. However, in Table 14.16, the 1994 financial statements of Dobson Park Industries provide an example of a company that does capitalise development expenditure. The charge to the profit and loss account is analysed between amortisation of the capitalised development costs and the immediate write-off of other non-capitalised research and development expenditure.

Table 14.16 – Dobson Park Industries plc – Annual Report & Accounts – 1 October 1994

Accounting Policies (extract)

Research and Development Expenditure

Expenditure on research and development is charged to the profit and loss account in the year in which it is incurred with the exception of expenditure on the development of certain major new product projects where the outcome of those projects is assessed as being reasonably certain as regards viability and technical feasibility. Such expenditure is capitalised and amortised over a period not longer than five years commencing in the year sales of the product are first made.

- The fact that the amount of unamortised development expenditure is not to be treated as a realised loss for the purposes of calculating distributable profits.

- The circumstances that the directors relied upon to justify their decision not to treat the unamortised development expenditure as a realised loss.

[Sec 269(2)(b)].

Computer software

14.225 There is considerable diversity in practice in respect of accounting for the costs of computer software, both as regards software for internal use and software that is incorporated into products under development. Many companies write off the cost of their computer software immediately to the profit and loss account. However, an increasing number of companies have capitalised their computer software costs as either tangible fixed assets or intangible fixed assets.

14.226 FRS 10 has an important bearing on the treatment of the costs of internal-use software. The FRS does not permit internally developed intangible assets to be capitalised (except for those that have a readily ascertainable market value, which in practice is few, if any). Therefore, the FRS would not permit any internal costs of developing computer software for internal use to be capitalised as an intangible fixed asset. FRS 10 recognises that the rules restricting the recognition of internally developed intangible assets potentially create a problem for computer software costs. It explains that such costs should be treated as part of the cost of the related hardware (and, hence, as a tangible, rather than intangible, asset) where they are *"directly attributable to bringing a computer system or other computer-operated machinery into working condition for its intended use within the business"*. [FRS 10 para 2].

14.227 Computer software development costs may arise in several ways. Consider the following four situations:

- A company purchases computer software externally (including, for example, packages for applications such as payroll, or general ledger or other similar packages to be used on the company's own computer). The company should capitalise the cost of such software as a tangible fixed asset. This is because the software complies with the Act's definition of a fixed asset, as the company will generally purchase it to use on a continuing basis in the company's activities.

  The company should depreciate this software, in common with its other fixed assets, over its estimated useful life. Where a company purchases a software package specifically to run on a particular computer, the software's estimated useful life should generally not exceed the computer's remaining useful life.

Where a company incurs subsequent expenditure to upgrade or enhance the software (so that its service potential is increased), it could either write this expenditure off immediately or capitalise it if it has a policy of capitalising software development costs. If this expenditure is capitalised it should be written off over the remaining useful life of the software package. However, where the improvement costs lead to an extension of the software's useful life, the company will need to revise the depreciation charge, because the asset's life has been extended.

UITF Abstract 20 addresses the specific issue of the treatment of software modification costs incurred to achieve year 2000 compliance. Capitalisation of such costs is only permitted where an entity already has an accounting policy for capitalising software costs and to the extent that the service potential of an asset is enhanced rather than merely maintained.

- A company employs programmers to develop software for the company's own use. In this situation, two problems exist, namely that:
  - The company will need to analyse the programmers' time and other expenses in order to identify the costs of developing the software.
  - If the software is not operational at the time the financial statements are prepared, the company will have to provide evidence to demonstrate that the software will be completed successfully and have a value to the business.

  Provided that it can overcome both of these problems, a company may capitalise this type of computer software cost as a tangible fixed asset if it meets the criteria in FRS 10 (see para 14.226 above). If the software is to be capitalised, but is not fully developed, it should be included under the balance sheet heading of 'Payments on account and assets in the course of construction'.

  SSAP 13 criteria are not relevant in assessing whether this expenditure should be capitalised, because the expenditure is not part of a commercial project. The company is merely producing its own fixed assets. However, it will be necessary to ensure that the definition of an asset is met, namely that the expenditure provides access to future economic benefits – which means that the development must be capable of being assessed as viable. Costs that might fall to be treated as tangible assets in this way include the costs of developing electronic dealing systems and websites, where ongoing activities are associated with those assets.

- A company buys computer software to incorporate into a product that it is developing. This could include software that an external software house writes and that the company will include in computer-controlled equipment it will produce and sell.

  This expenditure is a form of development expenditure and so the question of whether this can be capitalised is covered by the criteria included in SSAP 13. Provided that these criteria are satisfied, the company may capitalise the expenditure and amortise it over the product's estimated useful life.

- A company's own programmers write software that the company will include in its products. The question of capitalisation will again depend on whether the criteria set out in SSAP 13 are satisfied.

14.228 An example of a company that capitalises major software purchases is The Automobile Association (Table 14.17).

Table 14.17 – The Automobile Association – Annual Report and Accounts – 31 December 1996

Accounting policies (extract)

Software
Software costs are written off as incurred, except for purchases from third parties in respect of major systems. In such cases, the costs are written off over a maximum of five years from the date of implementation.

Comparison with IASs

14.229 IAS 38 'Intangible assets' was published in September 1998. Research and development costs are within its scope. IAS 38 requires that an intangible asset should be recognised if, and only if:

- It is separately identifiable from goodwill.

- It is controlled – for example, by legal rights.

- It is probable that economic benefits will flow from it – for example, from revenue or from cost savings.

- Its cost can be measured reliably.

14.230 Additional criteria for recognising internally generated intangible assets preclude the recognition of internally generated brands, mastheads, publishing titles, customer lists and items similar in substance. Expenditure on research, start-up activities, training and advertising should also be expensed as incurred. Development costs should be recognised as intangible assets if specified criteria are met, which include evidence of technical feasibility and of future economic benefits. Costs previously expensed cannot be reinstated as intangible assets.:

14.231 Intangible assets acquired in a business combination should be recognised separately from goodwill if their cost (that is, fair value) can be measured reliably. Where there is no active market for the asset, the standard permits the use of other valuation techniques that are used in the relevant industry to estimate fair values, such as multiples of turnover and discounted cash flows.

14.232 Intangible assets should be amortised over the best estimates of their useful lives. There is a rebuttable presumption that the useful life does not exceed 20 years. If a longer life is chosen, the reasons should be disclosed. However, an indefinite life (that is, non-amortisation) is not permitted. If a period of more than 20 years is chosen, the intangible asset must be tested annually for impairment.

14.233 Historical cost is the benchmark treatment for intangible assets. Revaluation of intangible assets would only be permitted (as an allowed alternative treatment) if there is an active market and market prices are available to the public (in practice, few exist).

Chapter 15

Leases and HP contracts

Chapter 15

Leases and HP contracts

Introduction

15.1 This chapter considers the accounting treatment and disclosure of leased assets in a company's financial statements and discusses some of the practical issues concerning lease accounting. The UK accounting requirements for lease transactions for both lessees and lessors are set out in SSAP 21, 'Accounting for leases and hire purchase contracts'. Additionally, those lease transactions which form part of a complex arrangement or which contains options, conditional provisions and guarantees also fall under the scope of FRS 5. As explained in FRS 5, where a transaction falls under the scope of both FRS 5 and SSAP 21 the standard containing the more specific provision will apply. In general, SSAP 21 contains the more specific provisions, relating to stand-alone leases. The exception to this in Application Note B of FRS 5, which deals specifically with sale and repurchase transactions including the treatment of options.

15.2 Under SSAP 21, a 'lease' is defined as a contract between the lessor and the lessee for the hire of a specific asset. The lessor retains ownership of the asset, but conveys to the lessee the right to use the asset in return for paying specific rentals. In addition, the definition of a lease in the standard includes other arrangements not described as leases, in which one party retains ownership but conveys to another the right to use the asset for an agreed period of time in return for specific rentals.

15.3 In broad terms, SSAP 21 requires that, where a company finances a significant amount of its capital investment through leasing, its financial statements should properly reflect the commercial effect of those transactions. Thus, where the substance of those transactions is akin to the lessee purchasing the asset, financed by borrowings drawn from the lessor (a 'finance lease'), the standard requires the lessee's balance sheet to show both an asset, reflecting the lessee's rights in the leased asset, and a liability, reflecting the future financial obligations under the lease. However, where the lease does not have the commercial effect of a financing arrangement for the acquisition of an asset (an 'operating lease') the lessee need only account for the rental expense through its profit and loss account.

15.4 Similarly, from the lessor's perspective, leases that have similar characteristics to other forms of lending ('finance leases') are classified in the balance sheet as receivables; whereas assets held for use in operating leases are treated in a similar way to other tangible fixed assets.

15.5 Thus, the accounting treatment of a lease depends on the commercial substance of the lease. The accounting distinction between a finance lease and an operating lease is, therefore, a crucial one.

15.6 The paragraphs below consider the factors to be taken into account when classifying leases. The following two sections consider the appropriate treatment from the perspective of the lessee and lessor, respectively, once the lease has been classified.

Classification of leases

15.7 Under SSAP 21, a finance lease is defined as *"...a lease that transfers substantially all the risks and rewards of ownership of an asset to the lessee".* [SSAP 21 para 15]. Thus, a finance lease is an arrangement that has the substance of a financing transaction for the lessee to acquire effective economic ownership of an asset.

15.8 An operating lease, under SSAP 21, is simply *"...a lease other than a finance lease".* [SSAP 21 para 17]. In practice, this means that an operating lease does not pass substantially all the risk and rewards of ownership to the lessee: a significant element of risk must, therefore, remain with the lessor or some party other than the lessee. Consequently, an operating lease is usually for a period substantially shorter than the asset's useful economic life and the lessor will be relying on recovering a significant proportion of his investment from either the proceeds from the asset's sale or the asset's further hire after the end of the lease term.

15.9 Whether or not a lease passes substantially all the risks and rewards of ownership to the lessee will normally be self-evident from the terms of the lease contract and an understanding of the commercial risks taken by each party. Where the lessor takes little or no asset-related risk, other than a credit risk on the lessee, the agreement will obviously be a finance lease. Similarly, where the lessor is exposed to significant levels of risks relating to movements in the asset's market value, utilisation, or performance, such as on a short-term hire agreement, the agreement will be easily classified as an operating lease. The difficulty, therefore, tends to emerge on classifying leases where the lessor recovers most of his investment through the terms of the lease, but retains some element of risk relating to the asset's residual value at the end of the lease term.

15.10 In order to provide guidance on when such risks and rewards could be reasonable presumed to have passed, SSAP 21 sets a simple test:

> *"It should be presumed that such a transfer of risks and rewards occurs if at the inception of a lease the present value of the minimum lease payments, including any initial payment, amounts to substantially all (normally 90 per cent or more) of the fair value of the leased asset".* [SSAP 21 para 15].

15.11 In essence, the present value test is a measure of the risk that the lessor (or other third party) is taking in relation to the asset's residual value at the end of the lease term. Where the lessor (or other third party) is assuming a significant level of residual value risk (ten per cent or more in present value terms) then it is presumed that substantially all the risks of ownership could not have passed to the lessee. As a yardstick for measuring risk the present value test is somewhat crude, but it was seen as a reasonable test of risk at the time SSAP 21 was introduced. It was, however, never intended to provide a strict mathematical definition of a finance lease. Thus, SSAP 21 provides that the presumption can be overridden where there is demonstrable evidence to support doing so.

15.12 One of the principal criticisms of SSAP 21 is that it lead to practices under which lessors would structure leases in a way that apparently gives a present value result below the 90 per cent threshold, often marginally so, in order to provide lessees with a source of off-balance sheet finance. In July 1987, the ICAEW took the unusual step of issuing a Technical Release, TR 664, to clarify the rules in SSAP 21. TR 664 seeks to dissuade preparers of financial statements from standing behind the present value test in determining whether a leased asset should be on- or off-balance sheet by emphasising that the leases should be classified according to an informed judgement as to what is the true substance of the leasing transaction. Thus, while the present value test sets a presumption, it should be overridden where the circumstances justify it.

15.13 The publication of FRS 5, 'Reporting the substance of transactions', in 1994 further reinforces the message of TR 664, because it requires emphasis to be placed on those aspects and implications of a transaction that are likely to have a commercial effect in practice. Moreover, FRS 5 is particularly relevant in interpreting leases containing options, guarantees and conditional provisions where it provides more specific guidance than SSAP 21.

15.14 Consequently, although the present value test may be a useful yardstick for measuring the lessor's risk in a lease, it is by no means conclusive of where the risks and rewards lie. A proper interpretation of the classification of a lease, therefore, requires the exercise of judgement to determine the agreement's true nature. In this matter, the terms dealing with: the contractual lease period, the cancellation provisions, the renewal options and the rights and obligations of each party in relation to the asset at the end of the lease term are particularly important.

Lease term

Under SSAP 21, the lease term includes both of the following:

- The period for which the lessee has a contractual obligation to lease the asset.

- Further periods for which the lessee has the option to continue to lease the asset, with or without further payments, and it is reasonably certain at the inception of the lease that the lessee will exercise that option.

[SSAP 21 para 19].

Those parts of the lease that deal with: the lease's minimum contractual period (sometimes referred to as the 'primary period'); cancellation (or 'break') clauses; exchange and upgrade conditions; and options to extend the lease must, therefore, be considered carefully.

15.15 If a lease contains a clean break clause, that is, where the lessee is free to walk away from the lease agreement after a certain time without penalty, then the lease term for accounting purposes will normally be the period between the inception of the lease and the earliest point at which the break option is exercisable by the lessee. Thus, the inclusion of a break clause can significantly reduce the minimum lease payments for the purpose of the present value test with the effect that the present value of the minimum lease payments falls below the 90 per cent threshold and the lease is classified as an operating lease. This, however, is not an unreasonable result if there is a genuine commercial possibility that the lessee might exercise the option resulting in the realisation of the lessor's unrecovered investment in the leased asset being subject to market risk.

15.16 If a lease contains an early termination clause that requires the lessee to make a termination payment to compensate the lessor (sometimes referred to as the 'stipulated loss value') such that the recovery of the lessor's remaining investment in the lease was assured, then the termination clause would normally be disregarded in determining the lease term.

15.17 Where, however, there are break clauses that transfer some economic risk to the lessor, but at the same time give the lessor some protection from financial loss, the interpretation becomes more difficult. For example, certain computer lessors include right to exchange clauses in leases that would otherwise be classified as finance leases. These give lessees the right to return equipment, or a proportion of the equipment, at certain times during the primary lease term, but normally on condition that a replacement lease is entered into on the new and remaining equipment. These right to exchange clauses need to be considered very carefully.

15.18 On the one hand, the effect may be the replacement of one finance lease by another, analogous to an outright purchase of equipment with a right to trade in for new equipment at a future date. This will be particularly so where the commercial loss on early termination (the difference between market value and the lessor's book value) is effectively rolled into the new lease agreement either through higher rentals or through an extension of the term on the remaining pool of assets not subject to the exchange. On the other hand, if the lessor takes a genuine residual value risk under the exchange conditions and such losses are not passed on to the lessee in the way described, this may justify classification as an operating lease.

15.19 Renewal clauses can cause similar problems of interpretation as break clauses. Where the terms of renewal are set at what is anticipated to be significantly below a fair market rental then it is reasonable to assume that the lessee will act in his own commercial interests and extend the lease. In these situations, the lease term would include both the minimum period and the renewal period. Where, however, the rentals in the secondary period are based on a fair market basis, such that there is no compelling commercial reason why the lessee must extend the lease, then the lease term will normally exclude the secondary period.

15.20 Other factors that may need to be considered in determining whether secondary periods should be included in the lease term are other forms of commercial compulsion such as penalties. For example, if the lessee is subject to a penalty for failing to renew a lease or exercise a purchase option, or if the return conditions stipulated in the lease are unduly penal, it may be to the lessee's advantage to continue to lease the asset. Similarly, if the lessee's business is dependent on the asset such that the cost of its removal and disruption of business are disproportional to the costs of continuing the lease, the secondary period should be included in the lease term.

Minimum lease payments

15.21 Once the lease term is determined, the lessee's minimum lease payments can be calculated. These are the payments that the lessee is committed to make during the lease term, and include:

- Any initial payment the lessee makes.
- The minimum rentals over the lease term (excluding charges in respect of services, such as maintenance, and VAT).
- Any amounts guaranteed by the lessee, or by a party related to him, to the lessor in respect of the realisation of the asset at the end of the lease term.

[SSAP 21 para 20].

15.22 From the lessor's perspective, the minimum lease payments may be different from that defined above since the lessor's minimum lease payments includes all the above and further amounts that are guaranteed by third parties in relation to the asset's future realisation. Thus, if the manufacturer originally supplying the asset agreed to repurchase the asset from the lessor, or guaranteed the sales proceeds, at the end of the lease term, then this amount would be included in the lessor's minimum lease payments. Consequently, in these circumstances, the lessee and lessor may well classify the lease quite differently.

15.23 The inclusion of 'residual guarantees' in lease agreements and related documentation will have an important impact on the way leases are classified by both lessors and lessees.

15.24 Obviously, if the lessee guarantees the whole of the asset's expected residual value at the end of the lease term the lessor would not be taking any of the risks relating to the performance or market value of the asset and the transaction would be clearly a finance lease. It would also mean that, by definition, the present value of the minimum lease payments would be equal to 100 per cent of the asset's fair value.

15.25 However, it is not uncommon in certain leases for the lessee and lessor to share both the downside risks and potential upside benefits associated with the asset's market value at the end of the lease term such that the lessee is taking some, but not all, the residual risk. For example, in certain leases the terms of the agreement provide for the asset to be sold at the end of the lease term and any profit and loss arising against anticipated values is shared between the lessor and lessee. However, the profit and loss sharing arrangements are usually unevenly balanced between the parties, with the lessee often taking the first tranche of loss up to a stipulated amount, with the lessor (or other third parties) only taking losses beyond that sum. In these circumstances, the amount of losses the lessee guarantees is normally set at such an amount that the inclusion of the guaranteed amount in the minimum lease payments does not cause the 90 per cent test to be breached.

15.26 Interpreting these types of agreement can be particularly difficult. The lessor may have a residual risk of ten per cent in present value terms, but if this implies that residual values have to fall to a level substantially below that anticipated to occur in practice, even under the most pessimistic circumstances, then the lessor's risk is remote and all the real commercial risks must rest with the lessee. In these circumstances, there is a strong argument for overriding the results of the present value test and classifying the lease as a finance lease.

Example

A lease of a car for two years has built into it an assumed residual value for the car of 45% of original cost. The market's perception is that the likely range of the residual value is

40-50% of cost. The terms of the lease provide that the lessee takes the risks and rewards regarding the residual down to a residual of 20% of cost. Below 20%, the lessor bears the loss.

It is clear under the combination of SSAP 21 and FRS 5 that the lessor's taking of risk below 20% of cost should not be taken into account in classifying the lease. The lessee takes the residual risk in all likely outcomes of residual value. Therefore, subject to any other terms in the lease, a finance lease is indicated.

15.27 However, in practice, the facts as illustrated above are rarely so simple. For example, under certain aircraft leases the lessee is offered a range of options under which he can terminate, or not renew, the leasing agreement. If he terminates the lease the residual sharing arrangements can be complex with the residual risk being shared by a number of parties including the lessor, lessee, supplier and residual insurer in a complex series of tranches. Interpreting these types of complex lease arrangements can be particularly difficult and the general principles and specific provisions of FRS 5 will need to be applied to determine the nature of transactions. For example, implementing FRS 5 had a dramatic impact on British Airways' accounting for certain aircraft leases (see Table 15.1).

Table 15.1 – British Airways Plc – Report & Accounts – 31 March 1995

Notes to the accounts

1 CHANGES IN ACCOUNTING POLICIES (extract)

Adoption of new accounting standard (extract)

The Group has adopted the provisions of Financial Reporting Standard 5 'Reporting the Substance of Transactions' with effect from 1 April 1994 and corresponding amounts have been adjusted accordingly. As a consequence, the leases on twenty-four aircraft previously accounted for as operating leases are now accounted for as if they were finance leases and are aggregated with finance leases in the various disclosures in theses accounts. The effect of this change on the balance sheet at 31 March 1995 has been to increase tangible fixed assets by £870 million (1994: £1,006 million) and borrowings by £905 million (1994: £1,041 million) and to reduce opening reserves by £52 million (1994: £45 million). The effect on the results for the year ended 31 March 1995 has been to increase operating profit by £53 million (1994: £43 million) and to increase interest payable by £54 million (1994: £52 million), thereby reducing profit before taxation for the year by £1 million (1994: £9 million).

15.28 In some agreements relating to car fleets, the assessment of the commercial effects of these residual sharing arrangements can be further complicated by terms that mitigate a lessor's risk by providing for any residual losses on individual assets to be pooled against profits on others in the same portfolio. Again, these types of arrangement will need to be considered carefully to determine the nature of the risks borne by the lessor (and other third parties) and those transferred to the lessee. As a general rule, for instance, losses on some assets should not be set against profits on others.

The interest rate implicit in the lease

15.29 The rate of interest used for the present value test should be the interest rate implicit in the lease. This is the discount rate that, when applied at the inception of the lease to the amounts that the lessor expects to receive and retain from his investment in the lease, produces a present value equal to the leased asset's fair value. The amounts that the lessor expects to receive and retain comprise:

- The lessee's minimum lease payments.
- Any further amounts guaranteed by third parties in respect of the asset's residual value.
- The asset's expected residual value at the end of the lease, which is not guaranteed by the lessee or any other party.
- Less any amounts for which the lessor will be accountable to the lessee (for example, a rental rebate at the end of the lease based on the proceeds from the assets' sale).

[SSAP 21 para 24].

15.30 In more simple terms, the interest rate implicit in the lease is the lessor's internal rate of return from the lease taking into account the normal cash price of the leased asset, rentals and the amount he expects to recover from the residual value. In practice, the interest rate implicit in the lease is unlikely to be stipulated in the agreement and, unless the lessor volunteers the information to the lessee, the lessee will need either to derive an estimate of the rate from the information available to him or to use an approximation based on a similar lease.

15.31 A lessee can normally derive a reasonable estimate of the interest rate implicit in a lease where he either knows, or can make a reasonable estimate of, the cost of the asset and the anticipated residual value of the asset at the end of the lease term.

The present value calculation

15.32 The present value calculation is performed by discounting the minimum lease payments and comparing the resulting present value to the fair value of the leased asset. In most circumstances, the fair value will be the normal cash price at which the lessee could otherwise purchase the asset. A potentially misleading result can arise if the comparison is made against an amount that is not representative of the fair value, for example, a list price where substantial discounts are normally given to customers purchasing assets.

15.33 As indicated above, the present value test can also be misleading where the results of the present value test are engineered to provide a result marginally below the 90 per cent threshold. Such engineering can arise through the uses of break clauses, renewal clauses, and residual guarantees. Where there is evidence that the amount of residual risk taken by the lessor (or other unrelated parties) is insignificant or remote then there will be reasons to believe that substantially all the risks and rewards of ownership have passed to the lessee. In these circumstances, the results of the present value test should be overridden and the lease classified as a finance lease.

Property leases

15.34 Under the standard, leases of land and buildings are subject to the same accounting requirements as other leased assets. This means that they should either be classified as finance leases or as operating leases and should be accounted for accordingly. However, the present value test is difficult to apply to property leases and can sometimes be misleading. This is partly because of the practical difficulties of ascertaining the true interest rate implicit in the lease and partly because of the commercial nature of most UK institutional property leases.

15.35 Most UK institutional 'short' leases are for periods up to 25-30 years, and contain clauses that adjust lease payments to market rates at a regular interval (for example, five-yearly or three-yearly rent reviews). The lessor is often an institution that is seeking long-term rental and capital growth and is, therefore, taking most of the risks and rewards associated with changes in the property market. Although part of the investor's return may be protected by 'upward only' rental review clauses the overall return is dependent on market conditions, which may be substantially less or greater than originally anticipated. In this sense, the nature of the lessor's return is very different from a 'lender's return', which is based on the lender's cost of money plus margin.

15.36 However, it does not necessarily follow that all leases that look like institutional 'short' leases are operating leases. In recent years the lack of rental growth in the property market has led to the development of a number of hybrid leasing structures which, though in the legal form of a short lease, have many of the characteristics of financing arrangements.

15.37 Again the principles of FRS 5 and, in particular, whether the lender achieves a lenders' return, will help determine the true nature of the lease. An example could be a building with a relatively short life, perhaps built to a customer's specification or for a specific use, or certain types of sale and leaseback arrangements where the commercial objective is for the lessee to repurchase the property at an early option date.

15.38 Long leases (usually 99-999 years) are more likely to be finance leases. Such leases often involve the payment of a large lease premium with only a small annual ground rent. In these situations, the lease premium is normally capitalised and depreciated over the lease term. While, strictly, the present value of the ground rent should also be capitalised and an obligation set up, these amounts are often ignored as being immaterial.

Accounting by lessees

Accounting for finance leases

15.39 The standard requires that a finance lease should be recorded in a lessee's balance sheet both as an asset and as an obligation to pay future rentals. At the inception of the lease, the sum to be recorded both as an asset and as a liability should be the present value of the minimum lease payments, derived by discounting them at the interest rate implicit in the lease. [SSAP 21 para 32].

15.40 An asset leased under a finance lease should be depreciated over the shorter of the lease term and its useful life. [SSAP 21 para 36]. The lease term, as defined in SSAP 21, is the period for which the lessee has contracted to lease the asset plus any further optional periods, which are at the lessee's option and which are reasonably certain to be exercised. [SSAP 21 para 19]. With a hire purchase contract that has the characteristics of a finance lease, the asset should be depreciated over its useful life. [SSAP 21 para 36].

15.41 The lease is deemed to commence on the earlier of the date on which the asset is brought into use by the lessee and the date from which rentals first accrue. Therefore, if a lease provides for a rent-free period at the start of the lease, the lessee should treat the inception date as the date on which he started to use the asset.

15.42 Rentals payable should be apportioned between the finance charge and a reduction of the outstanding obligation for future amounts payable. The total finance charge under a finance lease should be allocated to accounting periods during the lease term, so as to produce either a constant periodic rate of charge on the remaining balance of the obligation for each accounting period or a reasonable approximation to it. [SSAP 21 para 35].

Example

Cost of leased asset	£100,000
Lease term	5 years
Rental six-monthly in advance	£12,000
Expected residual on disposal at the end of the lease term	£10,000
Lessee's interest in residual proceeds	97%
Economic life	8 years
Inception date	1 January 19X4
Lessee's financial year end	31 December

In this example, the lease must obviously be a finance lease because the lessor has only a 3% interest in the residual value. There is, therefore, little point in performing the 90% test.

The amounts the lessor expects to receive and retain comprise the rentals, plus 3% of the residual at the end of the lease term. These amounts can be used to determine the interest rate implicit in the lease and the present value of the lessee's minimum lease payments as follows:

	Present value factor	Present value at 4.3535%
		£
Lessee's minimum lease payments (10 × £12,000)	8.3170	99,804
Lessor's residual (£10,000 – £9,700)	0.6533	196
Fair value		100,000

The interest rate that amortises these amounts is 4.3535%, compounded on a six-monthly basis.

The amount that is capitalised as both an asset and an obligation at the inception of the lease is, therefore, £99,804. Alternatively, it could be simply assumed that, because the lessor's residual was so immaterial, the fair value was a reasonable approximation of the present value of the lease payments and this would generally be allowed in such a case. If this approach was adopted, the amount that would be capitalised at the inception of the lease as an asset and an obligation would be £100,000.

The finance charge can now be allocated to each accounting period. In this example the actuarial method has been used:

Period commencing	Obligation at start of period £	Rental paid £	Obligation during period £	Finance charge at 4.3535% £	Obligation at end of period £
January 19X4	99,804	(12,000)	87,804	3,823	91,627
June 19X4	91,627	(12,000)	79,627	3,467	83,094
January 19X5	83,094	(12,000)	71,094	3,095	74,189
June 19X5	74,189	(12,000)	62,189	2,707	64,896
January 19X6	64,896	(12,000)	52,896	2,303	55,199
June 19X6	55,199	(12,000)	43,199	1,881	45,080
January 19X7	45,080	(12,000)	33,080	1,440	34,520
June 19X7	34,520	(12,000)	22,520	980	23,500
January 19X8	23,500	(12,000)	11,500	500	12,000
June 19X8	12,000	(12,000)	–	–	–
		(120,000)		20,196	

The finance charges for each year and, by deduction, the capital repayment element of the rental can now be summarised as follows:

	Rental £	Finance charges £	Capital repayment £
19X4	24,000	7,290	16,710
19X5	24,000	5,802	18,198
19X6	24,000	4,184	19,816
19X7	24,000	2,420	21,580
19X8	24,000	500	23,500
	120,000	20,196	99,804

In this example, the lessee's financial year end coincides with the end of a rental period and so no interest accrual is necessary.

Depreciation can now be calculated as follows:

Lease term = 5 years
Economic life = 8 years
Lessee's interest in the proceeds of the residual = £9,700

Therefore, the depreciation charge on a straight line basis is:

$$\frac{£99{,}804 - £9{,}700}{5 \text{ years}} = £18{,}021 \text{ per annum}$$

Where the lessee's interest in the anticipated proceeds of the residual is immaterial, the residual can be ignored for the purposes of calculating depreciation.

The effects on the lessee's balance sheet and profit and loss account for each year can now be summarised as follows:

	Obligations under finance leases £	Net book value of leased assets £	Depreciation £	Finance charges £	Total charges £
Start	99,804	99,804			
19X4	83,094	81,783	18,021	7,290	25,311
19X5	64,896	63,762	18,021	5,802	23,823
19X6	45,080	45,741	18,021	4,184	22,205
19X7	23,500	27,720	18,021	2,420	20,441
19X8	–	9,700	18,020	500	18,520
			90,104	20,196	110,300

The above example illustrates that, in addition to its impact on the lessee's balance sheet, lease capitalisation may also have a significant impact on the lessee's profit and loss account. For example, the lease rentals are £24,000 per annum, but the combined charge for depreciation and interest varies from £25,311 to £18,520 per annum. These differences between rental payments and profit and loss charges will be more pronounced on assets subject to long economic lives and leases with short primary lease periods, but which may have secondary periods at peppercorn rents.

Accounting for operating leases

15.43 Operating leases should not be capitalised and the lease rental should be charged on a straight-line basis over the lease term, unless another systematic and rational basis is more appropriate. This applies even if the payments are not made on such a basis. [SSAP 21 para 37].

Reverse lease premiums

15.44 Prospective lessees are sometimes given incentives to sign operating leases for office or retail property. These incentives may include either rent-free or reduced-rent periods at the start of the lease or even contributions toward fitting out costs. Such incentives were common in the late 1980s and early 1990s when developers, faced with surplus rental property, attempted to obtain tenants in a competitive market.

15.45 In February 1994, the FRRP published a press notice on its consideration of reverse lease premiums in the financial statements for the year ended 31 December 1992 of Pentos plc. Pentos had a stated accounting policy of taking the net income from reverse premiums to income over two accounting periods in order to match income received and start-up costs incurred for new shops. The FRRP believed that the policy was not clearly stated. The directors of Pentos agreed to clarify this accounting policy and the information presented about such premiums in the financial statements for the year ended 31 December 1993. However, the

FRRP also noted that the requirements in law and accounting standards that existed at that time did not provide unequivocal guidance as to the correct accounting treatment of reverse premiums.

15.46 The FRRP brought this deficiency to the attention of the ASB and, as a result the UITF considered the matter and issued Abstract 12, 'Lessee accounting for reverse premiums and similar incentives', in December 1994. UITF Abstract 12 expands and clarifies the requirements of paragraph 37 of SSAP 21 with regard to incentives for lessees to sign leases. These incentives may take many different forms. Examples of such incentives include: contributions to relocation or start-up costs; the assumption of liabilities, such as the rentals under the an old lease which would otherwise fall to be a vacant property; or the gift of an asset such as the lessor bearing directly all the costs of fitting out the property to the lessee's specifications. However, the abstract details the same treatment for all incentives regardless of their form or cash flow effect.

15.47 The UITF consensus is that benefits received and receivable by a lessee as an incentive to sign a lease in whatever form should be spread by the lessee on a straight-line basis over the lease term, or, if shorter than the full lease term, over the period to the review date on which the rent is first expected to be adjusted to the prevailing market rent. [UITF 12 para 8]. This requirement seeks to ensure that the profit and loss account reflects the true effective rental charge for the property irrespective of the particular cash flow arrangements agreed between the two parties. The lessor will seek to recover a market rental over the lease term. Therefore, the existence of an up-front incentive creates the presumption that the subsequent rental levels will be set at higher than the prevailing market level until either the end of the lease or until the review date when the rent is adjusted to the market level. In requiring that the incentive should be spread over the lease term or to the first rent review to market value if earlier, the abstract amended paragraph 16 of the guidance notes to SSAP 21, which had stated merely that incentives should be spread over the period in which the asset is in use.

15.48 In exceptional circumstances, where the presumption that an incentive (however structured) is in substance part of the lessor's market return can be rebutted, the abstract permits another systematic and rational basis to be used to spread the incentive. However, if another basis is used, the following must be disclosed:

- An explanation of the specific circumstances that render spreading the incentive on a straight line basis over the lease term or period to the first review date misleading.

- A description of the basis used and the amounts involved.

- A note of the effect on the result for the current and corresponding period of any departure from the standard treatment.

[UITF 12 para 8].

15.49 In addition, if a method of spreading the incentive other than on a straight- line basis is considered to more accurately adjust the rents paid to the prevailing market rate, then that method may be used, but the disclosures detailed in paragraph 15.48 above would apply. [UITF 12 para 9].

Lessee disclosure requirements

15.50 In respect of finance leases, SSAP 21 requires the following information to be disclosed in the lessee's financial statements:

- The gross amount, the related accumulated depreciation and the total depreciation allocated for the period, analysed by each major class of asset capitalised under finance leases. [SSAP 21 para 49].

- Alternatively, this information may be included within the totals disclosed by each major class of asset for owned assets. However, where this alternative is adopted, the total of the net amount of assets held under finance leases and the total amount of depreciation allocated for the period in respect of finance leases, need to be disclosed separately. [SSAP 21 para 50]. An example of this disclosure is in Table 15.2 on page 16.

- The liability for net obligations under finance leases (net of finance charges allocated to future periods), shown separately from other liabilities. This liability should be disclosed either on the face of the balance sheet or in the notes to the financial statements (see Table 15.3 on page 17). [SSAP 21 para 51].

- The liability for net obligations under finance leases, analysed between amounts payable in the next year, amounts payable in the second to fifth years inclusive from the balance sheet date and the aggregate amounts payable after the fifth year. [SSAP 21 para 52]. For example, Table 15.3 illustrates this disclosure. The detailed disclosure requirements for such creditors are also contained in chapter 17.

- Where the lessee discloses the analysis of obligations under finance leases separately, he may, as an alternative to analysing the net obligations, analyse the gross obligations and show future finance charges as a separate deduction from the total (see Table 15.5 on page 19). [SSAP 21 para 52].

- The aggregate finance charge allocated to the period. [SSAP 21 para 53]. This disclosure is often made as part of the interest charge for the year as illustrated in Table 15.4 on page 19.

- The commitments under finance leases existing at the year end that have been entered into, but whose inception occurs after the year end. [SSAP 21 para 54]. This requirement is analogous to the legal requirements in paragraph 50(3) of Schedule 4 in respect of commitments for capital expenditure (see chapter 20). Zeneca Group, for example, includes such disclosure in the leases note (see Table 15.5 on page 19).

Table 15.2 – British Airways Plc – Report & Accounts – 31 March 1995

Notes to the accounts (extract)

	Group	
£ million	**1995**	1994
5 OPERATING PROFIT (extract)		
a Operating Profit is arrived at after charging:		
Depreciation of Group tangible fixed assets		
Owned assets	**263**	258
Finance leased aircraft	**109**	117
Hire purchased aircraft	**63**	48
Other leasehold interests	**23**	24
	458	447

15 TANGIBLE ASSETS (extract)

				Group total	
£ million	Fleet	Property	Equipment	**1995**	1994
Net Book Amounts					
31 March 1995	5,155	801	207	**6,163**	
31 March 1994	5,127	484	200		5,811
Utilisation at 31 March					
Assets in current use					
Owned	1,883	734	165	**2,782**	2,631
Finance leased	1,436			**1,436**	1,623
Hire purchased arrangements	1,445			**1,445**	1,274
Progress payments	377	65	42	**484**	257
Assets held for resale	14	2		**16**	26
	5,155	801	207	**6,163**	5,811

Table 15.3 – Cable and Wireless plc – Report and Accounts – 31 March 1995

Balance sheets (extract)

at 31 March	Note	Group 1995 £m	Group 1994 Restated £m
Creditors: amounts falling due within one year	21		
Loans and obligations under finance leases		**321.4**	359.5
Other creditors		**1,423.8**	1,318.8
		1,745.2	1,678.3
Creditors: amounts falling due after more than one year	22		
Convertible bonds		**149.5**	154.5
Other loans and obligations under finance leases		**1,190.2**	1,022.4
Other creditors		**33.4**	34.2
Provisions for liabilities and charges			
Deferred taxation	23	**130.0**	126.8
Other provisions	24	**89.5**	28.8
		1,592.6	1,366.7

21. Creditors: amounts falling due within one year (extract)

	Group 1995 £m	Group Restated 1994 £m
Loans and obligations under finance leases		
Banks loans and overdrafts	**39.2**	32.6
Bills payable	**15.2**	31.1
Current instalments due on loans	**253.8**	287.4
Obligations under finance leases	**13.2**	8.4
	321.4	359.5

22. Creditors: amounts falling due after more than one year (extract)

	Group	
		Restated
	1995	1994
	£m	£m
Loans and obligations under finance leases		
Sterling repayable at various dates up to 2019	**353.2**	161.1
Hong Kong dollars repayable at various dates up to 1995	**200.9**	220.9
US dollars repayable at various dates up to 2041	**775.1**	838.8
Other currencies repayable at various dates up to 1997	**56.7**	63.6
	1,385.9	1,284.4
Less: Current instalments due	**253.8**	287.4
	1,132.1	997.0
Net obligations under finance leases	**71.3**	33.8
Less: Current instalments due	**13.2**	8.4
	58.1	25.4
Total loans and net obligations under finance leases	**1,190.2**	1,022.4
Total loans and net obligations under finance leases are payable as follows:		
Between one and two years	**130.7**	56.7
Between two and five years	**259.6**	289.3
In five or more years	**799.9**	676.4
	1,190.2	1,022.4

Table 15.4 – Racal Electronics Plc – Annual Report & Accounts – 31 March 1994

Notes on the financial statements (extract)

5 NET INTEREST RECEIVABLE (extract)	1994	
	£000	£000
Interest receivable:		
Interest receivable on loans and deposits		12,283
Interest receivable on finance leases		3,499
		15,782
Less interest payable:		
Bank overdrafts, loans and other borrowings repayable within five years	(13,034)	
Loans and other borrowings repayable wholly or in part after five years	(405)	
Finance charges on hire purchase contracts and finance leases	(710)	
		(14,149)
		1,633

Table 15.5 – Zeneca Group PLC – Annual Report and Accounts – 31 December 1994

Notes relating to the accounts (extract)

6 LEASES

The total rentals under operating leases, charged as an expense in the profit and loss account, are disclosed below.

	1994 £m	1993 £m
Hire of plant and machinery	8	6
Other	28	29
	36	35

Commitments under leases to pay rentals during the year following the year of these accounts are given in the table below, analysed according to the period in which each lease expires.

Obligations under operating leases comprise		
Land and buildings		
Expiring within 1 year	3	1
Expiring during years 2 to 5	3	3
Expiring thereafter	4	4
	10	8
Other assets		
Expiring within 1 year	7	4
Expiring during years 2 to 5	6	12
Expiring thereafter	–	–
	13	16
Obligations under finance leases comprise		
Rentals due within 1 year	2	4
Rentals due during years 2 to 5	6	5
Rentals due thereafter	2	2
Less interest element	(2)	(2)
	8	9

Obligations under finance leases are included in other creditors (Note 18).

The Group had commitments totalling £6m (1993 £nil) under finance leases at the balance sheet date which were due to commence thereafter.

15.51 In respect of operating leases, SSAP 21 requires the following information to be disclosed:

- The total of operating lease rentals charged as an expense in the profit and loss account, and analysed between amounts payable both in respect of hire of plant and machinery and in respect of other operating leases. [SSAP 21 para 55]. An example of this disclosure is included in Table 15.5 above.

- The payments that the lessee is committed to make during the next year, analysed between: those in which the commitment expires within that year; those in which the commitment expires within the second to fifth years inclusive; and those in which the commitment expires more than five years after the balance sheet date. This analysis should show the commitments in respect of land and buildings separately from those of other operating leases. [SSAP 21 para 56]. This requirement is sometimes misunderstood; the intention is to show only the annual commitment not the total amount that will be payable until the end of the lease as illustrated in Table 15.5 above.

15.52 In respect of both finance leases and operating leases, the accounting policies that the lessee has adopted must be disclosed in the financial statements. [SSAP 21 para 57]. For example, Table 15.6 contains such an accounting policy.

Table 15.6 – Cable and Wireless plc – Annual report and Accounts – 31 March 1998

Statement of Accounting Policies (extract)

j) Leased assets

Where assets are financed by leasing agreements that give rights approximating to ownership, the assets are treated as if they had been purchased outright. The amount capitalised is the present value of the minimum lease payments payable during the lease term. The corresponding lease commitments are shown as obligations to the lessor. Lease payments are split between capital and interest elements using the annuity method. Depreciation on the relevant assets and interest are charged to the profit and loss account. All other leases are operating leases and the annual rentals are charged to operating profit on a straight line basis over the lease term.

15.53 In addition to the standard's disclosure requirements, the Guidance Notes to the standard indicate that other details about a company's leases may need to be disclosed in order to give a true and fair view of the company's state of affairs. These include for example: contingent rentals; profit participation arrangements; significant restrictions on future borrowing or leasing; and contingent liabilities. The information will depend on whether the user's appreciation of the company's state of affairs would be affected if he was aware of that information. The criteria to be applied to that information are no different from those to be applied to any other information about the company's financial affairs.

Sale and leaseback transactions

15.54 A sale and leaseback transaction arises when a vendor sells an asset and immediately re-acquires the use of the asset by entering into a lease with the buyer. Such transactions are a popular method of releasing cash funds for new investment as an alternative to borrowing. Under SSAP 21, the accounting treatment depends on the type of lease entered into. It also depends on whether the sale and the subsequent leaseback are on a strictly arm's length basis.

Finance leasebacks

15.55 Where the seller enters into a finance lease, the leaseback is essentially a financing operation. In essence, the seller/lessee never disposes of the risks and rewards of ownership of the asset and so he should not recognise a profit or loss on the sale. Accordingly, any apparent profit or loss on the transaction (that is, the difference between the sale price and the previous carrying value) should be deferred and amortised over the shorter of the lease term and the asset's useful life. [SSAP 21 para 46]. This treatment will have the effect of adjusting the overall charge to the profit and loss account for the depreciation of the asset to an amount consistent with the asset's carrying value before the leaseback.

15.56 Normally, a fixed asset's carrying value before a sale and finance leaseback will not be more than the leased asset's fair value. Indeed, if it were, and the fall in value was other than temporary, a provision would need to be made in order to comply with the requirements of Schedule 4 to the Act. Any such adjustments to the asset's carrying value should be made before determining the apparent profit or loss on the sale and leaseback transaction. The apparent profit or loss that is deferred and amortised over the lease term will then represent the difference between the sale price and the revised carrying value (the fair value). In these circumstances, such a difference would arise only if the sale proceeds and the subsequent rentals were determined other than on an arm's length basis.

15.57 Where the carrying value before the sale is significantly below the fair value, it may be appropriate to revalue it. The apparent profit or loss to be deferred and amortised over the shorter of the lease term and the economic life would then be the difference between the proceeds of sale and the revalued amount. In these circumstances an apparent profit or loss would arise only if the sale proceeds and the subsequent rentals were determined other than on an arm's length basis.

15.58 One problem that SSAP 21 does not address is the problem of the values that should be attributed to the lease obligation and the leased asset on a leaseback where the proceeds of sale are determined other than on an arm's length basis. Normally, under a finance lease the amount capitalised as an asset and the amount capitalised as an obligation are the same (namely, the present value of the minimum payments). Another, and perhaps simpler, way of looking at the accounting treatment of a sale and finance leaseback would be to treat the transaction not as a sale and repurchase, but simply as a source of finance, like raising a secured loan on an existing asset. Proceeds could then be simply credited to a liability account (representing the present value of the obligation under the finance leases), and there would be no need to show a disposal and a re-acquisition of an asset. In effect, the apparent profit or loss on the transaction would be reflected in higher or lower finance charges over the lease term. It can be argued that this treatment better reflects the commercial substance of this transaction because it is only the legal form of the transaction that represents a disposal of the underlying asset. This treatment is, therefore, consistent with the principles underlying FRS 5 (which are considered further in chapter 4).

15.59 A question arises as to whether the revaluation surplus on the asset becomes realised or not on a sale and finance leaseback. The accounting principles upon which SSAP 21 is based argue that the seller/lessee does not dispose of the risks and rewards of ownership under a sale and finance leaseback arrangement. Section 262(3) of the Act states that whether profits are realised or not depends on

"...principles generally accepted, at the time when those accounts are prepared, with respect to the determination for accounting purposes of realised profits or losses". Because in accounting terms there is no genuine disposal of the asset by the seller/lessee, it is considered that the revaluation surplus does not become realised immediately.

Operating leasebacks

15.60 Where the seller enters into a sale and operating leaseback, he effectively disposes of substantially all the risks and rewards of owning the asset in the sale transaction; and may re-acquire some of the risks and rewards of ownership in the leaseback, but does not re-acquire substantially all of them. Accordingly, under the specific requirements of SSAP 21, the transaction should be treated as a disposal and any profit or loss on the transaction should be recognised. It is interesting to note that in this respect the specific requirements of SSAP 21 are different to the general principles of FRS 5. This is because SSAP 21 recognises assets and liabilities on an all or nothing basis. FRS 5, however, will only recognise a disposal of an asset in its entirety when all significant rights or other access to benefits and all exposures to risks have been transferred. However, in a sale and leaseback transaction rights and obligations are retained by the seller-lessee. In this case, however, as SSAP 21 contains the more specific requirements the SSAP 21 treatment would prevail. Under SSAP 21, the calculation of the profit or loss will depend on whether the sale proceeds and the rentals under the subsequent lease were determined on an arm's length basis.

15.61 Where the sale transaction is established at the fair value, any profit or loss on the sale should be recognised immediately. Consequently, no further adjustment is necessary. [SSAP 21 para 47].

15.62 Where the sale price is above the fair value, the excess of the sale price over the fair value does not represent a genuine profit. This is because the rentals payable in future years will almost certainly be inflated above the market value. Accordingly, the excess of the sale proceeds over the fair value should be deferred and amortised over the shorter of the remainder of the lease term and the period to the next rent review. [SSAP 21 para 47]. This treatment will have the effect of reducing the annual expense for rentals to a basis consistent with the fair value of the asset.

15.63 Where the sale price is below the fair value, the standard requires that any profit or loss should be recognised immediately. This requirement recognises the fact that the company, perhaps motivated by the need to raise cash quickly, may simply have negotiated a poor bargain. An exception is made, however, where a loss is compensated by future rentals that are below market levels. In such a circumstance, the standard requires the loss (to the extent that it is compensated by future rentals below market levels) be deferred and amortised over the remainder of the lease term (or, if it is shorter, the period during which the reduced rentals are chargeable). [SSAP 21 para 47]. This practice may seem to go against the prudence principle. In effect, however, it merely reverses the effect of an artificial loss created by establishing, in an artificial way, the sale price and the subsequent rental. Rather strangely perhaps, the standard does not require a similar adjustment where the profit that is made is lower than would be expected if the sale proceeds and the subsequent rentals were established on an arm's length basis.

Sale and leasebacks with repurchase options

15.64 The use of put and call options in sale and leaseback transactions involving properties has become popular as a method to enable a company to raise medium-term finance to the value of the property that it owns. Under such arrangements, the seller/lessee may have an option to repurchase the property (call option), or the buyer/lessor may have an option to require the seller/lessee to repurchase the property (put option), or there may be a combination of options.

15.65 These types of arrangements fall within the ambit of Application Note B of FRS 5. The substance of the transaction needs to be considered very closely in order to classify the lease correctly as a finance or operating lease. In essence, the objective is to determine whether the commercial effect of the transaction is that of a genuine sale or that of a secured loan.

15.66 If the repurchase price contained in an option to repurchase is the market value of the asset at the date of exercise, it is probable that the buyer/lessor acquires both the opportunity to benefit from any increase in the value of the asset and the risk of loss if there is a fall in its value. In this situation the option is a 'genuine' option and will not influence the way the lease is classified.

15.67 If, however, the repurchase price is predetermined so that, when exercised it assures the buyer/lessor of a return of his original purchase price together with his required rate of return, this may well be indicative of a finance lease. A key issue will be whether there is a genuine commercial possibility that the option will fail to be exercised and, in that event, what further conditions protect the buyer/lessor's return. For example, if the conditions of the leaseback were such that the rental rate increased to a rate substantially in excess of a commercial rate should the lessee fail to exercise his repurchase option, this could well have the effect of a penalty which would force the exercise of the option. Consequently, it is important to understand properly the commercial objectives for the inclusion of a repurchase option in the leaseback and the commercial effect it will have in practice.

Accounting by lessors

Accounting for finance leases

15.68 The amount due from the lessee under a finance lease should be recorded in the lessor's balance sheet as a debtor at the amount of the net investment in the lease, after making provisions for items such as bad and doubtful rentals receivable. [SSAP 21 para 38].

15.69 At the inception of a finance lease, the lessor's net investment in the lease is the cost of the asset to the lessor. Over the lease term, rentals will be apportioned between a reduction in the net investment in the lease and gross earnings.

15.70 At any point in time during the lease term, the net investment in the lease will be represented by the remaining minimum lease payments (the amounts the lessor is guaranteed to receive under the lease from either the lessee or third parties), less that part of the minimum lease payments that is attributable to future gross earnings (namely, interest and the lessor's profit). The lessor's net investment in the lease may also include an unguaranteed residual value. The unguaranteed residual value, which will be small in a finance lease, represents the amount the lessor expects to recover from the value of the leased asset at the end of the lease term that is not guaranteed in any way by either the lessee or third parties.

15.71 SSAP 21 requires that the total gross earnings under a finance lease be allocated to each accounting period during the lease term in such a manner as to produce a constant rate of return (or a reasonable approximation to it) on each period's net *cash* investment. [SSAP 12 para 39]. The net cash investment in a lease represents the total cash invested after taking into account all of the cash flows associated with the lease. It differs, therefore, from the amount of the net investment in the lease that is shown in the balance sheet. This is because it takes account of other cash flows. The most important of these other cash flows relates to the tax effects of the lease.

15.72 One of the reasons why SSAP 21 requires that gross earnings should be allocated to accounting periods on the basis of the net cash investment is that the gross earnings will then be properly matched with the interest costs of funding the net cash investment in the lease. Consequently, SSAP 21 permits alternative methods of allocating gross earnings which allocate gross earnings so that net earnings (gross earnings less estimated interest costs) are recognised on a systematic basis. This means that an allocation of gross earnings is first made to each accounting period to cover the estimated costs of finance. The remaining balance of gross earnings is then allocated to accounting periods on a systematic basis (for example, by using the sum-of-the-digits method).

15.73 A finance company will normally allocate gross earnings from a hire purchase contract to give a constant periodic rate of return on its net investment (ignoring any tax effects). This is because the tax effects of a hire purchase contract are rarely significant as the lessee takes all of the benefit and so the company's net investment in a hire purchase contract will approximate to its net cash investment in that contract.

15.74 The most popular methods for allocating gross earnings to accounting periods that are used in practice in the leasing industry are the 'actuarial after-tax method' and the 'investment period method'. Below, we briefly describe the actuarial after-tax method and illustrate its application.

The actuarial after-tax method

15.75 The basis of the actuarial after-tax method is that rentals are allocated between interest (gross earnings) and capital (amortisation) in each accounting period in such a way that the anticipated after-tax profit (gross earnings less interest expense and tax) will emerge as a constant periodic rate of return on the lessor's average net cash investment in the lease. The accounting entries for 'amortisation' and 'gross earnings' for each period during the lease is, therefore, based on the forecast cash flows made at the start of the lease.

Example

Lease term	Seven years from 31 March 19X4
Rental payments	£1,787.00 payable annually in advance
Asset cost	£10,000.00
Lessor's year end date	31 March
Lessor's tax payment date	Nine months after the year end (1 January)
Cost of money	8.5% per annum
Reinvestment rate	3.0% per annum
Interest assumptions	calculated daily in arrear (annual compounding)
Tax rate 33%	
Capital allowances	25% writing down allowance
Balancing allowance (assumed)	31 March 19Y1

The first step, is to calculate the after-tax profit-take-out rate using the forecast lease cash flows. This is the rate at which the lessor could theoretically withdraw profit from the lease measured as a constant rate on the average daily net cash investment balance for each period. It is calculated by a computer program using an iterative process that involves a succession of trial-and-error estimates of the rate until the net cash investment balance becomes zero at the end of the cash flows. In this example the profit-take-out rate is calculated at 0.8458% per annum.

Date	Net cash investment start of period	Rental	Tax	Interest paid/ (received)	Profit taken out	Net cash investment end of period
	£	£	£	£	£	£
31 March 19X4	10,000.00	(1,787.00)	–	–	–	8,213.00
1 January 19X5	8,213.00	–	(823.38)	–	–	7,389.62
31 March 19X5	7,389.62	(1,787.00)	–	681.04	67.76	6,351.42
1 January 19X6	6,351.42	–	(253.79)	–	–	6,097.63
31 March 19X6	6,097.63	(1,787.00)	–	536.03	53.34	4,900.00
1 January 19X7	4,900.00	–	(51.24)	–	–	4,848.76
31 March 19X7	4,848.76	(1,787.00)	–	415.44	41.34	3,518.54
1 January 19X8	3,518.54	–	104.57	–	–	3,623.10
31 March 19X8	3,623.11	(1,787.00)	–	301.24	29.97	2,167.32
1 January 19X9	2,167.32	–	229.26	–	–	2,396.58
31 March 19X9	2,396.58	(1,787.00)	–	188.97	18.80	817.35
1 January 19Y0	817.35	–	331.57	–	–	1,148.92
31 March 19Y0	1,148.92	(1,787.00)	–	76.62	7.62	(553.84)
1 January 19Y1	(553.84)	–	417.60	–	–	(136.24)
31 March 19Y1	(136.24)	–	–	(13.56)	–	(149.80)
1 January 19Y2	(149.80)	–	152.07	–	–	2.27
1 January 19Y2	2.27	–	1.12	(3.39)	–	–
		(12,509.00)	107.78	2,182.39	218.83	

The lessor's initial net cash investment in the lease is the cost of the leased asset (£10,000).

Interest paid is calculated at 8.5% per annum on the daily net cash investment balances. Similarly profit-taken-out is calculated at the profit-take-out rate of 0.8458% on the daily net cash investment balances. Thus interest of £681.04 and profit-take-out of £67.76 for the period to 31 March 19X5 is based on net cash investment balances of £8,213.00 for 276 days and £7,389.62 for 89 days.

Interest received is calculated at a conservative rate of 3.0% per annum on the daily cash surplus balances. No profit-take-out arises when the net cash investment is in surplus (after 31 March 19Y0).

Tax is payable/receivable on 1 January each year, based on rentals, interest paid, interest received, and capital allowances in the previous accounting year, as follows:

Year to 31 March	Accrued rental	Capital allowances	Interest	Total	Tax payable (receivable)
	£	£	£	£	£
19X4	4.90	(2,500.00)	–	(2,495.10)	(823.38)
19X5	1,786.99	(1,875.00)	(681.04)	(769.05)	(253.79)
19X6	1,787.01	(1,406.25)	(536.03)	(155.27)	(51.24)
19X7	1,787.00	(1,054.69)	(415.44)	316.87	104.57
19X8	1,787.00	(791.02)	(301.24)	694.74	229.26
19X9	1,786.99	(593.26)	(188.97)	1,004.76	331.57
19Y0	1,787.01	(444.95)	(76.62)	1,265.44	417.60
19Y1	1,782.10	(1,334.83)	13.56	460.83	152.07
19Y2	–	–	3.39	3.39	1.12
	12,509.00	(10,000.00)	(2,182.39)	326.61	107.78

In order to simplify the calculations of the tax cash flows, it has been assumed that the amount of expenditure unrelieved after five years' writing-down allowances is relieved in the computation for the year ending 31 March 19Y1. Where the lessor does not anticipate recovering the remaining unrelieved expenditure by the end of the lease term it may be appropriate for him to delay recognising some of his gross earnings.

A further simplification is that the cash flows are deemed to terminate at the last tax payment date relating to the above. Thus interest for the period 1 April 19Y1 to 1 January 19Y2 and tax thereon is deemed to be paid on 1 January 19Y2.

The apportionment of gross earnings to each period for accounting purposes is derived from the cash flows by working backwards from the anticipated after-tax profit as follows:

Year to 31 March	Anticipated after-tax profit	Derived pre-tax profit	Anticipated interest	Derived apportionment of gross earnings
	£	£	£	£
19X4	–	–	–	–
19X5	67.76	101.14	681.04	782.18
19X6	53.34	79.60	536.03	615.63
19X7	41.34	61.70	415.44	477.14
19X8	29.97	44.73	301.24	345.97
19X9	18.80	28.06	188.97	217.03
19Y0	7.62	11.38	76.62	88.00
19Y1	–	–	(16.95)	(16.95)
	218.83	326.61	2,182.39	2,509.00

The anticipated after-tax profit is derived from the cash flows by time apportioning the profit-take-out. In this example, because the lease was written on 31 March and because it has been assumed interest is to be taken daily in arrear, the profit-take out on the cash flow matches the figures accrued for accounting purposes. An alternative basis would be to accrue one day's income and interest expense for the year to 31 March 19X4 and to adjust each year's figures by one day.

The pre-tax profit is derived by grossing-up the anticipated after-tax profit for each period by the appropriate tax rate. The tax rate is 33% and so the factor by which the after-tax profit is grossed up to arrive at the pre-tax profits is 1/(1 – 0.33).

The anticipated interest is derived from the cash flow summary in a similar way. In this example no interest accrual is necessary.

The derived apportionment of gross earnings is simply the sum of the derived pre-tax profit and anticipated interest.

For the purpose of calculating gross earnings for accounting purposes the small amount of interest receivable of £3.39 in the cash flows for the period to 31 March 19Y2 and tax thereon has been treated as arising in the year to 31 March 19Y1. This is a simplification for illustration purposes in order to limit the period over which gross earnings are spread. More sophisticated systems may well spread the gross earnings over a period extending beyond the lease term to take full account of the interest effects associated with tax cash flows arising beyond the end of the lease term.

The effect of allocating gross earnings in this way can be summarised as follows:

Profit & Loss Account

	19X4	19X5	19X6	19X7	19X8	19X9	19Y0	19Y1
	£	£	£	£	£	£	£	£
Rent receivable	4.90	1,786.98	1,787.02	1,787,00	1,787.00	1,786.98	1,787.02	1,782.10
Amortisation	4.90	1,004.80	1,171.39	1,309.86	1,441.03	1,569.95	1,699.02	1,799.05
Gross earnings	–	782.18	615.63	477.14	345.97	217.03	88.00	(16.95)
Interest costs	–	681.04	536.03	415.44	301.24	188.97	76.62	(16.95)
Pre-tax profit	–	101.14	79.60	61.70	44.73	28.06	11.38	–
Tax:								
Current	(823.38)	(253.79)	(51.24)	104.57	229.26	331.57	417.60	153.19
Deferred	823.38	287.17	77.50	(84.21)	(214.50)	(322.31)	(413.84)	(153.19)
Post-tax profit	–	67.76	53.34	41.34	29.97	18.80	7.62	–

Balance sheet	19X4	19X5	19X6	19X7	19X8	19X9	19Y0	19Y1
	£	£	£	£	£	£	£	£
Assets								
Lease receivables	8,213.00	7,208.18	6,036.81	4,726.95	3,285.92	1,715.95	16.95	–
Group relief	823.38	253.79	51.24	–	–	–	–	–
Cash	–	–	–	–	–	–	553.84	153.19
	9,036.38	7,461.97	6,088.05	4,726.95	3,285.92	1,715.95	570.79	153.19
Liabilities								
Borrowings	8,213.00	6,351.42	4,900.00	3,518.54	2,167.32	817.35	–	–
Deferred tax	823.38	1,110.55	1,188.05	1,103.84	889.34	567.03	153.19	0.00
Current tax	–	–	–	104.57	229.26	331.57	417.60	153.19
	9,036.38	7,461.97	6,088.05	4,726.95	3,285.92	1,715.95	570.79	153.19

For the purpose of illustrating the profit and loss and balance sheet the actual interest charges have been assumed to match precisely those anticipated in the cash flows and the post-tax profit is assumed to be fully distributed. Consequently, in this example the net cash investment balances per the anticipated cash flows will match the borrowing/cash position in the balance sheet. In practice, actual cash flows will almost certainly vary from those forecast, but this will not be sufficient reason by itself, to reassess the allocation of gross earnings.

Lease receivables at 31 March 19X5 of £7,208.18 represents future rentals of £8,935 less future gross earnings of £1,782.12. Alternatively, it can be proven as the cost of the leased asset of £10,000 less accumulated amortisation of £1,009.70 less prepaid rent of £1,782.12.

Accounting for operating leases

15.76 SSAP 21 requires that a lessor should record as fixed assets the assets held for leasing under operating leases. It also requires that the lessor should depreciate those assets over their useful economic lives. [SSAP 21 para 42]. This requirement has not been followed by Brammer Plc in its financial statements for the year ended 31 December 1994. In these financial statements, the directors included rental assets, consisting of electronic instruments, in stock at the lower of amortised cost and net realisable value on the grounds that these assets were circulating capital. The FRRP rejected the directors' views and argued that SSAP 21 required such assets to be classified as fixed assets as they were held for use in operating leases. Accordingly, in the company's 1995 Annual Report the rental inventory was reclassified as fixed assets and the 1994 comparative figures were adjusted as indicated in Table 15.7 below.

15.77 Where assets held for use in operating leases are recorded as fixed assets, the lessor should recognise his rental income from operating leases (excluding charges for services such as insurance and maintenance) on a straight-line basis over the period of the lease, irrespective of when the payments are due. This requirement does not apply, however, if another systematic and rational basis is more representative of the time pattern in which the lessor receives the benefit from the leased asset (for example, the time pattern of the related depreciation charge). [SSAP 21 para 43].

Table 15.7 – Brammer plc – Annual Report – 31 December 1995

Accounting policies (extract)

Change of accounting policy – rental inventory

As explained in the financial review on page 14, the company has agreed with the Financial Reporting Review Panel that rental inventory, previously classified as current assets, should be reclassified as fixed assets. As a result of effecting this change:

- proceeds from the disposal of previously rented instruments are excluded from turnover and included in the profit on sale of fixed assets in the profit and loss account.

- rental inventory is classified as fixed assets and is valued at cost less depreciation on a straight line basis over the expected economic lives of the assets (generally 2 to 6 years) taking account of estimated residual values, less any necessary provision for permanent diminution in value.

- the depreciation charge for the year on rental inventory is added back to operating profit in arriving at net cash inflow from operating activities in the cash flow statement.

The accounts carrying value of rental inventory is unchanged and, accordingly, the change of classification does not affect the profit for the year in any year or the shareholders' equity at the end of the year. The figures in the 1994 consolidated profit and loss account, balance sheet and cash flow statement have been reclassified as a result of this change.

[The next page 15031.]

Lessor disclosure requirements

15.78 In respect of finance leases (including hire purchase contracts that have similar characteristics) the following needs to be disclosed:

- The net investment in finance leases and hire purchase contracts at the balance sheet date. [SSAP 21 para 58].

- The costs of assets acquired in the period (whether by purchase, finance lease or hire purchase) for the purpose of letting under finance leases or hire purchase contracts. [SSAP 21 para 60(c)].

Table 15.7A contains an example of these disclosure requirements.

Table 15.7A – Inchcape plc – Annual Report & Accounts – 31 December 1994

notes to the accounts (extract)

17 Debtors (extract)

	Group	
	1994	1993
	£m	£m
Net investment in finance leases and hire purchase contracts comprises:		
Total amounts receivable	**79.9**	64.0
Less: Interest allocated to future periods	**(11.3)**	(10.0)
	68.6	54.0
Finance leases and hire purchase contracts:		
Rentals receivable during the year	**33.8**	27.9
Assets acquired during the year	**32.5**	32.4

15.79 In respect of operating leases (including hire purchase contracts that have similar characteristics), the gross cost and the accumulated depreciation of the assets held for use under operating leases or hire purchase contracts that have similar characteristics need to be disclosed. [SSAP 21 para 59]. Companies may make this disclosure by including a separate column for assets held for operating leases in the fixed asset note or by making a statement in the fixed asset note. Inchcape, for example, gives such a statement in their fixed asset note (see Table 15.8).

Table 15.8 – Inchcape plc – Annual Report and Accounts – 31 December 1994

notes to the accounts (extract)

14 Fixed assets – tangible assets (extract)	**1994 £m**	1993 £m
The book value of tangible fixed assets held for rental to customers under operating leases amounted to:		
– cost	**35.3**	47.5
– less depreciation	**(13.2)**	(13.0)
	22.1	34.5

15.80 In respect of both finance leases and operating leases (including hire purchase contracts that have similar characteristics), the following need to be disclosed also:

- The policy adopted for accounting for operating leases and finance leases and, in detail, the accounting policy adopted for recognising finance lease income. [SSAP 21 para 60(a)]. Table 15.9 contains an example of such a policy.

- The aggregate rentals receivable in the accounting period, analysed between amounts receivable under finance leases and amounts receivable under operating leases. [SSAP 21 para 60(b)]. For example, Gestetner Holdings includes this information in the analyses of trading profit (see Table 15.10).

Table 15.9 – Automated Security (Holdings) PLC – Report and Financial Statements – 30 November 1994

ACCOUNTING POLICIES (extract)

2. FIXED ASSETS

The cost of equipment on contract hire installed by Group companies is capitalised. Costs comprise materials, labour and attributable overheads relating to identifiable and recoverable equipment. All other costs are written off as they are incurred.

On the acquisition of installed systems from third parties, a fair value is placed on installed equipment acquired.

6. EQUIPMENT LEASED TO CUSTOMERS

Equipment leased to customers under finance leases is deemed to be sold at normal selling value which is taken to turnover at the inception of the lease. Debtors under finance leases represent outstanding amounts due under these agreements less finance charges allocated to future periods. Finance lease interest is recognised over the primary period of the lease so as to produce a constant rate of return on the net cash investments. Equipment leased to customers under operating leases is capitalised in accordance with 2 above. Operating lease income is accounted for on a straight line basis with any rental increases recognised during the period to which they relate.

Table 15.10 – Gestetner Holdings PLC – Report and Accounts – 31 December 1994

Notes to the accounts (extract)

Note 2 Trading profit (extract)	**1994 £m**	1993 £m
Rental receivable under		
operating leases	**(21.7)**	(24.9)
finance leases	**(10.2)**	(12.3)
Equipment acquired for sale under finance leases	**73.4**	70.0

[The next paragraph is 15.83.]

15.83 The Guidance Notes to SSAP 21 indicate that the lessor may also need to disclose further information about his leases and hire purchase contracts that is of particular significance to the users of the financial statements. This includes, for example, details of arrangements that could affect his future profitability, such as contingent rentals or new-for-old guarantees.

Implications of the Act on the disclosure lessors make

15.84 Although some banks carry out leasing activities themselves, many banks prefer, for tax reasons, to carry out their leasing through separate subsidiaries. Consequently, many lessors, whether they are related to a bank or not, will not be a banking company within the meaning of the Banking Act 1987 and so they will have to comply with the requirements of Schedule 4 to the Act for the purpose of their own statutory financial statements. However, at the same time those leasing companies with banking parents will need to provide information to their parent companies for consolidation purposes to comply with Schedule 9.

15.85 The balance sheet formats set out in Schedule 4 do not show any specific category for leased assets. Paragraph 3(2) of Schedule 4, however, permits (with certain exceptions) a company's balance sheet or profit and loss account to include an item that is not otherwise covered in the formats. SSAP 21, however, requires that amounts due from lessees under finance leases be recorded as a debtor and assets held for use in operating leases as a fixed asset.

15.86 As a category of debtors, amounts due under finance leases will need to be analysed in the notes to the financial statements between amounts receivable within one year and those receivable after more than one year. However, where the amounts due over one year are particularly material in the context of net current assets such that a reader might misinterpret the financial statements, UITF 4 requires the amounts over one year to be disclosed on the face of the balance sheet (see further chapter 17).

15.87 The turnover of a leasing company will consist of its 'gross earnings' from finance leases and rentals from operating leases.

15.88 Those leasing companies, or parents of leasing companies, that are banks will need to comply with the requirements relating to the form and content of financial statements of banking companies as set out in Parts I to III of Schedule 9. Under these formats, finance leases would be shown either under 'Loans and advances to customers' or 'Loans and advances to banks' as appropriate and gross earnings from finance leases would be included under interest receivable. The treatment of operating leases and related income under the formats is less clear. A strict interpretation would be to classify: operating leases under 'Tangible fixed assets'; operating rentals under 'Other income'; and depreciation of operating leased assets under 'Depreciation and amortisation'.

15.89 However, where a bank has significant amounts of operating leases and a significant amount of the bank's interest costs relate to the financing of such activities it could be argued that this treatment gives a misleading picture of the true net interest income from banking activities. Some banks have, therefore, taken the view that operating lease rentals less related depreciation is in effect a form of 'interest receivable' and have treated it in this way. Thus, net interest income will reflect both net income from operating leasing and the related interest expense, while the bank's depreciation expense will reflect only those tangible fixed assets other than operating leases. While this form of presentation has considerable merit there is an element of doubt as to whether it strictly accords with the Act's requirements.

Direct costs

15.90 SSAP 21 states that initial direct costs may be apportioned over the period of the lease on a systematic and rational basis (or may alternatively be written off immediately). In allowing either of these treatments SSAP 21 draws no distinction between those initial direct costs from finance leases and those from operating leases.

15.91 SSAP 21 defines initial direct costs as:

> "*...those costs incurred by the lessor that are directly associated with negotiating and consummating leasing transactions, such as commissions, legal fees, costs of credit investigations and costs of processing documents for new leases acquired.*" [SSAP 21 para 30].

15.92 SSAP 21 gives no further guidance on the interpretation of the words 'directly associated' with these activities, although the Guidance Notes indicate that it is not intended to exclude salespersons' costs. This, therefore, leaves these words open to interpretation.

15.93 In contrast, the US accounting standard's definition of initial direct costs, while based on the same principles, is considerably more detailed and helpful. From a UK perspective, FAS 13 (as modified by FAS 91) has no authority in the UK, but it is nonetheless a useful starting point when seeking to interpret those costs that are 'directly associated with' these activities. FAS 91 identifies two types of direct costs:

- External independent third party costs that result directly from and are essential to acquire the lease and would not have been incurred had the leasing transaction not occurred (for example, third party commissions and legal costs).

- Certain costs directly relating to specific activities:

  - Evaluating and recording guarantees, collateral and other security arrangements.

- Negotiating lease terms.
- Preparing and processing lease documentation.
- Closing the transaction.

15.94 In this latter situation, the list of activities is almost identical to those identified by SSAP 21. In practice, UK lessors have generally adopted one of three different approaches:

- Write off all direct costs immediately.
- Defer only significant incremental costs (usually external commissions are the most significant and easily identifiable direct cost although internal salesmen's commission may also be included).
- Defer commissions and other direct costs including an estimate of the overheads relating to specific activities.

15.95 Generally, the most appropriate, systematic and rational basis for deferring initial direct costs will be the same pattern used for recognising income. For finance leases this can be achieved by either deducting initial direct costs from total gross earnings before the net amount is allocated to accounting periods, or recognising sufficient gross earnings in the first year to absorb the costs and allocating the balance of gross earnings over the lease term. For operating leases, a straight-line basis of deferral over the lease term will usually be the most appropriate method.

Rental variation

Tax variation clauses

15.96 Major changes in tax rates can create significant accounting issues for lessors. This is because many finance leases contain tax variation clauses that vary the rental the lessee pays in the event of a tax rate change in order to preserve the lessor's post-tax rate of return.

15.97 In simple terms, if tax rates are reduced lessors pay less future tax, but will instead receive reduced rentals under their existing leases. Under SSAP 15, deferred tax is provided to the extent that tax liabilities are expected to crystallise in the future. Thus, deferred tax is provided at the corporation tax rate at which it is expected to be paid. Consequently, the 'windfall' gain from a reduction in corporation tax rates will be reflected in the tax charge or credit in the profit and loss account in the year in which the tax changes are announced. However, the related reductions in rentals will generally occur over the remaining periods of the leases and, therefore, reduce future pre-tax income. The reduction in future rental income means that the carrying value of the lease receivable has been impaired. This impairment should be recognised immediately as a charge to pre-tax income. Although the impairment loss may not be exactly offset by the tax credit arising from the reduction in corporation tax rate, the difference may not be significant in terms of preserving the lessor's post-tax rate of return. This treatment will ensure that the lessors do not report material future losses on their leases. The previous practice, widely used in the leasing industry, of 'grossing up' tax savings would not comply with the principles of UITF Abstract 16.

[The next paragraph is 15.101.]

Variations in interest rates

15.101 Normally, when a finance lessor apportions his gross earnings, he does this on the basis of the forecast he prepares, at the start of the lease, of his future cash flows under the lease. The amount of gross earnings he releases to the profit and loss account in subsequent periods will then follow the forecast, even though his actual cash flows may vary from those he initially anticipated.

15.102 Minor variations in interest costs from those expected in the original cash flows evaluation will almost certainly occur. The interest charged to the lessor's profit and loss account in the period will be the actual interest cost for the period, thus, any differences from that originally anticipated will be reflected in the profit and loss account in the period in which they occur.

15.103 To mitigate interest rate risk, the lease facility may provide for a specifically calculated periodic adjustment for the difference between the actual rate of interest incurred on the borrowings and the rate of interest initially used in the cash flow to determine the level of lease rentals. Such adjustments are made periodically in arrears by applying, for example, the difference in interest rates on the first day of each quarterly period to the amount of the lessor's cash investment in the lease.

Construction periods

15.104 Often, where a leased asset is constructed over a period of time, the terms of the lease provide for rentals to commence only when the lessee brings the asset into use. In effect, the lessor finances the asset during the period of construction and recovers his costs out of his rentals over the remaining lease term. In order to match his gross earnings from the lease with his interest costs, the lessor will need to spread his gross earnings over the whole lease term (including the construction period). Where he adopts this treatment, however, the lessor will need to consider carefully his potential risks of loss from cancellation or default.

Manufacturer/dealer lessors

15.105 SSAP 21 distinguishes manufacturer/dealer lessors from other lessors. Although the term is not defined in the standard, it is discussed in the context of a business that has a manufacturing or dealing activity which can be distinguished from its leasing activities. What makes the manufacturer/dealer lessor different from a normal lessor is the cost at which he acquires an asset for lease. Because he obtains the asset at his cost of manufacture or at a wholesale price his cost will be below a normal arm's length selling price. The accounting issue is whether he should recognise a normal sale profit and this will depend on the accounting classification of the lease.

15.106 Where the manufacturer/dealer enters into an operating lease, he should not recognise a selling profit when he leases the asset. [SSAP 21 para 45]. This is because the risks and rewards associated with the asset's ownership have not passed to the customer. Consequently, the manufacturer/dealer will account for the lease in the same way as any other operating lessor does. He will capitalise the asset at its cost and depreciate it over its remaining economic life. In addition, he will recognise rentals on a straight-line basis over the period of the lease.

15.107 Where a manufacturer/dealer enters into a finance lease with a customer, the manufacturer/dealer may be able to recognise a normal selling profit. This is because the risks and rewards associated with the ownership of the asset have passed to the customer. The gross earnings under the lease (namely, the difference between what the manufacturer/dealer expects to receive and retain and the normal selling price) would be allocated over the lease term in the normal way. For example, the accounting policy of Automated Security (Holdings) indicates that the company takes what it deems the 'normal selling value' to turnover at the inception of the lease (see Table 15.9 on page 15032).

15.108 In most circumstances, where the sales price is known, determining the split between selling profit (recognised immediately) and gross earnings from finance leasing (spread over the lease term) is relatively easy. Where, however, a manufacturer/dealer does not sell the asset separately he may have difficulty in determining a true arm's length sales price. In these circumstances, some lessors have sought to determine the sales profit by assuming a deemed selling price (of fair value) being the present value of the minimum lease rentals discounted at a commercial rate.

15.109 The practice of calculating the sales profit in this way does not contradict the spirit of the SSAP 21, but can be lead to abuse and excessive front-end profits unless the present values are calculated prudently. For example, understating the true commercial lease rate or including overly optimistic residual values in the present value calculation will overstate sales profit. For this reason, this method needs to be applied with care.

15.110 Even when the normal sales price is known, it does not necessarily follow that the full normal sales profit should be recognised at the lease's inception. In order to promote sales, a manufacturer/dealer lessor may offer finance leasing arrangements at concessionary rates. When it does this it should restrict its initial selling profit to an amount that will allow it to recognise its gross earnings at the normal commercial rate over the lease term.

Back-to-back and sub-leases

15.111 The term 'back-to-back' can be used to describe a variety of different agreements, each of which has different legal and tax implications. It is, therefore, difficult to prescribe specific accounting treatments for each variation. The Guidance Notes to SSAP 21, however, set out the broad principles that a lessor should follow when accounting for back-to-back leases and sub-leases. In addition, FRS 5 provides the more detailed rules on the treatment of non-recourse finance that can be applied to these types of arrangement (see further chapter 4).

15.112 For convenience, the Guidance Notes terms are used below. These refer to the three parties to a lease agreement as: the head lessor; the intermediate party (who may be either a lessor under a sub-lease to the lessee or merely an agent for the head lessor); and the lessee.

The head lessor

15.113 The head lessor's accounting is straightforward. Unless the original lease agreement between the head lessor and the intermediate party is replaced by a new agreement, the head lessor's accounting should not be affected if the intermediate party enters into a sub-lease.

The intermediate party

15.114 The intermediate party's accounting, however, is more complex. The form it takes will depend on the nature of the intermediate party's contract with the head lessor and the substance of the transaction.

15.115 If the intermediate party's role is genuinely in substance that of a broker or agent for the head lessor, such that the intermediate party has no significant commercial benefits or risks associated with the sub-leases, it should not include either the asset or the obligation on its balance sheet. Such a view would be consistent with the principles for recognising and ceasing to recognise assets set out in FRS 5 and the guidance given in the Guidance Notes to SSAP 21. [FRS 5 paras 20, 22; SSAP 21 para 165].

15.116 Where, however, the intermediate party enters into a lease with the head lessor, and that lease requires him to make payments to the head lessor regardless of whether he receives payments from the lessee under a sub-lease (a full 'recourse' arrangement) or he bears other significant risks such as 'slow payment' risk, he should account for the arrangement as two separate transactions. Such a view is supported by paragraph 21 of FRS 5 and paragraph 166 of the Guidance Notes to SSAP 21. This is because the intermediate party's liability under the head lease remains in effect and needs to be reflected in his accounting treatment. Where the intermediate party's lease with the head lessor is a finance lease, the intermediate party will need to record the obligation as a liability on his balance sheet. He will also need to record an asset on his balance sheet for the sub-lease to the ultimate lessee. Where the sub-lease is a finance lease the intermediate party should record the asset as a receivable. Where the sub-lease is an operating lease he should record the asset as a fixed asset.

15.117 The above explains the accounting treatment where the intermediate party acts purely as an agent or where the head lessor has full recourse to the intermediate party. Between these extremes, there are arrangements that might qualify under paragraphs 23 to 25 of FRS 5 as 'special cases' for partial de-recognition or which might qualify under paragraphs 26 and 27 of FRS 5 for 'linked presentation'. These are particularly difficult to interpret. The guidance in FRS 5 is discussed in detail in chapter 4.

15.118 Where the effect of the arrangement is to transfer all the risks and benefits relating to a separately identifiable benefit stream (for example, the rentals) to the head lessor, but retain others (for example, marketing rights); or to transfer a proportion of the benefit stream (for example, the sub-lease rentals less a margin, but no more) to the head lessor, it may be appropriate for the intermediate party to simply recognise a new asset, which reflects his remaining and distinctly separate parcel of rights in the arrangement. Such an approach would only be appropriate where the transaction met the 'special case' conditions of paragraphs 23 to 25 of FRS 5 concerning 'partial de-recognition'.

15.119 The way in which the intermediate party recognises his income will also depend on the nature of the agreement. Where the intermediate party accounts for a separate liability and asset, the treatment he applies both to his gross earnings from his sub-lease and to the finance charges that are due on the head lease, will follow the normal requirements of SSAP 21. Where the intermediate party uses the linked presentation, the 'net' earnings will be included in the profit and loss account with separate disclosures of the gross earnings and finance charges in the notes to the financial statements. Where the intermediate party acts an 'agent', the Guidance Notes state that he should recognise his income on a systematic and rational basis. For example, he could recognise a pure commission immediately, but he should spread a guarantee fee over the period at risk.

Residuals

15.120 Residual values will need to be recognised by lessors when they are a fundamental component to the profitability of the lease transaction. However, it is important that they are recognised prudently. This need for prudence is reflected in the Finance & Leasing Association's own definition of a residual:

> *"The amount initially estimated by the lessor as the 'sales proceeds' which he can safely expect and which he does not, therefore, need to recover by way of rentals..."*

15.121 The amount that the lessor 'can safely expect' is difficult to assess. If the lessor is too optimistic in his residual estimates he carries a risk of incurring a loss. If he is excessively conservative in his estimates his rental rates may prove uncompetitive. How he estimates residuals will depend on specific factors:

- The nature of the asset under consideration.
- The known volatility of second-hand values.
- The rate of technological change.
- Competitive conditions.
- The asset's economic life relative to the lease's primary period.
- The degree to which the lessor can spread his risks.

15.122 The accounting treatment of a residual will largely depend on the nature of the lease. This is because SSAP 21 recognises two different types of leases, finance and operating leases, and prescribes a very different accounting treatment for each.

Residuals under operating leases

15.123 Under an operating lease, the lessor's revenue (rental income) is normally allocated over the lease term on a straight-line basis to reflect the time pattern of the performance of the service he is providing. In the lessor's balance sheet, assets leased to customers are shown as fixed assets, which are depreciated over the assets' economic life to their expected residual values. Different estimates of residual value obviously give rise to different levels of depreciation and, therefore, different levels of profit being recognised over the lease term.

15.124 Where the lessor values his future residuals conservatively, an eventual profit is likely to emerge at the end of the lease term on the sale of the asset, which would be represented by the sales proceeds less residual value and related selling costs.

15.125 While depreciation methods can vary, the method most widely used by operating lessors is the straight-line method. Thus, under operating leases, gross profit (rentals less depreciation) is normally recognised on a straight-line basis.

Residuals under finance leases

15.126 While finance leases are treated for accounting purposes by the lessor as though they are financial products akin to lending, there can, of course, still be a small element of residual risk. This risk is often disregarded as it will represent, at most, less than ten per cent of the lessor's investment at the inception of the lease. However, even variations in a component as small as ten per cent of the original investment can have a significant effect on a lessor's profitability because, although the residual is a small part of the total investment, it may amount to a substantial proportion of the expected gross earnings from the lease.

Fluctuations in anticipated residual values

15.127 Where the amount of residual values is significant the lessor will need to monitor the second-hand market closely and continuously. He will need to do this both to ensure that he has based his current rental pricing structure on up-to-date estimates and to ensure that he is accounting for the residual values correctly. Where the lessor identifies market conditions that indicate that there has been a permanent fall in residual values, he will need to account for the deterioration.

15.128 If the lease is an operating lease he should calculate new depreciation rates for his leased assets in order to ensure the remaining book value of the leased asset is amortised to its anticipated residual value over its remaining useful life. In some circumstances, however, the lessor's future rental income less his operating costs of assets on lease may be insufficient to absorb the additional depreciation that will arise from his revised depreciation rates. Where such a situation arises, the lessor should write down his leased assets to their recoverable amounts immediately, by charging an additional amount for depreciation in the current period's profit and loss account.

15.129 Similarly, if the lease is a finance lease, the lessor may need to write down the future residual value and recalculate the remaining future earnings to be recognised over the lease term. Where the write down of the future residual exceeds the expected future profit in the lease, the excess should be written off immediately to profit and loss account.

15.130 Many lessors also adhere to the principle that residual values should not be revised upwards. While this is not a strict requirement of SSAP 21 or SSAP 12, it is good practice and is a requirement under the US accounting standard FAS 13.

15.131 There are no specific disclosure requirements in the UK for lessors to provide additional information concerning the quantification of residual value estimates within the financial statements of leasing companies. However, given the recent publicity associated with the failures of certain prominent leasing companies and the public's natural concern over the role of residual values and residual accounting treatment, it could be argued that leasing companies should give additional information in their financial statements so that the users of such financial statements can properly assess the impact of residual exposures on the lessor's financial position. For example, where material, a lessor could give an analysis of the gross future residual values used in the calculation of the net book values of finance leases and operating leases with sufficient detail to assist the user to assess the relative concentrations of residual exposure by major product categories.

Tax-free grants

15.131.1 Grants are normally paid to the owner of the asset upon which the grant is claimed. When a lessor receives such a grant on an asset that is subject to a finance lease, it is usual for the lessor to pass the benefit of the grant to the lessee either in the form of a lump sum payment (a negative rental) or in lower rentals over the lease term. The benefit of the grant comprises not just the cash amount of the grant, but also the fact that it is non-taxable. The tax benefit arises because, although the grant reduces the net cost of the asset to the lessor, he can still claim capital allowances on the full gross cost of the asset. If the lessor passes the tax benefit of the grant back to the lessee in one of the two ways mentioned above, it could have the effect of reducing the total rentals payable by the lessee below the net cost of the leased asset. Thus the lessor shows an accounting loss in pre-tax terms, but a profit after tax.

15.131.2 Under paragraph 21 of SSAP 14, a lessor could choose to treat the grant in the profit and loss account in either of the following ways:

- As a non-taxable income reflecting the fact that the grant has borne no tax.
- As a grossed-up amount as if the grant was a larger taxable amount that suffered a tax charge and increasing the tax charge accordingly. This treatment would eliminate the apparent anomaly of showing a pre-tax loss and an after tax profit.

15.131.3 However, as discussed in chapter 13, UITF Abstract 16, issued on 13 February 1997, prohibits the grossing-up of income and expenses that are non-taxable or taxed at a rate other than the standard rate of tax. In order to ensure consistency of treatment between leasing and other kinds of transactions, the ASB issued an amendment to SSAP 21 on the same date which eliminates the second alternative discussed above.

15.131.4 Therefore, tax-free grants that are available to the lessor against the purchase-price of assets acquired for leasing should be spread over the period of the lease and dealt with by treating the grant as non-taxable income. [SSAP 21 para 14]. This amendment is effective for financial statements relating to accounting periods ending on or after 22 June 1997. Earlier adoption is encouraged, but not required.

[The next paragraph is 15.132.]

Future developments

15.132 SSAP 21 was introduced in 1984. Since then there have been developments in both the leasing industry and in financial reporting that result in the SSAP showing its age. Indeed, the ASB accepts that SSAP 21 needs to be revisited when its work programme permits, although this is not currently on the ASB's agenda.

15.133 The application of SSAP 21 has caused difficulty in practice in two areas:

- The classification of leases.
- Lessor income recognition.

Lease classification

15.134 Since SSAP 21 was introduced, there has been a growth in leases that claim to be operating leases and even pass the present value test detailed in paragraph 15.10 above, but that, in reality, pass most of the risks and rewards of ownership to the lessee. A mechanistic approach to the present value test is not in keeping with the spirit of SSAP 21, which clearly states that the present value test may be overridden in exceptional circumstances. [SSAP 21 para 16]. Indeed, the ICAEW Technical Release on the 'Implementation of SSAP 21' issued in 1987 emphasised that the present value test was not a strict mathematical definition of a finance lease. FRS 5, while not in itself changing the accounting treatment of the majority of straight-forward leasing transactions, has also served to emphasise that the substance of the agreement is paramount in determining its classification as a finance lease or an operating lease. Nevertheless, the classification of leases is an area that is subject to manipulation.

15.135 In March 1992, the FRAG produced a report for the ASB on the major practical problems of SSAP 21 (FRAG 9/92). Much of the report addressed this difficult issue of lease classification and although no conclusions were reached, put forward three alternatives for lease capitalisation:

- Capitalise all contractual obligations.
- Capitalise all contractual obligations extending beyond an arbitrary period (for example, over 12 months).
- Capitalise all assets where the entity bears substantially all the risks and rewards of ownership (the SSAP 21 approach).

15.136 In addition, the FRAG looked at many of the practical problems associated with the existing methodology of the SSAP 21 approach. In particular, the paper suggested that if this methodology is retained, the present value test should be abandoned in favour of an approach based on qualitative tests.

15.137 The ASB's draft Statement of principles will also influence any revision to SSAP 21. The draft Statement of principles indicates that all leases give rise to rights and obligations that should be reflected in the financial statements:

> *"In principle, a transaction gives rise to an asset at the time at which the entity has the right to require the other party to perform and a liability at the point when the entity can be compelled to perform by the other party."*

[The next page is 15045.]

> *"Under a lease agreement performance consists of placing the property at the disposal of the lessee. Once the property is delivered, there is no significant doubt that the lessee will be required to pay the rentals required by the lease. Accordingly, the lessee should recognise an asset – the rights to use the leased property – and a liability – the obligation to pay the rentals – at the time of delivery."* [DSP chp 4 paras 18,19].

15.138 The implementation of this principle in the form of an FRS would represent a major change from existing practice. Although the ASB has indicated that it will take account of the financial community's desire for evolutionary rather that revolutionary change, it does indicate the ASB's view that all leases give rise to rights and obligations that should be reflected on the balance sheet. Whilst the ASB may be in favour of capitalising all leases, not just finance leases, it realises that it will face considerable resistance to change.

15.139 FRS 5, unlike SSAP 21, is more in line with the thinking in the draft Statement of principles. However, FRS 5 states that where a transaction falls within the scope of another standard, the standard giving the more specific provision should be applied. [FRS 5 para 13]. Where FRS 5 overlaps with SSAP 21, SSAP 21 would generally contain the more detailed guidance and would, therefore, apply. An exception to this rule applies to sale and leasebacks where FRS 5 may contain more detailed guidance. However, such demarcation rules would not be necessary if both standards gave the same result.

15.140 Although both standards are based on the concept of substance, FRS 5 analyses assets and liabilities differently from SSAP 21. Under FRS 5 an asset may not simply be the asset itself, but a proportional interest in an asset or certain rights in an asset. Under SSAP 21, either the company has substantially all the risks and rewards of ownership or it does not; either it has an asset to record or it does not. A new standard on leasing will need to be consistent with FRS 5's partial derecognition rules.

Lessor income recognition

15.141 Recent corporate failures such as Atlantic Computers and Sound Diffusion have highlighted problems with lessors recognising too much profit at the front-end of transactions. SSAP 21 gives some guidance on the treatment of the sales profits that may be recognised by manufacturers or dealers who are also lessors and this is discussed from paragraph 15.105 above. However, the guidance is very limited and does not relate specifically to the types of complex arrangements that may be entered into by, for example, specialist computer lessors.

15.142 FRAG 9/92 also recognises this difficulty and recommends that, at the very minimum, a revised leasing standard should clarify that entities are not allowed to recognise a pre-tax profit in the early years and a loss in later years in respect of the same lease. Also, gross earnings should be calculated under a finance lease using a commercial rate of interest, with any remaining element of total profit being taken as sales profit.

15.143 The failure of Atlantic Computers also highlighted the difficulties of accounting for residual values. FRAG 9/92 suggested that a revised leasing standard should define residual value and provide guidance on the re-evaluation of residual values and how such adjustments should be reflected in the profit and loss account. Therefore, further guidance on this complex area would be expected to be included in a revision of SSAP 21 in the future.

Future developments

15.144 In April 1994 the ASB approved the Finance & Leasing Association for the development of a SORP on lessor accounting. In January 1998, the Finance & Leasing Association (FLA) issued a draft SORP on 'Accounting issues in the asset finance and leasing industry'. The principal objective of the draft SORP is to harmonise the accounting treatment adopted by lessors in respect of income recognition and other related issues. It is intended to apply only to lessors that are members of the FLA, but non-members are encouraged to follow its recommendations.

15.145 The draft SORP endorses the requirements of SSAP 21 and FRS 5 that lease transactions should be accounted for and presented in accordance with their substance and not merely their legal form. In determining this substance, the draft SORP sets out a number of questions which, whilst not intended to be a comprehensive list, the lessor should consider.

15.146 Consistent with SSAP 21, the draft SORP requires that gross earnings under a finance lease should be allocated to accounting periods to produce a constant periodic rate of return on the net cash investment in the lease. As a result, the alternative method described in paragraph 40 of SSAP 21 and explained in paragraph 15.72 above would no longer be allowed. Where the tax consequences of a lease form a material and integral part of the overall return on the lease, finance lessors should recognise gross earnings in accordance with the actuarial after tax method explained from paragraphs 15.75 above, as this is the preferred method. Other methods such as the investment period method or the sum of digits method may be used provided certain conditions are met. Where the tax effects of a lease are not considered a material and integral part of the lease, the actuarial before tax method should be used in preference to the sum of the digits method.

15.147 Estimates of residual values may form an important part of the pricing of a lease transaction. The draft SORP sets out a number of factors which the lessor should consider in assessing the residual values. It also recommends estimates of residual values to be reviewed regularly. For finance leases, diminution in the estimate of residual values should be recognised either over the remaining term of the lease or immediately under certain circumstances, such as where the leasing balance is not recoverable. As regards operating lessors, a similar approach is appropriate. Where an after tax method is used to recognise the profit from the operating lease, the same method as for finance leases should be applied in accounting for a diminution. If already written down, an uplift in the estimate of the residual value can be recognised provided that the value does not exceed the value estimated at the inception of the lease.

15.148 The draft SORP provides guidance on how manufacturer/dealer lessors can determine the initial sales profit on writing a finance lease. Under a finance lease, the manufacturer/dealer can recognise a sales profit immediately provided the sales price can be quantified with reasonable certainty. Any profit recognised should be restricted to the excess of the fair market value of the asset over the manufacturer's/dealer's costs. Where the normal sales price cannot be determined, profit should be calculated by reference to the present value determined by discounting the lessor's minimum lease payments.

15.149 The draft SORP sets out a number of disclosure requirements, in addition to those already required by SSAP 21 and the Act. Significant amongst these are the disclosures by lessors of the aggregate of residual value. In addition, for each type of asset, the residual values used in calculating the gross value of finance and operating leases should be analysed by year in which the exposure is expected to mature:

- Within one year.
- Between one and two years.
- Between two and five years.
- More than five years.

The policy for monitoring residual value exposure and providing for anticipated shortfall in residual values should also be disclosed. Manufacturer/dealer lessors should disclose both the amount of the initial selling profits and the basis of determining sales price for the purposes of calculating initial selling profits.

Comparison with IASs

15.150 The IASC has revised its original standard IAS 17, 'Accounting for leases', which came into force in 1984. IAS 17 (revised), 'Accounting for leases', is effective for accounting periods beginning on or after 1 January 1999. The revision was based on a review conducted in the context of those issues considered essential to complete a core set of standards acceptable to the IOSCO for cross-border funding and stock exchange listing. The IASC Board has agreed to undertake a more fundamental reform in the area of lease accounting standards.

15.151 The broad approach of the revised IASC and UK rules on lease accounting is similar. However, there are many differences of detail, which are discussed below under the following headings:

- Classification of leases.
- Income recognition by lessors.
- Disclosures by lessees and lessors.

Classification of leases

15.152 Under both SSAP 21 and IAS 17 (revised), a finance lease is one that transfers to the lessee *"substantially all the risks and rewards incident to ownership of an asset"*. [IAS 17 para 3]. Although SSAP 21 is based on the principles of substance over form, there is not enough guidance in SSAP 21, other than the numerical 90 per cent test that may be rebutted in certain circumstances, on the classification of leases. IAS 17 (revised), on the other hand, sets out a host of circumstances and additional factors which would normally lead to a lease being classified as a finance lease.

Income recognition by lessors

15.153 The key issue that the IASC Board had to decide when revising the standard was on the allocation of finance income by the lessor. The original IAS 17 provided a free choice of method in the allocation of finance income by a lessor, namely the recognition of income based on a constant periodic rate of return on either the lessor's net cash investment or the net investment. The IASC Board decided that lessors should recognise finance income on one method for all contracts with no exceptions. As a result, the IASC Board eliminated the net cash investment method and IAS 17 (revised) now requires lessors to use the net investment method. In contrast, SSAP 21 favours the net cash investment method. Indeed, as discussed above, the draft SORP also supports this method.

Disclosure by lessees and lessors

15.154 Under the original IAS 17, the disclosures required by lessees and lessors were less onerous than under SSAP 21. Following the revision of IAS 17, the balance has tipped in favour of IAS 17. IAS 17 (revised) added a host of new disclosures in respect of operating and finance leases for both lessees and lessors, which go beyond SSAP 21 disclosures. For example, some of the new disclosures in IAS 17 (revised) which are not included in SSAP 21 include, in addition to enhanced general descriptive disclosure of lessees' and lessors' operating and finance leasing arrangements, the following:

- The total of minimum lease payments reconciled to the present values of lease liabilities in three periodic bands: not later than one year; later than one year and not later than five years; and later than five years (required of a lessee).

- The total gross investment in the lease reconciled to the present value of minimum lease payments receivable in three periodic bands: later than one year; later than one year and not later than five years; and later than five years (required of a lessor).

- The total of future minimum sub-lease payments expected to be received under non-cancellable sub-leases at the balance sheet date by lessees.

- The unguaranteed residual values accruing to the benefit of, and the accumulated allowance for uncollectible minimum lease payments receivable by, lessors

- Contingent rents recognised in income by lessors.

Lease accounting – a fundamental review

15.155 The IASC board has indicated that it will carry out a more fundamental review of lease accounting, for example capitalisation of all leases with a term of more than one year, including leases currently classified as operating leases. This approach was explored in a discussion paper, 'Accounting for leases: A new approach', developed jointly by the Accounting Standards Boards in Australia, Canada, New Zealand, the UK, the USA and the IASC. Indeed, the ASB in the UK is very much involved in this project and is currently developing a paper that will consider new approaches for lease capitalisation.

Chapter 16

Investments

Chapter 16

Investments

Scope of chapter

16.1 This chapter considers the disclosure required for all types of investments, including investments in subsidiary undertakings where consolidated financial statements are not prepared. These requirements are included in Schedule 5 to the Act, which deals with the disclosure in companies' financial statements of information concerning related undertakings. The Schedule is divided into two parts. The first part sets out the disclosure requirements for undertakings that are not required to prepare consolidated financial statements and the second part deals with the disclosure requirements for those undertakings that must prepare consolidated financial statements. The latter requirements are covered in chapter 21.

16.2 On the whole, the current reporting requirements for investments are to be found in the Act. For listed companies, however, the requirements of the Stock Exchange's Listing Rules are also relevant. There is, as yet, no UK accounting standard in place dedicated to investment accounting, although SSAP 19, published in 1981, deals with investment properties. However, the chapter does consider the proposals put forward by the ASC in 1990 in ED 55, 'Accounting for investments', as well as the practical difficulties that have worked against the exposure draft's subsequent conversion into an accounting standard.

Definition of investments

16.3 The Act does not provide a formal definition of investments although the model formats for the balance sheet include a heading for 'Investments' under the general heading of both 'Fixed assets' and 'Current assets'. Moreover, there are separate sub-headings for investments under both the fixed and the current categories:

- The sub-headings identified for fixed asset investments are:
  - Shares in group undertakings.
  - Loans to group undertakings.
  - Participating interests.
  - Loans to undertakings in which the company has a participating interest.
  - Other investments other than loans.

- Other loans.
- Own shares.

■ The sub-headings identified for current asset investments are:

- Shares in group undertakings.
- Own shares.
- Other investments.

The potential difficulties that the Act's narrow definition of fixed assets causes, with regard to treating certain categories of investments as fixed assets, are discussed briefly in chapter 14.

16.4 While there is no specific UK accounting standard in place dealing with the subject of investments, ED 55 defined an investment in general terms as "*...an asset that is characterised by its ability to generate economic benefits in the form of distributions and/or appreciation in value*". This definition is relatively broad and should cover all types of investments, such as:

- Shares.
- Debentures.
- Interest-bearing securities.
- Loan stock.
- Bonds and other debt instruments.
- Warrants and options.
- Commodities (other than those to be used in the enterprise's activities).
- Futures contracts.
- Rights to subscribe for any of these.

16.5 ED 55 also provided a negative definition as well as a positive definition of an investment. It stated that an investment is not an asset that the enterprise holds with a view to realising future benefits through its use, such as plant and equipment, land or buildings, or intangible assets, such as, patents or brands. However, where such assets are held solely with a view to profit through appreciation, that is, they are not used to generate profit through the activities of the enterprise, then they may also be deemed to be investments. Although stock held in connection with the business activities of an enterprise is not generally considered to be an investment, those enterprises that hold investments of the type listed in paragraph 16.4 as part of their businesses would generally be expected to account for them using the normal rules for investments and this was also envisaged in ED 55. ED 55 did, however, specifically excluded investment properties from its scope since these were already governed by SSAP 19. The accounting for such properties is considered in chapter 14.

16.6 In determining how to account for an investment in shares, the amount of control that the shareholding gives the investing company is particularly important. For example, where the investing company controls more than 50 per cent of the voting rights of an entity's shares, the entity will be a subsidiary. In this case, the investing company will generally be required to prepare consolidated financial statements consolidating the results and financial position of its subsidiary. The rules concerning subsidiaries and consolidated financial statements are dealt with in chapter 21. Where the company's control of an entity is between 50 per cent and 20 per cent and the company has significant influence, the entity will generally either have to be accounted for in the company's consolidated financial statements as an associate using the equity method of accounting, or as a joint venture and either be equity accounted or proportionately consolidated. These rules are discussed in chapter 28. Even where the investing company prepares consolidated financial statements which include the share of results and assets and liabilities of subsidiaries, associates and joint ventures, the investing company still has to prepare its own individual balance sheet. In its individual balance sheet, the company will include its interests in subsidiaries, associates and joint ventures as part of its investments. The rules relating to the measurement and disclosure of these interests together with other investments are dealt with in the paragraphs that follow.

Classification

16.7 Under the Act, a company can treat investments in its balance sheet as either fixed asset investments or current asset investments depending on how it intends to use them. A company's investments that are *"...intended for use on a continuing basis in the company's activities"* should be classified as fixed assets in the company's financial statements. Generally, investments should be classified as fixed where the company intends to hold them for the long-term and this intention can clearly be demonstrated. Furthermore, such a situation might arise where the company's ability to dispose of an investment is restricted for a particular reason. If a company's investments do not fall within the category described above and are, therefore, not considered to be fixed asset investments, they will fall to be classified as current asset investments.

16.8 Whether a company intends to use an investment on a continuing basis (that is, hold it for the long-term) will often be obvious from the nature of the investment. Treatment as a fixed asset might also arise where there are practical restrictions on an investor's ability to dispose of the investment. Fixed asset investments will, therefore, comprise:

- Equity shareholdings in, or loan to, subsidiaries and associates.
- Investments arising from other trading relationships.

- Investments that either cannot be disposed of or cannot be disposed of without a significant effect on the operations of the investing company.

- Investments that are intended to be held for use on a continuing basis by investing companies whose objective is to hold a portfolio of investments to provide income and/or capital growth for their members.

[ED 55 para 24].

16.9 It should be remembered, however, that the mere fact that an investment has been held for a long time does not necessarily make it a long-term asset, unless it also falls within one of the categories indicated in paragraph 16.8.

Measurement rules

16.10 The paragraphs below consider the measurement rules that apply to fixed asset investments and to current asset investments. Such investments can either be recorded in the financial statements in accordance with the Act's historical cost accounting rules or its alternative accounting rules, which allow such assets to be recognised in the financial statements at a valuation. How these rules apply to all assets (including investments) is considered in detail in chapter 5 and is summarised in the paragraphs that follow. When determining the amount at which an investment should be recognised in the financial statements, each individual investment should be determined separately. [4 Sch 14]. This means that a 'portfolio' basis of valuation (that is, treating a number of investments as a single asset) cannot be used for an investment portfolio; each investment has to be considered separately.

Fixed asset investments

Historical cost accounting rules

16.11 Under the Act's historical cost accounting rules, fixed asset investments, like other fixed assets, are required to be recognised in the financial statements at their purchase price or production cost. [4 Sch 18]. Clearly, production cost is not relevant for fixed asset investments and hence they should be recorded at their purchase price. Where a fixed asset investment has diminished in value the diminution may be provided for in the profit and loss account, thereby reducing the investment to its recoverable amount. [4 Sch 19(1)]. Therefore, in a similar way for other fixed assets, permanent diminutions in value must be taken to the profit and loss account, but also temporary diminutions in value of fixed asset investments (which would include market value fluctuations) can also be charged to the profit and loss account.

16.12 Where a diminution in value of a fixed asset investment has been charged to the profit and loss account, but the circumstances giving rise to the diminution have reversed to any extent (for example, the investment's market value has increased) the provision should be written back to the extent that it is no longer necessary. Any amounts of this nature written back should be shown in the profit and loss account. [4 Sch 19(3)]. (See further chapter 5.)

16.13 Purchase price for such investments includes their cash cost together with any incidental costs of purchase. [4 Sch 26(1)]. In some circumstances, for example, with the purchase of an investment in a subsidiary, the incidental costs of purchase can be quite high. The costs incurred in such a transaction will include the costs associated with issuing shares and other capital instruments to finance the acquisition. The definition of 'issue costs' and their accounting treatment is set out in FRS 4, 'Accounting for capital instruments', and is considered in detail in chapter 18. In summary, issue costs of capital instruments must either be deducted from the instrument itself to arrive at its net proceeds (which is the rule applied for debt instruments), or be written off to the share premium account or other reserves (which is the rule applied for shares). There may, however, be other costs associated with an acquisition that do not fall within the definition of issue costs, which is tightly drawn. These other costs can generally be added to the cost of the investment as long as this does not arrive at a value that exceeds the investment's worth, which would then require a provision for diminution to be made.

16.14 It must also be remembered that for investments in shares, the underlying company's net asset value will not necessarily be a good indication of the worth of the investment, because this does not place any value on the goodwill that might attach to that company's business.

Alternative accounting rules

16.15 Under the Act's alternative accounting rules, fixed asset investments can be included in the balance sheet at either:

- their market value determined as at the date of their last valuation; or
- at a value determined on any basis that appears to the directors to be appropriate in the company's circumstances.

[4 Sch 31(3)].

Where a directors' valuation is used, the particulars of the method of valuation adopted and the reasons for adopting it must be disclosed in the notes to the financial statements.

16.16 Where the alternative accounting rules have been applied, the amount of any profit (or loss) arising on the revaluation must be credited to (or debited to) the revaluation reserve. Then the normal rules regarding the use of that reserve apply (see further chapter 5). Slightly different rules apply to investment companies (as defined in section 266 of the Act) who are allowed to take revaluation gains and losses to another reserve other than the revaluation reserve. In addition, they are allowed to take permanent diminutions in the value of fixed asset investments to that same reserve, whereas other companies have to take such losses to the profit and loss account (as explained in chapter 5).

16.17 The market value to be used where there is a quoted price for the investment would normally be the middle market price (that is the average of the bid and offer prices). But, where a company holds marketable securities of another company and the size and nature of the holding is such that the market is not capable of absorbing a sale of the investment without a material effect on its quoted price, the current market price may not be indicative of the true market value of the investment. In this type of situation, the market price should generally be adjusted to reflect the proceeds that the enterprise could realistically expect to raise by disposing of the holding in the ordinary course of business.

16.18 In certain situations, a holding of a size sufficient to affect market price, if sold, may not always be indicated by a large percentage ownership of shares. For example, where only a portion of the total is actively traded, a much smaller percentage holding could affect the market price significantly. Where this is so, the investment should normally be valued at the amount that could be raised if it was disposed of in smaller tranches, taking into account, for example, the higher transaction costs.

16.19 There may, however, be situations where an investor controls, say, five per cent of a very large enterprise. In this situation, the market price may be higher than the quoted price, because the quoted price usually reflects the trading of much smaller tranches of shares. Indeed, there may be a premium attached to such an influential stake. In this case, the quoted price would be lower than 'market' and should normally be used for valuation purposes. This would be required because any 'premium' price would not be attainable on short notice.

16.20 Where an investment is not quoted, the directors may still wish to record the investment at a value in the financial statements. As mentioned above, it is acceptable under the Act for them to carry out their own valuation as long as the disclosures set out in paragraph 16.15 are complied with. There are a number of valuation techniques that can be applied in these circumstances. One of the common approaches is to find a similar listed company to the unquoted company to be valued and apply the listed company's PE ratio to the unquoted company's earnings to arrive at a price. The valuation of unquoted investment is of great importance to certain industries, particularly the investment trust industry. Some investment trusts specialise in making high risk venture capital investments (often in management buyouts) and the British Venture Capital Association issued some guidelines in November 1993 of the valuation and disclosure of venture capital portfolios.

16.21 The rules and techniques for valuing investments that apply under that Act's alternative accounting rules are the same as those that apply when an investment is acquired as part of the acquisition of a subsidiary. The rules for fair valuing investments on such an acquisition are considered in Part II of chapter 23.

Current asset investments

Historical cost accounting rules

16.22 Current asset investments are required under the Act to be recorded at the lower of cost and net realisable value. [4 Sch 22,23]. Therefore, where a current asset investment's net realisable value is lower that its cost an amount should be provided in the profit and loss account for the diminution in value. Where the reason for making the provision has ceased to apply to any extent, the provision should be written back through the profit and loss account to that extent. [4 Sch 23].

Alternative accounting rules

16.23 Under the Act's alternative accounting rules, current asset investments may be included in the balance sheet at their current cost. Current cost is, in effect, the value to the business of the asset and for current asset investments will often be the investment's market value, unless the investment is unquoted, when the directors can determine its value. In a same way as the rule applies for fixed asset investments, any profit or loss arising from the valuation of current asset investments must be credited or debited to the revaluation reserve. [4 Sch 34].

16.24 The rules concerning the market value to be attributed to current asset investments are the same as the rules discussed for fixed asset investments in paragraphs 16.17 to 16.20 above.

Marking to market

16.25 Many companies, particularly those that actively trade in their current asset investments, mark their investments to market value (known as, 'marking to market') where they are considered to be readily marketable. Those readily marketable investments that it is appropriate to mark to market have the following characteristics:

- An active market in the investment that is both open and accessible and for which the prices are known and openly quoted.

- The price quoted is an accurate indicator of the price at which the security could be sold.

16.26 There are a number of reasons why marking to market is considered by many accountants to be a sound, supportable, approach for valuing current marketable investments and some of these were summarised in ED 55 as follows:

- Marketable securities represent a store of liquidity; movements in their value represent a realised profit or loss for the period and should be recognised as such in the profit and loss account.

- Management performance is best reflected by recognising gains and losses in the value of marketable securities.

- Market value is an objective measurement.

- Marking to market eliminates the opportunity to manipulate earnings through the timing of disposals.

- The market value of such investments is their most significant attribute.

- Marking to market eliminates the valuing of identical assets at different prices due to different acquisition dates.

16.27 The current acceptability of marking to market and the legal problems associated with it are considered in detail in chapter 5.

Disclosure requirements

All investments

16.28 As mentioned above, a company can treat its investments in its balance sheet as either fixed asset investments or current asset investments depending on how it intends to use them. The model formats for the balance sheet include a heading for 'Investments' under the general heading of both 'Fixed assets' and 'Current assets'. Moreover, there are separate sub-headings for investments under both the fixed and the current categories.

16.29 For each of the sub-headings of fixed asset investments, a company has to disclose the information required for other fixed assets under Schedule 4 paragraphs 42(1)(2). These include disclosure of the aggregate amount of that item at both the beginning and the end of the financial year and certain other information about the purchase and sale of those investments. These requirements are discussed in chapter 14.

16.30 In addition, Schedule 4 paragraph 42(3) requires details to be disclosed about any provisions made in respect of each fixed asset investment category. Again the rules are the same as for other fixed assets as discussed in chapter 14.

16.31 Furthermore, the Act requires the notes to the financial statements to include certain information about any investments a company holds (irrespective of whether these are shown as fixed assets or as current assets). In particular, the notes must disclose:

- The total amount that relates to all listed investments.
- The aggregate market value of listed investments where it differs from the amount at which they are stated in the balance sheet.
- Both the market value and the stock exchange value of any listed investments must be disclosed, where the former value is taken as being higher than their stock exchange value. This disclosure is required because the market value and the stock exchange value may differ according to the size of the investment and its marketability. For example, a controlling stake could be worth proportionately more than a minority interest in a company, because stock exchange prices traditionally reflect the values of small parcels of shares.

[4 Sch 45(1)(2) as amended by SI 1996/189].

16.32 For this purpose, a 'listed investment' means any investment that is listed either on a 'recognised investment exchange' other than an overseas investment exchange within the meaning of the Financial Services Act 1986 or on any stock exchange of repute outside Great Britain. [4 Sch 84]. All other investments are to be regarded as unlisted and no additional information is required to be disclosed for these investments. A 'recognised investment exchange' means any body of persons that is a recognised investment exchange for the purposes of the Financial Services Act 1986. Currently, the only bodies designated in Great Britain as recognised investment exchanges are:

- The London Stock Exchange (the Stock Exchange).
- LIFFE Administration & Management.
- The International Petroleum Exchange of London Limited (IPE).
- The London Commodity Exchange (1908) Limited (LCE).
- The London Metal Exchange Limited (LME).
- OMLX, The London Securities and Derivatives Exchange Limited.
- Tradepoint Financial Networks plc (Tradepoint).

16.33 There is no definition of 'stock exchange of repute' in the Act. In practice, whether a stock exchange outside Great Britain is reputable or not will depend both on its status in its own country and on the circumstances surrounding its operation.

16.34 The disclosure requirements for *listed* investments outlined above are best illustrated by an example:

Example

Details of investments held:

	Co	Balance sheet value £'000	Market Value £'000	Stock exchange value £'000
Listed on the London Stock Exchange (a recognised investment exchange)	A	100	250	300
	B	150	110	110
	C	130	150	125
	D	75	25	20
		455	535	555
Listed on the New York Stock Exchange (a stock exchange of repute outside Great Britain)	E	190	200	225
	F	65	110	100
	G	15	25	25
		270	335	350
Traded on AIM		30	70	75
Total of investments		755	940	980

This disclosure may be summarised in the notes to the financial statements as follows:

Listed investments	£'000
Balance sheet value	725
Market value	870

Listed investments include certain investments for which the market value is considered to be higher than the stock exchange value. The market value of these investments is £285,000 (that is £150,000 + £25,000 + £110,000) and their stock exchange value is £245,000 (that is £215,000 + £20,000 + £100,000). The investment in the company traded on AIM has been excluded from this disclosure as companies traded in this way are not listed investments.

16.35 In Table 16.1, Lonrho provides an analysis for 'other' fixed asset investments.

Table 16.1 – Lonrho Plc – Annual Report and Accounts – 30 September 1994

Notes to the Accounts (extract)

16. Other investments - fixed assets	**Group**	Investments £m	Loans £m	Provisions £m	Total £m
	At 30 September 1993	26	3	(12)	17
	Additions/advances	1	2		3
	Disposals/repayments	(1)	(1)		(2)
	Provisions			(3)	(3)
	Transfers		(1)		(1)
	At 30 September 1994	**26**	**3**	**(15)**	**14**

Net book value of investments shown above:-

	1994 £m	1993 £m
Listed – on the London Stock Exchange	1	1
– on overseas stock exchanges	2	2
Unlisted	8	11
	11	14
Value at 30 September:		
Listed (market value)	11	8
Unlisted (Directors' valuation)	28	28

Company	Investments £m	Provisions £m	Total £m
Cost:			
At 30 September 1993 and 1994	10	(8)	2

Net book value of investments shown above:-

	1994 £m	1993 £m
Listed – on the London Stock Exchange	1	1
Unlisted	1	1
	2	2
Value at 30 September:		
Listed (market value)	1	1
Unlisted (Directors' valuation)	1	1

Significant holdings greater than 20 per cent

16.36 Where a company at the end of its financial year has a 'significant holding' of shares of any class in another undertaking, other than a subsidiary undertaking, the Act requires the company to disclose certain information. [5 Sch 7].

16.37 For the purposes of the disclosure requirements, it is necessary to consider the meanings of the terms 'significant holding', 'undertaking' and 'shares'.

- The Act defines a 'significant holding' as a holding of 20 per cent or more of the nominal value of any class of shares in the undertaking, or a holding that exceeds one fifth of the amount of the company's assets as disclosed in its balance sheet. [5 Sch 7(2) as amended by SI 1996/189].

- 'Undertaking' means a body corporate or partnership or an unincorporated association carrying on a trade or business, with or without a view to profit. [Sec 259(1)].

- Reference to 'shares' is taken to mean:

  - The allotted shares in relation to an undertaking that has a share capital. This applies to bodies corporate with a share capital.

  - The rights to share in the capital of an undertaking which has capital, but has no share capital. This would apply to partnerships.

  - Interests that confer any right to share in the profits, or liability to contribute to the losses, of the undertaking, or that give rise to an obligation to contribute to the debts or expenses of the undertaking in the event of it being wound up. This includes most other undertakings that are not bodies corporate or partnerships.

[Sec 259(2)].

Basic information

16.38 The notes to the financial statements of the investing company must disclose in respect of such undertakings:

- Its name.

- Its country of incorporation, where it is incorporated outside Great Britain.

- If it is unincorporated, the address of its principal place of business.

- The identity of each class of shares the investing company holds.

- The proportion of the nominal value of the shares of each class that the investing company holds.

[5 Sch 8, 24 as amended by SI 1996/189].

16.39 Table 16.2 illustrates the type of information that should be disclosed. Corresponding amounts are not required to be disclosed. [4 Sch 58(3)].

Table 16.2 – Whitbread PLC – Annual Report and Accounts – 26 February 1994

Notes to the accounts (extract)

16 Participating interests

In accordance with the Companies Act 1985 the investments below, which comprise more than 20% of the equity capital of the undertakings, are described as "Participating Interest". Because Whitbread PLC continues not to participate in the commercial or financial policy decisions of the undertakings, they are not regarded as associated undertakings. They are, therefore, included as cost and not equity value. As described in note 32, these investments were sold after the year end.

	Total equity per value (a)	Group holding of (a)	Total loan capital (b)	Group holding of (b)	Latest reported net assets	Latest reported pre-tax profit
The Boddington Group PLC	£30.3m ord	20%	£0.7m	-	£220.4m	£41.2m
Marston, Thompson & Evershed PLC	£22.2m ord	21%	£15.5m	-	£229.4m	£20.1m

The above companies are registered in England, which is also the main area of operations.

16.40 In interpreting the Act's disclosure requirements, shares held on behalf of the company by any person should be attributed to it. However, shares held on behalf of a person other than the company should not be attributed to it. Furthermore, shares held by a company (company A) by way of security should be treated as held by the company providing them as security (company B), where both the following conditions apply:

- The rights attached to the shares (other than the right to exercise them for the purpose of preserving the security or of realising it) are exercisable only in accordance with the instructions of company B.

- Where the shares are held by way of security in connection with the granting of loans by way of normal business activities, those rights (other than the right to exercise them for the purpose of preserving the security or of realising it) are exercisable only in the interests of company B.

[5 Sch 13(3)(4)].

16.41 The particulars to be disclosed may relate *inter alia* to either an undertaking that is established under the law of a country outside the UK or an undertaking that carries on its business outside the UK. Where, in either of these two situations, the directors believe that disclosure of the information detailed in paragraph 16.38 above would be seriously prejudicial to the business of that undertaking, or to the business of the company or any of its subsidiary undertakings, and the company has obtained the Secretary of State's agreement, that information need not be disclosed. [Sec 231(3)]. Earlier legislation had a similar exemption that applied if, in the opinion of the directors, disclosure would be harmful to the business of the company or any of its subsidiaries. The wording in the current legislation has been tightened to apply in situations where disclosure would be seriously prejudicial. Where advantage is taken of this exception, this must be stated in the notes to the financial statements. [Sec 231(4)].

16.42 Where a company has a significant holding in a number of undertakings and, in the directors' opinion, compliance with the above disclosure requirements would mean that particulars of excessive length would have to be disclosed in the financial statements, the company is not required to disclose the information detailed above for every undertaking. In this circumstance, the directors have to give in the notes to the financial statements the information relating to those undertakings whose results or financial position principally affect the figures shown in the company's financial statements and similar information for those undertakings excluded from consolidation under section 229(3) or 229(4). [Sec 231(5)(a)(b)].

16.43 Where a company takes advantage of the exemption outlined in the above paragraph, the financial statements must state that the information is given only for those investments that principally affect the company's annual financial statements. [Sec 231(6)(a)]. In addition, the full information (including both the information that is disclosed in the notes to the financial statements and the information that is not) should be annexed to the company's next annual return. [Sec 231(6)(b)]. Where a company fails to annex this information to its next annual return, the company and any officer of it who is in default is liable to a fine, and for continued contravention, to a daily default fine. [Sec 231(7)]. Obviously, under these provisions, the information required to be given in the annual return could be lengthy and company secretaries should take care in compiling this information.

Information concerning profit, capital and reserves

16.44 The following information should be given in the financial statements in addition to the information set out in paragraph 16.21 above:

- The aggregate amount of the capital and reserves of the undertaking at the end of its relevant financial year.

- The profit or the loss of that undertaking as disclosed by those financial statements.

[5 Sch 9(1), 28(1) as amended by SI 1996/189].

16.45 These amounts are to be ascertained from the undertaking's financial statements prepared for the year ending with, or last before, the company's financial year. [5 Sch 9(5)]. British Aerospace included more than the minimum information about the results of its investment in Hutchison Telecommunications (UK) Limited (see Table 16.3).

Table 16.3 – British Aerospace Public Limited Company – Annual Report – 31 December 1994

Notes to the accounts (extract)

13 Fixed Assets – Investments (extract)

Included within investments of the Group and Company is a 30% interest in the ordinary share capital of Hutchison Telecommunications (UK) Limited, a company registered in England and Wales; the remaining shares are controlled by Hutchison Whampoa Limited (65%) and Barclays Bank PLC (5%). In view of this shareholding structure the investment is not accounted for as an associated undertaking. The latest published consolidated accounts available for Hutchison Telecommunications (UK) Limited are for the year ended 31st December, 1993 and show an aggregate deficit on capital and reserves of £325 million and a retained loss for the year of £240 million. This loss is stated after charging exceptional costs of £182 million relating to withdrawal of the public telepoint service, write down of goodwill relating to the cellular services division, provision for mobile data development costs and provision for other restructuring costs. During 1994, the Company replaced guarantees with interest bearing shareholder loans of £247 million to Hutchison Telecommunications (UK) Limited. These loans are included within the above addition to loans.

16.46 If this additional information is immaterial, it need not be disclosed. [5 Sch 9(4)]. Also, the exemptions in paragraphs 16.41 and 16.42 above are available but the information required by paragraph 16.43 above must still be given in the company's next annual return.

16.47 Moreover, the additional information in paragraph 16.44 above does not need to be given in either of the following two situations where:

- The company is exempt by virtue of section 228 from the requirement to prepare consolidated financial statements (see below). But for this exemption to apply, the company's investment in all such undertakings must be shown, in aggregate, in the notes to the company's financial statements by way of the equity method of valuation (that is, by stating the company's share of the undertaking's net assets).

  Section 228 exempts a company from the requirement to prepare consolidated financial statements in the following circumstances, provided certain other conditions are satisfied (see chapter 21):

- The company is a wholly-owned subsidiary of EU parent.
- The company is a subsidiary of an EU parent and that parent holds more than 50 per cent of the shares in the company and notice requesting the company to prepare financial statements has not been served on the company by shareholders holding in aggregate more than half of the remaining shares or five per cent of the total shares in the company.

- The company's investment is in an undertaking that is not required by any of the Act's provisions to deliver a copy of its balance sheet to the Registrar of Companies and it does not otherwise publish that balance sheet in Great Britain or elsewhere. Where this situation exists, the information need not be given, provided the company's holding is less than 50 per cent of the nominal value of the shares in the undertaking.

[5 Sch 9(2)(3)].

Participating interests

16.48 'Participating interest' is defined in section 260(1) of the Act as "*...an interest held by an undertaking in the shares of another undertaking which it holds on a long-term basis for the purpose of securing a contribution to its activities by the exercise of control or influence arising from or related to that interest*". The term was introduced by the Companies Act 1989 and derives from a category of investments that the Companies Act 1981 introduced as 'shares in related companies'. The term 'related companies' was removed by the Companies

Act 1989. In its place the Act now refers to 'undertakings in which the company has a participating interest'.

16.49 A holding of 20 per cent or more of the shares of an undertaking is presumed to be a participating interest, unless the contrary is shown. With regard to the disclosures set out in paragraph 16.54 below, for this purpose, a participating interest does not include an interest in a subsidiary undertaking. It will, however, include associates and joint ventures as defined in both the Act and FRS 9 (see para 16.55 below).

[The next paragraph is 16.51.]

16.51 The Companies Act 1989 introduced the term 'associated undertaking' which is dependent on holding shares which give 'voting rights'. In the definition of an associated undertaking, an undertaking is presumed to exercise significant influence if it holds 20 per cent or more of the *voting* rights in another undertaking, unless the contrary is shown. However, following the introduction of FRS 9, this assumption can be rebutted where significant influence is not exercised in practice (see further chapter 28).

16.52 The term 'associated undertaking' is defined in the Act for consolidated financial statements purposes. Consequently, this term does not appear in any of the balance sheet formats of an individual company. Therefore, where an investing company that is not required to prepare consolidated financial statements holds 20 per cent or more of the shares, whether voting or non-voting, in another undertaking, that investment will generally be shown as a 'participating interest' in the company's balance sheet. Participating interests will include associates and joint ventures as defined in FRS 9. If, however, the company is included in the consolidated financial statements of a larger group, in the group's consolidated balance sheet, any holding of 20 per cent or more of the voting shares in an undertaking (that is, in an associate or a joint venture) will be shown under the sub-heading 'interests in associated undertakings', and any holding of 20 per cent or more of the non-voting shares in an undertaking will be shown under the sub-heading 'other participating interests'.

16.53 The further information about participating interests set out in paragraph 16.54 below is required to be disclosed in the investing company's financial statements in addition to the information about investments outlined in paragraph 16.44 above.

16.54 'Participating interests' and 'loans to undertakings in which the company has a participating interest' appear as separate sub-headings under the fixed asset main heading of 'investments' in both balance sheet formats. Also, both balance sheet formats require the disclosure of 'amounts owed by undertakings in which the company has a participating interest' under 'debtors', and the disclosure of 'amounts owed to undertakings in which the company has a participating interest' under 'creditors'. In addition, 'amounts owed by and to undertakings in which the company has a participating interest' that are due for payment within one year must be shown separately from amounts due after one year. [Notes 5 and 13 to the balance sheet formats]. These format requirements effectively prohibit companies from showing participating interests and investments in associates and joint ventures as one figure, including the cost of the shares in the undertakings, loans to them and after deducting loans from them. The same argument applies to investments in subsidiaries. This disclosure also fulfils the requirements contained in paragraph 55 of FRS 9, with the exception that the standard requires such balances to be analysed further between amounts relating to loans and amounts relating to trading balances.

Associates, joint ventures and other joint arrangements

16.55 As stated in paragraph 16.49 above, participating interests include investments in associates and joint venture entities. Companies that have investments in associates and joint venture entities have to comply with the requirements of FRS 9 for accounting periods beginning on or after 23 June 1998.

16.56 Investments in associates and joint ventures should be shown in the investing company's own financial statements as follows:

- Income from associates and joint ventures should be shown as dividends received and receivable.
- Unless it is shown at a valuation, the amount at which the investing company's interests in associates and joint ventures should be shown is the cost of the investment less any amounts written off. [FRS 9 paras 20, 26].

The treatment of an investing group's interests in associates and joint ventures is covered in chapter 28.

16.57 If the investing company does not prepare consolidated financial statements because it has no subsidiaries, then it only has to report its own profit and loss account and balance sheet. The only income that can properly be included in that profit and loss account will be dividends received from the associate or joint venture.

Inclusion of dividends rather than share of earnings is necessary because of the Act's requirement that only realised profits can be included in a company's profit and loss account. For this reason FRS 9 requires that a company should show its share of its associate's or joint venture's results and net assets by presenting a separate proforma profit and loss account in addition to its own profit and loss account. Alternatively, the company could add the information in supplementary form to its own profit and loss account in such a way that its share of the associate's or joint venture'sprofits is not treated as realised for the purposes of the Act, as illustrated below. [FRS 9 para 48].

Example

The supplementary information could be included on the face of the profit and loss account or in the notes to the company's financial statements.

Company profit and loss account

(All figures relate to continuing activities)	Company	*Proforma information* Joint ventures & Associates	Total
	£'000	£'000	£'000
Turnover	200	120	320
Cost of sales	120		
Gross profit	80		
Administrative expenses	40		
Operating profit	40	54	94
Interest	(20)	(22)	(42)
Profit on ordinary activities before tax	20	32	52
Tax on profit on ordinary activities	5	7	12
Profit for the financial year	15	25	30
Equity dividends	4		4
Retained profit for the year	11		26

16.57.1 In order to comply with FRS 9, it would also be necessary for the proforma information concerning joint ventures and associates to be further analysed in the notes between amounts relating to joint ventures and amounts relating to associates. It is also necessary to give additional information concerning the company's share of items appearing in the joint venture's or associate's statement of total recognised gains and losses and cash flow statement. These issues are considered further in chapters 28 and 30.

[The next paragraph is 16.58.]

16.58 Similarly, as the company's balance sheet will carry the investment at cost less amounts written off, FRS 9 requires that a separate proforma balance sheet should be given in which the associate or joint venture is presented on the equity method of accounting. Alternatively, the information could be added in supplementary form to the company's own balance sheet as illustrated below. [FRS 9 para 48].

Example

Company balance sheet

	Company	*Proforma information* Company including associates & joint ventures
	£'000	£'000
Fixed assets		
Tangible assets	898	898
Investments:		
Company	238	
Joint ventures:		
Share or gross assets		2,359
Share of gross liabilities		1,448
		911
Associates		67
Other investments		82
		1,060
	1,136	1,958
Current assets		
Stocks	321	321
Debtors: amounts falling due after one year	10	10
Debtors: amounts falling due within one year	229	229
Cash at bank and in hand	43	43
	603	603
Creditors: amounts falling due within one year	520	520
Net current assets	83	83
Total assets less current liabilities	1,219	2,041
Creditors: amounts falling due after more than one year	647	647
Borrowings and other creditors	35	35
Provisions for liabilities and charges	204	204
	886	886
Net assets	333	1,155
Capital and reserves		
Called up share capital	200	
Share premium account	500	
Profit and loss account	(367)	
Total shareholders' funds – all equity	333	

16.59 Furthermore, the FRS 9 requires more detailed information to be given for associates and joint ventures in aggregate and individually where they are particularly material to the company. This information is dealt with in chapter 28. The requirements of the standard need not be complied with if the investing company is exempt from preparing consolidated financial statements, or would be exempt, if it had subsidiaries, because in that situation, the investing group's interest in the associate or joint venture will be accounted for on the equity basis in the ultimate group's consolidated financial statements. [FRS 9 para 48]. However, where the information on associates and joint ventures is not given for this reason, the additional disclosures required by the Act outlined in paragraph 16.44 above apply. These concern the disclosure of the profit for the financial year and the aggregate amount of capital and reserves of the associates and joint ventures.

16.60 FRS 9 also deals with the accounting requirements that apply to joint arrangements that are not entities and to structures with the form, but not the substance of, a joint venture. For both of these types of joint arrangements, the standard requires that the investing company should account in its individual financial statements for its share or part of the assets, liabilities and cash flows stemming from the arrangement. [FRS 9 paras 18, 24]. The accounting requirements explained above for associates and joint ventures do not apply to these types of joint arrangements. Such joint arrangements and their accounting requirements are considered in detail in chapter 28.

[The next paragraph is 16.62.]

[The next page is 16021.]

Subsidiary undertakings

16.62 Where, at the end of a financial year, a company does not prepare consolidated financial statements, but has subsidiary undertakings, the investing company's financial statements have to disclose the information outlined in paragraph 16.38 above for each of its subsidiary undertakings. [5 Sch 1, 2(1)]. For this purpose, an undertaking is a subsidiary of a parent undertaking where any of the following five situations apply. The parent:

- Holds a majority of the voting rights in the undertaking.
- Is a member of the undertaking and can appoint or remove directors having the majority of the votes on the board.
- Has a right to exercise a dominant influence over the undertaking by virtue of provisions either in its memorandum or articles, or in a 'control contract'.
- Is a member of the undertaking and controls the majority voting rights in it *via* an agreement with other shareholders.
- Owns a participating interest in the undertaking and actually exercises a dominant influence or operates unified management.

The five situations are considered in detail in chapter 21.

16.63 The disclosure requirement in the last two points of paragraph 16.38 above is extended to include, in addition, the shares held by any subsidiaries of the investing company. Consequently, the identity and nominal values of the shares in each class that the investing company and its subsidiaries hold in a subsidiary undertaking has to be shown, distinguishing between those held by the company itself and those held by any of its subsidiaries. [5 Sch 2(2)]. It is not sufficient to show just the identity and the proportion of shares that the investing company holds in the subsidiary undertaking.

16.64 The Act also requires the company to state the reasons for not preparing consolidated financial statements. [5 Sch 1(4)]. If the reason why the company is not required to prepare consolidated financial statements is that its subsidiary undertakings fall within the exclusions from consolidation provided for in section 229, the reason for exclusion should be stated for each subsidiary undertaking. [5 Sch 1(5)]. Section 229 exclusions are covered in detail in chapter 21.

16.65 Except where one of the conditions below is satisfied, the information outlined in paragraph 16.44 above must also be given for each subsidiary. [5 Sch 3(1)].

- The company is exempt by virtue of section 228 from the requirement to prepare consolidated financial statements (see para 16.47 above). [5 Sch 3(2)].

- The company's investment is in a subsidiary undertaking which is included in the company's financial statements (that is, the balance sheet) using the equity method of valuation. [5 Sch 3(2A) inserted by SI 1996/189].

- The company's investment is in a subsidiary undertaking that is not required by any provision of the Act to deliver a copy of its balance sheet to the Registrar of Companies and that does not otherwise publish that balance sheet in Great Britain or elsewhere. Where this situation applies, the information need not be given, provided the company's holding is less than 50 per cent of the nominal value of the shares in the subsidiary undertaking. [5 Sch 3(3)].

- The information to be disclosed is not material. [5 Sch 3(4)].

16.66 In addition, the company need not give the information outlined in paragraphs 16.38 and 16.44 where the information would be seriously prejudicial or would be of excessive length as explained in paragraphs 16.41 and 16.42 respectively. Where the company has taken exemption by virtue of paragraph 16.42 above, the full information must still be given in the company's next annual return (see para 16.43).

16.67 Directors are under an obligation to ensure that the financial years of the group's subsidiaries coincide with that of the parent, unless there are good reasons for a subsidiary's year end to be different. But where the financial year of a subsidiary undertaking does not coincide with that of the company and the company is not exempt from the giving the information set out in paragraph 16.44 above (see para 16.65), the notes to the company's financial statements must disclose the date on which the subsidiary's last financial year ended.[5 Sch 4 as amended by SI 1996/189].

[The next paragraph is 16.71.]

16.71 Both the balance sheet formats specify the place where the aggregate amounts should be shown of any amounts owed to and from, and any interests in, group undertakings. In addition, a parent or a subsidiary must disclose separately (either on the face of the balance sheet or in the notes to the financial statements) any item required to be shown in the balance sheet formats in relation to group undertakings, split between the amounts owed to or from, and any interests in:

- Any parent or any fellow subsidiary.
- Any subsidiary.

[4 Sch 59].

16.72 Because amounts owed by and to group undertakings have to be shown in specific positions in the formats, it is not acceptable for undertakings to net these balances off and to disclose the net balance, together with the cost of the investments, in the balance sheet as 'Investments in subsidiaries'. Such offset is also precluded by FRS 5 paragraph 29. This applies even where a note to the financial statements gives additional information that explains the net balance.

16.73 Moreover, the amounts owed and owing have to be ascertained on an undertaking by undertaking basis. [4 Sch 5]. Consequently, for accounting presentation purposes, amounts that one subsidiary owes to the parent cannot be offset against amounts the parent owes to another subsidiary. Set-off can be allowed only where the offset criteria in FRS 5 are met (see further chapter 4).

16.74 Furthermore, undertakings have to analyse 'amounts owed by (and to) group undertakings' between amounts that will fall due within one year and amounts that will fall due after more than one year. [Notes 5 and 13 on the balance sheet formats]. The results of this analysis will largely depend both on the way in which group undertakings are financed and on the terms of any agreements between the undertakings.

16.75 In addition to the requirements of the Act, the Stock Exchange Listing Rules require listed companies to disclose the name of the principal country in which each subsidiary operates. [LR 12.43(f)]. However, where the number of such undertakings is large, particulars with regard to those of less importance can be omitted in line with the relaxation allowed by Part II of Schedule 5 to the Act.

Parent company information

16.76 Where, at the end of a financial year, a company is a subsidiary of another undertaking, certain information concerning the name and country of incorporation, etc., should be disclosed with respect to the company (if any) regarded by the directors as the company's ultimate parent company. In addition, similar information relating to potentially two further parent undertakings in the same group may have to be disclosed where the ultimate parent company does not prepare consolidated financial statements. The rules concerning these disclosures are complex and are considered in detail in chapter 21 in relation to companies that are required to prepare consolidated financial statements (that is, those covered by Part II of Schedule 5 to the Act). Furthermore, these rules apply in the same way to companies that are not required to prepare consolidated financial statements (that is, those covered by Part I of Schedule 5 to the Act) as the legislation is duplicated in paragraphs 11 and 12 of Schedule 5.

Membership of a qualifying undertaking

16.77 Where at the year end the company is a member of a qualifying undertaking, it has to give the following information in its financial statements:

- The name and legal form of the undertaking.
- The address of the undertaking's registered office or, if it does not have such an office, its head office.

[Sch 5 9A(1)(2)].

16.78 In addition, where the qualifying undertaking is a qualifying partnership one of the following must also be stated:

- That a copy of the latest financial statements of the undertaking has been, or is to be, appended to the copy of the company's financial statements sent to the Registrar under section 242 of the Act.

- The name of at least one body corporate (which may be the company) in whose consolidated financial statements the undertaking has been, or is to be, dealt with by the method of full consolidation, proportional consolidation or the equity method of accounting.

[5 Sch 9A(3)].

16.79 For the purpose of these rules, 'qualifying undertakings', can either be companies or partnerships. A qualifying company (or qualifying partnership) is an unlimited company (or partnership) incorporated in (or governed by the laws of any part of) Great Britain if each of its members is:

- a limited company; or
- another unlimited company, or a Scottish firm, each of whose members is a limited company.

The references to limited company, another unlimited company and Scottish firm also encompasses any comparable undertakings incorporated in, or formed under the law of, any country or territory outside Great Britain. [SI 1993/1829 Reg 3, 9].

16.80 The information required to be disclosed in the second bullet point of paragraph 16.78 need not be given if the partnership is dealt with either by consolidation, proportional consolidation or equity accounting in the consolidated financial statements prepared by:

- a member of the partnership that is established under the law of a member State; or
- a parent undertaking of such a member established in the same way.

[SI 1993/1820 Reg 7(1)].

16.81 The exemption can only be taken, however, where the following two conditions are complied with:

- The consolidated financial statements are prepared and audited under the law of the member State in accordance with the provisions of the 7th Directive.

- The notes to those consolidated financial statements disclose that advantage has been taken of the exemption.

[SI 1993/1820 Reg 7(2)].

[The next paragraph is 16.84.]

Own shares and shares in own parent

16.84 The main heading of 'investments' has a sub-heading 'own shares'. When a company purchases its own shares, it must cancel them at the time it purchases them. [Sec 160(4), 162(2)]. Thus, unlike the practice that is generally permitted both in the USA and also by the 2nd Directive, a company cannot purchase its own shares and then treat them as 'treasury shares' until the time it resells them.

16.85 A company will generally hold its own shares only where it has acquired them by forfeiture, or by surrender in lieu of forfeiture, or by way of gift. The Act sets out certain rules to govern situations where companies hold their own shares. In particular, a public company that acquires shares by forfeiture must generally dispose of them within three years. Otherwise, it must cancel them and so effectively bring about a capital reduction (see also chapter 6). [Sec 146].

16.86 A subsidiary company cannot normally own shares in its parent company. [Sec 23(1)]. However, this prohibition does not apply where the subsidiary is acting as a personal representative for a third party, or as trustee and the holding company or a subsidiary of it has no beneficial interest under the trust. [Sec 23(2)]. This provision also does not extend to market makers. [Sec 23(3)]. However, the prohibition does include those shares that might be held on behalf of the subsidiary by another person as its nominee. [Sec 23(7)].

16.87 Where a body corporate becomes a subsidiary company because of the changes in the definition of subsidiaries included in section 736 of the Act, it may retain any shares that it already held in its parent. However, where shares are held in this way, they will carry no right to vote at company meetings. [Sec 23(4)].

16.88 In certain situations, a subsidiary may find that it does hold shares in its parent. This may arise, for example, where the parent has recently acquired the subsidiary which owned shares in the parent before it became a group member. Before the introduction of the Companies Act 1989, such holdings may have been in breach of section 23(1) of the Act. Now, however, where a company acquires shares in its parent after the commencement of the new section 23(1), but before it becomes a subsidiary of the parent, it may retain those shares. Also in this circumstance, those shares will carry no right to vote at company meetings. [Sec 23(5)].

16.89 The notes to the parent's financial statements must disclose the number, description and the amount of the shares that subsidiaries or their nominees hold. [5 Sch 6(1) as amended by SI 1996/189]. This information is not required, however, where the subsidiary holds the shares as personal representative or as trustee. [5 Sch 6(2) as amended by SI 1996/189]. However, the exemption for a subsidiary acting as a trustee will not be available if the company or any of its subsidiaries is beneficially interested under the trust, unless the beneficial interest is by way of security for the purpose of a transaction entered into by it in the ordinary course of business, which includes the lending of money. [5 Sch 6(3) as amended by SI 1996/189].

16.90 In recent years, some companies have established employee share ownership plans (ESOP), because of the tax advantages that they afford employees. ESOPs can be set up in a variety of ways. However, normally the sponsoring company establishes an ESOP trust which provides a warehouse for its shares. Shares are acquired by the trust and sold or transferred to employees in the future. The trustees will generally purchase those shares out of funds supplied by the sponsoring company by way of cash, loans or by third party bank loans, often guaranteed by the sponsoring company. The UITF issued Abstract 13 in June 1995, which details how such plans should be accounted for to comply with FRS 5. It concluded that FRS 5 requires that the sponsoring company of an ESOP trust should recognise certain assets and liabilities of the trust as its own whenever it has *de facto* control of the shares held by the ESOP trust and bears their benefits and risks. Where this is judged to be the case and it is determined that the shares are held for the continuing benefit of the sponsoring company's business they have to be recognised by the sponsoring company as 'own shares' within fixed assets, otherwise they should be classified as 'own shares' within current assets. UITF Abstract 13 is considered in more detail in chapter 4.

Loans for acquisition of own shares

16.91 Where any outstanding loans made in respect of the acquisition of the company's shares under either section 153(4)(b) [(bb)] or (c) or section 55 of the Act (various situations of financial assistance by a company for purchase of its own shares) are included under any item in the balance sheet, these must be disclosed in aggregate for each item. [4 Sch 51(2)]. The acquisition by a company of its own shares is considered in chapter 40.

Other investments

16.92 The category 'other investments' will normally include the following items (other than investments in subsidiaries and companies in which the investing company has a participating interest):

- Listed and unlisted securities.
- Life assurance policies.
- Joint ventures and partnerships, if they are not subsidiaries or participating interests.

16.93 Building society deposits and bank deposits could be included either as 'other investments' (either under fixed assets or under current assets - depending on the nature of the deposits) or as 'cash at bank and in hand'. If the amount is material, the accounting policies should disclose where such items are included.

ED 55

16.94 As was indicated in paragraph 16.2, ED 55, 'Accounting for investments', was published in 1990, but has not been converted into an accounting standard. The exposure draft deals primarily with the valuation of investments. It also provides a definition of the term 'investments' (see paras 16.4 to 16.5), as well as listing examples, which include shares, debentures, interest-bearing securities, bonds and various other investment instruments.

16.95 As ED 55 was written in general terms, it does not specifically address accounting for complex capital issues or accounting for hedged transactions. The exposure draft would have applied, however, to the treatment of investments in associates and subsidiaries in the parent company's financial statements.

16.96 ED 55 identifies market makers and other dealers in investments and investment companies as falling into this group of enterprises. Justification for this is given in the following manner:

"However, the ASC considers that the asset that is being traded in such cases has the same underlying characteristics as it has when held either by the enterprise which sells an investment to the dealer or by the ultimate purchaser. Therefore, it is intended that investments held for trading purposes by market makers or other dealers should be accounted for in accordance with the proposed statement." [ED 55 para 6].

16.97 This approach has a certain degree of consistency in that enterprises derive benefits from investments in one or both of two forms: distributions and capital appreciation. This is so even where enterprises hold investments as stock. Therefore, the definition of investment in ED 55, albeit with certain exclusions, hinges on the form of future benefit, that is the nature of the asset, rather than on whether or not it is the entity's trading stock.

Entities covered

16.98 ED 55 was intended to apply to all enterprises which are normally subject to accounting standards. Thus, it would have included those enterprises for which the trading of investments forms a significant portion of the business of the enterprise. The ASC concluded that neither the nature of the enterprise nor its volume of investing activity should determine a particular accounting treatment.

16.99 ED 55 recognised that certain of its proposals (described below) could cause practical problems for certain enterprises, particularly insurance companies, which do not distinguish between current and long-term assets. This did not, however, lead the ASC to exclude such companies from ED 55. Instead, in the preface, the ASC indicated that it would welcome comments on whether such enterprises should be excluded from the scope of the proposed statement. In addition, in the explanatory note, it is stated that the development of this standard would not preclude the development of specific guidance for particular groups of enterprises or industries.

Proposed accounting treatment

16.100 The principal proposals of ED 55 are as follows:

- Current asset investments should be separated into two categories, those that are readily marketable and those that are not. Readily marketable investments should be 'marked to market', that is, carried at current market value. The adjustments resulting from marking to market should be recorded in the profit and loss account.

- Current investments that are not readily marketable may be valued at the lower of cost and net realisable value or, if the company wishes, they may be carried at current value with any revaluation surplus taken to a revaluation reserve.

- Fixed asset investments may be carried at original cost, less any provision for permanent impairment in value, or they may be revalued, on an annual basis, by following the provisions of ED 51, 'Accounting for fixed assets and revaluations'.

- Gains or losses on the sale of investments should be calculated by reference to the carrying value and recorded in the profit and loss account. Where a fixed asset investment is carried at a revalued amount, any amount remaining in the revaluation reserve in respect of the disposed investment will be transferred to the profit and loss reserve.

16.101 Whilst many of the exposure draft's recommendations were in line with the Act's requirements and existing practice, its recommendations in respect of gains or losses on the disposal of revalued investments and marking to market were seen by many as controversial. These proposals are considered in detail in chapter 5.

Recognising gains and losses on disposal

16.102 In the period since ED 55's publication, the ASB has issued FRS 3, 'Reporting financial performance'. This standard has effectively implemented the proposals of ED 55 in terms of recognising gains and losses on the disposal of revalued assets, including investments. FRS 3 requires that the profit and loss on disposal of an asset should be accounted for in the profit and loss account for the period in which the disposal occurs as the difference between the net sale proceeds and the net carrying amount, whether carried at historical cost (less any provisions made) or at a valuation. [FRS 3 para 21]. The requirements of FRS 3 are considered in detail in chapter 7.

Comparison with IASs

16.103 On the whole, the IASC rules in this area (in IAS 25) are similar to the UK rules. One difference is that fixed asset marketable securities should be valued at the lower of cost and market, determined on a portfolio basis. [IAS 25 para 23]. In parent company accounts, subsidiaries can be accounted for by the equity method which is not allowed in the UK. [IAS 27 para 22].

16.104 There are no UK rules on the transfer of fixed asset investments to current asset status. However, IAS 25 has rules on these transfers, depending on how current assets are held by the reporting entity. Transfers should be made at:

- the lower of cost and carrying amount, if the current investments were held at the lower of cost or market; or

- carrying amount, if the current investments were carried at market value.

[IAS 25 para 36].

Chapter 17

Current assets and liabilities

Page

Chapter 17

Current assets and liabilities

Introduction

17.1 This chapter deals with the accounting treatment and disclosure of current assets (other than current asset investments which are considered in chapter 16) and liabilities including provisions.

17.2 At first sight, current assets may seem to be an uncomplicated area as accounting for stocks, debtors and cash is normally relatively straightforward. However, there are areas that give rise to difficulties, for instance accounting for long-term contracts. Also FRS 5, 'Reporting the substance of transactions', has had considerable implications for current assets in areas such as factored debts, consignment stocks and sale and repurchase arrangements where current assets are retained on balance sheet either in full or as an interest in a residual.

17.3 FRS 5 has also had implications for liabilities, requiring many financings that were previously treated as off-balance sheet to be brought on. In addition to the above areas, examples include discounted bills of exchange and trade loans where companies bear the risks relating to loans taken out by customers.

17.4 In September 1998, the ASB published FRS 12, 'Provisions, contingent liabilities and contingent assets'. This introduces significant new rules governing what should be recognised as provisions in the balance sheet and it supersedes SSAP 18, 'Accounting for contingencies'. Only liabilities that exist at the balance sheet date can be recognised, which means that companies will not be able to carry general provisions or to provide for future expenditure that they can avoid by their future actions. The new rules apply form March 1999 year ends. They are not yet reflected comprehensively in this chapter except that a summary is given in paragraph 17.290.

17.5 In particular, this chapter deals with:

- The carrying value of stocks and complex transactions involving stock such as consignment stock and sale and repurchase of stocks.

- The treatment of long-term contracts including the carrying value of the contract and profit recognition.

- Accounting for transfers from current assets to fixed assets.
- Disclosure of debtors including long-term and factored debts.
- The definition and disclosure of cash at bank and in hand.
- Disclosure of certain current liabilities including trade creditors, bills of exchange and trade loans.
- The recognition of provisions for liabilities such as redundancies, onerous leases and environmental liabilities (pre-FRS 12).
- A summary of the new rules on provisions introduced by FRS 12 for periods ending on or after 23 March 1999.

Stocks

17.6 Stocks include goods or other assets purchased for resale, consumable stores, raw materials and components purchased for incorporation into products for sale, products and services in intermediate stages of completion, long-term contract balances and finished goods. [SSAP 9 para 16].

17.7 The amount at which stocks are stated in the financial statements should be the total of the lower of cost and net realisable value of the separate items of stock or of groups of similar items. [SSAP 9 para 26]. These items should be considered individually, as to compare the total realisable value of stocks with the total cost would result in an unacceptable setting off of foreseeable losses against unrealised profits. [4 Sch 14].

Definition of cost of stocks

17.8 Cost is defined as being that expenditure that has been incurred in the normal course of business in bringing the product or service to its present location and condition. This expenditure should include, in addition to cost of purchase, such costs of conversion as are appropriate to that location and condition. [SSAP 9 para 17]. Cost of purchase comprises purchase price including import duties, transport and handling costs and any other directly attributable costs, less trade discounts, rebates and subsidies. [SSAP 9 para 18].

17.9 Costs of conversion comprise:

- Costs that are specifically attributable to units of production, for example, direct labour, direct expenses and sub-contracted work.

- Production overheads, that is, those incurred in respect of materials, labour or services for production, based on the normal level of activity, taking one year with another.

- Other overheads, if any, attributable in the particular circumstances of the business to bringing the product or service to its present location and condition.

[SSAP 9 para 19].

17.10 The Act also allows interest to be included in cost if it relates to capital borrowed to finance the production of the asset insofar as it arises in the period of production. This is discussed in more detail in chapter 5.

17.11 Appendix 1 to SSAP 9 contains some guidance on the inclusion of overheads in cost of conversion. The adoption of a prudent approach to the valuation of stocks has sometimes been used to argue against the inclusion of overheads. SSAP 9 states that prudence will be taken into account in determining net realisable value and is not a reason for excluding overheads from the cost of stock. Having said that, the overheads that should be included are those arising from normal activity. All abnormal conversion costs (such as exceptional spoilage, idle capacity and other losses), which are avoidable under normal operating conditions, should be excluded.

17.12 The classification of overheads for the purpose of the allocation takes the function of the overhead as its distinguishing characteristic (for example, whether it is a function of production, marketing, selling or administration), rather than whether the overhead varies with time or with volume. The costs of general management, as distinct from functional management, are not directly related to current production and are, therefore, excluded from cost of conversion.

17.13 The Act states that distribution costs may not be included in production cost. [4 Sch 26(4)]. This means that a company should not include external distribution costs such as those relating to the transfer of goods from a sales depot to an external customer. It may, however, include a proportion of the costs that a company incurs in distributing goods from its factory to its sales depot as these are costs incurred in bringing the product to its present location.

17.14 An example of a retail company disclosing its methods of determining cost of sales and distribution costs is illustrated in Table 17.1. Cost of sales includes costs of transfer to the point of sale. For retailers, costs of transfer to the point of sale will often include a proportion of normal warehouse costs. Distribution costs include holding costs at the point of sale and costs of transfer to the customer.

Table 17.1 – Safeway plc – Annual Report and Accounts – 29 March 1997

Statement of Accounting Policies (extract)

Cost of sales and distribution costs

Cost of sales represents the purchase cost of goods for resale and includes the cost of transfer to the point of sale.

Distribution costs represent the cost of holding goods at the point of sale, selling costs and the costs of transferring goods to the customer and include store operating expenses.

Determination of cost

17.15 It is often not possible to relate expenditure to specific units of stock and so a near approximation has to be ascertained. This gives rise to two problems:

- The selection of an appropriate method for relating costs to stocks, for example:
  - Job costing.
  - Batch costing.
  - Process costing.
  - Standard costing.
- The selection of an appropriate method for calculating the related costs where a number of identical items have been purchased or made at different times.

17.16 The Act allows companies to use certain methods for arriving at the purchase price or the production cost of stocks and other 'fungible items'. For this purpose, 'fungible items' are those items that are indistinguishable one from another (for example, identical nuts and bolts). [4 Sch 27(6)].

17.17 Under the Act a company may adopt any of the following methods (but the method chosen must be the one which appears to the directors to be appropriate in the circumstances of the company):

- First-in, first-out (FIFO).
- Last-in, first-out (LIFO).
- Weighted average price.
- Any other similar method.

[4 Sch 27(1)(2)].

17.18 An example of a company using an average cost method is Cadbury Schweppes (see Table 17.2).

Table 17.2 – Cadbury Schweppes plc – Annual Report – 31 December 1997

Accounting Policies (extract)

(j) Stocks Stocks are valued at the lower of average cost and estimated net realisable value. Cost comprises direct material and labour costs together with the relevant factory overheads (including depreciation) on the basis of normal activity levels. In the case of cocoa, cost also reflects the use of the futures market on the basis of forecast physical requirements.

17.19 Under the FIFO method, the cost of stock is calculated on the basis that the quantities in hand represent the latest purchases or production. An example of a company using the FIFO method is Bass (see Table 17.3).

Table 17.3 – Bass PLC – Annual Report – 30 September 1994

Accounting Policies (extract)

Stocks

The basis of valuation is as follows:

i) Raw materials, bought-in-goods and consumable stores at the lower of cost and net realisable value on a first in, first out basis.

ii) Work in progress and finished stocks at the lower of cost, which includes an appropriate element of production overhead costs, and net realisable value.

Cost includes all expenditure incurred in bringing each product to its present condition and location. Net realisable value is based on estimated selling prices less further costs expected to be incurred in bringing the stocks to completion and disposal.

17.20 The example below illustrates the calculation of the value of stocks on both a FIFO basis and a weighted average price basis.

Example

Two companies, A and B, have identical opening and closing stocks and purchases in a particular year, as follows:

		Units	Values £
Opening stocks		100	835
Purchases	March	50	500
	July	100	1,150
	September	50	600
	December	150	2,000
Closing stocks		250	

Company A chooses to determine the value of its closing stocks by the FIFO method, and company B does so by the 'weighted average price' method. In these circumstances, the amount to be included in the balance sheets would be calculated as follows:

		£
Company A:		
150 @ £2,000 ÷ 150	=	2,000
50 @ £600 ÷ 50	=	600
50 @ £1,150 ÷ 100	=	575
		3,175
Company B:		
$\frac{835 + 500 + 1{,}150 + 600 + 2{,}000}{100 + 50 + 100 + 50 + 150}$ × 250 =		2,825

Either £3,175 or £2,825 is an acceptable answer even though significantly different. The selected method must be applied consistently in which case the difference, on a year on year basis, will matter less.

17.21 When choosing a method, the directors must ensure that the method they choose provides the fairest practicable approximation to 'actual cost'. SSAP 9 considers that the LIFO method (where the quantities in hand represent the earliest purchases or production) does not usually bear a reasonable relationship to actual cost and so LIFO is not an acceptable method of valuation in the UK.

17.22 Similarly, a base stock method is also not normally an acceptable method of stock valuation as it often results in stocks being stated in the balance sheet at amounts that bear little relationship to recent cost levels. Under this method, the cost of stocks is calculated on the basis that a fixed unit value is ascribed to a predetermined number of units of stock, any excess over this number being valued on the basis of some other method.

17.23 An example of a company that used LIFO and base stock methods for certain stocks but which changed to FIFO as it considered that departure from SSAP 9 was no longer justified is Cookson (see Table 17.4).

Table 17.4 – Cookson Group plc – Annual Report – 31 December 1993

Notes to the accounts

1 ACCOUNTING POLICIES (extract)

Stocks

All stocks are stated in the Group balance sheet at the lower of cost and net realisable value on the first in first out method. Cost comprises expenditure directly incurred in purchasing or manufacturing stocks together with, where appropriate, attributable overheads based on normal activity levels.

20 PRIOR YEAR ADJUSTMENTS (extract)

(c) Stock valuation

In previous years the valuation of certain stocks for the Group profit and loss account differed from that required by Statement of Standard Accounting Practice No. 9 (SSAP 9). These stocks were valued in the profit and loss account on the Base Stock or, for certain overseas subsidiaries, the Last In First Out (LIFO) method. As the market prices of the materials in question could fluctuate widely over a period, and because those companies were processors and not traders, the effects of such variations in stock values were not operating profits or losses. The use of the Base Stock and LIFO methods, together with covering arrangements for quantities in excess of Base Stock level, caused the profit and loss account to be charged with the current costs of the material consumed.

In recent years, as a result of the combined effects of changes in some of the products concerned, in procurement and also in the composition of the Group, the Directors believe that it is no longer warranted to apply policies for these stocks which differ from that required by SSAP 9. Accordingly all Group stocks are now valued on the basis explained in the Accounting Policies in Note 1 and in accordance with SSAP 9.

The results for 1992 have been restated in the Group profit and loss account, reducing the operating profit for that year by £3.7m. Had the previous policy been applied for 1993, the effect on the results would have been negligible.

17.24 Costs are often allocated to stocks by the use of a standard costing method. The cost of stocks is calculated on the basis of periodically predetermined costs derived from management's estimates of expected levels of costs and operational efficiency. The standard costs should be based on normal levels of operations and any abnormal costs or costs arising from inefficiencies should be written off in the period. Where standard costs are used they need to be reviewed frequently to ensure that they bear a reasonable relationship to actual costs arising during the period.

17.25 The method of arriving at cost by applying the latest purchase price to the total number of units in stock is unacceptable in principle because it is not necessarily the same as actual cost and, in times of rising prices, will result in the taking of profit that has not been realised.

17.26 One method of arriving at cost is the use of selling price less an estimated profit margin. This is acceptable only if it can be demonstrated that it gives a reasonable approximation of the actual cost. This method is often used by retailers with a large number of rapidly changing individual items in stores, for example, Tesco (see Table 17.5).

Table 17.5 – Tesco PLC – Annual report and financial statements – 28 February 1998

Accounting policies (extract)

Stocks
Stocks comprise goods held for resale and development properties, and are valued at the lower of cost and net realisable value. Stocks in stores are calculated at retail prices and reduced by appropriate margins to the lower of cost and net realisable value.

17.27 In industries where the production process results in minor by-products, the costs of the main products are calculated after deducting the net revenue from sales of the by-products. An example of this treatment is found in the accounts of Lonrho (see Table 17.6).

Table 17.6 – Lonrho Plc – Annual Report and Accounts – 30 September 1997

Statement on Accounting Policies (extract)
Stock and work in progress (extract)

Platinum group metal stock is valued using the by-product costing basis. Cost is allocated to platinum and rhodium stock based on the annual cost of production, less revenue from by-products, apportioned according to the quantities of each of the two metals produced.

Net realisable value of stocks

17.28 SSAP 9 requires that the figure of stocks disclosed in the financial statements should be the total of the lower of cost and net realisable value of the separate items of stock or of groups of similar items. [SSAP 9 para 26].

17.29 If there is no reasonable expectation of sufficient future revenue to cover cost incurred, the irrecoverable cost should be charged to revenue in the year under review. Net realisable value is the actual or estimated proceeds from the sale of items of stock (net of trade discounts, but before settlement discounts) less all further costs to completion and less all costs to be incurred in marketing, selling and distributing directly related to the items in question.

17.30 The principal situations in which net realisable value is likely to be less than cost are where there has been:

- An increase in costs or a fall in selling price.
- Physical deterioration of stocks.
- Obsolescence of products.
- A decision as part of a company's marketing strategy to manufacture and sell products at a loss.
- Errors in production or purchasing.

17.31 The initial calculation of provisions to reduce stocks from cost to net realisable value may often be made by the use of formulae based on predetermined criteria. The formulae normally take account of the age, movements in the past, expected future movements and estimated scrap values of the stock, as appropriate. Whilst the use of such formulae establishes a basis for making a provision which can be consistently applied, it is still necessary for the results to be reviewed in the light of any special circumstances that cannot be anticipated in the formulae, such as changes in the state of the order book.

17.32 Where a provision is required to reduce the value of finished goods below cost, the stocks of the parts and sub-assemblies held for the purpose of the manufacture of such products, together with stocks on order, need to be reviewed to determine if provision is also required against such items.

17.33 Events occurring between the balance sheet date and the date of completion of the financial statements need to be considered in arriving at the net realisable value at the balance sheet date (for example, a subsequent reduction in selling prices). However, a reduction is not necessary when the realisable value of material stocks is less than the purchase price, provided that the goods into which the materials are to be incorporated can still be sold at a profit after incorporating the materials at cost price.

Disclosure

17.34 The Act requires that stocks should be analysed between the following four categories:

- Raw materials and consumables.
- Work in progress.
- Finished goods and goods for resale.
- Payments on account – this represents the payments a company makes on account of stocks and not the payments it receives from customers.

[4 Sch formats].

17.35 A company should follow this categorisation so long as it produces true and fair financial statements. However, in certain circumstances, the special nature of a company's business may mean that the company needs to adapt the formats. Table 17.7 shows a company that has included additional categories for showhomes and part exchange properties within stocks.

Table 17.7 – Bellway p.l.c. – Annual Report – 31 July 1997

NOTES TO THE ACCOUNTS

10 Stocks	**1997**	1996
	£000	£000
Group		
Work in progress and stocks	**317,440**	281,793
Grants	**(13,061)**	(13,231)
Payments on account	**(4,986)**	(3,129)
	299,393	265,433
Showhomes	**14,560**	14,926
Part exchange properties	**5,760**	7,569
	319,713	287,928

17.36 The accounting policy that has been applied to stocks should be stated and applied consistently within the business and from year to year. [SSAP 9 para 32]. There is no requirement to state the methods used in calculating cost and net realisable value, but this is often done as best practice as illustrated above in Table 17.2 on page 5, Table 17.3 on page 5 and Table 17.4 on page 7.

Replacement value of stocks

17.37 Paragraph 27 of Schedule 4 says that, where the historical cost of stocks or fungible assets is calculated using a method permitted by the Act (that is, FIFO, LIFO, weighted average or any similar method), and that valuation differs materially from the 'relevant alternative amount' of those items, then the difference should be disclosed in a note to the financial statements.

17.38 The 'relevant alternative amount' will normally be the amount at which the assets would have been disclosed if their value had been determined according to their replacement cost as at the balance sheet date. [4 Sch 27(4)]. The replacement cost of these types of assets will normally be their current cost. However, a company may instead determine the relevant alternative amount according to the most recent actual purchase price or the most recent actual production cost of assets of that class before that date. But it can do this only where this method gives a more appropriate standard of comparison for assets of the class in question. [4 Sch 27(5)]. The Act leaves it to the company's directors to form an opinion as to whether the method does this. An example of the disclosure of replacement cost is found in the accounts of BP (see Table 17.8).

Table 17.8 – The British Petroleum Company p.l.c. – Annual Report and Accounts – 31 December 1997

Notes on accounts

21 Stocks

		£ million
	1997	1996
Petroleum	**2,003**	2,407
Chemicals	**253**	272
Other	**74**	64
	2,330	2,743
Stores	**251**	266
	2,581	3,009
Replacement cost	**2,621**	3,039

17.39 The example below considers the disclosure of the replacement cost of stocks. It uses the details from the previous example:

Example

Two companies, A and B, have identical opening and closing stocks and purchases in a particular year, but company A chooses to determine the value of its closing stocks by the FIFO method, and company B does so by the 'weighted average price' method. In these circumstances, the amount to be included in the balance sheets would be calculated as follows:

Company A:	£3,175
Company B:	£2,825

The value of the stocks at replacement cost is, say, £3,300.

If the difference between the balance sheet value of stocks and their replacement cost is material in the context of their balance sheet value, it must be disclosed under the requirement outlined in paragraph 17.37. The difference for company A is £125 (£3,300 – £3,175), which is unlikely to be considered material. The difference for company B is £475 (£3,300 – £2,825), which is likely to be considered material. If it is, it must be disclosed.

17.40 Counsel has advised that a 'method' is not used when stocks are valued at either their actual purchase price or their production cost. It would appear, therefore, that where companies value their stocks at actual purchase price or production cost, they do not need to disclose, in their financial statements, the difference between this value and the replacement value of those stocks.

17.41 In many situations, it is likely that some items of stocks will be valued by one of the methods mentioned above and that other items will be valued at actual purchase price or production cost. Where a company does this, the company will need to disclose not only the difference between the figure of stocks valued by a method and their replacement cost, but also the actual purchase price or production cost of the stocks it has valued by that method. Otherwise, it could be misleading for the company to disclose the figure that represents the difference, without also giving an indication of the proportion of the total stock value to which this difference relates.

Sale and repurchase of stocks

17.42 Sometimes stock is sold with an option to buy it back. The detailed terms of such options vary and indeed the options may sometimes be expressed at market value such that it is by no means certain that the options will be exercised. Perhaps more commonly, however, the option is constructed so that it is reasonably certain that it will be exercised. The arrangement may run for months, or even years, during which time the company that sold the stock will use the sale proceeds as a form of finance. The stock and the related purchase obligation (that is, the liability to repay the finance provided by the temporary holder of the stock) were often excluded from the balance sheet in the past.

17.43 Such arrangements are now covered by FRS 5 and are considered in detail in chapter 4. In summary, the true commercial effect of a transaction is a sale if the seller genuinely relinquishes control of significant benefits and transfers the exposure to significant risks associated with the asset to the buyer (for example, if the repurchase price is market value at the date of repurchase). However, a transaction structured so that in practice the purchaser secures a lender's return on the purchase price without genuine exposure to, or benefit from, changes in value of the underlying assets (for example, if the repurchase price is predetermined as original sale price plus an increment based on interest rates applied to the finance provided) should be treated as a financing arrangement.

Example

A company sells stock in year one for £100,000 and at the same time enters into an agreement to repurchase it a year later for £110,000. The £10,000 should not be treated as part of the cost of the stock, but represents interest, and should be charged to the profit and loss account.

If the company's year end fell halfway through the transaction, the company should initially show in its balance sheet stock of £100,000 and a financing liability of £100,000. Interest should be calculated at a constant rate on the carrying value of the liability although, if there was no significant difference, it could be assumed to accrue evenly throughout the period. In this case, interest of £5,000 should be accrued and charged to the profit and loss account.

Consideration would also need to be given as to whether the stock was slow moving and might, therefore, require a provision to reduce it to net realisable value.

17.44 FRS 5 recognises that, in more complex situations, it may be determined that a sale and repurchase agreement is not in substance a financing transaction and that the seller only retains access to some of the benefits of the original asset. In this circumstance, the partial derecognition rules in paragraph 23 of the standard might apply. If, for example, the buyer receives more than merely a lender's return, as other benefits and risks associated with the asset have been transferred to the buyer, the seller will not have retained the original asset. In this situation, the original asset should be derecognised and the analysis should determine whether another asset should be recognised in its place. For example, the seller might have an interest in the asset's residual value at the end of its life, in which case this asset should be recognised in the seller's balance sheet. An example of this can be found in the accounts of J Bibby & Sons, where FRS 5 has resulted in equipment sold with repurchase obligations being included in stocks as 'residual interests in equipment' (see Table 17.9).

Table 17.9 – J. Bibby & Sons PLC – Annual Report and Accounts – 24 September 1994

FINANCIAL REVIEW (extract)

FRS 5

The implementation of FRS 5 (Reporting the Substance of Transactions), which applies to accounting periods ending after 22nd September 1994, has resulted in bills and leases discounted with recourse and repurchase obligations for equipment sold being included on the balance sheet. All the transactions which gave rise to these items were entered into entirely within the normal course of business and have been included in debtors or stocks on the one hand and creditors on the other hand. The amounts are as follows:

	1994			1993		
	Total £000's	Recourse commitments £000's	Repurchase obligations £000's	Total £000's	Recourse commitments £000's	Repurchase obligations £000's
Under one year	25,477	21,241	4,236	27,195	25,296	1,899
Over one year	12,593	508	12,085	6,989	1,253	5,736
	38,070	21,749	16,321	34,184	26,549	7,635

The repurchase obligations enable our Capital Equipment and Materials Handling Divisions to re-acquire equipment, which has usually been maintained by themselves, at the end of primary periods thus providing opportunities in the used equipment market.

NOTES TO THE ACCOUNTS (extract)

9 Stocks (extract)	**1994 £000's**	1993 £000's
Raw materials	**20,183**	22,080
Work in progress	**8,470**	9,722
Finished goods	**67,985**	73,115
Livestock	**142**	7,530
Residual interests in equipment	**16,321**	7,635
	113,101	120,082

17.45 The notes to the financial statements should include the following information concerning all sale and repurchase transactions:

- The transaction's principal features. [FRS 5 App B paras B19 and B21].

- The asset's status. [FRS 5 App B paras B19 and B21].

  For example, disclosure that an asset has been legally sold to another party, but has been retained on balance sheet.

- The relationship between the asset and the liability. [FRS 5 App B paras B19 and B21].

Again, where an asset has been legally sold, but has been retained on balance sheet because the transaction is considered to be a financing arrangement, the notes should explain how the finance is connected with the asset (for example, whether it is non-recourse).

17.46 An example of stock retained on balance sheet where it has been legally sold is seen in Table 17.10.

Table 17.10 – Galliford plc – REPORT AND ACCOUNTS – 30 June 1995

NOTES TO THE ACCOUNTS

21 Business Expansion Scheme

Since entering into a commitment on 23 March 1993 to promote a Business Expansion Scheme ('BES'), the group has sold interests in 101 properties to a BES company, B.EXBES I Plc. Under the terms of the scheme, the group has guaranteed a minimum return to investors in the BES company through the payment on 5 April 1998 of £5.9m for either its entire issued share capital or for the properties transferred.

The BES properties are held in the balance sheet at their original cost (including attributable overheads) as 'BES assets' within stocks (see note 14), and the sale proceeds recieved from the BES company as a deferred creditor (see note 17).

The finance charge implicit in the BES arrangements, calculated by reference to the difference between the sale proceeds received and the guaranteed payment to the BES investors to be made on 5 April 1998 (as explained above), has been determined and an accrual for an appropriate proportion to date has been made in these accounts (see note 7).

The net rental income arising from the BES properties is disclosed in note 4.

14 Stocks	Parent		Group	
	1995	1994	**1994**	1993 Restated
	£'000	£'000	**£'000**	£'000
Raw materials and consumables	**10**	7	**1,580**	1,724
Work in progress	–	–	**29,147**	22,347
BES assets (note 21)	–	–	**4,137**	4,137
Finished goods and goods for resale	–	–	**364**	1,282
	10	7	**35,228**	29,490

17 Creditors: amounts falling due after more than one year (extract)

	Parent		Group	
	1995	1994	**1995**	1994
	£'000	£'000	**£'000**	£'000
Bank loan	**–**	–	**187**	250
Monies advanced under BES arrangements (note 21)	**–**	–	**4,543**	4,543
Trade creditors	**–**	–	**296**	445
Other creditors	**10**	21	**442**	379
	10	21	**5,468**	5,617

17.47 Where the substance of the transaction is that the seller has a different asset, then, in addition to the disclosure set out in paragraph 17.45, 17.45, the terms of any provision for repurchase (including any options) and of any guarantees should be disclosed. [FRS 5 App B para B21]. Disclosure of repurchase obligations in respect of residual interests in equipment is shown in Table 17.9 on page 14.

Consignment stock

17.48 Arrangements where goods are supplied from a manufacturer to a dealer on a consignment basis are common in certain industries, particularly in the motor vehicle trade. Application Note A to FRS 5 shows how the principles of recognising assets and liabilities should be applied to these arrangements.

Objective of consigning stocks

17.49 The objective of both parties to a consignment stock arrangement is to enable the dealer to sell as many units of the product as possible. The dealer is often given some incentive by the manufacturer through various bonus schemes to ensure that the volume of items sold is as high as possible. The consignment arrangement serves to achieve this objective and benefit both parties.

17.50 However, under such arrangements the manufacturer (or a financier) generally retains title to the goods supplied to the dealer until some predetermined event occurs. This may be when the dealer sells the goods or has held them for a set period, or some other event triggers the dealer's adoption of the goods (that is, when he pays for them and acquires title). But the date that title transfers tends to be some time after the date that the stock item is physically transferred to the dealer. Title will generally pass on receipt of cleared funds (but not to the dealer if he has already sold the vehicle on).

17.51 The standard's application note seeks to determine the point at which the dealer has in substance acquired an asset that should be recognised on its balance sheet (that is, whether it is when legal title passes or at some other time).

Principal sources of benefits and risks

17.52 In practice, the terms of consignment agreements vary considerably in important respects, for example: the right of return by the dealer; the determination of the sale price, known as the transfer price; and the terms under which deposits are required to be made by the dealer to the manufacturer or a requirement for the dealer to pay interest (which is in substance indicative of an advance of finance). These are normally the most important factors to be considered in the analysis. Other aspects of consignment transactions such as rights of inspection, responsibility for damage and loss or theft and related insurance are of less importance.

17.53 The standard analyses the principal benefits and risks associated with consignment stock arrangements from the point of view of the dealer to determine whether the stock should appear on the dealer's balance sheet. The application note identifies four principal sources of benefits and risks, which need to be considered in the analysis:

- Manufacturer's right of return.
- Dealer's right of return.
- Stock transfer price and deposits.
- Dealer's right to use stock.

17.54 These principal sources of benefits and risks are then considered in detail in the application note and the principles stemming from that discussion are summarised in a table. The summary table is reproduced below, but with the principal sources of benefits and risks added as headings; also included are references to the paragraphs of the application note that give the narrative explanation:

Indicates stock is not an asset of the dealer at delivery	**Indicates stock is an asset of the dealer at delivery**
Manufacturer's right of return [App A para A5].	
Manufacturer can require the dealer to return stock (or transfer stock to another dealer) without compensation, or	Manufacturer cannot require dealer to return or transfer stock, or
Penalty paid by the dealer to prevent returns/transfers of stock at the manufacturer's request.	Financial incentives given to persuade dealer to transfer stock at manufacturer's request.

Dealer's right of return [App A para A6].	
Dealer has unfettered right to return stock to the manufacturer without penalty and actually exercises the right in practice.	Dealer has no right to return stock or is commercially compelled not to exercise its right of return.
Manufacturer bears obsolescence risk, for example: – obsolete stock is returned to the manufacturer without penalty; or – financial incentives given by manufacturer to prevent stock being returned to it (for example, on a model change or if it becomes obsolete).	Dealer bears obsolescence risk, for example: – penalty charged if dealer returns stock to manufacturer; or – obsolete stock cannot be returned to the manufacturer and no compensation is paid by manufacturer for losses due to obsolescence.
Stock transfer price and deposits	
Stock transfer price charged by manufacturer is based on manufacturer's list price at date of transfer of legal title. [App A para A7].	Stock transfer price charged by manufacturer is based on manufacturer's list price at date of delivery. [App A para A7].
Manufacturer bears slow movement risk, for example: – transfer price set independently of time for which dealer holds stock, and there is no deposit. [App A para A8].	Dealer bears slow movement risk, for example: – dealer is effectively charged interest as transfer price or other payments to manufacturer vary with time for which dealer holds stock; [App A para A8]. or – dealer makes a substantial interest-free deposit that varies with the levels of stock held. [App A para A9].

17.55 One of the principal sources of benefits and risks is not dealt with in the table above and that concerns the dealer's right to use the stock. The existence of a right by the dealer to use consignment stock will not normally of itself require the stock to be recorded on the dealer's balance sheet. However, once that right is exercised and the dealer uses the stock (for example, as a demonstration model) and once he has paid for it this generally causes the legal title to be transferred to the dealer and thus the stock to be recognised on its balance sheet.

17.56 The analysis of a consignment stock agreement will often give conflicting indications, as some aspects of the transaction might indicate that the stock should be put on the dealer's balance sheet while other aspects might indicate that it should remain off. In such a circumstance, one of the important factors will be to determine who pays the finance/interest cost of holding the stock. If the dealer pays an interest cost or another charge that varies with the time the stock is held (sometimes referred to by some other name, for example, display charge) then this strongly indicates that the dealer has an obligation and hence a liability that should be recognised in the dealer's financial statements. The related asset may only be an 'interest in consignment stock', but should be recorded as such until the dealer adopts the stock when that interest will convert to recognising the actual consignment stock on balance sheet. These principles are explained more fully in the example in paragraph 17.61.

Accounting treatment

17.57 The accounting treatment in the dealer's books specified in the standard is as follows. If the analysis shows that the asset should be recorded on the dealer's balance sheet then the double entry is:

Dr Stock or interest in stock	£10,000	
Cr Liabilities – trade creditors		£10,000

To record the consignment stock brought onto the dealer's balance sheet.

17.58 Where the dealer has paid a deposit to the manufacturer for the consignment then this amount should be deducted from the liability to the manufacturer and the balance shown within trade creditors (assuming the asset and liability comply with the offset rules in FRS 5.

17.59 The notes to the financial statements should give the following information:

- An explanation of the nature of the arrangement.
- The amount of the consignment stock.
- The main terms under which the consignment is held.
- The terms of any related deposit.

[FRS 5 App A para A12].

17.60 Where the analysis of the transaction indicates that the stock should remain off the dealer's balance sheet, then the dealer should still give in the notes to the financial statements the information set out in paragraph 17.59. If the dealer has paid a deposit to the manufacturer, then this should be included within 'other debtors' on the balance sheet.

Example of required analysis

17.61 Application Note A does not give any examples of how to apply the analysis, but the example that follows illustrates the types of feature that might underlie a typical consignment arrangement and how the analysis under FRS 5 would determine how to account for the arrangement.

Example

A motor manufacturer enters into an arrangement with its dealers to consign stock to them. The agreement is the same for each dealer in the network. The basic principles of the consignment are as follows:

- The dealer orders and is allocated stock by the manufacturer under a consignment agreement and, in most cases, the stock is physically located at the dealer's premises. The manufacturer can reward or penalise dealers through the allocation of consignment stock.

- Title to the stock does not pass until the dealer has paid for the stock. The obligation to pay will arise on the earlier of:

  - The date of sale of the vehicle to the customer.
  - The date of adoption of stock (for example, as a demonstration model).
  - 180 days.

- A third party finance house has a separate agreement with the manufacturer and dealer, whereby the manufacturer receives a payment from the finance house, by way of a deposit, for all vehicles consigned to the dealer. The dealer has to pay a funding cost to the finance house based on the value of the vehicles consigned to it, which is set at 3% above LIBOR. There is a free stocking period of two months, where there is no finance charge to the dealer for the consignment stock (the finance cost being paid by the manufacturer).

- At any point, until the dealer adopts the stock or sells it or the 180 days has passed, the stock may be returned to the manufacturer, exchanged or transferred to another dealer in the manufacturer's network. This ensures that the dealer has access to the complete range of manufacturer's stock. In practice, stock is rarely returned to the manufacturer (only about 1% of vehicles consigned). In rare circumstances the manufacturer will request the return of a vehicle to fulfil a particular order elsewhere. In this situation no benefit accrues to the dealer. However, as much as 30% of stock is transferred between dealers generally by receiving a similar model in exchange.

- If a model is not selling well, then approaching its adoption date, the dealer can take one of the following actions:

- Exchange it or transfer it to another dealer who may have a demand for that particular vehicle.
- Negotiate an extension of the adoption date with the manufacturer.
- Give an incentive to sell the stock, which might be supported by the manufacturer where the model is performing badly (for example, giving one year's free insurance).

- The transfer price is set at the adoption date by reference to the manufacturer's list price. However, prices on older models may be held to enable the dealer to discount his selling price.

It can be seen that such agreements can be very complex and very difficult to analyse in practice. Considering the principal benefits and risks the transaction can be analysed as follows:

	Off B/sheet	**On B/sheet**
Manufacturer's right to return		
Manufacturer can require dealer to return stock or transfer stock without compensation.	✓	
Dealer's right to return		
Dealer does have a right to return stock to the manufacturer without penalty, but because of the incidence of transfers between dealers, does not need to effect this right often.	✓	
Financial incentives are given by the manufacturer to prevent stock being returned in the event that a model becomes obsolete.	✓	
Regular exchanges or transfers between dealers.	✓	
Consignment period extended with agreement of the manufacturer.	✓	
Stock transfer price and deposits		
Stock transfer price is based on the manufacturer's list price at the date of adoption of the vehicle.	✓	

After the initial stocking period, which is interest free, the dealer pays the finance house a finance cost which varies with the level of stock held and as a consequence bears slow movement risk.		✓

It is necessary to consider the results of the analysis very carefully. It is not merely a matter of counting the ticks in the left hand column and those in the right hand column to determine which presentation wins. It is a matter of determining which of the parties bears the benefits and risks of ownership. It would appear that the manufacturer has retained the risk of obsolescence in this example, but the risk of slow movement falls to the dealer. This is a real risk as interest is paid following the period of free stocking. Therefore, after the free stocking period is complete (that is, after two months), the dealer has a risk which gives rise to an obligation that needs to be recognised by the dealer. Analysing this risk using the standard's definition of a liability, it is clear that the obligation should be recorded in the dealer's balance sheet as such at the end of the free stocking period and at an amount that equates to the deposit on which the interest is being paid. The corresponding asset could be disclosed as an 'interest in consignment stock' and would be recorded at the same amount. When the consignment stock is adopted it should then be recorded as stock of the dealer. Adoption will either take place for demonstration purposes or for onward sale.

17.62 As illustrated in the example, the interest payments in this particular transaction represent an obligation to transfer economic benefits and, as a consequence, a liability for them arises, which is in substance a loan. Under the standard, the loan should be recognised in the financial statements if it can be measured with sufficient reliability. The 'loan' would, therefore, be recorded in the dealer's balance sheet and an asset recognised which represents the dealer's interest in the consignment stock. In a study carried out for the motor industry on the impact of FRED 4, the exposure draft that preceded FRS 5, this test was seen as the primary test and has been termed the 'liability test'.

17.63 Alternatively, the analysis might have indicated that the dealer bore the risks and rewards of ownership of the stock and, as a consequence, the consignment stock itself (rather than just an interest in it) should be recorded on the dealer's balance sheet and the related finance recorded as a liability (known as the 'asset test'). Consequently, an asset (either the vehicle or an interest in it) and the corresponding liability should be accounted for on balance sheet at the earlier of: (a) the date the asset test is passed; and (b) the date the liability test is passed. However, the figure for the interest in stock recorded following the liability test will not necessarily be the same amount as the consignment stock recognised following the asset test.

Manufacturer's position

17.64 There is no discussion in the standard of the accounting treatment in the manufacturer's financial statements and its treatment cannot be assumed to be the reverse of that adopted in the dealer's books. For example, the manufacturer might recognise the physical stock in its financial statements while the dealer recognises an interest in that stock. Furthermore, there are no specific disclosures required to be given by the manufacturer in its financial statements other than the general requirement of paragraph 30 of FRS 5, which requires that the disclosure should be sufficient to enable the user of the financial statements to understand the transaction's commercial effect.

17.65 Revenue recognition by the manufacturer has to be decided on its own merits. The date that the dealer records the interest in the stock in its financial statements is not necessarily the date from which the manufacturer would recognise its revenue on sale of the stock. In the example in paragraph 17.61, the effect is that:

- In the period prior to the end of the free stocking period the manufacturer holds 'stock' whilst the dealer has no asset. The manufacturer will benefit from the deposit advanced by the finance company and pay interest to the finance company.

- In the period between the end of the free stocking period and the adoption date the manufacturer holds 'stock' whilst the dealer also holds an 'interest in consignment stock'. In this period the manufacturer will benefit from the deposit advanced by the finance company and will not pay interest to the finance company as this is paid by the dealer.

- In the above example, the manufacturer recognises revenue at the date the consignment stock is adopted (which is when all the risks and rewards of ownership are transferred).

Conclusion

17.66 Obviously, as mentioned above, the terms of consignment stock agreements differ significantly. It must be stressed, therefore, that the analysis of these transactions needs to be undertaken very carefully in conjunction with the detailed application note in FRS 5.

Goods with reservation of title

17.67 It is quite common for companies that sell goods to other companies to have reservation of title clauses included in their contracts. This enables the selling company to retain ownership of those goods until the purchaser has paid for them. Such clauses are often known as 'Romalpa clauses' following the Romalpa case (*Aluminium*

Industrie Vaassen B.V. v Romalpa Aluminium Limited [1976] 1 WLR 676) in 1976, which was concerned with contractual relationships. The main effect of trading with reservation of title is that the position of the unpaid seller may be improved if the purchaser becomes insolvent. However, whether an effective reservation of title exists depends upon the construction of the particular contract.

17.68 Even if there is an effective reservation of title clause, on a going concern basis it is common practice for the purchaser to recognise such stocks in its balance sheet, although the supplier retains legal title to the goods. The liability to the supplier is also recognised. This was first recommended in guidance issued by ICAEW in 1976, 'Accounting for goods subject to reservation of title'. It is consistent with FRS 5 as it is the purchaser who bears the risks and benefits from the rewards of the asset.

17.69 The ICAEW guidance recommended that where the financial statements are materially affected by the accounting treatment adopted in relation to sales or purchases subject to reservation of title, the treatment should be disclosed and a note indicating the amount of liabilities that are subject to reservation of title clauses be given, where quantifiable. An example of such disclosure is given in Table 17.11.

Table 17.11 – CHARNOS plc – Annual Report and Accounts – 31 December 1988

Notes on the accounts

16 Creditors – amounts falling due within one year (extract)

Part of the amount owing to trade creditors is or may be secured by the reservation by the supplier of legal title to the goods supplied and to the proceeds of their sale. The amount secured in this way depends on the legal interpretation of individual contracts and cannot readily be determined. In the opinion of the directors, the maximum amount likely to be involved is £1,150,000 (group) and £400,000 (company).

17.70 However, in practice, this note is often not given where the purchasing company is a going concern such that the likelihood of the reservation of title clause crystallising is remote. Whether or not disclosure is necessary in order to give a true and fair view will be a matter for judgement. FRS 5 requires sufficient details of a transaction to be given to enable the user to understand its commercial effect. [FRS 5, para 30]. It also requires an explanation where the nature of assets and liabilities differs from those items normally included under the relevant balance sheet headings. An example would be where the company did not have legal title to assets and disclosure of this fact was necessary for a true and fair view to be given.

Long-term contracts

17.71 Long-term contracts need to be considered separately, because of the length of time taken to complete such contracts. The main accounting issue is the allocation of turnover and costs to the accounting periods in which work is carried out. To defer recording turnover and not to take account of profit until completion of the contract may result in the profit and loss account reflecting not so much a fair view of the results of the activity of the company during the year, but rather a view of the results relating to contracts that have been completed in the year. It is, therefore, appropriate to take credit for ascertainable turnover and profit while contracts are in progress.

Definition of long-term contracts

17.72 A 'long-term contract' is defined in SSAP 9 as follows:

> *"A contract entered into for the design, manufacture or construction of a single substantial asset or the provision of a service (or of a combination of assets or services which together constitute a single project) where the time taken substantially to complete the contract is such that the contract activity falls into different accounting periods. A contract that is required to be accounted for as long-term by this accounting standard will usually extend for a period exceeding one year. However, a duration exceeding one year is not an essential feature of a long-term contract. Some contracts with a shorter duration than one year should be accounted for as long-term contracts if they are sufficiently material to the activity of the period that not to record turnover and attributable profit would lead to a distortion of the period's turnover and results such that the financial statements would not give a true and fair view, provided that the policy is applied consistently within the reporting entity and from year to year."* [SSAP 9 para 22].

17.73 A situation where a contract of duration of less than one year might be treated as long-term is, for example, when a company completes a material short-term contract just after the year end, but a substantial amount of work on the contract had been completed before the year end. If an element of turnover and profit is not attributed to the current period, this might distort that period's turnover and results to such an extent that they do not give a true and fair view.

Accounting treatment of long-term contracts

17.74 Long-term contracts should be assessed on a contract by contract basis and reflected in the profit and loss account by recording turnover and related costs as contract activity progresses. Turnover is ascertained in a manner appropriate to the stage of completion of the contract, the business and the industry in which it operates. [SSAP 9 para 28].

17.75 Where it is considered that the outcome of a long-term contract can be assessed with reasonable certainty before its conclusion, the prudently calculated attributable profit should be recognised in the profit and loss account as the difference between the reported turnover and related costs for that contract. [SSAP 9 para 29].

Turnover

17.76 No definition of turnover is provided in SSAP 9; it merely states that turnover is ascertained in a manner appropriate to the stage of completion of the contract, the business and the industry in which it operates and it is left to individual companies to determine according to their own circumstances. However, amounts taken through the profit and loss account in an accounting period would normally relate to separate or measurable parts of the contract completed within that period. Appendix 1 to the standard states that turnover may sometimes be ascertained by reference to the valuation of work carried out to date. In other situations, there may be specific points during a contract where individual elements of work done will have separately ascertainable sales values, where costs can be identified and, therefore, turnover can be recorded as appropriate. This could be, for example, when delivery or when customer acceptance takes place.

17.77 Although there is no definition of turnover in the revised standard, the standard does require that, in particular, the means of ascertaining turnover, should be disclosed as an accounting policy. [SSAP 9 para 32]. An example of such disclosure is found in the accounts of Rolls-Royce, (see Table 17.12) and Wimpey (see Table 17.16 on page 39).

Table 17.12 – Rolls-Royce plc – Annual Report – 31 December 1994

Notes to the Financial Statements

Accounting policies (extract)

Turnover

Turnover excludes value added tax. Long-term contracts are included in turnover on the basis of the sales value of work performed during the year by reference to the total sales value and stage of completion of these contracts.

Recognition of profit

17.78 The profit and loss account should only include profit when the outcome of a particular contract can be ascertained with reasonable certainty (that is, where it is reasonable to foresee profits in advance of the completion of a contract). This is often a difficult exercise to undertake in practice. In addition, the standard comments that this judgement of future profitability should be exercised with prudence. [SSAP 9 para 29].

17.79 In some businesses, long-term contracts for the supply of services or goods exist where the prices are determined and invoiced according to separate parts of the contract. IAS 11, 'Construction contracts', contains guidance on when a long-term contract should be accounted for as separate stages. Each stage should be treated as a separate contract where:

- Separate proposals have been submitted for each stage.
- Each stage has been subject to separate negotiation and the contractor and customer are able to accept or reject that part of the contract.
- The costs and revenues of each stage can be identified.

[IAS 11 para 8].

17.80 In these businesses the most appropriate method of reflecting profits on each contract is usually to match costs against performance of the separable parts of the contract, treating each such separable part as a separate contract. In such instances, however, future revenues from the total contract need to be compared with future estimated costs and provision made for any foreseeable loss. [SSAP 9 app 1 para 22].

17.81 More commonly, the separate stages of a long-term contract will fall to be treated as a single contract. The separate stages should be treated as a single contract when:

- The stages are negotiated as a single package.
- The stages are so closely interrelated that they are, in effect, part of a single project with an overall profit margin.
- The stages are performed concurrently or in a continuous sequence.

17.82 The procedure to recognise profit is to include an appropriate proportion of total contract value as turnover in the profit and loss account as the contract activity progresses. The costs incurred in reaching that stage of completion are matched with this turnover, resulting in the reporting of results that can be attributed to the proportion of work completed.

17.83 The turnover recognised on a particular contract will depend on the state of completion of that contract. For example, when, in the contract's early stages, it is not possible to foresee its outcome with reasonable certainty, turnover will normally equal the costs incurred that are charged to cost of sales. Therefore, no profit will be recognised in the profit and loss account. However, when in the later stages of a contract, the outcome can be assessed with reasonable certainty, turnover should include profit prudently recognised as earned at that stage of completion.

17.84 In practice, there appear to be two basic approaches to determining attributable profit:

- The actual profit calculated by comparing the priced 'bill of quantities' to a contractor's own internal costing of the project. The 'bill of quantities' is a document prepared at the tender stage showing specifications set out in terms of quantities and values.

- By calculating total anticipated profit to completion of the contract and 'attributing' a reasonable portion to the work carried out. This might be done by reference to the cost of work incurred to date and the cost estimated to complete the contract ('the percentage of completion method').

17.85 In addition, some companies prefer to take a more prudent approach, and show profit only on that portion of work inspected and accepted by the contracting parties.

17.86 The figures to be included in the year's profit and loss account will be both the appropriate amount of turnover and the associated costs of achieving that turnover, to the extent that these exceed amounts recognised in previous years. The estimated outcome of a contract that extends over several accounting years will nearly always vary in the light of changes in circumstances and for this reason the result of the year will not necessarily represent the profit on the contract which is appropriate to the amount of work carried out in the period. It may also reflect the effect of changes in circumstances during the year that affect the total profit estimated to accrue on completion. This is illustrated in the following example.

Example

A construction contractor has a fixed price contract for £11,500. The initial estimate of costs is £7,500 and the contract is expected to take four years. In year two the contractor's estimate of total costs increases to £8,000. Of the £500 increase, £300 is to be incurred in year three and the remainder in year four.

The contractor determines the stage of completion of the contract by comparing the costs of work to date with the estimated total costs.

	Year 1 £	Year 2 £	Year 3 £	Year 4 £
Turnover agreed in contract	11,500	11,500	11,500	11,500
Contract costs incurred to date	3,000	4,500	6,675	8,000
Contract costs to complete	4,500	3,500	1,325	–
Total estimated costs	7,500	8,000	8,000	8,000
Estimated profit	4,000	3,500	3,500	3,500
Stage of completion	40%	56.3%	83.4%	100%
	(3,000 ÷ 7,500)	(4,500 ÷ 8,000)	(6,675 ÷ 8,000)	

The amount of turnover, costs and profit recognised in the profit and loss account in the four years is as follows:

	To date	Prior years	Current year	Margin
Year 1				
Turnover (11,500 × 40%)	4,600		4,600	
Costs (7,500 × 40%)	3,000		3,000	
Profit	1,600		1,600	(35%)
Year 2				
Turnover (11,500 × 56.3%	6,475	4,600	1,875	
Costs (8,000 × 56.3%)	4,504	3,000	1,504	
Profit	1,971	1,600	371	(20%)

Year 3				
Turnover (11,500 × 83.4%)	9,591	6,475	3,116	
Costs (8,000 × 83.4%)	6,672	4,504	2,168	
Profit	2,919	1,971	948	(30%)
Year 4				
Turnover	11,500	9,591	1,909	
Costs	8,000	6,672	1,328	
Profit	3,500	2,919	581	(30%)

The profit margin in year two (that is, 20%) is lower than in the subsequent years (that is, 30%) because it takes account of the fact that in the light of the revised estimates, too much profit has been taken in year one when the total estimated costs were lower.

If the initial cost estimates had been £8,000, then the percentage completion at the end of year one would have been 37.5% (that is, 3,000 ÷ 8,000). This means that turnover of £4,313 (£11,500 × 37.5%) would have been attributed to the costs incurred to date of £3,000 giving a profit of £1,313 compared with the reported profit of £1,600. The turnover recognised in year two is that attributed to the total costs incurred to date, calculated on the basis of the revised estimates, less the turnover of £4,600 reported in year one. Therefore, the results in year two reflect the fact that an adjustment is necessary in respect of year one.

17.87 Contract costs are usually recognised as an expense in the period in which the work to which they relate is performed. Only if the costs relate to future activity should they be carried forward as work in progress. Equally, if costs incurred to date are used to determine the percentage completion, then turnover attributed to work carried out should not be increased to offset additional costs incurred where these represent inefficiencies. SSAP 9 states that the profit accounted for needs to reflect the proportion of the work carried out at the accounting date and to take into account any known inequalities of profitability in the various stages of a contract. [SSAP 9 para 9]. This is illustrated by the following example.

Example

A construction contractor has a fixed price contract for £11,500. The initial estimate of costs is £7,500 the contract is expected to take four years. In year two the contractor's estimate of total costs increases to £8,000 as a result of inefficiencies in year two.

The contractor determines the stage of completion of the contract by comparing the costs of work to date with the estimated total costs.

Method one

	Year 1	Year 2	Year 3	Year 4
	£	£	£	£
Turnover agreed in contract	11,500	11,500	11,500	11,500
Contract costs incurred to date	3,000	5,000	6,875	8,000
Contract costs to complete	4,500	3,500	1,125	–
Total estimated costs	7,500	8,000	8,000	8,000
Estimated profit	4,000	3,500	3,500	3,500
Stage of completion	40%	62.5%	85.9%	100%
	(3,000 ÷ 7,500)	(5,000 ÷ 8,000)	(6,875 ÷ 8,000)	

The amount of turnover, costs and profit recognised in the profit and loss account in the four years under this method would be as follows:

	To date	Prior years	Current year	Margin
Year 1				
Turnover (11,500 × 40%)	4,600		4,600	
Costs (7,500 × 40%)	3,000		3,000	
Profit	1,600		1,600	(35%)
Year 2				
Turnover (11,500 × 62.5%)	7,188	4,600	2,588	
Costs (8,000 × 62.5%)	5,000	3,000	2,000	
Profit	2,188	1,600	588	(23%)
Year 3				
Turnover (11,500 × 85.9%)	9,879	7,190	2,689	
Costs (8,000 × 85.9%)	6,872	5,000	1,872	
Profit	3,007	2,190	817	(30%)
Year 4				
Turnover	11,500	9,879	1,621	
Costs	8,000	6,872	1,128	
Profit	3,500	3,007	493	(30%)

Under this method the profit in year two is reduced as a result of the inefficiencies. However, part of this inefficiency is being spread forward into years three and four as is evident from the reduced profit margins of 30% compared with 35% in the initial estimates.

In view of the fact that the increased costs result from inefficiencies in year two, there is an argument that it is not prudent to spread the effect of this.

Method two

	Year 1	Year 2	Year 3	Year 4
	£	£	£	£
Contract costs incurred to date	3,000	5,000	6,875	8,000
Total estimated costs	7,500	8,000	8,000	8,000
Stage of completion (Ignoring inefficiencies of £500)	40%	60%	85%	100%
	(3,000 ÷ 7,500)	(4,500 ÷ 7,500)	(6,375 ÷ 7,500)	

The amount of turnover, costs and profit recognised in the profit and loss account in the four years under this method would be as follows:

		To date	Prior years	Current year	Margin
Year 1					
Turnover (11,500 × 40%)		4,600		4,600	
Costs (7,500 × 40%)		3,000		3,000	
Profit		1,600		1,600	(35%)
Year 2					
Turnover (11,500 × 60%)		6,900	4,600	2,300	
Costs:	normal (7,500 × 60%)	4,500	3,000	1,500	
	inefficiencies	500	–	500	
		5,000	3,000	2,000	
Profit		1,900	1,600	300	(13%)
Year 3					
Turnover (11,500 × 85%)		9,775	6,900	2,875	
Costs:	normal (7,500 × 85%)	6,375	4,500	1,875	
	inefficiencies	500	500	–	
		6,875	5,000	1,875	
Profit		2,900	1,900	1,000	(35%)
Year 4					
Turnover		11,500	9,775	1,725	
Costs		8,000	6,875	1,125	
Profit		3,500	2,900	600	(35%)

This method is preferred because the inefficiencies are charged to the period in which they are incurred leaving a 'normal' contract profit margin in the subsequent periods.

17.88 No matter what method of determining attributable profit is adopted, it should be applied consistently and from year to year. Paragraph 32 of SSAP 9 requires that the method of ascertaining attributable profits should be stated in the accounting policies. This means that the basis of calculation should be disclosed. An example of a company with an accounting policy note giving details of the method of ascertaining attributable profit is Verson International Group which uses the percentage of completion method (see Table 17.13).

Table 17.13 – Verson International Group plc – Annual Report – 31 January 1994

Accounting Policies (extract)

f) *Stocks and long-term contracts*

In the case of long-term contracts where the group's involvement is principally as a manufacturer, rather than contract manager, turnover represents the estimated contract revenues on work during the year. Contract revenues and profits are computed on the percentage of completion method, primarily by reference to labour hours, profits being determined after making reserves against all anticipated costs including possible warranty claims.

Where the group's involvement in a long-term contract is principally as a contract manager, turnover reflects costs incurred to date in establishing and managing the contract plus the directors' best estimate of profits attributable to the work performed to date. For this purpose the directors' estimate of attributable profits will include a proportion of the total profits anticipated to be made on the contract, to the extent that their realisation is reasonably foreseeable, and after making provision for all future costs including all possible warranty claims.

Long-term contract balances included in stocks comprise costs incurred on long-term contracts, net of amounts transferred to cost of sales, after deducting foreseeable losses and related payments on account. Costs include all direct material and labour costs incurred in bringing a contract to its state of completion at the year end, including an appropriate proportion of indirect expenses. Provisions for estimated losses on contracts are made in the period in which such losses are foreseen. Long-term contract balances do not include attributable profit.

The excess of payments received over amounts recorded as turnover is classified under creditors due within one year. Amounts recoverable on contracts, being the amount by which recorded turnover is in excess of payments on account, is classified under debtors.

Other stocks are stated at the lower of cost and net realisable value.

Provision is made for obsolete, slow-moving or defective items where appropriate.

Determination of future costs

17.89 When a company determines the amount of attributable profit to be included in turnover, it should take account of the company's type of business, the nature of the contract and the contractual relationship with its customer. Appendix 1 to SSAP 9 states that when estimating profit:

> *"It is necessary to take into account not only the total costs to date and the total estimated further costs to completion ... but also the estimated future costs of rectification and guarantee work, and any other future work to be undertaken under the contract. These costs are then compared with the total sales value of the contract."* [SSAP 9 App 1 para 25].

17.90 The definition of attributable profit requires that it should be calculated, specifically, after estimating 'remedial and maintenance costs'. [SSAP 9 para 23]. In practice, for example, these costs will include the usual snagging clause of a building contract (that is, the clauses covering completion of the finishing touches to a building). They would also include provision for costs incurred under a 'guarantee' period for maintenance that is part of the original contract.

17.91 In considering future costs, it is necessary to have regard to likely increases in wages and salaries, to likely increases in the price of raw materials and to rises in general overheads, so far as these items are not recoverable from the customer under the terms of the contracts. Also, if interest on borrowings financing specific long-term contracts is capitalised (see chapter 5), then the calculation of total cost should include future interest costs.

Variations and claims

17.92 A variation is an instruction by the customer for a change in the scope of the work to be performed under the contract. Examples are changes in the specifications or designs of an asset and changes in the contract's duration.

17.93 Where approved variations have been made to a contract during its course and the amount to be received in respect of these variations has not yet been settled and is likely to be a material factor in the outcome, it is necessary to make a conservative estimate of the amount likely to be received and this is then treated as part of the total sales value. On the other hand, allowance needs to be made for foreseeable claims or penalties payable arising out of delays in completion or from other causes.

17.94 A claim is an amount that the contractor seeks to collect from the customer or another party as reimbursement for costs not included in the contract price. A claim may arise from, for example, errors in the initial specifications and delays caused by the customer

17.95 The settlement of claims arising from circumstances not envisaged in the contract or arising as an indirect consequence of approved variations is subject to a high level of uncertainty relating to the outcome of future negotiations. In view of this, it is generally prudent to recognise receipts in respect of such claims only when negotiations have reached an advanced stage and there is sufficient evidence of the acceptability of the claim by the customer, with an indication of the amount involved also being available. Trafalgar House provides an example of an accounting policy for claims on contracts (see Table 17.14). Another example is shown in Table 17.16 on page 39.

Table 17.14 – Trafalgar House Public Limited Company – Report and Accounts – 30 September 1994

Principal accounting policies (extract)

g) Long-term contracts (extract)

Amounts recoverable on contracts (other than small works) are valued at anticipated net sales value of work done after provision for contingencies and anticipated future losses on contracts. Claims are included in the valuation of contracts and credited to the profit and loss account when entitlement has been established.

Losses on contracts

17.96 If it is expected that there will be a loss on a contract as a whole, all of the loss should be recognised as soon as it is foreseen (in accordance with the prudence concept). [SSAP 9 para 11].

17.97 Foreseeable losses are defined as losses which are currently estimated to arise over the duration of the contract (after allowing for estimated remedial and maintenance costs and increases in costs so far as not recoverable under the terms of the contract). This estimate is required irrespective of:

- Whether or not work has yet commenced on such contracts.
- The proportion of work carried out at the accounting date.
- The amount of profits expected to arise on other contracts.

[SSAP 9 para 24].

17.98 Where unprofitable contracts are of such magnitude that they can be expected to utilise a considerable part of the company's capacity for a substantial period, related administration overheads to be incurred during the period to the completion of those contracts should also be included in calculating the provision for losses. [SSAP 9 para 11].

Cost of sales

17.99 The associated costs of achieving the turnover that is recorded in the profit and loss account on a contract by contract basis is deducted from the total costs incurred to date and charged in the profit and loss account as 'cost of sales'. Consequently, the reported result is attributed to the proportion of work completed.

17.100 Cost of sales will include costs that relate directly to the specific contract and also other costs that can be allocated to the contract. Costs that relate directly to the contract may include:

- Site labour costs.
- Costs of materials used in construction.
- Transport costs of plant and equipment to and from the site.
- Depreciation of plant and equipment used on the site.
- Design and technical costs related to the contract.
- The estimated costs of rectification and guarantee work.

17.101 Other costs that may be allocated to the contract include insurance, construction overheads and supervision costs.

17.102 Cost of sales will also normally include provisions made in respect of a loss making contract. An example of provisions for losses on contracts shown within cost of sales is shown in Table 17.15.

Table 17.15 – Trafalgar House Public Limited Company – Report and Accounts – 30 September 1993

Notes to the Accounts

2 Exceptional items (extract)

Total exceptional items included in continuing operations have been allocated to the following statutory headings:

	Note	**1993** **£m**	1992 £m
Cost of sales			
Current asset write downs			
Commercial developments	*(f)*	**(87.2)**	(0.9)
Residential developments	*(g)*	**(16.7)**	(38.9)

(*f*) Commercial development properties have been valued by the directors at the lower of cost and net realisable value. The write downs of commercial developments relate principally to the following items:

- US business parks where, during the year, the directors have decided to accelerate the group's withdrawal from this activity and have therefore written down the developments to estimated disposal values expected to be achieved.

- The Paddington Basin developments where the directors believe there is now insufficient certainty that the development can be completed within the timescale previously envisaged and have therefore written down the development to the current value of the group's interests in the site, having regard to the group's obligations under the terms of its developments agreement with British Waterways Board.

(*g*) The write downs of residential developments reflect the effect of the decision, taken by the directors during the year, to withdraw from the group's activities in Portugal and a provision in respect of UK residential development.

Amounts recoverable on contracts

17.103 Amounts recorded as turnover in respect of a contract are treated as debtors to the extent that they are unpaid and amounts recorded as costs of sales are deducted from the balance sheet work in progress figure. This is based on the theory that once a transaction has been recorded as turnover, it cannot then also be carried as stocks and must, consequently, be a receivable.

17.104 The treatment of turnover in respect of a contract as a debtor to the extent that it is unpaid resolved a conflict between the original requirement in SSAP 9, before revision in 1988, to include attributable profit in work in progress and the Act's requirement to show stocks (including work in progress) at the lower of cost and net realisable value.

17.105 The ASC realised that there was concern over the treatment and sought Counsel's opinion before issuing the revised standard. Counsel's opinion stated that there was nothing in the proposals that conflicted with the law. A long-term contract bears the characteristics of any legally binding contract so that the contractor may sue for any monies rightfully owed by the customer. This implies that amounts receivable for work completed under a long-term contract can, correctly, be regarded as realisable. Consequently, to regard amounts recoverable on contracts as a debtor is not contrary to the Act and the balance may be disclosed separately under debtors in the balance sheet formats. In addition, there is no necessity to disclose any further details, such as the profit element included in the debtor, in the notes to the financial statements.

Disclosure

17.106 Long-term contracts should be disclosed in the balance sheet as follows:

- The amount by which recorded turnover is in excess of payments on account should be classified as 'amounts recoverable on contracts' and separately disclosed within debtors.

- The balance of payments on account (in excess of amounts matched with turnover, and offset against long-term contract balances) should be classified as 'payments on account' and separately disclosed within creditors.

- The amount of long-term contracts, at costs incurred (net of amounts transferred to cost of sales) after deducting foreseeable losses and payments on account not matched with turnover, should be classified as 'long-term contract balances' and separately disclosed within the balance sheet heading 'stocks'. The balance sheet note should disclose separately the balances of:

  - Net cost less foreseeable losses.
  - Applicable payments on account.

- The amount by which the provision or accrual for foreseeable losses exceeds the costs incurred (after transfers to cost of sales) should be included within either 'provisions for liabilities and charges' or 'creditors' as appropriate.

[SSAP 9 para 30].

17.107 'Payments on account' are defined as all amounts received and receivable at the accounting date in respect of contracts in progress. [SSAP 9 para 25].

17.108 The accounting policies that have been applied to long-term contracts, in particular the method of ascertaining turnover and attributable profit, should be stated and applied consistently within the business and from year to year. [SSAP 9 para 32]. An example of typical disclosure for long-term contracts is Wimpey (see Table 17.16).

Table 17.16 – George Wimpey PLC – Annual Report – 31 December 1994

ACCOUNTING POLICIES (extract)

Turnover

Contracting turnover comprises the value of work executed during the year including the settlement of claims arising from previous years, amounts received on management fee contracts funded by the client and the Group's share of unincorporated joint venture turnover. Other turnover is based on the invoiced value of goods and services supplied during the year and includes house and land sales completed, trading and investment property sales completed and rental income. Turnover excludes value added tax and intra-group turnover.

Profit

Operating profit comprises the results of contracting, the provision of goods and services, private housing development, land sales, property development and investment. It includes the results attributable to contracts completed and long-term contracts in progress where a profitable outcome can prudently be foreseen, after deducting amounts recognised in previous years and after making provision for foreseeable losses. Claims receivable are recognised as income when received or if certified for payment. Estate development profit is taken on the number of houses of an estate in respect of which legal completions have taken place.

Long-term contracts

The amount of long-term contracts, at costs incurred, net of amounts transferred to cost of sales, after deducting foreseeable losses and payments on account not matched with turnover, is included in work in progress and stock as long-term contract balances. The amount by which recorded turnover is in excess of payments on account is included in debtors as amounts recoverable on long-term contracts. Payments in excess of recorded turnover and long-term contract balances are included in creditors as payments received on account on long-term contracts. The amount by which provisions or accruals for foreseeable losses exceed costs incurred, after transfers to cost of sales, is included within either provisions for liabilities and charges or creditors, as appropriate.

17.109 Each of the above balance sheet disclosure requirements is illustrated in the examples that follow:

Turnover exceeds payments on account

Example

	£'000
Turnover (value of work done)	52
Cumulative payments on account	45
Excess – *included in debtors*	7
Balance of costs on this contract not transferred to cost of sales – *included in stocks*	10

Balance sheet (extract)

Stocks	
Work in progress	
Net cost less foreseeable losses	10
Debtors	
Amounts recoverable on contracts	7

17.110 In the above example, the value of work included in turnover for the particular contract exceeds the progress payments received and receivable to date on that same contract. In accordance with SSAP 9, the excess amount is classified as 'amounts recoverable on contracts' and is shown separately under the heading 'debtors' in the balance sheet formats. The balance of costs not transferred to cost of sales is shown as work in progress.

Payments on account exceed turnover

Example

	£'000
Turnover (value of work done)	52
Cumulative payments on account	60
Excess – *reduces stocks*	8
Balance of costs on this contract not transferred to cost of sales – *included in stocks*	10

Balance sheet (extract)	
Stocks	
Work in progress	
Net cost less foreseeable losses	10
Applicable payments on account	(8)
	2

17.111 In this example, there is nothing to be included as 'amounts recoverable on contracts', because all turnover has been invoiced as payments on account and so will either be included in trade debtors or will have been received.

17.112 The amount included in work in progress comprises the total costs incurred to date less:

- Amounts transferred to cost of sales in the profit and loss account in respect of work carried out to date.
- Any foreseeable losses.
- Any applicable payments on account, that is, those in excess of turnover.

The balance sheet note should disclose separately both the net cost less foreseeable losses and the applicable payments on account.

Payments on account exceed turnover and balance of costs on contracts

Example

	£'000
Turnover (value of work done)	52
Cumulative payments on account	60
Excess – *part reduces stocks/and part included in creditors*	8
Balance of costs on this contract not transferred to cost of sales – *included in stocks*	5
Balance sheet (extract)	
Stocks	
Work in progress	
Net cost less foreseeable losses	5
Applicable payments on account	(5)
	–
Creditors	
Payments on account (£8,000 – £5,000)	3

17.113 In the this example, payments on account exceed both the amount of recorded turnover and the balance of costs incurred to date included in stocks. The excess amount is classified as 'payments on account' and separately disclosed in 'creditors'.

17.114 An example of balance sheet disclosure for long-term contracts is provided by Wimpey (see Table 17.17). The accounting policy note is shown in Table 17.16 on page 39.

Table 17.17 – George Wimpey PLC – Annual Report – 31 December 1994

NOTES ON THE ACCOUNTS

15 Work in Progress and Stock	**Group**	
	1994	1993
	£m	£m
Long-term contract balances – net cost less foreseeable losses	**11.8**	11.6
– less applicable payments on account	**(11.2)**	(11.4)
Net valuation	**0.6**	0.2
Land development and construction	**504.8**	473.3
Other stock	**20.6**	20.0
	526.0	493.5

17 Debtors (extract)	**Group**		**Parent**	
	1994	1993	**1994**	1993
	£m	£m	**£m**	£m
Receivable within one year:				
– trade debtors	**80.1**	78.7	**–**	–
– amounts recoverable on long-term contracts	**62.1**	56.0	**–**	–
– amounts owed by subsidiary undertakings	**–**	–	**140.4**	186.6
– amounts owed by associated undertakings	**2.1**	1.7	**–**	–
– prepayments and accrued income	**8.2**	5.9	**0.2**	–
– corporate taxation	**9.2**	12.2	**2.1**	–
– other	**15.7**	13.1	**–**	–
	177.4	167.6	**142.7**	186.6

18 Creditors Falling Due Within One Year	Group		Parent	
	1994	1993	**1994**	1993
	£m	£m	**£m**	£m
Finance debt (Note 20)	**17.3**	14.2	**3.5**	0.3
Trade creditors	**313.5**	309.1	**–**	–
Payments received on account on long-term contracts	**53.2**	53.7	**–**	–
Amounts owed to subsidiary undertakings	**–**	–	**86.7**	173.0
Amounts owed to associated undertakings	**0.4**	0.1	**–**	–
National insurance, VAT and other taxes	**9.9**	9.1	**–**	–
Accruals and deferred income	**12.8**	10.6	**–**	–
Corporate taxation	**36.2**	30.3	**3.4**	5.0
Proposed dividend (Note 6)	**12.6**	11.7	**12.6**	11.7
Other	**13.4**	11.1	**1.9**	1.6
	469.3	449.9	**108.1**	191.6

Provision for foreseeable losses

17.115 The amount transferred to the profit and loss account for a particular contract is the costs incurred to date in reaching that contract's stage of completion recognised in turnover. In most circumstances, this amount represents the cost of sales figure for a contract. However, where a provision is made for foreseeable losses, this charge also becomes part of cost of sales.

Example

	£'000
Turnover (value of work done)	52
Cumulative payments on account	45
Excess – *included in debtors*	7
Total costs on this contract	50
Transferred to cost of sales	40
Balance – *included in stocks*	10
Provision/accrual for foreseeable losses – *included in cost of sales in the profit and loss account. In the balance sheet part reduces stocks and part is included in liabilities*	30
Profit and loss account (extract)	
Turnover	52
Cost of sales (£40,000 + £30,000)	(70)
Loss	(18)

Balance sheet (extract)

Stocks	
Work in progress	
Net cost less foreseeable losses	
(£10,000 – £10,000)	=
Debtors	
Amounts recoverable on contracts	7
Liabilities	
Provision/accrual	
(£30,000 – £10,000 deducted from stocks)	20

17.116 In this example, foreseeable losses exceed the total costs incurred after transfers to cost of sales by £20,000 and the excess should be included in either accruals or provisions, as appropriate.

17.117 SSAP 9 provides no guidance on when these losses should be shown as an accrual and when they should be shown as a provision. The treatment used would appear to depend on the contract's state of completion at the time the financial statements are finalised. A provision is defined in the Act as:

> *"...any amount retained as reasonably necessary for the purpose of providing for any liability or loss which is either likely to be incurred, or certain to be incurred but uncertain as to the amount or as to the date on which it will arise."* [4 Sch 89].

17.118 The definition of a provision given in the Act implies that there is some argument for disclosing a loss as an accrual if a loss can be quantified with certainty. Losses that cannot be calculated with accuracy at the time of signing the financial statements should be disclosed as a provision. Provisions are considered in more detail from paragraph 17.204.

Transfers from current assets to fixed assets

17.119 The Act defines a fixed asset as one intended for use on a continuing basis in the company's activities and any which are not intended for such use are current assets. [Sec 262(1)]. Where, at a date subsequent to its original acquisition, a current asset is retained for use on a continuing basis in the company's activities, it becomes a fixed asset and the question arises as to the appropriate transfer value. An example is a property that is reclassified from trading properties to investment properties.

17.120 A problem arises as a result of the different rules for valuing fixed and current assets. Fixed assets are carried at depreciated cost less any provision for permanent diminution in value whereas current assets are carried at the lower of cost and net realisable value (that is, after writing down for both temporary and permanent diminutions in value). The different rules gave rise to concerns that companies could avoid charging the profit and loss account with write downs to net realisable value arising on unsold trading assets. This could be done by transferring the relevant assets from current assets to fixed assets at above their net realisable value, as a result of which any later write down might be debited to the revaluation reserve as a temporary diminution.

17.121 One company that decided to retain its development properties rather than sell at unattractive prices was Trafalgar House. In its financial statements for the year ended 30 September 1991 the properties were transferred from current assets to fixed assets. The write down was taken to the revaluation reserve rather than to the profit and loss account as a result of which the company faced criticism from the financial press and analysts. Although arguably at the time this was legally acceptable.

17.122 This criticism attracted the attention of the FRRP, which in February 1992 notified the company that it was considering certain matters in connection to the 1991 financial statements, including the reclassification of properties. The company argued against the FRRP's view, but the FRRP evidently held its ground and eventually the directors of Trafalgar House agreed to make the changes in order to avoid litigation. The FRRP issued a strongly worded Press Notice that stated:

> *"On the basis of independent legal and accounting advice the directors of Trafalgar House have hitherto not accepted the Review Panel's view on the two principal matters in contention. The Review Panel has therefore been minded to make an application to the court under section 245B of the Companies Act 1985 for an order requiring the directors of the company to prepare revised accounts. However the directors of the company have now undertaken to make appropriate changes and adjustments in the accounts of the company for the year ended 30 September 1992 to meet the Review Panel's concerns, and on this undertaking the Review Panel will not be proceeding with the section 245B court application."*

17.123 As a result of this case, the UITF was requested to produce rules dealing with such reclassification. In July 1992, UITF Abstract 5, 'Transfers from current assets to fixed assets', was issued. This states that where assets are transferred from current to fixed, the current asset accounting rules should be applied up to the effective date of transfer, which is the date of management's change of intent.

Consequently, the transfer should be made at the lower of cost and net realisable value and, accordingly, an assessment should be made of the net realisable value at the date of transfer and if this is less than its previous carrying value the diminution should be charged in the profit and loss account, reflecting the loss to the company while the asset was held as a current asset. [UITF 5 para 5].

17.124 The timing of the transfer of current assets to fixed assets should reflect the timing of management's change of intent and should not be backdated (for example, to the start of the financial year). This change of intent will need to be evidenced, for instance in board minutes. Since the date of the management's decision is unlikely to correspond with the balance sheet date, at which a full review of carrying values would be made, consideration must be given to the appropriate amounts at which such assets should be transferred at the time of transfer.

17.125 Whether assets are transferred at cost or at net realisable value in accordance with UITF 5, the fixed asset accounting rules will apply to the assets subsequent to the date of transfer. In cases where the transfer is at net realisable value, the asset should be accounted for as a fixed asset at a valuation (under the Act's alternative accounting rules) as at the date of the transfer. At subsequent balance sheet dates it may or may not be revalued, but in either event the disclosure requirements appropriate to a valuation should be given. These disclosure requirements are discussed in chapter 5.

17.126 The abstract deals only with situations where current assets are included in the balance sheet at the lower of cost and net realisable value under paragraphs 22 and 23 of Schedule 4 to the Act. Therefore, it does not apply to current assets that are accounted for under the alternative accounting rules, for example, investments.

17.127 As a result of the challenge by the FRRP, the prior year figures in the 1992 financial statements of Trafalgar House were restated. Property write downs previously charged to the revaluation reserve were reflected in the profit and loss account for the year. This is shown in Table 17.18

Table 17.18 – Trafalgar House Public Limited Company – Report and Accounts – 30 September 1992

CHAIRMAN'S AND GROUP CHIEF EXECUTIVE'S REPORT (extract)

Financial Reporting (extract)

In February 1992 the Financial Reporting Review Panel notified the company that it was considering certain matters in connection with the company's accounts for the year ended 30th September 1991. The Panel's principal concerns related to the reclassification of certain properties from current assets to fixed assets and the amount of ACT carried forward in the balance sheet.

On the basis of independent legal and accounting advice, your Board was of the view that the treatment of those matters in the 1991 accounts was in accordance with accounting standards and complied with the Companies Acts. However, the Panel continued to express concern and, after due consideration, and in order to avoid the delays and uncertainties which would have resulted from prolonged litigation, your Board agreed to make certain changes and adjustments in the 1992 accounts and to the comparative figures for 1991 in these accounts. The Panel did not require the 1991 accounts to be reissued.

We agreed to adopt, early, the requirements of Urgent Issues Task Force Abstract 5, issued on 22nd July 1992, in our 1992 accounts. Consequently, the 1991 comparative figures show deficits on revaluations of property of £102.7m as a charge to the profit and loss account rather than to reserves. We also agreed to write off £20.0m of ACT to the prior period.

NOTES TO THE ACCOUNTS

1 Basis of preparation

The accounts and notes are prepared in accordance with applicable accounting standards. The particular accounting policies adopted are described in Note 2.

In particular, in these accounts:

* FRS 3 (Reporting financial performance) has been adopted;
* UITF 3 (Treatment of goodwill on disposal of a business) has been adopted; and
* In accordance with the agreement reached with the Financial Reporting Review Panel, UITF 5 (Transfer from current assets to fixed assets) has been adopted early and ACT amounting to £20m has been written off to the prior period.

Comparative figures have been restated to reflect these changes in the basis of preparation of the accounts. This can be summarised as follows:

	Shareholders' Funds at 30th September 1991 £million
September 1991 published accounts	704.6
ACT write off as described above	(20.0)
September 1992 accounts – comparatives	684.6

	Year ended 30th September 1991 Profit/(loss) for the financial year £million
September 1991 published accounts (before dividends)	44.9
Property write downs previously charged to revaluation reserve, now reflected in the profit and loss account in accordance with UITF 5	(102.7)
ACT write off as described above	(20.0)
Goodwill reflected in loss on disposal of discontinued operations in accordance with UITF 3	(21.6)
September 1992 accounts – comparatives	(99.4)

Debtors

Disclosure

17.128 The Act requires that all debtors should be disclosed as current assets, no matter when they fall due for payment. [Schedule 4 balance sheet formats]. The Act draws a distinction only between fixed assets and current assets. If a company intends to use assets on a continuing basis in its activities, then they are fixed assets. If the assets do not comply with this definition, they are deemed to be current assets. [Sec 262(1)].

17.129 The Act requires that debtors should be analysed into the following categories:

- Trade debtors.
- Amounts owed by group undertakings.
- Amounts owed by undertakings in which the company has a participating interest.
- Other debtors.
- Called-up share capital not paid.
- Prepayments and accrued income.

[4 Sch formats].

17.130 An item representing an asset that is not covered by the prescribed format may be shown separately. [4 Sch 3(2)]. Examples of debtors that are sometimes shown as separate categories within total debtors are factored debts and finance lease receivables.

Presentation of long-term debtors

17.131 The amount of each item to be shown under the heading 'Debtors' must be split between those receivable within one year of the balance sheet date and those receivable later than that. [Schedule 4 note 5 to the balance sheet formats]. For this purpose, a debtor is considered to be receivable on the earliest date on which payment is due, rather than on the earliest date on which payment is expected.

17.132 The Act does not require this disclosure to be given on the face of the balance sheet. However, this means that there is an imbalance between the treatment of long-term debtors and long-term creditors where the latter are disclosed as long-term on the face of the balance sheet and not included in net current assets. There will be some instances where the absence of disclosure of long-term debtors on the face of the balance sheet may mean that users misinterpret the financial statements.

17.133 As a result of this imbalance, UITF Abstract 4, 'Presentation of long term debtors in current assets', requires disclosure of debtors due after more than one year on the face of the balance sheet if the amount is material in the context of net current assets. [UITF 4 para 3]. The Abstract gives pension fund surpluses recognised as prepayments and long-term trade debtors of lessors as examples where this additional disclosure may be appropriate. The debtor will still be included in current assets, but will be shown separately on the face of the balance sheet.

17.134 This disclosure is normally given by including an additional line item 'Debtors: amounts falling due after more than one year' in the current assets section of the balance sheet. An example of a company with such disclosure is Williams Holdings which has a long-term debtor that includes a large pension prepayment (see Table 17.19).

Table 17.19 – Williams Holdings PLC – Annual Report – 31 December 1994

Consolidated Balance Sheet (extract)

	Notes	**1994** **£m**	1993 £m
Current assets			
Stocks		**213.6**	185.7
Debtors:			
Falling due within one year	15	**266.6**	213.4
Falling due after more than one year	15	**185.4**	180.0
		452.0	393.4
Investments and other assets for sale		**5.6**	8.3
Cash		**191.8**	76.2
		863.0	663.6

Notes to the financial statements (extract)

15 Debtors (extract)	**Group**		**Company**	
	1994	1993	**1994**	1993
	£m	£m	**£m**	£m
Amounts falling due after more than one year:				
Pension fund prepayment (note 28)	**127.6**	129.3	**–**	–
Amounts owed by subsidiary companies	**–**	–	**496.0**	407.9
Amounts owed by associated companies	**–**	2.0	**–**	–
Other debtors and prepayments	**22.6**	15.2	**17.3**	15.0
Corporate taxation recoverable	**11.9**	9.5	**43.8**	9.5
Deferred taxation	**23.3**	24.0	**–**	–
	185.4	180.0	**557.1**	432.4

17.135 Prior to the issue of UITF 4, some companies chose to show long-term debtors of this type as a separate category between fixed and current assets on the grounds that compliance with the Schedule 4 formats, that is, including the long-term debtors within current assets, did not give a true and fair view. We consider that, following UITF 4, the inclusion of such an additional asset category on the balance sheet could only be achieved by using the true and fair override and that in most situations a true and fair view will be given by following the disclosure requirements of UITF 4. Therefore, long-term debtors should not normally be shown in a separate category between fixed and current assets. If a company wished to depart from the Act's formats it would have to justify this and give the disclosures required by UITF Abstract 7 (see chapter 2).

Valuation

17.136 The Act requires current assets to be shown at the lower of cost and net realisable value. [4 Sch 22,23]. This means that debtors should be stated after any provision for bad or doubtful debts.

17.137 One problem that arises with the valuation of debtors is where a company issues pro-forma invoices to customers at provisional prices that may be higher than the prices that eventually will be agreed. The company will have to make provision against part of the balance invoiced. The provision is normally deducted from debtors in respect of the same customer and the net amount is recorded as sales. This accounting treatment is acceptable. The provision of the Act that prohibits set-off (that is, paragraph 5 of Schedule 4), does not inhibit normal accounting for assets and liabilities. Debts should be shown net of provisions to reduce them to their net realisable value.

17.138 This situation may also arise where a company gives a discount to its debtors for the early settlement of debts, although this type of discount would not normally be deducted from sales, but would normally be included under 'administrative expenses' or 'interest payable and similar charges' if it was considered to be more in the nature of a finance charge.

Debt factoring

17.139 Factoring is a transaction which is capable of different accounting treatments. It involves raising money from the sale of a company's debtor balances before the debt is collected. Debt factoring is considered in Application Note C of FRS 5 and encompasses also invoice discounting. Factoring arrangements come with many different features; at their simplest they might, for example, feature a clean sale of debts at a fixed price without recourse. More complex arrangements might feature a sale of debts on terms where there is both recourse to the seller in respect of non-payment (bad debt or credit risk) and the price received for the debts varies according to the actual period the debts remain unpaid (slow payment risk).

17.140 In the former case, the seller has no further interest in the debts so they can be removed from the balance sheet by crediting them with the proceeds from the factor. In the latter case, the seller clearly retains a significant economic interest in the underlying debts and the arrangement should be accounted for as a financing with the debts remaining on balance sheet. In addition, there is now a middle ground where significant, but not all, benefits and risks have been transferred to the factor. In such a transaction, the company might be eligible to use the linked presentation where the conditions in paragraph 27 of FRS 5 (see chapter 4) are met. Partial derecognition is not an option for such transactions, because they are financing arrangements.

17.141 Some of the arguments contained in the application note for and against asset recognition are finely balanced and there are likely to be grey areas in practice. Therefore, individual arrangements will need to be carefully reviewed. The three accounting treatments that might apply are:

- Derecognition – where no significant benefits or risks are retained.

- Linked presentation – where the company retains significant benefits and/or risks associated with the factored debts, but the downside exposure to loss is limited to a fixed amount and the other conditions for use of the linked presentation are met.

- Separate presentation – showing the factored debts and the related finance separately (not linked) on the balance sheet, where the company retains significant benefits and/or risks relating to the assets and the conditions for the linked presentation cannot be met.

17.142 The application note lists the main benefits and risks of factoring arrangements as:

- The benefit arising from the future cash flows due to the payment of the debts.
- The risk of slow payment.
- The risk of non payment – credit risk.

[FRS 5 App C para C5].

Main benefits and risks

17.143 The main benefits and risks set out above are considered in detail in the application note and the principles stemming from that discussion are then summarised in a table. The summary table is reproduced below, but with the main benefits and risks added as headings; also included are references to the paragraphs of the application note that give the narrative explanation:

Indicates derecognition	**Indicates linked presentation**	**Indicates separate presentation**
Cash flow benefit and slow payment risk		
Transfer is for a single, non-returnable fixed sum. [App C para C6].	Some non-returnable proceeds received, but seller has rights to further sums from the factor (or *vice versa*) whose amount depends on whether or when debtors pay. [App C para C15].	Finance cost varies with speed of collection of debts, for example: - by adjustment to consideration for original transfer [App C para C8]; or - subsequent transfers priced to recover costs of earlier transfers. [App C para C8].
Credit risk		
There is no recourse to the seller for losses. [App C para C9].	There is no recourse for losses, or such recourse has a fixed monetary ceiling. [App C para C15].	There is full recourse to the seller for losses. [App C para C9].

Other indicators		
Factor is paid all amounts received from the factored debts (and no more). Seller has no rights to further sums from the factor. [App C para C12].	Factor is paid only out of amounts collected from the factored debts, and seller has no right or obligation to repurchase debts. [App C para C15].	Seller is required to repay amounts received from the factor on or before a set date, regardless of timing or amounts of collections from debtors. [App C para C6].

17.144 Debt factoring, as opposed to just invoice discounting, not only involves the discounting of invoices, but often includes the factor administering the sales ledger and collecting the debts on behalf of the company. Generally, for debt factoring the administration arrangements will not affect the analysis of the transaction significantly for accounting purposes provided they are at arm's length. However, with arrangements where the factor is only administering the sales ledger (that is, service-only factoring), the seller will retain access to the benefits and risks associated with the debts and hence they should remain on balance sheet.

17.145 In order for factored debts to be derecognised (that is, completely taken off the balance sheet), the seller cannot retain any significant benefits or risks associated with those debts. Derecognition is, therefore, only appropriate where all of the following apply:

- The transaction takes place at an arm's length price for an outright sale.

- The transaction is for a fixed amount of consideration and there is no recourse either implicit or explicit.

  Warranties given in respect of the conditions of the debts (for example, to their existence) at the time of transfer are allowed, but warranties concerning the condition of the debts in the future or their future performance (for example, payment or speed of payment) are not allowed.

- The seller will not benefit or suffer if the debts perform better or worse than expected.

[FRS 5 App C para C12].

17.146 Derecognition cannot be used where the seller retains significant benefits or risks, but in such a situation it might be possible to use the linked presentation. The linked presentation would normally be appropriate where the downside exposure to risk is limited to a fixed monetary amount and where the conditions for the linked presentation are met. However, the linked presentation should not be used where the factored debts cannot be separately identified.

17.147 It is possible in factoring arrangements where the linked presentation is used, for old debts to be replaced by new debts as long as the conditions in FRS 5, paragraph 27(b) (no recourse to other assets) and 27(f) (finance to be repaid out of the cash receipt from debt) are satisfied. The practical problems associated with achieving the linked presentation in this situation are explained in relation to credit card receivable securitisations in chapter 4.

Accounting treatment

Derecognition

17.148 If, after analysing the transaction, it is determined that the assets can be derecognised, a loss (and in certain circumstances a profit) will arise which will simply be the difference between the carrying value of the debts and the net proceeds received from the factor. [FRS 5 App C para C18]. This amount will generally represent a finance cost and should be included within interest in the profit and loss account.

Linked presentation

17.149 Where the conditions for linked presentation are met, the finance should be deducted from the related debts on the face of the balance sheet, after providing for any bad debts. The interest element of the factor's charge should be accrued as it is incurred. In addition, the notes to the financial statements should include the following information:

- The main terms of the arrangement. [FRS 5 App C para C19].

- The gross amount of the outstanding factored debts at the balance sheet date. [FRS 5 App C para C19].

  Although not stated explicitly in the FRS, the amount to be disclosed is presumably before deducting bad debt provisions as otherwise this additional disclosure would appear unnecessary, because the amount of the debts factored (after deducting bad debt provisions) will be disclosed anyway in the balance sheet linked presentation, although at some point a bad debt must be written off and, therefore, eliminated from both sides.

- The factoring charges recognised in the period, analysed between interest and other charges. [FRS 5 App C para C19].

- A statement by the directors that the company is not obliged and does not intend to support any losses beyond the recourse to the specific debts linked under the scheme. [FRS 5 para 27(c)].

- A note that the factor has agreed in writing that it will seek recourse to both principal and interest only to the extent that sufficient funds are generated by the specific debts it has financed. [FRS 5 para 27(d)].

17.150 An example of disclosure of the statements in the last two bullet points above is seen in Table 17.20 in relation to hire purchase trade debtors discounted with banks, subject to strictly limited recourse.

Table 17.20 – Inchcape plc – Annual Report & Accounts – 31 December 1994

Consolidated balance sheet (extract)

		1994		1993
	£m	**£m**	£m	restated £m
Current assets:				
Stocks		**1,112.1**		876.8
Debtors		**1,379.1**		1,220.5
Trade debtors subject to limited recourse financing	**34.8**		36.3	
less: non-returnable amounts received	**(24.8)**		(26.1)	
		10.0		10.2
Cash at bank and in hand		**427.3**		354.9
		2,928.5		2,462.4

17 Debtors (extract)

Trade debtors subject to limited recourse financing represent hire purchase debtors discounted with banks in the ordinary course of business, subject to strictly limited recourse so that the majority of cash received by the Group on discounting is not returnable, and which carry interest at variable rates. The returnable element of the proceeds is recorded as bank loans and overdrafts due within one year and after one year as appropriate. The Group will not make good any losses over and above the agreed recourse limit and the relevant banks have confirmed their acceptance of this position in writing.

The Group figures also include the effects of implementing FRS5 in respect of bills of exchange, trade debtors and hire purchase debtors discounted with recourse, at variable rates of interest, to banks and finance houses in the ordinary course of business. These balances have been included within trade debtors due within one year £6.0m (1993 – £32.2m) and net investment in finance leases and hire purchase contracts £0.4m due within one year and £4.0m due after one year respectively (1993 – £0.4m and £3.7m).

Separate presentation

17.151 Where the analysis indicates that separate presentation should be used for the transaction, the amount of the debts factored should remain in debtors on the balance sheet (net of any provisions for bad debts). The proceeds received from the factor should be recorded as a liability under the heading of, for example, 'amounts due in respect of factored receivables'. In addition, the interest element of the factor's charges should be accrued and shown as interest in the profit and loss account. Also the notes to the financial statements should show the amount of the factored debts outstanding at the balance sheet date. [FRS 5 App C para C20].

17.152 An example of disclosure of trade debtors and hire purchase debtors discounted with recourse is seen in Table 17.20 above.

Examples of required analysis

17.153 The application note provides two examples of factoring arrangements: one where the factor has recourse and continued recognition is required; and another where the factor has limited recourse and the linked presentation is used.

17.154 The following example, which is not one of those included in the application note, also illustrates the FRS 5 principles as they apply to factoring arrangements:

Example

A company has a number of large trade debtors totalling £1m, which are very unlikely to default, but are long-dated. The company decides to sell these debtors to a factoring company. Because the debtors are sound companies, there are unlikely to be any bad debts and the risk of slow payment is minimal. Even so, the seller has given the factor a guarantee of up to 10% of the debtors' balance if they do not pay. In past experience, over the last ten years, the company has never had to provide against any balances with these customers.

Some might try to argue that such a transaction should be accounted for as a sale of assets and recognition of a new asset or liability (partial derecognition). In this case, the recognition would be of an obligation to repay the factor if the debtors go bad (which is extremely unlikely). This argument appears to be supported by paragraph 73 of FRS 5 which illustrates a similar situation; *"... an entity may sell equipment subject to a warranty in respect of the condition of the equipment at the time of sale, or subject to a guarantee of its residual value. This would normally transfer all significant rights to benefits and some significant exposure to risks to the buyer ..., but leave the seller with some significant risk in the form of obligations relating to the equipment's future performance or residual value. The seller would therefore cease to recognise the equipment as an asset, but would recognise a liability for its warranty obligation or guarantee (with the liability being accounted for in accordance with the provisions of SSAP 18)"*. This paragraph would seem to support the argument that the obligation in the example is so remote that it does not need to be recognised and, as a consequence, the transaction can be treated as an outright sale. However, there is one primary objection to this argument, which is that partial derecognition is not available for financing transactions and this transaction is clearly a financing arrangement. In any case, paragraphs 12 and 13 of Application Note C only allow three possible accounting treatments for debt factoring: full derecognition where the transaction is an outright sale and there is no recourse; linked presentation where there is recourse and the conditions for that presentation are met; and separate presentation. *Partial derecognition is not an option.*

Therefore, using the principles of Application Note C, the benefits and risks of the transaction can be analysed as follows:

	Off B/sheet	**Linked**	**On B/sheet**
Cash flow benefit and slow payment risk The transfer is for a fixed sum, but part may have to be repaid if the guarantee is called.		✓	
Credit risk The factor has recourse via the guarantee to the company for losses, which has a fixed monetary ceiling, but is unlikely to be called.		✓	
Other indicators The factor is only paid out of the amounts collected from the debtors and the seller has no right or obligation to repurchase the debtors.		✓	

The company has retained significant risks associated with the debtors, because it is still liable to fund bad debts up to a limit of 10%. The company might contend, in practice, that its risk of bad debts is nil (because of past experience). This is true, but it still has retained the same significant risk that it had prior to undertaking the transaction, because it is exposed to the risk of bad debts on the gross amount of the debtors it has transferred. It has merely transferred to the factor the risk of catastrophe (the risk of bad debts exceeding the 10% limit). Consequently, the analysis above indicates that the linked presentation is the appropriate accounting treatment for this transaction, but it can only be used where the conditions for its use are met. If those conditions cannot be met, then separate presentation must be used.

The accounting treatment using the linked presentation would be as follows:

Balance sheet (extract)	£'m	£'m
Current assets		
Debtors		
Trade debtors (say)		10.0
Trade debtors subject to financing arrangements	1.0	
Less: non-returnable amounts received	0.9	
		0.1
Total trade debtors		10.1
Creditors		
Financing of trade debtors		0.1
(comprising the amount of finance with recourse)		

Bills of exchange

17.155 Even with a relatively simple transaction such as a bill of exchange the accounting treatment following FRS 5 has changed. A company might, for example, receive a bill of exchange from a customer in respect of a trade debtor balance. The company might then decide to discount the bill with a bank. Before FRS 5, the company would typically have accounted for this by transferring the amount from debtors to cash, charging the discount to the profit and loss account and noting a contingent liability in respect of the bank's recourse to the company in the event that the bank was not paid by the customer.

17.156 Under the provisions of FRS 5, however, where such a bill is discounted with a bank and the bank has full recourse to the company, then the company has not transferred all the risks related to the payment from the debtor. Therefore, following the standard, the debtor should remain on the company's balance sheet and the cash received for discounting the bill should also be shown as an asset with a corresponding liability for the finance provided (with recourse) by the bank. This follows the same principles as for factoring of debts. Even where a bill is settled after the year end, this does not constitute an adjusting event and would not affect how the bill should be accounted for at the balance sheet date.

17.157 Because bills of exchange can be short-term or long-term, care needs to be taken in the balance sheet in classifying the debtors and the liability to the bank so that the correct maturity period is reflected.

17.158 An example of a company restating its figures as a result of FRS 5 is English China Clays which has included bills of exchange discounted with recourse in trade debtors and, on the creditors side, in bank loans and overdrafts (see Table 17.21).

Table 17.21 – English China Clays plc – Annual Report & Accounts – 31 December 1994

Notes to the Accounts

11 Debtors (extract)

Following the adoption of FRS 5, Reporting the Substance of Transactions, trade debtors and bank loans and overdrafts (included within Note 12 below) as at 31st December 1994 include £12.1M of bills discounted with recourse. The 1993 figures have been restated to include bills discounted with recourse of £9.5M.

17.159 An alternative presentation for the creditors side is that of Burmah Castrol which includes bills discounted with recourse as a separate line item within creditors (see Table 17.22).

Table 17.22 – Burmah Castrol plc – Annual Report – 31 December 1994

NOTES TO THE ACCOUNTS

19 Creditors (extract)

	Amounts falling due within one year		Amounts falling due after more than one year	
	1994 £ million	1993 £ million (as restated)	**1994 £ million**	1993 £ million (as restated)
Group				
Convertible capital bonds			**56.0**	56.0
Bank loans and overdrafts	**115.2**	76.8	**64.4**	95.7
Other loans wholly repayable within five years				
Other loans	**83.6**	111.2	**110.9**	107.9
Obligations to banks under trade loan guarantees			**100.9**	106.8
Bills discounted with recourse				
Payments received on account	**7.8**	16.1	**67.7**	44.2
Trade creditors	**6.8**	6.9		
Amounts owed to companies in which the group	**1.1**	3.0		
has a participating interest	**343.8**	275.6	**0.1**	
Taxation and social security				
Dividends	**0.9**	0.7	**0.3**	1.0
Other creditors	**89.2**	76.6		
Accruals and deferred income	**64.3**	21.7		
	57.9	50.4	**9.7**	13.9
	111.2	107.7	**2.5**	1.7
	881.8	746.7	**412.5**	427.2

Prepayments and accrued income

17.160 Prepayments and accrued income may be disclosed in one of two alternative positions. [Note 6 on the balance sheet formats]. They may be disclosed either as a category of debtors or as a separate category in their own right. Where prepayments and accrued income are disclosed under debtors, the Act requires them to be analysed by age. If, however, they are included as a separate category, then strictly under the Act no such analysis is required. However, UITF Abstract 4, requires separate disclosure of debtors due after more than one year where the amount is material in the context of the total net current assets. We consider that this applies to prepayments and accrued income regardless of whether the total is included in debtors or shown as a separate category.

17.161 An example of disclosure of long-term prepayments within debtors can be seen in the accounts of Seton Healthcare Group (see Table 17.23).

Table 17.23 – Seton Healthcare Group plc – Annual Report – 28 February 1994

NOTES TO THE FINANCIAL STATEMENTS

16 DEBTORS: AMOUNTS FALLING DUE AFTER MORE THAN ONE YEAR

	Group		Company	
	1994	1993	**1994**	1993
	£'000	£'000	**£'000**	£'000
Other debtors	**1,779**	1,913	**–**	–
Prepayment	**453**	753	**453**	753
	2,232	2,666	**453**	753

Included within other debtors are £153,000 of deferred tax recoverable on the exceptional losses in 1992 and a £1,626,000 debt arising from the disposal of the USA businesses repayable over 5 years.

The prepayment of £453,000 is an advance payment relating to products to be supplied under a 5 year manufacturing agreement ending September 1996.

Deferred costs

17.162 Costs should only be deferred and carried forward as a prepayment where the matching principle is not overridden by prudence. According to the ASB's draft Statement of principles, prudence dictates that it should be assumed that any expenditure incurred should be written off immediately unless there is evidence that it will contribute to the generation of future benefits. If there is such evidence, the expenditure may be deferred only if it meets the ASB's definition of an asset. In general, therefore, this means that costs incurred should only be carried forward where they will be recovered from future related revenues or where they give rights to obtain services in a future period.

17.163 The following examples illustrate the types of principle that must be considered before costs can be deferred.

Example 1

A company introduces new technology and incurs redundancy costs. It wishes to defer these and match them against the future benefits to be obtained from the new technology.

Redundancy costs cannot meet the definition of an asset. Although costs are incurred with a view to increasing profitability *via* a reduction in the ongoing level of operating costs, they do not contribute to the generation of future revenues. Consequently, there is no basis for matching such costs with revenues in future periods. They should be expensed immediately.

Example 2

A company negotiated a long-term facility and pays a commitment fee. It wants to defer this cost and amortise it over the term of the facility.

According to FRS 4, such costs are not assets as defined in the ASB's draft Statement of principles, because they do not provide access to any future economic benefits. FRS 4 requires costs of negotiating sources of finance to be written off to the profit and loss account as incurred. Such costs may be deferred only if they qualify as a cost of issuing a debt instrument; the costs should then be shown as part of the net proceeds (that is, deducted from the liability) and be amortised over the term of the related debt.

Example 3

A company has capitalised internally developed software for use in its own business. It now wishes to capitalise 'installation' costs which include a large element of staff training costs.

The cost of training staff to use the software should generally not be capitalised as there is no clear matching of such costs against future revenue. On the grounds of prudence they should be written off as incurred.

17.164 An example of a company writing off internally funded project-related education expenditure is British Aerospace (see Table 17.24).

Table 17.24 – British Aerospace Public Limited Company – Annual Report – 31 December 1997

Accounting Policies (extract)

Launch costs

The costs of launching an aircraft project fall into three principal categories: design and development; education; and jigs and tools.

Design and development and education – In the case where the project is fully funded by the Group, design and development and education expenditure is charged to the profit and loss account as incurred. In the case where the project has external funding, design and development and education expenditure is carried forward within stocks and amortised by reference to an assessment of sales.

Jigs and tools – Expenditure on jigs and tools is capitalised into fixed assets and depreciated over its useful economic life.

Example 4

A company is preparing to open a new retail branch outlet. It proposes to adopt a policy of deferring revenue costs incurred prior to opening the branch and amortising such expenditure over three years from the date that trading commences.

The commercial viability of the new outlet must be reasonably assured before deferral of such costs is possible. The costs incurred in setting up the branch must be expected to contribute to an increase in future revenues and provided there is sufficient evidence that the costs will be recovered, they may, in principle, be deferred and amortised under the matching principle against the revenues generated by the new branch. Care should be taken to ensure that only costs directly related to the set-up are carried forward where the circumstances justify this. Generally, however, the majority of such costs should be written off to the profit and loss account on the grounds of prudence.

17.165 Tables 17.25 and 17.26 give examples of companies that disclose accounting policies for deferring certain expenditure.

Table 17.25 – The Rank Group Plc – Directors' Report and Accounts – 31 December 1997

ACCOUNTING POLICIES (extract)

4 Deferred expenditure

Deferred expenditure comprises (a) those costs incurred prior to the commencement of trading which are regarded as a prepayment against future profits to be earned, (b) other amounts deferred including rights acquired and (c) advance payments on supply contracts. The expenditure is included in prepayments and is written off over periods of three to eight years, the period over which the related benefits are expected to arise.

Table 17.26 – Ladbroke Group PLC – Report and Accounts – 31 December 1997

Accounting Policies (extract)

Deferred expenditure

Pre-opening expenditure incurred up to the date of commencement of full trading in new hotel developments is, where appropriate, deferred and expensed to profit and loss account over a period of five years.

17.166 The deferral of start-up costs is an area that often attracts adverse comment, mainly because it is not considered to be prudent and it is open to manipulation. It has already attracted the attention of the FRRP which raised the accounting treatment of start-up costs with the directors of Associated Nursing Services plc. The press notice issued in August 1992 by the FRRP stated that *"The Panel has noted that the directors have reviewed the company's policy in respect of start-up costs and intend to incorporate the results of that review in the company's accounts for the year ended 31 March 1992. It welcomes their decision to include a clear and finite time limit to the capitalisation of these costs"*. The revised accounting policy for capitalised internal costs is shown in Table 17.27.

Table 17.27 – Associated Nursing Services plc – Annual Report – 4 April 1992

NOTES TO THE FINANCIAL STATEMENTS (extract)

1 ACCOUNTING POLICIES (extract)

e) CAPITALISATION OF INTERNAL COSTS

During the course of major refurbishment and extension of existing homes, costs directly attributable to building works are capitalised. Normal running costs which are incurred whilst a home is below capacity because of capital works are written off immediately to the profit and loss account.

For new homes all costs and revenues up to the earlier of three months from the date of Registration or the date that the break even level of occupancy is achieved are capitalised. Previously all costs and revenues up to the projected break even level of occupancy were capitalised. The directors have made this change of accounting policy because they consider the new policy to be more prudent.

Cash at bank and in hand

Definition of cash

17.167 Schedule 4 to the Act requires cash at bank and in hand to be included as a separate line item within current assets. The Act does not define cash and this has resulted in inconsistencies in practice.

17.168 FRS 1, 'Cash flow statements' revised in October 1996, defines cash as *"Cash in hand and deposits repayable on demand with any qualifying financial institution, less overdrafts from any qualifying financial institution repayable on demand. Deposits are repayable on demand if they can be withdrawn at any time without notice and without penalty or if a maturity or period of notice of not more than 24 hours or one working day has been agreed. Cash includes cash in hand and deposits denominated in foreign currencies"*.

17.169 Therefore, the FRS 1 definition of cash includes deposits repayable on demand with any bank or other financial institution and so would include, for example, accounts with Building Societies. The definition excludes any term deposits with banks or other financial institutions.

17.170 An example of a company that excludes short-term deposits from cash at bank is The Boots Company (see Table 17.28). Cash at bank on the balance sheet totals £14.6 million at 31 March 1995. This all qualified as cash and cash equivalents (under the original FRS 1) in addition to a further amount of £1,002.7 million of short-term deposits included under 'investments and deposits' in the balance sheet.

Table 17.28 – The Boots Company PLC – Report and Accounts – 31 March 1995

Balance sheets (extract)

	Notes	**Group 1995 £m**	Group 1994 £m	**Parent 1995 £m**	Parent 1994 £m
Current assets (extract)					
Investments and deposits	16	**1,015.6**	491.9	**986.8**	251.8
Cash at bank and in hand		**14.6**	11.5	**.1**	304.7

16 Current asset investments

	Group 1995	Group 1994	**Parent 1995**	Parent 1994
Listed investments	**.6**	.6	**.5**	.5
Short term deposits	**1,003.7**	479.8	**975.0**	239.8
Certificates of tax deposit	**11.3**	11.5	**11.3**	11.5
	1,015.6	491.9	**986.8**	251.8
Market value of investments issued on The London Stock Exchange	**1.8**	.6	**1.7**	.5

23 Notes to the group cash flow statement (extract)

b Analysis of cash, cash equivalents, investments and borrowings	**Cash and cash equivalents £m**	**Investments and borrowings £m**	Cash and cash equivalents £m	Investments and borrowings £m
Cash at bank and in hand	**14.6**	–	11.5	–
Current asset investments (note 16):				
– Listed investments	–	**.6**	–	.6
– Short term deposits	**1,002.7**	**1.0**	196.0	283.8
– Certificates of tax deposit	–	**11.3**	–	11.5
	1,017.3	**12.9**	207.5	295.9
Borrowings (note 19):				
– Due within one year	**(253.0)**	**(35.8)**	(128.2)	(38.3)
– Due after more than one year	–	**(224.2)**	–	(267.9)
	(253.0)	**(260.0)**	(128.2)	(306.2)
	764.3	**(247.1)**	79.3	(10.3)
Net cash		**517.2**		69.0

Cash equivalents are highly liquid deposits which are readily convertible into known amounts of cash and which were within three months of maturity when acquired, less advances from banks repayable within three months from the date of advance.

Investments and borrowings have original maturities of more than three months.

17.171 In contrast, another interpretation used in practice for the balance sheet heading 'cash at bank and in hand' is the total amount of money on deposit with a bank or other financial institution. This includes amounts on current account that can be withdrawn on demand and amounts in a deposit account, available after due notice has been given. This is a wide definition and does not restrict cash at bank to those deposits which are available on demand.

17.172 An example of a company that appears to classify cash at bank using this wider definition is Hanson (see Table 17.29). Cash at bank on the balance sheet totals £6,734 million at 30 September 1994. Of this total, only £2,500 million qualified as cash/cash equivalents for the purpose of the cash flow statement. This presumably means that term deposits of £4,234 million with periods exceeding three months are included in the line item 'cash at bank and in hand'.

Table 17.29 – Hanson PLC – Annual Report – 30 September 1994

BALANCE SHEETS (extract)

	Consolidated		Company	
	1994 £ million	1993 £ million	**1994 £ million**	1993 £ million
Current assets (extract)				
Cash at bank	**6,734**	8,019	**48**	89

NOTES TO THE ACCOUNTS (extract)

23 Analysis of changes in cash, overdrafts and deposits utilised in investing activities

	Cash £ million	Overdraft £ million	Net £ million	Deposits £ million
Balance at October 1, 1992	**2,170**	**(765)**	**1,405**	**6,269**
Effect of exchange fluctuations	28	(16)	12	–
Net cash inflow (outflow)	3,132	–	3,132	(3,580)
Balance at October 1, 1993	**5,330**	**(781)**	**4,549**	**2,689**
Effect of exchange fluctuations	(208)	105	(103)	(4)
Net cash inflow (outflow)	(2,622)	315	(2,307)	1,549
Balance at September 30, 1994	**2,500**	**(361)**	**2,139**	**4,234**
Deposits per above	4,234			
Cash at bank per balance sheet	**6,734**			

17.173 A more restrictive definition is to include only money on deposit with a bank that can be withdrawn on demand. This excludes balances on deposit with other financial institutions such as Building Societies. This interpretation seems unduly harsh. If the purpose of the split between current asset investments and cash at bank is to give an indication of liquidity of the asset then a reasonable interpretation would seem to be the one in paragraph 17.169, that is, the money on deposit with a bank or other financial institution which can be withdrawn on demand.

Right of set-off of bank balances

17.174 Assets and liabilities are only allowed to be offset against one another in financial statements where there is a legally enforceable right of set-off between the balances. This stems from the requirement in paragraph 5 of Schedule 4 to the Act, which states that amounts in respect of items that represent assets or income may not be offset against amounts in respect of items that represent liabilities or expenditure, or *vice versa*.

17.175 FRS 5, 'Reporting the substance of transactions', expands upon this and sets out conditions that have to be met in order for offset to apply. The standard's rules require offset where the balances do not constitute separate assets and liabilities and where the following conditions are met:

- The company and other party owe each other determinable monetary amounts denominated either in the same currency or in different but freely convertible currencies.

  A freely convertible currency is one for which quoted exchange rates are available in an active market that can rapidly absorb the amount to be offset without significantly affecting the exchange rate.

- The company has the ability to insist on net settlement.

  Any such right to insist on net settlement should only be taken into account if the company is able to enforce net settlement in all situations of default by the other party. This would obviously include the other party's liquidation, but also includes all other situations that might arise during the term of the transactions. Therefore, generally in a normal trading company, if it has debit and credit balances with a bank and the bank can insist on net settlement, but the company cannot, then the company will not be able to offset these balances in its financial statements.

- The company's ability to insist on net settlement is assured beyond reasonable doubt and would survive the insolvency of the other party.

- The debit balance matures no later than the credit balance.

  This condition will be met if the company can ensure that result by accelerating the maturity of the deposits with the other party or deferring the maturity of the credit balance with that party.

[FRS 5 para 29].

17.176 Extreme care needs to be taken in consolidated financial statements, where it may be difficult to arrange for an amount that one group company owes to another party (such as a bank) to be offset against the amount of a deposit that another member of the group has lodged with that party. However, where a bank funds members of a group of companies this situation would be different if both of the following conditions applied:

- Each individual depositing company in the group has a joint and several liability to pay the same debts as the borrowing companies (that is, each is deemed to be a principal debtor for the same debts).

- The bank has a liability to each individual depositing company in respect of its deposit.

17.177 In these circumstances such assets and liabilities may be offset against each other if all the criteria are met. Tesco has bank deposits at subsidiary undertakings which have been offset against borrowings in the parent company under a legal right of set-off (see Table 17.30).

Table 17.30 – Tesco PLC – Annual Report and Accounts – 25 February 1995

Note 14 Creditors – amounts falling due within one year (extract)

	Group		**Company**	
	1995	1994	**1995**	1995
	£m	£m	**£m**	£m
Bank loans and overdrafts (a)	**298**	8	**878**	505

(a) Bank deposits at subsidiary undertakings of £614m (1994 – £505m) have been offset against borrowings in the parent company under a legal right of set-off.

17.178 An example of a company that had to change its treatment of bank balances as a result of FRS 5 is Gestetner Holdings (see Table 17.31).

Table 17.31 – Gestetner Holdings PLC – Report and Accounts – 31 December 1994

Financial review (extract)

Off balance sheet finance (extract)

Cash Offsetting and Back to Back Arrangements

In instances where cross company cash pooling arrangements are in place with certain banks, or where bank lending is secured by cash deposits, the accounting treatment in previous years has been to net down cash balances against borrowings. Under FRS 5, unless the Group subsidiary as well as the bank has a legal right to offset these balances, netting down is not permitted.

This grossed up the Group's balance sheet (cash and borrowings) by £69m at 31 December 1994 (1993: £128m).

Notes to the accounts (extract)

	Group		Company	
Note 14 Cash at bank and in hand	**1994 £m**	1993 £m	**1994 £m**	1993 £m
Fixed deposits	**57.3**	70.7	–	–
Call deposits	**69.5**	29.0	–	–
Cash and bank balances	**15.8**	98.2	–	0.2
	142.6	197.9	–	0.2

Of the above, £48.3m (1993 – £53.5m) is secured against loans and overdrafts granted by various banks where they have a legal ability to insist on a net settlement in all situations of default but Group undertakings do not have an equal and opposite right. The related liability is included as secured bank borrowings in Note 16, Loans and Overdrafts. This represents a change of accounting policy, following the introduction of Financial Reporting Standard 5, Reporting the Substance of Transactions, and the 1993 balance sheet has been restated (see Note 37). In previous years, such balances were netted off against the respective loans.

In addition to the above, £6.6m (1993 – £3.9m) is subject to exchange controls.

Treatment of uncleared items

17.179 Traditionally, balances at bank are included in the financial statements of companies at the balance shown in the cash book, and the uncleared cheques and lodgements are reconciled to the balance shown in the bank statements. In normal situations, this would represent the prudent view, in that the company is anticipating the bank's clearance of its cheques. Cheques issued are usually no longer in the control of the issuing company and the balance at bank is deemed to be the balance shown in the cash book. Debtors and creditors are likewise reflected as though outstanding cheques or lodgements have in fact been cleared.

17.180 In certain situations, however, there may be an abnormal period of time between the date on which the cheques are drawn and recorded in the company's cash book and the date on which they are cleared through the bank account. Some companies, therefore, choose to include in their financial statements the balance shown on the bank statement. This raises the question of the appropriate form of presentation for uncleared banking items (that is, cheques issued or received before the year end, but not cleared by the bank).

17.181 Where the company's policy is to show the bank statement balance in the financial statements, cheques issued or received before the year end, but not cleared by the bank should normally be included in creditors and debtors respectively. The rationale for this treatment is that the company is not recognising the cash transaction until it is reflected by the bank. An alternative treatment that may be appropriate if the amounts are material would be to disclose such uncleared cheques as 'Cash in transit' or 'Uncleared banking items'. The effect of this treatment is that the balance at bank is shown as the balance on the bank statement, and creditors and debtors are shown after reflecting cheques issued or received respectively before the year end and the net amount being processed by the bank is shown as 'Cash in transit' or 'Uncleared banking items'.

17.182 For the purposes of disclosure in the financial statements, either method is acceptable, provided that a company uses the same method from one year to the next. If a company changes its method, it should, in that year, adjust the comparatives and give an explanation. If the balance at bank is the balance shown on the bank statements, it is desirable that this fact is noted in the accounting policies.

Restricted cash balances

17.183 Cash at bank and in hand will sometimes include balances that can only be used for a specific purpose or where access is restricted. If these amounts are material then they should be disclosed, normally in the notes to the financial statements. Examples of such disclosure are found in the accounts of John Mowlem (cash balances subject to legal charges, see Table 17.32), Cable & Wireless (cash balances subject to exchange regulation, see Table 17.33) and ICI (short-term deposits and cash held by insurance subsidiaries, see Table 17.34).

Table 17.32 – John Mowlem & Company PLC – Annual Report and Accounts – 31 December 1994

NOTES TO THE ACCOUNTS

18 Cash

At 31 December 1994, cash balances with banks include £6.4 million (1993 £4.4 million) of cash deposits which are subject to either a legal assignment or a charge in favour of a third party. It is expected that they will be released in 1995.

Table 17.33 – Cable and Wireless plc – Annual report and Accounts – 31 March 1998

Notes to the Accounts

21. SHORT-TERM DEPOSITS AND CASH AT BANK AND IN HAND

Of the total amounts shown, £21m (1997 – £34m) is held in countries subject to exchange regulations which may delay repatriation.

Table 17.34 – Imperial Chemical Industries PLC – Annual Report and Accounts – 31 December 1997

Notes relating to the accounts

17 Current asset investments and short-term deposits (extract)

Included in unlisted investments and short-term deposits and cash are amounts totalling £206m (1996 £191m) held by the Group's insurance subsidiaries. In 1997 £24m (1996 £14m) was readily available for the general purposes of the Group.

Creditors

Disclosure

17.184 All items included under creditors must be analysed between amounts that will fall due within one year of the balance sheet date and amounts that will fall due after more than one year. [Schedule 4 balance sheet formats]. The Act requires that creditors should be analysed into the following categories:

- Debenture loans.
- Bank loans and overdrafts.
- Payments received on account.
- Trade creditors.

- Bills of exchange payable.
- Amounts owed to group undertakings.
- Amounts owed to undertakings in which the company has a participating interest.
- Other creditors including taxation and social security.
- Accruals and deferred income.

[4 Sch formats].

17.185 An item representing a liability that is not covered by the prescribed format may be shown separately. [4 Sch 3(2)]. Examples of creditors that are sometimes shown as separate categories within total creditors are amounts due in respect of factored debts or bills of exchange discounted with recourse, finance lease payables and deferred consideration in respect of acquisitions.

17.186 Both the Act and FRS 4 specify a considerable amount of detail that a company should disclose in its financial statements in respect of its indebtedness. These disclosure requirements are considered in detail in chapter 18.

17.187 For the purpose of the Act, a loan falls due for repayment (or an instalment falls due for payment) on the earliest date on which the lender could require repayment (or payment) if the lender were to exercise all options and rights available to him. [4 Sch 85]. This definition is also included in FRS 4, which provides guidance on its interpretation including the implications of underlying borrowing facilities. The maturity of debt is discussed in detail in chapter 18.

17.188 Where any item that is shown under the heading 'Creditors' includes liabilities for which the company has given security, these liabilities must be disclosed in aggregate. Also, the notes must give an indication of the nature of the securities given. [4 Sch 48(4)]. For this requirement to be meaningful, the financial statements should show some disaggregation of the relevant liabilities. This is because it could be misleading merely to disclose the aggregate of securities compared with the aggregate of liabilities.

Debentures

17.189 There is no precise definition of a debenture, either in law or in practice. In legal terms it is generally construed as formal acknowledgment of a debt. However, section 744 of the Act refers to debentures as including *"debenture stock, bonds and any other securities of a company, whether constituting a charge on the assets of the company or not"*. This definition is very wide. It does not distinguish clearly between a debenture loan and any other loan. Whether a particular loan is a debenture or not will depend on the documentation. A formal loan agreement, whether containing security or not, will often constitute a debenture. Although a bank loan may be a debenture loan, the balance sheet formats distinguish between bank loans and other debenture loans.

17.190 For accounting measurement and disclosure purposes, there is no difference between debentures, loans and other debt instruments. They are all capital instruments issued for raising finance and are dealt with in detail in chapter 18.

Trade creditors

17.191 Trade creditors normally represents amounts owed to suppliers of goods and services. It could comprise either all items included in the creditors ledger or simply those items that relate to the cost of sales. If companies classify all creditors ledger items as trade creditors, such treatment could distort the cost of sales/trade creditors ratio. A company should ensure that, whatever treatment it adopts, it is consistent from year to year.

Obligations in respect of trade loans

17.192 Trade loans are common in a number of industries, a typical example being the brewing industry. Trade loans are often given by brewers to their tied houses and in consideration for the loan the tied house will agree to take a certain quantity of beer from the brewer. Such arrangements can be financed in a variety of ways, for example, by advances from the brewer, or from a bank. FRS 5 requires the substance of the arrangement to be accounted for and so, depending on the circumstances of the particular agreement, the obligation in respect of the trade loans may have to be shown on the brewer's balance sheet.

17.193 From the 1994 financial statements of Bass, it can be seen that the trade loans and related obligations have been brought on balance sheet following the introduction of FRS 5 (see Table 17.35). The liability has been included within the total for 'other borrowings'.

Table 17.35 – Bass PLC – Annual Report – 30 September 1994

Accounting Policies (extract)

iii) Investments

Fixed asset investments are stated individually at cost less any provision for permanent diminution in value. Fixed asset investments comprise trade loans and advances, trade investments in the equity of other undertakings, quoted securities and debentures. Trade loans are principally advances made to operators of UK on-licensed outlets by the Brewing division, either directly or through an arrangement with a bank. They are advanced in order to obtain a beer supply agreement and are generally cancellable at three months' notice.

Notes to the Financial Statements

13 Fixed asset investments (extract)

To comply with FRS 5 arrangements entered into by the Group with a number of banks to advance loans to third party outlets are now incorporated within both fixed asset investments and borrowings (see note 20). Trade loans and advances cost at 30 September 1993 has been restated accordingly by £80m.

17.194 An example of a company in a different industry recognising obligations in respect of trade loans to third parties, as a result of FRS 5, is Burmah Castrol (see Table 17.36). Obligations to banks in respect of the provision of financial assistance to customers in the group's fuel and marketing operations have been brought on balance sheet. The liability is shown as a separate item 'obligations to banks under trade loan guarantees' within creditors (see Table 17.22 on page 59).

Table 17.36 – Burmah Castrol plc – Annual Report – 31 December 1994

FINANCIAL REVIEW (extract)

Accounting policies (extract)

The group's lubricants and fuels marketing operations sometimes entail entering into agreements whereby customers receive financial assistance from banks. The group has an obligation to banks in respect of such loans, which are normally serviced and repaid by the withholding of sales rebates. At 31 December 1994, the total amount outstanding under such obligations was £76 million (1993, £60 million). In accordance with FRS5, which came into effect in 1994, these amounts have been incorporated into the group's consolidated balance sheet, both as an asset under trade advances and similar arrangements, and as a liability under obligations to banks in respect of trade advances. The costs and benefits to the group of these arrangements continue to be included in operating profit.

NOTES TO THE ACCOUNTS

2 Changes to corresponding figures (extract)

(b) In compliance with FRS5, certain obligations relating to the provision of financial assistance to third parties have been included in the group's consolidated balance sheet. Corresponding figures for 1993 have been adjusted, increasing fixed asset investments by £60.3 million, creditors falling due within one year by £16.1 million and creditors falling due after one year by £44.2 million. Also, retained on balance sheet are bills discounted with recourse, which at 31 December 1993 amounted to £6.9 million. Current assets and creditors falling due within one year have been adjusted by this amount.

17.195 As mentioned above, there are various forms that trade loans can take and some will clearly be on balance sheet and some clearly off balance sheet. However, there are a number of grey areas where the risks and rewards will have to be considered very carefully to determine whether such loans are on or off balance sheet. Consider the following situations using brewers as an example:

Example 1

A bank makes a loan to a brewer and the brewer makes a loan to its tied house at a lower interest rate than that charged by the bank.

In such circumstances, it is clear that both loans should be on the brewer's balance sheet, one as an asset and the other as a liability.

Example 2

A bank makes a loan to the tied house which is guaranteed by the brewer. In consideration for the guarantee, the tied house agrees to take a certain quantity of beer from the brewer on normal commercial terms.

This type of transaction is likely to be off the brewer's balance sheet, because the fact that it has guaranteed the loan would not of itself result in a liability that needs to be recorded on its balance sheet. The guarantee would be disclosed as a contingent liability in accordance with SSAP 18.

Example 3

The facts are the same as the example above, but the brewer subsidises part of the interest cost on the loan to the tied house. This is done either by making payments direct to the bank or by making payments to the tied house.

It can be argued that the substance of this arrangement is a subsidised loan made from the brewer to the tied house. Consequently, the brewer's position is no different from the situation where the bank makes a loan to the brewer and the brewer then lends those funds to the tied house at a subsidised rate (example 1). The risks and rewards to the brewer are identical. If the tied house defaults on the loan then the bank has full recourse *via* the guarantee to the brewer. The brewer also bears the interest differential. Alternatively, it can be argued that this transaction is similar to example 2 above and its substance is that of a contingent liability arising from the guarantee and the interest subsidy is a way of giving the tied house a trade discount. These are finely balanced arguments and strictly in accordance with FRS 5 this type of arrangement should probably be accounted for as a financing transaction.

Example 4

The bank makes a loan to the tied house which is guaranteed by the brewer. The brewer does not subsidise the interest payments, but the tied house agrees to take a certain quantity of beer from the brewer and is given a trade discount (which is not normally available).

Again, the substance of such a transaction would have to be considered very carefully. If the substance is similar to that in example 3 above, because there is a strong correlation between the amount of the loan and the amount of business (such that the amount of the trade discount is similar to the amount which would have been paid as interest subsidy), then there seems to be an argument for saying that the substance is a financing and the full amount of the loan should be recorded as a liability on the brewer's balance sheet. If, however, there is little or no correlation between the amount of business and the loan, such that the discount given differs from the amount that would have been paid as interest subsidy, then there is an argument for saying that the substance has changed and the loan should not be recognised on the brewer's balance sheet.

17.196 Alternatively, there may be ways whereby the trade loans can be structured so that the risks to the brewer are capped. If, for example, the brewer's portfolio of trade loans was £100 million and the bank advances (say) £80 million of non-recourse finance, the bank would be protected if the bad debts on the portfolio are expected to be only £5 million. The brewer is still exposed to the bad debt risk, but its downside risk is capped at £20 million and the bank is exposed merely to the unlikely risk of catastrophe. In this circumstance, it might be possible to use the linked presentation. The non-recourse finance could then be deducted from the trade loans it finances on the face of the balance sheet; the difference (£20 million in the example) less a provision for bad debts (say £5 million) is the asset included in the balance sheet totals. The presentation would be as follows:

	£m	£m
Trade loans	95	
Less: Non-recourse finance	80	
		15

17.197 This presentation could only be justified, however, if the finance is to be repaid from the specific item it finances and there is no possibility whatsoever of a claim on the brewer being established other than against funds generated by the trade loans. Furthermore, the strict linked presentation conditions in paragraph 27 of FRS 5 would also have to be met before this approach could be used (see chapter 4).

Other creditors including taxation and social security

17.198 The line 'other creditors including taxation and social security' must be analysed between other creditors, and taxation and social security. [Note 9 on the balance sheet formats]. These headings should include the following items:

- Other creditors.
  - Dividends.
  - Any creditor items that cannot appropriately be analysed elsewhere.

- Taxation and social security.
  - Corporation tax.
  - VAT.
  - ACT payable on dividends.
  - Social security and other amounts (such as PAYE owed in respect of wages and salaries).
  - Excise duty.

17.199 'Other creditors including taxation and social security' contrasts with the line under provisions for 'taxation, including deferred taxation'. The latter item will comprise all deferred tax liabilities.

Dividends and related ACT

17.200 Schedule 4 requires the disclosure in the profit and loss account of the aggregate amount that is recommended for distribution by way of dividend. [4 Sch 3(7)(b)]. Paragraph 51(3) of Schedule 4 requires the proposed dividends to be disclosed also in the balance sheet or in the related notes. Dividends are not specifically referred to in either of the balance sheet formats. A proposed dividend is not a liability in law until it has been declared, and so it would not be appropriate to include it within any of the items listed in the formats. In practice, as indicated above, it is normally included as a separate item under 'creditors'. Dividends and other appropriations are considered further in chapter 19.

17.201 Furthermore, SSAP 8 requires that proposed dividends should be included in creditors without the addition of the related ACT. The ACT payable on proposed dividends (whether recoverable or irrecoverable) should be included under 'taxation and social security'. ACT is considered further in chapter 13.

Accruals and deferred income

17.202 In the same way that 'prepayments and accrued income' may be shown in either of two positions in the formats, the item 'accruals and deferred income' may be disclosed either as a category of creditors or as a separate category in its own right. [Note 10 on the balance sheet formats]. Where 'accruals and deferred income' is disclosed under creditors, it must be analysed between those amounts that will fall due within one year and those amounts that will fall due after more than one year. [Note 13 on the balance sheet formats]. No such analysis is required if 'accruals and deferred income' is included as a separate category.

17.203 'Accruals and deferred income' could include government grants of a capital or revenue nature that are accounted for as deferred credits. These are discussed in chapter 14.

Provisions for liabilities

Introduction

17.204 The accounting treatment of provisions has been a matter of some debate, particularly the timing of such provisions. Many companies that have carried out restructuring programmes in recent years have set up large provisions. These so-called 'big-bath' provisions have sometimes been criticised because it has not always been clear what they contain and there has been concern that they may be used to manipulate a company's future results. It has also been argued that an intention to incur expenditure did not represent a change in the economic position of the entity and, therefore, was not a basis for recognising a provision.

17.205 This criticism and the fact that there is no consistent treatment has attracted the attention of standard setters. In previous years, the ASB has introduced some rules for provisions in specific circumstances. Under FRS 3, 'Reporting financial performance', provisions for losses on termination of an operation can be made only when the company is demonstrably committed to the termination and cannot realistically withdraw. Under FRS 7, 'Fair values in acquisition accounting', provisions or accruals for reorganisation and integration costs expected to be incurred as a result of the acquisition can no longer be included in the fair value exercise and have to be treated as post-acquisition. For reorganisations, this still left the questions of the timing of the charge to the profit and loss account and what could be included in this charge. The ASB has published FRS 12, 'Provisions, contingent liabilities and contingent assets', which rules that provisions should be recognised only when an entity has an obligation(legal or constructive) to transfer economic benefits as a result of a past event. Where the entity can avoid future expenditure by its future actions, it does not have a liability for that expenditure and so no provision is recognised.

17.206 In the following sections we consider the position prior to the introduction of FRS 12 for the definition of provisions, the disclosure requirements and the accounting treatment for specific types of provisions. The new rules in FRS 12 are summarised in paragraph 17.290.

Definition

17.207 There is sometimes confusion whether items should be disclosed under provisions, or creditors or accruals. In this connection, the treatment of provisions for current taxation has already been considered under 'Other creditors including taxation and social security' (see paragraph 17.198). For some provisions (for example, those for bad and doubtful debts), it is correct to net them against the assets to which they relate. This treatment is correct because the assets have to be stated, in accordance with the statutory accounting rules, at their net realisable value. [4 Sch 23(1)].

17.208 'Provisions for liabilities or charges' is defined in the Act as:

> *"Any amount retained as reasonably necessary for the purpose of providing for any liability or loss which is either likely to be incurred, or certain to be incurred but uncertain as to amount or as to the date on which it will arise."* [4 Sch 89].

17.209 Creditors, by contrast, normally comprise those amounts that are actually owing to third parties and not amounts provided for other liabilities or losses that are likely to be incurred. Also, accruals generally include those amounts representing costs and charges already incurred (possibly apportioned at the balance sheet date) that are not yet actually owing to third parties.

Disclosure

General

17.210 The Act requires 'Provisions for liabilities and other charges' to be analysed into the following categories:

- Pensions and similar obligations.
- Taxation, including deferred taxation.
- Other provisions.

[4 Sch formats].

17.211 An item representing a provision that is not covered by the prescribed format may be shown separately. [4 Sch 3(2)]. Examples of such provisions are those set up in relation to restructurings, integration of acquisitions, self-insurance and environmental liabilities.

17.212 Where there has been any transfer to or from any provision for liabilities or charges other than a transfer from that provision for the purpose for which that provision was set up, the Act requires certain information to be disclosed in respect of each provision that is shown either on the face of the balance sheet or in the notes. This information is as follows:

- The aggregate amount of the provision at both the beginning and the end of the financial year.
- Any amounts transferred either to or from the provision during the financial year.
- The source and the application of any amounts so transferred.

[4 Sch 46(1)(2)].

An example of such a disclosure is given in Table 17.37.

Table 17.37 – Trafalgar House Public Limited Company – Report and Accounts – 30 September 1994

Notes to the accounts

22 Provisions for liabilities and charges

	Ration-alisation £m	Insurance funds £m	Other £m	Group total £m	Company £m
As at 1 October 1993 *(restated)*	34.4	49.3	300.2	383.9	23.5
Exchange translation differences	(0.4)	–	(1.9)	(2.3)	–
Profit and loss account	16.8	7.3	60.5	84.6	0.2
Transfer from creditors	–	–	29.7	29.7	–
Expenditure	(18.0)	(10.3)	(68.4)	(96.7)	(6.8)
As at 30 September 1994	32.8	46.3	320.1	399.2	16.9

Other provisions at 30 September 1994 include amounts in respect of contract related provisions (£150.1 million), environmental liabilities (£24.2 million), rent guarantees (£15.0 million), onerous lease commitments (£42.8 million) and an overseas pension fund (£10.4 million). Group and company provisions include a provision for the premium payable on early repurchase of debt of £10.7 million.

Pensions and similar obligations

17.213 The Act requires the following disclosure in respect of pensions provisions:

- Any pension commitments included under any provision shown in the company's balance sheet.
- Any such commitments for which no provision has been made.

[4 Sch 50(4)].

17.214 In addition, SSAP 24, 'Accounting for pension costs', contains extensive disclosure requirements in respect of pensions, including the disclosure of any provisions or prepayments in the balance sheet resulting from a difference between the amounts recognised as cost and the amounts funded or paid directly. [SSAP 24 para 88(f)]. Pensions and similar obligations are considered in detail in chapter 12.

Taxation provisions

17.215 If the provision for liabilities and charges includes any provision for taxation (other than deferred taxation) it must be disclosed separately. [4 Sch 47].

17.216 Deferred taxation should be included under the balance sheet heading 'Taxation, including deferred taxation' within provisions. In addition, both the Act and SSAP 15 require any provision for deferred taxation to be shown separately. The deferred tax balance, its major components, and transfers to and from the deferred tax account should be disclosed in the notes to the financial statements. [SSAP 15 paras 37, 38].

17.217 Where a company does not provide for some or all of any deferred tax (because the directors do not consider that a liability will crystallise), paragraph 40 of SSAP 15 requires that the total amount of any unprovided deferred tax should be disclosed in a note to the financial statements, analysed into its major components. Deferred taxation is dealt with in chapter 13.

Other provisions

17.218 Where an amount is shown under 'Other provisions', and it includes any individual provision that is itself material, particulars must be given in respect of each such provision. [4 Sch 46(3)]. Possible examples are provisions for future rationalisation, redundancies, dilapidations, or warranty claims. Examples of such disclosure are found in the financial statements of Trafalgar House (see Table 17.37 above on page 80) and Pilkington (see Table 17.38).

Table 17.38 – Pilkington plc – Directors' Report and Accounts – 31 March 1995

Notes on the Financial Statements

27 Provisions for Liabilities and Charges (extract)

Other provisions at 31st March 1995 include £13 million (1994 £13 million) for tank repairs, £16 million (1994 £16 million) for exceptional provisions on the termination of operations and the restructuring of continuing operations, £15 million (1994 £15 million) for holiday pay provisions, £9 million (1994 £6 million) for insurance claims provisions and £19 million (1994 £22 million) for warranty claims.

Acquisition provisions

17.219 FRS 6 'Acquisitions and mergers' requires movements on provisions or accruals for costs related to an acquisition to be disclosed and analysed between the amounts used for the specific purpose for which they were created and the amounts released unused. [FRS 6 para 32]. Such disclosure should be given separately for each material acquisition and for other acquisitions in aggregate. [FRS 6 para 23]. The disclosure is considered in more detail in chapter 23.

Recognition of provisions

17.220 FRS 12, 'Provisions, contingent liabilities and contingent assets', which is effective for years ending on or after 23 March 1999 has introduced rules for the recognition of provisions. Prior to this, in order to determine when a provision should be recognised in financial statements it has been necessary to consider the underlying principles for recognition of liabilities and losses.

17.221 The Act states that *"...all liabilities and losses which have arisen or are likely to arise in respect of the financial year to which the accounts relate or a previous financial year shall be taken into account, including those which only become apparent between the balance sheet date and the date on which it is signed on behalf of the board of directors"*. [4 Sch 12(b)].

17.222 Under SSAP 2, the concept of prudence requires provision to be made for all known liabilities (expenses and losses) whether the amount of these is known with certainty or is a best estimate in the light of information available. [SSAP 2 para 14].

17.223 Liabilities are not defined in the Act but are now defined in the draft Statement of principles and in FRS 5 as *"an entity's obligations to transfer economic benefits as a result of past transactions or events"*. The standard states that whilst most obligations are legally enforceable, a legal obligation is not a necessary condition for a liability. The notion of obligation implies that the entity is not free to avoid an outflow of resource. Where an entity is unable to avoid an outflow, whether for legal or commercial reasons, it will have a liability. The event giving rise to the obligation must already have taken place, although in some cases the obligation may only crystallise into a legal liability on the happening of some future event.

17.224 FRS 5 requires a liability to be recognised if:

- there is sufficient evidence of the existence of the item (including, where appropriate, evidence that a future outflow of benefit will occur); and
- the item can be measured at a monetary amount with sufficient reliability.

17.225 Paragraphs 17.223 and 17.224 take a balance sheet approach to provisions, that is, the provision is made when a liability exists. This is the approach taken in FRS 3 in respect of provisions for terminations, where demonstrable commitment is required before making a provision. However, an alternative view is to consider whether it is appropriate to record a loss (the profit and loss account approach). Under this approach, costs are expensed in the period in which they are incurred, unless they are carried forward to match against related income or they are provided for in advance on the grounds of prudence. The latter is the approach used in practice prior to the introduction of FRS 12, for provisions such as restructuring costs and environmental costs and is consistent with the prudence concept in SSAP 2.

17.226 FRS 12 has now introduced rules for the recognition of provisions that confirms the balance sheet approach. The FRS defines a provision as *"a liability of uncertain timing or amount"*. [FRS 12 para 2]. A provision should be recognised when an entity has a present obligation (legal or constructive) as a result of a past event and it is probable that a transfer of economic benefits will be required to settle the obligation and a reliable estimate of that obligation can be made. [FRS 12 para 14].

17.227 The definition of provisions as a category of liabilities is a change from current practice where the Act refers to provisions for liabilities and losses. SSAP 18 also refers to providing for losses. This change appears to have been made so that provisions fit into one of the defined elements of the balance sheet in the draft statement of principles. This change will impact on current practice in areas such as reorganisation provisions (currently often provided when there is a firm decision) and maintenance provisions (often provided for over a period before there is an obligation). The paragraphs that follow consider current practice for specific types of provisions prior to the introduction of FRS 12. The new rules are summarised in paragraph 17.290.

Redundancy provisions

17.228 An area that often results in significant provisions is redundancies. The timing of such provisions is considered below by looking at the various stages involved.

Compulsory redundancies

17.229 The process of making compulsory redundancies usually involves several stages:

- The decision.
- Identifying employees to be made redundant in terms of numbers.
- Identifying employees to be made redundant in terms of individuals.
- Informing employees.
- Making the redundancy payments.

Situation 1

17.230 Where all the above steps have been taken by the balance sheet date the cost of the redundancy programme will be reflected in the financial statements of the year. This is because the liability has been incurred and settled.

Situation 2

17.231 Where the first four steps have been completed by the balance sheet date (that is, employees have been informed) provision should be made in the financial statements for the year. This is because a clear obligation has been incurred to specific employees. It is probable that there will be an outflow of resources and the cost can be measured with reliability.

17.232 Some may argue that the liability and obligation are not 'in respect of the year or past years', but are in respect of next year. However, FRS 5 makes it clear that an obligation does not have to be legally binding at the time that it is recognised. In this case the decision, coupled with the fact that employees have been identified and told, constitutes the assumption of an obligation by the company in the current year.

17.233 Another argument for it being a liability of the current year is that the obligation to make a redundancy payment is a legal liability. This is normally not recognised as a liability by companies because it is contingent and is usually a remote contingency where accounts are prepared on a going concern basis. However, when a decision is made to make redundancies and employees are told, the contingency crystallises into an actual liability.

17.234 It is sometimes argued that the contingency represents only the amount that is legally payable to employees and that *ex-gratia* amounts, paid over and above the legal minimum, need not be provided. This may be an argument in some cases where it has not been the company's practice in the past to make such *ex-gratia* payments. However, if it is established practice in the company to make *ex-gratia* payments and the decision has been made to pay such extra amounts in the particular case it is arguable that an obligation has been assumed for the additional payments as well. This would be so if the employees had terms in their contracts that provided for such extra amounts, or if the employees included directors who are entitled to such extra amounts under their service contracts. In general, it is considered that the full amount of redundancy payments should normally be provided and not just the legal minimum.

Situation 3

17.235 Where the first three stages have been completed and the employees have been identified both in terms of numbers and individuals, it is considered that the arguments are the same as in situation 2 and that provision should be made. Under current accounting practice (that is, pre-FRS 12) the fourth stage, that is, informing the employees, does not seem to be relevant to the question of whether or not provision should be made.

Situation 4

17.236 In this situation only a decision has been made and the numbers to be made redundant have been identified, but not the specific employees (the first two stages above). If the employees are known to be all of the same category and the provision would be the same whichever employees are identified, the conclusion under current accounting practice (that is, pre-FRS 12) would be that provision should be made.

17.237 If there is a choice between different classes of employees and different age groups it may not be possible to quantify exactly the amount of the provision required. However, part of the liability may be reliably quantified. For instance, it may be possible to determine accurately the minimum amount of the redundancy payments that will be required to be made by law. This should be provided and an estimate should be made of the *ex-gratia* amounts and this estimate should also be provided.

Situation 5

17.238 In this situation only a decision has been made by the balance sheet date to make redundancies, but the numbers and the individuals have not been quantified. It is likely that in a situation like this, a liability could not be quantified. If not, then no provision should be made. However, if subsequent to the year end and before the financial statements are signed further information is obtained, for example, because of actual redundancies made as a result of the decision, then provision should be made to the extent made possible by the further information.

17.239 This is suggested because the Act requires provision to be made for liabilities of the year that only become apparent between the balance sheet date and the date on which it is signed. The liability at the year end is evidenced by the decision and the information gained after the year end enables the liability to be reliably measured. However, it should be noted that this argument will no longer be possible under FRS 12, 'Provisions, contingent liabilities and contingent assets', which is effective for years ending 23 March 1999.

Voluntary redundancies

17.240 The same principles apply to voluntary redundancies. In general, provision should be made for the expected amount of the redundancy payment. However, if a decision has been made by the balance sheet date to reduce the workforce but the board does not know how much of the reduction will come from voluntary redundancies, how much from natural wastage, and how much from compulsory redundancies, it is possible that any liability that arises as a result of the decision will not be capable of being reliably measured.

17.241 Although this suggests that no provision should be made for the full liability, there may be minimum amounts that can be estimated reliably. For instance, it may be possible to estimate the maximum number of people that could be lost through natural wastage and, therefore, to estimate the numbers who would be made redundant, whether voluntarily or compulsorily. If the latter numbers could be determined it might be possible to quantify the legal minimum that would have to be paid in redundancy pay and provide for that.

17.242 A further factor that may make it impossible to quantify a liability reliably is if the reduction in employees is to take place over an extended period. If the programme is over an extended period, this could, for instance affect the numbers of employees who would be lost through natural wastage and thus make more difficult the estimates of how many would be made redundant. In such a case, where the amounts cannot be reliably measured, no provision should be made.

Restructuring provisions

Termination of operations

17.243 Restructurings that involve the termination of an operation are dealt with by FRS 3. The standard requires provision for any losses to be made if a decision to close has been made and the decision is evidenced by a detailed formal plan for termination from which the reporting entity cannot realistically withdraw. [FRS 3 para 18]. Evidence of the commitment might be the public announcement of specific plans, the commencement of implementation or other circumstances effectively obliging the reporting entity to complete the termination.

17.244 The provision required by the standard should include direct costs of the termination and any operating losses of the operation up to the date of termination, after taking account of any future profits of the operation or from disposal of its assets. [FRS 3 para 18]. It should be noted that FRS 3 is amended by FRS 12 (effective for accounting periods ending on or after 23 March 1999) to preclude profits on disposals of assets from being taken into account in measuring such provisions. Provisions for losses on termination of operations are discussed in detail in chapter 7.

Restructuring of continuing operations

17.245 Companies often make provisions for restructurings as part of their continuing operations or as a result of a fundamental change to the nature and focus of the operations. Prior to the introduction of FRS 12, these provisions have typically included redundancy costs (see above), costs of disposal of assets and facilities, relocation costs and costs of surplus leased properties (see below). Recent examples of large restructurings, which illustrate the types of costs included in the provisions, are seen in Grand Metropolitan (see Table 17.39) and British Gas (see Table 17.40 and Table 17.41).

Table 17.39 – Grand Metropolitan Public Limited Company – Annual Report – 30 September 1994

Notes (extract)

22 PROVISIONS FOR LIABILITIES AND CHARGES (extract)

(b) Acquisition and restructuring provisions of £307m, comprising £48m (1993 – £23m) for the integration and reorganisation costs arising on the restructuring of acquired businesses and £259m (1993 – £118m) in respect of the exceptional restructuring costs.

6 EXCEPTIONAL ITEMS (extract)

(i) Operating costs

The £272m disclosed in the profit and loss account as exceptional operating costs comprises restructuring costs of £143m in respect of the Drinks sector (£100m for the closure and disposal of production facilities, £31m for the rationalisation of support structures and £12m for process re-engineering and other actions), £55m in respect of the European operations of the Foods sector (£18m for restructuring production facilities, £19m for the rationalisation of support structures and £18m for Häagen-Dazs shops and the closure of field offices), £31m in respect of Burger King to extend the re-engineering programme initiated during 1993 and £43m principally in respect of the writedown of group properties and the consolidation and rationalisation of corporate support structures.

Operating costs in 1993 included £175m of reorganisation costs to restructure the group's overhead and operational base, including plant rationalisation at Green Giant and store closures at Pearle, and a £50m writedown in respect of the group's UK properties, most of which related to the Brick Lane former brewery site in East London.

Table 17.40 – British Gas plc – Annual Report and Accounts – 31 December 1994

Notes to the Accounts

21 Provisions for liabilities and charges (extract)

	As at 1 January 1994 (as restated) £m	Disposal of subsidiary undertakings £m	Transfers £m	Profit and loss charge £m	Paid £m	**As at 31 December 1994 £m**
Group						
Abandonment costs	153	(18)	(1)	19	(1)	**152**
Pension costs	448	–	–	196	(49)	**595**
Environmental costs (see note 6, page 43)	151	–	–	90	(8)	**233**
Restructuring costs (see note 6, page 43)	1,411	–	–	105	(338)	**1,178**
Deferred petroleum revenue tax	305	–	–	125	–	**430**
Deferred taxation	61	(36)	(5)	20	–	**40**
Other	56	–	5	12	(1)	**72**
	2,585	(54)	(1)	567	(397)	**2,700**

6 Exceptional charges

The 1994 results include provisions for exceptional charges amounting to £195m (1993 £1,683m which comprised £1,650m in respect of restructuring costs within the UK Gas Business and a £33m environmental provision).

£105m has been provided for relocating staff from the corporate centre to locations outside London and for relocating research staff to Loughborough. The provision comprises £65m relating to the vacation of surplus properties. £29m relating to the relocation of corporate centre staff and £11m for the relocation of research staff. At 1 January 1994 the restructuring costs provision was £1,411m and this year's charge of £105m, less a spend in 1994 of £338m, leaves a closing provision of £1,178m.

A further £90m has been allocated to clean contaminated gas manufacturing sites. This activity, though costly, is essential environmentally and if the Company is to release the value of these surplus sites. At 1 January 1994 the environmental provision was £151m and this year's charge of £90m, less a spend in 1994 of £8m, leaves a closing provision of £233m.

Table 17.41 – British Gas plc – Annual Report and Accounts – 31 December 1993

Notes to the Accounts

4 Exceptional charges

The results for 1993 include an exceptional charge of £1 650M for the major restructuring of the UK Gas Business. This restructuring, into five separate business streams: Transportation and Storage, Public Gas Supply, Contract Trading, Servicing and Installation, and Retailing, will ensure that the Company's UK Gas Business will be leaner, more competitive and more commercially focused at a time when the gas market in Great Britain is undergoing radical change. The cash effect of these initiatives will be borne largely over the next three years (£61M was paid during 1993). The exceptional charge includes severance, pension and relocation costs as well as other incremental costs that will be required to implement the restructuring, such as training, property related costs and information technology costs. The 1992 restructuring costs of £195M comprised a £70M provision for restructuring the Company's headquarters and a £125M provision for refocusing UK Gas Business operations.

In 1992, an environmental provision of £125M was made for the estimated costs of dealing with the Company's statutory obligations relating to contamination at old gas manufacturing sites. Further survey work has been undertaken resulting in an additional provision of £33M for 1993.

17.246 Provisions for restructurings have been the subject of debate partly because it is often not clear what is included and because there is a concern that they can be used to manipulate a company's future results, for instance if they are timed to match exceptional profits from asset sales. There is also concern that the provisions may be loaded with normal operating costs thereby benefiting future operating profits.

17.247 These concerns and the fact that there is no consistent treatment have attracted the attention of standard setters both in the UK and abroad. In the US, the SEC expressed concerns that companies were including the costs of ordinary operations, for example advertising and legal settlements, in the restructuring provisions. Such was its concern that it wrote to around 60 companies that had reported large restructuring charges warning that the charges would be carefully scrutinised.

17.248 Following on from this, the US Emerging Issues Task Force issued Abstract 94-3 'Liability recognition for certain employee termination benefits and other costs to exit an activity (including certain costs incurred in a restructuring)'. Under this Abstract, an obligation in respect of an exit plan arises when:

- Management approves and commits the entity to an exit plan.
- The exit plan identifies all significant actions to be taken and the expected date of completion.
- Actions required by the exit plan will begin as soon as possible after the commitment date and the period of time to complete the plan indicates that significant changes are not likely.

17.249 Therefore, until recently, the rules for restructurings of continuing operations in the US have been more restrictive than in the UK. The US Abstract requires the company to demonstrate its commitment to the restructuring before making a provision. This is similar to the UK rules for terminations dealt with in paragraph 17.243. For restructurings of continuing operations, in the UK it has been normal to make provision when a firm decision has been made to carry out a restructuring, but there is no requirement for the matters in the last two bullet points of paragraph 17.248 to be evidenced. However, in practice there is normally some degree of evidence and quantification of the amount of the provision required and if the amount involved is material then the provision would have to be explained in the financial statements (see Tables 17.39 on page 87 and 17.40 on page 88) and it would be normal for the restructuring to be discussed in the Operating and financial review.

17.250 Examples of provisions being made on the basis of decisions taken by the directors can be found in the financial statements of Trafalgar House (see Table 17.42) and British Steel (see Table 17.43). In Trafalgar House, provision is made for decisions taken by directors during the year. In British Steel, rationalisation costs are provided in respect of decisions taken prior to the finalisation of the financial statements.

Table 17.42 – Trafalgar House Public Limited Company – Report and Accounts – 30 September 1994

Notes to the accounts

2 Exceptional items (extract)

c The charge of £24.4 million for rationalisation programmes includes costs incurred and provisions made for decisions taken by the directors during the year to reduce the cost base of the group's businesses by closing certain facilities, reducing management and administrative headcount, and relocating certain businesses.

Table 17.43 – British Steel plc – Report and Accounts – 1 April 1995

Accounting policies (extract)

III Rationalisation and related measures

The revenue costs of rationalisation and related measures are provided for in respect of decisions taken prior to the finalisation of the accounts and are included under operating costs.

17.251 The differences in treatment of restructuring costs is highlighted in the UK to US GAAP reconciliation of Grand Metropolitan (see Table 17.44). Of the £272 million exceptional restructuring costs in 1994, £134 million is added back under US GAAP. This is explained by the company as follows:

Table 17.44 – Grand Metropolitan Public Limited Company – Annual Report – 30 September 1994

INFORMATION FOR US SHAREHOLDERS

Notes on differences between UK and US GAAP (extract)

(f) Restructuring costs

Under UK GAAP restructuring costs are charged to the profit and loss account in the period in which the decision has been made to restructure a part of the group's business. The timing of the recognition of certain types of restructuring costs differs from US GAAP which requires a number of specific criteria to be met including the requirement to recognise the expense in the statement of income in the period when the obligation to incur costs first exists.

17.252 FRS 12 has now introduced specific rules for the recognition of provisions for restructuring costs. Examples of a restructuring include a sale or termination of a line of business; the closure or relocation of business locations, changes in management structure (for example, eliminating a layer of management) and fundamental reorganisations that have a material effect on the nature and focus of the entity's operations. [FRS 12 para 75].

17.252.1 Under FRS 12, provisions for reorganisations should only be recognised if there is an obligation at the balance sheet date. A constructive obligation arises only if the entity has a detailed formal plan and has raised a valid expectation in those affected by it that the restructuring will be carried out (for example, by starting to implement it or by announcing it in sufficient detail). [FRS 12 para 77]. A management or board decision to restructure taken before the balance sheet date does not in itself give rise to a constructive obligation at the balance sheet date.

17.252.2 The detailed formal plan for the restructuring should identify at least:

- The business or part of a business concerned.
- The principal locations affected.
- The location, function, and approximate number of employees who will be compensated for terminating their services.
- The expenditures that will be undertaken.
- When the plan will be implemented.

[FRS 12 para 77].

17.252.3 If it is expected that there will be a long delay before the restructuring begins or that the restructuring will take an unreasonably long time, it is unlikely that the plan will raise a valid expectation on the part of others that the entity is at present committed to restructuring, because the timeframe allows opportunities for the entity to change its plans. [FRS 12 para 79].

[The next paragraph is 17.253.]

17.253 Prior to FRS 12 there were no rules concerning the costs that should be included in a restructuring provision, although it would normally include costs incurred as a direct result of the restructuring that are incremental to other costs incurred by the company. Redundancy and relocation costs fall into this category. Also included would be costs representing contractual obligations that will either continue after the restructuring with no economic benefit to the entity or involve a penalty to cancel the contractual obligation. An example of the latter would be a lease cancellation fee that the company pays in respect of a leased property. An example of the former would be where the company is not permitted to cancel the lease and is unable to use the property in its continuing operations. The onerous lease will need to be provided for in the restructuring provision. Onerous leases are discussed in more detail from paragraph 17.256 below.

17.254 Disclosure of the costs included in the restructuring provision is given by British Gas in Table 17.41 on page 89. The exceptional charge includes severance, pension and relocation costs as well as other incremental costs that will be required to implement the restructuring, such as training, property related costs and information technology costs.

17.254.1 FRS 12 now specifies that a restructuring provision should include only the direct expenditures arising from the restructuring, which are those that are both:

- necessarily entailed by the restructuring; and
- not associated with the ongoing activities of the entity.

17.254.2 Expenditures included in a restructuring provision will include costs of making employees redundant; costs of terminating leases and other contracts, the termination of which results directly from the reorganisation; and expenditure to be made in the course of the reorganisation such as the remuneration of employees engaged in dismantling plant and disposing of surplus stocks. However, FRS 12 states that retraining or relocating continuing staff, marketing, or investment in new systems and distribution networks should not be included in the restructuring provision.[FRS 12 para 86]. Gains on the expected disposal of assets are not taken into account in measuring a restructuring provision, even if the sale of assets is envisaged as part of the restructuring. [FRS 12 para 88].

[The next paragraph is 17.255.]

17.255 These new rules are similar to US guidance, under which the restructuring provision should not include costs that are part of normal continuing operations. The types of costs that are excluded from restructuring costs in the US as they benefit continuing operations are:

- Costs incurred to develop new computer software to enable the remaining staff to work more efficiently.
- Costs of hiring outside consultants to identify future corporate strategy and organisational structures.
- Advertising costs promoting a new company image.
- Costs of retraining and relocating existing employees.

Vacant leasehold property

17.256 Where a company has a head lease on a property it has a continuing obligation to pay the landlord for the rents due under the lease. However, if the property is vacant the company may not be able to recover any of that cost in the future unless it can find a sub-lessee for the unoccupied premises.

17.257 The UITF issued a draft Abstract in June 1993 which proposed that, when a property substantially ceased to be used for the purposes of the business, a provision should be made to the extent that the recoverable amount of the interest in the property was insufficient to cover the future obligations relating to the lease. However, in a statement issued in July 1993, the UITF decided not to proceed with the subject. It concluded that the existing accounting standards and principles did not provide a sufficient basis for it to develop a ruling in general terms that would ensure appropriate treatment for all the diverse circumstances that existed in practice.

17.258 The statement made it clear that in reaching its conclusion the UITF was in no way discouraging the use of the proposed accounting treatment, that is, provision for the outstanding obligation, by an company that found it to be appropriate to its circumstances. The UITF also encouraged disclosure of the accounting policies followed for vacant leasehold property (including property that is only partly occupied), where this materially affects results.

17.259 Therefore, although the UITF did not issue a final ruling, the issue has not gone away and it is necessary to consider the specific circumstances and apply normal accounting principles.

17.260 Where a leased property is vacant, there is a liability that may have no corresponding economic benefit in the future. Although the liability will be settled over a number of years, the future payments represent a contingent loss at the balance sheet date, that is, contingent upon the property not being used or sub-let. SSAP 18 requires that *"...a material contingent loss should be accrued in financial statements where it is probable that a future event will confirm a loss which can be estimated with reasonable accuracy at the date on which the financial statements are approved"*. In other words, SSAP 18 requires that where the accruals concept is no longer appropriate, because there is no economic benefit in the future to match against future costs, the prudence concept should be applied and provision should be made immediately.

17.261 An example of a company that discloses an accounting policy for vacant leasehold property is Cordiant (see Table 17.45).

Table 17.45 – Cordiant plc – Report and Accounts – 31 December 1994

Accounting Policies (extract)

Long term property provisions

Provision is made for the future rental and related costs of leasehold property where it is vacant or surplus to the Group's requirements, the sublease is not coterminous with the Group's lease commitment or the leasehold property has been sublet at a loss.

Notes to the accounts

14 Provision for liabilities and charges (extract)

Analysis of leasehold property provisions by years:	**31 Dec 1994** £ million	31 Dec 1993 £million
Under one year	13.6	16.8
One to two years	13.1	12.1
Two to five years	29.7	28.3
Over five years	66.4	81.0
	122.8	**138.2**

17.262 A number of different situations arise in which a company may have vacant properties. Not all of these will give rise to the need for a provision, either because it is reasonable to believe that the properties will be used in the business in the future, or because there is a future economic benefit that can be identified that relates to the empty property. Several situations are considered below.

Example 1

A company relocates to a new head office. The old premises are now empty and will not be used in the business. The company will suffer lease costs on the properties until the lease expires in ten years and the lease costs are material.

In this example, there are no future economic benefits and so the recoverable amount of the interest in the property is insufficient to cover the obligation and provision should be made for the liability. The cost would be included in arriving at operating profit and would be disclosed as exceptional if necessary.

Example 2

A business has been disposed of, but several properties have been retained. The properties are now empty and will not be used in the business. The company will suffer lease costs on the properties until the leases expire in ten years and the lease costs are material. In this example, the properties cannot be said to be part of the company's continuing operations and, consequently, provision should be made for the onerous lease. The provision would normally be included in the profit or loss on disposal of the business.

The above examples are at one extreme where: the property is empty; does not form part of the company's on-going operations; and there is no benefit, direct or indirect, that will be obtained from the property.

Example 3

A company has a large number of retail branches that are on short or long leases. At any one point in time some of the branches are unoccupied. Some of the empty properties may be sold; some may be refurbished and reopen for business; and some may continue unoccupied until the end of the lease.

In a situation like this the existence of unoccupied branches may not require a provision for onerous leases, if the company's branches are viewed as a portfolio. It could be argued that the portfolio as a whole is part of the continuing business of the company and that it is part of the normal operations to have some unoccupied properties. Therefore, all lease costs should be expensed as they occur, because to provide up front for onerous leases would ignore the benefit of other favourable leases and may be impracticable as the use of particular branches might vary over the period of the lease.

An exception to this treatment would be where there was a limited number of branches and stores and it was clear that certain identifiable stores were vacant and would remain so. An example would be where a retail group closed down a particular sector of its business, or reduced it considerably, such that the stores that were vacant as a result were clearly no longer part of the continuing operations. In such a case, provision would be made for the onerous leases.

Example 4

In this situation, a company has moved out of a major property on which it now has an onerous lease, because it will no longer use the property in its operations. Normally, provision would be made for the onerous lease. However, the company has received an incentive from the landlord of its new premises which is designed specifically to compensate it for the costs of the old lease. The incentive is a lower than market rent on the new premises. Taking the rent on the old premises together with the rent on the new premises and spreading the total over the period of the old lease gives a charge which is equivalent to a market rent on the new premises.

The incentive received will normally be spread over the period to the first rent review to market rentals in accordance with UITF 12. Care would need to be exercised before allowing the onerous lease liability to be spread. Unless the new landlord obtains right of occupation of, or the right to sublet, the old premises it is unlikely that the 'incentive' is really linked to the old lease. Instead it is likely that the incentive would have had to be paid whether or not there was the old onerous lease, in which case the costs of the onerous lease should not be spread, but should be provided immediately. If, however, the new landlord obtains rights over the old premises, such as the right to occupy or sublet it, the spreading treatment set out above could be adopted, subject to the total cost being spread not exceeding a market rent on the new premises.

Although simplistic, this example recognises that where the cost of an onerous lease is to some extent specifically compensated for by beneficial terms of a new lease, the liability for the onerous lease may be reduced by taking account of the benefit in the new lease, provided that the new lessor obtains genuine rights over the old lease. Although it may be difficult to quantify the benefit, professional advice from valuers or estate agents may enable a reasonable estimate to be made.

Example 5

The company leases five floors of a building. It occupies three floors, but the other two floors are vacant. It was the original intention that the company would grow and in due course would occupy all five floors.

In the situation where a company is expanding and in due course may occupy the vacant space, the vacant property will eventually form part of the company's operations and so the lease costs should be charged to the profit and loss account as they occur.

Where, however, there is unlikely to be a situation where the vacant floors are used in the company's operations, provision should be made for the onerous liability. It will be necessary to exercise judgement in some cases to decide which of the situations referred to above has occurred, particularly where it is argued that, 'by spreading people round' all five floors, it could be said to be used in the business. Such an argument might be refuted, for instance, if the two 'unoccupied' floors are being advertised for letting.

In addition, where it is known that there will be a minimum period during which the floors will be empty, provision should be made in respect of this minimum period.

Example 6

The company is an investment property company which leases an office block. It has not managed to sublet the office block to tenants, because there is an excess supply of office property in the area.

In this situation, the company is required to carry its properties at market value by SSAP 19. The valuer will attribute a lower or negative value to the property if he considers that the rent payable by the client exceeds the property's open market rental (which is likely if the client is unable to sublet the property). Hence any reduction in value will be taken care of and no further provision need be made.

17.263 When it has been decided that a provision is required in respect of an onerous lease, the amount of the provision needs to be determined. Measurement of the provision required will depend on the particular circumstances. In some cases it may reasonably be expected that a sublessee will be found within say two years. Such an assumption might be supported, for instance, by a chartered surveyor's opinion. In such a case, the provision could be reliably measured at the value of the two years' rentals.

17.264 However, it might be that the view was taken that the premises could not be sublet (for instance if the location has become blighted) or used again in the business. In such a situation, the provision might be the value of the rentals until the end of the lease (say ten years), discounted if appropriate as a proxy for the amount that the company would have to pay now to persuade someone to take over the lease.

17.265 Both of the above assume that the company does not sublet the property. If, however, the company took on a sublessee at a rental below that which the company was paying for, say, a ten year lease the amount of the provision would be the difference between the two rentals for ten years, discounted if appropriate. However, if the property had not been sublet at the time of assessing the provision, there would have to be evidence that the company had identified a lessee or could readily obtain one and intended to do so.

17.266 Any provision for an onerous lease should also take account of obligations in respect of business rates and other similar expenses such as security, insurance and dilapidations.

17.266.1 FRS 12 requires that a provision should be recognised if an entity has a contract that is onerous. [FRS 12 para 71]. An onerous contract is one in which the unavoidable costs of meeting the obligations under it exceed the economic benefits expected to be received. [FRS 12 para 2]. An example of such a contract would be vacant leasehold property where the rentals payable exceed the amount expected to be recovered from subletting to another party.

17.266.2 The unavoidable costs under a contract reflect the least net cost of exiting from the contract, that is, the lower of the cost of fulfilling it and any compensation or penalties arising from failure to fulfil it. [FRS 12 para 73].

17.266.3 Before a separate provision for an onerous contract is established, an entity recognises any impairment loss that has occurred on assets dedicated to that contract. [FRS 12 para 74].

[The next paragraph is 17.267.]

Self-insurance losses

17.267 If a company takes out insurance to cover potential future losses, the cost is accounted for annually on the basis of the premium paid. However, if a company does not take out insurance cover, but instead decides to self-insure, often by means of a separate captive insurance subsidiary, the question arises as to how this should be accounted for.

17.268 There are different views as to how self-insurance should be accounted for. One view is that if the self-insured losses are likely to occur then these should be provided for on an on-going basis on the grounds of prudence. The provision would be an actuarial best estimate, based on previous experience of claims. An example of such a policy is found in the financial statements of National Grid (see Table 17.46).

Table 17.46 – The National Grid Company plc – Annual Report and Accounts – 31 March 1994

Accounting policies (extract)

j. Self-insurance
A provision is made in the accounts in respect of future losses which may arise from certain uninsured risks. The charge against profits in respect of this provision is based on advice received from the Group's external insurance adviser.

17.269 However, there is also a view that the group, taken as a whole, does not incur a loss until an incident occurs and so provision should only be made for any known or likely claims as this is when an obligation arises. This reflects the fact that the group does not have external insurance cover and, therefore, incurs losses when the event giving rise to the claim occurs. A company that states in its accounting policy note that it provides for claims in excess of costs expended on related incidents is NFC (see Table 17.47).

Table 17.47 – NFC plc – Annual Report & Accounts – 1 October 1994

Accounting policies (extract)

m Insurance Provisions Provision for the amount by which the costs of self-insured claims are estimated to exceed sums immediately expended on the occurrence of any related incident is made in each year of risk by discounting such estimated costs to present value by reference to the anticipated period over which the claims will be settled. In subsequent years the provision for each year of risk is increased by interest calculated at an appropriate rate. Full provision or accrual is made for the estimated costs of claims or losses falling otherwise outside the limits of insurance policies.

17.270 At present, both treatments are found in practice. The most appropriate accounting policy will depend upon the types of risks that are self-insured. If the risks are of a type that the group would normally provide for on the basis of best estimates in the light of information available, for example, environmental liabilities or product warranties, then provision should be made on the basis described in paragraph 17.268. On the other hand, if the self-insured risk is one that would not normally be provided for in the group until an incident occurs, for example, employers' liability risk, then provision should be made on the basis described in paragraph 17.269.

17.270.1 It should, however, be noted that FRS 12 will only allow a provision to be recognised if there is an obligation at the balance sheet date (effective for accounting periods ending on or after 23 March 1999). Where an entity self-insures there is no obligation to another party until an accident occurs and so provision of a larger amount than the cost of the actual accidents is not be permitted. Therefore, any provision under FRS 12 will comprise the expected cost of all accidents that occurred before the balance sheet date, including those for which the other party has yet to make a claim. The new rules in FRS 12 are discussed further from paragraph 17.290.

[The next paragraph is 17.271.]

Environmental liabilities

17.271 In April 1995 ICAEW issued a discussion paper, FRAG 12/95, 'Financial reporting of environmental liabilities', that considered the key issues relating to the financial reporting of environmental costs, liabilities and impaired assets. In broad terms, the paper concluded that the accounting for such costs is covered by existing accounting requirements and that most of the issues involved are not particularly contentious. However, the application of certain principles may be difficult due to the more extended timeframes that need to be considered and the degree of judgement required.

17.272 Although the ICAEW discussion paper concluded that the issues are not particularly contentious, the accounting treatment of environmental liabilities has been the subject of debate. The ASB exposure draft, FRED 14, proposed that provisions for environmental liabilities should be recognised at the time that the entity becomes obliged, legally or constructively, to rectify environmental damage or to perform restorative work on the environment. These proposals have now been implemented in FRS 12 which will have an impact on the timing of recognition of other environmental liabilities such as those for decommissioning costs. This is considered in more detail from paragraph 17.280. In the following paragraphs we consider the current accounting treatment of provisions for other environmental costs.

17.273 In general, environmental costs can be split into four categories:

- Costs incurred at the company's option.
- Costs required to be incurred because of existing or new legislation.
- Costs that have to be incurred because of environmental damage caused by the company.
- Fines relating to environmental damage.

17.274 Accounting for environmental liabilities can be said to be a specific application of normal accounting rules. Where a company has an obligation in respect of environmental costs, provision should be made in the balance sheet if the expenditure is probable and the amount can be estimated with a reasonable degree of accuracy.

17.275 Where it is known at the outset that there is an environmental cost associated with an operation, prior to FRS 12, provisions have been made over the life of the activity to build up the liability, for example decommissioning. The full provision is, therefore, only recognised in the balance sheet at the end of the life of the activity. Costs required to be incurred because of legislation would fall into this category. It would also include costs incurred at the company's option where the decision to incur these was taken at the outset. Examples of policies where the provision is built up over a period are found in Severn Trent (see Table 17.48) and Attwoods (see Table 17.49).

Table 17.48 – Severn Trent Plc – Annual report and accounts – 31 March 1998

Notes to the financial statements

Accounting Policies (extract)

j **Landfill restoration costs**

Provision for the cost of restoring landfill sites is made over the operational life of each landfill site and charged to the profit and loss account on the basis of the usage of void space.

k **Environmental control and aftercare costs**

Environmental control and aftercare costs are incurred over the operational life of each landfill site and may be incurred for a considerable period thereafter. Provision for such costs is made over the operational life of the site and charged to the profit and loss account on the basis of the usage of void space.

Table 17.49 – Attwoods plc – Annual Report & Accounts – 31 July 1994

Statement of Accounting policies (extract)

Site clean-up, remediation and other environmental costs

Accruals are made for the costs of landfill engineering, restoration and reinstatement together with costs in respect of leachate management, gas control and site management and monitoring incurred during and after the operational life of landfill sites. Such accruals are provided in respect of operational and closed landfill sites together with a contingency reserve to provide a fund in the unlikely event of a significant unexpected environmental liability. These accruals are built up by charges against profits at rates calculated by reference to the airspace consumed and based on management's judgement and past experience of the appropriate levels of such accruals.

17.276 Where an obligation arises because of a particular event of which management were not aware at the beginning of the project, then such provision should be made and the obligation recognised as it arises. Costs that have to be incurred because of environmental damage caused by the company and fines relating to environmental damage would fall into this category. It may also include costs required to be incurred because of changes to legislation and costs that the company has decided to incur where these relate to past operations. An example of a policy where the provision is charged when the expenditure is probable and can be reasonably estimated is found in ICI (see Table 17.50).

Table 17.50 – Imperial Chemical Industries PLC – Annual report and accounts – 31 December 1997

accounting policies (extract)

Environmental liabilities

The Group is exposed to environmental liabilities relating to its past operations, principally in respect of soil and ground water remediation costs. Provisions for these costs are made when expenditure on remedial work is probable and the cost can be estimated within a reasonable range of possible outcomes.

17.277 Accounting policies for both types of costs are found in the financial statements of BP, which has separate policy notes for abandonment costs (allocated over accounting periods) and environmental liabilities (costs recognised when they are probable and can be reasonably estimated). The accounting policies are shown in Table 17.51.

Table 17.51 – The British Petroleum Company p.l.c. – Annual Report and Accounts – 31 December 1997

Accounting policies (extract)

Decommissioning
Provision is made for the decommissioning of production facilities in accordance with local conditions and requirements on the basis of costs estimated as at balance sheet date. The provision is allocated over accounting periods using a unit-of-production method based on estimated proved reserves.

Changes in unit-of-production factors
Changes in factors which affect unit-of-production calculations are dealt with prospectively, not by immediate adjustment of prior years' amounts.

Environmental liabilities
Environmental expenditures that relate to current or future revenues are expensed or capitalised as appropriate. Expenditures that relate to an existing condition caused by past operations and that do not contribute to current or future earnings are expensed.

Liabilities for environmental costs are recognised when environmental assessments or clean-ups are probable and the associated costs can be reasonably estimated. Generally, the timing of these provisions coincides with the commitment to a formal plan of action or, if earlier, on divestment or on closure of inactive sites.

17.278 Environmental liabilities are often long-term and so any provisions will be no more than best estimates. This means that it is necessary to keep the provisions under review in the light of experience and changing requirements. This is illustrated in the 1992 financial statements of ICI, which include an exceptional charge following a reassessment of environmental provisions to reflect current experience and tightening worldwide requirements (see Table 17.52).

Table 17.52 – Imperial Chemical Industries PLC – annual report and accounts – 31 December 1994

NOTES RELATING TO THE ACCOUNTS

3 EXCEPTIONAL ITEMS (extract)

Owing to the material impact that exceptional items have had on the reported results for the year, these items have been disclosed separately on the face of the profit and loss account so that their overall effect may be better appreciated.

	Group	
	1992	1991
	£m	£m
Charged in arriving at trading profit		
Provisions for environmental liabilities	**(148)**	–
Re-assessment to reflect current experience and tightening worldwide requirements. Provisions to remediate impaired sites, principally relating to potential soil and groundwater contamination, have been increased to a more prudent level within the range of possible outcomes.		

17.279 In certain situations, a company may be able to recover some of the environmental costs that it incurs. Generally, these expected recoveries should not be taken into account when assessing the liability for future environmental expenditure. The liability and the expected recovery normally have their own associated risks and uncertainties and so they should be evaluated and presented separately in the balance sheet, unless a legal right of set-off exists and the offset criteria in paragraph 29 of FRS 5 are met. Furthermore, the more stringent criteria for recognising contingent gains will apply and so the inclusion of the recovery asset in the balance sheet will depend on the degree of certainty involved (this is considered further in chapter 20). An example of gross presentation is found in Attwoods (see Table 17.53).

Table 17.53 – Attwoods plc – Annual Reports & Accounts – 31 July 1994

Statement of Accounting Policies (extract)

Cost of environmental litigation

Accruals are made, based on estimates made by the directors, for costs which the Group expects to incur in resolving environmental litigation under US "Superfund" law. These costs include legal fees and site remediation expenses. Any amounts which are expected to be recovered from third parties such as former owners of businesses acquired by the Group and insurance companies, are recognised as other debtors.

Abandonment and decommissioning costs

Definition

17.280 Abandonment is the term used in the Petroleum Act 1987 to describe: the plugging and abandonment of wells; the dismantlement of wellhead; production and transportation facilities; and restoration of producing areas in accordance with the licence requirements and the relevant legislation. It normally commences at the date when the facility ceases to produce, treat, transport or store saleable quantities of oil or gas.

17.281 Similar costs are incurred in other industries such as: decommissioning costs in the electricity and nuclear industries; abandonment costs in the mining and extractive industries; clean up and restoration costs of landfill sites; and environmental clean up costs in a number of industries.

Current accounting practice

17.282 The underlying issue is whether, on developing a facility (such as drilling an oil well, excavating a mine or commissioning a power station), the liability that will arise in the future to abandon or decommission should be recognised in full as a liability on day one or should be recognised gradually by spreading over a period.

17.283 The current accounting practice for abandonment and other similar costs is to build up the eventual liability over the working life of the facility (see Table 17.48 on page 101 and Table 17.51 on page 102). The costs are normally allocated to accounting periods on a unit of production basis. The periodic charge is based on current requirements as to scope, currently available technology and current price levels and is not normally computed on a discounted basis. Changes in estimates of the eventual liability are accounted for as more information becomes available.

17.284 The liability recognised in the balance sheet, therefore, represents the accumulation of periodic charges, less any costs incurred to date. An example of an accounting policy for abandonment costs is disclosed by LASMO (see Table 17.54). In the notes to the financial statements the company also discloses the total estimated liability.

Table 17.54 – LASMO plc – annual report and accounts – 31 December 1994

STATEMENT OF ACCOUNTING POLICIES (extract)

Abandonment provisions

Provision is made for the cost of abandonment of Group-owned assets using the unit of production method based on proven and probable reserves on an entitlement basis. Such provision represents the Group's share of the estimated liability for costs which may be incurred in removing production platforms and facilities at the end of the producing life of each field.

Effect of changes in estimates

The effect of revisions of previous estimates of proven and probable oil and gas reserves and of costs is taken up prospectively in unit of production calculations.

NOTES TO THE ACCOUNTS

18 Provisions for liabilities and charges (extract)

The provisions for abandonment represent the accumulated amount of the Group's share of abandonment costs of £39 million (1993 £65 million) for all North Sea fields in which the Group has an interest and which are currently in production and £4 million (1993 £3 million) for similar costs in Nova Scotia. The total estimated liability for the Group's share of abandonment costs is currently forecast at £88 million (1993 £162 million).

17.285 The current treatment in the UK is consistent with present practice in the US. However, some argue that US accounting principles suggest that dismantlement, restoration and abandonment costs are liabilities that should be recorded immediately. The FASB is working on a project on nuclear decommissioning costs which could also affect the financial statements of oil and gas companies. There are new rules which will change the current treatment in the UK as described below.

OIAC proposals

17.286 In January 1995, the Oil Industry Accounting Committee (OIAC) issued a discussion paper dealing with the application of FRS 5 to future abandonment costs. The paper proposed that the obligations in respect of abandonment of production infrastructure at the end of its useful life should be recognised as a liability in full, as soon as the relevant facility is in place. It proposed that this could be done on a discounted basis.

17.287 Under these proposals, the expected cost of abandonment would be regarded as part of the costs of the development of the facility (in this situation, the oil and gas reserves) and, therefore, capitalised as a fixed asset and depreciated over the useful life of the facility.

[The next paragraph is 17.289.]

17.289 The OIAC proposals for recording an asset and liability up front attracted widespread criticism and the OIAC did not proceed with the issue. However, the ASB produced similar proposals in FRED 14. An application note proposed that provisions for decommissioning costs are recognised when the entity becomes obliged to rectify the environmental damage – which will normally be when the damage is inflicted. The amount provided should be the entity's best estimate of the total amount that will be required to settle its obligation, discounted where this has a material effect. Where the costs meet the test of providing access to economic benefits, it is proposed that they should be capitalised as part of the cost of the facility. As a result, the costs will be charged as an expense over the facility's useful economic life, subject to any need to recognise an impairment of the facility. These proposals have been controversial, but have recently been implemented by FRS 12 and are effective for accounting periods ending on or after 23 March 1999.

FRS 12

17.290 In September 1998, the ASB published FRS 12, 'Provisions, contingent liabilities and contingent assets'. This introduces significant new rules governing what should be recognised as provisions in the balance sheet and it supersedes SSAP 18, 'Accounting for contingencies'. It is effective for accounting periods ending on or after 23 March 1999, with earlier adoption encouraged.

17.291 The objective of FRS 12 is to ensure that appropriate recognition criteria and measurement bases are applied to provisions, contingent liabilities and contingent assets and that sufficient information is disclosed in the notes to the financial statements to enable users to understand their nature, timing and amount. The FRS defines a provision as *"a liability of uncertain timing or amount"*. [FRS 12 para 2]. It means that any provisions that have previously been included within creditors or accruals will have to be reclassified to provisions and will be subject to the detailed disclosure requirements. A summary of the new rules is set out below.

Scope

17.291.1 The FRS covers provisions, contingent liabilities and contingent assets. It excludes from its scope financial instruments that are carried at fair value, executory contracts except where these are onerous and contracts with policyholders in insurance entities' accounts. [FRS 12 para 3]. But the new rules do not apply to provisions that are covered by more specific standards (for example, long-term contracts, deferred tax and pension costs) or to items such as depreciation, impairment of assets or doubtful debts that are adjustments to the carrying amounts of assets. [FRS 12 paras 8, 9].

Recognition

17.291.2 A provision should be recognised when an entity has a present obligation (legal or constructive) as a result of a past event and it is probable that a transfer of economic benefits will be required to settle the obligation and a reliable estimate of that obligation can be made. [FRS 12 para 14]. An entity will normally be able to determine a range of possible outcomes sufficient to enable it to make a reliable estimate of an obligation. [FRS 12 para 25].

17.291.3 A constructive obligation is defined as an obligation that derives from an entity's actions whereby an established pattern of past practice, published policies or a sufficiently specific current statement, the entity has indicated to other parties that it will accept certain responsibilities; and as a result, the entity has created a valid expectation on the part of those other parties that it will discharge those responsibilities.

17.291.4 A past event that leads to a present obligation is called an obligating event. This is an event that creates a legal or constructive obligation that results in an entity having no realistic alternative to settling the obligation. Only liabilities that exist at the balance sheet date can be recognised. Where an entity can avoid future expenditure by its future actions, it does not have a present liability and a provision cannot be recognised. [FRS 12 paras 17, 18]. Therefore, the new rules prohibit provisions for future repairs and maintenance of own assets and for future costs such as Year 2000 costs.

17.291.5 A board decision does not give rise to a constructive obligation at the balance sheet date, unless that decision has been communicated before the balance sheet date in sufficient detail to create a valid expectation in other parties that the entity will discharge the obligation. [FRS 12 para 20].

17.291.6 A past event is deemed to give rise to a present obligation if it is more likely than not that a present obligation exists at the balance sheet date. [FRS 12 para 15]. If not, then it is a contingent liability. A contingent liability is either:

- a possible obligation arising from past events whose existence will be confirmed only by the occurrence of one or more uncertain future events not wholly within the entity's control; or
- a present obligation arising from past events that is not recognised because it is not probable that a transfer of economic benefits will be made or because it cannot be measured with sufficient reliability. [FRS 12 para 2].

17.291.7 Contingent liabilities should not be provided for, but should be disclosed unless remote. [FRS 12 paras 27, 28]. Similarly, contingent assets should not be recognised but should be disclosed if an inflow of economic benefits is probable. [FRS 12 paras 31, 34].

Measurement

17.291.8 The amount recognised as a provision should be the best estimate of the expenditure required to settle the present obligation at the balance sheet date. [FRS 12 para 36]. The best estimate should take account of any risks and uncertainties. [FRS 12 para 42].

17.291.9 Where the effect of the time value of money is material, the amount of a provision should be the present value of the expenditures expected to be required to settle the obligation. [FRS 12 para 45]. The unwinding of the discount should be included within interest (with separate disclosure). [FRS 12 para 48].

17.291.10 The discount rate should be a pre-tax rate that reflects current market assessments of the time value of money and the risks specific to the liability. It should not reflect risks for which future cash flow estimates have been adjusted. [FRS 12 para 47].

17.291.11 Gains from the expected disposal of assets should not be taken into account in measuring a provision. [FRS 12 para 54]. This new rule has resulted in an amendment to paragraph 18 of FRS 3, 'Reporting financial performance', which previously required such gains to be taken into account in calculating a provision for losses on termination of an operation.

Other rules

17.291.12 When an obligation recognised as a provision (for example, decommissioning costs) gives access to future economic benefits then an asset should also be recognised. Otherwise, the provision should be charged immediately to profit and loss account. [FRS 12 para 66].

17.291.13 Provisions should be reviewed at each balance sheet date and adjusted to reflect the current best estimate. If it is no longer probable that a transfer of economic benefits will be required, then the provision should be reversed. [FRS 12 para 62].

17.291.14 A provision should be used only for the expenditures for which it was originally recognised. [FRS 12 para 64].

17.291.15 A liability and any expected reimbursement (for example, insurance recoveries) should be shown gross in the balance sheet. The asset resulting from the reimbursement should only be recognised when its recovery is virtually certain and should not exceed the amount of the provision. [FRS 12 para 56]. This is a change to SSAP 18 where provision was made for the net loss. However, in the profit and loss account, the expense relating to settlement of the liability and the reimbursement may be presented net. [FRS 12 para 57].

Disclosure

17.291.16 The FRS contains disclosure requirements for provisions and contingent liabilities and contingent assets. These are detailed and include disclosure of movements on provisions, a description, details of uncertainties and any expected reimbursements.

Specific applications

17.291.17 Provisions should not be recognised for future operating losses (although assets may have to be written down for impairment). [FRS 12 para 68]. However, a provision should be recognised if an entity has a contract that is onerous. [FRS 12 para 71]. An onerous contract is one in which the unavoidable costs of meeting the obligations under it exceed the economic benefits expected to be received. [FRS 12 para 2].

17.291.18 No obligation arises for the sale of an operation until the entity is committed to the sale, that is, there is a binding sale agreement. [FRS 12 para 83].

17.291.19 Provisions for reorganisations should only be recognised if there is an obligation at the balance sheet date. A constructive obligation arises only if the entity has a detailed formal plan and has raised a valid expectation in those affected by it that the restructuring will be carried out (for example, by starting to implement it or by announcing it in sufficient detail). [FRS 12 para 77]. This is unlikely to be the case if there is a long time-frame. [FRS 12 para 79]. The provision for restructuring costs should not include costs associated with ongoing activities (such as relocation or retraining costs). [FRS 12 paras 85 and 86].

Implementation rules

17.291.20 Where a provision is being recognised for the first time as a result of the new rules (for example, decommissioning costs) or where it is being removed from the balance sheet because it does not represent an obligation at that date under the new rules (for example, certain restructuring provisions) then this will be a change in policy and, if material, should be accounted for using a prior year adjustment. [FRS 12 para 101].

17.291.21 Where an existing provision qualifies for recognition under the new rules, but its amount is revised as a result of the new measurement rules (for example, discounting) then this is a change to an accounting estimate and should be dealt with in the profit and loss account for the period, with the effect stated where material. [FRS 12 para 101].

[The next paragraph is 17.292.]

17.292 As noted above, the FRS includes specific rules for the measurement of provisions. The amount recognised as a provision should be the best estimate of the expenditure required to settle the present obligation at the balance sheet date and this estimate should take account of any risks and uncertainties. Uncertainties surrounding the amount to be recognised as a provision are dealt with by various means according to the circumstances. Where the provision being measured involves a large population of items (for example a warranty provision), the obligation is estimated on the basis of expected values – in other words, having regard to all possible outcomes weighted by their associated probabilities. [FRS 12 para 39]. This is illustrated by the following example:

Example

An entity sells goods with a warranty for the repair of any manufacturing defects that become apparent within the first six months after purchase. If minor defects were detected in all products sold, repair costs of £1 million would result. If major defects were detected in all products sold, repair costs of £4 million would result. The entity's past experience and future expectations indicate that, for the coming year, 75% of the goods sold will have no defects, 20% of the goods sold will have minor defects and 5% of the goods sold will have major defects. The expected value of the cost of repairs is £400,000 (that is (75% of nil) + (20% of £1m) + (5% of £4m)).

17.293 However, where a single obligation is being measured, the individual most likely outcome may be the best estimate of the liability. However, even in such a case, the entity should consider other possible outcomes and where other possible outcomes are either mostly higher or mostly lower than the most likely outcome, the best estimate will be a higher or lower amount. [FRS 12 para 40].

17.294 Appendix III of the FRS illustrates the application of the FRS with some specific examples. These include:

- Warranties – a provision is recognised for the best estimate of the costs of making good under the warranty products sold before the balance sheet date.

- Contaminated land – where legislation is virtually certain to be enacted or where the entity has a constructive obligation to incur the expenditure, a provision is recognised for the best estimate of the costs of the clean-up.

- Decommissioning costs (oilfield) – a provision is recognised for the best estimate of the eventual costs that relate to the restoration of damage caused at the outset. These costs are included as part of the cost of the asset (oil rig).

- Sales refunds – where a store has a constructive obligation because its conduct has created a valid expectation on the part of its customers that it will refund purchases, then a provision is recognised for the best estimate of the costs of refunds.

- Training costs – the obligating event is considered to arise when the training takes place and so provisions for training costs are not permitted.

- Guarantees – the obligating event is the giving of the guarantee (which is a legal obligation). A provision is recognised if it is probable that a transfer of economic benefits will be required under the guarantee. If it is not probable, then the guarantee is disclosed as a contingent liability unless the probability of any transfer is regarded as remote.

- Repairs and maintenance – the cost of major refurbishments of an owned asset cannot be provided for, because no obligation is considered to exist independent of the entity's future actions. Instead of a provision being recognised, the depreciation of the asset should take account of its consumption. The refurbishment costs then incurred are capitalised and depreciated.

- Self-insurance – the example in the FRS says that no provision is recognised and that there is no present obligation, because there is no other party involved in insuring the risks. This is unclear because an obligation arises as a result of an incident and not as a result of being able to recover the costs from a third party. Therefore, provision should be made for known incidents that have occurred before the balance sheet date, including those for which a claim has yet to be made (so-called incurred but not reported (IBNR) claims).

17.295 Examples of companies that are likely to be most affected by the new rules are:

- Companies that have previously provided for restructuring costs prior to announcement or implementation – even if the provisions were in a prior year (in which case comparatives may have to be restated so that costs are charged in the period that there was an obligation).
- Any companies with reorganisation provisions that include relocation costs (including integration costs on an acquisition) or retraining costs.
- Companies with environmental liabilities required to be recognised in full under the new rules (for example, decommissioning costs) where these have previously been accrued over a period.
- Utility companies or other companies with large provisions for future maintenance costs.
- Companies with contingent liabilities that have been offset against expected recoveries (for example, litigation losses and insurance recoveries).
- Companies with significant self-insurance provisions where these do not represent obligations at the balance sheet date.

Chapter 18

Capital instruments

Chapter 18

Capital instruments

Introduction

18.1 During the 1980s there was considerable growth in the range of capital instruments available for raising finance. The development of such instruments had a sound economic purpose and provided issuers and investors with significant benefits. However, until the publication of FRS 4, 'Capital instruments', in December 1993, there was no UK accounting standard that dealt with their accounting treatment. However, as investors and issuers became more sophisticated, the instruments became more complex with the result that accounting failed to keep pace with their development.

18.2 For straightforward capital instruments, the distinction between debt and share capital was based on their legal form. The Act's provisions dealt with their treatment and disclosure in the financial statements and these rules were generally considered as adequate. In the case of complex capital issues, however, the accounting treatment adopted was either too simplistic to reflect new features, or too complex for readers to understand.

18.3 Given the lack of published guidance in this complex area, the Technical Committee of the ICAEW issued TR 677, 'Accounting for complex capital issues' in 1987. The paper attempted to lay down some general principles, which it recommended should be applied when accounting for any form of complex capital issue. But it dealt with relatively simple forms of capital instruments and it did not address the central issue of accounting for instruments that have both debt and equity features. Accounting for such instruments has not been uniform and a variety of arguments has been advanced to justify differing treatments. For example, many people argued that a redeemable preference share is, in substance, more akin to debt than equity and should be treated as such irrespective of its legal nature. Also, a bond that gives the holder the option to redeem or convert into ordinary shares was sometimes argued to be more in the nature of equity than debt.

18.4 Given that equity and debt are fundamentally different, the question as to whether instruments having characteristics of both debt and equity should be accounted for on the basis of their economic substance or their legal form came under increasing scrutiny and the need for guidance on this central issue became evident. Indeed, the UITF's first pronouncement dealt with one of these issues, namely, the accounting treatment of supplemental interest and premiums payable on convertible bonds.

18.5 The first step towards developing an accounting standard was taken in December 1991 when the ASB issued a discussion document on capital instruments. The paper dealt with a wide range of issues, in particular the circumstances in which capital instruments should be reported as debt (that is, as liabilities), or as shares. It also considered the way in which such instruments and related transactions, such as payments of interest and issue costs, should be dealt with in the financial statements. Disclosure requirements in respect of capital instruments were also considered.

18.6 The principal proposals in the discussion paper were generally well received and formed the basis of FRED 3, which was issued in December 1992. Finally, in December 1993, the ASB issued FRS 4. Its requirements were almost unchanged from those proposed in FRED 3.

18.7 FRS 4 takes a rather legalistic approach towards accounting for capital instruments by ignoring the economic substance of the instruments and merely reflecting their legal form, a point that concerned many respondents on both the discussion document and FRED 3. In particular, it was pointed out that FRS 4's provisions were inconsistent with FRED 4, 'Reporting the substance of transactions', issued in February 1993 (which was subsequently turned into FRS 5, 'Reporting the substance of transactions') and with E48, 'Financial Instruments', issued by the IASC in January 1994 (the disclosure proposals have now been turned into an accounting standard IAS 32, 'Financial instruments: disclosure and presentation', but the measurement issues are still being considered by the IASC). Examples of inconsistency cited were the requirement to report convertible debt as a liability where conversion was highly likely and the inclusion of redeemable non-equity shares within shareholders' funds rather than as a liability, where in both cases the substance of the instruments would arguably require a different treatment. In their defence, the ASB argued that there were practical and legal difficulties in the UK in accounting for such instruments in accordance with their economic substance. The ASB's arguments are documented in paragraphs 25 to 27 of appendix III to the standard.

18.8 Nevertheless, the standard provided guidance on many aspects of accounting for share capital, debt and minority interests that were the subject of differing treatments and interpretations prior to its publication. The standard prescribes methods that should be used to determine the amounts to be attributed to capital instruments and their associated costs and specifies how the instruments should be disclosed.

FRS 4's objectives

18.9 The principal objective of FRS 4 is to enhance the usefulness of financial statements by providing a coherent and consistent approach to accounting for capital instruments. It does this by requiring all capital instruments to be classified as either debt, equity shares or non-equity shares. [FRS 4 para 1]. Hybrid instruments having a combination of debt and equity features (for example, convertible debt) are classified as liabilities if they contain an obligation to transfer economic benefits, even if the obligation is contingent.

18.10 Prior to FRS 4's issue, there was little guidance on accounting for costs associated with capital instruments and a variety of treatments was encountered, which permitted either write off of such costs to the profit and loss account or to the share premium account or, in certain circumstances, capitalisation. The standard describes how finance costs of each class of capital instrument are to be calculated and for redeemable instruments requires them to be allocated to the profit and loss account on a fair basis over the period the instrument is in issue.

18.11 Given the variety and complexity of capital instruments currently in existence and those that may evolve, the standard requires extensive disclosures. The disclosures go beyond those required by the Act and the Stock Exchange's Listing Rules. The additional disclosures were intended to facilitate users' understanding of the actual and potential impact that these instruments have on the reporting entity's assets, liabilities, commitments and associated risks that may arise from dealing in these instruments. Although the standard contains extensive disclosure requirements, in practice few companies are likely to have in issue all the various kinds of capital instruments discussed in the standard and, accordingly, only some of the disclosure requirements will apply to them.

18.12 The accounting treatments specified in the standard are applicable to all forms of capital instruments including those denominated in foreign currencies. The definition of capital instruments is considered in paragraph 18.23. The accounting principles are also sufficiently general to apply to new instruments as they are developed in the future. Furthermore, the large number of disclosures that are required together with the discussion recommended by the ASB's Statement on 'Operating and financial review' on capital structure and treasury policies (see chapter 33) have gone a long way in meeting the needs of investors and other users of financial statements in this complex aspect of financial reporting.

Scope

18.13 FRS 4 applies to all financial statements intended to give a true and fair view of a reporting entity's financial position and profit or loss (or income and expenditure) for the period. Although the standard was written primarily for companies, its provisions apply to other entities, which should adapt the terminology used in the statement as appropriate. [FRS 4 para 18].

18.14 The standard's requirements apply to issuers of capital instruments and not to investments in capital instruments issued by other entities. [FRS 4 para 19]. Furthermore, its requirements apply to all capital instruments as defined in the standard (see para 18.23 below) apart from:

- Warrants issued to employees under employee share schemes.
- Leases, which should be accounted for in accordance with SSAP 21.
- Equity shares issued as part of a business combination that is accounted for as a merger.

[FRS 4 para 21].

18.15 Capital instruments that are issued at the same time in a composite transaction should be considered together. They should be accounted for as a single instrument unless they can be transferred, cancelled or redeemed independently of each other. [FRS 4 para 22]. For example, debt is sometimes issued with a warrant attached. Where the debt and the warrants are capable of being transferred independently, they should be accounted for separately (see further para 18.224).

Transitional provisions

18.16 The standard applied to financial statements relating to accounting periods ending on or after 22 June 1994. However, there are no transitional provisions contained in the standard and its requirements apply to all transactions and to all instruments that come within its scope irrespective of the date at which they were issued. This means that the standard applies not only to new issues of capital instruments, but also to any existing issue.

Classification of capital instruments

18.17 Practice before FRS 4's introduction was to account for debts and shares having simple and conventional structures in accordance with their legal form and to classify them in the balance sheet as liabilities or shareholders' funds respectively. Similarly, interest paid on debt was treated as a charge in arriving at profit before tax in the profit and loss account, whilst dividends on all forms of shares were shown as an appropriation of profits. However, many instruments exist that have characteristics of both debt and equity.

18.18 Some people argue that the traditional distinction between liabilities and shares was not relevant for classifying instruments having both debt and equity features. It was argued that because such instruments could not be placed in either category, they should be shown in a separate part of the balance sheet, sometimes described as 'mezzanine', which could appear above 'minority interests', but below 'capital and reserves'. This presentation would have the effect of showing these hybrid instruments as quasi shareholders' funds. Others argued that the only sensible way to account for the hybrid nature of these instruments was to treat the equity and the debt components separately in the balance sheet. This approach, which reflects the instrument's commercial substance rather than its legal form, is often described as 'split accounting' and is the method required for 'compound financial instruments' by IAS 32 published by the IASC in July 1995.

18.19 Neither of the above arguments found much favour with the ASB. They rejected a separate categorisation as mezzanine finance because it is not permitted by the Act's balance sheet formats. Split accounting was fully explored in the discussion paper that preceded the standard's publication and was considered to be too complex, although as mentioned it is required for compound financial instruments in IAS 32 (see also paras 18.60).

18.20 In developing the accounting treatment for capital instruments, the ASB maintained the traditional distinction between liabilities and shareholders' funds as a basis for classifying capital instruments. This basis of categorisation is consistent both with the ASB's draft Statement of principles under which liabilities and shares are defined as distinct elements of financial statements and with existing legal requirements. Thus, in terms of the draft Statement of principles any instrument reflected in the financial statements as a source of finance must either be a liability or a share or minority interests.

18.21 The FRS, therefore, requires all capital instruments to be accounted for in the balance sheet within one of the following categories:

- Liabilities.
- Shareholders' funds.
- Minority interests, in the case of consolidated financial statements.

[FRS 4 para 23].

18.22 Given the diversity of capital instruments, the standard also requires for certain instruments separate disclosure of their carrying amount within the major categories listed above. The disclosure requirements for shares and debt are considered in detail from paragraph 18.131 and from paragraph 18.176, respectively. The paragraphs that follow consider the definition and classification of capital instruments and discuss the different types of shares and debt that may be issued by companies. Also considered below from paragraph 18.69 is how minority interests should be classified, following FRS 4's requirements.

Definition

18.23 Prior to FRS 4's issue, there was no formal definition of capital instruments. Instead the term 'financial instruments' has been generally used in the past to mean not only shares and debt instruments, but also financial derivative products like futures, forward rate agreements, options, interest rate caps and swaps. The term 'financial instruments' is now formally defined in IAS 32 as "*... any contract that gives rise to both a financial asset of one enterprise and a financial liability or* *equity instrument of another enterprise"*. The term, therefore, encompasses not only primary instruments like cash, receivables, payables and equity securities, but also secondary or derivative instruments like the ones mentioned above.

18.24 The definition of capital instruments contained in the FRS is not as wide as the IAS 32 definition of financial instruments, but is restricted to primary instruments like shares and debt as well as options and warrants to obtain such instruments. Consequently, derivative instruments that are issued for managing foreign exchange and interest rate risks rather than for raising finance are outside FRS 4's scope. Derivative instruments were not considered on the grounds that their additional complexity might have delayed the standard's issue. The ASB has subsequently indicated that it is dealing with derivatives in a separate project. Capital instruments are defined in FRS 4 to mean:

> *"All instruments that are issued by reporting entities as a means of raising finance, including shares, debentures, loans and debt instruments, options and warrants that give the holder the right to subscribe for or obtain capital instruments. In the case of consolidated financial statements the term includes capital instruments issued by subsidiaries except those that are held by another member of the group included in the consolidation."* [FRS 4 para 2].

18.25 It follows from the above definition that the instrument's principal purpose must be for raising finance. An instrument may come within the above definition whether or not the consideration given for its issue takes the form of cash. For example, the consideration may be a specified amount of commodity (commodity linked instruments) or other capital instruments. Furthermore, a capital instrument may take the form of contracts between two parties (for example, a borrower and its bank). [FRS 4 para 68].

Classification of share capital

18.26 Capital instruments that *do not* contain an obligation to transfer economic benefits are required by FRS 4 to be reported within shareholders' funds (or minority interests in the case of consolidated financial statements). Capital instruments that *do* contain an obligation to transfer economic benefits should be classified as liabilities. [FRS 4 para 24]. Certain types of shares have an obligation to transfer economic benefits (for example, because they are redeemable and have a predetermined fixed dividend) and their features under the above provision might lead them to be treated as liabilities. However, paragraph 24 specifically excludes shares from the requirement to classify such instruments as liabilities. One of the reasons for this is that the standard is closely based on the balance sheet formats contained in Schedule 4 to the Act. But there is also a distinction between redeemable shares and debt in that debt carries an unconditional obligation to repay principal or pay interest, whereas with shares, redemption or payment of dividends may be dependent on sufficient distributable profits being available or the proceeds of a fresh issue of shares made at the same time as the redemption. Therefore, under FRS 4 all types of shares should be recorded within shareholders' funds whether or not they are in substance similar to debt. It is not possible to show shares that are akin to debt elsewhere in the balance sheet, for example, in a mezzanine level (as discussed in para 18.18) or in creditors, except in the one situation where the group has an obligation to transfer economic benefits in respect of shares issued by a subsidiary (see para 18.70).

18.27 Shares can be divided into many different types, including ordinary shares, preference shares, non-voting shares and redeemable shares. Only some of these types of shares will form the company's equity capital. In law, the classification between equity and non-equity capital depends upon the rights that the shares are given in the company's memorandum and articles of association. When setting up a company it is important to consider the share structure very carefully in order to issue shareholders with the type of share that properly reflects the rights they are intended to have. For example, a financial institution might be more interested in a defined exit route than in participating in the company's control. In such a circumstance, a redeemable preference share might be appropriate. The rights attaching to the share will determine the degree of shareholders' participation in, and control over, the company.

18.28 By varying the rights attaching to shares it is possible to change their substance dramatically. For example, it is possible to give a share rights to make it redeemable in (say) five years and to set its dividend as a rate of return on the capital that is linked to (say) the movement in LIBOR. In such a situation, the nature of the share is in many ways more like debt than share capital. The standard distinguishes these types of shares from pure equity by referring to them as 'non-equity', which as mentioned above must nevertheless be reported within shareholders' funds. The distinction is made clear by requiring the total of shareholders' funds to be analysed between equity interests and non-equity interests. [FRS 4 paras 37, 40].

Distinction between equity and non-equity

18.29 *Equity shares* are defined in the Act as the issued share capital of a company excluding any part which, neither as respects dividends nor as respects capital, carries any right to participate beyond a specified amount in a distribution. [Sec 744]. Equity shares represent the residual interests in a company and as such confer on their holders the right to share in the company's net assets (after settling any prior claims). Such shares are normally termed ordinary shares, but it is quite possible for a preference share to be constructed in such a way that it meets the Act's definition of equity.

18.30 The Act's definition of equity is of less importance now, from an accounting viewpoint, than it was before the introduction of the Companies Act 1989. Before the 1989 Act was enacted, equity capital was the main criterion used to determine whether a company was a subsidiary of another. If a company owned more than 50 per cent of another company's equity share capital then the latter company was its subsidiary. However, since the Companies Act 1989, the main criterion for determining whether a company is a subsidiary of another has changed from looking at the ownership of equity capital to considering whether a company has voting control over the shares in that other company (see further chapter 21). The Act's definition of equity share capital is, however, still used, for example, to determine whether the company is eligible for merger relief and may still be used in legal documents, such as debenture trust deeds.

18.31 Under FRS 4's provisions, an analysis of shareholders' funds has to be made between those funds attributable to *equity interests* and the funds attributable to *non-equity interests*. The standard provides a definition of *non-equity* shares rather than adopting the Act's definition of equity share capital. Equity shares are defined as a residual category of shares, which is those shares other than non-equity shares. [FRS 4 para 7].

18.32 The definition given in FRS 4 of non-equity shares is as follows:

> *"Shares possessing any of the following characteristics:*
>
> *a) any of the rights of the shares to receive payments (whether in respect of dividends, in respect of redemption or otherwise) are for a limited amount that is not calculated by reference to the company's assets or profits or the dividends on any class of equity share.*
>
> *b) any of their rights to participate in a surplus in a winding up are limited to a specific amount that is not calculated by reference to the company's assets or profits and such limitation had a commercial effect in practice at the time the shares were issued or, if later, at the time the limitation was introduced.*

c) *the shares are redeemable either according to their terms, or because the holder, or any party other than the issuer, can require their redemption." [FRS 4 para 12].*

18.33 Whereas the Act defines equity share capital and non-equity share capital becomes a residual class, the standard defines non-equity share capital and equity share capital becomes a residual class. However, the standard's definition of non-equity shares is not consistent with the legal definition. The principal difference appears to be that in the standard's definition a share is non-equity if it carries limited distributions of *either* dividends or capital, whereas in the legal definition a share is non-equity only if there are limitations on the distribution of *both* dividends and capital. It follows that under FRS 4 non-equity is a broader category and, therefore, residual equity is a narrower category than under the Act.

18.34 In practice it is often difficult to determine whether or not a share is non-equity. For example, the definition of non-equity shares given above states that shares will be non-equity if *"any of the rights of the shares to receive payments (whether in respect of dividends, in respect of redemption or otherwise) are for a limited amount..."*. This can be read as meaning that where a share has more than one right to the payment of dividends each of these separate rights should be considered individually in determining whether or not the share is non-equity. Even if only one of these rights is restricted, the share will be non-equity. This principle also applies to rights to participate in a surplus on a winding up, where a share might be entitled to more than one right. The principle is illustrated in the example that follows:

Example

A company has issued participating preference shares that carry a right to a fixed dividend of 5% and a further right to a participating dividend of 10% of profit after tax, less the fixed dividend.

Taken together the dividend rights of the shares are not for a limited amount and, therefore, it may appear that the shares fall outside the definition of non-equity. However, because one of the separate rights of the shares is to receive a fixed rate of dividend, the shares do satisfy FRS 4's definition and, accordingly, they should be classified as non-equity.

18.35 The definition of non-equity shares in FRS 4 has been deliberately widely drawn so that any right to a dividend, to a redemption payment, or to participate in a winding up, that is for a limited amount will require the share to be treated as non-equity. Consequently, it is quite possible for a company to issue (say) a preference share that is classified as equity share capital under the Act, but which is a non-equity share for the purposes of the analysis of shareholders' funds under FRS 4. This situation would arise where, for example, a preference share, which has a fixed dividend, has unrestricted rights to distribution on winding up. The share might, for instance, have a right on liquidation to share in a fixed percentage of the balance on the company's share premium account. The FRS acknowledges this possibility in paragraph 85 and states that where in accordance with FRS 4 the share is classified as non-equity, but under the Act it falls within the definition of equity share capital and this would mislead or confuse the user of the financial statements, further explanation is necessary in the financial statements. [FRS 4 para 85]. An example of the type of disclosure that might be made is given in Table 18.1.

Table 18.1 – Granada Group PLC – Annual Report and Accounts – 1 October 1994

Notes to the accounts (extract)

	1994 £m	1993 £m
21 Called up share capital (extract)		
Ordinary Shares		
Authorised: £209.704 million (1993: £156.199 million) comprising 838,817,302 (1993: 624,798,158) Ordinary Shares of 25p each		
Issued: 580,854,706 (1993: 467,948,775) Ordinary Shares of 25p each, fully paid	**145.2**	116.9
Convertible Preference Shares		
Authorised: £17.549 million (1993: £17.554 million) comprising 175,491,391 (1993: 175,539,251) Convertible Preference Shares of 10p each		
Issued: 175,491,391 (1993: 175,539,251) Convertible Preference Shares of 10p each, fully paid	**17.5**	17.6
New Convertible Preference Shares		
Authorised: £3.247 million (1993: £3.247 million) comprising 32,465,354 (1993: 32,465,354) New Convertible Preference Shares of 10p each		
Issued: nil (1993: nil)	**–**	–
At 1 October 1994	**162.7**	134.5

b The Convertible Preference Shares may be converted into fully paid Ordinary Shares on the basis of 33⅓ Ordinary Shares for every 100 Convertible Preference Shares. Conversion may only take place on a conversion date, which is 30 April in each year up to and including 2003. Between 1 July 2003 and 31 January 2009 the Company has the right to redeem at any time any outstanding shares for £1 per share; any shares outstanding on 31 January 2009 shall be redeemed by the Company on the same terms. The Convertible Preference Shares fall within the definition of non-equity shareholders' funds for accounting purposes. However, they meet the definition of equity shares for Companies Act purposes because the rights on a winding up are not limited to a specific amount. In the period ended 1 October 1994 a total of 47,860 issued Convertible Preference Shares of 10p each fully paid were converted into 15,938 issued Ordinary Shares of 25p each fully paid and 3,206 authorised but unissued Ordinary Shares of 25p each.

18.36 Paragraph b) of the definition of non-equity shares given in paragraph 18.32 above relates to the rights that shares have on winding up. For the purposes of determining whether a share is a non-equity share when analysing shareholders' funds, FRS 4 points out in paragraph 86 that rights to participate on a winding up are not usually taken into account, because financial statements are normally prepared on a going concern basis.

18.37 Paragraph c) of the definition of non-equity shares in paragraph 18.32 means that all redeemable shares are classified as non-equity for the purposes of analysing shareholders' funds under FRS 4. Such shares do not have a residual interest in the company. As the amount at which they are redeemed is inevitably fixed before redemption, their rights on redemption are restricted and, consequently, they fall within the category of non-equity. [FRS 4 para 87].

18.38 One effect of the FRS 4 definition of non-equity shares in practice is that it is quite possible for a company not to have any equity shares (per the FRS 4 definition). This is often the case in split capital investment trusts, for example. (See further paragraph 18.274.)

Types of equity shares

18.39 As mentioned in paragraph 18.29, ordinary shares are the main form of equity share capital and normally confer on their holders the residue of the rights of the company, which have not been conferred on other classes. Therefore, subject to the rights of other classes (which are normally, though not always, limited), the rights attributed to the ordinary shares are generally unlimited. Ordinary shares also normally carry the company's voting power. It is quite possible for a company to have more than one type of ordinary share in issue and where two such share types are in issue, these are generally named A and B ordinary shares.

18.40 For financial reporting purposes under FRS 4's provisions, ordinary shares generally represent part of the equity interests in shareholders' funds. In certain circumstances, companies issue shares that have deferred rights. For example, such a share might only entitle its holder to a dividend once the normal ordinary shareholders have received a certain level of dividend (for example, £2 million per annum) on their shares. A further deferred right on liquidation could, for example, be for the deferred shareholders to receive no return of capital or surplus reserves until the ordinary shareholders have received their capital and a fixed amount of reserves (for example, £50 million). Where the rights of deferred shares are restricted in this way, they should normally be classified as equity, because typically they rank behind ordinary shares and neither their rights to dividends nor their rights to capital on a winding up are restricted once the participation level has been reached.

Types of non-equity shares

Preference shares

18.41 Preference share is the name given to any share that has some preferential rights in relation to other classes of shares, particularly in relation to ordinary shares. These preferential rights are of great variety, but refer normally to the right to a *fixed dividend*, although they could also refer to the right on winding up to receive a fixed part of the *capital* or otherwise to participate in the distribution of the company's assets (shares with such rights are often known as participating preference shares). Preference shares generally do not carry any voting rights, although they can be constructed to do so. Some preference shares carry voting rights if their dividend is not paid. Also they can be constructed to be equity share capital under the Act.

18.42 For financial reporting purposes, under FRS 4's provisions preference shares will always represent part of the non-equity interest in shareholders' funds whether constructed to be equity share capital or non-equity share capital under the Act.

Redeemable shares

18.43 There are strict rules in the Act that govern the purchase by a company of its own shares. However a company may, if authorised to do so by its articles, issue shares that are redeemable at the option of the company or the shareholder. But a company can only issue such shares where there are also non-redeemable shares in issue. [Sec 159]. One stipulation before this type of share can be redeemed is that it must be fully paid up. Subject to the general rules regarding the purchase or redemption by a company of its own shares in sections 159-181 of the 1985 Act, redemption of shares may be made on such terms and in such a manner as the Articles provide. [Sec 161(3)].

18.44 The Government proposed an amendment by inserting section 159A into the Act which would require the terms of redemption to be specified in the Articles before the shares were issued. However, this was considered to be over-restrictive and it is unlikely, therefore, that section 159A will now be brought into force.

18.45 The general rules governing the redemption of redeemable shares are very similar to the rules that apply when a company purchases its own shares as explained in chapter 40.

18.46 Under the Act, redeemable shares form part of the company's non-equity share capital. In addition, under FRS 4's provisions, redeemable shares represent part of the non-equity interests in shareholders' funds.

Auction market preferred shares

18.47 Auction market preferred shares (AMPS) are a particular type of preference share for which dividends are determined in accordance with an auction process between a panel of investors. The shares are transferred to the investor who will accept the lowest dividend. Dividends may be passed without giving holders any

[The next page is 18013.]

further rights, for example, to demand repayment. The shares are redeemable at the issuer's option, usually at the issue price.

18.48 In accordance with FRS 4, AMPS should be reported within shareholders' funds as non-equity shares, because they are redeemable at a fixed price and because their dividend rights are limited. The finance cost of each period should be the dividend rights accruing in respect of that period. This is the position illustrated in Table 18.2.

Table 18.2 – Cadbury Schweppes plc – Annual Report - 31 December 1994

Notes on the Accounts (extract)

18 Capital and Reserves

(a) Share Capital of Cadbury Schweppes plc	1994	1993
Authorised Share Capital:	£m	£m
Attributable to equity interests:		
Ordinary shares (1,100 million of 25p each)	275.0	275.0
Attributable to non-equity interests:		
US$ Preference shares (750 of US$1,000 each)	0.4	0.4
Can$ Preference shares (150 of Can$1,000 each)	0.1	0.1
	275.5	275.5
Allotted and called up Share Capital:		
Attributable to equity interests:		
Ordinary shares (833.9 million of 25p each, fully paid) (1993: 829.8 million)	208.5	207.5
Attributable to non-equity interests:		
US$ Preference shares (455 of US$1,000 each)	0.2	0.2
Can$ Preference shares (150 of Can$1,000 each)	0.1	0.1
	208.8	207.8

(f) Cumulative Perpetual Preference Shares

In 1990 the Company issued 105 US$ Cumulative Perpetual Preference Shares (Series 1) and 150 Can$ Cumulative Perpetual Preference Shares (Series 2) at a price of US$500,000 and Can$500,000 respectively. For the first five years the dividend rate on the Series 1 shares is a floating rate set at 80% of 3 month US$ LIBOR, and that on the Series 2 shares is a floating rate set at 80% of 90 day Canadian Bankers' Acceptance rates. These rates were increased from 75% of the respective indices in 1993 as a result of the change in the rate of UK tax credit available to investors. At the end of the five year period the dividend rate is subject to renegotiation. Also in 1990 the Company issued 350 US$ Auction Preference Shares (Series 3 to 6) at the same issue price. The dividend rate on each of Series 3 to 6 shares is reset at auctions normally held every 28 days.

For the US dollar shares the rates of dividend paid during 1994 ranged between 2.70% and 4.80% and at 31 December 1994 the weighted average rate payable was 5.33%. For the Canadian dollar shares the rates of dividend paid during 1994 ranged between 3.13% and 5.07% and at 31 December 1994 the average rate was 4.81%. The preference shares are redeemable at any time only at the Company's option and at 31 December 1994 the redemption value was £180.1m (1993: £192.0m).

Classification of debt instruments

18.49 The ASB's draft Statement of principles defines liabilities as *"an entity's obligations to transfer economic benefits as a result of past transactions or events"*. It follows that all capital instruments (whether or not redeemable) should be accounted for as liabilities if they contain an obligation to transfer economic benefits. [FRS 4 para 24]. But as explained in paragraph 18.26 above, shares are specifically excluded from this requirement. For conventional debt, the obligation that makes it a liability usually consists of payments for debt servicing and the ultimate repayment to the holder of the instrument.

18.50 For debt, the obligation to repay covers a number of different aspects of the loan. For example, it covers the basic obligation to repay the debt, the interest obligation and any premium payable on redemption or as supplemental interest. Also, the obligation need not be discharged in cash, it could be discharged by transfer of other kinds of property (for example, a specified quantity of a commodity). However, the way in which the obligation is described or characterised in the instrument, or the form in which it is actually settled, should not affect the instrument's classification. As long as the instrument involves an obligation to transfer economic benefits, it should be classified and accounted for as a liability.

18.51 The obligation to transfer economic benefits need not be actual, it may be contingent on the occurrence of a future event. [FRS 4 para 72]. This means that an instrument should be classified as a liability if it embodies an optional or conditional feature that would require the issuer to transfer assets to the holder if the option were exercised or the conditional event occurred. For example, convertible debt imposes a contractual obligation on the issuer to deliver cash or to issue shares, contingent on the exercise of an option by the holder. This type of instrument falls to be classified as a liability, because until the option is exercised, the contingent obligation to transfer benefits remains.

18.52 Obligations to transfer economic benefits that are contingent only on the insolvency of the issuer should be ignored. [FRS 4 para 72]. This is rather obvious because different rights and obligations associated with capital instruments come into effect at insolvency, that would not otherwise be triggered during the ordinary course of business. Obligations to transfer economic benefits in the event that lending covenants are violated should also be ignored as long as the possibility of a breach is remote. For example, as a consequence of breaching loan covenants, the borrower might be required to transfer economic benefits to the lender (say, pay a penalty) in order to restore the original conditions and continue to enjoy the benefit of the original financing. These transfers of economic benefits should not be taken into account either in the instrument's classification or in determining its carrying value so long as the issuer is expected to be able to comply with the covenants. [FRS 4 para 72].

18.53 Capital instruments that are classified as debt come in various forms. They may be: straightforward debentures and loan capital; convertible into shares; subordinated to other borrowings; perpetual in nature; or sometimes issued on terms that the lender's recourse is limited. The features of these type of instruments are examined below.

Types of debt instruments

Debentures and loan capital

18.54 There is no precise definition of a debenture, either in law or in practice. In legal terms it is generally construed as a formal acknowledgement of a debt. However, section 744 of the Act refers to debentures as including *"... debenture stock, bonds and any other securities of a company, whether constituting a charge on the assets of the company or not"*. This definition is very wide. It does not distinguish clearly between a debenture loan and any other loan. Whether a particular loan is a debenture or not will depend on the documentation. A formal loan agreement, whether containing security or not, will usually constitute a debenture in the context of company law. A bank loan may also be a debenture loan, but the balance sheet formats distinguish between bank loans and other debenture loans.

18.55 For accounting measurement and disclosure purposes, there is no difference between debentures, loans and other debt instruments. They are all capital instruments issued for raising finance and can be transferred, cancelled or redeemed. Accordingly, they fall to be treated as liabilities.

Convertible debt

18.56 A conventional convertible bond gives the bondholder the option to exchange the bond for a number of shares in the issuing company at a future date. Because of the option the coupon on the bond is usually set at a lower rate than straight debt. It, therefore, provides not only a cheaper form of financing, but also gives the issuer the opportunity to increase equity rather than repay cash at maturity. The advantage to the bondholder is that it provides not only a specified amount of interest, but also an opportunity to gain from share price appreciation and some protection from downside risk by promising a fixed payment at maturity.

18.57 Given that the bondholder receives regular interest payments and can also exercise his option voluntarily, he may simply prefer to hold the security. This is one of the reasons why almost all types of convertible debt provide for a call price. The call feature enables the company to call the debt for redemption and to force conversion if the need arises. In practice, companies usually issue convertible debt with the full expectation that these securities will be converted within a certain period of time. Few convertible securities are ever redeemed unless there is a significant reduction of share prices as happened after 'Black Monday'.

18.58 A variant is to issue the convertible bond with a premium put feature. The put option allows the bondholder to require the issuing company to repurchase the bond at a premium (the put price) as an alternative to exercising his rights to convert the bond into the company's shares. The repurchase takes place either at:

- a single put price and at a single exercise date or several exercise dates (convertible debt with a single premium put); or
- at a series of put prices and exercise dates (convertible debt with a rolling premium put).

18.59 Whatever the bond's structure, it is clear that the conversion option gives the otherwise redeemable bond its equity features. Given this compound feature of debt and equity, the question is whether issuers should account for these instruments as being either entirely a liability instrument or entirely an equity instrument; or as consisting of a liability component and an equity component that should be accounted for separately.

18.60 Some favour accounting for convertible debt as entirely a liability until it is either converted or redeemed, because the debt and the conversion option remain physically inseparable until conversion. It is, therefore, effectively a single instrument under which the issuer is obligated to pay, and the bondholder entitled to receive, periodic interest payments. Others argue that convertible debt should be shown as part of, or next to, shareholders' funds once conversion is considered to be the probable outcome. This follows the substance over form argument. Yet others favour accounting for the debt and the equity components separately (referred to as 'split accounting') and consider that the holder of a convertible debt owns a bond and a call option on the company's shares similar to a share warrant. They argue that because the bond and the call option can be valued separately, there is no reason why the accounting should not reflect what is in effect the convertible bond's true substance.

18.61 Given the above three approaches for accounting for convertible debt, the ASB's choice was largely influenced by the legal distinction between share capital and debt as recognised in the UK. Instruments that are legally debt cannot be shown under capital and reserves. Therefore, as already explained, the ASB opted for the first approach. Accordingly, convertible debt should be reported within liabilities irrespective of the probability of future conversion. [FRS 4 para 25]. The other two approaches, probability-based accounting and split accounting, were considered to be too complex and subjective.

Bonds with detachable warrants

18.62 Although split accounting is not considered to be suitable for accounting for convertible debt, the method is required by FRS 4 for compound instruments where the share capital and the debt components are capable of being transferred, cancelled or redeemed independently of each other. [FRS 4 para 22]. An example is a bond issued with a warrant where the owner of the bond-warrant package can exercise the warrant and buy shares for cash and keep the bond, unlike an owner of a convertible bond who has to give up the bond in order to exercise the option. The accounting treatment of debt issued with a detachable warrant is further considered from paragraph 18.224.

Subordinated debt

18.63 Some debt instruments are subordinated to other creditors. The intended effect of the subordination is to rank the subordinated debenture holders behind other unsecured creditors with respect to claims on the company's assets. In the event of liquidation, subordinated debenture holders should receive settlement only if all unsecured and secured creditors are paid the full amount owed to them. However, subordinated debentures still rank ahead of equity and non-equity shareholders.

18.64 Because subordinated debentures are subordinated to all existing and future debts, they can work to the advantage of senior debenture holders that have a priority claim on the company's assets. The senior debenture holders, therefore, view subordinated debentures in much the same way as equity. For this reason, subordinated debt is sometimes referred to as 'quasi-equity'.

18.65 In practice, a variety of subordination methods is used. But whatever the means of subordination, the subordinated debenture holders do not forgo the right to be repaid, rather the repayments are effectively postponed under certain conditions. It follows that irrespective of the method of subordination, the company has an obligation to repay and, therefore, subordinated debts should be classified as liabilities.

Perpetual debt

18.66 Sometimes debts can be issued on terms with no redemption date, but on which interest payments are made, usually at a constant rate or at a fixed margin over LIBOR in perpetuity. Because the instrument's economic substance is similar to a preference share with no fixed redemption date, it is sometimes suggested that a perpetual debt should not be recorded as a liability. However, under the principles stated in the standard, perpetual debt constitutes an obligation to transfer economic benefits in the form of interest payments in perpetuity and hence should be accounted for as a liability. Well known examples of perpetual debts are Consols and War loans, irredeemable British Government stock on which interest is paid in perpetuity. The accounting treatment of perpetual debt is considered in paragraph 18.227.

Limited recourse debt

18.67 Companies sometimes raise debt on terms that give the provider of the finance limited recourse. Recourse by the lender, in the event of default by the company as borrower, is limited only to the particular asset the lender has financed or a particular security that is identified in the loan agreement and not to the company's other resources. Such non-recourse financing is usually common in equipment financing and some property developments.

18.68 Limited recourse debt constitutes an obligation on the part of the company to repay and, therefore, should be accounted for as a liability. However, FRS 5 allows in certain limited circumstances non-recourse debt to be shown as a deduction from the gross amount of the asset it finances on the face of the balance sheet within a single asset caption. This is referred to as a 'linked presentation' (see further chapter 4).

Shares issued by subsidiaries

General treatment

18.69 Normally, shares issued by subsidiaries to persons outside the group are accounted for as minority interests both under the normal rules of preparing consolidated financial statements and under paragraph 17 of Schedule 4A to the Act. FRS 4 also generally requires this treatment. Paragraph 17 requires the amount of capital and reserves attributable to such shares to be shown under minority interests. Such interests are disclosed both in the profit and loss account formats and in the balance sheet formats as 'minority interests'. The accounting implications of FRS 4 for minority interests including the need to analyse the interests between equity and non-equity are considered in detail in chapter 24.

Classification as debt

18.70 There is one situation under FRS 4 where shares issued by subsidiaries to persons outside the group should be classified as liabilities rather than minority interests. This is where the group (taken as a whole) has an obligation to transfer economic benefits in connection with those shares. In this circumstance, the shares are required by the standard to be accounted for in the consolidated financial statements not as minority interest, but as liabilities (for example, see Table 18.3). [FRS 4 para 49]. This is one of a few situations in the standard where the transaction's substance prevails over its legal form.

Table 18.3 – Smith & Nephew plc – Annual Report and Accounts – 31 December 1994

Accounting policies (extract)

Restatement of comparatives Comparative figures have been restated in accordance with Financial Reporting Standard No 4 ("Capital Instruments") so as to reclassify the convertible preference shares issued by Smith & Nephew Finance NV from minority interests to net borrowings. Dividends payable on these preference shares have been reclassified from minority interests to interest payable. All the preference shares were converted or redeemed in full by 31 December 1994.

18.71 The rationale for this treatment is that the group is a single reporting entity and may have an obligation in respect of shares of certain subsidiaries held outside the group and that obligation is not abated even where the subsidiary itself has insufficient resources to meet it. For example, a member of the group might give a guarantee to pay amounts in respect of those shares, such as dividends or amounts due on their redemption; or another group member might undertake to purchase the shares in the event that the subsidiary issuing them fails to make the expected payments. Where this is so, the outside shareholders will look to the guarantor if the subsidiary has defaulted. Consequently, in such a situation the group as a whole is unable to avoid the transfer of economic benefits. Accordingly, the standard states that it would be incorrect for the shares to be shown as part of minority interests and they should instead be shown as liabilities. This will also be the case where the shares are issued by a subsidiary incorporated in a country whose laws, unlike in the UK, do not require that dividend payments or redemption amounts are financed primarily out of distributable profits. [FRS 4 para 89].

Example

A company's subsidiary had issued preference shares to third parties. The third parties had an option to put the preference shares back to the company for cash in five years' time. Because of this option the group as a whole had an obligation and in its consolidated financial statements the preference shares were shown as debt rather than as minority interests. However, the company has subsequently agreed that its subsidiary will pay the third parties an additional dividend in the future in exchange for the third parties giving up their option and the third parties have agreed. In this case, because the obligation has now been released, the preference shares should now be reported as minority interests and not as debt.

18.72 Where shares issued by a subsidiary to persons outside the group are guaranteed on a subordinated basis, the treatment will depend on the nature of the subordination agreement. This is because the degree of subordination varies widely in practice and particular care is necessary in assessing the effect of the subordination. Consider, for example, a situation where the parent company has guaranteed the redemption of a subsidiary's redeemable preference shares, but the terms of the guarantee are subordinated to other borrowings. It is possible that the terms of the subordination have the effect that the guarantee gives the preference shareholders no better rights than they would have enjoyed had the shares been issued by the parent. In other words, any payments for the shares can be avoided by all companies in the group in all the circumstances where avoidance would be possible if the shares were issued by the parent.

18.73 The intended effect of the subordination then is to ensure that the rights attaching to the redeemable shares of the subsidiary are the same as if they had been issued by the parent company. As preference shares issued by the parent are not treated as liabilities, it follows that shares issued by the subsidiary having identical rights as those of the holder of preference shares of the parent should similarly not be treated as liabilities. Instead, the redeemable preference shares of the subsidiary should be treated as non-equity minority interests. [FRS 4 para 90]. FRS 4 does not allow the instrument to be shown as part of shareholders' funds.

18.74 In practice, it is often difficult to evaluate the terms of a subordinated guarantee or to know precisely how the subordinated rights will be enforced. Even if the rights of the holders of shares in a subsidiary against the group can be made equivalent to those of a class of shares in the parent, there is a risk that future events may indicate that the presumed equivalence does not exist. Where it cannot be established that the subordination will have the desired effect of making the shares in the subsidiary equivalent to those issued by the parent, the subsidiary's shares should be accounted for as if the subordination has no effect, that is, the shares should be treated as liabilities and not as minority interests. [FRS 4 para 90]. This treatment should also be adopted where it is clear that the subsidiary's shares rank behind all other debts but before any shares issued by the parent. In some situations, the subordination may be effective only when the parent is wound up. As this does not prevent the subsidiary's shareholders from claiming under the guarantee in any other circumstance, the shares should be reported as liabilities and not as minority interests.

18.75 The requirement to show shares issued by subsidiaries to persons outside the group as liabilities and not as minority interests, where the group taken as a whole has an obligation to transfer economic benefits, might appear to conflict with the requirements of paragraph 17 of Schedule 4A to the Act. Hence, it might appear that the adoption of the treatment specified by the standard would involve recourse to the 'true and fair override' provisions in the Act. The ASB, however, takes the view that paragraph 1 of Schedule 4A, in requiring that group accounts are prepared as if the group were a single company, provides the necessary authority for the treatment required by the standard. This argument, which is considered in paragraph 4 of Appendix 1 to FRS 4 dealing with the legal requirements, is based on the premise that the reclassification of the shares in question as debt simply reflects the adoption of the group perspective and embraces all aspects of the arrangement. Because the treatment specified by the standard accounts entirely for the arrangement as a liability from a group perspective, there will be no amount remaining that represents an interest in the capital and reserves of the subsidiary. Accordingly, the ASB concluded that recourse need not be made to the true and fair override when adopting the treatment specified in the standard.

18.76 Where any part of minority interests is determined under FRS 4 to represent a liability, the general rules relating to debt will apply to the instrument (see para 18.70). That is, the debt should be recorded as a liability and its related issue costs should be netted against the liability. Finance costs are calculated in the same way as for other debt instruments and this is explained from paragraph 18.79. The finance costs will include the dividends payable which would previously have been treated as part of minority interests. Now, as they are regarded as the finance costs relating to a capital instrument that is treated as debt, they will be charged in the group profit and loss account as interest and added to the outstanding debt. In addition, as mentioned above in relation to unguaranteed non-equity shares, if such debt is repayable at a premium, an accrual for the redemption premium will be made each year as part of the finance costs.

18.77 FRS 4 requires that for non-equity minority interests where there is some form of guarantee as outlined above, that any rights of holders of the shares against other group companies should be described in the notes to the financial statements. [FRS 4 para 61].

18.78 In certain situations, the guaranteed non-equity shares that are classified as debt might be convertible. Where this is so, not only have they to be treated as liabilities, but, where material, they will have to be separately disclosed as convertible on the face of the balance sheet. Examples of such disclosures are given in Tables 18.4 and 18.5. Other companies, post FRS 4, have revoked any guarantees given previously in order to ensure that minority interests remain shown in that position and are not reclassified as debt.

Table 18.4 – Coats Viyella Plc – Annual report and accounts – 31 December 1992

Balance sheet (extract)

		Group		Company	
		1992	1991 Restated	**1992**	1991
At 31 December 1992	Notes	**£m**	£m	**£m**	£m
Creditors – amounts falling due after more than one year					
Other creditors	18	**(289.3)**	(268.6)	**(144.6)**	(244.9)
Redeemable convertible preference shares in Coats Viyella Finance NV	18	**(115.8)**	(109.9)	**-**	-
		(405.1)	(378.5)	**(144.6)**	(244.9)
Provisions for liabilities and charges	20	**(115.6)**	(139.3)	**-**	-
Net assets		**756.8**	687.8	**(325.2)**	357.0

Notes to the accounts (extracts)

7 Interest payable and similar charges

	1992	1991
	£'000	£'000
Debentures	**0.2**	0.1
Loans	**25.3**	18.7
Bank overdrafts and other borrowings	**20.6**	20.6
Finance leases	**4.5**	4.8
	50.6	44.2
Cost of financing convertible debt (note 18)		
- dividends	**7.1**	7.1
- supplemental redemption premium	**5.8**	5.2
	12.9	12.3
Total interest payable and similar charges	**63.5**	56.5

18 Creditors (amounts falling due after more than one year)

	Group 1992	Group 1991	Company 1992	Company 1991
Debentures, loans and loan stock (note 19)	**226.3**	210.6	**0.8**	0.9
Amounts owed to subsidiaries	**-**	-	**143.8**	244.0
Other creditors	**3.1**	0.8	**-**	-
Accruals and deferred income	**17.8**	13.2	**-**	-
Finance lease obligations	**42.1**	44.0	**-**	-
	289.3	268.6	**144.6**	244.9

The amounts owed to subsidiaries have no specified dates of repayment but are only repayable on receipt of twelve months' notice and do not bear interest.

Finance lease obligations are repayable as follows:		
Within one year	**6.1**	8.6
Between two and five years inclusive	**18.8**	19.7
Over five years	**23.3**	24.3
	48.2	52.6
Convertible debt		
Called up redeemable convertible preference share capital of subsidiary (see note *below*)	**115.8**	109.9

Note

On 14 June 1989, Coats Viyella Finance NV, a subsidiary company incorporated in the Netherlands Antilles, issued 98,000 7.25% Guaranteed Redeemable Convertible Preference Shares with a paid up value of £1,000 per share. The shares are guaranteed on a subordinated basis by Coats Viyella Plc and are convertible into its Ordinary Shares at a price of 196p per Ordinary Share at any time prior to 7 June 2004. The shares then outstanding will be redeemed on 14 June 2004 at their issue price or in certain circumstances upon earlier revocation of the guarantee. The preference shareholders may require the shares to be redeemed on 14 June 1994 at a redemption price of 128.5% of the paid up value thereof subject to the issuer's right to seek deferral of the redemption by electing to pay dividends at a higher level. Provision is made for the possible premium on redemption. At 31 December 1992 the amount accrued was £17.8m (1991: £11.9m). This is now included along with the paid up value of the shares.

Table 18.5 – THORN EMI plc – Annual Report – 31 March 1994

Notes to the accounts (extract)

15. Borrowings	Group		Company	
	1994	1993	**1994**	1993
	£m	£m	**£m**	£m
Long-term borrowings				
US dollar private placements	**67.6**	152.3	**27.0**	26.5
Auction Preferred Stock	**-**	132.4	**-**	-
Other US dollar	**182.3**	171.6	**57.1**	-
Other currencies	**89.9**	95.4	**4.9**	3.5
Finance leases	**9.8**	11.8	**-**	-
Less repayable within one year	**(1.6)**	(2.0)	**(0.4)**	(0.3)
Total long-term borrowings	**348.0**	561.5	**88.6**	29.7

Short-term borrowings				
Loans and overdrafts:				
US dollar	**96.6**	111.4	**0.2**	70.4
Other currencies	**70.0**	106.5	**-**	7.4
Finance leases	**1.4**	3.9	**-**	-
Short-term element of long-term loans	**1.6**	2.0	**0.4**	0.3
Convertible debt:				
Redeemable Convertible Preference Shares	**-**	103.0	**-**	-
Total short-term borrowings	**169.9**	326.8	**0.6**	78.1
Total borrowings	**517.6**	888.3	**89.2**	107.8

At 31 March 1993, THORN EMI America Finance Inc., a wholly-owned subsidiary registered in Delaware, USA, had in issue 200 shares of Auction Preferred Stock of US$1m each. Funds raised from this issue were loaned to other Group companies and repayment was guaranteed by the Company and certain other UK subsidiaries. The Auction Preferred Stock was repaid and cancelled in January and February 1994.

The 5¾ per cent Guaranteed Redeemable Convertible Preference Shares 2004 (RCPS) were issued by THORN EMI Capital NV, a wholly-owned subsidiary registered in the Netherlands Antilles. On 18 August 1993, THORN EMI plc gave notice of the revocation of its guarantee in respect of the RCPS. At 1 April 1993 there were 20,596 RCPS outstanding, of which 105 were redeemed and 20,491 were converted into 14,309,258 Ordinary Shares of THORN EMI plc, in accordance with the terms and conditions of the issue.

Finance costs

18.79 One of the main principles of FRS 4, which follows the basis first set out in TR 677, is to charge the finance costs (as defined) of a capital instrument to the profit and loss account over the instrument's term. (The term of a capital instrument is considered from para 18.92.) This basic principle applies to the finance costs on non-equity shares, debt and non-equity minority interests. Finance costs are defined in the standard as:

> *"The difference between the net proceeds of an instrument and the total amount of the payments (or other transfers of economic benefits) that the issuer may be required to make in respect of the instrument."* [FRS 4 para 8].

18.80 For non-equity shares the finance costs include issue costs, the total dividend payments to be made on the shares over the term and the difference between any premium on issue and any redemption premium (this is considered further from para 18.114 – see for example Table 18.6). Similarly for debt, the finance costs include issue costs, interest payments over the term, any redemption premium and any discount on issue (as explained further from para 18.151). The implications of FRS 4 on the calculation of minority interests is considered in chapter 24.

Table 18.6 – Pearson plc – Annual Report – 31 December 1997

Notes to the Accounts (extract)

1 Accounting policies (extract)

m) Capital instruments

Capital instruments are included at cost, adjusted for discount accretion or premium amortisation where the intention is to hold them to maturity. Interest receivable thereon and the premium or discount where relevant is taken to the profit and loss account so as to produce a constant rate of return over the period to the date of expected redemption.

Forward foreign exchange contracts and other off-balance sheet instruments are valued at the market prices prevailing at the balance sheet date. Borrowing is classified according to the maturity date of the respective individual holdings.

Accounting treatment

18.81 In accordance with the principle of matching, the finance cost should be recognised over the instrument's life. The simplest method of accounting would be to recognise finance costs on a straight line basis. However, although this method of allocation is simple, it fails to reflect the true cost of finance. This is because the amount charged each year does not necessarily bear any relationship to the outstanding obligation; that is, the method ignores the time value of money which is clearly relevant for financial decisions. For this reason, the ASB rejected the straight line method of allocation and opted instead for a more sophisticated method.

18.82 Under the method adopted by FRS 4, finance costs are charged to the profit and loss account at a constant rate on the carrying amount of the instrument. The constant rate is the discount rate that equates the present value of the net proceeds of the instrument with the present value of the total amount repaid on the instrument. It is better known as 'the internal rate of return' or sometimes referred to as 'the effective periodic rate' or 'the effective yield'; and it is equivalent to 'the rate implicit in the lease' under SSAP 21. It may be found by mathematical techniques involving an iterative process or by using a financial calculator or computer. Various examples are included in this chapter that illustrate the allocation of finance costs to accounting periods using this method.

18.83 Therefore, generally, it will not be acceptable to use the straight line method to allocate finance costs, unless this produces a similar result to a basis which achieves a constant rate. In this respect the standard adds that in certain instances the nominal interest rate on debt will not be materially different from the amount required by the FRS to achieve a constant rate and in those circumstances the nominal interest rate can be charged in the profit and loss account instead. [FRS 4 para 75]. This will often be so where the issue costs on a debt instrument are immaterial and there is no redemption premium to be accrued over its term. Consequently, for simple debt, such as straightforward bank loans and overdrafts where issue costs are immaterial or do not feature, the actual interest charged on the debt should be the amount recorded in the profit and loss account. Otherwise a basis similar to that illustrated in the examples in paragraphs 18.115 and 18.153 should be used.

18.84 Although the FRS requires that the finance cost should be charged to the profit and loss account over the instrument's term, it does not preclude capitalising those costs. Where it is appropriate to capitalise finance costs as part of the cost of an asset, the costs should still initially be written off to the profit and loss account as part of the interest cost, but should also be credited simultaneously to the profit and loss account and debited to the asset in order to record the capitalisation. [FRS 4 para 76]. As a result, the interest charge shown on the face of the profit and loss account would be the net amount and in the notes this would be expanded to show the gross amount and the amount capitalised deducted. However, for assets of the company being constructed, only the finance costs incurred during the period of construction of the asset can be capitalised (see further chapter 5).

Elements making up finance cost

18.85 Finance costs can be split into three separate elements:

- Dividends or interest.
- The difference between any premium received on the issue of an instrument and any redemption premium; or the discount on issue added to any redemption premium.
- Issue costs.

Dividends or interest

18.86 Where the dividend or interest is floating rather than fixed, it will not be possible to determine it in advance. Therefore, it will not be possible to calculate the total finance cost, but that should not cause a difficulty, because the floating rate interest charge or dividend appropriation made each year will be the correct amount to be shown in the profit and loss account for that year. Contingent payments of this nature are dealt with further in paragraphs 18.130 and 18.157.

Issue and redemption premiums

18.87 There may be circumstances where it is difficult to establish what the final redemption value of a capital instrument will be. For example, it may be linked in some way to future profits or to the market price of the company's shares, or it might be difficult to determine when the redemption might occur. These issues are considered further in paragraphs 18.157 and 18.217.

Issue costs

18.88 The ASB considers that issue costs are incurred to provide funds over a period of time and to charge those costs in full to the profit and loss account in the year of issue is not in accordance with the matching concept. However, deferral of such costs as some form of prepayment is not appropriate because the Act does not allow these costs to be carried forward nor does the prepayment qualify as an asset as defined in the ASB's draft Statement of principles. Accordingly, issue costs are accounted for as a deduction from the amount of the consideration received. This will result in issue costs for non-equity shares and debt being written off over the instrument's life. If it became clear that the instrument would be redeemed early, the amortisation of the issue costs and any discount on issue would need to be accelerated. Where the instrument does not have a term, for example, equity shares and perpetual debt, costs incurred in their issue would not be amortised (see paras 18.104 and 18.227). The types of costs that should be treated as issue costs are considered from paragraph 18.237.

18.89 Following the publication of FRS 4, it is now not generally possible to write off issue costs to the profit and loss account in the year an instrument is issued. The only exceptions will be:

- Where issue costs are immaterial, the provisions of FRS 4 do not apply and, therefore, they can be charged to the profit and loss account immediately.
- If the term is only one year or less.
- Where the costs associated with an issue do not fall within the strict definition of issue costs.
- Where the costs, if spread, would give rise to an excessively high finance cost on the instrument, which is out of line with that expected to be charged.

The last two points are considered in the paragraphs that follow.

18.90 FRS 4 states in paragraph 96 that costs that do not qualify as issue costs should be written off to the profit and loss account. However, this statement is made as part of the explanatory section rather than in the FRS standard section and seems to be dealing with the basic situation where a company is simply raising finance for its continuing operations or organic growth. It does not seem to be intended to preclude a company that has issued capital instruments to fund an acquisition of another company from capitalising as part of its cost of investment external costs it has incurred in connection with the acquisition, which do not fall within the strict definition of 'issue costs'. Capitalisation of such costs can be made even where merger relief is taken, but where merger accounting is used for the acquisition, FRS 6, 'Acquisitions and mergers', requires such costs to be expensed (see further chapter 27).

18.91 Finance costs might be overstated where a company is in financial difficulties and in order to raise finance to continue trading it incurs material costs related to the issue. If may be imprudent for such a company to spread these excessive issue costs forward. In this type of situation, it would be prudent for the company to recognise some or all of the issue costs as an exceptional finance cost in the year that they are incurred.

Term of capital instruments

18.92 Capital instruments come with various terms, which might be fixed, varying or indeterminate. A capital instrument's term is not necessarily the same period as its life. A capital instrument might have a number of different dates during its life when it can be redeemed or converted. These rights of redemption or conversion can be at the behest of the holder or the issuer of the instrument and are often granted by the use of options. The life of the instrument might extend for (say) ten years, but the impact of the options, if they are exercised, might be to shorten or lengthen the term considerably.

18.93 Under FRS 4 it is necessary to determine the term of an instrument for two reasons. First, the calculation of finance costs may depend on the term. For example a ten year bond might have an option to redeem after (say) five years at a premium of 20 per cent, but if not redeemed until year ten, the premium might reduce to (say) ten per cent. One of these premiums should be treated as part of the finance costs of the instrument, but the question is which one and this will depend on the instrument's term. Therefore, it is important to establish whether the term is five or ten years. Secondly, once determined, the finance costs are required by FRS 4 to be amortised over the instrument's term.

Definition of term

18.94 The term of capital instruments is defined in FRS 4 in the following way:

> *"The period from the date of issue of the capital instrument to the date at which it will expire, be redeemed, or be cancelled.*

If either party has the option to require the instrument to be redeemed or cancelled and, under the terms of the instrument, it is uncertain whether such an option will be exercised, the term should be taken to end on the earliest date at which the instrument would be redeemed or cancelled on exercise of such an option.

If either party has the right to extend the period of an instrument, the term should not include the period of the extension if there is a genuine commercial possibility that the period will not be extended." [FRS 4 para 16].

Implications of options

18.95 In many situations it will be obvious what the instrument's term is and this will in the majority of cases be the life of the instrument. However, where there are options built into the instrument the term becomes complicated. As can be seen from the second paragraph of the definition, where there is an option to redeem or cancel, the term is taken to end on the earliest date on which the option can be exercised. Paragraph 73 of FRS 4 goes on to comment that if there is an option for early redemption, the term should be taken to end on the earliest date the option could be exercised, unless there is *no* genuine commercial possibility that the option will be exercised. This requirement might at first sight seem a little odd, but it is based on the premise that options are normally granted for a purpose, for instance to allow a borrower to repay the debt early if the borrower either no longer needs debt or finds its interest rate unattractive.

18.96 There is one exception to the general rule that an instrument's term should end on the earliest date an option for redemption can be exercised. The exception given in UITF Abstract 11 relates to issuer call options. An issuer call option arises where the issuer (but not the investor) has a right to redeem the instrument early on the payment of a premium. The effect of an issuer call option on the instrument's term is considered from paragraph 18.250. That section also considers how options affect the allocation of finance costs over an instrument's term.

18.97 The requirement to take the term of the instrument, where an option (apart from an issuer call option) to redeem or cancel exists, to be up to the earliest date the option can be exercised has some odd consequences in practice. For example, in a typical management buyout (MBO), options for early repayment of redeemable shares and debt will often feature in the terms of those instruments. These may well operate to allow repayment of the finance at any time after the instrument has been issued. Where this is the case, unless it can be shown that there will be *no* genuine commercial possibility that the option will be exercised, the term will be less than one year (in effect it will be the notice period required). Thus, the whole of the finance costs should be written off to the profit and loss account in the year the instrument is issued and treated as an exceptional interest cost (or an exceptional appropriation if the instrument is a non-equity share) separately disclosed where material. The finance cost so written off will include the interest cost (or dividend cost) for the period and any issue costs. Finance costs should also include the difference between any premium on issue and any redemption premium. In the next year, if the instrument continues to be outstanding, the finance costs charged to the profit and loss account will merely be the interest cost or dividend cost for the period.

Term extended

18.98 As indicated in the definition, the term should not include any period for which the instrument might be extended, unless at the time the instrument is issued it is virtually certain that the term will be extended. [FRS 4 para 73]. Consequently, the economic interests of the parties to the instrument are important in determining its term. The FRS cites as an example the situation where a zero coupon bond is issued. If the terms of the bond are such that on early redemption the lender receives merely the original issue price, then the lender is unlikely to require early redemption unless there is a severe deterioration in the creditworthiness of the borrower. Therefore, at the outset, the bond's term should be taken to extend to its final maturity. [FRS 4 para 74].

18.99 These principles are illustrated in the two examples that follow:

Example 1

A company issues £1 million 10% preference shares. The terms are that £500,000 is redeemable in 19X2 and the balance is redeemable at the company's option in any year up to 19X9, when the balance must be redeemed. If the £500,000 is not redeemed in 19X2 additional dividends of 5% will accrue on that amount. The company is in financial difficulties and is unlikely to be able to redeem the shares in 19X2.

If there is no genuine possibility that redemption of the £500,000 will occur in 19X2, the term should be taken to be to the year 19X9 for the whole of the £1 million preference shares. This means that the finance costs should include the additional dividends on the £500,000 that will not be redeemed in 19X2. The additional dividends should be accrued for over the whole of the instrument's term.

Example 2

A company has issued a bond to raise money from a securities house pending a flotation. The bond is convertible into shares when the company is floated. It has a low coupon at first, but if the company is not floated, it is repayable at a fixed date in the future at a premium.
The term should be taken to be up to the date that is fixed for repayment in the event that the company is not floated. The total finance costs, including the premium should be amortised over this period to give a constant periodic rate of charge.

Term shortened

18.100 During an instrument's life, it is possible that its term could be shortened, for example, if for some reason the instrument is to be redeemed early in a way that was not foreseen. In this situation, the amortisation of issue costs and any discount on issue, or premium on redemption, should be accelerated over the remaining period of the shortened term. [FRS 4 para 94].

Indeterminate term

18.101 If the life of an instrument is indeterminate (for example, a perpetual bond) then FRS 4 comments that the benefit of the issue costs is reflected in the terms of the financing indefinitely. [FRS 4 para 95]. Where, for example, a perpetual bond of £100,000 is issued by a company and it incurs £2,000 of issue costs, the issue costs should reduce the carrying amount of the debt shown in the company's balance sheet. They would only be charged to the profit and loss account if and when the instrument is repurchased from the lender and would form part of the eventual profit or loss arising on the repurchase.

Shareholders' funds – measurement and disclosure

18.102 The term 'shareholders' funds' is not used in the balance sheet formats in the Act, but is defined in FRS 4 as the *"aggregate of called up share capital and all reserves, excluding minority interests"*. [FRS 4 para 15]. The term is used to describe the total shown in most financial statements of the items within the balance sheet format caption of 'capital and reserves' as set out in Schedule 4 to the Act, that is:

- Called up share capital.
- Share premium account.
- Revaluation reserve.
- Other reserves, which include:
  - Capital redemption reserve.
  - Reserve for own shares.
  - Reserves provided for by the articles.
  - Other reserves.
- Profit and loss account reserve.

Equity and non-equity shareholders' funds

18.103 FRS 4 changed the way that companies accounted for both equity and non-equity shares. Although the basic principles of the standard are relatively simple in nature, the measurement and accounting required to implement its principles can be complex. There are two basic requirements. The first is to require companies to report all shares and warrants as part of shareholders' funds. [FRS 4 para 37]. The second is to analyse the total amount of shareholders' funds between the amount that is attributable to equity interests and the amount that is attributable to non-equity interests. [FRS 4 para 40]. The FRS 4 definitions of equity interests and non-equity interests are considered earlier in paragraph 18.29.

Measurement and accounting

Equity share issues

18.104 FRS 4 requires the net proceeds from the issue of equity shares (using the FRS definition of equity) to be credited directly to shareholders' funds. [FRS 4 para 45]. It goes on to say that the amount that is attributable to shares should not be subsequently adjusted to reflect changes in the shares' value. Shares are recorded and stated in the financial statements at their nominal value with any surplus received on their issue taken to the share premium account (unless merger relief applies in which case the premium is taken to the merger reserve). Net proceeds is defined as *"the fair value of the consideration received on the issue of equity shares after deduction of issue costs"*. [FRS 4 para 11]. Issue costs are further defined as *"the costs that are incurred directly in connection with the issue of a capital instrument, that is, those costs that would not have been incurred had the specific instrument in question not been issued"*. [FRS 4 para 10]. The difficult question of the type of costs that can be treated as issue costs is discussed from paragraph 18.237.

18.105 Before the introduction of FRS 4, a company could choose where it debited the costs it incurred in issuing its shares. If it had a share premium account or issued the shares at a premium, it could charge the issue costs straight to that account, which as illustrated below, it still can under the provisions of FRS 4. Alternatively, if the company, for example, acquired an investment in a subsidiary or an unincorporated business, it could debit the costs of issuing any shares made in full, or in part, consideration for the acquisition to its cost of investment. This treatment is now precluded by FRS 4, because as explained above the standard requires that issue costs are regarded as part of the net proceeds of issuing the shares. However, other acquisition costs may still be added to the cost of investment (see para 18.90).

18.106 In addition, before the provisions of FRS 4 applied, if a company did not have a share premium account and was not acquiring an investment, it had to write off the costs it incurred in issuing its shares to the profit and loss account as an expense of the year. This treatment now appears to be no longer allowable under the standard, because issue costs have to be treated as part of the net proceeds of the issue. However, there are four situations where costs of this nature might be charged to the profit and loss account in the year they are incurred and these are considered in paragraph 18.89.

Treatment of issue costs where share premium exists

18.107 Assume that a company issues 100,000 £1 equity shares at a premium of 10p per share and the costs of issue are £2,000, then the net proceeds of issue are £108,000 (that is, £100,000 + £10,000 – £2,000). Where the company has a share premium account or there is a premium on the issue of the shares, then one option still available under the FRS is for the costs of issue to be written off to the share premium account. The double entry in this example would be as follows:

	£	£
Dr Cash (capital issued)	110,000	
Cr Share capital		100,000
Cr Share premium account		10,000
Cr Cash (issue costs)		2,000
Dr Share premium account	2,000	

To record the issue of shares at a premium and issue costs written off to the share premium account.

This treatment accords with FRS 4's provisions, because the net proceeds have been credited to shareholders' funds, namely the share capital of £100,000 plus the share premium of £10,000 less the issue costs of £2,000.

18.108 The movement shown in the reconciliation of shareholders' funds (a note required by FRS 3) will be the net proceeds of the shares issued. In the example, that is £108,000. However, it seems sensible to make the analysis clear to the reader and show also the gross components of the figure of net proceeds in this statement as follows:

Reconciliation of shareholders' funds

	£	£
Profit for the year		69,275
Dividends		13,000
		56,275
Proceeds of issue of equity shares	110,000	
Costs of share issue written off to share premium account	(2,000)	
Net proceeds of share issue		108,000
Net addition to shareholders' funds		164,275
Opening shareholders' funds		367,908
Closing shareholders' funds		532,183

Treatment of issue costs where no share premium exists

18.109 Where a company does not have a share premium account, it is still required by FRS 4 to credit the net proceeds of an issue of equity shares to shareholders' funds. Furthermore, as explained above, the company can no longer charge costs it incurs in issuing those shares to the profit and loss account or to the cost of investment in another undertaking the acquisition of which it has financed by the share issue. Although the standard does not state so explicitly, the most logical way to comply with its provisions, where the company does not have a share premium account, is to charge the issue costs to another reserve. Unless a more suitable reserve is available, the profit and loss account reserve would appear to be the most appropriate. Hence, if a company issues 100,000 £1 ordinary shares and incurs costs on issue of £2,000 and it does not have a share premium account, the double entry would be as follows:

	£	£
Dr Cash (capital issued)	100,000	
Cr Share capital		100,000
Cr Cash (issue costs)		2,000
Dr Profit and loss account *reserve*	2,000	

To record the issue of shares and issue costs written off to the profit and loss account reserve.

18.110 In this situation, the movements in the reconciliation of shareholders' funds will be the same as those shown in paragraph 18.108 above, except that it will show 'costs of share issue written off to the profit and loss account reserve' as one of the components of net proceeds.

Non-equity share issues

18.111 FRS 4 requires shareholders' funds to be analysed between equity interests and non-equity interests (see further para 18.137 below). However, this analysis is not the only reason why it has to be established which shares are non-equity. The standard changed the accounting requirements and disclosure requirements that applied to non-equity shares. The additional disclosure requirements for such shares are considered in chapter 19 whilst the accounting requirements are considered in the paragraphs that follow.

18.112 Initially, the standard's requirements for non-equity shares are similar to those for equity shares, as the FRS states that immediately after the issue of non-equity shares the amount of non-equity shareholders' funds attributable to those shares should be the net proceeds of the issue. [FRS 4 para 41]. For example, a company issues 100,000 £1 non-equity shares at a premium of 10p per share. It incurs issue costs of £2,000 related to the issue. The non-equity shares have a fixed cumulative dividend of 5 per cent a year and are redeemable in five years at a premium of 20 per cent. The net proceeds of the issue are £108,000 (that is, proceeds of £110,000 – issue costs of £2,000). The double entry for the issue would be as follows:

	£	£
Dr Cash (capital issued)	110,000	
Cr Share capital		100,000
Cr Share premium account		10,000
Cr Cash (issue costs)		2,000
Dr Share premium account or other reserve	2,000	

To record the issue of shares at a premium and issue costs written off to the share premium account or directly to other reserves (generally the profit or loss account reserve).

18.113 As can be seen in the example, the same rules concerning the issue costs that apply to equity shares explained in paragraphs 18.104 to 18.109 also apply to the issue of non-equity shares. However, for non-equity shares the standard goes on to require that the net proceeds should then be increased by the finance costs in respect of the period and reduced by dividends or other payments made in respect of the instrument in that period. [FRS 4 para 41]. Other payments would include, for example, the difference between any premium received on issue and any premium that might arise on redemption of a non-equity share.

18.113.1 The FRRP issued a press release in December 1995 regarding the financial statements of Caradon plc for the year ended 31 December 1994 concerning the analysis of shareholders' funds. The financial statements showed an amount for non-equity interests of £24.3 million, whereas the amount attributable to non-equity interests calculated in accordance with FRS 4 was £163.1 million. The £24.3 million represented the nominal value of the non-equity shares issued, but they were issued at a substantial premium. The related share premium was cancelled in the same year, after the approval of the high court and the special reserve thereby created was used to write off goodwill arising on an acquisition. The FRRP pointed out that the cancellation of the share premium account did not affect the requirement in FRS 4 to show as non-equity interests the net proceeds from the issue (including the share premium account).

18.113.2 A similar situation arose in the financial statements of First Choice Holdings plc for the year to 31 October 1994 and it made an adjustment which was reported in its interim statement issued in June 1995. The company reported in its interim statement that *"following developments in the application of FRS 4, the directors have reviewed the disclosure for equity and non-equity shareholders' funds and decided to restate the split to allocate all goodwill against equity shareholders' funds. Following a subsequent enquiry by the Financial Reporting Review Panel (FRRP), the directors understand that this revised treatment accords with the FRRP's views".*

Treatment of finance costs

18.114 Finance costs for non-equity shares are calculated on the same basis as finance costs for debt and are also defined in the same way (see para 18.147 onwards). [FRS 4 para 42]. Therefore, in the example illustrated above, the finance cost for the non-equity shares is calculated as follows:

	£	£
Amount payable on redemption:		
Capital repaid	100,000	
Premium on redemption	20,000	120,000
Dividends over the life of the instrument:		
£100,000 x 5% x 5 years		25,000
		145,000
Net proceeds of share issue		108,000
Finance costs		37,000

18.115 The standard then requires that the finance costs for non-equity shares should be allocated to periods over the term of the shares at a constant rate on the carrying amount and should be shown as an appropriation in the profit and loss account. [FRS 4 para 42, 28]. The table below shows the allocation of the finance charge of £37,000 in the above example to achieve a constant rate over the term of the non-equity instrument compounded semi-annually. An interest rate of 6.544 per cent can be calculated to allocate the finance cost over the term to provide a constant rate assuming that the dividend is paid half-yearly. One way of finding the rate is to use a spreadsheet model. In such a model the rate is varied up and down until an interest rate is found that produces a balance at the end of year five of £120,000.

[The next page is 18037.]

Interest rate 5% compounded semi-annually. Overall finance cost 6.544%							
Year	Balance b/f	Finance cost 6 mths	Interim divi.	Balance	Finance cost 6 mths	Final divi.	Balance c/f
1	108,000	3,534	(2,500)	109,034	3,567	(2,500)	110,101
2	110,101	3,603	(2,500)	111,204	3,638	(2,500)	112,342
3	112,342	3,676	(2,500)	113,518	3,715	(2,500)	114,733
4	114,733	3,754	(2,500)	115,987	3,795	(2,500)	117,282
5	117,282	3,837	(2,500)	118,619	3,881	(2,500)	120,000
		18,404	(12,500)		18,596	(12,500)	
					18,404	(12,500)	
Total finance costs and dividends					37,000	(25,000)	

18.116 As can be seen from the calculation above, the dividend paid each year does not equal the finance cost for the year. For example, in year one the dividend cost is £5,000, whereas the finance cost is £7,101. The difference is made up of the proportion charged in the year of the issue costs of £2,000 and the allocation of the excess of the premium payable on redemption compared to that received on issue, which is £10,000 (that is, £20,000 – £10,000). The effect is noted in the accounting policy reproduced in Table 18.7.

Table 18.7 – AMEC p.l.c. – Annual report and accounts – 31 December 1994

Financial highlights and review (extract)

Accounting standards (extract)

Two new accounting standards, FRS 4 – 'Capital Instruments' and FRS 5 – 'Reporting the Substance of Transactions', came into effect during 1994 and have been adopted in the preparation of these accounts. FRS 4 introduced a new analysis of shareholders' funds and its application also affects the accounting treatment of the preference dividend. This is now stated in the profit and loss account at a slightly higher amount, reflecting the amortisation of the discount at which such shares were issued, relative to their redemption value. This treatment has no effect on the level of dividend payments made to preference shareholders.

Notes to the accounts (extract)

2 Adoption of new accounting standards (extract)

FRS 4 requires that :

finance costs of non-equity shares, including dividends, premium on redemption and issue costs, are charged at a constant rate in the profit and loss account as an appropriation of profit.

In addition, FRS 4 requires the analysis of shareholders' funds to be apportioned between amounts attributable to equity shareholders and non-equity shareholders.

The effect of the introduction of FRS 4 is a small increase in the cost of the ordinary and preference dividends.

18.117 The standard states that where the finance costs for non-equity shares are not equal to the dividends the difference should be accounted for in the profit and loss account as an appropriation of profits. [FRS 4 para 44]. Consequently, the £5,000 will be recorded in the profit and loss account as a dividend and the balance of the finance costs of £2,101 in year one will also be shown as an appropriation. The disclosure could be made in the following way:

Profit and loss account extract (year 1)	£	£
Profit for the financial year		69,275
Dividends and appropriations		
Preference share dividend	5,000	
Preference share appropriation	2,101	
Non-equity appropriation	7,101	
Ordinary dividend	13,000	20,101
Retained profit for the financial year		49,174

18.118 The double entry to record the allocation of the finance costs and treatment as an appropriation in year one is as follows:

		£	£
Dr	Profit and loss account appropriation	7,101	
Cr	Cash		5,000
Cr	Profit and loss account reserve		2,101

To record the finance costs as an appropriation, to provide for the redemption premium on the shares together with the issue costs which have already been written off to the share premium account or to another appropriate reserve.

18.119 The double entry may appear rather cosmetic in that the appropriation for issue costs and redemption premium is debited to the profit and loss account (appropriations section) and credited to the profit and loss account reserve. The entry is necessary because the objective is to show the full cost of non-equity shares in the profit and loss account, so as to reflect properly the profit for the year that belongs to the equity shareholders (see for example Table 18.8). As far as the issue costs are concerned, they would have been debited to the share premium account or another reserve at the time of payment, so the only entries now necessary are those that concern the allocation of results and shareholders' funds between equity and non-equity interests.

Table 18.8 – Granada Group PLC – Annual Report and Accounts - 1 October 1994

Notes to the accounts (extract)

	1994 £m	1993 £m
9 Dividends		
Equity shares:		
Interim dividend of 3.33p (1993: 3.025p) per share, paid 3 October 1994	19.3	14.1
Final proposed dividend of 6.67p (1993: 5.725p) per share, payable 3 April 1995	38.7	26.8
	58.0	40.9
Non-equity shares:		
Dividend of 7.5p per share, paid in two instalments on 31 January and 31 July 1994	13.2	13.2
Finance credit (FRS 4)	(1.1)	(1.0)
	12.1	12.2
	70.1	53.1

	Share capital £m	Share premium £m	Revaluation reserve £m	Merger reserve £m	Profit and loss account £m	Total 1994 £m	Total 1993 £m
23 Reconciliation of movements in shareholders' funds (extract)							
a Group							
Balance at 2 October 1993	134.5	175.6	138.1	(344.8)	360.9	464.3	561.5
Retained profit for period for equity shareholders	-	-	-	-	121.9	121.9	73.2
Other finance costs of non-equity shares	-	-	-	-	(1.1)	(1.1)	(1.0)
Adjustments in respect of shares for dividend scheme	-	-	-	-	2.2	2.2	1.3
Shares issued in period (net)	28.2	3.0	-	584.1	-	615.3	150.8
Share issue costs	-	(20.9)	-	-	-	(20.9)	-
Currency adjustments	-	-	-	-	(0.9)	(0.9)	0.1
Net movement on goodwill	-	-	-	(656.1)	(22.4)	(678.5)	(325.0)
Transfers	-	-	(0.4)	-	0.4	-	-
Surplus on property revaluations	-	-	-	-	-	-	3.4
At 1 October 1994	162.7	157.7	137.7	(416.8)	461.0	502.3	464.3

18.120 The element of the finance cost that equates to the difference between the premium received on the issue of the non-equity shares and the premium payable on their redemption is treated in the same way as the issue costs, that is, as an appropriation. The credit for this cost could be made to a redemption reserve as an alternative to being made to the profit and loss account reserve, because it represents a gradual building up of the premium that will be paid on redemption. Even if this treatment is adopted, only part of the redemption premium would be credited to this reserve over the life of the instrument, namely the difference between the premium on the issue of the non-equity shares (in the example £10,000) and the redemption premium (in the example £20,000). Hence, an additional amount of £10,000 would have to be charged to the profit and loss account reserve when the non-equity shares are finally redeemed. This additional amount which is always equal to the premium received is not required to be set aside over the life of the instrument, although it could be set aside as a reserve movement. (Furthermore, it should not be forgotten that under the Act the share capital itself when redeemed will have to be repurchased out of distributable profits or out of the proceeds of a fresh issue of shares (see further chapter 40).)

18.121 It may be simpler, rather than to credit part of the redemption premium to a separate redemption reserve over the life of the non-equity share, to leave it in the profit and loss account reserve as illustrated in paragraph 18.118. Then, at the end of the instrument's term, the whole of the redemption premium and the nominal value of the shares can be paid out of the profit and loss account reserve.

18.122 If the non-equity shares were issued at the beginning of the year, then at the year end the necessary entries would be reflected in the reconciliation of shareholders' funds in the following way:

Reconciliation of shareholders' funds		
	£	£
Profit for the year		69,275
Dividends and appropriations		20,101
		49,174
Proceeds of issue of non-equity shares	110,000	
Costs of share issue written off to share premium account	(2,000)	
Net proceeds of share issue		108,000
Reversal of non-equity appropriations		2,101
Net addition to shareholders' funds		159,275
Opening shareholders' funds		367,908
Closing shareholders' funds		527,183

Non-equity dividends

Accrual of dividends

18.123 As explained above, dividends on non-equity shares form part of the instrument's overall finance costs. To the extent they are shown as an appropriation in the profit and loss account, they are notionally added to the non-equity shareholders' funds and when they are declared, they reduce the non-equity shareholders' funds and are transferred to creditors. [FRS 4 para 41]. In practice, this process is reflected in the financial statements by recording the dividend proposed as a creditor (unless it cannot be paid) and reducing non-equity shareholders' funds.

18.124 Where dividends on non-equity shares are calculated by reference to time, the dividends should be accounted for on an accruals basis except in those circumstances where ultimate payment will be remote. [FRS 4 para 43]. Ultimate payment of dividends will be remote where there are insufficient distributable profits and the dividends are non-cumulative. Accruals will always have to be made for dividends that are cumulative even in the absence of sufficient distributable profits. The accounting treatment of cumulative dividends is considered further in paragraphs 18.126 and 18.127.

18.125 The question then arises as to how to treat accruals of dividends on non-equity shares that have been proposed at the company's year end, but that are not paid until after its year end. Paragraph 30 of FRS 4 is helpful here, because it allows finance costs, to the extent that they have been accrued in one period and will be paid in the next, to be included in the balance sheet as an accrual. Therefore, where a dividend on a non-equity share is outstanding at the year end, but is to be paid in the next accounting period, it should be included in accruals within current liabilities and thereby reduce the amount of shareholders' funds that is attributable to non-equity interests (see further para 18.137 below).

Cumulative dividends in arrears

18.126 Often non-equity shares have cumulative dividends that accrue to the non-equity shareholders even where there are no distributable reserves available out of which to make a distribution. Before FRS 4 came into effect, arrears of cumulative dividends were merely noted in the financial statements and no accounting entries were made for them until they were paid. The accounting treatment for such cumulative dividends changed following FRS 4's publication. As with other dividends on non-equity shares, cumulative dividends form part of the finance costs of the share. As such, in accordance with the standard, cumulative dividends are charged to the profit and loss account with other finance costs to achieve a constant rate on the outstanding instrument as explained in paragraph 18.115.

18.127 The standard is, however, silent as to what should be done with the credit that arises as a result of charging the cumulative dividend to the profit and loss account as an appropriation when the company has no distributable profits. It could, for example, be credited to liabilities as a dividend payable, but this does not seem to be the right answer as the dividend cannot be declared as there are no distributable reserves from which to make the payment. A better treatment would be to credit it back to the profit and loss account reserve and to note the arrears as required by the Act (see para 18.135). Then, to comply with analysis of shareholders' funds required by FRS 4, the arrears of dividend would increase the non-equity interests in shareholders' funds and decrease the equity interests in shareholders' funds. When sufficient distributable profits have been earned, from which the arrears of dividend can be paid, then the double entry will be to credit creditors when the dividend is declared and to debit the profit and loss account reserve with the amount of dividend declared. In addition, it would seem necessary in order to comply with the Act to show the dividend paid in the profit and loss account. The example below suggests how this can be achieved.

Example

A company issues cumulative preference shares at the beginning of year 1. The shares carry a cumulative dividend of 5%, which in year 1 gives rise to a dividend of £10,000. The company has no distributable reserves and no other reserves. The equity shares in issue have a nominal value of £5,000 and the non-equity shares in issue have a nominal value of £200,000. The loss in year 1 is £2,000 (the reserves brought forward are nil). The total shareholders' funds at the year end is £203,000 (that is, equity shares £5,000 + non-equity shares £200,000 – profit and loss account reserve deficit £2,000) before accounting for the cumulative dividend.

Under FRS 4 (as explained above) the company should accrue for the cumulative dividend of £10,000 as an appropriation in the profit and loss account.

Profit and loss account extract (year 1)	£
Loss for the financial year	(2,000)
Dividends and appropriations	
Preference share appropriation	(10,000)
Retained loss for the financial year	(12,000)

The dividend should then be shown as part of non-equity shareholders' funds rather than as a creditor as the company has no distributable profits. The effect of this on the analysis of shareholders' funds is that the amount attributable to non-equity shareholders would be increased by £10,000, with the equity shareholders' funds decreased by £10,000. At the end of year 1 the balance of shareholders' funds disclosed in the financial statements, that is, attributable to equity shareholders would be calculated as follows:

Total shareholders' funds	£
Equity share capital	5,000
Non-equity share capital	200,000
Profit and loss account reserve	(2,000)
Total shareholders' funds	203,000
Shareholders' funds allocated to non-equity	
Non-equity share capital	200,000
Cumulative dividend not yet declared	10,000
	210,000
Shareholders' funds allocated to equity	
Difference between total shareholders' funds and amount allocated to non-equity interests	(7,000)
Made up as follows:	
Equity shares	5,000
Profit and loss account reserve	(2,000)
Cumulative dividend due to non-equity shareholders	(10,000)
	(7,000)

If the company makes (say) £12,000 of distributable profits in the next year and the dividend is declared, the entry would be to debit non-equity shareholders' funds and to credit creditors with £10,000 to reflect the fact that the company now has an obligation to pay the preference shareholders. The profit and loss account for the year should show the previous year's dividend proposed to be paid to accord with the Act as well as the dividend for year 2 that is to be paid (say) £2,000 (although the directors could decide in this example to pay up to £4,000, that is, for the current year the total amount of distributable profits) and the balance of the cumulative dividend due (that is £8,000) as an appropriation.

Profit and loss account extract (year 2)	£	£
Profit for the financial year		12,000
Dividends and appropriations		
Preference share dividend arrears	10,000	
Appropriated in previous year	(10,000)	
	-	
Preference share dividend current year	2,000	
Preference share appropriation	8,000	10,000
Retained profit for the financial year		2,000

18.128 The treatment of cumulative dividends in arrears is illustrated in Table 18.9.

Table 18.9 – Queens Moat Houses P.L.C. – Annual Report and Accounts – 2 January 1994

Accounting Policies (extract)

(b) Accounts presentation

The company has adopted the provisions of Financial Reporting Standard 4 'Capital instruments' ("FRS 4") which requires the amount of shareholders' funds attributable to equity and non-equity interests to be separately disclosed. Dividends for the year on the company's convertible cumulative redeemable preference shares have been appropriated through the profit and loss account. However, as the company does not have sufficient distributable reserves in order to pay such preference share dividends, these dividends have been credited back within profit and loss account reserves. To be consistent with this treatment, a prior year adjustment has been made for the appropriation through the profit and loss account of preference share dividends in respect of 1992, and these dividends have been credited back within 1992 profit and loss account reserves. Issue costs incurred in connection with debt instruments issued prior to the beginning of the financial year have not been reflected in the carrying value of the debt instruments as these are not material.

9 Dividends and appropriations (extract)

	1993 £m	1992 £m
Preference shares (non-equity) dividends		
7.0% convertible cumulative redeemable preference shares	**0.3**	0.3
7.5% convertible cumulative redeemable preference shares	-	10.5
	0.3	10.8
Preference shares (non-equity) appropriations		
7.0% convertible cumulative redeemable preference shares	**0.3**	0.3
7.5% convertible cumulative redeemable preference shares	**14.1**	3.6
	14.4	3.9
	14.7	14.7
Ordinary shares (equity) dividends		
Interim dividend nil pence per share (1992 – 1.395 pence per share)	-	12.9

In accordance with the provisions of FRS 4, the company has appropriated through the profit and loss account preference share dividends for the year on the company's 7.0% and 7.5% convertible cumulative redeemable preference shares of £0.3 million and £14.1 million respectively. However, as the company does not have sufficient distributable reserves in order to pay such preference share dividends, these dividends have been credited back within profit and loss account reserves (note 20). A prior year adjustment has been made for the appropriation of preference share dividends in respect of 1992 on the company's 7.0% and 7.5% convertible cumulative redeemable preference shares of £0.3 million and £3.6 million respectively, and these dividends have been credited back within 1992 profit and loss account reserves.

20 Reserves (extract)

Group	Share premium account £m	Revaluation reserve £m	Profit and loss account £m
At 1 January 1993	464.6	65.8	(1,162.7)
Retained loss for the year	-	-	(59.1)
Currency translation adjustments	-	(1.1)	7.5
Preference shares appropriations (note 9)	-	-	14.4
Surplus arising on revaluation of tangible fixed assets (note 11)	-	49.8	-
Transfers of revaluation surplus realised	-	(4.4)	4.4
Goodwill on disposals	-	-	0.4
At 2 January 1994	**464.6**	**110.1**	**(1,195.1)**

Redemption premiums

18.129 FRS 4 requires that where there is a premium payable on the redemption of preference shares this should be accrued over the term of the preference shares. If there was also a premium on issue of the shares then the amount to be accrued over the life as part of the finance cost is the difference between the premium on issue and the premium on redemption. It might in a particular case appear that accruing this premium over the term of the share as an appropriation has the effect of reducing distributable reserves to nil, in which case the result would be that no dividend could be paid. However, the annual appropriation in respect of the premium is matched by an equivalent credit to reserves (probably to the profit and loss account reserve or to a redemption reserve). The effect on the company's legally distributable reserves is, therefore, neutral and a dividend can still be paid if there are in other respects sufficient distributable reserves. However, if the dividend is paid the company's ability ultimately to redeem the preference shares may be affected as the redemption can only be made out of distributable profits or from the proceeds of a fresh issue of shares (see further chapter 40).

Calculation of finance costs

18.130 In many situations it will not be possible to determine the total finance costs for a non-equity share at the outset. This is because either the dividend will not be a fixed amount (for example, a dividend calculated by reference to an index), or the term of the instrument will not be determinable (for example, the share is not redeemable). In such situations the dividend element of the finance cost charged as an appropriation each year will merely be the dividends paid and accrued as payable in that year. Furthermore, where shareholders waive a dividend in the year, no charge will be made for that dividend in the profit and loss account as part of the finance costs.

18.130.1 The FRRP issued a press notice in February 1996 concerning Securicor Group Plc's September 1994 financial statements. The company has cumulative participating preference shares. These are classified as non-equity presumably because they have a right to a fixed dividend of 4.55 per cent (net). In addition, the shares have a right to a further participating dividend of 4.725 per cent (gross) for every one per cent gross dividend on the ordinary shares. On winding up, the preference shares participate in surpluses (25 per cent) after various priority payments. In 1994 the company disclosed equity shareholders' interests of £174 million and non-equity interests of £25 million. The nominal value of the preference shares was £677,000 and the company had no share premium account. The company explained that calculating the finance costs and dividends over the life of the instrument was impractical and it was considered that an equity/non-equity analysis based on the division of profits gave a more true and fair view of the respective interests. This argument was not accepted by the FRRP which required the company to restate its figures so that the comparatives in its 1995 financial statements are now shown as equity shareholders' interests of £200 million and non-equity interests of £677,000. There is a footnote stating that as the non-equity shares are entitled to dividends equal to a fixed proportion of the ordinary dividends, a distribution to ordinary shareholders would require further dividends to be paid on the preference shares with a consequent decrease in equity interests.

Disclosure

Profit and loss account appropriations

18.131 The Act requires that the aggregate amount of dividends paid and proposed should be disclosed in the profit and loss account after the profit and loss for the financial year as an appropriation. [4 Sch 3(7)(b); FRS 4 para 43]. However, the appropriations made in the profit and loss account under FRS 4 will include not only the dividends paid and proposed on equity and non-equity shares, but will also include:

- Other elements of finance costs on non-equity shares (for example, issue costs and premiums). [FRS 4 para 44].
- Cumulative dividends on non-equity shares, which cannot yet be proposed or paid because the company has insufficient distributable reserves. [FRS 4 para 43].

18.132 In addition, FRS 4 requires that the aggregate dividends are disclosed for each class of shares. This analysis by class should sub-total to the amounts in respect of dividends on equity shares, participating dividends and other dividends on non-equity shares. [FRS 4 para 59]. Participating dividends are defined in paragraph 13 of FRS 4 as:

> *"A dividend (or part of a dividend) on a non-equity share that, in accordance with a company's memorandum and articles of association, is always equivalent to a fixed multiple of the dividend payable on an equity share."*

Participating dividends will be very rare and, therefore, most companies will need merely to give the sub-totals for equity and non-equity dividends.

18.133 Furthermore, any additional amounts of finance costs on non-equity shares (that is, premiums payable on redemption or issue costs) treated as appropriations in accordance with FRS 4 must be separately disclosed. [FRS 4 para 59].

18.134 An example of the type of disclosure necessary to satisfy the requirements is given below (see also Table 18.10 and Table 18.8 on page 39).

[The next page is 18047.]

> *

Profit and loss account (extract)

	Note	1995 £'000	1994 £'000
Profit/(loss) for the financial year		1,918	(5,524)
Dividends (including dividends and other appropriations in respect of non-equity shares)	15	(1,051)	(946)
Retained profit/(loss) for the year		867	(6,470)

15 Dividends and appropriations

	1995 £'000	1994 £'000
Dividends on equity shares:		
Ordinary – Interim paid of 0.75p per share (1994: 0.5p)	299	194
Ordinary – Final proposed of 1.7p per share (1994: 1.75p)	677	678
	976	872
Dividends on non-equity shares:		
Preference 5.6% paid	67	67
Appropriation for premium payable on redemption and issue costs	8	7
	75	74
	1,051	946

Table 18.10 – Tate & Lyle Public Limited Company – Annual Report – 24 September 1994

Group Profit and Loss Account (extract)

For the 52 weeks to 24 September 1994

	Notes	**1994 £ million**	1993 £ million
Profit for the period		**171.1**	149.2
Dividends paid and proposed	6	**65.5**	60.3
of which – on equity shares		***51.8***	*46.5*
- on non-equity shares		***13.7***	*13.8*
Retained profit		**105.6**	88.9

Notes to the Financial Statements (extract)

6 Dividends Paid and Proposed

Dividends on non-equity shares – 6½% cumulative preference shares	**0.1**	0.1
- 7.25p convertible cumulative redeemable preference shares of 12.5p each	**13.6**	13.7
	13.7	13.8
Dividends on equity shares – ordinary shares	**51.8**	46.5
	65.5	60.3

The total ordinary dividend is 14.4p made up as follows:
Interim dividend paid 19th July 1994 – 4.6p (1993 – 4.3p)
Final dividend proposed payable 7th February 1995 – 9.8p (1993 – 8.7p)

18.135 Where a class of shares carries a fixed cumulative dividend that is in arrears, the Act requires that the financial statements should disclose in a note the amount of the arrears. The Act also requires the period for which the dividend is in arrears to be disclosed and where there is more than one class in arrears the period for each class should be given. [4 Sch para 49]. The accounting treatment of cumulative dividends that cannot be paid because of insufficient distributable profits is explained in paragraph 18.126. When such a dividend is paid, it would seem sensible to disclose the cumulative dividend in arrears that has now been settled and to show the amount declared to be paid on the face of the profit and loss account to comply with the Act's requirement to disclose the aggregate amount of any dividends paid and proposed (see the example in paragraph 18.122).

Share capital

18.136 The disclosure that has to be made in a company's financial statements concerning its share capital, which is detailed in FRS 4, the Act and the Stock Exchange's listing rules, is explained in chapter 19.

Shareholders' funds

18.137 The total of shareholders' funds has to be disclosed on the face of the balance sheet and analysed between the amount that is attributable to equity interests and the amount that is attributable to non-equity interests. [FRS 4 paras 38, 40]. Where the non-equity interest's share of shareholders' funds is immaterial the disclosure may be given in the notes as long as the caption on the balance sheet makes it clear that non-equity interests are included. [FRS 4 paras 54, 100]. For example, the balance sheet caption for the total of shareholders' funds could read 'Shareholders' funds (including non-equity interests)'. It is not, however, acceptable to split only the share capital on the face of the balance sheet between equity shares and non-equity shares, even where the only non-equity interest is the non-equity shares in issue.

18.138 It is important to remember that the analysis of shareholders' funds is of a memorandum nature only and is required to be disclosed on the face of the balance sheet to give readers a better understanding of the share of net assets that are attributable to the two categories of shares in issue. It is not necessary in order to arrive at the amounts to be disclosed to allocate reserves on a specific basis to either equity or non-equity interests, because FRS 4 requires only analysis of the total, not of each component. However certain companies do analyse their reserves in this way although this is not a requirement of the standard as illustrated in Table 18.11.

Table 18.11 – Cadbury Schweppes plc – Annual Report – 31 December 1994

Balance Sheets (extract)
At 31 December 1994

Notes		Group		Company	
		1994 £m	1993 £m	**1994 £m**	1993 £m
	Capital and Reserves				
	Attributable to equity interests				
18	Called up share capital	**208.5**	207.5	**208.5**	207.5
18	Share premium account	**717.5**	704.4	**717.5**	704.4
18	Revaluation Reserve	**95.7**	95.3	**1.3**	1.5
18	Profit and loss account	**319.0**	199.0	**269.3**	183.4
	Attributable to non-equity interests				
18	Called up share capital	**0.3**	0.3	**0.3**	0.3
18	Share premium account	**158.0**	158.0	**158.0**	158.0
		1,499.0	1,364.5	**1,354.9**	1,255.1
	Equity minority interests	**128.0**	145.0	**-**	-
		1,627.0	1,509.5	**1,354.9**	1,255.1

18.139 For the analysis of shareholders' funds, it is necessary first to calculate the amount of shareholders' funds that is attributable to non-equity interests. This is done by working out the amount of shares in, and reserves of, the company that is attributable to all classes of non-equity shares (including warrants for non-equity shares). [FRS 4 para 40]. The amounts of shares and reserves to be treated as part of non-equity interests in shareholders' funds are considered from paragraph 18.111. Then the amount of equity interests in shareholders' funds is the difference between total shareholders' funds and the total amount attributable to non-equity interests. [FRS 4 para 40].

18.140 The amount of shareholders' funds disclosed on the face of the balance sheet that is attributable to non-equity interests has to be split further in the notes to the financial statements between each class of non-equity share and series of warrants for non-equity shares. [FRS 4 para 55]. There is, however, no equivalent requirement to analyse the amount of shareholders' funds attributable to equity interests between the different classes of equity shares in issue.

18.141 An example of the disclosure of the split of shareholders' funds between equity interests and non-equity interests is given in Table 18.12.

Table 18.12 – The Rank Organisation Plc – Directors' Report and Accounts 31 October 1994

BALANCE SHEETS (extract)

		Group		Company	
At 31st October 1994	*Note*	**1994**	1993	**1994**	1993
Capital and reserves		**£m**	£m	**£m**	£m
Called up share capital	20	**128.5**	127.3	**128.5**	127.3
Share premium account	20	**514.4**	483.3	**514.4**	483.3
Capital redemption reserve	20	**1.3**	1.3	**1.3**	1.3
Revaluation reserves	20	**143.4**	172.8	**152.0**	152.0
Other reserves	20	**771.2**	701.0	**763.0**	694.9
Shareholders' funds		**1,558.8**	1,485.7	**1,559.2**	1,458.8
Equity interests		**1,349.5**	1,278.5	**1,349.9**	1,251.6
Non-equity interests		**209.3**	207.2	**209.3**	207.2
Minority interests (including non-equity interests)	21	**47.8**	47.1	**-**	-
		1,606.6	1,532.8	**1,559.2**	1,458.8

18.142 The analysis of shareholders' funds between equity interests and non-equity interests does not necessarily give an indication of the amount that would be payable to the respective shareholders on a liquidation. Neither does the analysis necessarily reflect the shareholders' rights to reserves as set out in the company's memorandum and articles of association. For example, if a company issues 100,000 £1 redeemable preference shares at a premium of ten per cent, then it is quite possible on a liquidation that the premium on the redeemable shares would be attributable to the equity shareholders and would form part of their funds on liquidation. Under the FRS, this premium is attributed in the analysis of shareholders' funds to non-equity shareholders' interests. However, this example is simplistic and the actual outcome in practice on liquidation would depend upon the terms of the ordinary shares and redeemable preference shares of the particular company concerned.

18.143 Companies need to keep additional records to show how they have determined the allocation of shareholders' funds to non-equity interests (the balance being attributable to equity interests).

18.144 In the example used in paragraph 18.112, a company issued 100,000 £1 non-equity shares at a premium of 10p per share. It incurred issue costs of £2,000 related to the issue. The non-equity shares had a fixed cumulative dividend of 5 per cent a year and were redeemable in five years at a premium of 20 per cent. In the example the amount of shareholders' funds initially attributable to non-equity shareholders is the net proceeds of the issue £108,000 (that is, £100,000 nominal value of non-equity shares issued + £10,000 premium on issue – £2,000 issue costs). This amount is increased each year by the finance cost in respect of the period and reduced by the dividends and other payments made in respect of the instrument. [FRS 4 para 41]. In other words, as illustrated below, the finance cost excluding the dividend element (because this is either paid or recorded as a liability) is added to non-equity shareholders' funds each year until redemption.

Year	Balance b/f	Finance cost less dividend	Balance c/f
1	108,000	2,101	110,101
2	110,101	2,241	112,342
3	112,342	2,391	114,733
4	114,733	2,549	117,282
5	117,282	2,718	120,000
Total finance costs less dividends		12,000	

Immediately before redemption in year five the amount attributable to non-equity shareholders' interests will be the total amount to be redeemed. On redemption, the £120,000 will have to be paid out of distributable profits or from the proceeds of a fresh issue of shares (see chapter 40).

18.145 In certain situations where a company has cumulative preference shares in issue, it is possible for the non-equity interests to be such that they reduce the equity interests to nil. Consider the following example.

Example

A company has 100,000 £1 preference shares in issue with a cumulative dividend rate of 5% and its equity capital is £8,000. In year 19X1 the dividend on the preference shares is in arrears for one year as the company's other reserves are nil. In this situation, the equity/non-equity split would be as follows:

	£'000
Equity interests	3
Non-equity interests	105
Total shareholders' funds	108

The dividend of £5,000 will have been appropriated in the profit and loss account (see further para 18.126) and is attributable to the non-equity interests. The effect of this adjustment is to recognise that the preference shareholders have a preferred right to £105,000, which would on a liquidation mean that only £3,000 is attributable to the equity shareholders.

In 19X2 the company made no profit or loss and so cannot pay any of the cumulative dividend for the year. If £5,000 of dividend is appropriated in the profit and loss account, the equity/non-equity split would be as follows:

	£'000
Equity interests	(2)
Non-equity interests	110
Total shareholders' funds	108

Opinions vary as to whether this presentation is helpful. On the one hand it shows the extent to which the company has to make and retain profit before the equity shareholders start to have any entitlements. On the other hand, it can be argued to be misleading in that it might (wrongly) imply that the equity shareholders would contribute £2,000 in order that the non-equity shareholders could be paid out in full. Whichever approach is adopted, it is important that the balance sheet presentation taken together with the notes to the financial statements fully explain the relative entitlements of the two groups.

18.146 In addition to the provisions of FRS 4 explained above, FRS 3 requires that a note should be given in the financial statements presenting a reconciliation of opening and closing shareholders' funds for the period (see further chapter 7). [FRS 3 para 28].

Debt instruments – measurement and disclosure

18.147 The paragraphs below examine the ways in which debt instruments should be recognised and disclosed in the financial statements.

Measurement and accounting

Initial recognition

18.148 The first question that arises in accounting for debt instruments is the value that should be attributed to the instrument on initial recognition. Before the publication of FRS 4, it was standard practice to record debt initially at its nominal value. This did not take into account transaction costs associated with the issue, such as commissions or other debt issue expenses. These costs were either written off to an existing share premium account as permitted by the Act or, in the absence of a share premium account, written off to the profit and loss account. Such costs cannot be carried forward as an asset because recording issue costs as an asset is not permitted by the Act. [4 Sch 3(2)(b)].

18.149 Recording debt at its nominal value was also quite common where debt was issued at a discount (or repayable at a premium). This point is addressed in the Act, which states that where the amount repayable on any debt owed by a company is greater than the value of the consideration originally received, the amount of the difference may be treated as an asset. [4 Sch 24(1)]. The Act goes on to state that this asset should be written off by reasonable amounts each year and must be completely written off before repaying the debt. [4 Sch 24(2)(a)]. Although the discount was always amortised over the life of the loan, some companies chose to follow the treatment permitted by the Act and recorded the discount separately as an asset. Other companies, however, chose to net it off against the gross amount of the debt. In the case of debt redeemable at a premium, the practice was not to set up the premium initially as a liability, rather it was common to accrue for the premium over the life of the debt and to record it separately from the debt's carrying value. Consequently, in either situation, the debt was usually recorded at the nominal value at each balance sheet date until the debt was ultimately cancelled or redeemed.

18.150 Under FRS 4, recording debt at its nominal value is not considered to be an appropriate accounting basis. Instead, FRS 4 requires that immediately after issue, debt should be stated at the amount of the net proceeds (for example, see Table 18.13). [FRS 4 para 27]. The net proceeds are defined as the fair value of the consideration received on the issue of a capital instrument after deducting issue costs. [FRS 4 para 11]. Where debt is issued at a discount, the discount cannot be treated any longer as an asset, rather the debt should be recorded at the fair value of the consideration received net of any discounts given. The ASB considers that this treatment does not conflict with paragraph 24 of Schedule 4 to the Act which, as stated above, permits (but does not require) the discount to be treated as an asset.

Table 18.13 – Bass PLC – Annual Report – 30 September 1994

Borrowings

All borrowings are initially stated at the fair value of the consideration received after deduction of issue costs. Issue costs together with finance costs are charged to the profit and loss account over the term of the borrowings and represents a constant proportion of the balance of capital repayments outstanding. Accrued finance costs attributable to borrowings where the maturity at the date of issue is less than 12 months are included in accrued charges within current liabilities. For all other borrowings, accrued finance charges and issue costs are added to the carrying value of those borrowings.

Treatment of finance costs

18.151 Having established that debt should be recognised initially at the amount of the net proceeds, the next question to consider is the value at which the debt should be stated in balance sheets drawn up at dates between the original issue of the debt and its redemption. The answer lies essentially in how payments are accounted for between the date of issue and redemption and the recognition of finance costs.

18.152 Finance costs are considered from paragraph 18.79 and, for debt, comprise the interest payable over the instrument's life, the repayment of the principal amount, the difference between any premium received on issue and any premium payable on redemption and any discount allowed on the debt's issue. Clearly, the finance cost is not necessarily equal to the amount of interest payable. The following example illustrates the issues that arise.

Example 3

A company issues 5% debentures having a nominal value £100,000 at a discount of 10% repayable in five years' time at a premium of 20%. Debt issue costs amounted to £5,000 and interest is payable annually in arrears.

	£	£
Net proceeds received:		
Nominal value		100,000
Discount on issue @ 10%		(10,000)
Issue costs		(5,000)
		85,000
Total amount payable:		
Interest @ 5% for 5 years		25,000
Redemption premium		20,000
Nominal value		100,000
		145,000

Finance cost		
Interest	25,000	
Issue costs	5,000	
Discount on issue	10,000	
Redemption premium	20,000	
		60,000

18.153 As explained in paragraph 18.81, the finance cost should be recognised over the term of the loan, that is, five years at a constant rate on the outstanding obligation. In the example used above, the rate can be found to be 12.323 per cent. If the finance costs are allocated to accounting periods using this rate, the movements on the loan would be as follows:

Interest rate 5% compounded annually. Overall finance cost 12.323%				
Year	Balance b/f	Finance cost @ 12.323%	Interest paid	Balance c/f
1	85,000	10,474	(5,000)	90,474
2	90,474	11,149	(5,000)	96,623
3	96,623	11,906	(5,000)	103,529
4	103,529	12,757	(5,000)	111,286
5	111,286	13,714	(5,000)	120,000
Total finance costs and interest		60,000	(25,000)	

18.154 The effective interest rate of 12.323 per cent is higher than the nominal interest rate of 5 per cent because of the incidence of issue costs, the discount on issue and the premium payable on redemption. As explained in paragraph 18.81, in some circumstances the nominal interest rate may not be materially different from the effective interest rate, in which case the nominal interest rate may be used.

18.155 The Act allows issue costs on debentures to be written off to the share premium account, which seems to conflict with the provisions of FRS 4. However, although FRS 4 requires issue costs on debt to be charged to the profit and loss account over the term of the debt as part of the finance costs, it does not preclude the subsequent charging of those issue costs to the share premium account. [FRS 4 para 97]. Therefore, when part of the issue costs are charged to the profit and loss account in a particular year, a reserve transfer of the same amount can be made from the profit and loss account reserve to the share premium account (see for example Table 18.14). This treatment may be adopted where issue costs are material in order to protect distributable reserves.

Table 18.14 – Cable and Wireless plc – Annual report and accounts – 31 March 1998

Statement of Accounting Policies (extract)

l) Debenture issue costs
The costs of issue of capital instruments such as bonds and debentures are charged to the profit and loss account on an annual basis over the life of the instrument. A corresponding amount is subsequently transferred from the share premium account to the profit and loss account reserve.

Subsequent recognition and carrying value

18.156 Once the effective interest rate on the debt has been calculated by reference to the initial carrying value and the future cash outflows, it is a relatively simple matter to arrive at the carrying value of debt at each period end. As evident from the table above, the carrying value at the end of each period is obtained by adding to the carrying value at the beginning of the period the finance cost in respect of the reporting period (calculated by applying the effective interest rate to the carrying value at the beginning) and deducting any payments made in respect of the debt in that period. [FRS 4 para 28]. In fact, the carrying value at each balance sheet date is the discounted amount of the future payments specified in the debt instrument using the effective interest rate inherent in the amount at which the debt was initially recognised. The requirement to record the carrying value of debt at a discounted amount in financial statements is relatively new in UK financial reporting, although discounting is widely used in investment appraisals.

Contingent payments

18.157 The effective interest rate and, hence, the carrying value of debt is relatively easy to calculate where the cash outflows specified in the instrument are known or fixed at the outset. However, where the future cash outflows are not known in advance, but are variable, an effective interest rate cannot be calculated. For example, in the case of floating rate notes where the amount of periodic payments of interest is calculated by reference to a particular formula or by reference to LIBOR, say LIBOR plus two per cent, the interest payments over the instruments' life are not known in advance. Another example is that of index linked loans, which may be redeemable at the principal amount multiplied by an index. The effect of each is that the effective interest rate of the instrument over its life is not only unknown, but also changes every time there is a change in circumstance. The most practical way of accounting for such instruments is not to try to anticipate the change in circumstance, but to take account of it in the period in which the change occurs.

18.158 Therefore, the standard requires that where the amount of payments required by a debt instrument is contingent on uncertain future events such as changes in an index, those events should be taken into account in calculating finance costs and the carrying amount once they have occurred. [FRS 4 para 31]. In other words, the initial accounting for the instrument should take no account of those events, but the carrying value of the instrument at each subsequent balance sheet date should be recalculated to take account of the changes that have occurred in the period. The resulting change in carrying amount should be accounted for as an adjustment to the finance cost for the period. The treatment specified in the standard is illustrated by reference to a floating rate instrument below. Another example where the principal amount of a capital instrument varies (for example, in the case of index linked bonds) rather than interest, is illustrated from paragraph 18.217 onwards.

Example

A company borrows £1,000,000 from a bank repayable in five years' time. Interest is paid annually in arrears at a rate equal to the bank's prime rate plus 1%. Due to arrangement fees and bank commission, the company receives a net amount of £980,000. The bank's prime rate in years 1 and 2 remains at 5%. At the beginning of year 3, the prime rate rises to 6%.

As an effective interest rate cannot be calculated at inception without advanced knowledge of the change in future rates, the finance cost in each period would need to be calculated by reference to the actual rate prevailing in that period. The example is slightly complicated because of the incidence of issue costs of £20,000. The amortisation of the issue costs over the five year period can either be carried out if immaterial on a straight line basis (or written off to the profit and loss account immediately), or when they are material, on a constant interest rate basis by regarding them as being similar to a discount on issue. On the latter basis, the interest rate for amortising the issue costs over the five year period is 0.4049%. The additional finance cost which is the interest element would be charged in the period at the actual rate incurred.

Year	Balance b/f	Finance cost Issue cost 0.4049%	Interest for period	Total charge	Interest paid	Balance c/f
1	980,000	3,968	60,000	63,968	(60,000)	983,968
2	983,968	3,984	60,000	63,984	(60,000)	987,952
3	987,952	4,000	70,000	74,000	(70,000)	991,952
4	991,952	4,016	70,000	74,016	(70,000)	995,968
5	995,968	4,032	70,000	74,032	(70,000)	1,000,000
Total costs		20,000	330,000	350,000		

18.159 It is doubtful whether the above treatment can be applied to all situations where the amount of cash outflows on the instrument is not known in advance. Consider a situation, where a shareholder makes a non-interest bearing loan to his company which is redeemable at the end of three years at a premium determined by applying a known percentage to the aggregate profits for a three year period in excess of a benchmark amount. In this situation, the premium payable on redemption is contingent on the company achieving profits in excess of the benchmark amount and this amount will only be known at the end of the third year. If the wording of the standard is read literally, no amount of the premium payable will fall to be accrued in the first two years, but the whole amount will be charged in the profit and loss account in the third year, thus distorting the results for that year. Clearly this treatment does not accord with the spirit of FRS 4. Therefore, a 'best estimate' of the likely premium payable on redemption should be made at the outset and a proportion provided for every year. The provision would require adjustments in years two and three when the outcome becomes clearer and eventually known.

18.160 If, in the situation explained above, the company had incurred some issue costs and the loan was interest bearing, these components of finance costs should be charged to the profit and loss account at a constant rate, thus leaving the unknown element to be dealt with in the manner specified above.

Repurchase of debt

18.161 Companies sometimes have the opportunity to repurchase their own debt or settle debt early at an amount that differs from the amount at which the debt is stated in their balance sheet at the time. For example, a company may decide to take advantage of falling interest rates by repurchasing its existing long-term fixed interest debt, even though this may involve payment of a premium. The question arises as to how the difference on the repurchase or early settlement should be accounted for. Accounting for repurchase of debt was first addressed by UITF Abstract 8, which was subsequently superseded by FRS 4.

18.162 Some accountants support the view that the difference on repurchase should be deferred on the grounds that the opportunity to repurchase the debt at a gain or loss is created principally by movements in interest rates. In effect, the economic decision to repurchase the debt is neutral, because the gain or loss is effectively counterbalanced by a corresponding increase or decrease in interest costs in the future. Therefore, they argue that the accounting for the effect of the repurchase should also be neutral and, accordingly, the gain or loss should be deferred. The UITF, however, reached the conclusion that the gain or loss on repurchase should be taken to the profit and loss account in the period in which the repurchase occurs. The UITF reached this conclusion on the grounds that the finance cost reported by an entity should normally reflect only its current borrowing arrangements and should not be influenced by any arrangement that previously existed, but that had now been terminated.

18.163 FRS 4 follows the UITF's ruling, and accordingly, requires that gains or losses should be recognised in the profit and loss account in the period during which the repurchase or early settlement is made. [FRS 4 para 32]. The gain or loss should be disclosed in the profit and loss account as separate items within or adjacent to 'interest payable and similar charges'. [FRS 4 para 64]. An example where a company has followed this disclosure requirement is given below in Table 18.15.

Table 18.15 – Scottish Power plc – Directors' Report and Accounts 31 March 1994

Group Profit and Loss Account (extract)

For the year ended 31 March 1994

	Note	1994	1993
	1		(restated)
		£m	£m
Profit on ordinary activities before interest		**359.7**	316.5
Net interest charge	6	**(8.6)**	(9.0)
Net premium charge on loan redemptions	7	**-**	(10.4)
Profit on ordinary activities before taxation		**351.1**	297.1

Notes to the Accounts (extract)

7 Net premium charge on loan redemptions

On 15 December 1992 the group repurchased the £142 million 11.856% bond due in 2005 from HM Treasury at a premium of £18.4 million. The net premium charge on loan redemptions for the year ended 31 March 1993 reflects that payment less £8 million in respect of the write back of the unamortised balance of discount from earlier loan redemptions.

18.164 Therefore, the general rule is that any gain or loss on the repurchase of debt should be credited or charged in the profit and loss account in the year the repurchase is made. The only time that it might be possible to argue that no profit or loss has arisen in the period is (following the principles of FRS 5) where in substance there is no repurchase and the old debt being repurchased has been replaced by new debt, which in effect gives the same economic result as the old debt. This is the argument followed in UITF Abstract 8 (see below), but it rests on the foundation that the new debt must give the same economic result as the old debt. In the majority of situations in practice this is unlikely to be the case, because there will always be a commercial reason compelling the change; otherwise why would the company repurchase? Consider the following example:

Example

A company repays £150,000 debt early and incurs a penalty of £5,000 which is specified in the agreement, but replaces it with a new loan of £150,000 from the same party. The terms of the loan and the loan covenants are very similar. The company is willing to pay this penalty, because the new loan is a variable rate loan, whereas the old loan is fixed rate. Therefore, although the loan is very similar in nature, the cash flows related to interest payments are different and because the penalty is pre-determined it does not reflect accurately the difference between the fixed rate of interest and the current and expected future variable interest rates. It seems clear in this situation that there has been a change in substance in relation to these loans and that as a result the £5,000 penalty should be charged in the profit and loss account in the year of repurchase.

18.165 UITF Abstract 8 was developed at the time that certain major utility companies were repurchasing their Government debt to help reduce the Government's public sector borrowing requirement. Some of these repurchases were special in nature and required different rules to normal repurchases. The Abstract was withdrawn on FRS 4's issue, but remains a good source of guidance to help determine those exceptional cases where in substance there has been no repurchase. UITF Abstract 8 made two exceptions to the requirement for immediate recognition of a gain or loss arising on the repurchase of debt. The exceptions, which are considered below are referred to in appendix III of FRS 4 which deals with the standard's development. The two exceptions are where:

- The agreement to repurchase the debt is also connected with its refinancing on substantially the same terms (other than interest costs). This would apply where the original debt is fully replaced by new debt which gives the same economic result as the original debt, that is, there has been no change of substance in the debt. For this to be the case, as a minimum the following conditions must be satisfied:

    - The replacement debt and the original debt are both fixed rate.

    - The replacement debt is of a comparable amount to the original debt.

    - The maturity of the replacement debt is not materially different from the remaining maturity of the original debt.

    - The covenants of the replacement debt are not materially different from those of the original debt.

  A refinancing may fall within this exception whether or not the lender of the replacement debt is the same as the lender of the original debt.

- The agreement to repurchase the debt is not carried out on a fair value basis because the overall finance costs of the replacement debt are significantly different from market rates. This condition has been introduced to prevent recognition of an artificial profit, compensated by higher costs in the future.

18.166 Where either of the above exceptions apply, the gain or loss should be spread forward either over the remaining maturity of the original debt or, if not significantly different, over the maturity of the replacement debt. In addition, the circumstances should be disclosed, together with the method of accounting adopted and the principal terms of the original and replacement borrowing.

Renegotiation of debt

18.167 A company that is experiencing financial difficulties and is unable to meet its scheduled debt repayments may seek to renegotiate the terms of its debt obligations with its lenders. As a result of the negotiations, the lender may agree to a reduction or a deferral of the payments due to him. Since the company's obligations are significantly reduced, a gain may arise. The recognition and measurement of this gain are central to the accounting for renegotiation of debt.

18.168 The accounting for renegotiation of debt is not included in the standard, but the ASB's initial proposals, first published for public comment in a bulletin issued in July 1993 (which are also discussed in paragraphs 41 to 44 of appendix III of the FRS), are examined here.

18.169 Accounting for the effects of the renegotiation (the concession granted by the lender) involves two particular issues, namely:

- The way in which the concession should be recognised. That is, whether the finance costs should be reduced over the remaining period in which the debt is in issue or whether the gain should be recognised at the time of the renegotiation.

- If it is considered that a gain arises, the way in which the gain should be determined. That is, whether market interest rates prevailing at the time of renegotiation should be used or whether the revised payments should be discounted at the rate inherent in the original debt.

18.170 With respect to the first point above, some support deferral of the gain on the grounds that they consider it paradoxical to recognise a gain that relates primarily to a deterioration of the company's financial condition. They believe that no gain should be recognised, but the benefit of the reduction should be recognised over the term of the replacement loan by way of a reduced interest burden. Others argue that the recognition of the gain at the time of renegotiation reflects the economic consequences of the concession granted by the lender. It also ensures that both liabilities and finance costs for subsequent periods are shown at amounts that properly represent the agreement then in force. The ASB supported the latter view and proposed that in principle the gain should be recognised in the period in which the renegotiation was concluded.

18.171 The ASB argued that the renegotiation was a transaction that effectively resulted in the original loan being replaced by a new loan giving rise to revised payments and, therefore, the amount relating to the old, superseded, debt was no longer relevant. Accordingly, the ASB proposed that the debt should be stated at its market value at the time of renegotiation, because this treatment best reflected the economic circumstances prevailing at that time. As the debt would generally not be traded, its market value would often be determined by discounting the revised payments by reference to the rate of interest which the company would have expected to pay on a loan of similar characteristics to that resulting from the renegotiation. Any change in the company's credit rating since the original loan was made, as well as changes in the general level of interests rates, would be reflected in that rate. Several respondents objected to this aspect of the ASB's proposal. Their objections can best be illustrated by an example.

Example

A company took out a long-term bank loan of £1,000,000 on 1 January 19X0 at a fixed rate of 8% per annum for 10 years. Interest on the loan is paid yearly in arrears. As a result of deteriorating financial condition, the company successfully agreed with its bankers to reduce the yearly interest payments from £80,000 to £20,000 per annum with effect from 1 January 19X4, but the loan is still repayable at the original amount on 31 December 19X9. At 1 January 19X4, the company would have paid 15% per annum on a loan of similar characteristics to that resulting from the renegotiation. Had the company's credit rating not declined, the interest rate on similar borrowings would have been 10% per annum.

	Original rate	Market rate excluding decline in credit rating	Market rate including decline in credit rating
Rate (%)	8.00%	10.00%	15.00%
	£'000	£'000	£'000
Original loan	1,000	1,000	1,000
PV of revised repayments	723	652	508
Gain on renegotiation	277	348	492

Future finance costs			
31 December 19X4	57	65	76
31 December 19X5	61	70	85
31 December 19X6	64	75	94
31 December 19X7	68	80	106
31 December 19X8	71	86	118
31 December 19X9	76	92	133
Total finance costs	397	468	612
Less: interest payments	120	120	120
Gain	277	348	492
Carrying value			
31 December 19X4	761	697	564
31 December 19X5	802	747	629
31 December 19X6	846	802	703
31 December 19X7	894	862	788
31 December 19X8	944	928	887
31 December 19X9	1,000	1,000	1,000

18.172 Under the ASB's proposal, the carrying value of the loan of £1,000,000 immediately after renegotiation, calculated by discounting the revised payments by reference to the market rate for new borrowings that takes account of the decline in the company's credit standing, would be restated at £508,000 giving rise to a gain of £492,000 that would be recognised immediately. This gain would reverse as finance costs are recognised at a higher amount of £612,000 over the subsequent six years compared with the actual interest payments of £120,000 over the same period, as indicated above. However, as is evident from the table above, the gain of £492,000 under the ASB's proposals is made up of three components:

- A gain of £277,000 (that is, £1,000,000 – £723,000) which is equal to the present value of the actual reduction in financing costs from £80,000 to £20,000, that is, £60,000 per annum for six years discounted at eight per cent.
- A gain of £71,000 (that is, £723,000 – £652,000) attributable to the change in market rate of interest from eight per cent to ten per cent.
- A gain of £144,000 (that is, £652,000 – £508,000) attributable to the decline in the credit standing of the company.

18.173 Many argue that in most cases the combined effect of the above components will mean that the more distressed the company's financial condition is, the greater will be the gain on renegotiation as a consequence of using a higher discount rate as the

ASB proposed. This is highly imprudent and rather anomalous. Also, the second element of the gain is not considered to be suitable under existing accounting framework. Furthermore, the ASB's own draft Statement of principles recognises this anomaly when considering how to deal with changes in the market value of liabilities that result from changes in market interest rates. A footnote to paragraph 26 of chapter 5 of the ASB's draft Statement of principles states:

> "*Some would wish to take account only of changes in the general rates of interest rather than in the rate applicable to the entity, since otherwise an entity will report gains and losses relating to changes in its own perceived creditworthiness. It is particularly questionable whether it is appropriate to reflect a gain relating to a decrease in creditworthiness, because the compensating loss is usually a change in future earning power, or the value of assets, some of which are not reflected in the financial statements.*"

Accordingly, opponents of the ASB's proposals believe that if a gain is recognised, it should be calculated by reference to the future expected cash flows as modified by the renegotiation, but discounted at the effective rate of interest inherent in the original loan.

18.174 Because of the above concerns, the ASB decided not to address the accounting for renegotiation of debt in the standard, but may revisit the matter at a later date. In the absence of adequate guidance, it is regarded as preferable not to recognise the gain, but the effects of the renegotiation should be treated as an interest subsidy. It may be necessary to disclose the nature and amount of the renegotiation to give a true and fair view of the company's financing arrangements. This means that the debt would remain in the balance sheet at £1,000,000 and the new finance cost of £20,000 would be charged each year giving an effective interest rate of two per cent from the date of renegotiation to date of maturity. This is the most prudent approach and is the one adopted under US GAAP (FAS 15). Under FAS 15, a gain would be recognised only if the total future cash payments (that is, £1,120,000 in this example) are less than the carrying value of the debt at the time of the renegotiation.

18.175 Some would argue that a gain should be recognised, but based only on discounting the revised payments at the original interest rate of eight per cent (that is, the gain of £277,000 in the above example). The effect would be to restate the carrying value of the loan at £723,000 at the time of the renegotiation. In subsequent periods, the effective rate of interest charged in the profit and loss account is eight per cent on the new carrying value of the loan (which is increased in each period by the difference between the interest charged at eight per cent and the actual interest paid of £20,000). The method of discounting using the original inherent rate is the one preferred by the IASC's measurement proposals in E48. Furthermore, they argue that as a reduction in a liability is considered to be a realised profit, the gain of £277,000 should be reported in the profit and loss account. However, although this method is acceptable, it is less prudent because it leads to recognising a future gain arising from the reduction of future interest charges when the company is in financial distress.

Disclosure

18.176 Both the Act and the standard specify a considerable amount of detail that a company's financial statements must give in respect of its borrowings. In addition, companies listed on the Stock Exchange are required to give further information. These disclosure requirements are considered below.

General disclosure

18.177 Under the Act, capital instruments in the form of debentures, loans and debt instruments fall to be included under the general heading of 'Creditors'. All items included under creditors must be analysed between amounts that will fall due within one year of the balance sheet date and amounts that will fall due after more than one year. [Note 13 on the balance sheet formats].

18.178 In distinguishing between the above two categories, a loan is regarded as falling due for repayment (or an instalment is regarded as falling due for payment) on the earliest date on which the lender could require repayment (or payment) if he were to exercise all options and rights available to him. [4 Sch 85]. The classification of debt between current and non-current is further examined from paragraph 18.189 below.

18.179 For each item shown under creditors (whichever balance sheet format is adopted) there must be disclosed separately the aggregate amounts of debts falling into the two categories below:

- Debts that are payable or repayable otherwise than by instalments and falling due for payment or repayment after the end of the five year period beginning with the day after the end of the financial year.
- Debts that are payable or repayable by instalments, any of which will fall due for payment after the end of that five year period.

[4 Sch 48(1) as amended by SI 1996/189].

The requirement is to disclose one figure showing the aggregate of the above two items, but the aggregation of instalment and non-instalment debts results in a figure that is rather meaningless. The DTI's intention seems to have been to require disclosure of the amount of debts and instalments which are payable in over five years, to bring the disclosure in line with that required by Article 43(1)(6) of the 4th Directive. In practice, it seems sensible to give the intended disclosure as this is more meaningful.

18.180 The terms of payment or repayment and the applicable rate of interest for each debt covered by the disclosure under the preceding paragraph must also be given. [4 Sch 48 (2)]. Where the number of debt instruments is such that, in the directors' opinion, this requirement would result in a statement of excessive length, this information need be given only in general terms. [4 Sch 48(3)].

18.181 Where any item that is shown under the heading 'Creditors' includes debts for which the company has given security, these debts must be disclosed in aggregate. Also, the notes must give an indication of the nature of the securities given. [4 Sch 48(4)]. For this requirement to be meaningful, the financial statements should show some disaggregation of the relevant liabilities. This is because it could be misleading merely to disclose the aggregate of a basket of securities compared with the aggregate of a basket of liabilities. However, in practice, companies often describe the charge in general terms, referring, for example, to 'mortgages on freehold land and buildings' rather than specifying the particular properties involved.

18.182 A brief description should be given of the legal nature of any instrument included in debt where it is different from that normally associated with debt. [FRS 4 para 63]. An example when this type of disclosure is relevant is where shares are issued by a subsidiary undertaking that are classified as debt in accordance with the FRS (see further from para 18.76). Other examples of unusual debt include subordinated debt and limited recourse debts. For all such debts, a brief description of the obligations and legal arrangements should be given. [FRS 4 para 63].

18.183 Where the amount ultimately payable on the debt, or the claim that would arise on a winding up, are significantly different from the debt's balance sheet carrying value, that amount should be stated. [FRS 4 para 63]. An example is a deep discounted debt. The disclosure is also likely to be relevant in the early years of a long-term debt instrument where the carrying value may often be significantly different from the amount finally payable on redemption or the claim that could arise on winding up.

18.184 If a company has issued any debentures (see further para 18.54) during the financial year, the notes to the financial statements must disclose:

- The classes of debentures issued.
- The amount issued and the consideration the company received in respect of each class of debentures issued.

[4 Sch 41(1) as amended by SI 1996/189].

Convertible debt

18.185 A company that has debenture loans must split them between convertible and non-convertible loans. [Note 7 on the balance sheet formats]. Hitherto, this analysis has usually (but not always) been given in the notes as required by the Act. The standard now requires that the amount attributable to convertible debt should be stated on the face of the balance sheet separately from that of other liabilities. [FRS 4 para 25]. In some cases, however, on grounds of immateriality, this information may be disclosed in the notes. Where this is done, the caption on the face of the balance sheet should indicate that convertible debt is included. [FRS 4 para 54]. In assessing materiality in connection with convertible debt, consideration should be given not only to the carrying amount, but also to the implications of conversion.

18.186 In addition to disclosing convertible debt on the face of the balance sheet, the following details should be given:

- In respect of the redemption option, the dates of redemption and the amount payable on redemption.
- In respect of the conversion option:
  - The number and class of shares into which the debt may be converted.
  - The dates at, or the periods within, which the conversion may take place.
  - A statement as to whether conversion is at the option of the issuer or that of the holder.

[FRS 4 para 62].

See for example Table 18.16.

Table 18.16 – Inchcape plc – Annual Report & Accounts – 31 December 1994

consolidated balance sheet AS AT 31st DECEMBER 1994 (extract)

Notes (pages 44-66)		£m	1994 £m	£m	1993 restated £m
	Net current assets		**308. 9**		323. 3
	Total assets *less* current liabilities		**1,121. 1**		1,178. 0
20(b)	**Creditors – amounts falling due after more than one year:**				
20, 21	Borrowings	**(57.1)**		(54.2)	
20	6¼% Convertible Subordinated Bonds Due 2008	**(125.0)**		(125.0)	
	Other	**(80.9)**		(74.4)	
		(263.0)		(253.6)	
22	**Provisions for liabilities and charges**	**(109.5)**		(52.1)	
			(372.5)		(305.7)
	Net assets		**748. 6**		872. 3

Notes to the accounts (extract)

20 Creditors (extract)

The £125m 6¼% Convertible Subordinated Bonds Due 2008 are convertible at the option of the holder, on or prior to 3rd May 2008, into fully paid ordinary shares of 25p each of Inchcape plc at 689 pence per share. Interest is payable semi-annually on 10th May and 10th November. None of the bonds were converted during the year. If the conversion rights attaching to the bonds outstanding at 31st December 1994 were exercised 18,142,235 ordinary shares of 25p each of Inchcape plc would fall to be issued. Unless previously redeemed or converted, the bonds will be redeemed at par on 10th May 2008. The bonds may be redeemed at the option of the Company, in whole or in part, at par at any time after 30th May 1988 or earlier if certain conditions are met.

[The next paragraph is 18.188.]

18.188 Where the number of debt instruments for which the disclosure requirements of paragraphs 18.182, 18.183, and 18.186 apply is large, it is sufficient to summarise the relevant information rather than give the information for each debt instrument. [FRS 4 para 63]. However, the standard states that if the brief summaries cannot adequately provide the information necessary to understand the commercial effect of the instruments, that fact together with the particulars of where the relevant information may be obtained should be stated, but it also requires that the principal features of the instruments should nevertheless be given. [FRS 4 para 65]. The Operating and financial review could complement these disclosures if further information is necessary to understand the instrument's commercial effect.

Maturity analysis of debt

18.189 Before the introduction of FRS 4, only companies that were listed on the Stock Exchange were required to state in respect of the company's (or group's) bank loans and overdrafts and separately for other borrowings, the aggregate amounts repayable:

- In one year or less, or on demand.
- Between one year and two years.
- Between two and five years.
- In five years or more.

Of these, only the second and third items represent analysis additional to that required by the Act. FRS 4 extended the above debt maturity analysis to apply to all companies whether or not they are listed on the Stock Exchange. [FRS 4 para 33]. As a consequence, the Stock Exchange's requirement has been deleted. Therefore, companies now only have to give this analysis in aggregate for all debt and do not have to analyse bank loans and overdrafts separately from other borrowings. Similar analysis is still separately required for finance lease obligations as required by SSAP 21 (see further chapter 15). The required maturity analysis is illustrated in Table 18.17 although giving more information concerning currency exposure than is required. Table 18.18 shows the same analysis for finance leases obligations which is required by SSAP 21, although SSAP 21 does not require the band between one and two years.

Table 18.17 – Reed Elsevier -Annual Review – 31 December 1997

Notes to the Combined Financial Statements (extract)

20. ANALYSIS OF NET BORROWINGS (extract)

£ million	Less than 1 year	1-2 years	2-5 years	5-10 years	Over 10 years	1997	1996
US dollar	**315**	**157**	**152**	**167**	**181**	**972**	1,188
Sterling	**298**	**–**	**–**	**–**	**–**	**298**	56
Guilder	**12**	**23**	**9**	**–**	**–**	**44**	29
Other currency	**160**	**–**	**–**	**–**	**–**	**160**	64
Total	**785**	**180**	**161**	**167**	**181**	**1,474**	1,337

Borrowings less than 1 year include US commercial paper and other short term borrowings which are supported by available committed facilities. At 31 December 1997 a total of £602m (1996 £334m) of committed facilities was available, all of which matures in over 1 year (1996 £276m). £8m of borrowings are secured under finance leases (1996 £11m).

Table 18.18 – Coats Viyella Plc – Annual report and accounts – 31 December 1997

Notes to the accounts (extract)

18 Creditors (amounts falling due after more than one year) (extract)

	Group	
	1997 **£m**	1996 £m
Finance lease obligations are repayable as follows:		
Within one year	**4.6**	4.6
Between one and two years	**4.5**	4.6
Between two and five years inclusive	**15.1**	14.2
Over five years	**22.6**	22.6
	46.8	46.0

18.190 For the purposes of the above analysis, the standard requires that the maturity of debt should be determined by reference to the earliest date on which the lender can require repayment. [FRS 4 para 34]. This measure of maturity is consistent with that prescribed by the Act for the purposes of classifying debts in the balance sheet formats between current (due within one year) and non-current (due after more than one year – see para 18.177 above).

18.191 The maturity analysis of debt is relatively straightforward for debentures and loans with fixed repayment terms. However, in practice there other debts can cause more difficulty.

Example

A company receives a loan of £500,000 from its bank which is repayable in equal instalments over a five year period. A letter from the bank states that it is the bank's current intention that the loan will run to maturity. However, the letter goes on to state that all amounts outstanding under the loan are repayable on demand which may be made by the bank at its sole discretion.

The bank probably intends that the loan should be long-term as evidenced by the schedule of repayments over the five year term. However, the clause giving extensive powers to the bank cannot be disregarded. It is likely in this type of situation that the loan should be shown as short-term to accord with FRS 4's provisions, unless the company can negotiate with its bankers to amend the clause so that it becomes a specific adverse change clause. Then it might be possible to get the bank to confirm at the year end that no adverse change has taken place and then it might be possible to show the loan as long-term.

18.192 Companies sometimes issue debt that is 'revolving' in nature and backed up by committed long-term facilities. For these types of revolving debts, companies often used to base the maturity analysis by reference to the facilities that back up the borrowing rather than on the term of the borrowing itself. As a consequence, debts that might be legally short-term in nature were disclosed as long-term on the grounds that the substance of the borrowing agreement is long-term. This type of presentation was often used by companies to disclose short-term borrowings under a commercial paper programme as long-term, even where, as often happens, the facilities in existence were unconnected with the original borrowings.

18.193 The ASB, however, took a more rigid view on the substance of the borrowing arrangements in place. They argued that a back-up facility could not justify the reclassification of short-term borrowings as long-term if it merely permitted finance to be raised from a second source in the event that the company was unable to raise finance from the first source. In the context of borrowings under a commercial paper programme, companies that regarded such borrowings as long-term normally expected to be able to refinance those borrowings by further issues of commercial paper and not rely on the back-up facilities. The facility merely acts as a safeguard to protect the company from the possibility that it may be unable to finance the redemption of commercial paper from a fresh issue, for example, if the market dries up. However, if the lender and the granter of the long-term back-up facility are the same party (a situation that is uncommon under commercial paper borrowings), the facility is in effect merely an extension of the borrowing from the same source, a condition that the ASB believes effectively falls within the requirement of paragraph 85 of Schedule 4. These rules are illustrated in Table 18.19.

Table 18.19 – TI Group plc – Annual Report – 31 December 1995

Notes to the financial statements (extract)

21 LOANS AND OTHER BORROWINGS FALLING DUE AFTER MORE THAN ONE YEAR

Loans repayable partly or wholly after five years include debts of $105m and $100m privately placed by TI Group Inc with major US institutional investors. These debts have fixed coupons of 8.52% and 8.853% respectively, with final maturity during 1996 but where committed facilities from the same lender are in place until 2002. Similarly, £92.6m of unsecured bank and other loans repayable wholly within five years (1994 £98.8m) comprise revolving credit facilities with drawings maturing during 1996 but where committed facilities from the same lender are in place until 2000. All these drawings are therefore shown as due for repayment on maturity of the facilities, comprising £nil between one and two years (1994 £83.5m), £92.6m between two and five years (1994 £15.3m), and £22.5m after five years (1994 £nil).

18.194 The standard, therefore, requires that where committed facilities are in existence at the balance sheet date that permit the refinancing of the debt for a period beyond its maturity, the earliest date at which the lender can require repayment should be taken to be the maturity date of the longest refinancing permitted by a facility. [FRS 4 para 35]. However, this treatment is only permitted where all of the following conditions are met:

- The debt and the facility are under a single agreement or course of dealing with the same lender or group of lenders. [FRS 4 para 35(a)]. This means that either the facility is directly related to the debt or the facility taken out in the normal course of dealing can be used for other purposes in addition to the refinancing of the debt. For this purpose lenders should be regarded as part of the same group if they are parties to the same agreement or course of dealing, even though some individual members of the group may not have actually participated in the financing. This may be so for some multi-option facilities.

- The financing cost for the new debt is not significantly higher than that of the existing debt. [FRS 4 para 35(b)]. This requirement would appear to reinforce the previous condition that the facility and the borrowings in question must be related. This is because if refinancing was only permitted on terms that were considerably more expensive, the company would probably in practice resort to other cheaper unconnected facilities for refinancing, hence defeating the condition that the debt and the facility should be related. Where the interest rate specified in the facility is determined by reference to a base rate (such as LIBOR), an increase in that base rate should not be regarded as an increase in the level of finance costs.

- The obligations of the lender (or group of lenders) are firm. That is, the lender is not able legally to refrain from providing funds except in circumstances that can be demonstrated to be remote. [FRS 4 para 35(c)]. This condition must be assessed with particular care. For example, facility agreements usually contain a clause that further funds would be withheld if the financial condition of the borrower suffered an adverse change. In order to rely on borrowings under the facility being available, the clause must be precisely defined and not open to any subjective interpretation. If the adverse change clause is not precisely defined, there is a presumption that the lender's obligation is not firm and, accordingly, the borrowings would fall to be disclosed as short-term.

- The lender (or group of lenders) is expected to be able to fulfil its obligations under the facility. [FRS 4 para 35(d)]. This condition is rather obvious if the borrower is to rely on the facility for its refinancing needs. Accordingly, the facilities must be committed and funds under the facility must be available, if required.

18.195 It follows from the above that the maturity of debt must always be assessed by reference to the contractual maturity of the actual debt outstanding at the time or by reference to the maturity of the facility where a 'linkage' exists between the original lender and the group of lenders providing the backing facility. In practice, borrowings backed up by facilities that are provided by parties who are not the original lenders (as for example with commercial paper) do not satisfy all the conditions in paragraph 18.194. Consequently, they must be classified as short-term even if backed up by long-term facilities as illustrated in Table 18.20 below.

Table 18.20 – Reed Elsevier – Annual Review – 31 December 1997

NOTES TO THE COMBINED FINANCIAL STATEMENTS (extract)

20 ANALYSIS OF NET BORROWINGS (extract)

Borrowings less than 1 year include US commercial paper and other short term borrowings which are supported by available committed facilities. At 31 December 1997 a total of £602m (1996 £334m) of committed facilities was available all of which matures in over 1 year (1996 £276m).

18.196 Where debts have been stated in the maturity analysis by reference to refinancing facilities in accordance with paragraph 18.194, the amounts of the debt so treated, analysed by the earliest date on which the lender could demand repayment in the absence of the facilities, should also be disclosed. [FRS 4 para 36]. Consider the situation where the earliest date on which a lender could demand repayment of a debt instrument of £200 million is at the end of two years from the balance sheet date of the borrower, but the debt can be refinanced under an existing facility taken out with the same lender and which expires after five years from the balance sheet date. In this situation, the debt should be included in the maturity analysis in the five year or more band, but with an additional note stating that in the absence of existing related facilities, the earliest date on which the lender could demand repayment of the debt of £200 million is two years. See Table 18.19 on page 18072.

18.197 The maturity analysis required by the Act coupled with the maturity analysis required by the standard raises the question as to whether the maturity analysis of debt should be stated by reference to the gross value (nominal value) or by reference to the net value (carrying value net of, for example, issue costs or discounts). There is no specific requirement in the Act to state debt at nominal value, but it may be argued that this is what the Act requires. There is a contention that the rule prohibiting netting assets off against liabilities together with the fact that issue costs cannot be treated as an asset (but the discount on issue or the premium payable on redemption can be so treated) implies that debt should be recorded at nominal value.

18.198 The ASB, however, takes a rather different line. Issue costs are not regarded as assets either under the Act or under the ASB's draft Statements of principles and, therefore, their deduction from gross proceeds is not regarded by the ASB as an infringement of the Act's netting rules. On the treatment of any discount on issue or premium payable on redemption as an asset, the ASB considers that, as this treatment is not mandatory, the treatment required by FRS 4 in respect of these items is also not in conflict with the Act. Furthermore, as the maturity profile is not altered whether debt is shown at the net or gross amount and, as the figures stated in the balance sheet under FRS 4 are always net of future finance costs, it would appear that recording debt at the net amount in the maturity analysis of borrowings is a logical extension of the balance sheet presentation. In addition, the standard requires that where debt is stated in the balance sheet at an amount that is significantly different from the amount that would be payable on its redemption or the claim that would arise on a winding up, that amount should also be stated. [FRS 4 para 63].

Market value of debt

18.199 FRED 3 proposed that where the market value of a class of debt security can be readily obtained, the market value at the balance sheet date should be disclosed. Although this requirement as not included in FRS 4, the ASB still believes that market value information may be useful to users of financial statements. Accordingly, it encourages companies to provide this information on a voluntary basis.

Accounting for specific instruments

18.200 Having discussed the way in which capital instruments generally can be classified and recognised in the issuer's balance sheet, the paragraphs below examine how FRS 4's accounting requirements can be applied to specific types of capital instruments. Many of the instruments considered below are discussed in the application notes to the standard, but are further explained and analysed here.

Convertible debt

18.201 As explained from paragraph 18.56 convertible debt of any kind should be accounted for as a liability. The paragraphs that follow examine the accounting treatment that companies should adopt on the initial issue and on subsequent redemption or conversion of convertible debt.

18.202 For any type of convertible debt (with a call or put option), the following general principles apply:

- On initial issue, the debt should be stated at the amount of the net proceeds after deducting any issue costs.

- The finance costs should be calculated at a constant rate on the carrying amount, on the assumption that the debt will never be converted, and charged to the profit and loss account over the term of the security. In this situation, the finance cost will generally include any issue costs, the periodic interest payments, any premium payable on redemption less any premium on issue, and plus any discount on issue.

- The term of the convertible debt with an option should be taken to end on the earliest date on which the debt can be redeemed or cancelled as a result of an option being exercised.

- At subsequent balance sheet dates, the debt's carrying amount should be increased by the finance cost in respect of the reporting period and reduced by payments made in respect of the debt in that period.

- Convertible debt should be stated separately on the balance sheet from other liabilities. Information on convertible debt should be disclosed in accordance with the requirements discussed from paragraph 18.185.

- If convertible debt is redeemed, the amount payable on redemption will generally be equal to the carrying value at the time of redemption. Where this is not the case, any gain or loss on redemption should be recognised in the profit and loss account in the period in which the redemption takes place.

- If, on the other hand, the debt is converted, the amount recognised in shareholders' funds in respect of the shares issued should be the amount of the carrying value of the security as at the date of conversion. The nominal value of the shares issued should be credited to called up share capital and the difference between the carrying value of the security and the nominal value of the shares issued will be credited to the share premium account, although there is some doubt as to whether the difference represents a section 130 premium arising on the issue of shares. In certain circumstances, all or part of the difference may not legally be required to be taken to the share premium account. If the share premium account is not used, however, the difference should be credited to a suitable non-distributable reserve. For the avoidance of doubt, it is probably sensible to credit the difference to a suitable undistributable reserve. No gain or loss should be recognised on conversion. The conversion of such an instant is illustrated in Table 18.21.

Table 18.21 – GKN plc – Report and Accounts – 31 December 1994

NOTES ON THE ACCOUNTS (extract)

21 SHARE CAPITAL (extract)

As part of the funding for the Group's acquisition of Westland, holders of GKN plc ordinary shares on the register at 4th February 1994 were offered the right to subscribe for 1 unit of non-interest bearing unsecured loan stock (automatically convertible into new ordinary shares) for every 5 ordinary shares held at 480p per stock unit, payable in two equal instalments. The stock units were converted into ordinary shares on 11th May 1994. The difference between the nominal value and the issue price of the stock units allotted net of issue costs (£194.7 million) has been accounted for as a non-distributable reserve.

22 RESERVES (extract)

Group	SHARE PREMIUM ACCOUNT £m	REVAL- UATION RESERVE £m	OTHER RESERVES £m	PROFIT AND LOSS ACCOUNT £m	TOTAL £m
At 1st January 1994	143.0	67.6	(106.9)	288.0	391.7
Prior year adjustment for FRS 5 (note 1)	-	-	-	(1.6)	(1.6)
As restated	143.0	67.6	(106.9)	286.4	390.1
Transfer from profit and loss account	-	-	-	17.8	17.8
Currency variations	-	1.0	(6.3)	2.7	(2.6)
Net premium on share issues	128.4	-	-	3.1	131.5
Net premium on issue of stock units (note 21)	-	-	194.7	-	194.7
Subsidiaries and associated companies acquired and sold	-	-	(281.4)	-	(281.4)
Transfers between reserves	-	(2.7)	(45.2)	47.9	-
Other movements	-	-	(3.0)	6.0	3.0
At 31st December 1994	**271.4**	**65.9**	**(248.1)**	**363.9**	**453.1**
Parent company and subsidiaries	271.4	65.9	232.0	328.5	897.8
Associated companies	-	-	9.1	35.4	44.5
Goodwill arising on consolidation	-	-	(489.2)	-	(489.2)
	271.4	**65.9**	**(248.1)**	**363.9**	**453.1**

18.203 The way in which the above principles can be applied to a convertible bond is illustrated in the example below.

Example

On 1 January 19X4, a company issued a 6% convertible bond having a face value of £1,250. Issue costs amounted to £50. The bond is convertible at any time into ordinary shares of £1 each of the company at 335p per share. This price represents a 16% premium over the market price of the shares at the time of issue. In addition, the bondholders may elect in January 19X9 to redeem the bond and at the same time require the company to pay supplemental interest on the bonds. Such interest, if paid, would increase the interest rate on the bonds from 6% to 11.6% per annum over the five years to January 19X9. The company also has the option to require conversion so as to ensure exchange into ordinary shares either during January 19X9, or at any time, subject to the price of the ordinary shares exceeding certain levels.

18.204 It is clear from the above terms that either the bondholders will elect for conversion or the company will force conversion before the redemption date of January 19X9. This is based on the assumption that the performance of the company and, hence its share price, will not be subject to volatile changes. Therefore, as it is very unlikely that redemption will occur in normal circumstances, it was sometimes argued in the past that no supplemental interest would become payable. In fact, prior to the issue of UITF Abstract 1, which required accrual for any supplemental interest payable on redemption, it was common practice not to accrue for such interest. That treatment is no longer allowed.

18.205 Applying the principles set out in paragraph 18.202 above, the accounting should be based on the assumption that the bond will never be converted, even if it is probable that it will be as in this example, and the term of the bond is taken to be the earliest date on which redemption would take place, that is January 19X9. This means that the supplemental interest payable on redemption has to be accrued from the date of issue to the date of redemption. The carrying values and the finance charges over the life of the bond are shown below.

Amounts payable on redemption	1,250
Interest payments: £1,250 @ 6% x 5 =	375
Supplemental interest: £1,250 @ (11.6% – 6%) x 5 =	350
Total amount payable	1,975
Net proceeds at issue (£1,250 - £50) =	1,200
Finance cost	775
Effective interest rate = 11.55%	

	Balance b/f	Finance cost	Interest paid	Balance c/f
1 January 19X4	1,200			
31 December 19X4	1,200	139	(75)	1,264
31 December 19X5	1,264	146	(75)	1,335
31 December 19X6	1,335	154	(75)	1,414
31 December 19X7	1,414	163	(75)	1,502
31 December 19X8	1,502	173	(75)	1,600
Total finance costs and interest		775	(375)	

18.206 Assuming that the bondholders opt for redemption, the bond will be redeemed at £1,250 + £350 = £1,600, which is the carrying value of the bond prior to redemption.

18.207 If the bond is converted at any time prior to 31 December 19X8, the shares issued are recorded at the carrying value of the bond as at the date of conversion, which will include accrued interest. Assuming that the bond is converted at 31 December 19X7 at the price of 335p per share, the company would have to issue 373 shares (that is, £1,250/3.35). The shares would be recorded at £1,502, the carrying value of the bond at conversion date. Therefore, £373 would be credited to called up share capital and the balance of £1,129 credited either to the share premium account or to a suitable non-distributable reserve (see para 18.202). No gain or loss is recognised on conversion.

18.208 Given that the term of a convertible debt is always taken to end on the earliest date on which the holder has the option to require redemption and that conversion should never be anticipated, the actual accounting for the convertible debt is no different from straight or redeemable debt. In fact, all types of convertible debt, however designed, (the standard provides examples of various types) will fall to be treated as debt and accounted for in the manner illustrated above.

Convertible preference shares

18.209 Convertible preference shares are similar to convertible debt in that they usually have a redemption or a conversion option. These shares may either be issued by the parent company or by a subsidiary, but convertible into ordinary shares of the parent. Sometimes these convertible preference shares may be issued with a premium put, so that if the redemption option is chosen, an enhanced dividend will become payable. As the dividend rights on these shares are limited and they are redeemable, they will fall to be treated as non-equity shares.

18.210 Because convertible preference shares are non-equity shares they should be accounted for in a similar way to debt. Therefore, the accounting treatment of the conversion of such shares is no different from convertible debt discussed above. That is, they should be accounted for on the basis that conversion will never take place. Because they are shares, the dividends and any premium will be shown as an appropriation of profits. If they incorporate a premium put option, the premium should be included as part of the finance cost of the instrument and accordingly accrued over its term. On conversion, the proceeds of the shares issued should be deemed to be the carrying amount of the preference shares immediately prior to conversion including any accrued premium in the same way as for convertible debt explained above.

Deep discount bonds

18.211 A deep discount bond is a redeemable bond which is issued at a substantial discount to its par value or maturity value. The bond carries a low nominal interest so that the discount together with the interest represent the cost of finance to the borrower. Zero coupon bonds are an extreme form of deep discount securities where no coupon is paid at all; the discount comprises the whole of the return to the investor. Deep discount bonds and zero coupon bonds are often used in the Eurobond market. Sometimes, medium-term commercial paper may be issued at a deep discount.

18.212 Under the principles of FRS 4, accounting for a deep discount bond is relatively straightforward. A simple example follows:

Example

A company issues a five year bond of £100,000 nominal value at a price of £65,000. The bond carries interest at 2% per annum and is repayable at par. The profile of the finance cost and the carrying value of the bond over the five year period is stated below.

Interest on £100,000 @ 2% x 5	10,000
Redemption amount	100,000
Total payments	110,000
Proceeds of bond	65,000
Finance cost	45,000

Effective interest rate = 11.617%

Date	Balance b/f	Finance cost	Interest paid	Balance c/f
31 December 1994	65,000	7,551	(2,000)	70,551
31 December 1995	70,551	8,196	(2,000)	76,747
31 December 1996	76,747	8,916	(2,000)	83,663
31 December 1997	83,663	9,720	(2,000)	91,383
31 December 1998	91,383	10,617	(2,000)	100,000
Total finance cost and interest		45,000	(10,000)	

18.213 It can be seen from the above table that the total finance cost is the sum of the discount on issue of £35,000 and interest cost of £10,000 giving an effective interest rate of 11.617 per cent over the life of the bond. The debt would be recorded at the balance sheet in each period at the amount of the ending balance stated above. The previous practice of recording the debt at the nominal value of £100,000 and the discount of £35,000 as an asset is no longer permitted.

Stepped interest bonds

18.214 A stepped interest bond is one where the interest rate is not fixed, but where it increases progressively in a predetermined way over the life of the bond. In this situation, the true cost of borrowing in any period during the time the bond is in issue cannot be determined from the actual interest cost paid in that period. This is because a lower interest charge in one period is compensated by a higher interest charge in another.

18.215 Under the principles of FRS 4, the pattern of interest payments in cash flow terms should not affect the allocation of finance costs, which should be based on the overall effective interest rate. The effective interest rate can be easily calculated because the variations, and hence the total amount of payments, are known in advance. Once the effective interest rate is calculated, the finance cost in each accounting period is calculated to achieve a constant rate on the outstanding debt. Any payments made during the period will reduce the finance cost and any balance remaining (positive or negative) will be adjusted against the outstanding obligation. The effect of this is to ensure that the bond is stated in the balance sheet, just prior to redemption, at the amount at which it will be redeemed.

18.216 In practice, it may not be necessary to calculate the effective interest rate by reference to future cash outflows. In some instances, an average interest rate is much simpler to calculate and will produce results that are not materially different from that obtained by using discounting techniques, as the following example shows.

Example

A company issues a bond of £100,000 redeemable at par at the end of year 10 on which interest of 5% is payable for the first two years and increases by steps of 2% every second year until maturity. The interest cost, therefore, rises from £5,000 in year 1 to £13,000 in year 10, a total of £90,000 over the full term.

The effective interest rate calculated on a discounted basis and the finance costs and the carrying value over the life of the bond are as follows:

Effective interest rate: 8.3644%				
Year	Balance b/f	Finance cost	Interest paid	Balance c/f
1	100,000	8,364	5,000	103,364
2	103,364	8,646	5,000	107,010
3	107,010	8,951	7,000	108,961
4	108,961	9,114	7,000	111,075
5	111,075	9,291	9,000	111,366
6	111,366	9,315	9,000	111,681
7	111,681	9,341	11,000	110,022
8	110,022	9,203	11,000	108,225
9	108,225	9,052	13,000	104,277
10	104,277	8,723	13,000	100.000
Total finance and interest costs		90,000	90,000	

On a straight line basis

(5+7+9+11+13) x 2 ÷ 10 = 9%

The interest rate on a straight line basis is 9% compared with the effective interest rate of 8.3644%. Provided the amount of the debt is not large, it would be acceptable, indeed permitted by FRS 4, to use the straight line interest rate of 9%, to allocate the finance cost. It would be necessary to make full disclosure about the terms of the instrument in the financial statements.

Bonds with variable interest rates or redemption payments

18.217 Sometimes bonds may be issued on terms whereby the amounts payable in respect of interest and principal over the bond's life are not only variable, but the variations, unlike a stepped interest bond, are not known in advance. A classic example is a bond where the interest rate on the instrument is calculated by reference to a benchmark rate such as the London inter-bank offered rate (LIBOR) or a bank's prime rate. Another example is where the principal amount payable under the instrument varies in relation to an index.

18.218 Where the interest rate or the redemption value is contingent on uncertain events such as changes in an index, the finance cost for a period should be adjusted to reflect those events once they have occurred. This means that the initial interest rate or the carrying value will take no account of those future events, but will require adjustment once those events have taken place. The adjustment should be accounted for by increasing or decreasing the finance costs for the period in which the event occurs. The provisions of the standard dealing with contingent payments and the accounting treatment of an index linked bond have already been examined in detail from paragraph 18.157.

18.219 The accounting treatment of an instrument where the principal amount is linked to any index is very similar to a debt that is issued in a foreign currency. Under SSAP 20, the foreign currency borrowing outstanding at the balance sheet date would need to be retranslated to sterling at the rate of exchange ruling at that date. The difference between the sterling amount prior to recalculation and the amount as recalculated at the balance sheet date is the exchange adjustment that is taken to the profit and loss account of the period. This recalculation is performed at each balance sheet date until the debt is repaid. Similarly, where the principal amount of a bond is repayable based on an index, the carrying value of the bond is recalculated when the index changes. The difference between the previously recalculated value and the current recalculated value is included as part of the interest cost for the period. This recalculation will be performed each time there is a change in the index until the debt is repaid. An example is given in the standard's application notes.

Warrants

18.220 The basic principle in FRS 4 concerning warrants is that they should be reported as part of shareholders' funds. This is on the basis that the only obligation associated with the instrument is to issue shares at a fixed price to the warrant holder. The standard requires that the net proceeds from the warrant's issue should be reported in the year of issue in the reconciliation of shareholders' funds. [FRS 4 paras 37, 45]. The warrant proceeds can be regarded as a part payment for the share capital that will be issued should the warrant be exercised. The difficulty of determining how much should be attributed to a warrant where it is issued attached to another capital instrument is discussed from paragraph 18.224.

18.221 In the analysis of shareholders' funds, warrants for non-equity shares should be included in the amount of non-equity shareholders' funds. [FRS 4 para 40]. The standard does not explain where warrant proceeds should be shown in the balance sheet. If the amount is immaterial it could be aggregated with other reserves. If it is material it should be shown separately and described as 'warrant proceeds' or by some other suitable term.

18.222 If a warrant expires unexercised, then FRS 4 requires that the amount previously recognised in shareholders' funds should be shown in the statement of total recognised gains and losses and not credited to the profit and loss account. [FRS 4 para 47]. This is on the basis that the credit is not a gain arising from the company's operations, but from a transaction with potential shareholders. The amount can then be credited to the profit and loss account reserve as a reserve movement as it represents a realised profit.

18.223 If alternatively the warrant is exercised, the amount previously recognised within shareholders' funds should be treated as part of the net proceeds of the shares issued. [FRS 4 para 46]. The standard does not, however, address where this additional amount of consideration should be credited once the shares have been issued. It would seem logical that it should be treated as share premium and non-distributable, although legally it is not a section 130 premium arising on the issue of shares. If the share premium account is not used then it should be credited to another non-distributable reserve.

Bonds issued with detachable warrants

18.224 Companies may issue a bond with a warrant attached to subscribe for equity shares in the company. Immediately after issue, the warrant can be detached and traded separately. As a result, the cost of debt is reduced because the holder accepts a lower coupon in return for a separately tradeable asset.

18.225 As stated in paragraph 18.62, each element of a compound instrument consisting of distinct instruments that are capable of being transferred, cancelled or redeemed separately should be accounted for separately. This is an example of split accounting where the proceeds on the issue of the bond/warrant package are allocated between the debt and the warrant and the two instruments accounted for separately thereafter. This contrasts with convertible debt which is accounted for as a single instrument.

18.226 The allocation of the initial proceeds between the debt and the warrant can be determined by reference to the market values for the debt and the warrant immediately after issue, where they are available. If not, then some other basis of allocation would need to be used. For example, the company could estimate the value of a loan having the same terms and cash flow profile as the bond by reference to market rates of interest. The value of the warrant can then be found by deducting the derived value of the loan without the warrant from the total proceeds. Once the proceeds have been allocated, the bond should be accounted for in the normal way (for example, see Table 18.22). Accounting for warrants is considered from paragraph 18.220.

Table 18.22 – Pilkington plc – Directors' Report and Accounts – 31 March 1994

Notes on the Financial Statements (extract)

28 Called Up Share Capital (extract)

In April 1993 the company issued £80 million 7.5% bonds at an issue price of £95 million to finance the acquisition of the United Kingdom glass processing and merchanting businesses of Heywood William Group PLC. The bonds were issued with 78.2 million warrants, each warrant entitling the holder to procure up to 4 May 1998 the allotment of one share in Pilkington plc at a price of 120p.

The capital amount attributable to the warrants is £16.4 million and is included in other reserves (note 29).

Perpetual bonds

18.227 Where a company issues a perpetual bond, the bond should be recorded initially at the amount of the net proceeds. If interest is paid at a constant rate, the cash outflow in respect of each period remains constant for each year to perpetuity. The present value of this series of cash flows to perpetuity discounted at the stated interest rate will obviously be equal to the gross proceeds. However, discounting at the effective rate would arrive at the net proceeds. The finance charge for each period will be the actual coupon payable for each period and the debt will remain in the balance sheet at the amount of the net proceeds. This means that the difference between the gross proceeds and the net proceeds, that is, any issue cost or discount on issue, is never amortised, but reflected in the carrying value indefinitely. This treatment will also apply where the interest is variable, for example, at a fixed margin over LIBOR. Put another way, since the debt is never going to be repaid there is no need to adjust its initial carrying value and the finance cost will be equal to the actual interest paid in each period to perpetuity.

18.228 Where a company has issued perpetual debt, the details of the arrangement should be disclosed in the financial statements. If the amount payable on a winding up is different from the carrying value, that amount should be disclosed.

Repackaged perpetual bonds

18.229 Sometimes perpetual bonds are repackaged in such a way that the principal amount is effectively repaid. One way of achieving this is to pay a high rate of interest for a number of years (the primary period), which then falls to a negligible figure. If the interest were simply charged to the profit and loss account, the company would bear an artificially high rate during the primary period and then would suffer no significant profit and loss charge for the rest of the life of the perpetuity. Such treatment might reflect the form of the loan agreement, but it would not deal with its substance. The substance of such transactions, in practice, is that the excessive interest the bond yields is intended to pay back the bond's nominal value over the primary interest period. Consider the following example:

Example

A company issues a perpetual bond for £100,000 on which interest at 14% is paid for the first ten years and thereafter at a nominal rate of 0.125%. Consequently, at the end of the first ten years, the bond has little value.

The capital element of the bond is, in effect, repaid over the initial ten year primary period of high interest payments. Consequently, the interest payment during the primary period represents a payment of interest and a repayment of capital. The total payments of £140,000 – £100,000 = £40,000 is the effective finance cost over the primary period. This amount should be allocated over the ten year period at a constant rate on the carrying amount, which works out to be 6.6374%. Therefore, the profit and loss account would only bear an interest charge based on 6.6374% and the balance of the 14% interest represents a repayment of capital.

Although the carrying value of the bond at the end of the ten year period will be nil, there is still an actual liability of £100,000 that may crystallise should the company go into liquidation. In practice, however, there will usually be arrangements to enable the company to repurchase the bond for a nominal amount and, therefore, extinguish any liability on it.

Stapled shares

18.230 For tax reasons, overseas shareholders of a UK parent company sometimes prefer to take their dividends on the company's shares from their own tax jurisdiction rather than that of the parent. Such an arrangement is put in place by issuing shares (usually preference shares) of a foreign subsidiary (typically operating in the country of residence of the overseas shareholders) to the overseas shareholders of the parent, which are linked with equity shares of the parent denominated in sterling (usually of a different class). The effect is that the two shares are 'stapled' together and cannot be traded separately, thus forming a single unit. The basic dividend payable on the foreign subsidiary's preference shares is fixed and is normally a small proportion of the total dividend payable on the whole unit as the major part is the participating element. In some arrangements, the dividends receivable on the stapled shares are equal in gross terms to the dividends receivable from the parent. Sometimes the arrangement may give the overseas shareholders the option to receive dividends from the foreign subsidiary or from the parent. Other rights of the stapled share, for example, voting rights and rights arising on liquidation are comparable with the parent's equity shares. In substance, therefore, the shares issued by the foreign subsidiary are little different from the equity shares in the UK parent, except that the dividends will not have a tax credit attaching to them.

18.231 Current practice is to account for stapled shares on the basis of their economic substance. There is a strong argument in support of the view that the economic substance of the stapled unit is to create two equivalent equity share classes with equivalent voting, dividend and capital rights on which dividends can be paid in a tax efficient manner to both domestic and overseas shareholders. The stapling of the foreign subsidiary's shares with that of the parent is the mechanism by which this is achieved. The shares issued by the subsidiary, which are held by persons who are also holders of the parent's equity shares, are an integral component of the stapled unit and as they cannot be traded separately on their own, they do not have a separate existence independent of the parent's equity shares.

18.232 Consequently, the shares issued by the subsidiary are regarded for accounting purposes as being no different from the equity shares issued by the parent and are reported in the consolidated financial statements as part of the shareholders' funds rather than as minority interests. Furthermore, as the primary purpose of the arrangement is to ensure that overseas shareholders of the parent company receive dividends in a tax efficient manner and as this purpose is achieved by paying dividends on the stapled shares from profits attributable to the parent, the dividends on the subsidiary's shares are similarly reported as part of the group dividends.

18.233 Stapled share arrangements are not common and few companies have such arrangements in place. Also, the structure of such arrangements differs from company to company. However, the principles of FRS 4 can be applied to a stapled share arrangement. Paragraph 22 of the standard states that capital instruments that are issued at the same time in a composite transaction should be accounted for as a single instrument, unless they are capable of being transferred, cancelled or redeemed independently of each other. Although paragraph 22 was probably written in the context of capital instruments that are issued in a composite transaction by the same entity (for example, where an entity issues debt with warrants attached) its provisions can in the context of consolidated financial statements reasonably be applied to stapled shares that are regarded as being issued by the group in a composite transaction.

18.234 Based on the above analysis, it would appear that the foreign subsidiary's share forming part of the stapled unit could be shown within the shareholders' funds of the group and not as minority interest without offending FRS 4. As far as disclosure under FRS 4 is concerned, it could be argued that the foreign subsidiary's part of the stapled share unit is a non-equity share and, therefore, that the group would need to analyse further its shareholders' funds into equity and non-equity components. Similarly, on this basis the total dividends payable on the stapled shares would need to be analysed further into its preferential non-equity element and the participating element and disclosed separately in accordance with paragraph 59 of FRS 4. In addition, full disclosure should be given of the stapled share arrangement to accord with paragraph 56 of FRS 4.

18.235 Because shares issued by a subsidiary forming part of a stapled unit are not reported in the consolidated financial statements as minority interests, the question arises as to whether this treatment would require use of the Act's true and fair override provisions. A similar argument to that explained in paragraph 18.75, for treating shares issued by a subsidiary to parties outside the group as debt and not as minority interest without invoking the true and fair override, can be applied to the stapled share arrangement. The argument is based on the premise that the Act requires consolidated financial statements to be prepared as if the group were a single reporting entity. The subsidiary's shares forming part of the stapled units are regarded from a group perspective as shares effectively issued by the parent on which dividends are paid to shareholders of the parent from profits attributable to the parent. The shares are reported as part of group shareholders' funds and, therefore, there will be no amount remaining that would fall to be disclosed as minority interests. Accordingly, the Act's requirements are effectively met and the true and fair override provisions need not be invoked where the accounting treatment specified above is adopted.

Practical issues

18.236 Paragraphs 18.237 to 18.276 consider a number of practical issues that arise from FRS 4's application such as issue costs, facility fees, scrip dividends and capital contributions.

Issue costs

18.237 The accounting treatment of issue costs has been dealt with from paragraph 18.88. This section considers the type of issue costs that may arise in practice which fall to be treated as part of an instrument's finance costs. Issue costs are defined in the standard as:

> *"The costs that are incurred directly in connection with the issue of a capital instrument, that is, those costs that would not have been*

incurred had the specific instrument in question not been issued." [FRS 4 para 10].

18.238 Clearly this definition is intended to be restrictive and the first point to note is that it excludes indirect costs. Consequently, the costs have to be directly related to the issue of the capital instrument before they fall to be treated as issue costs. This is rather obvious, otherwise inclusion of other indirect costs incurred on the issue as part of the cost of the instrument would only serve to defer those costs to future periods by overstating the finance cost charged in each period. Therefore, care needs to be taken in determining which costs fall to be treated as part of the cost of issuing the instrument.

18.239 In particular, the standard explains that the definition of issue costs does not allow the inclusion of costs incurred in:

- Researching sources of finance.
- Negotiating sources of finance.
- Ascertaining the suitability or feasibility of particular instruments.

[FRS 4 para 96].

18.240 Furthermore, the standard does not allow a company to allocate a proportion of its internal costs that would have been incurred had the instrument not been issued. This exemption would preclude, for example, management remuneration to cover their time involved with the issue from being treated as issue costs. [FRS 4 para 96]. Prudence should be exercised to ensure that only those costs that can be demonstrated to relate directly to the issue of the financial instrument are treated as issue costs.

18.241 The rules mentioned above relating to the types of costs that should be treated as issue costs are very similar to the rules concerning the costs that can be written off to the share premium account on the issue of shares or debentures. And for all practical purposes, issue costs can be regarded as the same as the costs that can be charged to the share premium account. Use of the share premium account is governed by the Act and it can only be used for specific purposes, namely to:

- Pay up fully paid bonus shares.
- Write off preliminary expenses.
- Write off expenses of any issue of shares or debentures.
- Write off commission paid or discount allowed on any issue of shares or debentures.
- Provide for the premium payable on any redemption of debentures.

[Sec 130(2)].

18.242 There are certain direct costs of issuing shares and debt that are clearly able to be written off against share premium and should be treated under FRS 4 as issue costs. These costs include underwriting fees, registration fees and certain legal, merchant bank and accounting fees where these are incurred solely in the production of a prospectus offering shares to the public or incurred in relation to documentation drawn up to cover a debt instrument. In a straightforward issue of new shares to the public where a company already has a listing it is quite possible that all the costs incurred will be issue costs.

18.243 Lawyers fees in a complex financing (such as a management buyout) could cover general corporate finance work and tax advice, but will also inevitably include fees to cover drafting of legal documentation in relation to the issue of capital instruments. These latter costs are issue costs, but the former are less likely to be unless they are incurred directly in relation to the issue of shares or debt. Accountants' fees will also cover a wide variety of work and unless specifically related to the issue of the capital instruments will not be issue costs. However, where a company can make a reasonable allocation of such fees, as between those attributable to the issue of shares (for instance, costs of preparing and advising on a rights issue document), those attributable to the issue of the debt and those attributable to the other aspects of the financing, only the last of these will not fall to be treated as issue costs.

18.244 As to how a reasonable allocation can be made in practice, it may be possible for the company to ask its advisors to indicate on their invoices the amount of costs that are attributable to each area of the advisors' work. However, the invoices may not be definitive. If no such allocation is possible, but there is a list of the work which the professional advisors have done, then an analysis of the invoices would have to be made to segregate costs associated with the issue from other costs. If there is neither an allocation nor an analysis of professional advisors' costs, an estimate of the extent to which advisors' costs have been incurred on the issue, on some reasonable basis, would have to be made.

18.245 The fees charged by banks and other financial institutions for finance will be charged in two ways. First there is an arrangement fee, which is normally a fixed percentage of the finance raised, and secondly, the finance interest coupon. The arrangement fee, as it relates to the specific instrument, should normally be treated as an issue cost as it can be regarded as part of the overall finance cost, having the effect of increasing the coupon. Syndication fees are charged by banks and financial institutions to arrange for other banks and financial institutions to participate in funding capital instruments (sub-participation). Again, these costs seem clearly to fall within the definition of issue costs.

18.246 Where several classes of equity, non-equity shares or debt are issued at once, it would be reasonable to make an apportionment of the total issue costs to each category on the basis of gross proceeds.

18.247 With regard, however, to costs incurred in connection with a financial restructuring or renegotiation, paragraph 96 of FRS 4 states that they do not qualify as issue costs. These costs are regarded under the FRS as relating to previous sources of finance even where a new instrument is issued following the restructuring or renegotiation. So costs incurred in negotiating with a financial institution to extend the term or change the interest rate on debt would be disallowed, even where a new debt instrument is issued. This also follows from paragraph 32 of the FRS which requires that gains and losses arising on the repurchase of early settlement of debt should be recognised in the profit and loss account in the period during which the repurchase or early settlement is made. But where an offer document is issued in relation to raising new debt or shares, the relevant costs of the offer should be regarded as issue costs, even though the debt so raised might be used to pay off previous borrowings.

Facility fees

18.248 Where a company negotiates with a bank or other financial institution for a loan facility, the institution will charge a facility fee at the time of putting the loan facility in place. For example, such an arrangement might provide for the total facility to be £20 million which can be drawn down in specified or unspecified tranches over the life of the facility. The facility gives the company financial flexibility to draw down a range of finance from the full amount of the facility to nothing at all. Facility fees are very similar in nature to issue costs. Prior to the issue of FRS 4, facility fees of this nature were generally written off to the profit and loss account as incurred. Now only costs that are directly incurred in connection with the issue of a capital instrument fall to be treated as issue costs and included in the calculation of finance costs. The facility fee is a cost of negotiating a source of finance, which represents the cost the company is prepared to incur in order to obtain the necessary financial flexibility. The fee is not related to any specific loan. Consequently, in accordance with paragraph 96 of the standard, facility fees do not generally qualify as issue costs and should be written off to the profit and loss account as incurred.

18.249 As mentioned, the costs do not relate to a specific loan, as no loan is necessarily issued when the facility is granted. But where, for example, a facility was granted for £20 million and £5 million of the facility was drawn down immediately, then it could be argued that a quarter of the facility fee represents an issue cost of the £5 million loan. If, however, the initial draw down does not occur shortly after the facility is put in place or occur in a different accounting period from the one in which the facility fee is paid, the full fee should be written off to the profit and loss account when it is incurred. It is not possible to carry forward (say) half of the facility fee on the basis that £10 million is anticipated to be drawn down in three years' time.

Effect of options on an instrument's term

18.250 As mentioned above in paragraph 18.95, where an instrument includes an option to redeem or cancel it, its term is taken to end on the earliest date on which the option can be exercised, unless there is no genuine commercial possibility that the option will be exercised. [FRS 4 paras 16, 73]. Therefore, because most options will have a genuine commercial reason, instruments' terms will often be determined to end on the earliest date on which an option can be exercised.

18.251 For example, a company might have a ten year £100,000 redeemable fixed rate five per cent bond which is redeemable at a premium of ten per cent and on which its costs of issue amounted to £2,000. In addition as part of the terms of the instrument, the company might hold an option to redeem the bond after year five and incur a premium of 15 per cent if early redemption is taken. If interest rates move down sufficiently, then it might pay the company to redeem the instrument early and this is a decision that the company will take in year five. The option, therefore, does have an economic purpose and under the provisions of FRS 4 it appears that the option should be taken into account when determining the instrument's term, because it cannot be said that there is *no* genuine commercial possibility that the option will not be exercised.

18.252 Companies believed that this rule was too harsh, because they argued that in this circumstance the option is merely a right of the issuer (but not the investor) to redeem the instrument early on the payment of the premium (known as an issuer call option). In the example, the company will make the decision to refinance the debt in year five and any additional costs (such as the premium) should rightly be borne in the year the decision is taken. This issue was taken up with the UITF who agreed that the amount of premium payable under an issuer call option is not a payment *"that the issuer may be required to make in respect of the instrument"* and, consequently, does not fall within the definition of 'finance costs'.

18.253 The UITF, as a consequence, issued Abstract 11, 'Capital instruments: issuer call options', in September 1994 which concluded that where an instrument includes a call option that can be exercised only by the issuer, the payment required on exercise of that option does not form part of the instrument's finance costs. [UITF 11 para 6]. Therefore in the example given above, the premium of 15 per cent that could be payable in year five does not form part of the instrument's finance costs although it might seem to under a strict interpretation of FRS 4. But the Abstract's consensus can only be applied to genuine options and, as a consequence, does not apply to situations where it is clear that the issuer would be commercially obliged to exercise the call option. The UITF cites an example of such a case where the instrument's terms and conditions give the issuer the option of early redemption, but it is clear from the outset that in all conceivable circumstances it would be advantageous for the issuer to exercise the option rather than to allow the debt to remain in issue. [UITF 11 para 8].

18.254 Furthermore, the UITF also commented that where an instrument has an issuer call option the exercise of which is uncertain, the instrument's term will end on the date on which the option is exercisable. [UITF 11 para 7]. This statement is somewhat anomalous, because although the Abstract allows in the example above the 15 per cent premium to be excluded from finance costs, the instrument's term is still determined as five years. This means in practice that the costs of issuing the instrument have to be written off over the period to the option date (in the example five years and not the full ten years). It has been argued that the requirement that the term should end on the date the option is exercisable implies that all of the instrument's finance costs should be written off to the profit and loss account over this period, including any premium payable on the instrument's eventual redemption (a premium of ten per cent in the example payable in year ten). We do not believe that the UITF intended this outcome as it seems totally wrong to accrue ten years' interest and the £10,000 premium in the example over the first five years of the instrument and, therefore, not to accrue any finance cost over the last five years of the instrument's term. We, therefore, consider in this type of situation that issue costs should be charged to the profit and loss account over the shorter term, but interest cost and any redemption premium payable on the instrument's eventual redemption should be accrued over its full term.

18.255 Continuing with the example in paragraph 18.251, under UITF Abstract 11's provisions and our interpretation given above, the finance costs to be allocated to the first five years would be £32,000, comprising the fixed interest cost of £25,000 plus half of the premium arising on the eventual redemption of £10,000 plus the whole of the issue costs of £2,000. The example assumes that interest is paid semi-annually in arrears. The finance cost is allocated to accounting periods at a constant rate on the outstanding balance and for the first five years this rate is calculated to be 6.3385 per cent.

Interest rate compounded semi-annually. Overall finance cost 6.3385%							
Year	Balance b/f	Finance cost 6 mths	Interest 6 mths	Balance	Finance cost 6 mths	Interest 6 mths	Balance c/f
1	98,000	3,106	(2,500)	98,606	3,125	(2,500)	99,231
2	99,231	3,145	(2,500)	99,876	3,165	(2,500)	100,541
3	100,541	3,186	(2,500)	101,228	3,208	(2,500)	101,936
4	101,936	3,231	(2,500)	102,666	3,254	(2,500)	103,420
5	103,420	3,278	(2,500)	104,198	3,302	(2,500)	105,000
		15,945	(12,500)		16,055	(12,500)	
					15,945	(12,500)	
Total finance and interest costs					32,000	(25,000)	

18.256 For the second five years of the term, the interest rate reduces slightly to 5.6 per cent because all of the issue costs have been amortised over the first five year term. The total finance costs over the ten years come to £62,000, which is made up of interest of £50,000, redemption premium of £10,000 and issue costs of £2,000.

Interest rate compounded semi-annually. Overall finance cost 5.6%							
Year	Balance b/f	Finance cost 6 mths	Interest 6 mths	Balance	Finance cost 6 mths	Interest 6 mths	Balance c/f
6	105,000	2,940	(2,500)	105,440	2,953	(2,500)	105,893
7	105,893	2,965	(2,500)	106,358	2,978	(2,500)	106,836
8	106,836	2,992	(2,500)	107,328	3,005	(2,500)	107,833
9	107,833	3,020	(2,500)	108,353	3,034	(2,500)	108,887
10	108,887	3,049	(2,500)	109,436	3,064	(2,500)	110,000
		14,966	(12,500)		15,035	(12,500)	
					14,966	(12,500)	
Total finance and interest costs					30,000	(25,000)	

18.257 The UITF made one exception to the general rule concerning issuer call options where the effective rate of interest increases after the date on which the option is exercisable. [UITF 11 para 9]. This type of circumstance arises where the economics of the instrument are such that the premium payable on exercising the option compensates the investor for forgoing the increase in interest due after the option date. In this circumstance, the finance costs calculation must include the redemption premium payable on exercising the option; and the term would remain, in the example, five years.

18.258 Where in the example in paragraph 18.251, the option is a put option, the instrument's term should be taken to be five years. In this case, the finance cost over the first five years is £42,000 comprising the fixed interest cost of £25,000 plus the early redemption premium of £15,000 and issue costs of £2,000. The example assumes that interest is paid semi-annually in arrears. The finance cost is allocated to accounting periods at a constant rate of 7.9923 per cent on the outstanding balance.

Interest rate compounded semi-annually. Overall finance cost 7.9923%							
Year	Balance b/f	Finance cost 6 mths	Interest 6 mths	Balance	Finance cost 6 mths	Interest 6 mths	Balance c/f
1	98,000	3,916	(2,500)	99,416	3,973	(2,500)	100,889
2	100,889	4,032	(2,500)	102,421	4,093	(2,500)	104,014
3	104,014	4,157	(2,500)	105,670	4,223	(2,500)	107,393
4	107,393	4,292	(2,500)	109,184	4,363	(2,500)	111,048
5	111,048	4,438	(2,500)	112,985	4,515	(2,500)	115,000
		20,834	(12,500)		21,167	(12,500)	
					20,834	(12,500)	
Total finance and interest costs					42,000	(25,000)	

18.259 If, however, the option is not taken up in year five, then depending upon the terms of the instrument the finance cost for the next period of five years until the instrument is ultimately redeemed will be less than for the first five years. This is because a higher redemption premium has been accrued over the first five year period. This is illustrated in the table below which shows the allocation of the finance costs of £20,000 for the latter five year term. The finance cost is made up of £25,000 of interest plus £10,000 premium payable on redemption less £15,000 of premium already accrued.

Interest rate 5% compounded semi-annually. Overall finance cost 3.5454%							
Year	Balance b/f	Finance cost 6 mths	Interest 6 mths	Balance	Finance costs 6 mths	Interest 6 mths	Balance c/f
6	115,000	2,039	(2,500)	114,539	2,030	(2,500)	114,069
7	114,069	2,022	(2,500)	113,591	2,014	(2,500)	113,105
8	113,105	2,005	(2,500)	112,610	1,996	(2,500)	112,106
9	112,106	1,987	(2,500)	111,593	1,978	(2,500)	111,071
10	111,071	1,969	(2,500)	110,540	1,960	(2,500)	110,000
		10,022	(12,500)		9,978	(12,500)	
					10,022	(12,500)	
Total finance and interest costs					20,000	(25,000)	

Scrip dividends and enhanced scrip dividends

18.260 Many listed companies choose to make arrangements for ordinary shareholders to elect to receive their dividends in the form of additional shares rather than in cash. The share equivalent is sometimes referred to as a scrip dividend or a stock dividend and consists of shares fully paid up out of the company's reserves. The advantages of issuing scrip dividends are that, in the short term, the company's cash position is improved. Secondly, no ACT is payable in respect of those dividends taken in the form of shares.

18.261 Scrip dividends can be of significant benefit to the company where ACT would otherwise be irrecoverable, so much so that in recent years enhanced scrip dividends have been offered by companies. Enhanced scrip dividends give the shareholder an incentive to elect to take the shares rather than the cash dividend. For example, the cash dividend might be worth £100 to an individual investor, but the shares issued as an alternative might be worth £150. This means that the shareholder will invariably opt for the share alternative rather than the cash. In addition, a number of third party financial institutions have, in conjunction with the paying company, offered placing facilities to shareholders taking the scrip, such that if a shareholder opts to take (say) £150 of shares they will immediately be placed for cash of (say) £140. This makes it virtually certain that the shareholder will elect to take the shares rather than the dividend alternative (for example, see Table 18.23).

Table 18.23 – Cadbury Schweppes plc – Annual Report – 31 December 1994

Notes on the Accounts (extract)

18 Capital and Reserves (extract)

(b) Ordinary shares (extract)

On 26 January 1995, the Company declared a second interim dividend on its Ordinary Shares for the year ended 31 December 1994, instead of a final dividend. The company offered to Shareholders an Underwritten Enhanced Scrip Dividend Alternative (UESDA) under which Shareholders could elect to receive Ordinary Shares instead of the cash dividend. The Company made arrangements for Shareholders accepting the UESDA to be able to sell their Ordinary Shares arising under the UESDA at a price of not less than 340p per Ordinary Share. The UESDA was accepted in respect of 88.2% of Ordinary Shares and resulted in the Company retaining £80.9m which would otherwise have been paid out as dividends.

(c) Movements on capital and reserves – Company (extract)

	Preference Shares £m	Ordinary Shares £m	Share premium £m	Revaluation reserve £m	Retained profits £m
At beginning of year	0.3	207.5	862.4	1.5	183.4
Share options exercised	-	0.7	7.7	-	-
Share dividends	-	0.3	5.4	-	-
Profit for financial year	-	-	-	-	135.3
Dividends to Ordinary Shareholders	-	-	-	-	(130.5)
Adjustment for UESDA (see (b) above)	-	-	-	-	80.9
Realised on disposals	-	-	-	(0.2)	0.2
At end of year	0.3	208.5	875.5	1.3	269.3

18.262 The paragraphs that follow consider the way that such dividends, and the corresponding issue of additional shares, should be accounted for in the company's financial statements.

18.263 FRS 4 requires that where shares are issued, or proposed to be issued, in lieu of a dividend, the value of the shares should be deemed to be the amount receivable if the cash alternative had been chosen.

18.264 Whether or not shares are offered in lieu of a final dividend, prudence requires that full provision for the dividend payment in cash should be made on all allotted shares at the year end and, in accordance with FRS 4, the provision should be made at the amount of the cash dividend (for example, see Table 18.24). [FRS 4 para 48]. This treatment is necessary because the number of shareholders who will accept the offer is unknown. After the year end when some shareholders accept the offer to take additional shares instead of the cash dividend, the remaining balance of the dividend provision relating to those shareholders has to be dealt with.

Table 18.24 – Grand Metropolitan Public Limited Company – Annual Report - 30 September 1994

Notes (extract)

1 ADOPTION OF NEW ACCOUNTING STANDARDS (extract)

FRS 4 requires that where scrip dividends are issued or proposed, the value of such shares, deemed to be the amount of the cash dividend alternative, should be treated as an appropriation of profits. The effect of complying with this requirement has been to increase the 1993 dividends by £20m with a corresponding increase in creditors and decrease in the profit and loss reserve at 30th September 1993. It is estimated to have had a similar effect on the 1994 results and year end balance sheet. In addition, FRS 4 requires that borrowings should generally be classified according to the maturity of the financial instrument and not according to the maturity of the available committed facilities. The analysis of borrowings at 30th September 1993 has been restated to reclassify £1,661m of commercial paper and other borrowings, which were previously classified according to the maturity of available back-up committed facilities, as due within one year. The equivalent figure at 30th September 1994 was £621m, which has been classified as due within one year.

18.265 There are two alternative bases that can be adopted, the bonus issue method and the re-investment method and there are published examples of both methods being used in practice, which are illustrated in Table 18.25 and Table 18.26. The choice of which method should be used depends, however, on whether there are any provisions relating to scrip dividends in the company's articles of association. It should also be noted that the 'bonus issue' basis maximises the level of distributable reserves that remain available after the issue. The two methods are explained below.

Bonus issue method

18.266 This approach is based on dividing the scrip dividend into two separate events, namely the waiver of the dividend by the shareholder; and the subsequent issue of bonus shares to that shareholder by the company. In this situation, the total remaining provision is written back to the profit and loss account reserve, then the bonus issue is made out of reserves (usually the share premium account or the revaluation reserve) at its nominal value. [FRS 4 para 99].

Example

A company proposes to pay a dividend of £100,000 and offers as an alternative shares with a nominal value of £50,000, but a market value of £150,000. At its year end, it does not know who will take up the scrip, but after the year end, 80% of the shareholders take up the scrip offer.

The double entry at the year end to set up the proposed dividend is set out below:

	£	£
Dr Profit and loss account appropriation	100,000	
Cr Creditors dividends payable		100,000

To record the dividend at its full cost and to show the whole amount of the dividend as a liability.

The double entry in the next year would be:

	£	£
Dr Creditors	20,000	
Cr Cash		20,000
Dr Creditors	80,000	
Cr Profit and loss account reserve		80,000
Dr Share premium account	40,000	
Cr Share capital		40,000

To record the payment of 20% of the dividend in cash, to record the reversal of the provision of 80% of the dividend to reserves and to show the capitalisation of an appropriate reserve to create the share capital at its nominal value.

Table 18.25 – Enterprise Oil plc – Annual Report and Accounts – 31 December 1994

NOTES TO THE FINANCIAL STATEMENTS (extracts)

10. DIVIDENDS	**1994 £m**	1993 £m
Ordinary shares:		
Interim paid, 6.5p (1993 – 9.5p) per share	**32.0**	45.4
Final proposed, 9.5p (1992 – 6.5p) per share	**46.8**	32.0
Preference shares	**16.0**	16.2
	94.8	93.6

Amounts shown in respect of the interim dividend for 1993 reflect the cash dividend of 9.5 pence per share. An enhanced scrip dividend alternative to the interim dividend was also offered, with the result that only £1.1 million of the interim dividend liability for 1993 was paid in cash.

20. SHAREHOLDERS' FUNDS (extract)	Group		Company	
(i) Movement in shareholders' funds	**1994 £m**	1993 £m	**1994 £m**	1993 £m
Profit for the financial year	**71.0**	94.7	**134.5**	172.6
Dividends	**(94.8)**	(93.6)	**(94.8)**	(93.6)
Retained profit/(deficit) for the financial year	**(23.8)**	1.1	**39.7**	79.0
Other recognised gains and losses related to the year	**(5.1)**	(5.4)	**-**	-
New equity share capital subscribed (net of issue costs)	**0.2**	0.8	**0.2**	0.8
Cash dividend retained under scrip alternative	**-**	44.3	**-**	44.3
Associate's share of Enterprise Oil dividend	**3.5**	8.7	**-**	-
	(15.0)	49.5	**39.9**	124.1
Shareholders' funds at 1 January	**951.3**	901.8	**794.9**	670.8
Shareholders' funds at 31 December	**936.3**	951.3	**834.8**	794.9

Re-investment method

18.267 This approach is based on the premise that the issue of shares under a scrip dividend scheme is not the issue of bonus shares. In substance, the issue of shares can be regarded as the payment of cash dividends with shareholders simultaneously reinvesting the proceeds in an issue of new shares. The dividend forgone by the shareholder in electing to take a scrip dividend of shares may, therefore, be treated as being the consideration paid for those new shares. Normally the consideration for the new shares will exceed their nominal value. Accordingly, the nominal value of the shares issued would be credited to the share capital account and the balance of the deemed consideration credited to the share premium account. The whole of the deemed consideration would be charged against the remaining provision.

Example

This example follows that given for the bonus method and uses the same facts.

The double entry at the year end to set up the proposed dividend would be the same as the previous example, but the double entry in the next year would be as follows:

Dr Creditors	20,000	
Cr Cash		20,000
Dr Creditors	80,000	
Cr Share capital		40,000
Cr Share premium account		40,000

To record the payment of 20% of the dividend in cash, to record the provision of 80% of the dividend being satisfied by the shares issued and a premium arising on their issue.

18.268 It can be seen in the example that, even where an enhanced scrip dividend is made, the share premium arising on the issue is calculated by reference to the creditor forgone and not the market value of the shares (which in the example is £120,000). This is because the fair value of the consideration received for the issue of the shares is the amount of the dividend written back. Furthermore, the fair value of the consideration would not include any ACT benefit gained from the share issue.

Table 18.26 – The Boots Company PLC – Report and Accounts – 31 March 1995

Notes Relating to the Financial Statements

22. Share capital (extract)	Number of shares 1995 million	Number of shares 1994 million	1995 £m	1994 £m
Ordinary shares of 25p each:				
Authorised	1,200	1,200	**300.0**	300.0
Allotted, called up and fully paid	949	1,041	**237.2**	260.2

Shares allotted/(repurchased) during the year	Number million	Nominal value £m	Consideration £m
Scrip dividends	1.8	.4	9.5
Option schemes	2.4	.6	6.2
Share repurchase	(96.1)	(24.0)	(507.8)
	(91.9)	(23.0)	(492.1)

During the year approximately 22% of shareholders owning 6% of shares elected to take all or part of their dividends in shares.

21. Capital and reserves (extract) Group	Called up share capital £m	Share premium account £m	Revaluation reserve £m	Capital redemption reserve £m	Profit and loss account £m	Total £m
At 1st April 1994	260.2	204.6	304.9	-	838.9	1,608.6
Profit retained	-	-	.2	-	492.8	493.0
Movement on goodwill (see below)	-	-	-	-	413.1	413.1
Revaluation surplus	-	-	6.6	-	-	6.6
Revaluation surplus realised on disposals	-	-	(1.0)	-	1.0	-
Issue of shares	1.0	14.7	-	-	-	15.7
Share issue expenses	-	(.3)	-	-	-	(.3)
Repurchase of shares (note 22)	(24.0)	-	-	24.0	(511.3)	(511.3)
Currency adjustments on:						
- Goodwill (see below)	-	-	-	-	(33.6)	(33.6)
- Assets and results	-	-	-	-	(23.7)	(23.7)
- Borrowings and currency swaps	-	-	-	-	38.8	38.8
At 31st March 1995	**237.2**	**219.0**	**310.7**	**24.0**	**1,216.0**	**2,006.9**

18.269 The accounting for the receipt of scrip dividends is considered in chapter 3.

Capital contributions

18.270 One of the application notes in FRS 4 deals with the accounting treatment of capital contributions and these are also considered in detail in chapter 3.

[The next paragraph is 18.273.]

Merger accounting

18.273 The provisions of the standard do not apply to equity shares issued as part of a business combination that is accounted for as a merger. [FRS 4 para 21(c)]. In such a situation it is not possible to report the fair value of the net proceeds on an issue of shares in the reconciliation of movements in shareholders' funds. This is because the premium that arises on the issue is not accounted for in either the parent's financial statements or the group's financial statements. Only the nominal value of the shares issued is recorded in the group's shareholders' funds and, therefore, shown in the reconciliation of movements in shareholders' funds. The question then arises as to whether this exemption extends to situations where non-equity shares as well as equity shares are issued in a business combination accounted for as a merger. In certain situations where the non-equity shares are issued as part of a section 131 arrangement, they also attract merger relief. Consequently, where this is the case, in the merged group's financial statements the movement on shareholders' funds related to the non-equity shares will also merely be the nominal value of the shares issued and not the fair value of the shares issued. It is not clear why the exemption only relates to equity shares issued in connection with a merger.

Company with no equity shares

18.274 The difference between the definition of equity share capital given in the Act and that of equity shares given in FRS 4 can lead to situations in practice where a company may not have any equity shares (FRS 4 definition) in issue. In the standard's definition, a share is non-equity if it carries limited distributions of either dividends or capital, whereas in the legal definition a share is non-equity only if there are limitations on the distribution of both dividends and capital.

18.275 Consider then a company that might have 'A' and 'B' ordinary shares in issue together with a cumulative redeemable preference share. Normally the ordinary shares would be expected to be equity and the cumulative redeemable preference share non-equity. However, if both of the types of ordinary share have a fixed dividend (even if it is cumulative), they are classified under FRS 4 as non-equity. Consequently, in this case all of the company's share capital is non-equity. This will mean that in the analysis of shareholders' funds required by FRS 4 the total amount of shareholders' funds will be allocated to the non-equity shareholders, as there are no equity shareholders. Because this type of situation will be very unusual in practice, it would be helpful to users if an explanation is given at the foot on the balance sheet along the following lines:

Example

Under Financial Reporting Standard No 4, each class of the company's share capital falls under the description 'non-equity'. A further analysis of shareholders' rights is given in note 10 to the financial statements.

18.276 Another problem arises in this type of situation because paragraph 55 of the standard requires that an analysis should be given of the total amount of non-equity interests in shareholders' funds relating to each class of non-equity shares and series of warrants. This requirement seems to imply that because *all* reserves are attributable to non-equity shares they should be allocated to each class of share in the analysis of shareholders' funds by class of non-equity shares. However, it does not seem possible to allocate reserves such as the profit and loss account reserve and the goodwill write off reserve to classes of share on any meaningful basis. In this circumstance, it seems more sensible to allocate those amounts that are specifically applicable to the non-equity shares (as envisaged by FRS 4), which is any premium on issue plus the finance costs for the period less any dividends paid or proposed in the period. Any other reserves could be disclosed in the note in aggregate as illustrated in the example below.

Called up share capital (note 10)

	Shares of £1 each	
	1994	1993
	£'000	£'000
Authorised, allotted, called up and fully paid		
100,000 'A' ordinary shares (note (a))	100	100
50,000 'B' ordinary shares (note (b))	50	50
500,000 Cumulative redeemable preference shares	500	500
	600	600

The rights relating to each class of share in issue at 31 December 1994 are as follows:

(a) The 'A' ordinary shares have a fixed cumulative dividend of 10% commencing on the date on which all of the cumulative redeemable preference shares are redeemed. In the event of winding up the company, they rank below the other classes of share. They carry one vote per share.

(b) The 'B' ordinary shares have a fixed dividend of 15%. In the event of winding up the company they rank after repayment of the cumulative redeemable preference shares. They carry one vote per share.

(c) The cumulative redeemable preference shares have a fixed cumulative dividend of 10%. In the event of winding up the company, they rank first and would be paid 125% of the original subscription price plus any arrears of dividend. They have no voting rights. The shares are redeemable at a premium of 15%, as follows.

	Nominal value	Cash to be paid
1 January 1995	250,000	287,500
1 January 1996	250,000	287,500
	500,000	575,000

Under the Companies Act 1985, both the 'A' ordinary shares and the 'B' ordinary shares are classified as equity share capital, because they have a right to participate beyond a specified amount on liquidation in addition to their fixed dividend entitlement. However, under FRS 4 these shares are classified as non-equity. Therefore, all of the shareholders' funds are attributable under FRS 4 to non-equity interests. The interests relating to each class of share at 31 December 1994, are set out below

	1994 £'000	1993 £'000
'A' ordinary shares	120	120
'B' ordinary shares	60	60
Cumulative redeemable preference shares	562	543
	742	723
Profit and loss account reserve	823	145
Goodwill write off reserve	(200)	(200)
	1,365	668

Chapter 19

Share capital and reserves

Page

Chapter 19

Share capital and reserves

Introduction

19.1 This chapter deals with the general disclosure requirements for share capital and reserves. The effect of FRS 4, 'Capital instruments', on the measurement and disclosure of share capital and shareholders' funds is discussed in detail in chapter 18.

19.2 This chapter also deals with realised and distributable profits. Companies may make a distribution to their shareholders only out of profits that are available for distribution. Part VIII of the Act, 'Distribution of profits and assets', imposes conditions that companies must satisfy before they can make distributions. Some of these conditions apply only to public companies. Also, special provisions apply to investment companies and insurance companies.

19.3 Part VIII of the Act is concerned with the profits that may legally be distributed by way of dividend. The actual payment of dividends must be made in accordance with the company's memorandum and articles. The articles may also contain special provisions regarding dividends.

19.4 In addition to the statutory rules in Part VIII of the Act, directors may have to consider other restrictions on their ability to make distributions. For example, under the common law, dividends cannot be paid out of capital. The directors must also consider their duty to act in the company's best interests. They must, for example, consider the future cash needs of their company, even if they have profits that are distributable under Part VIII.

Share capital

Types of shares

19.5 Shares can be divided into numerous different types including: ordinary shares, preference shares, non-voting shares, and redeemable shares. The classification depends on the rights that the shares are given in the company's memorandum and articles of association.

19.6 The Act defines equity share capital as the issued share capital of a company except for any shares that, neither in regard to dividends nor in regard to capital, carry any right to participate beyond a specified amount in a distribution. [Sec 744]. In general, ordinary shares meet this definition, although it is possible to design preference shares that qualify as equity share capital in terms of the Act.

19.7 For tax purposes, ordinary share capital has a special meaning that differs from the company law definition of 'equity share capital'. Ordinary shares are defined in the Income and Corporation Taxes Act 1988 as *"...in relation to a company, all the issued share capital (by whatever name called) of the company, other than capital the holders of which have a right to a dividend at a fixed rate, but have no other right to share in the profits of the company"*. [ICTA 1988 Sec 832]. Consequently, preference shares cannot be ordinary share capital for tax purposes where they carry the right to a fixed dividend.

19.8 FRS 4 has had a significant impact both on the classification of shares into equity or non-equity and on their presentation and disclosure in financial statements. For example, the definition of non-equity share capital in FRS 4 is not the opposite of the definition of equity share capital given in the Act. The effect of FRS 4 on share capital is discussed in detail in chapter 18.

19.9 There are strict rules in the Act that govern the purchase by a company of its own shares. The rules governing the redemption of redeemable shares are very similar to the rules that apply when a company purchases its own shares. A company may, if authorised to do so by its articles, issue shares that are redeemable at the option of the company or the shareholder. However, a company can only issue such shares where there are also non-redeemable shares in issue. [Sec 159]. The classification of redeemable shares according to FRS 4 is considered in chapter 18 and the rules concerning the purchase of own shares, including redeemable shares, are detailed in chapter 40.

Measurement of share capital

19.10 The memorandum must state the amount of the nominal share capital and the nominal value of each type of share. Shares can be issued for consideration which is greater than their nominal value. This premium over the nominal value forms the share premium account (unless merger relief is available, see chapter 26). Shares can be traded, either on the Stock Exchange or otherwise, at their market value. However, shares are recorded in the balance sheet at nominal value plus any premium and the subsequent value of a company's share does not affect the amount at which it is stated in the financial statements.

19.11 Public or private companies may allot shares, including any premium, for money or for other items which can be valued in money such as goodwill or know-how. [Sec 99]. However, the Act prevents shares being allotted at a discount. If shares are allotted at a discount by mistake, the allottee must pay the company an amount equal to the discount plus interest. [Sec 100].

19.12 Shares do not have to be paid for in full at the time of issue. For a private company there are no rules to determine the minimum amount of consideration that must be paid or how the consideration paid should be divided into the nominal value of share capital and share premium. For example, a private company can issue (say) a 20p share at £1 and have only 30p paid up. A public company must, however, have paid up at least a quarter of the nominal value plus the whole of any premium. [Sec 101]. Consequently, in the example, the minimum amount paid up would represent 85p (that is 20p × ¼ + premium of 80p). Shares issued by a public company to the subscribers to the memorandum, however, must be fully paid in cash including any premium. [Sec 106].

19.13 A public company must not accept an undertaking for services to be performed as payment for shares or share premium. If the company treats the undertaking of services as payment for shares, then the holder of the shares is liable to pay the company an amount equal to the nominal value of the shares and any share premium and also pay interest on this amount. [Sec 99].

19.14 A public company that intends to accept non-cash consideration (other than services) for the allotment of shares must have the consideration independently valued under section 108. [Sec 103]. This valuation report must be made for the company, during the six months before the allotment, by a person qualified to be the company's auditor who may seek assistance from any suitably qualified and independent valuer. [Sec 108]. The valuer's report should contain sufficient information to allow the amount of the paid up share capital and any premium to be readily apparent. The report must state in particular:

- The nominal value of the shares to be wholly or partly paid for by the consideration being valued.
- The amount of any premium payable on the shares.
- The description of the consideration.
- The extent to which the nominal value of the shares and any premium are to be treated as paid up either by the consideration that has been valued or by cash.

[Sec 108(4)].

The report must also state that, on the basis of the valuation of the consideration, together with any cash paid, the amount of the nominal value of the share capital (plus the whole of any premium) that is to be treated as paid is not less than the valued consideration plus any cash paid. [Sec 108(6)(d)]. A copy of the report must be sent to the proposed allottee. [Sec 103(1)(c)].

19.15 A valuation report is not required where a public company uses the credit balance on a reserve account such as the profit and loss account reserve or a revaluation reserve to allot shares, including any premium on the shares, to any members of the company (known as a bonus issue). [Sec 103(2)]. Amounts are to be transferred from the reserve to share capital and share premium in accordance with the articles and memorandum and the terms of the issue.

19.16 In addition, a valuation report is not necessary if shares are issued in consideration for the transfer or cancellation of shares in another company provided that the arrangement is open to all the other company's shareholders or all the shareholders of the class of shares in the other company being transferred. [Sec 103(3)(4)]. Shares issued in connection with a proposed merger, where the issuing company will take over all the assets and liabilities of another company in exchange for the issue of shares with or without any cash payment, also do not require a valuation report. [Sec 103(5)].

Fair value of consideration received

19.17 FRS 4 requires the net proceeds from the issue of shares to be credited to shareholders' funds. Net proceeds is defined as the "*...fair value of the consideration received on the issue of a capital instrument after deduction of issue costs*". [FRS 4 para 11]. Issue costs and their treatment are considered further in chapter 18. The fair value of the consideration received on the issue of share capital will represent the nominal value of the shares and the amount of the share premium. Difficulties can sometimes arise in determining the fair value of the consideration that arises as a result of the conversion of another capital instrument as considered in the following examples.

Example 1

As part of a restructuring, a debt of £5 million has been converted into ordinary shares with a nominal value of £100,000. There is no formal waiver of the loan and the shares probably have a market value of about £100,000. What share premium should be recorded?

Proceeds are defined as the fair value of the consideration received. Whilst it might be argued that the fair value is only £100,000, this does not appear reasonable given that, in the absence of a specific forgiveness of the loan, this treatment would result in £4.9 million being credited to the profit and loss account. Where no formal waiver of the loan is made, a premium of £4.9 million should be set up.

Example 2

A company has a loan obligation of £8 million. A bank has agreed to accept nil coupon preference shares redeemable in 5 years at £8 million in settlement of the loan. The nominal value of the shares is £4 million. How much share premium should be recorded?

The fair value of the consideration for the issue of the preference shares is the £8 million loan discounted by the rate of interest that the company would expect to pay on an equivalent loan of £8 million over 5 years. (If the loan is immediately repayable or is repayable on demand, there is no discount). The premium would then be the difference between the nominal value of the shares and this discounted amount.

This will result in a profit being initially recorded as the difference between the discounted amount and the £8 million liability previously recorded in the company's balance sheet. However, the premium on redemption will have to be accrued over the 5 years as an appropriation of profits. The treatment of the premium on the redemption of shares is discussed in chapter 18.

If, on the other hand, the company was in financial difficulties, it would be more prudent to treat the nil coupon in the same way as a waiver of interest. In that case, no profit would be recognised on the transaction and the consideration given for the preference shares would be the full £8 million un-discounted. In this case, a share premium of £4 million would arise on the transaction.

Disclosure of share capital

Statutory requirements

19.18 The amount of allotted share capital and the amount of called up capital that has actually been paid up must be shown separately in the financial statements. These amounts must be shown either under the heading 'called up share capital' in the balance sheet, or in a note to the financial statements. [Note 12 on the balance sheet formats]. 'Called up share capital' means:

- That proportion of a company's share capital as equals the aggregate amount of the calls made on its shares (whether or not those calls have been paid).
- Any share capital that has been paid up without being called.
- Any share capital that is to be paid on a specified future date under the Articles of Association, or under the terms of allotment, or any other arrangements for paying for those shares.

[Sec 737(1)].

19.19 The following example illustrates the disclosure requirements for called up share capital:

Example

On 30 November 19X1, a company allots 100,000 ordinary shares of £1 each. By 31 December 19X1, the company has made calls amounting to 75p per share. At 31 December 19X1, the holders of 10,000 shares have not paid the last call of 25p per share. In the financial statements at 31 December 19X1, the company would have to make the following disclosures:

Allotted share capital	100,000
Called up share capital	75,000
Paid-up share capital	72,500
Called up share capital not paid	2,500

19.20 Called up share capital is part of the double entry, and it will appear under capital and reserves (KI in Format 1 or AI in Format 2). Similarly, called-up share capital not paid forms part of the double entry, and it will appear in the balance sheet format either as a separate item (A in Format 1 or 2) or under debtors © II 5 in Format 1 or 2). Neither the allotted share capital nor the paid-up capital forms part of the double entry. However, they must still be disclosed either on the face of the balance sheet or in a note to the financial statements.

19.21 The notes to the financial statements must also show the amount of a company's authorised share capital. In addition, where shares of more than one class have been allotted, the notes must show the number and the aggregate nominal value of the shares of each class that have been allotted. [4 Sch 38(1)]. In practice, companies will generally be able to refer to share capital that is 'allotted, called up and fully paid', because these items will often be the same amount.

19.22 It is not appropriate to accrue for the issue of shares. The correct time to record the issue is when the shares are allotted. This is because share capital is a residual interest. The normal reasons for making accruals, to allocate a cost or revenue to the correct period or to recognise an asset or a liability at the appropriate time, do not therefore apply.

Example

At its year end, a company had committed itself to issue shares as a result of an underwritten rights issue although it is not known whether the shares will be issued to individuals or the underwriter. How should the 'shares to be issued' be shown in the financial statements?

The financial statements should not show the rights issue in share capital since the shares have not been issued. However, the issue should be disclosed as part of a post balance sheet event note and a proforma balance sheet could be prepared to reflect the issue.

[The next page is 19007.]

19.23 The Act requires certain information to be disclosed concerning redeemable shares in addition to what is required by FRS 4. The notes to the financial statements must show:

- The earliest and the latest dates on which the company may redeem those shares.

- The fact whether or not the company is obliged to redeem those shares, or either it or the holder merely has an option to do so.

- The amount of any premium payable on redemption, or the fact that no such premium is payable.

[4 Sch 38(2)].

FRS 4 disclosure requirements

19.24 FRS 4 requires a brief summary of the rights that attach to each class of non-equity shares (using the FRS 4 definition of non-equity) including:

- The rights to dividends.
- The dates on which the shares are redeemable and the amounts payable on redemption.
- Their priority and the amounts receivable on a winding up.
- Their voting rights.

[FRS 4 para 56].

Where the rights disclosed vary according to certain circumstances, those circumstances and the variation should be further explained.

19.25 Similar disclosures are not generally required for equity shares (using the FRS 4 definition) where they have:

- No right to dividends other than those that may be recommended by the directors.

- No redemption rights.

- Unlimited rights to share in the surplus remaining on a winding up after all liabilities and participation rights of other classes of shares have been satisfied.

- One vote per share.

[FRS 4 para 57].

Consequently, no additional disclosure will normally arise for ordinary shares. Table 19.1 gives an example of the disclosures required by the Act and FRS 4 for share capital.

Table 19.1 – Tate & Lyle Public Limited Company – Annual report – 24 September 1994

Notes to the Financial Statements (extract)

22 Share Capital	**1994 £ million**	1993 £ million
Authorised share capital of Tate & Lyle PLC		
2,394,000 6½% Cumulative preference shares of £1 each	**2.4**	2.4
603,057,915 Ordinary shares of 25p each	**150.8**	150.8
214,732,170 7.25p (net) dividend convertible cumulative redeemable preference shares of 12.5p each	**26.8**	26.8
	180.0	180.0
Allotted and fully paid		
2,394,000 6½% cumulative preference shares of £1 each (1993 2,394,000)	**2.4**	2.4
359,796,209 Ordinary shares of 25p each (1993 – 357,908,564)	**89.9**	89.5
187,728,160 7.25p (net) dividend convertible cumulative redeemable preference shares of 12.5p each (1993 – 187,849,079)	**23.5**	23.5
	115.8	115.4

Details of shares allotted during the year are given in the Directors' Report.

The rate of dividend of the 6½% cumulative preference shares is 4.55% plus the associated tax credit. On a return of capital on a winding-up, the holders shall be entitled to £1 per share, in preference to all other classes of shareholders. Holders of these shares are entitled to vote at meetings, except on the following matters: any question as to the disposal of the surplus profits after the dividend on these shares has been provided for, the election of directors, their remuneration, any agreement between the directors and the Company, or the alteration of the Articles of Association dealing with any of such matters.

The convertible preference shares may be converted into fully paid ordinary shares of 25p each on 28th February in any of the years 1995 to 2008 on the basis of 11.299 ordinary shares for every 25 convertible preference shares. The Company will be entitled at any time after 1st September 2008, and will be obliged on 28th February 2013, to redeem at £1 per share any convertible preference shares then in issue. On a return of capital on a winding-up, the holders of convertible preference shares are entitled to £1 per share, after payment of all amounts due to the holders of 6½% cumulative preference shares, but in priority to holders of ordinary shares. No voting rights attach to these shares unless the dividend on the shares is six months in arrears or a resolution is proposed affecting the rights of this class of shareholders.

In 1991 the Company issued 37,200 warrants to acquire shares. The proceeds were credited to a non-distributable reserve. At 24th September 1994 all such warrants were still outstanding, each of which entitles the holders to subscribe for 866 ordinary shares during the period to March 2001. The exercise price per warrant is £4,185.25 until 20th March 1995, increasing in annual increments to £5,143.75 from 21st March 2000. Alternatively, a warrant may be exercised by the surrender of one 5¾% Guaranteed Bond 2001 with a principal amount of £5,000. The maximum number of shares that could be issued under these warrants is 32,215,200.

At 24th September 1994, options had been granted and were still outstanding under the Company's share option schemes. These options are exercisable for a total of 8,695,000 ordinary shares in periods between now and 2004 at prices ranging from 107.75p to 438p per share. The number of shares issuable and the subscription prices have been adjusted in accordance with the rules of each scheme to take account of the rights issue made in May 1988 and the share split in January 1989. During the year, options for 923,750 shares were granted under the executive share options schemes and for 734,439 shares under the SAYE share option scheme.

Directors' Report (extract)

Share Capital – Ordinary Shares – The Company issued 1,887,645 ordinary shares during the year of which 54,650 were issued on the conversion of preference shares, 594,290 as share alternative dividends and 1,238,705 on the exercise of employee share options. The total value of ordinary shares issued at the issue price was £5.2 million.

19.26 Following the disclosure required by FRS 4, it should generally be clear why a class of share has been classified as equity or non-equity (using the FRS 4 definitions) for the purpose of analysing the total of shareholders' funds. However, where this is not so, the FRS requires that additional information is given to explain the position. [FRS 4 para 56].

Allotment of shares during the financial year

19.27 The Act requires that where a company has allotted any shares during the financial year, the notes to the financial statements must state:

- The classes of shares allotted.
- The number of shares allotted, their aggregate nominal value, and the consideration received in respect of each class of shares allotted.

[4 Sch 39 as amended by SI 1996/189].

19.28 In addition to the particulars required by the above paragraph, the Stock Exchange's Listing Rules require certain information where a listed company (or its unlisted major subsidiary) has allotted shares for cash and the allotment has neither been made to the company's shareholders in proportion to their shareholdings nor specifically authorised by the company's shareholders. The requirement is for the following information to be disclosed:

- The names of the allottees, if less than six in number, and in the case of six or more allottees, a brief generic description of them.

- The market price of the securities concerned on a named date, being the date on which the terms of the issue were fixed.

[LR 12.43(o)].

19.29 Furthermore, information has to be given about any 'contingent rights to the allotment of shares' that may exist. These rights could be options to subscribe for shares, or rights on the conversion of loan stock or any other rights where a person may require the allotment of shares (whether, in the latter case, the rights arise on conversion of any other type of security, or otherwise). The information to be given is:

- The number, the description and the amount of the shares in respect of which the right is exercisable.
- The period during which the right is exercisable.
- The price to be paid for the shares allotted.

[4 Sch 40].

Hence, the financial statements have to include details of the rights of conversion of convertible loan stock or issues required by share option schemes.

19.30 Table 19.1 above illustrates the disclosures necessary when shares have been issued in the year and where there are contingent rights for the issue of shares.

Serious loss of capital

19.31 If the value of a public company's net assets falls to half or less than half of its called up share capital, the directors have a duty to convene an extraordinary general meeting in order to consider whether any, and if so, what action to take to deal with the situation. Proper notice must be given, and the directors must convene the meeting not later than 28 days from the earliest date the serious loss of capital was known to a director. The meeting itself must be held within 56 days of that earliest date. If the company fails to convene the meeting, each of the directors of the company permitting the failure is liable to a fine. [Sec 142].

19.32 The Act defines called up share capital as including so much of its share capital as equals the aggregate amount of calls made on its shares (whether or not those calls have been paid), and other paid up share capital to be paid on a specified future date. [Sec 737]. Depending on the terms on which shares are allotted, the directors may make calls on shares so that shareholders become immediately liable to the nominal value of the shares allotted, together with any premium that the shareholders have agreed to pay. Calls are sometimes paid by instalments. In situations where the dates for payment of calls is specified, the called up share capital would be the same as the nominal value of, and share premium payable on, the shares in question.

19.33 However, if shares are issued at a premium, an amount equal to this premium must be transferred to the share premium account. [Sec 130]. This implies that the share premium is not part of a company's paid-up share capital. Also, the balance sheet formats in Schedule 4 show separate captions for called up share capital and for share premium account. Consequently, for the purposes of determining whether a company has suffered a serious loss of capital under section 142, called up share capital is generally taken in practice to exclude the share premium account.

Multi-currency share capital

19.34 In recent years a number of companies have issued share capital denominated in foreign currencies. One of those companies was the Scandinavian Bank Group Plc. In 1986 it petitioned the court for confirmation of a special resolution to cancel part of its existing sterling share capital in order to increase its share capital to £30m, $30m, SFr 30m and DM 30m (see *Re Scandinavian Bank Group plc*, [1987] BCLC 220).

19.35 The court confirmed that a company can have shares in more than one currency. Any particular share, however, must be denominated in one particular currency, but different shares can be denominated in different currencies. This does not conflict with the requirement in the Act because section 5(a) states that *"...the memorandum must...state the amount of the share capital...and the division of the share capital into shares of a fixed amount"*. By fixed amount the Act does not mean a fixed value in sterling terms.

19.36 However, sections 117 and 118 of the Act require a public company to have an authorised minimum allotted share capital of £50,000. This requirement stems from Article 6 of the 2nd Directive. Accordingly, the court held (obiter) that this 'authorised minimum' must be in pounds sterling.

19.37 Consequently, a private company can issue any amount of shares in a foreign currency. However, a public limited company can only express its shares in more than one currency if at least £50,000 of its share capital is in sterling. The question of whether foreign currency share capital should be translated at the year end and how any resulting exchange differences should be treated is discussed in chapter 29.

Reserves

19.38 Companies may have any of the following reserves and accounts in the balance sheet. These headings must be shown on the face of the balance sheet:

- Profit and loss account reserve.
- Share premium account.
- Revaluation reserve.
- Other reserves.

19.39 The heading 'Other reserves' may combine the following reserves:

- Capital redemption reserve.
- Reserve for own shares.
- Reserves provided for by the articles of association.
- Other reserves.

19.40 Other reserves include all reserves, both realised and unrealised, that do not fit elsewhere in the formats. If they are material, they should be specifically described.

Profit and loss account

19.41 Many companies do not use the wording 'profit and loss account'. They use instead terms such as 'revenue reserves' or 'retained profits'. The possibility of changing the wording of headings from those prescribed in the formats is discussed in chapter 6. The general rule is that the Act does not allow different wording to be used. The term 'revenue reserves', however, is generally accepted and understood in the UK. This applies equally to those companies such as investment trusts that wish to publish a 'revenue account', instead of a 'profit and loss account'. However, investment trusts are soon to be governed by an AITC SORP, which will give further advice in this area.

Share premium account

19.42 The share premium account records the difference between the nominal value of shares issued and the fair value of the consideration received. The use of the share premium account is governed by the Act, which provides that it can only be used for specific purposes, namely to:

- Pay up fully paid bonus shares.
- Write off preliminary expenses.
- Write off expenses of any issue of shares or debentures.

- Write off commission paid or discount allowed on any issue of shares or debentures.
- Provide for the premium payable on any redemption of debentures.

[Sec 130(2)].

19.43 The preliminary expenses that may be written off to share premium should be limited to the legal costs and fees relating to a company's incorporation. For example, solicitors' fees, registration fees and the costs of printing the memorandum and articles are expenses that may reasonably be written off to the share premium account. However, other costs, such as pre-incorporation trading losses, should not be written off to the share premium account.

19.44 The expenses of, the commission paid and the discount allowed on the issue of shares and debentures which may be written off to the share premium account are discussed in detail in chapter 18. The effect of FRS 4 on providing for premiums payable on redemption of debt instruments on the share premium account is also considered in chapter 18.

19.45 However, although the share premium account can only be used for specific purposes, it is treated as forming part of a company's capital for the purposes of the reduction of share capital. As such, it can be reduced under section 135 of the Act by application to the court. Share premium reductions are detailed in chapter 23.

Revaluation reserve

19.46 Where a company has valued an item in accordance with one of the alternative accounting rules, the Act states that the revaluation surplus or deficit must be credited or debited to a revaluation reserve. [4 Sch 34(1)].

19.47 Furthermore, a company can transfer an amount from the revaluation reserve to the profit and loss account, if the amount was previously charged to that account or represents a realised profit. A company is also permitted to apply the whole or a part of the revaluation reserve in wholly or partly paying up unissued shares in the company to be allotted to the members as fully or partly paid shares. The revaluation reserve will also be reduced by any amounts transferred to it that are no longer necessary for the purpose of the valuation method that the company has adopted. [4 Sch 34(3)]. Furthermore, it is possible to transfer from the revaluation reserve an amount in respect of the taxation relating to any profit or loss credited or debited to that reserve. [4 Sch 34(3)(b) inserted by SI 1996/189]. This applies for example to the deferred tax arising on a revaluation.

19.48 The revaluation reserve must be disclosed on the face of the balance sheet. However, it may be described by a different name, although it is generally preferable for companies to keep to the terminology in the Act. [4 Sch 34(2)].

19.49 Where an amount has been credited or debited to the revaluation reserve, its treatment for taxation purposes must be disclosed in a note to the financial statements (see chapter 13). [4 Sch 34(4)].

19.50 The revaluation reserve and some of the problems surrounding it are considered in the discussion of the alternative accounting rules in chapter 5. The use of the revaluation reserve to write off goodwill is considered in chapter 23.

Other reserves

Capital redemption reserve

19.51 Unless a private company is making an acquisition of its own shares out of capital, the Act requires companies to maintain their capital after the redemption or purchase of their own shares. This generally means that companies have to make a transfer to a capital redemption reserve of an amount equal to the nominal value of the shares that they acquire. [Sec 170(1)]. But where the acquisition is funded by an issue of new shares (a 'fresh issue' of shares) the amount that is required to be transferred to the capital redemption reserve is the difference between the proceeds of the fresh issue and the nominal value of the shares being purchased if it is greater. [Sec 170(2)]. In this situation, where the acquisition is funded by a fresh issue, the capital of the company is still maintained, although some of the capital may now be represented by share premium and an amount transferred to the capital redemption reserve. The purchase by a company of its own shares is discussed in detail in chapter 40. The use of the capital redemption reserve to write off goodwill is considered in chapter 23.

Merger reserve

19.52 A merger reserve may be created when a company acquires another company and the consideration includes the issue of shares. If merger relief is available on the issue of shares, then the difference between the fair value of the shares issued and their nominal value can be credited to a merger reserve (as opposed to a share premium account) or need not be recorded. Merger relief is discussed in detail in chapter 26. The merger reserve could be used to write off goodwill on consolidation before FRS 10 came into effect and prevented goodwill from being written off to reserves immediately on acquisition. Any old goodwill that is not recapitalised under the transitional arrangements in FRS 10 can continue to be offset against the merger reserve. This is considered in chapter 23.

[The next paragraph is 19.54.]

Disclosure

19.54 Certain information must be included in the notes to the financial statements in respect of movements on each reserve that is shown either on the face of the balance sheet or in the notes to the financial statements. This information is as follows:

- The amount of the reserve at the beginning and end of the year.
- The amounts transferred to or from the reserve during the year.
- The source and application of any amounts so transferred.

[4 Sch 46(1)(2)].

19.55 Companies may either give the information for each reserve in a separate note or prepare a combined note. Combining reserves helps clarify reserves movements when there are transfers between different reserves (see Table 19.2).

Table 19.2 – Grand Metropolitan Public Limited Company – Annual Report – 30 September 1994

Notes (extract)

25 RESERVES ATTRIBUTABLE TO EQUITY SHAREHOLDERS

	Share premium £m	Revaluation £m	Goodwill £m	Profit and loss £m	Total £m
At 30th September 1993	628	578	(2,652)	4,631	3,185
Accounting policy changes (note 1)	-	-	-	(41)	(41)
As restated	628	578	(2,652)	4,590	3,144
Retained profit for year	-	-	-	158	158
Exchange adjustments	-	(4)	128	(171)	(47)
Premiums on share issues, less expenses	48	-	-	-	(48)
Share dividend transfer	(20)	-	-	20	-
Goodwill written off during the year	-	-	(320)	-	(320)
Transfer of goodwill on disposal	-	-	34	-	34
Deficit on revaluation of properties in associate	-	(10)	-	-	(10)
Realisation of revaluation reserves	-	(430)	-	430	-
At 30th September 1994	656	134	(2,810)	5,027	3,007

> Goodwill is stated net of £62m of merger reserve and £426m of special reserve. The merger reserve arose in 1992 on the issue of shares at a premium in connection with an acquisition. The special reserve was created, with shareholder and Court approval, in 1988 by a transfer from the share premium account. Aggregate goodwill written off, net of disposals, is £3,298m (1993 -£3,140m).
>
> Of the £320m goodwill written off during the year, £194m arose on the acquisition of Food – branded businesses, including £119m on Martha White, and £123m arose on the acquisition of Drinks businesses, including £66m on Glen Ellen.
>
> Included in the revaluation reserve is £38m (1993 – £68m) representing the unrealised reserve on the transfer of the tenanted pub estate to Inntrepreneur Estates Ltd. £10m of the reduction in the year arose from the deficit on revaluation of investment properties in IEL (see note 16).
>
> The exchange adjustments include losses of £116m in respect of local currency borrowings by overseas companies and £53m in respect of other currency borrowings.

Realised and distributable reserves

19.56 The Act contains no specific requirement for reserves to be disclosed as either realised or unrealised, or as distributable or non-distributable. However, there may be differences between the balance on a company's profit and loss account and the amount that is realised (and so is distributable in law). Where there is a material difference between the balance on the profit and loss account and the amount that is legally distributable the financial statements may need to disclose the amounts of distributable and undistributable reserves respectively, in order to give a true and fair view.

19.57 Although distributions are made from the distributable reserves of individual companies, rather than groups, users of financial statements may nonetheless draw inferences from the amount shown on the consolidated profit and loss account reserve. It would be misleading if consolidated financial statements gave the impression that subsidiary companies' distributable profits were readily available for distribution outside the group through payments to the parent when there were significant restrictions on their distribution to the parent. SSAP 2 states that where significant statutory, contractual or exchange control restrictions exist that materially limit a parent company's access to the distributable profits of its subsidiaries, the nature and extent of the restrictions should be disclosed.

19.58 Indeed, users of consolidated financial statements may wish to know how much a parent could distribute if all the subsidiaries in the group were to pay up their realised profits by way of dividends to the parent. Some groups specifically disclose this amount or state in their reserves note any amounts that are not available for distribution. For example, the financial statements of Coats Viyella include a note that clarifies the reserves that are, or are not, available for distribution by the company. Coats Viyella's note also details the distributable reserves of the group, that is the reserves that would be available if all the subsidiaries paid up their reserves as dividends to the parent company (see Table 19.3).

Table 19.3 – Coats Viyella Plc – Annual report and accounts – 31 December 1997

Notes to the accounts (extract)

	Group		Company	
25 Total reserves	**1997**	1996 Restated	**1997**	1996 Restated
	£m	£m	**£m**	£m
Available for distribution	**196.1**	256.7	**345.4**	203.0
Not available for distribution	**328.6**	327.0	**241.8**	241.9
	524.7	583.7	**587.2**	444.9

19.59 Companies may also consider it necessary to give such disclosure when the size of a dividend paid or proposed is substantial, as compared to the total of distributable reserves of the company, and there is the risk that the shareholders may be under the mistaken impression that the same level of dividends can be maintained in the future.

Statement of movement on reserves

19.60 As stated in paragraph 19.54 a reserves note is required by the Act to show movements in each reserve and movements between reserves. Therefore, it is not possible to substitute for share capital and for the movements in the reserves note a figure such as the total recognised gains and losses for the year. That figure, which summarises several different types of reserve movements, must be broken down into its component parts in the reserves note, and transfers between reserves must also be shown in the note. For example, the reserves note is required to show movements between the revaluation reserve and the profit and loss account reserve in respect of previous revaluation surpluses that have been realised in the year. This movement would not be evident from either the profit and loss account or the statement of total recognised gains and losses.

19.61 FRS 3 requires an additional statement or note reconciling movements in shareholders' funds. This reconciliation between opening and closing shareholders' equity should include the components of the total recognised gains and losses of the year. The reconciliation will also include dividends as a deduction from the profit or loss for the year and other movements in shareholders' funds such as goodwill written off and share capital issued or redeemed. Since the reconciliation can be provided in the form of a note or in the form of a primary statement, considerable flexibility is given to where this statement appears and thus to the prominence or lack of prominence given to it.

19.62 It may, however, be appropriate to combine the statement of movements on reserves with the reconciliation of movements in shareholders' funds. This can be done by including a column for the total shareholders' funds brought forward from the previous year and carried forward for the year in the reserves note. Siebe plc provides a reconciliation of movements in shareholders' funds that also serves as the reserves note (see Table 19.4).

Table 19.4 – Siebe plc – Report and Accounts – 1 April 1995

Consolidated Balance Sheet (extract)

		Group		Company	
		1995	1994 Restated Note 1	**1995**	1994
	Notes	**£m**	£m	**£m**	£m
Capital and reserves					
Called up share capital	25	**107.1**	106.9	**107.1**	106.9
Share premium account	26	**393.4**	390.1	**393.4**	390.1
Other reserves	26	**(10.3)**	24.7	**217.3**	222.2
Revenue reserve	26	**476.0**	428.4	**64.1**	59.0
Shareholders' funds – equity		**966.2**	950.1	**781.9**	778.2
Minority interests – equity		**79.0**	63.3	**-**	-
		1,045.2	1,013.4	**781.9**	778.2

26 Reconciliation of movements in shareholders' funds (extract)

	Share capital £m	Share premium account £m	Merger reserve £m	Exchange variation reserve £m	Other reserves Total other reserves £m	Revenue reserve £m	Total £m	1994 Total £m
Group								
At 3 April 1994	106.9	390.1	-	24.7	24.7	428.4	950.1	742.6
Profit attributable to the members of Siebe plc	-	-	-	(35.0)	(35.0)	160.3	125.3	127.0
Dividends	-	-	-	-	-	(51.9)	(51.9)	(47.1)
Rights issue	-	-	-	-	-	-	-	184.3
New share capital subscribed	0.2	3.3	-	-	-	-	3.5	3.1
Goodwill written off	-	-	-	-	-	(60.8)	(60.8)	(59.8)
At 1 April 1995	107.1	393.4	-	(10.3)	(10.3)	476.0	966.2	950.1

The cumulative amount of goodwill resulting from acquisitions which has been written off between 1 April 1984 and 2 April 1994 is £228.9 million, of which £218.6 million has been charged to Merger Reserve and £10.3 million to Revenue Reserve.

Distinction between realised and unrealised profits

19.63 Although section 263(3) of the Act provides that a company's available profits for distribution are *"...its accumulated, realised profits ... less its accumulated, realised losses"*, the exact meaning of the term 'realised' is not defined in the Act (see also section 742(2)). Section 262(3) merely gives an indication of the interpretation of the term. It says that *"...references to realised profits and realised losses, in relation to a company's accounts, are to such profits or losses of the company as fall to be treated as realised in accordance with principles generally accepted, at the time when the accounts are prepared, with respect to the determination for accounting purposes of realised profits or losses"*.

19.64 Not only is the definition somewhat circular, there is also little indication in case law of what is meant by 'realised'. The few cases that there have been mainly relate to tax law, rather than to company law. All that can really be derived from the cases is that the judges have interpreted 'realised' as meaning something wider than 'realised in cash', and also that they, like the legislature, see realisation as an accounting rather than a strictly legal concept.

19.65 Because of these difficulties of interpretation, the CCAB issued, in September 1982, the following guidance statements:

- TR 481 – The determination of realised profits and the disclosure of distributable profits in the context of the Companies Acts 1948 to 1981.
- TR 482 – The determination of distributable profits in the context of the Companies Acts 1948 to 1981.

These two guidance statements are reproduced as annexes to chapter 3. Although they both refer to the Companies Acts 1948 to 1981, they apply equally to the Companies Act 1985 (as amended by the Companies Act 1989), and all references below refer to the equivalent sections of the 1985 Act.

19.66 The ASB's draft Statement of principles also refers to the concept of realisation without seeking to define it. It states:

> *"The concept of realisation is difficult to define precisely, but is usually taken to require that the gain has been, or is confidently expected to be, evidenced by the receipt of cash or of another asset than can be expected with reasonable certainty to be converted into cash."* [DSP chp 6 para 22].

Technical release 481

19.67 The main purpose of TR 481 is to give guidance on the interpretation of the term 'principles generally accepted', as used in section 262(3) of the Act. The phrase is not defined in the Act, but it has been given a judicial interpretation, as being *"...principles which are generally regarded as permissible or legitimate by the accountancy profession. That is sufficient even though only one company actually applies it in practice".* [*Lord Denning, MR, in Associated Portland Cement Manufacturers Ltd v Price Commission.* [1975] ICR 27]. The main conclusions that TR 481 sets out are detailed in the following paragraphs.

19.68 Unless an Accounting Standard specifically indicates that a profit should be treated as unrealised, a profit that is required by an Accounting Standard to be recognised in the profit and loss account should normally be treated as a realised profit. For example, SSAP 9, 'Stocks and long-term contracts', requires that attributable profit should be included in the value of long-term contracts (see chapter 17). Consequently, this attributable profit should be treated as realised.

19.69 A profit may be recognised in the profit and loss account in accordance with an accounting policy that is not the subject of an accounting standard, or (exceptionally) that is contrary to a standard. Such a profit will normally be a realised profit if the accounting policy is consistent with the two concepts of accruals and prudence as set out in both SSAP 2 and Schedule 4 to the Act (see chapter 3).

19.70 Where, in special circumstances, financial statements could not give a true and fair view (even if they provided additional information) without including an unrealised profit in its profit and loss account, the Act requires a company to include that unrealised profit. Moreover, where the directors have special reasons for doing so, Schedule 4 allows them to include an unrealised profit in the profit and loss account. Where unrealised profits are thus recognised in the profit and loss account, a note to the financial statements must give particulars of this departure from the statutory accounting principles, the reasons for it and its effect. [4 Sch 15]. The disclosures detailed in UITF Abstract 7 clarify these requirements of the Act (see chapter 2).

19.71 For example, according to SSAP 20 exchange gains that arise on long-term monetary items are not realised, but there is a 'special reason' for a company to include them in its profit and loss account. The special reason is that the company needs to treat exchange gains and losses symmetrically. Exchange gains can be determined no less objectively than can exchange losses. However, a true and fair override is necessary if such unrealised profits are taken to the profit and loss account.

[The next page is 19021.]

Technical release 482

19.72 TR 482 gives guidance on the way in which a company should determine distributable profits in the context of current legislation. It states that, in general, companies are allowed to make distributions only out of realised profits, less realised losses (as outlined in paragraph 19.76). In addition, a public company must deduct any net unrealised losses from net realised profits before making a distribution.

19.73 When determining the profits from which a company is allowed to make distributions, the starting point (the *"...accumulated realised profits ... less accumulated realised losses"*) will normally be the accumulated balance on the profit and loss account. This figure may need adjusting to take into account any items that the company is required to exclude in determining its distributable profits (such as, any unrealised gains that have been included in the profit and loss account; or the additional restrictions imposed on public companies referred to above).

19.74 TR 482 also considers the effect of revaluations, development costs and dividends receivable within a group on distributable profits. These issues and other difficulties concerning the determination of distributable profits are considered in remainder of this chapter.

Distributable profits

Definition of distribution

19.75 For the purposes of Part VIII of the Act, 'distribution' is defined as any distribution of a company's assets to its shareholders (whether or not it is made in cash), other than a distribution that is made by way of any one of the following:

- The issue of either fully-paid or partly-paid bonus shares.
- The redemption or the purchase of any of the company's own shares, either out of capital, or out of the proceeds of a fresh issue of shares, or out of unrealised profits in accordance with Part V, Chapter VII of the Act.
- The reduction of share capital by either of the following means:
  - Extinguishing or reducing the liability in respect of share capital that is not paid up.
  - Paying off paid-up share capital.
- The distribution of assets to shareholders on a winding-up.

[Sec 263(2)].

Conditions applying to companies (other than investment companies)

19.76 Any company (whether public or private) may make a distribution only out of *"profits available for the purpose"*. [Sec 263(1)]. In this sense, the word 'make' means 'pay'. Therefore, a company must have available sufficient profits at the time it pays a dividend not just at the time it declares one.

19.77 For any company other than an investment company or an insurance company, profits available for distribution are the company's accumulated realised profits that have not previously been either distributed or capitalised, less its accumulated realised losses (insofar as they have not been previously written off in either a reduction or a re-organisation of capital). [Sec 263(3)]. The origin of these profits and losses may be either revenue or capital. [Sec 280(3)].

19.78 In general, provisions for depreciation or diminution in value of assets and provisions that are necessary to provide for a liability or a loss must be treated as realised losses for the purpose of determining the amount of distributable profits [Sec 275(1)]. The exception to this rule is where a provision in respect of a diminution in value of a fixed asset is found to be necessary when all the fixed assets of the company (or all the fixed assets other than goodwill) are revalued. This exception is discussed from paragraphs 19.97 and 19.125.

Additional conditions applying to public companies

19.79 In addition to the condition that it can make a distribution only out of profits available for the purpose, a public company can make a distribution only to the extent that the distribution does not reduce the amount of the company's net assets below the aggregate of its called-up share capital (see para 19.18) plus its undistributable reserves. [Sec 264(1)].

19.80 In this context, 'undistributable reserves' include:

- The share premium account.

- The capital redemption reserve.

- The excess of accumulated unrealised profits that have not previously been capitalised over accumulated unrealised losses that have not previously been written off by a reduction or a re-organisation of capital. For this purpose, capitalisation includes the issuing of bonus shares, but it excludes transfers of profits to the capital redemption reserve that have been made after 22 December 1980.

- Any reserve that the company, for any other reason, is prohibited from distributing.

[Sec 264(3)].

19.81 The effect of this additional condition is that whereas a private company can make a distribution provided only that it has realised profits available, a public company can do so only if it has profits available after it has provided for any net unrealised losses.

19.82 The table below, which sets out extracts from the balance sheets of four companies, gives examples of the method of calculating distributable profits.

Examples of distributable profits in private and public companies

	Company 1		Company 2		Company 3		Company 4	
	£	£	£	£	£	£	£	£
A Share capital		1,000		1,000		1,000		1,000
B Unrealised profits	150		150		150		-	
C Unrealised losses	-		(200)		(200)		(200)	
D Net unrealised profits		150		-		-		-
E Net unrealised losses		-		(50)		(50)		(200)
F Realised profits	300		300		300		300	
G Realised losses	-		-		(120)		(120)	
H Net realised profits		300		300		180		180
I Share capital and reserves		1,450		1,250		1,130		980
Maximum distributable profit:								
Private company (H)		300		300		180		180
Public company (H-E)		300		250		130		Nil

Provisions relating to investment companies

19.83 Investment companies may make a distribution either on the basis of the *capital maintenance* test applicable to all public companies (see para 19.79) or on the basis of an *asset ratio* test (see para 19.86). However, where a distribution reduces an investment company's net assets below the aggregate of its called up capital and undistributable reserves, this fact must be disclosed in the notes to the financial statements. [4 Sch 72(1)].

19.84 Subject to the conditions listed in paragraph 19.85 below, an investment company may make a distribution at any time out of those of its accumulated realised *revenue* profits that have not previously been either distributed or capitalised, *less* its accumulated *revenue* losses (realised and unrealised, and only insofar as they have not been previously written off in a reduction or re-organisation of capital). The advantage of this is that capital losses may be ignored, although the other side of the coin is that realised capital profits cannot be included and the asset ratio test in paragraph 19.86 below must be satisfied. An investment company is, therefore, able to satisfy the Inland Revenue condition of non-retention of income, because it may make distributions even where the value of its investments has fallen.

19.85 The conditions which must be satisfied before an investment company may make a distribution on this basis are:

- The company's shares must be listed on a recognised investment exchange other than an overseas investment exchange within the meaning of the Financial Services Act 1986. [Sec 265(4)(a)].

- During the period beginning with the first day of the accounting reference period immediately preceding that in which the proposed distribution is to be made (or, where the distribution is proposed to be made during the company's first accounting reference period, the first day of that period) and ending with the date of that distribution, the company must not have:

  - Distributed any of its capital profits.

  - Applied any unrealised profits or capital profits (whether realised or unrealised) in paying up debentures or any amounts unpaid on any of its issued shares. This means that company may not distribute indirectly any amounts that are not available for distribution directly.

  [Sec 265(4)(5)].

- The company must have given the Registrar of Companies the notice required in section 266(1) at one of the following times:

  - Before the beginning of the period referred to in the point immediately above.

- As soon as reasonably practicable after the date on which the company was incorporated.

  [Sec 265(6)].

  This condition is necessary to prevent companies adopting investment company status merely for a particular distribution and who might then revoke that status only to adopt it again for the purpose of the next distribution.

- The amount of the company's assets must be at least 50 per cent greater than the aggregate of its liabilities. [Sec 265(1)(a)]. In this context, 'liabilities' includes any provision other than for depreciation of diminution in the value of assets. [Sec 265(2), 4 Sch 89]. However, the company must not include any uncalled share capital as an asset in those financial statements that are used to determine the legality of any distribution. [Sec 265(3)].

19.86 Where all the above conditions are satisfied, an investment company may make a distribution, but only to the extent that the distribution does not reduce the company's assets below 150 per cent of the aggregate of its liabilities. [Sec 265(1)(b)].

19.87 The following example sets out extracts from the balance sheets of four companies. The example shows how investment companies calculate their distributable profits and contrasts this with how other companies calculate their distributable profits:

Examples of distributable profits in private and public companies

	Company 1		Company 2		Company 3		Company 4	
	£	£	£	£	£	£	£	£
A Share capital		1,000		1,000		1,000		1,000
B Share premium		100		100		100		100
C Unrealised capital profits	600		600		600		600	
D Unrealised revenue profits	-		-		100		100	
E Unrealised capital losses	-		(700)		(700)		(700)	
F Unrealised revenue losses	-		(250)		(250)		(250)	
G Net unrealised reserves		600		(350)		(250)		(250)
H Realised revenue profits	1,200		1,200		1,200		1,200	
I Realised capital profits	-		-		100		100	
J Realised capital losses	-		-		-		(600)	
K Realised revenue losses	-		-		(150)		(150)	
L Net realised reserves		1,200		1,200		1,150		550

	Company 1	Company 2	Company 3	Company 4
	£	£	£	£
M Share capital and reserves	2,900	1,950	2,000	1,400
N Total liabilities	1,300	1,300	1,300	1,300
O Total assets	4,200	3,250	3,300	2,700
Maximum distributable profits – Special rules for an investment company				
(i) per section 265 The lower of:				
(a) Realised revenue profits (H) less accumulated revenue losses (K + F)	1,200	950	800	800
(b) 150 per cent asset test, O – (1½ × N)	2,250	1,300	1,350	750
Amount distributable	1,200	950	800	750
Normal rules for a public company (ii) per section 264 (the lower of L and (L+G))	1,200	850	900	300

Effect of revaluations on distributable profits

19.88 The revaluation of fixed assets can affect the amounts recorded in the profit and loss account and distributable profits in the following ways:

- Depreciation on revalued assets passes through the profit and loss account.

- The profit on revalued assets that are subsequently sold may not pass through the profit and loss account.

- The revaluation itself may involve writing off depreciation that has previously been charged to the profit and loss account.

- Diminutions in value of assets may need to be taken to the profit and loss account.

Depreciation of revalued assets

19.89 When assets are revalued, depreciation charged to the profit and loss account must in accordance with SSAP 12 be based on the carrying value of the asset rather than the original cost. Provisions for the depreciation of revalued fixed assets require special treatment to the extent that they *exceed* the amounts that would have been provided if the assets had not been revalued. For the purpose of calculating the amount of profit that is legally available for distribution, a company is required to treat an amount equivalent to the excess depreciation on the revaluation surplus as a realised profit. [Sec 275(2)]. In this way, the provision for depreciation that is charged in the profit and loss account is reduced to the amount that would have been charged on the asset's original cost.

19.90 As a result, when fixed assets have been revalued, the depreciation of the 'surplus element' will not normally affect the amount of a company's accumulated distributable profits. However, it will affect its annual profits as stated in the published financial statements since the depreciation charge in the profit and loss account will included the 'surplus element'.

Example

Ignoring the effect of taxation, a revaluation would have the following effect on the profit and loss account:

Example of depreciation adjustment for revalued fixed assets

	Cost	Valuation	Difference between cost and valuation
	£	£	£
Fixed assets	1,000	2,500	1,500
Profit before depreciation	5,000	5,000	N/A
Depreciation at 10% a year	100	250	150
Profit after depreciation	4,900	4,750	150

Therefore, without the requirement of section 275(2) to treat an amount equal to the difference between the depreciation of the asset at cost and at a valuation as a realised profit, the distributable profit would be £4,750. This is because the profit in the financial statements is the profit after charging depreciation on the revalued amount. The effect of section 275(2) is to add back the additional depreciation of £150 (that arises because the assets have been revalued) in determining the profits available for distribution.

Without this requirement of the Act, companies might be discouraged from revaluing their fixed assets, because the extra depreciation charged on the revalued amount would have the effect of reducing their profits available for distribution. (Of course, companies might be discouraged from revaluing their assets despite this, because of the effect of the additional depreciation on their reported profits.)

19.91 The difference between the depreciation based on the historical costs and on revalued amounts should also form part of the note of historical cost profits and losses required by FRS 3. This is illustrated in Table 19.6. NFC plc adjusts for the 'surplus depreciation' in both its historical cost profits and losses note and in its reserves note.

Table 19.6 – NFC plc – Annual Report & Accounts – 1 October 1994

Group Historical Cost Profits and Losses

	1994	1993
		As restated
	£m	£m
Profit on ordinary activities before taxation	**105.6**	104.9
Revaluation surpluses realised on sale of properties	**5.1**	3.5
Difference between depreciation based on historical costs and on revalued amounts	**1.2**	1.2
Historical cost profit on ordinary activities before taxation	**111.9**	109.6
Historical cost retained profit for the year	**30.6**	53.7

Notes to the Accounts (extract)

25 Reserves (extract)

	Revaluation reserve £m	Profit and loss account £m
Profit for the financial year	-	73.4
Dividends	-	(49.1)
	-	24.3
Elections for shares under share dividend plans	-	1.4
Unrealised deficit on revaluation of properties	(5.7)	-
Transfer of revaluation surpluses realised on disposals of properties	(5.1)	5.1
Transfer of difference between depreciation based on historical costs and on revalued amounts	(1.2)	1.2
Goodwill written off		(13.6)
Translation differences on net investment in non-sterling assets	(0.1)	2.6
Movements in the year	(12.1)	21.0
At 2 October 1993 as previously reported	83.5	144.2
Prior year adjustment (note 9)	-	(1.4)
At 1 October 1994	71.4	163.8

The revaluation reserve arises in respect of the revaluation of certain properties.

Subsequent sale of revalued assets

19.92 Reserve adjustments are also required for items taken to reserves that may properly be included in determining distributable profits. For example, an unrealised profit on an asset revaluation will originally be included in the statement of total recognised gains and losses and credited to a revaluation reserve. When the asset is subsequently disposed of, the whole profit is clearly realised, notwithstanding the fact that all or part of it may not have been passed through the profit and loss account. However, since the gain was previously recognised in the statement of total recognised gains and losses, it is considered inappropriate to recognise it again in the profit and loss account when it is realised. The gain or loss on the disposal of the asset must be calculated by reference to its carrying value rather than its original cost in accordance with FRS 3 paragraph 21.

19.93 The note of historical cost profits and losses provides users of accounts with details of all profits that have been earned in the period based on historical cost figures regardless of whether the profits have previously been recognised as unrealised. Therefore, this note should contain an adjustment to restate profits and losses on the sale of assets onto the historical cost basis. This same adjustment will also need to be made as a transfer between the revaluation reserve and the profit and loss account reserve so that the profit and loss account reserve contains the realised profit. For example, Table 19.6 includes such an adjustment in both its note of historical cost profits and its reserves note.

19.94 In addition, where a revalued asset is disposed of, any deficit below cost that has previously been treated as unrealised should be redesignated as a realised loss. For example, if a revaluation of an investment property resulted in a diminution in value below cost that the directors believed was temporary then, in accordance with the ASB's amendment to SSAP 19 issued in July 1994, the deficit would be taken to the revaluation reserve and reported in the statement of total recognised gains and losses rather than being included in the profit and loss account. When the asset is subsequently sold, the profit or loss on disposal should be calculated based on the carrying value and the deficit on the revaluation reserve relating to the asset should be transferred to the profit and loss account reserve.

Example

An investment property that originally cost £10 million was revalued down to £8 million in previous years. The directors considered that the decrease in value was temporary and the deficit was included in the revaluation reserve. During the year the property was sold for £9 million. The table below shows the profit and loss account and the profit and loss account reserve for the sale of the revalued property and the sale of the property if the revaluation had not taken place.

Loss based on historical cost and revalued amount

	Historical cost £'m	Revalued amount £'m
Proceeds	9	9
Cost/carrying value	10	8
Profit and loss account for the year	(1)	1
Transfer from revaluation reserve	-	(2)
Effect on profit and loss account reserve	(1)	(1)

The realised loss recorded in the profit and loss account reserve of £1m is the same regardless of whether the temporary diminution in value had previously been recorded.

19.95 Where an asset's original cost is not known, or where it is not possible to ascertain it without unreasonable delay or expense, its cost is taken to be the value shown in the company's earliest available record of its value. [Sec 275(3)].

Revaluations and previously charged depreciation

19.96 The CCAB guidance statement, TR 482, discusses the writing back of past depreciation when an asset is revalued. However, opinion is divided as to whether the amount of depreciation written back represents a realised or an unrealised surplus, and the guidance statement gives no firm guidance. SSAP 12 paragraph 22 comments that this depreciation should not be written back to the profit and loss account, except to the extent that it relates to a provision for permanent diminution in value which is subsequently found to be unnecessary. However, this comment does not necessarily answer the question of whether the profit is realised or not. Where a company places reliance on such a profit being realised in order to make a distribution, the directors may find it appropriate to seek legal advice.

Provision for diminution in the value of assets

19.97 A provision for depreciation or diminution in value of an asset, to the extent that it does not offset a previous revaluation surplus on that asset, must normally be treated as a realised loss. Such a realised loss cannot be reduced by being offset (either wholly or in part) against revaluation surpluses on other assets (whether or not they are of the same class). There is, however, an exception to this contained in section 275. The provisions of this section of the Act are complicated and are considered from paragraph 19.125.

Foreign currency translation

19.98 SSAP 20 requires that a company should translate those of its currency transactions that are outstanding at the end of the year (for example, creditors for fixed assets purchased from overseas and currency loans) using the rate of exchange at the balance sheet date (that is, the closing rate). Where, however, the rate of exchange is fixed under the terms of the relevant transaction, the company should use that rate. Where an outstanding trading transaction is covered by a related or a matching forward contract, the rate specified in that contract may be used. [SSAP 20 para 48].

19.99 Exchange gains and losses will arise both on the currency transactions a company completes during the year and on its short-term monetary items. The company should include all such exchange differences in its profit or loss account. However, not all exchange gains on the translation of currency transactions that are included in the profit and loss account are realised. There is a conflict here with paragraph 12 of Schedule 4 to the Act, which states that *"...only profits realised at the balance sheet date shall be included in the profit and loss account"*.

19.100 Where exchange gains and losses arise on short-term monetary items, their ultimate cash realisation can normally be assessed with reasonable certainty. Therefore, gains and losses on such items are considered to be realised gains and losses in accordance with the prudence concept defined in SSAP 2. Accordingly, the inclusion of these gains in the profit and loss account does not conflict with paragraph 12 of Schedule 4 to the Act.

19.101 Exchange gains that arise on long-term monetary items may or may not be considered to be realised depending on the circumstances and these issues are considered further in chapter 29.

Capitalisation of development costs

19.102 The Act states that where development costs are shown as an asset in the financial statements, any amount in respect of those costs should be treated as a realised loss, unless there are special circumstances justifying the directors' decision not to treat the costs as a realised loss and certain statements are made in the notes to the financial statements. [Sec 269]. Where development costs are capitalised in accordance with SSAP 13 (see chapter 14), these special circumstances generally exist. The note to the financial statements that states the special circumstances that permit the company to capitalise development costs must state also that the development costs have not been treated as a realised loss and the justification (the special circumstances contained in SSAP 13) the directors used for adopting this treatment. [Sec 269(2)]. However, this requirement does not apply to any part of the amount in the balance sheet that represents an unrealised profit on a revaluation of the development costs.

19.103 TR 482 notes that companies that carry forward costs in accordance with SSAP 13 will normally be able to justify these costs not being treated as a realised loss.

Goodwill

19.104 When goodwill arises on consolidation, there is no effect on the realised and distributable profits because it is individual companies that make distributions not groups. However, where goodwill arises in a company, questions arise as to whether and how any write-off of goodwill would affect distributable profits.

19.105 Where goodwill is capitalised in a company's balance sheet, any amortisation or impairment charges reduce its distributable profits.

19.105.1 Where goodwill pre-dating FRS 10 remains written off to a company's reserves under the standard's transitional arrangements, the goodwill write-off should be transferred from unrealised to realised reserves over its estimated useful economic life. This will reduce realised reserves on a systematic basis in the same way as if the company had capitalised and amortised the goodwill. [FRS 10 appendix V para 2].

[The next paragraph is 19.106.]

19.106 Where negative goodwill pre-dating FRS 10 remains credited to reserves, a company should credit it initially to an unrealised reserve.. The company may then transfer the negative goodwill from that unrealised reserve to realised reserves. This transfer should be in line with the depreciation or the realisation of the assets acquired in the business combination that gave rise to this negative goodwill. [FRS 10 appendix V para 3]. The treatment of pre-FRS 10 goodwill that remains in reserves, including suitable reserves to be used for writing it off, is discussed in detail in chapter 23.

Transactions within the group

19.107 Where consolidated financial statements are prepared, the relevant distributable profits will be the parent company's realised profits. This is because distributable profits must be established for individual companies and not for groups of companies.

19.108 Consequently, a situation may arise where the group has sufficient distributable profits in aggregate to make a desired distribution, but the parent company itself has insufficient distributable profits. In this situation, a distribution may not be made to the parent company's shareholders without distributions first being made from the subsidiaries to the parent company to pass the distributable profits to the parent. The parent company must then prepare *relevant accounts* that account for the receipt of these distributions in order to justify a distribution to its shareholders (see from para 19.114 below). However, these relevant accounts need only include the parent company's financial statements (not the consolidated financial statements), because it is the parent company that will make the distribution.

19.109 If a parent company or a subsidiary has assets that have been revalued in accordance with the alternative accounting rules, the revaluation reserve is unrealised. However, if the company sells these revalued assets to another company within the same group the revaluation reserve appears to have been realised in the company. It then appears *prima facie* that these reserves are available for distribution. Similarly, a parent company could sell one of its subsidiaries to another subsidiary to create distributable reserves. If these transactions are carried out at arm's length, settled in cash or cash equivalents and are supported by proper legal documentation, the resulting surpluses appear to be realised. The fact that a transaction is undertaken between companies in the same group need not prevent the profit on the transaction being realised and therefore distributable. However, transactions undertaken at other than fair value and transactions undertaken when one of the parties to the transaction has net liabilities or no distributable reserves may be unlawful. Such transactions are considered from paragraph 19.156.

19.110 If the transaction is artificial it may be unlawful to make a distribution from the resulting profit. This point has not yet been tested in the courts. As an example, however, Counsel has advised that, where the consideration is left outstanding because the group company that was purchasing the asset did not have sufficient funds to complete the transaction, then the transaction would not be effective for the purpose of creating realised profits. In addition, where the vendor does not retain the cash proceeds which are immediately, through a pre-ordained arrangement, returned to the purchaser, this would not be effective for creating a realised profit, unless and until the resulting loan was settled by the purchaser in cash, with the vendor then retaining the cash. It may, therefore, sometimes be difficult in practice to determine whether a transaction results in realised profits. Where a company wishes to create distributable profits by an intra-group transaction, it would be advisable to obtain legal advice regarding the legality of the proposed distribution.

19.111 Such transactions also create problems on consolidation.

Example 1

A subsidiary has a property that originally cost £100,000, but it has been revalued in the subsidiary's books to £500,000. Ignoring any depreciation, the revaluation reserve balance is £400,000. The subsidiary then sells the property to a fellow subsidiary in an arm's length transaction for cash of £500,000 (its open market value). Consequently, the subsidiary will transfer to its profit and loss account reserve the surplus on disposal of the property of £400,000. If the transaction results in a distributable profit, the subsidiary may then distribute this realised profit to its parent company. However, as far as the group is concerned, there is no disposal. Therefore, on consolidation, the revaluation surplus that has been realised should be reinstated as a revaluation reserve. An additional problem may arise if the parent company

[The next page is 19035.]

decides to distribute these funds to its shareholders. In these circumstances, funds have left the group, and the transaction may need to be explained further if the consolidated financial statements are to give a true and fair view.

Example 2

The situation is similar to that described above, except that the realised profit in the subsidiary represents pre-acquisition reserves. Pre-acquisition reserves are a company's retained earnings at the date on which that company becomes a subsidiary of another company. Before the enactment of the Companies Act 1981, where a subsidiary paid a dividend to its parent company out of its pre-acquisition profits, the parent company would treat the dividend received as a reduction of the cost of its investment in that subsidiary. Consequently, dividends the subsidiary paid to the parent company out of pre-acquisition profits were not available for distribution to the parent company's shareholders.

However, the Companies Act 1981 amended paragraph 15(5) of the then Schedule 8 to the Companies Act 1948. This change had the effect that where a subsidiary now pays a dividend to its parent company out of pre-acquisition profits, that dividend need not necessarily be applied as a reduction in the cost of the investment in the subsidiary. [FRS 6 Appendix 1 para 16]. Such a dividend should be applied to reduce the carrying value of the investment to the extent that it is necessary to provide for a diminution in value of the investment in the subsidiary as stated in the parent company's financial statements. To the extent that this is not necessary, it appears that the amount received will be a realised profit in the hands of the parent company. However, in this example, on consolidation, any part of the dividend received by the parent company that has not been applied to reduce the cost of the investment, will need to be adjusted on consolidation by taking out of the parent company's realised reserves an amount that will cause the goodwill on consolidation to remain the same as in previous years. If, as in the first example, the parent company decides to distribute these funds to its shareholders, the transaction may need to be explained further if the consolidated financial statements are to give a true and fair view.

The consequences of intra-group transactions are also discussed in detail in chapter 22.

Pre-combination profits

19.111.1 Pre-combination profits are those profits earned by a subsidiary company before it is acquired by a group. Following a change brought about by the Companies Act 1981, in certain circumstances, it is now possible for a parent company to distribute to its shareholders pre-combination profits arising in its subsidiaries. The treatment of pre-combination profits is discussed in detail in chapter 26.

[The next paragraph is 19.112.]

Other transactions

19.112 A bed and breakfast transaction is one in which a company agrees to sell certain assets (such as securities) to a third party (normally a broker) and arranges to repurchase them, or identical assets, shortly thereafter, usually overnight, for the same price. Such transactions are normally undertaken to crystallise a capital gain or loss for tax purposes. They may also be undertaken in an attempt to turn an unrealised revaluation gain on investments into realised and therefore distributable profits. Bed and breakfast transactions are examples of sale and repurchase transactions to which the provisions of FRS 5 apply. In general, they are unlikely to create realised profits. Chapter 4 considers the implications of such transactions.

19.113 Marking to market – the revaluation of readily marketable current asset investments to market value – may give rise to a realised profit in some circumstances. The implications of marking to market are also considered in detail in chapter 5.

Relevant accounts

19.114 The Act states that, in order to determine whether a company has profits available, and (if it is a public company) whether the additional condition in paragraph 19.79 above has been satisfied, reference must be made to certain items in the company's 'relevant accounts'. [Sec 270(2)].

19.115 The items to be referred to in the 'relevant accounts' are:

- Profits, losses, assets and liabilities.
- Provisions (as discussed in chapter 17).
- Share capital and reserves (including undistributable reserves).

[Sec 270(2)].

19.116 The 'relevant accounts' are normally the company's latest audited financial statements that have been laid before the company in general meeting. [Sec 270(3)]. However, where a distribution would exceed the amount that is distributable according to the latest audited financial statements, *interim accounts* must be prepared and used in addition to the latest financial statements to justify the payment. These additional financial statements are necessary to enable a proper judgement to be made of the amounts of any of the relevant items referred to in paragraph 19.115. [Sec 270(4)(a)]. These interim accounts are different to those required under the Stock Exchange's Listing Rules.

19.117 Furthermore, *initial accounts* must be prepared and used where a company proposes to make a distribution during its first accounting reference period or before the date on which it lays its first audited financial statements before its shareholders. [Sec 270(4)(b)]. These initial accounts must be such as to enable a reasonable judgement to be made of the amounts of the items mentioned in paragraph 19.115.

19.118 This legislation, although of importance to all companies, is particularly important for investment trusts because they are required to distribute the majority of their reserves each year. Consequently, an interim dividend is unlikely to be covered by the retained reserves included in their last financial statements. Therefore, generally, such companies will need to prepare interim accounts in order to pay an interim dividend legally.

19.119 The Act lays down strict requirements in respect of the relevant accounts used for the purposes of testing the legality of a distribution. Failure to comply with these requirements will mean that the distribution will be illegal. [Sec 270(5)]. The shareholders cannot agree to waive the requirements. [*Re Precision Dippings Ltd v Precision Dippings Marketing Ltd* [1985] Ch 447]. The requirements set out in paragraph 19.120 do not apply to a private company's interim or initial accounts and, as a consequence, they can use management accounts for this purpose to support a distribution.

[The next page is 19037.]

However, as mentioned above the Act requires a private company to prepare such accounts to enable the directors to make a reasonable judgement as to the profits available for distribution. [Sec 270].

19.120 The requirements for relevant accounts, that is annual financial statements of all companies and *interim and initial accounts* of public companies, are as follows:

- They must be 'properly prepared', or they must be so prepared at least to the extent that is necessary in order to decide whether or not a proposed distribution is legal. In particular, the items referred to in paragraph 19.115 above must be determined. [Sec 271(2), 272(2), 273(2)].

  For annual financial statements, 'properly prepared' means that they must comply with Part VII of the Act. For either *interim or initial accounts*, it means that they must comply with section 226 of the Act (that is, they must comprise a balance sheet, profit and loss account and related notes as required by that section and Schedule 4). However, directors' reports (required by Schedule 7) and cash flow statements (which are not required by the Act) need not be included. It also means that the balance sheet comprised in those accounts has to be signed by the directors in accordance with section 233 of the Act. [Sec 272(3), 273(3)].

- They must give a true and fair view of both the state of the company's affairs and its profit or loss. [Sec 271(2), 272(3), 273(3)].

- They must not include, for a public company, any uncalled share capital as an asset. [Sec 264(4)].

- With annual financial statements, the auditors must have given their opinion on them in accordance with section 235 of the Act. [Sec 271(3)]. So far as *initial accounts* are concerned, the auditors must have reported whether, in their opinion, those accounts have been properly prepared. [Sec 273(4)]. *Interim accounts* need not be audited.

- If the auditors have qualified their opinion on annual or initial accounts, they must state, in writing, whether the subject matter of their qualification is material, by reference to the items listed in paragraph 19.115, 19.115, in determining the legality of the proposed distribution.
  [Sec 271(3)(4), 273(4)(5)].

- With annual financial statements, this statement will suffice if it relates to distributions of the same description as the distribution proposed (see para 19.134 below). [Sec 271(5)]. Such statements must have been laid before the shareholders in general meeting. [Sec 271(4)].

- With *initial accounts*, a copy of those accounts, together with a copy of the auditors' report and such statement (where applicable), must have been delivered to the Registrar of Companies before the proposed distribution is made. [Sec 273(6)].

- With *interim accounts*, a copy of the accounts must be delivered to the Registrar of Companies before the proposed distribution is made. [Sec 272(4)].

19.121 If any document in a set of accounts that must be delivered to the Registrar of Companies is in a foreign language, a certified translation (see chapter 21 for an explanation) of that document must also be delivered to the Registrar of Companies. [Secs 242(1), 272(5), 273(7)]. However, the Registrar of Companies will, by concession, accept financial statements in a currency other than sterling, provided that they include the exchange rate between that currency and sterling at the balance sheet date.

19.122 A company may find that it does not have sufficient distributable reserves shown in its last relevant accounts to justify paying an interim dividend. Where this is so, the company will have to prepare *interim accounts* and, with a public company, will have to deliver them to the Registrar of Companies (in the way outlined above) to justify the payment of the interim dividend. Also if the company is listed on the Stock Exchange, the company should also release the interim accounts to the Stock Exchange as they may contain price-sensitive information. The Listing Rules include a general requirement that such information should be released to the Stock Exchange as soon as it is available. The Listing Rules also require that the company notify the Company Announcements Office of any decision to make a distribution. [LR 12.40(c)].

19.123 A particular set of financial statements may have been used to determine whether a distribution can be made. If it is proposed to determine the legality of a subsequent distribution by reference to the same financial statements, the amount of the proposed distribution must be notionally increased by the amount of the earlier distribution. [Sec 274(1)]. The object of this requirement is to prevent a company avoiding the restrictions by making several small distributions that are permissible individually, but which, when taken in aggregate, exceed the amount available for distribution.

19.124 Similarly, a set of financial statements used to determine whether a distribution can be made must be adjusted by the amount of financial assistance for the purchase of own shares out of distributable profits or certain payments in respect of, or in connection with, the purchase of own shares if the assistance was provided since the financial statements were prepared. [Sec 274(2)].

Treatment of revalued assets in relevant accounts

19.125 Paragraph 19.76 sets out the basic conditions for establishing profits available for distribution, that is, a company's accumulated realised profits less its accumulated realised losses, and that provisions for depreciation of assets must be treated as realised losses. Section 275(1) of the Act permits, as an exception, that a provision for depreciation or diminution in value of an asset, to the extent that it does not offset a previous revaluation surplus on that asset, may not need to be treated as a realised loss. However, a company needing to rely on the complicated provisions of section 275 in order to have sufficient distributable profits to pay a dividend, is likely to have other difficulties and would be well advised to seek legal advice before relying on section 275. The provisions of this section of the Act are complicated and the purpose of the following section is to clarify these requirements.

19.126 Surprisingly, where a company revalues all of its fixed assets and takes advantage of section 275, then even where an actual revaluation shows an overall deficit, the diminution in value of the asset that is being accounted for can still be treated as an unrealised loss for distribution purposes, even if it has been accounted for through the profit and loss account for the period. However, the diminution in value of the asset that is being accounted for will reduce a public company's distributable profits if, as a result of the provision, there is a net deficit on the revaluation reserve. This is because a public company's distribution must not reduce its net assets to less than its share capital plus undistributable reserves (see para 19.79 above).

19.127 In determining whether a revaluation of a company's fixed assets has taken place for the purposes of the exception from section 275(1), the directors' *consideration* of the value at any particular time of any fixed asset may be treated as a revaluation. [Sec 275(4)]. 'Consideration' does not necessarily mean the directors must value each asset as an individual item. It simply means that the directors should have addressed themselves to the question of the asset's value for the purpose of determining the legitimacy of distributions. However, a company may take advantage of the exception from section 275(1) only where the conditions below are satisfied.

19.128 The conditions referred to in paragraph 19.127 above that must be satisfied are as follows:

- All the company's fixed assets (or all those other than goodwill) have been revalued, either by an actual revaluation or by the directors' consideration of their value.

- The directors' consideration of the value of those fixed assets that have not actually been revalued must take place at the same time as, and must consider the value at the same date as, the revaluation that recognised the particular asset's diminution in value.

- Where there has been no actual valuation, the directors are satisfied that the aggregate value of the fixed assets that they have treated as having been revalued by virtue of their considering the assets' value at the time in question, is not less than the aggregate amount at which those assets are, for the time being, stated in the company's financial statements. [Sec 275(5)]. (See para 19.130 for the statement to be made in the notes to the financial statements.)

19.129 For example, Table 19.7 contains such disclosures made by Berisford International as well as a reconciliation of the profit and loss reserve to the distributable reserves.

Table 19.7 – Berisford International plc – Annual Report & Accounts – 30 September 1992

Notes to the accounts (extract)

24. Revaluation reserve	**1992**		1991	
	Group £m	**Company £m**	Group £m	Company £m
The movement for the year comprised:				
At 1 October	-	**328.2**	84.2	585.2
Revaluation in year				
investments in subsidiary entities *(Notes 12 & 25)*	-	**(46.7)**	-	(257.0)
tangible fixed assets *(Note 11)*	-	-	(1.0)	-
Transfers to profit and loss account on disposal of subsidiary entities	-	**(4.7)**	(83.2)	-
At 30 September	-	**276.8**	-	328.2

25. Profit and loss account (extract)	**1992**		1991	
	Group £m	**Company £m**	Group £m	Company £m
The movement for the year comprised:				
At 1 October	**81.5**	**(246.7)**	(93.1)	(338.4)
(Loss) profit for the financial year (i)	**(67.1)**	**(20.5)**	62.1	74.8
Currency realignment	**(0.8)**	**(2.3)**	2.9	(10.2)
Transfer from other reserves and revaluation reserve (Notes 23 & 24)	**-**	**4.7**	114.0	27.1
Share of goodwill written off by associated undertakings	**(1.6)**	**-**	(4.4)	-
At 30 September	**12.0**	**(264.8)**	81.5	(246.7)

(i) The Directors have revalued the Company's investments in subsidiary entities at 30 September 1992 to their underlying net asset values. The Directors have considered the value of the remaining fixed assets and are satisfied that these are worth, in total, not less than the aggregate amount at which they are stated in the Company's accounts. Accordingly, in accordance with Section 275 of the Companies Act 1985 the aggregate provision does not fall to be classified as a realised loss and therefore distributable reserves of the Company are £12.0m (1991 £81.5m) as analysed below:

	1992 £m	1991 £m
Profit and loss account	(264.8)	(246.7)
Provisions against investments in subsidiary entities		
Excess of provisions over surpluses on revaluation of investments in subsidiary entities	332.4	396.9
	(55.6)	(68.7)
Distributable reserves	12.0	81.5

19.130 In addition, the directors will not be able to use this consideration to justify treating a provision as unrealised unless the notes to the relevant accounts state that:

- The directors have considered the value of some of the company's fixed assets, without actually revaluing those assets.
- The directors' consideration of the value of those assets that have not been revalued took place at the same time as, and considered the values at the same date as, the revaluation that recognised the particular asset's diminution in value.
- The directors are satisfied that the aggregate value of those assets whose value they have considered was not less than the aggregate amount at which those assets are or were stated in the company's accounts.
- The asset or assets that have diminished in value are recorded in the company's relevant accounts after providing for that diminution in value.

[Sec 275(6)].

19.131 The examples below serve to illustrate the effect of section 275 in different situations.

Values of all a company's fixed assets

	Book value	Market value	Deficit
	£000	£000	£000
Land and buildings	1,000	750	250
Plant and machinery	50	40	10
	1,050	790	260

Example 1

The market value of all the fixed assets has been determined by a professional valuation. The diminutions in value may, therefore, be treated as unrealised losses, even though there is an overall deficit of £260,000. The reason for this is that the deficit results from a revaluation of all the fixed assets. [See 275(1)].

Example 2

The market value of the land and buildings has been determined by a professional valuation, but the market value of the plant and machinery results from the directors' consideration of its value. Because the aggregate value of the assets that the directors have considered is £40,000, which is less than their book value of £50,000, the directors cannot claim to be satisfied that those assets' aggregate value is not less than their book value. The directors are, therefore, not able to rely on the exception from section 275(1) and so they must treat the deficit on the revaluation of the land and buildings as well as the deficit on the plant and machinery as a realised loss. [Sec 275(5)]. However, if the directors had *valued* the assets rather than merely considering their value, both deficits would result from a revaluation of all the fixed assets and the diminutions in value would be treated as unrealised losses. [Sec 275(1)].

Example 3

If the directors considered that the plant and machinery's market value was £60,000 (not £40,000), then they would be able to treat the deficit on the land and buildings of £250,000 as unrealised. This applies even though the fixed assets have an overall deficit of £240,000.

However, in both the first and the third examples, if the company were a public company, it might still be prevented from making a distribution even if it could treat the loss as unrealised. This is because a distribution must not reduce the amount of a public company's net assets below the aggregate of its called-up share capital plus its undistributable reserves. [Sec 264(1)].

Interpreting section 275

19.132 The interpretation of the provisions of section 275 may cause difficulties in certain circumstances. The responses to the questions discussed below are based on guidance given by Counsel.

Question 1

Where a provision has been charged to realised profits, and it is subsequently released, does this restore the realised profits in question?

Where an asset has been either written down or provided against and it is then written up again, the initial reaction is that the write-up constitutes a profit that *prima facie* appears to be unrealised. However, it seems correct that the write-up should be treated as a realised

[The next page is 19043.]

profit to the extent that the previous reduction was charged to realised profits. (This view is supported by *Bishop v Smyrna and Cassaba Railway Co.* [1895] 2 Ch 596, in particular at 601, and by *Stapley v Read Bros.* [1924] 2 Ch 1.) Furthermore, paragraph 19(3) of Schedule 4 requires a company to write back such a provision no longer required to the profit and loss account. The write-back to the profit and loss account will fall to be treated as realised.

Question 2

In what order should releases of provisions be applied where provisions have been made in previous years, and where some of these have been treated as realised losses and some as unrealised losses?

The principle expressed above is easy enough to apply when all provisions have been charged against the same reserve and where the whole of a particular provision is restored at the same time. It seems that there is no established authority or principle that lays down any rule where the position is less simple. The best solution would seem to be to apply common sense. This approach leads to the conclusion that the more recent parts of the provision should normally be regarded as being released before the earlier parts.

Question 3

What is the meaning of the words 'value' and 'the company's accounts' in sections 275(4) and 275(5) respectively?

It seems clear that the word 'value' in section 275(4) means market value, and not book value.

The question arises whether the 'company's accounts' that are referred to in section 275(5), are those financial statements (to, say, 30 September 19X5), which are in the course of preparation, and in which the directors have adjusted the assets' book values (by taking into account depreciation, for example), or the previous financial statements (that is, those to 30 September 19X4).

When section 275(4) is relied on, section 275(6) deals with the contents of the note to the financial statements where the directors have considered the value of any of the company's fixed assets, without actually revaluing those assets. Section 275(6)(b) requires the notes to state:

> *"That they (the directors) are satisfied that the aggregate value of those assets at the time in question is or was not less than the aggregate amount at which they are or were for the time being stated in the company's accounts."*

This note makes it clear that the company's accounts for the purpose of section 275(5) are those in which the revaluation is incorporated. Thus the directors must compare actual values with the values at which the relevant assets are to be incorporated in the accounts.

This view is supported by the fact that the section 275(4) procedure, including the requirement for a section 275(6) note, applies also to *initial accounts* being prepared.

Question 4

If no dividend is to be paid by reference to the relevant accounts, but the directors have considered the value of the company's fixed assets in accordance with section 275(4), does section 275(6) require that the note that is needed if a distribution is to be made to be included in those relevant accounts?

Relevant accounts are those financial statements that contain the entries that justify a particular distribution, either because they show adequate distributable profits or because they have been specially prepared in order to justify the distribution. (This interpretation seems clear from section 270 generally and, in particular, from subsections (2) and (3) and the introductory words of sections 271(1), 272(1) and 273(1).)

Consequently, it appears to follow that, if a company does not propose to justify a particular distribution by reference to a particular set of financial statements, section 275(6) does not require those financial statements to contain the special note, because those financial statements are not *relevant accounts*.

Accordingly, it seems that the note that section 275(6) requires need not appear in the financial statements either for the year in which the section 275(4) revaluation took place, or for a subsequent year, unless those financial statements are to be relied upon for the purpose of justifying a distribution.

However, if the note is excluded from the financial statements, the directors cannot use those financial statements to justify a distribution in the future. Although the directors may have no plans at that time to make a distribution, they may wish to do so at some time before the next audited financial statements are prepared. If they have not included the note required by section 275(6) in their last set of financial statements, then they will need to prepare *interim accounts* to justify the proposed distribution. Consequently, it will be sensible to include in the financial statements the note that section 275(6) requires, even where the directors do not intend at that time to make a distribution.

However, for a private company, the note need not appear in the *interim* or the *initial accounts* that the directors rely upon to justify making a distribution. This is because sections 272 and 273 do not apply to private companies.

Question 5

Where the note that section 275(6) requires is not included in a company's financial statements, does this omission convert a provision on a revaluation that is made in those financial statements into a realised loss for all future financial statements that are to be used as relevant accounts?

It appears that any financial statements that are used to justify a distribution are *relevant accounts*. And, for the purposes of section 275(6), they are the relevant accounts, even if the directors do not need to rely on the particular section 275(4) revaluation in order to justify a current distribution. Accordingly, if a set of financial statements that does not contain a note relating to a section 275(4) revaluation that took place in either that year or a previous year, become *relevant accounts* (because they are used to justify a distribution), it seems that the provision that is made on that revaluation becomes, and must remain, a realised loss. Where it becomes necessary to rely on section 275(4) to justify a subsequent distribution, it will be too late to include the section 275(6) note in a subsequent set of financial statements.

This last point, however, is a difficult issue and it is still the subject of debate. Consequently, this is another reason why it is advisable to include in any financial statements the note that section 275(6) requires, even where a distribution is not to be made by reference to those financial statements.

Summary of action relating to section 275

19.133 To summarise, therefore, when the directors have some of the company's assets valued, and provisions for diminution in value arise that affect the company's ability to pay a dividend, the directors, after taking legal advice, may wish to:

- Consider the value as at the same date of all other assets (excluding goodwill) themselves at the same time that the valuation of the assets that shows the deficit is made.
- Include the note referred to in paragraph 19.130 above in the financial statements for the year in which the valuation took place. The directors should do this even if they do not intend to rely on their consideration of the value to justify a distribution.
- Repeat that note in all subsequent financial statements, because they may become *relevant accounts* for the purpose of making a distribution in the future.

If the directors take these three steps, any provisions that arise from a revaluation of the company's assets may be treated as unrealised for the purpose of ascertaining the profits available for distribution unless the value of the assets considered, but not revalued, by the directors is less than their book value. (see para 19.131 example 2).

Qualified audit reports and distributions

19.134 If the auditors have qualified their opinion and the company is proposing to pay a dividend based on those financial statements as the relevant accounts, the auditors must state in writing whether the subject matter of their qualification is material in determining the legality of the proposed distribution.

[Sec 271(3)(4), 273(4)(5)]. This statement must be laid before the company in general meeting. [Sec 271(4)]. A qualified audit report is a report that is not a report without qualification to the effect that, in the auditors' opinion, the financial statements have been properly prepared in accordance with the Act. [Sec 271(3), 273(5)].

19.135 Therefore, for an audit report that contains an explanatory paragraph referring to a fundamental uncertainty, but is unqualified, there would appear to be no legal requirement for the auditors to make a statement under section 271(4). However, in some instances, if there is a fundamental uncertainty about, for example, going concern, it may also be uncertain whether the directors would be acting in the best interests of the company if they pay a dividend and they would be wise to seek legal advice in such circumstances.

19.136 Many companies pay interim dividends and the annual financial statements that the auditors report on will constitute the *relevant accounts* for the purposes of those interim dividends. Accordingly, auditors should, whenever possible, word their statement to cover any future distributions. If the statement is not worded to cover future distributions but only covers the final dividend proposed in the annual financial statements, the auditors will need to make a further statement in respect of any interim dividends.

19.137 The implication of a qualified audit report may be either *favourable* or *unfavourable*. An audit qualification may be material for distribution purposes, but in a favourable sense. For example, it may be possible to say that if any adjustment was to be made to eliminate the need for the qualification, it could have the effect only of increasing the company's net assets or realised profits. In this situation, the qualification is regarded as *favourable* for distribution purposes. An *unfavourable* qualification means that the profits available for distribution could be less than the amount shown in the financial statements.

19.138 Where the effect of the auditors' qualification is *favourable,* the auditors could include the following additional statement in their report:

> *"In our opinion, the qualification is not material for the purpose of determining whether any distribution payable by reference to these financial statements is permitted under Sections 263 (and 264 for public companies only) of the Companies Act 1985."*

19.139 Where the auditors can quantify the effect of an audit qualification that is *unfavourable* but not material for the purpose of determining a distribution up to a certain amount, they could word the additional statement in their report as follows:

"In our opinion, the qualification is not material for the purpose of determining whether distributions not exceeding £X in total payable by reference to these financial statements are permitted under Sections 263 (and 264 for public companies only) of the Companies Act 1985."

19.140 If the auditors can word their statement on these lines and not restrict it to the legality of the proposed final dividend only, they will not need to make a further statement in respect of the next interim dividend. If, however, the auditors do have to make a further statement, the company will have to hold a general meeting to lay the statement before the shareholders.

Other matters

Bonus issues

19.141 Companies can use the revaluation reserve in order to issue bonus shares. In this situation, the revaluation reserve would be debited with the nominal value of the shares issued and the share capital would be credited with an equivalent amount.

19.142 Section 264(3) of the Act defines a company's undistributable reserves as including *"the amount by which the company's accumulated unrealised profits, so far as not previously utilised by capitalisation ... exceed its accumulated, unrealised losses (so far as not previously written off in a reduction or reorganisation of capital duly made)"*. Capitalisation is defined as including every description of capitalisation except a transfer of the company's profits to its capital redemption reserve on or after 22 December 1980. This definition implies that a company may utilise its undistributable reserves, such as a revaluation reserve, for bonus issues. In addition, there is no specific provision in the Act that requires the revaluation reserve to be reinstated if it has been utilised in a manner the law permits.

19.143 Companies may not make bonus issues unless their articles of association expressly permit them to do so. Therefore, newly-incorporated companies must take express power in their articles to make bonus issues out of unrealised profits (for example, as detailed in article 110 of Table A). However, companies that existed before 22 December 1980 need not alter their articles to do this if immediately before that date they had power under their articles to capitalise unrealised profits. With companies that existed at 22 December 1980, this means that a power in the articles to make bonus issues out of profits available for dividend will be deemed to include a power to make bonus issues out of unrealised profits. [Sec 278].

Amounts unpaid on debentures and shares

19.144 A company may not apply an unrealised profit to pay up debentures or any amounts that are unpaid on its issued shares. [Sec 263(4)]. The purpose of this prohibition is to prevent profits that are not available for distribution being made available indirectly for dividend purposes.

Profits and losses made before 22 December 1980

19.145 The commencement date of the 1980 Companies Act was 22 December 1980. This Act introduced statutory distribution rules including concepts of realised and unrealised profits, for the first time. As a result, transitional measures were required.

19.146 Where, after making all reasonable enquiries, the directors are unable to determine whether a profit or a loss that was made before 22 December 1980 is realised or unrealised, they may treat the profit as realised and the loss as unrealised. [Sec 263(5)]. This provision prevents problems occurring if no record exists of the original cost of an asset or the amount of a liability.

Memorandum and articles of association

19.147 Distributions are not only influenced by the provisions of the Act: they may also be subject to any enactment, or any rule of law or any provision in the memorandum or articles of association that may restrict either the amounts available for distribution or the circumstances in which a distribution may be made. [Sec 281]. For example, investment companies are restricted by their memorandum and articles of association from distributing realised capital profits.

19.148 It is important, therefore, for the directors to have regard to the memorandum and articles, as well as to the statutory rules, before making a distribution. Also, it would probably be unlawful as a matter of general law to pay a dividend if, as a result, the company either became insolvent, or had insufficient working capital to carry on its business in the foreseeable future.

Distributions in kind

19.149 A company may make a distribution that includes or comprises a non-cash asset. Where the asset to be distributed has been included in the relevant accounts, and part of the amount at which it is stated represents an unrealised profit, the Act allows that profit to be treated as realised for the purpose of the distribution.

[Sec 276(a)]. However, the company's articles must contain a power to make such distributions. Table A contains this power in article 105, and it requires the dividend to be approved at a general meeting. The dividend is declared as a cash amount, and it is for the directors to satisfy themselves as to the asset's value.

19.150 The directors may have difficulty in determining a value to be placed on the asset that is being distributed. They could value the asset that is being distributed at its fair value in order to show the dividend at its fair value. The asset's fair value would, in most situations, be its open market value and the asset should, therefore, be valued at arm's length. Consequently, a surplus or a deficit (which is the difference between the asset's net book value and its fair value) may have to be accounted for in the company's financial statements. Any deficit would be reflected in the company's profit and loss account as an amount written off investments. A surplus would be taken to revaluation reserve. The amount taken to revaluation reserve may then be transferred to profit and loss account as a 'transfer from reserves' after the format line 'profit for the financial year', and the full fair value of the distribution would then be reflected as a demerger dividend.

19.151 In practice, book values are often used to value the asset that is being distributed. For example, in a demerger of a subsidiary, the parent company may record a demerger dividend in specie at an amount equal to the book value of the investment and the group may record the same dividend in specie at the amount of the net assets of the subsidiary at the date of the demerger. For example, Pearson recorded the demerger of Royal Doulton at different values in the company and in the group. (See Table 19.8).

Table 19.8 – Pearson plc – Annual Report & Accounts – 31 December 1993

Notes on the accounts (extract)

20 Notes on the company balance sheet (extract)

The company demerger dividend *in specie* of £134.2 million is the historical cost of the investment in Royal Doulton.

The group demerger dividend *in specie* of £111.8 million is the net assets of Royal Doulton at the date of demerger and goodwill written back on disposal.

19.152 The company should not show the dividend as a deduction from reserves, because paragraph 3(7)(b) of Schedule 4 to the Act requires it to be shown in the company's profit and loss account.

Liability for an unlawful distribution

19.153 Any shareholder of a company who receives an unlawful distribution is liable to repay it to the company if, at the time he received it, he knew, or he had reasonable grounds to believe, that it was made in contravention of the Act. [Sec 277(1)]. This provision is without prejudice to any other liability of a shareholder to repay distributions that have been unlawfully made to him. [Sec 277(2)]. In addition, if the directors make an unlawful distribution they may be in breach of their fiduciary duties to the company.

19.154 Even where a distribution has been made that is apparently permitted by the relevant accounts, the directors may be personally liable in respect of payments made out of undistributable reserves. This situation may arise where the company makes a distribution that is covered by the distributable reserves shown in the last relevant accounts, but the company no longer has distributable reserves because they have been consumed by losses the company has made since those accounts were drawn up.

19.155 If the company subsequently goes into liquidation, the liquidator could apply to the court for an order to compel the directors to compensate the company for their having misapplied the company's property by making the unlawful distribution. The directors should not only refer to the relevant accounts when they authorise a dividend: they should also take into account the company's results since the date on which those accounts were drawn up.

Aveling Barford

19.156 The judgment given by Hoffmann J in *Aveling Barford v Perion Ltd and others* [1989] BCLC 626 is relevant to transactions not undertaken at market value. In that case, the plaintiff company sold property at considerably less than its fair value to a company controlled by the company's sole shareholder at the time when it had no distributable reserves. In delivering his judgment, the judge stated that:

> *"The sale to Perion was not a genuine exercise of the company's power under its memorandum to sell its assets. It was a sale at a gross undervalue for the purpose of enabling a profit to be realised by an entity controlled and put forward by its sole beneficial shareholder. This was as much a dressed-up distribution as the payment of excessive interest in Ridge Securities or excessive remuneration in Halt Garage. The company had at the time no distributable reserves and the sale was therefore ultra vires and incapable of validation by the approval or ratification by the shareholder."*

19.157 In this case, since the company had large negative reserves, it was not in a position to make a distribution. The sale of property was at a significant undervalue and as the company had no distributable reserves, the sale effectively amounted to an unauthorised return of capital.

19.157.1 Company distribution rules are dealt with in section 270 of the Act. There is an argument that the Act does not permit any transfer of an asset at book value which constitutes a distribution to take place unless the asset is first written up to its full value and section 276 applies. The contrary view is that a transfer may take place at book value provided care is taken to avoid an unlawful reduction of capital (see 19.157.2 below). This is a complex area where legal advice should be sought.

19.157.2 The Aveling Barford case confirmed that where a company undertakes a transaction at an undervalue at a time when the company has no distributable reserves (or inadequate reserves to cover the shortfall), this amounts to an unlawful reduction in capital. It follows that the transaction is incapable of validation by the approval of, or ratification by, the shareholders. The Aveling Barford case does not discuss the effects of the distribution of provisions of the Act.

19.157.3 A transfer of an asset at a consideration less than its proper value will *prima facie* involve a breach of duty by the directors and the transferor company. But for certain transfers between group companies this might not be so. This may be the case where, for example, the transferor and transferee are UK companies within the same group and wholly owned, the objects of the transferor company allow assets to be disposed of for such a consideration as is thought fit, the transfer is approved by the shareholders of the transferor company and the transaction does not place in any doubt the solvency of any of the parties to it.

[The next paragraph is 19.158.]

19.158 The implications of the Aveling Barford ruling can be summarised as follows:

- Where an asset is transferred at an undervalue for a consideration that is less than its book value when the transferor company does not have sufficient distributable profits to cover the undervalue, then this amounts to an unlawful reduction of capital.

- Where an asset is transferred at an undervalue, but for a consideration at least equal to its book value (such that the transfer does not affect the transferor company's distributable reserves) it is sufficient that the transferor company has some distributable reserves.

- Where an asset is transferred for a consideration less than its market value but equal to or above book value at a time when the transferor company has accumulated losses that exceed the difference between the book value and the transfer value, this amounts to an unlawful reduction of capital because the surplus on realisation of the asset will be insufficient to make good the accumulated losses.

- If a transfer takes place for consideration of more than the market value of the asset, the company receiving the asset must have distributable reserves at least equal to the excess of the consideration over the market value. These distributable reserves would need to be sufficient to allow the asset to be written down to its market value and still leave the company with distributable reserves.

19.159 In addition, depending on the circumstances, the provisions of section 151 of the Act or section 238 of the Insolvency Act 1986 may apply to transactions not at market value if carried out in connection with the acquisition of its shares. Section 151 prohibits a company from giving financial assistance for the acquisition of its own shares. The prohibition does not apply to a lawful dividend. [Sec 153(3)]. Section 238 of the Insolvency Act 1986 applies if an administration order is made in relation to the company or the company goes into liquidation and permits the liquidator or administrator to apply to the court to have a transaction at undervalue (which would include the payment of a dividend) set aside.

19.160 The company law consequences are dependent on the precise circumstances of each situation. In addition to the issues discussed above, a transaction not at market value may also have one or more of the following company law consequences as it may be:

- Ultra vires.
- In breach of the directors' fiduciary duties.
- A fraud on the minority.

19.161 Directors of both the vendor and purchaser companies should, therefore, obtain proper advice as to the value of the assets, as well as appropriate legal advice, before they decide upon implementing a transaction that may not be at market value if the companies involved do not have sufficient distributable reserves. This advice should be obtained even if the vendor and purchaser are wholly-owned members of the same group.

19.162 Examples of typical transactions not undertaken at market value include the following:

- The sale of an asset at an undervalue.

- The purchase of an asset at an overvalue – for example, the transfer of a subsidiary intra-group without warranties and indemnities normally given on third party sales and purchases.

- Book/tax written down value transfers where these do not correspond to market value.

- Sale for debt in certain circumstances, for example, where the debt is not repayable on demand and does not bear interest, or where the purchaser does not have a realistic prospect of settling the debt.

- Capitalising or subordinating debt.

- Waivers of debt.

- Capital contributions – UK company law is silent about such contributions, but essentially these are gifts.

- Interest-free loans or loans with excessive rates of interest.

- Non-payment for the surrender of group relief and ACT.

- Assumption of an inherent tax liability under the Taxation of Capital Gains Act 1992, section 171 – when an asset is transferred by one member of a capital gains group to another member, the transferee inherits the transferor's base cost and, therefore, is liable to corporation tax on the increase in value of the asset that accrued during the transferor's period of ownership.

Chapter 20

Contingencies, commitments and post balance sheet events

Page

Chapter 20

Contingencies, commitments and post balance sheet events

Introduction

20.1 The accounting treatment and disclosure of significant contingencies (such as litigation) or post balance sheet events (such as a major restructuring) can be of critical importance to users in assessing a company's state of affairs. However, there are particular difficulties in dealing with these. The outcome of contingencies is dependent on uncertain future events and this necessitates the use of estimates. Also, in many cases the details are commercially sensitive. Significant post balance sheet events have to be distinguished between those that require inclusion in the reported figures and those that require disclosure. The appropriate level of disclosure is often a matter for judgement and may involve the use of pro-forma figures.

20.2 The principal accounting and disclosure requirements in relation to contingencies and post balance sheet events have been contained in two SSAPs; namely SSAP 18, 'Accounting for contingencies' (but see next paragraph) and SSAP 17, 'Accounting for post balance sheet events', together with paragraph 50 of Schedule 4 to the Act, which deals with commitments and contingent liabilities. In addition, Schedule 7 to the Act specifies the disclosures required in the directors' report concerning post balance sheet events.

20.3 In September 1998, the ASB issued FRS 12, 'Provisions, contingent liabilities and contingent assets'. This supersedes SSAP 18 and is effective for accounting periods ending on or after 23 March 1999. The following sections look at the accounting and disclosure requirements under SSAP-17 and SSAP 18. The new rules on provisions and contingencies in FRS 12 are summarised in chapter 17.

Contingencies

20.4 The accounting treatment and disclosure of contingencies is governed by Schedule 4 paragraph 50(2) to the Act and SSAP 18. A contingency is defined by SSAP 18 as *"...a condition which exists at the balance sheet date, where the outcome will be confirmed only on the occurrence or non-occurrence of one or more uncertain future events. A contingent gain or loss is a gain or loss dependent on a contingency"*. [SSAP 18, para 14].

20.5 The Act requires that where a contingent liability exists that has not been provided for in the financial statements, the notes must disclose:

- The amount, or estimated amount of that liability.
- Its legal nature.
- Whether any valuable security has been provided by the company in connection with that liability. Where this is so, details of the security provided must be given.

[4 Sch 50(2)].

20.6 It should be noted that the disclosure requirements under Schedule 4 paragraph 50(2) relate to contingencies other than those that result from a charge on the company's assets to secure the liabilities of any other person (that is, guarantees). The disclosures that are required in respect of guarantees are discussed in paragraph 20.33 below.

20.7 The accounting treatment of a contingent liability under SSAP 18 depends on whether the expected outcome is probable, possible or remote. Where it is *probable* that a future event will confirm a loss that can be estimated with reasonable accuracy at the date on which the board of directors approves the financial statements, a provision should be made. Where it is *possible* that a loss will arise, disclosure should be given by way of a footnote. If the likelihood of loss is *remote* no disclosure is required.

20.8 Contingent gains should not be accrued in the financial statements. A material contingent gain should be disclosed in the financial statements only if it is probable that the gain will be realised. [SSAP 18 para 17].

20.9 The accounting treatment of contingencies is summarised in the following table:

Summary of accounting treatment of contingencies

	Accounting treatment	
Probability of outcome	*Contingent gain*	*Contingent Loss*
Reasonably certain	Accrue	Accrue
Probable	Disclose	Accrue
Possible	Do not disclose	Disclose
Remote	Do not disclose	Do not disclose

20.10 To comply with SSAP 18, the notes to the financial statements must state:

- The nature of the contingency.
- The uncertainties that are expected to affect the ultimate outcome.

- A prudent estimate of the financial effect, or a statement that such an estimate is not practicable. For this purpose, the amount to be disclosed is the potential financial effect (before taking account of taxation) after deducting any amounts accrued and the amounts of any contingencies that have only a remote possibility of loss.

[SSAP 18 paras 18, 19, 20].

Accounting estimates

20.11 The explanatory note to SSAP 18 (para 1) states that it is not intended that uncertainties connected with accounting estimates should fall within the standard's scope. Hence the following estimates that are necessarily inherent in drawing up financial statements are not normally regarded as being contingencies:

- The lives of fixed assets.
- The amount of bad debts.
- The net realisable value of inventories.
- The expected outcome of long-term contracts.
- The valuation of properties.
- The value of foreign currency balances.

Practical considerations

Gross or net presentation

20.12 In situations where a contingent liability exists, but there are related counter claims or claims against a third party (for example, insurance claims), it is normally appropriate to reduce any accrual, or the amount to be disclosed in the notes to the financial statements, by taking into account the probable outcome of such claims. [SSAP 18 para 6]. It will be necessary, however, to separately assess the likely success and probable amount of the claim and counter claim respectively. Separate disclosure may be required depending on the circumstances. For example, it would be necessary to assess whether an insurance claim was recoverable.

20.13 Once the liability ceases to be contingent (because, for example, a claim has been agreed), the normal recognition rules will apply. Hence in such circumstances, it will only be appropriate to offset assets and liabilities if the offset conditions of FRS 5 paragraph 29 are met (see further chapter 4).

20.14 There is an argument that the offset rules contained in FRS 5 should also be applied to contingencies that are either accrued or disclosed in the notes to the financial statements; such that contingent assets and contingent liabilities are not offset unless the FRS 5 conditions are met. However FRS 5 states that *"where a transaction falls within the scope of both the FRS (FRS 5) and another accounting standard or statute,* *whichever contains the more specific provisions should be applied"*. [FRS 5 para 43]. For this reason we consider that the provisions of SSAP 18 should be followed in relation to contingencies. It may, therefore, be appropriate to offset related claims in determining the amount to be accrued or disclosed as a contingent liability depending on the circumstances.

20.15 An example of where it is not appropriate to offset an anticipated recovery under an insurance programme is in relation to investigation and compensation in respect of pension transfers and opt outs. FRAG 2/95 'Pension transfers and opt outs' issued by the ICAEW states that:

> *"Any anticipated recovery should be disclosed separately as an asset and not offset against the provision, in accordance with the requirements of FRS 5."* [FRAG 2/95 para 26].

20.16 It should be noted that SSAP 18 is superseded by FRS 12 (effective for accounting periods ending on or after 23 March 1999). This requires a liability and any anticipated reimbursement (such as an amount recoverable from an insurance company) to be recognised separately. Offset is allowed only where the reporting entity no longer has an obligation for the part of the expenditure that is to be met by the third party.

Contingent or actual liability

20.17 When considering whether a liability is contingent or actual, FRS 5 provides some guidance to assist in this. FRS 5 defines liabilities as:

> *"An entity's obligations to transfer economic benefits as a result of past transactions or events."* [FRS 5 para 4].

20.18 An entity, therefore, has a liability if it has an obligation that will result in an outflow of funds. Such an obligation will exist if the entity is unable to avoid either legally or commercially an outflow of benefits. [FRS 5 para 18]. Where an entity's obligation is contingent on the outcome of one or more uncertain future events, a liability should not necessarily be recognised. [FRS 5 para 58].

20.19 The ASB's draft statement of principles states that where the amount or timing of a liability, or the identity of the party to which the obligation is owed, is subject to a significant degree of uncertainty it is usual to report the estimated amount as a provision for the liability. [DSP chp 3 para 23]. However, it goes on to say that:

> *"Obligations that are not expected to result in a transfer of economic benefits such as the guarantee of another entity's debt where that entity is expected to remain solvent are also liabilities, although they may not be recognised in financial statements"*. [DSP chp 3 para 24].

20.20 How obligations which are not expected to result in a transfer of economic benefits meet the ASB's definition of a liability is *prima facie* unclear. However, it does seem clear that such obligations will, in general, meet the SSAP 18 definition of a contingency and should, therefore, be disclosed as such, unless the amounts are immaterial.

20.21 A useful distinction between liabilities and contingent liabilities is made in a recent IFAC Public Sector Committee publication, *'Accounting for and reporting liabilities'*, which states:

> *"What distinguishes a liability from a contingency is the uncertainty related to its existence. It is not simply uncertainty in and of itself that distinguishes a contingent liability from a liability as there may be considerable uncertainty about the measurement of certain liabilities. Indeed, some liabilities can be measured only by using a substantial degree of estimation, such as liabilities for pension obligations. But in that case, it is the measurement of the existing obligation that involves certain assumptions and estimation. In the case of a contingency, it is the event or events creating the obligation that is uncertain, in addition to any measurement uncertainty."*

20.22 To summarise:

- If the entity has a known obligation to transfer economic benefits as a result of past transactions or events, this represents an actual liability and will be reported as a creditor.

- If the entity has an obligation to transfer economic benefits as a result of past transactions or events, the timing or amount of which is uncertain, then the estimated amount will be reported as a provision for the liability.

- If the entity may have an obligation to transfer economic benefits as a result of past transactions or events, the existence of which is uncertain, then this represents a contingent liability and is treated in accordance with SSAP 18 as discussed in paragraph 20.8 above.

Litigation claims

20.23 Except where it is not practicable (and that fact is disclosed) SSAP 18 requires disclosure of an estimate of the financial effect of a contingency. [SSAP 18 para 18]. For contingent losses, the SSAP states that the disclosure of the potential financial effect should be reduced by any amounts accrued and by the amounts of any components where the possibility of loss is remote, with only the net amount required to be disclosed. [SSAP 18 para 19]. A particular application of such a contingency is litigation claims. An example of disclosure of the potential financial effect of a contingent loss arising from a legal claim is given in Table 20.1, which discloses the amount of the claim against a company but which goes on to say that the board believes that the company has good defences to the claim.

> **Table 20.1 – Tarmac PLC – Annual Report – 31 December 1996**
>
> **Note to the Accounts (extract)**
>
> **23 Contingent liabilities (extract)**
>
> At 31st December 1996 the Group had a 20 per cent interest in the Transmanche-Link ("TML") joint venture, which is in the course of proceedings before the panel constituted under the terms of the contract for construction of the Channel Tunnel to rule on claims between the contractor (TML) and Eurotunnel, as employer. Eurotunnel has claimed the equivalent of approximately £980 million from TML in relation to the procurement of rolling stock for the Channel Tunnel and the panel ruling is expected in the second quarter of the year. On the basis of legal advice received, the Board believes that TML has good defences to the claims and also that it has valid counterclaims against Eurotunnel.
>
> The Group is the subject of certain other legal proceedings which are regarded as unlikely to succeed or to have a material effect on the Group's financial position.

20.24 Preparers of financial statements may consider disclosure of a litigation claim to be potentially prejudicial to the claim's outcome. However, where the facts are such that the directors are able to state that in their opinion the claim's outcome will not have a significant effect on the company's financial position, it may not be necessary to disclose the amount of the potential financial effect. An example of an instance where this form of disclosure has been used is British Airways as illustrated in Table 20.2 below.

> **Table 20.2 – British Airways Plc – Report and Accounts – 31 March 1995**
>
> **Notes to the accounts (extract)**
>
> **33 LITIGATION**
>
> **a** A number of legal claims have been made against the Company by Virgin Atlantic Airways Limited. Having regard to legal advice received, and in all the circumstances, the Directors are of the opinion that these claims will not give rise to liabilities which will in the aggregate have a material effect on these accounts.
>
> **b** There are a number of further identified legal and other claims which emanate from international airline operations and other activities of the Group for which the Directors have made what they believe is appropriate provision.
>
> **c** In addition, experience with litigation and regulation has led the Directors to conclude that it is prudent to continue to carry forward £22 million of a provision made in prior years.

20.25 In situations where it is not practicable to disclose an estimate of the financial effect of the outcome of a contingent liability, that fact must be disclosed. In addition, details of the nature of the contingency and the uncertainties expected to affect the outcome should be given. An example of such disclosure is given in Table 20.5 on page 9 where NFC refers to a potential material adverse effect resulting from federal taxes.

Bills of exchange

20.26 Often companies receive bills of exchange from their customers in respect of trade debtor balances and subsequently discount them with banks. Before FRS 5, such a company would most probably have accounted for this by transferring the amount from debtors to cash, and by charging the discount to the profit and loss account. Where the bank had recourse to the company, in the event the customer did not honour the bill on maturity, the company would have noted this as a contingent liability.

20.27 Under the provisions of FRS 5, however, where such a bill is discounted with a bank and the bank has full recourse to the company, then the company has not transferred all the significant risks related to the payment from the debtor. Therefore, following the standard, the debt should remain on the company's balance sheet and the cash received for discounting the bill should also be shown as an asset with a corresponding liability for the finance provided (with recourse) by the bank. The treatment of bills of exchange is discussed further in chapter 17.

Taxation

20.28 SSAP 15, 'Accounting for deferred tax', requires that deferred tax should be accounted for to the extent that it is probable that a liability or asset will crystallise. [SSAP 15 para 25]. The ASC obtained legal advice that unprovided deferred tax is a contingent liability, except where the prospect of it becoming payable is too remote that it does not amount to a contingent liability at all. [SSAP 15 para 53].

20.29 In addition, where the potential amount of deferred tax on an asset that has been revalued is not shown (because the revaluation does not constitute a timing difference), this fact (but not necessarily the amount) should be stated in the financial statements (see further chapter 13).

20.30 Similarly, where the value of an asset is shown in a note to the financial statements (because it differs materially from its book amount), the note should show the tax effects, if any, that would arise if the asset were realised at that value at the balance sheet date. [SSAP 15 para 42]. In this situation 'tax effect' means that the potential amount of tax should be disclosed. An example of the disclosures made in practice is illustrated in Table 20.4 below.

Table 20.3 – Tarmac PLC – Annual Report 1996 – 31 December 1996

Notes to the Accounts (extract)

21 Deferred taxation (extract)

No provision has been made for any taxation which may arise in the event of any assets which are included in the accounts at a figure in excess of their original cost being realised at that higher figure. These assets are held for the purposes of the Group's business and, as regards those owned by undertakings located in the UK, it is considered that any notional liability which might arise on their disposal would be subject to deferment under the provisions of the Taxation of Chargeable Gains Act 1992 (S.152). As a result of the provisions of that Act (S.35), it is anticipated that the notional liability so deferred would be minimal in most cases. It is unlikely that such deferment would be available in respect of assets held by undertakings located outside the UK. The amount of notional liability to taxation cannot readily be calculated but would not exceed £10.0 million (1995 – £10.0 million).

20.31 Accounting for deferred taxation is considered in more detail in chapter 13.

20.32 Examples of disclosure of contingent liabilities is respect of disputes with tax authorities are given in Tables 20.4 and 20.5. Racal Electronics discloses details of a dispute with the Inland Revenue and quantifies the amount that the company may be liable to pay if it loses its appeal. NFC discloses details of a potential liability due to an unresolved ruling from the US Internal Revenue Service. It is unable to quantify the effect, but warns that it may have a material adverse effect if the ruling goes against the company.

Table 20.4 – Racal Electronics Plc – Annual Report and Accounts – 31 March 1996

Notes on the financial statements (extract)

33 CONTINGENT LIABILITIES (extract)

On appeal the High Court found in favour of the Inland Revenue in the dispute over the deductibility of certain payments made in connection with the buy-out minority interests in Racal Cellular Limited in 1986. Leading Tax Counsel has advised the Company that it has strong grounds for appealing this decision. Accordingly the Company has appealed and no provision has been made in respect of this matter. If the dispute was finally determined in favour of the Inland Revenue, the Company would become liable to pay in the order of £12 million.

Table 20.5 – NFC plc – Annual Report and Accounts – 30 September 1996

Notes to the accounts (extract)

22 CONTINGENT LIABILITIES (extract)

In December 1992, the US Internal Revenue Service issued a private letter ruling that sub-contractors engaged as truck providers and drivers by Merchants Home Delivery Service, Inc should be classified as employees and, therefore, should be subject to federal income and other payroll taxes. In January 1996, the US Internal Revenue Service withdrew its ruling citing significant unresolved and conflicting facts making it inappropriate to rule on the case at the present time. The employment status of a different segment of sub-contractors is also being examined by the Internal Revenue Service. NFC is unable at this time to quantify its potential liability, if any, for such federal taxes. Failure by NFC to prevail could have a material adverse effect on the Group's results.

Guarantees

20.33 The notes to the financial statements must give details of:

- Any charge on the company's assets that has been given in order to secure the liabilities of any other person.
- The amounts so secured (where practicable).

[4 Sch 50(1)].

Borrowings

20.34 Examples of guarantees that are required to be disclosed as contingent liabilities often include situations where a company has guaranteed the borrowings of a subsidiary or an associated undertaking irrespective of whether a charge over the company's assets has been given by way of security. Where a loss is foreseen, a liability will need to be recognised in the financial statements, being the estimated amount of the loss that is expected to arise.

20.35 Therefore, where, for example, a company has guaranteed a subsidiary's overdraft to the extent of £10 million by way of a charge on the company's assets, the actual overdraft of the subsidiary at the year end should be disclosed (up to a maximum, in this situation, of £10 million). If the overdraft outstanding at the balance sheet date was less than £10 million, disclosure of the maximum amount guaranteed, that is £10 million, as well as the actual amount outstanding at the balance sheet date would be required.

20.36 In addition to the requirement to disclose details of any charge on the company's assets, paragraph 50(2) of Schedule 4 to the Act (other contingent liabilities) requires the notes to disclose whether any valuable security has been provided.

20.37 Examples of disclosures made in relation to guarantees are shown in Tables 20.6 to 20.8 below.

Table 20.6 – Inchcape plc – Annual Report and Accounts – 31 December 1996

Notes to the accounts (extract)

11 Contingent liabilities (extract)

The company has given guarantees in respect of various subsidiaries' bank facilities totalling £354.2m at 31 December 1996 (1995 – £326.0m). £17.5m (1995 – £nil) has been drawn against these facilities. Other guarantees, mainly in respect of associated companies, amounted to £91.6m (1995 – £35.9m).

Table 20.7 – British Aerospace Public Limited Company – Annual Report – 31 December 1994

Contingent Liabilities and Operating Lease Commitments (extract)

Contingent liabilities (extract)

The Group's investment in the Orionsat project gives rise to gross contingent liabilities under a guarantee structure of £105 million (1993 £118 million). The Orion satellite was successfully launched on 29th November, 1994 and entered into commercial operation on 20th January, 1995. The Directors are of the opinion that no material loss will arise under this guarantee structure.

At 31st December, 1993 the Company had provided bank guarantees of £156 million arising from the Company's investment in Hutchison Telecommunications (UK) Limited. During the year, these guarantees were replaced by a £247 million interest bearing shareholder loan by the Company to Hutchison Telecommunications (UK) Limited. The Company is committed to provide up to approximately £30 million of further funding through the remaining investment phase of the Orange mobile phone business.

Table 20.8 – B.A.T Industries p.l.c. – Directors' Report and Accounts – 31 December 1996

Notes on the accounts (extract)

40 Contingent liabilities and financial commitments (extract)

B.A.T Industries has guaranteed borrowings by subsidiary undertakings of **£2,594 million** 1995 £2,766 million and borrowing facilities of **£4,489 million** 1995 £4,910 million which were not utilised at the balance sheet date. Performance guarantees given to third parties in respect of Group companies were **£103 million** 1995 £140 million.

Employee share ownership plans (ESOPs)

20.38 Prior to the publication, in June 1995, of UITF Abstract 13, 'Accounting for employee share ownership plans', where a company had guaranteed the external borrowings of its ESOP trust (in order to enable the trust to purchase shares) this was typically disclosed as a guarantee by way of a footnote.

20.39 To meet the requirements of UITF Abstract 13, in most instances, such borrowings will instead now need to be recognised in the sponsoring company's financial statements. The requirements of UITF Abstract 13 are considered further in chapter 4.

Complex guarantees

20.40 The required accounting treatment and disclosures in respect of straightforward guarantees are generally clear. However, considerable care is needed in considering the substance of more complex arrangements in order to determine the appropriate accounting treatment.

20.41 In certain circumstances, the commercial effect of a guarantee may give rise to liabilities that are required to be recognised in the financial statements.

Example

A company finds a customer some equipment. The company buys the equipment and sells it to a third party, which grants an operating lease to the customer. The third party has recourse to the company for the rentals if the customer were to become insolvent, but the company has no obligation to purchase the equipment at the end of the operating lease.

Under FRS 5, the substance of the transaction appears to be that the company has disposed of the residual, but has kept the risks relating to the operating lease rentals. The company should de-recognise the equipment asset (and it could take a dealer's profit on the sale to the third party). However, it should recognise an asset and a liability in respect of the operating lease rentals. The matched asset would be shown in debtors. The matched asset and the liability would reduce to zero over the period of the operating lease.

20.42 From the above examples it can be seen that the treatment of guarantees can be complex, particularly where assets or liabilities were previously recognised in the financial statements. This is discussed in more detail in chapter 4.

Commitments

General

20.43 The Act requires the notes to the financial statements to disclose details, where practicable, of:

- Capital commitments.
- Pension commitments.
- Other financial commitments.

[4 Sch 50(3)-(5)].

Capital commitments

20.44 Where practicable details must be disclosed of the aggregate amount or estimated amount of capital expenditure contracted for, but not provided for, at the balance sheet date. It is no longer necessary to disclose the aggregate amount or estimated amount of capital expenditure authorised by the directors, but not contracted for, at the balance sheet date. [4 Sch 50(3) as amended by SI 1996/189].

20.45 In circumstances where a business is highly capital intensive and the capital commitments are of particular significance in the context of the financial statements as a whole, it may be considered appropriate to provide more information as to the extent and nature of the commitments. An example of the more detailed disclosures made by British Airways is illustrated below in Table 20.9.

Table 20.9 – British Airways Plc – Report & Accounts – 31 March 1997

Notes to the accounts (extract)

15 CAPITAL EXPENDITURE COMMITMENTS

Capital expenditure authorised and contracted for but not provided in the accounts amounts to £3,030 million for the Group (1996: £3,788 million) and £2,871 million for the Company (1996: £3,788 million).

The outstanding commitments include £2,539 million which relates to the acquisition of Boeing 747-400 and Boeing 777 aircraft scheduled for delivery during the next four years and £255 million which relates to the acquisition of Boeing 757-200 and Boeing 737-300 aircraft scheduled for delivery during the next year. It is intended that these aircraft will be financed partially by cash holdings and internal cash flow and partially through external financing, including committed facilities arranged prior to delivery.

> At March 31, 1997 British Airways had an unused long term secured aircraft financing facility of US$2.31 billion and unused overdraft and revolving credit facilities of £40 million, and undrawn uncommitted money market lines of £229 million and US$45 million with a number of banks. In addition, British Airways had arranged a £150 million bank-guaranteed facility from the European Investment Bank to assist in funding the airline's ongoing longhaul fleet replacement programme.
>
> The Group's holdings of cash and short-term loans and deposits, together with committed funding facilities and net cash flow, are sufficient to cover the full cost of all firm aircraft deliveries due in the next two years.

Pension commitments

20.46 The notes to the financial statements must give details of:

- Any pension commitments included under any provision shown in the company's balance sheet.
- Pension commitments that have not been provided.

20.47 Such commitments in relation to pensions payable to past directors of the company must be separately disclosed. [4 Sch 50(4)]. This principally relates to unfunded pension arrangements.

20.48 The Act does not specify the basis a company should use to measure pension costs or pension commitments that it has not provided for. However extensive guidance is given by SSAP 24 and, except in relation to disclosure of any commitments to pay pensions to past directors, compliance with SSAP 24 is considered to be sufficient to meet the Act's requirements. The provisions of SSAP 24 are considered in chapter 12.

20.49 In addition UITF Abstract 6, 'Accounting for post-retirement benefits other than pensions', noted that where employers had not yet applied SSAP 24 to post-retirement benefits other than pensions, and, therefore, these had not been recognised as a liability, such obligations would constitute financial commitments required to be disclosed under paragraph 50(5) of Schedule 4 to the Act (see para 20.50 below). It should be noted, however, that UITF 6 requires SSAP 24 principles to be applied for accounting periods ending on or after 23 December 1994. The application of SSAP 24 principles to post-retirement benefits is discussed further in chapter 12.

Other financial commitments

20.50 The Act requires details to be disclosed of any other financial commitments which:

- Have not been provided for.
- Are relevant to assessing the company's state of affairs.

[4 Sch 50(5)].

20.51 However, the Act does not define financial commitments nor does it give guidance as to the nature of the commitments that are required to be disclosed.

20.52 Part 4 of SSAP 21 sets out the Act's requirements that are relevant to the standard's application. The legal requirements referred to include paragraph 50(5) of Schedule 4 to the Act thereby implying that a commitment under a lease is an example of an 'other financial commitment'.

20.53 Chapter 2 of the ASB's draft Statement of principles, 'The qualitative characteristics of financial statements', provides some further guidance, insofar as it considers what information would generally be regarded as being relevant in the context of financial reporting. It states *"Information has the quality of relevance when it has the ability to influence the decisions of users by helping them evaluate past, present or future events or by confirming, or correcting, their past evaluations"*. [DSP chp 2 para 8].

20.54 On this basis, commitments such as short-term purchase commitments made in the ordinary course of business are unlikely to be relevant. Hence, in practice such unprovided commitments are not normally required to be disclosed under this subsection of the Act.

20.55 Conversely, commitments that represent an unusual risk to the reporting entity, either because of their nature or their size or duration, are likely to be considered relevant to an assessment of the reporting entity's state of affairs. Examples of such contracts could include significant long-term purchase contracts and forward exchange or commodity contracts that do not hedge existing commitments. ICI and PowerGen are examples of companies that disclose details of purchase commitments, as shown in Tables 20.10 and 20.11 below.

Table 20.10 – Imperial Chemical Industries PLC – Annual Report and Accounts – 31 December 1997

Notes relating to the accounts (extract)

41 Commitments and contingent liabilities (extract)

Significant take-or-pay contracts entered into by subsidiaries are as follows:

(i) the purchase of electric power, which commended April 1993, for 15 years. The present value of the remaining commitment is estimated at £688m.

(ii) the purchase of electric power, which will commence in the second quarter of 1998, for 15 years. The present value of this commitment is estimated at £141m.

Table 20.11 – PowerGen plc – Report and Accounts – 30 March 1997

Notes to the Accounts (extract)

29 COMMITMENTS AND CONTINGENT LIABILITIES (extract)

c) Future purchase commitments
The Company has a number of coal supply contracts which when signed required it to purchase coal above market price. These contracts end no later than 31 March 1998. The prices under these contracts have declined in real terms over their lives. These coal purchase commitments are secured by back to back contracts for differences with the Regional Electricity Companies. The contracts comprise a five year contract entered with BCC (now assigned to RJB Mining (UK) Ltd) and a number of smaller supply contracts of differing lengths with other UK coal suppliers.

At 30 March 1997 the Group's future commitment for the supply of coal under all its contract arrangements, including the above, totalled approximately £900 million.

The supply of gas to the Group's three CCGT power stations is provided predominantly via long term gas supply contracts expected to expire between 2008 and 2021. The Company is also committed to purchase gas under various other long term gas supply contracts held by its subsidiary Kinetica Limited. At 30 March 1997 the estimated minimum commitment for the supply of gas under all these contracts totalled approximately £9.6 billion.

Environmental clean up costs

20.56 In a number of industries, such as oil, mining, electricity generation (particularly nuclear) and landfill sites, significant clean up costs are generally required to be incurred once operation of the facility has ceased. It is likely, therefore, that such commitments will be considered relevant to an assessment of the company's state of affairs and hence, will be required to be disclosed as an *'other financial commitment'* to the extent such costs have not been provided for.

20.57 The question as to whether the liability in relation to clean up costs that will arise once the facility is abandoned or decommissioned should be recognised at the outset is discussed in chapter 17.

20.58 An example of the disclosure of environmental commitments is shown in Table 20.12 below.

Table 20.12 – The British Petroleum Company p.l.c. – Annual Report and Accounts – 31 December 1996

Notes on accounts (extract)

40 Contingent liabilities (extract)

The group is subject to numerous national and local environmental laws and regulations concerning its products, operations and other activities. These laws and regulations may require the group to take future action to remediate the effects on the environment of prior disposal or release of chemical or petroleum substances by the group or other parties. Such contingencies may exist for various sites including refineries, chemical plants, oil fields, service stations, terminals and waste disposal sites. In addition, the group may have obligations relating to prior asset sales or closed facilities. The ultimate requirement for remediation and its cost is inherently difficult to estimate. However, the estimated cost of known environmental obligations has been provided in these accounts in accordance with the group's accounting policies. While the amounts of future costs could be significant and could be material to the group's results of operations in the period in which they are recognised, BP does not expect these costs to have a material effect on the group's financial position or liquidity.

Forward foreign exchange commitments

20.59 As noted in paragraph 20.55 above, in certain circumstances disclosure of unprovided commitments arising on forward contracts may be considered relevant to an assessment of the reporting entity's state of affairs. A number of companies have made detailed disclosures of commitments under forward contracts, for example, British Airways Plc (see Table 20.13).

Table 20.13 – British Airways Plc – Report and Accounts – 31 March 1997

Notes to the accounts (extract)

35 FORWARD TRANSACTIONS (extract)

The Group had outstanding forward transactions to hedge foreign currencies in fuel purchases as follows:

	in currency		Sterling equivalents	
	1997	1996	**1997**	*1996*
Group				
Maturing within one year:				
– to cover future capital commitments in US Dollars	**US$590m**	*US$300m*	**£362m**	*£197m*
– to hedge future currency revenue in US Dollars	**US$39m**	*US$35m*	**£24m**	*£23m*
– to hedge future currency revenues in other currencies			**£48m**	*£35m*
– to hedge future operating payments in US Dollars	**US$31m**	*US£135m*	**£19m**	*£88m*
– to hedge future fuel costs in US dollars	**US$165m**		**£101m**	
– to hedge future operating payments in other currencies			**£60m**	*£4m*
Maturing after one year:				
– to cover future capital commitments in US Dollars	**US$140m**	*US$75m*	**£86m**	*£49m*
– to hedge future currency revenues in other currencies			**£1m**	

20.60 The accounting treatment of forward contracts is discussed further in chapter 29. The disclosure of these and other derivative instruments is considered further in chapter 41.

Accounting for post balance sheet events

Introduction

20.61 Almost invariably, it will not be practicable for preparers to finalise financial statements without a period of time elapsing between the balance sheet date and the date on which the financial statements are approved by the directors. The question, therefore, arises as to the extent to which events occurring between the balance sheet date and the date of approval, that is, 'post balance sheet events', should be reflected in the financial statements.

Accounting requirements

20.62 The Act requires material post balance sheet events to be disclosed in the directors' report, but does not specify to what extent such events should be adjusted for in preparing the financial statements. [7 Sch 6(a)]. The disclosures required in the directors' report are discussed in chapter 31. SSAP 17 distinguishes between events that require changes in the amounts to be included in the financial statements ('adjusting events') and events that only require to be disclosed ('non-adjusting events').

Adjusting events

20.63 A material post-balance-sheet event requires changes in the amounts to be included in financial statements where either of the following applies:

- It is an adjusting event (that is, it is an event that provides additional evidence relating to conditions that existed at the balance sheet date).
- It indicates that it is not appropriate to apply the going concern concept to either the whole or a material part of the company.

[SSAP 17 para 22].

20.64 In certain instances custom and statutory requirements require post balance sheet events that are *prima facie* considered to be 'non-adjusting' to be treated as 'adjusting' events. These include:

- Proposed dividends.
- Amounts appropriated to reserves.
- The effects of changes in taxation.
- Dividends receivable from subsidiary and associated companies.

[SSAP 17 para 11].

20.65 Separate disclosure of adjusting events is not normally required since such events simply provide additional evidence in support of the items in the financial statements. An exception to this might arise where, in exceptional circumstances, a 'non-adjusting' event is treated as an 'adjusting' event to comply with the prudence concept. In such situations, disclosure of the circumstances is normally required to be made.

Non-adjusting events

20.66 Conversely, a material post balance sheet event does not require changes in the financial statements, but it does require to be disclosed in the notes to the financial statements, in either of the following situations:

- It is a non-adjusting event. That is, it is an event that arises after the balance sheet date concerning conditions that did not exist at that time and it is of such materiality that its non-disclosure would affect the ability of users of the financial statements to reach a proper understanding of the financial position.

- It is either a reversal or a maturity after the year end of a transaction entered into before the year end and the substance of that transaction was primarily to alter the appearance of the company's balance sheet (that is, window dressing).

[SSAP 17 para 23].

20.67 In such circumstances, the information to be disclosed in the financial statements is the nature of the event and an estimate of its financial effect. The estimate of the financial effect should be disclosed before taking account of taxation, although the taxation implications should be explained where necessary for a proper understanding of the financial position. Where it is not possible to make an estimate of an event's financial effect, that fact must be disclosed. [SSAP 17 para 24].

20.68 The appendix to SSAP 17 sets out examples of adjusting and non-adjusting post balance sheet events that illustrate the principles outlined in the standard:

Adjusting events

- Fixed assets: The subsequent determination of the purchase price or of the proceeds of sale of assets purchased or sold before the year end.
- Property: A valuation which provides evidence of a permanent diminution in value.
- Investments: The receipt of a copy of the financial statements or other information in respect of an unlisted company that provides evidence of a permanent diminution in the value of a long-term investment.
- Stocks and work in progress:
  - The receipt of proceeds of sales after the balance sheet date or other evidence concerning the net realisable value of stocks.
  - The receipt of evidence that the previous estimate of accrued profit on a long-term contract was materially inaccurate.
- Debtors: The renegotiation of amounts owing by debtors, or the insolvency of a debtor.
- Dividends receivable: The declaration of dividends by subsidiaries and associated companies relating to periods prior to the balance sheet date of the parent company.
- Taxation: The receipt of information regarding rates of taxation.
- Claims: Amounts received or receivable in respect of insurance claims that were in the course of negotiation at the balance sheet date.
- Discoveries: The discovery of errors or frauds that show that the financial statements were incorrect.

Non-adjusting events

- Mergers and acquisitions.
- Reconstructions and proposed reconstructions.
- Issues of shares and debentures.
- Purchases and sales of fixed assets and investments.
- Losses of fixed assets or stocks as a result of a catastrophe such as fire or flood.
- Opening new trading activities or extending existing trading activities.
- Closing a significant part of the trading activities if this was not anticipated at the year end.
- Decline in the value of property and investments held as fixed assets, if it can be demonstrated that the decline occurred after the year end.
- Changes in rates of foreign exchange.
- Government action, such as nationalisation.
- Strikes and other labour disputes.
- Augmentation of pension benefits.

[SSAP 17 appendix].

20.69 The appropriate accounting treatment for a post balance sheet event can normally be readily determined by reference to the underlying principle of SSAP 17 (that is, that material events arising after the balance sheet date need to be reflected in financial statements if they provide additional evidence of conditions that existed at the balance sheet date). This can be illustrated by the following examples.

Example 1

Consider the situation where an adverse movement on the foreign exchange rate post year end has had the effect that the exchange differences arising on the retranslation of the bank overdraft that existed at the balance sheet date at the current exchange rate (as compared to the rate at the balance sheet date), exceed the profit for the period under review. How should this be reflected in the financial statements?

Although the bank overdraft existed at the balance sheet date, the conditions that gave rise to the loss did not. The exchange rate fluctuation occurred subsequent to the balance sheet date. Accordingly, we consider that, in normal circumstances, the effect of the exchange rate fluctuations should not be adjusted for in the financial statements. Exchange rate changes are included in the list of non-adjusting post balance sheet events set out in the Appendix to SSAP 17. The effect of the exchange rate fluctuations should be referred to in the directors' report as a post balance sheet event. If the fluctuations are of such a materiality that non-disclosure would affect the true and fair view then they should also be quantified (as at the latest date before the financial statements are approved by the directors) and disclosed by way of note to the financial statements as a non-adjusting post balance sheet event.

Example 2

A further example that often arises in practice is where the company has a holding of shares in a listed company and these were included in the balance sheet at market value at the balance sheet date. Subsequently, the listed company has disclosed financial problems and the holding is now worth less than at the balance sheet date. Such an event is generally regarded as being non-adjusting, because the loss has arisen subsequently and it would have been possible for the holding to be sold at the balance sheet date for its then market value.

20.70 In practice, however, if the diminution in value was severe and likely to be permanent a provision would generally be made to write down the investment to its realisable value on the grounds of prudence. This is entirely consistent with the comment made in the Appendix to SSAP 17 that in exceptional circumstances the prudence concept may require a normally 'non-adjusting' event to be treated as an 'adjusting event'. In such circumstances, full disclosure would be required.

20.71 A major stock market movement after the balance sheet date, such as the fall in values that occurred on 'Black Monday' in October 1987, would be an example of a decline in value that is considered to have occurred subsequent to the balance sheet date. Such a 'crash' would, therefore, generally be regarded as being a 'non-adjusting' event.

20.72 There may be circumstances in which a change in the value of an investment subsequent to the year end falls to be treated as an 'adjusting' event. This would arise, for example, where there is evidence that the conditions that gave rise to the fall in value existed at the year end.

Sale or revaluation of assets

20.73 Where either a current or fixed asset is sold at a loss or revalued downwards subsequent to the balance sheet date, this will generally provide additional evidence of a diminution in value that existed at the balance sheet date and should, accordingly, be regarded as an 'adjusting' event. The Appendix to SSAP 17 also includes as an example of an 'adjusting' event a valuation providing evidence of a permanent diminution in value.

Example

Consider the situation where, prior to the approval of the financial statements but subsequent to the balance sheet date, a company in trading difficulties obtained a valuation of its properties for the purpose of providing additional security to its bankers. In view of its trading difficulties, the company is also considering selling certain properties to generate cash. The amount shown by the valuation is materially lower than the amount attributed to the properties at the balance sheet date based on a valuation carried out three years ago at the height of the property boom. How should this be reflected in the financial statements?

We consider that the valuation provides evidence of a diminution in value that had occurred prior to the balance sheet date. Unless it can be shown that the diminution is temporary, the revaluation should be regarded as being an 'adjusting event' with the values attributed to the properties in the balance sheet being adjusted accordingly. It appears unlikely in this situation that the diminution in value can be considered as temporary since the properties were last valued at the height of the property boom and it is envisaged that some may be sold in the short term.

20.74 However, where the circumstances are such that it can be clearly demonstrated that the change in value occurred subsequent to the balance sheet date or, in relation to a fixed asset revaluation, the diminution can be shown to be temporary in nature and the fixed asset is to be held for the foreseeable future, it may be appropriate to regard the change in value as a non-adjusting event.

Operations to be closed

20.75 Where a decision to close an operation is made after the balance sheet date, this will constitute an 'adjusting' event if it indicates that applying the going concern concept to the whole or a material part of the company is not appropriate. In such situations, a provision for any losses that are anticipated to arise following the closure would be required to be made. [SSAP 17 para 22]. This is illustrated by the following extracts from the accounts of Huntingdon International Holdings plc.

Table 20.14 – Huntingdon International Holdings plc – Annual report and Accounts – 30 September 1994 (extract)

CHIEF EXECUTIVE'S REVIEW (extract)

EXCEPTIONAL LOSSES (extract)

On the change of control of the Travers Morgan group, HIH had made a provision of £10,368,000. This comprises the anticipated failure to recover any of the intercompany balances due to it and other HIH Group companies, plus the fact that HIH has also guaranteed the overdraft facilities drawn down by the Travers Morgan group under the group facilities arranged between HIH Group and National Westminster Bank plc.

NOTES ON THE ACCOUNTS (extract)

2. ACCOUNTING POLICY IN RESPECT OF THE TRAVERS MORGAN GROUP

As discussed in the Chief Executive's Review, joint administrators were appointed to Travers Morgan Limited, on December 15 1994. The Travers Morgan group has been accounted for as follows:

(i) The results of the Travers Morgan group for the twelve months to 30 September 1994 have been included in the Consolidated Profit and Loss account as discontinued activities.

(iii) The assets and liabilities of the Travers Morgan group have been included in the Consolidated Balance Sheet. Provision has been made to reflect intercompany and other balances that it is anticipated may not be recovered by the Company following the appointment of joint administrators to the Travers Morgan group.

Upon granting of the administration order, control of the realisation of the assets and settlement of liabilities passed from the Company to the Administrator. Accordingly it is not possible for the Directors to estimate the extent of any further adjustments that would be made to restate the accounts of the Travers Morgan group on a break-up basis, or to reflect the final effect of the administration of the Group.

TRAVERS MORGAN GROUP BALANCE SHEET

The balance sheet of the Travers Morgan Group, shown below, has been used in preparing the Consolidated Balance Sheet as at 30 September 1994.

Upon granting of the administration order, control of Travers Morgan Limited (see note 2) passed to the administrators. The administrator is now responsible for the management of the business and optimising the realisation of the Travers Morgan Group. The Directors of the company have no control over the manner in which the administration will be conducted and therefore cannot be certain of the amount that will be realised or the manner in which realisation will occur. The Directors have, in principle, agreed to supply standby funding to the administrator on a fully secured basis.

	At 30 September 1994 used for the purposes of Consolidation £000's
Fixed Assets	
Tangible fixed assets	3,147
Investments	8
	3,155
Current Assets	
Stocks	2,612
Debtors	13,285
Cash at bank and in hand	493
	16,390
Creditors	
Amounts falling due within one year	
Bank loans and overdrafts	5,994
Trade and other creditors	7,239
Amounts due to parent undertaking	5,651
	18,884
Net current liabilities	(2,494)
Total assets less current liabilities	661
Creditors	
Amounts falling due after more than one year	
Long term loans	60
Provisions for liabilities and charges	1,878
Total assets less liabilities	(1,277)
Provision made on consolidated balance sheet	10,368

33 POST BALANCE SHEET EVENT

On 15 December 1994 joint administrators were appointed to Travers Morgan Limited. The accounting treatment of this appointment is discussed in note 2. Further details of this event are included in the Chief Executive's Review.

20.76 The treatment of provisions for losses on closure of operations under FRS 3, 'Reporting financial performance', is discussed further in chapter 7.

Window dressing

20.77 As noted in paragraph 20.66 above, paragraph 23 of SSAP 17 requires the disclosure of transactions entered into before the balance sheet date that subsequently reverse or mature after the balance sheet date, where the substance of the transaction is primarily to alter the appearance of the company's balance sheet.

20.78 In certain instances, for example the sale and repurchase of assets, disclosure alone may not be sufficient to comply with the provisions of FRS 5. Rather it is likely that, under FRS 5, it would not be appropriate to exclude the asset from the balance sheet where the substance of the transaction was such that significant risks and rewards were retained by the company throughout the period between the 'sale' and subsequent 'repurchase'. An example might be where the transaction is primarily a financing arrangement. The requirements of FRS 5 in relation to sale and repurchase arrangements are discussed further in chapter 4.

Stock Exchange Listing Rules

20.79 The Listing Rules for listed companies require any change in directors' interests occurring between the end of the period under review and a date not more than one month prior to the date of the notice of the general meeting at which the annual financial statements are to be laid before the company to be disclosed. Furthermore, if there has been no such change, that fact should be disclosed. [LR 12.43(b)(ii)].

20.80 Similarly, details of major interests in a company's share capital need to be disclosed as at a date not more than one month prior to the date of the notice of general meeting. [LR 12.43(1)].

20.81 The detailed requirements in relation to directors' interests in shares and major interests in shares are discussed in chapter 31.

Major financing restructuring

20.82 Where a company is in the process of negotiations in relation to major financial restructuring at the balance sheet date that are subsequently completed prior to the approval of the financial statements, disclosure of the terms of the financial restructuring is likely to be a post balance sheet event of such significance to shareholders that disclosure is essential.

20.83 An extract from the extensive disclosures made by Queens Moat Houses is illustrated in Table 20.15 below. The Queens Moat Houses' financial statements also include a pro-forma balance sheet showing the effect of the restructuring. The disclosure of pro-forma information is discussed in chapter 6.

Table 20.15 – Queens Moat Houses P.L.C. – Annual Report & Accounts – 1 January 1995

Notes to the Accounts (extract)

1 Post balance sheet events

The company and certain of its subsidiary undertakings have entered into various agreements with the group's principal lenders as part of a financial restructuring of the group's share capital and borrowings. These arrangements are conditional, inter alia, upon the approval of shareholders and debenture stockholders at meetings to be convened for 28 April 1995 and 27 April 1995, respectively, as well as upon the approval of the High Court of Justice to a scheme of arrangement to effect the reorganisation of the share capital of the company. It is expected that the financial restructuring will become effective on or around 18 May 1995. Assuming that the above conditions are fulfilled, the reorganisation of the share capital of the company and the financial restructuring will include the following:

Reorganisation of share capital

Under the scheme of arrangement, the existing ordinary shares in the company will effectively be consolidated on the basis of one new ordinary share for every ten existing ordinary shares; the 7.0% and 7.5% convertible cumulative redeemable preference shares in the company will effectively be converted into new ordinary shares at conversion rates equivalent to approximately 2.94 times their existing conversion rates, to reflect their current preferential rights, and the share capital of the company will be reduced. The special non-voting deferred redeemable shares in the company will be cancelled.

Open offer and debt conversion

All existing shareholders will be offered the opportunity to subscribe for the new ordinary shares in the company in proportion to their existing holdings. The proceeds of new ordinary shares subscribed by existing shareholders under the open offer will principally be used to repay indebtedness to the group's lenders and the number of new ordinary shares to be issued to the group's lenders will be reduced accordingly. Approximately £199.4 million of the group's indebtedness will effectively be converted into new ordinary shares in the company.

Term debt

Approximately £332.8 million of the group's indebtedness will be converted into term debt, repayable by instalments between 31 December 1996 and 31 December 2000, and bearing no interest until 1 July 1995 (except in respect of certain holders of existing security and one other lender). The borrowers will be the company and three of its German subsidiaries. The company's payment obligations will be guaranteed by certain of its subsidiary undertakings. The approximate amount of indebtedness is based on exchange rates as at 1 January 1995. The precise amount of indebtedness will depend upon the exchange rates prevailing when the financial restructuring becomes effective.

Junior term debt

Approximately £241.1 million of the group's indebtedness will be converted into junior term debt, repayable not later than 31 December 2006 and bearing no interest (except in respect of certain holders of existing security) until 1 July 1999 (unless a dividend is paid on any class of the company's shares). Part of this debt will be convertible into new ordinary shares if the company goes into liquidation and, at that time, would otherwise have been insolvent. The borrower will be the company and its payment obligations will be guaranteed by certain of its subsidiary undertakings. The approximate amount of indebtedness is based on exchange rates as at 1 January 1995. The precise amount of indebtedness will depend upon the exchange rates prevailing when the financial restructuring becomes effective.

Junior convertible debt

Approximately £97.7 million of the group's indebtedness will be converted into junior convertible debt, repayable not later than 31 December 2008, and bearing no interest unless a dividend is paid on any class of the company's shares. Conversion of the junior convertible debt into new ordinary shares is possible either if the company goes into liquidation and, at that time, would otherwise have been insolvent, or at any time at the option of the board of directors of the company if it considers it in the interest of shareholders. The approximate amount of indebtedness is based on exchange rates as at 1 January 1995. The precise amount of indebtedness will depend upon the exchange rates prevailing when the financial restructuring becomes effective.

Interest

Certain outstanding interest prior to the effective date of the financial restructuring will be waived by the group's lenders. This amounts to approximately £46.0 million as at 1 January 1995.

Debenture stocks

The terms of the two series of first mortgage debenture stocks in the company will be amended to waive existing events of default and to reduce the risk of events of default arising in the future. Debenture stockholders will continue to receive interest at the current rates and the maturities of the debenture stocks will not be altered.

Finance leases

Finance lease arrangements relating to eight UK hotels, one French hotel and two office blocks in the UK will be restructured. Full ownership of the UK properties will revert to the original lessors, who will also receive allocations of new ordinary shares and the various debt instruments described above in place of the amounts owed under the finance leases. The UK hotels will remain under the management of the group. An overseas subsidiary undertaking has also agreed to convert the finance lease over a hotel into a short term operating lease. As a result of these transactions, tangible fixed assets will be reduced by approximately £73.3 million and the group's indebtedness will be reduced by approximately £96.7 million.

Austria

Queens Moat Houses (Germany) Holdings GmbH ("QMH Germany") and its Austrian subsidiary, Autel Hotelbetriebsgesellschaft mbH ("Autel"), have agreed to a restructuring of the borrowings of Autel, under which QMH Germany has the option to dispose of its interest in Autel, and guarantees given by QMH Germany in respect of Autel's borrowings will be released.

Other

Other debt renegotiations and restructurings have been agreed with several lenders to the group, including those in Continental Europe.

Reserves

In conjunction with the scheme of arrangement, whereby there will be a reduction of the share capital of the company, the company's share premium account will be cancelled. The aggregate of these amounts will be applied in reducing the deficit on the company's profit and loss account reserve.

The terms of the financial restructuring and the reorganisation of the share capital of the company are described in detail in a circular to shareholders and listing particulars to be issued by the company in relation to the financial restructuring.

Acquisition and disposals

20.84 Acquisitions and disposals that are made subsequent to the balance sheet date are examples of post balance sheet events that are frequently disclosed in financial statements. Where the impact of the acquisition or disposal is significant companies often illustrate its impact by disclosing proforma information. The use of proforma information is discussed further in chapter 6. Examples of disclosures made are shown in Tables 20.16 and 20.17 below.

Table 20.16 – TI Group plc – Annual Report – 31 December 1994

NOTES TO THE FINANCIAL STATEMENTS (extract)

32 POST BALANCE SHEET EVENT

On 27th July 1994 TI Group and SNECMA Group of France announced that final agreement had been reached to establish a joint venture between their respective aircraft landing gear businesses, Dowty Landing Gear, based in the UK and Canada, and Messier, based in France. The joint venture became fully operational on 1st January 1995 through a holding company. Messier-Dowty International Ltd (Messier-Dowty), owned equally by TI Group and SNECMA. Accordingly TI Group will deconsolidate Dowty Landing Gear and account for its investment in Messier-Dowty as an associated undertaking with effect from 1st January 1995.

The table below sets out an illustrative proforma statement of the net assets of TI Group as at 31st December 1994 after adjustments to reflect the formation of Messier-Dowty. The book value of the net assets deconsolidated by TI Group was £69.9m at end 1994 exchange rates, with no goodwill arising on the transaction. The initial shareholder loans from TI and SNECMA were replaced by external finance in February 1995 so reducing TI Group's investment in the joint venture to £31.4m and reducing TI Group's external net debt by £38.2m.

Messier-Dowty intends to pursue a full distribution policy and TI Group's share of the joint venture's profit after tax will be received as a cash dividend. In each of the first three years. TI Group is entitled to a share of Messier-Dowty's dividends in excess of 50%. For 1995 the proportion will be 90%, for 1996 80%, and for 1997 62.5%, after which dividends will be shared equally. TI Group's share of Messier-Dowty's profit before tax will reflect this entitlement and will be included within "associated undertakings". TI Group will also benefit from reduced interest charges as a result of lower external debt following the repayment of the shareholder loans.

	TI Group 31 Dec 1994	Deconsolidate Dowty Landing	Messier-Dowty Formation	TI Group Pro-Forma Net Assets
	£m	£m	£m	£m
Fixed assets	**370.6**	(61.4)	–	309.2
Investments	**15.0**	–	31.4	46.4
	385.6	(61.4)	31.4	355.6
Net current assets excluding net cash	**222.4**	(30.3)	–	192.1
Other creditors falling due after more than one year	**(34.3)**	19.8	–	(14.5)
Net borrowings	**(84.6)**	2.1	38.2	(44.3)
Provisions for liabilities and charges	**(132.9)**	0.2	–	(132.7)
Total shareholders' funds	**356.2**	(69.6)	69.6	356.2

Table 20.17 – Rolls-Royce plc – Annual Report – 31 December 1994

Notes to the Financial Statements (extract)

28 Other commitments

Acquisition of Allison Engine Company, Inc. (Allison)

On November 21, 1994 Rolls-Royce announced that it had agreed to acquire Allison from Clayton, Dubilier and Rice, Inc, subject to the necessary regulatory approvals.

Allison had profit before tax of £4m and retained profit of £2m for the year ended December 31, 1994 which after estimated adjustments to reflect Rolls-Royce accounting policies amounted to £2m and £1m respectively. These figures have been derived from Allison's unaudited financial statements for the year ended December 31, 1994.

Acquisition of Rolls-Royce & Partners Finance Limited (RRPF)

Rolls-Royce is considering acquiring the remaining 60% of the shares of RRPF which it does not already own. RRPF had profit before tax of £4m and retained profit of £3m for the year ended December 31, 1994. These figures have been derived from RRPF's unaudited financial statements for the year ended December 31, 1994.

Proforma statement of net assets of the enlarged group

The following illustrative proforma statement of the combined net assets of the enlarged group is based on the December 31, 1994 unaudited consolidated balance sheets of Allison and RRPF. The proforma balance sheet has been prepared as if the interests had been acquired by Rolls-Royce on December 31, 1994. No fair value adjustments have been made.

	Rolls-Royce Group £m	Allison £m	RRPF £m	Adjustments £m	Enlarged Rolls-Royce Group £m
Tangible fixed assets	907	184	104	12	1,207
Short-term deposits and cash	681	82	1	(21)	743
Borrowings	(396)	(122)	(60)	109	(469)
Other assets and liabilities	63	(84)	(11)	(5)	(37)
	1,255	60	34	95	1,444

The proforma consolidated balance sheet includes adjustments reflecting the following:

i) the issue of ordinary Rolls-Royce shares to fund the acquisition of Allison and repay Allison's borrowings,

ii) the payment of cash consideration with respect to the acquisition of RRPF and adjustments in respect of existing arrangements with Rolls-Royce.

iii) adjustments to reflect significant differences between the accounting policies of Allison and Rolls-Royce including; treatment of intangible assets, depreciation of tangible fixed assets, valuation of inventory, basis of calculation of provisions and deferred taxation.

Dividends receivable

20.85 SSAP 17 makes the point that there are certain post balance sheet events that, because of statutory requirements or customary accounting practice, are treated as adjusting events. These events include proposed dividends. The list of adjusting events in the appendix to SSAP 17 includes dividends receivable – for instance, the declaration of dividends by subsidiaries and associated companies relating to periods prior to the balance sheet date of the parent company.

20.86 A recent development in this area means that it is necessary to consider whether dividends receivable from subsidiaries by UK and other EC companies are realised profits. This issue is relevant for both accounting and tax purposes. A recent EC legal judgement ('Tomberger') concerning payment of dividends in Germany could call into question the established UK practice of a parent recognising as income at, say, 31 December a dividend proposed by the subsidiary in its financial statements to the same date. If the subsidiary has held its AGM and approved its financial statements before the parent approves its own financial statements, there is no problem. But the matter is potentially open to challenge if, as is more likely, the subsidiary's financial statements have not been finalised in that way.

20.87 Where the subsidiary paying the dividend is wholly-owned, its approval of the dividend before its parent's financial statements are approved will generally be less of an issue as the parent is the only shareholder. Where minority interests are involved, the problem can be overcome if the dividend from the subsidiary is treated as an interim (or second interim) dividend and paid by reference to its relevant financial statements (see chapter 19) before the parent's financial statements are approved.

New developments

20.88 In September 1998, the ASB issued FRS 12, 'Provisions contingent liabilities and contingent assets', which deals with recognition, measurement and disclosure of provisions, together with new rules that replace SSAP 18. It is effective for accounting periods ending on or after 23 March 1999, with earlier adoption encouraged.

20.89 FRS 12 requires that a provision should be recognised when an entity has a present obligation as a result of a past event and it is probable that a transfer of economic benefits will be required to settle the obligation and a reliable estimate of that obligation can be made. [FRS 12 para 14]. A past event is deemed to give rise to a present obligation if it is more likely than not that a present obligation exists at the balance sheet date. [FRS 12 para 15]. If not, then it is a contingent liability.

20.90 A contingent liability is defined in FRS 12 as either:

- a possible obligation arising from past events whose existence will be confirmed only by the occurrence of one or more uncertain future events not wholly within the entity's control; or
- a present obligation arising from past events that is not recognised, because it is not probable that a transfer of economic benefits will be made or because it cannot be measured with sufficient reliability.

[FRS 12 para 2].

20.91 Contingent liabilities should not be provided for, but should be disclosed unless remote. [FRS 12 paras 27 and 28].

20.92 Contingent assets should not be recognised, but should be disclosed if a inflow of economic benefits is probable. [FRS 12 paras 31 and 34].

20.93 A liability and any expected reimbursement (for example, insurance recoveries) should be shown gross in the balance sheet. The asset resulting from the reimbursement should only be recognised when its recovery is virtually certain and should not exceed the amount of the provision. [FRS 12 para 56]. This is a change to SSAP 18 where provision was made for the net loss. However, in the profit and loss account, the expense relating to settlement of the liability and the reimbursement may be presented net. [FRS 12 para 57].

Chapter 21

The group and its structure

Chapter 21

The group and its structure

Introduction

21.1 Companies have performed consolidations since the early 1900s in the US and they were in evidence in the UK by the 1920s. Since then, the methods of consolidation have continued to be revised in recent years and will continue to evolve. In the UK, group accounts were first required by law in the Companies Act 1947 and these provisions were incorporated into the Companies Act 1948. That Act specified when group accounts were required and what form they should take. It allowed group accounts to be prepared in several ways, one of them being consolidated financial statements. These options were removed by the Companies Act 1989, which requires that group accounts should be presented in a single set of consolidated financial statements of the company and its subsidiaries. Underlying the present rules on consolidations in the UK is the 'parent company concept' which is one of the three group concepts explained below.

21.2 This chapter considers the purpose of consolidated financial statements. It also considers those entities that are required to prepare consolidated financial statements and those entities that are required to be consolidated as subsidiaries. Furthermore, it looks at the reasons parents must exclude certain subsidiary undertakings from their consolidated financial statements and the additional disclosures that then apply. It also sets out the disclosure required in the consolidated financial statements concerning all subsidiary undertakings.

21.3 In this chapter the terms 'subsidiary' and 'subsidiary undertaking' are used interchangeably and unless otherwise stated, 'subsidiary' is used to mean 'subsidiary undertaking' as defined in section 258 with regard to preparing consolidated financial statements and not as defined in section 736 (see further para 21.175).

Concept of the group

21.4 The 'group' is defined in the Act to mean *"a parent undertaking and its subsidiary undertakings"*. [Sec 262(1)]. However, three concepts have evolved since the first consolidations were made that concern how the group is established and how the financial statements of the companies forming the group are consolidated. The three concepts are the:

- Proprietary concept.
- Entity concept.

- Parent company concept.

21.5 Each of these concepts is explained in the paragraphs that follow.

Proprietary concept

21.6 The proprietary concept considers the group as if the parent's members are only concerned with the proportion of the assets and liabilities of the group that they own. Consequently, it takes a very narrow view of the group. The members are, therefore, not concerned with the control they might have over the proportion of assets (and liabilities) that are owned, in effect, by minorities.

21.7 Under this concept the consolidated balance sheet deals only with the proportion of assets and liabilities that the parent owns in a subsidiary. Similarly, the profit and loss account would deal with only an equivalent proportion of revenues and expenses of such a subsidiary. Consequently, no minority interests would be shown in the consolidated financial statements.

21.8 This concept of accounting is not generally used in the UK, although it may be seen as a foundation for the equity method and for proportional consolidation. Partnerships in the UK are sometimes consolidated on a proportional basis, which similarly takes account only of the investor's share of the assets and liabilities and profits and losses. Equity accounting and proportional consolidation are considered further in chapter 28.

Entity concept

21.9 The entity concept considers the group as a single entity. Consequently, any companies that are controlled by the parent would be consolidated. Therefore, unlike the proprietary concept, this concept requires 100 per cent consolidation of all subsidiaries even if the parent has less than 100 per cent of the shares in the subsidiary. Furthermore, intra-group profits would be eliminated 100 per cent.

21.10 Minority interests are sometimes recognised under this concept, but they are treated as part of the shareholders' funds, thereby emphasising the control that the parent and its shareholders have over a subsidiary. The entity concept is not used in the UK, and minority interests are not treated as part of shareholders' funds. However, this concept has been used in Germany.

Parent company concept

21.11 The parent company concept takes an intermediate view between the two concepts mentioned above. The concept still retains 100 per cent consolidation of all controlled subsidiaries as its base, but recognises that the interest of the parent company's members is limited to the parent's shareholding in subsidiaries. Consequently, minority interests are not recognised as shareholders' funds, but are shown separately either before or after shareholders' funds.

21.12 This concept developed in the UK and stems from the early days of consolidation when the consolidated balance sheet was seen as a supplement to the parent company's balance sheet. The US also uses a similar concept, but in contrast the consolidated balance sheet is seen in the US as a substitute for the parent's balance sheet.

21.13 The basis of consolidation to be used under the Act is defined in section 262(1). The section defines the term 'included in consolidation' to mean the *"undertaking is included in the accounts by the method of full (and not proportional) consolidation"*. Furthermore paragraph 17(2) of Schedule 4A requires minority interests to be disclosed separately in the consolidated balance sheet and profit and loss account.

Background to the accounting rules

21.14 As mentioned above, although group accounts were prepared since the 1920s in the UK, they were first required by law in the Companies Act 1947 and these provisions were incorporated into the Companies Act 1948. These Acts, however, did not include any detailed rules regarding the preparation of group accounts, apart from specifying when subsidiaries could be excluded from them. Also, under those Acts a holding company could choose between several options in presenting its group accounts. However in practice, group accounts were normally presented as consolidations. But even where a holding company did not prepare group accounts in the form of consolidated financial statements, it still had to give either the same or equivalent information as it would have disclosed if it had prepared consolidated financial statements.

21.15 The first accounting standard on the subject outside the US was IAS 3, 'Consolidated Financial Statements', published in 1976 by the IASC. Whilst being generally in accordance with the law and practice in the UK, IAS 3 did differ in some respects. (IAS 3 has subsequently been superseded by IAS 27, 'Consolidated financial statements and accounting for investments in subsidiaries' and IAS 28 'Accounting for investments in associates'.) The publication of the international standard made it desirable for there to be a domestic standard on the subject. That standard, SSAP 14, 'Group accounts', was issued in 1978.

21.16 SSAP 14 enhanced the provisions of the Companies Acts in force at that time, which were eventually themselves combined into the Companies Act 1985. In particular, SSAP 14 narrowed the 1948 Act's requirements by specifying that where group accounts were required by law they should be in the form of consolidated

consolidated financial statements on an item-by-item basis, eliminating intra-group balances and transactions and unrealised intra-group profits and losses, was well understood in the UK. Consequently, the statement was not intended to be a detailed text on the principles of consolidations. The standard did, however, lay down some of the basic principles underlying consolidations, such as adopting uniform accounting policies, the grounds for excluding subsidiaries from consolidation and determining the effective date of acquisition or disposal of subsidiaries.

21.17 The EC 7th Directive on group accounts (see appendix 4) was adopted by the Council of Ministers in June 1983 as part of the EC company law harmonisation programme. It was not required to be brought into the legislation of member states until the end of 1987 and even then only with effect from 1990. The key areas dealt with by the 7th Directive are as follows:

- The requirement to prepare group accounts and exemptions from that requirement.
- The form of group accounts, that is, consolidated financial statements.
- Definitions of subsidiaries, which place the emphasis on control and inclusion of unincorporated undertakings.
- Subsidiaries exempted from inclusion in consolidated financial statements.
- The treatment of associates and joint ventures.

21.18 The 7th Directive was implemented in the UK by Part I of the Companies Act 1989. Part I of that Act amended the Companies Act 1985 and was effective from 1 April 1990, but applied to accounting periods commencing on or after 23 December 1989. Following the introduction of the Companies Act 1989, SSAP 14 was no longer entirely consistent with company legislation.

21.19 The need to amend SSAP 14 to make it consistent with the changes in the law provided an opportunity to conduct a thorough review of the standard. This review was carried out by the ASC and ED 50, 'Consolidated accounts', was issued in July 1990. Its proposals were to bring together SSAP 1 and SSAP 14, to deal with the conflicts between these standards and the new legislation and to provide additional guidance on new provisions in the legislation not previously dealt with by a standard. Some of the proposals in this exposure draft were intended to restrict the application of certain of the Companies Act's new provisions. In July 1990 the ASC was disbanded and replaced by the ASB.

21.20 In December 1990, the ASB issued its first pronouncement entitled 'Interim Statement: consolidated accounts'. This statement had immediate effect to coincide with the introduction of the accounting provisions of the Companies Act 1989. It was issued by the ASB to deal with some of the conflicts between both SSAP 1 and SSAP 14 and the legislation. In addition, it included a definition of the term 'actually exercises a dominant influence'. This is an expression used in the Companies Act as part of one of the definitions of subsidiary, which was not defined in the legislation itself (see further para 21.115).

21.21 The Interim Statement also made mandatory certain accounting treatments permitted by the Act. For example, the Act permits but does not require exclusion of subsidiaries from consolidation in certain circumstances. The Interim Statement tightened the conditions for exclusion and then made exclusion mandatory where those conditions were met (see further para 21.179).

21.22 It was the ASB's intention to issue an FRS on the subject of consolidated financial statements, dealing with subsidiaries, associates and joint ventures. However, due to the complexity of the subject and the recognition of the need to issue a standard dealing with accounting for subsidiaries at the earliest possible date the ASB decided to issue FRS 2, 'Accounting for subsidiary undertakings', and to leave accounting for associates and joint ventures for a subsequent FRS. FRS 2 is very closely based on the Interim Statement and supersedes it except for those parts that relate to associates and joint ventures. FRS 2 supersedes SSAP 14 entirely. The accounting practices set out in FRS 2 became standard practice in respect of consolidated financial statements relating to periods ending on or after 23 December 1992.

Draft statement of principles

21.23 The draft statement of principles on the reporting entity (chapter 7) sets out the conditions that determine whether an entity should prepare consolidated financial statements. It says that parent entities prepare consolidated financial statements to provide financial information about the economic activities of their groups. It goes on to say that consolidated financial statements reflect a parent's control of the assets and liabilities of its subsidiaries by consolidation, a process that aggregates the assets, liabilities and results of the parent and its subsidiaries using the same accounting bases.

21.24 The statement comments that the boundary of a group (that is, the entities which form the group) which are the subject of a set of consolidated financial statements is set by the extent of control. It then explains that control is the power to direct and that there are two aspects to control:

- The ability to deploy the economic resources, whether assets or entities.

- The ability to benefit by (or to suffer from) their deployment.

To have control it comments that an entity must have both these abilities. A group has control of another entity where it directs the operating and financial policies of that entity with a view to gaining economic benefits from its activity. This is the essence of control and control of the operating and financial policies forms the basis of the definitions of subsidiaries found in FRS 2 as explained below.

Accounting for investments

21.25 At present in the UK there are a number of ways a company may account for an investment in another undertaking, which depend upon the size of the investment and the control or influence the investing company has over the entity in which it is investing. These different situations are summarised below:

- Where the investing entity does not exercise significant influence over the operating and financial policies of the other undertaking (normally holdings of below 20 per cent), its investment is recorded at:
  - cost unless there is a permanent diminution in its value; or
  - market value.
- Where the investing entity does exercise significant influence over the operating and financial policies of the other undertaking (normally holdings of over 20 per cent), its investment is accounted for using equity accounting, unless the entity is a joint arrangement in which case, another method of accounting should be used (see further chapter 28).
- Where the investing entity controls the operating and financial policies of the other undertaking (normally holdings of more than 50 per cent) its investment is consolidated in full and any minority interests are recognised.

21.26 There are, therefore, three ways in which an undertaking can be consolidated into the financial statements of the investing undertaking primarily in its consolidated financial statements:

- Equity accounting – the investing undertaking incorporates its share of the assets and liabilities and profits and losses before tax of the entity in which it has invested on a one line basis in its consolidated balance sheet (netting assets and liabilities) and its consolidated profit and loss account (netting profits and losses), respectively. In the profit and loss account, the investing group's share of taxes is also shown proportionately. Only dividends received are recorded in the investing entity's cash flow statement. Where the investing undertaking does not prepare consolidated financial statements the equivalent information has to be given in the notes to the financial statements. Equity accounting is explained in chapter 28.

- Proportional consolidation – in this method, the investing undertaking consolidates into its financial statements its share of assets and liabilities, profits and losses and cash flows of the entity in which it has invested line by line in its consolidated balance sheet, its consolidated profit and loss account and its consolidated cash flow statement, respectively. As only the investing company's share of assets and liabilities are consolidated, this method does not result in recognising any minority interests. Proportional consolidation is mentioned in more detail in chapter 28 in relation to accounting for joint arrangements.

- Full consolidation – the investing undertaking consolidates in full 100 per cent of the assets and liabilities, profits and losses and cash flow of the entity in which it has invested on a line by line basis in its consolidated balance sheet, its consolidated profit and loss account and its consolidated cash flow statement, respectively. Where the investing undertaking's interest is less than 100 per cent, a minority interest is recognised representing the minority's share of assets and liabilities and profits and losses on a net basis. The rules that apply to preparing consolidated financial statements are considered in chapter 22.

Purpose of consolidated financial statements

21.27 The explanatory section of FRS 2 provides the following justification for requiring parents to prepare consolidated financial statements:

> *"For a variety of legal, tax and other reasons undertakings generally choose to conduct their activities not through a single legal entity but through several undertakings under the ultimate control of the parent undertaking of that group. For this reason the financial statements of a parent undertaking by itself do not present a full picture of its economic activities or financial position. Consolidated financial statements are required in order to reflect the extended business unit that conducts activities under the control of the parent undertaking."* [FRS 2 para 59].

Scope of the Act's and FRS 2's provisions

21.28 The Companies Act 1985 (as amended by the Companies Act 1989) requires *parent companies*, subject to certain exemptions, to prepare consolidated financial statements and it sets out the form that those financial statements should take. [Sec 227].

21.29 The provisions of FRS 2 go further and apply to *all parent undertakings*, not just parent companies. Subject to certain exemptions, FRS 2 requires *all parents* preparing financial statements that are intended to give a true and fair view of the financial position and profit or loss of the group to prepare them in the form of consolidated financial statements (see further para 21.43). [FRS 2 para 18].

21.30 FRS 2 also directs a parent that uses one of the exemptions from the requirement to prepare consolidated financial statements, but prepares individual financial statements intended to give a true and fair view, to include certain additional disclosure (see para 21.80). FRS 2 does not otherwise deal with the individual financial statements of a parent.

21.31 FRS 2 was drafted within the framework of the Act and, although it does not conflict with it, there are circumstances where the standard is more restrictive than the Act. Furthermore, the standard states that:

> *"Parent undertakings that do not report under the Act should comply with the requirements of the FRS, and of the Act where referred to in the FRS, except to the extent that these requirements are not permitted by any statutory framework under which such undertakings report".* [FRS 2 para 19].

21.32 By referring to sections of the Act and applying them to parents that are not subject to the Act, the FRS achieves a single set of rules that apply to parents preparing consolidated financial statements, whether or not they are companies.

Parent and subsidiary undertakings

21.33 The Companies Act 1989 introduced important changes to the definitions of parent and subsidiary. Although these changes were fundamental in principle, they did not in practice affect the composition of most groups (see further para 21.86).

21.34 The Act refers throughout to 'parent undertaking' and 'subsidiary undertaking'. These terms stem directly from the EC 7th Directive. The term 'undertaking' is defined in the Act and FRS 2 as follows:

> *"... a body corporate or partnership, or an unincorporated association carrying on a trade or business, with or without a view to profit."* [Sec 259(1); FRS 2 para 16].

21.35 Consequently, a *parent undertaking* could be a partnership or an unincorporated business. However, under the Act consolidated financial statements have only to be prepared where, at the end of a financial year, an undertaking is a parent company. [Sec 227(1)]. Therefore, parent undertakings that are not companies are not required by the Act to prepare consolidated financial statements, but as explained above they are required to do so in certain circumstances by FRS 2 (see further para 21.43).

21.36 However, *subsidiary undertakings* (including both partnerships and unincorporated associations) are required to be consolidated into the group's consolidated financial statements. Such entities are normally required to be fully consolidated and any minority interests (see chapter 24) are shown separately in the consolidated balance sheet.

21.37 The Act and FRS 2 require as a starting point that all subsidiary undertakings should be included in the consolidated financial statements. [Sec 229(1); FRS 2 para 23]. The FRRP commented in July 1993 that the Report and Accounts of Breverleigh Investments plc for the year ended 30 June 1992 did not include its subsidiary The Banyan Tree of Key West Inc. in its consolidated financial statements. Following discussions with the FRRP this subsidiary was consolidated in accordance with the Act and FRS 2 in the group's consolidated financial statements for the year to 30 June 1993 and comparatives were amended accordingly. There are, however, a number of situations where subsidiary undertakings may, or should, legitimately be excluded from consolidated financial statements and may be accounted for in some other way. These situations are covered in the provisions of both the Act and FRS 2.

21.38 The provisions of both the Act and FRS 2 that relate to the definitions of subsidiary undertakings and the exemptions from the requirement to consolidate certain subsidiary undertakings are considered in detail below (see paras 21.84 and 21.179 respectively).

Requirement to prepare consolidated financial statements

21.39 Whether or not there is a legal or regulatory obligation for a parent to prepare consolidated financial statements will depend on how the parent is constituted.

Parent companies

21.40 As mentioned above, where a *company* is a parent company at the end of a financial year the directors of the company are required by the Act, subject to certain exemptions, to prepare consolidated financial statements as well as individual company financial statements for the financial year. [Sec 227(1)]. The consolidated financial statements must comply with the Act's requirements. [Sec 227(4)].

21.41 The consolidated financial statements prepared by a parent company are also required by law to give a true and fair view. [Sec 227(3)]. In order to comply with the true and fair requirement, the parent should comply with the provisions of FRS 2.

Small and medium-sized groups

21.42 A parent company need not prepare consolidated financial statements if the group headed by it qualifies as a small group or a medium-sized group, provided it is not an ineligible group. [Sec 248(1)]. An ineligible group is one that includes one or more of the following:

- A public company or a body corporate that is able lawfully to issue shares or debentures to the public.
- An authorised institution under the Banking Act 1987.
- An insurance company to which Part II of the Insurance Companies Act 1982 applies.
- An authorised person under the Financial Services Act 1986.

[Sec 248(2)].

These exemptions and the conditions that need to be fulfilled are explained further in chapter 36.

Other parent undertakings

21.43 Whether or not an unincorporated parent undertaking is *required* to prepare consolidated financial statements will depend on the statutory framework under which that undertaking was established. If that framework requires the undertaking to prepare *consolidated* financial statements and to prepare financial statements that give a *true and fair view* (and, as a consequence, require it to comply with FRS 2), then that undertaking will be *required* to prepare consolidated financial statements (providing it is not entitled to an exemption). [FRS 2 para 18].

21.44 For example, a partnership that owns a subsidiary company is not required by the Act to prepare consolidated financial statements as it is not itself a parent *company*. However, if there is a requirement in the partnership deed for the partnership to prepare consolidated financial statements and for it to prepare financial statements that give a true and fair view (and, therefore, comply with FRS 2) the partnership would be required to prepare consolidated financial statements in accordance with FRS 2.

21.45 The basic rule is that any parent preparing consolidated financial statements purporting to give a true and fair view is required to comply with FRS 2, unless it is specifically exempt from preparing such financial statements. [FRS 2 paras 18, 19].

21.46 The extent to which certain specialised businesses are required to comply with FRS 2 is considered in the table below.

Partnerships

- Companies Act – does not apply.
- Other statutes or regulations – normally reference is made only in the partnership deed.
- Compliance with FRS 2 – only where the partnership's consolidated financial statements are intended (or required by the partnership deed) to give a true and fair view.

Limited partnerships

Requirements as for partnerships.

Trusts

- Companies Act – does not apply.
- Other statutes or regulations – normally only in the trust deed.
- Compliance with FRS 2 – only where the trust's consolidated financial statements are intended (or required by the trust deed) to give a true and fair view.

Unit trusts

- Companies Act – does not apply.
- Other statutes or regulations – included in the trust deed, the unit trust SORP and SIB regulations.
- Compliance with FRS 2 – do not need to comply, as unit trusts are not allowed to have subsidiaries.

Pension schemes

- Companies Act – does not apply.
- Other statutes or regulations – The Occupational Pension Scheme (Requirement to obtain Audited Accounts and a Statement from the Auditor) Regulations 1996 (SI 1996/1975) require for accounting periods ending on or after 6 April 1997 that pension scheme financial statements should state whether they have been prepared in accordance with the SORP 'Financial reports of pension schemes' issued by the Pensions Research Accountants Group (PRAG). Paragraph 3.32 of the SORP requires consolidation of subsidiaries in accordance with FRS 2.
- Compliance with FRS 2 – required by the pension schemes SORP.

Unincorporated associations

- Companies Act – does not apply.
- Other statutes or regulations – the constitution of an unincorporated association will rarely lay down any specific duties concerning the preparation of financial statements.
- Compliance with FRS 2 – if the constitution requires the undertaking or the undertaking decides to prepare consolidated financial statements that give a true and fair view then the parent must comply with FRS 2, otherwise it need not comply.

Friendly societies

- Companies Act – does not apply.
- Other statutes or regulations – sections 69 and 70 of the Friendly Societies Act 1992 require such undertakings to prepare consolidated financial statements that give a true and fair view in accordance with The Friendly Societies (Accounts and Related Provisions) Regulations 1994 (SI 1994/1983).
- Compliance with FRS 2 – as the consolidated financial statements must give a true and fair view, FRS 2 should be complied with.

Industrial & provident societies

- Companies Act – does not apply.
- Other statutes or regulations –
  - Section 13 of the Friendly and Industrial and Provident Societies Act 1968 and the Industrial and Provident Societies (Group Accounts) Regulations 1969 (SI 1969/1037) require group accounts to be prepared giving a true and fair view although these may be in formats other than consolidated financial statements if the society's committee consider this to be preferable.
  - The definition of subsidiary under the Friendly and Industrial and Provident Societies Act 1968 depends upon legal ownership, rather than control.
  - Societies conducting insurance business are subject to the Insurance Accounts Directive (Miscellaneous Insurance Undertakings) Regulations 1993 (SI 1993/3245).
- Compliance with FRS 2 – in general, the requirements of FRS 2 will apply, although depending on the circumstances, the regulations governing the society might override the requirements of FRS 2.

Building societies

- Companies Act – does not apply.
- Other statutes or regulations – Under sections 72 and 73 of the Building Societies Act 1986 consolidated financial statements must show a true and fair view and must be prepared in the format prescribed by the Building Society (Accounts and Related Provisions) Regulations 1991 (SI 1991/2705). The Building Societies Act 1986 (Modifications) Order 1991 (SI 1991/2086) substituted 'subsidiary undertaking' for 'subsidiary' in the Building Societies Act.
- Compliance with FRS 2 – as the Building Societies Act requires consolidated financial statements to give a true and fair view, the provisions of FRS 2 should be complied with.

Housing associations

- Companies Act – only applies to associations incorporated under that Act.
- Other statutes or regulations – if the association is incorporated under the Industrial and Provident Societies Acts 1965 to 1978 it has a specific duty to prepare a revenue account and balance sheet giving a true and fair view.
- Compliance with FRS 2 – the Housing Association SORP requires compliance with FRS 2.

Charities

- Companies Act – only applies to charities that are registered as companies.
- Other statutes or regulations – The Charities (Accounts and Reports) Regulations 1995 (SI 1995/2724) require for accounting periods beginning on or after 1 March 1996 that all charities that are not companies state in their financial statements whether or not they have been prepared in accordance with applicable accounting standards and the SORP 'Accounting by charities' issued by the Charity Commissioners. Paragraph 54 of the SORP requires charitable and non–charitable subsidiaries to be consolidated in accordance with the requirements of FRS 2.
- Compliance with FRS 2 – required by the charities SORP.

Form of consolidated financial statements

21.47 Both the Act and FRS 2 require the financial statements of a group to be in the form of consolidated financial statements, unless the parent is exempt.

21.48 FRS 2 defines consolidated financial statements as *"the financial statements of a group prepared by consolidation"* and it defines consolidation as *"the process of adjusting and combining financial information from the individual financial statements of a parent undertaking and its subsidiary undertakings to prepare consolidated financial statements that present financial information for the group as a single economic entity"*. [FRS 2 paras 4, 5].

21.49 The Act requires that for parent companies consolidated financial statements should include:

- A consolidated balance sheet dealing with the state of affairs of the parent and its subsidiary undertakings.
- A consolidated profit and loss account dealing with the profit or loss of the parent and its subsidiary undertakings.
- Notes to the consolidated financial statements dealing with additional disclosure requirements.

[Sec 227(2)(4)].

These provisions are explained further in chapter 6.

21.50 FRS 3 now also requires the consolidated financial statements to include a consolidated statement of total recognised gains and losses, a consolidated note of historical cost profits and losses and a consolidated reconciliation of movements in shareholders' funds. Entities preparing such consolidated financial statements are not required to publish equivalent statements for the parent entity itself. The provisions of FRS 3 concerning these statements are considered in detail in chapters 6 and 7.

21.51 In addition, subject to certain exemptions, FRS 1 requires all undertakings preparing financial statements that are intended to give a true and fair view to prepare a cash flow statement. Undertakings preparing consolidated financial statements should prepare a consolidated cash flow statement and related notes; they are not then required to prepare an entity cash flow statement. The detailed requirements of FRS 1 are dealt with in chapter 30.

21.52 Both the Act and FRS 2 state that the consolidated financial statements should include the parent and all its subsidiaries, except for those subsidiaries that are required to be excluded. The provisions relating to exclusion of subsidiaries are considered further in paragraph 21.179.

Parent's profit and loss account

21.53 When a parent company prepares consolidated financial statements in accordance with the Act, it is not required to include its own profit and loss account and related notes if the financial statements satisfy the following requirements:

- The notes to the parent company's individual balance sheet show the company's profit or loss for the financial year determined in accordance with the provisions of the Act. [Sec 230(1)(b)].

  The figure to be given is the profit or loss reported in the parent's profit and loss account format line item 'profit or loss for the financial year', which is before any consolidation adjustments or dividends.

- The parent company's board of directors must approve the company's individual profit and loss account in accordance with the rules concerning approval of the company's financial statements. [Sec 230(3)].

- The notes to the financial statements disclose the fact that the parent company has taken advantage of this exemption. [Sec 230(4)].

21.54 Where the consolidated financial statements do not include the company's profit and loss account, the consolidated financial statements need not include certain supplementary information when presented to the Board for their approval. [Sec 230(2)]. The information that can be excluded is specified in paragraphs 52 to 57 of Schedule 4 to the Act, which includes the following:

- Certain items of income and expenditure including:

  - Interest and similar charges.
  - Amounts set aside for the redemption of shares and loans.
  - Income from listed investments.
  - Rents from land.
  - Hire of plant and machinery.

  [4 Sch 53].

- Detailed particulars concerning tax. [4 Sch 54].
- Disaggregated information concerning turnover. [4 Sch 55].
- Particulars of the average number of staff. [4 Sch 56].
- Certain miscellaneous matters including:

  - The effect of including any preceding year's items in the current year's profit and loss account.
  - Particulars of extraordinary income or extraordinary charges.
  - The effect of any exceptional items.

  [4 Sch 57].

21.55 Suitable wording for a note to be included in the consolidated financial statements when the parent's profit and loss account is not reproduced would be:

> *"As permitted by section 230 of the Companies Act 1985, the parent company's profit and loss account has not been included in these financial statements and its profit/loss for its financial year amounted to £X."*

21.56 In certain situations an intermediate parent, for example, might wish voluntarily to prepare consolidated financial statements even though it might comply with the conditions that would allow it not to prepare consolidated financial statements (see para 21.63). In this situation, it might not wish to include its individual company profit and loss account in those consolidated financial statements. However, the wording of section 230 of the Act would only seem to allow the exemption where the company is *required* to prepare consolidated financial statements. The solution to this technical issue is for the intermediate parent deliberately not to comply with one of the conditions outlined in paragraph 21.68. For example, one of those conditions is that the company must disclose that it is exempt from the requirement to prepare consolidated financial statements in its financial statements. If it does not make this disclosure, then it is strictly required by the Act to prepare consolidated financial statements and, therefore, can take the exemption outlined above from presenting its own profit and loss account.

True and fair view

21.57 It is an overriding requirement of the Act that a company's consolidated financial statements must give a true and fair view of the state of affairs as at the end of the financial year and of the profit or loss for the financial year, of the undertakings included in the consolidation. [Sec 227(3)].

21.58 Where, however, compliance with the disclosure provisions of the Act (including Schedule 4A to the Companies Act 1985) would not be sufficient to give a true and fair view, then additional information should be given in the financial statements or in the notes to the financial statements. [Sec 227(5)]. This additional information needs to be of sufficient detail to ensure that its disclosure enables the financial statements to give a true and fair view.

21.59 There is a further provision concerning the true and fair view, which provides that if in 'special circumstances' compliance with the Act's provisions would be inconsistent with the requirement to give a true and fair view, the directors of the company must depart from the Act's provisions. Where such a departure is necessary, the particulars of the departure, the reasons for it and its effect must be given in a note to the financial statements. UITF Abstract 7 requires that these provisions of the Act should be interpreted as follows:

- 'Particulars of any such departure' should be interpreted to mean a statement of the treatment which the Act would normally require in the circumstances and a description of the treatment actually adopted.
- 'The reasons for it' should be interpreted to mean a statement as to why the treatment prescribed would not give a true and fair view.
- 'Its effect' should be interpreted to mean a description of how the position shown in the financial statements is different as a result of the departure, normally with quantification, except:
  - where quantification is already evident in the financial statements themselves; or
  - whenever the effect cannot reasonably be quantified, in which case the directors should explain the circumstances.

These provisions are considered further in chapter 2.

21.60 The true and fair override given by section 227(6) cannot be used to justify not consolidating a subsidiary; it merely entitles the directors to depart from the other requirements of the Act with respect to the matters to be included in the consolidated financial statements. In interpreting the Act's provisions the court would be bound to give effect so far as possible to the provisions of the EC 7th Directive. In the EC 7th Directive (see appendix) the true and fair override in article 16(5) (included in section 227(6) of the Companies Act) applies only to specific articles of the directive (that is, articles 17 to 35 and 39). It does not apply to the articles which set out the conditions for consolidation. Therefore, the override cannot be used to override provisions relating to the composition of consolidated financial statements so as to exclude a subsidiary undertaking from consolidation.

21.61 This requirement of the law has been reinforced by the ASB in FRS 2. The ASB consider that for consolidated financial statements to give a true and fair view they must present information about the group that is complete and, for this reason, the conditions set out in the Act for exclusion of subsidiaries from consolidation have been further restricted in the standard. These restrictions are considered from paragraph 21.179 onwards.

Exemptions from preparing consolidated financial statements

21.62 There are three situations where a parent may be exempt from the general requirement to prepare consolidated financial statements. The exemptions are for:

- Parents of small and medium-sized groups.
- Certain parents that are also subsidiaries (that is, intermediate parents – see para 21.63).
- Parents, all of whose subsidiaries are permitted or required to be excluded from consolidation (see para 21.78).

[FRS 2 para 21].

The provisions concerning small and medium-sized groups are explained in chapter 36.

Intermediate parent exemption

21.63 An intermediate holding company is not required to prepare consolidated financial statements, where it is wholly owned by its immediate parent undertaking that is established under the law of a member state of the European Economic Area (EEA – see para 21.75 below). [Sec 228 (1)(a); Sec 2 European Economic Area Act 1993]. Before the introduction of the Companies Act 1989, a parent had to be incorporated in Great Britain for this exemption to apply. However, there are a number of conditions that must apply before the exemption can be taken and these are summarised below in paragraph 21.68.

21.64 Furthermore, this exemption extends to the situation where the parent (established under the law of any EC member state) holds more than 50 per cent of the shares by number in the company and no notice has been served on the company to prepare consolidated financial statements. Such notice has to be made by either of the following:

- Shareholders holding in aggregate more than half of the remaining shares in the company.
- Shareholders holding in aggregate five per cent of the total shares in the company.

[Sec 228(1)(b)].

21.65 The notice has to be served within six months of the end of the previous financial period (that is, normally within the first six months of the financial year for which the consolidated financial statements are being prepared). [Sec 228(1)]. Consequently, the onus is clearly on the minority shareholders to serve such notice if they require consolidated financial statements to be prepared for a sub-group.

21.66 FRS 2 extends the scope of the relevant sections of the Act outlined above to apply also to unincorporated parents.

21.67 For the purposes of determining whether the company is wholly owned or whether the parent holds more than 50 per cent of the shares of the company, the rules below apply:

- Shares held by directors to comply with their share qualification requirements should be disregarded when determining whether a company is wholly owned in paragraph 21.63. [Sec 228(4)].
- In determining whether the parent holds more than 50 per cent of the shares of the company in paragraph 21.64, shares held by a parent's wholly owned subsidiary should be attributed to the parent undertaking. Also shares held on behalf of the parent, or by or on behalf of a wholly-owned subsidiary, should be attributed to the parent undertaking. [Sec 228(5)].

Conditions for exemption

21.68 Both the exemptions outlined above in paragraphs 21.63 and 21.64 only apply, however, where the following conditions have been followed:

- The company is included in the consolidated financial statements of a larger group drawn up to the same date (or an earlier date in the same financial year

– see para 21.69) by a parent established (that is, incorporated) in the EEA (see para 21.75). [Sec 228(2)(a)].

'Included in' for this purpose means by way of full consolidation; equity accounting or proportional consolidation is not sufficient.

- The consolidated financial statements of the parent must be drawn up and audited, and the parent's financial statements must be drawn up, in accordance with the provisions of the EC 7th Directive (where applicable as modified by the provisions of the Bank Accounts Directive or the Insurance Accounts Directive). [Sec 228 (2)(b); SI 1992/3178; SI 1993/3246].

- It must be noted in the company's individual financial statements that it is exempt from preparing and delivering to the Registrar of Companies consolidated financial statements. [Sec 228(2)(c)].

- The name of the parent that prepares the consolidated financial statements must be noted in the company's individual financial statements stating one of the following:

    - The parent's country of incorporation, if it is incorporated outside Great Britain.

    - Whether the parent is registered in England and Wales or in Scotland, if it is incorporated in Great Britain.

    - The address of the parent's principal place of business, where it is unincorporated.

  [Sec 228(2)(d)].

- The company must deliver to the Registrar of Companies within the period allowed for delivering its individual financial statements a copy of the parent's consolidated financial statements and a copy of the parent's annual report together with the audit report thereon (see further para 21.72). [Sec 228(2)(e)].

- Where any of the documents delivered to the Registrar of Companies in accordance with the previous requirement is not in English, a copy of a translation must be annexed to those documents. The translation has to be certified in the prescribed manner to be a correct translation (see further para 21.70). [Sec 228(2)(f)].

- The company cannot have any securities listed on any stock exchange in an EC member state. [Sec 228(3)]. For this purpose, 'securities' include shares and stocks, debentures (including debenture stock, loan stock, bonds, certificates of deposit and other similar instruments), warrants and similar instruments and certain certificates and other instruments that confer rights in respect of securities. [Sec 228(6)].

Relevant dates

21.69 The relevant dates specified in the first condition in paragraph 21.68 can cause particular problems in practice as explained in the example that follows:

Example

A parent company acquires the whole of the company S sub-group in June 19X1 during its current financial year and after the acquisition the group has the following structure.

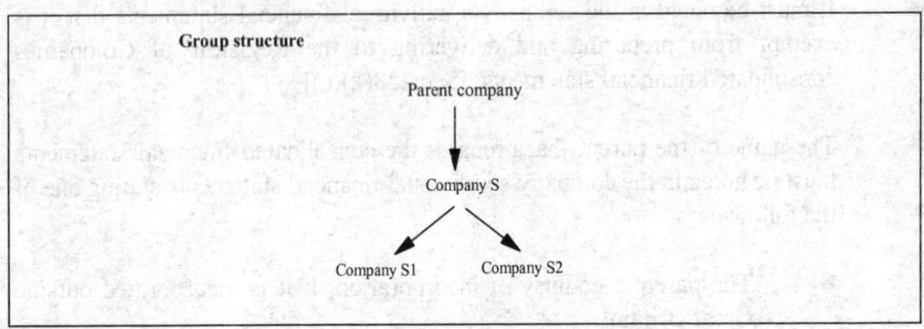

The parent company's year end is 31 December, but the year end of the company S sub-group is 30 September. The question then arises as to whether company S can take advantage from the exemption to prepare consolidated financial statements for its sub-group (that is including both company S1 and company S2). If it complies with the other conditions in paragraph 21.68 it will fail on the first condition in the year of acquisition (that is, 19X1). This is because at its year end, 30 September 19X1, it will not have been included in the parent's consolidated financial statements drawn up to the same date (that is, 30 September 19X1) or to an earlier date in company S's financial year. The company S sub-group will only be included in the parent's consolidated financial statement as at 31 December 19X1. In 19X2, company S does comply with this condition, because its results will be consolidated into its parent's financial statements to an earlier date in its financial year to 30 September 19X2 (that is, its parent's consolidated financial statements for the financial year to 31 December 19X1). Therefore, in 19X1 company S will have to prepare consolidated financial statements, but in 19X2 if it complies with the other conditions it will not have to prepare them. The simple way round this problem is for company S to change its year end from 30 September to 31 December.

Certified translations

21.70 The term 'certified translation' used in the penultimate bullet point above means a translation made by any of the following:

- A notary public.

- A solicitor if the translation was made in the UK.
- A person authorised in the place where the translation was made to administer an oath or any of the British officials mentioned in section 6 of the Commissioners for Oaths Act 1889 for translations made overseas. This includes British Ambassadors, envoys, ministers, chargés d'affaires and secretaries of embassies and every British consul-general, consul, vice-consul, acting consul, pro-consul, consular agent, acting consul-general, acting vice-consul, and acting consular agent exercising his functions in any foreign place, including anyone with the diplomatic rank of counsellor.
- Any person certified by any of the above to be known to him to be competent to translate the document into English.

[SI 1990/572 para 5(1)].

21.71 In practice, if the translation is to be made in the UK, a notary or a solicitor should be asked to arrange for a translation to be made and certified.

Practical problems in taking the exemption

21.72 A problem that may occur in practice arises from the requirement for the parent's annual report to be drawn up in accordance with its own country's law and the provisions of the EC 7th Directive. Many of the member states have been slow to bring the provisions of the EC 7th Directive into their own legal and accounting framework. An undertaking wishing to take the exemption should, therefore, ensure that:

- The EC 7th Directive applies in the country in which the parent is established.
- It is effective for the relevant accounting period.
- The parent's annual report and consolidated financial statements have indeed been prepared and audited in accordance with the law of its own country and in accordance with the provisions of the EC 7th Directive.
- It is possible to obtain a certified translation of the parent's financial statements in time for filing with the parent's individual financial statements.

21.73 It should also be remembered that the conditions set out above also apply where the immediate parent is established in the UK. For example, a wholly-owned UK subsidiary of a UK parent that is also itself a parent company will also have to file a copy of its parent's consolidated financial statements with its own to comply with the requirement. To ensure that the Registrar of Companies files the financial statements correctly it is necessary for the wholly-owned subsidiary's company number to be clearly written on the front cover of the parent's consolidated financial statements to ensure that they are filed on the subsidiary's file at Companies House and not the parent's file by mistake.

21.74 Situations might arise in practice where, for example, a group's ultimate parent is established in Germany (within the EEA) where it wholly owns a subsidiary established in Switzerland (outside the EEA), which in turn owns a group of companies established in the UK (within the EEA). Even where the ultimate parent prepares consolidated financial statements in accordance with the 7th Directive that include the UK group, the UK group will still have to prepare consolidated financial statements, because its immediate parent is not established under the laws of a member state of the EEA. [Sec 228(1)].

The European Economic Area

21.75 The European Economic Area (EEA) came into effect on 1 January 1994 and extends the European Community single market to participating states. The term, therefore, now covers the non-EU countries of Norway, Iceland and Liechtenstein as well as the EU countries of Austria, Belgium, Denmark, Finland, France, Germany, Greece, Republic of Ireland, Italy, Luxembourg, The Netherlands, Portugal, Spain, Sweden and the UK.

21.76 The provisions of the EC 7th Directive were partly enacted into the laws of Austria and Finland in 1994. However, Finland and Austria have only approximately enacted both the 4th and the 7th Directives. This means that if a parent in one of these countries prepares its consolidated financial statements strictly in accordance with its national laws they will not satisfy the requirements of the EC 7th Directive as required by section 228(b) of the Act (explained in para 21.68 above). As a consequence, any subsidiaries of such a parent who are themselves intermediate parent companies will have to prepare consolidated financial statements for their sub-groups. To overcome this problem, it is possible for parent companies in Austria and Finland to go further than their national laws require and comply fully with the EC 7th Directive.

21.77 Italy implemented the EC 7th Directive from 1 January 1994 and Sweden did so in 1995. All the other members of the EU implemented the EC 7th Directive before January 1993. However, it remains important to check that the parent's consolidated financial statements do comply with the EC 7th Directive before the exemption is taken.

All subsidiaries excluded from consolidation

21.78 Where all of a parent's subsidiaries are permitted or required to be excluded from consolidation by section 229 of the Act (as restricted by FRS 2), that parent is exempt from the requirement to prepare consolidated financial statements. The conditions for exclusion of subsidiaries from consolidation are considered in detail in paragraph 21.179.

Accounting treatment

21.79 Where a parent makes use of any of the above exemptions not to prepare consolidated financial statements, it should treat in its individual financial statements its interests in subsidiaries as fixed asset investments except for those held exclusively with a view to resale. Subsidiaries held exclusively with a view to resale should be recorded as current asset investments at the lower of cost and net realisable value (see further para 21.196).

Disclosure

21.80 Where a parent makes use of any of the exemptions and does not prepare consolidated financial statements, FRS 2 requires that parent to:

- Comply with the disclosure requirements of Part 1 of Schedule 5 to the Act in respect of parent companies not required to prepare consolidated financial statements.

- State that its financial statements present information about it as an individual undertaking and not about its group. The statement should include or refer to the note giving the grounds on which the parent undertaking is exempt from preparing consolidated financial statements, as required by Schedule 5 paragraph 1(4).

[FRS 2 para 22].

21.81 The disclosure requirements set out in Part 1 of Schedule 5 to the Act are extensive. They cover the following subjects:

- Reason for not preparing consolidated financial statements.

- Details about subsidiaries including: name; country of incorporation or registration; proportion of shares held; profit/loss for the year; aggregate capital and reserves at the year end; details about non-coterminous year ends; qualified audit reports; and holdings in shares and debentures of the parent.

- Details about significant holdings of greater than 10 per cent in undertakings other than subsidiary undertakings including: name; country of incorporation; proportion of shares held.

- Additional information about significant holdings of greater than 20 per cent in undertakings other than subsidiary undertakings including: aggregate capital and reserves and profit or loss for the year.

- Details of arrangements attracting merger relief.

- Details about parents including: name of ultimate parent; name of largest group of undertakings for which consolidated financial statements are drawn up of which the undertaking is a member; and the name of the smallest such group.

21.82 The disclosure requirements of Part I of Schedule 5 that relate to subsidiaries are explained in detail in chapter 16.

Suggested wording for exempt parents

21.83 In practice, it is likely that many parent undertakings will be exempt from the requirement to prepare consolidated financial statements. Set out below are examples of wording that may be included in the accounting policies of parent undertakings that use one of the exemptions from preparing consolidated financial statements.

Example

Intermediate parent undertaking

Accounting policy extract – company

The financial statements contain information about GAAP UK Limited as an individual company and do not contain consolidated financial information as the parent of a group. The Company is exempt under section 228 of the Companies Act 1985 from the requirement to prepare consolidated financial statements as it and its subsidiary undertakings are included by full consolidation in the consolidated financial statements of its parent, [GAAP (UK) plc/ FRGAAP SA], a company [registered in England and Wales/registered in Scotland/ incorporated in (for example) France].

Accounting policy extract – unincorporated undertaking

The financial statements contain information about GAAP & Co as an individual undertaking and do not contain consolidated financial information as the parent of a group. The [Partnership/Trust/ or other undertaking as applicable] is exempt under paragraph 21 [(b) or (c) as applicable] of Financial Reporting Standard No. 2 from the requirement to prepare consolidated financial statements as it is included by full consolidation in the consolidated financial statements of its parent, [GAAP & Co/GAAP (UK) plc, a [partnership whose principal place of business is at [insert address]/company registered in England and Wales].

All subsidiaries excluded from consolidation

Accounting policy extract – company

The financial statements contain information about GAAP UK Limited as an individual company and do not contain consolidated financial information as the parent of a group. The Company is exempt under section 229(5) of the Companies Act 1985 from the requirement to prepare consolidated financial statements as the directors consider that all the company's subsidiaries [may/should] be excluded from consolidation for the reasons set out [below/in note x].

Accounting policy extract – unincorporated undertaking

The financial statements contain information about GAAP & Co as an individual undertaking and do not contain consolidated financial information as the parent of a group. The [Partnership/Trust/ or other undertaking as applicable] is exempt under paragraph 21(d) of Financial Reporting Standard No. 2 from the requirement to prepare consolidated financial statements as the [directors/corresponding officers] consider that all its subsidiaries [may/should] be excluded from consolidation for the reasons set out [below/in note x].

Subsidiary undertakings

Introduction

21.84 Before the parent of a group of companies can start to prepare consolidated financial statements, it is important to decide exactly which undertakings form the group and should, therefore, be included in the consolidation. In addition, it is important to determine whether any subsidiaries should be excluded from the group under the exemptions allowed or required by the legislation and FRS 2.

21.85 Consequently, determining which undertakings are the parent's subsidiaries and should, therefore, be consolidated is fundamental to the preparation of consolidated financial statements and this section considers the rules that govern whether an undertaking is a subsidiary for this purpose.

Implications of the EC 7th Directive

21.86 The Companies Act 1989 implemented most of the provisions of the EC 7th Directive with regard to the definitions of subsidiary undertakings. The definitions included in the 7th Directive are based on control, whereas the definitions that applied under the old rules in the Companies Act 1985 were based principally on the legal ownership of a company. Although the changes in some of the definitions were fundamental, they have not affected significantly the companies that are consolidated by groups. This is because, for example, the majority of 100 per cent *owned* subsidiaries that were consolidated under the old legislation, are also 100 per cent *controlled* and, consequently, are also consolidated under the provisions in the Companies Act 1989.

Meaning of subsidiary undertaking

21.87 As mentioned above, a subsidiary undertaking can mean any of the following undertakings:

- A body corporate.
- A partnership.
- An unincorporated association carrying on a trade or business for profit.
- An unincorporated association not trading for profit.

[Sec 259(1); FRS 2 para 16].

21.88 Consequently, any undertakings included in the above list may fall to be consolidated with the financial statements of the parent if they are subsidiary undertakings.

21.89 It appears that the definition of 'undertaking' in section 259 of the Act is wide enough to include trusts. Case law refers to 'association' meaning a combination of persons or of firms carrying on a particular venture, which seems to encompass trusts. The distinction in case law between associations and undertakings is that undertakings carry on business for gain. However, the definition in section 259 is not restricted to there being a profit or gain resulting from the association's activities. Therefore, it would seem that generally trusts are associations that fall within the definition of undertaking in section 259.

21.90 The Act provides the definitions of parent and subsidiary. FRS 2 uses the same definitions as those given in the Act and builds on them by giving additional guidance on their interpretation. There are five situations where an undertaking may be a subsidiary of a parent undertaking and these are where the parent:

- Holds a majority of the voting rights in the undertaking.

- Is a member of the undertaking and has the right to appoint or remove directors holding a majority of the voting rights at meetings of the board on all, or substantially all, matters.

- Has a right to exercise dominant influence over the undertaking by virtue of provisions either in its memorandum or articles, or in a control contract. (Note that no shareholding is necessary.)

- Is a member of the undertaking and controls alone, pursuant to an agreement with other shareholders or members, a majority of the voting rights in the undertaking.

- Has a participating interest in the undertaking and:

- actually exercises dominant influence over it; or
- the parent and the undertaking are managed on a unified basis.

[Sec 258(2)(4), 10A Sch 3(1)].

21.91 The common feature of these definitions is that of control by the parent (or the parent and its subsidiaries) over the subsidiary. The definitions are considered in detail in the paragraphs that follow.

21.92 Where an undertaking is determined not to be a subsidiary undertaking under the Act and FRS 2 it may still require to be consolidated if it is a quasi-subsidiary. A quasi-subsidiary is defined in FRS 5 as *"a company, trust, partnership or other vehicle that, though not fulfilling the definition of a subsidiary, is directly or indirectly controlled by the reporting entity and gives rise to benefits for that entity that are in substance no different from those that would arise were the vehicle a subsidiary"*. [FRS 5 para 7]. Where a quasi-subsidiary is identified, it is accounted for in the same way as other subsidiaries, that is, by way of full consolidation. Quasi-subsidiaries and how to account for them are considered in chapter 4 (see also para 21.161).

Expressions used by unincorporated undertakings

21.93 Although subsidiaries can now include other unincorporated undertakings such as partnerships, various parts of the legislation use expressions that are common to companies only. Consequently, the Act provides the following provision:

> *"Other expressions appropriate to companies shall be construed, in relation to an undertaking which is not a company, as references to the corresponding persons, officers, documents or organs, as the case may be, appropriate to undertakings of that description."* [Sec 259(3)].

21.94 This provision will apply in a number of situations, but a good example of its effect concerns the expressions used by limited partnerships. A limited partnership is made up of a 'general partner' and a number of 'limited partners'. The general partner manages the business and the limited partners cannot be involved in the day to day business of the partnership. The partnership itself does not have a board of directors, but the equivalent to the board is the general partner himself. Consequently, if a company is a general partner in a limited partnership, then it will control the board of the limited partnership (see para 21.103) and the partnership will, therefore, be a subsidiary under section 258(2)(b) (see further para 21.112).

21.95 Section 259(3) is also important because various disclosure provisions concerning subsidiary undertakings detailed in Schedule 5 to the Act are expressed using terms that are only relevant to companies. These disclosure requirements are considered further in paragraph 21.230.

Majority of voting rights

21.96 An undertaking is a subsidiary where the parent undertaking holds a majority of its voting rights. [Sec 258(2)(a); FRS 2 para 14(a)].

21.97 This is the definition of a subsidiary that is applied most frequently in practice to identify subsidiaries. While ownership (equity) and voting rights are usually held in equal proportions, there are situations where an undertaking may own a majority of the equity in another undertaking and yet not hold a majority of the voting rights in it. In such a situation, the undertaking will not be a subsidiary (unless it is a subsidiary by virtue of one of the other definitions).

21.98 The example that follows illustrates how these provisions work in practice. Company A owns 100 ordinary shares in company B and company C owns 100 five per cent preference shares in company B. Company B has no other share capital.

Example

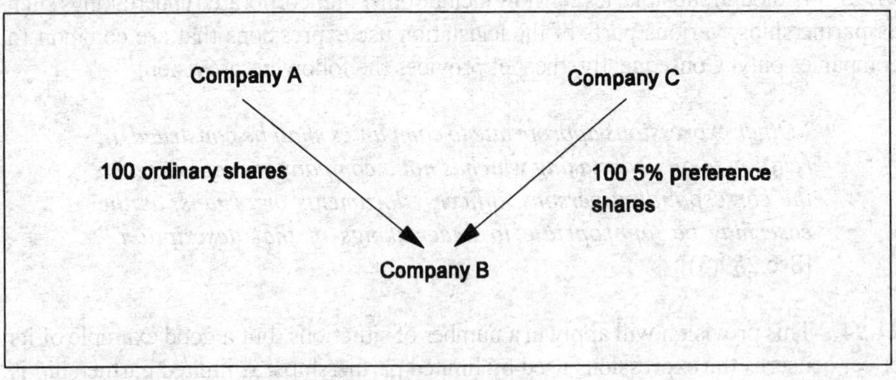

The rights attached to company B's shares are as follows:

- Ordinary shares:
  - 100 £1 ordinary shares.
  - All dividends after payment of preference dividends.
  - Right to all surplus assets on a winding up of the company after repayment of 5% preference shares.
  - Right to vote on all matters at any meetings of the company.

- Preference shares:
  - 100 £1 preference shares.
  - Fixed preference dividend.
  - Right on winding up to the repayment of par value and up to 25% of any sum standing to the credit of the share premium account.
  - No rights to vote at company meetings.

The ordinary shares carry a right to participate beyond a specified amount in the winding up of the company and are, therefore, 'equity' share capital in law. In addition, the preference shares are similarly equity under the Act because they also carry a right to participate beyond a specified amount in a winding up. (However, under FRS 4 they would be classified as non-equity shares, because they have a fixed dividend (see further chapter 18)). The classification of shares between equity share capital and non-equity share capital was crucial in determining whether a company was a subsidiary of another under the pre Companies Act 1989 rules. Consequently, in this example, because both types of share rank as equity in law, company A only owns 50% of the equity share capital of company B. Company B would, therefore, not have been a subsidiary of company A under those rules.

Under the Companies Act 1989 rules, however, the distinction between equity share capital and other share capital is irrelevant in determining whether an undertaking is a subsidiary of another. The 1989 Act definition looks at who controls the 'voting rights' in the undertaking. The preference shares have no voting rights, while the ordinary shares do. Consequently, under the 1989 Act rules, company B is a subsidiary of company A, but is not a subsidiary of company C. This of course ignores who has the right to appoint the majority of the board of directors.

21.99 The Act and FRS 2 provide considerable guidance on the interpretation of the term 'voting rights', both in the context of companies and in the context of unincorporated undertakings.

21.100 'Voting rights' means the rights conferred on shareholders in respect of their shares to vote at the undertaking's general meetings on all, or substantially all, matters. [10A Sch 2(1); FRS 2 para 17]. Similarly, where an undertaking does not have a share capital, voting rights also mean the rights conferred on members to vote at the undertaking's general meetings on all, or substantially all, matters. [10A Sch 2(1); FRS 2 para 17]. If the undertaking does not have general meetings where matters are decided by exercising voting rights, 'voting rights' will mean having the right under the undertaking's constitution to direct its overall policy, or to alter the terms of its constitution. [10A Sch 2(2)].

21.101 In determining whether an undertaking holds a majority of the voting rights, certain common rules apply and these are explained further in paragraph 21.168. In particular, options will generally only be taken into consideration, for the purposes of determining whether any party has a majority of voting rights or control of the board, when the option *has been exercised* (see further 21.170).

21.102 In addition, the total voting rights in an undertaking have to be reduced where any rights are exercisable by the undertaking itself. [10A Sch 10]. This means, for example, that where an undertaking holds any of its own shares they should be excluded from the total voting rights taken into account in deciding whether the undertaking is a subsidiary.

Appointment or removal of majority of board

21.103 An undertaking is a subsidiary where the parent is a member of that undertaking and has the right to appoint or remove a majority of its board of directors. [Sec 258(2)(b); FRS 2 para 14(b)]. The meaning of the term 'member' is discussed in paragraph 21.164.

21.104 In this circumstance, *"the right to appoint or remove the majority of the board of directors"* means the right to appoint or remove directors that have a majority of the voting rights at board meetings on all or substantially all matters (without the need for any other person's consent or concurrence, except in the case where no other person has the right to appoint or, as the case may be, remove in relation to that directorship). [10A Sch 3(1)(3)]. In these circumstances, an undertaking should be treated as having the right to appoint a person to a directorship where:

- The person's appointment follows directly from his appointment as a director of the investing undertaking.

- The directorship is held by the investing undertaking itself.

[10A Sch 3(2)].

21.105 Certain common rules apply to the expression 'rights' used in paragraph 21.103 above and these are explained further in paragraph 21.168.

21.106 The operation of this definition of subsidiary is illustrated by the example that follows. In this example, the structure is the same as that described in the example in paragraph 21.98 above and illustrated in the diagram. However, in this example the rights attaching to the two different types of share are as follows:

Example

- Ordinary shares:
  - 100 £1 ordinary shares.
  - All dividends after payment of preference dividends.
  - Right to all surplus assets on a winding up of the company after repayment of 5% preference shares.

- Right to vote on all matters at any meetings of the company.
- Power to appoint two directors of the company with one vote each.

- Preference shares:

  - 100 £1 preference shares.
  - Fixed preference dividend.
  - Right on winding up to the repayment of par value and up to 25% of any sum standing to the credit of the share premium account.
  - No rights to vote at company meetings.
  - No voting rights, but where the preference dividend payment is passed the shareholders have the power to appoint two directors with two votes each.

Initially, company A holds the majority of the voting rights of company B and by virtue of section 258(2)(a) (as explained in para 21.98 above) company B is a subsidiary of company A. However, if the preference dividend is in arrears and as a consequence the preference shareholders appoint their two directors, company B becomes a subsidiary of company C by virtue of section 258(2)(b), as company C then has the right to appoint or remove directors holding a majority of the voting rights at company B's board meetings.

21.107 The situation described in the example is unusual and it is likely that in this situation as soon as company C is able to control the board of company B, company A will lose effective control and will have to exclude company C from its consolidated financial statements. In this regard, FRS 2 states that where more than one undertaking is identified as a parent in such a situation, only one of those parents can have control in practice. [FRS 2 para 62]. In practice, when the arrears of dividend are paid the directors appointed to company B by company C might cease to hold office, in which case control would again reside with company A.

21.108 Where severe long-term restrictions exist on the rights or the ability of one of the parents to exercise control and where this is so the subsidiary is required under FRS 2 to be excluded from consolidation (see para 21.185). Alternatively, in a situation where there is effectively deadlock in voting rights there might be common control, in which case this might indicate the existence of a joint venture (see chapter 28). [FRS 2 para 63].

21.109 Where an undertaking has the right to appoint a director with a casting vote in the event of a board deadlock and that undertaking controls half of the voting rights on the board, it will effectively control the board as it holds the casting vote and can, therefore, control any board decision.

21.110 In practice a further complication can arise. Many 50/50 joint ventures are set up in the form of companies with each party owning 50 per cent of the equity, holding 50 per cent of the voting rights in general meeting and having the right to appoint directors with 50 per cent of the votes on the board. In order to avoid total deadlock in the event of disagreement a 'rotating' chairman is appointed with a casting vote. The chairman, who is chosen from the directors, is appointed in alternate years by each party to the joint venture. Therefore, in theory, by virtue of the casting vote, in years one, three and five the undertaking is the subsidiary of one of the venturers while in years two, four and six it is a subsidiary of the other.

21.111 Clearly it does not make sense for each party to consolidate in alternate years. Consequently, using the provision in paragraph 62 of FRS 2 mentioned in paragraph 21.107, such problems can be resolved in practice by considering the substance of the arrangement. It is likely that the arrangement outlined above would be treated as a joint venture with shared control, that is, both parties might equity account, or if the joint venture were an unincorporated undertaking proportionately consolidate, their interests.

Limited partnerships

21.112 As mentioned in paragraph 21.94 above a limited partnership is made up of a 'general partner' and a number of 'limited partners'. The general partner manages the business and the limited partners cannot be involved in the day to day business of the partnership. The partnership itself does not have a board of directors, but the equivalent to the board is the general partner himself. Consequently, if a company is a general partner in a limited partnership, then it will control the equivalent of the board and the partnership will, therefore, be a subsidiary. Treating such limited partnerships as subsidiaries can cause particular problems in practice, especially where a company's investment in a limited partnership is as the general partner and is only nominal in amount.

21.113 Venture capitalists have made extensive use in recent years of limited partnerships (for tax reasons) and under the provisions of the Act appear to have to consolidate such undertakings, even where they are merely the general partner. However, as explained below in paragraph 21.179, the Act does allow subsidiaries not to be consolidated in certain circumstances. One such circumstance is where the interest of the parent is acquired and is held exclusively with a view to subsequent resale. This might appear to be a let out for venture capitalists, because their investments in limited partnerships are generally held for resale. However, the ASB in its Interim Statement on consolidated accounts restricted the use of the Act's exemption for such venture capital investments, because although such investments are argued to be held exclusively with a view to subsequent resale, they are generally held for longer than one year and under the Statement a subsidiary could not be excluded on these grounds unless it was expected to be sold within one year. This provision of the ASB's Interim Statement was included in paragraph 11 of FRS 2 (see para 21.196).

21.114 The result of consolidating such a limited partnership could be very odd. For example, where a venture capital investment is only (say) one per cent as a general partner, full consolidation of the limited partnership would be required showing a minority interest of 99 per cent. Consequently, this seems an ideal situation where the true and fair override should apply to avoid full consolidation. It might be justifiable in such circumstances to proportionately consolidate (see further chapter 28) the company's share of the assets and liabilities and profits and losses of the limited partnership; this represents an override of the requirement in paragraph 1 of Schedule 4A to the Act which requires consolidation in full of those results and assets and liabilities. If such an override is used, the particulars, reasons and effect should be given in the notes in accordance with the Act and UITF Abstract 7 (see para 21.57 and chapter 2). This illustrates the point that a group cannot override those sections of the Act that specify the composition of the group; but it can override the detailed provisions of (in this case) Schedule 4A as to how a subsidiary is to be consolidated. An example of a company that has adopted proportional consolidation to account for its limited partnership subsidiaries is Electra Investment Trust P.L.C, which is given in Table 21.1.

Table 21.1 – Electra Investment Trust P.L.C – Report & Accounts – 30 September 1994

STATEMENT OF ACCOUNTING POLICIES (extract)

Limited Partnership Funds

The Group consolidates its attributable proportion, as a limited partner, of the assets and liabilities and income and expenditure of the limited partnership funds which it manages as a general partner.

Such funds fall within the definition of subsidiary undertakings contained in the Companies Act 1985, as amended by the Companies Act 1989, and Financial Reporting Standard No. 2. The Act and the Standard require the consolidation of all subsidiary undertakings. The two limited partnership funds, Electra Private Equity Partners ("EPEP") and Electra Innvotec Limited Partnership ("Innvotec"), in which the Company has invested and which are managed by companies within the Group, technically fall within the definition of subsidiary undertakings. However, the Directors do not consider the Accounts would present a true and fair view if the EPEP and Innvotec funds were to be fully consolidated with the interests of the other investors (representing respectively at 30 September 1993 57.9% and 72.7% of the EPEP and Innvotec funds) accounted for as minority interests. The Directors have not accounted for these funds as subsidiary undertakings as they consider the accounts would not give a true and fair view if the assets of the other limited partners were to be consolidated with the assets of the Group. The effect of full consolidation is shown in Note 25.

Dominant influence

21.115 The Act uses the term dominant influence in two of its definitions of subsidiaries. These definitions, which are considered in detail later in this chapter, are as follows; an undertaking is a subsidiary of a parent if the parent:

- Has a *right to exercise a dominant influence* over the undertaking by virtue of provisions either in its memorandum or articles, or in a control contract (see para 21.118).

- Owns a participating interest in the undertaking and *actually exercises a dominant influence* over it (see para 21.124).

21.116 The Act defines the term 'right to exercise a dominant influence', but it does not define 'actually exercises a dominant influence'. Furthermore, the Act specifically states that its definition of 'right to exercise a dominant influence' should *"not be read as affecting the construction of the expression 'actually exercises a dominant influence'"*. [10A Sch 4(3)]. The two definitions appear somewhat contradictory, but the right sought in the first bullet point above is a contractual right, whereas with the latter definition, it is the control that the investing entity actually has in practice that is important. The contractual right to exercise a dominant influence was introduced into the EC 7th Directive to deal with situations that arose in another EC member state; although it was also included in the UK legislation, it may not be effective in the UK (see further para 21.123).

21.117 FRS 2 first defines 'dominant influence' and then provides definitions for *'right to exercise a dominant influence'* and *'actually exercises a dominant influence'*. Dominant influence is defined as:

> *"Influence that can be exercised to achieve the operating and financial policies desired by the holder of the influence, notwithstanding the rights or influence of any other party."*
> [FRS 2 para 7].

21.118 By defining 'dominant influence', as well as the two longer expressions in the Act containing the term, FRS 2 is, in effect, linking the two expressions. The common thread is the implementation by the subsidiary of the operating and financial policies desired by the holder of the influence, that is, the parent.

Right to exercise a dominant influence

21.119 As stated above, an undertaking will be a subsidiary where the parent has the right to exercise a dominant influence in either of the following two ways:

- By provisions contained in the undertaking's memorandum or articles of association.

- By a 'control contract' with the undertaking.

[Sec 258(2)(c)].

21.120 A 'control contract' is a contract in writing that confers such a right that is authorised by the memorandum or articles of the undertaking in relation to which the right is exercisable and is permitted by the law under which that undertaking is established. [10A Sch 4(2)].

21.121 It should be noted that for this definition of a subsidiary the parent need not have an interest in the subsidiary.

21.122 Both the Act and FRS 2 state that the right to exercise dominant influence over another undertaking shall not be regarded as exercisable unless:

> "*... it has a right to give directions with respect to the operating and financial policies of that other undertaking which its directors are obliged to comply with whether or not they are for the benefit of that other undertaking.*"[10A Sch 4(1); FRS 2 para 7(a)].

21.123 It is thought that 'the right to exercise a dominant influence' is unlikely to apply to UK subsidiary companies as, in the UK, directors have a duty under common law to act in the best interests of the company. There is some doubt whether the directors of a UK subsidiary could be obliged to comply with the directions of the holder of the influence if to do so would not be for the benefit of the subsidiary as this might leave them in breach of their duties as directors.

Participating interest and dominant influence

21.124 An undertaking is a parent in relation to another undertaking, its subsidiary, if it owns a *participating interest* in the undertaking and *actually exercises a dominant influence* over it. [Sec 258(4)(a); FRS 2 para 14(e)].

21.125 This definition of subsidiary, like the others, has been taken directly from the EC 7th Directive. Although its implementation by member states into their national laws was optional, it was incorporated into the UK legislation by the Companies Act 1989 deliberately to catch a number of off balance sheet schemes that used special purpose companies to avoid consolidation (see further chapter 4).

21.126 A participating interest is presumed to exist where an interest in the shares (by number) of an undertaking is more than 20 per cent, unless the contrary is shown. [Sec 260(2)]. A participating interest is defined as:

> "*.....an interest held by an undertaking in the shares of another undertaking which it holds on a long-term basis for the purpose of securing a contribution to its activities by the exercise of control or influence arising from or related to that interest.*"
> [Sec 260(1) and FRS 2 para 15].

21.127 For the purposes of this definition, references to shares in relation to:

- An undertaking with a share capital, are to allotted shares.
- An undertaking with capital in a form other than share capital, are to rights to share in the capital of the undertaking.
- An undertaking without capital, are to interests:
  - conferring any right to share in the profits or the liability to contribute to the losses of the undertaking; or
  - giving rise to an obligation to contribute to the debts or expenses of the undertaking in the event of a winding up.

[Sec 259(2)].

21.128 The references to shares, therefore, include all types of shares and not just ordinary shares.

21.129 References to an interest in shares include an interest that is convertible into an interest in shares and an option to acquire shares or any interest that is convertible into shares. [Sec 260(3); FRS 2 para 15(b)]. For the purpose of determining whether a company has a participating interest in another company, it does not matter whether the options can be exercised now or in the future, their mere existence is taken into account whether or not they are currently exercisable (which is not the case when determining whether the entity is a subsidiary *via* control of its voting rights – see further para 21.170). An interest or option in shares falls within this definition even if the shares to which it relates, until conversion or the exercise of the option, are unissued. [Sec 260(3)]. Interests held on behalf of an undertaking or by, or on behalf of, any of its subsidiary undertakings should be treated as held by it. [Sec 260(4),(5)(a); FRS 2 para 15(c)]. Consider the following example.

Example

A parent has a 10% long-term holding in an undertaking and a subsidiary of the parent has a 15% long-term holding in the same undertaking. The subsidiary is unlikely to have a participating interest in the undertaking as it only holds 15% of the shares, but the parent is deemed to have a 25% holding in the undertaking and is, therefore, presumed to hold a participating interest, unless shown otherwise.

21.130 It should be remembered that it is quite possible for a holding of 20 per cent or below in an undertaking to be a participating interest and in certain circumstances require consolidation, as explained below.

Actually exercises a dominant influence

Definition

21.131 Neither the Act nor the EC 7th Directive define the term 'actual exercise of a dominant influence' used in this definition of a subsidiary. The first proposal for a definition of the term was set out in ED 50 in July 1990. This was shortly followed by the first formal definition in the Interim Statement. When FRS 2 was issued, it redefined 'actual exercise of dominant influence' as follows:

> *"The actual exercise of dominant influence is the exercise of an influence that achieves the result that the operating and financial policies of the undertaking influenced are set in accordance with the wishes of the holder of the influence and for the holder's benefit whether or not those wishes are explicit. The actual exercise of dominant influence is identified by its effect in practice rather than by the way in which it is exercised."* [FRS 2 para 7 (b)].

21.132 The definition above hinges on the term 'dominant influence'. Dominant influence is defined in FRS 2 in terms of the influence that can be exercised to achieve the operating and financial policies desired by the holder of the influence (see para 21.117). [FRS 2 para 7].

21.133 The interpretation of the term 'actual exercise of dominant influence' has proved to be most difficult in practice, principally because of the degree of judgement involved.

21.134 An illustration of a group that consolidates subsidiaries because of dominant influence is given in Table 21.2.

Table 21.2 – BET Public Limited Company – Annual Report – 2 April 1994

Accounting policies (extract)

(b) Basis of consolidation (extract)

SUBSIDIARY UNDERTAKINGS (extract)

All companies over which the group is able to exercise a dominant influence are consolidated as subsidiary undertakings. Dominant influence is defined as the right to give directions with respect to operating and financial policies.

Operating and financial policies

21.135 The operating and financial policies of an undertaking will normally be set by the board of directors (in the case of a company) or a similar body for unincorporated undertakings. Usually, a parent would have a *right* to control the board by having the power to appoint or remove a majority of the board and would, therefore, be a parent by virtue of section 258(2)(b) of the Act.

21.136 The 'actual exercise of dominant influence' definition of a subsidiary, discussed above, is intended to apply to those undertakings that, although effectively controlled by the parent, are not specifically caught by other definitions of the Act.

21.137 The operating and financial policies of a typical business would cover (but may not be limited to) the following subjects:

- Overall strategy.
- Financial.
- Marketing.
- Production.
- Personnel.

Effect in practice

21.138 Heavy emphasis is placed on the effect of the influence in practice to ensure that only undertakings genuinely controlled by the parent are defined as subsidiaries under this section. Theoretical powers, that would never be likely to be exercised or to influence the decisions of those in day-to-day control of the operating and financial policies of the undertaking, could not by themselves form a basis for actual exercise of dominant influence. It is what happens in practice that is important.

Power of veto and other reserve powers

21.139 A power of veto (or other reserve power) that has the necessary effect in practice may give the holder a basis for actually exercising a dominant influence. However, the nature of the power of veto will be of critical importance. In general, a power of veto will only have the necessary effect if:

- it is held in conjunction with other rights or powers; or
- it relates to the day-to-day activities of the undertaking and no other party holds a similar veto.

21.140 For example, if an undertaking has shares carrying less than 50 per cent of the votes, but has over 75 per cent of the equity share capital of a company, it may only be able to block business that requires a special resolution. Such a power of veto is not, alone, sufficient to give the undertaking control, but would clearly have to be taken into account with other factors in determining whether the undertaking has the requisite control over the other party.

Commercial relationships

21.141 Certain undertakings can become very dependent on others by virtue of the commercial relationship between them. Examples include undertakings with:

- Only one customer.
- Only one possible supplier.
- Large borrowings from a bank.

21.142 In each of the above examples there may be situations where the undertaking concerned may be significantly influenced by the desires of the other party. With this in mind FRS 2 states that *"Commercial relationships such as that of supplier, customer or lender do not of themselves constitute dominant influence"*. [FRS 2 para 72].

21.143 These relationships will not, generally, give rise to dominant influence unless some other factors are involved. For example, in the situation where undertakings only have one customer or supplier, if the customer or supplier concerned has a substantial participating interest in the undertaking, but it is not quite sufficient to control the undertaking on the grounds of his interest alone, the participating interest and the customer/supplier relationship taken together could be sufficient to give the customer/supplier the required control.

Active or passive

21.144 A parent may actually exercise its dominant influence in an interventionist or non-interventionist way. The parent may wish to be involved in the detailed day-to-day operating and financial policies of its subsidiary, or it may prefer to take more of a 'back seat' approach and merely outline the results it desires while leaving the subsidiary's management to deal with day-to-day decisions.

21.145 The 'day-to-day' approach is likely be more common where a parent with considerable management experience in a particular market purchases a participating interest in a poorly managed undertaking trading in the same sector.

21.146 The 'back seat' approach is likely be more common where a parent purchases a participating interest in a well managed and profitable undertaking trading in a market in which the parent's management has little experience. In practice, it may be difficult to obtain evidence of dominant influence exercised in this manner.

21.147 Equally, a parent's management may change between the 'day-to-day' and the 'back seat' approaches depending upon the circumstances prevailing at any particular time.

21.148 Because of the variety of ways in which dominant influence can be exercised, the FRS states that *"evidence of continuous intervention is not necessary to support the view that dominant influence is actually exercised"*. [FRS 2 para 73]. It may be that rare intervention on a critical matter will be sufficient evidence. But if no intervention takes place, there is no actual exercise of dominant influence.

Two parents

21.149 If an undertaking is a subsidiary of one parent, for example, by virtue of controlling the voting rights in general meeting, then it might also be a subsidiary of another parent by virtue of that parent holding a participating interest and actually exercising a dominant influence if the first parent's control is subject to severe long-term restrictions. The situation where two parents are identified by the Act is considered further in paragraphs 21.107.

Ceasing to exercise a dominant influence

21.150 As interpretation of the term 'actual exercise of dominant influence' is subjective it might be seen as an opportunity, by some, to manipulate profit or gearing. In theory, at least, a parent might consolidate the results of a subsidiary in some years and exclude them in others, on the grounds that the parent either does, or does not, actually exercise dominant influence in a particular year. FRS 2 recognises that this may cause problems and states that:

> *"Once there has been evidence that one undertaking has exercised a dominant influence over another, then the dominant undertaking should be assumed to continue to exercise its influence until there is evidence to the contrary. However, it is still necessary for the preparation of the consolidated financial statements to examine the relationship between the undertakings each year to assess any evidence of change in status that may have arisen."* [FRS 2 para 73].

21.151 If an undertaking has demonstrated that it actually exercises a dominant influence by, for example, vetoing a board decision or removing a chief executive then that undertaking will be presumed to continue to actually exercise dominant influence. This will continue to apply, even if the veto is not exercised again, unless there is some change in status of the relationship between the two undertakings.

21.152 Once an undertaking has been treated as a subsidiary of another, because the other actually exercises dominant influence over it, the general principle is that it should continue to be treated as a subsidiary until there is persuasive evidence that the relationship between the two undertakings has changed.

Summary

21.153 To decide whether or not, in practice, an undertaking actually exercises a dominant influence over another a number of different factors have to be considered. Therefore, it is important that the full circumstances of each situation are considered, including the effect of any formal or informal agreements between the undertakings. Any decision in this respect is likely to be judgemental and should take into account the following:

- The degree of board representation.
- The degree of day-to-day influence over the financial and operating policies of the undertaking.
- The extent of any powers of veto (or other reserve powers) held by the investor.
- Evidence of intervention to ensure that the investor's preferred operational and financial policies are implemented by the undertaking.
- Powers held by other investors or third parties that affect the degree of influence of the investor over the undertaking.
- Evidence of decisions *not* being taken in accordance with the investor's wishes.
- Other contrary evidence that indicates that dominant influence is not held.

Disclosure

21.154 Where an undertaking is a subsidiary only because its parent undertaking has a participating interest in it and actually exercises a dominant influence over it, the consolidated financial statements should disclose the basis of the parent's dominant influence. [FRS 2 para 34].

Participating interest and managed on a unified basis

21.155 An undertaking is a parent in relation to another undertaking, a subsidiary, if it has a participating interest in the undertaking and it and the undertaking are managed on a unified basis. [Sec 258(4)(b); FRS 2 para 14(e)].

21.156 The Act provides no definition of 'managed on a unified basis', however, FRS 2 defines it as follows:

> *"Two or more undertakings are managed on a unified basis if the whole of the operations of the undertakings are integrated and they are managed as a single unit. Unified management does not arise solely because one undertaking manages another."*
> [FRS 2 para 12].

21.157 The application of this definition in practice will, as for dominant influence, require considerable judgement. The definition seems to suggest unified management at all levels in the undertakings. Characteristics of unified management could include:

- Adoption of an overall management strategy for the group which includes the undertaking in question.
- The group treating the undertaking as if it were a subsidiary, for example by determining its dividend policy.
- Common management teams, both at board level and operationally.
- Common employees.
- Common administrative functions, for example, accounting, personnel and marketing.
- Common premises.

Control governed by an agreement

21.158 An undertaking will be a subsidiary where the parent is a member of it and controls alone, following an agreement with other shareholders or members of the undertaking, a majority of its voting rights. [Sec 258(2)(d); FRS 2 para 14(d)].

21.159 The term 'voting rights' in this context means the same as the term explained in paragraph 21.100 above.

Parent but no control

21.160 It is possible for an undertaking to be identified by the tests of the Act as the parent of another undertaking (its subsidiary), without the parent having control over the subsidiary. In that situation the subsidiary is required by the Act to be consolidated unless it meets one of the requirements for exclusion from consolidation. In the situation where a parent does not control a subsidiary it is likely that, unless the lack of control is temporary, it will meet the requirements for exclusion from consolidation on the grounds of severe long-term restrictions (see para 21.185).

Control but not the parent

21.161 In certain situations, an undertaking will control another and yet not be defined by the Act as the parent of that other undertaking. In this situation it is likely that the other undertaking will be a quasi-subsidiary. Many off balance sheet schemes have, until recently, been constructed around the use of special purpose vehicles (SPV's) which, although legally not subsidiaries, are nevertheless effectively controlled by another undertaking. Consolidation of the assets and liabilities of non-subsidiary SPV's has been avoided in the past as they were not subsidiary undertakings. The implications of quasi-subsidiaries and their definition are considered in detail in chapter 4. Lonrho has a 19 per cent interest in an entity which it considers to be a quasi-subsidiary, as illustrated in Table 21.3.

Table 21.3 – Lonrho Plc – Annual Report and Accounts – 30 September 1994

Notes to the Accounts (extract)

14. Quasi-subsidiary (extract)

The Lonrho Group has a 19 per cent interest in Masterdrive Limited, a vehicle leasing company which is considered to be a quasi-subsidiary under the terms of FRS 5. The assets and liabilities of the company are consolidated in the 1994 accounts and the comparative figures restated accordingly.

Control contrasted with shared control

21.162 There is an important distinction to be drawn between the control that identifies the parent/subsidiary relationship and shared control. Shared control is the principal feature of a joint venture. A parent that has sole control over its subsidiary's resources can exercise that control to use the subsidiary's resources in a similar way to its own. The ability of an undertaking that shares control of the operating and financial policies of an undertaking is limited by the need to take account of the wishes of the other parties that share control. Shared control may indicate the presence of a joint venture and such ventures are considered further in chapter 28.

Common expressions and interpretations

21.163 In the definitions of subsidiaries explained above there are a number of common expressions and interpretations and these are considered in the paragraphs below.

Parent and subsidiary undertakings

21.164 The subscribers of a company's memorandum are deemed to have agreed to become members of the company and are entered as such in the company's register of members. Every person who agrees to become a member of a company and whose name is entered in its register, is a member of the company. [Sec 22]. A person holding preference shares in a company is a member of that company for this reason.

21.165 In the definitions of subsidiaries a parent undertaking is treated as a member of another undertaking if any of the parent's subsidiaries are members of that other undertaking. [Sec 258(3)(a); FRS 2 para 14]. Furthermore, this is also so if any shares in the other undertaking are held by a third party on behalf of the parent or its subsidiaries. [Sec 258(3)(b); FRS 2 para 14]. These provisions, however, do not extend to the situation where an undertaking is consolidated for the reason that its parent has a participating interest and exercises dominant influence over it, or manages it on a unified basis, although similar attribution provisions can be found in section 260(4)(5) (see para 21.129).

Example

A parent's subsidiary company B may be a member of company C. In this circumstance, even where the parent is not a member of company C itself (for the purposes of determining whether company C is a subsidiary of the parent), the parent is treated as a member of company C by virtue of section 258(3).

21.166 In addition, where a group has intermediate parent undertakings (which can either be companies or unincorporated undertakings), their subsidiaries will also be regarded as subsidiaries of any parent undertakings further up the group structure. [Sec 258(5)]. Consequently, subsidiaries of all parent undertakings within a group are deemed by this provision to be subsidiaries of the ultimate parent company.

21.167 In the situation where an undertaking is not a company, the Act provides no specific guidance on what constitutes membership of that undertaking. The Act does, however, provide general guidance on interpreting expressions used by companies that are not used by unincorporated undertakings. These provisions are discussed in paragraph 21.93.

Provisions concerning rights

21.168 There are a number of common provisions that explain how to treat rights in different situations. These rules apply to voting rights (see para 21.96 and 21.158 above) and rights to appoint or remove the majority of the board of directors (see para 21.103 above).

21.169 In determining whether rights should be attributed to a parent, rights held by a subsidiary undertaking should be treated as if they are held by the parent. [10A Sch 9(1)].

21.170 Rights exercisable in certain circumstances should only be taken into account when those circumstances have arisen and only for as long as they continue. [10A Sch 5(1)(a)]. Furthermore, such rights should also be taken into account where the circumstances are in the control of the person having the rights. [10A Sch 5(1)(b)]. In this respect, it is obvious that where the option *has been exercised* the shares must be taken into account in determining whether any party has a majority of voting rights or control of the board. However, where an option to acquire shares has not yet been exercised, but can be freely exercised by its holder (that is, the option is within its exercise period) the rights in the shares under option (such as the voting rights) do not vest with the holder until the option is actually exercised. Where a bargain purchase option exists, in certain situations the holder of the option might, in effect, have a power of veto. For example, if control of the voting rights can be obtained by exercising an option for £1, this might indicate that the holder can actually exercise a dominant influence (using FRS 2's definition of that term) and the entity would be a subsidiary under section 258(4).

21.171 In addition, rights that the undertaking can normally exercise, but that are temporarily incapable of being exercised, should continue to be taken into account. [10A Sch 5(2)].

21.172 Rights should not be treated as held by a person (which includes an undertaking) if they are held in a fiduciary capacity. [10A Sch 6]. Similarly, rights held by a person as nominee should not be treated as held by him. Such rights will be considered held 'as nominee' for another person if they can only be exercised on his instructions or with his consent or concurrence. [10A Sch 7]. However, this provision cannot be used to require rights held by a parent to be treated as held by any of its subsidiaries. [10A Sch 9(2)].

21.173 Rights that are attached to shares held as security shall be treated as held by the person providing the security where those rights (excluding any right to exercise them to preserve the value of the security, or to realise it) are only exercisable in accordance with his instructions. This rule applies where the shares are held in connection with granting loans in the normal course of business and, except where they are exercisable to preserve the value of the security or to realise it, the rights are exercised only in the interests of the person providing the security. [10A Sch 8]. This provision, however, cannot be used to require rights held by a parent to be treated as held by any of its subsidiaries. [10A Sch 9(2)]. Furthermore, rights should be treated as being exercisable in accordance with the instructions, or the interests of, an undertaking if they are exercisable in accordance with the instructions of, or in the interests of, any group undertaking. [10A Sch 9(3)].

Provisions concerning capital

21.174 References to shares in an undertaking with a share capital are to allotted shares. [Sec 259(2)(a)]. In an undertaking that has capital, but no share capital, shares mean the rights to share in the capital of the undertaking. [Sec 259(2)(b)]. For example, in the case of a partnership, this would mean the relevant partners' share in the capital of the partnership. For an undertaking that has no capital, shares mean an interest conferring any right to share in the profits, or to contribute to the losses, of the undertaking. In this situation, it could also mean an interest giving rise to an obligation to contribute to the debts or expenses on winding up the undertaking. [Sec 259(2)(c)].

Meaning of subsidiary used elsewhere in the legislation

21.175 Whereas the paragraphs above explain the definitions of subsidiary undertaking used in the Act to determine which undertakings should be included in consolidated financial statements, section 736 of the Act explains the meaning of 'subsidiary', 'holding company' and 'wholly-owned subsidiary' used elsewhere in the legislation; and the definitions of subsidiary differ. Section 736 is narrower than section 258 (which defines the undertakings to be included in the consolidation) in that section 736 only includes some of the definitions of subsidiaries discussed above. Section 736 does not include the following definitions used for consolidation purposes:

- Rights to direct operating and financial policies (see para 21.119).
- Dominant influence or unified management (see paras 21.124 and 21.155).

21.176 The notion of 'equity share capital' used before the introduction of the Companies Act 1989 as the main criterion in determining whether a company was a subsidiary of another, does not now apply either when determining whether an undertaking is a subsidiary for the purposes of consolidation or as part of the section 736 definitions of subsidiary for other purposes within the Act. However, the term remains in the Act as it is used elsewhere in the legislation.

21.177 Loan stock deeds often refer to the parent and its subsidiaries as defined by section 736 in determining borrowing restrictions. However, in this particular circumstance, section 144(6) of the Companies Act 1989 will allow the old definition based on equity share capital to remain in operation for trust deeds executed before the Companies Act 1989 came into effect.

Examples of practical situations

21.178 The examples that follow illustrate the type of situations that might arise in practice.

Example 1

A group takes an interest in a company that has £500,000 net liabilities in the hope that it can turn the company around. The group's interest is £100,000 preference shares and the preference shares are convertible at any time into 51% of the company's equity carrying 51% of the company's voting rights. The group also has an option to acquire the other 49% of the company's equity shares. In addition, the group has a power of veto over the operating policy.

The group, therefore, has an interest of over 20% in the company by virtue of its interest in preference shares and the option. This interest is deemed to be a participating interest unless otherwise shown. However, although it is clear there is a participating interest, it would still be necessary in practice to establish whether the company exercises dominant influence over the company or manages it on a unified basis before it is deemed to be a subsidiary. The mere existence of the power of veto over the company's operating policy does not necessarily give the group the required control; this will depend on how control is exercised in practice. If it is determined that the undertaking is a subsidiary, the group will consolidate fully the assets and liabilities of the company and will show a significant minority interest. Such a situation could be very confusing for a reader of the financial statements and, as a consequence, some additional disclosure might be necessary.

Although the existence of the option is taken into account in determining whether the group has a participating interest in the company, it is not taken into account until the option is exercised in determining whether the group controls more than 50% of the subsidiary's voting rights. When the option is exercised, the company will become a subsidiary on the latter basis (if it is not already one through dominant influence) as the group will then control more than 50% of the subsidiary's voting rights.

Example 2

A UK group has a 50% interest in an overseas joint venture company and the other 50% is held by another overseas company incorporated in the same overseas country. Representation on the board and the share of income is split equally. Any disputes are referred to an arbitrator or to the High Court. The joint venture company manufactures goods only for the UK group and sells these goods at a price that is designed to provide a fixed return to the joint venture. The managing director of the joint venture is also an employee of the UK group.

Although the joint venture appears to have been set up as a 'deadlock' company the commercial arrangements suggest that it may be managed on a unified basis with the UK group and that the UK group might have dominant influence over the joint venture. The UK group clearly has a participating interest in the joint venture (which is presumed where the interest is greater than 20 per cent). In order to determine the extent of the influence, it would be necessary to establish if the joint venture's board is independent of the UK group. If, for example, the managing director reports to the board of the UK group and that board decides on, for instance, production levels and other management issues, then the joint venture may well be a subsidiary of the UK group.

Example 3

A group decides to dispose of a subsidiary to its management. After the disposal the group retains 49% of ordinary shares, management has 30% and outsiders have 21%. The group, management and outsiders also have convertible shares, which are convertible into the same proportions of ordinary shares. Those of the group are convertible after five years without any conditions, but those of the management are convertible only if certain profit targets are met. If they are not met management's shares will not be converted and the conversion of the group's shares will result in the company becoming a subsidiary again.

It is necessary to decide whether in practice the group has dominant influence or manages the subsidiary on a unified basis. If that is so, the company would remain a subsidiary throughout. If the group does not have dominant influence over the company or manage it on a unified basis, a view has to be taken as to whether it is probable and there is reasonable evidence that the profit targets will be met. If it is considered probable that they will be met, the company would not be treated as the group's subsidiary and, consequently, would not be consolidated. However, full details of the conversion rights should be disclosed in the group's consolidated financial statements.

Subsidiaries excluded from consolidation

21.179 As mentioned in paragraph 21.37 above, the general rule under both the Act and FRS 2 requires that all subsidiary undertakings should be included in the consolidated financial statements. [Sec 229(1); FRS 2 para 23]. The Act *permits* exclusion of a subsidiary from consolidation where:

- Inclusion is not material for the purposes of giving a true and fair view. [Sec 229(2)].
- The information necessary for the preparation of consolidated financial statements cannot be obtained without disproportionate expense or undue delay. [Sec 229(3)(b)].
- There are severe long-term restrictions over a parent's rights in respect of a subsidiary. [Sec 229(3)(a)].
- The parent's interest is held exclusively with a view to resale and has not previously been included in consolidated financial statements prepared by the parent. [Sec 229(3)(c)].

21.180 Furthermore, the Act *requires* exclusion of a subsidiary from consolidation where its activities are so dissimilar from the rest of the group that inclusion would be incompatible with the obligation to give a true and fair view. [Sec 229(4)].

21.181 Within the constraints of the statutory framework set out in the Act, FRS 2 refined the conditions for exclusion so that they identify those undertakings which, although defined by the Act as subsidiaries, are not controlled by the parent in a way that would in principle justify consolidation. Having identified such subsidiaries, FRS 2 *requires* their exclusion from consolidation.

21.182 FRS 2 points out that exclusion of a subsidiary from consolidation is not the only way of clarifying the effect on the group of circumstances affecting some of its subsidiaries. For instance, it suggests that in some situations segmental reporting can give better information concerning restrictions or activities with special risks, than exclusion from consolidation of the subsidiaries concerned. Exclusion should only be used exceptionally.

Inclusion not material

21.183 As mentioned above, a subsidiary undertaking need not be consolidated where its inclusion in the consolidation would have an immaterial effect. Two or more undertakings may only be excluded using this provision where taken together they are still not material to the consolidation. [Sec 229(2)]. As Financial Reporting Standards deal only with material items, this exemption is not found in the main body of FRS 2, but is dealt with and permitted by paragraph 78(a) of the explanatory section of FRS 2. However, materiality needs to be judged carefully, as Alliance Trust was commented on by the Financial Reporting Review Panel (FRRP) in April 1995 for not consolidating its banking subsidiary. In its financial statements for the year to 31 January 1994, Alliance Trust had excluded its subsidiary on the grounds of immateriality, but has consolidated it in the subsequent year following discussions with the Stock Exchange and the FRRP (see Tables 21.4 and 21.5).

Table 21.4 – The Alliance Trust PLC – Report and Accounts – 31 January 1994

NOTES ON THE ACCOUNTS (extract)

1. ACCOUNTING POLICIES (extract)

f The accounts of Alliance Trust (Finance) Limited have not been consolidated with those of the Company as the directors consider that the amounts involved are not material and that their inclusion would detract from the clarity of the accounts in respect of the principal activity of the Company as an authorised investment trust. A separate statement of the affairs of Alliance Trust (Finance) Limited is on page 23.

Table 21.5 – The Alliance Trust PLC – Report and Accounts – 31 January 1995

REPORT OF THE DIRECTORS (extract)

The consolidated accounts, which are provided for the first time this year, include the results of our banking and savings subsidiary, Alliance Trust (Finance) Limited. These have been produced in the light of developing accounting standards, which will lead shortly to adoption of a Statement of Recommended Practice for investment trusts, and after discussion with the Financial Reporting Review Panel, the Company having raised the issue of consolidation with the Stock Exchange. Full information on the subsidiary has previously been included separately within the accounts. Relevant information continues to be given in note 12.

Disproportionate expense or undue delay

21.184 Although the Act allows a subsidiary that is material in the context of the group to be excluded on the grounds that the information necessary for the preparation of the consolidated financial statements cannot be obtained without disproportionate expense or undue delay, this is not permitted by FRS 2. [Sec 229(3)(b); FRS 2 para 24]. FRS 2 takes the view that mere expense or undue delay are not sufficient grounds to exclude a material subsidiary and, therefore, in practice this reason for exclusion cannot be used. The ASB's view is that if the subsidiary is material, it must be included and the consolidated financial statements cannot give a true and fair view without its inclusion.

Severe long-term restrictions

Basis of exclusion

21.185 Consolidation of a subsidiary undertaking is *not required* by the Act where severe long-term restrictions substantially hinder the exercise of the parent company's rights over the assets or over the management of the undertaking. [Sec 229(3)(a)]. The rights that must be restricted for this exclusion to apply are those that would result in the undertaking being a subsidiary of the parent and without which it would not be a subsidiary (see para 21.168). [Sec 229(3); FRS 2 para 25(a)]. They include all such rights attributed to the parent undertaking under section 229(3). Table 21.6 illustrates a situation where certain subsidiaries are excluded from consolidation because of severe long-term restrictions.

Table 21.6 – BM Group PLC – Annual Report – 30 June 1993

NOTES TO THE FINANCIAL STATEMENTS (extract)

15. Investments (extract)

The net assets of certain African subsidiaries of the Group have been excluded from consolidation on the basis that severe long term restrictions are in place which hinder the exercise of the Group's rights over the assets employed. The subsidiaries concerned are Blackwood Hodge (Kenya) Ltd, Blackwood Hodge (Cote d'Ivoire) SarL. Blackwood Hodge (Tanzania) Ltd, Blackwood Hodge (Ghana) Ltd (60% owned) and Blackwood Hodge (Sierra Leone) Ltd.

21.186 The ASB considers, however, that where the parent's rights are restricted in this way the subsidiary concerned *should* be excluded from consolidation. The important difference is that the Act *permits* exclusion on these grounds whereas FRS 2 *requires* exclusion. However, FRS 2 states that in order to justify not consolidating a subsidiary the effect of the restrictions must be that the parent does not *control* its subsidiary.

21.187 Furthermore, severe long-term restrictions are identified by their effect in practice rather than by the way in which the restrictions are imposed. For example, a subsidiary should not be excluded because restrictions are threatened or because another party has the power to impose them unless such threats or the existence of such a power has a severe and restricting effect in practice in the long-term on the parent's rights. [FRS 2 para 78(c)].

21.188 There are a number of situations where a parent's control over its subsidiary *may* be subject to severe long-term restrictions. These include situations where the following exist:

- A power of veto is held by a third party.
- Severe restrictions exist over remittances.
- Insolvency or administration procedures are in progress.
- Two parent undertakings are identified under the definitions in the Act, but one does not control the subsidiary undertaking or exercise joint control.

An example of a situation where a company holds a majority of the subsidiary's voting rights, but its ability to exercise those rights is restricted, is given in Table 21.7.

Table 21.7 – British Steel plc – Report and Accounts – 2 April 1994

ACCOUNTING POLICIES (extract)

1. BASIS OF CONSOLIDATION (extract)

The Company holds a majority of the voting rights in UES Holdings Limited (UES), but is restricted in its ability to exercise those rights under an agreement with the other shareholder. Consequently, the investment has not been consolidated in these accounts but has been included based on the Group's share of its results and net assets.

21.189 In general, restrictions are better dealt with by disclosure rather than by exclusion. However, the overriding principle is that a parent *should not* consolidate a subsidiary that it does not control. Consider the following example, which deals with a power of veto and restrictions over remittances.

Example

A parent has a subsidiary overseas. The subsidiary is owned and managed by the parent, but the host government has the power to:

- Veto the sale of the parent's interest in the subsidiary to an overseas investor.
- Veto any board decisions that are not in the interests of the local community.
- Restrict or prevent the remittance of funds from the subsidiary to the UK.

The parent company does not intend to sell the subsidiary and it has never experienced a veto of a board decision or restrictions of remittances by the host government. In practice, the parent's and the host government's objectives are the same and it is, therefore, extremely unlikely that the veto will be used or the restrictions over remittances imposed.

Although the host government has a power of veto over a sale and certain board decisions and can restrict remittance of funds to the UK, it has never used these powers and it is assumed, from the facts given, that it is unlikely to do so. Furthermore, as the parent's objectives and those of the local government are similar, it is unlikely that the threat of the veto or restrictions have any effect on the manner in which the subsidiary is managed by the parent. This would, therefore, appear to be a situation where the veto and restrictions have little effect in practice and consolidation would be required. The potential restrictions over distributions should then be disclosed in accordance with paragraph 53 of FRS 2.

21.190 FRS 2 specifically considers the situation where a subsidiary undertaking is subject to an insolvency procedure in the UK. Where control over that undertaking has passed to a designated official (for example, an administrator, an administrative receiver or a liquidator), the effect will be that severe long-term restrictions are in force. A company voluntary arrangement does not necessarily lead to loss of control and in some overseas jurisdictions formal insolvency procedures may not amount to loss of control. [FRS 2 para 78(c)].

Example

An intermediate holding company's parent is in administration and is unlikely to produce consolidated financial statements. It therefore appears that the intermediate holding company will have to prepare consolidated financial statements as it will not be able to avail itself of the exemption from preparing consolidated financial statements given in the Companies Act (see para 21.63). Most of the intermediate parent's subsidiaries have been sold since the year end because of the group's need to realise assets. There is also a problem in obtaining information from the purchasers of those companies.

If it can be demonstrated that there are significant restrictions imposed on the intermediate parent by the administrator such that the intermediate parent was unable to exercise its rights over the assets and management of the subsidiaries then that would be a justifiable reason for non-consolidation.

Accounting treatment

21.191 Where a parent's control over a subsidiary is subject to severe long-term restrictions, that subsidiary should be excluded from consolidation and treated as a fixed asset investment. If the subsidiary was acquired with the restrictions, the investment should be carried initially at cost. However, if the restrictions came into force at a later date, the investment should be carried at a fixed amount calculated using the equity method at the date on which the restrictions came into force. While the restrictions are in force the parent should make no further accruals for the profits or losses of the undertaking. But if it continues to exercise significant influence over the undertaking it should account for its investment as an associate using equity accounting (see chapter 28). [FRS 2 para 27].

21.192 A review of the value of subsidiary undertakings subject to severe long-term restrictions should be carried out to assess whether the carrying value of the investment has suffered an impairment. Where any impairment has occurred, this should be reflected by providing against the carrying amount of the relevant subsidiary and charging the provision to the consolidated profit and loss account. It may then be necessary also to make a provision against the carrying value of the investment in the undertaking holding the investment and charge that provision to that undertaking's profit and loss account. In assessing impairment, each subsidiary should be considered individually. The intra-group balances with subsidiary undertakings excluded on the grounds of severe long-term restrictions should also be reviewed and written down, if necessary. [FRS 2 para 27].

21.193 When the severe long-term restrictions cease and the parent undertaking's rights are restored, the amount of the profit or loss for that subsidiary that accrued during the period of restriction should be separately disclosed in the consolidated profit and loss account for the period in which the control is resumed. Any amount previously charged as an impairment that is written back as a result of restrictions ceasing should be separately disclosed. [FRS 2 para 28]. An example of this situation is given in Table 21.8 on page 21056.

21.194 It should be remembered, however, that where a subsidiary is liquidated during or after the year end, it should still be consolidated up to the point that the restrictions come into force. Such a subsidiary should only be excluded from consolidation after the date on which it has gone into liquidation.

21.195 It is possible that restrictions may lift sufficiently for a subsidiary that has previously been treated as an investment to be equity accounted as an associated undertaking, because the parent now has significant influence over that undertaking, but does not exercise sufficient control to justify full consolidation. In practice this is likely to be rare, but should it occur, the *group's share* of the profit or loss that accrued during the period of the restriction should be dealt with in the consolidated profit and loss account of the period in which significant influence is resumed. The amount should be separately disclosed if it is material.

Interest held exclusively with a view to subsequent resale

Basis of exclusion

21.196 Consolidation of a subsidiary undertaking is *not required* where the interest of the parent company was acquired and is held exclusively with a view to subsequent resale. [Sec 229(3)(c)]. In this situation, the 'interests' of the parent company are the interests attributed to it under the definition of 'parent undertaking' (see para 21.168). Again, this exemption is repeated in FRS 2, but with the important difference that the Act *permits* exclusion on these grounds whereas FRS 2 *requires exclusion*. [FRS 2 para 25(b)].

21.197 The standard defines an interest held exclusively with a view to subsequent resale as:

> *"a An interest for which a purchaser has been identified or is being sought, and which is reasonably expected to be disposed of within approximately one year of its date of acquisition*; or
>
> *b An interest that was acquired as a result of the enforcement of a security, unless the interest has become part of the continuing activities of the group or the holder acts as if it intends the interest to become so."* [FRS 2 para 11].

21.198 FRS 2 gives specific guidance on the interpretation of disposal 'within approximately one year'. An interest for which a sale is not completed within one year of its purchase may still meet the requirement if, at the time the financial statements are signed:

- The terms of sale have been agreed.
- The process of disposing of the subsidiary is substantially complete.

[FRS 2 para 78(d)].

21.199 FRS 2 includes only 'enforcement of a security' and excludes other methods of involuntary acquisition (unless they meet the first definition's requirements). Typically 'enforcement of a security' will apply to banks that have made secured loans to undertakings that have subsequently defaulted on their loans and which are, therefore, controlled by the banks. Provided such an undertaking has not become part of the continuing activities of the bank's group and the bank does not act as if it intends it to become so, the undertaking should not be consolidated.

21.200 FRS 2 draws attention to paragraph 8 of Schedule 10A to the Act which provides that *rights* that are *"attached to shares held as security"* should be treated as held by the *"person providing the security"* where those rights are only exercisable in accordance with his instructions. The right of the holder of the security to exercise the rights to preserve the value of the security or to realise it does not affect the above provision. This rule applies where the shares are held in connection with granting loans in the normal course of business and, apart from the purpose of preserving the value of the security or of realising it, the rights are exercisable only in the interests of the provider of the security.

Example

A bank has acquired over 50% of the voting rights of a company as a result of a reconstruction whereby it and other lenders converted debt into equity. The bank intends to dispose of the equity when it gets the opportunity.

The company is technically a subsidiary of the bank, but it would not require to be accounted for on a full consolidation basis in the bank's consolidated financial statements as it is held for resale. It should, therefore, be excluded from consolidation and accounted for in the way described below.

21.201 An illustration of a company excluding a subsidiary from consolidation on this ground is given in Table 21.8.

Table 21.8 – Barclays PLC – Report and Accounts – 31 December 1993

Notes to the accounts (extract)

54 Subsidiary and associated undertakings (extract)

Certain subsidiaries not consolidated in previous years are now included in these accounts because, in the opinion of the Directors, the long-term restrictions which hindered the exercise of the rights of the Group over their assets or management have ceased. After allowing for dividends received and foreign exchange adjustments, there were no unrecognised profits or losses accruing during the period of restriction.

During 1992, the Group acquired a 100% interest in Imry Holdings Limited (Imry), a company registered in England, as a result of enforcing security against a loan to Chester Holdings (UK) Limited, the parent company of Imry. The interest is held exclusively with a view to subsequent resale and therefore has not been consolidated. The Group holds all the issued shares of Imry and all of the £100m zero coupon preference shares in its subsidiary, Imry Jersey Limited. The shareholdings were valued at £56m at 31st December 1993 (1992 £56m). At 31st December 1993, the capital and reserves of Imry amounted to £79m (1992 £71m). The profit before taxation of Imry for the year ended 1993 was £8m. There were outstandings of £81m (1992 £85m) due to the Group, secured by a fixed and floating charge on the assets of Imry. During the year, Barclays Mercantile Limited paid £2,147,000 in rentals to Imry under a lease. Imry paid £675,000 to Barclays Bank PLC in exchange for the Bank providing a guarantee for the rental obligations of Barclays Mercantile Limited under its lease, and £385,000 to Barclays Property Holdings on behalf of Barclays Mercantile Limited to cover the cost of repair work required under the terms of the lease. There were no other material transactions between Imry and the Group during the year.

Accounting treatment

21.202 A subsidiary held exclusively with a view to resale and not previously consolidated, although controlled by its parent, does not form part of the group's continuing activities. The parent's control is temporary and is not used to deploy the underlying assets and liabilities of that subsidiary as part of the group's continuing activities and for the parent's benefit. The subsidiary should, therefore, be excluded from consolidation on these grounds and should be treated as a current asset investment, included in the group balance sheet at the lower of cost and net realisable value. [FRS 2 paras 29, 79(b)]. Where the subsidiary has still not been sold within approximately one year of the acquisition, it should be consolidated and fair values attributed to its individual assets and liabilities as at the date of acquisition (see further chapter 23). [FRS 7 para 18]. An example of a subsidiary excluded on these grounds is given in Table 21.12 on page 21065.

Dissimilar activities

Basis of exclusion

21.203 A further exemption from consolidation applies where the activities of one or more subsidiaries are so different from those of the other undertakings included in the consolidated financial statements that their inclusion would be *"incompatible with the obligation to give a true and fair view"*. [Sec 229(4)].

21.204 This requirement is mandatory, whereas the old provision in the unamended Companies Act 1985 was optional. In addition, previously under the old provision the Secretary of State's permission was required if this reason was used to exclude a subsidiary from consolidation. The Secretary of State's permission is no longer necessary.

21.205 FRS 2 repeats the Act's provision and states that it is exceptional for such circumstances to arise and that the ASB has not found it possible to identify any particular contrast of activities where the necessary incompatibility with the true and fair view generally occurs. [FRS 2 para 25(c)].

21.206 The provisions in the Act and FRS 2 go on to state that this exemption does not apply merely because some of the undertakings are industrial, or some are commercial and some provide services, or because they carry on industrial or commercial activities involving different products or provide different services. [Sec 229(4); FRS 2 para 25(c)]. This paragraph is taken directly from the EC 7th Directive and its intention is to restrict significantly the undertakings to which the exemption applies.

21.207 In the US, SFAS No 94, 'Consolidation of all majority-owned subsidiaries' was issued in October 1987. This statement requires that all majority-owned subsidiaries should be consolidated unless control is temporary or does not rest with the majority owner. The statement requires consolidation of all majority-owned subsidiaries even if they have 'nonhomogeneous' operations (that is, dissimilar activities in UK terminology). Previously in the US before the introduction of this SFAS, subsidiaries with dissimilar activities were excluded from consolidation. A similar change has recently been made in International Accounting Standards. There has been a general shift in the views of many accountants throughout the world towards consolidation of the majority of subsidiaries whether they have dissimilar activities or not and this is borne out in the US. Furthermore, this change of views coincided with the provision of more segmental information of the different aspects of a group's business (see further chapter 8).

21.208 In practice, instances of subsidiaries excluded from consolidation on the grounds of dissimilar activities are now rare and the FRS states that it would be misleading to link, in general, the circumstances where this exemption applies to any particular contrast of activities. Indeed, it specifically considers the contrast between Schedule 9 companies (banking and insurance companies and groups) and other companies and states that of itself this contrast is not sufficient to justify non-consolidation. It also states that the contrast between profit and not-for-profit undertakings is also insufficient to justify non-consolidation.

21.209 Groups do now consolidate banking and insurance subsidiaries, but rather than aggregate insurance assets and liabilities with those of other trading activities, they are often shown separately. For example B.A.T presents separately on the face of the balance sheet its commercial and corporate activities, its financial services general business and its financial services life business. This presentation is considered to be a departure from the requirements of the Act, which the directors consider necessary to give a true and fair view (see Table 21.9). An alternative presentation has been used by Hambro Countrywide of its life business. It shows a separate column in its balance sheet for its life activities (see Table 21.10).

Table 21.9 – B.A.T Industries p.l.c – Directors' Report and Accounts – 31 December 1994

Accounting Policies (extract)

1 The Group accounts (extract) have been prepared in accordance with applicable accounting standards and combine the accounts of Group undertakings at 31 December. As permitted by the Companies Act 1985 the accounts formats have been adapted, as necessary, to give a true and fair view of the state of affairs and profit of the commercial activities of the Group and to present the insurance activities in accordance with the provisions of that Act applicable to insurance companies. The accounts are on an historical cost basis as modified to include certain insurance assets at market value.

Accordingly, the accounts formats have been developed to reflect most appropriately the operations of the Group. All the assets and liabilities of the Group's businesses are included in the consolidated balance sheet. To equity account for either tobacco or financial services would not give a true and fair view of the total Group. However, given the differences between the two main businesses of the Group and the constraints of the regulatory environment within which insurance companies operate, the assets and liabilities are shown separately under headings covering commercial and corporate activities, financial services general business and financial services life business. This approach has been reflected in preparing separate cash flow statements for the three businesses as the regulatory environment in insurance limits the availability of cash flows between businesses. The Directors are of the opinion that this approach, where it differs from the Companies Act 1985 and applicable accounting standards as described further in the Finance Director's Review in the Annual Review and Summary Financial Statement, is necessary to present a true and fair view of the Group.

Group Profit and Loss Account

for the year ended 31 December

REVENUE		Notes	**1994 £m**	1993 £m
Commercial activities		1	**12,171**	11,778
Financial Services:	general business	2	**3,081**	3,108
	life business	3	**3,136**	2,993
Share of associates *page 55*			**2,748**	2,888
Continuing operations			**21,136**	20,767
PROFIT				
Commercial activities before exceptional items			**1,011**	979
Reorganisation of acquired business		1,5	**(191)**	
Profit on exchange of brands		1,6		138
Costs of rationalisation		1,7		(73)
Commercial activities after exceptional items		1	**820**	1,044
Financial services:	general business	2	**523**	544
	life business	3	**319**	321
Share of associates *page 55*			**266**	183
Continuing operations			**1,928**	2,092
Discontinued operations		2,8		(141)
Operating profit *page 9 note 5*			**1,928**	1,951
Profit on sale of discontinued operations		8	**57**	9
Profit on ordinary activities before interest			**1,985**	1,960
Investment income		9	**111**	102
Interest payable		9	**(294)**	(253)
Profit on ordinary activities before taxation			**1,802**	1,809
Taxation on ordinary activities		10	**(486)**	(548)
Profit on ordinary activities after taxation			**1,316**	1,261
Minority interests including non-equity		33	**(111)**	(92)
Profit for the year *page 13*		33	**1,205**	1,169
Capital reserve transfer *page 9 note 6*			**151**	(26)
			1,356	1,143
Dividends:				
	base dividend	11	**(675)**	(618)
	additional payments	11	**(167)**	
Retained profit			**514**	525
Earnings per share		12		
	Net basis on profit for the year		**39.1p**	38.5p
	Nil basis on profit for the year		**34.5p**	36.5p
Dividends per share:				
	base dividend	11	**21.9p**	20.1p
	additional payments	11	**5.4p**	–

Balance sheets (extract)

31 December

ASSETS		Notes	GROUP 1994 £m	GROUP 1993 £m	COMPANY 1994 £m	COMPANY 1993 £m
	Commercial and corporate activities					
	Tangible fixed assets	20	**1,684**	1,487	**4**	5
	Investments in Group companies	22			**2,596**	1,930
	Other investments and long term loans	23	**76**	81		
	Fixed assets		**1,760**	1,568	**2,600**	1,935
	Stocks	24	**2,146**	1,991		
	Debtors	25	**1,269**	953	**3,357**	2,990
	Current investments	26	**188**	333	**3**	
	Short term deposits		**971**	503	**59**	
	Cash and bank balances		**99**	135		1
			6,433	5,483	**6,019**	4,926
	Financial services general business					
	Interest in underwriting associations	27	**1,497**	1,583		
	Investments	28	**3,870**	3,956		
	Associates	28	**34**	34		
	Tangible fixed assets	29	**324**	342		
	Other assets	30	**1,905**	2,115		
	Cash and bank balances		**50**	43		
			7,680	8,073		
	Financial services life business					
	Investments	28	**22,679**	23,227		
	Securitised mortgages	28	**245**	290		
	Non-recourse financing	28	**(245)**	(290)		
			–	–		
	Associates	28	**33**	19		
	Interest in life businesses		**1,009**	1,020		
	Tangible fixed assets	29	**102**	99		
	Other assets	30	**1,167**	1,278		
	Cash and bank balances		**116**	121		
			25,106	25,764		
	Investments in associates	31	**766**	614		
	Total assets		**39,985**	39,934	**6,019**	4,926

Certain comparative figures have been restated as explained in accounting policy 1 on page 8 and details of these changes are given in the individual notes to which they relate.

Table 21.10 – Hambro Countrywide PLC – Annual Report and Accounts – 31 December 1994

GROUP BALANCE SHEET
at 31 December

Note		1994* Consolidated (except Life) £000	1994* Life £000	1994 Group £000	1993* restated Consolidated (except life) £000	1993* restated Life £000	1993 restated Group £000
	Fixed assets						
15	Tangible assets	**20,733**	**4,530**	**25,263**	11,470	3,310	14,780
16	Investment in Life Assurance Activity	**59,284**	–	–	58,423	–	–
17	Investments	**183**	**16,777**	**16,571**	4,814	33,253	37,729
		80,200	**21,307**	**41,834**	74,707	36,563	52,509
37	Long Term Business Fund	–	**41,191**	**41,191**	–	28,926	28,926
18	Value of Life Assurance business	–	**34,758**	**34,758**	–	17,509	17,509
	Current assets						
19	Debtors	**35,647**	**7,793**	**38,783**	20,032	7,497	19,856
20	Cash at bank	**8,661**	**2,205**	**10,866**	2,439	3,363	5,802
		44,308	**9,998**	**49,649**	22,471	10,860	25,658
	Current liabilities						
21	Creditors: amounts falling due within one year	**(38,288)**	**(6,204)**	**(39,808)**	(24,115)	(6,614)	(23,080)
	Net current assets	**6,020**	**3,794**	**9,841**	(1,644)	4,426	2,578
	Total assets less current liabilities	**86,220**	**101,050**	**127,624**	73,063	87,244	101,522
22	**Creditors** Amounts falling due after more than one year	**(178)**	–	**(178)**	(43)	–	(43)
37	Long Term Business Fund	–	**(41,191)**	**(41,191)**	–	(28,926)	(28,926)
23	**Provisions for liabilities and charges**	**(8,132)**	**(680)**	**(8,812)**	–	–	–
	Net Assets	**77,910**	**59,179**	**77,443**	73,020	58,318	72,553
	Capital and reserves						
24	Called up share capital	**17,661**	**40,600**	**17,661**	16,455	40,550	16,455
25	Share premium account	**14,783**	–	**14,783**	3,946	–	3,946
25	Capital redemption reserve	**1,250**	–	**1,250**	1,250	–	1,250
25	Other reserves	**26,497**	–	**26,030**	27,707	–	27,240
25	Profit and loss account	**17,719**	**18,579**	**17,719**	23,662	17,768	23,662
	Total shareholders' funds	**77,910**	**59,179**	**77,443**	73,020	58,318	72,553

Approved by the Board of Directors on 7 March 1995 and signed on its behalf by:

C H Sporborg
M C Nower

The notes on pages 29 to 45 form part of the accounts

* Life comprises Hambro Guardian Ltd and its subsidiary companies including Hambro Guardian Assurance plc, Consolidated (except Life) includes the Life Assurance Activity under the equity method of accounting. (See Note 1(a) (ii)).

NOTES TO THE ACCOUNTS

1 Accounting policies (extract)

(a) Basis of preparation (extract)

(ii) The assets and liabilities of Hambro Guardian Ltd and its subsidiaries including Hambro Guardian Assurance plc, which carry out the Group's life assurance activities, have been separately identified on the Group Balance Sheet. Further details of this activity are given in note 37 on page 45.

The financial information in respect of Hambro Guardian Assurance plc is derived from the financial statements of that company which are prepared in accordance with the requirements of Section 255 of, and Schedule 9 to, the Companies Act 1985. In the consolidated balance sheet a value is placed on the shareholders' interest in the in-force policies of the life assurance fund of Hambro Guardian Assurance plc. This value is a prudent estimate of the net present value of the profits inherent in these policies. Changes in this value are included within the profit of the Life Assurance Activity in the consolidated profit and loss account. The net present value of the pre-tax surpluses and of the related tax charges are calculated separately in order to arrive at the appropriate profit before tax and tax charge. Future taxation has only been provided to the extent that, in the opinion of the Directors, such taxation will become payable, based on prudent assumptions relating to the level of future expenses.

21.210 The balance sheet and profit and loss account formats will change dramatically for insurance companies when they adopt the formats included in Schedule 9A to the Act. There are many similarities between those formats and the formats included in Schedule 4 (as amended for groups by Schedule 4A). Most of the Schedule 4 items are included in the Schedule 9A formats. Therefore, it might be easier in future to consolidate a subsidiary that prepares its financial statements in accordance with Schedule 9A within the group's consolidated financial statements prepared in accordance with Schedules 4 and 4A, without having to resort to the true and fair override. This, however, might not be possible where a group has a banking subsidiary, because the formats in Schedule 9 for banks are very different to those in Schedule 4.

21.211 Where consolidation of a subsidiary with dissimilar activities might appear to be incompatible with the obligation to give a true and fair view, consideration should be given to the general provisions of the Act in respect of true and fair view (see para 21.57 above).

21.212 The different activities within a group are best dealt with by consolidation and providing segmental analysis rather than by exclusion.

21.213 Table 21.11 shows a situation where the underwriting activities of a subsidiary are no longer considered so material and so dissimilar to warrant exclusion from consolidation.

Table 21.11 – C.E. Heath Public Limited Company – Report and Accounts – 31 March 1994

Notes to the accounts
for the year ended 31 March 1994 (extract)

1. Principal accounting policies (extract)

Consolidation of underwriting activities

The group accounts consolidate the results of underwriting activities, which in previous years were excluded from full consolidation. The prior year comparatives have been restated accordingly. Following the disposal of a majority interest in C E Heath International Holdings Limited during the prior year and the continuing reduction in the scale of the group's underwriting activities, the directors consider that the group's underwriting activities are no longer so material and so dissimilar that, as was considered to be the case in previous years, consolidation would be misleading and incompatible with the obligation for the accounts to show a true and fair view.

The effect of this change in accounting policy has been to reclassify amounts previously shown net in the profit and loss account and balance sheet and include them within the relevant captions. Operating profit and net assets remain unaltered.

Accounting treatment

21.214 Subsidiaries that are excluded on the grounds of dissimilar activities are controlled by the parent and contribute to the wealth and performance of the group. The results, assets and liabilities should, therefore, be included in the consolidation, but as full consolidation is inappropriate the equity method of accounting should be used. [4A Sch 18; FRS 2 para 30].

Disclosure for subsidiaries excluded from consolidation

21.215 Schedule 5 to the Act sets out certain information about subsidiaries that companies that prepare consolidated financial statements have to give; these general requirements are considered in paragraph 21.230 below. Also, companies that do not prepare consolidated financial statements have to give information about their subsidiaries and this information is similarly set out in Schedule 5 to the Act. These provisions are considered in chapter 16.

21.216 The additional disclosure required by Schedule 5 to the Act and FRS 2 concerning subsidiaries that have been excluded from consolidation where consolidated financial statements are prepared is extensive. Although, in general, the disclosures relate to individual subsidiaries excluded from consolidation, there are circumstances where it may be possible to provide the information on an aggregated basis for some or all of the subsidiaries concerned. FRS 2 extends the Act's disclosure requirements for subsidiaries excluded from consolidation (including those that are unincorporated subsidiaries).

The Act's requirements

21.217 Where a subsidiary is excluded from consolidation, the notes to the consolidated financial statements must disclose:

- The reasons why the subsidiary or the subsidiaries are not dealt with in the consolidated financial statements. [5 Sch 15(4)]. The reason disclosed would have to be one of those explained above.

- The aggregate amount of the subsidiary's capital and reserves at the end of its relevant financial year and its profit or loss for the period. This information need not be given, however, where either of the following conditions is satisfied:

  - The group's total investment in its subsidiaries' shares is included in the consolidated financial statements by the equity method of valuation (see chapter 28).

  - The undertaking is not required under the Act to file its balance sheet with the Registrar of Companies or publish it in Great Britain or elsewhere. Exemption is only allowed under this provision, however, if the group's holding in the undertaking is less than 50 per cent of the nominal value of that undertaking's shares. [5 Sch 17(1)(2)].

An example of the type of disclosure required where a subsidiary has been excluded on the grounds of being held exclusively for resale is illustrated in Table 21.12.

Table 21.12 – Airtours plc – Annual report and accounts – 30 September 1993

Notes to the financial statements (extract)

10) Fixed asset investments (extract)

All of the subsidiary undertakings, with the exception of Moon Leasing Limited, have been consolidated in the Group financial statements. The financial statements of Moon Leasing Limited have not been consolidated as it is being held exclusively for resale.

The aggregate amount of the capital and reserves of Moon Leasing Limited was £149,808 at 30th September 1993. The profit for the year was £149,807.

21.218 References to 'relevant financial year' above are to the subsidiary's financial year ending with the parent's year end or the last financial year ending before that date. [5 Sch 17(4)].

21.219 The information required by paragraph 17 of Schedule 5 to the Act need not be given if it is not material.

Additional requirements of FRS 2

21.220 In addition to the disclosures required by Schedule 5 to the Act, the following information should be given in the consolidated financial statements for subsidiaries not included in the consolidation:

- Particulars of the balances between the excluded subsidiaries and the rest of the group.
- The nature and extent of transactions of the excluded subsidiaries with the rest of the group.
- For an excluded subsidiary carried other than by the equity method, any amounts included in the consolidated financial statements in respect of:
  - Dividends received and receivable from that subsidiary.

  - Any write-down in the period in respect of the investment in that subsidiary or amounts due from that subsidiary.

- Guarantees in respect of subsidiary undertakings excluded from consolidation have to be treated in the same way as guarantees given by members of the group to third parties. [FRS 2 para 79(d)]. The detailed disclosure in respect of commitments and guarantees is set out in paragraph 50 of Schedule 4 to the Act and is discussed in detail in chapter 20.

- For subsidiaries excluded because of different activities, the separate financial statements of those subsidiaries. Summarised information may be provided for subsidiaries that individually, or in combination with those with similar operations, do not account for more than 20 per cent or more of the group's:

  - operating profits;
  - turnover; or
  - net assets.

  The group amounts should be measured by including all excluded subsidiaries. [FRS 2 para 31].

Aggregation of disclosures

21.221 The general disclosure requirements listed above are required for individual excluded subsidiaries. However, if the information about excluded subsidiaries is more appropriately presented for a sub-unit of the group made up from more than one excluded subsidiary, the disclosures may be made on an aggregate basis. The sub-units for which these disclosures should be given are to be made up from subsidiary undertakings *"excluded under the same sub-section of section 229"*. [FRS 2 para 32]. The four permitted or required exclusions are dealt with in section 229 as follows:

- Not material (see para 21.183 above).
- Severe long-term restrictions (see para 21.185 above).
- Held for subsequent resale (see para 21.196 above).
- Dissimilar activities (see para 21.203 above).

21.222 As FRS 2 does not deal with immaterial matters the disclosures are not required for subsidiaries excluded from consolidation on the grounds of immateriality.

21.223 A strict interpretation of paragraph 32 of FRS 2 suggests that aggregation of the information concerning subsidiaries excluded because of severe long-term restrictions and subsequent resale is permitted as they are both dealt with by the Act in section 229(3). However, as the subsidiaries concerned are excluded for different reasons this may lead to some confusion. To avoid such confusion, aggregation might be given under the following headings:

- Severe long-term restrictions.
- Held for subsequent resale.
- Dissimilar activities.

21.224 However, individual disclosures should be made for any excluded subsidiary, including its sub-group where relevant, that alone accounts for more than 20 per cent of any one or more of the group's:

- Operating profits.
- Turnover.
- Net assets.

[FRS 2 para 32].

21.225 The group amounts in paragraph 21.224 should be measured by including all excluded subsidiaries. [FRS 2 para 32].

General exemptions from disclosure requirements

21.226 The information required to be disclosed under the Act concerning subsidiaries excluded from consolidation outlined above (except for that required by paragraphs 5(2), 6, 9A, 20 and 28A of Schedule 5 to the Act) need not be disclosed if, in the directors' opinion, its disclosure would be seriously prejudicial to the subsidiary's business or to the business of the parent or any of its subsidiaries. This exemption applies where the particulars relate to a subsidiary that is established under the law of a country outside the UK or where its business is carried on outside the UK. However, the Secretary of State has to agree that the disclosure need not be made and the fact that advantage is taken of this exemption has to be disclosed. [Sec 231(3)(4)]. It is then questionable whether this exemption extends to disclosures required by FRS 2 and this is considered further in paragraph 21.252.

21.227 An example of an occasion when it would be allowable not to disclose this information would be when a company has trading subsidiaries in two countries and those two countries are either in conflict, or have trade embargoes between them. In these two situations where these subsidiaries are excluded from consolidation on one of the grounds considered above, the disclosure of the UK group's investment in each subsidiary might impair its trading ability in those countries.

21.228 The general exemption from the disclosure requirements of Schedule 5 to the Act (where certain information is not required if the number of undertakings is such that the resulting disclosure is, in the opinion of the directors, excessively lengthy) does not apply to subsidiaries that are excluded from consolidation. [Sec 231(5)(b)].

21.229 In addition, where a subsidiary has been excluded from consolidation as outlined from paragraphs 21.179 above, the Act requires that the information outlined below from paragraph 21.230 should be given. Also, where a holding company prepares consolidated financial statements, the information set out in chapter 16 concerning details of intercompany balances, etc. must be given in respect of any subsidiaries that are not consolidated.

Disclosure requirements concerning subsidiaries and investments

21.230 Certain additional information has to be given for all subsidiaries and this is detailed in Schedule 5 to the Act. Considered below are the disclosure requirements concerning the information required for subsidiaries that are included in consolidation and these requirements are supplemented by FRS 2. The information required about subsidiaries when the parent does not prepare consolidated financial statements is considered in chapter 16.

Place of origin and reason for consolidation

21.231 The Act requires disclosure of the following information concerning subsidiary undertakings:

- Name of each subsidiary undertaking.
- The country of incorporation, if incorporated outside Great Britain.
- The address of the principal place of business if the undertaking is unincorporated.
- Whether the subsidiary is included in the consolidation, and if not, the reasons for excluding it.

[5 Sch 15(1) to (4) as amended by SI 1996/189].

These disclosures are illustrated in Tables 21.13 and 21.14.

Table 21.13 – Whitbread PLC – Annual Report and Accounts – 25 February 1995

Notes to the accounts (extract)

14 Investment in subsidiary undertakings (extract)

	Principal activity	Country of incorporation or registration	Country of principal operations	% of equity and votes held
Churrasco Steak-Restaurant GmbH.*	Restaurants	Germany	Germany	100
Country Club Hotels Ltd.	Hotels	England	England	100
Keg Restaurants Ltd.*	Restaurants	Canada	Canada	100
Keg Restaurants U.S. Inc.	Restaurants	U.S.A.	U.S.A.	100
Whitbread Restaurants (Australia) Ltd.	Restaurants	England	Australia	100

Shares in the above are all held directly by Whitbread PLC except those marked with an asterisk. All subsidiary undertakings have the same year end as Whitbread PLC. All the above companies have been included in the group consolidation. The companies listed above include all those which materially affect the amount of profit and the assets of the Group. A full list of subsidiary and associated undertakings will be annexed to the next annual return of Whitbread PLC to be filed with the Registrar of Companies in August 1995.

Table 21.14 – Guinness PLC – Report and accounts – 31 December 1994

Principal subsidiary and associated undertakings and joint ventures (extract)

6. The registered addresses of partnerships in which the group has an interest are:

Schieffelin & Somerset Co	2 Park Avenue, 17th Floor, New York, NY10016, USA.
Asbach GmbH & Co.	AM Rottland 2-10, 65385 Rudesheim am Rhein, Germany.
Bundaberg Rum Company	Whittred Street, Bundaberg, Queensland 4670, Australia.

21.232 Furthermore, it is necessary to disclose the particular definition of 'subsidiary undertaking' that makes an undertaking a subsidiary under the provisions of the Act. [5 Sch 15(5)]. However, there is an exemption where the undertaking is a subsidiary because the parent holds a majority of its voting rights and it holds the same proportion of shares in the subsidiary as it holds voting rights. This will obviously be the reason for consolidating most subsidiaries and, consequently, disclosure will only be required for other subsidiary undertakings, of which there will be relatively few.

21.233 FRS 2 supplements the above disclosures by requiring the following additional information to be given for subsidiaries:

- The proportion of voting rights held by the parent and its subsidiary undertakings.
- An indication of the nature of the subsidiary's business.

[FRS 2 para 33].

21.234 FRS 2 also requires that where an undertaking is a subsidiary because its parent has a participating interest in it and it actually exercises dominant influence over it (see para 21.124), the financial statements should indicate the basis of the parent's dominant influence (for example see Table 21.3 on page 43). [FRS 2 para 34].

Holdings in subsidiary undertakings

21.235 The following information has to be given separately (where different) concerning the subsidiary's shares held by the parent and the group:

- The identity of each class of shares held.
- The percentage held of the nominal value of each of those classes of shares.

[5 Sch 16].

21.236 Shares that are held on the parent's or group's behalf by any other person should be treated for this purpose as if they are held by the parent. [5 Sch 32(1)(2)(a)(3)]. However, shares held on behalf of a third party other than the parent or the group should be disregarded for this purpose. [5 Sch 32(3)].

Financial years of subsidiaries

21.237 Where a subsidiary's financial year, for which financial statements are drawn up for consolidation purposes (that is, either statutory financials or management accounts), does not coincide with its parent's financial year, FRS 2 requires that the notes should disclose, for each principal subsidiary that has a different accounting date, its name, its accounting date and the reasons for using a different accounting date. If a principal subsidiary's accounting period is of a different length from that of its parent, this accounting period should also be stated. [FRS 2 para 44].

[The next paragraph is 21.239.]

21.239 The requirements concerning non-coterminous year ends are considered further in chapter 22.

Company shares and debentures held by subsidiaries

21.240 A subsidiary company cannot generally own shares in its parent company. [Sec 23(1)]. This prohibition also applies equally to subsidiaries incorporated overseas. This provision extends to sub-subsidiaries holding shares in their immediate parent companies and also their ultimate parent companies. It also includes any shares held on behalf of the subsidiary by another person as its nominee. [Sec 23(7)]. However, the prohibition does not apply where the subsidiary is acting as a personal representative for a third party, or as a trustee. This exemption only applies, however, where the subsidiary or a parent company is not beneficially interested under the trust. [Sec 23(2)]. An exemption is also given to market makers. [Sec 23(3)].

21.241 For the purposes of section 23, the definitions of holding company and subsidiary given in section 736 of the Act are relevant and not those given in section 258 (see further para 21.175).

21.242 Where a corporate body became a subsidiary company because of the changes to the definition of subsidiaries included in section 736 of the Act (as amended by the Companies Act 1989), it may continue to retain any shares that it already held in its parent. However, where shares are held in this way, they will carry no right to vote at company meetings. [Sec 23(4)].

21.243 In certain situations a subsidiary may find that it does hold shares in its parent. This may arise, for example, where the parent has recently acquired a subsidiary which owned shares in the parent before it became a group member. Before the introduction of the Companies Act 1989, the effect of section 23(1) of the Act was unclear. Now, section 23 expressly provides that, where a company acquires shares in its parent, but before it becomes a subsidiary of the parent, it may retain those shares. In this circumstance also, those shares will carry no right to vote at company meetings. [Sec 23(5)].

21.244 The notes to a parent's financial statements must disclose the number, the description and the amount of any of its shares or debentures that subsidiaries or their nominees hold. [5 Sch 20(1)]. This information is not required, however, where the subsidiary holds the shares or debentures as personal representative or as a trustee. [5 Sch 20(2)]. However, the exemption for a subsidiary acting as a trustee will not be available if the company or any of its subsidiaries is beneficially interested under the trust, unless the beneficial interest is by way of security for the purpose of a transaction entered into by it in the ordinary course of a business which includes the lending of money. [5 Sch 20(3)].

21.245 In the parent's consolidated financial statements any shares that its subsidiaries hold in it will be shown as 'own shares' in the balance sheet. The implications for a parent's shares held under an Employee Share Ownership Plan by a trust are considered in chapter 4.

Significant investment holdings of the parent or group

21.246 Where the parent or any of its subsidiaries has *significant holdings* in undertakings, certain additional information has to be given in the consolidated financial statements. A 'significant holding' means one where the investment in the undertaking concerned amounts to twenty per cent or more of the nominal value of *any class* of shares in the undertaking. [5 Sch 23(2)(a),26(2)(a) as amended by SI 1996/189]. (Joint ventures and associated undertakings are considered separately in chapter 28.)

21.247 The disclosure is also required where the holding by the parent or its subsidiaries exceeds twenty per cent of the amount of the parent's, or the group's, assets. [5 Sch 23(2)(b),26(2)(b) as amended by SI 1996/189]. The information to be disclosed is as follows:

- The name of the undertaking.
- The country of incorporation of the undertaking, if it is incorporated outside Great Britain,
- The address of its principal place of business, if it is unincorporated.
- The identity of each class of shares held.
- The percentage held of the nominal value of each of those classes of shares.

[5 Sch 24, 27 as amended by SI 1996/189].

21.248 Furthermore, additional information is required to be disclosed as follows:

- The aggregate amount of the capital and reserves of the undertaking at the end of its 'relevant year'. Relevant year means the year ending with, or last before, that of the company.
- Its profit or loss for the year.

[5 Sch 25(1)(4),28(1)(4) as amended by SI 1996/189].

21.249 This additional information need not be disclosed if the undertaking is not required by the Act to deliver to the Registrar of Companies a copy of its balance sheet and does not otherwise publish it (for example, a partnership). However, this exemption only applies where the company's holding is less than 50 per cent of the nominal value of the undertaking's shares. [5 Sch 25(2),28(2)]. Consequently, this exemption is likely to apply to investments in partnerships where the interest in the partnership is less than 50 per cent. The information is also not required if it is immaterial.

21.250 For investments in unincorporated undertakings with capital, 'shares' for the purposes of the paragraphs above means the rights to share in the capital of the undertaking, by virtue of section 259(2)(b). In respect of an undertaking that does not have capital, the term 'shares' refers to any right to share in the profits or liability to contribute to losses of the undertaking, or an obligation to contribute to its debts or expenses on winding up. [Sec 259(2)(c)].

Interpretation of 'shares held by the group'

21.251 In the paragraphs above, reference to shares held by the group are to shares held by the parent company or any of its subsidiaries, or to shares held on their behalf. However, such references do not include shares held on behalf of third parties. [5 Sch 32(3)]. Furthermore, shares held by way of security must be treated as held by the person providing the security where both the following apply:

- The rights attached to the shares are exercisable only in accordance with that person's instructions (apart from the right to exercise them for the purpose of preserving the value of the security or of realising it).
- The shares are held in connection with granting loans as part of normal business activities and the rights attached to the shares are exercisable only in that person's interest (apart from the right to exercise them for the purpose of preserving the value of the security, or of realising it).

[5 Sch 32(4)].

Disclosure 'seriously prejudicial'

21.252 In certain circumstances, the information required by Schedule 5 concerning subsidiaries and other significant holdings in undertakings (summarised above) need not be given where the undertaking is established under the law of a country outside the UK, or carries on business outside the UK. [Sec 231(3)]. The situations where this exemption will apply are where, in the directors' opinion, disclosing information would be *seriously prejudicial* to the business of that undertaking, or to the business of the parent company, or to any of the parent's subsidiaries. Permission to exclude the information also needs to be obtained from the Secretary of State before advantage can be taken of this exemption. A group that takes advantage of this exemption is required under section 231(4) to disclose this fact in its financial statements.

21.252.1 The section 231(4) statement that exemption has been taken is required to be given irrespective of whether the group has taken advantage of section 231(5) (see para 21.254 below), which only requires information for subsidiaries that principally affect the group's reported figures to be given in its financial statements. Under section 231(5) the full information for all subsidiaries must be annexed to the company's next annual return, but where the Secretary of State has granted exemption under section 231(3), this need not include the information regarding the subsidiary excluded on seriously prejudicial grounds.

21.253 The exemption does not apply, however, to the information required by paragraph 20 of Schedule 5, which is summarised in paragraph 21.244 above.

Disclosure of excessive information

21.254 There is a further relaxation of the disclosure requirements of Schedule 5 that applies if, in the directors' opinion, the resulting disclosure would be excessively lengthy. This will often be the situation where the group has a significant number of subsidiaries. Where this is so, the directors need only give the required information concerning the undertakings whose results or financial position principally affect the figures shown in the company's annual accounts. [Sec 231(5)]. However, the directors are required to give the necessary information that relates to undertakings excluded from consolidation, except where they are excluded on the ground of materiality (see para 21.183).

21.255 Where the directors take advantage of this exemption, they have to note in the financial statements that the information given is only in respect of principal subsidiaries and significant investments. [Sec 231(6)(a)]. In addition, the full information (including that disclosed in the financial statements) has to be annexed to the parent's next annual return. [Sec 231(6)(b)].

Disclosure of parent company

21.256 The Act deals with the disclosures concerning a company's parent (or parents) in Schedule 5 to the Act. Part I of Schedule 5 sets out the disclosures to be made where a company is not required to prepare consolidated financial statements, whereas Part II deals with the disclosure requirements concerning those companies that are required to prepare consolidated financial statements. These requirements are identical. The paragraphs that follow summarise these disclosures and make reference to the paragraphs of Schedule 5 that are duplicated.

21.257 Where, at the end of a financial year, a company is a subsidiary, or where the company is a parent company and is itself a subsidiary, it should disclose concerning its *ultimate parent company* its name and if incorporated outside Great Britain the country of its incorporation (if known). 'Company' includes any corporate body in this context. [5 Sch 12, 31 as amended by SI 1996/189].

21.258 An example of the disclosures required by the Act is given in Table 21.15.

[The next page is 21075.]

Table 21.15 – Dunhill Holdings PLC – Report and Accounts – 31 March 1993

NOTES TO THE ACCOUNTS (extract)

28 ULTIMATE HOLDING COMPANY

The Company is a subsidiary of Rothmans International p.l.c., which is incorporated in England and Wales. Copies of the accounts of Rothmans International p.l.c. are available from 15 Hill Street, London, W1X 7FB.

The Directors consider the Company's ultimate holding company to be Compagnie Financière Richemont AG, which is incorporated in Switzerland. Copies of that company's accounts are available from its registered office at Rigistrasse 2, CH-6300 Zug, Switzerland.

21.259 Furthermore, where the parent company is itself a subsidiary, similar information has to be disclosed (whether or not it prepares consolidated financial statements) for the parent undertaking that heads the following:

- The largest group of undertakings that prepares consolidated financial statements which include the sub-group either by consolidation or by equity accounting.
- The smallest group of undertakings that prepares consolidated financial statements which include the sub-group either by consolidation or by equity accounting.

[5 Sch 11(1), 30(1)].

21.260 The information to be disclosed in respect of both these undertakings is similar to that required by paragraph 21.257 above:

- The name of the parent undertaking.
- The country of incorporation of the undertaking, if it is incorporated outside Great Britain.
- The address of its principal place of business, if it is unincorporated.
- If copies of the undertaking's consolidated financial statements are available for the public, then the address where copies of the financial statements can be obtained.

[5 Sch 11(2)(3)(4), 30(2)(3)(4) as amended by SI 1996/189].

21.261 Where the ultimate parent company prepares consolidated financial statements, the information in paragraph 21.260 disclosed in the sub-group parent's financial statements need be given only for the ultimate parent and for the smallest group of undertakings that prepare consolidated financial statements which include the sub-group (if such an undertaking exists) (see for example Table 21.16). [5 Sch 11(1), 30(1)].

Table 21.16 – The Telegraph plc – Annual Report and Accounts – 31 December 1994

Notes to the accounts (extract)

32. Ultimate parent company

Hollinger Inc., incorporated in Canada and listed on the Toronto, Montreal and Vancouver stock exchanges, is regarded by the directors of the company as the company's ultimate parent company.

The largest group in which the results of the company are consolidated is that of which Hollinger Inc. is the parent company. The consolidated accounts of Hollinger Inc. may be obtained from Montreal Trust Company of Canada, 151 Front Street West, 8th Floor, Toronto, Ontario, Canada M5J 2N1.

The smallest such group is that of which DT Holdings Limited is the parent company, whose consolidated accounts may be obtained from 21 Wilson Street, London EC2M 2TQ. DT Holdings Limited is registered in England and Wales.

21.262 However, where the ultimate parent does not prepare consolidated financial statements, the information in paragraph 21.257 above has to be disclosed in the sub-group parent's financial statements. In addition, the information set out in paragraph 21.260 may also be required to be disclosed concerning the largest and smallest groups that prepare consolidated financial statements which include the sub-group.

21.263 These provisions can be very confusing and are best illustrated by an example. Consider the group structure set out in the diagram below.

Example

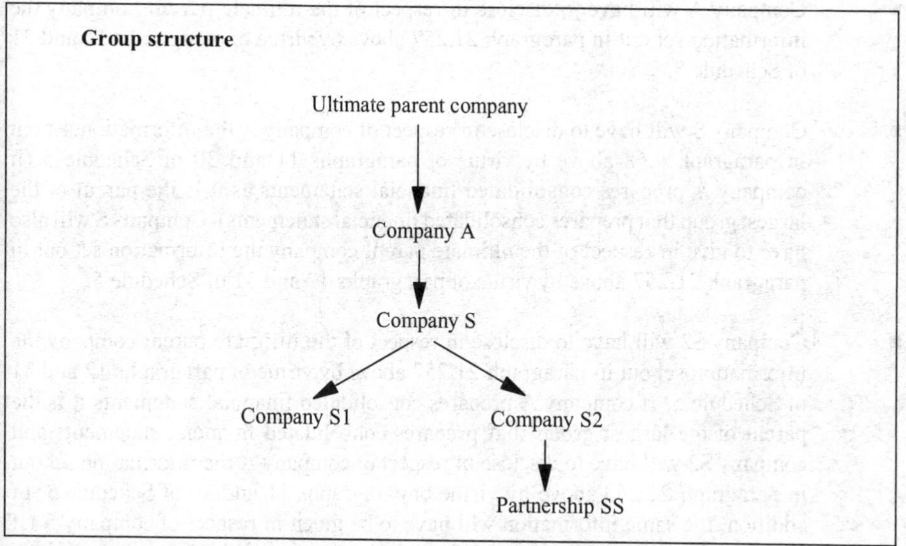

In the situation where the ultimate parent company *does prepare* consolidated financial statements, the following disclosure applies:

- Company A will have to disclose in respect of the ultimate parent company (being the largest group parent) the information set out in paragraphs 21.257 and 21.260 above by virtue of paragraphs 11, 12, 31 and 30 of Schedule 5.

- Company S will have to disclose in respect of company A the information set out in paragraph 21.260 above by virtue of paragraphs 11 and 30 of Schedule 5 (if company A prepares consolidated financial statements as it is the parent of the smallest group that prepares consolidated financial statements). Company S will also have to give in respect of the ultimate parent company (being also the largest group parent) the information set out in paragraphs 21.257 and 21.260 above by virtue of paragraphs 11, 12, 31 and 30 of Schedule 5.

- Company S2 will have to disclose in respect of the ultimate parent company (being also the largest group parent) the information set out in paragraphs 21.257 and 21.260 above by virtue of paragraphs 11, 12, 31 and 30 of Schedule 5. If company S prepares consolidated financial statements, then company S2 will also have to disclose in respect of company S (being the parent of the smallest group that prepares consolidated financial statements) the information set out in paragraph 21.260 above by virtue of paragraphs 11 and 30 of Schedule 5. Where company S does not prepare consolidated financial statements, then company S2 has to give the same information in respect of company A (if company A prepares consolidated financial statements as it is the parent of the smallest group that prepares consolidated financial statements).

In the situation where the ultimate parent company *does not* prepare consolidated financial statements, the following disclosure applies:

- Company A will have to disclose in respect of the ultimate parent company the information set out in paragraph 21.257 above by virtue of paragraphs 12 and 31 of Schedule 5.

- Company S will have to disclose in respect of company A the information set out in paragraph 4.68 above by virtue of paragraphs 11 and 30 of Schedule 5 (if company A prepares consolidated financial statements as it is the parent of the largest group that prepares consolidated financial statements). Company S will also have to give in respect of the ultimate parent company the information set out in paragraph 21.257 above by virtue of paragraphs 12 and 31 of Schedule 5.

- Company S2 will have to disclose in respect of the ultimate parent company the information set out in paragraph 21.257 above by virtue of paragraphs 12 and 31 of Schedule 5. If company A prepares consolidated financial statements it is the parent of the largest group that prepares consolidated financial statements and company S2 will have to disclose in respect of company A the information set out in paragraph 21.260 above by virtue of paragraphs 11 and 30 of Schedule 5. In addition, the same information will have to be given in respect of company S (if company S prepares consolidated financial statements as it is the parent of the smallest group that prepares consolidated financial statements). This means that in the situation described, company S2 is required to disclose information concerning three parent companies. Furthermore the situation might arise, for example, where another intermediate parent undertaking exists in the group structure between company S and company A. Even where such an undertaking prepares consolidated financial statements company S2 is still only required to give information concerning company A, company S and its ultimate parent. This is because the legislation only requires the information concerned to be disclosed in respect of the largest and smallest groups preparing consolidated financial statements and is not concerned with other intermediate parents in between that prepare consolidated financial statements.

21.264 In practice in the majority of situations, these provisions will mean that the information required by paragraph 21.260 above will have to be given for the next parent undertaking in the group that prepares consolidated financial statements that included the sub-group, and will also have to be given for the ultimate parent company that prepares consolidated financial statements.

Membership of a qualifying undertaking

21.265 Where at the year end a parent company or group is a member of a qualifying undertaking, it has to give the following information in its financial statements:

- The name and legal form of the undertaking.
- The address of the undertaking's registered office or, if it does not have such an office, its head office.

[Sch 5 28A(1)(2)].

21.266 In addition, where the qualifying undertaking is a qualifying partnership one of the following must also be stated:

- That a copy of the latest financial statements of the undertaking has been, or is to be, appended to the copy of the company's financial statements sent to the Registrar under section 242 of the Act.

- The name of at least one body corporate (which may be the company) in whose consolidated financial statements the undertaking has been, or is to be, dealt with by the method of full consolidation, proportional consolidation or the equity method of accounting.

[5 Sch 28A(3)].

21.267 For the purpose of these rules, 'qualifying undertakings' can either be companies or partnerships. A qualifying company (or qualifying partnership) is an unlimited company (or partnership) incorporated in (or governed by the laws of any part of) Great Britain if each of its members is:

- a limited company, or
- another unlimited company, or a Scottish firm, each of whose members is a limited company.

The references to limited company, another unlimited company and Scottish firm also encompass any comparable undertakings incorporated in, or formed under the law of, any country or territory outside Great Britain. [SI 1993/1820 Reg 3, 9].

21.268 The information required to be disclosed in the second bullet point of paragraph 21.266 need not be given if the partnership is dealt with either by consolidation, proportional consolidation or equity accounting in the consolidated financial statements prepared by:

- a member of the partnership that is established under the law of a member State; or

- a parent undertaking of such a member established in the same way.

[SI 1993/1820 Reg 7(1)].

21.269 The exemption can only be taken, however, where the following two conditions are complied with:

- The consolidated financial statements are prepared and audited under the law of the member State in accordance with the provisions of the 7th Directive.

- The notes to those consolidated financial statements disclose that advantage has been taken of the exemption.

[SI 1993/1820 Reg 7(2)].

Other disclosure issues

Realised and distributable reserves

21.270 The restrictions on distributions contained in the Act apply to individual companies and not to groups. This is because individual companies make distributions, whereas groups do not. However, users of consolidated financial statements may wish to know the amount the holding company could distribute if all the group's subsidiaries were to pay up their realised profits by way of dividends to the parent company. Many groups specifically disclose the amount of their distributable reserves and this issue is discussed in chapter 19. In addition, FRS 3 now requires companies and groups to include in their financial statements a note of the historical cost profits and losses for the year. [FRS 3 para 26]. Consequently, groups are required by this FRS to show the historical cost profit or loss for the year, which will typically be exactly or approximately the group's realised profit or loss for the period.

21.271 Furthermore, FRS 2 requires that, where significant statutory, contractual or exchange control restrictions exist which materially limit the distributions a subsidiary undertaking can make and, therefore, the parent undertaking's access to distributable profits, the nature and extent of the restrictions should be disclosed (see for example Table 21.17). [FRS 2 para 53].

Table 21.17 – The BOC Group plc – Report and Accounts – 30 September 1994

Notes on Financial Statements (extract)

12. Dividends and equity (extract)

The undistributed profits of Group undertakings may be liable to overseas and/or UK tax (after allowing for double tax relief) if distributed as dividends. There are exchange control restrictions in certain countries on the remittance of funds to the UK. Provision has been made against those dividends declared by overseas undertakings currently "blocked". Goodwill written off against reserves in respect of continuing businesses amounts to £318.0 million.

21.272 The parent company's ability to distribute pre-acquisition reserves of its subsidiaries is discussed in chapter 3.

Tax on the accumulated reserves of overseas subsidiaries

21.273 SSAP 15 'Accounting for deferred tax' provides some guidance on the treatment of overseas retained earnings. Its provisions require that deferred tax should be computed using the liability method. [SSAP 15 para 24]. Furthermore, tax deferred (or accelerated) by the effect of timing differences should be accounted for to the extent that it is probable that a liability (or asset) will crystallise. [SSAP 15 para 25]. More specifically, SSAP 15 suggests that retained earnings overseas only constitute a timing difference in certain situations; and FRS 2 adds to the disclosure requirements. These matters are considered in chapter 13.

Comparison with IASs

21.274 The IASC's rules in this area are to be found in IAS 27, 'Consolidated financial statements and accounting for investments in subsidiaries, which came into force in 1990. These rules are less detailed than those of FRS 2 and the Companies Act. For example, there are no instructions in IAS 27 requiring disclosures relating to excluded subsidiaries or cessation of subsidiaries.

21.275 FRS 2's large number of exemptions from parents preparing consolidated financial statements are not found in IAS 27, which merely exempts parents that are wholly-owned subsidiaries or (with the approval of minorities) virtually wholly-owned subsidiaries. [IAS 27 para 8].

21.276 IAS 27's definition of a subsidiary is simply *"an enterprise that is controlled by another"*. [IAS 27 para 6]. That is, the complex definitions introduced into the UK by the Companies Act 1989 are not found in IAS 27.

21.277 In a parent's financial statements IAS 27 allows the option to account for subsidiaries using the equity method. [IAS 27 para 29]. This is the practice in several countries, including the Netherlands and Denmark.

21.278 IAS 27 does not allow the exclusion of a subsidiary on the grounds of dissimilarity. In practice, this may also be the effect of the provisions in FRS 2 as explained earlier.

Chapter 22

Consolidation rules

Page

Consolidation rules

Introduction

22.1 Consolidated financial statements must give a true and fair view of the state of affairs and the profit or loss of the company and those of its subsidiaries included in the consolidated financial statements as a whole, so far as concerns the parent company's shareholders. [Sec 227(3)]. As with individual financial statements, this is an overriding requirement. This overriding requirement is explained in chapter 2.

22.2 In addition to the overriding requirement to give a true and fair view, the Act and FRS 2 include accounting rules that apply to consolidated financial statements. In general, the Act's provisions correspond to those that apply to an individual company's financial statements. Consequently, consolidated financial statements must comply with the requirements of Schedule 4 to the Act both as to their form and content and as to the information they must disclose in the notes (to the extent that this Schedule applies to consolidated financial statements). The historical cost accounting rules and the alternative accounting rules set out in Schedule 4 to the Act apply equally to consolidated financial statements as they do to individual companies' financial statements. These rules are considered in detail in chapter 5.

22.3 Furthermore, the Companies Act 1989 introduced a new Schedule 4A to the Companies Act 1985. This Schedule details the rules concerning the form and content of consolidated financial statements and introduced into UK company law the majority of the 7th Directive's provisions. One exception to these consolidation rules is that if any member of a group is a banking or an insurance company the Schedule 4 and 4A formats are not appropriate. Banks have to comply with Schedule 9 of the Act which was completely revised by the Companies Act 1985 (Bank Accounts) Regulations 1991 (SI 1991/2705). Insurance companies have to comply with Schedule 9A to the Act as revised by the Companies Act 1985 (Insurance Companies Accounts) Regulations 1993 (SI 1993/3246). The accounting requirements that apply to banking and insurance companies are not within the scope of this book.

22.4 If, at the end of the financial year, a company has one or more subsidiaries, consolidated financial statements must be prepared in addition to the parent company's individual financial statements. The consolidated financial statements should deal with the state of affairs and the profit or loss of the company and its subsidiaries. [Sec 227(2)].

22.5 FRS 2 extends the Act's provisions to require that consolidated financial statements should be prepared also where a parent undertaking is an entity other than a company and its financial statements are to give a true and fair view. [FRS 2 para 18].

22.6 The only exceptions to the general rules outlined in paragraph 22.4 above are considered in chapter 21.

22.7 The particular provisions in Schedule 4A to the Act and the provisions in FRS 2 that form the basic consolidation rules are explained below, together with other rules that have become generally accepted accounting principles through their general use in preparing consolidations.

Generally accepted accounting principles

22.8 Consolidated financial statements have to incorporate all of the information contained in the individual financial statements of the undertakings included in the consolidation. [4A Sch 2(1)]. However, this provision is subject to adjustments authorised by Schedule 4A and to any adjustments that are necessary in order to accord with *"generally accepted accounting principles or practice"*. [4A Sch 2(1)]. Although the term in the Act incorporates the word 'practice', the term is more often referred to by accountants as 'Generally Accepted Accounting Principles' (GAAP). The term UK GAAP is one that means generally accepted accounting principles that apply to UK companies and groups and that encompass UK law, accounting standards, UITF Abstracts, the Stock Exchange accounting requirements (if appropriate) and other generally accepted accounting practices (see further chapter 2).

22.9 The accounting principles that are used in the consolidation process should be disclosed in the accounting policies note to the consolidated financial statements. This note generally covers the following matters relating to consolidations:

- The methods of accounting used to consolidate new subsidiaries, that is either of the following:
  - Acquisition accounting (see chapter 23).
  - Merger accounting (see chapter 26).
- The treatment of any goodwill arising on consolidation, and the treatment of other differences arising on consolidation (see further chapter 23).

- The translation of overseas subsidiaries' financial statements (see chapter 29).
- How minority interests are dealt with (see chapter 24).
- How associated companies and joint ventures are dealt with (see chapter 28).
- How the trading between non-coterminous year ends of the parent and subsidiary are dealt with (see para 22.28).
- The treatment of intra-group transactions (see para 22.38 below).

Procedure for consolidation

22.10 As mentioned in paragraph 22.8 above, the Act specifies that the consolidated balance sheet and the consolidated profit and loss account should incorporate in full the information contained in the individual financial statements of the undertakings included in the consolidation, subject to certain consolidation adjustments. [4A Sch 2(1)]. However, it does not specify how the aggregation of this information should be undertaken.

22.11 FRS 2 makes no comment on the process of consolidation and SSAP 14, its predecessor, only commented that the method for preparing consolidated financial statements on an item by item basis, eliminating intra-group balances and transactions and unrealised intra-group profit, was well understood and did not deal further with the matter. IAS 27, 'Consolidated financial statements and accounting for investments in subsidiaries', mentions that, in preparing consolidated financial statements, the financial statements of the parent and its subsidiaries are combined on a line by line basis by adding together like items of assets, liabilities, income and expenses. [IAS 27 para 13]. IAS 27 then goes on to mention some of the steps in the consolidation process. These are very similar in nature to the matters mentioned in paragraph 22.9 above.

22.12 In practice, there are two methods of preparing consolidated financial statements. In the first method the individual financial statements of subsidiaries are aggregated centrally by adding together the profit and loss account and balance sheet figures on a line by line basis. These aggregate figures taken from the subsidiaries' statutory financial statements are then amended to deal with consolidation adjustments. Such adjustments would be necessary in order to:

- Adjust individual figures in the financial statements of subsidiaries to bring them onto common accounting policies (see para 22.15 below).

- Achieve the consolidation by, for example, dealing with goodwill and minority interests (see para 22.22 below).

22.13 A second method, more suitable for large groups, is for each subsidiary to prepare a consolidation return. The consolidation return is made up from the individual subsidiary's financial statements which are:

- Adjusted to common accounting policies.
- Edited into a format and analysis that makes the consolidated process easier.

These returns are then aggregated to form the group's consolidated financial statements. Even using this basis, there may still be a need to make consolidation adjustments. For example, company A would not know how much intra-group profit to eliminate on goods sold to its subsidiary company B, because it would not know how much of that stock company B had sold. In some companies such forms are electronic and input *via* group networks to update central consolidation packages.

Consolidation adjustments

22.14 There are a number of reasons why a parent may have to make consolidation adjustments to its subsidiaries' financial statements in preparing the group's consolidated financial statements. Some of these reasons and the rules relating to such adjustments are considered in the paragraphs that follow.

Uniform accounting polices

22.15 Except in exceptional situations, which are explained below, uniform group accounting policies should be used to determine the amounts to be included in the consolidated financial statements. This may require adjustment, on consolidation, of the amounts that have been reported by subsidiaries in their individual financial statements. [4A Sch 3(1); FRS 2 para 40].

22.16 In practice, a group that operates wholly within the UK is unlikely to have to make such adjustments because:

- All UK companies are expected to follow UK GAAP.
- In situations where UK GAAP permits the use of different accounting policies, the parent is likely to impose the group policy on each of its subsidiaries.

22.17 The Act specifically requires consolidation adjustments to be made where a subsidiary undertaking's assets and liabilities have been valued using accounting rules that differ from those used by the group. [4A Sch 3(1)]. For example, the need for such an adjustment would arise where a subsidiary values its stocks using a LIFO method of valuation. In the UK LIFO stock valuations are not allowed for UK corporation tax purposes and are considered in SSAP 9 to be likely to be incompatible with the requirement to give a true and fair view. Such valuations are, however, allowed for both tax and accounting purposes in other countries, for example South Africa and the US, and, consequently, subsidiaries that operate in those countries may value their stocks on that basis. Clearly, when such subsidiaries are consolidated, an adjustment will be required to bring the stock valuations onto a basis acceptable in the UK (for example, FIFO or average cost).

22.18 However in certain situations, the parent's directors might consider that there are special reasons for retaining the different accounting rules adopted by the subsidiary. Where this is so, the Act's and FRS 2's provisions require that particulars of the departure, the reasons for it and its effect should be disclosed in the notes to the consolidated financial statements. [4A Sch 3(2); FRS 2 para 41]. UITF Abstract 7 interprets the information the Act requires in such a situation and its implications are considered further in chapter 2.

22.19 It may also be that the accounting policies used by the parent in its individual financial statements differ from those of the group. However, this is less common. While the law does not require the policies of the parent and the group to be the same, it requires disclosure of any differences in the notes to the consolidated financial statements and of the reason for the differences. [4A Sch 4]. An example of where such a difference could arise is where the parent records its fixed asset land and buildings at historical cost, but the group carries them at revalued amounts, but in practice this is unlikely to happen.

22.20 Where a new subsidiary is acquired by a group and the two have different accounting policies, the new subsidiary has sufficient reason to change its accounting policy and make a prior-year adjustment in accordance with FRS 3. Alternatively, the new subsidiary may continue with its original accounting policy in its entity financial statements, in which case the group would need to make an adjustment on consolidation to reflect the subsidiary's results in accordance with the group's accounting policy.

22.21 Problems can arise with overseas subsidiaries in applying uniform accounting policies. Where the subsidiaries are subject to either company law or tax law that is different from that in the UK, it may not always be practicable for the parent to insist that the subsidiaries change their accounting policies to bring them into line with the group's accounting policies. For example, in many European countries depreciation is calculated in accordance with local tax regulations rather than by reference to the estimated useful life of the asset. However, in order to obtain the tax relief, the tax-based depreciation figure must be shown in the subsidiary's individual financial statements. In order to comply with FRS 2 and the

Act an adjustment must then be made on consolidation to both the depreciation charge for the year and the accumulated depreciation to bring them into line with UK (and the group's) practice. In this situation, an adjustment to deferred taxation may also be required. Table 22.1 illustrates a situation where local legislation prevents the subsidiaries adopting the group's accounting policies.

Table 22.1 – GKN plc – Report & Accounts – 31 December 1997

NOTES ON THE ACCOUNTS (extract)

1 Basis of Consolidation

Accounting policies

The Group's accounting policies are shown in the notes on pages 37 to 51. Local legislation prevents certain overseas subsidiaries from conforming with the accounting policies adopted by the Group. Where appropriate, adjustments are made on consolidation so that the group accounts are presented on a uniform basis.

Other consolidation adjustments

22.22 Consolidation adjustments are required for a variety of reasons and the group's accounting policies will often describe the areas where adjustments are made as detailed in paragraph 22.9 above. The elimination of pre-acquisition reserves, although it would not generally be dealt with specifically in the accounting policies note, is another adjustment that is fundamental to the consolidation process (see further chapter 23).

22.23 A consolidation adjustment may also be necessary where a material 'subsequent event' occurs in a subsidiary between the date when the subsidiary's directors sign the subsidiary's own financial statements and the date when the holding company's directors sign the consolidated financial statements. If the 'subsequent event' is material to the group and is an 'adjusting event' (which is a post balance sheet event that provides additional evidence of conditions that exist at the balance sheet date), a consolidation adjustment should be made for it in the consolidated financial statements.

22.24 It is debatable, however, whether some other adjustments that are made 'on consolidation', but which do not relate to the process of consolidation are permissible. For example, a group might wish to set up a provision on consolidation for redundancies in a subsidiary that it intends to run down. In this situation, it would be unlikely that the subsidiary's financial statements could give a true and fair view without that provision being reflected in them.

Subsidiary year ends

22.25 The financial statements of all subsidiaries to be used in preparing the consolidated financial statements should, wherever practicable, be prepared to the same financial year end and for the same accounting period as those of the parent. [FRS 2 para 42]. The directors have an obligation under section 223(5) of the Act to secure that the financial year of each of its subsidiary undertakings coincides with the parent company's own financial year, unless in their opinion there are good reasons for this not to be so.

22.26 The Act requires that the financial statements of a subsidiary may not be consolidated if its accounting period ends more than three months before that of its parent. [4A Sch 2(2)(a)]. If the subsidiary's financial year ends before this period, it has to prepare interim financial statements to coincide with the end of the parent company's financial year. [4A Sch 2(2)(b)].

Interim financial statements

22.27 However, FRS 2 takes a stricter approach and requires that where the financial year of a subsidiary undertaking differs from that of the parent, interim financial statements should be prepared to the same date as those of the parent for use in preparing consolidated financial statements (see for example Table 22.2). If it is *not practicable* to use such interim financial statements, the subsidiary's financial statements should be used, providing that its year ended not more than three months before the relevant year end of the parent. In this situation, any changes that have taken place in the intervening period that materially affect the view given by the financial statements should be taken into account by adjusting the consolidated financial statements. [FRS 2 para 43]. In certain circumstances, such adjustments might be considered to be immaterial as illustrated in Table 22.3.

Table 22.2 – Abbey National plc – Directors' Report and Accounts – 31 December 1994

Accounting policies (extract)

Basis of consolidation

The group accounts comprise the accounts of the Company and its subsidiary undertakings made up to 31 December, with the exception of a number of leasing and investment subsidiaries and the companies within the HMC group, which, because of commercial considerations, have various accounting reference dates. In addition, WF Company Ltd, which was acquired on 21 December 1994, currently has an accounting reference date other than 31 December. The accounts of these subsidiaries have been consolidated on the basis of interim accounts for the year to 31 December 1994.

Table 22.3 – National Westminster Bank Plc – Annual Report and Accounts – 31 December 1997

Notes to the accounts (extract)

1 PRINCIPAL ACCOUNTING POLICIES (extract)

(ii) **Basis of consolidation (extract)**

To avoid undue delay in the presentation of the Group's accounts, the accounts of certain subsidiary undertakings have been made up to 30 November. There have been no changes in respect of these subsidiary undertakings, in the period from their balance sheet dates to 31 December, that materially affect the view given by the Group's accounts. Details of principal subsidiary undertakings are given in note 25.

22.28 Consolidation adjustments of this nature might be required for dividends paid by the subsidiary to the parent and settlement of intra-group balances outstanding at the subsidiary's year end, which would obviously have to be dealt with as part of the consolidation process. Other transactions might not be so obvious, such as a post balance sheet event in the subsidiary. For example, an adjustment would have to be made for a substantial loss on a contract undertaken by a subsidiary that has occurred in between the subsidiary's year end and that of its parent. Another example, where the subsidiary is incorporated overseas, is where there has been a devaluation of the currency in which it trades between its year end date and that of its parent.

22.29 FRS 2 is, therefore, restricting the legislation by giving preference to the requirement to prepare interim financial statements and only permitting the use of the subsidiary's own financial statements if the preparation of interim financial statements is *not practicable*. One practical reason sometimes given for having different year ends is to avoid delays in presenting the consolidated financial statements (for example, see Table 22.3 above and Table 22.4 on the next page).

Table 22.4 – Blue Circle Industries PLC – Annual Report & Accounts – 31 December 1997

Accounting Policies (extract)

2 *Consolidation*

The Group accounts incorporate the results of the Company and its subsidiary and principal associated undertakings. In these accounts, these entities are referred to as subsidiaries and related companies respectively. To avoid delay in the presentation of the accounts the accounting period of one overseas subsidiary ends on 30 November. The results of related companies are based upon statutory or management accounts for periods ending on either 30 November or 31 December. Where subsidiaries and related companies are acquired or disposed of during the year, results are included from the date of acquisition or to the date of sale.

22.30 The example below illustrates the options that are available when consolidating a subsidiary with a non-coterminous year end.

Example

A parent company has a year end of 31 December 19X1. One of its subsidiaries has a year end of 30 June 19X1 and another has a year end of 30 September 19X1. What figures may the parent include in its consolidated financial statements in respect of these subsidiaries?

In the first situation the subsidiary must prepare interim financial statements covering the year ended 31 December 19X1 (that is, coinciding with that of its parent). It may not prepare interim financial statements to, for example 30 November, despite this date being within three months of the parent's year end. Under no circumstances (unless the subsidiary is immaterial) may the parent consolidate the subsidiary's own statutory financial statements as the subsidiary's year end is more than three months before that of the parent.

In the second situation the parent should consolidate interim financial statements prepared by the subsidiary for the year ended 31 December 19X1, but if this is not practicable it may consolidate the financial statements of the subsidiary for the year ended 30 September 19X1 (as it ends no more than three months prior to the parent's year end). If the financial statements for 30 September 19X1 are used, consideration should be given to the requirement to adjust for transactions between the subsidiary's year end and that of the parent.

22.31 The interim financial statements are not required by the Act to be audited. However, they would have to be audited at least to the group materiality to satisfy the requirement that the group's consolidated financial statements have to give a true and fair view.

Disclosure where year ends differ

22.32 The following information should be given for each material subsidiary that is included in the consolidated financial statements on the basis of information prepared to a different date or for a different accounting period from that of the parent:

- Its name.
- Its accounting date or period, including the date on which its last financial year ended.
- The reason for using a different accounting date or period, including why the directors consider that the subsidiary's financial year should not end with that of its parent.

[5 Sch 19; FRS 2 para 44].

These disclosures are illustrated in Table 22.5.

Table 22.5 – Imperial Chemical Industries PLC – Annual report and accounts – 31 December 1994

notes relating to the accounts (extract)

1 Composition of the Group

The Group accounts consolidate the accounts of Imperial Chemical Industries PLC (the Company) and its subsidiary undertakings, of which there were 363 at 31 December 1994. Owing to local conditions and to avoid undue delay in the presentation of the Group accounts, 62 subsidiaries made up their accounts to dates earlier than 31 December, but not earlier than 30 September; one subsidiary makes up its accounts to 31 March but interim accounts to 31 December are drawn up for consolidation purposes.

principal subsidiary undertakings (extract)

	Class of capital	Held by ICI %	Principal activities
OTHER COUNTRIES (extract)			
AECI Explosives Ltd Republic of South Africa	Ordinary	51†	Manufacture of industrial explosives and initiating systems

ICI Australia Ltd Australia (Accounting and reporting date 30 September)	Ordinary*	62†	Manufacture and distribution of chemicals and other products including fertilisers and crop care, industrial and specialty chemicals, consumer and effect products, plastics and performance of related services
ICI China Hong Kong and China	Ordinary	100†	Merchanting of ICI and other products
ICI India Ltd India (Accounting date 31 March; reporting date 31 December)	Equity*	51	Manufacture of industrial explosives, paints, agrochemicals, pharmaceutical, polyurethanes, catalysts, rubber chemicals and surfactants

* Listed

† Held by subsidiaries

The country of principal operations and registration or incorporation is stated below each company. The accounting dates of principal subsidiary undertakings are 31 December unless otherwise stated.

Practical problems

22.33 Problems often arise in deciding what accounting periods to include in the consolidation when subsidiaries have different accounting year ends to their parent. The example below illustrates the type of situation that can arise in practice.

Example

Financial statements consolidated

19X2

	Start	End
Parent	1/4/X1	31/3/X2
Subsidiary	1/1/X1	
Consolidation		

19X1

	Start	End
Parent	1/4/X0	31/3/X1
Subsidiary	1/1/X0	31/12/X0
Consolidation		

A parent whose year end is 31 March has for a number of years consolidated a subsidiary's financial statements drawn up to 31 December. It has now decided to use the subsidiary's management accounts to 31 March 19X2 for consolidation with the group's financial statements to 31 March 19X2. The situation can be illustrated as set out below:

The consolidated financial statements for the year to 31 March 19X2 would include 16 months of the subsidiary's trading. By comparison, the group's published financial statements for the year to 31 March 19X1 include 12 months of the subsidiary's trading ending on 31 December 19X0. Therefore, the consolidated financial statements prepared for the year to 31 March 19X2 include comparatives which are not truly comparable. Also, if the subsidiary was particularly material to the group, it might be misleading to describe the group's consolidated financial statements as representing the group's trading for merely 12 months. However, it would be wrong, in the group's consolidated financial statements to 31 March 19X2, to leave out of account the subsidiary's trading for the period from 1 January 19X1 to 31 March 19X1.

Consequently, if the subsidiary's trading is particularly material to the group, the consolidated financial statements should indicate clearly that they include the financial statements of the parent (and other subsidiaries) for the year to 31 March 19X2, but the result of the material subsidiary for the 16 month period ending on the same date. Then it would be necessary to show the impact that the additional three months has on the reported results. This can be done in a variety of ways, the best approach would be to split the trading into three columns and show the subsidiary's trading for the 3 months to 31 March 19X1 in one column, the trading for the 12 months to March 19X2 (including the subsidiary) in the next column and a total column. The comparatives would remain unchanged. This method gives users clear disclosure of the group's most recent 12 months trading which may assist in their projections of future comparable trading periods. It also satisfies the Act's requirements concerning consolidations. Some would argue that this basis still does not solve the problem as the comparatives are not truly comparable. To resolve this issue it would also be necessary to disclose the subsidiary's trading for the 3 months to 31 March 19X2. We consider that this additional disclosure is generally unnecessary and the need for it will depend on the individual circumstances.

Parent's period differs from group

22.34 Similar difficulties to those explained above arise where the parent has recently been incorporated and acquires subsidiaries which have different reporting periods to that of the parent.

Example

A parent is incorporated on 1 September 19X1 and acquires a group of subsidiaries on 1 January 19X2. Acquisition accounting is adopted. The parent's first financial statements cover the 16 month period to 31 December 19X2. December is the year end of the group of subsidiaries.

The question then is should the group's financial statements be prepared to cover the same 16 month period. This is certainly one answer, but poses problems because the subsidiaries' financial years run from 1 January. The solution to this problem is to prepare the consolidated financial statements for the 16 month period to 31 December 19X2 including the parent's results for the 16 months (of which the first three months may well be immaterial, because the company will have been set up to acquire the subsidiaries and will not have traded in that period) and the results of the subsidiaries for 12 months, that is, from the date of acquisition. Appropriate disclosure of the basis adopted would be necessary. Proforma comparatives comprising the subsidiaries' results for the 12 months to 31 December 19X1 may be given for information.

22.35 A similar type of situation arose in Chubb Security Plc, where a new parent was incorporated on 17 August 1992 and acquired Chubb International Holdings Limited (CIHL) on 5 October 1992. The group's financial statements ended 31 March 1993 show proforma accounts for 1993 and 1992 as if the group had existed independently for those two years. The statutory financial information is given as a separate column and includes the results of CIHL from the date of its acquisition in October 1992 to 31 March 1993. The balance sheet shows the statutory group balances for the year to 31 March 1993 and proforma information as comparatives (see Table 22.6).

Table 22.6 – Chubb Security Plc – Annual Report & Accounts – 31 March 1993

Notes to the Accounts

1 **BASIS OF REPORTING**

Chubb Security Plc was incorporated on 17 August 1992. During 1992 all companies within the Security Division of Racal Electronics Plc (Racal) which were not already owned by Chubb International Holdings Limited (CIHL), formerly Racal Security Limited, were transferred into its ownership and companies owned by CIHL which were not part of the Security Division were transferred out of its ownership. CIHL was then transferred into the ownership of Chubb Security Plc which was demerged from Racal on 5 October 1992.

The proforma financial statements include the results for the Group as currently constituted and show the results that would have been presented if Chubb Security Plc had been an independent company throughout the two years ended 31 March 1993. The results for the year ended 31 March 1992 are as previously presented in the Introduction to the Official List (Listing Particulars) circulated to Racal shareholders in September 1992.

The statutory financial statements for the period ended 31 March include the results for the Group for the 21 weeks from 10 October 1992 (the closest date to the demerger up to which management accounts had been prepared) to 31 March 1993. It was not practical to adjust these management accounts by the results for the period 5 to 9 October 1992.

Consolidated Profit and Loss Account (extract) for the Period and Year Ended 31 March 1993

Note		1993 Proforma £000	1992 Proforma £000	1993 Statutory £000
2	Turnover	**674,402**	668, 943	**330,880**
2 & 3	Operating profit before exceptional items	**75,602**	53,326	**40,078**
4	Exceptional items	**(7,822)**	(5,943)	**(2,248)**
	Trading profit	**67,780**	47,383	**37,830**
5	Group interest payable less investment income	**3,577**	8,311	**1,995**
	Profit on ordinary activities before taxation	**64,203**	39,072	**35,835**

Consolidated Balance Sheet (extract) at 31 March 1993

Note			1993 Statutory	1992 Proforma	
		£000	**£000**	£000	£000
	FIXED ASSETS				
13	Tangible assets		**123,671**		121,935
14	Investments		**1,624**		4,154
			125,295		126, 089

22.36 In the reorganisation of Rothmans International in 1993, a new parent company was incorporated to acquire the tobacco business of the group, but here the principles of merger accounting were applied (see Table 22.7). In this case, the parent company's accounting period (28 July 1993 to 31 March 1994) was shorter than that of the subsidiaries acquired and group accounts were prepared including the new parent's results for the period 28 July 1993 to 31 March 1994, but incorporating the results of the subsidiaries for their full financial year, that is, for the year to 31 March 1994 in accordance with the principles of merger accounting. Comparatives for the group were the results of the subsidiaries for the year to 31 March 1993.

Table 22.7 – Rothmans International p.l.c. – Annual Report and Accounts – 31 March 1994

DIRECTORS' REPORT (extract)

INCORPORATION AND CHANGE OF NAME The Company was incorporated on 28th July 1993 as New Rothmans plc. On 25th October 1993 the Company changed its name to Rothmans International plc.

STATEMENT OF ACCOUNTING POLICIES (extract)

BASIS OF PREPARATION As part of the amalgamation and reconstruction of the tobacco and luxury goods interests of Rothmans International p.l.c. ('old Rothmans'), Compagnie Financière Richemont AG ('Richemont') and Dunhill Holdings PLC ('Dunhill') in October 1993, the tobacco businesses of old Rothmans and certain tobacco trade marks owned or controlled by Dunhill and by Richemont, were transferred to two new listed companies, Rothmans International plc (formerly New Rothmans plc) and Rothmans International N.V. (together, 'new Rothmans'). Rothmans International plc acquired the UK based tobacco business of old Rothmans and the Dunhill tobacco trade marks. Rothmans International N.V. acquired the non UK based tobacco business of old Rothmans and certain tobacco trade marks owned or controlled by Richemont. The luxury goods interests of old Rothmans, comprising its 58 per cent interest in Dunhill and its 47 per cent indirect interest in Cartier Monde S.A., were transferred to form part of a new separate listed group under the name Vendôme Luxury Group. Shareholders in old Rothmans received units in new Rothmans, each comprising one Rothmans International plc share and one Rothmans International N.V. share, in exchange for their shares in old Rothmans which were transferred to that group, and a payment of cash, representing funds not required by new Rothmans. Units in new Rothmans were also issued to the shareholders in Dunhill and to Richemont representing the tobacco trade marks transferred to new Rothmans. Pursuant to the reconstruction, old Rothmans is in voluntary liquidation.

The consolidated financial statements of the Rothmans International plc group have been prepared using the principles of merger accounting. As a result, although the reconstruction did not take effect until 23rd October 1993, the financial statements are presented as if the reconstruction had taken place on 1st April 1992, except for the exchange of shares, which took place on 23rd October 1993, the return of surplus cash on 1st November 1993 and certain other transactions connected with the reconstruction. The results of the UK based tobacco business of old Rothmans for the year ended 31st March 1993 and for the full year ended 31st March 1994 have been included in these consolidated financial statements except that net dividends received from companies which are now in the Rothmans International N.V. group and dividends received from Dunhill have been excluded from the profit and loss account and are shown as a movement in reserves.

The consolidated accounts include the accounts of Rothmans International plc and its subsidiary undertakings together with the Group's share of the profits and retained post-acquisition reserves of associated undertakings.

22.37 Non-coterminous accounting periods are also considered in chapter 27 which looks at the problems that can arise in merger accounting.

Elimination of intra-group transactions

22.38 Until the Companies Act 1989, there were no laid down rules concerning how to eliminate intra-group transactions. Nevertheless, it has been accepted accounting practice to eliminate transactions between group members in the consolidated financial statements. SSAP 14 stated that such eliminations should be made, but did not detail how, apart from stating that the method was well understood. However, the Act specifically requires *"debts and claims"* (that is, debtors and creditors) between group undertakings to be eliminated on consolidation. Also, income and expenditure relating to transactions between group undertakings should be eliminated on consolidation. [4A Sch 6(1)].

22.39 Similarly, profits and losses resulting from transactions between group undertakings included in the value of assets retained at the year end should be eliminated. [4A Sch 6(2)]. The Act, but not FRS 2 (see below), permits the elimination of such profits and losses to be made in proportion to the group's interest in the undertaking's shares. [4A Sch 6(3)]. Prior to the Companies Act 1989, companies generally eliminated 100 per cent of such transactions.

22.40 The rules set out in FRS 2 are consistent with the Act except that they are further restricted as follows:

- Profits or losses on any intra-group transactions, to the extent that they are reflected in the book value of assets to be included in the consolidation, should be eliminated in full.

- Intra-group debtors and creditors should be eliminated.

- The elimination of profits or losses relating to intra-group transactions should be set against the interests held by the parent and its other subsidiaries and against the minority interest in proportion to their respective holdings in the undertaking whose individual financial statements recorded the eliminated profits or losses.

- All transactions that would be eliminated if they were between undertakings included in the consolidation should also be eliminated if one party is a subsidiary excluded because of its different activities (see further chapter 21).

[FRS 2 para 39].

22.41 The rationale for full elimination of unrealised profits or losses even where the related transactions are between subsidiary undertakings with minority interests is set out below.

22.42 Transactions between subsidiaries included in the consolidation are wholly within the control of the parent company, whether or not the subsidiaries are wholly owned. All the assets and liabilities of a subsidiary and transactions between subsidiaries are brought into the consolidation in full, again whether or not they are wholly owned. Therefore, as the group includes 100 per cent of all the subsidiaries' assets and liabilities, intra-group transactions that give rise to profits or losses that are unrealised at the balance sheet date are wholly unrealised to the group and do not represent any increase or decrease in the group's net assets. They should, therefore, be eliminated in full, even where the transactions involve subsidiaries with minority interests.

Elimination calculations

22.43 The following examples deal with the elimination of intra-group profit on the sale of assets by a subsidiary to its parent and the elimination of intra-group profit on sale of assets by a parent to its subsidiary.

Example 1

A parent owns 60% of a subsidiary. The subsidiary sells some stock to the parent for £70,000 and makes a profit of £30,000 on the sale. The stock is in the parent's balance sheet at the year end.

The parent must eliminate 100% of the unrealised profit on consolidation. The stock will, therefore, be carried in the group's balance sheet at £40,000 (£70,000 – £30,000). The profit and loss account will show a corresponding reduction in profit of £30,000. The minority interest in the profit and loss account for the year will be credited with the minority's share of the unrealised profit, £12,000 (40% × £30,000).

The double entry on consolidation is as follows:

	£'000	£'000
Dr Profit before taxation	30	
Cr Stock		30
Being the elimination of 100% of the unrealised profit from the balance sheet.		
Dr Balance sheet minority interest	12	
Cr Profit and loss account minority interest		12
Being the allocation to the minority of its 'share' of the elimination of the unrealised profit.		

The effect on the profit and loss account and balance sheet is as follows:

Profit and loss account	Results of sub (say)	Adjustment	Results consolidated
	£'000	£'000	£'000
Profit before taxation	100	(30)	70
Minority interests	(40)	12	(28)
Profit for the financial year	60	(18)	42

Consolidated balance sheet	Before adjustment (say)	Adjustment	After adjustment
Stock	800	(30)	770
Other shareholders' funds	400	-	400
Profit and loss account	275	(18)	257
Minority interests	125	(12)	113
	800	(30)	770

In other words, from the group's point of view, no profit has been recognised. The stock is retained at cost to the group of £40,000. The profit before tax also does not include any of the profit of £30,000 on the stock in question. This reflects the fact that the group as an entity has not made a profit on selling stock to itself. Since in this method, the objective is to eliminate the entire profit, it is necessary to show the effect of the subsidiary in question earning £30,000 less profit. The effect of this is that the group has earned £18,000 less (60% x £30,000). Hence the adjustment of £12,000 shown above in the minority's line.

Example 2

The situation is as above except that, on this occasion, it is the parent that makes the sale. The parent owns 60% of a subsidiary. The parent sells some stock to the subsidiary for £70,000 and makes a profit of £30,000 on the sale. The stock is in the subsidiary's balance sheet at the year end.

The parent must eliminate 100% of the unrealised profit on consolidation. The stock will, therefore, be carried in the group's balance sheet at £40,000 (£70,000 – £30,000). The profit and loss account will show a corresponding reduction in profit of £30,000. As the minority has no interest in the company that made the profit (the parent) there will be no element of the elimination attributed to the minority.

The double entry on consolidation is as follows:

	£'000	£'000
Dr Profit before taxation	30	
Cr Stock		30
Being the elimination of 100% of the unrealised profit from the balance sheet.		

The effect on the profit and loss account and balance sheet is:

Consolidated profit and loss account	Before adjustment (say)	Adjustment	After adjustment
	£'000	£'000	£'000
Profit before taxation	100	(30)	70
Minority interests	(40)	-	(40)
Profit for the financial year	60	(30)	30
Consolidated balance sheet	Before adjustment (say)	Adjustment	After adjustment
Stock	800	(30)	770
Other shareholders' funds	400	-	400
Profit and loss account	275	(30)	245
Minority interests	125	-	125
	800	(30)	770

Profit elimination from fixed assets

22.44 The rules explained above apply equally to any profit that might be included in the group's fixed assets (including investments) as a result of one group company selling assets to another group company at a profit. Before the introduction of FRS 2 many companies did not eliminate such profits immediately from their fixed assets, but eliminated them over the life of the asset *via* higher depreciation charges. This method is not acceptable under FRS 2 and such intra-group profits must be eliminated in full.

Losses

22.45 Where a company makes a loss selling assets to another group company, no consolidation adjustment should be necessary at the year end. This is because it would be wrong to reinstate the asset at a value above its recoverable amount.

Subsidiaries excluded from consolidation

22.46 The elimination of intra-group transactions in the context of subsidiaries excluded from consolidation requires special consideration. Transactions with subsidiaries excluded from consolidation because of dissimilar activities, which would be eliminated if the subsidiaries were included in the consolidation, should also be eliminated. [FRS 2 para 83]. Subsidiaries excluded on this ground are required by FRS 2 to be included in the consolidation using the equity method of accounting (see further chapter 21).

22.47 Profits or losses arising on transactions with undertakings excluded from consolidation because they are held exclusively with a view to subsequent resale or because of severe long-term restrictions need not be eliminated, except to the extent appropriate where significant influence is retained and the subsidiary is treated as an associate (that is, equity accounted). However, it is important to consider whether it is prudent to record any profit arising from transactions with subsidiaries excluded on these grounds (see the examples in para 22.49 below). [FRS 2 para 83].

22.48 The adjustments required to eliminate the effects of intra-group trading between a group and an undertaking included in the consolidation by the equity method are straightforward. The elimination of intra-group profits or losses should be in proportion to the group's interest.

22.49 To eliminate the profits or losses of such undertakings in proportion to the group's share is logical as it ensures that only profits that are actually recorded in the profit and loss account are eliminated. It would clearly be wrong to eliminate a greater proportion of profit than was recorded originally. Two examples below deal with whether or not any adjustments are necessary when intra-group profits are made on sales of assets to subsidiaries that have been excluded from consolidation. In the first example, the two subsidiaries have been wholly excluded. In the second example, the subsidiary is equity accounted as significant influence is retained.

Example 1

A group has a subsidiary that manufactures office equipment. It also has two subsidiaries that are not included in the group's consolidated financial statements either by full consolidation or by equity accounting. The first of these subsidiaries is profitable and has not been consolidated as it is being held exclusively with a view to subsequent resale and the second has been excluded due to severe long-term restrictions (remittances to the UK are virtually impossible). At the year end the consolidated financial statements show substantial debtor balances due from each of the excluded subsidiaries. Are any consolidation adjustments necessary?

As neither of the debtor balances are with subsidiaries included in the consolidation the balances do not require elimination as intra-group transactions. However, consideration should be given to whether it would be prudent to recognise any element of profit included in those balances.

The first of the subsidiaries is profitable and provided there is no reason to believe that the debt will not be settled there is no reason to make an adjustment to eliminate the profit included in the debtor.

The second subsidiary has been excluded on the grounds that remittances to the UK are virtually impossible. It would clearly be imprudent for the group to recognise a profit on a sale to such a company until the debt was settled. Indeed, in this situation it may be necessary to provide for the whole debt in the group's profit and loss account.

Example 2

Company H prepares its consolidated financial statements to 31 December 19X1. It has a 60% holding in a subsidiary (company S) which has been excluded on the grounds of severe long-term restrictions, but it retains significant influence and accounts for the subsidiary under the equity method of accounting. During the year company H purchased stock amounting to £1 million on which company S made a profit of £500,000. At the year end half of this stock remained unsold to third parties. Company H's consolidated financial statements would initially record its share of this profit under the equity method at £300,000 (60% x £500,000) and the unrealised element of this should be eliminated. The unsold stock amounts to £500,000 on which there is £250,000 unrealised profits. The elimination journal in the consolidation would be to debit share of the subsidiary's profit £150,000 (60% x £250,000), and to credit stock £150,000.

22.50 Where an undertaking that is fully consolidated makes a sale to an undertaking that is included in the consolidation under the equity method, a profit may arise in the group. The undertaking's assets that are equity accounted will be overstated by the profit element if the asset is held at the year end. Consequently, an adjustment is required on consolidation to reduce the group's share of the associate's net assets by the same amount. But in this case, the group's profit will not be eliminated in full as the element of profit which is attributable to the minority's share is not recorded in the balance sheet. This is because under the equity method the group's balance sheet will only include its percentage share of the net assets of the subsidiary. Therefore, for a 60 per cent subsidiary that is equity accounted, 40 per cent of the group's profit on the transaction (that is, the element of the profit that is attributable to the third party shareholders) will be recorded in the consolidated profit and loss account and 60 per cent eliminated.

Example

A parent company sells stock worth £100,000 to a 60% owned subsidiary which has been excluded from consolidation on the grounds of lack of control because of severe long-term restrictions. The profit on the transaction is £20,000 and the subsidiary retains the stock at the year end. The results of the subsidiary are equity accounted with those of the group. The profit to be eliminated is 60% of the £20,000, that is, £12,000. The stock included in the net assets that are equity accounted before the profit elimination would be £60,000 (that is, £100,000 x 60%). The stock would, therefore, be reduced to £48,000. The double entry on consolidation is as follows:

	£'000	£'000
Dr Profit before taxation	12	
Cr Net assets of equity accounted subsidiary		12

Being the elimination of the group's share of 60% of the unrealised profit included in the balance sheet by the equity method of accounting.

Chapter 23

Acquisitions

Page

Chapter 23

Acquisitions

Introduction

Business combinations

23.1 There are two accounting methods that might be applicable in a business combination. Groups will generally have to use acquisition accounting, but in certain exceptional circumstances merger accounting *must* be used to account for the business combination. There are now strict conditions that must be satisfied before merger accounting may be adopted.

23.2 The Act contains rules on acquisition accounting and merger accounting, an area which had before the Companies Act 1989 traditionally been left to accounting standards and practices. The 1985 Act (as amended by the Companies Act 1989) states that an acquisition should be accounted for by the acquisition method of accounting, unless the conditions for accounting for it as a merger are met and the merger method of accounting is adopted. [4A Sch 8]. Merger accounting is, therefore, optional under the Act's provisions, but must be used where the merger accounting conditions set out in FRS 6 are met (see further chapter 27).

Comparison of acquisition accounting to merger accounting

23.3 Before considering the detailed accounting requirements that apply to business combinations it is useful to understand the three main differences between acquisition accounting and merger accounting, which are explained in the paragraphs below.

23.4 In acquisition accounting, the consolidated financial statements reflect the acquired company's results from the date of acquisition only. However, in merger accounting, the consolidated financial statements incorporate the combined companies' results as if the companies had always been combined. Consequently, under merger accounting, the consolidated financial statements reflect both companies' full year's results, even though the business combination may have occurred part of the way through the year. Under merger accounting, the corresponding amounts in the consolidated financial statements for the previous year should reflect the results of the combined companies, even though the business combination did not occur until the current year.

23.5 In acquisition accounting, the acquiring group should attribute fair values to the assets and liabilities of the acquired business at the date of acquisition and these are used as the initial carrying values (or 'cost') in the acquiring group's balance sheet. However, in merger accounting, the group does not restate any assets and liabilities at their fair values. Instead, the group incorporates the assets and liabilities at the amounts recorded in the books of the combined companies, adjusted only to achieve harmonisation of accounting policies.

23.6 Acquisition accounting may give rise to goodwill on consolidation. However, goodwill does not arise in merger accounting. Merger accounting may lead to differences on consolidation. For example, in merger accounting, there may be a difference between the nominal value of the shares issued together with the fair value of any additional consideration given, and the nominal value of the other company's shares that have been acquired. However, such differences are not goodwill as defined in FRS 10, because they are not based on the fair values of both the consideration given and the identifiable assets and liabilities acquired.

23.7 An example that demonstrates the difference between acquisition accounting and merger accounting is given in chapter 27. It is somewhat artificial in that the two methods are not alternatives in accounting for the same transaction and hence it is merely illustrative.

Acquisitions

23.8 The rules governing how to account for the acquisition of a subsidiary are now contained in FRS 2, FRS 6, FRS 7, FRS 10 and the Act. This chapter considers all of the requirements that determine how a company should account for the acquisition of a subsidiary including the disclosure requirements and fair valuing rules.

23.9 Section I of this chapter considers primarily the accounting treatment that should be adopted when a subsidiary is acquired and also considers some of the problems that arise with piecemeal acquisitions. Many investments that end up as subsidiaries start out as much smaller interests in the undertakings concerned and may be treated in the group's financial statements in a variety of ways before they actually become subsidiaries. The most common way for an undertaking to become a subsidiary of another is by acquisition. It is also possible for a parent to gain a subsidiary other than by acquisition, for example:

- By gaining control without acquiring a further interest in an undertaking, perhaps by virtue of an agreement with another shareholder.
- By enforcement of a security by a lender where a creditor defaults on a loan.
- By the company purchasing and cancelling its own shares held by third parties.

- By changes to the voting rights attached to shares.

23.10 These issues are fully explained in section I of this chapter, which also outlines the disclosure that is required in the year that a company acquires a subsidiary.

23.11 Section II of this chapter looks at the rules concerning fair valuing assets, liabilities and consideration in detail and discusses many of the practical issues relating to FRS 7.

23.12 Section III of this chapter considers accounting for goodwill. Goodwill is one of the most hotly debated subjects in accounting and the publication of FRS 10 was a major event, particularly for acquisitive companies. FRS 10 also deals with intangible assets and the question of whether assets such as brands should be separated from goodwill in the financial statements.

Merger relief and group reconstruction relief

23.13 It is extremely important in any business combination to understand how merger relief might impact the accounting treatment. Merger relief is a relief given under the Act from the need to transfer to a share premium account the difference between the nominal value of any shares issued by the company to acquire shares in another company and the fair value of those issued shares. Merger relief does not only apply to business combinations accounted for as mergers, it also applies to those accounted for using acquisition accounting techniques. By obtaining merger relief a group may be able to distribute pre-acquisition profits which would otherwise be locked in the subsidiary it acquires. The rules as they apply to both acquisitions and mergers are considered in chapter 26.

23.14 Group reconstruction relief can be taken in certain situations where assets are transferred around the group and where the subsidiaries concerned are wholly owned. This relief applies to the transfer of both shares in wholly-owned group companies and other assets where the consideration is shares issued by the group company acquiring the assets. Chapter 26 explores this complex area and explains in detail how the minimum premium value is calculated on such transactions, being the amount that it is necessary to credit to the share premium account on the share issue.

- By changes to the voting rights attached to shares.

23.10 These issues are fully explained in section I of this chapter, which also outlines the disclosure that is required in the year that a company acquires a subsidiary.

23.11 Section II of this chapter looks at the rules concerning fair valuing assets, liabilities and consideration in detail and discusses many of the practical issues relating to FRS 7.

23.12 Section III of this chapter considers accounting for goodwill. Goodwill is one of the most hotly debated subjects in accounting and the publication of FRS 10 was a major event, particularly for acquisitive companies. FRS 10 also deals with intangible assets and the question of whether assets such as brands should be separated from goodwill in the financial statements.

Merger relief and group reconstruction relief

23.13 It is extremely important in any business combination to understand how merger relief might impact the accounting treatment. Merger relief is a relief given under the Act from the need to transfer to a share premium account the difference between the nominal value of any shares issued by the company to acquire shares in another company and the fair value of those issued shares. Merger relief does not only apply to business combinations accounted for as mergers, it also applies to those accounted for using acquisition accounting techniques. By obtaining merger relief a group may be able to distribute pre-acquisition profits which would otherwise be locked in the subsidiary it acquires. The rules as they apply to both acquisitions and mergers are considered in chapter 25.

23.14 Group reconstruction relief can be taken in certain situations where assets are transferred around the group and where the subsidiaries concerned are wholly-owned. This relief applies to the transfer of both shares in wholly-owned group companies and other assets, where the consideration is shares issued by the group company acquiring the assets. Chapter 25 explores this complex area and explains in detail how the minimum premium value is calculated in such transactions, being the amount that it is necessary to credit to the share premium account on the share issue.

Section I – Accounting rules

Introduction

23.15 As explained above, there are two methods that a parent company can use to account for a business combination in its consolidated financial statements. But following the introduction of FRS 6 the vast majority of business combinations are in practice accounted for using acquisition accounting techniques and only a small minority are required to use merger accounting.

23.16 The rules concerning acquisition accounting are contained in FRS 2, FRS 6, FRS 7 and FRS 10, as well as the Act. Although FRS 6 primarily defines the situations where merger accounting must be used, it does in addition bring together in one standard most of the disclosure requirements that must be followed for all business combinations whether accounted for as acquisitions or mergers (including those required by the Act). However, most of the disclosure requirements concerning goodwill arising on an acquisition are set out in FRS 10.

Date of changes in group membership

Background

23.17 The date on which an undertaking becomes or ceases to be a subsidiary marks the point at which a new accounting treatment for that undertaking in the group's consolidated financial statements applies. The Act does not define the effective date of acquisition or disposal. However, the Act does state that undertakings *controlled* by the group should be consolidated and those that are *not controlled* should not be consolidated. FRS 2, therefore, contains a definition which is based entirely on the passing of control.

Definition

23.18 The date of change in group membership is the date on which control of that undertaking passes to its new parent undertaking. Furthermore, this date is said in FRS 2 to be the date of acquisition for the purposes of Schedule 4A paragraph 9, (which is the Act's requirement to account for the purchase of a subsidiary using acquisition accounting). [FRS 2 para 45]. The date, therefore, hinges on 'control' passing and control is defined as:

> *"The ability of an undertaking to direct the financial and operating policies of another undertaking with a view to gaining economic benefits from its activities."* [FRS 2 para 6].

23.19 The definition of control refers to 'gaining economic benefits'. This is not intended to be interpreted restrictively and covers a wide range of situations in practice, including gaining benefits:

- In the form of current or future profits.
- By preventing another competitor from buying the business.
- By preventing a key supplier or distributor from going out of business.
- By reducing losses of the acquiring group.

For undertakings that are not formed for the purpose of making profits, for example charities, the economic benefits will not necessarily be profit related.

23.20 The date of change in group membership under FRS 2 should also be taken as the date on which an undertaking becomes or ceases to be a subsidiary under section 258 of the Act. In practice, although it may often be difficult to determine, the date on which control passes is a matter of fact and cannot be backdated or artificially altered. [FRS 2 para 84]. Consequently, as with previous definitions of the effective date of acquisition, the definition under FRS 2 applies even if the acquiror has a right to profits from a date earlier than the effective date of acquisition.

23.21 The following factors could, for example, indicate that the acquiror has gained control of an undertaking:

- The acquiror starts to direct the operating and financial policies of the acquired undertaking.

- The acquiror starts to benefit from the economic benefits arising from the undertaking. However, this does not cover the situation where a potential acquiror is given a right to profits from a date which is conditional on the completion of the purchase at some later date. Equally, it does not apply to an agreement giving the acquiror rights to past profits.

- The date the consideration is paid. The payment date for the consideration will often in simple acquisitions be the date on which control passes, but in practice this cannot be assumed, because this date can easily be manipulated. Furthermore, payment of consideration is often made by instalments and, as a consequence, may have little relevance to when control passes.

23.22 In practice, control might pass in a number of ways, which will often depend on whether the offer for the entity is made to the public (a public offer) or is a private sale (a private treaty) or is effected by the issue or cancellation of shares.

23.23 Where control is transferred by a public offer, the date control is transferred is the date the offer becomes unconditional. This will usually be the date on which a sufficient number of acceptances (that is, over 50 per cent) are received to enable the new parent to exercise control over the undertaking. [FRS 2 para 85]. Under a private treaty, the date control is transferred is generally the date an unconditional offer is accepted. [FRS 2 para 85].

23.24 It can be seen that in both a public offer and a private treaty, the key to control passing is dependent on acceptance of *unconditional* terms. The negotiations to purchase or sell a subsidiary may take place over a considerable period and there may be considerable delays between the time when agreement is reached in principle and the time when the legal formalities are completed. Other conditions, such as third party or shareholder approval may also take time to be satisfied. Until such time as agreement is reached and all conditions are satisfied the transaction cannot be regarded as unconditional.

23.25 Where an undertaking becomes a subsidiary through an issue of shares or by a cancellation of shares, the date that control will be transferred is the date on which those shares are issued or cancelled. [FRS 2 para 85].

Effective date post balance sheet

23.26 Where the effective date of acquisition of a subsidiary is after the parent's year end, but before the consolidated financial statements are approved and signed on behalf of the board, the transaction should be treated as a non-adjusting post balance sheet event in accordance with the requirements of paragraph 23 of SSAP 17, 'Accounting for post balance sheet events'. If the group wishes to show the effect that this post balance sheet acquisition will have, it will be necessary for it to prepare proforma accounts in addition to its statutory financial statements.

Consolidation of a new subsidiary

23.27 The Act sets out the basic requirements for consolidating a subsidiary when it is first acquired. It specifies that:

- The identifiable assets and liabilities of the subsidiary acquired should be included in the consolidated balance sheet at their fair values as at the date of acquisition.

- The income and expenditure of the undertaking acquired should be brought into the consolidated financial statements from the date of the acquisition.

- The interest of the group in the adjusted capital and reserves of the undertaking acquired should be offset against the acquisition cost of the group's interest in the shares of the undertaking. The difference if positive represents goodwill and if negative represents a negative consolidation difference (that is, negative goodwill).

[4A Sch 9].

23.28 Consequently, on an acquisition it is necessary to ascertain the following elements in respect of the undertaking acquired in order to account for that undertaking as a subsidiary on consolidation:

- Acquisition cost.
- Adjusted capital and reserves.
- Identifiable assets and liabilities.
- Date for recognising profits or losses from operations.

Each of these elements of acquisition accounting is considered in the paragraphs that follow.

Acquisition cost

23.29 Under the Act the 'acquisition cost' incurred in acquiring a subsidiary includes the amount of any cash consideration paid and the fair value of any other consideration (such as shares and debentures), together with fees and other expenses of the acquisition. [4A Sch 9(4)]. FRS 7 deals with the fair value issues that arise when determining the cost of acquisition and these issues are considered in detail in section II of this chapter.

23.30 When a company issues shares as part of the consideration to acquire a subsidiary, the difference between the fair value of the consideration and the nominal value of the shares issued has to be credited to the share premium account, unless the company is eligible for merger relief. Consequently, the fair value of the consideration has a direct bearing on the amount that has to be credited to the share premium account. Eligibility for merger relief is considered in detail in chapter 26. If the company can obtain merger relief on the issue, then the difference between the fair value of the shares issued and their nominal value can be credited to a merger reserve (as opposed to a share premium account) or need not be recorded. Where a merger reserve is used, the parent's investment will be recorded in its financial statements at an amount equal to the fair value of the consideration received.

23.31 Where a merger reserve is not set up on an acquisition, the investment will be recorded in the parent's financial statements at the nominal value of shares issued plus the fair value of any other consideration given in the acquisition. FRS 4, 'Capital instruments', requires that the fair value of the consideration received on the issue of shares should be reported in the reconciliation of movements in shareholders' funds. In double entry terms, in order to achieve this requirement, the standard implies that, as shareholders' funds are credited with the fair value, then the cost of investment must be debited with the fair value of the consideration also. This would seem to preclude a company that can claim merger relief from recording the investment merely at the nominal value of the shares it issues plus other consideration and thereby not having to set up a merger reserve. However, the ASB has indicated that this result was not the intention of FRS 4 and that the standard should not restrict the reliefs given under the Act. As a consequence, it is still acceptable, where a company obtains merger relief on the shares it has issued to acquire a subsidiary, to record its investment at the nominal value of the shares issued plus the fair value of any other consideration given as part of the acquisition.

23.32 Unlike the merger reserve, the share premium account can only be used for the following specific purposes:

- To pay up fully paid bonus shares.
- To write off preliminary expenses.
- To write off expenses of any issue of shares or debentures.
- To write off commission paid or discount allowed on any issue of shares or debentures.
- To provide for the premium on any redemption of debentures.

[Sec 130(2)].

Fees and expenses of acquisition

23.33 The fees and expenses of an acquisition have to be analysed. Some may relate to the issue of any capital instruments (that is, shares or debt) given as part of the consideration. Issue costs are defined in FRS 4 as:

> *"The costs that are incurred directly in connection with the issue of a capital instrument, that is, those costs that would not have been incurred had the specific instrument in question not been issued."* [FRS 4 para 10].

Once ascertained the issue costs have to be accounted for in accordance with the requirements of FRS 4. For debt this means deducting them from the debt and amortising the costs (as part of the overall finance costs) to the profit and loss account over the term of the debt. For equity shares and for non-equity shares issue costs should be charged to the share premium account or to the profit and loss account reserve. Then for non-equity shares a notional amortisation of these costs is required as an appropriation in the profit and loss account and they are then credited back to reserves. The definition of issue costs is restrictive and their accounting treatment complex: further guidance on issue costs is given in chapter 18.

23.34 Certain fees and expenses of acquisition that do not relate to the issue of capital instruments can be added to the cost of an investment and these are considered further in paragraph 23.445.

Adjusted capital and reserves acquired

23.35 The Act requires that the adjusted capital and reserves is set off against the acquisition cost of the acquired subsidiary in order to ascertain the figure of goodwill (or negative goodwill) arising on the acquisition. In this context 'adjusted capital and reserves' means the subsidiary's capital and reserves at the date of acquisition after adjusting the undertaking's identifiable assets and liabilities to fair values. [4A Sch 9(4)]. This is equivalent to 'adjusted net assets'. Consequently, the subsidiary's adjusted capital and reserves will be made up of its capital and reserves disclosed in its books of account adjusted for any changes in the value of net assets determined in fair valuing its assets and liabilities. The following example illustrates this provision of the legislation.

Example

Company A acquires 80% of company B on 22 November 1998. The acquisition cost is £50m and at the date of acquisition, the reserves of the subsidiary are determined as follows:

Capital and reserves of company B	
	£m
Share capital	2
Share premium account	1
Revaluation reserve	10
Profit and loss account	15
Total capital and reserves	28

Company A carries out a fair value exercise on Company B as at 22 November 1998 and ascertains that its fixed assets and stocks have values in excess of their book values of £12m and £3.5m respectively.

Adjusted capital and reserves of company B	
	£m
Capital and reserves (as above)	28.0
Fair value adjustment	15.5
Total capital and reserves	43.5

Consequently, the difference arising on consolidation (goodwill) would be calculated as follows:

Difference arising on consolidation	
	£m
Acquisition cost	50.0
Adjusted capital and reserves (£43.5m × 80%)	(34.8)
Goodwill	15.2

Identifiable assets and liabilities

23.36 The Act requires that the subsidiary's identifiable assets and liabilities must be included in the consolidated balance sheet at their fair values, as at the date of acquisition. [4A Sch 9(2)]. There is no guidance in the Act on how to determine the fair values of assets and liabilities, but rules on fair valuing are now detailed in FRS 7 and these are considered in detail in section II of this chapter. For this purpose the Act defines 'identifiable assets and liabilities' to mean the:

> "*...assets or liabilities which are capable of being disposed of or discharged separately, without disposing of a business of the undertaking.* " [4A Sch 9(2)].

FRS 7, which also applies to entities other than companies, contains an equivalent definition.

23.37 The test to establish whether an asset should be included in the category of identifiable assets, is whether the asset can be identified and sold separately without disposing of a business as a whole. In this context, goodwill is clearly not separable from a business as a whole. Such assets, however, may well include other intangible assets (including trade marks and brands) and their valuation is considered in more detail in chapter 14. Ascertaining the fair values of identifiable assets is very difficult in practice and substantial problems can arise and these issues are considered in detail in section II of this chapter.

Recording adjustments to fair values

23.38 Although an acquiring company has to carry out a fair value exercise as at the date of acquisition, there is no general requirement to record these values in the books of account of the subsidiary (unless, for example, they relate to permanent diminutions in the value of assets). Equally, there is nothing generally to stop the adjustments being made in the subsidiary's books of account and this may happen in practice. But it is not normally possible for UK subsidiaries to record their stocks at a fair value that exceeds cost, because the Act and SSAP 9 require stocks to be valued at the lower of cost and net realisable value. [4 Sch 23; SSAP 9 para 26]. Consequently, in the previous example in paragraph 23.35 only the £12m in respect of fixed assets could be recorded in the subsidiary's books of account.

Treatment of goodwill

23.39 Any difference between the total of the subsidiary's acquisition cost (that is, the fair value of the purchase consideration plus expenses) and the group's share of the subsidiary's adjusted capital and reserves represents purchased goodwill arising on consolidation (or, if negative, negative goodwill, termed a negative consolidation difference in the Act). [4A Sch 9(5); FRS 10 para 2; FRS 6 para 20]. The treatment of both goodwill and negative goodwill arising on consolidation is considered in section III of this chapter.

The parent company's financial statements

23.40 Where one company acquires another company, the identifiable assets and liabilities acquired from the point of view of the acquiring company will be the shares in the acquired company, not the individual assets and liabilities of the acquired company. Consequently, when one company acquires another company, purchased goodwill will not arise in the parent's balance sheet.

23.41 However, goodwill will arise on consolidation because the fair value of the consideration given is not in general the same as the aggregate fair value of the acquired company's identifiable assets and liabilities.

Example

Company H acquires a listed company S for £10m, even though the Stock Exchange capitalisation of company S prior to its being acquired was only £9m and the value of its adjusted capital and reserves (which equates to its identifiable net assets) is £8m. The total market capitalisation is based on the number of shares multiplied by the market price. However, the market price is the price for only small parcels of shares. The market may put a different value on a controlling interest in the company. Consequently, the £10m consideration is more likely to represent the fair value of the shares that the holding company has acquired. Therefore, purchased goodwill will not arise in the holding company's financial statements but, in this example, £2m of goodwill will arise on consolidation.

23.42 The parent's investment in the subsidiary should be recorded in the parent's books at cost. In the example above, the investment would be recorded in the parent's books of account at £10 million. This is so unless merger relief applies (see further para 23.31).

23.43 FRS 10 does not require an adjustment to be made in the parent's financial statements to the carrying value of the shares in the subsidiary in respect of any consolidation goodwill written off either in the consolidated financial statements or in the subsidiary's own financial statements. An exception is that, where consolidation goodwill is written off because it is impaired, FRS 10 requires the carrying value of the parent's investment also to be reviewed for impairment. [FRS 10 para 42]. The parent company will in normal circumstances only write down the investment's carrying value to reflect any permanent diminution in value. As a result, it is not unusual to see groups where the reserves of the parent are greater than those of the group, because the latter take into account goodwill write-offs on consolidation.

Pre-acquisition and post-acquisition reserves

23.44 In the past, an important element of consolidations was whether profits of a subsidiary should be treated as pre-acquisition or post- acquisition. In particular, this was important because it had a bearing on how dividends paid by the subsidiary were treated in the parent's financial statements. If, for example, a subsidiary paid a dividend out of pre-acquisition profits to a parent, the parent would reduce its investment in the subsidiary by this amount (assuming that the net worth of the subsidiary had decreased by a similar amount). The parent could not treat this amount as realised and could not distribute it.

23.45 Paragraph 15(5) of the original Schedule 8 to the Companies Act 1948, which was the source of the above treatment, was amended by the Companies Act1981. As a result of this change, when a dividend is paid out of pre-acquisition profits by a subsidiary, it need not be applied in reducing the carrying value of the investment in the subsidiary in the parent's books. It should be taken to the profit and loss account. Only if the underlying value of the subsidiary does not support the amount at which the parent carries its investment in the subsidiary following the dividend, does the parent have to make a provision against its investment if that diminution in value is expected to be permanent. This accords with the legal requirements included in Schedule 4, paragraph 19(2), which requires a company to make provision for any permanent diminution in value of any fixed asset. Consider the following example.

Example

Company A has an investment in its subsidiary company B. Company A acquired the subsidiary for £22m. The net assets of the subsidiary at that time were £18m. In the following year, the subsidiary's net assets are £20m and it decides to pay a dividend to its parent of £1m. It is unclear whether this dividend is made out of pre-acquisition reserves or post-acquisition reserves. Company A should take the dividend it receives from company B to its profit and loss account. However, company A then has to consider whether it is necessary to make a provision against the carrying value of its investment in company B. This assessment will take into account not only the net asset value of company B (which after the dividend payment has reduced to £19m), but also any additional value that the shares in company B have. When it was acquired, this additional value was £4m, which equates to the goodwill arising on consolidation. If company A considers that the premium on the value of company B's shares has not diminished, then the worth of company B is in excess of £23m.

On this basis company A does not need to make a provision against its investment in company B and can treat the dividend received as realised and, consequently, distributable.

This provision as it applies to merger relief is considered in chapter 26.

Date for recognising trading

23.46 The Act states that income and expenditure of the subsidiary should only be brought into the consolidated financial statements from the date of acquisition. [4A Sch 9(3)]. The date of acquisition is discussed under the heading of 'date of changes in group membership' above from paragraph 23.17 onwards. Similarly, FRS 6 requires that the results and cash flows of the acquired company should be brought into the consolidated financial statements only from the date of acquisition. [FRS 6 para 20].

23.47 It is, therefore, necessary on an acquisition to apportion the results between pre-acquisition and post-acquisition on a reasonably accurate basis. In practice, this is often achieved by using the subsidiary's management accounts or completion accounts, if any, prepared as at the date of acquisition. However, there may be rare situations where there is no alternative but to use a time apportionment method. Where such a method is used, however, it will be necessary to identify any profit and loss account items that do not arise evenly over the accounting period. For such items a time apportionment would not be acceptable. For example, this may be the situation with exceptional items. Such items would, therefore, need to be analysed into the period in which they arose and treated accordingly as either being pre-acquisition or post-acquisition.

23.48 Following the introduction of FRS 3, the operating results of continuing operations have to be shown separately from those of discontinued operations. Furthermore, acquisitions in the period have to be shown separately as a component of continuing operations. As a minimum on the face of the profit and loss account turnover and operating profit have to be analysed between continuing operations, acquisitions as a component of continuing operations and discontinued operations. In addition, this analysis has also to be given in the notes (if not given on the face of the profit and loss account) for each of the profit and loss account format line items between turnover and operating profit. The provisions of FRS 3 are dealt with in detail in chapter 7.

23.49 Although the method of consolidating the results in the profit and loss account outlined above has to be adopted, groups may still wish to give their members an idea of what the results of the new group would have looked like for a whole period's trading. Clearly, the shareholders will not be able to ascertain this picture entirely from the consolidated results as presented, although for 'substantial acquisitions' as defined in FRS 6 a summarised profit and loss account and statement of total recognised gains and losses has to be given for the subsidiary acquired from the beginning of its last accounting reference period to the date of acquisition (see further para 23.91). [FRS 6 para 36]. There is no reason, however, why the group should not also include in its consolidated financial statements a pro-forma consolidated profit and loss account by way of a note showing the combined results of all subsidiaries for the entire period of trading, regardless of when they were acquired. In addition, the group may wish to disclose a pro-forma earnings per share by way of note based on the pro-forma consolidated profit and loss. In this way it is possible for a group to account for its acquisition using acquisition accounting in its statutory financial statements, but retain some of the benefits of the merger accounting principles, namely of reporting the trends of the enlarged group as if the subsidiary has always been combined with the rest of the group.

23.50 Where the group decides to include this type of additional information in its consolidated financial statements, it should not give the pro-forma accounts more prominence than its statutory accounts.

Increases in stake

Introduction

23.51 Many accounting problems can arise on increasing a stake in an undertaking. Such acquisitions arise where the investing company starts off with a small stake in an undertaking and gradually increases its investment. Initially the interest in the undertaking may be no more than an investment that will be either valued at cost (less any provisions for diminution in value of the investment) or at a valuation (under the alternative accounting rules).

23.52 Once the interest in the undertaking becomes 20 per cent or more of the equity voting rights of a company and the investor actually exercises significant influence, then the investment is likely to have to be treated in the consolidated financial statements as an associate in accordance with the requirements of FRS 9. In certain circumstances an interest in an undertaking can be treated as an associate where the investment is below 20 per cent and equally interests in excess of 20 per cent may, in certain circumstances, be treated as investments.

23.53 Similarly, once an interest in the undertaking is over 50 per cent of the voting rights of a company, then the investment has to be treated in the consolidated financial statements as a subsidiary to accord with the Act and FRS 2. However, in special circumstances an interest below 50 per cent might be regarded as a subsidiary, where control over the undertaking is exercised in some other way.

Accounting principles

23.54 The basic principles of accounting for acquisitions set out in the Act apply equally to increases in stake. FRS 2 provides specific guidance on interpreting the Act in the context of changes in stake. The principles that apply are as follows:

- The identifiable assets and liabilities of the subsidiary acquired should be included in the consolidated balance sheet at their fair values at the acquisition date, that is, the date it becomes a subsidiary. [4A Sch 9(2); FRS 2 para 50].

- The income and expenditure of the undertaking acquired should be fully consolidated into the consolidated financial statements from the date the undertaking first becomes a subsidiary. [4A Sch 9(3)].

- The interest of the group in the adjusted capital and reserves of the undertaking acquired should be offset against the acquisition cost of the group's interest in the shares of the undertaking. The difference if positive represents goodwill and if negative represents a negative consolidation difference (that is, negative goodwill). [4A Sch 9(5)].

23.55 Paragraph 9 of Schedule 4A to the Act requires goodwill to be calculated as the difference between the following two amounts:

- The fair value, at the date an undertaking becomes a subsidiary, of the group's share of its identifiable assets and liabilities.

- The total acquisition cost of the interests held by the group in that subsidiary.

23.56 This approach, a one-off exercise at the time the undertaking becomes a subsidiary, is required by the Act even where the interests have been purchased at different dates. FRS 2 points out that that approach will provide a practical means of applying acquisition accounting in most cases, because it does not require retrospective fair value exercises to be performed. [FRS 2 para 89]. However, FRS 2 notes that, in special circumstances, not using fair values at the dates of earlier purchases, while using an acquisition cost part of which relates to earlier purchases, may result in accounting that is inconsistent with the way the investment has previously been treated in the group's consolidated financial statements. It suggests that the inconsistency may lead to the treatment required by the Act failing to give a true and fair view. [FRS 2 para 89].

23.57 FRS 2 considers two examples of such inconsistency that might lead to failure to give a true and fair view:

- An acquisition of a further interest in an undertaking that has already been treated as an associate by the group is acquired so that the undertaking becomes a subsidiary. Using the method set out above to calculate goodwill will lead to the group's share of post acquisition profits, losses and reserve movements of its associated undertaking being reclassified as goodwill (usually negative goodwill). This situation is considered in detail in paragraph 23.69 below.

- A group has substantially restated an investment that subsequently becomes its subsidiary. For example, where a provision has been made against such an investment for an impairment, the effect of using the Act's method of calculating goodwill would be to increase reserves and create goodwill. This situation is considered in detail in paragraph 23.63 below.

[FRS 2 para 89].

23.58 In such situations, where the calculation of goodwill in accordance with the Act's provisions would be misleading, the FRS states that goodwill should be calculated as the sum of the goodwill arising from each purchase of an interest in the relevant undertaking adjusted as necessary for any subsequent impairment. [FRS 2 para 89]. The goodwill arising on each purchase should be calculated as the difference between the cost of that purchase and the fair value *at the date of that purchase* of the identifiable assets and liabilities attributable to the interest purchased. The difference between the goodwill calculated using the true and fair override and that calculated in accordance with paragraph 9 of Schedule 4A to the Act is shown in reserves. [FRS 2 para 89].

23.59 Adopting this alternative treatment requires the use of the section 227(6) true and fair override as it does not comply strictly with the requirements of the Act. The Act provides that in this type of situation, *"If in special circumstances compliance with any of those provisions is inconsistent with the requirement to give a true and fair view, the directors shall depart from that provision to the extent necessary to give a true and fair view. Particulars of any such departure, the reasons for it and its effect shall be given in a note to the accounts"*. The disclosures required when the true and fair override is used are explained further in UITF Abstract 7. Table 23.1 gives an example of such disclosure in respect of accounting for an associated company that has become a subsidiary.

Table 23.1 – THORN EMI plc – Report and accounts – 31 March 1995

Notes to the accounts (extract)
30. Purchase of businesses (extract)

TOEMI – On 3 October 1994, THORN EMI plc increased its shareholding in TOEMI from 50 to 55 per cent. TOEMI became a consolidated subsidiary on this date, having previously been accounted for as an associated company.

The transaction was effected by a redemption of shares owned by the joint venture partner, Toshiba Corporation, and funded by TOEMI's cash reserves in which the Group already had a 50 per cent beneficial interest. The indirect cost to the Group was therefore Yen 3.75 billion (£24.1m).

The Companies Act 1985 normally requires goodwill arising on the acquisition of a subsidiary undertaking to be calculated as the difference between the total acquisition cost of the undertaking and the fair value of the Group's share of the identifiable assets and liabilities at the date it became a subsidiary undertaking.

FRS 2 recognises that, where an investment in an associated undertaking is increased and it becomes a subsidiary undertaking, in order to show a true and fair view goodwill should be calculated on each purchase as the difference between the cost of that purchase and the fair value at the date of that purchase.

If goodwill had been calculated in accordance with the basis set out in the Companies Act 1985, £61.2m of the Group's share of the retained earnings of TOEMI would have been reclassified as goodwill and in total negative goodwill of £63.9m would have been recognised.

Practical examples

23.60 There are three basic situations that might arise with a piecemeal acquisition, as follows:

- An undertaking has an investment in another undertaking and increases its stake in the undertaking so that it becomes a subsidiary.
- An undertaking has an investment in an associate and increases its stake in the undertaking so that it becomes a subsidiary.
- A parent has an investment in a subsidiary and acquires part or all of the minority's interest.

Each of these situations is explained in the paragraphs that follow.

An investment becomes a subsidiary

23.61 This is the simplest situation to account for. The rules that apply in determining the date upon which an undertaking becomes a subsidiary are considered from paragraph 23.17.

23.62 The initial investment will be recorded in the parent's accounting records at either its cost (less provisions) or at a valuation (in accordance with the alternative accounting rules). With creeping acquisitions, up to the date of acquisition the parent will only have accounted for dividend income received from the undertaking. On acquisition, the goodwill arising on the acquisition has to be ascertained and this will be the difference between the fair value of the consideration given for the subsidiary (including the cost of the investment to date, any revaluation being ignored) and the fair value of the parent's share of net assets acquired. Consider the following example:

Example

A group made an investment of 10% in a company in 1992. The investment cost £2.5m and has subsequently been revalued to £5m. In 1998 it makes a further investment in the company of 50% to bring its total investment to 60%. The fair value of the consideration given for the 50% is £25m. The net assets of the company acquired stand in its books at the date of acquisition at £20m. The fair value exercise shows that the company's net assets are worth £35m, which is also the adjusted capital and reserves. The goodwill on acquisition and minority interest would be calculated in the following way:

Cost of acquisition	
	£m
Original investment in company (at cost)	2.5
Fair value of consideration given	25.0
Total consideration	27.5
Consolidation goodwill	
Total consideration	27.5
Adjusted capital and reserves (being 60% of £35m)	21.0
Goodwill	6.5
Minority interests	
Share capital (40% of £5m)	2.0
Reserves (40% of £30m)	12.0
Minority interests	14.0

The only additional adjustment that is required in this example, in contrast to a straight acquisition of a subsidiary, is to reduce the value of the original investment from its revalued amount to cost. The entry on consolidation would be to debit the revaluation reserve with £2.5m and credit the investment £2.5m. Whether the parent decides to make this adjustment in its own balance sheet might depend on whether the total cost of the subsidiary including the valuation adjustment exceeds the parent's share of the subsidiary's worth (including goodwill). Consequently, in this example the total consideration paid for the subsidiary together with the book value of the original investments is £30m (that is, £25m + £5m). If 60% of the subsidiary (including goodwill) is worth more than £30m, then no provision will have to be made in the parent's books of account against the carrying value of its investment.

23.63 As already mentioned, a further complication can arise where a provision has been made against an investment for permanent diminution in value. Consider the following example:

Example

A parent acquired a 10% interest in a property company in 1993 for £11m. At that time the fair value of the net assets of the property company was £100m. The parent has subsequently provided for a permanent diminution in value of its investment and written it down from £11m to £4m. In 1998 the other shareholder sold its 90% holding to the parent for £40m. At that time the fair value of the net assets of the property company were £50m.

Calculation of goodwill – applying the provisions of paragraph 9 of Schedule 4A

Cost of acquisition	£m
Original investment 10% in 1993	11
Final investment 90% in 1998	40
Total consideration	51

Calculation of goodwill	£m
Total consideration	51
Less: adjusted capital and reserves at date property company became subsidiary	(50)
Goodwill arising on acquisition of subsidiary	1

The double entry on consolidation is as follows:

	£m	£m
Dr Investment	7	
Cr Profit and loss account reserve		7

Being the restatement of the original investment to original cost.

Dr Capital and reserves of subsidiary	50	
Dr Goodwill	1	
Cr Investment		51

Being the capitalisation of goodwill

In practice some of the provision for permanent diminution of £7m may be written back through the parent's profit and loss account, as the parent's cost of investment (after provision for permanent diminution in value) is £44m compared to underlying net assets of £50m. Let us suppose, for example, that £6m of the provision is written back through the parent's profit and loss account. The write-back of £6m should then be credited to the consolidated profit and loss account (as it was originally charged to the consolidated profit and loss account) and the remaining £1m credited to the consolidated profit and loss account reserve with the corresponding debit shown as goodwill arising on the acquisition.

23.64 The method just described gives a figure for positive goodwill by, in effect, reinstating the provision for permanent diminution in value and offsetting it against a substantial negative goodwill figure which arose on the second tranche. However, in substance the effects of the transactions are:

- A substantial holding loss on the original investment.
- A purchase at a discount.

23.65 The substance of the transaction is more closely represented by the following approach, which uses the true and fair override in calculating the goodwill arising on consolidation.

Example

Calculation of goodwill – using the true and fair override		
Cost of acquisition		£m
Original investment 10% in 1993		11
Final investment 90% in 1998		40
Total consideration		51
Consolidation goodwill		
Total consideration		51
Less: adjusted capital and reserves at dates of original investments		
10% × £100m	10	
90% × £50m	45	55
Negative goodwill		(4)
The double entry on consolidation is as follows:	£m	£m
Dr Investment	7	
Cr Profit and loss account reserve		7
Being the restatement of the original investment to original cost.		

Dr Capital and reserves of subsidiary	50	
Cr Cost of investment		51
Cr Negative goodwill		4
Dr Profit and loss account reserve	5	

Being the recognition of negative goodwill arising on consolidation and the reduction in the underlying net assets of £5m attributable to the original 10% investment between its acquisition date in 1993 and the date the undertaking became a subsidiary (10% × (£100m – £50m)).

As above, in practice, some of the provision for permanent diminution may be written back through the parent's profit and loss account, as the parent's cost of investment (after provision for permanent diminution in value) is £44m compared to underlying net assets of £50m. Again let us suppose that £6m of the provision is written back through the parent's profit and loss account. Only £1m of the £6m provision also reported in the consolidated profit and loss account in previous years could be credited back through the consolidated profit and loss account, because in effect £5m of that provision has already been adjusted to reserves in the calculation to arrive at the goodwill arising on the acquisition of the 10% interest.

23.66 If the true and fair override is adopted, the particulars of the departure from the requirements of paragraph 9 of Schedule 4A, the reasons for it and its effect should be disclosed in a note to the financial statements. [Sec 227(6)]. In addition, the disclosure provisions of UITF Abstract 7 must be complied with (see chapter 2).

An associate becomes a subsidiary

23.67 When an associate becomes a subsidiary the accounting treatment is not as straightforward as in the previous example. The main difference lies in the fact that a proportion of the associate's results have already been dealt with in the consolidated profit and loss account and consolidated balance sheet. In addition, goodwill will have been calculated on the acquisition of the interest in the associate and will have been either written off to reserves or amortised over its useful economic life.

23.68 The method set out in the Act still applies and the goodwill arising on the acquisition of the subsidiary should be calculated as the difference between the following two amounts:

- The fair value, at the date an undertaking becomes a subsidiary, of the group's share of its identifiable assets and liabilities.

- The total acquisition cost of the interests held by the group in that subsidiary.

23.69 Using this method to calculate goodwill leads to the group's share of post acquisition profits, losses and reserve movements of its associated undertaking becoming reclassified as goodwill, thus reducing goodwill or creating negative goodwill on the acquisition. FRS 2 recognises that this accounting treatment is inconsistent with the way the investment has previously been treated and that this inconsistency could lead to a failure to give a true and fair view.

Example

A group made an investment of 20% in a company in 1992. The investment cost £12m and the book value (also fair value) of the associate's net assets at that date was £50m. In 1998 it makes a further investment in the company of 50% to bring its total investment to 70%. Goodwill on the acquisition of the associate was written off directly against reserves in the year of acquisition which was prior to the implementation of FRS 10. The net assets of the associate stand in its books at £68m on the date it becomes a subsidiary. The associate would be treated as follows up to the date of acquisition:

Acquisition of associate	
	£m
Original investment in company	12.0
Fair value of net assets acquired (20% × £50m)	10.0
Goodwill arising	2.0
Consolidation of associate up to date of increased investment	
Share of net assets	
Date of acquisition	10.0
Post acquisition profits (being (£68m – £50m) × 20%)	3.6
	13.6

The fair value of the consideration given for the additional 50% is £42m. The fair value exercise shows that the company's net assets are worth £75m, which is also the adjusted capital and reserves. The group must include the whole amount of the fair value of the subsidiary's net assets in the consolidated balance sheet. The goodwill on acquisition and minority interest would be calculated as follows:

Associate becomes a subsidiary – applying the provisions of the Act

Cost of acquisition as shown in the parent's books

	£m	£m
Original investment in company		12.0
Fair value of consideration given for new investment		42.0
Total investment in subsidiary		54.0
Consolidation goodwill		
Total consideration		54.0
Adjusted capital and reserves		
being 20% of £75m	15.0	
being 50% of £75m	37.5	52.5
Total goodwill arising on the acquisition		1.5
Goodwill previously written off		2.0
Balance of goodwill (negative)		(0.5)
Minority interests		
Share capital (30% of £5m)		1.5
Reserves (30% of £70m)		21.0
Minority interests		22.5

The problem with this method of calculating the goodwill is that it treats the post acquisition profits and reserve movements of the undertaking while it was an associate of the group as a deduction from goodwill. The amount of the undertaking's profits while it was an associate have to be 'removed' from the profit and loss account reserves as part of the double entry on consolidation, as follows:

	£m	£m
Dr Profit and loss account reserve	3.6	
Cr Investment		3.6
Being the restatement of the original investment to original cost.		

This method gives a figure of negative goodwill of £0.5m, which is the difference between the goodwill arising on the acquisition of £1.5m less the goodwill of £2m previously written off on the initial acquisition of the associate interest. However, the goodwill of £1.5m is understated because the total interest of 70% has been applied to the fair value of the net assets at the date the undertaking becomes a subsidiary (which method complies with the Act) and does not take into account the fact that when the 20% interest was acquired the fair value of the net assets was less. Therefore, if the difference is material, it is necessary to adopt the Act's true and fair override in order to arrive at the correct amount of goodwill arising on the acquisition.

Associate becomes a subsidiary – adopting true and fair override		
Cost of acquisition as shown in the parent's books		£m
Original investment in company		12.0
Fair value of consideration given for new investment		42.0
Total investment in subsidiary		54.0
Consolidation goodwill		
Total consideration		54.0
Adjusted capital and reserves		
being 20% × £50m	10.0	
being 50% × £75m	37.5	47.5
Goodwill		6.5
Goodwill previously written off		2.0
Balance of goodwill		4.5
Minority interests		
Share capital (30% × £5m)		1.5
Reserves (30% × £70m)		21.0
Minority interests		22.5

In this case, the goodwill figure that emerges is instinctively correct as it reflects the fact that a premium of £4.5m arises on the acquisition of the additional 50% (that is, £42m – (£75m × 50%)). The results since the date of acquisition of the associate are attributable to the group and as such are correctly treated as post-acquisition.

There is one further adjustment that is required to be made on consolidation in this example. There is a difference of £5m between the fair values of the net assets consolidated (that is, £75m) and the adjusted capital and reserves taken into account above (that is, £47.5m + £22.5m = £70m). The amount relates to two items. Part relates to the post acquisition profits of £3.6m taken into account since the acquisition of the associate (that is, 20% × (£68m – £50m)). The other part relates to the increase in net assets of £7m from their book value of £68m to their fair value of £75m. In the above example 30% of that increase is reflected in the minority's interest and 50% is taken into account in calculating goodwill. The other 20% (that is, £1.4m) is the further adjustment that will need to be credited to the consolidated revaluation reserve. This represents a revaluation (not a fair value adjustment) of the assets that were already included in the consolidated balance sheet by virtue of the inclusion of the associate interest.

The double entry on consolidation is as follows:

	£m	£m
Dr Profit and loss account reserve	3.6	
Cr Investment		3.6
Being the restatement of the original investment to original cost.		
Dr Share capital and reserves	75.0	
Cr Minority interest		22.5
Cr Cost of investment		54.0
Cr Revaluation reserve		1.4
Cr Profit and loss account reserve		3.6
Dr Goodwill written off to reserves*	2.0	
Dr Goodwill capitalised*	4.5	
Being the adjustment necessary to reflect minority interests and goodwill		

* Even though the goodwill arising on the original acquisition of the associate interest was written off to reserves, which was allowed prior to the introduction of FRS 10, the goodwill arising on the further transfer of shares acquired must be capitalised in accordance with FRS 10.

A parent acquires part or all of the minority

23.70 FRS 2 states that when a group increases its interest in an undertaking that is already its subsidiary, the identifiable assets and liabilities of that subsidiary should be revalued to their fair value and goodwill arising on the increase in interest should be calculated by reference to those fair values. This rule is additional to the general rule in FRS 2 that requires a fair value exercise to be carried out when an entity becomes a subsidiary. However, the standard goes on to say that such a revaluation is not required if the difference between net fair values and carrying amounts of the assets and liabilities attributable to the increase in stake is not material. [FRS 2 para 51].

23.71 When a group increases its stake in a subsidiary the consideration it pays may not equal the fair value of the identifiable assets and liabilities acquired from its minority. If the net assets of the subsidiary, which are already included in the consolidation, were not revalued to up to date fair values before calculating the goodwill arising on the change in stake, the difference between the consideration paid and the relevant proportion of the carrying value of the net assets acquired would be made up in part of goodwill and in part of changes in value. For that reason FRS 2 requires that the assets and liabilities of the subsidiary be revalued to their fair value at the date of the increase in stake, unless the difference between the fair values and the carrying amounts of the share of net assets acquired is not material. [FRS 2 para 90].

Example

A parent acquired a 60% interest in an undertaking in 1992 for £50m. At that time the fair value of the net assets of the subsidiary was £60m. In 1998 the parent purchased a further 30% interest in the subsidiary for £40m. At that time the fair value of the net assets of the subsidiary was £150m; the increase in fair value of net assets between the original investment date and 1995 is due to revaluation increases of £70m and profits of £20m.

Assuming that the difference between the fair values and carrying values of the net assets acquired is material the acquisition will be dealt with as follows:

Cost of acquisition	£m	£m
Original investment 60% in 1992		50
Additional investment 30% in 1998		40
Total consideration		90
Consolidation goodwill		£m
Total consideration		90
Less: share of adjusted capital and reserves		
60% × £60m	36	
30% × £150m	45	81
Goodwill		9

The profits of the subsidiary company between 1992 and 1998 will have already been reflected in the assets and liabilities in the consolidated balance sheet. The treatment of the £70m revaluation element will depend on whether it has already been reflected in the consolidated balance sheet. If the revaluation had been booked prior to the purchase of the second tranche of shares the entries would have been:

	£m	£m
Dr Net assets	70	
Cr Revaluation reserve		42
Cr Minority interests		28

On the acquisition of the additional 30% the minority's share of the revaluation, £21m (30% × £70m) would be transferred from minority interests to the cost of control account together with the other elements of minority interests that relate to the 30% interests (that is, share capital, profit and loss account and other reserves).

If, on the other hand, the revaluation had not been reflected in the consolidated balance sheet the entries to reflect the revaluation would be:

	£m	£m
Dr Net assets	70	
Cr Revaluation reserve		42
Cr Minority interests		7
Cr Cost of control account†		21

† The entries in the cost of control account are shown below:

Cost of control account

Dr		Cr	
Original cost of investment	50	Share of adjusted capital and reserves in 1992 (£60m × 60%)	36
		Goodwill on original acquisition	14
	50		50
Additional cost of investment	40	Share of adjusted capital and reserves in 1998 (£60m + £20m × 30%)	24
		Share of revaluation reserve	21
Negative goodwill	5		
	95		95

The effect of these entries is that not only is there a fair valuation of the 30% acquired, but also a revaluation of the 60% which represents the share of assets previously owned (credited to the group's revaluation reserve) and a revaluation of the share still attributable to minority interests of 10%. It can also be seen that the goodwill of £9m is made up of £14m on the original acquisition and negative goodwill of £5m arising on the increase in stake.

An alternative view is that the proportion of assets of the subsidiary held prior to the acquisition of the minority (60% in this case) need not be revalued when the minority interest is acquired. If this approach is adopted the result will be that only the additional 30% of assets acquired will be subject to fair value at the date of acquisition of the 30% minority, the bulk of the assets will be held at their original cost to the group.

Change in stake not material

If the difference between the carrying values of the assets of the subsidiary and their fair values was not deemed to be material and the change in stake was not considered significant there would have been no requirement to revalue the assets of the subsidiary in the consolidation and the calculations would be as follows:

Cost of acquisition		£m
Original investment 60% in 1992		50
Final investment 30% in 1998		40
Total consideration		90
Consolidation goodwill		£m
Total consideration		90
Less: share of adjusted capital and reserves		
60% × £60m	36	
30% × (£60m + £20m) net assets in balance sheet prior to revaluation	24	60
Goodwill		30

The goodwill of £30m is made up of £14m on the original acquisition and £16m arising on the increase in stake (cost of £40m less net assets of £24m) attributable to the 30% purchased.

Becoming a subsidiary other than by a purchase or an exchange of shares

23.72 Some investments that end up as subsidiaries start out as much smaller interests in the undertakings concerned and may be treated in the group's financial statements in a variety of ways before they actually become subsidiaries. The most common way for an undertaking to become a subsidiary of another is by acquisition, but it is also possible for a parent to gain a subsidiary other than by acquisition, for example:

- By gaining control without acquiring a further interest in an undertaking, perhaps by virtue of an agreement with another shareholder.
- By enforcement of a security by a lender where a creditor defaults on a loan, such that under an arrangement the loan is converted into a holding of shares, which is sufficient to make it a subsidiary of the lender.
- By the subsidiary company purchasing and cancelling its own shares held by third parties.
- By changes to the voting rights attached to shares.

23.73 Where an undertaking becomes a subsidiary other than as a result of a purchase or exchange of shares, not only should its name be disclosed as required by paragraph 21(a) of FRS 6, but also FRS 2 paragraph 49 requires the circumstances to be explained.

Reverse takeovers

23.74 A reverse takeover occurs when a company that is 'being acquired' actually becomes the new parent because it issues shares in consideration for the combination. Problems arise in practice because when one company becomes the legal subsidiary of another, there is a natural tendency to assume that the new legal parent company has acquired the other company. Reverse takeovers often involve companies of significantly different sizes. A common motive for a reverse takeover is to acquire a stock exchange listing or other privilege in an indirect, less onerous, way.

23.75 In such cases, IAS 22 requires that the entity issuing the shares (that is, the legal parent) is deemed to be acquired by the other (that is, the legal subsidiary) and the fair value exercise is carried out on that basis. FRS 6 'Acquisitions and mergers', notes that this treatment is incompatible with the Companies Act. It had been suggested in the light of this that it was not possible to invoke the Act's true and fair override in order to fair value the acquiror rather than the acquiree. This issue was considered by the UITF and in its information sheet no 17 published in July 1996 the UITF concluded that, whilst each case should be considered on its merits, there are some instances where it would be appropriate to use the true and fair override and apply 'reverse acquisition accounting'. It also agreed this is simply an application of the general requirement of the true and fair override that may be invoked in the circumstances prescribed by the Act and as a consequence did not propose to publish an Abstract on this issue.

Disclosure for acquisition accounting

23.76 Schedule 4A to the Act sets out various details that have to be disclosed in the consolidated financial statements in the year that a subsidiary is acquired. These disclosure requirements concern business combinations that are accounted for using either acquisition accounting or merger accounting. In addition, FRS 6 repeats these requirements and includes further disclosure requirements relating both to acquisitions and mergers. Those relating to merger accounting are dealt with in chapter 27. The disclosures relating to the treatment of goodwill that arises on an acquisition are detailed in section III of this chapter. The disclosures related to fair valuing on an acquisition have been consolidated into FRS 6 and include disclosures of post-acquisition reorganisation costs which are discussed in section II of this chapter. The disclosures required where the group has taken merger relief on the issue of its shares in an acquisition are given in chapter 26. The paragraphs that follow outline the general disclosure requirements that apply to business combinations that are accounted for as acquisitions.

23.77 With the exception of goodwill, the disclosures concerning acquisitions can now be found in one standard, FRS 6. This standard encompasses the disclosure requirements of the Act. FRS 6 also repeats some of the disclosure requirements contained in FRS 1 and FRS 3, and expands the latter in an important respect.

23.78 A group may make several acquisitions in an accounting period. There is no exemption from disclosure on the grounds of excessive information, although information relating to non-material acquisitions can be aggregated. For acquisitive groups the disclosure resulting from FRS 6 and the Act is extensive.

General requirements

23.79 The acquiring company should disclose certain information in respect of all acquisitions. The parent must disclose in the consolidated financial statements that deal with the period in which the acquisition occurs:

- The names of undertakings acquired during the financial year, or where a group of companies is acquired, the name of the group's parent. [4A Sch 13(2)(a); FRS 6 para 21(a)].

- That the company has adopted acquisition accounting. [4A Sch 13 (2)(b); FRS 6 para 21(b)].

- The date of the acquisition (that is, the date on which control passes). [FRS 6 para 21(c)].

23.80 As described in the following paragraphs, FRS 6 requires certain additional disclosures to be given in respect of each *material acquisition*, and in aggregate for other acquisitions that are individually not material. Whilst the FRS 6 disclosures encompass those required by the Act, where the corresponding disclosures apply *"in relation to an acquisition which significantly affects the figures shown in the group accounts"* they go further than the Act [4A Sch 13(2)]. FRS 6 indicates that an acquisition should be judged to be material when *"the information relating to the acquisition might reasonably be expected to influence decisions made by the users of general purpose financial statements"*. [FRS 6 para 84]. However, FRS 6 also introduces a new class of *substantial acquisitions*, which are defined by reference to a size test and lead to certain enhanced disclosures.

23.81 If in the directors' opinion the disclosure of any of the information in para 23.79 above and paras 23.82 to 23.91 below that is required by the Act (relating to an undertaking established under the law of a country, or one that carries on a business, outside the UK) would be seriously prejudicial to the business of the undertaking, its parent or its fellow subsidiaries, it need not be given if the Secretary of State's permission is obtained. [4A Sch 16].

Purchase consideration

23.82 The following information should be disclosed for each material acquisition and for other non-material acquisitions in aggregate:

- The composition and the fair value of the consideration for the acquisition given by the parent and its subsidiaries. [4A Sch 13(3); FRS 6 para 24].
- Where applicable, a statement that the attributed fair value of the purchase consideration has been determined on a provisional basis at the end of the accounting period in which the acquisition took place. Any material adjustments in subsequent periods should be disclosed and explained. [FRS 6 para 27].
- The nature of any purchase consideration where settlement is deferred or where the amount is contingent on future events. [FRS 6 para 24].
- The range of possible outcomes and the principal factors that might affect the amount of contingent purchase consideration that may become payable in the future. [FRS 6 para 24].

23.83 Fair valuing the purchase consideration, including deferred and contingent consideration, is considered in section II of this chapter.

Fair values of identifiable assets and liabilities

23.84 The following information should be disclosed for each material acquisition and for other non-material acquisitions in aggregate:

- A table of assets and liabilities acquired, including a statement of the amount of goodwill or negative goodwill arising on the acquisition (see para 23.85 below). [4A Sch 13(5); FRS 6 para 25].
- Where applicable, a statement that the attributed fair values at the end of the accounting period in which the acquisition took place are provisional, together with the reasons. Any material adjustments made to those provisional fair values in the next financial statements should also be disclosed and explained. [FRS 6 para 27]. (See para 23.231 for discussion and example.)

Table of assets and liabilities acquired

23.85 The Act and FRS 6 require the book values and fair values of each class of assets and liabilities of the undertaking or group acquired to be stated in tabular form. The book values to be shown in the table are those recorded in the books of the acquired entity immediately before the acquisition and before any fair value adjustments. [FRS 6 para 25 (a)]. The book values of assets and liabilities of a group acquired must include all the necessary consolidation adjustments within that group. [4A Sch 13(7)].

23.86 The table should also detail the fair value adjustments of those same categories of assets and liabilities at the date of acquisition. FRS 6 also requires the fair value adjustments to be analysed between the following:

- Revaluations.
- Adjustments to bring accounting polices of the subsidiary onto the same basis as those of the group.
- Any other significant adjustments, including reasons for the adjustments.

[FRS 6 para 25(b); 4A Sch 13(5)].

23.87 The FRRP published a statement in November 1997 in connection with the financial statements of Stratagem Group plc concerning the adequacy of the information and explanations given in respect of fair value adjustments. The Panel was concerned that the company had not analysed such adjustments into the components specified above.

23.88 The table should also include a statement of the amount of goodwill or negative goodwill arising on acquisition. [FRS 6 para 25; 4A Sch 13 (5)]. Table 23.2 gives an example of a fair value table showing a material acquisition separately and other acquisitions in aggregate.

Table 23.2 – Hanson PLC – Annual Report – 30 September 1995

Notes to the accounts (extract)

20 Acquisitions, demerger and disposals (extract)

Acquisitions

Eastern was acquired on September 18, 1995 and included in the consolidated balance sheet at September 30, 1995. For the period since acquisition, sales of £74mn and operating profit of £7mn are included within the consolidated profit and loss account as continuing operations – acquisitions.

On September 18, 1995 the acquisition of Eastern was declared unconditional. The purchase consideration was £2.5bn. The operating assets and liabilities of Eastern, Carter Mining and other acquisitions during the year were as follows:

	Eastern Book value £ million	Others Book value £ million	Total Book value £ million	Total Adjustments £ million	Total Fair value £ million
Fixed assets	1,118	211	1,329	625	1,954
Stock	12	49	61	(1)	60
Debtors	364	16	380	(11)	369
Cash	264	1	265	–	265
Unlisted investments	251	–	251	295	546
Creditors	(411)	(15)	(426)	–	(426)
Loans and finance leases	(688)	(16)	(704)	–	(704)
Provision for liabilities	(113)	(49)	(162)	(497)	(659)
	797	197	994	411	1,405
Accrued purchase consideration					2,495
Cash consideration					299
Consideration (Eastern £2,496mn and others £298mn)					2,794
Goodwill (Eastern £1,377mn and others £12mn)					(1,389)
					1,405

Of the provisions for liabilities above, £88mn was provided by Eastern for reorganisation costs in the year up to acquisition.

The following fair value adjustments which relate principally to Eastern and Carter Mining were made to the book value of the assets and liabilities of the above acquisitions:

	Eastern £ million	Others £ million	Total £ million
Revaluations			
Tangible fixed assets	242	383	625
Unlisted investments	295	–	295
Alignment of accounting policies			
Liabilities in respect of mining reclamation	–	(94)	(94)
Black lung excise tax liability	–	(183)	(183)
Other			
Liabilities in respect of purchase contracts	(129)	–	(129)
Taxation	(86)	–	(86)
Other liabilities	–	(17)	(17)
	322	89	411

The above figures reflect a preliminary allocation of the purchase consideration to the net assets and liabilities of Eastern and other acquisitions of the year. The preliminary allocation will be reviewed based on additional information up to September 30, 1996. The directors do not believe that any net adjustments resulting from such review would have a material adverse effect on Hanson.

For the year ended March 31, 1995, Eastern reported an audited post-tax profit of £141mn. For the period ended September 18, 1995 the unaudited operating profit before exceptional items was £80mn and the unaudited post-tax loss after exceptional items was £19mn based on its then accounting policies.

23.89 Because of the intention of FRS 7 to curtail provisioning as part of the fair value exercise (as explained in section II of this chapter) FRS 6 requires that any provisions for reorganisation and restructuring costs which have been included in the liabilities, or related asset write-downs, of the acquired entity to be identified separately in the table. This is, however, only required where the provisions were made in the twelve months up to the date of acquisition. [FRS 6 para 26]. The example in Table 23.2 discloses the existence of such provisions.

23.90 This disclosure is an anti-avoidance measure (see para 23.176). To a very limited extent, some reorganisation provisions may be properly regarded as pre-acquisition liabilities of the acquired company where, for example, the acquired company was already committed to the expenditure before the acquisition was in prospect. By requiring separate disclosure of any such provisions in the fair value table, the ASB is seeking to ensure that the spirit of FRS 7 is observed. The disclosure of such provisions in the fair value table is likely to be a sensitive matter. Accordingly, the directors of the acquiring group may wish to include a statement explaining why the provision is valid.

Pre-acquisition activities of material acquisitions

23.91 For each *material acquisition* (but for *substantial acquisitions*, see para 23.95 below) the notes should disclose the following:

- The profit or loss after tax and minority interests of the undertaking or group acquired for the period from the beginning of its financial year up to the date of acquisition.
- The profit or loss after tax and minority interests of the undertaking or group acquired for its previous financial year.
- The date on which the acquired undertaking's or group's financial year before the acquisition began.

[FRS 6 para 35].

23.92 FRS 6 incorporates the disclosure that was previously required by the Act (before it was deleted by SI 1996/189) and defines the level of profit or loss as 'profit or loss after tax and minority interests'.

23.93 FRS 6 is silent on the question of whether the disclosed profit or loss of the acquired undertaking should be adjusted to comply with the accounting policies of the acquiring group. It would be consistent with the disclosures for substantial acquisitions (see para 23.100 below) for this information to be reported on the basis of the acquired undertaking's accounting policies prior to the acquisition, although the directors of the acquiring group may wish to disclose additional adjusted figures.

23.94 The above disclosures are not required to be given in aggregate for non-material acquisitions.

Pre-acquisition activities of substantial acquisitions

23.95 The ASB was anxious to meet the concerns of users who were interested in assessing the performance of acquisitions in the acquiring group, by requiring a more detailed analysis of the pre-acquisition results of significant acquisitions than was previously required by the Act. The objective was to enable users to put together something of a track record for the acquisition before and after it enters the group, given that in most acquisitions it is continuing businesses that are acquired. Such information has the effect of complementing the layered format for the profit and loss account required by FRS 3, which provides separate disclosure of the post-acquisition results of acquisitions made during the year.

23.96 FRS 6 requires, for each acquisition that meets the following size tests, disclosure of additional information about the pre-acquisition results of the acquired entity for its financial year in which the acquisition takes place.

23.97 The size tests are:

- 'Class 1' or 'Super Class 1' acquisitions, where the acquirer is listed on the Stock Exchange. It should be noted that the 'Class 1' category was abolished by the Stock Exchange in an amendment to the Listing Rules in August 1995. UITF Abstract 15, issued in January 1996, confirmed that the size test in FRS 6 should continue to be based on the former 'Class 1' criteria. UITF 15 requires references to Class 1 transactions in FRS 6 to be interpreted as meaning acquisitions where any of the figures (as used in the Listing Rules to define Super Class 1 transactions), expressed as a percentage exceed 15%:

    - The net assets of the acquired entity divided by the net assets of the listed company.

    - The profits of the acquired entity divided by the profits of the listed company (profits are defined as profits before tax and extraordinary items).

    - The consideration divided by the net assets of the listed company.

    - The consideration divided by the aggregate market value of all the equity shares of the listed company.

    - The gross capital of the company or business being acquired divided by the gross capital of the listed company. [LR 10.4(c)].

- For other acquiring entities, if either of the following conditions are met:

  - The net assets or operating profits of the acquired entity (as shown its last statutory financial statements before the date of acquisition) exceed 15 per cent of those of the acquiring entity. For this purpose, the amount of net assets is determined after adding any purchased goodwill that has been written off to reserves as a matter of accounting policy and not charged in the profit and loss account.

  - The fair value of the consideration given exceeds 15 per cent of the net assets of the acquiring entity.

- Other exceptional cases where an acquisition does not meet the above criteria, but is nevertheless of such significance that the disclosure is necessary in order to give a true and fair view.

[FRS 6 para 37].

23.98 For each substantial acquisition as defined above, the disclosures required in the financial statements of the acquirer for the financial year in which the acquisition took place are:

- For the period from the beginning of the acquired entity's latest financial year to the date of acquisition:

  - A summarised profit and loss account of the acquired entity, disclosing as a minimum the turnover, operating profit, any exceptional items falling within paragraph 20 of FRS 3, profit before taxation, taxation, minority interests, and extraordinary items.
  - A summarised statement of total recognised gains and losses of the acquired entity.

  - The date on which the period began.

- For the acquired entity's previous financial year, the profit or loss after tax and minority interests. This is the same as the disclosure required for each material acquisition (see para 23.91 above).

[FRS 6 para 36].

23.99 The principal components of the statement of total recognised gains and losses would usually be:

- Profit or loss for the period.
- Exchange gains or losses taken direct to reserves.

- Revaluation surpluses or deficits booked in respect of asset revaluations in the period.
- Total recognised gains or losses.

23.100 The information described above may in some situations be of limited practical use to analysts. Firstly, the period for which the more detailed summary of the results of the acquired entity is included will vary according to the timing of the acquisition in relation to the financial year end of the target and may be very short. Secondly, FRS 6 requires the results of the acquired entity to be shown on the basis of its own accounting policies prior to the acquisition. [FRS 6 para 36].

23.101 Where harmonisation of accounting policies on to the acquiring group's own policies gives rise to a material restatement of the results of the acquired company, their disclosure on the old basis may be misleading when compared to the disclosure of post-acquisition performance on the basis of the new policies. However, the standard explains that management may in those circumstances wish voluntarily to disclose, as additional notes, the same information restated on to the basis of the accounting policies of the acquiring group. [FRS 6 para 89]. Although this is sensible, it could give rise to excessive disclosure in the acquirer's consolidated financial statements.

23.102 There may be practical difficulties in complying with the disclosure requirements where a business (for example, the trade and assets of a division) rather than a subsidiary is acquired. Information about pre-acquisition results may not be readily available to the acquirer. Furthermore, profitability may have been distorted by intra-group charges under previous ownership, or matters such as taxation may not have been dealt with at a divisional level. In such circumstances, the acquirer should comply as far as is practically possible. The disclosure note may need to explain how the figures have been derived. Tables 23.3, 23.4 and 23.5 illustrate different solutions to the disclosure problem in practice. In Table 23.5, the acquirer disclosed that the information could not be given.

Table 23.3 – Reckitt & Colman plc – Report and Accounts – 31 December 1994

Notes to the accounts (extract)

27 **ACQUISITION OF BUSINESSES**

The 1994 full year trading result and statement of recognised gains and losses of L&F Household, as reported on the US accounting basis used by the business as part of Kodak, were as follows:

	1994 US$m
Net sales	809.13
Operating profit	105.87
Profit before tax	101.62
Taxation	(40.65)
Profit after tax	60.97
Foreign currency translation adjustments	3.36
Other	4.88
Total recognised gains and losses relating to the financial year	69.21

In 1993 profit after tax was $53.49m. The taxation affairs of L&F Household were treated integrally with those of Kodak, and the above figures include a charge of 40% of profit before taxation. There were no minority interests.

There is no material difference in the result when calculated using Reckitt & Colman's accounting policies.

Table 23.4 – SmithKline Beecham plc – Annual Report & Accounts – 31 December 1994

NOTES TO THE FINANCIAL STATEMENTS **(extract)**

Acquisitions (extract)

Acquisitions consist of Diversified Pharmaceutical Services, Inc., which was acquired from United HealthCare on 27 May 1994 and the worldwide consumer healthcare business of Sterling Winthrop Inc.,which was acquired from Eastman Kodak on 31 October 1994.

From 1 January 1994 to 27 May 1994 Diversified had sales of £74 million and a trading profit of £31 million; profit before taxation was £16 million and taxation £6 million. The profit after tax for Diversified for the year to 31 December 1993 was £17 million. There is no difference between profit after tax and the recognised gains and losses for the period.

From 1 January 1994 to 31 October 1994 Sterling had sales of £379 million and a trading profit of £66 million. The trading profit for Sterling for the year to 31 December 1993 was £80 million. The trading profit is presented before corporate and other charges, interest and taxation, as all financing items and US taxation matters were dealt with on a group basis by Eastman Kodak, and no meaningful allocation of such items can be made.

Table 23.5 – Scottish & Newcastle plc – Annual Report & Accounts – 28 April 1996

NOTES TO THE ACCOUNTS **(extract)**

25 ACQUISITION OF THE COURAGE BUSINESS (extract)
The Courage business was acquired from the Foster's Brewing Group on 16 August 1995.

Prior to acquisition the Courage business was part of Courage Limited. However, only certain of the assets and liabilities of Courage Limited were acquired. In these circumstances, it is not practical to provide details of profits or recognised gains and losses for the Courage business for financial periods before acquisition. Since acquisition the operations of the Courage business have been integrated into the existing Beer Division. As a result it is impractical to isolate the cashflows of the Courage business.

Post-acquisition activities

FRS 3 layered formats

23.103 FRS 6 repeats the requirements of FRS 3 concerning the reporting of the results of acquisitions made during the financial year of the acquiring group. The results of acquisitions excluding those that are also discontinued in the period, should be disclosed separately in aggregate as a component of the group's continuing operations. As with the other continuing operations the minimum analysis given on the face of the profit and loss account should be turnover and operating profit. The analysis of each of the other profit and loss account headings between turnover and operating profit may be given in a note, instead of on the face of the profit and loss account. In addition, where an acquisition has a material impact on a major business segment this should be disclosed and explained.

23.104 FRS 3 recognises that sometimes it may not be possible to determine post-acquisition results of an acquired operation to the end of the period. This might occur, for instance, where the business of an acquired subsidiary is transferred to another group company and merged with the existing business of that company shortly after the acquisition. If the results of the acquisition cannot be obtained the standard requires an indication to be given of the contribution of the acquisition to turnover and operating profit of the continuing operations. If that is also not possible, this fact and the reason should be explained. An illustration of this latter situation is given in Table 23.6 on page 23042, where the operations of the continuing and acquired businesses were merged for the latter part of the reporting period.

23.105 FRS 6 has added an important new interpretation of the requirements of FRS 3 as summarised above. It requires the post-acquisition results of businesses acquired in the financial year to be disclosed separately for each material acquisition and for other acquisitions in aggregate. [FRS 6 para 23]. This new interpretation – FRS 3 only refers specifically to separate disclosure of the aggregate results of acquisitions – is explained, in the appendix to the standard that deals with its development, as a clarification of FRS 3.

23.106 The FRS 3 presentation is considered in more detail in chapter 7, together with examples from published financial statements.

Exceptional items

23.107 The results of acquired companies disclosed for the first period after acquisition may not be entirely indicative of the ongoing performance of such companies. This is because, for example, they may be distorted significantly by fair value adjustments made on acquisition. Alternatively, they may be affected by changes introduced by the acquirer soon after the acquisition. FRS 6 indicates that exceptional profits or losses that arise as a result of fair valuing the assets and liabilities of acquired companies should be disclosed in accordance with FRS 3 and should be identified as relating to the acquisition. Once again, such disclosure should be given separately for each material acquisition and for other acquisitions in aggregate. [FRS 6 para 30].

23.108 The standard gives examples of circumstances where such disclosures may be necessary:

- Abnormal trading margins resulting from the revaluation of stocks to fair values on acquisition.

- Material profits resulting from the acquirer turning a loss-making long-term contract into a profitable contract.

- Material profits or losses resulting from contingent assets or liabilities crystallising at amounts different from their attributed fair values.

[FRS 6 para 85].

23.109 The above examples are considered in the sections in section II of this chapter that deal with fair valuing stocks and contingencies.

Post-acquisition reorganisation and integration

23.110 FRS 6 requires the profit and loss account or notes to the financial statements of periods following an acquisition to disclose the costs incurred in those periods in reorganising, restructuring and integrating the acquisition. [FRS 6 para 31]. Such disclosure should be given separately for each material acquisition, and for other acquisitions in aggregate. [FRS 6 para 23].

23.111 Such costs are restrictively defined in the standard. The practical implications of this requirement are considered in detail from paragraph 23.165.

Acquisition provisions

23.112 FRS 6 requires movements on provisions or accruals for costs related to an acquisition to be disclosed and analysed between the amounts used for the specific purpose for which they were created and the amounts released unused. [FRS 6 para 32]. Such disclosure should be given separately for each material acquisition and for other acquisitions in aggregate. [FRS 6 para 23]. This disclosure is considered from paragraph 23.207.

23.113 Table 23.6 provides extracts from the accounts of Glaxo Wellcome plc and illustrates the extensive profit and loss account disclosure required where a group makes a material acquisition and other acquisitions during the financial year. In addition, the group changed its year end from 30 June to 31 December, thus presenting its results for an 18 month period.

Table 23.6 – Glaxo Wellcome plc – Annual Report and Accounts – 31 December 1995

Consolidated Profit and Loss Account

	Notes	12 months to 30.6.95		6 months to 31.12.95			18 months to 31.12.95	12 months to 30.6.94 (restated)
		Glaxo continuing business	Acquisitions	Merged business	Combined business	Integration	Total	
		£m	£m	£m	£m	£m	£m	£m
Turnover	26	5,834	638	4,018	10,490	–	10,490	5,656
Operating costs	5	3,863	438	2,592	6,893	1,215	8,108	3,839
Trading profit	26	1,971	200	1,426	3,597	(1,215)	2,382	1,817
Profit on disposal of business	7	35	–	–	35	–	35	–
Share of profits/(losses) of associated undertakings	8	(8)	26	39	57	–	57	(3)
Profit before interest		1,998	226	1,465	3,689	(1,215)	2,474	1,814
Net (interest payable)/investment income	9	130	(96)	(121)	(87)	–	(87)	21
Profit on ordinary activities before taxation	26	2,128	130	1,344	3,602	(1,215)	2,387	1,835
Taxation	10	627	53	417	1,097	(230)	867	524
Profit on ordinary activities after taxation		1,501	77	927	2,505	(985)	1,520	1,311
Minority interests		39	5	18	62	–	62	12

	Note							
Profit attributable to shareholders		1,462	72	909	2,443	(985)	1,458	1,299
Dividends	12	1,004	–	526	1,530	–	1,530	823
Retained(loss)/ profit	23	458	72	383	913	(985)	(72)	476
Earnings per Ordinary Share	11	47.8p			74.6p		44.5p	42.7p
Weighted average number of shares in issue (millions)		3,056			3,274		3,274	3,040
Dividends per Ordinary Share	12				45.0p		45.0p	27.0p

The basis of analysis between Glaxo continuing business, Acquisitions, Merged business and Integration is set out in Note 1 on the Accounts.

Notes to the Accounts (extract)

1 Presentation of Accounts (extract)

Presentation of Profit and Loss Account

The Company has presented the profit and loss account in columnar form to illustrate the respective effect on the results for the period of the acquisitions during the period and their subsequent integration. This analysis is consistent with the way the business was managed and reported during the period. The analysis by column is defined as follows:

Glaxo continuing business reflects the results of the Glaxo business for the 12 months to 30th June 1995. Net investment income is stated as if Glaxo's investment funds had been available for investment throughout the period.

Acquisitions reflects the trading results of the acquisitions from their respective dates of acquisition to 30th June 1995. Interest payable on acquisitions represents the interest costs on borrowings taken out to finance the acquisitions, as if none of the combined Group's investment funds had been utilised to reduce borrowings. Taxation is stated at the rates applicable to the acquired businesses and to the interest costs.

Merged business reflects the results for the six months from 1st July 1995, from which date the continuing and acquired businesses were effectively merged and managed on a unified basis. It is therefore not feasible to identify and report separately the acquired businesses from 1st July 1995.

Integration reflects the costs charged relating to the integration of the continuing and acquired businesses. Taxation is stated at the rates applicable to integration costs and internal restructuring.

5 Operating costs (extract)

	12 months to 30.6.95		6 months to 31.12.95	18 months to 31.12.95			12 months to 30.6.94 (restated)
	Glaxo continuing business	Acquisitions	Merged business	Combined business	Integration	Total	
	£m	£m	£m	£m	£m	£m	£m
Cost of sales	1,037	115	654	1,806	558	2,364	1,004
Selling, general and administrative expenditure	1,986	227	1,368	3,581	400	3,981	1,988
Research and development expenditure	852	103	585	1,540	257	1,797	858
Other operating income	(12)	(7)	(15)	(34)	–	(34)	(11)
	3,863	438	2,592	6,893	1,215	8,108	3,839

Costs expected to be incurred in integrating the businesses of Glaxo and Wellcome are estimated at £1,215 million, comprising severances and other cash costs of £763 million and losses on disposal of fixed assets of £452 million. Costs of £384 million had been incurred by 31st December 1995 and provision for further costs of £831 million has been made at that date.

Operating and Financial Review (extract)

Acquisitions

The results of Wellcome have been consolidated into the Group results from 16th March 1995. In the period to 30th June 1995 Wellcome sales added £628 million to Group turnover and £204 million to trading profit; this represents a trading margin of 32 per cent.

The consolidation of Glaxo Korea Limited added £10 million to sales in this period but made no contribution to trading profit. The consolidation of Affymax N.V. added £4 million to operating costs.

Integration

Plans and financial targets for integration, as developed by the integration task forces in the period to 30th June 1995, were referred to in the Second Interim Report sent to shareholders in September 1995. The plans and targets were updated in November and December 1995 and form the basis of the figures reflected in this Annual Report and Accounts. Compared with the separate forward plans of Glaxo and Wellcome prior to Glaxo's bid for Wellcome, the new plan for the combined Group envisaged the achievement of cost savings year by year amounting to £700 million per year by the end of 1998, and progress is being made towards this objective.

The costs expected to be incurred in achieving these savings are forecast at £1,215 million. Some £452 million of the costs relate to potential losses on asset disposals resulting from site closures.

Cumulative savings are expected to achieve payback of total costs by around the end of 1997. In terms of the cash costs of £763 million, payback will be achieved earlier. The proceeds of asset disposals will reduce the net cash costs of integration.

To recognise the impact of integration activities, the anticipated costs of £1,215 million have been charged in the Accounts at 31st December 1995. The charge comprises costs incurred by 31st December 1995 of £384 million, and a provision for a further £831 million of costs. Taxation relief on integration amounts to £230 million. In calculating the attributable taxation, no taxation relief has been assumed on asset write downs.

Cash flow statement

23.114 Where a group acquires a subsidiary, FRS 1 requires the cash flows relating to the purchase consideration to be reported under 'acquisitions and disposals' in the consolidated cash flow statement. The amounts of cash and overdraft acquired should be shown separately along with the gross consideration paid for the acquisition.

23.115 A group's consolidated cash flow statement should be consistent with the rest of its consolidated financial statements, that is, cash flows should be included from the date of acquisition. Recording the gross consideration separately along with the cash and overdraft balances acquired means that the assets and liabilities of the acquired subsidiary at the date of acquisition, excluding cash and overdraft, would need to be eliminated so as to avoid double counting. For example, stock, debtors and creditors acquired would need to be eliminated from the total balance sheet changes in stock, debtors and creditors in the reconciliation of operating profit to operating cash flows.

Disclosures

23.116 FRS 1 requires a significant amount of disclosure to be made in respect of the cash flow effects of subsidiaries acquired during the financial year. These disclosure requirements are also referred to in FRS 6. The information should be disclosed for each material acquisition and for other non–material acquisitions in aggregate. These disclosure requirements are considered in chapter 30.

Section II – Fair valuing

Introduction

23.117 Consolidated financial statements are prepared on the principle that the reporting entity and its subsidiary undertakings are a single economic entity. Thus, the activities, assets and liabilities of all the undertakings in a group are included within the consolidation.

23.118 When a group extends its activities through the purchase of a new business entity, the purchase price is seldom negotiated on the basis of the values of the individual assets and liabilities of the entity being acquired. Instead, it is more likely to be determined by reference to the purchase of a stream of future profits or cash flows, so that a value is arrived at for the entity as a whole. Nevertheless, for the purposes of the consolidated financial statements the transaction has to be 'looked through' in order to determine initial carrying values for the underlying assets and liabilities of the acquired entity. This is sometimes described as a process of allocating the purchase price to the underlying net tangible and intangible assets to arrive at a 'cost' to the group. Establishing initial carrying values for those assets and liabilities, as a proxy for their cost, also provides a basis for reporting the performance of the enlarged group from the date the new entity is acquired.

23.119 The elements of accounting for a typical business acquisition can be demonstrated as follows:

Purchase consideration

Add: Expenses of acquisition

=

Cost of acquisition

Less: Fair valued assets and liabilities

=

Goodwill on acquisition

23.120 Fair values are a key part of acquisition accounting because:

- The fair value of the purchase consideration determines the cost of acquisition of the investment to the acquiring company.

- The fair value of the identifiable net assets acquired will be used as the carrying amounts for the newly acquired assets and liabilities in consolidated financial statements.

- The difference between the cost of acquisition and the sum of the fair values of the identifiable assets less liabilities is goodwill.

23.121 The principle of fair valuing assets and liabilities in acquisition accounting has been recognised for many years, both in the UK and internationally. The principle is also recognised in the Act, which requires that a newly acquired subsidiary's identifiable assets and liabilities must be included in the consolidated balance sheet at their fair values, as at the date of acquisition. [4A Sch 9(2)].

23.122 While the principle is relatively simple, agreeing how it should be applied in practice has proved a difficult matter. The ASB, and its predecessor body the ASC, spent several years developing an accounting standard on how the principle should be applied in practice. It was not until September 1994 that FRS 7, 'Fair values in acquisition accounting', was published, after a development process that included two discussion papers (from the ASC in June 1988 and the ASB in April 1993) and two exposure drafts (ED 53 in July 1990 and FRED 7 in December 1993).

23.123 Following the increase in acquisitions and mergers during the 1980s, it became clear that the principles underlying fair valuing were not sufficiently well defined in existing standards to ensure that the treatment of assets and liabilities in acquisition accounting was consistent or fair. In particular, there was widespread concern among many observers over the apparent ease with which an acquired entity's liabilities could legitimately be inflated – for example, by making provisions for losses or costs expected to be incurred after an acquisition – or its asset values minimised. Such practices enabled acquirers to present post-acquisition performance in the best possible light.

23.124 The ASB had stated its concerns about previous acquisition accounting practices in no uncertain terms during the development of the standard. When the ASB first outlined its proposals on fair value accounting in a discussion paper in April 1993, Chairman Sir David Tweedie said that *"acquisition accounting has been described as the 'black hole' of financial reporting in the UK"*. When FRS 7 was published he said that *"Accounting for acquisitions has long been seen as fertile ground for manipulating figures. This is in no-one's interest as it creates an atmosphere of suspicion and it puts unfair pressure on the many companies that try to present their results honestly"*.

23.125 In FRS 7 the ASB has introduced a more rigorous framework for acquisition accounting. Where the acquisition method of accounting is applied, FRS 7 sets out the principles that an acquirer should use both to identify and attribute fair values to the assets and liabilities of an acquired company or business and to determine the cost of acquisition. The fair values ascribed to the identifiable assets and liabilities in aggregate directly affect the amount recognised as purchased goodwill or negative goodwill on an acquisition.

Scope and basic principles of FRS 7

Scope

23.126 FRS 7 deals with fair value in the context of the acquisition of subsidiary undertakings by a parent company that prepares consolidated financial statements. Acquired subsidiary undertakings can include unincorporated entities, such as partnerships. The principles of the FRS also apply where a group or an individual company acquires the trade and assets of an unincorporated business (including a division of a company), when it is necessary for the acquirer to account for the cost of acquisition by recognising the underlying assets, liabilities and goodwill of the acquired business in its own financial statements. [FRS 7 para 4].

23.127 Other transactions that require fair value accounting, and the calculation of goodwill, include:

- The purchase of an additional interest in an existing subsidiary from a minority shareholder. FRS 2 states that when a group increases its interest in an undertaking that is already its subsidiary, the identifiable assets and liabilities of that subsidiary should be revalued to their fair values and goodwill arising on the increase in interest should be calculated by reference to those fair values (except where the effect of changes in value is not material). [FRS 2 para 51]. (See para 23.70 above.)
- The purchase of interests in associated undertakings and joint ventures which are accounted for under the equity method or gross equity method in accordance with FRS 9. [FRS 9 para 31].

The principles of FRS 7 are relevant to accounting for the above transactions in the acquirer's consolidated financial statements.

Purchase of business or assets

23.128 The definition of an 'acquisition' in FRS 7 derives from the definition of a 'business combination', which is framed as *"the bringing together of separate entities into one economic entity as a result of one entity uniting with, or obtaining control over the net assets and operations of, another"*. [FRS 7 para 2].

23.129 In some purchase transactions, it is necessary to determine whether the substance of the transaction is really the acquisition of a business or simply the purchase of assets or other payment. In the latter case, the transaction does not give rise to goodwill in the acquirer's financial statements, but results in the recording of any identified assets at their cost, as evidenced by the purchase price.

23.130 The above definitions imply that, for acquisition accounting to be applicable, the acquired entity must be more than a collection of assets and liabilities. It would normally be carrying out a continuing trade with an identifiable turnover, which means that the assets and liabilities of the acquired entity interact with each other and, importantly, with the people who operate the assets as a business.

Objective

23.131 The standard's overriding objective is twofold:

- All the assets and liabilities that existed in the acquired entity at the date of acquisition should be brought into the acquirer's financial statements at fair values reflecting their condition at that date.

- All changes to the acquired assets and liabilities, and the resulting gains or losses, that arise after control has passed to the acquirer are reported as part of the post-acquisition financial performance of the acquiring group.

[FRS 7 para 1].

23.132 By restricting the assets and liabilities recognised in the fair value exercise to those that already existed in the acquired entity, and by limiting the extent to which future events may be anticipated in arriving at fair values, the ASB has established a strict framework for determining whether revenues and costs should be treated as pre-acquisition (that is, reported within the pre-acquisition assets and liabilities of the target) or post-acquisition (that is, reported as profits or losses) in the acquirer's consolidated financial statements.

23.133 Consistent with its stated objective, the FRS precludes an acquirer from recognising any costs of planned post-acquisition reorganisation in the fair value exercise and, as a result, in the calculation of purchased goodwill, because they were not liabilities of the acquired entity at the date of acquisition. This framework has introduced a significant change from previous acquisition accounting practices, where it had been accepted that initial fair values could be adjusted to take account of changes anticipated by the acquirer when bidding for control.

Fair value of identifiable assets and liabilities

Overriding principles

23.134 The objective of FRS 7 is reflected in the two stated principles that underpin the standard for determining initial fair values for the assets and liabilities of an acquired entity, which are:

- The identifiable assets and liabilities to be recognised should be those of the acquired entity that existed at the date of the acquisition. [FRS 7 para 5].

- The recognised assets and liabilities should be measured at fair values that reflect the conditions at the date of the acquisition. [FRS 7 para 6].

Identifying the assets and liabilities acquired

Definitions of assets and liabilities

23.135 Identifiable assets and liabilities are defined as:

> *"The assets and liabilities of the acquired entity that are capable of being disposed of or settled separately, without disposing of a business of the entity"*. [FRS 7 para 2].

This definition is for all intents and purposes the same as the definition in the Act. [4A Sch 9(2)].

23.136 An acquiring company should review its acquisition and determine all the identifiable assets and liabilities as soon as possible after making the purchase. Goodwill is not an identifiable asset, because it cannot be sold separately from a business.

23.137 Definitions of assets and liabilities have been developed by the ASB in its draft Statement of Principles, and have been incorporated into FRS 5 'Reporting the substance of transactions'. These definitions are implicitly embodied in the principles of FRS 7. Assets are defined as:

> *"Rights or other access to future economic benefits controlled by an entity as a result of past transactions or events."* [FRS 5 para 2].

Liabilities are defined as:

> *"An entity's obligations to transfer economic benefits as a result of past transactions or events."* [FRS 5 para 4].

23.138 When applied to acquisition accounting the 'entity' is the acquired entity. The past transactions or events giving rise to the rights or obligations (including those that are contingent) of the acquired entity must have occurred before the date of acquisition if they are properly to be regarded as pre-acquisition.

23.139 Therefore, to qualify for recognition in the fair value exercise, FRS 7 requires that, in the case of assets, the rights to future benefits must have been obtained by the acquired entity before the date of acquisition. In the case of liabilities, there must have been a commitment by the acquired entity before the date of acquisition to transfer economic benefits.

23.140 The definitions of assets and liabilities quoted above are wide ranging and encompass most items that would usually be recognised in the balance sheet of an acquired entity under conventional accounting principles. For example, the definition of assets would generally include prepayments or deferred costs, where payments have been made which give the acquired entity rights to obtain future services or access to future benefits. Similarly, the definition of liabilities would generally include, in addition to creditors and accruals, items of deferred income, where the entity has still to incur costs in respect of future obligations relating to payments that have been received. These items, which would normally be recognised in the financial statements of the acquired entity, should also be taken into account in the fair value exercise.

Inclusion of additional assets and liabilities

23.141 Not all items that meet the above definitions of assets and liabilities are necessarily recorded in the financial statements as soon as they are identified. Consequently, some identifiable assets and liabilities may need to be recognised by the acquirer although they have not been recognised in the financial statements of the acquired entity. The FRS refers to over-funded or under-funded pension schemes and contingent assets as examples. Where no acquisition is involved, the recognition in the financial statements of some assets and liabilities is deferred, either on grounds of prudence or because other standards require gradual recognition over several financial years. In the pensions example, an underlying surplus or deficiency may already exist at the date of acquisition but, in accordance with SSAP 24, they may not yet have been booked as an asset or a liability by the acquired entity.

23.142 However, an acquisition requires a fair value allocation to be made, so far as is practically possible, over all the existing assets and liabilities of the acquired entity, irrespective of whether they have been recognised under the acquired entity's accounting policies. The standard states that if this is not done, the reporting of post-acquisition performance is distorted by changes in assets and liabilities not being recognised in the correct period. [FRS 7 para 36].

23.143 Examples of liabilities that may not previously have been booked in the acquired company's financial statements, but would be included as fair value adjustments, include provisions for the following:

- Environmental clean-up obligations related to past activities of the acquired company.
- Unfunded post-retirement healthcare or other benefits.
- Onerous leasing commitments, such as future rentals payable on properties that were unoccupied by the acquired company.
- Onerous financial contracts entered into by the acquired company, such as forward, futures and options contracts, where the provision is calculated by reference to current market values of the relevant financial instruments.
- Contingent losses, provided that the contingency was in existence before the acquisition (see para 23.329 for further discussion of contingencies).
- Losses arising from pre-existing contractual arrangements, such as 'poison pill' clauses in shareholder agreements or compensation clauses in directors' service contracts, that are triggered in the event of a change of ownership, that is, where the crystallisation of the liability is independent of any decision or action of the acquirer. This type of identifiable liability is referred to in the explanation section of the standard. [FRS 7 para 37].

23.144 In each of the above examples, the item meets the criteria for recognition in the fair value exercise because either the obligation had been incurred before the acquisition or the underlying contingency giving rise to the provision was in existence before the acquisition and, in the last case, the outcome was not dependent on the acquirer's intentions. Various practical examples are considered in paragraph 23.153 below.

23.145 FRS 7 makes specific reference to onerous contracts and commitments:

> *"Identifiable liabilities include items such as onerous contracts and commitments that existed at the time of acquisition, whether or not the corresponding obligations were recognised as liabilities in the financial statements of the acquired entity".* [FRS 7 para 38].

Whilst the standard does not define what 'onerous' means, this should generally be interpreted with reference to its basic principles. Firstly, a contract must have been onerous to the acquired entity at the date of acquisition and not have become onerous as a result of the acquirer's actions. Secondly, whether or not a contract is onerous can often reasonably be interpreted as meaning whether or not the obligation exceeds the current (that is, at date of acquisition) market value.

23.146 Examples of potentially onerous contracts include long-term supply contracts for commodities such as oil, gas and electricity, where the price to which the acquired company is committed exceeds the current market price for such contracts. They should usually be capable of being bought and sold in an arm's length transaction. They would not be recognised on the acquired entity's balance sheet unless, unusually, it had a policy of marking such contracts to market. The 'losses' derived from fair valuing such commitments – the value at which a contract for a similar product, a similar amount and for a similar future delivery date could be entered into at the date of acquisition – would be recognised as identifiable liabilities in the fair value exercise.

23.147 An important consideration in fair valuing long-term purchase commitments is that there should be consistency of treatment. This means that where long-term purchase commitments are recognised as identifiable liabilities, all such commitments, whether onerous or favourable, should be recognised. Thus where commitments have been entered into at prices lower than current market prices for equivalent commitments, the 'gains' derived from valuing them at fair value should be recognised as assets in the fair value exercise.

23.148 Tables 23.2 (on page 33) and 23.7 give examples of onerous purchase contracts recognised as fair value adjustments.

Table 23.7 – United Utilities PLC – Annual Report & Accounts – 31 March 1996

Notes to the accounts (extract)

12 **Purchase of subsidiary (extract)**

The Group acquired NORWEB plc on 8 November 1995 and the acquisition method of accounting has been adopted. The analysis of net assets acquired and the fair value to the Group is as follows:

	Book value £m	Revaluation £m	Accounting policy alignment £m	Other £m	Fair value to Group £m
Tangible fixed assets	779.3	234.9	–	–	1,014.2
Investments	147.4	247.6	–	–	395.0
Stocks	68.4	–	(3.7)	–	64.7
Debtors	248.2	–	(14.7)	(21.1)	212.4
Cash and cash equivalents	254.9	–	–	–	254.9
Creditors falling due within one year	(281.0)	(48.0)	–	4.0	(325.0)
Creditors falling due after more than one year	(517.7)	(32.5)	–	–	(550.2)
Provisions for liabilities and charges	(44.2)	(1.0)	(1.3)	(217.9)	(264.4)
Net assets before special dividend	655.3	401.0	(19.7)	(235.0)	801.6
Special dividend, including advance corporation tax	(195.6)	–	–	–	(195.6)
Net assets	459.7	401.0	(19.7)	(235.0)	606.0
Consideration:					
Cash					1,463.2
Shares allotted					197.0
Share option obligations					22.7
Total consideration					1,682.9
Goodwill arising					1,076.9

Explanations of the major fair value adjustments in the above table are given in the financial review on pages 12 and 13.

The fair value adjustment of £217.9 million relating to provisions for liabilities and charges includes £173.2 million in respect of onerous gas and electricity contracts.

The fair value adjustments are provisional and may be subject to revision in the 1996/97 accounts. Any adjustments made will be reflected in the goodwill calculation.

Financial review (extract)

Acquisition of Norweb (extract)

Norweb's net assets acquired, excluding the special dividend and associated advance corporation tax, amounted to £801.6 million. This was after a net increase of £146.3 million for provisional fair value adjustments.

The **distribution network** was revalued upward on the basis of the return being earned on those assets increasing the net book value by £248 million.

The **investments** in the National Grid and Pumped Storage Business were revalued upward by £199.6 million, net of £48.0 million tax provisions, reflecting the net proceeds received on disposal.

Provision was made for **gas and electricity contracts** of £173.2 million mainly in relation to long term power purchase agreements, where the recent collapse in gas prices and reduced capacity costs resulted in onerous conditions compared to prices available in November 1995, the date the fair valuation was made. The provisions are of a long term nature and, in any event, will not be utilised prior to 1998. Also included is a small element relating to short term take or pay gas purchase contracts.

Other adjustments are given in note 12 to the accounts.

The fair value adjustments will be reviewed again during the course of 1996/97 and amended as necessary in the light of subsequent knowledge or events.

Exclusion of certain assets and liabilities

23.149 Conversely, certain items recognised by the acquired entity may not be recognised by the acquirer. An obvious example is where purchased goodwill is recognised as an asset in the acquired entity's balance sheet in respect of its previous acquisitions. That purchased goodwill is by definition not an identifiable asset and would be subsumed within the calculation of goodwill arising on the acquisition in the acquirer's consolidated financial statements. Another example is development expenditure capitalised in the accounts of the acquired entity. In the fair value exercise it may, for example, be impossible to arrive at a reliable fair value relating to the balance of unamortised deferred development expenditure; alternatively, deferral of development costs may be inconsistent with the accounting policies of the acquiring group. In those circumstances, it would be necessary to reflect the value of all past research and development expenditure in goodwill.

23.150 Where the acquired entity has booked provisions for expenditure not yet incurred, the standard requires the circumstances to be considered very carefully in order to determine whether the provisions are proper pre-acquisition liabilities. It states that "*only if the acquired entity was demonstrably committed to the expenditure whether or not the acquisition was completed would it have a liability at the date of acquisition*". [FRS 7 para 40]. Any provisions that fail this test do not meet the definition of identifiable liabilities and should be added back to the net assets of the acquired entity in the fair value exercise. This issue is considered further in paragraph 23.178.

Adjustments for different accounting policies

23.151 FRS 7 requires that, subject to the detailed rules that apply its principles to specific types of assets and liabilities of an acquired business, recognition and measurement should be determined in accordance with the acquirer's accounting policies for similar assets and liabilities. [FRS 7 para 8].

23.152 Examples where fair value adjustments may be necessary to achieve consistency with the acquirer's accounting policies include: current assets affected by different revenue recognition policies; and liabilities for product warranties affected by different provisioning policies. One of the effects of these examples is that post-acquisition performance is not distorted purely by accounting policy differences.

Examples – identifiable liabilities or post-acquisition costs

23.153 Some examples of items that would be included in pre-acquisition liabilities and items that would be treated as post-acquisition costs are considered below:

Example 1 – Vacant leasehold property

An acquired company has a lease on a property that it no longer occupies. The acquirer decides to move out of one of its existing properties, which it also leases, and occupy the surplus property leased by the acquired company. The acquirer decides to incur the costs of early termination of its existing lease.

The UITF considered the general question of whether the rent payable and other expenses of vacant leasehold property should be provided for when such property ceases to be used. Although the UITF decided not to issue a ruling on this matter, in July 1993 it issued a statement saying that in some circumstances full provision would be required. These circumstances would include the situation where a property has ceased to be used for the purposes of the business and is unlikely to be reoccupied or sublet.

Following the principles of FRS 7, the acquired company's obligations in respect of the lease on the vacant property is likely to be an identifiable liability that existed at the date of acquisition. If provision is appropriate in the circumstances of the acquired company at the date of acquisition, it should be recognised as a fair value adjustment if it has not already been provided for in the acquired company's financial statements.

The reoccupation of the property leased by the acquired company and the abandonment of the property leased by the acquirer are part of the post-acquisition reorganisation of the combined group and, therefore, the financial effects of the relocation would be included in the consolidated profit and loss account. Thus any provision recognised as an identifiable liability at the date of acquisition would be written back and the cost of terminating the acquirer's lease would be written off, with both items being treated as post-acquisition.

Example 2 – Vacant leasehold property

An acquired company had occupied a rented warehouse. After the acquisition the acquiring group rationalised its distribution facilities and the warehouse occupied by the acquired company was vacated. The group is making provision for the rentals payable under the unexpired lease.

Under FRS 7 the abandonment of the property should be accounted for as a post-acquisition event. The provision for rent payable on the property being vacated should be charged in the profit and loss account as part of the cost of post-acquisition reorganisation.

Example 3 – Property lease at above market rent

An acquired company leases its head office on an operating lease. The rent for the next 15 years is fixed at a level that is in excess of the rents payable on leases of comparable buildings that are on the market at the time of the acquisition. Can provision be made in the fair value exercise for the onerous lease, that is, the difference between the committed lease payments over the term of the lease and those that would reflect current market rents?

There are alternative approaches to this question. One argument is that operating leases are not recognised as liabilities under standard accounting practice, neither does FRS 7 specifically indicate that they should be recognised in acquisition accounting. Rents payable under operating leases are required by SSAP 21 to be expensed on a straight-line basis over the term of the lease; the method of expensing is not accelerated (or decelerated) as market rentals fluctuate. Only timing differences between the amount of rentals expensed and rentals paid are recognised as prepayments or accruals. Consequently, the onerous element of the lease is not an identifiable liability and no provision should be recognised in the fair value exercise. The actual lease payments would continue to be expensed in the acquirer's consolidated profit and loss account. The benefit of lower market rentals would not be reflected in the profit and loss account unless, and until, the acquirer renegotiates the lease.

A counter argument is that recognising a provision for the onerous element of the lease is consistent with the principles of FRS 7 that underlie the identification of the acquired company's existing obligations and with the concept of fair value underlying the specific rules. Some companies do revalue leasehold property interests in their financial statements, including short-term operating leases. Guidelines for the valuation of property assets for the purposes of financial statements, contained in statements of asset valuation practice published by the Royal Institution of Chartered Surveyors, indicate that a leasehold interest may have a negative value (that is, it is a liability to a company) where, for example, the rent reserved under the lease exceeds the open market rental value. Such a value represents an estimated open market value of the lessee's existing commitment. Some companies include such negative values as liabilities in their financial statements. Furthermore, paragraph 64 of FRS 7 states, in the context of contingencies, "*in rare cases where a commitment....is of a kind that is normally assumed or acquired in an arm's length transaction...., its fair value would reflect the market price for such transactions*".

The conclusion can be drawn from the above that, in some circumstances, negative values of operating leases could be included as identifiable liabilities in the fair value exercise. It would be permissible for an acquiring company to have an accounting policy of fair valuing the leases of an acquired company. Of course, if this treatment is adopted, it should be applied consistently in the valuation of all leasehold interests acquired, to include, where applicable, any favourable operating leases (that is, where the rent under the lease is below the current open market rental value) as assets in the fair value exercise. Equally, an acquiring company can have a policy for not making fair value adjustments for leases in an acquired company. The acquiring company should apply one of these policies consistently to all acquisitions.

Example 4 – Relocation costs

Company A acquired a subsidiary of company B. The subsidiary occupied premises that it shared with other operations in B's group. As part of the purchase agreement the new subsidiary was required to vacate those premises. Company A is making a provision in the accounts of the subsidiary for the estimated costs of relocation.

Under FRS 7 the relocation costs were not an identifiable liability of the acquired subsidiary at the date of acquisition. The relocation is a post-acquisition event and is not, for example, an action that the subsidiary was committed to whether or not the acquisition was completed, nor the crystallisation of a pre-existing contingent liability. The provision should, therefore, be charged as a post-acquisition revenue cost in company A's consolidated financial statements.

Example 5 – Golden parachute

The directors of the target company have clauses in their contracts that entitle them to receive twice their basic salary, together with an amount in respect of loss of pension benefits, if they decide to terminate their contracts within 28 days of an offer for more than 50% of the company's share capital being declared unconditional. The company has been taken over and the directors have exercised their rights to terminate their contracts and claim compensation.

In this example, a so-called golden parachute, the acquirer has no control over the decision to terminate the service contracts of the acquired company's directors and incur the consequential costs. As the change of ownership clauses were already in existence before the acquisition took place, those directors had the right to claim compensation regardless of the acquirer's intentions towards the acquired company. It is, therefore, appropriate to treat the compensation costs as identifiable liabilities resulting from the crystallisation of a pre-acquisition contingency, that is, to include them as fair value adjustments under the principle in paragraph 37 of FRS 7.

In contrast, if the acquirer decided to fire the directors of an acquired company where those directors had no such rights to terminate their contracts as a result of an acquisition, it would not be appropriate to accrue for the ensuing compensation costs in the fair value exercise. That is because paragraph 7 of FRS 7 requires changes resulting from the acquirer's intentions or actions after the acquisition to be treated as post-acquisition costs. Similarly, the costs would be post-acquisition if artificial arrangements were made between acquirer and target to put in place such clauses during the negotiations for the acquisition.

Example 6 – Redundancy costs

Company A has acquired company B. Company A has the management capacity to integrate the operations of company B into its own operations without taking on the majority of B's employees. The purchase price for B of £20m has been negotiated in contemplation of redundancy costs of £2m being incurred after the acquisition. The employees to be made redundant, and their costs, had been identified during the course of negotiations and a formal plan had been drawn up and agreed between the acquirer and vendor. The balance sheet in the completion accounts of B included a provision of £2m in respect of the anticipated redundancy costs.

In accordance with paragraph 40 of FRS 7, the redundancy costs of £2m should be treated as post-acquisition costs in company A's consolidated financial statements. Despite the fact that provision was included in the completion accounts of company B, the provision was clearly made for the purposes of reaching an agreed purchase price with company A, and did not reflect expenditure that company B was committed to whether or not the acquisition was completed.

Example 7 – Redundancy costs and vendor refunds

Facts as in the previous example except that, instead of a provision being included in the completion accounts, the purchase price payable on completion is £22m and the vendor has undertaken to refund up to £2m as and when the employees of company B are made redundant after the acquisition. In addition, company B is currently making losses and the agreement says that up to £1m should be refunded in respect of future operating losses of company B.

In accordance with paragraph 7 of FRS 7, both the future redundancy costs and the future operating losses should be treated as post-acquisition in the consolidated profit and loss account of company A because they are not identifiable liabilities of company B at the date of acquisition. Amounts up to £3m refunded by the vendor of company B would be applied by company A to reduce the purchase consideration, that is, the cost of investment in company B and goodwill.

Some accountants would argue that the amounts refunded should be matched with the costs and losses to which they relate, that is, that they should be credited in the profit and loss account. However, the net purchase price of £19m payable to the vendor reflects the fact that the acquired business is loss-making and requires management action to turn it around. Such action involves incurring revenue costs. Following the principles in FRS 7, the short-term operating losses and the costs of reorganisation should all be shown as part of post-acquisition performance.

Intangible assets

23.154 FRS 7 makes only the briefest of references to identifiable intangibles. It merely states that "*where an intangible asset is recognised, its fair value should be based on its replacement cost, which is normally its estimated market value*". [FRS 7 para 10].

23.155 A number of companies have included a variety of intangibles in their fair value exercises in recent years. Such intangibles have included brand names, publishing titles, the embedded value of life insurance, milk quotas and even company names. Intangibles can constitute very significant proportions of a company's consolidated balance sheet. For example, a substantial portion of the capital employed of Reed Elsevier comprises intangibles identified on past acquisitions, see Table 23.8.

Table 23.8 – Reed Elsevier plc – Annual Review – 31 December 1996

Accounting policies (extract)

Intangible fixed assets

Publishing rights and titles, databases, exhibition rights and other intangible assets are stated at fair value on acquisition and are not subsequently revalued. Having no finite economic life, no systematic amortisation is applied, but provision is made for any permanent impairment in value. Internally developed intangibles are not carried on the balance sheet. Intangible assets are only recognised on more significant acquisitions.

Combined Balance Sheet (extract)

£ million	1996
Fixed assets	
Intangible assets *note 13*	2,550
Tangible assets *note 13*	323
Investments *note 14*	180
	3,053
Current assets	
Stocks	139
Debtors: amounts falling due within 1 year *note 15*	667
Debtors: amounts falling due after more than 1 year *note 16*	147
Cash and short term investments *note 17*	1,141
	2,094
Creditors: amounts falling due within 1 year *note 18*	(2,146)
Net current (liabilities)/assets	(52)
Total assets less current liabilities	3,001

23.156 This treatment has reflected the increased commercial importance of brands and similar assets in the context of many acquisitions. This is because the most significant value is often in intangible benefits rather than in the tangible assets of the acquired entity. The practice has attracted much attention among preparers and users of accounts, while standard setters in the UK struggled for many years to develop principles for recognising intangibles. The debate centred around two problem areas: first the problem of establishing which intangibles are truly identifiable assets; and secondly the problem of how to value them.

23.157 The problem of accounting for intangibles was eventually settled with the publication of new rules on goodwill in FRS 10. The ASB considered that, because some intangibles, such as brand names, are very similar to goodwill, the most important principle was that the accounting treatment should be the same irrespective of whether intangibles are labelled separately on the balance sheet or subsumed within goodwill. Lack of comparability had been perceived as a major problem when, on the one hand, goodwill was written off to reserves immediately on acquisition whilst, on the other hand, intangibles could be recognised on the balance sheet. The problem was exacerbated because identifying and measuring such intangibles to separate their value from goodwill can be subjective.

23.158 Since FRS 10 requires purchased goodwill to be capitalised and accounted for alongside intangible assets, the separate recognition of intangibles has become less of an issue. Nevertheless, the standard sets three thresholds that must be passed before an intangible asset of an acquired business can be capitalised separately from goodwill:

- Separability.
- Control.
- Reliable measurement.

23.159 First, FRS 10's definition of an intangible asset requires it to be identifiable. Identifiability is a basic concept in FRS 7 and the Act for recognising any asset and liability in an acquisition (see para 23.135). Separability is a key component of the definition of an identifiable asset. FRS 10 explains that an asset is not identifiable if it *"can be disposed of only as part of the revenue-earning activity to which it contributes"*. [FRS 10 para 2].

23.160 These words do little to clarify the issue – some intangibles are more clearly separable than others, but defining the cut remains subjective. In practice, the standard admits a wide range of intangibles such as those specifically mentioned in the balance sheet formats in the Act (concessions, patents, licences, trademarks and similar rights) as well as quotas, publishing titles, franchise rights and brands. But not all such items would necessarily be identifiable in all circumstances; to some extent this depends on how fundamental the intangible item is to the continuation of the acquired business. A business name is much less likely to qualify as identifiable.

23.161 Secondly, an identifiable intangible must be controlled through custody or legal rights which secure an entity's access (and restrict the access of others) to the benefits that are expected to derive from it. In practice, this rules out recognition of items such as a skilled workforce or a customer list because, whilst they may be extremely valuable to a business, the business does not control them and, hence, their value is part of its goodwill.

23.162 Thirdly, an intangible should be recognised if (and only if) its initial fair value can be measured reliably. [FRS 10 para 10]. The FRS refers to two categories of intangibles:

- Intangibles with a readily ascertainable market value.
- Intangibles that are unique to the business.

23.163 In practice, hardly any intangibles fall into the first category. The FRS defines them as belonging to a homogeneous population of assets that are equivalent in all material respects and where there are frequent transactions in an active market. These are very strict conditions, because the FRS also allows intangibles of this type only to be revalued and to be recognised where they have been self-developed. The FRS suggests that some operating licences, franchises and quotas might meet these conditions (although many of these will in fact be unique).

23.164 The ASB has been sceptical about the reliability of valuations of unique intangibles such as brands and publishing titles where there is no market value as such. The standard accepts, however, that certain entities that regularly buy and sell them have developed reliable valuation techniques that would allow them to be capitalised separately from purchased goodwill as a result of an acquisition. This implies that those entities that are not in that position may legitimately choose not to attempt to value such intangibles and may subsume them within goodwill. An element of the ASB's scepticism remains in FRS 10, because the standard specifically precludes intangibles (other than those with a readily ascertainable market value) from being recognised to the extent that their valuation would increase the net assets of the acquired business above the purchase price to give rise to negative goodwill. The accounting treatment and valuation of intangibles is discussed in chapter 14.

Post-acquisition reorganisation and integration costs

23.165 FRS 7 specifically requires the following items to be *excluded* from the fair value exercise and treated as post-acquisition items in the acquirer's consolidated financial statements:

- The accounting effects of changes to the acquired entity resulting from the acquirer's intentions or future actions.

- Impairments in asset values, or other changes, resulting from events subsequent to the acquisition.
- Provisions for future operating losses.
- Provisions or accruals for reorganisation and integration costs expected to be incurred as a result of the acquisition, whether they relate to the acquired entity or to the acquirer.

[FRS 7 para 7].

Background

23.166 In recent years there has been much criticism of the use of provisions and the making of excessive asset write-downs in fair valuing acquisitions. By setting up provisions in the fair value exercise, in the post-acquisition period, companies could offset subsequent costs that would otherwise have to be charged in the profit and loss account, against those provisions. On the other hand, if provisions are not set up as fair value adjustments, these costs of reorganisation will flow through to the profit and loss account in the subsequent periods and will, therefore, adversely affect the earnings per share of the combined group.

23.167 Previous guidance on setting up acquisition provisions was given in ED 53, issued by the ASC in 1990. ED 53 proposed that provision should not be made for future trading losses of continuing businesses. It proposed that provisions for reorganisation costs could be made, but only if the following conditions were met:

- There was a clearly defined programme of reorganisation and those costs for which provisions were to be made had been specified in reasonable detail.
- There was evidence that in formulating its offer, the acquirer had taken account of plans or proposals for such reorganisation and associated costs.

23.168 The ASB considered and rejected ED 53's approach to the recognition of reorganisation provisions. The ASB's reforms attracted strong support from the investment community and strong opposition from companies. While the ASB has openly stated that the principal reason for introducing the reforms in FRS 7 is to eliminate, or at least to significantly curtail, the scope for exploiting the flexibility afforded by previously accepted principles, it has also taken great pains to justify its approach on conceptual grounds. The section of FRS 7 that describes the development of the standard contains a lengthy analysis of the ASB's reasons for adopting this approach and for rejecting the arguments from those who opposed this approach and preferred the approach in ED 53.

23.169 The principal objection that was raised by many companies to the treatment of reorganisation costs in the manner prescribed by FRS 7 was that, in their view, it does not reflect commercial reality. In their view, where an acquiring company has taken account of the costs of future reorganisation in arriving at a price it is prepared to pay, those costs should be reflected as capital costs. They argue that such costs should be included in the fair value exercise and should not be charged as revenue costs in the profit and loss account in subsequent periods. This view was supported by one ASB member in a 'dissenting view' published with the standard.

23.170 One of the ASB's main arguments for the approach taken in FRS 7 has been that financial statements should treat the costs and benefits of reorganisations related to acquisitions in the same manner as reorganisations of continuing operations. The benefits derived from realising synergy, and from implementing other post-acquisition restructuring and investment programmes, add post-acquisition value to the acquiring group by improving its profitability. Consequently, the costs of achieving such improvements should also be treated as post-acquisition. Those costs should be treated as revenue or capital according to normal accounting principles. The ASB has also stated that the approach adopted in FRS 7 is consistent with its developing Statement of Principles and with the profit and loss account formats introduced by FRS 3.

Post-acquisition activities

23.171 There are many reasons why companies seek to expand by acquisition. These might include:

- Gaining access to new markets.
- Diversification into a new business or a different product line.
- Expanding market share or protecting an existing market position.
- Acquiring production or distribution facilities, market skills or other expertise.
- Achieving economies of scale by rationalising facilities.
- Securing the supply of a key component or service.
- Financial reasons such as securing the utilisation of unrelieved tax losses and allowances.

23.172 A successful acquisition will normally involve:

- A thorough investigation of the target before the acquisition is completed.
- A detailed post-acquisition integration plan for maximising the value of the acquisition to the acquiring group.

23.173 In other words, few companies buy blind. They have commercial and strategic plans underlying their acquisitions, conduct a detailed evaluation and due diligence exercise and develop a strategy for getting the required or best return out of the enlarged operation. Frequently, this means that the integration plans are already at an advanced stage of development, even before the acquisition contract is signed.

23.174 The post-acquisition plan would examine how the combining organisations are to be fitted together. It would identify opportunities to:

- Integrate activities, for example by harmonising systems and strategies. This would include activities such as consolidating marketing and advertising functions, financial control systems, data processing and other administrative systems.
- Achieve cost savings by reducing management and other overheads.
- Rationalise activities through closure of facilities that are surplus to the combined group.
- Invest in the development of the target company's business.

23.175 FRS 7 does not permit provisions to be made in the fair value exercise to cover the costs of such post-acquisition activities, even where these costs were taken into account by the acquirer when negotiating the acquisition price, because they were not liabilities of the acquired entity at the date of acquisition. The following are examples of items, as disclosed in companies' financial statements, that have been included as acquisition provisions in arriving at the fair value of net assets acquired, under pre-FRS 7 practices. Under FRS 7 these items should be treated as post-acquisition costs.

- Redundancy costs.
- Closure of head office and certain branches of acquired company.
- Costs of restructuring and strategically realigning operations to acceptable levels of efficiency.
- Cost of implementing strategic changes subsequent to acquisition.
- Costs of implementing the acquirer's quality standards, including training.
- Costs of converting and integrating acquired retail outlets into the acquirer's chain.
- Plant and other fixed assets written off as part of post-acquisition reorganisation.

- Rationalisation and reorganisation of existing business as a consequence of the acquisition.

Anti-avoidance measures

23.176 FRS 7 contains measures specifically addressed at a potential loophole concerning the timing of provisions for future reorganisation. Provisions for the type of expenditure to be incurred in reorganisation plans are generally booked before the relevant expenditure is incurred. Most acquisitions do not involve hostile bids, but are agreed between willing buyers and willing sellers. The ASB has been concerned that, particularly in the case of 'friendly' takeovers, there could be scope for provisions for reorganisation planned by the acquirer to be booked by the acquired company during the course of negotiations with the acquirer, and before the date of acquisition. Those provisions would then be entered as pre-acquisition liabilities when the newly acquired company is consolidated. An example is where reductions in excessive manpower in the acquired company are 'negotiated' during the course of the acquisition. Potentially a significant principle of the standard could relatively easily be circumvented.

23.177 The FRS (together with FRS 6, which contains the relevant disclosure provisions) deals in three ways with the problem of provisions made by the acquired company shortly before the acquisition. The explanation states that:

- Only if the acquired entity was demonstrably committed to the expenditure whether or not the acquisition was completed would it have a liability at the date of acquisition. [FRS 7 para 40].

- If obligations were incurred by the acquired entity as a result of the influence of the acquirer, it would be necessary to consider whether control had been transferred at an earlier date and, consequently, whether the date of acquisition under FRS 2 should also be taken to be an earlier date. [FRS 7 para 40].

- *Disclosure* is required in the fair value table of any provisions for reorganisation and restructuring costs made within the 12 months preceding the date of acquisition that are included in the identifiable liabilities acquired, together with related asset write-downs. [FRS 7 para 40; FRS 6 para 26].

23.178 As mentioned in paragraph 23.150 above, a pre-condition for inclusion in the identifiable liabilities at the date of acquisition is that the acquired entity must have been *committed* to a particular course of action by the date of acquisition.

23.179 This approach to the recognition of certain liabilities is already embodied in FRS 3, where principles are set out in respect of setting up provisions for losses on businesses to be sold or terminated. That standard requires a provision to be made if, but not before, a decision has been made to close an operation *and* the commitment is evidenced by a detailed formal plan from which the reporting entity cannot realistically withdraw.

23.180 It follows from the above that, if a reorganisation provision set up by the acquired entity before the date of acquisition relates to a reorganisation that is only implemented because of the acquisition, the provision should not be treated as an identifiable liability of the acquired entity in the fair value exercise. This is because the acquired entity is not committed to the expenditure before the acquisition, as it is conditional on the acquisition taking place.

23.181 Similarly, if a reorganisation provision set up by the acquired entity before the date of acquisition relates to its plans as a stand-alone operation, but those plans are subsequently cancelled by the acquirer before they have been implemented, the provision should not be treated as an identifiable liability of the acquired entity. That is because the acquired entity could not have been demonstrably committed to the expenditure regardless of whether or not the acquisition was completed.

23.182 In practice, it may be unlikely that management of a company being acquired could commit the company irrevocably to a particular course of action at the request of an acquiring company unless the completion of the acquisition was a foregone conclusion. If they did bind the acquired company, this might suggest that the acquirer had *de facto* already obtained control.

23.183 If the acquirer has gained control, the date of acquisition should be brought forward and the new subsidiary should be consolidated from the earlier date. Hence, the profits and losses (including the reorganisation provisions) would be brought into the acquirer's consolidated profit and loss account from that earlier date. Identifying the date of acquisition for the consolidated financial statements is dealt with in FRS 2 and is considered in section I of this chapter. It should be stressed that all aspects of the relationship between the acquirer and the target would need to be considered before the date of acquisition is brought forward. Where, for example, completion of the acquisition is conditional on the approval of the shareholders of the acquirer, it is unlikely that, in practice, control could have passed at an earlier date. It is equally unlikely in such a case that the acquired company could, in fact, commit itself irrevocably to the reorganisation.

23.184 The effect of the above anti-avoidance measures is that any commitments entered into by the acquired company at the request of the acquirer may well be deemed to be post-acquisition in substance. However, it is not unusual for a vendor to reorganise a business that is to be put up for sale in order to make the business more attractive to a potential purchaser. The purchase price would then reflect the business in its reorganised or semi-reorganised state. Thus reorganisation costs may be incurred by a company shortly before it is sold and there may be some provisions related to the reorganisation that are properly regarded as pre-acquisition liabilities.

23.185 The ASB also seeks to ensure that the spirit of FRS 7 is observed, in respect of reorganisation provisions, by requiring disclosure, in the fair value table, of any reorganisation provisions that were made by the acquired company in the 12 months immediately preceding the date of acquisition and which are included in its pre-acquisition liabilities. The example in Table 23.2 on page 23033 discloses the existence of such provisions.

Disclosure of post-acquisition reorganisation costs

23.186 FRS 7 requires that all post-acquisition reorganisation costs should be charged in the profit and loss account of the acquiring group. The ASB believes that, where they are material, separate disclosure of such costs is important for a proper assessment of post-acquisition performance to be made, particularly in the context of the 'information set' style of the profit and loss account under FRS 3. To some extent these disclosures may mitigate the adverse effect of the new accounting requirements in the eyes of preparers.

23.187 All the disclosure requirements relating to acquisitions, including those stemming from FRS 7, are consolidated in FRS 6. FRS 6 *requires* the following disclosure regarding reorganisation costs to be made in the financial statements of an acquiring group for each material acquisition, and for other acquisitions in aggregate:

- The profit and loss account or notes to the financial statements of periods following the acquisition should show the costs incurred in those periods in reorganising, restructuring and integrating the acquisition. [FRS 6 para 31].
- If material, these costs should be shown as exceptional items, and disclosed separately from other exceptional items, whether they relate to a fundamental restructuring or not. [FRS 6 para 86].

23.188 FRS 6 explains that post-acquisition integration, reorganisation and restructuring costs, including provisions in respect of them, would, if material, be reported as exceptional items under FRS 3. If, and only if, a reorganisation or restructuring is fundamental, having a material effect on the nature and focus of the *enlarged* group's operations, would the costs be included as one of the items required by paragraph 20 of FRS 3 to be shown separately on the face of the profit and loss account after operating profit and before interest. [FRS 6 para 86].

23.189 Tables 23.6 on page 23042, 23.9, 23.10, and 23.11 show examples of different methods that have been used to present acquisition reorganisation costs in the profit and loss account.

Table 23.9 – SmithKline Beecham plc – Annual Report and Accounts – 31 December 1994

CONSOLIDATED PROFIT AND LOSS ACCOUNT (extract)

	Notes	Comparable business £m	Acquisitions (note 1) £m	Business performance £m	One-off items (note 1) £m	1994 £m
Sales						
Continuing operations		5,877	194	6,071	–	**6,071**
Discontinued operations		421	–	421	–	**421**
	1	6,298	194	6,492	–	**6,492**
Cost of goods sold		(2,109)	(95)	(2,204)	(243)	**(2,447)**
Gross profit		4,189	99	4,288	(243)	**4,045**
Selling, general and administrative expenses	2	(2,261)	(85)	(2,346)	(320)	**(2,666)**
Research and development expenditure	2	(620)	(1)	(621)	(17)	**(638)**
Trading profit						
Continuing operations	1&2	1,224	13	1,237	(580)	**657**
Discontinued operations	1&2	84	–	84	–	**84**

NOTES TO THE FINANCIAL STATEMENTS (extract)

One-off items

A restructuring provision, to be utilised over three years, of £580 million has been established and is included under a separate column headed 'one-off items' on the profit and loss account. This provision is to cover the cost of closing Sterling's New York headquarters; the integration of the Sterling and existing Consumer Healthcare operations; the establishment of an integrated Pharmaceutical and Consumer Healthcare International business; the creation of shared services across all of the business operations and the reorganisation of the Group's supply chain.

The 'one-off items' column also includes the tax charge arising on the reorganisation of Sterling in connection with the sale by SB of Sterling's North American business and a credit associated with the deferred tax asset arising on the creation of the restructuring provision. (see note 5).

Table 23.10 – Reckitt & Colman plc – Report & Accounts – 31 December 1994

Group profit and loss account (extract)

Notes		1994 £m	1993 £m
3	**Sales to customers:**		
	Continuing operations	**2,070.78**	2,068.09
	Discontinued operations	**8.17**	27.56
	Total sales to customers	**2,078.95**	2,095.65
3	Cost of sales	**(1,073.22)**	(1,048.26)
	Gross profit	**1,005.73**	1,047.39
	Net operating expenses	**(834.67)**	(735.94)
3	**Operating profit:**		
	Continuing operations[1]	**169.35**	305.22
	Discontinued operations	**1.71**	6.23
4	**Total operating profit**	**171.06**	311.45

[1] In 1994 operating profit from continuing operations is stated after charging exceptional reorganisation costs of £56.00m in Europe and £83.10m in connection with the L&F Household integration in the USA.

Table 23.11 – Scottish Power plc – Annual Report & Accounts – 31 March 1996

Group Profit and Loss Account (extract)

	Before acquisitions 1996 £m	Acquisitions 1996 £m	Total before reorganisation costs 1996 £m	Reorganisation costs 1996 £m	Total 1996 £m	Total 1995 £m
Turnover from continuing operations	**1,832.1**	**439.4**	**2,271.5**	–	**2,271.5**	1,715.8
Cost of sales	**(1,091.3)**	**(283.7)**	**(1,375.0)**	–	**(1,375.0)**	(1,011.8)
Gross profit from continuing operations	**740.8**	**155.7**	**896.5**	–	**896.5**	704.0
Transmission and distribution costs	**(152.4)**	**(49.8)**	**(202.2)**	**(1.0)**	**(203.2)**	(141.9)
Administrative expenses	**(199.6)**	**(28.6)**	**(228.2)**	**(41.7)**	**(269.9)**	(188.0)
Other operating income	**7.8**	**3.1**	**10.9**	–	**10.9**	6.0
Operating profit from continuing operations	**396.6**	**80.4**	**477.0**	**(42.7)**	**434.3**	380.1

The group profit and loss account includes under Acquisitions the results of Manweb for the period 6 October 1995 to 31 March 1996.

23.190 Where a post-acquisition reorganisation does not qualify as fundamental in the context of the operations of the enlarged group, the costs should be charged in arriving at the profit or loss on ordinary activities before tax and shown under the statutory format headings to which they relate. In practice, this means that reorganisation costs that qualify as exceptional items (but are not fundamental) would be shown in arriving at operating profit or loss. In accordance with FRS 3 the amount should be disclosed separately by way of note, or on the face of the profit and loss account if that is necessary to give a true and fair view.

23.191 FRS 6 *suggests* that, for major acquisitions where post-acquisition reorganisation is expected to extend over more than one period, management may wish to disclose in the notes the total expenditure expected to be incurred and the nature of the expenditure. This suggested disclosure analyses the total: between amounts charged in the profit and loss account and further amounts expected to be incurred; and between cash expenditure and asset write-offs. [FRS 6 para 87].

23.192 The above-mentioned suggested disclosures were in response to users who believed that it is important to be able to ascertain the total expected costs relating to an acquisition. They also enable management to present what they believe to be the true total acquisition cost, that is, the consideration given for the acquisition plus, for example, the planned costs of turning the acquisition around and integrating it into the acquiring group. Appendix IV to FRS 6 gives an example of the type of disclosure that the ASB had in mind.

23.193 Many companies already give significant disclosures about the progress of recent acquisitions, details of post-acquisition integration plans and their associated costs in the part of the annual report in which the Board reviews the group's activities for the year. The ASB's own recommendations for the content of an Operating and Financial Review (OFR) contain some specific references to acquisitions. For example it recommends that the OFR should discuss significant features of operating performance, including the effects of material acquisitions and it states that "*the discussion should comment on the extent to which the expectations at the time of acquisition have been realised*". [OFR para 10]. Clearly, discussion of post-acquisition reorganisation plans and their likely future benefits, together with the subsequent monitoring of those costs and benefits, would form an integral part of this disclosure.

23.194 For listed companies it is always open to them to give an additional earnings per share figure that adds back exceptional post-acquisition reorganisation costs. FRS 3 and FRS 14 permit EPS to be calculated at other levels of profit, provided that such other calculations are made on a consistent basis over time and are reconciled to the basic EPS figure required by FRS 14.

23.195 There are two practical issues regarding the disclosure of exceptional post-acquisition reorganisation costs required by FRS 6:

- What is *fundamental* in the context of the enlarged group?
- Which costs should be included in the captions that are required to be separately disclosed as costs of *reorganising, restructuring and integrating the acquisition*?

Fundamental reorganisation or not

23.196 Identifying a fundamental reorganisation under FRS 3 is considered in chapter 7. FRS 6 makes it clear that whether a post-acquisition reorganisation is fundamental must be judged in relation to the enlarged group. It is not automatic that such costs would be shown as a non-operating exceptional item. Clearly, the use of judgement is required to determine whether a particular reorganisation is fundamental or not. However, by requiring the reorganisation to have a material effect on both the nature and focus of the enlarged group's operations, it is implicit that the reorganisation should encompass the whole or a substantial part of the enlarged group's total operations and should not be a reorganisation of only one among many different operations of the enlarged group.

23.197 At one end of the spectrum, a group may acquire a new subsidiary and run it as a stand alone operation. The acquired subsidiary may be reorganised to achieve cost savings, but the existing operations of the subsidiary and the group are essentially left intact. The reorganisation would not be fundamental to the enlarged group, nor even probably to the acquired subsidiary. In this situation, the reorganisation costs should be charged in arriving at operating profit and, if material, separately identified. FRS 3 already requires the profit and loss account of an acquiring group to disclose separately (in aggregate) the operating results attributable to acquisitions made in the year, as a component of the group's continuing operations.

23.198 At the other end of the spectrum, a group may make a substantial acquisition in its core business. Soon after the acquisition the business of the new subsidiary is subsumed into the existing operations of the acquiring group. The post-acquisition plan for the enlarged group involves material expenditure in respect of both integrating the combining operations and repositioning their market focus. This results in the enlarged group withdrawing from certain market sectors and investing in those that are core to the group's future strategy. The restructuring goes to the root of the enlarged group's operations and the repositioning process includes significant asset disposals from both the pre-existing and acquired operations. In these circumstances, the post-acquisition reorganisation is likely to be fundamental and the costs would be shown separately after operating profit.

23.199 However, in the majority of cases it is likely that post acquisition reorganisation costs will be included as part of the acquiring group's operating results and not as fundamental reorganisation or restructuring. Although the integration of combining operations may require significant reorganisation across the enlarged group, this fact alone does not make the reorganisation fundamental. A fundamental reorganisation must involve a material change in the nature and focus of the enlarged group's operations – that is, the combined operations of the acquirer and acquired business after the acquisition – and this would need to result in the repositioning of its products or services in their markets.

Nature of reorganisation costs

23.200 The nature of reorganisation costs is important because requiring post-acquisition reorganisation costs to be shown in the profit and loss account would not, of itself, remove the often publicised possibilities under previous practices for flattering the operating results following an acquisition. In practice, the headline reporting of performance tends to focus on a company's operating results. If the amount shown under exceptional reorganisation costs (in particular, fundamental costs) were inflated by items that should properly be shown as normal operating costs, the operating result would also be inflated.

23.201 FRS 6 gives, in the standard section, a strict definition of which costs are permitted, as a matter of principle, to be included in the captions of costs relating to reorganising, restructuring and integrating an acquisition. It states that such costs are those that:

- Would not have been incurred had the acquisition not taken place.
- Relate to a project identified and controlled by management as part of a reorganisation or integration programme set up at the time of acquisition or as a direct consequence of an immediate post-acquisition review.

[FRS 6 para 31].

23.202 Subject to meeting the criteria in the above paragraph, examples of costs that might be included under this definition are:

- Employee redundancy and early retirement costs.
- Costs of relocating facilities as part of an integration plan.
- Contract cancellation costs.
- Plant closure costs, including costs of eliminating duplicate facilities.
- Write-off of fixed assets and stocks relating to the reorganisation.

(The write-down of assets is mentioned in paragraph 87 of FRS 6 as a potential component of reorganisation costs, which suggests that the profit and loss charge is properly shown under reorganisation costs rather than as, for example, losses on the disposal of fixed assets.)

- Incremental costs incurred in converting branches of the acquired company into the format of the acquiring group.
- Incremental costs incurred in implementing the administrative and management information systems of the acquiring group into the acquired company.
- Costs of retraining the workforce of the acquired company.

23.203 FRS 6 refers to costs of integrating as well as reorganising and restructuring the acquisition. Consequently, it appears that some integration costs admitted under this caption could relate to the acquirer's own business, provided that the costs are incurred as a direct consequence of the acquisition and relate directly to the activities being integrated. Such costs might include the following:

- Costs of closing facilities in the acquiring group that are duplicated in the enlarged group in preference to closing those of the acquired company.
- Costs of redundancies in the acquiring group resulting from the merging of head office functions.

23.204 Where other activities of the acquiring group are reorganised following an acquisition, the costs would not be admitted into the FRS 6 definition.

23.205 The following items would not appear to qualify as costs of reorganising, restructuring and integrating the acquisition. They should be included in the relevant headings in normal operating costs:

- Ongoing salaries of staff to be made redundant, unless they have effectively been made redundant, that is they have ceased to provide services to the group.
- Operating costs of running facilities to be merged or closed pending the implementation of the reorganisation plan.
- Internal management costs relating to time spent on developing and implementing the reorganisation plan.

23.206 It might be argued that some of the above items, for example, the 'additional' costs of running two departments rather than one, should be included as reorganisation costs because they are additional costs incurred from the time of the acquisition to the date of the implementation of the reorganisation. Arguments against this are: first, it does not reflect what happened after the acquisition, because the fact is that two departments did exist and their operating costs were incurred; secondly, it is probable that each of the departments in fact carried out a necessary task up to the date that the reorganisation was implemented and, therefore, until that time the costs incurred were not, in fact, 'additional' costs.

Disclosure of acquisition provisions

23.207 FRS 6 *requires* movements on provisions or accruals for costs related to an acquisition to be disclosed and analysed between the amounts used for the specific purpose for which they were created and the amounts released unused. [FRS 6 para 32]. The information should be disclosed separately for each material acquisition and for other non-material acquisitions in aggregate.

23.208 This requirement is similar to the disclosure previously required by SSAP 22 in respect of provisions related to acquisitions. The difference is that, whereas the provisions disclosed under SSAP 22 were generally made as fair value adjustments, the provisions disclosable under FRS 7 would generally have been charged to the post-acquisition profit and loss account. The disclosure would include the run-off of any existing provisions related to acquisitions accounted for under the old rules of SSAP 22. An example is given in Table 23.12.

Table 23.12 – Glaxo Wellcome plc – Annual Report and Accounts – 31 December 1995

Notes on the Accounts (extract)

19 Provisions for liabilities and charges (extract)	Integration costs	Pensions and other post-retirement benefits	Deferred taxation	Other provisions	Total
	£m	£m	£m	£m	£m
At 1st July 1994 as previously stated	–	90	139	64	293
Prior period adjustment	–	26	(9)	–	17
At 1st July 1994 restated	–	116	130	64	310
Exchange adjustments	–	3	(3)	2	2
Acquisition of subsidiary undertakings	–	92	187	75	354
Charge/(credit) for the period	1,215	138	(251)	67	1,169
Applied	(384)	(34)	(33)	(67)	(518)
At 31st December 1995	831	315	30	141	1,317

The provision for integration costs at 31st December 1995 represents the costs expected to be incurred in integrating the businesses of Glaxo and Wellcome.

23.209 The words 'accruals for costs' have been added to the previous standard. This is interpreted to mean that the information should be given in respect of all material costs accrued and shown in the profit and loss account as costs of reorganising, restructuring and integrating an acquisition and not just those that are shown in the balance sheet under the caption of provisions.

23.210 FRS 6 and 7 set out requirements for identifying and disclosing post-acquisition reorganisation costs. They do not provide any guidance on the principles for setting up provisions for such costs where they are expected to be incurred over more than one period. Recognition and measurement rules that apply to provisions for restructuring costs generally are contained in FRS 12. These rules affect the amount of 'one-off' acquisition reorganisation provisions that can be charged in the immediate post-acquisition period. Where costs relating to a post-acquisition reorganisation and integration programme are charged over more than one period, FRS 6 suggests that management may wish to disclose the total expected costs, indicating the extent to which they have been charged in the profit and loss account, in order to give a fuller picture of the progress of the post-acquisition plan. [FRS 6 para 87]. Appendix IV to the standard provides an illustration, in tabular form, of how this information might be presented by analysing details of amounts charged and amounts still to be charged.

Measuring fair values of identifiable assets and liabilities

Meaning of fair value

23.211 FRS 7 defines fair value as:

> *"The amount at which an asset or liability could be exchanged in an arm's length transaction between informed and willing parties, other than in a forced or liquidation sale".* [FRS 7 para 2].

23.212 This basic definition of fair value, or similar versions of it, is well recognised in accounting literature. The problem in accounting for business combinations is that many of the assets and liabilities to be recognised in an acquisition are not regularly exchanged in arm's length transactions. Consequently, the definition is of limited practical use in measuring fair values for this purpose.

23.213 Before FRS 7, it had been accepted practice for acquisitions to be fair valued from the perspective of the acquiring company. The perspective of the acquirer was favoured because it took into account the acquirer's plans for the future and its style of operation. It was also consistent with the concept of the acquirer's perspective that provisions for reorganisation costs included in those plans should be taken into account in the fair value exercise.

23.214 The ASB considered that the notion of a 'fair value to the acquiring company' seemed to contradict the basic definition of fair value, which is a market value concept reflecting both buyers and sellers. The ASB also argued that, as a general principle, management intent is not a sufficient basis for recognising changes to an entity's assets and liabilities; and in the context of acquisition accounting, the acquirer's intentions regarding the future use of acquired assets are not necessarily relevant to determining their cost.

23.215 Consequently, FRS 7 rejected the acquirer's perspective as a principle for determining fair values. Instead, the standard attempts to adhere to the definition of fair value by requiring that:

- Fair values should reflect the conditions at the date of acquisition.
- Fair values should *not* reflect:
  - Changes resulting from the acquirer's intentions or future actions.
  - Impairments, or other changes, resulting from events subsequent to the acquisition.

[FRS 7 paras 6, 7].

23.216 The basic concept of fair value in FRS 7 is, therefore, free from any particular 'perspective'. It attempts to establish what the price paid for a whole business represented, taking into account the conditions of the acquired business, including its existing cost structures, that existed at the time of acquisition.

23.217 The last part of the definition of fair value in paragraph 23.211 indicates that fair values of individual assets and liabilities should generally be valued on a going concern basis, even if the business was acquired cheaply in a fire sale from, for example, a vendor who was in financial difficulty. In circumstances where the acquirer has obtained a bargain purchase as a result of a forced or liquidation sale, the fair values of the identifiable net assets may well exceed the cost of acquisition, with negative goodwill arising on consolidation.

23.218 The standard provides a detailed framework for establishing fair values for individual categories of assets and liabilities. Although the concept of fair value as described above is intended to prevail, there are several exceptions or modifications to the concept when applied in practice to certain assets and liabilities where market values do not exist. This framework draws heavily on the chapter of the ASB's draft Statement of Principles, 'Measurement in Financial Statements', that deals with valuations in financial statements generally. This describes the concept of deprival value or 'value to the business' that in many cases corresponds to fair value under FRS 7.

23.219 The overall framework can be summarised as follows:

- Fair values are indicated by market values where similar assets are bought and sold on a readily accessible market.

[The next page is 23079.]

- Where market values are not available, or are inappropriate to the circumstances of the acquired company, fair values should be based on replacement cost, reflecting the acquired company's normal buying process and the sources of supply and prices available to it (but see below).

- The fair value of an asset should not exceed its recoverable amount. Therefore, where the fair value of an asset is based on its depreciated replacement cost, the recoverable amount will also need to be considered.

  The recoverable amount of an asset is in effect the maximum discounted cash flows that can be obtained from the asset, either by selling it or by continuing to use it (see para 23.261 below).

- A valuation of an asset at recoverable amount should reflect its condition on acquisition, but not any impairments or enhancements resulting from subsequent events or actions of the acquirer.

- The accounting policies of the acquiring group should be adopted where they affect fair values attributed to assets and liabilities.

23.220 The attribution of fair values is not determined from the 'acquirer's perspective', in the sense that the acquirer's intentions for the future use of assets do not affect the valuation of the business as it stood when it was acquired. However, fair values can only be arrived at under the system described in paragraph 23.219 after a detailed investigation of the acquisition by the acquirer. Therefore, in several cases fair values would represent the acquirer's judgement of the worth of the underlying assets in their existing state.

23.221 Examples of situations where considerable judgement needs to be exercised by the acquirer include:

- Review of useful lives of fixed assets, for determining depreciated replacement cost.

- Compilation of cash flow projections for the business being acquired, for determining the recoverable amount of assets where the business is unable to recover the depreciated replacement cost.

- Review of provisions against the value of slow-moving stock, for determining net realisable value.

- Review of the recoverability of debtors.

23.222 In carrying out the fair value exercise, it would be appropriate to work at a fairly detailed level and, therefore, to assign fair values to individual assets or small groups of assets. For example, if a property portfolio is being fair valued, it would usually be necessary to carry out the exercise on individual assets. Clearly, this may not be possible where stocks are concerned. Also, where a business of the acquired company is to be resold soon after acquisition, the standard requires the whole business unit to be valued as a single item (see further para 23.301).

Period for completing the fair value exercise

23.223 The standard requires that fair values of assets and liabilities should be based on conditions at the date of acquisition. They should not generally be affected by matters arising after this date. In practice, sufficient time is required to enable an acquirer to examine the acquisition in order to identify all the assets and liabilities existing at the date of acquisition and to perform a full and reliable fair value exercise.

23.224 As far as the assets and liabilities of the acquired company are concerned, the fair value exercise should, if possible, be completed by the date on which the board of the acquirer approves for publication the acquiring group's first annual financial statements following the acquisition. [FRS 7 para 23].

23.225 However, the standard recognises that some acquisitions need more time to be properly investigated. Situations where this is likely to arise include the following:

- The acquisition is complex and is completed late in the financial year of the acquirer.

- The acquired company has assets and liabilities where more evidence is required before they can be valued reliably – examples include evaluating environmental liabilities and contingent liabilities involving legal claims.

23.226 In circumstances where the fair value exercise cannot be completed in time for publication of the acquirer's first post-acquisition financial statements, FRS 7 requires *provisional* fair values to be included. These provisional fair values should be amended, if necessary, in the next financial statements with a corresponding adjustment to goodwill. [FRS 7 para 24].

23.227 The cut-off point for making fair value adjustments is, therefore, the date of approval of the acquirer's second annual financial statements after the acquisition. By basing the investigation period on the financial year of the acquirer rather than on an absolute time limit, there could in practice be significant differences in the time available for completing the fair value exercise in respect of different acquisitions. The time available depends on the timing of an acquisition in relation to the financial year end of the acquirer and could, in theory, extend for over two years.

Subsequent amendments to fair values

Amendments after investigation period has expired

23.228 Amendments may still be necessary to fair values after the investigation period, as described above, has expired. Because the standard does not allow any further goodwill adjustments to be made, the effect of such amendments should, where applicable, be dealt with in the profit and loss account for the year. If material, they may require separate disclosure as exceptional items.

23.229 The only exception to the above treatment is where amendments discovered outside the permitted investigation period result from fundamental errors in the fair value exercise rather than from the normal process of revising estimates that is inherent in financial reporting. An example is where hidden problems relating to past activities of the acquired company are only discovered later by the acquirer. In these circumstances, the fundamental errors would, in accordance with FRS 3, be treated as prior period adjustments, that is by adjusting the goodwill arising on the acquisition.

23.230 An example of adjustments that have been treated as fundamental errors was contained in the accounts of Ferranti (see Table 23.13).

Table 23.13 – Ferranti International Signal plc – Annual report & accounts (revised) – 31 March 1989

Notes to the accounts (extracts)

1 Bases of accounting

For the reasons given in paragraphs 2 to 4 of the Report of the Directors the accounts of the group and the parent company for the year ended 31 March 1989, despatched to shareholders on 11 August 1989, have been withdrawn and revised to write off assets in respect of certain suspect contracts (as defined in the Report of the Directors) and incorporate a consequential adjustment to the fair value of the net tangible assets of International Signal & Control Group PLC ("ISC") at the date of acquisition by the company, 16 November 1987, and a restatement of the comparative amounts shown for the year ended 31 March 1988. No credit has been taken for any amounts which may be recoverable from third parties in respect of the suspect contracts. The Revised Accounts also reflect other adjustments for post balance sheet events occasioned by the extension of the date of approval of the Accounts from 13 July 1989 to 16 November 1989 and reflecting additional evidence relating to conditions in the group existing at 31 March 1989.

Note 20 Reserves (extract)

	Share premium £M	Merger £M	Revaluation £M	Profit & loss £M	Total £M
Group					
As previously reported at 31 March 1988	3.8	73.5	38.9	152.4	268.6
Adjustment in respect of acquisitions other than ISC		17.0		(17.0)	–
Adjustment to the fair value of the net tangible assets of ISC as at the date of acquisition		(90.5)		(50.9)	(141.4)
Adjustment to retained profit:					
Operating profit previously taken on suspect contracts				(13.5)	(13.5)
Consequential tax effects				4.7	4.7
Currency translation effects	–	–	–	12.1	12.1
As restated at 31 March 1988	3.8	–	38.9	87.8	130.5
Deficit for the year				(6.6)	(6.6)
Premium on allotments	1.0				1.0
Goodwill arising on acquisitions (note 21)				(4.0)	(4.0)
Sale of revalued property			(0.4)		(0.4)
Currency translation	–	–	–	(5.0)	(5.0)
At 31 March 1989	4.8	–	38.5	72.2	115.5

Amendments within investigation period

23.231 Where fair values attributed to the assets and liabilities of an acquired company are considered provisional in the acquirer's first post-acquisition financial statements, FRS 6 requires this fact to be stated and the reasons to be given. It also requires any material adjustments made to those fair values in the next financial statements, with corresponding adjustments to goodwill, to be disclosed and explained. [FRS 6 para 27].

23.232 The FRRP published a statement in April 1997 in connection with the financial statements of Reckitt & Colman plc concerning the adequacy of the disclosure of final adjustments to provisional fair values. The Panel noted that in its view this second stage requires a similar level of disclosure and explanation so as to comply with the requirements of paragraph 25 of FRS 6 and paragraph 13(5) of Schedule 4A to the Act and should include an analysis of the adjustments and an explanation of the reasons for them.

23.233 An example of a provisional fair value allocation and subsequent goodwill adjustment is taken from the accounts of RJB Mining PLC (see Table 23.14).

Table 23.14 – RJB Mining PLC – Annual Report and Accounts – 31 December 1995

NOTES TO THE FINANCIAL STATEMENTS (extract)

23 Goodwill on acquisition of English Coal	Provisional fair value to the Group 1994 £'000	Completion and hindsight period adjustments 1995 £'000	Final fair value to the Group 1995 £'000
Fixed assets	643,818	(84,258)	559,560
Stock & WIP			
Coal stock	189,407	6,121	195,528
Stores	54,927	(8,278)	46,649
Work in progress	95,271	(11,781)	83,490
Debtors	2,395	(1,604)	791
Creditors	(28,264)	(1,568)	(29,832)
Provisions for liabilities and charges			
Concessionary coal	(29,041)	–	(29,041)
Claims	(43,500)	1,673	(41,827)
Surface damage	(28,439)	–	(28,439)
Restoration and closure costs (opencast)	(41,580)	–	(41,580)
Restoration and closure costs (deep mines)	(8,832)	(1,380)	(10,212)
Draglines maintenance	(3,597)	2,508	(1,089)
Deferred taxation	(17,000)	38,441	21,441
	785,565	(60,126)	725,439
Purchase consideration	844,289	(1,074)	843,215
Goodwill written off	58,724	59,052	117,776

The principal adjustments to fair value to the group are in respect of the Asfordby colliery which has been written down to a nominal carrying value following a reassessment due to the difficult geological conditions and consequent operational problems associated with safe and economic extraction of coal from these reserves. The other adjustments to fair value in the hindsight period relate to agreement of the final acquisition cost and to asset and liability valuation and existence assessments in the period.

1. Asfordby	£77.8m
2. Revaluation of deferred opencast assets	£11.5m
3. Other	£8.2m
4. Deferred tax on adjustments	(£38.4m)

23.234 FRS 7 indicates that fair values should not be considered provisional in the first post-acquisition financial statements unless it has not been possible to complete the investigation of fair values by then and the fact is disclosed in those financial statements. This would suggest that, where an acquirer has completed its investigation of the acquisition by the date of approval of the financial statements for the year in which the acquisition took place, and obtained all the evidence considered necessary at that time to arrive at reliable estimates of fair values based on information then available, no further adjustments should be made to those fair values (and goodwill) in the subsequent financial year.

23.235 Even if additional information is obtained in the next financial year which causes previous estimates to be changed, those changes would usually be dealt with in the profit and loss account of the period in which they are identified. This principle is consistent with normal practice in financial statements, where items relating to prior periods, which arise from corrections and adjustments that are the natural result of estimates inherent in accounting and in the periodic preparation of financial statements, are dealt with as they arise and are not adjusted retrospectively.

23.236 However, there may be exceptional situations where fair values and goodwill would need to be adjusted retrospectively in the acquirer's second post-acquisition financial statements, even where the fair values attributed to the acquired company at the previous balance sheet date had not been declared provisional in the previous financial statements.

23.237 For example, paragraph 57 of the explanatory section in FRS 7 discusses the treatment of exceptional stock profits arising after the date of acquisition. It states that, if exceptional profits appear to have been earned on the realisation of stocks after the date of acquisition, it will be necessary to re-examine the fair values determined on acquisition and, if necessary, to make an adjustment to these values and a corresponding adjustment to goodwill. It goes on to state that, if, alternatively, the profit is attributable to post-acquisition events, it should be disclosed as an exceptional item in the post-acquisition profit and loss account.

23.238 Paragraph 57 is clearly addressing a potential source of abuse, because errors made in calculating the fair value of stocks quickly feed through into the profit and loss account. If the fair value attributed to stocks is understated, post-acquisition profits are inflated by their realisation in the post-acquisition period.

Fair valuing fixed assets

23.239 If there are separately identifiable asset transactions in an acquisition, the bargained price would normally provide the initial fair value, that is, actual cost, assuming the price is a proper arm's length value. In other cases, fair values should be estimated using conventional measurement principles, that is, market value, replacement cost or recoverable amount. FRS 7 requires the choice of valuation basis to be determined by a structured analysis of the circumstances, as summarised in paragraph 23.219 above.

Market value

23.240 Where there is a ready market in the types of fixed assets held by the acquired company, market values should generally be used. Such assets would include properties in which an active market exists. Properties that are sometimes referred to as *non-specialised* properties may be included in this category – examples include shops, offices, and general purpose warehouses that could be occupied by a number of different users. Professional valuers would normally be required to value such assets.

23.241 Where assets are sold shortly after the acquisition, the price obtained will often provide the most reliable evidence of fair value at the date of acquisition.

23.242 There may be some confusion as to what market value means, because variants are used in practice when properties are included in accounts at valuations. The most commonly used bases are open market value and existing use value. Until a consistent framework or guidelines are established for revaluing properties generally, it is not possible to be dogmatic about the question of market value in the fair value exercise.

23.243 Guidelines for the valuation of property assets for the purposes of financial statements are presently contained in the RICS Appraisal and Valuation Manual, published by the Royal Institution of Chartered Surveyors (RICS).

23.244 Open market value (without qualification) as defined in those statements reflects the value for any use to the extent to which that value is reflected in the price obtainable in the open market, assuming that a reasonable period of time is allowed for marketing and selling the asset. This definition corresponds closely to the definition of fair value in FRS 7, and is the basis generally used for valuing investment properties, properties held for future development and surplus properties.

23.245 Existing use value, until recently referred to by the RICS as 'open market value for existing use', is the basis normally used for valuing properties that are occupied in the company's business and that have not been declared surplus. It is based on open market value, but the valuation reflects an important assumption that the property can be used for the foreseeable future only for the existing use. It is intended to represent the cost of replacing the remaining service potential of a property.

23.246 Neither open market value nor existing use value include any value attributable to the goodwill generated by the business that occupies the property with the following exception. A variation of existing use value is 'existing use as a fully operational business unit'. This basis applies to properties that invariably change hands in the open market at prices based directly on trading potential for a strictly limited use. Examples of such properties include hotels, private hospitals and nursing homes, public houses, cinemas, theatres, bingo clubs, gaming clubs, petrol filling stations, licensed betting offices and specialised leisure and sporting facilities. The valuation includes the value of the trading potential which runs with the property, but should not include any goodwill which has been created by the owner and which would not remain with the property should it be sold.

23.247 In acquisition accounting, properties that would normally be valued, under the alternative accounting rules, on an existing use value basis in the acquired company's financial statements (that is, those occupied for the purpose of its business) would also usually be valued on this basis in the fair value exercise. That is because FRS 7 requires fair values to reflect the conditions of the acquired company at the date of acquisition. If an acquirer determines to change the use of an acquired property, subsequently carrying out the necessary planning and redevelopment procedures, any resulting change in value is attributable to the acquirer's actions and, consequently, treated as post-acquisition as required by paragraph 7 of FRS 7.

23.248 FRS 7 discusses the use of market values in secondhand assets. It states that where a fair value is based on a market price, it is important to ensure that such price is appropriate to the circumstances of the acquired business. [FRS 7 para 44].

23.249 Fixed assets that can be traded in secondhand markets include cars, commercial vehicles, computer equipment and certain plant and machinery. Where, for example, a company operates a fleet of vehicles, the market price of a used vehicle that is not due for replacement may be irrelevant to the business if, as is usually the case, it would never consider replacing vehicles in the secondhand market. In this situation the standard indicates that the fair value of a vehicle should be taken to be the current purchase price of a new vehicle, depreciated to reflect its age and condition. For certain used assets the depreciated replacement cost could be significantly different from the value in the secondhand market owing to a different pattern of depreciation in value.

23.250 As a general rule, depreciated replacement cost should be used for such assets unless the acquired business is genuinely able to consider the purchase of secondhand equipment as a viable alternative to purchasing new replacement assets.

Depreciated replacement cost

23.251 Where market values are not applicable, FRS 7 explains that depreciated replacement cost should be used as a proxy for fair value, provided it does not exceed the recoverable amount.

23.252 Depreciated replacement cost should reflect the acquired business's normal buying process and the sources of supply and prices available to it. [FRS 7 para 9].

23.253 Depreciated replacement cost is normally used by professional valuers for valuing *specialised* properties. These are defined in the RICS valuation manual as those properties which, due to their specialised nature are rarely, if ever, sold on the open market for single occupation for a continuation of their existing use, except as part of a sale of the business in occupation. Depreciated replacement cost would also generally be the appropriate basis of valuation of such properties in a fair value exercise. Examples of properties that might be valued on this basis include chemical installations, power stations, docks, breweries and other special purpose factories.

23.254 Depreciated replacement cost is the proper basis for fair valuing most items of plant and machinery. This may be viewed as the cost of replacing an asset with one having a similar service potential.

23.255 In principle, all fixed assets should be fair valued. The carrying value in the financial statements of an acquired company should not be used in the fair value exercise unless there is a reasonable basis for concluding that the current depreciated replacement cost is not materially different.

23.256 The gross replacement cost of an asset may be determined by reference to sources of information such as:

- Suppliers' quotations and current price lists.
- Recent purchases of the same or similar assets.
- Expert knowledge of the industry, which might include expert opinion.
- Relevant specific price indices for indexing historical cost.
- Cost of modern equivalent assets.

23.257 To arrive at the depreciated replacement cost, an appropriate amount of depreciation should be deducted to reflect the age and condition of the asset. FRS 7 explains that when the acquirer is assessing the remaining useful lives and, where applicable, residual values of fixed assets for the purposes of arriving at an estimate of their depreciated replacement cost, the *acquirer's* own policies for determining depreciation rates for similar assets should be used where these differ from the acquired company's. This is consistent with the general principle in FRS 7 that accounting policies should be harmonised by way of fair value adjustments, so that post-acquisition profit and loss accounts are not distorted by this type of non-performance adjustment.

23.258 Where government grants would be available to the acquired company for the replacement of fixed assets, it would be consistent with the principles of FRS 7 for allowance to be made for such grants in the calculation of a depreciated replacement cost to the acquired company. The fair value would be reduced by the notional grant; the amount of grant deducted would normally be calculated as an amortised amount that matches the amount of depreciation deducted from the gross replacement cost in order to reflect the acquired asset's age and condition. (Any deferred income in the books of the acquired company relating to grants previously received for the purchase of fixed assets would be eliminated on consolidation.)

23.259 Fair valuing by one of the techniques referred to above is inherently a process of estimation and as a practical measure it seems acceptable to use an appropriate level of aggregation for valuing groups of similar assets rather than valuing each asset separately.

Recoverable amount

23.260 Although depreciated replacement cost places a cap on the fair values that a purchaser can ascribe, fair value should not exceed the asset's recoverable amount. In fact, the RICS guidelines require a valuer to qualify every valuation prepared on a depreciated replacement cost basis as being subject to the adequate potential profitability of the business having due regard to the value of the total assets employed and the nature of the operation.

23.261 'Recoverable amount' is defined in FRS 7 as *"the greater of the net realisable value of an asset and, where appropriate, the value in use"*. 'Value in use' is defined as *"the present value of the future cash flows obtainable as a result of an asset's continued use, including those resulting from the ultimate disposal of the asset"*. [FRS 7 para 2]. In other words the fair value attributed to a fixed asset should not exceed the net cash flows the business can recover from the asset, either by disposing of it or by continuing to use it. This is one of the most difficult and subjective areas of valuation in practice.

23.262 FRS 7 explains that an asset is impaired when its replacement cost is not recoverable in full. The recoverable amount should be assessed to reflect the condition of the asset on acquisition, but not any impairments resulting from subsequent events or actions of the acquirer. [FRS 7 para 47]. Thus, for example, if an acquirer decides to close a profitable factory occupied by the acquired company in order to rationalise the enlarged group's manufacturing facilities, any asset write-downs related to the closure (to reduce the assets' carrying values to net realisable value) should be charged in the post-acquisition profit and loss account and should not be included in the attributed fair values.

23.263 Recoverable amount needs to be considered in situations where it is unlikely that a fixed asset would be worth replacing at its current replacement cost because, even with the most efficient and profitable use of the asset, the business could not generate sufficient cash flows to earn an adequate return on the investment. Examples might include businesses owning major infrastructure assets whose replacement cost could not be recovered in full from the cash flows of the acquired business. In such situations, fair values reflecting lower recoverable amounts would need to be estimated.

23.264 The recoverable amount of fixed assets also needs to be reviewed in circumstances where the fair value exercise gives rise to negative goodwill, that is, where the fair values assigned to the identifiable assets and liabilities exceed, in aggregate, the cost of acquisition. FRS 10 requires the fair values of the acquired assets to be tested for impairment and the fair values of the acquired liabilities checked carefully to ensure that none has been omitted or understated. [FRS 10 para 48].

23.265 Where negative goodwill arising on an acquisition is material, after reviewing the assets' recoverable amounts, this may indicate that the acquirer has made a genuine bargain purchase, for example as a result of a distress sale. However, under FRS 7, negative goodwill may arise in other circumstances. For example, the purchase consideration for an acquisition may be lower than the fair value of the net assets acquired, because the acquired business is in need of reorganisation. The purchase price may reflect the fact that the acquirer has to incur reorganisation costs after the acquisition. FRS 7 does not allow the anticipated reorganisation costs to be recognised as an identifiable liability in the fair value exercise; it requires the reorganisation costs to be expensed in the profit and loss account of the acquiring group.

23.266 Where the recoverable amount of an asset is estimated by reference to the 'value in use', that is *via* projected future cash flows, those cash flows should be discounted to their present value. Any valuation based on future cash flows is inherently very subjective.

23.267 One problem is that it is often very difficult to attribute cash flows to individual fixed assets. In estimating future cash flows for determining recoverable amount, FRS 7 allows assets to be considered as a group where they are used jointly. [FRS 7 para 49]. The grouping of assets by reference to cash flows is also inevitably subjective. One approach would be for such grouping to be taken as the smallest group of assets for which cash flows can be identified that are broadly independent of the cash flows of other assets or groups of assets. This approach has been adopted in FRS 11, 'Impairment of fixed assets and goodwill', which specifies methods for measuring value in use when fixed assets are reviewed for impairment. Such impairment reviews are usually carried out at the level of 'income-generating units' which comprise groups of assets, liabilities and associated goodwill that generate cash flows that are largely independent of an entity's other income streams.

23.268 FRS 7 gives no guidance on the choice of discount rate to be applied to the future cash flows in arriving at a value in use. The following two documents contain guidance on discounting and illustrate the emerging methodologies that may be useful for the purposes of estimating fair values of fixed assets by reference to recoverable amounts:

- A working paper entitled 'Discounting in financial reporting' issued by the ASB in April 1997.

- FRS 11 'Impairment of fixed assets and goodwill' published in July 1998.

23.269 The working paper explains the concepts involved in discounting where long-term assets and liabilities are measured by reference to future cash flows. The value of future cash flows is affected not only by the time value of money, but also by the variability (risk) associated with the cash flows. The paper specifically considers the value in use calculations that are required to estimate an asset's recoverable amount. The principle is that value in use represents the cash flows expected by the entity discounted at a market rate that takes account of the riskiness of the cash flows. The risk adjustment should be based on the market's price for risk. In effect, value in use is intended to simulate the market value of the cash flows expected by the entity.

23.270 Although it does not specifically deal with acquisition accounting, FRS 11 sets out in considerable detail the methodology for estimating cash flows and choosing a risk-adjusted discount rate for the purpose of calculating value in use when reviewing fixed assets for impairment. Some relevant points are summarised below.

- All relevant cash flows attributable to the group of assets or operation being valued should be taken into account, including an allocation of central overheads. Interest payments and other costs of capital are not included since these are taken into account in the discount rate.

- Cash flow forecasts should be based on reasonable and supportable assumptions and be consistent with budgets and plans that have been formally approved by management. Beyond the period covered by formal budgets and plans, the projections should generally assume a steady or declining growth rate.

- The cash flows used for estimating the value in use of income-generating units or individual fixed assets in their current condition should not include:

  - the costs or benefits that are expected to arise from a future reorganisation for which provision has not yet been made; or

  - the effects of future capital expenditure that is expected to enhance the assets from their current condition.

- The discount rate should be an estimate of the rate of return that the market would expect on an equally risky investment. Therefore, the riskiness of the cash flows, taking into account any significant uncertainties about their amount or timing, will affect the risk factor built into the discount rate. There may be a variety of means of estimating this rate including reference to:

  - The rate implicit in market transactions of similar assets.

- The weighted average cost of capital of a listed company whose cash flows have a similar risk profile to those of the asset.

- The weighted average cost of capital for the entity, but only if adjusted for the particular risks associated with the asset or the operation in which the asset is employed.

- FRS 11 requires that value is use is measured, for the purpose of impairment reviews, using cash flow forecasts that do not include tax cash flows. The pre-tax cash flows are discounted using a pre-tax discount rate.

23.271 The net present value that emerges from the discounted cash flow exercise will represent, in aggregate, the recoverable amount of all the identifiable assets less liabilities of the group of assets that generates the cash flows on which the calculation is based. If the recoverable amount is lower than their aggregate book value immediately before the acquisition, a fair value adjustment is required.

23.272 Any fair value adjustment to reduce aggregate book values to a lower recoverable amount will need to be allocated on a rational basis to the identifiable assets of the acquired business. FRS 11 could be used for guidance in the context of a fair value exercise. It proposes that, unless a specific asset is obviously impaired, assets with the most subjective valuations should be written down first. Any capitalised intangibles would thus be written down first; thereafter, tangible assets would be written down on a pro rata or more appropriate basis. However, no intangible asset that has a reliably ascertainable market value should be written down below its net realisable value; and no tangible asset with a net realisable value that can be measured reliably should be written down below its net realisable value.

23.273 Table 23.15 gives an example where assets acquired (on the acquisition by RJB Mining PLC of the principal coal mining activities of British Coal Corporation in England) have been fair valued at recoverable amounts.

Table 23.15 – RJB Mining PLC – Annual Report and Accounts – 31 December 1994

Notes to the Financial statements (extract)

13 Tangible fixed assets (extract)

	Land and buildings £'000	Mineral rights £'000	Mines and surface works £'000	Assets in course of construction £'000	Plant and machinery £'000	Total £'000
Group						
Cost or valuation						
At 1 January 1994	3,511	4,150	–	420	63,556	71,637
Additions	1,125	–	12,560	11,773	9,759	35,217
Acquired with Monckton	723	–	–	–	6,607	7,330
Acquired with English Coal						
Disposals	52,795	–	412,846	151,774	26,403	643,818
Reclassification	(220)	(65)	–	(699)	(6,121)	(7,105)
	–	(988)	485	988	(485)	–
At 31 December 1994	**57,934**	**3,097**	**425,891**	**164,256**	**99,719**	**750,897**

On acquisition, book values of collieries assets have been adjusted to net recoverable amounts. These amounts have been arrived at, following existing mining plans, by estimating future cash flows, net of all costs of running collieries, including capital expenditure, an allocation of central overheads and closure restoration costs and discounting these to their present values. The discount rate used has been based on the weighted cost of capital and taking into account appropriate risk. The methodology used to value fixed assets on acquisition is in accordance with Financial Reporting Standard 7 and Technical Release 773 issued by the Institute of Chartered Accountants in England and Wales.

Fair valuing stocks

23.274 Fair values of stocks and work-in-progress are determined using the same measurement principles as for fixed assets, that is by reference to open market value, replacement cost or net realisable value, according to the circumstances. 'Value in use' is not an issue in the valuation of stocks, because stocks are held for resale and not for their continued use in the business.

23.275 The application of 'value to the business', or deprival value, principles to stocks mean that, in general, the valuation relates to the acquired company as a buyer rather than a seller. Consequently, in contrast to the proposals made in ED 53, FRS 7 does not require a profit element to be included in the fair value of finished and partly finished stocks. This means that, where stocks are revalued to market value or replacement cost, the consequent reduction in post-acquisition profits (assuming stock values move up rather than down) when the revalued amounts feed through into cost of sales is limited to the effect of market price or input price changes during the period the stocks were held by the acquired company. Often, where the turnover period is short, the effect of price changes will be immaterial and no revaluation will be necessary. Consequently, the post-acquisition operating profit of the acquired company will not be reduced in the acquirer's consolidated financial statements by the application of replacement cost principles.

23.276 If fair values are attributed to stocks, and these values are in excess of historical cost to the acquired company, it would seem that the provisions of SSAP 9 would not allow the fair values to be incorporated in the financial statements of the acquired company. This is because the standard requires that stocks, other than long-term contracts, should be recorded at the lower of cost and net realisable value. [SSAP 9 para 26]. Fair values should be incorporated in the consolidated financial statements because they represent cost to the group, but not in the acquired company's financial statements if they are in excess of cost to that company.

23.277 It will again be necessary for the group to keep separate records of any stocks that are recorded at fair values in excess of cost to the acquired company.

[The next page is 23093.]

A consolidation adjustment will be necessary to adjust the profits and stocks of the acquired company for the effect of the fair value exercise, for so long as the stocks remain unsold.

23.278 Whether market value, replacement cost or net realisable value is used, FRS 7 stresses that the basis of valuation must be consistent with the circumstances pertaining to the acquired company at the date of acquisition. Thus, for example:

- Market values are relevant where stocks are replaced by purchasing in a ready market to which the acquired entity has access. [FRS 7 para 52].

- Replacement cost should reflect the acquired company's normal buying process, the sources of supply available to it and its current cost of manufacture. [FRS 7 paras 12, 53].

- Estimates of net realisable value should be justified by the circumstances of the acquired entity before acquisition. [FRS 7 para 57]. However, the standard's definition of fair value does not permit stocks to be written down to values that would reflect a forced or liquidation sale.

Open market value

23.279 Fair values would normally be based on open market values in the following cases:

- Commodity and dealing stocks.
- Land and buildings held as trading stock.
- Land and buildings held for development.

Replacement cost

23.280 FRS 7 explains that for most manufactured stocks, fair value is represented by the current cost to the acquired company of reproducing the stocks. Account should be taken of the way the acquired company purchased or manufactured the stocks. [FRS 7 paras 52, 53].

23.281 The implications for the valuation of raw materials, work in progress and finished goods are as follows:

- Raw materials should be valued at replacement cost, reflecting the acquired company's normal sources of supply and current prices available to it.

- Manufactured work in progress and finished goods should be valued at the current cost of bringing the stocks to their present location and condition, reflecting the acquired company's own cost structures at the date of acquisition. Current standard costs would be used where these are available and reliable.

- Properties in the course of development would usually be valued at the replacement cost to the acquired company of the land and the development at its current stage of completion.

- Bought-in finished goods should be valued at replacement cost, reflecting the acquired company's normal sources of supply and current prices available to it.

23.282 In times of low inflation in manufacturing input prices, it is likely that the difference between historical cost and current replacement cost of most short-term manufactured stocks would not be material. In such circumstances no fair value adjustments would be necessary. There is an existing Companies Act requirement to disclose any material difference between the historical cost of stocks and their current replacement cost. [4 Sch 27(3)].

23.283 FRS 7 explains how these principles should be applied to determine the replacement cost of certain long-term maturing stocks, such as distillery products and growing timber. As an example, a whisky distiller holds stocks of whisky at different stages of maturity; there is also a market in semi-matured whisky. In a fair value exercise the question is whether such stocks should be valued at a market price or at the acquired company's own replacement cost.

23.284 FRS 7 indicates that market prices should be used if the acquired company normally purchases stocks in the market. If it does not replace stocks by purchasing in the market, then market prices would not be used. Where, as is likely to be the case, there is market trading at the margin, but the market is very thin compared to the volumes of stocks held, the standard indicates that market prices would not be appropriate. Where replacement by manufacture would not be possible in the short term, the standard suggests that a surrogate for replacement cost may be found in the historical cost of the stocks, together with an interest cost in respect of holding the stock. [FRS 7 para 55].

23.285 An example of fair valuing long-term maturing stocks is taken from the financial statements of Guinness PLC when it accounted for the acquisition of Distillers. (Table 23.16). The policy described appears to correspond to the method suggested by FRS 7.

Table 23.16 – Guinness PLC – Annual Report – 31 December 1986

Notes to the consolidated accounts (extracts)

15 Effect of the acquisition of Distillers on the Consolidated Balance Sheet (extract)

(ii) Stocks

Stocks have been included at fair value which has been determined by taking account of costs of production, including financing costs, and after writing off surplus stocks and providing for costs of realisation.

18 Stocks

	1986 £m	1985 £m
Raw materials and consumables	127	52
Work in progress	11	8
Stocks of maturing whisky	788	82
Finished goods	118	55
Goods purchased for resale	77	55
	1,121	**252**

The estimated replacement cost of all stocks is not materially different from the above figures.

In accordance with the Group's accounting policy, stocks of maturing whisky include an appropriate proportion of financing costs in determining production costs. At 31 December 1986 the total cost of £788m included £360m as a result of the application of this policy, of which £62m arose during the period. The balance of £298m represents the amount remaining of the accumulated financing costs taken into account in the Group's assessment of fair value at date of acquisition and is stated after a reduction of £46m in respect of sales during the period.

The net adjustment to stocks of £16m during the period, resulting from the increase of £62m and the reduction of £46m as set out above, has been credited to the profit and loss account as described in Note 7.

23.286 The emphasis on valuing stocks according to the existing cost structures of the acquired company means that one potential source of fair value adjustment is avoided. An acquiring company might consider that it could reduce the cost base of the acquired company and, accordingly, lower its cost of sales, by reorganising its manufacturing operations and negotiating discounts with its suppliers. Under FRS 7 the acquirer is not allowed to reduce the fair value of the acquired company's stocks if it believes it could have produced those stocks more cheaply. Thus, the benefit of lower cost of sales would not feed into the acquirer's post-acquisition operating results until stocks produced after the post-acquisition reorganisation (that is, at a lower cost) are sold.

Net realisable value

23.287 The principles for determining net realisable value of stocks are set out in SSAP 9. The calculation of provisions to reduce stocks from cost to net realisable value is often subjective and involves the use of different criteria by different companies. Where an acquisition is involved, the acquirer should review the book values of slow-moving, excess or obsolescent stocks and, if necessary, make adjustments to those values to reflect the application of its own criteria as represented by its own accounting policies.

23.288 FRS 7 explains that any material write-down in the fair value exercise should be justified by the circumstances of the acquired company before acquisition. [FRS 7 para 57]. As with any other impaired assets, the fair value attributed to stocks should not reflect any impairments resulting from post-acquisition events, such as stock written off in a post-acquisition reorganisation.

Example 1

The management of a company that is acquired may have certain stocks that are slow moving, but which they hope to sell after conducting an advertising campaign. They may, therefore, value these stocks at cost. The management of the acquirer may decide, on investigating the company, that an advertising campaign would not work and that consequently, the stocks are unsaleable. The management of the acquirer would, therefore, attribute a lower fair value to the stocks, as the impairment in value existed at the date of acquisition.

Example 2

An acquired company has stocks relating to a continuing product range, which have been turning over within a reasonable period. The management of the acquired company considered that the net realisable value exceeded cost. The management of the acquirer decides to discontinue that product range and reduces the selling price of the product in order to achieve a quick clearance of the remaining stocks. A provision is then necessary to reduce the cost of the stocks to their new net realisable value. Under FRS 7 the fall in net realisable value is attributable to the post-acquisition actions of the acquirer and, accordingly, the provision should be charged against post-acquisition profits and not as a fair value adjustment.

23.289 Although the above examples show a clear distinction between a stock provision that is allowed as a fair value adjustment and a stock provision that should be charged against post-acquisition profits, some situations will be less clear cut.

23.290 Paragraph 57 of the explanatory section of the FRS indicates that some hindsight should be applied in situations where exceptional margins appear to have been earned in the post-acquisition period, that is, within the period allowed for making fair value and goodwill adjustments. First, the attributed fair values would need to be re-examined in the light of actual experience and adjusted if they are found to have been materially understated. Secondly, if the profits are attributable to post-acquisition events, there may need to be disclosed as an exceptional item as required by paragraph 30 of FRS 6.

23.291 Although the standard discusses the implications of exceptional post-acquisition profits, there is no reason why the same logic should not be used where stocks are realised at a loss in the post-acquisition period, that is, fair values should be re-examined within the permitted hindsight period and adjusted if they are found to have been overstated.

Long-term contracts

23.292 The presentation of long-term contracts under SSAP 9, as revised in 1988, is convenient for FRS 7, because amounts recorded as turnover in respect of a contract are treated as debtors and not as work-in-progress. Amounts included as work-in-progress are generally very small. Consequently, the application of replacement cost principles is unlikely to be an important issue for long-term contracts in a fair value exercise.

23.293 A 'long-term contract' is defined in SSAP 9 as *"a contract entered into for the design, manufacture or construction of a single substantial asset or the provision of a service..... where the time taken substantially to complete the contract is such that the contract activity falls into different accounting periods"*. [SSAP 9 para 22].

23.294 Although such contracts usually extend for more than one year, some contracts with a shorter duration than one year should be accounted for as long-term contracts if they are sufficiently material to the activity of the period that not to record turnover and attributable profit would lead to distortion of the period's turnover and results such that the financial statements would not give a true and fair view, provided that the policy is applied consistently within the reporting entity and from year to year.

23.295 In acquisition accounting, the acquirer first needs to identify those contracts that fulfil the criteria in the definition described above. By applying the principles of accounting for long-term contracts in SSAP 9, the turnover and profit attributable to such contracts are allocated to the pre-acquisition and post-acquisition periods, as well as to discrete financial years, on a basis that matches the progress of the contracts.

23.296 As the guidance in SSAP 9 is very general, methods of calculating turnover and recognising attributable profit (or foreseeable losses) on long-term contracts vary between different companies and different industries and, of course, between different countries. Some companies in the UK take a more prudent approach to profit recognition than others.

23.297 The main source of fair value adjustments under FRS 7 is likely to be in the area of harmonising the methods of accounting in the acquired company with those of the acquirer. If, for example, both the acquiring and acquired companies took a similar approach to identifying long-term contracts, calculating turnover and determining attributable profit, no fair value adjustments would be necessary to the balances shown as amounts recoverable on contracts.

23.298 Additionally, an acquirer would wish to make a critical review of the estimated outcome of each long-term contract, in order to ensure that adequate provisions have been made by the acquired company's management for any foreseeable losses as required by SSAP 9. Fair value adjustments would be made, as necessary, where the acquirer considered existing provisions to be inadequate or excessive, taking into account the circumstances of the acquired company before the acquisition.

23.299 Where exceptional margins or deficits appear to have been earned on acquired long-term contracts post acquisition, the principles described in paragraph 23.290 above should be applied. First, previously attributed fair values should be re-examined and, if necessary, adjusted. Secondly, if the profit or loss is attributed to post-acquisition activities, the acquirer should consider whether the profit or loss should be disclosed as an exceptional item in the profit and loss account. An example of a potential exceptional item given in paragraph 85 of FRS 6 is the release of a provision in respect of an acquired loss-making long-term contract that the acquirer makes profitable.

23.300 The following question sometimes arises in connection with fair valuing long-term contracts, where contracts are acquired that are similar in nature to contracts already being carried out by the acquirer. If the contracts undertaken by the acquired company are less profitable than those of the acquirer, the acquirer may consider that provisions should be made in the fair value exercise so that the contracts acquired will then give similar margins to those of the acquirer. Clearly such a practice would be contrary to the principles of FRS 7 because, even though the contracts may not be as valuable as the acquirer would like, they are not loss-making contracts. Whereas SSAP 9 requires provision to be made for contracts that are expected to result in a loss as soon as the loss is foreseen, it does not permit provision to be made for sub-normal future profits. Consequently, such contracts cannot be identifiable liabilities of the acquired company.

Disposals of business segments

23.301 There have been many examples of acquisitions where the acquirer has subsequently disposed of unwanted portions of the acquired business, sometimes recouping the major part of his initial outlay in the process.

23.302 FRS 2 had already dealt in a limited way with the treatment of interests in subsidiaries held exclusively with a view to subsequent resale. Such an interest is defined as *"an interest for which a purchaser has been identified or is being sought, and which is reasonably expected to be disposed of within approximately one year of* *its date of acquisition"*. [FRS 2 para 11]. FRS 2 requires such a subsidiary to be excluded from consolidation (provided it has not previously been consolidated) and to be shown in the acquirer's consolidated financial statements as a current asset at the lower of cost and net realisable value. [FRS 2 para 29].

23.303 FRS 7 has extended this treatment to any business operation acquired and held exclusively with a view to subsequent resale, whether a separate subsidiary or not, provided that its assets, liabilities, operating results and activities are clearly distinguishable, physically, operationally and for financial reporting purposes, from the other assets, liabilities, results of operations and activities of the acquired entity. [FRS 7 para 16]. In other words, the treatment only applies to a discrete business unit, including a business that operates as a division of an acquired company, which should be accounted for in the fair value exercise as a single identifiable asset instead of a collection of underlying assets, liabilities and goodwill. Additionally, the operation must be sold as a single unit.

23.304 The accounting treatment described in this section only applies to business operations sold. If an acquirer decides to *close* an operation of the acquired business, the assets, liabilities and results of that operation should be fully consolidated from the date of acquisition. Fair values should be attributed individually to identifiable assets and liabilities according to the normal rules of FRS 7. Closure costs and asset write-downs would have to be charged in the profit and loss account to the extent that they do not relate to identifiable liabilities that already existed or to assets that were already impaired at the date of acquisition. The treatment of disposals by means of sale is, therefore, inconsistent with the treatment of disposals by closure and with the general principles of FRS 7, which do not allow the acquirer's intentions regarding the acquired business to affect the fair valuing process.

23.305 FRS 7 requires the fair value of businesses sold or held exclusively with a view to subsequent resale to be determined as follows:

- Where the business has been sold by the time the first post-acquisition accounts are approved, fair value is based on the net proceeds of the sale, adjusted for the fair value of any assets or liabilities transferred into or out of the business. [FRS 7 para 16].

  Such transfers would include items such as dividends from and capital contributions to the business between the date of acquisition and the date of disposal.

- Where the business has not been sold by the time the first post-acquisition financial statements are approved, fair value is based on the estimated net proceeds of sale. [FRS 7 para 17].

23.306 Where the business has not been sold by the time the first post-acquisition financial statements are approved, for it to be excluded from consolidation the acquirer must be able to demonstrate that:

- A purchaser has been identified or is being sought.
- Disposal is reasonably expected to occur within approximately one year of the date of acquisition.

Otherwise, normal consolidation of the assets, liabilities and results of the business according to the general requirements of FRS 2 and FRS 7 is required.

23.307 The effect of the prescribed period for disposing of the business is that the disposal must have occurred within the period allowed in FRS 7 for completing the fair value exercise, because that period extends for more than one financial year. Any provisional fair value in the first post-acquisition financial statements (based on estimated net proceeds) should be adjusted in the subsequent period, with a corresponding adjustment to goodwill.

23.308 The FRS requires that if the business is not, in fact, sold within approximately one year of the acquisition, it should be fully consolidated, with fair values attributed to the individual assets and liabilities as at the date of acquisition. [FRS 7 para 18]. This means that a prior period adjustment would be necessary, as a change of accounting policy, in order to 'backdate' the consolidation to the date of acquisition, and to re-work the fair value exercise. The prior period adjustment would involve replacing the previously identified single asset. That is, the current asset investment in the subsidiary or business would be replaced by fair values of individual assets and liabilities (and goodwill). The profit and loss account of the previous period would be adjusted to include the results of that operation from the date of acquisition. These accounting adjustments would need to be accompanied by adequate management explanation.

23.309 It is interesting to consider what would happen in the opposite scenario – where an acquired business that was consolidated in the immediate post-acquisition period (because it was not then up for sale) is actually sold in the next financial year and within a year of its acquisition. In that situation, once consolidated, a business would continue to be consolidated right up to the date of disposal, as required by FRS 2, because the exclusion from consolidation of subsidiaries held exclusively for resale does not apply where the subsidiary has previously been consolidated. There is no question of altering the previous treatment and restating comparative figures.

23.310 The choice of net realisable value as fair value at the date of acquisition is justified by the ASB on the grounds that the resale value of a business in an arm's length transaction shortly after the valuation date would normally provide the most reliable evidence of its fair value at the date of acquisition. Otherwise, if a low fair value were placed on a business segment and it were subsequently sold at a profit it would be tempting to argue that the profit is entirely due to the expertise of the new management.

23.311 FRS 7 states that fair value should not be based on net realisable value in the follow cases:

- Where the adjusted net proceeds are *demonstrably* different from the fair value at the date of acquisition *as a result of a post-acquisition event.*

- Where the acquirer has made a material change to the acquired business before disposal.

- The disposal is completed at a reduced price for a quick sale.

[FRS 7 paras 16, 69].

23.312 In each of the above circumstances the proceeds from disposal may be materially different from fair value at the date of acquisition as defined in the standard. It would then be necessary to estimate separately fair values at the date of acquisition and record a profit or loss on disposal in the post-acquisition profit and loss account. An example is where there is a collapse in the market for one of the subsidiary's products, which is attributable to an identifiable post-acquisition event.

Example 1

An acquisition of a group of companies included a coffee trading subsidiary that the acquirer intends to sell. Since the acquisition date, but before the first consolidated accounts following the acquisition were completed, the price of coffee has risen by 100%, thus increasing the value of the subsidiary's stocks and the market value of the company.

If there is evidence of a post-acquisition increase in value which is reflected in the price obtained for the subsidiary, the increase should not be included in the fair value attributed to the subsidiary; it should be accounted for as a profit on the sale of an operation in the post-acquisition profit and loss account of the acquiring group.

Example 2

An acquirer has carried out a reorganisation of an acquired subsidiary prior to its resale. In such a case the net realised value would in all likelihood be above the fair value of the subsidiary at the date of acquisition. The costs of reorganisation borne by the subsidiary, and the increase in value that could reasonably be attributed to the reorganisation would (because the subsidiary is excluded from consolidation) in effect be combined and shown as a post-acquisition profit on sale, which would be disclosed as a post-operating exceptional item.

23.313 An explanatory paragraph to FRS 7 also states that where the effect is material, the net proceeds from disposal would be discounted to obtain their present value at the date of acquisition. [FRS 7 para 65]. The effect of discounting is to shelter the post-acquisition profit and loss account from any notional or actual interest cost in respect of financing the purchase of the subsidiary or business operation during the period it is held by the group. It may, therefore, be appropriate to discount the net proceeds at a debt rate of interest.

23.314 An example of an acquisition including businesses held for resale is shown in Table 23.17.

Table 23.17 – De La Rue plc – Annual Report – 31 March 1995

Notes to the Accounts (extract)

23 **Acquisitions (extract)**

On 6 February 1995 the Group acquired the entire issued share capital of Portals Group plc (Portals) for a consideration, including expenses, of £716.7m. The acquisition has been accounted for using the acquisition method.

On 7 March 1995 the Group announced its intention to dispose of all the Portals non-security papermaking businesses. These businesses are held as assets for disposal and their results are excluded from the operating profit of the Group. The book values of the assets and liabilities of the retained Portals businesses immediately prior to the acquisition and the fair value adjustments required in recognition of the change of ownership are as follows:

	Book value prior to acquisition £m	Revalu -ations £m		Accounting policy alignment £m	Assets for disposal £m	Fair value to the Group £m
Tangible fixed assets	48.8	2.7	a	–	–	51.5
Stocks	11.1	–		(0.8)b	–	10.3
Debtors	8.3	0.6	c	–	–	8.9
Assets held for disposal	–	–		–	158.0d	158.0
Cash at bank and in hand	23.1	–		–	–	23.1
Bank loans and overdrafts	(6.9)	–		–	–	(6.9)
Creditors due within one year	(8.4)	–		–	–	(8.4)
Taxation	(2.1)	–		–	–	(2.1)
Deferred taxation	0.8	(0.8)	c	(8.5)e	–	(8.5)
Provisions for liabilities and charges	(5.1)	2.5	c	–	–	(2.6)
Net assets acquired	**69.6**	**5.0**		**(9.3)**	**158.0**	**223.3**
Consideration						
Cash						402.8
Shares issued (at market value)						295.4
Loan notes						18.5
Total consideration						**716.7**
Fair value of net assets acquired (as above)						**223.3**
Goodwill						**493.4**

Notes:

a The revaluations of plant and machinery employed in the security papermaking businesses are based upon depreciated replacement cost.

b The value of maintenance stocks has been adjusted as a result of applying De La Rue's accounting policies.

c The Portals pension scheme was revalued on acquisition. The assumptions upon which this revaluation is based are stated in note 24.

d The assets for disposal represent the anticipated net sale proceeds, as estimated by the Directors of De La Rue plc, discounted to their present value at the date of acquisition (see note 13).

e Deferred taxation has been provided for timing differences in accordance with the tax provisioning policy of De La Rue.

13 **Assets Held for Disposal**

Assets held for disposal represents the Group's investment in those companies listed as "Businesses held for resale" on page 62. These companies, all of which were subsidiaries of Portals Group plc when the Group acquired Portals Group plc, are held exclusively with a view to resale. They are held at the Directors' valuation of anticipated net sales proceeds discounted to their present value at 31 March 1995.

Included within other creditors is £3.3m owing to these businesses by the rest of the Group as at 31 March 1995, representing £2.6m of cash received and £0.7m of trading items. Apart from these transactions, during the period from acquisition to 31 March 1995 there were no material transactions between these businesses and the rest of the Group, and there were no dividends received or receivable from them.

23.315 Tucked away in the small print of the explanation is a sentence stating that the principles set out in the FRS for attributing expenses to the cost of an acquisition would also apply to the costs of disposals. [FRS 7 para 65].

23.316 Where fair value is based on net realised value, it is arrived at after deducting costs incurred in disposing of the business. The rules on acquisition costs restrict expenses that can be capitalised to fees and similar incremental costs that would not have been incurred had the acquisition not taken place (see para 23.445). They do not permit any allocation and capitalisation of internal costs that would have been incurred anyway. In the same way that the FRS takes a restrictive view on acquisition costs to avoid overstating the cost of acquisition, it takes a similarly restrictive view on disposal costs and prevents internal costs from being taken out of the profit and loss account and deducted from the disposal proceeds and, as a result, from increasing goodwill.

Fair valuing monetary assets and liabilities

23.317 The fair value of most short-term receivables and payables is usually not significantly different from their book values, because they reflect amounts expected to be received or paid in the short term. Fair value adjustments would usually be limited to those arising from the acquirer's different estimates of amounts recoverable or payable.

Example – Debtors

A significant debtor of an acquired company has gone into liquidation between the date of acquisition and the completion of the group accounts. No provision was made against the debtor in the acquired company's books. Is the provision now required as a fair value adjustment in the group accounts?

Any new evidence that comes to light before the fair value exercise is completed and that concerns the condition, as at the date of acquisition, of the acquired company's assets, would be taken into account in arriving at fair values. The adequacy of bad debt provisions is one area where a certain amount of hindsight is usually necessary.

SSAP 17 cites the insolvency of a debtor between the balance sheet date and the date of approval of a company's financial statements as an example of an adjusting post balance sheet event. An adjusting event is, according to SSAP 17, an event that provides additional evidence relating to conditions existing at the balance sheet date. This principle is consistent with FRS 7's principle of reflecting conditions at the date of acquisition. Although the debtor was not in liquidation at the date of acquisition, it is likely that it was in financial difficulties, even if those only became apparent after the date of acquisition. On this basis we consider that the provision is a fair value adjustment.

23.318 For long-term monetary items, the time value of money also needs to be taken into account. The fair value of most long-term receivables and payables is represented by their face values where a market rate of interest is paid during the term the item is outstanding. However, fair values of long-term receivables and payables may be materially different from their book or face values where they either carry no interest or carry interest at rates significantly different from prevailing market rates at the date of acquisition. Long-term monetary items would include finance lease receivables and payables.

23.319 For example, the fair value today of £1m receivable in one year's time is obviously less than £1m. Similarly, the fair value today of a five year loan of £1m carrying a fixed rate of interest of 12 per cent is greater than £1m if the current rate for similar borrowings is 6 per cent.

23.320 In these circumstances, FRS 7 requires the items to be recognised at fair values, which are deemed to be one of the following:

- Market prices, where these are available.
- Current prices at which the business could acquire similar assets or enter into similar obligations.
- Discounted present values.

[FRS 7 para 14].

23.321 The effect of making such fair value adjustments is that the post-acquisition profit and loss account of the acquiring group shows finance charges or interest receivable that equate to market rates of interest at the date of acquisition.

23.322 The standard gives the following guidance on the choice of discount rate to be used for discounting items to their present values:

- Long-term borrowings: based on current lending rates for an equivalent term, the credit standing of the issuer and the nature of any security given.
- Long-term debtors: based on current lending rates, after any necessary bad debt provisions have been made.

[FRS 7 para 61].

23.323 The fair value of assets would be measured by their market value if an active market for them exists. For example, if an acquired company has invested in long-term debt issued by an entity that the market perceives to be at risk of default, there may be a secondary market in which the debt is traded at a discount to its face value. This discounted value may be the best available evidence of fair value.

23.324 Similarly, the fair value of any quoted debt securities issued by the acquired entity would usually be measured by their market values at the date of acquisition. However, an explanatory paragraph to the standard makes an exception where the acquired company is perceived to be at risk of defaulting on its debt obligations and the pre-acquisition market value of issued securities is reduced from its face value to reflect this risk. The standard states that such a reduction in the value of debt would not be recognised in the fair value allocation if the debt was expected to be repaid at its full amount after the acquisition. [FRS 7 para 63].

23.325 By making this exception to its general principles of fair valuing, the standard is recognising that, in such circumstances, the acquired company still has a liability to repay the gross amount of its debt. The acquired company is not absolved from its debt obligations where the market value of its debt is discounted to reflect market concerns. Accordingly, when attributing fair values to such debt in the financial statements of the acquiring group, the acquirer should recognise either the gross amount or, if the rates of interest on such debt are significantly different from current market rates, a present value that reflects current market rates, but not distress rates. If this were not done, recognising such debt in the fair value exercise at its (discounted) market value would mean a pre-acquisition gain would be attributed to the acquired company, followed by a post-acquisition loss attributed to the acquiring group, whereas, in fact, no such gain or loss has arisen.

23.326 It could also be inferred from the exception described above that a similar approach should be adopted where the debt issued by an acquired company that is in financial difficulty is not quoted, notwithstanding the reference to *"the credit standing of the issuer"* as mentioned in paragraph 23.322 above. To be consistent, and for the same reasons, we consider that it would be inappropriate to fair value the debt at a deep discount to its face or book value if the total payments (capital and interest) the acquired company is required to make under the terms of the debt are expected to be made.

23.327 This approach is consistent with the discussion in the ASB's draft Statement of Principles (Chapter 5) relating to determining the current value of liabilities. The market interest rate applicable to a particular loan may alter because of a change in the perceived risk of the specific business, rather than because of a general change in market rates. An increase in business risk will increase the interest rate applicable to the entity, thus reducing the market value of its loans. This applies in particular to long-term fixed rate debt. The ASB recognises in the draft Statement of principles that it is particularly questionable whether it is appropriate to reflect a gain relating to a decrease in creditworthiness. In fair value accounting, we consider that fair values of unquoted debt obligations should not, in general, be reduced to reflect any deteriorations in the creditworthiness of the acquired company since the debt was issued, if the debt is expected to be repaid at its full amount.

23.328 FRS 7 also requires the fair values of accruals and provisions to be determined by taking into account the amounts expected to be paid and their timing. [FRS 7 para 14]. It gives discounting to present value as one of the options for determining the fair values of monetary assets and liabilities generally. Accounting practices relating to the measurement of long-term provisions have previously varied according to the nature of the liability. However, FRS 12 introduced rules that apply to measuring all provisions – they should be measured at present values of expected expenditures where the effect of the time value of money is material. The discount rate should be a pre-tax rate that reflects current market assessments of the time value of money and the risks specific to the liability. Alternatively, the expected future cash outflows may be adjusted (that is, increased) for risk and discounted by using a risk-free rate (such as a government bond rate). Care should be taken to ensure the effect of risk is not double-counted – that is, risk should be taken into account either in estimating the (undiscounted) future expenditures or by adjusting (that is, reducing) the discount rate, but not both. The measurement basis required by FRS 12 should generally be consistent with the principles for determining fair values of provisions in FRS 7.

Fair valuing contingencies

23.329 The treatment of contingent purchase consideration is considered later in paragraph 23.426. The paragraphs that follow consider contingencies that affect the value of identifiable net assets.

Identification of contingencies

23.330 SSAP 18 defines a contingency as *"a condition which exists at the balance sheet date, where the outcome will be confirmed only on the occurrence or non-occurrence of one or more uncertain future events"*. The standard explains that *"a contingent gain or loss is a gain or loss dependent on a contingency"*. [SSAP 18 para 14].

23.331 In acquisition accounting, a pre-acquisition contingency would be a contingency of the acquired company which existed at the date of acquisition and which could result in a contingent asset or a contingent liability. For fair value exercises, the identifiable assets and liabilities of an acquired company must include contingent assets and liabilities that existed before the date of acquisition.

Measurement of contingencies

23.332 The normal rules in SSAP 18 for recognising and measuring contingencies in financial statements are as follows:

- Contingent losses should be accrued where it is probable that a future event will confirm a loss which can be estimated with reasonable accuracy at the date on which the financial statements are approved. A material contingent loss not accrued (because, for example, the loss is possible rather than probable) should be disclosed except where the possibility of loss is remote. [SSAP 18 paras 15,16].

- Contingent gains should not be accrued. A material contingent gain should be disclosed only if it is probable that the gain will be realised. [SSAP 18 para 17].

23.333 In acquisition accounting, the identifiable assets to be included in the fair value exercise include contingent gains as assets, even though they are not normally included in financial statements as gains until they are realised. Thus, contingent assets and contingent liabilities are treated in like manner. Recognition of contingent assets or liabilities in a fair value exercise has no immediate profit and loss account effect; instead it means all assets and liabilities that have value are recognised, with only the residual difference between the purchase price and the identified net assets being reported as goodwill. In contrast, omitting a pre-acquisition contingent gain in the fair value exercise would mean that a pre-acquisition asset may be recognised as a post-acquisition gain in succeeding financial statements.

23.334 FRS 7 requires all identifiable assets and liabilities to be recognised in the fair value exercise, provided they can be reliably valued. Fair values, representing the price at which such an item might be exchanged in an arm's length transaction, would rarely be ascertainable unless the contingent asset or liability were of a kind that is normally exchanged. Consequently, the standard allows reasonable estimates of the expected outcome to be used as the best approximation to fair value. [FRS 7 para 15].

23.335 For this purpose, the standard explains that the acquiring company's management's best estimate of the likely outcome should be used in place of any previous estimate, assuming that no post-acquisition events or other changes in circumstances are reflected in the valuation. [FRS 7 para 64].

23.336 The practical effect of recognising most contingent assets and liabilities at a best estimate of the likely outcome is that both would be recognised if they meet criteria similar to those that SSAP 18 lays down for the recognition of contingent liabilities. If contingencies are subsequently resolved at amounts recognised in the fair value exercise, there is no effect on the post-acquisition profit and loss account.

23.337 Many contingencies, such as legal claims, require a considerable amount of time to be investigated in order to make reliable predictions of the outcome. Often it may not be possible to incorporate reliable figures in the first set of consolidated financial statements following the acquisition. In such circumstances, the fair values would be declared provisional and adjustments would be made in the second post-acquisition group accounts if new information becomes available within the permitted hindsight period that enables the resolution of the contingency to be reliably predicted. In practice, such items are sometimes covered by warranties given by vendors or by insurance; if so, the accounting is less of an issue for the acquirer.

23.338 In accounting periods that follow the period in which the fair value exercise is completed, there may be changes in the amount of any contingent assets or liabilities that have been recognised. Such changes would be reflected in the profit and loss account for the period in which they are recognised in the same way as changes in estimates of other assets and liabilities are dealt with.

23.339 FRS 6 gives, as an example of a post-acquisition profit or loss that would require separate disclosure as an exceptional item in the financial statements of the acquiring group, the *"realisation of contingent assets or liabilities at amounts materially different from their attributed fair values"*. [FRS 6 para 85].

23.340 Where contingent assets are recognised on acquisition, but subsequently they do not materialise, there will be an adverse effect on the profit and loss account. In this respect, where a contingent asset is set up on acquisition, it will be necessary to consider in future periods whether there is a reduction in its value. Where there is, the asset should be written down, by providing an amount against post-acquisition profits. On the other hand, where a contingent gain is subsequently expected to be realised at an amount in excess of its attributed fair value on acquisition, the normal rules of SSAP 18 would preclude the recognition of any gain in the profit and loss account of the acquiring group until its realisation becomes reasonably certain.

23.341 Similarly, where contingent liabilities are recognised in the fair value exercise, they will have to be reconsidered in future periods to ascertain whether the provisions are adequate. Where they are not, an additional provision will have to be made and charged to the post-acquisition profit and loss account. On the other hand, where the amount accrued in the fair value exercise is subsequently found to be excessive, the excess provision would be written back in the post-acquisition profit and loss account.

23.342 If the outcome of a contingency in the acquired company cannot be reliably estimated from information available at the end of the period allowed for completing the fair value exercise, contingent gains or losses would not be recognised as assets or liabilities, but would be disclosed in the acquirer's consolidated financial statements as required by SSAP 18.

23.343 When evaluating pre-acquisition contingencies, in practice it is not always clear whether adjustments to the acquired company's financial statements should be reported as fair value adjustments or as post-acquisition events. The following examples illustrate the difficulties.

Example 1

An acquired publishing company has a publishing subsidiary which has been sued for libel. The company's counsel has advised that, in his opinion, the case could be successfully defended. Accordingly, no provision has been included in the acquired company's financial statements, other than for estimated legal fees. The management of the acquiring company decide that the case should be settled out of court in order to avoid a protracted court case and the risk that the company could lose. The overall settlement cost exceeds the provision in the acquired company's financial statements.

It could be argued that the acquired company's financial statements reflected the best estimate of the likely outcome and that no further fair value adjustment is required. The financial effect of the acquirer's decision not to defend the case would then be reflected as a current, that is, post-acquisition, event.

However, a different view is that as the settlement related to a contingency that was already in existence and as there has been no new information or change in circumstances relating to the contingency, the cost of settlement is an event that confirms the outcome of the contingency. Therefore, the cost should be reflected as a fair value adjustment. This seems to be the more sensible interpretation and reflects the acquiring company's management's best estimate of the likely outcome as explained in paragraph 64 of FRS 7.

Example 2

An acquired company was pursuing a claim for negligence against a firm of accountants who had provided investigation services in respect of a previous acquisition that failed. The claim amounted to £10m. The accountants strenuously denied acting negligently. However, they had made an offer of settlement of £2m, which the company had rejected. The case was, therefore, scheduled for a court hearing. The management of the acquiring company subsequently negotiated, and accepted, an out of court settlement of £3m.

In this example, it is likely to be impossible to arrive at any meaningful fair value without the benefit of hindsight, that is, unless the actual outcome of the claim is reflected. If the claim was settled within the period for completing the fair value exercise, the credit of £3m should probably be accounted for as a fair value adjustment, because it relates to a contingency that was already in existence. However, it would be tempting for the management to argue that the settlement was due to their own efforts and skills, or that changes in the litigious environment had favoured a higher settlement and that, accordingly, some or all of the credit should be reflected in the post-acquisition profit and loss account.

If the settlement is not reached by the time the period for completing the fair value exercise has expired, the treatment would depend on the information available at the end of that period. If the outcome of the claim could be reliably predicted at that time, a best estimate of the settlement amount would be included as a contingent asset, that is, as a fair value adjustment. Later, when a settlement is reached, any income would be credited in the profit and loss account in the period it is received. Of course, it would be reported as an exceptional item, if material.

23.344 Table 23.18 gives an example where the receipt after the acquisition date of a pre-existing claim by the acquired company has been partly recognised as a fair value adjustment (increasing the fair value of debtors) and partly as an exceptional post-acquisition profit.

Table 23.18 – GKN plc – Report & Accounts – 31 December 1994

NOTES ON THE ACCOUNTS (extract)

23 ACQUISITIONS

Westland (extract from fair value table)

	BOOK VALUE PRIOR TO ACQUISITION	ACCOUNTING POLICY ALIGNMENT	REVALUATIONS	OTHER	FAIR VALUE TO THE GKN GROUP
	£m	£m	£m	£m	£m
Debtors – joint venture termination	–	–	–	112.0	112.0
– other	120.2	–	–	–	120.2

The fair value adjustments made include:

(c) a debtor for the net cash received in June 1994 amounting to £112 million arising from an arbitration award against the Arab Organisation for Industrialisation (AOI) following the termination of a joint venture between AOI and Westland Helicopters Limited to manufacture Lynx helicopters under licence. This receipt was secured as a result of actions initiated by Westland prior to acquisition and has accordingly been referred back to 31st March 1994. A further final net receipt of £51 million was negotiated in August 1994 and has been treated as a post acquisition exceptional profit (see note 4). These items, taken together with the net £15 million received by Westland in December 1993, give a total net receipt of £178 million from the award.

4 EXCEPTIONAL ITEMS (extract)

	1994	
	CONTINUING OPERATIONS	**DISCONTINUED OPERATIONS**
	£m	**£m**
Subsidiaries		
Profits (£83.7 million) less losses (£109.1 million) on sale or closure of businesses:		
Westland joint venture termination (note 23c)	**50.9**	–
Reduction in shareholding in Chep UK	**22.2**	–
Sale of US and Australian rental businesses	-	**(34.0)**
Provision for loss on sale of UES Holdings	**(59.6)**	–
Other	**(7.4)**	**2.5**
	6.1	**(31.5)**

Pensions and other post-retirement benefits

Identification of assets and liabilities

23.345 Where an acquisition involves the assumption of pension schemes or other post-retirement benefit plans, FRS 7 requires the following to be recognised as identifiable assets or liabilities in the fair value exercise:

- A surplus in a funded scheme, to the extent that it is reasonably expected to be realised.
- A deficiency in a funded scheme.
- Accrued obligations in respect of an unfunded scheme.

[FRS 7 para 19].

23.346 FRS 7 does *not* permit companies to recognise, as adjustments in the fair value exercise, changes in pension or other post-retirement arrangements following the acquisition. The cost of such changes should be dealt with in the post-acquisition profit and loss account under the normal rules of SSAP 24. [FRS 7 para 20].

23.347 Defined contribution schemes do not pose any problems in acquisition accounting, because the employer's obligation at any point in time is restricted to the amount of contributions payable to date, including to the date of acquisition. A liability will exist in the acquired company's financial statements if all contributions due by it have not been paid to the scheme and an asset will exist where excess contributions have been paid.

23.348 Defined benefit schemes, however, pose greater problems because the employer's liability for future benefits payable is not, in the case of funded schemes, restricted to the amount of contributions paid to the scheme.

23.349 Arrangements for transferring pensions obligations when a change of ownership takes place are many, varied and often complex. They may include: the acquisition of all schemes in the acquired group, in the case of the takeover of a listed group of companies; the acquisition of part of the vendor's pension schemes, in the case of the purchase of a subsidiary from a parent company; or simply the transfer of assets from the vendor's scheme to the purchaser's scheme reflecting transfer values of the accumulated pension rights of individual employees.

23.350 The value of the assets of a scheme acquired may exceed the estimated liability for the benefits that have accrued to members at the date of acquisition and, therefore, there may be a surplus. Equally, if the assets are insufficient to cover future liabilities for pensions there would be a deficiency. The surplus (with exceptions – see para 23.356 below) or deficiency should generally be recognised as an identifiable asset or liability in the fair value exercise.

23.351 In the past, a problem faced by many companies, and particularly those that have acquired subsidiaries in the US, has been how to deal with post-retirement health care benefits, which were sometimes a substantial hidden liability of acquired subsidiaries. Both FAS 106 in the US and UITF Abstract 6 in the UK have introduced rules requiring such benefits to be accounted for on an accruals basis. UITF 6 requires SSAP 24 principles to be applied to all post-retirement benefits from 1994 calendar financial years onwards. Companies need to review acquisitions to ensure that any material post-retirement benefits are identified and appropriate liabilities recognised in the fair value exercise.

23.352 The appointed actuary, or an actuary acting for the acquirer in the due diligence exercise, will play a key role in determining the surplus or deficit position for pension schemes and in determining the UITF 6 requirement.

Measurement of assets and liabilities

23.353 FRS 7 does not prescribe any rules for measuring the amount of surplus or deficiency to be recognised. The standard merely explains that the actuarial valuation depends on several assumptions about the future; and the *acquirer* would apply its own judgement in determining these assumptions. [FRS 7 para 73].

23.354 Generally, therefore, an actuarial valuation should be carried out as at the date of acquisition using actuarial methods and assumptions that are consistent with those the acquirer normally uses for the purpose of determining pension costs. These may differ from those previously used by the acquired company. An accrued benefits method of valuing pension liabilities would usually be appropriate in a fair value exercise, since such methods value the pension obligations in respect of employees' past service.

23.355 However, the valuation should not take into account the cost of any retrospective changes in benefits and membership that are decided upon by the acquirer. Such costs should be written off in the acquirer's consolidated profit and loss account, normally by spreading over the remaining service lives of the employees of the acquired company as required by SSAP 24. The following are examples of items that should be treated as post-acquisition:

- Costs of benefit improvements following the acquisition.
- Pension effect of a significant reduction in the number of employees following a post-acquisition reorganisation.
- Cost of enhanced pensions initiated by the acquirer to induce early retirement.

23.356 FRS 7 places an important limitation on the amount of any surplus that should be recognised as an asset on consolidation. It should take into account *"the extent to which the surplus could be realised in cash terms, by way of reduction of future contributions or otherwise, and the timescale of such potential realisations*". [FRS 7 para 71].

23.357 Many defined benefit schemes are designed such that the employees pay a fixed rate of contribution and the employer has an obligation to fund the balance. If a scheme is in surplus, the employer may be able to suspend or reduce the normal level of contributions until the surplus is eliminated. Where a surplus in an acquired company's scheme is to be run off by a contribution holiday after the acquisition, the surplus at the date of acquisition should clearly be recognised as an asset in the fair value exercise. The same goes for amounts subsequently refunded to the employer.

23.358 Situations where it would be either inappropriate or imprudent to recognise the full amount of a surplus as an asset might include the following:

- It is a condition of the scheme that part of the surplus belongs to the employees.

- The employees share in a contribution holiday.

- The trust deed prevents a refund of surplus to the employer company, and the surplus is so large that even an extended employer contribution holiday would not recover the whole amount of the surplus in the foreseeable future. Accordingly, it may be prudent to recognise a smaller surplus in the fair value exercise, for example the present value of a contribution holiday.

23.359 One means of utilising a surplus is to allow it to finance benefit improvements to employees that would otherwise be funded by increased contributions. Because the standard is quite specific that the cost of changes in pension arrangements such as benefit improvements following an acquisition should be accounted for in the profit and loss account as post-acquisition variations, it appears that such costs should not be deducted from the amount of surplus recognised on acquisition. The costs (and corresponding reduction in surplus) would either be recognised gradually over the expected remaining service lives of current employees in the scheme or, more prudently, immediately as a write-down of the asset.

Post-acquisition accounting

23.360 Any accruals or prepayments existing in the financial statements of an acquired company as a result of its own pension cost accounting policies will be replaced on consolidation by any surpluses or deficiencies recognised on acquisition. The principles of SSAP 24 would not allow these fair values to be incorporated into the financial statements of the acquired company. This is because the normal spreading principles of the standard require surpluses or deficiencies to be recognised systematically over future periods.

23.361 It will again be necessary for the group to keep separate records to track the pensions balances that are recorded as fair values. Consolidation adjustments will be necessary to:

- Adjust the pension costs reported in acquired subsidiaries to exclude any variations relating to a pre-acquisition surplus or deficiency. The group profit and loss account is then charged with the ongoing regular cost; variations arising after the acquisition; and a credit or a cost in respect of interest on the surplus or deficiency.

- Substitute the amounts reported in the balance sheets of acquired subsidiaries with amounts derived from the initial balances calculated under FRS 7.

23.362 Table 23.19 below shows a pension surplus treated as an asset in a fair value exercise.

Table 23.19 – Trafalgar House Public Limited Company – Report and Accounts – 30 September 1991

Notes to the accounts (extracts)

16 Debtors (extract)	**1991 The Group £m**	1990 The Group £m
Amounts falling due after more than one year:		
Trade debtors	**10.0**	4.3
Net advance corporation tax recoverable (Note 21)	**55.0**	55.0
Other debtors	**20.0**	13.9
Pension prepayment (Note 4)	**75.4**	–
	160.4	73.2

4 Pension costs (extract)

The Group operates a number of pension schemes throughout the world under which contributions are paid by Group companies and employees. The assets of the schemes are held in trustee administered funds separate from the finances of the Group.

The rates at which the Group accounts for the main UK pension schemes are assessed in accordance with the advice of qualified actuaries. The projected unit method was used for all but the three smaller UK schemes, for which the attained age method was used, and the latest valuations of the various schemes were as at April 1988, 1989 and 1990. The valuations of the two principal UK schemes assumed an investment return of 2 per cent or 1½ per cent higher than the rate of inflationary salary growth and 5 per cent higher than the rate of increase of present and future pensions.

At the date of the latest actuarial valuations, all the main UK schemes were in surplus. The market value of their assets was £646 million which is a significant increase as a result of the acquisition of Davy Corporation plc. The actuarial value of the assets was sufficient to cover 126 per cent of the benefits that had accrued to members, after benefit improvements made following the valuations. £75.4m of the surplus, relating to Davy schemes, has been dealt with as described below and the remaining surplus is to be spread over the service lives of employees in the relevant schemes.

The three UK pension schemes operated by Davy have been assessed at the date of acquisition by the Company's actuaries on a basis consistent with that being used for Trafalgar House pension schemes. As part of the adjustments to arrive at fair value set out in Note 25 a sum of £75.4m has been included on the balance sheet, representing the funding surplus in respect of the Davy schemes. This surplus will be amortised in future periods.

Deferred taxation

Introduction

23.363 The guidance in FRS 7 for dealing with deferred taxation on acquisitions is very thin. It would not be surprising if some of the more complex issues that arise from combining the tax affairs of the parties to an acquisition result in varying interpretations. The main problem is that the concept of 'partial provision' in SSAP 15 is at odds with the principles on which FRS 7 is built, because both the identification and measurement of deferred tax liabilities in any company under SSAP 15 are heavily influenced by the management's intentions that may affect the likely pattern of future tax liabilities, including those relating to future capital expenditure, asset disposals, etc. Under FRS 7, with a few exceptions, the intentions of the acquirer's management are not supposed to affect fair values attributed at the date of acquisition.

23.364 A range of possible approaches to deferred tax accounting has been exposed during the development of the accounting standard on fair value accounting. In ED 53 the ASC had proposed a tax equalisation approach, in which fair value adjustments made to other assets and liabilities would have been accounted for as if they were timing differences. The effect of such proposals would have been to minimise distortions in the effective rate of tax after the acquisition when fair value adjustments fed through into the profit and loss account.

23.365 In the discussion paper that preceded FRED 7, the ASB had proposed a completely different approach that would have required deferred tax assets and liabilities of the acquired company to be recognised in the fair value exercise by considering the acquired company's own tax position as a separate entity before the acquisition. This approach would have been consistent with the ASB's approach to fair valuing other assets and liabilities.

23.366 In FRED 7, the ASB abandoned the approach taken in the discussion paper, which it considered would be unworkable in practice. The reason was that it would often not be possible to assess what the deferred tax liability of an acquired company would have been under SSAP 15 before the acquisition, because it would not have been possible for an acquirer to make or test assumptions about the future intentions of the acquired company's management. The ASB reached a pragmatic solution by proposing that the acquiring group should use SSAP 15 principles for establishing initial post-acquisition deferred tax balances for the enlarged group as a whole.

23.367 FRS 7 has adopted the same approach that was proposed in FRED 7. The standard requires the following:

- Deferred tax assets and liabilities recognised in the fair value exercise should be determined by considering the enlarged group as a whole. [FRS 7 para 21].

- The benefit to the group of any tax losses attributable to an acquired entity at the date of acquisition should be recognised in accordance with SSAP 15. [FRS 7 para 22].

23.368 The following paragraphs consider practical issues for implementing these broad requirements. The steps involved include:

- Considering the acquired company's own deferred tax position, in order to schedule the timing differences.
- Determining whether the fair value adjustments to the assets and liabilities of the acquired company should be accounted for as if they were additional timing differences.
- Assessing, from a group perspective, the amount of potential deferred tax liabilities and assets that will probably become payable or recoverable.

23.369 The ASB has a project underway to review SSAP 15. Any move away from partial provision to, for example, full provision would be likely to make the deferred tax aspects of acquisition accounting much more straightforward to apply than is presently the case with the combination of FRS 7 and SSAP 15.

Identifying timing differences

23.370 Timing differences arise when income and expenditure are recognised in financial statements in different periods from those in which they are recognised for tax purposes. When fair value adjustments are made to certain assets and liabilities, further differences may arise because gains or losses recognised in the financial statements relating to the pre-acquisition period are dealt with for tax purposes in post-acquisition periods. The ASB's discussion paper 'Accounting for tax' states that fair value adjustments are not timing differences as defined in SSAP 15 because they are not recognised as gains or losses in the financial statements of the combined entity. Instead, they are permanent differences. Nevertheless, it indicates that it is common practice in the UK to treat fair value adjustments as if they were timing differences. [DP 8.1.4,5].

23.371 Examples of fair value adjustments that may give rise to differences between accounting and tax profits in the financial statements of the enlarged group are as follows:

- Revaluation of stocks in the acquired company to replacement cost.

  If stocks are revalued above cost, the profit for the post-acquisition period will be the difference between the sale proceeds and the fair values of stocks sold, but the tax charge will be based on the difference between the sales proceeds and the cost of sales in the acquired company's books.

- Revaluation of land and buildings above cost.

Under SSAP 15, a revaluation will create a timing difference insofar as the profit that would result from disposal at the revalued amount would be taxable, unless a disposal and any subsequent replacement of the asset would not result in a tax liability, after taking account of any expected rollover relief.

- Revaluation of plant and machinery.

  Where depreciable assets are revalued to, for example, depreciated replacement cost, the depreciation charged in the post-acquisition period would increase, whereas capital allowances available to the acquired company would be unaffected by the revaluation.

- Assets or liabilities recognised in respect of pension surpluses or deficiencies of an acquired company.

  Tax relief on employers' pension contributions is generally granted in the period in which the contributions are paid. Where a pension asset or liability is recognised as a fair value adjustment, it might be treated as a timing difference for deferred tax purposes because the pension cost recognised in post-acquisition periods will differ from contributions paid. The asset or liability would reverse over the period the surplus or deficiency is eliminated, for example the period of reduced or enhanced employer contributions.

23.372 We consider that in many situations it would be appropriate for the acquiring group to recognise, as part of the fair value exercise, deferred tax on fair value adjustments. In our view, this treatment would reflect a proper allocation of the tax charge between the pre- and post-acquisition performance of the acquired company.

23.373 In the past, plant and machinery and stocks have not often been revalued upwards in most fair value exercises. In relation to stocks the tendency has been to make provisions against the book value rather than to revalue upwards. If, as a result of FRS 7, companies are more ready in the future to revalue plant and machinery and stocks upwards, then the tax effects will become more significant.

Enlarged group basis

23.374 FRS 7 requires the provision for deferred tax to be viewed from the overall position of the enlarged group. SSAP 15 requires the combined effect of timing differences to be considered when assessing whether a tax liability will crystallise. It also requires this assessment to be based on reasonable assumptions about the future. These should reflect the financial plans or projections of the enlarged group.

23.375 FRS 7 explains that the effect of moving from one set of assumptions (the acquired company) to another (the acquiring group) should be reflected in the fair value exercise rather than as post-acquisition tax charges or credits. Adjustments will, therefore, be required as part of the fair value exercise to restate the aggregate of the existing deferred tax balances in the acquiring and acquired entities to the deferred tax liability or asset of the enlarged group required by SSAP 15 immediately after the acquisition.

23.376 The following are examples of matters to be considered when assessing the combined deferred tax position and, accordingly, the adjustments that are necessary:

- Revalued properties.

  Under SSAP 15, the need for a deferred tax provision relating to a valuation of an asset above cost is normally determined when a decision is made to dispose of the asset. Therefore, the acquirer's intentions regarding holding or disposing of relevant assets in the acquired company need to be taken into account in assessing whether a deferred tax provision is required.

- Accelerated capital allowances.

  Where tax has been deferred in an acquired company due to accelerated capital allowances, the need for a deferred tax provision in the enlarged group should be determined by substituting the acquirer's capital expenditure plans for those of the acquired company on which any previous deferred tax liability was based. The effect of changed assumptions should be reported as fair value adjustments.

- Retained profits in overseas subsidiaries.

  SSAP 15 states that the retention of overseas earnings will create a timing difference only if there is an intention or obligation to remit them, and remittance would result in a tax liability after taking account of any related double tax relief. The acquirer's intentions will be relevant to assessing the deferred tax position in the enlarged group and any changes would be reported as fair value adjustments.

- Pensions and other post-retirement benefits.

  SSAP 15 (as amended in December 1992) permits either the full provision basis or the partial provision basis to be used in accounting for the deferred tax implications of timing differences relating to pension cost accounting. The deferred tax implications of assets or liabilities recognised in the fair value exercise in respect of pension surpluses, deficiencies or other obligations in the acquired company should, therefore, be recognised on a basis that is consistent with the accounting policy adopted by the acquiring group.

23.377 Other deferred tax implications arise from combining the tax affairs of the acquiring and acquired entities, including the operation of group relief arrangements.

Example 1

The acquirer has provided for a deferred tax liability, but the acquired company expects to have net originating timing differences in the future, which can be used to reduce the acquirer's tax liability.

In this situation, if the acquirer assesses that no deferred tax is likely to become payable in the enlarged group as a result of the acquisition, the adjustment of the acquirer's deferred tax liability to nil would be reported as a fair value adjustment in the acquirer's group accounts.

Example 2

An acquirer can demonstrate that it will be able to use tax losses carried forward to group relieve tax liabilities arising in the acquired company in future periods.

SSAP 15 requires a provision for deferred tax liabilities to be reduced by any deferred tax debit balances arising from separate categories of timing differences. In the context of the enlarged group, if there is a deferred tax liability in the acquired subsidiary's financial statements it would be reduced in the fair value exercise to the extent that the acquiring group is expected to be able to use its future tax losses to relieve any tax arising in the acquired company.

Tax losses

23.378 FRS 7 only deals specifically with tax losses in the *acquired* entity at the date of acquisition. The measurement of the asset is required to follow the criteria set out in paragraph 30 of SSAP 15 for recognising tax losses as deferred tax assets.

23.379 Hence, tax losses would be treated as follows in the fair value exercise:

- First, they would be set off against deferred tax liabilities, if any.

- Secondly, they would be recognised as deferred tax assets to the extent that their recovery is assured beyond reasonable doubt, taking account of evidence available up to the date that the fair value exercise is completed. Thus any tax losses recovered in the hindsight period would be recognised as deferred tax assets in the fair value exercise. It would be a matter of judgement as to how much, if any, of the losses carried forward to future periods would also be recognised as deferred tax assets.

- Thirdly, if they do not meet the SSAP 15 recognition criteria within the permitted hindsight period, no deferred tax asset would be recognised; instead, the tax losses would flow through into the profit and loss account of the acquiring group as and when they become recognisable.

23.380 In its 1985 financial statements, CH Beazer (Holdings) PLC included a deferred asset in respect of tax losses of a newly acquired company. This disclosure reflected the value of losses to be used up within a limited period of two years, with the value of remaining losses not being recognised. The deferred tax asset in Beazer's financial statements was £2,162,000 and is explained in Table 23.20.

Table 23.20 – CH Beazer (Holdings) PLC – Report and Accounts – 30 June 1985

Notes to the accounts (extract)

15. Deferred taxation (extract)

The acquired deferred tax losses reflect the value attributed at the time of acquisition to the tax losses of William Leech and its subsidiary companies to the extent that they are expected to be utilised in the period to 30th June 1987. This amount is taken into account in arriving at the goodwill written off on this acquisition.

Certain group companies have further tax losses of some £12,800,000 (1984 – £4,000,000), in aggregate, which are available for set off against those companies' future taxable profits. Of this sum, a total of approximately £11,400,000 relates to losses of Leech and its subsidiaries which were acquired during the year, the utilisation of which is not anticipated prior to 30th June 1987.

23.381 The treatment of previously unrecognised tax losses in the acquiring group is more problematical in terms of what should be reported as fair value adjustments and what should flow through into the post-acquisition profit and loss account. Although it is not dealt with in the standard, it appears reasonable to make a working assumption that the benefit to the acquiring group of losses utilised against post-acquisition profits of the acquired business would usually be taken in the post-acquisition profit and loss account, except to the extent that the losses are offset against deferred tax liabilities when the deferred tax position of the enlarged group is considered.

ACT

23.382 Similar considerations to the treatment of tax losses would apply to the treatment on acquisition of surplus ACT carried forward in the acquired company or the acquiring group.

23.383 The benefit to the group of any ACT carried forward in the acquired company at the date of acquisition would be recognised in accordance with SSAP 15. Therefore, provision for deferred tax liabilities, as adjusted, would be reduced by ACT which is available for offset against those liabilities. Any asset to be recognised in the fair value exercise (that is, as recoverable ACT) would be assessed by taking account of circumstances up to the end of the permitted hindsight period – normally recognising ACT whose recovery was assured beyond reasonable doubt, looking no further than the hindsight period and the succeeding accounting period. Any ACT that is not permitted to be recognised as an asset by SSAP 15 (irrecoverable ACT) at the end of the hindsight period would flow through into the post-acquisition profit and loss account as a credit to the tax charge in the period in which it becomes recoverable.

23.384 There may also be some circumstances where, following the principle that deferred tax should be determined on a group basis, surplus ACT in the acquiring group that was previously written off, but which becomes recoverable as a result of the acquisition, should be recognised in the fair value exercise rather than as post-acquisition credits.

23.385 One example is where a deferred tax liability is created or increased as a fair value adjustment and which can be reduced by such surplus ACT. The ACT offset against the deferred tax liability should also be increased as a fair value adjustment by bringing back surplus ACT at the appropriate rate of offset.

23.386 Another example is where a group acquires a company with a capacity to absorb ACT against profits earned in pre-acquisition periods, in circumstances that enable the acquiring group to recover surplus ACT.

23.387 Where, in contrast, a group with surplus ACT acquires a company which provides a future source of UK taxable profits against which the acquiring group expects to be able to surrender ACT, the accounting effects of any recovery of surplus ACT would generally be treated as post-acquisition.

Tax relief on goodwill arising on US acquisitions

23.388 Under US tax regulations, when a US company is acquired, it is possible in some circumstances for the group to obtain tax relief in the US on goodwill acquired. This arises, for example, where a purchaser is able to elect to treat a stock purchase as though it were a purchase of tangible and intangible assets including goodwill. The goodwill is amortised for tax purposes over a predetermined life.

23.389 The question is how this tax relief should be accounted for in the group accounts of the UK parent when, in common with most UK groups before FRS 10 came into effect, purchased goodwill was not recognised as an asset, but was eliminated on acquisition against reserves. Potential treatments include: allowing the tax credit to flow through annually into the profit and loss account, noted as an exceptional tax credit if material; or recognising a deferred tax asset on acquisition in respect of the anticipated future tax relief.

23.390 Under the flow through method there appears to be a mis-match in the acquirer's post-acquisition financial statements, because the tax relief relates to an 'asset' that has been written off directly to reserves under the accounting policies of the acquiring group.

23.391 Recognising the future tax relief as a deferred tax asset (or reducing deferred tax liabilities) treats the immediate write-off of goodwill as a timing difference. An analogy can be made with an asset which is written down in the financial statements to zero in year one, but which is written down for tax purposes, and attracts tax allowances, over several years.

23.392 It could be deduced from the requirement to consider the enlarged group as a whole that, in principle, a deferred tax asset should be set up in the fair value exercise. Applying SSAP 15 principles, a deferred tax asset should be recognised unless it is not recoverable without replacement by equivalent debit balances, or there is reasonable doubt about whether there will be sufficient future taxable profits to enable the asset to be recovered.

Disclosure of special circumstances affecting tax charge

23.393 Both FRS 3 and the Act require an explanation to be given in the financial statements of special circumstances affecting the tax charge for the period and for future periods. FRS 3 requires the individual effects of any special circumstances to be quantified.

23.394 There are a number of situations where the tax consequences of an acquisition can have a significant effect. Some of these have been mentioned in the preceding paragraphs. An obvious candidate is the effect on the tax charge of losses utilised or carried forward for relief in future periods, where they have not been recognised in the fair value exercise. When such losses are significant the effect on the tax charge and earnings per share in the post-acquisition consolidated financial statements can be material and should be disclosed.

Fair valuing the purchase consideration

Cost of acquisition

23.395 The Act and FRS 7 state that the acquisition cost of a subsidiary is made up of some or all of the following elements:

- Cash consideration.
- Fair value of other consideration.

- Expenses of acquisition.

[4A Sch 9(4); FRS 7 para 26].

23.396 Consequently, the objective of determining the fair value of the consideration given is to fix the acquisition cost of the investment. Where cash forms part of the consideration, the fair value will be the amount payable in respect of the item, unless settlement is deferred, where it may be necessary to discount it (see para 23.416 below).

23.397 Non-cash consideration may take the form of:

- The assumption of liabilities by the acquirer.
- Quoted securities issued.
- Unquoted securities issued.
- Consideration given in the form of non-monetary assets, including securities of another entity.

23.398 The assumption of liabilities by the acquirer may take the form of the repayment of borrowings in an acquired company owed to its former investors, including, in the case of the purchase of a subsidiary from its former parent, the repayment of an acquired company's intra-group debt.

23.399 The fair value would be the amount paid or payable, discounted to present value, if necessary, where settlement of the liabilities is due at a future date.

23.400 Securities issued by the acquirer may take the form of:

- Ordinary shares.
- Preference shares (convertible or non-convertible).
- Loan stock (convertible or non-convertible).
- Share warrants and other options relating to the securities of the acquiring company.

23.401 The various elements that make up the total consideration are considered further in the paragraphs that follow.

Quoted securities

23.402 The most common form of securities given as consideration is ordinary or equity shares. The standard states that the fair value would usually be taken to be the market price at the date of acquisition. For practical purposes, the mid-market price is normally used. There are two related issues:

- The point in time at which shares should be valued.

- The use of alternative valuations to a valuation based on the quoted market price.

23.403 Where control is transferred by a public offer, the fair value of securities given as consideration should be based on the market price of the security on the date on which the final successful offer becomes unconditional. This is in line with FRS 2 which defines this as the date on which an undertaking becomes a subsidiary. This price takes account of the market's reaction to a bid and movements in the share price of a bidder.

23.404 In order to avoid a major fluctuation in share price on a single day distorting the acquisition price, the standard states that market prices for a reasonable period before the date of acquisition, during which acceptances could be made, would need to be considered. It may then be appropriate to base the fair value on an average of market prices over a short period. Such method of valuation would, however, be the exception rather than the rule, because only in very unusual circumstances – for example, a market rumour causing a very temporary blip in the share price – would the actual market price on the date of acquisition fail to provide the most reliable measure of fair value.

23.405 Where the shares are quoted, but trade in them is infrequent, as in the case of some public companies with significant family shareholdings (close companies) and unprogressive dividend policies, market price could be an unreliable measure of fair value. In such circumstances, the approach applied for valuing unquoted securities, as set out below, may be more appropriate.

Unquoted securities

23.406 Where no market price is available for ordinary shares (or where the market price of quoted securities is inappropriate), the fair value should be estimated by traditional share valuation methods. For example, applying an appropriate capitalisation rate to earnings (P/E ratio), or discounting the cash flows of securities to their present value. The values of unquoted securities can sometimes be estimated by reference to securities with, and issued by enterprises with, similar characteristics.

23.407 In some cases it may not be possible to value the consideration given by any of the above methods. The cost of acquisition, in such circumstances, should be determined by valuing the business being acquired (that is, including its goodwill) rather than by valuing the securities issued.

Other securities

23.408 The general principles that apply to determining the fair value of ordinary shares can also be applied to other securities, such as preference shares, loan stock, share warrants and other options. Consequently, where there is a market price available, the market price on the date on which the successful offer finally becomes unconditional should be used. Where there is no market price, similar bases to those described above should be used. For convertible securities, such as convertible loan stock or preference shares, the fair value will include the value of the conversion rights and be related to the value of the security into which it can convert in the future.

Non-monetary consideration

23.409 FRS 7 states that where the purchase consideration takes the form of non-monetary assets, fair values would be determined by reference to market prices, estimated realisable values, independent valuations, or other available evidence. [FRS 7 para 80].

23.410 The purchase consideration may sometimes take the form of other assets, for example, where a company has an investment in a second company (which may be listed) and swaps that investment for a controlling interest in another company. In acquiring the holding in the new subsidiary, the consideration given will be the shares in the second company. Under FRS 7 it would be necessary to arrive at a current fair value of the holding in the second company and this would represent the cost of the holding in the new subsidiary.

23.411 If the fair value of the investment in the second company is greater than the carrying value, a difference will arise between the original carrying value of the second company and the cost of the investment in the new subsidiary. The question arises as to whether this difference represents a realised profit. The answer to this question would probably be that the profit should be treated as unrealised, because it will not be realised until the new subsidiary is disposed of.

Other consideration

23.412 There are certain forms of 'consideration' that for tax or other reasons are sometimes given. These include payments made for an agreement by a vendor not to compete with the acquirer for a number of years and bonus payments to vendors who continue to be directors of the acquired company after the acquisition. The standard mentions that in practice it will be necessary to look at the substance of the relevant transactions in order to determine the accounting treatment. If the payments represent compensation for post-acquisition services or profit sharing, they should be reported as post-acquisition revenue costs. If the payments are in substance consideration for the business acquired, they should be capitalised as part of the acquisition cost.

23.413 The accounting treatment should reflect the true commercial effect of the transactions, both the initial purchase consideration and subsequent payments, in the eyes of the acquirer and vendor. If, for example, payments are conditional on the recipients remaining with, and providing continuing future services to the acquired company, there would be a presumption that the post-acquisition payments should be charged as post-acquisition expenses in the profit and loss account of the acquiring group. On the other hand, if it can be clearly demonstrated that the purchase consideration has been reduced in anticipation of additional payments, and such payments are not conditional on the recipient providing future services to the company, the payments are likely in substance to be additional purchase consideration.

23.414 Purchase consideration can take the form of a special dividend paid by the acquirer after the date of acquisition. For example, as part of the offer a special dividend might be paid shortly after the acquisition to those members who became shareholders as a result of accepting the acquirer's offer for the shares of the acquired company, and the dividend may be equivalent to an interim or final dividend payable by the acquirer in respect of a period prior to the acquisition. This is not specifically mentioned in FRS 7, but in principle such dividends could be treated as part of the purchase consideration where it can be demonstrated that the payment was in substance part of the acquisition cost. An example of this treatment is shown in Table 23.21. Where a dividend is capitalised in this way, the acquirer would need to ensure that the cost of the dividend is not double-counted in arriving at the fair value of the total consideration. For example, the shares issued in consideration for the acquisition may need to be valued at an ex-div price.

Table 23.21 – Redland PLC – Report and Accounts – 31 December 1992

Notes to the accounts (extract)

6 Dividends

	Year ended 31.12.92 £million	Year ended 31.12.91 £million
Ordinary shares:		
Interim paid: 8.25p per share net (1991: 8.25p)	39.5	27.9
Final proposed 1992: 16.75p per share net (1991: 16.75p)	80.3	57.0
Total dividends on Redland PLC ordinary shares: 25.0p per share net (1991: 25.0p)	119.8	84.9
Less: transfer to cost of investment to Steetley plc	(8.6)	–
	111.2	84.9

Scrip dividends to the value of £5.1 million in respect of the 1991 final dividend and £1.9 million in respect of the 1992 interim dividend were taken instead of a cash payment.

23.415 For tax reasons, payments that are in substance a form of purchase consideration are sometimes made by the acquired company itself (subject to financial assistance considerations), rather than by acquirer. If the acquired company's financial statements include a provision in respect of such payments, on consolidation this provision should be regarded as part of the cost of acquisition rather than as a pre-acquisition liability of the acquired company. Accordingly, the obligation to make such payments should be treated in the fair value table as an element of the purchase consideration and not as a reduction in the net assets of the acquired company.

Deferred consideration

23.416 Part of the consideration for an acquisition may become payable at a date after the acquisition has been completed. Such deferred consideration could take the form of cash, shares or other consideration where the amounts are known with certainty. FRS 7 requires the fair value of all forms of consideration to be reflected in the cost of acquisition.

Deferred cash consideration

23.417 The fair value of deferred consideration payable in cash should be taken to be the amount of cash payable discounted to its present value. In addition, the present value of deferred cash consideration would be provided in the acquirer's financial statements as a liability. The standard states that the appropriate discount rate is the rate at which the acquirer could obtain a similar borrowing, taking into account its credit standing and any security given. [FRS 7 para 77].

23.418 The treatment of deferred consideration in FRS 7 is consistent with the treatment of the various forms of debt finance in FRS 4. The difference between the amount (fair value) at which the liability is stated at the acquisition date and the total amounts payable at future dates is a finance cost, analogous to the finance costs of debt in FRS 4, and should be charged as an interest expense in the acquirer's post-acquisition profit and loss account over the period the liability is outstanding. The 1994 financial statements of Verson International Group plc disclose deferred cash consideration that has been discounted to present value. The relevant extract is reproduced in Table 23.22.

Table 23.22 – Verson International Group plc – Annual Report – 31 January 1994

Notes to the accounts (extract)

16. Creditors – amounts falling due after more than one year (extract)

		Group	
		1994	1993
		£000	£000
Bank loans	– U.K. (secured)	**2,250**	2,750
	– overseas (secured)	**10,529**	10,204
Other loans		**2,023**	2,483
Deferred consideration		**6,554**	6,454
Hire purchase and finance lease creditors		**646**	1,306
Other long term creditors		**2,122**	1,923
		24,124	25,120

Deferred consideration includes an amount of £5,334,000 (1993 – £5,024,000) relating to the agreement to repurchase, on or before 8 September 1996, 42,094 non-voting preference shares in Clearing-Niagara Inc. (formerly Niagara Machine and Tool Works) held by the former owners, for a total amount of $9,500,000. The balance reflects amounts outstanding on the acquisition of a freehold property in the USA also acquired during 1993.

The deferred consideration in respect of the acquisition of Clearing-Niagara Inc. has been discounted from the anticipated settlement date at a rate of 6.875%. The difference between this present value and the mandatory purchase amount has been accrued through a charge to interest payable of £343,000 (1993 – £128,000) during the year.

Deferred share consideration

23.419 Where the deferred consideration is in the form of shares, the fair value should, in accordance with FRS 4, be credited directly to shareholders' funds. The most appropriate treatment is to disclose such deferred consideration under share capital as a separate caption with a heading such as 'shares to be issued'. In the analysis of shareholders' funds that is required by FRS 4, the recognised amount of deferred share consideration should be attributed to equity interests or non-equity interests as appropriate.

23.420 The valuation of deferred share consideration, and other deferred consideration in a form other than cash, would be based on the principles that apply to those forms of consideration as discussed above. Normally with shares, the amount of deferred consideration payable is fixed at the date of acquisition and the number of shares issued to satisfy that consideration varies according to the market price of the shares at the date the consideration is issued.

23.421 FRS 7 makes no reference to the question of discounting deferred share consideration. The ASB's discussion paper that preceded FRED 7 explained that deferred share consideration is analogous to the issue of warrants (which are covered by FRS 4) and that theoretically its fair value at the date of acquisition is the value of the right conferred upon the vendor to receive shares at a future date.

23.422 In theory, following the principles in FRS 4, deferred consideration in the form of *non-equity shares* would initially be recorded at a present value, where the discount rate would reflect the cost of capital implicit in the shares that are to be issued. However, the question of discounting deferred share consideration seems rather esoteric, especially as any finance cost reported during the period the consideration was outstanding would be shown as an appropriation and so would not affect reported profit. Consequently, it is likely to be ignored in practice.

[The next paragraph is 23.426.]

Contingent consideration

23.426 FRS 7 deals specifically with the treatment of deferred consideration where the amount payable is uncertain because it is contingent on the outcome of future events. The most common form of contingent consideration arises where the acquirer agrees to pay additional consideration if the acquired company achieves a certain level of performance.

23.427 The standard requires *"a reasonable estimate of the fair value of amounts expected to be payable in the future"* to be included in the cost of acquisition when the fair value exercise is undertaken. [FRS 7 para 27].

23.428 This amount will have to be adjusted, if necessary, when the final amount payable is determined, or when revised estimates are made. Such adjustments should continue to be made to the cost of acquisition and, therefore, to goodwill, until the consideration is finally determined. In contrast to fair valuing assets and liabilities acquired, there is no limit on the period in which this aspect of the fair value exercise must be determined.

23.429 Once a reasonable estimate has been made of the future consideration payable, the same principles of valuing the components of the consideration (including discounting estimated amounts to their present values) that are discussed in the above section on deferred consideration would be applicable in order to record the initial cost of acquisition at its estimated fair value.

23.430 In practice, the acquirer may need to look at profit forecasts for the acquired company on expected, best case and worst case scenarios. Provision for future consideration would normally be made on the basis of the expected outcome.

23.431 A practical problem is that it may be very difficult to make reliable estimates of the future consideration in some cases. For example, such consideration might depend on an average of profits of the acquired company for three years into the future and might not be payable at all unless the average exceeded a certain amount. The acquired company may be in a development phase where any forecasts are extremely subjective and unreliable. When the acquirer's first post-acquisition financial statements are prepared it could be very difficult to assess the probable amount, or indeed whether any amount will be payable. In those circumstances, the standard explains that at least those amounts that are reasonably expected to be payable would be recognised. [FRS 7 para 81].

23.432 If, for example, a minimum sum is guaranteed to be paid as part of contingent consideration, at least this minimum must be provided initially. Any further sums must be provided as soon as reasonable estimates can be made. It cannot be assumed that contingent consideration can adequately be dealt with by giving details of the contingency in a note to the financial statements, together with a range of possibilities. An example of a company that provided for contingent consideration is given in Table 23.23.

Table 23.23 – Logica plc – Annual Report – 30 June 1994

Notes to the accounts (extract)

12 Acquisitions

On 2 May 1994 Logica North American Inc, acquired the business of Precision Software Corporation for an initial consideration of £2,340,000. The balance sheet of Precision Software Corporation on acquisition was as follows.

	Book value at 2 May £000	Fair value adjustments £000	Fair value at acquisition £000
Intangible assets	1,381	(1,381)	0
Tangible assets	296	68	364
Work in progress	66	0	66
Trade debtors	87	(45)	42
Creditors – amount falling due within one year	(217)	(198)	(415)
Net assets acquired	1,613	(1,556)	57
Goodwill			3,582
Consideration			3,639
Satisfied by:			
Cash			2,200
Related costs of acquisition			140
Deferred consideration			1,299
			3,639

The fair value adjustments relate to the revaluation of a freehold property, a debtor provision, and the alignment of accounting policies with those of the Group.

The deferred consideration is payable upon the achievement of certain minimum targets. This represents the minimum amount that is reasonably expected to be payable. Further performance related payments up to a maximum of £4,545,000 may become payable between the date of acquisition and June 1998.

Initial estimates of the deferred consideration will be revised as further and more certain information becomes available with corresponding adjustments to goodwill.

Discounting contingent cash consideration

23.433 Following the principle in paragraph 77 of FRS 7 (see para 23.417 above), the fair value of contingent consideration payable in cash should be taken to be the estimated amount of cash payable discounted to its present value.

23.434 A practical problem arises, because when the contingent consideration becomes more certain as the time gets nearer to its payment, the previously estimated amount may prove to be incorrect. Where this is so, the amount provided should be revised as the outcome becomes more certain until the ultimate amount is known. These amendments will also affect the amount of goodwill recognised on the acquisition and similar adjustments should be made to the goodwill figure until the consideration is finally determined. The problem is how to account for the interest effect in each accounting period if the estimate (undiscounted) of the future consideration is continually revised – in effect, how to discount a moving target. Consider the following example.

Example

An acquisition is made on 1 January 19X1. Part of the consideration for the acquisition, payable in cash on 1 January 19X4, is subject to the achievement of specified performance levels in the acquired company over the next three years. The maximum consideration payable is £20m, and the directors of the acquirer have estimated that the final figure will be £10m. This figure of £10m, subject to discounting, is to be added to the cost of acquisition and included as a provision in the acquirer's consolidated financial statements. A discount rate of 10%, reflecting the acquirer's cost of debt, is to be used.

The fair value (that is, net present value) at 1 January 19X1 of the estimated deferred liability of £10m is £7,513,000. This figure is included in the cost of acquisition and the calculation of goodwill. An interest cost of 10% should be charged on the deferred liability, giving an interest charge of £751,300 for 19X1, which is added to the deferred liability. At 31 December 19X1 the deferred liability will stand at £8,264,300.

During the year ending 31 December 19X2, interest of £826,430 is charged and added to the deferred liability, which then stands at £9,090,730 in the acquirer's books.

The acquired company performs better than expected during 19X2. When preparing the financial statements for the year ending 31 December 19X2, the directors revise their estimate of contingent consideration upwards to £12,000,000.

A suggested way of dealing with this in the 19X2 financial statements is as follows. The present value at 31 December 19X1 of the new estimate of £12,000,000 is £9,916,800. The increase from £8,264,300 to £9,916,800, (that is, £1,652,500), is added to the cost of investment in the acquirer's books and, hence, to goodwill on consolidation. The interest charge for 19X2 would then be revised upwards from £826,430 to £991,680 and the book value of the deferred liability at 31 December 19X2 would be increased from £9,090,730 to £10,908,480.

(Interest would then be charged in 19X3 on the revised liability of £10,908,480, taking the book value of the liability to its nominal value of £12m at 31 December 19X3, assuming no further revisions of the consideration payable are made.)

An alternative method is to discount the revised estimate back only to 31 December 19X2; the present value is £10,908,000. This gives a goodwill adjustment of £10,908,000 less £9,090,730, (that is, £1,817,270). Interest would then be charged in 19X3 on the revised liability. However, in this case the interest charge for 19X2 would be understated, because it is based on the previous lower estimate of the consideration payable. It would, therefore, only seem to be acceptable to use this method where revised estimates do not have a material effect on the interest calculation in the year in which the revised estimates are recognised.

Consideration to be satisfied by either shares or cash

23.435 Often with deferred or contingent consideration, either the acquirer or the vendor has the option to take the consideration in the form of shares or cash. Consequently, at the date of acquisition it may not be possible to determine how the deferred consideration will be settled. In the past, where the acquirer had the option, the usual accounting treatment has been to reflect his intentions.

23.436 In keeping with the general principles of the standard, FRS 7 does not allow management intentions to dictate the accounting treatment where there are acquirer or vendor options:

- Where the *vendor* has the option to demand shares or cash, the deferred or contingent consideration should be reported as a liability until the consideration is settled.

- Where the *acquirer* has the option to settle consideration by issuing shares or paying cash, the deferred or contingent consideration should be reported as part of shareholders' funds until an irrevocable decision regarding the form of consideration has been taken.

[FRS 7 para 83].

Table 23.24 shows an example of the treatment of contingent consideration to be satisfied in shares or cash at the acquirer's option.

23.437 In either case, the amounts earmarked for settlement of consideration and held, as appropriate, within liabilities or shareholders' funds, will be adjusted during the period the consideration is outstanding, such that the settlement will be recorded at the amount of cash payable or the market value of the shares to be issued. The balance sheet treatment required by the standard also has a profit and loss effect over the period the consideration is outstanding. Whilst changes in estimates of the final value of contingent consideration will result in changes to the cost of acquisition and goodwill, the time value of the deferral of monetary consideration (not deferred share consideration) will also result in an interest cost in the profit and loss account.

23.438 If the vendor has the option to demand shares or cash, and subsequently elects to receive shares rather than cash, the acquirer will nevertheless have suffered an interest cost during the period the consideration was outstanding, because the deferred consideration should have been reported as a liability. Conversely, if the acquirer has the option to issue shares or to pay cash, and subsequently elects to pay cash rather than to issue shares, it appears that the acquirer will have avoided an interest cost in the profit and loss account, because the deferred consideration should have been reported as part of shareholders' funds, not as a liability.

Table 23.24 – Scottish & Newcastle plc – Annual Report and Accounts – 28 April 1996

GROUP AND COMPANY BALANCE SHEETS **(extract)**

	Notes	GROUP 1996 £m	GROUP 1995 £m	COMPANY 1996 £m	COMPANY 1995 £m
Capital and reserves					
Equity share capital	20	**180.5**	163.1	**180.5**	163.1
Non-equity share capital	20	**15.0**	16.6	**15.0**	16.6
Called up share capital		**195.5**	179.7	**195.5**	179.7
Contingent equity share capital	20	**21.1**	–	**21.1**	–

20 **SHARE CAPITAL (extract)**

	Authorised 1996 £m	Authorised 1995 £m	Issued and fully paid 1996 £m	Issued and fully paid 1995 £m
Equity share capital				
Ordinary shares of 20p each	**141.2**	141.1	**122.7**	106.8
Special deferred shares of 20p each	**57.8**	56.3	**57.8**	56.3
	199.0	197.4	**180.5**	163.1
Non Equity share capital				
Cumulative preference shares of £1 each				
4.6% + tax credit	**3.9**	3.9	**3.9**	3.9
6.425% + tax credit	**7.0**	7.0	**7.0**	7.0
7% convertible	**4.1**	5.7	**4.1**	5.7
	15.0	16.6	**15.0**	**16.6**

As contingent consideration for the acquisition of the Courage business there is contingent share capital of £21.1m representing ordinary shares to be issued to Foster's Brewing Group (note 25).

25 **ACQUISITION OF THE COURAGE BUSINESS (extract)**

The contingent consideration is that Scottish & Newcastle have agreed to pay to the Foster's Brewing Group in either 1999 or 2000 a sum equal to the increase in value of ten million of the Company's ordinary shares over 537p per share. Payment to the Foster's Brewing Group will be satisfied at Scottish & Newcastle's option either by the issue of ordinary shares or in cash. An estimate of the contingent consideration is shown in the fair value table above and in contingent share capital in note 20.

[The next paragraph is 23.442.]

Disclosure of contingent consideration

23.442 FRS 6 requires the following to be disclosed in respect of deferred or contingent purchase consideration:

- The nature of the consideration.
- The range of possible outcomes.
- The principal factors that affect the outcome.

[FRS 6 para 24].

23.443 This disclosure is required individually for each material acquisition, and in aggregate for other acquisitions. [FRS 6 para 23]. The example in Table 23.23 covers these requirements.

Consideration contingent on net assets

23.444 In some cases the amount of contingent consideration depends not on the future performance of the acquired company, but on the outcome of an uncertainty in the valuation of the net assets acquired, for example the settlement of a contingent liability. The outcome of the contingency may not be determined until after the hindsight period allowed for finalising the fair values of assets and liabilities has expired. FRS 7 does not deal with this situation. Clearly, the fair value of the purchase consideration and, hence, the cost of acquisition (and goodwill) should be adjusted to reflect any increase or decrease in the consideration payable. It also appears that the fair value of the contingent liability (and goodwill) should be adjusted by the same amount, in order to achieve a proper matching, despite the fact that this adjustment is outside the hindsight period, so that there is no net change in goodwill on the acquisition.

Example

A group has acquired a new subsidiary that had given warranties in respect of products it had sold in the past. A provisional amount of purchase consideration was payable in cash on completion. This amount is subject to revision at a future date. The revised figure depends on the extent to which costs relating to those warranties crystallise. If they exceed a level specified in the sale and purchase agreement, the vendor will refund the difference. If they are lower, the acquirer will pay the difference to the vendor. How should these aspects of the acquisition be accounted for?

A provision for warranty costs should be included in the consolidated financial statements as an identifiable liability of the acquired subsidiary at the date of acquisition. In common with other pre-acquisition obligations, the fair value would be determined by making a reasonable estimate of the costs that are likely to crystallise.

FRS 7 explains that the acquiring group's management's best estimate of the likely outcome should normally be used if this is different from any previous estimate. Therefore, if the estimate used in attributing a fair value to the provision is different from the amount specified in the agreement, the fair value of the purchase consideration should be increased or reduced by the difference. A debtor or a creditor for the future amounts expected to be refunded from, or paid to, the vendor would be set up. As the adjustment to the provision is matched by an adjustment to the purchase consideration, there is no net effect on goodwill.

When the warranty costs incurred by the acquired subsidiary crystallise in future accounting periods, further adjustments will be required in the acquiring group's post-acquisition financial statements if the costs incurred differ from the estimates used in the initial fair value allocation. The fair value of the purchase consideration and, hence, the cost of acquisition, should be adjusted to reflect the final revised consideration.

A matching adjustment needs to be made to the fair value of the identifiable net assets acquired, so that overall there is no net effect on goodwill or on the group's profit and loss account. This is achieved by increasing or decreasing the fair value of the warranty provision attributed to the acquired subsidiary at the date of acquisition.

Although FRS 7 requires the cost of acquisition to be revised without time limit where any part of the purchase consideration is contingent, it does not normally permit any further fair value adjustments to the acquired subsidiary's assets and liabilities after the specified investigation period.

However, in these particular circumstances, where a change in the outcome of a pre-existing contingent liability is offset by a matching revision to the purchase consideration, we believe that the matching treatment described above should be preserved even though the outcome of the contingency may not be determined until after the hindsight period normally allowed has expired, because there is no impact on goodwill.

Fees and other expenses of acquisition

23.445 Costs incurred in carrying out an acquisition need to be analysed into two elements.

- Costs of raising capital for the acquisition and of issuing capital instruments in consideration for the acquisition. Where these fall within the restrictive definition of 'issue costs' contained in FRS 4, they should be accounted for as a deduction from the proceeds of those capital instruments.

- Fees and similar incremental costs, excluding costs of raising capital, incurred directly in making an acquisition. These should be added to the cost of acquisition.

23.446 Costs of raising capital that do not qualify to be treated as issue costs under FRS 4, and other expenses that cannot be treated as part of the cost of acquisition under FRS 7 (see para 23.449 below), should be written off to profit and loss account as incurred.

23.447 First, it is necessary to allocate the expenses between those that relate to issuing capital instruments and those that relate to other aspects of negotiating and transacting the acquisition. The treatment of issue costs required by FRS 4 applies whether capital is raised to finance acquisitions or for any other purpose. Such costs might include underwriting, legal and other fees in connection with share issues, and arrangement fees payable to banks for providing loan finance. This will result in any issue costs associated with an acquisition being accounted for as follows (as required by FRS 4).

- Issue costs relating to bank loans and other forms of debt should be initially deducted from the liability and subsequently written off in the profit and loss account over the term of the debt.

- Costs of issuing equity shares should be debited against reserves. The share premium account would be available for the write-off of such issue costs.

- Costs of issuing non-equity shares should initially be debited against reserves, including share premium, and subsequently written off in the profit and loss account as part of the appropriation in respect of non-equity shares over the term of the shares.

23.448 Secondly, it is necessary to consider which of those expenses that do not qualify as issue costs under FRS 4 should be capitalised by adding them to the cost of acquisition as required by FRS 7. By treating expenses as part of the cost of acquisition, they are included in the calculation of goodwill and, if goodwill is written off directly to reserves, they are excluded from the post-acquisition profit and loss account.

23.449 FRS 7 also provides a narrow definition of costs that may be capitalised. They include *"fees and similar incremental costs incurred directly in making an acquisition"*, but must not include *"internal costs, and other expenses that cannot be directly attributed to the acquisition"*. [FRS 7 para 28].

23.450 Therefore, costs eligible for capitalisation might include fees payable to merchant banks, lawyers, accountants and other advisors for:

- Investigating and valuing the target.
- Auditing the completion accounts.
- Negotiating the price and completing the transaction.
- Undertaking due diligence work.

23.451 The treatment of fees in respect of searching for and identifying the business that was subsequently acquired is marginal. A finders' fee resulting from work commissioned to identify a suitable target might qualify to be capitalised where it relates to the business that was acquired; however, in general, other search and investigation fees incurred before a specific target has been identified would need to be written off.

23.452 Moreover, where such services are provided by in-house departments of the acquirer rather than by external advisors, FRS 7 does not allow the costs to be capitalised. Previously there was sometimes argument over whether allocations of costs such as time spent by a company's management on researching and negotiating an acquisition, or specific overtime payments related to work on the acquisition, could be capitalised. FRS 7 precludes capitalisation of *any* internal costs.

23.453 The ASB had exposed an alternative view in FRED 7 that would also have allowed costs to have been capitalised where they were incurred in respect of equivalent services provided by in-house departments, such as legal advice or acquisition search and investigation services. The ASB decided that the difficulty of satisfactorily defining eligible internal costs, and the consequent risk of allowing excessive costs to be capitalised, outweighed the anomalies in the restrictive approach taken in FRS 7.

23.454 In practice, the work carried out by advisors in respect of transacting the acquisition will overlap the work on raising capital. It may then be necessary to make reasonable allocations of advisors' expenses to determine which accounting treatment is appropriate.

Section III – Goodwill

Introduction

23.455 Goodwill has been one of the most hotly debated subjects in accounting. The most fundamental issue was whether purchased goodwill arising from acquisitions should or should not be treated as an asset in the balance sheet. During one of the longest running of accounting debates, deeply entrenched views were held on both sides. The publication of FRS 10 in December 1997 was a major event that would change the shape of the financial statements of acquisitive companies. For financial years from December 1998, purchased goodwill must be accounted for as an asset. Even the ASB was not unanimous in its support for the final standard; a dissenting view of one Board member was published with the FRS.

23.456 FRS 10 superseded SSAP 22, which had been the accounting standard on goodwill (produced by the ASC) since 1984. The ASC had started developing its standard in the early 1970s. SSAP 22 was the result of a compromise between those who supported capitalising purchased goodwill and eliminating it by gradual amortisation through the profit and loss account, and those who supported eliminating goodwill immediately on acquisition against shareholders' funds.

The move from immediate write-off to capitalisation

23.457 SSAP 22 had allowed a choice of methods, except that the immediate write-off option was preferred in the standard. The immediate write-off method was also the preferred method in practice with the overwhelming majority of listed companies using this method as opposed to capitalisation and amortisation.

23.458 The effect of immediate write-off has been that net assets have been reduced, but the profit and loss account has not had to bear any charge for goodwill, except on disposal. In contrast, capitalising and amortising goodwill has a positive balance sheet effect – increasing shareholders' funds and reducing gearing. But it has a negative effect on performance measures shown in the financial statements – reducing the rate of return on investments in new businesses and reducing earnings per share. It has even been argued by some that UK companies have had an advantage – say in a contested acquisition – over US bidders, because US bidders would have to recognise and amortise goodwill and so could not 'afford' to pay as much as UK bidders who could 'lose' goodwill from the balance sheet. Others have argued that users ignore goodwill in financial statements, because its accounting treatment has no relevance to future cash flows.

23.459 Previous attempts by the ASC to introduce a policy of capitalisation and amortisation into UK accounting (as proposed by ED 47 in 1990) foundered because they met a hostile response: companies argued that they should not be forced to charge amortisation (suggesting a loss of value of goodwill) when the acquired business was flourishing and, if anything, the value of the goodwill was increasing.

23.460 When the ASB took control of the project, it was determined that SSAP 22 should be replaced with a standard that prescribed one method only of accounting for goodwill. The development of FRS 10 took several years. It involved a wide-ranging discussion paper (1993) covering the pros and cons of several different methods based around capitalisation and elimination, public hearings on initial proposals on which it sought to build a consensus (1995), and an exposure draft FRED 12 (1996). The proposals submitted for the public hearings attracted sufficient support for the ASB to develop them into a draft accounting standard and, with only fine tuning, into the final standard.

23.461 The ASB's project did not find a conceptual solution to the goodwill problem. Goodwill does not meet ASB's own definition of an asset in its draft Statement of principles, because a company does not control the future benefits. However, the ASB settled on capitalisation of purchased goodwill, rather than elimination, for a number of reasons:

- Management accountability for the cost of goodwill on acquisitions is maintained (rather than lost) in the accounting treatment.
- Purchased goodwill and intangibles that are similar to goodwill are accounted for consistently.
- Capitalisation had become the accepted treatment internationally.

23.462 One of the key issues for the ASB was to develop an acceptable method of dealing with the amortisation problem. Just as there is a conceptual divide between treating the amount spent on goodwill as an asset and treating it as a reduction in shareholders' equity, so there is a divide between treating capitalised goodwill as a depreciable asset and treating it as an investment with continuing value. One view is that the original purchased goodwill is depleted over time and replaced by internally generated goodwill which cannot be recognised. Another view is that the cost of goodwill to the group should be treated consistently with the cost of investment by the parent, which is only written down if its carrying value is impaired, that is, not supported by the value of the future cash flows of the acquired business.

23.463 The ASB has been sympathetic to the investment argument and to the principle that goodwill should be written off in the profit and loss account only if, and when, its value is impaired and not gradually over an arbitrary period. But an important constraint is that the Act requires purchased goodwill to be fully amortised over a finite period if it is treated as an asset. It does not allow goodwill to be carried permanently as an asset. FRS 10's method of accounting for goodwill is, however, something of a hybrid between the automatic amortisation and impairment approaches. The constraints of law and practicality led the ASB to develop a method that would allow goodwill to be amortised quickly, slowly or not at all according to the circumstances. But the final standard steers companies firmly towards automatic amortisation over a maximum 20-year period, which is the same approach that had previously met such strong opposition from the corporate sector.

23.464 So it appears that the ASB cleverly managed to build enough support around an approach that is not very different to what was so strongly objected to before. In practice, the requirements that must be met to justify carrying goodwill or other intangibles indefinitely without amortisation are more likely to be achievable for a limited range of separable intangibles, such as durable brands, than for goodwill itself.

Scope of FRS 10

23.465 FRS 10 is really two standards rolled into one. It covers all goodwill (arising from business acquisitions and from acquisitions of equity accounted interests in associates and joint ventures) and, with a few exceptions, all intangible assets (including those identified in a business acquisition, those purchased separately and those developed internally). The ASB found it convenient to deal with both goodwill and intangibles in a single standard because they are closely related and the ASB decided the same accounting rules should apply to both.

23.466 Many intangibles and goodwill share similar characteristics. Accounting for intangibles is an important issue in acquisition accounting because any values ascribed to separate intangibles reduce the residual amount of goodwill. It is less of an issue, however, under FRS 10 than it was under SSAP 22 when, on the one hand, goodwill could be written off to reserves immediately on acquisition whilst, on the other hand, intangibles could be recognised as assets.

23.467 The rules relating to identifying intangible assets in acquisition accounting are discussed from para 23.154. The recognition and measurement rules that apply to purchased and internally developed intangible assets are discussed in chapter 14. The discussion in this section primarily considers purchased goodwill arising from business combinations. FRS 10's application to associates and joint ventures is discussed in chapter 28.

Definition of purchased goodwill

23.468 Purchased goodwill is simply an accounting difference. It is the amount by which the cost of a business entity as a whole exceeds the aggregate fair values of its identifiable assets and liabilities at the date of acquisition. Those fair values are determined by applying the rules in FRS 7 and they are used as the carrying amounts (a proxy for cost) for the newly acquired assets and liabilities in the acquirer's financial statements. If the aggregate fair values of the acquired business' identifiable assets and liabilities exceed the cost of acquisition, the difference is referred to as negative goodwill.

23.469 Purchased goodwill may arise in the acquirer's consolidated financial statements only (where a parent company acquires a new subsidiary), or in the acquiring entity's individual financial statements (where it purchases an unincorporated undertaking or a business and assets of another company).

Accounting for goodwill – summary

Internally generated goodwill

23.470 Internally generated goodwill may be viewed as the difference between the market value of a business entity and the aggregate fair value of its net assets. Neither the Act nor FRS 10 allows internally generated goodwill to be recognised on the balance sheet. The Act states that goodwill may be shown as an asset only if it was acquired for valuable consideration. [Note 3 on the balance sheet formats; FRS 10 para 8].

Purchased goodwill

23.471 FRS 10 requires purchased goodwill to be treated as an asset on the balance sheet. Its objective, in relation to capitalised goodwill, is:

- To ensure that goodwill is charged in the profit and loss account in the periods in which it is depleted.
- To ensure that disclosure is sufficient to enable users to determine the goodwill's impact on financial position and performance.

[FRS 10 para 1]

23.472 Goodwill should be amortised quickly, slowly or not at all according to the circumstances:

- Where goodwill has a limited useful economic life, it should be amortised systematically over that life.
- There is a rebuttable presumption that the useful economic life does not exceed 20 years.
- A longer life than 20 years, or an indefinite life, may be chosen where the value can be demonstrated to be more durable.
- Non-amortisation of goodwill is a 'true and fair override' of company law (which requires goodwill to be amortised down to zero) and so can only be adopted in special circumstances when following the basic rule of amortisation would not give a true and fair view.

23.473 If a company either amortises goodwill over more than 20 years or does not amortise goodwill at all, it has to carry out an annual impairment test. This is a thorough exercise which is aimed at demonstrating whether the present value of the future cash flows that the acquisition will earn are, or are not, enough to justify the carrying value of the goodwill. If they are not, an impairment write-down should be made.

23.474 If a company amortises goodwill over no more than 20 years, a recoverable amount check is required at the end of the first full financial year following the acquisition. This 'first year review' is intended to capture any overpayment for the acquisition or failure of the acquired business to meet expectations at the time of the acquisition. If the impairment review confirms that the carrying value of the goodwill is not recoverable, it should be written down. In other years an impairment test is required only if adverse events indicate that the amortised carrying value of the goodwill may not be recoverable, and an impairment write-down should be made if the test confirms this.

23.475 The details of the impairment tests are found in FRS 11 'Impairment of fixed assets and goodwill'. The tests are complex and subjective. This is particularly so for the not infrequent case where a group acquires a new subsidiary and integrates it into the group. In these situations it is not possible to isolate and track the cash flows attributable to the acquisition.

23.476 Goodwill cannot be revalued above original cost.

23.477 Amortisation or impairment charged in previous periods cannot be reversed in subsequent periods except in limited circumstances with respect to impairment.

Useful economic life

23.478 For each acquisition the useful economic life of the residual amount of purchased goodwill must be estimated.

Definition

23.479 The useful economic life of purchased goodwill is subtly defined, not in relation to the *original* purchased goodwill, but as *"the period over which the value of the underlying business acquired is expected to exceed the values of its identifiable net assets"*. [FRS 10 para 2].

23.480 Purchased goodwill is in effect treated as an element of the investment in the acquired business, that is, the premium over its net asset value. In theory, the useful economic life can be indefinite if management continue to invest in the acquired business so as to maintain the premium; furthermore, the above definition allows for goodwill to be continuously regenerated after the acquisition.

23.481 The definition of useful economic life has been a contentious issue during the development of FRS 10. The ASB has described its approach to amortisation as one which seeks to charge goodwill to the profit and loss account only to the extent that the carrying value of the goodwill is not supported by the *current* value of the goodwill within the acquired business. This allows for purchased goodwill to be carried permanently without amortisation in some circumstances.

23.482 This is different from SSAP 22 which required capitalised goodwill (that is, the *original* purchased goodwill) to be amortised in all circumstances. SSAP 22 specifically did not allow the useful economic life to be extended by the effects of subsequent expenditure or other circumstances subsequently affecting the acquired business. The reason was that they would have the effect of replacing the original purchased goodwill with internally generated goodwill, which cannot be recognised as an asset. The argument was that the benefits of purchased goodwill that existed (and was paid for) at the time of the acquisition are always consumed over a relatively short period; the continuing (or enhanced) premium over net asset value is eventually transformed into internally generated goodwill. This is also the approach adopted by international standards (IAS 22).

Rebuttable presumption of 20 years or less

23.483 Despite the opportunity given by FRS 10's definition to regard goodwill as having a very long or indefinite useful economic life, the practical emphasis in the standard is rather different. The standard explains that *"the transient nature of many business opportunities makes it appropriate for there to be a presumption that the* *'premium' that an acquired business has over its net asset value cannot be maintained indefinitely"*. [FRS 10 para 20]. The framework for determining goodwill's useful economic life is as follows:

- There is a rebuttable presumption that the useful economic life does not exceed 20 years.
- A useful economic life exceeding 20 years, or an indefinite life, may be chosen *only* if:
  - the durability of the acquired business for the longer (or indefinite) period can be demonstrated; and
  - the goodwill is capable of continued measurement (so that annual impairment reviews will be feasible).

[FRS 10 para 19].

23.484 One reason for having a presumed arbitrary upper limit on the useful economic life is that it would otherwise frequently be difficult to estimate it. A period of 20 years is a benchmark that has some significance internationally. However, the uncertainty involved in estimating useful lives does not allow 20 years to be automatically used by default, nor does it allow goodwill to be written off over an unrealistically short period. A company could not, for example, simply expense all goodwill as a one-off hit to earnings in the year of acquisition in order to avoid future amortisation charges. [FRS 10 paras 21, 22].

23.485 On the other hand, the FRS states that the 20-year upper limit *may* be rebutted if the conditions (that is, evidence of durability and continued measurability) are met. Furthermore, the standard's interpretation of those conditions make it improbable that a company could be forced to adopt a useful economic life of more than 20 years if it chose not to, even if the value of the goodwill was expected to be more durable. The assumptions used in forecasting become more vulnerable the longer the estimated life is. For example, in many industries the pace of developments means that consumer patterns cannot be predicted with much certainty over very long periods. Clearly the emphasis is on being prudent, without being unrealistically prudent.

23.486 The second condition for rebutting the 20-year upper limit, that the goodwill is capable of continued measurement, is important. The annual impairment reviews specified by FRS 11 have to be feasible and be expected to remain so for the foreseeable future. FRS 10 states that goodwill will not be capable of continued measurement if the cost of such measurement is viewed as being unjustifiably high. This clearly invites directors to opt not to rebut the presumption of a 20-year life if they judge that the cost of carrying out annual impairment reviews outweighs the benefits. The standard gives as an example the situation where businesses are integrated after acquisition so that the goodwill relating to the acquired business can no longer be readily tracked. Even if there are no such integration plans, the directors may not wish to rule out future reorganisations that could lose the separate identity of the acquired business. Other examples given are where the company's management information systems are not compatible with the detail of the impairment reviews required by the standard, and where the amounts of goodwill involved are not sufficiently material to justify the cost of carrying out the impairment reviews. [FRS 10 para 23].

Factors determining useful economic life

23.487 Apart from explaining the conditions for rebutting the 20-year threshold, FRS 10 gives little guidance on how to estimate the useful economic life. It gives examples of factors that contribute to the durability of goodwill and, since these will limit useful economic lives, they are also relevant for estimating lives that are considered to be 20 years or less. These factors refer to the nature of the business, the stability of the industry, the effects of future competition, the typical lifespans of the products of the acquired business and the extent to which the acquisition overcomes market entry barriers that will continue to exist. [FRS 10 para 20].

23.488 These factors often combine to present an overall picture of durability. A long life (20 years plus) will generally require a business, industry and products to have a long past track record of stability and achievement and to have high barriers to market entry. Added to this, of course, is the commitment of the new management to continue to invest in the acquired business for the long-term to maintain and enhance its value. Other businesses, industries and products may be relatively new, potentially much more volatile and possibly requiring a payback for the acquirer over a much shorter period. An amortisation period much shorter than 20 years may then be appropriate. This may be so for products with expected short life cycles or where there are few barriers to prevent new competitors from entering the market.

23.489 A group should assess the factors at the time it makes an acquisition. Examples of issues to consider are:

- Expected changes in products, markets or technology. A high technology company that only has one main product might have considerable goodwill while that product is leading the market, but if a competitor produces a better product, then the company's goodwill can diminish rapidly.

- Expected future demand, competition or other economic factors that may affect current advantages.

- The expected period of future service of certain employees or the retention period of key clients. An advertising agency's goodwill may be very dependent on key employees/clients and the agency's goodwill may depend significantly on their retention period.

- The extent to which goodwill is linked to the economic lives of intangible assets.

23.490 The last of the above is an important factor that is attached to the definition of useful economic life itself. Where intangible assets have been subsumed into the residual amount of goodwill, because they cannot be measured reliably, the useful economic life of the goodwill is linked to the lives of those intangibles. [FRS 10 para 2]. For example, an acquired company may have a licence to carry on a particular business for a finite period. If the licence were recognised as a separate intangible, it would be amortised over the licence period, unless the licence rights were renewable and renewal were assured. If the value of the licence were subsumed within purchased goodwill, the amortisation period should be the same, that is, aligned with the life of the underlying rights.

23.491 This factor could also work to demonstrate a long or indefinite useful economic life. For example, much of the value of goodwill on an acquisition may be in a brand name that does not meet the recognition criteria for a separate intangible asset. Nevertheless, the brand may have been well established for decades and an indefinite future life may be justifiable by linking the goodwill to the brand that is fundamental to maintaining the current value of the premium in the acquired business.

Accounting implications of life above or below 20 years

23.492 The accounting implications of choosing a useful economic life above or below 20 years are summarised below:

20 years or less	More than 20 years
Amortisation charge against earnings 5% or more	Amortisation charge against earnings less than 5%
	Nil amortisation requires true and fair override
Impairment review at end of first full year, thereafter only on exception basis	Detailed annual impairment reviews
Less exposure to future (unpredictable) impairment losses	Greater exposure to future (unpredictable) impairment losses
	Additional disclosure

23.493 FRS 10 requires disclosure of the amortisation periods and the reasons for choosing those periods. [FRS 10 para 55].

23.494 The additional disclosures required where the useful economic life is more than 20 years are as follows:

- the grounds for rebutting the 20-year presumption, including

- a reasoned explanation based on the specific factors contributing to the durability of the acquired business.

[FRS 10 para 58]

Indefinite life – true and fair override

23.495 The Act states that where goodwill is treated as an asset, it should be reduced by provisions for depreciation calculated to write it off in full (that is, to nil) systematically over a period chosen by the company's directors, which must not exceed its useful economic life. [4 Sch 21(2)(3)]. Therefore, whilst the Act permits goodwill to be amortised over a shorter period than its useful economic life, it does not allow either an indefinite useful economic life or any residual value to be assumed. The Act in effect reflects the traditional view of the useful economic life where the value of purchased goodwill is depleted over time and replaced by non-purchased goodwill generated by the new owners.

23.496 So, non-amortisation can be adopted only by invoking the 'true and fair override' of the Act's requirement for amortisation. Moreover, the Act's true and fair override provisions can only be invoked in 'special circumstances' when following the basic rule of amortisation would not give a true and fair view.

23.497 In the appendix to FRS 10 that explains its development, the ASB states that it believes there may be circumstances where a true and fair view will be given only if goodwill or an intangible asset is not amortised, but is instead subject to annual reviews for impairment. [FRS 10, Appendix III para 35]. But FRS 10 in effect restricts non-amortisation to exceptional circumstances in order to avoid being in conflict with the Act, since the 'true and fair override' cannot be applied indiscriminately. Restricting non-amortisation of goodwill to such 'special circumstances' means that it raises a number of policy issues for companies making acquisitions:

- Non-amortisation must be considered on an acquisition-by-acquisition basis – it cannot be adopted as a general accounting policy.

- The circumstances specified in FRS 10 regarding the indefinite durability of the acquired business place a clear onus on a company's directors to demonstrate that they can maintain (or enhance) the value of the premium paid for the acquisition indefinitely.

- Non-amortisation would be restricted to material acquisitions where amortisation charges would not give a true and fair view.

- The directors must be confident that they will always in the future be able to measure the current value of such goodwill with sufficient reliability to carry out the annual impairment reviews; future business reorganisations may have an impact on this.

- The reaction of analysts and other users needs to be considered if a company claims it has demonstrated no need for amortisation, but other companies in similar sectors chose to amortise their goodwill (and *vice versa*). In this regard, the Institute of Investment Management and Research (IIMR) at present excludes goodwill amortisation from its definition of 'headline earnings'. It will be interesting to see whether any change to this is made in view of the change in accounting rules in FRS 10.

23.498 The required disclosures, which must also comply with UITF 7, give considerable prominence to the 'true and fair override'. The disclosures, which are intended to convey to users the circumstances justifying its use, are:

- A statement that the financial statements depart from the specific requirement of the Act to amortise goodwill over a finite period.

- Particulars of the departure from the Act. This means a statement that the Act would normally require amortisation and a description of the treatment actually adopted.

- The reasons for the departure from the Act, which should include an explanation of the specific factors contributing to the durability of the acquired business. Also there should be a statement as to why amortisation would not give a true and fair view.

- The effect of the departure from the Act – however, this will not normally be possible to quantify, because where goodwill arising from a particular acquisition is assigned an indefinite life, there is no benchmark for calculating an amortisation charge required by the Act. The circumstances should, therefore, be explained.

- The disclosures above should either be included, or cross-referenced, in the note required by paragraph 36A of Schedule 4 (re compliance with accounting standards).

[FRS 10 para 59; UITF 7 paras 4, 7].

Goodwill with more than one useful economic life

23.499 An acquisition of a group of companies may comprise two or more lines of business whose activities differ significantly from one another. The question arises whether the goodwill that arises overall on the acquisition should be allocated to the separate lines of business and, if applicable, those components attributed different useful economic lives. If that is done, the amortisation charge would reflect the different economic lives of the different components.

23.500 Some would argue that, since there is only one acquisition, there is only one composite goodwill amount and one life.

23.501 Allocation of purchased goodwill to different businesses is, however, necessary in order to properly account for future business disposals and to perform the impairment reviews which are specified by FRS 11 'Impairment of fixed assets and goodwill'. FRS 11 requires capitalised goodwill to be allocated to income-generating units along with other assets and liabilities for the purpose of impairment reviews. It also requires goodwill on an acquisition comprising two dissimilar businesses to be reviewed separately for impairment. [FRS 11 para 34]. Therefore, an impairment loss in one business segment could not be offset against an increase in value of the other.

23.502 Although FRS 10 is silent as to whether goodwill can be divided into one or more elements for calculating amortisation periods, it would be consistent with FRS 11's impairment rules for goodwill attributable to dissimilar businesses to be amortised separately if they demonstrably have different useful economic lives. The resulting annual amortisation charge would also better reflect the estimated rate of depletion of the purchased goodwill than using, say, an average of the useful lives of different components.

Example

An acquisition comprises two different business segments. The total goodwill is £1m which is allocated £600,000 to segment A and £400,000 to segment B. The goodwill attaching to segment A is considered to have a useful life of 40 years, whereas the goodwill attaching to segment B has a useful life of 10 years.

One approach might be to estimate a weighted average of the useful economic life in aggregate, that is, 28 years. This may be shortened to 20 years if FRS 10's presumption of a maximum life of 20 years is not rebutted. A 20-year life would give an annual amortisation charge of £50,000; a 28-year life would give an annual amortisation charge of £35,714. However, this approach appears to be flawed, because averaging the short-life goodwill over a longer period means the amounts charged to the profit and loss account in the first 10 years (that is, the short life of segment B's goodwill) understates the amount by which the goodwill is in aggregate expected to be depleted. Therefore, this method may fail FRS 10's objective that goodwill is charged in the profit and loss account in the periods in which it is depleted.

A preferable approach is to amortise the goodwill attributable to the two segments separately. This in turn could lead to two different amortisation patterns.

The first is to amortise £600,000 in segment A over 40 years (£15,000 per annum) and £400,000 in segment B over 10 years (£40,000 per annum). This produces an annual amortisation charge of £55,000 for 10 years and £15,000 for the subsequent 30 years. This pattern matches the actual expected rate of depletion of the goodwill. However, the goodwill in segment A would be subject to annual impairment reviews.

The second is to amortise £600,000 in segment A over 20 years (£30,000 per annum) and £400,000 in segment B over 10 years (£40,000 per annum), if the company decides not to rebut FRS 10's presumption of a maximum life of 20 years. This produces an annual amortisation charge of £70,000 for 10 years and £30,000 for the subsequent 10 years.

23.503 It should be noted that allocating goodwill to different segments could not result in negative goodwill being attributed to one segment and positive goodwill being attributed to another, because neither FRS 10 nor the Act permit purchased goodwill (positive or negative) arising on a single acquisition to be divided into positive and negative components.

Comparison with US GAAP

23.504 In the US and Canada, the maximum period allowed to write off goodwill is 40 years and many corporations use that period. The question that arises for those UK companies that also report under US GAAP is whether different useful economic lives can be used for the same acquisition when reporting under UK and US GAAP.

23.505 Clearly, it is possible, subject to satisfying the conditions in FRS 10 for demonstrating durability and continued measurability, for the useful economic life of goodwill under UK GAAP to be longer than the 40 year maximum imposed by US GAAP. Where goodwill is given an indefinite life under FRS 10, it cannot have an indefinite life under US GAAP (or, for that matter, under IAS).

23.506 Of particular interest is the impact of the rebuttable maximum 20-year period in FRS 10 – can a life of 20 years be chosen for UK reporting purposes and a life of 40 years for US reporting purposes?

23.507 An argument for using the same useful economic life is based on consistency. Both UK and US rules contain similar guidance for the factors to be considered when estimating useful economic lives. In addition, as a general matter, reporting different lives for the same asset may confuse users.

23.508 However, although the differences between UK and US GAAP diminished as a result of FRS 10, significant differences remain. These are illustrated in the following table.

Useful life	
UK	**US**
No upper limit	40 years upper limit
20 years – rebuttable presumption	No equivalent
More than 20 years – requires purchased goodwill to be continually measured	No equivalent

Impairment reviews	
UK	**US**
20 years or less – only on exception basis where indicators of impairment	40 years or less – only on exception basis where indicators of impairment
More than 20 years – annually	No equivalent

23.509 Although US GAAP restricts the amortisation period to 40 years, it has no equivalent of FRS 10's rebuttable presumption of 20 years. A longer period than 20 years requires the ability and willingness of management to carry out annual impairment reviews. This means that the goodwill must be capable of being tracked through any subsequent reorganisations. There is no corresponding requirement for automatic annual impairment reviews under US GAAP. It is, therefore, possible that goodwill could be attributed a 40 year life for US GAAP purposes and a 20-year life (choosing not to override FRS 10's rebuttable presumption) for UK reporting, purely as a result of the GAAP differences.

Revisions of useful economic lives

23.510 Estimating useful economic lives of goodwill is very judgemental. FRS 10 requires that the useful economic lives should be reviewed at the end of each reporting period and revised if necessary. [FRS 10 para 33].

23.511 Useful lives may need to be revised to reflect previously unexpected events or changes in circumstances, such as a major technological change or a market being opened up to greater competition. Adverse factors that might lead to a write-off of goodwill (via the impairment review procedures) might similarly indicate that the remaining useful life of the balance has been shortened.

23.512 Where it is considered that previous estimates of useful economic lives need to be revised, the net book values at the date of revision should be amortised prospectively over the revised remaining useful economic lives. [FRS 10 para 33].

23.513 An estimated useful economic life may be shortened or increased. However, if it is increased from 20 years or less to more than 20 years from the date of acquisition, annual impairment reviews would be required thereafter in accordance with the normal rules for goodwill that is amortised over more than 20 years or not at all. Therefore, a 20-year life in effect remains a ceiling for those companies that are unable or unwilling to carry out annual impairment reviews.

23.514 Where a useful economic life is revised, the reason and the effect, if material, should be disclosed in the year of change. [FRS 10 para 56]. The effect of a change is the difference between the amortisation charge that results from applying the previous and the revised estimated useful lives (that is, how much more or less profit a company records as a result of changing useful economic lives).

Methods of amortising goodwill

23.515 Where goodwill is amortised, it must be amortised down to zero over its estimated useful economic life. No residual value is allowed to enter the calculation. [FRS 10 para 28; 4 Sch para 21(2)].

23.516 For example, it would not be permitted to identify a useful economic life of 20 years and yet charge little or no amortisation, because a significant residual value was expected at the end of 20 years. In that situation, the goodwill is in effect expected to be more durable than 20 years. A low or nil annual amortisation charge can only be arrived at if the presumption of a maximum 20-year life is rebutted and a longer or indefinite life is chosen. Of course, the goodwill would then be subject to annual impairment reviews. If the 20-year presumption is not rebutted, the goodwill must be amortised to zero over 20 years.

23.517 FRS 10 states that the method of amortising goodwill should reflect the expected pattern of its depletion. However, a straight-line method should be chosen, unless another method can be demonstrated to be more appropriate. [FRS 10 para 30]. Although arbitrary, specifying a benchmark method is a practical means of dealing with the difficulty of measuring depletion and it does promote comparability.

23.518 The FRS also explains that it is unlikely that methods that are less conservative than the straight-line method could be justified with sufficient evidence. It also states that interest methods, such as the 'reverse sum of digits' method, which have the effect of backloading the amortisation charge to later periods, are not appropriate methods of amortising goodwill because they are not related to its depletion. [FRS 10 paras 31, 32].

23.519 FRS 10 requires the methods of amortising goodwill to be disclosed. [FRS 10 para 55].

23.520 A company may conceivably wish to change its method of amortising goodwill, say, to revert to the straight-line method from some other method. Where this occurs, FRS 10 requires the reason and the effect, if material, to be disclosed in the year of change. The effect of a change is the difference between the amortisation charge that results from applying the previous and the revised amortisation methods (that is, how much more or less profit a company records as a result of changing amortisation methods).

Acquisition with contingent consideration

23.521 An important practical effect of the goodwill amortisation requirements arises where the consideration for an acquisition is deferred and contingent on the acquired company achieving a specified level of performance in future years. FRS 7 requires a reasonable estimate of the fair value of amounts expected to be payable in the future to be included in the cost of acquisition when the fair value exercise is undertaken. Any such amounts recognised increase the purchased goodwill that is recognised when the acquisition is first accounted for.

23.522 Amortising the whole amount of the estimated purchased goodwill on a straight-line basis from the date of acquisition results in full charges against earnings in the immediate post-acquisition periods, before the future contingent payments have fallen due or been finally determined and possibly before the specified levels of post-acquisition earnings have been achieved. This situation can only be avoided if an amortisation pattern can be justified that increases in line with the actual consideration payments. But, although FRS 10 does not rule this out, as mentioned above, the standard suggests that it is unlikely that there will be circumstances justifying an amortisation pattern that is less conservative than straight-line.

23.523 When contingent consideration is finally determined, any adjustments to the amounts estimated at the time of the acquisition would feed through as adjustments to purchased goodwill. The adjustments would have the effect of increasing or decreasing the annual amortisation charges over the goodwill's remaining useful economic life.

23.523.1 Where material adjustments are made to estimates of contingent consideration, a question arises as to what effect this has on the amortisation of goodwill. There are two possible ways of dealing with this:

- Amortise the revised carrying value prospectively.
- Restore the excess amortisation previously charged (crediting profit and loss account with the excess amount).

23.523.2 These methods are illustrated in the following example.

Example

An acquisition was made at the beginning of year 1. Consideration of £40m was paid on completion and further consideration was payable based on an earn-out formula relating to the performance of the acquired business over the next three years. £60m of further consideration was provided for in the acquirer's first post-acquisition accounts, giving an estimated cost of acquisition of £100m. Net assets were fair valued at £20m, leaving purchased goodwill of £80m. The goodwill is being amortised over five years (straight-line basis) – an amortisation charge of £16m was recognised in year 1, leaving a carrying value of £64m at the end of year 1.

The acquisition does not perform as well as expected. At the end of year 2, the estimate of further consideration payable is revised downwards from £60m to £20m, resulting in an adjustment reducing the carrying value of goodwill by £40m.

The two methods are illustrated in the following tables (a zero discount rate is assumed).

Method (a) – prospective amortisation

Year	1	2	3	4	5
Goodwill b/f	80	64	18	12	6
Adjustment		(40)			
		24			
Amortisation	(16)	(6)	(6)	(6)	(6)
Goodwill c/f	64	18	12	6	-

Method (b) – reversal of excess amortisation charged in previous year

Year	**1**	**2**	**3**	**4**	**5**
Goodwill b/f	80	64	24	16	8
Adjustment		(40)			
Amortisation reversal (credit P&L)		8			
		32			
Amortisation	(16)	(8)	(8)	(8)	(8)
Goodwill c/f	64	24	16	8	-

FRS 10 does not deal with a situation where the amount of goodwill relating to an acquisition is adjusted as a result of a revision of the estimated cost of acquisition. Apart from the reversal (in limited circumstances) of some impairment losses, FRS 10 states *"goodwill ... should not be revalued, either to increase the carrying value above original cost or to reverse prior period losses arising from impairment or amortisation"*. [FRS 10 para 45]. Thus, for example, where the useful economic life is revised, the carrying value at the date of revision should be amortised (prospectively) over the revised remaining useful economic life. [FRS 10 para 33]. This corresponds with method (a) above.

However, the issue described above is not a revaluation in the sense of paragraph 45. The carrying value of goodwill has to be adjusted downwards as a result of the revised estimate of the cost of acquisition. The question in the example above is whether the carrying value at the beginning of year 2 should be adjusted to 24 (method (a)) or to 32 (method (b)).

One of the objectives of FRS 10 is *"to ensure that...capitalised goodwill and intangible assets are charged in the profit and loss account in the periods in which they are depleted..."*. Neither method properly achieves this.

Method (a) overstates the cumulative depletion of goodwill, because an amount has previously been charged in the profit and loss account which, with hindsight, will not be paid for. It also arguably understates the cost of goodwill consumed over the remaining estimated useful economic life.

Method (b) better reflects the cumulative depletion of goodwill, but the current year's amortisation charge does not properly reflect the goodwill consumed in that year, because it is credited with the excess charge of the previous year.

It should also be noted that if the purchased goodwill was being accounted for in the accounts of an individual company, the reversal or non-reversal of past amortisation would directly affect the company's distributable profits.

Our view is that either method is acceptable. Whilst we would normally expect the prospective treatment in method (a) to be adopted where estimates are revised, method (b) could be used where the effect of the adjustment to the cost of acquisition is material to the pattern of goodwill amortisation. Whichever method is chosen, material debits should be treated consistently with material credits in respect of different acquisitions.

Presentation of amortisation and impairment charges

23.523.3 FRS 11 requires impairment losses recognised in the profit and loss account to be included within operating profit under the appropriate statutory heading, and disclosed as an exceptional item if appropriate. [FRS 11 para 67].

[The next paragraph is 23.524.]

23.524 FRS 10's note on legal requirements states that the formats in Schedule 4 to the Act prescribe the headings under which depreciation and other amounts written off tangible and intangible fixed assets are to be included in the profit and loss account. [FRS 10 appendix 1 para 16]. Amortisation and other amounts written off goodwill fall within those headings. Under Format 1, where expenses are classified by function, goodwill would normally be treated as an administrative expense. Under Format 2, where expenses are classified by type, there is a separate heading 'depreciation and amounts written off tangible and intangible fixed assets', which is an operating expense. Both amortisation and impairment losses in respect of goodwill should, therefore, be charged in arriving at operating profit.

23.525 In the financial year in which an acquisition is made, FRS 3 requires the operating results of the acquired business to be disclosed separately in the acquiring entity's profit and loss account. The amortisation or impairment of any goodwill related to the acquisition for that period should be attributed to the results of the acquisition rather than included with other goodwill amortisation charges that are attributable to the results of continuing operations excluding the acquisition.

23.526 Although goodwill write-offs should generally be included in arriving at operating profit or loss, companies that report earnings per share figures may wish to exclude goodwill write-offs in any additional EPS calculated on another level of earnings. The 'headline' earnings figure defined by the Institute of Investment Management and Research (IIMR) in its Statement of Investment Practice No 1, which seeks to produce a standardised measure of trading performance, states that *"goodwill should not affect earnings in any way"*. Consequently, the 'headline' earnings figure excludes any charges in respect of goodwill in its reconciliation of FRS 3 earnings to IIMR 'headline' earnings.

Reversals of past goodwill write-offs

23.527 The carrying value of purchased goodwill cannot be increased by revaluation or by reversing past amortisation charges. If goodwill is considered to have been amortised too quickly in the past, its useful economic life may be increased, but the carrying value should be amortised prospectively over the remaining revised useful life.

23.528 Impairment losses in respect of goodwill may be reversed (that is, credited back in the profit and loss account), but only in limited circumstances. These are where (a) an external event caused the original impairment loss, and (b) subsequent external events clearly and demonstrably reverse the effects of that event in a way that was not foreseen in the original impairment calculations. [FRS 10 para 44; FRS 11 para 60].

23.529 An impairment loss in FRS terminology is similar to provision for permanent diminution in value in the Act. Where there is a permanent diminution in the value of any goodwill held as an asset which is expected to be permanent, a provision should be made in the profit and loss account. [4 Sch 19(2)]. If the reasons for such a provision no longer apply, then the provision should be written back to the extent that it is no longer necessary. [4 Sch 19(3)]. For all practical intents and purposes the reversal criteria in FRS 10 and the Act are deemed to be the same.

23.530 The objective of restricting reversals of impairment losses is to prevent a goodwill write-off from being credited back to the profit and loss account if the credit is in effect attributable to the generation of new non-purchased goodwill. Consequently, situations that justify reversals are likely to be rare and in most cases amounts written off goodwill will stay written off. In this respect, the reversal criteria for goodwill (and most intangible assets) are stricter than those for tangible fixed assets, where impairment losses should be reversed in a much wider range of circumstances provided that subsequent increases in recoverable amount can be attributed to changed economic conditions. The reason given for the different approaches is that tangible fixed assets can in any case be revalued, whereas goodwill and most intangible assets cannot be.

23.531 One example of originating and reversing external events that would meet the reversal criteria for goodwill is the introduction of a new law that damages profitability (resulting in a goodwill write-off) and that is subsequently repealed by a new government. Another example is the confiscation of assets in an overseas territory (resulting in a goodwill write-off) that are subsequently released to allow the business to continue its operations. In both of these examples the original goodwill has been reclaimed.

23.532 The recoverable amount of an acquired business may increase in subsequent years after an impairment loss has been recognised, but the improvement will often be unrelated to the circumstances that gave rise to the original impairment. One example is where goodwill has been written off because a competitor has introduced a better product to the market; some years later, the company launches a new product of its own and regains its lost market share. Another example is where a business has been reorganised to curtail underperforming operations, resulting in a write-off of goodwill; in later years, the business may expand again as new market opportunities arise. In neither of these examples would the turnaround justify reversing the impairment loss relating to the goodwill if the recoverable amount of the business has increased above the balance sheet value of its net assets and goodwill, because the higher value of goodwill that now exists includes goodwill that has been generated internally since the original impairment.

23.532.1 It should be noted that if the net assets of a business included impaired carrying values for both purchased goodwill and tangible fixed assets, and their recoverable amount subsequently increased, the impairment losses relating to the tangible fixed assets would be reversed in circumstances such as those described above, unlike the goodwill. The situation where some impairment loss reversals are permitted (for tangible fixed assets) and others are not (for goodwill and most intangible fixed assets) may occur with business restructurings. Goodwill and tangible fixed assets of businesses in need of reorganisation may have to be written down (there is a concession, though, for recent acquisitions – see para 23.606.3 below); if their values are restored as a result of reorganisation, only the impairment losses relating to the tangible fixed assets may be written back in the profit and loss account.

[The next paragraph is 23.533.]

23.533 The amount that can be written back to reverse an impairment loss is restricted to an amount that increases the carrying value of the goodwill to the carrying value that would have been recognised had the original impairment not occurred. [FRS 11 para 61].

23.534 The following disclosures relate to reversals of past impairment losses:

- The Act requires provisions for permanent diminutions in value that are written back because they are no longer necessary to be disclosed in the profit and loss account or in a note to the financial statements. [4 Sch 19(3)].

- FRS 10 requires reversals of past impairment losses to be disclosed separately in the note that reconciles the movements between the opening and closing goodwill balances. [FRS 10 para 53].

- FRS 11 requires that the reason for the reversal of impairment losses in respect of fixed assets or goodwill should be disclosed, together with any changes in the assumptions upon which the calculation of recoverable amount is based. [FRS 11 para 70].

Allocation of purchased goodwill

23.535 Groups need to keep detailed records of the composition of the aggregate amount of purchased goodwill, that is, to which parts of the group it relates. Allocation of goodwill to business units is necessary in order to:

- Account for subsequent disposals.
- Carry out impairment reviews.
- Keep track of elements of goodwill with different useful economic lives (see para 23.499).

Disposals

23.536 Where businesses are disposed of, the net book value of any related goodwill has to be eliminated from the balance sheet and written off as part of the profit or loss on disposal.

23.537 Even where pre-FRS 10 goodwill was written off to reserves, profits or losses on disposals of businesses had to include any related goodwill that had not previously been written off in the profit and loss account. This continues to be a requirement in respect of pre-FRS 10 goodwill that remains written off to reserves under FRS 10's transitional arrangements.

23.538 It has always been recognised that there are practical difficulties with attributing goodwill to businesses disposed of. Traceability of purchased goodwill is an issue in complex group structures, particularly where an acquired business quickly loses its separate identity or when businesses undergo change and restructuring. The requirement in UITF 3 (since superseded by FRS 10) was that records should normally be sufficient to enable *"an appropriate estimate or apportionment"* of goodwill to be made. This implied that the amount of goodwill attributed to disposals is often likely to be a 'soft' number which is the product of a judgmental allocation exercise. Nevertheless, groups have generally managed to make reasonable allocations of goodwill to disposals.

Impairment reviews

23.539 Some allocation of purchased goodwill to separate businesses may also be necessary for carrying out the impairment reviews required by FRS 10. For example, impairment tests on goodwill relating to dissimilar businesses have to be performed separately on each dissimilar business.

23.540 Any goodwill that is amortised over more than 20 years (or not amortised at all) must be formally reviewed for impairment each year.

23.541 Even where goodwill is amortised over 20 years or less and, as a result, no annual impairment reviews are required, there is still a possibility that an impairment review will be required in the future. This will be the case if evidence emerges that the net book value may not be recoverable.

23.542 The details of impairment reviews are considered from paragraph 23.571.

Guidelines on allocating goodwill

23.543 On a group acquisition, the aggregate amount of goodwill may need to be allocated across a range of business units. In particular, goodwill will need to be disaggregated if a business in that group is sold or terminated. As far as is practical and consistent with the requirements of the impairment review, the objective should be to allocate goodwill balances to business units on a basis consistent with the group's management reporting structure.

23.544 In principle, goodwill should be allocated based on information and factors existing at the date of acquisition. A reasonable guideline is found in US GAAP, where such allocations to each business unit should be completed within the hindsight period for completing the fair value exercise.

Positive and negative goodwill

23.545 The acquisition of a group may give rise to positive goodwill overall. Where the acquisition includes a loss-making or marginally profitable business, the issue is whether negative goodwill can be attributed to that business, leaving a larger amount of positive goodwill attributable to the others. This could have a significant impact on disposal profits and losses.

23.546 Allowing both positive and negative goodwill to be recognised in respect of a single acquisition would introduce far more subjectivity into the allocation process than already exists. The ASB specifically prohibited such an approach in FRS 10, following the principle that goodwill (positive or negative) is a residual difference that arises from fair valuing the acquisition as a whole.

23.547 Businesses would, therefore, receive a zero allocation of goodwill where it is believed to be negative or nil at the date of acquisition. The overall goodwill on the acquisition would be allocated to those businesses where it is believed goodwill does exist.

23.548 Similarly, where an acquisition gave rise to negative goodwill overall, the negative goodwill would be allocated to those businesses where it is believed negative goodwill existed. No positive goodwill would be attributed to other businesses.

Allocation principles

23.549 There is no real guidance in accounting literature on allocating purchased goodwill to different business units. FRS 11's rules on measuring impairment of fixed assets and goodwill would both require assets, liabilities and goodwill associated with acquisitions to be allocated to separate business units which are identified to tie in with management information systems. But there is no guidance on how the allocation of goodwill should be done.

23.550 In the US, FAS 121 'Accounting for the impairment of long-lived assets and for long-lived assets to be disposed of', requires that when fixed assets are tested for recoverability, any related goodwill should be allocated to the business units on a pro-rata basis using the relative fair values of the fixed assets and recognised intangibles acquired at the acquisition date, unless there is evidence to suggest that some other method of associating the goodwill with those assets is more appropriate.

23.551 If the acquirer, when framing its offer, had assessed individually the value of different businesses in an acquired group, such valuations should be a good starting point for the allocation of goodwill. Thereafter, various methods could be adopted to apportion goodwill to different businesses (or income-generating units, as required for conducting impairment reviews in accordance with FRS 11). The choice should best reflect the basis on which the business would be valued by the market. Example methods are:

- Using discounted cash flow forecasts where these are available at the time of the acquisition.
- Pro-rata on the basis of a price-earnings formula, using cash flows or income streams projected at the acquisition date.
- Pro-rata on net asset value at the acquisition date (probably excluding interest-bearing debt and other financing liabilities).
- Pro-rata using the fair values of the fixed assets at the acquisition date.

23.552 Earnings-based methods (the first two bullet points above) may give a very different goodwill allocation from asset-based methods (the last two bullet points). The choice should be determined by ascertaining how the market rates businesses similar to those acquired – on an earnings or net assets basis. Earnings-based methods are, in general, likely to be appropriate for most acquisitions because asset-based methods do not generally reflect the relative profitability of different businesses. A cash flow/PE approach is also consistent with the rules in FRS 11 concerning measurement of the continuing value of purchased goodwill. An asset value basis would be appropriate for some asset-based acquisitions, such as property companies.

23.553 The choice of a price-earnings formula could be influenced by considering PE ratios of similar businesses that are quoted. For example, if an acquisition comprised a construction and a transport operation, the allocation would take account of the differing PE ratios relating to those sectors at the acquisition date.

23.554 No goodwill would be attributed to a business unit where management believe none existed when the group was acquired – for example, where a business is loss-making or operating at a low level of profitability that does not cover the cost of capital.

23.555 An example of different allocation methods is illustrated below.

Example – allocation of purchased goodwill

An acquisition of a group comprises three business segments A, B and C. Total purchase consideration was £450m. The fair value of the net assets in aggregate was £350m (as allocated in the table below), leaving goodwill of £100m. Different allocation methods are illustrated in the table below.

Business acquired	**A**	**B**	**C**	**Total**
Profit (estimated)	20	30	(5)	45
Net assets – fair value	200	100	50	350
Sector PE ratio	12	8		
Goodwill – earnings basis	22	78	Nil	100
Goodwill – net assets basis	67	33	Nil	100

Segment C (which is loss-making) receives a zero allocation of goodwill under both methods. Therefore, all of the goodwill has been allocated to A and B.

On an earnings basis, A and B are each valued at £240m (that is, 12 × £20m and 8 × £30m respectively), compared with fair valued net assets of £200m and £100m respectively. The purchased goodwill of £100m is allocated *pro rata* to the amount by which the values of A and B exceed the fair values of their net assets (£40m and £140m respectively) which results in £22m being allocated to A and £78m being allocated to B.

On a net assets basis, the purchased goodwill of £100m is allocated *pro rata* to the fair valued net assets of £200m in A and £100m in B, which results in £67m being allocated to A and £33m to B.

Integrated acquisitions

23.556 Tracing goodwill is more difficult, and allocations may become more arbitrary, where acquired businesses lose their separate identity as a result of post-acquisition integration with pre-existing operations and reorganisation.

23.557 However, it is usually possible to make such allocations on a reasonable basis, for example by tracking products, markets and key assets introduced by acquisitions. Subsequent business reorganisations would require a reallocation of goodwill balances.

23.558 Allocations can normally be readily achieved where branded activities were acquired, since these may be easily identifiable in current business units, especially if the products have not changed significantly over time. In other cases, more judgement is required. For example, where an established brand has been re-branded since its acquisition, the original purchased goodwill would (assuming the acquired operation is still continuing in some form) be attributed to the operation where the re-branded activity resides.

23.559 It should be noted that if a subsidiary is acquired and the business is subsequently transferred to another part of the group, leaving the subsidiary to be liquidated, no goodwill is transferred to the consolidated profit and loss account (as would happen if the business were sold), because the goodwill attaches to the retained business, not to the legal entity.

Impairment reviews

Purpose of impairment reviews

23.560 The impairment review is a recoverable amount check. It follows the long-established principle that an asset's balance sheet carrying value should not exceed its recoverable amount, which is measured by reference to the future cash flows that can be generated from its continued use or disposal. Impairment is defined in FRS 10 as *"a reduction in the recoverable amount of a fixed asset or goodwill below its carrying value"*.

23.561 Measuring the recoverable amount of purchased goodwill is complicated, because goodwill is by definition not a separable asset – it attaches to a business as a whole. The details of impairment reviews for fixed assets and goodwill are quite prescriptive and are contained in FRS 11 'Impairment of fixed assets and goodwill'.

When impairment reviews are required

23.562 The requirements for impairment reviews differ according to whether goodwill is amortised over more or less than 20 years, as illustrated below.

Impairment reviews	
Useful life 20 years or less	**Useful life more than 20 years**
End of first full year (simplified review)	Every year (detailed review)
Other years – high level check for impairment indicators detailed review only if impairment indicators are present	

23.563 Where goodwill is carried permanently as an asset or amortised over a very long period, there is a greater risk of impairment in the future. Where goodwill is written off over a shorter period, there is less risk of impairment, because its net book value in any case diminishes more quickly. A threshold of 20 years has been chosen, below which the impairment reviews are less onerous than for longer periods.

Useful life 20 years or less

First year review

23.564 A first year impairment review is required on all acquisitions where goodwill arises. This should be carried out at the end of the first full financial year following the acquisition. The timing of this review corresponds with the end of the investigation period in FRS 7, when the fair value exercise on the assets and liabilities of the acquired business should be completed and the final goodwill figure established. This review is intended to identify factors such as:

- Overpayment.
- Under performance compared with expectations.
- Material adverse changes to the acquired business in the immediate post-acquisition period.

23.565 The first year review has two stages. The first stage in effect requires management formally to consider whether the acquisition has lived up to expectations. This is done by comparing post-acquisition performance with the forecasts used in the acquisition appraisal and by considering whether there have been any other unexpected adverse events or changes in circumstances that throw doubt on the recoverability of the capitalised goodwill. If the acquisition passes this test, there is no need to go on to the second stage.

23.566 The second stage, which is a full impairment review (as described from para 23.571 below), is only necessary if the first stage indicates that there may be an impairment problem. [FRS 10 para 40].

Reviews in other years

23.567 After the first full year, management has to consider whether events or changes in circumstances indicate that the amortised carrying value of goodwill may not be recoverable. If there are no such indicators, no further work is required. In many situations it would be immediately apparent that there is no impairment. The goodwill will in any case be fully written off over 20 years at most.

23.568 FRS 11 gives a list of examples of situations that indicate fixed assets and goodwill may have been impaired. The list of impairment indicators is not intended to be exhaustive; management should consider the effect of any other material adverse changes to the business and the environment in which it operates. The main indicators relevant to capitalised goodwill are:

- Operating losses or net cash outflows incurred or expected.
- Adverse change in the business or market, such as the entrance of a major competitor.
- Adverse change in the statutory or regulatory environment.
- Commitment to a significant reorganisation.
- Major loss of key employees.
- Significant increase in market interest rates or rates of return.

23.569 If there are factors that indicate that the carrying value of goodwill may not be recoverable, a full impairment review has to be carried out and, if impairment is confirmed, the carrying value should be written down to the recoverable amount. This means the onus is then on management to demonstrate positively that assets have not been impaired if a write-down is to be avoided.

23.569.1 Some may find it curious that, in historical cost accounting, a company may be required to reduce the carrying value of fixed assets or purchased goodwill because interest rates have increased. However, FRS 11 emphasises that increases in short-term interest rates would not necessarily trigger an impairment review, because they may not affect the rate of return the market would require on long-term assets. [FRS 11 para 11].

[The next paragraph is 23.570.]

23.570 As a practical matter, a company may have opted to amortise goodwill over 20 years rather than a longer period, because it did not consider the annual impairment reviews that would then be required to be feasible. The company may not, therefore, have the records necessary to carry out a full impairment review as prescribed in FRS 11 some years after the acquisition if an impairment indicator arises, especially if the acquisition has been integrated into other operations and has lost its separate identity. Quantifying any impairment loss with an acceptable degree of reliability will then be difficult. In some extreme circumstances it would be prudent to write off a whole tranche of goodwill if there is evidence of impairment rather than to attempt arbitrary, and subjective, calculations that will be unreliable.

Detailed impairment review

23.571 A detailed impairment review is required in the following situations:

- Where goodwill is amortised over more than 20 years or carried permanently as an asset at each year end automatically (including the end of the year in which the acquisition took place).
- Where goodwill is amortised over 20 years or less:
  - At the end of the first full year following the acquisition, *only* if there is an indicator of impairment or if the first year review indicates that the post-acquisition performance has failed to meet pre-acquisition expectations.
  - In other years, *only* if there is an indicator of impairment.

23.571.1 The impairment review compares the carrying value of goodwill with its recoverable amount. The recoverable amount of goodwill is the higher of its net realisable value, if known, and its value in use. Value in use is defined as *"the present value of the future cash flows obtainable as a result of an asset's continued use, including those resulting from its ultimate disposal"*. [FRS 10 para 2]. To the extent that the carrying value exceeds the recoverable amount, goodwill is impaired and should be written down. In practice, unless a business is being sold, its goodwill does not have a net realisable value that can be determined objectively, and so its recoverable amount is normally its value in use.

[The next paragraph is 23.572.]

23.572 The details of the impairment review concerning the calculation of value in use differ according to whether:

- Goodwill *only* is being reviewed for impairment (for example, the mandatory annual review for goodwill with a useful life of more than 20 years, where there are no indicators of impairment).
- Goodwill *and* other fixed assets are being reviewed for impairment (for example, because there are indicators that an impairment may have occurred).

23.573 The differences relate to the level of aggregation at which groups of assets or businesses are reviewed for impairment, as explained in the following paragraphs.

23.574 In summary, the steps in the calculation of value in use are:

- Identifying separate income-generating units.
- Establishing balance sheets for each income-generating unit, comprising the net tangible and intangible assets plus allocated purchased goodwill.
- Forecasting the future cash flows of the income-generating unit and discounting them to their present value.
- Comparing the PV of the cash flows with the balance sheet net assets and recognising any shortfall as an impairment loss.

23.575 Where goodwill has to be reviewed annually for impairment, but is not actually expected to be impaired, the reviews in subsequent years after the first annual review can often be performed by updating the calculations performed for the first review. FRS 10 notes that if there have been no adverse changes since the first review, it may be possible to ascertain immediately that there has been no impairment. [FRS 10 para 38].

[The next paragraph is 23.577.]

Identifying income-generating units

23.577 Cash flows are normally generated by groups of assets (tangible and intangible) working together, usually by the whole range of assets used in a business. The recoverable amount of goodwill (or, indeed, of most fixed assets) cannot be determined in isolation. Therefore, a degree of aggregation is necessary in order to estimate value in use for complete groups of assets and associated goodwill.

23.578 FRS 11 requires that companies should divide their activities into 'income-generating units' and, in general, carry out impairment reviews at that level. An income-generating unit (IGU) is defined as:

> *"A group of assets, liabilities and associated goodwill that generates income that is largely independent of the reporting entity's other income streams. The assets and liabilities include those directly involved in generating the income and an appropriate portion of those used to generate more than one income stream".* [FRS 11 para 2].

23.579 Management has discretion to identify IGUs to fit their information systems within the following parameters set out in FRS 11:

- The groups of assets and liabilities should be as small as is reasonably practicable (consistent with the principle that assets should be valued separately).
- The income streams of each IGU should be largely independent of each other and should be capable of being monitored separately.
- IGUs are likely to be identified in a way that is consistent with the level at which management makes decisions about continuing or closing different lines of business.
- IGUs may be identified by reference to major products or services.
- Unique intangible assets (such as brands and mastheads) can often be used to identify IGUs because they may generate income independently of each other and are usually monitored separately.

[FRS 11 paras 27 to 29].

23.580 Several commentators on FRED 15 referred to the subjectivity involved in identifying IGUs and raised issues as to when income streams are really independent.

23.581 For example, in businesses that operate large numbers of retail outlets, such as stores, restaurants and financial services, different companies may take different views as to whether an IGU is an individual retail outlet or a group of outlets in a smaller or larger geographical region. Much depends on how they are managed and how independent or interdependent they are.

23.582 In general, the higher the level of aggregation the greater is the risk that impairment losses on unprofitable assets can be masked by unrecognised increases in value of profitable ones. Hence, impairment reviews should as a matter of principle be carried out at the lowest level that is practicable. FRS 11 does accept, though, on materiality grounds that in some cases the impairment review may be conducted at a level that combines a number of IGUs, that is provided that material impairments would not escape recognition by such aggregation. The FRS gives an example of a restaurant chain where, although each restaurant may be a separate IGU according to its definition, any impairment of individual restaurants is unlikely to be material. Hence, groups of restaurants that are affected by the same economic factors may be reviewed together for the purpose of identifying material impairments.

23.583 There are many situations where business units may appear to have independent income streams, but where they are not in fact economically independent. An example is a transport operator that may operate a number of unprofitable routes in order to have access to profitable ones – it could not obtain the benefits of the latter without incurring the cost of the former where it may be under contract to provide a specified minimum level of service. Each route may have its own dedicated assets and identifiable revenues and operating costs, but the cash flows are not independent in an economic sense. It would not make sense to review the assets of the unprofitable routes in isolation and incur write-downs on those assets when the business at a higher level is earning an adequate return on its assets. An IGU would then need to be identified at a level that grouped one or more profitable routes with dependent unprofitable routes.

23.584 In response to respondents' concerns about this issue, additional guidance was introduced into the FRS in the form of examples. One example is a transport company operating a trunk route fed by supporting routes (that is, similar to the example in the previous paragraph), which should be combined for the purposes of determining an IGU. The reasons given are that the cash flows of each route are not independent, and that economic decisions about continuing or closing the supporting routes are not based on their returns in isolation. Another example is a manufacturer that can allocate production across a number of facilities. One facility may be operating with surplus capacity and, hence, might be considered to be impaired if it were reviewed in isolation. However, there is not enough surplus capacity overall to enable any one manufacturing site to be closed. The FRS explains that, in this situation, the IGU should comprise all the sites at which the product can be made, because the cash inflows generated by any one site depend on the allocation of production across all sites. At the larger IGU level, there may be no impairment.

Aggregation for goodwill

23.585 Although impairment reviews for fixed assets, including recognised intangibles, should be carried out at the level of each IGU that is being tested for impairment, FRS 11 allows a higher level of aggregation for impairment reviews on goodwill.

23.586 IGUs may be combined for testing the recoverability of the related goodwill if:

- they were acquired as part of the same investment; and
- they are involved in similar parts of the business.

[FRS 11 para 34]

23.587 This means that if goodwill relating to the acquisition of a group of companies has to be reviewed annually for impairment only because it is being carried permanently as an asset or is being amortised over more than 20 years, and there are no reasons to suggest that either the goodwill or other assets have actually been impaired, the whole acquisition could be treated as one IGU if it comprises similar activities. Thus, the overall goodwill on the acquisition would not have to be sub-divided for the purpose of this impairment review.

23.588 If, however, there are indicators that the carrying values of goodwill or fixed assets may not be recoverable (see para 23.568), the impairment review is more complex. Individual reviews of each relevant IGU must then be carried out to consider whether other fixed assets have been impaired. This can be done with or without an allocation of the overall goodwill on the acquisition. If the review at IGU level is done without an allocation of goodwill, then a further review is required to test the recoverability of the goodwill. This may be done at the higher level of aggregation explained in the previous paragraph. The two different approaches are illustrated in the following example.

Example

An acquisition made some years ago comprised two IGUs, A and B. There has been an indicator that the carrying value of A may be impaired. The carrying values of the net assets and goodwill and the value in use are determined as follows:

Income generating unit	**A**	**B**	**Total**
	£m	**£m**	**£m**
Net assets	220	110	330
Goodwill	40	40	80
Total net assets	260	150	410
Value in use	200	180	380
Impairment	60		60

In this example, where purchased goodwill is allocated to the separate IGUs there is an impairment loss of £60m in A, reducing the carrying value of its net assets and goodwill to £200m. The impairment loss is attributed £40m to goodwill and £20m to other fixed assets (see para 23.610).

If A and B, which were acquired together in one investment, were involved in similar parts of the business, the calculations could be done as follows:

Income generating unit	A £m	B £m	Goodwill £m	Total £m
Net assets	220	110	80	410
Value in use	200	180		380
Impairment	20		10	30

First, segment A is reviewed for impairment without any allocation of goodwill. The value in use of £200m is compared with the carrying value of its net assets (excluding goodwill) of £220m. There is an impairment loss of £20m, reducing the carrying value of its net assets to £200m.

Secondly, A and B may be combined to assess the recoverability of the goodwill. The value in use of the combined units is £380m, which is compared with the aggregate carrying value of the net assets and goodwill, which is £390m (that is, £410m less the £20m written off the net assets of unit A). Therefore, a further impairment loss of £10m is recognised to write down the goodwill to £70m.

Under the first method there is an impairment loss of £60m; under the second method it is £30m. The second method in effect allows the impairment in the value of the impaired IGU to be partly offset against an increase in the value of the unimpaired IGU. This offset would not be allowed if A and B were involved in dissimilar activities.

It should be noted that if A or B were subsequently sold separately, an allocation of the carrying value of goodwill would be necessary to eliminate it from the balance sheet (that is, to write off as part of the profit or loss on disposal). Where the first method (allocating goodwill to separate IGUs) has been used to account for impairment, this is straightforward. Where the second method has been used, a further calculation will be required to disaggregate the remaining goodwill figure on some other basis. But as referred to earlier, it is good practice to allocate goodwill to business units on acquisition.

Allocating assets and liabilities to income-generating units

23.589 Balance sheets for individual IGUs need to be established for the purpose of impairment reviews. Three types of assets are involved:

- Assets and liabilities that are directly and exclusively attributable to a specific IGU.

- Assets and liabilities that are indirectly attributable to more than one IGU (that is, central assets).

- Capitalised goodwill (or negative goodwill).

23.590 The assets and liabilities attributed to IGUs should be consistent with the cash flows that are identified for calculating value in use. Liabilities that relate to financing the operations of IGUs (including interest-bearing debt, dividends and interest payable) are not allocated, because the related cash outflows are also excluded from the impairment calculations and such items are taken into account in the rate used to discount the future operating cash flows when calculating an IGU's value in use. Similarly, tax balances are not allocated, because the discounted cash flow forecasts are prepared on a pre-tax basis.

23.591 Where practicable, FRS 11 requires that indirect assets and liabilities, such as head offices and working capital, should be allocated to individual IGUs on a logical and systematic basis that reflects the extent to which those resources are applied to support each IGU. An example is given of pro-rating according to the net assets directly attributable to IGUs. The idea is that the carrying values of all IGUs in a group should add up to the carrying value of the group's net assets in aggregate (excluding tax and financing items).

23.592 This treatment of central assets may be problematical if companies' information systems do not readily provide such allocations. In addition, the basis for allocating central costs to operating units will need to be reviewed to ensure that the cash flows used for the impairment reviews are adjusted, if necessary, to put them on a basis that is consistent with the basis on which the central assets have been allocated. For example, if an IGU is allocated a portion of the book value of the group's head office, any rent payable to the group company that owns the head office would need to be excluded from the IGU's cash flows when comparing the IGU's value in use with the carrying value of its allocated net assets.

23.593 FRS 11 permits a less burdensome alternative approach to be used where central assets cannot readily be allocated on a meaningful basis. The alternative approach permits central assets to be reviewed for impairment on an aggregate basis similar to that described in paragraph 23.585 above for goodwill where there is no reasonable basis for allocating them to individual IGUs. This would require a two-tier impairment review:

- A review at the individual IGU level (a 'bottom up' review), where only the assets and liabilities directly involved are reviewed for impairment.

- A review at a higher level (a 'top down' review), where any central assets that contribute to the IGU are reviewed for impairment in aggregate with all other IGUs to which they contribute. This review compares the aggregate of the net assets of those IGUs and the central assets with their combined value in use.

23.594 As in the goodwill example in paragraph 23.588 above, the two methods may give different overall impairment results. The second method described above (the 'top down' review) could have the effect of allowing central assets to be allocated first to the more profitable IGUs, thus protecting less profitable IGUs from impairment losses. In these circumstances, the view would presumably be that the central assets are not impaired as long as the more profitable parts of the business can support their carrying values.

23.595 The two methods of dealing with central assets are illustrated in the following example.

Example

The facts are the same as in the example in paragraph 23.588 above, except that the group also has a head office with a book value of £30m.

The following table illustrates the impairment review assuming that both the head office and purchased goodwill are allocated fully to the two IGUs. The head office is allocated *pro rata* to the other net assets; thus £20m is allocated to A and £10m is allocated to B. There is now an impairment loss of £80m in A.

Income generating unit	**A £m**	**B £m**	**Total £m**
Net assets	220	110	330
Head office	20	10	30
Goodwill	40	40	80
Total net assets	280	160	440
Value in use	200	180	380
Impairment	80		80
Net assets as written down	200	160	360

The following table illustrates the impairment review assuming that the head office is allocated to the two IGUs, but goodwill is reviewed in aggregate, because it relates to a single acquisition and the two IGUs are involved in similar parts of the business.

The allocated net assets of unit A are impaired by £40m and the capitalised goodwill in aggregate is impaired by £20m, giving a total impairment loss of £60 million. This method in effect allows the impairment of goodwill to be offset by unrecognised internally generated goodwill of £20m in unit B. This offset would not be allowed if A and B were involved in dissimilar activities.

Income generating unit	A £m	B £m	Goodwill £m	Total £m
Net assets	220	110	80	410
Head office	20	10	—	30
Total net assets	240	120	80	440
Value in use	200	180		380
Impairment	40		20	60
Net assets as written down	200	120	60	380

The following table illustrates the impairment review if neither the head office nor purchased goodwill are allocated to the individual IGUs. Instead, two impairment reviews are carried out. The first review is at the individual IGU level, comparing value in use with the carrying value of the net assets directly involved in the businesses (that is, excluding central assets and goodwill). The second review brings in the head office and goodwill at an aggregate level.

Under this method, the value in use of units A and B should include an allocation of the head office occupancy costs – for example, being reduced by rent payable to the parent company. In this example, the present value of an economic rent payable by A and B is assumed to be £20m and £10m respectively, equal to the book value of the head office (reducing the value in use to £180m and £170m respectively).

The first review shows an impairment loss of £40m in unit A.

The second review compares the aggregate value in use (£380m) with the aggregate net asset value recognised after the first impairment review (£400m), comprising the impaired net assets of unit A (£180m), the net assets of unit B (£110m), the head office (£30m) and the capitalised goodwill (£80m). This results in a further impairment loss of £20m, which is allocated to the goodwill.

Income generating unit	A £m	B £m	Head office £m	Goodwill £m	Total £m
Net assets	220	110	30	80	440
Value in use	180	170	30		380
Impairment	40			20	60
Net assets as written down	180	110	30	60	380

The last two allocation methods have resulted in the same allocation of the impairment loss (£60m), because in both cases the same amount of £30m in respect of the head office has been allocated in the same way to the two IGUs. In the first case, an allocation was made to increase their net assets; in the second case, an economic rent was charged to reduce their value in use. If different figures were used, the two methods would give different results. For example, if no rent were charged to the two IGUs, their value in use would increase to £200m and £180m respectively, resulting in an impairment loss of only £20m in unit A and £40m in respect of goodwill. This also illustrates that the calculations can be significantly affected by subjective allocations of central assets or central costs.

23.596 The principles of allocating goodwill to individual IGUs are discussed from paragraph 23.543 above. A difficulty arises where an acquisition is broken up and integrated with other operations of the acquiring group. This is considered from paragraph 23.613 below.

Estimating value in use

23.597 Cash flow forecasts should be prepared for each IGU (or group of IGUs) being tested for impairment. The cash flow forecasts should be made on the basis of reasonable and supportable assumptions and projections; and should be consistent with budgets approved by management. [FRS 11 para 36]. However, the detailed requirements include some exceptions to that principle.

23.598 The cash flows should include allocations of central overheads. The assets of an IGU would be impaired if, for example, its own cash flows did not cover a contribution to central overheads.

23.599 The cash flows should exclude cash flows relating to financing (which include interest payments), since financing items are also excluded from the liabilities attributed to IGUs and because discounting picks up interest in a different way. Tax cash flows should also be excluded, because the FRS requires value in use to be calculated on the basis of discounting pre-tax cash flows at a pre-tax discount rate.

23.600 FRS 11 also imposes several important limitations on the cash flows that may be recognised in the calculation of value in use, including restrictions on the growth assumptions that can be built into long-term cash flow forecasts.

[The next paragraph is 23.602.]

23.602 In the period that is covered by formal budgets and plans, there are no restrictions as long as the period does not exceed five years. Therefore, in that initial period the cash flows will reflect the variability that is included in the explicit forecasts.

23.603 However, the cash flows for periods beyond those covered by formal budgets and plans should assume a steady or declining growth rate that does not exceed the long-term average growth rate for the country or countries in which the business operates. The UK's post-war average growth in gross domestic product, expressed in real terms, is stated to be 2.25 per cent. Only in exceptional circumstances may this growth constraint be overridden. [FRS 11 para 36]. Whilst this restriction is clearly aimed at preventing short-term difficulties from being offset by over-optimistic long-term forecasts, the theory is that in the long run a business has no right to assume it can out-perform the economy as a whole. The FRS gives an example of a situation where a higher long-term growth rate may be justified. This is where the specific industry is expected to grow faster than the country's economy in the long-term, and the business under review is expected to grow as rapidly as the industry as a whole, taking into account the prospects of increased competition.

23.604 This restriction has implications for impairment reviews carried out during economic recessions. If no economic recovery is assumed before the end of the period covered by the formal budgets, FRS 11 presupposes that the long-term rate of growth from the recessionary base should also be restricted. This could lead to impairment losses being recognised more readily than under the previous approach that was based on assessing whether diminutions in value were expected to be permanent or temporary.

23.605 FRS 11 states that only in exceptional circumstances should the period before a restricted or declining growth rate is assumed exceed five years. There are situations where it would be unrealistic to cap the growth assumptions after five years. For example, an acquired company with products under development may be expected to incur losses for two or three years and be followed by several years of significant growth as the new products reach the market.

23.606 If the period covered by explicit forecasts and before a steady or declining growth rate is assumed exceeds five years, FRS 11 requires the length of the longer period and the circumstances justifying it to be disclosed. [FRS 11 para 72].

23.606.1 Similarly, where the long-term growth rate for the period beyond that covered by explicit forecasts exceeds the long-term average for the country in which the business operates, the assumed growth rate and the circumstances justifying it must be disclosed. [FRS 11 para 73].

23.606.2 There is another important constraint concerning the assumptions relating to future reorganisation and capital investment. Value in use is supposed to reflect the value of assets or goodwill in their current condition. Hence, the future costs and benefits of future reorganisation should not be recognised in the cash flow forecasts unless related provisions have been made. This means in effect that if management is committed to carrying out a reorganisation, provisions would have been booked and the cash flow forecasts should be prepared on the basis that the reorganisation will proceed according to plan. If a planned reorganisation has not reached that stage and no provisions have been booked, it should not be taken into account in the cash flow forecasts either. Furthermore, the costs and benefits of future capital investment that is intended to improve or enhance the performance of the assets or business should not be taken into account in the cash flow forecasts. [FRS 11 para 38].

23.606.3 The above rules are modified, though, for the purpose of reviewing the value of goodwill arising on a recent acquisition. FRS 10 requires goodwill with a long (more than 20 years) or indefinite life to be reviewed for impairment at the end of each financial year, including the year immediately following the acquisition. Goodwill with a shorter life (20 years or less) should be reviewed for impairment at the end of the first full year following the acquisition.

23.606.4 FRS 11 allows the costs and benefits of planned reorganisation and capital investment relating to the newly acquired business to be taken into account for the purpose of impairment reviews in the initial years after the acquisition. In the case of planned reorganisation, this is irrespective of whether provisions have yet been made in the financial statements. However, the reorganisation or investment that is taken into account in those impairment reviews should be consistent with the budgets and plans that had been formulated by the end of the first full year after the acquisition. [FRS 11 para 39]. With tougher rules on reorganisation provisions introduced by FRS 12, this is a somewhat pragmatic approach. It is designed to avoid the situation where goodwill on a new acquisition might have to be deemed to be impaired (and, hence, written down immediately) if the benefits of future reorganisation and investment, which were taken into account by the acquirer in framing its offer, could not be reflected in the impairment reviews over the initial years. The FRS goes on to explain that the validity of this treatment would be called into question if the reorganisation or investment does not, in fact, proceed according to the acquisition plan. [FRS 11 para 40].

[The next paragraph is 23.607.]

23.607 The forecast cash flows are discounted at a rate described as *"an estimate of the rate that the market would expect on an equally risky investment"*. [FRS 11 para 41]. This means that assets are regarded as impaired if they are not expected to earn a market-related rate of return. The FRS suggests this rate can be estimated by a number of means:

- The rate implicit in market transactions of similar assets.
- The weighted average cost of capital (WACC) for a listed company with a similar risk profile.

- The WACC for the entity, adjusted up or down for the particular risks of the IGU being reviewed for impairment.

[FRS 11 para 42].

23.608 The choice of a discount rate is a subjective area. The result of an impairment review is also sensitive to variations in discount rates. Rates applicable to different business units, for example in different countries, may vary to reflect any risk factors that are specific to those units. The rate should be appropriate to the country in which the IGU operates rather than the country in which the finance is sourced. In general, the more uncertain the cash flows are, the more risky the investment is, and the greater the risk adjustment is to increase the discount rate. For example, an acquisition of the type referred to in paragraph 23.605, where higher (but uncertain) long-term growth rates are assumed in the cash flow forecasts, would warrant a higher discount rate to reflect those risks and uncertainties.

23.609 The FRS notes, however, that if the discount rates are derived from the entity's WACC, the weighted average of the rates applied to each IGU should equal the WACC of the entity as a whole. [FRS 11 para 43]. In addition, the discount rates derived from WACC need to be adjusted from a post-tax to a pre-tax basis, because the FRS requires value in use to be calculated by discounting pre-tax cash flows at a pre-tax discount rate.

23.609.1 If an impairment loss is recognised and is measured by reference to value in use of a fixed asset or IGU, the FRS also requires the discount rate to be disclosed in the financial statements. As an alternative to using a risk-adjusted discount rate, it may sometimes be more practicable to adjust the expected cash flows (downwards) for risk and to discount those risk-adjusted cash flows at a risk-free discount rate, such as a government bond rate. Where this is done, the FRS requires some indication of the risk-adjustments made to the cash flows to be disclosed. [FRS 11 para 69].

[The next paragraph is 23.610.]

Recognising impairment losses

23.610 If the carrying value of the net assets of an IGU (individually or in aggregate, depending on the type of review being carried out) exceeds the present value of the estimated future cash flows, the shortfall is an impairment loss that (unless it is obviously attributable to a specific asset) should be allocated to write down the assets in the following order:

- Purchased goodwill.
- Capitalised intangibles.
- Tangible assets, on a *pro rata* or more appropriate basis.

[FRS 11 para 48].

23.611 The reason is to ensure that the assets with the most subjective valuations are written off first. However, within this allocation framework no intangible asset with a readily ascertainable market value or tangible asset with a net realisable value that can be measured reliably should be written down below those values. [FRS 11 para 49].

Example

An IGU has attributed net assets of £500m, as set out in the table below. An impairment review estimates the present value of its future cash flows to be £300m. There is an impairment loss of £200m which is written off as shown.

	£m	Write-off £m
Purchased goodwill	150	(150)
Intangible assets	30	(30)
Net tangible assets	320	(20)
Net assets	500	(200)
Value in use	300	

23.612 When goodwill has been impaired, the remaining carrying value (if any) should be amortised over the remaining useful economic life. This should be reviewed and revised if necessary, that is, it may need to be shortened. [FRS 10 para 41; FRS 11 para 21].

Integration of acquired businesses

23.613 An impairment review of purchased goodwill may not be too complicated where an acquired business continues to be managed as a separate operation. A significant problem arises, however, where the acquired business is broken up and integrated with other operations of the acquiring group and, as a result, quickly loses its separate identity.

23.614 FRS 10 suggests that goodwill may not be capable of continued measurement when businesses are merged to such an extent that the goodwill associated with the acquired business cannot readily be tracked thereafter. It might appear that in such circumstances it is not possible to carry out an impairment review on the capitalised goodwill relating to the original acquisition. This would have the effect that groups that subsume their acquisitions would be less likely to rebut the presumption that the useful economic life does not exceed 20 years than those groups that run their acquisitions as stand-alone businesses.

23.615 FRS 11, however, sets out a method that should be applied to a combined IGU that contains both (capitalised) purchased goodwill relating to the acquired business and (unrecognised) internally generated goodwill that relates to the existing business. This method notionally preserves a distinction between the two types of goodwill in the IGU in order to prevent a potential impairment of the purchased goodwill from being avoided, because it is offset by unrecognised internally generated goodwill in the existing business with which the acquired business is merged.

23.616 FRS 11 requires that companies should value the internally generated goodwill of the existing business at the date of merging the businesses. This exercise requires the existing business to be valued separately before the integration. The internally generated goodwill should be calculated by deducting the fair value of the net assets (and any purchased goodwill) of the existing business from its estimated value in use before combining the businesses. [FRS 11 paras 50 to 52].

23.617 The internally generated goodwill as calculated should be added to the carrying value of the net assets of the combined IGU for the purpose of the impairment review as illustrated below:

Integrated income-generating unit

	Net assets	**Goodwill**
New acquisition	Fair value	Purchased
Existing business	Carrying value	Internally generated
		Purchased (re previous acquisitions, if any)

23.618 An impairment review of the combined IGU should be carried out immediately. If the aggregate carrying value of the net assets and goodwill, including the notional internally generated goodwill as illustrated above, exceeds the recoverable amount of the combined IGU, the impairment should be allocated wholly to the capitalised purchased goodwill relating to the acquired business and, hence, recognised in full in the consolidated profit and loss account. This is intended to ensure that, for example, any overpayment for the acquisition is identified and written off and is not offset against the unrecognised goodwill of the existing business.

23.619 Any goodwill impairments identified in subsequent years should be apportioned on a *pro rata* basis between the carrying value of the purchased goodwill and the notional carrying value of the internally generated goodwill. Only the impairment allocated to the capitalised purchased goodwill would be charged in the profit and loss account.

23.620 This is a complicated approach and somewhat artificial, but it appears to be a consequence of the possibility of carrying goodwill permanently as an asset or amortising it over very long periods.

Example

The combined balance sheet of an IGU formed by merging an acquired business with an existing business is set out in the following table. The figures in italics are those that include the notional value of (unrecognised) internally generated goodwill in the existing business.

The actual recognised net assets and purchased goodwill of the combined IGU amounts to £400m. Added to this is unrecognised internally generated goodwill in the existing business of £500m (which derives from the value that was estimated when the businesses were merged – see paragraph 23.616 above), making a notional total of £900m.

Impairment review of combined IGU	**Acquisition**	**Existing business**	**Combined**
Net assets	80	100	180
Goodwill	220	*500*	*720*
Total	300	*600*	*900*
Value in use			750
Impairment	46	*104*	*150*

An impairment review of the combined IGU compares its value in use (£750m) with its aggregate (notional) net assets (£900m).

Assuming that this impairment review takes place some years after the integration of the acquired business, the impairment loss of £150m is allocated *pro rata* between the purchased goodwill (acquisition) and the internally generated goodwill (existing business). This allocates £46m to the former and £104m to the latter.

Only the impairment loss of £46m allocated to the capitalised purchased goodwill is written off in the consolidated profit and loss account.

If, however, the impairment was identified when the businesses were merged, the whole loss of £150m would be allocated to the capitalised purchased goodwill relating to the acquisition and, hence, written off in the consolidated profit and loss account.

It should be noted that if this *pro rata* exercise were not required, in the above example no impairment loss would be recognised in the profit and loss account. That is because there would be no impairment of the combined IGUs recognised net assets, which amount only to £400m. The impairment of the goodwill in the acquired business would in effect be offset against the unrecognised internally generated goodwill (£500m) in the existing business. Hence, the recoverable amount of the combined IGU would have to fall below £400m before any impairment loss were recognised in the consolidated profit and loss account.

Subsequent monitoring of cash flows

23.621 FRS 11 contains a safety net to safeguard against companies continually using over-optimistic forecasts to defer impairment losses. Where an impairment review has been carried out and recoverable amount has been based on value in use, for the next five years the actual cash flows should be compared with those forecast in the impairment review. If actual post-acquisition cash flows are significantly less than those forecast in the impairment review, the calculations would have to be reworked by substituting actual cash flows for those previously forecast. If an impairment loss would have been recognised previously if the actual cash flows had been forecast, an immediate impairment write-down would have to be made in the current period, unless the impairment had reversed and the reversal met FRS 10's strict criteria for crediting reversals of goodwill impairments in the profit and loss account. [FRS 11 para 54]. Even if no impairment is recognised, the impairment that would have been recognised and its subsequent reversal should be disclosed. [FRS 11 para 71].

Parent's investment in subsidiaries

23.622 Where capitalised goodwill on consolidation is written down as a result of impairment, the carrying value of the parent company's investment in the relevant subsidiary should also be reviewed for impairment. [FRS 10 para 42].

23.623 The goodwill and other net assets in the consolidated financial statements that are attributable to an impaired subsidiary will usually differ from the subsidiary's carrying value in the parent's balance sheet as time goes by after the acquisition. The likelihood that the parent's investment has also been impaired will depend partly on its accounting policy, which may be:

- Cost less provision for permanent diminution in value.

- Cost (excluding share premium qualifying for merger relief or group reconstruction relief) less provision for permanent diminution in value.

- Net asset value (including unamortised goodwill).

- Estimated market value.

Negative goodwill

23.624 In some acquisitions, the fair value of the identifiable assets less liabilities may exceed the cost of acquisition, giving rise to negative goodwill.

[The next page is 23181.]

23.625 Negative goodwill is the mirror image of positive goodwill and is an even more difficult accounting conundrum. FRS 10 requires negative goodwill to be shown as a separate (negative) item on the asset side of the balance sheet immediately below positive goodwill, followed by a net sub-total, as illustrated below. [FRS 10 para 48]. If the amount of negative goodwill exceeds the amount of positive goodwill, there would be a net credit figure on the assets side.

Balance sheet extract (extract)

Fixed assets	£'000	£'000
Intangible assets		90
Goodwill	180	
Negative goodwill	(20)	160
		250
Tangible assets		150

23.626 Negative goodwill is generally attributed to one of two causes:

- The first is where the acquirer has made a genuine bargain purchase. This might occur as a result of a distress sale, for example, where the vendor is forced to sell the business quickly and cheaply to relieve cash flow problems.
- The second is where the purchase price is reduced to take account of future costs or losses, for example, where it is recognised that the acquirer will have to incur significant reorganisation costs to turn the business around. Such costs or losses are not identifiable liabilities of the acquired business at the date of acquisition.

23.627 FRS 10 seeks to restrict situations where negative goodwill is recognised. The first requirement where a fair value exercise appears to give rise to negative goodwill is that the fair values of the identifiable assets should be tested for impairment and the fair values of the identifiable liabilities should be checked carefully to ensure none has been omitted or understated. [FRS 10 para 48]. Any further reductions to the acquired net assets that need to be made as fair value adjustments as a result of this exercise will reduce or eliminate the negative goodwill.

23.628 The recoverable amount of the assets should be considered particularly carefully in the second of the situations mentioned in paragraph 23.626 above. Where the acquired business is loss-making or under-performing and in need of reorganisation, it must be questionable whether the fair values of the net assets in aggregate, which (as required by FRS 7) should be measured to reflect the conditions at the date of acquisition, are actually worth more than the price paid for the business as a whole. It should be noted that FRS 7 requires a valuation at recoverable amount to reflect the condition of the asset on acquisition (reflecting, for example, lack of profitability, under-utilisation or obsolescence). [FRS 7 para 47]. The ASB considers that much of any negative goodwill that would otherwise be attributed to future costs or losses would be eliminated by reducing the fair value of the assets in this way. [FRS 10 Appendix III para 57]. It follows that negative goodwill will most commonly arise in genuine bargain purchase situations.

23.629 A further restriction is that FRS 10 does not allow both negative goodwill and intangible assets to be recognised in respect of a single acquisition. It does this by capping the fair values attributable to any identifiable intangibles at an amount that does not give rise to negative goodwill overall, as illustrated below. [FRS 10 para 10].

	Valuation £m	**Restricted fair value £m**
Tangible net assets	200	200
Intangibles	400	300
	600	500
Cost of acquisition	500	500

23.630 The ASB's reason for this treatment is that valuations of intangibles are very subjective. Also, many intangibles are similar to goodwill and FRS 10 does not allow both positive and negative goodwill to be recognised on the same acquisition.

23.631 Negative goodwill that remains after the fair values of the acquired assets and liabilities have been re-checked should be accounted for as follows.

- Negative goodwill up to the fair values of the non-monetary assets acquired should be amortised to the profit and loss account in the periods in which the non-monetary assets are recovered, whether through depreciation or sale. [FRS 10 para 49].Non-monetary assets include stocks as well as fixed assets.

- Any negative goodwill in excess of the fair values of the non-monetary assets acquired should be recognised in the profit and loss account in the periods expected to be benefited. [FRS 10 para 50].

23.632 The standard does not specify where in the profit and loss account amounts of negative goodwill credited should be shown. It would be consistent with the treatment of positive goodwill to include negative goodwill as a negative component of goodwill amortisation charges that are treated as operating costs in arriving at operating profit or loss.

23.633 By matching the release of negative goodwill into the profit and loss account with the depreciation or cost of sales of the non-monetary assets acquired, a wide range of amortisation patterns is possible. No guidance on this is given in FRS 10. If the release of negative goodwill is matched first with the depreciation of the fixed assets, it will be credited, say, over the average useful life of the fixed assets acquired. Intuitively, this would seem to be a sensible treatment in most circumstances. It is also prudent, considering that fair valuing tangible fixed assets acquired can sometimes be as subjective as fair valuing intangible assets. If the release of negative goodwill is matched first with the cost of sales relating to the sale of the stocks acquired, it will be credited much more quickly. But, relative to fixed assets, stock is less likely to be subject to measurement uncertainty.

23.634 Situations where negative goodwill exceeds the fair values of the non-monetary assets acquired should be very rare indeed. If, for example, the only non-monetary assets were debtors, it would be logical to credit the excess negative goodwill in the profit and loss account over the period the debtors were collected.

23.635 The following disclosures are required in respect of negative goodwill:

- The aggregate movements on negative goodwill should be disclosed separately from those on positive goodwill, detailing additions, disposals and amounts written back to profit and loss account in the period. [FRS 10 para 53].

- The period(s) in which negative goodwill is being written back in the profit and loss account. [FRS 10 para 63].

- Where negative goodwill exceeds the fair values of the non-monetary assets (which should be very rare), details of its amount and source and the period(s) in which it is being written back. [FRS 10 para 64].

Pre-FRS 10 goodwill that remains in reserves

23.636 SSAP 22's preferred method of accounting for goodwill was immediate elimination against reserves. FRS 10's transitional arrangements permit, but do not require, previously eliminated goodwill to be reinstated on the balance sheet (see paragraph 23.681). Under the transitional options, unless all goodwill relating to pre-FRS 10 acquisitions is reinstated, one of the following amounts will remain eliminated against reserves:

- All goodwill written off before the adoption of FRS 10.

- All goodwill written off before the adoption of FRS 7 (which became effective in 1995.

- All goodwill written off before 23 December 1989 where its composition is not known.

Separate goodwill write-off reserve prohibited

23.637 Under the elimination method preferred by SSAP 22, there had been an increasing trend for groups to have a policy of writing goodwill off against a special reserve set up for the purpose. The reserve initially had a nil balance and so the reserve created would be negative and would equal the figure of goodwill written off. This was similar to a (prohibited) treatment known as a 'dangling debit' where goodwill would be carried on the balance sheet as a permanent debit deducted from shareholders' funds. One of the perceived advantages of this method was that the accounting treatment maintained some accountability for goodwill through its visibility in the financial statements, in contrast to writing goodwill off to, say, the profit and loss account reserve where it was 'lost'. The 'dissenting view' of one ASB member published with FRS 10 advocated an alternative approach to goodwill that was based on a separate goodwill reserve.

23.638 FRS 10 does not allow previously eliminated goodwill that is not reinstated on the balance sheet under the transitional arrangements to be carried forward in a separate goodwill write-off reserve. It requires such goodwill to be offset against the profit and loss account or another appropriate reserve. Furthermore, it does not allow such goodwill to be shown separately on the face of the balance sheet in any way, such as a separate component of the reserve to which it has been written off. [FRS 10 para 71(b)].

23.639 The ASB's justification for the decision to outlaw the goodwill write-off reserve is that, in the context of a new standard based on specific capitalisation, amortisation and impairment requirements, it could be misleading and confusing to have goodwill appearing in two different places on the balance sheet. Otherwise, some balance sheets would contain a permanent reminder of the transition. If continued accountability for the cost of past acquisitions is considered to be of overriding importance by companies, recapitalisation is the only method allowed to achieve this.

Reserves used for write-offs

23.640 The following reserves are the principal candidates for carrying goodwill that remains written off under FRS 10's transitional arrangements:

- Profit and loss account reserve.
- Merger reserve.
- Other non-distributable reserves (except those noted below).

23.641 The following reserves *cannot* be used to carry goodwill write-offs:

- Share premium account.
- Capital redemption reserve.
- Revaluation reserve.

Profit and loss account

23.642 Where more than one reserve is available to absorb the goodwill that is not recapitalised, no order of write-off is specified. Therefore, the profit and loss account can be used as a first choice or as a last choice to bear the goodwill write-off. In the latter case, the profit and loss account would absorb any balance of goodwill that cannot be offset against other reserves.

Merger reserve

23.643 A merger reserve arises on consolidation where a company issues shares as part of the consideration to acquire another company and it takes merger relief on the issue of those shares. The provisions of merger relief are explained fully in chapter 26. Where merger relief is available, the amount by which the fair value of the shares issued exceeds their nominal value results in a merger reserve on consolidation (rather than a share premium). Under the old rules for goodwill, a merger reserve could be used to write off goodwill that arose on the acquisition that gave rise to the reserve and it could also be used to write off any other goodwill. This was one of the key advantages of obtaining merger relief on the issue of shares to acquire another undertaking.

23.644 Where purchased goodwill is capitalised under FRS 10, the merger reserve can, of course, no longer be used to absorb goodwill write-offs on acquisition. But any old goodwill that is not recapitalised can continue to be offset against any existing merger reserve.

23.645 If a group wishes to use the merger reserve first to absorb any such goodwill, but the reserve is insufficient to offset all of the goodwill, the balance of goodwill would have to be offset against another reserve (that is, the profit and loss account reserve, if no other reserve is available). However, if the merger reserve subsequently increases as a result of a new share for share acquisition, there is nothing to prevent that balance of goodwill offset from being transferred from the other reserve to the increased merger reserve.

Other non-distributable reserves

23.646 Apart from the capital reserves that are governed by the Act (see below), neither the Act nor SSAP 22 restricted groups from writing off goodwill arising on consolidation against any other non-distributable reserves. Such reserves might include a special reserve created on a court-approved reduction of share premium which was carried out in the past specifically to enable goodwill to be written off against it on consolidation (see para 23.648 below).

Share premium account

23.647 The use of the share premium account is governed by the Act and so it can only be used for specific purposes, namely to:

- Pay up fully paid bonus shares.
- Write off preliminary expenses.
- Write off expenses of any issue of shares or debentures.
- Write off commission paid or discount allowed on any issue of shares or debentures.
- Provide for the premium payable on any redemption of debentures.

[Sec 130(2)].

23.648 However, although the share premium account can only be used for specific purposes, and writing off goodwill is not one of them, it does form part of a company's capital and, as such, can be reduced under section 135 of the Act by application to the court. Where groups make acquisitions by issuing shares (or a mixture of shares and other forms of consideration) the parent, unless it is eligible for merger relief, has to credit the difference between the fair value of the shares issued and their nominal value to its share premium account. Alternatively, a share premium account may exist from previous share issues. The parent company may then take steps to reduce its share premium account by a certain amount and that amount would in the consolidated financial statements be redesignated as another reserve to be used specifically to write off consolidation goodwill. A special resolution for the reduction is required and all of the relevant facts about the proposal must be set out in the documentation sent to shareholders.

23.649 Once the shareholders have passed the necessary special resolution, an application has to be made to the court to obtain its confirmation. Such confirmation is required by the Act and the court will be concerned in particular to ensure that the parent company's creditors are not prejudiced.

23.650 Share premium reductions of this nature were common when goodwill was eliminated against reserves. This route remains an option for groups that wish to write off all pre-FRS 10 goodwill against a reserve created by reducing share premium rather than against the profit and loss account reserve.

23.651 It should be remembered that the share premium account in such situations is that of the parent company. The reserve that is created from the share premium account is in most cases initially not available for distribution by the parent. It remains undistributable until certain conditions specified by the court have been satisfied, for instance, that the creditors that exist at the date of the reduction have been paid. Once these conditions have been fulfilled, the reserve becomes distributable. However, whether the reserve arising on the reduction is distributable is not relevant for consolidation purposes. Consolidation goodwill can be written off to the reserve created out of the parent's share premium account whether or not it is distributable by the parent.

Capital redemption reserve

23.652 Capital redemption reserves are set up for a specific purpose and will be utilised at some future date for that purpose. Therefore, their use is restricted. Furthermore, the normal provisions that apply to the reduction of share capital also apply to the capital redemption reserve. [Sec 170(4)]. Consequently, except where there has been a reduction confirmed by the court, this reserve is not available to write off goodwill arising on consolidation.

Revaluation reserve

23.653 The use of the revaluation reserve is restricted by the Act which states:

> *"An amount may be transferred from the revaluation reserve-*
> *(a) to the profit and loss account, if the amount was previously charged to that account or represents a realised profit, or*
> *(b) on capitalisation;*
> *and the revaluation reserve shall be reduced to the extent that the amounts transferred to it are no longer necessary for the purposes of the valuation method used.*
> *In sub-paragraph (b) 'capitalisation', in relation to an amount standing to the credit of the revaluation reserve, means applying it in wholly or partly paying up unissued shares in the company to be allotted to members of the company as fully or partly paid shares.*
> *The revaluation reserve shall not be reduced except as mentioned in this paragraph."*

[4 Sch 34(3)(3A)(3B)].

23.654 The wording of paragraph 34 was changed by the Companies Act 1989 specifically to ensure that goodwill arising on consolidation could no longer be written off against the consolidated revaluation reserve. Before that, the Act (by reference to the EC 4th Directive) prohibited goodwill arising in a company's individual financial statements from being written off against the company's revaluation reserve. However, this restriction did not extend to goodwill arising on consolidation.

23.655 The commencement order introducing part I of the Companies Act 1989 into the UK's legislation, however, included certain transitional provisions. One of these provisions concerned those groups that had in the past written off consolidation goodwill to their consolidated revaluation reserve. Where a group had previously written consolidation goodwill off against the revaluation reserve, it did not have to reverse this treatment. However, for any acquisitions that a group made following the change brought about by the Companies Act 1989 the treatment was no longer possible.

Effect on distributable profits – groups

23.656 Where, under the old rules, a group wrote off consolidation goodwill arising on the acquisition of subsidiaries immediately to reserves, the write-off did not affect the distributable profits of the parent or any individual group company. Since it is individual companies, not groups, that make distributions, the write-off of goodwill did not affect the amount of the total potential distributable profits of the group.

23.657 Consequently, whether pre-FRS 10 goodwill remains eliminated against the profit and loss account reserve or against unrealised reserves such as a merger reserve has no effect on distributable profits. Furthermore, a group does not need to transfer any amounts from unrealised reserves to realised reserves over the estimated useful economic life of such goodwill.

23.658 Although it is individual companies, not groups, that make distributions, users of consolidated financial statements may wish to know how much the parent could distribute if all the subsidiaries in the group were to pay up their realised profits by way of dividends to the parent. Some groups specifically disclose this amount. In the absence of such disclosure, users of the consolidated financial statements might mistakenly interpret the group's profit and loss account reserve as representing realised reserves.

Effect on distributable profits – companies

23.659 Where goodwill arises in a *company* as opposed to a group questions arise as to whether, or how, any write-off affects realised and distributable profits. This situation would arise where a company purchased the trade and assets (including goodwill) of an unincorporated business. SSAP 22 provided guidance on this issue which is reproduced in Appendix V to FRS 10, because it is still relevant for pre-FRS 10 goodwill that remains eliminated against a company's reserves under the transitional options.

23.660 The appendix states that to the extent that goodwill is considered to have suffered an actual diminution in value, the write-off should be charged against realised reserves; but realised reserves should not be reduced immediately where goodwill is written off as a matter of accounting policy and there is no actual diminution in value. It goes on to explain that immediate depletion of realised reserves can be avoided by eliminating goodwill initially to a suitable unrealised reserve. The amount eliminated against the unrealised reserve should then be transferred to realised reserves over the goodwill's useful economic life so as to reduce realised reserves on a systematic basis in the same way as if the company had amortised goodwill.[FRS 10 appendix V para 2]. A transfer to realised reserves would also have to be made if the carrying value of goodwill deducted from the unrealised reserve was found to have been impaired because, for example, an adverse event damaged the profitability of the acquired business.

23.661 The availability of suitable unrealised reserves is, however, limited. Merger relief reserves (if recognised by the company), negative goodwill and other capital reserves (except for share premium, capital redemption and revaluation reserves) can be used. However, FRS 10's prohibition of carrying goodwill in a separate (negative) goodwill write-off reserve applies to companies as well as groups. The profit and loss account reserve can, therefore, no longer be protected from goodwill write-offs by carrying a separate negative reserve. If pre-FRS 10 goodwill remains eliminated against reserves, it has to be eliminated against the profit and loss account reserve to the extent that no other reserves are available. The appendix does not specifically address the question whether goodwill that is actually eliminated against the profit and loss account reserve has the effect of reducing a company's realised reserves.

23.662 We consider that the elimination of goodwill does not become a realised loss just because it is offset against the profit and loss account reserve instead of, say, being carried as a separate negative reserve. This is primarily a matter of presentation. The principle remains that goodwill only becomes a realised loss to the extent that it is amortised or considered to have suffered an actual diminution in value. Therefore, FRS 10's prohibition of a separate goodwill write-off reserve should make no difference to the basis on which a company had previously been allocating such goodwill from unrealised to realised reserves, that is, over its estimated useful economic life as determined under SSAP 22. It should be noted that SSAP 22 defined useful economic life differently from FRS 10 and did not allow goodwill to be carried in the balance sheet as a permanent item.

23.663 Where purchased goodwill has been offset against a company's profit and loss account reserve, it would be important to disclose in the notes the amount of goodwill offset that is an unrealised loss in order to give a clear picture of the company's distributable profits.

Goodwill on disposals

23.664 FRS 10 retains the rules previously set out in UITF Abstract 3. Where goodwill attributable to a past acquisition remains eliminated against reserves (and, hence, has not been previously charged in the profit and loss account) it must be transferred to the profit and loss account when the business is subsequently disposed of, by treating it as part of the profit or loss on disposal. The attributable goodwill is credited in reserves and debited in the profit and loss account. The amount of goodwill included as a component of the profit or loss on disposal should be separately disclosed. [FRS 10 para 71(c)]. The disclosure could be either on the face of the profit and loss account or in the notes.

23.665 An exemption from this treatment is given if the business disposed of was acquired before 1 January 1989 and it is impracticable or impossible to ascertain the attributable goodwill that was originally written off. In this situation the facts and the reasons should be stated. This exemption coincides with the transitional provisions of the Companies Act 1989, before which there was no necessity to keep detailed records of goodwill eliminated against reserves.

Impairment of goodwill

23.666 Where goodwill is capitalised, timely recognition of impairment losses is a key feature of FRS 10's rules. However, neither FRS 10 nor its predecessors have dealt with the issue of whether goodwill that is eliminated against reserves and has lost its value should be charged in the profit and loss account earlier than on disposal of the acquired business. FRS 11's rules for measuring and recognising impairments of capitalised goodwill specifically do not apply to old goodwill that remains written off to reserves. [FRS 11 para 7]. In some situations, either as a matter of accounting policy or as part of the accounting for an impending disposal, goodwill may be written off in the profit and loss account earlier to recognise a permanent diminution in value. This issue is discussed in chapter 7. Any impairment that has been written off in the profit and loss account does not pass through the profit and loss account again on disposal of the business.

Disclosures

23.667 FRS 10's transitional provisions contain some specific disclosure requirements that relate to goodwill that remains eliminated against reserves.

Accounting policy

23.668 The accounting policy relating to that goodwill should be separately disclosed. [FRS 10 para 71(a)(i)]. It would be useful for companies to indicate what the balance eliminated against reserves comprises by reference to the transitional option they adopted: all goodwill eliminated before FRS 10 was adopted, or all goodwill eliminated before FRS 7 was adopted, or goodwill relating to acquisitions made before 23 December 1989.

[The next page is 23191.]

23.669 Another policy issue that might be considered for disclosure is the basis on which such goodwill is charged in the profit and loss account, that is, on disposal or (if applicable) when a permanent diminution in value is identified.

Cumulative amounts written off

23.670 The notes to the financial statements should disclose the cumulative amount of positive goodwill eliminated against reserves, net of any goodwill attributable to businesses disposed of before the balance sheet date. If both positive and negative goodwill have been taken to reserves, the cumulative amounts of each should be disclosed separately. [FRS 10 para 71 (a)(ii)].

23.671 The notes should also state that this goodwill has been eliminated as a matter of accounting policy and would be charged or credited in the profit and loss account when the businesses to which it relates are subsequently disposed of. [FRS 10 para 71(a)(iii)]. Not all of the disclosable cumulative amount of goodwill may in fact be chargeable in the profit and loss account on disposal. For example, some of this goodwill may already have been written off in the profit and loss account, because the company has a policy of recognising impaired goodwill earlier. Another example is where the identity of goodwill relating to acquisitions made before 1 January 1989 is unknown and, hence, by virtue of the exemption in FRS 10, may never pass through the profit and loss account

23.672 The Act also requires the cumulative amount of goodwill written off that results from acquisitions in the current year and in earlier years to be disclosed. [4A Sch 14(1) as amended by SI 1996/189]. The amount disclosed should also be stated net of any goodwill attributed to an undertaking that has subsequently been sold. [4A Sch 14(2)]. This requires disclosure of the aggregate of amounts written off directly to reserves, but not the amounts amortised through the profit and loss account.

23.673 The FRRP published a statement in December 1995 in connection with the financial statements of Ferguson International Holdings PLC confirming that, where advantage is taken of the merger relief provisions of the Act, the figures disclosed for goodwill arising on acquisitions in the year and the cumulative amount of goodwill written off should be the gross amounts before deducting merger relief.

23.674 The Act, however, does not require the gross amount of goodwill written off to be disclosed in certain circumstances where an undertaking that is established outside the UK or that carries on its business outside the UK has obtained the permission of the Secretary of State. [4A Sch 16]. Similarly the transitional provisions on the introduction of the Companies Act 1989 do not require the amount to be disclosed in certain situations where it is not possible to ascertain the figure for goodwill written off that has arisen on acquisitions made prior to the introduction of the Companies Act 1989 and to do so would cause unreasonable expense or delay. In these situations the financial statements must state that the gross figure disclosed does not include an amount on these grounds.

Pre-FRS 10 negative goodwill that remains in reserves

23.675 SSAP 22 required negative goodwill to be credited directly to reserves. Under FRS 10's transitional arrangements, some or all negative goodwill attributable to pre-FRS 10 acquisitions may remain credited to reserves.

23.676 SSAP 22 did not require a group to set up a separate reserve for negative goodwill, but some companies and groups did so. FRS 10 does not allow the amount by which any reserve has been increased by the addition of negative goodwill to be shown separately on the face of the balance sheet. [FRS 10 para 71(b)]. To be consistent with positive goodwill, this implies that negative goodwill should also not be carried as a separate reserve if it an be credited to another appropriate reserve. Therefore, negative goodwill arising on consolidation may either be credited to a capital reserve, if any is available (excluding the statutory share premium, capital redemption and revaluation reserves), or to the consolidated profit and loss account reserve. In the former case, it would normally be included under 'other reserves' in the balance sheet format.

23.677 Such negative goodwill as remains credited to reserves should be transferred to the profit and loss account when the business to which it relates is sold or closed, by inclusion in the calculation of the profit or loss on disposal. The amount of negative goodwill transferred should be separately disclosed as a component of the profit or loss on disposal.

23.678 The cumulative amount of negative goodwill added to reserves, net of any attributable to businesses disposed of before the balance sheet date, should be disclosed in the notes, together with the fact that this would be credited in the profit and loss account on subsequent disposal of the business to which it related. If both positive and negative goodwill have been taken to reserves, the cumulative amounts of each should be disclosed separately. [FRS 10 para 71(a)].

Effect on distributable profits – companies

23.679 Where negative goodwill arises in a company, it should credit it initially to an unrealised reserve. The company may then transfer the negative goodwill from that unrealised reserve to realised reserves. This transfer should be in line with the depreciation or the realisation of the assets acquired in the business combination that gave rise to the goodwill in question. [FRS 10 appendix V para 3].

23.680 Unlike negative goodwill arising on consolidation, negative goodwill in an individual company should not be credited immediately to the profit and loss account reserve, because it is not a realised profit. It would have to be shown under the heading 'other reserves' in the company's balance sheet.

Implementing FRS 10 – transitional arrangements

Options for reinstating goodwill eliminated against reserves

23.681 FRS 10 must be applied to goodwill relating to acquisitions first accounted for in financial years ending on or after 23 December 1998. Where goodwill relating to earlier acquisitions has been eliminated against reserves, the standard permits, but does not require, the goodwill to be recapitalised as an asset on the balance sheet. There are effectively four options for dealing with old goodwill eliminated against reserves:

- Leave all goodwill eliminated against reserves.
- Reinstate all goodwill previously written off to reserves.
- Reinstate all goodwill relating to post-23 December 1989 acquisitions (where the information on earlier acquisitions cannot be obtained without unreasonable expense or delay), leaving the balance eliminated against reserves.
- Reinstate all goodwill eliminated since the adoption of FRS 7, leaving the balance eliminated against reserves.

[FRS 10 para 69].

23.682 Each of the reinstatement options requires a prior period adjustment for a change of accounting policy from immediate write-off to capitalisation.

23.683 The transitional options represent a compromise between consistency and practicality. Whilst the standard notes that ideally all goodwill would be reinstated as a prior period adjustment, the ASB considered that this could present practical difficulties in some cases – for example, where acquisitions were made many years ago it might be difficult to reflect judgements that would have been made about economic lives or impairments, had goodwill been capitalised from the outset.

23.684 The two options for reinstating some (but not all) of the goodwill relating to previous acquisitions take natural cut-off points. FRS 7 did not require fair values and goodwill relating to earlier acquisitions to be restated retrospectively, and so goodwill eliminated before FRS 7 was implemented may have been calculated on quite a different basis from goodwill eliminated in respect of acquisitions since FRS 7 was adopted. The 23 December 1989 cut-off date stems from transitional provisions in the Act.

23.685 Other than as described above, the standard does not permit goodwill to be reinstated on a selective basis, (such as, recapitalising goodwill relating to an unusually large acquisition and leaving the balance relating to smaller acquisitions eliminated against reserves).

23.686 Matters to be considered when choosing one of the transitional options include:

- Achieving consistency (or otherwise) within the financial statements.
- Maintaining accountability for the cost of goodwill on past acquisitions.
- The positive balance sheet effect of reinstating goodwill compared with the negative effect on future earnings.
- The possibility of capitalising some goodwill without amortisation, balanced against the risk of incurring future impairment losses.
- Reducing the amount of goodwill to be accounted for on future business disposals by capitalising goodwill net of amortisation or impairment attributable to past periods.
- The practical difficulties of accounting retrospectively for acquisitions made many years ago.
- The balance as between positive and negative goodwill (that is, companies would generally prefer not to carry net negative goodwill on the assets side of the balance sheet).

Requirements where goodwill is reinstated

23.687 Where some or all goodwill that has previously been eliminated against reserves is capitalised, this represents a change of accounting policy requiring a prior period adjustment. The goodwill should be capitalised at cost less amortisation or impairment attributable to previous periods, which would need to be assessed for each acquisition. Reinstating goodwill requires, for each acquisition, an estimate to be made of the amortisation attributable to periods since the date of acquisition. A useful economic life should be determined as at the date of acquisition – in accordance with the mainstream requirements of FRS 10, there would be a rebuttable presumption that this does not exceed 20 years.

23.688 FRS 10 also requires useful economic lives to be reviewed at the end of each reporting period and revised if necessary. [FRS 10 para 33]. In practice, such reviews would be very difficult to perform retrospectively for the purpose of establishing transitional written down values, but companies may wish to make a realistic assessment of remaining useful economic lives looking forward from the implementation date. Different assumptions about original economic lives and subsequent revisions would lead to different amounts of amortisation being attributed to prior periods and, hence, different amounts to be charged against future earnings. If, however, a current estimate of the remaining useful economic life increases it to more than 20 years from the date of acquisition (for example, where a business was bought many years ago and is still thriving), the relevant amounts of capitalised goodwill would then be subject to the FRS's rules requiring annual impairment reviews where goodwill is amortised over more than 20 years.

23.689 The FRS requires any impairment attributed to prior periods to be determined in accordance with FRS 11. [FRS 10 para 70]. FRS 11 gives several examples of events and other factors that indicate that goodwill or other fixed assets may have been impaired. These are typically adverse changes that would have resulted in a material decline in the performance of an acquired business, or in its future prospects, since its acquisition. Examples are:

- Actual deterioration in operating performance.
- Significant adverse changes in the business, its markets, competitor activity or the regulatory environment.
- Undertaking significant reorganisation.
- Major loss of key employees.

23.690 FRS 11's rules for measuring the recoverable amount of goodwill should form the basis of the calculation of any impairment loss. If such impairment occurred in the current year or the previous year, the impairment loss would be charged in the current or comparative profit and loss account respectively, together with the amortisation charge for those periods. If the impairment occurred in earlier years, the loss would be included in the adjusted reserves brought forward at the beginning of that period. Evidence is, therefore, required to support any impairment of goodwill being attributed to prior years.

23.691 If the parent company's policy is to carry investments in subsidiaries at cost less provision for permanent diminution in value, attributing an impairment of goodwill to prior years would be expected to be evidenced by a write-down of the related investment in a previous year. However, other evidence may be strong enough to support attributing the goodwill impairment to previous years even where there has been no write-down of the related investment. One reason why the investment might not have been written down in the past is that the impairment review required by FRS 11 may be more stringent than reviews carried out in the past. For example, FRS 11 requires estimated future cash flows to be discounted to their present value when comparing them with the investment's carrying value; previously there was no such requirement for discounting. Other evidence will also be required where the parent's investment in the subsidiary has been protected from write-down, because the acquisition qualified for merger relief and the carrying value excludes the premium on consideration shares issued.

23.692 If reinstated goodwill is found to have been impaired and no previous write-down of the parent's investment has been made, the investment should be written down if it has also been impaired. However, unlike the reinstated goodwill on consolidation, FRS 11 would not allow the impairment loss on the investment to be charged in the parent's own financial statements as a prior period adjustment. FRS 11 requires such impairment losses that are recognised when the impairment standard is implemented for the first time to be treated as a change in accounting estimate (and charged to the profit and loss account of that year) and not as a change of accounting policy. It should be noted that where the recoverability of the parent's investment had previously been assessed by reference to undiscounted future cash flows, this would in future have to be done by reference to discounted cash flows.

23.693 The FRS also requires amounts attributed to prior period amortisation and prior period impairment to be disclosed separately in the notes in the year the standard is adopted. [FRS 10 para 70].

23.694 The capitalised written down value established as a prior period adjustment should subsequently be accounted for by applying the FRS's rules for amortisation and impairment reviews. The reinstated amount should be amortised against earnings over the remaining useful economic lives relating to each underlying acquisition and will be subject to impairment reviews where applicable. If goodwill attributable to a major acquisition is considered to have an indefinite economic life (and its recoverable amount can still be measured reliably), it would be capitalised at its cost and be reviewed annually for impairment, subject to the 'true and fair override' disclosures (see para 23.495).

23.695 When a business is subsequently sold or closed, the capitalised net book value of the attributable goodwill is written off as part of the profit or loss on disposal. Any amortisation or impairment written off as part of the prior period adjustment to recapitalise goodwill has, by virtue of the prior period adjustment, already been written off in the profit and loss account. That part of the goodwill does not pass through the profit and loss account again on disposal of the business.

23.696 Companies that wish to reinstate their old goodwill are not required to go further and separately identify any intangibles that may have been subsumed within the balance of goodwill originally written off to reserves. [FRS 10 para 70].

Requirements where goodwill remains eliminated against reserves

23.697 Goodwill relating to old acquisitions that remains written off to reserves when FRS 10 is adopted should not be shown as a debit balance on a separate goodwill write-off reserve but should be offset against the profit and loss account or another appropriate reserve. [FRS 10 para 71]. Therefore, companies that have previously carried such reserves will have to transfer them to another reserve. This would be accomplished as a prior period adjustment. The reason given by the ASB for this requirement is to avoid goodwill appearing in two different places on the face of the balance sheet.

23.698 The FRS also prohibits companies from showing separately on the face of the balance sheet the amount by which a reserve has been reduced by goodwill write-offs, thus precluding, for example, showing separate totals for the profit and loss account reserve before and after goodwill written off. However, the cumulative goodwill eliminated against reserves must still be disclosed in the notes. [FRS 10 para 71]. There is nothing to prevent a company from analysing, in the notes, the balance of the reserve to which goodwill has been written off between goodwill and other.

23.699 Except for the presentation issue described above, FRS 10 does not change the accounting rules in respect of goodwill that remains eliminated against reserves. Goodwill need not be recognised in the profit and loss account until the acquired business is sold or closed. The attributable goodwill should then be charged (and shown separately) as part of the profit or loss on disposal or closure. [FRS 10 para 71(c)].

Negative goodwill

23.700 SSAP 22 required negative goodwill to be credited directly to reserves. FRS 10 requires it to be recognised on the balance sheet below positive goodwill. FRS 10's transitional arrangements do not specify how to deal with negative goodwill, but it would be good practice for goodwill and negative goodwill to be treated consistently when choosing one of the transitional options.

23.701 Therefore, where a group has both positive and negative goodwill eliminated against and credited to reserves respectively, a prior year adjustment to recapitalise goodwill would encompass both elements. Negative goodwill would be brought on to the face of the balance sheet (shown separately as a deduction from positive goodwill) at its original value less amortisation attributed to previous periods.

23.702 Where a group has previously credited negative goodwill to reserves and has no positive goodwill (or has a smaller amount of positive than negative), a prior period adjustment is still an option. Negative goodwill would be eliminated from reserves and shown on the face of the balance sheet (in the position where goodwill would be shown, but as a negative figure). Whilst this treatment would have a negative balance sheet effect (reducing net assets and shareholders' funds), it would have a positive effect on future earnings. That is because under FRS 10 negative goodwill should generally be credited in the profit and loss account in the periods in which the non-monetary assets of the acquired business are depreciated or sold.

23.703 If a group does not make a prior period adjustment, negative goodwill relating to previous acquisitions will remain added to reserves until the acquired business is disposed of. It should then be credited in the profit and loss account and shown separately as part of the profit or loss on disposal.

Treatment of previously capitalised goodwill and intangibles

23.704 Any intangible assets and goodwill that had already been capitalised before the adoption of FRS 10 would thereafter be subject to the recognition, amortisation and impairment rules of the FRS. Several issue arise:

- Previously capitalised intangibles may not meet FRS 10's recognition criteria.
- Previously capitalised intangibles that do not have a readily ascertainable market value may have been revalued since their acquisition and may, therefore, have to be written down.
- An impairment may be identified when the new procedures for carrying out impairment reviews are adopted.
- Companies may wish to modify their amortisation policy, for example to comply with FRS 10's rebuttable presumption of a maximum useful economic life of 20 years.

Intangibles not meeting FRS 10's recognition criteria

23.705 As FRS 10 does not permit internally developed intangibles to be capitalised (except for those intangibles that are excluded from the scope of the standard), any such items appearing on a company's balance sheet should be written off as a prior period adjustment.

23.706 Some intangibles recognised separately from goodwill when previous acquisitions were fair valued may not satisfy all the elements of FRS 10's definition of intangible assets. Customer lists and similar items may fall into this category. Such intangibles should also be eliminated as a prior period adjustment, that is, they should be subsumed within goodwill. The increased amount of goodwill relating to the relevant acquisitions would then, if it has previously been eliminated against reserves, be subject to the transitional arrangements described above, being either reinstated on the balance sheet as goodwill or left written off to reserves.

Previously revalued intangibles

23.707 Where any purchased intangibles have been revalued since their acquisition and are not of the rare type that has a readily ascertainable market value, FRS 10 does not permit them to be carried at valuations. The revaluations should, therefore, be reversed as a prior period adjustment, in order to restate the intangibles at cost (that is, fair value attributed on acquisition) less amortisation or impairment attributed to previous periods.

Impairment losses

23.708 FRS 10 specifically requires that any impairment loss relating to previously capitalised goodwill and intangible assets that is recognised when the FRS is first adopted (that is, when the specified impairment reviews are first applied), should be charged as an expense in the current period and not as a prior period adjustment. This is consistent with the transitional rules in FRS 11 that apply to all fixed assets and goodwill. The reason is that any impairment is regarded as having resulted from a change of estimate of an asset's recoverable amount and not from a change of accounting policy. This treatment does not apply where goodwill that has previously been written off to reserves is reinstated.

Change of amortisation policy

23.709 A company may decide to adopt a more prudent amortisation policy for previously capitalised goodwill and intangibles, as a result of FRS 10. For example, a company may have previously not amortised certain intangibles because their useful economic lives had been deemed to be indefinite. On implementing FRS 10, the company may consider they should be amortised over a period of 20 years from the date of acquisition in view of FRS 10's tougher rules for adopting a longer period. One reason is that the company may not be able or willing (owing to the unjustifiably high costs) to carry out the additional impairment review procedures that are required if a longer amortisation period is chosen. Therefore, the intangibles might not be capable of continued measurement in the context of FRS 10's requirements for determining useful economic lives and so FRS 10's presumed maximum life of 20 years would not be rebutted.

23.710 The question arises whether this is a change of accounting policy or a revision of the intangible asset's useful economic life. If it is a change of accounting policy, the intangible would be restated net of amortisation attributed to the period since its purchase; the 'backlog' amortisation would be treated as a prior year adjustment and would not affect current or future earnings. If it is a revision of the asset's useful economic life, the whole of the previous carrying value would be amortised prospectively against earnings over the remaining portion of the 20-year life (which could be a short period if the intangible was bought many years ago).

23.711 A prior year adjustment for a change of accounting policy would be justified if the company's amortisation policy was changed purely as a result of FRS 10's new rules for determining asset lives rather than because there had been a genuine revision of the asset's useful life in the context of the previous policy.

Additions to goodwill in existing subsidiaries

Increases in stake

23.712 If a parent company increases its stake in an existing subsidiary by purchasing additional shares from the minority, goodwill may arise on the purchase. The new goodwill must be capitalised if the purchase is accounted for when FRS 10 is effective. The old goodwill (pre-dating FRS 10) may or may not be capitalised, depending on whether or not it was reinstated under the transitional options. Therefore, it is possible that goodwill relating to one subsidiary may appear in two different places. The more recent purchase will appear on the balance sheet and be subject to the amortisation and impairment rules, whereas the older purchase will remain eliminated against reserves.

Earnout consideration

23.713 Sometimes an acquirer agrees to pay additional consideration for an acquisition that depends on its future performance. The additional consideration may give rise to more goodwill. In this situation, however, the additional goodwill does not relate to a new acquisition or to the acquisition of a further tranche of shares. It is an adjustment to the goodwill on the previous acquisition. FRS 7 in fact requires estimates of future performance-related consideration to be provided for when the acquisition is first accounted for. Therefore, any additional goodwill should always be treated in the same way as the goodwill that was accounted for when the acquisition was made.

Comparison with IASs

23.714 The IASC rules are to be found in IAS 22, 'Business combinations', (as revised in 1998). As in UK practice, acquisitions are the normal form of business combinations. The limited 1998 revision to IAS 22 has reduced the extent of the differences between UK and international standards relating to determining fair values and accounting for goodwill, but some important differences remain.

23.715 The principles for recognising and fair valuing the identifiable assets and liabilities of an acquired business are similar, but there is one important difference. Although IAS 22 requires the assets and liabilities recognised in the fair value exercise to be restricted to those of the acquired business that existed at the date of acquisition, there is one specific exception to this which is not permitted by FRS 7. A provision for restructuring costs should also be recognised as an identifiable liability acquired if certain specific criteria are met. Provision as part of the fair value exercise is restricted to those situations where restructuring is an integral part of the acquirer's plan for the acquisition. Conditions are specified that require the acquirer to have developed and announced the main features of the plan at, or before, the date of acquisition, and to have developed those main features into a detailed formal plan by the earlier of three months after the date of acquisition and the date on which the financial statements are approved. The costs that may be included in such a provision are limited to those relating to terminating or reducing the activities of the acquired business, not those of the acquirer. [IAS 22 para 31].

23.716 Goodwill arising on an acquisition must be treated as an asset and should be amortised over its useful life. FRS 10's definition of the useful life of goodwill allows for purchased goodwill to be replaced by internally generated goodwill over time, whereas IAS 22 does not. There is a rebuttable presumption that the useful life does not exceed 20 years. If a longer life is chosen (IAS 22 emphasises that this would occur only in rare cases), the reasons should be disclosed. However, unlike FRS 10, an indefinite useful life cannot be assigned to goodwill. If a period of more than 20 years is chosen, the goodwill must be tested annually for impairment.

23.717 The revised IAS 22 requires negative goodwill to be presented as a deduction from positive goodwill, which is consistent with FRS 10. The previous benchmark treatment of eliminating negative goodwill by reducing the fair values of identifiable assets acquired is no longer permitted. Negative goodwill should be recognised in income on a different basis from FRS 10. To the extent that negative goodwill relates to expectations of future losses and expenses that are identified in the acquirer's plan for the acquisition (which are not recognised as identifiable liabilities), it should be recognised as income when those future losses and expenses are recognised - FRS 10 does not allow negative goodwill to be credited to income in this way. To the extent that negative goodwill does not relate to future losses and expenses, it should be recognised as income over the remaining average useful life of the non-monetary assets acquired. Negative goodwill in excess of the fair values of the non-monetary assets acquired should be recognised as income immediately. [IAS 22 paras 59 to 64].

23.718 For the calculation of minority interests on acquisition IAS 22 has a benchmark of showing them at a proportion of pre-acquisition book values and an alternative of having a complete fair value exercise, as in the UK. [IAS 22 paras 32, 34].

Chapter 24

Minority interests

Page

Chapter 24

Minority interests

Introduction

24.1 Under the parent company concept of accounting for groups (explained in chapter 21), which is the basis adopted for consolidations in the UK, minority interests are shown separately either before or after shareholders' funds and therefore, unlike under the entity concept, do not form part of shareholders' funds. Minority interests represent the share of net assets of subsidiaries consolidated into the group's consolidated financial statements that are financed by shareholders who are not members of the group and are outside third parties.

24.2 Until the publication of the 1989 Companies Act, there was nothing in accounting standards or the law that indicated how minority interests should be determined. However, in practice the method of calculating minority interests was generally accepted and had been explained in depth in accounting text books. The 1989 Act's provisions stated for the first time in UK law that minority interests represent the amount of capital and reserves attributable to the shares in subsidiaries held by persons other than the parent and its subsidiaries. Also the Act specifies where in the balance sheet and profit and loss account formats minority interests should appear. The 1989 Act's provisions were encompassed within, and expanded upon in, FRS 2, 'Accounting for subsidiary undertakings'. This standard defines 'minority interests' and includes additional guidance on their calculation.

24.3 These provisions were further embellished by FRS 4 'Accounting for capital instruments' which was issued in December 1993. As its title indicates, FRS 4 details how companies should account for capital instruments (that is, broadly a company's shares and debt), but it does also include specific provisions that relate to the disclosure and calculation of minority interests. First, there is a general requirement that the minority interests recognised in the profit and loss account and in the balance sheet should be analysed between equity interests and non-equity interests. Secondly, in certain circumstances where the group guarantees either the dividends or redemption of the minority's shares, the minority interests are an obligation of the group and as such have to be shown, in accordance with their substance, as a liability.

24.4 This chapter considers the general accounting and disclosure requirements that apply to minority interests now to be found in the Companies Act 1985 (as amended), FRS 2 and FRS 4. It also explains the situation where minority interests should be classified according to their substance, as debt (see para 24.33). The latter half of the chapter concentrates on the problems associated with calculating minority interests and considers:

- Direct and indirect holdings (see para 24.43).
- Treatment of minority interests on acquisition (see para 24.45).
- Treatment of dividends (see para 24.47).
- Acquisition of minority interests (see para 24.48).
- Shares with differing rights (see para 24.51).
- Loss making subsidiaries (see para 24.52).

Definition

24.5 'Minority interests' is defined in the Act to mean *"the amount of capital and reserves attributable to shares in subsidiary undertakings included in the consolidation held by or on behalf of persons other than the parent company and its subsidiary undertakings"*. [4A Sch 17(2)]. The effect of the legislation is, for example, that where a parent owns 70 per cent of a subsidiary, it has to consolidate 100 per cent of the subsidiary's results and net assets and show minority interests of 30 per cent.

24.6 FRS 2 also defines minority interests based on the Act's definition, but the standard's definition recognises also that a parent need not be a company. It states that the minority interest in a subsidiary is:

> *"The interest in a subsidiary undertaking included in the consolidation that is attributable to the shares held by or on behalf of persons other than the parent undertaking and its subsidiary undertakings."* [FRS 2 para 13].

24.7 The definition in FRS 2 and the Act's requirements can be seen reflected in companies' accounting policies, for example see Table 24.1 which shows GEC's policy for minority interests.

Table 24.1 – The General Electric Company, p.l.c. – Annual Report and Accounts – 31 March 1994

Notes to the Accounts (extract)

5 MINORITY INTERESTS

Minority interests represent the share of the profits less losses on ordinary activities after taxation attributable to the interests of shareholders in subsidiaries which are not wholly owned by the Company or its subsidiaries.

24.8 The term 'minority interests' was originally introduced into company law at a time when consolidation was based on equity ownership rather than control. Under the current provisions of the Act, where consolidation is based on control, it is possible, although fairly uncommon, for minority interests to be more than 50 per cent. Indeed there are situations where minority interests might be considerably higher than 50 per cent (see further para 24.10).

24.9 With regard to the disclosure of minority interests, Article 21 of the EC 7th Directive on group accounts states that minority interests should be shown as a separate item (with an appropriate heading) in the company's capital, reserves and results brought forward. The Companies Act 1989 brought this requirement into UK law and, therefore, specifies where minority interests should be shown in both the consolidated balance sheet formats and the consolidated profit and loss account formats (see further para 24.20).

Minority or majority interests

24.10 Under the revised definitions of subsidiary brought into company law by the Companies Act 1989, a company has to be treated as a subsidiary where its parent has a participating interest in its shares and either exercises dominant influence over it or manages it on a unified basis (see further chapter 21). Consequently, it is quite possible for a parent to own only (say) 20 per cent of the equity of an undertaking and exercise dominant influence over it or manage it on a unified basis. Where this is so, it is also quite possible that the minority shareholders will hold (say) 80 per cent of the equity of the undertaking. Accordingly, the minority interests shown in the consolidated financial statements will be calculated using this percentage. This could result, for example, in the group consolidating 100 per cent of the assets and liabilities of the subsidiary, but showing also minority interests of 80 per cent of those assets and liabilities. A similar situation could arise where the parent owns a majority of the voting rights, but owns (say) only 20 per cent of the total equity.

24.11 Where these types of situation arise, it is unlikely that this is a good enough reason for the term 'minority interests' to be amended to (say) 'majority interests'. Furthermore, we consider that it is unlikely that circumstances would exist where using the term 'minority interests' would affect the true and fair view and, therefore, justify using another term. In the situation described above, the minority although owning the majority of capital will be in a minority position with regard to controlling the company and, consequently, the term 'minority interests' still describes the outside interest fairly. However, we consider that in this type of situation it is necessary to explain the relationship with the subsidiary fully in the consolidated financial statements in order that they should give a true and fair view. In particular, FRS 2 requires that where the parent has a participating interest in the subsidiary and actually exercises a dominant influence over it, the consolidated financial statements should disclose this fact and should explain the basis of the parent's dominant influence. [5 Sch para 15(5); FRS 2 para 34].

Basis of recognising minority interests

24.12 FRS 2 states that the effect of the existence of minority interests on the returns to investors in the parent is best reflected by presenting the net identifiable assets attributable to minority interests on the same basis as those attributable to group interests. The same general approach applies to the balance sheet where the group's assets and liabilities, whether they are attributable to minorities or to the parent, should be presented on a consistent basis. This is logical as the group includes 100 per cent of the assets and liabilities of a subsidiary in its consolidated balance sheet (after consolidation eliminations) whatever the parent's holding in the subsidiary. As explained briefly above, this basis is consistent with the parent company concept.

24.13 This consistency of approach does not extend, however, to all of the goodwill of the subsidiary. When a parent purchases a controlling, but not 100 per cent, interest in a subsidiary, goodwill may arise (see chapter 23). The goodwill that arises on consolidation relates only to the parent's share of the subsidiary and not to the minority's share. Although it might be possible to estimate a goodwill figure for minority interests by extrapolation or valuation, it would be inappropriate to include that amount in the balance sheet as the minority is not party to the group's transaction to acquire the subsidiary. To include an amount for goodwill would, from the group's point of view, represent the recognition of inherent goodwill, which is not permitted by the Act or FRS 10. The requirement that goodwill arising on acquisition should only be recognised with respect to the part of the subsidiary undertaking that is attributable to the interest held by the parent and its other subsidiaries is summarised in paragraph 38 of FRS 2. This would be the situation, for example, where company P acquires 70 per cent of sub-group A. The net assets of sub-group A would be fair valued on consolidation (ignoring any goodwill recognised in sub-group A) and the minority would be given their share of those net assets. However, a subsidiary (company A) of parent (company P) has acquired a sub-subsidiary (company B), any goodwill arising on the acquisition of company B which in company A's consolidated financial statements is capitalised and amortised (as opposed to written off immediately to reserves) will have an effect on the calculation of any minority interests in company A recognised in the parent's consolidated financial statements (see further para 24.44).

Measurement of minority interests

24.14 As explained above shares issued by subsidiaries to persons outside the group are normally accounted for as minority interests. But in situations where the group guarantees the payment of the minority's dividends or the repayment of its capital, the minority's interests should be classified as debt. The measurement of such debt and its disclosure is considered from paragraph 24.33. Where there is no such guarantee, minority interests in both the profit and loss account and the

[The next page is 24005.]

balance sheet should be analysed between equity minority interests and non-equity minority interests. For this purpose FRS 4 defines non-equity shares as:

"*Shares possessing any of the following characteristics:*

a) any of the rights of the shares to receive payments (whether in respect of dividends, in respect of redemption or otherwise) are for a limited amount that is not calculated by reference to the company's assets or profits or the dividends on any class of equity share.

b) any of their rights to participate in a surplus in a winding up are limited to a specific amount that is not calculated by reference to the company's assets or profits and such limitation had a commercial effect in practice at the time the shares were issued or, if later, at the time the limitation was introduced.

c) the shares are redeemable either according to their terms, or because the holder, or any party other than the issuer, can require their redemption." [FRS 4 para 12].

For example, any preference share that has a fixed dividend will be a non-equity share under this definition. Equity shares are defined as any shares other than non-equity shares. As a consequence, the definition of equity shares under FRS 4 differs from the definition under the Act. This and other issues concerning these definitions are considered in detail in chapter 18.

24.15 The analysis of minority interests between equity interests and non-equity interests is considered in the paragraphs that follow.

Non-equity minority interests

24.16 The basic requirement in FRS 4 is that the amount shown in the balance sheet as minority interests should be analysed between that attributable to equity interests and that attributable to non-equity interests. [FRS 4 para 50]. This attribution is done on the same basis as the analysis of shareholders' funds between equity and non-equity interests required by FRS 4 and explained in chapter 18. These rules have the effect that amount of capital and reserves attributable to non-equity minority interests equals the net proceeds on issue of the shares to the minority plus finance costs less payments made (such as dividends). [FRS 4 para 91]. The net proceeds on issue is equal to the value of the shares issued less any issue costs. Issue costs are defined in FRS 4 and the types of costs that can be included within issue costs is fully explored in chapter 18. The total finance costs on a non-equity share can be found by deducting the net proceeds on issue from the gross amounts payable on the instrument throughout its term. This includes payments for dividends and redemption (including any redemption premium). The finance costs are then, under FRS 4, required to be spread to achieve a constant rate on the outstanding balance of the instrument and these rules are the same as those that apply when analysing shareholders' funds between equity and non-equity interests (explained in chapter 18).

Example

A subsidiary's only minority interest is a redeemable preference share of £100,000 issued to a person outside the group at a premium of £10,000 with a redemption premium of £20,000 payable on redemption in ten years' time. (The issue costs have been assumed to be immaterial, but if they were material, they would reduce the net proceeds and, therefore, represent part of the finance costs as explained above.) Prior to FRS 4, some companies might have been tempted to show simply the nominal value of £100,000 as the minority interest. However, this would not have been very realistic, as it did not properly reflect the full entitlement of the holders of those shares on redemption. Under FRS 4, it is clear that it is necessary to attribute to the non-equity minority interests the actual interests of the holders, that is, the nominal value plus the premium received plus an accrual of additional premium payable on redemption. Under this approach, the group presents a larger figure for minority interests (non-equity) and a smaller figure for shareholders' funds. This properly represents the entitlements of the various holders.

The £110,000 represents the initial investment, and therefore entitlement, of the non-equity shareholders in the subsidiary. At the end of the first year the minority interests included in the balance sheet would be £111,000 (that is, shares of £100,000 plus the premium on issue of £10,000 and an accrual of the redemption premium of £1,000 (assuming this amount equates to an amount calculated to produce a constant rate on the outstanding balance – see also chapter 18). The £111,000 represents the amount to which the entitlement of those shareholders has grown. At the end of the term, the non-equity minority interests will be shown at £120,000, which is the amount at which they will be redeemed.

24.17 The mechanics of the consolidation process will mean that the non-equity minority will be allocated part of the group's reserves in addition to the nominal value of the non-equity shares (that is, figures varying from £110,000 to £120,000 as above). Consequently, the group's reserves will be reduced by £10,000 over the period until redemption.

24.18 Two examples that follow in paragraphs 24.51 and 24.58 illustrate the calculation of non-equity minority interests.

Equity minority interests

24.19 For the analysis of minority interests in the balance sheet the calculation of equity minority interests is more straightforward. Equity minority interests are merely represented by the net proceeds on issue of the equity shares (that is, net of issue costs) plus the equity minority shareholders' percentage interest in the other reserves of the company. An example of the calculations and disclosures of equity and non-equity interests is given in the examples that follow from paragraph 24.39.

Presentation in financial statements

Balance sheet

24.20 In the balance sheet Format 1 'minority interests' should be shown either directly above or below 'capital and reserves'. Because it is possible to total the format 1 balance sheet in different positions, it is possible to:

- Draw a total before capital and reserves which includes minority interests.
- Draw a total before capital and reserves and minority interests, showing minority interests either before or after capital and reserves.

Chapter 6 includes a summary of Format 1 which shows the positioning of 'minority interests'.

24.21 In Format 2 the disclosure of 'minority interests' should be made under 'liabilities' between the headings 'capital and reserves' and 'provisions for liabilities and charges'. [4A Sch 17(1)(2); FRS 2 para 35].

24.22 In determining how the disclosure of minority interests can be changed or adapted in the consolidated balance sheet, the Act states that the item should be treated in the same way as if a letter were assigned to it. [4A Sch 17(5)(a)]. But in practice even under the Act's strict criteria there are a number of ways of presenting minority interests to emphasise different balance sheet totals as illustrated in the examples that follow. For example, in Table 24.2 MEPC plc which uses a Format 2 balance sheet shows minority interests after drawing a total for shareholders' interests. This is probably the most common position for presenting minority interests whether the Act's Format 1 or Format 2 balance sheets are used. Table 24.3 shows Bass PLC's balance sheet which is Format 1, but it has presented minority interests in the alternative position before capital and reserves and has also totalled net assets to include the deduction for minority interests. This is perfectly acceptable under the Act's rules, because although the order of items in the formats can only be changed within certain defined parameters, there are no rules on where the balance sheet totals can be struck. From Table 24.4 it can be seen that ICI's balance sheet is also Format 1 and that it has used a similar positioning to Bass PLC, but has totalled in a different place showing 'total assets less current liabilities'.

Table 24.2 – MEPC plc – Report and Financial Statements – 30 September 1997

1997 Balance sheets (extract)
as at 30 September

Note		Group 1997 £m	1996 £m	MEPC 1997 £m	1996 £m
	Fixed assets				
	Tangible assets				
14	Investment and development properties	**4,127.7**	3,423.7	**277.6**	276.0
15	Other fixed assets	**9.9**	8.4	**7.4**	6.4
		4,137.6	3,432.1	**285.0**	282.4
	Investments				
16	Subsidiary undertakings	–	–	**1,829.6**	1,512.9
17	Other investments	**77.0**	55.6	**6.8**	11.0
		4,214.6	3,487.7	**2,121.4**	1,806.3
	Current assets				
18	Trading properties	**13.1**	33.3	–	–
19	Debtors				
	Due after more than one year	**14.6**	11.0	**2,405.1**	2,333.9
	Due within one year	**136.0**	154.3	**70.4**	60.8
20	Investments	**314.8**	297.0	**36.6**	4.3
21	Cash	**125.3**	321.6	**57.5**	246.5
		603.8	817.2	**2,569.6**	2,645.5
		4,818.4	4,304.9	**4,691.0**	4,451.8
	Capital and reserves				
	Equity share capital	**104.8**	104.7	**104.8**	104.7
	Non-equity share capital	**2.2**	2.2	**2.2**	2.2
22	Called up share capital	**107.0**	106.9	**107.0**	106.9
23	Share premium account	**480.7**	480.5	**480.7**	480.5
23	Revaluation reserve	**373.9**	116.1	**110.6**	87.9
23	Other reserves	**965.7**	956.8	**593.2**	588.0
23	Profit and loss account	**158.5**	225.6	**397.5**	436.2
	Shareholders' funds	**2,085.8**	1,885.9	**1,689.0**	1,699.5
	Minority interests				
	Equity	**58.3**	19.8		
29	Non-equity	**252.0**	260.0		
		310.3	279.8		
24	**Provisions for liabilities and charges**	**51.6**	–	**2.0**	–
25	**Creditors**				
	Due within one year	**866.4**	823.2	**421.5**	413.4
	Due after more than one year	**1,504.3**	1,316.0	**2,578.5**	2,338.9
		2,370.7	2,139.2	**3,000.0**	2,752.3
		4,818.4	4,304.9	**4,691.0**	4,451.8

1997 Group profit and loss account (extract)

for the year ended 30 September

Note		*Before restructure and swap terminatio n charges £m*	*Exceptional restructure and swap termination charges £m*	*Total 1997 £m*	*Total 1996 £m*
10	**Profit on ordinary activities before taxation**	**166.8**	**(82.7)**	**84.1**	140.2
11	Taxation	**(37.1)**	**24.7**	**(12.4)**	(28.8)
	Profit on ordinary activities after taxation	**129.7**	**(58.0)**	**71.7**	111.4
29	Minority interests				
	Equity	**(2.2)**		**(2.2)**	(1.3)
	Non-equity	**(14.3)**		**(14.3)**	(14.9)
		(16.5)		**(16.5)**	(16.2)
12	Dividend on preference shares	**(0.1)**		**(0.1)**	(0.1)
	Profit attributable to ordinary shareholders'	**113.1**	**(58.0)**	**55.1**	95.1

1997 Notes to the accounts (extract)

29 **Subsidiary undertakings' preference shares and non-equity minority interests**

The group currently has five public US$ preference share issues made by MEPC International Capital, L.P., MEPC Overseas Finance Limited, UK-American Properties Inc. and subsidiaries of MEPC American Holdings Inc.

The classification of the instruments for the purposes of financial statements has been determined on the following basis:

(a) Minority interests:
(i) The capital outstanding and the dividends payable are classified as non-equity minority interests in both the balance sheet and profit and loss account, where the issue does not represent a contingent obligation on the parent undertaking or a Group company under guarantees in respect of letters of credit supporting the issue.

(ii) The capital outstanding and the dividends payable are classified as non-equity minority interests in both the balance sheet and profit and loss account, respectively, where although there is no contingent obligation under guarantees in respect of letters of credit supporting the issue, there is a guarantee such that the subsidiary undertaking's preference shareholders rank pari passu with MEPC plc's preference shareholders. Details of the rights of the parent undertaking's preference shareholders are in note 22.

(b) Creditors:
(i) The capital outstanding is classified as subsidiary undertakings' preference shares within creditors in the balance sheet and the dividends payable included in finance costs in the profit and loss account where the parent undertaking or a Group company has a contingent obligation under guarantees either directly or in respect of letters of credit supporting the issue.

Details of outstanding preference share issues are:
(1) Two separate issues of Dutch Auction Rate Transferable Securities (DARTS) totalling US$280m are currently outstanding. These shares are regarded as tax advantaged securities in the US market due to special local tax concessions as regards dividends received by the owners. A US$100m issue made in 1989 is a non-credit supported issue and is classified as described in (a)(i) above. A US$180m credit supported issue made in 1988 is classified as described in (b)(i) above.

(2) A non-credit enhanced perpetual issue of US$250m of preference shares made in April 1996 carries a parent undertaking guarantee and is classified as described in (b)(i) above and included in creditors due after more than one year, net of unamortised issue costs.

(3) As part of the acquisition of the net assets of American Property Trust in December 1993 the Group assumed an on-going obligation for an issue of US$99m money market preference shares. These are presently non-credit supported, trade in a structured stand-alone special purpose vehicle and are classified as described in (a)(i) above.

(4) During September 1995 an issue of US$215m 9⅛% Quarterly Income Preferred Shares (QUIPS) was made by MEPC International Capital, L.P., a special purpose limited partnership which is non-credit supported. The preferred shares have been structured to provide a guarantee by the parent undertaking such that the holders are effectively in the same position as the holders of the parent undertaking's preference shares with respect to payment of dividends and amounts upon liquidation, dissolution and winding-up. These are classified as described in (a)(ii) above, net of unamortised issue costs.

The US$250m preference share issue in (2) above is the subject of a currency swap agreement into sterling and the US$215m 9⅛% QUIPS issue was converted into sterling. The three other issues are used in the USA and the proceeds are largely invested in investment grade securities which are classified as current asset investments in the balance sheet.

A summary of outstanding subsidiary preference share issues (gross) is:

Issuer	*Minority interests*	*Creditors*	*Total*	*Instrument*
MEPC International Capital	215	–	215	QUIPS
UK – American Properties	99	–	99	Preferred shares
MEPC Overseas Finance	–	250	250	Preferred shares
MEPC Capital Corp	100	180	280	DARTS preferred shares
Total US$	414	430	844	
£m equivalent	257	266	523	

Table 24.3 – Bass PLC – Annual Report – 30 September 1994

Balance sheets (extract)

30 September 1994	Note	Group **1994 £m**	Group 1993 £m	Company **1994 £m**	Company 1993 £m
Total assets less current liabilities		**4,942**	4,834	**3,700**	3,685
Creditors: amounts falling due after more than one year	18	**(1,268)**	(1,288)	**(1,286)**	(1,273)
Provisions for liabilities and charges		**(62)**	(85)	**-**	-
Minority equity interests	19	**(30)**	(48)		-
Net assets	21	**3,582**	3,413	**2,414**	2,412
Capital and reserves – equity interests					
Called up share capital	22	**218**	217	**218**	217
Share premium account	23	**539**	517	**539**	517
Revaluation reserve	23	**1,007**	1,051	**-**	-
Capital reserve	23	**-**	-	**241**	241
Profit and loss account	23	**1,818**	1,628	**1,416**	1,437
Shareholders' funds		**3,582**	3,413	**2,414**	2,412

Table 24.4 – Imperial Chemical Industries PLC – Annual report and accounts – 31 December 1994

balance sheets (extract)
at 31 December 1994

	Notes	Group 1994 £m	Group 1993 £m	Company 1994 £m	Company 1993 £m
Total assets less current liabilities		**6,396**	6,777	**3,964**	4,648
FINANCED BY					
Creditors due after more than one year					
Loans	20	**1,522**	1,717	**200**	263
Other creditors	19	**95**	123	**1,141**	1,190
		1,617	1,840	**1,341**	1,453
Provisions for liabilities and charges	21	**675**	680	**40**	51
Deferred income: Grants not yet credited to profit		**30**	39	**1**	1
Minority interests – equity		**338**	330		
Shareholders' funds – equity					
Called-up share capital	22	**724**	722	**724**	722
Reserves					
Share premium accounts		**569**	561	**569**	561
Revaluation reserve		**37**	46	**-**	-
Associated undertakings' reserves		**60**	66		
Profit and loss account		**2,346**	2,493	**1,289**	1,896
Total reserves	23	**3,012**	3,166	**1,858**	2,457
Total capital and reserves attributable to parent company (page 14)		**3,736**	3,888	**2,582**	3,179
		6,396	6,777	**3,964**	4,684

24.23 FRS 4 has added the requirement that the minority interests disclosed in the balance sheet should be further analysed between the aggregate amounts attributable to equity interests and amounts attributable to non-equity interests. [FRS 4 para 50]. Generally this analysis has to be given on the face of the balance sheet unless the amount attributable to non-equity minority interests is immaterial. Even so, where the non-equity interests are immaterial, the caption on the face of the balance sheet should indicate that the figure includes non-equity interests and the split should be given in the notes. The analysis between equity and non-equity interests is considered in paragraph 24.14.

24.24 Table 24.2 shows the balance sheet of MEPC plc which gives the typical analysis of minority interests between equity and non-equity interests on the face of the balance sheet. Bass, ICI and Marks and Spencer plc do not have any non-equity minority interests, but for the sake of clarity have specified on the face of the balance sheet (see Table 24.5) that their minority interests are all equity. BTR plc (Table 24.6) also has not given the analysis on the face of the balance sheet, but indicate on the face that the minority interests include non-equity interests, those interests being analysed further in the notes.

Table 24.5 – Marks and Spencer p.l.c. – Annual Report and Financial Statements – 31 March 1995

Consolidated profit and loss account (extract)
FOR THE YEAR ENDED 31 MARCH 1995

	Notes	1995 52 weeks £m	1994 53 weeks Restated £m
PROFIT ON ORDINARY ACTIVITIES BEFORE TAXATION	2	**924.3**	851.5
Tax on ordinary activities	6	**(299.5)**	(272.2)
PROFIT ON ORDINARY ACTIVITIES AFTER TAXATION		**624.8**	579.3
Minority interests (all equity)		**(1.0)**	(1.1)
PROFIT FOR THE FINANCIAL YEAR	7	**623.8**	578.2

Balance sheets (extract)
AT 31 MARCH 1995

	Notes	THE GROUP 1995 £m	THE GROUP 1994 £m	THE COMPANY 1995 £m	THE COMPANY 1994 £m
CAPITAL AND RESERVES					
Called up share capital	21	**699.0**	696.2	**699.0**	696.2
Share premium account		**190.1**	162.3	**190.1**	162.3
Revaluation reserve		**455.4**	457.0	**464.0**	465.6
Profit and loss account		**2,370.4**	2,008.5	**2,579.7**	2,279.4
SHAREHOLDERS' FUNDS	22	**3,714.9**	3,324.0	**3,932.8**	3,603.5
Minority interests (all equity)		**20.8**	19.4	**-**	-
TOTAL CAPITAL EMPLOYED		**3,735.7**	3,343.4	**3,932.8**	3,603.5

Table 24.6 – BTR plc – Report & Accounts – 31 December 1994

CONSOLIDATED PROFIT AND LOSS ACCOUNT (extract)

FOR THE YEAR ENDED 31 DECEMBER 1994

£ millions	**1994**	**1994**	1993	(Restated) 1993	Notes
Profit on ordinary activities before taxation		**1,412**		1,274	1
Taxation		**(395)**		(355)	8
Profit on ordinary activities after taxation		**1,017**		919	
Minority interests (including non-equity interests)		**(146)**		(117)	9
Profit for the financial year		**871**		802	

CONSOLIDATED BALANCE SHEET (extract)

AT 31 DECEMBER 1994

£ millions	**1994**	1993	Notes
FINANCED BY			
Capital and reserves			
Called up share capital	**909**	870	21
Share premium account	**578**	234	23
Revaluation reserve	**128**	137	23
Current equalisation account	**(110)**	(122)	23
Profit and loss account	**1,185**	928	23
Shareholders' funds	**2,690**	2,047	
Minority interests (including non-equity interests)	**1,175**	1,151	24
	3,865	3,198	

Notes

£ millions	Consolidated **1994**	1993
24 MINORITY INTERESTS		
Equity interests: minorities' share of net assets of subsidiaries	**974**	961
Non-equity interests: preference shares	**201**	190
	1,175	1,151

BTR Australia Ltd Cumulative Redeemable Preference Shares, amounting to £198 million (£183 million), are redeemable at par on 31 March 1999 or, at the option of either the investor or the issuer, on 31 March 1995. BTR Australia Limited has given notice that it intends to redeem these shares on 31 March 1995.

The prior year comparatives have been restated in accordance with UITF 6.

Profit and loss account

24.25 For the profit and loss account formats the Act requires two additional lines to be added for minority interests. The first line requires the disclosure of minority interests in the profit or loss excluding extraordinary items, and in Format 1 and Format 2 this item should be included after 'profit or loss on ordinary activities after taxation'. In addition, the Act specifies that the item should be described 'minority interests'. For Format 3 and Format 4 minority interests should be included under 'charges' or 'income' as appropriate, in the same position after striking the 'profit or loss on ordinary activities after taxation'. [4A Sch 17(3); FRS 2 para 36]. This presentation can be seen in many of the extracts from the financial statements reproduced in this chapter, for example see Table 24.2.

24.26 The second line required to be disclosed by the legislation is the minority's share of any extraordinary items. [4A Sch 17(4)]. However, the introduction of FRS 3 (see chapter 7) has, in effect, stopped the use of extraordinary items as a caption for presentation in the profit and loss account. Consequently, the position of the minority's share of extraordinary items is no longer relevant.

24.27 The consolidated profit and loss account disclosure for 'minority interests' under Format 1 is illustrated in chapter 6.

24.28 There is in principle more scope to adapt and combine the minority interests disclosure in the consolidated profit and loss account than there is in the balance sheet. This is because the Act states that minority interests shall be treated as if they have been assigned an Arabic number. [4A Sch 17(5)(b)]. This means that the minority interests disclosure in the profit and loss account can be adapted where the special nature of the group's business requires such adaptation. [4 Sch 3(3)]. It is, in practice, difficult to imagine when this particular provision would apply apart from perhaps in the circumstance of stapled stock (see para 24.36).

24.29 In a similar way to the presentation of minority interests in the balance sheet, FRS 4 requires the amount of minority interests in the profit and loss account to be analysed between equity interests and non-equity interests. [FRS 4 para 60]. However, this disclosure need not be given on the face of the profit and loss account, but can be relegated to the notes.

24.30 The range of analysis that companies now typically give on the face of the profit and loss account under FRS 4 is illustrated in Tables 24.2, 24.5 and 24.6.

24.31 FRS 3, 'Reporting financial performance', requires that the notes to the financial statements should include information regarding the effect on any minority interests of the three non-operating exceptional items specified in that standard, which are:

- Profits or losses on the sale of termination of an operation.
- Costs of a fundamental reorganisation or restructuring having a material effect on the nature and focus of the reporting entity's operations.
- Profits or losses on the disposal of fixed assets.

[FRS 3 para 20].

24.32 Table 24.7 shows an extract from Unitech plc's annual report and accounts which has shown the minority's share of a non-operating exceptional.

Table 24.7 – Unitech plc – Annual report and accounts – 31 May 1993

Notes (extract)

2 Segment information (extract)

The gains arising on the sale of buildings include a £1,225,000 gain, less tax of £55,000, on the disposal of buildings owned by Nemic-Lambda in Israel, of which the minority interest share is £578,000.

Classification as debt

24.33 There is one situation under FRS 4 where shares issued by subsidiaries to persons outside the group should be classified as liabilities rather than minority interests. This is where the group (taken as a whole) has an obligation to transfer economic benefits in connection with those shares. In this circumstance, the shares are required by the standard to be accounted for in the consolidated financial statements not as minority interest, but as liabilities. [FRS 4 para 49]. This is one of a few situations in the standard where the substance of the transaction prevails over its legal form. These implications are considered in detail in chapter 18.

Auction market preferred shares

24.34 Auction market preferred shares (AMPS) are a particular type of preference share for which dividends are determined in accordance with an auction process between a panel of investors. The shares are transferred to the investor who will accept the lowest dividend. Dividends may be passed without giving holders any further rights, for example to demand repayment. The shares are redeemable at the option of the issuer, usually at the issue price.

24.35 In accordance with FRS 4, AMPS issued to outside third parties should generally be reported as non-equity minority interests because they are redeemable at a fixed price and because the dividend rights are limited. The finance cost of each period should be the dividend rights accruing in respect of that period. If, however, their redemption or dividend payment is guaranteed by the parent of other members of the group then they would not be classified as minority interests, but would represent an obligation which would have to be shown as a liability in the group's consolidated financial statements (see further chapter 18).

Stapled shares

24.36 Another example of where the minority interests in the balance sheet might need to be shown in another position in order to give a true and fair view is where shareholders in the parent have been issued with shares in a subsidiary that have been 'stapled' with their shares in the parent. This method of share issue is often used where the subsidiary is resident overseas for tax purposes to ensure that distributions from it are not subject to UK ACT rules. Therefore, depending upon the circumstances and the rights attaching to the subsidiary's shares, those shares might, in substance, be more akin to shareholders' funds than to minority interests. Stapled shares are considered in more detail in chapter 18.

Directors' interests

24.37 It is often a requirement of a company's articles of association for the company's directors to acquire nominee shareholdings in the company's shares. Generally these shareholdings are very small and the directors have no beneficial interest in them. Where such a situation arises in a subsidiary company, clearly the directors' shareholding from the group's perspective does not constitute a minority interest in the company as the shares are normally held on the parent company's behalf.

24.38 Other situations arise in practice where directors have beneficial interests in the company's shares. These situations need to be considered very carefully to determine whether the shareholding constitutes a minority interest or should be recognised for accounting purposes in some other way. For example, if a director is given shares in his/her company and the company's parent arranges to reacquire those shares at a future date, the substance of the transaction might be to remunerate the director. Where this is so, the cost to the company should be charged to the profit and loss account as staff costs over the term of the arrangement and disclosed as directors' emoluments. Alternatively, the substance of the transaction could be quite different, for example, it might be a way of acquiring intellectual property rights or expert knowledge that the director has or has some right to. In such a situation it could be argued that the transaction relates to the acquisition of that right or knowledge and as such represents an intangible asset and should be accounted for as such. Clearly, transactions with directors of this nature need to be considered very carefully and inevitably where they are not accounted for as minority interests additional disclosure will be necessary, because the transaction is likely to be material to the director (see further chapter 34) and it will be a transaction with a related party (see chapter 35).

Calculation of minority interests

24.39 Minority interests included in the consolidated balance sheet should represent the total amount of capital and reserves attributable to shares in the subsidiary held by or on behalf of persons other than the parent and its other subsidiaries. [4A Sch 17(2)]. Similar wording is also used to indicate how to calculate the minority's interest in the profit and loss for the period. [4A Sch 17(3)(4)]. The Act's basic requirements were expanded by the publication of FRS 4, which, as outlined above, specifies the measurement rules for equity and non-equity minority interests. In practice, the calculation of minority interests is fraught with complications. These complications can arise because of the payment of dividends, changes in stake, different rights attaching to shares in the subsidiary and the treatment of losses. The examples that follow illustrate each of these problems.

Profit and loss account calculation

24.40 The minority interests in a subsidiary's profit for the year is calculated by taking the profit after taxation and calculating the proportion of the profit that is attributable to the minority. Consider the following simple example.

Example

A parent owns 80% of a subsidiary's ordinary share capital (there are no other classes of capital). The subsidiary's profit and loss account is as follows:

	£'000
Operating profit	1,000
Non-operating exceptional item	1,250
Profit on ordinary activities before taxation	2,250
Tax on profit on ordinary activities	(280)
Retained profit for the financial year	1,970

The figures that would be brought into the consolidated financial statements in respect of the subsidiary (ignoring any intra-group profit elimination) are:

	£'000
Operating profit	1,000
Non-operating exceptional item	1,250
Profit on ordinary activities before taxation	2,250
Tax on profit for the financial year	(280)
Profit on ordinary activities after taxation	1,970
Minority interests (20% × £1,970,000)	(394)
Retained profit for the year	1,576

Balance sheet calculation

24.41 The calculation of the balance sheet minority interests follows directly from the definition. In a simple situation involving only equity shares, the balance of the minority interests at the year end is the minority's interest in the capital and reserves of the subsidiary. An example of the calculation of the balance sheet minority interests is shown below:

Example

Following on from the example above, the subsidiary's balance sheet is as follows:

		£'000
Net assets		3,820
Equity share capital		250
Share premium		500
Revaluation reserve		300
Profit and loss account	800	
Retained profit for the year	1,970	2,770
Equity shareholders' funds		3,820

The minority interests in the capital and reserves of the subsidiary are calculated as follows, assuming that issue costs are immaterial (if they were material the relevant proportion should be deducted from the minorities' equity share capital):

		£'000	£'000
Equity share capital	20% × 250,000		50
Share premium	20% × 500,000		100
Revaluation reserve	20% × 300,000		60
Profit and loss account b/f	20% × 800,000	160	
Minority's interest in the profit after taxation		394	554
Minority interests			764

24.42 This is clearly a very straightforward example and would be made more complicated by, for example, a share structure involving different classes of shares (particularly if one or more of those classes is a non-equity share) or where there are intra-group transactions that require elimination.

Indirect holdings

24.43 Where a parent holds an indirect interest in a subsidiary the treatment of minorities becomes more complicated. Before the minority interests can be calculated it is first necessary to establish whether the entity is a subsidiary of the parent and, therefore, should be consolidated.

Example

Consider the following group structure:

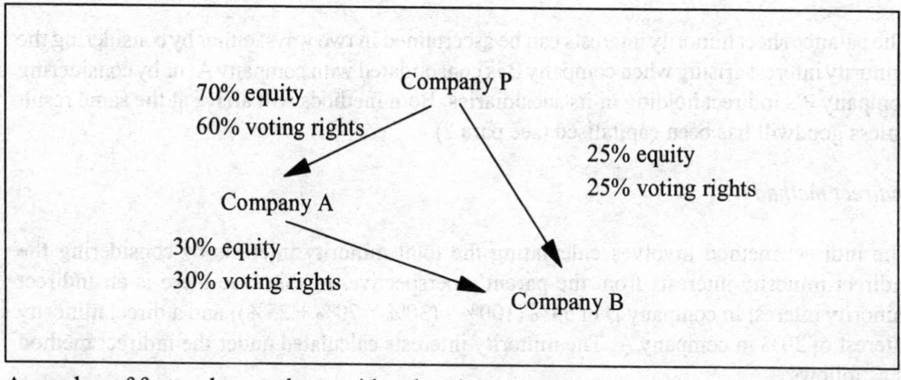

A number of factors have to be considered to determine whether company B is a subsidiary of company P. These matters are fully discussed in chapter 21. However, in the example company P owns 70% of the equity of company A and 60% of the voting rights of company A. Company A is, therefore, a subsidiary of company P, because company P controls more than 50% of the voting rights of company A.

Minority interests

Company P owns 25% of the equity and voting rights in company B, while company A owns 30% of the equity and voting rights in company B. Company B is not a direct subsidiary of company A as company A only controls 30% of its votes (assuming company B is not a subsidiary of company A for other reasons, for example, dominant influence – see further chapter 21). However, company P controls 25% of the votes in company B directly and, by virtue of its control of company A, 30% of the votes in company B indirectly. Company B is, therefore, a subsidiary of company P as company P controls in total 55% of the voting rights in company B. On the other hand, if company A had not been a subsidiary of company P, then company P would not have controlled company B and, as a consequence, company B would not have been a subsidiary of company P either.

The summarised balance sheets of each of the group companies is as follows:

Summarised balance sheets	Co P	Co A	Co B
	£'000	£'000	£'000
Investment in subsidiaries	60*	30	-
Net assets	190	120	200
	250	150	200
Equity share capital	100	50	100
Profit and loss account	150	100	100
Equity shareholders' funds	250	150	200

* The investment in subsidiaries represents the investments in company A and company B, which were acquired for their nominal value.

The balance sheet minority interests can be ascertained in two ways: either by considering the minority interest arising when company B is consolidated with company A; or by considering company P's indirect holding in its subsidiaries. Both methods will arrive at the same result unless goodwill has been capitalised (see para ?)

Indirect method

The indirect method involves calculating the total minority interests by considering the indirect minority interests from the parent's perspective. In this case there is an indirect minority interest in company B of 54% (100% - (30% × 70% + 25%)) and a direct minority interest of 30% in company A. The minority interests calculated under the indirect method is as follows:

Minority interest in group – indirect method	£'000
Minorities' share of net assets of company A	
net assets × direct minority interest (£120,000 × 30%)	36
Minorities' share of net assets of company B	
net assets × indirect minority interest (£200,000 × 54%)	108
	144

Direct method

The direct method of calculating the minority interests involves consolidation of the minority interests of company B with company A and then consolidating company A with company P. The calculation is as follows:

Minority interest in group – direct method	£'000
Company B consolidated into company A	
Equity share capital of company B (£100,000 × 70%)	70
Reserves of company B (£100,000 × 70%)	70
Minority interest in group A	140
Group A consolidated into company P	
Equity share capital of company A (£50,000 × 30%)	15
Reserves of company A (£100,000 × 30%)	30
Reserves of company B ((£100,000 – £70,000) × 30%)*	9
Adjustment to eliminate 25% of company B owned directly by company P†	
Equity share capital of B (£100,000 × 25%)	(25)
Reserves of B (£100,000 × 25%)	(25)
	144

* The minority in group A will take their proportion of the reserves of company B that have been consolidated with company A's reserves.

† The adjustment is necessary because the 70% minority interest in company B consolidated into company A includes the 25% held by company P.

24.44 The two methods arrive at the same result, unless goodwill is capitalised on acquisition. Assume in the example above that company B becomes a subsidiary of company A after company A has been acquired by company P. If company A capitalised goodwill arising on the acquisition of company B, as opposed to writing it off immediately to reserves which is allowed under the transitional provisions of

FRS 10 for goodwill arising before that standard's introduction, higher reserves would arise in company A's consolidated financial statements. The minority interests in company P should be allocated their share of this increase in reserves. Consequently, capitalising goodwill on acquisition will result in the direct method giving a higher figure for minority interests than the indirect method, therefore, we would recommend groups use the direct method of calculating minority interests.

Treatment of minority on acquisition

24.45 When a subsidiary is acquired it is necessary to allocate to the minority its share of the net assets of the subsidiary. This is normally done in the consolidation process by allocating to the minority its share of the adjusted capital and reserves of the subsidiary (that is, after fair value adjustments). However, they are not allocated any goodwill (see para 24.13). The example that follows illustrates these principles.

Example

At the end of year 1, company P acquires company S. Immediately before the acquisition the summarised balance sheets of both companies are as follows:

Summarised balance sheets	Co P	Co S
	£'000	£'000
Net assets	500	100
Equity share capital	200	20
Share premium account	100	-
Profit and loss reserve	300	80
Equity shareholders' funds	500	100

On the acquisition company P issues 10,000 £1 equity shares to the shareholders of company S to acquire 80% of its issued capital. The fair value of the consideration is valued at £150,000 and the fair value of the net assets of company S at the date of acquisition are determined to be £160,000. Consequently, the companies' balance sheets will look as follows after the acquisition:

Summarised balance sheets	Co P		Co S	
	£'000	£'000	£'000	£'000
Investment in subsidiary		150		-
Other net assets	500		100	
Fair value adjustment	-	500	60	160
		650		160

Equity share capital	210	20
Share premium	240	-
Profit and loss account	200	80
Revaluation reserve	-	60
Equity shareholders' funds	650	160

The goodwill arising on acquisition and the minority interests are calculated as follows:

Cost of control account/goodwill

	£'000		£'000
Investment	150	Equity share capital (£20,000 × 80%)	16
		P&L reserve (£80,000 × 80%)	64
		Revaluation reserve (£60,000 × 80%)	48
			128
		Goodwill	22
	150		150

Minority interests account

	£'000		£'000
Balance		Equity share capital (£20,000 × 20%)	4
	32	P&L reserve (£80,000 × 20%)	16
		Revaluation reserve (£60,000 × 20%)	12
	32		32

The consolidated balance sheet for the group immediately after the acquisition would be as follows:

Summarised consolidated balance sheet	Group
	£'000
Goodwill	22
Net assets (£500,000 + £160,000)	660
	682
Equity share capital	210
Share premium account	240
Profit and loss account reserve	200
Equity shareholders' funds	650
Minority interests	32
	682

24.46 In certain situations it might appear that there is a minority to recognise at the year end, where one should not be recognised. Such a situation might arise, for example, where the investing company makes an offer before the year end and receives (say) 90 per cent of acceptances before the year end. If it were to acquire the remaining 10 per cent soon after the year end, then it would be acceptable for the group not to record a minority interest in its consolidated financial statement, but explain in the notes the circumstances.

Treatment of dividends

24.47 Even where there is a minority interest, the group's consolidated profit and loss account should include all of the profits and losses that are attributable to a subsidiary. The minority's share of these profits and losses is then either deducted from or added to the group's consolidated profit or loss. Where the subsidiary has paid or proposed a dividend, whether or not this has been accounted for as received or receivable in the parent, certain adjustments will have to be made on consolidation. Consider the following example, which builds on the information given in the example in paragraph 24.45 above.

Example

Company P acquires company S at the year end and the facts for year 1 remain the same as in the previous example in paragraph 24.45. However, in year 2 company P makes a profit of £150,000, which includes a dividend receivable from company S of £16,000. Company S has made a profit of £100,000 during the year and has provided a dividend payable of £20,000, giving a retained profit of £80,000. The summarised balance sheets of both companies at the end of year 2 are set out below:

Summarised balance sheets	Co P		Co S	
	£'000	£'000	£'000	£'000
Investment in subsidiary		150		-
Other net assets		634		260
Dividend receivable/(payable)		16		(20)
		800		240
Equity share capital		210		20
Share premium		240		-
Profit and loss account	200		80	
Profit for the year	150	350	80	160
Revaluation reserve		-		60
Equity shareholders' funds		800		240

The cost of control account and goodwill arising on acquisition remain the same as in the previous example; the minority interests are calculated as follows:

Minority interests account

	£'000		£'000
Balance	48	Equity share capital (£20,000 × 20%)	4
		P&L reserve (£160,000 × 20%)	32
	—	Revaluation reserve (£60,000 × 20%)	12
	48		48

The consolidated profit and loss account would be arrived at in the following way:

Extract from profit and loss accounts	Co P £'000	Co S £'000	Group £'000
Trading profit	134	100	234
Dividend received	16	-	-
Profit on ordinary activities	150	100	234
Minority interest (£100,000 × 20%)	-	-	(20)
Dividend	-	(20)	-
Retained profit	150	80	214

The consolidated balance sheet for the group at the end of year 2 would be as follows:

Summarised consolidated balance sheet		Group
	£'000	£'000
Goodwill		22
Net assets (£634,000 + £260,000)		894
Dividend payable (to minority)*		(4)
		912
Equity share capital		210
Share premium account		240
Profit and loss account reserve (see previous example)	200	
Retained profit for the year	214	414
Equity shareholders' funds		864
Minority interests		48
		912

* A dividend payable of £4,000 arises on consolidation, which represents the difference between the dividend payable in company S's accounts of £20,000 and the amount shown as receivable in company P's accounts of £16,000. Before the introduction of FRS 4, dividends of this nature might have been included with the balance of minority interests. Dividends due to minorities are obligations of the group and as such under both FRS 4 and FRS 5 should be recognised as liabilities in the financial statements and not as part of minority interests.

Acquisition of minority interests

24.48 Where a holding company acquires more shares in a subsidiary either by buying them from the minority or by subscribing for a fresh issue of shares in the subsidiary itself, the goodwill arising on the acquisition will need to be recalculated. The identifiable assets and liabilities of the subsidiary should be revalued to fair value and the goodwill arising on the increase in interest should be calculated by reference to those fair values. This revaluation is not required if the difference between net fair values and the carrying amounts is not material. [FRS 2 para 51]. An example of a group acquiring a minority interest is given in Table 24.8.

Table 24.8 – Tesco PLC – Annual Report and Accounts – 25 February 1995

Notes to the financial statements (extract)

Note 29 Acquisitions

The company acquired a controlling interest in the Hungarian food retailer Global TH ('Global') on 28 June 1994.

On 2 September 1994 the company also acquired the UK food retailer Win Low & Company PLC ('WM Low'). WM Low results from this date until 25 February 1995 have been consolidated within the group profit and loss account. In the year ended 2 September 1994 the WM Low group made a profit after taxation of £15m (1993 – £17m).

During the year the group also acquired the remaining ordinary share capital of Ets. Catteau S.A. ('Catteau') for a consideration of £9m, increasing its holding from 95% to 100%.

All of the group's acquisitions have been accounted for using acquisition accounting.

The acquisitions of Global, Wm Low and the remaining share capital of Catteau have been consolidated into the Tesco group balance sheet as follows:

	Balance sheet at acquisition			
	Wm Low	**Other**	**Fair value adjustments**	**Fair value balance sheet**
	£m	**£m**	**£m**	**£m**
Fixed assets	240	5	27	272
Working capital	(13)	1	(2)	(14)
Taxation	(2)		-	(2)
Net short term borrowings	(51)	19	-	(32)
Minority interests	-	(8)	-	(8)
Shareholders' funds	174	17	25	216
Goodwill				65
Total purchase consideration				281

The purchase consideration for Wm Low includes £181m that was settled by the issue or ordinary shares in Tesco PLC. The remaining consideration for Wm Low and other acquisitions was settled by cash of £100m.

The net outflow of cash and cash equivalents for the purchase of subsidiary undertakings comprises:

	£m
Cash consideration	100
Cash at bank and in hand acquired	(26)
Bank overdrafts of acquired subsidiary undertakings	58
	132

Fair values at acquisition, total purchase consideration and goodwill are analysed as follows:

	Fair value balance sheet £m	Total purchase consideration £m	Goodwill £m
Wm Low	199	257	58
Global	14	15	1
Catteau	3	9	6
	216	281	65

Fair value adjustments

All fair value adjustments relate to the acquisition of Wm Low.	£m
Revaluation (a)	27
Accounting policy alignment	(1)
Other	(1)
	25

a) The principal adjustment relates to the revaluation of the property portfolio totalling £30m following advice from independent chartered surveyors.

There were no provisions for reorganisation or restructuring made in the accounts of Wm Low in the year ended 2 September 1994.

No fair value exercise

24.49 The example below is a continuation of the two previous examples in paragraphs 24.45 and 24.47 and considers how to account for a reduction in the minority interests.

Example

On the first day of year 3 company P subscribes for a further 20,000 £1 equity shares in company S for cash amounting to £40,000. The minority interests in the subsidiary are, therefore, reduced from 20% to 10%. During the year company P makes a profit of £200,000, which includes a dividend receivable from company S of £9,000. In the same period company S makes a loss of £20,000 and as a consequence reduces its dividend to £10,000, which is provided for in its financial statements. Immediately prior to the share issue the fair value of company S's net assets was £260,000 compared to a book value of £250,000. As this difference is not material, company P does not intend to fair value the net assets attributable to company S included in the consolidation.

The balance sheets of company P and company S at the end of year 3 are as follows:

Summarised balance sheets	Co P		Co S	
	£'000	£'000	£'000	£'000
Investment in subsidiary		190		-
Other net assets				
Company P (634 + 16 + 200 – 9 – 40)		801		-
Company S (260 – 20 + 40 – 20)		-		260
Dividend receivable/(payable)		9		(10)
		1,000		250
Equity share capital		210		40
Share premium		240		20
Profit and loss account	350		160	
Profit for the year	200	550	(30)	130
Revaluation reserve		-		60
Equity shareholders' funds		1,000		250

The goodwill arising on acquisition and the minority interests are calculated below:

Cost of control account/goodwill

	£'000			£'000
Investment		Equity share capital		
(£150,000 + £40,000)	190	(£20,000 × 80%)		16
		Acquired in year		20
		Total capital (£40,000 × 90%)		36
		P&L reserve		
		(£80,000 × 80%)	64	
		(£160,000 × 10%)	*16	80
		Revaluation reserve		
		(£60,000 × 80%)	48	
		(£60,000 × 10%)	* 6	54
		Share premium		
		(£20,000 × 90%)		18
				188
Negative goodwill	20	Initial goodwill		22
	210			210

* It is only necessary to bring into the cost of control account pre-acquisition reserves. Consequently, the additional percentage acquired need only be applied to the reserve

balances at the date of acquisition, which in the example is the first day of the year. Therefore, the balances at the previous year end date have been used (see example in para 24.47).

Minority interests account

	£'000		£'000
Balance	25	Equity share capital (£40,000 × 10%)	4
		Share premium (£20,000 × 10%)	2
		P&L reserve (£130,000 × 10%)	13
		Revaluation reserve (£60,000 × 10%)	6
	–		
	25		25

The consolidated profit and loss account would be arrived at in the following way:

Extract from profit and loss accounts	Co P £'000	Co S £'000	Group £'000
Trading profit/(loss)	191	(20)	171
Dividend received	9	-	-
Profit on ordinary activities	200	(20)	171
Minority interest (£20,000 × 10%)	-	-	2
Dividend	-	(10)	-
Retained profit	200	(30)	173

The consolidated balance sheet for the group at the end of year 3 would be as follows:

Summarised consolidated balance sheet

	Group	
	£'000	£'000
Goodwill	22	
Negative goodwill	(20)	
		2
Net assets (£801,000 + £260,000)		1,061
Dividend payable (to minority)*		(1)
		1,062
Equity share capital		210
Share premium account		240
Profit and loss account reserve (see previous example)	414	
Profit for the year	173	587
Equity shareholders' funds		1,037
Minority interests		25
		1,062

* As in the previous example, a balance of £1,000 arises on consolidation, which represents the difference between the dividend payable in company S's accounts of £10,000 and the amount shown as receivable in company P's accounts of £9,000 (see further the explanation in the previous example).

Consequences of fair valuing

24.50 The example that follows is exactly the same as the example above in paragraph 24.49, except that immediately prior to the share issue at the beginning of year 3 the fair value of company S's net assets is £410,000 compared to a book value of £250,000. As this difference is material to company P's consolidated financial statements it must fair value the net assets attributable to company S included in the consolidation.

Example

The balance sheets of company P and company S at the end of year 3 are as follows:

Summarised balance sheets	Co P		Co S	
	£'000	£'000	£'000	£'000
Investment in subsidiary		190		-
Other net assets				
Company P (634 + 16 + 200 – 9 – 40)		801		-
Company S (260 – 20 + 40 – 20 + 160)		-		420
Dividend receivable/(payable)		9		(10)
		1,000		410
Equity share capital		210		40
Share premium		240		20
Profit and loss account	350		160	
Profit for the year	200	550	(30)	130
Revaluation reserve		-		220
Equity shareholders' funds		1,000		410

The goodwill arising on acquisition and the minority interests are calculated below:

Cost of control account/goodwill				
	£'000			£'000
Investment		Equity share capital		
(£150,000 + £40,000)	190	(£20,000 × 80%)		16
		Acquired in year		20
		Total capital (£40,000 × 90%)		36
		P&L reserve		
		(£80,000 × 80%)	64	
		(£160,000 × 10%)	*16	80
		Revaluation reserve		
		(£60,000 × 80%)	48	
		(£220,000 × 10%)	*22	70
		Share premium		
		(£20,000 × 90%)		18
				204
Negative goodwill	36	Initial goodwill		22
	226			226

* See the explanation in the previous example.

Minority interests account

	£'000		£'000
Balance	41	Equity share capital (£40,000 × 10%)	4
		Share premium (20,000 × 10%)	2
		P&L reserve (£130,000 × 10%)	13
		Revaluation reserve (£220,000 × 10%)	22
	41		41

The consolidated profit and loss account is the same as that given in example 6. The consolidated balance sheet for the group at the end of year 3 would be as follows:

Summarised consolidated balance sheet	Group	
	£'000	£'000
Goodwill	22	
Negative goodwill	(36)	
		(14)
Net assets (£801,000 + £420,000)		1,221
Dividend payable (to minority)*		(1)
		1,206
Equity share capital		210
Share premium account		240
Profit and loss account reserve b/f	414	
Profit for the year	173	587
Revaluation reserve (80% × £160,000)		128
Equity shareholders' funds		1,165
Minority interests		41
		1,206

* See explanation in the previous example.

Minority acquires shares with differing rights

24.51 When a minority acquires shares that have different rights to other shares in the subsidiary, then the calculation of minority interests is complicated by this fact. This situation often arises where the minority holds preference shares in a subsidiary. Such shares do not normally carry any rights to participate in the capital of the subsidiary on winding up beyond the amount of preference capital itself. In this type of situation the rights attached to the minority's share capital have to be considered very carefully before calculating the minority interests. In addition, such shares are likely to be non-equity shares and to accord with the requirements of FRS 4. The disclosure of minority interests in the financial statements has to show the split between equity and non-equity interests (see further para 24.16). Consider the example that follows, which again progresses from the example in paragraph 24.49.

Example

On the first day of year 4, company S issues £40,000 10% redeemable preference shares to its minority shareholders for cash of £60,000 (issue costs are immaterial). The rights attached to the preference shares are that they carry a fixed dividend payable in one instalment after the year end and are redeemable in five years at a premium of £35,000. On liquidation, the preference shareholders are entitled only to repayment of the nominal value of their capital (that is, £40,000). These shares are non-equity under FRS 4. During year 4, company P makes a profit of £300,000 which includes a dividend receivable from company S of £18,000. Company S returns to profit in the year and makes a profit of £50,000 from which it proposes an ordinary dividend of £20,000 and a preference dividend of £4,000. In accordance with FRS 4, it accrues as an appropriation an additional finance cost on the preference shares of £2,739 and credits this to a separate redemption reserve. This amount represents the accrual of the redemption premium less the premium received on issue of the shares (that is, £35,000 – £20,000 = £15,000) over the term until its redemption, which is in five years time. It is calculated on an actuarial basis. (The calculation of such appropriations on non-equity shares in considered in detail in chapter 18.) The balance sheets of company P and company S at the end of year 4 are given below:

Summarised balance sheets	Co P		Co S	
	£'000	£'000	£'000	£'000
Investment in subsidiary		190		-
Other net assets				
Company P (801 + 9 + 300 – 18)		1,092		-
Company S (260 – 10 + 50 + 60)		-		360
Dividend receivable/(payable)		18		(24)
		1,300		336

Equity share capital		210		40
Non-equity share capital		-		40
Share premium				
Brought forward	240		20	
Premium on non-equity issue	-	240	20	40
Profit and loss account				
Brought forward	550		130	
Profit for the year	300		26	
Additional appropriation	-	850	(3)	153
Redemption reserve		-		3
Revaluation reserve		-		60
		1,300		336

The goodwill arising on acquisition remains the same as in the previous example in paragraph 24.50. The minority interest will change in order to take account of the issue of the preference share capital.

Minority interests account

	£'000		£'000
Balance	90	Attributable to equity shares	
		Share capital (£40,000 × 10%)	4
		Share premium (20,000 × 10%)	2
		P&L reserve	
		(£153,000 × 10%)	15
		Revaluation reserve	
		(£60,000 × 10%)	6
			27
		Attributable to non-equity shares	
		Preference shares	40
		Share premium	20
		Redemption reserve	3
	90		90

* The minority are allocated all of the preference share capital and under FRS 4 all of the share premium arising on those shares, even though they are not entitled to this reserve on a liquidation. Furthermore, the non-equity minority is also allocated appropriations for finance costs which have not yet been paid at the balance sheet date. In the example, this amount is the balance on the redemption reserve, but also could be part of the profit and loss account reserve, if the appropriation were credited back to the profit and loss account reserve instead of to a separate redemption reserve (see further chapter 18).

The consolidated profit and loss account would be arrived at in the following way:

Extract from profit and loss accounts	Co P £'000	Co S £'000		Group £'000
Trading profits	282	50		332
Dividend receivable	18	-		-
Profit on ordinary activities	300	50		332
Minority interests*				
Equity interests			(4)	
Non-equity interests	-	-	(7)	(11)
Dividend		(24)		-
Appropriation	-	(3)		-
Retained profit	300	23		321

* The equity minority interests share of the profit for the year is calculated by applying their interest to the profit for the year of company S after deducting the preference dividend paid to the non-equity minority and the non-equity appropriation (that is, (£50,000 - £4,000 – £3,000) × 10% = £4,300) say £4,000). The non-equity minority interests are £7,000, which is made up of the preference dividend of £4,000 and the appropriation of £3,000. These two amounts represent under FRS 4 the finance costs for the year of the minority non-equity shareholders. The minority interests in the profit and loss for the period has to be analysed between equity and non-equity interests (as shown above), but this analysis may alternatively be given in the notes to the financial statements. The disclosure is seldom seen on the face of the profit and loss account. [FRS 4 para 60].

The consolidated balance sheet for the group at the end of year 4 would be as follows:

Summarised consolidated balance sheet	Group	
	£'000	£'000
Goodwill	22	
Negative goodwill	(20)	
		2
Net assets (£1,092,000 + £360,000)		1,452
Dividend payable		(6)
		1,448
Share capital		210
Share premium account		240
Profit and loss account reserve (see previous example)	587	
Profit for the year	321	908
Shareholders' funds		1,358
Minority interests *		
Equity interests	27	
Non-equity interests	63	90
		1,448

* FRS 4 requires balance sheet minority interests to be analysed between equity and non-equity interests. Where this analysis is not given on the face of the balance sheet on the grounds of materiality, the balance sheet must indicate whether the minority interests figure includes non-equity minority interests, and if so, give the analysis in the notes to the financial statements.

Loss making subsidiaries

24.52 The treatment of minority interests requires special attention for subsidiaries that have made losses in the current year or in previous years. As seen above, minority interests for profitable subsidiaries are shown as a deduction in the profit and loss account and, consequently, reduce the group's profits transferred to shareholders' funds. Conversely, minority interests in a loss making subsidiary are, if recognised, added to the consolidated profit and account, thereby reducing the loss transferred to shareholders' funds.

24.53 The balance sheet minority interests in respect of a loss making subsidiary will be a credit if the subsidiary has net assets and will be a debit if it has net liabilities. Debit minority interests recognised in the balance sheet need careful consideration and FRS 2 requires the group to consider making a provision against such a balance where it arises. A provision should be made to the extent that the group has an obligation (whether formal or implied) to provide finance that may not be recoverable in respect of the accumulated losses attributable to the minority interests. [FRS 2 para 37]. For example, where a parent issues a letter of support to its subsidiary, the existence of the letter would indicate that there is a legal or commercial obligation on the parent to make good the losses of its subsidiary. Consequently, in these circumstances, a provision would need to be made against any debit minority interests arising on consolidation.

24.54 In situations where no provisioning is necessary it is argued that not recognising a debit minority interest balance in the consolidated balance sheet obscures the comparison between the assets and liabilities attributable to the minority interests and those attributable to group interests. This is particularly true where over a period of time accumulated losses accrue and are then made good by subsequent profits. Accumulated losses of this nature do not necessarily require funding by the parent, but, as mentioned above, a provision should be made in the consolidated balance sheet where funding is likely to be required. A debit balance does not represent an amount receivable from a minority, but rather the net liabilities attributable to the shares held by the minorities in that subsidiary.

24.55 FRS 2 makes it clear that the group should provide for any commercial or legal obligation, whether formal or implied, to provide finance that may not be recoverable in respect of the accumulated losses attributable to the minority interests. Any provision made with respect to minority debit balances should be set directly against the minority interests shown in the profit and loss account and in the balance sheet.

24.56 Provisions of this sort would go beyond merely providing against a debit balance and could include the minorities' share of any liability guaranteed by the group, or any liability that the group itself would be likely to settle for commercial or other reasons, if the subsidiary could not do so itself. This is born out by the requirement in FRS 4 to show any guaranteed obligation that the group has to its minority as a liability and not as minority interests. [FRS 4 para 49].

24.57 As losses are incurred by a subsidiary the minority's share of these losses will:

- First, be set against the minority's share of the subsidiary's reserves.
- Secondly, be set against the minority's share of the subsidiary's capital.
- Finally, be recognised as a debit balance in the consolidated balance sheet to the extent that the group does not have a commercial or legal obligation in respect of the losses attributable to the minority interests.

The above process should be reversed when profits attributable to the minority start to make good the losses incurred previously.

24.58 The following example illustrates the treatment of minority interests in a loss-making subsidiary, which eventually start to reverse.

Example

A parent company P owns 90% of the ordinary share capital and 20% of the non-redeemable cumulative preference share capital of its subsidiary company S. The summarised results of company S for four years are set out below:

	Year 1	Year 2	Year 3	Year 4
	£'000	£'000	£'000	£'000
Summarised profit and loss accounts				
Loss on ordinary activities after taxation	(202)	(535)	(675)	200
Preference dividend *	(8)	(8)	(8)	(8)
Ordinary dividend	(50)	-	-	-
	(260)	(543)	(683)	192
Summarised balance sheets				
Net assets	1,147	554	(121)	79
Dividend payable	(58)	-	-	-
	1,089	554	(121)	79
Equity share capital	500	500	500	500
Non-equity share capital	100	100	100	100
Profit and loss account	489	(54)	(737)	(545)
Other reserves				
Cumulative preference shares*	-	8	16	24
	1,089	554	(121)	79

* The preference dividend is cumulative and, to accord with FRS 4, continues to be appropriated even where the company has no distributable reserves from which to pay it, as it represents the finance costs on the preference shares. But while the cumulative dividend cannot be paid (as in years 2 to 4), it is credited back to the profit and loss account reserve or to another reserve (as in the example). This treatment is explained further in chapter 18.

In each year company P's consolidated profit and loss account will show 100% of company S's losses on ordinary activities before taxation and 100% of company S's taxation charge/credit. The consolidated balance sheet will show 100% of the net assets/liabilities of company S. The minority interests shown in the consolidated profit and loss account and balance sheet will be as follows:

Year 1

Profit and loss account

Minority interests:	
Equity interests:	£
10% of the loss after preference dividends, increased by the preference dividend (£(202,000) + £(8,000) × 10%)	(21,000)
Non-equity interests: 80% of preference dividend (£8,000 × 80%)	6,400
	(14,600)

Balance sheet

Minority interests	£
Equity interests:	
10% of ordinary share capital (£500,000 × 10%)	50,000
10% of profit and loss account reserves (£489,000 × 10%)	48,900
	98,900
Non-equity interests: 80% of preference share capital (£100,000 × 80%)	80,000
	178,900

If either the ordinary or the preference dividend is outstanding (that is, not paid) at the year end the creditor for dividends payable to the minority would, to the extent that it is paid in the next accounting period, be shown under creditors as explained previously.

Year 2

Profit and loss account

Minority interests	£
Equity interests: 10% of the loss after preference dividends (£(535,000) + £(8,000) × 10%)	(54,300)
Non-equity interests: 80% of preference dividend (8,000 × 80%)	6,400
	(47,900)

Balance sheet

Minority interests	£	£
Equity interests:		
10% of ordinary share capital (£500,000 × 10%)	50,000	
10% of profit and loss account reserves (£(54,000) × 10%)	(5,400)	44,600
Non-equity interests:		
80% of preference share capital (£100,000 × 80%)	80,000	
80% of cumulative dividend reserve (£8,000 × 80%)	6,400	86,400
		131,000

Reconciliation of minority interests	Equity £	Non-equity £	Total £
Minority interests brought forward	98,900	80,000	178,900
Profit and loss account	(54,300)	6,400	(47,900)
Minority interests carried forward	44,600	86,400	131,000

In year 3, the minority interests might appear, at first glance, to be 10% of the loss after preference dividends and appropriations. However, the loss for the year will be taken first by the ordinary shareholders and then, when the losses are sufficient to fully offset the ordinary share capital, by the preference shareholders including their cumulative entitlement to preference dividends.

The minority interest in the loss for the year will be 10% of that element of the loss which fully eliminates the ordinary share capital and then 80% of the losses which eliminate the preference share capital. Any further losses (that is, losses that move the subsidiary into a net liability position) will then be borne by the ordinary shareholders.

Year 3

Profit and loss account

Minority interests	Loss for the year £	Minority interests £
Equity interests:		
10% of losses on ordinary capital ((£(500,000) – £(54,000)) × 10%)	(446,000)	(44,600)
10% of further losses increased by the preference dividends due to the minority: ((£(675,000) + £(8,000) – £(446,000) – £(100,000)) × 10%)	(137,000)	(13,700)
Add back losses used to eliminate preference dividends (see below)		12,800
		(45,500)
Non-equity interests:		
80% of losses on preference share capital (£(100,000) × 80%)	(100,000)	(80,000)
80% of preference dividend (8,000 × 80%)	8,000	6,400
Share of losses to eliminate preference dividends		(12,800)
		(86,400)
	(675,000)	(131,900)

Balance sheet

Minority interests		
Equity interests:		
10% of ordinary share capital (£500,000 × 10%)		50,000
10% share of profit and loss account deficit (£(500,000) × 10%)		(50,000)
Remaining profit and loss account deficit ((£137,000 × 10%) – £12,800 re preference dividend – see below)		(900)
		(900)
Non-equity interests:		
80% of preference share capital (£100,000 × 80%)	80,000	
80% share of profit and loss account deficit (£(100,000) × 80%)	(80,000)	
80% of cumulative dividend reserve (£16,000 × 80%)	12,800	
Further share of profit and loss account deficit to eliminate cumulative dividends	(12,800)	-
Debit minority interests *		(900)

Reconciliation of minority interests	Equity	Non-equity	Total
	£	£	£
Minority interests brought forward	44,600	86,400	131,000
Profit and loss account	(45,500)	(86,400)	(131,900)
Minority interests carried forward	(900)	-	(900)

* For the purposes of this example it has been assumed that the parent has no legal or commercial obligation (whether formal or implied) to provide finance that may not be recoverable in respect of the accumulated losses attributable to the minority interests. Had the parent been obliged to provide such finance a provision would have been required. The provision would be set off in the profit and loss account and the balance sheet against the minority interests up to £900 and thereafter charged to the profit before taxation and set up as a provision in the balance sheet. Furthermore, the debit balance of minority interests has all been allocated to the equity minority interests, because the non-equity minority have in effect no further interest in the company and until the company returns to profit the non-equity minority interests will remain nil.

If in the example the parent had provided a guarantee to the preference shareholders, in the event of winding up the subsidiary, the minority interests credit balance would not have been reduced by the losses attributable to the preference share capital of £80,000. However, in this circumstance, the non-equity minority interests would not be recorded in the balance sheet as minority interests, but would be shown as a liability in accordance with FRS 4 (see further para 24.33).

In year four, the subsidiary makes a profit of £200,000, which turns its net assets positive. The profits reverse the previous losses and affect the minority by reversing the losses set against the preference share capital before reversing those set against the ordinary capital. In addition, the cumulative preference dividends have been reinstated as reserves allocated to the non-equity minority interests.

Year 4

Profit and loss account

Minority interests	Profit for the year £	Minority interests £
Equity interests:		
Reversal of share of 10% of further losses taken in previous year (£137,000 × 10%)	137,000	13,700
Reversal of losses used to eliminate preference dividends (see below)		(12,800)
		900
Non-equity interests:		
80% of reversal of part of the losses on preference share capital (£55,000 × 80%)	55,000	44,000
80% of preference dividend (£8,000 × 80%)	8,000	6,400
Reversal of share of losses to eliminate preference dividends		12,800
		63,200
	200,000	64,100

Balance sheet

Minority interests		
Equity interests:		
10% of ordinary share capital (£500,000 × 10%)		50,000
10% share of profit and loss account deficit (£(500,000) × 10%)		(50,000)
		-
Non-equity interests:		
80% of preference share capital (£100,000 × 80%)	80,000	
80% share of profit and loss account deficit (£(45,000) × 80%)	(36,000)	
80% of cumulative dividend reserve (£24,000 × 80%)	19,200	63,200
Minority interests		63,200

Reconciliation of minority interests	Equity	Non-equity	Total
	£	£	£
Minority interests brought forward	(900)	-	(900)
Profit and loss account	900	63,200	64,100
Minority interests carried forward	-	63,200	63,200

24.59 The example above illustrates the complexities that can arise where there are different classes of shares in issue held by minorities and the company in which the minority interests is held starts to make losses. FRS 4 does not explain in detail how the split between equity and non-equity minority interests would be calculated in these circumstances and therefore there may by other ways of calculating the split. Whatever method is used, it should still be based on the basic objective of FRS 4 which is to *"provide a clear, coherent and consistent treatment of capital instruments"*.

Chapter 25

Disposals of subsidiaries

Page

Chapter 25

Disposals of subsidiaries

Introduction

25.1 Typically, an undertaking will cease to be a subsidiary of another when the group sells it or reduces its percentage interest in the undertaking. Equally a parent may lose control over an undertaking because of changes in the rights it holds or in those held by another party in that undertaking or because there is a change in some other arrangement that gave the parent its control (see further chapter 21).

25.2 A reduction in percentage interest may arise from a direct disposal (for example, the sale of shares in a company) or from a deemed disposal (for example, the exercise of share options by another party). A gain or loss will normally arise on both a disposal and a deemed disposal (for example, see Table 25.1).

Table 25.1 – Forte Plc – Report and Accounts – 31 January 1994

Notes to the Accounts (extract)

7 Profit on disposal of discontinued operation
The profit on disposal of discontinued operations, amounting to £122m, relates to the flotation of the Group's interest in its Airport Services Division (now called ALPHA Airports Group Plc – "ALPHA") on 25 January 1994 and the sale of the Group's interest in Kentucky Fried Chicken (Great Britain) Ltd on 2 December 1993. Proceeds amounting to £155m from the ALPHA disposal were outstanding at the year end and were received on 10 February 1994. The Group has retained a 25% interest in ALPHA.

14 Fixed assets – investments (extract)
ALPHA
Following the flotation of the Group's Airport Services Division in January 1994, the Group retained 25% of the ordinary shares of the new holding company, ALPHA Airports Group Plc. In addition the Group holds 46,000 6.5% cumulative redeemable preference shares of £1 each. The Group's share of the net assets of ALPHA as at 31 January 1994, calculated using Forte's accounting policies, amounted to £12m. ALPHA shares were listed on 10 February 1994 at a price valuing this interest at £53m.

25.3 Where a parent loses control because of changes in its rights or the rights of other parties, or because of changes in some other arrangement, neither a gain nor a loss will arise in the consolidated profit and loss account, unless there is a payment for the transfer of the control. This is because there will be no change in the net assets attributable to the group's holding in the former subsidiary. [FRS 2 para 86]. See further paragraph 25.24. However, a gain or loss (albeit normally unrealised) can arise where, for example, a company (company P) disposes of shares it holds in its subsidiary (company S) in exchange for shares in another company (company A). The subsidiary (company S) will often then become a subsidiary of the acquiring company (company A). The acquiring company will also often become a subsidiary of the original parent (company P). An example of this type of arrangement is given in paragraph 25.26.

25.4 The disposal of a business has to be accounted for in much the same way as a disposal of a subsidiary. Therefore, many of the principles explained in this chapter apply equally to the disposals of businesses as they do to disposals of subsidiaries. Furthermore, the disclosures that have to be given are also similar. Disposals of businesses are not dealt with in the Companies Act, but the provisions in FRS 2, FRS 3 and FRS 10 are the same for disposals of businesses and subsidiaries.

The accounting rules

Rules in FRS 2

25.5 Accounting for an undertaking that ceases to be a subsidiary is often as complex as accounting for the acquisition of a subsidiary. The matters that need to be considered when an undertaking ceases to be a subsidiary include both how to account for trading in the period after the implementation of the decision to dispose of the subsidiary and how to account for the cessation itself.

25.6 Where an undertaking ceases to be a subsidiary during a period, the consolidated profit and loss account for that period should include, to the extent that they have not already been provided for in the consolidated financial statements:

- The results of the subsidiary up to the date it ceases to be a subsidiary.
- The gain or loss arising on the cessation.

[FRS 2 para 46].

25.7 The calculation of the gain or loss arising on cessation (whether it is the result of a direct disposal, a deemed disposal or another event) is the difference between the following two amounts:

- The carrying amount of the net assets of the subsidiary attributable to the group's interest before the cessation (including any attributable goodwill - see para 25.10).

- Any remaining carrying amount attributable to the group's interest after the cessation (including any attributable goodwill), together with any proceeds received.

[FRS 2 para 47].

25.8 In many sales an element of contingent performance-related consideration is included as part of the proceeds. This element would normally be treated as a contingent gain under SSAP 18; consequently it would not be recognised in the profit and loss account until it became receivable and until then it would merely be disclosed the notes to the financial statements. Where consideration is simply deferred (and, hence, not contingent on future performance), the amount receivable may need to be discounted to its present value at the disposal date depending on the length of time over which it has been deferred and whether or not it bears interest.

25.9 There may be other losses or gains that arise as a result of an undertaking ceasing to be a subsidiary that need to be recognised (for example, provisions for guarantees). Such gains or losses are not directly part of the profit or loss on the disposal, but where they need to be provided for, if they are quantifiable, they should normally be included as part of the profit or loss on disposal. If for some reason they are not provided for, they might need to be disclosed to show the full effect of the cessation. [FRS 2 para 87].

FRS 10

25.10 The value of net assets used to calculate the profit or loss on disposal (see para 25.7) should include any related goodwill (including any negative goodwill) not previously written off through the profit and loss account. [FRS 2 para 47]. The requirement in FRS 2 to include such goodwill not previously written off through the profit and loss account was first required by UITF Abstract 3 and this is repeated in the transitional provisions of FRS 10. The effect of this requirement in practice is that goodwill (or negative goodwill), arising before the introduction of FRS 10, which has remained written off (or credited) directly to reserves on acquisition following FRS 10's transitional provisions [FRS 10 para 71(c)], and any goodwill that has been capitalised but not yet amortised, must be charged (or credited) to the profit and loss account on disposal. This treatment is considered necessary to ensure that purchased goodwill (or negative goodwill) having been written off (or credited) to reserves prior to the implementation of FRS 10 does not bypass the profit and loss account completely. The requirement applies whether the disposal is a direct disposal, a deemed disposal or another event.

25.11 The practical impact of the provisions of both FRS 2 and FRS 10 means that groups have to keep detailed records of how the aggregate amount of goodwill written off direct to reserves prior to the implementation of FRS 10 is made up and to which parts of the group it relates. Because of the difficulties this can cause, particularly where the acquisition took place many years ago, there is some relief given, but this is subject to disclosure. In such a situation, it is necessary to state that goodwill has not been included in the calculation of the profit or loss arising on the sale and to explain the reason why this is so (see also para 25.41). [FRS 10 para 71(c)]. The requirement to include the attributable goodwill when calculating the profit or loss on sale of a subsidiary does pose particular problems. Consider the following examples:

Example 1

A group acquired another group of companies some years ago before the introduction of FRS 10. The consideration was £100m and the fair value of the net assets acquired was £40m. The resultant goodwill of £60m was written off to reserves on acquisition. The acquired group consists of five companies and the goodwill was allocated between them on the basis of a price earnings formula. The allocation was positive goodwill of £70m relating to four of the companies and negative goodwill of £10m relating to the fifth. The group is now disposing of the company in respect of which the negative goodwill arose.

Prior to FRS 10, companies could apportion the goodwill arising on acquisition in this way and, therefore, on the sale of the part of the group that gave rise to the negative goodwill, the negative goodwill would have been taken into the calculation of the profit or loss on the sale. However, for acquisitions arising following FRS 10's introduction purchased goodwill on a single transaction should not be divided into positive and negative components. In this situation, using the same facts as in the example, the £60m of goodwill should still be allocated over the five companies. However, because of the new rules in FRS 10 the original allocation would need to be changed. This would mean allocating a figure of nil to the first company and £60m of goodwill over the other four companies. As a result, goodwill of nil would be attributed to the company being disposed of.

Example 2

A group disposes of a subsidiary after the year end and there is a binding contract before the financial statements are approved. The net assets are £100m and proceeds will be £50m. The group proposes to make a provision at the year end for the loss on sale. However, there is negative goodwill of £60m on the original acquisition of the subsidiary which arose before the introduction of FRS 10 and had been taken to reserves. The negative goodwill needs to be taken into account in calculating the provision. If this is done there is a profit on disposal, and hence no need for a provision.

The provision for loss on sale is £50m before taking into account goodwill. If the negative goodwill is taken into account in full, then there will be a profit of £10m. However, as the sale has not actually taken place at the year end the £10m is unrealised and should not be brought into the profit and loss account. Only £50m of the negative goodwill should be taken into account at the year end resulting in a nil profit or loss. However, reserves will fall by £50m (because the negative goodwill has been reduced to £10m) and there will be a corresponding provision against the net assets of the subsidiary included in provisions. In the following year the gain of £10m would be recognised in the profit and loss account. If on the other hand the overall position taking into account the goodwill previously written off to reserves was a loss of £10m rather than a profit of £10m, this would have to be provided for in the current year.

25.12 As explained in chapter 23, prior to the introduction of FRS 10 it was acceptable to write goodwill off against the merger reserve and this continues to be acceptable practice for goodwill arising prior to FRS 10's implementation. On the sale of a subsidiary, as explained above, it is necessary to include in the calculation of any profit or loss on sale any goodwill written off direct to reserves on the original acquisition. Where an amount was credited to a merger reserve on the acquisition, that reserve would at the time be unrealised. On disposal the merger reserve arising on the acquisition becomes realised. The question then arises as to whether it is acceptable to take that part of the merger reserve to the profit and loss account on the sale of the subsidiary to mitigate the goodwill charged there. This is not, however, an acceptable treatment, because the intention of FRS 2 and FRS 10 is to measure the profit or loss on the sale by reference to its cost. The original cost for this purpose is represented by the fair value of the consideration, that is the nominal value of the shares issued plus the merger reserve. To take the release of the merger reserve to the profit and loss account would mean that the loss on sale of the subsidiary was not calculated by reference to this amount. Therefore, any merger reserve that is realised should instead be transferred to the profit and loss account reserve as a reserve movement.

Implications of FRS 3

25.13 FRS 3 requires the profit or loss on the sale of an asset to be calculated by reference to the carrying value of that asset. [FRS 3 para 21]. This requirement might seem to conflict with the FRS 2 calculation explained in paragraph 25.10 above, which requires goodwill written off to reserves in the past prior to FRS 10's implementation to be brought back into the calculation of the profit or loss on the sale of a subsidiary. The explanation of this apparent inconsistency is that the write-off of goodwill direct to reserves was not regarded as a recognised loss and, therefore, when the write-off was initially made it did not appear in the statement of total recognised gains and losses. Because it has not been 'recognised' in the past it follows that it must be recognised on disposal of the subsidiary by inclusion in the profit or loss recognised in the profit and loss account.

25.14 The treatment of profits and losses on disposals of operations, including the rules concerning loss provisions, is considered in detail in chapter 7.

Discontinued operations

25.15 Where an operation is sold, its results up to the date of sale should be disclosed as part of operating profit under either the heading 'discontinued operations' or, if it does not qualify as a discontinued operation (see para 25.16), as 'continuing operations'. The profit or loss on sale should be shown as an exceptional item after operating profit and before interest and should also be disclosed as relating to 'discontinued operations' or, if it does not qualify, it should be disclosed as relating to 'continuing operations'. [FRS 3 para 20]. It is quite possible for a business or a subsidiary that is being sold not to qualify as a discontinued operation under FRS 3 (see for example Table 25.2).

Table 25.2 – Grand Metropolitan Public Limited Company – Annual Report – 30 September 1996

Consolidated profit and loss account (extract)
for the year ended 30th September 1996

	Notes	1996 Before exceptional items £m	1996 Except -ional items £m	1996 Total £m	1995 Before exceptional items £m	1995 Except-ional items £m	1995 Total £m
Turnover							
Continuing operations		8,727		8,727	7,733		7,733
Discontinued operations		247		247	292		292
Total turnover	3	8,974		8,974	8,025		8,025
Operating costs	4	(7,866)		(7,866)	(6,993)	(122)	(7,115)
Operating profit							
Continuing operations		1,096		1,096	1,009	(122)	887
Discontinued operations		12		12	23	-	23
Total operating profit		1,108		1,108	1,032	(122)	910
Share of profits of associates	5	47	(24)	23	48	(15)	33
		1,155	(24)	1,131	1,080	(137)	943
Continuing operations							
Disposal of fixed assets			(3)	(3)		(9)	(9)
Sale of businesses	6		27	27		(44)	(44)
Provisions for losses on sale of businesses	6		(250)	(250)		-	-
Discontinued operations							
Sale of businesses	6		(327)	(327)		198	198
			(553)	(553)		145	145
Interest payable (net)	7	(190)	-	(190)	(168)	-	(168)
Profit on ordinary activities before taxation		965	(577)	388	912	8	920

Notes (extract)

6 Sale of businesses

	1996		1995
	Profit/(loss) on sale of businesses £m	Provisions set up for businesses to be sold £m	Profit/(loss) on sale of businesses £m
Continuing operations			
National food businesses in Europe (note (a))	35	(250)	-
Green Giant processing	-	-	(42)
Other	(8)	-	(2)
	27	(250)	(44)
Discontinued operations			
Pearle (note (b))	(291)	-	-
Betting and gaming (note (c))	(36)	-	-
Alpo Petfoods	-	-	198
	(327)	-	198

(a) The sale of the German food business, Erasco, was completed on 30th September for a consideration of £134m; provisions of £250m have been set up in respect of the remaining national food businesses in Europe. The profit on sale and the provisions are after charging goodwill previously written off attributable to the businesses of £222m.

(b) The sale of Pearle for a consideration of £138m was agreed on 25th September 1996 and was completed on 15th November 1996. The loss on sale was after charging goodwill previously written off attributable to Pearle of £270m.

(c) The £36m in respect of betting and gaming relates to a £118m downward adjustment to the consideration for the group's former retail betting operation, which was sold in December 1989 for £685m, offset by £82m which remained outstanding from The William Hill Group Ltd in relation to the sale. This disposes of the major aspect of a dispute with the purchaser, but there are other ongoing claims arising from the sale which have yet to be resolved.

25.16 FRS 3 defines discontinued operations as those operations that satisfy all of the following conditions:

- The sale or termination is completed either in the period or before the earlier of three months after the commencement of the subsequent period and the date on which the financial statements are approved.
- If a termination, the former activities have ceased permanently.
- The sale or termination has a material effect on the nature and focus of the reporting entity's operations and represents a material reduction in its operating facilities resulting either from its withdrawal from a particular market (whether class of business or geographical) or from a material reduction in turnover in the reporting entity's continuing markets.

- The assets, liabilities, results of operations and activities are clearly distinguishable, physically, operationally and for financial reporting purposes.

[FRS 3 para 4].

25.17 The very strict definition of 'discontinued operations' and the detailed disclosure requirements of both continuing and discontinued operations are considered in detail in chapter 7. Any reorganisation or restructuring of continuing operations resulting from a sale should be treated as part of the continuing operations. [FRS 3 para 17].

Date of sale

25.18 The date of sale is the date on which a binding legal agreement for the sale of an operation is entered into (see further chapter 7). The date on which an undertaking ceases to be another undertaking's subsidiary is the date on which control passes. [FRS 2 para 45]. Where control is transferred by public offer the relevant date is usually when an offer becomes unconditional. Where it is transferred by private treaty the date is usually where an unconditional offer is accepted. The signing of a binding legal agreement for the sale of an operation would, therefore, appear to be the date on which an offer becomes unconditional and is accepted and, therefore, should be the date from which the disposal is accounted for as having occurred. [FRS 2 para 85]. The effective date for accounting for changes in group membership is discussed in detail in chapter 23.

Impact of FRS 1

25.19 The provisions of FRS 1, 'Cash flow statements', require that where a group disposes of a subsidiary, the amounts of cash and overdrafts transferred as part of the disposal should be shown separately from the gross consideration received for the disposal. [FRS 1 para 23(a)]. Where a subsidiary is disposed of during the year, the cash flows of the group should include the cash flows of the subsidiary up to the date of sale. [FRS 1 para 43]. The provisions of FRS 1 are explained in detail in chapter 30 and the disclosure requirements relating to disposals are summarised in paragraph 25.39.

Accounting for the sale of a subsidiary

Full disposal

25.20 The most common transaction that results in an undertaking ceasing to be a subsidiary is a straight disposal. The consolidated profit and loss account should include the trading results of the undertaking up to the date of its ceasing to be a subsidiary, disclosed, where appropriate, as discontinued operations as explained above. Any gain or loss arising on disposal would be included in the profit and loss account on the basis explained above.

25.21 In effect, the profit or loss on disposal of all or part of a subsidiary will be the difference at the date of sale between the following amounts:

- The proceeds of the sale.
- The group's share of the subsidiary undertaking's net assets disposed of, together with any premium or discount on acquisition (apportioned if necessary to that element of the net assets sold) that has not been written off through the profit and loss account.

25.22 The calculation of the profit or loss on sale is illustrated by the following examples. The example below looks at the calculation of the gain on disposal of a subsidiary where the group capitalised goodwill arising on the initial acquisition and amortises that goodwill over its useful life.

Example

A parent purchased an 80% interest in a subsidiary for £80,000 during 19X1 when the fair value of the subsidiary's net assets was £87,500. Goodwill on consolidation that arose on the acquisition is being amortised over its estimated useful life of ten years and a full year's charge for amortisation was made in the consolidated financial statements to 31 December 19X1. The parent sold its investment in the subsidiary on 31 December 19X4 for £100,000. The book value of the subsidiary's net assets on the date of the sale was £112,500.

The parent's profit and loss account for 19X4 would show a gain on the sale of the investment of £20,000 calculated as follows:

	£'000
Sale proceeds	100
Less: cost of investment in subsidiary	(80)
Gain on sale in the parent's accounts	20

However, the group's profit and loss account for 19X4 would show a gain on the sale of the subsidiary of £4,000 calculated as follows:

		£'000	£'000
Sale proceeds			100
Less:	share of net assets at date of disposal (£112,500 × 80%)	(90)	
	goodwill on consolidation unamortised at date of sale*	(6)	(96)
Gain on sale in the group's accounts			4

* The unamortised goodwill on consolidation is calculated as follows:

		£'000
Fair value of consideration at date of acquisition		80
Less:	fair value of net assets of subsidiary at date of acquisition (£87,500 × 80%)	70
Goodwill arising on consolidation		10
Amortisation (4 years × £1,000)		4
Unamortised goodwill at 31 December 19X4		6

The difference between the gain in the holding company's profit and loss account and the gain reported in the group's consolidated profit and loss account is £16,000 (that is, £20,000 - £4,000). This difference represents the share of post-acquisition profits retained in the subsidiary of £20,000 (that is, (£112,500 - £87,500) × 80%) that have been reported in the group's profit and loss account up to the date of sale, less goodwill of £4,000 that has been written off in the group's profit and loss account.

25.23 The next example looks at the calculation of the gain or loss on disposal where the group on acquisition, prior to the implementation of FRS 10, wrote off the goodwill arising on purchasing the subsidiary direct to reserves.

Example

The facts are identical to those in the example in paragraph 25.22 except that the goodwill that arose on consolidation was written off direct to reserves in the year of acquisition.

As before, the parent's profit and loss account for 19X4 would show a gain on the sale of the investment of £20,000. The group's profit and loss account for 19X4 would show no gain or loss on the sale of the subsidiary calculated as follows:

		£'000	£'000
Sale proceeds			100
Less:	share of net assets at date of disposal (£112,500 × 80%)	(90)	
	goodwill written off directly to reserves *	(10)	(100)
			–

* The goodwill on consolidation is calculated as follows:

		£'000
Fair value of consideration at date of acquisition		80
Less:	fair value of net assets of subsidiary at date of acquisition (£87,500 × 80%)	70
Goodwill arising on consolidation		10

The difference between the gain in the parent's profit and loss account and the gain reported in the group's consolidated profit and loss account is £20,000. This difference represents the share of post-acquisition profits retained in the subsidiary of £20,000 (that is, (£112,500 – £87,500) × 80%) that have been reported in the group's profit and loss account up to the date of sale. The goodwill is required by FRS 2 and FRS 10 to be written back to reserves on sale of the subsidiary and charged as part of the overall profit or loss on the disposal (see further para 25.10).

Ceasing to be a subsidiary other than by sale or exchange of shares

25.24 An undertaking may cease to be a subsidiary undertaking as a result of loss of control. Such loss of control could occur, for example, because of: changes in voting rights attaching to shares held; changes in the power to appoint or remove directors or their voting rights; or the parent no longer actually exercising dominant influence (see further chapter 21). In these situations no profit or loss will arise in the consolidated financial statements, unless there is a payment for loss of control, because there is no change in the net assets attributable to the group's holding in the former subsidiary undertaking.

25.25 Where loss of control arises in this way, the former subsidiary undertaking should not be consolidated, but should be shown instead at its net asset value as an associated undertaking (see chapter 28) or as an investment depending on the degree of influence retained. In addition, the circumstances that resulted in the undertaking ceasing to be a subsidiary should be explained in a note to the consolidated financial statements. [FRS 2 para 49].

Sale of a subsidiary for shares

25.26 Disposals often arise where a parent sells a subsidiary for shares in another undertaking, which results in the acquiring company becoming either an associate or a subsidiary of the vendor. Therefore, at the same time as the disposal there is an acquisition. The transaction can be regarded as a swap although in some situations cash may pass and often a difference will arise on consolidation. This difference arises because the net assets given up in the swap are brought into the calculation at book value, whereas the net assets acquired are brought into the equation at fair value. The difference should be adjusted to goodwill. The example below illustrates a transaction where the acquirer becomes a subsidiary of the vendor and the accounting implications.

Example

Company A has a wholly-owned subsidiary company B. Company A sells its subsidiary company B to company C, a listed company, for shares in company C and ends up owning 75% of company C's shares (as illustrated in the diagram).

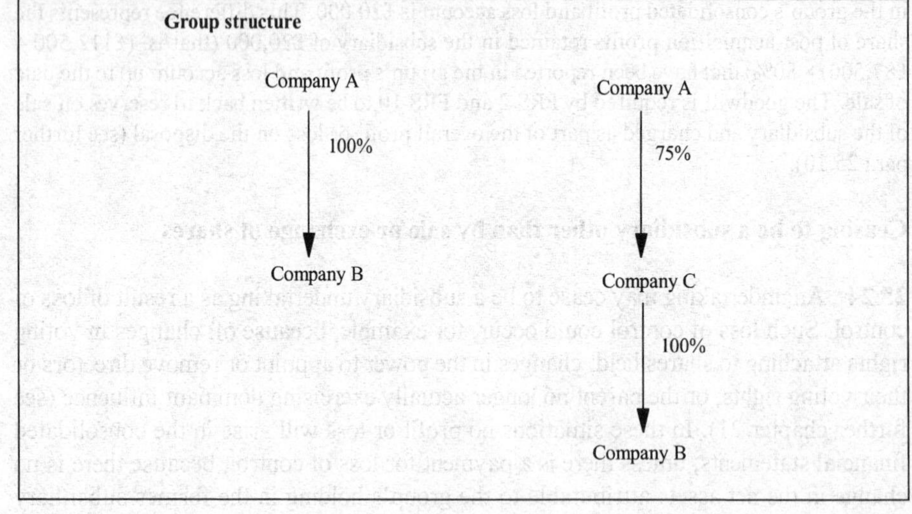

The net assets of company B prior to the disposal are £1 million and goodwill previously capitalised is £600,000 (for simplicity, goodwill has not been amortised in this example); the carrying value of company B in company A's books is £1.5 million. At the date of its acquisition by company A, company B's profit and loss account reserve was £400,000 and has since made £100,000 post acquisition profits. The position prior to the transaction was, therefore, as follows:

Consolidation of companies A and B before transaction

	Co A £'000	Co B £'000	Consol £'000
Goodwill	-	-	600
Investment in subsidiary	1,500	-	-
Net assets	10,000	1,000	11,000
	11,500	1,000	11,600
Equity share capital	2,000	500	2,000
Profit and loss account reserve	9,500	100	9,600
– pre acquisition reserves	-	400	-
	9,500	500	9,000
Equity shareholders' funds	11,500	1,000	11,600

The goodwill arising on the acquisition by company A of company B is calculated as follows:

Cost of control account/goodwill

	£'000		£'000
Investment	1,500	Equity share capital	500
		P&L reserve	400
	1,500		900
		Goodwill	600
			1,500

The net assets of company C prior to its acquisition of company B are £380,000. Company C then issues shares worth £1.75 million (which is the fair value of the consideration given for the sale), being £600,000 nominal value and £1.15 million share premium. The balance sheets of the three companies directly after the issue of shares by company C are as follows:

Summarised balance sheets	Co A £'000	Co B £'000	Co C £'000
Investment in subsidiary	1,500	-	1,750
Net assets	10,000	1,000	380
	11,500	1,000	2,130
Equity share capital	2,000	500	800
Merger reserve	-	-	1,150
Profit and loss account reserve	9,500	500	180
Equity shareholders' funds	11,500	1,000	2,130

The parent, company A, had an interest in company B that cost £1.5 million, and has in effect swapped this for an interest in company C's group. The cost to company A remains £1.5 million, although this investment has a market value of £1.75 million.

With regard to company A's consolidated financial statements, it is necessary to compare the carrying values of net assets and attributable goodwill before and after the transaction.

Calculation of difference arising on transaction

	£'000	£'000
Net assets and proceeds after transaction		
75% of net assets of company B (£1m × 75%)	750	
75% of goodwill (£600,000 × 75%)	450	
	1,200	
75% of net assets of company C (£380 × 75%)	285	
Proceeds (in this example nil)	-	1,485
Less: net assets before transaction		
Net assets of company B	1,000	
Goodwill	600	1,600
Difference arising		115

The difference of £115,000 represents new goodwill arising on the transaction. Goodwill remaining on the original acquisition of the 75% of company B is £450,000 (that is, £600,000 × 75%). The total goodwill carried forward is, therefore, £565,000.

Some might argue that this transaction should be accounted for as two separate components (rather than a swap) – a disposal of 25% of company B and an acquisition of 75% of company C. If this argument is pursued, a gain would arise on the disposal and goodwill would arise on the acquisition. But if such a calculation is made, both the gain and goodwill are dependent on the figure placed on the consideration. If the consideration is increased both the gain and goodwill increase; they are inextricably linked. The gain would reflect in part the difference between the book value of the assets given up and the fair value of the assets acquired, which is not a realised gain. In addition, part of the gain relates to internally generated goodwill not previously recognised which is given up in the transaction. Consequently, where in substance such a transaction represents a swap of net assets, we consider that any difference should not be treated as a gain or a loss and should be adjusted to goodwill.

The consolidated position following the transaction is given below:

Consolidation of companies A, B and C after the transaction

	Co C £'000	Co B £'000	B&C Consol £'000	Co A £'000	A,B&C Consol £'000
Goodwill	-	-	750	-	565
Investment in subsidiaries	1,750	-	-	1,500	-
Net assets	380	1,000	1,380	10,000	11,380
	2,130	1,000	2,130	11,500	11,945
Equity share capital	800	500	800	2,000	2,000
Merger reserve	1,150	-	1,150	-	-
Profit and loss account	180	500	180	9,500	9,600
Minority interest	-	-	-	-	345
Equity shareholders' funds	2,130	1,000	2,130	11,500	11,945

The goodwill on the consolidation of company C with company B is calculated as follows:

Cost of control account/goodwill

	£'000		£'000
C's investment in B	1,750	B's equity share capital	500
		B's P&L reserve	500
	1,750		1,000
		Goodwill	750
			1,750

The minority interests calculation arising on the further consolidation of company A with companies B and C is shown below:

Minority interests account

	£'000		£'000
C's investment in B (£1.75m × 25%)	437	B's equity share capital (£500,000 × 25%)	125
		B's P&L reserve (£500,000 × 25%)	125
		C's Equity share capital (£800,000 × 25%)	200
		C's Merger reserve (£1.15m × 25%)	287
Balance	345	C's P&L reserve £180,000 × 25%)	45
	782		782

Partial disposals

25.27 Partial disposals arise where a parent disposes of part of its interest in a subsidiary (for example see Table 25.4). The remaining interest of the parent in the undertaking might result in the undertaking continuing to be a subsidiary or it might become an associate or an investment.

Table 25.4 – Cable and Wireless plc – Report and Accounts – 31 March 1993

Notes to the Accounts (extract)

9 **Exceptional items: profit on partial sale of subsidiaries**	£m	1993 £m	1992 £m
Consolidation adjustment arising as a result of the sale of 20% of Mercury Communications Limited to BCE Inc.	166.0		
Less: Goodwill previously written off to reserves (Note 25)	48.3		
		117.7	-
Profit arising on the sale of shares in Hong Kong Telecommunications Limited as a result of the exercise of warrants	63.6		
Less: Goodwill previously written off to reserves (Note 25)	3.5		
		60.1	-
		177.8	-

There was no taxation or minority interest charge or credit applicable to the exceptional items shown above.

25.28 The basic principles that apply to disposals also apply to partial disposals. Therefore, where a group reduces its stake in an undertaking any profit or loss should be calculated as the difference between the following:

- The carrying amount of the net assets of that subsidiary attributable to the group's interest before the reduction.
- The carrying amount attributable to the group's interest after the reduction together with any proceeds received.

The net assets compared should include any related goodwill not previously written off through the profit and loss account.

25.29 Where the undertaking continues to be a subsidiary after the disposal, the minority interests in that subsidiary should be increased by the carrying amount of the net identifiable assets that are now attributable to the minority interests because of the decrease in the group's interest. However, as explained in chapter 24, no amount for goodwill that arose on the acquisition of the group's interest in that subsidiary should be attributed to the minority interests.

25.30 Three examples follow that illustrate the consequences of a partial sale where the subsidiary undertaking after the sale:

- Remains a subsidiary, but with a reduced interest (see para 25.31).
- Becomes an associate (see para 25.32).
- Retains a small shareholders' interest (see para 25.33).

Remaining a subsidiary

25.31 The example that follows illustrates the calculation of the gain or loss arising on a partial disposal, where the undertaking remains a subsidiary.

Example

A parent purchased a 100% subsidiary for £500,000 during 19X1 when the fair value of the subsidiary's net assets was £400,000. Goodwill arising on the acquisition prior to the implementation of FRS 10 was written off direct to reserves in the year of acquisition. The parent sold 40% of its investment in the subsidiary in December 19X4 for £450,000. The book value of the subsidiary's net assets on the date of the sale was £800,000. The parent's profit and loss account for 19X4 would show a gain on the sale of the investment of £250,000 calculated as follows:

	£'000
Sale proceeds	450
Less: cost of investment in subsidiary (£500,000 × 40%)	(200)
Gain on sale in the parent's accounts	250

However, the group's profit and loss account for 19X4 would only show a gain on the sale of the subsidiary of £90,000 calculated as follows:

	£'000	£'000
Net assets and proceeds after disposal:		
Share of net assets (£800,000 × 60%)	480	
Goodwill written off directly to reserves (£100,000 × 60%)	60	
Sale proceeds	450	990
Less: net assets before disposal		
Net assets	800	
Goodwill written off directly to reserves *	100	900

* The goodwill on consolidation is calculated as follows:	
	£'000
Fair value of consideration at date of acquisition	500
Less: fair value of net assets of subsidiary at date of acquisition	400
Goodwill arising on consolidation	100

The difference between the gain in the parent's profit and loss account and the gain reported in the group's consolidated profit and loss account is £160,000. This difference represents the share of post-acquisition profits retained in the subsidiary of £160,000 (that is, (£800,000 – £400,000) × 40%) that have been reported in the group's profit and loss account up to the date of sale.

The minority interests immediately after the disposal will be 40% of the net carrying value of the subsidiary included in the consolidated balance sheet of £800,000, that is, £320,000.

Becoming an associate

25.32 The next example illustrates the calculation of the gain or loss on a partial disposal where the subsidiary becomes an associate.

Example

The facts of this example are the same as the example in paragraph 25.31 except the group disposes of a 60% interest for £675,000, leaving the parent with 40% and significant influence. The parent's profit and loss account for 19X4 would show a gain on the sale of the investment of £375,000 calculated as follows:

	£'000
Sale proceeds	675
Less: cost of investment in subsidiary (£500,000 × 60%)	(300)
Gain on sale in the parent's accounts	375

However, the group's profit and loss account for 19X4 would only show a gain on the sale of the subsidiary of £135,000 calculated as follows:

	£'000	£'000
Net assets and proceeds after disposal:		
Share of net assets (£800,000 × 40%)	320	
Goodwill written off directly to reserves (£100,000 × 40%)	40	
Sale proceeds	675	1,035
Less: net assets before disposal		
Net assets	800	
Goodwill written off directly to reserves *	100	900
Gain on sale to the group		135

In this situation, after the sale the undertaking will no longer be treated as a subsidiary, but rather as an associate and equity accounted. It will be included in the consolidated balance sheet as an investment in an associated undertaking of £320,000 (40% × £800,000) using the equity method of accounting. Goodwill relating to the associate of £40,000 has already been written off to reserves and will remain there.

Becoming an investment

25.33 The example below considers the situation where a parent disposes of part of its interest in a subsidiary such that it merely has a small remaining investment in the undertaking.

Example

The facts of this example are the same as the previous two examples above, except that the group disposes of a 90% interest for £855,000, leaving the parent with a 10% investment.

The parent's profit and loss account for 19X4 would show a gain on the sale of the investment of £405,000 calculated as follows:

	£'000
Sale proceeds	885
Less: cost of investment in subsidiary (£500,000 × 90%)	(450)
Gain on sale in the parent's accounts	405

However, the group's profit and loss account for 19X4 would only show a gain on the sale of the subsidiary of £45,000 calculated as follows:

	£'000	£'000
Net assets and proceeds after disposal:		
Share of net assets (£800,000 × 10%)	80	
Goodwill written off directly to reserves (£100,000 × 10%)	10	
Sale proceeds	855	945
Less: net assets before disposal		
Net assets	800	
Goodwill written off directly to reserves	100	900
Gain on sale to the group		45

In this situation the undertaking will no longer be treated as a subsidiary, but rather as an investment. It will be included in the consolidated balance sheet at 'cost' determined on an equity basis as £80,000 (£800,000 × 10%). The investment, however, is only recorded in the parent at £50,000 (that is, £500,000 × 10%). The double entry needed to ensure that the consolidation reserves reconcile on consolidation would be as follows:

	£'000	£'000
Dr Investment	40	
Cr Reserves		40

To recognise the group's share of post-acquisition reserves previously recognised in the consolidated financial statements which relates to the 10% investment retained.

Dr Reserves	10	
Cr Investment		10

To recognise the group's share of the goodwill arising on the acquisition of the original investment which relates to the 10% investment retained.

The reserves of £40,000 have already been recognised in the consolidated reserves as they represent the share retained of the post-acquisition reserves that have arisen from the subsidiary's original acquisition up to the date of sale. It can be argued that this is the only adjustment required and that the investment should be recorded at £90,000 in the consolidated financial statements. However, it is more prudent to show the goodwill investment value reduced by the amount of goodwill that has previously been written off to reserves.

The parent could in this circumstance revalue the investment from its cost of £50,000 to £80,000 to show the same figure as that shown in the group. It is necessary, of course, to consider whether the £80,000 is substantiated by the group's remaining share of the underlying value of the undertaking. If it is not, a provision would be required to write it down to the investment's underlying value.

Deemed disposals

25.34 An undertaking may also cease to be a subsidiary, or the group may reduce its percentage interest, as a result of a deemed disposal. A deemed disposal may arise, *inter alia*, where:

- The group does not take up its full allocation of rights in a rights issue.
- The group does not take up its full share of a scrip dividend.
- Another party exercises its options or warrants.
- The subsidiary issues shares to other non-group parties (for example, see Table 25.5).

[FRS 2 para 87].

Table 25.5 – Capital and Regional Properties plc – Report and Accounts – 25 December 1993

Notes to the Accounts (extract)

27. Deemed disposal on flotation of CenterPoint

The flotation of CenterPoint on the American Stock Exchange reduced the Group's effective interest in its operations (excluding the additional shares acquired directly by the Group at the flotation) from approximately 60% to 18.8%. The reduction in the Group's effective interest is a deemed disposal within the meaning of Financial Reporting Standard No. 2 and resulted in a loss of £90,000, which has been dealt with as an exceptional item in the profit and loss account:

	£000
Group share of CenterPoint net assets at the date of deemed disposal	12,360
Loss arising on deemed disposal	(90)
Market valuation of shares retained in CenterPoint following flotation (see note 15)	12,270

No goodwill has been dealt with previously in reserves. US operations contributed £652,000 to the Group profit before taxation up to the date of the deemed disposal. The reduction in value of £6,582,000 arising on the US properties up to the deemed disposal is explained in note 13.

25.35 Deemed disposals have the same effect as changes in ownership by disposal and should be accounted for in the same way. Such disposals fall into three categories for accounting purposes:

- Another party subscribes for shares in an undertaking and the parent does not increase its investment (see Table 25.6 and example below).

  This might arise, for example, where another party exercises options or warrants, or it subscribes for rights in a rights issue, but the parent does not. It may also arise where another party subscribes for new shares in the subsidiary.

- Another party subscribes for shares in an undertaking and a proportionally smaller number of shares are subscribed for by the parent (see example in para 25.37).

- Another party subscribes for shares in an undertaking and the parent sells its right to subscribe to a third party (see example in para 25.38).

Table 25.6 – Daily Mail and General Trust plc – Annual Report – 2 October 1994

Notes to the Accounts (extract)

7 Surplus on the Reduction of Interest in Subsidiary

	1994 £m	1993 £m
	15.9	-

In May 1994, Euromoney Publications raised cash of £23.1 million through a market placing of shares in which the Group could not participate for technical reasons. The Group has reported its share of the increase arising in its net assets as exceptional profit, as required by FRS 2.

Example

In January 19X4 a group had a 60% interest in a subsidiary with share capital of 100,000 £1 ordinary shares. The goodwill arising on the acquisition of £40,000 was written off directly to reserves in the year of acquisition prior to FRS 10's introduction. On 31 December 19X4 the 40% minority shareholder exercised an option to subscribe for a further 50,000 £1 ordinary shares in the subsidiary at £12 per share. The net assets of the subsidiary prior to the exercise of the option were £900,000.

Shareholdings	Before		After	
	No	%	No	%
Group	60,000	60	60,000	40
Other party	40,000	40	90,000	60
	100,000	100	150,000	100
Net assets	£'000	%	£'000	%
Group's share	540	60	600	40
Other party's share	360	40	900	60
	900	100	1,500	100

Calculation of group loss on deemed disposal	£'000	£'000
Net assets and proceeds after deemed disposal		
Net assets	600	
Goodwill written off directly to reserves*	27	
Proceeds	-	627
Less: net assets before deemed disposal		
Net assets	540	
Goodwill written off directly to reserves*	40	580
Profit on deemed disposal		47

* A loss of goodwill has been attributed to the deemed disposal, because the minority has in effect bought part of the goodwill in the price it has paid for its increased stake in the company. The group's interest is now 40% and, provided that the parent exercises significant influence over its former subsidiary, it will be treated as an associate and equity accounted. The goodwill attributable to the interest in the subsidiary was previously written off to reserves when the entity was originally acquired and consolidated. Part of this goodwill, £13,333 (that is £40,000 ÷ 60% × 20%) is attributable to the deemed disposal and must be taken to the profit and loss account as part of the profit on sale of £47,000. The remaining goodwill of £26,667 is now attributable to the interest in the entity after the deemed disposal and under equity accounting the remaining goodwill would continue to be written off against reserves.

25.36 An illustration of such a deemed disposal is given in Table 25.1 on page 1. In that situation, although the group's interest is diluted, a profit arises on the deemed disposal as the dilution took place by a public offer of shares.

25.37 The next example considers a deemed disposal that arises from the parent subscribing for proportionally fewer rights in a rights issue.

Example

At the beginning of the year a group had a 55% interest in a subsidiary company. The goodwill arising on the acquisition of £450,000 was written off directly to reserves in the year of acquisition, which was prior to the implementation of FRS 10. The subsidiary's share capital was £2 million (ordinary £1 shares) and its net assets were £10 million immediately prior to the rights issue. During the year the subsidiary made a 1 for 2 rights issue priced at £6 per share. The group exercised its rights to 100,000 shares and neither exercised nor sold its remaining rights. All the minority shareholders exercised their rights.

The group owned 55% of the share capital prior to the rights issue, that is, 1,100,000 shares. As it exercised rights to 100,000 shares it owns 1,200,000 shares after the rights issue.

Shareholdings

The number of shares of the subsidiary in issue following the rights issue was:

2,000,000 + 100,000 + (2,000,000 × 0.45 × ½) = 2,550,000 shares

	Before		After	
	No	%	No	%
Group	1,100,000	55	1,200,000	47
Other party	900,000	45	1,350,000	53
	2,000,000	100	2,550,000	100

Net assets

The net assets of the company post rights issue were:

£10,000,000 + (550,000 × £6) = £13,300,000

	£'000	%	£'000	%
Group's share	5,500	55	6,251	47
Other party's share	4,500	45	7,049	53
	10,000	100	13,300	100

Calculation of group profit on deemed disposal	£'000	£'000
Net assets and proceeds after deemed disposal		
Net assets	6,251	
Goodwill written off directly to reserves*	383	
Cost of subscribing for rights	(400)	6,234
Less: net assets before deemed disposal		
Net assets	5,500	
Goodwill written off directly to reserves*	450	5,950
Profit on deemed disposal		284

* A loss of goodwill has been attributed to the deemed disposal as the minority have subscribed for their rights issue at full market price. Assuming the voting rights follow the share capital the company would no longer be a subsidiary of the group and would be treated as an associated company and, therefore, equity accounted. The goodwill attributable to the interest in the subsidiary was £450,000 and was previously written off to reserves when the

entity was originally acquired and consolidated. Therefore, an adjustment needs to be made for that goodwill figure as a result of the deemed disposal. The group has disposed of an interest of 8% and this equates to goodwill of £66,942 (that is, £450,000 ÷ 55% × 8%). This amount is written off to the profit and loss account and included in the net profit on disposal of £284,000. The residual £383,058 of goodwill will remain written off against reserves on equity accounting the retained associate interest of 47%.

25.38 The next example considers the situation where a deemed disposal arises from the sale by the parent of its rights in a rights issue.

Example

At the beginning of the year a group had a 55% interest in a subsidiary company. The goodwill arising on the acquisition of £450,000 was written off directly to reserves in the year of acquisition, which was prior to the implementation of FRS 10. During the year the subsidiary made a 1 for 2 rights issue priced at £6 per ordinary £1 share. The group did not exercise its rights, but sold them to a third party for £200,000. The third party then exercised those rights as did other minority shareholders owning 40% of the remaining 45% of the company's share capital. The rights issue was, therefore, taken up by 95% of the shareholders. The subsidiary's share capital was £2 million (ordinary £1 shares) and its net assets were £10 million immediately prior to the rights issue.

The group owned 55% of the share capital prior to the rights issue, that is, 1,100,000 shares. As it exercised no rights it also owned 1,100,000 shares following the issue.

Shareholdings

The number of shares of the subsidiary in issue following the rights issue was:

2,000,000 + (2,000,000 × 0.95 × ½) = 2,950,000 shares

	Before		After	
	No	%	No	%
Group	1,100,000	55	1,100,000	37
Other party	900,000	45	1,850,000	63
	2,000,000	100	2,950,000	100

Net assets

The net assets of the company post rights issue were:

£10,000,000 + (950,000 × £6) = £15,700,000

	£'000	%	£'000	%
Group's share	5,500	55	5,809	37
Other party's share	4,500	45	9,891	63
	10,000	100	15,700	100

Calculation of group profit on deemed disposal	£'000	£'000
Net assets and proceeds after deemed disposal		
Net assets	5,809	
Goodwill written off directly to reserves*	303	
Proceeds from sale of rights	200	6,312
Less: net assets before deemed disposal		
Net assets	5,500	
Goodwill written off directly to reserves*	450	5,950
Profit on deemed disposal		362

* A loss of goodwill has been attributed to the deemed disposal as the parent's percentage interest has reduced. As with the previous two examples, assuming the voting rights follow the share capital the company would no longer be a subsidiary of the group and would be treated as an associated company and, therefore, equity accounted. The goodwill attributable to the interest in the subsidiary previously written off to reserves was £450,000 when the entity was originally acquired and consolidated. Therefore, an adjustment needs to be made for that goodwill figure as a result of the deemed disposal and the group has in effect disposed of an 18% interest, which equates to goodwill of £147,272 (that is, £450,000 ÷ 55% × 18%). This goodwill write off is charged to the profit and loss account as part of the net profit on the deemed disposal of £362,000. The balance of the goodwill will remain written off to reserves on equity accounting the associated interest.

Disclosure requirements

25.39 Where, during the period, an undertaking has ceased to be a subsidiary and this significantly affects the figures shown in the consolidated financial statements the following should be disclosed in the notes to the financial statements:

- The name of the undertaking that has ceased to be a subsidiary. In the case of a group of undertakings ceasing to be subsidiaries, the name of the parent of that group. [4A Sch 15(a); FRS 2 para 48].

- The Act requires disclosure of the extent to which the profit or loss shown in the consolidated profit or loss account is attributable to the undertaking or group that has been disposed of. [4A Sch 15(b)]. In addition, FRS 3 requires that the results up to the date of sale should be disclosed as a discontinued operation assuming that the criteria are met. [FRS 3 para 14]. Therefore, if there is only one sale of an undertaking or group of undertakings during a period, the Act's requirement would be fulfilled by the FRS 3 disclosure of discontinued operations. However, if there is more than one undertaking or group disposed of during the year then the profit or loss attributable to each undertaking or group of undertakings disposed of would appear to require to be separately disclosed, as the Act refers to the profit or loss attributable to *"that undertaking or group"*.

- The profit or loss on disposal shown as a non-operating item below operating profit and described 'Profit or loss on sale of discontinued operation' (see for example para 25.15). [FRS 3 para 20].

- The amount of purchased goodwill (or negative goodwill) attributable to the business disposed of included in the profit or loss on disposal, separately disclosed as a component of the profit or loss on disposal. [FRS 10 para 71(c)(ii)]. Where the item is presented as two components there should be, in addition, a single subtotal showing the total profit or loss on disposal. This disclosure can either be given on the face of the profit and loss account or in a note to the financial statements.

- The amount of any ownership interest retained in any material undertaking that has ceased to be a subsidiary in the period. [FRS 2 para 48].

- Where any material undertaking has ceased to be a subsidiary other than by the disposal of at least part of the interest held by the group, the circumstances should be explained. [FRS 2 paras 48, 49].

- A note to the cash flow statement should show a summary of the effects of disposals indicating how much of the consideration was made up of cash. [FRS 1 para 45].

- Where the disposal has had a material effect on the amounts reported under each of the standard headings in the cash flow statements (such as operating, capital expenditure and financial investments, financing, etc.), the effect should be disclosed as a note to the cash flow statement. This information can be given by segregating cash flows between continuing and discontinued operations. [FRS 1 para 45]. However, the information need only be given in the period the disposal is made. [FRS 1 para 48].

- Where part of the consideration for the disposal is other than cash (such as, shares), it should be disclosed in the notes to the cash flow statement where this is necessary to fully understand the transaction. [FRS 1 para 46].

25.40 The Act provides that where the directors consider that the disclosure required by paragraph 15 of Schedule 5 to the Act (bullet points one and two above) would be seriously prejudicial to the business of any undertaking in the group and the subsidiary being sold is established, or carries on business, outside the UK, the information is not required to be given. However the Secretary of State's permission is required. [4A Sch 16]. The Secretary of State's permission would only be given in certain extreme circumstances. For example, his permission might be given not to disclose the name of the subsidiary disposed of where it operates in a politically sensitive country.

Where the Secretary of State's permission is being sought in this way, the company's case might be helped if the company's letter to the Secretary of State is accompanied by a letter from its auditors supporting the non-disclosure. Although FRS 2 does not appear to extend this exemption to apply to its disclosure requirements, it would seem that it was not the ASB's intention to restrict this exemption and it should, therefore, be assumed that the exemption, if agreed by the Secretary of State for the Companies Act disclosures, also applies to the disclosures required by paragraph 48 of FRS 2 outlined above. It is probably best if the letter to the Secretary of State covers also the FRS 2 disclosures that are proposed not to be given.

25.41 In order to give the disclosure required in the third bullet point of paragraph 25.39 and to calculate the total profit or loss arising on a disposal, companies need to maintain detailed records of the cumulative amount of goodwill written off to reserves (net of disposals) and records of the parts of the group to which it relates. In practice, it may be necessary to estimate or apportion goodwill written off to the part of the business being disposed of. However, it is recognised in the Act and FRS 10 that there may be situations where it is not practicable to make a reasonable estimate of the purchased goodwill attributable to the business being disposed of. This situation might arise, for example, where the part of the group being disposed of was acquired many years ago prior to the implementation of FRS 10. In such a situation where it is not possible to ascertain the goodwill that was acquired before 1 January 1989 attributable to the disposal, or to make a reasonable apportionment of the goodwill arising on the acquisition of that part of the business, this fact and the reason should be explained in the financial statements. [FRS 10 para 71(c)].

Chapter 26

Merger relief and group reconstruction relief

Page

Chapter 26

Merger relief and group reconstruction relief

Introduction

26.1 Chapter III of Part V of the Act sets out rules that relate to the creation of share premium on an issue of shares and also to the way in which that premium may be used. The basic rule is detailed in section 130(1), and it says that, where a company issues shares at a premium (whether for cash or otherwise), a sum equal to the aggregate amount or value of the premium must be transferred to a share premium account. This section is derived from section 56 of the Companies Act 1948 and, until the Companies Act 1981 came into effect, there was no relief from the provisions of that section. The Companies Act 1981 introduced certain merger and group reconstruction relief provisions that modified the effect of section 56 of the Companies Act 1948. These provisions are currently set out in sections 131 and 132 of the Companies Act 1985.

Share premium account

26.2 Where a company issues shares at a value that exceeds their nominal value, a sum equal to the difference between the issue value and the nominal value must be transferred to a share premium account. [Sec 130(1)]. For example, if a company issues 100,000 £1 shares at £1.50 each, then it must credit £50,000 to a share premium account.

26.3 Once a share premium account has been established, it may only be used for certain specified purposes. Apart from these specific uses, the share premium account has to be treated as if it were part of the paid-up share capital of the company. Consequently, the provisions of the Act that apply to the reduction of share capital apply also to the share premium account. [Sec 130(3)].

Implications of *Shearer v Bercain Ltd.*

26.4 The tax case of *Shearer v Bercain Ltd.* questioned the construction of section 56 of the Companies Act 1948, which is now section 130 of the Companies Act 1985. [*Shearer v Bercain Ltd.* [1980] 3 AER 295].

26.5 Before *Shearer v Bercain Ltd.*, it was widely thought that there were two legally acceptable methods of accounting for certain types of business combinations, as discussed below:

- The first method, the acquisition method, which the majority of companies used, required that the shares transferred to the purchasing company should be recorded in that company's books at their fair value. Where that value exceeded the nominal value of any shares issued in exchange, the excess had to be recorded as a share premium (in accordance with the requirements of section 56 of the 1948 Act). This treatment had the effect of treating the acquired company's reserves as pre-acquisition and, therefore, as undistributable.

- The second method, the merger method, which few companies used, required that the shares transferred to the purchasing company as part of a merger should be recorded in the purchasing company's books at the nominal value of the shares that it issued in exchange. Consequently, the only difference that had to be dealt with on consolidation was the difference between the nominal value of the shares issued as consideration and the nominal value of the shares transferred to the purchasing company. The distributable reserves of all the companies involved in the merger remained distributable by the parent, provided they could be passed up to it by way of dividend.

26.6 The merger method was seldom used in practice, because its legality was uncertain. However, it was more attractive than acquisition accounting because it gave companies freedom to distribute, in effect, both companies' distributable reserves (subject to the rules concerning distributions contained in the Act).

26.7 In *Shearer v Bercain Ltd.*, the court had to consider whether company law permitted companies to use the 'merger' method as an alternative to the 'acquisition' method.

26.8 The court held that where shares were issued at a premium, whether for cash or otherwise, section 56 of the 1948 Act required the premium to be carried to a share premium account in the issuing company's books, and the premium could be distributed only if the procedure for reducing capital was carried through.

26.9 This judgment gave authority to the interpretation of section 56 of the 1948 Act that required a company to set up a share premium account in any transaction where it acquired another company's shares in return for the allotment of its own shares and the fair value to it of the shares it acquired exceeded the nominal value of the shares it issued.

26.10 *Shearer v Bercain Ltd.* was not directly concerned with the actual accounting treatment of acquisitions. But the legal effect of requiring that a share premium account should be set up in such circumstances was to prohibit the merger method of accounting. It meant also that it was not lawful for the acquiring company to distribute the acquired company's pre-acquisition profits paid to it by a dividend. Consequently, companies that had previously used merger accounting, and had then regarded the acquired company's pre-acquisition profits as distributable, had contravened the law.

26.11 Following the court's decision, the Government made it known that it considered that there were certain circumstances in which a company's failure to set up a share premium account was unobjectionable. Accordingly, the Government introduced legislation that relieved companies, in certain circumstances, from the obligation to carry any share premium to a share premium account. The provisions that give this relief appear in sections 131 and 132 of the 1985 Act.

Merger relief

26.12 The essence of merger relief is that, where appropriate conditions are met, section 130 of the 1985 Act does not apply. Merger relief, despite its name, is in effect relief from the need to set up a share premium account. It is a relief that affects the accounting in the issuing company's own accounts. Although there are rare exceptions, it is normally a pre-condition that the parent is able to benefit from *merger relief* (or group reconstruction relief which is dealt with later in this chapter)before the group may use *merger accounting* on consolidation, but the two are not the same.

26.13 The situations in which companies can obtain merger relief are those in which the transaction satisfies the following three conditions:

- A company (known either as the issuing company or the acquiring company) secures at least 90 per cent of the nominal value of each class of the equity share capital of another company (the acquired company) as a result of an arrangement.
- The arrangement provides for the allotment of equity shares in the issuing company. (Such allotment will normally be made to the acquired company's shareholders.)
- The consideration for the shares so allotted is either: the issue, or the transfer, to the issuing company of equity shares in the acquired company; or the cancellation of those of the equity shares in the acquired company that the issuing company does not already hold.

[Sec 131(1)(5)].

26.14 In determining whether a particular transaction satisfies the above conditions, the following rules apply:

- Any shares in the acquired company that are held by other companies in the same group (other than associates) as the issuing company, or their nominees, should be treated as being held by the issuing company. [Sec 131(6)].

- An 'arrangement' means any agreement, scheme or arrangement, including an arrangement that is sanctioned under either section 425 of the Act (company compromise with creditors and members) or section 110 of the Insolvency Act 1986 (liquidator accepting shares, etc., as consideration for the sale of the company's property). [Sec 131(7)].

- A company will be treated as having secured a 90 per cent holding in another company as part of an arrangement, irrespective of whether or not it actually acquired, under that arrangement, all the equity shares that it holds. [Sec 131(4)]. This rule means that, in determining whether or not a company has obtained a 90 per cent holding in another company, prior holdings can be taken into account.

- 'Company' includes any body corporate, except where reference is made to the issuing company (the acquiring company). [Sec 133(4)].

- In any provisions that relate to a company's acquisition of shares in another company, shares that a nominee of a company acquired are to be treated as having been acquired by the company itself. Similarly, the issue, or the allotment or the transfer of any shares to or by a company's nominee is to be regarded as if the shares were issued, or allotted or transferred to or by the company itself. [Sec 133(2)].

- 'Equity share capital' is a company's issued share capital, excluding any part that (as regards dividends and capital) does not carry a right to participate beyond a specified amount in a distribution. [Sec 744, 131(7)]. 'Non-equity shares' are all other shares. In particular, preference shares will generally not form part of a company's 'equity share capital'. (Note that this is the Act's definition. The FRS 6 and FRS 4 definition is different – see chapter 27.)

- The transfer of a company's shares includes the transfer of a right to be included in the company's register of members in respect of those shares. [Sec 133(3)].

26.15 The examples that follow illustrate the application of these provisions:

Example 1

Company A issues equity shares and acquires 90% of company B's equity shares in a share-for-share exchange. This is the most obvious application of the provisions. In these circumstances, company A is entitled to the relief from section 130 of the Act.

Example 2

Company C owns 60% of company D's equity shares. The members of company D agree to a cancellation of the equity shares that company C does not hold, in return for the allotment to them of equity shares in company C. In this situation, also, company C is entitled to the relief from section 130. There are two reasons for this:

- The effect of cancelling the remaining shares is to increase company C's 60% holding to a 100% holding (and so over the 90% threshold).
- The consideration for the allotment of company C's equity shares is the cancellation of those of company D's shares that it does not already hold.

For this purpose, it is irrelevant that the acquiring company did not acquire the original 60% holding as part of the arrangement. To be entitled to the relief, a company (whether newly formed or otherwise) needs only to acquire shares sufficient either to secure or increase its holding to at least 90%. However, company C is entitled to the relief only on the shares it is now issuing in consideration for the cancellation of the shares in company D that it does not hold. It cannot retrospectively write back any share premium that it set up on any shares it issued when it acquired the 60% holding.

Example 3

Company E acquires all of company F's 'A' equity shares. Company F also has 'B' equity shares in issue, but company E holds none of these. In this situation, company E is not entitled to the relief from section 130 of the Act, because section 131 requires the issuer to secure a 90% holding of each class of equity shares in the acquired company. This applies even if the 'B' shares represent in total only 10% or less of the nominal value of company F's equity share capital.

Example 4

Company G acquires 95% of company H's equity shares. The consideration for these shares is, in equal proportions, equity shares in company G and cash. In this situation, company G is entitled to the relief from section 130. This is because there is no 'cash limit' criterion in the merger conditions. The section states only that the consideration received for the shares allotted should be equity shares. It does not stipulate any minimum proportion of the consideration that should consist of shares.

Application of merger relief

26.16 Where an issue of shares satisfies the conditions referred to in paragraph 26.13, the Act provides relief from the application of section 130. In these circumstances, section 130 will not apply to any premium that attaches to the shares that the issuing company allots as part of the arrangement. [Sec 131(2)].

26.17 In addition, where a transaction satisfies the conditions referred to in paragraph 26.13 the relief will extend to shares issued for either the acquisition, or the cancellation, of non-equity shares. The relief extends to cover an arrangement that provides for the allotment of any shares in the issuing company in return for either of the following:

- The issue or the transfer to the issuing company of non-equity shares in the acquired company.
- The cancellation of any shares in the acquired company that the issuing company does not hold.

In such circumstances, section 130 will not apply to any premium that attaches to the shares that the issuing company allots for this purpose. [Sec 131(3)].

26.18 In this connection, it is important to note that where a transaction satisfies those conditions, which as stated in paragraph 26.13 must include the issue of equity shares, the issuing company can also allot any of its shares in return for either the acquisition of non-equity shares or the cancellation of shares in the acquired company. This means that the issuing company may itself also allot non-equity shares for the acquisition of non-equity shares or the cancellation of shares not held by the issuing company and take merger relief on the non-equity shares that it issues.

26.19 Merger relief can be used by the parent company where either acquisition accounting or merger accounting is used on consolidation. Consequently, where a company has to acquisition account for a subsidiary, but can take merger relief on the issue of its shares, a merger reserve (instead of a share premium account) and goodwill arise on consolidation. The accounting treatment of the investment in the parent company's entity accounts is described in chapter 27.

Relief in respect of group reconstructions

26.20 The decision in *Shearer v Bercain Ltd.* also made it clear that the issuing company should transfer any premium on the issue of its shares to a share premium account, not only where a 'third party' acquisition occurs, but also where a group reconstruction occurs. The Act provides some relief from this requirement. But it does not dispense altogether with the requirement to set up a share premium account. The merger relief provisions of section 131 (which have been discussed in paragraphs 26.13 to 26.19 above) are not available for group reconstructions. [Sec 132(8)]. The relief in respect of group reconstructions is contained in section 132 of the Act. The group reconstructions to which the Act applies are different from those defined in FRS 6 (see further chapter 27) and are those that satisfy the following conditions:

- A wholly-owned subsidiary (the issuing company) allots some of its shares either to its holding company or to another wholly-owned subsidiary of its holding company. [Sec 132(1)].

- The allotment is in consideration for the transfer to it of any assets (other than cash) of its holding company or of another wholly-owned subsidiary of its holding company. [Sec 132(1)].

- 'Company' includes any body corporate except where reference is made to the issuing company (that is, the acquiring company). [Sec 133(4)].

26.21 For example, the allotment may be in consideration for the transfer to the issuing company of shares in another subsidiary (which is not necessarily wholly-owned) that the holding company holds. Diagrammatically, the situation before and after such a reconstruction would be as shown below.

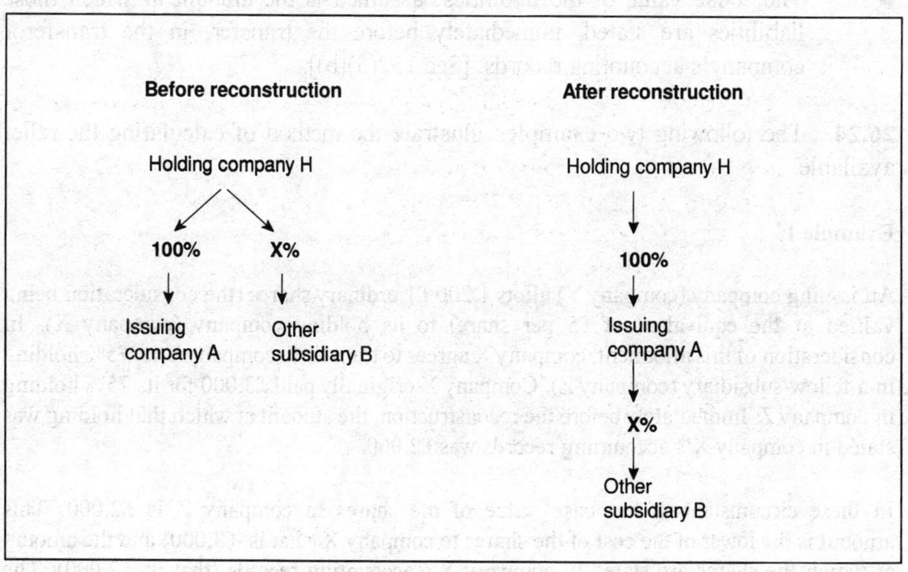

26.22 Where those shares in the issuing company that relate to the transfer are issued at a premium, the issuing company need only transfer to the share premium account an amount equal to the 'minimum premium value'. [Sec 132(2)].

26.23 For this purpose, the following definitions apply:

- The 'minimum premium value' is the amount, if any, by which the base value of the consideration that the issuing company receives exceeds the aggregate nominal value of the shares that it allots in consideration for the transfer. [Sec 132(3)].

- The 'base value' of the consideration that the issuing company receives is the amount by which the base value of the assets transferred to it exceeds the base value of any liabilities that the issuing company assumes as part of that consideration. [Sec 132(4)].

- The 'base value of the assets transferred' is the lower of:

  - The cost to the transferor company of those assets.
  - The amount at which the assets are stated, immediately before the transfer, in the transferor company's accounting records.

  [Sec 132(5)(a)].

- The 'base value of the liabilities' assumed is the amount at which those liabilities are stated, immediately before the transfer, in the transferor company's accounting records. [Sec 132(5)(b)].

26.24 The following two examples illustrate the method of calculating the relief available:

Example 1

An issuing company (company Y) allots 1,200 £1 ordinary shares (the consideration being valued at the equivalent of £5 per share) to its holding company (company X). In consideration of this allotment, company X agrees to transfer to company Y its 75% holding in a fellow-subsidiary (company Z). Company X originally paid £3,000 for its 75% holding in company Z. Immediately before the reconstruction, the amount at which that holding was stated in company X's accounting records was £2,000.

In these circumstances, the base value of the shares in company Z is £2,000. This amount is the lower of the cost of the shares to company X (that is, £3,000) and the amount at which the shares are stated in company X's accounting records (that is, £2,000). The nominal value of the shares that company Y allots in respect of the transfer is £1,200. Therefore, the minimum premium value is £800. This amount is calculated as the base value of the shares in company Z (that is, £2,000) less the nominal value of the shares company Y allots (that is, £1,200). Consequently, the amount of £800 must be transferred to company Y's share premium account. (Without the relief given by section 132, the company would have had to transfer £4,800 to its share premium account. This amount is calculated as the difference between the value of £5 and the nominal value of £1 for each of the 1,200 shares.)

Example 2

A holding company (company H) has a wholly-owned subsidiary (company S). Company H has, as part of its assets, land that originally cost £110,000. This land has subsequently been revalued and it is currently included in the company's accounting records at £175,000. In addition, the purchase of the land was partly financed by a loan of £40,000 that is secured on the land and is still outstanding. The land is currently valued at £200,000. It is proposed that company S allots to company H 25,000 of its ordinary £1 shares in consideration for the transfer to it of the land that company H currently owns. In addition, company S will assume the liability for the loan of £40,000 that is secured on the land.

If the Act did not provide relief from section 130 in respect of group reconstructions such as the above, company S would need to transfer £135,000 to a share premium account. This premium is calculated as follows:

	£	£
Nominal value of shares allotted		25,000
Fair value of consideration received:		
Current value of the land	200,000	
less: liability assumed	40,000	160,000
Premium on the shares allotted		135,000

However, because of the relief from section 130 that section 132 of the Act gives, the company needs only to transfer £45,000 (which is the 'minimum premium value') to a share premium account. This minimum premium value is calculated as follows:

	£
Base value of the land transferred (being the lower of the original cost of £110,000 and the amount at which it currently stands in company H's books, £175,000).	110,000
Base value of the liability that company S assumes	40,000
Base value of the consideration that company S receives for the shares it allots	70,000
Nominal value of the shares that company S allots	25,000
Minimum premium value	45,000

26.25 The principal difference between the relief that relates to group reconstructions and merger relief is that, with group reconstruction relief, the need may arise to set up a share premium account; with merger relief, there is no such requirement.

[The next paragraph is 26.33.]

Pre-combination profits

26.33 Paragraph 15(5) of the pre-1981 Schedule 8 to the Companies Act 1948 provided that a subsidiary's pre-acquisition profits were not to be treated as the holding company's profits. However, the Companies Act 1981 repealed this requirement. One effect of this is that a holding company is, in principle, able to distribute to its shareholders the subsidiary's pre-combination profits. This applies in general, that is, whether or not merger relief is available and whether merger or acquisition accounting is used on consolidation. However, in general the advantage comes into play when merger relief under sections 131 to 133 is taken, that is when the investment is recorded at the nominal value of the shares issued. If the 1981 Act had not repealed this requirement, one of the principal advantages of merger relief would have been lost, because the distributability of the subsidiary's pre-combination profits would still have been restricted.

[The next page is 26013.]

26.34 In merger accounting, the subsidiary's pre-combination profits are normally available for eventual distribution to the parent company's shareholders. However, this may not always be the case. Furthermore, prior to the merger relief provisions being enacted, pre-combination profits were not available for distribution where acquisition accounting was used. For example, where the new subsidiary pays a dividend out of its pre-combination profits, the holding company may have to treat some of it as income and some as a reduction in, or recovery of, the capital investment. There are two ways in which this can be reflected in accounting terms. First, the whole of the dividend received could be taken as income in the recipient's profit and loss account. The recipient would then need to consider the carrying value of its investment; and if it was not recoverable in full, it should be written down through the profit and loss account. The alternative approach, which has the same overall effect, is to apply the dividend to reduce the carrying value of its investment to the extent that it is necessary in order to provide for a diminution in that carrying value, with the remainder being available to be treated as income. This second approach is the one described in FRS 6. [FRS 6 appendix 1 para 16]. The following example illustrates the way in which companies that use merger accounting should apply this rule:

Example

The abbreviated balance sheets of company H and company S before the merger are as follows:

	Co H £'000	Co S £'000
Net tangible assets	1,000	935
Share capital	800	10
Profit and loss account	200	925
	1,000	935

Company H issues shares with a nominal value of £600,000 in exchange for the shares in company S. The abbreviated balance sheets of company H, company S and the group after the merger are as follows:

	Co H £'000	Co S £'000	Group £'000
Other net assets	1,000	935	1,935
Investment	600	-	-
	1,600	935	1,935
Share capital	1,400	10	1,400
Profit and loss account*	200	925	535
	1,600	935	1,935

* The group profit and loss account balance is made up as follows:

	£'000
Profit and loss account balance of company H	200
Profit and loss account balance of company S	925
	1,125
Excess of carrying value of investment over nominal value of shares acquired (that is, £600,000 – £10,000)	(590)
	535

Suppose that company S pays all of its profit and loss account balance (that is, £925,000) to company H. Then company S is left with share capital of £10,000 and net assets of £10,000.

If the £10,000 of net assets represents the value of company H's investment in company S, then company H should reduce the carrying value of its investment in company S to £10,000. Paragraph 16 of the appendix to FRS 6 indicates that company H should use £590,000 of the dividend that it receives, in order to provide for the diminution in the carrying value of its investment in company S. The remaining £335,000 of the dividend represents realised profits to company H. The abbreviated balance sheets of company H, company S and the group after the distribution are then as follows:

	Co H £'000	Co S £'000	Group £'000
Other net assets	1,925	10	1,935
Investment	10	-	-
	1,935	10	1,935
Share capital	1,400	10	1,400
Profit and loss account	535	-	535
	1,935	10	1,935

However, the £10,000 of net assets might not represent the value of company H's investment in company S, because company S may have hidden reserves. For example, there may be unrecorded intangibles that are the source of earnings. Alternatively, company S's tangible fixed assets might have a net book value of £5,000, but a current value of, say, £150,000. Company S would then have a hidden reserve of £145,000 and the value of company H's investment in company S would be £155,000 – not £10,000. Consequently, company H need use only £445,000 of the dividend that it receives, in order to provide for the diminution in the carrying value of its investment in company S. The remaining £480,000 of the dividend represents realised profits to company H. The abbreviated balance sheets of company H, company S and the group are then as follows:

	Co H £'000	Co S £'000	Group £'000
Other net assets	1,925	10	1,935
Investment	155	-	-
	2,080	10	1,935
Share capital	1,400	10	1,400
Profit and loss account	680	-	535
	2,080	10	1,935

Company H's profit and loss account is greater than the group's profit and loss account. The group profit and loss account balance is made up as follows:

	£'000
Profit and loss account balance of company H	680
Profit and loss account balance of company S	-
	680
Excess of carrying value of investment over nominal value of shares acquired (that is, £155,000 – £10,000)	(145)
	535

[The next paragraph is 26.36.]

26.36 Where acquisition accounting is being used on consolidation, merger relief may nonetheless be available to the parent or issuing company, provided the conditions set out in paragraph 26.13 above are satisfied. Accounting for this can take two forms. First, the premium can be disregarded altogether, in which case the considerations regarding pre-combination dividends are as described above in the context of merger accounting. [Sec 133]. Secondly, the parent or issuing company could record the shares issued and the investment at fair value, with the premium being credited to a merger reserve instead of to a share premium account. In this situation, where a dividend is paid to the parent by its subsidiary an equivalent amount of the merger reserve becomes realised. If there is a need to write down the carrying value of the investment this write down should be made to the profit and loss account. However, an equivalent amount can be transferred from the merger reserve to the profit and loss account reserve.

Comparison with IASs

26.37 There are no rules on group reconstructions. The relevant document (IAS 27) is not sufficiently detailed to cover this area. IAS 22 excludes from its scope transactions among enterprises under common control.

Chapter 27

Merger accounting

Chapter 27

Merger accounting

Introduction

27.1 Chapter 23 considers various matters concerning acquisition accounting. This hapter looks at the other accounting method a company must use in certain ircumstances when preparing consolidated financial statements, namely merger ccounting.

27.2 Although there are rare exceptions, a prerequisite for merger accounting is ormally that shares issued as consideration for the combination must be eligible for nerger relief or for group reconstruction relief. The legal provisions relating to these eliefs are described in chapter 26 and this chapter assumes knowledge of those rovisions. Merger or group reconstruction relief may also be obtained where cquisition accounting rather than merger accounting is required for a combination. 'his is because the conditions for merger accounting are more restrictive than the onditions for obtaining merger or group reconstruction relief.

7.3 In April 1985, the ASC issued SSAP 23 which was the result of a long debate n acquisition and merger accounting that had taken place since the ASC originally ublished ED 3, 'Accounting for acquisitions and mergers', in 1971. The ASC ublished ED 3 to try to standardise the method of merger accounting that was eveloping at the time. However, some people believed that merger accounting might onflict with the requirement in section 56 of the Companies Act 1948 (now section 130 f the Companies Act 1985) to set up a share premium account. On the grounds that ere was insufficient agreement on the legal implications of merger accounting, the SC decided not to convert ED 3 into an accounting standard.

7.4 It is important to remember that the Companies Act 1985 originally only ontained provisions regarding the application of merger relief to companies and did not ecify any provisions concerning merger accounting. SSAP 23, on the other hand, ealt with merger accounting in consolidated financial statements and did not apply to dividual companies' financial statements. There was, however, a significant overlap etween the concept of merger relief and merger accounting.

7.5 SSAP 23 laid down certain rules that determined whether a holding mpany should use acquisition accounting or merger accounting in its consolidated nancial statements. These rules were further supplemented by the provisions of the ompanies Act 1989. The new provisions have been incorporated into Schedule 4A to e Companies Act 1985 and include certain conditions that must apply to an acquisition before it can be accounted for as a merger. Furthermore, Schedule 4A to the Act includes certain additional disclosure requirements that apply where an acquisition is accounted for as a merger.

27.6 There had been considerable dissatisfaction with the criteria in SSAP 23 as they were generally considered to allow merger accounting to be used too frequently. In any case the standard needed to be updated in light of the 1989 Act changes. Hence, in February 1990 the ASC issued ED 48, 'Accounting for acquisitions and mergers', which proposed significant changes in the rules relating to merger accounting. ED 48 proposed that the conditions that had to be satisfied before merger accounting was allowed should be much narrower than those in SSAP 23. As a result the opportunities to merger account would become fewer. In addition, where the conditions set down in ED 48 were satisfied merger accounting would no longer be optional, it would be required.

27.7 The ASC was succeeded as the principal UK standard setting body in 1990 by the ASB. The ASB did not convert the proposals in ED 48 directly into a standard, but instead published FRED 6 on 'Acquisitions and mergers'. FRED 6 took the same line as ED 48 by introducing much more stringent criteria than those in SSAP 23 and by requiring merger accounting to be adopted in those situations where the criteria were met.

27.8 In September 1994 the ASB issued FRS 6, 'Acquisitions and Mergers', which substantially repeated the proposals in FRED 6. The provisions of both the Act and FRS 6 are considered in detail in the paragraphs that follow.

Merger accounting conditions

27.9 The objectives of FRS 6 are:

- To ensure that merger accounting is used only for those business combinations that are not, in substance, the acquisition of one entity by another, but the formation of a new reporting entity as a substantially equal partnership where no party is dominant.
- To ensure the use of acquisition accounting for all other business combinations.
- To ensure that in either case the financial statements provide relevant information concerning the effect of the combination.

27.10 To this end the FRS defines a merger as:

> *"A business combination that results in the creation of a new reporting entity formed from the combining parties, in which the shareholders of the combining entities come together in a partnership for the mutual sharing of the risks and benefits of the combined entity, and in which no party to the combination in substance obtains control over any other, or is otherwise seen to be dominant, whether by virtue of the proportion of its shareholders' rights in the combined entity, the influence of its directors or otherwise."* [FRS 6 para 2].

27.11 If a business combination satisfies the conditions for merger accounting outlined in the Act and the combination meets the definition of a merger under FRS 6 then the group must use merger accounting to account for it. To meet the definition of a merger in FRS 6 the combination *must* satisfy certain conditions which are described below. If the business combination fails to satisfy the conditions for merger accounting, then the group *must* use acquisition accounting for the business combination. [4A Sch 8]. Situations may arise where the Act's conditions are satisfied, but those of FRS 6 are not. Where this arises, merger accounting should not be used. This is because the Act says the adoption of the merger method of accounting must accord with generally accepted accounting principles or practice (which now means the conditions contained in FRS 6). [4A Sch 10(1)(d)]. Similarly, if FRS 6's conditions are satisfied, but those of the Act are not, merger accounting should not be used.

27.12 The conditions contained in the Act and FRS 6 require certain tests to be satisfied as follows:

- Offer to shareholders test.
- 90 per cent holding test.
- Immaterial cash or non-equity consideration test.
- No identifiable acquirer or acquiree test.
- Joint participation in management test.
- Relative size test.
- Full participation in future performance test.

27.13 Each of these tests is considered in the paragraphs that follow and the provisions of the Act and FRS 6 are contrasted.

Offer to shareholders test

27.14 The Act requires that the shares acquired as a result of the acquisition must be obtained by an arrangement providing for the issue of equity shares by the parent or any of its subsidiaries. [4A Sch 10(1)(b)]. Furthermore, FRS 6 requires that all but an immaterial proportion of the consideration must be in the form of equity shares as defined in FRS 4. (See 'Immaterial cash or non-equity consideration test' below.) The definitions of equity and non-equity shares in FRS 4 are repeated in FRS 6. [FRS 6 para 2]. The definition of equity in both FRS 4 and FRS 6 is much more restrictive than the Act's definition. The reason for adopting the more restrictive definition in FRS 6 is to prevent the Act's condition, that the offer is satisfied by the issue of equity shares, being met by the use of shares that, although within the legal definition of equity, have nonetheless characteristics that are closer to non-equity shares. The difference between equity as defined in the Act and as defined in FRS 6 is described below.

27.15 Equity shares are defined in the Act as the issued share capital of a company excluding any part which, neither as respects dividends nor as respects capital, carries any right to participate beyond a specified amount in a distribution. [Sec 744]. Equity shares represent the residual interests in a company and as such confer on their holders the right to share in the net assets of the company (after settling any prior claims). Such shares are normally termed ordinary shares, but it is quite possible for a preference share to be constructed in such a way that it meets the Act's definition of equity.

27.16 FRS 6 provides a definition of non-equity shares rather than adopting the Act's definition of equity share capital. Equity shares are defined as a residual category of shares, which is those shares other than non-equity shares. [FRS 6 para 2].

27.17 The definition given in FRS 6 of non-equity shares is as follows:

> *"Shares possessing any of the following characteristics:*
>
> *(a) any of the rights of the shares to receive payments (whether in respect of dividends, in respect of redemption or otherwise) are for a limited amount that is not calculated by reference to the company's assets or profits or the dividends on any class of equity share;*
>
> *(b) any of their rights to participate in a surplus in a winding up are limited to a specific amount that is not calculated by reference to the company's assets or profits and such limitation had a commercial effect in practice at the time the shares were issued or, if later, at the time the limitation was introduced;*

(c) *the shares are redeemable, either according to their terms or because the holder, or any party other than the issuer, can require their redemption."*
[FRS 6 para 2].

27.18 Whereas the Act defines equity share capital and non-equity share capital as a residual class, the standard defines non-equity share capital and equity share capital becomes a residual class. However, the standard's definition of non-equity shares is not consistent with the legal definition. The principal difference appears to be that in the standard's definition a share is non-equity if it carries limited distributions of either dividends or capital, whereas in the legal definition a share is non-equity only if there are limitations on the distribution of both dividends and capital. It follows that under FRS 6 non-equity is a broader category and, therefore, residual equity is a narrower category than under the Act.

27.19 The definition of non-equity shares in FRS 6 has been deliberately widely drawn so that any right to a dividend or to a redemption payment that is for a limited amount will require the share to be treated as non-equity. Consequently, it is quite possible for a company to issue (say) a preference share which is classified as equity share capital under the Act, but the preference share would be non-equity under FRS 6, for example, for the purposes of determining whether all but an immaterial proportion of the consideration given in a business combination is in the form of equity shares.

27.20 This situation could arise for instance where a company issued as consideration for a business combination preference shares which had a fixed dividend and unrestricted rights to distributions on winding up. The shares might, for instance, have a right on liquidation to share in a fixed percentage of the balance on the company's share premium account. Whereas these shares would qualify under the Act as equity because the limitations on distributions apply only to dividends and not to capital, they would not qualify as equity under FRS 6, because a limitation on either dividends or capital means they are non-equity under the standard. Therefore, although they qualify as equity for the purpose of obtaining merger relief under the Act, they do not count as equity under FRS 6 for the purpose of determining whether all but an immaterial proportion of the consideration is in the form of equity shares. (See 'Immaterial cash or non-equity consideration test' below.)

Ninety per cent holding test

27.21 The Act requires that at least 90 per cent of the nominal value of the 'relevant shares' in an undertaking acquired as a result of an arrangement must be held by or on behalf of the parent and its subsidiaries. [4A Sch 10(1)(a)]. In this context, 'relevant shares' means those shares in the acquired company that carry unrestricted rights to participate both in its distributions and in its assets upon liquidation. [4A Sch 10(2)]. This is in effect 'super-equity', and would include most ordinary share capital, but would exclude most other forms of participating preference shares (although these shares are often equity shares as defined in the Act). In this sense, therefore, the Act's definition of 'relevant shares' is similar to FRS 6's definition of equity.

27.22 The Act also states that the proportion referred to in paragraph 27.21, that is 90 per cent of the nominal value of the relevant shares, must be attained pursuant to an arrangement providing for the issue of equity shares. [4A Sch 10(b)]. However, this does not mean that, in order to merger account, the parent and its subsidiaries cannot hold more than 10 per cent of the nominal value of the relevant shares before the acquisition. It merely means that as a result of the offer the company must have reached at least a 90 per cent holding in the relevant shares (taking into account any prior holdings). For this purpose, 'relevant shares' has the same meaning as explained in paragraph 27.21 above.

27.23 Similarly under FRS 6 there is no limit on prior holdings, although the nature of the consideration given for the prior holding *is* relevant. As an example a company might hold 25 per cent of the relevant equity shares in another company that it acquired over two years before (see para 27.26 below) and might then obtain a further 65 per cent of the relevant shares of that other company as a result of an offer. In such a situation, and provided that all the other conditions for merger accounting were met, the existence of a prior holding of 25 per cent would not prevent merger accounting being adopted. This contrasts with SSAP 23, which prohibited merger accounting where there was a prior holding of 20 per cent or more that had been acquired at any time in the past.

Immaterial cash or non-equity consideration test

27.24 Where merger accounting is adopted, the consideration given for the relevant shares can include other consideration such as debentures and cash. However, the provisions of the Act restrict significantly the other consideration that can be given where the merger accounting method is to be used. The fair value of such other consideration given by the parent and its subsidiaries cannot exceed more than 10 per cent of the *nominal value* of the equity shares issued as part of the consideration pursuant to the arrangement. [4A Sch 10(c)].

27.25 The provisions of the Act contrast with the requirement included in FRS 6 where the following conditions must apply:

- Under the terms of the combination or related arrangements the consideration received by equity shareholders of each party to the combination, in relation to their equity shareholding, comprises primarily equity shares in the combined entity; and any non-equity consideration, or equity shares carrying substantially reduced voting or distribution rights, represents an immaterial proportion of the fair value of the consideration received by the shareholders.

- Where one of the combining entities has, within the period of two years before the combination, acquired equity shares in another of the combining entities, the consideration for this acquisition should be taken into account in determining whether this criterion (that is, the immaterial cash or non-equity consideration test) has been met.

- For the purposes of the above provisions, the consideration should not be taken to include the distribution to shareholders of:

  - an interest in a peripheral part of the business of the entity in which they were shareholders and that does not form part of the combined entity; or

  - the proceeds of the sale of such a business, or loan stock representing such proceeds.

A 'peripheral part of the business' is one which can be disposed of without having a material effect on the nature and focus of the entity's operations. [FRS 6 paras 9, 10].

27.26 Under these requirements in FRS 6, the fair value of the total consideration that the offeror gives should include also the fair value of the consideration that the offeror gave for shares that it acquired within two years before the offer. [FRS 6 para 9]. (In contrast, it is not necessary to take prior holdings into account in calculating the Act's limit mentioned in paragraph 27.21.)

27.27 It should be noted that the non-equity restriction in the Act relates to ten per cent of the *nominal* value of equity shares issued, whereas the restriction in FRS 6 relates to an immaterial proportion of the *fair* value of the consideration.

27.28 In some circumstances this may mean that the conditions of the Act are more restrictive than those of the standard as the following example demonstrates.

Example

A company issues equity shares in connection with a business combination, which have a nominal value of £100,000 together with £15,000 in cash. The fair value of the shares issued is £1,485,000. In this situation the business combination does not qualify for merger accounting under the Act, because the cash element is greater than 10% of the nominal value of the equity shares issued. The combination would however satisfy the condition in FRS 6, that not more than immaterial proportion of the fair value of the consideration is in the form of non-equity consideration, because in this case it represents only 1% of the fair value. Because the Act's requirement also has to be satisfied, however, merger accounting would not be possible in this case.

If in the above example the consideration had been £100,000 nominal value of equity shares and £10,000 cash, the conditions of the Act would have been satisfied and merger accounting would be permitted under both the Act and FRS 6. This might be so even if the fair value of the consideration had been only £110,000, that is if the shares had been issued at par (the lowest possible amount for which they could be issued) because even then the cash element of the total fair value would have been less than 10% of the total fair value. This conclusion is based on the assumption that 'immaterial' in FRS 6 may be interpreted as less than 10%. However, interpretations may vary as discussed below.

27.29 Although the ten per cent condition in the Act appears more restrictive than the condition of FRS 6, the Act does not require holdings acquired before the offer, and which are not part of the arrangement through which the 90 per cent holding is acquired, to be taken into account in determining the cash or non-equity element of the consideration. In contrast, FRS 6 requires that any acquisition by one of the combining parties of equity shares in the other within two years before the combination should be taken into account in determining whether or not non-equity consideration represents more than an immaterial proportion of the total consideration. Where such acquisitions have taken place the conditions of FRS 6 may be more restrictive than those of the Act as the following example demonstrates.

Example

Company B has share capital of 1,000 £1 equity shares. Company A has previously acquire 100 shares in company B for £5,000 (that is, £50 per share). These shares were acquire entirely for cash 18 months ago and were not acquired as part of an arrangement to acquir over 90% of company B. Company A now wishes to acquire the remaining 900 shares i company B. The value of company B has decreased since company A acquired its previou holding and the 900 shares are valued at £45 per share. The consideration for these 90 shares is to be given entirely by an issue of company A's equity shares. A's equity shares t be issued have a nominal value of £20,000 and fair value of £40,500.

The fair value of the total consideration that company A will have given is:

	£
Cash	5,000
Fair value of shares (namely, 900 × £45)	40,500
Total consideration	45,500

Company A makes its offer for 90% of the relevant shares of company B and because this offer is wholly for shares, the Act's provisions on the cash limit explained above do not apply. It, therefore, does not matter that the £5,000 cash exceeds 10% of the £20,000 nominal value of the A shares that are issued. However, because the previous acquisition was made within two years of the current offer and the non-equity element represents 10.9% of the fair value of the total consideration given in the acquisition, the non-equity element is material. The limit set out in FRS 6 is, therefore, exceeded and merger accounting cannot be used.

27.30 As explained in paragraph 27.15 above the definitions of equity in FRS 6 and the Act are different. The ASB has deliberately chosen to adopt the FRS 4 meaning of 'equity' to ensure that this test cannot be avoided by the use of shares that are 'equity' under the Act, but are not so in substance. This difference may also affect the determination of whether the limitations placed on the proportion of non-equity consideration by the Act and FRS 6 have been exceeded. The following example illustrates how this might occur.

Example

Company A issues 100,000 ordinary shares and 250,000 participating preference shares as consideration for acquiring 100% of the equity shares of company B. The nominal values of the ordinary shares and the participating preference shares are £100,000 and £250,000 respectively and their fair values are £1,000,000 and £250,000 respectively. The participating preference shares have the right to a fixed dividend of 5% and, in addition, they receive a proportion of the dividends paid on the ordinary shares. They qualify as equity under the Act, because they carry a right to participate beyond a specified amount in a distribution, but they do not qualify as equity under FRS 6. This is because one of the rights of the participating preference shares is to a fixed dividend of 5% and the definition of non-equity shares in FRS 6 states that a share qualifies as non-equity if *"<u>any</u> of the rights of the shares to receive payments (whether in respect of dividends, in respect of redemption or otherwise) are for a limited amount that is not calculated by reference to the company's assets or profits or the dividends on any class of equity share"*. [FRS 6 para 2].

27.31 Under the Act, the whole of the consideration in this example qualifies as equity and, therefore, the ten per cent limitation for non-equity is not breached. Under FRS 6, however, the participating preference shares are non-equity and as they amount to 20 per cent of the total fair value of the consideration the limit in FRS 6 that requires not more than an immaterial amount of the consideration to be in the form of non-equity, is breached.

27.32 In the above examples it has been suggested that the FRS 6 reference to immaterial might be interpreted as meaning less than ten per cent. No numerical figure is placed on the term 'immaterial' in FRS 6, but in practice it is often assumed that amounts representing less than five per cent are not material, between five and ten per cent may or may not be material and over ten per cent are material. As the Act uses a ten per cent limit for non-equity consideration compared to the nominal value of equity shares, it seems reasonable to assume that in the context of the FRS 6 condition, a non-equity element that represents over ten per cent of the total fair value of the consideration should be regarded as material.

Disposal of peripheral part of business

27.33 The consideration for a business combination should not include the distribution to shareholders of an interest in a peripheral part of a business of an entity in which they were shareholders and that does not form part of the combined entity. Nor should it include the distribution of the proceeds of sale of such a business or loan stock representing such proceeds. The implication of this is that where such a distribution or sale is not peripheral, then it should be counted as part of the consideration.

27.34 This situation might occur where two entities decide to merge, but there are certain businesses which do not fit in and that the two parties decide should be disposed of prior to the merger taking place. FRS 6 makes it clear that the disposal of such businesses must not materially affect the nature and focus of the disposing entity's operations. This seems rather a harsh condition as a group might well wish to merge certain of its operations only with another entity whilst allowing its shareholders to receive shares in the remainder of the group by, for instance, a distribution in kind. Provided that the operations to be merged with the other entity have a proper track record and are independent of the rest of the group there seems to be no good reason why the combination of that part of the group with another entity should not be eligible for merger accounting. However, FRS 6 would prohibit merger accounting in such a case, if the operations retained by the shareholders of the group and, therefore, excluded from the merger, materially affected the nature and focus of the original group's operations.

27.35 There is a similar prohibition in the Explanation section of FRS 6 which states that merger accounting is not appropriate for a combination where one entity divests itself of part of its business, which is then combined with another entity. The reason given in that section is that the divested business will not have been independent for a sufficient period to establish itself as being a party separate from its previous owner. The section continues that only once the divested business has established a track record of its own can it be considered as a party to a merger.

27.36 This condition is rather strange and appears over-restrictive. Many large groups have businesses that are run by their own management as quasi-independent entities under the group 'umbrella'. It is relatively straightforward to establish a trading record for such businesses. Evidence that this is so is the number of stock market flotations of businesses in recent years, which were hived off or demerged from larger groups.

Vendor placings and vendor rights

27.37 In recent years, under the rules laid down by SSAP 23, it was possible to merger account for a business combination even where a vendor placing or a vendor rights was made to effect the combination.

27.38 The use of vendor rights or vendor placings enabled the target company's shareholders to receive cash whilst the acquiring company, because technically it had issued its own shares in exchange for shares in the target, was able not only to obtain merger relief, but also to merger account, provided all the other conditions of SSAP 23 were satisfied. Vendor placings and vendor rights are described briefly below.

27.39 A vendor placing normally works as follows. The acquiring company will offer its shares to the target company's shareholders in exchange for their shares in that company. If there are any shareholders of the target company who do not wish to retain the consideration shares of the acquiring company, then the acquiring company will arrange for its financial adviser (for example, a merchant bank) to place those consideration shares. The financial adviser will put together a placing list (that will normally include institutions such as pension funds and insurance companies) so that the target company shareholders may dispose of their consideration shares in the acquiring company for cash.

27.40 So after the vendor placing has occurred, cash has been transferred from the institutions, *via* the financial adviser (acting in his capacity as a broker) to some or all of the target company's shareholders. In return, the institutions now own shares in the acquiring company and the acquiring company now owns the target company. The acquiring company has issued shares, rather than paying cash, for the target company and, therefore, prior to FRS 6, as long as the offer complied with both the Act's and SSAP 23's merger conditions, the acquiring company could use merger accounting on consolidation.

27.41 The vendor rights normally work as follows. The acquiring company will offer its shares to the target company's shareholders in exchange for their shares in that company. If any shareholders of the target company do not wish to retain their consideration shares of the acquiring company, then the acquiring company will arrange for its financial adviser to place those consideration shares. Up to this point, the vendor rights method is the same as a vendor placing. However, as part of the placing agreement the acquiring company's shareholders will have an option to buy ('claw back') some of the consideration shares from the placees. They will be entitled to buy back at the placing price a certain proportion of the placed shares on a *pro rata* basis.

27.42 Therefore, after the vendor rights method is completed, cash has been transferred from the acquiring company's shareholders, *via* the financial adviser, to some or all of the target company's shareholders. In return, the acquiring company's shareholders now have a stake in a larger group, because the acquiring company now owns the target company. The acquiring company has issued shares, rather than paying cash, for the target company, and so, prior to FRS 6, it could use merger accounting on consolidation.

27.43 Even under SSAP 23, however, there were many who argued that vendor placings and vendor rights did not meet the spirit of SSAP 23, which stated in its Explanatory Note that *"Merger accounting is considered to be an appropriate method of accounting when two groups of shareholders continue, or are in a position to continue, their shareholdings as before but on a combined basis"*. Although in a vendor rights at least the acquiree's shareholders are technically in a position to continue as shareholders, many people felt that the very structure of the consideration as a vendor rights or vendor placing indicated that many of the shareholders did not intend to continue investing in the combined entity.

27.44 FRS 6 resolves the possible contradiction between the offer of vendor placing or rights and the spirit of merger accounting by saying that equity shareholders would be considered to have disposed of their shareholdings for cash where any arrangement is made in connection with the combination that enables them to exchange or redeem the shares they receive for cash or other non-equity consideration. Such arrangements will include a vendor placing or a vendor rights. All arrangements made in conjunction with the combination must be taken into account, but a normal market transaction or a privately arranged sale by a shareholder is not deemed to be made in conjunction with the combination and does not prevent the immaterial cash or non-equity consideration criterion being met. [FRS 6 para 71].

27.45 Any convertible shares or loan stock that are outstanding at the time of the offer should not normally be regarded as equity for the purposes of satisfying the merger conditions. The only exception to this is where the convertible stock is converted into equity as a result of the business combination. [FRS 6 para 12].

No identifiable acquirer or acquiree test

27.46 Under SSAP 23 it was not relevant whether one party to a business combination was perceived as the dominant party. The approach adopted in FRS 6, however, is that in order to qualify for merger accounting, a business combination must represent a genuine partnership between the combining entities in which none of the parties dominates the other party or parties. No party to the combination should be portrayed as either acquirer or acquiree either by its own board or management or by that of another party to the combination. [FRS 6 para 6]. This is the principle that underlies the definition of a merger in the standard (see para 27.10 above).

27.47 The standard sets out a number of factors that may be evident in a business combination and which could indicate that one or other party is dominant. It makes clear that for merger accounting to be possible all of these factors must be absent.

27.48 The most straightforward of these factors is if one or other party is portrayed either by itself or by another party to the acquisition as the acquirer, or as having the subservient role of being acquired. One party's portrayal as acquirer or as acquiree is particularly likely to be a factor present in a contested bid, where one party attempts to gain control against the wishes of the other party's management.

27.49 As mentioned in paragraph 27.11 above, where all the conditions for merger accounting are satisfied the business combination must be accounted for as a merger. It is not an optional treatment. However, it is pointed out in paragraph 9 of the 'Development' section of FRS 6 that it would be relatively easy for merging parties to ensure that one of the conditions was not met, without fundamentally altering the commercial substance of the transaction, if they did not want to use merger accounting. This condition, that no party should be portrayed as an acquirer or as being acquired, seems to be probably the most susceptible to such manipulation.

27.50 FRS 6 lists a number of other aspects of a transaction that could indicate whether or not one party was dominant. These include:

- The form by which the combination was achieved.
- The plans for the combined entity's future operations (for instance whether any closures or disposals relate more to one party than to another).
- The proposed corporate image (such as name, logo, and location of headquarters and principal operations).

- In a publicly quoted company, the content of its communications with shareholders.

[FRS 6 para 62].

27.51 If any of these indicates that one party to the combination dominates the other or has the subservient role of being acquired, merger accounting is not permitted.

27.52 The standard indicates that where one party is seen to be paying a premium over the market value of the shares acquired, this is evidence that that party has assumed the role of acquirer, unless there is a clear explanation for the premium, other than its being a premium to acquire control. [FRS 6 para 61].

27.53 This condition is not always easy to put into operation. It appears to apply to cases where offers are made for listed companies which at the date of the offer represent a substantial premium to the market price. However, during the course of the offer the target company's share price will often rise to the offer price level or even above. It is not clear from the standard at which point the comparison with market price should be made in order to determine whether or not it is a premium to market price and, if so, whether it is a premium to acquire control. However, even if this is a difficult condition of the standard to interpret, it should be clear from other circumstances of the offer whether or not there is a premium paid for control. It is also important that whilst the market's perception might be that there is a premium being paid for control and this might be demonstrated by a significant difference between the market price at the date of an offer and the offer price, the standard's test of whether or not one party is portrayed as dominant is determined by how the parties to the combination portray themselves, not how the market portrays them.

Joint participation in management test

27.54 The FRS requires that the boards of all the combining parties or their appointees should participate in setting up the management structure for the combined entity and in selecting the management personnel. They should set up this structure and select the management personnel on the basis of consensus decisions between the combining parties rather than purely by exercise of voting rights. [FRS 6 para 7].

27.55 This does not mean that the management structure and personnel have to be equally divided between the combining parties. Indeed it could be that one party provides most of the management. This would not contravene the joint participation rule provided that it reflected the wishes of all the parties to the merger.

27.56 In determining whether the condition of joint participation is satisfied consideration has to be given not just to the structure, but also to the identity of all persons involved in the main financial and operating decisions and the way in which the decision making process operates in practice. For instance, if all financial and operating decisions had to be approved by the managing director and only one of the parties to the combination could appoint the managing director, that party might be presumed to exert undue dominance over the management. As explained above, however, if that was in accordance with the wishes of all the parties it would not breach the 'joint participation' condition.

27.57 Sometimes there may be arrangements made at the date of combination whereby there is joint participation in management for a limited period only, with other arrangements being made thereafter. If at the outset there is such an agreement for short-term joint participation, but it is agreed that at the expiry of that period, one party may assume control of management whether or not the other party agrees, then that arrangement would probably breach the joint participation rule and merger accounting would not be permitted. Where, however, arrangements for the period that followed a short period of joint participation provided that management should be selected on the basis of merit only, such arrangements would not breach the joint participation rule, provided that all parties agreed to the policy at the outset.

27.58 The standard makes clear that only decisions made about management structure and personnel at the outset of the merger need be considered in determining whether there is joint participation, but as illustrated above both the short-term and long-term consequences of those decisions need to be evaluated.

Relative size test

27.59 The standard requires that the relative sizes of the combining entities are not so disparate that one party dominates the combined entity by virtue of its relative size. [FRS 6 para 8].

27.60 As to what constitutes dominance in terms of size the standard says that one party should be presumed to dominate if it is more than 50 per cent larger than each of the other parties to the combination. The test of size should be made by reference to the proportion of the equity of the combined entity attributable to each of the combining parties.

27.61 However the presumption of dominance, where one party is more than 50 per cent larger than each of the other parties, may be rebutted if it can be clearly shown that there is no such dominance. In some circumstances, for instance, there may be agreements between the parties that determine voting rights or other matters, such as powers of veto, which mean that the apparent dominance due to size is not effective in practice. Any such circumstances should be disclosed and explained.

Example 1

Company A is listed and has 100 million equity shares of £1 in issue which have a market value of £1,000 million. Company B is also listed and has 100 million 5p equity shares in issue with a market value of £600 million. Company A makes an agreed offer for company B and the offer is valued at £750 million, that is company A will issue 75m shares.

In this situation if the relative sizes pre-merger are considered company A is more than 50% larger than company B. However, this is not relevant for determining whether or not the relative size test is satisfied. It is the relative proportions of equity of the combined entity that are relevant. Comparison of A's share of the combined equity of £1,750 million with B's share, shows that the company A shareholders own 100 million shares (that is, 57% of the combined entity), which is not more than 50% larger than that of company B shareholders' interest of 75 million shares (that is 43% of the combined entity). By reference to the size test alone, therefore, the combination would be entitled to be merger accounted. However, consideration would then have to be given as to whether the substantial premium of £150 million paid by company A was a premium to acquire control (see paras 27.52 and 27.53 above).

Example 2

Company A is unlisted and has 15,000 equity shares in issue. There is no quoted market value available, but the company has net assets of £150,000. Company B is also unlisted and has 3,000 equity shares in issue. Its net assets are £50,000. Company A issues 5,000 equity shares to the shareholders of company B in consideration for their equity shares in that company.

A comparison of the respective holdings of the former shareholders of company A (15,000 shares) and the former shareholders of company B (5,000 shares) shows that the former shareholders of company A have a holding of 75% in the combined entity that is more than 50% larger than that of the former shareholders of company B who own 25%. Therefore, it is presumed that company A is dominant and merger accounting is not permitted (unless the presumption can be rebutted in some way).

Example 3

Company A has 10,000 equity shares in issue that have a market value of £500,000. Company B has 1,000 equity shares in issue having a market value of £200,000. Company A is in a period of low profitability and its markets are mature and declining. The shares in company B are owned by a dynamic individual Mr X who also manages that company and has built its business up rapidly. Company A wishes to retain the services of that individual to run the combined business. In turn he wishes to retain an effective say in the running of the business whilst enjoying the benefits of a larger organisation. Company A issues 4,000 shares to acquire company B. At the same time it enters into an agreement with Mr X as a shareholder in the combined entity. The agreement specifies that decisions on all major operational and financial matters must be agreed by shareholders representing at least 75% of the equity. In this way control is effectively shared between the shareholders in the old company A and Mr X, the shareholder of the former company B.

In this situation, although the former shareholders of company A hold over 50% (71%) more of the enlarged equity than the former shareholder of company B (29%) the shareholders' agreement means that control is effectively divided equally between the two. In such a situation, the presumption that company A is dominant can be rebutted and if all the other conditions for merger accounting are satisfied merger accounting would be required. The financial statements would have to disclose the reasons why company A was not considered to be dominant.

Full participation in future performance test

27.62 The FRS requires that no equity shareholders of any of the combining entities retain any material interest in the future performance of only part of the combined entity. [FRS 6 para 11].

27.63 A situation where different shareholders might retain material interests in different parts of a combined entity might be as follows:

Example 1

Company A and company B combine by means of a new holding company, company C, issuing shares to the former shareholders of companies A and B. The shares issued to the former shareholders of company A (A shares) are entitled to 80% of the profits of the former company A businesses and the shares issued to the former shareholders of company B (B shares) are entitled to 80% of the profits of the former company B businesses. All other profits are shared equally between the two sets of shareholders. Assuming that there are an equal number of A and B shares and that the company A businesses make £100,000 in the first year and the company B businesses make £50,000 the A shares would be entitled to £80,000 of the profits from the company A businesses while the B shares would be entitled to £40,000 from the company B businesses. The balance of £30,000 of the total profits would be shared equally.

Because, in this example, certain of the equity shareholders retain a material interest in only part of the future performance of the combined entity the condition of full participation in future performance would not be satisfied and merger accounting would not be permitted for the combination.

Similarly, where there is an earnout or similar performance related arrangement the condition would not be met.

Example 2

Company A and company B combine by means of shares issued by company A to company B shareholders. Part of the consideration (to be settled in shares) is deferred and is contingent on the performance of the company B businesses over the next three years. The potential amount of the contingent consideration is material.

Because the shareholders of company B have a material interest in only one part of the combined business, the issue of further equity shares to them depends solely on the performance of the company B businesses.

It might be argued that once the earnout is completed, then all shareholders will participate fully, but the standard appears to be concerned to ensure that the condition of full participation is satisfied based on conditions existing at the date of the combination.

An exception is where at the date of the combination there is uncertainty about the value of a specific asset or liability contributed by one of the parties, such as the eventual outcome of a legal action against one of the parties, or the eventual sales value of an asset owned by one of the parties. An agreement for the allocation of the consideration between the combining parties that depend on the eventual outcome of the uncertainty would not invalidate the full participation rule.

Example 3

At the date of a business combination between company A and company B, company A has not resolved a claim made by it against various former customers who have failed to take delivery of goods manufactured for them under contract. No account of any potential gain has been taken in determining the consideration to be allocated to company A shareholders at the date of the combination, but it has been agreed that those shareholders will be entitled to 80% of any subsequent gain arising from the claim.

In these circumstances, the participation of the company A shareholders in any future gain arising from the claim would not infringe the condition of full participation, because the outcome does not depend on the future performance of the combined business, but rather on the outcome of an uncertainty existing at the date of the combination.

27.64 The full participation in future performance test is not met where there is a material minority, that is ten per cent or more, of shareholders of one of the combining parties that has not accepted the offer. This is because if there is such a minority then it retains an interest in only part of the combined entity and the condition that no equity shareholders of the combining entities should retain a material interest in the future performance of only part of the combined entity, is not met. It is also unlikely that, if there was such a large minority, the other conditions for merger accounting could be met.

Merger accounting principles

27.65 The principles of acquisition accounting are explained in chapter 23 and the principles of merger accounting are considered in greater detail below. Whereas FRS 6 has changed the criteria for when merger accounting is used, it has not changed the principles or methods of merger accounting from those described in SSAP 23.

27.66 When a group uses merger accounting to account for a business combination, the group does not need to incorporate into its consolidated financial statements the fair values of the subsidiary's assets and liabilities. [FRS 6 para 16]. Therefore, no goodwill arises in a merger and the group should incorporate into its consolidated financial statements the assets and liabilities at the amounts at which the subsidiary recorded them in its books before the combination. [4A Sch 11(2)].

27.67 One exception to this principle is that a group should adopt uniform group accounting policies for consolidation purposes in accordance with the Act and FRS 2. Consequently, if the acquired company's accounting policies are not the same as the acquiring company's, then adjustments should be made to achieve uniformity. One way of doing this might be for the subsidiary to make these adjustments in its own records. It could restate the amount of its assets and liabilities in its books to reflect the change in accounting policy. Alternatively, if it is not practicable for the acquired company to change its accounting policies, adjustments may be made on consolidation to the values of the acquired company's assets and liabilities that are stated in its books.

27.67.1 An example of disclosure of adjustments to conform accounting policies is Table 27.1. It is worth noting that changes to the policies of either party to the merger may be made depending on which of the combining parties' policies the enlarged entity chooses to adopt.

Table 27.1 – Royal & Sun Alliance Insurance Group plc – Directors' Report and Accounts – 31 December 1996

Accounting policies (extract)

Effects of merger on Group financial statements
On 19th July 1996, Sun Alliance Group plc (Sun Alliance) was renamed Royal & Sun Alliance Insurance Group plc and became the Parent Company of the new Group formed by the merger of Royal Insurance Holdings plc (Royal Insurance) and Sun Alliance. Merger accounting principles have been used and the results have been presented as if the new Group had been established throughout the current and prior years.

Alignment of accounting policies and presentation
The new Group's accounting policies are set out on pages 17 to 19. The process of aligning policies and presentation across the new Group has resulted in the following principal changes:

a) General business is accounted for on an annual basis. Previously Sun Alliance used a fund basis of accounting for London market marine and aviation business.
b) Overseas revenue transactions are translated at rates ruling at the year end. Previously Royal Insurance used average rates of exchange during the year to translate revenue transactions.
c) The reinsurers' share of technical provisions is presented on the assets side of the balance sheet. Previously Royal Insurance presented these amounts on the liabilities side of the balance sheet in arriving at net technical provisions.
d) Balances arising from insurance broking transactions are presented gross. Previously Sun Alliance took advantage of the transitional provision within Financial Reporting Standard 5 permitting the offset of balances between insurance brokers and the Group.
e) The value of long term business, being the value of the shareholders' interest in the long term funds in excess of that recognised under the modified statutory solvency basis of reporting long term business, is included within investments in the consolidated balance sheet. Previously Sun Alliance did not include this value in the financial statements but disclosed it in the Group Chief Executive's review.
f) British Aviation Insurance Company Ltd is accounted for as a subsidiary of the Group. Previously this company was an associated undertaking of both Royal Insurance and Sun Alliance.
g) Sun Alliance and Royal Insurance Australia Holdings Ltd is accounted for as a subsidiary of the Group. This company was previously an associated undertaking of Royal Insurance and a subsidiary of Sun Alliance.
h) Scrip acceptances received under the scrip dividend alternative are subsequently added back to reserves. Previously Sun Alliance made no adjustment to reserves for scrip dividend acceptances which were accounted as shares issued at a premium.
i) Goodwill arising on acquisitions is written off to other reserves in the consolidated balance sheet along with the merger reserve arising on consolidation of Royal Insurance and Sun Alliance. Previously Sun Alliance wrote goodwill off against the consolidated profit and loss account reserve.

[The next paragraph is 27.68.]

27.68 The group's consolidated financial statements for the period in which the business combination takes place should include the subsidiary's income and expenditure and cash flows for the entire period. [4A Sch 11(3); FRS 6 para 17]. That is to say, they should include the subsidiary's results for the part of the period before the business combination, as well as the results of the subsidiary for the part of the period after the business combination. These results should be consolidated on a line by line basis in the profit and loss account and the cash flow statement as if the subsidiary had always been part of the group. In addition, the corresponding amounts in the consolidated financial statements should reflect the position that would have arisen if the companies had been combined throughout the previous period and also at the previous balance sheet date. [4A Sch 11(4)].

27.69 The aim of the consolidated financial statements in merger accounting is to show the combined companies' results and financial positions as if they had always been combined. Consequently, even the share capital issued during the year for the purposes of the merger has to be shown as if it had always been issued.

Example

In 19X1 company A and company B combine and the combination is eligible for merger accounting. The share capital of company A (which has remained unchanged since the beginning of 19X0) is 100,000 equity shares of £1 each prior to the merger and that of company B is 200,000 shares of 50p each. Company A issues 100,000 equity shares in consideration for the acquisition of company B the fair value of which is £1 million and incurs merger expenses of £10,000. Profits of company A for the year 19X0 were £150,000 and for 19X1 they were £200,000. Profits of company B for 19X0 were £190,000 and for 19X1 they were £100,000 to the date of merger and £75,000 for the post-merger period. There were no adjustments required to achieve uniformity of accounting policies.

The profits of the combined group would be presented as if company A and company B had always been combined. Thus the group profit and loss account would show profits for 19X0 of £340,000 (£150,000 + £190,000) and for 19X1 the profits would be £375,000 (£200,000 + £100,000 + £75,000), before merger expenses.

The share capital of company A would be adjusted so as to show the shares issued in respect of the merger as if they had been in existence at the start of 19X0. Therefore, company A's share capital at the beginning of 19X0 would be shown at £200,000. There would be no difference arising on consolidation as the nominal value of shares issued as consideration is equal to the nominal value of shares acquired. The merger expenses of £10,000 would be written off to the group profit and loss account for 19X1. (Although there might seem to be an argument for charging these expenses in 19X0 the standard specifically requires them to be charged at the date of the merger as reorganisation or restructuring expenses in accordance with paragraph 20 of FRS 3, that is as a post-operating profit exceptional item.)

27.70 The examples that follow illustrate some of the problems that can arise with the principles of merger accounting.

Example 1

Company A combines with company B during the year and merger accounts for the combination. Company A has large tax losses and has never had a tax charge. Company B paid tax last year and it is proposed that the two companies' results should be combined and the tax charge of company B excluded from the comparatives on the basis that if the companies had always been combined, this tax charge would never have arisen.

In this type of situation, it would be carrying the principles of merger accounting too far to eliminate the tax charge. The tax has been paid and cannot be recovered now that company B has joined the group. Consequently, the tax charge should be shown as a

[The next page is 27021.]

comparative in the merged profit and loss account. Company A could of course add a note to explain why the tax charge has arisen.

Example 2

A company combines with another and will use merger accounting. The company's year end is 31 December and the subsidiary's year end is 30 June. The company wishes to know how to deal with the difference in year ends.

The company should consolidate the results of the subsidiary for the 12 months ended 31 December. It should take the second six months from the year to 30 June and add the following six months of trading. This treatment is necessary to comply with the Act's requirements concerning the accounting period of the subsidiary that must be consolidated.

Example 3

A listed company with a December year end combines with a company with a June year end. Merger accounting is to be used. The second company had a subsidiary that made losses to June, but it disposes of its loss-making subsidiary before the date of merger which is in November.

The results of the loss-making subsidiaries should be included in the consolidation, because, although technically they never become subsidiaries of the listed company, the spirit of FRS 6 requires that the merged companies should incorporate the unaltered results of the two companies for the full year. The results of the subsidiaries that are sold should, if material, be shown separately and disclosed as discontinued operations, but they should still be included in the consolidated profit and loss account of the merged companies.

Applicability to business combinations achieved by using a new parent company

27.71 Often business combinations are effected by incorporating a new company which then issues shares to two or more combining companies. The accounting treatment in such cases will depend on the substance of the arrangement. This often means that the new parent should be ignored and the tests for merger accounting should be applied to the combining entities other than the new parent, (except insofar as it is necessary to bring in the new parent as, for instance, in satisfying the 'offer to shareholders', '90 per cent holding' and 'immaterial cash or non-equity consideration' tests).

27.72 If the substance is that a combination of the entities would have been a merger, merger accounting should be used. However, if the substance is that an acquirer can be identified, acquisition accounting should be used. In the latter case the new parent company and the acquirer should be accounted for by using merger accounting and then the other parties to the combination should be acquisition accounted. [FRS 6 para 14].

27.73 Where a new parent is used to effect a business combination and merger accounting is to be used it is advisable to ensure that the accounting period of the new parent company is the same as that of the combining companies and that the new parent has been in existence for the whole of the combining companies' current accounting periods (see para 27.106 below).

Applicability to group reconstructions

27.74 Merger accounting may be used for group reconstructions, even where there is no business combination that meets the definition of a merger. However, this is conditional on:

- The use of merger accounting not being prohibited by companies legislation.
- The ultimate shareholders remaining the same and the rights of each such shareholder, relative to other shareholders, being unchanged.
- No minority's interest in the net assets of the group being altered by the combination.

[FRS 6 para 13].

27.74.1 The conditions for merger accounting under the Companies Act and FRS 6 have been discussed above from paragraph 27.12. In the case of a group reconstruction only the Act's requirements need to be met. The additional conditions imposed by FRS 6 for merger accounting are not required to be met. The Act's conditions which are explained in more detail from paragraph 27.12 above, are:

- At least 90 per cent of the nominal value of the relevant shares in the undertaking acquired is held by or on behalf of the parent company and its subsidiary undertakings.
- The proportion referred to above was attained pursuant to an arrangement providing for the issue of equity shares by the parent company or one or more of its subsidiary undertakings.
- The fair value of any consideration other than the issue of equity shares given pursuant to the arrangement by the parent company and its subsidiary undertakings did not exceed ten per cent of the nominal value of the equity shares issued.
- Adoption of the merger method of accounting accords with generally accepted accounting principles or practice.

[4A Sch 10(1)]

[The next paragraph is 27.75.]

27.75 The definition of a group reconstruction in FRS 6 extends the meaning of the term to include several types of business combination which would not have been considered to be group reconstructions in the past. Indeed it includes several types of combination which would be eligible for merger relief rather than group reconstruction relief under the Act. The definition is:

> *"Group reconstruction:-*
>
> *Any of the following arrangements:*
>
> *(a) the transfer of a shareholding in a subsidiary undertaking from one group company to another;*
>
> *(b) the addition of a new parent company to a group;*
>
> *(c) the transfer of shares in one or more subsidiary undertakings of a group to a new company that is not a group company but whose shareholders are the same as those of the group's parent;*
>
> *(d) the combination into a group of two or more companies that before the combination had the same shareholders."*
>
> [FRS 6 para 2]

[The next page is 27023.]

27.76 Where any of the above forms of combination is planned it will be necessary to determine whether group reconstruction relief or merger relief is applicable. These reliefs are explained in chapter 26.

Example 1

Company A is the parent company of a group. It is proposed to form a new parent company, company B. Company B is formed as an independent company, not as a subsidiary of company A. Company B issues shares in exchange for all the shares in company A.

In this situation company B does not qualify for group reconstruction relief, because it is not the wholly-owned subsidiary of company A, but it does qualify for merger relief.

Example 2

Company A is the US parent company of a group which has a number of UK subsidiaries. It is proposed to form a new UK parent company for the UK subsidiaries. Company B is formed as a wholly-owned subsidiary of the US parent. It issues shares to the US parent in exchange for the US parent's holdings in the UK subsidiaries.

In this situation, company B is eligible for group reconstruction relief, because it is the wholly-owned subsidiary of the US parent and issues shares to that parent in exchange for the transfer to company B of the parent's holdings in the UK subsidiaries.

27.77 In both of the above situations merger accounting is permitted by law, the ultimate shareholders remain the same as do their rights and there is no minority interest affected by the combination. Accordingly, merger accounting is permitted.

27.78 It is noticeable that FRS 6 does not make merger accounting compulsory in the case of group reconstructions, in contrast to other business combinations. However it is likely that, in most cases where there is a group reconstruction and the conditions set out above for merger accounting are satisfied, companies will wish to use merger accounting.

27.79 Example (d) in the definition of group reconstructions covers a situation where there is a so called 'horizontal' group. This is a group where the companies involved are not part of a legal group for Companies Act purposes, but are under the common ownership of an individual or individuals. Where this situation exists it would clearly be somewhat severe if the combination had to satisfy all the stringent tests for merger accounting that apply to combinations other than group reconstructions. For instance, the 'relative size test' and the 'no identifiable acquirer or acquiree tests' are not really relevant in this situation.

Example

Mr X and his family interests own the whole of the share capital of three companies – company A, company B and company C – which have net assets of 10, 100 and 1,000 respectively. It is decided that the three companies should be combined and company C issues shares to Mr X and his family interests in exchange for their shares in company A and company B. In this case, group reconstruction relief is not applicable, but company C is able to take merger relief. In addition, the combination is treated as a group reconstruction for the purposes of FRS 6 and the standard's conditions for merger accounting in the case of group reconstructions are satisfied. The conditions that FRS 6 sets out for business combinations that are not group reconstructions are not relevant. Thus it does not matter if company C is portrayed as the acquirer or that company C is much larger than the other two parties to the combination.

27.80 One of the conditions for merger accounting for a group reconstruction is that no minority's interest in the net assets of the group is altered by the transfer. A minority's interest may be unaffected, for instance, where a subsidiary undertaking is transferred within a subgroup that has a minority shareholder, but is likely to be affected if a subsidiary is transferred into or out of such a group.

Example

Company B is the intermediate parent company of subsidiary companies C, D and E. There is a minority interest of 10% in company B the remainder of whose shares are owned by the ultimate parent company, company A. Company A has a further direct subsidiary company X. Company B enters into two transactions, first it transfers ownership of company C to company E in exchange for shares in company E (which are issued to company B). Second, it transfers company E, (which now owns company C), to company X for shares. Both company E and company X prepare consolidated financial statements.

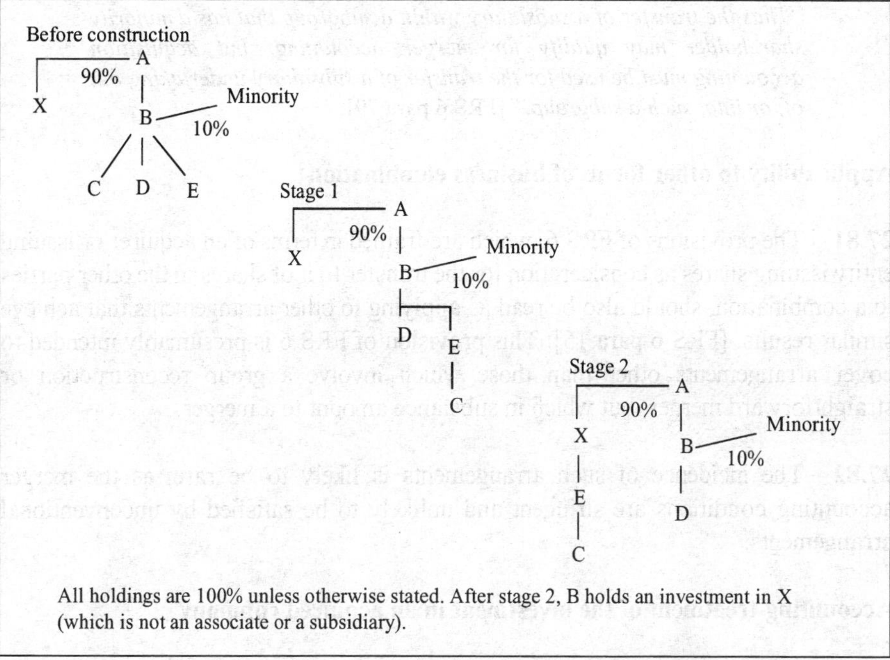

All holdings are 100% unless otherwise stated. After stage 2, B holds an investment in X (which is not an associate or a subsidiary).

In the first transaction, the transfer of company C to company E, the minority interest is not affected because the composition of the subgroup headed by company B remains unchanged. In company E's consolidated financial statements, therefore, the combination with company C could be merger accounted.

In the second transaction company E and its subsidiary company C move out of the company B subgroup and company B's investment in company E (and its subsidiary company C) is replaced by an investment in company X (but company X does not thereby become a subsidiary of company B).

If the investment in company X is recorded in company B's consolidated financial statements at the same value as it had previously recorded the net assets of company E and company C (ignoring goodwill), the minority's share of net assets will be unchanged. In terms of the carrying values, this transaction might seem to satisfy the condition that the minority's interest in the net assets is not altered. However, the explanation section of the standard says:

> *"If a minority has effectively acquired, or disposed of, rights to part of the net assets of the group, the FRS requires the transfer to be accounted for by using acquisition accounting rather than merger accounting."* [FRS 6 para 79].

As the minority has indeed disposed of part of the company B group in this situation it appears that company X must acquisition account for the combination with company E and company C. This would appear to be so because the 'group' referred to in quotation above must be the company B subgroup. This interpretation is reinforced by a further quotation from the explanation section of the standard:

> *"Thus the transfer of a subsidiary within a subgroup that has a minority shareholder may qualify for merger accounting; but acquisition accounting must be used for the transfer of a subsidiary undertaking out of, or into, such a subgroup."* [FRS 6 para 79].

Applicability to other forms of business combination

27.81 The provisions of FRS 6, which are framed in terms of an acquirer or issuing entity issuing shares as consideration for the transfer to it of shares in the other parties to a combination, should also be read as applying to other arrangements that achieve similar results. [FRS 6 para 15]. This provision of FRS 6 is presumably intended to cover arrangements other than those which involve a group reconstruction or straightforward merger, but which in substance amount to a merger.

27.82 The incidence of such arrangements is likely to be rare, as the merger accounting conditions are stringent and unlikely to be satisfied by unconventional arrangements.

Accounting treatment of the investment in an acquired company

27.83 The Companies Act 1985 clarifies the accounting treatment of an investment in an acquired company that should be used in an issuing company's balance sheet where there is:

- Merger relief under section 131.
- Group reconstruction relief under section 132.

27.84 In these circumstances, the amount at which the issuing company carries its investment in the acquired company does not need to include an amount corresponding to the premium (or the part of the premium) that the issuing company has not credited to its share premium account. [Sec 133(1)]. That is, the issuing company has a choice. Disregarding other considerations such as cash, the issuing company can record both the shares it issues and the investment in the new subsidiary at either:

- the nominal value of the shares issued and any section 132 minimum premium; or

- the fair value of the shares issued, with the premium credited to a merger reserve instead of to a share premium account.

27.85 Although the Act says that the value of the investment shown in the balance sheet need not include the premium, it at first sight appears that the application of FRS 4 would require it to do so, where merger relief or group reconstruction relief is taken, but acquisition accounting is adopted for the business combination. This is because FRS 4 requires that the net proceeds from the issue of equity shares should be credited to shareholders' funds. 'Net proceeds' are defined as *"the fair value of the consideration received on the issue of a capital instrument after deduction of issue costs"*. [FRS 4 para 11].

27.86 Therefore, where acquisition accounting is adopted on consolidation for the business combination, FRS 4 would appear to require the shares issued by the acquiring company to be recorded at fair value. This does not mean that the difference between the nominal value and the fair value would be credited to share premium account. Only the minimum premium value, where group reconstruction relief is taken, would be credited to that account. The balance of the difference (all of it, if merger relief is taken) would be credited to a separate reserve, normally called a merger reserve.

27.87 As the shares issued would then be recorded at fair value it follows that the investment would also have to be recorded at fair value in these circumstances.

27.88 However, where merger accounting is adopted for the business combination on consolidation the requirements of FRS 4 do not apply to equity shares issued. There is an exception in FRS 4 for equity shares issued as part of a business combination that is accounted for as a merger. At first sight this exception appears only to apply to equity shares that are issued and not to non-equity shares that are issued.

27.89 Despite the apparent requirements of FRS 4 in this regard it has become clear since the issue of FRS 4 that it was not the ASB's intention to restrict the reliefs available under section 133 where either acquisition or merger accounting is adopted. As evidence of this the Appendix to FRS 6, 'Note on Legal Requirements', states: *"The FRS deals only with the method of accounting to be used in group accounts; it does not deal with the form of accounting to be used in the acquiring or issuing company's own accounts and in particular does not restrict the reliefs available under Sections 131-133 of the Companies Act"*. In addition in FRS 7 the ASB has included a paragraph in the legal requirements section stating: *"Where (if the merger relief provisions apply) the premiums are disregarded, the cost of investment in the parent company's books will be different from the cost of acquisition for the purpose of para 9(4) of Sch 4A"*.

27.90 Therefore, the apparent requirements of FRS 4 may be disregarded both when acquisition accounting and merger accounting is adopted. This does not of course prevent a company recording the shares issued and the investment acquired at fair value where acquisition accounting is adopted, if it wishes, but does leave it a choice.

27.91 Where merger (or acquisition) accounting is adopted on consolidation and the investment shown in the holding company's balance sheet does not include the premium it is debatable whether the investment should be described as being at cost, because the amount shown in the balance sheet may be quite different from the actual cost. It could be argued that the 'true' cost of the shares issued is their fair value and not their nominal value. Consequently, the company may need to choose some appropriate wording other than 'cost' to describe the investment (for example, 'at nominal value of shares issued').

Example

A company owns 40% of another company that it acquired for cash several years ago. It decides to acquire the remaining 60% in an exchange for shares. Merger accounting does not apply, but merger relief is available. The company wonders how it should record its investment in the parent company's financial statements.

Even though merger accounting is not available, the parent can record its investment at the nominal value of the shares it issues in exchange for the 60% interest, plus the existing cost of the investment. Alternatively, the fair value of the shares issued can be added to the previous investment cost. The difference between the fair values of the shares issued and their nominal value would then be shown as a merger reserve (as opposed to share premium).

Difference on consolidation

27.92 In merger accounting under the Act the parent's balance sheet will generally show its investment in the subsidiary at the nominal value of the shares that it issued as consideration plus the fair value of any additional consideration.

27.93 A difference may then arise on consolidation between the value at which the parent carries its investment in the subsidiary and the aggregate of the nominal value of the subsidiary's shares that the parent acquires together with any share premium account and capital redemption reserve of the subsidiary (these being the parts of the subsidiary's shareholders' funds that need to be eliminated on consolidation, that is the subsidiary's distributable reserves flow through into the consolidated reserves). The value of the investment will represent the aggregate of the following:

- The nominal value of the 'qualifying shares' issued by the parent in consideration for the acquisition of the shares in the subsidiary. [4A Sch 11(5)(a)]. 'Qualifying shares' means those shares where merger relief is obtained and, consequently, no share premium has to be recorded on them or those shares where group reconstruction relief applies and where, consequently, the appropriate amount is the nominal value together with any minimum premium value as defined in section 132 of the Act. [4A Sch 11(7)].

- The fair value of any other consideration given for the acquisition determined at the date of acquisition. [4A Sch 11(5)(b)].

27.93.1 In the extract from the Movement in Shareholders' Funds statement given in Table 27.2 below, the difference arising on consolidation is shown as £494 million. This has been calculated as the difference between the nominal value of 706 million 25p shares issued by Sun Alliance, that is £176 million, and the share capital and share premium account of the subsidiary Royal Insurance amounting to £670 million.

Table 27.2 – Royal & Sun Alliance Insurance Group plc – Directors' Report and Accounts – 31 December 1996.

Movement in Shareholders' Funds (extract)

	Notes	Share capital/ premium £m	Revaluation reserve £m	Other reserves (see below) £m	Profit and loss account £m	1996 £m	1995 £m
Shareholders' funds at 1st January as previously reported by							
Royal Insurance		670	991	(381)	1,396	**2,676**	1,882
Sun Alliance		377	1,752	–	511	**2,640**	1,768
Merger reserve adjustment		(494)	–	494	–	–	–
Accounting policy alignment	*1d*	–	869	(286)	287	**870**	702
Merged shareholders' funds at 1st January		553	3,612	(173)	2,194	**6,186**	4,352

Other reserves as restated at 1st January represent the cumulative amount of goodwill written off (adjusted for disposals) of £667m and the merger reserve of £494m arising as a result of the merger of Royal Insurance and Sun Alliance on 19th July 1996. As at 31st December 1996 the cumulative amount of goodwill written off (adjusted for disposals) is **£675m**.

Note 31 (extract)
On 14th June 1996 the authorised share capital was increased by the creation of 1,00,000,000 ordinary shares of 25p each. Pursuant to a scheme of arrangement, 706,252,430 shares were issued on 19th July 1996 to former shareholders of Royal Insurance on the basis of 1,067 ordinary shares of 25p each in the Company for every 1,000 Royal Insurance shares of 25p each held.

[The next paragraph is 27.94]

27.94 On consolidation, the inclusion of the subsidiary's share premium account and capital redemption reserve in the set off reflects the fact that these accounts are effectively part of the capital of the subsidiary. Because these amounts are included in the set off, the effect is that the share premium and capital redemption reserve in the consolidated balance sheet will comprise only the amounts from the parent's balance sheet.

27.95 The group should adjust the differences arising on consolidation against other reserves on consolidation and should show the movement in reserves in the reconciliation of movements in shareholders' funds. [4A Sch 11(6); FRS 6 para 18].

27.96 Where the investment's carrying value is less than the nominal value of the shares (plus any share premium and capital redemption reserve of the subsidiary) that the parent company has acquired, the group should treat the difference as an 'other reserve' that arises on consolidation. Where the investment's carrying value is greater than the nominal value of the shares (again plus any share premium and capital redemption reserve) acquired, the difference represents the extent to which the group has effectively capitalised its reserves as a result of the merger. Consequently, the group should reduce its 'other reserves' by the amount of the difference.

27.97 The two examples that follow show how these consolidation differences arise and how they should be treated:

Example 1: Where the carrying value is less than nominal value

Company A acquires all of company B's £200,000 nominal share capital. The purchase consideration consists of new shares that company A issues and these have a nominal value of £190,000. The business combination satisfies all the merger conditions and the group uses merger accounting. The respective balance sheets, after the merger, of the individual companies and the group are as follows:

	Co A	Co B	Group
	£'000	£'000	£'000
Net tangible assets	1,500	1,400	2,900
Investment in subsidiary	190	–	–
	1,690	1,400	2,900
Share capital	400	200	400
Profit and loss account	1,290	1,200	2,490
Difference on consolidation	–	–	10
	1,690	1,400	2,900

The difference on consolidation of £10,000 is calculated as follows:

	£'000
Nominal value of shares acquired	200
Parent company's carrying value of investment	190
Difference on consolidation	10

The group should treat the difference on consolidation as a reserve that arises on consolidation, because the investment's carrying value is less than the nominal value of the shares acquired.

Example 2: Where the carrying value is greater than nominal value

The facts in this example are the same as those in example 1 above, except that the purchase consideration consists of new shares with a nominal value of £250,000. In this example, the respective balance sheets, after the merger, of the individual companies and the group are as follows:

	Co A	Co B	Group
	£'000	£'000	£'000
Net tangible assets	1,500	1,400	2,900
Investment in subsidiary	250	–	–
	1,750	1,400	2,900
Share capital	460	200	460
Profit and loss account	1,290	1,200	2,490
Other reserves	–	–	(50)
	1,750	1,400	2,900

The difference on consolidation of £50,000 is calculated as follows:

	£'000
Nominal value of shares acquired	200
Parent company's carrying value of investment	250
Difference on consolidation	(50)

The investment's carrying value is greater than the nominal value of the shares acquired, and so the group should reduce its reserves by the amount of the difference.

Merger expenses

27.98 Expenses of the merger must not be included in the calculation of the difference arising on consolidation. Merger expenses should instead be charged in the profit and loss account of the combined entity as reorganisation or restructuring expenses in accordance with paragraph 20 of FRS 3. [FRS 6 para 19]. This means that such expenses should be charged as a non-operating exceptional item, if material. An example of this is Table 27.3 which also shows exceptional operating costs arising from reorganisation as a pre-operating profit item.

Table 27.3 – United News & Media plc – Annual Report and Accounts – 31 December 1996

Group profit and loss account (extract)

	Notes	Before exceptional items 1996 £m	Exceptional items (note 4) 1996 £m	Total 1996 £m
Turnover	1			
Continuing operations		1,917.5		1,917.5
Acquisitions		21.0		21.0
		1,938.5		1,938.5
Discontinued operations		52.2		52.2
		1,990.7		1,990.7
Operating costs	2	(1,710.0)	(112.5)	(1,822.5)
Operating profit				
Continuing operations		268.9	(94.4)	174.5
Acquisitions		0.7	(18.1)	(17.4)
		269.6	(112.5)	157.1
Discontinued operations		11.1	–	11.1
		280.7	(112.5)	168.2
Income from interests in associated undertakings		21.2	(62.5)	(41.3)
Income from other fixed asset investments	3	2.2	–	2.2
Total operating profit	1	304.1	(175.0)	129.1
Continuing operations				
Merger expenses			(31.0)	(31.0)
Profit on the disposal of fixed asset investments			11.6	11.6
Discontinued operations				
Profit (loss) on sales and closure of businesses			138.0	138.0
Profit on ordinary activities before interest		304.1	(56.4)	247.7
Net interest expense	5	(13.9)	–	(13.9)
Profit on ordinary activities before tax		290.2	(56.4)	233.8
Tax on profit on ordinary activities	6	(88.6)	12.7	(75.9)
Profit on ordinary activities after tax		201.6	(43.7)	157.9
Minority interests		(5.5)	–	(5.5)
Profit for the year	7	196.1	(43.7)	152.4
Dividends	8			(115.3)
Retained profit for the year	23			37.1
Earnings per share after exceptional items	9			31.1p
Earnings per share before exceptional items	9			40.0p

27.99 The standard does not prohibit such expenses from being subsequently charged to share premium account by means of a reserve transfer from profit and loss account reserve to the share premium account provided the expenses are eligible to be charged to share premium account under section 130 of the Act. The relevant expenses that could be charged subsequently to the share premium account include, for example: the expenses of the issue of shares by the acquiring company; the preliminary expenses of any new parent company formed to effect the merger; and any commission paid on the issue of the shares.

27.100 The question of how merger expenses should be accounted for in the financial statements of the parent company that effects the combination is not dealt with in the standard. If the parent company has a share premium account and wishes to set eligible expenses against that account, it would seem reasonable that it should mirror the treatment on consolidation, by passing the expenses through its own profit and loss account and then making a transfer from the profit and loss account reserve to the share premium account. It could also adopt the treatment required in acquisition accounting by FRS 4 and FRS 7 and write such costs off direct to share premium or to other reserves.

27.101 However, where there is no share premium account or the parent does not wish to write the eligible costs off against that account, there would appear to be a further alternative to writing these and other costs relating to the merger off to the profit and loss account. Because the parent has acquired an asset, the shares in the other party to the combination, it should record that asset at its purchase price and to the purchase price should be added any expenses incidental to its acquisition. [4 Sch 17 and 26(1)].

27.102 The carrying value of the investment in the acquired entity may, therefore, be included in the parent company's balance sheet at the nominal value of shares issued plus the fair value of any other consideration given (where group reconstruction relief is obtained there may be some premium included) plus the expenses that are incidental to the merger. These expenses will of course have to be disregarded when comparing the carrying value of the investment with the nominal value of shares issued in order to determine the difference arising on consolidation that is discussed above. Also in the consolidated financial statements the costs will be charged to the group profit and loss account.

27.103 Any difference between the treatment of merger expenses in the parent's financial statements and those of the group will need to be disclosed in a note to the financial statements together with the reasons for the difference. [4A Sch 4]. An example of such a note where such expenses have been capitalised in the parent is shown below.

Example

Merger expenses of £5 million have been included in the parent company's financial statements as part of the carrying value of the investment in X plc. On consolidation in accordance with the requirements of FRS 6, 'Acquisitions and Mergers', these expenses have been charged to the consolidated profit and loss account. The difference in accounting treatment arises because such expenses may be included in the carrying value of the investment under the provisions of the Companies Act 1985, but must be written off to the profit and loss account on consolidation under the provisions of FRS 6.

27.104 Where relevant merger expenses are added to the carrying amount of investment in the parent's balance sheet care will need to be taken to ensure that the resultant carrying amount does not exceed the investment's recoverable amount. If it did, a provision would be needed against the investment. This might occur if the expenses were very large in relation to the value of the entity with which the parent is combining. However, the fact that the shares issued are recorded at their nominal value, rather than at their fair value, should usually mean that the carrying

[The next page is 27033.]

value including expenses is well below the recoverable amount of the investment and thus no provision will normally be needed.

27.105 The alternative treatment described above of costs that are eligible to be written off against share premium account, that is adding such costs to the carrying value of the investment, differs from the treatment of such costs prescribed by FRS 7 where acquisition accounting and fair valuing are required (see chapter 23). However, as the treatment of expenses on consolidation also differs between merger and acquisition accounting this difference is considered acceptable.

Accounting periods

27.106 Where a new parent company is formed to effect a merger between two companies or to effect a group reconstruction whereby it becomes the parent company of an existing group, problems can arise if the accounting period of the new parent differs from that of the other combining entities. Three examples are given below and two other examples are given above in paragraph 27.70.

Example 1

A new parent company is formed 1 July 19X1 and issues equity shares in exchange for the equity shares of company A. Company A's accounting reference period is the 12 months to December 19X1. The first reference period of the new parent company is fixed as the 6 months to 31 December 19X1. The combination satisfies the conditions for merger accounting.

The question arises as to what figures for company A should be included in the consolidated financial statements, which themselves must cover the period from 1 July to 31 December 19X1.

One argument would be that the consolidated financial statements should include the results of company A for the period from 1 July to 31 December 19X1 with comparatives for the period 1 July to 31 December 19X0. However, this would mean that the group financial statements would omit the 6 months trading of company A from 1 January 19X1 to 30 June 19X1. This would not be consistent with the principle of merger accounting, which is explained in FRS 6 as follows:

> *"In merger accounting the financial statements of the parties to the combination are aggregated, and presented as though the combining entities had always been part of the same reporting entity".* [FRS 6 para 41].

Paragraph 2 of Schedule 4A of the Act requires that the consolidated balance sheet and profit and loss account shall incorporate in full the information contained in the individual financial statements of the undertakings included in the consolidation, subject to the adjustments authorised or required by the Schedule and to such other adjustments as may be appropriate in accordance with generally accepted accounting principles or practice.

Based on this provision of the Act, and because there do not appear to be any adjustments that would be required by the Schedule or generally accepted accounting principles or practice, we consider that in the situation described above the results of company A should be included in the consolidated financial statements for the full accounting reference period of company A. Thus the consolidated financial statements for the 6 months to 31 December 19X1 would include the results of the new parent for 6 months and the results of company A for 12 months. The comparative figures for the consolidated financial statements under merger accounting would comprise the profit and loss account, cash flow statement and balance sheet of the new subsidiary for the year to 31 December 19X0.

Example 2

A similar approach would be adopted if the new parent company were formed on 1 October 19X0 and had its first year end on 31 December 19X1, a 15 month accounting period.

In this case the consolidated financial statements for the 15 months to 31 December 19X1 would include the new parent for 15 months from 1 October 19X0 and company A's results for its accounting reference period of one year from 1 January 19X1 to 31 December 19X1. Comparative figures would most sensibly be for the year to December 19X0 as this would give a continuous record for the combined group. (There would be no duplication of the new parent company's results on the reasonable assumption that it will not have traded in the period to 31 December 19X0.)

27.107 As the above two examples demonstrate, the apparent problems that arise, where the accounting periods of the new parent and the other combining entity are different, can be overcome. It is obviously much simpler, however, to arrange that where a new parent company is to be formed and merger accounting is to be adopted it should have the same accounting period as the company that it combines with.

27.108 Where no new parent company is involved, but the year ends of the combining companies differ, again problems may arise.

Example

Company A, which has a year end of 31 December, combines with company B which has a year end of 30 September. Company A is preparing consolidated financial statements for the year ended 31 December 19X5, the year in which the merger took place. There are three apparent possibilities at first sight in respect of inclusion of company B's results.

(i) Include the results of company B for the year ended 31 December 19X5 based on interim accounts prepared by company B for the 12 months to that date. This is permitted by Schedule 4A paragraph 2(b) to the Companies Act 1985 which states:

"If the financial year of a subsidiary undertaking included in the consolidation differs from that of the parent company, the consolidated accounts shall be made up –

> *(a) from the accounts of the subsidiary undertaking for its financial year last ending before the end of the parent company's financial year provided that year ended no more than three months before that of the parent company, or*
>
> *(b) from interim accounts prepared by the subsidiary undertaking as at the end of the parent company's financial year."*

The comparatives for the year ended 31 December 19X4 would similarly include the results of company B for the year ended on that date based on interim accounts for 12 months.

(ii) Include the results of company B for the 15 months ended 31 December 19X5 with the comparative figures for the year ended 31 December 19X4 including company B for the 15 months ended on that date again based on interim accounts. This approach is not appropriate as it would involve double counting of company B's results for the period from September 19X4 to December 19X4.

(iii) Include the results of company B for the 12 months to September 19X5 with the comparatives similarly including the results of company B for the 12 months to September 19X4. Although permitted by the Act (because the year end of company B is not more than three months before that of the parent) it should be noted that FRS 2 requires that interim accounts should be prepared to 31 December, the parent's year end, unless it is impracticable to do so. Therefore, this approach should only be adopted in the rare circumstances where it is impracticable to prepare interim accounts.

Of the three possibilities, therefore, (i) is the appropriate treatment in all cases except where it is impracticable in which case (iii) would be adopted. The treatment in (ii) should not be adopted.

Comparison of acquisition accounting with merger accounting

27.109 FRS 6 highlights the following three main differences between acquisition accounting and merger accounting:

- In acquisition accounting, the consolidated financial statements reflect the acquired company's results from the date of acquisition only. However, in merger accounting, the consolidated financial statements incorporate the combined companies' results and cash flows as if the companies had always been combined. Consequently, under merger accounting, the consolidated financial statements reflect both companies' full year's results, even though the business combination may have occurred part of the way though the year. Under merger accounting, the corresponding amounts in the consolidated financial statements for the previous year should reflect the results of the combined companies, even though the business combination did not occur until the current year.

- In acquisition accounting, the acquiring group should account for the assets it acquired at the cost to the acquiring group. The acquiring group determines that cost by attributing a fair value to the assets and liabilities that it acquires. However, in merger accounting, the group does not restate any assets and liabilities at their fair values. Instead, the group incorporates the assets and liabilities at the amounts recorded in the books of the combining companies. As in the profit and loss account presentation, merger accounting shows the position of the combining companies as if the companies had always been combined.

- Acquisition accounting may give rise to goodwill on consolidation. However, goodwill does not arise in merger accounting. Merger accounting may lead to differences on consolidation. For example, in merger accounting, there may be a difference between the nominal value of the shares issued together with the fair value of any additional consideration given, and the nominal value of the other company's shares that have been acquired (see paras 27.92 to 27.97). However, such differences are not goodwill as defined in SSAP 22 (revised), because they are not based on the fair values of both the consideration given and the identifiable assets and liabilities acquired.

27.110 The following example illustrates the difference between acquisition accounting and merger accounting. The example is somewhat artificial in that it shows both methods applying to the same situation whereas in practice under FRS 6 there is no choice between the methods of accounting. The combination will either have to be acquisition accounted or it will have to be merger accounted. The method will depend on whether or not all the conditions for merger accounting in FRS 6 are met.

Example

Company H (the issuing company) acquires the whole of company A's equity share capital. The effect of the acquisition will be to merge the interests of company H and company A.

Company A's shareholders accept an offer from company H of 400,000 shares in company H for the 410,000 issued shares in company A as at 31 December 19X0. The value at 31 December of the 400,000 of company H's £1 shares that are offered to company A's shareholders is £6.4 million, (that is, £16 per share). The fair value of company A's net assets is £6.1 million (that is, £90,000 above their net book value). The difference of £300,000 is attributable to goodwill. On 31 December 19X0, before the acquisition, the summarised balance sheets of the two companies are as follows:

	Co H	Co A
	£'000	£'000
Net assets	5,000	6,010
Share capital (shares of £1 each)	500	410
Reserves	4,500	5,600
	5,000	6,010

The summarised consolidated balance sheets of the issuing company and its subsidiary under the two methods of accounting are as follows:

	Notes	Acquisition accounting £'000	Merger accounting £'000
Goodwill on consolidation	(a)	300	–
Net assets	(b)	11,100	11,010
		11,400	11,010
Share capital	(c)	900	900
Distributable reserves	(e)	4,500	10,100
Merger reserve	(d)	6,000	
Other reserves	(f)	–	10
		11,400	11,010

Notes to the example above:

(a) Goodwill on consolidation is the amount by which the purchase consideration (that is, 400,000 shares at £16, or £6.4 million) exceeds the fair value of the underlying net assets acquired (that is, £6.1 million).

(b) Net assets are the two companies' total net assets. In acquisition accounting, the assets acquired are included at their fair value, as required by the Act and FRS 2. In merger accounting the assets of the combining companies are not fair valued.

(c) The share capital consists of the 500,000 shares originally in issue, together with the 400,000 shares allotted when company H combined with company A.

(d) The amount credited to the merger reserve taking merger relief under section 131 of the Act is £6 million (that is, 400,000 shares issued at a premium of £15 per share).

(e) Under merger accounting there is no requirement to transfer to a merger reserve the premium on the shares allotted to the acquired company's shareholders. Consequently, both companies' distributable reserves are pooled. In accordance with the Act and paragraph 16 of FRS 6 the excess of the fair value of company A's net assets over their book value (that is, £90,000) need not be incorporated into the consolidated financial statements.

(f) Under merger accounting the difference between the nominal value of shares issued (that is, £400,000) and the nominal value of shares received as consideration (that is £410,000) is credited to other reserves. Had the carrying value of the investment exceeded the nominal value of the shares received as consideration the difference would be debited to reserves.

27.111 The example that follows illustrates the differences between using acquisition accounting and using merger accounting in a group reconstruction where the group reconstruction qualifies for relief under section 132.

Example

In 19X1, company A acquired all of company C's issued share capital (100,000 £1 shares) for £390,000. Company C had no reserves at that time. On 31 December 19X5, another wholly-owned subsidiary (company B) allots 100,000 £1 shares to company A. In return for the allotment, company A transfers to company B the shares in company C that it owns. Subsequently, company A is to be liquidated, and its shareholders will receive shares in company B. At the time of the reconstruction, company B's shares that are issued to company A are worth £400,000 (that is, £4 per share) and the fair value of company C's recorded net assets is £360,000 (the difference of £40,000 being attributed to goodwill). The fair value of company A's and company B's net assets is equal to their book value.

Diagrammatically, the reconstruction is as follows:

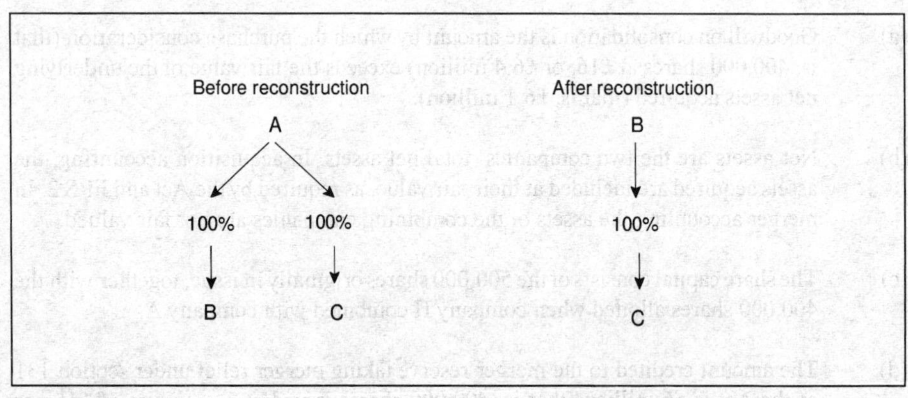

The individual balance sheets of the three companies as at 31 December 19X5 before the reconstruction are as follows:

	Co A £'000	Co B £'000	Co C £'000
Investment in B*	210	–	–
Investment in C*	320	–	–
Net assets	–	700	350
	530	700	350
Share capital (shares of 1 each)	150	200	100
Reserves	380	500	250
	530	700	350

*The investments are stated at the cost of shares to company A, reduced for company A's investment in company C by a write-down of £70,000 made in 19X2.

After the reconstruction, the summarised consolidated balance sheet of company B and its subsidiary company C is as follows:

	Notes	Acquisition accounting £'000	Merger accounting £'000
Goodwill on consolidation	(a)	40	–
Net assets	(b)	1,060	1,050
		1,100	1,050
Share capital	(c)	300	300
Share premium account	(d)	220	220
Merger reserve	(e)	80	–
Reserves	(f)	500	530
		1,100	1,050

Notes to the example above:

(a) Goodwill on consolidation is the amount by which the purchase consideration (that is, 100,000 shares at £4, or £400,000) exceeds the fair value of the underlying assets acquired (that is, £360,000). Under merger accounting, goodwill does not arise, because the net assets' fair value need not be incorporated in the consolidated financial statements.

(b) Company C's net assets are included at their fair value when they are accounted for as an acquisition. But when they are accounted for as a merger, they are included at their book value.

(c) The share capital consists of the 200,000 shares originally in issue, together with the 100,000 shares allotted on company B's acquisition of company C.

(d) Under section 132 of the Act, the issuing company is required to transfer to the share premium account only an amount equal to the minimum premium value. The minimum premium value is calculated as the amount by which the base value of the shares in company C, that are transferred from company A to company B, exceeds the aggregate nominal value of the shares that company B allots in consideration for the transfer. The amount of the transfer to the share premium account is calculated as follows:

	£'000	£'000
The base value of shares in company C is the lower of:		
The cost of the shares to company A	390	
The amount at which those shares are stated in company A's accounting records immediately before the transfer	320	
		320
Less: Nominal value of the shares company B allotted in respect of the transfer		100
Transfer to the share premium account		220

(e) The amount credited to the merger reserve under acquisition accounting is the amount of the premium that is not required to be taken to the share premium account because of section 132 relief (that is, 100,000 shares issued at a premium of £3, or £300,000 less £220,000 required to be taken to share premium under section 132).

(f) Under acquisition accounting, the amount to be included in other reserves is the amount of company B's reserves (that is, £500,000). Under section 132 of the Act (which gives the relief in respect of group reconstructions) other reserves are made up as follows:

	£'000
Reserves of company B	500
Reserves of company C less minimum premium value (that is, £250,000 – £220,000)	30
	530

Disclosure for merger accounting

Consolidated financial statements

27.112 The issuing company should disclose certain information in respect of all material mergers. The parent must disclose in the consolidated financial statements that deal with the period in which the merger occurs:

- The names of the merging companies (other than the reporting entity). [4A Sch 13(2)(a); FRS 6 para 21 (a)]. The Act goes on to add that where the issuing company has merged with a group of companies, only the name of the group's parent needs to be disclosed.

- That the company adopted merger accounting for the combination. [4A Sch 13(2)(b); FRS 6 para 21(b)].

- The effective date of the merger. [FRS 6 para 21(c)].

27.113 In addition, further information is required to be disclosed for mergers that significantly affect the figures shown in the consolidated financial statements. The FRS 6 disclosures listed below do not apply to group reconstructions (but the Act's disclosure requirements *do* apply even where they are the same as in FRS 6). [FRS 6 para 82]. These requirements are as follows:

- The composition and the fair value of the consideration given by the parent and its subsidiaries. [4A Sch 13(3); FRS 6 para 22(c)].

- An explanation of any significant adjustments made to the assets and liabilities of the undertaking or group acquired. This should include a statement of any resulting adjustment to the consolidated reserves (including a restatement of opening consolidated reserves). [4A Sch 13(6); FRS 6 para 22(f)]. The figures above should be disclosed after taking into account the consolidation adjustments required by the Act. [4A Sch 13(7)]. This would include for example adjustments to achieve uniform accounting policies.

- The nature and the amount of significant accounting adjustments made to the net assets of any party to the merger to achieve consistent accounting policies and an explanation of any other significant adjustments made to the net assets of any party to the merger as a consequence of the merger. [FRS 6 para 22(e)].

- The aggregate book value of the net assets of each party to the merger at the effective date of the merger. [FRS 6 para 22(d)].

27.114 If in the directors' opinion the disclosure of any of the information above that is required by the Act (relating to an undertaking established under the law of a country, or one that carries on a business, outside the UK) would be seriously prejudicial to the business of the undertaking, its parent or its fellow subsidiaries, it need not be given if the Secretary of State's permission is obtained. [4A Sch 16].

27.115 In addition in respect of a material merger, other than a group reconstruction, the issuing company should disclose the following information in its financial statements that deal with a year in which a merger occurs:

- An analysis of the principal components of the current year's profit and loss account and statement of total recognised gains and losses into:
    - amounts relating to the merged entity for the period after the date of the merger; and
    - for each party to the merger, amounts relating to that party for the period up to the date of the merger.
- An analysis between the parties to the merger of the principal components of the profit and loss account and statement of total recognised gains and losses for the previous financial year.

[FRS 6 paras 22(a)(b)].

27.116 The standard specifies the headings that comprise the principal components of the profit and loss account and statement of total recognised gains and losses for the purposes of the disclosure requirements. These are:

- Turnover analysed between continuing operations (with acquisitions disclosed separately) and discontinued operations.
- Operating profit analysed in the same way as turnover.
- Exceptional items analysed in the same way as turnover.
- Profit before taxation.
- Taxation and minority interests.
- Extraordinary items (highly unlikely under FRS 3).

[FRS 6 para 22].

27.117 The principal components of the statement of total recognised gains and losses, whilst not specified in the FRS, would usually be:

- Profit for the financial year.
- Exchange gains or losses taken direct to reserves.
- Revaluation surpluses or deficits.
- Total recognised gains or losses.

27.118 In relation to the category of revaluation surpluses or deficits, the standard makes it clear that the requirement for disclosure does not mean that revaluations carried out at the end of a financial year would need to be repeated at the effective date of merger.

[The next paragraph is 27.121]

Example

An example of the extensive disclosure that might result from compliance with the requirements of the FRS and the Act is as follows:

XYZ plc merged with ABC plc on 30 June 19X1 and has accounted for the combination using merger accounting. The consideration was satisfied by the issue of £400,000 equity shares with a nominal value of £1 each. The fair value of the consideration was £5m based on the market price of XYZ plc shares at 30 June 19X1. No significant adjustments were made to the assets and liabilities of ABC plc which have been recorded at their book values immediately prior to the merger and no adjustments were made to the net assets of XYZ plc. The book value of net assets of XYZ plc and ABC plc at the date of the combination were £1.2m and £1m respectively. The difference of £50,000 arising on consolidation between the nominal value of XYZ plc shares issued (£400,000) and the nominal value of ABC plc shares acquired (£450,000) has been credited to reserves. ABC's financial year began on 1 January 19X1.

The analysis of the principal components of the profit and loss accounts and statements of total recognised gains and losses is as follows:

19X1	**Combined post merger £m**	**XYZ plc pre merger £m**	**ABC plc pre merger £m**	**Total for the year £m**
Profit and loss account				
Turnover				
Continuing	27	12	13	52
Acquisitions	4	—	1	5
Total continuing	31	12	14	57
Discontinued	1	1	—	2
	32	13	14	59

Operating profit				
Continuing	4	2	1	7
Acquisitions	1	–	–	1
Total continuing	5	2	1	8
Discontinued	(1)	–	–	(1)
	4	2	1	7
Exceptional items				
Discontinued operations				
Loss on sale of subsidiaries	(1)	–	–	(1)
Profit before taxation	3	2	1	6
Taxation	1	1	–	2
Profit after taxation and for the financial period	2	1	1	4
Total recognised gains and losses				
Profit after taxation and for the financial period	2	1	1	4
Exchange (losses)/gains	1	(1)	–	–
Revaluation surplus	3	–	–	3
Total recognised gains	6	–	1	7

The equivalent analysis for the previous year is as follows:

19X0	**XYZ plc £m**	**ABC plc £m**
Profit and loss account		
Turnover		
Continuing	20	23
Discontinued	3	–
	23	23
(There were no acquisitions in 19X0)		
Operating profit		
Continuing	3	4
Discontinued	(1)	–
	2	4
(there were no post operating profit exceptional items in 19X0)		
Profit before taxation	2	4
Taxation	–	1
Profit after tax and for the financial year	2	3
Total recognised gains and losses		
Profit after tax and for the financial year	2	3
Exchange (losses)/gains	(1)	1
Revaluation surpluses	3	4
Total recognised gains	4	8

27.121 Interest has been ignored in the above example. Also the totals for 19X1 are not required as they appear in the profit and loss itself, but have been given above to enable the figures for the pre-acquisition and post-acquisition periods to be reconciled. Further disclosure requirements that may apply if a merger has occurred are set out in chapter 26.

27.121.1 A further example of the disclosures described above is Table 27.4.

Table 27.4 – United News & Media plc – Annual Report and Accounts – 31 December 1996

Accounting policies (extract)

Merger with MAI plc On 8 February 1996, United News & Media plc (United) and MAI plc (MAI) announced plans for the merging of their respective businesses. The merger was to be effected by way of offers made by United for the whole of the issued share capital of MAI. These offers became unconditional on 2 April 1996. The merger has been accounted for using the merger accounting principles set out in Financial Reporting Standard 6. Accordingly, the financial information for the current period has been presented, and that for the prior year restated, as if MAI had been owned by United throughout the current and comparative accounting periods.

Note 24

24. Merger adjustments The merger adjustments reflect the alignment of accounting policies following the merger:

(a) Intangible assets – in previous periods publishing rights and titles had been stated at directors' valuation. These are now stated at fair value on acquisition and are not revalued. The effect of this restatement is a debit adjustment to the revaluation reserve of £73 million. The comparative figures for 1995 have been restated.

(b) Consolidation – on acquisition of subsidiary undertakings, business or associated undertakings the purchase consideration is allocated between underlying assets on a fair value basis. Any goodwill arising is written off direct to reserves. Previously in MAI the goodwill relating to certain associates was amortised over its expected economic life. The effect of this restatement is a debit adjustment to goodwill of £27.7 million. The comparative figures for 1995 have been restated.

Note 29

29.Business merger As explained in the accounting policies, on 8 February 1996, United and MAI announced plans for the merging of their respective businesses. The merger was to be effected by way of offers made by United for the whole of the issued share capital of MAI, being 332,718,123 ordinary shares of 5 pence each and 120,956,330 preference shares of 5 pence each, for a consideration of 242,090,550 ordinary shares of 25 pence each, the fair value of which amounted to £1,560.3 million. These offers became unconditional on 2 April 1996. The merger has been accounted for using the merger accounting principles set out in Financial Reporting Standard 6. Accordingly the financial information for the current period has been presented, and that for the prior periods restated, as if MAI had been owned by United throughout the current and prior accounting periods.

The book value of net assets at the time of the merger together with adjustments arising from the alignment of accounting policies were:

	£m
United	
Book value of net assets at time of merger	238.0
Merger adjustment (note 24)	(73.0)
Restated net assets at time of merger	165.0
MAI	
Book value of net assets at time of merger	224.6
Merger adjustment (note 24)	(27.7)
Restated net assets at time of merger	196.9

29. Business merger continued

An analysis of contribution to the profit attributable to shareholders made by the combining groups in the period prior to the merger date on 2 April 1996, the principal components of the profit and loss accounts and statements of total recognised gains and losses is as follows:

	United pre merger	MAI pre merger	Combined post merger	Total
Profit and loss account	£m	£m	£m	£m
Turnover				
Continuing operations	268.8	196.9	1,451.8	1,917.5
Acquisitions	2.7	–	18.3	21.0
Discontinued operations	6.8	14.6	30.8	52.2
	278.3	211.5	1,500.9	1,990.7
Operating profit				
Continuing operations	21.4	23.5	129.6	174.5
Acquisitions	0.7	–	(18.1)	(17.4)
Discontinued operations	0.2	4.0	6.9	11.1
	22.3	27.5	118.4	168.2
Income from interests in associated undertakings	1.9	3.9	(47.1)	(41.3)
Income from other fixed asset investments	0.6	–	1.6	2.2
Total operating profit	24.8	31.4	72.9	129.1
Merger expenses	–	–	(31.0)	(31.0)
Profit on the disposal of fixed asset investments	–	11.6	–	11.6
Profit on sales and closure of businesses	–	–	138.0	138.0
Profit on ordinary activities before interest	24.8	43.0	179.9	247.7
Net interest expense	(4.0)	(1.0)	(8.9)	(13.9)
Profit before tax	20.8	42.0	171.0	233.8
Tax	(6.8)	(14.0)	(55.1)	(75.9)
Profit after tax	14.0	28.0	115.9	157.9
Minority interest	–	(0.2)	(5.3)	(5.5)
Profit for the year	14.0	27.8	110.6	152.4
Total recognised gains and losses				
Profit for the year	14.0	27.8	110.6	152.4
Exchange gains	–	–	1.4	1.4
	14.0	27.8	112.0	153.8

The equivalent analysis for the year ended 31 December 1995 is as follows:

Profit and loss account	United £m	MAI £m	Total £m
Turnover			
Continuing operations	1,032.9	768.2	1,801.1
Discontinued operations	37.7	52.6	90.3
	1,070.6	820.8	1,891.4
Operating profit			
Continuing operations	111.2	89.1	200.3
Discontinued operations	3.9	12.8	16.7
	115.1	101.9	217.0
Income from interests in associated undertakings	0.9	12.9	13.8
Income from other fixed asset investments	3.3	–	3.3
Total operating profit	119.3	114.8	234.1
Loss on sales and closures of businesses	(2.9)	–	(2.9)
Profit on ordinary activities before interest	116.4	114.8	231.2
Net interest expense	(11.9)	(4.0)	(15.9)
Profit before tax	104.5	110.8	215.3
Tax	(34.3)	(36.0)	(70.3)
Profit after tax	70.2	74.8	145.0
Minority interest	(1.5)	1.4	(0.1)
Profit for the year	68.7	76.2	144.9
Total recognised gains and losses			
Profit for the year	68.7	76.2	144.9
Exchange losses	(0.5)	–	(0.5)
	68.2	76.2	144.4

[The next paragraph is 27.122.]

The holding company's financial statements

27.122 The appendix to FRS 6 entitled 'Legal requirements' states that the FRS does not deal with the form of accounting to be used in the acquiring or issuing company's own financial statements. However, this is discussed above in paragraphs 27.83 to 27.91. Chapter 26 deals with the disclosure requirements relating to the holding company's financial statements where merger relief is taken under the Companies Act.

Chapter 28

Associates, joint ventures and joint arrangements

Page

Chapter 28

Associates, joint ventures and joint arrangements

Introduction

28.1 The Accounting Standards Committee (ASC) issued its first Statement of Standard Accounting Practice (SSAP 1) on accounting for associated companies in 1971. The ASC at that time recognised that where a company conducts an important part of its business through the medium of other companies, the mere disclosure of dividend income from those companies was unlikely to be sufficient to give adequate information regarding the sources of income and the manner in which their funds were being employed. This concern gave birth in the UK to the equity method of accounting for associate interests. This basis of accounting recognises that through the investor's long-term significant influence over its associate it has a measure of direct responsibility for the return on its investment. Furthermore, that basis also recognises that the investor has an interest in its share of the reserves of its associate and is not merely interested in a dividend stream.

28.2 The equity accounting method required by SSAP 1 called for the investing group to reflect its share of its associates' profits and losses in the group's consolidated profit and loss account. This was supplemented by the investor's share of its associates' tax and, where the associate was material, additional information such as share of turnover was required to be given in the notes to the financial statements. The investing group's share of its associates' net assets and premium or discount arising on acquisition was also required to be included in the group's consolidated balance sheet as a one line item, which was then, in certain circumstances, expanded in the notes where the associates were particularly material to the group.

28.3 Equity accounting for associates has stood the test of time with only minor amendments over the years and it was further endorsed by its incorporation into international accounting in November 1988 by the issue of International Accounting Standard (IAS) No. 28, 'Accounting for investments in associates'.

Participating interests

28.4 The Companies Act 1981 introduced a term 'related companies', which was very similar to the term 'associated companies' as defined in SSAP 1. However, it was possible to have a related company that was not an associate and vice versa. The term 'related companies' was replaced in the Companies Act 1989 by the term 'undertakings in which the company has participating interests'. On consolidation, this item is further split under the Companies Act between 'interests in associated undertakings' and 'other participating interests'. Consequently, the legislation still envisages that there could be situations where a participating interest may be held in an undertaking that is not an associated undertaking, although in practice this is rare.

28.5 The meaning of the term 'participating interest' under the Act has become integral in determining whether or not an investment is an associated undertaking. A participating interest in an undertaking is necessary before it could be judged to be an associate. Furthermore, it is presumed under the Act, unless otherwise shown, that a participating interest exists where the investing company holds more than 20 per cent of the voting rights in another undertaking.

Companies Act 1989 and interim statement

28.6 The Companies Act 1989, which incorporated the EU's 7th Directive into UK company law, brought with it the statutory requirement to equity account associated undertakings and most joint ventures. Following the introduction of that Act, the Accounting Standards Board (ASB) issued an Interim Statement as a temporary measure to deal with the anomalies that existed between the legislation and SSAP 14 and SSAP 1. The anomalies concerning consolidations were dealt with when SSAP 14 was superseded by FRS 2, but certain paragraphs of the Interim Statement amending those of SSAP 1 remained in existence.

28.7 Joint ventures had not previously been dealt with in legislation prior to the 1989 Act. Until that time there had only been a fleeting reference in SSAP 1 to joint ventures and no detail as to how they should be accounted for. Following the Companies Act 1989, it was possible for groups to account for their unincorporated joint ventures on a proportional consolidation basis (although equity accounting was also allowed under the Act for such investments). Proportional consolidation is the consolidation on a line by line basis of the parent's proportionate share of the investee undertaking's individual assets and liabilities as well as its profits and losses. The 1989 Act, however, required all incorporated joint ventures to be equity accounted in the same way as for associated undertakings.

28.8 The term 'joint venture' was not defined in SSAP 1 and at that time the ASB decided that the Act's general description could usefully be supplemented by a definition, which it included in its Interim Statement. The Interim Statement also mentioned that in the Act a joint venture is described essentially as an undertaking jointly managed by one undertaking included in the consolidation with one or more undertakings not included in the consolidation. It went on to say that the Act's term 'joint management' could more aptly be described as 'joint control'. It pointed out that the Act's provisions do not require the joint venturers to be involved in the day-to-day operations of the venture's business. Also, the Act does not preclude the venture being managed by a single operator.

ASB discussion paper

28.9 Following the introduction of the 1989 Act, there had been growing concern regarding whether equity accounting was still appropriate for certain interests. These concerns, together with the need to revise SSAP 1 to update it for the changes made in the Interim Statement, culminated in a project by the ASB to undertake a fundamental review of how associates and joint ventures should be accounted for. The ASB had been concerned for some time that SSAP 1 was increasingly being interpreted as requiring equity accounting at the 20 per cent investment threshold instead of there being a proper assessment of whether of not the investor actually exerted significant influence over its investee. It was also concerned that the information given by the equity method of accounting, particularly the one line presentation in the balance sheet, was inadequate and equity accounting was being used as a form of off balance sheet finance.

28.10 The ASB's initial proposals were issued in the form of a discussion paper on 'Associates and joint ventures', published in August 1994, which proposed some radical changes to the way in which associates and joint ventures should be accounted. It proposed a notion of 'strategic alliances', a term that encompassed partnership interests, joint ventures and a significantly restricted set of associates that had similar characteristics. The paper suggested that only 'strategic alliances' should be equity accounted and their results included within operating activities. The intention was to reduce significantly the set of interests that could be accounted for as associates. The ASB believed at the time that it was unsatisfactory to include in the investor's profit and loss account its share of profits of its associate if the two were relatively uninvolved with each other and in particular if the investor had little or no access to the cash flows of the associate beyond the dividend. Equity accounting was favoured for all strategic alliances and proportional consolidation was not – even for joint ventures. In addition, the proposals were to extend significantly the note disclosures.

28.11 Many commentators criticised the proposals, although there was sympathy for narrowing the set of interests that would be regarded as associates, but not to the extent of getting out of line with international practice, which required a wider set of associates to be equity accounted (equivalent to those equity accounted under SSAP 1). Also some of the disclosures proposed were criticised as being excessive and unnecessary.

28.12 One of the main issues where commentators on the discussion paper expressed concern was with the proposals for accounting for the increasing number of joint ventures. The only reference in SSAP 1 stated that equity accounting *"need not be* *applied to interests in partnerships or non-corporate joint ventures where such arrangements have features which justify accounting for a proportionate share of individual assets and liabilities as well as profits and losses"* (that is, proportional consolidation). Many commentators supported this approach.

FRED 11

28.13 FRED 11, 'Associates and joint ventures', was published by the ASB in March 1996. It represented a significant move away from the radical proposals made in the ASB's discussion paper. The FRED 11 proposals were more in line with SSAP 1, except that there were certain conditions that had to be complied with in determining whether the investor had significant influence over its associate. Under the proposals it would no longer be assumed that a holding of 20 per cent or more would lead automatically to an associate relationship. Generally, joint ventures would be equity accounted.

28.14 The form of equity accounting proposed in FRED 11 was to include the share of associates' operating profit within the group's operating result and then in the line items that follow to require the inclusion of the group's share of its associates. Respondents to the FRED pointed out that this looked like a form of proportional consolidation in the profit and loss account. They also pointed out that the profit and loss account interest included the share of associates' interest, which meant that the profit and loss account did not articulate with the balance sheet, as the related debt was included only as part of the one line share of associates' net assets. In addition, the FRED proposed extensive disclosures, which were to apply depending on whether or not associates and joint ventures in aggregate or individually exceeded certain thresholds.

28.15 Although there was general acceptance that equity accounting should be used for associates and the move back to the wider set of interests this covered rather than the strategic alliance approach, many respondents to the FRED fundamentally disagreed that this basis should also be used to account for joint ventures (whether incorporated or not). The only reason put forward in the FRED for rejecting proportional consolidation appeared in the development section, where the ASB said that: *"Proportional consolidation is inappropriate for most joint ventures because the venturer controls its investment in the joint venture, its share of the venture, rather than controlling its share of each of the individual assets and liabilities of the joint venture"*. This argument ran counter to the recognition of assets in FRS 5 where it has become more common to recognise interests in assets, which includes the recognition of a proportionate share of an asset. Also, proportional consolidation overcame the criticism levelled at equity accounting; that is, it could be used as an off balance sheet financing technique. So, many accountants believed that proportional consolidation was a preferable method of accounting for all joint ventures and did not agree with the ASB's arguments for rejecting it.

28.16 The ASB's proposals in the FRED only required proportional consolidation in one particular situation. The one exception related to shared facilities and in this respect the ASB was considering proposing a change to the law to allow proportional consolidation of a small number of incorporated joint ventures. The responses to FRED 11, however, confirmed that many accountants believed that such a change to the law should have been extended to all incorporated joint ventures.

Associated Nursing Services plc

28.17 There was also another reason for clarifying the definition of a joint venture. Following concerns stemming from the Financial Reporting Review Panel's (FRRP) press notice on Associated Nursing Services plc it was unclear whether Associated Nursing Services' joint ventures would have been classified as such under the definition in FRED 11. This was an important issue, because many accountants knowing very little about the detail of this case were confused by the ruling. For example, it was unclear how joint venture agreements interact with the statement in FRS 5 paragraph 34, which states that *"where the financial and operating policies of a vehicle are in substance pre-determined, contractually or otherwise, the party possessing control will be the one that gains the benefits arising from the net assets of the vehicle"*. A party having control in such a situation would have had to consolidate the joint venture in full as a subsidiary and show a minority interest, which was what was required of Associated Nursing Services plc. This issue is considered from paragraph 28.197.

FRS 9

28.18 FRS 9 was published by the ASB on 27 November 1997. Following from the proposals in FRED 11, under FRS 9 associates are slightly more restrictively defined than in SSAP 1 and a new definition of joint venture entities is introduced. The standard's objective is to reflect the effect on an investor's financial position and performance of its interests in two special kinds of investments – associates and joint ventures – for whose activities it is partly accountable, because of the closeness of its involvement:

- In associates, as a result of its participating interest and significant influence.
- In joint ventures, as a result of its long-term interest and joint control.

[FRS 9 para 1].

The FRS also deals with joint arrangements that do not qualify as associates or joint ventures, because they are not entities.

28.19 Under FRS 9 all associates and joint venture entities are required to be equity accounted. But the distinction between associates and joint ventures is now important, because the standard requires a different type of presentation for joint ventures called the 'gross equity method' and separate disclosure for associates and joint ventures. Proportional consolidation does not feature at all in the standard even for shared facilities; instead a new category of investment – a joint arrangement that is not an entity – is introduced. Consequently, it is also necessary to identify these joint arrangements separately from associates and joint ventures, as a new set of accounting requirements apply to them.

28.20 The 'gross equity' method is a new requirement in the standard having not been previously exposed for comment. Under this method, the investor's share of joint ventures' turnover must be disclosed (equivalent disclosure for associates is optional). In addition, under the gross equity method the investor's share of joint ventures' gross assets and gross liabilities must be shown on the face of the balance sheet before the investor's share of associates' net assets. Other than these two additional disclosures, the gross equity accounting requirements are identical to those for associates using the normal equity accounting method.

28.21 Another change to the proposals in FRED 11 is that the investor's share of investees' operating results is now required to be included immediately after the group operating result, not before it as proposed in FRED 11. In addition, the investor's share of super-exceptionals, interest and tax must be separately disclosed.

28.22 Similar disclosure thresholds are used to those outlined in FRED 11, but the required disclosures are slightly less onerous. Additional disclosures arise where the investor's share in its associates in aggregate (or in its joint ventures in aggregate) exceeds 15 per cent, or individually 25 per cent, of the group's: gross assets; gross liabilities; turnover; or operating results (on a three-year average).

28.23 As mentioned above, a new category of investment – joint arrangement that is not an entity – was introduced in FRS 9 and the accounting requirements had not been exposed for comment before the standard was published. An investor in such an entity should account for its own transactions in accordance with the terms of the agreement. Similarly, a participant in a joint venture structure used as a framework within which each participant carries on its own business should also account for its own transactions in accordance with the terms of the agreement.

28.24 This chapter considers in detail the distinction between associates and joint ventures and then from paragraph 28.67 looks at how to account for them. Other joint arrangements and their accounting requirements are considered from paragraph 28.169.

Scope

28.25 FRS 9's requirements apply to all financial statements that are intended to give a true and fair view of the reporting entity's financial position and profit or loss (or income and expenditure) for the period. [FRS 9 para 2]. The standard is effective for accounting periods ending on or after 23 June 1998, although early adoption is encouraged. [FRS 9 para 59].

28.26 A new issue arising for the first time in this standard is how to apply the standard's provisions to small entities now that the Financial Reporting Standard for Smaller Entities (FRSSE) applies to them. The FRS states that such entities are exempt from the standard's requirements, unless they prepare consolidated financial statements. Somewhat surprisingly it then goes on to state that, where the entity does prepare consolidated financial statements, it should apply the accounting standard that is required to be used by the FRSSE *currently in issue*. [FRS 9 para 3]. The FRSSE currently in issue requires such entities to adopt SSAP 1. Therefore, until such time as the FRSSE is updated to incorporate the requirements of FRS 9, small companies to which the FRSSE applies can ignore the effective dates noted in the paragraph above and continue to account for associates and joint ventures using the provisions of SSAP 1. As small companies are unlikely to prepare consolidated financial statements, this will only affect the information reported concerning associates and joint ventures in the company's individual financial statements.

Investment funds

28.27 For a number of years prior to FRS 9's introduction, problems had arisen in the venture capital industry, where companies often invest in high risk start-up ventures and look for capital growth rather than an income return. As a consequence, the industry views valuation information as relevant and equity accounting as irrelevant. This issue led to a number of companies in that sector adopting the Act's true and fair override in order not to equity account such investments, which was a requirement of both the Act and SSAP 1. Following consultation with the Association of Investment Trust Companies (AITC) and others, the ASB now accepts that in such entities, whilst the interests held by the investor and the rights attaching to those interests vary according to particular circumstances, the investor's relationship to its investment tends to be that of a portfolio investor. [FRS 9 para 50]. The standard now requires that, in these circumstances, the stake is properly accounted for as an investment using the same accounting policy as that applied to other investments in the entity's investment portfolio, rather than accounting for the interests as associates or joint ventures. This applies even where the investor has significant influence or joint control. [FRS 9 paras 49, 50].

28.28 The standard explains that: *"Investments are held as part of an investment portfolio if their value to the investor is through their marketable value as part of a basket of investments rather than as media through which the investor carries out its business"*. [FRS 9 para 49]. Consequently, investments of this nature are specifically exempted from FRS 9's requirements to equity account associates and joint ventures. However, it does appear that such investments might still fall to be treated as associates under the Act. This will depend on whether or not the investor has significant influence. Significant influence is defined in FRS 9 (see para 28.37) and this definition applies also to associated undertakings under the Act. The investor will exercise significant influence if it is actively involved and influential in the direction of its investee. In those situations where a company adopts FRS 9's relaxation in respect of its associates and joint ventures included in its investment portfolio, if the investor still exercises significant influence over those undertakings after the introduction of FRS 9, it should still recognise a departure from the Act by giving the particulars, reasons and effect as required by the Act and expanded upon in UITF Abstract 7, 'True and fair override disclosures' (see further chapter 2). Now, however, the reason should include the fact that FRS 9 specifies the accounting treatment to be adopted.

28.29 Investment companies might also have investments that should be treated as joint ventures and associates that are held outside their investment portfolio. Such joint ventures and associates often carry on businesses which are similar or complementary to those of the investor. In these circumstances, the provisions of FRS 9 should be applied and such joint ventures and associates should be equity accounted in accordance with the normal rules as explained below.

Classification as associates and joint ventures

28.30 As mentioned above, equity accounting applies to both associates and joint venture entities. However, under FRS 9 joint venture entities must give slightly more information using the 'gross equity method' of accounting than associates. Therefore, the distinctions between the two types of arrangement are important and the paragraphs below explain the definitions that apply in determining whether an investment is an associate or a joint venture entity.

Definition of associate

28.31 The term associate is defined in both the Companies Act and in FRS 9. The definition in FRS 9 seeks to reduce the number of entities which would have fallen before its introduction to be equity accounted under the Act and SSAP 1. The Act's definition hinges on the investing company having a participating interest and exercising significant influence.Under the legislation a participating interest is presumed to exist where the investing company holds more than 20 per cent of the voting rights in the other undertaking. This presumption is rebutted under FRS 9, which sets out a more stringent test to determine whether there is a participating interest. But where the Act's presumptions are rebutted the investor should explain the facts in the financial statements (see para 28.100 below).

28.32 An 'associated undertaking' is defined in the Act in the following terms:

> *"... an undertaking in which an undertaking included in the consolidation has a participating interest and over whose operating and financial policy it exercises a* significant influence, *and which is not-*
> *(a) a subsidiary undertaking of the parent company, or*
> *(b) a joint venture dealt with in accordance with paragraph 19."*
> [4A Sch 20(1)].

28.33 'Participating interest' is defined in section 260(1) of the Act to mean *"... an interest held by an undertaking in the shares of another undertaking which it holds on a long-term basis for the purpose of securing a contribution to its activities by the exercise of control or influence arising from or related to that interest"*.

28.34 The meaning of 'shares' in the definition is explained in section 259(2) of the Act. For this purpose, references to shares in relation to:

- An undertaking with a share capital, are to allotted shares.
- An undertaking with capital in a form other than share capital, are to rights to share in the capital of the undertaking.
- An undertaking without capital, are to interests:
  - conferring any right to share in the profits or the liability to contribute to the losses of the undertaking; or
  - giving rise to an obligation to contribute to the debts or expenses of the undertaking in the event of a winding up.

[Sec 259(2)].

28.35 In addition, it is quite clear under the Act that a participating interest includes an option to acquire shares or any interest that is convertible into shares. [Sec 260(c)]. For this purpose, it does not matter whether the options can be exercised now or in the future, their mere existence is taken into account whether or not they are currently exercisable. An interest or option in shares falls within this definition even if the share to which it relates, until conversion or the exercise of the option, is unissued. [Sec 260(3)]. In addition, interests held on behalf of an undertaking or by, or on behalf of, any of its subsidiary undertakings should be treated as held by it. [Sec 260(4), (5)(a)].

28.36 The definition of 'participating interest' is also applicable to other participating interests that the group might have (see para 28.4) and, furthermore, applies to the definition of subsidiary for consolidation purposes where the group exercises dominant influence or manages the undertaking on a unified basis (see further chapter 21).

28.37 The definition of 'associated undertakings' in the Act is consistent with that given in FRS 9 for an associate. The definition in FRS 9 is also expressed making reference to the need for both a participating interest and the exercise of significant influence as follows:

> *"An entity (other than a subsidiary) in which another entity (the investor) has a* participating interest *and over whose operating and financial policies the investor* exercises a significant influence.*"* [FRS 9 para 4].

28.38 Therefore, it is essential to have both a participating interest and be able to exercise significant influence and these two terms are also defined in the standard. A participating interest is:

> *"An interest held in the shares of another entity on a long-term basis for the purpose of securing a contribution to the investor's activities by the exercise of control or influence arising from or related to that interest. The investor's interest must, therefore, be a beneficial one and the benefits expected to arise must be linked to the exercise of its significant influence over the investee's operating and financial policies. An interest in the shares of another entity includes an interest convertible into an interest in shares or an option to acquire shares."* [FRS 9 para 4].

The term 'shares' in the definition has the same meaning as explained in paragraph 28.34 above.

28.39 As mentioned above, the Act presumes there is a participating interest where the investor holds 20 per cent or more of the shares in the undertaking. However, whilst both the Act and FRS 9 require the interest to be for the long term, FRS 9 introduces a very restrictive interpretation of the meaning of 'long-term'. Under FRS 9, an interest held on a long-term basis is one that is *not* 'held exclusively with a view to subsequent resale' and the latter term is defined in the standard as: *"...(a) an interest for which a purchaser has been identified or is being sought, and which is reasonably expected to be disposed of within approximately one year of its date of acquisition; or (b) an interest that was acquired as a result of the enforcement of a security, unless the interest has become part of the continuing activities of the group or the holder acts as if it intends the interest to become so"*.[FRS 9 para 4]. Table 28.1 includes an example of an associate which is held for resale. The standard comments that 'enforcement of a security' should be interpreted to include other arrangements that, in substance, have the same effect.

Table 28.1 – Granada Group PLC – Annual report and accounts – 27 September 1997

Notes to the accounts (extract)

12 Investments

e The investment in Savoy comprises 69.7% of the 'A' shares and 12.6% of the 'B' shares, representing 68.4% of the equity of Savoy and 42.1% of the voting rights. During the period Savoy was accounted for as an investment as it is not the Group's intention to hold this investment for the long term. As at 31 December 1996, Savoy had share capital and reserves amounting to £372.1 million and the loss for the financial year then ended amounted to £26.8 million.

28.40 The effect of the requirement for the investment to be for the long term on short-term property development investments, which might run for (say) up to 18 months, is considered in paragraph 28.177.

28.41 The 20 per cent presumption in the Act is also rebutted where the interest is a non-beneficial one. In judging whether an interest is, or is not, a beneficial one, dividends are not the only way that a beneficial interest might be enjoyed. There may be other ways of extracting benefits, for example, through a management contract with a fee that is based on performance, which would make the receiver of the fee more than just a manager.

28.42 The other essential element to the definition of an associate is that the investor must exercise a 'significant influence' over the entity's financial and operating policies for there to be an associate relationship. The Act similarly presumes that the investor will have significant influence where the investor holds more than 20 per cent of the voting rights in the undertaking. [4A Sch 20(2)]. Whilst the Act does not define 'significant influence' FRS 9 does. The definition in FRS 9 is more stringent than in its predecessor SSAP 1 and is the chief reason why fewer undertakings than before will now qualify as associates. The definition of 'significant influence' in FRS 9 is as follows:

> *"The investor is actively involved and is influential in the direction of its investee through its participation in policy decisions covering aspects of policy relevant to the investor, including decisions on strategic issues such as:*
> *(a) the expansion or contraction of the business, participation in other entities or changes in products, markets and activities of its investee; and*
> *(b) determining the balance between dividend and reinvestment."*
> [FRS 9 para 4].

28.43 It is often difficult in practice to determine whether there is an associate relationship with an undertaking. FRS 9 indicates that significant influence over a company essentially involves participation in the financial and operating policy decisions of that company, but the standard is looking for a higher level of participation than might have arisen under the old definition of an associate in SSAP 1. It mentions that for significant influence to exist it must generally have a substantial basis of voting power and a holding of 20 per cent of more of the voting rights does not in itself ensure this level of influence. [FRS 9 para 16]. That is, even where the investing group holds more than 20 per cent of the voting rights it might not have significant influence. This situation could also arise where one or more other large shareholders could prevent the group exercising 'significant influence'. This might arise, for example, where the investor holds 25 per cent of the shares, but another entity holds the remaining 75 per cent (see for example Table 28.2). On the other hand, FRS 9 also confirms that it is not necessary to control those policies for an associate relationship to exist (otherwise the investment would be a subsidiary). In order to gain the level of influence necessary, representation on the board of directors (or its equivalent for unincorporated entities) is essential in most circumstances, unless it is clear that there are other arrangements in place that would allow the investor to participate effectively in policy-making decisions. [FRS 9 para 16].

Table 28.2 – Galliford plc – Annual Report & Accounts – 30 June 1997

Notes to the Accounts (extract)

25 Associated undertakings and other participating interests (extract)

The group's 25% interest in Rapid Transport International plc has not been treated as an associated undertaking as the company is controlled by its majority shareholders and, in the opinion of the directors, the group does not, at present, exercise significant influence over its operations.

28.44 In order to obtain significant influence, the investor needs an agreement or understanding, formal or informal, with its associate to provide the basis for its significant influence. The investor must be actively involved in the operating and financial policy decisions – a passive role is clearly not sufficient. The type of relationship that is necessary is one whereby the investor uses its associate as a medium through which it conducts a part of its activities, although it is not envisaged that the associate need be in the same business as the investor. The associate's policies over time should accord with (and not be contrary to) the investor's strategy. Consequently, if an investee persistently implements policies that are inconsistent with its investor's strategy, no associate relationship exists. [FRS 9 para 14].

28.45 Significant influence means that the investor must be involved in strategic decisions, for example, determining the balance between dividend and reinvestment.

Furthermore, the investor should not only be interested in maximising the payment of dividends, but should also be concerned that the entity's future cash flows are compatible with the investor's objective of reinvestment. The investor's participation in policy decisions should be with a view to gaining economic benefits from the entity's activities, but this involvement should also expose the investor to the risk that those activities might be loss-making. [FRS 9 para 15].

Example

A group has a 30% investment in a company at the beginning of the year. It has previously been treated as an associated company in the group's financial statements. Another shareholder increases his shareholding in the company during the year from 40% to 60%. The group no longer wishes to treat its investment in the undertaking as an associate.

As explained above following the stricter definitions introduced in FRS 9, where the investment in another undertaking is greater than 20%, it will no longer be presumed that the undertaking is an associate. In this situation, if the group can demonstrate that it no longer has a significant influence over the undertaking then it may be necessary to treat the investment as a trade investment rather than as an associate.

28.46 A practical problem arises in judging the amount of influence the investor has over its investment where the investment has only just been made. In these circumstances the actual relationship usually becomes clear fairly soon after an investment is acquired. In the intervening period the number of board members the investor may nominate and the proposed decision-taking process may be used to evaluate the relationship before its record is established. [FRS 9 para 17]. If the actual relationship were to develop differently from that assumed from the arrangements on acquisition, it would be necessary subsequently to change the way in which the investment is accounted. For example, if it looked at the outset as if the entity were an associate, then it would have been equity accounted in the first financial statements produced post acquisition. If subsequently it was judged that this analysis did not prove to be correct in practice, then it would be necessary to treat the interest in the entity as an investment. This might, therefore, indicate that there was a fundamental error in accounting for the investment as an associate in the previous year and require a prior year adjustment. However, in practice, this is only likely to arise when the investment is made close to the investor's year end, in which case the profits brought in in error would be small.

28.47 Furthermore, where an investing group treats an undertaking as an associate where it controls less than 20 per cent of the votes, it is even more important following FRS 9's publication to ensure that it can clearly demonstrate that it has significant influence. But it is undoubtedly possible even under FRS 9's stricter definitions for significant influence to exist where the investing group controls less than 20 per cent of the voting shares. An example of an investment below 20 per cent which has been treated as an associate because of significant influence prior to FRS 9's introduction is given in Table 28.5 on page 28032.

28.48 An associate relationship can also arise where a company was initially legally a subsidiary of its investor, but the investor no longer controls the operating and financial policies of the undertaking. This could occur, for example, where the investor's interest is 40 per cent and in the past it has exercised dominant influence over the undertaking and it was, as a consequence, a subsidiary under the Act. Although there is no change in the shareholding, the investor's influence has reduced and it now exerts only significant influence and is, therefore, an associate. A similar situation is illustrated in Table 28.3 and contrasted with an example of a less than 50 per cent interest and dominant influence making the undertaking a subsidiary.

Table 28.3 – Lonrho Plc – Annual Report and Accounts – 30 September 1996

Principal Group companies
Including Associates (extract)

* LOMACO is a subsidiary under the Companies Act, but, because the company represents an equal joint venture between the Government of Mozambique and the Lonrho Group, the investment has been accounted for under the equity method of accounting.

** John Holt Plc. is a 45 per cent owned company in which the Group's interest is considered to be long-term and substantial, and in which the Group is in a position to exercise, through representation on the board, a dominant influence on commercial and financial policy decisions. As such the company is considered to be a subsidiary undertaking under the provisions of the Companies Act 1985.

Treatment of voting rights

28.49 The Act gives a significant amount of guidance on when to take into account voting rights in order to determine whether an associate relationship exists between two undertakings. The paragraphs that follow summarise the guidance given in the Act.

28.50 For the purposes of the definition of an associated undertaking, 'voting rights in the undertaking' means the rights conferred on the shareholders in respect of their shares to vote at general meetings of the undertaking on all, or substantially all, matters. It can also mean, in a situation where the undertaking has no share capital, any other rights conferred on members to vote at the undertaking's general meetings on all, or substantially all, matters. [4A Sch 20(3)].

28.51 Voting rights should not be treated as held by a person (which includes an undertaking) if they are held in a fiduciary capacity. [4A Sch 20(4), 10A Sch 6]. Similarly, voting rights held by a person as nominee should not be treated as held by him. Such voting rights will be considered held 'as nominee' if they can only be exercised on the instructions or with the consent of another person. [4A Sch 20(4), 10A Sch 7(2)]. It is not possible to treat voting rights held by a parent undertaking as held by a subsidiary by using nominee holdings. [4A Sch 20(4), 10A Sch 9(2)].

28.52 Voting rights that are attached to shares held as security shall be treated as held by the person providing the security where those voting rights (excluding any right to exercise them to preserve the value of the security, or to realise it) are only exercisable in accordance with his instructions. This rule applies where the shares are held in connection with granting loans in the normal course of business and the rights are exercised only in the interest of the person providing the security. [4A Sch 20(4), 10A Sch 8]. This provision cannot be used to require voting rights held by a parent to be treated as held by any of its subsidiaries. [4A Sch 20(4), 10A Sch 9(2)]. Furthermore, voting rights should be treated as being exercisable in accordance with the instructions, or the interests of, an undertaking if they are exercisable in accordance with the instructions of, or in the interests of, any group undertaking. [4A Sch 20(4), 10A Sch 9(3)].

28.53 The voting rights in an undertaking have also to be reduced by any voting rights held by the undertaking itself. [4A Sch 20(4), 10A Sch 10].

Definition of joint venture entities

28.54 Although joint ventures are required under FRS 9 to be equity accounted, the level of detail that investors in joint ventures are required to give in their consolidated financial statements is greater than for investments in associates. Therefore, it is important that investors categorise their investments correctly between those in associates and those in joint ventures. FRS 9 makes a distinction between joint venture entities and joint arrangements that are not entities. Joint arrangements that are not entities are not equity accounted and their accounting requirements and how to distinguish them from other forms of joint venture are considered from paragraph 28.169.

28.55 Particular care needs to be taken in assessing whether an undertaking is a joint venture entity or a joint arrangement (under FRS 9), or a subsidiary undertaking (under FRS 2), or a quasi-subsidiary (under FRS 5). As mentioned earlier an FRRP ruling in February 1995 concerned joint ventures which were determined to be quasi-subsidiaries. The implications of this case for joint ventures and joint arrangements is considered from paragraph 28.197. The paragraphs that follow look at the definitions found within both the Act and FRS 9 concerning joint ventures.

28.56 Under the Act, paragraph 19(1) of Schedule 4A refers to a joint venture arising in a situation where an *undertaking* manages another undertaking jointly with one or more other undertakings that are not included in the consolidation. Consequently, the Act places emphasis on the undertaking's *joint management*. But the Act's provisions concerning joint ventures do not apply if the joint venture undertaking is a limited company, as proportional consolidation for joint ventures is only allowed for unincorporated undertakings under the Act. Also, the Act's provisions concerning joint ventures do not apply where the undertaking is a subsidiary for consolidation purposes under the definitions in the Act (see further chapter 21). [4A Sch 19(1)].

28.57 FRS 9 defines a joint venture in the following terms:

> *"An entity in which the reporting entity holds an interest on a long-term basis and is* jointly controlled *by the reporting entity and one or more other venturers under a contractual arrangement."* [FRS 9 para 4].

28.58 As can be seen from the definition, the interest must be held on a long-term basis and this is to be judged in the same way as for associates (see para 28.39 above). The definition also hinges on the term 'joint control' which is defined in FRS 9 as follows:

> *"A reporting entity jointly controls a venture with one or more other entities if none of the entities alone can control that entity but all together can do so and decisions on financial and operating policy essential to the activities, economic performance and financial position of that venture require each venturer's consent."* [FRS 9 para 4].

28.59 This definition can be contrasted with 'control', which was originally defined in FRS 2 and is repeated in FRS 9 as: *"The ability of an entity to direct the operating and financial policies of another entity with a view to gaining economic benefits from its activities"*. [FRS 9 para 4].

28.60 Although to be treated as a joint venture partner the investor must have joint control with its other investors, the standard envisages the situation whereby *one* of the parties to a joint venture might not share control with the other joint venturers. In this type of situation, the investor that does not share control would account for its interest as an investment. [FRS 9 para 10]. The other venturers would gross equity account for their interests in accordance with the standard.

28.61 The standard explains that in a true joint venture the venturers exercise their joint control for their mutual benefit, each conducting its part of the contractual arrangement with a view to its own benefit. The venturers must play an active role in setting the operating and financial policies of the joint venture. However, their involvement can be at quite a high level, for example, setting the general strategy of the venture. [FRS 9 para 11]. But their interest should not necessarily only occur at the outset of a venture, for example, in setting the general policies to be included within a partnership agreement. If this were to be the case, then the financial and operating policies might be predetermined, in which case the entity could be a joint arrangement or a quasi-subsidiary (see further para 28.197).

28.62 It seems clear from the definition that it is quite possible to have a joint venture between investors where the venturers do not have equal shares in the entity, as long as they control the entity jointly together. For example, it would be possible to have an arrangement whereby the investors' interests were 30:35:35 or 25:35:40. But there must be joint control including the ability for one party to veto the wishes of the other parties. For example, the 25 per cent shareholder would have to have the ability to veto the financial and operating policies being advocated by the other two venturers owning 75 per cent of the shares. In this type of situation, one of the parties might manage the venture under a management agreement and, in this circumstance, it is important to establish clearly that the veto can be applied in practice.

28.63 The standard also does not preclude a venturer from managing the joint venture provided that the venture's principal operating and financial policies are collectively agreed by the venturers and the venturers have the power to ensure that those policies are followed. [FRS 9 para 11]. This is often the case in the venture capital industry, where it is common for the venture capitalist investor to have an interest in the joint venture, but also to manage the venture *via* a separate management agreement.

28.64 The standard also points out that in some cases an investor may qualify as the parent of an entity under the definition of a subsidiary in the Act and FRS 2, but contractual arrangements with the other shareholder mean that in practice the shareholders have joint control over their investee. [FRS 9 para 11]. For example, a company might control over 50 per cent of the entity's voting rights, but the joint venture agreement might significantly restrict this control. It could, for example, require unanimous agreement between the venturers before it could: pay a dividend; change direction of the company's business; incur capital expenditure over a specified level; pay its directors and other employees; change other major operating and financial policies, etc. In this type of situation, the interests of the minority shareholder (the other joint venture partner) would amount to 'severe long-term restrictions' that would substantially hinder the exercise of the parent's rights over the assets or management of its legal subsidiary. In such cases, following from the requirements in FRS 2, the standard requires that the subsidiary should not be consolidated, but should instead be treated as a joint venture and be gross equity accounted. [FRS 9 para 11]. For example, see Table 28.3 on page 28014. However, this type of situation is unlikely to arise frequently in practice, because even where there is such a shareholders' agreement, unless it does impose a significant restriction (which it will not if the agreement means the subsidiary follows the parent's wishes) it will remain a subsidiary.

28.65 Joint control of high-level strategic decisions will entail each venturer having a veto on those decisions. Such a veto distinguishes a joint venturer from a minority shareholder in a company, because the latter has no veto and, consequently, is subject to majority rule. [FRS 9 para 12]. It is the practical application of this which is important and, hence, it is not necessary that the consent to strategic decisions is set out in the joint venture agreement, although in many instances this will be the case in practice. One indication that the arrangement might be a joint venture is where the joint venture agreement sets out arbitration procedures in the event the parties to the venture cannot agree.

28.66 IAS 31, 'Financial reporting of interests in joint ventures', issued in January 1991 defines a joint venture in similar terms to those used in FRS 9: *"a contractual arrangement whereby two or more parties undertake an economic activity which is subject to joint control"*. IAS 31 comments that it is this contractual arrangement that distinguishes a joint venture from an associate and without a contractual arrangement to establish joint control a joint venture does not exist. Such a contractual arrangement can be evidenced in a number of ways, for example, by: contract; minutes of discussions between the venturers; or incorporation in the joint venture's articles or other by-laws. The matters that such an agreement might deal with are:

- The joint venture's activity, duration and reporting obligations.
- The appointment of the joint venture's board of directors or equivalent governing body and the voting rights of the venturers.
- Capital contributions by the venturers.
- The sharing by the venturers of the joint venture's output, income, expenses and results.

[IAS 31 para 5].

Equity method of accounting

Introduction

28.67 FRS 9 specifies that equity accounting is the method that should be used to reflect investors' interests in both associates and joint ventures. The form of presentation under this method has been extended for joint ventures and this is referred to in FRS 9 as the 'gross equity method'. The requirements for equity accounting are more extensive than previously required by SSAP 1 and also differ from the form of equity accounting required by IAS 28, 'Accounting for investments in associates'. The Act also stipulates that associated undertakings should be accounted for by the 'equity method' of accounting, but leaves it to the accounting standard to specify what this method entails. [4A Sch 22(1)].

28.68 There is now an extensive definition in FRS 9 which explains what the equity method of accounting involves. It describes the equity method as:

> *"A method of accounting that brings an investment into its investor's financial statements initially at its cost, identifying any goodwill arising. The carrying amount of the investment is adjusted in each period by the investor's share of the results of its investee less any amortisation or write-off for goodwill, the investor's share of any relevant gains or losses, and any other changes in the investee's net assets including distributions to its owners, for example by dividend. The investor's share of its investee's results is recognised in its profit and loss account. The investor's cash flow statement includes the cash flows between the investor and its investee, for example relating to dividends and loans."* [FRS 9 para 4].

28.69 The 'gross equity method' is identical in most respects with the normal equity method, but it requires in addition that the investor's share of the aggregate gross assets and liabilities underlying the net equity investment be shown on the face of the balance sheet [FRS 9 para 4]. Consequently, it is not adequate to disclose this information in the notes to the consolidated financial statements. In addition, in the profit and loss account, the investor's share of the investee's turnover has to be given. [FRS 9 para 4].

28.70 The disclosures required for both the equity method and the gross equity method have to be given separately. The information relating to the investor's share in its joint ventures must be given separately and before that relating to its share in its associates.

Profit and loss account

28.71 Under FRS 9's requirements, there are a number of line items in the profit and loss account for which the investor's share of its joint ventures' and its associates' results have to be included and disclosed. The requirements cover primarily:

- Turnover (but optional disclosure for associates).
- Operating profit.
- Super-exceptional items as specified in paragraph 20 of FRS 3.
- Interest.
- Taxation.

Turnover

28.72 As explained above, the gross equity method requires that the investor's share of turnover for joint ventures must be shown. [FRS 9 para 21]. Equivalent disclosure for associates is not required, but may be given where it is helpful to give an indication of the size of the business as a whole. [FRS 9 para 27]. The standard specifically states that joint ventures' and associates' turnover cannot be shown as part of group turnover, because the Act requires turnover to be disclosed excluding amounts attributable to associates and joint ventures. [Sec 262(1)]. So it is important that the turnover is shown in such a way that the group turnover excluding joint ventures and associates is clearly disclosed. Table 28.4 shows how this might be done. The example is pre-FRS 9, but shows joint ventures and other associated companies separately.

Table 28.4 – The General Electric Company, p.l.c. – Annual Report and Accounts – 31 March 1998

Consolidated Profit and Loss Account (extract)

For the year ended 31st March, 1998		Note	**1998 £ million**	1997 £ million
Turnover				
Group turnover	– retained business	2	**5,875**	5,458
	– disposals	2	**394**	1,039
Share of turnover of:				
Joint ventures		11	**4,514**	4,438
Associates			**318**	212
		1	**11,101**	11,147

28.73 In addition, in the segmental analysis required by SSAP 25, the joint ventures' turnover (and associates' turnover where disclosed voluntarily) should be distinguished clearly from that of the group. [FRS 9 paras 21, 27]. Segmental reporting is dealt with in chapter 9.

Operating results

28.74 The share of operating results of joint ventures and associates must be included *immediately* after the group's operating result. [FRS 9 paras 21, 27]. Before the introduction of FRS 9, SSAP 1's requirements were not as specific and it was possible to show the share of associates' and joint ventures' results before or after operating profit.

28.75 Unlike goodwill arising on an acquisition of a subsidiary, there is nothing in the Companies Act that specifies where goodwill arising on the acquisition of an interest in a joint venture or an associate should be amortised in the profit and loss account. As a consequence, the ASB has determined in FRS 9 that any amortisation or write-down of goodwill (that arose on the acquisition of a joint venture or an associate) should be charged at the same point as the share of operating results of associates and joint ventures. [FRS 9 para 21, 27]. This would seem to allow any amortisation or write-down of goodwill to be aggregated with the share of operating results on the face of the profit and loss account as a single item. But where this is done, the goodwill amortised or written off must be separately disclosed in the notes to the financial statements.

Super-exceptional items

28.76 The investor's share of joint ventures' and associates' super-exceptional items appearing after operating profit must be shown with the group's super-exceptionals, but separately from them. [FRS 9 paras 21, 27]. The super-exceptional items specified in FRS 3 are know as 'paragraph 20 items' and cover:

- Profits or losses on the sale or termination of an operation.
- Costs of a fundamental reorganisation or restructuring having a material effect on the nature and focus of the reporting entity's operations.
- Profits or losses on the disposal of fixed assets.

Other line items

28.77 The standard also specifies that the investor's share of joint ventures' and associates' interest must be shown separately from the amounts of the group. [FRS 9 para 21, 27]. In addition, for the line items that appear in the Act's formats at and below the level of profit before tax, the standard specifies that the investor's share of its joint ventures' and associates' equivalent line items must be included within the amounts for the group. This would include, for example, the investor's share of its joint ventures' and associates' taxation. Although the standard says that these amounts should be included with those of the group, it still requires separate disclosure of the investor's share of each such item for its joint ventures and its associates.

How the Act's requirements are satisfied

28.78 In addition to FRS 9's requirements, the Act indicates the position in the profit and loss account formats where associated undertakings (which includes joint venture entities) should be dealt with. In the profit and loss account formats shown in Schedule 4 to the Act, for the purposes of consolidated financial statements, the item 'income from shares in related companies' is replaced by 'income from interests in associated undertakings' and 'income from other participating interests'. [4A Sch 21(3)]. Although the position is specified in the formats, companies can draw their operating profit line before 'income from interests in associated undertakings'.

This is because the formats do not contain a line item for operating profit. However, as can be seen from the explanation above, FRS 9 requires the line item in the Act to be split between share of: operating result (which must be shown immediately after the group's operating profit or loss); three super-exceptional items; interest; taxation and any further line items below profit before tax. There is nothing in the standard that explains how this anomaly is overcome, but appendix IV example 1 explains that the amounts shown for associates and joint ventures are subdivisions of the item for which the statutory prescribed heading is 'Income from interests in associated undertakings'. Paragraph 3(1) of Schedule 4 to the Act allows format line items to be shown in greater detail than required by the profit and loss account format adopted and there is nothing in the legislation that specifies that such additional analysis needs to be summed to show the total for the particular line item required by the formats.

Ability to aggregate and relegate to the notes

28.79 It is not at all clear from the standard which elements of the disclosures considered above have to be shown on the face of the profit and loss account and which can be relegated to the notes. The only help on this issue is again given in appendix IV example 1 which notes that subdivisions for which the statutory prescribed heading is 'Income from interests in associated undertakings' may be shown in a note rather than on the face of the profit and loss account. This seems to imply that all the disclosures specified above can be relegated to the notes and yet the example in FRS 9 that directly follows the note shows each of the required disclosures with the exception of taxation on the face of the profit and loss account (albeit the example does not include any super-exceptional items). In addition, all of these disclosures show the share of joint ventures' and associates' results separately on the face of the profit and loss account, which for many groups would be impracticable because of printing space constraints. To further compound the issue, the Act requires that 'Income from interests in associated undertakings' in the formats should be treated as if it is preceded by an Arabic numeral. Under the format rules, which are discussed in chapter 6, items preceded by an Arabic numeral can be relegated to the notes.

28.80 We therefore suggest the following practical solution to the issues raised above:

- The share of joint ventures' turnover should be shown separately from that of the group on the face of the profit and loss account in order to comply with the Act's requirements (as explained in para 28.72 above). It is also possible, however, to show a total figure for turnover including joint ventures, as long as joint ventures' turnover and the group's turnover excluding that of its joint ventures is clearly shown.

- Where the share of associates' turnover is disclosed voluntarily, it should be shown on the face of the profit and loss account, but may be combined with that of joint ventures, but must be separately analysed in the notes. It is also possible to give a total for the group's turnover including both joint ventures and associates as long as the group's turnover excluding that of its associates and joint ventures is clearly shown.

- Share of operating results of joint ventures and associates should be shown on the face of the profit and loss account, but may be combined in a single line item 'share of joint ventures and associates operating profit' as long as they are shown separately in the notes, with the share of joint ventures' operating results shown first.

- Amortisation or the write-down of goodwill arising on the acquisition of joint ventures or associates should be included within 'share of joint ventures and associates operating profit'. There should be separate disclosure of this item in the notes.

- Share of each super-exceptional item of joint ventures and associates should be shown separately on the face of the profit and loss account below any super-exceptional items of the group. (Immaterial amounts should be aggregated with the share of their operating results.) For each super-exceptional item, the investor's share of joint ventures' and associates' figures may be combined in a single line item suitably styled on the face of the profit and loss account, but should be shown separately in the notes, with the joint ventures' share shown first.

- Share of interest and format line items below the level of profit before tax should be included within the amounts shown on the face of the profit and loss account for the group. The share should then be separately disclosed in the notes, with the share of joint ventures' items shown first.

- In addition, the share of results of associates and joint ventures have to be analysed between continuing activities (including acquisitions) and discontinued activities as required by FRS 3 (see further chapter 7).

Illustrative example

28.81 An illustration of this type of disclosure is given below:

Consolidated profit and loss account

		Continuing operations			Discontinued operations	
			Acquisitions	Total		Total
	Notes	£m	£m	£m	£m	£m
Turnover including share of joint ventures and associates		250	50	300	20	320
Less: Share of joint ventures and associates turnover	1	105	10	115	5	120
Group turnover		145	40	185	15	200
Cost of sales		89	23	112	8	120
Gross profit		56	17	73	7	80
Administrative expenses		28	4	32	8	40
Group operating profit (loss)		28	13	41	(1)	40
Share of operating profit of joint ventures and associates	2	52	3	55	(1)	54
Operating profit including joint ventures and associates		80	16	96	(2)	94
Sale of operations:						
Group					20	20
Joint ventures and associates	3	—	—	—	(15)	(15)
		—	—	—	5	5
Profit on ordinary activities before interest		80	16	96	3	99
Interest						(42)
Profit on ordinary activities before tax	5					57
Tax on profit on ordinary activities						12
Profit on ordinary activities after tax						45
Minority interests						6
Profit for the financial year						39
Equity dividends						10
Retained profit for the year						29

The notes to the financial statements would analyse the line items above to give the disclosures required by the standard as follows:

1. Turnover (extract)	Continuing operations			Discontinued operations	
		Acquisitions	Total		Total
	£m	£m	£m	£m	£m
Share of joint ventures' turnover	30	10	40	–	40
Share of associates' turnover	75	–	75	5	80
	105	10	115	5	120
2. Operating profit (extract)					
Share of joint ventures' operating profit	27	3	30	–	30
Share of associates' operating profit	25	–	25	(1)	24
	52	3	55	(1)	54
3. Profit/loss on sale of operations (extract)					
Share of joint ventures' profit on sale of operations				21	21
Share of associates' loss on sale of operations				(36)	(36)
				(15)	(15)
4. Interest (extract)				£m	£m
Interest receivable (group)					6
Interest payable:					
Group				(26)	
Joint ventures				(10)	
Associates				(12)	(48)
					(42)
5. Taxation (extract)		3			£m
Group					(5)
Joint ventures					(5)
Associates					(2)
					(12)

Statement of total recognised gains and losses

28.82 The investors' share of its joint ventures' and associates' other gains and losses included in the statement or total recognised gains and losses (STRGL) must also be disclosed where they are material. The requirement would apply, for example, to the investor's share of any revaluation surpluses of its joint ventures and associates reported in their STRGLs. Here the standard is more helpful in that it states specifically that such amounts should be: *"shown separately under each heading, if the amounts are material, either in the statement or in a note that is referred to in the statement"*. [FRS 9 paras 21, 28]. The requirement is still to disclose separately the investor's share of joint ventures' relevant amounts from those of its associates and in that order, but this detail can be given in the notes to the financial statements.

Statement of total recognised gains and losses

	Notes	£m
Profit for the financial year		39
Unrealised surplus on revaluation of properties	6	25
Currency translation differences on foreign net investment		(8)
Other recognised gains and losses relating to the year		17
Total recognised gains and losses for the year		56

Notes to the financial statements

6 Fixed assets (extract)

The revaluation gains arising in the year are analysed as follows:

Group	19
Joint ventures	(8)
Associates	14
	25

Balance sheet

28.83 Unless it is shown at a valuation, the amount at which the investing company's interest in its joint ventures or its associates should be shown in the investing company's own financial statements is the cost of the investment less any amounts written off, as explained in chapter 16. [FRS 9 paras 20, 26].

28.84 The amount at which the investing group's interests in joint ventures and associates should be shown in the group's consolidated balance sheet is the value under the 'equity method' of accounting, being the total of:

- The investing group's share of the net assets (other than goodwill) of the joint ventures and associates, stated after attributing fair values to the net assets at the time the interests in the joint ventures and associates were acquired.

- The goodwill (or negative goodwill) arising on the acquisition of the interests in the joint ventures and associates, insofar as it has not already been written off or amortised.

[FRS 9 paras 21, 29].

28.85 It is not appropriate, once the balance sheet interest has been ascertained using the equity method of accounting as explained above, to then revalue the investment in the associate or joint venture to its market value, even where the entity is listed. This method was adopted by Foreign and Colonial Investment Trust plc before the introduction of FRS 9. The FRRP issued a press notice in April 1996 in respect of the company's December 1994 financial statements. At issue was the adequacy of the *explanation* given for a departure from equity method of accounting in the balance sheet treatment of an associate, which was carried at a directors' valuation. Following discussions with the FRRP, the directors gave a fuller explanation of the departure and its effect in their 1995 financial statements. The departure from SSAP 1 was explained in the 1995 group accounts as follows:

> *"Hypo Foreign and Colonial Management (Holdings) Limited ('HFCM'), the group's associated undertaking, is accounted for in the revenue account using the equity method prescribed in SSAP 1. The carrying value is restated in the consolidated balance sheet at directors' or market valuation, to be consistent with the group's accounting policy for investments.*
>
> *As the investment in HFCM forms part of the group's investment portfolio, the directors believe adoption of the equity method in the balance sheet would not show a true and fair view. The effect of this departure from SSAP 1 is set out in note 12 on the accounts."*

We considered at the time that this was an odd ruling, because whilst criticising the disclosure the FRRP appeared to be condoning adoption of a policy for the balance sheet (that is, valuation) that was inconsistent with the policy adopted for the revenue account (that is, equity accounting). We consider that such a treatment would be an unacceptable departure from SSAP 1 and now from FRS 9. In addition, FRS 9 has special rules that apply to investment funds. Investments included within their investment portfolio should be accounted for using the same policy that applies to other investments included in the portfolio, namely cost or market value and not equity accounted (see further para 28.27).

Goodwill

28.86 Any goodwill carried in the balance sheet of the joint venture or associate on acquisition is excluded from the calculation of goodwill arising on the acquisition and is, therefore, not recognised separately on consolidation. [FRS 9 para 31]. It is acceptable to aggregate the above two disclosures on the face of the balance sheet, but where this is done the standard requires that the balance of goodwill after amortisation and any write-downs should be disclosed separately. [FRS 9 para 29]. Furthermore, it is necessary to show a reconciliation of movements in the year on the goodwill arising on joint ventures and associates in a table in order to accord with FRS 10 (Goodwill and intangible assets). [FRS 10 para 53]. Although it is necessary to disclose this reconciliation separately from the reconciliation relating to goodwill arising on the consolidation of the group's subsidiaries, it does not seem necessary to analyse the movements between goodwill attributable to joint ventures and goodwill attributable to associates. It is only necessary to analyse the closing balance of goodwill between joint ventures and associates.

28.87 In addition, the Act requires that any goodwill arising on the acquisition of the associated undertaking (including joint venture entities) should be dealt with in accordance with the rules in Schedule 4, which require amortisation of capitalised goodwill to nil on a systematic basis over a period chosen by the directors. [4A Sch 22(1); 4 Sch 21(2)]. The rules in FRS 10 also apply to goodwill that arises on the acquisition of an associate. Under FRS 10 the required treatment is to capitalise goodwill and amortise it over its useful life, which would normally not exceed 20 years. There are special rules that apply where the goodwill life exceeds 20 years or is indeterminate. In certain special circumstances it is possible not to amortise goodwill, but this requires use of the true and fair override and specific impairment tests then apply. The rules in FRS 10 are considered in detail in chapter 23 and apply equally to goodwill arising on the acquisition of a joint venture or an associate. FRS 10 also includes transitional provisions that allow companies either to capitalise goodwill previously written off directly to reserves prior to the standard's introduction, or allow it to remain written off against reserves. Where goodwill remains written off against reserves, the financial statements must state:

- The accounting policy followed in respect of that goodwill.
- The cumulative amounts of positive goodwill eliminated against reserves and negative goodwill added to reserves, net of any goodwill attributable to businesses disposed of before the balance sheet date.
- The fact that this goodwill had been eliminated as a matter of accounting policy and would be charged or credited in the profit and loss account on subsequent disposal of the business to which it related.

[FRS 10 para 71(a)].

Gross equity method

28.88 Investors have also to supplement the disclosure in paragraph 28.84 where they have interests in joint ventures. To accord with the gross equity method of accounting, the investor's share of both the aggregate gross assets and liabilities underlying the net amount included for the investment must be shown on the face of the balance sheet. [FRS 9 paras 4, 21]. In this situation, the standard is clear that this disclosure cannot be relegated to the notes to the financial statements and must appear on the face of the balance sheet.

Illustrative example

28.89 An illustration of the required disclosure is given below:

Consolidated balance sheet (extract)

	Group £'000
Fixed assets	
Goodwill	130
Intangible assets	898
Tangible assets	31,082
Investments:	
Investments in joint ventures:	
Share of gross assets	1,273
Share of gross liabilities	(1,014)
	259
Investments in associates	148
Other investments	617
	1,024
	33,134

28.90 The balance sheet formats in the Act also require long-term loans to associates and joint ventures to be shown as a separate line item. One way of complying with this disclosure is to give a columnar presentation in the notes to the financial statements, where the column headings are the line items found in the formats, as illustrated in the example below:

8 Fixed asset investments (extract)

Group	Joint ventures £'000	Associates £'000	Subsidiary excluded from consolidation £'000	Loans £'000	Own shares and other investments £'000	Total £'000
Cost or valuation						
At 31 March 1997						
Goodwill	66	43	–	–	–	109
Other	172	121	654	120	352	1,419
	238	164	654	120	352	1,528
Additions	–	–	–	–	151	151
Share of retained profit	33	7	–	–	–	40
At 31 March 1998						
Goodwill	66	43	–	–	–	109
Other	205	128	654	120	503	1,610
	271	171	654	120	503	1,719

Amounts written off						
At 31 March 1997						
Goodwill	10	15	–	–	–	25
Other	–	–	654	–	6	660
	10	15	654	–	6	685
Amortisation of goodwill	2	3	–	–	–	5
Impairment of goodwill	–	5	–	–	–	5
At 31 March 1998						
Goodwill	12	23	–	–	–	35
Other	–	–	654	–	6	660
	12	23	654	–	6	695
Net book value						
At 31 March 1998						
Goodwill	54	20	–	–	–	74
Other	205	128	–	120	497	950
	259	148	–	120	497	1,024
Net book value						
At 31 March 1998						
Goodwill	56	28	–	–	–	84
Other	172	121	–	120	346	759
	228	149	–	120	346	843

Investor's individual financial statements

28.91 For investments in both joint ventures and associates, in the investor's individual financial statements, the investments should be treated as fixed asset investments and shown either at cost, less amounts written off, or at valuation. [FRS 9 paras 20, 26].

Cash flow statement

28.92 FRS 9 also details how the results of associates and joint ventures should be dealt with in the cash flow statement and the standard makes a number of amendments to FRS 1, 'Cash flow statements'. The revised requirements are considered in chapter 30.

Consolidated financial statements not prepared

28.93 The standard requires that where an investor does not prepare consolidated financial statements, because it is not a parent company, it should still present the relevant amounts for joint ventures and associates using equity accounting. Such an entity would prepare a separate set of financial statements including the equity accounting information or give this information as additional information to its own individual financial statements. However, companies that are exempt from preparing consolidated financial statements, or would be exempt if they had subsidiaries, do not need to comply with this requirement. An example of the information and disclosure such an entity should give is explained in chapter 16.

Additional disclosure

General requirements

28.94 Schedule 5 to the Act includes certain additional information that has to be disclosed in the consolidated financial statements about an undertaking's investments in its joint ventures and associates. Some of this information is also required to be given by FRS 9. Investors have to give the following information:

- The name of the principal joint ventures and associates.
- If the joint venture or associate is incorporated outside Great Britain, the country of its incorporation.
- Where the joint venture or associate is unincorporated, the address of its principal place of business.
- In respect of shares held by the parent company or by other members of the group:
  - The identity of each class of shares.
  - The proportion held of the nominal value of each class.
  - Any special rights or constraints attaching to each class.

  The disclosures in the first two bullet points have to be split between those held by the parent and those held by the group.
- The accounting period or date of the joint venture's or the associate's financial statements used if they differ from those of the investing group.
- An indication of the nature of the joint venture's or the associate's business.

[5 Sch 22 as amended by SI 1996/189; FRS 9 para 52].

This type of information for associates is illustrated in Table 28.5.

Table 28.5 – Cable and Wireless plc – Annual Report & Accounts – 31 March 1997

Principal subsidiary and associated undertakings and trade investments (extract)

	Associated undertakings held by the Company (extract)	*Issued share Capital m*		*Percentage holding and class*	*Country of incorporation*	*Area of operation*
a)	Bahrain Telecommunications Company B.S.C.***	Dinar	80	20 Ordinary	Bahrain	Bahrain
a)	Fiji International Telecommunications Limited†	Fiji$	7	49 Ordinary	Fiji	Fiji
a)	Asia Satellite Telecommunications Company Limited†***	HK$	39	23 Ordinary	Hong Kong	Asia
a)	International Digital Communications Inc.†*	Yen	31,200	18 Ordinary	Japan	Japan

* The Group regards International Digital Communications Inc. as an associated undertaking because it exercises significant influence

*** These companies had a financial year end of 31 December 1996 due to the requirements of the shareholders' agreements.

† These companies are audited by firms other than KPMG International member firms.

28.95 The information required by Schedule 5 above need not be disclosed where the joint venture or associate is established under the law of a country, or carries on a business, outside the UK, if in the directors' opinion the disclosure would be seriously prejudicial to the business of the joint venture or associate, or to the investor's business or any of its subsidiaries. But this information may only be withheld in this type of situation where the Secretary of State agrees that it need not be disclosed and this fact must be stated in the notes to the financial statements. [Sec 231(3)].

28.96 Where the company's directors are of the opinion that the number of undertakings in respect of which the company is required to disclose the above information required by Schedule 5 would result in excessive disclosure being given, the information need only be given in respect of joint ventures and of associates whose results or financial position, in the opinion of the directors, principally affected the figures shown in the financial statements. Where advantage is taken of this provision the notes to the financial statements should state that the information is given only with respect to principal joint ventures and associates and should state that the full information (both that disclosed in the notes and that which is not) will be annexed to the company's next annual return. [Sec 231(5)].

28.97 In addition, information is required to be disclosed concerning the trading balances with joint ventures and associates. The amount of loans owing and owed between an investor and its joint ventures or its associates must be disclosed (for example, see the illustration in para 28.90). [FRS 9 para 55]. Also, balances that arise from unsettled normal trading between joint ventures or associates and other group members should be included under current assets and current liabilities and disclosed separately if material. [FRS 9 para 55].

28.98 Furthermore, the standard requires other matters to be disclosed that are material in understanding the effect on the investor of its investments in its joint ventures and its associates. [FRS 9 para 53]. For example, this covers any notes of particular significance included in the joint venture's or associate's own financial statements. It also covers explanations of matters that should have been noted had the investor's accounting policies been applied. In addition, the investor's share in contingent liabilities incurred jointly with other venturers or investors should be given and its share of joint venture's, or associate's, capital commitments should be disclosed. It would seem to follow from the disclosure requirements given earlier in the standard that this information should be shown separately for joint ventures and associates.

28.99 If there are any significant statutory, contractual or exchange control restrictions on a joint venture's or an associate's ability to distribute its distributable reserves, the extent of the restrictions should be disclosed. [FRS 9 para 54]. This type of situation could arise where, for example, the associate is situated in a country where there are exchange control restrictions, which restrict the associate's ability to pay dividends out of that country.

28.100 A note of explanation is required in two situations where the Companies Act's presumptions concerning the definition of associates (including joint ventures) are rebutted. The first situation is where the presumption is rebutted that an investor holding 20 per cent or more of the voting rights of another entity exercises significant influence over its operating and financial policies. The second is where the presumption is rebutted that an investor holding 20 per cent or more of the shares of another entity has a participating interest. [FRS 9 para 56].

15 and 25 per cent threshold information

28.101 Additional disclosures arise where the investor's share in its associates in aggregate, or in its joint ventures in aggregate, exceeds 15 per cent of certain thresholds. In addition, where the investor's share in any of its individual joint ventures and associates exceeds 25 per cent of certain thresholds individually, then additional disclosures have to be given for that entity. The thresholds should be applied by comparing the investor's share for either its associates in aggregate or its joint ventures in aggregate (or its individual associates or joint ventures) of the following:

- gross assets;
- gross liabilities;
- turnover; or
- operating results (on a three-year average),

with the corresponding amounts for the group (excluding joint ventures and associates). If any of the thresholds are breached the additional disclosures detailed below have to be given. [FRS 9 para 57].

28.102 Where the 15 per cent threshold is exceeded for all associates the aggregate of the investor's share in its associates of the following must be given:

- Turnover (unless it is already included as a memorandum item).
- Fixed assets.
- Current assets.
- Liabilities due within one year.
- Liabilities due after one year or more.

[FRS 9 para 58(a)].

28.103 Similar information is required for joint ventures in aggregate where the 15 per cent threshold is exceeded for all joint ventures. But, in this case, the turnover will already have been given as one of the requirements of gross equity accounting. [FRS 9 para 58(b)].

28.104 Where the 25 per cent threshold is exceeded for an individual associate or joint venture, the associate or joint venture should be named and the investor's share of the following should be disclosed for that entity:

- Turnover.
- Profit before tax.
- Taxation.
- Profit after tax.
- Fixed assets.
- Current assets.
- Liabilities due within one year.
- Liabilities due after one year or more.

[FRS 9 para 58(c)].

28.105 However, where the individual joint venture or associate accounts for nearly all of the amounts included for that class of investment, only the aggregate, not the individual, information in paragraph 28.104 need be given, provided that this is explained and the associate or joint venture identified. [FRS 9 para 58(c)].

28.106 In addition to the disclosure requirements outlined above, the standard requires further analysis to be given where this is necessary to understand the nature of the amounts disclosed. The headings to be given under the disclosure requirements detailed above will not conform with those used by some joint ventures and associates. This might be because they are, for example, banks, insurance companies or investment companies. In this situation it is necessary to consider the nature of the joint venture's or associate's business in deciding the most relevant and descriptive balance sheet amounts to be disclosed. Furthermore, the standard says that it may be important to give an indication of the size and maturity profile of the liabilities held. [FRS 9 para 58].

Optional disclosure for joint ventures

28.107 For joint ventures, the ASB adopted equity accounting (albeit a slightly expanded version, the 'gross equity method') as it did not consider that proportional consolidation should be used for joint ventures. Its main reason for rejecting proportional consolidation was that it believed that it would be misleading to represent each venturer's joint control of a joint venture as being in substance equivalent to it having sole control of its share of each of that entity's assets, liabilities and cash flows. This becomes particularly apparent when considering the impact of proportional consolidation in the cash flow statement, which would lead to the venturer's share of the joint venture's cash flows being treated as direct cash flows of the investor.

28.108 However, the ASB believes that it is important to encourage experimentation concerning how best to report the results and operations of joint ventures, particularly where they are a significant part of a group's activities. The ASB is happy for groups to give additional information concerning their joint ventures provided that it is in a form that is consistent with the gross equity method of accounting. To this end, the ASB includes an illustration of an optional presentation in appendix IV to the standard. Two illustrative presentations are given below of the profit and loss account and the balance sheet showing memorandum information, which is based on the previous examples shown on pages 28024 and 28029. One of the major constraints on this type of disclosure is purely a practical one and concerns how much information it is possible to get onto a printed page. Another issue concerns whether or not users will fully understand the implications of the additional information, which amounts to proportional consolidation.

Consolidated profit and loss account

	Continuing operations			Discontinued operations		*Proforma information*	
		Acquisitions	Total		Group	Joint ventures	Total
	£m	£m	£m	£m	£m	£m	£m
Turnover including share of joint ventures and associates	250	50	300	20	320		
Less: Share of joint ventures and associates	105	10	115	5	120		
Group turnover	145	40	185	15	200	40	240
Cost of sales	89	23	112	8	120	8	128
Gross profit	56	17	73	7	80	32	112
Administrative expenses	28	4	32	8	40	2	42
Group operating profit (loss)	28	13	41	(1)	40	30	70
Share of operating profit of:							
Joint ventures	27	3	30	–	30		
Associates	25	–	25	(1)	24		24
Operating profit including joint ventures and associates	80	16	96	(2)	94		94
Sale of operations:							
Group	–	–	–	20	20		
Joint ventures and associates	–	–	–	(15)	(15)		
	–	–	–	5	5		
Profit on ordinary activities before interest	80	16	96	3	99		
Interest					(42)		
Profit on ordinary activities before tax					57		
Tax on profit on ordinary activities					12		
Profit on ordinary activities after tax					45		
Minority interests					6		
Profit for the financial year					39		
Equity dividends					10		
Retained profit for the year					29		

The proforma information given in the box is of a memorandum nature only and is presented to give an indication of the effect of the group's share of the trading of its joint ventures on the results of the group.

Consolidated balance sheet

	Group	*Proforma information* Joint ventures	Total
	£'000	£'000	£'000
Fixed assets			
Goodwill	130	–	130
Intangible assets	898	–	898
Tangible assets	31,082	835	31,917
Investments:			
Investments in joint ventures	259	(259)	–
Investments in associates	148	–	148
Other investments	617	23	640
	1,024		788
	33,134		33,733
Current assets			
Stocks	7,821	230	8,051
Debtors: amounts falling due after one year	510	22	532
Debtors: amounts falling due within one year	9,029	127	9,156
Investments	166	–	166
Cash at bank and in hand	843	36	879
	18,369	415	18,784
Creditors: amounts falling due within one year	8,520	530	9,050
Net current assets (liabilities)	9,849	(115)	9,734
Total assets less current liabilities	42,983	743	43,467
Creditors: amounts falling due after more than one year			
Borrowings and other creditors	7,851	380	8,231
Provisions for liabilities and charges	10,035	104	10,139
	17,886	484	18,370
Net assets	25,097		25,097
Capital and reserves			
Called up share capital	11,161		
Share premium account	1,512		
Revaluation reserve	5,426		
Profit and loss account	5,503		
Total shareholders' funds – all equity	23,602		
Minority interests – equity	1,495		
	25,097		

The proforma information shows the group's share of the gross assets and liabilities of its joint ventures and the effect on the group's assets and liabilities if it were to be proportionally consolidated. The figure of £259,000 represents the elimination of the group's share of its joint ventures' net assets included within the group column.

Equity accounting principles

Introduction

28.109 The principles concerning how to equity account for joint ventures and associates mainly follow those that apply to the consolidation of subsidiaries. These principles concern, for example, the date from which to equity account an interest in a joint venture or associate, how to determine goodwill and the types of consolidation adjustments that are necessary. The primary difference between an associate interest, or a joint venture interest, and an interest in a subsidiary is the level of the investor's control. An investor controls its subsidiaries, and therefore has access to the information necessary for carrying out certain consolidation procedures, but it exercises only significant influence over its associates or jointly controls its joint ventures. Consequently, this might mean that access to information necessary to make the required consolidation adjustments is limited. Where this is so, the standard states that estimates may be used. But such a limitation in itself might call into question the investor's relationship with its associate or joint venture. Where the information available is extremely limited, the investor will need to reassess whether or not it actually has significant influence over, or whether or not it jointly controls, its investment. [FRS 9 para 35].

28.110 Furthermore, the standard mentions that regulations on the dissemination of information could possibly restrict the extent to which the financial statements of an investor might contain information about its joint ventures and its associates, unless such information is available to other interested parties at the same time. [FRS 9 para 37]. This is of particular importance where the associate is itself listed (as explained in para 28.129 below). Investors should, therefore, consider how to satisfy any regulations that apply concerning publishing price sensitive information about its joint ventures and its associates.

28.111 The paragraphs that follow consider the consolidation rules that apply to equity accounting both associates and joint ventures, starting with examining how the share to be equity accounted is ascertained.

Share

28.112 Before it is possible to equity account for joint ventures and associates, it is necessary to establish what share the group owns. There are a number of matters that need to be considered in determining what is the appropriate share, as in many situations the percentage will not be easily ascertained. Paragraphs 28.33 to 28.36 above explain how to determine whether or not the investor has a participating interest in the joint venture or the associate and paragraphs 28.49 to 28.53 consider what voting rights should be taken into account. These rules also apply in determining what percentage share the group has in the joint venture or associate.

28.113 Where the investor is a group, its share of its associate or joint venture is the aggregate of the parent's interest and the interest of its subsidiaries in that entity. [FRS 9 para 32]. Therefore, it is the group's aggregate interest in the joint venture or associate which needs to be ascertained and this is the appropriate percentage which should be applied in equity accounting. But the holdings of any of the group's other associates or joint ventures should be ignored for this purpose. [FRS 9 para 32].

28.114 In a simple situation where the investor only has an interest in the equity share capital of the associate or joint venture it is easy to ascertain the share to be equity accounted: it will normally be the number of shares held divided by the total number of equity shares in issue. This amount will equate to the investor's entitlement to dividends and other distributions. Complications arise where the investee has different classes of shares or where the entitlement to dividends, or capital on winding up, vary. For example, the investor might have an interest in the non-equity capital as well as the equity capital. Clearly in this type of situation, the rights attaching to each class of share need to be considered carefully to determine the appropriate percentage to be brought into the equity interest calculation. It is a matter of looking at the substance of the respective rights to establish the appropriate accounting treatment.

Example

A group has an interest in the equity shares of its associate and owns all of the other class of the company's shares in issue, which is cumulative preference shares. The group owns 45% of the equity shares and 500,000 6% cumulative preference shares with a nominal value of £1 each. Dividends have been in arrears on the preference shares for two years and although these have been appropriated in the associate's financial statements (to accord with the requirements of FRS 4), they have been added back to reserves rather than being shown as a liability. The net assets of the associate are £1m.

The reserves of the associate include an appropriation of £60,000 which is solely attributable to the investor's interest in the cumulative preference shares. The investor's share of net assets is determined by adding together its entitlement to cumulative dividends and its interest in the preference shares before calculating its share of the remaining net assets. Ignoring fair values and goodwill, the investor's share of net assets would be £758,000 (that is, £60,000 + £500,000 + 45% (£1,000,000 – £500,000 – £60,000)).

28.115 In many situations the share to be taken into account will be derived from the percentage holding in shares, but in other situations the economic interest might differ from the shareholding, but will be the appropriate interest to take into account. For example, although the shareholding in a joint venture might be 50/50, the venturers might share profits in the ratio 40:60. Therefore, in this circumstance it will be appropriate to equity account for the economic share rather than the equity participation. Consequently, considerable care needs to be taken in establishing the appropriate share to be equity accounted.

Options, convertible shares and convertible debt

28.116 Where the investor holds options, convertibles or non-equity shares in its joint venture or its associate, the standard says that these should be taken into account in determining the investor's share where the conditions attaching to such holdings indicate that this is appropriate. The standard goes on to say that, in such cases, the costs of exercising the options or converting the convertibles, or future payments in relation to the non-equity shares, should also be taken into account. It also states that the necessary calculation depends on the relevant circumstances in any particular case, but notes that care should be taken not to count any interest twice. For example, such double counting would occur where an investor included a greater share of its associate under the equity method than that which would arise on the basis of the investor's existing equity holding, while simultaneously writing up the value of options held in the associate to reflect an increase in market value. [FRS 9 para 33]. It is not easy to see what these requirements mean in practice and these issues are explored in the paragraphs that follow.

28.117 The standard's section 'The development of the FRS' says that the basis of paragraph 33 outlined above is the requirement in FRS 5 that the substance of transactions should be reported. In particular, paragraph 14 of FRS 5 specifies that *"in determining the substance of a transaction, all its aspects and implications should be identified and greater weight should be given to those more likely to have a commercial effect in practice"*. FRS 9 goes on to say that the investor should, therefore, account for the substance of its interests in its joint ventures or its associates in cases where this is affected by its holdings of options, convertibles or non-equity shares. It gives one example where the existence of such a holding might affect the share. This is where the price of exercising or converting options or convertibles is so low that there is commercially near certainty that they will be exercised or converted. It is, therefore, quite clear from this explanation that the ASB considers that the share to be equity accounted should in certain special circumstances be adjusted to take account of the existence of options and convertibles.

28.118 As mentioned earlier, it is clear under the Act that a participating interest, which is defined in section 260, includes an option to acquire shares or any interest that is convertible into shares. [Sec 260(c)]. For this purpose, it does not matter whether the options or other interests can be exercised now or in the future; their mere existence is taken into account whether or not they are currently exercisable. An interest or option in shares falls within this definition even if the shares to which it relates, until conversion or the exercise of the option, are unissued. [Sec 260(3)]. In addition, interests held on behalf of an undertaking or by, or on behalf of, any of its subsidiary undertakings should be treated as held by it. [Sec 260(4), (5)(a)].

28.119 These rules apply in determining whether or not an investor has a participating interest in an entity and, as a consequence, are important in establishing whether or not the entity is a joint venture or an associate. But the question arises as to whether such interests should be taken into account in determining the share to be equity accounted. Clearly for this purpose, having an option interest or a convertible interest is very different from holding the shares to which they relate. For example, it seems clear that if the options or convertible interests are not within their exercise or conversion period, it is unlikely that they should be brought into account in determining the investor's interest in the associate, unless they are exercisable at a purely nominal figure and it appears in the circumstances that it would be in the investor's interest to exercise them. However, where they are within their option period and exercisable at a fair market price and the holder can exercise them at any time unconditionally then whether or not they fall to be treated as part of the investor's interest will depend on a number of factors. It would be highly unusual to take options and convertible interests into account in determining the share before they have been exercised, so the circumstances would have to be considered very carefully before adjusting the share to be equity accounted for such interests. One issue to consider is the distribution policy of the associate. If, for example, the associate was planning to pay an enhanced dividend this would need to be taken into account. The example that follows illustrates some of these issues.

Example

A group has a 25% interest in its associate's equity share capital of £100,000. It also has options which it has held for a number of years to acquire a further 5,000 shares of £1 each from the company at £14 per share. The options, which cost £1 per share, are traded and have been valued in the group's financial statements at £2 per share. The net assets of the associate at the year end are £1m.

Ignoring fair values, the investor's equity interest in its associate's net assets is worth £250,000 which would normally be consolidated in the group's balance sheet. In addition, the group has shown the interest in the options at a value of £10,000. If the group had exercised its options at the year end and paid the £14 per share, the associate's net assets would increase by £70,000 (that is, 5,000 × £14) to £1,070,000 and the investor's interest would increase from 25% to 28.57% (that is, 30,000 ÷ 105,000 × 100). Therefore, the investor's share of the net assets and goodwill on the increase in stake would be £325,000. This is made up of the share of net assets of £305,700 (that is, £1,070,000 × 28.57%) and goodwill arising on the increase in stake of £19,300. The goodwill is the difference between the consideration of £75,000 (that is, the cost of the additional shares of £70,000 plus the initial cost of the options of £5,000) and the additional share of net assets of £55,700. Clearly, if this increased interest is booked in the consolidated balance sheet, then it would be necessary to eliminate the revaluation of the options of £5,000 in order to avoid double counting. In addition, it would be necessary to make a provision for the purchase of the additional shares, which would cost £70,000.

Consequently, in this example the net assets relating to the associate without taking into account the exercise of the options are £260,000 (that is, £250,000 + £10,000), but after taking into account the exercise of the options, the share of net assets of £325,000 (that is, share of net assets of £305,700 plus goodwill of £19,300) less a provision for consideration of £70,000 gives a total of £255,000; a net decrease of £5,000.

Following the introduction of FRS 10, because goodwill is capitalised the amount paid for an acquisition always equates to the increase in net assets plus goodwill recognised on consolidation (the fair value exercise only determining how the consideration figure is split between assets and goodwill). Consequently, anticipating an acquisition by providing for the consideration to be paid has a nil effect on the share of net assets plus goodwill shown on consolidation. In this example, the decrease in net assets of £5,000 is merely due to the reversal of the revaluation of £5,000 relating to the options recognised in the balance sheet.

28.120 Whether or not the investor would take into account an interest in options in ascertaining its share of its joint ventures and associates will depend on the facts of each case. The investor's intentions are, therefore, important. For example, if the options were exercisable at market value, the investor might intend to wait until the share price falls before it exercises its options or might intend to exercise them for other strategic business reasons. Where the investor does intend to exercise the options (say, shortly after the year end) then FRS 9 implies in paragraph 33 that it should take this into account in reflecting its interest in its joint venture or associate. But, as mentioned above, the circumstances that would justify adjusting the company's share for such options are not likely to arise very often in practice.

28.121 In certain situations the investor's intentions might be more obvious. This will be the case, in particular, where a fixed price put and call option exists. In this situation, either the investor or the investee is assured to exercise the option, as it will be in one of their economic interests to do so. However, care needs to be taken, because the effect of exercising options might not be obvious even where they are exercisable at below their market value. Consider the following example.

Example

If in the previous example the investor's options were exercisable at £2 per share as opposed to £14 per share, then the effect on the group's net assets would be as follows.

The investor's share of the net assets and goodwill on the increase in stake would be £265,000. This is made up of the share of net assets of £288,557 (that is, £1,010,000 × 28.57%) less negative goodwill arising on the increase in stake of £23,557. The goodwill is the difference between the consideration of £15,000 (that is, the cost of the additional shares of £10,000 plus the initial cost of the options of £5,000) and the additional share of net assets of £38,557. Consequently, if the exercise of the options is taken into account, the share of net assets of £265,000 (that is, share of net assets of £288,557 less negative goodwill of £23,557) less a provision for consideration of £10,000 gives a total of £255,000; a net decrease of £5,000.

The net assets recognised is the same as in the previous example. This is no coincidence and is the effect of having to recognise purchased goodwill or negative goodwill on the balance sheet. As mentioned in the previous example, the increase in net assets recognised on consolidation always equates to the amount paid for the acquisition. Similarly in this example, anticipating an acquisition by providing for the consideration to be paid has a nil effect on the net assets on consolidation. Again in this example the decrease in net assets of £5,000 is due to the reversal of the revaluation of £5,000 relating to the options recognised in the balance sheet.

28.122 As can be seen from the previous two examples, the exercise price has no impact on the net assets recognised before or after acquisition, the net assets will remain the same. However, there would be an impact on the gross assets and liabilities recognised.

28.123 Another situation which arises in practice is where the investor has options over shares in the joint venture or associate which are held by third parties. Again the facts of the situation will have to be considered carefully. The intention of the investor might be influenced by the purchase price compared to the increased interest and possibly by the additional influence this gives the investor.

28.124 Problems can also arise at the margins, because the existence of options might tip the balance at the opposite extremes of the associate/joint venture spectrum. At one end an investment might become an associate by taking into account options (as discussed in para 28.118 above). At the other end of the spectrum exercising options might turn a joint venture or an associate into a subsidiary. Generally, however, for this to happen, the investor would have to actually exercise dominant influence over the entity or manage it on a unified basis with its own activities. The issues concerning when such an interest becomes a subsidiary are considered in detail in chapter 21.

Convertible shares

28.125 The standard applies the same rules to convertible shares as it specifies for options as explained in paragraph 28.116 above. Therefore, it is necessary to establish whether or not the convertible shares are within their conversion period. If they are, the next step is to consider whether the investor intends to convert. The investor's intention will depend on similar factors to those considered above for options. Only if it is clear that the investor intends to convert and no significant distributions will be made before it does so should the conversion be taken into account in determining the share to be equity accounted. Also it will be necessary to take into account any costs of conversion to ensure that there is no double counting.

Example

A group has a 25% interest in its associate's equity share capital of £100,000. It also holds 100,000 convertible redeemable preference shares of 25p. These are convertible into 10,000 £1 equity shares between 1 January 1998 and 31 December 1999. The net assets of the associate at the year end are £1m. There is no cost of conversion, but if there was, then it would have to be provided for.

Ignoring fair values and goodwill, the investor's equity interest in its associate's net assets before conversion is £268,750 (that is, (£1,000,000 – £25,000) × 25% + £25,000), which would be consolidated in the group's balance sheet. If the group had exercised its options to convert at the year end, the investor's interest would increase from 25% to 31.82% (that is, 35,000 ÷ 110,000 × 100). Therefore, the investor's share of the net assets will increase to £318,200 (that is, £1,000,000 × 31.82%).

Convertible debt

28.126 Similar issues arise if the investor has invested in convertible debt of its joint venture or associate. The investor's intention is the key to determining whether conversion of the debt should be anticipated. In principle, we consider that conversion should not be anticipated, unless the circumstances are very unusual, because such anticipation would run counter to FRS 4, which takes the view that where convertible debt is in issue conversion should not be anticipated. Also, anticipating conversion would have no impact on the net assets of the group as illustrated in the following example.

Example

A group has a 25% interest in its associate's equity share capital of £100,000. It also holds £100,000 of convertible debt. The debt is convertible into 15,000 £1 equity shares between 1 January 1998 and 31 December 1999. The net assets of the associate at the year end are £1m. There is no cost of conversion, but if there was, then it would have to be provided for.

Ignoring fair values, the investor's equity interest in its associate's net assets before conversion is £250,000 (that is, £1,000,000 × 25%) and it also has a loan to the associate of £100,000. Therefore, its total interest before conversion is £350,000. If the group had converted its debt at the year end, the investor's interest would increase from 25% to 34.78% (that is, 40,000 ÷ 115,000 × 100). The associate's net assets increase by the £100,000 of debt which would be transferred to share capital and to share premium on conversion. Therefore, the investor's share of the net assets and goodwill after the conversion also comes to £350,000. This is made up of the share of net assets of £382,580 (that is, £1,100,000 × 34.78%) less negative goodwill arising on the increase in stake of £32,580. The negative goodwill is the difference between the consideration of £100,000 (that is, the value of the loan given up) and the additional share of net assets of £132,580.

As mentioned in the previous examples, the increase in net assets recognised on consolidation always equates to the amount paid for the acquisition. In this example, the group's net assets have remained the same, because the loan of £100,000 has been replaced by an increased share of net assets offset by negative goodwill.

28.127 Problems can also arise where other investors in the associate hold converting interests, which might have the effect of diluting the share of the associate to be equity accounted. Again it is necessary to consider carefully the implications and the substance of the transaction to determine whether or not the equity share should be adjusted.

Example

A group has a 38% interest in its associate's equity share capital. The associate has convertible debt in issue which is held by third parties. This debt will convert into equity shares of the associate in two years' time and it is almost certain that the debt-holders will opt for conversion. Once converted the investor's interest will decrease to 35%.

In this case, although it is almost certain that the debt will convert and conversion is not within the control of the investor, the investor should still equity account for its 38% interest until the conversion takes place. Only after conversion has taken place should the investor account using the 35%, because this is the actual date of the deemed disposal (see further para 28.163). However, because conversion is likely, the investor should provide for any losses (but not profits) in relation to the change in interest from 38% to 35%. It is, therefore, necessary to calculate the loss or gain on the deemed disposal. The gain or loss is calculated by comparing the share of net assets before the deemed disposal with the share of net assets after the deemed disposal (adjusted for any proceeds on the conversion of the debt). This calculation would also have to take into account a share of the goodwill given up on the deemed disposal, which would reduce any profit or increase any loss. If there is a resulting loss this would have to be provided for in the consolidated profit and loss account.

Crossholdings

28.128 One complicated issue that arises with equity accounting is how to deal with crossholdings of shares between the investor and its investee. This situation can arise whereby one company (the investor) issues shares to another company in exchange for shares in that other company. Obviously, without some adjustment there will be an element of double counting if the investor equity accounts for its share of the investee's net assets, which includes the holding of shares in the investor company. Therefore, this crossholding needs to be eliminated as explained in the following example.

Example

Company H takes a 25% stake in company A, which has net assets of £1m. The market value of the associate's shares is £1.5m. For simplicity, the net asset value and the fair value of the net assets is the same, that is, £1m. Company H issues shares with a value of £375,000 to acquire its interest.

In the simple situation where the investor issues its shares to the owners of the associate in exchange for the 25% interest, company H's share capital and share premium would increase by £375,000, being its investment in company A. On consolidation, the investment in company A of £375,000 is simply allocated between the group's share of the fair value of its net assets (that is, £250,000) and goodwill arising on the acquisition of £125,000 (that is, £375,000 – £250,000).

But now assume there is an equity swap, such that the investor issues shares worth £375,000 to the associate in consideration for the associate issuing the investor new shares. The associate's net assets increase by £375,000, the cost to it of the shares it holds in company H. Consequently, company A's worth has increased to £1,875,000 and it has net assets of £1,375,000. Company H's share of company A's increased net assets is £343,750 (that is, £1,375,000 × 25%), but this includes the value of the interest in its own shares of £93,750 (that is, 25% × £375,000). Company A's goodwill is still worth £500,000, of which company H's share is still £125,000. So it might appear that on consolidation the value of company H's interest in its associate should be £468,750 (that is, £1,875,000 × 25%), but company H's consolidated net asset (including goodwill) should not exceed £375,000, the value of the shares it has issued. If the group had recognised its share as £468,750 instead, it would have inflated its consolidated balance sheet by recognising some value for its own internally generated goodwill.

Therefore, to avoid double counting for the self-investment it is then necessary to split the interest in the associate of £375,000 between the share of the fair value of the net assets acquired and goodwill. It seems appropriate to reduce the value of company H's investment in company A's net assets by £93,750 to £250,000 and state goodwill at £125,000. The rationale is that the net assets are reduced to eliminate the crossholding and this also ensures that purchased goodwill in company A is recorded at the appropriate value. A problem arises if company A subsequently sells its interest in company H – an adjustment is required to bring company H's investment in its consolidated financial statements back up to the increased share of net assets of company A (that is, to £468,750). The double entry would be to credit the group's revaluation reserve with the increase in value of the associate interest.

In the consolidated profit and loss account, company H's share of company A's results should be included excluding any portion of those results attributable to company A's investment in company H. However, it should include a share of any dividends paid by company H to company A.

Financial statements used

28.129 The financial statements used for the purpose of including the results of joint ventures and associates should be either coterminous with those of the group (which for an associate with a different year end would involve preparing special financial statements to the same date as the investor's year end) or, where this is not practicable, made up to a date that is not more than three months before the investing group's period end. [FRS 9 para 31(d)].

28.130 If a joint venture or an associate is listed on a recognised stock exchange, only published information should be disclosed in the group's consolidated financial statements. This can cause particular problems in practice where, for example, there is more than six months between the year end of the associate and that of the group. In the situation where the use of financial statements drawn up for a period ending not more than three months before the investor's period end would release price-sensitive information, FRS 9 allows instead financial statements prepared for a period that ends not more than six months before the group's period end to be used. [FRS 9 para 31(d)]. Any changes after the period end of the associate or joint venture and before that of the investor that are material, should be taken into account by adjustment.

Example

A group draws up its consolidated financial statements to 31 December 1998. It has an investment in a listed associate, which it equity accounts on consolidation. The associate's last year end was 31 January 1998.

It is not possible for the group to consolidate results of its associate made up to coincide with its period end 31 December 1998, because this would entail publishing information concerning its associate that has not been made available to the public. It is also not possible to equity account for the associate's results to 31 January 1999, the period ending shortly after that of the group (this was possible under the provisions of SSAP 1, but is not allowed under FRS 9). In addition, it is not possible to equity account for the previous year to 31 January 1998, as this is precluded by FRS 9. Under the Stock Exchange's requirements, the listed associate will have to prepare interim accounts. Assuming it reported at the half year, the accounts that should be equity accounted in this case are those for the year to 31 July 1998, the interim period end of the associate. This will entail taking into account the results for the second half of the associate's previous year and the first half of its current year, which together constitute the year to 31 July 1998.

Consolidation adjustments

28.131 Adjustments similar to those required for the purposes of including subsidiaries in the consolidated financial statements should be made when the associates or joint ventures are incorporated into the group's consolidated financial statements. The type of adjustments that may be necessary cover the following matters:

- To achieve consistency of accounting policies.
- To set up goodwill arising on the associate's or joint venture's acquisition and to deal with fair value adjustments.
- To deal with abnormal transactions that arise between an associate's or joint venture's year end and its parent's year end.
- To eliminate the effects of intra-group trading.
- To translate the results of overseas associates or joint ventures.

28.132 These types of adjustments are considered in respect of consolidations of subsidiaries in detail in chapter 22 and the translation rules are considered in chapter 29. Those principles can be applied equally to the consolidation adjustments that are required when equity accounting joint ventures and associates. Some specific issues are considered in the paragraphs that follow.

Consistent accounting policies

28.133 The standard states that in arriving at the amounts to be included by the equity method of accounting, the same accounting policies as those of the investor should be applied. [FRS 9 para 31(c)]. This will entail making adjustments to the joint venture's or associate's results to harmonise accounting policies. However, in practice, such adjustments will not always be possible, because the information necessary to make them may not necessarily be available. Where this situation arises, the standard offers no guidance. However, this is also another area where the investor's relationship with its associate (that is, significant influence), or with its joint venture (that is, joint control), would be called into question, if the appropriate information is not available.

Goodwill and fair values

28.134 The standard requires that when an entity acquires a joint venture or an associate, fair values should be attributed to the investee's underlying assets and liabilities. [FRS 9 para 31(a)]. These fair values should be ascertained in accordance with the principles of FRS 7, 'Fair values in acquisition accounting', and adjustments should be made to conform with the investor's accounting policies. Again, as explained in the previous paragraph, where it is not possible to ascertain fair values on acquisition of a joint venture or an associate interest, this would call into question whether or not the entity fulfils the definitions of joint venture or associate, because it could suggest that the appropriate level of control or interest has not been achieved in practice.

28.135 For joint ventures and associates, it is unlikely that any necessary fair values adjustment would be booked in the joint venture's or associate's books of account, but nevertheless the fair value of assets should provide the basis for subsequent depreciation that is reflected in the investor's share of the results. The standard requires that both the consideration paid in the acquisition and the goodwill arising should be calculated in the same way as on the acquisition of a subsidiary. These issues are considered in detail in chapter 23. As explained in paragraph 28.86 above, the investee's assets used in calculating the goodwill arising on acquisition should not include any goodwill carried in the balance sheet of the joint venture or associate. Goodwill arising on the acquisition of joint ventures or associates has now to be accounted for in accordance with the provisions of FRS 10, 'Goodwill and intangible assets'. These requirements are fully explained in chapter 23.

28.136 Paragraph 31(a) in FRS 9, which specifies the above rules, deals with the measurement issues that arise when the equity accounting method is used, but it does not specify what disclosure requirements apply on acquisition. Therefore, for acquisitions of joint ventures and associates we do not consider that the disclosure requirements specified in FRS 6, 'Acquisitions and mergers', for acquisitions of subsidiaries apply. Consequently, there is no need to give the fair value table information required by that standard, although some companies do give this type of information – see Table 28.6. The disclosures required for joint ventures and associates are considered from paragraph 28.94 above.

Table 28.6 – British Telecommunications plc – Report & Accounts – 31 March 1995

Notes to the financial statements (extract)

13 Fixed asset investments (extract)

(b) MCI Communications Corporation
On 30 September 1994 the company purchased a 20% interest in MCI Communications Corporation (MCI). The consideration of £2,842m comprised £2,316m cash, and the conversion of the company's holding of MCI preferred shares, with a book value of £526m, purchased in June 1993. MCI is the second largest carrier of long-distance telecommunication services in the USA.

The acquisition of the interest in MCI comprised:

	£m
Group share of original book value of net assets	1,121
Fair value adjustment to achieve consistency of accounting policies	(230)
Revaluations	(10)
Fair value to the group	881
Goodwill	1,961
Total cost	**2,842**

At 31 March 1995, the group's 20% share of the net assets of MCI, calculated in accordance with group accounting policies, amounted to £907m. This value comprised tangible fixed assets of £994m, short-term investments of £346m and other assets of £394m, from which are deducted borrowings of £377m and other liabilities of £450m.

Abnormal transactions between year ends

28.137 Care should be taken where the joint venture's or associate's year end does not coincide with that of the investing undertaking to ensure that there are no material events that have occurred since the joint venture's or associate's year end. Where such events have taken place, then if the effect is material it will be necessary to make adjustments to the results and net assets of the associate before they are consolidated with the group's financial statements. [FRS 9 para 31(d)]. For example, the associate might sell fixed assets to the group (or *vice versa*) during this period. Another example is where the group increases loans made to the joint venture or associate after the joint venture's or associate's year end.

Elimination of intra-group trading

Profits and losses included in assets

28.138 The method used to eliminate intra-group trading with joint ventures and associates may be different from that adopted for subsidiaries. The normal method of adjustment for a subsidiary company would be to eliminate profits and losses fully. However, the Act specifies that the elimination of profits and losses resulting from transactions between group undertakings, which have been included in the value of assets, may be eliminated in proportion to the group's interest in the shares of the undertaking. [4A Sch 6(3)]. The implication of this method of elimination as it applies to subsidiaries is restricted by FRS 2 and is considered further in chapter 22. Although only brought into the legislation by the introduction of the Companies Act 1989, this method of eliminating profits had been used for joint ventures and associates being equity accounted for some time before that date. This treatment is confirmed in FRS 9, which states that where profits and losses resulting from transactions between an investor and its associate, or its joint venture, are included in the carrying amount of assets in either entity, the part relating to the investor's share should be eliminated. [FRS 9 para 31(b)]. In addition, the standard notes that where the transaction provides evidence of the impairment of those assets or any similar assets, this should be taken into account. Blue Circle eliminate profits in this way as explained by their accounting policy (see Table 28.7).

Table 28.7 – Blue Circle Industries PLC – Annual Report & Accounts – 31 December 1996

1 Accounting Policies (extract)

2 Consolidation

The Group accounts incorporate the results of the Company and its subsidiary and principal associated undertakings. In these accounts, these entities are referred to as subsidiaries and related companies respectively. To avoid delay in the presentation of the accounts the accounting periods of some overseas subsidiaries end on 30 November. The results of related companies are based upon statutory or management accounts for periods ending on either 30 November or 31 December. Where subsidiaries and related companies are acquired or disposed of during the year, results are included from the date of acquisition or to the date of the sale.

> **12 Property (extract)**
> Sales of properties are recognised when a legally binding and unconditional contract for sale has been exchanged. Where properties are sold to related companies or joint ventures, profits are only recognised in proportion to third parties' interests in these entities. The remaining profits are recognised when the properties are sold by the related company or the joint venture to unrelated parties.

28.139 The following example explains how the adjustment should be made.

Example

Company H prepares its consolidated financial statements to 31 December 1998. It has a 25% investment in an associate. During the year company H purchased an investment from the associate for £120,000. The associate made £50,000 profit on the sale. On consolidation, using the equity method of accounting, that element of the associate's profit should be reduced to the extent of the group's investment in it (that is, reduced by 25%). Consequently, the share of the associate's profit consolidated with the group would be reduced by £12,500 (that is, 25% × £50,000), thereby, eliminating the group's share of that profit. In addition, to complete the double entry, the value of the investment shown in the group's consolidated balance sheet should be reduced by £12,500 to £107,500.

28.140 This type of adjustment is logical for joint ventures and associates, because the consolidated financial statements only include the group's share of the profits and losses of joint ventures and associates and, consequently, it would be wrong to eliminate a greater proportion of the profit. Furthermore, in the situation where a group member makes a sale to a joint venture or an associate, then a profit will arise in the group to the extent of the outside interest in the joint venture or associate. Similarly, the joint venture's or associate's assets will also, in this situation, be overstated by the profit element. Consequently, a similar adjustment will be required on consolidation to reduce the group's share of the joint venture's or associate's assets by the same amount.

Transfers of assets to a joint venture

28.141 The requirement to eliminate such profits applies equally to transfers of assets or liabilities to set up a joint venture or to acquire an initial stake in an associate as well as to all other transactions during the life of the associate or joint venture. [FRS 9 para 36].

Example

A group enters into a 50/50 joint venture with a third party. The joint venture is to be set up in a limited company and the group is to contribute assets worth £1,000,000 to the joint venture. The other party is to contribute cash for its 200,000 £1 shares. In consideration for the assets the group receives 200,000 £1 shares, loan stock of £600,000 and cash of £200,000 (which the joint venture has received from its other shareholder).

The amount of the profit on the disposal of the group's property to the joint venture to be eliminated on consolidation depends upon the proportion of capital invested by the group and the other party to the venture. The proportions are as follows:

	Group	Other JV partner	Total capital
	£'000	£'000	£'000
Shares	200	200	400
Loan stock	600	–	600
	800	200	1,000

If the group made a profit on the disposal of the property to the joint venture, it should eliminate 80% of that gain, being the proportion of its interest it still retains in the asset. Only 20% can be regarded as being realised. The elimination entry would be to debit the group's profit and loss account with the proportion of the gain being eliminated and credit the group's interest in the joint venture's assets shown on the face of the balance sheet following the gross equity method of accounting. Alternatively, the credit could be treated as deferred income, particularly where the assets will be realised subsequently. If the loan stock is subsequently repaid, the proportion to be eliminated would change to 50%.

In the individual entity making the disposal, the amount of the profit and any revaluation reserve being treated as realised will not depend on the capital invested in the joint venture, but will depend on the cash received under the transaction.

	Group	Asset value	Proportion
	£'000	£'000	
Cash received	200	1,000	20%
Loan Stock	600		
	800	1,000	80%

The proportion of the profit that can be recognised if only £200,000 is received in cash is 20%. If the loan stock is repaid, the proportion of the profit that can be recognised is 80%.

Intra-company trading transactions

28.142 The standard also makes the point that because associates and joint ventures are not part of the group, balances between the investor and its associates or joint ventures should not be eliminated and, therefore, unsettled normal trading transactions should be included as current assets or liabilities. [FRS 9 para 36]. Similarly, with the exception of turnover, normal trading transactions between the group and its joint ventures or its associates do not require elimination. These principles are illustrated in the two examples that follow:

Example 1

A group sells goods to a distribution joint venture (owned 50/50) which in turn sells on to third parties at a margin. In the period the group makes sales of £10m to the joint venture which cost £5m to produce. The joint venture in turn sells the goods to third parties for £12m and it cost of sales is £10m.

The turnover required to be disclosed under the Companies Act is that of the group excluding its joint venture (that is, £10m) and the standard requires the group's share of its joint ventures' turnover to be shown. It would clearly be misleading to show a total group turnover including joint ventures of £16m. Hence it is necessary to eliminate £5m relating to intra-group trading. The question then arises as to which figure of turnover to eliminate the £5m against. The £5m represents the group's share of the joint venture's cost of sales and it would be logical to eliminate this against the group's turnover reducing it to £5m and to show as share of joint venture's turnover £6m. This gives the correct total of, £11m, but does not comply with the Act's requirements, as the group's turnover, which must be disclosed under the Act, is £10m. Therefore, we suggest that the elimination is made against the share of the joint venture's turnover. This would result in the following presentation:

Consolidated profit and loss account (extract)	
	£m
Turnover including share of joint venture	11
Less: Share of joint venture	1
Group turnover	10
Cost of sales	5
Group operating profit	5
Share of operating profit of joint venture	1
Operating profit including share of joint venture	6

Depending on how material the group's share of its joint venture turnover is, it may be necessary to indicate that the reported share of joint venture turnover is stated after eliminating intra-group turnover of £5m.

Example 2

A group has a 50% interest in a joint venture. The group charges the joint venture interest of £10,000 on a loan it has made to the joint venture. Therefore, the group has interest income in its profit and loss account of £10,000 and the joint venture has an interest expense of £10,000.

On consolidation the group would show for these items interest income of £10,000 and share of joint venture's interest payable of £5,000. Overall, therefore, the group has only recognised net income of £5,000, which represents the interest charged by the group to the other investor.

28.143 It can be seen from the examples that, with the exception of turnover, under equity accounting it is not necessary to eliminate inter-company trading on a line-by-line basis. Therefore, generally for trading transactions no consolidation adjustments are necessary as the group's share of the transaction is taken up in the share of its joint venture's or its associate's results. Consolidation adjustments are only necessary, as explained above, where profits and losses resulting from transactions between the investor and its joint venture, or its associate, are included in the carrying value of assets in either the group or the joint venture or associate and also to eliminate intra-group turnover.

Partnerships that are joint venture entities

28.144 Under the standard's provisions, a partnership may be either a joint venture entity or a joint arrangement that is not an entity. How to determine which type of joint arrangement an undertaking is it considered from paragraph 28.169 below.

28.145 An issue arises with the accounting requirements for partnerships that are joint venture entities. In the group's consolidated financial statements, such partnerships should be equity accounted using the gross equity method. However, the question arises how the partnership should be accounted for in the investor's individual financial statements. The standard is silent as regards the treatment in the investor's own profit and loss account, but requires that, in the investor's own balance sheet, its interests in joint ventures should be treated as fixed asset investments and shown either at cost, less any amounts written off, or at valuation. It follows from this that in the company's profit and loss account only the investment income should be accounted for. Before the introduction of FRS 9, some partnerships of this nature were accounted for using proportional consolidation, or were equity accounted, in the investor's individual financial statements. Proportional consolidation is no longer possible following FRS 9's introduction. However, where there are no restrictions on the distribution of profits from the partnership, it may still be appropriate to record the investor's share of the results of its partnership. It could do this by showing its share of the results on one line representing its investment income rather than merely the distributions received from the partnership. In the balance sheet, the investment would be valued on the basis of the investor's share of the partnership's net assets. The accounting requirements that apply to partnerships that are joint arrangements are considered from paragraph 28.195 below.

Where the associate itself is a group

28.146 Where the associated undertaking (including joint ventures) is a group of undertakings, the Act requires that the net assets and the profits or losses that should be taken into account on equity accounting the associate should be those of the associate consolidated with its subsidiary undertakings. [4A Sch 22(2)]. This requirement is added to by FRS 9, which requires that the net assets and profits or losses to be dealt with should include the joint venture's or associate's share of the net assets and profits or losses of investments it may itself have in its own joint ventures or associates. [FRS 9 para 32].

Interests in losses and net liabilities

28.147 A problem may arise where a joint venture or an associate starts to make losses, particularly where those losses are such that the undertaking has net liabilities. Where this is so, the investing group should normally continue to record changes in carrying amounts of its joint ventures or associates in its consolidated balance sheet even where this results in recognising its share of any deficiency in a joint venture or an associate. [FRS 9 para 44]. This would apply, for example, where the investment is still regarded by the group as long-term (an essential condition of the definition of a joint venture or an associate).

28.148 The standard states that the only exception to equity accounting for such deficits is where there is sufficient evidence that an event has irrevocably changed the relationship between the investor and its investee, marking its irreversible withdrawal from its joint venture or associate. [FRS 9 para 44]. Consequently, where, for example, there is no intention to support the undertaking, then only the liabilities that the group will incur if the undertaking should cease to trade would need to be provided for in full in the consolidated financial statements. However, mere intention alone will not be adequate and the standard is looking for a demonstrable commitment to the withdrawal including a public statement to that effect. In particular, such a commitment will arise where the direction of the joint venture's or the associate's operating and financial policies has become the responsibility of its creditors (including bankers), for example where the joint venture or associate is in liquidation. Where the interest in a joint venture or an associate is in net liabilities, the amount recorded should be shown as a provision or a liability. [FRS 9 para 45].

[The next page is 28055.]

Example

A company has an interest of 25% in an associate. The associate has net liabilities at the year end of £3.5m. The net liabilities include a loan of £2.5m from the investor. In the investor's individual financial statements a provision of £1.5m has been made against the loan.

In the group's consolidated financial statements, the investment in the associate is made up of its share of net liabilities together with any loan made to the associate. The group's share of the associate's net liabilities is £875,000 (that is, £3.5m × 25%). But of the net liabilities of £3.5m, the group has already made a provision of £1.5m against its loan. Consequently, it has, in effect, already made a provision against its share of net liabilities of £375,000 (that is, £1.5m × 25%) Therefore, the group only needs to provide for a further £500,000 on consolidation. This provision would also be made against the loan, giving a net investment in the associate of £500,000.

28.149 Often where a joint venture or an associate is making losses, there may be a significant diminution in the joint venture's or associate's value. Where there is any permanent diminution in value of any goodwill attributable to an investment in a joint venture or an associate, a provision should be made to write down that goodwill. [FRS 9 para 38]. A provision for any further impairment in the associate's net assets would not normally be required in the group's consolidated financial statements, because such an impairment in value would generally be reflected in the associate's net asset value. Where there is an impairment in goodwill, FRS 9 requires that the amount written off in the period should be separately disclosed. [4 Sch 19(2); FRS 9 para 38].

28.150 In certain circumstances, a group may have a material investment in an associate that has a significant deficit of net assets that exceeds the group's share of net assets of its other associates. In this type of situation, it is necessary to decide how to show the deficit in the consolidated financial statements. The most appropriate caption on the balance sheet within which to show the group's share of the deficiency is 'other provisions', although the standard states it should be shown as a provision or a liability. [FRS 9 para 45]. However, it would not be appropriate in this circumstance to net the positive interest in associates against the negative interest to show a net provision. Consequently, the group's interest in the other associates' net assets should be shown separately from the provision made for the group's share of negative net assets of its associates that are in deficit.

28.151 Table 28.8 shows a group that has treated its interest in negative net assets of an associate in a similar way to that described above.

Table 28.8 – Airtours plc – Annual report and accounts – 30 September 1995

Notes to the financial statements

19) Provisions for liabilities and charges (extract)

Other provisions			Aircraft	
		Pension	maintenance	
	Total	provisions	provisions	Other
	1995	1995	1995	1995
The Group	£000	£000	£000	£000
At 1st October 1994	27,764	4,259	19,347	4,158
Provided during the year	13,430	680	12,750	–
	41,194	4,939	32,097	4,158
Utilised in the year	(5,339)	(102)	(5,237)	–
Exchange differences	589	357	–	232
Transfer from investments in associated companies	(3,179)	–	–	(3,179)
At 30th September 1995	33,265	5,194	26,860	1,211

The other provision represents the Group's share of deficiency in net assets within an associated company (see note 12).

Joint and several liability

28.152 FRS 9 makes the important point that, where unincorporated undertakings are treated as joint ventures or associates, a liability could arise in excess of that taken into account when accounting for the group's share of the joint venture or associate. In this case it is important that all such liabilities with respect to that entity are reflected appropriately in the financial statements. [FRS 9 para 46] The example given in the standard is that of joint and several liability in a partnership. [FRS 9 para 47]. Where such a potential liability exists (or a similar type of support agreement exists) it is necessary to consider whether a provision should be made for the possibility that the other party to the agreement may be unable to meet its obligations under that agreement.

28.153 In circumstances where it is clear that the other party is able to honour such an agreement, it is still necessary under the Act, FRS 9 and SSAP 18 for the group to disclose the existence of its potential commitment as a contingent liability and clearly explain the circumstances in which the liability might crystallise. [FRS 9 para 47]. Table 28.9 shows the extent of guarantees given in respect of bank borrowings and funding of associates.

Table 28.9 – Trafalgar House Public Limited Company – Report and Accounts – 30 September 1992

NOTES TO THE ACCOUNTS (extract)

31 Contingent liabilities (extract)

The group has contingent liabilities in respect of building and other agreements entered into in the normal course of business and in respect of litigation arising therefrom. In addition there are guarantees as follows:

	1992		1991	
	The Company £m	**The Group £m**	The Company £m	The Group £m
Guarantees given in respect of bank borrowings of subsidiaries	**240.7**	–	328.3	–
Guarantees and undertakings given in respect of bank borrowings and funding of associates	**114.4**	**114.4**	230.7	230.7

Minority interests

28.154 Where the associate is held by a subsidiary that is partly held by a minority, the minority's share of the associate's results should be shown as part of minority interests in the consolidated financial statements.

Acquisitions and disposals

Effective date of acquisition or disposal

28.155 The effective date of acquisition of an associate is the date on which the investor begins to fulfil the two essential elements of the definition of an associate, that is, holding a participating interest and exercising significant influence. Similarly, the effective date for the acquisition of a joint venture interest is the date on which the investor begins to control that entity jointly with the other venturers. [FRS 9 para 40]. These requirements are equivalent to those in FRS 2, which states that for subsidiaries, the date on which an undertaking becomes a subsidiary is the date on which control passes to the parent. [FRS 2 para 45]. In addition, the investment must be a long-term interest, that is, it is not held for subsequent resale.

28.156 It follows, therefore, that the date on which an investment ceases to be an associate is the date on which it ceases to fulfil either element of the definition mentioned above. Similarly, the date on which an investment ceases to be a joint venture is the date on which the investor ceases to have joint control. [FRS 9 para 40].

28.157 Once the investment has qualified as a joint venture or an associate, minor temporary changes in the relationship between the investor and its joint venture or associate should not affect its status. In a similar way to the rules that apply to interests in subsidiaries, once the investor has accounted for its investments as associates or joint ventures, it should continue to equity account for them whether or not the investor intends to keep its interest or dispose of it. [FRS 9 paras 7, 43]. The investor should only stop equity accounting when the investment ceases to be a joint venture or an associate.

Acquisition rules

28.158 Often an investment in a joint venture or an associate is acquired in stages. Where this happens, FRS 9 states that the rules specified in paragraphs 50 to 52 of FRS 2 should be applied. [FRS 9 para 41]. These provisions require that where a group increases its interest in an undertaking that is already an associate or a joint venture, the identifiable assets and liabilities of that entity should be revalued to fair values and goodwill should be calculated only on the increase in interest by reference to those fair values. Consequently, a new fair value exercise will need to be carried out for each tranche of shares acquired, unless the difference between the fair values and the carrying amounts of the net assets attributable to the increase in stake is immaterial. For piecemeal acquisitions of subsidiaries, complying with FRS 2's requirements can conflict with the Act, because the Act requires the identifiable assets and liabilities of subsidiaries to be included in the consolidation at their fair value at the date of acquisition. This means that under the Act's provisions goodwill is calculated at the time the entity becomes a subsidiary, ignoring the effect of acquiring previous tranches. However, the conflict with the Act does not arise in accounting for piecemeal acquisitions of associates or joint ventures, because the Act does not deal with how to account for the acquisition of associates or joint ventures. Consequently, the rules in FRS 2 should be followed.

28.159 The provisions of FRS 2 concerning piecemeal acquisitions are explained in detail in part I of chapter 23, which describes various situations that might arise. One of those situations is where an investment in an undertaking is increased such that it becomes an associate. An undertaking might become an associate in a number of ways (whereas joint ventures tend to be set up as such from the outset), for example:

- The investing group acquires an additional investment in the undertaking to bring its voting rights to over 20 per cent.

- The investing group has an investment of over 20 per cent, but previously did not have board representation or significant influence over the financial or operating policy decisions of the undertaking. It has now gained significant influence.

28.160 The treatment of an investment becoming an associate is illustrated in the example that follows.

Example

A group made an investment of 10% in a company a few years ago. The investment cost £25,000 and has subsequently been revalued to £50,000. It makes a further investment of 15% to bring its total investment to 25%. The fair value of the consideration given for the additional investment is £250,000. The net assets of the investee stand in its own books at the date of the second acquisition at £800,000. A fair value exercise has been undertaken at the date of acquisition which shows a fair value of net assets of £1.1m (including capitalised goodwill in the associate of £100,000). The adjusted capital and reserves of the associate are, as a consequence, £200,000 share capital and £900,000 reserves (which includes a £200,000 revaluation reserve). The associate has goodwill recognised in its balance sheet of £100,000. The goodwill arising on acquisition and the balance sheet treatment in the group would be as follows:

Cost of acquisition	£'000
Original investment	25
Fair value of consideration given	250
Total consideration	275
Consolidation goodwill	£'000
Total consideration	275
Adjusted capital and reserves excluding capitalised goodwill of £100,000 (being, 25% × (£1.1m – £100,000 goodwill))	250
Goodwill	25
Balance sheet (extract)	£'000
Interest in associated undertakings	
Share of net assets excluding goodwill (being, 25% × £1m)	250
Goodwill on acquisition	25
	275

The only adjustments that would be required in this example are to reduce the value of the original investment from its market value to cost and to eliminate the goodwill recognised in the associate. Consequently, the entries on consolidation would be to debit the revaluation reserve of the investor with £25,000 and credit the investment £25,000 and in the associate to credit goodwill £100,000 and debit reserves with £100,000. The goodwill arising on acquisition of £25,000 would be dealt with in accordance with FRS 10 (see chapter 23).

Alternatively, the goodwill arising on the acquisition of the additional 15% interest can also be calculated separately.

Goodwill arising on acquisition of the additional 15% interest	£'000
Fair value of consideration	250
Adjusted capital and reserves after elimination of goodwill arising in the associate (15% × (£1.1m – £100,000))	150
Goodwill	100

If goodwill of £100,000 is recognised, the difference between this amount and the goodwill of £25,000, being a credit of £75,000, calculated above represents a revaluation of the 10% interest and should be credited to the revaluation reserve. This calculation gives a fairer presentation of the goodwill arising on the increase in stake. At present, either method is acceptable.

28.161 In the example above, where an investment becomes an associate interest, it is possible to account for the increase in the investment in two ways. There are no specific rules in this area, so either method can be used. The technically correct method would be to calculate the goodwill arising on the acquisition of each tranche of the investment. However, this would generally not be practicable, because fair values would not necessarily be available at the time the original investment was made. The second method described above treats the increase in stake as a separate acquisition and gives a fairer result that the first method.

28.162 Although the second method described above is not required where an investment becomes an associate, it is necessary to consider each tranche separately where there is an increase in stake in an associate. FRS 2 requires that such a method is used for piecemeal acquisitions for subsidiaries and these same rules are applied *via* FRS 9 to increases in stake for associates. Consider the following example:

Example

A group made an investment in an associate of 20% in 1992. The investment cost £12m and the book value (also fair value) of the associate's net assets at that date was £50m. In 1998 it makes a further investment in the company of 20% to bring its total investment to 40%. Goodwill on the original acquisition of the associate was written off directly against reserves in the year of acquisition (following the rules that applied before the introduction of FRS 10). The net assets of the associate stand in its books at £68m on the date of the increase in stake. The associate would be treated as follows up to the date of the original acquisition:

Acquisition of associate	£m
Original investment in company	12.0
Fair value of net assets acquired (20% × £50m)	10.0
Goodwill arising	2.0

The fair value of the consideration given for the additional 20% is £16m. The fair value exercise shows that the company's net assets are worth £75m, which is also the adjusted capital and reserves. The goodwill on acquisition of the increase in stake would be calculated as follows:

Increase in stake in associate		
Cost of acquisition as shown in the investor's books	**£m**	**£m**
Original investment in company		12
Fair value of consideration given for new investment		16
Total investment in associate		28
Consolidation goodwill		
Total consideration		28
Adjusted capital and reserves		
being 20% × £50m	10	
being 20% × £75m	15	25
Goodwill		3
Goodwill previously written off		2
New goodwill arising on the increase in stake		1

The goodwill figure that emerges is instinctively correct as it reflects the fact that a premium of £1m arises on the acquisition of the additional 20% (that is, £16m – (£75m × 20%)). The results since the date of acquisition of the associate are attributable to the group and as such are correctly treated as post-acquisition. The alternative calculation of considering the total investment of £28m compared to the total share of net assets of £30m (that is, £75m × 40%) gives a total figure of negative goodwill of £2m and, as a consequence, negative goodwill of £4m arising on the increase in stake. This method understates the goodwill arising on the increase in stake and is not the method specified in FRS 2, but nevertheless may be used where the difference between the net fair values and the carrying amounts of the assets and liabilities attributable to the increase in stake is not material.

Disposal rules

28.163 The standard states that where an interest in a joint venture or an associate is disposed of, the profit or loss arising on disposal should be calculated after taking into account any related goodwill that has not previously been written off through the profit and loss account. [FRS 9 para 40]. For example, there may be a balance of unamortised goodwill that relates to the joint venture or associate which is capitalised as part of the interest in the investment. Alternatively, under FRS 10's transitional provisions, goodwill arising on the acquisition of joint ventures or associates that arose before the introduction of that standard may still be written off directly against reserves. Where this is so, the goodwill that applies to the proportion of the investment disposed of should be brought into account in calculating the profit or loss arising on the disposal.

28.164 When an entity ceases to be either a joint venture or an associate, the investor may retain all or some of its interest in that entity simply as an investment. In this circumstance, it is necessary to determine the carrying value of any remaining interest in the undertaking. This should be based on the percentage retained of the final carrying amount for the joint venture or associate at the date the entity ceased to qualify as a subsidiary or an associate. The remaining interest should also include any related goodwill. [FRS 9 para 42]. For example, if goodwill arising on the original acquisition of a 24 per cent interest in an associate was £50,000, then if the investment decreases to 12 per cent and the entity is no longer an associate, the carrying value of the investment should include 50 per cent of the goodwill arising on the original investment, that is, £25,000. The new carrying amount of the investment is a surrogate cost (not based on any consideration paid) and should be reviewed and written down, if necessary, to its recoverable amount. [FRS 9 para 42].

Example

A group has had an investment of 40% in an associate for a number of years. At the beginning of the accounting period, the balance sheets of the group excluding the associate and the group including the associate are as follows:

Summarised balance sheets

	Group excluding associate £'000	Associate £'000	Group including associate £'000
Fixed assets	500	230	500
Investment in associate:			
Cost	110	–	–
Equity accounting	–	–	125
Current assets	300	150	300
Current liabilities	(250)	(80)	(250)
	660	300	675
Share capital	300	100	300
Share premium	220	50	220
Profit and loss reserve	40	100	55
Other reserves	100	50	100
	660	300	675

The net assets of the associate at the date of acquisition of the 40% interest were £250,000. The goodwill that arose on the original acquisition of the associate is £10,000 (that is, £110,000 – (£250,000 × 40%)). The goodwill was capitalised on the acquisition of the associate to accord with FRS 10's requirements and £5,000 has been amortised to the profit and loss account since acquisition. Consequently, the group's investment in the associate of

£125,000 is made up of its share of net assets of £120,000 (that is, £300,000 × 40%) plus the balance of goodwill unamortised of £5,000.

The group's profit and loss reserve of £55,000 is made up of £40,000 less goodwill amortisation of £5,000 plus the share of the associate's post-acquisition reserves of £20,000 (that is, £50,000 × 40%).

During the year the group disposes of 50% of its investment in the associate and no longer has board representation. Consequently, the remaining interest of 20% is no longer considered to be that of an associate, but represents a simple investment. The proceeds received on the sale are £70,000 and the net asset value of the associate at the date of sale is £320,000. Consequently, up to the date of sale of part of the group's investment in the associate, it made a profit of £20,000. The associate, therefore, becomes an investment part way through the year. The profit and loss accounts of the group excluding the former associate, the former associate and the group adjusted to include the revised carrying amount of the investment in the former associate are given below:

Summarised profit and loss accounts

	Group excluding interest £'000	Former associate £'000	Group including interest £'000
Operating profit	40	30	40.0
Share of operating profit of associate (note (a))	–	–	8.0
Operating profit including associate	40	30	48.0
Profit on sale of interest in associate (note (b))	15	–	3.5
Profit for the financial year	55	30	51.5
Reserve brought forward	40	100	55.0
Reserve carried forward	95	130	106.5

(a) The income from interest in the associated undertaking of £8,000 is the group's share of the results of the undertaking before the disposal (that is, 40% × £20,000).

(b) The profit on the sale of the share of the associate in the company selling the interest is £15,000, which is calculated by deducting from the sale proceeds of £70,000 the cost of the investment of £55,000 (that is, £110,000 × 50%). The profit on sale to the group is £3,500, which is calculated by deducting from the sale proceeds of £70,000 a 20% share of the associate's net assets consolidated up to the date of sale of £64,000 (that is, £320,000 × 20%) and half of the balance of unamortised goodwill of £2,500 that arose on the original acquisition.

At the group's year end, the balance sheets of the group and the former associate, which is now an investment, are set out below:

Summarised balance sheets

	Group excluding interest £'000	Former associate £'000	Group including interest £'000
Fixed assets	530	250	530.0
Investment (cost)	55	–	66.5
Current assets	390	170	390.0
Current liabilities	(260)	(90)	(260.0)
	715	330	726.5
Share capital	300	100	300.0
Share premium	220	50	220.0
Profit and loss reserve	95	130	106.5
Other reserves	100	50	100.0
	715	330	726.5

The investment in the former associate of £66,500 represents the share of net assets and goodwill retained by the group at the date of disposal (that is, (£320,000 × 20%) + (£5,000 × 50%)). The share of goodwill remaining is shown as part of the investment. The result is curious, because the investment in the company holding the interest is shown at a cost to that company of £55,000, but the group shows a cost to the group for the investment of £66,500. The difference of £11,500 represents the results of the associate recorded by the group which include retained reserves of £14,000 (that is, (£320,000 – £250,000) × 20%) less goodwill amortisation of £2,500. It is necessary to ensure that the carrying value of the investment in the group is not impaired, but as long as this is not the case, it would be possible in the company to revalue the investment to £66,500 the same value as shown in the group and credit to the revaluation reserve with the difference of £11,500.

28.165 An example of a disposal of a part interest in an associate is given in Table 28.10.

Table 28.10 – Flextech p.l.c. – Report and accounts – 31 December 1996

Notes to the accounts (extract)

23 Acquisitions and disposals (extract)

(d) On 30 July 1996, HIT Entertainment PLC ("HIT") became listed on the Alternative Investment Market. Flextech p.l.c. did not acquire any additional shares and, as a result, its shareholding reduced from 28% to 23.39%. The dilution of the investment in HIT has been treated as a deemed disposal by Flextech p.l.c. and the profit of £506,000 arising on the disposal of the 4.61% has been taken to the profit and loss account.

A joint venture becomes an associate

28.166 An interest in an entity that ceases to be a joint venture may still qualify as an associate. In this case, a profit or loss will arise on disposal, but the same rules, that is, equity accounting, will apply to the remaining interest, albeit disclosure is no longer required of the share of the associate's gross turnover or gross assets and gross liabilities on the face of the balance sheet. In addition, a joint venture can become an associate where the investor does not dispose of any interest in the entity. This would arise where the degree of influence the investor has over its investee changes from joint control to mere significant influence. In this situation, there will be no change to the share to be equity accounted only the level of disclosure will decrease from the 'gross equity' requirements to the less detailed normal equity accounting disclosures.

A subsidiary becomes an associate

28.167 Acquisitions of associates are considered from paragraph 28.158 above, but an associate can also arise from the disposal of an interest in a subsidiary, for example:

- The investing group sells a share of a subsidiary company, which has reduced the group's shareholding to below 50 per cent of the undertaking's voting rights although the group has retained significant influence and, accordingly, it is now an associate.
- A subsidiary issues shares to a third party such that the investing group's shareholding reduces below 50 per cent of the undertaking's voting rights, although significant influence is retained.
- The investing group ceases to have dominant influence at, for example, the 40 per cent level, but continues to have significant influence.

28.168 The treatment of a subsidiary becoming an associate is illustrated in the example that follows.

Example

A group has had an investment of 80% in a subsidiary for a number of years. At the beginning of the accounting period, the balance sheets of the group excluding the subsidiary and the group including the subsidiary are as follows:

Summarised balance sheets

	Group excluding sub. £'000	Sub. £'000	Group including sub. £'000
Goodwill	–	–	10
Fixed assets	500	230	730
Investment in subsidiary	220	–	–
Current assets	300	150	450
Current liabilities	(250)	(80)	(330)
	770	300	860
Share capital	300	100	300
Share premium	220	50	220
Profit and loss reserve	150	100	180
Other reserves	100	50	100
Minority interests	–	–	60
	770	300	860

The goodwill that arose on the original acquisition of the subsidiary is £20,000 and is calculated as set out below. The goodwill was capitalised on the acquisition of the subsidiary to accord with the requirements of FRS 10 and £10,000 has been amortised to the profit and loss account since acquisition.

Cost of control account/goodwill

Investment	220,000	Share capital (80% × 100,000)	80,000
		Share premium (80% × 50,000)	40,000
		Pre-acq. profit and loss reserve (80% × 50,000)	40,000
		Other reserves (80% × 50,000)	40,000
		Balance, *viz* goodwill	20,000
	220,000		220,000

The minority interests at the beginning of the year are calculated as follows:

Minority interests account

Minority interests	60,000	Share capital (20% × 100,000)	20,000
		Share premium (20% × 50,000)	10,000
		Profit and loss reserve (20% × 100,000)	20,000
		Other reserves (20% × 50,000)	10,000
	60,000		60,000

The group's profit and loss reserve of £180,000 is made up of £150,000 less goodwill amortisation of £10,000 plus the subsidiary's post-acquisition reserves of £40,000 (that is, £50,000 × 80%).

During the year the group disposes of 50% of its investment in the subsidiary. The proceeds received on the sale are £140,000 and the net asset value of the subsidiary at the date of sale is £320,000. Consequently, up to the date of sale of part of the group's investment in the subsidiary, it made a profit of £20,000. The subsidiary, therefore, becomes an associate part way through the year. The profit and loss accounts of the group excluding the associate, the associate, and the group including the associate using the equity method of accounting are given below:

Summarised profit and loss accounts

	Group excluding assoc. £'000	Assoc. £'000	Group including assoc. £'000
Operating profit (note (a))	40	30	60
Share of operating profit of associate (note (b))	–	–	4
Operating profit including associate	40	30	64
Profit on sale of interest in subsidiary (note (c))	30	–	7
Operating profit	70	30	71
Minority interests (note (d))	–	–	4
Profit for the year	70	30	67
Reserve brought forward	150	100	180
Reserve carried forward	220	130	247

(a) The operating profit for the group of £60,000 represents the profit of the group of £40,000, (excluding the associate's profit) plus the profit of the subsidiary up to the date of sale of the 40% interest (which is £20,000).

(b) The income from interests in associated undertakings of £4,000 is the group's share of the results of the undertaking after it became an associate (that is, 40% × £10,000).

(c) The profit on the sale of the subsidiary in the company selling the interest is £30,000, which is calculated by deducting from the sale proceeds of £140,000 the cost of the investment of £110,000 (that is, £220,000 × 50%). The profit on sale to the group is £7,000, which is calculated by deducting from the sale proceeds of £140,000 a 40% share of the subsidiary's net assets consolidated up to the date of sale of £128,000 and half of the balance of unamortised goodwill that arose on the original acquisition of £5,000. The net assets of the subsidiary are made up of the net assets at the last balance sheet date of £300,000 plus the profit on ordinary activities to date of sale of £20,000. The group's share of those assets is £128,000 (that is, £320,000 × 40%).

(d) The minority interest figure of £4,000 is the minority's share of the profits of the subsidiary up to the date of sale of the 40% interest and is calculated by applying the minority's share of 20% to the profits recognised of the subsidiary in the period (that is, £20,000).

At the group's year end, the balance sheets of the group and the former subsidiary, which is now an associate, are set out below:

Summarised balance sheets

	Group excluding assoc.	Assoc.	Group including assoc.
	£'000	£'000	£'000
Fixed assets	530	250	530
Investment in associate:			
Cost	110	–	–
Equity accounting	–	–	137
Current assets	460	170	460
Current liabilities	(260)	(90)	(260)
	840	330	867
Share capital	300	100	300
Share premium	220	50	220
Profit and loss reserve	220	130	247
Other reserves	100	50	100
Minority interest	–	–	–
	840	330	867

The investment in the associate of £137,000 represents the share of net assets and goodwill retained by the group at the date of sale (that is, (£320,000 × 40%) + (£10,000 × 50%)), together with the share of the associate's results that arose after the sale (that is, £10,000 × 40%). The goodwill is shown as part of the investment in the associate, but should also be separately disclosed in the notes to accord with FRS 9.

Joint arrangements

28.169 A 'joint arrangement' is a new term which encompasses the following types of undertakings:

- A joint arrangement that has its own trade or business. This is a joint venture and should be gross equity accounted in accordance with the provisions of FRS 9, as explained earlier in this chapter.

- A 'joint arrangement that is not an entity'. This is a joint activity undertaken by two or more participants, whereby the activity does not amount to the carrying on of its own trade or business.

- A structure with the form, but not the substance, of a joint venture.

28.170 This section deals with the last two types of arrangement, which are referred to below as 'joint arrangements'. Joint arrangements of this type are required to be accounted for in a different way from associates and joint ventures; that is, interests in such arrangements should not be equity accounted. Both of these types of arrangement are somewhat similar in nature to joint ventures in that they will be formed by two or more participants and there will be an agreement covering the arrangement. But they differ from joint ventures in other respects.

Joint arrangement that is not an entity

28.171 A 'joint arrangement that is not an entity' is defined as:

> *"A contractual arrangement under which the participants engage in joint activities that do not create an entity because it would not be carrying on a trade or business of its own. A contractual arrangement where all significant matters of operating and financial policy are predetermined does not create an entity because the policies are those of its participants, not of a separate entity."* [FRS 9 para 4].

28.172 For this purpose, the term 'entity' is defined in FRS 9 to mean:

> *"A body corporate, partnership or unincorporated association carrying on a trade or business with or without a view to profit. The reference to carrying on a trade or business means a trade or business of its* own *and not just part of the trades or businesses of entities that have interests in it."* [FRS 9 para 4].

28.173 The term 'undertaking' in the Act uses identical wording to that in the first sentence of the definition of 'entity', but does not include the second qualifying sentence. Consequently, an undertaking can be a 'joint arrangement that is not an entity'. Appendix I to the standard, which includes a note on the legal requirements, says clearly that a joint arrangement may qualify as an undertaking under the Act, even where it does not carry on its own trade. It goes on to say that in such cases the undertaking acts merely as an agent for the venturers. [FRS 9 Appendix I para 6].Therefore, a 'joint arrangement that is not an entity' can be an undertaking such as a limited company or a partnership or an unincorporated undertaking or may be a simple arrangement between the parties where a separate legal entity is not established, as it is the nature of its trading relationship that determines whether or not it will fall within the standard's definition, not how it is constituted. The term 'entity' is used to describe the substance rather than the legal form.

28.174 In contrast, for a joint arrangement to be a separate entity, that is, a joint venture, it must carry on a trade or business of its own and not just be part of its participants' trades or businesses. Such an entity will have some independence from its participants to pursue its own commercial strategy in buying and selling and will have access to the market in its own right for its main inputs and outputs. [FRS 9 para 8]. This independence must be allowed within the objectives set by the agreement governing the entity, for example, in the joint venture agreement. If, on the other hand, the objectives are predetermined in that agreement and in effect the business unwinds exactly as specified within that agreement, the undertaking is likely to be a joint arrangement.

28.175 As stated above, to be a joint arrangement the undertaking must not carry on a trade or business of its own. For this reason, cost-sharing or risk-sharing arrangements are likely to be classified as joint arrangements and the standard gives as examples the following types of arrangements:

- Joint marketing.
- Joint distribution.
- Shared production facilities.

For example, a joint marketing arrangement established by two parties whereby the participants fund a joint marketing campaign is likely to be a joint arrangement. In such a case, the joint arrangement does not have access to the market in its own right, but is merely an extension of each participant's trade.

28.176 It follows that a company can *only* be a joint arrangement where it acts as an agent for its joint venturers. In this circumstance, it will not have access to the market in its own right as it is merely acting on its principals' behalf. Consequently, in the example of the joint marketing arrangement mentioned above, if the joint marketing is conducted within a limited company, it would only amount to a joint arrangement where the company is acting as an agent for its principals, otherwise it will be a joint venture or an associate.

28.177 Repetition of buying and selling is indicative of an arrangement carrying on a trade or business. Conversely, where an arrangement carries out a single project, such as a single property joint development, the undertaking will not carry on a separate trade or business where it acts as an agent for its principals' businesses. The undertaking would fall to be treated as a joint arrangement. [FRS 9 para 9]. This would apply, for example, to a short-term property development undertaken as a partnership. However, it appears that where a short-term property development is undertaken in a limited company, then it will not be a joint arrangement, unless the company is acting as an agent for its principals. Where an agency arrangement does not exist, such a company would fall within the definitions of an associate or a joint venture even where, for example, it only runs for 18 months. This is because in this situation the investment would be deemed to be held for the long term. Long term is defined in the standard by reference to whether or not the investment is held with a view to subsequent resale and not in relation to the length of time the undertaking will exist to fulfil its purpose. [FRS 9 para 4].

28.178 The standard mentions two further examples of joint arrangements that are not entities. The first is where the participants derive their benefit from products or services taken in kind, rather than by receiving a share in the results of trading. [FRS 9 para 8(a)]. This could, for example, be a joint research arrangement, whereby each of the participants benefits from the research, but are not billed a royalty specifically by the research company for using that patented research. The participants would fund the research through some other means. In addition, the standard states that joint arrangements can cover situations where the participants take their share of the joint product in cash where that commodity is actively traded. [FRS 9 para 8(a)]. This might arise, for example, in the oil and gas industry where two or more producers form a joint distribution arrangement.

28.179 The second situation described in the standard is where each participant's share of the output or result of the joint activity is determined by its supply of key inputs to the process producing that output or result. [FRS 9 para 8(b)]. An example might be where it is possible to segregate the activities of the entity so that each of the participants' results can be separately seen. This is very similar to the standard's description of a joint arrangement that has the form, but not the substance, of a joint venture (see further para 28.183).

28.180 The nature of a joint arrangement might change over time. For example, it might start out as such an arrangement whereby it is just an extension of its participants' trades, such as with the development and use of an oil or gas pipeline. But if the joint arrangement starts to trade with third parties that are not participants in the joint arrangement, then it may well take on the form of a joint venture entity and require to be gross equity accounted. [FRS 9 para 9].

28.181 In practice, it will often be difficult to judge whether or not an undertaking is a joint arrangement or a joint venture. The following examples illustrate two different structures.

Example 1

Three venturers form a company to supply IT services to a customer. The parties to the arrangement each own 33% of the company's shares. The venturers supply different IT products, with one supplying the software, another the hardware and the third supplying the systems expertise. The sole purpose for the company is to allow the parties to invoice the customer in one name. The supplier of the systems expertise manages the provision of the hardware and software supply and gives a performance guarantee to the customer. The hardware supply represents 50% of the company's turnover, the software accounts for 20% and the system development 30%. The operation of the company is governed by a shareholder agreement with the company and sub-contract agreements with the venturers. The company makes no margin on the on-billing of the hardware, software and systems development, any administrative expenses being recharged to the participants.

In this situation, it is clear that the financial and operating policies of the company are predetermined by the shareholder agreement and the other agreements surrounding the arrangement. In addition, the undertaking does not have access to the market in its own right as it is merely a facility through which the participants' businesses are conducted and, as a consequence, is acting as their agent. Therefore, the undertaking would be judged to be a joint arrangement rather than a joint venture under FRS 9's provisions.

Example 2

Three venturers form a company to bid for the provision of healthcare services to a Health Trust under the Private Finance Initiative (PFI). The parties to the venture are a construction company, a service provider and an equity investment fund. Each of the venturers owns 33% of the company's shares. The company constructs a hospital, which is financed in part by the equity venturers and also by bank funding secured on the payments to be made by the Health Trust (that is, the unitary payment). In substance the construction and the service provision are sub-contracted to two of the venturers. The unitary payment made by the Health Trust varies depending upon the delivery performance under the terms of the PFI contract. The property has been judged to be on balance sheet of the company. There is a shareholder agreement with the company and sub-contract agreements with the venturers. Under the shareholder agreement, profits or losses of the company are shared equally between the venturers and all decisions have to have full agreement of the venturers (there are also arbitration procedures specified in the agreement). The amount the service provider receives is dependent upon its performance and this is detailed in its sub-contract agreement.

For the service provider, the arrangement could be either a joint venture or a joint arrangement. At first sight, the structure has many of the features of a joint arrangement. For example, most of the financial and operating policies are predetermined in the agreements (these include, the PFI agreement, the shareholder agreement, the loan agreement with the bank and the sub-contract agreements with the venturers). Also, it could be argued that the company does not have access to the market in its own right, because it only has one customer under the PFI agreement and its relationship with the Health Trust was established in the agreements. But this argument ignores the fact that the company is carrying on a business of its own, which is the provision of an *integrated* service to the Health Trust, and is not acting as an agent in this respect. In addition, the company could provide a similar service for other customers in the future and, as a consequence, has access to the market in its own right. Therefore, the facts of this case indicate that the undertaking falls within the definition of a joint venture, which should be accounted for under the gross equity accounting method by its venturers rather than falling to be treated as a joint arrangement.

28.182 It can be seen from the above examples that joint arrangements are unlikely to be common in practice. They are likely to be limited to agency type arrangements, where it is clear that the undertaking's business is just an extension of the separate businesses of its venturers and where it does not have access to the market in its own right.

Joint venture with the substance of a joint arrangement

28.183 Another type of joint arrangement identified in the standard is an undertaking that has the form of a joint venture, but not the substance of one. Such an arrangement would arise where the joint venture undertaking is used only as a means for each participant to carry on its own business. [FRS 9 para 24]. In this type of situation the venturers would operate their own businesses separately within the structure. The framework entity would act merely as an agent for each of the venturers, who are able to identify their own share of the assets, liabilities and cash flows within the framework. [FRS 9 para 25]. Where such an arrangement exists and is conducted through a limited company, the undertaking will only be a joint arrangement if it acts as an agent for its principals. [FRS 9 Appendix I para 5].

28.184 Some securitisation special purpose vehicles work in this way. Each of the originators/participants in the special purpose vehicle will be able to identify the assets (such as, mortgage receivables) that it has contributed to the venture and its benefits and risks arise directly from those assets and their related finance.

Accounting for joint arrangements

28.185 FRS 9 requires the same accounting treatment for both the types of joint arrangements identified above. The only requirement specified in the standard is that the participants in such a joint arrangement should account for their own assets, liabilities and cash flows, measured according to the terms of the agreement governing the arrangement. [FRS 9 paras 18, 24].

28.186 In practice this requirement gives rise to a number of interpretation problems. First, the requirement does not specifically state that the participants must account also for the trading impact of those transactions, but this is implied because this will be the effect of accounting for the changes in assets and liabilities. In addition, appendix III to the standard says the accounting should be for the investor's *"own* share *of the assets, liabilities and cash flows"* as compared to the standard itself which makes no mention of the word 'share'. [FRS 9 Appendix III para 8]. Consequently, how to account for the transactions might not be obvious. In most situations the amounts to be accounted for will not be governed by the participant's equity share, but will be dependent upon the economic sharing arrangements under the arrangement. For example, a joint billing arrangement might be conducted through an undertaking where the equity share is 50/50, but where one of the participants generates 80 per cent of the transactions, in which case it should recognise its own transactions undertaken by the joint arrangement. In this type of situation it will be necessary to consider carefully how any residual profit or loss in the joint arrangement is dealt with. In other situations, it might be more appropriate to account for the underlying transactions that specifically relate to the particular investor, rather than a share of the joint arrangement's transactions.

28.187 The paragraphs that follow consider how participants in different types of joint arrangement should account for their underlying transactions.

Joint agreements between participants

28.188 Joint arrangements that are merely agreements between the participants where there is no undertaking involved are easily dealt with under the standard's provisions. It is relatively simple for the participants to account for their share of the assets and liabilities and cash flows under the arrangement in their individual financial statements. Indeed, this is how transactions of this nature were accounted for before FRS 9 became standard practice and, if this is how a participant has accounted for the transactions in the past, no prior year adjustment is required on implementing the standard.

28.189 Joint arrangements of this nature encompass jointly controlled operations and jointly controlled assets. These have already been dealt with in IAS 31, 'Financial reporting of interests in joint ventures' and FRS 9 follows the same path. Because

IAS 31 has more detailed guidance than FRS 9, the explanation that follows draws heavily on IAS 31's provisions. In these types of arrangements, the venturers use their own assets and resources rather than establishing a company, partnership or other entity. Examples given in IAS 31 of jointly controlled operations include the manufacture, marketing and distribution jointly of a particular product, such as an aircraft. Different parts of the manufacturing process are carried out by the venturers, which bear their own costs and take a share of the revenues of the aircraft in accordance with the joint agreement. The accounting for jointly controlled operations under FRS 9 is the same as under IAS 31, with each of the venturers recognising in its individual financial statements and in its consolidated financial statements:

- The assets that it controls and the liabilities that it incurs.
- The expenses that it incurs and its share of the income that it earns from the sale of goods or services by the joint venture.

No consolidation adjustments or other consolidation procedures are necessary, because the assets, liabilities, income and expenses are already recognised in each of the joint venturers' financial statements. [IAS 31 para 10].

Example

Two companies decide to undertake a joint road construction project. They agree to supply different assets and staff to the joint arrangement. The joint arrangement has a separate bank account. The participants charge rental for their plant used in the project to the bank account and also have an agreed staff cost per hour, which is also charged to that account. The participants fund the account and invoice the customer in their joint names. Any surplus is shared 50/50.

The joint arrangement transactions that need to be reflected in each participant's accounts are unlikely to be a straight share of those transactions, but will depend on the costs that the participants have borne themselves. Therefore, although a participant is charging a rental to the joint arrangement for the use of its plant, that plant is already accounted for as a fixed asset in that participant's balance sheet and its profit and loss account will already bear a normal depreciation charge for the asset's use. Hence, the rental to the joint arrangement should be eliminated. Similarly, the participant will have charged its actual staff costs in its profit and loss account, so it will need to eliminate any charge made to the joint arrangement on a different basis. The joint arrangement will bill its customers for the work undertaken by the venture and it would be appropriate for the participant to recognise its share (50% in this case) in its turnover. In order to arrive at the correct profit share in the participant's profit and loss account, it will be necessary to book an equalisation charge or credit in order to take into account that the actual costs incurred by the participant might be different from its share of the joint arrangement's costs. Consequently, the participant may in part be funding the costs of its joint arrangement partner (or vice versa).

28.190 Many activities in the oil, gas and mineral extraction industries involve the use of jointly controlled assets. An often cited example is where a number of venturers jointly control and operate an oil pipeline. Typically in such arrangements, each venturer uses the pipeline to transport its own product, in return for which it bears an agreed proportion of the expenses of operating the pipeline. Again the accounting under FRS 9 for such ventures is the same as required under IAS 31. Each venturer shows in its individual financial statements and in its consolidated financial statements:

- Its share of the jointly controlled assets, classified according to the nature of the assets rather than as an investment. For example, a share of a jointly controlled oil pipeline is classified as property, plant and equipment.
- Any liabilities that it has incurred, for example, those incurred to finance its share of the asset.
- Its share of any liabilities incurred jointly with other venturers.
- Any income from the sale or use of its share of the output, together with its share of any expenses incurred.
- Any expenses which it has incurred in respect of its interest in the venture, for example those related to financing the venturer's interest in the assets and selling its share of the output.

As with joint operations, no consolidation adjustments or other consolidation procedures are necessary, because the assets, liabilities, income and expenses are already recognised in each of the joint venturers' financial statements. [IAS 31 para 15].

Joint arrangements in unincorporated undertakings including partnerships

28.191 FRS 9 goes further than IAS 31 and identifies that joint arrangements can arise in unincorporated undertakings, such as partnerships. FRS 9 requires that participants who enter into joint arrangements that are carried out in unincorporated undertakings and in partnerships should similarly account for their share of the assets, liabilities and cash flows under the arrangement in their individual financial statements and, as a consequence, these transactions will find their way into the group's consolidated financial statements.

28.192 Two legal issues arise from this accounting treatment. First, whether on consolidation the Companies Act allows a company to account for its joint arrangement entity's results in this way. Before the introduction of FRS 9, it was quite acceptable in the group's consolidated financial statements to proportionately consolidate the results of unincorporated joint ventures such as partnerships, as this is an option under the legislation (equity accounting also being permissible under the Act). The Act's rules remain unchanged following the introduction of FRS 9, so it would appear possible to continue to adopt proportional consolidation for such entities under the Act. To all intents and purposes in the group's consolidated financial statements, proportional consolidation gives the same result as FRS 9's requirement to account for the participant's share of the assets and liabilities and cash flows under the arrangements.

28.193 The second issue arises in the participant's individual financial statements. The issue is whether or not it is legal to include the appropriate share of the joint arrangement's transactions, which arise in a separate legal entity, in the financial statements of the participant, which will generally be a limited company. Where the joint venture entity is a partnership, it will be possible for the partners to record their share of the partnership's transactions in their individual financial statements. It is generally appropriate to do this, however, only where there is no restriction on the distribution of the partnership's profits and reserves. This basis of accounting is the same as that used prior to the introduction of FRS 9 for many partnership arrangements of this nature.

28.194 Furthermore, where the joint arrangement is acting as an agent of each of the participants (which might arise, for example, where the joint arrangement entity is on-billing goods for each participant), the share of the transactions should rightly be included in each principal's (that is, each participant's) books. Whether the transactions will be recorded in the agent's (that is, the joint arrangement entity's) books, or will be recorded at nil value, depends upon whether or not the entity is acting as a disclosed or an undisclosed agent (see chapter 36).

Joint arrangements in limited companies

28.195 Because of the definition of a joint arrangement, it is quite possible under FRS 9 for a limited company to be a joint arrangement. As for other joint arrangements FRS 9 requires that participants who invest in limited companies that are joint arrangements should account for their share of the assets and liabilities and cash flows under the arrangement in their individual financial statements and, as a consequence, in their group's consolidated financial statements.

28.196 As explained in paragraph 28.176 above, joint arrangements will not arise in a company, unless the undertaking acts as an agent of its participants. Consequently, where the joint arrangement company acts as either a disclosed agent or an undisclosed agent, the appropriate share of transactions undertaken by the agent should rightly be included in each principal's (that is, each participant's) books. Consequently, the participant's share of the joint arrangement's transactions would appear in its individual financial statements and, as a result, in its consolidated financial statements. This accounting treatment complies with FRS 9 and also with the Act. Furthermore, whether or not the transactions are also recorded in the agent's (that is, the joint arrangement undertaking's) books will depend on whether the joint arrangement is a disclosed agent or an undisclosed agent (see further chapter 36).

Joint arrangements versus quasi-subsidiaries

28.197 As mentioned in paragraph 28.17, following the FRRP ruling made against Associated Nursing Services plc there has been confusion concerning the distinction between a joint venture and a quasi-subsidiary and, therefore, concerning the entities that need to be consolidated in full or accounted for in some other way in the group's consolidated financial statements. The ruling was made in February 1997, before FRS 9's publication and that confusion has now been compounded by the advent of joint arrangements. The FRRP ruling noted that Associated Nursing Services had entered into joint ventures with two partners and it had treated the joint ventures as associated undertakings in its 1995 and 1996 financial statements under the rules in SSAP 1 prior to FRS 9's publication.

28.198 In one case, which involved a joint venture with a bank, the board of the joint venture company in question was 'deadlocked'. It was the FRRP's view that the financial and operating policies of that company were substantially predetermined by underlying agreements; and through its interest in the joint venture Associated Nursing Services gained benefits arising from the net assets of the company, such that it had control. In the other case a venture capital arrangement with five venture capital funds had been set up through an intermediary. In the FRRP's view the financial and operating policies of that company were again substantially predetermined by underlying agreements. Even though in that case Associated Nursing Services held only a minority of the ordinary share capital, the investor's interests were effectively limited and the FRRP took the view that Associated Nursing Services gained benefits arising from the company's net assets, such that it had control.

28.199 In the FRRP's view, therefore, the substance of the arrangements was that the joint venture companies were in fact quasi-subsidiaries as defined by FRS 5. Consequently, they should not have been accounted for by the equity method, but should have been treated, as FRS 5 requires, as if they were subsidiaries. The ruling hinges on paragraph 34 of FRS 5 which states that: *"where the financial and operating policies of a vehicle are in substance pre-determined, contractually or otherwise, the party possessing control will be the one that gains the benefits arising from the net assets of the vehicle"*.

28.200 The wording in paragraph 34 of FRS 5 uses similar terminology to that used in the definition of a 'joint arrangement that is not an entity' in paragraph 4 of FRS 9. Part of the joint arrangement definition says that: *"A contractual arrangement where all significant matters of operating and financial policy are predetermined, does not create an entity because all the policies are those of its participants, not of a separate entity"*. The feature which distinguishes a joint arrangement from a quasi-subsidiary seems to be that although in both a joint arrangement and a quasi-subsidiary the financial and operating policies may be predetermined, in a quasi-subsidiary the investor must gain substantially all of the benefits arising from the net assets of the vehicle. This is because for an investment to meet the definition of a quasi-subsidiary the investment must give substantially the same benefits and risks to the investor as if it were an actual subsidiary.

Example

An entity is established to undertake a property development. There are two parties to the arrangement each providing 50% of the equity. The property development activities of the venture are all predetermined in the agreements with the venturers setting up the undertaking and with the providers of finance, including the profit-sharing arrangements. Where the profit-sharing arrangements are 50/50 between the parties, this type of venture would seem to fall within the joint arrangement category of investment under FRS 9. The investor would then account for its share of the arrangement, as considered in the paragraphs above. However, where the profit-sharing arrangements are not in line with the venturers' equity investment and, for example, one of the parties is given (say) 90% of the profits generated by the business, then this would indicate that that party gains the benefits arising from the net assets of the vehicle. If this is the case, then the venture is a quasi-subsidiary of that investor and should be consolidated in its financial statements. Where the profit sharing arrangements are (say) 60:40 judgment will be needed to decide whether to account for the arrangement as a joint arrangement or as a quasi-subsidiary.

Limited partnerships

28.201 As explained above, whether or not an undertaking is a joint arrangement depends on whether it has a trade or business of its own, not on how it is constituted legally. Consequently, a limited partnership can be a joint arrangement in particular circumstances. For example, a limited partnership might be set up to raise finance for the investor or to achieve some tax advantage. In these types of situations, the limited partnership will not have a trade or business of its own and should be accounted for as a joint arrangement.

28.202 As explained in chapter 21, limited partnerships are made up of a 'general partner' and 'limited partners'. The general partner manages the business and the limited partners are precluded from involvement in the day-to-day management of the undertaking. The partnership itself does not have a board of directors, but the equivalent to the board is the general partner himself. Consequently, where the general partner is a company, that company will control the board and under the Act's provisions the limited partnership will be a subsidiary. The company would, therefore, have to consolidate the limited partnership in its consolidated financial statements.

28.203 However, despite the fact that under the Act a limited partnership will be a subsidiary of a company if that company is its general partner, where the financial and operation policies are predetermined and the general partner merely manages the unwinding of the business in accordance with those predetermined policies, the partnership might be a joint arrangement. Where the limited partnership is judged to be a joint arrangement, in the investing company's financial statements FRS 9 requires the investor's share of the joint arrangement to be accounted for. But on consolidation, following FRS 9 would result in the investor's share of the joint arrangement being included within the consolidated financial statements. This results, in effect, in the company proportionately consolidating the limited partnership in its consolidated financial statements, whereas the Act would require full consolidation. This is a similar to the situation that arises in the investment management industry, where companies acting as general partners in limited partnerships have proportionally consolidated their investment rather than consolidating it in full. But where this is done, these groups have invoked the Act's true and fair override (see chapter 21). A similar override is necessary in order to comply with FRS 9's requirements in the consolidated financial statements where the investor is a general partner in a limited partnership, which fulfils the definition of a joint arrangement.

Prior year adjustments on implementation

28.204 FRS 9 introduces a number of changes from the requirements of SSAP 1. Consequently, on introduction of the standard groups will need to consider a number of issues some of which will give rise to prior year adjustments and some of these issues are considered below.

Classification

28.205 Some investments that were classified as associates under SSAP 1 will not qualify as such under FRS 9 and a prior year adjustment is needed on the standard's introduction. Such investments will no longer be required to be equity accounted and should instead be accounted for using the normal policy for the group's long-term investments.

28.206 It will be necessary to classify the remaining associates between associates and joint ventures as the standard has introduced special requirements for joint ventures. Those associates that are now judged to be joint ventures will have to be gross equity accounted.

28.207 The standard has introduced two new categories of joint arrangements. Equity accounting can no longer be used for these investments, as the investor has to record its interest in the assets, liabilities and cash flows of such joint arrangements. This might entail a prior year adjustment on consolidation, but a number of undertakings such as partnerships have often been accounted for in a similar way in the past and adjustments may not be needed where they have previously been proportionately consolidated.

28.208 Unincorporated joint venture entities carrying on a trade or business of their own have to be gross equity accounted under the FRS and, if they were previously proportionately consolidated, a prior year adjustment should be made on implementation.

Equity method of accounting

28.209 The equity method of accounting required by FRS 9 is very different in the profit and loss account from that previously required by SSAP 1. It will be necessary on the standard's introduction to adjust comparatives to give the equivalent new disclosures.

28.210 As mentioned above, the gross equity method of accounting now applies to joint ventures which requires turnover to be included in the profit and loss account and separately disclosed and requires gross assets less liabilities to be shown on the face of the balance sheet. Similar disclosures will have to be given for comparatives on the standard's introduction.

Equity accounting principles

28.211 Under FRS 9 goodwill is calculated on a different basis and the requirements of FRS 10 will apply to the remaining balance. Goodwill on the acquisition of a joint venture or an associate is the difference between the fair value of the consideration paid and the fair value of the investor's share of the net assets of the joint venture or associate acquired excluding any goodwill that is carried in the joint venture's or associate's own financial statements. Previously under SSAP 1, any goodwill arising in the joint venture's or associate's financial statements was disclosed separately and was not treated as part of the goodwill arising on acquisition. Consequently, it would now seem appropriate to treat such goodwill in the same way as the balance of acquired goodwill arising on the acquisition. This may necessitate a prior year adjustment, for example, to eliminate old goodwill against reserves if the balance of acquisition goodwill had been eliminated there.

28.212 In addition, prior to FRS 9's introduction, goodwill arising on an acquisition was accounted for in accordance with the requirements of SSAP 22. This meant that acquisition goodwill could be written off to reserves immediately or amortised. The vast majority of groups opted for immediate write-off. Two issues now arise. First, for a group adopting FRS 9 prior to the implementation of FRS 10, goodwill arising on acquisitions prior to FRS 10's implementation date can still be accounted for in accordance with SSAP 22 and no prior year adjustments arise. FRS 10 applies to accounting periods ending on or after 23 December 1998, although earlier adoption is encouraged. Secondly, for a company that has adopted FRS 9 and FRS 10, the full ramifications of FRS 10's transitional provisions apply and the group will need to consider whether to reinstate any goodwill relating to its joint ventures and associates that has previously been written off direct to reserves. If it decides to do so, this will require a prior year adjustment. Part III of chapter 23 considers FRS 10's transitional provisions in detail.

Additional disclosures

28.213 On implementing the standard it will also be necessary to include comparative information for the detailed disclosures that are required where the disclosure thresholds are breached for: joint ventures in aggregate; associates in aggregate; individual joint ventures; and individual associates.

Comparison with IASs

28.214 Associates and joint ventures are covered by IAS 28, 'Accounting for investments in associates', and IAS 31, 'Financial reporting of investments in joint ventures'.

28.215 Under IAS 28, the definition of associate is similar to that given in FRS 9, although FRS 9's definition is more restrictive. Consequently, some associates under IAS 28 would not be classified as such under FRS 9. Under IAS 28's requirements associates are required to be equity accounted in a group's consolidated financial statements. There is, however, no notion of gross equity accounting, which is required for joint venture entities under FRS 9.

28.216 In the parent's individual company financial statements, UK practice is to treat associates as investments. However, IAS 28 allows the use of the equity method of accounting. [IAS 28 para 12]. Where there are no consolidated financial statements, again IAS 28 allows the associate to be shown in the parent's individual financial statements using the equity method of accounting or using cost, with a note of the amounts that would have been shown under the equity method.

28.217 The IASC rules do not include the detailed disclosure requirements of FRS 9, in particular, the extensive additional disclosure required in aggregate or individually where certain measurement thresholds are exceeded.

28.218 For joint ventures, IAS 31 distinguishes between: jointly controlled 'entities'; and jointly controlled operations or assets. FRS 9 makes a similar distinction, but jointly controlled operations or assets fall within the FRS 9 category of joint arrangements that are not entities. 'Entities' under IAS 31 can be corporations, partnerships or other enterprises. This is similar to FRS 9, with the exception that such undertakings will not fall to be treated as joint ventures in the UK, unless they carry on their *own* trade or business.

28.219 Under IAS 31, the entity controls the assets of the joint venture and shares in its results. An entity maintains its own accounting records and prepares financial statements. 'Operations' involve the venturers in joint activities which are nevertheless recorded in detail as assets, expenses, etc. of the venturers. 'Assets' are jointly controlled or owned.

28.220 For entities, IAS 31 has a benchmark treatment of proportional consolidation where relevant, but permits the use of the equity method as an allowed alternative treatment. [IAS 31 paras 25 and 32]. This is different to FRS 9 where in the UK proportional consolidation of joint venture entities is not allowed and such investments must be accounted for using the gross equity method.

Chapter 29

Foreign currencies

Chapter 29

Foreign currencies

Introduction

29.1 Businesses conducted by UK companies are not simply confined within national boundaries. The globalisation of markets for goods and services as well as capital makes it imperative for companies to engage in international trade, cross-border alliances and joint ventures if they are to survive and grow in today's competitive business environment. The ways in which companies enter the international market place are varied. First, companies directly undertake transactions of buying goods and services from overseas suppliers and selling goods and services to overseas customers. Secondly, they may extend their international business by conducting their affairs through overseas subsidiaries, branches and associates.

29.2 In the first situation, transactions undertaken by the UK company will often be expressed in foreign currencies and the results of these transactions will need to be translated into sterling for financial reporting purposes. In the second situation, it is usual for the foreign enterprise to maintain its accounting records in its local currency. In order to prepare consolidated financial statements, the complete financial statements of the foreign enterprise will need to be translated into sterling.

29.3 Accounting for foreign currencies is primarily concerned with this translation process – a process whereby financial data denominated in one currency are expressed in terms of another currency. It is important to note that the translation process in no way changes the essential characteristics of the assets and liabilities measured. It merely restates assets and liabilities, initially valued in a foreign currency unit, to a common currency unit by applying a rate of exchange factor. It does not restate historical cost.

29.4 Translation would be a relatively simple matter if exchange rates between currencies remained constant. However, as exchange rates do not remain constant, but fluctuate over time, a method of translation must be established that adequately measures the effect of changes in exchange rates on financial statements. There has been considerable debate among accountants on how best to achieve this objective. The debate centres on two major aspects of the translation process: which rate of exchange is appropriate for restating foreign currency revenue, expenses, assets and liabilities; and how best to treat the resulting exchange gains and losses in the financial statements.

29.5 The selection of an appropriate exchange rate is not a simple matter because there are different translation rates that may be used depending on circumstances. These are:

- The historical rate – the rate of exchange ruling at the date the transaction occurred.
- The closing rate – the rate ruling at the balance sheet date.
- The average rate ruling during the year.

29.6 The average rate is generally confined to income and expenditure items. The rates used for balance sheet items will depend on the types of assets and liabilities being translated in individual company financial statements and upon the method of translation used for branches or consolidation of subsidiaries, namely the closing rate/net investment method or the temporal method. These methods are discussed in detail later in this chapter.

29.7 In addition to the difficulties in choosing an appropriate translation method, the treatment of exchange differences that arise on translation raises a number of questions, such as: the extent to which exchange gains and losses from different sources can be offset; whether some exchange differences should be recognised immediately whilst others should be deferred; and whether the recognition should be through the profit and loss account or through reserves. These and other vexing issues, such as the extent to which inflation in overseas countries should be taken into account in the translation process, remained unresolved both in the UK and internationally for many years.

29.8 The complexity of the subject is highlighted by the fact that SSAP 20, 'Foreign currency translation' published in April 1983, was preceded by no fewer than three exposure drafts – ED 16 (September 1975), ED 21 (September 1977) and ED 27 (October 1980). The standard was published after wide consultation by the ASC with several major companies with significant involvement in foreign trade, with banks, the Department of Trade, ASC's legal advisers, the IASC, FASB and the Canadian Institute of Chartered Accountants. The situation in the US was no different with the result that the FASB withdrew SFAS 8 (temporal method) published in 1975 and replaced it with SFAS 52 (closing rate method) in December 1981. Finally, the IASC published IAS 21, 'Accounting for the effects of changes in foreign exchange rates' in July 1983. IAS 21 is broadly similar to SSAP 20 and SFAS 52, although there are a number of differences in detail.

29.9 SSAP 20 has been successful in narrowing the range of permissible alternatives by stipulating that the closing rate/net investment method or, in some situations, the temporal method should be used for translating the financial statements of foreign enterprises. In spite of this, the standard is flexible and offers a range of choices both in the selection of exchange rates and in the treatment of the exchange differences in individual and consolidated financial statements.

However, SSAP 20 does not cover all the problem areas in accounting for foreign currencies. This is to be expected because of the complexity of the subject matter. For example, it fails to provide adequate guidance on accounting for forward contracts and the treatment of inflation, both of which are adequately covered in SFAS 52 which was issued two years prior to SSAP 20. The latter shortcoming has, to some extent, been rectified by the publication of UITF Abstract 9, 'Accounting for operations in hyper-inflationary economies'.

29.10 This chapter deals with the provisions of SSAP 20 and UITF Abstract 9. It covers many of the problem areas that are not adequately dealt with in SSAP 20, in particular, accounting for hedged transactions with forward contracts and currency options. This is an important area as many companies now manage their exposure to foreign exchange risks by adopting hedging strategies. In this context, reference has been made, where applicable, to the treatments specified in SFAS 52. However, the chapter does not deal with other currency instruments and derivative products which have experienced tremendous growth over the last few years. The accounting for financial derivative products and their disclosure in financial statements is a complex area which is on the ASB's agenda.

SSAP 20

Scope

29.11 SSAP 20 sets out the standard accounting practice for foreign currency translation and applies to any entity that comes within the scope of statements of standard accounting practice and engages in foreign currency operations. The standard does not deal with the method of calculating profits or losses arising from a company's normal currency dealing operations. Consequently, all currency forward contracts, currency buying and selling activities, and cash balances that are associated with those activities are excluded from the standard's scope. However, when accounting for its currency dealing operations, a company should comply with the spirit of SSAP 20. The standard does not deal with how to determine distributable profits, although applying its provisions could give rise to problems with respect to distributability. This is considered further from paragraph 29.142.

Objectives

29.12 The translation objectives of SSAP 20 are as follows:

- To produce results that are generally compatible with the effects of rate changes on a company's cash flows and its equity.

- To reflect in consolidated financial statements the financial results and relationships as measured in the foreign currency financial statements prior to translation.
- To ensure that the financial statements present a true and fair view of the management's actions.

[SSAP 20 para 2].

The above objectives may appear to be relatively simple, but their achievement, in practice, is fraught with difficulties. In some situations, these objectives may well conflict as will be apparent later in this chapter.

Procedures

29.13 SSAP 20 deals with the procedures that should be adopted when accounting for foreign currency operations in two stages, namely:

- The translation of foreign currency transactions by individual companies.
- The translation of foreign currency financial statements for consolidation purposes.

[SSAP 20 para 3].

The individual company stage

General rules for translation

29.14 The general rules that a company should follow in recording foreign currency transactions undertaken during an accounting period are as follows:

- Each asset, liability, revenue or cost arising from a transaction denominated in a foreign currency should be translated into the company's local currency at the exchange rate in operation on the date on which the transaction occurred.
- If rates do not fluctuate significantly, an average rate for a period *may* be used as an approximation.
- Where the transaction is to be settled at a contracted rate, that rate should be used.
- Where a trading transaction is covered by a related or matching forward contract, the rate of exchange specified in the contract *may* be used.

[SSAP 20 para 46].

The above rules appear to be relatively straightforward, but their application in practice may create a number of problems, for instance: determining the date of transaction may not always be that obvious; determining an average rate as an approximation to the actual rate; and the selection of an appropriate rate for translating foreign currency transactions where there is more than one rate in operation.

Date of transaction

29.15 There is no specific guidance in SSAP 20 as to whether the transaction date should be taken as the date on which the contract for the purchase or sale was signed, or the date of delivery, or the date when the invoice is received, or the date of payment. However, the standard does state that a difference may arise if a transaction is settled at a rate that is different from that used when the transaction was initially recorded. [SSAP 20 para 7]. It seems reasonable to assume, therefore, that the date on which a transaction is recorded under normal accounting rules should be taken as the transaction date. SFAS 52 supports this as it defines the transaction date as *"the date at which a transaction (for example, a sale or purchase of merchandise or services) is recorded in accounting records in conformity with generally accepted accounting principles"*.

Determining the average rate

29.16 The standard permits the use of an average rate for a period for recording foreign currency transactions as a proxy to the actual rate prevailing at the date of each transaction, provided that there is no significant change in rates during that period. An average rate is unlikely to be used by companies undertaking few transactions in a foreign currency. It is also unlikely to be used for translating large, one-off transactions which would be recorded at the actual rate as illustrated in Table 29.1 below. The flexibility allowed in the standard is likely to be most beneficial to companies that enter into a large number of transactions in different currencies, or that maintain multi-currency ledgers. However, no guidance is provided in the standard as to how such a rate should be determined.

Table 29.1 – Trafalgar House Public Limited Company – Report and Accounts – 30 September 1994

Principal accounting policies (extract)

c) Foreign currencies

Trading results denominated in foreign currencies are translated into sterling at average rates of exchange during the year except for material exceptional items which are translated at the rate on the date of the transaction.

Assets and liabilities are translated at the rates of exchange ruling at the year end except where rates of exchange are fixed under contractual arrangements.

Differences on exchange arising from the translation of the opening net assets of foreign subsidiaries and branches and ships denominated in foreign currency and of any related loans are taken to reserves together with the differences between profit and loss accounts translated at average rates and rates ruling at the year end. Other exchange differences are taken to the profit and loss account when they arise.

29.17 The determination of an average rate and its use in practice will depend on a number of factors, such as: the nature of the company's accounting systems; the frequency and value of transactions undertaken; the period over which the rate will apply; and the acceptable level of materiality. The choice of the period to be used for calculating the average rate will depend on the extent to which daily exchange rates fluctuate in the period selected. If exchange rates are relatively stable over a period of say, one month, then the average exchange rate for that month can be used as an approximation to the daily rate. If, however, there is volatility of exchange rates, it may be appropriate to calculate an average rate for a shorter period such as a week. Whatever period is chosen, materiality is likely to be an important consideration.

29.18 Depending on the circumstances, a company may use an actual average rate or an estimated average rate. An actual average rate is likely to be used where there is some delay between the date when the transactions occurred and the date when they are recorded. In other situations, it may be necessary for a company to use an estimated average rate for a period rather than wait for the period to end in order to calculate an actual average rate. This estimate may be based on the average of daily exchange rates for the previous period or the closing rate of the previous period. Whichever basis is used, it will be necessary to ensure than the estimated average rate is a close approximation of the actual rates prevailing during the period. If it is not, the rate should be revised accordingly.

Dual rates or suspension of rates

29.19 Some countries may operate more than one exchange rate. In that situation, the question arises as to which rate should be used to translate and record the transaction. SSAP 20 provides no guidance. Obviously, where there is a marginal difference between the two rates, it does not matter which rate is used. But where the difference is considered to be significant, we suggest that companies should consider following the relevant provision in SFAS 52. This states that *"the applicable rate at which a transaction could be settled at the transaction date shall be used to translate and record the transaction. At a subsequent balance sheet date, the current rate (closing rate) is that rate at which the related receivable or payable could be settled at that date"*. In some situations, it may be prudent to use the less favourable rate.

Example

The Nigerian budget in January 1995 made changes to the foreign exchange market. From that date all commercial foreign exchange transactions take place at the autonomous rate of exchange (say Niara 65 to US$1) rather than at the official rate of exchange (say Niara 22 to US$ 1). This means that all imports and exports and remittances of profits, dividends and technical services and other fees will take place at the autonomous rate of exchange.

Therefore, when retranslating foreign exchange transactions and monetary amounts receivable and payable in the financial statements of an individual company, the autonomous rate rather than the official rate of exchange should be used. This would also apply to the translation of the results and net assets of Nigerian subsidiary companies in consolidated financial statements.

29.20 From time to time, countries may experience economic conditions that affect the free-market convertibility of the local currency. As a result, the exchangeability between two currencies may be temporarily lacking at the transaction date or a subsequent balance sheet date. SSAP 20 is silent on this point, but SFAS 52 requires companies to use the rate on the first subsequent date at which exchanges could be made.

Treatment of non-monetary items

29.21 Non-monetary items are all items other than monetary items. Non-monetary items are generally physical in nature, such as properties, plant and equipment, stocks and equity investments. In some instances, however, it may not be readily apparent whether an item should be regarded as a monetary item or a non-monetary item. The ambiguity can usually be resolved if it is considered whether the item represents an amount to be received or paid in money, in which case it would fall to be treated as a monetary item. Otherwise, it should be treated as a non-monetary item.

29.22 SSAP 20 requires that where a non-monetary item has been translated at the rate ruling when it was originally recorded, no subsequent translation of the asset is normally required. [SSAP 20 para 47]. This effectively means that such assets are recorded at historical cost. However, in certain circumstances, this treatment will not apply to foreign equity investments. These special circumstances are considered from paragraph 29.79 below.

Treatment of monetary items

29.23 Monetary items, as the name imply, are money held and amounts to be received or paid in money. [SSAP 20 para 44]. Obvious examples include cash and bank balances, loans, debtors and creditors. Monetary items can be categorised as short term or long term. Short-term monetary items are those that fall due within one year of the balance sheet date and long-term monetary items are those that fall due more than one year after the balance sheet date.

29.24 SSAP 20 requires that a company should translate its monetary assets and liabilities denominated in foreign currencies outstanding at the end of the year using the closing rate. [SSAP 20 para 48]. An example is given in Table 29.1 on page 6. The closing rate is the exchange rate for spot transactions ruling at the balance sheet date and is the mean of the buying rate and the selling rate at the close of business on the day for which the rate is to be ascertained. [SSAP 20 para 41]. Where, however, the rate of exchange is fixed under the terms of the relevant contract, the company should use that rate. Where an outstanding trading transaction is covered by a related or matching forward contract, the rate specified in that contract may be used. [SSAP 20 para 48]. An example of a company that uses forward contracted rates is given in Table 29.2 below.

Table 29.2 – British Aerospace Public Limited Company – Annual Report – 31 December 1997

Notes to the Accounts

1 Accounting Policies (extract)

Foreign currencies

Transactions in overseas currencies are translated at the exchange rate ruling at the date of the transaction or, where forward cover contracts have been arranged, at the contracted rates. Monetary assets and liabilities denominated in foreign currencies are retranslated at the exchange rates ruling at the balance sheet date or at a contracted rate if applicable and any exchange differences arising are taken to the profit and loss account.

For consolidation purposes the assets and liabilities of overseas subsidiary and associated undertakings are translated at the closing exchange rates. Profit and loss accounts of such undertakings are consolidated at the average rates of exchange during the year. Exchange differences arising on these translations are taken to reserves.

Treatment of exchange gains and losses

29.25 An exchange gain or loss will arise if a currency transaction is settled during an accounting period at an exchange rate which differs from the rate used when the transaction was initially recorded, or, where appropriate, the rate that was used at the last balance sheet date. An exchange gain or loss will also arise on unsettled transactions if the rate of exchange used at the balance sheet date differs from that used previously. All exchange gains and losses, whether arising on settled transactions or on unsettled transactions, should be reported as part of the profit or loss for the year from ordinary activities. The only exception to this rule is that an exchange difference on a currency transaction that is itself treated as an extraordinary item should be included as part of that item, but such items will be very rare following the issue of FRS 3 'Reporting financial performance'. The classification of exchange differences in the profit and loss account formats is dealt with in paragraph 29.140.

Settled transactions

29.26 Where a transaction is *settled* at an exchange rate that differs from the rate used when the transaction was initially recorded, the exchange difference will be recognised in the profit and loss account of the period in which the settlement takes place. The rationale for this treatment is that, as the exchange difference will have been reflected in the cash flow at the time of the settlement, it is appropriate to recognise such exchange differences as part of the profit or loss for that year.

Example 1

In March 19X4, a UK company purchases plant for use in the UK from a French company for FF 425,000. At the date the company purchases the plant, the exchange rate is £1 = FF 8.50. The purchase price is to be settled in three months time, although delivery is made immediately. The UK company should record the plant in its accounting records at £50,000. The company will not need to translate the plant again. At the settlement date, the exchange rate is £1 = FF 8.75 so the actual amount the UK company pays is £48,571. The company should include the gain on exchange of £1,429 (that is, £50,000 - £48,571) in arriving at its profit or loss on ordinary activities.

Example 2

In March 19X4, a UK company purchases plant for use in the UK from a German company for DM 750,000. The transaction is contracted to be settled at £1 = DM 2.50. The UK company should record the plant in its accounting records at £300,000. The company will not need to translate the plant again, and no exchange differences will arise.

Example 3

In January 19X5, a UK company sells goods to a Dutch company for Fl 405,000. The Dutch company pays for the goods in March 19X5. At the time of the sale, the exchange rate is £1 = Fl 2.7, and at the time of the payment, the exchange rate is £1 = Fl 2.9. The UK company, however, covers the transaction by a matching forward contract to sell Dutch Guilders. The exchange rate specified in the forward contract is £1 = Fl 2.75. The relevant translations are as follows:

Fl 405,000 at Fl 2.7 (transaction rate) =	£150,000
Fl 405,000 at Fl 2.9 (settlement rate) =	£139,655
Fl 405,000 at Fl 2.75 (forward contract rate) =	£147,273

The UK company could record the sale in one of the following ways:

- It could record the sale and the debtor at £150,000, that is, at the exchange rate ruling at the date of the sale. Because the company has entered into a matching forward contract, the amount received from the debtor is Fl 405,000 which is sold for £147,273. Consequently, the company would have a loss on exchange on the transaction of £2,727 (that is, £150,000 - £147,273) to include in its profit or loss on ordinary activities.
- It could record the sale and the debtor at £147,273, that is, at the exchange rate specified in the matching forward contract. Because the company has entered into a matching forward contract, the amount receivable and ultimately received from the debtor is £147,273. Consequently, the company would not recognise a loss on exchange on the transaction.

Whichever method the company chooses to record the sale (that has been settled in the same period), its profit or loss on ordinary activities will be the same. Forward contracts are dealt with in more detail from paragraph 29.118.

Unsettled transactions

29.27 Where the transaction remains *outstanding* at the balance sheet date, an exchange difference arises as a consequence of recording the foreign currency transaction at the rate ruling at the date of the transaction (or when it was translated at a previous balance sheet date) and the subsequent retranslation to the rate ruling at the balance sheet date. Such exchange differences arise on monetary items (for example, foreign currency loans, debtors and creditors). To the extent that exchange differences relate to short-term monetary items, they will be soon be reflected in cash flows and, therefore, they should be reported as part of the profit or loss for the year from ordinary activities.

Example

In January 19X4, a UK company purchases equipment from a Spanish company for Pts 11,250,000. At the date the company takes delivery of the equipment, the exchange rate is £1 = Pts 225. Therefore, the company initially records both the equipment and the creditor at £50,000 (Pts 11,250,000 @ 225). At 31 March 19X4, the balance sheet date, the creditor is still outstanding. No further translation of the equipment is necessary, but the creditor should be retranslated using the rate of exchange at the balance sheet date, which is £1 = Pts 240. The company should include the gain on exchange of £3,125 (that is, £50,000 - £46,875) in its profit or loss on ordinary activities.

29.28 Where exchange differences arise on the retranslation of unsettled long-term monetary items, SSAP 20 requires that these exchange differences should be reported as part of the profit or loss for the year on ordinary activities, even though they may not be reflected in cash flows for a considerable time. SSAP 20 argues that the treatment of these long-term items on a simple cash movements basis would be inconsistent with the accruals concept and goes on to state:

> *"Exchange gains on unsettled transactions can be determined at the balance sheet date no less objectively than exchange losses; deferring the gains whilst recognising the losses would not only be illogical by denying in effect that any favourable movement in exchange rates had occurred but would also inhibit fair measurement of the performance of the enterprise in the year. In particular, this symmetry of treatment recognises that there will probably be some interaction between currency movements and interest rates and reflects more accurately in the profit and loss account the true results of currency involvement."* [SSAP 20 para 10].

29.29 Paragraph 12 of Schedule 4 to the Act states that *"only profits realised at the balance sheet date shall be included in the profit and loss account"*. Exchange gains that arise on long-term monetary items are not realised profits, but SSAP 20 generally requires them to be recognised in the profit and loss account. Paragraph 15 of Schedule 4 permits a departure from paragraph 12 of that Schedule if there are special reasons for such a departure. The need to give a true and fair view of the results, referred to in paragraph 29.28, 29.28 is considered to constitute a special reason for departure. It will be necessary to disclose particulars of the departure, the reasons for it and its effect, in accordance with UITF Abstract 7 'True and fair override disclosures'. A company that discloses the use of the override for exchange gains on long-term liabilities is Thames Water (see Table 29.3). The impact of foreign currency translation on distributable profits is dealt with from paragraph 29.142.

Table 29.3 – Thames Water Plc – Annual Report and Accounts – 31 March 1995

Notes to the accounts

1 Principal accounting policies (extract)

j Foreign currencies All transactions denominated in foreign currencies are translated into sterling at the actual rate of exchange ruling on the date of the transaction. Assets and liabilities, including long term liabilities, in foreign currencies are translated into sterling at rates of exchange ruling at the balance sheet date. All exchange differences arising are dealt with in the profit and loss account. This treatment is required by Statement of Accounting Practice (SSAP) number 20 in order to give a true and fair view of the Group's results. Compliance with SSAP 20 overrides Schedule 4 Paragraph 12 of the Companies Act 1985 which states that only profits realised at the balance sheet date should be included in the profit and loss account. The effect of currency retranslation is disclosed in note 4. The results of overseas subsidiary undertakings are translated at average rates of exchange for the year. Differences arising from the translation of year end assets and liabilities at closing rates together with the restatement of opening balance sheets of overseas subsidiary undertakings at closing rates are dealt with through reserves together with exchange differences on the translation of foreign currency borrowings funding such investments.

4 Operating costs (extract)	**1995**	1994
	Continuing operations	
	£m	£m
Foreign currency gains (see note 1j)	**(2.1)**	-

(iii) The foreign currency gains are net of unrealised gains and losses of £3.6m and £0.9m respectively.

29.30 In certain exceptional situations, however, a company may have doubts as to either the convertibility or the marketability of the currency of a long-term monetary item outstanding at the end of the year. Where this is so, on the grounds of prudence such a company should restrict the amount of any gain (or the amount by which any gain exceeds past exchange losses on the same item) that it recognises in its profit and loss account. [SSAP 20 para 50].

29.31 Doubts as to convertibility may arise if, for example, a UK company makes a long-term currency loan to, say, an overseas supplier, but restrictions on the remittance of funds are imposed by the overseas country sometime prior to the maturity of the loan. Such restrictions would probably arise if there is political upheaval or severe exchange control regulations in the overseas country. In that situation, the company should consider the loan's realisable value in the light of such restrictions and limit any exchange gains arising on the retranslation that is taken to the profit and loss account. The following example illustrates this type of situation.

Example

In April 19X4, company A, which is incorporated in the UK, used surplus currency to make a long-term loan of FC 20m (FC being a fictional currency) to its overseas supplier. The loan was made when the exchange rate was £1 = FC 5.00. Initially, the loan would be translated and recorded in company A's books at £4m. The amount that company A will ultimately receive will depend on the rate of exchange ruling on the date when the loan is repaid.

At 31 March 19X5, company A's year end, the exchange rate is £1 = FC 4.00. If the loan of FC 20m was translated at this rate it would give an asset of £5m and an exchange gain of £1m. There are, however, doubts as to the convertibility of FC. Therefore, company A considers that, on the grounds of prudence, it should limit the gain so that the sterling value of the loan is shown at its present estimated realisable value of £4,500,000. Accordingly, company A restricts the exchange gain that it includes in its profit and loss account for the year ended 31 March 19X5 to £500,000.

Transactions between group companies

29.32 Where transactions take place between companies in a group, exchange differences are likely to arise in one or other company since the transaction is likely to be carried out in the local currency of one of the companies in question. SSAP 20 requires that exchange gains and losses arising on such transactions should normally be reported in the individual company's financial statements as part of the profit or loss for the year in the same way as gains and losses arising from transactions with third parties. [SSAP 20 para 12].

The consolidation stage

Introduction

29.33 Translation of foreign currency financial statements is necessary so that the financial statements of overseas subsidiaries may be consolidated with the holding company's sterling financial statements. The method of translation in consolidated financial statements should be such as to reflect the financial and other operational relationships that exist between the investing company and its foreign enterprises. In this context, a foreign enterprise includes not only a foreign subsidiary, but also an associated company or branch whose operations are based in a currency other than that of the investing company or whose assets and liabilities are denominated mainly in a foreign currency. [SSAP 20 para 36].

29.34 The standard requires that, normally, a company should use the 'closing rate/net investment' method for translating the financial statements of its foreign enterprises. However, in certain specified circumstances, the temporal method should be used. [SSAP 20 para 14].

Closing rate/net investment method

29.35 The closing rate/net investment method is based on the premise that a foreign enterprise generally operates as a separate or quasi-independent entity. Such an entity normally conducts its day to day affairs in its local currency, is likely to be financed wholly or partly by local currency borrowings, and is not normally dependent on the investing company's reporting currency. If a foreign enterprise is relatively independent then what is at risk from the investing company's perspective is the net worth of the investment rather than the individual assets and liabilities of that enterprise. The investing company may or may not receive regular dividend income, but the net investment remains until the business is liquidated or the investment is sold.

29.36 Accordingly, it is important to retain the financial and operational relationships existing in the foreign entity's financial statements prior to translation in order to produce results that are meaningful at the consolidation stage. Use of a constant rate of exchange for all items maintains such a relationship in the retranslated financial statements of the reporting currency as existed in the foreign currency financial statements. Therefore, for example, fixed assets would be the same proportion of long-term liabilities.

29.37 Although this method is widely supported both in the UK and internationally, it is not without its critics. Critics attack the method as being inconsistent with the objective of consolidation to present the results of the parent company and its dependent subsidiaries as if the group were a single entity. Furthermore, when the closing rate is applied to items stated at historical cost, such as fixed assets, the result is an accounting model which at best is a hybrid of historical costs.

29.38 Proponents of the closing rate/net investment method claim that the method acknowledges the fact that operations which are conducted in currencies and in economic environments other than those of the parent are essentially different from the parent's own operations. Accordingly, it clearly reflects the true economic facts, because stating all items at the closing rate presents the foreign enterprise's true earnings at that time, particularly since from the investor's point of view the only real earnings are those that can actually be distributed. The translation of the historical cost financial statements at closing rates is merely a restatement of assets and liabilities for the purposes of consolidation and does not constitute a revaluation.

29.39 Under the closing rate/net investment method:

- All items in a foreign subsidiary's balance sheet at the year end should be translated at the closing rate of exchange into the parent's reporting currency.

- On consolidation, the exchange differences that arise when the parent retranslates its opening net investments in the foreign subsidiary to the closing rate should be treated as a movement on consolidated reserves. Exchange differences may also arise where the closing rate differs from that ruling on the date of a subsequent capital injection (or reduction). Such exchange differences should also be dealt with as a movement in reserves. The rationale for taking such exchange differences to reserves is explained in paragraph 19 of SSAP 20, which states:

  > *"If exchange differences arising from the retranslation of a company's net investment in its foreign enterprise were introduced into the profit and loss account, the results from trading operations, as shown in the local currency financial statements, would be distorted. Such differences may result from many factors unrelated to the trading performance or financial operations of the foreign enterprise; in particular, they do not represent or measure changes in actual or prospective cash flows. It is therefore inappropriate to regard them as profits or losses and they should be dealt with as adjustments to reserves."*

  SSAP 20, unlike SFAS 52, does not require companies to maintain a separate reserve for exchange differences, but some companies do so.

- The profit and loss account of a foreign subsidiary may be translated either at the closing rate or at an average rate for the period. Although the use of a closing rate is more likely to achieve the objective of translation, stated in paragraph 29.12 above, of reflecting the financial results and relationships as measured in the foreign currency financial statements prior to translation, the use of an average rate reflects more fairly the profits or losses and cash flows as they accrue to the group throughout the period. Therefore, the standard permits the use of either method, provided that the one selected is applied consistently from period to period. [SSAP 20 para 17]. Where the average rate is used, the company should record, as a movement on consolidated reserves, the difference between translating the profit and loss account at the average rate and translating it at the closing rate. [SSAP 20 para 54].

An example of a company that uses the closing rate/net investment method is given in Table 29.4 below.

Table 29.4 – The Peninsular and Oriental Steam Navigation Company – Annual Report and Accounts – 31 December 1997

Accounting Policies (extract)

Foreign currencies
Transactions in foreign currencies are recorded at the rate of exchange ruling at the date of the transaction. Profits and losses of subsidiaries, branches and associates which have currencies of operation other than sterling are translated into sterling at average rates of exchange except for material exceptional items which are translated at the rate ruling at the date of transaction. Assets and liabilities denominated in foreign currencies are translated at the year end exchange rates.

Exchange differences arising from the retranslation of the opening net assets of subsidiaries, branches and associates which have currencies of operation other than sterling and any related loans are taken to reserves together with the differences arising when the profit and loss accounts are translated at average rates and compared with rates ruling at the year end. Other exchange differences are taken to the profit and loss account.

29.40 The net investment which a company has in a foreign enterprise is its effective equity stake and comprises its proportion of such foreign enterprise's net assets; in appropriate circumstances, intra-group loans and other deferred trading balances may be regarded as part of the effective equity stake. [SSAP 20 para 43]. It follows from the above definition that the net investment is the amount at which the group states the net assets of the subsidiary in the consolidated balance sheet. It is not (for example) the amount at which the net assets are recorded in the subsidiary's financial statements which may be different if the group has restated the assets at fair value at the time of acquisition. Nor is it the market value of the foreign subsidiary.

Illustration of the closing rate/net investment method

29.41 The closing rate/net investment method is illustrated by the following example.

Example

Company A, a UK company, whose accounting period ended on 30 September 19X4, has a wholly-owned US subsidiary, S Corporation, that was acquired for US$ 500,000 on 30 September 19X3. The fair value of the net assets at the date of acquisition was US$ 400,000. The exchange rate at 30 September 19X3 and 19X4 was £1=US$ 2.0 and £1=US$ 1.5 respectively. The weighted average rate for the year ended 30 September 19X4 was £1=US$ 1.65.

The summarised profit and loss account of S Corporation for the year ended 30 September 19X4 and the summarised balance sheets at 30 September 19X3 and 19X4 in dollars and sterling equivalents, are as follows:

S Corporation: Profit and loss account for the year ended 30 September 19X4

	$'000	Closing rate £'000	Average rate £'000
Exchange rate £1 =		$1.50	$1.65
Operating profit	135	90.0	81.8
Interest paid	(15)	(10.0)	(9.0)
Profit before taxation	120	80.0	72.8
Taxation	(30)	(20.0)	(18.2)
Profit after taxation	90	60,0	54.6
Dividends paid in the year	(14)	(9.3)	(8.5)
Retained profit	76	50.7	46.1

Balance sheets of S Corporation

	19X4 $'000	19X3 $'000	19X4 £'000 P&L closing	19X4 £'000 P&L average	19X3 £'000
Closing exchange rate £1 =			$1.50	$1.50	$2.00
Fixed assets:					
Cost (19X4 additions: $30)	255	225	170.0	170.0	112.5
Depreciation (19X4 charge: $53)	98	45	65.3	65.3	22.5
Net book value	157	180	104.7	104.7	90.0
Current assets:					
Stocks	174	126	116.0	116.0	63.0
Debtors	210	145	140.0	140.0	72.5
Cash at bank	240	210	160.0	160.0	105.0
	624	481	416.0	416.0	240.5
Current liabilities:					
Trade creditors	125	113	83.3	83.3	56.5
Taxation	30	18	20.0	20.0	9.0
	155	131	103.3	103.3	65.5
Net current assets	469	350	312.7	312.7	175.0
Loan stock	150	130	100.0	100.0	65.0
Net assets	476	400	317.4	317.4	200.0

Share capital	200	200	100.0	100.0	100.0
Retained profits	276	200	217.4	217.4	100.0
	476	400	317.4	317.4	200.0

The analysis of retained profits under the closing rate and the average rate method is as follows:

	$'000	Closing rate £'000	Average rate £'000
Exchange rate £1 =		$1.50	$1.65
Pre-acquisition profit brought forward	200	100.0	100.0
Profit for the year	76	50.7	46.1
Exchange difference	-	66.7	71.3
Retained profits	276	217.4	217.4
Analysis of exchange difference:			
Arising on retranslation of opening net investments:			
at opening rate – $400,000 @ $2 = £1		200.0	200.0
at closing rate – $400,000 @ $1.5 = £1		266.7	266.7
Exchange gain on net investment		66.7	66.7
Exchange gain arising from translating profit and loss account at average rate (£46.1) rather than closing rate (£50.7)		-	4.6
Total exchange difference		66.7	71.3

Note: On consolidation, the above exchange differences will be included in consolidated reserves and shown in the statement of total recognised gains and losses.

It is further assumed that parent company A does not trade on its own and its only income is dividends received from S Corporation. The summarised balance sheets of company A at 30 September 19X3 and 19X4 are as follows:

Company A – Balance Sheets	19X4	19X3
	£'000	£'000
Investments in subsidiary ($500,000 @ 2.0)	250	250
Cash	208	200
Net assets	458	450
Share capital	450	450
P&L account (dividend received: $14,000 @ 1.75*)	8	–
	458	450

* actual rate on date dividend received

Where company A uses the closing rate/net investment method, it may use either the closing rate or the average rate for translating the results of S Corporation. The summarised consolidated profit and loss account for the year ended 30 September 19X4 drawn up on the two bases and the summarised consolidated balance sheet at that date are as follows:

Consolidated profit and loss account for the year ended 30 September 19X4

	Closing rate £'000	Average rate £'000
Operating profit of S Corporation	90.0	81.8
Operating profit of company A	8.0	8.0
	98.0	89.8
Elimination of inter company dividend*	(9.3)	(8.5)
Net operating profit	88.7	81.3
Interest paid	(10.0)	(9.0)
Profit before taxation	78.7	72.3
Taxation	(20.0)	(18.2)
Retained profit	58.7	54.1

* The exchange difference arising on the inter-company dividend, being the difference between the dividend calculated at the date of receipt and at the closing rate or at the average rate, is included in the profit and loss account.

Consolidated balance sheet at 30 September 19X4

	Closing rate £'000	Average rate £'000
Fixed assets	104.7	104.7
Current assets:		
Stocks	116.0	116.0
Debtors	140.0	140.0
Cash (S Corporation: £160; company A £208)	368.0	368.0
	624.0	624.0
Current liabilities:		
Trade creditors	83.3	83.3
Taxation	20.0	20.0
	103.3	103.3
Net current assets	520.7	520.7
Loan stock	100.0	100.0
Net assets	525.4	525.4
Share capital	450.0	450.0
Reserves:		
Retained profit	58.7	54.1
Exchange difference on opening net assets	66.7	66.7
Exchange difference on P&L account	–	4.6
Goodwill written off ($100,000 @ 2.0)	(50.0)	(50.0)
	525.4	525.4

In the above illustration goodwill has been translated at the rate ruling on the date of acquisition on the grounds that it arises only on consolidation and is not part of the net assets of the foreign enterprise. An alternative treatment is to regard the goodwill as a currency asset which is retranslated at the closing rate. In this situation, an exchange difference would arise on the opening net investment including the goodwill (see further para 29.78).

The temporal method

29.42 As stated in paragraph 29.34 above, SSAP 20 acknowledges that the use of the closing rate/net investment method may not be appropriate in certain circumstances. The circumstances relate to situations where the foreign enterprise's operations are so closely interlinked with those of the investing company that it no longer seems appropriate to regard the foreign currency as being that on which the foreign enterprise is dependent. In such a situation, the foreign enterprise's local currency is deemed to be that of the investing company and the temporal method should be used for translating the foreign enterprise's financial statements. Under the temporal method all of the foreign enterprise's transactions are treated as if they had been entered into by the investing company itself and all of the foreign enterprise's assets and liabilities are treated as though they belong directly to the investing company.

29.43 SSAP 20 acknowledges that it is not possible to select one factor which would indicate the temporal method should be used. All available evidence must be considered in determining which currency is the local currency (referred to in SFAS 52 as the 'functional currency') of each foreign enterprise respectively. SSAP 20 defines a company's local currency as *"the currency of the primary economic environment in which it operates and generates net cash flows"*. [SSAP 20 para 39].

29.44 The standard specifies a number of factors that need to be taken into consideration in determining the dominant currency. The factors, which are listed below, should be considered both individually and collectively before deciding on the appropriate method of translation. In those situations, where the indicators are mixed and the dominant currency is not obvious, considerable management judgment will be required.

- The extent to which the cash flows of the enterprise have a direct impact upon those of the investing company, for example, whether there is regular and frequent transfer of funds between the two companies or whether there are only occasional remittances of dividends.

- The extent to which the functioning of the enterprise is dependent directly upon the investing company, for example, whether major decisions are taken by the parent company, whether pricing decisions are based on local competition and costs or are part of a worldwide decision process.

- The currency in which the majority of the trading transactions are completed, for example, the sales market is mostly in the parent's country of origin or sales invoices are denominated in the parent's currency.

- The major currency to which the operation is exposed in its financing structure, for example whether the operation is dependent on finance raised locally or from the parent.

[SSAP 20 para 23].

29.45 Examples of situations where the temporal method may be appropriate are where the foreign enterprise:

- Acts as a selling agency receiving stocks of goods from the receiving company and remitting the proceeds back to the company.

- Produces a raw material or manufactures parts or sub-assemblies which are then shipped to the investing company for inclusion in its own products.

- Is located overseas for tax, exchange control or similar reasons to act as a means of raising finance for other companies in the group.

[SSAP 20 para 24].

It should be noted that the above are extreme situations where the use of the temporal method is rather obvious. In practice, this will rarely be so and determining the local currency will need to be made in the light of the above factors and the management's judgement.

29.46 SSAP 20 states that the mechanics of the temporal method are identical to those used in preparing the financial statements of an individual company. [SSAP 20 para 22]. This is probably true to a degree, but applying this method in practice requires detailed and additional record keeping that is not required under the closing rate method and is far more complicated as illustrated in the example below. The similarity of the temporal method with the method used in individual financial statements implies that under the temporal method:

- All transactions should be translated at the rate ruling at the transaction date or at an average rate for the period if this is not materially different.

- Non-monetary items, such as fixed assets and stocks measured at historical cost or valuation, are translated at the exchange rate in effect at the date to which the historical cost or valuation pertains. They are not retranslated at each balance sheet date.

- Monetary items, whether short-term or long-term, are translated using the closing rate at the balance sheet date.

- All items in the profit and loss account are translated at the historical rate. An average rate may be used where it is not materially different from the rate ruling at the transaction date, except for depreciation and stocks which must be included at historical rate.

- All exchange gains and losses including those arising on the retranslation of opening monetary items should be taken to the profit and loss account for the year as part of the profit or loss from ordinary operations.

29.47 It should be noted that the temporal method was originally expounded in the US and later included in SFAS 8 in 1975 in response to the existence in practice of several significantly different methods of accounting for the translation of foreign currency transactions and financial statements at that time. It was also permitted when ED 21 was issued by the ASC in September 1977. However, it was recognised that although the method met the objective of consolidation, that is, of treating the group as a single economic unit, the results produced did not reflect the underlying economic reality of foreign operations. For example, since inventory is translated at the historical rate, a loss could be reported during the period in which the foreign currency actually strengthened against the reporting currency. Moreover, using the historical rate to translate fixed assets, whilst translating long-term debt used to finance those assets at current rate (closing rate), may be inappropriate and may result in large gains and losses which will not be realised for a long time. Furthermore, the inclusion of all exchange gains and losses in the profit and loss account means that the profit for the period will be adversely impacted by the volatility of exchange rates, leading to a distortion in long-term trends. It is for these valid reasons that the method was discarded by the FASB when it replaced SFAS 8 by SFAS 52 and by the ASC when it issued ED 27, which was based on the closing rate/net investment concept. The temporal method is now only used in circumstances mentioned in paragraph 29.42 above.

Illustration of the temporal method

29.48 The way in which the temporal method is used in practice is illustrated by the following example.

Example

The facts and the data are the same as that used in the closing rate method in paragraph 29.41 above, except that further details on exchange rates at the dates of acquisition of fixed assets and stocks are given, together with an analysis of operating profit.

Company A, a UK company, whose accounting period ended on 30 September 19X4, has a wholly-owned US subsidiary, S Corporation, that was acquired for US$ 500,000 on 30 September 19X3. The fair value of the net assets at the date of acquisition was US$ 400,000. The exchange rate at 30 September 19X3 and 19X4 was £1=US$ 2.0 and £1=US$ 1.5 respectively. The weighted average rate for the year ended 30 September 19X4 was £1=US$ 1.65.

S Corporation: Profit and loss account for the year ended 30 September 19X4

	$'000	Exchange rate	£'000
Sales	3,760	Average -$1.65	2,278.8
Opening stock	126	Historical -$2.0	63.0
Purchases	3,620	Average – $1.65	2,193.9
Closing stock	(174)	Historical -$1.6	(108.8)
Cost of sales	3,572		2,148.1
Gross profit	188		130.7
Depreciation	53	Historical -$2.0/1.85*	26.8
Operating profit	135		103.9
Interest paid	(15)	Average -$1.65	(9.1)
Exchange gain	-	Balance	16.8
Profit before taxation	120		111.6
Taxation	(30)	Average -$1.65	(18.2)
Profit after taxation	90		93.4
Dividends paid in the year	(14)	Actual	(8.5)
Retained profit	76		84.9

* The charge for depreciation is translated as follows; on original assets ($45,000 @ 2 = £22,500) and on additions ($8,000 @ 1.85 = £4,300) = £26,800.

Balance sheets of S Corporation

	19X4 $'000	Exchange Rate	19X4 £'000	19X3 $'000	Exchange Rate	19X3 £'000
Fixed assets:						
Cost (i)	255	$2.0/1.85	128.7	225	$2.0	112.5
Depreciation (ii)	98	$2.0/1.85	49.3	45	$2.0	22.5
Net book value	157		79.4	180		90.0
Current assets:						
Stocks	174	$1.6	108.8	126	$2.0	63.0
Debtors	210	$1.5	140.0	145	$2.0	72.5
Cash at bank	240	$1.5	160.0	210	$2.0	105.0
	624		408.8	481		240.5

Current liabilities:						
Trade creditors	125	$1.5	83.3	113	$2.0	56.5
Taxation	30	$1.5	20.0	18	$2.0	9.0
	155		103.3	131		65.5
Net current assets	469		305.5	350		175.0
	626		384.9	530		265.0
Loan stock	150	$1.5	100.0	130	$2.0	65.0
Net assets	476		284.9	400		200.0
Share capital	200	$2.0	100.0	200	$2.0	100.0
Retained profits	276	Balance	184.9	200	Balance	100.0
	476		284.9	400		200.0

(i) Fixed assets are translated at the historical rate which, in this example, will be the exchange rate at the date of acquisition (£1 = $2.0) or, for subsequent additions, the actual rate at the transaction date (say £1 = $1.85). The translated amount at 30 September 19X4 is ($225,000 @ 2.0 = £112,500) + ($30,000 @ 1.85 = £16,200) = £128,700.

(ii) Cumulative depreciation is translated as follows; on original assets ($90,000 @ 2.0 = £45,000) and on additions ($8,000 @ 1.85 = £4,300) = £49,300.

Analysis of exchange difference included in the profit and loss account

	Opening monetary items $'000	Closing monetary items $'000
Debtors	145	210
Cash at bank	210	240
Trade creditors	(113)	(125)
Taxation	(18)	(30)
Loan stock	(130)	(150)
	94	145

Opening monetary items at opening rate – $94 @ $2	47.0	
Opening monetary item at closing rate – $94 @ $1.5	62.7	15.7
Increase in monetary items at closing rate – $51 @ $1.5	34.0	
Increase in monetary items at average rate – $51 @ $1.65	30.9	3.1
Exchange gain		18.8
Exchange difference arising on acquisition of fixed asset:		
Cash outflow on non-monetary items at actual rate $30 @ 1.85	16.2	
Cash outflow on non-monetary items at average rate $30 @ 1.65	18.2	
Exchange loss		(2.0)
Total exchange difference included in profit and loss account		16.8

It is further assumed that parent company A does not trade on its own and its only income is dividends received from S Corporation. The summarised balance sheets of company A at 30 September 19X3 and 19X4 are as follows:

Company A – Balance Sheets	19X4 £'000	19X3 £'000
Investments in subsidiary ($500,000 @ 2.0)	250	250
Cash	208	200
Net assets	458	450
Share capital	450	450
P&L account (dividend received: $14,000 @ 1.75*)	8	-
	458	450

* actual rate on date dividend received

The summarised consolidated profit and loss account for the year ended 30 September 19X4 drawn up on the temporal method and the summarised consolidated balance sheet at that date are as follows:

Consolidated profit and loss account for the year ended 30 September 19X4	
	£'000
Profit before taxation of S Corporation	111.6
Profit before taxation of company A	8.0
	119.6
Elimination of inter company dividend	(8.5)
Net operating profit	111.1
Taxation	(18.2)
Retained profit	92.9

Consolidated balance sheet at 30 September 19X4

	Average rate £'000
Fixed assets	79.4
Current assets:	
Stocks	108.8
Debtors	140.0
Cash (S Corporation: £160; company A £208)	368.0
	616.8
Current liabilities:	
Trade creditors	83.3
Taxation	20.0
	103.3
Net current assets	513.5
Total assets less current liabilities	592.9
Loan stock	100.0
Net assets	492.9
Share capital	450.0
Reserves:	
Retained profit	92.9
Goodwill written off ($100,000 @ 2.0)	(50.0)
	492.9

Calculation of Goodwill	£'000
Consideration £500,000 @ 2.0	250.0
Net assets per balance sheet at date of acquisition	200.0
Goodwill written off	50.0

Foreign branches

29.49 Where a UK company conducts its foreign operations through a foreign branch, the translation method adopted would depend on the nature of the branch operations. A foreign branch may be a legally constituted enterprise located overseas or a group of assets and liabilities which are accounted for in foreign currencies. [SSAP 20 para 37]. Where the foreign branch operates as an extension of the company's trade and its cash flows have a direct impact upon those of the company, the temporal method described in paragraphs 29.42 to 29.48 above should be used. Where the foreign branch operates as a separate business possibly with local finance it should be accounted for under the closing rate/net investment method. [SSAP 20 para 25]. This applies in the individual entity financial statements in addition to the consolidated financial statements.

29.50 The following are examples of situations given in TR 504, 'Statement by the ASC on the publication of SSAP 20 – Foreign currency translation', where a foreign branch consists of a group of assets and liabilities that should be accounted for under the closing rate/net investment method:

- A hotel in France financed by borrowings in French francs.
- A ship or aircraft purchased in US dollars – with an associated loan in US dollars – which earns revenue and incurs expenses in US dollars.
- A foreign currency insurance operation where the liabilities are substantially covered by the holding of foreign currency assets.

29.51 In each of the above situations the local operation's currency is not the investing company's currency, since the branch operates as a separate business with local finance. Therefore, it is not appropriate to use the temporal method and the closing rate/net investment method should be used. The net investment is likely to be represented by a Head Office Account with the branch which should be translated using the closing rate. Any exchange differences arising from this retranslation process will be taken to reserves. An example of the accounting treatment followed by British Airways, which treats aircraft financed by foreign currency borrowings as a separate group of assets and liabilities is given in Table 29.5 below.

Table 29.5 – British Airways Plc – Report & Accounts – 31 March 1995

ACCOUNTING POLICIES

Tangible fixed assets (extract)

Aircraft which are financed in whole or in part in foreign currency, either by loans, finance leases or hire purchase arrangements, are regarded together with the related liabilities as a separate group of assets and liabilities and accounted for in foreign currency. The amounts in foreign currency are translated into Sterling at rates ruling at the balance sheet date and the net differences arising from the translation of aircraft costs and related foreign currency loans, except for those loans which are hedged, are taken to reserves. The costs of all other aircraft is fixed in Sterling at rates ruling at the date of purchase.

Other matters

29.52 This section deals with a number of important practical matters that arise at the consolidation stage, but which are not adequately dealt with in SSAP 20. Where relevant guidance or treatment in the UK is lacking or non-existent, appropriate references have been made to SFAS 52.

Determining the average rate

29.53 As stated in paragraph 29.39 above, SSAP 20 permits the profit and loss account of a foreign enterprise to be translated at an average rate for the period. SSAP 20 intentionally does not prescribe any definitive method of calculating the average rate on the grounds that the appropriate method may justifiably vary as between individual companies. However, the standard suggests that the determination of an appropriate average rate will include such matters as the company's internal accounting system, the extent of any seasonal trade variation and the desirability of using a weighting procedure. [SSAP 20 para 18].

29.54 There is a large number of methods under which an average rate can be calculated, ranging from simple monthly or quarterly averages to more sophisticated methods using appropriate weighting that reflects changes both in exchange rates and in the volume of business. Where the results of an overseas subsidiary are affected by seasonal factors, it may be necessary to weight the average exchange rate used in the calculation by applying an average rate for a shorter period than the whole year. But whatever method a company uses, it should calculate it by the method it considers is most appropriate to the foreign undertaking's circumstances. [SSAP 20 para 54]. An example of an averaging method employed in practice is given in Table 29.6 below.

Table 29.6 – The Boots Company PLC – Report and Accounts - 31 March 1998

Accounting Policies (extract)

Foreign currencies (extract)

The results and cash flows of overseas subsidiaries are translated into sterling on an average exchange rate basis, weighted by the actual results of each month. Assets and liabilities including currency swaps are translated into sterling at the rates of exchange ruling at the balance sheet date.

29.55 In recent years many companies have moved away from using the closing rate to using an average rate for translating the profit and loss accounts of foreign enterprises. In fact, a large majority of companies now use the average rate method. The fact that the use of an average rate reflects more fairly the results and cash flows as they arise throughout the accounting period and permits aggregation of interim results appears to outweigh the relative simplicity of the closing rate method. Where a company decides to change from the closing rate method to the average rate method, the change in method represents a change of accounting policy and not a refinement of accounting policy in view of the conceptual difference between the two methods. As a consequence, a prior year adjustment is required in accordance with FRS 3 if the amounts involved are material. It may be reasonably easy for a company to justify changing its accounting policy to move to an average rate of exchange on the grounds that it is using a better method. However, it would generally be much harder for such a company to justify a move back to year end rates, especially where the move to an average rate has only occurred recently. An example of a company which has recently changed from the closing rate method to the average rate method is given in Table 29.7 below.

Table 29.7 – The Peninsular and Oriental Steam Navigation Company – Annual report and accounts – 31 December 1994

Notes to the accounts

2 Change in accounting policy for foreign currencies

Profits and losses of subsidiaries, branches and associates which have currencies of operation other than sterling are translated into sterling at average rates of exchange except for material exceptional items which are translated at rates ruling on the date of transaction. Previously such profits and losses were translated at the exchange rates ruling at the year end. The accounting policy has been changed because the directors consider the new policy gives a fairer presentation of the Group's results and cash flows as they arise during the course of an accounting period. The effect of this change in accounting policy on the results for the year ended 31 December 1994 is to increase operating profit by £2.0m (1993 £1.5m decrease), increase the interest charge by £1.1m (1993 £0.3m decrease) and increase profit before tax by £0.9m (1993 £1.3m decrease).

Dual rates or suspension of rates

29.56 The problems of dealing with dual rates or suspension of rates in the context of individual financial statements have already been discussed in paragraph 29.19 above. The same principles also apply to consolidated financial statements when determining which rate should be used to translate results of foreign enterprises using the closing rate/net investment method. There is no guidance on this subject in SSAP 20. However, SFAS 52 states that the rate used in the translation should be that applicable to dividend remittances. The rate applicable to dividend remittances is considered more meaningful than any other rate, because this is the rate indicative of ultimate cash flows from the entity to the investing company.

Local currency

29.57 As discussed in paragraph 29.43, SSAP 20 defines a company's local currency as the *"currency of the primary economic environment in which it operates and generates net cash flows"*. [SSAP 20 para 39]. Where the closing rate/net investment method is used, the currency of the country in which the foreign enterprise operates will usually be its local currency. Similarly, where the temporal method is used, the investing company's currency will usually be the local currency. However, this will not always be the case.

29.58 In some circumstances, a foreign entity's local currency might not be the currency of that country. For example, a UK company may have a subsidiary in Amsterdam that deals in oil. Since the international oil market is conducted in US dollars, it is likely that the US dollar is the currency in which the subsidiary operates and generates net cash flows. If the majority of the transactions are recorded locally in US dollars rather than the Dutch Guilder or pound sterling, no particular problem arises as the US dollar financial statements can be translated into sterling using the closing rate/net investment method. However, where the transactions are recorded in Dutch Guilders, it would be necessary to first restate the financial statements in US dollars using the temporal method and then retranslate the US dollar financial statements to pounds sterling using the closing/rate net investment method.

Change from the temporal method to the closing rate method or vice-versa

29.59 A company can change the basis of translating the financial statements of a foreign enterprise from the temporal method to the closing rate method or *vice versa* if the financial and other operational relationships that exist between the investing company and its foreign enterprises change so as to render the method currently used inappropriate. However, as the change is brought about by changed circumstances, it does not represent a change in accounting policy and, therefore, a prior year adjustment under FRS 3 is not necessary. It follows that the effect of the change should be accounted for prospectively from the date of change. If this date is difficult to determine, the change may be accounted for generally as from the beginning of the period as an approximation of the date of change. No guidance is given in SSAP 20 as to how any prospective adjustments should be made, but guidance is provided in SFAS 52.

29.60 SFAS 52 states that where a company changes from the temporal method to the closing rate method, the adjustment attributable to translating non-monetary items, previously included at historical rate, to the closing rate should be dealt with as a reserve movement.

Example

A foreign subsidiary of a UK parent purchases an equipment having an useful life of 10 years for FC 100,000 (fictitious currency) in 1 January 19X0 when the rate of exchange was FC 8 = £1. Under the temporal method, the asset would be recorded in the consolidated financial statements at £12,500. At 31 December 19X4, the equipment has a net book value of FC 50,000 in the subsidiary's books and £6,250 in the parent's consolidated financial statements.

On 1 January 19X5 the subsidiary acquires a significant local operation financed by borrowings raised locally. Under these circumstances, the parent considers that the temporal method is no longer appropriate and changes to the closing rate method. The fixed asset remains in the subsidiary's financial statements at FC 50,000, but on consolidation the asset will have to be retranslated at the closing rate of say FC 10 = £1, which is £5,000. The difference in the carrying value using the historical exchange rate and the closing rate, that is an exchange loss of £1,250, should be debited to consolidated reserves.

29.61 Where a company changes from the closing rate method to the temporal method, because the operations of the foreign subsidiary has become significantly dependent on the parent's reporting currency, the translated amounts for non-monetary assets at the end of the prior period become the accounting basis for those assets in the period of the change and in subsequent periods. This means that there is no need to restate non-monetary assets at rates ruling when those assets were originally acquired by the foreign enterprise. Any cumulative exchange adjustments for prior periods that have been taken to reserves remain in reserves and need not be reflected in the profit and loss account of the period of change.

Intercompany dividends

29.62 Where a foreign subsidiary pays a dividend to its parent company, the dividend income should be recorded by the parent company at the rate of exchange ruling at the date when the dividend is declared payable, or at the year end rate if the dividend is proposed at that date. An exchange gain or loss will arise if the rate of exchange moves between the date of declaration (or proposal) and the payment date. This exchange difference will be reported in the parent's profit and loss account as a normal inter-company transaction exchange gain or loss.

29.63 Where the temporal method is used in the group financial statements, the dividend payment should be translated at the same rate, that is, the rate of exchange ruling at the date of declaration (or proposal at the year end). This means that both the dividend payment and receipt and the related exchange differences will be eliminated on consolidation.

29.64 Under the closing rate method, it is likely that the dividend, particularly an interim dividend, recorded in the financial statements of the foreign subsidiary will be translated either at the closing rate or at an average rate. On consolidation, the translated amount recorded in the subsidiary's profit and loss account will not cancel with the amount at which the dividend is recorded in the parent's profit and loss account because of the exchange difference. Consider the following example:

Example

A foreign subsidiary declared an interim dividend of FC 100,000 on 30 June 19X4 and proposed a final dividend of FC 150,000 for the year ended 31 December 19X4. The interim dividend was paid on 15 July 19X4 and the final dividend on 15 January 19X5. The parent prepares consolidated financial statements for the year ended 31 December 19X4 and uses the average rate for translating the results of the foreign subsidiary. The relevant exchange rates are as follows:

30 June 19X4 FC 1.50 = £1
15 July 19X4 FC 1.60 = £1
31 December 19X4 FC 1.75 = £1
Average for the year FC 1.55 = £1
15 January 19X5 FC 1.80 = £1

The interim dividend will be recorded in the translated profit and loss account of the foreign subsidiary and in the parent as follows:

Subsidiary's translated financial statements	£
Profit and loss account	
Interim paid FC 100,000 at average rate – FC 1.55	64,516
In parent's profit and loss account	
Initially recorded at rate when dividend is declared – FC 1.5	66,667
Exchange loss in the profit and loss account	(4,167)
Amount recorded at rate when interim dividend paid – FC 1.6	62,500
On consolidation	
Parent's P&L – dividend received	66,667
Subsidiary's P&L – dividend paid	64,516
Exchange gain on consolidation	2,151

The overall exchange difference in the consolidated financial statements is a loss of £2,016 comprising the loss of £4,167 in the parent's financial statements and the gain of £2,151 arising on cancellation of the inter-company dividends.

As can be seen from the above example, the cancellation of the inter-company dividends on consolidation gives rise to a further exchange difference, in this example, a gain of £2,151. Some argue that in order for the consolidated financial statements to retain the same financial relationships shown in the subsidiary's own financial statements, the results of the subsidiary should be translated at an average rate and the exchange gain arising on cancellation of the dividends should be taken to reserves. However, we prefer the argument that the exchange difference should be taken to the consolidated profit and loss account. This means that the consolidated profit and loss account reflects the economic effect, namely:

- Profits distributed by the subsidiary are included at the sterling amount remitted. The net exchange loss of £2,016 in the consolidated profit and loss account reflects the difference between the amount remitted translated at an average rate (£64,516) and the actual rate (£62,500).

- Profits retained by the subsidiary are translated at an average exchange rate.

An exchange difference will also arise if the dividend remained outstanding at the year end. In that situation, the parent will record an exchange loss of £9,524 being the amount at which the dividend was initially recorded, that is, £66,667 and the year end receivable of £57,143 (FC 100,000 @ 1.75). Again, such difference should be reported as part of consolidated results, together with the gain of £2,151 arising when the recorded dividends are eliminated on consolidation.

29.65 In the case of a proposed dividend, the dividend payable in the subsidiary's profit and loss account will be translated for consolidation purposes at an average rate (if the group translates the results of subsidiaries at the average rate). The amount payable in the balance sheet will be recorded at the closing rate resulting in an exchange difference that is taken to reserves under the closing rate/net investment method. The parent will record the dividend receivable at the closing rate both in the profit and loss account and in the balance sheet. On consolidation, the inter-company accounts will cancel out, but the dividends will not cancel out in the consolidated profit and loss account because of exchange differences. As explained above, this exchange difference should remain in the consolidated results. For instance, in the above example:

Example

The proposed dividend will be recorded in the translated profit and loss account of the foreign subsidiary and in the parent as follows:

Subsidiary's translated financial statements	£
Profit and loss account	
Proposed dividend FC 150,000 @ 1.55	96,774
In parent's P&L account	
Dividend receivable FC 150,000 @ 1.75	85,714
On consolidation	
Parents P&L – dividend receivable	85,714
Subsidiary's P&L – dividend payable	96,774
Exchange loss	11,060

The cancellation of the inter-company dividends on consolidation gives rise to an exchange loss of £11,060. As explained above, we prefer the argument that this exchange difference should be included in the consolidated profit and loss account such that the profits being remitted to the parent are translated at the rate at which they are remitted. When the final dividend is paid after the year end, a further exchange loss of £2,381 ((FC 150,000 @ 1.80 = £83,333) – £85,714) will arise in the parent's financial statements in that year.

29.66 Given that exchange differences can arise on any transaction where the settlement date is different from the date when the transaction is recorded, it may be appropriate, particularly where there is a likelihood of an exchange loss arising, to ensure that inter-company dividends are paid on the same date as they are declared. In practice, this may not always be possible, so it is not uncommon for a parent company to mitigate exchange differences arising by taking out appropriate forward contracts.

Example

A company has an overseas subsidiary that declares a dividend at the year end. At that date the parent takes out a forward contract to sell foreign currency equal in amount to the dividend that will be remitted, thereby hedging the remittance. The forward sale will be deliverable at the same date as the remittance. Considering the treatment in the parent's financial statements:

- The parent could record the dividend receivable both in the profit and loss account and in the balance sheet at the contracted rate in which case no exchange difference will arise when the cash is received, which is clearly the reason for taking out the forward contract.

- The parent could record the dividend receivable at the year end rate in the profit and loss account, but the debtor at the contracted rate. The exchange difference arising is then taken to profit and loss account.

Although the dividend recorded in the profit and loss account is the not the same under the above methods, the overall effect on the profit and loss account is the same. Since the purpose of taking out the forward contract is to eliminate the effect of exchange fluctuations on the overall profit for the year, both methods achieve this objective and are, therefore, acceptable. Forward contracts are dealt with in more detail from paragraph 29.118.

In the consolidated financial statements there may still be an exchange difference when the dividends are eliminated on consolidation, depending upon the translation policy. If the parent records the dividend receivable at the contracted rate and translates the results of its subsidiaries at an average rate then there will be a difference on consolidation which, as explained in the example in paragraph 29.64, we believe should be included in the consolidated profit and loss account.

Intra-group trading transactions

29.67 Where normal trading transactions take place between group companies located in different countries, exchange differences will arise which will not be eliminated on consolidation. As the transactions will probably be recorded in the local currency of one of the companies in question, exchange differences will arise, which should be reported in the profit and loss account of the enterprise in the same way as gains or losses on transactions arising with third parties. On consolidation, the net exchange gain or loss will have affected group cash flows and, therefore, it is proper that it should be included in consolidated results for the year. The exchange difference arising simply reflects the risk of doing business with a foreign party, even though that party happens to be a group member.

Example

A UK parent company has a wholly-owned subsidiary in the US. During the year ended 31 December 19X4, the US company purchased plant and raw materials to be used in its manufacturing process from the UK parent. Details of the transactions are as follows:

	Exchange rate
Purchased plant costing £500,000 on 30 April 19X4	£1 = US$ 1.48
Paid for plant on 30 September 19X4	£1 = US$ 1.54
Purchased raw materials costing £300,000 on 31 October 19X4	£1 = US$ 1.56
Balance of £300,000 outstanding at 31 December 19X4	£1 = US$ 1.52
Average rate for the year	£1 = US$ 1.55

The following exchange gains/losses will be recorded in the profit and loss account of the US subsidiary for the year ended 31 December 19X4.

	US$	US$
Plant costing £500,000 @1.48	740,000	
Paid £500,000 @ 1.54	770,000	
Exchange loss	(30,000)	(30,000)
Raw materials costing £300,000 @1.56	468,000	
Outstanding £300,000 @1.52	456,000	
Exchange gain	12,000	12,000
Net exchange loss recorded in P&L account		(18,000)

The inter-company creditor of US$ 456,000 in the US subsidiary's balance sheet will be translated into sterling at the closing rate to £300,000 and will be eliminated against the debtor recorded in the UK parent's inter-company account. The net exchange loss of US$ 18,000 will either be translated at the average rate or the closing rate depending on whether the UK parent uses the average rate or the closing rate to translate the profit and loss account of the US subsidiary. The resulting sterling figure for exchange losses will not be eliminated on consolidation and will be reported as part of the consolidated results of the group.

Unrealised profit on stocks

29.68 It is generally accepted that intra-group profit arising from the transfer of assets between companies in the group should be eliminated in full where such assets are still held in the undertakings included in the consolidation at the balance sheet date, because it does not represent profit to the group. No guidance is given in SSAP 20 as to the exchange rate at which the profit should be eliminated, although SFAS 52 requires elimination at the actual rate ruling at the date of the transaction or at a weighted average rate.

Example

The facts are the same as in the previous example except that the raw materials purchased for £300,000 by the US subsidiary are still in stock at 31 December 19X4. These goods cost the UK parent £270,000.

Therefore, unrealised profit of £30,000 would need to be eliminated on consolidation. However, elimination of this unrealised profit of £30,000 will not necessarily result in the stocks being included in the consolidated balance sheet at cost to the group where the closing rate method is used as illustrated below.

The amount for raw materials included in stock in the balance sheet of the US company at the transaction date is US$ 468,000. Under the closing rate method, the stock would be retranslated at the year end rate of 1.52 to £307,895. Therefore, the stock will be recorded in the consolidated balance sheet as follows:

	£
Cost of stock US$ 468,000 @ 1.52	307,895
Unrealised profit	(30,000)
Stock carried in consolidated balance sheet	277,895

The difference of £7,895 represents the exchange difference arising on the retranslation of the stock in the subsidiary's financial statements to the year end rate under the closing rate/net investment method, that is, £307,895 less the cost to the subsidiary of £300,000.

If, on the other hand, the parent has purchased the raw materials from the US subsidiary for US$ 468,000 at 31 October 19X4, which cost the US subsidiary US$ 421,200, and these items were still in the parent's stock at the year end, a problem arises as to what rate the unrealised profit of US$ 46,800 should be eliminated.

As stated above, if the guidance in SFAS 52 is followed, the profit will be eliminated at the actual rate and the stock will be recorded in the consolidated balance sheet as follows:

	£
Cost of stock US$ 468,000 @ 1.56	300,000
Unrealised profit US$ 46,800 @1.56	(30,000)
Stock carried in consolidated balance sheet	270,000

The amount of stock recorded in the balance sheet represents the original cost to the group of US$ 421,200 translated at the rate ruling at the date of the intra-group transaction. This is the method required by SFAS 52, but it will only be appropriate under UK GAAP if the results of the subsidiary are translated at weighted average rates (that is, approximating to actual rates).

This method will not be appropriate under UK GAAP if the results of the subsidiary are translated at closing rate. In this situation the amount of profit to be eliminated is that attributable to the subsidiary in the group profit and loss account, that is, US$ 46,800 @ 1.52 = £30,789.

	£
Cost of stock US$ 468,000 @ 1.56	300,000
Unrealised profit US$ 46,800 @ 1.52	(30,789)
Stock carried in consolidated balance sheet	269,211

In practice, a majority of companies use an average rate for translating the results of foreign operations under the closing rate/net investment method. In this situation, the amount of profit to be eliminated should be calculated using that average rate.

	£
Cost of stock US$ 468,000 @ 1.56	300,000
Unrealised profit US$ 46,800 @ 1.55	(30,194)
Stock carried in consolidated balance sheet	269,806

In any event, the amount of stock recorded in the consolidated balance sheet under the closing rate/net investment method will not be the same as the actual cost to the group.

Under the temporal method, the transaction would be recorded at actual rates and, therefore, any intra-group profit eliminated will automatically bring the amount of the stock back to its cost to the group.

29.69 Even if intra-group transactions do not give rise to intra-group profit, there could still be an effect on asset values as the following example illustrates.

Example

A UK parent has a wholly-owned subsidiary in Pololand where the currency is Polos. The net assets of the group at 31 March 19X4 are £54,000; consisting of cash £24,000, held in the UK parent and stock held in the Pololand subsidiary costing Pols 3m, which was included in the consolidated balance sheet at the closing rate of £1 = Pols 100. On 30 September 19X4, the subsidiary transfers the goods to its UK parent at cost price when the rate of exchange is £1 = Pols 125. The transaction is settled in cash and the goods are included in parent's stock at £24,000. At 31 March 19X5, the goods are still in stock. The Polos has weakened further against sterling and the exchange rate at the balance sheet date is £1 = Pols 150.

No gain or loss is recorded by either company on the transfer, hence there are no inter-company profits to be eliminated.

		31 March 19X4
		£
Net assets:		
Stock 3m @ 100 (held by sub)		30,000
Cash (held by parent)		24,000
		54,000
		31 March 19X5
		£
Net assets:		
Stock (held by parent)		24,000
Cash 3m @ 150 (held by sub)		20,000
		44,000
Exchange difference on retranslation of opening net assets of foreign subsidiary:		
3m @ 100 =	30,000	
3m @ 150 =	20,000	10,000
		54,000

In this example, no exchange difference falls to be included in the consolidated profit and loss account as there is no trading gain or loss, but the effect of switching stock round the group affects the carrying value of the assets. If the stock had not been transferred the net assets would still have to be decreased by £10,000 but the reduction would have been entirely in the stock value with the cash balance unchanged. However, the result of moving the stock around the group is that there is a decrease of £6,000 in the stock value and a decrease of £4,000 in the group's cash position. This reflects the fact that the group's foreign currency exposure is centred on different assets.

Intra-group long-term loans and deferred trading balances

29.70 The recording of intra-group loans made by one group member to another in a currency which is different from the local currency of the borrower is no different from the recording of any other foreign currency monetary items. The borrower will initially record the foreign currency loan at the rate of exchange ruling at the date the loan is made. At each balance sheet date thereafter, until it is repaid, the loan will be translated at the closing rate and any exchange difference will be reported in the profit and loss account. On consolidation, the intra-group loan account will cancel out, but the exchange difference reported in the borrower's profit and loss account will flow through in the consolidated profit and loss account. The same principles apply to an unsettled inter-company account that arises from trading transactions, for example, where a parent finances the acquisition of a fixed asset by the foreign subsidiary through the inter-company account.

29.71 In certain circumstances, however, the parent may decide, because of tax or other benefits, to finance a foreign subsidiary with long-term loans and deferred trading balances rather than wholly with equity. In those situations, it may not be appropriate to treat such financing as an ordinary monetary item and to include the resulting exchange differences in the consolidated profit and loss account when exchange difference arising on equivalent financing with equity capital would be taken to consolidated reserves. SSAP 20 recognises this situation and states:

> *"Although equity investments in foreign enterprises will normally be made by the purchase of shares, investments may also be made by means of long-term loans and inter-company deferred trading balances. Where financing by such means is intended to be, for all practical purposes, as permanent as equity, such loans and inter-company balances should be treated as part of the investing company's net investment in the foreign enterprise; hence exchange differences arising on such loans and inter-company balances should be dealt with as adjustments to reserves."* [SSAP 20 para 20].

The definition of net investment is stated in paragraph 29.40 and includes long-term loans and deferred trading balances.

29.72 The inclusion of long-term loans and deferred trading balances as part of net investment is only permitted where the parent regards them as being as permanent as equity. The parent will effectively regard them as permanent if there is no intention that such balances will be repayable in the foreseeable future. In practice it is likely that a long-term loan of say, 15 to 20 years, would be designated by the parent as being part of the effective equity stake in the foreign enterprise. It is also likely that a short-term loan that is allowed to be continuously rolled over and not intended to be repaid, whether or not the subsidiary is able to repay it, would be regarded for all practical purposes as permanent as equity. The same principle applies to inter-company balances arising from normal trading transactions. Where it is not intended that such balances will be settled in cash for the foreseeable future, they could be regarded as part of the effective equity stake.

29.73 Where exchange differences on long-term loans and deferred trading balances which are regarded as permanent are taken to reserves on consolidation, the question arises as to whether a similar treatment can be adopted in the financial statement of the individual company. Consider the following example:

Example – currency loan made by parent to overseas subsidiary

A UK parent is preparing its financial statements to 30 June 19X5. It has a loan receivable from its German subsidiary of DM 1m which has been outstanding for some time. The parent notified the German subsidiary at the previous year end that no repayment of the amount will be requested for the foreseeable future.

The relevant exchange rates are as follows:

		30 June 19X4	30 June 19X5
£1	=	DM 2.45	DM 2.20

In the financial statements of the parent company, the following exchange difference will arise if the loan is retranslated at the closing rate:

UK parent: **Exchange difference on long-term loan**	£
DM 1m @ 2.45	408,163
DM 1m @ 2.20	454,545
Exchange gain	46,382

On consolidation, the retranslated long-term loan will be regarded as part of the net investment in the foreign subsidiary and, therefore, the related exchange gains will be taken to reserves under the closing rate/net investment method. It should be noted that there will also be a corresponding exchange loss included in reserves, arising as part of the retranslation of the net assets (which include the DM loan creditor) of the German subsidiary.

The question arises as to how the long-term loan should be treated in the financial statements of the parent company. Some take the view that the loan should be regarded as a monetary item and any exchange difference taken to the profit and loss account. This is because the definition of net investment in SSAP 20 applies to consolidated and not entity accounts. However, we consider that this is a restrictive interpretation.

The parent is exposed to foreign currency risk on the DM loan but, as it does not expect any repayment for the foreseeable future or until the investment is sold, the exchange risk is potentially eliminated. If the long-term loan can be regarded as a permanent investment on consolidation then it is reasonable to treat it in a similar manner in the parent's financial statements. This means that the long-term loan will not be retranslated in the books of the parent, but will be carried at the historical rate of exchange such that no exchange difference arises in the parent's financial statements. This reflects the substance of the loan.

The situation is more complicated if the long-term loan is financed by foreign borrowings in the parent company in which case the long-term loan would be retranslated to offset currency differences on the borrowings. This is dealt with in detail from paragraph 29.79.

Another problem that might arise is the appropriate treatment that should be adopted in the year in which the parent decides to designate any long-term loans or deferred trading balances as effective equity stakes. In the above example, the long-term DM loan was designated as being part of the parent's net investment in the German subsidiary from the beginning of the accounting period. If the parent did this part way during the year, say, at 31 December 19X4, it would be appropriate for the parent to treat the long-term loan as a monetary item up to that date and take any exchange difference arising to its profit and loss account. The exchange rate at the date that the loan is designated as permanent equity will be regarded as the historical rate for the purpose of translating the non-monetary asset and so no further exchange differences on the long-term loan will arise in the parent's financial statements.

29.74 In the above example, where the foreign currency loan is regarded as being as permanent as equity, there is no exchange difference in the profit and loss account of the parent company or in the group profit and loss account. However, the situation will differ where the loan is denominated in sterling such that it is the subsidiary that is exposed to the currency risk as there will be an exchange difference in the subsidiary's profit and loss account. Consider the following example:

Example – sterling loan made by parent to overseas subsidiary

A UK parent is preparing its financial statements to 30 June 19X5. It has a deferred trading balance of £200,000 owed by its French subsidiary.

The relevant exchange rates are as follows:

		30 June 19X4	30 June 19X5
£1	=	FF 8.14	FF 7.71

In the financial statements of the individual companies, the following exchange differences will arise if the deferred trading balance is retranslated at the closing rate.

UK parent
There is no exchange difference in the parent's financial statements in respect of the deferred trading balance as this is denominated in sterling.

French subsidiary
Exchange difference on deferred trading balance

£200,000 @ 8.14	FF 1,628,000
£200,000 @ 7.71	FF 1,542,000
Exchange gain	FF 86,000
Exchange gain translated at closing rate (@ 7.71)	£11,154

The exchange gain of FF 86,000 on the deferred trading account should be taken to the profit and loss account of the French subsidiary. This is because the trading transactions were originally carried out in the parent's currency and the subsidiary was exposed to the foreign currency risk. Therefore, it is appropriate to take the exchange difference to the subsidiary's profit and loss account.

On consolidation, the exchange gain in the subsidiary's profit and loss account will be translated into sterling (£11,154 assuming that the group uses the closing rate to translate its subsidiaries' results). The normal treatment would be to include this exchange gain in the consolidated profit and loss account. However, as the long-term loan is regarded as part of the net investment in the subsidiary, the exchange gain of £11,154 should be taken to reserves in the consolidated financial statements. There will be a corresponding exchange loss included in reserves arising as part of the retranslation of the net assets of the French subsidiary. The effect is that the consolidated profit and loss account will not reflect any exchange difference on the deferred trading balance, which is consistent with the fact that the deferred trading balance has no impact on group cash flows.

29.75 The two examples above consider the accounting implications when a loan is made by the parent company to an overseas subsidiary. In the case of a foreign currency upstream loan, that is, a borrowing by a UK parent company from the subsidiary in the subsidiary's local currency, the treatment of exchange differences in the consolidated financial statements will depend on the treatment in the parent company's own financial statements. Such loans are often regarded as hedging transactions because they reduce the net foreign currency investment in the subsidiary (see further para 29.90). If the borrowing is accounted for in the parent's financial statements as a hedge under the SSAP 20 offset procedure (see para 29.81 for details) then exchange differences on the borrowing are taken to reserves (insofar as they offset exchange differences on the investment being hedged) and do not appear in the parent company's profit and loss account. A similar treatment will apply in the consolidated financial statements.

Goodwill arising on consolidation

29.76 Goodwill may arise on consolidation where a company acquires the equity share capital of a foreign subsidiary. Under SSAP 22, this goodwill may either be written off to reserves or capitalised as an intangible asset and amortised through the profit and loss account over its useful economic life. Where the foreign investment is accounted for under the closing rate/net investment method, the question arises as to whether or not the goodwill, once calculated at acquisition, should be retranslated each year at closing rate.

29.77 In the example illustrating the application of the closing rate method in paragraph 29.41 above, goodwill is translated at the rate ruling on the date of acquisition and written off to reserves. It is not included in the retranslation of the opening net assets on the grounds that it arises only on consolidation and is not part of the net assets of the foreign enterprise. This view would appear to be supported by the ASC when it issued TR 504 on the publication of SSAP 20. Paragraph 21 of TR 504 indicates that the goodwill element of an investment would not be treated as a foreign currency asset for the purpose of the offset procedure in consolidated financial statements. Under this view the goodwill is regarded as a sterling asset whose carrying amount does not fluctuate when the rate of exchange changes.

29.78 An alternative treatment is to regard the goodwill as a currency asset which is retranslated at the closing rate. In this situation, an exchange difference would arise on the opening net investment including the goodwill. This treatment is required by SFAS 52. This view is perhaps closer to business reality because it regards goodwill not as a sterling asset that is measured at a specific point in time and valid only at that time and in the circumstances then prevailing, but as one that resides in the foreign entity's business which generates income in foreign currency. We support this view and consider that this treatment (whereby the goodwill is regarded as a foreign currency asset) can be adopted whether goodwill is accounted for by the immediate write off method or by the method of capitalisation and amortisation. Where the immediate write off method is adopted, however, we believe that the amount that can be treated as a foreign currency asset should ideally be restricted to the amount that would remain on balance sheet had a policy of capitalisation and amortisation been adopted. We consider that this approach is justified by the ASB's statement that goodwill, when written off, is not a recognised loss and by the statement in SSAP 22 that the write off of goodwill as a matter of accounting policy does not necessarily mean it has lost its value. Whilst the above reference to TR 504 indicates that this view was not taken at the time that the technical release was issued, the date of issue (April 1983) preceded the issue of SSAP 22, UITF 3 and FRS 3. Also the technical release does not form part of SSAP 20 and so we consider that the alternative view is not a departure from that standard. An example of a company that has adopted this policy, but which has retranslated the full amount of goodwill written off is given in the Table 29.8 below.

Table 29.8 – Automated Security (Holdings) PLC – Report and Financial Statements – 30 November 1994

Accounting Policies (extract)

10. FOREIGN EXCHANGE

Foreign currency assets and liabilities of Group companies are translated into sterling at the rates of exchange ruling at the balance sheet date. The trading results of overseas subsidiaries and associated undertakings are translated at the average exchange rate ruling during the year, with the adjustment between average rates and the rates ruling at the balance sheet date being taken to reserves. The difference arising on the restatement of the opening net investment, including goodwill, to overseas subsidiary and associated undertakings, and of matching foreign currency loans and foreign currency swap facilities, are dealt with as adjustments to other reserves. All other exchange differences are dealt with in the profit and loss account.

NOTES TO THE FINANCIAL STATEMENTS

21. RESERVES (extract)	Group £'000	Company £'000
(d) OTHER RESERVES		
At 1st December 1993	(87,560)	80
Goodwill in the year written off (note 24)	(20,193)	-
Goodwill of associated undertakings transferred to profit and loss account	17,365	-
Exchange adjustments on:		
Net investments including goodwill	(6,945)	-
Hedging arrangements	2,136	-
Goodwill	4,516	-
At 30th November 1994	(90,681)	80

24 GOODWILL	Cost of goodwill eliminated £'000	Exchange adjustments £'000	Total £'000
Eliminated to 30th November 1993	196,496	7,482	203,978
Acquisitions in the year			
- Associated undertakings	17,466	-	17,466
- Other businesses acquired	1,769	-	1,769
Adjustments to previous year's acquisitions	535	-	535
Share of goodwill movements of associated undertakings	423	-	423
	20,193	-	20,193
Transferred to profit and loss account	(17,365)	-	(17,365)
Exchange adjustments (note 21 (d))	-	(4,516)	(4,516)
Eliminated to 30th November 1994	199,324	2,966	202,290

Foreign equity investments financed by foreign borrowings

Treatment in individual company

29.79 As stated in paragraph 29.22, in certain circumstances the normal rule that non-monetary items should be carried in the balance sheet at their historical cost at the exchange rate ruling when they were originally acquired without further retranslation, does not apply to foreign equity investments. The exception arises in circumstances where a company or a group has used foreign currency borrowings to finance foreign equity investments, or to provide a hedge against the exchange risk associated with existing foreign equity investments.

29.80 If the normal rules of translation of monetary and non-monetary items are applied to the circumstances mentioned above, any exchange gain or loss on the borrowings would be taken to the profit and loss account, while no exchange gain or loss would arise on the equity investments. SSAP 20 recognises that in such circumstances, as no economic gain or loss would in fact arise where there is a movement in exchange rates, it would be inappropriate to recognise any accounting profit or loss. [SSAP 20 para 28].

29.81 Therefore, provided the conditions set out in the paragraph below apply, the company *may* denominate its equity investments in the appropriate foreign currency. This means that the investment will be regarded as a currency investment and the company will need to translate the carrying amount at the closing rate each year for inclusion in its financial statements. Where a company treats investments in this way, it should take direct to reserves any exchange differences that arise when the investments are retranslated. It should also take the exchange differences on the related foreign currency borrowings to reserves and not to the profit and loss account to be offset against those exchange differences. [SSAP 20 para 51]. This is known as the 'cover' method or 'offset' procedure.

29.82 The conditions for offset, all of which must apply, are as follows:

- In any accounting period, exchange gains or losses arising on the borrowings may be offset only to the extent of exchange differences arising on the equity investments.
- The foreign currency borrowings, whose exchange gains or losses are used in the offset process, should not exceed, in the aggregate, the total amount of cash that the investments are expected to be able to generate, whether from profits or otherwise.
- The accounting treatment adopted should be applied consistently from period to period.

[SSAP 20 para 51].

Offset restriction

29.83 The first condition deals with situations where there is not an exact match between the borrowings and the investments (either in amount or currency or both) and greater exchange gains or losses arise on the loans than are available for offset against the investments. Since the excess gains or losses are deemed to be speculative in nature they are not allowed to be used for offset in reserves and must be taken to the profit and loss account. Therefore, only that portion of the total gains or losses on the loans which is matched by an opposite exchange movement on the investments falls to be taken to reserves for offset purposes.

29.84 Whilst it is to be expected that for the cover to operate, exchange gains or losses on the borrowings would be matched by opposite exchange losses or gains arising on the investments, it is possible, particularly where investments are managed on a pool basis and financed by a basket of loans in different currencies, for both the borrowings and the investments to show either exchange gains or losses. In this context, it should be noted that the cover method need not be restricted to individual investments and borrowings. It can also be applied to a group of investments financed by a variety of different currencies. However, where an investment or a number of investments has been financed by a specific borrowing the offset should be applied on an individual matched basis, rather than putting them in a general pool.

Example

A UK company is preparing its financial statements for the year ended 30 June 19X5. On 31 December 19X4 it raised a loan of US$ 2m in order to finance two equity investments, one in France costing FF 1,500,000 and the other in Germany costing DM 2,500,000. The relevant exchange rates are:

31 December 19X4	£1 = US$ 1.48 = FF 8.89 = DM 2.45
30 June 19X5	£1 = US$ 1.55 = FF 8.39 = DM 2.54

	Exchange difference £	P&L account £	Reserves £
Exchange difference on investment in French company			
31/12/X4 – FF 1,500,000 @ 8.89	168,729		
30/06/X5 – FF 1,500,000 @ 8.39	178,784		
Exchange gain	10,055		
Exchange difference on investment in German company			
31/12/X4 – DM 2,500,000 @ 2.45	1,020,408		
30/06/X5 – DM 2,500,000 @ 2.54	984,252		
Exchange loss	(36,156)		
Net exchange loss on equity investments	(26,101)		(26,101)
Exchange difference on US$ loan			
31/12/X4 – US$ 2m @ $1.48	1,351,351		
30/06/X5 – US$ 2m @ $1.55	1,290,323		
Exchange gain	61,028	34,927	26,101

In this example, the amount of the exchange gain on the loan that the company can offset as a reserve movement against the exchange loss on the investments is limited to £26,101. The excess gain of £34,927 is deemed to be speculative and, therefore, is taken to the profit and loss account.

29.85 If, in the example, there had been a loss on exchange on the loan for the year ended 30 June 19X5 of, say, £65,000 and a net gain on exchange on the investments of, say, £35,000, the amount of the exchange loss on the loan that the company could have offset as a reserve movement against the exchange gain on the investment would have been limited to £35,000. The company would have had to include the balance of the exchange loss on the loan (that is, £30,000) in its profit or loss on ordinary activities for the year.

29.86 On the other hand, if in the example there had been either a net gain on exchange on the retranslation of the equity investments as well as an exchange gain on the loan (or a net loss on exchange on the retranslation of the equity investments as well as an exchange loss on the loan) the company would have had to take the whole of the gain or loss on exchange on the equity investments to reserves and the whole of the gain or loss on the loan to its profit or loss on ordinary activities for the year. This is because the offset conditions place no limit on the amount of gain or loss on investments that may be taken to reserves, but limit the amount of the gain or loss on borrowings that may be taken to reserves to the amount of the loss or gain on the investments.

Borrowing restriction

29.87 The second condition is designed to ensure that the hedge is genuine by requiring that the borrowing is not greater than the total amount of cash generated from the investment. However, no guidance is given as to how the cash generation is to be measured or how long the foreign undertaking is given to generate profits. The condition should not cause any undue problem where a borrowing that is invested in a profitable company is sufficiently long-term to enable that company to generate sufficient profits to cover the borrowing. However, where the foreign enterprise is unprofitable or earns negligible profits not sufficient to cover the cash outflows on the borrowings, the expected cash generated will be represented by the net realisable value of the investment at the balance sheet date. To the extent that the net realisable value is less than the book value of the investment, the borrowing used for offset should be restricted accordingly. Restriction might also apply where the foreign enterprise is subject to severe exchange control restrictions such that the expected cash generated from the investment is considered to be insufficient to cover the borrowing. The next example illustrates this provision.

Example

Some years ago, a UK company raised a foreign currency loan in Argentina to finance the acquisition of a company in that country. Both at 31 March 19X4 and at 31 March 19X5, the loan amounted to Peso 5m, and the equity investment amounted to Peso 7m. The company is preparing its financial statements to 31 March 19X5 and considers that the total amount of cash that the investment is able to generate will be 4m Argentinean Pesos. The exchange rates are as follows:

31 March 19X4	£1 = Peso 1.6
31 March 19X5	£1 = Peso 1.4

In this example, the maximum amount of borrowings that can be used for offset purposes is limited to the net realisable value of the investment.

	Exchange difference £	P&L account £	Reserves £
Exchange difference on loan			
31/03/X4 – Peso 5m @ 1.6	3,125,000		
31/03/X5 – Peso 5m @ 1.4	3,571,429		
Exchange loss	(446,429)	(89,286)	(357,143)
But restricted to net realisable value of investment			
31/03/X4 – Peso 4m @ 1.6	2,500,000		
31/03/X5 – Peso 4m @ 1.4	2,857,143		
Exchange gain			357,143

In this example, the amount of the exchange loss arising on the loan that can be offset in reserves against the exchange gain arising on the investment is £357,143. The remaining exchange loss on the loan of £89,286 must be taken to the profit and loss account.

In addition, the company will also have to write down the investment for permanent diminution in value of Peso 3m as illustrated below.

	£	P&L account £
Equity investment		
Opening carrying value Peso 7m @ 1.6	4,375,000	
Permanent diminution Peso 3m @ 1.6	(1,875,000)	1,875,000
	2,500,000	
Retranslation gain (taken to reserves)	357,143	
Realisable value Peso 4m @ 1.4	2,857,143	

Therefore, the total charge in the profit and loss account for the year is £1,964,286 comprising permanent diminution of £1,875,000 and excess exchange loss on retranslation of the loan of £89,286.

29.88 Although, in the above example, it has been assumed that the company is able to determine the amount of the cash which the investment is expected to generate, in practice, it may be difficult or impractical to forecast the total cash to be generated from the investment, both from profits and from its ultimate realisation because of the speculative nature of long-term cash flow projections. It may also be that the investment cash flows are never converted into the currency of the borrowing because they are expected to be reinvested. In that situation, as a practical expediency the alternative would be to consider the amount that would be raised if the investment were sold immediately. If this amount is equal to the book value of the investment, then the whole of the book value is available for use in the offset calculation.

Consistent accounting treatment

29.89 Given that the application of the cover method is fairly flexible the third condition outlined in paragraph 29.82 above is simply designed to ensure that a company does not change its accounting treatment depending on the way in which exchange rates move, but adopts a consistency policy as laid down in SSAP 2. For example, where exchange rate movements give rise to exchange losses on borrowings, and the first two conditions apply, it is obviously advantageous for a company to be able to use the offset procedure. If, however, in a subsequent year, exchange rate movements give rise to exchange gains on those borrowings, and the first two conditions still apply, the company must still use the offset procedure. It cannot include the exchange gains in its profit on ordinary activities.

Hedging by means of upstream loans

29.90 It is sometimes appropriate for a UK direct or indirect parent company to borrow from its overseas subsidiary. If the borrowing is in the subsidiary's local currency and the borrowed funds are converted into sterling or invested elsewhere in the business, this reduces the group's net assets in the foreign currency and, therefore, has the same affect that an external borrowing in the currency, used in the same way, would have had. This means that in the parent's individual accounts, the intra-group borrowing can be treated as a hedge against the equity investment under the provisions of paragraph 51 of SSAP 20, that is, exchange differences on the loan can be offset (subject to the criteria in the standard) against exchange differences on the investment which is treated as a currency asset and retranslated. Companies entering into such transactions with their overseas subsidiaries should seek specialist taxation advice as the rules in this area are complex.

Termination of hedging during the year

29.91 The application of the consistency principle becomes particularly relevant where hedging is terminated during the year following either the repayment of the foreign currency borrowing or the sale of the foreign equity investment. In those situations, the offset procedure should be applied up to the date of repayment of the loan or the date of sale of the investment and not stopped at the previous year end. Termination of a hedge is considered in the example below.

Example

A UK company, which prepares its financial statements to 30 June each year, borrowed US$ 2m to finance the acquisition of a company in Hong Kong costing HK$ 12m (£1,049,869) some years ago. The company's accounting policy is to take unrealised exchange differences on long-term borrowings, that are matched with currency equity investments, direct to reserves. On 31 December 19X4, the company repaid the borrowing which resulted in an exchange gain. How should the gain arising on the repayment be treated in its financial statements for the year ended 30 June 19X5 and at what value should the equity investment be recorded in the balance sheet at 30 June 19X5?

The relevant exchange rates are as follows:

30 June 19X4	£1 = US$ 1.54	£1 = HK$ 11.93
31 December 19X4	£1 = US$ 1.56	£1 = HK$ 12.10
30 June 19X5	£1 = US$ 1.59	£1 = HK$ 12.31

	Exchange difference	P&L account	Reserves
Equity investments	£	£	£
30/06/X4 – HK$ 12m @ 11.93	1,005,868		
31/12/X4 – HK$ 12m @ 12.10	991,736		
Exchange loss	(14,132)		(14,132)
Loan			
30/06/X4 – US$ 2m @1.54	1,298,701		
31/12/X4 – US$ 2m @1.56	1,282,051		
Exchange gain	16,650	2,518	14,132

Given that the hedging continues up to the date of repayment of the borrowing and ceases thereafter, the company should continue with its consistent policy of taking the exchange gain on the loan to reserves to be matched with the exchange loss on the equity investment until 31 December 19X4. Since the amount of the exchange gain to be offset in reserves is limited to £14,132, the balance of £2,518 should be included in the profit and loss account for the year.

As far as the carrying value of the investment at 30 June 19X5 is concerned, the investment should be recorded at £991,736, its carrying value at the date when cover ceased (that is, 31 December 19X4). The rationale is that after the cover has been removed the investment ceases to be a currency asset and should thereafter be treated as a non-monetary asset without any further retranslation until such time as another loan is taken out to provide a hedge.

Some would argue that the investment should be recorded at the carrying value at the previous balance sheet date, that is £1,005,868 on the grounds that, as there are no borrowings at the year end, the cover is deemed to have ceased at the beginning of the period. But this treatment fails to recognise the fact that the hedging continued until the date of repayment of the loan. Others might opt to record the investment at its historical cost of £1,049,869. The effect of this would be to reverse cumulative exchange differences of £58,133 (£1,049,869–£991,736) on the investment that had been taken to reserves. This treatment ignores the fact that hedging on the investment ever took place.

29.92 If the foreign currency investment is sold, but the borrowing is retained, no particular problem arises. The company should apply the offset procedure up to the date of sale of the investment and not stop at the previous year end. At the date of sale, the borrowing changes its nature and becomes a borrowing that is not a hedge. Therefore, any movement from that date to the balance sheet date should be taken to the profit and loss account. Even if that were to show a loss while a hedge, and a profit while not an hedge, that would still be the proper treatment.

Borrowings taken out before or after the investment

29.93 The standard permits the cover method to apply to borrowings that have been taken out before or after the investment is made, because they can be designated as hedges against a new investment or an existing equity investment. In these situations, the period during which the borrowings are in place is different from the period during which the investments are held. Although no guidance is provided in the standard as to how the cover method should operate in these circumstances, it would appear that for the cover method to operate sensibly, the exchange differences on the borrowings that may be offset against the investments should be those that arise during the period when the hedge is effective.

Example

Some years ago, a UK company acquired all the share capital of a French company for FF 10m when the rate of exchange was £1 = FF 10. The investment was carried at historical cost of £1m. On 30 June 19X4, the directors considered the investment to be worth FF 12m and took out a long-term loan of FF 12m to provide a hedge against the investment. The proceeds of the loan were used to reduce an existing sterling borrowing. The relevant exchange rates at 30 June 19X4 and 31 December 19X4 are £ 1= FF 8.4 and £1 = FF 8.00 respectively. How should the company apply the cover method for the year ended 31 December 19X4?

The company can apply the cover method in the following ways:

The most straightforward method and the one which recognises the economic rationale of taking out the hedge is to record the investment at directors' valuation of FF 12m (£1,428,571) at 30 June 19X4. The difference between this value and the historical cost, that is, £428,571 is taken to the revaluation reserve. Since the investment and the borrowing are now perfectly matched after 30 June 19X4, the exchange differences arising on the retranslation of both the investment and the loan will cancel out in reserves and no exchange difference on the loan will fall to be taken to the profit and loss account.

Alternatively, if the company does not wish to record the investment at the directors' valuation of FF 12m then, under the approach set out in paragraph 29.93 above, the exchange difference on the investment that arises during the period in which it is hedged is regarded as being available for offset against the exchange differences arising on the loan during the same period. To achieve this, the investment is first treated as a currency asset at 30 June 19X4, the date the loan was taken out, and recorded at £1,190,476 (FF 10m @ 8.4), the exchange gain of £190,476 being taken directly to reserves as it represents a revaluation surplus. Once the investment has been established as a currency asset and its value determined for offset purposes, no further problem arises and the normal rules apply as indicated below.

	Exchange difference	P&L account	Reserves
Equity investment	£	£	£
30/06/X4 – FF 10m @ 8.4	1,190,476		
31/12/X4 – FF 10m @ 8.0	1,250,000		
Exchange gain	59,524		59,524
Loan			
30/06/X4 – FF 12m @ 8.4	1,428,571		
31/12/X4 – FF 12m @ 8.0	1,500,000		
Exchange loss	(71,429)	(11,905)	(59,524)

It can be seen that a proportion of the exchange loss on the loan remains unutilised and is taken to the profit and loss account. If the directors had revalued the investment to FF 12m and followed the first approach outlined above, all of the exchange difference would have been taken to reserves. The first approach is considered to be superior as it better reflects the transaction's underlying purpose.

29.94 The situation where a borrowing is taken out before the investment is made is relatively straightforward. The cover should only apply for the period when the hedge is effective. This means that any exchange difference arising on the borrowing prior to the date that the investment is made should be taken to the profit and loss account. Thereafter, the normal rules of offset apply.

Carrying value of foreign equity investment

29.95 Paragraph 51(a) of SSAP 20 allows exchange gains and losses on foreign currency borrowings to be offset in reserves only to the extent of exchange differences arising on the foreign equity investments. Therefore, where companies use foreign currency borrowings to finance or provide a hedge against foreign equity investments, it may be necessary to consider the accounting policy for the carrying value of those investments. Furthermore, as this is likely to have taxation implications and the rules are complex in this area, specialist tax advice may be necessary.

29.96 The appropriate accounting policy is likely to be influenced by the treasury policy, for instance whether the company chooses to hedge against the investment's cost, the subsidiary's underlying net assets or the underlying fair value. The choices of policy for the carrying value include the following:

- Cost (reduced to net recoverable amount in the event of any permanent diminution in value).
- Net asset value (annual revaluation). It should be noted that if this policy is adopted, the carrying amount of the investment immediately after an acquisition will be reduced by any amount relating to goodwill. It may, however, be an appropriate policy if the subsidiaries were acquired a number of years ago or were set up by the parent, such that the net asset values being hedged are significantly in excess of original cost.
- Directors' valuation (periodic as required). This could be based on cost plus retained post-acquisition profits, or an estimate of the realisable value in the market place.

29.97 Whichever policy is adopted, it must be applied consistently from year to year. Any change in policy would have to be justified on the grounds that the new policy is preferable to the one it replaces, because it will give a fairer presentation of the reporting entity's results and financial position. [FRS 3 para 62].

29.98 Where an investment is designated as a foreign currency asset and is carried at a valuation, it will be necessary to analyse separately the effect of exchange rate movements on the opening value of the investment and the effect of a revaluation of the foreign currency carrying value.

Example

A UK company has an investment in a US subsidiary which is financed by US$ borrowings. It adopts a policy of net asset value for the carrying value of the investment.

	31 December 19X0	31 December 19X1
Net asset value of subsidiary	$100m	$110m
Exchange rate	2.0	1.67
Net asset value in sterling	£50m	£66m

The increase in value of £16m is analysed as follows:

	£m
Exchange gain on retranslation of opening net assets ($100m @ 1.67 – $100m @ 2.0) – taken to reserves for offset with exchange loss on borrowings	10
Gain on revaluation at the year end ($110m – $100m = $10m @ 1.67) – taken to revaluation reserves	6
	16

In the above example, it has been assumed that the whole of the increase in net assets of $10m arising from the increase in profits arose at the end of the year. In practice, however the profits will arise throughout the year. Therefore, it may be possible to split the $10m increase between a real revaluation gain that is taken to the revaluation reserve and a further exchange difference that recognises the fact that the increase in net assets occurs not on the last day of the year, but over the course of the year. For example, if the average exchange rate is £1= $1.85, the increase in the value of £16m could be analysed as follows:

	£m
Exchange gain on retranslation of opening net assets ($100m @ 1.67 – $100m @ 2.0) – taken to profit and loss reserves for offset with exchange loss on borrowings	10.0
Exchange gain arising on the increase in net assets from use of average rate ($10m @ 1.67 – $10m @1.85) – taken to profit and loss reserves for offset with exchange loss on borrowings	0.6
Gain on revaluation = increase in net assets at average rate ($10m @ 1.85) – taken to revaluation reserves	5.4
	16.0

Although the effect of the above calculation is to squeeze out a further amount of exchange difference from the overall revaluation increase that may properly be taken to profit and loss account reserve for offset against the exchange loss on the borrowings, there is nothing in the standard to suggest that this treatment is inappropriate. Indeed, it makes good sense and is consistent with what actually happens in practice, that is, the company is hedging its net investments at the end of each year, provided of course the offset and the borrowing restrictions discussed above are not breached.

Partial hedges

29.99 Paragraph 51 of SSAP 20 refers to a company using foreign currency borrowings to finance its foreign equity investments, but it is not specific as to the extent to which an asset has to be financed in this way. We consider that the general interpretation should be that the investment is entirely or mostly financed by foreign currency borrowings as it would be contrary to the spirit of the standard if a low level of borrowings, say five per cent of the asset amount, could result in the asset being regarded as a foreign currency asset and, consequently, the exchange differences on the borrowings being taken to reserves rather than to the profit and loss account.

29.100 However, there may be circumstances where a less restrictive interpretation is appropriate. For instance, if a group has an overall balance sheet gearing of say 30 per cent and as a matter of policy wants to borrow, for all major subsidiaries, 30 per cent of the asset's carrying value in the relevant currency, then it would seem reasonable to regard the investment as a foreign currency asset. The question then arises as to the appropriate treatment for translation of the partially hedged investment.

29.101 One view is that the whole amount of the partially hedged investment is regarded as a foreign currency asset even though the borrowing in the relevant currency is only, say, 30 per cent of the carrying value of the investment. The effect of regarding such investments as foreign currency assets is that differences on the retranslation of the whole investment go to reserves, but they are only partially matched by differences on a smaller amount of borrowings. Some take the view that this is preferable to the alternative of regarding 30 per cent of the investment as a foreign currency asset and 70 per cent as a sterling asset.

29.102 However, there is also an argument in favour of this alternative treatment which is that the purpose under the offset procedures of retranslating the investment is solely to allow the exchange difference on the borrowings to be relieved, to reflect the fact that there is no economic risk. Taking this view, it would, therefore,

[The next page is 29057.]

make sense to limit the exchange difference recognised on the investment to that on the borrowing. We believe that either method is acceptable provided that it is consistently applied to all investments that are partially hedged.

Intermediate holding companies

29.103 A UK parent company may hold shares in an overseas intermediate holding company that holds investments in further overseas subsidiaries in various countries. A common example is for an intermediate holding company to be based in the Netherlands. If the UK parent company has taken out foreign currency borrowings to finance or hedge its investment then the SSAP 20 offset procedures will apply. At first sight, the UK parent would have a Dutch Guilder investment. However, economically, the investment is a multi-currency asset, that is, its value depends on fluctuations of the currencies in which the underlying subsidiaries operate. In this situation, the investment in the overseas intermediate holding company can be accounted for as a multi-currency asset such that exchange differences on foreign currency borrowings used as hedges can be offset against the exchange differences on each component of the multi-currency asset.

Example

A UK company holds subsidiaries in Germany, Hong Kong and Australia through an intermediate Dutch Holding company. The original cost of the investment in the Dutch company was Dfl 276m (equivalent to £90m). The Dutch company has no assets other than shares in the three subsidiaries. The UK company borrows DM 150m to hedge the German subsidiary and HK$ 360m to hedge the Hong Kong subsidiary, but does not hedge the investment in the Australian subsidiary. The relevant figures are as follows:

	German Co DM m	Australian Co A$ m	Hong Kong Co HK$ m
Cost	100	80	400
Net asset value			
- on acquisition	70	40	350
- post acquisition retained profits	100	10	(30)
- total	170	50	320
Financed by borrowings	150	—	360

All the assets of the Dutch company are shares in the overseas subsidiaries and, therefore, the investment in the Dutch company can be regarded as a multi-currency asset. In order to offset the exchange differences on the borrowings, it will be necessary for the UK company to establish a multi-currency carrying value in the relevant currencies by looking through the Dutch company and building up the carrying value by reference to the appropriate carrying value of the subsidiaries. Possible choices include the following:

- Cost – this would be DM 100m + A$ 80m + HK$ 400m (reduced to a lower value if the reduction in reserves is regarded as representing a permanent diminution in value). However, a carrying value of cost is insufficient to allow the exchange differences on the whole of the DM 150m borrowing to be taken to reserves.

- Net asset value – this would be DM 170m + A$ 50m + HK$ 320m. However, this policy does not allow exchange differences on the whole of the HK$ 360m borrowing to be taken to reserves.

- Directors' valuation – a number of different bases could be adopted as a policy, for example, a valuation based on net asset value, cost plus retained post-acquisition reserves or a valuation based on the earnings stream.

In this example, the Australian investment is not hedged, and the implications of this need to be considered. If the UK company directly held the three subsidiaries then the DM and HK$ investments that are hedged could be regarded as foreign currency assets whereas the A$ investment would remain a sterling investment. Where there is a Dutch intermediate holding company that has no other assets then it is possible to look through this company and split the investment into its component parts so that the same result is obtained as if the subsidiaries were directly held.

If the UK company's policy is to record investments at cost, the DM and HK$ investments would retain a fixed cost in DM and HK$ but this would be retranslated each year into varying sterling amounts and exchange differences would be taken to reserves (offset against exchange differences on the related borrowings). The A$ investment would retain a fixed sterling cost.

If the UK company's policy is to record investments at a valuation, say, net asset value, the above distinction between currency and sterling investments does not seem to apply. For the DM and HK$ investments, the net assets figure would be a DM or HK figure and this would be retranslated into sterling for the purpose of the UK company's entity financial statements. For the (unhedged) A$ investment, the objective would be to establish an up to date sterling figure for net asset value. But this could only sensibly be done by considering the net assets in A$ and translating them into sterling at the closing rate. The process seems to be the same. This is odd given that two are regarded as foreign currency investments and one regarded as a sterling investment, but appears not to matter.

If we assume that the UK company adopts a policy of cost plus retained post-acquisition profits for the carrying value of its investments and that during the year the retained profits are DM 20m, A$ 10m and HK$ 15m, the opening and closing positions will be as follows:

	DM	A$	HK$	Total £m
Opening exchange rate	2.2	2.4	11.0	
Closing exchange rate	2.4	2.0	12.0	
Opening carrying value in currency	200	90	370	
Closing carrying value in currency	220	100	385	
Opening carrying value in £	90.9	37.5	33.6	162.0
Closing carrying value in £	91.7	50.0	32.1	173.8
Increase/(decrease) in carrying value	0.8	12.5	(1.5)	11.8

As the A$ investment is a sterling asset, the whole increase in value is regarded as a revaluation gain and taken to revaluation reserve. However, it will be necessary to split the changes in value of the currency assets between revaluation gains and exchange differences in order to offset the exchange differences on the borrowings.

		DM £m	HK £m
Revaluation gains (increase in currency value @ closing rate)		8.3	1.3
Exchange losses on investments (opening net assets retranslated at closing rates)	[A]	(7.5)	(2.8)
		0.8	(1.5)
Currency borrowing		DM 150.0	HK$ 360.0
Opening value in £		68.2	32.7
Closing value in £		62.5	30.0
Exchange gains on borrowings	[B]	5.7	2.7
Net exchange loss taken to reserves [A – B]		1.8	0.1

29.104 The above example uses the illustration of an overseas intermediate holding company. This is a foreign equity investment that is regarded as being denominated in different currencies than the actual currency of the shares in which the investment is made. However, where the intermediate holding company is a UK company, it is not itself a foreign equity investment. The question then arises as to whether the SSAP 20 offset procedures can be applied where the ultimate parent has currency borrowings taken out to finance the overseas subsidiaries held by the UK intermediate holding company. Our view is that where the UK intermediate holding company has no other assets and liabilities other than the investments in the overseas subsidiaries, it can be regarded as a foreign equity investment and valued by reference to its multi-currency component parts.

Treatment in consolidated financial statements

29.105 The offset procedure described above is available also in consolidated financial statements. Within a group, foreign currency borrowings are often used either to finance, or to provide a hedge against, equity investments in foreign undertakings. Where this is so and also the conditions set out below have been complied with, exchange differences on the borrowings *may* be offset, as a movement on consolidated reserves, against exchange differences that arise when the opening net investment in the foreign subsidiary is retranslated for consolidation purposes. But the offset procedure is optional and, if it is not used, the effect is that exchange differences on the net investment are taken to reserves, whilst those arising on the borrowings used to finance the investment are taken to the profit and loss account. Our view is that where a group is covered in economic terms and not exposed to any exchange risk, it is preferable to adopt the offset procedure and, indeed, arguably inappropriate to record an accounting profit or loss when exchange rates change.

29.106 The conditions for offset, all of which must apply, are as follows:

- The relationships between the investing company and the foreign undertakings concerned should justify the use of the closing rate/net investment method of translation for consolidation purposes.

- In any accounting period, exchange differences on the borrowings may be offset only to the extent of the exchange differences arising on the net investments in foreign enterprises.

- The foreign currency borrowings, whose exchange gains or losses are used in the offset process, should not exceed, in aggregate, the total amount of cash that the net investments are expected to be able to generate from profits or otherwise.

- The accounting treatment adopted should be applied consistently from period to period.

[SSAP 20 para 57].

29.107 The last three conditions stated above are similar to those relating to the offset conditions for individual companies as set out in paragraph 29.82 above. These conditions are explained above and the explanations apply equally to consolidated financial statements. The first condition is necessary because the offset applies to any foreign equity investments at the entity level, but applies only to those foreign enterprises that fall to be accounted for under the closing rate/net investment method at the consolidation level. It is for this reason that where a foreign investment is accounted for under the temporal method, the offset rules cannot be applied to that investment on consolidation and all exchange gains and losses on the foreign borrowings must be taken to the profit and loss account.

29.108 Despite the similarities between the offset conditions that apply in the individual company's financial statements and that apply on consolidation, it will usually be necessary to reverse the entries made at an entity level and recompute the adjustments on a consolidated level for the following reasons:

- At the entity level, the offset applies to *all* foreign equity investments, whereas on consolidation foreign enterprises accounted for under the temporal method are excluded. For these investments, exchange differences on foreign borrowings that have been taken to reserves in the individual company's financial statements must be reversed and reflected in the consolidated results for the year.

- At the entity level, only borrowings of the investing company may be used for offset purposes, whereas on consolidation borrowings of any group company may be included.

- At the entity level, the exchange difference arising each year on the carrying value of the investment translated at the closing rate is used for offset, whereas on consolidation the exchange difference used is that arising through retranslation of the opening net investment.

29.109 There is one situation in which there is no need to reverse the entry. The standard states that in the case of a foreign enterprise that is neither a subsidiary nor an associated company the same offset procedure that has been applied in the individual company's financial statements may be applied in the consolidation financial statements. [SSAP 20 para 58]. This is logical, as it merely acknowledges that where there is a genuine hedge of a simple equity investment at the entity level the hedge does not cease to exist at the consolidation level. Despite this, there may nonetheless be occasions where there is a different treatment on consolidation. An example would be where there was a relevant borrowing in the group, but not one in the investing entity.

29.110 As the next example shows, even where offset procedures are used, it does not always follow that the whole of the exchange difference on the borrowing can be offset in reserves against an exchange difference on the net investment.

Example

A UK company is preparing its consolidated financial statements for the year ended 30 June 19X5. On 31 December 19X4 it raised a loan of US$ 2m in order to finance two wholly-owned subsidiaries, one in France costing FF 1,500,000 and the other in Germany costing DM 2,500,000. The net assets of the two subsidiaries at the date of acquisition are FF 2m and DM 2,750,000. The relevant exchange rates are:

31 December 19X4	£1 = US$ 1.48 = FF 8.89 = DM 2.45
30 June 19X5	£1 = US$ 1.55 = FF 8.39 = DM 2.54

	Exchange difference	P&L account	Reserves
	£	£	£
Exchange difference on net assets in French company at acquisition			
31/12/X4 – FF 2m @ 8.89	224,972		
30/06/X5 – FF 2m @ 8.39	238,379		
Exchange gain	13,407		
Exchange difference on net assets in German company at acquisition			
31/12/X4 – DM 2,750,000 @ 2.45	1,122,449		
30/06/X5 – DM 2,750,000 @ 2.54	1,082,677		
Exchange loss	(39,772)		
Net exchange loss on net investments	(26,365)		(26,365)
Exchange difference on US$ loan			
31/12/X4 – US$ 2m @ 1.48	1,351,351		
30/06/X5 – US$ 2m @ 1.55	1,290,323		
Exchange gain	61,028	34,663	26,365

In this example, the amount of the exchange gain on the loan that the company can offset as a reserve movement against the exchange loss on the net investments is limited to £26,365. The excess gain of £34,663 is deemed to be speculative and, therefore, is taken to the consolidated profit and loss on ordinary activities for the year.

Goodwill on consolidation

29.111 As stated in paragraph 29.78 above, there is some support among UK companies for regarding goodwill arising on consolidation as a currency asset residing in the foreign enterprise, so that any exchange difference arising on its retranslation is included with those arising on the retranslation of the opening net investment and taken to consolidated reserves. In the context of the cover method, the question arises as to whether the exchange difference arising on the goodwill is available for offset against exchange differences on group borrowings. The question is relevant because the availability of any exchange gain arising on the goodwill element may reduce or even eliminate exchange losses on borrowings not fully covered by exchange gains on the opening net investment, which would otherwise have been taken to the profit and loss account.

29.112 If goodwill can be regarded as a currency asset, there is no reason why the exchange difference arising on the goodwill cannot be used in applying the cover method. This is consistent with economic reality that the group is covered in economic terms against any movements in exchange rates. The cover method can be applied even if goodwill on acquisition has been written off to reserves, insofar as it would not have been amortised had a policy of capitalisation and amortisation been adopted, as the write off is a consequence of following an accounting policy not because of the fact that the goodwill has lost its value.

UITF Abstract 19

29.112.1 Under current tax legislation, exchange gains and losses on foreign currency borrowings that are used by a company to finance or hedge its investment in a foreign enterprise may be taxable. Some examples of circumstances where tax may be payable are as follows:

- A matching election for tax purposes is not made by the company irrespective of whether or not it has followed the SSAP 20 offset procedure in its financial statements.
- The foreign investment and the borrowings are located in different companies in a group and, although an economic hedge may exist for consolidated financial statements, the matching election is not available. A tax matching election may be made only where the foreign investment and the related currency borrowings are held within the same company.
- A matching election is made by the company, but under the SSAP 20 offset restriction excess exchange gains or losses on the borrowings fall to be reported in the profit and loss account. Under the tax rules, a liability is matched by an asset at any time only to the extent that the value of the liability is matched by the value of the asset at that time.

29.112.2 The question then arises as to how the tax effects of any exchange gains and losses on the borrowings that have been offset in reserves under the SSAP 20 offset procedures and reported in the statement of total recognised gains and losses should be recognised.

29.112.3 It is already current practice to account for the tax effects of transactions recognised directly in reserves also in reserves. The UITF adopts this principle in Abstract 19, 'Tax on gains and losses on foreign currency borrowings that hedge an investment in a foreign enterprise', which was issued on 20 February 1998 and is effective for accounting periods ending on or after 23 March 1998. The Abstract states that where exchange differences on foreign currency borrowings that have been used to finance, or provide a hedge against, equity investments in foreign enterprises are taken to reserves and reported in the statement of total recognised gains and losses, in accordance with paragraphs 51, 57 and 58 of SSAP 20 and paragraph 27 of FRS 3, tax charges and credits that are directly and solely attributable to such exchange differences should also be taken to reserves and reported in that statement.

29.112.4 The UITF also considered how such tax effects reported in the statement of total recognised gains and losses and in reserves would impact on the restriction on the amount of exchange differences on foreign currency borrowings that can be offset in reserves in accordance with paragraphs 51(a) and 57(b) of SSAP 20. The Abstract concludes that the restriction should be applied after taking account of any tax attributable to those exchange differences – that is, the net-of-tax exchange difference on borrowings should be offset only to the extent of exchange difference arising on the equity investment. The offset restriction is considered in detail from paragraph 29.83. Similarly, the comparison with the total amount of cash that the investments are expected to be able to generate and the exposure created by the borrowings (paragraphs 51(b) and 57(c) of SSAP 20) should be considered in after-tax terms.

29.112.5 Consistent with SSAP 20's requirement to disclose the amount of exchange gains or losses on borrowings that are taken to the statement of total recognised gains and losses, the abstract requires disclosure of any related tax charges and credits accounted for as described above, in addition to the gross amount of the exchange differences.

29.112.6 The way in which UITF Abstract 19 is likely to apply in practice is illustrated in the following example.

Example

A UK company's financial year ends on 31 March. On 31 March 19X7 it raised a loan of DM 840,000 to finance an equity investment in Germany costing DM 840,000. Assume UK tax rate is 30%. The relevant exchange rates are as follows:

31 March 19X7 £1 = DM 2.80
31 March 19X8 £1 = DM 2.90

The company adopts the offset procedure in SSAP 20 in its financial statements for the year ended 31 March 19X8. Therefore the exchange difference on the DM borrowing that is offset in reserves before considering any tax consequences is as follows:

31 March 19X7 – DM 840,000 @ 2.80	=	£300,000
31 March 19X8 – DM 840,000 @ 2.90	=	£289,655
Gain on borrowing		£ 10,345

Matching election claimed

If the company claims the tax matching election, there are no tax consequences. This is because the sterling value of the liability is fully matched by the sterling value of the asset and the exchange gain on the loan is fully matched with the exchange loss in reserves.

Matching election not claimed

If the company does not make a matching election, it would have to pay tax of £3,104 at 30% on the exchange gain of £10,345. Applying UITF Abstract 19, the company would offset £10,345 – £3,104 = £7,241of net exchange gain on the borrowing against the exchange loss of £10,345 in reserves. Both the exchange difference of £10,345 and the attributable tax of £3,104 would be disclosed.

29.112.7 The above example is fairly simple and does not demonstrate the complications that can arise in the tax treatment of exchange gains and losses. The tax rules on matching election are complex and specialist taxation advice should be sought.

[The next paragraph is 29.113.]

Hedging transactions

Identification of a hedge

29.113 Companies enter into hedging transactions primarily to reduce risks, including those associated with exchange rate movements, that can have an adverse effect on their financial position and results. A diverse range of financial instruments, such as forward exchange contracts, futures contracts, currency swaps and currency options, are available for reducing foreign exchange risk. These instruments are often referred to as 'derivative products' because their values are derived from an underlying security, an index, an interest rate, or another financial instrument.

29.114 The word *hedge* is used in a variety of ways by derivatives traders, accountants and regulators and there appears to be no single accepted definition. However, most definitions are based on the notion of reducing exposure to price risk, interest rate risk or currency risk. For instance, in its exposure draft E48 'Financial instruments', the IASC identifies a financial instrument as a hedge when:

- The position to be hedged is specifically identified and exposes the enterprise to risk of loss from price changes.

- The instrument is specifically designated as a hedge.

- It is highly probable that changes in the fair value of the instrument designated as a hedge and opposite changes in the fair value of the position being hedged will have a high degree of correlation so that the hedging instrument will be effective as a hedge, that is, it eliminates or reduces substantially the risk of loss from the position being hedged.

[E48 para 133].

29.115 Hedging in an economic sense concerns the reduction or elimination of the effects of market risk, interest rate risk or currency risk, each of which may be present to some extent in a financial instrument. It involves entering into a transaction in the expectation that it will reduce an enterprise's exposure to loss from price risk, often with the additional consequence of reducing the potential for profit. A financial instrument is generally viewed as a hedge when an enterprise has a specifically identified position that is exposed to the risk of loss as a result of adverse price changes in financial markets and the effect of holding the instrument is to mitigate that risk of loss. A hedge is achieved by taking a position exposed to effects of price changes that move inversely and with a high degree of correlation with the effects of price changes on an existing or expected position.

29.116 A position to be hedged can be interpreted fairly broadly. A financial instrument may be accounted for as a hedge when it has an exposure to price risk that is equal but opposite to that of a group of financial instruments or a portion of one instrument. Furthermore, it is not necessary for hedges to be specifically matched with individual items being hedged. However, because different types of assets and liabilities have substantially different exposures to potential gain or loss, the items constituting a group of financial instruments must be similar at least to the extent of the common price risk being hedged.

29.117 Accounting for derivative products is complex and the subject is currently on the ASB's agenda. However, in the context of foreign exchange transactions, the paragraphs that follow consider two hedging tools that are commonly in use and which are not dealt with in SSAP 20. These are forward exchange contracts and currency options.

Forward exchange contracts

29.118 A forward exchange contract is a legal agreement under which a company contracts to buy or sell a specified amount of foreign currency at a specified exchange rate (which is the forward rate), but with delivery and settlement at a specified future date. One of the parties to a forward contract assumes a long position and agrees to buy the underlying currency on a specified future date at the forward rate. The other party assumes a short position and agrees to sell the currency on the same date for the same forward rate.

29.119 The duration of the contract is usually fixed, for example, one month, three months or six months. The forward rate specified in the contract is stated at a premium or discount to the spot rate based upon current market conditions and expectations, but it is not an estimate of what the spot rate will be at the end of the

[The next page is 29065.]

contract. Since the alternative to a forward contract is to buy (or sell) the required currency now, the amount of the premium or discount to the spot rate is principally based on:

- The interest rate differentials between the relevant currencies.
- The duration of the contract.

The following example (simplified) illustrates how forward exchange rates are calculated:

Assumptions	
UK interest rate	9%
US interest rate	6%
Spot rate at beginning of year	£1 =
One year forward rate	US$1.55
	To determine
Company borrows £1m for one year	£
Amount payable	
Principal	1,000,000
Interest @ 9% for one year	90,000
Total payable	1,090,000
Company converts £1m to US dollars at the spot rate, invests the dollars for one year and takes out a one year forward contract to sell the original dollars and interest for sterling.	
Amount payable	US$
Principal £1m @1.55	1,550,000
Interest @ 6%	93,000
Total payable	1,643,000

Ignoring any transaction costs, the one year forward rate at inception of the contract would be calculated on the basis that the company is indifferent between choosing the above two strategies. For this to occur, the one year forward rate must be US$ 1,643,000/£1,090,000 = 1.50734. In fact, the forward rate can be determined arithmetically by applying the interest rate differential ruling between the two currencies in question to the spot rate.

$$\text{Forward rate} = 1.55 \times \frac{1.06}{1.09} = 1.50734$$

A further factor would need to be built into the calculation if the period was other than one year.

Forward rates are usually quoted as being either at a discount or premium to the spot rate. To arrive at the forward rate for US dollars the discount is added to the spot rate and a premium is deducted from the spot rate.

29.120 Forward exchange contracts are frequently used by companies to protect them from experiencing exchange gains or losses from existing positions and on anticipated transactions. They offer the advantage that they can be specifically tailored in terms of amount, currency and maturity date to any hedging situation. There is no initial deposit or margin to pay and settlement is made at maturity. The disadvantage is that there is no benefit from favourable exchange rate movements.

29.121 Accounting for forward contracts is dealt with only briefly in SSAP 20. Two viewpoints have been advanced to account for foreign exchange contracts:

- All aspects are viewed as part of a single transaction (the 'one transaction' view). That is, the commitment to buy or sell currency necessary to settle a foreign currency payable or receivable is viewed as part of the purchase or sale transaction and the forward contract rate is used to record that transaction. This is the approach adopted in SSAP 20.

- The transaction to settle a foreign currency payable or receivable is treated separately from the forward contract (the 'two transaction' view). In addition, the premium or discount on the forward contract is accounted for separately and spread over the life of the contract. The forward contract is marked to market as the contract progresses (for example, at the balance sheet date it is marked to the rate effective on that day). This is the treatment adopted by SFAS 52.

The above viewpoints are illustrated below in some of the typical situations where a company enters into a forward contract for hedging purposes.

Forward exchange contracts taken out at the transaction date

29.122 This is the only situation that is dealt with in SSAP 20. The standard states that the rate specified in the forward contract *may* be the appropriate rate to use for the translation of trading transactions denominated in a foreign currency (or the monetary assets or liabilities arising from such transactions) where these are covered by a related or matching forward contract. This treatment recognises that the purpose of such transaction is to hedge any exchange risk involved in foreign currency operations and that no economic gain or loss will therefore arise. Therefore, under this approach, the premium or discount on a forward contract is immediately recognised in the profit and loss account.

Example

A company is preparing its financial statements to 31 December 19X5. In October 19X5, the company sells goods to a Dutch company for Fl 405,000. The Dutch company pays for the goods in March 19X6. At the time of the sale, the exchange rate is £1 = Fl 2.7, and at the balance sheet date the exchange rate is £1 = Fl 2.9. The UK company, however, covers the transaction by a matching forward contract to sell Dutch Guilders. The exchange rate specified in the six month forward contract is £1 = Fl 2.6. The relevant translations are as follows:

10/X5 – Fl 405,000 @ 2.7 (transaction rate) =	£150,000
12/X5 – Fl 405,000 @ 2.9 (balance sheet rate) =	£139,655
03/X6 – Fl 405,000 @ 2.6 (forward contract rate) =	£155,769

The UK company could record the sale in one of the following ways:

- It could record the sale and the debtor at £155,769, that is, at the exchange rate specified in the matching forward contract. Because the company has entered into a matching forward contract, the amount receivable and ultimately received from the debtor is Fl 405,000 which is sold for £155,769. Consequently, the company would not recognise a loss on exchange on the transaction and no further accounting entries are required. This approach is permitted by SSAP 20.

- A second method is to view the sale and the debtor separately from the commitment to sell foreign currency under the six month forward contract. Therefore, the sale and the debtor would be initially recorded at £150,000. At 31 December 19X5, the debtor would be translated at the exchange rate ruling at that date, that is £139,655. The loss on exchange of £10,345 would be taken to the profit and loss account. This would be matched by an equivalent gain on the forward contract, which is computed by taking the difference between the foreign currency amount of the forward contract translated at the spot rate at the date of inception of the forward contract (Fl 405,000 @ 2.7 = £150,000) and the amount translated at the balance sheet date (Fl 405,000 @ 2.9 = £139,655).

  In addition, the premium or discount on the contract should be accounted for separately. This will give rise to a profit or loss on the forward contract, calculated by taking the difference between the foreign currency amount of the forward contract translated at the spot rate at the date of inception of the forward contract (Fl 405,000 @ 2.7 – £150,000) and the contracted forward rate (Fl 405,000 @ 2.6 = £155,769). In this situation, there is a profit of £5,769 which should be amortised over that period. Accordingly, £2,885 should be taken to the profit and loss account for the year ended 31 December 19X5 and the balance should be recognised in the following year. This is the approach favoured by SFAS 52.

The effect of the two methods can be summarised as follows:

	Method 1	Method 2
	£	£
Balance sheet at 31 December 19X5		
Debtor	155,769	139,655
Forward contract	-	13,230
Profit and loss account for year ended 31 December 19X5		
Included in profit on sale of goods	5,769	-
Exchange loss on retranslation of debtor	-	(10,345)
Exchange gain on forward contract	-	10,345
Amortisation of profit on forward contract	-	2,885
	5,769	2,885
Profit and loss account for year ended 31 December 19X6		
Amortisation of profit on forward contract	-	2,884

29.123 Although SSAP 20 allows the first method, it does not rule out the use of the alternative method discussed above. The advantage of the first method is its simplicity, whilst the second method takes a completely different approach and is perhaps theoretically correct. It treats the forward contract as a separate instrument and attributes a value to it. The rationale for this treatment is that the revenue is determined by the original sale transaction and not by any subsequent agreement to exchange currencies.

Hedging an existing asset or liability with forward exchange contract

29.124 Companies may sometimes enter into a forward exchange contract to hedge an existing monetary asset or a liability.

Example

A company is preparing its financial statements to 31 December 19X4. It took out a foreign currency loan of FC 1m at fixed interest rate of 10% on 1 July 19X4 with a maturity date of one year. Interest is payable on 31 December and 30 June. The company immediately enters into two forward contracts as follows

Contract No 1, to purchase FC 50,000 (half-yearly interest on FC 1m) for payment on 31 December 19X4 at a fixed contract price of £1 = FC 1.50.

Contract No 2, to purchase FC 1,050,000 (principal of FC 1m + half-yearly interest of FC 50,000) for payment on 30 June 19X5 at a fixed contract price of £1 = FC 1.46.

The relevant spot rates are as follows:

1 July 19X4	£1 = FC 1.54
31 December 19X4	£1 = FC 1.47

The illustration that follows views the loan and the commitment to purchase foreign currency under the forward contracts separately.

		P&L account	Balance sheet
Loan	£	£	£
Exchange difference on loan			
1/7/X4 – FC 1m @ 1.54 (transaction rate)	649,351		
31/12/X4 – FC 1m @ 1.47 (balance sheet rate)	680,272		(680,272)
Exchange loss	(30,921)	(30,921)	
Forward contracts			
Exchange gain on forward contract No 1			
31/12/X4 – Value at settlement FC 50K @ 1.47	34,014		
1/7/X4 – Value at inception date FC 50K @1.54	32,467		
Exchange gain on settled contract*	1,547	1,547	
Premium payable on contract No 1			
1/7/X4 – FC 50,000 @ 1.54 (spot rate)	32,467		
1/7/X4 – FC 50,000 @ 1.50 (forward rate)	33,333		
Premium payable*	(866)	(866)	
Interest FC 50,000 @ 1.47 paid on 31/12/X4		(34,014)	
		(33,333)	
Forward contract No 2			
Exchange gain on forward contract (principal amount only)			
31/12/X4 – Value at year end FC 1m @ 1.47	680,272		
1/7/X4 – Value at inception date FC 1m @ 1.54	649,351		
Exchange gain on outstanding contract	30,921	30,921	30,921
Premium payable on contract No 2			
1/7/X4 – FC 1.05m at @ 1.54 (spot)	681,818		
1/7/X4 – FC 1.05m at @ 1.46 (forward)	719,178		
Premium payable (half deferred)	(37,360)	(18,680)	(18,680)

Cash			
Loan proceeds	649,351		
Interest paid	(34,014)		
Net settlement on contract No 1 (gain – premium)*	681		
Cash balance	616,018		616,018
Net charge to P&L account		(52,013)	52,013
			-

*The net settlement on contract No 1 amounting to £681 can also be calculated as the difference between the forward contract amount at the spot rate at the date of settlement, being £34,014 (FC 50,000 @1.47) and the contracted rate, being £33,333 (FC 50,000 @ 1.50).

As can be seen from the above table, the exchange loss on the loan is matched by an equivalent gain on the outstanding forward contract No 2. This gain is calculated on the principal amount of FC 1m. The balance of the forward contract (FC 50,000) is not included because it is hedging a future commitment. This is dealt with in detail from paragraph 29.125.

As contract No 1 matured during the year, the premium payable is taken to the profit and loss account. The premium payable on contract No 2 is amortised over its life, half the amount being charged during the year ended 31 December 19X4. As stated earlier, the above approach is theoretically correct as it attributes a value to the contract.

If the treatment permitted by SSAP 20 is followed, the half-yearly interest charged to the profit and loss account is translated at the forward rate being £33,333 (FC 50,000 @ 1.5). The loan is translated at the forward rate at the balance sheet date, being £684,932 (FC 1m @1.46) and the difference between this amount and the amount at which it was initially recorded (£649,351), being an exchange loss of £35,581 is taken to the profit and loss account. This exchange loss represents the total premium on the portion of the forward contract relating to the loan principal, that is FC 1m @ 1.46 (contract rate) less FC 1m @ 1.54 (inception). Under this method no part of this premium is deferred.

Hedging a foreign currency commitment

29.125 Companies may also use forward exchange contracts to hedge anticipated future transactions, such as a foreign currency payable or receivable, or to a hedge a foreign currency commitment, such as an agreement to buy goods from or sell goods to a foreign entity at some time in the future. In these situations, the gain or loss arising on the forward contract is deferred until the actual date the commitment is fulfilled. This is an example of the 'one transaction' approach (see para 29.121) because both the transaction and the forward contract taken out to hedge it are future commitments. The example illustrated below deals with a future commitment. An anticipated future foreign currency payable or receivable would be treated in a similar manner.

Example

A company's financial year ends on 31 December 19X1. It intends to renovate part of its plant and enters into an agreement with a foreign supplier on 30 September 19X1 to purchase an improved version of the equipment for FC 1m. The equipment is to be delivered on 31 March 19X2 and the price is payable on 30 June 19X2. In order to hedge the commitment to pay FC 1m, the company enters into a forward contract on 30 September 19X1 to purchase FC 1m on 30 June 19X2 at a fixed exchange rate of £1 = FC 1.51.

The relevant spot rates are as follows:

Inception date	30 September 19X1	£1 = FC 1.54
Year end date	31 December 19X1	£1 = FC 1.47
Transaction date	31 March 19X2	£1 = FC 1.45
Settlement date	30 June 19X2	£1 = FC 1.43

As before, there are two possible treatments:

Method 1

If the treatment permitted by SSAP 20 is followed, then no accounting entries are required at the year end and the company will simply disclose the financial commitment in its balance sheet. On 31 March 19X2, both the equipment and the liability to pay the supplier will be recorded at the forward contract rate, being £662,252 (FC 1m @ 1.51).

Method 2

Method 2 is based on the two transaction approach. No entries are made in respect of the equipment at 31 December 19X1. At 31 March 19X2, the equipment and the liability to the supplier would be initially recorded at £689,655 (FC 1m @ 1.45 – transaction rate). The amount payable to the supplier at 30 June 19X2 is £699,301 (FC 1m @ 1.43 – spot rate at settlement). The exchange loss of £9,646 arising on the settlement will be charged in the profit and loss account for the year ended 31 December 19X2, but will be offset by a corresponding gain on the forward contract (see below).

The forward contract would be accounted for as a separate transaction as follows:

Exchange gain on forward contract	£
Gain up to balance sheet date	
30/09/X1 – FC 1m @ 1.54 (spot – inception date)	649,351
31/12/X1 – FC 1m @ 1.47 (spot – balance sheet date)	680,272
Gain on forward contract	30,921
Gain from balance sheet date to transaction date	
31/12/X1 – FC 1m @ 1.47 (spot – balance sheet date)	680,272
31/03/X2 – FC 1m @ 1.45 (spot – transaction date)	689,655
Gain on forward contract	9,383
Total gain to transaction date (deferred)	40,304
Gain from transaction date to settlement date	
31/03/X2 – FC 1m @ 1.45 (spot – transaction date)	689,655
30/06/X2 – FC 1m @ 1.43 (spot – settlement date)	699,301
Gain on forward contract	9,646
Total exchange gain on forward contract	49,950
Premium payable on forward contract	
30/09/X1 – FC 1m @ 1.54 (spot rate at inception)	649,351
30/09/X1 – FC 1m @ 1.51 (forward rate)	662,252
Premium payable	12,901

The gain or loss arising on the forward contract from the date of inception up to the transaction date is not recognised in the profit and loss account, but is deferred. The amount deferred at 31 December 19X1 is £30,921. The total amount deferred at the transaction date as indicated above is £40,304 and this amount will subsequently be reflected in the asset value.

During the hedging period, between the transaction date and the settlement date, the exchange gain arising on the contract matches the exchange loss arising on the liability to the supplier, reflecting that the position is hedged. These exchange differences are offset in the profit and loss account.

As far as the premium on the contract is concerned, there are two possible treatments that will have an effect on asset values. The first treatment is to amortise the premium payable over the life of the contract. Therefore, half the premium, that is £6,451, would be charged to the profit and loss account for the year ended 31 December 19X1, the balance will be deferred and charged in the following year. If this treatment is followed, only the gain on the forward contract will have an effect on the asset value. The effect is that the asset will be recorded in 19X2 at the spot rate ruling at the date the forward contract was taken out as indicated below.

Asset	£
Initially recorded at transaction date – FC 1m @1.45	689,655
Less deferred gain on forward contract	(40,304)
Value – FC 1m @ 1.54 (spot rate at inception of contract)	649,351

Alternatively, the premium that relates to the commitment period may be deferred and included in the related foreign currency transaction. The effect is that the asset will be recorded at the forward rate as indicated below.

Asset	£
Initially recorded at transaction date – FC 1m @1.45	689,655
Less deferred gain on forward contract	(40,304)
Plus deferred premium	12,901
Value – FC 1m @ 1.51 (forward rate)	662,252

Although both treatments are acceptable, it is preferable to use the second alternative as the company 'locked in' the cost of the equipment at £662,552 by entering into the forward contract. It should be noted that SFAS 52 requires the second method when the contract is designated as a hedge and the forward commitment is firm. An intention to enter into a commitment is not sufficient.

Hedging net investment

29.126 A company may decide to hedge against the effects of changes in exchange rates in the company's net investment in a subsidiary. This may be done by taking out a foreign currency borrowing to hedge a foreign equity investment, which is recognised by SSAP 20 and discussed from paragraph 29.105. However, SSAP 20 does not deal with the situation of using forward exchange contracts to hedge foreign equity investments. The question then arises as to how the forward contract should be dealt with in the consolidated financial statements.

29.127 To be consistent with the treatment of the exchange differences on borrowings that are taken out as a hedge, we consider that any gain or loss arising on a forward contract may be taken to reserves to match the movement in the net investment being hedged. This treatment is sensible as it recognises the economic rationale of taking out the forward contract. The premium on the contract should be taken to the profit and loss account, because it represents the interest rate differential between the currencies being exchanged.

Hedging future results of foreign investments

29.128 A company can also take out a forward contract as a hedge against the future results of a foreign subsidiary. Where this is done, the gain or loss on the contract should be included in the profit and loss account for the period being hedged. If the results are translated at the closing rate and the contract is for the whole year, the inclusion of the gain or loss on the contract will ensure that the results are stated at the contracted rate. Where the contract is not for a full year, the results up to the date of contract will effectively be hedged and reflected at the contracted rate. If the contract remains outstanding at the end of the year, the gain or loss on the contract from the date of inception up to the balance sheet date should be recognised in the profit and loss account and the related value of the contract included in the balance sheet. If the results are translated at an average rate and the contract is for less than a year, it may be appropriate to translate the results of that part of the year covered by the contract at the contracted rate and the balance at the average rate.

29.129 Where a company takes out a forward contract to hedge the future results of a foreign subsidiary (for example, the results of the following year) or where there is a rolling hedge so that at the year end there are contracts outstanding to hedge future results, a considerable degree of prudence should be observed in assessing whether or not the future results will be sufficient to ensure that the contract is not an excessive hedge. If projections of the results of the foreign subsidiary are too optimistic or the subsidiary suffers a deterioration in its performance, some of the contract could become speculative with the result that any potential loss should be provided for immediately. Consider the following example:

Example

A company has forward contracts outstanding at the year end for the sale of FC 20m at a contract rate of FC 1.60. The future trading results of the subsidiary for next year were originally estimated at FC 21m but at the year end have been revised to FC 15m. The relevant spot rate at the year end is FC 1.40.

The revised forecasts indicate that the company will have to purchase FC 5m in order to meet its commitment under the sales contract. At the exchange rates current at the year end, this will result in a loss of £446,429 (FC 5m @ 1.40 less FC 5m @1.60) which should be provided on the grounds of prudence.

29.130 Some take the view that hedge accounting may not be appropriate for forward contracts that are taken out to hedge future results and that such contracts are in fact speculative. It is possible that UK rules will be tightened when the ASB issues its proposals on derivatives.

Speculative forward contracts

29.131 A speculative forward contract is a contract that does not hedge an exposure. Because of the risks involved, companies do not normally enter into such speculative contracts and it is inadvisable for them to do so. However, where a company does enter into a forward contract as a speculative transaction, a gain or loss will arise during the period from inception to maturity. If this period straddles the company's year end it is necessary to deal with the gain or loss that arises for the year. Again SSAP 20 does not deal with this situation. For trading companies, such gains or losses can be regarded as contingent and, consequently, provision should be made for losses, whereas gains would normally be deferred until they crystallise. Other companies (for example, banks) that have a policy of marking to market would recognise both gains and losses. Two possible methods of accounting for the contract are illustrated in the example below.

Example

A company is preparing its financial statements to 31 December 19X1. It enters into a forward contract on 1 October 19X1 to purchase FC 1m 180 days forward on 31 March 19X2 at a contracted rate of £1= FC 1.52. At the year end, the 90 day forward is £1 = FC 1.46. The relevant spot rates are as follows:

1 October 19X1	£1 = FC 1.54
31 December 19X1	£1 = FC 1.47

Method 1

Exchange gain on speculative forward contract	£
Gain up to balance sheet date	
01/10/X1 – FC 1m @ 1.54 (spot – inception date)	649,351
31/12/X1 – FC 1m @ 1.47 (spot – balance sheet date)	680,272
Gain on forward contract	30,921
Premium payable on forward contract	
01/10/X1 – FC 1m @ 1.54 (spot rate at inception)	649,351
01/10/X1 – FC 1m @ 1.52 (forward rate)	657,895
Premium payable	(8,544)
Proportion recognised (half)	(4,272)
Net amount taken to P&L account	26,649

This method is the same as that used for a forward contract that is taken out as a hedge. It has the effect of recognising the exchange gain to 31 December 19X1, but deferring part of the premium.

Method 2

No separate recognition is given to the premium on the speculative contract and instead the gain or loss is calculated by taking the difference between the foreign currency amount of the forward contract at the forward rate at the balance sheet date for the remaining maturity of the contract and the contracted forward rate (or the forward rate last used to measure an earlier gain or loss on the contract). This is the method recommended by SFAS 52.

Gain on speculative forward contract	£
Gain up to balance sheet date	
FC 1m @ 1.52 (forward rate – contracted)	657,895
FC 1m @ 1.46 (forward rate – remaining maturity)	684,932
Gain on forward contract	27,037

The second method has the effect of anticipating all the gain on the contract in the year to 31 December 19X1. The first method has the effect of only recognising the gain to 31 December 19X1 but carrying forward part of the premium. Either approach appears acceptable as presumably if the contract was closed out at 31 December 19X1 a gain would arise. As stated above, trading companies would normally defer any gain until it crystallised on maturity of the contract.

Foreign currency options as a hedge

29.132 An option is a contract conveying the right, but not the obligation, to buy (call) or the right to sell (put) a specified item at a fixed price (known as the strike or exercise price). A foreign currency option, therefore, is a right to buy or sell a foreign currency. A company acquiring an option will have to a pay a non-refundable premium to the option seller in exchange for the right to buy or sell a fixed amount of currency. The option premium represents the market's perception of the value of the option, which essentially consists of two parts:

- Intrinsic value – which for a call option is the excess of the market price of the underlying item over the option's strike price.

- Time value – which is the difference between the price paid for the option (the premium) and the intrinsic value.

The intrinsic value represents the benefit to the holder if the option was exercised immediately. The time value is associated with the remaining term to maturity of the option and reflects the income foregone from not holding the underlying item, the cost avoided by not having to finance the underlying item and the value placed on the possibility that the option's intrinsic value will increase prior to its maturity due to future volatility in the fair value of the underlying item.

29.133 If the spot exchange rate is lower than the strike rate, a foreign exchange call will not be exercised and the option is said to be 'out-of-the-money'. If it is advantageous to exercise the option, it is said to be 'in-the-money'. Where the strike rate is equal to the spot rate, the option is said to be 'at-the-money'. Therefore, unlike a forward foreign exchange contract, an option buyer will be able to gain from favourable exchange rate movements.

29.134 Accounting for currency options is not dealt with in SSAP 20. The general principle is that losses in the underlying item being hedged are offset by gains in the option position. It should be noted, however, that the maximum loss that the company can incur on an option is the premium as it will not exercise the option if the exchange rate movements are unfavourable. Due to the nature of a currency option, it would not be appropriate to record the item being hedged at the rate in the related currency option as it may never be exercised. Therefore, the asset or liability being hedged should be treated separately from the premium. The premium should initially be recorded as an asset. At the balance sheet date, the underlying currency amount under the option should be translated at the current rate and compared with the amount translated at the option rate. The resulting gain or loss should be treated as follows:

- If there is a gain, the gain less the cost of the option may be recognised provided that the loss on the item being hedged is also recognised. If a corresponding loss is not recognised, for instance, because the option is hedging a future transaction, then the gain should be carried forward to be matched with the loss when this is recognised.

  If the option is speculative, that is, it is not taken out as a hedge, the gain would normally be deferred unless the company adopts a policy of marking to market. However, it is generally accepted that entering into speculative option contracts is inadvisable as companies have suffered losses in the past where they have taken out such contracts.

- If there is a net loss, the whole of the premium should be written off. If the loss is less than the premium paid then the premium should be written off to the extent of the loss.

29.135 Alternatively, the premium on the hedging option could be 'marked to market' to the current premium at the balance sheet date. If the premium has increased in value there is a gain on the contract indicating that the option is in the money. On the other hand if the premium has fallen in value such that the option is unlikely to be exercised, there will be loss on the contract.

Disclosures

Requirements of the Act

29.136 The Act does not include any provisions that deal with either the translation of foreign currency transactions or the translation of foreign currency financial statements, other than to require the basis on which sums are translated into sterling to be stated. [4 Sch 58(1)]. The Act does require disclosure of financial commitments to the extent that they are relevant to a proper understanding of the company's state of affairs. [4 Sch 50(5)]. Therefore, where a company has outstanding forward contracts the amounts outstanding under the forward contracts should be disclosed. An example where a company has disclosed outstanding forward contracts is given in Table 29.9 below.

Table 29.9 – British Airways Plc – Report & Accounts – 31 March 1995

Notes to the accounts

15 TANGIBLE ASSETS (extract)

f Forward Transactions in Foreign Currency

The Group and the Company had the following forward contracts outstanding

	in currency		Sterling equivalent	
	1995	*1994*	**1995**	*1994*
Group				
Maturing within one year:				
to cover future capital commitments in US Dollars	**US$720m**	*US$158m*	**£442m**	*£107m*
to hedge future currency revenue in US Dollars	**US$11m**	*US$29m*	**£7m**	*£20m*
to hedge future currency revenues in Sterling	**£45m**	*£79m*	**£45m**	*£79m*
to hedge future operating payments in US Dollars	**US$132m**	*US$173m*	**£81m**	*£117m*
to hedge future operating payments in other currencies			**£2m**	*£4m*
Maturing after one year:				
to cover future capital commitments in US Dollars	**US$274m**	*US$32m*	**£168m**	*£22m*
to hedge future operating payments in US Dollars	**US$8m**		**£5m**	

Company				
Maturing within one year:				
to cover future capital commitments in US Dollars	**US$720m**	*US$158m*	**£442m**	*£107m*
to hedge future currency revenues in US Dollars	**US$11m**	*US$29m*	**£7m**	*£20m*
to hedge future currency revenues in Sterling	**£45m**	*£79m*	**£45m**	*£79m*
to hedge future operating payments in US Dollars	**US$42m**	*US$85m*	**£26m**	*£57m*
to hedge future operating payments in other currencies			**£2m**	*£4m*
Maturing after one year:				
to cover future capital commitments in US Dollars	**US$274m**	*US$32m*	**£168m**	*£22m*

Requirements of the standard

29.137 In addition to the above disclosure, SSAP 20 requires a number of other disclosures which are considered below. Furthermore, following the guidance on publication of the 'Operating and financial review' companies now tend to give much more information on their foreign currency operations. The following paragraphs deal with the disclosures required to be made both in individual financial statements and in consolidated financial statements.

29.138 The methods used in translation of the financial statements of foreign enterprises and the treatment accorded to exchange differences should be disclosed in the financial statements. [SSAP 20 para 59]. These disclosure requirements are illustrated in Table 29.10 below.

Table 29.10 – Reuters Holdings PLC – Annual Report – 31 December 1997

Accounting Policies (extract)

Foreign currency translation

Where it is considered that the functional currency of an operation is sterling the financial statements are expressed in sterling on the following basis:

a. Fixed assets are translated into sterling at the rates ruling on the date of acquisition as adjusted for any profits or losses from related financial instruments.

b. Monetary assets and liabilities denominated in a foreign currency are translated into sterling at the foreign exchange rates ruling at the balance sheet date.

c. Revenue and expenses in foreign currencies are recorded in sterling at the rates ruling for the month of the transactions.

d. Any gains or losses arising on translation are reported as part of profit.

For other operations and associated undertakings, assets and liabilities are translated into sterling at the rates ruling at the balance sheet date. Revenue and expenses in foreign currencies are recorded in sterling at the rates ruling for the month of the transactions and gains or losses arising on translation are dealt with through reserves.

Treasury

Reuters receives revenue and incurs expenses in more than 60 currencies and uses financial instruments to hedge a portion of its net cash flow and operating profit. Profits and losses from hedging activities are matched with the underlying cash flows and profits being hedged. Those relating to trading cash flows are reported as part of profit and those relating to Reuters capital expenditure programme are adjusted against the cost of the assets to which they relate.

Reuters uses financial instruments to hedge a portion of its interest exposure. Profits and losses on financial instruments are reported as part of profit for the period to which they relate.

Financial instruments hedging the risk on foreign currency assets are revalued at the balance sheet date and the resulting gain or loss offset against that arising from the translation of the underlying asset into sterling.

29.139 The standard requires disclosure of the net amount of exchange gains and losses on foreign currency borrowings less deposits, identifying separately:

- The amount offset in reserves under the provisions of paragraphs 51, 57 and 58 of SSAP 20. This applies to exchange differences included in the offset process. Examples of this disclosure are included in Table 29.11 and Table 29.12 below.

- The net amount charged/credited to the profit and loss account.

In addition, disclosure is required of the net movement on reserves arising from exchange differences. [SSAP 20 para 60].

Table 29.11 – Reckitt & Colman plc – Report & Accounts – 31 December 1994

Notes to the accounts

32 **OTHER RESERVES**

	Group £m	Subsidiary undertakings £m	Parent £m
At beginning of year as previously reported	**542.32**	**395.74**	**146.58**
Prior year adjustment for post-retirement benefits other than pensions	(35.38)	(35.38)	-
At beginning of year restated	**506.94**	**360.36**	**146.58**
Movements during the year:			
Profit for the financial year	81.89	27.54	54.35
Ordinary dividends	(75.99)	-	(75.99)
Net exchange loss on foreign currency loans	(0.35)	-	(0.35)
Exchange differences arising on translation of net investments in overseas subsidiary undertakings	(22.58)	(13.83)	(8.75)
Dividend adjustment (Note 8)	3.09	-	3.09
Goodwill and acquisition costs written off	(206.41)	(206.41)	-
Goodwill reinstated	6.54	6.54	-
	293.13	**174.20**	***118.93**

As permitted by s.230 of the Companies Act 1985, no profit and loss account is presented for Reckitt & Colman plc.

The cumulative amount of goodwill written off to reserves since 1984 in respect of the acquisition of continuing businesses is £536m (1993, £336m).

* The reserves of subsidiary undertakings have generally been retained to finance their businesses. There were statutory or other restrictions on the distribution of £109m (1993, £81m) of the reserves of subsidiary undertakings at 31 December 1994.

Table 29.12 – Imperial Chemical Industries PLC – Annual report and accounts – 31 December 1994

notes relating to the accounts

23 Reserves (extract)

	Share premium account £m	Revaluation £m	Associated under-takings £m	Profit and loss account £m	**1994 Total £m**	1993 Total £m
GROUP						
Reserves attributable to parent company						
At beginning of year as previously stated						3,572
Prior year adjustment (note 2)						(89)
At beginning of year as restated	561	46	66	2,493	**3,166**	3,483
Profit/(loss) retained for year			(63)	52	**(11)**	(433)
Amounts taken direct to reserves						
Share premiums	8				**8**	59
Goodwill				(48)	**(48)**	80
Exchange adjustments		(6)	(11)	(79)	**(96)**	(23)
Share of other reserve movements of associated undertakings and other items			(9)	2	**(7)**	-
	8	(6)	(20)	(125)	**(143)**	116
Other movements between reserves		(3)	77	(74)		
At end of year	569	37	60	2,346	**3,012**	3,166

In the Group accounts, £33m of net exchange gains (1993 losses £26m) on foreign currency loans have been offset in reserves against exchange losses (1993 gains) on the net investment in overseas subsidiaries and associated undertakings.

29.140 Apart from the item mentioned in paragraph 29.139, there is no requirement to disclose the amount of exchange gains and losses taken to the profit and loss account. Nonetheless, the profit and loss account formats in Schedule 4 to the Act distinguish between operating income and expenses and other income and expenses. Therefore, a company will need to consider the nature of each exchange difference. A company should normally show gains and losses that arise from trading transactions as 'other operating income/charges'. Where arrangements that can be considered as financing give rise to exchange gains and losses, a company should disclose these separately as part of 'other interest receivable and similar income' or as part of 'interest payable and similar charges'. Exchange gains and losses that arise from events that themselves fall to be disclosed as exceptional items should be included as part of such items. Similarly, exchange gains and losses that arise from events that fall to be treated as extraordinary items should be included as part of such items (though, in practice these will be rare following the introduction of FRS 3).

29.141 The guidance on the 'Operating and financial review', issued by the ASB recommends a number of disclosures that are relevant to foreign currency operations. In particular, it recommends discussion of the operating results for the period (including the effect of changes in exchange rates) and factors which may have a major effect on future results (possibly including exchange rate fluctuations). Furthermore, the financial review section of the OFR which explains the capital structure and financial position, recommends discussion on the state of the capital funding, the treasury policies and objectives. These should include management of exchange rate risk and the extent to which foreign currency net investments are hedged by currency borrowings and other hedging instruments. Many listed companies are now adhering to these recommendations by disclosing the ways in which they manage their foreign currency exposures and treasury activities. Examples of these types of disclosures are included in Table 29.13 and in chapter 33 that deals with the OFR.

Table 29.13 – British Airways Plc – Report & Accounts – 31 March 1995

Operating and financial review of the year (extract)

Foreign currency exposure

The Group does business in some 140 foreign currencies which account for approximately 60 per cent of Group revenue and approximately 50 per cent of operating expenses. The Group generates a surplus in most of these currencies. The principal exceptions are the US Dollar and the pound Sterling in which the Group has a deficit arising from capital expenditure and the payment of some leasing costs, together with expenditure on fuel, which is payable in US Dollars, and the majority of staff costs, central overheads and other leasing costs, which are payable in pounds Sterling. However, the broad spread of currencies in the business – many of which are linked to the US Dollar and the pound Sterling – gives the Group a measure of protection against exchange rate movements and reduces the overall sensitivity of the Group's results to exchange rate fluctuations. Nonetheless, the Group can experience adverse or beneficial effects. For example, if Sterling weakened against the US Dollar and strengthened against other major currencies, the overall effect would be likely to be adverse, while the reverse would be likely to produce a beneficial effect.

The Group seeks to reduce its foreign exchange exposure arising from transactions in various currencies through a policy of matching, as far as possible, receipts and payments in each individual currency. Surpluses of convertible currencies are sold, either spot or forward for US Dollars and pounds Sterling.

The Group's forward transactions in foreign currency are detailed in Note 15f to the accounts.

In addition to the primary effects outlined above, exchange rate movements can affect demand for services, especially from leisure travellers whose decision whether and where to travel may alter as a result of exchange rate movements. While it is not possible to quantify this effect, British Airways does monitor exchange rate movements in an attempt to anticipate likely changes in the pattern of demand.

Effect that foreign currency translation has on distributable profits

29.142 Companies can only make a distribution to their shareholders out of profits that are available for that purpose. The amount of distributable profits is calculated by reference to the financial statements of an individual company and the rules differ for private and public companies. The rules relating to calculating distributable profits are considered in detail in chapter 19. In order to determine distributable profits, it is necessary to distinguish between realised and unrealised profits and losses. This can be a particularly complex area when dealing with foreign currency translation.

29.143 In an individual company, the exchange gains and losses that arise both on the currency transactions that the company completes during the year and on its outstanding short-term monetary items (as defined in para 29.23), are taken to the profit and loss account. Paragraph 12 of Schedule 4 to the Act states that *"...only profits realised at the balance sheet date shall be included in the profit and loss account"*. Where exchange gains and losses arise on short-term monetary items, their ultimate cash realisation can normally be assessed with reasonable certainty. For companies that prepare financial statements in accordance with Schedule 4, monetary items should be categorised as either short-term or long-term items. Short-term monetary items are those that fall due within one year of the balance sheet date. Therefore, gains and losses on such items are considered to be realised gains and losses in accordance with the prudence concept defined in SSAP 2. Accordingly, the inclusion of these gains in the profit and loss account does not conflict with paragraph 12 of Schedule 4 to the Act.

29.144 Exchange gains that arise on outstanding long-term monetary items are not realised profits. However, as discussed in paragraph 29.28, SSAP 20 requires these gains to be included in the profit and loss account. This requirement conflicts with paragraph 12 of Schedule 4 to the Act and so involves the use of the true and fair override (see chapter 2).

29.145 Where exchange gains on long-term monetary items are included in the profit and loss account, they will be unrealised to the extent that they exceed past losses on the same items. Where exchange losses on long-term monetary items are included in the profit and loss account, they will be realised to the extent that they exceed past unrealised gains on the same items. To illustrate this, consider the following example.

Example

In 19X1, a UK company took out a long-term US dollar loan. It did not use the loan to finance a foreign equity investment. Consequently, the company must include in its profit and loss account the exchange gains and losses that arise when the loan is retranslated at the closing rate. (There are no doubts as to either the convertibility or the marketability of US dollars.) Consider the table below.

Exchange gains and losses

Year ended 31 December	Exchange gain/(loss) included in profit and loss account	Unrealised	Realised	Note
	£	£	£	
19X1	250,000	250,000	-	(a)
19X2	(300,000)	(250,000)	(50,000)	(b)
		-	(50,000)	
19X3	75,000	25,000	50,000	
		25,000	-	(c)
19X4	50,000	50,000	-	(d)
		75,000	-	

Notes to the example above:

(a) The company must treat the whole of the exchange gain as unrealised.

(b) On the basis that the exchange loss reverses the previous exchange gain on the loan, it would appear equitable that the company can treat £250,000 of the loss as unrealised. The company must treat the balance of the loss as realised.

(c) The company can treat the gain as realised to the extent that it reverses a past loss on the loan. It must treat the balance of the gain as unrealised.

(d) The company must treat the whole of the exchange gain as unrealised.

29.146 In order to identify unrealised exchange gains on the translation of long-term monetary items, a company will need to keep detailed records of the exchange gains and losses that arise over the life of each long-term monetary item.

29.147 Where the exchange difference on a long-term monetary item such as a borrowing is a loss, SSAP 20 requires this to be included in the profit and loss account, unless the foreign borrowing is being used to finance or provide a hedge against a foreign equity investment (and the conditions in paragraph 51 of SSAP 20 are met). This means that the loss should generally be treated as a realised loss (except to the extent that it represents a reversal of accumulated unrealised exchange gains on the same loan). This is because it is the current best estimate of the probable loss that will be incurred when the borrowing is repaid.

29.148 Where an individual company has a foreign currency borrowing that is being used to finance or provide a hedge against a foreign equity investment held by that same company then SSAP 20 permits the exchange loss on the borrowing to be offset in reserves against the exchange gain on the investment (subject to the conditions in paragraph 51 of SSAP 20 being met). Although in broad terms there is a hedge and no overall gain or loss, a problem may arise if there is:

- a gain on the investment;
- a loss on the borrowing; and
- a need to repay the borrowing before realising the investment.

29.149 The exchange loss on the borrowing is normally regarded as a realised loss (except to the extent that it represents a reversal of accumulated unrealised exchange gains on the same loan). This is because, as stated above, it is the current best estimate of the probable loss that will be incurred when the borrowing is repaid. In addition, repaying the borrowing will crystallise the loss prior to the realisation of the gains on the investment. It is, therefore, prudent to regard the loss on the borrowing as realised. In contrast, the corresponding gain on the investment will be unrealised.

29.150 However, there may be situations where the exchange loss on the long-term borrowing would not be considered to be a realised loss. One such situation is where the terms of the borrowing provide that:

- The lender may demand repayment of the borrowing only when the company disposes of its foreign equity investment.

- Repayment of the borrowing at the requirement of the lender may be made only out of the disposal proceeds of the investment.

29.151 In this situation, an exchange loss can be regarded as unrealised even if the company had the right to repay the borrowing at any time. The rationale for this is that the lender cannot force the company to crystallise a loss. The company could decide to repay early if there was a gain on the borrowing. Even if the company decided to repay early when there was a loss on the loan, we would regard the loss as being realised at the time the company decided to repay early. However, if sufficient distributable profits for the purpose of paying a dividend exist only as a result of the company offsetting a loss on its long-term borrowings against an unrealised gain on its related foreign equity investments, it may be appropriate for the directors to take legal advice.

29.152 Another situation where the exchange loss on the long-term borrowing would not be considered to be a realised loss is where it is hedging a foreign equity investment that is in the form of a long-term loan and the maturity terms of the asset and liability are the same. If this is the case, then no net realised exchange gain or loss will arise on translation. This is because, if the asset and liability have the same maturity as well as the same currency, there is an economic hedge and no real gain or loss arises. In contrast, if the maturity periods of the asset and liability differ, a separate gain or loss will arise on each transaction and it is necessary to consider whether they are realised. If the asset and liability have the same maturity date but are for different amounts, the same argument applies to the amounts that match, but it will be necessary to consider whether a gain or loss on the unmatched asset or liability is realised.

29.153 In practice, the financing and hedging of foreign equity investments can be complicated and may involve a number of group companies. For instance, the external borrowing may be held by the ultimate parent company, which then makes loans to an intermediate parent company that holds the foreign investments. It is necessary to consider the impact of the treasury arrangements on the distributable profits of each entity. Where the asset and liability are both intra-group then it may be possible to structure the transactions so that there is no mismatch of realised and unrealised gains and losses. However, where the borrowing is external it may be difficult to achieve this and distributable profits could be reduced by exchange losses on the borrowing.

Hyper-inflation

29.154 Where a foreign subsidiary or an associate operates in a country in which a very high rate of inflation exists, the closing rate/net investment method is not considered to be suitable for translating the financial statements of the foreign enterprise for inclusion in the consolidated financial statements. This is because an asset acquired in foreign currency is worth very little in sterling terms at a time of high inflation when the foreign currency has weakened considerably against sterling, leading to a large debit to group reserves. At the same time, the results of the foreign enterprise are included at an inflated amount in the group's profit and loss account (whether from high interest income on deposits in a rapidly depreciating foreign currency or from trading operations which could be considered to reflect unrealistically high profitability).

29.155 The above problems were recognised by SSAP 20 which states:

> *"Where a foreign enterprise operates in a country in which a very high rate of inflation exists it may not be possible to present fairly in historical cost accounts the financial position of a foreign enterprise simply by a translation process. In such circumstances the local currency financial statements should be adjusted where possible to reflect current price levels before the translation process is undertaken."* [SSAP 20 para 26].

29.156 SSAP 20 does not provide guidance on what is meant by a high rate of inflation and when or how this guidance should be applied in practice. As a result, the UITF considered this matter and issued Abstract 9, 'Accounting for operations in hyper-inflationary economies', in June 1993. The question of what constitutes hyper-inflation is judgemental. There is some guidance in IAS 29 'Financial reporting in hyper-inflationary economies' which describes a number of characteristics of the economic environment of a country that indicate hyper-inflation. These are as follows:

- The general population prefers to keep its wealth in non-monetary assets or in a relatively stable foreign currency. Amounts of local currency held are immediately invested to maintain purchasing power.

- The general population regards monetary amounts not in terms of the local currency but in terms of a relatively stable foreign currency. Prices may be quoted in that currency.

- Sales and purchases on credit take place at prices that compensate for the expected loss of purchasing power during the credit period, even if the period is short.

- Interest rates, wages and prices are linked to a price index.

- The cumulative inflation rate over three years is approaching, or exceeds, 100 per cent.

29.157 The UITF reached a consensus that adjustments are required where the distortions caused by hyper-inflation are such as to affect the true and fair view given by the group financial statements. In any event adjustments must be made where the cumulative inflation rate over three years is approaching, or exceeds, 100 per cent and the operations in the hyper-inflationary economies are material. [UITF 9 para 5].

29.158 The Abstract is not clear whether the word 'cumulative' is intended to mean that the three-year inflation rate should be calculated by simply adding up the inflation rates for each of the three years or by computing the compound inflation rate over the three years. Consider the following example:

Example

The following data are relevant to a country operating in a hyper-inflationary economy:

	19X1	19X2	19X3	19X4
Inflation rate		30%	28%	34%
General price level	120	156	200	268

Based on simple addition the cumulative inflation rate for the years 19X2 to 19X4 is 92% (30+28+34).

Compounded annually (using the index at the end of 19X1 as the base), the cumulative inflation for 19X2 to 19X4 is (268 – 120) ÷ 120 = 123%.

In our view, the cumulative three-year inflation rate should be compounded, because it provides a measure of inflation for the three years taken as a whole.

29.159 The determination of whether a country has experienced cumulative three-year inflation of approximately 100 per cent or more should be based on an internationally or locally recognised general price-level index for that country. Countries that have recently experienced cumulative three-year inflation of 100 per cent or more, include amongst others, Argentina, Brazil, Nigeria, Sudan, Zaire, Turkey, Poland and Romania. Information on inflation rates in various countries is available in International Financial Statistics, issued monthly by the Bureau of Statistics of the International Monetary Fund.

29.160 Although SSAP 20 suggested the use of a local price-level index for adjusting the financial statements of a local enterprise before translation, it may not always be possible to obtain a reliable local index. UITF Abstract 9, therefore, allows an alternative method that is similar to that required by SFAS 52. The two methods, that are now considered to be acceptable and, therefore, consistent with SSAP 20 are as follows:

- Adjust the local currency financial statements to reflect current price levels before the translation process is undertaken as suggested in paragraph 26 of SSAP 20. This includes taking any gain or loss on the net monetary position through the profit and loss account.

- Using a relatively stable currency (which would not necessarily be sterling) as the functional currency (that is, the currency of measurement) for the relevant foreign operations. For example in certain businesses operating in Latin American territories the US dollar acts effectively as the functional currency for business operations. The functional currency would in effect be the 'local currency' as defined in paragraph 39 of SSAP 20. In such circumstances, if the translations are not recorded initially in that stable currency, they must first be remeasured into that currency by applying the temporal method described in SSAP 20 (but based on the dollar or other stable currency rather than sterling). The effect is that the movement between the original currency of record and the stable currency is used as a proxy for an inflation index.

[UITF 9 para 6].

29.161 If neither of the above methods is considered appropriate for material operations, then the reasons should be stated and alternative methods to eliminate the distortions should be adopted. [UITF 9 para 7]. In practice, companies tend to follow one or the other method described above as illustrated in the examples below.

29.162 Where group operations in areas of hyper-inflation are material in the context of group results or net assets, the accounting policy adopted to eliminate the distortions of such inflation should be disclosed. [UITF 9 para 8].

Table 29.14 – Courtaulds plc – Report and Accounts – 31 March 1995

Statement of accounting policies (extract)

Foreign currencies

The accounts of overseas subsidiaries are translated into sterling at the rates at which the currencies could have been sold at the date of the Group balance sheet. Gains or losses arising on these transactions are dealt with in reserves. Other assets and liabilities denominated in foreign currencies are translated into sterling at year end rates and differences arising are dealt with in the profit and loss account. The results of subsidiaries in hyper-inflationary economies are dealt with in accordance with UITF 9 using the US$ as the functional currency.

Table 29.15 – Reckitt & Colman plc – Annual Report & Accounts – 3 January 1998

Accounting policies (extract)

Foreign currency translation

Transactions denominated in foreign currencies are translated at the rate of exchange on the day the transaction occurs or at the contracted rate if the transaction is covered by a forward exchange contract.

Assets and liabilities denominated in a foreign currency are translated at the exchange rate ruling on the balance sheet date or, if appropriate, at a forward contract rate. Exchange differences arising in the accounts of individual undertakings are included in the profit and loss account except that, where foreign currency borrowing has been used to finance equity investments in foreign currencies, exchange differences arising on the borrowing are dealt with through reserves to the extent that they are covered by exchange differences arising on the net assets represented by the equity investments.

The accounts of overseas subsidiary and associated undertakings are translated into sterling on the following basis:

Assets and liabilities at the rate of exchange ruling at the year-end date except for tangible fixed assets of undertakings operating in countries where hyper-inflation exists which are translated at historical rates of exchange.

Profit and loss account items at the average rate of exchange for the financial year. An inflation adjustment is charged in arriving at local currency profits of undertakings operating in hyper-inflation countries before they are translated to reflect the impact of the hyper-inflation on the undertakings' working capital requirements.

Exchange differences arising on the translation of accounts into sterling are recorded as movements on reserves. Where foreign currency borrowing has been used to finance equity investments in foreign currencies, exchange differences arising on the borrowing are dealt with through reserves to the extent that they are covered by exchange differences arising on the net assets represented by the equity investments.

Multi-currency share capital

29.163 It is not uncommon for a UK company to issue shares in a currency other than sterling. The legal aspects are dealt with in chapter 19. The question arises as to how such foreign currency share capital should be translated for reporting purposes at the company's year end. This is not dealt with either in SSAP 20 or FRS 4 'Capital instruments'. There are two possible treatments:

- The shares could be maintained at the historical rate at the date the shares were issued.
- The shares could be retranslated at each year end at the closing rate of exchange.

In the latter case, exchange differences would normally be taken directly to reserves (but see example in para 29.164 below). Overall, both methods have the same effect on shareholders' funds.

29.164 For equity shares either method is acceptable. For non-equity shares we consider that the substance of the instrument should be considered. If the non-equity shares are, for instance, redeemable preference shares then these are similar in nature to debt. Long-term debt is normally retranslated by using the closing rate at each year end. The most appropriate treatment, therefore, would appear to be to retranslate the preference shares at each year end at the closing rate. This is considered further in the following example:

Example

A company has issued preference shares denominated in dollars. These are redeemable at par in 19X9. How should the shares be recorded in the company's sterling financial statements and how should the exchange differences, if any, be dealt with?

The redeemable preference shares are economically similar to debt. Long-term debt is normally retranslated by using the closing rate of exchange at each year end, with exchange gains and losses taken into the profit and loss account. The most appropriate treatment, therefore, would appear to be to retranslate the preference shares at each year end at the closing rate.

FRS 4 requires the finance costs for non-equity shares to be calculated on the same basis as the finance costs for debt. Exchange gains or losses on debt or non-equity shares would fall within the definition of finance costs in FRS 4. In addition, paragraph 68 of SSAP 20 indicates that exchange differences on debt should be disclosed separately as part of interest payable and similar charges.

Since these are non-equity shares rather than debt, the exchange gains or losses would be taken to the profit and loss account, but would be shown separately as an appropriation of profit along with the preference dividends, instead of being charged or credited in arriving at the profit for the year. The exchange differences would then be added to or subtracted from the amount attributed to non-equity interests in the analysis of shareholders' funds that is required by FRS 4, so that the resulting figure is the retranslated sterling amount.

An exception to the treatment described above is where the preference shares were issued to finance or provide a hedge against, for example, an equity investment in the US. In those circumstances it would be acceptable to use the offset method in SSAP 20. Under this method the investment would be designated as a dollar asset. Both the investment and the preference shares would then be retranslated at each year end at the closing rate. The exchange differences on the preference shares would then be offset, as a reserve movement, against the exchange differences on the investment. Application of the conditions for offset in paragraphs 51 and 57 of SSAP 20 would result in exchange gains or losses on the preference shares being offset only to the extent of exchange differences arising on the foreign equity investments. Any surplus exchange differences on the preference shares would then be shown as an appropriation in the profit and loss account as described above.

Whichever method is chosen to account for the exchange differences on the preference shares, the amount attributable to non-equity interests in the analysis of shareholders' funds would be the same, that is, the retranslated sterling amount.

The European single currency – the euro

Introduction

29.165 Economic and Monetary Union (EMU) and the proposed introduction of the single currency – the euro – scheduled for 1 January 1999 will bring radical changes to how companies do business in Europe. Basically, companies that operate in a Member State that will join EMU, or trade with a company within one of those States, will be affected. In fact, the weight of the European Union as a trading block is such that each one of its trading partners, whether they join the EMU or not in the first wave, will have to adapt to the euro. This applies particularly to those companies in the UK, which is not joining the EMU in the first wave, with cross-border operations or with operations based in Member States participating in the EMU. These companies will have to adapt their operations and information systems to accommodate the euro.The financial sector, including both banking and insurance, the retail industry and government agencies will be particularly affected, although all commercial organisations based in or with operations in Europe will have to carefully consider the impact of EMU. The situation for small and medium-sized enterprises will not differ much from larger companies as the same considerable changes need to be made to adapt to the euro.

29.166 Apart from the treatment of the wide variety of additional costs arising from the introduction of the euro, there are other issues that have accounting implications. The UITF issued Abstract 21, 'Accounting issues arising from the proposed introduction of the euro', on 5 March 1998, which considers the three issues discussed below. The Abstract is consistent with the relevant guidance included in the paper, 'Accounting for the introduction of the euro', published by the European Commission in June 1997.

Costs associated with the introduction of the euro

29.167 The UITF considered the issue as to whether internal and external costs incurred in connection with the introduction of the euro should be expensed or capitalised as an asset and what disclosure would be appropriate. The Abstract notes that many of the costs of preparing for the euro, such as administrative planning, staff training, the provision of information to customers, etc will not give rise to assets and should be expensed as incurred.

29.168 Where costs are incurred to make the necessary modifications to existing assets, such as vending machines, cash registers or banks' automatic teller machines, the considerations are very similar to those arising in respect of year 2000 costs discussed in chapter 14. Therefore, such costs should be written off except in those cases where the entity already has a policy of capitalising assets of the relevant type. In that situation, the costs should be capitalised and depreciated only if the expenditure clearly enhances the asset's service potential beyond that originally assessed rather than merely maintaining its service potential.

29.169 Regarding the timing of recognition of a provision for costs associated with the introduction of the euro, the considerations relating to the timing of recognition of year 2000 related costs considered in chapter 14 apply. That is, no provision would be made for estimated future costs and such costs would be recognised in the accounting period in which the work is carried out.

29.170 The Abstract requires that costs incurred in connection with the introduction of the euro and regarded as exceptional should be disclosed in accordance with FRS 3. Particulars of commitments at the balance sheet date in respect of costs to be incurred (whether to be treated as capital or revenue) should be disclosed where they are regarded as relevant to assessing the entity's state of affairs. Where the potential impact is likely to be significant to the entity, the Abstract indicates that information on estimated total costs and some discussion of the impact should be given. This information may be located either in the directors' report or in the OFR or other statement included in the annual report. An example is given in the Table 29.16 below.

Table 29.16 – The British Petroleum Company p.l.c. – Annual Report and Accounts – 31 December 1997

FINANCIAL REVIEW (extract)

The Euro
BP is adapting its commercial and financial processes so that its European operations can do business in the Euro after it is introduced in some countries on 1 January 1999. The capability to conduct business in national currencies will be retained as long as necessary. The costs associated with these changes are estimated at $100 million. We do, however, see the introduction of the Euro primarily as a business opportunity.

Cumulative foreign exchange translation differences

29.171 As a result of the introduction of the euro, conversion rates between the currencies of participating Member States and the euro will be legally and irrevocably fixed. Where both a parent and its subsidiary companies report at present in different national currencies of participating Member States, exchange differences arising from the retranslation of the subsidiary's financial statements at each balance sheet date under the closing rate/net investment method would have been taken to consolidated reserves and reported in the statement of total recognised gains and losses. Following the introduction of the euro, no further gains and losses will arise and no further accounting entries will be required in respect of these foreign exchange differences. The Abstract follows the principles of FRS 3 and makes it clear that such items have already been reported once in total recognised gains and losses and should not be reported a second time through the profit and loss account, even though they have crystallised. Consequently, the exchange differences should remain in reserves and not be recycled through the profit and loss account.

29.172 There will be no change from the current treatment for UK parent companies with subsidiaries in participating Member States. Although exchange differences between the sterling and the national currencies of the participating Member States will disappear on 1 January 1999, UK parent companies will still be exposed to exchange rate risk: the sterling will continue to fluctuate against the euro just as it does today against say the German mark or the French franc.

Anticipatory hedges existing at the date of introduction of the euro

29.173 Foreign exchange contracts, such as forwards, options and swaps are often used to hedge currency risk. As stated above, following the introduction of the euro the exchange risk between currency units of two participating Member States will disappear. As a result, the hedging effect of contracts in existence after the introduction of the euro will cease to have any effect. The question arises as to what should happen to those exchange gains and losses on such open contracts arising up to the date of introduction of the euro.

29.174 There is no accounting standard dealing with anticipatory hedges. As explained in the example in paragraph 29.125, current practice is to defer gains and losses on anticipatory hedges and recognise them in the profit and loss account in the same period as the related income or expense or asset or liability being hedged. The Abstract states that the introduction of the euro would have no impact on the accounting treatment adopted at present and, accordingly, gains and losses arising on open contracts up to the date of introduction of the euro would continue to be deferred.

under the closing rate/net investment method, would have been taken to consolidated reserves and reported in the statement of total recognised gains and losses. Following the introduction of the euro, no further gains and losses will arise and no further accounting entries will be required in respect of these foreign exchange differences. The Abstract follows the principles of FRS 3 and makes it clear that such items have already been reported once in total recognised gains and losses and should not be reported a second time through the profit and loss account, even though they have been realised. Consequently, the exchange differences should remain in reserves and not be recycled through the profit and loss account.

29.172 There will be no change from the current treatment for UK parent companies with subsidiaries in participating Member States. Although exchange differences between the sterling and the national currencies of the participating Member States will disappear on 1 January 1999, UK parent companies will still be exposed to exchange rate risk; the sterling will continue to fluctuate against the euro just as it does today against, say the German mark and French franc.

Anticipatory hedges existing at the date of introduction of the euro

29.173 Foreign exchange contracts, such as forwards, options and swaps are often used to hedge currency risk. As stated above, following the introduction of the euro the exchange risk between currency units of two participating Member States will disappear. As a result, the hedging effect of contracts in existence after the introduction of the euro will cease to have any effect. The question arises as to what should happen to those exchange gains and losses on such open contracts arising up to the date of introduction of the euro.

29.174 There is no accounting standard dealing with anticipatory hedges. As explained in the example in paragraph 29.125, current practice is to defer gains and losses on anticipatory hedges and recognise them in the profit and loss account in the same period as the related income or expense or asset or liability being hedged. The Abstract states that the introduction of the euro would have no impact on the accounting treatment adopted at present and, accordingly, gains and losses arising on open contracts up to the date of introduction of the euro would continue to be deferred.

Chapter 30

Cash flow statements

Page

Chapter 30

Cash flow statements

Introduction

30.1 The success, growth and survival of every reporting entity depends on its ability to generate or otherwise obtain cash. Cash flow is a concept that everyone understands and with which they can identify. Reported profit is important to users of financial statements, but so too is the cash flow generating potential of an enterprise. What enables an entity to survive is the tangible resource of cash not profit, which is merely one indicator of financial performance. Thus, owners look for dividends, suppliers and lenders expect payments and repayments, employees receive wages for their services, and the tax authorities are legally entitled to tax revenues due.

30.2 Yet the provision of cash flow information by UK companies, as part of their external reporting function, is a relatively new phenomenon. Until the issue of FRS 1, 'Cash flow statements', in September 1991, which came into effect for accounting periods ending on or after 23 March 1992, there was no requirement in the UK to prepare a cash flow statement. Instead, UK companies provided a funds statement under SSAP 10, 'Statements of source and application of funds'.

Limitations of SSAP 10

30.3 SSAP 10 was issued in 1975 and required that audited financial statements should include a statement of source and application of funds. However, there was little formal prescription concerning the structure and content of the funds statement. Consequently, in practice, a wide variety of different presentations were found, some of which were very informative while others were less so. This flexibility in funds statement reporting practices had the effect of reducing comparability between statements and, therefore, their usefulness.

30.4 Perhaps the principal shortcoming of SSAP 10 was that the statement simply provided an analysis of the sources and application of funds (however defined) in terms of the movements in assets, liabilities and capital that had taken place during the year, rather than in terms of how the various activities of the business had either generated or absorbed funds. The result was that the funds statement merely listed the changes in balance sheet totals, thereby giving little, if any, additional information and so explained little about a company's ability to meet obligations or to pay dividends or about its need for external financing.

30.5 Numerous interpretations of the word 'funds' were used in practice. Narrowly defined, funds were taken to mean net liquid funds, the only term defined in SSAP 10, whilst at the other extreme funds included all the financial resources of the company. In between these two extremes fell definitions such as working capital and net borrowings. The effect was that there was very little comparability between the funds statements of different companies.

Development of cash flow reporting under FRS 1

30.6 The advent of cash flow reporting was a direct consequence of the shortcomings of the funds flow reporting practices adopted under SSAP 10. These shortcomings were further exposed by the much publicised failures of some reputable listed companies during the late 1980s that had been widely regarded as profitable. In order to address these shortcomings, and also to keep pace with the significant international developments that had already taken place in cash flow reporting particularly in the USA and Canada, the ASC, prior to its demise, published ED 54, 'Cash flow statements', in July 1990.

30.7 ED 54 proposed that a cash flow statement should be required in place of the funds flow statement under SSAP 10. The exposure draft proposed that cash flows should be classified according to the operating, investing and financing activities of the business. Although the exposure draft provoked much comment, it was generally felt that the quality of the information provided by a cash flow statement was superior to that produced by a funds flow statement. The ASB took over this project as one of its top priorities and published FRS 1 in September 1991.

30.8 Whilst retaining the general thrust of ED 54, FRS 1 made significant changes to the structure of the cash flow statement proposed in ED 54 and introduced two additional standard headings, 'Returns on investments and servicing of finance' and 'Taxation'. It also exempted a larger number of reporting entities from preparing cash flow statements.

FRS 1 in practice

30.9 The ASB's first financial reporting standard has been in operation for about five years. It was generally well received and many listed companies saw advantages in FRS 1 and adopted the statement early. However, as preparers and users became accustomed to the standard, a number of practical matters, some more fundamental than others, arose.

30.10 The original standard required that the cash flow statement should include all the reporting entity's inflows and outflows of cash and cash equivalents. Although the concept of cash was readily understood, it was the definition of cash equivalents that caused the greatest difficulty in practice. The standard classed deposits with more than three months to maturity when acquired as investments, not cash equivalents. Critics argued that their exclusion from cash equivalents failed to capture their substance. Company treasurers normally take a longer view of their cash management function and do not draw a distinction between investments and cash in the way envisaged by the old FRS 1, or if they do they draw a different distinction. As a result, they believed that the three month rule was of little or no relevance to their treasury management operations and of limited use in assessing the true liquidity position of the company. Critics also argued that a narrow definition of cash equivalents was not consistent with the objective of FRS 1, which asserted that the purpose of the cash flow statement was to assist users of the financial statements in their assessment of the reporting entity's liquidity, viability and financial adaptability.

30.11 In practice, companies chose to deal with the shortcomings of the definition of cash equivalents in a variety of ways. Generally companies have tended to follow the strict definition of cash and cash equivalents in preparing their cash flow statements, but have also adapted the format and/or given additional information that reflects the way in which they manage their cash flows. For example, some companies have chosen voluntarily to disclose the movements of net cash/net debt, which they regard as more useful information than the movements in cash and cash equivalents, because it gives a better indication of the liquidity of the business. Others have taken a more radical approach by including short-term investment movements in financing on the grounds that they manage their borrowings and investments as an integrated treasury operation, making investments when rates are good and drawing down on borrowings when rates are low. These companies consider it misleading to show such investments as part of investing activities.

30.12 The ASB was aware of the concerns expressed above. Indeed when FRS 1 was first issued, the ASB indicated that it would review the standard after its first two years of operation. It kept its promise by calling for comments in March 1994 on how the standard could be improved. On 7 December 1995, after a long period of deliberation, the ASB issued FRED 10, 'Revision of FRS 1 Cash flow statements', which proposed significant changes to FRS 1.

Revision of FRS 1

30.13 The ASB worked hard to find a suitable alternative definition of cash equivalents, but found it impossible to reach a consensus. According to the ASB, preferred maturity periods for cash equivalents varied from as short as one month to as long as a year. Some suggested measuring the maturity of short-term investments from the balance sheet date (residual maturity) in place of the standard's measure of original maturity. In the end, the ASB went down a completely different route and proposed to overhaul significantly the way companies report their cash flows.

30.14 FRED 10 proposed to drop cash equivalents and to use only cash (cash in hand and at bank, less overdrafts) as the basis of the cash flows reported in the cash flow statement. A new format for the statement was proposed. Dividends paid and capital expenditure would be shown differently, in a way that would highlight free cash flows. The movements in former cash equivalents, which often formed part of a company's treasury activities, were proposed to be included under a new heading that deals with the management of liquid resources. In addition, FRED 10 proposed to split the 'investing activities' into two: 'capital expenditure' and 'acquisitions and disposals'. The proposals also firmly linked the cash flow statement with the profit and loss account and the balance sheet by introducing a reconciliation of cash flows to the movement in net debt as well as to operating profit.

30.15 The proposals in FRED 10 were novel and represented what is arguably the world's first pure cash flow statement. It picked up many of the suggestions that were made in response to the ASB's invitation to comment on FRS 1. It was a major improvement on the current version of the standard. The notion of 'cash equivalents' always was arbitrary and so it seemed sensible to move to a narrower measure of simply cash and to a broader measure of net debt. Both are measures that businesses use and understand.

30.16 It is, therefore, not surprising that the proposals in FRED 10 received a favourable response from all quarters. The revised standard, which was issued on 30 October 1996 and which is effective for accounting periods ending on or after 23 March 1997, is therefore closely based on FRED 10. Reference in this chapter to FRS 1 should be read as reference to the revised standard.

30.17 One possible drawback is that the revised FRS 1 moves the UK away from international practice. Both the international standard, IAS 7, and the US standard, SFAS 95, involve reporting changes in 'cash and cash equivalents' and allocate the cash flows into three headings. So a UK change that abandons cash equivalents and moves from five headings to nine (increased from the revised eight headings to nine in November 1997 following publication of FRS 9, which is effective for accounting periods ending on or after 23 June 1998) hardly sounds like harmonisation. It isn't, but in this particular case, the UK is right to experiment with the new approach and, if successful, the IASC and other countries might consider it.

Objectives and scope of FRS 1

Objectives

30.18 The principal objective of FRS 1 is to require reporting entities falling within its scope to:

- Report their cash generation and cash absorption for a period by highlighting the significant components of cash flow in a way that facilitates comparison of the cash flow performances of different businesses.

- Provide information that assists in the assessment of their liquidity, solvency and financial adaptability.

[FRS 1 para 1].

30.19 The above objective is consistent with the draft 'Statement of principles for financial reporting' being developed by the ASB. Chapter 1 of the exposure draft dealing with 'The objective of financial statements' makes it clear that a cash flow statement provides an additional perspective on the performance of an enterprise by indicating the amounts and principal sources of its cash inflows and outflows. This information is useful in assessing the implications for future cash flows of the enterprise's performance and is particularly relevant to an assessment of financial adaptability.

30.20 The form of cash flow reporting required under FRS 1 provides useful information on liquidity, solvency and financial adaptability that is additional to that provided by the profit and loss account and balance sheet. A combination of profitability and liquidity data enables users of financial statements to view both sides of the same coin when assessing corporate viability over time (business survival depends on both profits from operations and sound cash management). Reporting historical cash flows also helps management to discharge its stewardship function by showing an enterprise's past cash flows, solvency and liquidity performance. Although historical cash flow is not necessarily a good indicator of future cash flows, it may nevertheless help users to review the accuracy of their previous predictions and, therefore, act as a base for assessing future cash flow performance and liquidity.

30.21 The standard also sets out how cash flow information should be presented and how extensive it should be. A standard format results in uniform presentation of cash flow information and makes such information much more comparable among companies. This comparability should, as with the original FRS 1, make the information useful to investors, creditors and other users of financial statements.

Scope

30.22 There is no statutory requirement for companies to prepare a cash flow statement. However, FRS 1 requires all reporting entities that prepare financial statements intended to give a true and fair view of their financial position and profit or loss (or income and expenditure) to include a cash flow statement as a *primary* statement within their financial statements, unless specifically exempted. [FRS 1 paras 4, 5].

Available exemptions

30.23 The following entities are exempt from preparing a cash flow statement.

Subsidiary undertakings

30.24 A subsidiary undertaking, 90 per cent or more of whose voting rights are controlled within a group, is exempt from producing a cash flow statement, provided the consolidated financial statements in which the subsidiary undertaking is included are publicly available. [FRS 1 para 5(a)]. It should be noted that the original standard only exempted wholly-owned subsidiaries of EC parent companies from preparing a cash flow statement provided certain other conditions were satisfied. The revised standard extends the exemption to cover 90 per cent or more owned subsidiaries of any parent undertaking and also substantially relaxes the other conditions, such that the only condition is that consolidated financial statements in which the 90 per cent or more owned subsidiary undertaking is included are publicly available. Unlike the original standard, there is no requirement for the parent undertaking to prepare and make publicly available a consolidated cash flow statement that includes the cash flows of the subsidiary undertaking. This exemption is, therefore, similar to the 90 per cent or more exemption included in FRS 8, 'Related party disclosures' (see chapter 35).

30.25 Clearly, the extensions will allow a much wider range of subsidiary undertakings to claim the exemption than hitherto. In particular, all 90 per cent or more owned UK subsidiaries of parent companies incorporated outside the EC will be able to take the exemption from preparing a cash flow statement provided the parent's consolidated financial statements in which the subsidiary is included are publicly available. However, not all countries have a requirement to make financial statements available to the public. Publicly available normally means disclosure in a registry or by publication in a register or gazette. Laws requiring disclosure to shareholders alone are not laws requiring public disclosure. It would, therefore, appear that UK subsidiaries of say, a US parent that is not an SEC registrant, would not be able to claim the exemption, because there is no requirement in the US for such a private company to publish or otherwise make available its financial statements to the public.

Mutual life assurance companies

30.26 Mutual life assurance societies that are owned by policy holders and friendly societies that carry on mutual life assurance business are exempt from producing a cash flow statement. [FRS 1 para 5(b)].

Pension schemes

30.27 The SORP, 'Financial reports of pension schemes', does not require pension schemes to produce a cash flow statement. This is because information about the cash flows of the scheme is normally provided by the fund account and net asset statement. Although the fund account adopts an accruals basis of accounting rather than a strict cash flow basis, re-presenting the information in the format of a cash flow statement would generally not provide any significant additional information for the readers of pension scheme financial statements. The original FRS 1 did not specifically exempt pension schemes from its scope, but the revised standard grants exemption for pension schemes from preparing a cash flow statement, which is consistent with the SORP.

Open-ended investment funds

30.28 The standard exempts open-ended investment funds from producing a cash flow statement provided certain conditions are satisfied. For this purpose, the standard defines an investment fund by using three of the four conditions for qualifying as an investment company as set out in section 266(2) of the Act. [FRS 1 para 2]. The fourth condition, which prohibits capital profits from being distributed, is intentionally left out of the standard's definition so as to allow unauthorised unit trust type vehicles (often used for unquoted or venture capital investments) and certain investment entities whose trust deeds or articles do not prohibit distribution of capital profits to claim the exemption from preparing a cash flow statement.

30.29 Clearly, the exemption is broad and means that a wide range of authorised and unauthorised investment vehicles will not have to prepare cash flow statements. However, the exemption is conditional on meeting all of the following criteria:

- Substantially all of the entity's investments are highly liquid.
- Substantially all of the entity's investments are carried at market value.
- The entity provides a statement of changes in net assets.

[FRS 1 para 5(d)].

Most investment vehicles should have little difficulty in meeting the above conditions.

Building societies

30.30 Building societies, as defined by the Building Societies Act 1986, are currently required by section 72(1)(c) of that Act to produce a statement of source and application of funds in a prescribed format. The original standard exempted building societies from preparing a cash flow statement on the grounds that a cash flow statement, in addition to the statutorily prescribed statement, would result in the duplication of much of the information that could not be justified on cost-benefit grounds. The ASB believes that the exemption for building societies should be ended because of the similarity of their operations with banks, which are not given any exemption from producing cash flow statements. However, as the proposal depends on changes in building society legislation and related aspects of financial reporting for banks and building societies, the revised standard extends the exemption for building societies for two years from the effective date of its introduction. [FRS 1 para 5(e)].

Small companies and groups

30.31 Small (but not medium-sized) companies entitled to file abbreviated financial statements with the Registrar under section 246 of the Act need not prepare a cash flow statement. [FRS 1 para 5(f)]. Generally, a company qualifies as small if it meets the relevant conditions and the size criteria specified in the Act (see further chapter 36). A small company is not actually required to file abbreviated financial statements, but merely has to be entitled to do so in order to claim the exemption from preparing a cash flow statement. However, the exemption is not available where the small company is a public company, a banking company, an insurance company, an authorised person under the Financial Services Act 1986, or a member of a group containing one or more of the above mentioned entities.

30.32 The FRSSE encourages, but does not require, smaller entities to prepare a cash flow statement. Where a smaller entity voluntarily produces a cash flow statement, the statement should be prepared using the indirect method as discussed in paragraph 30.71. This is because the indirect method is helpful in understanding the connection between the cash generated during the period and the resulting profit.

30.33 Where a small company is also the parent company of a small group and the parent company claims the exemption under section 248 from preparing consolidated financial statements, a consolidated cash flow statement need not be prepared. Although this would appear to be obvious, the exemption is not specifically mentioned in FRS 1 as it only makes reference in paragraph 5(f) of FRS 1 to the exemptions for *small companies when filing accounts with the Registrar*. Nevertheless, it will have the effect of applying in practice. This is because if a parent company of a small group can claim the exemption from having to prepare consolidated financial statements, then it is certain that the parent company and each of its subsidiary undertakings will qualify as small companies in their own right and will individually be exempt from preparing a cash flow statement. Consequently, where a small parent claims the section 248 exemption from preparing consolidated financial statements, it will not have to include a consolidated cash flow statement or its own cash flow statement when preparing its individual financial statements.

30.34 Similarly, a consolidated cash flow statement is not required, for the reasons stated above, where the small group voluntarily prepares consolidated financial statements, although it may make sense to include a consolidated cash flow statement in this situation.

Medium-sized companies and groups

30.35 Medium-sized companies are not exempt from producing cash flow statements irrespective of whether or not they choose to file abbreviated financial statements with the Registrar.

30.36 For medium-sized groups, however, the position is not so clear cut. Generally, where a medium-sized group is entitled to claim the section 248 exemption from having to prepare consolidated financial statements and does so, a consolidated cash flow statement need not be prepared. But where a medium-sized group voluntarily chooses to prepare consolidated financial statements, it will have to produce a consolidated cash flow statement.

30.37 A particular problem faces the parent company of a medium-sized group where the parent company itself meets the small size criteria, but nevertheless is deemed to be a medium-sized company under section 247A(3) of the Act. Where such a group claims the exemption from producing consolidated financial statements, the question arises as to whether the parent company can dispense with the need to produce a cash flow statement as part of its individual financial statements. The standard does not specifically exempt such a parent from producing a cash flow statement as part of its individual financial statements, because it does not fall to be treated as a small company under section 246(5) of the Act. Therefore, a small parent of a medium-sized group will have to prepare a cash flow statement as part of its individual financial statements where consolidated financial statements are not prepared. Furthermore, its 90 per cent or more owned subsidiary undertakings, which are unlikely to meet the small-size criteria, will have to include a cash flow statement as part of their individual financial statements. This is for two reasons. First they are unable to claim the small company exemption in their own right. Secondly, there is no exemption available to the subsidiary undertakings, because the parent does not produce consolidated financial statements that are publicly available.

Small unincorporated entities

30.38 Entities that are unincorporated, but would satisfy the criteria for small company exemptions had they been incorporated under the Act are exempt from preparing a cash flow statement. [FRS 1 para 5(g)]. They are, nevertheless, encouraged to prepare one if they consider it appropriate on cost-benefit grounds.

Other entities

30.39 Except for the above exemptions, the provisions of the FRS apply across all industry groups since cash flow is relevant to all businesses. This means that banks, insurance companies and other financial institutions have to present cash flow information. Because of the special nature of their businesses, FRS 1 requires slightly different formats for banks and insurance companies. Appendix I to the standard provides illustrations of amended layouts for cash flow statements for a bank and an insurance group.

Preparation of cash flow statements

30.40 It is consistent with the objective stated in paragraph 30.18 above that a cash flow statement should focus on identifying the cash effects of transactions with parties that are external to the reporting entity and their impact on its cash position. Only those transactions that involve a *cash flow* should be reported in the cash flow statement. [FRS 1 para 6]. *Cash flow*, not surprisingly, is defined as an increase or decrease in an amount of cash. [FRS 1 para 2].

Definition of cash

30.41 As the cash flow statement only reflects movements in cash, the definition of cash is central to its proper preparation. The standard does not define cash as used in common parlance, but extends the definition to include overdrafts that are repayable on demand. Overdrafts are included in the definition because they are generally viewed as negative cash balances and effectively repayable on demand. Thus cash includes:

- Cash in hand, and also deposits, including those denominated in foreign currencies, *repayable on demand* with any bank or other qualifying financial institutions.

- Overdrafts from any bank or qualifying financial institutions repayable on demand.

[FRS 1 para 2].

For this purpose, a qualifying financial institution is an entity that as part of its business receives deposits or other repayable funds and grants credits for its own account. [FRS 1 para 2].

30.42 One impact of the definition of cash is that monies transferred between deposits that qualify as cash do not result in cash inflows and outflows, but are merely movements within the overall cash balance. For instance, a transfer from a deposit account to reduce the company's overdraft would not be reflected in cash flows as it is an intra cash movement. However, all charges and credits on accounts qualifying as cash, such as bank interest, bank fees, deposits or withdrawals other than movements wholly within them, represent cash inflows and outflows of the reporting entity.

Meaning of 'repayable on demand'

30.43 In order to qualify as cash, deposits must be *'repayable on demand'*, which they are if they meet one of the following criteria:

- They can be withdrawn at any time or demanded without notice and without penalty.
- A period of notice of no more than 24 hours or one working day has been agreed.

[FRS 1 para 2].

Without notice implies that the instrument would be readily convertible into known amounts of cash on demand, that is, not subject to any time restriction. Therefore, monies deposited in a bank account for an unspecified period, but which can only be withdrawn by giving notice of more than 24 hours or one working day would not fall to be treated as cash under the definition. However, such funds can always be withdrawn by paying a penalty. In some situations, this penalty payment may not be significant enough to cause any appreciable change in the capital amount withdrawn. Nevertheless, the standard makes it clear that cash is repayable on demand if it is in practice available within 24 hours *without penalty*. Therefore, repayable on demand implies both withdrawal without penalty and without notice, or if a notice period has been agreed it must not exceed 24 hours or one working day.

Definition of liquid resources

30.44 As can be seen from the above, the definition of cash is sufficiently narrow to exclude investments, however liquid or near maturity. Nevertheless, companies normally use a range of such investments like term deposits, gilts, money market instruments, listed equity securities, Euronotes, not for their investment potential, but for managing their overall cash or net debt position. If the focus of the cash flow statement is to report movements in pure cash, the question arises as to where in the cash flow statement movements in such investments which do not qualify as cash, but which are nevertheless used increasingly in cash management and treasury operations, should be reported.

30.45 The revised standard creates a separate heading 'management of liquid resources' within the cash flow statement for reporting the cash flows arising on such liquid investments. This heading differentiates investments that are effectively used in managing the entity's net debt or net funds position from those that are held for their investment potential. However, to qualify as a liquid resource, the investment must be held as a readily disposable store of value. To be held as a readily disposable store of value, the investment must be held as a current asset investment. Fixed asset investments, therefore, do not qualify, because by definition these are held for use on a continuing basis and so are not readily disposable. For this purpose, a readily disposable investment is one that is not only disposable by the entity without curtailing or disrupting its business, but also satisfies either of the following criteria:

- It is readily convertible into known amounts of cash at or close to its carrying amount.

- It is traded in an active market.

[FRS 1 para 2].

30.46 The first criterion is particularly relevant for classifying investments in short-term deposits. Although a measure of liquidity, or a maturity period, is not specifically mentioned in the definition, the standard explains that the criterion that the deposit should be readily converted into cash at or near its carrying amount would tend to exclude any that are more than one year from maturity on acquisition. [FRS 1 para 52]. A period of one year would also be consistent with the investment's classification in the balance sheet as a current asset investment, a condition that is necessary for the investment to qualify as a liquid resource.

30.47 Liquid resources meeting the first condition are likely to encompass investments held with qualifying financial institutions that are short-dated and on which there are very little price fluctuation between the time the deposit was made and its ultimate conversion into cash. Therefore, it does not matter whether a term-deposit can be withdrawn by giving notice of more than 24 hours or whether the deposit can be withdrawn prior to its maturity by payment of a penalty, provided the penalty is not significant to cause any appreciable change in capital value. It does not also matter whether the maturity period is of a short duration (say three months) or medium duration (say six months to a year). As long as the deposit is readily convertible into a known amount of cash at or near its carrying amount and there are no restrictions as to the investor's ability to dispose of the investment without curtailing the business, it will qualify as a liquid resource. Deposits intended to be held for a long term, say between one and two years, are unlikely to qualify, even though they may be used by the entity in managing its overall cash or debt position. This is because, according to the definition, they are not sufficiently liquid. Therefore, any movements in them would fall to be reported under capital expenditure and financial investments.

30.48 The second condition allows current asset investments such as government securities, equity and debt instruments in other entities and derivative instruments to be treated as liquid resources, provided they are traded in an active market. Where an active market exists, the inference is that the instruments are easily exchangeable into known amount of cash and, hence, will represent readily disposable stores of value. Therefore, unlisted investments held as current assets are unlikely to qualify as liquid resources.

30.49 As explained in paragraph 30.14, the scrapping of the former 'cash equivalents' and the introduction of 'liquid resources' represents a neat solution to the major drawback in the former standard. No regard normally needs be paid to when investments will mature or whether they are convertible into known amounts of cash without notice (that is, effectively available immediately at face value) or whether they are subject to any capital value risk. Provided they represent readily disposable stores of value, and meet either of the conditions set out in paragraph 30.45, a wide range of current asset investments will qualify as liquid resources. The emphasis now is on a wider measure of liquidity rather than the type of the investment. The standard does not *require* all readily disposable investments to be classified as liquid resources. An entity can *choose* which of its current asset investments will be treated as liquid resources. However, it would need to explain its policy and any changes to its policy (see further para 30.106).

Treatment of borrowings

30.50 Borrowings, whether short or long-term, do not qualify as liquid resources, although bank overdrafts repayable on demand are included in cash (see para 30.41). It follows that, except for bank overdrafts, cash flows arising from all forms of borrowings, including commercial paper, should be included within the financing section of the cash flow statement. This is a change from the original standard under which short-term bank advances repayable within three months from the date of advance were included within cash equivalents.

Format of cash flow statements

30.51 To achieve the objective of providing information to help investors, creditors and others in making assessments about the liquidity, viability and financial adaptability of an entity, the standard requires cash flows to be classified under the following standard headings:

- Operating activities.
- Dividends from joint ventures and associates.
- Returns on investments and servicing of finance.
- Taxation.
- Capital expenditure and financial investments.
- Acquisitions and disposals.
- Equity dividends paid.

- Management of liquid resources.
- Financing.

30.52 The cash flows for each of the headings should be listed in the order set out above. However, the last two headings may be combined under a single heading relating to the management of liquid resources and financing provided the cash flows relating to each are shown separately and separate subtotals are given. [FRS 1 para 7]. Some companies that manage their liquid investments and borrowings as an integrated treasury operation, making investments when rates are good and drawing down on borrowings when rates are low, and matching investments with borrowings, may find this ability to combine the two headings particularly useful (see Table 30.0.2).

30.53 Striking a subtotal after any of the above headings is neither required or prohibited. Therefore, it is possible to strike a subtotal, for instance, after capital expenditure and before acquisitions and disposals. Indeed, some entities may consider it appropriate to highlight this figure as it indicates a measure of 'free cash flow' that their businesses have generated and over which they have discretionary spending ability. An example is given in Table 30.0.1 below. Although this measure does not necessarily distinguish between discretionary capital expenditure for expansion from that incurred for routine replacement and presumes that acquisitions and, more importantly, disposals are discretionary, which may not be the case, it may nevertheless be useful. Some may find it preferable to strike a subtotal after equity dividends paid as indicated in Table 30.0.2 below. Others may find it useful to draw a sub-total before financing as shown in Table 30.0.3 below. The ability to strike a subtotal at any level will, therefore, enable entities to highlight cash flows that they consider appropriate to their particular circumstances.

Table 30.0.1 – Coats Viyella Plc – Annual Report and Accounts – 31 December 1996

Analysis of free cash flow

For the year ended 31 December 1996	1996 £m	1995 Restated £m
Net cash inflow from operating activities	205.6	198.5
Returns on investments and servicing of finance	(37.8)	(35.7)
Tax paid	(54.4)	(46.5)
Capital expenditure and financial investment	(72.2)	(66.2)
Free cash flow	**41.2**	50.1

Table 30.0.2 – Bass PLC – Annual Report and Financial Statements – 30 September 1996

GROUP CASH FLOW STATEMENT

For the year ended 30 September 1996	Note	**1996 £m**	**1996 £m**	1995 £m	1995 £m
Operating activities	25		**992**		885
Interest paid		**(127)**		(128)	
Dividends paid to minority shareholders		**(5)**		(4)	
Interest received		**51**		57	
Returns on investments and servicing of finance			**(81)**		(75)
UK corporation tax paid		**(92)**		(112)	
Overseas corporate tax paid		**(19)**		(39)	
Taxation			**(111)**		(151)
Tangible fixed assets		**(547)**		(372)	
Trade loans		**(60)**		(65)	
Other fixed asset investments		**(56)**		(68)	
Paid		**(663)**		(505)	
Tangible fixed assets		**24**		97	
Trade loans		**85**		96	
Other fixed asset investments		**45**		28	
Received		**154**		221	
Capital expenditure and financial investment			**(509)**		(284)
Consideration for acquisitions	24	**(246)**		(306)	
Cash for overdrafts acquired		**12**		-	
Acquisitions			**(234)**		(306)
Equity dividends			**(205)**		(189)
Net cash flow	25		**(148)**		(120)
Management of liquid resources and financing	26		**154**		123
Movement in cash and overdrafts			**6**		3

Table 30.0.3 – TI Group plc – Annual Report – 31 December 1997

CASH FLOW STATEMENT (extract)

FOR THE YEAR ENDED 31ST DECEMBER 1997 (extract)

	Notes	1997 £m	1996 £m
Net cash inflow from operating activities	23	**241.4**	218.1
Dividends received from joint ventures and associates	23	**10.6**	11.6
Returns on investments and servicing of finance	24	**(13.3)**	(4.7)
Taxation	25	**(73.5)**	(61.5)
Capital expenditure and financial investment	26	**(59.6)**	(50.0)
Acquisitions and disposals	27	**(13.7)**	(175.4)
Equity dividends paid		**(69.6)**	(55.2)
Management of liquid resources	28	**(94.0**	60.8
Cash flow before financing		**(71.7)**	(56.3)
Issue of shares		**5.8**	12.8
Capital element of finance leases		**(0.4)**	(0.7)
Increase/(decrease) in loans		**26.7**	64.2
Financing		**32.1**	76.3
(Decrease)/increase in cash		**(39.6)**	20.0

30.54 There is also a degree of flexibility allowed in the reporting of the individual elements of cash inflows or outflows that make up each of the standard headings. Although these individual cash inflows or outflows should not be netted against each other, except in certain circumstances as explained in paragraph 30.59 below, they could either be reported gross on the face of the cash flow statement under the appropriate standard headings or shown in the notes. This means that it is acceptable to include merely the (net) totals for each of the above headings on the face of the cash flow statement, which would obviously avoid clutter on the face of the cash flow statement and possibly make it easier to understand. An example of such a presentation is shown in Table 30.1 below.

[The next page is 30015.]

Table 30.1 – Acatos & Hutcheson plc – Annual Report – 29 September 1996

Consolidated Cash Flow Statement (extract)

52 weeks ended 29th September 1996

	Notes	*1996* *£000*	*1995* *£000*
Cash flow statement			
Net cash inflow from operating activities		**20,133**	6,885
Returns on investment and servicing of finance	24	**191**	581
Taxation paid		**(2,323)**	(4,206)
Capital expenditure and financial investment	24	**(11,421)**	(6,477)
Acquisitions and disposals	24	**(6,218)**	(4,256)
Equity dividends paid		**(3,809)**	(3,272)
Cash flow before use of liquid resources and financing		**(3,447)**	(10,745)
Management of liquid resources and financing	24	**316**	27,197
Increase/(decrease) in cash during the period		**(3,131)**	16,452
Reconciliation of net cash flow to movement in net funds/(debt)			
Net funds/(bank borrowings) at beginning of period		**8,101**	(8,351)
Increase/(decrease) in cash (above)		**(3,131)**	16,452
Net funds at end of period		**4,970**	8,101

24 Notes to the consolidated cash flow statement

Analysis of gross cash flows	*1996* *£000*	*1995* *£000*
Returns on investment and servicing of finance		
Interest received	**581**	680
Interest paid	**(386)**	(85)
Other financing costs	**(4)**	(14)
	191	581
Capital expenditure and financial investment		
Purchase of tangible fixed assets	**(13,085)**	(7,212)
Proceeds of sale of tangible fixed assets	**1,634**	636
Decrease in own shares held in trust	**30**	99
	(11,421)	(6,477)
Acquisitions and disposals		
Investment in joint venture	**(10,601)**	(1,918)
Cost of businesses acquired	**-**	(2,338)
Cash received from businesses sold	**4,383**	-
	(6,218)	(4,256)
Management of liquid resources and financing		
Proceeds from issue of ordinary share capital	**316**	27,408
Expenses of share issues	**-**	(211)
	316	27,197

Classification of cash flows

30.55 A cash flow statement must classify cash receipts and cash payments under each of the nine standard headings. The classification of cash flows into reasonably distinct groups provides useful analysis about the relative importance of each of these groups and the inter-relationship between them. It should also provide useful information for comparison purposes across reporting entities.

30.56 The standard provides specific guidance for classifying cash flows. It sets out each individual element of cash inflows and outflows that should be included under a particular standard heading. Enterprises are required to disclose separately, where material, the individual categories of cash flows within each standard headings, either in the cash flow statement or in a note [FRS 1 para 8]. The way in which elements of cash flow are attributed to each standard heading is considered from paragraphs 30.67 below.

30.57 There are other elements of cash flows, not considered in the standard headings, that may cause classification difficulties. Clearly, it is not possible for the standard to provide an exhaustive list of all types of different cash flows. Consequently, the standard stipulates that where a cash flow is not specified in the categories set out in the standard headings, it should be shown under the most appropriate standard heading in accordance with the transaction's substance. [FRS 1 para 10]. Since the transaction's substance also determines the way in which it is normally reported in the profit and loss account and the balance sheet, it follows that there should be consistency of treatment in the cash flow statement and in the other primary statements. This requirement for consistency, which was not included in the original standard, would eliminate subjectivity in classifying cash flows not identified as specific items under the standard headings. [FRS 1 para 57]. Therefore, following this general principle, cash outflows relating to development expenditure that are capitalised in the balance sheet would fall to be shown under capital expenditure in the cash flow statement. Similarly, where the expenditure is written off as part of operating profit in the profit and loss account, the cash outflows would fall to be included in operating cash flows. Another example is the receipt of a government grant. To the extent that the grant is made as a contribution towards fixed assets, the substance argument would require the cash receipt to be shown under capital expenditure in the cash flow statement, irrespective of whether it is reported in the balance sheet as a deduction from the cost of the specific asset or included as deferred income and amortised over the expected useful economic life of the asset. Similarly grants given as a contribution towards revenue expenditure should be included in operating cash flows to match their treatment in the profit and loss account.

30.58 There is one situation where the general rule of classifying cash flows according to the transaction's substance is not considered appropriate. This applies to interest paid that is capitalised, for instance, as part of the construction cost of an asset in the balance sheet. Following the general rule would require reporting the interest paid under capital expenditure in the cash flow statement. However, all interest paid is specifically required to be shown under 'returns on investments and servicing of finance' heading, regardless of whether or not it is capitalised in the balance sheet. [FRS 1 para 10].

Gross or net cash flows

30.59 Generally cash inflows and outflows under each of the standard headings should be reported gross, whether on the face of the cash flow statement or in a note to it. However, there are some exceptions. These are as follows:

- The reporting of gross cash flows does not apply to operating activities where the indirect method is followed (see para 30.71).
- Cash inflows and outflows relating to the management of liquid resources or financing may be netted against each other provided the inflows and outflows meet either of the following conditions:
  - They relate in substance to a single financing transaction which satisfies all the four conditions set out in paragraph 35 of FRS 4.
  - They are due to short maturities and high turnover occurring from rollover or reissue (for example, a commercial paper programme or short-term deposits).

[FRS 1 para 9].

30.60 The ability to net cash inflows and outflows relating to the management of liquid resources or financing is a significant improvement over the strict requirements of the original standard. Many large industrial and commercial companies raise funds by issuing commercial paper in the form of unsecured promissory notes with fixed maturity between seven and 364 days. Normally these are issued at a discount to the face value and provide a cheaper source of finance than other means of borrowing. A commercial paper programme may involve issues and redemptions throughout the financial year and often these are backed up by committed bank facilities. Prior to the revision of the standard, all movements in cash flows (issues and redemptions) during the year should strictly have been reported gross in the financing section of the cash flow statement. In practice, these were often shown net. Many argued that it is not only desirable, but necessary for a better understanding of the financing cash flows to report these potentially large inflows and outflows, for what may in substance be a continuing source of finance, on a net basis.

30.61 The ASB accepted the above argument and the revised standard accordingly introduces a requirement for net reporting for the limited class of items that fulfils either of the two conditions above. The FRS 4 conditions are discussed in detail in chapter 18.

An example of a company that has reported the net change in the obligation under a commercial paper programme is given in Table 30.1.1 below.

Table 30.1.1 – Bass PLC – Annual Report & Financial Statements – 30 September 1996

NOTES TO THE FINANCIAL STATEMENTS (extract)

26 Management of liquid resources and financing	**1996 £m**	1995 £m
New borrowings	**854**	932
Net commercial paper repaid	**(84)**	(60)
Other borrowings repaid	**(846)**	(894)
	(76)	(22)
Ordinary shares issued	**28**	27
Financing	**(48)**	5
Liquid resources*	**202**	118
Total financing and liquid resources	**154**	123

* Liquid resources primarily comprise short-term deposits of less than one year and short-term investments in commercial paper.

30.62 Similarly, short-term funds that are continuously rolled over by successive deposits and withdrawals will fall to be reported net under the second condition. A question arises as to whether netting is permissible in circumstances where withdrawals from short-term deposits and payments into short-term deposits are effected with different parties. The standard is silent on this point, but in practice, treasurers often withdraw funds from one party and place them on deposits with another party to increase the overall returns on those funds. Therefore, as long as the short-term deposit is constantly renewed or rolled over, whether with the same party or with a different party, it is acceptable to report the cash inflows and outflows on a net basis.

30.63 The ability to report net cash flows in relation to rollover and reissue transactions effectively brings the UK standard in line with IAS 7 and the US FAS 95. The alternative of showing the gross amounts for raising and repaying money under a commercial paper programme or constantly renewable short-term deposits would not add very much to users' understanding of a company's treasury activities.

Additional classification

30.64 The individual items of cash inflows and outflows set out under each of the standard headings in FRS 1, other than operating activities, should not be regarded as depicting a rigid set of classification rules. The analysis under each heading merely refers to those items that would normally fall to be included under that heading and, hence, prescribe a minimum acceptable level of disaggregation of cash flow information. The individual items may be further sub-divided or new items added, if appropriate, to give a full description of the activities of the business or to provide segmental information. [FRS 1 para 8]. Indeed, the standard encourages entities to disclose additional information relevant to their particular circumstances. [FRS 1 para 56]. For example, repayments of amounts borrowed may be sub-divided further to show payments made on the redemption of debentures and other repayments of long-term borrowings. Another example would be to divide the cash flows from operating activities into those relating to continuing activities and those relating to discontinued operations (see further para 30.168).

30.65 Whatever level of detail is disclosed, it must be sufficient and relevant so that the user is able to understand the relationship between the entity's different activities and the way in which they generate and expend cash. On the other hand, too much information can cloud or obscure key issues. The problem is one of striking a balance between what the entity needs to report and how much explanation is required by the users. There is no definitive solution to this problem, because so much depends on the reporting entity's circumstances and the specific needs and expertise of the users.

Departure from the standard presentation

30.66 Prior to its revision, the original standard acknowledged that there might be circumstances where the standard presentation would not give a fair representation of the reporting entity's activities. In such rare situations, the standard called for the exercise of informed judgement to devise an appropriate alternative treatment. In practice, however, companies have rarely, if ever, departed from the standard presentation. As a result, the need to devise an appropriate alternative presentation has been deleted from the revised standard. Therefore, entities can add new items within each of the standard headings, but can no longer use a different heading, or depart from the format headings, unless there are grounds for invoking the true and fair override.

Classification of cash flows by standard headings

Cash flow from operating activities

30.67 Cash flows from operating activities generally include the cash effects of transactions and other events relating to the operating or trading activities of the enterprise. The net cash flow from operating activities, therefore, represents the movements in cash resulting from the operations shown in the profit and loss account in arriving at operating profit. In addition, cash flows relating to any provision in respect of operating items, whether or not the provision was included in operating profit, should also be included as part of operating cash flows. For example, cash flows in respect of redundancy payments provided as part of the cost of a fundamental reorganisation or closure of operations that is reported outside operating profit in accordance with FRS 3 'Reporting financial performance', will fall to be included in operating cash flows (see para 30.114). Similarly, operating cash flows will also include cash flows in respect of provision for integration costs following an acquisition. [FRS 1 para 11].

[The next page is 30019.]

[The next paragraph is 30.69.]

30.69 Operating cash flows may be reported on the gross or net basis (also known as the direct method and the indirect method respectively). [FRS 1 para 7]. Under the direct method, the major classes of gross operating cash receipts (for example, cash collected from customers) and gross operating cash payments (for example, cash paid to suppliers and employees) are reported on the face of the cash flow statement under operating activities. An example of the direct method of presentation for net operating cash flow is illustrated in Table 30.2.

Table 30.2 – Marks and Spencer p.l.c. – Annual Report and Financial Statements – 31 March 1996

Consolidated cash flow statement (extract)

FOR THE YEAR ENDED 31 MARCH 1996

	Notes	1996 £m	*1995 £m*
OPERATING ACTIVITIES			
Received from customers		**7,046.0**	*6,665.0*
Payments to suppliers		**(4,741.9)**	*(4,426.3)*
Payments to and on behalf of employees		**(928.4)**	*(782.8)*
Other payments		**(566.9)**	*(547.1)*
Net cash inflow from operating activities	24	**808.8**	*908.8*

Notes to the financial statements (extract)

24 RECONCILIATION OF OPERATING PROFIT TO NET CASH INFLOW FROM OPERATING ACTIVITIES

	THE GROUP 1996 £m	*1995 £m*
Operating profit	**940.2**	*896.5*
Depreciation	**160.4**	*150.7*
Increase in stocks	**(45.8)**	*(22.4)*
Increase in customer balances	**(190.2)**	*(144.5)*
Increase in other debtors	**(109.6)**	*(22.7)*
Increase in creditors	**53.8**	*51.2*
Net cash inflow from operating activities	**808.8**	*908.8*

Operating profit has increased by £43.7m whereas the net cash inflow from operating activities of £808.8m is £100.0m lower than last year. This reflects the £90.0m payment in respect of the pension scheme deficit (see note 10A) together with an increase of £45.7m in the movement of customer balances within Financial Services.

30.70 The ASB allows, but does not require, reporting entities to provide information on gross operating cash flows. [FRS 1 para 58]. However, the standard makes it mandatory to provide a reconciliation between operating profit and net cash flow from operating activities as discussed in paragraph 30.72 below, *even where the direct method is adopted* as indicated in Table 30.2 above. For this reason and because of the additional burden of producing gross cash flow information where these figures are not directly available from the accounting system, the direct method has not been very popular with companies despite its theoretical soundness.

30.71 Under the indirect method, the same operating cash flows as under the direct method are reported except that the net figure is produced by adjusting operating profit for non-cash items (such as depreciation) and changes in working capital (such as accruals and prepayments) and bringing in cash flows relating to any provision in respect of operating items, whether or not the provision was included in operating profit. However, in keeping with the objective that a cash flow statement should only include items of pure cash flows, the standard requires that under the indirect method the cash flow statement should start with the net cash flow from operating activities.

Reconciliation of operating profit to net cash flow from operating activities

30.72 The reconciliation of operating profit to net cash flow from operating activities is not part of the cash flow statement. However, companies may choose whether to present the reconciliation as a supplementary note to the cash flow statement, or adjoining the cash flow statement. This latter approach, absent from the original standard, has been introduced to counter criticism that the positioning of this reconciliation far away from the cash flow statement itself is not very helpful. However, if the latter approach is adopted, the reconciliation statement should be separately identified and clearly labelled to maintain the distinction that it is not part of the primary cash flow statement. [FRS 1 para 12]. This is because the reconciling items are not themselves cash flows and to report them as part of the cash flow statement itself would be inappropriate. However, we do not regard it ideal for the reconciliation to introduce the cash flow statement as illustrated in example 1 in Appendix 1 to the standard. The reconciliation statement in that example is presented immediately under the general heading 'Cash flow statement' and appears to be part of the cash flow statement itself, which is clearly not the intention. It is also confusing to have two headings for cash flow statement on the same page. A way of dealing with this is to entitle the page something along the lines 'Information on cash flows'. The term 'Cash flow statement' could then be used to describe the statement itself. A way of avoiding the problem is to position the reconciliation either under the cash flow statement or in a note immediately following it.

30.73 The reconciliation should disclose separately the movements in stock, debtors and creditors related to operating activities and other differences (for example, depreciation including profit or loss on sale of fixed assets included within operating profit, provisions, etc.) between cash flow and operating results (see worked example at the end of the chapter).

30.74 For the reconciliation to be properly carried out, it will be necessary to analyse the movements in opening and closing debtors and creditors in order to eliminate those movements that relate to items reported in the standard headings other than operating activities. For example, a company may purchase a fixed asset prior to the year end on credit. In this situation, the closing creditor balance would need to be adjusted to eliminate the amount owing for the fixed asset purchase before working out the balance sheet movements for operating creditors. It follows that movements in working capital included in the reconciliation would not be the same as the difference between the opening and the closing balance sheet amounts. Indeed, under FRS 1 this is rarely the case except in very simple situations. This is because the balance sheet movements in stock, debtors, and creditors may be affected by such items as acquisitions and disposals of subsidiaries during the year (see para 30.134), exchange differences on working capital of foreign subsidiaries (see example para 30.156) and other non-cash adjustments for opening and closing accruals of non-operating items.

30.75 A question arises as to whether the eliminated items within each balance sheet movement of working capital need to be reported separately so that the overall movement between the opening and closing balance sheet amounts is readily understandable. For example, a company could identify the total balance sheet movement in creditors and then separately itemise the operating element and the other movements. The standard is silent on this point and in practice, this is rarely done; only the operating movement is reported. An example where a company has provided a detailed reconciliation between the movements in operating working capital reported in the reconciliation of operating profit to operating cash flows and the corresponding balance sheet movements is given in Table 30.3. Whether shareholders, investors and other users of financial statements are really interested in this degree of detail is debatable as it serves no more than a mere arithmetical check. The contrary view is that if a reconciliation is presented, it will be beneficial only if the amounts are capable of being individually traced back to the amounts shown under the equivalent captions in the balance sheet.

Table 30.3 – BTR plc – Report and Accounts – 31 December 1995

NOTES (extract)

	Consolidated	
£ millions	**1995**	1994
26 CASH FLOW STATEMENT (extract)		
a) Reconciliation of operating profit before interest and tax to net cash inflow from operating activities		
Profit before interest and tax	**1,673**	1,546
Depreciation	**413**	389
Reorganisation provisions in respect of acquisitions	**64**	
Investment income	**(32)**	(35)
Net movement in working capital (trade and other):		
Inventories	**(134)**	(60)
Debtors	**(91)**	(103)
Creditors	**25**	22
Movement in provisions for liabilities and charges	**(126)**	(66)
Profits on disposal of subsidiaries and investments	**(170)**	(99)
Profit on disposal of properties	**(1)**	
	1,621	1,594

b) Balance sheet movement reconciliation

1995

	Movement of cash	Acquisitions less divestments	Non-cash movements	Exchange movements	Balance sheet movement
Inventories	134	33		(5)	162
Debtors	91	62	32	(11)	174
Creditors	(25)	(81)	42	10	(54)
Provisions for liabilities and charges	126	(20)	(143)	(18)	(55)
Working capital and provisions movement	326	(6)	(69)	(24)	227
Cash	342	32		28	402
Bank overdrafts	(1,173)	(25)		(17)	(1,215)
Finance leases and bills of exchange	19	(3)		(3)	13
Loans	(484)	(259)		(32)	(775)
Assets held under contract for sale			34		34
Movement on net debt	(1,296)	(255)	34	(24)	(1,541)
Other balance sheet items					
Tangible assets	614	27	(415)	21	247
Investments	(29)		(48)	(3)	(80)
Interest	(4)				(4)
Dividends	542		(608)		(66)
Taxation	474	5	(417)	4	66
Minority interests	261	485	(54)	46	738
Total movements	888	256	(1,577)	20	(413)

Dividends from joint ventures and associates

30.75.1 This is a new heading introduced into FRS 1 (Revised) following the changes made to the standard by FRS 9, 'Associates and Joint ventures', published in November

1997 and effective for accounting periods ending on or after 23 June 1998. Prior to FRS 9, dividends received from equity accounted entities were reported either within operating cash flows where their results were included as part of group operating profit or under returns of investments and servicing of finance where their results were reported outside group operating profit. Under FRS 9, the investor's share of the results of its equity accounted entities is included immediately *after* group operating profit rather than in group operating profit. Consistent with this treatment, the option of including dividends within operating cash flows is no longer available. The ASB also rejected the alternative of including dividends from equity accounted entities under returns on investments and servicing of finance because it felt that such dividends have a different significance from the normal returns on investments. As a result, the cash flows relating to dividends received from joint ventures and associates are reported under a new heading, between operating activities and returns on investment and servicing of finance. [FRS 1 para 12A].

[The next paragraph is 30.76.]

Returns on investments and servicing of finance

30.76 'Returns on investments and servicing of finance' are receipts resulting from the ownership of an investment and payments to providers of finance, non-equity shareholders and minority interests, excluding those items that are specifically required by the standard to be classified under another heading. [FRS 1 para 13].

30.77 This heading was introduced by the original FRS 1 following the controversy that surrounded the classification of interest and dividends paid in the cash flow statement proposed by ED 54. ED 54 proposed that dividends paid by an enterprise should be classified under financing activities whereas interest received and paid and dividends received should be shown under operating activities. However, many commentators on the exposure draft felt that a reasonable case could be made for an alternative classification as both were payments to providers of capital. As there was no consensus on the preferred treatment both in the UK and internationally, the ASB dealt with the controversy by simply requiring all interest and dividends paid and received to be shown under a separate heading in the cash flow statement. The controversy appears to have resurfaced, although not in the same context as before. The ASB's consultation revealed that there was general support for at least equity dividends paid to be taken out of 'returns on investments and servicing of finance' and located further down the statement after 'acquisition and disposals' on the grounds that such payments are more discretionary than, say, dividends on non-equity shares and interests payments on debt, which have to be made. As a result, equity dividends paid are no longer included under this heading.

30.78 Cash inflows in respect of returns on investments include the following items that should be separately disclosed:

- Interest received, including any related tax recovered.
- Dividends received net of any tax credits (except dividends from equity accounted entities).

[FRS 1 para 14].

30.79 Similarly, cash outflows from servicing of finance include:

- Interest paid (even if capitalised), including any tax deducted and paid to the relevant tax authority.
- Cash flows that are treated as finance costs under FRS 4 (this will include issue costs on debt and non-equity share capital).
- The interest element of finance lease rental payments.
- Dividends paid on non-equity shares of the entity
- Dividends paid by subsidiaries to equity and non-equity minority interests.

[FRS 1 para 15].

Table 30.4 below provides a good illustration of the type of items that should be included under returns on investments and servicing of finance.

Table 30.4 – Airtours plc – Annual Report and Accounts – 30 September 1996

Group cash flow statement

Year ended 30th September 1996	Notes	1996 £000	1996 £000	Restated 1995 £000
Net cash inflow from operating activities	24		**111,218**	95,018
Returns on investments and servicing of finance				
Interest received		**19,988**		11,838
Interest paid		**(5,440)**		(5,570)
Preference dividends paid		**(3,220)**		(3,226)
Interest element of finance leases		**(2,100)**		(726)
Minority interests		**(127)**		3
Net cash inflow from returns on investments and servicing of finance			**9,101**	2,319

30.80 Investment income included under this heading will include income from current asset investments, irrespective of whether they are regarded as liquid resources, and on fixed asset investments other than equity accounted entities whose results are included as part of operating profit.

30.81 The standard requires that the cash flow effect of any tax relating to interest should be shown as part of the interest. This applies to tax deducted at source on interest received as well as to tax withheld on interest paid. This means that the actual cash received (or paid) in respect of interest must be shown, but where tax has been deducted at source (or withheld) and is subsequently recovered (or paid), it should also be included under this heading as part of interest received (or paid) at the time of receipt (payment). For example, where there is a timing difference between the actual interest received (or paid) and the settlement of the tax, the net interest received (or paid) would fall to be shown in the period in which the cash is received (or paid), whereas the cash flow effect of any tax deducted at source (or withheld) would fall to be shown in the period in which the tax is recovered (or paid).

30.82 Interest paid should be the actual amount of interest paid during the period, irrespective of whether it is charged to the profit and loss account or capitalised in the balance sheet. Similarly, the interest paid on finance lease obligations should be reported under this heading.

30.83 Unlike the treatment of tax on interest in the cash flow statement, the tax credits on dividends received or the ACT on dividends paid is not reported as part of dividends received or paid. Rather, the net amount of any ACT paid during the period is reported under taxation (see para 30.86 below). This is because under the imputation system of company taxation no withholding tax is actually deducted on dividends paid or tax actually paid on dividends received by a UK company, ACT generally represents an advance payment of tax (see further chapter 13).

30.84 The cash flows relating to finance costs for non-equity shares and debt should be reported under this heading. Therefore, in addition to reporting finance costs such as dividends paid on non-equity shares and interest paid on debt instruments, this heading would also include any payments made for the issue of non-equity shares and debt instruments. Furthermore, the cash flow effects of items such as discounts and premiums on debt instruments and non-equity shares, which are treated as finance costs under FRS 4, would also fall to be included under this heading (see para 30.180).

30.85 The segregation of interest and dividends received and interest paid under the heading 'returns on investments and servicing of finance' is relevant particularly to non-financial companies, as these items are normally shown after operating profit. However, many investment companies and financial institutions show interest received and dividends received in their profit and loss account prior to arriving at their operating profit. Banks and insurance companies also include interest paid in operating profit.

Where the special nature of the business requires the inclusion of items relating to interest and dividend in operating profit, the cash flows relating to these items should remain as part of the operating cash flows. If any interest paid clearly relates to financing, then it should be included under 'returns on investments and servicing of finance'. [FRS 1 para 60].

Taxation

30.86 The treatment of taxation cash flows arising from revenue and capital profits proposed in ED 54 was another area that generated a significant amount of controversy. ED 54 proposed that such taxation cash flows should be shown as operating activities unless material elements of cash flows related to investing and financing activities, in which case they should be reported under the relevant headings. Many commentators on the exposure draft felt that, in practice, it may be inappropriate and rather misleading to require allocation between the three economic activities. As payment of corporation tax involves only one cash flow based on taxable income arising from all sources, including chargeable capital gains, and not a collection of individual taxation cash inflows and outflows, any apportionment based on the activities that gave rise to them could in some cases only be done on an arbitrary basis. Consequently, any allocation that attempted to segregate the taxation cash flows in this manner may result in the reporting of hypothetical figures in the cash flow statement. This argument was felt to be sufficiently strong and convincing for the ASB to require all taxation cash flows arising from revenue and capital profits to be disclosed in a separate section within the cash flow statement entitled 'taxation'.

30.87 Reporting entities need to include under this heading the following items in respect of taxation relating to revenue and capital profits:

- Cash receipts from the relevant tax authority of tax rebates, claims or returns of overpayments.
- Cash payments for corporation tax, including payments of ACT.

For a subsidiary undertaking, payments received from or made to other members of the group for group relief should be included under this heading. [FRS 1 paras 17, 18].

30.88 It should be noted that cash flows relating to VAT or other sales taxes, employees income taxes, property taxes and any other taxes not assessed on revenue and capital profits should not be shown under the heading of 'taxation'. [FRS 1 para 16].

30.89 Generally, payments or receipts of VAT or other sales taxes should be netted against the cash flows that gave rise to them. For example, payments for fixed assets should be shown net of VAT under capital expenditure. However, where the VAT falls to be irrecoverable, because the entity carries on an exempt or partially exempt business, or incurs VAT on items that are disallowed (for example, VAT on purchase of motor vehicles), the cash flows should be shown gross of the irrecoverable tax. If this is not practicable for any reason, the irrecoverable tax should be included under the most appropriate standard heading. [FRS 1 para 39].

30.90 The net movement on the VAT payable to, or receivable from, Customs & Excise should be allocated to cash flows from operating activities unless it is more appropriate to allocate it to another heading. [FRS 1 para 39]. Generally, the majority of the VAT transactions would be relevant to operating activities, but where a significant proportion of the VAT payments (or receipts) relate to other cash flow headings, such as 'capital expenditure and financial investments' or 'acquisitions and disposals', it may be appropriate to include the net payment (or receipt) under that heading. The effect of including the net movement on the VAT account in operating cash flows means that there will be no need to eliminate the amount of VAT included in opening and closing debtors or creditors when carrying out the reconciliation between operating profit and net cash flow from operating activities.

30.91 Taxation cash flows excluding those in respect of tax on revenue and capital profits, VAT or other sales taxes should be included in the cash flow statement under the same standard headings as the cash flow that gave rise to the taxation cash flows. [FRS 1 para 40]. For example, employers' national insurance contributions and amounts paid in respect of PAYE to the tax authorities should be included in operating activities. Where the direct method is followed, they will be included in the amounts shown as paid to or on behalf of employees.

Capital expenditure and financial investment

30.92 'Capital expenditure and financial investment' is a new heading that resulted from the need to split the former 'investing activities' into two new headings, the other being 'acquisitions and disposals' which is considered from paragraph 30.98 below. The cash flows included in 'capital expenditure and financial investment' include the cash effects of transactions relating to the acquisition and disposal of any fixed asset (including investments) and current asset investments not regarded by the enterprise as liquid resources. For this purpose, fixed asset investments exclude a trade or business, or investment in an entity that is an associate, joint venture or a subsidiary undertaking. The cash flows relating to the acquisitions and disposals of these fixed asset investments are reported under 'acquisitions and disposals'. Therefore, cash flows relating to acquisitions and disposals of certain financial investments, for example long-term investments in gilts or other financial investments that are held purely for investment purposes and not for the management of liquid resources, would be reported under this heading, but returns on them would be reported under 'returns on investments and servicing of finance'. If no cash flows relating to financial investments fall to be included under this heading, the caption may be reduced to 'capital expenditure'. [FRS 1 para 19].

30.93 Cash inflows in respect of 'capital expenditure and financial investments' include the following items that should be separately disclosed:

- Receipts from sales or disposals of property, plant or equipment.
- Receipts from the repayment of the reporting entity's loans made to other entities or sale of other entities' debt instruments other than receipts forming part of an acquisition or disposal or a movement in liquid resources.

[FRS 1 para 20].

30.94 Cash outflows in respect of 'capital expenditure and financial investments' include the following items that should be separately disclosed:

- Payments to acquire property, plant or equipment.
- Loans made by the reporting entity and payments to acquire debt instruments of other entities other than payments forming part of an acquisition or disposal or a movement in liquid resources.

[FRS 1 para 21].

30.95 The amount paid in respect of tangible fixed assets during the year may not be the same as the amount of additions shown in the tangible fixed asset note. The difference may be due to a number of reasons. For example, tangible fixed assets may be purchased on credit, in which case the amounts for additions shown in the fixed asset note would need to be adjusted for the outstanding credit to arrive at the cash paid. Furthermore, the change in fixed asset creditors should be eliminated from the total change in creditors, to arrive at the movement in operating creditors, a figure needed for the reconciliation of operating profit to net cash flow from operating activities. Another example is where fixed assets have been acquired in foreign currencies. In this situation, the sterling equivalent of the foreign currency amount paid that is reported in the cash flow statement is not necessarily the same as the sterling equivalent of the cost recorded at the date of the transaction and included in the balance sheet, because of changes in exchange rates. In addition, where interest has been capitalised during the period, the figure for interest would need to be deducted to arrive at the correct amount of cash paid for the acquisition or construction of a fixed asset. The amount of interest capitalised and paid during the period would be shown under 'returns on investments and servicing of finance'.

30.96 A further example arises where assets have been acquired during the year under finance leases. Most companies do not show assets acquired under finance leases separately, but include them in the total additions figure for the year in their fixed assets movements note. Since assets acquired under finance leases do not involve any cash outlay at the inception of the lease, it will be necessary to eliminate the fair value of the leased assets that is included in the figure for fixed assets additions so that the true cash outflow for fixed assets actually purchased can be reflected in the cash flow statements (see worked example, para 30.192, 30.192). The finance lease rental payments should be analysed between interest and capital, with the interest element shown under 'returns on investments and servicing of finance' and the capital element shown under 'financing'.

30.97 Companies may invest to maintain their existing level of operations (for example, routine replacement of plant and machinery for normal wear and tear) or to expand that level of operations (for example by investing in new products, services or businesses). The original FRS 1 recognised that it may be difficult to distinguish clearly between these two types of capital expenditure in the light of constantly changing technologies, markets and processes, but nevertheless encouraged disclosure where such a distinction could be made. In practice, such disclosures were rarely, if ever, made. So the revised standard neither requires nor encourages their disclosure. However, it does require cash flows to be analysed between capital expenditure and acquisitions and disposals. This is a useful split, but should not be interpreted as reflecting replacement expenditure on the one hand and expenditure for expansion on the other because, depending on circumstances, expansion may be included under either heading.

Acquisitions and disposals

30.98 As already discussed in paragraph 30.97 above, 'acquisitions and disposals' is a new heading that is a subset of the former 'investing activities'. The cash flows under this heading are those related to the acquisition or disposal of any trade, business or an entity that is an associate, joint venture or a subsidiary undertaking. [FRS 1 para 22].

30.99 Cash inflows from 'acquisitions and disposals' include:

- Receipts from sales of investments in subsidiary undertakings, showing separately any balances of cash and overdrafts transferred as part of the sale (see further para 30.133).

- Receipts from sales of investments in associates or joint ventures.

- Receipts from sales of trades or businesses.

[FRS 1 para 23].

30.100 Similarly, cash outflows from 'acquisitions and disposals' include:

- Payments to acquire investments in subsidiary undertakings, showing separately any balances of cash and overdrafts acquired (see further para 30.133).
- Payments to acquire investments in associates and joint ventures.
- Payments to acquire trades or businesses.

[FRS 1 para 24].

Cash flows arising under this standard heading are discussed from paragraph 30.125 dealing with consolidated cash flow statements.

Equity dividends paid

30.101 As explained in paragraph 30.77, equity dividends paid by the reporting entity should be disclosed separately. These are dividends paid on the reporting entity's, or, in a group, the parent's equity shares. For this purpose, equity shares are those that fall to be treated as equity under FRS 4. The dividends paid should be the cash dividend paid and excludes any advance corporation tax. [FRS 1 para 25]. Dividends paid by subsidiaries to shareholders outside the group, both in respect of equity and non-equity interests must be reported under 'returns on investments and servicing of finance'. Therefore, equity dividends paid to minority interests should not be shown under this heading.

Management of liquid resources

30.102 The 'management of liquid resources' is a new heading that arises as a result of the abolition of former 'cash equivalents', which, as already explained in paragraph 30.10, was considered to be the main defect in the original standard. The revision, which drops cash equivalents and changes the focus of the cash flow statement to report only movements in cash, effectively deals with the concerns of company treasurers and others by requiring treasury activities to be reported under this new heading. This heading, therefore, includes cash flows relating to items that were formerly classified as cash equivalents and most liquid items that fell outside cash equivalents and which, by default, were reported as investing cash flows. The type of liquid resources that should be reported under this heading are considered from paragraph 30.44.

30.103 Cash inflows in management of liquid resources include:

- Withdrawals from short-term deposits not qualifying as cash – to the extent that they do not relate to deposits that qualify for net reporting under a rollover or reissue transaction as explained in paragraph 30.59.

- Inflows from disposal or redemption of any other investments held as liquid resources.

[FRS 1 para 27].

30.104 Cash outflows in management of liquid resources include:

- Payments into short-term deposits not qualifying as cash to the extent that they do not relate to deposits that qualify for net reporting under a rollover or reissue transaction as explained in paragraph 30.59.

- Outflows to acquire any other investments held as liquid resources.

[FRS 1 para 28].

30.105 Only cash flows relating to short-term deposits that are not repayable on demand and, therefore, do not meet the definition of cash would fall to be included under this heading. Generally, the gross cash inflows and outflows should be reported, unless the deposit is one that is continuously rolled over, in which case the net cash flows may be shown as explained further in paragraph 30.59.

30.106 Cash outflows and inflows relating to a wide range of other non-cash current investments would also fall to be reported under this heading provided they are easily and promptly convertible into cash through an active market without curtailing or disrupting the entities business as explained in paragraph 30.48. Although many such current asset investments may qualify as liquid resources, not all of them may be used in the entity's treasury activities. Some current asset investments may be held purely for investment purposes. Others may be held for trading purposes, although this would generally apply to banks and investment companies. Given that there is a choice as to which current asset investment can be used for managing the net funds or net debt position, the standard requires entities to explain what it includes as liquid resources and any changes in its policy. [FRS 1 para 26]. This is a sensible requirement as an investment initially acquired for investment purposes in one year could be designated as a liquid resource in the following year depending on the company's circumstances. A change in policy regarding the use of a particular investment would not give rise to any cash flows in the year of change, but would need to be reported as a non-cash movement in the reconciliation and analysis of net debt (see para 30.119). An example of a company that explains what it includes as liquid resources is given in Table 30.4.1 below.

30.107 The reporting of cash flows relating to the management of liquid resources is a significant improvement over the original standard as cash flows relating to treasury activities can now be viewed as a whole and kept separate from other investing decisions. The previous practice of reporting large volatile cash flows from short-term investing activities with the normal flows from long-term investing activities relating to the acquisitions and disposals of fixed assets and businesses merely served to distort the investing section of the cash flow statement and was not particularly useful.

Table 30.4.1 – Unilever Group – Annual Accounts – 31 December 1996

Notes to the consolidated accounts (extract)

23 Analysis of cash flows for headings netted in the cash flow statement (extract)	**£ million 1996**	1995
Capital expenditure and financial investment		
Purchase of tangible fixed assets	**(1 169)**	(1 214)
Disposal of tangible fixed assets	**134**	86
Acquisition/disposal of fixed investments	**(22)**	1
Purchase of own shares (employee share schemes)	**(20)**	(41)
	(1 077)	(1 168)
Acquisitions and disposals		
Acquisition of group companies 21	**(1 246)**	(798)
Cash balances of businesses acquired	**31**	67
Consideration paid in respect of acquisitions made in previous years	**(1)**	(9)
Disposal of group companies 21	**344**	96
Cash balances of businesses sold	**1**	(2)
Consideration received in respect of disposals made in previous years	**3**	21
	(868)	(625)
Management of liquid resources		
Purchase of current investments	**(409)**	(383)
Sale of current investments	**342**	547
(Increase)/decrease in cash on deposit	**(226)**	94
	(293)	258
Financing		
Issue of ordinary share capital (employee share schemes)	**-**	3
Issue of shares by group companies to minority shareholders	**14**	14
Debt due within one year:		
Increases	**1 381**	1 529
Repayments	**(1 473)**	(1 790)
Debt due after one year:		
Increases	**507**	315
Repayments	**(135)**	(148)
	294	(77)

Included as liquid resources are term deposits of less than one year, government securities and AI/PI rated corporate commercial paper.

Financing

30.108 Financing cash flows comprise receipts from or repayments to external providers of finance. [FRS 1 para 29]. They will generally include the cash effects of transactions relating to the manner in which the operating and investing activities of the enterprise have been financed. However, only cash flows that relate to the principal amounts of finance are dealt with under this heading, since the cash flows relating to the servicing of finance (that is, dividends and interest) are dealt with under returns on investments and servicing of finance heading and equity dividends paid.

30.109 Cash inflows in respect of financing include the following items:

- Receipts from issuing shares or other equity instruments.

- Receipts from issuing debentures, loans, notes and bonds, and from other long and short-term borrowings (other than bank overdrafts).

[FRS 1 para 30].

30.110 Cash outflows in respect of financing include the following items:

- Repayments of amounts borrowed (other than overdrafts). The treatment of discounts and premiums on debt instruments is considered in paragraph 30.180 below.

- The capital element of finance lease rental payments.

- Payments to re-acquire or redeem the entity's shares.

- Payments of expenses or commissions on any issue of equity shares.

[FRS 1 para 31].

Table 30.5 shown below provides an illustration of the items that are normally included under this heading.

Table 30.5 – Coats Viyella Plc – Annual Report and Accounts - 31 December 1996

32 Notes to the cash flow statement (extract)

b Analysis of financing cash flows		1996 £m	1995 £m
Issue of ordinary share capital		2.5	2.6
Issue of shares to minorities		1.7	0.5
Redemption of minorities		(0.1)	-
		4.1	3.1
(Decrease)/increase in borrowings:	– new long-term loans	1.9	69.2
	– new short-term loans	111.5	153.3
	– repayment of amounts borrowed	(127.9)	(127.2)
	– redemption of convertible debt	-	(6.7)
	– capital element of finance lease rental payments	(4.7)	(6.4)
		(19.2)	82.2
Net cash (outflow)/inflow from financing		(15.1)	85.3

30.111 The cash flows under financing can be shown in a single section with those under 'management of liquid resources', provided that separate subtotals for each are given. [FRS 1 para 29]. The flexibility to report cash flows relating to liquid resources and financing under a combined heading may appeal to a number of companies that manage their borrowings and liquid investments as an integrated treasury operation (See Table 30.0.2 on page 1).

Exceptional and extraordinary cash flows

30.112 Where cash flows relate to items that are classed as exceptional, these exceptional cash flows should be shown under the appropriate standard heading, according to the nature of each item. The exceptional cash flows should be separately identified in the cash flow statement or a note to it and the relationship between the cash flows and the exceptional item should be explained. [FRS 1 para 37].

30.113 FRS 3 requires three exceptional items to be reported after operating profit:

- Profits or losses on the sale or termination of an operation.
- Profits or losses on sale of fixed assets.
- Costs of a fundamental reorganisation or restructuring.

The first two items are not themselves cash flows, but the net cash proceeds from the sale of operations will fall to be included under 'acquisitions and disposals', and those arising from the sale of fixed assets under 'capital expenditure and financial investment', irrespective of where the gain or loss is charged in the profit and loss account (see further paras 30.182 to 30.185).

30.114 The disclosure of cash flows relating to costs of a fundamental reorganisation or restructuring that is reported outside operating profit is not so clear. In general, the cash outflows are likely to include an amalgam of items, such as:

- Redundancy costs.
- Costs associated with the elimination and reduction of product lines.
- Costs to consolidate or relocate plant facilities.
- Costs for new systems developments or acquisition.
- Costs to retrain employees to use newly deployed systems.
- Losses on asset impairments and disposal of assets.

However, as stated in paragraph 30.67 above, the standard makes it clear that the cash flows relating to any operating items should be reported in operating cash flow, whether or not the costs are included in operating profit. This means that the nature of each item included within the total reorganisation costs needs to be analysed, with the result that some cash flows fall to be reported under operating activities, some under capital expenditure and some under acquisitions and disposals.

30.115 The original standard had no clear rules and so in the past the analysis mentioned above was rarely done. Companies tended to include the total cash flow effect of a fundamental reorganisation or restructuring within operating cash flows by disclosing it either separately on the face of the cash flow statement (see Table 30.6), or showing the amounts expended as a separate line item in the note of the reconciliation of operating profit to net operating cash flows (see Table 30.7). Given the new requirement that cash flows relating to operating items should be included in operating cash flows, irrespective of where the costs are reported in the profit and loss account, it is doubtful whether companies will be able to use the presentation given in Table 30.6 and Table 30.7 without carrying out a proper analysis. The cash flow effect of reorganisation provisions arising on an acquisition of a subsidiary is considered in paragraph 30.186 below.

Table 30.6 – Imperial Chemical Industries PLC – Annual report and accounts – 31 December 1995

statement of group cash flow (extract)
for the year ended 31 December 1995

	Notes	**1995 £m**	1994 £m
Cash inflow from operating activities			
Net cash inflow before exceptional items	26	**1,277**	1,032
Outflow related to exceptional items	27	**(86)**	(144)
Net cash inflow from operating activities		**1,191**	888

[The next page is 30035.]

notes relating to the accounts (extract)

27 Outflow related to exceptional items

This includes expenditure charged to exceptional provisions relating to business rationalisation and restructuring and for sale or closure of operations, including severance and other employee costs, plant demolition and site clearance. The major part of the 1995 expenditure related to provisions raised in 1992 and 1994.

Table 30.7 – Bass PLC – Annual Report – 30 September 1993

GROUP CASH FLOW STATEMENT (extract)

(I) RECONCILIATION OF PROFIT ON ORDINARY ACTIVITIES BEFORE INTEREST TO NET CASH INFLOW FROM OPERATING ACTIVITIES	1993 £m	1992 £m
PROFIT ON ORDINARY ACTIVITIES BEFORE INTEREST	**590**	519
Depreciation	**180**	178
Loss on disposal of fixed assets	**10**	11
Loss/(surplus) on disposal of operations	**3**	(3)
Decrease/(increase) in stocks	**59**	(7)
(Increase)/decrease in debtors	**(11)**	36
Decrease in creditors	**(20)**	(64)
Amortisation of and provisions against investments	**24**	20
Cost of fundamental reorganisation provided	**-**	75
Provisions expended:		
Acquisition	**(41)**	(50)
Reorganisation	**(44)**	(80)
NET CASH INFLOW FROM OPERATING ACTIVITIES	**750**	635

NOTES TO THE FINANCIAL STATEMENTS (extract)

16 PROVISIONS FOR LIABILITIES AND CHARGES (extract)

Reorganisation provisions were created over a number of years in relation to a major programme of fundamental reorganisation which established the present divisional structure and led to rationalisation within the Brewing, Pubs and Leisure divisions designed in part to reduce the operational cost bases and in part to improve efficiency. Acquisition provisions were created in connection with the purchase of the Holiday Inn Business in North America and Granada Leisure to reflect the costs of integrating these businesses into the Group.

30.116 There may be instances where the cash flows are exceptional because of their size or incidence, but are not related to items that are treated as exceptional in the profit and loss account. These exceptional cash flows should also be disclosed and sufficient explanation given to explain their cause and nature. [FRS 1 para 38]. An example cited in the explanatory paragraph of the standard is that of a large prepayment against a pension liability which is not reported as part of an exceptional or extraordinary item in the profit and loss account. [FRS 1 para 63]. Disclosure of exceptional cash flows where there is no corresponding exceptional item in the profit and loss account is likely to arise where the provision to which the cash flows relates was reported as an exceptional item in a previous period.

30.117 It follows from the requirements explained in paragraphs 30.112 and 30.116 that the cash flow statement should disclose separately any cash flows that are exceptional because of their size or incidence, irrespective of whether or not they relate to items that are reported as exceptional in the profit and loss account. Sufficient disclosure of the nature of the exceptional item and the related cash flows should also be given in a note to the cash flow statement so that users may gain an understanding of how these transactions have affected the reporting entity's cash flows.

30.118 Cash flows from extraordinary items would be reported in a similar manner. [FRS 1 paras 37]. In practice, however, such cash flows will rarely arise, if at all, following the virtual abolition of extraordinary items under FRS 3 (see further chapter 7).

Reconciliation with balance sheet figures

Reconciliation to net debt

30.119 One of the objectives of the cash flow statement is to provide information that is useful in assessing the liquidity, solvency and financial adaptability of an enterprise. Critics of the original standard argued that this objective was not met by a cash flow statement that focused only on the changes in cash and cash equivalents. Indeed, many companies chose to give additional information that highlighted the movement in net funds or net debt, which they regarded as more useful than the movements in cash and cash equivalents in providing a better indication of the liquidity and solvency of their businesses. In its revision of FRS 1, the ASB acknowledged that the movement in net debt, which is a widely used financial indicator, can provide useful information about changes in liquidity on a broader basis than that provided solely by the movement in cash balances.

30.120 The revised standard, therefore, requires a note that reconciles the movement of cash in the period with the movement in *net debt* for the period. The changes in net debt should be analysed from the opening to the closing component amounts as shown in the opening and closing balance sheets. The reconciliation is not part of the cash flow statement and, if adjoining the cash flow statement (for example, presented at the foot of the statement), it should be clearly labelled and kept separate. [FRS 1 para 33]. For this purpose, net debt is defined to include the borrowings of the reporting entity (comprising debt as defined in FRS 4, together with related derivatives and obligations under finance leases), less cash (including overdrafts) and liquid resources. Where cash and liquid resources exceed the borrowings of the entity, reference should be made to 'net funds' rather than to 'net debt'. [FRS 1 para 2].

30.121 The reconciliation should begin with the increase or decrease in cash for the period as shown at the bottom of the cash flow statement. Because this movement in cash includes cash flows relating to management of liquid resources and cash flows relating to borrowings included in financing, these cash flows should be added back to give the total change in net debt resulting from cash flows during the period. These separate components of cash flows should be separately disclosed in the reconciliation where material. There may be other changes in net debt for the period that do not arise from cash flows. Typically these non-cash movements may relate to items such as exchange differences, acquisition of assets under finance leases, loans and finance leases acquired as part of an acquisition and other movements that have an effect on the closing figure for net debt. These non-cash changes in net debt should also be disclosed in the reconciliation, if material. [FRS 1 para 33]. The way in which this reconciliation should be carried out is shown in the worked example on page 77.

30.122 The total change in net debt arising from both cash flows and non cash items should then be reconciled with the opening and closing net debt amounts. In particular, the standard requires the following reconciling items to be disclosed, where material:

- The cash flows relating to the separate component of net debt as explained above.
- The acquisition or disposal of subsidiary undertakings. These relate to borrowings acquired or transferred as part of the acquisition or disposal of a subsidiary undertaking because these are not reflected in the financing section of the cash flow statement, but have an effect on the closing amount of net debt.
- Other non-cash changes – an example being the acquisition of fixed assets under finance leases.
- The recognition of changes in market value and exchange rate movements. For example, changes in market values relating to current asset investments that are treated as liquid resources do not have any cash flow impact during the period, but may affect the carrying value of those investments at the balance sheet date (for example, if the company has a policy of marking to market such investments). Similarly, exchange rate adjustments arising from the ret ranslation of opening foreign currency cash and borrowings and those arising from translating the cash flows of subsidiaries at rates other than the year end rate, do not give rise to any cash flows, but form part of the carrying values of cash and borrowings at the period end.

[FRS 1 para 33].

30.122.1 An example of a reconciliation required by the standard is given in Table 30.8 below.

Table 30.8 – Airtours plc – Annual Report and Accounts – 30 September 1996

Notes to the financial statements

25) **Reconciliation of net cash flow to movement in net funds**

	1996 £000	Restated 1995 £000
(Decrease)/increase in cash in the year	(26,310)	53,544
Cash outflow/(inflow) from decrease/(increase) in debt and lease financing	15,142	(83,459)
Cash outflow/(inflow) from increase/(decrease) in liquid resources	156,928	(41,801)
Changes in net debt resulting from cash flows	145,760	(71,716)
Loans and finance leases acquired with subsidiary undertakings	(15,040)	(1,606)
Transfer to accruals	-	29,641
New unsecured loan notes	-	(9,000)
Provisions	-	(38)
Exchange differences	(5,142)	2,074
Movement in net funds in the year	125,578	(50,645)
Net funds at 1st October	223,005	273,650
Net funds at 30th September	**348,583**	223,005

[The next paragraph is 30.123.]

Analysis of changes in net debt

30.123 Where the opening and closing amounts of net debt shown in the above reconciliation are not readily apparent, because they are included under different balance sheet headings, sufficient details should be shown to enable the cash and other components of net debt to be respectively traced back to the amounts shown under the equivalent caption in the balance sheet. [FRS 1 para 33]. For example, bank loans and overdrafts included as a single figure within current liabilities would need to be identified separately because overdrafts, unlike other borrowings, are included within the cash component of net debt. Another example where separate identification may be necessary relates to the situation where some current asset investments are used for managing liquid resources, but others are not. This additional note is also necessary to enable the movements in net debt for the period to be readily understood. For example, the reclassification of an amount of debt from long-term to current categories in the balance sheet would not appear in the reconciliation to net debt, because it is a movement within the same component of net debt, but would need to be separately identified in the analysis of the changes in net debt for the closing amount of current and non-current debt to be readily identified with balance sheet figures. The ways in which an analysis of net funds or net debt can be presented are shown in Table 30.8.1 and Table 30.8.2 below.

Table 30.8.1 – Airtours plc – Annual Report and Accounts – 30 September 1996

Notes to the financial statements

26) Analysis of net funds

	At 1st October 1995 £000	Cash flow £000	Acquisitions £000	Other non-cash changes £000	Exchange movements £000	30th September 1996 £000
Cash at bank and in hand	142,416	(26,378)	-	-	(4,491)	**111,547**
Term deposits	162,088	151,953	-	-	-	**314,041**
Overdrafts	(65)	68	-	-	(3)	**-**
Debt due within one year	(35,216)	130	-	(185)	44	**(35,227)**
Debt due after one year	(43,958)	-	-	185	13	**(43,760)**
Finance leases	(7,012)	15,012	(15,040)	-	(705)	**(7,745)**
Current asset investments	4,752	4,975	-	-	-	**9,727**
	223,005	145,760	(15,040)	-	(5,142)	**348,583**

Table 30.8.2 – Bass PLC – Annual Report and Financial Statements - 30 September 1996

NOTES TO THE FINANCIAL STATEMENTS (extract)

29 Net debt 30 September 1996	**Cash and overdrafts**			**Other borrowings**			
	Cash at bank and in hand £m	**Over-drafts £m**	**Total £m**	**Current asset invest-ments £m**	**Due within one year £m**	**Due after one year £m**	**Total £m**
At 30 September 1995	69	(47)	22	684	(392)	(1,177)	(863)
Net cash flow (note 25)	(151)	3	(148)	-	-	-	(148)
Financing and liquid resources movement	154	-	154	(202)	69	7	28
Other borrowings acquired	-	-	-	-	(36)	(7)	(43)
Exchange adjustments	-	-	-	(1)	(4)	(4)	(9)
At 30 September 1996	**72**	**(44)**	**28**	**481**	**(363)**	**(1,181)**	**(1,035)**

30.124 It should be noted that the reconciliation of the movement in cash to the movement in net debt and the analysis of changes in net debt effectively combines the notes on the analysis of the changes in cash and cash equivalents, and the analysis of changes in financing that were required by the original standard. Moreover, the reconciliation to net debt and the corresponding analysis note is relevant only to non-financial companies. Banks and insurance companies are not required to give a reconciliation of net debt because the concept of net debt is not really applicable to them. Banks should, therefore, continue to give the notes reconciling the movements in cash and changes in financing with the related items in the opening and closing balance sheet. It should be noted that this requirement for banks is not explicitly stated in the standard, but is illustrated in example 3 in appendix I to FRS 1. Insurance companies, on the other hand, are required to give an equivalent note that analyses the movement in portfolio investments less financing, either adjoining the cash flow statement or in a note. [FRS 1 para 35]. A note linking the movements to the related balance sheet amounts for portfolio investments and financing is also required. [FRS 1 para 36].

Consolidated cash flow statements

30.125 The form and content of cash flow statements discussed above apply equally to any group of enterprises where consolidated financial statements are prepared. Therefore, a parent company of a group that is required to prepare a consolidated balance sheet and a consolidated profit and loss account should also prepare a consolidated cash flow statement reflecting the cash flows of the group. In preparing consolidated cash flow statements, adjustments should be made to eliminate those cash flows that are internal to the group. Only those cash receipts and payments that flow to and from the group as a whole should be included. [FRS 1 para 43]. Many important issues arise in preparing consolidated cash flow statements and these are considered below.

Minority interests

30.126 Where there are minority interests in any subsidiary that is consolidated as part of a group, the treatment of the minority interest in the consolidated cash flow statement should be consistent with the overall approach followed in preparing the group's financial statements. Companies are required by law and FRS 2 to eliminate intra-group balances and intra-group transactions in the consolidated financial statements. Therefore, they should do the same in preparing a consolidated cash flow statement even where minority interests, which may be substantial, are involved. (For example, where a subsidiary is consolidated because the parent has a participating interest of say 40 per cent and exercises a dominant influence, the minority interest could be 60 per cent.) Intra-group transactions should be eliminated because the group, including partly owned subsidiaries, is a single entity for financial reporting purposes. Therefore, in this situation, only cash flows that are external to the group, which includes those with minorities, should be reflected in the cash flow statements. In particular, the standard requires dividends to minorities to be shown under the heading 'returns on investments and servicing of finance', in the same place as non-equity dividends and separately disclosed.

30.127 FRS 4 requires minority interests to be shown as liabilities where the parent or any fellow subsidiary undertaking has guaranteed their dividends or redemption, or undertaken to purchase the minority shares if the subsidiary fails to make the expected payments. If minority interests are classified as liabilities, the dividends paid on those shares should be shown as part of the interest charge in the consolidated profit and loss account. It follows that, in the consolidated cash flow statement, the dividends paid should similarly be shown as interest paid and not as dividends to minorities; but they would still be included under the heading 'returns on investments and servicing of finance'.

Investments accounted on the equity method

30.128 Where a group has investments in associated undertakings or joint ventures that are included in the consolidation under the equity method, the consolidated cash flow statement should include only the cash flows between the group and those entities, but not the cash flows of those entities. [FRS 1 para 44]. This means that only the following cash flows should be included:

- Cash flows from investments in, and dividends from, the associated undertakings or joint ventures.

- Cash flows from sales or purchases between the group and the associated undertakings or joint ventures.

The same treatment will apply to any non-consolidated subsidiaries that are included in the consolidation using the equity method.

30.129 Specifically, the following information should be disclosed separately for equity accounted entities:

- Dividends received from these entities should be shown under their own heading. [FRS 1 para 12A].
- Cash flows relating to acquisitions and divestments should be shown under acquisitions and disposals. [FRS 1 paras 23, 24].
- Financing cash flows received from or paid to equity accounted entities should be shown under financing. [FRS 1 para 32].

Investments in joint arrangements

30.130 As stated in chapter 28, a company may have an investment in a joint arrangement, which does not carry on a trade or business in its own right and is merely an extension of its participants' trades or businesses. In that situation, the participants in the joint arrangement should account for their own assets, liabilities and cash flows, measured according to the terms of the agreement governing the arrangement, that is, the investor's share of the relevant cash flows of the joint arrangement will be included in the related line items for the investing company. Adjustments may have to be made to eliminate cash transactions between the investor and the joint arrangement.

[The next paragraph is 30.132].

Acquisitions and disposals of subsidiaries

30.132 When a parent undertaking acquires or disposes of a subsidiary undertaking during a financial year, the cash flows relating to the consideration should be reported under acquisitions and disposals in the consolidated cash flow statement.

30.133 The standard specifies the treatment of cash and overdrafts acquired or transferred on acquisition, or disposal, of a subsidiary. It requires that the amounts of cash and overdrafts acquired or transferred to be shown separately along with the gross consideration paid or received for the acquisition or disposal. [FRS 1 paras 23(a), 24(a)]. This is a change from the previous treatment under the original standard that required such amounts to be netted off against the gross consideration. It is hard to understand the basis for such a change. Presumably, the rationale for separate presentation is that the cash and overdraft balances acquired with, or disposed of with, the subsidiary undertaking are part of the subsidiary undertaking's working capital and, therefore, different in substance from the gross cash that is expended or generated by the group in the acquisition and disposal of that undertaking. An example is given in Table 30.8.3 below.

Table 30.8.3 – Airtours plc – Annual Report and Accounts – 30 September 1996

Group cash flow statement **(extract)**

Year ended 30th September 1996	Notes	1996 £000	1996 £000	Restated 1995 £000
Acquisitions				
Purchase of subsidiary undertakings		**(18,350)**		(41,384)
Acquisition expenses		**(2,337)**		(786)
Cash at bank and in hand acquired with subsidiaries		**8,509**		5,931
Net cash outflow from acquisitions			**(12,178)**	(36,239)

30.134 Recording the gross consideration separately along with the cash and overdraft balances transferred means that any fixed assets, working capital excluding cash and overdrafts, and borrowings of the subsidiary at the date of acquisition or disposal would need to be eliminated so as to avoid double counting. For example, stock, debtors and creditors acquired or disposed of would need to be eliminated from the total balance sheet changes in stock, debtors and creditors in the reconciliation of operating profit to operating cash flows. Similarly, borrowings including finance lease obligations taken over or transferred would need to reflected in the reconciliation to net debt and the note that analyses the changes in net debt during the period. The worked example at the end of this chapter shows the disclosure and the adjustments that need to be made for an acquisition (see page 80).

30.135 Where the consideration for the acquisition or disposal has been discharged partly in *cash* and partly by the issue of *shares*, the cash flow statement would show only the cash element of the consideration paid or received. This would be shown as a single item (along with any cash and overdrafts of the subsidiary acquired or disposed of) under the heading 'acquisitions and disposals'. The shares that are issued as part of the consideration in exchange for net assets acquired do not give rise to any cash flows and, consequently, they should not be shown in the cash flow statement, but disclosed as a major non-cash transaction in a note to the cash flow statement (see para 30.165 below).

Example

A parent company pays £20,000 in cash and issues £40,000 in shares and £50,000 in loan notes to acquire a subsidiary with cash balances of £30,000, borrowings of £60,000 and other net assets including goodwill of £70,000.

In this situation, the cash flow statement would show a cash outflow of £20,000 and a cash inflow of £30,000 under acquisitions and disposals, despite it being an acquisition. The loan notes of £50,000 issued and the borrowings of £60,000 acquired would be reported in the reconciliation statement that analyses the changes in the balance sheet amounts making up net debt. The shares and loan notes would be disclosed in the note giving details of material non-cash transactions (see para 30.165). A note summarising the effects of the acquisition indicating how much of the consideration comprised cash is also required (see para 30.137).

30.136 Where acquisitions and disposals take place during a financial year the cash flows of the group should include the cash flows of the subsidiary for the same period as the group profit and loss account includes the subsidiary's results (see further chapter 23). [FRS 1 para 43]. This is rather obvious, but care should be taken to eliminate all cash flows between the group and the subsidiary acquired or disposed of for the period that the subsidiary is included within the consolidated figures.

[The next page is 30043.]

30.137 The standard also requires significant amounts of other disclosures to be made in respect of the cash flow effects of a subsidiary acquired or disposed of during the financial year. First, a note to the cash flow statement should show a summary of the effects of acquisitions and disposals indicating how much of the consideration comprised cash. [FRS 1 para 45]. In order to show the effects of the acquisition and disposal fully, it is necessary to disclose separately the assets and liabilities of the subsidiary acquired or disposed of. In practice, the summary of the effects of acquisitions and disposals required by the standard can be combined with that required by the Act and FRS 6. An example of the relevant disclosures is given in Table 30.9 below.

30.138 Secondly, reporting entities are required to disclose, as far as practicable and where material, the extent to which the amounts reported under each of the standard headings have been affected by the cash flows of the subsidiary acquired or disposed of during the year. This information can be given by segregating cash flows between continuing and discontinued operations and acquisitions. [FRS 1 para 45]. Consequently, users of financial statements will be able to ascertain the amount of the contribution to the group's cash flows that has been made by an acquired subsidiary and how much the group's cash flows have been depleted as a result of a disposal. This information need only be given in the financial statements for the period in which the acquisition or disposal occurs. [FRS 1 para 48]. In practice, it may be difficult, if not impossible, to give this information, particularly where the business of the acquired subsidiary has been integrated with the group. Therefore, unless the post-acquisition cash flows of the acquired subsidiary are clearly identified and segregated, it may be difficult to attribute cash flows as being strictly related to the acquisition. An example where a company has been able to disclose the material effects of an acquisition on the amounts reported under each standard heading is shown in Table 30.10.

Table 30.9 – Bowater PLC – Annual Report – 31 December 1993

NOTES TO THE CASH FLOW STATEMENT (extract)

	Acquisitions		Disposals	
IV EFFECTS OF ACQUISITION AND DISPOSALS OF SUBSIDIARY UNDERTAKINGS AND BUSINESSES	**1993**	1992	**1993**	1992
	£m	£m	**£m**	£m
Tangible assets	**162.7**	144.6	**10.9**	11.2
Business for resale	**13.5**		**13.5**	
Associates	**1.3**	1.5	**0.1**	0.1
Associates goodwill eliminated		(0.7)		
Equity holding in associate	**(16.6)**			
Surplus properties	**0.2**			
Working capital	**44.2**	50.3	**(1.5)**	3.9
Current and deferred taxation	**8.5**	10.2		
Provisions	**(49.5)**	(65.2)	**1.1**	1.5
Cash and cash equivalents	**14.5**	(48.6)	**(2.3)**	(0.1)
Loan capital	**(89.6)**	(176.9)	**(3.0)**	
Finance leases	**(0.3)**	(3.6)		(0.8)
Minority interests	**(1.0)**	(0.3)		
Goodwill	**239.8**	326.0	**47.4**	16.9
Surplus/(deficiency) on disposal			**10.3**	(0.6)
	327.7	237.3	**76.5**	32.1
Consideration: cash	**312.3**	226.0	**76.5**	32.1
deferred	**26.7**	11.3		
Taxation relief	**(11.3)**			
	327.7	237.3	**76.5**	32.1

V ANALYSIS OF MOVEMENTS OF CASH AND CASH EQUIVALENTS IN RESPECT OF ACQUISITIONS AND DISPOSALS OF SUBSIDIARY UNDERTAKINGS AND BUSINESSES	**1993**	1992	**1993**	1992
	£m	£m	**£m**	£m
Cash consideration	**312.3**	226.0	**76.5**	32.1
Cash and cash equivalents	**(14.5)**	48.6	**2.3**	0.1
	297.8	274.6	**78.8**	32.2

Table 30.10 – Bowater PLC – Annual Report – 31 December 1993

NOTES TO THE CASH FLOW STATEMENT (extract)

III CASH FLOW MOVEMENTS ARISING FROM BUSINESSES ACQUIRED AND DISPOSED DURING THE YEAR

	1993	1992
Acquisitions:	£m	£m
Net cash inflow from operating activities	**56.4**	53.7
Returns on investments and servicing of finance	**(4.9)**	(3.2)
Taxation paid	**(1.4)**	(2.3)
Investing activities	**(20.2)**	(39.2)
Net cash inflow before financing	**29.9**	9.0
Disposals have not had a material impact.		

Foreign currency

30.139 A company may engage in foreign currency operations in two main ways:

- First, it may enter directly into business transactions that are denominated in foreign currencies.
- Secondly, it may conduct its foreign operations through a subsidiary, associated company or branch whose operations are based in a country other than that of the investing company or whose assets and liabilities are denominated in a currency other than that of the investing company (a 'foreign enterprise').

30.140 The results of foreign currency transactions and the financial statements of the foreign enterprise will need to be translated into the currency in which the company reports. This translation process should produce results that are compatible with the effect of exchange rate changes on a company's cash flows and its equity. The accounting treatment of foreign currency operations in cash flow statements can be complex and, even though the standard has been revised, there is still little guidance on the subject. The guidance that follow deals with the treatment of exchange differences in individual companies first, followed by their treatment in consolidated financial statements.

Individual companies

30.141 Where an individual company has cash receipts or makes cash payments in a foreign currency, it is consistent with the objectives of cash flow statements that those receipts and payments should be translated into the reporting currency at the rate ruling at the date on which the receipt or payment is received or paid.

30.142 Exchange differences may, therefore, arise because of a rate change between the transaction date (the date at which the transaction is recorded) and the settlement date. Exchange differences also arise where a transaction remains unsettled (that is, not realised in cash) at the balance sheet date and is required to be retranslated at that date. Such differences relate to the retranslation of monetary assets and liabilities.

Settled transactions

30.143 Where a transaction is *settled* at an exchange rate which differs from that used when the transaction was initially recorded, the exchange difference will be recognised in the profit and loss account of the period in which the settlement takes place. To the extent that the settled transaction relates to operations, the gain or loss would be included in arriving at operating profit. This exchange gain or loss would also have the effect of increasing or decreasing the reporting currency equivalent of amounts paid or received in cash settlement. Consequently, no adjustment for the exchange gain or loss is necessary in the reconciliation of operating profit to operating cash flow. Consider the following example:

Example

A UK company was set up in January 19X5 and raised £200,000 by issuing shares. It purchased goods for resale from France in February 19X5 for FF992,500 when the exchange rate was £1 = FF7.94. It entered the purchase in its stock records as: FF992,500 @ 7.94 = £125,000. Under the terms of the contract, the company settled the debt in October 19X5 when the exchange rate was £1 = FF8.58. The amount paid in settlement was: FF992,500 @ 8.58 = £115,676. The company would, therefore, record an exchange gain of £125,000 – £115,676 = £9,324 in arriving at its operating profit for the year.

Assuming that there are no other transactions during the year and the stock remained unsold at the balance sheet date at 31 December 19X5, a simplified cash flow statement is given below:

Cash flow statement		
	£	£
Net cash flow from operating activities		(115,676)
Financing		
Issue of shares		200,000
Increase in cash		84,324
Workings		
Proceeds of share issue	200,000	
Less: payment for stocks	(115,676)	
Increase in cash		84,324

Reconciliation of operating profit to net cash flow from operating activities	
Net operating profit	9,324
Increase in stocks	(125,000)
Net cash flow from operating activities	(115,676)

It is obvious that the net cash flow from operating activities comprises the payment of £115,676 for the stock. Because the outstanding creditor for £125,000 was settled during the year for £115,676, the exchange gain of £9,324 is already reflected in the payment and, therefore, no adjustment for the exchange gain is necessary in the reconciliation of operating profit to operating cash flow as illustrated above. Therefore, as a general rule, exchange differences on settled transactions relating to operations will not appear as a reconciling item in the reconciliation of operating profit to net cash flow from operating activities.

In the above example, had the settlement rate of £1 = FF 8.58 been the rate under a forward foreign exchange contract taken out to pay for the stock on the due date, the stock could have been recorded at the forward rate. In that situation, no exchange difference would be reported in the profit and loss account and the amount shown for the stock movement in the reconciliation would be at the forward rate, that is, £115,676.

30.144 Where a settled transaction does not relate to operations and the exchange gain or loss is included in the profit and loss account, but not within operating profit, the exchange gain or loss will be included as part of the cash flows arising from the settlement. An example would be income receivable from a foreign investment. In this situation, the sterling equivalent of foreign cash actually received would be shown under 'returns on investments and servicing of finance', and would include any exchange gain or loss that arises at the time of receipt reported in the profit and loss account below operating profit.

Unsettled transactions

30.145 Where the transaction remains *outstanding* at the balance sheet date, an exchange difference arises as a consequence of recording the foreign currency transaction at the rate ruling at the date of the transaction (or when it was translated at a previous balance sheet date) and the subsequent retranslation to the rate ruling at the balance sheet date. This exchange difference will generally be included in the profit and loss account. Normally such exchange differences arise on monetary items (for example, foreign currency loans, debtors and creditors). In the context of an individual company's operations, these exchange gains or losses will ultimately be reflected in cash flows. However, the way in which they affect the cash flow statement will depend upon the nature of the monetary assets or liabilities, that is, whether they are short-term or long-term.

30.146 Where they relate to short-term monetary items such as debtors and creditors, no adjustment for the exchange difference arising on their retranslation at the balance sheet date is necessary in the reconciliation of operating profit to net cash flow from operating activities, even though they do not involve any cash flows. This is because increases or decreases in the debtor or creditor balances will include exchange differences on their retranslation at the balance sheet date, and the total movement in debtors and creditors would form an adjusting item in the reconciliation of operating profit to operating cash flows. The effect is that the net cash flow from operating activities will not be distorted by such retranslation differences as illustrated in the following example.

Example

The facts are the same as in the previous example except that at the company's year end 31 December 19X5 the account had not been settled. At 31 December 19X5 the exchange rate was £1 = FF8.25 so that the original creditor for £125,000 would be retranslated at FF992,500 @ 8.25 = £120,303. The gain on exchange of £125,000 – £120,303 = £4,697 would be reported as part of operating profit for the year. The cash flow statement would be as follows:

Cash flow statement	£
Net cash flow from operating activities	Nil
Financing	
Issue of shares	200,000
Increase in cash	200,000
*Represented by closing cash balances	200,000

Reconciliation of operating profit to net cash flow from operating activities:

Net operating profit	4,697
Increase in stocks	(125,000)
Increase in creditors	120,303
Net cash flow from operating activities	Nil

It is clear that the exchange difference included in operating profit and in the year end creditor balance cancels each other with the result that operating cash flows are not affected. Therefore, as a general rule balance sheet movements in foreign currency trade debtors and creditors, except where they relate to foreign subsidiaries (see example below), will include the impact of exchange differences reported in operating profit and no adjustments for such exchange differences are necessary in the reconciliation.

30.147 Exchange differences on long-term monetary items such as long-term loans would normally be reported as part of the profit or loss for the financial year. To the extent that such differences are included in operating profit, they need to be eliminated in arriving at the net cash flows from operating activities. This is because the actual movement on long-term monetary items which includes the relevant exchange difference is not reported in the reconciliation of operating profit to operating cash flow. Whether or not the exchange differences are reported within operating profit, they should, nevertheless, fall to be included in the reconciliation to net debt and the note that analyses the changes in the balance sheet amounts making up net debt. Consider the following example:

Example

The opening balance sheet at 1 October 19X5 of a company consists of cash of £100,000 and share capital of £100,000. The company takes out a long-term loan on 31 March 19X6 of US$270,000 when the rate of exchange is £1 = US$1.8. The proceeds are immediately converted to sterling, that is, £150,000. There are no other transactions during the year. The exchange rate at the balance sheet date 30 September 19X6 is £1 = US$1.5.

The summarised balance sheet at 30 September 19X6

	£'000
Cash	250
Long-term loan ($270,000 @ 1.5)	(180)
Net assets	70
Share capital	100
P&L account	(30)
	70

The foreign currency loan having been translated at the rate ruling at the date of receipt to £150,000 (US$270,000 @ 1.8), is retranslated at the balance sheet date to £180,000 (US$270,000 @ 1.5). The exchange loss of £30,000 is recognised in operating profit for the year. The cash is made up of £100,000 received from the share issue and £150,000 received on converting the currency loan immediately to sterling.

Simplified cash flow statement

	£'000
Net cash flow from operating activities	-
Financing	
Receipt of foreign currency loan	150
Increase in cash	150

Notes to the cash flow statement

Reconciliation of operating profit to net cash flow from operating activities

Operating loss	(30)
Adjustment for exchange loss	30
Net cash flow from operating profit	-

Reconciliation on net cash flow to movement in net funds

Increase in cash in the period	150
Cash inflow from increase in debt	(150)
Change in net funds resulting from cash flows	-
Net funds at 1 October 19X5	100
Exchange difference on loan	(30)
Net funds at 30 September 19X6	70

Analysis of net funds

	At 1 Oct 19X5 £'000	Cash Flows £'000	Exchange movement £'000	At 30 Sept 19X6 £'000
Cash	100	150	-	250
Loans	-	(150)	(30)	(180)
Total	100	-	(30)	70

It is apparent from the above illustration that the exchange loss of £30,000 does not have any cash flow effect and, therefore, needs to be eliminated from operating profit. A similar adjustment would be necessary if the loan remains outstanding at 30 September 19X7. However, if the exchange loss of £30,000 is included outside operating profit, for example in 'other interest receivable/payable and similar income/expense', the exchange difference would only fall to be reported in the reconciliation and the analysis of net funds during the year.

30.148 Similarly, where exchange differences arise on the retranslation of foreign currency cash balances, they will not appear in the cash flow statement. This is because they are non-cash movements within the cash balances and will not form part of the increase or decrease in cash for the financial year. They do, however, form part of the reconciliation of opening to closing balances and will, therefore, appear in the reconciliation to net debt and the note that analyses the changes in net debt during the year.

Borrowings used for hedging equity investments

30.149 Where a company has used foreign currency borrowings either to finance, or to provide a hedge against, its foreign equity investments, exchange differences on the borrowings may have been taken directly to reserves in accordance with paragraph 51 of SSAP 20. These exchange differences will have no cash flow impact and will not be included in the cash flow statement or in the reconciliation of operating profit to net cash flow from operating activities. They must, however, be included in the reconciliation to changes in net debt and the note that analyses the changes in net debt during the year (as illustrated in the example above). Similarly, the exchange difference on retranslating the hedged equity investment (taken to reserve) has no cash flow effect.

Group companies

30.150 Where a group conducts part of its business through a foreign entity, different considerations arise from those for individual transactions discussed above. This is because the cash flows of the foreign entity are considered as a whole rather than as a series of single transactions. There are two commonly accepted methods of translation, the temporal method and the closing rate/net investment method. The latter method is generally used for translation purposes, unless the foreign entity's operations are regarded as being more dependent on the economic environment of the investing company's currency, when the temporal method is used (see further chapter 29).

Temporal method

30.151 Under the temporal method, all non-monetary items and profit and loss account items of the foreign subsidiary or branch are translated at the rate ruling on the transaction date or at an average rate for a period if this is not materially different. Where the reporting entity uses the temporal method to translate the financial statements of the foreign enterprise, then the only exchange differences that arise will be those relating to monetary items and these will be reported as part of operating profit.

30.152 By using the temporal method, the consolidated financial statements reflect the transactions of the foreign enterprise as if they had been entered into by the reporting entity itself. Accordingly, the treatment of exchange differences in the consolidated cash flow statement will be similar to that explained above for exchange differences arising in individual companies.

Net investment method

30.153 Under the closing rate/net investment method, the profit and loss account of the foreign entity is translated at the closing rate or at an average rate for the period. [SSAP 20 para 54]. FRS 1 requires that the same rate that is used for translating the results of activities in the profit and loss account of the foreign subsidiary should also be used for translating the cash flows of those activities for inclusion in the consolidated cash flow statement. [FRS 1 para 41]. This means that *all* the cash flows of the foreign subsidiary (not just those arising from its operating activities) must be included in the consolidated cash flow statement using the same exchange rates (average or closing) as were used for translating the results of its activities in the consolidated profit and loss account.

30.154 Where the group uses the closing rate method of translating the financial statements of a foreign entity, then all exchange differences relating to the retranslation of the opening net assets of the foreign enterprise to the closing rate will have been taken directly to reserves. As such exchange differences have no actual or prospective cash flow effect, they will not be included in the consolidated cash flow statement. However, where the opening net assets include foreign currency cash, overdrafts and loan balances then, to that extent, the exchange difference arising on their retranslation at the closing rate for the current period will have been reflected in the closing balances. Such translation differences should not be reported in the cash flow statement itself, but should be included in the effect of exchange rate movements shown as part of the reconciliation to net debt. [FRS 1 para 33(d)].

30.155 Where the group translates the foreign entity's profit and loss account at an average rate, a further translation difference between the result as translated at the average rate and the result translated at the closing rate will have been taken to reserves. This difference will include the exchange rate effect of the movement in foreign currency cash and overdrafts from the average rate to the closing rate. Under FRS 1, this exchange difference will be included with the exchange differences arising on the retranslation of the opening foreign currency cash, overdrafts and loan balances (as stated in the preceding paragraph) in the note that provides a reconciliation between the movements of cash to net debt. [FRS 1 para 33(d)].

30.156 In summary, the treatment specified in the standard has the effect of removing all exchange differences from the cash flow statement that do not have any cash flow impact in the reporting period. The treatment of foreign currency exchange differences in the consolidated cash flow statement can be fairly complex and the following example illustrates the application of the principles discussed above.

Example

Company A, a UK company, whose accounting period ended on 30 September 19X5, has a wholly-owned US subsidiary, S Corporation, that was acquired for US$600,000 on 30 September 19X4. The fair value of the net assets at the date of acquisition was US$500,000. The exchange rate at 30 September 19X4 and 19X5 was £1 = US$2.0 and £1 = US$1.5 respectively. The average rate for the year ended 30 September 19X5 was £1 = US$1.65.

The summarised balance sheet at 30 September 19X4 and 19X5 and an analysis of the retained profit for the year ended 30 September 19X5 of S Corporation, extracted from the consolidation returns, in dollars and sterling equivalents, are as follows:

Balance sheets of S Corporation

	19X5 $'000	19X4 $'000	**19X5 £'000 P&L closing**	**19X5 £'000 P&L average**	19X4 £'000
Exchange rate £1 =			**$1.50**	**$1.65**	$2.00
Fixed assets:					
Cost (19X5 additions: $30)	255	225	170.0	170.0	112.5
Depreciation (19X5 charge: $53)	98	45	65.3	65.3	22.5
Net book value	157	180	104.7	104.7	90.0
Current assets:					
Investments	250	100	166.6	166.6	50.0
Stocks	174	126	116.0	116.0	63.0
Debtors	210	145	140.0	140.0	72.5
Cash at bank	240	210	160.0	160.0	105.0
	874	581	582.6	582.6	290.5
Current liabilities:					
Bank overdraft	150	-	100.0	100.0	-
Trade creditors	125	113	83.3	83.3	56.5
Taxation	30	18	20.0	20.0	9.0
	305	131	203.3	203.3	65.5
Net current assets	569	450	379.3	379.3	225.0
Loan stock	150	130	100.0	100.0	65.0
Net assets	576	500	384.0	384.0	250.0

Share capital	300	300	150.0	150.0	150.0
Reserves:					
Pre acquisition	200	200	100.0	100.0	100.0
Post acquisition	76	-	50.7	46.1	-
Exchange difference					
Net assets ($500/1.5 – $500/2.0)	-	-	83.3	83.3	-
Increase ($76/1.5 – $76/1.65)	-	-	-	4.6	-
	576	500	384.0	384.0	250.0

Analysis of retained profit for year ended 30 September 19X5

	$'000	Closing rate £'000	Average rate £'000
Operating profit	135	90.0	81.8
Interest paid	(15)	(10.0)	(9.0)
Taxation	(30)	(20.0)	(18.2)
Dividends paid in the year	(14)	(9.3)	(8.5)
Retained profit	76	50.7	46.1

It is further assumed that company A does not trade on its own and its only income is dividends received from S Corporation. The summarised balance sheet of company A at 30 September 19X4 and 19X5 is as follows:

Company A – Balance sheets	**19X5 £'000**	**19X4 £'000**
Investments in subsidiary ($600,000 @ 2.0)	300	300
Cash	208	200
Net assets	508	500
Share capital	500	500
P&L account (dividend received: $14,000 @ 1.75*)	8	-
	458	500

* actual rate on date dividend received

Where company A uses the closing rate/net investment method, it may use either the closing rate or the average rate for translating the results of S Corporation. The summarised consolidated profit and loss account for the year ended 30 September 19X5 drawn up on the two basis and the summarised consolidated balance sheet at that date are as follows:

Consolidated profit and loss account for the year ended 30 September 19X5	**£'000 Closing rate**	**£'000 Average rate**
Operating profit of S corporation	90.0	81.8
Operating profit of Company A	8.0	8.0
	98.0	89.8
Adjustment – inter company dividend	(9.3)	(8.5)
Net operating profit	88.7	81.3
Interest paid	(10.0)	(9.0)
Taxation	(20.0)	(18.2)
Retained profit	58.7	54.1
Consolidated balance sheet as at 30 September 19X5		
Fixed assets	104.7	104.7
Current assets:		
Investments	166.6	166.6
Stocks	116.0	116.0
Debtors	140.0	140.0
Cash (S Corporation: £160; Company A £208)	368.0	368.0
	790.6	790.6
Current liabilities:		
Bank overdraft	100.0	100.0
Trade creditors	83.3	83.3
Taxation	20.0	20.0
	203.3	203.3
Net current assets	587.3	587.3
Loan stocks	100.0	100.0
Net assets	592.0	592.0
Share capital	500.0	500.0
Reserves:		
Retained profit	58.7	54.1
Exchange difference on opening net assets	83.3	83.3
Exchange difference on P&L account	–	4.6
Goodwill written off ($100,000 @ 2.0)	(50.0)	(50.0)
	592.0	592.0

In the above illustration goodwill has been translated at the rate ruling on the date of acquisition on the grounds that it arises only on consolidation and is not part of the net assets of the foreign enterprise. An alternative treatment is to regard the goodwill as a currency asset which is retranslated at the closing rate. In this situation, an exchange difference would arise on the opening net investment including the goodwill.

Given the above information, the consolidated cash flow statement drawn up in accordance with the exchange rate used in the profit and loss account and the related notes to the cash flow statement are as follows:

Consolidated cash flow statement for the year ended 30 September 19X5	**£'000 Closing**	**£'000 Average**
Net cash flow from operating activities	56.7	52.2
Returns on investments and servicing of finance		
Interest paid ($15,000 @ 1.5 and 1.65)	(10.0)	(9.1)
Taxation		
Overseas tax paid ($18,000* @ 1.5 and 1.65)	(12.0)	(10.9)
Capital expenditure		
Purchase of fixed assets ($30,000 @ 1.5 and 1.65)	(20.0)	(18.1)
Management of liquid resources		
Purchase of current asset investments ($150,000 @ 1.5 and 1.65)	(100.0)	(90.9)
Financing		
Issue of loan stock ($20,000 @ 1.5 and 1.65)	13.3	12.1
Decrease in cash	(72.0)	(64.7)

* Overseas tax paid relates to settlement of previous year's liability

Reconciliation of net cash flow to movement in net funds	**£'000 Closing**	**£'000 Average**
Decrease in cash for the period	(72.0)	(64.7)
Cash flow from increase in liquid resources	100.0	90.9
Cash flow from increase in debt	(13.3)	(12.1)
Change in net fund resulting from cash flows	14.7	14.1
Translation difference (see note 2)	29.9	30.5
Movement in net funds in the period	44.6	44.6
Net funds at 1 October 19X4	290.0	290.0
Net funds at 30 September 19X5	334.6	334.6

Notes to the cash flow statement

1 Reconciliation of operating profit to net cash inflow from operating activities

	Closing rate £'000	Average rate £'000
Operating profit	88.7	81.3
Depreciation ($53,000 @ 1.5 and 1.65)	35.3	32.1
Increase in stocks ($48,000 @ 1.5 and 1.65)	(32.0)	(29.1)
Increase in debtors ($65,000 @ 1.5 and 1.65)	(43.3)	(39.4)
Increase in creditors ($12,000 @ 1.5 and 1.65)	8.0	7.3
Net cash flow from operating activities	56.7	52.2

The movement in working capital in note 1 above could also be obtained by taking the difference between the closing and the opening balance sheet figures and adjusting the result to eliminate the non-cash effects of exchange rate adjustments. But this method is rather cumbersome as illustrated below for stocks:

	Closing rate £'000	Average rate £'000
Stocks at 30 September 19X5 ($174 @ 1.5)	116.0	116.0
Stocks at 30 September 19X4 ($126 @ 2.0)	63.0	63.0
Increase in stocks ($48)	53.0	53.0
Exchange difference:		
On opening balance ($126 @ 1.5 – $126 @ 2.0)	(21.0)	(21.0)
On movement ($48 @ 1.5 – $48 @ 1.65)	-	(2.9)
Increase in stocks included in reconciliation above	32.0	29.1

2 Analysis of net funds – Closing rate method

	1 Oct 19X4 £'000	Cash flow £'000	Exchange difference £'000	30 Sep 19X5 £'000
Cash				
Cash at bank	305.0	28.0	35.0	368.0
Bank overdraft	-	(100.0)		(100.0)
	305.0	(72.0)	35.0	268.0
Liquid resources				
Current asset investments	50.0	100.0	16.6	166.6
Debt				
Loan stock	(65.0)	(13.3)	(21.7)	(100.0)
Net funds	290.0	14.7	29.9	334.6

Analysis of net funds – Average rate method

	1 Oct 19X4	Cash flow	Exchange difference	30 Sep 19X5
	£'000	£'000	£'000	£'000
Cash				
Cash at bank	305.0	26.2	36.8	368.0
Bank overdraft	-	(90.9)	(9.1)	(100.0)
	305.0	(64.7)*	27.7	268.0
Liquid resources				
Current asset investments	50.0	90.9	25.7	166.6
Debt				
Loan stock	(65.0)	(12.1)	(22.9)	(100.0)
Net funds	290.0	14.1	30.5	334.6

* Note:

Movements in cash – (S Corp $30 @ 1.65 = £18.2 + A Ltd £8)	£26.2
Movement in overdraft (S corp $150 @ 1.65)	£90.9

See workings below for calculation of exchange differences

The effect of foreign exchange rate changes on net funds may be reconciled as follows.

	Closing rate	Average rate
	£'000	£'000
Cash at bank		
Opening balance ($210 @ 1.5 – $210 @ 2.0)	35.0	35.0
Increase in the period ($30 @1.5 – $30 @ 1.65)	-	1.8
	35.0	36.8
Bank overdraft:		
Opening balance	-	-
Increase in the period ($150 @ 1.5 – $150 @ 1.65)	-	(9.1)
	-	(9.1)
Liquid resources – current asset investment		
Opening balance ($100 @ 1.5 – $100 @ 2.0)	16.6	16.6
Increase in the period ($150 @ 1.5 – $150 @ 1.65)	-	9.1
	16.6	25.7

Debt – loan stock		
Opening balance ($130 @ 1.5 – $130 @ 2.0)	(21.7)	(21.7)
Increase in the period ($20 @ 1.5 – $20 @ 1.65)	-	(1.2)
	21.7	(22.9)

30.157 As can be seen from the above example, in practice, a reporting entity will find it simpler to require each of its foreign subsidiaries to prepare a cash flow statement with supporting notes, in its domestic currency. This cash flow statement can then be translated into sterling either at the average rate or the closing rate, whichever rate is used for translating the profit and loss account of the foreign subsidiary for consolidation purposes. The sterling equivalent of each subsidiary's cash flow statement can then be consolidated with the cash flow statement of the reporting entity after eliminating intra-group items such as dividends and inter-group loans.

Intra-group transactions

30.158 Transactions between members of a group located in different countries may not cancel out on consolidation because of exchange differences. As explained in chapter 29, these exchange differences are usually reported in the consolidated profit and loss account, particularly if they relate to intra-group trading transactions and dividends. Such exchange differences may have an effect on group cash flows. For consolidated cash flow statements, these intra-group cash flows may not cancel out unless the actual rate at the date of transfer is used for translation. In the previous example, the only intra-group transaction that took place between the parent and the subsidiary was in respect of a dividend payment. The consolidated operating profit after cancellation of the inter-company dividend is shown below for the two situations where the subsidiary's profit and loss account has been translated at the closing rate and the average rate.

Consolidated profit and loss account for the year ended 30 September 19X5	**£'000 Closing rate**	**£'000 Average rate**
Operating profit of S corporation	90.0	81.8
Operating profit of Company A	8.0	8.0
	98.0	89.8
Adjustment – inter company dividend	(9.3)	(8.5)
Net operating profit	88.7	81.3

30.159 As can be seen the amount of £9,300 and £8,500 is used to cancel the dividend paid by the subsidiary and not the £8,000 received by the parent. It would, therefore, appear that an exchange difference has been left in operating profit, which would need to be eliminated in the reconciliation of operating profit to operating cash flow. However, this is not the case. Deducting the amount for the dividend paid by the subsidiary in the consolidated profit and loss account at the same amount included in the subsidiary's profit and loss account translated at closing rate or average rate, cancels the dividend paid, and so ensures that the consolidated profit and loss account reflects the dividends received by the parent at the sterling amount received. In the consolidated cash flow statement, the same approach is adopted. In effect, the subsidiary's cash flows are reported at the closing rate or average rate, except that the dividend payment is reversed at that same rate and included at the sterling amount actually received by the parent. As a result, no further adjustment for the exchange difference is necessary in the reconciliation of operating profit to operating cash flow, or in the reconciliation to net debt. Indeed, this is to be expected as the transaction was settled during the year, any exchange difference already being reflected in cash flows. The standard, therefore, permits the use of an actual rate, or an approximation thereto, to translate intra-group cash flows in order to ensure that they cancel out in the preparation of the consolidated cash flow statement. [FRS 1 para 41].

30.160 If, on the other hand, the amount of £8,000 received by the parent had been used to cancel the intra-group dividend, the consolidated operating profit would have increased as shown below.

Consolidated profit and loss account for the year ended 30 September 19X5	**£'000 Closing rate**	**£'000 Average rate**
Operating profit of S corporation	90.0	81.8
Operating profit of Company A	8.0	8.0
	98.0	89.8
Adjustment – inter company dividend	(8.0)	(8.0)
Net operating profit	90.0	89.8

30.161 Using identical amounts to cancel the intra-group dividend in the consolidated profit and loss account does not mean that the exchange difference has been eliminated in the cash flow statement. The effect of using the actual amount received in the cancellation process means that the profits remitted by the subsidiary are being translated at the closing rate or the average rate. As a result the intra-group dividend paid and received does not cancel out in the consolidated cash flow statement. The difference of £1,300 for the closing rate or £500 for the average rate then needs to be eliminated. The standard states that if the rate used to translate intra-group cash flows is not the actual rate, any exchange rate differences should be included in the effect of the exchange rate movements shown as part of the reconciliation to net debt. [FRS 1 para 41]. It could be argued that it makes more sense to report this exchange rate difference in the reconciliation of operating profit to operating cash flows. This is because the subsidiary's cash has gone down by £9,300 and the holding company's cash has gone up by £8,000, resulting in a real economic loss to the group which normally falls to be recognised in the consolidated profit and loss account as explained in chapter 29. However, the treatment required by the standard ensures that the profit and loss account and the cash flow statement are treated in a consistent way. Because, in the above example, operating profit does not include any exchange difference on the intra-group dividend, it follows that no adjustment for the exchange difference is necessary in the reconciliation of operating profit to operating cash flows. The only other place to report this exchange difference is in the reconciliation to net debt.

Hedging transactions

30.162 Hedging transactions are normally undertaken by entities to protect themselves from financial loss, especially loss that would occur if prices or exchange rates were to vary. For example, an entity may purchase or sell a hedging instrument, such as a futures contract or a forward contract, in order to protect itself from price fluctuations that may arise in connection with the sale or purchase of stocks. The question arises as to how cash flows that result from the purchase or sale of the hedging instrument should be classified in the cash flow statement. Should these be shown under capital expenditure and financial investments or classified in the same category as the cash flows of the items being hedged, for example, under operating activities?

30.163 The standard provides that cash flows that result from transactions undertaken to hedge another transaction should be reported under the same standard heading as the transactions which are the subject of the hedge. [FRS 1 para 42]. This is a sensible treatment because it links the cash flows from hedging instruments that are accounted for as hedges with the cash flows arising from the items being hedged. The treatment required by the standard for hedging transactions applies only to futures contracts, forward contracts, options and swaps that are taken out as hedges of identifiable transactions or events. For example, the reporting entity may purchase a futures contract in order to reduce its exposure to increases in the price of a planned stock purchase and, therefore, any cash flows arising on the futures contract should be reported in operating cash flows. It should be noted that the ASB has decided to take a pragmatic approach on hedging because it is currently working on a project on derivatives which will consider all aspects of hedging.

30.164 The treatment required by the standard for hedged transactions cannot apply to situations where the reporting entity hedges a net investment in a foreign subsidiary with a borrowing that is denominated in the same currency as the net investment being hedged (the hedged situation explained in SSAP 20, see chapter 29). Accounting for the borrowing as a hedge is incidental; it cannot change the basic fact that it is still a borrowing. Furthermore, the foreign subsidiary may have contributed to group cash flows reported under each of the standard headings. Since the cash flows from the borrowings cannot be identified with any specific cash flows from that subsidiary, it follows that the cash flows from the borrowing can only be classified in the cash flow statement under financing.

Notes to the cash flow statements

Specific disclosures

30.165 In addition to the cash flow statement itself, the standard requires a number of explanatory notes to the cash flow statements. The positioning of these notes within the financial statements varies from company to company, but in general they are either presented immediately after the cash flow statement itself or are included in the notes to the financial statements with appropriate cross-references to the cash flow statement. Many of the specific disclosures that are necessary to supplement the information presented in the cash flow statement have already been discussed and illustrated by practical examples, but are restated below for completeness.

- A note showing the reconciliation between operating profit and net cash flow from operating activities should be provided. This reconciliation should disclose all differences between operating cash flows and operating profits (see para 30.72). This reconciliation should be presented either adjoining the cash flow statement or in a note to the statement.

- A reconciliation of the movement in cash to the movement in net debt should be provided showing the changes in net debt during the year and the way in which such changes are related to the opening and closing balance sheet figures. This reconciliation, like the previous one, may be presented either adjoining the cash flow statement or in a note to the statement. Where several balance sheet items or parts thereof have to be combined to permit a reconciliation, sufficient detail should be shown to enable the movements to be understood. This detail should be given in a note to the statement (see para 30.123).

- Where a group acquires or disposes of a subsidiary undertaking, the notes to the cash flow statements should show a summary of the effects of the acquisition or disposal. Disclosure should also be made of the extent to which the amounts reported under each of the standard headings have been affected by the cash flows of the subsidiary acquired or disposed of during the year (see paras 30.137 and 30.138).

- Major non-cash transactions should also be disclosed. Such transactions do not involve any cash flow, but have the same effect as if several cash transactions were made together. For example, conversion of debt to equity can be viewed as the equivalent of repaying debt in cash and then receiving cash on the issue of new shares. Because there are no actual cash flows, the transaction would not feature in the cash flow statement. But important information would thereby remain undisclosed merely because, in effect, a notional cash outflow has been cancelled by an equal and opposite notional cash inflow. Therefore, in order to report the activities of an enterprise in full, material non-cash transactions should be disclosed in a note to the cash flow statement if disclosure is necessary for an understanding of the underlying transactions.

Supplementary disclosures

30.166 In addition to the specific disclosures identified above, the standard *encourages* reporting entities to provide additional information relevant to their particular circumstances. [FRS 1 para 56]. The additional information that may be presented is considered below.

Reporting of gross operating cash flows

30.167 Entities are allowed to provide information on gross operating cash receipts and gross operating cash payments. [FRS 1 para 7]. Clearly, presentation of such information produces a cash flow statement in its purest form with new information that is not otherwise available from the profit and loss account or the balance sheet. The way in which such information should be presented is illustrated in Table 30.2 above on page 19.

Cash flows from discontinued operations

30.168 Entities are encouraged to distinguish between net cash flows from continuing operating activities and those arising from discontinued operations. [FRS 1 para 56]. Although not specifically required in the standard section of FRS 1, the analysis is given in example 2 of the illustrative examples included in the FRS. This disclosure is consistent with the separate disclosure in the profit and loss account of the results of continuing activities from those relating to discontinued operations required by FRS 3. Many companies have not given this analysis, but an example of a company that has separately analysed its net cash flows from operating activities between continuing and discontinued operations is shown in Table 30.11 below.

Table 30.11 – Pearson plc – Directors' Report and Accounts – 31 December 1996

Notes to the Accounts (extract)

25 Notes to consolidated statement of cash flows

a) Reconciliation of operating profit to net cash inflow from operating activities	**Continuing 1996 £m**	**Discontinued 1996 £m**	**Total 1996 £m**	Continuing 1995 £m	Discontinued 1995 £m	Total 1995 £m
Operating profit	**146.0**	**35.3**	**181.3**	237.6	22.0	259.6
Depreciation charges	**56.8**	**6.4**	**63.2**	54.7	6.8	61.5
Share of profit of partnerships and associated undertakings	**(53.1)**	**-**	**(53.1)**	(43.3)	-	(43.3)
Dividends from partnerships and associated undertakings	**33.5**	**-**	**33.5**	30.7	-	30.7
Decrease/(increase) in stocks	**4.6**	**1.9**	**6.5**	(34.6)	(1.9)	(36.5)
Decrease/(increase) in debtors	**21.8**	**(1.0)**	**20.8**	(80.3)	(0.2)	(80.5)
Increase/(decrease) in creditors	**59.9**	**1.0**	**60.9**	20.2	(2.0)	18.2
(Decrease)/increase in operating provisions	**1.6**	**(3.5)**	**(1.9)**	29.2	(0.2)	29.0
Exchange adjustments	**(7.7)**	**-**	**(7.7)**	2.8	-	2.8
Other	**(10.6)**	**(1.7)**	**(12.3)**	(5.1)	-	(5.1)
Net cash inflow from operating activities*	**252.8**	**38.4**	**291.2**	211.9	24.5	236.4
Purchase of fixed assets and finance leases	**(85.9)**	**(5.0)**	**(90.9)**	(97.6)	(4.3)	(101.9)
Sale of operating tangible fixed assets	**6.5**	**0.4**	**6.9**	31.6	0.5	32.1
Other	**10.0**	**1.8**	**11.8**	(20.1)	-	(20.1)
Operating cash flow	**183.4**	**35.6**	**219.0**	125.8	20.7	146.5

* Cash inflow for 1996 includes a £20.9m outflow relating to exceptional items charged in 1996 and £12.5m outflow relating to exceptional items charged in prior years.

Commentary on cash flows in operating and financial review

30.169 It is acknowledged that the assessment of liquidity, viability and financial adaptability of an enterprise requires more information than just a statement of cash flows. The provision of such additional information is now recommended by the ASB's voluntary statement 'Operating and financial review' (OFR), which is discussed further in chapter 33. The OFR provides opportunities for listed companies and other large corporations where there is a public interest in their financial statements to provide a commentary on their cash flows. The OFR recommends discussion in the 'financial review' section of 'funds from operating activities and other sources of cash' and 'current liquidity'. Many companies have taken advantage of this opportunity to provide further information on their cash generating potential and liquidity position that go beyond that required by the standard. An example is given in Table 30.12 below.

Table 30.12 – THORN EMI plc – Annual Report – 31 March 1996

Financial review (extract)

Cash flow and borrowings

Borrowings increased from £363.3m at 31 March 1995 to £391.4m at 31 March 1996. The principal factors were the inflow of free cash of £159.8m which more than covered the outflow of £143.4m on dividends. However, this net inflow was more than offset by a foreign exchange translation increase of £44.8m which resulted from our policy of protecting shareholders' funds by hedging foreign currency assets with foreign currency borrowings.

[The next page is 30065.]

Several movements contributed to the £43.1m reduction in free cash flow compared to 1995. The detail of the free cash inflow of £159.8m is shown in the table below. On the positive side, operating profit was £191.5m higher and fixed asset disposals increased by £42.3m. On the negative side, non-cash movements were lower reflecting the higher level of operating exceptional provisions taken in 1995, and provision utilisation was £23.2m higher due to spend on the withdrawal from UK electrical retailing.

Working capital increased by £131.4m, due largely to significant shipments by EMI Music in late March, settlement of the Dillons trade creditors, and a reduction in creditors as a result of the withdrawal from electrical retailing in the UK. Capital expenditure was £35m higher, mostly in EMI Music as it continued to invest in additional CD capacity and IT systems. Finally, tax payments grew by £45.2m as a consequence of both increased profit and the higher tax rate.

Free cash flow

	1996 **£m**	1995 £m
Operating profit	**520.0**	328.5
Non-cash movements	**579.7**	616.2
Provisions utilised	**(101.8)**	(78.6)
(Increase) decrease in working capital	**(58.7)**	72.7
Net cash inflow from operating activities	**939.2**	938.8
Capital expenditure	**(687.7)**	(652.2)
Sale of tangible fixed assets	**123.0**	80.7
Interest	**(34.9)**	(36.8)
Taxation	**(175.8)**	(130.6)
Other	**(4.0)**	3.0
Free cash flow	**159.8**	202.9
Free cash flow per share	**37.2p**	47.6p

30.170 In discussing the cash generated from operations and other cash inflows during the period, the OFR encourages companies to disclose and discuss segmental cash flows where they are significantly out of line with segmental profits, because of the impact of capital expenditure. [OFR para 31]. In fact, FRS 1 also encourages enterprises to give a segmental breakdown of their cash flows, but does not specify how this information should be given. [FRS 1 para 8]. Many companies, following SSAP 25, 'Segmental reporting', already give segmental information about their operations in terms of turnover, profits, capital employed, etc. The extension of segmental information to cash flows enables users to understand the relationship between the cash flows of the business as a whole and those of its component parts.

30.171 The type of segmental cash flow information that should be reported is not specifically identified by FRS 1 or the OFR, but ED 54 proposed that, as a minimum, an entity should give an analysis of the most important elements of operating cash flows between the major reportable segments. Clearly, there may be problems of allocation, such as common costs and interest, but they could be allocated between segments in the same way as other segmental information. Guidance on the allocation of common costs and interest is given in SSAP 25 and discussed in chapter 9. An example of a company that has given a segmental analysis of operating cash flows is shown in Table 30.13 below.

Table 30.13 – Bass PLC – Annual Report and Financial Statements – 30 September 1996

NOTES TO THE FINANCIAL STATEMENTS (extract)

28 Operating cash flow		**1996 £m**	1995 £m
Hotels:	Holiday Inn Worldwide	**184**	115
Leisure retailing:	Bass Taverns	**114**	204
	Bass Leisure	**(22)**	19
Branded drinks:	Bass Brewers*	**139**	160
	Britvic Soft Drinks	**43**	41
Other activities*		**(9)**	24
		449	563

* Figures for 1995 have been restated to include in Bass Brewers operating cash flow related to its overseas brewing operations which was previously included in other activities; this restatement amounts to £28m outflow.

30.172 Some companies are also disclosing 'cash flow per share' (see Table 30.12 above where Thorn EMI has disclosed an amount for free cash flow per share). Although ED 54 did not recommend the disclosure of cash flow per share on the grounds that it could be regarded as comparable to earnings per share and could be regarded as a substitute for it, there is, in principle, nothing wrong with disclosing this information. Indeed, there is no such prohibition in FRS 1. Cash flow per share information presented over time would reveal the trend of cash flows and, when compared to earnings per share, would demonstrate the quality of profits earned.

30.173 In discussing current liquidity, the OFR calls for disclosure and comments on the level of borrowings including seasonality, peak borrowing levels and maturity profile of both borrowings and committed borrowing facilities. [OFR para 32]. At present, financial statement disclosure about actual borrowings at the year end is provided by analysing bank and other borrowings by maturity period of up to one year, one to two years, two to five years and beyond five years. However, there is no requirement to disclose the amount of undrawn borrowing facilities (both committed and uncommitted). Disclosure of an entity's borrowing facilities together with its ability to access further resources will, no doubt, go a long way in providing useful information about the entity's viability and financial adaptability. However, the level of disclosure is left entirely to the company for obvious reasons. For example, companies could resist such disclosure on the grounds that it provides too much competitive information. Also the company's main bankers could object because disclosure may provide competitors with valuable information on their lending policies.

30.174 The discussion on borrowings suggested by the OFR should also refer to any restrictions on the ability of the group to transfer funds from one part of the group to another and restrictions and breaches of borrowing covenants. [OFR paras 34, 35]. The disclosure of the amounts of cash that are not freely remittable to the parent company coupled with sufficient information on the restrictions (for example, exchange controls) provides useful information for users of financial statements to make an assessment of the probable future effect of the restriction on the company's cash flows. As discussed in paragraph 30.175, the revised standard has now introduced required disclosures on the treatment of cash that is subject to restriction. Similarly, information on assets and liabilities denominated in foreign currencies, which incidentally is not directly relevant for supplementing information reported in the cash flow statement, may be useful for making assessments of a company's liquidity and financial viability. Information on any restrictive financial covenants on current borrowing agreements and breaches or likely breaches of covenants is equally important in assessing its viability and financial adaptability.

Restrictions on remittability

30.175 Sometimes cash may be held in a separate blocked account or an escrow account to be used only for a specific purpose, or held by subsidiaries operating in

[The next page is 30067.]

countries where exchange control restrictions are in force such that cash is not freely transferable around the group. The standard requires that where restrictions prevent the transfer of cash from one part of the business or group to another, a note to the cash flow statement should disclose the amount and explain the nature of the restriction. [FRS 1 para 47]. This is consistent with that recommended by the OFR as discussed in paragraph 30.174 above. However, disclosure is required only in circumstances where the restriction is imposed by external factors outside the company's control. Restrictions arising from a specific purpose designated by the reporting entity need not be disclosed. A typical example of disclosure is where a foreign subsidiary is prevented from remitting funds to its overseas parent, because of local exchange control regulations. [FRS 1 para 68]. Other examples given in the standard where disclosure may be relevant, depending on the regulatory environment, relate to cash balances in escrow, deposited with a regulator or held within an employee share ownership trust. The treatment of cash subject to restriction is considered from paragraph 30.190.

Comparative figures

30.176 Comparative figures should be given for all items reported in the cash flow statements and in the supplementary notes. Comparative figures are required for the reconciliation of the movement of cash to the movement in net debt, but not for the note that analyses the changes in the balance sheet amounts making up net debt. Nor are comparative figures required for the amounts included under each of the standard headings in respect of the cash flows of subsidiaries acquired or disposed of during the year. [FRS 1 para 48].

30.177 Normally, it is a relatively simple matter to provide comparative figures for all items reported in the cash flow statement itself. However, disclosure of comparative amounts for all items reported in the notes to the cash flow statement may cause some practical difficulties in interpreting this requirement. For example, the illustrative example in the standard provides a detailed breakdown of the assets and liabilities of subsidiaries acquired or disposed of during the year, together with an analysis of the net consideration paid or received in the transfer. Normally, such disclosures are also required by the Act and FRS 6, but only in the year of acquisition or disposal. If the strict wording of the standard is to be followed, then comparative figures would be required. Many companies do not provide such comparative information, although it is arguable that where an acquisition or disposal has taken place both in the current and the preceding year, the analysis of the net consideration should be given for both years in the notes as illustrated in Table 30.9 above on page 44.

Practical application of FRS 1

30.178 This section attempts to clarify some of the practical problems that may arise in interpreting and applying the revised standard. Although the revision of the standard has eliminated many of the problems encountered previously, nevertheless there are some issues that require consideration. No doubt others will arise in due course when companies have become accustomed to the new standard.

Balance sheet cash versus FRS 1 cash

30.179 The strict definition of cash used for the purposes of cash flow reporting explained in paragraph 30.41 above is unlikely to accord with the interpretation of cash used in the balance sheet classification 'cash at bank and in hand'. Although some companies follow a narrow interpretation of cash by including only cash held in current accounts and short-term deposits repayable on demand (former cash equivalents) under the balance sheet heading, others follow a wider interpretation by including the total amount of money on deposit with a bank or financial institution without regard to whether the deposit was short or long-term. If the wider interpretation was followed previously, the movements in cash as reported in the cash flow statement are now unlikely to agree with the movements in cash as disclosed in the balance sheet caption, because of the narrow definition of cash included in the revised standard. The differences are likely to be for those short-term deposits that are regarded as liquid resources and whose movements are reported under 'management of liquid resources' and for other long-term deposits that are not regarded as liquid resources whose movements are reported under 'capital expenditure and financial investment'. It may be that following the revision of FRS 1, some companies may change their balance sheet presentation of cash to accord with the strict definition used in the standard. An example is given in Table 30.14 below. It may also be that companies generally will use the term 'liquid resources' as a new item within the balance sheet classification of current asset investments.

Table 30.14 – TI Group plc – Annual Report – 31 December 1996

Notes to the financial statements (extract)

	The Group		The Company	
	1996	1995	**1996**	1995
Cash at bank and in hand	**85.4**	75.0	**23.4**	10.7
	298.6	345.4	**200.1**	260.5

Following the adoption of the revised FRS1, cash at bank and in hand now includes overnight deposits of £35.2m (1995 £21.2m) for the Group, and £23.4m (1995 £10.7m) for the Company, previously included in short term bank deposits.

Discounts and premiums

30.180 Where a deep discounted bond is redeemed or a premium is paid on the redemption of a debt security, the question sometimes arises as to where in the cash flow statement the premium should be reported. An intuitive response may be to include it within financing together with the other principal amount repaid on the instrument. However, under FRS 4 the discount on issue and the redemption premium form part of the finance cost of the instruments, which is reported in the profit and loss account as interest expense over the life of the instruments. The revised standard takes a similar approach. It requires that the cash flow effects of these items should be reported within 'returns on investments and servicing of finance' when the instruments are redeemed in order to provide a link between the

[The next page is 30069.]

profit and loss account and the cash flow statement as illustrated in the following example.

Example

A company issues a ten year zero coupon bond with a face value of £100,000 at a discount of £61,446. Its issue price is, therefore, £38,554 and the effective yield is 10%. How should the transaction be reflected in the cash flow statement?

At the issue date, the proceeds of £38,554 would be shown as a cash inflow in financing. The discount of £61,446 represents a rolled-up interest charge which would be amortised to the profit and loss account as an interest expense over the life of the bond while the bond remains outstanding. However, there would be no cash flow in these periods, because no cash has been paid.

On maturity, the discount of £61,446, which is part of the finance cost under FRS 4, should be shown under 'returns on investments and servicing of finance' separately classified, if material, as premium paid on redemption of bond in accordance with paragraph 15(a) of the standard. The balance of £38,554 should be shown under financing as repayment of the bond. The result is that a decrease in cash of £100,000 would be reported at the end of the cash flow statement. It should be noted that although the discount has been accrued over the years when the bond was in issue, the repayment of the discount on redemption means that the accrual should be adjusted as a non-cash change in the reconciliation to net debt as shown below:

Reconciliation to net debt	£'000
Decrease in cash in the period	(100,000)
Cash flow from decrease in debt financing	38,554
Change in net debt from cash flows	(61,446)
Other non cash changes – reversal of accrual for discount	61,446
Movement in net debt for the period	-
Opening net funds (say cash of £150,000 less bond of £100,000)	50,000
Closing net funds (cash of £50,000)	50,000

It is clear from the above example that accruals for finance costs would need to be reported as other non-cash changes in the reconciliation to net debt. This adjustment should be made both in the year(s) in which the accrual arises (as an increase in net debt) and in the year in which it reverses, otherwise the movement in net debt for the period cannot be reconciled with the opening and closing component of net debt.

A similar treatment would apply to the investor. The investor should record the payment for the bond of £38,554 as part of cash outflow in financial investment. On maturity, the receipt of £100,000 should be split and shown as to £38,554 under financial investment and £61,446 under 'returns on investments and servicing of finance'.

0.181 Where debt instruments are redeemed at a premium, it will also be necessary to separate the principal and the interest element of the amounts paid on redemption.

For example, where supplemental interest is paid on convertible bonds that are redeemed rather than converted, the whole amount of the supplemental interest accrued over the life of the bond and paid at redemption should be reported under 'returns on investments and servicing of finance'. Similar arguments would apply to non-equity shares that are redeemed at a premium. See further chapter 18.

Gains and losses

30.182 It is consistent with the objective of cash flow reporting that gains and losses that do not give rise to any cash flows should be excluded from the cash flow statement. Gains and losses are reported in the profit and loss account or in the statement of total recognised gains and losses of the reporting entity. To the extent that these are included in arriving at operating profit, they should be adjusted (gains should be deducted and losses added) in the reconciliation to arrive at the net cash flow from operating activities. For example, a gain on the sale of plant and machinery that has been included in operating profit (as a depreciation adjustment) should be excluded from cash flow from operating activities. The gain is not a cash flow as such, but forms part of the proceeds from the sale that are disclosed under capital expenditure in the cash flow statement.

30.183 A similar treatment would apply to gains and losses on investments. However, where investments are used for trading activities (typically by a bank or a financial institution), any gain or loss arising on their disposal during the year would be included in operating profit. In this situation, operating profit need only be adjusted for the movement in investments and not for the gain or loss arising (which is realised) to arrive at the net cash flow from operating activities.

30.184 Gains and losses on current asset investments that are regarded as liquid resources, would need to be eliminated from operating profit, if the gain or loss is also reported as part of operating profit, to give the correct cash flow from operating activities. Irrespective of whether or not the gain or loss is reported within operating profit, the gain or loss would need to be reported as a non-cash item in the reconciliation to net debt.

30.185 In relation to debt securities, a further question arises as to whether a gain or loss that arises on the early settlement of a debt security issued by a reporting entity should be reported as part of the finance cost under 'returns on investments and servicing of finance' or as part of the capital repayment under 'financing'. Consider the following example.

Example

The facts are the same as in the previous example except that the company has decided to redeem the bond early at the beginning of year 4 for £55,000.

The carrying value of the bond in the balance sheet at the end of year 3 is calculated as follows:

	£'000	£'000
Proceeds at beginning of year 1		38,554
Interest accrued in year 1 – 10% on £38,554	3,854	
Interest accrued in year 2 – 10% on £42,408	4,241	
Interest accrued in year 3 – 10% on £46,649	4,665	12,760
Carrying value (capital value of bond £100,000 less unamortised discount of £61,446 – £12,760 = £48,686)		51,314
Loss on redemption:		
Redemption payment		55,000
Less carrying value		51,314
		3,686

The loss should be allocated to interest paid, giving £16,446 (£12,760 + £3,686) to be reported under returns on investments and servicing of finance and £38,554 to be reported as capital repayment under financing. This treatment is appropriate because the total cash cost of the finance is reflected in the cash flow statement. Under FRS 4, the difference between the net proceeds of an instrument (in this example, £38,554) and the total amount of the payments made (£55,000) is finance cost (£16,446). As explained before, FRS 1 also requires the cash flow effect to be treated in a similar way. The alternative of reporting the loss incurred as part of the capital repayment, giving £42,240 (£38,554 + £3,686) to be reported under financing and £12,760 to be reported as interest paid under returns on investments and servicing of finance, is not considered acceptable.

Reorganisation costs following an acquisition

30.186 Where a company undertakes to reorganise the business of a recently acquired subsidiary, it may incur costs that are provided for in periods prior to the actual disbursement of cash. The question arises as to whether the subsequent cash outflow in respect of the amount provided should be disclosed as part of operating activities or 'acquisitions and disposals'.

30.187 Prior to the issue of FRS 7, 'Fair values in acquisition accounting', in September 1994, such costs were often provided for as part of the fair value exercise on acquisition, but FRS 7 now requires them to be reported in the post acquisition profit and loss account of the acquiring group. The cash outflows should, therefore, be reported under operating activities if such costs are also reported in the post acquisition profit and loss account in arriving at operating profit. Where the costs are reported as a non-operating exceptional item in accordance with FRS 3 and FRS 6, 'Acquisition and mergers', (that is, if the reorganisation is fundamental to the enlarged group), the exceptional cash flows would also fall to be reported separately under operating activities as discussed in paragraph 30.115 above.

Refinancing of borrowings

30.188 Companies may renegotiate their existing borrowings on terms that are different from those that were in place prior to the renegotiation. For example, as part of the renegotiation, a significant part of the company's current overdraft balance may be converted into a long-term loan. The question arises as to how such a reclassification should be dealt with in the cash flow statement.

30.189 The answer depends on whether the renegotiation gives rise to any cash flows. If the renegotiation is undertaken with the same bankers, it is likely that no cash flows are involved. In that situation, the proper treatment would be to reclassify the relevant portion of the overdraft balance from cash to financing in the notes that analyse the changes in net debt during the year. On the other hand, if the refinancing is carried out with a different bank, such that the proceeds of the new loan are utilised to settle all or part of the old overdraft balance, a cash inflow and outflow have taken place. Consequently, the new loan would be shown in financing with the result that the net movement in the overdraft balance will automatically be reflected in the increase or decrease in cash for the period.

Cash subject to restriction

30.190 The treatment of cash subject to restriction in the cash flow statement is not specifically covered by the standard, although disclosure is required, where access is severely restricted (see para 30.175). Nevertheless, the question arises as to how they should be dealt with in the cash flow statement itself. Consider the following example.

Example

A property company has secured development finance of £10m from its bankers during the year ended 31 December 19X5. The funds are held in a special blocked account to be used only for a specific development. Development on the property commenced during the year and by the end of its financial year the company had expended £2m. At 31 December 19X5, there was a balance of £8m in the blocked account.

- There is a view that the balance of £8m in the blocked account should not be included in cash, because to do so would create a distorted impression of the company's liquidity position. In that situation, the company would show the net cash outflow of £2m from operating activities, a cash inflow of £10m in financing with the balance of

£8m as fixed deposits under capital expenditure and financial investment. Adequate disclosure on the restrictions should also be given in a note if funds can only be drawn down with the banker's permission.

- An alternative treatment might be to treat the £8m balance as part of cash with a clear explanation of the nature of the restriction given either on the face of the cash flow statement or in the note that analyses the changes in net debt with balance sheet amounts.

The first presentation is correct because the definition of cash is not met in the second presentation. Cash held in a special blocked deposit account does not meet the narrow definition of cash as set out in the standard (see para 30.41, 30.41).

30.191 In general, the treatment of cash subject to restriction should depend on the nature of the item and the restriction in force. For example, client money is not generally available for business's own use and falls outside the definition of cash, even though it may be reported in the balance sheet along with the related liability. Another situation is where a company is required to give a bond or a guarantee to a third party, for example, a bond may be held by Customs & Excise for the clearance of imported merchandise. In that situation, the payment to Customs would form part of operating cash flows. Where there are restrictions on the transfer of cash from a foreign subsidiary to the parent in the UK because of exchange control restrictions, the cash balances held in the foreign subsidiary would be treated as part of group cash in the cash flow statement, provided they meet the definition of cash in the foreign subsidiary that owns them. Furthermore, this restriction would need to be disclosed as stated in paragraph 30.175.

Worked example

30.192 A worked example showing how a cash flow statement would be prepared for a group in accordance with the standard is given below. In order to prepare a consolidated cash flow statement for Alphabeta Plc, the consolidated profit and loss account, the consolidated balance sheet and certain other information related to the company are given. The starting point in the preparation of a cash flow statement is to compute all the increases and decreases in balance sheet amounts between the current period and the preceding period. Once the increases and decreases have been identified, each one must be analysed to determine its effect, if any, on the net cash provided or used in operating activities, returns on investments and servicing of finance, taxation, capital expenditure and financial investment, acquisitions and disposals, equity dividends paid and financing. If any increase or decrease affects more than one of the standard headings, each one must be separately analysed. In the example, each figure in the cash flow statement can be traced to the profit and loss account or balance sheet (via workings) by following the note references shown on the cash flow statement. The example does not deal with foreign currency operations as they have been covered in an earlier example (see para 30.156). Comparative figures for the cash flow statement have not been presented. The presentation of the cash flow statement and the related notes follow the illustrative example given in the standard.

Example

Summarised below is the consolidated profit and loss account of Alphabeta Plc for the year ended 31 December 19X5, together with the consolidated balance sheets as at 31 December 19X5 and 19X4. A cash flow statement for the group for the year ended 31 December 19X5 including notes to that statement is also given. The detailed workings supporting the figures in the cash flow statement follow immediately after the notes.

Alphabeta Plc
Consolidated profit and loss account for the year ended 31 December 19X5

	£'000
Turnover	47,852
Cost of sales	35,889
Gross profit	11,963
Distribution costs	2,814
Administrative expenses	5,250
Group operating profit	3,899
Income from interests in associated company	230
	4,129
Investment income	126
Interest payable and similar charges	(465)
Profit on ordinary activities before taxation	3,790
Taxation	1,600
Profit on ordinary activities after taxation	2,190
Minority interest	425
Profit for the financial year	1,765
Dividends	800
Retained profit for the year	965

Alphabeta Plc
Consolidated balance sheets

		19X5 £'000	19X4 £'000
Fixed assets			
Intangible assets	1	398	200
Tangible assets	2	17,082	12,800
Investments	6	1,230	833
		18,710	13,833
Current assets			
Stocks	3	6,586	6,821
Debtors	4	7,975	4,790
Investments		166	197
Cash at bank and in hand		2,541	2,050
		17,268	13,858
Creditors: amounts falling due within one year	5	10,909	8,085
Net current assets		6,359	5,773
Total assets less current liabilities		25,069	19,606

Creditors: amounts falling due after more than one year			
Debenture and other long-term loans	9	1,200	650
Obligations under finance leases	5	614	676
Provisions for liabilities and charges			
Pensions	10	426	103
Deferred tax	5	1,182	725
		3,422	2,154
Net assets		21,647	17,452
Capital and reserves			
Called up share capital	8	13,800	12,000
Share premium account	8	1,525	600
Revaluation reserve		600	392
Profit and loss account		4,225	3,260
Shareholders' funds		20,150	16,252
Minority interests	7	1,497	1,200
		21,647	17,452

Alphabeta Plc

Consolidated cash flow statement for the year ended 31 December 19X5

	Note	**£'000**	**£'000**
Net cash flow from operating activities	**I**		4,829
Dividends from joint ventures and associates	**6b**		150
Returns on investments and servicing of finance	**II**		(507)
Taxation	**5d**		(879)
Capital expenditure and financial investment	**II**		(3,888)
Acquisitions and disposals	**II**		(115)
Equity dividends paid	**5j**		(700)
Cash outflow before management of liquid resources and financing			(1,110)
Management of liquid resources	**II**		(439)
Financing	**II**		
Issue of ordinary shares		925	
Increase in debt		331	1,256
Decrease in cash in the period			(293)

Reconciliation of net cash flow to movement in net debt (note III)

	£'000	£'000
Decrease in cash in the period	(293)	
Cash outflow from increase in liquid resources	439	
Cash inflow from increase in debt and lease financing	(331)	
Change in net debt resulting from cash flows		(185)
New finance lease		(228)
Movement in net debt in the period		(413)
Net funds at 1 January 19X5		47
Net debt at 31 December 19X5		(366)

Notes to the cash flow statement

I Net cash flow from operating activities

		£'000
Operating profit		3,899
Amortisation of intangible fixed assets	**1b**	152
Depreciation on tangible fixed assets	**2a**	1,345
Gain on sale of tangible fixed assets	**2c**	(45)
Decrease in stocks	**3a**	600
Increase in trade debtors	**4a**	(2,432)
Increase in prepayments and accrued income	**4b**	(249)
Increase in trade creditors	**5b**	996
Decrease in amounts owed to associated company	**5c**	(50)
Increase in other taxation and social security	**5e**	254
Increase in accruals	**5f**	36
Increase in pension provisions	**10a**	323
Net cash flow from operating activities		4,829

II Analysis of cash flows for headings netted in the cash flow statement

		£'000
Returns on investments and servicing of finance		
Interest received	**4c**	102
Interest paid	**5g**	(236)
Interest element of finance lease rentals	**5h**	(120)
Premium paid on redemption of debentures	**5i**	(125)
Dividends paid to minorities	**7a**	(128)
Net cash outflow for returns on investments and servicing of finance		(507)
Capital expenditure and financial investment		
Purchase of patents	**1a**	(40)
Purchase of tangible fixed assets	**2b**	(3,974)
Sale of tangible fixed assets	**2d**	503
Purchase of fixed asset investments	**6a**	(377)
Net cash outflow for capital expenditure		(3,888)
Acquisitions and disposals	**Note IV**	
Purchase of subsidiary undertaking		(175)
Cash acquired with subsidiary		60
Net cash outflow for acquisitions and disposals		(115)
Management of liquid resources*	**Note III**	
Cash placed on short-term deposit		(470)
Sale of government securities		31
Net cash outflow from management of liquid resources		(439)
Financing		
Issue of ordinary shares	**8b**	1,000
Expenses paid in connection with share issue	**8a**	(75)
Issue of shares		925
New secured loans	**9a**	750
Repayment of debentures	**9b**	(200)
Principal payment under finance lease	**5a**	(219)
Increase in debt		331
Net cash inflow from financing		1,256

* Alphabeta Plc includes term deposits and government securities held as current asset investments as liquid resources.

III Analysis of net debt

	1 Jan 19X5	Cash flow	Other non-cash changes	31 Dec 19X5
	£'000	£'000	£'000	£'000
Net cash:				
Cash at bank and in hand:	2,050			2,541
Less: deposits treated as liquid resources	(780)			(1,250)
	1,270	21		1,291
Bank overdraft	(700)	(314)		(1,014)
	570	(293)		277
Liquid resources:				
Deposits included in cash	780	470		1,250
Current asset investments	197	(31)		166
	977	439		1,416
Debt:				
Finance leases	(850)	219	(228)	(859)
Debts falling due after one year	(650)	(550)	-	(1,200)
	(1500)	(331)	(228)	(2,059)
Net debt	47	(185)	(228)	(366)

Analysed in Balance Sheet	1 Jan 19X5	31 Dec 19X5
Cash at bank and in hand	2,050	2,541
Current asset investments	197	166
Bank overdraft	(700)	(1,014)
Finance leases		
within one year	(174)	(245)
after one year	(676)	(614)
Debentures and other long-term loans		
after one year	(650)	(1,200)
	47	(366)

IV Acquisition of Zeta Limited

On 1 March 19X5, a new wholly subsidiary, Zeta Limited, was acquired by the issue of 1,200,000 ordinary shares of £1 each, whose fair market value was deemed to be £1.50 per share and £175,000 in cash. The fair values of Zeta Limited's identifiable assets and liabilities at the date of acquisition (including goodwill) were as follows:

Net assets acquired	**£'000**
	310
Goodwill	1,550
Fixed assets	365
Stocks	480
Debtors	60
Cash at bank and in hand	(655)
Trade creditors	(135)
Accruals	1,975
Satisfied by	
	1,800
Shares allotted	175
Cash	1,975

Zeta Limited contributed £482,000 to the group's net operating cash flows, paid £75,000 in respect of net returns on investments and servicing of finance, paid £127,000 in respect of taxation and utilised £250,000 for capital expenditure.

V Major non-cash transactions

(a) During the year the group entered into a finance lease arrangement in respect of equipment with a capital value at the inception of the lease of £228,000.

(b) Part of the consideration for the purchase of Zeta Limited comprised shares. Further details of the acquisition are set out in note 4.

Cash flow statement workings

1 Analysis of intangible fixed assets

		£'000	**£'000**
Net book value at 31 December 19X4			
Net book value of patents and trade marks		50	
Goodwill net of amortisation		150	200
Additions during the year			
Patents and trade marks	**a**	40	
Goodwill arising on Zeta Ltd		310	350
Amortisation for the year			
On patents		10	
On goodwill	**b**	142	(152)
Net book value at 31 December 19X5			398

2 Analysis of tangible fixed assets

		£'000	£'000
Net book value at 31 December 19X4			12,800
Addition in respect of new subsidiary			1,550
Additions			4,327
Surplus on revaluations			208
Net book value of disposals			(458)
Depreciation for the year	**a**		(1,345)
Net book value at 31 December 19X5			17,082

Additions during the year include a warehouse constructed by the group for £1,925,000 of which £125,000 related to interest capitalised and new equipment purchased on a finance lease with a fair value of £228,000. Included in administrative expenses is £45,000 for the gain arising on sale of fixed assets.

Additions as above		4,327
Less: leased assets		(228)
Less: capitalised interest (see workings note 5)		(125)
Cash paid	**b**	3,974
Net book value of disposals		458
Gain arising on sale	**c**	45
Proceeds of sale	**d**	503

3 Stocks

		£'000
At 31 December 19X5		6,586
At 31 December 19X4		(6,821)
Decrease		(235)
Less: arising from acquisition of Zeta Ltd		(365)
Net decrease included in reconciliation (note I)	**a**	(600)

4 Analysis of debtors

	19X5	19X4
	£'000	**£'000**
Trade debtors	7,327	4,415
Prepayments and accrued income	648	375
	7,975	4,790

Trade debtors are stated net of provisions for bad debts of £960,000 in 19X5 and £485,000 in 19X4 respectively. The group wrote off £175,000 in bad debts and recognised an additional provision of £650,000 in administrative expenses.

Trade debtors		**£'000**
Trade debtors at 31 December 19X5		7,327
Trade debtors at 31 December 19X4		(4,415)
Increase		2,912
Less: arising on acquisition of Zeta Ltd		(480)
Net increase included in reconciliation (note I)	**a**	2,432

Note: The provision of £650,000 arising in the year has been included in the net movement on trade debtors and not separately identified.

Prepayments and accrued income

Included in prepayments and accrued income is interest receivable of £47,000 and £23,000 for 19X5 and 19X4 respectively.

		£'000	£'000
At 31 December 19X5		648	
Less: interest receivable		(47)	601
Less:			
At 31 December 19X4		375	
Less: interest receivable		(23)	(352)
Net increase included in reconciliation (note I)	**b**		249

Interest received		£'000
Receivable at 31 December 19X4		23
Investment income per P&L account		126
Receivable at 31 December 19X5		(47)
Cash received	c	102

5 Analysis of creditors

	19X5	19X4
	£'000	£'000
Bank loans and overdrafts	1,014	700
Obligations under finance leases	245	174
Trade creditors	6,004	4,353
Amounts owed to associated companies	193	243
Corporation tax	746	575
Advance corporation tax	267	234
Other taxation and social security	440	186
Accruals	1,200	920
Dividends payable	800	700
	10,909	8,085

Bank loans and overdrafts for 19X5 and 19X4 are all repayable on demand and included in cash.

Obligations under finance leases		£'000	£'000
Obligations at 31 December 19X4			
Less than one year		174	
More than one year		676	850
New capital lease			228
Obligations at 31 December 19X5			
Less than one year		245	
More than one year		614	(859)
Principal payment under finance leases	a		219

Trade creditors		£'000
At 31 December 19X5		6,004
At 31 December 19X4		(4,353)
Increase		1,651
Less: arising on acquisition of Zeta Ltd		(655)
Net increase included in reconciliation (note I)	b	996

Amounts owed to associated company			£'000
At 31 December 19X5			193
At 31 December 19X4			(243)
Net decrease	c		(50)

Amounts owed to the associated company arise on trading activities

Taxation		**£'000**	**£'000**
Balance at 31 December 19X4			
Corporation tax		575	
ACT		234	
Deferred tax		725	1,534
Tax charged per accounts:			
UK Corporation tax		980	
Transfer to deferred tax		457	
Prior year underprovision		103	
		1,540	1,540
Associated company		60	
Tax charged in P&L account		1,600	
Balance at 31 December 19X5			
Corporation tax		746	
ACT		267	
Deferred tax		1,182	(2,195)
Tax paid	d		879

Other taxation and social security			£'000
At 31 December 19X5			440
At 31 December 19X4			(186)
Net increase included in reconciliation (note I)	e		254

Accruals

Included in accruals at 31 December 19X5 and 19X4 is interest payable of £154,000 and £45,000 respectively.

		£'000	**£'000**
At 31 December 19X5		1,200	
Less: interest payable		(154)	1,046
Less:			
At 31 December 19X4		920	
Less: interest payable		(45)	(875)
Net increase			171
Less: arising on acquisition of Zeta Ltd			(135)
Net increase included in reconciliation (note I)	f		36

Interest paid on loans and finance leases:		£'000	£'000
Interest accrued at 31 December 19X4			45
Charge per P&L account:			
On overdrafts, bank and other loans		220	
On finance leases		120	
On premium paid on debenture redemption		125	465
Interest capitalised (see workings note 2)			125
Interest accrued at 31 December 19X5			(154)
Cash paid			481
Interest paid on overdrafts, bank & other loans	**g**		236
Interest paid on finance leases	**h**		120
Premium paid on debenture redemption	**i**		125
			481

Dividends paid by holding company		£'000
Balance at 31 December 19X4		700
Per P&L account		800
Balance at 31 December 19X5		(800)
Cash paid	**j**	700

6 Investments

		Associated company £'000	Listed Investments £'000	Total £'000
Balance at 31 December 19X4		603	230	833
Share of retained profits		20	-	20
Additions	**a**	-	377	377
Balance at 31 December 19X5		623	607	1,230
Share of associated company's profits (£230) less tax (£60)		170		
Less profits retained		20		
Dividends received	**b**	150		

Current asset investments

Current assets investments, which relate to British Government Securities, are classified as liquid resources by the group.

7 Minority interests

		£'000
Balance at 31 December 19X4		1,200
Profit for the year		425
Balance at 31 December 19X5		(1,497)
Dividends paid to minority shareholders	**a**	128

8 Share capital and share premium

		£'000	£'000
At 31 December 19X5			
Share capital		13,800	
Share premium		1,525	15,325
At 31 December 19X4			
Share capital		12,000	
Share premium		600	(12,600)
Net increase			2,725
Less: issued for purchase of Zeta Ltd			(1,800)
Add: share issue expenses written off	**a**		75
Balance issued for cash	**b**		1,000

9 Debentures and other loans

		£'000
At 31 December 19X5		1,200
At 31 December 19X4		(650)
Net increase		550
Increase consists of:		
New secured loans	**a**	750
Repayment of debentures (nominal value)	**b**	(200)
		550

10 Provisions for liabilities and charges

		£'000
Pensions		
At 31 December 19X5		426
At 31 December 19X4		
Increase included in reconciliation (note I)	**a**	(103)
		323

Comparison with IASs

30.193 The IASC rules are to be found in IAS 7, 'Cash flow statements', which was revised in 1992. These rules are significantly different from those included in the revised FRS 1. The principal differences, which are dealt with in appendix II to the standard, are summarised below:

- IAS 7 has none of the exemptions that allow many enterprises not to prepare cash flow statements under FRS 1.

- IAS 7 requires cash flows to be reported under three sections: operating, investing and financing, whereas FRS 1 requires cash flows to be reported in far greater detail under nine standard headings.

- The cash flows to be reported under IAS 7 relate to movements in cash and cash equivalents (defined as short-term highly liquid investments that are readily convertible into known amounts of cash and subject to insignificant risk of changes in value). The revised FRS 1 has dropped the notion of cash equivalents and requires the movement of cash (defined as cash in hand and deposits repayable on demand, less overdrafts) to be reported in the cash flow statement. Cash flows relating to former cash equivalents are reported under a new heading 'management of liquid resources'.

- IAS 7 requires most cash flows to be shown gross, whereas FRS 1 allows operating cash flows to be reported net or gross. [IAS 7 para 21]. IAS 7 requires net reporting of cash flows relating to customers where the cash flows reflect the activities of the customer rather than those of the entity. There is no equivalent provisions in FRS 1.

- IAS 7 does not require a reconciliation of movements in cash flows to the movement in net debt.

30.194 In 1994, the International Organisation of Securities Commission (IOSCO) recommended IAS 7 for the preparation of cash flow statements for cross-border listings. This has been followed by official endorsement of this by the SEC for filing of financial statements in the US by foreign registrants.

Chapter 31

Directors' report

Page

Chapter 31

Directors' report

Introduction

31.1 The directors' report is one of the documents that is included with a company's annual financial statements, laid before the company in general meeting and delivered to the Registrar of Companies. [Sec 241(1); 242(1)].

31.2 The duty to prepare a directors' report is contained in section 234 of the Act. However, section 234 does not contain all the disclosure requirements, but refers, instead, to Schedule 7 which contains much of the information that should be included in the directors' report.

31.3 It should be noted that the directors have a responsibility to prepare the report even if none of the directors, at the time the report is produced or laid before the company in general meeting, were directors during the period covered by the report. They cannot avoid this responsibility simply because they were not responsible for all or some of the activities that are being reported on.

31.4 The principal objectives of the directors' report are not only to supplement the financial information in the profit and loss account and the balance sheet with discussions and explanations about the company's activities and its future, but also to provide details of other non-financial matters. The purpose of the narrative information is to give the user of the financial statements a more complete picture of the company than he would otherwise obtain.

31.5 Although the extent of the detail to be included in the report depends on the nature and size of the company, most companies tend to comply only with the minimum statutory requirements. Listed companies regard the annual financial statements as an important mode of communication with shareholders. They, therefore, take the opportunity presented by statute and the Stock Exchange's Listing Rules to provide the shareholders with information about all aspects of the company's activities and the environment in which it operates, the company's objectives and its values. However, much of this information is generally presented outside the statutory directors' report, for example, in the chairman's statement or in a separate statement that deals specifically with the operating and financial review of the business (see further chapter 33). An example directors' report is given on page 3 of GAAP UK Plc – Example annual reports (see appendix I).

Matters to be dealt with in the directors' report

Principal activities

31.6 The principal activities of both the company and of its subsidiaries during the year, and details of any significant change in those activities, should be stated. [Sec 234(2)].

31.7 The term 'principal activities' is not defined in the Act, but is generally taken to mean the diverse industry segments or classes of business in which the entity operates. Guidance is provided in SSAP 25, 'Segmental reporting', which defines a separate class of business as the distinguishable component of the entity that provides a separate product or service or a separate group of related products or services. [SSAP 25 para 11]. Distinguishable components of an entity may include, for example, mining, textiles, electrical etc. Broad categories such as *manufacturing, wholesaling, retailing* are not indicative of the industries in which the entity operates. Those terms should not generally be used to describe an entity's industry segments without identification of the products or services.

31.8 Therefore, the categories of principal activities described in the directors' report should as far as possible be consistent with the information that is provided for segmental reporting purposes. There are various factors that should be taken into account when deciding whether or not an entity operates in different industry segments and these are discussed further in chapter 9 on segmental reporting. However, no single set of characteristics is universally applicable in determining industry segments of all entities, nor is any single set of characteristics likely to be relevant in all cases. Consequently, determining the industry segments in which the entity operates must depend to a considerable extent on the directors' judgment.

31.9 Furthermore, judgment is required in deciding whether differing types of business are sufficiently significant to require separate disclosures. Although no precise rules have been laid down in this respect, it is suggested that where there are significant differences between categories of activity, such that they cannot reasonably be treated as a single class, entities should follow the size criterion (the ten per cent rule) discussed in chapter 9, in determining whether an activity is significant enough to require separate disclosure.

31.10 A change in activity should be reported whenever there has been a commencement of a new activity or a complete withdrawal from a previous activity rather than a change in the degree of the activity undertaken. Such a change may be brought about by the acquisition or disposal of a subsidiary undertaking. In order to provide meaningful disclosure of the changes in activities, the extent to which the acquisition or disposal has impacted on any resultant change in the group's activities should be considered. Indeed, FRS 3 requires that if an acquisition, a sale or a termination has a material impact on a major business segment, this impact should be disclosed and explained. [FRS 3 para 53].

31.11 The degree of detail that should be given under principal activities will obviously depend upon the nature of the company's business. For companies operating in one or two business segments, the relevant information is normally given in the directors' report. Multinational corporations engaged in a wide range of business activities tend to include the relevant details elsewhere in the financial statements, for example, in a separate statement that sets out a detailed review of their operations. Where this is done, a reference should be given in the directors' report to where the necessary information can be found. Table 31.1 provides an illustration of the disclosure of, and changes in, principal activities.

Table 31.1 – Airtours plc – Annual report and accounts – 30 September 1994

Directors' report (extract)

Principal activities

Airtours is a fully integrated Group of Companies operating within the leisure travel industry.

The Group consists of the United Kingdom's second largest chain of retail travel agents, the second largest tour operating business and a substantial charter airline dedicated to servicing the requirements of the in-house tour operator.

On 2nd June 1994 the Group acquired SAS Leisure AB, which is the largest tour operator in Scandinavia, and which also owns or manages 14 resort hotels mainly operating under the Sunwing brand name.

During the year the Group's activities have been expanded further by its entry into the fly-cruise market. On 28th April 1994 the Group announced its proposed acquisition of the MS Southward, to be re-named the MS Seawing, and on 17th October 1994 announced its proposed acquisition of the MS Nordic Prince, to be re-named the MS Carousel.

A review of the Group's activities and its financial position at 30th September 1994 are reported in the Chairman's statement and in the financial, operational and business reviews on pages 4 to 21.

Review of business

31.12 The directors must include in their report a fair review of the development of the business of the company and its subsidiaries during the financial year and of their position at the end of it. [Sec 234(1)(a)].

31.13 The Act does not indicate the form that this review of the business should take, nor does it indicate the degree of detail the directors must include in their review. The only requirement is that the information presented must be fair. The provision is expressed in broad terms only, so as to allow directors as much freedom as possible to decide how best to meet the requirement. Consequently, in practice, both the format and content of this review vary considerably.

31.14 However, in July 1993, the ASB issued a statement entitled 'Operating and financial review' (OFR) containing guidance on matters that should be included in the annual report. This guidance is not an accounting standard; rather it aims to build on the foundation of existing disclosures by providing a range of subjects that the directors may consider in discussing the main factors underlying the company's financial performance and position. Although the statement does not seek to prescribe a particular format for the OFR, it encourages directors to develop the presentation in a way that best complements the style and layout of their annual report. Consequently, it is for the directors to decide how and where the information should best be presented. The contents of the OFR are considered further in chapter 33.

Likely future developments

31.15 The Act also requires the directors' report to contain an indication of likely future developments in the business of the company and its subsidiaries. [7 Sch 6(b)]. As with the provisions relating to a review of the company's business during the year, the Act contains no amplification as to the extent and the scope of this commentary on likely business developments. In practice, directors tend to interpret this requirement by providing information that will have a significant impact on future earnings and profitability of the company or the group. For example, information on such matters as development of new products or services, business expansion or rationalisation plans, capital expenditure plans and proposed disposals and acquisitions, is fairly common.

31.16 The guidance on OFR recommends that directors should discuss known events, trends and uncertainties that are expected to have an impact on the business in the future together with details of the company's investment for the future. In discussing such trends and uncertainties, the directors should explain their significance to the business, rather than include a forecast of the outcome of such uncertainties or include anything that may be construed to be a profit forecast.

31.17 As stated in paragraph 31.5 above, many listed companies do not, in practice, include in their directors' report the review of the business and indications of likely future developments. Instead, they include the required information either in the chairman's statement or the chief executive's report or in a separate, stand-alone section that deals with a detailed review of operations. Provided that the directors' report refers to the place where the information appears, it still complies with the Act. An example of such a disclosure is given in Table 31.2 below.

Table 31.2 – Vodafone Group Plc – Annual Report & Accounts – 31 March 1998

REPORT OF THE DIRECTORS (extract)

Review of the Group's business
The Company and its subsidiary and associated undertakings are involved principally in mobile telecommunications services. A review of the development of the business of the Company and its subsidiary and associated undertakings is contained in the Chairman's statement on pages 4 to 6 and the operating and financial reviews on pages 8 to 33.

FUTURE DEVELOPMENTS
The Group is currently involved in the expansion and development of the cellular telecommunications and related businesses as detailed in the Chairman's statement on pages 4 to 6 and the operating and financial reviews on pages 8 to 33.

Implications for listed companies

31.18 For listed companies, the wording for the note on future developments will have to be chosen very carefully. Otherwise, there is the danger that the note could, at some later stage, be construed as a profit forecast. Paragraph 12.26 of the Listing Rules provides the following guidance:

> *"A form of words which expressly or by implication states a minimum or maximum for the likely level of profits or losses for a period subsequent to that for which the audited accounts have been published, or contains data from which a calculation of an approximate figure for future profits or losses may be made, is a profit forecast or estimate, even if no particular figure is mentioned and the word 'profit' is not used."*

31.19 The City Code on Take-Overs and Mergers states that, if a company has issued any statement that constitutes a profit forecast and that forecast relates to a period during which a takeover bid arises, then that forecast must be repeated in any offer or defence document and accountants must report on it.

31.20 In the circumstances in paragraph 31.19, if the directors' report of a listed company is construed as including a profit forecast or an estimate, it would have the following consequences:

- Accountants would be required to report that the forecast or estimate has been properly compiled on the basis stated and that it is presented on a basis consistent with the accounting policies of the company or group in question. [LR 12.22].

- The following year's financial statements will have to explain any differences if the actual results for the period reported in those financial statements differ by ten per cent or more from any published forecast or estimate made by the company for that period. [LR 12.43(b)].

Dividends

31.21 The amount (if any) that the directors recommend should be paid as dividend must be stated. [Sec 234(1)(b)]. Where the directors do not propose a dividend then it is customary to state this fact. An example of the relevant disclosure is given in Table 31.3 below.

Table 31.3 – Rolls-Royce plc – Annual Report – 31 December 1993

Report of the Directors (extract)

Results for the year (extract)

...The directors recommend a final dividend of 3.00p a share. With the interim dividend of 2.00p a share, paid on January 10, 1994, this will make a total dividend of 5.00p a share for the year (1992 5.00p). Subject to approval of the recommended final dividend, the total cost of dividends for 1993 is £56m. If approved, the Company will pay the final dividend on July 4, 1994 to shareholders registered on April 14, 1994. Consequently £7m has been added to Group reserves.

The Chairman's Statement, the Chief Executive's Review of Activities and the Finance Director's Review together give information relating to the year's operations, research and development activities and future prospects.

Post balance sheet events

31.22 Particulars of any *important* events affecting the company or any of its subsidiaries that have occurred since the end of the financial year must be disclosed. [7 Sch 6(a)]. This requirement gives rise to two potential conflicts between the law and SSAP 17, 'Post balance sheet events', which are considered further in chapter 20.

- SSAP 17 distinguishes between events that require adjustments to the amounts disclosed in the financial statements ('adjusting events') and events that only require to be noted ('non-adjusting events' and the reversal of window dressing transactions). However, the Act does not make such a distinction and thus must be construed as requiring disclosure of important post balance sheet events whether adjusting or non-adjusting. In practice, only non-adjusting events are normally commented on in the directors' report, although disclosure in the financial statements of the financial effects of material non-adjusting post balance sheet as proforma information is not uncommon as indicated in Table 31.4 below.

- The Act requires material post balance sheet events to be disclosed in the *directors' report*, whereas SSAP 17 requires disclosure of non-adjusting events only in the *notes to the financial statements*. Where a post balance sheet event requires disclosure under both the Act and the standard, then theoretically disclosure ought to be made both in the directors' report as well as in the notes to the financial statements. In practice, however, companies normally disclose the information only in one place so as to avoid duplication. Where the information is disclosed in the notes, there should be a cross-reference to the directors' report, and vice versa.

Table 31.4 – Guinness PLC – Report and Accounts – 31 December 1993

Report of the Directors (extract)

POST BALANCE SHEET EVENT

At an Extraordinary General Meeting of shareholders held on 25 February 1994, approval was given for the Group to restructure its interest in LVMH. The Group has agreed, subject to the satisfaction or waiver of certain conditions, to sell its indirect 24% interest in LVMH held through Jacques Rober and Christian Dior to the Arnault Group for £1,323 million, to acquire a direct 34% shareholding in Moët Hennessy, the wines and spirits business of LVMH for £902 million and to enter into a shareholders agreement with LVMH to govern their interests in Moët Hennessy. LVMH has agreed, subject to the completion of the sale and acquisition referred to above, to reduce its shareholding in Guinness from 23.85% to 20% by 30 June 1995.

The pro forma financial effects of these transactions are shown in Note 29 to the Group accounts on page 51.

Research and development activities

32.1 An indication of the activities (if any) of the company and its subsidiaries in the field of research and development should be provided in the directors' report. [7 Sch 6(c)].

32.2 As the Act does not indicate how much detail needs to be given, the extent of disclosure varies considerably in practice. Some companies, particularly those in the pharmaceutical sector, give significant details about their research and development activities whilst others give a fairly minimal amount of disclosure on the subject. As research and development activities are particularly sensitive matters, companies are understandably reluctant to disclose too much information on the subject. However, in order to meet the Act's requirements, the statement need not be technically elaborate or esoteric. A broadly-based note that considers the commercial aspects of the research and development activities and their impact on the activities of the company or group would be sufficient in most situations. An illustration of this disclosure is shown in Table 31.5.

Table 31.5 – Cable and Wireless plc – Report and accounts – 31 March 1995

Report of the Directors (extract)

Research and development

Although the Group does not have a central research and development facility, research is carried out within its regional business. Many technical trials are currently being implemented throughout the Group, with the objective of maintaining Group engineering and service skills at the forefront of communications technology. Consistent with the federal approach, the results of these trials will be shared throughout the Group.

Through Mercury's association with BCE Inc., the Group continues to have access to Bell Northern Research, one of the foremost telecommunications laboratories in the world. The Group also continues to maintain associations with and support key universities around the world who have relevant research capabilities.

32.3 The requirement to give an indication of the research and development activities of the company and its subsidiaries does not mean that the accounting policy for research and development should be disclosed in the directors' report. The statement required by the Act should instead supplement the accounting policy and the other disclosure requirements of SSAP 13, 'Accounting for research and development' (see also chapter 14).

(The next paragraph is 31.27.)

Differences between market and balance sheet value of land

31.27 Substantial differences between the market value and the balance sheet value of any interest in land held by the company or the group should be disclosed in the report, if in the opinion of the directors the difference is of such significance that it should be brought to the shareholders' or debenture holders' attention. 'Land' includes the buildings and other structures. [Sch 1 Interpretation Act 1978]. The difference has to be shown with such degree of precision as is practicable. [7 Sch 1(2)]. An example is given in Table 31.6 below. Although there is no requirement to make a negative statement that the difference is not significant, many companies do make this statement where there might otherwise be doubt.

31.28 It is recommended that where there are several interests in land, the aggregate market value and the aggregate book value should be compared to see if the difference is substantial. When it is considered that a substantial difference exists, it is preferable to state both the aggregate market value and the basis on which the market value has been arrived at. In this regard, SSAP 15 also requires disclosure of the tax effects, if any, that would arise if the asset were realised at a price equal to the estimated market value. [SSAP 15 para 42]. An independent professional valuation is not required if the directors are competent to arrive at the market value themselves, but the wording should make the position clear in this respect. Where property is situated overseas, especially in territories subject to political unrest or where the remittance of currencies is restricted, it may not always be practicable, and may be misleading, to give the information required. In such circumstances, the wording should make this clear.

Table 31.6 – Lloyds Bank Plc – Directors' Report and Accounts -31 December 1994

Directors' report (extract)

Premises

The directors have reviewed the current value of premises and are of the opinion that, compared with the balance sheet amount, there is a shortfall of £114 million *(1993: £162 million)*, of which £109 million *(1993: £155 million)* relates to UK premises and £5 million *(1993: £7 million)* to overseas premises. The directors are of the opinion that this shortfall, an average of some 10 per cent *(1993: 13 per cent)*, will not prove to be permanent and no adjustment has been made in the balance sheet.

Details of directors

31.29 Disclosure is required of the names of the persons who were directors of the company at any time during the financial year. [Sec 234(2)]. This can be achieved either by listing the names of the directors in the report or by referring to the page where this information may be found (for example, see Table 31.7 below). In group financial statements, disclosure is required of the names of the parent company's directors only.

31.30 Although not required by the Act, it has become customary to include the following information:

- The dates of appointments or resignations of directors occurring during the financial year.
- Changes in the directors since the end of the financial year.
- Retirement of directors at the AGM and whether they offer themselves for election.

Non-executive directors for listed companies

31.31 Listed companies must disclose the identity of independent non-executive directors, together with a short biographical note on each. [LR 12.43(i)]. However, many companies go beyond this minimum disclosure requirement by including biographical details for executives as well as non-executive directors and identifying the roles of the respective directors within the board (see Table 31.7 below).

31.32 The disclosures concerning the roles of directors gained prominence when the Cadbury Report on the Financial Aspects of Corporate Governance came into effect on 30 June 1993. The Cadbury Report, which is explained further in chapter 32, expanded the role of non-executive directors in setting and maintaining standards of corporate governance. The report recommends that all boards should include, as a minimum, three non-executive directors of sufficient calibre and independence. Independence means that they should be independent of management and free from any business or other relationships. Details of the non-executive directors and the various committees on which they sit (for example, the audit committee and the remuneration committee) need not be given in the directors' report, provided a reference is given to where that information can be found.

Table 31.7 – Bass PLC – Annual Report – 30 September 1994

Directors' Report (extract)

Directors
The names of the present directors of the Company, together with brief career details, are shown on pages 26 and 27.

Hamish Swan and Charles Darby retired on 29 June 1994 and 31 July 1994 respectively, both having reached the age of 60. Richard North was appointed a director on 1 September 1994.

Richard North, having been appointed during the year, retires and offers himself for re-appointment. The directors retiring by rotation are Sir Michael Perry and Tony Portno who, being eligible, offer themselves for re-appointment. Richard North and Tony Portno have service agreements with the Company requiring two and three years' notice of termination respectively, subject to retirement at age 60. Sir Michael Perry does not have a service contract.

> In October 1994, the executive directors agreed to convert their service agreements from a three to a two year notice period without compensation, with effect from 1 January 1995. In view of his relative proximity to normal retirement age, Tony Portno remains on three years' notice.Details of the directors' interests in the Company's shares are shown in note 7 on page 46.
>
> No director was materially interested in any contract of significance to the Group's business, other than a service contract. Ian Prosser, however, is a non-executive director of Lloyds Bank Plc, which provides commercial banking and share registration services to the Company. Bryan Langton is a non-executive director of Wachovia Bank of Georgia NA, which provides lines of credit to Holiday Inns, Inc. Philip Bowman is a director of British Sky Broadcasting Group Plc, which provides satellite TV programming to Bass Taverns Limited.
>
> During the year the Company maintained liability insurance for its directors and officers.

Directors' service contracts for listed companies

31.33 The directors' report for listed companies must state the unexpired term of the directors' service contracts of any director who is proposed for re-election at the forthcoming AGM (see Table 31.7 above). If the directors proposed for re-election do not have service contracts, the directors' report must state that fact. [LR 16.8, 16.12]. Directors' service contracts for this purpose are defined by reference to section 318 of the Act and, essentially, exclude contracts expiring or determinable within one year by the employing company without payment or compensation other than statutory compensation. Copies of the service contracts are required to be made available for inspection at the company's registered office and at the AGM. [LR 16.9].

31.34 The Cadbury Code recommends that service contracts for directors should not exceed three years without shareholders' approval. If a service contract does not specify a term, the term can be ascertained in one of the following ways:

- If the contract is determinable on the giving of notice, the expiration of the notice period will indicate the earliest date at which the contract could end.
- If no notice period is stated in the contract, there may be a custom or practice as to the length of the notice.

- In the absence of an express provision as to duration or expiry or a customary arrangement, there is a presumption at common law that (subject to the statutory minimum entitlements to notice) every contract of employment is terminable on reasonable notice by either party.

Where the length of the unexpired period of a director's service contract has been determined in one of the ways above, the details should be fully disclosed in the directors' report.

31.35 The notice of AGM of listed companies must give the place where, and the time at which, copies of service contracts can be examined. If there are no such contracts, the notice must state the fact. [LR 14.20].

31.36 Directors' service contracts available for inspection must disclose or have attached to them the following information:

- The name of the employing company.
- The date of the contract, the unexpired term and details of any notice periods.
- Full particulars of the directors' remuneration including salary and other benefits.
- Any commission or profit sharing arrangements.
- Any provision for compensation payable upon early termination of the contract.
- Any other matters necessary to enable investors to estimate the possible liability of the company upon early termination of the contract.

[LR 16.11].

Directors' interests

31.37 Disclosure should be made in respect of directors' interests in shares or debentures of the company or any body corporate of the same group. All directors have a duty to notify their interests in writing to the company when they become interested in shares in, or debentures of, the company or any body corporate in the same group. [Sec 324]. Every company has an obligation to keep a register of directors' interests notified under section 324. [Sec 325].

31.38 Section 324 provides for the term 'interests in shares or debentures' to be interpreted in accordance with Schedule 13 to the Act. The following basic rules apply:

- An interest in shares or debentures includes any interest of any kind whatsoever in shares and debentures. [13 Sch 1(1)].

- Any restraints or restrictions on the exercise of any right attached to the interest are disregarded. [13 Sch 1(2)].

- Persons having a joint interest are deemed to each have that interest. [13 Sch 7].

- It does not matter for disclosure purposes that shares or debentures in which a person has an interest cannot be specifically identified. [13 Sch 8].

- The interests of a director's spouse and infant children (other than their interest if they are also directors of the company) are to be treated as the interest of the director. [Sec 328].

Schedule 13 also contains further specific rules for determining the interests that should be included in and excluded from the disclosure requirements stated below.

31.39 Disclosure of information set out in paragraphs 31.40 and 31.41 below must be given in the directors' report with respect to each person who was a director of the company, or in the case of a group, of the parent company at the end of the financial year. The information regarding directors' interests may alternatively be disclosed in the notes to the financial statements. [7 Sch 2(1)]. For the purposes of disclosure, interests in shares or debentures has the same meaning as in section 324. [7 Sch 2A(4)]. The information disclosed should be based on the information contained in the register the company maintains in accordance with section 325 of the Act.

Interests in shares and debentures

31.40 The following information must be given in respect of each person who was a director of the company at the end of the financial year:

- A statement as to whether or not the director, according to the register, had an interest in either that company or any body corporate in the same group (that is, the company itself, or parent company, or a subsidiary, or a fellow subsidiary) *at the end of the financial year*. This is taken to mean that also the name of the company or companies in question must be stated. [7 Sch 2A(1)].

- If the director has such an interest, the number of shares in, and the amount of debentures of, the particular company at that date must also be disclosed. [7 Sch 2A(2)]. Disclosure must be given in respect of each class of shares or debentures that the director holds. [Sec 324(1); 325(2)].

- If the director was interested in shares or debentures at the end of the year, information corresponding to that required by the two points above should also be given as *at the beginning of the financial year.* [7 Sch 2A(3)].

31.41 If he became a director during the financial year, the information stated in the last point above should be given on the date he became a director. [7 Sch 2A(3)]. If a person was appointed a director on more than one occasion during the year, the information should be given as at the date he was first appointed. [7 Sch 2A(5)]. This requirement covers a situation where, for example, a person is appointed a director between the end of the preceding financial year and the date of the AGM. Under article 79 of Table A (if applicable), this person (if appointed by the directors) would have to be reappointed as a director at the AGM. However, the financial statements should give the information required under the last point of paragraph 31.40 above as at the date he was first appointed.

Interests in options

31.42 Where the interests of the directors in the company's shares take the form of a 'put' or 'call' option that a director holds otherwise than under a trust, the information set out in paragraph 31.40 and 31.41 above should be disclosed. The disclosures apply where the director has a right to call for delivery of, or a right to acquire, or under an obligation to take, an interest in the shares, or debentures. [13 Sch 6(1)]. The right or obligation need not be unconditional. [13 Sch 6(1)].

31.43 It should be noted that a *right to acquire, or an obligation to take, an interest in the shares* or debentures does not include *a right or obligation to subscribe for shares* or debentures. [13 Sch 6(2)]. Rights to subscribe for shares may include, for example, options granted by the company to its employees including directors under a saving related or executive share scheme. Consequently, the disclosure requirements of paragraph 31.40, that is, disclosure of opening and closing figures, that apply to rights or options to acquire shares does not apply to rights or option to *subscribe* for shares, although such disclosure requirements are now recommended by UITF Abstract 10 'Disclosure of directors' share options' (see further chapter 11). In any event, details of rights or options to subscribe for shares or debentures must be included in the register of directors' interests maintained in accordance with section 325(3).

31.44 Although the Act does not require disclosure of the opening and closing figures where a company has granted rights or options to subscribe for shares, it does require disclosure where any such rights or options have been granted or exercised by the director during the financial year. The required disclosures are as follows:

- A statement should be given in respect of each director whether, according to the register, any right to subscribe for shares in, or debentures of, the company or another body corporate in the same group was granted to, or exercised by, the director or member of his 'immediate family' during the financial year.

- If any such rights were granted or exercised during the financial year, the number of shares or the amount of debentures should be stated, also disclosing the name of the company involved.

[7 Sch 2B(1)(2)].

A director's 'immediate family' includes a spouse and infant children, including step-children. In Scotland the term 'infant' means a pupil or minor. [7 Sch 2B(3)]. 'Immediate family' does not include a person who is also a director of the company. [7 Sch 2B(4)].

31.44.1 There is no requirement under the Act for the disclosure of the price at which a director can exercise a share option, if he has any. However, the Act requires public companies to disclose, as part of directors' emoluments, the aggregate amount of gains made by directors on the exercise of options on shares (whether allotted or not) in the company or a member of a group. But disclosure of price information is recommended by UITF Abstract 10 (see further chapter 11). In any event, the notes to the financial statements must disclose, in summary, both the option price at which, and the period during which, any options to subscribe for shares are exercisable in respect of the company's shares (see further chapter 19). [4 Sch 40].

[The next paragraph is 31.45.]

Interests in contracts

31.45 The Act also requires disclosure of transactions and arrangements in which the director of a company has, directly or indirectly, a material interest (for example, contracts between a director and a company for the sale of non-cash assets). The disclosure requirements of contracts or substantial property transactions in which a director has a material interest are considered in detail in chapter 34.

Additional disclosure for listed companies

31.46 The Listing Rules require a listed company to disclose the following information in respect of its directors' interests in the company's shares or debentures.

- A statement as at the end of the financial year showing by way of note any change in the interests of each director of the company between the end of the financial year and a date not more than one month before the date of the notice of the general meeting at which the financial statements are to be laid before the company. If there has been no such change, that fact should be stated.
- The changes in interests to be disclosed occurring in the period mentioned above include not only the directors' interests disclosed to the company under section 324, but also spouses and children's interests disclosed under section 328, together with any rights to subscribe for shares in, or debentures of the company. The interests that are disclosed must also distinguish between beneficial interests and non-beneficial interests. Normally, an interest should be shown as non-beneficial only if the director, his spouse and infant children have no beneficial interest.

[LR 12.43(k)].

31.47 The Cadbury Report also called for full and clear disclosure of directors' share options in the context of directors' emoluments, but was silent on the relevant disclosure requirements. The disclosure issue was finally resolved with the publication of UITF Abstract 10. The UITF accepted that granting of share options gave rise to a benefit under the Act which should be included in the aggregate directors' emoluments. However, the UITF concluded that it was not practicable to specify an appropriate valuation method for options as a benefit in kind. Instead, the UITF recommended a level of disclosure that would be consistent with the recommendation of the Cadbury Report. The provisions of UITF Abstract 10 are considered in detail in chapter 11. In practice, the disclosure of directors' interests in shares and options are generally combined and presented in a tabular manner. An illustration of how a company discloses its director's interests in accordance with the Act, the Listing Rules and UITF Abstract 10 is given in Table 31.8 below. Further examples are included in chapter 11, which deals with directors' emoluments.

Table 31.8 – Attwoods plc – Annual Report & Accounts – 31 July 1994

Report of the Directors (extract)
for the year ended 31 July 1994

DIRECTORS' INTERESTS IN SHARES

The interests as defined by the Companies Act 1985, of the Directors in the shares of the Company and in the guaranteed redeemable convertible preference shares of Attwoods (Finance) NV are as follows:

	31 July 1994		1 August 1993 (*or date of appointment)	
	The Company	**Attwoods (Finance) NV**	The Company	Attwoods (Finance) NV
	Ordinary shares	**Guaranteed redeemable convertible preference shares**	Ordinary shares	Guaranteed redeemable convertible preference shares
The Lord Lane of Horsell	**10,000**	-	10,000	-
M K Foreman	**780,536**	-	780,536	-
E D Johnson	**14,450**	-	14,450	-
T J Penfold	**158,450**	**10,000**	158,450	10,000
M H J Radcliffe	**2,000**	-	-*	-*

[The next page is 31017.]

In addition Messrs J R Bullock, I R Cairns and L W Haworth had a non-beneficial interest in 84,270,906 ordinary shares of the Company and 47,856,351 guaranteed redeemable convertible preference shares of Attwoods (Finance) NV at both of the above dates by virtue of them being officers of Laidlaw Inc.

Other than the above, the Directors had no non-beneficial interests in the shares of any company in the Group.

During the period 1 August 1994 to 14 October 1994 there have been no changes in the interests of the Directors in the share capital of any company in the Group.

DIRECTORS' INTERESTS IN SHARE OPTIONS

Directors names	Number of options At 1.8.93	During the year Granted	Exercised	At 31.7.94	Exercise price	Date from which exercisable	Expiry date
M K Foreman	233,348			233,348	197.087p	22.12.92	22.12.99
		100,000		100,000	112.000p	27.4.97	27.4.04
E D Johnson	100,000			100,000	117.000p	28.4.95	28.4.99
		75,000		75,000	112.000p	27.4.97	27.4.01
T J Penfold	33,355			33,355	96.238p	25.11.90	25.11.97
	93,340			93,340	197.087p	22.12.92	22.12.99
	80,000			80,000	117.000p	28.4.95	28.4.02
		75,500		75,000	112.000p	27.4.97	27.4.04

No options lapsed during the year. The market price of the shares at 31 July 1994 was 118p and the range during the financial year was 103p to 164p with an average price over the period of 129.03p

31.48 The Listing Rules require disclosure of particulars of any contract of significance (including substantial property transactions) subsisting during the period under review, to which the company, or one of its subsidiary undertakings, is a party and in which a director of the company is, or was, materially interested. [LR 12.43(q)]. In this context, 'a contract of significance' is one which represents in value a sum equal to one per cent or more, calculated on a group basis where relevant, of:

- The aggregate of the group's share capital and reserves for a capital transaction or for a transaction of which the principal purpose is the granting of credit.

- The group's total purchases, sales, payments or receipts, as appropriate for other transactions.

[LR 12.44].

Exemption from disclosure

31.49 Where a director of a wholly-owned subsidiary is also a director of the parent company, which is itself required to keep a register under section 325(1), The Companies (Disclosure of Directors' Interests) (Exceptions) Regulations 1985

(SI 1985/802) give relief from section 324 and hence from the disclosure requirements in paragraphs 31.40 to 31.44 above. In this situation, the director's interest needs to be disclosed only in the parent company's financial statements and not in the subsidiary's.

31.50 Furthermore, those same regulations exempt a director from notifying interests in shares to his company where that company is a wholly-owned subsidiary of a body incorporated outside Great Britain. The exemption extends to interests in shares in, or debentures of, a parent company that is incorporated outside Great Britain, or any other body incorporated outside Great Britain. Consequently, such interests are not required to be disclosed in a company's financial statements, because they are not required to be notified to the company.

Purchase of own shares

31.51 Where the company has an interest in its own shares, Part II of Schedule 7 to the Act requires the directors' report to include certain information. The directors' report must contain the details set out in paragraph 31.52 below where any of the following circumstances occur:

Acquisition of shares by the company

- A company purchases its own shares or otherwise acquires them by forfeiture, or by surrender in lieu of forfeiture, or by way of a gift, or redemption, or in a reduction of capital duly made, or by order of the court. [7 Sch 7(a), Sec 143(3)].

Acquisition of shares in a public company by another person

- A nominee of a public company acquires shares in the company from a third party without the company providing any financial assistance directly or indirectly and the company has a beneficial interest in those shares. [7 Sch 7(b); Sec 146(1)(c)].

- Any person acquires shares in a public company with the financial assistance of the company and the company has a beneficial interest in those shares. [7 Sch 7(b); Sec 146(1)(d)].

Lien or charges on own shares held by the company

- A company takes a lien or a charge (either express or implied) on its own shares for any amount that is payable in respect of those shares. [7 Sch 7(c); Sec 150(2)].

- A company that remained an 'old public company' after 22 March 1982, and did not apply before that date to be re-registered under section 8 of the Companies Act 1980 as a public company, holds a lien or a charge (either express or implied) on its own shares, and that lien or charge existed on 22 March 1982. [7 Sch 7(c); CC(CP) Sec 6(3)].

- A company that either existed on 2 November 1862 or was formed after that date in pursuance of either any Act of Parliament (other than the 1985 Act) or letters patent, or was otherwise legally constituted and has registered or re-registered under section 680 of the Act as a public company (see section 685), holds a lien or a charge (either express or implied) on its own shares, and that lien or charge existed immediately before the company applied to be re-registered or registered as a public company. [7 Sch 7(c); Sec 150(4)].

31.52 Where any of the above circumstances has occurred, the directors' report must state the following details:

In respect of shares purchased

- The number and the nominal value of the shares that have been purchased in the financial year and the percentage of the called-up share capital which shares of that description represent.

- The aggregate amount of consideration paid and the reasons for their purchase.

An example is given in Table 31.9 below.

In respect of shares acquired other than by purchase or charged

- The number and the nominal value of any shares that have been otherwise acquired (whether by the company or by its nominee or any other person) or charged at any time during the financial year.

- The maximum number and the nominal value of shares which, having been so acquired or charged (whether or not during the year) are held at any time during the financial year.

- The number and the nominal value of such shares that were disposed of by the company (or any other person holding them on behalf of the company) during the year, or that were cancelled by the company during the year.

- The percentage of the called-up share capital which shares of that description represent.
- The amount of any charge.

In addition to the above, there should be disclosed the amount or the value of any consideration for any shares that either the company or the other person disposed of during the financial year that the company or the other person acquired for money or money's worth.
[7 Sch 8].

Table 31.9 – Redrow Group plc – Annual Report and Accounts - 30 June 1994

Directors' Report (extract)

Repurchase of shares
In the process of floatation, Redrow Group plc repurchased 2,147,000 of its own ordinary shares of 10 p each, representing 1.0% of the post-flotation share capital, for an aggregate consideration of £282,000.

1,900,000 were purchased from the Redrow Staff Pension Scheme thereby bringing its level of self-investment within the limits set for listed companies.

247,000 were purchased from P L Pedley who wished to realise part of his investment.

Additional disclosures for listed companies

31.53 The directors' report of a listed company must give the following additional information concerning purchases or proposed purchases of the company's own shares:

- Particulars of any authority given by the shareholders in general meeting for the company to purchase its own shares that is still effective at the year end (that is, authority that has not yet been exercised and has not expired).
- In relation to purchases other than through the market or by tender or by partial offer to all shareholders, the names of the sellers of the shares that have been purchased, or are to be purchased, by the company.
- If the company has purchased any of its own shares since the year end, or has either been granted an option or entered into a contract to purchase its own shares since the year end, then the directors' report should disclose the

equivalent information to that required under the Act as detailed in paragraph 31.52 above.
[LR 12.43(n)].

Examples of the relevant disclosures are given in chapter 40 dealing with the acquisition by a company of its own shares.

Employee information

31.54 Parts III, IV and V of Schedule 7 require the directors' report to contain information regarding the company's policy in respect of the employment of disabled persons, of the health, safety and welfare at work of employees, and of the involvement of employees in the management of the company.

31.55 If a company is required to prepare consolidated financial statements, the directors' report needs to contain the employee information required by Schedule 7 only in respect of the parent company. However, in practice, most parent companies include the required employee information in respect of the whole group.

Employment of disabled persons

31.56 If the company employed, on average, 250 or more employees in the UK in each week of the financial year, the directors' report must contain a statement that describes the company's policy during the year in respect of the following:

- Giving full and fair consideration (having regard to the persons' particular aptitudes and abilities) to applications for employment that disabled persons (as defined in the Disabled Persons (Employment) Act 1944) make to the company.

- Continuing the employment of, and arranging appropriate training for, any of the company's employees who have become disabled during the period in which the company employed them.

- Otherwise providing for the training, the career development and the promotion of those disabled persons the company employs.

[7 Sch 9].

An illustration of this disclosure is given in Table 31.10 below.

Table 31.10 – Wellcome plc – Annual report – 31 December 1994

Directors' Report (extract)

EMPLOYMENT OF DISABLED PERSONS

It is the policy of the Group in the United Kingdom that disabled people, whether registered or not, should receive full and fair consideration for all job vacancies for which they are suitable applicants. Employees who become disabled during their working life will be retained in employment wherever possible and will be given help with any necessary rehabilitation and retraining. The Group is prepared to modify procedures or equipment, wherever this is practicable, so that full use can be made of an individual's abilities.

Employee involvement

31.57 The directors' report should describe the action the company has taken during the financial year to introduce, maintain, or develop arrangements aimed at:

- Providing employees systematically with information on matters of concern to them as employees.
- Consulting employees or their representatives on a regular basis, so that the company can take the views of employees into account in making decisions that are likely to affect their interests.
- Encouraging the involvement of employees in the company's performance through (for example) an employees' share scheme.
- Achieving a common awareness on the part of all employees of the financial and the economic factors that affect the company's performance.

[7 Sch 11(3)].

31.58 The above requirements apply only to the directors' report of a company that employs, on average, more than 250 employees in the UK each week during the financial year. [7 Sch 11(1)]. Table 31.11 gives an example of the information to be shown.

Table 31.11 – Dixons Group plc – Annual Report – 2 May 1998

Directors' Report (extract)

Employee involvement The Group maintains its commitment to pro-active programmes for involving its employees in Group affairs. This is achieved in a variety of ways, including the regular publication of newsletters and staff newspapers, audio tapes, video presentations, staff briefings and by consultation with recognised trade unions and staff committees. Regular staff attitude surveys are undertaken and a number of suggestion schemes are in operation, providing a regular flow of ideas for improving efficiency and performance.

The Company's philosophy is to offer highly incentivised pay systems and focused training programmes to enable staff to perform well and to develop their full potential.

The Group has recently established the Dixons Group Forum. This is a body of formally elected employee representatives through which the Company aims to consult with employees throughout the Group to ensure that their views are taken into account in making decisions that will affect the business and its employees.

Creditor payment policy

31.59 A provision of the Act introduced by the Companies Act 1985 (Miscellaneous Accounting Amendments) Regulations 1996 (SI 1996/189) and amended by the Companies Act 1985 (Directors' Report) (Statement of Payment Practice) Regulations 1997 (SI 1997/571) requires a company to disclose its payment policy for its suppliers. The provision applies to plcs and large private companies (that is, neither small nor medium-sized companies) which are members of a group whose parent is a plc. The provisions apply at a company level and not to the group as a whole. The requirement is for the directors to state with respect to the financial year *following* that covered by the annual report whether it is the company's policy to follow any code or standard on payment practice. Only where a company follows a particular code does it have to give the name of the code or standard together with an indication of where information about, and copies of, the code or standard can be obtained. [7 Sch 12(2)(a) inserted by SI 1997/571]. The directors also have to state whether it is the company's policy in respect of some or all of its suppliers:

- To settle the terms of payment with those suppliers when agreeing the terms of each transaction.
- To ensure that those suppliers are made aware of the terms of payment.
- To abide by the terms of payment.

[7 Sch 12(2)(b) inserted by SI 1997/571].

31.60 Where the company's policy is different in respect of some or all of its suppliers from that outlined above, the directors must also state the company's policy in respect of those suppliers. In addition, where the company's policy is different for different suppliers or classes of suppliers, the directors must identify in their report the suppliers or classes of suppliers to which the different policy applies. [7 Sch 12(2) inserted by SI 1997/571]. Examples of payment policies are given in Tables 31.12, 31.12A and 31.12B.

31.60.1 The Companies Act 1985 (Directors' Report) (Statement of Payment Practice) Regulations 1997 (SI 1997/571) introduced a further provision which requires that the directors' report should state the number of days represented by trade creditors falling due for payment within one year at the year end (for example, balance sheet Format 1 item E4) compared to the total amounts invoiced to suppliers during the year. The requirement is to disclose the number of days that bears to the number of days in the financial year the same proportion as X bears to Y where:

- X = the aggregate of the amounts that were owed to trade creditors at the end of the year.
- Y = the aggregate of the amounts invoiced by suppliers during the year.

[7 Sch 12(3) as inserted by SI 1997/571].

31.60.2 The calculation of the number of creditor days is illustrated in the example below.

Example

Trade creditors at the end of the year are £30 million. Amounts invoiced during the year by suppliers are £300 million. Number of days in the financial year is 365.

$$\frac{30}{300} \times 365 = 36.5 \text{ days}$$

31.60.3 For the purposes of the above provisions, a person will be a supplier of the company at any time if:

- At the time, the person is owed an amount in respect of the goods and services supplied.
- The amount owed would be included within trade creditors (item E4 in Format 1) if the financial statements were prepared at that time, were prepared in accordance with Schedule 4 and that format was adopted.

[7 Sch 12(4) as inserted by SI 1997/571].

31.60.4 If a company does not draw up its accounts under balance sheet Format 1 in Schedule 4, it still has to comply with the disclosures outlined above. If, for example, the company is an insurance company, the disclosure has to be given in respect of creditors for goods and services which would have been included under trade creditors, had the company drawn up its financial statements in accordance with Schedule 4. Therefore, for an insurance company, although insurance and reinsurance creditors would not be classified as trade creditors, creditors for stationery and rent would be and the required disclosure has to be given in respect of these creditors.

Table 31.12A – Cable and Wireless plc – Annual report and accounts – 31 March 1997

Directors' report (extract)

Payments to suppliers

In the United Kingdom the Group agrees payment terms with its suppliers when it enters into binding purchase contracts. The Group seeks to abide by the payment terms agreed with suppliers whenever it is satisfied that the supplier has provided the goods or services in accordance with the agreed terms and conditions. The Group does not have a standard or code which deals specifically with the payment of suppliers.

The Company had 29 days purchases outstanding at 31 March 1997 based on the average daily amount invoiced by suppliers during the year ended 31 March 1997.

Table 31.12B – Marks and Spencer p.l.c. – Annual Report and Financial Statements – 31 March 1998

REPORT OF THE DIRECTORS (extract)

CREDITOR PAYMENT POLICY

The Company's policy concerning the payment of its trade creditors is as follows:

In the UK, General Merchandise is automatically paid for 11 working days from the end of the week of delivery. Foods are paid for 13 working days from the end of the week of delivery (based on the timely receipt of an accurate invoice).

UK distribution suppliers are paid monthly, for costs incurred in that month, based on estimated annual contracts, and payments are adjusted quarterly to reflect any variations to estimate.

Trade creditor days of the Company for the year ended 31 March 1998 were 14.9 days (10.6 working days), based on the ratio of Company trade creditors at the end of the year to the amounts invoiced during the year by trade creditors.

Suppliers to overseas subsidiaries (for merchandise and distribution) and foreign merchandise suppliers of the UK Company are paid on average within 30 days of the receipt of invoice or delivery documentation.

For trade creditors, it is the Company's policy to:

- agree the terms of payment at the start of business with that supplier,
- ensure that suppliers are aware of the terms of payment,
- pay in accordance with its contractual and other legal obligations.

31.60.5 To assist companies to honour their contract payment terms, the CBI has developed a Code of practice for buyers. The Code requires that responsible companies should:

- Have a clear, consistent policy that they pay bills in accordance with the contract.
- Ensure that the finance and purchasing departments are both aware of this policy and adhere to it.
- Agree payment terms at the outset of a deal and stick to them.
- Not extend or alter payment terms without prior agreement.
- Provide suppliers with clear guidance on payment procedures.
- Ensure that there is a system for dealing quickly with complaints and disputes and advise suppliers without delay when invoices, or parts of invoices, are contested.

[The next paragraph is 31.61.]

Environmental issues

31.61 In recent years there has been a growing tendency on the part of listed companies to comment on environmental issues in their annual report and accounts. Amongst smaller companies, the practice is relatively rare. Although environmental reporting, like health and safety, is not specifically required by the Act or the Listing Rules, public pressures matched by recent legislation, in particular the Environmental Protection Act 1990 and various EC Regulations, have been instrumental in many companies submitting their environmental practice to external scrutiny. There is also increasing recognition by international organisations, such as the United Nations and The International Chamber of Commerce, that environmental protection measures are a significant reporting issue for companies.

31.62 Because disclosure of environmental issues is currently voluntary, it is not surprising that the level of disclosure in annual reports varies from company to company. However, not all companies in the industrial sector discuss the impact their businesses have on the environment. Some companies are good at identifying environmental impacts and risks that are most relevant to their circumstances and the way in which they are addressing, or intend to address, those concerns. An example is given in Table 31.13 below. Some leading companies, for example, Imperial Chemical Industries Plc, go even further and publish separate environmental reports. Others are merely keen to emphasise the good works they do for the community and the environment. Meaningful reporting of environmental performance is still in its infancy, but guidance on what is regarded as good practice can be found in 'Statement of good practice – Environmental Reporting in Annual Accounts', issued by the Hundred Group of finance directors in September 1991.

Table 31.13 – Rentokil Group PLC – Report and Accounts – 31 December 1993

Report of the Directors (extract)

ENVIRONMENT

Rentokil is committed to the provision of services and products which improve the quality of life, for both our customers and the community, using working practices designed to protect the environment.

Heightened awareness of environmental issues and increased legislation provide a focal point for developing greener techniques and solutions to problems, both in our more traditional businesses and also in offering opportunities to develop new businesses.

The Rentokil fumigation bubble uses acceptable atmospheric gases to eradicate pests. The 'sharps' disposal service – the safe disposal of used hypodermic needles and scalpels – meets public concern over the spreading of AIDS and Hepatitis B. Anti-bacterial deep cleaning of both industrial and commercial premises, in particular high risk areas such as washrooms, drains and food production and preparation areas, has been developed to meet increased legislation and concern as to health and food safety. Water and Ventilation services were born from new awareness of both Legionnaires' disease and sick building syndrome. Pest Control services use electronically controlled infra red 'mouse alert' systems in high risk areas such as food production and preparation, which eliminate the need for more traditional methods.

It is the responsibility of the company and all employees to ensure that all services and products are procured, produced, packaged and delivered, and waste materials are ultimately disposed of, in ways which are appropriate from an environmental viewpoint. It is the responsibility of our employees to carry out their work in a manner that will not cause damage to the environment.

[The next paragraph is 31.65.]

Political and charitable donations

31.65 If a company that is not the wholly-owned subsidiary of another company incorporated in Great Britain has given money for either political purposes or charitable purposes during the year, and the amount given for both purposes exceeds £200 in aggregate, the company must disclose certain information in its directors' report. [7 Sch 3(1)(2)].

31.66 The information that must be disclosed is as follows:

- The amount given for both political purposes and charitable purposes. These amounts must be disclosed separately. [7 Sch 3(2)(a)].
- If the company has given money for political purposes (including a subscription to a political party), the name of each person or political party to whom the company has donated more than £200 during the year, together with the actual amount donated. [7 Sch 3(2)(b)].

An example of such a disclosure is given in Table 31.15 below.

Table 31.15 – Rolls-Royce plc – Annual Report – 31 December 1993

Report of the Directors (extract)

Donations

During 1993 the Company made charitable donations amounting to £208,000. The annual donations budget is administered by a committee of the Board and by local site committees to a policy predominantly directed towards assisting military services benevolent associations and charities associated with engineering, scientific and educational objectives as well as objectives connected with the Group's business and place in the community.

A political contribution of £60,000 was made to the Conservative and Unionist Party.

31.67 For the purposes of paragraph 31.66, the following applies:

- A company is to be treated as giving money for political purposes if, directly, or indirectly, it gives a donation or subscription to a political party in the UK or any part of it; or it gives a donation or subscription to a person who, to the company's knowledge, is carrying on, or proposing to carry on, any activities that can, at the time at which the donation or subscription was given, reasonably be required as likely to affect public support for such a political party as is mentioned above.

[The next page is 31027.]

- Money given for 'charitable purposes' means any money it gives for purposes that are exclusively charitable. [7 Sch 5(4)]. Donations for purposes that include either a political or a commercial element do not come within the definition. The definition also excludes charitable donations a company gives to a person who, at the time of the gift, was ordinarily resident outside the UK.

[7 Sch 5].

31.68 With a group (again where the parent is not a wholly-owned subsidiary of another company incorporated in Great Britain), the parent company directors' report needs to give the information in paragraph 31.66 above only in respect of the group as a whole. It has to give the information only if the amount the company and its subsidiaries have given for both political purposes and charitable purposes exceeds £200 in aggregate. [7 Sch 4]. Furthermore, some companies consider it good practice to seek shareholders' approval for such donations although this is not required by the Act.

Disclosure of overseas branches

31.69 Companies (other than an unlimited company) must give an indication of the existence of branches that they operate outside the UK. [7 Sch 6(d)]. This requirement was introduced by SI 1992/3178 and came into effect for accounting periods beginning on or after 1 January 1993. For this purpose, a branch is defined in section 698 to mean only branches within the EC (see further chapter 37). Therefore, branches operated in the US, for example, would not require disclosure. It should be noted that disclosure is required only of the company's branches, not those of its subsidiaries. This means that the directors' report of a parent company need only refer to the existence of branches which it operates outside the UK, and not to those that are operated outside the UK by its subsidiaries. Branches operated by its subsidiaries would fall to be disclosed in the subsidiaries' directors' reports.

Directors' responsibility statements

31.70 The main duties and responsibilities, particularly of a financial or accounting nature, that directors owe to their company are codified in the Act. However, until 1993 there was no requirement, legal or otherwise, for directors to make a specific statement about their responsibilities in the company's annual financial statements. The inclusion of a directors' responsibility statement (either free standing or included in the directors' report) in a company's financial statement is a recent innovation, first recommended by the Cadbury Report. The Report, issued in December 1992 with a Code of Best Practice that became effective for financial years ending after 30 June 1993, recommends that financial statements of listed companies should contain a separate statement of responsibilities by auditors and directors.

31.71 The notes to the Code of Best Practice set out the matters that should be covered in the statement of directors' responsibilities. These are:

- The legal requirement for directors to prepare financial statements for each financial year which give a true and fair view of the state of affairs of the company (or group) as at the end of the financial year and of the profit and loss for that period.
- The responsibility of the directors for maintaining adequate accounting records, for safeguarding the assets of the company (or group), and for preventing and detecting fraud and other irregularities.
- Confirmation that suitable accounting policies, consistently applied and supported by reasonable and prudent judgement and estimates, have been used in the preparation of the financial statements.
- Confirmation that applicable accounting standards have been followed, subject to any material departures disclosed and explained in the notes to the financial statements.

31.72 The Cadbury recommendation to include a directors' responsibility statement was effectively extended to unlisted companies by SAS 600, 'Auditors' Reports on Financial Statements', which was issued in May 1993 and became effective for audits of financial statements for periods ending on or after 30 September 1993. In developing SAS 600, the APB took the view that the distinction between the responsibilities of those who prepare financial statements and those who audit them is essential to achieve an understanding of the nature and context of the opinion expressed by the auditors. As a result, SAS 600 introduced a new form of audit report containing a statement distinguishing the respective responsibilities of directors and auditors. An example wording for the statement of directors' responsibilities is included in Appendix 3 to SAS 600.

31.73 It should be noted, however, that whilst the example given in the Cadbury Report calls for confirmations that suitable accounting policies have been consistently applied and accounting standards followed, the example in SAS 600 merely requires a statement that directors are responsible for doing so. Therefore, the Cadbury example appears to serve a different purpose to SAS 600 as it does not formally acknowledge all the directors' responsibilities. In practice, companies are divided. Many companies are simply content in stating the directors' responsibilities by following the example given in SAS 600 (see Table 31.16). Others follow the Cadbury recommendations and include various confirmations (see Table 31.17).

Table 31.16 – The BOC Group plc – Report and Accounts – 30 September 1994

Responsibility of the Directors for preparation of the financial statements

Company law requires the directors to prepare financial statements for each financial year which give a true and fair view of the state of the affairs of the Company and of the Group for that period. In preparing those financial statements, the directors are required to:

- select suitable accounting policies and then apply them consistently;
- make judgements and estimates that are reasonable and prudent;
- state whether applicable accounting standards have been followed, subject to any material departures disclosed and explained in the financial statements;
- prepare the financial statements on the going concern basis unless it is inappropriate to presume that the Group will continue in business.

The directors are responsible for keeping proper accounting records which disclose with reasonably accuracy at any time the financial position of the Company to enable them to ensure that the financial statements comply with the Companies Act 1985. They are also responsible for safeguarding the assets of the Group and hence for taking reasonable steps for the prevention and detection of fraud and other irregularities.

Table 31.17 – Thorn plc – Annual Report and Accounts – 31 March 1997

STATEMENT OF DIRECTORS' RESPONSIBILITIES IN RESPECT OF THE ACCOUNTS

Company law requires the Directors to prepare accounts for each financial year which give a true and fair view of the state of affairs of the Company and of the Group, and of the profit or loss of the Group for that period. In preparing those accounts, the Directors are required to:

- select suitable accounting policies and then apply them consistently;
- make judgements and estimates that are reasonable and prudent; and
- state whether applicable accounting standards have been followed, subject to any material departures disclosed and explained in the accounts.

The Directors confirm that they have complied with the above requirements in preparing the accounts.

The Directors are responsible for keeping proper accounting records which disclose with reasonable accuracy at any time the financial position of the Group and enable them to ensure that the accounts comply with the Companies Act 1985. They are also responsible for safeguarding the assets of the Group and hence for taking reasonable steps for the prevention and detection of fraud and other irregularities.

31.74 There is also variation in practice as to the actual positioning of the directors' statement of responsibilities within the financial statements. The Cadbury Code requires that directors should explain their responsibility for preparing the accounts next to a statement by the auditors about their reporting responsibilities. [Cadbury 4.28, Code 4.4]. Following the publication of SAS 600, auditors refer to their audit responsibilities in the audit report. The intention is that the two statements will complement each other. Whilst many companies issue a separate statement of directors' responsibilities which precedes the auditors' report, a large number also include the statement within the Directors' Report which is not always placed next to the auditors' report. To the extent that the directors' responsibilities are set out in a separate statement in the financial statement, the audit report need only cross-refer to the page on which it appears. Only if the directors do not include such a statement or where there is inadequate description of their responsibilities would the auditors be required to include a description in their own report.

Re-appointment of auditors

31.75 It is customary, but not a statutory requirement, to state at the end of the directors' report that a resolution will be put to the general meeting, regarding the appointment or re-appointment of the auditors. Where a private company has elected to dispense with the requirement to appoint auditors annually in accordance with section 386, such a statement will of course not be relevant. In that situation, companies may wish to include a statement indicating that in the absence of a notice proposing that the appointment be terminated, the auditors will be deemed to be re-appointed for the next financial year.

Additional matters for listed companies

31.76 The directors' report of listed companies should give information on further matters in addition to those already discussed above. These additional matters are considered in the paragraphs that follow.

Major interest in company's shares

31.77 A statement should be given of particulars of the nature and extent of the interests of any person, in any holding of three per cent or more of the nominal value of any class of capital carrying rights to vote in all circumstances at general meetings of the company. The statement must be made at a date not more than one month prior to the date of notice of the annual general meeting. [LR 12.43 (l)].

31.78 The particulars to be disclosed include the names of the persons and the amount of their interests. The interests which are to be stated are those contained in the register the company maintains under section 211 of the Act. If there is no such interest, that fact should also be stated. [LR 12.43]. It is customary to give this information in the directors' report. An example is given in Table 31.18 below.

31.79 The rules for the disclosure of interests by a shareholder to the company are contained in Part VI of the Act and are very complex. Generally, when a person comes under an obligation to notify his interest in a public company's relevant share capital under section 198, he must do so in writing within two days of the obligation to notify arising so that the interest can be included in the company's register. [Sec 202(4)]. The term 'interest' is widely drawn and includes both family and corporate interests.

31.80 The provisions contained in Part VI were significantly amended by The Disclosure of Interests in Shares (Amendment) Regulations 1993 (SI 1993/1819) to take account of the EC Directive 88/627/EEC, the 'Major Shareholdings Directive' dealing with market transparency. The new Regulations came into force on 18 September 1993. The Act distinguishes between material interests and non-material interests in the nominal share capital carrying voting rights (relevant share capital). The following interests in relevant share capital must be notified:

- Material interests of three per cent or more. [Sec 199(2)(a)]. A material interest means any interest other than a non-material interest.

- Non-material interests of ten per cent or more (including any material interests not exceeding three per cent). [Sec 199(2)(b)]. Section 199(2A) provides a list of interests that are regarded as non-material interests. For example, the interest of a person authorised to manage investments belonging to another, or the interest of an operator of an authorised unit trust scheme, which were previously exempt from notification, will now fall to be notified as non-material interest when the ten per cent threshold is reached.

31.81 Not all interests in the relevant capital need to be notified provided they do not include voting rights. Particulars of interests which are to be disregarded and, hence exempt from notification, are contained in section 209. For example, an interest held by virtue of holding units (as defined in section 75 of the Financial Services Act 1986) in an authorised unit trust scheme need not be notified provided it does not include voting rights. [Sec 209(5)].

31.82 It should be noted that the DTI has issued a consultative document that seeks to amend Part VI of the Act dealing with the disclosure of interests in shares. The DTI accepts that the disclosure requirements are unnecessarily complex, and there is a need to redress gaps and anomalies in the present requirements. The intention is to make the disclosure requirements less onerous, but to do so in a way that still achieves the basic objective of enabling companies to know who might be in a position to influence their affairs through having a significant interest in their shares.

Table 31.18 – Allied-Lyons PLC – Report and Accounts – 5 March 1994

Report of the Directors (extract)

Substantial interests

The directors have been notified that as at the date of this report Suntory Limited was materially interested in 4.25% of the issued ordinary share capital of the company.

Save for the above, no person has reported any material interest of 3% or more or any non-material interest exceeding 10% of the issued ordinary share capital of the company.

The close company provisions of the Income and Corporation Taxes Act 1988 do not apply to the company.

Transactions with a controlling shareholder

31.83 The directors' report should disclose particulars of any contract of significance between the company (or one of its subsidiary undertakings) and a controlling shareholder (previously referred to as 'corporate substantial shareholder') subsisting during the year. [LR 12.43(r)]. For this purpose, a 'contract of significance' is one which is determined in accordance with the rules set out in paragraph 31.48 above. An example is given in Table 31.19 below.

31.84 A 'controlling shareholder' is defined as any person who is:

- entitled to exercise, or control the exercise of, at least 30 per cent of the voting power at the company's general meetings; or
- is in a position to control the composition of a majority of the company's board of directors.

[LR 3.12].

31.85 In addition, the directors' report should disclose details of any contract with a controlling shareholder (as defined above) to provide services to the company or to one of its subsidiaries (see Table 31.19 below). This information is not required if the shareholder is providing services that it normally provides as part of its principal business and it is not a contract of significance that is required to be disclosed. [LR 12.43 (s)].

Table 31.19 – The Telegraph plc – Annual Report and Accounts - 31 December 1994

Directors' Report (extract)

Contracts of significance

In addition to the service agreement referred to in note 26(c) to the accounts, on 23 June 1992 the company entered into a co-operation agreement with Hollinger under which Hollinger has undertaken that, subject to specified exceptions and so long as it controls the company, it and the companies under its control (other than companies in the Telegraph group) will not, without the prior consent of the company, carry on or hold an interest of 3 per cent or more in a company carrying on a media business in the United Kingdom, the rest of the European Community, Australia or New Zealand. The company has undertaken that, subject to specified exceptions and so long as it is controlled by Hollinger, it and the companies under its control will not, without the prior consent of Hollinger, carry on or hold an interest of 3 per cent or more in a company carrying on a media business in the United States of America, Canada, the Caribbean, or Israel.

Mr Black has entered into an agreement with the company on 23 June 1992 which provides that he will serve as an executive chairman of the company while he is chairman and chief executive officer of Hollinger, or until his appointment is terminated by the company. Mr Black has agreed that while he remains an executive of the company he will not, without written consent of the company, carry on or be interested in carrying on a media business within the United Kingdom, the rest of the European Community, Australia or New Zealand except through a holding of less than 3 per cent.

Following approval of the shareholders of the Telegraph at the extraordinary general meeting held on 13 April 1993, The Telegraph entered into a joint venture agreement with Hollinger in consequence of which each of the two companies acquired a 50 per cent indirect interest in 14,290,000 common shares in Southam Inc. ("Southam"), Canada's largest newspaper publisher. Between 21 and 23 November 1994, the Telegraph and Hollinger each acquired a further 250,000 common shares in Southam Inc. to bring their total joint holding to 14,790,000 common shares representing approximately 19.5 per cent of Southam's outstanding share capital. Another shareholder in Southam, Power Corporation of Canada, also increased its interest to 19.5 per cent in November 1994. Under arrangements entered into with Southam, the joint venture company is entitled to three seats on Southam's board, and two of those appointees, Mr Black and Mr Jarislowsky, are directors of The Telegraph (as also is Mr Radler, a third director of Southam). The Telegraph directors believe that Hollinger, The Telegraph and Power, with aggregate shareholdings of 39 per cent, together represent a powerful force for change at Southam and a commitment to enhance shareholder value. They expect The Telegraph to continue to contribute its particular experience and skills to enhance the performance of Southam's businesses.

NOTES TO THE ACCOUNTS (extract)

26. Commitments (extract)

(c) Service agreement

Under the terms of a services agreement with Hollinger Inc., for as long as Mr Black remains chairman of the board, The Telegraph will bear 66.7% of the cost of the office of the chairman incurred by Hollinger or such other proportion as may be agreed from time to time by the Audit Committee. Other services will be provided at cost and may include the arrangement of insurance, assistance in the arrangement of finance and assistance and advice on acquisitions, disposals and joint venture arrangements. Charges to the company in respect of Mr Black's office and these and other services amounted to £871,192 in 1994 *(1993: £1,044,000)*.

Waiver of dividends

31.86 Particulars of any arrangements under which any shareholder has waived or agreed to waive any dividends should be disclosed. This requirement applies to waivers of future dividends as well as to waivers of dividends payable during the past financial year. Waivers of dividend of less than one per cent of the total value of any dividend may be disregarded provided that some payment has been made on each share of the relevant class during the year. [LR 12.43(e)].

Close company status

31.87 The requirement to state whether, so far as the directors are aware, the company is a 'close company' or 'close investment holding company' for taxation purposes has been deleted as a result of the amendment to the Listing Rules in August 1995.

Cadbury Code of Best Practice

31.88 Listed companies are required to give a statement that they have complied with the Cadbury Code of Best Practice. A company is required to comply with specific paragraphs of the Code. Where a company has not complied with the Code, or has complied with only part of the Code or (in the case of requirements of a continuing nature) complied for only part of the accounting period, it must specify the paragraphs with which it has not complied and give reasons for any non-compliance. [LR 12.43(j)]. This means that companies are not expected to comment separately on each item of the Code, but areas of non-compliance will have to be dealt with individually.

31.89 The statement of compliance with the Code can either be made in the directors' report or included in a separate statement that deals with the more general aspects of corporate governance in the annual report. The statement of compliance must also be reviewed by the company's auditors. An example is given in Table 31.20 below. Corporate governance is considered in detail in chapter 32.

Table 31.20 – Abbey National plc – Directors' Report and Accounts - 31 December 1994

Directors' Report (extract)

Corporate Governance

The Stock Exchange requires directors to report on compliance with the recommendations set out in the Code of Best Practice published by the Committee on Financial Aspects of Corporate Governance ("the Code"). The directors have carefully considered these and confirm that Abbey National plc meets, in the light of the Company's particular circumstances, the Code's recommendations.

As required by the Code, specific statements are provided below on the application of the concept of "going concern" in the accounts, and on internal control on page 25.

In order to comply with the Code, the directors confirm that they are satisfied that the Group has adequate resources to continue in business for the foreseeable future. For this reason, they continue to adopt the going concern basis in preparing the accounts.

The auditors, Coopers & Lybrand, have reviewed the statement on compliance with the Code in accordance with Auditing Practices Board guidance. They have confirmed that the directors' comments on going concern and internal financial control are not inconsistent with the information of which they are aware based on their normal audit work, and provide the disclosures required by paragraphs 4.5 and 4.6 of the Code (as supplemented by the related guidance). They have also reported to the Company that the statement appropriately reflects the Company's compliance with the other paragraphs of the Code specified by the London Stock Exchange for their review.

The required procedures performed during this normal audit work do not encompass the specific steps that would be necessary to give an opinion on the directors' statement that the Company has adequate financial resources to continue in operational existence for the foreseeable future. In view of the significant additional work and cost that would be involved to enable such an opinion to be given and the limited assurance this would provide, the directors do not consider that such cost is justified. Accordingly, the auditors do not give an opinion on the adequacy of the Company's financial resources. They are not required to carry out the additional work necessary to, and do not, express an opinion on the effectiveness of either the Company's system of internal financial control or its corporate governance procedures.

Special business

31.90 Holders of listed securities who are sent a notice of a meeting, that is to occur on the same day as an AGM, which includes business that is considered not to be routine business of an AGM must be provided with an explanation in the directors' report of such business, unless an explanatory circular accompanies the notice. [LR 14.17]. An example of matters that are regarded as special business in an AGM is given in Table 31.21 below.

Table 31.21 – Coats Viyella Plc – Annual report and accounts – 31 December 1994

DIRECTORS' REPORT (extract)

ANNUAL AND EXTRAORDINARY GENERAL MEETINGS

Accompanying this report is the Notice of Annual General Meeting, which sets out the resolutions for the ordinary business of the meeting. A separate notice of an Extraordinary General Meeting (to be held on the same day) sets out certain special business resolutions which are explained in a letter from the Chairman incorporated with the Notice of Extraordinary General Meeting. This notice relates to the following matters:

- amendment to the Articles of Association
- approval of Senior Management Incentive Plan
- Authorisation of share dividends – 1994/95
- renewal of the Directors' authority for the Company to purchase its own shares
- renewal of the authority of the Directors to allot relevant securities
- dis-application of preemption rights

Disclosure exemptions for small companies

31.91 Small companies and groups headed by a small company are exempt from disclosing certain information in their directors' report. The exemptions are contained in section 246(4) of the Act (inserted by SI 1997/220). The disclosure exemptions for small companies are dealt with in chapter 36.

Approval and signing of directors' report

31.92 The board of directors must formally approve the directors' report and it must be signed on behalf of the board by a director or the secretary of the company. [Sec 234A(1)].

31.93 Every copy of the directors' report that is laid before the company in general meeting, or that is otherwise circulated, published or issued, must state the name of the person who signed it on behalf of the board. [Sec 234A(2)]. A copy of the directors' report that is to be delivered to the Registrar of Companies must also be signed on behalf of the board by a director or secretary of the company. [Sec 234A(3)].

Liability for contravention

31.94 Every person who was a director of the company at the end of the period within which the company's financial statements must be laid before the company in general meeting and be delivered to the Registrar of Companies may be guilty of an offence if the directors' report fails to comply with the Act's requirements (see further chapter 38). This offence is punishable by a fine. [Sec 234(5)].

31.95 It is a defence in such a situation for a director to prove that he took all reasonable steps to ensure that the directors' report complied with all the Act's requirements. [Sec 234(6)].

31.96 Furthermore, where the company does not comply with the requirements for the approval and signing of the directors' report as set out in paragraphs 31.92 and 31.93 above, the company and every officer of it who is in default will be guilty of an offence and liable to a fine. [Sec 234A(4)].

Chapter 32

Corporate governance disclosures

Chapter 32

Corporate governance disclosures

Introduction

32.1 The Cadbury Committee defined corporate governance as "*the system by which companies are directed and controlled*" (Cadbury Report para 2.5). Whilst noting that it was somewhat restrictive, the Hampel Committee endorsed the definition. In addition, it focussed on the processes by which enterprises are directed and controlled in response to the rights and aspirations of shareholders and other stakeholders.

32.2 Most UK companies have a single 'unitary' board of directors. Corporate governance in the UK corporate sector is, therefore, primarily concerned with:

- The procedures adopted by the board and its committees to discharge its duties (for example, membership of the board; frequency of, and procedures at, board meetings; the role of non-executive directors; constitution and terms of reference of audit and remuneration committees; and the role of the company secretary).
- The board's accountability to shareholders and other stakeholders (for example, annual reporting; use of AGMs and shareholder voting rights).
- The manner in which the board controls the company or group (for example, management structures; group legal structure; and internal control philosophy and practice).

32.3 Corporate governance potentially covers a very wide range of issues and disciplines from company secretarial and legal, through business strategy, executive and non-executive management and investor relations, to accounting and information systems.

32.4 Governance went higher up the corporate agenda in the early 90's partly in response to a series of scandals, fuelled by the recession. Business failures heightened concerns about effective governance and led amongst other things to the development of corporate governance disclosures.

32.5 The importance of such disclosures is that, provided the information can be relied upon, it should help determine a company's value and be useful to stakeholders wishing to assess their risk exposure before deciding whether to commit resources to, or withdraw resources from, a company. Company failures have highlighted the need for stakeholders to obtain assurance on governance. They have also heightened the need for directors to be able to give such assurance if they are to continue to attract funds.

32.6 Some governance issues have attracted significant political and public interest, because they strike at the root of the objectives of companies – none more so than the accountability of boards to shareholders in relation to executive pay.

32.7 Improvements in governance disclosures over the last few years have meant that UK public companies are among the most accountable of organisations. In addition to publishing their results and having their financial statements audited, public companies are required to disclose detailed information about their operations, relationships, remuneration and governance.

32.8 There has been criticism from some sources that this emphasis on accountability has been at the expense of what should be considered as a board's primary responsibility, namely to enhance the prosperity of the business and the investment of their shareholders. Recent developments in the field of corporate governance, in particular the Hampel Committee report, have helped to refocus attention on these dual aims of accountability and prosperity.

The development of corporate governance disclosures

32.9 The response to the scandals and failures of the late 1980s was a series of committees, reports and recommendations. The first of these was the Committee on the Financial Aspects of Corporate Governance, generally referred to as the Cadbury Committee, after its chairman Sir Adrian Cadbury. Its report was issued in December 1992 as a result of which major changes were made in the way in which governance was viewed by companies as well as in the disclosures that they give.

32.10 Whilst board remuneration was one of a number of issues addressed by Cadbury, it was not the main focus. Nonetheless, the level of board remuneration continued to attract a high profile, particularly in relation to levels of pay in privatised utilities. In response to this a separate group was set up to study the matter and the result was 'Directors' remuneration: report of a study group chaired by Sir Richard Greenbury'. This is known as the Greenbury report and was published in July 1995. The Greenbury Report led to additional disclosure requirements being included in the Listing Rules. These are discussed in chapter 11.

32.11 One of Cadbury's recommendations was that a successor body should be set up to review progress and it identified a number of issues which that body might consider. The successor body, 'The Committee on Corporate Governance' (the 'Hampel committee' – note: not the *financial* aspects of corporate governance) was set up in November 1995 under the chairmanship of Sir Ronald Hampel.

32.12 The final version of the Hampel report was published in January 1998. Whilst the Hampel report included 56 conclusions and recommendations, many of those involved supporting conclusions previously arrived at by Cadbury and Greenbury. The recommendations aim to ensure a balance between business prosperity and accountability.

32.13 Following the completion of its report, the Hampel Committee co-operated with the Stock Exchange in publishing 'The Combined Code – Principles of Good Corporate Governance and Code of Best Practice' in June 1998. The Combined Code was derived from the Committee's Final Report and from the Cadbury and Greenbury Reports. The final version of the Combined Code includes a number of changes made by the London Stock Exchange, with the Committee's agreement, following the consultation undertaken by the Exchange on the Committee's original draft.

32.14 The Combined Code contains both principles and detailed code provisions and is in two parts, Part 1, 'Principles of good governance' and Part 2, 'Code of best practice'. Each part of the Combined Code is split into two sections. Section 1 contains the corporate governance principles applicable to all listed companies incorporated in the UK. Section 2 contains the principles and code provisions applicable to institutional shareholders with regard to their voting, dialogue with the company and evaluation of governance arrangements.

32.15 The London Stock Exchange has appended the Combined Code to its Listing Rules (although it does not form part of those rules) and has introduced a new listing rule that requires companies to include a two part disclosure statement in their annual report describing *how* they have applied the principles of the Combined Code and whether or not they have complied with its detailed provisions throughout the accounting period with details of any non-compliance. This new listing rule applies to accounting periods ending on or after 31 December 1998. Although the changes to the Listing Rules issued by the London Stock Exchange in June 1998 only address the principles and Combined Code provisions in Section 1, the Hampel Committee regards Section 2 as an integral part of the recommendations and it encourages institutions to make voluntary disclosure to their clients and the public based on these recommendations.

32.16 The Combined Code is not mandatory for listed companies whose accounting periods end before 31 December 1998 and the previous rules and related guidance remain in place for those companies until the new Stock Exchange Listing Rules come into effect. The commentary that follows concentrates on explaining the requirements of the Combined Code and discussing how this will impact companies reporting on their own compliance. The Stock Exchange disclosure requirements relating to the requirements of the Combined Code concerning directors' remuneration are considered in detail in chapter 11. The new Combined Code is considered from paragraph 32.29.

The Hampel Report

Objectives

32.17 The Committee on Corporate Governance, chaired by Sir Ronald Hampel (the Hampel Committee), was set up following the recommendations of the Cadbury and Greenbury Committees that a new committee should review the implementation of their findings. Following consultation, the final report of the committee, the Hampel Report, was issued in January 1998.

32.18 The Hampel Committee's remit was to:

> *"Seek to promote high standards of corporate governance in the interests of investor protection and in order to preserve and enhance the standing of companies listed on the Stock Exchange."*

This included reviewing the previous reports by Sir Adrian Cadbury on the financial aspects of corporate governance and by Sir Richard Greenbury on boardroom pay.

32.19 Hampel supported the contribution that Cadbury and Greenbury made to recent improvements in the accountability of public companies and endorsed the overwhelming majority of the findings of the two earlier committees. As a result, Hampel did not attempt to go over every point raised by Cadbury and Greenbury, but chose to approach corporate governance from a different perspective. The Hampel Committee considered that public interest over the past few years had concentrated on accountability at the expense of the role corporate governance could make to business prosperity and wished to see the balance corrected.

32.20 Hampel considered that Cadbury and Greenbury were responses to actual and perceived governance failures and as a result concentrated on prevention of abuse and on the accountability of the companies to their shareholders. Although both reports have been successful, with the London Stock Exchange adopting their recommendations and listed companies for the most part implementing both Codes fully, smaller listed companies have found it harder to comply with the requirements.

'Box ticking'

32.21 Hampel argued for more flexibility when considering corporate governance standards and a proper regard for the individual circumstances of the companies concerned. Too often companies' experience of Cadbury and Greenbury was that the Codes had been treated as sets of prescriptive rules with shareholders and their advisors following a 'box ticking' approach focussing only on whether a rule had been complied with rather than the particular circumstances involved.

32.22 In Hampel's view this 'box ticking' approach did not take account of the diversity of circumstances and experience among different companies and within the same company. Although Hampel agreed with Cadbury that there are guidelines that are appropriate in most cases, Hampel considered that there will often be valid reasons for exceptions and companies should not be penalised for this. The focus by those considering corporate governance arrangements on 'box ticking' draws attention away from the diligent pursuit of corporate governance objectives and becomes an objective in itself. Compliance with every Code requirement does not guarantee that the business will not fail. It is possible for a company to arrange matters so that the letter of every governance rule is complied with, but not the substance.

Objectives of listed companies

32.23 These views led Hampel to broaden the Cadbury Committee's definition of corporate governance as *"the system by which companies are directed and controlled"*. Hampel considered that this definition excluded many activities involved in the management of a company which were also vital to the success of the business.

32.24 The Hampel Committee considered that the single overriding objective shared by all listed companies is the preservation and enhancement of their shareholders' investment. Ultimately this is the responsibility of all boards and their policies and corporate governance arrangements should reflect this.

Shareholders/stakeholders

32.25 Hampel recognised that the board's relationship with the company's shareholders is different to that with other stakeholders. The board of directors is responsible for relations with stakeholders, but because the shareholders elect the directors the board is accountable to the shareholders. Although the directors' primary responsibility is to the shareholders, both present and future, different types of companies will have different relationships with stakeholders and the objective of enhancement of long term shareholder value can only be met by directors developing and sustaining their relationship with stakeholders.

Recommendations

32.26 The Hampel Report identified a small number of broad principles directed largely at the process of corporate governance. The Hampel Report distinguished between principles of corporate governance and the more detailed guidelines in the Cadbury and Greenbury Codes.

32.27 The Hampel Report recommended that companies include a narrative statement, in their annual reports, of how they applied the broad principles of corporate governance to their particular circumstances. The Hampel Report did not prescribe the form or content of this statement, but recommended a number of principles that it felt could contribute to good governance expecting companies to explain their governance policies and any circumstances where departure from best practice was justified.

32.28 The Hampel Committee recommended that those tasked with the evaluation of governance practices should apply the principles flexibly, with common sense and due regard to the company's individual circumstances. Hampel stated that *"box ticking is neither fair to companies nor likely to be efficient in preventing abuse"*.

The Combined Code

Overview

32.29 Much of the Combined Code retains the substance of the Cadbury and Greenbury recommendations. The process of consolidation has included some changes, for example the Cadbury requirement that the remuneration committee report directly to the shareholders has been replaced by the Combined Code requirement for the Committee to report to the board who then report to the shareholders. In addition, more information needs to be published about companies' governance arrangements and there are sufficient changes in the detail to warrant companies reviewing carefully the provisions of the Combined Code to see how they are affected.

32.30 The Combined Code contains both principles and detailed code provisions and is in two parts: Part 1 deals with 'Principles of good governance' and Part 2 includes the 'Code of best practice'. The 17 principles in the Combined Code are fairly general statements that expound the ideals of transparency and openness in disclosure about a company's corporate governance arrangements. The Hampel Committee considered that if companies do not let their investors know what they are doing and how, the investors will look elsewhere for information on whether or not the Board is managing the company's affairs well. Inevitably investors will draw erroneous conclusions and as it is the investors who influence the market value of the company it is in the directors' interests to be open and transparent.

32.31 This underlying philosophy is responsible for the inclusion of a section in the Combined Code on institutional shareholders. Transparency and openness are less effective if the communication is a one way process. Investors have duties and responsibilities too. To this effect Hampel has included in section 2 of the Combined Code three principles relating to institutional shareholders. These cover voting, dialogue with companies and evaluation of governance disclosures. Although the Stock Exchange has little authority over institutional investors and they are not included in the 14 principles that the company is required to apply, Hampel thought this issue to be of sufficient note to include them in the Combined Code. This issue is discussed further from paragraph 32.72.

32.32 Although the Hampel Committee's intention was to consolidate, this entailed review and some clarification of existing provisions. There are in fact a number of differences between the Combined Code and its predecessors. The key change from the Cadbury-derived regime concerns internal control where the Combined Code says:

> *"The directors should, at least annually, conduct a review of the effectiveness of the group's system of internal controls and should report to shareholders that they have done so. The review should cover all controls, including financial, operational and compliance controls and risk management."*

As before, this does not extend to making a statement about whether the board found the controls to be effective – it merely requires the board to say that they have reviewed them. But a significant extension is that the review should now cover the effectiveness of all internal controls each year and not just financial controls. Boards will need to review and, if necessary, extend their internal policies and consider how to respond both internally and in public to the findings.

32.33 The Combined Code does not, however, contain the principle included in the Hampel committee's final report, which proposed that auditors should report independently to shareholders in accordance with statutory and professional requirements and independently assure the board on the discharge of its responsibilities for financial reporting and internal control. Hampel and the Stock Exchange consider that it is for the APB to issue guidance on the auditor's involvement with governance issues.

32.34 The Hampel Committee's Report and Combined Code have increased the interest in corporate governance issues and require companies to take actions to establish compliance with the provisions.

Contents of the Combined Code

32.35 Each part of the Combined Code is split into two sections as follows:

- Section 1 – Companies:
  - A – Directors.
  - B – Directors' remuneration.
  - C – Relations with shareholders.
  - D – Accountability and audit.
- Section 2 – Institutional shareholders:
  - E – Institutional investors.

32.36 Section 1 contains the corporate governance principles (Part 1 of the Code) and the best practice provisions (Part 2 of the Code) applicable to all listed companies. It is this section that is covered by the two part statement by the company required by the Listing Rules (see further para 32.76). Section 2 contains principles (Part 1 of the Code) and code provisions (Part 2 of the Code) applicable to institutional shareholders with regard to their voting, dialogue with companies and evaluation of a company's corporate governance arrangements. The committee did not regard it as appropriate for the Listing Rules to include any disclosure of compliance with section 2 of these requirements, but it hoped that at least the major institutions would voluntarily disclose to their clients and the public the extent to which they are able to give effect to the Code's provisions.

32.37 Part 1 of the Combined Code sets out the principles of good governance that companies and institutional investors should follow and in Part 2 expands on each of these principles in the detailed code of best practice. It looks at four areas concerning: the company's relationship with its directors; their remuneration; the company's relationship with its shareholders; and the board's accountability and relationship with its auditors. These sections of the code are considered in the paragraphs that follow. The Code's principles (included in Part 1) are explained, followed by the detailed provisions included in the code of best practice (Part 2 of the Code).

Actions required by listed companies

32.38 Although there are few changes from the rules governing Cadbury and Greenbury disclosures, because of the timing of the issue of the Combined Code and the application by the London Stock Exchange to accounting periods ending on or after 31 December 1998, the new rules apply to periods that were already almost half way through when the requirements were published.

32.39 As a matter of urgency, companies should:

- Review the details of their compliance with the Combined Code.
- Ensure the Combined Code's principles are embedded within their governance procedures.
- Identify any gaps that they need to address.

32.40 This review should not only deal with compliance, but should also deal with how good corporate governance procedures can contribute to business success and shareholder value enhancement.

32.41 Ten actions that directors should take to apply the Combined Code are summarised in the following table.

Action by directors of listed companies

1 Reassess the existing process for reviewing the effectiveness of internal control. In addition to financial control, the new code requires this review to cover operational and compliance controls and risk management. In securing compliance companies may wish to reappraise their approach and procedures, which may have become 'tired' or bureaucratic.

2 Commission a point by point review of compliance with the 45 detailed provisions of the Combined Code and report back to the board on any actions required to comply.

3 Commission preparation of a draft statement for the annual report explaining application of the 14 principles in the Combined Code and justifying any departures from the code.

4 Review board structure and balance of appointments between executive and non-executive directors. Review the contribution of individual directors to the board's overall objectives and effectiveness.

5 Consider who is the 'senior independent non-executive director'.

6 Reconsider or confirm the independent status of non-executive directors.

7 For companies of all sizes, reconsider the need for an internal audit department.

8 Establish training arrangements for new directors on appointment.

9 Consider how and when directors' service contracts may be reduced to periods of one year.

10 Review the relevance, quality and timeliness of information received by the board. The chairman has an explicit responsibility to ensure that all directors are properly briefed.

Directors

32.42 The Combined Code's principles cover the board and appointments and re-election to it, responsibilities of the chairman and the chief executive officer (CEO), the balance between executive and non-executive directors and their information needs.

The board

32.43 The first principle is that every listed company should be headed by an effective board that should lead and control the company. [CC Sec 1A.1]. The best practice provisions relating to this principle require that:

- The board should meet regularly.

- The board should have a formal schedule of matters specifically reserved to it for decision.

- The board should agree a procedure for directors, in the furtherance of their duties, to take independent professional advice if necessary, at the company's expense.

- All directors should have access to the advice and services of the company secretary, who is responsible to the board for ensuring that board procedures are followed and that applicable rules and regulations are complied with. Any question of the company secretary's removal should be a matter for the board as a whole.

- All directors should bring an independent judgement to bear on issues of strategy, performance, resources (including key appointments) and standards of conduct.

- Every director should receive appropriate training on the first occasion that he or she is appointed to the board of a listed company and subsequently as necessary.

[CC Sec 1A.1].

32.44 The Combined Code reinforces training and development of directors as an important part of good governance. It is the board's responsibility to ensure that this training is available for directors.

Chairman and chief executive officer

32.45 The second principle comments that there are two key tasks at the top of every public company – the running of the board (undertaken by the chairman) and the executive responsibility for the running of the company's business (undertaken by the CEO). There should be a clear division of responsibilities at the head of the company to ensure a balance of power and authority, to ensure that no one individual has unfettered powers of decision. [CC Sec 1A.2].

32.46 The best practice provisions underlying this principle require that a decision to combine the posts of chairman and chief executive officer in one person should be publicly justified. Whether the posts are held by different people or by the same person, there should be a strong and independent non-executive element on the board, with a recognised senior member other than the chairman to whom concerns can be conveyed. The annual report should clearly identify the chairman, the chief executive and the senior independent director. [CC Sec 1A.2.1].

32.47 The requirement in the Combined Code that a senior independent non-executive director should be appointed and identified in the annual report is a change from the previous requirements. This role, while not precisely defined, is expected to provide an additional route for concerns to be conveyed to the board and/or an early warning system for poor management. This now applies even where the chairman and chief executive's roles are split. Many companies do not currently have a recognised senior non-executive and will need to identify one.

Board balance

32.48 The third principle is that the board should include a balance of executive and non-executive directors (including independent non-executives) in order that no individual or small group of individuals can dominate the board's decision taking. [CC Sec 1 A.3]. The best practice provisions underlying this principle require that:

- The board should include non-executive directors of sufficient calibre and number for their views to carry significant weight in the board's decisions. Non-executive directors should comprise not less than one-third of the board.

- The majority of non-executive directors should be independent of management and free from any business or other relationship that could materially interfere with them exercising independent judgement. The annual report should identify the non-executive directors considered by the board to be independent.

[CC Sec 1 A.3.].

32.49 The main area of non-compliance with the Cadbury Code, particularly amongst smaller listed companies, was the requirement to appoint at least three non-executive directors. The combined code requirement for non-executives to comprise at least one third of the board may make it even more difficult to report compliance. In addition, the recommendations of the Combined Code regarding independent non-executives may also prove difficult for smaller companies to comply with given the practical difficulty of attracting and retaining high quality independent non-executives.

Supply of information

32.50 The fourth principle concerning directors is that the board should be supplied in a timely manner with information in a form and of a quality appropriate to enable it to discharge its duties. [CC Sec 1A.4]. The best practice provision associated with this principle requires that management has an obligation to provide the board with appropriate and timely information, but information volunteered by management is unlikely to be enough in all circumstances and directors should make further enquiries where this is necessary. Furthermore, the chairman should ensure that all directors are properly briefed on issues arising at board meetings. [CC Sec 1 A.4.1]

32.51 The effectiveness of the board is dependent on the information it receives from management and the Combined Code recognises the obligation of management to provide the board with information and the importance of the the role of the chairman.

32.52 Companies should from time to time consider reviewing the effectiveness of the information provided to the board and, because chairmen have an explicit responsibility to consider this, they may want to commission a specific review.

Appointments to the board

32.53 The Combined Code principle relating to board appointments requires that there should be a formal and transparent procedure for the appointment of new directors. [CC Sec 1A.5]. The best practice provisions dictate that unless the board is small, a nomination committee should be established to make recommendations to the board on all new board appointments. A majority of the members of this committee should be non-executive directors and the chairman should either be the chairman of the board or a non-executive director. The annual report should identify the chairman and the members of the nomination committee. [CC Sec 1 A.5.1].

32.54 Although there is no guidance as to when a board is regarded as small many companies without a nomination committee will now need to establish one.

Re-election

32.55 The Combined Code principle on re-election of directors requires that all directors should be required to submit themselves for re-election at regular intervals and at least every three years. [CC Sec 1A.6]. The best practice provisions require:

- Non-executive directors to be appointed for specified terms subject to re-election and to Companies Act provisions relating to the removal of a director. Furthermore, reappointment should not be automatic.
- All directors should be subject to election by shareholders at the first opportunity after their appointment and to re-election at intervals of no more than three years. The names of directors submitted for election or re-election should be accompanied by sufficient biographical details to enable shareholders to make an informed decision on their election.

[CC Sec 1 A.6]

32.56 This represents a change to the Cadbury Code's recommendation that only executive directors should submit themselves for re-election at least every three years. The Combined Code has extended this to include all directors, including non-executives. In addition, the Combined Code recommends that directors' service contracts or notice periods should not be greater than one year. Boards should set this as an objective, but the Report recognised that this may not be achieved overnight.

Directors' remuneration

32.57 The Combined Code's principles concerning the level and make-up of remuneration, the procedure for developing policy on executive directors' remuneration and the resulting disclosure in the financial statements are as follows:

- Levels of remuneration should be sufficient to attract and retain the directors needed to run the company successfully, but companies should avoid paying more than is necessary for this purpose. A proportion of executive directors' remuneration should be structured to link rewards to corporate and individual performance. [CC Sec 1 B.1]

- Companies should establish a formal and transparent procedure for developing policy on executive remuneration and for fixing the remuneration packages of individual directors. No director should be involved in deciding his or her own remuneration. [CC Sec B.2]

- A statement of remuneration policy and details of the remuneration of each director should be included in the company's annual report. [CC Sec 1 B.3]

32.58 Although the Combined Code substantially mirrors the Greenbury Committee requirements, the following additional recommendations were made as part of the best practice provisions:

- The performance related elements of remuneration should form a significant proportion of the total remuneration package of executive directors and should be designed to align their interests with those of the shareholders and to give those directors keen incentives to perform at the highest levels.

- Remuneration committees should consider what compensation commitments (including pension contributions) their directors' contracts of service, if any, would entail in the event of early termination. In particular, they should consider the advantages of providing explicitly in the initial contract for such compensation commitments, except in the case of removal for misconduct.

32.59 The Code also includes two additional schedules offering further guidance:

- Schedule A – Provisions on the design of performance-related remuneration.
- Schedule B – Provisions on what should be included in the remuneration report.

The Combined Code's principles and best practice provisions concerning directors' remuneration are considered in more detail in chapter 11.

Relations with shareholders

32.60 The Combined Code specifies the type of dialogue that companies should have with their institutional shareholders, and includes the principle that companies should be ready, where practicable, to enter into a dialogue with institutional shareholders based on the mutual understanding of objectives. [CC Sec 1 C.1] Furthermore, the Combined Code's principles on relations with shareholders require that boards should use the annual general meeting to communicate with private investors and encourage their participation. [CC Sec 1C.2].

32.61 These principles are supplemented by the following best practice provisions:

- Companies should count all proxy votes and, except where a poll is called, should indicate, for each resolution after it has been dealt with on a show of hands, the level of proxies lodged and the balance for and against the resolution.

- Companies should propose a separate resolution at the annual general meeting on each substantially separate issue and should in particular propose a resolution at the annual general meeting relating to the report and accounts.

- The chairman of the board should arrange for the chairmen of the audit, remuneration and nomination committees to be available to answer questions at the annual general meeting.

- Companies should arrange for the Notice of the annual general meeting and related papers to be sent to shareholders at least 20 working days before the meeting.

[CC Sec 1.C.2]

32.62 The changes to the format of shareholder meetings introduced by the Combined Code are intended to encourage shareholder involvement and in particular the requirement for companies to announce all proxy votes lodged and the manner in which they voted after any show of hands is designed to encourage shareholder voting. In addition, following criticism of the 'bundling' of different proposals into one resolution the Combined Code now requires each separate issue to be voted on individually.

Accountability and audit

32.63 The Combined Code also covers how directors should present financial information to their shareholders and their responsibilities concerning internal control, as well as their relationship with external auditors. The principle concerning financial reporting requires that the board should present a balanced and understandable assessment of the company's position and prospects. [CC Sec 1D.1]. The best practice provisions indicate that to achieve this:

- The directors should explain their responsibility for preparing the financial statements and there should be a statement by the auditors about their reporting responsibilities.
- The board's responsibility to present a balanced and understandable assessment extends to interim and other price-sensitive public reports and reports to regulators as well as to information required to be presented by statutory requirements.
- The directors should report that the business is a going concern, with supporting assumptions or qualifications as necessary. Reporting on going concern is discussed further from paragraph 32.89.

[CC Sec 1.D.1].

Internal control

32.64 The Combined Code sets out the principle that the board should maintain a sound system of internal control to safeguard shareholders' investment and the company's assets. [CC Sec 1D.2]. The best practice provisions provide that:

- The directors should, at least annually, conduct a review of the effectiveness of the group's system of internal controls and should report to shareholders that they have done so. The review should cover all controls, including financial, operational and compliance controls and risk management.
- Companies that do not have an internal audit function should from time to time review the need for one.

[CC Sec 1.D.2]

32.65 The importance of internal control to good governance is well recognised and the Combined Code now requires all companies, regardless of their size, to consider the need for an internal audit department. Modern internal audit should be focussed on all aspects of internal control including business risk assessment and response, financial management, safeguarding assets and compliance with laws and regulations. In addition, internal audit can also add value to the organisation as well as providing assurance on the control environment.

32.66 The Combined Code requires that the directors should at least annually review the effectiveness of all controls, including operational, financial compliance and risk management. This represents a significant change from the Cadbury requirement, as interpreted by the guidance issued to directors in December 1994 (the so-called Rutteman guidance) only to review internal *financial* controls.

32.67 The purpose of this review is to ensure that there is a strong control framework through which the organisation can both protect and increase shareholder value. Some companies will have already decided that financial controls can be difficult to distinguish from other types of control and are already covering all types of controls in their review. But for many companies this change may be the most onerous aspect of the Combined Code and will require the active involvement of senior management. This is discussed further from paragraph 32.110.

32.68 The requirement for companies to review the effectiveness of all controls also affects the company's auditors who are currently required by the Stock Exchange Listing Rules to report on the company's compliance with that provision of the Combined Code. This is discussed further from paragraph 32.157.

Audit committee and auditors

32.69 The Combined Code includes the principle that the board should establish formal and transparent arrangements for considering how they should apply the financial reporting and internal control principles and for maintaining an appropriate relationship with the company's auditors. [CC Sec 1D.3].

32.70 The best practice provisions underlying this principle provide that:

- The board should establish an audit committee of at least three directors, all non-executive, with written terms of reference that deal clearly with its authority and duties. The annual report should include the names of the members of the committee, a majority of whom should be independent non-executive directors.

- The duties of the audit committee should include keeping under review the scope and results of the audit and its cost-effectiveness and the auditors' independence and objectivity. Where the auditors also supply to the company a substantial volume of non-audit services, the committee should keep the nature and extent of such services under review, seeking to balance the maintenance of objectivity and value for money.

[CC Sec 1 D.3]

32.71 The Combined Code places more emphasis on the role of the audit committee including for example monitoring the application of the financial reporting and internal control principles. In addition, the requirement that the majority of the audit committee's members must be independent non-executives is a change on which boards must focus.

Institutional shareholders

32.72 The Combined Code includes in Section 2 of both Part 1 and Part 2 certain recommendations for institutional shareholders concerning their relationship with listed companies. The first of the three Combined Code principles relating to institutional investors states that institutional shareholders have a responsibility to make considered use of their votes. [CC Sec 2 E.1].

32.73 The best practice provisions concerning the institutional shareholders' responsibility to make considered use of their votes require that institutional shareholders should:

- Endeavour to eliminate unnecessary variations in the criteria that each applies to the corporate governance arrangements and performance of the companies in which they invest.
- Make available to their clients on request information on the proportion of resolutions on which votes were cast and non-discretionary proxies lodged.
- Take steps to ensure that their voting intentions are being translated into practice.

[CC Sec 2 E.1].

32.74 The two remaining principles relating to institutional investors recommend that institutional shareholders should be ready, where practicable, to enter into a dialogue with companies based on the mutual understanding of objectives. [CC Sec 2 E.2]. Furthermore when evaluating companies' governance arrangements, particularly those relating to board structure and composition, institutional investors should give due weight to all relevant factors drawn to their attention. [CC Sec 2 E.3].

32.75 The principles and detailed Combined Code provisions relating to institutional shareholders are not matters which are appropriate for the Listing Rules to include within the disclosure requirement. The Hampel Committee did, however, regard Section 2 of the Combined Code, relating to institutional shareholders, as an integral part of the committee's recommendations and hoped that at least the major institutions would voluntarily disclose to their clients and to the public the extent to which they are able to give effect to these provisions.

Compliance statement

32.76 The Stock Exchange requirements take effect for accounting periods ending on or after 31 December 1998. A listed company has to include in its annual report and accounts a two part statement on corporate governance. In the first part the company is required to make a narrative statement explaining how it has applied the principles set out in Section 1 of the Combined Code (that is, the part that applies to companies). This statement should provide sufficient explanation to enable the company's shareholders to evaluate how the principles have been applied. [LR 12.43A(a)].

32.77 In the second part listed companies have to report whether or not the company has complied throughout the accounting period with the provisions set out in Section 1 of the Combined Code. Where a company has not complied with the Code's provisions, or has only complied with some of the Code's provisions or (in the case of provisions whose requirements are of a continuing nature) has complied for only part of an accounting period, the compliance statement must specify the Code provisions with which the company has not complied. In addition, where it is relevant it should also disclose for what part of the period such non-compliance continued and give reasons for any such non-compliance. [LR 12.43A(b)].

32.78 There are no requirements specifying where the statement of compliance should be located within the annual report. Under the previous requirements it would not normally be included within the audited financial statements. The corporate governance statement would commonly have been included within a separate section dealing with corporate governance just before the directors' report, or within the directors' report itself. Occasionally, it is dealt with or referred to within the chairman's statement.

32.79 In support of the compliance statement, boards or audit committees would generally expect to see a paper that sets out how the company complies with each aspect of the Combined Code, supported by relevant documentation. It is helpful for the board or audit committee to minute its approval of such a paper.

Statements of non-compliance

32.80 Any element of non-compliance with the Combined Code for any part of the period must be identified, giving reasons. The specific aspect of the Combined Code must be identified. This does not mean that the paragraph number in the Combined Code must be used, although some companies might do so. It would not be adequate simply to list the paragraph numbers of the Combined Code, because the reader would have to refer elsewhere to discover the significance of the statement.

32.81 Statements of non-compliance might become quite lengthy where there is significant non-compliance. But it would be very rare indeed for a company to fail to comply with all aspects. For example, few boards would wish to suggest that they do not *"meet regularly"*, *"bring an independent judgement to bear on issues of strategy, performance, resources (including key appointments) and standards of conduct"*, or that the annual report does not *"... set out the company's policy on executive directors' remuneration"* [CC Sec 1 A.1.1, A.1.5, B.3.2].

32.82 The shortest way to make a statement of non-compliance is to provide a list of areas of non-compliance with individual provisions or overall reasons for non-compliance. However, such a minimalist approach will be very negative, because it focuses on the areas of non-compliance. It is preferable to give a more balanced statement which gives information on compliance and/or on areas where the company is moving towards compliance. Although at the date of writing there are no published examples of such a statement, a statement of a similar type made under the Cadbury Code is given in Table 32.1.

Table 32.1 – Toad Plc – Annual Report and Accounts – 31 March 1997

Corporate Governance (extract)

Whilst the Board fully supports the highest standards in corporate governance, the level of corporate activity in the last year, culminating in the transactions announced today, has meant that the Group has been unable to implement all of the various procedures envisaged by the Code of Best Practice published by the Committee on the Financial Aspects of Corporate Governance (the "Cadbury Committee") since its full listing on the London Stock Exchange in January 1997. The Board is committed to remedying the situation as soon as is practicable, and sets out below the areas of non-compliance and the remedial action proposed.

The Board has yet to implement formal procedures for conducting its business and, in particular, no schedule of matters specifically reserved for the Board has been adopted and implemented by the Board as required by Section 1.4 of the Code.

An initial review of the effectiveness of the system of internal financial control was carried out by David Baynes at the time of the full listing on the Stock Exchange in January 1997 and was subsequently reviewed by the Board. However, the system has not been subject to any further formal review by the full Board. Accordingly, the directors cannot report that they have reviewed the Company's system of internal control as required by Section 4.5 of the Code.

There is no written procedure for directors in the furtherance of their duties to take independent professional advice if necessary, at the Company's expense, as required by Section 1.5 of the Code.

The Group has no formal procedures for the selection and the appointment of non-executive directors as required by Section 2.4 of the Code.

No written terms of reference had been prepared which deal clearly with the authorities and duties of the audit committee as required by Section 4.3 of the Code.

In the light of current developments and in the spirit of the code the Board is committed to taking the following actions:

- reviewing the membership of the Board and bringing in such additional executive and non-executive members as may be required to run the enlarged group;
- agreeing a schedule of matters specifically reserved for the Board;
- carrying out regular formal reviews of the Group's systems of internal financial control;
- formalising the procedure for directors in the furtherance of their duties to take independent advice, if necessary, at the Group's expense;
- formalising the procedure for the selection and appointment of non-executive directors; and
- agreeing written terms of reference which will define the authorities and duties of the Audit Committee

Board composition

The board currently comprises two non-executive directors and one full-time and one part-time executive director, plus the chairman, and is responsible for the management of the Group.

Board and other committees

One or both of the executive directors and other senior members of the management team meet at least weekly, setting and monitoring Group strategy, reviewing trading performance and formulating policy on key issues.

The Audit Committee comprises all the non-executive directors and is chaired by Dr Evans. It is programmed to meet twice a year and assists the Board in ensuring that the Group's published financial statements give a true and fair view. The Committee meets as necessary with and receives reports from the external auditors.

The Remuneration Committee comprises all of the non-executive directors and is chaired by Dr Evans. It meets as necessary and is responsible for making recommendations to the Board on the remuneration of senior executives and all directors.

32.83 Compliance with the Combined Code throughout the period is likely to be difficult for the first year. Although the Combined Code was issued in June 1998, companies with December 1998 year ends are expected to report compliance for the whole of the year then ending. This could lead to some fairly convoluted reports in the first year as non-compliance with certain provisions for certain periods has to be described.

32.84 There could be valid reasons why some of the provisions have not yet been followed or some alternative procedures may have been adopted. As long as the company explains and has reasonable justification for any non-compliance with specific aspects and governance is effective in practice, in the spirit of transparency, it is hoped that the market will react in a positive way.

32.85 The London Stock Exchange recommended that shareholders and others monitoring compliance with the Combined Code should do so with flexibility, common sense and with regard to the individual company's circumstances, particularly in the first year of reporting compliance with the Combined Code.

32.86 Stating non-compliance under Cadbury has clearly been unattractive for major listed companies – nearly all top 100 companies stated full compliance with the Cadbury Code. Many listed companies went well beyond the minimum requirements of the Cadbury Code, commonly devoting a whole page in the annual report to corporate governance, in addition to certain other disclosures resulting from compliance with the Cadbury Code. Certain bodies also made voluntary disclosures, principally financial services companies and public interest bodies such as the BBC, housing associations and universities.

Reporting on going concern

Combined Code requirement

32.87 Compliance with the Combined Code requires that *"the directors should report that the business is a going concern, with supporting assumptions or qualifications as necessary"*. [CC Sec 1 D1.3]

32.88 This is unchanged from the requirement under the Cadbury Code and should be interpreted in the light of the guidance, 'Going concern and financial reporting' (GCFR), which was published by a joint working group in November 1994. The going concern statement became a separate requirement of the Listing Rules effective for accounting periods beginning on or after 31 December 1995 and this is unchanged by the amendment to the Listing Rules following the Combined Code. [LR 12.43(v)]. Examples of this type of statement are shown in Tables 32.2 and 32.3.

Table 32.2 – GKN plc – Report and Accounts – 31 December 1997

Financial Review (extract)

Going concern
In view of the strength of the year-end balance sheet and in the light of future funding requirements, the Directors are of the opinion that it is appropriate for the accounts to be prepared on a going concern basis. The auditors have reported on this on page 55.

Table 32.3 – Allied Domecq Plc – Report and Accounts – 31 August 1997
Corporate governance statement (extract) GOING CONCERN After making enquiries, the directors have formed a judgement, at the time of approving the financial statements, that there is a reasonable expectation that the company and the group have adequate resources to continue in operational existence for the foreseeable future. For this reason, the directors continue to adopt the going concern basis in preparing the financial statements.

32.89 The guidance describes procedures that companies may undertake so that the directors are in a position to express a positive opinion on going concern and sets out what the disclosure should include.

Form of disclosure

32.90 The form of disclosure depends on the directors' conclusions having undertaken procedures in relation to going concern. There are three basic conclusions:

- they have a reasonable expectation that the company or group will continue in operational existence for the foreseeable future; or
- they have identified factors that cast doubt on the ability of the company or group to continue in operational existence, but they consider it appropriate to use the going concern basis in preparing the financial statements; or
- they consider that the going concern basis is not appropriate.

32.91 Most companies fall into the first category. The guidance suggests the appropriate form of words in this case:

> *"After making enquiries, the directors have a reasonable expectation that the company has adequate resources to continue in operational existence for the foreseeable future. For this reason, they continue to adopt the going concern basis in preparing the accounts."* [GCFR para 49].

32.92 This form of disclosure has been adopted by most companies, although a significant number of blue chip companies, especially in the financial services sector, have chosen to be rather more positive, for example see Table 32.4.

Table 32.4 – Abbey National plc – Directors' Report and Accounts – 31 December 1997

Going concern

The directors confirm that they are satisfied that the Group has adequate resources to continue in business for the foreseeable future. For this reason, they continue to adopt the going concern basis in preparing the accounts.

32.93 The guidance places emphasis on the fact that 'going concern' is a fundamental accounting concept with a technical meaning defined by SSAP 2 that the enterprise will continue in operational existence for the foreseeable future. The guidance requires directors to state that they believe it appropriate to continue to use the going concern basis, not to guarantee that the company will not fail.

32.94 The guidance recommends that the disclosure should be located in the operating and financial review (OFR) recognising that the OFR provides a context for a going concern statement. Despite this, and recognising that some listed companies do not publish an OFR, it is quite common for the going concern statement to be included within the corporate governance statement with a separate sub-heading.

32.95 The guidance provides very limited indication of what might constitute *"factors which cast doubt"* on the company's or group's ability to continue in operational existence. An example is given of a company that is in breach of its loan covenants and where negotiations are continuing.

32.96 Where there are factors that cast doubt, directors are expected to perform more detailed work to determine the extent of the problem. The directors will then need to *"explain the circumstances so as to identify the factors which give rise to the problems"* and explain how they intend to deal with them.

32.97 The guidance gives an example of such a disclosure:

> *"The company is in breach of certain loan covenants at its balance sheet date and so the company's bankers could recall their loans at any time. The directors continue to be involved in negotiations with the company's bankers and as yet no demands for repayments have been received. The negotiations are at an early stage and, although the directors are optimistic about the outcome, it is as yet too early to make predictions with any certainty.*
>
> *In the light of the actions described elsewhere in the Operating and Financial Review, the directors consider it appropriate to adopt the going concern basis in preparing the accounts."* [GCFR para 51].

32.98 South West Water, in their 1997 annual report, gave a conventional going concern statement. However, as an illustration of non-standard wording we reproduce in Table 32.5 the statement South West Water made in 1995, regarding the impact of regulatory price limits that may affect the company's ability to finance its functions.

Table 32.5 – South West Water PLC – Annual Report & Accounts – 31 March 1995

CORPORATE GOVERNANCE (extract)

GOING CONCERN

As reported as part of the Chairman's interim statement issued in November 1994, the Director General of Water Services had set price limits for South West Water Services Limited for the next ten years which the Directors concluded may not enable that company properly to finance its functions and could jeopardise the company's ability to meet its obligations, and the reasonable expectations of its customers for quality and service. For this reason, the Directors of South West Water Services Limited formally notified the Directors General in September of the company's requirement for him to refer this Determination to the Monopolies and Mergers Commission.

The Water Industry Act 1991 provides that the Director General (or, upon a reference, the Monopolies and Mergers Commission) shall secure that companies holding appointments under this Act as water or sewerage undertakers are able to finance the proper carrying out of their functions. The Directors therefore consider that the Monopolies and Mergers Commission process is not inconsistent with continuing the adoption of the going concern basis.

The Directors consider, after making appropriate enquiries, that the Company and the Group have adequate resources to continue in operational existence for the foreseeable future. For this reason they continue to adopt the going concern basis in preparing the financial statements.

32.99 If the directors conclude that the company is unlikely to continue in operational existence for the foreseeable future, a non-going concern basis will be required in preparing the financial statements and this will require disclosure. Directors will generally wish to take legal advice before making such a disclosure, in particular in relation to whether the directors may be liable for wrongful trading.

32.100 None of these disclosures obviate the need to make the disclosures relating to a non-going concern basis required by the Companies Act and accounting standards within the financial statements (see chapter 2).

Application to groups

32.101 The guidance requires directors of a parent company to make disclosures in relation to both the parent and the group as a whole. This does not mean that each individual company in the group is a going concern, but it does mean that the directors' procedures will need to consider the impact of any difficulties in subsidiaries on the group as a whole.

Procedures

32.102 The guidance specifies a series of procedures that directors may wish to adopt in considering whether it is appropriate to adopt the going concern basis for the financial statements. It recognises that appropriate procedures will vary according to circumstances. The effect of the guidance is that the board should expect to see a paper that pulls together the evidence available from such procedures and any additional procedures that may be deemed necessary in the circumstances identified. The directors will need to consider this and other evidence available to them to determine whether it is appropriate to make the proposed statement on going concern.

32.103 The procedures, which are explained more fully in an appendix to the guidance, cover the following areas:

- Forecasts and budgets.
- Borrowing requirements.
- Liability management.
- Contingent liabilities.
- Products and markets.
- Financial risk management.
- Other factors.
- Financial adaptability.

Foreseeable future

32.104 The guidance explains that directors should make their statement on the basis of information available to them at the date they approve the financial statements. In practice, the review procedures will be undertaken to an earlier date and then reviewed for any changes up to the date of approval.

32.105 During the drafting of the guidance there was significant discussion of how far forward the directors should look in considering whether the business is expected to remain a going concern. The guidance observes that any such consideration is inherently uncertain and can only represent a judgement at a point in time that may subsequently be overturned. The guidance requires directors to consider all information of which they are aware at the time of approval. Events expected more than, say, a year beyond approval should not, therefore, be ignored.

32.106 The guidance seeks to avoid specifying a minimum period, but requires that *"where the period considered by the directors has been limited, for example, to a period of less than one year from the date of approval"*, the directors should consider whether additional disclosure should be made to explain this limitation. SAS 130 published by the APB requires that:

> *"If the period to which the directors have paid particular attention in assessing going concern is less than one year from the date of approval of the financial statements, and the directors have not disclosed that fact, the auditors should do so within the Section of their report setting out the basis of their opinion"* [SAS 130 para 45].

32.107 Most directors will find such a reference by auditors unattractive and, therefore, for practical purposes, companies will want to ensure that the period given active consideration is at least a year from the date of approval (or the directors themselves have to explain why this is inappropriate). For some companies this will mean extending budgets and cash flows, at least at group level, beyond the end of the following financial period to cover 12 months from the date of approval.

Reporting on internal control

Combined Code requirement

32.108 Compliance with the Combined Code requires that:

> *"The directors should, at least annually, conduct a review of the effectiveness of the group's system of internal controls and should report to the shareholders that they have done so. The review should cover all controls, including financial, operational and compliance controls and risk management".* [CC Sec 1 D2.1]

32.109 The requirement for directors to review the effectiveness of all controls goes further than the previous Cadbury requirement to review *financial* control and will require the active involvement of senior management.

32.110 For many companies that have already accepted that in practice it is difficult to distinguish financial from other controls, this wider risk and control review may already be well established. For others, this change may require a significant extension of the work previously done to review and report on internal financial control. Past experience shows that the review of internal financial control was one of the more onerous requirements of Cadbury. It has also been one of the more fruitful where undertaken effectively.

32.111 However, for many listed companies the previous review may have become something of a bureaucratic process, which recently has failed to engage management and added little real value to the business. The requirement of the Combined Code for the review now to cover risk management and operational, financial and compliance controls provides an ideal opportunity to review the effectiveness of the existing processes, taking into account the significant developments in risk management thinking that have occurred since Cadbury was introduced. High level integrated risk management approaches that take account of strategy, organisation and people as well as business processes are now seen by leading corporates as offering clear potential for enhancing shareholder value.

Guidance for directors

32.112 The Cadbury report recognised that companies would find it difficult to comply with the paragraph of the Cadbury Code relating to internal control until necessary guidance had been developed, and set up a joint working group, comprising individuals put forward by the Hundred Group of Finance Directors, the Institute of Chartered Accountants in England and Wales and the Institute of Chartered Accountants of Scotland, chaired by Paul Rutteman, to provide guidance to directors. The guidance for directors, 'Internal control and financial reporting' (ICFC), was finalised in December 1994 and was effective for accounting periods beginning on or after 1 January 1995.

32.113 At the date of writing no further guidance has been issued to directors covering the wider review required by the Combined Code and yet the Listing Rule requirement to report in accordance with the Code on the review of internal control remains in place. The ICAEW is shortly expected to constitute a new working group to review whether there is a need for new guidance for directors on internal control, and to consider what this might be. It is likely that any further guidance will be based on the initial guidance and the following paragraphs provide an explanation of the guidance available to directors in 'Internal control and financial reporting'. In the absence of new guidance for directors concerning their wider responsibilities companies will have to work with the existing guidance, but apply it to all aspects of their internal control.

Internal control and financial reporting

32.114 The foreword to the Rutteman guidance, written by the Cadbury Committee, makes it clear that compliance with the guidance constitutes compliance with the Cadbury Code requirement regarding internal financial control.

32.115 The guidance requires that the directors make a statement containing:

> *"(a) acknowledgement by the directors that they are responsible for the company's system of internal financial control;*
>
> *(b) explanation that such a system can provide only reasonable and not absolute assurance against material misstatement or loss;*
>
> *(c) description of key procedures that the directors have established and which are designed to provide effective internal financial control; and*

(d) confirmation that the directors (or a board committee) have reviewed the effectiveness of the system of internal financial control." [ICFR para 11].

32.116 The first two requirements are relatively straightforward and will follow fairly standard wording. Paragraph 11(c) leads to a significant amount of disclosure, commonly up to half a page and should be specific to the business. The most challenging disclosure, however, is usually that required by paragraph 11(d). Although the disclosure itself is straightforward, there is a significant amount of work required so that the board or a committee thereof (commonly the audit committee) can confirm that it has reviewed the effectiveness of internal financial control. Both the description of key procedures and the review procedures are dealt with below.

32.117 Notice that, although the guidance requires the directors to confirm that they have *reviewed* the effectiveness of internal financial control, it does not require them to state whether control is effective. That is, it does not generally require them to disclose the conclusions drawn from their review. The guidance does, however, give this option, stating that *"directors may also wish to state their opinion on the effectiveness of their system of internal financial control"*. We would generally advise against making this additional disclosure as it may unnecessarily add to the directors' legal exposure. Almost all companies, especially those with listings in the US, have to date felt it best not to make this disclosure. There is also a risk of setting a precedent that could be difficult to follow in subsequent years if significant control failings emerge.

32.118 The disclosure may be located within:

- a general statement on corporate governance;
- the statement of directors' responsibilities;
- the directors' report; or
- the OFR.

32.119 The last option recognises that there is a link between the discussion of risks within the OFR and the risk assessment procedures that form part of the internal control framework. However, within the statement of corporate governance is the more normal location and if the statement is not placed there then a cross-reference to where it is to be found should be included in the statement on corporate governance. [ICFR para 7].

32.120 The Rutteman guidance draws heavily on the equivalent US guidance 'Internal control – integrated framework' written for the Committee of Sponsoring Organisations of the Treadway Commission (COSO) by Coopers & Lybrand in the US.

Scope of reporting

32.121 Drawing on COSO, Cadbury recognises the objectives of internal control as being to provide assurance in three areas:

- Effective and efficient operations.
- Internal financial control.
- Compliance with laws and regulations.

32.122 The guidance only requires directors to report in relation to internal *financial* control which it defines as:

> *"The internal controls established in order to provide reasonable assurance of:*
>
> *(a) the safeguarding of assets against unauthorised use or disposition; and*
>
> *(b) the maintenance of proper accounting records and the reliability of financial information used within the business or for publication."* [ICFR para 2].

32.123 In practice, this is a fairly wide definition including, for example, the reliability of monthly management accounts as well as published annual financial statements. It is not always possible to draw a clear boundary around internal *financial* control and the guidance recognises that consideration of its effectiveness may have to include consideration of certain operational and compliance controls. It is commonly these controls whose failure can have severe financial consequences.

Application to groups

32.124 The directors' statement is required to deal with the period of the financial statements and take account of material developments after the balance sheet date, such as a significant control failing coming to light.

32.125 In the case of a parent preparing consolidated financial statements the disclosures should relate to the group as a whole. This can be very significant for a group with many subsidiary and overseas operations and implies that directors must have a clear view on how they exercise control over the whole group. In the case of associates and joint ventures, the nature of that control will be different from that for subsidiaries. However, the directors should still consider whether they have appropriate mechanisms in place to protect the group's exposure to actions of the associate or joint venture business.

32.126 The guidance is concerned with the *high level* control framework and not, in the first instance, with detailed controls of either an accounting or an operational nature. This is clear from paragraph 8(d) of ICFR which requires the *directors* to have reviewed the effectiveness of control and from paragraph 11 which refers to *"the specific high level procedures used by the company/group"*. Whilst the review should, therefore, begin at a high level, for most groups of companies, it will be necessary to conduct some level of review and/or confirmation of control effectiveness at operating company level.

Review of internal financial control

32.127 The guidance stipulates that, in reviewing the effectiveness of internal financial control, the directors should have regard to a series of criteria under five headings drawn directly from the US COSO guidance. [ICFR para 11]. COSO also contains significantly more detailed evaluation tools in each of these areas.

- *The control environment* is the tone set from the top of the organisation. It includes the response to control failures, the organisational structure, ethical policies and the structure of incentives.

- *Risk assessment* is the process to identify and evaluate major business risks including the likelihood of their crystallising and their potential financial impact. It is in this area that most companies have had significant work to undertake in order to comply. The guidance states that *"in assessing the effectiveness of a system, attention should be directed to whether the material risks have been identified and have been given the requisite attention, as well as the nature of the action taken"*. The guidance also suggests the option of providing a brief explanation of the major financial risks identified.

- *Information systems* include annual budgeting, monthly reporting and comparisons with budgets and forecasts. They include non-financial key performance indicators in relation to key business objectives and risks.

- *Control procedures* are the activities that have more commonly been given attention in relation to control and include authorisation procedures, segregation of duties, reconciliations and supervisory checks.

- *Monitoring procedures* are those high level procedures employed to assure the board that the system is effective in managing the key risks identified. They may include the audit committee, management reviews, self-certification, internal audit and/or reports from independent accountants.

32.128 The starting point for a review of internal financial control is often a paper to the board or audit committee that takes each of the detailed criteria under the five headings above and documents against each:

- An assessment of the group's current state of compliance.
- Additional action proposed to meet the criteria in a way appropriate to the business.

32.129 The guidance is deliberately written in a flexible, non-prescriptive manner recognising that risks and control structures vary from business to business. It is not, therefore, possible to treat the criteria as a simple checklist. What matters is that the directors form a view on whether the procedures that they have in relation to the five areas above are appropriate and sufficient to give them assurance that the business is effectively controlled. This is a matter of judgement and what is appropriate will depend on the particular risks facing the business and the board's philosophy and approach to controlling the business.

32.130 At a minimum boards or audit committees require papers that demonstrably cover the five criteria for control. In our experience, a more satisfactory and worthwhile analysis will be achieved if the businesses' directors and senior management participate in a rigorous exercise to identify the major financial and non-financial risks facing the business and then map against these responsibilities, control procedures and monitoring procedures. Properly structured, such an exercise can add real value to the business by helping focus board and management attention on areas that may require improvement or which must not be allowed to slip.

Description of key procedures

32.131 A description of the key procedures that directors have established to provide effective internal financial control will deal with high level procedures. It will follow naturally from the review described above.

32.132 Companies are advised to draft disclosures that describe actions and monitoring procedures specific to their organisation. Statements that are full of platitudes or that have clearly been copied directly from other companies may well be read as implying that the directors have not given any real attention to internal control.

32.133 The description is required to have regard to the five criteria described in paragraph 32.127 above. Those headings may, therefore, be used to provide a structure to the statement.

32.134 Some of the following may be relevant to be included within the statement:

- Management and control philosophy (for example, decentralised v centralised).
- Board and audit committee remit and action on control.
- Organisation, levels of authority, division of responsibilities.
- Code of conduct/ethics.
- Personnel policies – selection, training and control.
- Business planning and strategy process.
- Management reporting cycle.
- Risk identification and management.
- Financial accounting function.
- Written financial and operating policies and procedures.
- Self-assessment/certification.
- Internal audit – programme and findings.
- External auditors – reports to management arising from audit of financial statements.

32.135 The following are examples of descriptive statements on internal financial control.

Table 32.6 – Scottish Power plc – Annual Report & Accounts – 31 March 1998

Corporate Governance (extract)

Internal financial control

The Board of Directors is responsible for the group's system of internal financial control and for monitoring its effectiveness. It must be recognised that any such system can provide only reasonable and not absolute assurance of the safeguarding of assets, the maintenance of proper accounting records and the reliability of financial information. The key features of the control system which has been established, and which is designed to ensure effective internal financial control, are as follows:

Control environment

The company is committed to ensuring that a proper control environment is maintained. There is a commitment to competence and integrity, and the communication of ethical values and control consciousness to managers and employees. Human Resources policies underpin that commitment by a focus on enhancing job skills and promoting high standards of probity amongst staff. In addition the appropriate organisational structure has been developed within which to control the businesses and to delegate authority and accountability having regard to acceptable levels of risk. Business managing directors report regularly on operating performance to the relevant executive director with line responsibility, and the performance of each business is reviewed monthly by the Chief Executive's Committee.

Risk assessment and control procedures
The company's strategy is to follow a prudent risk policy, effectively managing exposures where appropriate.

The Board has undertaken a specific exercise to review and assess its key risks at a group level and to ensure that it is receiving appropriate information to monitor the management of those risks. The Board has required each of the businesses to complete a similar exercise to define key risks, controls and monitoring procedures utilising a well defined and consistent methodology. It is a key requirement of the procedures that a written certificate is provided annually by the managing director and financial manager of each business confirming that they have reviewed the effectiveness of the system of internal financial controls during the year. Periodic detailed review by the Finance Director of the accounting records of each business reinforces a focussed approach to control throughout the group's finance functions.

Audit of controls
Operation of the group's control and monitoring procedures is reviewed and tested by the group's internal audit function under the supervision of the Head of Internal Audit, reporting directly to the Finance Director. Internal audit reports and recommendations on the group's procedures are reviewed regularly by the Audit Committee. As part of their external audit responsibilities, the external auditors also provide reports to the Audit Committee on the operation of the group's internal financial control procedures.

The directors confirm that they have reviewed the effectiveness of the system of internal financial controls utilising the procedures set out above.

Table 32.7 – Carlton Communications Plc – Annual report & accounts – 30 September 1997

Corporate Governance (extract)

Internal financial controls
The Company has established financial and managerial procedures. Such a system can provide only reasonable and not absolute assurance against any misstatement or loss. These can be summarised as follows:

Control environment – clear management responsibilities are established for the executive directors and the directors of each of the operating companies. These are laid down in the Company's Management Policies.

Risk management – operating company management have a clear responsibility for the identification of risks facing each of the businesses, and for putting in place procedures to mitigate and monitor risks. Each operating company is required to prepare a risk assessment which is reviewed by the internal audit function. The executive directors together with the rest of the Board monitor this process.

Information and control systems – the Group has a comprehensive process of annual budgets and detailed monthly reporting together with weekly cash reporting. The annual budget of each operating company is reviewed by the executive directors and the Board approves the overall Group budget as part of its normal responsibilities.

Monitoring system – the financial controls are monitored by management review, the internal audit function and by the audit committee. All operating companies are required to certify to the Board that a comprehensive system of financial controls was in place throughout the period. The audit committee has reviewed the effectiveness of the internal financial controls of the Group for the period 1 October 1996 to 30 September 1997.

Disclosure of material weaknesses

32.136 In respect of control weaknesses, disclosure is only required where weaknesses in internal financial control *"have resulted in material losses, contingencies or uncertainties"* which *"require disclosure in the financial statements or in the auditors' report"*. The additional requirement is to:

- describe what corrective action has been taken or is intended to be taken; or
- explain why no changes are considered necessary.

[ICFR para 12].

32.137 Where directors are aware of control failures or of potential weaknesses they will clearly wish to take mitigating action. They will also need to ensure that the statement does not give a misleading impression by being overly positive about the state of internal financial control.

General statements on corporate governance

32.138 The Cadbury report recommended that companies may *"wish to go beyond the strict terms of the London Stock Exchange rule and make a general statement about the corporate governance of their enterprises"*. This is not specifically dealt with in the Combined Code and at the date of writing there are no examples of such statements relating to the Combined Code. Reproduced in Table 32.8 is an example of a report made under the Cadbury Code.

Table 32.8 – SmithKline Beecham plc – Annual Report and Accounts – 31 December 1997

Directors' report (extract)

Corporate Governance

In 1996, the Company complied with all aspects of the Code of Best Practice contained in the Report on the Financial Aspects of Corporate Governance prepared by the Cadbury Committee.

Board of Directors

Directors meet regularly and retain full and effective control over the Company. SB has a non-executive Chairman and a separate Chief Executive. The Board comprises a majority of non-executive directors, who are independent of management. All directors have access to the advice and services of the Company Secretary, who is responsible for ensuring that board procedures and applicable rules and regulations are observed. There is an agreed procedure for directors to take independent professional advice, if necessary, at the Company's expense. Executive directors have agreed to service contracts that run for 24 months or less.

Board Committees

SB has a Remuneration and Nominations (R&N) Committee, an Audit Committee and a Finance Committee. The R&N and Audit Committees consist wholly of non-executive Directors. The Audit Committee receives reports regularly from the Company's internal audit department and ensures that an objective and professional relationship is maintained between the Board and the external auditors. The Audit Committee also meets with internal and external auditors, without executive management being present. The Finance Committee is responsible for implementing Treasury policies, approving capital expenditure and other corporate investment proposals up to agreed limits, approving the quarterly trading results and declaring interim dividends. The members of these committees are set out on page 32 of this Report.

Internal control

The directors are responsible for the Company's system of internal financial control. The system of internal financial control is designed to provide reasonable but not absolute assurance against material misstatement or loss. The Company has an established framework of internal financial controls, the operation and effectiveness of which has been reviewed by the Audit Committee in 1997:

- Financial reporting: there is a comprehensive budgeting system with an annual plan approved by the Directors. The results of operating units are reported monthly and compared to the plan. Forecasts are prepared regularly throughout the year. The Company reports to shareholders on a quarterly basis.
- Quality and integrity of personnel: one of the Company's five core values is integrity. The Company's policies are detailed in a Corporate Policy Manual. Written confirmation of compliance with internal financial control policies is obtained from the Finance Directors and General Managers of all operating units annually.
- Operating unit controls: financial controls and procedures including information systems controls are detailed in policies and procedures manuals. Operating units complete Self-Certification Questionnaires confirming compliance with these procedures. These questionnaires are reviewed by both the Company's internal and external auditors.
- Functional speciality reporting: the Company assesses the risks facing the business on an ongoing basis and has identified a number of key areas which are subject to regular reporting to the Board, such as Treasury Operations, Environmental, Legal and Risk Management matters.

- Investment appraisal: the Company has clearly defined guidelines for capital expenditure. These include annual budgets, detailed appraisal and review procedures, levels of authority and due diligence requirements where businesses are being acquired. Post-investment appraisals are performed for major investments.

Going concern

The Directors have reviewed the Group's budget for 1998 and the medium-term plans for 1998 to 2000. After taking into account the cash flow implications of the plans, including proposed capital expenditure and restructuring costs, and after comparing these with the Group's committed borrowing facilities and projected gearing ratios, the Directors are satisfied that it is appropriate to produce the Group and Company accounts on a going concern basis.

Directors' responsibilities

The Directors are required by the Companies Act 1985 to prepare financial statements for each financial year which give a true and fair view of the state of affairs of the Company and the Group as at the end of the financial year and of the profit or loss for the financial year.

The Directors consider that in preparing the financial statements, the Group has used appropriate accounting policies, consistently applied and supported by reasonable and prudent judgements and estimates.

All accounting standards which they consider to be applicable have been followed, subject to any explanations and material departures disclosed in the notes to the financial statements.

The Directors have responsibility for ensuring that the Company and the Group keep accounting records which disclose with reasonable accuracy the financial position of the Company and the Group and which enable them to ensure that the financial statements comply with the Companies Act 1985.

The Directors have general responsibility for taking such steps as are reasonably open to them to safeguard the assets of the Group and to prevent and detect fraud and other irregularities.

Sir Christopher Hogg
Chairman
Audit Committee
26 February 1998

32.139 Companies should draft such a statement to describe what the directors believe to be the most important features of their governance. It is of no great value simply to reiterate areas of the Combined Code with which they comply. To the extent that directors are not already aware of the practice described, the board or audit committee would expect to have supporting papers evidencing the statement proposed.

32.140 The general statement would usually begin with the two part statement of compliance with the Combined Code. Other items of disclosure commonly dealt with on the same page as a general statement are internal financial control, going concern, and a description of the auditors' review.

Smaller listed companies

32.141 Amongst smaller listed companies, a significant number initially chose to state non-compliance with the Cadbury Code, but gradually many smaller listed companies brought their procedures into line with the Cadbury Code. The most common area of non-compliance was in relation to the Cadbury Code's requirement to appoint three non-executive directors to the board (a majority of whom should be independent). The Combined Code's requirement for at least third of the board to be non-executive increases the pressure on companies to find and retain non-executives.

32.142 The City Group for Smaller Companies (CISCO) has explicitly recognised that some aspects of the Cadbury Code were drafted more with larger listed companies in mind. It has published 'The financial aspects of governance – Guidance for smaller companies' with a foreword by Sir Adrian Cadbury recommending certain modifications of the Cadbury Code for application to smaller listed companies. These recommendations do not change the requirement of the London Stock Exchange to state non-compliance with any aspects of the original Code, but they may be cited by companies as evidence of support for the stance they are taking. This is particularly relevant to companies coming to the market who are discussing their governance arrangements with sponsors.

Non-listed organisations

32.143 Where non-listed organisations choose voluntarily to report on compliance with the Combined Code, we recommend that they report fully as though they were listed. We, therefore, advise against phrases such as:

> *"We comply with all aspects of the Combined Code relevant to the Institution."*

This form of disclosure on its own provides the reader with no indication of what aspects of the Combined Code the institution has considered relevant and, therefore, is of no real value. Some organisations, such as the National Health Service Management Executive, have issued their own code of governance. In these situations, reference will of course be made to such codes instead.

32.144 Although non-listed companies are encouraged to aim at meeting the requirements of the Combined Code, outside of public interest organisations and financial services companies this has been rare to date.

32.145 Companies that are considering the possibility of a listing will need to consider establishing appropriate governance procedures well in advance of coming to the market. In particular, they should review and, if necessary, improve their systems of internal control. In seeking a listing, companies will be expected to make a statement of 'support' for the principles of the Combined Code. It is also usual to describe the steps the company has taken to comply in the areas of non-executive directors, audit remuneration and nomination committees (describing their composition and principal functions), even if they have only recently been appointed or established. The sponsors will also normally expect to see significant moves to compliance in other areas. In their first period following listing, the Stock Exchange has generally permitted new registrants to make a statement of compliance for the period from the date of listing only rather than for the full accounting period. Nevertheless, it will be important to be well prepared, because certain procedures can take some time to implement.

Statements of directors' and auditors' responsibilities

32.146 The Cadbury Code introduced the requirement for directors of listed UK companies to make a statement of their responsibilities. This has been slightly modified by the Combined Code to read as follows *"the directors should explain their responsibility for preparing the accounts and there should be a statement by the auditors about their reporting responsibilities"*. [CC Sec 1D 1.1].

32.147 This is a relatively formal statement. Appendix 3 to the Cadbury report specified the minimum content:

> *"(a) the legal requirement for directors to prepare financial statements for each financial year which give a true and fair view of the state of affairs of the company (or group) as at the end of the financial year and of the profit and loss for that period;*
>
> *(b) the responsibility of the directors for maintaining adequate accounting records, for safeguarding the assets of the company (or group), and for preventing and detecting fraud and other irregularities;*
>
> *(c) confirmation that suitable accounting policies, consistently applied and supported by reasonable and prudent judgements and estimates, have been used in the preparation of financial statements;*
>
> *(d) confirmation that applicable accounting standards have been followed, subject to any material departures disclosed and explained in the notes to the accounts."*

32.148 Subsequent to publication of the Cadbury report, the APB published SAS 600, 'Auditors' report on financial statements'. The effect of this is to extend to all audited financial statements the requirement to include a statement of directors' responsibilities.

The minimum content is almost identical to that in the Cadbury report with the addition of the requirement to explain that the financial statements are required to be prepared on the going concern basis, unless a separate statement on going concern is included elsewhere in the annual report. Also, whereas the Cadbury Report recommends specific confirmation of certain matters (see para 32.147 above) the version in SAS 600 does not. Accordingly, listed companies should adapt the SAS 600 version to give the specific confirmations, see for example Table 32.8 on page 32035.

32.149 SAS 600 gives a specimen wording that has been widely, but not universally, adopted, which is reproduced below.

SAS 600 – Auditors' report on financial statements – May 1993

Appendix 3

Example wording of a description of directors' responsibilities for inclusion in a company's financial statements.

Company law requires the directors to prepare financial statements for each financial year which give a true and fair view of the state of affairs of the company and of the profit or loss of the company for that period. In preparing those financial statements, the directors are required to:

- select suitable accounting policies and then apply them consistently;
- make judgements and estimates that are reasonable and prudent;
- state whether applicable accounting standards have been followed, subject to any material departures disclosed and explained in the financial statements[6];
- prepare the financial statements on the going concern basis unless it is inappropriate to presume that the company will continue in business[7];

The directors are responsible for keeping proper accounting records which disclose with reasonable accuracy at any time the financial position of the company and to enable them to ensure that the financial statements comply with the Companies Act 1985. They are also responsible for safeguarding the assets of the company and hence for taking reasonable steps for the prevention and detection of fraud and other irregularities.

[6] Large companies only.

[7] If no separate statement on going concern is made by the directors.

32.150 The requirement of the Combined Code to include a statement by the auditors about their reporting responsibilities is currently met by the illustrative auditors' report on the annual financial statements as specified by SAS 600 for all audited financial statements. This report includes a brief statement of the auditors' responsibilities:

> *"As described on page x, the company's directors are responsible for the preparation of financial statements. It is our responsibility*

to form an independent opinion, based on our audit, on those statements and to report our opinion to you."

32.151 There is no longer a requirement under the Combined Code that the statement of directors' responsibilities should be *next to* the statement by the auditors. The directors' statement is commonly included as a separate statement, within the directors' report or at the end of the corporate governance statement.

Early adoption of Listing Rule

32.152 Although the Listing Rule only comes into effect in respect of accounting periods ending on or after 31 December 1998, some companies may consider reporting under the Combined Code and new Listing Rule for earlier periods (for example, companies with September year ends). Whilst a proactive approach to corporate governance developments should be encouraged there are a number of problems with early adoption of the Combined Code. It would be preferable for companies to report under the existing regime for such earlier periods even though they may be implementing many of the additional or expanded provisions of the new Code during these periods.

32.153 The following points are relevant when considering the question of early adoption:

- A number of the Combined Code requirements are new and it is likely that companies will not have complied with all of the provisions for the whole of the period of review. In its statement, the company has to note all areas of non-compliance. Directors may not want to report a long list of areas where provisions were not in place for the full year.

- Directors are now to conduct, at least annually, a review of the effectiveness of *all* internal controls (including financial, operational, compliance, risk management). As mentioned in the previous section the existing guidance for directors on internal financial control dates from 1994 and no formal recognised framework for conducting the broader review envisaged by the Combined Code exists. More guidance is expected to be considered soon, but the outcome is uncertain. The directors will, therefore, have to take a view of the robustness and coverage of their existing control reviews. Many directors will not want to make a public statement on the wider scope before the requirement is effective, preferably when the broader review of their systems has been completed.

- There is uncertainty on the auditor's role in the new regime (as discussed from para 32.157). The initial proposals were to ask the auditors to review the company's statements on the objective provisions of the Code, of which there are only seven. The Auditing Practices Board (APB) is considering what up to date guidance is now required This aspect is considered in more detail from paragraph 32.162.

32.154 In view of these factors, it may not be advantageous for companies to attempt to adopt early the reporting aspects of the new Listing Rule. Companies should, however, implement any new corporate governance practices required as soon as possible.

Auditor reporting on compliance with the Combined Code

Listing Rule requirement

32.155 The Listing Rules require that the company's statement of compliance with the Combined Code required under Listing Rule 12.43A(b) (see para 32.77 above) must be reviewed by the auditors before publication, but only insofar as it relates to the following Code provisions:

- The board should have a formal schedule of matters specifically reserved to it for decision. [CC Sec 1A.1.2].

- There should be a procedure agreed by the board for directors in the furtherance of their duties to take independent professional advice if necessary, at the company's expense. [CC Sec 1A.1.3].

- Non-executive directors should be appointed for specified terms subject to re-election and to Companies Act provisions relating to the removal of a director, and reappointment should not be automatic. [CC Sec 1A.6.1].

- All directors should be subject to election by shareholders at the first opportunity after their appointment and to re-election thereafter at intervals of no more than three years. The names of directors submitted for election or re-election should be accompanied by sufficient biographical details to enable shareholders to take an informed decision on their election. [CC Sec 1A.6.2].

- The directors should explain their responsibility for preparing the financial statements and there should be a statement by the auditors about their reporting responsibilities. [CC Sec 1D.1.1].

- The directors should, at least annually, conduct a review of the effectiveness of the group's system of internal controls and should report to shareholders that they have done so. The review should cover all controls, including financial, operational and compliance controls and risk management. [CC Sec 1D.2.1].

- The board should establish an audit committee of at least three directors, all non-executive, with written terms of reference that deal clearly with its authority and duties. The members of the committee, a majority of whom should be independent non-executive directors, should be named in the report and accounts. [CC Sec 1D.3.1].

32.156 Furthermore, the scope of the auditors' report on the financial statements must cover certain disclosure requirements concerning directors' remuneration. These include the disclosures required by Listing Rule 12.43A(c)(ii), (iii), (iv), (ix) and (x) (see further chapter 11). The auditors must state in their report if in their opinion the company has not complied with the disclosures specified above and, where this information has not been given, must include in their report, so far as they are reasonably able to do so, a statement giving the required information. [LR 12.43A].

Changes to the provisions reviewed by the auditors

32.157 The seven provisions of the Combined Code recommended for review by the company's auditors are those that are capable of independent verification and do not cover the principles or the directors' statement in general. Although the provisions are similar to those which the auditors reviewed under Cadbury, the detail has changed slightly in some cases.

32.158 Now in addition to the Cadbury requirements, the auditors must review the directors statement of compliance that:

- All directors are subject to election and full biographical details are included in the election resolution.

- The internal control report covers review of all controls, including financial, operational and compliance and risk management.

- The majority of the members of the audit committee are independent and all members are named in the report and accounts.

32.159 Concern has been expressed by the APB that users may not appreciate the limitations of the auditors' role under the Combined Code. Users will read an auditors' report on the Combined Code and assume that it covers all or substantially all of the 45 provisions not just the seven required for review under the Listing Rule requirement.

APB proposal

32.160 Rather than suggest the approach outlined in the paragraph above remains, in June 1998 the APB published a proposal 'Auditors' responsibility statements and auditors' reports on corporate governance'. This proposed an alternative option, whereby, instead of a limited and possibly misunderstood report on a few corporate governance provisions, the company should instead include in its annual report a comprehensive auditors' responsibility statement, that explains, in plain English, the auditors' responsibilities towards the entire annual report's content. An illustrative statement is provided in the APB's proposal.

32.161 It is hoped that the way forward will be decided before the effective date for the Listing Rule amendment. If it is decided to keep a report on specific provisions, it is expected that the APB will issue up to date guidance on how this can be undertaken.

32.162 If companies intend to adopt the amendment early, there is, as noted above, a problem as to the auditors' role. If the company insists on reporting under the new Combined Code this year an auditor could report privately to the board, but might want to resist reporting publicly in advance of the APB's deliberations. Despite the guidance referred to below there is no compulsion at the moment to publish the auditors' governance report.

Form of auditors' report under Cadbury

32.163 For years ending before 31 December 1998, there is no change to the requirements regarding auditor reporting on corporate governance matters. Auditors' should report in accordance with the APB's published guidance for auditors on the conduct and reporting of such reviews: 'Disclosures relating to corporate governance (revised)' [Bulletin 1995/1 updated by Supplement 1996/3]. The guidance recommends that companies should publish a separate report from the auditors setting out the scope and findings of their review which will normally be as follows [App 3 to the 1996/3 Supplement]:

Example

Report by the auditors to XYZ plc on corporate governance matters

In addition to our audit of the financial statements, we have reviewed the directors' statements on pages ... concerning the company's compliance with the paragraphs of the Cadbury Code of Best Practice specified for our review by the London Stock Exchange and their adoption of the going concern basis in preparing the financial statements. The objective of our review is to draw attention to non-compliance with Listing Rules 12.43 (j) and 12.43(v).

We carried out our review in accordance with guidance issued by the Auditing Practices Board. That guidance does not require us to perform the additional work necessary to, and we do not, express any opinion on of the effectiveness of either the company's system of internal financial control or its corporate governance procedures nor on the ability of the company to continue in operational existence.

Opinion

With respect to the directors' statements on internal financial control on page …, and going concern on page …, in our opinion the directors have provided the disclosures required by the Listing Rules referred to above and such statements are not inconsistent with the information of which we are aware from our audit work on the financial statements.

Based on enquiry of certain directors and officers of the company, and examination of relevant documents, in our opinion the directors' statement on page … appropriately reflects the company's compliance with the other aspects of the Code specified for our review by Listing Rule 12.43(j).

ABC & Co Address
Chartered Accountants Date

32.164 This report is commonly published immediately following the company's statement on corporate governance. Alternatively, the directors may include within their corporate governance statement a description of the auditors' review. The form of such a statement, which should be agreed with the auditors, is as follows:

Example

The auditors have confirmed that, in their opinion: with respect to the directors' statements on internal financial control on page …, and going concern on page ..., the directors have provided the disclosures required by the Listing Rules of the London Stock Exchange and such statements are not inconsistent with information of which they are aware from their audit work on the financial statements; and that the directors' other statements on pages(s) … appropriately reflects the company's compliance with the other aspects of the Cadbury Code specified for their review by Listing Rule 12.43(j). They were not required to perform the additional work necessary to, and did not, express any opinion on the effectiveness of either the company's system of internal financial control or its corporate governance procedures nor on the ability of the company to continue in operational existence. [App 6 to the 1996/3 Supplement].

Early adoption

32.165 If a company insists on adopting the Combined Code early *and* insists on an auditors' review under the Listing Rules amendment, then in the absence of any other guidance, it would appear that auditors will have to carry out the review in accordance with the APB Bulletin 1995/1 and Supplement 1996/3, which is not ideal as it relates to the old regime and requires, for example, an opinion on the directors' going concern statement, which is not covered under the new Code (as it is covered under separate Listing Rule requirements). Auditors will have to ensure that when reporting, the scope of their work is clear.

32.166 One major current problem is the directors' report on internal control. The APB Bulletins state that if the directors make a statement about effectiveness of control beyond internal *financial* control, this statement is outside the auditors' scope and so should be excluded from the opinion. Therefore, if reporting before the various auditing issues are resolved, the opinion is likely to have to be along the lines of *'we have reviewed ... A.1.1, A.1.3, A.6.1, A.6.2, D.1.1, D.2.1 other than the statements going beyond internal financial control, and D.3.1 ...'*. This is clumsy and would be very much an interim measure. Also, in the absence of any new guidance it will not be able to be used after December 1998 as it does not comply with the new Listing rules (which, if they apply for December 1998 year ends onwards without further amendment, would require auditors to look at statements going beyond internal financial control).

12.156 One major current problem is the directors' report on internal control. The APB Bulletins state that if the directors make a statement about effectiveness of control beyond internal *financial* control, this statement is outside the auditors' scope and so should be excluded from the opinion. Therefore, if reporting before the various auditing issues are resolved, the opinion is likely to have to be along the lines of 'we have reviewed A.1.1, A.1.2, A.1.3, A.6.1 and 2, D.1.1, D.2.1 other than the statements going beyond internal financial control, and D.3.1'. This is clumsy and would be very much an interim measure. Also, in the absence of any new guidance it will not be able to be used after December 1998 as it does not comply with the new Listing Rules (which, if they apply for December 1998 year ends onwards without further amendment, would require auditors to look at statements going beyond internal financial control).

Chapter 33

Operating and financial review

Chapter 33

Operating and financial review

Introduction

33.1 Whilst the Accounting Standards Board has devoted most of its efforts since its formation to improving accounting standards, it has not lost sight of the fact that, for many users of financial statements, the most interesting and useful information is given by narrative explanations and analysis of business operations and performance. As financial statements grow more complex with the introduction of new accounting standards, the need for clear and objective commentary on the results becomes more important. At the same time users are increasingly interested in the strategy and development of businesses in which they invest, as the number and risk of opportunities for conquering new markets and expanding through new products or acquisitions increase. To meet the twin goals of providing informed comment on financial performance and explaining the development of a company's operations in the context of its overall strategy, the ASB decided that a fresh, structured approach to the narrative explanations and analysis was required. As explained below, for the best companies this amounts to a codification of existing practice, for others it represents an opportunity to improve dramatically their communication with shareholders and the market.

33.2 The ASB published in July 1993 a statement entitled 'The operating and financial review' (OFR). The statement is unusual in that, despite being developed and issued by the ASB, it is not an accounting standard. The OFR is persuasive rather than mandatory; it is designed as a formulation and development of best practice and is intended for use by listed companies and other large corporations where there is a legitimate public interest in their financial statements. To this end, the ASB has indicated that its use is commended by the FRC, the Hundred Group of Finance Directors and the Stock Exchange.

33.3 Other large corporations where there is a legitimate public interest might include:

- Nationalised industries and similar bodies.
- Major UK subsidiaries of international groups.
- Major UK unlisted companies that are of a size comparable to listed companies.

33.4 Whilst the ASB acknowledges that it is the major corporations that are best placed to lead the way in developing the OFR as a form of communication with shareholders, it adds that *"...other listed companies, especially smaller ones or those operating in specialised or highly competitive industries, are urged to follow the spirit of the Statement and use their best endeavours to adapt the detailed guidance to their own circumstances"*. This seems to accept that the larger groups not only have more complexity and, therefore, more to say, but also are in a better position to develop the OFR than smaller ones.

33.5 While most of the ASB's work is concerned with improving financial statements themselves, in its statement on the OFR it has widened its remit. It takes the view that, useful though the financial statements are, the annual report as a whole is more useful if the directors provide a narrative review of the company's operations and financial position in a more structured way.

33.6 The idea of companies producing an OFR is not completely new. There is relevant US experience with the 'Management discussion and analysis' (MD&A), which has to be produced by companies registered with the SEC. Even in the UK, before the issue of the ASB's statement, companies already gave a variety of information additional to that included in the financial statements themselves:

- Companies are required by law to publish a *directors' report*. The legal requirements are that directors should give:

  - A description of the principal activities of the company and its subsidiaries during the year and of any significant changes in those activities. [Sec 234(2)].

  - A fair review of the development of the business of the company and its subsidiaries during the year and of their position at the end of the year. [Sec 234(1)(a)].

  - An indication of likely future developments in the business of the company and its subsidiaries. [Sec 234(4), 7 Sch 6(b)].

  - Particulars of any important events affecting the company or its subsidiaries which have occurred since the end of the year. [Sec 234(4), 7 Sch 6(a)].

  The standard and content of directors' reports vary, but in general they are relatively brief documents that are not expanded into extensive commentaries. But while commentaries under the headings mentioned above tend to be brief, many larger companies cross-refer to other statements, such as the chairman's statement, where further details are given.

- Listed companies and some other large public interest companies publish a *chairman's statement*. In some cases these are brief, but others, particularly those issued by the larger listed companies, are quite extensive and wide-ranging. One characteristic that is often found, however, is that chairman's statements tend to stress the good news and downplay, or do not mention, the setbacks. In part, this is natural and is what might be expected. Again, practice varies considerably in this regard. Some chairmen's statements are relatively balanced and neutral while others are clearly regarded as public relations exercises.

33.7 The directors' report and the chairman's statement are relatively unaffected by the ASB's recommendations for an OFR. The main impact of the ASB's recommendations has been on two other documents that major companies produced (and in some cases still do):

- Some listed and similar companies published a *chief executive's review,* often in addition to a relatively short chairman's statement. This might typically be done where the chairman was non-executive. Chief executives' reviews were often factual commentaries on the business as a whole and its major segments, but even these could be biased towards discussion of the good news. Sections of annual reports were sometimes given over to the chief executives of major divisions.

- In addition, some listed companies published a *finance director's review*. This tended to focus, as might be expected, on interpretation of the accounts and sometimes discussion of liquidity, gearing, dividend cover and policy and similar matters.

33.8 Essentially, the ASB's recommendations regarding OFRs sought to bring all listed and similar companies up to the standard of the best. A company that published all of the documents listed above, and wrote them in a full, factual and balanced way, was probably close to publishing an OFR already, in broad terms. It might not be called an OFR; it might not be formatted as a single document; but most of the content recommended by the ASB was probably given in one place or another.

33.9 The ASB's recommendations in fact made it clear that companies could decide whether to deal with the matters addressed in the statement in a new, stand-alone, document or whether to deal with them in existing documents such as those referred to above, that is, the chief executive's review or the finance director's review. Therefore, there was no need to change the existing structure of the report and accounts. Many companies have indeed adopted this approach and still give two separate reviews. This is not surprising as often the knowledge needed to describe the operational and financial circumstances lies with different people in an organisation.

33.10 A further relevant feature of the OFR is that, having set out the recommended content of the statement, it acknowledges that some of the recommended disclosures could give rise to problems of commercial confidentiality for some companies. As the OFR is not a mandatory statement, it is not necessary for it explicitly to give an exemption from disclosures on confidentiality grounds (such as is contained in SSAP 25, 'Segmental reporting', for example). The way it is dealt with is that the introduction acknowledges that directors will be concerned that the benefits of the disclosures to users and, therefore, to the company are not outweighed by commercial damage through sensitive information becoming available to competitors. It points out that the emphasis is on matters of significance to the business as a whole, and "*...it is expected that in most cases directors will be able to provide a reasonably comprehensive and informative OFR whilst avoiding disclosures of a confidential or sensitive nature*".

Summary of the recommendations

33.11 As the ASB sees the OFR, it should include a discussion and interpretation of the business. It should deal both with the main factors – uncertainties as well as positive features – that underlie it and with the structure of its financing. It is a report on the year under review, not a forecast of future results, but should draw out those aspects of the year under review that are relevant to an assessment of future prospects.

33.12 This approach builds on the ASB's general objective of having companies set out historical information in such a way that it helps users of accounts to make their own forecasts of future results and cash flows. This theme runs through the ASB's draft Statement of principles, and underlies, for example, the separate disclosure required by FRS 3, 'Reporting financial performance', of continuing activities, acquisitions and discontinued activities.

33.13 The essential features of an OFR are discussed in the paragraphs that follow.

Clear and succinct

33.14 The statement starts by saying an OFR "*...should be written in a clear style and as succinctly as possible, to be readily understandable by the general reader of annual reports, and should include only matters that are likely to be significant to investors*". [OFR para 3].

33.15 Whereas sophisticated investors study the financial statements comprehensively, it is well established that the less sophisticated – for example, many private investors – tend to read the chairman's statement with most interest. This position is likely to continue because, partly as a result of the ASB's other work, financial statements themselves continue to become more complex. The ASB clearly wishes, with the OFR, to expand and make more useful the non-technical part of the annual report.

33.16 The reference to 'investors' in paragraph 3 of the OFR statement is somewhat odd. The ASB refers, in its draft Statement of principles, to accounts being for a wide range of users. Users such as customers, suppliers, employees and others are likely to share with private investors the characteristic of finding the chairman's statement and the OFR relatively accessible and the financial statements less so. Hence it is hard to see why the ASB should have in mind investors only.

Balanced and objective

33.17 The ASB says that an OFR should also be *"...balanced and objective, dealing even-handedly with both good and bad aspects"*. [OFR para 3].

33.18 This is clearly a somewhat idealistic aim, because it is human nature that when accounting to others for one's actions the good points are stressed. Nevertheless, there is considerable evidence that companies are prepared to deal more readily with the negative aspects of performance within the framework of the OFR than they were before. This is perhaps because the OFR provides a relatively dispassionate list of 'things to cover' which inhibits over-exuberance about good news whilst at the same time allowing negative news to be referred to in a relatively low key fashion. In other words, the 'format' facilitates communication of both good and bad news.

Previous comments

33.19 Thirdly, the ASB says that OFRs should *"...refer to comments made in previous statements where these have not been borne out by events"*. [OFR para 3].

33.20 This wording should not be read restrictively. Whilst it refers to those comments that have not been borne out by events, it is helpful if OFRs are running commentaries, from one year to the next, of the progress of the business. In this context it is more balanced if an OFR refers back to previous comments in connection with events that did bear out those comments as well as those that did not.

33.21 Examples of matters that might be discussed under this heading are:

- Trends in sales and margins.
- Expansion of production facilities.
- Sales and closures of businesses.
- New product launches.

- Intended refinancings.

Analytical discussion

33.22 The fourth essential feature of an OFR is that *"...it should contain analytical discussion rather than merely numerical analysis"*. [OFR para 3].

33.23 The idea here is that it should add to the information contained in the financial statements, not just reproduce it in another form. For example, a good OFR would not merely report a time series of gearing ratios, based on numbers drawn from the balance sheet. It would in addition, explain, where relevant:

- Why gearing has gone up or down.
- What the board regards as the target level or range of gearing.

33.24 Again, an OFR should not just report, for example, that US sales of product A increased by x per cent last year and y per cent in the current year. It should explain:

- Why sales have gone up.
- Whether that is considered good or bad given the growth or decline in the industry.
- To what extent the reported numbers reflect, for example, real price increases or decreases, volume changes, inflation or exchange rate movements.

Top-down structure

33.25 ASB says that an OFR should *"...follow a 'top-down' structure, discussing individual aspects of the business in the context of a discussion of the business as a whole"*. [OFR para 3].

33.26 The intention here is that the OFR should provide an overview of the business as a whole, whilst at the same time giving the reader an indication of how individual segments of the business have performed. Typically, the OFR of a major company may be split into: a general review of the business followed by separate reviews of major operating segments, but the general review of the business might be presented separately in the chairman's statement or chief executive's review, with detailed analysis of major segments given in a separate operating review. The review of individual operating segments may be by geographical or business segment or sometimes both, depending on how the business is organised. For example, a retail company with operations in several geographical areas might prefer to discuss its operations by geographical area, whilst a conglomerate of several different types of business operations might set out its operations review by business segment, but discuss each geographic area within the section dealing with the specific business segment being discussed.

Change in accounting policy

33.27 The statement also indicates that an OFR *"...should explain the reason for, and effect of any changes in accounting policies"*. [OFR para 3].

33.28 This is not so much an 'essential feature', but a specific disclosure item and is discussed below in the context of the operating review.

Ratios

33.29 The statement indicates that an OFR should *"...make it clear how any ratios or other numerical information given relate to the financial statements"*. [OFR para 3].

33.30 Some, but not all, ratios and numerical information given in an OFR will be based on figures in the financial statements. Where this is so, any figures quoted should be drawn from the financial statements. If, exceptionally, different figures are used, that fact should be made clear.

33.31 The following are examples of relating OFR figures to the financial statements:

- Some figures might be discussed in an OFR that are not drawn from the financial statements. Examples are the volume growth in sales, or the monetary amount of sales growth excluding the effects of changes in exchange rates. If these figures are used, the basis of their calculation should be explained if there is any ambiguity about their meaning.

- Some figures, like growth in sales, or current assets divided by current liabilities (the current ratio) are self-evident and require no elaboration, provided they are indeed based on the figures in the financial statements.

- Ratios like gearing, although generally drawn from figures on the balance sheet, can be calculated in a number of different ways. Hence it is not adequate merely to quote a gearing figure without explaining the basis of its calculation.

33.32 A good example of this last point is SmithKline Beecham's tables of financial ratios (see Table 33.1). For example, they indicate that gearing is defined as net borrowings divided by total capital employed. Net borrowings is defined as *"...loans and overdrafts less investments and cash"* which is cross-referenced to a note to the financial statements.

Table 33.1 – SmithKline Beecham plc – Annual Report and Accounts – 31 December 1994

Financial ratios

			1994	1993 (restated) [5]
Profitability[1]				
Gross margin	Gross profit / Sales	%	**66.3**	67.1
Trading margin	Trading profit / Sales	%	**20.4**	19.1
Return on trading assets	Trading profit / Average trading assets[2]	%	**33.7**	40.9
Return on trading assets (excl. intangibles)	Trading profit / Average trading assets	%	**47.8**	41.3
Productivity				
Sales per employee	Sales / Average number of employees	£'000	**124**	117
Trading profit per employee	Trading profit / Average number of employees	£'000	**25**	22
Cover[1]				
Interest cover	Trading profit / Net interest charge	times	**24.0**	78.7
Dividend cover (Total)	Profit attributable to shareholders / Dividends payable	times	**2.24**	2.39
Dividend payout ratio (UK Basis)	Dividends per A share / Earnings excluding exceptional items	%	**39.9**	37.5
Gearing ratios				
Statutory balance sheet	Net borrowings[3] / Total capital employed	%	**205.6**	2.5
Pro-forma balance sheet	Net borrowings[4] / Total capital employed	%	**98.6**	-

Dividends per share			
Dividends per A Share	p	**12.9**	10.9
Dividends per Equity Unit	cents	**25.23**	20.46

(1) The profitability and cover ratios have been calculated on continuing operations, including acquisitions, but before exceptional and one-off items.
(2) Trading assets principally represent intangible and tangible fixed assets, stocks, debtors and creditors after excluding net borrowings, taxation, dividends and creditors falling due after more than one year (see note 1).
(3) Net borrowings represent loans and overdrafts less investments and cash (see note 25).
(4) Net borrowings following completion of the sale of the Animal Health business.
(5) The 1993 ratios have been restated to incorporate the borrowings of the ESOT in the balance sheet (page 48).

25 NET BORROWINGS

	1994 £m	1993 (restated) £m
Investments held as current assets	440	1,032
Cash	202	148
Loans and overdrafts falling due within one year	(1,892)	(373)
Loans falling due after more than one year	(1,086)	(852)
	(2,336)	(45)

33.33 Earnings per share (EPS) figures are particularly important in this context. Following FRS 3, it is now common for companies to publish the basic EPS figure together with an additional figure. This is permissible provided that companies reconcile the figure to the FRS 3 figure and certain other conditions are met (see chapter 8). Although some companies publish a figure of their own design, others voluntarily publish a figure based on the 'Headline' earnings defined by the Institute of Investment Management and Research (IIMR) in their paper 'The definition of IIMR headline earnings'. If the additional figure is on the IIMR basis, it will be helpful to state that either in the financial statements or in the OFR.

33.34 The financial statements themselves show the reconciliation of the two figures and the definition of the additional figure. Therefore no additional definition is needed in the OFR. What *is* needed is for companies either:

- to quote both EPS figures whenever they quote EPS; or
- if (less preferably) they quote one EPS figure, to specify which one they are quoting.

33.35 Quoting both EPS figures is preferable, because FRS 3 says that the additional figure should not be any more prominent than the basic FRS 3 figure. To quote the additional figure alone does make it more prominent. To do so would be simply against the standard if the standard applied to the OFR. However, it applies only to the financial statements themselves. Nevertheless, the spirit of the standard would be to apply it to the annual report as a whole and that is why it is preferable for companies to quote both figures whenever they discuss EPS.

Trends

33.36 Finally, the statement indicates that an OFR:

> *"...should include discussion of:*
>
> - *trends and factors underlying the business that have affected the results but are not expected to continue in the future; and*
>
> - *known events, trends and uncertainties that are expected to have an impact on the business in the future."* [OFR para 3].

33.37 In this context, the ASB indicates that an OFR should explain the significance to the business of trends and uncertainties, but adds that *"...it is not intended that the OFR should necessarily include a forecast of the outcome of such uncertainties; nor is it suggested that the OFR should contain anything of the nature of a profit forecast"*. [OFR para 4].

33.38 This again is consistent with the ASB's approach of having companies provide information from which users can make their own forecasts.

33.39 Examples of how this approach might be put into practice are:

- If the business relies on a patent that will expire shortly, that fact should be disclosed, including the date on which it expires.

- If new customers have been found towards the end of the year, such that a major division is now considerably more profitable than before, that should be disclosed. The provision of this information would then enable users to make their own estimates of the profitability of the next full year, but neither the financial statements nor the OFR would themselves give a quantified forecast.

- If there is a legal claim against the business, that should be disclosed, but without necessarily speculating about the chances of success. (Note, however, that in such a case there would probably be either note disclosure of the contingent liability or provision made for a potential loss.)

The operating review

Introduction

33.40 The OFR statement contains a considerable amount of detailed guidance, relating to both the operating and the financial parts of an OFR, so much so that it appears to be very prescriptive. It would be wrong, however, to interpret the OFR as being prescriptive, even for a company that intends to follow it fully. First, the ASB indicates that *"...the detailed guidance should not be regarded as a comprehensive list of all matters that might be relevant, nor are all items listed relevant to all businesses. The OFR should focus on those matters that are of greatest significance to that business"*. [OFR para 7].

33.41 As regards the operating review, the ASB notes that its *"...principal aim ... is to enable the user to understand the dynamics of the various lines of business undertaken – that is, the main influences on the overall results and how these interrelate. Thus the OFR needs to identify and explain the main factors that underlie the business, and in particular those which have varied in the past or are expected to change in the future"*. [OFR para 8].

33.42 The ASB statement discusses six main headings under which companies are encouraged to comment. These are dealt with in the paragraphs that follow.

Operating results for the period

33.43 It is envisaged that an OFR would include under this heading a discussion of operating performance. However, it evidently does not literally mean 'operating', as it refers to a discussion *"...covering all aspects of the profit and loss account to the level of profit on ordinary activities before taxation"*. It refers to focusing on the overall business, but also on *"...those segments or other divisions that are relevant to an understanding of the performance as a whole"*. [OFR para 9]. In practice, this may amount to a discussion of the overall results plus a discussion of the results of those segments that are disclosed separately under SSAP 25, 'Segmental reporting'.

33.44 The ASB asks for discussion of *"...changes in the industry or the environment in which the business operates, developments within the business, and their effect on the results"*. [OFR para 9].

33.45 The statement then gives the following as *examples* of the matters that might be discussed under this heading:

- Changes in market conditions.
- New products and services introduced or announced.

- Changes in market share or position.
- Changes in turnover and margins.
- Changes in exchange rates and inflation rates.
- New activities, discontinued activities and other acquisitions and disposals.

[OFR para 9].

33.46 While these are useful as a means of illustrating the general principles, it should be remembered that they are just examples. If, for example, the businesses operate in the UK, it may well be that the effect of exchange rates and inflation rates is immaterial, in which case no comment is necessary, although companies could comment to that effect if they wished. Note also the application of the exemption in relation to confidentiality (see para 33.10). The second bullet point refers only to new products and services that have been introduced or announced. Information about new products about to be launched would no doubt be of interest to investors and other readers, but could be commercially very harmful and thus need not be given.

33.47 Examples of actual disclosures for each of the matters listed in paragraph 33.45 are given in Tables 33.2 to 33.10 below. The extracts have been deliberately kept short but in most of them, reference to the full OFR provides further elaboration of the details given in the extracts.

33.48 Table 33.2 illustrates disclosure of changes in market conditions.

Table 33.2 – Coats Viyella Plc – Annual report and accounts – 31 December 1994

Operating Review (extract)

THREAD (extract)

The overall performance was affected by substantial movements in two major markets – Brazil and Turkey – caused by macro-economic changes. In Brazil, the success of the economic plan launched in July and confidence in the new President elected later in the year caused a substantial and sustained improvement in demand. The business was able to benefit from both the resultant increase in demand and its lower cost base, following rigorous reductions in previous years. The key issue for 1995 will be the continued success of government policy and the settled level of demand once the economic boom is over. Turkey was adversely affected by the devaluation early in the year; this affected not only the results on translation but the level of demand in the market. Management acted with urgency and vigour to address the cost base, and generated very strong cash flow in difficult circumstances. The economic and political outlook in Turkey remains uncertain and the performance of the business in 1995 will depend largely on external factors.

33.49 Table 33.3 illustrates a new product being introduced.

Table 33.3 – Whitbread PLC – Annual Report and Accounts – 25 February 1995

Chief Executive's review (extract)

Pushing back the frontiers

It is not very often that a technical development creates newspaper headlines but that's what happened earlier this year when Whitbread launched its 'widget in a bottle' – the world's first device to enable draught quality beer to be served from a bottle. It was the result of two years of intensive work by Whitbread's Research & Development department (R&D) and followed their earlier success with the 'draughtflow' system for cans which has helped transform the take-home market and the sales of Boddingtons bitter and other premium brands.

Although technology and a hospitality business may seem like strange bedfellows, in fact R&D plays a big part in the company's innovation programmes whether they are directed at product development or in helping us become a far more efficient operator.

As well as inventing new ways of packaging beer, R&D created a whole series of new brands – the New Classic Ales portfolio – including Fuggles Chocolate Mild which intrigued beer drinkers all over the world.

Other recent projects have included the development of a touch-screen wine selection system for Thresher and the application of technology to improve operational efficiency and the working environment in the 3,500 kitchens in Whitbread's pubs, restaurants and hotels. Here extensive research and development has resulted in state-of-the-art ergonomic kitchen layouts and this work continues in conjunction with the investigation of exciting new technologies for cooking food.

R&D has been working for many years with all the company's businesses on managing the use and controlling the cost of gas, electricity and water. Considerable progress has been made in reducing costs and, equally importantly, in making our operations more environmentally friendly.

33.50 Table 33.4 discloses changes in market share. In this table the disclosure relates to market share in a particular product.

Table 33.4 – Argos plc – Directors' Report and Accounts – 31 December 1994

operating review (extract)

With the exception of DIY and sports, Argos gained market share in all ranges. The most notable gains were in furniture, jewellery and toys. Especially good growth in toys – helped by some very competitive pricing, a strong Christmas offer, and the inclusion of 'pocket money' toys – meant Argos retained the number one toy retailer slot which it had achieved in the first six months of the year.

33.51 Table 33.5 illustrates market share for the business as a whole and also discloses details of changes in turnover and margins. The summary included illustrates increase in turnover, split between that attributable to old stores and that attributable to new stores, the effect of inflation on sales and information on margins.

Table 33.5 – J Sainsbury plc – Annual Accounts – 11 March 1995

J Sainsbury Supermarkets (extract)

Our supermarket business traded strongly in a challenging economic climate, with sales growing by 8.3% of which 7.2% came from net new sales area. Sales in like-for-like stores grew by 1.1%, giving a small volume gain after deducting sales inflation of 0.8% for the year. The weekly number of customers increased to around 9 million and our market share, including Savacentre food sales, increased from 11.4% to 11.7% on the basis of Central Statistical Office figures.

Operating profit increased by 12.5% to £784.3 million. Net operating margin increased by 0.31% of sales to 8.17% despite the fact that gross margins declined slightly. Operating profit increased by 18.2% in the second half of the year, compared to 7.7% in the first half.

33.52 Table 33.6 illustrates changes in exchange rates and Table 33.7 refers to the effects of inflation and is an interesting example of where the commentary in the Business Overview is based on constant exchange rates.

Table 33.6 – Inchcape plc – Annual Report and Accounts – 31 December 1994

financial review (extract)

Results are also affected by movements in exchange rates on underlying business transactions. A substantial percentage of the goods the Group sells is sourced from Japan, so the Yen has a significant influence on gross profits. The Yen was more stable compared to last year, but its continuing strength has caused upward pressure on selling prices with a consequent effect on volumes and significantly increased advertising and promotional expenditure to hold market positions. The gross (net of hedging actions but prior to selling price adjustments) financial impact on Motors cost of sales of all significant currency movements at the transactional level on our subsidiaries was approximately £45m compared to 1993; our associates suffered a gross impact of around £10m.

Group operating margin* for the year of 3.4% was some 0.3% below last year. Motors overall operating margin fell from 4.2% to 3.5% in 1994. Japanese franchises generally suffered significant margin erosion whereas other franchises and the retail business were both stronger that last year. Lower Motors margins were partially offset by Marketing increasing from 2.5% to 3.2% and Services up from 7.0% to 7.3%.

The table below demonstrates the effect of exchange rate movements on the activities of the Group by showing the change in profits at the previous year's rates (ie constant rates) and also the impact of translation into Sterling of overseas results.

	1994 £m	Exchange Translation Effect £m	Change at Constant Rates £m	1993 £m
Motors	**143.0**	(1.2)	(29.5)	173.7
Marketing	**75.4**	(1.4)	18.6	58.2
Services:				
Insurance	**21.4**	(0.2)	2.6	19.0
Shipping	**15.8**	(0.6)	2.4	14.0
Testing	**21.5**	(2.2)	3.3	20.4
Buying	**2.0**	0.1	3.1	(1.2)
Total services	**60.7**	(2.9)	11.4	52.2
Other	**3.4**	-	1.6	1.8
Discontinued operations	**5.6**	0.3	(13.9)	19.2
Central charges	**(15.0)**	-	0.3	(15.3)
Adjusted total operating profit	**273.1**	(5.2)	(11.5)	289.8
Reverse Insurance and Shipping interest receivable	**(12.4)**	-	(2.2)	(10.2)
Net interest	**(30.1)**	0.5	(3.4)	(27.2)
IIMR profit before tax	**230.6**	(4.7)	(17.1)	252.4

Return on capital employed* of 24.6% is 1.2% lower than last year (restated for FRS5) on lower profits and increased assets due to higher working capital.

* *Definitions are shown on page 71 of the Report and Accounts*

Table 33.7 – Unilever PLC – Annual Accounts – 31 December 1994

Business Overview (extract one)

Unilever's results are published in the currencies of the two parent countries, namely the guilder and the pound sterling. Fluctuations between currencies can lead to markedly different trends for the same business. This is why we normally comment on performance at constant exchange rates (i.e. the same rates as in the preceding year), thus eliminating one variable over which we have no control. We also use constant exchange rates for the management of the business. In 1994, the year on year performance in guilders and pounds at current exchange rates happens to be the same and only marginally different from constant rates.

Business Overview (extract two)

Latin America – In a single year, Brazil experienced the extremes of hyperinflation in the first half year and relative price stability in the second half, with the new currency actually strengthening against the United States dollar. In such conditions our Brazilian companies did well to grow volume by 11% and maintain profit at last year's record level under the harsh light of daily constant price accounting.

33.53 The ASB also refers specifically to the need to discuss acquisitions and exceptional items. In relation to acquisitions, the OFR calls for comment on the extent to which expectations at the time of an acquisition have been realised and for comment where the acquired business is seasonal. Table 33.8 refers to the acquisition of a major new subsidiary and the expected benefits. Elsewhere in the OFR details are given of the exceptional item for reorganisation costs associated with the acquisition.

Table 33.8 – B.A.T Industries p.l.c. – Directors' Report and Accounts – 31 December 1994

Finance Director's Review (extract)

Changes in the Group (extract)

On 22 December B.A.T Industries acquired **American Tobacco Company** (ATCo) for US$1 billion, an acquisition which will bring both financial and strategic benefits for the Group. It will strengthen B&W's position in the US domestic market and give the Group worldwide ownership of Lucky Strike and Pall Mall, key US international brands (which we already own outside the US), as well as the rights to Silk Cut outside Europe. The integration of ATCo with B&W is now well underway.

33.54 Tables 33.9 and 33.10 discuss new activities (a recurring theme in 1994 and 1995 has been moves to establish business in China), and discontinued activities respectively. In the example of discontinued activities the reason for the discontinuance is given in the Chairman's statement with details given in a separate section headed 'discontinued operations' in the OFR.

Table 33.9 – Zeneca Group PLC – Annual Report and Accounts – 31 December 1994

Operational review (extract)

Pharmaceuticals (extract)

The expanding $4 billion Chinese medicines market represents a clear opportunity, provided intellectual property rights become more reliable. 'Diprivan', 'Zoladex', 'Tenormin' and 'Zestril' were launched in China in 1994, and during 1995 the emphasis will be placed on successful commercialisation of this portfolio. This process will be facilitated by the 75% Zeneca-owned joint venture with Sinopharm, the State Pharmaceutical Administration of China. This agreement will enable the partners to share good practice, facilitate technology transfer and enhance access to the Chinese markets.

Table 33.10 – Dawson International PLC – Annual Report – 1 April 1995

Chairman's Statement (extract)

Since the end of the financial year the principal assets and business of Dawson Home Fashions have been sold to Springs Industries, Inc., a much larger player in the home fashions market, who will be able to achieve and derive synergies that were not available to us.

Review of Operations (extract)

DISCONTINUED OPERATIONS

	1994/95			1993/94	
	Sales	Operating profit/loss		Sales	Operating profit/(loss)
		before exceptionals	after exceptionals	*restated*	*restated*
	£million	£million	£million	£million	£million
Fabrics – Premier Fabrics	**6.7**	**(0.2)**	**(0.4)**	6.7	0.1
US Apparel – fleece & jersey	**25.5**	**(5.8)**	**(5.8)**	61.0	(21.1)
Utilisation of termination provisions	**-**	**5.8**	**5.8**	-	-
US Home Fashions	**54.5**	**(4.5)**	**(16.5)**	57.4	(3.6)
Intra-group sales	**(0.9)**	**-**	**-**	(2.8)	-
	85.8	**(4.7)**	**(16.9)**	122.3	(24.6)

FABRICS – PREMIER FABRICS

The sale of Premier Fabrics, the Group's specialist UK weaving business, to Yorklyde plc for £2.6 million in cash, was completed on 28 April 1995. The consideration equated to the net asset value of the business at the year end. In addition, £0.6 million of capital reserves arising from the original acquisition of the business in 1980, which were previously added direct to reserves, will be recorded as income in the profit and loss account for the financial year to 30 March 1996.

US APPAREL – FLEECE & JERSEY

Following the decision announced in March 1994 to withdraw from the fleece and jersey businesses, all inventories have been liquidated and the ten manufacturing plants and southern distribution centre closed. The Leesport plant was subsequently sold during the financial year and the distribution centre leased to a third party on a two year basis at a market rental with an option to purchase at a predetermined price. The net written down book value of fixed assets, including the distribution centre, remaining at the end of the financial year was £12.1 million (US$19.8 million),

Since the end of the financial year, detailed negotiations have commenced to dispose of six of the remaining nine plants.

In view of uncertainties over the likely selling prices for the remaining properties and certain liabilities not previously forecast, a further exceptional provision of £1.9 million (US3.0 million) has been made.

US HOME FASHIONS

On 30 May 1995 the sale of the principal assets and business of the Dawson Home Fashions shower curtain and bathroom accessories business to Springs Industries, Inc., was completed. The proceeds of the sale, which comprised the Sardis manufacturing facility, inventories and receivables, have been estimated at US$41.4 million, of which US$37.2 million was received in cash at completion. The balance is due following a completion audit. Dawson Home Fashions is discharging all remaining liabilities and is in the process of selling all residual assets including the Ohio manufacturing facility for which a conditional sales contract has been signed. An exceptional charge of £9.7 million (US$15.0 million) has been made in the 1994/95 financial statements to cover the maximum total estimated loss on the exit from the business. The £12.0 million disposal provision made in 1993/94 was released earlier in the year and replaced by an equivalent restructuring provision.

33.55 It is apparent from examining the OFRs produced by companies within different industry sections and with different geographical spreads of business, that the matters listed in paragraph 33.45 above, have varying relevance for different companies. In highly competitive industry sectors such as retailing or package holidays, changes in market share, turnover and margins are of prime importance, whilst in a business with a broad geographical spread of operations, changes in exchange rates and rates of inflation may be the factors that particularly affect group performance. Several of the examples above bear this out.

Dynamics of the business

33.56 The OFR addresses the issue of identifying the factors that particularly affect the business in a separate section 'Dynamics of the business', and this is discussed below.

33.57 The phrase 'dynamics of the business' is somewhat vague, but sounds neutral. The ASB indicates that it wants this part of the OFR to include a discussion of the *"...main factors and influences that may have a major effect on future results, whether or not they were significant in the period under review"*. This too sounds neutral and one would expect the resultant disclosures to be evenly balanced between good and bad news. However, the ASB goes on to say that this would include a discussion identifying *"...the principal risks and uncertainties in the main lines of business, together with a commentary on the approach to managing these risks and, in qualitative terms, the nature of the potential impact on results"*. [OFR para 12]. The examples given continue this sense of bad news, risks and uncertainties:

- Scarcity of raw materials.
- Skill shortages and expertise of uncertain supply.
- Patents, licences or franchises.
- Dependence on major suppliers or customers.
- Product liability.
- Health and safety.
- Environmental protection costs and potential environmental liabilities.
- Self-insurance.
- Exchange rate fluctuations.
- Rates of inflation differing between costs and revenues, or between different markets.

[OFR para 12].

33.58 Although the ASB's OFR suggests items to be discussed under the different headings 'Operating results for the period' and 'Dynamics of the business' it is clear that there may be a considerable degree of overlap. A major environmental disaster, for instance, could well have serious effects on the operating result as well as being a factor that would be mentioned under dynamics of the business when discussing product liability or health and safety. For this reason, many OFRs in practice do not divide themselves into compartments but, instead, deal with the main factors affecting both the business generally and the year's performance in particular, in one place.

33.59 The points listed in paragraph 33.57 are put forward as *"...examples of matters that might be relevant, depending on the nature of the business"*. So it is important not to read them too prescriptively. If some of them have no relevance they should be left out and if there are other factors of more importance, those other factors should be added. Also, the emphasis given to the various factors should reflect their importance. Equal emphasis should not be given to unimportant factors as is given to those that are important.

33.60 The ASB points out that some of these matters will be referred to in the contingent liabilities note, but indicates that the OFR discussion should cover a wider range of risks and uncertainties relating to the business.

33.61 It appears, in this section of the OFR, that the ASB is not in line with its overall approach of asking for balanced reporting. If the ASB had wanted merely a discussion of risks and uncertainties of the type indicated by its list of examples above, it has clouded the issue by referring to the 'dynamics of the business'. Another interpretation is that it is using the term 'risks' in the same way as FRS 5, 'Reporting the substance of transactions', where it means potential for gain as well as exposure to loss. Similarly, uncertainties can result in either good or bad outcomes. We prefer this interpretation and would, therefore, encourage companies to discuss the items in the above list that are relevant, but also items such as:

- Potential opportunities to expand activities into new territories. An example would be in the US where regulators may currently restrict some financial services to a single state rather than the whole country, yet there is the prospect of relaxation.

- Potential for reduction of cost, or cost reductions that have been identified, but not yet put into practice. This could include re-engineering of processes or input substitution, as well as reductions in the costs of existing supplies.

33.62 Some of the points in the ASB's own list (see para 33.57) can also be interpreted neutrally or beneficially, even though the whole tone is negative. For example, fluctuations in exchange rates or differences in inflation rates, could give rise to either gains or losses or could have been hedged.

33.63 A negative factor for one company may be a positive factor for another. In 1994, companies whose principal raw materials were paper and pulp suffered from steeply rising costs, which they had to try to pass on to customers. An example of this is given in Table 33.11. Companies that manufactured these raw materials, however, saw sales volumes and profits rise. Table 33.12 is an example of a company that has benefited as a result of increased demand for its pulp and paper products. To some extent, companies may also hedge the risk of rising raw material prices by owning businesses that produce the raw materials as well as businesses that produce the finished product using that raw material. In Table 33.12, an increase in the usage of the pulp for paper making resulted in a fall of five per cent in external pulp sales.

Table 33.11 – Bowater PLC – Annual Report – 31 December 1994

Finance Director's Operating and Financial Review (extract)

PERFORMANCE OF BUSINESS SECTORS

During 1994 world demand for paper and resin, Bowater's principal raw materials, increased sharply resulting in some shortages. The effect has been to increase the prices of these raw materials by up to 100% during the year. Most price increases did not occur until the second half of the year, led by pulp and paper costs in the third quarter while plastic resin costs accelerated rapidly in the fourth quarter. The effect of these increases was more pronounced in Europe than in North America. The Group has generally been successful in passing on these price increases, although there have been some timing delays. Sales have increased by approximately £50m as a result of raw material inflation being passed on to our customers in 1994. In a full year this figure is likely to be in excess of £200m.

Table 33.12 – Arjo Wiggins Appleton p.l.c. – Directors' Report and Financial Statements – 31 December 1994

Financial review (extract)

Associated companies

The strong recovery in pulp prices and further volume growth in paper production resulted in SOPORCEL making a profit at the pre-tax level in 1994, the first time since 1990. Our share of this pre-tax profit was £11.7 million, compared with a share of losses amounting to £17.4 million in 1993, of which £14.7 million was caused by unrealised exchange losses; such losses did not recur in 1994.

Paper sales volume increased by 12%, accompanied by a richer product mix, higher selling prices and the productivity improvements initiated in 1993. However, this also led to a greater proportion of total pulp output being used in the paper-making activity, resulting in a fall of 5% in external pulp sales.

33.64 In some industries, patents and licences are particularly important and loss of a patent may have serious effects on the businesses. In the pharmaceutical industry, the success or failure of a patent application or licence for a new drug is particularly significant. Table 33.13 illustrates this point.

Table 33.13 – Zeneca Group PLC – Annual Report and Accounts – 31 December 1994

Chief Executive's review (extract)

Pharmaceutical companies have developed different responses to these challenges, but whichever route is chosen, the first and absolute requirement for future success is to maintain R&D capable of producing a steady stream of innovative medicines. At Zeneca's inception we stated that we intended, on average, to launch one new therapy each year. In September 1994 'Merrem', our new broad spectrum antibiotic, was launched in Italy and during the year we also filed for regulatory approval for a new oral prostate cancer treatment, 'Casodex', in a number of countries. Filings should be made for three further products ('Arimidex' and 'Tomudex' anti-cancer therapies and the anti-asthma compound 'Accolate') in 1995 and for our schizophrenia therapy 'Seroquel' in 1996. I am confident that Zeneca has the requisite skill to maintain our high quality new product pipeline and that we shall exceed by some margin our target of launching one new therapy each year.

33.65 Although not mentioned in the list in paragraph 33.57, for many companies in the food and drinks industry, brands are at the root of their success. Consequently, many such companies give considerable comment in their OFR, and in the financial statements, on their leading brands. Table 33.14 demonstrates that, for some companies, brand development is the key to progress.

Table 33.14 – Grand Metropolitan Public Limited Company – Annual Report – 30 September 1994

Chief Executive's Review (extract)

PROSPECTS (extract)

In my statement to you last year, I said that I saw my role as Chief Executive of GrandMet very clearly. I said that I believed my mission was to create a climate within which GrandMet, now a highly focused, branded food and drinks business, can flourish.

I also set out for you the four ways in which we intend to grow this business – namely by supporting our leading brands, by developing new and innovative brands, by making relevant add on acquisitions and by expanding into new developing markets around the world.

33.66 Dependence upon major suppliers or customers would generally not be a risk factor for large listed companies, which usually have a wide range of customers and suppliers and, therefore, such disclosure is not common. One example of disclosure, however, is given in Table 33.15, the company which (as stated in its OFR) won an award for the best annual report and the Grand Prix for best UK Investor Relations. One other obvious example where a major customer could be a risk factor is in the defence industry, where the receipt and timing of orders from the Ministry of Defence can be critical to business performance.

Table 33.15 – Coats Viyella Plc – Report and Accounts – 31 December 1994

Financial Review (extract)

The Group's largest customer in 1994 remained Marks & Spencer plc. Turnover with Marks & Spencer is predominantly UK based and was £285m (£265m).

33.67 Product liability and health and safety are generally considered to be minor risks for most businesses and in the majority of cases are not given particular mention in OFRs. This is perhaps understandable as few companies would wish to admit that their products could risk harming customers or affect health and safety and indeed companies that had such products would not survive long.

33.68 Disclosure of environmental protection costs and potential environmental liabilities ranges from extensive to minimal. Among the best examples of disclosure is ICI, which produces a separate environmental performance report that describes how four main environmental objectives were set in 1990 and what progress was made in the year towards achieving the objectives. The report discloses that about £430 million was spent on safety, health and the environment in 1994 of which about £210 million was spent on the environment. At the other end of the scale some companies, where some description of environmental matters would be expected to be seen, make very little disclosure.

33.69 Table 33.16 combines disclosure of environmental risks with disclosure of other operational risks and goes on to disclose when the company has not taken out insurance cover against risks.

Table 33.16 – Monument Oil and Gas plc – Annual Report and Financial Statements – 31 December 1994

Financial review (extract)

Risk management (extract)

Monument's oil and gas activities are subject to a wide range of operational and financial risks which can have a significant adverse effect on its performance. Action can be taken to limit the financial consequences of such risks through insurance and treasury activities. The Group's overall approach to managing these exposures is to be risk averse on a cost effective basis.

Operational risks include equipment failure, well-blowouts, pollution, bad weather and fire. An insurance programme appropriate to the Group's assets is maintained and is reviewed by the Board annually. Some of the effects of operational risks cannot be reasonably insured against and others are judged to be not cost-effective: at present the Group does not have any business interruption cover. Its insurance policies also contain overall limits and deductibles.

33.70 Whilst in some cases a company may have a deliberate policy of not insuring where the cost is not economic, other companies use captive insurance companies for certain risks which effectively means that they make provisions for the likely cost of those risks crystallising into liabilities. An example is included in Table 33.17 under 'hazard risk'. This example also deals with overall financial risk management, foreign exchange risk, liquidity risk and debt management and interest rate risk.

Table 33.17 – Inchcape plc – Annual Report and Accounts – 31 December 1994

financial review (extract)

Financial Risk Management Policy The Board has set clear policies for the management of the Group's material financial risks, including foreign exchange, liquidity, interest rate and hazard risks. These policies form the basis of a detailed controls framework, compliance with which is monitored by Group Internal Audit.

The Corporate Finance Committee oversees implementation of these policies and the setting of the Group's various risk management strategies. It reports to the Board on a quarterly basis, or more frequently where necessary.

Operating units are required to transact all significant financial instruments either through Group Treasury in London or Hong Kong, or under its guidance where central dealing is impractical. Financial instruments, including derivatives, may only be used in pursuance of clearly defined and approved foreign exchange and interest rate hedging strategies, and are subject to ongoing monitoring and control to ensure that they do not give rise to incremental risks.

The Group also seeks to limit counter-party risk by conducting most of its banking and dealing activities with a limited number of major international banks, whose status is kept under constant review.

In addition, in order to ensure that the Group is managed on a financially prudent basis, the Board has laid down a comprehensive framework of financial condition measures. These measures include fixed charge cover*, interest cover*, and capital gearing*, with control levels being set well within any externally imposed covenants or constraints.

Foreign Exchange Risk Foreign exchange rate volatility can have a material impact on both the Group's earnings and its foreign currency assets and liabilities. The Group seeks actively to manage these risks by employing a clearly defined risk management methodology.

The Group's major transaction exposures arise from the activities of its Motors businesses. The exposures are primarily to the Yen, but there are also significant exposures in Deutschemarks, Sterling and US Dollars. Operating units are required to hedge transaction exposures as they are committed. In addition, during the course of the year, more attention has been focused on developing strategies to manage individual operating units' pre-transaction exposures.

All pre-transaction hedging decisions are approved by the Corporate Finance Committee, with any resultant transactions being undertaken in accordance with the policy noted above.

The Group manages the majority of its remitted earnings with the initial aim of protecting their budgeted Sterling value, this objective being refined throughout the year to that of improving on the average translation rate. These hedges are effected using financial instruments such as options and forward contracts.

The Group's policy is to remit full dividends from subsidiaries subject to tax and legal considerations. There are no funds of any materiality subject to exchange control or other restrictions as to their remittability. However, equivalent net cash of some £13m in Inchcape Berhad (a 63% owned publicly quoted company on the Singapore Stock Exchange) is subject to the normal considerations of a subsidiary with minority ownership.

To the extent that earnings remain unremitted, they are not specifically hedged, as the Group considers it to be inappropriate potentially to incur a cash cost, resulting from the use of hedging instruments, to cover a non-cash exposure. These amounts are, therefore, translated into Sterling from underlying currencies at the average rates for the year.

To the extent that the Group has not been able to reduce its foreign currency asset base by the dividend remittance policy described above, it seeks further to reduce translation risk on the residual net assets by hedging centrally via foreign currency borrowing and swap arrangements, subject to economic and tax considerations. The principal net asset exposures of the Group arise in respect of US Dollar and Dollar related currencies in Singapore Dollars.

Liquidity Risk and Debt Management The Group manages its liquidity risks in order to ensure that adequate facilities are available to cover both short-term and medium-term funding requirements.

Working capital is primarily funded by a combination of short-term bank overdrafts and loans, short-term trade credit from principals or their related finance arms as part of normal commercial arrangements, and trade credit from other finance companies in respect of specific shipments of goods.

Longer term funding requirements are satisfied by the 6¼% Subordinated Convertible Bonds issued in 1993 and due to mature in 2008, and by £300m of committed medium-term standby facilities which remain unutilised.

Furthermore, the Group seeks to minimise its long-term commitment of funds to fixed asset investments whose return on capital employed is below our target level. This is achieved by leasing property and other fixed assets wherever it is both practical and consistent with operational and economic considerations. Including the costs for hire of plant and net operating lease rental payments, the Group's fixed charge cover* has declined to 2.9 times, compared to 3.1 times in 1993.

Year end net borrowings for gearing purposes were £462.1m of which £280.0m falls due in less than one year. This compares to £303.1m in 1993, after adjusting for the impact of FRS5, which included £123.9m due in less than one year. The year on year increase was largely due to the Hogg acquisition and increased working capital resulting from the downturn in the Motors businesses. This latter effect continues to exert upward pressure on the Group's borrowing levels. Capital gearing* was 61.7% at the end of 1994 (of which the acquisition of Hogg accounts for 28pts) compared with an adjusted 34.7% in 1993.

The effect of applying FRS5 increased year end capital gearing* by 3.1pts, and 10.0pts last year, primarily in relation to debtors discounted with recourse. Also, stocks and creditors have increased by £113.1m (1993 – £72.4m) because of FRS5, primarily in respect of re-purchase commitments given on the sale of certain motor vehicles.

Interest Rate Risk The Group's interest rate exposures are centrally managed on an active basis in order to minimise the risk of interest rate movements having an unfavourable effect on the Group's earnings, and a variety of financial instruments such as options, swaps and forward rate agreements are used.

The definition of interest cover* was changed during the year to recognise that interest earned on funds held on behalf of third parties is income freely available to the Group. These interest earnings are now more significant following the Hogg acquisition. This revised definition is more readily accessible to users of the accounts. On the revised basis, interest cover* declined from 10.3 times to 8.7 times reflecting the reduction in year on year profits and the higher net interest charge. On the previous basis, interest cover would have been 8.4 times (1993 – 6.8 times).

Hazard Risks The Group, like any other, is exposed to many external risks, ranging from political and economic instability to specific hazards such as fire, flood and earthquake. The Group aims progressively to reduce its exposure to such risks through strategies agreed by the Board.

Business Streams are responsible for the active management and economic reduction of risk whilst the Group's risk management advisers provide guidance and recommendations on risk reduction through periodic risk audits.

Risks to assets and potential liabilities to customers or the public, which are significant and identifiable, are insured with international insurers and the Group's own captive insurance company. Risks of controllable magnitude are self-insured where financially beneficial.

* *Definitions are shown on page 71 of the Report and Accounts.*

Investment for the future

33.71 This section of the OFR is aiming for disclosure of both capital and revenue investment. The general point is that, although the OFR is not a forecast, it is an opportunity to convey some information about the future. A discussion of investment, both made and planned, is an important part of that review.

33.72 As regards capital investment, the ASB is saying that the OFR should discuss the current level of capital expenditure together with planned expenditure. Planned expenditure should include both committed, and authorised but not committed. Where disclosure of such plans would be confidential, it need not be given. The discussion should indicate the geographical area and business segment involved and, for material parts of the total, the major projects. The discussion should include the benefits from the capital expenditure, both those starting to be achieved from expenditure incurred and benefits expected from future capital projects. This discussion is generally straightforward.

33.73 The ASB also calls for disclosure of what has been called 'revenue investment'. This is a more difficult and controversial area. In the course of developing FRS 3, 'Reporting financial performance', the ASB issued FRED 1 of the same title. The FRED proposed that companies should be required to disclose details of 'revenue investment', which was defined as *"...those material categories of expenses which have been charged to the profit and loss account of a period having been incurred wholly or partly in order to enhance future profitability and which can be varied within a relatively wide range without significantly affecting current trading".* [FRED 1 para 8]. The ASB proposed in FRED 1 that companies should disclose revenue investment, showing separately research and development, training, advertising and major maintenance and refurbishment. Changes in the level of expenditure from year to year would be explained. The ASB's idea was that such disclosure would enable users to see: the extent of such investment in absolute terms, which would give users an idea of future profitability; and the variation in the expenditure, that is, whether or to what extent a downturn in operating performance has been masked by a cutback in revenue investment. This is not to say that businesses should not make savings in revenue investment in recessions; it is merely that users would be able to form their own view on the extent of cutbacks and the merits of such policies. There was a considerable amount of objection to this proposal and the ASB agreed to drop it in the eventual standard FRS 3.

33.74 The same general idea has re-emerged in the OFR, although the term 'revenue investment' is not used. ASB says that:

> *"In addition to capital expenditure, many other activities and expenditure can be regarded, to a greater or lesser extent, as a form of investing in the future."*

[OFR para 16].

33.75 The ASB goes on to say that the nature of this expenditure will vary from company to company and that the absolute level of such expenditure is less important than changes in it, and the effect of those changes on the current and future profitability.

33.76 Again, the ASB provides a list of examples of what might fall under this heading:

- Marketing and advertising campaigns.
- Training programmes.
- Refurbishment and maintenance programmes.
- Pure and applied research that may lead to potential new products and services.
- Development of new products and services.
- Technical support to customers.

[OFR para 17].

33.77 There are many good examples of disclosure of capital investments made and planned by companies in the OFRs so far published. This is one area where companies are very willing to discuss their plans for the future although understandably the descriptions of planned investment are not always accompanied by the quantification of the amounts involved. Of particular note are the number of joint venture projects being initiated overseas, particularly in the Far East. It is clear from a cursory glance at the OFRs of the major British groups that China and the Far East are considered to be major growth markets of the future. An example of this disclosure is given in Table 33.18. In this example, the Chief Executive's Review refers to investments in Poland and China and the level of expenditure is indicated in the Financial Review. There is also discussion of the investment in the reviews of the individual Beverages and Confectionery businesses, which are not reproduced in the example.

33.78 Table 33.18 also gives some indication of marketing expenditure and the increase in the year. For certain industries, marketing and advertising expenditure is particularly important. These tend to be the industries that rely heavily on branded products. The food and drinks industry is an obvious example, but industries such as vehicle dealers, pharmaceuticals and household products are others.

Table 33.18 – Cadbury Schweppes plc – Annual Report – 31 December 1994

Group Chief Executive's Review (extract)

Development

In last year's Annual Report I drew attention to actions that we were taking to strengthen our international position by expanding activity into selected developing markets where we believe prospects for growth are attractive.

In November 1994 we began the manufacture of Piasten and Cadbury chocolate in our new factory in Poland and are currently investing to build our presence in this market. In Russia confectionery sales have risen dramatically to 26,000 tonnes sourced from the UK, Germany, South Africa, Ireland, Spain, Egypt and India. In beverages the Crush brand is now being bottled locally in Moscow.

Construction of the joint venture confectionery factory in China is on track as is installation of a chocolate manufacturing facility at Cadbury Stani in Argentina. Both new plants will supply their respective markets later in 1995.

In India, where Cadbury has long established strength in confectionery, investment programmes and good market growth have brought strong and continuing progress in profitability. We have established our first licence agreement to introduce a number of our soft drinks brands into India in 1995.

These examples illustrate some of the investment that the Group is making to ensure that the seeds of future growth are both sown and nurtured.

Financial Review (extract)

Investment in the Business

Marketing expenditure increased by 10% to £467m and represented 11.6% of sales compared with 11.4% in 1993. A significant part of the increase, in both the amount and the percentage, reflected the acquisition of A&W Brands where, as with all our franchise businesses, the ratio of marketing to sales is much higher than in manufacturing operations.

Capital expenditure rose by 8% to £239m. 61% of the total was spent on confectionery businesses and 39% on beverages. The confectionery total includes expenditure of £25m on new factories in Poland and China and a further £18m on new capacity in Argentina and India.

33.79 Training and the use of new technology to assist both customers and staff are significant factors in improving the efficiency and the reputation of a business, particularly one that provides services to the public. Table 33.19 illustrates disclosure of those factors.

Table 33.19 – Hambro Countrywide PLC – Annual Report and Accounts – 31 December 1994

Operating and Financial Review (extract)

We continue to invest in technology, to maintain and improve our market share through improved service to our clients. We have invested in point-of-sale systems for our financial consultants which will enhance client advice and speed the transmission of data to shorten policy processing times, to the benefit of both clients and consultants. After a successful pilot we have started to roll out the Quest IT system to our residential and mortgage valuation surveyors. This system likewise enables speedier communication between our surveyors and our clients and helps to cut down the time taken to issue a mortgage offer. We also continue to invest in training, development and other measures to improve the quality of service we provide to our customers.

33.80 The OFRs published to date give surprisingly good disclosure in relation to research and product development. Whilst understandably the disclosure is of a general nature so as to preserve confidential information, it appears to be considered by companies to be an opportunity to demonstrate that confidence in the future of the business is justified. An example of such disclosure is given in Table 33.20.

Table 33.20 – Courtaulds plc – Report and Accounts – 31 March 1995

Research and Product Development

Courtaulds research and product development objectives are currently twofold: to provide higher performance, value for money products, and to develop more reliable and cost efficient processes. Environmental considerations loom large in both cases.

In Marine coatings, large scale supply started in 1994 of non tar containing ballast tank coatings. In the Yacht business new products included Toplac gloss finishes for the do-it-yourself market and interfill fillers and Interspray 900 finishes for large superyachts. Powder continues to be the most environmentally friendly type of coating. Thinner film coatings based on a patented new technology have been launched as well as higher exterior durability powders for the architectural and automotive markets. The new automotive exterior trim powder is being specified by major manufacturers such as Ford of Europe. Work continues on PVC-free and water-based coatings for the packaging market, while in Aerospace a new high solids coating Desothane HS was launched for aircraft such as Boeing 777 and new lightweight sealants with improved corrosion inhibition properties based on Permapol polymers were introduced. The range of coil coatings has been extended with new products for consumer electronics.

Recyclability is a major issue in packaging. Courtaulds position has been strengthened with the introduction of all plastic laminate tubes which are easier to recycle. Novel polymer blends to improve the barrier properties of toothpaste tubes have also been developed. Performance Films is introducing a new solvent-free colouring technology and has also made a breakthrough in flexible circuitry materials.

In Fibres & Chemicals, process improvement is often as important as new product development. In this context, a new acetate flake manufacturing process has been successfully commissioned. In Fine Chemicals, new processes are being developed for manufacturing the chemical intermediates required by pharmaceutical companies.

Development has continued on the superabsorbent Oasis fibre, in conjunction with Allied Colloids, and on fibres with special properties for wound dressings which significantly speed up healing. Significant as these activities are, however, a high proportion of the development work is focused on Tencel. Process improvements have significantly reduced the capital cost per tonne and there has been considerable progress both in improving the processability of the fibre and in developing its aesthetic characteristics.

33.81 Despite the good examples of disclosure in the Tables above, the general level of disclosure of revenue investment, particularly of refurbishment or maintenance programmes, is patchy. It may be that those who have increased expenditure on revenue investment are more willing to disclose than those who have reduced it. A fall in profits coupled with an increase in revenue investment may be seen as acceptable, an increase in profits coupled with a reduction in revenue investment might take more explaining. There may also be a reluctance by some companies to give information of this nature, either for competitive reasons or because they do not wish readers to see the extent to which they 'manage' their results by deferring or accelerating such expenditures.

Profit for the financial year, total recognised gains and losses and shareholders' perspective

33.82 Under this heading, the ASB believes the OFR should discuss *"...the overall return attributable to shareholders, in terms of dividends and increases in shareholders' funds, commenting on the contributions from the operating performance of the various business units and on other items reported as part of total recognised gains and losses"*. [OFR para 19].

33.83 Although the ASB does not refer explicitly to FRS 3 in this context, it is clearly intended that the data generated by FRS 3 should be discussed here. The ASB refers to information on revaluation gains and losses that, prior to FRS 3, were previously merely put to reserves, but are now also shown with more prominence in the statement of total recognised gains and losses (SORG). It points out that for certain businesses, in particular investment businesses, revaluation gains and losses are an important part of overall performance and should be discussed as such. This is certainly true: for example in the case of a property company, the changes in value of the properties may be at least as important as the revenue result for the year – although this was equally true before FRS 3.

33.84 In practice, most companies do not seem to discuss total recognised gains in great detail. Instead, the heading used is often 'Operating results' or 'Profit for the year'. This is probably because the majority of companies do not have significant recognised gains or losses other than those that are reflected in the profit and loss account. Companies such as investment property companies also tend to keep a clear distinction between revenue, that is rental income, and increase in net asset value, which results primarily from regular property valuations. The distinction is usually made by having quite separate sections of the OFR dealing with revenue on the one hand and revaluations of property on the other. The idea of combining a discussion of the profit for the year with a discussion of 'capital' items such as revaluations, as if they were like items within total performance, does not seem to have gained much acceptance so far. For this reason, the SORG does not seem to be fulfilling its intended purpose as a measure of total performance.

33.85 It is also notable that in the vast majority of cases the discussion of profit for the year is contained in the financial review section rather than in the operating review section of the OFR. This seems to be a more logical place for the discussion.

Profit for the financial year, dividends and earnings per share

33.86 There appears to be some overlap between this and the previous heading, and in practice companies combine these sections of their OFR.

33.87 The ASB envisages that an OFR would discuss the comparison between the profit for the financial year and dividends, both in total and in per share terms. 'Profit for the financial year' is the result shown at the foot of the profit and loss account, but before dividends. It is therefore not quite the same figure as the basis for calculation of earnings per share, which is after deducting preference dividends. In many situations the two will not be significantly different. However, where they are, it will be advisable to discuss:

- The profit for the financial year.
- The profit after preference dividends and thus the amount that is the basis for the EPS calculation and that remains for ordinary shareholders.

It is only after preference dividends that a valid comparison can be made between the profits available and that part which is being distributed to ordinary shareholders.

33.88 Under this heading, the ASB also calls for discussion of the company's overall dividend policy. This can be a tricky area for companies. Dividend policy is a complex matter. Many companies may have a general policy of paying out, for example, 40 per cent of available profits on the basis of their expectation of medium-term levels of profitability. But there are also shorter-term, tactical issues. For example, if there are losses or very low profits in a particular year, should the company maintain its dividend, cut it or pass it? This will depend partly on market expectations, partly on what other companies are doing and partly on how confident the directors are about an early return to the normal level of profitability. Therefore, directors are sometimes reluctant to be too precise in an OFR about their dividend policy.

33.89 Generally, therefore, statements appear which are rather bland, along the lines of *"the dividend has been increased by X per cent this year in line with the Board's policy of maximising returns to investors over the long term"*.

33.90 A notable exception to this type of rather superficial disclosure is given in Table 33.21. This extract indicates the seriousness with which the Board has considered the question of dividend policy and indicates the Board's future intentions and the factors on which the future achievement of their aims may depend.

Table 33.21 – Pearson plc – Directors' Report and Accounts – 31 December 1994

Financial Review (extract)

Dividend policy

Institutional investors have rightly been rather critical of the vagueness with which corporate dividend aspirations are often expressed. The Pearson Board has reconsidered its policy in this area, which has been to pay steady increases subject to earnings and the immediate outlook in terms of both profits and liquidity. Studies of the UK equity market over many decades confirm that dividends generally make a greater contribution than capital growth to total shareholder return. Yet Pearson's existing dividend yield is materially less than that for the FT-SE 100 as a whole, even if based on a share price that excludes the notional value of our holding in BSkyB. So our intention now is to increase dividends at a rate sufficiently greater than the historic 2% long-term real growth for the market in order to put Pearson's yield on a par with the market's over the medium-term. Clearly, our ability to carry out this policy and the speed with which it can be implemented will depend on our continuing to maintain and improve the high level of cash generation we have achieved in recent years; the mix of profits between the UK and the rest of the world will also have a bearing. Both factors will be influenced by economic conditions, including inflation, at home and in our main overseas markets.

33.91 The ASB also calls for discussion where additional figures of EPS are given, as permitted by FRS 3. Where a company gives an additional figure of EPS (such as one based on the IIMR headline earnings, discussed in paragraph 33.33 above), it will often be because it believes the basic figure required by FRS 3 and SSAP 3 (revised) is too volatile and is neither helpful in divining trends nor a good predictor of future EPS. Therefore, it may make sense to link discussion of the additional EPS figure with discussion of the trend of financial performance. However, this will not in general involve any explicit prediction of future results, as the OFR falls short of calling for any forecast information.

Accounting policies

33.92 In this section of the statement, the ASB calls for discussion in the OFR where, in applying the accounting policies, there are subjective judgements to which the financial statements are particularly sensitive. Examples might include:

- The recognition of profit on long-term contracts.
- The recognition of both cost and revenue in software development companies.

- Judgements about the economic life for depreciation purposes of certain high-technology assets.

- Judgements about what development costs should be carried forward.

33.93 There is no suggestion in the OFR that companies should calculate the numbers on a different basis, or discuss the range of possible outcomes had other judgements been taken. It is just a matter of highlighting that there are areas where the accounting numbers are relatively soft. In this section, any changes of accounting policy that have been made in the year should also be disclosed (see para 33.27 above), though in practice this is more often done in the financial review.

The financial review

Introduction

33.94 The ASB explains that the principal aim of this section of an OFR *"...is to explain to the user of the annual report the capital structure of the business, its treasury policy and the dynamics of its financial position – its sources of liquidity and their application, including the implications of the financing requirements arising from its capital expenditure plans"*. [OFR para 23]. It adds that *"...the discussion should concentrate on matters of significance to the position of the business as a whole"*. [OFR para 24]. It should be a narrative commentary supported by figures, that is, the opposite emphasis to the financial statements themselves.

Capital structure and treasury policy

33.95 Under this heading, the ASB calls for a wide-ranging discussion, both in terms of policy and objectives and also actual implementation of the policy, of a number of related issues. The ASB's recommendations are laid out in a rather repetitive way, but seem to come down to the following:

- Capital structure, that is, types of capital instrument used.

- Maturity profile of debt.

- Currency of both borrowings and cash and cash equivalents, and the management of exchange rate risk.

- Interest rate structure and risk. This would include discussion of the extent to which borrowings (and, presumably, also deposits) are at a fixed rate. It would also include discussion of the effect of interest costs on profits and the potential impact of interest rate changes.

- The use of financial instruments for hedging purposes; specifically, the extent to which foreign currency net investments are hedged by currency borrowings and other hedging instruments.

- The manner in which treasury activities are controlled.

33.96 The ASB indicates that discussion of these matters should include referring to ratios such as interest cover and gearing (debt/equity ratios) and should also deal with financing transactions, both during the year and post balance sheet, up to the date of approval of the financial statements.

33.97 For many listed companies, this section of the OFR could be relatively complex. The issues will often be inter-linked. For example, a discussion could:

- Start with a description of the gearing and capital structure at the beginning of the year.

- Observe that the gearing level was lower than normal.

- Discuss the capital expenditure plans.

- Explain that ten year debt was raised to finance that expenditure.

- Explain that long-term debt was raised because the investment was in long-term assets, but also acknowledge that:

  - the group was overly reliant on short-term debt; and

  - the group wanted to take advantage of the historically low rate of interest on long-term debt.

This could lead to a discussion of the group's policy regarding fixed or floating rate finance. If interest rate swaps had been taken out as part of this policy, they could be summarised.

33.98 In other circumstances, a group might have overseas subsidiaries and might have changed the way in which they are financed. For example, the discussion could deal with the opening position, which might be that all funding was in sterling, and explain that the directors had decided during the year that, particularly in the light of their ambitions for overseas expansion, this gave rise to unduly high exchange rate exposure. The discussion could add that the directors had, therefore, decided to re-finance the overseas operations by a mixture of US dollar and ECU borrowings. Alternatively, it might be explained that the group had retained its sterling borrowings, but taken out derivative contracts to hedge the overseas investments.

33.99 An example of disclosure relating to capital structure is Table 33.22. Although only the section of the OFR on capital structure is reproduced in the example. There are other sections dealing with 'Capital expenditure and cash flow' and 'Treasury and risk management'.

Table 33.22 – Marks and Spencer p.l.c. – Annual Report and Financial Statements – 31 March 1995

Financial review (extract)

CAPITAL STRUCTURE

A process of simplification was completed in 1994. The Company's two small preference share issues were redeemed following resolutions at last year's AGM, and the last £15m of outstanding debentures were repaid.

The increase in issued ordinary share capital results from shareholder scrip dividend schemes, employee profit sharing, savings and share option schemes. Further information on these plans is available in the relevant notes to the financial statements.

The new Marks & Spencer Life Assurance Company – which has begun to trade since the 1994/95 year end – was capitalised within the Financial Services group of companies by the subscription of £38m.

Overseas, our policy is to match our assets with overseas borrowings, thereby reducing foreign exchange exposure. Such borrowings are normally short term, the exception being a US$450m Promissory Note taken out at the time of the acquisition of Brooks Brothers in 1988. This Note is due in 1998, and short-term dollar investments of US$320m have been established to go towards neutralising the potential foreign exchange transaction risk of that repayment.

It will be seen from note 26 to the financial statements that Cash and Cash Equivalents declined in value by £26.8m because of foreign exchange movements. This is matched by a decline of the same amount in the value of our US$ long-term borrowings, which include the Promissory Note (see note 27). The Group does not enter into foreign exchange contracts to hedge translation exposure in the balance sheet and profit and loss account.

Two Eurobonds, US$150m due 1996 and £150m due 1998 complete the list of longer term borrowings, and are used to provide funding for general corporate purposes including Financial Services. Currency swaps have been arranged for the first of these and interest rate swaps are in place for each so that, in both cases, short-term sterling funding is provided at rates below LIBOR. The balance of financial services borrowing requirements is met either through the short-term sterling market or by inter-company lending.

Marks and Spencer p.l.c. is rated AAA/Aaa long term and A+/P1 short term by Standard & Poor's and Moody's.

33.100 An example of discussion of treasury management is in Table 33.23. In this table, only the text is reproduced, but in the financial statements there are charts which show the currency exposure of the group for both 1994 and 1993.

Table 33.23 – Reuters Holdings PLC – Annual Report – 31 December 1994

Review of Financial Needs, Resources and Treasury Management (extract)

Treasury management

A substantial portion of Reuters revenue is committed under two-year or four-year contracts and over 80% is denominated in non-sterling currencies. Net cash flows are converted into sterling and are mainly invested in sterling money market instruments with financial institutions holding strong credit ratings. The use of sterling instruments minimises currency exposure.

The risk from a fall in sterling interest rates is managed using a mix of financial instruments which commence and mature at various dates through March 1998. The risk that foreign currencies might weaken against sterling is also hedged.

Hedging is undertaken within parameters laid down by the Board. The priority in treasury policy is to reduce risk to acceptable levels while allowing a degree of flexibility to take advantage of market movements. During 1994 the Board agreed a revised mandate for Treasury. This reduced the period of foreign exchange cover from 30 months to 24 months. In summary the main principles underlying hedging policy are as follows:

- committed hedging cannot exceed the underlying exposure;
- options can only be written against an underlying exposure;
- levels of cover for currency hedging cannot exceed 90% of underlying exposure for the first 12 months and 70% for the following 12 months.

The gain/(loss) on hedging activities for the three years to 31 December 1994 and the fair value of the unrecognised loss on the hedging book at the end of 1994 are summarised below. The interest rate hedging benefit is calculated by comparing the achieved yield with the yield that would have been obtained from three-month sterling certificates of deposit in respect of sterling investments and three-month Treasuries in respect of US dollar investments. The unrecognised gains/(losses) shown below are based on fair values at the end of 1994 and include certain realised items which have been deferred because they relate to future periods.

	Recognised gain/(loss)			Unrecognised gain/(loss) at 31 December 1994	
	1992 £m	1993 £m	**1994 £m**	Relating to 1995 £m	Total £m
Currency hedging	4	(34)	**(22)**	(21)	(25)
Interest hedging	7	26	**28**	9	9
	11	(8)	**6**	(12)	(16)

33.101 The ASB called for disclosure of how treasury activities are controlled and Table 33.23 above also illustrates this disclosure. This recommendation no doubt stems from the well-publicised losses that have occurred from time to time as a result of treasurers or dealers over-extending themselves and either not being controlled by authority limits or going beyond those limits, from hedging into speculation. A number of companies currently spell out their policy in this area, no doubt following concerns about corporates delving too deeply into risky rather than risk-reducing, derivative contracts. For example, THORN EMI PLC states *"Treasury continues to operate as a cost centre and will not undertake any speculative activities. Controls and monitoring systems are in place to ensure that all Treasury activities are undertaken within the parameters laid down by the Board"*. This point is related to recommendation 1.4 of the Cadbury Code of Best Practice that the board should have a formal schedule of matters specifically reserved to it for decision. That is, the OFR could state the level of transactions above which board approval is required.

Taxation

33.102 The ASB recommends that where the overall tax charge differs significantly from the standard tax charge, the main components of the reconciliation between the actual and standard tax charges should be discussed. The standard charge in this context means the normal UK tax rate applied to the profit before taxation.

33.103 This provision of the OFR complements existing requirements in company law and accounting standards. The Act requires there to be disclosed *"...particulars ... of any special circumstances which affect liability in respect of taxation of profits, income or capital gains for the financial year or liability in respect of taxation of profits, income or capital gains for succeeding financial years"*. [4 Sch 54(2)]. Similarly, FRS 3 requires note disclosure of *"...any special circumstances that affect the overall tax charge or credit for the period, or that may affect those of future periods"*. [FRS 3 para 23]. In practice, companies are tending to increase disclosure in the notes to the financial statements, by way of more extensive tax reconciliations, rather than by increasing disclosure in the OFR.

33.104 Table 33.24 is an example of OFR disclosure. The company also provides in a note (not reproduced) a detailed list of special factors affecting the year's tax charge.

Table 33.24 – Coats Viyella Plc – Annual report and accounts – 31 December 1994

Financial Review (extract)

The Group tax rate for 1994 was 39.2% (32.9%). The loss on disposals attracted minimal tax relief so, had the businesses been retained, the tax rate would have fallen to 27.0%. This was primarily due to reductions in UK tax resulting from the enhanced scrip and Foreign Income Dividend (FID) initiatives. The impact of these was to lower the overall tax rate before provision for loss on sale of operations by 8.8% and enable £9.2m ACT previously written off to be utilised. The results have also benefited from a lower overseas tax rate mainly due to the utilisation of losses in Brazil. Going forward, the ability to maintain a low tax rate will depend largely on further profit improvement in the UK but the Group's intention is to continue to pay the interim dividend as a FID, thereby continuing to make inroads into the ACT surplus.

Funds from operating activities and other sources of cash

33.105 This is the reference in the OFR which is, presumably, intended to encourage companies to give a commentary on the cash flows of the business. In referring to *"...the cash generated from operations and other cash inflows during the period"*, it appears to be restricted to inflows. It is doubtful if this is what is intended, for it goes on to say that, although segmental analysis of profit may be indicative of the cash flow generated by each segment, this will not necessarily be the case, for example, because the pattern of capital expenditure may be different.

33.106 A more useful interpretation, therefore, is that there should be a general discussion of the overall cash flows – inflows and outflows – of the business focusing on all categories of cash flow and with specific commentary by segment where this is different from the profit by segment. It should be noted that analysis of cash flow by segment is not presently a requirement of FRS 1, although SSAP 25 and company law do require various analyses of turnover, profit and net assets by segment.

33.107 Examples of disclosure under this heading clearly indicate the degree of dissatisfaction amongst companies with the FRS 1 definition of 'cash and cash equivalents'. Many companies have defined an alternative cash measurement figure that they consider is more appropriate to their business and this is the figure which they discuss in the OFR. However, in October 1996, the ASB revised FRS 1. The revision abolished cash equivalents and reformed cash flow reporting to bring it more into line with business practice. As a result, companies can now report their cash flow performance in the OFR in the way they think fit. Chapter 30 contains further discussions on the reporting of cash flows information in the OFR.

[The next paragraph is 33.109.]

Current liquidity

33.109 The ASB calls for discussion of a range of issues relating to liquidity. First the liquidity at the end of the period, which "*...should include comment on the level of borrowings at the end of the period under review, the seasonality of borrowing requirements, indicated by the peak level of borrowings during that period, and the maturity profile of both borrowings and committed borrowing facilities*". [OFR para 32].

33.110 Secondly, companies should refer to the funding requirements for capital expenditure commitments and authorisations. Comment on this could sensibly be linked to the discussion of capital expenditure plans (see para 33.72 above).

33.111 Thirdly, if there are restrictions on the group's ability to transfer funds to meet the obligations of another part of the group, this should be discussed. But this would apply only where the restrictions "*...represent or might foreseeably come to represent...*" a significant restraint on the group. The restrictions could be in the form of legal barriers such as exchange controls that preclude or limit repatriation of profits, or they could be commercial obstacles such as where funds could be repatriated, but unduly high rates of withholding or other taxes would have to be paid. In some cases, for example, where the balance sheet gives an impression of considerable liquidity, but most of it is locked in certain countries by exchange controls, it may be necessary to give some information to that effect in the financial statements themselves, in order to give a true and fair view. However, it is not appropriate to use the OFR to help the financial statements give a true and fair view – they must do that by themselves. The OFR is a separate commentary, outside the financial statements.

33.112 Finally, the ASB makes recommendations for disclosure when borrowing covenants are in place and "*...negotiations with the lenders on the operation of these covenants are taking place or are expected to take place*". ASB then goes on to say that "*where a breach of a covenant has occurred or is expected to occur, the OFR should give details of the measures taken or proposed to remedy the situation*". The meaning of the second quote is clear, although there is clearly some judgement involved in assessing whether a breach of covenant is expected to occur. But the wording of the first quote is somewhat odd. It seems to recommend disclosure when negotiations are being held, perhaps to change the covenants, in a situation where there is no breach nor any expectation of breach. An example might be where a covenant is being renegotiated, not because of financial difficulty, but following the introduction of a new accounting standard that alters the ratios without any change in the underlying economic position. It is hard to see what benefit such a disclosure would bring.

33.113 Companies may find difficulty with some of the ASB's recommendations in the area of liquidity. A company that is soundly financed will tend to have little difficulty with them, for it will be able to report that (say) year end borrowings were £100,000, the seasonal peak was £150,000 and the facilities available were £500,000. Moreover, it would be happy to disclose the (long) maturity of its facilities. But a company that is weaker financially may be unwilling to disclose publicly that (say) its year end borrowings were £100,000, its peak borrowings in the year were £550,000 and its facilities were £500,000, that is, it had temporarily exceeded its borrowing facilities and perhaps also breached its covenants. The ASB's recommendation in such circumstances would have the company go on to give details about *"...measures taken or proposed to remedy the situation"*. This could lead to some awkward disclosures if the company and its bankers have not agreed what those measures might be. Disclosure in those latter circumstances is of course exactly what the ASB is aiming for and exactly what investors would welcome. But if this type of disclosure is given only by the strong, then arguably the OFR will not have been a total success. On the other hand, if most companies give satisfactory disclosures under this heading, the market and users generally will presumably soon come to realise that no comment by the directors represents danger signals. It is also possible, as with some of the Cadbury recommendations, that the very fact of focusing attention on the area will lead companies to review their position, for example, to put in place longer-term facilities of a type that they are happy to disclose publicly.

33.114 An example of disclosure of current liquidity is shown in Table 33.26.

Table 33.26 – Cordiant plc – Report and Accounts – 31 December 1994

Operating and Financial Review (extract)

Current liquidity
At the end of 1994, the Group had £77m of undrawn credit facilities. Those facilities are in part required for the cyclical working capital needs of the Group and in part provide a margin to finance any unforeseen contingency. Cyclical needs arise both during each month, derived from the media payment cycles in each country, and during the year as periods of high advertising activity seasonally improve the Group's cash position.

[The next page is 33043.]

The Group has significant cash balances in its international operations. These balances are required primarily to finance the working capital cycles of the individual country operations and, in certain cases, to provide the required level of working capital to allow the agencies to buy media on behalf of their clients. There are no material legal restrictions on transfers of funds in excess of those requirements.

Acquisition commitments, at £13 million over the period to 1999, are not significant.

After making enquiries, the Directors have a reasonable expectation that the Company has adequate resources to continue in operational existence for the foreseeable future. For this reason, they continue to adopt the going concern basis in preparing the financial statements.

Going concern

33.115 As the ASB notes, the Cadbury Code of Best Practice calls for directors of listed companies to state in their annual report their opinion regarding the company being a going concern. Cadbury recommended that guidance should be developed on the form that such a report might take. ASB observed that, *"...subject to what such guidance says when available, the going concern confirmation may appropriately be made as part of the OFR discussion of financial position"*.

33.116 Guidance on the form of going concern statement that companies might use was published in November 1994 in a document entitled 'Going concern and financial reporting – Guidance for directors of listed companies registered in the UK'. An example of disclosure given in the document was:

> *"After making enquiries, the directors have a reasonable expectation that the company has adequate resources to continue in operational existence for the foreseeable future. For this reason, they continue to adopt the going concern basis in preparing the accounts".*

33.117 Because a statement on this subject is now required if listed companies are to be able to say that they have complied with the Cadbury Code, it is now almost universally made by such companies. An example is included in Table 33.26 above.

33.118 Whilst most going concern statements do no more than reproduce with minor variations the suggesting wording of the guidance, Table 33.27 is an example that points out, in addition, that future events are inherently uncertain.

Table 33.27 – Tesco PLC – Annual report and accounts – 28 February 1998

Going concern

The directors consider that the Group and the company have adequate resources to remain in operation for the foreseeable future and have therefore continued to adopt the going concern basis in preparing the financial statements. As with all business forecasts the directors' statement cannot guarantee that the going concern basis will remain appropriate given the inherent uncertainty about future events.

Balance sheet value

33.119 After a series of 'shoulds', the ASB becomes more tentative and states that *"the OFR* ***could*** *also give a commentary on strengths and resources of the business whose value is not reflected in the balance sheet (or only partially shown in the balance sheet). Such items* ***could*** *include brands and similar intangible items.* ***Where considered appropriate****, the value of such items, and increases or decreases in their overall value,* ***could*** *be discussed"*. [OFR para 37, emphasis added]. The ASB was clearly less confident, or less agreed among itself, about these disclosures than about the rest of the OFR. This is a shame, as there is merit in companies giving information about the value of assets on a supplementary basis. Whilst we are not against including revaluations in financial statements, we take the view that an alternative way of conveying information about value is through either note information or through some kind of supplementary statement. This could show both the values (or revaluation surpluses) of assets that are carried at cost and the values of assets that are not carried on the balance sheet at all.

33.120 The ASB goes on to say that *"...it is not intended that an overall valuation of the business be given, nor, in the case of listed companies, for net asset value to be reconciled to market capitalisation"*. [OFR para 37). Whilst we would agree that this should not be mandated, we believe it is an area in which experimentation should be encouraged. A possible layout that companies might wish to consider is as follows:

	£m
Net asset value per the balance sheet	10
Revaluations of assets on the balance sheet	
Land and buildings	3
Other	2
Valuation of assets not on balance sheet	
Brands	5
Other	2
Total current value of separable net assets	22
Total goodwill of the business	5
Market capitalisation	27

33.121 These are soft numbers and better lend themselves to an OFR than to audited financial statements. An objection to the statement is that the £27 million of market capitalisation is merely the value on one day, and, in any case, is the product of multiplying up a figure that relates only to a small parcel of shares rather than to the business as a whole. This point is valid and some companies may wish to stop at the total value of the separable assets. Another response is to give a range of the market capitalisation during the year and since the year end.

33.122 An advantage of a table of this nature is that it focuses attention on the difference, both in concept and in amount, between the value of the assets and the value of the business as a whole. In doing so, it gives information about the *current* value of the *total goodwill* of the business, as judged by the market, rather than about the historical cost of the purchased part of the goodwill.

33.123 Table 33.28 is an example where a company discloses the amount of shareholders' equity funds, the movement in the share price during the year and the market capitalisation at the end of the year. Similar disclosure is made by a growing number of companies. The range of share price movement in this example indicates how volatile the movements in market capitalisation can be and reinforces the view that any attempts to estimate the total goodwill of a business as in paragraph 33.120 above would need to be based on an average of share prices over a period.

Table 33.28 – Sears plc – Annual Report and Accounts – 31 January 1995

Operating and Financial Review (extract)

Shareholders' Return and Value
Ordinary shareholders' equity funds increased from £1,129.3 million to £1,191.6 million.

The increase in attributable profits to £114.3 million has allowed the Board to recommend a final dividend of 2.90 pence per share, up by 8.2%. This will provide a dividend cover of 1.91 times for the year.

The Company's share price fluctuated in the range of 98.5 pence to 131.5 pence during the year. At 31st January 1995, the mid-market price of an Ordinary share was 98.5 pence and the Company's equity market capitalisation was £1,493 million.

Position of the auditor

33.124 The OFR is envisaged as being unaudited, in line with the chairman's statement, chief executive's review, finance director's review and similar documents that it to some degree replaces or formalises. Auditors have a statutory responsibility to review the directors' report (and any information referred to from the directors' report) for consistency with the financial statements, but an OFR is not part of the directors' report, so in a legal sense the auditor's responsibility does not extend to it in the same way. Nevertheless, as a practical matter, auditors will, in general, review an OFR to ensure that the views expressed and any financial information given are neither misleading nor incompatible with the financial statements and may offer advice to the directors on its contents. It will, therefore, be helpful if auditors are given an early opportunity to read the draft OFR. This approach is consistent with SAS 160 'Other information in documents containing audited financial statements', which requires that auditors review any other information (for example, that contained in the chairman's statement or five year summary) for consistency with the audited financial statements.

Chapter 34

Loans and other transactions involving directors

Page

Chapter 34

Loans and other transactions involving directors

Introduction

34.1 The common law imposes on directors the obligation not to put themselves into a position where their personal interest and the interest of their company conflict. Directors are, as a consequence, only permitted to contract with their company to the extent permitted by the articles of association or to the extent approved by shareholders. However, to prevent a complete waiver of the common law rules by a company, which would not benefit shareholders, certain statutory restrictions have been imposed.

34.2 The 1985 Act imposes restrictions on dealings between a company and its directors by making certain loans and credit-related transactions and arrangements unlawful. The purpose of these restrictions is to prevent directors taking advantage of their position. Certain transactions, such as substantial property transactions, have to be approved by shareholders. In addition, the Act requires transactions and arrangements with the company in which a director is interested to be declared to the board and most have to be disclosed in the company's financial statements whether they are lawful or not.

34.3 The restrictions imposed by the Act relating to transactions and arrangements between the company and its directors or officers are, perhaps, the main legal safeguard available against directors or officers abusing their position in a company. The disclosure requirements, in particular, ensure that shareholders and others that have an interest in the company (for example, creditors) will be informed about all the significant transactions the company enters into with those responsible for the company's management that might (either directly or indirectly) benefit those individuals. The intention is to encourage directors and officers to take care before entering into such transactions and arrangements, because the shareholders will be fully informed of them.

34.4 There has been a degree of uncertainty surrounding the extent of the disclosure to be made in the financial statements for directors' transactions and, consequently, the disclosure requirements that are dealt with in Part II to Schedule 6 to the Act may be clarified by further legislation. This is, however, unlikely to lead to less disclosure.

34.5 Listed companies may be required to make additional disclosures of transactions between a company and its directors or their related parties to comply with the Stock Exchange Listing Rules Chapter 11 - Transactions with Related Parties (see from para 34.113). In addition, the disclosures required by FRS 8, 'Related party disclosure', will soon be required in connection with transactions with directors (see chapter 35).

34.6 The annex to this chapter contains decision tables that determine whether a loan, quasi-loan or credit transaction to or for a director is prohibited by the Act. These tables should be read in conjunction with this chapter.

34.7 This chapter deals, first, with loans, quasi-loans and credit transactions as they apply to relevant and non-relevant companies. It explains their legality, the disclosure requirements for transactions with directors and officers and the sanctions imposed if the rules are breached. It deals, secondly, with the procedural and disclosure requirements of other types of transactions or arrangements involving a company and a director, including transactions in which the director has a material interest. Thirdly, it deals with the special provisions for such transactions that apply exclusively to money lending companies and banking companies. Lastly it mentions sanctions for non-disclosure.

Definitions

34.8 The definitions that follow are essential to an understanding of the types of transaction that the Act regulates.

Director

34.9 The word 'director' as used in the Act includes any person who occupies the position of director by whatever name called. [Sec 741(1)]. This means that it is the person's responsibilities and duties and not his title that determines whether or not he is a director. A director is a person who actively takes part in board meetings and votes at them. 'Directors' may be called governors, managers or trustees.

34.10 Directors can be of three kinds: *de jure* directors (that is, directors who have been validly appointed as such); *de facto* directors (that is, directors who assume to act as directors without having been appointed validly or at all); and shadow directors. Shadow directors and *de facto* directors are considered below.

Shadow director

34.11 A 'shadow director' is a person in accordance with whose instructions the directors are accustomed to act. [Sec 741(2)]. A recent case, *Re Hydrodan (Corby)*

Ltd [1994] BCC 161, considered the question of shadow directors and distinguished them from de facto directors. The judge said *"A shadow director lurks in the shadows, sheltering behind others who, he claims, are the only directors of the company to the exclusion of himself. He is not held out as a director by the company."* To show a person is a shadow director it will be necessary to prove:

- Who are the directors of the company, whether *de facto* or *de jure* (see para 34.10 above).
- That the person directed those directors how to act in relation to the company, or that he was one of the persons who did so.
- That those directors acted in accordance with such directions.
- That they were accustomed so to act.

The judge emphasised that what is needed is a board of directors claiming and purporting to act as such and then a pattern of behaviour in which the board did not exercise any discretion or judgment of its own, but acted in accordance with the directions of others.

34.12 In his judgment it was possible (although it was not alleged in the case) that the directors of a parent company as a collective body gave directions to the directors of its subsidiary company and that the directors of the subsidiary were accustomed to act in accordance with such directions. If they had given such directions as directors of the parent, acting as the board of the parent, they did so as agents for the parent and the result is to constitute the parent, but not the directors, as shadow directors of the subsidiary.

34.13 Section 741(2) also contains an exception *"A person is not deemed a shadow director by reason only that the directors act on advice given by him in a professional capacity."* It is suggested that the courts will take a narrow view of what constitutes 'professional capacity'. The Financial Law Panel in its Paper on Shadow Directorships published in 1994 is of the view that the exemption would only apply to professions, such as solicitors and accountants, where the following factors exist:

- Entry is by examination.
- The members of the profession subscribe to a common ethical code and discipline their members.

The Paper goes on to say that if the advice is given as part of the contractual duties of the person concerned, and for which a fee is paid, the exemption clearly applies.

If any of these factors is absent, it will be more difficult to demonstrate that the adviser is acting in a professional capacity.

34.14 The law relating to shadow directors remains unclear, because of the lack of case law. However, it is thought that certain classes of persons who deal with the affairs of a company could be shadow directors. These could include, for instance: banks, which seek to control certain aspects of an insolvent company's management; parent companies, which impose policy and decisions on their subsidiaries controlling shareholders; venture capitalists who participate in the running of the company; company doctors; and locum managers (see *re Tasbian Ltd (No 3)* [1992] BCC 358). These aspects are discussed in greater detail in the Financial Law Panel Paper mentioned above.

Example

The principal shareholder (owning 60%) of a company ceased to be a director before the beginning of the year, but continues to direct the operations of the company as he still controls and dominates the company.

The principal shareholder falls within the definition of a shadow director and should be treated as a director of the company. Any transactions that he enters into that are covered by the Act's requirements should, therefore, be disclosed.

De facto director

34.15 The distinction between a *de facto* director and a shadow director has been clarified in *Re Hydrodan* mentioned above. The judge considered that they were alternatives and in most, and perhaps all, cases are mutually exclusive. He stated that a *de facto* director is a person who assumes to act as director. Such a person is *held out* as a director by the company and claims and purports to be a director, although never actually or validly appointed as such. To be a *de facto* director it must be shown that the person undertook functions which could properly be discharged only by a director. It is not sufficient to show that he was concerned in the management of the company's affairs or undertook tasks that can properly be performed by a manager below board level. A shadow director, on the other hand, does not claim or purport to act as a director. He will act through the directors (see para 34.11 above).

Alternate director

34.16 The position of an 'alternate director' is determined by the articles of association of a company. If the articles adopted are those of Table A, the alternate director has the following position:

- He is appointed and can be removed by the same director of the company.

- If the potential alternate director is not already a director, his appointment must be approved by a resolution of the board.

- If the director who appointed the alternate director ceases to be a director, the appointment of the alternate ceases immediately.

- The alternate director is, unless the articles provide otherwise, a director of the company, and can, at meetings of the board, fulfil all the functions of the director appointing him, in the absence of that director. Attendance and voting at board meetings is only permitted when the appointing director is absent.

34.17 Where the term 'director' is used in this chapter, it includes references to directors (both *de facto* and *de jure*), shadow directors, and alternate directors.

Connected persons

34.18 A 'connected person' is a person who is connected with a director of a company and is either an individual or a legal person (for example, a company). A connected person is defined by section 346 to include any of the following:

(a) The director's spouse, child (including an illegitimate child), or step-child, but excluding any child who has reached 18 years of age. [Sec 346(2)(a),(3)(a)].

(b) A body corporate with which the director is associated (except in certain contexts). [Sec 346(2)(b)]. (See further para 34.19.)

(c) A person acting in his capacity as a trustee of any trust in either of the following situations:

  - The trust includes as a beneficiary the director, his spouse, children, step children, or a body corporate with which he is associated.

  - The trust confers a power on the trustees that may be used to benefit the director, his spouse, children, step children, or a body corporate with which he is associated. [Sec 346(2)(c)].

  However, a person acting as trustee of either an employee share scheme or a pension scheme is not to be regarded as connected with a director merely by virtue of that trusteeship. [Sec 346(3)(b)].

(d) A partner of the director or of a person who is connected with him under (a), (b) or (c) above. [Sec 346(2)(d)].

(e) A Scottish firm in which one of the following applies:

- The director is a partner, or persons connected with him under (a), (b) or (c) above, are partners.

- Another Scottish firm is a partner, and the director or any such connected persons are partners of that other Scottish firm. [Sec 346(2)(e)].

In Scotland a firm is a legal person distinct from the partners of whom it is composed, but each partner can still be compelled to pay the firm's debts.

However, none of the above persons are connected if they themselves are also directors of the company. [Sec 346(2)].

Body corporate with which a director is associated

34.19 A director is 'associated' with a body corporate if, and only if, the director, together with the persons connected with him satisfy either of the following two conditions:

- They are *interested* (according to the rules set out in Part I of Schedule 13) in at least 20 per cent of its equity share capital.

- They are entitled to *exercise or control the exercise* of more than 20 per cent of the voting power at any general meeting.

[Sec 346(4)].

For simplicity, a body corporate (that is, an entity incorporated in Great Britain or elsewhere, but excluding a Scottish firm) is referred to below as a company. It should be remembered, however, that a person connected with a director can be a foreign-registered company.

34.20 For the purposes of establishing whether a director is 'associated' with a company, a director's *interest* in at least 20 per cent of the equity share capital, or his ability to *exercise or control the exercise* of 20 per cent of the voting power, may be either *direct* (that is, he or his connected parties own the shares or control the votes) or *indirect* (that is, a company that he or his connected parties 'control' owns the shares or controls the votes). These rules are set out below.

Control of shares or votes

34.21 In determining whether the director and those connected with him can *control the exercise* of more than 20 per cent of the voting power of a company in general meeting, any votes held *indirectly* by a director through another company are to be included in the calculation, but only if the director 'controls' that second company. [Sec 346(8)]. A director of a company is deemed to 'control' that second company if, but only if, *both* the following two conditions in section 346(5) are satisfied:

- He or any person connected with him is *interested* in any part of the equity share capital of that second company, or is entitled to *exercise or control the exercise* of any part of the voting power at any general meeting of that company.
- That director, the persons connected with him and the other directors of that company, together, are *interested* in more than 50 per cent of the second company's share capital or are entitled to *exercise or control the exercise* of more 50 per cent of that voting power.

[Sec 346(5)].

Sub-sections 346(4) and (5) are illustrated in example 4 in paragraph 34.24 below.

Interests in shares

34.22 Under the above provisions, a director's *interests* in shares must be aggregated with those of his connected persons. The Act lays down rules in Schedule 13 for determining whether a person is interested in shares. These provide, *inter alia*, that a person, is to be treated as interested in shares if a company is interested in them and either of the following two conditions are met:

- The person is entitled to exercise or control the exercise of more than 50 per cent of that company's voting power at general meetings.
- That company or its directors are accustomed to act in accordance with his directions or instructions.

[13 Sch 4].

See also examples 2 and 3 in paragraph 34.24 below.

Limits on aggregation

34.23 For the purpose *only* of determining whether a company is associated with a director, another company with which the director is associated is not regarded as a connected person (see para 34.18 above), except where that company is:

- A partner of the director or of a person who is connected with the director under (a), (b) or (c) in paragraph 34.18 above [Sec 346(6)(a)]; or

- A trustee of a trust the beneficiaries of which include, or may include the persons mentioned in (c) of paragraph 34.18. [Sec 346(6)(b)]

Further, a trustee of a trust the beneficiaries of which include (or may include) a company with which a director is associated is not to be treated as connected with a director by reason only of that fact [Sec 346(6)(b)]. Section 346(6) is referred to in example 1 below.

34.24 The following examples illustrate the operation of the rules mentioned in the above paragraphs to establish whether a director is associated with a company -firstly, an 'association' through an interest in shares and, secondly, an 'association' through control of voting power:

Association through an interest in shares

Example 1

Mr. Jones owns 18% of company A's equity share capital, and he also owns 25% of company B's equity share capital. Company B owns 19% of company A's equity share capital.

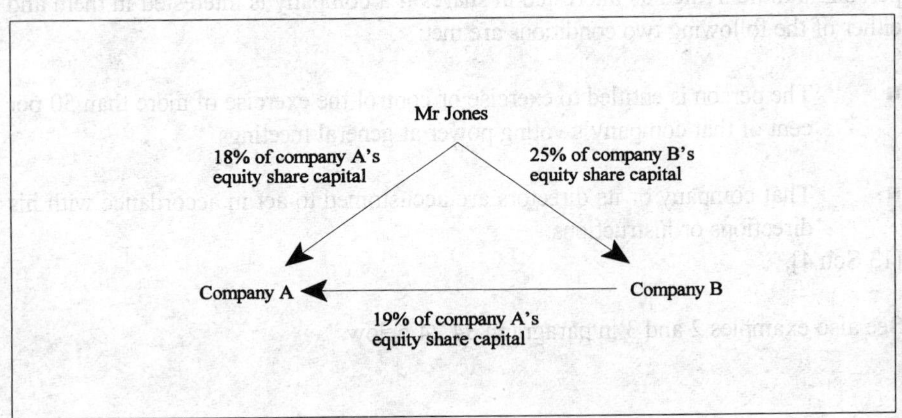

Mr. Jones is associated with company B, because he has an *interest* in more than 20% of the equity share capital of that company. [Sec 346(4)].

In the situation of company A, despite Mr Jones having an effective holding of 22.75% (that is, 18% + 25% x 19% = 22.75%), company A is *not associated* with him. This is because in deciding whether company A is associated with Mr Jones, company B's interest in company A's shares should be ignored. The reason for this is that, although company B is associated with Mr. Jones, its interest in company A cannot be aggregated with Mr Jones' own interest for the purposes of section 346(4). Company B is *not connected with* him for these purposes, because company B is not a partner or trustee of Mr. Jones. [Sec 346(6)].

Example 2

The facts are the same as in example 1 except that Mr Jones owns 5% of company A and he also owns 51% of company B.

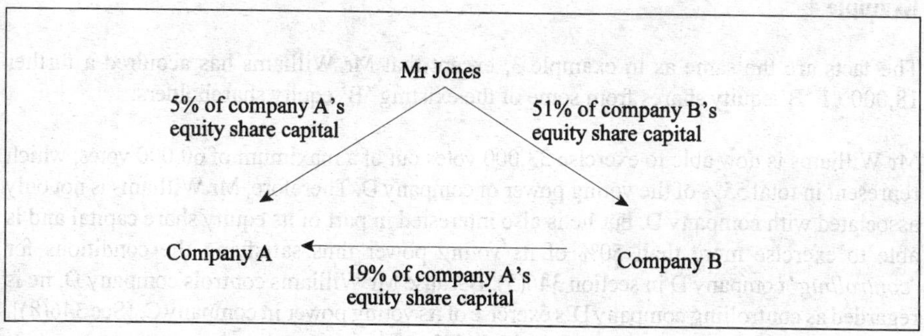

In this situation, although Mr Jones has an effective holding of 14.69% (that is, 5% + 51% x 19% = 14.69%), company A *is associated* with him. This is because, although company B's interest in company A's shares should be ignored by virtue of section 346(6), nevertheless, Mr. Jones is taken to be *interested* in the shares of company A held by company B, because he is entitled to exercise, or control the exercise of, more than 50% of the voting power of company B. [13 Sch 4]. Consequently, company A is *connected with* Mr. Jones via the operation of section 346(4)(a), because he has an interest in 24% (all of the 19% and not a proportion of it, together with a direct holding of 5%) that is greater than 20% of company A's equity share capital.

Association through control of voting power

Example 3

Mr. Williams owns 2% of company C's equity share capital. He also owns 100% of company D's £1 'A' equity shares, but none of the £1 'B' equity shares. The issued share capital of company D consists of 5,000 £1 'A' equity shares and 45,000 £1 'B' equity. Each 'A' share carries 3 votes and each 'B' share carries 1 vote. Company D owns 25% of company C's equity share capital (which represents 25% of company C's votes).

Although Mr. Williams holds only 10% of the equity share capital of company D, he is able to exercise 15,000 votes out of a maximum of 60,000 votes, which represent in total 25%

of the voting power. Therefore, Mr Williams is associated with company D, because he is able to control more than 20% of the voting power of that company. [Sec 346(4)(b)].

In determining whether company C is associated with Mr Williams, the interest of company D in the shares of company C should be disregarded. [Sec 346(6)(a)]. However, unlike in the second example above, Mr. Williams is also not taken to have an interest in the shares in company C held by company D for the purposes of the operation of paragraph 4 of Schedule 13, because he is only *entitled to exercise, or control the exercise of, 25% of the voting power* of company D. Because Mr Williams neither controls nor is presumed to control company D, company C is *not associated* with Mr. Williams by the operation of section 346(4).

Example 4

The facts are the same as in example 3, except that Mr Williams has acquired a further 18,000 £1 'B' equity shares from some of the existing 'B' equity shareholders.

Mr Williams is now able to exercise 33,000 votes out of a maximum of 60,000 votes, which represent in total 55% of the voting power of company D. Therefore, Mr Williams is not only associated with company D, but he is also interested in part of its equity share capital and is able to exercise more than 50% of its voting power thus satisfying the conditions for *'controlling'* company D in section 346(5). Because Mr Williams controls company D, he is regarded as controlling company D's exercise of its voting power in company C. [Sec 346(8)]. Because company D's *voting power exceeds 20%* of the potential voting power at company C's general meeting, company C is regarded as being *associated* with Mr Williams by the operation of section 346(4)(b).

Relevant company

34.25 A 'relevant company', for the purpose of the provisions of the Act that relate to directors' transactions, is either of the following types of company:

- A public company.
- A company that belongs to a group in which either the parent company or any subsidiary is a public company. [Sec 331(6)].

A non-relevant company is effectively a residual class, which includes all companies other than relevant companies.

Company

34.26 A 'company' is a company formed and registered under the Companies Act 1985 or any of the former Companies Acts. [Sec 735 (1)].

Holding company and subsidiary

34.27 These terms are defined in section 736. A company is a 'subsidiary' of another company, its 'holding company', if that other:

- Holds a majority of the voting rights in it, or
- Is a member of it and controls the board or a majority of voting rights in it.

It will also be a subsidiary if it is a subsidiary of a company which is itself a subsidiary of that other company. This is different from the definition of 'parent company' used for accounting purposes.

Body corporate

34.28 This term includes a company incorporated elsewhere than in Great Britain. It does not include a corporation sole or a Scottish firm (see para 34.18(e)).

Prohibited transactions

34.29 Section 330 of the Act prohibits a company from entering into certain types of transactions (listed below) for the benefit of its directors (see para 34.17) or persons connected with those directors, unless they fall within the exemptions provided in sections 332 to 338. These transactions are:

- Loans.
- Quasi-loans.
- Credit transactions.
- Guarantees or securities in connection with any of the above transactions made by another person.
- Assignments or assumptions of rights, obligations or liabilities under the above types of transactions.
- Indirect arrangements for the above.

The extent of the prohibitions affecting these transactions varies according to whether or not the company concerned is a relevant company. The transactions prohibited by section 330 and the exemptions to them for relevant and non-relevant companies, and money-lending and banking companies are considered in detail in this chapter.

Loans

Definition

34.30 Although the expression 'loan' is not defined in the Act, it was interpreted in a case brought under the Companies Act 1948. In that case it was held that the dictionary definition should be applied. The dictionary definition of a loan is *"a sum of money lent for a time to be returned in money or money's worth"*. [*Champagne Perrier-Jouet S.A. v H.H. Finch Ltd.* [1982] 1 WLR 1359]. It is, therefore, apparent that a loan arises wherever monies are advanced on the understanding that they will be repaid.

Value of loans

34.31 The value of a loan is the principal amount of the loan. [Sec 340(2)]. For these purposes, the interest due on the loans may be ignored. If the value cannot be ascertained as a specific sum, it is deemed to exceed £100,000 [Sec 340(7)]. The value is relevant for ascertaining the 'relevant amounts' to be aggregated for the purpose of establishing whether a proposed transaction is within the exemption for small loans. [Sec 339].

General prohibition

34.32 The general prohibition for making loans to directors and persons connected with them in section 330(2) is as follows:

- Relevant companies.

  A relevant company must not make a loan to either any of its own directors or its holding company's directors or a person connected with such directors. [Sec 330(2)(a), 330(3)(b)].

  Equally, a relevant company must not enter into any guarantee or indemnity, or provide any security, in connection with the loan a third party makes to either a director of the company or a director of its holding company or a person connected with such directors.
  [Sec 330(2)(b), 330(3)(c)].

- Non-relevant companies.

  A non-relevant company must not (a) make a loan or (b) enter into a guarantee or provide any security in connection with a loan made by a third party, to or for either a director of the company or a director of its holding company. [Sec 330(2)(a)(b)]. However, a non-relevant company is not prohibited by these provisions from making a loan to a person who is connected with a director.

Exemptions

Small loans

34.33 There is a general exemption for small loans. A company (whether relevant or non-relevant) is not prohibited from making a loan to a director of either the company or its holding company, provided that the aggregate of the 'relevant amounts' immediately after the loan is made to him does not exceed £5,000. [Sec 334].

34.34 The relevant amounts to be aggregated are:

(a) The value of the *proposed transaction.*

(b) The amount outstanding under *any existing transaction* made under the small loans exception for a person mentioned in paragraph 34.35 by any of the following:

- The *company* or a *subsidiary* (but see the limitation referred to in para 34.36).
- Where the proposed transaction or arrangement is to be made for a director of the company's holding company or a person connected with him, by that holding company or any of its subsidiaries (but see the limitation referred to in para 34.36). [Sec 339(2)(b)].

The amount outstanding is the value less any amount by which the value has been reduced. [Sec 339(2)(c) and (6)].

(c) The value of *any existing arrangement* within section 330(6) or (7) (described in paras 34.54 to 34.61 - for instance, an assignment to a company of rights or obligations) entered into under the small loans exception for the persons mentioned in paragraph 34.35 by any of the companies mentioned in the bullet points in (b) above.

[Sec 339(2)].

34.35 The amounts outstanding under *any existing transaction* referred to in sub-paragraph (b) above and the value of *any existing arrangement* referred to in sub-paragraph (c) above that have to be taken into account are those made for the following persons:

- The director for whom the proposed transaction or arrangement is to be made or any person connected with that director.

- Where the proposed transaction or arrangement is for a person connected with the director, that director or any person connected with him.

[Sec 339(3)].

Example

A subsidiary wishes to loan £3,000 to the director of its parent company, which has already lent him £2,500. It is unsure whether this proposed loan is legal.

Section 339(2) requires that amounts lent by the parent company or any subsidiary should be added to any proposed additional loan to the director of the parent company in order to determine whether the new loan falls within any available exemption. In this situation, the small loans exemption is £5,000, which is less than the total of the two loans combined (£3,000 plus £2,500). Assuming that the amount outstanding on the parent company's loan is still £2,500, the subsidiary should restrict its proposed loan by £500 to fall within the small loans exemption.

34.36 There is the following limitation for the purposes of calculating the relevant amounts. Transactions entered into by a company which at the time of entering into the transactions was a subsidiary or fellow-subsidiary, but which at the time when the calculation under section 334 has to be done, is no longer a subsidiary or fellow subsidiary, need not be taken account into such calculation. [Sec 339(5)].

34.37 The small loans exemption in section 334 *does not apply* to loans that *relevant* companies make to persons who are connected with a director. They remain caught by the prohibition. In the same way, the exemption also does not apply to guarantees, indemnities or securities that relevant companies provide for directors or their connected persons. [Sec 334].

34.38 A foreign subsidiary (that is, one incorporated outside Great Britain) of a company formed and registered under the Companies Act 1985 is not prohibited by section 330 from making a loan to a director of its British parent, provided that the parent or any British subsidiary does not compensate the foreign subsidiary for making the loan or guarantee it. This is because a foreign subsidiary does not fall within the definition of 'company' (see para 34.26). Such a foreign subsidiary may, however, be subject to restrictions under the laws of its home state.

Groups

34.39 The second exemption relates to inter-company loans in the same group (meaning a holding company and its subsidiaries). A relevant company is not prohibited from making a loan or quasi-loan to another company within the same group by reason only that a director of one of the group companies is associated with another group company. This also applies where the relevant company enters into a guarantee, or provides any security in connection with a loan or quasi-loan made by any person to another group company. [Sec 333].

Other loans not prohibited by section 330

34.40 A holding company, whether relevant or non-relevant, is not prohibited by section 330 from making loans to a director of its subsidiary. Similarly, a subsidiary may be able to lend to a director of a fellow subsidiary. However, in these instances the subsidiary or the fellow subsidiary must not be a party to any indirect arrangement under which they provide any benefit or compensation to the lending company. [Sec 330(7)]. Indirect arrangements are described in paragraph 34.58. The transaction might also be a related party transaction under the Listing Rules (see para 34.113 below).

34.41 In addition, although the Act prohibits loans to directors, a loan made before a person becomes a director does not automatically become prohibited. However, it would become disclosable as a loan to a director when he becomes a director.

Quasi-loans

Definition

34.42 A quasi-loan is a transaction where one party (the creditor) either:

- agrees to pay, or pays, a sum *for another* (the borrower); or
- agrees to reimburse, or reimburses, expenditure another party incurs for another (the borrower); and

either of the following two conditions apply:

- The transaction's terms are such that the borrower (or a person on his behalf) will reimburse the creditor.

- The circumstances surrounding the transaction give rise to a liability on the borrower to reimburse the creditor.

[Sec 331(3)].

The liabilities of a borrower under a quasi-loan include the liabilities of any person who has agreed to reimburse the creditor on the borrower's behalf. [Sec 331(4)].

The following are common examples of a quasi-loan:

Example 1

A director uses a company credit card to buy goods and he does so on the understanding that the company will settle the liability and he will reimburse the company at a later date.

Example 2

Companies in a group pay for goods and services for the personal use of a director of the parent company, on the basis that he will reimburse those companies at a later date.

Value of quasi-loans

34.43 The value of a quasi-loan is the amount, or maximum amount, that the person to whom it is made is liable to reimburse the creditor. [Sec 340(3)]. If the value is not ascertainable as a specific sum it is deemed to exceed £100,000. [Sec 340(7)]. The value is relevant in connection with the disclosure of quasi-loans to be made in the company's financial statements (see paras 34.79 and 34.139).

General prohibition - relevant companies

34.44 The general prohibition in section 330(3) on making quasi-loans to directors and persons connected with them applies only to relevant companies. A relevant company must not:

- Make a quasi-loan to either a director of the company or its parent company, or to any person connected with such a director. [Sec 330(3)(a)(b)].

- Must not enter into a guarantee or provide security for a quasi-loan a third party makes to such a director or a person connected with him [Sec 330(3)(c)].

34.45 The above prohibitions do not apply to a non-relevant company. Non-relevant companies are not prohibited by section 330 from making quasi-loans to the company's directors or its parent company's directors, or to the connected persons of such directors. Similarly they are not prohibited by section 330 from entering into a guarantee or providing security in connection with a quasi-loan to such a person.

Exemptions

Small, short-term quasi-loans

34.46 A relevant company (the creditor) is not prohibited from making a quasi-loan to a director provided the following two conditions are satisfied:

- The terms of the quasi-loan require its repayment within two months.

- The aggregate of the amount of the proposed quasi-loan and the amounts outstanding under existing relevant quasi-loans do not exceed £5,000.

[Sec 332(1)].

A quasi-loan is relevant for these purposes if it was made to the director under this exemption by the creditor or by its subsidiary, or, if the director is a director of the creditor's holding company, by any other subsidiary of the holding company. [Sec 332(2)]. This exemption does not extend to quasi-loans to persons connected with a director. They remain prohibited for relevant companies.

Groups

34.47 Where a relevant company is a member of a group, it is not prohibited either from making a quasi-loan to another member of that group, or from entering into a guarantee or providing security for any such quasi-loan, by reason only that a director of one of the group companies is associated with another group company. [Sec 333].

Credit transactions

Definition

34.48 A credit transaction is any transaction where a one party (the creditor):

- Supplies any goods or sells any land under either a hire purchase agreement or a conditional sale agreement.

- Leases or hires any land or any goods in return for periodic payments.

- Otherwise disposes of land, or supplies goods or services, on the understanding that payment (whatever form it takes) is to be deferred.

[Sec 331(7)].

'Services' means anything other than goods or land. [Sec 331(8)].

Value of credit transactions

34.49 The value of a credit transaction is the price that it would be reasonable to expect could be obtained for the goods, land or services to which the transaction relates if they had been supplied in the ordinary course of the company's business and on the same terms (apart from price). [Sec 340(6)]. If the value of the transaction cannot be ascertained, it is deemed to exceed £100,000. [Sec 340(7)]. The value is relevant in connection with the exemption for business transactions (see para 34.53), for ascertaining the 'relevant amounts' in connection with the exemption for minor transactions (see para 34.52), and in connection with the information relating to credit agreements to be disclosed in the company's financial statements (see para 34.79).

General prohibition - relevant companies

34.50 The general prohibition in section 330(4) on entering into credit transactions for directors applies only to relevant companies. A relevant company is prohibited from entering into:

- A credit transaction, as creditor, for a director of the company or its holding company, or a person connected with such a director. [Sec 330(4)(a)].

- Any guarantee or providing any security in connection with a credit transaction made by a third party for a such director or a person connected with him. [Sec 330(4)(b)].

34.51 Non-relevant companies are not affected by the above rules relating to credit transactions.

Exemptions

Minor transactions

34.52 Section 330(4) does not prevent a relevant company entering into a transaction if the aggregate of the value of the proposed transaction and the relevant amounts under other credit transactions, guarantees and securities and arrangements within sections 330(6) and 330(7) relating to such transactions and made for any one director or his connected persons, does not exceed £10,000. [Sec 335(1)]. (Arrangements that fall within sections 330(6) and (7) are discussed in paras 34.54 and 34.58.)

The 'relevant amounts' to be aggregated are set out in paragraph 34.34. In the context of this exception, the reference in that paragraph to the small loans exception should be read as a reference to the exception for minor transactions.

Business transactions

34.53 Section 330(4) does not prevent a relevant company entering into a transaction for a person if:

- The transaction in question was entered into in the ordinary course of its business; and

- The value and the terms on which the company enters into the transaction are no more favourable, for the person for whom it is made, than those the company would have normally offered to a person who was of similar financial standing, but was unconnected with the company.

[Sec 335(2)].

The value of a credit transaction is considered in paragraph 34.49 above.

Assignment or assumption of rights, obligations or liabilities

General prohibition

34.54 Both *relevant companies* and *non-relevant companies* are prohibited by section 330(6) from arranging for the assignment to them, or the assumption by them, of any rights, obligations or liabilities under transactions which, had they, themselves, *entered into* them, would have been unlawful under sections 330(2), (3) or (4). The transactions mentioned in these sub-sections are loans, quasi-loans and credit transactions (and guarantees, indemnities and the provision of security in respect of such loans, quasi-loans or credit transactions).

34.55 For the purposes of section 330 and the other provisions relating to loans, quasi-loans and credit transactions in sections 331 to 347, the transaction will be treated as having been *entered into* on the date of the arrangement for the assignment or assumption of rights, obligations or liabilities mentioned above. [Sec 330(6)].

34.56 An illustration of an 'assignment' is given in example 1 below, and an illustration of an 'assumption of liabilities' in example 2 below:

Example 1

A third party makes a loan to a director of a company and, subsequently, the director's company purchases the third party's rights to the loan. In this situation, the company has (illegally) paid out resources to acquire an asset and the company purports to become a creditor of the director just as if it had advanced the loan itself.

Example 2

A third party guarantees a loan that a fourth party makes to a director of a company and, subsequently, the director's company enters into an arrangement with the third and the fourth parties, whereby the third party is released from his guarantee, and the company purports to assume the liability under the guarantee. Again, in this situation, the company's resources are (illegally) tied up by a contingent liability when the company purports to assume the guarantee on behalf of the director.

Value of assignment or assumption

34.57 The value of this type of arrangement is the value of the transaction to which the arrangement relates less any amount by which the liabilities of the person for whom the transaction or arrangement was made have been reduced. [Sec 340(5)]. If the value of the transaction cannot be ascertained as a specific sum, it is deemed to exceed £100,000. [Sec 340(7)]. The value is relevant in connection with the information regarding the arrangement to be disclosed in the company's financial statements and in the calculation of 'relevant amounts' (see para 34.34).

Indirect arrangements

General prohibition

34.58 Indirect arrangements are prohibited by section 330(7). Thus, a company cannot take part in an arrangement whereby another person:

- enters into a transaction that would have contravened section 330 (2),(3),(4) and (6) had the company itself entered into it; and

- that other person has obtained, or is to obtain, under the arrangement a benefit of any kind from the company, its holding company, its subsidiary or its fellow subsidiary. [Sec 330(7)].

34.59 This provision expressly prevents a company's resources from being used to procure another person to provide one of the various forms of prohibited credit without the company itself either entering into, or subsequently becoming a party to, the transaction.

34.60 As a consequence, the provision is very widely drafted and is intended to cover the wide variety of forms that these types of arrangement can take. For example, it covers the situation where a company agrees to make a loan to another company's director in return for that other company making a loan to one of the first company's directors. It also covers the situation where a director persuades a bank to make a loan on favourable terms to him in return for his company placing business with the bank.

Value of indirect arrangements

34.61 The value of an indirect arrangement is ascertained in the same way as the value of an assignment or an assumption of rights considered in paragraph 34.57 above. The value is relevant for the same purposes.

General exemptions for loans and similar transactions

34.62 In addition to the exemptions that apply only to particular types of transactions (for example, the *de minimis* exemption for loans totalling not more than £5,000), the Act includes more general exemptions in respect of:

- Transactions between a subsidiary and its parent company.
- Directors' business expenditure.

Transactions between a subsidiary and its parent company

34.63 The following transactions between a subsidiary and its parent company are not affected by the restrictions that section 330 of the Act imposes on loans, quasi-loans and credit transactions:

- A loan or a quasi-loan a company makes to its holding company, or a company's guarantee or provision of security to a third person who has made a loan or quasi-loan to the company's holding company.
- A credit transaction a company enters into as creditor for its holding company, or a guarantee or security that a company provides in connection with a credit transaction a third party makes for the company's holding company.

[Sec 336].

This exemption would apply, for instance, where the holding company is a director of the subsidiary. Transactions which fall within the above provisions are, therefore, not prohibited by section 330.

Directors' business expenditure

34.64 Section 330 does not prohibit a company providing a director with funds to meet expenditure incurred or to be incurred by him for the purposes of the company, or to enable him to perform his duties properly as an officer of the company. [Sec 337(1)]. Furthermore, the company is not prohibited from doing anything to enable a director to avoid incurring expenditure of the kind described in section 337(1). [Sec 337(2)]. The company may provide these funds by way of a loan, or a quasi-loan or a credit transaction, or by any other similar arrangement. This exemption applies, subject to the overall limit for relevant companies mentioned below, if one of the following two conditions is satisfied:

- The transaction has been approved in advance by the company in general meeting. [Sec 337(3)(a)]. At that general meeting, the purpose of the expenditure, the amount of funds to be provided, and the extent of the company's liability under the transaction and any connected transaction must all be made known. [Sec 337(4)]. Where the company is a charity this approval is ineffective without the prior written consent of the Charity Commissioners. [Charities Act 1993 Sec 66].

- It is a condition of the transaction that, if the company does not subsequently approve the transaction at, or before, the next annual general meeting, the director will discharge, within six months, any liability that arises under the transaction. [Sec 337(3)(b)].

34.65 A relevant company cannot enter into such a transaction if the aggregate of the relevant amounts exceeds £20,000. [Sec 337(3)]. However, with non-relevant companies there is no upper limit specified by the section on transactions of this type. The relevant amounts to be aggregated are those referred to in paragraph 34.34. In the context of this exception, the reference in that paragraph to the small loans exception should be read as a reference to the exception for business expenditure.

34.66 The most common form of transaction of this nature relates to travelling expenses between different places of business. Another form of transaction of this nature is a bridging loan a company gives to a director, who changes location within the company and so is required to move house.

34.67 Section 337 of the Act only applies to transactions which amount to 'loans'. It does not restrict advances of an amount appropriate to the specific business expenditure it is anticipated the director will incur. An Audit Brief on Directors' Loans published in 1985 by the Auditing Practices Committee (the predecessor to the APB) may be of help in establishing the type of transaction involving the provision of expenses to directors which might not constitute a loan.

> *"The reason is that ordinary expense advances are not intended to be repaid by the recipient; the intention is that the recipient should use the amount advanced in his capacity as agent for the company for the benefit of the company. ... However, it should be borne in mind that in circumstances where the amount is clearly excessive or remains unspent for an unduly long time, then the recipient is likely to have derived some personal benefit. In fact, the transaction takes on the nature of a loan and if the recipient is a director it is disclosable and if the sum advanced is large, it may be illegal."*

Consequently, transactions which do not amount to loans or (in the case of relevant companies) quasi-loans are not required to be approved in general meeting.

Criminal sanctions and civil remedies

34.68 The sanctions and remedies which the Act imposes when a company enters into an illegal loan or other transaction described in section 330 with a director are set out in detail in paragraph 34.175.

Disclosure requirements

Introduction

34.69 The Act requires considerable detail to be disclosed regarding loans, quasi-loans and credit transactions with directors. It requires a director to declare his interest in any proposed contract with the company to the board of directors. [Sec 317]. He is likely also to have a duty to disclose his interest under the company's articles of association. These disclosure requirements are discussed from paragraph 34.163 onwards. In addition, the Act requires particulars of the transactions to be disclosed in the notes to a company's financial statements *whether they are lawful or not*. The circumstances in which disclosure is required in the financial statements and the particulars regarding disclosure are set out in Part II of Schedule 6 to the Act. The disclosure requirements relating to transactions with officers are set out in Part III of Schedule 6. [Sec 232(1)(2)]. Banking companies may, however, take advantage of a relaxation in the disclosure requirements by virtue of paragraph 2 of Part IV of Schedule 9 (as amended by the Companies Act 1985 (Bank Accounts) Regulations 1994 (SI 1994/233).

34.70 Details of the transactions that are required to be disclosed must be given in the notes to the consolidated financial statements of a holding company (or if it is not required to prepare consolidated financial statements, its individual financial statements), or in the financial statements of any company other than a holding company. Such transactions are required to be disclosed for shadow directors as well as for other directors. [6 Sch 27(2)].

Disclosure in financial statements

34.71 Any transaction or arrangement of a type described in section 330 (that is, loans, quasi-loans, credit transactions, related guarantees, assignments and indirect arrangements) and agreements to enter into such transactions must, unless they are specifically exempted (see para 34.81) be disclosed in the notes to the financial statements. [6 Sch 15(a)(b), 16(a)(b)].

34.72 The transactions, arrangements and agreements which are required to be disclosed in their financial statements by all reporting companies (relevant and non-relevant) are those entered into by the reporting company and (if it is a holding company) by its subsidiaries:

- For a person who was a director at any time during the financial year of either the company or its holding company.

- For a person who was connected with such a director. [6 Sch 15(a)(b), 16(a)(b)].

34.73 The disclosure provisions apply irrespective of whether or not:

- The transaction is either prohibited by section 330 of the Act, or falls within one of the exemptions given in sections 332 to 338.

- The person for whom the transaction was made was a director, or was a person connected with a director, at the time the transaction was made. What is relevant is that the person should have been a director at some time during the financial year.

- The company that entered into the transaction was a subsidiary of the company of which the person was a director at the time the transaction was made.

[6 Sch 19].

Information to be disclosed for all transactions

34.74 The following information must be given in the notes to the financial statements for each disclosable transaction, arrangement or agreement:

- Particulars of its principal terms. [6 Sch 22(1)]. The 'principal terms' will include those terms that relate to the provision of either the cash or the non-cash asset and also the arrangements for repaying the value of that asset (including any interest component, together with any related security or guarantees).

- A statement that the transaction either was made during the financial year or existed during that period. [6 Sch 22(2)(a)].

- The name of the director concerned in the transaction and where applicable, the name of the connected person. [6 Sch 22(2)(b)].

- The additional disclosures, as appropriate, set out below.

Additional disclosure for loans

34.75 For any loan, any agreement for a loan, or any arrangement relating to a loan under section 330(6) or (7), the following information has to be disclosed:

- The amount of the liability (in respect of both principal and interest), both at the beginning and the end of the financial year.
- The maximum amount of the liability during that period.
- The amount of any interest due but unpaid.
- The amount of any provision that the company has made against the failure or the anticipated failure of the borrower to repay the whole, or any part, of the principal or interest.

[6 Sch 22(2)(d)].

[The next paragraph is 34.77.]

Additional disclosure for guarantees or securities

34.77 For any guarantee or security, or any arrangement under section 330(6) relating to any guarantee or security, the following information has to be disclosed:

- The amount of the liability of the company or its subsidiary, both at the beginning and the end of the financial year.
- The maximum amount for which the company or its subsidiary may become liable.

- Any amount the company or its subsidiary has paid, and any liability it has incurred, either in fulfilling the guarantee or in discharging the security. [6 Sch 22(2)(e)].

The 'value' of such a guarantee or security is the amount guaranteed or secured [Sec 340(4)].

34.78 The above disclosure requirements are illustrated in Table 34.2.

Table 34.2 - British Aerospace Public Limited Company - Annual Report - 31 December 1994

Notes to the accounts (extract)

Transactions

Under a housing loan scheme operated by the Company, Mr M J Turner has a bank loan, bearing interest at 5% per annum, incurred in buying his house and entered into prior to him becoming a Director of the Company, as a result of relocating at the Company's request. At 31st December, 1994 the amount of principal outstanding under this loan was £23,883 (1993 £25,208) and the accrued interest outstanding was £43 (1993 £66). Mr Turner's loan is secured on his house and certain insurance policies and is repayable not later than September 2010. For the duration of the loan the Company maintains with the bank a deposit equal to the amount outstanding under the loan, such deposit bears interest at 3.75% per annum and is available as additional security for the loan.

Additional disclosure for quasi-loans and credit transactions

34.79 For quasi-loans, credit transactions and related arrangements for assignment and indirect arrangements under section 330(6) and (7) or agreements for such transactions, disclosure has to be made of the 'value' of the transaction or arrangement, or the 'value' of the transaction or arrangement to which the agreement relates. [6 Sch 22(f)]. The effect of this provision is to require, for example, the disclosure of:

- The amount, or the maximum amount, to be reimbursed in respect of a quasi-loan. [Sec 340(3)].

- The value, that is, the arm's length price of any goods and services purchased, of a credit transaction. [Sec 340(6)].

- For an arrangement for assignment or an indirect arrangement, the value of the transaction to which that arrangement relates, less any amount by which the liabilities under the arrangement have been reduced. [Sec 340(5)].

If the value is not capable of being ascertained as a specific sum, it is deemed to exceed £100,000. The meaning of 'value' is discussed in greater detail in connection with the specific type of transaction or arrangement concerned.

Exemptions for certain intra-group loans

34.80 Some of the additional information outlined in the above paragraphs need not be disclosed for loans and quasi-loans where:

- A company ('lender') makes or agrees to make them to or for a body corporate ('borrower') of which the lender is a wholly-owned subsidiary, or to or for a fellow wholly-owned subsidiary or the lender's wholly-owned subsidiary; and
- The information would not have been disclosable in the lender's financial statements if the borrower had not been *associated with* a director of the lender. For the meaning of a company being associated with a director (see para 34.18(b)).

[6 Sch 23].

But where this type of transaction does exist, the financial statements still have to give particulars of the transaction's principal terms, a statement that the transaction was made or existed during the year, and the name of the body corporate concerned (see para 34.74 above). This exception means that, where certain intra-group loans are made by the company, only those details are required to be disclosed.

Transactions excluded from disclosure

34.81 The disclosure requirements in Schedule 6 Part II set out above in respect of loans, quasi-loans and credit transactions and related guarantees and security and indirect arrangements and assignments, do not apply to the transactions, arrangements and agreements ('transactions') referred to below.

- A transaction between two companies, where a director of one of the companies (or of its subsidiary or its holding company) is interested *only* by virtue of the fact that he is also a director of that other company [6 Sch 18(a)]. This exemption means that, among other things, details of many general *intra-group trading* transactions between companies are not required to be disclosed.

- A transaction that was not entered into during the period to which the financial statements relate and that did not exist at any time during that period. [6 Sch 18(c)].

- A transaction of the kind mentioned below made by a company or its subsidiary for a person who, at any time during the financial year, was a director of the company or its holding company, or was connected with any such director, provided that the aggregate of the amounts outstanding (see below) under each such transaction did not exceed £5,000 at any time during the period. These transactions are:

  - Credit transactions.

  - Guarantees or securities relating to credit transactions.

  - Assignments, or assumptions or indirect arrangements of the type referred to in sections 330(6) and (7) of the Act relating to credit transactions.

  - Agreements to enter into credit transactions.

  The 'aggregate amount outstanding' mentioned above means the following in relation to the limit of £5,000 for a particular director. The aggregate of the values of all such transactions made for him or for any person connected with him, less any amount by which the liability of the person for whom the transaction was made has been reduced. [6 Sch 24(1)]. The value of a transaction is discussed above in connection with that kind of transaction.

[6 Sch 24(1)(2)].

34.82 Without this threshold limit, a company's financial statements would sometimes contain an excessive amount of information about directors' transactions. Petty credit transactions involving deferred payment by directors are very common and it is not the Act's intention to require disclosure of these. The Act intends that disclosure should prevent abuse where the transactions involve larger sums. It should be noted however, that this exclusion does not extend to loans or quasi-loans. Even small loans must be disclosed.

Penalties for failure to disclose transactions with directors

34.83 The penalties which apply when directors do not disclose the information required by Schedule 6 Part II are set out from paragraph 34.171 onwards.

Transactions in which directors have material interests

Introduction

34.84 Section 232 requires the information specified in Schedule 6 Part II regarding certain dealings in favour of directors to be disclosed in a company's financial statements. The paragraphs above have described the disclosure requirements relating to loans, quasi-loans and similar transactions specified in section 330 together with agreements for such transactions. The following paragraphs describe the disclosure requirements for other dealings in favour of directors. These are transactions and arrangements with the company (or a subsidiary of it) in which a director of the company or its holding company had, directly or indirectly, a *material interest*. A director of a company or its holding company is also treated as having a material interest where the transaction is between the company and a person connected with the director.

34.85 A holding company must disclose in its consolidated financial statements or, if it is not required to prepare consolidated financial statements, in its individual financial statements, such transactions or arrangements with it or with a subsidiary of it. A company which is not a holding company must disclose such transactions or arrangements in its financial statements.

34.86 Schedule 6 paragraph 15(c) and 16(c) requires disclosure where the director has directly or indirectly a *material* interest. For these purposes, the Act in paragraph 17(2) of Schedule 6 says that an interest in a transaction or arrangement is not 'material' if in the board's opinion it is not material; but this is without prejudice to the question whether or not such an interest is material in a situation where the board has not considered the matter. 'The board' means the directors of the company who prepare the financial statements, but it excludes the particular director who has the interest in the transaction.

34.87 Although paragraph 17(2) of Schedule 6 does not say so explicitly, it is, of course, implicit that the directors' opinion on the materiality of a director's interest in a transaction must have been formed reasonably and in good faith. Where the directors have not considered the question of materiality, the materiality will be a matter of fact. This does not mean that the director's interest in a transaction will be regarded as material. It simply means that, in the absence of an opinion from the directors, it cannot be presumed not to be material.

Interpretation of 'material interest'

34.88 In practice, the interpretation of the words 'material interest' has caused considerable debate. Although the test of materiality is not clear, two tests, the 'relevant' test and the 'substantial' test, are regarded as having some authority. The 'relevant' test considers a director's interest to be material if the transaction is likely to be of interest or relevance either to the shareholders or to the other users of the financial statements. The 'substantial' test considers a director's interest to be material if the director's interest in the transaction is substantial whether or not it is of significance to shareholders or creditors.

The 'substantial' test can be illustrated by the following example:

Example

Where a director buys a bar of chocolate in the company's shop, he is the other party to the contract, and accordingly his interest in the transaction (his purchase of the bar of chocolate from the company) is material.

34.89 The expression 'material' has not yet been interpreted in case law in the context of directors' transactions. However, of the two tests referred to above, Counsel has advised that the 'relevant' test is to be preferred. Counsel has said that the correct approach should be to find out whether the existence of the arrangement would be significant to a shareholder. It could be significant either because it is one of importance to the company or because it is one of importance to the individual director. Where the transaction is of importance either to the company or to the individual director, then a material interest does exist, and it should be disclosed. On the other hand, it should be borne in mind that other Counsel have advised that the substantial test is preferred. However, there is also a view that both tests may serve a complementary function. Some of the extreme implications of the 'substantiality' test have been removed by the exemptions added in 1984 - see bullet points 6 and 7 in paragraph 34.97.

34.90 Because of this confusion, the Law Society's Standing Committee on Company Law proposed an amendment to paragraph 17(2) of Schedule 6 to the Act (see para 34.86) to try to clarify the meaning of 'material interest'. It suggested that the definition should be altered to include the following:

> *"An interest is material if, and only if, knowledge thereof might reasonably be expected to influence the judgement:*
>
> *(a) of a person in determining whether he will enter into any transaction or arrangement with the relevant company and, if so, upon what terms or whether he will deal in securities of the company; or*
>
> *(b) of a member of the company in determining whether he will exercise any of his rights in that capacity."*

No amendment on these lines has yet been adopted.

34.91 There is still considerable uncertainty about the meaning of this term. Therefore, if a director has an interest in a transaction that may or may not be material, legal advice should be taken.

34.92 Certain other types of transaction involving a director (or the persons connected with him) and the company may not be regarded as material, and if so, they do not have to be disclosed in the financial statements. These are considered in paragraph 34.98 below.

Disclosure requirements

Introduction

34.93 The Act requires considerable detail to be disclosed regarding transactions in which a director has, directly or indirectly, a material interest. It requires a director to declare his interest in a proposed transaction to the board of directors. [Sec 317; Table A regulation 85]. This is discussed in connection with matters to be notified to the board. The Act requires disclosure of such interests in the notes to the company's financial statements. [6 Sch 15(c), 16(c)]. In addition, a listed company may be required to comply with the disclosure requirements of the Stock Exchange Listing Rules (see para 34.113).

Disclosure in financial statements

34.94 The Act requires disclosure of any transaction or arrangement with the company or (if it is a holding company) its subsidiary in which a person who at any time during the financial year was a director of the company or its holding company had, either directly or indirectly, a material interest. [6 Sch 15(c), 16(c)]. This requirement also applies if the transaction or arrangement is with a person who is connected with a director: it is then treated as one in which the director is interested. [6 Sch 17(1)].

34.95 A company must disclose the necessary particulars in its individual financial statements, unless it is a holding company preparing consolidated financial statements, when it must disclose them in its consolidated financial statements. [Sec 232(1)(2); 6 Sch 15, 16]. Where a company with subsidiaries has not prepared consolidated financial statements (either because it is a wholly-owned subsidiary or because its subsidiaries are excluded from consolidation), the notes to its individual financial statements must give the equivalent information that would have been given if it had prepared consolidated financial statements. [6 Sch 15]. Such transactions are required to be disclosed for shadow directors as well as for other directors. [6 Sch 27(2)]. Where a company has entered into a transaction or arrangement of the type described in paragraph 34.94 above that is required to be disclosed in the financial statements, the financial statements must contain the following information:

- Particulars of the principal terms of the transaction or arrangement. [6 Sch 22(1)]. The 'principal terms' will include those terms that relate to the provision of either the cash or the non-cash asset and also the arrangements for repaying the value of that asset (including any interest component, together with any related security or guarantees).
- A statement that the transaction or arrangement either was made during the financial year or existed during that period. [6 Sch 22(2)(a)].
- The name of the director concerned in the transaction. Where a transaction is made for a director's connected person, the name of the connected person and the director concerned have to be given. [6 Sch 22(2)(b)].
- The name of the director who has the material interest in the transaction, and the nature of the interest. [6 Sch 22(2)(c)].
- The 'value' of the transaction or arrangement or, where applicable, the value of the transaction or arrangement to which the agreement relates. This is the arms' length price of the goods, land or services to which the transaction or arrangement relates. [Sec 340(6)].

34.96 The above disclosure requirements for transactions in which a director has a material interest are illustrated in Tables 34.3 and 34.4.

Table 34.3 - The Royal Bank of Scotland Group plc - Report and Accounts - 30 September 1994

Notes to the accounts (extract)

51 Transactions with directors, officers and others

Dr G.R. Mathewson, a director of the company and the Bank has a right to repurchase from the Bank his former dwellinghouse which the Bank purchased from him and his wife in May 1988 at a price of £125,000. The right will become exercisable (1) in the event that Dr Mathewson ceases to be an executive director of the company or its subsidiaries; or (2) 31st May 2008 in the event that he remains an executive director at that date; or (3) on such earlier date as the directors of the company may allow. Any repurchase is to be at the higher of the purchase price paid by the Bank or a price determined by independent professional valuation at the time of repurchase.

The dwellinghouse is at present let by the Bank on a commercial basis, with any rental payments being received wholly by the bank.

Table 34.4 - Abingworth plc - Annual Report - 30 June 1989

Directors' report (extract)

Board of directors (extract)

Certain Directors of the Company were the principal promoters of and are shareholders in Interven Capital S.A., Interven II S.A., Tetraven Fund S.A. and Biotechnology Venture Fund S.A. ("the Luxembourg companies") to each of which Abingworth Management Limited provides investment advice, under the terms of separate investment advisory contracts, for which it is remunerated on the basis of cost plus ten per cent thereof. Each such contract subsisted throughout the course of the year. Details of the Directors' approximate percentage interests in the equity capital of each of the Luxembourg companies at 30 June 1989 are shown below:

	Interven Capital S.A.	Interven II S.A.	Tetraven Fund S.A.	Biotechnology Venture Fund S.A.*
Hon A.T.S. Montagu	7.63	5.90	5.69	3.61
P.F. Dicks	7.50	5.30	5.17	3.33
S.M. Gray	2.56	2.05	0.63	0.36
Dr N.W. Horne	-	0.13	0.13	0.08
D.F.J. Leathers	-	-	-	5.00
D.J. Morrison	-	0.13	1.75	1.13
D.W. Quysner	0.54	3.65	4.10	2.38
Sir James Spooner	1.50	1.30	0.31	0.15

* Fully diluted for committed subscriptions outstanding

On 17 August 1989, the Company entered into a conditional contract for the sale of Abingworth Management Limited to a company owned by Messrs. Montagu, Bunting, Dicks, Leathers, Morrison and Qusyner. The sale was approved by shareholders at an Extraordinary General meeting held on 13 September 1989, at which time the Company also entered into a revised Investment Advisory Agreement with Abingworth Management Limited.

Save as disclosed, there was no contract of significance subsisting during the year ended 30 June 1989 in which a Director of the Company had no material interest.

34.97 In addition to the statutory disclosure requirements outlined above, the Stock Exchange Listing Rules require listed companies to give particulars in their statutory financial statements of any contract of significance in which a director was materially interested and which existed during the financial year. [LR 12.43(q)]. The Stock Exchange requirements are dealt with in paragraph 34.113.

Exemptions from disclosure under the Act

34.98 The disclosure requirements set out in paragraph 34.95 above do not apply to the following transactions and arrangements:

- A transaction between two companies, where a director of one of the companies (or of its subsidiary or its holding company) is interested only by virtue of the fact that he is also a director of that other company [6 Sch 18(a)]. This exemption means that, among other things, details of many general intra-group trading transactions between companies are not required to be disclosed.

- A contract of service between a company and one of its directors, or a director of its holding company, or between a director of the company and any of its subsidiaries. [6 Sch 18(b)]. The inspection of such contracts by the company's members is regulated by section 318 of the Act. A listed company must also disclose details of certain service contracts under the requirements of the Stock Exchange Listing Rules. [LR 12.43(u),16.12]. This requirement is considered in chapter 31. There is a distinction between a *contract of service,* where a director is employed by the company, and a *contract for services,* where a director is an independent contractor. There is *no exemption* from disclosure for the latter type of contract.

- A transaction that was not entered into during the period to which the financial statements relate and that did not exist at any time during that period. [6 Sch 18(c)].

- There is a *de minimis* exception for any transactions with a company or any of its subsidiaries in which a director of the company or its holding company had, directly or indirectly, a material interest if the aggregate value did not exceed £1,000 at any time during the relevant period. The aggregate value is the aggregate of the following:

  - The value of each such transaction which was made after the commencement of the financial year.

  - The value of each such transaction that was made before the commencement of the financial year, less the amount (if any) by which the liability of the person for whom the transaction was made has subsequently been reduced.

  Alternatively, if that value did exceed £1,000, no disclosure is required if the aggregate value did not exceed the lower of £5,000 and one per cent of the value of the company's net assets as at the end of the financial year [6 Sch 25]. For this purpose, 'net assets' are the aggregate of the company's assets less the aggregate of its liabilities (including provisions for liabilities and charges). This minimum figure is flexible in order that it should take account of the needs of different sizes of company. The Secretary of State has power to increase by statutory instrument the financial limits mentioned above.

- Transactions that, in the opinion of the board, are not material (see para 34.86 and 34.87 above).

- Transactions involving other members of the same group which are entered into by those group companies in the ordinary course of their business and at arm's length and which would otherwise be disclosable under Schedule 6, paragraphs 15(c) or 16(c) (that is, those transactions outlined in para 34.94 above). [6 Sch 20(a)(b)]. There is some confusion on the interpretation of paragraph 20 of Schedule 6 and it has been suggested that the exemption can be read as applying even where there is no group. If this interpretation is correct (it is in line with the interpretation of the paragraph as stated in the Explanatory Note published with the Companies (Accounts) Regulations 1984 (SI 1984/1860)), the exemption will apply whether or not the company entering into the transaction is a member of a group. This would mean that any transaction in which a director has a material interest is exempted from disclosure under paragraph 15(c) or 16(c) if the transaction is entered into by the reporting company or by a company in the same group at arms' length and in the ordinary course of its business.

- A transaction or arrangement that would otherwise be disclosable under paragraph 15(c) or 16(c) of Schedule 6 because the director had a material interest, but only on account of the fact that he was associated with the company. ('Associated' is defined in para 34.19). This exemption applies only if the company is a member of a group of companies and if one of the following situations exists:

  - The company is a wholly-owned subsidiary.

  - No company within the same group, other than the company itself or one of its subsidiaries, was a party to the transaction or arrangement.

  [6 Sch 21].

  These conditions mean that the exemption from disclosure is available only if minority interests in the company are not affected. The effect of this provision is that, provided the conditions are satisfied, a director who is associated with the company and who would, therefore, have an interest in every contract that the company is party to that may be disclosable, does not have to disclose that interest in the financial statements.

Penalties for failure to disclose transactions with directors

34.99 The penalties for failure to disclose in the financial statements a transaction in which a director has a material interest are dealt with from paragraph 34.171 onwards.

Substantial property transactions

Introduction

34.100 Most loans, quasi-loans and credit transactions between a company and its directors (for relevant companies at least) are, as described above, *prima facie* unlawful under section 330. In addition, a company's ability to contract with a director is further restricted where it wishes to enter into certain substantial property transactions. This means that a company (whether a relevant company or not) is prohibited from entering into an arrangement for the acquisition of substantial non-cash assets from (or their transfer to) a director of the company or its holding company or a person connected with the director, unless the prior approval by resolution of the company in general meeting is given. [Sec 320(1)]. Consequently, unless such prior approval is given or the arrangement is affirmed by resolution of the company in general meeting within a reasonable period the transaction is voidable by the company.

34.101 Stricter rules apply to companies which are charities. In this case the approval or affirmation by the company in general meeting of a substantial property transaction under section 320, is ineffective unless the prior written consent of the Charity Commissioners is obtained. [Charities Act 1993 Sec 66].

34.102 Substantial non-cash assets are those whose value is not less than £2,000 and also exceeds the lesser of £100,000 and 10 per cent of the company's asset value. [Sec 320(2)]. For this purpose, 'asset value' means the value of the company's net assets as disclosed in its latest financial statements laid before shareholders. Alternatively, where there are no such financial statements, 'asset value' means the amount of the company's called-up share capital (as defined in section 737(1)). [Sec 320(2)].

34.103 In this context, 'non-cash asset' means any type or form of property, or any interest in property other than cash. (For this purpose, 'cash' includes foreign currency.) The acquisition or transfer of a non-cash asset also includes the creation or extinction of an interest in property (for example, a lease) and the discharge of any person's liability other than a liability for a liquidated sum. [Sec 739(1)(2)]. For illustrations of 'non-cash assets' see Table 34.5 below and the example in paragraph 34.111.

Shareholders' approval of transactions

34.104 As stated in paragraph 34.100, the Act requires that any arrangement for the acquisition of non-cash assets should first be approved by resolution of the company in general meeting (for an example, see Table 34.5 below). [Sec 320(1)]. In addition, if the arrangement is with a director of the holding company or a person connected with him, it must also be first approved by a general meeting of the holding company. [Sec 320(1)].

34.105 The arrangements that this section of the Act covers are those where:

- A director of the company or its holding company, or a person connected with such a director, acquires (or is to acquire) a non-cash asset from the company.

- A company acquires (or is to acquire) a non-cash asset from a director of the company or its holding company, or from a person connected with such a director. [Sec 320(1)]. An example of this is given in the example in paragraph 34.111.

34.106 The same rules apply to substantial property transactions of this nature that involve a shadow director or a person connected with the shadow director. [Sec 320(3)].

34.107 Section 320 also affects certain intra-group transactions. Where, for example, a director of a company owns or controls a certain percentage of the shares in another group company, that other group company may fall within the definition of a connected person (see para 34.18). In these circumstances all dealings between the company and any company that falls within the definition of a person connected with a director will require prior approval of the company in general meeting (see para 34.109 for the exemptions).

34.108 An example of a substantial property transaction is given in Table 34.5.

Table 34.5 - Fine Art Developments p.l.c. - Annual Report & Accounts - 31 March 1993

Directors' Report (extract)

Proposed transaction with an associated party

In accordance with their policy to dispose of businesses which are not considered core to the group, the directors have decided there should be a sale of Herbert Walker & Son (Printers) Limited. This company is engaged in commercial printing and, if it was retained, would require considerable investment in plant and equipment in the near future.

The profit before tax of Herbert Walker in the year to 31 March 1993 amounted to £66,450 and its net assets on completion of a sale are estimated to be £664,000. The independent directors have concluded that a fair value of the company would be £764,000. In reaching this conclusion it has been assumed that the group will continue to purchase printed products from Herbert Walker on normal commercial terms of no less than an annual total purchase price of £1.5m in each of the three years following completion of a sale. The independent directors have sought advice from BDO Binder Hamlyn who consider that the terms of the proposed disposal, taking into account all relevant factors, are fair and reasonable so far as concern the shareholders of Fine Art Development p.l.c.

Mr K Chapman, a director, has agreed to purchase and Britannia Products Limited, a subsidiary of Fine Art Developments p.l.c. and the holder of the whole of the issued share capital of Herbert Walker, has agreed to sell the whole of such capital for a cash consideration of £764,000 payable on completion, subject to approval of the transaction by shareholders in general meetings as required under Section 320 of the Companies Act 1985. The contract for sale will contain a provision that Fine Art Developments p.l.c. shall procure that the group place orders for printed products with Herbert Walker on the terms referred to above.

An ordinary resolution to approve the sale is set out in the notice of annual general meeting on page 11.

Exemptions from obtaining approval

34.109 Although the company will still have to comply with the disclosure requirements set out in paragraph 34.112, the shareholders' approval is not required for a substantial property transaction of the type described in paragraph 34.100 where one of the exceptions from section 320 set out below applies:

- The value of the non-cash asset at the time of the arrangement is less than £2,000 or (if the value is greater than £2,000), it is less than the lower of £100,000 and 10 per cent of the company's asset value. [Sec 320(2)].

- The body corporate in question is neither a company formed and registered under the 1985 Act nor a company which, although not formed under the Act, is capable of registration and is registered under section 680. [Sec 321(1)].

- The company in question is a wholly-owned subsidiary of any company, wherever incorporated. [Sec 321(1)]. In these circumstances, in practice, the holding company's directors have control over the subsidiary's directors.

- The non-cash asset is to be acquired:

  - By a holding company from any of its wholly-owned subsidiaries.
  - By a wholly-owned subsidiary from its holding company.

- By a wholly-owned subsidiary from a fellow wholly-owned subsidiary. [Sec 321(2)(a)].

  In effect, this exemption relieves companies that would otherwise be required by section 320 of the Act to obtain approval at a general meeting for intra-group transactions that take place in a wholly-owned group.

- The arrangement is entered into by a company that is being wound up, and the winding-up is not a members' voluntary winding-up. [Sec 321(2)(b)].

- The following two conditions are satisfied:

  - A member of the company acquires an asset from the company.
  - The arrangement was made with that person (for example, a director of the company or the holding company or a person connected with such a director) in his capacity as a member of the company.

  [Sec 321(3)].

- The transaction is effected on a recognised investment exchange by a director, or a person connected with him, through an independent broker. [Sec 321(4)].

Liabilities for contravention of section 320

34.110 An arrangement for which the shareholder approval required by section 320 has not been obtained (and any transaction pursuant thereto) may be treated as voidable by the company unless one of the following three conditions is satisfied:

- It is impossible to obtain restitution of the subject matter of the transaction, or the company has been indemnified for any loss or damage it has suffered.

- A third party has acquired rights, *bona fide* and for value, and without having notice of the contravention, which would be affected.

- The arrangement is affirmed by the company in general meeting (and by the holding company, as the case may be) within a reasonable period of the arrangement being made. [Sec 322(1)(2)].

34.111 A director who contravenes section 320 of the Act may incur civil penalties. The director and the person connected with him who entered into the arrangement, and any director who authorised it may all be liable to account to the company for any gain they have received. They may also be liable to indemnify the company from any resultant loss or damage it has incurred. [Sec 322(3)]. This liability is without prejudice to any other liability which may have been incurred and arises whether or not the arrangement has been avoided [Sec 322(4)]. However, a director will not be liable if the arrangement was made with a person connected with him, and if he himself took all reasonable steps to ensure that the company obtained the required approval [Sec 322(5)]. A person connected with a director or a director who authorised the transaction will not be liable if they can show that they did not know the relevant circumstances that formed the contravention. [Sec 322(6)].

Example of a voidable transaction

C was a director and shareholder of a company A, which it was accepted was connected to C for section 320 purposes. Company A agreed to buy a property for £495,000 and paid a deposit of £49,500. On completion the property was conveyed to another company, X, of which C was also a director. Company X paid the balance of the purchase price and reimbursed company A the deposit. Company X then sought to avoid the transaction, as the value of the property had subsequently fallen in value, on the ground that it had not been approved by the members of company X. The Court of Appeal held that the transfer to company X of the benefit of A's interest in the purchase contract was a non-cash asset of a value of £49,500. Since 10% of company X's net assets as shown in its last financial statements was £44,399, this was a non-cash asset of the requisite value under section 320. Consequently the transaction was voidable. [*Re a Company No 0032314 of 1992. Duckwari plc v Offerventure Ltd* [1995] BCC 89].

Disclosure requirements under the Act

34.112 A substantial property transaction is likely to require disclosure as a transaction in which a director has a material interest. Consequently, the disclosure requirements outlined in paragraph 34.93 onwards for transactions in which a director has a material interest, that is, disclosure by way of notification to the board of directors and disclosure in financial statements, apply equally to substantial property transactions and arrangements of a kind described in paragraph 34.100 above. The requirements apply irrespective of whether the transactions and arrangements have been approved by the company in general meeting. In addition, the penalties for failure to comply with the disclosure requirements and the auditors' responsibility for reporting transactions which are contrary to law are set out from paragraph 34.171 onwards.

Stock Exchange disclosure requirements

34.113 The Stock Exchange Listing Rules for listed companies, and the Alternative Investment Market Rules for small, young and growing companies traded on the Alternative Investment Market (AIM companies) contain further rules and disclosure requirements for substantial property transactions and other transactions with directors which come within following categories:

- Transactions with related parties (which include directors).
- Contracts of significance with directors (not AIM companies).

In addition, FRS 8 requires disclosure of transactions with related parties. Although there is a fair amount of overlap, related party transactions in the Listing Rules are defined slightly differently from those in FRS 8. Chapter 35 deals with related party disclosure under FRS 8.

34.114 The Listing Rules provide certain safeguards to prevent directors and other related parties from taking advantage of their position. These are based on disclosure, primarily to shareholders, and are set out in chapter 11 of the Listing Rules - Transactions with related parties. They apply to listed companies unless they do not have any equity securities listed. Added to these requirements, disclosure of information regarding contracts of significance with directors must be made in the financial statements. Related party transactions and contracts of significance under the Listing Rules and AIM Admission Rules (which affect directors) are discussed in chapter 35 in the context of related party disclosures in general.

[The next paragraph is 34.121.]

Invalidity of certain transactions involving directors

General rule

34.121 Where a company proposes to enter into a transaction with a director of the company or its holding company, the board of directors will need to ensure that, in doing so, they are not exceeding any limitation on their powers under the company's constitution, that is, its articles of association, any resolution of the company or any agreement between members. If they exceed their powers the transaction is voidable at the option of the company unless it is ratified by the shareholders. [Sec 322A]. This also applies where the party to the transaction includes a person connected with a director (including a company with which he is associated).

Effects of contravention

34.122 Whether or not the transaction is avoided, the director or connected person concerned, and any director who authorised the transaction, is liable to account to the company for any gain and indemnify the company against any loss or damage it suffers as a consequence. Nothing in the rules set out in this paragraph and in the paragraph above, however, affects any other rule of law under which the transaction may be called into question or under which liability to the company may arise (for instance, if it is an illegal loan). [Sec 322A (3),(4)]. A person other than a director of the company is not liable to account or to indemnify the company if he can show that at the time the transaction was entered into he did not know that the directors were exceeding their powers. [Sec 322A(6)].

34.123 The company may treat the transaction as voidable unless one of the following conditions is satisfied:

- Restitution of the money or other asset which was the subject of the transaction is no longer possible.

[The next page is 34045.]

- The company is indemnified for any loss or damage resulting from the transaction.

- Rights acquired *bona fide* for value and without actual notice of the directors' exceeding their powers by a person who is not a party to the transaction would be affected by the avoidance.

- The transaction is ratified by the company in general meeting by ordinary or special resolution or otherwise as the case may require.

[Sec 322A (5)].

34.124 However, the Act provides for the situation where the transaction is voidable under section 322A, but is valid under section 35A (power of directors to bind the company free of any limitation under the company's constitution). Where the person dealing with the company (not being a director of the company or its holding company or a person connected with him) has acted in good faith, the court may (on the application of that person or the company) make an order either confirming, severing, or setting aside the transaction, on such terms as appears to the court to be just. [Sec 322A(7)].

34.125 Where the company enters into a transaction which is outside the directors' powers and thus voidable under section 322A, it will be disclosable under Schedule 6 Part II as a contract in which a director has, directly or indirectly, a material interest (see para 34.93 onwards).

Transactions with directors who are sole members

34.126 There are special requirements for a single member company to document transactions with a director who is also its sole member. Where a private company with a sole member who is also a director (or shadow director) contracts with that director it must ensure that the terms of the contract are set out in a written memorandum or are recorded in the minutes of the first meeting of directors of the company following the making of the contract. This requirement does not apply where the contract is in writing or is entered into in the company's ordinary course of business. [Sec 322B].

34.127 Failure to comply with this requirement does not affect the validity of the contract. However, it is a criminal offence and the company and every officer in default is liable to a fine.

34.128 A sole director also has a duty to comply with the statutory provisions of section 317 which requires him to declare at a meeting of the directors the nature of his interest in any contract or proposed contract with the company. This was established by *Neptune (Vehicle Washing Equipment Ltd v Fitzgerald* [1995] 1 BCLC 352 where the judge said that he was satisfied that for the purpose of section 317 there can be a directors meeting in the case of a sole directorship. The requirements of section 317 are described in paragraph 34.163.

Transactions with officers

Transactions to be disclosed

34.129 In contrast to the substantial number of provisions in the Act relating to directors' transactions with their company, section 232 of the Act requires less disclosure of similar transactions with officers who are not directors. The requirements set out in Part III of Schedule 6 (described in paragraph 34.130) apply to the following types of transactions, arrangements and agreements made by the company or any of its subsidiaries for persons who at any time during the financial year were officers of the company (but not directors or shadow directors):

- Loans (including any guarantees and securities for loans), arrangements of the types described in section 330(6) or (7) of the Act relating to loans, and agreements to enter into any such transactions.

- Quasi-loans (including any guarantees and securities for quasi-loans), arrangements of the types described in section 330(6) or (7) of the Act relating to quasi-loans, and agreements to enter into any such transactions.

- Credit transactions (including any guarantees and securities for credit transactions), arrangements of the types described in section 330(6) or (7) of the Act relating to credit transactions, and agreements to enter into any such transactions. [Sec 232(2); 6 Sch 28].

For this purpose, the term 'officer' includes the company secretary and the company's senior managers. [Sec 744]. There is also little doubt that a person appointed to hold the office of auditor of a company is an officer of the company. [*R v Shacter* [1960] 2 QB 252].

Information to be disclosed

34.130 A statement containing the following information relating to transactions with officers of the kind mentioned in the paragraph above must be made in a holding company's consolidated financial statements (or, if it does not prepare consolidated financial statements, in its individual financial statements), or in the financial statements of a company other than a holding company:

- The aggregate amounts outstanding at the end of the financial year under such transactions, made by either the company or (if it is a holding company) its subsidiaries. The aggregate amounts must relate to each category of transaction described above.

In this respect, 'amount outstanding' means the amount of the outstanding liabilities of the person for whom the transaction was made. With a guarantee or a security, it means the amount guaranteed or secured. [6 Sch 30].

- The number of officers for whom transactions in each category were made. [6 Sch 29(1)].

Exemptions from disclosure

34.131 No statement need be given in respect of the transactions outlined in paragraph 34.129 made by the company for an officer of the company where the aggregate amount outstanding at the end of the financial year for that officer does not exceed £2,500. [6 Sch 29(2)]. The Secretary of State has power to increase this limit by statutory instrument. [6 Sch 29(3)].

Penalty for failure to disclose transactions with officers

34.132 If the directors approve accounts in which they have failed to make the disclosure the Act requires in respect of transactions with a company's officers in the company's financial statements, they will be guilty of an offence and liable to a fine. [Sec 233(5)]. In addition, the auditors must include a statement in their audit report giving the required particulars, so far as they are reasonably able to do so [Sec 237(4)]. (See para 34.171 onwards.)

Money-lending and banking companies

Introduction

34.133 The Act defines a 'money-lending company' as *"a company whose ordinary business includes the making of loans or quasi-loans, or the giving of guarantees in connection with loans or quasi-loans"*. [Sec 338(2)]. Money-lending companies are not necessarily banking companies under the Banking Act 1987, but banking companies fall within the definition of 'money-lending companies' for this purpose.

34.134 A banking company is defined as *"a company which is authorised under the Banking Act 1987"*. [Sec 744]. Authorisation under the Banking Act 1987 permits a company to conduct a deposit-taking business in the UK. A deposit-taking business is one where money received in the course of business by way of deposit is lent to others or used to finance any other activity of the business. Unless otherwise indicated, the term 'money-lending company' where used below will include a company which is a banking company.

34.135 The transactions prohibited by section 330 and the relevant exemptions to the prohibitions (see para 34.29 onwards) that apply to relevant and non-relevant companies also apply to relevant and non-relevant money-lending companies.

34.136 Money-lending companies (both relevant and non-relevant) may, however, take advantage of a further exemption relating to loans, quasi-loans and guarantees of loans and quasi-loans. This exemption and the disclosure requirements for money-lending companies (including banking companies) and those specifically for banking companies are considered in the paragraphs that follow.

Exemption for money lending companies

Loans on commercial terms

34.137 Section 338(1) of the Act exempts (subject to certain conditions) money-lending companies (whether relevant or non-relevant) from the general prohibition in section 330 regarding loans and quasi-loans. Consequently a money-lending company is not prohibited from:

- Making a loan or quasi-loan to any person (for instance, to a director of the company or its holding company or a person connected with the director); or
- Entering into a guarantee for a loan or quasi-loan.

The exemption is only available if the following two conditions are satisfied:

- The money-lending company makes the loan or quasi-loan or enters into the guarantee in the ordinary course of its business. [Sec 338(3)(a)].
- The amount of the loan or quasi-loan or the amount guaranteed is not greater than, and the terms of that transaction are not more favourable, in the case of the person for whom the transaction is made, than those that the company might reasonably be expected to have offered to, or in respect of, a person of the same financial standing who was unconnected with the company. (In other words, the facility is offered on the money-lending company's normal commercial terms.) [Sec 338(3)(b)].

Further condition for relevant money-lending companies

34.138 A relevant money-lending company that is not a banking company is subject to the further condition in section 338(4). Such a company must not make a loan, quasi-loan or enter into a guarantee if the aggregate of the '*relevant amounts*' (see para 34.139) exceeds £100,000. [Sec 338(4)]. In determining the aggregate of relevant amounts, any loans, quasi-loans and guarantees to or for a company with which the director is connected, but which he does not control may, be excluded. This is because the company is not deemed to be connected with him. [Sec 338(5)]. A director will control a company where he holds more than 50 per cent of the share capital or voting power. However, see section 346(1) to (8) for full details of the circumstances in which a director will be deemed to 'control' a company.

34.139 The '*relevant amounts*' to be aggregated for the purposes of the exemption for relevant (non-banking) money-lending companies in section 338(1) are referred to in paragraph 34.34. In the context of this exception the reference in that paragraph to the small loans exception should be read as a reference to the exemption for money-lending companies under section 338. For these purposes, the value of a loan is the amount of its principal, and the value of a quasi-loan is the amount, or the maximum amount, which the person to whom the quasi-loan is made is liable to reimburse the creditor. The value of a guarantee or security is the amount guaranteed or secured. [Sec 340(2)(4)]. The value of an arrangement under section 330(6) or (7) is the value of the transaction to which the arrangement relates less any amounts by which the liabilities under the arrangement of the person for whom the transaction was made have been reduced. [Sec 340 (5)]. If the value is not capable of being expressed as a specific sum, it is deemed to exceed £100,000. [Sec 340(7)].

Transactions to which the exemption is not applicable

34.140 It should be noted, however, the exemption for money-lending companies in section 338(1) which relates to loans, quasi-loans and guarantees for them (see paragraph 34.137), does not extend to the following types of transaction:

- The provision of security in connection with a loan or a quasi-loan.
- Credit transactions, or the provision of a guarantee or security in connection with them.
- The assignment of rights or obligations or assumption of liabilities under the above types of transaction.
- Indirect arrangements under the above types of transaction.

These transactions will remain caught by the general prohibition in section 330 for relevant companies. Consequently, in these situations, money-lending companies are subject to the same rules as any other company, and the provisions set out in sections 330 to 337 of the Act (as outlined in paras 34.29 to 34.68) apply to them.

Relaxation for loans on beneficial terms for house purchase

34.141 The second condition set out in paragraph 34.137 (that the exemption applies only where the loan is made on normal commercial terms) is relaxed where a money-lending company makes a loan to one of its directors or a director of its holding company for the purpose of house purchase or improvement (housing loan). [Sec 338(6)]. Consequently, a money-lending company (whether relevant or non-relevant) is not prevented by that condition from making a loan (but not a quasi-loan or a guarantee) to such a director on *beneficial* terms provided that all the following conditions are satisfied:

- The loan is to assist the director either to purchase or to improve his only or main residence, or land enjoyed with it. This type of loan will also include a loan made by the company in substitution for a loan that another person has made to the director.

- The company ordinarily makes similar loans of that type available to its employees on no less favourable terms.

- The aggregate of the relevant amounts does not exceed £100,000.

[Sec 338(6)].

34.142 The aggregate of the relevant amounts mentioned above for the exemption for housing loans on beneficial terms under section 338(6) is determined for money-lending companies and banking companies as follows:

- Relevant money-lending company

  The value of the following transactions must be aggregated with the principal amount of the proposed housing loan for the purpose of determining the relevant amounts:

  - Any existing housing loans on *beneficial* terms made under the exemption for money-lending companies in section 338(6), less any amount by which that value has been reduced.

  - Any existing loans, quasi-loans or guarantees of loans made on *commercial* terms under the exemption for money-lending companies under section 338(3)(b), less any amount by which that value has been reduced. [Sec 339(6)].

  - Any arrangements falling within section 330(6) or (7) relating to loans, quasi-loans or guarantees made under the exemption for money-lending companies in section 338(1).

The values of these types of transactions are referred to in paragraph 34.139. Consequently, a relevant money-lending company (which is not a banking company) is not prohibited from making a director a house purchase loan on beneficial terms or a loan on commercial terms to the value of £100,000, or any combination of them, provided that the aggregate of the relevant amounts for the transactions relating to that director does not exceed £100,000.

- Non-relevant money-lending company

  The same consideration applies to non-relevant companies as above. However, since no limit is imposed on non-relevant companies by the exception for loans on *commercial* terms, the limit of £100,000 applies to a non-relevant company which wishes to make a housing loan to a director on *beneficial* terms.

  It may then go on to make loans on commercial terms to any value. But, if a non-relevant company makes a loan on commercial terms to the value of £100,000 first, it cannot then make a housing loan on beneficial terms. The reason for this is that the £100,000 limit for 'relevant amounts' allowable under section 338(6) will then have been exhausted. It should be noted that this does not necessarily mean that directors of such companies are free to grant unrestricted loan facilities to themselves. There may be other limitations upon their powers. The transaction might also be disclosable as a transaction in which a director has a material interest.

- Banking company

  Banking companies may ignore loans made on *commercial* terms in computing whether or not a housing loan it proposes to make to a director on *beneficial* terms falls within the £100,000 limit. Therefore, only the amount of any existing housing loans on beneficial terms that are still outstanding should be brought into the aggregation. [Sec 339(4)]. In effect, a banking company may make housing loans to either its directors or its holding company's directors on beneficial terms provided the aggregate of the principal amounts of such loans less the amounts repaid does not exceed £100,000. The exemption imposes no restriction on the size of loans banking companies may make to such directors on commercial terms. [Sec 339(4)]

Disclosure requirements - money lending companies

34.143 A money-lending company (unless it is a banking company or the holding company of a credit institution - see definition below) is required to disclose the particulars required by Parts II and III of Schedule 6 in connection with loans, quasi-loans and other dealing with directors and other officers in the same way as any other company.

34.144 'Credit institution' is defined in section 262. This section refers to the definition in article 1 of the 1st Directive on the coordination of laws, regulations and administrative provisions relating to the taking up and pursuit of the business of credit institutions (77/780/EEC), that is to say, an undertaking whose business is to receive deposits or other repayable funds from the public and to grant credits for its own account. A credit institution would, therefore, include an institution, wherever incorporated, carrying on banking-type business.

34.145 A 'banking company' is defined in section 744 (see para 34.131) and, refers to the subset of credit institutions incorporated in Great Britain, which are authorised under the Banking Act 1987 to conduct a deposit-taking business in the UK.

34.146 In addition, a company which is a credit institution will come within the definition of a money-lending company as defined in section 338(2) (see para 34.133), because a credit institution makes loans in the ordinary course of its business. However, a money-lending company will not be a credit institution, unless the money-lending company, in addition to making loans, receives deposits or other repayable funds from the general public in the ordinary course of its business.

Disclosure requirements - banking company or group

Disclosure in financial statements

34.147 A banking company, or a company which is the holding company of a credit institution, may exempt itself from some of the disclosure requirements that apply to other companies. Section 255B(2) provides that the provisions in Schedule 6 relating to the disclosure of information in the financial statements concerning loans, quasi-loans and other dealings with directors have effect subject to Part IV of Schedule 9.

34.148 Part IV of Schedule 9 was amended by the Companies Act 1985 (Bank Accounts) Regulations 1994 (SI 1994/233) with effect from 28 February 1994. This Part now provides that a banking company or a company which is the holding company of a credit institution does not have to comply with Part II of Schedule 6 in the following respects. It need not disclose the detailed information outlined in paragraphs 34.74 to 34.79 (for loans, quasi-loans credit transactions and related dealings) in relation to a transaction or arrangement of a kind mentioned in section 330, or an agreement to enter into such a transaction or arrangement to which that banking company or credit institution is a party. [9 Sch Part IV, 2]. A banking company or company which is the holding company of a credit institution is not exempted by these provisions from disclosing transactions in which a director has a material interest (see Table 34.3 on page 32).

34.149 Where, however, a company takes advantage of these exemptions it must (i) include a statement in relation to the specified transactions in its financial statements, (ii) keep a register of the specified transactions and (iii) make a special statement including particulars of those transactions available to members.

Statement of transactions

34.150 Where a banking company or company which is the holding company of a credit institution takes advantage of the above provisions, it must instead comply with the provisions of Part III of Schedule 6. This means that it must include in its financial statements a statement of the information outlined below in respect of certain transactions, arrangements and agreements. These relate to quasi-loans, credit transactions and related guarantees, securities, arrangements of the kind described in section 330(6) and (7) and agreements to enter into such transactions and arrangements made by that banking company or credit institution for:

- A director or a shadow director of the company preparing the financial statements, or a person connected with such a director.
- A person who was a chief executive or manager (within the meaning of the Banking Act 1987) of that company or its holding company.

[9 Sch Part IV 3].

34.151 The Banking Act 1987 defines a chief executive as *"a person who, either alone or jointly with one or more persons, is responsible under the immediate authority of the directors for the conduct of the business of the institution"*. If the principal place of business is outside the UK, the chief executive also includes a person who alone or jointly with other persons, is responsible for the conduct of its business in the UK. [BA 1987 Sec 105(7)(8)].

34.152 A manager is defined by the Banking Act as a person (other than a chief executive) who, under the immediate authority of a director or chief executive of the institution, undertakes one of the following tasks:

- Exercises managerial functions.
- Is responsible for maintaining accounts or other records of the institution.

[BA 1987 Sec 105(6)].

34.153 The statement in the financial statements must contain the following details:

- The aggregate amounts outstanding at the end of the financial year, analysed under loans, quasi-loans and credit transactions.

- The number of persons (that is, of the directors and shadow directors of the company and persons connected with them and chief executive of the company or its holding company) for whom transactions in each of the above categories were made by the banking company.

[6 Sch Part III paras 28, 29; 9 Sch Part IV para 3].

An illustration of this disclosure is given in Table 34.6.

Table 34.6 - TSB Group plc - Annual Report and Accounts - 31 October 1994

Notes to the accounts (extract)

7 Directors' and officers' loans

At 31 October 1994 the aggregate amounts outstanding under transactions, agreements and agreements entered into by the Group's banking subsidiaries with directors, persons connected with directors, and officers were

	Directors and connected persons			Officers	
	Loans	Quasi loans	Guarantees	Loans	Quasi loans
Number of persons	4	5	1	3	2
Amounts £000	568	7	30	433	2

34.154 For the purpose of these provisions:

- In so far as they relate to loans, quasi-loans and credit transactions, a body corporate that a person does not control should not be treated as being connected with him. [9 Sch Part IV para 3(4)]. For the meaning of a director 'controlling' a company, see section 346 and para 34.21.
- The interpretation of a person connected with a director or controlling a body corporate is given in section 346 (see also para 34.35). [9 Sch Part IV, para 3(5)].
- References to officers in Part III are to be construed as including the persons mentioned in paragraph 34.150. [9 Sch Part IV para 3(2)].

Register of transactions

34.155 Where a company which is a banking company or holding company of a credit institution takes advantage in a financial year of the relaxation in paragraph 2 of Part IV of Schedule 9 relating to the disclosure requirements, it must keep a register. This register must been required to be disclosed in company's financial statements or consolidated financial statements. (See the disclosure rules in para 34.71 onwards.)

34.156 The register must contain these particulars for that financial year and for each financial year in the preceding ten years where it has taken advantage of these provisions. If the transaction, arrangement or agreement is not recorded in writing, the register must contain a written memorandum setting out its terms. [Sec 343(1)(2)(3) as amended by the Companies Act 1985 (Bank Accounts) Regulations (SI 1994/233) with effect from 28 February 1994].

34.157 No copies or memoranda, however, need be kept in the register where the outstanding aggregate value of those transactions, arrangements or agreements made by the company or a subsidiary for a director of the company or its holding company, or a person connected with such a director, did not exceed £2,000 at any time during the financial year. [Sec 344(1)].

Special statement for members

34.158 In addition, the following must be complied with unless the company is a banking company which is a wholly-owned subsidiary of another UK company [Sec 344(2)]. Where the company takes advantage of paragraph 2 of Part IV of Schedule 9 (see para 34.155) in relation to the last complete financial year preceding its annual general meeting, it must, before that meeting, make a statement. This statement must be available at its registered office and include particulars of the transactions, arrangements and agreements which it would, but for that paragraph, have had to disclose in its financial statements or consolidated financial statements for that financial year. This statement must be made available at the company's registered office for inspection by the company's members for at least 15 days before the annual general meeting and also at the meeting itself. [Sec 343(4)(5)].

34.159 The auditors must examine this statement before it is made available to members. They must also submit a report to the members stating whether in their opinion all the particulars that section 343(4) requires have been included in the statement. Where, in their opinion, it does not, the auditors must include a statement of the required particulars in their report (so far as they are reasonably able to do so). Their report must be annexed to the special statement. [Sec 343 (6)(7)].

34.160 The disclosure of particulars in the special statement need not be made where the outstanding aggregate value of those transactions, arrangements or agreements for a director or a connected person did not exceed £2,000 at any time during the financial year. [Sec 344(1)].

34.161 For the purpose of the provisions of section 343 insofar as they relate to loans and quasi-loans, a company that a person does not control should not be treated as being connected with him. [Sec 343(9)].

Liability for contravention

34.162 It is an offence where a company fails to comply with the following requirements:

- To keep a register with copies of transactions (see para 34.155); or
- To make the special statement and auditors' report available for inspection by members at its registered office and at its annual general meeting (see para 34.158).

Any person who is a director at the time of the failure is guilty of the offence. It will be a defence for a person to show that he took all reasonable steps to ensure that the company complied with the requirements. Also a person will not be guilty of an offence by virtue only of being a shadow director. [Sec 343(8)].

Other matters

Notification to the board

Declaration of interest under section 317

34.163 Section 317 is an indication of the importance in company law of the principle that a company should be protected against a director who has a conflict in interest and duty. Where a director is in any way interested in a contract that involves the company, section 317 of the Act imposes a specific duty on the director to declare the precise nature of his interest in the contract at a meeting of the company's directors. A contract for this purpose includes any transaction or arrangement. This applies whether the director is either directly or indirectly interested in the contract, or the proposed contract, with the company. A director must disclose his interest in a proposed contract at one of the following:

- At the directors' meeting at which the contract is first considered.
- If, however, the director acquires an interest in the contract at a later date, he must disclose his interest at the first meeting held after he became interested.

[Sec 317(2)].

34.164 When a director is, for example, a member of another company that might enter into transactions with the company, he can give a general notice to the directors that he is to be regarded as interested in any future contract with that other company. If he does this, it will be regarded as giving sufficient notice to cover all further transactions with that company. [Sec 317(3)]. The director must either give the notice at a meeting of the directors or take reasonable steps to ensure that it is brought up and read at the next directors' meeting. [Sec 317(4)].

34.165 These notification requirements apply to all transactions and arrangements in which a director (or a person connected with him) has a direct or indirect interest, including loans, quasi-loans and credit transactions covered by section 330 (see para 34.29). [Sec 317(6)]. Consequently, a director, for example, must declare at a directors' meeting his interest in any loan that he, or one of the persons connected with him, receives from the company. Again, a general notice of his interest in any contract with a specified person who is connected with him may be given.

34.166 The general principles of section 317 apply also to shadow directors. However, a shadow director must disclose his interest by notice, in writing, to the directors, not at a meeting of the directors. Such notice can be in either one of the following forms:

- Specific, and given before the date of the meeting at which he would have been required to declare his interest, had he been a director.
- General (as described in para 34.164).

[Sec 317(8)].

34.167 In a recent case, *Neptune (Vehicle Washing Equipment) Ltd v Fitzgerald* [1995] 1 BCLC 352 Lightman J held that the object of section 317 is to ensure that the interest of any director and of any shadow director in a contract shall be an item of business at a meeting of the directors. He also held that section 317 secured that three things should happen. First, all the directors should know of the interest; secondly, the making of the declaration should be the occasion for a statutory pause for thought about the existence of the conflict of interest and of the duty to prefer the interests of the company; thirdly, the disclosure had to be a distinct happening at the meeting which had to be recorded in the minutes of the meeting.

34.168 If a director fails to disclose an interest in accordance with section 317 of the Act, this will be a criminal offence and he will be liable to a fine. [Sec 317(7)]. Also, this section does not prejudice the operation of any rule of law that may restrict a director from being interested in contracts with the company, for instance, any restriction under the articles. [Sec 317(9)]. This means that the contract may be voidable, and the director may be liable to account to the company for any gain he has made as a result of the transaction, and to indemnify the company for any loss it incurs.

Notification to board by sole director

34.169 The Neptune case mentioned above considered whether section 317 applied to a sole director. The judge was satisfied that for the purpose of section 317 there can be a directors' meeting in the case of a sole director. Consequently, a sole director is under a duty to comply with section 317 which requires him to declare his interest in any contract or proposed contract with the company at a meeting of the board. The minutes should record such declaration which, if there was no person other than the director attending the board meeting, need not be out loud. [*Neptune (Vehicle Washing Equipment) Ltd. v Fitzgerald* [1995] 1 BCLC 352].

Disclosure required by the articles of association

34.170 To overcome the general rule restricting contracts between directors and their companies, a company's articles of association will generally contain specific requirements for the disclosure to the board by a director of his interest in a contract with the company. If these requirements are not followed, the director risks being accountable to the company for any benefit he derives from the contract. For example, Table A of the Companies (Tables A to F) Regulations 1985 (1985/805) deals, in articles 85 and 86, with directors' material interests in contracts. The requirements of these articles are as follows:

> *"Subject to the provisions of the Act, and provided that he has disclosed to the directors the nature and extent of any material interest of his, a director notwithstanding his office -*
>
> *(a) may be a party to, or otherwise interested in, any transaction or arrangement with the company or in which the company is otherwise interested;*
>
> *(b) may be a director or other officer of, or employed by, or a party to any transaction or arrangement with, or otherwise interested in, any body corporate promoted by the company or in which the company is otherwise interested; and*
>
> *(c) shall not, by reason of his office, be accountable to the company for any benefit which he derives from any such office or employment or from any such transaction or arrangement or from any interest in any such body corporate and no such transaction or arrangement shall be liable to be avoided on the ground of any such interest or benefit.*

For the purposes of [the above] regulation 85

(a) a general notice given to the directors that a director is to be regarded as having an interest of the nature and extent specified in the notice in any transaction or arrangement in which a specified person or class of persons is interested shall be deemed to be a disclosure that the director has an interest in any such transaction of the nature and extent so specified; and

(b) an interest of which a director has no knowledge and of which it is unreasonable to expect him to have knowledge shall not be treated as an interest of his." [Table A articles 85, 86].

Penalties for failure to disclose certain transactions

34.171 Section 232 of the Act requires companies to give the information specified in Schedule 6 Part II and III regarding transactions with directors and officers in the notes to their financial statements. The required information relates to:

- Loans, quasi-loans, credit transactions and related dealings described in section 330 in favour of directors and connected persons.
- Agreements to enter into any such transactions.
- Transactions in which directors and connected persons have, directly or indirectly, a material interest.
- Transactions by a company or a subsidiary with officers who are not directors.

It is the duty of a director and any person who has been an officer of the company within the preceding five years to give the company any of the information necessary for it to comply with Schedule 6. Failure to do so is an offence. [Sec 232(4)].

34.172 The Act also imposes a penalty on the company's directors for failure to disclose the information about directors' and officers' transactions referred to above in the company's financial statements. If the financial statements that are approved by the directors do not comply with the Act by not disclosing the required information, then every director of the company who is party to their approval and who knows that they do not comply or is reckless as to whether they comply is guilty of an offence. [Sec 233(5)].

34.173 Moreover, where the financial statements do not disclose the information required by the Act, the auditors must include, in their report (so far as they are reasonably able to do so), a statement giving the details that have been omitted.

[Sec 237(4)]. In addition, the auditors have certain responsibilities for considering any transactions to which the company was a party which may have been illegal or in breach of applicable regulations. [SAS 120]. Non-compliance refers to acts of omission or commission by the company being audited (either intentional or unintentional) that are contrary to law (comprising common law or statute) or regulations.

34.174 Auditors may, during their audit, become aware of information indicating that there may be non-compliance with law or regulations that they may need to refer to in their report. They may, therefore, need to include an explanatory paragraph in their report if they conclude that the view given by the financial statements could, as a result of the non-compliance, be affected by a level of uncertainty which is fundamental. If, however, they conclude that the non-compliance has a material affect on the financial statements and they disagree, for instance, with the accounting treatment or the disclosure, they may have to issue an adverse or qualified opinion. If they are unable to determine whether non-compliance has occurred because of a limitation in the scope of their work, they may have to issue a disclaimer or a qualified opinion. [SAS 120 para 51,52].

Criminal sanctions and civil remedies under section 330

34.175 The penalties the Act imposes on a company that enters into a transaction or arrangement that contravenes section 330 vary according to whether or not the company is a relevant company. A relevant company and its directors will incur both criminal and civil liability, whereas a non-relevant company and its directors will incur only civil liability.

34.176 Section 342 deals with criminal liability. A relevant company that enters into a transaction or arrangement ('transaction') for one of its directors or a director of its holding company in contravention of section 330 of the Act will be guilty of an offence. A director of a relevant company will be guilty of an offence if he either authorises or permits the company to enter into a transaction contravening section 330. A similar offence is committed if another person procures the company to enter into such a transaction. In these two situations, the state of mind of the director or the other person is relevant in deciding whether an offence has been committed. To be guilty of an offence, he must have known, or have had reasonable cause to believe, that the transaction contravened section 330. A relevant company may escape liability if it can prove that it did not know of the facts at the time it entered into the transaction.

34.177 A company may, as a civil remedy under section 341(1), seek to treat an unlawful transaction as voidable. This means that a company does not need to regard itself as bound by any agreement that it has entered into with the director or any other person. However, because a transaction is not actually void, a company may wish to elect to affirm the agreement instead. Also, the company will not be entitled to treat the transaction as voidable if the subject matter of the transaction cannot be restored (for example, where the sum a company has lent to a borrower who is unable to repay has been used to buy goods which have been consumed), or if the person who benefited under the transaction has indemnified the company.

34.178 Similarly, a transaction will not be voidable if a third party has, *bona fide* for value and without actual notice of the contravention, acquired rights under the agreement and these rights would be affected if the company avoided the liability. [Sec 341(1)(b)].

34.179 Moreover, whether or not an unlawful transaction has been avoided, the person who benefited from the unlawful transaction and any other director who authorised the transaction have a statutory duty to reimburse the company. They are, consequently, liable to account to the company for any gain they have made (whether directly or indirectly) and also to indemnify the company for any loss or damage resulting from the transaction. [Sec 341(2)]. Their liability may, however, be limited if either of the following applies.

- Where the transaction in question was made for a person connected with a director of the company or its holding company, that director is not liable to account to the company or to indemnify it if he shows that he took all reasonable steps to ensure that the transaction did not contravene section 330. [Sec 341(4)].

- A connected person (and a director who authorised the transaction) will avoid civil liability if he can show that, at the time the company entered into the transaction, he did not know of the circumstances that amounted to a contravention. [Sec 341(5)].

34.179.1 In a recent case, a company made a loan in excess of £5,000 (and, therefore, an illegal loan) to one of its directors. After he ceased to be a director, the company demanded repayment of the loan. The director alleged that it had been agreed that the loan was to be repaid from dividends, and that because the company had paid none, the loan was not repayable, at least not at this stage. The Court of Appeal held that the effect of section 341 was to render the loan voidable and that the company was entitled to immediate repayment irrespective of the terms on which the loan was made, which may specify a different date.

[The next paragraph is 34.180.]

Future developments

34.180 The DTI was due to publish a consultation document on the reform of the 1985 Act Part X (Enforcement of fair dealing by directors) and Schedule 6 (Disclosure of information: Emoluments and other benefits of directors) at the beginning of 1995. The publication of this document was held back as the Department felt that it was out of date in the light of the concerns and controversy relating to directors' pay, which were reported during the early part of 1995. One area of concern is that the existing provisions for the enforcement of fair dealing and disclosure under the Companies Act 1985 do not effectively require sufficient disclosure of payments or benefits that directors are awarded by their companies.

34.181 However, further consultation may result from the Government's recently announced wide-ranging review of company law. One aspect which will be considered by the review is the complexity of certain parts of the Companies Act 1985. An example is Part X (that is, sections 311 to 347) of the 1985 Act relating to the enforcement of fair dealing by directors.

Annex - Directors' loans decision tables

Decision table 1: Loans - relevant company

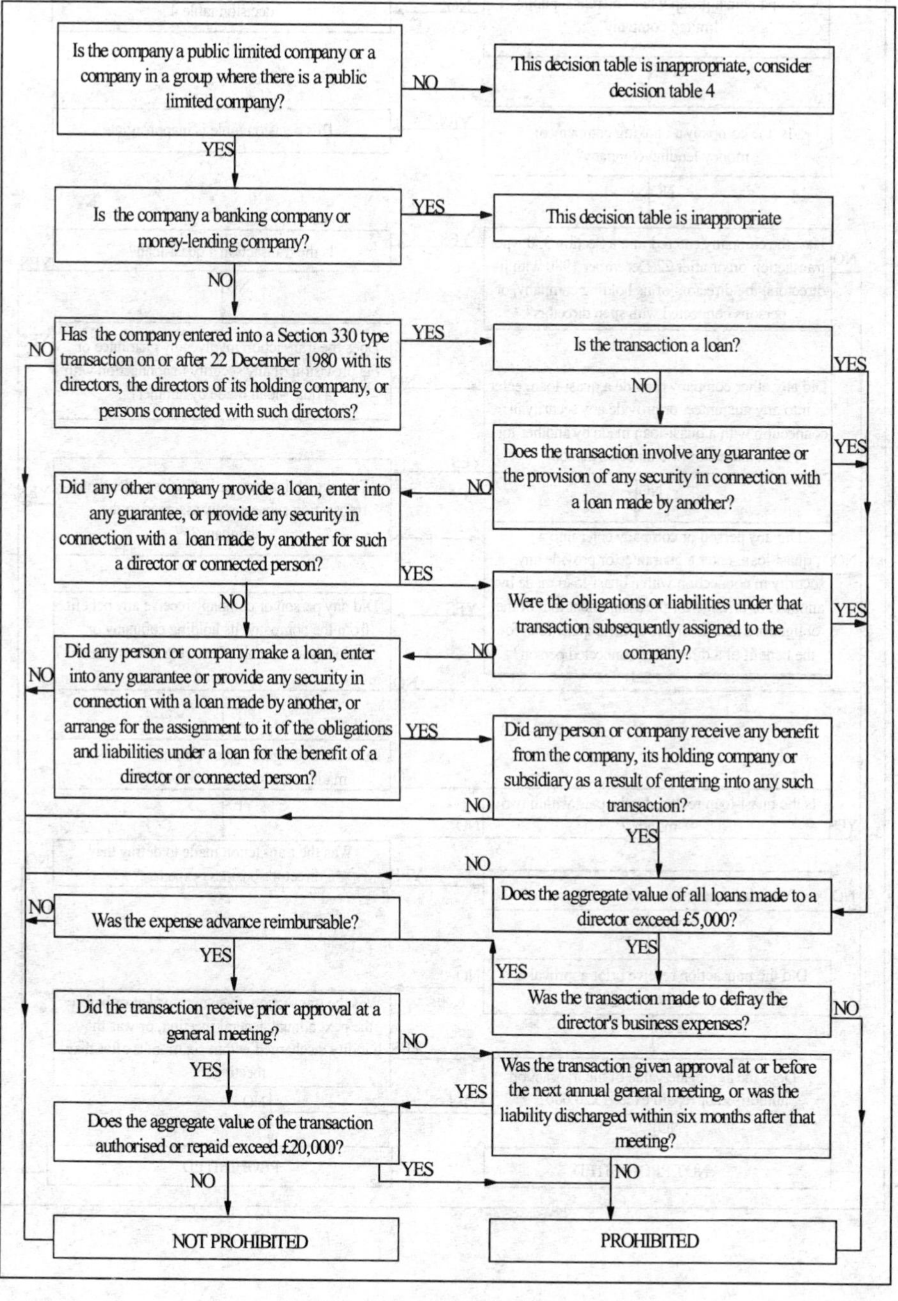

[The next page is 34063.]

Decision table 2: Quasi-loans - relevant company

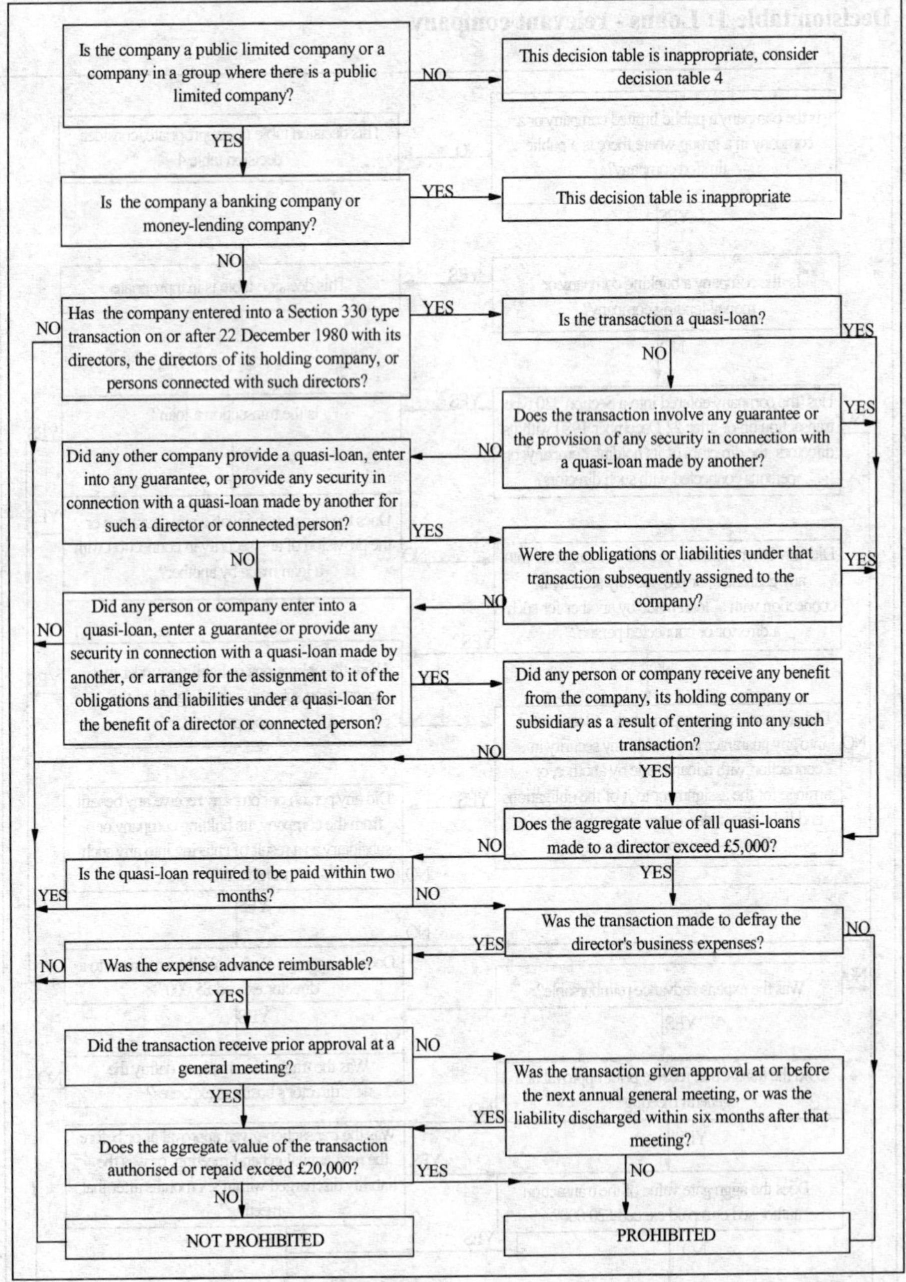

Decision table 3: Credit transactions - relevant company

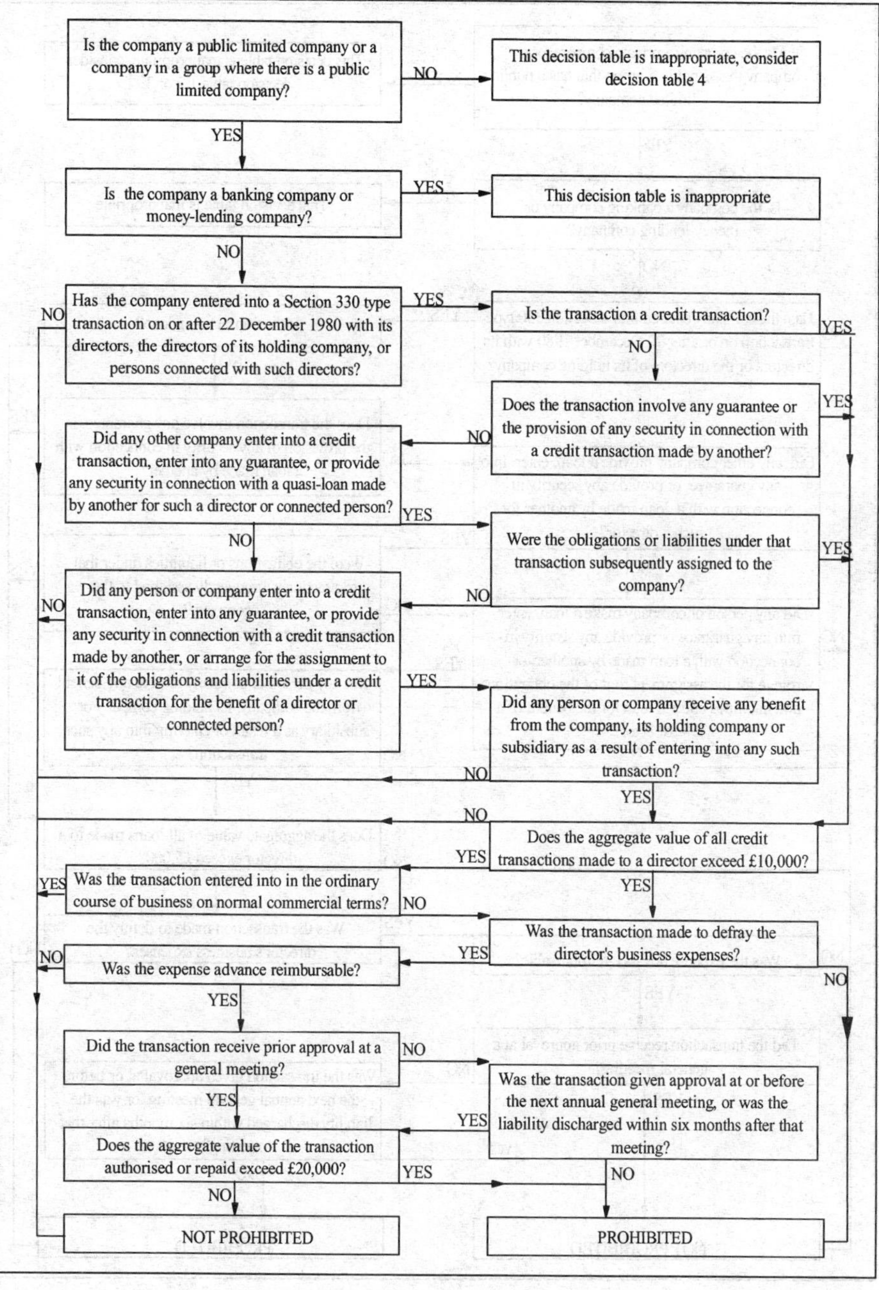

Decision table 4: Loans - non-relevant company

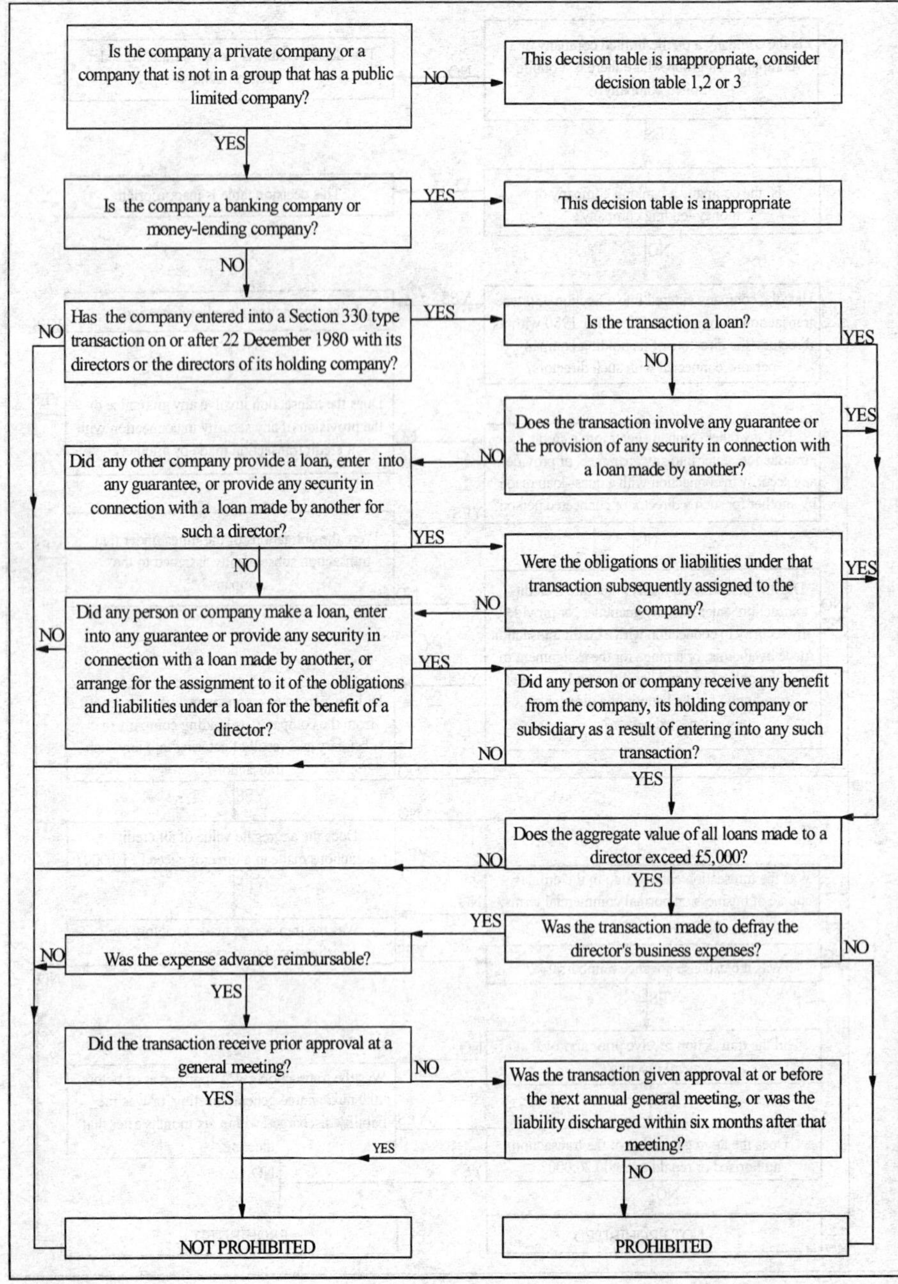

Chapter 35

Related party disclosures

Chapter 35

Related party disclosures

Introduction

Background

35.1 Related party transactions can take a variety of forms. Many of them include transactions in the normal course of business, for example, purchase or sale of goods at market values. Others include:

- Transferring fixed assets between related parties. The transfer may be at a fair value on an arm's length basis or it may be at book value or some other amount that differs from market prices.
- Outright gifts and capital contributions.
- Provision of accommodation or management services. This could be charged at a reasonable fee for the services provided or it may be without charge or at a fee that is unrelated to market value.

35.2 Although there are extensive Companies Act and Stock Exchange requirements and reliefs regarding the disclosure of transactions with related parties, neither the scope of the legislation nor the requirements of the Stock Exchange is considered comprehensive. For example, the Act places considerable emphasis on disclosing transactions with directors and the disclosure of group companies. Similarly, the Stock Exchange requires listed companies to disclose certain additional details about transactions with substantial shareholders. These provisions are designed to highlight the stewardship nature of a director's duties. FRS 8 closes some of the gaps in disclosure.

35.3 The need for enhanced disclosures has long been recognised. The lack of information about transactions with related parties, particularly ones which were not carried out on normal commercial terms, has been a recurrent theme of DTI reports on investigations into company failures over the past 20 or so years. In practice, it was often extremely difficult to work out whether related party transactions were involved. On some occasions, transactions with related parties were deliberately concealed from auditors or inaccurate information was given to auditors. As a consequence, both the financial statements and the auditors' report often failed to disclose relevant information. Furthermore, disclosure in the context of related party transactions has raised particular problems for auditors as they need to consider whether related parties and their transactions have been properly identified and disclosed in the financial statements by the directors. This in turn led to the development by the APB of standards and guidance for auditors on both auditing related party transactions and establishing the ultimate controlling party. This is to be found in SAS 460, 'Related parties'.

35.4 The disclosures required by FRS 8 (published in October 1995) are, therefore, intended to complement the existing statutory and Stock Exchange disclosure requirements. FRS 8's perspective is somewhat broader in that it concentrates on the relevance of the information to the users of financial statements. It extends the amount of disclosure that has to be given in some instances and also requires disclosure of additional transactions and relationships. The Stock Exchange's Listing Rules use the term 'related party' in relation to a listed company, but the definition of related parties in FRS 8 is different from the definition given in the Listing Rules. There are, however, related parties, such as directors and their families, which are common to both definitions.

35.5 FRS 8 applies to all financial statements that are intended to give a true and fair view of the reporting entity's financial position and profit or loss (or income and expenditure) for a period.

35.6 In summary, the standard requires the following information to be disclosed in a reporting entity's financial statements about its related parties:

- The name of the party that controls the reporting entity and, if different, the name of the ultimate controlling party (whether or not any transactions have taken place with those parties).
- Details of material transactions between the reporting entity and any related parties.
- Details of balances due to, or from, related parties at the balance sheet date.

35.7 Under the standard, two or more parties are related parties when:

- one party has direct or indirect control of the other party; or
- the parties are subject to common control from the same source; or
- one party has influence over the other party; or
- the parties are subject to influence from the same source.

Implementation

35.8 FRS 8 states that its accounting practices should be adopted for all financial statements relating to accounting periods commencing on or after 23 December 1995. Earlier adoption was encouraged, but was not required.

Development of FRS 8

35.9 The subject of related party transactions was under consideration by the Accounting Standards Committee (ASC) for many years before it published ED 46 in April 1989. The main proposal of ED 46 was for companies to report *abnormal* related party transactions. The exposure draft's other proposals were the disclosure of the existence and nature of controlling related party relationships whether or not any transactions had taken place between the parties, and the disclosure of economic dependence.

35.10 FRED 8, 'Related party disclosures', which superseded the proposals in ED 46, was published by the ASB in March 1994. In line with international practice, this proposed that *all* material related party transactions (not just abnormal ones) should be disclosed. This fundamental change came about because the ASB considered that it was necessary to report all control relationships and material related party transactions in order to draw attention to the possibility that the financial statements might have been affected by the relationship. The exposure draft no longer contained the proposed disclosure of economic dependence on the basis that this was not relevant in a standard dealing with related parties, since a customer or a supplier is not normally regarded as a related party.

35.11 FRS 8 adopted the proposals of FRED 8 with a few minor amendments.

Objective of FRS 8

35.12 FRS 8's stated objective is to ensure that financial statements contain the disclosures necessary to draw attention to the possibility that the reported financial position and results may have been affected by the existence of related parties and by material transactions with them.

35.13 The ASB has given an indication of its reasoning for requiring disclosure of all material related party transactions (rather than just abnormal ones) by explaining the effect on a reporting entity of the existence of related party relationships. This may be summarised as follows:

- In the absence of contrary information, it is assumed that a reporting entity has power over its resources and transactions and acts independently of the interests of its owners, managers and others. Transactions are presumed to have been undertaken on an arm's length basis.

- These assumptions may not be justified where related party relationships exist, because free market dealings may not occur. Sometimes disclosure of the relationship alone may be sufficient to make users of the financial statements aware of the possible implications of related party relationships. This is why transactions between 90 per cent subsidiary undertakings and other group members need not be disclosed in the subsidiary's financial statements (see further para 35.144).

- The reporting of material arm's length transactions between related parties is useful information, because such transactions are more susceptible to alteration. Although related party relationships sometimes preclude arm's length transactions, non-independent parties can deal at arm's length; for instance, where a parent places no restrictions on two subsidiaries, giving them complete freedom in their dealings with each other. However, financial statements should not imply that related party transactions were entered into on arm's length terms unless the parties have conducted the transactions in an independent manner.

[FRS 8 paras 8-10].

Related parties

The reporting entity

35.13.1 FRS 8 requires material transactions between the reporting entity and its related parties to be disclosed in its financial statements. The reporting entity will be the company, where it is preparing its individual financial statements. However, if the company is a parent company and is preparing consolidated financial statements, the reporting entity will be the group headed by the parent company. A parent company must under section 227 of the 1985 Act prepare group accounts, that is, consolidated financial statements comprising itself and its subsidiaries. 'Group' is defined in section 262 of the Act as *"a parent undertaking and its subsidiary undertakings"*. The criteria to establish related party relationships between a company and its related parties and the group and its related parties should, therefore, be applied at individual company level and, in the case of consolidated financial statements, at group level.

[The next paragraph is 35.14.]

Criteria for related party relationships

35.14 A related party can be an individual or an entity, such as a company or unincorporated business. Where a group of individuals or entities act in concert to divert a reporting entity from pursuing its own separate interests, each individual or entity in the group will be a related party.

35.15 A related party is a party that has a relationship with the reporting entity which affects the pursuit of separate interests of either the reporting entity or the related party itself. This related party relationship arises because transactions between the parties could have a significant effect on the financial position and operating results of the reporting entity. The reporting entity can be any of the parties that are involved in the transaction or the group of which they are a member.

35.16 The FRS sets out four criteria for establishing whether certain parties are related parties as follows.

> *"Two or more parties are related parties when at any time during the financial period:*
>
> *(i)* *One party has direct or indirect control of the other party; or*
>
> *(ii)* *The parties are subject to common control from the same source; or*

[The next page is 35005.]

(iii) *One party has influence over the financial and operating policies of the other party to an extent that that other party might be inhibited from pursuing at all times its own separate interests; or*

(iv) *The parties, in entering a transaction, are subject to influence from the same source to such an extent that one of the parties to the transaction has subordinated its own separate interests."*

[FRS 8 para 2.5(a)].

35.17 These criteria, which give rise to a related party relationship, may be summarised as: control; common control; influence; and common influence. These terms are discussed below from paragraph 35.18. There are, in addition, certain relationships that the standard automatically regards as related party relationships. These are described from paragraph 35.30.

Control

35.18 FRS 8's definition of 'control' as used in paragraph 35.16 above is similar to the definition of control found in paragraph 6 of FRS 2, 'Subsidiary undertakings'. The accounting concept of control is explained in FRS 2 in connection with identifying parent and subsidiary undertakings in the context of consolidation. [FRS 2 paras 62-67]. The definition in FRS 8 (given below) differs in that the ability to control can be held by an individual as well as an 'undertaking'. 'Control' is defined as:

> *"The ability to direct the financial and operating policies of an entity with a view to gaining economic benefits from its activities."*
> [FRS 8 para 2.2].

35.19 This appears to have the effect that control exists, for the purpose of FRS 8, where, for example, another company or an individual holds more than half a company's voting rights, whether or not that voting power is *actually* used to direct the company's policies. There must also be some potential economic benefit for the controlling party as a result of this direction. For instance, venture capitalists with 50 per cent or more of the shares with voting rights in a company will have 'control' of that company. Another example where control would exist would be where a company or individual has less than 50 per cent of voting rights, but actually exercises dominant influence over a company with or without the agreement of the other shareholders.

35.20 The definition of control encompasses control by individuals and, for example, partnerships, as well as parent companies. An example of control by a partnership would be where a limited partnership controls over 50 per cent of the voting rights in a reporting entity. This is discussed further in paragraph 35.105. The question of control in relation to a trust is discussed from paragraph 35.104.

35.21 Where control exists, even though no transactions have taken place, the disclosure required by FRS 8 may go further than that required by the 1985 Act. Schedule 5 to the 1985 Act requires disclosure of the ultimate parent company. In addition, under Schedule 7 the reporting entity must disclose the shareholdings of its directors, including shares held by their spouses and minor children (see para 35.176). These matters are illustrated by the following examples.

Example 1

Mr X, director of a family company, is a trustee of a trust which has controlling interest in the company's shares. The shares are held in trust for the director's infant children. He does not want the children to be named as controlling parties, for example, for security reasons. Schedule 7 of the Act requires directors' share interests in his company to be disclosed in the directors' report. These are deemed by section 328 to include the share interests of his minor children. Therefore, the controlling party for FRS 8 purposes could be described as the family interests of Mr X.

Example 2

A young businessman who is a director of a company might be influenced by his father. This would make the father a related party of the reporting entity and any transactions with the father would need to be disclosed, if material. If the father owns the majority of the shares he would also be a controlling shareholder. This is on the grounds that, as controlling shareholder, he directs, or has the ability to direct, the undertaking's financial or operating policies with a view to gaining economic benefits from its activities. Therefore, disclosure of control would be required, even if in practice he did not actively control the company.

35.22 Bearer shares cannot be issued to avoid disclosure of the controlling party. In addition to creating an auditing problem, it is difficult to see how this would be effective where the directors in practice know for whom they are working and to whom dividends are paid.

Common control

35.23 Entities subject to common control from the same source are included in the definition of a related party, because of the potential effect on transactions between them and on their financial position. Common control arises, for example, when two entities are subject to common control by an individual. Common control is also deemed to exist when both parties are subject to control from boards having a controlling nucleus of directors in common (for an example see para 35.28).

Influence

35.24 'Influence' as used in the definition of related party in paragraph 35.16 is where one party has influence over the financial and operating policies of another party to the extent that the other party *might* be inhibited from pursuing at all times its own separate interests. The difference between control and influence is that control involves the ability of the party that exercises control to cause the controlled party to subordinate its separate interests (that is, to possibly disregard its own interests in favour of those of the other party), whereas the effect of influence is less certain.

Common influence

35.25 Where the parties that enter into a transaction are subject to influence from the same source (that is, common influence) to the extent that one of the parties to the transaction has put its own separate interests after those of the other party (that is, has subordinated them), they are deemed to be related parties. The requirement for one of the parties to have subordinated its separate interests was considered necessary by the ASB otherwise a subsidiary in a large group, not qualifying for exemption, might not be aware that it had had transactions with a related party which was an associate of the group. Thus, in the absence of common control, two related parties of a third entity are not necessarily related parties of each other. Examples of arrangements that do *not* necessarily create related party relationships are given below:

- Where one party, B, is subject to control from A, and the other party, C, is subject only to influence from the same source, A, the two parties, B and C, are not necessarily related parties of each other. Since C is subject only to influence rather than control, the relationship between B and C would not normally justify being treated as related parties of each other (see diagram on page 35009).

- Entities are not related parties of each other if their only connection is by being associated companies of the same investor. The parties are subject only to influence (rather than common control) and that relationship is normally too tenuous to justify them being treated as related parties of each other.

- Two entities are not related parties simply because they have a director in common (see diagram on page 35009).

However, FRS 8 states that in all circumstances it will be appropriate to consider whether one or both transacting parties, subject to control and influence from the same source or to common influence, has put its own interests after those of the other parties in entering into that transaction. If either has, they will be related parties for the financial year and disclosure will be required of that transaction and all other transactions undertaken in the year.

Establishing influence and common influence

35.26 FRS 8 requires disclosure of transactions between parties where the relationship results from *influence* (as defined in para 2.5(a)(iii) of FRS 8). It is sometimes not clear whether one party influences another party to the extent that it might be inhibited from pursuing at all times its own separate interests. Our view is that the fact that one party has the right or power to inhibit the other is sufficient. It does not have to use this power or to prevent the other at all times from pursuing its own interests. Where one party has the ability to influence the other at any time during the financial period, transactions between them for the whole year become disclosable.

35.27 Where, on the other hand, two parties are subject to *common influence* (as defined in para 2.5(a)(iv) of FRS 8), transactions between those two parties become disclosable only where influence is actually exerted. It must have been exerted so that one or both transacting parties have subordinated their own separate interests in entering into a transaction. It is necessary to look at the facts of each transaction to assess whether there has been subordination of a party's own separate interests (that is, placing its own interests after those of others). Transactions where the price is above or below the commercial rate would generally mean a subordination; but it also might arise if one party is obliged to contract with a particular party or for a particular purpose, as that party would not have bargained knowledgeably and freely, unaffected by any relationship between the parties. Where two associated companies are directed to transact business with each other, this could mean a subordination of their separate interests.

35.28 Illustrations of these related party relationships, for instance, where A and B, and A and C, are related parties and B sells goods to C, can be shown diagrammatically as follows:

Common control

Control is the ability to direct the financial and operating policies gaining economic benefits from its activities.

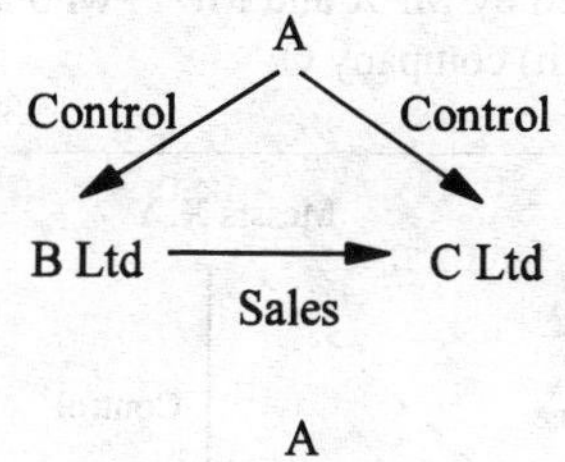

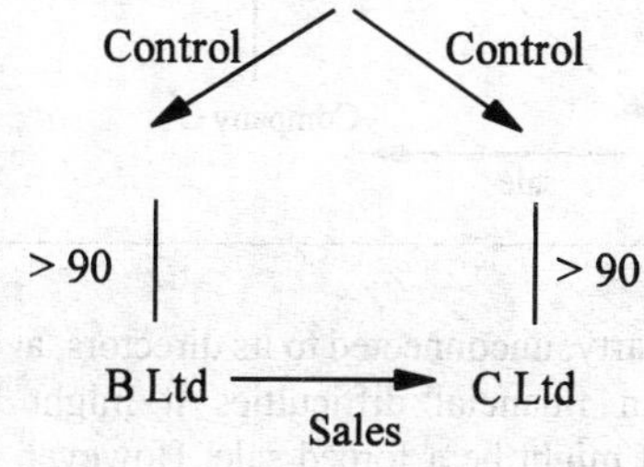

Common influence

Influence exists where B or C might be inhibited from pursuing at all times their own separate interests.

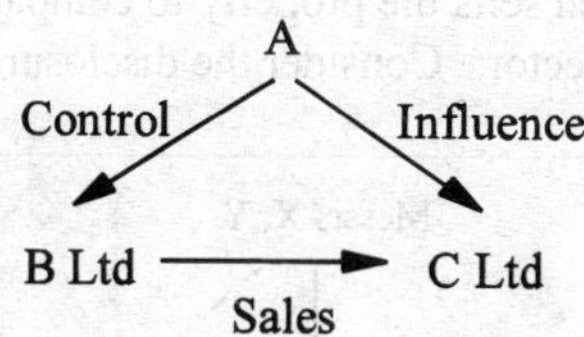

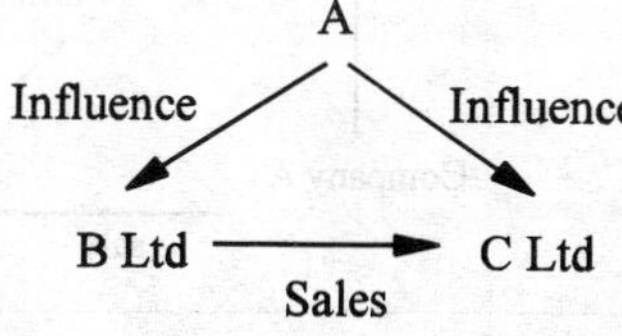

Controlling nucleus of directors in common

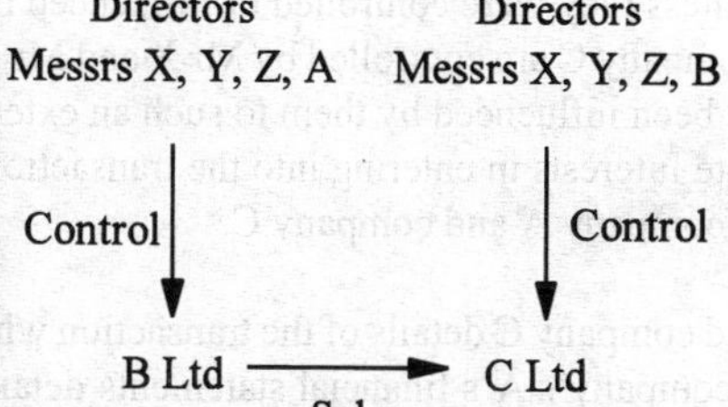

B and C are related parties in the above examples.

One director in common

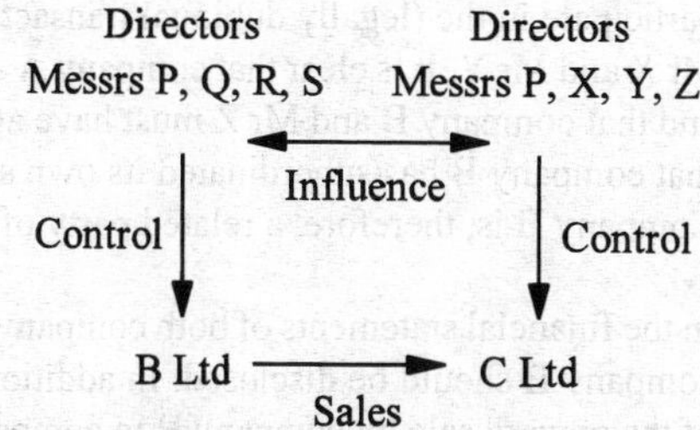

B and C are not related parties unless eith B or C or both have put their own separat interests after the other's in entering into sales transaction.

Examples of control or influence from same source

35.29 Transactions between parties subject to control or influence from the same source will be caught by the standard's disclosure requirements (see below).

Example

Company A is owned by Mr X and Mr Y who are its only directors and the company is in financial difficulties. Company A sells a property with a book value of £100,000 to company B, which is owned by Mr Z who is also B's sole director, for £50,000. Company B then sells the property to company C which is also owned by Mr X and Mr Y, who are its directors. Consider the disclosure in (i) company A and (ii) company C.

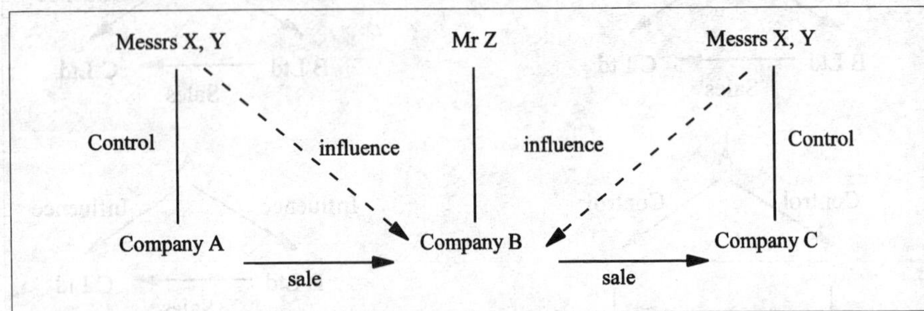

Company A has ostensibly sold a property to a third party, unconnected to its directors, at an undervalue. On the basis that the company is in financial difficulties it might be understandable that the sale is at an undervalue as it might be a forced sale. However, as company B makes neither profit or loss on the deal and appears to be an agent or intermediary for the transfer from A to C, it is very probable that Mr Z and company B are related parties of both A and C. This is because company B and Mr Z are unlikely to have agreed to participate in the (legally dubious) transaction unless they were controlled or influenced by Mr X and Mr Y. It is clear that company A and company C are controlled by Mr X and Mr Y and that company B and Mr Z must have at least been influenced by them to such an extent that company B has subordinated its own separate interests in entering into the transaction. Company B is, therefore, a related party of both company A and company C.

In the financial statements of both company A and company C details of the transaction with company B should be disclosed. In addition, in company's A's financial statements details of the onward sale by company B to company C should be disclosed with details of the fact that company C has the same shareholders and directors as company A. Similarly, in company C's financial statements, additional details of the sale by company A to company B should be disclosed, with disclosure also of the fact that company A is under common control with company C. This would be because the standard requires disclosure of *"any other elements of the transactions necessary for an understanding of the financial statements"*.

In practice, the directors and shareholders of company A and company C may, if the transaction is dubious, be very reluctant to disclose details and it may be for the auditors first to detect and then to insist on disclosure of the transactions. If Mr Z was close family o

Mr X or Mr Y, for instance his brother, the fact that Mr Z could be influenced by his brother in dealings with the reporting entities would mean that company B was a related party of both company A and company C, due to the fact that they are under the common control of Mr X and Mr Y. The gathering of audit evidence relating to close family could, however, be difficult for auditors who may sometimes need to make inquiries into private lives.

Effect of the group being the reporting entity

35.29.1 Group undertakings will all be presumed to be related to each other (see para 35.31), but their inter-group transactions are not required to be disclosed under FRS 8 at group level as they will be eliminated on consolidation (see para 35.141). They will also be exempt from disclosure in the parent's own financial statements if those financial statements are presented together with its consolidated financial statements (see para 35.143), and at subsidiary company level if the exemption for 90 per cent subsidiaries applies (see para 35.144).

35.29.2 On the other hand, transactions between a subsidiary undertaking and its related parties outside the group may be disclosable at group level if material even if not disclosable in the subsidiary's financial statements. For instance, an associate of a subsidiary undertaking will also be an associate of the group and transactions between the associate and the group will be disclosable at group level if material to the group. However, if FRS 8 paragraph 3(c) applies, any transactions between the subsidiary and the associate will be exempt from disclosure in the subsidiary's financial statements (see para 35.130). In addition, a director of a subsidiary would be a related party of the group if he came within the definition of key management of the group. Material transactions between him and the subsidiary would be disclosable at both company and group level.

[The next paragraph is 35.30.]

Related parties which are specified by FRS 8

35.30 The criteria referred to above are amplified in the FRS by two lists giving examples of related parties of the reporting entity. As has been mentioned, the reporting entity will either be the individual entity or the group in the case of consolidated financial statements. The related parties of a company may also be the related parties of the group.

35.30.1 The first list gives examples of parties that *are* related parties (because control or influence is deemed to exist) and the other list gives examples of parties that are *presumed* to be related parties because influence is presumed to exist in certain circumstances. Additionally, parties 'connected' to individual related parties may also be related parties of the reporting entity. However, the examples in the two lists and their connected parties are *not* intended to be exhaustive. These listings are considered in the paragraphs that follow.

[The next paragraph is 35.31.]

Parties deemed to be related

35.31 The first list of related parties set out in FRS 8 includes parties that control or are controlled by the reporting entity or that are under control from the same source as it. The term 'reporting entity' should be read as referring to the individual undertaking where individual financial statements are being prepared and to the group where consolidated financial statements are being prepared. FRS 8 states that, for the avoidance of doubt, the following *are* related parties of the reporting entity:

- Its ultimate and intermediate parent undertakings, subsidiary undertakings, and fellow subsidiary undertakings.
- Its associates and joint ventures.
- The investor or venturer in respect of which the reporting entity is an associate or a joint venture.
- Directors of the reporting entity and the directors of its ultimate and intermediate parent undertakings.
- Pension funds for the benefit of employees of the reporting entity or of any entity that is a related party of the reporting entity.

Each of these related parties is discussed in turn in the paragraphs below.

Parent, subsidiary and fellow subsidiary undertakings

35.32 The ultimate and intermediate parent undertakings, subsidiary undertakings and fellow subsidiary undertakings of the reporting entity are its related parties.

35.33 There is no definition of parent undertaking and subsidiary undertaking in the FRS, but it is reasonable to assume that the terms have the same meaning as in paragraph 14 of FRS 2, which in turn is based on section 258 of the Act. It should be noted that the definition refers to undertakings, not just companies. Entities in a group, whether unincorporated or incorporated, will be related parties.

Associates and joint ventures

35.34 A reporting entity's associates and joint ventures are its related parties. [FRS 8 para 2.5(a)]. Again, it is reasonable to assume, that the definitions in FRS 9 and paragraph 20 of Schedule 4A to the Act regarding associated undertakings would apply. Broadly, an associate is an undertaking (which is not a subsidiary undertaking or a joint venture) in which the investing company has 20 per cent or more of its voting rights and exercises a significant influence over its operating and financial policy. For an example of disclosure see Table 35.7 on page 35044. FRS 9 which applies to accounting periods ending on or after 23 June 1998, however, states that the 20 per cent holding must be held on a long-term basis and be a beneficial interest. The Act presumes that where an investor holds more than 20 per cent of the shares in an undertaking that this is a participating interest and, as a consequence, an associate relationship exists. However, under FRS 9's definition of an associate, the Act's presumption can be rebutted when the investor does not in practice have significant influence over the undertaking. See further chapter 28.

35.35 A joint venture, on the other hand, is an undertaking that the investing company manages jointly with other investors. [4A Sch 19]. Under FRS 9 a joint venture is defined as:

> *"An entity in which the reporting entity holds an interest on a long-term basis and is jointly controlled by the reporting entity and one or more other ventures under a contractual arrangement."* [FRS 9 para 4].

Investors and venturers

35.36 An investor or venturer in respect of which the reporting entity is an associate or a joint venture is a related party of that reporting entity. For an example of disclosure of joint venture agreements see Table 35.7 on page 35044 and Table 35.4 on page 35035.

35.37 There is nothing in the FRS to suggest that the venturers or investors in the same undertaking are themselves related parties by reason of their joint venture or investment.

Example 1

This situation may be illustrated by the following example in which D is a related party of each of A, B and C as it is an associate of these. A sells goods to B, and C provides services to B.

[The next page is 35013.]

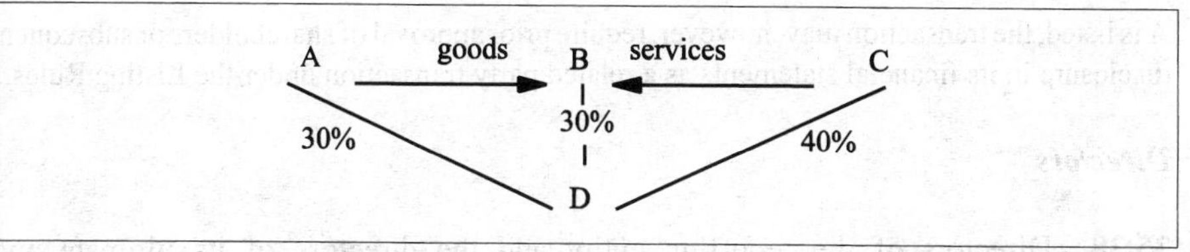

A, B and C are also each related parties of D, but not of each other. Consequently, the transactions between A and B and between C and B would not be disclosable.

Example 2

Company A owns 70% of the shares in company B which it consolidates. Company X owns the remaining 30% of the shares in company B. Company B sells a large property to company X at its market value established by outside valuation. Company X, being an investor in company B, is a related party of company B. Company B will, therefore, have to disclose details of the transaction in its financial statements, including any other elements of the transaction necessary for an understanding of the financial statements. As the sale is to a minority interest, such an element would include an indication that the property was sold at its market value.

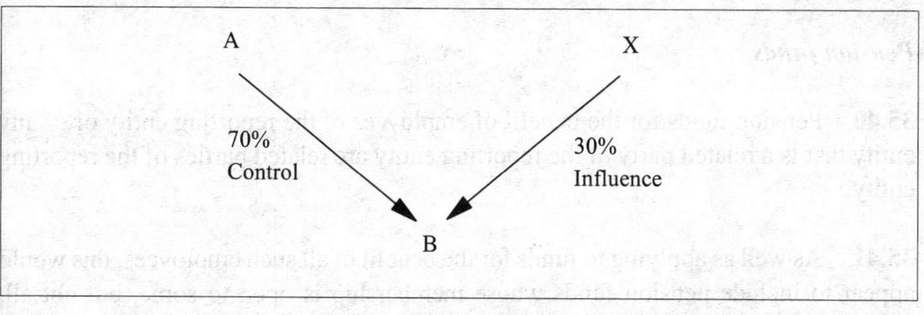

The question also arises whether company X is a related party of company A's group for the purpose of disclosing the transaction in the group's consolidated financial statements. However, the fact that company A and company X have an investment in the same company, company B, does not by itself make company A and company X related parties of each other as there would appear to be no related party relationship between them. [FRS 8 para 12]. Company A's *group* and company X will be related parties of each other only if they fall within the definition of related parties in FRS 8 paragraph 2.5(a), that is, if there is the necessary control or influence.

For instance, if company A's group was influenced by company X such that company X persuaded company A's group to dispose of the property to company X at below its market value (that is, company X exerted influence over company A), they would be related parties because company A subordinated its interests in entering into the transaction. This is a question of fact, but as the transaction was at market value, the question of one party having subordinated its interests is unlikely. Consequently, in this situation company A and company X would not be related parties and no disclosure would be necessary under FRS 8. If company

A is listed, the transaction may, however, require prior approval of shareholders or subsequent disclosure in its financial statements as a related party transaction under the Listing Rules.

Directors

35.38 Directors of the reporting entity and the directors of its ultimate and intermediate parent undertakings are its related parties.

35.39 The FRS states that directors include 'shadow directors'. 'Shadow directors' are defined in section 741 of the Act as *"persons in accordance with whose directions and instructions the directors of the company are accustomed to act"*. It should be noted, however, that, as for the disclosures required by Schedule 6 to the Act, directors of subsidiary undertakings as such are not related parties and transactions with them are not required to be disclosed. However, under the Listing Rules, a transaction between a company and a director of a subsidiary undertaking would be a transaction with a related party. Under the FRS, such directors may, however, be related parties through control or influence, for instance through shareholdings, or, possibly, by being key management either of the individual reporting entity or the group, but not because they are merely directors of the subsidiary.

Pension funds

35.40 Pension funds for the benefit of employees of the reporting entity or of any entity that is a related party of the reporting entity are related parties of the reporting entity.

35.41 As well as applying to funds for the benefit of all such employees, this would appear to include pension funds whose membership is open to some, but not all, employees, for instance, those open to directors and senior managers only. On the other hand, it is understood that industry-wide pension schemes would not be regarded as related parties of a reporting entity under this definition. The fact that pension funds are related parties is not intended to call into question the independence of the trustees of the scheme. Transactions between the reporting entity and the pension fund may be in the interest of members but nevertheless need to be reported in the reporting entity's financial statements. [FRS 8 para 15].

35.42 'Pension fund' may need to be interpreted widely to include funds maintained by employers to pay pensions to employees disabled at work. An example of this may be seen in Table 35.6 on page 35041.

Pension funds and their investment manager

35.43 The investment manager for a pension fund is a related party of the pension fund. Paragraph 2.67 of the SORP for pension scheme accounts states that:

> *"Entities engaged by the trustees to manage the pension scheme or its assets, including any scheme administrator or investment managers, should be presumed to be related parties."*

35.44 However, the employer would not be a related party of the fund's investment managers by reason only of the investment managers acting for the fund. But if the company paid the investment managers' fees, this would, if material, be disclosable by the company as a related party transaction on behalf of the fund (because the fund is a related party of the company under FRS 8). See Table 35.1 below, Table 35.3 on page 35019, Table 35.4 on page 35035, and para (c) of Table 35.5 on page 35037.

Table 35.1 – The Burton Group plc – Annual report and accounts – 30 August 1997

Notes to the accounts (extract)

25 Related party transactions

The Group recharges the Burton Group Pension Schemes with the costs of administration and independent advisors borne by the Group. The total amount recharged in the period to 30 August 1997 was £1.9 million (1996 – £1.8 million).

Parties presumed to be related

35.45 The second list of parties related because of the existence of influence is reproduced below and comprises parties that *are presumed* to be related parties unless it can be demonstrated that neither party has influenced the financial and operating policies of the other in such a way as to inhibit the pursuit of separate interests:

- The key management of the reporting entity and key management of its parent undertaking or undertakings (see para 35.48, 35.48).
- A person owning or able to exercise control over 20 per cent or more of the reporting entity's voting rights, whether directly or through nominees.
- Each person acting in concert in such a way as to be able to exercise control or influence over the reporting entity (see para 35.51).
- An entity managing or managed by the reporting entity under a management contract.

[FRS 8 para 2.5(c)].

- Persons connected to an individual related party (see para 35.55). [FRS 8 para 2.5(d)].

35.46 The presumption that such parties are related will, therefore, apply unless it can be demonstrated otherwise. The reporting entity will have to produce the necessary evidence to rebut the presumption and may need evidence from the other party if its own evidence is inadequate.

35.47 As an example, the rebuttable presumption acknowledges that, whilst, in general, shareholders holding 20 per cent of the voting rights would have the required level of influence to make them related parties, this is not necessarily the case. For instance, a shareholder may not actively associate himself with the company because he lives abroad and is not involved in the business world. He would be presumed to be a related party unless it could be demonstrated that he had not influenced the company's financial and operating policies so as to inhibit the pursuit of separate interests.

Key management

35.48 The term 'key management' is defined in the standard as follows:

> *"Key management are those persons in senior positions having authority or responsibility for directing or controlling the major activities and resources of the reporting entity."* [FRS 8 para 2.3].

35.49 It is not entirely clear who the ASB intends to catch by this definition as the people who have the authority and responsibility mentioned would normally be directors. However, the ASB's intention must be to catch more than just directors and shadow directors of the reporting entity or its parent, otherwise it would not have included an additional definition. We have assumed, therefore, that the definition covers people who are not appointed directors, but whose activities appear to encompass duties normally carried out by directors or who report directly to the board. We have also assumed that it will catch people who have responsibilities for the administration or direction of reporting entities, such as trusts, which are not incorporated.

35.50 As a reporting entity can be a group as well as an individual entity, key management must also be considered in relation to directing or controlling the group's resources. Whilst the term 'key management' could include a divisional director or the director of a subsidiary, such a person would need to direct or control a major part of the activities and resources of the group or the company.

Persons acting in concert

35.51 The term 'persons acting in concert' used in paragraph 35.45 above is defined in the standard to mean:

> *"Persons who, pursuant to an agreement or understanding (whether formal or informal), actively co-operate, whether by the ownership by any of them of shares in an undertaking or otherwise, to exercise control or influence over that undertaking."* [FRS 8 para 2.4].

35.52 The FRS states that 'influence' means influence over the financial and operating policies of the other party to an extent that that other party *might* be inhibited from pursuing at all times its own separate interests. Each person acting in concert will be a related party.

35.53 The question arises whether a small group of shareholders constitutes a concert party and, therefore, potentially a controlling party. For example, the shares in a company might be held by a husband and wife or two (or three or four etc) brothers, or two or more parties in a normal joint venture. In the absence of one party influencing the other(s) in a 'close family' context (for instance, they are husband and wife) the fact that they co-operate or vote the same way would not make them concert parties. They would just be shareholders working in the normal way for their collective benefit. We consider that acting in concert must mean more than this, that is, it must relate to a sub-group of the total shareholder base who, for example, meet and agree a common line before meetings of the board or shareholders. However, from an auditing perspective it might be presumed that, for example, members of the same household act in concert unless it can be demonstrated they do not.

Management contracts

35.54 Entities managing or managed by the reporting entity under a management contract are presumed to be related parties unless it can be shown that neither influenced the financial and operating policies of the other in such a way as to inhibit the pursuit of separate interests. Investment managers that manage a fund are likely to be related parties to the fund. For instance, a unit trust or investment trust is managed under a management contract. The managers are likely to have the required influence, because the unit trust has no separate voice and they effectively decide upon and manage all its investment activities. Consequently, the manager will be a related party. See Table 35.2 below and Table 35.9 on page 35048 for an example of disclosure.

Table 35.2 – The Scottish Mortgage & Trust PLC – Annual Report and Accounts – 31 March 1997

Notes to the accounts (extract)

3	INVESTMENT MANAGEMENT FEE – *all charged to revenue*		
	Investment management fee	3,415	3,125
	Irrecoverable VAT thereon	450	411
		3,865	3,536

Baillie Gifford & Co are employed by the Company as Managers and Secretaries under a management agreement which is normally terminable on not less than twelve months notice. For the year to 31 March 1997 Baillie Gifford & Co's annual remuneration was calculated at 0.05% of shareholders' funds per quarter plus 9.00% per annum of earnings attributable to shareholders for the preceding year, and is subject to VAT at the appropriate rate. The capital component of the fee is levied on all assets, including holdings in unit trusts managed by Baillie Gifford & Co. However, in respect of such holdings the Company is rebated the fees charged within the unit trusts. The investment management fee above is shown after crediting such rebates, which amounted to £833,000 (1996-£606,000).

Persons connected to a related party

35.55 In addition, FRS 8 also catches persons (including individuals, companies and other entities) who are connected to a related party. Because of their relationship with certain parties that are, or are presumed to be, related parties of a reporting entity, the following are also *presumed* to be related parties of the reporting entity:

- Members of the close family of any individual who is, or is presumed to be, a related party.
- Partnerships, companies, trusts or other entities in which any individual, or member of the close family of any individual who is or is presumed to be a related party, has a controlling interest.

[FRS 8 para 2.5(d)].

35.56 A party falling into one of the categories in paragraph 35.55 will be presumed to be a related party of the reporting entity. For instance, a company controlled by a director of the reporting entity would be its related party. See Table 35.3 below and Table 35.9, sub-note 6 on page 35048 and for examples of disclosure.

Table 35.3 – The Rank Group Plc – Annual Report and Accounts – 31 December 1996

Notes to the Accounts (extract)

32 RELATED PARTY TRANSACTIONS

The Group recharges The Rank Group UK Pension Schemes with the costs of administration and independent advisers borne by the Group. The total amount recharged in the year ended 31 December 1996 was £1,112,000 (1995 £1,016,000).

In December 1996 the Group sold the Shearings businesses (UK and continental coach holidays and UK holiday hotels) for a consideration of £75 million to Shearings Group Limited, a new company formed by NatWest Ventures Limited, and Shearings' management team. Mr.H.A. Crichton-Miller was a Director of The Rank Organisation Plc until 11 July 1996 and became a Director of Shearings Group Limited on 18 December 1996.

Close family

35.57 The term 'close family' used in paragraph 35.55 above is defined in the standard as follows:

> *"Close members of the family of an individual are those family members, or members of the same household, who may be expected to influence, or be influenced by, that person in their dealings with the reporting entity."* [FRS 8 para 2.1].

35.58 This definition will apply to make close family of directors, key managers and other individual related parties, themselves related parties of the reporting entity, but only where influence can be expected to exist. The definition can be compared with the similar provisions of the Act and the Listing Rules. The disclosure requirements of Part II of Schedule 6 to the Act apply to transactions involving directors of the reporting company or of its holding company and their 'connected persons', encompassing their spouses and children under 18 (including step-children and illegitimate children). Under the Listing Rules, 'family' in relation to a related party is defined to be the same. However, whereas Schedule 6 only covers directors of the reporting company and its holding company, related parties under the Listing Rules include directors of subsidiary, parent and fellow subsidiary undertakings and individual shareholders holding at least ten per cent of the voting rights.

35.59 'Close family' under the FRS, not being limited to spouses and minor children, catches a wider range of family members. Such family could include, for example, brother, adult child, parent and mother-in-law. In addition, the definition extends to members of the same household as the related party (for example, a co-habitee).

Partnerships, companies, trusts or other entities

35.60 The words 'controlling interest' are not themselves defined, but can be interpreted to mean an interest that gives, or results from, 'control', as defined. Consequently, it seems that to have a 'controlling interest' the individual related party must have an interest enabling him to direct the financial and operating policies of an undertaking and obtain economic benefits as a result of that direction.

35.61 The following is an example in diagrammatic form of a situation where a trust may be a related party because of the existence of a controlling interest and the influence that brings.

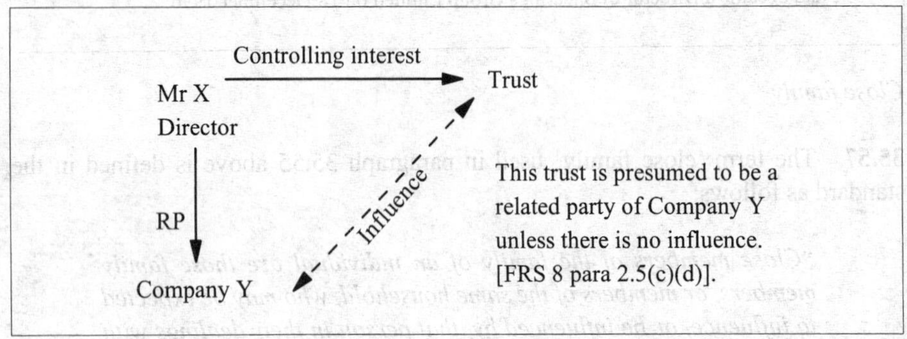

35.62 In this situation, one or more directors of a reporting entity has a controlling interest in a trust. The trust would, it seems, be presumed to be a related party of the reporting entity by virtue of its relationship with the directors. This interpretation would, for example, mean that where directors of the sponsoring company have a controlling interest in an employee share trust, the trust would generally be a related party under these provisions. Control in relation to a trust is discussed in paragraph 35.97.

Identification of related parties

35.63 The extent of the definition of related parties may give rise to difficulties regarding identifying related parties and transactions with them. As part of their corporate governance responsibilities directors will, therefore, need to ensure that the reporting entity has adequate accounting and internal control systems to enable them to give the appropriate related party disclosures in their financial statements. Directors will also need to satisfy their auditors that the information identifying material related parties and transactions with them is complete. The implications for directors are discussed further from paragraph 35.82.

Related party transactions

Definition of related party transactions

35.64 A 'related party transaction' is defined in FRS 8 as follows:

> *"The transfer of assets or liabilities or the performance of services by, to or for a related party irrespective of whether a price is charged."* [FRS 8 para 2.6].

Related party transactions specified by FRS 8

35.65 The following are examples of related party transactions that require disclosure by a reporting entity in the period in which they occur:

- Purchases or sales of goods (finished or unfinished).
- Purchases or sales of property and other assets.
- Rendering or receiving of services.
- Agency arrangements (see para 35.67).
- Leasing arrangements.
- Transfer of research and development.
- Licence agreements.
- Provision of finance (including loans and equity contributions in cash or in kind) (see Table 35.6 on page 35041).
- Guarantees and the provision of collateral security.
- Management contracts (see para 35.54).

[FRS 8 para 19].

It is clear that the definition of related party transaction is very wide ranging and that these are just examples, not a definitive list.

35.66 The definition envisages that some related party transactions might not be entered into a company's accounting records or might not involve any consideration passing. Examples of such transactions are:

- Management services provided by one company to another free of charge.
- Goods manufactured under a patent owned by a fellow subsidiary which makes no charge.
- Guarantees to third parties in respect of other group companies; interest free loans (the principal would be entered into the accounting records, but no interest would be). See paragraph 35.135 for guarantees by directors.

- Rent free accommodation or the loan of vehicles or other assets at no charge.
- Reporting entities' information systems must, therefore, be able to capture data that may not be in the accounting records for disclosure as related party transactions.

Agency arrangements

35.67 The standard specifically states that agency arrangements are disclosable. So, where a related party performs services as agent for the reporting entity, or the reporting entity performs services as agent for a related party, there is a related party transaction to disclose even where no commission is charged. For instance, if a company controlled by a director of the reporting entity paid the reporting entity's suppliers on its behalf and was reimbursed by it, these payments are likely to constitute agency arrangements which should be disclosed if material. If the reporting entity made the payment to the agency company before it settled the invoices, the arrangement could constitute a loan to a director.

35.68 Furthermore, section 234(2) of the 1985 Act requires the directors' report to state the principal activities of a company during the year. Consequently, disclosure of the fact that the reporting entity acts as agent will be required if this is one of the principal activities of the agency company.

35.69 Transactions entered into by the agents on behalf of their principals during the year under the agency arrangements and any balances with the principal are, therefore, disclosable. However, certain transactions and balances entered into by an agent with its principal may come within the exemptions from disclosure. For instance, the standard does not require disclosure of transactions and balances in the agent's financial statements if the agent is a subsidiary of its principal and comes within the exception for 90 per cent subsidiaries (see para 35.144).

35.70 A parent company preparing consolidated financial statements does not have to show in those financial statements transactions or balances with its agent that have been eliminated on consolidation (see para 35.141). If the third parties with whom the principal has contracted, via the agency, are themselves its related parties (for instance, the third parties and the principal are under common control), these transactions will also fall to be disclosed in the principal's financial statements as related party transactions, unless they are themselves exempted.

35.71 An example of the disclosure of agency arrangements can be found in Table 35.3 on page 35035.

Materiality

35.72 As noted above, earlier proposals concerning related party disclosures were for disclosure of *abnormal* transactions with related parties. FRS 8 in contrast calls for disclosure of *all* transactions with related parties provided that they are *material*. The principal reason for this is that it would be very difficult in practice to define what is normal and what is abnormal. Because potentially all related party transactions are disclosable, the interpretation of what is material in this context is particularly important.

35.73 The FRS defines 'material' in the following way::

> *"Transactions are material when their disclosure might reasonably be expected to influence decisions made by the users of general purpose financial statements."* [FRS 8 para 20].

Whilst this does not explicitly say *"only disclose transactions that are abnormal"*, it does appear to exempt from disclosure those transactions that would be of no interest to users. For example, a director buying a chocolate bar in the staff canteen is not of interest, but the director or his close family buying a six-bedroom house from the company for £25,000 certainly would be. Where the director bought a house from the company at its market value, the situation, interpreted by reference only to the above, requires further consideration.

35.74 The FRS, however, goes on to provide that:

> *"The materiality of related party transactions is to be judged, not only in terms of their significance to the reporting entity, but also in relation to their significance to the other related party when that party is:*
>
> *(a) a director, key manager or other individual in a position to influence, or accountable for stewardship of, the reporting entity; or*
>
> *(b) a member of the close family of any individual mentioned in (a) above; or*
>
> *(c) an entity controlled by any individual mentioned in (a) or (b) above."*
>
> [FRS 8 para 20].

35.75 The FRS explains that these words address the perspective that needs to be considered when a related party transaction has been undertaken directly or indirectly with an individual who is in a position to influence, or accountable for stewardship of, the reporting entity. [FRS 8 app IV para 19]. Consequently, in the examples given above, not only the significance to the company, but the transaction's significance to the director would need to be considered in order to form a judgement as to whether the transaction involving the purchase of the house was material. The transaction could be small to the company, but a major investment for the director. We believe the intention of the FRS is that transactions of the type and size shown in the example in paragraph 35.73, that is, the purchase of a house at market value, would be regarded as material to the director and, therefore, disclosable.

35.76 Although it is clear that the purchase of a house is material from the director's point of view and that the purchase of a chocolate bar is not, there will in practice be a number of transactions in between these two extremes whose materiality is borderline. It is not possible to be definitive about how materiality should be established, as much will depend on the facts of each case. However, at the margin, a transaction being at arm's length and on normal commercial terms would contribute to its being regarded as immaterial. Equally, a transaction that is on terms advantageous to the director would contribute to its being regarded as material and, therefore, disclosable.

General purpose financial statements

35.77 The definition of 'materiality' refers to users of general purpose financial statements. These are described in the introduction to the exposure draft, 'Statement of principles for financial reporting', issued by the ASB. The introduction says that general purpose financial statements are directed towards the common information needs of a wide range of users. Chapter one of the statement lists users as including present and potential investors, employees, lenders, suppliers and other trade creditors, customers, governments and their agencies and the public, and sets out some of their different needs.

35.78 Chapter one of the statement acknowledges that the information needs of all types of users mentioned above cannot be met by general purpose financial statements, but that there are needs that are common to all users. All users have some interest in the financial position, performance and financial adaptability of the reporting entity as a whole. Hence, when considering whether disclosure of a particular related party transaction is 'material', the interest of a wide range of users in information on such matters should be considered.

Comparison with 'materiality' under the Companies Act 1985

35.79 Under Part II of Schedule 6 to the Act, disclosure must be made of transactions in which a director has a material interest. In this context, an interest will not be material if the board of directors has honestly and reasonably concluded that it is not material. Two tests for deciding what is material have been suggested, which are discussed in paragraph 35.173.

35.80 The criterion in the FRS for determining materiality of transactions with related parties is expressed not only in terms of their significance to the reporting entity, but also in relation to their significance to the director or other individual related party.

35.81 However, the FRS contains no specific exemption similar to the exemption in paragraph 20 of Schedule 6 (see para 35.174) for material transactions with directors that are in the ordinary course of the company's business and at arm's length. As a result, it is likely to result in greater disclosure of transactions with directors as it is fair to assume that even relatively small transactions between directors (or their close family) and the company might be regarded as material, as described above. In addition, if a director enters into several small transactions in a financial year, they will need to be aggregated. If these transactions are material when aggregated, then they will need to be disclosed in accordance with the FRS.

Practical implications for directors

35.82 Inevitably, the wide definition of 'related parties' is likely to cause difficulties and directors should be implementing new procedures to identify related parties and related party transactions. The auditing standard, SAS 460, describes some of the problems facing directors as stemming from the fact that it may not always be self-evident to management whether a party is related. Furthermore, it says that many accounting systems are not designed to either distinguish or summarise related party transactions and that management may have to carry out additional analysis of the accounting records to identify related party transactions. [SAS 460 para 6].

35.83 The SAS points out that directors are responsible for the identification, approval and disclosure of related party transactions in the financial statements. The responsibility for disclosure arises because companies legislation, accounting standards and the Listing Rules require certain related party transactions and control of the entity to be disclosed in the financial statements. The directors should implement adequate accounting and internal control systems to ensure that related parties and related party transactions are adequately identified in the accounting records and disclosed in the financial statements. [SAS 460 paras 14 and 19].

35.84 These systems may include formal policies and codes of conduct dealing with relationships with related parties which cover the approval, recording and reporting of related party transactions entered into, on behalf of the entity, by directors and employees. [SAS 460 para 20].

35.85 The following types of transactions may be evidence of the existence of related party relationships:

- Transactions with abnormal terms of trade, such as unusual prices, interest rates, guarantees and repayment terms (see para 35.138 example 1 and para 35.137).

- Transactions that appear to lack a logical business reason for their occurrence (see para 35.29).

- Transactions in which substance differs from form (see the example in para 35.125).

- Transactions processed or approved in a non-routine manner or by personnel who do not ordinarily deal with such transactions.

- Unusual transactions that are entered into shortly before or after the end of the financial period (see the example in para 35.125)

- Transactions not recorded in the accounting records, such as the receipt or provision of management services at no charge (see para 35.66).

[SAS 460 para 27].

Auditors' involvement

35.86 The directors may be asked to give written representations to the auditors concerning the completeness of information on the related party and control disclosures in the financial statements. If the auditors are unable to obtain sufficient evidence of related parties, they may have to issue a qualified opinion, because of a limitation on the scope of their audit. If, however, they conclude that the disclosure of related party transactions or the controlling party is not adequate, they may have to issue a qualified opinion because of disagreement with the disclosure and include in the opinion section of their report, wherever practicable, the missing information. [SAS 460 para 37].

Disclosure requirements

Summary

35.87 Where a reporting entity's financial statements are intended to give a true and fair view the standard requires the following information to be disclosed in a reporting entity's financial statements about its related parties:

- The name of the party controlling the reporting entity and, if different, the name of the ultimate controlling party (whether or not any transactions have taken place).

- Details of material transactions between the reporting entity and any related parties.

- Details of balances due to, or from, related parties at the balance sheet date.

Disclosure of control

35.88 Where the reporting entity is controlled by another party, disclosure should be made of:

- the name of the controlling party; and
- if different, the name of the ultimate controlling party.

In both instances, the related party relationship should also be disclosed. [FRS 8 para 5].

35.89 These disclosures have to be made whether or not there have been any transactions between the parties. If the controlling party or ultimate controlling party of the reporting entity is not known, that fact should be disclosed. [FRS 8 para 5]. Disclosure is only required where there is control, as defined, and the above information is not required to be given where there is merely influence.

35.90 The explanation given in FRS 8 for requiring the disclosure of control is as follows. Where the reporting entity is controlled by another party, whether or not transactions have taken place with that party, the control relationship prevents the reporting entity from being independent, in the sense of being able to pursue its activities independently of the interests of its individual owners and others. The FRS sees identification of the controlling party as being important because it may establish the entity's standing in the business community, with consequent effects upon sources and types of products, and may affect the allegiance of the reporting entity's management. [FRS 8 para 18].

35.91 The controlling related party could be an individual, partnership or other entity. Alternatively, it could be a group of individuals or entities acting in concert if the individuals or entities, although each with small shareholdings, were able to control the entity by active co-operation.

35.92 The disclosure of the existence of control by a parent company is called for even if the reporting entity is a wholly-owned subsidiary. The exemption for 90 per cent subsidiaries that applies to the disclosure of transactions and balances with other group companies does not apply to disclosure of controlling relationships. However, in practice, this requirement is partially satisfied by the disclosure, currently required by Schedule 5 to the Act, which requires a company to give the name of the company regarded by its directors as its ultimate parent company.

Ultimate controlling party

35.93 If the party disclosed under Schedule 5 as the ultimate parent company is also the ultimate controlling party, the disclosure will need to make clear, for the purposes of the standard, that that company is also the ultimate controlling party and give the related party relationship.

35.94 However, where the ultimate parent company is itself controlled by, say, an individual or a trust, the ultimate controlling party would be that individual or trust. In this case, a higher level of control will fall for disclosure under FRS 8 than merely the Act's requirement to disclose the ultimate parent company. As a result, where a reporting entity is owned by, say, a German private company, the name of any controlling shareholder of the German private company will need to be given, even if not disclosed in the German company's financial statements, if this information is known to the reporting entity or its directors.

Source of control or ownership

35.95 Where no ultimate parent company has been disclosed, because the company is directly controlled by, say, an individual or a trust (rather than a parent company), disclosure of the identity of the controlling party and the nature of the relationship is required by the standard. Where the controlling party is a trust, it will be necessary to consider whether the trust itself is controlled by a person or persons who will, therefore, need to be disclosed as the ultimate controlling party (see also para 35.97). Where the controlling party or the ultimate controlling party is not known, this fact must be stated.

35.96 In special circumstances, section 231 of the Act permits a company to claim an exemption from disclosing information required by Schedule 5, including the identification of the ultimate parent company. Where a subsidiary carries on business outside the UK and, in the opinion of the directors, disclosure of the ultimate parent company would be seriously prejudicial to its business, the company can, with the consent of the Secretary of State, avoid the disclosure in its financial statements. It would seem unlikely that FRS 8 intends to require disclosure of the controlling party where specific permission for non-disclosure has been given by the Secretary of State. However, these situations are likely to be rare in practice.

Trusts

35.97 As has been mentioned previously, the definition of control comprises two elements:

- the ability to direct the financial and operating policies; and
- the ability to benefit from their direction.

Consequently, the question of establishing whether control exists is particularly difficult in relation to trusts. Trusteeship may be viewed as an example of where the two aspects of control are divided between two parties. The trustee has the power to deploy the trust assets: the beneficiary benefits from their deployment. In what may be called a pure trust, neither the trustee nor the beneficiary controls the trust. Not all vehicles created in the legal form of a trust will fall into the category of a pure trust and the rights and duties of the trustees and beneficiaries may be divided differently where the trust is not a pure trust. In fact, the UITF recently held that many employee share trusts were controlled by the sponsoring company, and FRS 5, 'Reporting the substance of transactions', also identifies trusts among the categories of entity that may qualify as quasi-subsidiaries, where they are in substance controlled by one party. In a pure trust, however, it is possible to argue that there is no controlling party of the trust, because neither the trustees nor the beneficiary have both elements of control. The question of whether or not control exists over a trust is one that will need particular care and scrutiny of the facts of each individual case.

35.98 Consequently, because of the above argument, where a 'pure trust' holds shares in the reporting entity it would follow that, other than disclosure of the trust as the controlling party, there would be no further requirement to disclose an ultimate controlling party.

35.99 However, many trusts may not be set up along the lines of a 'pure trust'. In these circumstances, there are difficulties in determining whether the trustees or any outside parties have control over the reporting entity through the trust for the purposes of establishing its ultimate controlling party. In the case of some trusts, trustees may be acting on occasions in accordance with the wishes of the settlor, the beneficiaries or the entity's directors or shadow directors. In others the settlor may have the power to appoint or remove trustees in certain circumstances, or the trustees may need to refer to the settlor before doing certain things. If these matters do not interfere with the general independence of the trustees, it may not be necessary to regard the existence of those rights as giving the settlor (or any other party, as the case may be) control over the trustees, or the trust, in the sense that control (as opposed to influence) is used in the standard. Alternatively, there may be no evidence of the trustees having given independent consideration to matters relevant to the reporting entity in the light of independent advice. These circumstances may point to trustees allowing outside parties, such as settlors or beneficiaries, in a position to do so, to exercise unfettered control. If they do exercise control, such parties would then need to be disclosed as the ultimate controlling party of the reporting entity.

35.100 As mentioned in paragraph 35.97, an ESOP trust is an example of a trust which a party other than the trustees will be deemed to control under FRS 5, 'Reporting the Substance of Transactions'. UITF Abstract 13, 'Accounting for ESOP Trusts', states:

> *"Although the trustees of an ESOP trust must act at all times in accordance with the interests of the beneficiaries under the trust, most ESOP trusts (particularly those established as a means of remunerating employees) are specifically designed to serve the purposes of the sponsoring company, and to ensure that there will be minimal risk of any conflict arising between the duties of the trustees and the interest of the company. Where this is so, the sponsoring company has de facto control and there will be nothing to encumber implementation of its wishes in practice."*

35.101 It would seem that similar reasoning can be applied to ascertaining the party, if any, to be disclosed as the controlling party of a trust for the purposes of FRS 8. That is, the controlling party is likely to be the party that both:

- has the ability to direct the trust, or ensure the implementation of its wishes concerning the trust's financial and operating policies; and
- derives the principal economic benefit, whether or not that party is a named beneficiary under the trust.

35.102 Where a party controls a trust that holds shares in the reporting entity, that party will need to be disclosed as the ultimate controlling party. The purpose for which a trust is established may, therefore, often indicate who the ultimate controlling party is, or whether there is one at all. For instance, where the reporting entity is a special purpose vehicle and a trust is established as a parent undertaking of the reporting entity as part of a securitisation, this will indicate that the trust and the reporting entity are probably controlled by one or other party to the securitisation.

35.103 Another complex situation would be where a director or other related party is a trustee of a trust that holds shares in the company (and the director or related party controls the trust), the shares held by the trust should be added to those held directly by the director for the purpose of establishing where control lies. Where a director or other related party – such as an adult or a minor child – is a beneficiary, but not a trustee, under a trust it would appear to be a question of establishing, on the facts of each case, whether the trustees administer the trust independently or whether the director or other related party control it.

Unit trusts

35.104 Although the unit trust SORP is silent on the requirements of FRS 8, we consider that it applies as the Securities and Investments Board (SIB) regulations require unit trust accounts to give a true and fair view. Consequently, unit trusts should disclose their controlling party. A unit trust will have a controlling party if a unit-holder or unit-holders acting in concert hold at least 75 per cent of the units (subject to certain regulatory restrictions on voting rights). This proportion effectively gives the unit-holders the ability to direct the financial and operating policies of a unit trust. If there is no such holding, the unit trust investment manager and the trustee acting in concert will be the controlling party, as together they will have the ability to exercise control over the unit trust. The ultimate controlling party in the former example would be the ultimate controlling party of the unit-holder(s), ad in the latter example would be the ultimate controlling party of the unit trust investment manager and trustee if they were members of the same group.

Limited partnerships

35.105 Where a limited partnership in the form of a managed fund controls over 50 per cent of the shares with voting rights in a reporting entity, the question arises as to who controls the reporting entity. The limited partnership holds the majority of the voting rights in the reporting entity and would control it. As the general partner has control of a limited partnership the general partner of the investing partnership would, it seems, be the reporting entity's controlling party. However, the general partner may, itself, have a parent undertaking or ultimate controlling party which it discloses in its financial statements. This would mean that the reporting entity would have to disclose that party as its ultimate controlling party.

Disclosure of transactions and balances

Material transactions

35.106 The FRS states that financial statements should disclose material transactions undertaken by the reporting entity with a related party. [FRS 8 para 6]. What is meant by material in this context is considered from paragraph 35.72. All *material* transactions, not just abnormal ones, must be disclosed. This is because the ASB considers that when transactions with related parties are material in aggregate, they are of interest whatever their nature. [FRS 8 app IV para 18]. This disclosure should be made irrespective of whether a price is charged. The information to be disclosed should include all the following:

- The names of the transacting related parties.
- A description of the relationship between the parties.
- A description of the transactions.

- The amounts involved.
- Any other elements of the transactions necessary for an understanding of the financial statements.

[FRS 8 para 6(a) to (e)].

35.107 FRS 8 gives an example of an appropriate disclosure of *"any other elements"* (required by the last bullet point above) as the need to give an indication that the transfer of a major asset has taken place at an amount materially different from that obtainable on normal commercial terms. [FRS 8 para 22]. The ASB believes that the absence of this information could reasonably be expected to influence decisions made by users of the financial statements. [FRS 8 app IV para 20]. The reference to a 'major asset' and 'materially different' in the example gives rise to the possible interpretation that such disclosure would be required only in respect of an unusual transaction or of a large number of transactions where the price difference could be of significance. A statement giving an indication that such sales or purchases or other transfers have taken place at amounts materially different from that obtainable on normal commercial terms may then be necessary for an understanding of the financial statements.

35.108 Disclosure of 'other elements' could also be necessary, for example, to give an indication that premises owned by the reporting entity are occupied by an associate company at a rent that is considerably lower than the market rent.

35.109 There is no requirement to disclose the actual difference between the fair value and the transacted amount. On the other hand, it should not be implied that the transactions were effected at arm's length, unless the related parties concerned acted in an independent manner. [FRS 8 para 10]. The FRS states that transactions are presumed to have been undertaken on an arm's length basis when they have been undertaken on terms such as could have been obtained in a transaction with an external party, in which each side bargained knowledgeably and freely, unaffected by any relationship between them. [FRS 8 para 8].

35.110 *"Any other elements of the transaction"* might also include disclosure of the profit made on a transaction if this was necessary for an understanding of the financial statements. However, in normal circumstances the requirement to disclose the *"amounts involved"* would be met by disclosure of the turnover or invoiced amount and would not seem to extend to separate disclosure of the profit made.

Balances between related parties

35.111 In addition to the information described above concerning transactions, the standard also requires the following information regarding *balances* to be disclosed:

- The amounts due to or from related parties at the balance sheet date and provisions for doubtful debts due from such parties at that date.

- Amounts written off in the period in respect of debts due to or from related parties.

[FRS 8 para 6(f)(g)].

35.112 The need to give the balances referred to arises independently of the requirement to disclose details of specific transactions undertaken during the year. For example, a balance may arise from a prior year transaction. If, after what may be an unusually long credit period, a balance due from a related party is written off, that information could be significant for users and is, presumably, an example of what the disclosure requirement is directed at. The disclosure of balances due to and from fellow subsidiaries is considered in paragraph 35.116.

Aggregation of transactions

35.113 To reduce the volume of disclosures of transactions with related parties, the FRS allows disclosure of details of transactions and details of balances to be made on an aggregated basis unless disclosure of an individual transaction or connected transactions (or balances) is either:

- necessary for an understanding of the impact of the transactions on the financial statements of the reporting entity; or
- required by law.

[FRS 8 para 6].

35.114 As a consequence, similar transactions and similar balances may be aggregated by type of related party. However, aggregation should not result in either of the following:

- Aggregation should not be done in such a way as to obscure the importance of significant transactions.

- Material related party transactions should not be concealed in an aggregated disclosure.

[FRS 8 para 21].

35.115 An example of aggregation given in the FRS is that purchases or sales with other group companies may be aggregated and described as such in the individual financial statements of a group company. Purchases or sales of goods should not, however, be aggregated with purchases or sales of fixed assets as this would obscure the importance of significant transactions. [FRS 8 para 21]. It seems clear from these examples that sales cannot be aggregated with purchases and that, therefore, the netting of transactions is not permitted. In addition, a material related party transaction with an individual should not be concealed in an aggregated disclosure. [FRS 8 para 21].

35.116 If intra-group transactions comprise different categories of transactions, for instance, purchases or sales of stock, or purchases or sales of fixed assets, individual balances for such categories of transactions will need to be separately disclosed. This is because, under the requirements of FRS 8, dissimilar transactions and balances cannot be aggregated. Generally, the Act requires the disclosure of balances with other group entities in the balance sheet formats. This will satisfy the standard's requirements for the disclosure of balances only if the amounts contain transactions which are similar.

35.117 Where permitted, aggregation may be made by type of related party. It does not necessarily require the individual names of the related parties to be disclosed. The extent of detail to be disclosed will depend on materiality. For example, when sales to all other group companies (that is, including parents, fellow subsidiaries and subsidiaries) are material but do not dominate the company's trading, then one total would suffice. But if such sales do constitute the majority of the trading, then analysis into (say) (i) ultimate and intermediate parent (ii) fellow subsidiaries and (iii) subsidiaries would be appropriate. In addition, transactions with associates and joint ventures would normally be separately disclosed. An example of separate disclosure of transactions is in Table 35.4 below.

Table 35.4 – British Aerospace Public Limited Company – Annual Report – 31 December 1996

Notes to the Accounts (extract)

30 Related party transactions

Related party	Sales to related party £m	Purchases from related party £m	Amounts owed by related party £m	Amounts owed to related party £m	Balance of cash advanced to the Group £m	Operating costs funded during the year £m
Airbus Industrie GIE	665	-	89	-	160	-
Panavia Aircraft GmbH	92	137	16	-	-	-
Eurofighter Jagdflugzeug GmbH . . .	126	-	9	20	-	-
BAeSEMA Ltd	1	2	1	-	-	-
Matra BAe Dynamics SAS	13	3	3	-	58	-
Aero International (Regional) SAS . .	1	1	4	5	-	32

Airbus Industrie GIE
The Group shares in the results of Airbus Industrie GIE and participates in Airbus programmes which are effectively carried out on a joint venture basis. Guarantees given by the Group relating to Airbus Finance Company Limited are given in note 21. Amounts owed by, and cash advanced by Airbus Industrie GIE to the Group are shown within trade debtors and creditors respectively.

Panavia Aircraft GmbH
The Group has a 42.5% share in Panavia Aircraft GmbH.

Eurofighter Jagdflugzeug GmbH
The Group has a 33% share in Eurofighter Jagdflugzeug GmbH.

BAeSEMA Ltd
The Group has a 50% share in BAeSEMA Ltd. The Group has a guaranteed obligation of BAeSEMA Ltd under a counter indemnity of £12 million.

Matra BAe Dynamics SAS
The Group has a 50% share in Matra BAe Dynamics SAS. Matra BAe Dynamics SAS was set up during the year as a joint venture between the Group and the Lagardère Group (note 12).

Aero International (Regional) SAS
The Group has a 33% share in Aero International (Regional) SAS, which acts as disclosed agent in respect of sales by the Group of regional aircraft to third party operators. Guarantees given by the Group in respect of Aero International (Regional) SAS are given in note 21.

British Aerospace Pension Scheme
British Aerospace Pension Fund Investment Managers Ltd (BAPFIM), a wholly owned subsidiary, provides investment advice to the British Aerospace Pension Scheme (the Scheme) on a day to day basis. During the year, BAPFIM charge the Scheme £2 million for such advice.

Transactions with directors

35.118 Special considerations arise in connection with directors' transactions. In general, it seems that the standard does not permit the aggregation of material transactions with directors. This is certainly the case when directors' transactions are unusual or unique. For example, separate disclosure is needed where a director of a company buys a property from the company.

35.119 However, aggregation may be an acceptable approach in cases such as the following:

- A situation sometimes arises where all directors have material transactions with the company. For example, where the company is an association or co-operative serving all its members, the members may put all or most of their turnover or purchases through the company. Some of the members are elected directors for certain periods and they enter into similar transactions to all other members and on the same terms. Here it is thought acceptable to aggregate the transactions for disclosure purposes. However, this approach cannot be used to conceal unusual transactions.

- In other circumstances, some or all directors may enter into transactions with the company that are or may be material, but less material than the transactions described in the previous bullet point. An example would be insurance policies taken out by directors of insurance companies on normal or staff terms. Here again it seems reasonable to aggregate the transactions for disclosure purposes. However, this approach would not apply to unusual contracts or heavily discounted policies. See, for example, para (d) of Table 35.4 below.

Table 35.5 – General Accident plc – Annual Report and Accounts – 31 December 1996

Notes to the Accounts (extract)

Transactions involving Directors

During the year transactions with related parties arose as follows:

(a) The group's interest in General Accident Insurance Company Kenya Limited was sold to a director of that company. S.Shah, who previously held 49% of the issued share capital of the company. The consideration for the sale was £0.9 million and the value of the group net assets was £1.0 million. As at 31st December 1996, the amount due by Mr Shah to the Group was £0.7 million. This disposal is not reported as a discontinued business as the amounts involved are not material in the context of the trading, assets or liabilities of the Group.

(b) Under a put option agreement General Accident Insurance Company Puerto Rico Limited and General Accident Insurance Agency Inc. from Gomez Holdings Incorporated, a minority shareholder and a company in which Luis A. Gomez, Jr., the chairman and chief executive officer of General Accident purchased Mr Hermes Vargas' holding in General Accident Life Assurance Company of Puerto Rico Inc., for a consideration of US$3.3 million. Mr Vargas is the president and chief operating officer of General Accident Life Assurance Corporation of Puerto Rico Inc,. The difference between the consideration and the minority interests in the net assets of the operations has been recognised as goodwill and written off to reserves.

(c) Group companies act as administrators of a number of employee related trusts and group pension schemes for which the fees chargeable are not significant. The Group's internal investment fund managers provide investment management services to the Group's pension funds. The funds under management are approximately £1.3 billion and fees are charged on the basis of a scale previously negotiated with the pension fund trustees.

(d) Members of the board may purchase insurance and other savings products on terms and conditions to other staff in the UK. The aggregate premiums payable by members of the board in respect of group products was £0.1 million.

35.120 In contrast to these two cases, consider the following example. Some directors of a house-building company may, over a period of a few years, buy houses from that company for their own or family use. However, given the nature of house purchases, they are likely to be less frequent than is the case with the insurance policy example. Moreover, they would be more clearly material to the directors. Hence in this example we do *not* believe that aggregation is an appropriate approach, even where house-building is the company's normal business and the transactions are on normal commercial terms.

Comparatives

35.121 The standard is silent on comparatives. The normal rule is that they are required for all amounts stated in the notes to the financial statements. This rule should, therefore, be applied to all financial statements to which the standard applies. Comparatives are not required for the first year in which the standard applies but are required for accounting periods beginning on or after 23 December 1996. Prior to FRS 8 disclosure of directors' transactions under Schedule 6 Part II were exempted by paragraph 58(3) of Schedule 4 to the Act from giving comparatives. This exemption is overridden by the standard.

Interaction with disclosures required by the Act

35.122 The Act requires disclosure in financial statements of certain details about section 330 transactions. Section 330 transactions are principally loans, quasi-loans and credit transactions with directors. It appears that the information required in connection with the above disclosure will in general suffice for the purposes of disclosure of such transactions under FRS 8. For example, neither the Act nor FRS 8 specifically requires disclosure of the rate of interest of a loan. Disclosure of that information, however, seems implicit in the Act's phrase *"the principal terms of the transactions"* and the words of the FRS *"description of the transactions"* or *"the amounts involved"*. [6 Sch 22(l); FRS 8 para 6].

35.123 In addition to loans and similar transactions, paragraphs 15(c) and 16(c) of Schedule 6 to the Act require disclosure of certain transactions in which a director has a material interest. If disclosure is required by the Act, the information it requires to be disclosed, which includes the transaction's principal terms will in general give sufficient information for the purposes of FRS 8 for such transactions. As discussed in paragraph 35.174, the Act gives exemption for transactions with directors in the normal course of business and at arm's length. However, these are now disclosable under FRS 8 if they are material, even though they may be exempted from disclosure under the Act.

35.124 There is, however, one aspect where the disclosure of information required by FRS 8 for related party transactions may go further than the existing disclosures required by the Act. Paragraph 6(e) requires disclosure of *"any other elements of the transactions necessary for an understanding of the financial statements"*. The FRS gives as an example of this: the need to given an indication that the transfer of a major asset has taken place at an amount materially different from that obtainable on normal commercial terms. However, the disclosure required in each instance will depend on the facts.

Examples of related party transactions

Transactions between companies under common control

35.125 FRS 8's requirements extend to the disclosure of transactions even where these might have been reversed because of the accounting implications of FRS 5.

Example

Company A, which is owned by Mr X, has slow-moving stock and a large overdraft from its bank. Prior to the year end it sells some of the stock to company B at a price that is below its market value. Company B pays for the goods before company A's year end and company A pays the proceeds into its bank account with its bank. Company A thus shows a lower overdraft in its year end financial statements. After the year end the transaction is reversed. No fee is payable to company B as it has agreed that company A will do a similar favour for company B at its (different) year end. Does FRS 8 affect the transaction?

The transaction should not be shown as a sale of stocks in company A's financial statements as under FRS 5 it is not a proper sale and the cash received from company B should be treated as a short-term loan. Thus, although the overdraft will still show a reduced balance, stocks will remain as before and there will be an additional creditor for the amount owed to company B.

Whilst FRS 5 also requires that disclosure of the transactions should be sufficient to enable a user to understand its commercial effect, FRS 8 may require further disclosures if company B is a related party of company A.

If, for instance, company A and company B are under common control, or if the owner of company B is a member of the close family of the owner of company A, disclosure would be required of the names and relationship of the related parties, details of the transaction, amounts, balances at the year end and the implications for the financial statements.

This might be as follows for company A with a 31 December year end:

> *"On 30 December 19X6 the company sold goods with a book value of £100,000 to company B limited, a company controlled by Mr Smith, the brother-in-law of the company's principal shareholder Mr Jones, for £80,000. This amount was received as cash and has been shown in the financial statements as a reduction in bank overdrafts which without the benefit of the transaction would be shown at £263,000 which is in excess of the company's present overdraft limit of £250,000. Subsequent to the year end, the goods were repurchased by the company for the original sale price of £80,000. In these financial statements, in accordance with FRS 5, the transaction has been recorded as a secured loan rather than as a sale and, accordingly, the financial effects of the transactions have been to decrease the overdrafts by £80,000 as described above and to increase creditors by the same amount, which is separately disclosed as 'amounts due to company B limited' in the balance sheet. There were no such transactions in 19X5."*

Subsidiaries acquired and disposed of during the year

35.126 Questions arise as to what transactions are disclosable in consolidated and individual financial statements where a group has acquired or disposed of a subsidiary during the year. It is considered that disclosure should be made on the following basis.

Consolidated accounts

- Where a group has acquired a subsidiary, transactions between the members of the acquiring group and the acquired subsidiary prior to the date of acquisition are disclosable in the consolidated financial statements. This is because an acquired subsidiary is deemed to be a related party of the group for the entire period, but only transactions prior to acquisition are disclosable as post-acquisition transactions are eliminated on consolidation.

- Where a group has disposed of a subsidiary during the year, only post-disposal transactions between the members of the group and the subsidiary disposed of are disclosable in the consolidated financial statements as pre-disposal transactions are eliminated on consolidation.

Entity accounts

- If the company disposed of was a 90 per cent subsidiary of a group at its previous year end, but is no longer a 90 per cent subsidiary of that group at its current year end, all transactions for the whole period with the group of which the company was formerly a subsidiary are disclosable in the company's financial statements. This is because the company is unable to use the exemption in paragraph 3(c) of FRS 8 as it is no longer a subsidiary of the former group at its year end.

- Where a company is acquired during the year, all transactions for the whole period with the other companies in the new group are disclosable in the financial statements of the acquired company, unless the company is 90 per cent owned at the year end, in which case transactions with group companies are exempt from disclosure.

35.127 An example of disclosure of transactions with a company after disposal can be found in Table 35.6 below.

Table 35.6 – George Wimpey PLC – 31 December 1996

Notes to the Accounts (extract)

31 Disclosure of related party transactions

The following disclosures are required under Financial Reporting Standard 8.

Transactions with Tarmac (ex-Wimpey companies)
In the period from 1 March to 31 December 1996, the Group continued to trade, in the normal course of business, with those companies disposed of to the Tarmac group. The amounts involved are not considered material to either party.

The Wimpey Staff Personal Accident Scheme
George Wimpey PLC funds the Staff Personal Accident Scheme which provides discretionary personal accident benefits to the members of the Wimpey Staff Pension Scheme. There is an interest free loan from The Scheme to the Group which is repayable at one month's notice. The balance owed by the Group to The Scheme was £0.5 million throughout the year.

Morrison Land Development Inc.
As a result of the asset swap with Tarmac on 1 March 1996, George Wimpey Canada Ltd., a former Group company sold to Tarmac, has legal title to land and other housing related assets in Canada on behalf of Morrison Land Development Inc., a Group company that has beneficial ownership of those assets. The balance owed by George Wimpey Canada Ltd. to the Group as a result of this arrangement was C$17.5 million on 1 March 1996 and C$15.2 million at the year end which represents the net book value of those assets held by George Wimpey Canada Ltd.

Quasi-subsidiary undertakings

35.128 FRS 5 defines 'quasi-subsidiary' as *"a company, trust, partnership or other vehicle that, though not fulfilling the definition of a subsidiary is, directly or indirectly controlled by the reporting entity and gives rise to benefits for that entity that are in substance no different from those that would arise were the vehicle a subsidiary".*

35.129 Where a company qualifies as a quasi-subsidiary and has transactions with its group, FRS 8 applies as follows:

- In consolidated financial statements no disclosure is necessary for transactions between group companies and quasi-subsidiaries, because the latter are treated as group entities and the transactions are eliminated on consolidation. [FRS 8 para 3(a)].

- In the parent's financial statements no disclosure is required, because group financial statements are prepared. [FRS 8 para 3(b)].

- In the quasi-subsidiaries' financial statements the exemption in FRS 8 paragraph 3(c) for 90 per cent subsidiaries does not apply, because quasi-subsidiaries are not legally subsidiary undertakings. Therefore, they need to disclose details of transactions and balances with the group, although sensible aggregation is permitted.

Associates and joint ventures

35.130 In general, any material transactions between the investing company and the associate or joint venture are disclosable by both parties. The situation can become more complicated in a group where the transaction may be between a subsidiary of the investing company and the associate of the investing company. The implications for disclosure are illustrated in the example below:

Example

Company H has a subsidiary, company S, and an associate, company A.

If company H transacts with company A and assuming that the transaction is material, then the disclosure in the relevant financial statements will be as follows:

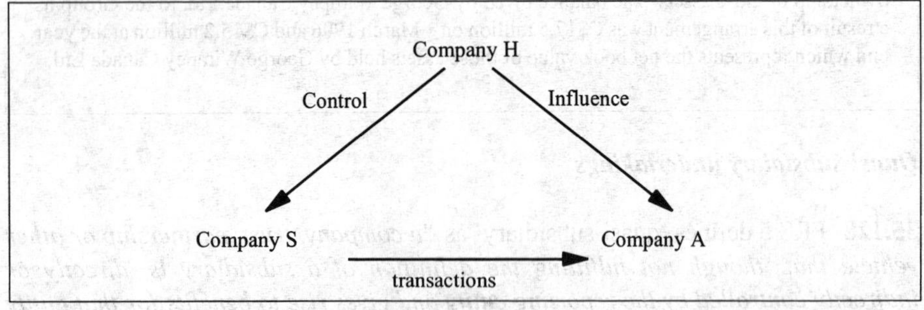

- *Company A's financial statements* – company H is a related party of company A and so company A will be required to disclose details of the transaction.

- *Company H's consolidated financial statements* – company A is a related party of company H and H's group, being an associate of both; so company H will be required to disclose details of the transaction.

If the transaction is between company S and company A, then the position is more complicated. Company H controls company S, but exercises influence over company A. Both company S and company A are related parties of company H, but are not necessarily related parties of each other. During the financial year they transact business. The questions arise whether those transactions are related party transactions that should be disclosed: in the individual financial statements of company S; in the consolidated financial statements of company H; and in the individual financial statements of company A.

Company S and company A would be related parties if either or both of them had put their own separate interests below those of the other parties (that is, subordinated their separate interests) in entering into those transactions. The following table considers the situations where they are and where they are not related parties for the purposes of disclosure of the transactions undertaken during the financial year.

Financial statements	Transactions where S and A are *not* related parties.	Transactions where S and A *are* related parties.
Company S	No disclosure	No disclosure as company S takes exemption for 90% subsidiaries for transactions with subsidiaries and associates of the group. [FRS 8 para 3(c)].
H's group	Disclosure as company A is related party of H's group. (see note below)	Disclosure as A is not a group entity and balances are not eliminated on consolidation. [FRS 8 para 3(a)].
Company A	No disclosure	Disclosure as A is not a 90% subsidiary and so not entitled to exemption.

Company H's consolidated financial statements – Although in this instance company A may not be a related party of company S, as it is an associate of company H it is by definition a related party of the reporting entity (that is, company H's group). So company H will be required to disclose details of transactions between the members of the group and company A in the consolidated financial statements.

Pension funds

35.131 Transactions with pension funds for the benefit of the reporting entity's employees or any related party (other than contributions paid) will be related party transactions. Table 35.7 below illustrates this type of disclosure.

Table 35.7 – Shanks & McEwan Group PLC – Annual Report and Accounts – 30 March 1996

Notes to the Accounts (extract)

26 Related party transactions

The Group has identified the following transactions which fall to be disclosed under the terms of FRS 8 following the early adoption of the standard:

Pension fund

The company leases offices at 22/23 Woodside Place, Glasgow from the Shanks & McEwan Group PLC Retirements Benefit Scheme. Normal commercial terms, including the current rent payable of £61,500 per annum, apply to the lease which runs for 25 years to 2015. Independent advice was taken regarding the terms of the lease at inception.

Joint venture and associated company

The Group, through the subsidiary company Land Fill Gas Ltd, participates in a joint venture with Norweb Generation Ltd and holds a 50% shareholding in the associated company Norweb Land Fill Gas Ltd where the remaining shares are owned by Norweb Generation Ltd. The purpose of the joint venture and the associated companies is the exploitation of landfill gas for power generation at third party landfill sites. In the year ended 30 March 1996, Group companies supplied gas field services at normal commercial rates to the associated company, Norweb Land Fill Gas Ltd, which were included in turnover for the year ended 30 March 1996 at £139,000 (1995 £344,000).

Shareholders

35.132 Transactions with shareholders holding at least 20 per cent are not disclosable as related party transactions under the Listing Rules if they are revenue transactions in the ordinary course of business or if they are very small transactions (see from para 35.177). However, these transactions may become disclosable under FRS 8.

Directors

35.133 The following are examples of related party transactions with directors.

Directors' share transactions

35.134 Purchases and sales of shares by a director in the market that do not involve the company as a party to the transaction are not disclosable as related party transactions. Subscriptions for shares in the company will be related party transactions and disclosable. But shares acquired in a capitalisation or rights issue on the same basis as all shareholders and of an amount to which the director's disclosed shareholding entitles him, would generally not be material to the company or to the director and, therefore, not disclosable. Subscriptions in other situations and share buy-backs will generally be sufficiently unusual as to require disclosure as related party transactions. (Chapter 31 discusses the requirements of the Act and Listing Rules to disclose certain share interests of directors.) See Table 35.8 below for disclosure of share options under FRS 8.

Table 35.8 – Wolseley plc – Annual Report and Accounts – 31 July 1996

Notes to the Accounts (extract)

28. RELATED PARTY TRANSACTIONS

Pursuant to an arrangement in place on the acquisition of Brossette in 1992, Mr G Pinault, who was appointed a director on 1 August 1994, held call and put options in relation to 7,000 shares in Brossette BTI. Having exercised the call option in early 1994, and paid the appropriate price, Mr Pinault exercised the put option during the year. Due to certain changed circumstances occurring during the period from the grant of the option to exercise, amendments to the original put option were agreed. Mr Pinault subsequently sold his entire share holding in Brossette BTI to an intermediary holding company at an agreed price of £508.40 per share. The company's auditors, Price Waterhouse, have reported to the directors that the terms of the amendment of the original put option were fair and reasonable as far as the members of Wolseley plc are concerned.

There are no other related party transactions requiring disclosure in this year's accounts in accordance with FRS8 (Related Party Disclosures).

Guarantees by directors

35.135 Guarantees are given as one of the examples of related party transactions in paragraph 19 of the standard. Personal guarantees by directors of the borrowings of the reporting entity would, therefore, be disclosable. It is probable that a director's personal guarantee is a material item both to him and the company. Financial Reporting Standard for Smaller Entities (para 15.2) specifically makes it clear that small companies should disclose such guarantees in the notes.

Dividends paid to directors

35.136 Although, in principle, dividends paid to directors are related party transactions, we believe that, since details of directors' shareholdings (including those of their spouses and minor children) and the rate of dividend are already disclosed in an annual report, this is sufficient disclosure in most cases. Where shares are held by other close family, our view is that in general no additional disclosure is necessary, unless it is considered necessary for the true and fair view. For example, if the directors own few or no shares and their adult children (who are not directors) hold the majority, disclosure is necessary. See Table 35.9 on page 35048 for an example of disclosure of dividends paid to directors.

Close family

35.137 Transactions with adult children and other 'close family' (as defined) of a director or a shareholder holding at least 20 per cent of the voting rights, and persons connected with them, will be disclosable, as illustrated below. In this example, there would be no disclosure under the 1985 Act as there are no 'connected parties' and no common directors.

Example

Mr Y's father owns 100% of the shares in company A Ltd. Mr and Mrs Y own 100% of the shares and are the only directors of company B. Mrs Y's sister provides book-keeping services from time to time to company B, but is not an employee. Company A has increased its loan of £150,000 to company B to £200,000 during the year, for which company A charges an advantageous rate of interest.

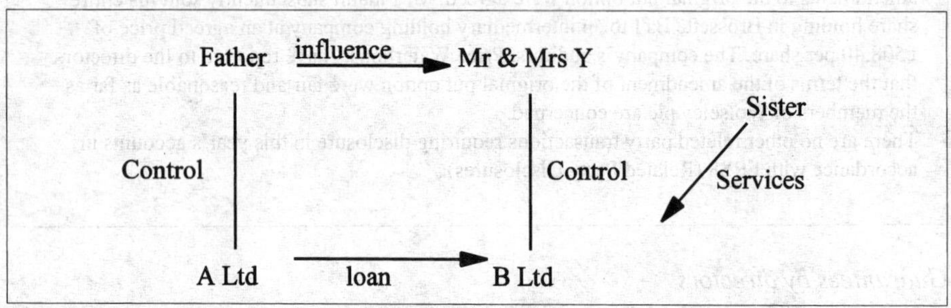

Under FRS 8, Mr Y's father and Mrs Y's sister will be related parties of company B if either may be expected to influence or be influenced by Mr or Mrs Y in dealings with company B. It seems that Mr Y's father could be expected to exert some influence over Mr and Mrs Y. It is, however, unlikely that Mrs Y's sister influences or is influenced by Mr or Mrs Y in dealings with company B. It can, therefore, be assumed for this example that Mr Y's father is a related party of company B and that Mrs Y's sister is not. Mr Y's father has a controlling interest in company A. It follows, therefore, that company A will be a related party of company B.

Both companies will need to disclose the necessary details regarding the increase in the loan to £200,000 in their financial statements. In addition, if any part of the existing loan of £150,000 and the additional loan of £50,000 is outstanding at the balance sheet date, company A will need to disclose the amounts due to it from company B on that date, together with any provisions and amounts written off. Company B will need to disclose the amount it owes to company A at the balance sheet date.

35.138 The following example is of a transaction that escaped disclosure under the 1985 Act before the introduction of FRS 8, but which is now caught.

Example

A company sells a property to the brother of a director. The brother is regarded as 'close family' as defined in FRS 8. The sale is at an arm's length price of £100,000.

> *"In April 19X6, the company sold a property for £100,000 to Mr X, the brother of Mr Y, a director of the company. Half of the price was payable in July 19X6 and the other half was paid after the year end in January 19X7. No interest was charged on this transaction. The balance owing to the company by Mr X was £50,000 at the year end (19X6: no transactions or balances)."*

Key management

35.139 The examples given from paragraph 35.134 of transactions with directors would also apply to key management.

Exemptions from disclosure

Introduction

35.140 The FRS does *not* require disclosure of related party transactions and balances in certain circumstances. These are considered in the paragraphs that follow. It is necessary to consider the following exemptions in the light of the fact that the reporting entity may prepare individual company financial statements or consolidated financial statements.

Intra-group transactions or balances eliminated on consolidation

35.141 In consolidated financial statements, disclosure is not required of any transactions or balances between group entities that have been eliminated on consolidation. The following points should be considered in relation to this exemption.

- Small and medium-sized groups which currently take advantage of the exemption in section 248 not to prepare consolidated financial statements are not able to use this exemption.

- Disclosure of control is not exempted.

35.142 For an example of disclosure where transactions presumably are not eliminated see Table 35.9 below.

Table 35.9 – Associated British Foods plc – Report and Accounts – 14 September 1996

Notes to the Accounts (extract)

31. RELATED PARTY TRANSACTIONS

The Associated British Foods plc group's ("ABF") related parties, as defined by Financial Reporting Standard 8, the nature of the relationship and the extent of transactions with them are summarised below:

	Sub note	1996 £'000
Management charge from Wittington Investments Limited, principally in respect of directors and staff paid by them	1	550
Charges to Wittington Investments Limited in respect of services provided by ABF and its subsidiaries	1	(40)
Dividends paid by ABF and received in a beneficial capacity by:		
(i) Trustees of the Garfield Weston Foundation	2	3,221
(ii) Directors of Wittington Investments Limited who are not Trustees of The Foundation		520
(iii) Directors of ABF who are not Trustees of The Foundation and are not directors of Wittington Investments Limited	3	28
(iv) a member of the Weston family employed within the ABF group	4	284
		£m
Sales to fellow subsidiaries on normal trading terms	5	7
Purchases from fellow subsidiaries on normal trading terms	5	-
Amounts due from fellow subsidiary undertakings	5	1
Sales to George Weston Limited on normal trading terms	6	1
Sales to associated undertakings on normal trading terms	7	39
Purchases from associated undertakings on normal trading terms	7	(4)
Amounts due from associated undertakings	7	5
Amounts due to associated undertakings	7	(1)

Sub notes

1. At 14 September 1996 Wittington Investments Limited held 458,342,290 ordinary shares (1995 – 458,142,290) representing in aggregate 50.9% (1995 – 50.9%) of the total issued ordinary share capital of ABF.

2. The Garfield Weston Foundation ("The Foundation") is an English charitable trust which was established in 1958 by the late Mr W Garfield Weston. The Foundation has no direct interest in ABF but as at 14 September 1996 held 683,073 shares in Wittington Investments Limited representing 79.2% of that company's issued share capital and is, therefore, ABF's ultimate controlling party. The Trustees of the Foundation comprise six of the late Mr W Garfield Weston's children, including Garry H Weston who acts as Chairman of the Board of Trustees, and four of Garry H Weston's children.

3. Details of the directors of ABF are given on page 2. Their beneficial interests, including family interests, in ABF and its subsidiaries are given on page 47. Directors' remuneration, including options, is disclosed on pages 34 and 35.

4. A member of the Weston family who is employed by the group and is not a director of ABF or Wittington Investments Limited and is not a Trustee of the Foundation.

5. Fellow subsidiary companies are Aughton Limited, which was disposed of during the year, and Fortnum & Mason plc.

6. George Weston Limited is a Canadian listed company in which Mr W G Galen Weston has a controlling interest.

7. Details of the group's principal associated undertakings are set out on page 46.

Parent's own financial statements

35.143 No disclosure is necessary in a parent's own financial statements when those statements are presented together with its consolidated financial statements. Thus, in these circumstances, under the FRS, disclosure of who controls the entity or of transactions or balances need not be given by the parent as a separate entity.

Ninety per cent subsidiaries

35.144 In the financial statements of subsidiary undertakings, 90 per cent or more of whose voting rights are controlled within the group, no disclosure is required by the standard of transactions or balances with entities that are part of the group or investees of the group qualifying as related parties, provided that the consolidated financial statements in which that subsidiary is included are publicly available. However, certain information regarding subsidiaries has to be given as the balance sheet formats under the Act require the disclosure of amounts owed by group undertakings and amounts owed to group undertakings. The disclosure of control is still required.

35.145 For this purpose, investees of the group qualifying as related parties include associates and joint ventures of group companies with whom the reporting subsidiary has transacted in circumstances where they are subject to influence from the same source to such an extent that one of the parties has put its own interest after those of the other party. For an example see paragraph 35.130.

35.146 This exemption permits 90 per cent subsidiary undertakings with, for instance, a small external holding in the equity or with third-party non-voting preference shareholders to take advantage of it.

35.147 No definition is given in the FRS of the phrase 'publicly available', but it seems clear that it means available to the public in general and not, for instance, just to shareholders. Section 240 of the 1985 Act refers to publication of accounts and states:

> *"For the purposes of this section a company shall be regarded as publishing a document if it publishes, issues or circulates it or otherwise makes it available for public inspection in a manner calculated to invite members of the public generally, or any class of members of the public, to read it."*

35.148 We consider that 'publicly available' may be interpreted in this way. However, the test should in practice be judged by reference to whether a copy of the consolidated accounts can be acquired relatively easily. The accounts may be on a public register, for example, but if the accounts themselves cannot be easily obtained, they would not be regarded as publicly available. Where there is no public register but the address from which they may be obtained is given, the accounts would be regarded as publicly available.

35.149 The Act requires a company that is a subsidiary undertaking to give the name of the largest group and the smallest group of undertakings of which the company is a member and for which consolidated financial statements are drawn up. In addition, if copies of those financial statements are available to the public, the addresses from which they can be obtained must be stated in the notes to its financial statements. If no such address is given in its financial statements, it will be difficult for a subsidiary company to argue that consolidated financial statements in which it is included are publicly available. [1985 Act, 5 Sch 11, 30]. These provisions are illustrated in the examples that follow.

Example 1

A UK company is 100% owned by a private US group. The US parent also has a subsidiary in Canada. The UK company sells finished goods to the Canadian company at prices that are not typically arm's length. Do these transactions have to be disclosed?

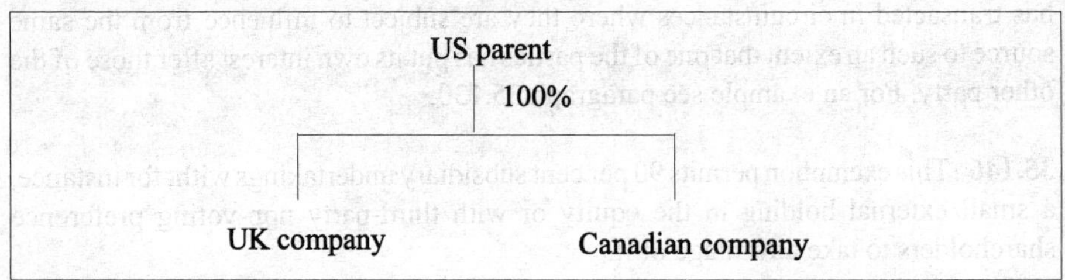

In this example, it is clear from paragraph 3(c) of the standard that the transactions between the UK company and the Canadian company would be disclosable. This is because the US parent, being privately owned, would not publish its financial statements. If the US parent made its consolidated financial statements publicly available, for example, by filing them with the SEC or publishing the address from which they can be obtained, the position would be different: the intra-group transactions in the UK company would not then need to be disclosed.

Example 2

This example is similar to Example 1, except that there is a UK sub-group, as shown in the next diagram. Here, the UK *subsidiary* sells finished goods to the Canadian company at prices that are not typically arm's length. Do these transactions have to be disclosed?

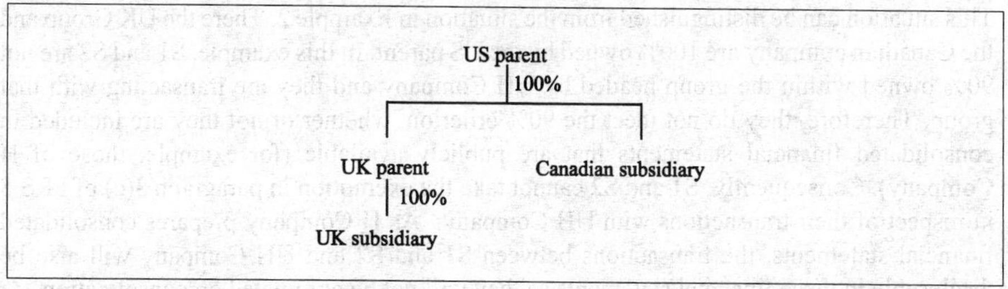

The wording of paragraph 3(c) of the standard indicates that in the financial statements of the UK subsidiary, transactions with entities that are part of the group (for example, the Canadian company) need not be disclosed provided the consolidated financial statements in which the UK subsidiary is included are publicly available. The financial statements of the US group are *not* publicly available, as it is privately owned. However, the UK parent has to prepare a UK consolidation in which the financial statements of the UK subsidiary are included. Because of this, the transactions with the Canadian company need not be disclosed in the financial statements of the UK subsidiary (and this is so, even though the Canadian company is outside the UK group). This, however, is not the full picture, because the disclosure question also arises in the context of the consolidated financial statements of the UK parent, and in that context, the exemption is not available. Hence the transactions and any balances with the Canadian company *would* be disclosable in the UK consolidated financial statements.

Example 3

A sub-group, headed by H Company, is less than 90% owned by UH Company plc, a company registered in England. Some subsidiaries in the sub-group, S1 and S2, enter into transactions with UH Company. UH Company and H Company prepare consolidated financial statements. Do these transactions have to be disclosed in S1 and S2's and H Company's financial statements?

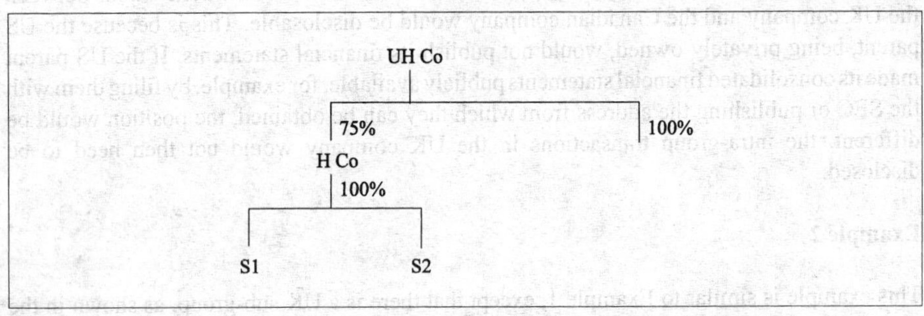

This situation can be distinguished from the situation in Example 2. There the UK Group and the Canadian company are 100% owned by the US parent. In this example, S1 and S2 are not 90% owned within the group headed by UH Company and they are transacting with that group. Therefore, they do not meet the 90% criterion, whether or not they are included in consolidated financial statements that are publicly available (for example, those of H Company). Consequently, S1 and S2 cannot take the exemption in paragraph 3(c) of FRS 8 in respect of their transactions with UH Company. As H Company prepares consolidated financial statements, the transactions between S1 and S2 and UH Company will also be disclosable in these financial statements as they will not be eliminated on consolidation.

If S1 and S2 had transacted with X, a 100% subsidiary of UH Company which is outside the sub-group headed by H Company, the disclosures in S1, S2 and the H Company consolidated financial statements would be the same, for the same reasons.

35.150 A company that is part of a small or medium-sized group where the parent company does not prepare consolidated financial statements, will not be able to take advantage of this exemption and will have to disclose intra-group transactions and balances in its own financial statements.

35.151 It is only transactions and balances between 90 per cent subsidiary undertakings and group related parties (including associates and joint ventures) that are exempted by the standard. Disclosure would, therefore, be required of transactions and balances with related parties of the reporting subsidiary other than those that are excluded by the exemption. [FRS 8 para 17]. In addition, disclosure of the party controlling the subsidiary undertaking is still required.

35.152 Reporting entities that take advantage of the exemption for 90 per cent subsidiaries not to disclose intra-group transactions, are required to state that fact. The ASB considers disclosure of the fact that the exemption has been invoked is sufficient to alert the reader of the financial statements to the possible existence of related party transactions.

Pension contributions

35.153 Pension contributions paid to a pension fund are not required to be disclosed, but other transactions and balances with the fund still need to be disclosed by the reporting entity, for instance refunds of contributions. In addition, any balances of pension contributions due but not paid at the year end are disclosable, as effectively they would constitute a loan from the pension fund.

Emoluments for services

35.154 No disclosure is required of emoluments in respect of services as an employee of the reporting entity. This exemption covers payments 'in respect of services' and it, therefore, does not cover any *ex gratia* payment or other payment not in respect of services as an employee. For instance, payments under consultancy arrangements are not covered by the exemption.

35.155 Although it is not clear from the standard, it appears that the intention is to exclude from disclosure payments made or costs incurred in respect of persons employed under contracts of service, which are included in staff costs and disclosed in the profit and loss account or the notes. What constitutes staff costs is set out in paragraph 94 of Schedule 4 to the 1985 Act.

35.156 Executive directors, who perform management functions, will usually have contracts of service; non-executive directors will usually have contracts for services. In each case it is a question of fact as to which type of contract they have. Amounts paid to directors under contracts for services should not be included in staff costs and, therefore, would seem to fall within the scope of FRS 8. However, extensive disclosure of directors' emoluments and their emoluments for services in connection with the management of the affairs of the company is already required, primarily, by Part I of Schedule 6 to the 1985 Act, with directors' share options disclosed under UITF Abstract 10. These disclosures are likely to satisfy the disclosures which would be required by FRS 8 in respect of any directors' remuneration that is not covered by this exclusion. In addition, following the Greenbury Report, the Listing Rules require listed companies to give the amount of each element in the remuneration package of each director by name for all accounting periods ending on or after 31 December 1995. [LR 12.43(x)].

Duty of confidentiality

35.157 Related party disclosure will also not be required by the FRS if disclosure would conflict with the reporting entity's duties of confidentiality arising by operation of law (but not from contractual provisions relating to confidentiality). Thus, banks that, by law, have to observe a strict duty of confidentiality about their customers' affairs will not have to disclose details concerning related parties which would be in conflict with that duty. [FRS 8 para 16].

Small and medium-sized companies

35.158 The ASB considered whether or not to exempt small companies (as defined by the Act) from the standard's disclosure requirements, but eventually decided not to do so. Although the ASB exempts smaller companies from some standards, FRS 8 did not appear to be a candidate for exemption, on the grounds that the related party disclosures may be more than usually important in small companies.

35.159 Small companies may file abbreviated financial statements under Schedule 8A to the Companies Act 1985. Abbreviated financial statements need not comply with the disclosure provisions of FRS 8, as they are not intended to give a true and fair view. As a result, a small company, by filing abbreviated financial statements, will be able to avoid the disclosures required by FRS 8 as to its controlling or ultimate controlling party as well as the disclosure of transactions and balances. Financial statements prepared for shareholders as either full financial statements or shorter form financial statements will, however, have to give the disclosures required by FRS 8.

35.160 The position with regard to the accounts of *medium-sized* companies is not as clear. However, some argue that, even though the abbreviated financial statements of medium-sized companies are only very slightly abbreviated, they are not required to give a true and fair view and, therefore, need not comply with FRS 8.

Additional relaxation of disclosure requirements

35.161 The FRS does not require disclosure of the relationship and transactions and balances between the reporting entity and the parties listed below simply as a result of their role as:

- Providers of finance in the course of their business in that regard.
- Utility companies.
- Government departments and their sponsored bodies.
- A customer, supplier, franchiser, distributor or general agent with whom an entity transacts a significant volume of business.

[FRS 8 para 4].

35.162 Disclosure is not required of the relationship and details of transactions and balances between the reporting entity and the parties in the first three bullet points above, even though the parties may circumscribe the freedom of action of an entity or participate in its decision-making process. This provision has the effect that the parties listed above do not become related parties of a reporting entity just as a result of the four relationships specified.

35.163 The paragraph 4 exemptions appear to be transaction based, which means that, for example, a bank providing a loan would not be treated as a related party merely because it could exert its influence by calling in the loan or charging a higher than normal rate of interest. However, the position is different where one of these parties is a related party for some other reason. For example, a venture capitalist, as a provider of finance, may provide debt finance to the reporting entity and also have an equity stake which exceeds 20 per cent and thereby be a related party. In this situation we consider that all transactions with that related party are disclosable by the reporting entity, including any transactions that arise out of the related party's role as, for example, a provider of finance.

35.164 This view has significant implications for quasi-government and health bodies as it would mean that all transactions between those bodies and the government or with other quasi-governmental or health bodies could become disclosable. It appears that if such entities report on a true and fair basis they would have to comply with FRS 8. Guidance has been issued by HM Treasury on the assumptions to be made in connection with FRS 8.

Example

A reporting company might be heavily dependent on a supply of gas from a gas company. But that does not, by itself, result in the gas company becoming a related party of the reporting company.

However, there may already be a related party relationship between a utility and another company. For example, a gas utility may have a 30% interest in a consulting company which it treats as an associated company. The two companies are, therefore, related parties, and, in the financial statements of the consulting company, transactions with the gas utility would be disclosable; they would not, for example, be eliminated on consolidation and would not, therefore, be exempted under paragraph 3(a) of the standard. The paragraph 4 exemption does not help in this context either, because the two are already related and the normal rules apply. However, bills for gas supply would not need to be disclosed if the transactions were immaterial (see para 35.73). It will presumably be easier for the gas company to argue immateriality in relation to disclosure in its financial statements of its transactions with the purchasing company.

35.165 The reporting entity and major suppliers or customers are not related parties by virtue of that connection alone, because the reporting entity is still able to make decisions in its own interests. It is clear that this would not be so where the relationship between them affects the pursuit of their separate interests. For instance, this might arise where a director of the reporting entity is also the controlling shareholder of the supplier.

Overriding requirement to give a true and fair view

35.166 Sections 226 and 227 of the 1985 Act oblige the directors of a company to prepare individual and consolidated financial statements that give a true and fair view. The view expressed by the ASB in its Foreword to accounting standards is that the requirement to give a true and fair view may in special circumstances require a departure from accounting standards. However, it envisages that only in exceptional circumstances will such a departure be necessary in order for the financial statements to give a true and fair view. [ASB Foreword para 18].

35.167 There may be circumstances, however, where, in order to give a true and fair view, it is necessary to give certain disclosures that would be exempt from disclosure under FRS 8. Such additional disclosure would not be a departure from the standard, because even though the standard may not specifically require the particular disclosure, it does not prohibit such disclosure being made.

35.168 Such a situation might arise where, in a group of companies suffering from financial difficulties, cheques are passed from one group company to another through a series of different banks (that is, by cheque kiting), in order to give the bankers the impression of high liquidity and of trading activities that do not actually exist. Because the subsidiaries are wholly-owned and the transactions are eliminated on consolidation, the exemption in respect of 90 per cent subsidiaries whose parents' consolidated financial statements are publicly available, would apply. However, in order to give a true and fair view, it would, in our view, be necessary for the extent and nature of the artificial payments and receipts to be disclosed both in the subsidiaries and the group's consolidated financial statements.

Directors' and officers' transactions under the 1985 Act

35.169 The Act does not use the term 'related party'. The provisions in Part II of Schedule 6 to the Act require disclosure of certain transactions with directors and persons connected with directors. A person connected with a director falls broadly into the following categories:

- A director's spouse or minor children.
- A body corporate in which a director owns at least 20 per cent of the shares or which is controlled by a director or the persons connected with him.
- A trustee of a trust of which the director or any persons connected with him are beneficiaries.

- A partner of the director (or a person connected with the director) in his capacity as partner.

[Sec 346].

35.170 The disclosures that the Act requires to be made concerning related party transactions are considered briefly in the paragraphs that follow. The annex to this chapter summarises the Act's sections that require such disclosures and makes reference to where the provisions are considered in more detail in this Manual chapter.

Loans and other similar transactions with directors

35.171 Details of directors' loans, quasi-loans, credit transactions, guarantees and security given for such transactions and other related assignments and arrangements are disclosable under Part II of Schedule 6. Disclosure extends to transactions entered into by the reporting company or any subsidiary with a director of the company or its holding company or with persons connected with such directors.

Loans and other similar transactions with officers

35.172 A statement must be given of the aggregate amounts outstanding at the end of the financial year in relation to the types of transactions mentioned in paragraph 35.171 with officers of the company who are not directors. This does not apply to transactions that do not exceed £2,500. [6 Sch 28-30].

Transactions in which a director has a material interest

35.173 The transactions which should be disclosed are those entered into by the reporting company or a subsidiary in which the director of the company or its holding company (or a person connected with him) has a material interest. [6 Sch 15(c),16(c)]. This would include substantial property transactions under section 320. The Act says that an interest in a transaction is not material if in the opinion of the board of directors it is not so. However, they must consider the matter honestly and reasonably and come to a reasonable conclusion. Although 'material interest' is not defined by the Act, two tests have been suggested to interpret it. The first test of materiality is whether disclosure of the transaction is likely to be of relevance to shareholders or creditors. The second test is whether the director's interest in the transaction is substantial. The guidance given by FRS 8 on establishing materiality is broadly similar to the two tests mentioned above (see from para 35.73).

35.174 The main exception from disclosure under the Act is for transactions in the normal course of business and at arm's length. Although the wording of this exemption has caused confusion, it is normally interpreted as exempting transactions that the reporting company or a subsidiary company:

- Enters into in the ordinary course of its business.
- On terms that are not less favourable to the reporting entity or its subsidiary company than it would be reasonable to expect if the person with the material interest had not been a director of the company or its holding company.

[6 Sch 20].

35.175 Details of the disclosures required in the financial statements for transactions in which a director has a material interest are given in chapter 34.

Disclosure of directors' share interests

35.176 Certain details of the interests of directors, their spouses and minor children in shares or debentures of the company or a company in the group must be disclosed in the directors' report. The interests that must be disclosed are those shown on the register maintained by the company under section 325. The directors' report must include the details regarding share interests and options to subscribe specified in paragraphs 2 to 2B of Schedule 7. These requirements and the requirements of the Listing Rules are discussed in chapter 31.

Related party transactions under the Listing Rules

Usual requirements for transactions with related parties

35.177 Under chapter 11 of the Listing Rules, where a listed company (or any of its subsidiary undertakings) proposes to enter into a transaction with a related party, the usual requirements are as follows. The company must give the required details of the proposed transaction to the Company Announcements Office of the Stock Exchange, send a circular to shareholders with the required information and obtain their approval to the transaction. [LR 11.4]. If a circular is required, it must provide sufficient information to enable the recipient to evaluate the effect of the transaction. Chapter 11 applies to investment trusts (as well as to investment companies) and to venture capital trusts. Companies that do not have any listed equity shares (or listed securities convertible into equity shares) do not have to comply with these provisions.

Definition of transaction with a related party

35.178 The related party provisions in the Listing Rules with effect from 8 September 1997 include an expanded definition of a *"transaction with a related party"*. This phrase now means one of the following:

- A transaction (other than a transaction of a revenue nature in the ordinary course of business) between a company, or any of its subsidiary undertakings, and a related party.

- Any arrangements pursuant to which a company, or any of its subsidiary undertakings, and a related party each invests in, or provides finance to, another undertaking or asset.

- The entering into, amendment or termination of any contractual arrangements safeguarding the independence of the company between the company and a controlling shareholder (see para 35.180).

[LR 11.1(a)].

35.179 The provisions of the second bullet point in paragraph 35.178 would be likely to catch arrangements where directors who are related parties and subsidiaries of the listed company both invest in a venture capital fund. However, certain such arrangements are excluded. These are joint investment arrangements where the terms and circumstances of the investment by the company or any of its subsidiaries are, in the opinion of an independent adviser acceptable to the Stock Exchange, no less favourable than those applicable to the investment by the related party.

35.180 The contractual arrangements mentioned in the third bullet point above are the arrangements which a company must have in place to ensure that it carries on business on an arm's length basis and independently of any controlling shareholder where a potential conflict exists between the interests of the company and those of the controlling shareholder (or associate). [LR 3.12, 3.13]. Controlling shareholder is defined in paragraph 35.182

Definition of related party

35.180.1 A related party means:

- A substantial shareholder. This is any person who is, or was within the 12 months preceding the date of the transaction, entitled to exercise or control the exercise of ten per cent or more of votes to be cast on all or substantially all matters at general meetings of the company (or any company which is its parent, subsidiary or fellow subsidiary undertaking).

- In relation to a transaction with a related party mentioned in paragraph 35.180, the relevant controlling shareholder or shareholders.

- A director (including a shadow director and a person who was a director or shadow director within the 12 months preceding the transaction) of the company or any company which is its subsidiary undertaking or parent undertaking, or a fellow subsidiary undertaking of its parent undertaking.

- In relation to any investment company or investment trust, the investment manager of the investment company or the investment trust.

- In relation to any venture capital trust, any investment manager of the venture capital trust.

- An associate of a substantial shareholder, controlling shareholder or director. This includes the following:

  - A individual substantial shareholder's spouse or child who is under 18 years (together 'the individual's family').

  - The trustees of a trust of which the individual or any of the individual's family is a beneficiary, other than certain trusts which are occupational pension schemes or employees' share schemes.

  - Another company which is a corporate substantial shareholder's subsidiary undertaking or parent undertaking, or fellow subsidiary undertaking.

  - Any company whose directors are accustomed to act in accordance with a corporate substantial shareholder's directions or instructions.

  - A company in whose equity shares the substantial shareholder (being an individual or a company) and other related parties have an interest which enables them, directly or indirectly, to exercise or control the exercise of 30 per cent or more of votes at general meetings on all, or substantially all, matters; or appoint or remove directors holding a majority of voting rights at board meetings on all, or substantially all, matters.

[LR 11.1].

[The next paragraph is 35.181.]

Exempted transactions

35.181 The rules in chapter 11 do not apply to the following types of related party transactions.

- The issue of new securities for cash by the company made available to all shareholders on the same terms.
- Certain employees' share schemes and long-term incentive schemes.
- The granting of credit upon normal commercial terms in the ordinary course of business.
- The grant of an indemnity to, or maintenance, of an insurance contract for a director of the company or any of its subsidiary undertakings to the extent permitted by section 310.

35.181.1 In addition, small transactions are exempt from these requirements. A very small transaction (that is where each of the ratios based on net assets, profits, consideration to assets, consideration to market capitalisation and gross capital is equal to or less than 0.25 per cent) is exempted from any disclosure. [LR 11.7(i)]. Where, however, a company proposes to enter into either of the following types of small transactions it must inform the Stock Exchange in writing of details of the proposed transaction. These are:

- A transaction where each of the ratios mentioned above is less than 5 per cent, but one or more exceeds 0.25 per cent.
- An amendment of any contractual arrangement referred to in paragraph 35.180.

35.181.2 In addition, prior to completing any such transaction the company must provide the Stock Exchange with written confirmation from an independent adviser acceptable to it that the terms of the proposed transaction or the amendment of the contractual arrangements are fair and reasonable so far as the shareholders are concerned. It must also undertake in writing to include details of the transaction or amendment in its next financial statements, including the identity of the related party, the value of the consideration for the transaction and all other relevant circumstances. [LR 11.8]. The inclusion of these details in the financial statements is, in turn, required by paragraph 12.43(t) of the Listing Rules.

Aggregation

35.181.3 The Stock Exchange will require all transactions to be aggregated which are entered into by the company (or any of its subsidiary undertakings) with the same related party (and any of its associates) in any twelve-month period. This would not apply where they have been approved by shareholders or described in a circular. If the aggregate of the transactions would mean that they would be classified as Class 2 or larger, the Exchange may require the company to comply with the usual requirements mentioned in paragraph 35.177 for each of the transactions. [LR 11.9].

[The next paragraph is 35.182.]

Other disclosures under Listing Rules

Contracts of significance

35.182 Particulars must be given of any contract of significance that subsisted during the period under review between the listed company or one of its subsidiary undertakings and a controlling shareholder. [LR 12.43(r)]. A contract of significance is one representing an amount equal to one per cent or more, calculated on a group basis where relevant, of:

- in the case of a capital transaction or transaction the principal purpose or effect of which is the granting of credit, the aggregate of the group's share capital and reserves; or

- in other cases, the total annual purchases, sales, payments or receipts, as the case may be, of the group.

[LR 12.44].

A controlling shareholder is a person (or persons acting jointly by agreement whether formal or otherwise) who is entitled to exercise, or control the exercise of, 30 per cent or more of the rights to vote at general meetings, or who is able to control the appointment of directors able to exercise the majority of votes at board meetings of the listed company. [LR 3.12].

35.183 In addition, particulars must be given of any contract subsisting during the period under review for the provision of services to the company or any of its subsidiary undertakings by a controlling shareholder. However, a contract need not be disclosed if:

- it is for the provision of services which it is the principal business of the shareholder to provide; and

- it is not a contract of significance.

[LR 12.43(s)].

Directors interests in contracts

35.183.1 The Listing Rules 12.43(q) require the financial statements of a listed company to contain particulars of any contract of significance which existed during the period under review to which the company or one of its subsidiary undertakings was a party and in which a director of the company is or was materially interested. A 'contract of significance' is defined in paragraph 35.182. This disclosure is also covered in chapter 31.

[The next paragraph is 35.184.]

AIM companies

35.184 An AIM company must also notify transactions with related parties to the Company Announcement Office of the Stock Exchange. It must provide details of any transaction (other than a transaction of a revenue nature in the ordinary course of business) it enters into with a related party where any of the specified percentage ratios is five per cent or more. (The specified ratios are ratios based on net assets, profits, consideration to assets, consideration to market capitalisation and gross capital.) These details include the name of the related party concerned and the nature and extent of the related party's interest in the transaction. The notification must also include a statement from the directors of the AIM company (excluding any director who is involved in the transaction as a related party) that, in their opinion, having consulted with the company's nominated adviser, the terms of the transaction are fair and reasonable so far as the shareholders of the company are concerned.[AIM Admission Rules 16.24].

35.185 Details of any transaction with a related party (including the identity of the related party, the value of the consideration for the transaction and all other relevant circumstances) where any percentage ratio exceeds 0.25 per cent must be included in the company's next published annual consolidated financial statements, whether notified under rule 16.24 (mentioned above) or not. [AIM Admission Rules 16.25]. The definition of 'related party' in the AIM Admission Rules is similar to the definition in the Listing Rules, but excludes specific reference to investment managers and controlling shareholders.

Comparison with IASC rules

35.186 The IASC rules are to be found in IAS 24, 'Related party disclosures'. This contains very similar requirements and definitions to FRS 8. FRS 8 states in Appendix III that compliance with the FRS will ensure compliance with IAS 24 in all material respects, except for the exemption in relation to certain subsidiaries.

35.187 Under IAS 24 this exemption is narrower than the equivalent exemption in FRS 8 and further disclosure may be necessary. IAS 24 states that no disclosure of transactions is required in the financial statements of a wholly-owned subsidiary if its parent is incorporated in the same country and provides consolidated financial statements in that country.

35.188 FRS 8, on the other hand, permits subsidiary undertakings 90 per cent or more of whose voting rights are controlled within the group not to disclose transactions with entities that are related parties of the group or investees of the group qualifying as related parties, provided the consolidated financial statements in which the subsidiaries are consolidated are publicly available (see para 35.144).

35.189 The other exemptions in IAS 24 are similar to those in FRS 8, but do not include express exemptions (as given in FRS 8) for pension contributions paid to a pension fund and emoluments in respect of services as an employee of the reporting entity.

35.190 If there have been transactions between related parties, IAS 24 states that the reporting enterprise should disclose:

- The nature of the related party relationships.
- The types of transactions.
- The elements of the transactions necessary for an understanding of the financial statements.

35.191 IAS 24 states that the elements mentioned in the last bullet point would normally include the following:

- An indication of the volume of the transactions, either as an amount or as an appropriate proportion.
- Amounts or appropriate proportions of outstanding items.
- Pricing policies.

35.192 FRS 8 is more specific as to the information to be disclosed (see from para 35.5 onwards). However, FRS 8 also requires disclosure of any other elements of the transactions necessary for an understanding of the financial statements. The standard states that as an example of this would be the need to give an indication that the transfer of a major asset has taken place at an amount materially different from that obtainable on normal commercial terms. [FRS 8 para 22]. There is no specific requirement in FRS 8 to give the volume of transactions or pricing policies although in many cases they may be considered necessary for an understanding of the financial statements. The requirement in FRS 8 to disclose balances owing to or from related parties, provisions for doubtful debts and amounts written off would appear to satisfy the IAS 24 requirement to give the amounts of outstanding items.

35.193 IAS 24 requires disclosure of related party relationships where control exists whether or not there have been any transactions between the related parties. There is a similar requirement in FRS 8 to disclose the party controlling a reporting entity, but FRS 8 specifically requires the additional disclosure of the ultimate controlling party if there is one.

Annex – Main disclosure requirements of the Companies Act 1985 and the Stock Exchange Listing Rules

Disclosures regarding the related parties shown below include the following.

Related party	**Disclosures**	**Manual chapter No.**
Directors and officers		
1985 Act		
Section 232	**Notes to contain details of:**	
Schedule 6 – Part I	Directors' emoluments, pensions and compensation.	11
Part II	Loans by company or subsidiary to directors, and other transactions directly or indirectly for directors' benefit.	34
Part III	Aggregate loans by company or subsidiary to and credit transactions with officers	34
Section 234	**Directors' report to state:**	31
	Name of directors	31
7 Sch 2, 2A	Directors' share interests in company and group shown on register kept under section 325.	31
7 Sch 2B	Directors' rights to subscribe for options in company and group shown on register kept under section 325.	31
Stock Exchange	**Items to be included in financial statements**	
LR 12.43(k)	Any change in the share interests of director and family disclosed under section 324 and their rights to subscribe showing beneficial and non-beneficial interests occurring between year end and one month prior to date of notice of GM.	31
LR 12.43(q)	Particulars of any contract of significance for a director involving the company or a subsidiary.	34

Related party	Disclosures	Manual chapter No.
LR 12.43(d)	Directors' emoluments waived or to be waived.	11
LR.12.43(x)	The information required by LR 12.43(x) contained in a report to shareholders by remuneration committee. (For accounting periods ending on or after 31 December 1995)	11
LR 12.43(t)	Details of small related party transactions with directors.	34
Substantial shareholders		
Stock Exchange	**Items to be included in financial statements**	
LR 12.43(e)	Details of dividends waived or to be waived.	-
LR 12.43(l)	Shareholders with material interests of 3% plus of voting rights and number of shares disclosed under sections 198-208.	38
LR 12.43 (l)	Shareholders with notifiable interests of 10% plus of voting rights and number of shares disclosed under sections 198-208.	38
LR 12.43(r)	Particulars of contracts of significance with a controlling shareholder (eg. 30% plus of voting rights).	35
LR 12.43(s)	Particulars of contract for provision of services by a controlling shareholder.	35
LR 12.43(t)	Details of small related party transactions with shareholders.	35
1985 Act		
5 Sch 12, 31	Notes of subsidiary to disclose ultimate parent company.	21
Group companies and investees		
1985 Act		
Section 231	**Notes to financial statements to contain:**	
5 Sch 12,31	Disclosure by subsidiary of ultimate *parent company*	21

Related party	Disclosures	Manual chapter No.
5 Sch 1-6 and 15-20	Disclosure by parent of name and financial information for each *subsidiary undertaking.*	21
5 Sch 22	Disclosure details of investment of consolidated undertakings in and name of *associated undertakings* (20% plus of voting rights).	16
5 Sch 21	Name and information on *joint ventures* and their proportional consolidation.	28
5 Sch 7-9, 23-28	Name of and information on *significant holdings* of company or group in investees .	16, 21
5 Sch 9A, 28A	Details of membership of company or group in and name of unlimited company or partnership.	21
Schedule 4 4 Sch 59	**Formats** require separate disclosure of intra-group balances.	6
4 Sch – notes 15, 16 to the formats, 4A Sch 21	Notes to profit and loss account require separate disclosure of group income/interest.	6
Stock Exchange		
LR 12.43(g)	Certain additional details of associated undertakings:	16

Chapter 36

Small and medium-sized companies and groups

Page

Chapter 36

Small and medium-sized companies and groups

Introduction

36.1 Prior to the Companies Act 1981, statutory reporting requirements in the UK made little practical distinction between reporting entities. As a result, in broad terms, corporate entities were governed by identical public reporting and disclosure requirements, irrespective of their size, the industry they operated in, or the public's interest in them.

36.2 This was probably a justifiable and sustainable position for as long as reporting requirements were relatively undemanding. However, the past sixteen years or so have been marked by rapid and widespread developments in company law reporting requirements. Many of these developments are part of the EC company law harmonisation programme. This situation has been compounded by the proliferation of accounting standards, many of which seem primarily designed to meet the accounting needs of multinational corporations operating in an increasingly complex business world.

36.3 In the light of such developments, it is hardly surprising that a number of interested parties have questioned whether it is equitable to expect smaller, owner-managed and/or private companies to be burdened with the extensive reporting requirements which are relevant to, and govern, large plcs and multinationals. The accounting purist argued that accounting standards and company law are equally applicable to all corporate financial statements that purport to give a true and fair view. The opposite and more pragmatic camp called for either considerable exemptions for smaller companies or two separate rule-books, one for the larger reporting entity and one for the smaller reporting entity. This so-called 'Big GAAP/Little GAAP' debate, which continued over the last decade, began to gather momentum in the 1990s.

36.4 In November 1992, the government, keen to reduce the reporting burdens of smaller companies, issued a statutory instrument (SI 1992/2452) that allowed small companies to prepare financial statements for shareholders in a less extensive format and without many of the disclosure requirements of Schedule 4. Encouraged by this development, the ASB asked the CCAB to examine the issue and to recommend to the Board, on the basis of wide consultation, criteria for exempting certain types of entity from accounting standards on the grounds of size and relative lack of public interest.

36.5 After much research, the CCAB working party published in november 1994 a consultative document, 'Exemptions from standards on grounds of size or public interest'. The paper proposed that small companies as defined in the Act should be exempt from all accounting standards other than SSAP 4, 9, 13, 17 and 18 and UITF Abstract 7. Whilst the result of the consultation confirmed that the system whereby small entities were required to comply with almost all accounting standards was unsatisfactory, there was no clear support of piecemeal application of a limited number of standards. Consultees expressed strong views that there was a need for guidance, particularly on measurement, to determine whether the financial statements of smaller entities gave a true and fair view. Some suggested that a codification of all standards should be undertaken in the context of their application to smaller entities.

36.6 In May 1995, the DTI, as part of its deregulation initiative, published a consultative document, 'Accounting Simplification' that sought views, amongst others, on the level of accounting disclosures required of small companies. Prompted by the DTI initiative and the comments received on its 1994 consultative document, the CCAB Working Party published another consultative document 'Designed to fit', in December 1995. The paper's principal theme was that there should be a specific Financial Reporting Standard for Smaller Entities (the FRSSE) that meets their needs. A draft FRSSE was included to illustrate the proposed approach.

36.7 The responses to the December 1995 paper were generally positive. Accordingly, the CCAB recommended to the ASB that it should issue, as part of its due process, an exposure draft containing the proposed FRSSE, amended as appropriate to incorporate comments made on the draft contained in 'Designed to fit'. The ASB duly issued an exposure draft in December 1996 with a number of changes that included the extension of the FRSSE to small groups. Finally, in November 1997, the ASB issued the actual standard.

36.8 On the legislative side, commentators on the DTI's consultative paper, 'Accounting simplification', strongly supported the case to produce a 'stand-alone' small company Schedule. The government, encouraged by this response, issued The Companies Act 1985 (Accounts of Small and Medium-Sized Companies and Minor Accounting Amendments) Regulations 1997 (SI 1997/220), which came into force on 1 March 1997. The regulations include a new Schedule 8 which sets out in full the provisions of Schedule 4 that are relevant to small companies.

36.9 Thus, the new Schedule 8 and the FRSSE establish a clearly distinguishable regime for small companies. While the measurement rules in the FRSSE are the same as, or are a simplification of, those in existing accounting standards, disclosure requirements are reduced substantially. Indeed, the FRSSE creates a link with the provisions of Schedule 8. The effect is that financial statements prepared by small companies in accordance with Schedule 8 and the FRSSE are sufficient to give a true and fair view. This new regime for small companies effectively brings the Big GAAP/little GAAP debate to a satisfactory conclusion.

Scope of the chapter

36.10 This chapter does not comment on all the measurement and disclosure requirements contained in the FRSSE and in Schedule 8 and, to this extent, it is not a stand-alone chapter dealing with all the provisions applicable to small companies' financial statements. To do so would be to repeat substantially all of the measurement rules and disclosure requirements discussed in the main body of this manual. Rather, the section on small company financial statements deals mainly with the exceptions and, where applicable, cross refers the relevant provisions of the FRSSE to the appropriate chapters of this manual. In some instances, the disclosure requirements of the FRSSE are included. This chapter also considers the statutory requirements that affect medium-sized companies and groups and dormant companies in the UK. A detailed discussion on agency companies is also included as a logical extension to dormant companies.

The regulatory framework

Company law

36.11 It was the 1981 Act that first distinguished 'small and medium-sized companies' from the body of companies as a whole, in terms of the form and content of their statutory financial statements. Integral to the introduction of this distinction was the design and implementation of criteria for identifying qualifying companies. These criteria evaluate companies by reference to annual turnover levels, the amount of the company's assets and the size of its workforce. Once identified, the 1981 Act allowed:

- 'Small and medium-sized companies', as well as groups which satisfied the 'small and medium-sized companies' criteria, to file *modified* financial statements with the Registrar of Companies.
- Dormant companies qualifying as *small* to elect not to appoint auditors.

36.12 In this context, it should be emphasised that filing modified financial statements with the Registrar did not absolve the reporting entity from preparing full, non-modified financial statements for its shareholders. Thus, qualifying companies were permitted to file modified financial statements for this public scrutiny, provided that they also produced full financial statements for their shareholders. Alternatively, they could produce one full set of financial statements for shareholders that would also be publicly filed with the Registrar. In effect, the Act allowed the directors of a reporting entity to decide whether the additional costs that would be incurred in preparing modified financial statements for filing were justified on the grounds of the added confidentiality afforded by them.

36.13 The 1989 Act subsequently amended the 1985 Act (which consolidated the 1981 Act), in that:

- Minor changes were made to the rules established by the 1981 Act. These changes included revised terminology which now refers to *"abbreviated"* rather than *"modified"* financial statements for filing by small and medium-sized companies.

- A significant new exemption from consolidation was introduced for groups qualifying as small or medium-sized under new definitions that apply to groups.

36.14 In November 1992, The Companies Act 1985 (Accounts of Small and Medium-Sized Enterprises and Publication of Accounts in ECUs) Regulations 1992 (SI 1992/2452) came into force. This statutory instrument inserted new provisions in the 1985 Act under section 246 and Parts I and II of Schedule 8. These provisions introduced further important revisions to the reporting requirements of such entities. Specifically:

- While the employee numbers criterion remained unchanged, the annual turnover and balance sheet total thresholds for small and medium-sized companies and groups were increased by approximately 40 per cent.

- New *"special accounting exemptions"* were introduced allowing companies qualifying as *small* to prepare financial statements for shareholders in a less extensive format than that required for other reporting entities. These exemptions also enable qualifying companies to omit certain of the disclosures required in full financial statements from the directors' report.

36.15 The exemptions referred to above, together with those relevant to abbreviated financial statements, were set out in Schedule 8. This schedule mostly comprised a list of those paragraphs of Schedule 4 from which small and medium-sized companies were exempt. Hence, preparers of abbreviated or shorter-form financial statements were required to determine specifically which of the provisions relevant to larger companies applied and which did not. At times, this proved to be a complex and time-consuming exercise.

36.16 On 1 March 1997, The Companies Act 1985 (Accounts of Small and Medium-sized Companies and Minor Accounting Amendments) Regulations 1997 (SI 1997/220) came into force and these went some way towards simplification of the rules. These regulations introduced a revised Schedule 8 and a new Schedule 8A which set out in full those provisions of Schedule 4 which are applicable to small companies. Reference must still be made to other schedules and sections of the Act, and the exemptions therefrom, which are now contained in a revised section 246, although by removing the requirement to trawl through Schedule 4 a major hurdle has been removed.

36.17 The exemptions available to medium-sized companies are no longer included in Schedule 8, but are set out in a new section 246A.

36.18 There are no changes of substance to the form and content of abbreviated or shorter-form financial statements, although the directors' statements and the rules governing audit reports have been simplified.

36.19 There is a fundamental point to be emphasised here. The financial statements referred to in the second bullet point of paragraph 36.14 are those which a company prepares for its shareholders. In this chapter, such financial statements are referred to as 'shorter-form financial statements'. However, it should be noted that this term is not used in the Act or amending regulations, but is used in this chapter purely for convenience, in order to avoid confusion with the term 'abbreviated financial statements'. The definitions of the above terms as used in this chapter are as follows:

- 'Shorter-form financial statements' means the individual or group financial statements small companies are permitted to prepare for shareholders by virtue of section 246(2)-(4) of the 1985 Act.

- 'Abbreviated financial statements' mean the individual financial statements that small and medium-sized companies are permitted to file by virtue of sections 246(5) or (6) or 246A(3) of the 1985 Act.

36.20 There are major differences between the form and content of shorter-form and abbreviated financial statements. Shorter-form financial statements are prepared for shareholders and are required to give a true and fair view. In contrast, abbreviated financial statements do not purport to give a true and fair view and on commercial/confidentiality grounds they exclude financial information that is integral to the true and fair view. Hence, the disclosure exemptions available in respect of shorter-form financial statements are much less extensive than those available in respect of abbreviated financial statements.

36.21 It is also important for the owners/directors of a reporting entity to consider the commercial costs and benefits that might accrue from utilising the exemptions described above. For example:

- Producing abbreviated financial statements for filing with the Registrar of Companies will result in some additional cost to the company, because they will be additional to the financial statements prepared for shareholders.

Consequently, abbreviated financial statements should only be produced where it is determined to be worthwhile on confidentiality grounds.

- The exemption from consolidation may save time and expense in terms of preparing financial statements. However, in some instances, the parent company's shareholders require information about the activities of the group as a whole. In these circumstances the parent will need to prepare consolidated financial statements for its shareholders in spite of the available exemption.

36.22 For shorter-form financial statements, the concessions from the detailed disclosure requirements of Schedule 4 concerning the items to be disclosed in the formats and in the notes, at first sight appear extensive. But it must be remembered that small companies may not have many of the categories of item allowed to be aggregated under the rules and hence, the concessions have less impact in practice. For example, under the heading of intangible assets, developments costs, concessions and patents and payments on account are allowed to be aggregated under the single item 'other intangible assets'. Many small companies will not have such assets and, as a consequence, for them this concession is redundant.

Accounting standards

Small companies and groups

36.23 As stated in the introduction to the chapter, the ASB issued a Financial Reporting Standard for Smaller Entities (FRSSE) in November 1997. It is designed to provide small companies with a single reporting standard that is focussed on their particular circumstances. The FRSSE is not compulsory, but where a small company chooses to adopt the FRSSE, it is exempt from other accounting standards and UITF Abstracts, unless preparing consolidated financial statements, in which case certain other accounting standards and one UITF Abstract apply, as set out in paragraph ? below.

36.24 The CCAB working party had to consider whether the measurement rules in existing standards should be transferred effectively unaltered into the FRSSE or whether some should be deleted or amended. The working party, however, recognised that significant differences of measurement between larger and smaller companies would have to be considered very carefully. As a consequence, the general measurement rules were retained, but their application was simplified in certain respects. The FRSSE also imports those disclosure rules from existing standards that are considered to be relevant to small companies. Section C of the FRSSE contains definition of terms that apply to the accounting practices set out in the FRSSE. These terms have been imported from existing accounting standards suitably modified in certain cases.

36.25 Appendix V of the FRSSE analyses, in table format, each paragraph of the FRSSE and explains the source, and whether that source has been adopted in its entirety, or with minor amendments, or with major changes. Major changes are those where either a measurement rule has been simplified, or a disclosure requirement has been lifted. As a corollary, Appendix VI of the FRSSE sets out simplifications that have been made in the FRSSE as compared with the existing body of accounting standards and the UITF Abstracts.

36.26 There may be circumstances where a small company enters into transactions on which accounting guidance is not provided in the FRSSE. It may be that guidance on such transactions is provided in the accounting standards applying to larger entities. In that situation, it makes sense to follow a practice that has been clearly established and accepted, unless there are good reasons for a small company to depart from it. Indeed, the FRSSE takes the same view that for transactions and events not dealt with in the FRSSE, small companies should have regard to other accounting standards and UITF Abstracts, not as mandatory documents, but as a means of establishing current practice. [FRSSE App IV para 19]. In that situation, adequate disclosure should be made in the notes to the financial statements of the transaction or arrangement concerned and the treatment adopted. This requirement is implicit in paragraph 2.2 of the FRSSE. It follows that for transactions and events not dealt with in the FRSSE, but dealt with in other accounting standards and UITF Abstracts, a small company should have regard not only to the measurements rules, but also to any disclosure requirements relevant to those transactions.

36.27 The FRSSE will be revised and updated periodically to reflect developments in financial reporting. In this connection, the ASB has established a Committee on Accounting for Smaller Entities that will recommend to the ASB how new standards or revisions to existing standards apply to smaller entities. The Committee will also be responsible for reviewing the operation of the FRSSE. Any proposed changes to the FRSSE will be subject to public consultation. Revisions of the FRSSE will be formally approved and issued by the ASB.

Medium-sized companies and groups

36.28 There are no special accounting standards for medium-sized companies and groups. Therefore, all accounting standards and UITF Abstracts apply to them except for the following:

- SSAP 3 (revised), 'Earnings per share', is applicable to listed companies only (see chapter 8).

- SSAP 13 (revised), 'Accounting for research and development', excludes from profit and loss account disclosures private companies less than ten times the financial criteria defining a medium-sized company (see chapter 14).

- SSAP 25, 'Segmental reporting', excludes private companies as in SSAP 13 above from some of the more detailed segmental disclosures (see chapter 9).

- FRS 2, 'Accounting for subsidiary undertakings', mirrors the Act in allowing parents of small and medium-sized groups an exemption from preparing consolidated financial statements in most circumstances. Indeed, because of this exemption, such groups are also effectively exempt from complying with SSAP 22, FRS 6 and FRS 7 (see chapter 21).

36.29 As can be seen from the above, while the exemptions FRS 2 apply to small companies as defined in the Act, the exemptions allowed in SSAP 13 and SSAP 25 are based on size criteria, which serve to exempt far larger companies from compliance.

Audit requirements

36.30 As a further complication, The Companies Act 1985 (Audit Exemptions) Regulations 1994 (SI 1994/1935), came into force on 11 August 1994. This statutory instrument introduced into the 1985 Act new sections 249A-E, allowing qualifying companies to be exempt from the requirement for any external audit. Although, in the UK, audit had been compulsory for companies of all sizes (unless dormant) for many years, that was not the case in some other EC countries. Thus, the EC 4th Directive, which permitted national governments to dispense with the requirement for small companies to undergo an audit, influenced this change in UK statutory requirements. Further changes were made on 15 April 1997 when The Companies Act 1985 (Audit Exemption) (Amendment) Regulations 1997 (SI 1997/936) came into force. The changes are effective for financial years ending on or after 15 June 1997 and mean that:

- A qualifying company will be exempt from the need to have an audit if its annual turnover and balance sheet total for the year are not more than £350,000 and £1,400,000 respectively, and no notice has been received by the company from a member or members holding at least 10 per cent of the company's issued capital, or 10 per cent of any class of shares, requiring that the financial statements for a particular year should be audited.

- For charitable companies, the limit is reduced to £250,000 and an accountant's report, prepared by an independent reporting accountant, will be required where gross income is in the range £90,000 to £250,000.

- Companies with an annual turnover in excess of £350,000 (gross income of £250,000 in the case of a charitable company) will remain subject to annual audit, even where they fulfil the small company criteria set out elsewhere in the Act in respect of abbreviated and shorter-form financial statements .

36.31 The circumstances where companies that meet the size exemption criteria are still prevented from obtaining an audit exemption are set out in section 249B of the Act. This indicates that a company will not be entitled to the audit exemption conferred by section 249A if at any time during the financial year it was one of the following:

- A public company.
- A banking or insurance company
- A company enrolled in the list maintained by the Insurance Brokers Registration Council under section 4 of the Insurance Brokers (Registration) Act 1977.
- An authorised person or an authorised representative under the Financial Services Act 1986.
- A special register body as defined in section 117(1) of the Trade Union and Labour Relations (Consolidation) Act 1992 or an employers' association as defined in section 122 of that Act.
- A parent company or a subsidiary undertaking unless:
  - it is a subsidiary undertaking that qualifies as dormant under section 250 of the Act (although no special resolution under section 250 is required for it to qualify for this exemption); or
  - it is a parent or a subsidiary undertaking in a small group, provided that the turnover of the group is not more than £350,000 net or £420,000 gross and the group's balance sheet total is not more than £1.4 million net or £1.68 million gross and the group is not an ineligible group within the meaning of section 248(2) (see para 36.51).

[Sec 249B(1) and (1A) to (1C) amended by SI 1997/936].

36.32 Where a qualifying small company takes advantage of the exemption from audit, the balance sheet should include a statement by the directors to the effect that:

- For the year in question the company was entitled to the exemption under subsection (1) (subsection (2) for charitable companies where gross income is more than £90,000) of section 249A.

- No notice from members requiring an audit has been deposited under subsection (2) of section 249B in relation to the company's financial statements for the financial year.

In addition, the statement should state that the directors acknowledge their responsibilities for:

- Ensuring that the company keeps accounting records that comply with section 221.

- Preparing financial statements that give a true and fair view and which otherwise comply with the Act's requirements.

[Sec 249B(4)].

36.33 The requirements above apply both to companies that take advantage of the total exemption from audit and to those charitable companies that require a report by reporting accountants. The statement should appear above the directors' signature on the balance sheet. [Sec 249B(5) amended by SI 1996/198]. The unaudited financial statements can be full financial statements, but as the company will be a small company under the Act, it may choose to take advantage of the special provisions of section 246 concerning abbreviated or shorter-form financial statements.

Summary

36.34 As a result of the legislative changes referred to above, the options that are available to small and medium-sized companies under the Act for the preparation and audit of financial statements for filing and for shareholders are complex and are summarised in the annex to this chapter.

Categorisation of companies and groups

Small and medium-sized companies

Basic size tests

36.35 A company may qualify as small or medium-sized for a financial year if it satisfies *any two* of the three conditions under the applicable heading in the following table during that year:

	Small	Medium-sized
■ Annual turnover not exceeding	£2,800,000	£11,200,000
■ Balance sheet total not exceeding	£1,400,000	£5,600,000
■ Average number of employees not exceeding	50	250
[Sec 247(3)].		

36.36 Where a company has not prepared its financial statements in respect of a 12 month period, the turnover thresholds must be proportionately adjusted in order to establish whether the appropriate conditions have been satisfied. [Sec 247(4)]. For example, in the case of a company which prepares financial statements for a nine-month period, the turnover threshold will be £2,100,000 (that is, 9/12 × £2,800,000) for a small company, and £8,400,000 (that is, 9/12 × £11,200,000) for a medium-sized company. Neither the balance sheet threshold, nor the employee number threshold, is affected by shorter or longer accounting periods.

36.37 Where a company adopts Format 1 for its balance sheet, the 'balance sheet total' is the aggregate of the amounts shown under the headings that are preceded by the letters A to D inclusive in the formats shown in either Schedule 4 or Schedule 8. [Sec 247(5)(a) amended by SI 1997/220]. Where a company adopts Format 2 for its balance sheet, the 'balance sheet total' is the aggregate of the amounts shown under the general heading *Assets*. [Sec 247(5)(b)]. In either case, the effect is to equate 'balance sheet total' to gross assets.

36.38 The number of employees means the average number of persons employed by the company in the year, determined on a monthly basis. The method prescribed by paragraph 56(2) and (3) of Schedule 4 to the Act should be adopted for the calculation; that is, adding up those defined as employed for each month and dividing the total thereby derived by the number of months in the period. [Sec 247(6) amended by SI 1996/189].

36.39 The basic size parameters are subject to periodic amendment. The latest such amendment occurred in November 1992 when SI 1992/2452 increased the annual turnover and balance sheet total thresholds by approximately 40 per cent. It is important to ensure, therefore, that reference is made to the latest set of thresholds, and that advantage is taken of any transitional provisions that may apply.

Other qualification criteria

36.40 The application of the criteria for small and medium-sized companies can prove complex, because, in addition to satisfying the basic size tests referred to above, companies must also satisfy other qualification criteria which may be more difficult to interpret. For this reason, care needs to be exercised in determining whether or not a company is qualified to take advantage of the exemptions available to small or medium-sized companies.

36.41 The Act sets out the following additional criteria that must be applied in determining whether a company qualifies as small or medium-sized in relation to a financial year, for the purposes of filing abbreviated financial statements (small and medium-sized companies) or preparing shorter-form financial statements (small companies only):

- In respect of a company's first financial year, it will qualify as small or medium-sized, provided that it satisfies the appropriate size conditions under section 247(3) in that year. [Sec 247(1)(a)].

- In subsequent years, a company will qualify as small or medium-sized, provided that it satisfies the appropriate size conditions under section 247(3) in both the year in question and the preceding year. [Sec 247(1)(b)].

- A company that qualifies as small or medium-sized under section 247(3) in one year will be treated as qualifying in the following year, even if it fails to satisfy the size conditions in that following year. However, if it does not satisfy the qualifying conditions in the year after that, then, for that third year, it must produce its financial statements in a format appropriate to its size. On the other hand, if the company reverts to satisfying the qualifying conditions in this third year, then it may continue to take advantage of available accounting exemptions. [Sec 247(2)(a)(b)].

36.42 The application of these qualification criteria is best illustrated by way of an example:

Example

Consider the following details relating to two companies, S and M. While company S is incorporated on the first day of year 2, company M is a long-established entity that fulfilled the size conditions of a medium-sized company in the year immediately before year 1.

Company S	**Year 1**	**Year 2**	**Year 3**	**Year 4**
Turnover	–	£2.6m	£3.0m	£2.6m
Gross assets	–	£1.3m	£1.5m	£1.2m
Average number of employees	–	55	60	55

In year 2, its year of incorporation, company S fulfils the size criteria for qualification as a small company. This is because it fulfils the criteria both for turnover and gross assets, although not for average number of employees. As year 2 is its first financial year, company S qualifies as a small company by virtue of section 247(1)(a) of the Act. As such, it can file abbreviated financial statements and prepare shorter-form financial statements for its shareholders.

In year 3, company S has exceeded all three size criteria for small company qualification. However, by virtue of section 247(2)(a), it still qualifies as a small company, because it fulfilled the size conditions in the preceding year, which was its first financial year. It can, therefore, file abbreviated financial statements and prepare shorter-form financial statements for this year.

In year 4, company S satisfies the size criteria for qualification as a small company. Despite the fact that it did not satisfy the size conditions in year 3, it still qualifies as a small company by virtue of section 247(2)(b), because it was treated as so qualifying in year 3 and currently meets the qualifying criteria. It can, similarly, file abbreviated financial statements and prepare shorter-form financial statements for this year.

Company M	**Year 1**	**Year 2**	**Year 3**	**Year 4**
Turnover	£10.2m	£11.6m	£12.3m	£11.0m
Gross assets	£5.4m	£5.5m	£6.0m	£5.0m
Average number of employees	250	255	255	250

In year 1, company M fulfils all the size criteria that qualify it to be treated as a medium-sized company. Since it has fulfilled the size-conditions for two consecutive years, it can take advantage of the exemptions allowed to it to file abbreviated financial statements. As a medium-sized company it cannot prepare shorter-form financial statements as these are only available to small companies.

In year 2, company M ceases to fulfil the size conditions for a medium-sized company because both its turnover and its average number of employees exceed the specified thresholds. However, it still qualifies as a medium-sized company for abbreviated financial statements purposes by virtue of section 247(2)(a), in that it fulfilled the size criteria for qualification in the two previous years.

In year 3, company M fails to meet the size criteria for a medium-sized company for a second consecutive year. Consequently, it no longer qualifies as a medium-sized company and cannot, therefore, file abbreviated financial statements for year 3.

In year 4, company M reverts to fulfilling the size conditions of a medium-sized company. However, it does not qualify as a medium-sized company for abbreviated financial statements purposes, because it has not fulfilled the size criteria for qualification for two consecutive years. Should it meet these criteria in year 5, it would then be able to revert to filing abbreviated financial statements.

36.43 For parent companies, there is a further condition that they must satisfy before filing abbreviated financial statements. A parent company should not be treated as qualifying as a small or medium-sized company in relation to a financial year, unless the group headed by it qualifies also as a small or medium-sized group. [Sec 247A(3) inserted by SI 1997/220]. Consequently, if the parent is a small company, it can only file abbreviated financial statements if it is also the parent of a 'small group'. If it were the parent of a 'medium-sized group', it could only file abbreviated financial statements applicable to a medium-sized company. Similarly a medium-sized parent can only file abbreviated financial statements if it is the parent of a 'medium-sized group'. These rules are explained further from paragraph 36.143.

Small and medium-sized groups

Basic size tests

36.44 A group may qualify as small or medium-sized for a financial year (and, therefore, be exempted from the requirement to prepare consolidated financial statements) if it satisfies *any two* of the three conditions under the applicable heading in the following table during that year:

	Small	Medium-sized
■ Aggregate net turnover not exceeding	£2,800,000	£11,200,000
or		
Aggregate gross turnover not exceeding	£3,360,000	£13,440,000
■ Aggregate net balance sheet total not exceeding	£1,400,000	£5,600,000
or		
Aggregate gross balance sheet total not exceeding	£1,680,000	£6,720,000
■ Average number of employees not exceeding	50	250
[Sec 249(3)].		

36.45 For groups, the figures for turnover, balance sheet total and average number of employees are arrived at by adding together the relevant figures for each group company. The net figures refer to the relevant amounts after making consolidation adjustments for set-offs and other matters. As an alternative the gross figures can be applied to the relevant amounts before making such adjustments. [Sec 249(4)]. A company may satisfy the qualifying criteria on the basis of gross or net figures and in any year it is permissible to mix the use of gross and net figures.

36.46 If the financial year of a subsidiary company is not coterminous with that of the parent company, then the subsidiary's latest financial statements, for a year which immediately predates the financial year of the parent, should be used. [Sec 249(5)(b)].

However, if the subsidiary's figures cannot be ascertained without disproportionate expense or undue delay, the latest available figures may be used. [Sec 249(6)].

Other qualification criteria

36.47 The other qualification criteria outlined in paragraph 36.40 of this chapter relating to small and medium-sized companies, are mirrored by similar criteria affecting small and medium-sized groups. [Secs 249(1),(2)]. Thus, the Act states that a group qualifies as small or medium-sized in relation to a financial year, where:

- The size test conditions set out in section 249(3) are met and it is the parent company's first financial year. [Sec 249(1)(a)].
- In any subsequent financial year the size test conditions are met and were in the year immediately preceding. [Sec 249(1)(b)].
- The size test conditions were met in the preceding year, but are not met in the current year. [Sec 249 (2)(a)].
- The size test conditions are met in the current year but were not met in the previous year, yet the group still qualified on that occasion by virtue of the rule in section 249(2)(a). [Sec 249(2)(b)].

36.48 As in the case of individual companies, care needs to be taken to ensure that these criteria are complied with, before a group concludes that it qualifies to take advantage of any of the exemptions available to small and medium-sized groups.

36.49 The application of the qualification criteria is complicated and is illustrated in the example in paragraph 36.42. Furthermore, if a group qualifies as small or medium-sized on, say, a net basis in a particular year, it is not required to apply the same basis in the following year. In each year, it may apply the net basis, the gross basis or a mixture of the two (see para 36.44).

Excluded companies and groups

36.50 The concessions that allow small companies to prepare shorter-form shareholders' financial statements and small and medium-sized companies to file abbreviated financial statements exclude certain companies. These concessions are not available to any company, regardless of its size, that is, or was at any time during the financial year that the financial statements relate to, one of the following:

- A public company.

- A banking company, being a company which is authorised under the Banking Act 1987.

- An insurance company under Part II of the Insurance Companies Act 1982.This is deemed to include an EC company lawfully carrying on insurance business in the UK. This means an insurance company incorporated in or formed under the law of a member state other than the UK, whose head office is in that state and which is authorised in accordance with Article 6 of the first general insurance Directive or Article 6 of the first long-term insurance Directive.

- An authorised person under the Financial Services Act 1986.

- A member of an ineligible group. An ineligible group is a group in which any of its members is one of the types of companies stated in points one to four above. In addition, an ineligible group includes a body corporate as defined in section 740 that is able lawfully to issue shares or debentures to the public. This includes a foreign company with the legal authority and power under its constitution to offer its shares to the public.

[Sec 247A(1),(2) inserted by SI 1997/220].

36.51 Not surprisingly, the Act has similar exclusions in relation to groups when it legislates for small and medium-sized groups. Consequently, a parent company cannot take advantage of the exemptions from preparing consolidated financial statements in section 248 if the group headed by it is an ineligible group. In this respect, an ineligible group is one which has as its members any of the entities mentioned in paragraph 36.50 above. [Sec 248(2)].

36.52 However, these exclusions do not preclude a company being treated as small or medium-sized if it is a subsidiary of a large *private* company and all the other qualification criteria set out in paragraph 36.50 are met.

Small company financial statements

Available options

36.53 A small company has the following options in preparing and filing its statutory financial statements.

- It may prepare and file full financial statements like a large company in conformity with accounting standards and the Act's reporting rules and Schedule 4 formats discussed in the main body of this manual.

- It may prepare its annual financial statements in accordance with the FRSSE and the special provisions available to small companies under Schedule 8, or add additional Schedule 4 requirements to the Schedule 8 minimum, and file them.

- It may prepare either of the above financial statements for shareholders, but file abbreviated financial statements prepared in accordance with Schedule 8A.

36.54 The distinction between financial statements that are prepared for shareholders and those that are delivered to the Registrar of Companies has been discussed in paragraphs 36.19 to 36.21. In summary, where a small company delivers abbreviated financial statements to the Registrar of Companies, it must still prepare full or shorter-form financial statements for its members.

36.55 In practice, few small companies make greater public disclosure than they have to. Consequently, while the first reporting option in the paragraph above is available, it is not the preferred choice of many small companies. Accordingly, the option is not further discussed in this chapter. The paragraphs that follow consider financial statements prepared for shareholders in accordance with the FRSSE and Schedule 8. Abbreviated financial statements prepared in accordance with Schedule 8A for filing, insofar as they relate to qualifying small companies, are considered from paragraphs 36.117.

Form and content of shorter-form financial statements

36.56 The general provisions that relate to the form and content of small company financial statements are detailed in Schedule 8 to the Act. These provisions are supplemented by specific requirements of the FRSSE which provide a link with the Schedule 8 provisions. In preparing the financial statements, a small company is permitted to comply with the provisions of Schedule 8, or it may comply instead with one or more of the corresponding provisions of Schedule 4. Any reference in section 226 (duty to prepare individual company accounts) to compliance with the provisions of Schedule 4 is then construed accordingly. [Sec 246(2) inserted by SI 1997/220].

36.57 Section 246(3) gives further exemptions from the disclosure requirements of other schedules to the Act while section 246(4) gives exemptions from certain of the disclosures generally required for the directors' report. These exemptions are explained in paragraphs 36.94 and 36.108 respectively.

36.58 Three primary statements included within a small company's financial statements are:

- Profit and loss account.
- Statement of total recognised gains and losses.
- Balance sheet.

36.59 Schedule 8 sets out two alternative formats for the balance sheet; which are a simplification of those set out in Schedule 4 and four alternative formats for the profit and loss account, which are identical to those set out in Schedule 4. It also lays down certain general guidelines to be followed. In addition, the Schedule requires small companies to disclose in the notes to the balance sheet and in the notes to the profit and loss account many of the disclosure requirements that apply to the generality of companies. Indeed, the new Schedule 8 does not provide any overall reduction in the disclosure requirements applicable to small companies.

36.60 The Act does not require companies to include in their financial statements a statement of total recognised gains and loses. This primary statement is required by the FRSSE for all small companies financial statements that are intended to give a true and fair view. However, where the only recognised gains and losses are the results included in the profit and loss account no separate statement to this effect is required. [FRSSE para 4.1].

36.61 There is no requirement in the Act for companies to prepare a cash flow statement. The CCAB working party had made proposals in 'Designed to fit', for a simplified cash flow statement but, following overwhelming rejection by respondents to the discussion paper, this proposal was dropped. Nevertheless, the FRSSE, like FRS 1, encourages, but does not require, small entities to prepare a cash flow statement. Section D of the FRSSE sets out the voluntary disclosures relating to cash flow information.

The balance sheet

Formats

36.62 The balance sheet formats set out in Schedule 8 are simplifications of those set out in Schedule 4. The table below considers format 1 of the balance sheet and indicates how the Schedule 8 formats take those in Schedule 4 and combine certain of the headings preceded by Arabic numerals. Format 2 allows identical combination of headings.

Items in italic in column 1 are combined under the item in italic shown opposite in column 2. The items with Roman numerals remain unchanged.

	Format 1 per Schedule 4		**Format 1 per Schedule 8**
A	Called up share capital not paid	A	Called up share capital not paid
B	Fixed assets	B	Fixed assets
B 1	Intangible assets 3. Goodwill *1. Development costs* *2. Concessions...* *4. Payments on account*	B 1	Intangible assets 1. Goodwill *2. Other intangible assets*
B II	Tangible assets 1. Land and buildings *2. Plant and machinery* *3. Fixture, fittings...* *4. Payments on account...*	B II	Tangible assets 1. Land and buildings *2. Plant and machinery, etc*
B III	Investments *1. Shares in group undertakings* *3. Participating interests* *2. Loans to group undertakings* *4. Loans to undertakings, etc*	B III	Investments *1. Shares in group undertakings and participating interests* *2. Loans to group undertakings and undertakings in which the company has a participating interest*
	5. Other investments other than loans *6. Other loans* *7. Own shares*		3. Other investments other than loans *4. Other investments*
C	Current assets	C	Current assets
C I	Stocks *1. Raw materials, etc.* *2. Work in progress* *3. Finished goods/goods for resale* 4. Payments on account	C I	Stocks *1. Stocks* 2. Payments on account

C II	Debtors 1. Trade debtors *2. Amounts owed by group undertakings* *3. Amounts owed by undertakings in which the company has a participating interest* *4. Other debtors* *5. Called up share capital not paid* *6. Prepayments and accrued income*	C II	Debtors 1. Trade debtors *2. Amounts owed by group undertakings and undertakings in which the company has a participating interest* *3. Other debtors*
C III	Investments 1. Shares in group undertakings *2. Own shares* *3. Other investments*	C III	Investments 1. Shares in group undertakings *2. Other investments*
C IV	Cash at bank and in hand	C IV	Cash at bank and in hand
D	Prepayments and accrued income	D	Prepayments and accrued income
E	Creditors: amounts ... within one year 2. Bank loans and overdrafts 4. Trade creditors *6. Amounts owed to group undertakings* *7. Amounts owed to undertakings in which the company has a participating interest* *1. Debenture loans* *3. Payments received on account* *5. Bills of exchange payable* *8. Other creditors including taxation and social security* *9. Accruals and deferred income*	E	Creditors: amounts ... within one year 1. Bank loans and overdraft 2. Trade creditors *3. Amounts owed to group undertakings and undertakings in which the company has a participating interest* *4. Other creditors*
F	Net current assets (liabilities)	F	Net current assets (liabilities)
G	Total assets less current liabilities	G	Total assets less current liabilities

H	Creditors amounts ... after one year 2. Bank loans and overdrafts 4. Trade creditors *6. Amounts owed to group undertakings* *7. Amounts owed to undertakings in which the company has a participating interest* *1. Debenture loans* *3. Payments received on account* *5. Bills of exchange payable* *8. Other creditors including taxation and social security* *9. Accruals and deferred income*	H	Creditors: amounts ... after one year 1. Bank loans and overdrafts 2. Trade creditors *3. Amounts owed to group undertaking and undertakings in which the company has a participating interest* *4. Other creditors*
I	Provision for liabilities and charges *1. Pensions and similar obligations* *2. Taxation, etc* *3. Other provisions*	I	Provisions for liabilities and charges *(Items 1-3 need not be shown)*
J	Accruals and deferred income	J	Accruals and deferred income
K	Capital and reserves	K	Capital and reserves
KI	Called up share capital	KI	Called up share capital
KII	Share premium account	KII	Share premium account
KIII	Revaluation reserve	KIII	Revaluation reserve
KIV	Other reserves *1. Capital redemption reserve* *2. Reserve for own shares* *3. Reserves provided for by articles* *4. Other reserves*	KIV	Other reserves *(Items 1-4 need not be shown)*
KV	Profit and loss account	KV	Profit and loss account

36.63 The following additional exemptions are available:

- In the case of both formats 1 and 2, a small company need not show amounts falling due after more than one year separately for each item included under debtors if it discloses the aggregate amount of debtors falling due after more than one year in the notes. [8 Sch 8(5) inserted by SI 1997/220]. However, following UITF Abstract 4, in some instances where the amount of long-term debtors is so material the split might need to be given on the face of the balance sheet.

- In the case of format 2, a small company need not show separately the amounts falling due within one year and after one year for each of the items included under creditors if it discloses the aggregate amount of creditors falling due within one year and the aggregate amount falling due after more than one year in the notes. [8 Sch 8(10) inserted by SI 1997/220].

- Although the balance sheet formats do not include a separate line for creditors in respect of taxation and social security, this amount should be shown separately. [8 Sch 8(7) inserted by SI 1997/220].

Tangible fixed assets and depreciation

36.64 As is evident from the balance sheet formats, small companies are permitted to sub-analyse tangible fixed assets into land and buildings and other tangible fixed assets in aggregate. The valuation bases and the depreciation rules discussed in chapter 5 are equally applicable to small companies. The depreciation rules are dealt with in paragraphs 5.1 to 5.10 of the FRSSE.

36.65 The Act's disclosure requirements for fixed assets are dealt with in paragraphs 40 and 41 of Schedule 8. These disclosure requirements are a replica of the equivalent Schedule 4 disclosure requirements, which are discussed in chapter 14 of this Manual. In addition, the FRSSE also requires the following information to be disclosed in respect of depreciation for each of the two categories of fixed assets:

- The depreciation methods used.
- The useful economic lives or the depreciation rates used.
- Total depreciation charged for the period.
- The gross amount of depreciable assets and the related accumulated depreciation.

[FRSSE para 5.11].

36.66 There is no requirement for small companies to disclose the investment revaluation reserve relating to investment properties on the face of the balance sheet as required by paragraph 15 of SSAP 19. The information can be given by way of a note to the balance sheet. [FRSSE App V]. However, the revaluation reserve is a separate line item in the balance sheet formats in Schedule 8 and has to be shown on the face of the balance sheet.

36.67 In respect of government grants, the FRSSE does not provide any guidance for dealing with financial support grants. If a small company receives such a grant, it should follow the accounting treatment specified in SSAP 4 as current best practice.

Leases

36.68 The FRSSE modifies the recognition rules for finance leases in SSAP 21 for small companies. Where a small company leases an asset on a finance lease, both the asset and the corresponding lease obligations should normally be recorded at the fair value of the asset, rather than the present value of the minimum lease payments. [FRSSE para 6.2]. However, where the fair value of the asset does not give a reliable estimate of the cost of the asset to the lessee because, for example, the lessee has benefited from grants and capital allowances that had the effect of reducing the aggregate minimum lease payments to below the fair value of the asset, the asset and the obligation should be recorded at the present value of the minimum lease payments. A negative finance charge should not be shown. [FRSSE para 6.3].

36.69 Where a small company is a lessor of assets under finance leases, the total gross earnings should be recognised on a systematic and rational basis. In most cases, this would be achieved by allocating gross earnings so as to give a constant periodic rate of return on the lessor's net investment rather than the lessor's net cash investment. [FRSSE para 6.9].

36.70 The information to be disclosed by lessees and lessors is dealt with in paragraphs 6.16 to 6.18 of the FRSSE. They do not cover all the disclosure requirements given in SSAP 21 and discussed in chapter 15. In particular, small companies need *not* give the following information:

- For finance leased assets, the total depreciation for period by major class of asset. This is because small companies are only required to analyse tangible fixed assets into land and buildings and other tangible fixed assets, rather than by major class of asset.

- Analysis of net obligations under finance leases between amounts payable in the next year, amounts payable in the second to fifth year inclusive from the balance sheet date, and the aggregate amounts payable thereafter.

- Finance charges and operating lease rentals charged for the period.

- Analysis of operating lease commitments between land and buildings and other operating leases.

- Aggregate rentals receivable by lessors in the accounting period in relation to both finance and operating leases.

Intangible fixed assets

36.71 Small companies need only classify intangible assets into goodwill and other intangible assets. Other intangible assets may include development expenditure. Paragraphs 7.1 to 7.8 of the FRSSE deals with the accounting and disclosure requirements of research and development expenditure, which are imported from SSAP 13 and discussed in detail in chapter 14.

36.72 Small companies are *not* required to disclose:

- The total amount of research and development expenditure charged to the profit and loss account.

- Movements on deferred development expenditure.

36.73 On goodwill, the FRSSE imports all the recognition and measurement rules, but none of the disclosures, in SSAP 22. These rules are discussed in paragraphs 7.9 to 7.16 of the FRSSE. It should be noted that except for smaller entities applying the FRSSE, FRS 10, 'Goodwill and intangible assets', supersedes SSAP 22. Therefore, small entities can continue to write off goodwill against reserves until such time as the FRSSE is amended to reflect the provisions of FRS 10.

Stocks and long-term contracts

36.74 Many of the problems that small companies face in valuing stocks and long-term contracts are usually of a practical nature rather than matters of principle. The FRSSE recognises this and incorporates the whole of Appendix I of SSAP 9 dealing with further practical considerations in Appendix III. The valuation principles and the recognition rules relating to stocks and long-term contracts, which are dealt with in paragraphs 8.1 to 8.4 of the FRSSE, are discussed in chapter 17. Consistent with the balance sheet formats, small companies are not required to sub-analyse the amount of stock stated in the balance sheet.

Consignment stock

36.75 Small companies are likely to enter into arrangements where goods are supplied to them on a consignment basis. Therefore, the FRSSE provides a table, illustrating the factors that should be considered in deciding whether or not consignment stock is an asset, in Appendix III. This table is a replica of the one contained in Application Note A in FRS 5 and is reproduced in chapter 17 of this manual.

36.76 Where consignment stock is in substance an asset, a small company should recognise it in the balance sheet and show the amount due to the supplier, after deducting any deposits, as trade creditors. Where consignment stock is not in substance an asset, it should not be recognised. Any deposits paid should be shown in 'other debtors'. [FRSSE para 8.5].

Debt factoring

36.77 Debt factoring and invoice discounting arrangements provide an important source of finance for small companies. A small company will need to analyse whether or not it should continue to show factored debts as an asset in its balance sheet. Therefore, like consignment stocks, the FRSSE imports the table illustrating the considerations affecting the treatment of debt factoring from Application Note C of FRS 5 in Appendix III. This table is also reproduced in chapter 17.

36.78 Paragraphs 8.6 to 8.8 of the FRSSE provides guidance on the three accounting treatments, viz, derecognition, linked presentation and separate presentation, that might apply to debt factoring arrangements. These issues are also considered in detail in chapter 17.

Contingencies and post balance sheet events

36.79 Requirements relating to contingencies are dealt with in paragraphs 11.1 to 11.7, and those relating to post balance sheet events are dealt with in paragraphs 14.1 to 14.6 of the FRSSE. These rules are identical to those found in SSAP 18, 'Accounting for contingencies', and SSAP 17, ' Accounting for post balance sheet events', which are considered in detail in chapter 20.

Capital instruments

36.80 Capital instruments, other than shares, bank loans and overdrafts and leasing obligations, are unlikely to form a major source of finance for small companies. According, paragraphs 12.1 to 12.5 of the FRSSE deal with only the basic principles of FRS 4 relating to debt. The term 'debt' has been replaced in the FRSSE by borrowings, which is defined in the FRSSE to include all capital instruments that are classified as liabilities. A substantial part of FRS 4 including all the disclosure requirements has been omitted.

36.81 It is common for banks providing loans to small companies to charge arrangement fees. The accounting treatment of arrangement fees is not explicitly covered in FRS 4, so the FRSSE provides the following guidance:

- Where an arrangement fee is such as to represent a significant additional cost of finance in relation to the interest payable over the life of the instrument, it should be allocated to periods over the term of the instrument at a constant rate on the carrying amount of the instrument.

- Where the arrangement fee is not significant, it should be charged immediately to the profit and loss account.

[FRSSE para 12.4].

36.82 Furthermore, the term 'non-equity' is not mentioned in the FRSSE, except that the FRSSE provides that any amounts accrued in excess of any dividends paid or payable should be shown separately in shareholders' funds. This means that any premium payable on the redemption of preference shares should be accrued and shown separately in shareholders' funds. Any such accruals should be reported, along with any dividends, as appropriations of profits in the profit and loss account. [FRSSE para 12.5].

The profit and loss account

Formats

36.83 The Act permits small companies to use any one of the four alternative formats of the profit and loss account set out in Schedule 8 and it leaves the choice between these formats to the company's directors. In addition, the Act attaches to the formats certain notes and comments on specific profit and loss account items. Since the formats and the related notes set out in Schedule 8 are the same as those set out in Schedule 4, the discussions in chapter 6 relating to formats are relevant.

The effect of FRS 3 on the profit and loss account formats

36.84 FRS 3 contains supplementary provisions relating to the format of the profit and loss account, but its effect on the profit and loss account formats for small companies is not significant. This is because the FRSSE does not include the FRS 3 requirements for small companies to analyse turnover, costs, results and exceptional items into continuing operations, acquisitions and discontinued operations. There is also no requirement for small companies to produce a note of historical cost profits and losses or a reconciliation of movements in shareholders' funds.

36.85 The FRSSE, nevertheless, requires small companies to show all exceptional items, other than the three items imported from paragraph 20 of FRS 3 and included in paragraph 3.3 of the FRSSE, under the statutory format headings to which they relate, either in the notes or on the face of the profit and loss account if this is necessary in order to give a true and fair view. [FRSSE para 3.2].

Taxation

36.86 Paragraphs 9.1 to 9.21 of the FRSSE deal with the measurement and disclosure relating to taxation. These twenty-one paragraphs cover most of the measurement and disclosure provisions of SSAP 8 and SSAP 15 dealt with in chapter 13 of this manual, except for those provisions that are more relevant to larger entities such as deferred tax treatment of revaluations and unremitted earnings of overseas subsidiaries.

36.87 Although small companies are required to disclose any special circumstances that affect the overall tax charge or credit in accordance with paragraph 9.2, there is no specific reference in the FRSSE to disclose special circumstances affecting the tax attributable to the three non-operating exceptional items included in paragraph 3.3. In practice, however, it is likely that the explanation of the special circumstances affecting the overall tax charge or credit will include the tax effects of the three non-operating items.

Pensions

36.88 The FRSSE includes in paragraphs 10.1 to 10.10 those provisions relating to pensions in SSAP 24, which are likely to affect small companies. Consequently, the three exceptions to the general rule of spreading surpluses and deficits dealt with in paragraphs 81 to 83 of SSAP 24 and considered in detail in chapter 12 are excluded. Furthermore, the FRSSE does not contain any provisions for circumstances where a small company may operate more than one scheme or operate foreign schemes. Some of the disclosure requirements for defined benefit schemes have also been trimmed.

Foreign currencies

36.89 Paragraphs 13.1 to 13.11 of the FRSSE cover most of the provisions relating to measurement, but none of the disclosure requirements of SSAP 20. Foreign currencies are dealt with in chapter 20 of this manual.

Notes to the financial statements

Notes to the balance sheet

36.90 Schedule 8 to the Act requires small companies to disclose information which either supplements the information given with respect to any particular item shown in the balance sheet and the profit and loss account or is otherwise relevant to assessing the company's state of affairs in the light of the information so given. As indicated in paragraph 36.10 above, this Schedule was formerly set out as a list of exemptions from the disclosure requirements of Schedule 4, but it has been revised to act as a stand-alone Schedule for small companies. However, in order to provide a link between this chapter and the other chapters of this manual that deal with all the disclosures requirements of Schedule 4, 5 and 6 of the Act, the paragraphs that follow specify the relevant paragraphs of the three schedules with which a small company need not comply and hence which are not included in Schedule 8.

36.91 A small company need *not* give any of the information supplementing the balance sheet required by the following paragraphs of Schedule 4:

- Paragraph 40 – particulars of any contingent right to the allotment of shares in the company.
- Paragraph 41 – information regarding issues of debentures.
- Paragraph 44 – details of the company's freehold and leasehold properties.
- Paragraph 47 – the amount of any provision for deferred taxation.
- Paragraph 48(2) – the terms of repayment and interest rates for debts.
- Paragraph 48(4)(b) – the nature of securities given for debts.
- Paragraph 51(2) – the aggregate amount of loans provided by way of permitted financial assistance for the purchase of own shares, such as under an employees' share scheme.

36.92 Further exemptions and modifications that are permitted in respect of balance sheet information are as follows:

- Where the carrying value of stocks and fungible assets included in the financial statements is calculated by a permitted approximation methodology, such as FIFO, and that value differs materially from their relevant alternative amount, in effect replacement cost, the amount of the difference need not be disclosed.
- Disclosure of debts repayable in more than five years need not be made for each item included in "Creditors", if the required information is given in aggregate for all items.

Notes to the profit and loss account

36.93 A qualifying small company also receives disclosure exemptions in respect of certain supplementary information to the profit and loss account normally required by Schedule 4 to the Act. Accordingly, it need *not* make separate disclosure of:

- Paragraph 53(2) – details of interest payable or similar charges.
- Paragraph 54 – particulars of tax, including details of corporation and income tax charges, and special circumstances affecting the tax charge.

- Paragraph 55 – segmental particulars of turnover. If, however, the company has supplied geographical markets outside the UK, the notes must state the percentage of turnover attributable to those markets. In giving this information, the directors must consider the manner in which the company's activities are organised.

- Paragraph 56 – particulars of staff numbers and costs.

Other disclosure exemptions

36.94 Section 246(3) gives further exemptions from the disclosure requirements of other schedules to the Act. In particular, the following information from Schedule 6 regarding directors' emoluments need *not* be given:

- Paragraph 1(2)(b) – The numbers of directors exercising share options and receiving shares under long-term incentive schemes.

- Paragraph 2 – Details of the highest paid director's emoluments.

- Paragraph 7 – Details of directors' and past directors' excess retirement benefits.

[Sec 246(3)(b) inserted by SI 1997/220 and amended by SI 1997/570].

36.95 In summary, therefore, the information which *must still be given* in respect of directors' emoluments is as follows:

- The aggregate amount of directors' emoluments, amounts receivable under long-term incentive schemes and contributions paid or treated as paid to a money purchase pension scheme. A small company may disclose a single figure, being the aggregate of these three items, rather than disclose the items separately. [Sec 246(3)(a) inserted by SI 1997/220 and amended by SI 1997/570].

- Aggregate compensation to directors for loss of office.

- Sums paid to third parties for making available the services of directors.

36.96 Small companies are also entitled to omit the information required by paragraph 4 of Schedule 5 concerning financial years of subsidiary undertakings. [Sec 246(3)(b)(i) inserted by SI 1997/220 and amended by SI 1997/570].

36.97 It is interesting to note that no exemption from disclosure in the notes is given in respect of the standard audit fee disclosures required by section 390A(3). However, qualifying small and medium-sized companies are not required to disclose the amounts paid to auditors for non-audit services. Abbreviated financial statements filed with the Registrar may, on the other hand, omit disclosure of both audit and non-audit fees (see para 36.122).

Accounting principles and policies

36.98 The four fundamental accounting concepts in SSAP 2 that underlie the preparation of financial statements are not set out in the FRSSE. This is because these, together with the concept that requires assets and liabilities to be valued separately, are set out in Schedule 8 as the 'accounting principles' which are instead referred to in the FRSSE. However, paragraph 2.1 of the FRSSE makes it clear that small companies should also have regard to the substance of the transaction, or series of transactions, if the financial statements are to give a true and fair view.

36.99 Although there is no requirement for small companies to state whether the financial statements have been prepared in accordance with applicable accounting standards, both the Act and the FRSSE require them to disclose those accounting policies that are considered to be significant in determining the result or financial position of the company. [8 Sch 36; FRSSE para 2.5]. When a small company changes an accounting policy, because the new policy, is preferable to the one it replaces, the disclosure requirements of UITF Abstract 14, discussed in chapter 7, applies. [FRSSE para 2.8].

Related party disclosures

36.100 Related party transactions are generally more prevalent in smaller business. As a result, the FRSSE, recognising that the full requirements of FRS 8 would be unduly onerous for smaller entities, only requires disclosure of those related party transactions that are considered to be material to the small reporting entity. Without this concession, small companies would have been required to disclose related party transactions that were material in relation to the other related party, even when that related party was an individual. Such disclosures would have been unnecessarily burdensome for small companies. Because the FRSSE revises the requirements of FRS 8, the provisions of the FRSSE are considered in the paragraphs that follow.

36.101 Where a small reporting entity:

- purchases, sells or transfers goods and other assets or liabilities; or
- renders or receives services; or
- provides or receives finance or financial support;

(irrespective of whether a price is charged) to, from or on behalf of a related party, then any such material transactions (materiality to be judged in terms of its significance to the reporting entity) should be disclosed, including:

- The names of the transacting related parties.
- A description of the relationship between the parties.
- A description of the transactions.
- The amounts involved.
- Any other elements of the transactions necessary for an understanding of the financial statements.
- The amounts due to or from related parties at the balance sheet date and provisions for doubtful debts due from such parties at that date.
- Amounts written off in the period in respect of debts due to or from related parties.

[FRSSE para 15.1].

36.102 In addition, FRSSE clarifies that personal guarantees given by directors in respect of borrowings by the reporting entity should be disclosed. [FRSSE para 15.2]. Transactions can be disclosed on an aggregated basis (aggregation of similar transactions by type of related party), unless disclosure of individual transactions is necessary for an understanding of the impact of the transactions on the financial statements or is required by law. [FRSSE para 15.3]. FRS 8 does not require disclosure of related party transactions in certain circumstances which are considered in chapter 35. These circumstances are also listed in paragraph 15.4 of the FRSSE.

36.103 Where the reporting entity is controlled by another party, disclosure should be made of:

- The name of the controlling party.
- If different, the name of the ultimate controlling party.

In both instances, the related party relationship should also be disclosed. These disclosures should also be made whether or not there have been any transactions between the parties. If the controlling party or ultimate controlling party of the reporting entity is not known, that fact should be disclosed. [FRSSE para 15.5].

True and fair override disclosures

36.104 The directors of a small company may depart from any of the Act's accounting provisions in order to give a true and fair view. In that situation, particulars of the departure, the reasons for it and its effect shall be given in a note to the financial statements. [Sec 226(5), 8 Sch 15]. The FRSSE uses the principles of UITF Abstract 7 in providing guidance on how the statutory disclosure requirements should be interpreted. [FRSSE para 2.9].

Additional statement required by the Act and the FRSSE

36.105 Where the directors of a small company prepare shorter-form financial statements, those financial statements must contain a statement in a prominent position on the balance sheet, above the signature required by section 233 of the Act, that they are prepared in accordance with the special provisions of Part VII of the Act relating to small companies. [Sec 246(8)(a) inserted by SI 1997/220].

36.106 There is also a similar requirement in the FRSSE for a statement that the financial statements have been prepared in accordance with the FRSSE. [FRSSE para 2.3].

36.107 A suitable wording that combines both the above statements is included by way of a foot note to paragraph 2.3 of the FRSSE and is reproduced below.

Example

The financial statements have been prepared in accordance with the special provisions relating to small companies within Part VII of the Companies Act 1985 and with the Financial Reporting Standard for Smaller Entities.

Directors' report

36.108 Where a small company prepares shorter-form financial statements for shareholders, it is also allowed to omit certain of the disclosures required in full financial statements from its directors' report. As with the balance sheet and profit and loss account exemptions, these exemptions are not compulsory, so the company may give fuller disclosure than the Act requires if it so wishes.

36.109 Where advantage is taken of these exemptions, the directors' report need *not* disclose any of the information which is required by the following provisions:

- A fair review of the development of the business of the company and its subsidiary undertakings during the year and of their position at the end of it. [Sec 234(1)(a)].
- An indication of likely future developments in the business. [7 Sch 6(b)].
- The dividends recommended by the directors. [Sec 234(1)(b) amended by SI 1996/189].

- Substantial differences between the market value and book value of interests in land held as fixed assets. [7 Sch 1(2)].
- Particulars of important events that have occurred between the end of the financial year and the date of approval of the financial statements. [7 Sch 6(a)].
- An indication of the activities, if any, in the field of research and development. [7 Sch 6(c)].
- An indication of the existence of branches, as defined in section 98(2), of the company outside the UK. [7 Sch 6(d)].
- Any information in respect of employee involvement in the company where the average weekly number of employees during the year exceeded 250. [7 Sch 11].

[Sec 246(4) inserted by SI 1997/220].

36.110 The usefulness of the above exemptions will depend on the specific circumstances of the company concerned. Thus, a company that has little trading activity, no dividend payments, and only a few employees, will benefit little from these exemptions. Indeed, it is possible to draw the conclusion that, while shorter-form financial statements appear to offer a large number of exemptions to qualifying companies, the reality is that, on the whole, they put companies to a notable amount of bother for no great savings in disclosure. Also, many of the concessions given relate to disclosures that a small company might not have to comply with anyway, because its trading activities and business will be far simpler than larger companies who will be involved in the activities that require disclosure. This contrasts with the situation of abbreviated financial statements, which are much briefer than full financial statements and are, therefore, filed by many small companies to maintain business confidentiality.

36.111 Where the directors also take advantage of the exemptions in respect of the preparation of the directors' report, they must make a statement in a prominent position above the signature on the directors' report that the report has been prepared in accordance with the special provisions of Part VII of the Act relating to small companies. [Sec 246(8)(b) inserted by SI 1997/220].

36.112 Suitable wording for such a statement is as follows:

Example

This report has been prepared in accordance with the special provisions of Part VII of the Companies Act 1985 relating to small companies.

Auditors' report

36.113 In general, shorter-form financial statements prepared in accordance with section 246 are capable of giving a true and fair view. However, there may be instances where the use of the exemptions means that the financial statements do not give a true and fair view. For example, a particular item may be of such significance that the auditors consider that it should be disclosed separately, but instead it is combined with other items using the available exemptions.

36.114 Formerly, specific provisions in the Schedule 8 dealt with this situation. Auditors were only required to report that the financial statements were properly prepared in accordance with the provisions of the Act applicable to small companies. However, when Schedule 8 was revised by SI 1997/220, these provisions were not re-enacted. Now, therefore, where the shorter-form financial statements of a small company fail to give a true and fair view for any reason, including the use of the exemptions, the auditors will need to qualify their opinion in the same way as for a larger company.

36.115 The question also arises as to whether permitted non-compliance by small companies with the provisions of certain accounting standards impacts on the true and fair view. The following general guidance can be given:

- Where a matter of disclosure required by an accounting standard is specifically referred to in the Act, and the Act also allows exemption from that disclosure, it need not be given when preparing shorter-form financial statements for shareholders. [Foreward to accounting standards para 15]. However, the amendments to the Act introduced by SI 1996/189 removed from Schedule 4 many of the disclosures which were duplicated in accounting standards.
- Where an accounting standard requires sub-analysis of an item which is exempted from disclosure under the Act, that sub-analysis need not be given when preparing shorter-form financial statements for shareholders. For example, the sub-analysis of the tax charge between UK corporation tax, UK income tax, overseas tax, and transfers between deferred tax and corporation tax required by SSAPs 8 and 15, need not be given.

36.116 Except for the above categories of item, all other disclosures required by accounting standards should be included when preparing shorter-form financial statements for the shareholders of small companies.

Abbreviated financial statements for filing

36.117 Abbreviated financial statements contain much less extensive financial information than shorter-form financial statements. A *small* company may file abbreviated financial statements with the Registrar of Companies taking advantage of the following exemptions:

- It is not required to file a profit and loss account.
- It is not required to file a directors' report.
- It is permitted to file either an abbreviated or a shorter-form balance sheet and notes thereto.

[Sec 246(5) inserted by SI 1997/220].

36.118 It is also permitted to omit certain other information normally required to be given in the notes to financial statements, including any information relating to emoluments, pensions and compensation for loss of office paid or payable to the directors (see further para 36.122). [Sec 246(6) inserted by SI 1997/220].

36.119 The formats for an abbreviated balance sheet are set out in Schedule 8A. They adopt a similar layout to those in Schedule 4 (both Format 1 and Format 2), but disclose only those items preceded by either a letter or a Roman numeral. However, the aggregate amount of debtors and creditors falling due after more than one year must be shown separately from those falling due within one year, unless this information is given in the notes. [8A Sch 2 inserted by SI 1997/220].

36.120 A Format 1 balance sheet from Schedule 8A is shown in the table below.

BALANCE SHEET – FORMAT 1

A	Called up share capital not paid
B	Fixed assets
	I Intangible assets
	II Tangible assets
	III Investments
C	Current assets
	I Stocks
	II Debtors
	III Investments
	IV Cash at bank and in hand
D	Prepayments and accrued income
E	Creditors: amounts falling due within one year
F	Net current assets (liabilities)
G	Total assets less current liabilities
H	Creditors: amounts falling due after more than one year
I	Provisions for liabilities and charges
J	Accruals and deferred income

K	Capital and reserves
	I Called up share capital
	II Share premium account
	III Revaluation reserve
	IV Other reserves
	V Profit and loss account

36.121 As regards the information required by Schedule 4 to be given in the notes to the financial statements of larger companies, a small company need only include the following information by way of notes to its abbreviated financial statements:

- Accounting policies. [8A Sch 4 inserted by SI 1997/220].
- Details of share capital. [8A Sch 5 inserted by SI 1997/220].
- Particulars of allotments of shares. [8A Sch 6 inserted by SI 1997/220].
- A fixed assets table, so far as it relates to items to which a letter or Roman number is assigned in the adopted balance sheet format. [8A Sch 7 inserted by SI 1997/220].
- Details of indebtedness. [8A Sch 8 inserted by SI 1997/220].
- The basis used in translating foreign currency amounts into sterling. [8A Sch 9(1) inserted by SI 1997/220].
- Corresponding amounts in respect of each of the above, with the exception of fixed assets. [8A Sch 9(2) inserted by SI 1997/220].

36.122 Although the above information must be disclosed, the notes to the financial statements, whether abbreviated or not, need not include the following information normally required by other Schedules and sections of the Act (see further para 36.132):

- Paragraph 4 of Schedule 5 (financial years of subsidiary undertakings).
- Paragraph 6 of Schedule 5 (shares of company held by subsidiary undertakings).
- Part I of Schedule 6 (directors' emoluments, pensions and compensation for loss of office)
- Section 390A(3) (auditors' remuneration).

[Sec 246(6) inserted by SI 1997/220].

36.123 It is worth noting that a *small* company's abbreviated financial statements will not disclose the amount of its profit or loss for the year. As the company's profit and loss account will not be filed with the Registrar of Companies, it will not be available to the company's competitors. In fact, the closest that a reader can get to this figure will be by considering the difference between the profit and loss account in the balance sheet at both the beginning and the end of the period that the financial statements cover. This will only be an approximation for the profit for the year.

36.124 In view of the extensive range of exemptions allowed in abbreviated financial statements, it is clear that they cannot be held to give a true and fair view. Since they are not intended to present a true and fair view, there is no requirement for them to comply with the disclosure provisions contained in accounting and financial reporting standards. However, because such accounts are based on full shareholder accounts, the measurement methods adopted therein will be consistent with those set out in accounting standards.

Directors' responsibilities

36.125 The provisions of section 233 regarding the signing of the copy of the full balance sheet delivered to the Registrar apply equally to abbreviated financial statements filed in their place. Therefore, where abbreviated financial statements are filed, the balance sheet must be signed on behalf of the board by a director. [Sec 246(7) inserted by SI 1997/220].

36.126 Abbreviated financial statements filed by a small company must also contain a statement in a prominent position on the balance sheet, above the signature required by section 233, that they are prepared in accordance with the special provisions of Part VII of the Act relating to small companies. [Sec 246(8)(c) inserted by SI 1997/220].

36.127 A suitable wording for such a statement is as follows:

Example

The abbreviated financial statements have been prepared in accordance with the special provisions of Part VII of the Companies Act 1985 relating to small companies.

Auditors' responsibilities

36.128 Abbreviated financial statements delivered to the Registrar by a small company must be accompanied by a *special auditors' report*, unless the company is exempt from the requirement for an audit by virtue of sections 249A(1) or (2) or 250. This report must state that, in the auditors' opinion:

- The company is entitled to deliver abbreviated financial statements.
- The abbreviated financial statements are properly prepared in accordance with sections 246(5) and/or (6).

[Sec 247B(2) inserted by SI 1997/220].

36.129 An example of a special auditors' report is as follows:

Example

Report of the auditors to the directors of GAAP UK Limited under section 247B of the Companies Act 1985

We have examined the abbreviated financial statements on pages x to y together with the annual financial statements of GAAP UK Limited for the year ended 31 December 19XX.

Respective responsibilities of directors and auditors

The directors are responsible for preparing the abbreviated financial statements in accordance with section 246 of and Schedule 8A to the Companies Act 1985. It is our responsibility to form an independent opinion as to the company's entitlement to deliver abbreviated financial statements prepared in accordance with sections 246(5) and (6) of the Companies Act 1985 and whether the abbreviated financial statements are properly prepared in accordance with those provisions and to report our opinion to you.

Basis of opinion

We have carried out the procedures we considered necessary to confirm, by reference to the annual financial statements, that the company is entitled to deliver abbreviated financial statements and that the abbreviated financial statements are properly prepared from those financial statements. The scope of our work for the purpose of this report does not include examining or dealing with events after the date of our report on the annual financial statements.

Opinion

In our opinion the company is entitled to deliver abbreviated financial statements prepared in accordance with sections 246(5) and (6) of the Companies Act 1985 and the abbreviated financial statements to be delivered are properly prepared in accordance with those provisions.

Chartered Accountants and Registered Auditors
(Address)
(Date)

36.130 The above report assumes that the exemptions in both sections 246(5) and (6) are taken (see paras 36.117 and 36.118). If the exemptions in only one of the sections are taken the references in the report would be amended accordingly.

36.131 Prior to the amendments brought about by SI 1997/220, the auditors were required to include within their special report the full text of the report on the full or shorter-form financial statements made under section 235. This requirement has been removed. However, if the section 235 report was qualified then the special report must include the full text of that report, together with any further material necessary to understand the qualification. [Sec 247B(3)(a) inserted by SI 1997/220]. If the section 235 report contained a statement under section 237(2) (accounts, records or returns inadequate or accounts not agreeing with records and returns) or section 237(3) (failure to obtain necessary information and explanations) then that statement should be reproduced in full. [Sec 247B(3)(b) inserted by SI 1997/220].

Full financial statements for filing

36.132 A small company is not required to take advantage of any of the exemptions available under section 246. It may, if it wishes, prepare and file full financial statements. Alternatively, it may prepare full financial statements in accordance with Schedule 4 but omit the information specified in section 246(6) from the copy of the financial statements filed with the Registrar (see para 36.122). If advantage is taken of this exemption, the financial statements are considered to be abbreviated and must include the statements and special audit report discussed in paragraphs 36.125 to 36.131. [Sec 247B(1)(a) inserted by SI 1997/220].

Medium-sized companies

Accounting exemptions for medium-sized companies

36.133 The exemptions available to medium-sized companies are considerably less than those available to small companies. In effect:

- The individual financial statements of a medium-sized company need not comply with the requirements of paragraph 36A of Schedule 4 (disclosure with respect to compliance with accounting standards). [Sec 246A(2) inserted by SI 1997/220].

- Medium-sized companies are entitled to file financial statements with the Registrar of Companies in an abbreviated format. However, this format differs from that available to small companies, since medium-sized companies are permitted fewer disclosure exemptions. [Sec 246A(3) inserted by SI 1997/220].

- Unlike small companies, medium-sized companies are not entitled to prepare shorter-form financial statements for shareholders. Other than the exemption from paragraph 36A noted above, the financial statements prepared for the shareholders must comply in full with Schedule 4.

Abbreviated financial statements

36.134 The modifications that the Act permits in respect of the abbreviated financial statements that a medium-sized company may deliver to the Registrar of Companies relate principally to the profit and loss account. Consequently, the normal requirements for full directors' report, balance sheet and notes to the financial statements are generally unaffected.

36.135 The limited exemptions available to medium-sized companies allow the following profit and loss account items to be combined and shown as one item under the heading 'Gross profit or loss':

- In Formats 1 and 3: turnover, the cost of sales, gross profit or loss and other operating income.
- In Formats 2 and 4: turnover, the change in stocks of finished goods and in work in progress, own work capitalised, other operating income, raw materials and consumables, and other external charges.

[Sec 246A(3)(a) inserted by SI 1997/220].

36.136 In addition, the notes to the financial statements may omit the segmental analysis of turnover that would otherwise be required by paragraph 55 of Schedule 4. [Sec 246A(3)(b) inserted by SI 1997/220].

36.137 Since the concessions permitted to medium-sized companies by the Act are so limited, with the requirements for the balance sheet, related notes and the directors' report fundamentally the same as those for large companies, the additional cost of preparing abbreviated financial statements for medium-sized companies will tend to exceed the potential confidentiality benefits that might derive from them. Furthermore, it is not clear whether abbreviated financial statements filed by a medium-sized company must comply with the disclosure requirements of accounting standards. As abbreviated financial statements do not purport to give a true and fair view, it is arguable, as for small companies, that they do not need to comply with these disclosure requirements. If this is so, the benefit of avoiding certain disclosures, in particular those required by FRS 8, may sometimes outweigh the cost of preparing abbreviated financial statements.

Statements to be made where advantage is taken of the exemptions

36.138 Where the directors of a medium-sized company file abbreviated financial statements, those financial statements must contain a statement in a prominent position on the balance sheet, above the signature required by section 233 of the Act, that they are prepared in accordance with the special provisions of Part VII of the Act relating to medium-sized companies. [Sec 246A(4) inserted by SI 1997/220].

36.139 An example of such a statement would be:

Example

The abbreviated financial statements have been prepared in accordance with the special provisions of Part VII of the Companies Act 1985 relating to medium-sized companies.

Auditors' reports

36.140 The abbreviated financial statements filed by a medium-sized company must be accompanied by a special auditors' report. This report must state that, in the auditors' opinion:

- The company is entitled to deliver abbreviated financial statements.
- The abbreviated financial statements are properly prepared in accordance with section 246A(3).

[Sec 247B(2) inserted by SI 1997/220].

36.141 An example of a special auditors' report is shown below:

Example

Report of the auditors to the directors of GAAP UK Limited under section 247B of the Companies Act 1985

We have examined the abbreviated financial statements on pages x to y together with the annual financial statements of GAAP UK Limited for the year ended 31 December 19XX.

Respective responsibilities of directors and auditors

The directors are responsible for preparing the abbreviated financial statements in accordance with section 246A of the Companies Act 1985. It is our responsibility to form an independent opinion as to the company's entitlement to deliver abbreviated financial statements prepared in accordance with section 246A(3) of the Companies Act 1985 and whether the abbreviated financial statements are properly prepared in accordance with that provision and to report our opinion to you.

Basis of opinion

We have carried out the procedures we considered necessary to confirm, by reference to the annual financial statements, that the company is entitled to deliver abbreviated financial statements and that the abbreviated financial statements are properly prepared from those financial statements. The scope of our work for the purpose of this report does not include examining or dealing with events after the date of our report on the annual financial statements.

Opinion

In our opinion the company is entitled to deliver abbreviated financial statements prepared in accordance with section 246A(3) of the Companies Act 1985 and the abbreviated financial statements to be delivered are properly prepared in accordance with that provision.

Chartered Accountants and Registered Auditors
(Address)
(Date)

36.142 The matters discussed in paragraph 36.131 above, concerning qualification of the auditors' report on the full financial statements of a small company, apply equally to medium-sized companies.

Small and medium-sized parent companies

36.143 The fact that a company qualifies as a small or a medium-sized company does not preclude it from also being the parent company of a group. Consequently, some consideration needs to be given to this category of entity and how it is affected by the shorter-form and/or the abbreviated financial statement exemptions.

36.144 The Act provides specific guidance in this area by stating that:

- A parent company shall not be treated as qualifying as a small company in relation to a financial year, unless the group headed by it qualifies as a small group.
- A parent company shall not be treated as qualifying as a medium-sized company in relation to a financial year, unless the group headed by it qualifies as a medium-sized group.

[Sec 247A(3) inserted by SI 1997/220].

36.145 The criteria for determining small and medium-sized groups are considered in paragraphs 36.44 to 36.49, and the exclusions thereto in paragraphs 36.50 to 36.52. What they imply, however, is that parent companies that meet the general criteria for qualification as either small or medium-sized companies will need to undertake some form of group consolidation exercise in order to establish whether they meet the additional conditions set out in paragraph 36.144 above.

36.146 When considering the reporting position at an individual entity level, some guidance on interpretation may be of value:

- Where the group headed by a small parent company also qualifies as a small group, the parent may utilise the concessions generally available to small companies. Thus, it may opt to file abbreviated financial statements and prepare shorter-form financial statements for shareholders.

- Where the group headed by a small parent company does not qualify as a small group, but does qualify as a medium-sized group, the parent cannot take advantage of the concessions generally available to small companies. However, it will be entitled to utilise the concessions generally available to medium-sized companies in terms of filing abbreviated accounts. It is emphasised in this regard that the exemptions allowed therein are much less extensive than those allowed in small company abbreviated financial statements.

- Where the group headed by a small parent company fails to meet the criteria for determining small or medium-sized groups, the parent will not be allowed to avail itself of the exemptions generally available to small or medium-sized companies respectively. Thus, it cannot prepare shorter-form financial statements, nor can it file any form of abbreviated financial statements, or take the exemption not to prepare consolidated financial statements (see below).

- Where the group headed by a medium-sized parent company meets the criteria for determining a small group, the parent may take advantage of the concessions generally available to medium-sized companies, in terms of filing abbreviated financial statements. However, the fact that the group is a small group does not allow the parent to claim the reporting concessions generally available to small companies.

- Where the group headed by a medium-sized parent company meets the criteria for determining a medium-sized group, the parent may take advantage of the reporting concessions generally available to medium-sized companies. Thus, it may opt to file abbreviated financial statements in the permitted format.

- Where the group headed by a medium-sized parent fails to meet the criteria for determining small and medium-sized groups, the parent will not be allowed to avail itself of any of the concessions generally available to small or medium-sized companies, in terms of preparing shorter-form shareholder financial statements or filing abbreviated financial statements. Nor will it be able to take the exemption not to prepare consolidated financial statements (see below).

Small and medium-sized groups

36.147 In general terms, the Act requires parent companies to prepare consolidated financial statements and specifies the form which those financial statements should take. [Sec 227]. In addition, FRS 2, 'Accounting for subsidiary undertakings', requires parent companies preparing financial statements intended to give a true and fair view of the financial position and profit or loss of the group, to prepare them in the form of consolidated financial statements. [FRS 2 para 18]. Furthermore, the standard (but not the Act) applies to *"all parent undertakings"* [FRS 2 para 18], a term designated to include not just corporate parents, but also partnerships and unincorporated associations.

Exemptions from consolidation

36.148 Both the Act and the standard allow specific exemptions from the general requirement to prepare consolidated financial statements. Included in these exemptions is the exemption allowed to a parent company not to prepare consolidated financial statements, if the group of which it is parent is a small or medium-sized group as defined in section 248 of the Act and it is not an ineligible group. [Sec 248(1), FRS 2 para 21(a)]. The definitions of small and medium-sized groups and ineligible groups are covered in paragraphs 36.44 to 36.51. (The definition of an ineligible group in section 248(2) is the same as that in section 247A(2) inserted by SI 1997/220.)

36.149 It is worth clarifying at this point that although the definition of an ineligible group is the same in section 248(2) as in 247A(2), there is a subtle difference in the application of the exemptions. A small or medium-sized company is not entitled to the exemptions in section 246 or 246A with respect to abbreviated or shorter-form financial statements if it is, or was at any time during the financial year, a *member* of an ineligible group. A similar company is not entitled to the exemption from preparing consolidated financial statements in section 248(1) if, at the year end, it is a *parent* of an ineligible group. This is shown in the example below.

Example

Companies A to D are manufacturing companies. Company A is incorporated in the USA and company D is a public company. Company B is small in size, as is the sub-group of which it is parent.

Company B will not be entitled to file abbreviated financial statements as it is a member of an ineligible group (company D being a public company). It will, however, be entitled to exemption from the preparation of consolidated financial statements as the sub-group headed by it is not ineligible.

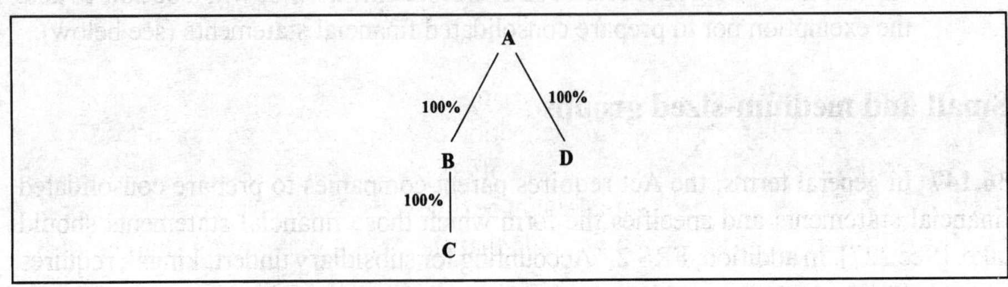

36.150 The Companies Act 1985 (Miscellaneous Accounting Amendments) Regulations 1996 (SI 1996/189) deleted the requirement for a company's auditors to make a specific report to the company's directors concerning whether or not the company is entitled to the exemption mentioned above. Instead, it requires the auditors to make a statement in their audit report only where they consider the company's directors are not entitled to take advantage of the exemption. [Sec 237(4A) inserted by SI 1996/189].

36.151 Where a parent company makes use of the exemption from consolidation, it is required to:

- Comply with the disclosure requirements of Part 1 of Schedule 5 to the Act in respect of parent companies not required to prepare consolidated financial statements. [Sec 231(2)].
- State that its financial statements present information about it as an individual undertaking and not about its group. [FRS 2 para 22]. The statement should include or refer to the note giving the grounds on which the parent undertaking is exempt from preparing consolidated financial statements, as required by Schedule 5 paragraph 1(4).

36.152 Set out below are two examples of an appropriate wording to be included in the accounting policies of a parent company or undertaking that uses the exemption from preparing consolidated financial statements for small and medium-sized groups:

Example 1 – parent company of a small group

The financial statements contain information about GAAP UK Limited as an individual company and do not contain consolidated financial information as the parent of a group. The company is exempt under section 248 of the Companies Act 1985 from the requirement to prepare consolidated financial statements as the group it heads qualifies as a small group.

Example 2 – unincorporated parent undertaking of medium-sized group

The financial statements contain information about GAAP UK Co as an individual undertaking and do not contain consolidated financial information as the parent of a group. The partnership is exempt under paragraph 21(a) of Financial Reporting Standard No. 2 from the requirement to prepare consolidated financial statements as the group it heads qualifies as a medium-sized group.

36.153 Insofar as the exemption from preparing consolidated financial statements for shareholders is concerned, there is *no* distinction drawn between small and medium-sized groups. Moreover, while the exemption offers potential cost savings, particularly to complex groups where consolidation might be time consuming, directors may choose not to take advantage of it, on the grounds that the parent company's shareholders require information about the activities of the group as a whole. Nonetheless, this does not prevent the parent company from filing abbreviated entity financial statements with the Registrar of Companies.

Abbreviated financial statements

36.154 As was discussed in paragraph 36.146 above, a parent company qualifying as small or medium-sized may file abbreviated financial statements if the group headed by it qualifies as a small or medium-sized group and is not ineligible. [Sec 247A(3) inserted by SI 1997/220]. However, any abbreviated financial statements filed with the Registrar of Companies must be abbreviated individual company financial statements, because abbreviated consolidated financial statements are not permitted. In such instances, therefore, it is implicit that the parent company must take advantage of the exemption from consolidation which is available to small or medium-sized groups in respect of those abbreviated financial statements. Non-statutory consolidated financial statements may still be prepared for the shareholders, but these must be accompanied by the appropriate statements set out in chapter 38.

Consolidated shorter-form financial statements

36.155 Where the small parent company of a small group has prepared individual shorter-form financial statements and is exempt from preparing consolidated financial statements under section 248, it may nevertheless choose to prepare and file such statements. If it does, it may adopt the shorter-format that is available to small companies in preparing their individual financial statements and directors' report, as suitably modified for consolidated financial statements. [Sec 248A(2) inserted by SI 1997/220].

36.156 Therefore, where a small parent company voluntarily prepares small group consolidated financial statements, it will have available to it the standard exemptions available to small companies, as explained in paragraphs 36.62 to 36.97. However, greater detail than that required by Schedule 8 must be given in respect of investments. Item B III.1 (shares in group undertakings and participating interests) in the balance sheet formats should be broken down as follows:

- Shares in group undertakings.
- Interests in associated undertakings.
- Other participating interests.

[Sec 248A(3) inserted by SI 1997/220].

36.157 Small companies voluntarily preparing consolidated financial statements are also entitled to take advantage of the FRSSE's provisions as discussed above. In addition, these consolidated financial statements should be prepared in accordance with the accounting practices and disclosure requirements set out in FRS 2, 6, 7 and, as they apply in respect of consolidated financial statements, FRS 5, SSAPs 1 and 22 and UITF Abstract 3. Both SSAP 1 and SSAP 22 continue to apply until the FRSSE is revised to incorporate FRS 9 and FRS 10. Where the reporting entity is part of a group that prepares publicly available consolidated financial statements, it is entitled to the exemptions given in FRS 8 paragraph 3(a)-(c). [FRSSE para 16.1].

36.158 As for individual company financial statements, the consolidated financial statements must include a statement in a prominent position above the signature on the balance sheet that they are prepared in accordance with the special provisions of Part VII of the Act relating to small companies (see paras 36.105 to 36.112) and in accordance with the FRSSE. [Sec 248A(5) inserted by SI 1997/220; FRSSE para 2.3].

36.159 As medium-sized companies are not permitted to prepare shorter-form financial statements, it follows that medium-sized groups cannot prepare shorter-form consolidated financial statements.

Dormant companies

36.160 The Act makes certain provisions regarding dormant companies. In particular, it allows a company to resolve not to appoint auditors when it has been dormant since its formation or when it has been dormant since the end of the previous financial year.

36.161 For this purpose, a 'dormant company' is defined as a company that had no significant accounting transactions during the period in question. A 'significant accounting transaction' is defined as any transaction that section 221 requires the company to enter into its accounting records. Section 221 requires, for example, the accounting records to contain entries on a daily basis of monies received and expended, a record of assets and liabilities, and statements of goods sold and purchased. A transaction that results from a subscriber to the memorandum taking shares in the company under his undertaking given in the memorandum can be disregarded. [Sec 250(3)].

36.162 Where a company has been dormant for any period, it immediately ceases to be dormant if any significant accounting transaction occurs. [Sec 250(3)].

Exemption from the need to appoint auditors

36.163 A dormant company may exclude the application of section 384 of the Act (company to appoint auditors at general meeting) by passing a special resolution resolving that auditors shall not be appointed.

36.164 A company may pass a special resolution exempting it from the need to have its financial statements audited and from the duty to appoint auditors. It may do so either at a general meeting of the company at any time after copies of the annual accounts for the previous financial year have been sent out to shareholders, or by written resolution. This resolution may be passed provided that the following three conditions are satisfied:

- The directors must have been entitled to prepare the company's individual financial statements for that year in accordance with the special provisions for small companies in section 246(2). However, this entitlement is extended to a company which would have qualified as small had it not been a public company or a member of an ineligible group, but does not extend to a bank, insurance company or a company authorised under the Financial Services Act 1986.

- The company is not required to prepare consolidated financial statements for that year.

- The company must have been dormant since the end of the previous financial year.

[Sec 250(1)(b) amended by SI 1997/220].

36.165 In this regard, where a non-trading subsidiary company with distributable reserves pays these up to its parent company, the subsidiary will have a significant accounting transaction in any year in which it accounts for the dividend. This means that it cannot then be dormant, will need to have its financial statements audited and hence will have to appoint auditors, unless it qualifies for exemption from audit under the provisions of section 249A (see para 36.176).

36.166 Another difficulty arises when companies, wishing to qualify as dormant and thereby avoid the need to appoint auditors, dispose of assets to other companies in their group in order to facilitate this. Sometimes, particularly where land is concerned, it is only the beneficial interest which is transferred, the company intending to retain only the legal interest or bare legal title. Such transfers are frequently conducted with the minimum of formality and paperwork. However, since 26 September 1989, with regard to land the legal position is that any contract for the sale or other disposition of an interest in land can only be made in writing and only by incorporating, in one document, all the terms which the parties to the transaction have expressly agreed. This document must be signed by or on behalf of each party to the contract. Transfers not complying with these provisions may not be legally effective to transfer land or the beneficial interest in such land. If the 'dormant' company will retain the land and, should that land generate income or incur costs, those will be transactions of the company. Thus, it may not be held to have been dormant during the periods in question.

36.167 Although section 250 of the Act empowers dormant companies to pass a special resolution not to appoint auditors, it is important to ensure that such a resolution would not contravene any provision in the company's articles of association. Companies that have adopted Table A as their articles, other than in the latest form which took effect from 1 July 1985, as well as many other companies incorporated before 1967, will have a clause in their articles that requires them to appoint auditors. Section 250 does not automatically override such a clause, because it relates only to the statutory requirement in section 384 to appoint auditors.

36.168 In this situation, the company should, in addition to passing the special resolution under section 250, consider whether it needs to pass a special resolution amending its articles to remove the clause concerning the appointment of auditors.

36.169 A company may not take advantage of the exemptions outlined in paragraph 36.163 if it is either a banking or insurance company, or an authorised person under the Financial Services Act 1986. [Sec 250(2) amended by SI 1996/189]. Before the Companies Act 1985 (Miscellaneous Accounting) Regulations 1996 (SI 1996/189) came into force on 2 February 1996, this prohibition also extended to public companies. Dormant public companies may now resolve, subject to the normal rules, not to appoint auditors.

36.170 The resolution not to appoint auditors need be passed only in the first year in which the company wishes to take advantage of the exemption. The company does not have to repeat the resolution in subsequent years. It will, however, have both to appoint auditors and to have financial statements audited in a year when it ceases to qualify as a dormant company, unless it remains exempt from the requirement for an audit in accordance with the provisions of sections 249A (see para 36.30).

36.171 Any company wanting to take advantage of these provisions of the Act should include a statement, such as the one set out below, in the directors' report attached to the financial statements that are to be laid before the next general meeting of the company. The notice of meeting must state *verbatim* the resolution to be proposed, and state that it is intended to propose it as a special resolution. [Sec 378].

Example

Auditors

In accordance with section 250 of the Companies Act 1985, a special resolution resolving that auditors shall not be appointed will be put to the annual general meeting.

36.172 The following example illustrates the situation in which a special resolution should be passed:

Example

A parent company prepares its financial statements to 31 December each year. On 30 June 19X5, one of its subsidiaries ceased trading and no significant accounting transactions took place thereafter. The next annual general meeting of the subsidiary is on 31 March 19X6. The directors wish to take advantage of the exemption not to appoint auditors. Assume the provisions of section 249A do not apply.

In order to qualify as a dormant company and, therefore, not appoint auditors, the following steps must be followed. The directors of the subsidiary must prepare the financial statements of the subsidiary for the year ended 31 December 19X5. In addition, the directors must be able to claim the exemptions available to small companies under section 246 when preparing those financial statements. These financial statements must be audited and laid before the general meeting on 31 March 19X6. As the company had been dormant since 31 December 19X5, a resolution not to appoint auditors can be tabled and passed at that meeting. The resolution remains effective for the financial year 19X6 and thereafter, provided the company remains dormant in each of the succeeding financial years commencing with 19X6.

Additional matters relating to dormant companies

36.173 Where a dormant company is exempt, at the end of its financial year, from the obligation to appoint auditors:

- It need only send a copy of its financial statements without an audit report to those persons entitled to receive copies of the financial statements under sections 238 and 239 (right to receive or demand the financial statements). [Sec 250(4)(a)].

- An auditors' report need not be laid before the company in general meeting. [Sec 250(4)(b)].

- An auditors' report need not be delivered to the Registrar of Companies. Where this is so, a statement must be included above the director's signature on the balance sheet to the effect that the company was dormant throughout the financial year in question. [Sec 250(4)(c) amended by SI 1996/189]. The directors' statement could take the following form:

The company was dormant (within the meaning of section 250 of the Companies Act 1985) throughout the year ended 31 December 1996.

- It is entitled to prepare and file financial statements in accordance with the special provisions for small companies contained in section 246. This requirement applies even where the dormant company is a member of an ineligible group. [Sec 250(4)(d) amended by SI 1997/220].

- The previous year's figures must be shown alongside for comparison, even if there are no items of income or expenditure for the current year. In addition, certain notes to the balance sheet must be included. Companies House has produced Notes for Guidance dealing with dormant company financial statements.

- The following statements and reports are not required:

  - The statement that would be required under section 246(8) that the financial statements are prepared in accordance with the special provisions of Part VII of the Act relating to small companies. [Sec 246(9) inserted by SI 1997/220].

  - The special report of the auditors that would be required by section 247B(2). [Sec 247B(1) inserted by SI 1997/220].

Ceasing to qualify as a dormant company

36.174 Where a company ceases, for any reason, to qualify as a dormant company, and it does not remain exempt from audit by virtue of the provisions of section 249A, the directors should appoint auditors at any time before the next general meeting at which the company's financial statements prepared under section 226 of the Act are laid before the company. Where this applies, those auditors hold office until the conclusion of that meeting. [Sec 388A(3)].

Comparison with audit exemption under section 249A

36.175 As discussed above, a qualifying dormant company may, by passing a special resolution, exempt itself from the requirement to appoint auditors. By definition, such a dormant company must have turnover of less than £350,000 so it may also be entitled to exemption from audit under section 249A (see from para 36.30). A special resolution would not be needed if the company was to take advantage of that exemption. [Sec 249A(6A) inserted by SI 1997/936].

Agency companies

36.176 The question often arises as to whether an agency company that acts for either a disclosed or an undisclosed principal is dormant and, therefore, entitled to take advantage of the audit exemption available to dormant companies. The over-riding principle is that a company may only be treated as dormant if it is not required to record any transaction in its accounting records during the reporting period in question.

36.177 From a practical point of view, many groups have reverted to operating on a divisional basis, rather than through a network of active subsidiaries. In such instances, divisionalisation tends to be achieved through transferring the trade of subsidiary companies to their parent company. Where this occurs, however, it is common for agency agreements to be drawn up, to the effect that the subsidiary continues to carry on trading in its own name and acts exclusively as an agent for its parent. This is often a preferred route post-acquisition, where the acquired subsidiary has an established reputation in a particular market-place or region, or where the subsidiary's name is synonymous with a branded product that it produces. Many such agency companies have been treated as dormant.

36.178 The situation regarding a subsidiary acting as an agent for an undisclosed principal is as follows. In legal terms, where an agent acts for an undisclosed principal without disclosing the existence of the principal, the agent is deemed to contract on its own behalf and is personally liable on the contract to the other party. As a consequence, it will have accounting transactions to record in its accounting records. The agent cannot then be a dormant company.

36.179 Where, however, the agent contracts on behalf of a disclosed principal (that is, it discloses the existence or identity of its principal), it is generally the principal who, by virtue of the agency, becomes a party to the contract. The transactions effected under the agency can, therefore, be shown in the principal's accounts. In this instance, to ensure that the agent avoids direct liability under the contract, all contactual documents must make it clear at the time of contracting that the agent is contracting as agent only. If the agent does not carry on any other business and earns no commission, it may not have any accounting transactions to record in its own accounting records.

36.180 Since an agency company may be treated as dormant only if it is not required to record any transaction in its accounting records, it may not qualify as a dormant company if it is involved in any one or more of the following types of activity:

- Receiving and expending monies.
- Disposing or acquiring of assets.
- Dealing in goods or stocks that it holds.

36.181 With any of the above activities, it will be a matter of fact as to whether a particular agency company performs any such activity. In the first instance, it is necessary to look to the agency agreement for guidance. This agreement defines the relationship between the principal company and the agency company, and it sets out the tasks the respective companies are to perform.

36.182 When considering the agreement, the following points may assist in determining whether the agency company is in fact 'dormant':

- Receiving and expending monies

  An agency company that is merely required to account to its principal for the amount (or the net amount) of the monies it has received for its principal in the course of the agency, is the owner of the monies it receives when acting as agent. The agency company should enter such receipts in its own accounting records. Where, however, the agency company is obliged to hand over to its principal the very monies it receives as agent, it will receive those monies as a trustee for its principal. It will then not be obliged to record those receipts in its own accounting records. Where the agent is a trustee, the agency company must pay the monies it receives on behalf of the principal into a separate bank account belonging to the principal.

  As regards expenditure, it is not sufficient that the principal indemnifies the agency company against any liabilities the company incurs in the course of acting as agent. The agency company must contract with third parties solely in its capacity as agent, and without assuming any liability on the resultant contract. It does not so contract if it does not disclose its principal. If the agency company does assume a liability on the contract, it would have a significant accounting transaction and it would not qualify as 'dormant'.

- Disposing or acquiring of assets

  An agency company might not, in fact, own any assets. However, care should be taken in situations where the agency company remains the legal owner of property. Provided that the agency agreement passed all the beneficial interests in freehold or leasehold property to the principal (see para 36.166) and has left only the legal title to that property in the name of the agency company, the subsequent transfer of that title would not constitute a transfer of assets. This is because a bare legal title that is held to the order of the principal cannot be said to be an asset of the agent.

- Dealing in goods or stocks that the agency company holds

  If the agent's sole business is that of trading for and on behalf of the principal, the agent is unlikely to 'hold' any stocks of its own.

36.183 It would, therefore, appear that there is no reason in principle why agency companies, in appropriate circumstances, should not qualify to be treated as dormant companies. Whether the agency company actually qualifies for the exemption available to dormant companies will, however, be a matter of fact in the light of both the appropriate agency agreement, the actual relationship between the two parties and whether that relationship is disclosed to third parties or not. Suppose, for example, that a parent company owns an agency company, but there is no formal agency agreement. The agency company may be able to avoid an audit if its board had minuted the company's appointment as agent by the parent and the terms of the agency. This would need to be backed up by the parent's board having minuted the fact that it had appointed the subsidiary as its agent to carry out the specified activities. If these documents provided satisfactory evidence of the arrangements, no formal agreement may be needed. However, the agency company would need to disclose that it is acting as agent in its dealings with third parties.

36.184 Where an agency is disclosed, there will generally be no significant accounting transactions to be recorded in its accounting records and, therefore, no transactions to be shown in its financial statements. As a consequence, such an entity may be in a position to prepare dormant financial statements and take advantage of the audit concessions.

36.185 Where an agency is undisclosed, the agent will have to account for its accounting transactions in its books of account. This then leads to the question of what should be shown in its statutory financial statements. Clearly, as it is contracting in its own name, it is likely to have at the balance sheet date debtor and creditor balances with the parties with which it has contracted. These balances should be reported in the agent's balance sheet. Consequently, at the balance sheet date the agent may have liabilities to third parties with which it has contracted on behalf of its principal, which will be reimbursed by the principal. Where the principal has given an indemnity, and subsequently settles these transactions before the agent's financial statements are signed, it can be argued that the value of any liabilities of the agency company are nil, because they have been settled by the principal. In addition, the agent may at the balance sheet date be owed money by third parties under contracts entered into on behalf of its principal. If the agent must hold such money in trust for its principal, it can be argued that the value of any assets of the agency company is nil, because they are held in trust for the principal and can be said to belong to the principal. If this argument is pursued, the agent has accounting transactions that need to be recorded in its accounting records albeit at nil value but, as a consequence, it could not be treated as dormant for filing or audit purposes.

36.186 What is reported in the profit and loss account might depend on the trading relationship between the principal and the agent. If the principal invoices the agent for goods that the agent sells on, and the agent in turn invoices the customer, then it is likely that the gross trading should be recorded in the profit and loss account. If, on the other hand, the agent invoices merely his commission, this should be recorded in the profit and loss account. However, in many divisionalisations the principal does not invoice the agent in this way and, as a consequence, it is possible that no trading will be shown through the profit and loss account as the transactions the agent undertakes are accounted for *via* its inter-company account with its principal.

Comparison with IASs

36.187 There are no IASC rules giving particular consideration to small, medium or dormant companies. The IASC takes the view that national jurisdictions can decide which enterprises should apply IASs.

Annex – choice of financial statements for shareholders and for filing

Decision table 1 – company without subsidiaries

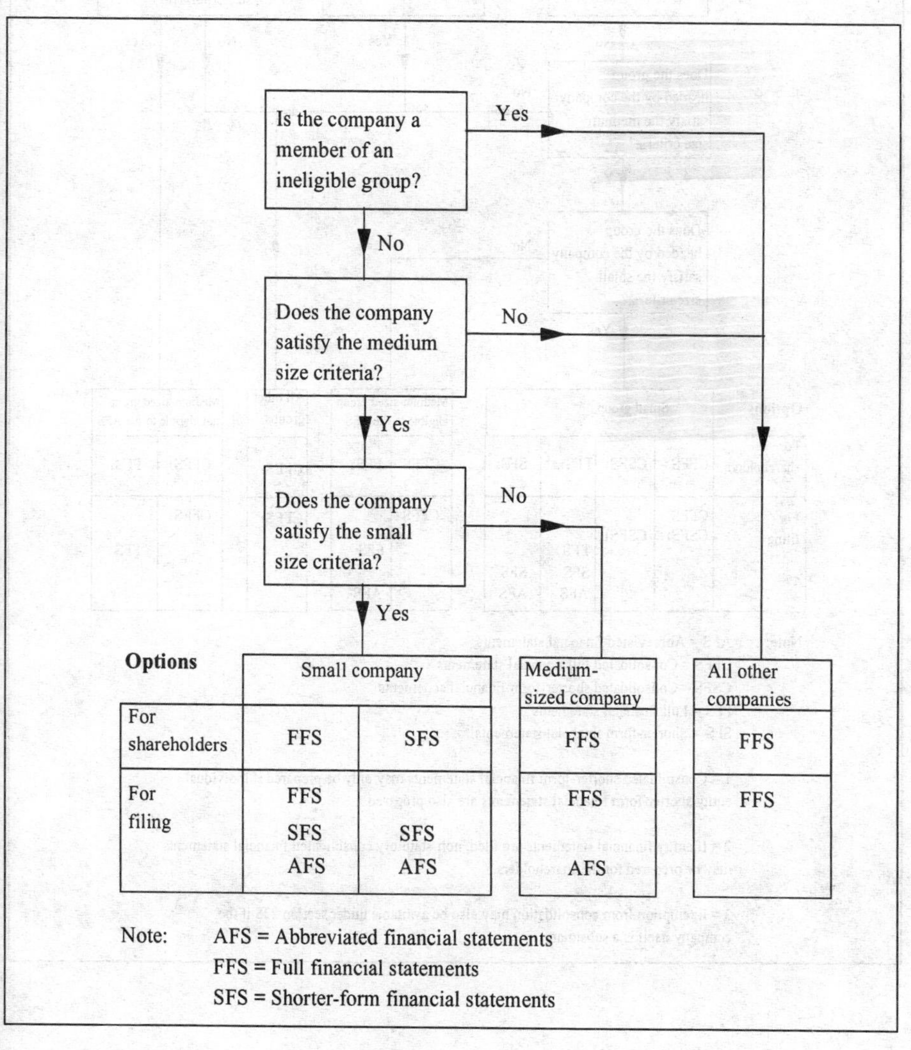

Decision table 2 – company with subsidiaries

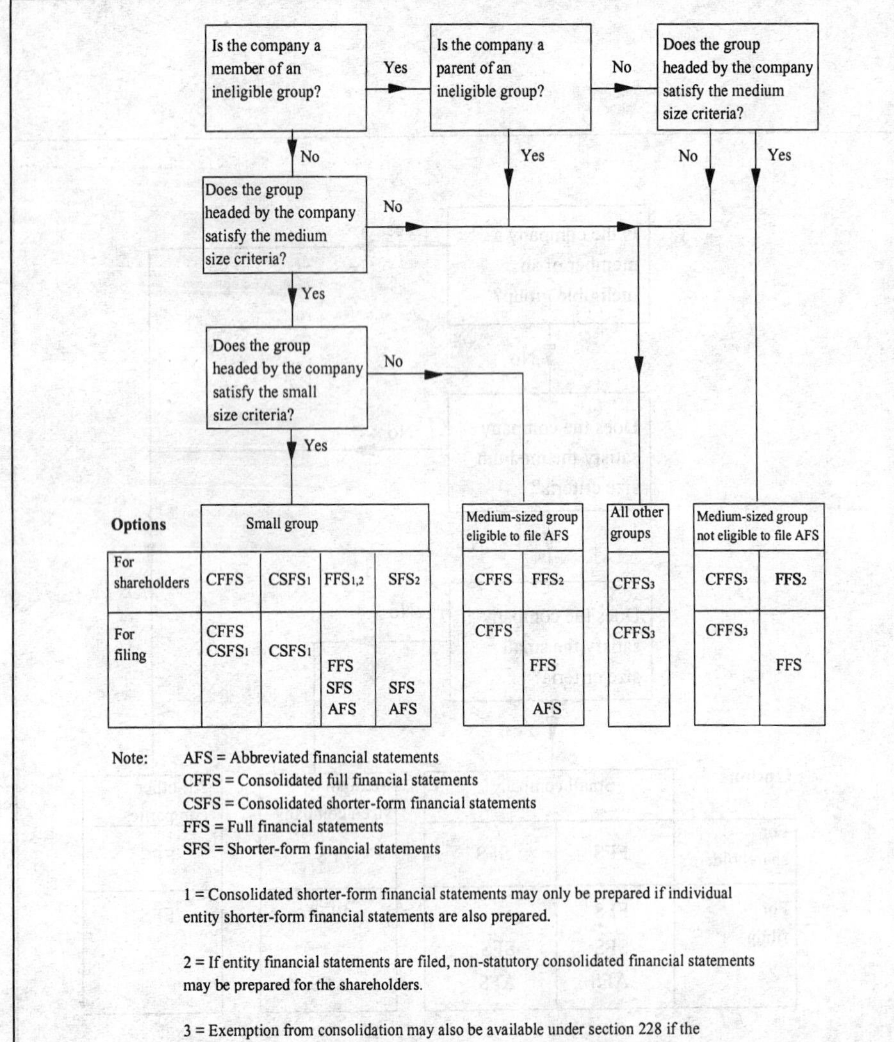

Options	Small group				Medium-sized group eligible to file AFS		All other groups	Medium-sized group not eligible to file AFS	
For shareholders	CFFS	CSFS[1]	FFS[1,2]	SFS[2]	CFFS	FFS[2]	CFFS[3]	CFFS[3]	FFS[2]
For filing	CFFS CSFS[1]	CSFS[1]	FFS SFS AFS	SFS AFS	CFFS	FFS AFS	CFFS[3]	CFFS[3]	FFS

Note: AFS = Abbreviated financial statements
CFFS = Consolidated full financial statements
CSFS = Consolidated shorter-form financial statements
FFS = Full financial statements
SFS = Shorter-form financial statements

1 = Consolidated shorter-form financial statements may only be prepared if individual entity shorter-form financial statements are also prepared.

2 = If entity financial statements are filed, non-statutory consolidated financial statements may be prepared for the shareholders.

3 = Exemption from consolidation may also be available under section 228 if the company itself is a subsidiary.

Chapter 37

Oversea companies

Page

Chapter 37

Oversea companies

Introduction

37.1 Companies incorporated outside Great Britain (meaning England, Wales and Scotland) frequently establish branches to trade in Great Britain. It is, therefore, necessary for the protection of the public that such companies are brought, to some extent, within the regulatory framework applicable to companies incorporated in Great Britain. This is done by requiring the registration of oversea companies with the Registrar of Companies, but extending wide exemptions to them so as not to discourage them from operating in Great Britain.

37.2 Oversea companies (defined in para 37.8) are regulated in accordance with Part XXIII of the Companies Act 1985. This provides for:

- Registration of oversea companies, including the regulation of names used by oversea companies.
- Preparation and filing of financial statements.
- Registration of charges. These provisions have not, at the time of writing, been brought into effect. Sections 409 and 424 still apply.
- Particulars to be delivered to the Registrar on winding up of a limited company incorporated outside the UK (meaning Great Britain and Northern Ireland) and Gibraltar with a branch in Great Britain.

37.3 The Act contains two regimes requiring an oversea company to register in Great Britain - the *place of business regime* and the *branch registration regime*. A company must register under one or other of these regimes. There is a fundamental difference between a place of business and a branch and the distinction between the two terms is considered in paragraphs 37.9 to 37.13 below.

37.4 Prior to 1 January 1993, an oversea company that had established a branch was regulated in the same way as an oversea company that had established a place of business in Great Britain. From 1 January 1993, however, new rules in relation to the registration and filing of financial statements and other corporate information were introduced for foreign companies (that is, companies incorporated outside the UK and Gibraltar) that conduct business in Great Britain through a branch. The need to introduce new rules for oversea companies that have a branch in Great Britain stems from the EC 11th Company Law Directive on Branch Accounts.

37.5 The EC 11th Directive deals with disclosures to be made in respect of a branch established in a particular member state where the limited company that controls it is established in another member state or a non-EC country. The Bank Branches Directive complements this by establishing special rules for filing of financial statements and reports and other corporate information of branches of credit or financial institutions in a member state whose head office is outside that state. Both directives were implemented in the UK by The Oversea Companies and Credit and Financial Institutions (Branch Disclosure) Regulations (SI 1992/3179). These provisions are now incorporated in Part XXIII of the Act.

37.6 The branch registration regime created by the new regulations complements the existing place of business registration scheme set out in Part XXIII of the Act. However, the new regulations make a number of amendments to Part XXIII, including the addition of four new schedules as follows:

- Regulation 2 and Schedule 1 of SI 1992/3179 implement the Bank Branches Directive and introduce a new Schedule 21C which sets out the requirements for delivering reports and financial statements of oversea companies that are credit or financial institutions to which the Bank Branches Directive (89/117/EEC) applies. For this purpose, a credit or financial institution is an entity that is incorporated or otherwise formed outside the UK and Gibraltar, has its head office outside the UK and Gibraltar, and has a branch in Great Britain. [Sec 699A].

- Regulation 3 and Schedule 2 of SI 1992/3179 implement the EC 11th Directive. It inserts three new schedules as follows:

  - Schedule 21A, which sets out the particulars to be disclosed under the branch registration regime by a limited company incorporated outside the UK and Gibraltar and which has a branch in Great Britain.

  - Schedule 21B, which provides for certain transitional arrangements where an oversea company moves from the place of business registration regime to the branch registration regime and *vice versa*.

  - Schedule 21D, which sets out the requirements for the reports and financial statements to be delivered by a limited company that is incorporated outside the UK and Gibraltar, has a branch in Great Britain and which is not an institution to which section 699A applies.

37.7 This chapter primarily deals with the accounting and the disclosure requirements for oversea companies that are not credit institutions engaged in deposit taking or lending, or financial institutions. As stated in paragraph 37.6 above, there are additional rules in Schedule 21C relating to the reports and financial statements to be delivered by credit and financial institutions as defined in section 699A. These rules are outside the scope of this chapter. All references in this chapter to an oversea company are to a company other than a credit or financial institution.

Definitions

Oversea company

37.8 An `oversea company' is defined as any `company' incorporated outside Great Britain (that is, England, Wales and Scotland) which has established a `place of business' in Great Britain. [Sec 744]. It includes unlimited as well as limited companies.

Place of business

37.9 There is no comprehensive statutory definition in English law of what constitutes a `place of business'. The Act merely states that the term includes a share transfer or share registration office. [Sec 744]. In general, if an oversea company performs functions in Great Britain that are only ancillary or incidental to the company's business as a whole (for example, warehouse facilities, administrative offices, internal data processing facilities), then the company has established a place of business in Great Britain rather than a branch. It follows that it is not necessary for the oversea company to carry out its main activities at the locality in Great Britain, but merely to restrict its activities there to matters incidental to its main business for it to have established a place of business. If this crucial test is met, the oversea company will be subject to the registration requirements under the place of business regime.

37.10 Whether a place of business has been established must be a question of fact in each particular circumstance. Guidance can be found by reference to decided cases that illustrate the following principles:

- A local habitation of its own.

  The company must have a "local habitation of its own". Accordingly, a company will not be regarded as having established a place of business if it carries on its activities through an agent. [*Lord Advocate v Huron & Erie Loan and Savings Co.* [1911] SC 612].

- Level of corporate activity required.

  It is sufficient that the company carries on some business activity at its representative office. It does not matter if that business is incidental and does not form a substantial part of its main activities. [*South India Shipping Corporation Limited v Export-Import Bank of Korea.* [1985] 1 WLR 585]. A share transfer or share negotiation office is a `place of business'. [Sec 744].

- Corporate presence of company officers.

  A hotel that a director frequently stays in when in Great Britain and from which he transacts the company's business is sufficient to denote an `established place of business'. [*Re. Tovarishestvo Manufactur Liudvig-Rabenek.* [1944] Ch 404]. However, the mere presence of the directors in their private residence will not make the residence a place of business. [*Re. Oriel Ltd.* [1986] 1 WLR 180].

Branch

37.11 The concept of a `branch' is one of Community law and has no ready counterpart in English law. Whilst the term `branch' is defined in section 699A, for the purposes of establishing whether a credit or financial institution is one to which section 699A applies, as "*a place of business which forms a legally dependent part of the institution and which conducts directly all or some of the operations inherent in its business*", there is no definition of the term for the purposes of the branch registration regime. As no definition of the term is given either in the EC 11th Directive or in the Act, it will ultimately be a question for the European Court of Justice to decide. Some guidance may, however, be found in the decisions of the Court. The Court considered the meaning of `branch or agency' in *Somafer SA v Saar-Ferngas Ag.* Case 33/78 [1979] 1 CMLR 490 and said that the concept of a branch or agency implies a place of business:

- Which has the appearance of permanency, such as the extension of a parent body.

- Has a management.

- Is materially equipped to negotiate business with third parties so that the latter, although knowing that there will if necessary be a legal link with the parent body, the head office of which is abroad, do not have to deal directly with such parent body, but may transact business at the place of business constituting the extension.

To indicate the approach that Companies House is taking to the legislation, it has issued a Guidance Note dated January 1993 entitled `Oversea companies: place of business and branch registration' which contains guidelines on its view on the definition of a branch and how it differs from a place of business.

37.12 In general, if the functions performed in Great Britain are not ancillary or incidental to the oversea company's business, but are conducted by the branch on behalf of the company, then the oversea company has established a branch. It should be noted, however, that the term `branch' is not used in the commonly understood sense of a local bank branch or an office branch at a single locality. It is closer in meaning to a subsidiary, although it will not be a separate body corporate.

37.13 Further, a single oversea company may set up more than one branch in Great Britain, if each branch has a separate management structure. This is important, since each `branch' has to be separately registered (see para 37.22 below).

Registration of oversea companies

37.14 There is no obligation upon a company incorporated outside Great Britain to register in Great Britain unless it has established a place of business or a branch here. However, where an oversea company has established a place of business or a branch, it must register in Great Britain either under the place of business registration regime or under the branch registration regime. An oversea company cannot have both a branch registration and a place of business registration in the UK at the same time. This is because every branch may comprise one or more places of business, but not every place of business is necessarily a branch.

37.15 It is, therefore, important for every oversea company wishing to establish a business activity in Great Britain to consider whether they should be registered under the branch or place of business regime and what sort of accounting disclosures should be made (see paras 37.38 to 37.50 below). Legal advice should be sought where there is doubt concerning the regime under which the oversea operations in Great Britain should be registered.

Place of business registration

37.16 As stated in paragraph 37.5 above, the scope of the EC 11th Directive is confined to disclosures to be made in respect of a branch established in a particular member state where the limited company that controls it is established in another member state or a non-EC country. The Directive does not deal with any disclosure member states may require from a foreign company with any lesser presence, such as a place of business, in their territory. Consequently, some companies continue to be subject to the old place of business registration regime if they have established a place of business in Great Britain. [Sec 691]. These companies, which cannot register under the new branch regime and remain subject to the place of business regime however large their operations, are as follows:

- *Unlimited* companies incorporated outside Great Britain (the EC 11th Directive applies only to limited companies incorporated outside the UK).
- Limited companies incorporated in Northern Ireland or Gibraltar. As Northern Ireland and Gibraltar are treated as being within the United Kingdom, the EC 11th Directive does not apply to companies incorporated in these regions if they open a branch in Great Britain. However, if such companies establish a place of business in Great Britain, they will be treated as oversea companies in Great Britain and, accordingly, become subject to the old place of business regime.
- Limited companies incorporated outside Great Britain that do not have a branch in Northern Ireland and whose presence in Great Britain is not sufficient to fall under the branch registration regime but is sufficient to fall within the place of business regime.

Branch registration

37.17 Every *limited* company, incorporated outside the UK and Gibraltar, which opens or has a branch in Great Britain is required to register under the branch registration regime. [Sec 690A]. All other oversea companies (see para 37.16 above) that do not qualify to be registered under the branch registration regime must register under the place of business regime. Whilst Channel Island companies and Isle of Man companies are also treated as oversea companies, a special regime applies to them under section 699 of the Act. However, for the purposes of the branch regime, they are treated as third countries, that is, not within the UK.

Change in registration regime

37.18 When an oversea company changes the nature of the business it conducts within Great Britain so that it moves from the place of business regime to the branch regime, or *vice versa,* it must re-register accordingly. [Sec 692A]. There are transitional provisions in relation to the change from one registration regime to the other. These are set out in Schedule 21B to the Act.

Particulars to be registered

Place of business regime

37.19 An oversea company that has established a place of business in Great Britain must, *within one month* of doing so, deliver to the appropriate Registrar of Companies (England & Wales, Companies House, Cardiff; Scotland, Companies House, Edinburgh), a return in the prescribed form (Form 691). In general, Form 691 requires details of the company's constitution and related documents and information on the company's directors and secretary. The detailed information and the particular documents to be filed are set out in section 691 of the Act.

37.20 Oversea companies incorporated in the Channel Islands or the Isle of Man that have a place of business in Great Britain are additionally treated, for the purpose of the provisions of the Act relating to documents to be forwarded, delivered or filed with the Registrar of Companies, as if they were registered in England and Wales or Scotland, subject to certain exceptions. [Sec 699].

Branch registration regime

37.21 An oversea company that has opened a branch in Great Britain must, *within one month* of doing so, deliver to the appropriate Registrar of Companies, a return in the prescribed form (Form BRA) containing particulars about the company and the branch. The detailed information and the particular documents to be filed are set out in Schedule 21A to the Act.

37.22 The branch registration requires certain information to be filed in respect of *each branch.* As a branch can operate from more than one place in Great Britain, it is necessary to consider whether each location constitutes a branch in its own right. The test is to establish whether each location has its own management structure, with distinct reporting lines back to the parent company. If that is the case, then each of these locations must be registered in its own right as a branch. If, however, the locations of the company in Great Britain are linked within a uniform management structure, through which reports are made to the parent company, then all the locations, no matter how numerous, count as one branch and require only one registration. The registration must be made with the Registrar of Companies for the appropriate jurisdiction (England & Wales or Scotland) according to the branch's principal place of business (for example, its head office or main office).

Accounting records

37.23 There are no provisions in the Act requiring an oversea company registered in Great Britain to keep adequate, or even any, accounting records. This is despite the detailed requirements to prepare and file financial statements considered in the paragraphs below. In practice, however, such records as are necessary for conducting the affairs of the oversea company are often kept.

Accounting reference period

Place of business regime

37.24 The accounting reference period of an oversea company subject to the place of business registration regime is determined in the same way as for a company incorporated under the Act, except that the equivalent of the date of incorporation of a company registered under the Act is the date on which an oversea company establishes a place of business in Great Britain. [Sec 701]. Accounting reference periods are considered further in chapter 38.

37.25 Furthermore, such an oversea company, unlike a company incorporated in Great Britain, is permitted to extend its accounting reference period even though more than five years have not elapsed since an earlier accounting period was extended by virtue of section 225. [Sec 701(3)].

Branch registration regime

37.26 The accounting reference period of an oversea company subject to the branch registration regime is the period for which the company is required or permitted by the law of the country in which it is incorporated to prepare financial statements. Consequently, section 701 does not apply to such companies.

Preparation of financial statements

37.27 The form of the reports and financial statements required to be prepared and delivered by an oversea company to the Registrar of Companies depends upon whether the company in question has established a place of business or a branch in Great Britain.

Place of business regime

37.28 Every oversea company that is subject to the place of business regime must prepare individual and (if appropriate) consolidated financial statements in respect of each accounting reference period. The basic rule is that these must be made up by reference to such dates and contain the same information as if the company had been formed and registered under the Act. [Sec 700(1)]. The Secretary of State, however, has taken advantage of the power contained in section 700(2) and (3) of the Act to modify these requirements or exempt oversea companies from some of them. The statutory instrument giving effect to the exemption is The Oversea Companies (Accounts) (Modifications and Exemptions) Order 1990 (SI 1990/440).

37.29 The financial statements, subject to the available exemptions set out in paragraph 37.33 below, have to comply with the requirements of sections 258 and 259 of and Schedule 9 to the Companies Act 1985 *before it was amended by the Companies Act 1989* as if the oversea companies were old special category companies insofar as those requirements applied. [SI 1990/440 para 2(1)(b)]. There is no requirement, however, to refer to the fact that the financial statements have been drawn up in compliance with section 258 or section 259 of, and Schedule 9 to, the unamended Companies Act 1985. [SI 1990/440 Sch 5]. The old Schedule 9 applied to banking and insurance companies, but in the context of the place of business regime for oversea companies, it applies to companies in all industry sectors.

37.30 Oversea companies are, of course, permitted to give additional information, including that required by Schedule 4 to the Act. Any information that an oversea company wants to include in its financial statements may alternatively be disclosed in a statement annexed to the financial statements.

37.31 Oversea companies may not take advantage of the exemptions available to small, medium-sized or dormant companies. [SI 1990/440 para 2(1)(c)].

37.32 An unlimited oversea company that, if it were a company registered in Great Britain, would be exempt from the requirement to deliver financial statements to the Registrar of Companies in respect of a particular accounting period under section 241(4) of the Companies Act 1985, is also exempt from the requirement to prepare (and hence deliver) such annual financial statements. [SI 1990/440 para 2(3)].

37.33 The exemptions referred to above allow oversea companies to omit the following information from their financial statements:

- An audit report (see also para 37.53).

- A directors' report.

- Taxation information:

  - The basis of computation and amount of any provision, or charge to revenue for UK corporation tax (ignoring double tax relief) and UK income tax.

  - The amount of any charge for taxation imposed outside the UK on profits, income and capital gains (to the extent that capital gains are credited to revenue).

- The amount of turnover and the method by which it is arrived at.

- Details in the parent company's financial statements of the identities of, the place of incorporation of, and particulars of the company's shareholdings in subsidiaries.

- Details of investments that exceed one-tenth of the nominal value of any class of the issued equity share capital of another body corporate and details of any investment that exceeds one-tenth of the company's own assets.

- Details of the name and place of incorporation of the company's ultimate parent company.

- Particulars of the chairman's and the highest-paid director's emoluments and the banding of all directors' emoluments.

- Details of any emoluments that directors have waived.

- Details of the bandings of higher-paid employees' emoluments.

- Particulars of loans and other transactions with directors and officers.

[SI 1990/440 Sch 2 - 6].

37.34 Where an oversea company avails itself of the above exemptions, the contents of its financial statements will be substantially different from those of a company incorporated in Great Britain. Consequently, it is recommended that any oversea company that takes advantage of the provisions of the regulation should disclose this fact in the notes to its financial statements. This recommendation applies whether or not those financial statements are audited. A suitable wording for inclusion in the basis of preparation note is:

Example

The financial statements have been prepared in accordance with the Companies Act 1985 applicable to oversea companies. The company has taken advantage of the modifications and exemptions from disclosure that are set out in the Oversea Companies (Accounts) (Modifications and Exemptions) Order 1990.

37.35 It should be noted that the financial statements prepared under section 700 of the Act must be the financial statements not of the UK operation, but of the legal entity incorporated overseas (containing the transactions of the UK operation as appropriate). Consequently, an oversea company with a place of business in Great Britain may have to disclose more information concerning its financial statements than is required by the laws of the country in which it is incorporated. In practice, however, the effect of the exemptions outlined above will generally mean that the oversea company can file its own statutory financial statements if they comply with the Act's provisions or amend them as necessary to comply with the Act's provisions.

[The next page is 37011.]

Branch registration regime

37.36 One of the principal purposes of the EC 11th Directive on Company Law is to protect companies operating in other EC countries from having to meet disclosure requirements in their financial statements that are more onerous than those required in their home state as discussed in the preceding paragraph. This relaxation in reporting rules, which was incorporated in the Companies Act when the EC 11th Directive was implemented in the UK by SI 1992/3179, allows an oversea company that is a foreign limited company (see para 37.6) to file the financial statements that have been prepared, audited and disclosed under its `parent law' together with a certified English translation. `Parent law' in this connection means the law of the country in which the company is incorporated.

37.37 The rules relating to the delivery of reports and financial statements by a foreign limited company that has established a branch in Great Britain are set out in Schedule 21D to the Act and are considered further in paragraphs 37.43 to 37.50 below.

Filing of financial statements with the Registrar

37.38 All oversea companies must deliver a copy of their financial statements for each accounting reference period to the Registrar of Companies irrespective of whether they have established a place of business or a branch in Great Britain. However, the form of the financial statements to be delivered and the period allowed for delivery to the Registrar are different for the two regimes.

Place of business regime

37.39 As discussed in paragraph 37.28 above, an oversea company that is subject to the place of business registration regime must prepare its financial statements in accordance with section 700 of the Act with the modifications and exemptions as allowed by SI 1990/440. There is no requirement that such financial statements must be circulated to shareholders, but copies must be delivered to the Registrar, together with a certified translation thereof where they are not written in the English language. [Sec 702(1)].

37.40 The period allowed for delivery to the Registrar is 13 months from the accounting reference date. [Sec 702(2)]. This is longer than the time limits for companies incorporated in Great Britain, which are allowed ten months for a private company, and seven months for a public company.

37.41 If the oversea company's first accounting reference period exceeds 12 months, the period allowed is 13 months from the first anniversary of the company establishing a place of business in Great Britain. [Sec 702(3)].

37.42 If the oversea company shortens its accounting reference period by giving notice under section 225 (alteration of accounting reference date), the period allowed for filing will be 13 months after the date on which the new accounting reference date ends or three months from the date of notice under that section, whichever expires last. [Sec 702(4)].

Branch registration regime

37.43 As stated in paragraph 37.37, 37.37 above, an oversea company that is a foreign limited company that has established a branch in Great Britain is required to deliver its reports and financial statements to the Registrar of Companies in accordance with Schedule 21D of the Act. These requirements are in some respects different from those applicable to companies merely establishing places of business in Great Britain. Furthermore, the form of the reports and the financial statements required to be delivered under Schedule 21D differ depending on whether the company in question is required to prepare, have audited and disclose its reports and financial statements under its parent law, or whether no such disclosure is required.

Disclosure required in state of incorporation

37.44 If the law of the state in which the oversea company is incorporated requires it to prepare, have audited and publicly disclose its financial statements it must, within one month of opening a branch, deliver to the Registrar of Companies with the return (Form BRA) for registration copies of its latest accounting documents prepared and disclosed in accordance with that law. [21D Sch 2(2)]. Publicly disclose means disclosure in a registry or by publication in a register, gazette or equivalent provision. Laws requiring disclosure to shareholders alone are not laws requiring public disclosure.

37.45 In the subsequent years after first registration, accounting documents prepared in relation to a financial period of the company must be delivered within three months of the date when they are first disclosed in accordance with the parent law. [21D Sch 4]. As a general rule the documents must be filed in respect of each branch. However, it is possible for a principal branch to file financial statements in respect of other branches provided this is specified in those branch returns. [21D Sch 3].

37.46 The accounting documents in relation to the financial period of the company referred to in the preceding paragraph consist of:

- The individual financial statements of the company.
- Its consolidated financial statements where it has subsidiaries.
- The directors' report for the period if any.
- The auditors' report on the financial statements.
- The auditors' report, if applicable, on the directors' report.

[21D Sch 6(2)].

A duly certified translation must also be provided of any document that is not in English. [21D Sch 2(4)].

37.47 If the parent law permits the company to disclose its accounting documents in a modified or abbreviated form, the oversea company may file these with the Registrar of Companies. [21D Sch 2(3)]. This is in contrast to an oversea company with a place of business in Great Britain that cannot take advantage of the modified financial statements provisions relating to small or medium-sized UK companies (see para 37.31 above).

37.48 A company incorporated outside the EC and required to file home country financial statements must notify the Registrar of Companies on registration of its accounting reference period and the date by which it is required to file its financial statements under its parent law. [21A Sch 2(2)].

Disclosure not required in state of incorporation

37.49 Where an oversea company with a branch is not required to prepare, have audited and make public disclosure of its financial statements under its parent law, it is required to prepare and deliver its financial statements in the same manner as an oversea company subject to the place of business regime as described above. Consequently, such companies will come within the scope of section 700 of the Act. This situation may apply, for example, to a private company incorporated in the US with a branch in Great Britain.

37.50 It follows that in order for financial statements prepared under a non-EC country's laws to be acceptable for filing in the UK, its parent law must *require* audited and publicly disclosed financial statements. It would not be sufficient, for example, if an oversea limited company with a branch in Great Britain whose country of incorporation did *not* require such financial statements, voluntarily drew up, had audited and disclosed financial statements in a form other than that required by the place of business regime. Such a company would still have to prepare financial statements under section 700 of the Act in order to comply with the UK filing requirements.

Listed overseas companies

37.51 Regardless of any of the exemptions or modifications referred to above, any oversea company that has obtained a listing on the Stock Exchange is bound by the requirements of the Listing Rules to circulate annual audited financial statements to all holders of its listed securities whose addresses are in the UK. [LR 17.46].

37.52 In general, a foreign company with a listing on the Stock Exchange must prepare its financial statements in accordance with its national law and, in all material respects, with UK Accounting Standards, US Accounting Standards or International Accounting Standards. However, financial statements prepared under a different standard from those referred to above may be accepted, if the Exchange is satisfied that those financial statements have been prepared to a standard appropriate for a company of international standing and repute. Reference must however be made to the Stock Exchange at an early stage. [LR 17.3, 17.4]. Furthermore, a company incorporated in a non-member state (of the EC) which is not required to draw up its financial statements so as to give a true and fair view must consult the Exchange to establish whether the standard to which they are drawn up will be sufficient. [LR 17.49]. Consequently, depending on the requirements that the Stock Exchange imposes, a listed oversea company may be unable to take advantage of many of the exemptions outlined above.

Audit requirements

37.53 No requirement for an audit is imposed by the Companies Act 1985 on oversea companies with a place of business in Great Britain, although the law of the oversea company's country of incorporation may still do so. This is subject to the obligations on overseas companies which are listed on the Stock Exchange as discussed in paragraphs 37.51 and 37.52 above.

Practical issue

37.54 Given that the financial reporting responsibilities of a limited company incorporated outside the UK under the place of business registration regime are fundamentally different from the branch registration regime, the question arises as to which of these two regimes provides the more effective environment for such a company to operate in Great Britain.

37.55 The answer depends firstly on the extent of the operations to be carried out by the oversea company in Great Britain. If the operations to be carried out in Great Britain are more than merely incidental to its main activities outside the UK, then the established operations would qualify as a branch rather than a place of business. Secondly, it is necessary to consider whether the oversea company is required to prepare, have audited and make public disclosure of its financial statements under its parent law. In that situation, it can meet the Act's filing requirements by simply filing its financial statements prepared under its parent law (including the transactions of the Great Britain branch) without any further modifications. On the other hand, if parent law does not require financial statements to be prepared, filed and audited then from the disclosure of financial statements point of view, it does not matter whether its operations in Great Britain are registered under the place of business registration regime or the branch registration regime. This is because, in either situation, the oversea company will have to prepare its financial statements (including the transactions of the Great Britain operation) under the old Schedule 9 rules with applicable disclosure exemptions, although these financial statements need not be audited.

37.56 However, in both situations, there is the disadvantage that the financial statements filed under the Act contain the transactions of the oversea operations as well as those of the Great Britain operations. It may be that the oversea company would prefer to file financial statements that deal only with its Great Britain operations, without divulging its identity or nature of its business carried on outside the UK. In that situation, the only route is to conduct the local operations through a UK subsidiary. Although there is a requirement to disclose in the financial statements of the UK subsidiary the identity and the country of incorporation of the ultimate parent, the subsidiary undertaking can take the exemption under section 231(3)(b) not to disclose such information, if it would, in the opinion of the directors, be seriously prejudicial to the business of its parent undertaking, or to its own or any of its subsidiaries, and the Secretary of State agrees that the information need not be disclosed. Indeed, some companies have taken advantage of this concession where its directors are of the opinion that disclosure of the ultimate or the immediate parent company's nationality would be unacceptable or offensive to its own customers.

Chapter 38

Secretarial matters

Page

Chapter 38

Secretarial matters

Introduction

38.1 The Act imposes certain duties and obligations regarding a company's financial management and administration on both the company and its directors. Many of these duties and obligations are of a secretarial nature and these are considered in this chapter and summarised in the paragraphs below.

38.2 The company's business letters and other documents must show the correct information regarding the company's name and other details. Furthermore, a company is under an obligation to keep proper accounting records and statutory books and to retain them for the appropriate period. From such records, the directors have to prepare financial statements for the company for each financial year. When a company's annual financial statements have been prepared in accordance with the Act's provisions, the company's directors are required to approve, sign and lay the financial statements and reports before the company in general meeting. The company's directors are required to deliver the financial statements to the company's members and other persons entitled to receive them and the Registrar of Companies.

38.3 This chapter considers the responsibilities of a company's directors for the company's financial statements and the role of its auditors. It discusses the accounting period that a company's financial statements must cover and the rules with which companies have to comply when they publish their financial statements. In addition, the rules for preparing summary financial statements and for revising defective financial statements (including defective directors' reports) are dealt with. These aspects of company law, together with the formalities regarding meetings and resolutions, including the right of private companies to elect to dispense with laying their financial statements before the company at a general meeting, are considered in detail in this chapter.

38.4 In many cases where the company or its directors fail to comply with the Act's provisions, they will be liable to a fine and in certain situations, the directors can be imprisoned. These types of penalties apply to criminal offences. Breach of other sections of the Act may involve directors or companies in civil penalties, for instance, section 242A imposes such a penalty on directors who breach the rules on the period allowed for filing their company's financial statements with the Registrar of Companies.

38.5 Penalties for breaching the Act's provisions are set out in full in Schedule 24 to the Act. In that Schedule the maximum fine for the offences on summary conviction is calculated by reference to the statutory maximum that may be imposed by a magistrate's court; and this is currently £5,000. On conviction on indictment there is no limit placed on the fine than can be imposed. The possible period of imprisonment on conviction, where such a penalty can be imposed, is set out in Schedule 24 to the Act.

Accounting records and statutory books

General requirements – accounting records

38.6 A company must ensure that it keeps proper accounting records. [Sec 221(1)]. A company's directors are under an obligation to present to the company's members, once a year, the company's annual financial statements, including the directors' report and the auditors' report on those statements. [Sec 241(1)]. The financial statements must include a profit and loss account for the financial year, together with a balance sheet prepared as at the last day of the financial year. [Sec 226(1)]. Schedule 4 to the Act lays down detailed rules that companies must follow in preparing their financial statements and Schedule 4A provides the rules for consolidated financial statements. (The rules in Schedule 4A are considered in detail in chapter 22.)

38.7 Furthermore, in preparing financial statements, companies have to consider other rules that are contained in FRSs, SSAPs and in other authoritative accounting statements (for example, SORPs and UITF Abstracts). In addition, if a company is listed on the Stock Exchange, it has to consider the accounting and disclosure requirements of the Listing Rules. Similarly, if the company's shares are traded on the Stock Exchange's AIM for small growing companies, it has to comply with the AIM Rules. The accounting records should be sufficient to enable the directors to prepare financial statements that comply with all these rules. What is sufficient will, in general, depend on the company's size and the nature and complexity of its business. This is discussed in more detail in paragraphs 38.9 to 38.24 below.

38.8 There may be other legislation that specifies the way in which particular companies should keep their accounting records. For example:

- The Housing Associations Act 1985 gives the Secretary of State power to prescribe accounting requirements for registered housing associations. The Secretary of State took advantage of this provision and has imposed certain accounting requirements by statutory instruments; Registered Housing Associations (Accounting Requirements) Order 1992 (SI 1992/512) applies to England. Housing associations have to comply with these requirements in order to ensure that their financial statements give a true and fair view.

- The Insurance Brokers (Registration) Act 1977 requires all insurance brokers to maintain accounting records that comply with the Insurance Brokers Registration Council (Accounts and Business Requirements) Rules Approval Order 1979 (SI 1979/489) (as amended by the Insurance Brokers Registration Council (Accounts and Business Requirements) (Amendment) Rules Approval Order 1981 (SI 1981/1630)).

- Friendly societies must keep accounting records and establish and maintain systems of control in accordance with section 68 of the Friendly Societies Act 1992. This section has superseded section 29 of the Friendly Societies Act 1974 with effect from January 1993. It extends the requirement in the 1974 Act to: have adequate systems of business control and inspection; to require the documentation of systems; and to cover systems for management information and control and report.

Proper accounting records

38.9 The Act's requirement that every company must keep proper accounting records is included in section 221(1). Section 221 is summarised below and Counsel has advised on the meaning of certain words and phrases used in that section, which are shown below in italics. Section 221 states that the accounting records must be sufficient to show and explain the company's transactions and, consequently, to:

- *Disclose* with reasonable accuracy the company's *financial position at any time.*

- Enable the directors to ensure that any balance sheet and profit and loss account prepared from the *accounting records* comply with the Act's requirements.

[Sec 221(1)].

38.10 A company's accounting records should detail the following:

- The *sums of money* the company received and expended on a day-to-day basis, together with explanations of the amounts it received and expended. [Sec 221(2)(a)].

- *A record of the assets and liabilities* of the company. [Sec 221(2)(b)].

- If the company deals in goods:

  - *Statements of stocks* the company held at the financial year end, together with supporting statements of stocktakes.

- *Statements of all goods sold and purchased* by the company, in sufficient detail to enable the goods and the buyers and sellers to be identified. (This requirement, however, does not apply to companies carrying on retailing.)

[Sec 221(3)].

Counsel's opinion

38.11 In March 1992 the Council of the ICAEW issued a guidance statement for members (published in Accountancy April 1992) on the obligation of companies to keep proper accounting records under the Act. This statement was settled in consultation with Counsel. The interpretation of section 221 of the 1985 Act set out below is based on that statement.

38.12 Section 221(1) obliges companies to keep accounting records. In addition, a parent company must also take reasonable steps to ensure that its subsidiary undertakings (which are not themselves companies) keep such accounting records to enable the parent company's directors to ensure that any balance sheet and profit and loss account prepared under Part VII of the Act comply with the Act's requirements. [Sec 221(4)].

Duty to keep accounting records

38.13 Accounting records should be made up of an orderly, classified collection of information capable of prompt retrieval, containing details of the company's transactions, assets and liabilities. An unorganised collection of vouchers and documents is not sufficient. The records must enable a trial balance to be constructed from them whatever their physical form. For example, where information is held in a computer database, the software should be capable of retrieving the appropriate data.

38.14 Whether a company is keeping the right kind of accounting records to meet the Act's requirements is a question of fact, which can only be decided on the facts of any particular case. In addition, the prevailing practice of the time in businesses of the type in question would be taken into account in determining whether proper accounting records have been kept. The records must also be sufficient to enable the directors to prepare annual financial statements that satisfy the Act's requirements. [Sec 221(1) and (4)].

38.15 The company's accounting records must be kept in a form that will enable it to comply with the retention period set in the Act. Accounting records must be preserved for six years for public companies or three years for private companies. [Sec 222(5)]. Furthermore, programmed instructions and supporting documentation in usable form, for example, from a computer database, and any necessary hardware, must be available for the same period.

Disclosure of the financial position at any time

38.16 In the requirement in section 221(1)(a), the words 'at any time' emphasise the obligation to keep accounting records up to date. This does not mean that transactions and events must be recorded instantaneously. It is sufficient if they are recorded within a reasonable time, which will depend upon the nature of the business and other circumstances. What is urgent for, say, a bank, may be less so for another business. In addition, records made to disclose the current financial position (including any stock records or memoranda, such as are referred to in paras 38.19 and 38.20) must be retained for the statutory period.

38.17 The Act requires the accounting records to be sufficient to disclose with reasonable accuracy, at any time, the company's financial position at that time. In doing so the legislation recognises that it is not practicable to keep accounting records in such a way so that financial statements can be prepared, giving a true and fair view, at every moment during the year. In other words, the Act does not expect a company to be able to reconstruct the financial statements as at any past date at random.

38.18 The directors should at any time be able to prepare a reasonably accurate statement of the company's financial position from the accounting records. The records should, therefore, contain the primary material on which a set of financial statements would be based. These records need not contain whatever additional items of information it would be necessary to know in order to make those financial statements true and fair. This is because the concept of 'true and fair' is extremely wide and embraces information not necessarily contained within the accounting records themselves. Furthermore, the financial position is not restricted to the cash position, it comprises the assets and liabilities including items such as those referred to in paragraph 38.20 below.

38.19 What constitutes a sufficient record of stocks will depend on the circumstances, for instance, the materiality of stock and stock movements. Continuous stock records can provide adequate information when they are supported by systematic physical checks. Furthermore, the information gathered from those physical checks would generally also be supplemented by accounting entries recording judgements of the stocks' realisable value and times of possible realisation. These entries may need to be in the form of memorandum as indicated in paragraph 38.20 below. Continuous records are not essential if the stock position can be assessed with sufficient reliability from other accounting records, for instance, interim stocktakings.

38.20 Provisions for depreciation, bad debts and other losses are often only made at the end of an accounting year, but section 221(1)(a) requires the records to disclose the financial position of the company with reasonable accuracy at any time during the financial year. This requirement can normally be satisfied if the company has a procedure to ensure that an adequate record is made and retained (for example, by way of memorandum), of any expected loss, liability or contingency material to the assessment of the stocks' current position. This type of memorandum would form part of the accounting records.

Sums of money

38.21 Section 221(2)(a) states that the accounting records must contain entries from day to day of all sums of money received and expended. The accounting records must, therefore, contain:

- The transaction date.
- The sums received and expended.
- The matters in respect of which the receipt and expenditure took place.

Such entries do not have to be made instantaneously, but must be made within a reasonable time (see para 38.16 above). Where a record of individual receipts is not necessary to explain the transactions (for example, in the daily cash takings of a shop), groups of transactions may be recorded rather than individual ones.

A record of the assets and liabilities

38.22 The accounting records must include details of all the company's assets and liabilities such as debtors, creditors, properties and plant. The records must show the dates of the transactions. The ASB's Statement of principles and FRS 5 contain definitions of assets and liabilities and rules for their recognition (see chapters 2 and 4).

Statements of stock

38.23 Where companies deal in goods, the statements of stock held at the end of each financial year are part of the accounting records. These statements and any statements of stocktakes supporting the year-end stock summary form part of the accounting records. Any continuous stock records or original stock sheets from a physical stocktake also have to be treated as part of the accounting records.

Statements of all goods sold and purchased

38.24 Where the company deals in goods, details of goods sold and purchased and of individual buyers and sellers must be recorded. However, this requirement does not apply to sales made by retailers.

Penalties and disqualification orders

38.25 Failure to comply with the provisions of section 221 is an offence. [Sec 221(5)(6)]. Furthermore, under section 9 of the Company Directors Disqualification Act 1986, the extent of a director's responsibility for the company's failure to comply with section 221 is one of the matters the courts must take into account on an application to disqualify the director (see para 38.76).

Directors' duty

38.26 The ICAEW issued a technical release (TR 723) in October 1988 that provides guidance on the main duties and responsibilities, particularly of a financial or accounting nature, that directors owe to their company and its shareholders and others. The guidance provided in TR 723 has been incorporated into section 1.401, 'Financial and accounting responsibilities of directors', of the ICAEW Members' Handbook.

38.27 This statement sets out what is considered to be best practice rather than what may be acceptable as the legal minimum. It has a section that deals with books of account and other accounting records. The statement gives the following guidance:

> *"In addition to the statutory requirement to keep proper accounting records, the directors have an overriding responsibility to ensure that they have adequate information to enable them to discharge their duty to manage the company's business."*

See also paragraph 38.78 below.

38.28 A company's normal books of account include:

- Cash books.
- Sales day book.
- Sales returns book.
- Purchase day book.
- Purchase returns book.
- Creditors ledger.
- Debtors ledger.
- Transfer journal.
- General ledger.

38.29 These books may be retained in book form, or on computer or in any other suitable readable form. Other books of account may be used to assist directors in preparing management accounts. These may include, for example, stock books to record continuous stock records used in a company's costing systems.

Auditors' duties and rights

38.30 In addition to the requirement that a company must keep proper accounting records, the company has a duty to appoint an auditor, unless it is a small company which may be exempt from this requirement. Small companies that meet the total exemption requirements set out in section 249A are exempt from having their financial statements audited. However, they may instead need to obtain the report of a reporting accountant. In addition, dormant companies that satisfy the conditions in section 250(1) may pass a special resolution under that section exempting them from having their financial statements audited. Apart from the exemptions for small companies and dormant companies, a company's auditors must normally examine any of the company's financial statements to be laid before the company in its general meeting. The auditors must also report to the members on those financial statements. [Sec 235(1)].

38.31 A company's auditors have a duty, in preparing their report, to carry out investigations that will enable them to form an opinion both on whether the company has kept proper accounting records and on whether they have received proper returns adequate for their audit from those branches they did not visit. [Sec 237(1)(a)]. They should also form an opinion on whether the company's financial statements are in agreement with the accounting records. [Sec 237(1)(b)]. If the company has not kept proper accounting records (including returns from branches), or if the financial statements are not in agreement with those records, then the auditors must state this fact in their report. In addition, if the disclosure required by Schedule 6 regarding directors' emoluments and other transactions that benefit directors is not made in the financial statements, the auditors must include in their report, so far as they are reasonably able to do so, a statement giving the required particulars. [Sec 237(2)-(4)].

38.32 Auditors have a right of access at all times to the company's books and accounting records. They also have a right to require such information and explanations from the company's officers as they believe they need in order to form an opinion on those financial statements. An officer of a company commits an offence if he knowingly or recklessly gives the company's auditors information or explanations that are misleading or false. A parent company must also take all reasonable steps to obtain from its subsidiaries incorporated in Great Britain such information and explanations as its auditors require. [Sec 389A].

Form of records

38.33 Any register, index, minute book or accounting record that a company is required to keep under the Act may be kept in a bound book or other similar form.

If the company maintains any of these items by recording the data otherwise than in a legible form (such as, in the form of a computer record), any duty imposed by the Act to allow the inspection of, or to provide a copy of, that data can be satisfied by reproducing that data in a legible form. But a company must take adequate precautions against falsification of such records. [Secs 722, 723].

Statutory books and records and their location

Accounting records

38.34 A company must keep its accounting records either at its registered office or at such other place as the directors think fit. The records have to be available for inspection by the company's officers at all times. [Sec 222(1)]. For this purpose, an officer includes a director, or a manager, or the company secretary. [Sec 744].

38.35 If the accounting records are kept outside Great Britain, then accounts and returns must be sent to and kept at an appropriate place in Great Britain (for example, the registered office), where they should be available for inspection at all times by the company's officers. [Sec 222(2)]. These accounts and returns should reflect the transactions recorded in the accounting records in order to:

- Disclose the company's financial position at intervals not exceeding six months.
- Enable the directors to ensure that the company's financial statements comply with the Act's requirements.

[Sec 222(3)].

38.36 The requirements as regards accounts and returns to be sent to Great Britain pose no problem for most companies that have branches overseas, because their overseas entities will usually return management accounts to Great Britain at regular intervals (normally, monthly). These management accounts will generally satisfy the requirements of section 222(3).

Statutory books and other records

38.37 The Act requires a company to keep the certain statutory books and records and specifies where these should be kept. The rules are considered in the paragraphs that follow.

38.38 The company's register of directors and secretaries must be kept at the registered office. The register must contain the particulars of the company's directors (including shadow directors) specified by section 289 and the particulars of the secretaries specified by section 290 of the Act. Any changes to these particulars must also be notified to the Registrar. The register must be open to inspection by members for no charge and by others on payment of a fee (currently set at £2.50 per hour). [Sec 288]. The Companies (Inspection and Copying of Registers, Indices and Documents) Regulations 1991 (SI 1991/1998) require a company to make the register, index or document available for inspection for two hours between 9am and 5pm on business days and to permit the person inspecting it to copy any information by taking notes.

38.39 The company's register of charges and copies of all instruments creating such charges must be kept at the registered office. [Secs 406, 407]. These sections were due to be replaced by similar provisions in section 101 of Part IV of the Companies Act 1989. At the time of writing, Part IV has not yet been brought into force. However, the DTI consulted at the end of 1994 on whether its proposals for reforming the law relating to company charges in Part IV of the 1989 Act should be implemented, whether the present legislation should remain, or whether more radical proposals for a new system based on notice filing should be adopted.

38.40 The minute books kept at the registered office must include minutes of the proceedings of a company's general meetings, decisions of sole members and records of written resolutions. Members are entitled to inspect and request copies of these minutes. [Secs 382, 382A, 383]. See also SI 1991/1998 mentioned above, which specifies the fee for copying minutes.

38.41 Minutes of meetings of directors or managers must also be entered into minute books, but the Act does not specify a place where these minute books must be kept. [Sec 382].

38.42

The register of members and, where the company has more than 50 members, an index of their names, must be kept at the registered office or can be kept at another location within England and Wales (for companies registered in England and Wales) and Scotland (for companies registered in Scotland) if this location had been notified to the Registrar. [Secs 352-354]. Members can inspect the register of members at no cost, but others have to pay a fee (currently set at £2.50 per hour). [Sec 356]. In addition, the company must provide members and others with a copy of the register if so requested. SI 1991/1998, mentioned in paragraph 38.38 above, provides that the fee for copies is £2.50 for the first 100 entries copied. Other amounts are specified where larger numbers of copies are required.

38.43 If a company keeps a register of debenture holders it must keep this at its registered office or can keep it at another location if this is notified to the Registrar. [Sec 190]. Debenture holders have the right to inspect and take copies of the register for no charge, but others are required to pay an inspection fee and a fee to copy the register. The fee for inspection and copying is the same as the fee for inspecting and copying the register of members (see SI 1991/1998 mentioned in para 38.38.)

38.44 The register of directors' interests in shares and debentures of group companies, together with the index must be either kept at the registered office or at the place where the register of members is kept. The Registrar must be notified of the place where the register is kept if other than the registered office. [Sec 325; 13 Sch 25-28]. The register is to be open for inspection by members without charge and by others on payment of the appropriate fee. For the right to inspect and require copies of the register, see SI 1991/ 1998 mentioned in paragraph 38.38 above.

38.45 For public companies, a register of persons interested in three per cent or more of the company's voting shares must be kept at the same location as the register of directors' interests is kept [Sec 211]. Shareholders are under an obligation to notify the company of their shareholdings when they have 'material interests' equal to or more than three per cent of the nominal value of the company's issued voting share capital. A 'material' interest is any interest in shares other than the interests specified in section 199(2A). The interests specified in section 199(2A) include the interest of an authorised investment manager. But for those 'non-material' interests, the obligation to notify the company applies when their interests are equal to or more than ten per cent of the nominal value of the company's voting share capital. [Sec 199]. For the right to inspect and require copies of the register, see section 219 and SI 1991/1998 mentioned in paragraph 38.38 above.

38.46 For public companies, reports of investigations into shareholdings made under section 214 must be kept at the registered office for six years. [Sec 215(7)]. For the right to inspect and take copies see also section 219 and SI 1991/1998 mentioned in paragraph 38.38 above.

38.47 A company will have specified the intended situation of its registered office on incorporation, but it may change its registered office by giving notice on the prescribed form to the Registrar. The change of address will take effect on registration of the notice. Documents held at the registered office must be transferred to the new registered office not more than 14 days after the company gives the notice to the Registrar. [Sec 287(3)(5)].

Company identification

Company name

38.48 A company's name is important not only for identification purposes, but also as a means of informing the public that it has limited liability status. Consequently, the Act contains several requirements regarding disclosure of company names and other details. Other legislation, such as the VAT legislation, may require a company to make additional disclosures, like the VAT registration number to be given on certain company documentation.

38.49 A company must state in legible characters on all of its business letters, notices and other official publications, order forms, invoices, cheques, receipts and other documents specified in section 349(1):

- The company's full corporate name.
- If the company is a charity, and its name does not include the word 'charity' or 'charitable', the fact that it is a charity. [Charities Act 1993 Secs 67, 68].

Failure to give the relevant information renders the company and the signatory liable to a fine. Furthermore, if a director or other officer of the company or a person on its behalf signs or authorises the signing of any of the documents referred to below in which the company's name is not mentioned, he is personally liable for the amount specified unless it is duly paid by the company. The documents are a bill of exchange, promissory note, endorsement, cheque or order for money or goods. [Sec 349(4)].

38.50 In addition, the following information is required to be stated on all of the company's business letters and order forms:

- The company's place of registration and registered number.
- The address of its registered office.
- For an investment company (as defined in section 266) that it is such a company.
- Even if a limited company is exempt under section 30 from the obligation to use 'limited' as part of its name, the fact that it is a limited company.

If the business letters or order forms contain any reference to the amount of the company's share capital, the reference must be to its paid up share capital. [Sec 351].

38.51 Business letters on which the company's name appears should not state the name of any of its directors (otherwise than in the text or as a signatory) unless the letter states the names of *all* of the company's individual or corporate directors. [Sec 305(1)]. This requirement extends to companies incorporated outside Great Britain that have an established place of business within Great Britain (see further chapter 37).

38.52 A company using the Welsh equivalent of plc or limited (cwmni cyfyngedig cyhoeddus or cyfyngedig) need no longer state in English that it is a public limited company or a limited company (whichever is appropriate) on all prospectuses, bill-heads, letter paper, notices and other publications of the company. [Welsh Language Act 1993 Sec 31].

Memorandum and articles of association

38.53 An up to date version of the company's Memorandum and articles of association must be filed with the Registrar and the directors must ensure that any alteration to it is filed with the Registrar within 15 days of its coming into force. Any alterations to the Memorandum and articles of association must be printed. [Sec 18]. Where the amendments are minor the Registrar allows, by concession, amendment slips to be inserted, provided these obscure the amended words.

Business name

38.54 Where a company carries on a business in Great Britain and uses a name that is not its corporate name, it must state in legible characters on all business letters, orders, invoices, receipts and written demands for payments both of the following:

- Its corporate name.
- An address in Great Britain where of any document relating to its business can be served effectively.

[BNA 1985 Secs 1,4].

Annual return

38.55 Section 139 of the Companies Act 1989 inserted new sections 363 to 365 into the 1985 Act. These sections instituted a new procedure for filing annual returns with the Registrar. The time for completion of the return was also altered and is no longer linked to the annual general meeting (AGM). Under new section 363 every company must submit to the Registrar an annual return (in the prescribed form) each year made up to the return date. The return date is a date not later than:

- the anniversary of the company's incorporation; or
- if the company's last return was made up to a different date, the anniversary of the date of the last return.

For filing company documents, reference is made in the rest of this chapter to filing at Companies House. It should be remembered, however, that the English and

Welsh, Scottish and Northern Irish registries are mutually exclusive for this purpose and documents sent to the inappropriate Companies House will be rejected.

38.56 There are three annual return forms prescribed by Regulations, which are needed because since 1991 the Registrar has been able to hold the register of companies on computer (see section 707A). In practice, Companies House now sends a computer generated form before the filing date based on information given by the company to the Registrar on other forms. The computer generated document needs to checked by the company on receipt and amended as necessary before returning to the Registrar.

38.57 A company may make its annual return to an earlier date than its last return date, but must deliver the return to Companies House within 28 days of the earlier date. Failure to deliver the return within the 28 days will mean that the company will not have complied with the 1985 Act and it will have to file another return made up to the original date and pay an additional filing fee.

38.58 The annual return form contains a box in which a company can insert a new return date that is less than 12 months from the date of the current return. Companies House will then send out the next return shortly before the date inserted. If no date is inserted, the next return will be sent out shortly before the anniversary of the current return.

38.59 The annual return in the prescribed form and containing the required information must be signed by a director or the company secretary. When it has been signed it must be delivered to the Registrar within 28 days after the date to which it is made up and be accompanied by a fee, which is currently £18. [Sec 363(2)].

38.60 The company's annual return form, must contain the following information, which is required by section 364:

- The address of the company's registered office as currently registered at Companies House.
- The type of company (for example, company limited by shares), and a description of its principal business activity, generally by reference to the VAT trade classification code.
- The name and address of the company secretary.
- Details of each of the company's directors, to include their full name, any former name, usual residential address, nationality, date of birth, business occupation and certain other UK directorships. Directors must disclose (in

the register of directors and hence in the annual return) the names of other UK companies of which:

- they are currently a director; or
- they have been a director at any time within the last five years;

unless those other companies are dormant or grouped with the company making the return. [Sec 289(1)(3)].

- If the director is a company or Scottish firm, its name and registered or principal office and particulars of other directorships should be given.

- The locations of the register of members and the register of debenture holders, if not kept at the registered office.

- If the company, being a private company, has elected to dispense with holding AGMs or laying its financial statements before general meetings, a statement to that effect.

38.61 A company having a share capital must also give on its annual return:

- Details of the company's issued share capital and each class of shares at the date to which the return is made up.

- The names and addresses of members and their holdings including persons who have ceased to be members since the last return and the number of shares transferred together with the date of registration of the transfers.

A full list of shareholders is required only every third year. In other years, a list of changes in membership and holdings suffices. [Sec 364A]. A leaflet, 'Notes for Completion of Annual Return', is available from Companies House to assist companies in completing their annual returns.

Members' lists

38.62 The Registrar has specified certain requirements, which are described briefly in paragraph 38.65 below, on the quality of documents filed at Companies House. These requirements apply also to the lists of shareholders which accompany annual returns as well as to filing annual financial statements. Guidance on document quality, print requirements, comfiche formats and acceptable magnetic tape systems and formats can be obtained from Companies House.

Penalties

38.63 A company that does not complete the annual return properly or fails to deliver it to the Registrar within the 28 days is guilty of an offence. Where the company is guilty of the offence every director and the company secretary will be liable also unless they can show that they took all reasonable steps to avoid committing the offence. [Sec 363(3) (4)]. Where a public company is late in filing its annual return, it appears that the Registrar may write to its directors at their home address (even if overseas) reminding them of their liability to prosecution.

Information annexed to annual return

38.64 In certain circumstances, a parent company may omit information required by Schedule 5 about certain of its subsidiaries, joint ventures and associates if its directors are of the opinion that it would otherwise result in information of excessive length being included its financial statements. [Sec 231(5)]. Where advantage is taken of this provision, the full information (including that disclosed in the notes to the financial statements and the information excluded from those statements) must be annexed to the company's next annual return. The next annual return is the return delivered to the Registrar after the financial statements in question have been approved under section 233. In addition, the financial statements themselves must contain a statement that the information is given only in respect of the undertakings whose results or financial position, in the opinion of the directors, principally affected the figures shown in the financial statements (including those undertakings excluded from consolidation). [Sec 231(6)]. The company and any of its officers who fail to comply with these disclosure requirements are liable to a fine. (See further chapters 16 and 21.)

Document quality

38.65 All documents that companies are obliged by statute to deliver to the Registrar (for instance, annual financial statements and lists of members accompanying annual returns and allotment forms) must comply with certain document quality requirements and they must:

- State in a prominent position the company's registered number.
- Comply with the requirements specified by the Registrar, including requirements to enable him to copy or read the document.

[Secs 706, 707].

The Registrar has a duty to make it possible to inspect the information contained in a document delivered to him and for a copy to be produced in legible form. As a consequence, the original documents filed must be clear to enable Companies House to photograph them so that the Registrar can produce a microfilm record for each company.

38.66 If the documents filed do not comply with sections 706 or 707, the Registrar may reject them and require the company to produce documents that do comply within 14 days. If a replacement complying with the relevant section is not delivered within a further 14 days, the original cannot be treated as having been delivered in time. The following requirements have been specified by the Registrar in relation to the legibility and the filmable quality of documents sent to Companies House for filing:

- Documents must be on paper that is white or otherwise of a background density not greater than 0.3.
- Documents must be on paper with a matt finish.
- Each page must be on A4 size paper.
- Each page must have a margin all round not less than 10mm wide. If the document is bound, the bound edge must have a margin of not less than 20mm.
- Letters must be clear, legible, and of uniform density.
- Letters and numbers must not be less than 1.8mm high, with a line width of not less than 0.25mm.
- Letters and numbers must be black or otherwise providing reflected line density of not less than 1.0.

38.67 Consequently, as documents should be black on white with a matt finish, as a rule glossy annual reports must not be filed at Companies House. Indeed, the Registrar has recently made it clear that glossy financial statements will be rejected. Companies House considers that a typed version or printer's proof is ideal provided it has been signed by the company's directors' and auditors' and where necessary by the company secretary.

Retention of accounting and other records

38.68 The Act requires that a private company should keep its accounting records for three years and a public company for six years from the date they are prepared. However, where a company is being wound up, this requirement is subject to any provision with respect to the disposal of records contained in the insolvency rules made under section 411 of the Insolvency Act 1986. [Sec 222(5)].

38.69 The period for which companies should keep their business documents in general (including their accounting records) is also governed by various other statutes. These include the Limitation Act 1980, the Latent Damage Act 1986, the Taxes Management Act 1970 and the Value Added Tax Act 1983. These may affect the retention of accounting records in the following ways:

- Limitation Act 1980 (as amended by the Latent Damage Act 1986 and the Consumer Protection Act 1987). This Act limits the time period during which an action can be brought as follows:

  - An action on a simple (non-specialty) contract or in tort (other than in respect of personal injuries) – six years from the date when the cause of the action arose, generally the breach.

  - An action on a contract under seal (specialty contracts) – 12 years from the date when the cause of the action arose.

  - A judgment debt – barred after six years.

  - Interest on a judgment debt – not recoverable more than six years after the date on which it accrued due.

  - Actions to recover land – 12 years from the date on which the right of action arose.

  - Actions for damages against manufacturers of defective products under Part I of the Consumer Protection Act 1987 – three years from the later of the date of the damage or injury or the date the plaintiff became aware of the cause of the damage or injury (subject to an overall period of ten years from the supply of the product).

- Taxes Management Act 1970. The Inland Revenue may generally assess within six years of the end of the chargeable period. Where there is fraudulent or negligent conduct, the limit is 20 years. The Taxes Management Act contains two further rules that may be relevant:

  - Production of accounts, books, documents and other information. The Inland Revenue may serve notice and require a company to deliver any documents within the company's possession (or power) that contain information relevant to any tax liability.

  - Time limit for recovery of penalties. Recovery of penalties may be commenced at any time within six years after the date on which the penalty was incurred or at any later time within three years of the amount of tax finally being determined on which the penalty is to be ascertained.

- Value Added Tax Act 1983 and VAT regulations. Those companies that are registered for VAT must keep their records and accounts and other related documents for a period of six years unless a shorter period has been agreed with HM Customs & Excise. These documents must be open to inspection by HM Customs & Excise at all times. There are special provisions relating to computerised records.

38.70 Consequently, the period of time for which a company should keep its accounting records depends primarily on the type of document involved. As a general rule, most accounting records should be kept for a period of at least six years. Some types of document may need to be kept for longer. Further guidance is available in the Accountants Digest, number 352, entitled 'Business documents -management and retention'.

38.71 To overcome the problems of storing accounting records, many companies now microfilm them and some store them in digital form. For VAT purposes, the Customs & Excise accepts records stored on microfilm, microfiche, and other modes of digital storage. However, prior clearance should be obtained from the Customs & Excise where a company intends to store accounting records in this way.

38.72 In court proceedings, a court will normally require the production of the original document. However, where the original document is not available, a court may accept other evidence of the document, but the company will need to establish that document's authenticity. For instance, where the document is on microfilm or is computer-produced, the relevant requirements of sections 4 to 6 of the Civil Evidence Act 1968 (in civil cases) or sections 69 to 72 of the Police and Criminal Evidence Act 1984 (in criminal cases) must in general be complied with in order for it to be admissible. The directors will, therefore, need to ensure that such documents are stored securely and that there are suitable procedures to enable the documents to be authenticated in accordance with the statutory provisions when the documents in question are required as evidence. A Code of Practice for legal admissibility of information stored on electronic document management systems has been developed and was published in early 1996 by the British Standards Institution. The Code does not guarantee legal admissibility, but it seeks to define the current best practice in relation to planning and procedures for the production and storage of documents on computer systems.

38.73 As a consequence, before a company destroys any documents that it has microfilmed or stored in digital form, it should consider very carefully whether it should retain the original document. It should remember that certain transactions (for example, a property lease) must be evidenced in writing and, therefore, it should not destroy the original document. Also, before a company destroys any accounting records, it should consult its auditors about whether the microfilmed or digitally stored records will provide them with sufficient audit evidence. The auditors will also want to satisfy themselves that the company imposes adequate controls over the microfilming process.

Penalties

38.74 If a company:

- does not keep proper accounting records sufficient to show and explain the company's transactions as required by section 221; or
- does not keep its accounting records in the places specified in section 222(1) and (2) or does not keep accounts or returns as required by section 222(3);

then, every officer in default will be guilty of an offence unless he can show that he acted honestly and that the default in question was excusable in the circumstances in which the company's business was carried on. [Secs 221(5)(6), 222(4)]. For this purpose, 'officer' includes a director, manager or secretary.

38.75 Similarly, where an officer fails to take all reasonable steps to ensure that the company keeps these accounting records for the period specified in section 222(5), (that is three years for private companies and six years for public companies), or intentionally causes any default by the company in observing this obligation, he will be guilty of an offence. [Sec 222(6)]. Failure to keep proper accounting records as required by section 221 may be attributable to negligence, incompetence or poor administration, but in some cases there may be fraudulent intent.

38.76 As mentioned in paragraph 38.25, the failure by directors to comply with their obligations to keep accounting records under section 221 is one of the matters which a court is required to take into account when considering disqualifying a director for being unfit to be a director. In *Re Firedart Ltd; Official Receiver v Fairall* [1994] 2 BCLC 340, the company's accounting records were held to be deficient in that the cash book, sales day book, the purchase day book and sales and purchase ledgers had not been written up for a period before the winding up order was issued. In addition, there was a lack of supporting vouchers and explanations for the company's expenditure recorded in the cash book. The judge found that failure to make these relevant entries was a breach of section 221 and that failure to maintain the evidence sufficient to explain the expenditure was equally a breach of that section.

38.77 The judge also considered that:

> *"When directors do not maintain accounting records in accordance with the very specific requirements of section 221, they cannot know their company's financial position with accuracy. There is therefore a risk that the situation is much worse than they know and that creditors will suffer in consequence. Directors who*

[The next page is 38021.]

permit this situation to arise must expect the conclusion to be drawn in an appropriate case that they are in consequence not fit to be concerned in the management of a company."

38.78 To guard against the possibility of trading whilst insolvent, directors should ensure that not only are proper accounting records kept, but that there are proper systems in place to provide the board with up-to-date information about the company's financial position on a regular basis. The absence of up-to-date information will be relevant to whether it was reasonable for directors to allow a company to continue trading at a time when it was unable to pay its debts. [*Re Grayan Building Services Ltd: Secretary of State for Trade and Industry v Gray & Anor* [1995] 3 WLR 1]. Directors may be guilty of wrongful trading if their company continues to trade when it is insolvent and may incur personal liability to compensate the company. [Insolvency Act 1986 Sec 214]. The amount which a director may be liable to contribute is likely to be calculated on the amount by which the company's assets can be seen to be depleted by the director's conduct. [*Re Produce Marketing Consortium Ltd (No. 2)* [1989] BCLC 520 at 553].

38.79 Sections 15 to 17 of the Theft Act 1968 impose penalties for obtaining property by deception and false accounting. False accounting includes dishonestly making in an account or record an entry which is misleading, false or deceptive in a material particular or omitting a material particular from such a document. Where a company has committed an offence under section 15, 16 or 17 of that Act with the consent or connivance of any director or other officer, he, as well as the company, will be criminally liable. [Theft Act 1968 Sec 18]. Also, it a criminal offence for any officer of a company to publish, with intent to deceive the company's members or creditors, any written statement or account that he knows is or may be misleading or false on a material point. [Theft Act 1968 Sec 19]. In this connection, any document has to be regarded as a whole. Moreover, even though each part of a statement is strictly true, that statement may be false if it conveys a false impression of the company's position, because material points have been omitted from it.

Data Protection Act 1984

38.80 The Data Protection Act has provided individuals with the right to inspect their personal data held on computer systems or other automatic processing systems and to have that information corrected if necessary. This legislation may, therefore, be an important influence on the information companies retain in their accounting records.

38.81 The Act seeks to ensure that personal data is:

- Obtained and processed fairly and lawfully.
- Held only for specified and lawful purposes.
- Not used or disclosed in a manner incompatible with the specified purposes.

- Adequate, relevant and not excessive in relation to specified purposes.
- Accurate and up to date.
- Not retained longer than necessary.
- Available for inspection and correction by the data subject.
  A data subject is an individual who is the subject of personal data. The individual need not be a UK resident. People in business on their own account, however, are individuals and, therefore, can be data subjects. A company cannot be a data subject, because it is not an individual.
- Secure against unauthorised access, or disclosure or destruction.

38.82 The Data Protection Registrar is able to issue notices ordering compliance with the principles of the Data Protection Act, or if necessary to suspend processing or restrict the transfer of data outside the UK. The Registrar possesses limited powers of access to buildings, to examine data, and in certain circumstances, to confiscate data.

38.82.1 This legislation impacts on each company that registers under it in different ways, depending on the type of records kept on computer and the purpose for keeping them. There is an exemption for personal data held by a company only for keeping accounts relating to its business or keeping records of purchases or sales, provided certain conditions are observed. Thus it is essential that professional advice is obtained before registration and subsequently, when records kept on computer are changed.

[The next paragraph is 38.83.]

Data Protection Act 1998

38.83 This new Act which is not likely to come into effect before early 1999 extends the terms of the present Act. Under the present Act individuals are given access to their personal data held on automatic processing systems; the new Act will extend this right to cover filing systems which include certain manual records. The data protection registrar will be renamed the data protection commissioner and will have wider enforcement powers. The changes are likely to affect a company's procedures relating to the collection of personal data, particularly data held in manual filing systems.

Accounting reference periods

38.83.1 The provisions of sections 224 and 225 relating to accounting reference periods and dates were amended by the Companies Act 1995 (Miscellaneous Accounting Amendments) Regulations 1996 (SI 1996/189). These regulations altered the method of calculating accounting reference dates for companies incorporated on or after 1 April 1996. They also widened the circumstances in which such dates may be changed; these provisions are also effective from 1 April 1996.

[The next paragraph is 38.84.]

Accounting reference date

38.84 A company incorporated before 1 April 1996 must within nine months of being incorporated, notify the Registrar of the date that it wishes to treat as the date each year when its accounting reference period comes to an end. [Sec 224(2)]. If a company does not give notice of this date, called the accounting reference date, to the Registrar within nine months of being incorporated, then, by default, its accounting reference date will become the end of the month in which its anniversary of incorporation falls. If it was incorporated before 1 April 1990 its accounting reference date will be 31 March, unless the company has registered a different date. [Sec 224(3)].

38.84.1 The accounting reference date of a company incorporated on or after 1 April 1996 is the last day of the month in which the anniversary of incorporation falls. [Sec 224(3A) inserted by SI 1996/189]. Its first and subsequent accounting reference periods will, therefore, end on that date, but this date can still be altered in the way permitted by the Act, which is described from paragraph 38.93.

[The next paragraph is 38.85.]

Financial year

38.85 The directors of a company must prepare financial statements for each financial year of their company. A company's first financial year begins on the first day of its first accounting reference period (see para 38.88 below) and ends either with:

- the last day of the first accounting reference period; or
- another date determined by the directors that is not more than seven days before or after the end of that period.

38.86 Subsequent financial years begin with the day immediately following the end of the company's previous financial year and end either with:

- the last day of its next accounting reference period; or
- a date determined by the directors not more than seven days before or after the end of that period.

[Sec 223].

This permits a company to end its financial year on the same day in the week rather than on the same date, if it wishes to. As a result, although a company's accounting reference period cannot exceed a period of 18 months, a financial year (and consequently the financial statements) may cover a slightly longer period.

38.87 A parent company's directors should ensure that, except where they consider there are good reasons for it, the financial year of any subsidiary undertakings coincides with the parent company's financial year. [Sec 223(5)]. The financial year of an undertaking that is not a company formed and registered under the Act refers to any period in respect of which a profit and loss account is required to be drawn up either by its constitution or by the law under which it is established. [Sec 223(4)].

Accounting reference periods

38.88 A company's first accounting reference period starts on the date of incorporation and ends on the accounting reference date. This period must not be less than six months and must not exceed 18 months. [Sec 224(4)].

38.89 Subsequent accounting reference periods will be for successive periods of 12 months. They will start immediately after the end of the previous accounting reference period and will end with its accounting reference date. [Sec 224(5)]. However, a company may alter its accounting reference date and shorten or lengthen its accounting reference period if it satisfies certain conditions (see para 38.94 below).

38.90 If a company's financial statements are not made up to its accounting reference date, or a date which is not more than seven days before or after this date, they will be rejected by the Registrar. The period for laying and delivering the financial statements to the Registrar is calculated by reference to the end of the relevant accounting reference period. [Sec 244]. The date a company chooses for its accounting reference date in the first year after incorporation can alter the accounting requirements considerably. The following three examples illustrate this:

Example 1

Company A is incorporated on 1 April 1996 and the company *did not* inform the Registrar of a change in accounting reference date. The company's accounting reference period, therefore, starts on the date of incorporation (that is, 1 April 1996), and ends 13 months later on 30 April 1997. [Sec 224(3)(b)].

Example 2

Company B is incorporated on 1 April 1996 and the company *did* notify the Registrar in accordance with section 225 that its accounting reference date is to be 31 December. Its first accounting reference period starts on the date of incorporation (that is, 1 April 1996), and it ends 9 months later on 31 December 1996. It cannot end on 31 December 1997 as this would mean a first accounting reference period of more than 18 months. The next accounting reference period is for 12 months, and it ends on 31 December 1997. [Sec 225].

Example 3

Company B is incorporated on 1 April 1996 and the company *did* notify the Registrar in accordance with section 225 that its accounting reference date is to be 31 August. The company's first accounting reference period, therefore, starts on the date of incorporation (that is, 1 April 1996), and ends 17 months later on 31 August 1997. It cannot end on 31 August 1996 as this would mean a first accounting reference period of less than 6 months. [Sec 224(4)].

38.91 Although a company's first accounting reference period should not be less than six months, it is possible to have a shorter period. The procedure for achieving a shorter reference period is illustrated in paragraph 38.98 below.

38.92 As soon as possible after its incorporation, a company should decide on a date that it wishes to treat as its accounting year end and it should inform the Registrar within the appropriate period allowed. The company should choose the date that is most convenient for it. For example, it should consider carefully the tax implications and also the peak workloads that the business may create (especially in a seasonal business), because it may be inconvenient to have to draw up financial statements at such a time. Unless a company wishes to change its accounting reference date, it is not required to make any further notifications to the Registrar.

Alteration of accounting reference date

38.93 The provisions below reflect the law with effect from 1 April 1996 when the Act was amended by statutory instrument 1996/189 as mentioned in paragraph 38.83.1.

Current and previous periods

38.94 A company may give notice to the Registrar that it wishes to alter its accounting reference date in relation to the company's current and subsequent accounting reference periods or its previous accounting reference period and subsequent periods. 'Previous accounting reference period' means the period immediately preceding its current accounting reference period. [Sec 225(1) as amended by SI 1996/189]. The period may be shortened or extended, but cannot be extended more than once in five years unless one of the following applies:

- The company is a subsidiary or parent of another EEA undertaking and the new accounting reference date coincides with that of the other undertaking or, where that undertaking is not a company, with the last day of its financial year.

- An administration order is in force under Part II of the Insolvency Act 1986.

- The Secretary of State directs that a company can extend its accounting reference period more often. He can do this in respect of a notice which has been given or which may be given.

[Sec 225(4) as amended by SI 1996/189].

An 'EEA undertaking' means an undertaking established under the law of any part of the UK or the law of another EEA state. [Sec 225(7) inserted by SI 1996/189].

38.95 The company must state on the notice given to the Registrar to alter the current or previous accounting reference date whether the accounting reference period is to be treated as shortened or extended. However, a company cannot extend an accounting reference period to make it exceed 18 months, unless the company is subject to an administration order under Part II of the Insolvency Act 1986. [Sec 225(6)].

Change of accounting reference date by listed company

38.95.1 A listed company which changes its accounting reference date must notify the Company Announcements Office immediately of the new date. If the effect of the change is to extend the accounting reference period to more than 14 months, the company must prepare and publish a second interim report or half-yearly report in respect of the second six months or of the last six months of the accounting period. These obligations have now been formally written into the Listing Rules with effect from 1 July 1996. The contents of half-yearly or interim reports are dealt with in chapter 39.

Previous periods

38.96 However, a notice may not be given to change the accounting reference date in relation to a previous accounting reference period if the period allowed by section 244 of the Act for laying and delivering financial statements in relation to that period has already expired. [Sec 225(5) as amended by SI 1996/189]. (The usual period within which a company must deliver is ten months for a private company and seven months for a public company, calculated from the end of the accounting reference period.)

38.97 The timing of the notice a company gives to the Registrar of a change in its accounting reference date is crucial to the acceptance of that new date, as the notice must reach the Registrar within the period allowed. Consider the following example.

Example

A private company's accounting reference date is 31 December. The company last completed and filed its financial statements for the 12 month period ended

[The next page is 38027.]

31 December 19X1. On 27 October 19X3, the company gives notice to the Registrar that it wishes to change its accounting reference date to 30 June in relation to its previous accounting period ended 31 December 19X2.

The company would then appear to have two choices: it may give notice either to lengthen its accounting reference period and prepare financial statements for the 18 month period to 30 June 19X3 provided the notice is not ineffective under section 225(4) (see para 38.94). Alternatively, it may seek to shorten its accounting reference period and prepare financial statements for the 6 month period to 30 June 19X2. However, if it does the latter, the company will be overdue in filing its financial statements by 6 months, because, by 27 October 19X3, it will be almost 16 months after the end of its new accounting reference period. This would be an offence under section 241 of the Act and so this option should not be used.

If the facts in the example given above remained the same, except that the company gave notice of the change of accounting reference date to the Registrar on 1 November 19X3, then this notice would not take effect. The reason for this is that the period for filing on the basis of the existing accounting reference date in relation to the previous accounting reference period (that is, 31 December 19X2), would have already expired (see para 38.96 above).

38.98 As stated in paragraph 38.91 above, a company's first accounting reference period cannot be less than six months. However, it is possible for the company to initially set a longer period and then reduce it by giving notice to the Registrar under section 225(1). The procedure is illustrated in the following example:

Example

Company C, a private company, is incorporated on 1 April 1996, and its accounting period will end on 30 April 1997, 13 months later. It then decides that seasonal factors require an accounting reference date of 30 June. The company may, at any time within the period to 30 April 1997, give notice to the Registrar that it wishes to alter its current accounting reference date to end on 30 June 1996, which gives a reference period of 3 months.

Preparing and approving financial statements

Directors' duty

38.99 The directors have a duty to prepare individual financial statements each financial year which consist of:

- A balance sheet as at the last day of the financial year giving a true and fair view of the company's state of affairs as at the end of the financial year. [Sec 226(1) and (2)].

- A profit and loss account giving a true and fair view of the company's profit or loss for the financial year. [Sec 226(1) and (2)].

- Additional information to be provided by way of notes. [Sec 226(3)].

- A statement of total recognised gains and losses. [FRS 3].

- A statement of cash flows. [FRS 1].

- A description of directors' responsibilities. [SAS 600]. This is not mandatory, but is generally included (see para 38.111).

- Additionally, for listed companies and major corporations (although not mandatory), an operating and financial review. [ASB Statement].

38.100 The directors must also ensure that:

- The company's individual financial statements comply with Schedule 4 as to the form and content of the balance sheet and profit and loss account and the additional information to be provided by way of notes.

- The information concerning related undertakings (section 231) and emoluments and other benefits of directors (section 232) is given in the notes to the financial statements.

- If compliance with the provisions of that Schedule and the other provisions of the Act would not be sufficient to give a true and fair view, the necessary additional information is included in the financial statements or in a note to them.

- If, in special circumstances, compliance with any of those provisions is inconsistent with the requirement to give a true and fair view, they must depart from that provision to the extent necessary to give a true and fair view. However, if they do so, the particulars of the departure, the reasons for it and its effect must be given in a note to the financial statements (see further chapter 2).

[Secs 226(2)-(6)].

The form and content of financial statements are discussed in more detail in chapter 6.

38.101 Where at the end of a financial year a company is a parent company, consolidated financial statements of the group must also be prepared on a similar basis, but complying with Schedule 4A as well as Schedule 4, and consisting of the same items. [Sec 227; FRS 1; FRS 3]. A parent company's individual profit and loss account may be omitted from its consolidated financial statements in certain situations (see para 38.106 below).

38.102 The board of directors has to approve the company's financial statements and they must be signed on the board's behalf by a company director signing the company's balance sheet. [Sec 233(1)(2)]. There is no legal requirement for the consolidated balance sheet to be signed in the same way, but this procedure is regarded as good practice. Every copy of the balance sheet laid before the company in general meeting, or otherwise circulated, published or issued, must state the name of the person who signed the balance sheet on behalf of the board. [Sec 233(3)]. In addition, the copy of the company's balance sheet that is to be delivered to the Registrar must be signed by a director on behalf of the board of directors. [Sec 233(4); 8 Sch 17(3)]. These provisions apply irrespective of whether the

[The next page is 38029.]

company is a small company filing abbreviated or shorter-form financial statements. Companies House has stated that a photostat or faxed signature is not acceptable in any circumstances.

38.103 In addition to the legal requirements in section 233 mentioned above, SSAP 17 paragraph 26 requires that the financial statements should disclose the date on which the board of directors approved the financial statements. The date of approval will normally be the date on which the board of directors formally approves a set of documents as the financial statements. The date of approval for consolidated financial statements is the date on which the board of directors of the parent company formally approve them.

38.104 The requirements of both the Act and SSAP 17 will be satisfied if the minutes of the board meeting at which the financial statements are considered record the directors' approval of the financial statements. The financial statements would then include, at the foot of the balance sheet, a note along the following lines:

Example

The financial statements on pages X to Y were approved by the board of directors on (date) and are signed on its behalf by:

(Name)

Director

38.105 The pages of the financial statements that are being approved would normally include, where applicable, any supplementary accounts or other financial statements (such as a value added statement or current cost information). The reason for this is that the directors should acknowledge their responsibility for all of the financial information that is presented at the meeting.

38.106 Where a parent company prepares consolidated financial statements in accordance with the Act, it is not required to include its own profit and loss account in the group's consolidated financial statements (see further chapter 6). In this situation, the company's individual profit and loss account must be approved by the board of directors and signed on behalf of the board by a director of the company in accordance with section 233(1). Also the financial statements must disclose that the exemption applies. [Sec 230].

Liability for approving defective financial statements

38.107 All financial statements (including consolidated financial statements) that are approved by the board must comply with the requirements of the Act (see para 38.99 onwards). If the financial statements do not comply with the Act, every director of the company who is party to their approval and who knows that they do not comply, or is reckless as to whether they comply, is guilty of an offence. For this purpose, every director of the company at the time the financial statements are approved is taken to be a party to their approval unless the director shows that he took all reasonable steps to prevent their approval. [Sec 233(5)].

38.108 There is, however, a statutory procedure (discussed in para 38.214) under which the directors can voluntarily revise any financial statements that they subsequently discover do not comply with the Act. This procedure also applies to a defective directors' report.

Liability if balance sheet is unsigned

38.109 The company and each of its officers that are in default will be guilty of an offence if either of the following applies:

- A copy of the balance sheet delivered to the Registrar has not been signed by a director as required by section 233 (see para 38.102).
- A copy of the balance sheet has been laid before the company in general meeting or is otherwise circulated, published or issued:
    - without the balance sheet being signed as required by section 233 (see para 38.102); or
    - without the required statement of the signatory's name being included (see para 38.102).

[Sec 233(6)].

38.110 In addition to the liabilities described in the paragraph above, delivering the financial statements to the Registrar without a signature on the balance sheet is likely to trigger a late filing penalty if the directors cannot rectify the omission before the filing deadline.

38.111 The Cadbury Committee's Code of Best Practice (discussed further in chapter 32) recommends that a brief statement explaining the directors' responsibilities for preparing the financial statements should appear in those statements immediately before the auditors' report. This recommendation has been reinforced by SAS 600 which now requires the auditors' report to distinguish between the auditors' responsibilities and those of the directors. Where a company's financial statements or directors' report do not include an adequate description of directors' relevant responsibilities, the auditors' report should include a description of those responsibilities. An example of such a description is included in

Appendix 3 of the SAS. Most companies now choose to include a similar description in their financial statements (see further chapter 32).

Directors' duties regarding their directors' report

Preparation and content

38.112 The directors must prepare a directors' report for each financial year which should include:

- A fair review of the development of the business of the company and its subsidiaries during the year and at the end of it.
- A statement of the amount of the dividend (if any) the directors are recommending to be paid and the amount to be carried to reserves.
- The names of the persons who were directors during the year, and the principal activities of the company and subsidiaries during the year and any significant change in those activities.
- The information required to be disclosed by Schedule 7, which sets out the detailed disclosures companies must make in their directors' reports.

[Sec 234].

Directors' reports are considered in detail in chapter 31.

38.113 It is an offence for the directors' report not to comply with the Act's provisions regarding its preparation and content. In this respect, each person who was a director immediately before the end of the period for laying and delivering the financial statements is guilty of an offence, unless he can show that he took all reasonable steps in trying to secure compliance with the Act's provisions. [Sec 234(5)(6)].

Approval and signing

38.114 The directors' report must be approved by the board of directors and be signed on the board's behalf by a director or by the company secretary. [Sec 234A(1)].

38.115 In addition, every copy of the directors' report that is laid before the company in general meeting, or that is otherwise circulated, published or issued, must state the name of the person who signed it on the board's behalf. The copy of the directors' report that is delivered to the Registrar must be signed on the board's behalf by a director or the company secretary. [Sec 234A(2)(3)]. The approval and signing of directors' reports are considered further in chapter 31.

38.116 If the directors' report is either laid before the company (or otherwise circulated, published or issued) without having been signed or without the signatory's name being stated, or delivered to the Registrar without being signed, the company and every officer who is responsible is guilty of an offence. [Sec 234A(4)]. However, the directors may revise any report they discover to be defective under the procedure for the revision of defective financial statements (see para 38.214).

Persons entitled to receive financial statements

38.117 Every member of the company, every debenture holder of the company and every person who is entitled to receive notice of general meetings is entitled to receive a copy of the annual financial statements (incorporating the directors' report and the auditors' report and any consolidated financial statements). A copy must be sent to them not less than 21 days before the date of the general meeting at which the financial statements are to be laid. [Sec 238(1)]. Certain people do not need to be sent copies and they are specified in section 238(2) and (3).

38.118 A copy of all such notices and other communications relating to general meetings must be given to the company's auditors. [Sec 390(1)]. In addition, the company's bankers may require that they should receive copies of the company's financial statements, and, although non-statutory, this requirement could be an enforceable term of either a loan agreement or a facility agreement. If all of the members who are entitled to vote at the general meeting are in agreement, the financial statements may be sent to members and others less than 21 days before the general meeting. [Sec 238(4)]. If the company is either listed on the Stock Exchange or traded on the AIM, the financial statements must be given to the members within six months from the end of the financial period to which they relate. [LR 12.42; AIMR 16.19(e)].

38.119 In addition to the right that a member has to be sent a copy of the annual financial statements (as mentioned in para 38.117 above), every member and debenture holder of the company is entitled (on demand and without charge) to be given, within seven days, a further copy of the company's last financial statements that were laid before the company in a general meeting. [Sec 239(1)-(3)].

38.120 Failure to comply with the provisions of section 238 to send a copy of the financial statements to members before a general meeting will render the company and every officer who is in default guilty of an offence. [Sec 238(5)]. Failure to supply a member on request with an additional copy of the financial statements within the seven days, will render the company and every officer who is in default guilty of an offence. If in proceedings concerning such an offence the issue arises whether a person had already been given a copy of the financial statements, the defendant bears the burden of proof. [Sec 239(4)].

Presentation of financial statements at general meetings

38.121 The directors have a duty to present the financial statements of the company before the shareholders each year at a general meeting of the company. [Sec 241(1)]. These financial statements must be laid before the company and filed with the Registrar before the end of the period allowed for doing so. This period is described in paragraph 38.140.

38.122 The financial statements do not necessarily have to be laid before the shareholders at the AGM; another general meeting will suffice. In practice, however, most companies do lay their annual financial statements before the shareholders at their AGM. The financial statements presented at that meeting should include the documents listed in paragraph 38.99, together with the directors' report and the auditors' report on the financial statements.

Election by private companies to dispense with AGM

38.123 A private company may (by elective resolution passed in accordance with section 379A), elect to dispense with certain formalities, such as the holding of an AGM and laying its financial statements before the company in a general meeting. [Secs 366A, 252]. This does not remove the requirement to send the financial statements to members. That is to say, such companies still have to prepare financial statements and send them to members, but they are exempt from holding an AGM and from presenting them at a general meeting. [Sec 252(1)]. Elective resolutions are discussed from paragraph 38.269.

38.124 Where such an election has been made and is in force, the following sections of the Act that refer to laying financial statements and other statements before members, should be read as meaning *sending* those financial statements to members, debenture holders and other people who are entitled to receive notice of general meetings:

- Section 235(1) – financial statements on which auditors are to report.
- Section 270(3) and (4) – financial statements by reference to which distributions are to be justified.
- Section 320(2) – financial statements relevant for calculating a company's net assets for the purpose of determining whether approval is required for certain transactions.

- Section 271(4) – statement made by the auditor where his opinion has been qualified and the company is proposing to pay a dividend.

[Sec 252(3)].

38.125 For instance, section 235(1) above refers to the requirement for auditors to report on all annual financial statements that are to be laid before the company in general meeting. Where an election is in force this would be read as still requiring the auditors to report on all annual financial statements that are to be sent to members.

38.126 The Act sets out the period during which the election applies. In the year that the election is made it applies to the financial statements for that year and to all subsequent years. [Sec 252(2)]. If the election is revoked, the financial statements for the year in which the election ceases to have effect and subsequent financial years must comply with normal requirements for the laying and delivering financial statements under section 241. [Sec 252(4)].

38.127 Where an election under section 252 is in force, copies of the financial statements must be sent to shareholders and others entitled to receive them, not less than 28 days before the end of the period allowed for laying and delivering financial statements. Where they are sent to a member of the company, they should be accompanied by a notice informing him of his right to require the financial statements to be laid before a general meeting. If a default is made in complying with these requirements, the company and every officer who is in default is guilty of an offence. [Sec 253(1)].

38.128 A member or the company's auditor has the right, by giving notice at the company's registered office, to require that a general meeting be held in order to lay the financial statements before the company. The notice must be sent to the company within 28 days beginning with the day on which the financial statements are sent out. [Sec 253(2)].

38.129 If the directors do not proceed to convene a meeting within 21 days from the date the notice is deposited with the company, the member or auditor may proceed to call a meeting himself. [Sec 253(3)]. Where a meeting is convened by the member or auditor it should be held within three months from the date the notice was deposited and should be convened in a similar manner as meetings convened by directors. [Sec 253(4)].

38.130 Where the directors do not convene a meeting, the person who deposited the notice may recover any reasonable expenses from the company that he incurs in convening the meeting himself. The company can recoup such expenses from the remuneration of the defaulting directors. [Sec 253(5)].

38.131 The directors are deemed not to have duly convened a meeting if the date chosen is more than 28 days after the date of the notice convening it. [Sec 253(6)]. Effectively this appears to give the directors 49 days in which to hold the meeting, since they have 21 days in which to proceed to convene a meeting after the notice is deposited by a shareholder or auditor.

Liability for not laying financial statements

38.132 The directors must ensure that they lay copies of the financial statements for each financial year at a general meeting of the company within the period allowed for laying and delivering financial statements to the Registrar (see section 244 and para 38.140 below). If they do not, every person who was a director of the company immediately before the end of that period may be guilty of an offence. [Sec 241].

38.133 It is a defence for a director in this situation to prove that he took all reasonable steps to ensure that the requirements would be complied with before the end of the period allowed. [Sec 241(3)]. However, it is not a defence that the financial statements had not been prepared. [Sec 241(4)].

Delivery to the Registrar

Individual and consolidated financial statements

38.134 In addition to laying the financial statements before the company in a general meeting, the company's directors also have a duty for each financial year to send a copy of the company's financial statements to the Registrar. The financial statements must comprise the individual financial statements required by section 226 and any consolidated financial statements required by section 227; including the directors' report and auditors' report on those financial statements. [Sec 242]. Financial statements in a language other than English must be accompanied by a translation certified in the prescribed manner. However, from 1 February 1994 financial statements in Welsh may be filed without an accompanying certified translation by unlisted companies whose registered office is in Wales. [The Companies (Welsh Language Forms and Documents) Regulations 1994 (SI 1994/117)].

Consolidated financial statements not prepared

38.135 Where a company is exempt under section 228 from preparing consolidated financial statements, a copy of the consolidated financial statements of its ultimate parent undertaking (which for these purposes must be established in the European Economic Area (EEA)) must be appended to the company's financial statements delivered to the Registrar. This exemption will only apply to a company in the following circumstances. The company must itself be a wholly-owned subsidiary of a parent undertaking established under the law of a member state of the EEA or, where such a parent holds more than 50 per cent of the shares in the company, no notice must have been served on the company by other shareholders to prepare consolidated financial statements. [Sec 228(1)]. If the ultimate parent does not prepare its financial statements in English, a translation of the parent's financial statements into English certified in the prescribed manner to be a correct translation must be appended. [Sec 228(2)(f)]. These provisions are explained further in chapter 21.

Subsidiaries excluded from consolidation

38.136 Special filing rules also apply where a parent company has a subsidiary undertaking that has been excluded from consolidation under section 229(4) on the grounds that its activities are different from those of the rest of the group. But this special rule only applies where the subsidiary is either a body corporate incorporated outside Great Britain without an established place of business in Great Britain or an unincorporated undertaking. [Sec 243(1)]. It should be mentioned that the exclusion of a subsidiary from consolidation on the ground of dissimilar activities will very rarely be possible since FRS 2 hardly ever allows exclusions on this ground. These provisions are further explained in chapter 21.

38.137 Under the Act's provisions, a copy of the excluded undertaking's latest individual financial statements and, if it is a parent, its latest consolidated financial statements, should be appended to the company's annual financial statements delivered to the Registrar. A copy of the auditors' report should also be appended if the financial statements are required by law to be audited. [Sec 243(2)]. Other requirements that must be complied with are as follows:

- The financial statements must be for a period ending not more than 12 months before the end of the financial year for which the parent company's financial statements are made up.
- If any document required to be appended is in a language other than English, a certified translation of that document should accompany it. This does not apply, however, to financial statements delivered in Welsh.

[Secs 243(3)(4), 710B(6)].

38.138 The requirements mentioned in paragraph 38.137 are, however, subject to the following qualifications:

- No financial statements need be specially prepared to satisfy the above requirements and if no such financial statements are prepared none need be appended.

- A document need not be appended if it is not otherwise required to be published, or made available for public inspection, anywhere in the world. The reason for not appending it should, however, be given in this circumstance.

- If a subsidiary undertaking and all *its* subsidiary undertakings (sub-subsidiaries) are excluded from consolidation under section 229(4), on the grounds that their activities are different from those of the rest of the group, the financial statements of any of the sub-subsidiaries that are included in the consolidated financial statements of the subsidiary need not be appended. This is because the subsidiary's consolidated financial statements that will be appended will include such a sub-subsidiary by consolidation.

[Sec 243(5)].

Period allowed for laying and filing

38.139 As stated above, the company's directors must lay the company's annual financial statements before the company in general meeting and must file them with the Registrar. These financial statements must be laid and filed before the end of the allowed period. [Sec 242(2)]. However, an unlimited company does not have to file its financial statements with the Registrar under certain conditions (see para 38.146 below).

38.140 The usual period allowed for laying and filing financial statements with the Registrar is:

- Ten months after the end of the relevant accounting reference period for a private company.
- Seven months after the end of that period for a public company.

[Sec 244(1)].

However, this period may be extended or shortened in the situations outlined in the paragraphs that follow.

38.141 If a company's *first* accounting reference period exceeds 12 months, the period allowed is the last to expire of the following.

- Ten months for a private company or seven months for a public company from the first anniversary of the company's incorporation.

- Three months from the end of the accounting reference period (see para 38.88 for the meaning of 'accounting reference period').

[Sec 244(2)].

38.142 The effect of this is that a new private company has to deliver its first financial statements within 22 months of incorporation and that a new public company will normally have 19 months.

Example

A public company is incorporated on 1 August 19X2, and its first accounting reference period ends on 31 December 19X3 (that is, 17 months later). The company must deliver its financial statements to the Registrar by 31 March 19X4. This is because the period allowed is the later of 3 months after the end of the accounting reference period, that is 31 March 19X4, and 7 months from the first anniversary of the inception of the company, that is, 28 February 19X4.

38.143 The period can be automatically extended by three months where the company carries on business or has interests outside the UK, the Channel Islands and the Isle of Man. For this to apply, the directors must give notice in the prescribed form to the Registrar before the end of the normal period allowed for laying and filing the financial statements. [Sec 244(3)].

38.144 A company may shorten its accounting reference period by notifying the Registrar under section 225 of the Act (see para 38.94 onwards). Where a company takes advantage of section 225 and shortens its accounting reference period, it must file its financial statements for this shorter period before the last to expire of the following.

- The period applicable under the relevant provision of section 244(1) to (3) described in paragraphs 38.140 to 38.143 above.

- Three months after the date on which the notice was given to the Registrar to change the accounting reference date.

[Sec 244(4)].

38.145 In exceptional circumstances the Secretary of State may extend the time for filing if application is made to Companies House before the expiry of the period allowed for filing the company's financial statements. Any such application will, however, need to give good reasons why the extension should be granted. [Sec 244(5)].

Filing exemption for unlimited companies

38.146 The directors of an unlimited company are not required under section 254 to file a copy of the company's financial statements with the Registrar provided the company was *not*, at any time during the relevant accounting reference period, any one of the following:

- A subsidiary company of a limited undertaking.
- A parent company of a limited undertaking.
- Subject to rights exercisable by or on behalf of two or more limited undertakings which, if exercised by one of them, would have made the company its subsidiary.
- A banking or insurance company or the parent company of a banking or insurance group.
- A qualifying company under the Partnerships and Unlimited Companies (Accounts) Regulations 1993 (SI 1993/1820). An unlimited company will be a qualifying company if each of its members is a limited company, or is another unlimited company or Scottish firm, each of whose members is a limited company.
- A company carrying on a business as the promoter of a trading stamp scheme (under the Trading Stamps Act 1964).

[Sec 254(1)(2)(3)].

38.147 Where an unlimited company is exempt from filing its financial statements under section 254, its statutory financial statements will be those prepared in accordance with Part VII of the Act and approved by the board of directors. If it publishes non-statutory financial statements, those financial statements must include a statement that the company is exempt from the requirement to deliver statutory financial statements. [Sec 254(4)]. See paragraph 38.155 where the meaning of publishing financial statements is explained.

Company's liability for late filing

38.148 Where a company does not deliver its annual financial statements to the Registrar within the period allowed, the Registrar has authority to require the company to pay a penalty. The penalties (which are set out in section 242A) are based on a sliding scale depending on the length of time between the date permitted by section 244 for filing and the actual date of delivery to the Registrar. The penalties are higher for public companies. The late filing penalties were introduced because of the legal duty imposed on directors to make public certain information about the company.

38.149 It should be noted that the Registrar is rigorously applying this provision of the Act and imposing late filing penalties even if the company is just over the filing deadline. Also it is the date the financial statements are received by the Registrar which counts, not the date of posting. The general rule the Registrar uses to calculate the seven or ten month period is based on the House of Lords decision in *Dodds v Walker* [1981] 1 WLR 1441. Thus the period ends upon the corresponding date in the appropriate month (that is, not necessarily the end of the month) or, where there is no corresponding date, the last day of that month. Consequently, a company with an accounting reference date of 30 September must file its financial statements with the Registrar by 30 April for a public company or by 30 July (not 31 July) for a private company.

38.150 These provisions came into force on 1 July 1992. Financial statements filed late after this date are liable to a penalty. Where the deadline falls on a bank holiday, the financial statements must be posted or be delivered by hand to arrive at Companies House on or before the last working day before the deadline. Companies House advise that financial statements should be delivered at least three weeks before the deadline.

38.151 The Registrar considers that the late filing penalties will extend to the situation where the court has declared that the striking of a company off the register is void and that the company is deemed to continue in existence as if it had never been struck off. The financial statements of a company restored to the Register at Companies House may, therefore, be liable to late filing penalties for the period during which the company was dissolved.

Directors' liability for late delivery

38.152 The late filing penalties mentioned above are quite separate from any offence of which the directors may be guilty for not delivering the annual financial statements to the Registrar before the end of the period allowed (see para 38.140). It is a defence for a director to prove that he took all reasonable steps for securing that the requirements to deliver the financial statements would be complied with before the end of the period allowed. It is not a defence that the documents were not in fact prepared.

38.153 In addition, if a company has not complied with the filing requirements within the period allowed for laying and filing financial statements, any member, or any of the company's creditors, or the Registrar may serve notice on the company requiring it to comply with the filing requirements. If the company's directors fail to make good the default within 14 days after this notice has been served, then the person who served the notice may apply to the court to make an order instructing the directors to comply with the filing requirements within a time the court specifies. The court order may also require the directors to bear the cost of the application. [Sec 242(3)].

38.154 The Company Directors (Disqualification) Act 1986 provides that if a director is persistently in default in filing any returns, financial statements or other document with the Registrar, he may be disqualified. Default may be conclusively proved if he has been adjudged guilty of three or more defaults in the five years ending with the application date. [The Company Directors (Disqualification) Act 1986 Sec 3(2)].

Publication of financial statements

Definition of publication

38.155 Section 240 sets out the requirements that companies have to comply with when they 'publish' their financial statements. A company will be regarded as 'publishing' financial statements if it publishes, issues or circulates them, or otherwise makes them available for public inspection in a manner calculated to invite members of the public (or any class of members of the public) to read them. [Sec 240(4)].

38.156 A company may publish the following categories of financial statements:

- Statutory financial statements:
  - Full financial statements.
  - Abbreviated financial statements.
  - Shorter-form financial statements for small companies.
  - Financial statements in ECUs.
- Summary financial statements.
- Non-statutory financial statements.
- Preliminary statements of annual results.
- Announcements of half-yearly results and reports of listed companies.

The definitions and the rules for publication of these categories of financial statements are discussed in the paragraphs that follow.

Statutory accounts

Full financial statements

38.157 Full financial statements are referred to in section 240(1) of the Act as a company's 'statutory accounts'. 'Statutory accounts' in that section means the company's individual financial statements or consolidated financial statements for a financial year, as required to be delivered to the Registrar under section 242. [Sec 240(5)]. Statutory accounts are referred to in the paragraphs that follow and throughout this book as statutory financial statements.

38.158 A company that publishes any of its statutory financial statements must include:

- The relevant auditors' report under section 235 or the report of a reporting accountant made for the purposes of section 249A(2). [Sec 240(1)].

- Its consolidated financial statements for the same year with its individual financial statements, if it is required to prepare consolidated financial statements by section 227. [Sec 240(2)].

38.159 If any of these requirements of section 240 are not complied with, the company and any officer of it who is in default will be guilty of an offence. [Sec 240(6)].

Abbreviated financial statements

38.160 Abbreviated (previously referred to in the Act as 'modified') financial statements are not full financial statements. They are prepared by some small companies that wish to take advantage of the special provisions for small companies. These permit a company that qualifies as small for a financial year to *file* abbreviated individual financial statements instead of full or shorter-form individual financial statements with the Registrar. [Sec 246(5)]. A company that qualifies as medium-sized may also file abbreviated individual financial statements under the special provisions for medium-sized companies. [Sec 246A(3)]. The intention of these special provisions is to provide small and medium-sized companies with greater privacy rather than to reduce the burden on them. A small or medium-sized company that takes advantage of the relevant provisions in the financial statements it can file, must still prepare full or shorter-form financial statements for its members.

38.161 Abbreviated financial statements in the form mentioned above that are filed with the Registrar will be 'statutory accounts' for the purposes of section 240 of the Act. If the financial statements that are being published are abbreviated financial statements the reference in section 240 to the auditors' report is to be read as a reference to the special auditors' report referred to in section 247B of the Act. [Sec 247B(5)]. The provisions relating to abbreviated financial statements are dealt with fully in chapter 36.

Shorter-form financial statements for small companies

38.162 A company that qualifies as a small company for a financial year is entitled under section 246(2) to *prepare* its annual financial statements (and if it does so, is entitled under section 248A to *prepare* any consolidated financial statements for that year) in one of the two special formats included in Schedule 8 to the Act. Section 246(3) and (4) permits certain information required by Schedules 5, 6 and 7 to be omitted from these financial statements.

38.163 These concessions were inserted into the Companies Act 1985 by the Companies Act 1985 (Accounts of Small and Medium-sized Companies and Minor Accounting Amendments) Regulations 1997 (SI 1997/220). They apply to annual financial statements approved by company boards on or after 1 March 1997. The concessions were subsequently amended by the Company Accounts (Disclosure of Directors' Emoluments) Regulations 1997 (SI 1997/570) for years ending on or after 31 March 1997.

38.163.1 If the company prepares shorter-form financial statements under section 246(2), they will be the company's annual financial statements. As a consequence, they must be authorised by the board of directors, laid before the company in general meeting and filed with the Registrar. The company may, however, instead of filing the shorter-form financial statements prepare abbreviated financial statements specifically for filing and file these instead (see para 38.160).

[The next paragraph is 38.164.]

38.164 Shorter form financial statements that are filed with the registrar will be the company's statutory financial statements for the purposes of section 240. Abbreviated financial statements which a small company can prepare for filing are much shorter than full financial statements. The formats provided for shorter-form financial statements, however, do not reduce greatly the number of items to be shown compared with full financial statements.

38.165 The accounting requirements concerning shorter-form financial statements are considered in detail in chapter 36.

Delivering and publishing financial statements in ECUs

38.166 From November 1992 companies have been permitted to publish their financial statements in ECUs. This may be done either by preparing annual financial statements in ECUs (in addition to the normal annual financial statements) or by including equivalent ECU information in the annual financial statements. The Act's wording seems to preclude a company only filing financial statements in ECUs. However, in both cases, the company must comply with the following conditions:

The amounts shown in ECUs must be translated at the relevant exchange rate prevailing on the balance sheet date.

The rate must be disclosed in the notes to the financial statements.

[Sec 242B(2) inserted by SI 1992/2452].

38.167 In addition, if a company wishes to publish, circulate or generally make available to the public copies of its financial statements which show the amounts in ECUs and which comply with the above:

- It must treat them as its statutory financial statements for the purposes of section 240 and the requirements of that section will apply to any publication of those financial statements.

- The auditors' report required by that section to accompany them is the auditors' report on the annual financial statements of which they are a copy.

[Sec 242B(4) inserted by SI 1992/2452].

38.168 'ECU' is defined as a unit equal to the value of the unit of account known as the ECU used in the European Monetary System. 'Relevant exchange' rate is defined as the rate used for translating the value of the ECU for the purposes of that system. [Sec 242B(5) inserted by SI 1992/2452].

38.169 Although not specifically dealt with in the Act, the Registrar has accepted annual financial statements prepared in a foreign currency, as long as the exchange rate to sterling is disclosed in the notes to financial statements. One major difference with this concession, however, is that equivalent sterling information is not required as it is where the financial statements have been prepared in ECUs. Currently it is not acceptable to file financial statements in Euros as this is not yet regarded as a foreign currency and there are no statutory concessions to allow this. However, on 1 January 1999 the euro will replace the ECU and national currencies in the EU member states joining the single currency.

Summary financial statements

Background

38.170 The Companies Act 1989 introduced summary financial statements by inserting a new section 251 into the 1985 Act. This is supplemented by regulations, currently the Companies (Summary Financial Statement) Regulations 1995 (SI 1995/2092). Listed public companies (that is, companies whose shares or debentures have been admitted to the Official List of the Stock Exchange), are able, in certain circumstances, to send summary financial statements to their members and debenture holders ('members') instead of the full financial statements otherwise required under section 238(1). [Sec 251(1)].

38.171 Summary financial statements have also been used by building societies, which are allowed to send such summaries to their members under section 76 of the Building Societies Act 1986 (amended by the Building Societies Act 1986 (Modifications) Order 1991 (SI 1991/1729)).

38.172 It has become evident that, since summary financial statements were introduced in 1990, only a small number of eligible companies have issued them. One reason why more companies have not done so may be due to the complexity of the regulations. In its consultative document 'Simpler procedures for summary financial statements' issued in March 1995, the DTI said that the purpose of summary financial statements is three-fold. That is:

[The next page is 38045.]

- To improve communication between companies and shareholders by allowing companies to provide key financial information in a form that is more accessible and easier to understand.

- To relieve companies of the cost of sending full sets of financial statements to members.

- To relieve shareholders of the burden of receiving long and complex documents, if they do not understand or have little interest in them.

38.173 As a result of the consultative document the Companies (Summary Financial Statement) Regulations 1995 (SI 1995/2092) were issued and replaced the Companies (Summary Financial Statement) Regulations 1992 (SI 1992/3075) with effect from 1 September 1995. However, listed companies other than insurance companies may continue to comply with the 1992 regulations for financial years beginning before 23 December 1994, and need not comply with the 1995 regulations. There are special transitional provisions for insurance companies.

38.174 The 1995 regulations are based on the 1992 regulations, but redrafted to make them easier to understand the main changes are:

- To simplify the manner in which listed companies ascertain whether members wish to receive summary financial statements instead of full financial statements.

- To permit the directors to choose the headings under which to give the information required by the regulations in the directors' report, summary profit and loss account and balance sheet.

38.175 However, against the potential benefits of summary financial statements must be set the extra cost of the preparation of an additional set of financial statements and their audit. The provisions relating to preparing and issuing summary financial statements are described below.

General conditions

38.176 A listed company will be prohibited from sending a summary financial statement to a member instead of full financial statements in the following circumstances:

- Where the company is prohibited from doing so by any provision in its memorandum or articles of association or in any of the company's debentures or trust deeds. [SI 1995/2092 Reg 3].

- Where the member has indicated that he wishes to receive full financial statements. [Sec 251(2)].

38.177 In addition, the company must not send summary financial statements for any financial year in place of copies of the full financial statements unless both the following conditions are satisfied:

- The period allowed for laying and delivering full financial statements under section 244 of the Act for that year has not expired.

- The summary financial statement has been approved by the board of directors and the original statement has been signed on behalf of the board by a director of the company.

[SI 1995/2092 Reg 4(4)].

38.178 Summary financial statements must be derived from the company's annual financial statements including the directors' report and comply with the requirements of section 251 [Sec 251(3)]. Provided that the summary financial statements sent to members comply with those requirements, the normal rules relating to publishing statutory and non-statutory financial statements in section 240 do not apply. [Sec 251(7)].

38.179 The requirements of section 251 fall into the following categories:

- The manner in which the wishes of members to receive full financial statements are to be ascertained. These provisions are set out in regulation 4 of SI 1995/2092.

- The statements to be included in the summary financial statement. [Sec 251(4)].

- The form and content of summary financial statements. [See SI 1995/2092 Regs 7 -10].

Unless these requirements are complied with, a listed company cannot sent out summary financial statements. These requirements are discussed in more detail below.

38.180 In addition to the above information, the Stock Exchange's Listing Rules require listed companies to disclose the earnings per share in summary financial statements. [LR 12.45].

Ascertaining wishes of members

38.181 A listed company cannot send a summary financial statement to a member in place of copies of its full financial statements unless it has ascertained that the member does not wish to receive copies of the full financial statements. A listed company has to ascertain whether a member wishes to receive full financial statements for a financial year (and future years) from one of the following.

- From a relevant notification in writing expressly given to the company by the member as to:

  - whether he wishes to receive copies of the full financial statements; or
  - whether, instead of full financial statements, he wishes to receive summary financial statements.

  A notification will be a relevant notification for a financial year if it relates to that year (whether given at the company's invitation or not) and is received by the company not later than 28 days before the first date on which copies of the full financial statements are sent out to members under section 238(1).

- Failing any express notification (that is, if a member has not replied to a consultation by notice or has not otherwise informed the company that he wishes to receive full financial statements), from a member's failure to respond to an opportunity to elect to receive copies of the full financial statements in response to one of the following:

  - To the company's consultation by notice.
  - As part of a relevant consultation by the company of his wishes.

[SI 1995/2092 Reg 4(1)-(3)].

Consultation by notice

38.182 This procedure, brought in by the 1995 Regulations (SI 1995/2092), is a simpler procedure by which companies may ascertain whether members wish to receive full financial statements or summary financial statements. It will enable a listed company to send to a member by post (or in any other manner authorised by the companies' articles) an advance notice which must comply with all the following. The notice must:

- State that for the future the member will be sent a summary financial statement for each financial year, unless he notifies the company in writing that he wishes to receive full financial statements.

- State that the summary financial statements will contain a summary of the company's or group's profit and loss account, balance sheet and directors' report for the year.

- State that the printed card or form accompanying the notice must be returned by the date specified in the notice. This date must be at least 21 days after the notice is sent out and not less than 28 days before the first date on which copies of the full financial statements for the next financial year are to be sent out to members under section 238(1).

- Include in a prominent position a statement that a summary financial statement will not contain sufficient information to allow as full an understanding of the results and state of affairs of the company (or group, as applicable) as would be provided by the full financial statements, and that members and debenture holders requiring more detailed information have the right to obtain, free of charge, a copy of the company's last full financial statements.

- State that the summary financial statement will contain a statement by the company's auditors as to whether:

  - the summary financial statement is consistent with the full financial statements for the year in question;

  - it complies with the requirements of section 251 of the Act and of the Companies (Summary Financial Statement) Regulations 1995 (SI 1995/2092); and

  - their report on the financial statements was qualified. (This is generally interpreted to mean that no reference to this point by the auditors is needed when the financial statements are unqualified – see para 38.182.1.)

[SI 1995/2092 Reg 5(1)].

38.182.1 In addition to the auditors' statement mentioned above, as mentioned in the third bullet point in paragraph 38.185, the company must state in the summary financial statement whether the audit report on the financial statements was unqualified or qualified. If the report was qualified, the company must set out the report in full and any further material needed to understand the qualification. In these circumstances auditors would generally cross refer to the statement included by the company. They will generally not include a cross-reference where their report on the financial statements was unqualified.

[The next paragraph is 38.183.]

38.183 The printed card or form accompanying the notice (mentioned above) must be worded so as to enable a member, by marking a box and returning the card or form, to notify the company that he wishes to receive full financial statements for the next financial year and for all future financial years he remains a member. Postage for the return of the printed card or form must be borne by the company, unless the member or debenture holder is outside the European Economic Area. [SI 1995/2092 Reg 5(2)(3)].

Relevant consultation

38.184 A 'relevant consultation' is an alternative option which companies may use to establish whether a member wishes to receive summary financial statements and also to establish whether any member who has chosen to receive full financial statements would like to change his mind. A relevant consultation of the wishes of

[The next page is 38049.]

a member is a notice given to a member by post (or in any other manner authorised by the company's articles) which complies with all the following:

- It states that in future the member will be sent a summary financial statement instead of full financial statements, unless he notifies the company in writing that he wishes to *continue* to receive the full financial statements.
- It accompanies a copy of the full financial statements.
- It accompanies a copy of a summary financial statement for the same year and this is identified in the notice as an example of the statement the member will receive in the future, unless he notifies the company otherwise.
- It is accompanied by the printed card or form which is so worded as to enable a member, by marking a box and returning the card or form, to notify the company that he wishes to receive full financial statements for the next financial year and for all future financial years he remains a member. Postage on the return of the card or form must be paid by the company unless the member or debenture holder is outside the European Economic Area. [SI 1995/2092 Reg 6].

Statements to be included in all summary financial statements

38.185 Every summary financial statement must:

- State that it is only a summary of information in the company's annual financial statements and directors' report.
- Contain a statement by the company's auditors of their opinion that the summary financial statement is consistent with the annual financial statements and directors' report and complies with the requirements of section 251 and regulations made under it, currently SI 1995/2092.
- State whether the auditors' report on the annual financial statements was unqualified or qualified and if it was qualified, set out the report in full together with any further material required to understand the qualification.
- State whether the auditors' report on the annual financial statements contained a statement concerning proper accounting records or inadequate returns under section 237(2), or failure to obtain certain necessary

information and explanations under section 237(3). If so, the statement will have to be set out in full.

[Sec 251(4)].

- State the name of the director who signed it on behalf of the board.

- Include, where the company is required to prepare consolidated financial statements, a statement in a prominent position that the summary financial statement does not contain sufficient information to allow as full an understanding of the results of the group and state of affairs of the company or of the group as would be provided by the full financial statements and reports; and that members and debenture holders requiring more detailed information have the right to obtain, free of charge, a copy of the company's last full financial statements and reports.

  Where a company *is not* required to prepare consolidated financial statements, a similar statement appropriately amended to refer solely to the company must be included in the summary financial statements.

- Contain a clear, conspicuous statement of how members and debenture holders:

  - can obtain, free of charge, a copy of the company's last full financial statements and reports; and

  - may elect in writing to receive full financial statements and reports in place of summary financial statements for all future financial years.

[SI 1995/2092 Reg 7].

Form and content of summary financial statement

38.186 Schedule 1 to the summary financial statement regulations specifies slightly different forms for summary financial statements that can be prepared by companies and by groups. (Schedules 2 and 3 to the regulations deal with the forms than apply to banking and insurance companies preparing financial statements under Schedule 9 and 9A of the 1985 Act.)

38.187 The paragraphs that follow outline the form and content of summary financial statements specified in the regulations which are applicable to listed companies that prepare consolidated financial statements (except banking, and insurance, companies and groups to which different rules apply).

38.188 Summary financial statements must contain the information prescribed by Schedule 1 in such order and under such headings as the directors consider appropriate. In addition, any other information necessary to ensure that the summary financial statement is consistent with the full financial statements and reports for the financial year in question must be given.

Summary directors' report

38.189 The information required to be included in the directors' report summary as taken from the directors' report in the company's full financial statements includes:

- A summary of the fair review of the development of the business as required by section 234(1)(a).

- A summary of the amount recommended to be paid as dividend, if not disclosed in the summary profit and loss account.

- A summary of the particulars of any important post balance sheet events, as required by paragraph 6(a) of Schedule 7.

- A summary of the indication given of likely future developments of the business, as required by paragraph 6(b) of Schedule 7.

- The list of the directors' names as required by section 234(2).

Summary profit and loss account

38.190 The format of the summary consolidated profit and loss account will depend on which of the four formats permitted for the full financial statements the company has adopted.

38.191 A Format 1 summary consolidated profit and loss account is illustrated below. The figures in brackets indicate references to the items in the format for the full consolidated profit and loss account (referred to in chapter 6), required by Schedule 4 and Schedule 4A, some of which are required to be aggregated. Comparative figures must be given in the summary profit and loss account for the immediately preceding year. Also as indicated, the aggregate of directors' emoluments has to be disclosed. As illustrated, the format will not add up from top to bottom. The items or combinations of items must be listed in the order set out in Schedule 1 of the regulations (which is as shown in the illustration) but they may appear under such headings as the directors consider appropriate.

Summary consolidated profit and loss account – Format 1		
Turnover	(1)	X
Income from interests in associated undertakings	(8)	X
Other interest receivable and similar income and interest payable and similar charges	(11+13)	X
Profit or loss on ordinary activities before tax		X
Tax on profit or loss on ordinary activities	(14)	X
Profit or loss on ordinary activities after tax	(15)	X
Minority interests	(16)	X
Extraordinary income and charges after tax and minority interests	(19+20+21)	X
Profit or loss for the financial year	(23)	X
Dividend paid and proposed		X
Directors' emoluments	(6 Sch 1(1))	X

In addition, as mentioned in paragraph 38.180 above, the Listing Rules require the disclosure of the earnings per share.

Summary balance sheet

38.192 A summary consolidated balance sheet is required to show, under such headings as the directors consider appropriate, a single amount for each heading to which letters are assigned in the format used for the full balance sheet in the order set out in that balance sheet. For example, the disclosure for a summary consolidated balance sheet under Format 1 would look as illustrated below. The letters in brackets refer to the items in the full Format 1 balance sheet as required by Schedule 4 and Schedule 4A referred to in chapter 6. Comparative figures are also required.

Summary consolidated balance sheet – Format 1

Called-up share capital not paid	(A)		X
Fixed assets	(B)		X
Current assets	(C)	X	
Prepayments and accrued income	(D)	X	
Creditors: amounts due within one year	(E)	(X)	
Net current assets/(liabilities)	(F)		X
Total assets less current liabilities	(G)		X
Creditors: amounts falling due after more than one year	(H)		X
Provisions for liabilities and charges	(I)		X
Accruals and deferred income	(J)		X
			X
Capital and reserves	(L)		X
Minority interests	(M)		X
			X

38.193 Where there are alternative positions in the formats for particular items (that is, 'prepayments and accrued income', 'accruals and deferred income' and 'minority interests'), then the summary balance sheet must use the same position used for the item as used in the full balance sheet.

Penalties

38.194 Default in complying with section 251 or the regulations renders the company and every officer of it who is in default, guilty of an offence. [Sec 251(6)].

Non-statutory accounts

38.195 Non-statutory accounts are not full financial statements. A company must comply with the provisions of section 240(3) when it *publishes* non-statutory accounts. 'Non-statutory accounts' means any balance sheet or profit and loss account of the company or the group that either relates to, or purports to deal with, a company's or group's full financial year, otherwise than as part of the company's statutory financial statements. [Sec 240(5)(a)(b)]. This means that where a full year's figures and a narrative explanation of those figures are recognisable as either a balance sheet or a profit and loss account of the company or the group, the rules that relate to non-statutory accounts are likely to apply. 'Publication' and 'statutory accounts' are discussed in paragraphs 38.155 and 38.157.

38.196 Where a company publishes non-statutory accounts, those accounts must be accompanied by a statement indicating:

- That the accounts are not the company's statutory accounts.
- Whether or not the statutory accounts have been delivered to the Registrar for the same year.
- Whether or not the auditors have reported under section 235 on the statutory accounts for that year.
- Whether or not the auditors' report was qualified or contained a statement under either of the following sections:
  - Section 237(2), where accounting records or returns have been inadequate, or the financial statements have not agreed with the records or returns.
  - Section 237(3), where necessary information and explanations have not been received.
- Where no auditors' report has been made and the company falls into the category of a small company, which is exempt from being audited under section 249A, whether the company's reporting accountant has made a report for the purposes of section 249A(2) on its statutory financial statements for that year.
- Where no auditors' report has been made, whether any report made for the purposes of section 249A(2) was qualified.

[Sec 240(3)].

38.197 Where a company publishes non-statutory accounts and the company's full financial statements are subject to audit, a statement along one or the other of the following lines (as appropriate) should be included in the non-statutory accounts.

Example 1

The figures and financial information for the year 19XX do not constitute the statutory financial statements for that year. Those financial statements have been delivered to the Registrar and included the auditors' report which was unqualified and did not contain a statement either under section 237(2) of the Companies Act 1985 (accounting records or returns inadequate or accounts not agreeing with records and returns), or section 237(3) (failure to obtain necessary information and explanations).

Example 2

The figures and financial information for the year 19XX do not constitute the statutory financial statements for that year. Those financial statements have not yet been delivered to the Registrar, nor have the auditors yet reported on them.

38.198 When a company publishes non-statutory accounts and the company is exempt from audit, but is subject to the requirement for a reporting accountant's report under section 249A, a statement along one or the other of the following lines (as appropriate) should be included in the non-statutory accounts.

Example 1

The figures and financial information for the year 19XX do not constitute the statutory financial statements for that year. Those financial statements have been delivered to the Registrar and included the reporting accountant's report for the purposes of section 249A(2) which was unqualified.

Example 2

The figures and financial information for the year 19XX do not constitute the statutory financial statements for that year. Those financial statements have not yet been delivered to the Registrar, nor has the reporting accountant made a report for the purposes of section 249A(2).

38.199 Where published non-statutory accounts deal with more than one year (for example, preliminary statements of the annual results of listed companies that must include comparative figures for the previous year), the one document may contain two sets of non-statutory accounts. Where this applies, the wording of the appropriate statement in paragraph 38.197 should be adapted to cover both sets of accounts.

38.200 A company that does not comply with the requirements for the publication of non-statutory accounts outlined above and any officer who is in default will be guilty of an offence. [Sec 240(6)].

38.201 Published non-statutory accounts must not include the auditors' report made in connection with the financial statements laid before members in accordance with section 235 or any report by a reporting accountant made for the purposes of section 249A(2) on the individual financial statements of a company which is exempt for the requirement to have an audit. [Sec 240(3)].

Stock Exchange requirements

Preliminary announcements

38.202 The Stock Exchange refers to these as preliminary statements of annual results. They are a requirement of the Listing Rules and must be notified to the Company Announcements Office of the Stock Exchange immediately after board approval. Preliminary announcements are generally considered to play a key part in the annual financial reporting cycle as they are the first public communication of companies' results for the whole year. Preliminary announcements are considered in more detail in chapter 39.

[The next paragraph is 38.204.]

Half-yearly reports

38.204 The Stock Exchange requires a company that has listed shares to prepare a half-yearly report, on a group basis where relevant, on its activities and profit or loss for the first six months of each financial year. [LR 12.46]. A half-yearly report must be published as soon as possible and in any event within four months of the end of the period to which it relates. [LR 12.48].

38.205 The company must publish the half-yearly report by notifying it to the Company Announcements Office without delay after board approval (release through the Regulatory News Service is deemed to be publication). However, in addition, the company must either send the half-yearly report to holders of its listed securities, or insert it as a paid advertisement in at least one national newspaper, no later than four months after the end of the period to which it relates. The contents of interim reports are dealt with in chapter 39.

[The next paragraph is 38.207.]

AIM companies

38.207 AIM companies must prepare a half-yearly report within four months of the end of the relevant period, make it available for inspection at a public address and send a copy to the Company Announcements Office [AIMR 16.19(f)]. The AIM opened on 19 June 1995.

Status of reports and announcements

38.208 Half-yearly reports that a listed company must issue or half-yearly reports that a company traded on the AIM must issue, are *prima facie* not considered to be non-statutory accounts. The reason for this is that the information they give relates to a six-month period and not to a full year. This also applied to announcements of half-yearly results that companies used to issue.

38.209 Where, however, the report includes, for comparative purposes, figures that relate to a full year, the company needs to consider the rules relating to non-statutory accounts. In these circumstances, much depends on whether the full year's comparative information is sufficiently comprehensive to be recognisable as either a balance sheet or a profit and loss account. For example, listed companies may give more detail in half-yearly reports than the Listing Rules require, by including profit and loss account and balance sheet information relating to the previous financial year. This is now a recommendation of the ASB's statement on interim reports. Companies that adopt this will need to give a summarised balance sheet and a summarised profit and loss account together with comparative figures, in the case of the summarised balance sheet, from the last annual financial statements and, in the case of the summarised profit and loss account for the previous full financial year. Where the information can be so recognised, the provisions that relate to non-statutory accounts (mentioned in para 38.195 above) apply. Interim reporting is dealt with more fully in chapter 39.

38.210 In contrast to half-yearly reports, preliminary statements of annual results that listed companies must issue are *prima facie* considered to be non-statutory accounts. This is because the preliminary results either relate to, or purport to deal with, a company's full financial year. Furthermore, the information that the Stock Exchange's Listing Rules require companies to give on a preliminary basis is capable of being recognised as a balance sheet or a profit and loss account. Consequently, where a listed company publishes a preliminary statement of annual results, the rules that relate to non-statutory accounts apply. In October 1997 the ASB published an exposure draft of a statement on preliminary announcements. The exposure draft states that the preliminary announcement should contain a statement that satisfies the provision of section 240 of the Companies Act regarding the publication of non-statutory accounts. The requirements for preliminary announcements are discussed more fully in chapter 39.

38.211 Another possible example of non-statutory accounts is the special reports that some companies prepare for employees. Much depends on whether the report either relates to, or purports to deal with, the company's activities during a full

[The next page is 38059.]

financial year, and also on whether it takes the form of a balance sheet or a profit and loss account.

38.212 It is not likely, however, that either five year or ten year summaries would be considered to be non-statutory accounts. The reason for this is that the purpose of such a summary is not to deal with a company's activities for any particular year. Rather its purpose is to put the company's current position in a larger perspective and to provide pointers for the future.

38.213 Where a listed company publishes preliminary statements of annual results or half-yearly reports (in the form of non-statutory financial statements or other statements meeting non-statutory criteria) they must comply with the rules for non-statutory financial statements and include the appropriate wording referred to in paragraphs 38.197 and 38.198 above.

Revision of defective financial statements

38.214 Before the Companies Act 1989, there was no legal provision for the revision of financial statements. In practice, when revisions took place the Registrar of Companies would accept the revised financial statements and put them on the company's file. However, there was no legal requirement for him to do so and the original financial statements were not removed from the file. The Companies Act 1989 amended the 1985 Act by introducing provisions which:

- Permit directors to prepare revised financial statements or a revised directors' report where it appears to them that the annual financial statements or the directors' report did not comply with the Act ('voluntary revision'). [Sec 245].

- Permit the Secretary of State (in the absence of a satisfactory explanation from the company's directors as to the question of whether the annual financial statements or the directors' report comply with the Act), to apply to the court for an order that revised financial statements or directors' report should be prepared. Such an application can only be made by the Secretary of State or a person authorised by the Secretary of State ('compulsory revision'). [Sec 245(A),(B)(C)]. The FRRP is authorised for this purpose. By agreement with the DTI, the normal ambit of the FRRP is public and large private companies, the DTI dealing with all other cases.

Voluntary revision

38.215 The detailed regulations governing preparing, auditing and issuing revised financial statements and directors' reports where the revision is voluntary, are contained in The Companies (Revision of Defective Accounts and Report)

Regulations (SI 1990/2570) as amended by the Companies (Summary Financial Statement) Regulations 1992 (SI 1992/3075) and the Companies Act (Audit Exemption) Regulations 1994 (SI 1994/1935). These regulations are described below.

38.216 If it appears to the company's directors that any financial statements (including the directors' report) did not comply with the Act's requirements, they may prepare revised financial statements or a revised report. [Sec 245(1)]. Where copies of the previous financial statements or report have been laid before the company in general meeting or delivered to the Registrar, section 245(2) requires the revisions to be confined to:

- Correcting those aspects in which the previous financial statements did not comply with the Act's requirements.
- Making any necessary consequential alterations.

It appears, therefore, that if the directors wish to revise the financial statements or directors' report after the financial statements are sent out to members, but before they are laid before the company in general meeting, the revisions do not have to be confined to the matters listed above.

38.217 Revision of the financial statements or directors' report may be made either by preparing replacement financial statements or directors' reports or by preparing a supplementary note indicating the corrections to be made to the original documents.

38.218 Where a decision has been made to replace the original financial statements or directors' report, they should be prepared in the normal way in accordance with the Act's provisions that were in force at the date on which the original financial statements and directors' report were approved. (And not, as might have been expected, the provisions in force at the company's year end date.) There could, therefore, be additional consequential amendments to be made as a result of changes in the Act between the company's year end and the date of approval of the original financial statements.

38.219 The regulations state that the Act's provisions relating to the matters to be included in a company's annual financial statements shall apply to the revised financial statements as if the revised financial statements were prepared and approved by the directors as at the date of approval of the original financial statements. [SI 1990/2570 Reg 3(1)]. Similar provisions for directors' reports are contained in regulation 3(4) of SI 1990/2570. The purpose of this is to exclude from consideration events that occur between the date of approval of the original financial statements and the date of approval of the revised financial statements or directors' report.

Approving and signing revised financial statements

38.220 The regulations provide that the revised financial statements must be approved by the board and signed by a director on the board's behalf. In the case of revision by supplementary note the signature should appear on the supplementary note.

38.221 Where the original financial statements have been sent to members, laid before the company in general meeting, or delivered to the Registrar, all the following must be stated in the financial statements that are revised by replacement.

- That the revised financial statements replace the original financial statements for the financial year (specifying it).

- That they are now the company's statutory financial statements for that financial year.

- That they have been prepared as at the date of the original annual financial statements (that is, the date on which the original financial statements were approved) and not as at the date of revision (that is, the date of approval of the revised financial statements) and, accordingly, do not deal with events between those dates.

- The respects in which the original financial statements did not comply with the Act's requirements.

- Any significant amendments made as a consequence of remedying the defects.

[SI 1990/2570 Reg 4(2)(a)].

38.222 Where the financial statements are revised by supplementary note the following statements must be made in the note:

- That the note revises in certain respects the company's original annual financial statements and is to be treated as forming part of those financial statements.

- That the annual financial statements have been revised as at the date of the original financial statements and not as at the date of revision (see point three in para 38.220) and, accordingly, do not deal with events between those dates.

[SI 1990/2570 Reg 4(2)(b)].

38.223 The date of approval of the revised financial statements must be given in those financial statements. In the case of revision by supplementary note, the date should be given in the note itself. [SI 1990/2570 Reg 4(2)].

Approving and signing revised directors' report

38.224 Similar considerations apply to a revised directors' report. The revised report must be approved by the board and signed on its behalf by a director or the company secretary. In the case of revision by supplementary note the note must be signed. Where the original directors' report has been sent to members, laid before the company in general meeting, or delivered to the Registrar, all the following must be stated in the report that is revised by replacement:

- That the revised report replaces the original report for the financial year (specifying it).
- That it has been prepared as at the date of approval of the original directors' report and not as at the date of approval of the revision and, accordingly, does not deal with any events between those dates.
- The respects in which the original directors' report did not comply with the Act's requirements.
- Any significant amendments made as a consequence of remedying the defects.

[SI 1990/2570 Reg 5(2)(a)].

38.225 Where the report is revised by supplementary note the note must state the following:

- That the note revises in certain respects the original directors' report of the company and is to be treated as forming part of that report.
- That the directors' report has been revised as at the date of approval of the original directors' report and not as at the date of approval of the revision and, accordingly, does not deal with events between those dates.

[SI 1990/2570 Reg 5(2)(b)].

38.226 The date of approval of the revised report must be given in the revised report (or in the supplementary note, if revision is made by supplementary note). [SI 1990/2570 Reg 5(2)].

Auditors' report

38.227 The report on the revised financial statements should be made by the company's current auditors. If, however, there has been a change of auditors between the date of the orginal financial statements and the date of the revised financial statements the directors of the company may resolve that the report will be made by the former auditors. In this case, the former auditors will have to agree to do so and be qualified for appointment as the company's auditors. [SI 1990/2570 Regs 6(1) and 7(1) as amended by SI 1996/315].

38.228 Whether the auditors' report as present or former auditors, the contents of the report must be the same. It must deal with all of the following matters:

- Whether in the auditors' opinion the revised financial statements have been properly prepared in accordance with the Act's provisions as they have effect under the regulations.
- Whether in their opinion a true and fair view, seen as at the date when the original financial statements were approved, is given by the revised financial statements of the state of the company's affairs at the end of the financial year, and of the profit or loss of the company for the financial year (or, in the case of consolidated financial statements, of the state of affairs of the company and the group at the end of the financial year and of the profit or loss of the group for the financial year).
- Whether in the auditors' opinion the original annual financial statements failed to comply with the Act's requirements in the respect identified by the directors:
  - in the situation where the revision is made by replacement, in the statement the directors are required to make in the revised financial statements (see the fourth point in para 38.221 above); and
  - in the situation where the revision is made by supplementary note, in the supplementary note.

[SI 1990/2570 Reg 6(3)].

38.229 The auditors must also consider whether the information in the original or, if it has been revised, the revised directors' report is consistent with the revised financial statements and, if it is not, they must state that fact in their report. On being signed the audit report replaces the audit report in the original financial statements. [SI 1990/2570 Reg 6(4)].

38.230 Where the financial statements are not being revised, but the directors' report is, the present or former auditors (as the directors decide) are not required to report on the financial statements. They must, however, report on the revised directors' report. Their report must state that they have considered whether the information in the revised report is consistent with the annual financial statements for the financial year and whether it is consistent. The auditors must also sign and date their report. [SI 1990/2570 Reg 7].

Reporting accountant's report

38.231 Certain categories of small company do not have to have their annual financial statements audited, by virtue of section 249A. Some very small companies are totally exempt under section 249A(1). Other small companies are, as a condition of the exemption, required to obtain a reporting accountant's report under section 249A(2) in respect of their individual financial statements. Where a reporting accountant has made a report for the purposes of section 249A(2) on the original financial statements, he has to make another report to the company's members on any revised financial statements. Alternatively, the directors may decide that the report should be made by someone who was not the original reporting accountant, but nevertheless is qualified to act as the company's reporting accountant. [SI 1990/2570 Reg 6A(1)(2)].

38.232 Where, as a result of the revisions, a company which was exempt from audit and a reporting accountant's report, but now requires a reporting accountant's report, it must obtain such a report on the revised financial statements in accordance with section 249C. Similarly, if as a result of the revisions it is no longer eligible to obtain an accountant's report, it must have the revised financial statements audited. [SI 1990/2570 Reg 6B(1)(2)].

38.233 On being signed by the reporting accountant, the further report will replace the report on the original financial statements. [SI 1990/2570 Reg 6A(4)]. The accountant's report or the auditors' report must be delivered to the Registrar within 28 days after the date on which the financial statements were revised. [SI 1990/2570 Reg 6B(3)].

Effects of revision

38.234 As soon as the revised financial statements or the revised directors' report (as the case may be) are approved by the directors, they become the annual financial statements or directors' report of the company in place of the original financial statements or report for all Companies Act purposes. For instance, regarding publishing statutory financial statements, the provisions in section 240(5) (see para 38.157 above) will then apply to the revised financial statements.

38.235 If the original financial statements and directors' report have already been sent to members and others entitled to receive copies, the directors must send copies of the revised financial statements and directors' report, together with the auditors' report, to those persons. The revised copy has to be sent not more than 28 days from the date of the directors' approval of the revised financial statements and report. Where, however, the revision has been by supplementary note the directors need only send the supplementary note and the auditors' report on the revised financial statements (or, as the case may be, on the revised report). The directors must also send a copy of the revised financial statements or report, together with the audit report within 28 days of approval of the revision to each person who, at the date on which the revised financial statements or report are approved, is:

- A member of the company.
- A holder of the company's debentures.
- A person who is entitled to receive notice of general meetings.

[SI 1990/2570 Reg 10].

Some of these people will not have been entitled to receive the financial statements at the time the original financial statements were sent out.

38.236 Where the original financial statements and directors' report have already been laid before members, the company will have to lay the revised financial statements and report, together with the auditors' report, before the next general meeting at which annual financial statements are laid, unless they choose to lay them before an earlier general meeting. [SI 1990/2570 Reg 11].

38.237 Where the original financial statements and directors' report have already been delivered to the Registrar, the directors must deliver the revised financial statements and report together with the auditors' report to the Registrar within 28 days of the date of their approval of the revised financial statements and report. Where the revision has been by supplementary note, only that note and the auditors' report on the revised financial statements (or as the case may be on the revised report) need be delivered. [SI 1990/2570 Reg 12].

Abbreviated financial statements

38.238 The regulations provide for the revision of abbreviated financial statements where these are affected by the revision of a company's full financial statements. In this case *either* the revised abbreviated financial statements should be delivered to the Registrar within 28 days with a statement as to the effect of the revisions made *or* the company must deliver a copy of the revised financial statements and directors' report together with the auditors' report. The latter alternative must be adopted, if, as a result of the revision, the company is no longer entitled to file abbreviated financial statements. Where abbreviated financial statements are not affected by the revision to the full financial statements, a note stating that the full financial statements have been revised in a respect that has no bearing on the abbreviated financial statements, together with a copy of the auditors' report on the revised financial statements, must be delivered to the Registrar. [SI 1990/2570 Reg 13]. A new section 13A inserted by the Companies (Revision of Defective Accounts and Report) (Amendment) Regulations 1996 (SI 1996/315) provides for the revision of abbreviated accounts which do not comply with the Act for reasons other than the revision of the full financial statements.

Companies exempted from audit

38.239 A dormant company that has passed a resolution under section 250 exempting itself from audit and a small company that is exempt from audit by virtue of section 249A(1) can apply the regulations as if they omitted any reference to an auditors' report.

38.240 Where a small company that is exempt from audit by virtue of section 249A(2) has obtained a report of a reporting accountant, regulations 10 to 13 of SI 1990/2570 have effect as if the references to an auditors' report were references to the report of the reporting accountant, and references to the auditors' report on the revised directors' report were omitted. The provisions of regulations 10 to 13 are described above and relate to sending the revised financial statements to members and others who received copies of the original financial statements (see para 38.235), laying and delivering the revised financial statements (paras 38.236 and 38.237) and small and medium-sized companies (para 38.238). [SI 1990/2570 Regs 14A, 15].

Summary financial statements

38.241 Where a summary financial statement has been sent to members, and its contents are affected by the revision of the annual financial statements, such that the original summary financial statement no longer complies with the Act, the company must prepare a revised statement. The revised summary financial statement must contain a short statement of the revisions and their effect. The company must send the revised statement to all those who received the original summary financial statement and to any person to whom the company would be entitled to send such a statement as at the date of preparing the revised statement. [SI 1990/2570 Reg 14(2)].

38.242 If, however, the original summary financial statement is not affected by the revision of the annual financial statements, the company must send a note stating that the annual financial statements or directors' report for the year have been revised in a respect that has no bearing on the summary financial statement for that year. This note should be sent to the same persons as mentioned in paragraph 38.241 above. If the auditors' report on the revised financial statements or directors' report has been qualified, a copy of that report must also be sent out attached to the note. However, the regulations do not provide for revision where the summary financial statement itself is defective. [SI 1990/2570 Reg 14(4)].

38.243 The revised summary financial statement or note must be sent within 28 days of the date of approval of the revised financial statements or directors' report.

[The next page is 38067.]

Compulsory revision

38.244 Responsibility in connection with the compulsory revision of defective financial statements is shared between the FRRP and the DTI. The FRRP's ambit is in respect of the financial statements of public and large private companies. The DTI remains responsible for all other companies. The FRRP operates under the aegis of the FRC. Its role is to examine the annual financial statements of public and large private companies to determine departures from accounting requirements of the Act. Within this framework, their main concern is stated to be material departures from accounting standards where such a departure results in the financial statements in question not giving a true and fair view as required by the Act. In practice, the FRRP concerns itself with a variety of matters within the framework. Where a company's financial statements are defective the Panel will endeavour to secure their revision by *voluntary* means, but if this approach fails it has the power to make an application to the court under section 245B for an order compelling a revision.

38.245 Since its inception in 1991 to the beginning of 1995, the FRRP has issued public statements in respect of its findings on some 25 companies. To date no court application has been pursued as the companies concerned have all agreed to make revisions on a 'voluntary' basis in line with the FRRP's opinion. Although such revisions are 'voluntary' in the terms of the Act, in practice many of the 25 companies went along with the FRRP's wishes very reluctantly, on the basis that doing so is preferable to being taken to court. The operations of the FRRP are discussed further in chapter 2.

38.246 There are no regulations governing preparing, auditing and issuing financial statements and directors' reports that are compulsorily revised, as the court is empowered to give directions as to these and other matters as it thinks fit.

Meetings and resolutions

Directors' meetings

38.247 The board of directors will generally have power to manage the company's business (see Table A Reg 70). On the question of how they should conduct their meetings, Table A provides, *"Subject to the provisions of the Act, the memorandum and the articles, the directors may regulate their proceedings as they think fit"*. [Table A Reg 88]. One of the factors in deciding how often the board should meet would be the nature of the company's business. Any of the company's directors can call a board meeting and the company secretary also has to call such meetings if he is requested to do so by a director. The company's articles usually specify the number of directors required to constitute a quorum at such meetings.

38.248 No specific notice period is necessary to call a board meeting provided the notice period is, in the circumstances in question, a reasonable one and the notice has been given to all directors. If some directors do not receive proper notice of a board meeting, the decisions taken at it will be invalid. A board meeting can be held informally, but a casual meeting will not be sufficient if all parties do not agree to treat it as a meeting.

38.249 The question sometimes arises as to whether the directors can hold a board meeting by telephone or other electronic means. Some doubt has been expressed about whether there can be a 'meeting' if the participants are not physically present in one place. The issue as to whether a meeting will be properly constituted if it is held by means of a conference call or video conferencing has not been tested in the English courts. It is, however, thought that provided there is a carefully worded provision permitting telephone meetings in the articles and the meeting is duly convened, the meeting would be valid. The articles of association of many companies now incorporate powers to permit telephone board meetings to occur.

General meetings

38.250 A company can hold the following types of general meetings of the company: AGMs; extraordinary general meetings; and class meetings. These meetings are regulated partly by statute and partly by the company's articles. The directors are generally given the power to call general meetings under the company's articles (see regulation 37 of Table A). If the directors have this power, and are required to do so by the company's members in accordance with the Act, they must immediately convene an extraordinary general meeting to be held not later than 28 days after the date of the notice convening the meeting. [Sec 368(8)]. The quorum required to be present at the meeting is usually specified in the articles. Where there is no mention in the articles, two members personally present will represent a quorum. [Sec 370(4)].

Annual general meetings

38.251 A company must hold an AGM each calendar year and not let more than 15 months elapse between one AGM and the next. The company must specify that the meeting is an AGM in the notices calling it. As long as a company holds its first AGM within 18 months of incorporation, it need not hold it in the year of incorporation or in the following year. [Sec 366(1)-(3)]. The annual financial statements, including the directors' report and auditors' report, are usually, but do not have to be, laid before the company at its AGM.

38.252 It is the directors who usually convene the AGM. [Table A Reg 37]. If the company fails to hold an AGM, the company and every director who is in default will be guilty of an offence. [Sec 366(4)]. In addition, the Secretary of State may, on the application of a member, call a meeting in default and give certain directions regarding the meeting. [Sec 367].

Notice

38.253 The directors are required to give at least 21 days notice in writing to call an AGM. [Sec 369]. For company meetings other than AGMs or meetings at which special resolutions are being proposed, 14 days notice in writing is required (or 7 days' notice for an unlimited company). It is possible to call company meetings on shorter notice if all members who are entitled to attend and vote at the meeting agree to the short notice. [Sec 369(3)]. The notice should be in writing and should state the time, place and date of the meeting and the general nature of the business to be transacted. For AGMs the notice must specify that it is an AGM. [Table A Regs 111, 38]. Business ordinarily conducted at AGMs comprises: receiving or adopting the financial statements; declaring a dividend; appointing and reappointing directors; and reappointing auditors and fixing their remuneration. The Stock Exchange adds the following to the list in its definition of 'ordinary business': the granting, renewing or varying of the directors' authority to allot certain shares under section 80 of the Act; or, within certain limitations, disapplying pre-emption rights under section 89 of the Act. [LR Definitions].

38.254 More detailed information should be given in the notice of the proposals to be considered at the meeting if business other than ordinary business is to be placed before shareholders. In relation to the notice convening the AGM of a listed company:

- It must state that there will be made available for inspection at the registered office, or transfer office, from the date of the notice to the date of the meeting and at the meeting, copies of, or a written memorandum of the terms of, all directors' service contracts with the company or any subsidiary (unless the contract of service will expire or is determinable by the company without payment of compensation, within one year). If there are no contracts, that fact is to be stated in the notice. [LR 14.20].

  However, no company may approve a director's service contract for more than five years unless a memorandum of the proposed terms under which a director's employment is to continue for that period was available at the general meeting itself and at the registered office for the 15 preceding days. The Cadbury Committee Report recommends that directors' service contracts should not exceed three years without shareholders' approval. Furthermore, the Greenbury Code now suggests that there is a strong case for setting service contacts for periods of one year or less and that where they exceed one year, the reasons for the longer notice period should be disclosed in the annual financial statements. [Greenbury Code para B 10].

- If business other than ordinary business (see para 38.253) is included, an explanatory circular must accompany the notice. The explanation may be included in the directors' report if it is to be considered at the AGM. Any circular should comply with the requirements of the Listing Rules. [LR 14.17, 14.18].

38.255 The notice periods required to be given for meeting often cause confusion in practice. The notice periods for shareholders' meetings must be 'clear' days. This means that it is necessary to disregard both:

- the date on which the notice is served or deemed to be served. Companies must consult their articles of association, but the notice period is usually 24 or 48 hours after posting; and
- the date of the meeting itself.

38.256 The notice period rules work in the way illustrated in the able below.

	'24 hour' articles	**'48 hour' articles**
Notices despatched	1st	1st
Notices deemed to be received	2nd	3rd
First day of the notice period	3rd	4th
Twenty-first day of the notice period	23rd	24th
AGM can take place on or after	24th	25th

Private company dispensing with AGM

38.257 Under section 366A a private company may, by elective resolution, elect to dispense with holding an AGM. The election has effect for the year in which it is made and for subsequent years, but does not affect any previous liability to hold an AGM. However, even where such an election is in place, any member may, by notice to the company not later than three months before the end of the year, require an AGM to be held. If this requirement is not complied with the company and the officers in default will be guilty of an offence.

38.258 Where an election to dispense with the AGM is in place, a company may also elect to dispense with laying its financial statements at an AGM. These provisions are discussed in paragraph 38.123.

Single member companies

38.259 Private companies limited by shares or guarantee with only one member should comply with the usual formalities relating to meetings with the necessary modifications for a single member company. For instance, when the single member takes a decision, which is of the nature that may be taken by a company in general meeting, that member must provide the company with a written record of that decision. [Sec 382B]. If the decision is taken by way of a written resolution, the resolution must be recorded in the same way as minutes of the proceedings of a general meeting (see para 38.275). [Sec 382A].

Extraordinary general meetings

38.260 Regulation 36 of Table A provides that all general meetings other than AGMs are extraordinary general meetings. Regulation 37 provides that the directors have the power to call an extraordinary general meeting (EGM), and that any director or any member may do so if there are insufficient directors in the UK to call one. If the articles make no provision for a meeting to be called, two or more members holding not less than one-tenth of the issued share capital may call a meeting. [Sec 370(3)]. EGMs are generally used when there is business that requires to be dealt with by the company's members before the next AGM. The business to be dealt with at the EGMs, like AGMs, must be set out in the notice calling the meeting.

38.261 The directors must call an EGM if members holding not less than one-tenth of paid up capital having voting rights require them to do so. The requisition by the members for such a meeting must state the objects of the requisition and be deposited at the company's registered office. If the directors do not call a meeting within 21 days (to be held not more than 28 days thereafter) the requisitionists may do so themselves within three months and claim expenses of holding the meeting from the company. [Sec 368].

Class meetings

38.262 Where a company's share capital is divided into different classes of shares, meetings of the different classes have to be held where required by the Act, the company's articles or the shares' terms of issue. Class meetings are most frequently required when it is proposed to vary the rights attached to a particular class of shares. [Sec 125].

Resolutions

38.263 Ordinary, special and extraordinary resolutions may be passed at general meetings. Regulation 46 of Table A provides that a resolution is to be decided on a show of hands, unless a poll is demanded on or before the result of the show of hands is declared. The articles may not require the number of members required to demand a poll to be greater than five members entitled to vote at the meeting. [Sec 373]. The procedure for a poll is usually set out in the articles. [Sec 373]. On a poll, every member shall have one vote for each share he holds. [Table A Reg 54].

38.264 Companies' articles of association frequently make it easier for shareholders to demand a poll by reducing the number of members or the proportion of shares below the maximum set out in section 373. Also the articles must be consulted to see whether they specify such matters as:

- Format of proxy cards.
- Adjournment of meetings.
- The chairman's right to demand a poll.
- Provisions concerning where and when any validly demanded poll can be conducted and the results announced.

38.265 There are often circumstances where it would be advisable for companies to appoint independent scrutineers, for example, if a close result is expected or where perhaps the resolution is particularly contentious. In certain situations a scrutineers' report is required, for example, at meetings held at the request of a court. The scrutineers need not be the company's auditors, unless the company's articles say they should be, which is rare.

Ordinary resolutions

38.266 An ordinary resolution is not defined in the Act. However, in *Bushell v Faith* [1970] AC 1099 at 1108, it was defined as follows.

> *"An ordinary resolution is in the first place passed by a bare majority on a show of hands by members entitled to vote who are present personally or by proxy and on such a vote each member has one vote regardless of his shareholding. If a poll is demanded then for an ordinary resolution still only a bare majority of votes is required."*

The Act requires an ordinary resolution, for example: for the removal of a director from office (section 303); to approve directors' service contracts for over five years (section 319); and to approve substantial property transactions which the company enters into with its directors (section 320).

Extraordinary resolutions

38.267 Extraordinary resolutions are principally used in a members' voluntary winding up and also in some instances a company's articles may require such a resolution for particular types of business. A resolution is an extraordinary resolution if it has to be passed by not less than three-quarters of the company's members who are entitled to vote and who vote personally or by proxy on the resolution. The intention to propose the resolution as an extraordinary resolution and the text of the resolution must be given in the notice of the general meeting at which it is to be considered. [Sec 378]. The notice periods specified in section 369 must be given (see para 38.253). A copy of every extraordinary resolution passed must be sent to the Registrar with 15 days [Sec 380].

Special resolutions

38.268 A special resolution is required by the Act for certain important transactions, for instance, alteration of a company's objects or articles (Secs 4, 9), reduction of share capital (Sec 135), and off-market purchase of its own shares (Sec 164). A special resolution requires the same majority as is required for the passing of an extraordinary resolution. In addition, however, not less than 21 days' notice, specifying the intention to propose the resolution as a special resolution at a general meeting, must have been given. [Sec 378(2)]. The intention to propose a resolution as a special resolution and the resolution itself must be given in the notice of the meeting. A copy of every special resolution must be sent to the Registrar within 15 days after it is passed. A copy of all such resolutions must also be attached to every copy of the articles subsequently issued. [Sec 380].

Elective resolutions

38.269 A private company may elect under section 379A to opt out of certain formalities in the 1985 Act by passing an elective resolution at a company's general meeting. For instance, under section 379A, it may elect to: dispense with laying financial statements before general meetings; to dispense with holding AGMs; and to dispense with appointing auditors annually.

38.270 At least 21 days notice must be given of the meeting, stating that an elective resolution is to be proposed and stating the resolution's terms. However, with effect from 19 June 1996 an elective resolution will be effective where less than 21 days' written notice has been given, provided that all the members entitled to attend and vote at the meeting so agree. [SI 1996/1471 Reg 2]. An elective resolution may be revoked by an ordinary resolution.

Written resolutions

38.271 Section 381A sets out a procedure where by a private company may pass a written resolution in place of an ordinary, special or elective resolution at a general meeting or at a class meeting. A written resolution must be signed by or on behalf of all the company's members entitled to attend and vote at the meeting were one to be held. The date of the resolution is when the resolution is signed by or on behalf of the last member to sign.

38.272 Where a director or the company secretary knows that it is proposed to seek the agreement of members to a written resolution and he knows the terms of the resolution, he must send the company's auditors a copy of, or otherwise inform them of, its contents. This is a new duty imposed by section 381B, as substituted by article 3 of the Deregulation (Resolutions of Private Companies) Order 1996 (SI 1996/1471) for resolutions first proposed on or after 19 June 1996. The director or secretary must do so no later than the time the resolution is supplied to a member for signature. This is required only if the company has auditors. If a director or secretary fails to notify the auditors he will be guilty of a criminal offence. However, it will be a defence if he can prove one of the following:

- The circumstances were such that it was not practicable for him to comply with the requirement to inform the auditors.
- He believed on reasonable grounds that a copy of the resolution had been sent to the auditors or that they had been informed of its contents.

The validity of the resolution is not affected. An appropriate record book of written resolutions (including the signatures) must be kept in the same way as minutes of general meetings. [Sec 382A].

38.273 For written resolutions first proposed before 19 June 1996, old section 381B required the company to send a copy of the proposed resolution to its auditors. If the resolution concerned them as auditors, the auditors could within seven days require the resolution to be considered at a general meeting. The resolution, however, did not take effect unless:

- The auditors notified the company that in their opinion the resolution:
  - did not concern them; or
  - did concern them, but need not be considered at a general meeting.
- The seven day period for the auditors to require a general meeting to be held had expired without the notice being given.

38.274 There are two situations where written resolutions cannot be used: to remove a director before the expiration of his period of office (Sec 303); and to remove an auditor before the expiration of his term of office (Sec 391). [15A Sch 1].

Records of meetings

38.275 The Act requires minutes of all proceedings of a company's general meetings, meetings of its directors and managers to be entered into books kept for that purpose and provides for penalties on default. [Sec 382]. Where minutes have been kept and have been signed by the chairman of the meeting or the next succeeding meeting they are evidence of those proceedings. Once those minutes have been signed, if any mistakes are found in them they should be rectified only by a further minute passed at a subsequent meeting.

38.276 The books containing the minutes of the proceeding of general meeting must be open to inspection by members at the registered office without charge. A member is entitled on payment of the prescribed fee to be provided with a copy of any such minutes within seven days of his request. Failure to do so by the company and any officer is an offence. In addition, the court may compel immediate inspection. [Sec 383]. The place where minute books can be kept is dealt with in paragraph 38.37 above.

Chapter 39

Interim reports and preliminary announcements

Page

Chapter 39

Interim reports and preliminary announcements

Introduction

39.1 For many years the Stock Exchange has required listed companies to produce interim reports on their activities and profit or loss for the first six months of each financial year. The Listing Rules detail the amount and type of information that must be included in the half-yearly report as well as the deadline for its publication.

39.2 The ASB published a statement on interim reports in September 1997. The process leading to the statement was initiated by the Cadbury Committee in 1992, which recommended clarification of the accounting principles to be adopted by companies when preparing their interim reports. In response to the Cadbury initiative, the Financial Reporting Committee of the ICAEW undertook a project on interim accounts, in particular, their content, measurement basis and extent of disclosure. The Committee published a consultative paper 'Interim Financial Reporting' in 1993, which led to formal proposals being presented to the ASB.

39.3 The ASB issued a draft statement on interim reports in November 1996, which was developed from the proposals and recommendations in the ICAEW paper. The process leading to the draft statement also involved consultation with the London Stock Exchange, preparers, users and auditors of financial statements.

39.4 The final statement closely resembles the draft statement, which received widespread support. The statement on interim reports is a voluntary statement of best practice, in the same manner as the statement 'Operating and Financial Review'.

39.5 The content and publication of preliminary announcements is also governed by the Stock Exchange. Following the publication of the ASB's statement on interim reports, the ASB turned its attention to establishing best practice for preliminary announcements and published its statement, 'Preliminary announcements' in July 1998. The statement is non-mandatory and in the same was as the ASB's statement on interim reports is designed to be a guide to best practice. Its use is encouraged by the ASB and commended by the FRC, the Hundred Group of Finance Directors and the London and Irish Stock Exchanges.

39.6 Companies are encouraged in the statement to issue their preliminary announcements within 60 days of the year end and to make these available to a wider audience using methods appropriate to their shareholder base. Such methods might include press advertisements, pre-registration schemes or electronic means, such as the Internet. The information in a preliminary announcement is expected to be consistent with the audited financial statements and so should be reliable and not subject to alteration. The statement notes that where the reliability of the information in the announcement is not compromised, it is accepted practice for the preliminary announcement to be issued when the audit is not completed, but has reached an advanced stage. The APB has subsequently issued guidance (Bulletin 1998/7) for auditors on the agreement of preliminary announcements.

39.7 These recommendations are a part of a larger long-term project in which the ASB is examining the whole annual reporting package and which may eventually see preliminary announcements supplanting the full statutory financial statements as far as the vast majority shareholders are concerned.

39.8 This chapter reviews the current Stock Exchange requirements and ASB recommendations for interim reporting and preliminary announcements. In addition, some of the practical problems that arise are addressed.

Interim reports

Stock Exchange requirements

39.9 The Stock Exchange's Listing Rules require a company that has listed shares to issue a report on its activities and profit or loss for the first six months of each financial year. (The Alternative Investment Market (AIM) also requires half-yearly reports.) For groups, this report must be prepared on a consolidated basis. The report must be published within four months after the end of the six month period, unless in exceptional circumstances the Stock Exchange grants an extension to this deadline. [LR 12.46, 12.48]. When a company changes its accounting reference date and prepares financial statements for a period of more than 14 months, the company must prepare and publish a second interim report in respect of the second six months of the accounting period or the period up to a date not more than six months prior to the new accounting reference date. [LR 12.60].

39.10 The Stock Exchange requires that the interim report must contain the following in table form:

- Net turnover.
- Profit or loss before taxation and extraordinary items.

- Taxation, with overseas tax and share of associates' tax being separately disclosed if material.
- Minority interests.
- Profit or loss attributable to shareholders before extraordinary items.
- Extraordinary items (net of tax) (although such items are now highly unlikely).
- Profit or loss attributable to shareholders.
- Rates of dividends paid and proposed and the amount absorbed thereby.
- Earnings per share expressed as pence per share.
- Comparative amounts, in respect of the above items, for the corresponding six month period in the preceding financial year.

[LR 12.52].

If any of the required headings are unsuitable to the company's activities, they may be adjusted as necessary. [LR 12.53].

39.11 The Stock Exchange may authorise omission of figures for turnover, profit or loss before tax and dividends, but only where disclosure of the information is considered by the company to be against the public interest, or seriously detrimental to the company. The company's reasons for requesting the omission must be sent in writing to the Stock Exchange. Authorisation for the omission will not be given if it is likely to mislead the public with regard to the information they need to assess the worth of the company's shares. [LR 12.58]. In practice, use of this authorisation is rare.

39.12 In addition, the report must contain an explanatory statement relating to the company's or group's activities and profit or loss during the six months. [LR 12.51]. This statement must include:

- Any significant information that enables investors to make an informed assessment of the trend of the activities and results.
- An indication of any special factor that has influenced those activities and results during the period.
- Sufficient information to enable a comparison to be made with the corresponding period of the preceding financial year.

- A reference to the prospects in the current financial year, so far as possible. [LR 12.56].

39.13 Very few interim reports are audited. This is because, the Stock Exchange does not require the half-yearly report to be audited. Generally, auditors' work on half yearly reports is limited to a review, but some companies request their auditors to undertake specific agreed-upon procedures as an alternative to a review or may approach auditors for advice on specific financial issues. Some companies do not involve their auditors in any way before issuing interim reports. If, however, there has been an audit then the auditors' report must be included in full, including any qualifications. [LR 12.54].

39.14 The APB published Bulletin 1993/1, 'Review of interim financial information', in November 1993, which provides guidance to auditors when reviewing and reporting on interim financial information. But given the variety of approach the APB believed that it may be difficult for listed companies to disclose, succinctly, the extent to which the interim report has been audited or reviewed. As a consequence, it issued Bulletin 1998/6 in June 1998, 'Review of interim financial information – supplementary guidance for auditors', which recommends that auditors agree to a statement that the interim financial information has been 'reviewed' only if a review in accordance with Bulletin 1993/1 has been carried out and the interim financial information is clearly identified within the interim report. Where the interim information is not clearly identified within the interim report or where the scope of the auditors' review is less than that set out in Bulletin 1993/1, the APB believes that the interim report should be described as *"neither audited nor reviewed"*.

39.15 Paragraph 12.47 of the Listing Rules requires that the accounting policies and presentation applied to the interim report must be consistent with those applied in the latest published annual financial statements except where:

- the policies and presentation are to be changed in the subsequent annual financial statements, in which case the new accounting policies and presentation should be adopted and the changes and the reasons should be disclosed in the half-yearly report; or

- the Stock Exchange otherwise agrees.

39.16 In general, companies are expected to follow the same accounting policies in their interims as in the last annual financial statements. A strict reading of the first bullet point in Listing Rule 12.47 above would suggest that where companies are to implement a new accounting standard, or change in presentation, in the next annual financial statements, they will have to implement it in their interims for that year. Even where new standards are published in the first six months, or before the interim report is approved, but are not effective until the year end, companies will have to adopt changes in the interim report. This may give companies little time to obtain the exact figures or decide on the exact details of proposed changes. Where it is impracticable for a company to adopt in its interims a new standard that will apply at its year end, it should consult the Stock Exchange.

39.17 Another difficulty may arise where the new standard contains options as to how it might be implemented. The company might not have decided, by the interim reporting date, quite how it will implement the new standard. Despite this uncertainty the new standard should be adopted at the half year. This does not preclude firming up the policy or the numbers in the annual financial statements; an analogy would be fair value accounting following an acquisition where the amounts initially applied can be provisional.

39.18 In circumstances where a new standard is published during the first half of the year, but does not require adoption until after the year end, a company could decide at its full year end to adopt the new standard before the required date on a voluntary basis. The company is not precluded from doing this merely because it did not adopt the standard in its interim report. Another circumstance is where a new standard (or, perhaps more likely, a UITF Abstract) is published in say July and applies to December year ends in the same year. In the case of a July publication date, it would be unreasonable to insist that a company must adopt the new ruling in its interim report to June if it was demonstrably impracticable to do so.

39.19 The second bullet point in paragraph 39.15 is expected to apply in the rare situations where proposed policies and presentations differ from those adopted at the previous year end and from those to be adopted at the forthcoming year end. That is, it would apply where companies adopt, for interim reporting, policies different to those used at either year end.

39.20 In exceptional circumstances, the Stock Exchange may allow the half-yearly report to include estimated figures for profit and loss with a statement, in the report, that the figures are estimates.

ASB Statement on interim reports

39.21 The ASB's statement was issued following recommendations from the Cadbury committee in respect of interim reporting. It also took account of the results of a project on interim financial reporting, undertaken by the Financial Reporting Committee of the ICAEW.

39.22 The statement's objective is to improve the consistency, comparability and quality of interim reporting within the constraints of cost and time. Compliance with the statement should promote best practice and increase comparability both between the interim reports of different companies and between interim reports and previously reported financial statements.

39.23 Interim reporting provides financial information about a company in the period between the release of the previous annual report and the next preliminary profit announcement. Interim reporting allows the company to discuss key issues affecting the business during the year and ensure that such information receives the widest possible circulation. Interim reports are not intended to be full statutory financial statements and are not intended, therefore, to give a true and fair view.

39.24 The ASB's statement recommends that:

- Interim reports should be drawn up using the same measurement and recognition bases as those used for annual reporting.

- The content of an interim report should include a:
  - Management commentary.
  - Summarised profit and loss account.
  - Statement of total recognised gains and losses, where relevant.
  - Summarised balance sheet.
  - Summarised cash flow statement.

[IR para 31].

Publication timescale

39.25 The statement encourages companies to make their interim reports available within 60 days of the interim period end. [IR para 3]. The current Stock Exchange requirement for interim reports to be published within four months of the interim date is one of the longest periods allowed among the large industrial countries. The average reporting time for the top 100 UK companies is less than 60 days, therefore, the statement will encourage those companies publishing interim reports more than 60 days after the end of the interim period to follow suit. The statement does not consider enforcement, as this is a matter for the Stock Exchange.

Basis of preparation

39.26 Two different approaches to preparing interim reports have developed over the years. One approach, commonly called the 'discrete period' approach, views the interim period in essentially the same manner as a full year – as a discrete, specific period. Under this method, figures are calculated and accruals and estimates made in exactly the same manner as would be the case at the year end. The other approach, called the 'integral' approach, treats the interim period as a component of the full year. Therefore, items are allocated to interim periods based on estimates of the total annual revenue and expenses. Under this approach, fluctuations in results are reduced rather than reflecting the possible uneven pattern of the business. In practice a full 'integral' approach would involve creating a separate series of accounting standards for interim reporting to formalise the criteria to be used for estimating the full year out-turn, dealing with uncertainty and other issues.

39.27 The ASB's statement advocates that the discrete approach should be used, that is, items of income and expenses should be measured and recognised on a basis consistent with that used in preparing the annual financial statements. [IR para 8]. The statement gives guidance in respect of annually determined items of income and expenditure, where the discrete approach is not appropriate.

39.28 Preparing financial information at any cut off date, even at the financial year end, involves making adjustments and estimates. Such judgements are necessary because no accounting period can be entirely independent; some items of income or expenditure will always be incomplete. At the interim period end, for specific items of income and expense that occur on an annual basis, it is necessary to take into account the estimated income or expense for the whole year to determine the appropriate amount to be recognised in the interim period. [IR para 8].

39.29 Taxation is an example of an annually determined item and the matters that need to be taken into consideration when determining the interim tax charge are discussed from paragraph 39.53 below.

39.30 The statement advocates that for items of income or expenditure determined on a formal basis once a year it will be necessary to determine whether an obligation (either contractual or constructive) exists at the interim period end. For example, a genuinely discretionary bonus given at the end of the year would be recognised only in the final full year financial statements. Other items such as a profit related bonus paid at the year end, although non-contractual, would be recognised in an earlier period, on the basis of profits earned in that period, if past practice indicated that there was a constructive obligation. [IR para 15].

39.31 The same principle would apply to other annually determined items of income and expenditure such as profit sharing, sales commissions and rent based on income or sales. For example, if a company receives (or grants) a volume discount based on the number of items purchased during a 12 month period a proportion of the estimated amount of discount for the year would be accrued in the earlier interim period, because this would be deemed to be a constructive obligation.

Example

A company has a December year end and only carries out one activity each year, an exhibition and conference that is held in March and which involves considerable costs being incurred such as advertising, booking of the venue and hire of equipment before the year end. Such a company will have an accounting policy with regard to recognising the income and expenditure on its activity, which is in accordance with SSAP 2's concepts of 'accruals' and 'prudence'. Some, if not all, of the direct costs of the exhibition and conference and any income received in advance should be carried forward at the year end to be matched with the income and further expenditure that will arise in March when the activity takes place, provided that the income is expected to exceed the costs.

The facts are the same as in the situation above except that the exhibition and conference takes place in September each year. The company must prepare an interim report as at the end of June.

This company should have an accounting policy for its interim reporting similar to that of the company in the situation above. The fact that it is preparing financial statements for an interim period rather than for the full year should not affect the accounting principles adopted.

Accounting policies

39.32 As mentioned in paragraph 39.15, the Listing Rules require that the accounting policies and presentation applied to the interim report must be consistent with those applied in the annual financial statements. The statement recommends that the accounting policies need to be stated and explained only where they differ from those previously adopted. [IR para 10]. For example, Ladbroke Group plc explains in its interim report that hotels and investment properties are not revalued for the interim reports (see Table 39.1). In all other cases, the interim report should include a statement that they are prepared on the basis of the accounting policies set out in the most recent set of annual financial statements. [IR para 10].

Table 39.1 – Ladbroke Group PLC – Interim results for the six months ending 30 June 1997

1 Basis of reporting

a The interim financial statements have been prepared on the basis of the accounting policies set out in the group's 1996 statutory accounts. The statements were approved by a duly appointed and authorised committee of the Board of Directors on 28th August 1997 and are unaudited. The auditors have carried out a review and their report is set out on page 11.

b The figures for the year ended 31st December 1996 have been extracted from the statutory accounts which have been filed with the Registrar of Companies. The auditors' report on those accounts was unqualified and did not contain any statement under section 237 of the Companies Act 1985.

c Hotels and investment properties are revalued annually at the year end and are therefore stated in the half year balance sheets at these preceding year end valuations.

Changes in accounting policy and prior year adjustments

39.33 The statement recommends that when it is known at the time the interim report is prepared that an accounting policy change will be made in the annual financial statements, the change should be implemented in the interim report. This ensures that the interim results are presented on the same basis as those for the full financial year. [IR para 11].

39.34 This recommendation is not as stringent as the Listing Rule requirement discussed above, which requires that known changes in accounting policies (or presentation changes) should be followed in the half-yearly report (see para 39.15). Consequently, the Listing Rules have precedent in this area, unless the Stock Exchange agrees otherwise. The extract from Zeneca's interim report, given in Table 39.2, illustrates the situation where changes in accounting policy, which will be adopted at the full year end, have been implemented at the half year to accord with these requirements.

Table 39.2 – Zeneca Group PLC – Half Year Results – 30 June 1998

Notes to the Interim Financial Statements (extract)

1 BASIS OF PREPARATION AND ACCOUNTING POLICIES

The unaudited results for the half year to 30 June 1998 have been prepared in accordance with UK generally accepted accounting principles. The accounting policies applied are those set out in the Group's 1997 Annual Report and Accounts except for changes in accounting arising from the adoption of Financial Reporting Standard No.9 "Associates and Joint Ventures" (FRS 9) and Financial Reporting Standard No. 10 "Goodwill and Intangible Assets" (FRS 10). Under FRS 9, certain investments previously accounted for as associates have been reclassified as joint ventures. Under FRS 10, goodwill arising on acquisitions made after 1 January 1998 is capitalised and amortised over its estimated useful life. Previously, all goodwill was written off to reserves on acquisition. The adoption of FRS 9 and FRS 10 has no impact on the Group's net assets as at 1 January 1998. The amortisation charge in respect of capitalised goodwill for the first half of 1998 was £3m ($5m).

39.35 The ASB's statement recommends that where a known accounting policy change in the current year is not implemented in the interim reports, an estimate of its effect should be shown and, if that is not possible, a statement of explanation should be included. [IR para 11].

39.36 Where there is a change in accounting policy, the amounts for the current and prior periods should be stated on the basis of the new policies. [IR para 12].

39.37 The cumulative effect on opening reserves of the new policy change should be disclosed at the foot of the statement of total recognised gains and losses of the period. Similar disclosures should be made in respect of other prior period adjustments, including those arising from the correction of fundamental errors. A description should be given to help users understand the nature of each change or adjustment. [IR para 12].

Materiality

39.38 Consistent with the discrete approach, the statement recommends that materiality should be assessed by reference to the results for the interim period rather than in relation to the expected results for the full year. [IR para 28]. For example, see exceptional items in paragraph 39.67.

Management commentary

39.39 The Stock Exchange's requirement for narrative in the half-yearly report is discussed in paragraph 39.12 above. The ICAEW consultation paper encouraged directors to look at the voluntary guidance in the ASB's operating and financial review (OFR) statement and consider whether comments on any of the items normally dealt with in an OFR should be included within the interim report to meet best the Stock Exchange's requirements. However, the commentary in the interim report was not expected to be as long or in as great a detail as that expected in the annual report. The ASB's statement adopted these proposals. It recommends that the commentary should be sufficient to enable users to appreciate the main factors influencing the company's performance during the interim period and its position at the period-end and should focus on areas of change since the last set of annual financial statements. [IR paras 34, 35, 36]. The OFR is discussed in chapter 33.

39.40 If the results of the business are seasonal, the commentary should describe the nature of the seasonal activity and, together with other disclosures, provide adequate information for the performance of the business and its financial position at the end of the period to be understood in the context of the annual cycle. The principles by which seasonal results are reflected in the interim report should be stated, particularly where there are any expected changes in the effects of seasonality. [IR para 37].

39.41 The commentary should draw attention to the summarised balance sheet and cash flow statement and should highlight and explain significant changes since the last annual financial statements particularly regarding movements in working capital, liquidity and net debt that are likely to be of value to users in their assessment of the business. [IR para 38]. Unilever's interim financial report in Table 39.3 below comments on balance sheet and cash flow information.

Table 39.3 – Unilever PLC – Second Quarter and Half Year Results 1998 – 30 June 1998

Unilever Results (extract)

Balance Sheet and Cash Flow

The main movement in the balance sheet at the half year compared to end 1997 is in working capital. This is mainly due to the seasonality of the business.

Net funds at the half year of £2,986 million are somewhat lower than end 1997, mainly reflecting higher outflows on working capital and payment of the final dividend. Net gearing remains zero.

Total Capital and Reserves increase by £644 million due to profits to the half year, partly offset by currency movements.

Cash flow from operating activities at £1,058 million is in line with the same period as last year.

39.42 The narrative commentary should also explain any other matter that management thinks would help users to understand the report. This would include for example, where relevant:

- Acquisitions and disposals of major fixed assets or investments during the period covered by the report.
- Changes in contingencies, commitments and off balance sheet financial instruments since the previous year end.
- Material changes in capital structure or financing.
- Events arising after the end of the period covered by the report.

[IR para 39].

39.43 Exceptional items are a further example of matters that should be explained in the management commentary.

Profit and loss account

39.44 The level of detail of profit and loss account disclosure in interim reporting has been the subject of Listing Rules requirements for many years. These requirements are detailed from paragraph 39.10 above.

39.45 Since interim reports should be prepared under accounting policies and presentation consistent with that applied in the latest published annual financial statements, according to the Listing Rules, then it is only reasonable that the terminology and principles underlying accounting standards are relevant for interim reports. The ASB's statement recommends that interim reports should include a summarised profit and loss account, which includes the following information where relevant:

- Turnover
- *Operating profit or loss*
- *Interest payable less interest receivable (net)*
- Profit or loss on ordinary activities before tax
- Tax on profit or loss on ordinary activities
- *Profit or loss on ordinary activities after tax*
- Minority interests
- Profit or loss for the period
- Dividends paid and proposed

[IR para 40].

39.46 In the above list the items shown in italics are those that are additional to the Listing Rules requirements (see para 39.10).

Acquisitions and discontinued operations

39.47 The ASB's statement recommends that turnover and operating profit of acquisitions and discontinued operations (as defined in FRS 3) should be separately disclosed on the face of the profit and loss account in the period in accordance with FRS 3. The statement recommends that where it is not practicable to determine the post-acquisition results of an operation to the end of the interim period, an indication should be given of the contribution of the acquisition to the turnover and operating profit of the continuing operations. [IR para 42].

39.48 The term 'discontinued', for the interim period, would have the same meaning as in FRS 3 paragraph 4, that is, operations would be regarded as discontinued, when the sale or termination is completed either in the interim period, or before the earlier of three months after the end of the interim period and the date on which the interim report is approved. Where, however, doubt exists regarding discontinuance within the time limits the related operations should be classified as continuing (see examples below). The statement recommends disclosure, either by way of note or management commentary, of the results of operations which, although not discontinued, are in the process of discontinuing or are expected to be classified as discontinued in the current year's financial statements. [IR para 42]. An example of a profit and loss account giving the recommended disclosures for discontinued operations is shown in Table 39.4 below.

Example 1

A listed company prepares its interim statement to 30 June. During the period it discontinued its coaches business (see chapter 7 for a definition of discontinued).

In this example the operation will be classed as discontinued in the interim report.

Example 2

As above except that the operation satisfies the conditions for discontinued operations in July of the same year, and the interim report is published in August.

In this example, the operation is discontinued before the earlier of approval of the interim report and three months after the interim period end and should, therefore, be classified as discontinued in the interim report.

Example 3

As above except that it is expected that the operation will satisfy the conditions for discontinued operations in January of the following year.

In this example, although the operation may qualify as discontinued for the full year's financial statements, it is certain at the date of publishing the interim report that it will not qualify as discontinued for the interim report. Consequently, the operation should be classified as continuing in the interim report. However, the disclosure referred to in paragraph 39.48 for operations in the process of discontinuing should be given.

Table 39.4 – TI GROUP PLC – Interim Statement 1998 – 30th June 1998

Consolidated profit and loss account (extract)

	Notes	6 months to 30th June 1998: Before goodwill amortisation and exceptional items £m	Goodwill amortisation £m	Exceptional items £m	Total £m	6 months to 30th June 1997 £m	12 months to 31st December 1997 £m
Turnover							
Total Group and share of joint venture	1	**1,008.7**	–	–	1,008.7	**932.6**	**1,870.4**
Less share of joint venture (discontinued)		(68.8)	–	–	(68.8)	(78.6)	(166.0)
Continuing operations		*881.7*	–	–	*881.7*	*837.3*	*1,670.0*
Acquisitions		*38.2*	–	–	*38.2*	–	–
Discontinued operations		*20.0*	–	–	*20.0*	*16.7*	*34.4*
Group		939.9	–	–	939.9	854.0	1,704.4
Operating profit	1						
Continuing operations		*115.6*	–	*(9.0)*	*106.6*	*111.0*	*216.1*
Acquisitions		*3.7*	*(3.0)*	–	*0.7*	–	–
Discontinued operations		*1.5*	–	–	*1.5*	*1.3*	*2.7*
		120.8	(3.0)	(9.0)	108.8	112.3	218.8
Joint venture and associates	2						
Continuing operations		*0.2*	–	–	*0.2*	*0.8*	*1.4*
Acquisitions		*1.0*	–	–	*1.0*	–	–
Discontinued operations		*7.7*	–	–	*7.7*	*7.1*	*16.8*
		8.9	–	–	8.9	7.9	18.2
Operating profit and joint venture and associates	1	129.7	(3.0)	(9.0)	117.7	120.2	237.0
Exceptional profit on disposal of operations	3	–	–	14.7	14.7	–	–
Exceptional loss on disposal of fixed assets	3	–	–	–	–	–	(1.9)
Profit before interest		**129.7**	(3.0)	5.7	132.4	**120.2**	**235.1**
Interest		(7.5)	–	–	(7.5)	(8.1)	(14.5)
Profit on ordinary activities before taxation							
Before exceptional items		**122.2**	(3.0)	–	119.2	**112.1**	**222.5**
Exceptional items (as above)		–	–	5.7	5.7	–	(1.9)
		122.2	(3.0)	5.7	124.9	112.1	220.6
Taxation	4	(37.9)	–	(5.6)	(43.5)	(34.8)	(68.8)
Profit on ordinary activities after taxation		84.3	(3.0)	0.1	81.4	77.3	151.8
Minority interests		(0.5)	–	–	(0.5)	(0.8)	(1.3)
Profit for the financial period		83.8	(3.0)	0.1	80.9	76.5	150.5

The Group adopted FRS 9 'Associates and Joint Ventures' in its financial statements for the 12 months to 31st December 1997 and accordingly the numbers for Joint ventures and associates and Interest for the 6 months to 30th June have been reanalysed.

39.49 The disclosure requirements in full year reports for acquisitions and disposals during a period in year end financial statements are extensive. The statement advocates that:

> *"Subject to the limited exceptions noted in this Statement, disclosures demanded by Financial Reporting Standards and Statements of Standard Accounting Practice are not generally required in the presentation of interim reports."* [IR para 57].

39.50 The recommendations of the statement will, therefore, be met by giving the split of acquisitions and discontinued operations on the face of the profit and loss account in accordance with FRS 3. In practice, however, many companies voluntarily give note disclosure, to varying degrees of detail, on acquisitions and disposals in the interim period.

Segmental information

39.51 The ASB's statement recommends that, to improve the quality of trend analysis and inter-company comparisons, companies that are required to present segmental information in their annual financial statements should adopt the same business and geographical classifications in their interim reports. They should disclose:

- Segment turnover, distinguishing inter-segment sales if significant.
- Segment profit or loss as disclosed in the annual financial statements, normally profit or loss before accounting for interest, taxation and minority interests.

[IR para 43].

39.52 Some companies also give information about segment net assets employed. However, the statement does not suggest disclosure of segmental net asset information. Presenting comparatives to any segmental information needs to considered in the light of the statement's recommendation that comparative amounts for the corresponding interim period and the previous full financial year should be given for the summarised profit and loss account (see para 39.95). By implication this recommendation extends to presenting similar comparative information for segmental analysis. An example of this type of disclosure is included in Table 39.5.

Table 39.5 – GKN plc – Interim Report for the 6 months to 27 June 1998

Segmental Analysis (extract)

	Sales			Operating Profit		
	First Half 1998 £m	First half 1997 £m	Full Year 1997 £m	**First Half 1998 £m**	First Half 1997 £m	Full Year 1997 £m
By business						
Automotive and Agritechnical products						
Subsidiaries	**1044**	938	1883	**117**	91	178
Joint ventures	**92**	81	166	**16**	15	30
	1136	1019	2049	**133**	106	208
Aerospace and Special Vehicles						
Subsidiaries	**409**	460	904	**47**	51	103
Industrial Services						
Subsidiaries	**21**	21	47	**7**	8	16
Joint ventures	**234**	187	383	**41**	34	74
	255	208	430	**48**	42	90
Total	**1800**	1687	3383	**228**	199	401
By region of origin						
United Kingdom						
Subsidiaries	**586**	644	1255	**62**	61	124
Joint ventures	**90**	79	166	**21**	17	36
	676	723	1421	**83**	78	160
Continental Europe						
Subsidiaries	**573**	536	1036	**84**	71	131
Joint ventures	**114**	81	160	**16**	13	28
	687	617	1196	**100**	84	159
The Americas						
Subsidiaries	**268**	187	438	**21**	11	30
Joint ventures	**97**	82	170	**16**	14	31
	365	269	608	**37**	25	61
Rest of the world						
Subsidiaries	**47**	52	105	**4**	7	12
Joint ventures	**25**	26	53	**4**	5	9
	72	78	158	**8**	12	21
Total	**1800**	1687	3383	**228**	199	401
Subsidiaries	**1474**	1419	2834	**171**	150	297
Joint ventures	**326**	268	549	**57**	49	104
Total	**1800**	1687	3383	**228**	199	401

Taxation

39.53 As noted in paragraph 39.29, taxation is an annually determined item and, accordingly, determining the tax charge will involve making an estimate of the likely effective tax rate for the year. The tax charge or credit cannot be properly determined until the end of the financial year when all allowances and taxable items are known. Calculating tax on the basis of the results of the interim period in isolation could result in recognising a tax figure that is inconsistent with the manner in which tax is borne by the company. Therefore, the calculation of the effective tax rate should be based on a prudent estimate of the tax charge or credit for the year expressed as a percentage of the expected accounting profit or loss. This percentage is then applied to the interim result, which results in tax being recognised ratably over the year as a whole, in common with other contractual, annually determined items of income and expenditure as noted in paragraph 39.28. [IR para 18].

39.54 The statement recommends that to the extent practicable and where more meaningful, a separate estimated effective annual tax rate should be determined for each material tax jurisdiction and applied individually to the interim period pre-tax income of each jurisdiction. Similarly, where different income tax rates apply to different categories of income, a separate rate should be applied to each category of interim period pre-tax income, where practical and material. It allows for weighted average rates to be used where they represent reasonable approximations of the effect of using more specific rates. [IR para 19].

39.55 The tax effect of exceptional items should not be included in the likely effective annual rate, but should be recognised in the same period as the relevant exceptional item. The estimated annual effective tax rate (excluding exceptional items) will in that case be applied to the interim profit or loss before exceptional items. [IR para 20].

39.56 Events and expenditure that are expected to fall in the second part of the year and would affect the effective annual tax rate should be brought into the estimate on a prudent basis. An event such as planned capital expenditure (see para 39.57) could be anticipated in calculating the effective tax rate for the year. It would not normally be appropriate, however, to take account of the tax effects of other significant events that, although expected to arise in the second part of the year, are subject to considerable uncertainty. [IR para 21].

Capital allowances

39.57 The likely level of capital expenditure may be readily apparent if such expenditure is planned and approved at the time the interim report is prepared. If not, then a prudent estimate should be made of the likely effect of capital expenditure in the second half year on the effective tax rate for the full year, if capital allowances are expected to have a material effect on the effective tax rate. [IR para 21].

39.58 The interim report should give a brief explanation of the basis of the effective tax rate in the narrative commentary where such events are anticipated. [IR para 22]. Most companies present information voluntarily about the effective tax rate used in the interim period and the effect of losses or overseas taxation, for example, on the rate.

Table 39.6 and Table 39.7 give examples of the type of voluntary information about taxation currently being included in notes to interim reports.

Table 39.6 – Elementis plc – Interim Report for the six months ended 30 June 1998

5. Tax

The tax charge of £5.9 million is based on an estimated effective tax rate on profit before exceptional items for the year to 31 December 1998 of 19.0 per cent. It includes overseas tax of £3.0 million (1997 – £2.1 million) (Year to 31 December 1997 – £5.7 million). The rate is lower than the standard UK corporation tax rate mainly due to the expected utilisation of surplus ACT written off in prior years and as a result of the impairment of fixed assets in 1997, tax depreciation now exceeding book depreciation.

Table 39.7 – Hammerson plc – Interim Report – 30 June 1998

3 TAXATION

Year ended 31 December 1997 £m		**Six months ended 30 June 1998 £m**	Six months ended 30 June 1997 £m
11.8	United Kingdom corporation tax at 31% (1997: 31.5%)	**6.5**	6.1
(0.5)	Advance corporation tax (written back)/written off	**(4.8)**	0.5
11.3		**1.7**	6.6
3.6	Overseas taxation	**0.8**	0.6
14.9		**2.5**	7.2

The tax change for the six months ended 30June 1998 takes into account the abolition of Advance Corporation Tax and is based on the projected effective tax rate for the full year.

Intra-period losses

39.59 The statement recommends that the general approach of making a prudent estimate of the effective tax rate for the year should be employed even where, for example, a company's result in the first half of the year is expected to be wholly or completely offset by its result in the second half of the year. The consequence of this approach is that, conceptually, even if the overall result for the year was expected to be a break even position, an effective rate of tax exists that needs to be applied to the interim period. [IR para 23]. This is outlined in the example below, which has been simplified to assume that the expected profit before tax is equal to the expected profit chargeable to corporation tax.

Example

Effective tax rate	Jan-June £'000	Jul-Dec £'000	Full year £'000
Profit/(loss) before tax	(10,000)	10,100	100
Tax credit/(charge)	3,300	(3,333)	(33)
Profit/(loss) after tax	(6,700)	6,767	67

The tax charge for the year is expected to be £33,000 and the profit for the year is expected to be £100,000, which results in an expected effective tax rate of 33% to be applied to the period ending in June.

39.60 The example indicates that the interim period will have a tax credit of £3,300,000 when the company is actually expected to suffer a tax charge of only £33,000. Expected effective tax rates should be applied to interim losses as well as to profits. However, prudence would dictate a more cautious approach to recognising tax credits. That is, if a tax credit arises with respect to a loss in the interim period and this 'relief' is merely the result of applying the expected effective rate of tax as outlined in the example above, then it should be recognised only if there is reasonable assurance that it will reverse in the foreseeable future. A history of losses in the first half of the year and then equal or larger profits in the second half would reinforce the argument that such a calculation is prudent. On the other hand, if the loss in the first half was unusual and unexpected there may be uncertainty regarding the likely results in the second half and, therefore, more difficulty in determining an expected effective rate of tax. In this situation, it would be prudent not to recognise a tax credit. [IR para 23].

39.61 If, however, losses are expected for the full year, then a deferred tax asset may only be carried forward at the interim date if it is expected to be recoverable without replacement by an equivalent debit balance. Therefore, unless the recovery of the 'relief' is reasonably assured, because for example the losses can be carried back, it should not be recognised as a current year credit in the interim period any more than it should be recognised in the annual financial statements. If, however, there were deferred tax liabilities, then the losses may be included in calculating the deferred tax provision.

39.62 In the example in paragraph 39.59 above, the tax credit (which could have just as easily been a tax charge if the profit allocation between the two periods were reversed) appears excessive in relation to the expected tax charge for the year as a whole. If the example had included disallowable items, then the effective rate of tax would have been higher and the effect of the disallowable items would have ratably increased the apparent tax credit. While this may seem to overstate the tax credit or tax charge for the interim period, it will allow users an insight into the expected tax rate for the full year and they will be able to compare this with the actual tax rate for the previous year. The effects of, for example, losses in the first half of the year and profits in the second on the tax borne should be discussed in the explanatory section of the report and the accounting policy used for calculating tax in the interim report should be disclosed.

Losses brought forward

39.63 In determining the amount of tax losses and recoverable ACT to recognise in the interim period, an estimate should be made of the utilisation expected over the whole tax year. The amount recognised in the interim period should be proportional to the profit before tax of the interim period and the estimated annual profit before tax, but limited to the amount recoverable for the year as a whole. [IR para 24]. This is outlined in the example below.

Example

A company has tax losses brought forward of £75,000, estimated first half-year taxable profits of £100,000 and an expected second half-year loss of £40,000.

The maximum annual utilisation of tax losses brought forward is £60,000, based on the expected taxable profits for the year. Tax losses of £60,000 could then be absorbed in the first half-year leaving £40,000 first half-year taxable profits to be set against second half-year losses of £40,000. This would result in a tax charge (at 30%) of £12,000 in the first half-year and a tax credit of £12,000 in the second half-year, resulting in an overall nil tax charge for the year.

Exceptional items

39.64 The FRS 3 paragraph 20 exceptional items, often called 'super exceptional' items or non-operating exceptional items, are those that are required by FRS 3 to be shown on the face of the statutory profit and loss account after operating profit and before interest and described as continuing or discontinued, as appropriate. These items are:

- Profits and losses on sale or termination of an operation.
- Costs of a fundamental reorganisation or restructuring having a material effect on the nature and focus of the reporting entity's operations.
- Profits or losses on the disposal of fixed assets.

39.65 The ASB's statement recommends that these are disclosed in interim reports in accordance with FRS 3. Any other exceptional items would also be disclosed separately. (The same would apply to extraordinary items, but it is reasonable to assume in the light of FRS 3 that such items will not occur.) Exceptional items rarely extend over more than one year and it is not generally appropriate to allocate their effect to different parts of the reporting period. Therefore, they should be recognised in the interim period in which they occur. [IR para 45].

Example 1

A listed company is to spend £10m during the year on a reorganisation of its operations. Should it provide for half of the reorganisation in its interim report?

If there is a demonstrable commitment to carry out the reorganisation, for example, if there is a detailed plan and a public announcement before the end of the first half year, a provision for the full amount should be made in the interim report. There would seem to be no logic in providing for half of the amount; there is either a commitment to carry out the reorganisation at the interim stage or merely an intention that does not trigger recognition of a provision.

Example 2

A listed company prepares its interim statement to 30 June. During the period to 30 June, a decision was taken to restructure and the costs of the resulting redundancies were paid. Can the cost of the redundancies be spread over the full year?

The cost should be recognised in full in the interim statement since the loss crystallises when the decision is made and the redundancies are paid. Once again, there is no logical reason to spread costs which result from actions undertaken in the interim period.

39.66 The types of exceptional item listed in paragraph 39.64 above should be disclosed separately on the face of the profit and loss account. The tax effects relating to these types of exceptional items should be shown as a separate element of the taxation charge either on the face of the profit and loss account or in a note to the interim report. [IR para 47]. Other exceptional items should be charged or credited in arriving at the profit or loss on ordinary activities by inclusion under the statutory headings to which they relate. They can be disclosed separately on the face of the profit and loss account or in a note, depending on their materiality. [IR para 46].

39.67 The materiality of such items at the half-yearly stage should be judged in the context of the interim period rather than the expected results for the full year. This view is consistent with the idea that exceptional items should be recognised as they arise. Communication with the users of interim reports, such as financial analysts, would be best served by highlighting any exceptional items so that the underlying trends can be appreciated.

Associates and joint ventures

39.68 The ASB's statement recommends that the share of results of associates and results of joint ventures should be disclosed if material. [IR para 40]. Regard should also be given to trends. For example, if income from interests in associated undertakings was immaterial in the previous year and was not disclosed separately in those financial statements, and is again immaterial in the interim period, then there seems to be no reason to disclose it separately in the interim report. On the other hand, if there has been a change in the business since the previous year end such that income from interests in associated undertakings will become material in the full financial year, then this could be highlighted by disclosing it separately at the interim stage, supported by commentary in the explanatory statement. This stance has been strengthened by the publication of FRS 9, 'Associates and joint ventures', which requires specific accounting treatments and disclosures for associates and joint ventures. These aspects are discussed in chapter 28.

Interest payable less interest receivable

39.69 The statement recommends that interest payable and interest receivable are disclosed net in the profit and loss account. [IR para 40]. Interest payable and interest receivable are disclosed separately in annual financial statements and separate disclosure was envisaged in the ICAEW proposals, however, separate disclosure is not considered by the ASB to be necessary at the half year. The net amount of interest payable or receivable provides sufficient information for users and is consistent with the idea of providing summarised information in the interim report. If further detail is required, then it could be included in a note or on the face of the profit and loss account depending on the importance attached to the components.

Foreign exchange

39.70 For annual financial statements, the results of foreign subsidiaries can be translated at either the closing rate or at the average rate for the year. The method adopted for interim reporting should be consistent with that used in the annual financial statements. That is, the exchange rate used should be that which relates to the interim period, either the period end rate or the average rate for the period, depending on the method used. [IR para 25].

39.71 In the past, some companies have used an exchange rate that related to the previous year. The use of an exchange rate for the previous year in isolation is inconsistent with the general approach proposed. Prior year rates would not relate to the interim period and would not be consistent with the approach adopted in the annual financial statements. Some companies may wish to show information translated at prior year rates to facilitate comparison and this is best dealt with in the explanatory section of the report where the underlying trends are being discussed. In Table 39.8, for example, the review of operations in Reed Elsevier's interim report includes calculations of turnover and operating profit at constant exchange rates to show the performance trends.

Table 39.8 – Reed Elsevier – Interim report for the six months ended 30 June 1997

Review of operations

Year ended 31 December 1996	£ million	Six months ended 30 June 1997	30 June 1996	% change	% change constant currencies
	Turnover				
553	Scientific	273	273	-	12%
1,037	Professional	519	518	-	7%
1,290	Business	665	682	-2%	5%
444	Consumer	207	203	2%	2%
3,324	Continuing operations	1,664	1,676	-1%	6%
57	Discontinued operations	14	24		
3,381	Total	1,678	1,700	-1%	6%

Year ended 31 December 1996	£ million	Six months ended 30 June 1997	30 June 1996	% change	% change constant currencies
	Operating profit				
231	Scientific	115	112	3%	16%
268	Professional	143	134	7%	14%
279	Business	155	165	-6%	1%
75	Consumer	33	29	14%	14%
853	Continuing operations	446	440	1%	10%
3	Discontinued operations	-	(1)		
856	Total	446	439	2%	10%

Discontinued operations comprise certain operations of Reed Books which have been divested by the date of this statement.

Following the reorganisation of certain businesses and the formation of the Reed Business Information and Elsevier Business Information groups which were effective 1 January 1997, certain operations have been transferred between the reporting segments. Comparative figures for the six months ended 30 June 1996 and the year ended 31 December 1996 have been restated accordingly. Unless otherwise stated, all figures quoted in the following commentary refer to percentage movements at constant currency rates, using 1996 full year average rates.

Earnings per share

39.72 The Listing Rules require listed companies to disclose earnings per share expressed as pence per share. Companies that publish an alternative earnings per share figure in their annual financial statements should publish it also in their interim report. Where a company does this, its reason for doing so should be disclosed as well as a reconciliation to the earnings per share calculated in accordance with FRS 14. [IR para 48].

Seasonality

39.73 It is recognised that, in certain businesses, there is significant and recurring variation between the levels of profit in the interim period and for the year as a whole. Such seasonal businesses might prefer a more integral approach to interim reporting where expenditure could be allocated to interim periods based on estimates of the total annual revenues and expenses. This would smooth the effect of the seasonality. For example, in regulated utility industries, the price charged to the consumer is generally fixed by the regulator and, to a greater or lesser extent, does not vary with the level of consumption. The cost to the utility of meeting the demand may be higher in the peak season, because it can vary with demand. For instance, electricity may cost the distributors more in the winter when demand is high. This would result in an actual profit profile similar to that shown in the example below.

Example

Actual profit profile	Apr-Sep £'m	Oct-Mar £'m	Year £'m
Revenue	100	200	300
Cost of sales	(50)	(130)	(180)
Gross profit	50	70	20
Gross profit percentage	50%	35%	40%

39.74 If the expected gross margin of 40 per cent were to be used for the interim period ending in September, then the reported profits would be £40 million which, if the expected margin was reasonably accurate, would be more in line with the actual results for the full year. This would also be the situation for a business which had its higher volume and lower margin season in the first six months where the margin would appear understated in the interim report, unless it were to be smoothed. The ASB's statement, however, takes the view that seasonality should be dealt with by disclosure rather than by smoothing of results. The recommendation to provide narrative explanation of significant effects of seasonality is discussed in paragraph 39.40.

39.75 In addition, the recommendation to disclose the results for the previous corresponding interim period and the previous year as discussed from paragraph 39.96 below would also help to inform users about the actual nature of the business and the recurring variation that can be expected. In a business with a regular and predictable seasonal pattern, a narrative explanation coupled with the disclosure requirements for comparatives will be sufficient to enable users to predict full year results. Even where there is not a regular and predictable seasonal pattern, the ASB's statement states that fluctuating revenues of seasonal businesses are generally understood by the market place and it is appropriate to report them as they arise. [IR para 16].

Balance sheet information

39.76 The Cadbury report recommended that interim reports should contain balance sheet *information* and the ASB's statement recommends that summarised balance sheet information should be disclosed. This includes disclosing the analysis of current assets. For consistency, similar classifications to those used in the annual financial statements should be adopted. For example, a Schedule 4 company or Schedule 4A group should give the following information:

- Fixed assets.
- Current assets.
  - Stocks
  - Debtors
  - Cash at bank and in hand
  - Other current assets
- Creditors: amounts falling due within one year.
- Net current assets/(liabilities).
- Total assets less current liabilities.
- Creditors: amounts falling due after more than one year.
- Provisions for liabilities and charges.
- Capital and reserves.
- Minority interests.

[IR para 52].

An example balance sheet format is set out in Table 39.9.

39.77 The format used in the statutory financial statements will influence the format of the interim balance sheet. For example, if 'prepayments and accrued income' and 'accruals and deferred income' are shown separately on the face of the balance sheet at the year end, then they would probably also be shown separately in the interim report. However, it would not be necessary to disclose the share of joint ventures gross assets and liabilities on the face of the interim balance sheet, because the balance sheet is a summary only. Similarly, if it is not necessary to disclose the components of any linked presentation – that is, the gross receivables from which the associated non-recourse finance is deducted. Immaterial items may be combined for the sake of clarity. An example balance sheet format is set out in Table 39.9.

39.78 More detailed information can be given about the components of any balance sheet item either in the notes or on the face of the balance sheet if this would be helpful to users. For example, where there are key indicators referred to in the narrative commentary, such as the level of debt and gearing, the summarised balance sheet would need to be sufficiently detailed to allow the net debt to be calculated or this figure would need to be disclosed in the notes.

Table 39.9 – Zeneca Group PLC – Half Year Results – 30 June 1998

Consolidated Balance Sheet (extract)

	Notes	30 June 1998 £m	31 Dec 1997 £m
Fixed assets			
Tangible fixed assets		2,113	1,951
Goodwill and intangible assets		262	81
Investments in joint ventures and associates		92	84
Other fixed asset investments		49	38
		2,516	2,154
Current assets			
Stocks		762	728
Debtors		1,697	1,399
Short-term investments	6	166	426
Cash	6	196	303
		2,821	2,856
Total assets		5,337	5,010
Creditors due within one year			
Short-term borrowings	6	(289)	(166)
Current instalments of loans	6	(8)	(17)
Finance leases	6	(3)	(4)
Other creditors		(1,631)	(1,676)
		(1,931)	(1,863)
Net current assets		890	993
Total assets less current liabilities		3,406	3,147
Creditors due after more than one year			
Loans	6	(505)	(510)
Finance leases	6	(10)	(12)
Other creditors		(11)	(13)
		(526)	(535)
Provisions for liabilities and charges		(418)	(420)
Net assets		2,462	2,192
Capital and reserves			
Called-up share capital		237	237
Share premium account		28	24
Merger reserve		285	285
Other reserves		152	132
Profit and loss account		1,731	1,482
Shareholders' funds – equity interests	5	2,433	2,160
Minority equity interests		29	32
Shareholders' funds and minority interests		2,462	2,192

39.79 Whether value changes of assets held at a valuation are recognised in the interim report depends on the nature of the assets and the difficulty of obtaining valuations. The ASB does not expect as a matter of course revaluations of properties for interim reports. The statement recommends that the valuations used in the previous annual financial statements would suffice, subject to the following:

- The most recent valuations available should be used. For example, see Table 39.1 on page 39008 where Ladbroke Group plc notes that hotels and investment properties are stated at the preceding year end valuations.

- Where valuations have been brought forward, without amendment from the previous annual financial statements, a statement to that effect should be given.

- Where significant, the directors are encouraged to comment on price movements since the last valuation. [IR para 26].

39.80 Whenever revaluations are undertaken and included in the interim report the effect on the statutory financial statements will need to be considered.

Example

A company revalued its properties for the purpose of its interim report and then sold them before the year end. Should the gain or loss be calculated by reference to the carrying values included in the previous year's annual financial statements or by reference to the values included in the interim report?

One view is that once a formal valuation has been carried out and the values included in financial information relating to the company, whether that be prospectus figures, interim figures or any other published financial information, it cannot be ignored. In the annual financial statements, therefore, the carrying values should first be adjusted to reflect the revaluation in the interim report and then the profit or loss on disposal should be calculated by reference to the revalued amount in accordance with FRS 3. Any gain or loss relating to the valuation would be recognised in the statement of total recognised gains and losses. Thus if the company had not revalued its properties at the interim stage, it would have reported a larger gain in the profit and loss account at the year end.

The alternative view is that, despite the importance of interim reports, annual financial statements have primacy and the results reported at the year end should not be affected by whether the company happened to have issued an interim report. Hence in the case of the sale of a revalued asset, the sale proceeds would be compared to the carrying value at the previous year end.

39.81 These two views clearly give different answers, which is unsatisfactory. The second view has support internationally, and so, at this stage, is the preferred approach.

39.82 Although revaluations are not required, impairments in the value of assets of which the directors are aware should be recognised in the interim report.

Example

A company has a property for sale. If it has not been sold during the current year it is likely that a provision will be needed at the year end against the carrying value. If the directors decide to make a provision at the half year stage, could they only provide for half the expected loss in value?

If there is an impairment in value at the half year, the whole of the impairment should be recognised in the interim report. There is no logical reason not to recognise the full impairment and to recognise only half would be meaningless.

39.83 Revaluations would be considered appropriate for certain assets for example in respect of quoted stocks carried at market value. This would be in accordance with the company's accounting policies. [IR para 26].

39.84 The statement recommends that it would not usually be necessary to obtain a new actuarial valuation for pension costs, unless a significant event, such as a change in benefits, has rendered the previous estimate misleading. If, however, a more recent actuarial valuation is available at an interim date, then this should be used in the interim report. [IR para 27]. We would expect that where a new valuation is available and a significant new variation has emerged, then this would be a matter which should be reported in the management commentary.

Stock

39.85 Stock is an area where difficulty could exist in preparing interim reports on the same basis as the annual financial statements. For example, companies may only perform a full stock count at the year end and rely on a standard costing system, continuous stock records or on calculations using gross profit ratios to determine the cost of stock at the interim date. If the basis used for determining the value of stock at the interim date differs from that used at the year end, then the method used at the interim date should be disclosed.

39.86 Companies that carry out long-term contracts may have similar difficulties accurately valuing their work in progress at the interim date. They may perform their most careful review of the probable outcome and profitability of individual contracts and the necessity for provisions against possible loss-making contracts for the annual financial statements. In addition, the year end value of work in progress is subject to audit. However, such companies must also review the progress of contracts throughout the year for their own management purposes. Therefore, sufficient information may be readily available to value work in progress at the interim date. If such information is not available, management will need to conduct reviews of individual contracts sufficient to satisfy themselves that the value of long-term work in progress is not materially misstated in the interim report.

39.87 Stock provisions should also be calculated in the same manner as for statutory financial statements. As a result, provisions for slow moving or obsolete stock might be calculated based on the expected usage in the period after the interim reporting date. However, if diminutions in the value of stock are a result of temporary factors, such as seasonality and the diminution is expected to reverse by the year end, it would be misleading to include a provision against this stock in the interim accounts. Therefore, stock diminutions resulting from a *permanent* decline in market prices or other deterioration in trading conditions need to be differentiated from *temporary* declines. Permanent diminutions must be recognised in the interim accounts, but those that are expected to be temporary, such that no provision would be required at a year end, should not be recognised.

39.88 There would need to be a regular seasonal pattern to stock levels and selling price reductions in order to establish that diminutions in value are temporary. In many such instances, provisions would not be required under generally accepted accounting principles if the diminution is considered temporary.

Example

A company that manufactures consumer electronics has a September year end. The majority of sales occur at Christmas, so the company always begins to increase the stocks of finished goods in September with the level of finished goods at its peak in November. At the interim date of 31 March, the company usually has relatively high stocks of component parts that it has purchased in preparation for the increase in manufacturing effort later in the year. It is possible that the stocks of components will not be completely exhausted until after Christmas. At the year end, the company has a policy of providing in full for any stock of components that exceed six months' expected usage. Since the technology changes every year, components that have not been used after the peak in production are unlikely ever to be used.

Strictly following the year end provisioning policy at the interim date would result in large provisions against stock that is expected to be used in the manufacture of finished goods that will be sold at or just after the year end. Since the company has an established pattern of stock build up and subsequent sales, it would give an incorrect result to apply a mechanistic formula at the interim date. However, any components that were provided against at the previous year end still in stock that are not expected to be used in the current year's production programme will need to be provided against at the interim date. This diminution is permanent.

39.89 The general rule must be that stock diminutions should be treated with the same level of scrutiny at the interim as at the year end. It is only in exceptional circumstances that seasonality or other factors might affect interim stock values to such an extent that the treatment may differ from that which would be expected in preparing statutory financial statements.

39.90 A further issue may arise for companies that use a standard costing system. Standards may be set that result in variances which require stock to be restated for the statutory financial statements. It is possible that companies presently use the standard cost of stock in their interim reporting to avoid any expense and time lost in restatement to actual cost. Under FASB rules it is acceptable for US companies to defer recognising variances from standard only if they are planned and expected to be absorbed by the year end. In general, variances that would be recognised at the year end should also be recognised in the interim report. The actual pattern of costs may not be smooth and financial reporting at the interim stage, and at the year end, needs to reflect actual trading conditions.

Cash flow information

39.91 The ASB's statement recommends that a summarised cash flow statement should be presented and, total amounts for the categories of cash flows specified by FRS 1, should be presented as follows:

- Net cash flow from operating activities.
- Dividends received from associates.
- Returns on investment and servicing of finance.
- Taxation.
- Capital expenditure and financial investment.
- Acquisitions and disposals.
- Equity dividends paid.
- Management of liquid resources.
- Financing.
- Increase/decrease in cash.

[IR para 53; FRS 9 para 61(f)].

39.92 The statement recommends that a reconciliation of operating profit to operating cash flow should be given in sufficient detail for users to appreciate its chief components. A reconciliation should also be given of the movement of cash in the period to the movement in net debt, as required by FRS 1, including the effect of movements on short-term and long-term borrowings, cash and other components of net debt, unless disclosed elsewhere. [IR para 54]. Table 39.10 illustrates an example of the voluntary disclosure of summarised cash flow information on the basis of FRS 1 and also discloses the reconciliation of operating cash flow and net cash (debt).

Table 39.10 – Reckitt & Colman plc – Interim Report – 4 July 1998

Group cash flow statement

for the half year ended 4 July 1998: unaudited	**1st half 1998 £m**	1st half 1997 £m	Full year 1997 £m
Cash flow from operating activities	**135.1**	165.7	392.2
Returns on investments and servicing of finance	**(27.2)**	(26.1)	(56.6)
Taxation	**(29.3)**	(70.2)	(83.4)
Capital expenditure and financial investment	**(18.5)**	(25.8)	(74.9)
Acquisitions and disposals	**(99.6)**	(5.1)	0.6
Equity dividends paid	**(35.8)**	(31.6)	(91.3)
Cash (outflow)/inflow before use of liquid resources and financing	**(75.3)**	6.9	86.6
Management of liquid resources	**11.7**	30.5	(68.2)
Financing	**10.5**	(25.9)	30.7
(Decrease)/increase in cash in period	**(53.1)**	11.5	49.1

Reconciliation of net cash flow to movement in net debt

	1st half 1998 £m	1st half 1997 £m	Full year 1997 £m
(Decrease)/increase in cash in period	**(53.1)**	11.5	49.1
Cash (inflow)/outflow from (increase in)/repayment of debt	**(6.6)**	29.1	(25.9)
Cash (inflow)/outflow from (decrease)/increase in liquid resources	**(11.7)**	(30.5)	68.2
Changes in net debt resulting from cash flows	**(71.4)**	10.1	91.4
Premium on shares allotted on conversion of convertible capital bonds	–	–	4.3
Translation differences	**9.5**	17.1	14.2
Movement in net debt in period	**(61.9)**	27.2	109.9
Net debt at beginning of period	**(535.5)**	(645.4)	(645.4)
Net debt at end of period	**(597.4)**	(618.2)	(535.5)
Net cash flow arising from ordinary operations	**24.3**	12.0	86.0

Management uses net cash flow arising from ordinary operations as a performance measure. This is defined as cash inflow before the use of liquid resources and financing, less acquisitions and disposals.

4. Reconciliation of operating profit to net cash flow from operating activities

	1st half 1998 £m	1st half 1997 £m	Full year 1997 £m
Operating profit	**179.8**	192.7	369.1
Non-cash items			
Depreciation	**34.3**	24.6	46.8
Other non-cash movements	**8.2**	2.0	4.1
Changes in working capital	**(85.2)**	(47.9)	(11.9)
Reorganisation provisions	**(2.0)**	(5.7)	(15.9)
Cash flow from operating activities	**135.1**	165.7	392.2

Statement of total recognised gains and losses

39.93 The ASB's statement recommends that a statement of total recognised gains and losses should be included where material gains or losses, other than operating profit or loss, are recognised in the period. [IR para 49]. If revaluations have taken place and are material, or if currency translation differences on foreign currency net investments are material, then a statement of total recognised gains and losses should be presented. Since interim reports are not required to meet all the disclosure requirements of accounting standards, there would not seem to be any need for a statement to be given that there are no recognised gains and losses for the period, other than the profit, if no total gains statement is presented. If, however, the company's accounting policy for statutory financial statements is to revalue assets on an annual, or a less frequent basis, then it should state that there have been no revaluations at the interim stage (see Table 39.1 on page 39008).

39.94 Similarly, where changes in capital and reserves during the interim period differ from the profit or loss for the period and any other recognised gains or losses, then a reconciliation of movements in shareholders' funds should be included in the interim report. [IR para 51]. For example Reckitt & Colman plc includes both a statement of total recognised gains and losses and a reconciliation of movements in shareholders' funds in its interim report shown in Table 39.11 below.

Table 39.11 – Reckitt & Colman plc – Interim Report – 4 July 1998

Other statements (extract)

Statement of total recognised gains and losses For the half-year ended 4 July 1998: unaudited	**1st half 1998 £m**	1st half 1997 £m	Full year 1997 £m
Profit for the period	**112.2**	118.1	215.8
Net exchange gain on foreign currency borrowings*	**8.0**	12.4	16.9
Exchange differences arising on translation of net investments in overseas subsidiary undertakings	**(25.5)**	(33.3)	(26.7)
Total recognised gains and losses relating to the period	**94.7**	97.2	206.0

* Net exchange gain on foreign currency borrowings is stated after deducting UK corporation tax

Reconciliation of movements in shareholders' funds for the half-year ended 4 July 1998: unaudited	**1st half 1998 £m**	1st half 1997 £m	Full year 1997 £m
Total recognised gains and losses relating to the period	**94.7**	97.2	206.0
Ordinary dividends	**(39.5)**	(35.3)	(97.6)
Ordinary shares allotted	**3.2**	5.3	14.0
Goodwill and acquisition costs written-off	**–**	(2.2)	(2.2)
Goodwill reinstated	**–**	–	12.5
Net increase/(decrease) in shareholders' funds	**58.4**	65.0	132.7
Total shareholders' funds at beginning of period	**910.1**	777.4	777.4
Total shareholders' funds at end of period	**968.5**	842.4	910.1

There is £4.5m of non-equity shareholders' funds included within total shareholders' funds.

Comparatives

39.95 The provision of corresponding amounts for the interim profit and loss account is governed by the Stock Exchange, which requires comparative figures for the corresponding six month period in the preceding financial year. [LR 12.52(j)].

39.96 The ASB's statement recommends the presentation of comparative figures for the corresponding interim period and the previous full financial year for the summarised profit and loss account, the statement of total recognised gains and losses where relevant and the summarised cash flow statement. [IR para 55].

39.97 The ASB believes, however, that the critical comparative figures for the balance sheet are those from the last annual financial statements. The statement indicates that these may be accompanied by those from the previous corresponding interim period to highlight the effect of seasonality. [IR para 56].

Non-statutory accounts

39.98 The Act includes rules that apply to the publication of non-statutory accounts, which are not part of the company's full statutory financial statements. Non-statutory accounts are the publication of:

- Any balance sheet or profit and loss account relating to or purporting to deal with a company's financial year.

- An account in any form which purports to be a balance sheet or profit and loss account for the group consisting of the company and its subsidiary undertakings relating to, or purporting to deal with, a company's financial year.

[Sec 240(5)].

Half-yearly reports, *prima facie* do not fall within this definition as the information they give relates to a six month period and not to a full year. If full year figures are given as comparatives, however, then that information could be construed as a non-statutory balance sheet or profit and loss account. Accordingly, the provisions that relate to non-statutory accounts will apply to that information. Further details about the rules concerning non-statutory accounts are included in chapter 38.

Additional information in the form of notes

39.99 Until the publication of the ASB's statement, interim reports of the largest listed companies were likely to contain a summary balance sheet and often contained a summary cash flow and some segmental information. However, they were less likely to encompass notes to the financial statements, such as explanations of significant accounting policies. The ASB's statement recommends including a statement in the interim report confirming that the accounting principles and practices adopted are consistent with those used in preparing annual financial statements. The policies adopted only need to be stated and explained where they differ from those previously adopted.

39.100 In addition to the statement described above, the statement recommends that the following additional information should be included in interim reports:

- The period covered by the interim report.
- The date on which the interim report was approved by the board of directors.
- The extent to which the information it contains has been audited or reviewed.

[IR para 58].

39.101 For an example of an interim report where this information has been included see Table 39.1 on page 39008 above.

Quarterly reporting

39.102 A number of UK companies, principally those whose shares are also listed in the US market, currently prepare quarterly reports as required in the US by the SEC. Quarterly information is more relevant to users since it is more up-to-date and also allows companies to improve control of the release and presentation of information. However, these benefits come at an increased cost in preparing, printing and distributing reports and the Stock Exchange already requires the disclosure of large acquisitions and other price sensitive information.

39.103 The ASB's statement does not address the issue of whether companies should be encouraged to report more frequently. It advises, however, that where companies choose to report quarterly, then the key principles of the statement, although designed in the context of a half-yearly reporting requirement, could also be applied to first and third quarters' statements. The content of first and third quarters' reports would not be expected to be as detailed as half yearly reports. Companies would also have to consider issues such as, for example, the selection of appropriate comparative data.

Preliminary announcements

39.104 Preliminary announcements are issued by companies as a first external communication, to the market, of their financial performance and position for the financial year.

39.105 Preliminary announcements originate from the Listing Rule requirement that quoted companies should notify the Stock Exchange of their preliminary statement of annual results and dividends immediately after board approval. The Stock Exchange requirements for preliminary statements of annual results are detailed below. The ASB issued a draft statement in October 1997, and a final statement 'Preliminary announcements' in July 1998. This statement is a voluntary statement of best practice, in the same manner as the statement on 'Interim reports' and is considered from paragraph 39.106.

Stock Exchange requirements

39.106 Listed companies are required to notify the Company Announcements Office without delay after board approval of certain matters relating to their preliminary statements of annual results and dividends. The Listing Rules require that the preliminary statement of annual results must:

- Have been agreed with the company's auditors.
- Show the figures in the form of a table, consistent with the presentation to be adopted in the annual financial statements for that financial year, including at least the items required for a half-yearly report (see para 39.9 above).
- If the auditor's report is likely to be qualified, give details of the nature of the qualification.
- Include any significant additional information necessary for the purpose of assessing the results being announced.

[LR 12.40(a)]

39.107 In respect of dividends, companies are required to notify the Stock Exchange of any decision to pay or make any dividend or other distribution on listed equity securities or to withhold any dividend or interest payment on listed securities. Details are required of:

- The exact net amount payable per share.
- The payment date.
- The record date (where applicable).
- Any foreign income dividend election, together with any income tax treated as paid at the lower rate and not repayable.

[LR 12.40(c)].

ASB's statement on preliminary announcements

39.108 Interim reports and preliminary announcements have much in common. They both communicate new information about the company's performance and position to the market. Both contain less detail than annual financial statements, but have a significant influence on the market's perception of the company and, accordingly, the information they contain needs to be sufficient, relevant, timely and reliable. Many companies choose to include more information in their preliminary announcements than is required by the Stock Exchange. The ASB has, therefore, published a statement on preliminary announcements, which is intended to promote best practice.

39.109 The objective of the statement is to improve the timeliness, quality, relevance and consistency of preliminary announcements within the constraints of reliability. Compliance with the statement both promotes best practice and increase comparability between preliminary announcements and previously published financial statements. [PA introduction].

Distribution

39.110 Although preliminary announcements tend to be targeted towards financial analysts and institutional shareholders, in principle, to be equitable, all shareholders should be entitled, on request, to have access to the preliminary announcement as soon as it becomes available. The statement notes that receiving a preliminary announcement after the market has reacted to that information is of limited use. It suggests, therefore, that access to preliminary announcement information may be given by use of electronic means, for example *via* the Internet, by pre-registration schemes, or by press advertisements. [PA paras 7, 8]. Indeed listed companies are under an obligation to notify the Stock Exchange of their preliminary announcements and the Exchange in turn disseminates this information using its Regulated News Service.

39.111 Use of the Internet as a means of communication to shareholders is in its infancy. However, although the ASB encourages its use because of its immediacy, it recognises that only a minority of shareholders will gain access to preliminary announcements *via* this route. Consequently, the ASB considers that it is important that all shareholders should, if they wish, be able to obtain a copy of the preliminary announcement as soon as it is issued. The methods that a company can choose to achieve the desired level of distribution include:

- Press advertisements summarising the essential details of the preliminary announcement.
- Pre-registration schemes (for example using reply cards that could be sent out with interim reports).
- Publicising an address or telephone number.
- Notifying shareholders (for example, in the interim report) of the announcement date, so that they can take appropriate action to receive the preliminary announcement

[PA para 8].

Publication timescale

39.112 The Stock Exchange's current requirement is for preliminary announcements to be notified to the Company Announcements Office without delay after board approval of the matters set out in paragraph 39.106 above. As there is a seven-month deadline for public companies to file their financial statements, preliminary announcements could be issued a long time after the year end. The ASB's statement encourages companies to make the information available within 60 days of the year end. It notes, however, that the benefits of early notification need to be balanced against the cost and reliability of collecting and processing such information. At present it is fairly common for preliminary announcements to be issued in the third month after the year end. The ASB statement suggests that companies should consider ways to accelerate their year end reporting timetable if it does not presently meet the 60 day deadline. [PA para 9].

39.113 The ASB's statement also encourages companies to issue their full report and financial statements as soon as practicable after the preliminary announcement has been issued. [PA para 10].

Reliability

39.114 Given that the Listing Rules require the preliminary announcement to have been agreed with the company's auditors before it can be published, there is an expectation that the information it contains will be consistent with that in the audited financial statements. In addition, before publication it is essential that the company's board formally approves the preliminary announcement. To ensure that the preliminary announcement is consistent with the unpublished financial statements the ASB's statement recommends that:

- The audit of the financial statements should be complete or should be at least at an advanced stage of completion at the date of the preliminary announcement.

- All the figures in the preliminary announcement should agree with figures in the audited financial statements or the draft financial statements on which the audit is at an advanced stage.

- The other information and commentary in the preliminary announcement should be consistent with the preliminary announcement itself and with the audited or draft financial statements.

[PA para 12].

39.115 There is a balance to be reached between timeliness of the preliminary announcement and the reliability of the information it contains. The overriding consideration should be that the information presented is reliable and not subject to subsequent alteration. The risk of late changes to the detail in the preliminary announcement is not completely removed unless the full financial statements have been approved by the directors and the auditors have signed their opinion on them when the preliminary announcement is made. [PA para 13]. However, in most cases the main figures and highlights can be released when the audit is at an 'advanced stage' without compromising the reliability of the information in the announcement. This will mean, in practice, that the figures can only be released when any outstanding audit matters are unlikely to have a material impact on the financial statements.

39.116 The Auditing Practices Board issued a bulletin, 'Bulletin 1998/7, The auditors' association with preliminary announcements', which gives guidance to auditors on interpreting the expression 'advanced stage'. The ASB statement does not require a preliminary announcement to include an auditors' report and the APB believes that this is appropriate. But to avoid possible misunderstanding and to make explicit the auditors' agreement to the preliminary announcement the bulletin recommends auditors to issue a letter to the company signifying their agreement with the preliminary announcement.

Non-statutory accounts

39.117 As explained above in paragraph 39.98, the Act includes rules that apply to non-statutory accounts as defined in section 240(5) of the Companies Act. Preliminary announcements clearly fall within the definition of non-statutory accounts and the Act's provisions with regard to publication apply to them. The Act requires a company to make a statement in the non-statutory accounts (that is, its preliminary announcement) whether or not its auditors have reported on the company's annual financial statements for that year. (Further details about the rules concerning non-statutory accounts are included in chapter 38.) Consequently, the ASB's statement recommends that preliminary announcements should clearly state that the audit report has yet to be signed if that is the case. [PA para 15]. The example given in Table 39.12 illustrates a statement when the audit is complete.

Table 39.12 – Racal Electronics plc – Preliminary results for the year ended 31 March 1998

J. Abridged accounts for The preliminary results for the year ended 31 March 1998 are unaudited. The financial information set out in the announcement does not constitute the Company's statutory accounts for the years ended 31 March 1998 or 31 March 1997. The financial information for the year ended 31 March 1997 is derived from the statutory accounts for that year which have been delivered to the Registrar of Companies. The auditors reported on those accounts; their report was unqualified and did not contain a statement under either Section 237 (2) or Section 237 (3) of the Companies Act 1985. The statutory accounts for the year ended 31 March 1998 will be finalised on the basis of the financial information presented by the directors in this preliminary announcement and will be delivered to the Registrar of Companies following the Company's Annual General Meeting.

Accounting policies and prior year adjustments

39.118 The ASB's statement specifies that the accounting policies and presentation adopted in the preliminary announcement should be consistent with that in the full financial statements. This will usually mean that the accounting policies adopted are the same as those used in the last published set of annual financial statements and a statement to this effect should be included in the announcement. If different accounting policies or presentations are used from those used in the last annual financial statements, the exceptions should be specified, even if the differences were adopted in the interim report. Where accounting policies have not been changed from the previous annual financial statements, they need not be repeated in the preliminary announcement.

39.119 If there is a change in accounting policy, the amounts for the current and prior years should be stated on the new policy. The cumulative effect of prior year adjustments resulting from changes in accounting policies or fundamental errors must be disclosed at the foot of the statement of total recognised gains and losses. A description should also be given to explain to users the nature of the change. [PA para 18].

Content

39.120 Although the Stock Exchange only requires preliminary announcements to include profit and loss information and any other significant information needed to assess the company's results, the ASB's statement notes that even prior to its publication, present practice showed a trend towards lengthier preliminary announcements driven by market demands and a desire by companies to communicate effectively and efficiently with their investors. Furthermore, analysts' briefings are now common and it is necessary that the preliminary announcement should include information at least equivalent to that included in such presentations for share price sensitivity reasons.

39.121 With this in mind, the statement advocates that the content of preliminary announcements should be the same as that recommended for interim statements, that is, a preliminary announcement should include:

- A narrative commentary.
- A summarised profit and loss account.
- A statement of total recognised gains and losses.
- A summarised balance sheet.
- A summarised cash flow statement.

[PA para 23]

39.122 Sufficient supplementary information should be given to permit an understanding of the significant items contained within the primary statements. For example, it may be useful to analyse fixed assets into component parts, provide detail on the company's borrowings or state equity and non-equity interests in shareholders' funds in accordance with FRS 4. [PA para 24]. Underlying figures supporting significant events or trends included in the announcement should be given either in the notes or on the face of the profit and loss account. [PA para 25].

Management commentary

39.123 The narrative commentary should explain the primary statements in the context of events and trends since the previous annual report and since the previous interim report. [PA para 22]. The purpose of the commentary is to enable users to appreciate the main factors influencing the company's performance during the year and its position at the year end.

39.124 Reasons for significant movements in key indicators should be explained and perceived trends identified. Whilst not as comprehensive as an operating or financial review (OFR) the commentary should still provide a balanced view to enable users to gain a better understanding of the business. This will include events and changes that are likely to have a significant effect on the succeeding year, even if they have relatively little impact in the current year. It will also cover the nature of any seasonal activity and the impact this has on the business and financial position. [PA paras 27-30].

39.125 The commentary should draw attention to the summarised balance sheet and cash flow statement and should explain significant changes from the last annual financial statements and from the interim report. [PA para 31]. This should include specific reference to movements in working capital, liquidity and net debt, where explanation of these movements is considered necessary for to assist users assessment of the business.

39.126 The preliminary announcement should explain any other matters that the directors believe users would find helpful to understand the report. This might include an explanation of:

- Acquisitions and disposals of major fixed assets and investments made during the year.
- Changes in contingencies, commitments and off balance sheet financial instruments since the previous year-end or since the interim report.
- Material changes in capital structure or financing.
- Events arising after the end of the period.
- The effect of foreign exchange movements during the period.
- The impact of revised actuarial valuations on pension costs.

[PA para 32].

Final interim period

39.127 The preliminary announcement has traditionally focused its attention on presenting the results of the year. However, the market tends to react to any new information or changes that relate to the second half (or fourth quarter if quarterly reporting is used). The second half results have not in the past been reported separately or particularly commented upon. But because of the market focus, the statement recognises that it is important that the salient events and features of the final interim period are referred to an explained as part of the management commentary. The statement, therefore, encourages preparers to include adequate management commentary on the final interim period's results. Furthermore, the statement encourages companies to include separate presentation of the final period figures if this is considered necessary to support the commentary and to assist understanding of the company's performance. [PA para 35]. An example where figures for a final (fourth quarter) interim period have been separately reported is set out in Table 39.13 on page 39043.

39.128 The statement recognises that it will not always be necessary to publish the separate results for the last interim period in tabular form, as it may be possible to give the salient numerical information as part of the narrative explanation. The narrative might include disclosure and explanation of significant changes to figures that were reported in the first period (or previous interim periods where quarterly reporting is used) and of significant changes in estimates of amounts that have been reported in the first interim period.[PA para 35]. This might arise where, for example, a change qualifies as a prior period adjustment and as a result affects the previously reported interim period.

Profit and loss account

39.129 The summarised profit and loss account in the preliminary announcement is the same as recommended for interim reports as set out below:

- Turnover
- Operating profit or loss
- Interest payable less interest receivable (net)
- Profit or loss on ordinary activities before tax
- Tax on profit or loss on ordinary activities
- Profit or loss on ordinary activities after tax
- Minority interests
- Profit or loss for the period
- Dividends paid and proposed

[PA para 36].

The preliminary announcement should distinguish between turnover and operating profit of acquisitions and discontinued operations on the face of the summary profit and loss account to accord with FRS 3. In addition, the statement recommends that there should be separate identification of significant amounts relating to associates and joint ventures. Also exceptional items, together with an explanation, should either be shown on the face of the summary profit and loss account or should be included in the notes. [PA para 40].

39.130 Where segmental information is of crucial importance to investors in aiding their understanding of a company's performance, this information should be disclosed in the notes to the preliminary announcement. The business and/or geographical classifications must follow those given in the full annual financial statements should include:

- Segment turnover, distinguishing inter-segment sales if significant.
- Segmental profit or loss on the same basis as in the annual financial statements.

[PA para 38].

39.131 Where there is a significant difference between the effective tax rate reported in the previous full financial statements and the current year's effective rate, an explanation of the change should be given. In addition, in certain situations it might be necessary to analyse the tax charge further into its significant components, where this aids an understanding of the current year's tax charge. [PA para 39].

39.132 The statement also requires the basic and diluted earnings per share figures to be disclosed calculated in accordance with FRS 14. [PA para41]. Where a company also gives an alternative per share figure in its annual financial statements, based on a different level of earnings, this should also be included in the preliminary announcement in accordance with the rules set out in FRS 3. (See further chapter 8.)

39.133 An example profit and loss statement is given in Table 39.13. This example shows interest receivable and interest payable separately. The ASB statement recommends only a net figure.

Table 39.13 – British Sky Broadcasting Group plc – Preliminary results for the year ended 30 June 1998 and the 3 months ended 30 June 1998

Consolidated results (extract)

	Notes	1998 Year Ended 30 June (audited) £m	1997 Year Ended 30 June (audited) £m	1998 3 months to 30 June (unaudited) £m	1997 3 months to 30 June (unaudited) £m
Turnover	1	1,434.1	1,249.3	374.0	350.1
Operating expenses, net	2	(1,093.5)	(875.3)	(289.1)	(235.9)
Operating profit		340.6	374.0	84.9	114.2
Share of results of joint ventures	3	(16.5)	(10.1)	(5.3)	(2.7)
Profit on ordinary activities before interest and taxation		324.1	363.9	79.6	111.5
Interest receivable and similar income		3.3	1.8	1.4	0.3
Interest payable and similar charges	4	(56.5)	(52.0)	(13.4)	(13.4)
Profit on ordinary activities before taxation		270.9	313.7	67.6	98.4
Taxation	5	(21.7)	(25.7)	(3.4)	(13.9)
Profit on ordinary activities after taxation		249.2	288.0	64.2	84.5

Statement of total recognised gains and losses

39.134 A statement of total recognised gains and losses should be included where material gains or losses, other than reported in the profit and loss account, are recognised in the period. [PA para 42]. An example is given in Table 39.14. A reconciliation of movements in shareholders' funds is only required if other movements need to be explained, for example, where the company has issued shares during the period.

Table 39.14 – Go-Ahead Group Plc – Preliminary results for the year ended 27 June 1998

Consolidated statement of total recognised gains and losses

	1998 £000	1997 £000
Profit for the financial year attributable to members of the parent company	25,745	15,576
Unrealised surplus on revaluation of properties	14,271	–
	40,016	15,576

Balance sheet

39.135 A summarised balance sheet is also recommended to be included in the preliminary announcement. The ASB statement suggests using the annual financial statement headings which accords with the presentation required in the interim report and for a Schedule 4 or 4A entity is as follows:

- Fixed assets.
- Current assets.
  - Stocks
  - Debtors
  - Cash at bank and in hand
  - Other current assets
- Creditors: amounts falling due within one year.
- Net current assets/(liabilities).
- Total assets less current liabilities.
- Creditors: amounts falling due after more than one year.
- Provisions for liabilities and charges.
- Capital and reserves.
- Minority interests.

[PA para 44].

39.136 If other major headings are used in the annual financial statements it is usual to include these in the summarised balance sheet. However, it is not necessary to disclose the detailed share of gross assets and liabilities for joint ventures or the elements of any linked presentation of debtors with the associated non-recourse creditors; these balances may be presented net. Any significant movements in key indicators should also be highlighted in the balance sheet. An example balance sheet format is set out in Table 39.15.

Table 39.15 – Allied Leisure plc – Preliminary results for the year ended 30 June 1998

Group balance sheet (extract)

		30 June 1998		30 June 1997
	£000	£000	£000	£000
Fixed assets				
Intangible assets		134		158
Tangible assets		46,805		43,783
Investments		800		–
		47,739		43,941
Current assets				
Stocks	1,180		1,062	
Debtors	3,838		2,385	
Cash at bank and in hand	197		291	
	5,215		3,738	
Creditors due within one year	(13,653)		(9,494)	
Net current liabilities		(8,438)		(5,756)
Total assets less current liabilities		39,301		38,185
Creditors due after more than one year	(13,821)		(12,253)	
Provisions for liabilities and charges	(601)		(1,273)	
		(14,422)		(13,526)
		24,879		24,659
Capital and reserves				
Called up share capital		5,945		5,902
Share premium account		14,412		14,338
Profit and loss account		4,522		4,419
Shareholders' funds – equity interests		24,879		24,659

Cash flow statement

39.137 Inclusion of cash flow information is recommended by the ASB statement and, where it is given, FRS 1 (revised 1996) should be followed for the preliminary announcements. [PA para 23]. This includes the following presentations:

- Net cash inflow/outflow from operating activities.
- Dividends received from joint ventures and associates.
- Returns on investments and servicing of finance.
- Taxation.
- Capital expenditure and financial investment.
- Acquisitions and disposals.
- Equity dividends paid.
- Management of liquid resources.

- Financing.
- Increase/decrease in cash.

[PA para 45.]

39.138 It is also recommended that other aspects of FRS 1 should be followed such as disclosing the reconciliation of operating profit to operating cash flow , which may be summarised, but should be given in sufficient detail for users to appreciate its chief components. Similarly, a reconciliation should also be given of the movement of cash in the period to the movement of net debt. This reconciliation should include the effects of movements on short-term and long-term borrowings, cash and other components of net debt. [PA para 46].

39.139 An example of a cash flow statement in preliminary announcements, together with the reconciliation of operating profit to operating cash flows and net cash flow to net debt is set out in Table 39.16.

Table 39.16 – PizzaExpress Plc – Preliminary results – 30 June 1998

Group cash flow statement (extract)

	Notes	1998 £'000	1997 £'000
Net cash inflow from operating activities	(1)	27,982	18,382
Returns on investment and servicing of finance			
Interest received		110	116
Interest paid		(417)	(94)
Investment income		21	32
Costs associated with non-equity share issues		(1)	(2)
		(287)	52
Taxation		(576)	(1,360)
Capital expenditure and financial investment			
Purchase of tangible fixed assets		(26,543)	(24,523)
Sale of tangible fixed assets		2,658	2,757
Redemption of shares in fixed asset investment		266	267
		23,619)	(21,499)
Acquisitions and disposals			
Acquisition of a subsidiary undertaking		(6,189)	–
Acquisition of businesses	(7)	(2,844)	(18,654)
Net overdraft and loan acquired with subsidiary		(884)	–
Purchase of interest in joint venture		(55)	–
		(9,972)	(18,654)
Equity dividends paid		(2,351)	(1,718)

Financing			
Issue of equity share capital		128	28,525
Expenses paid in connection with equity share issues		–	(960)
Issue of non-equity share capital		131	162
Redemption of loan notes		(1,045)	–
Capital element of finance lease rental payments		(28)	(46)
		(814)	27,408
(Decrease)/increase in cash	(2)	(9,637)	2,611

(1) Reconciliation of operating profit to operating cash flows

	1998 £'000	1997 £'000
Operating profit	22,561	15,408
Depreciation charges	3,837	2,199
Increase in stocks	(689)	(894)
Increase in debtors	(688)	(522)
Increase in creditors and provisions	2,961	2,191
Net cash inflow from operating activities	27,982	18,382

(2) Reconciliation of net cash flow to movement in net debt

	1998 £'000	1997 £'000
(Decrease)/increase in cash in the period	(9,637)	2,611
Cash outflow from reduction in debt and lease financing	1,080	(4,599)
Change in net debt resulting from cash flows	(8,557)	(1,988)
Net debt at 1 July	(2,649)	(661)
Net debt at 30 June	(11,206)	(2,649)

(3) Analysis of changes in net debt

	1-7-97 £'000	Cash flow £'000	Other non-cash changes £'000	30-6-98 £'000
Cash at bank and in hand	6,812	(1,430)	–	5,382
Overdrafts	(2,740)	(8,207)	–	(10,947)
	4,072	(9,637)	–	(5,565)
Debt due within one year	(6,645)	1,045	–	(5,600)
Finance leases	(76)	35	–	(41)
	(6,721)	1,080	–	(5,641)
TOTAL	(2,649)	(8,557)	–	(11,206)

Comparative figures

39.140 Comparative figures for the previous full financial year should be presented for all the summarised statements. [PA para 47].

Other disclosures

39.141 Other detailed disclosures required by accounting standards do not have to be given in the preliminary announcement. But the ASB's statement recommends that the preliminary announcement should state:

- The period covered by the report.
- The date on which it was approved by the board of directors.

[PA para 49].

Chapter 40

Acquisition of own shares

Page

Chapter 40

Acquisition of own shares

Introduction

40.1 The general rule that prevented a company acquiring its own shares was established in 1887 by the case of *Trevor v Whitworth* on the grounds that such action might amount to 'trafficking' in its own shares or operate as a reduction of capital. The general prohibition, now set out in section 143 of the Companies Act 1985, is that a company cannot acquire its own shares whether by purchase, subscription or otherwise, unless it falls within one of the exceptions specified in section 143(3). However, unlimited companies can reduce their capital or purchase their own shares without restriction if the company is authorised to do so by its articles. For other companies, an acquisition that does not come within the specified exceptions is void and, therefore, has no effect. In addition, there are criminal sanctions available against the company and its officers in such a circumstance.

40.2 The only situations where a company can acquire its own shares are as follows:

- The shares are purchased under section 162 of the Act.
- Redeemable shares are redeemed under section 159 of the Act.
- The acquisition of shares is an authorised reduction of capital under section 135 of the Act.
- The purchase of shares is made under a court order (for example, in a reconstruction).
- The shares are forfeited or surrendered as a result of calls on the shares not having been paid.
- The shares are acquired without the payment of any consideration (for example, a bequest or a gift).

[Sec 143(3)].

40.3 This chapter deals with the first two exceptions and is a practical guide to the accounting rules and the company law requirements concerning the purchase and redemption by a limited company of its own shares. The rules apply also to companies limited by guarantee that have a share capital. It does not, however, deal with the tax implications, which are complex and need to be considered thoroughly before a company embarks on acquiring its own shares.

40.4 If a company follows the statutory procedure when it purchases or redeems its own shares, the prohibition in section 143 will not apply. Non-compliance with that procedure results in a purchase or redemption being illegal and the purported acquisition having no effect. The law in this area is, however, complicated and this chapter gives general guidance by referring to the legal provisions to be considered; it primarily considers the accounting implications of such transactions. It is not, therefore, intended to be a substitute for taking legal advice on specific transactions.

Summary of requirements

40.5 A company's ability to purchase its own shares can have advantages, particularly for private companies. It was often difficult in the past to transfer shares in private companies, with the result that shareholders became 'locked in'. Since 1981, however, a company has been able to use the statutory procedure to purchase its own shares, for example, to remove a dissident shareholder or to enable an outside investor to realise his investment.

40.6 The advantages of being able to purchase own shares are, perhaps, less significant for public companies than for private ones, but they can nonetheless be of real benefit. In particular, public companies are able to return surplus funds to shareholders by purchasing and cancelling some of their shares. Some companies have purchased their own shares to boost their net asset value per share or earnings per share (see for example Table 40.1). Also, this ability provides public companies with flexibility both in ordering their capital structure and in matching that structure to their needs at any stage of their development.

Table 40.1 – Taylor Woodrow plc – Annual Report – 31 December 1994

DIRECTORS' REPORT (extract)

SHARE CAPITAL (extract)
Changes in the company's issued share capital during the year are set out in note 23 on the accounts.

In order to create a more efficient capital structure and enhance earnings per share, thus creating the potential for improved shareholder value in the future, the company implemented the authority granted by shareholders on 27 May 1994 to make market purchases of its own shares.

40.7 The procedural requirements for acquiring own shares are set out in two checklists in the annex at the end of this chapter. The first checklist specifies the general rules when a public or private company purchases its own shares and the second checklist applies to a private company that makes the purchase out of capital.

Redeemable shares

40.8 Many of the requirements in sections 159 to 181 of the Act apply to the redemption of redeemable shares as well as to purchases by a company of shares which are not issued as redeemable. In fact sections 159 to 161 specifically set out the rules that apply to the redemption of redeemable shares and then section 162(2) applies those same rules to the purchase by a company of its own shares. One rule, however, does not apply to a purchase, that is, the terms and manner of purchase need not be determined by the company's articles of association. A company may acquire any of its own shares either by initial agreement, as in the issue of redeemable shares, or by subsequent agreement to purchase, as with a purchase from an existing shareholder.

40.9 In order to issue redeemable shares a company must be authorised to do so by its articles of association. Redeemable shares are those shares that are specifically redeemable under the terms of their issue at the option of the company or the shareholder. [Sec 159]. In this respect, Table A of the Companies (Tables A to F) Regulations 1985 (SI 1995/805)) includes regulation 3 which states that *"subject to the provisions of the Act, shares may be issued which are redeemable or are to be liable to be redeemed at the option of the company or the holder on such terms and in such manner as may be provided by the articles"*. Redeemable shares include shares that are to be redeemed on a particular date, as well as shares that are merely redeemable at the option of either the company or the shareholder.

40.10 The terms and manner of redemption (including the amount payable on redemption and the redemption date) must be set out in the articles of association. [Sec 160 (3)]. Section 133 of the Companies Act 1989 inserted a new section 159A into the Companies Act 1985, but this has not yet been brought into force and is now unlikely to be implemented. In a consultative document in November 1993, the DTI proposed that the amendment contained in section 159A should be repealed and that no further substantive amendment should be made to the existing rules dealing with the redemption of redeemable shares.

40.11 As mentioned above, the provisions that apply to the acquisition of redeemable shares are in the main the same as those that apply to the acquisition of other shares. However, the legal procedures relating to both market and off-market purchases (defined in para 40.64) do not apply to redeemable shares. There are, however, a few additional provisions that apply to redeemable shares and where these apply they are mentioned in the text.

Initial matters to consider

40.12 A public or private company may purchase any of its own shares (including redeemable shares before their date for redemption), provided the company:

- Is authorised to do so by its articles of association, for example, by Regulation 35 of Table A of the Companies (Tables A to F) Regulations 1985 (No. 1985/805). If it has no such authority, a new article must be added by the company by a special resolution in a general meeting. [Sec 162(1)]. Before 1 July 1985 Table A did not contain the necessary authority.

- Is not prohibited from doing so by any pre-emptive provision in the company's articles of association or in a shareholders' agreement or by any similar restrictions on the transfer of its shares by members. This will apply particularly to a private company. Otherwise it will be necessary to seek consent.

- Complies with certain conditions (see para 40.13).

- Follows the appropriate procedure, which depends on whether it is a *market* or an *off-market* purchase (see from para 40.63) or the purchase of a right to purchase (a contingent purchase contract – see from para 40.89). [Secs 163-166].

Conditions for acquisition

40.13 A company must, after the purchase or redemption of its own shares, have other non-redeemable shares in issue. At least two shares must remain for a public company, although it must, after the purchase or redemption, have an allotted share capital which is not less than the authorised minimum (that is, £50,000). If the company is private or limited by guarantee, only one share need remain in issue. The company cannot purchase or redeem any of its own shares that are not fully paid. For example, it would not be possible to purchase a £1 redeemable preference share issued at a premium of £11, where only £5 has been paid on the share.

Consideration for the acquisition

40.14 The terms of purchase or redemption must provide for the shares to be paid for in cash at the time they are purchased or redeemed. They cannot, for example, be paid for by instalments. [Sec 159]. It is also thought that it would not be acceptable for, say, the seller of the shares to loan the company a sum of money equivalent to a deferred instalment on the shares being purchased or for the company to exchange a debenture for shares, because the shareholders have not effectively received payment for the shares.

40.15 It is generally accepted that the term 'purchase' in the context of a company purchasing its own shares, means a purchase of shares for cash. An exchange of shares for other forms of property, such as land, would not be a 'purchase' falling within sections 159 to 181 of the Act. Such a transaction might be possible, however, in the form of a reduction of capital, which would require the approval of the court under section 135.

Accounting and funding requirements

40.16 The accounting and funding requirements of purchases and redemptions of shares can be complex. A purchase or redemption can only be made out of:

- Distributable profits.
- Proceeds of a fresh issue of shares (up to the nominal value of the shares being purchased).
- Share premium (where there is a fresh issue at a premium and the shares being purchased were similarly issued at a premium).
- Capital (where the company is a private company and the above have been exhausted).

These rules are summarised in the paragraphs that follow and dealt with in detail in the body of the chapter.

Acquisition out of distributable profits or proceeds of fresh issue

40.17 Where a company purchases or redeems its own shares, the shares can only be purchased or redeemed out of distributable profits or out of the proceeds of a new issue of shares (called a 'fresh issue' in the Act) made for the purposes of the purchase or redemption. In addition, any premium payable on the purchase or redemption must be paid out of the company's distributable profits. However, if a premium arose on the original issue of the shares being acquired, the premium payable on their acquisition may be funded out of a fresh issue of shares made for that purpose (see further para 40.32). [Sec 160(1)]. 'Distributable profits' are defined in section 181(a) as those profits out of which a company could lawfully make a distribution equal in value to the payment. A private company can additionally fund a purchase out of its capital (see para 40.19).

40.18 Certain other payments relating to a purchase of shares can only be made out of distributable profits. For example, payments in consideration for varying a contract for an off-market purchase of a company's own shares (see para 40.70) or for the release of any obligations under a contract to purchase a company's own shares. [Sec 168(1)].

Payment out of capital

40.19 If the total distributable profits and the proceeds of a new issue of shares (if any) are not sufficient to meet the purchase or redemption price, a private company may make up the shortfall by a payment from 'capital' (that is, otherwise than out of its distributable profits or the proceeds of a fresh issue of shares). [Sec 171]. The conditions that must be complied with before a payment out of capital can be made are considered from paragraph 40.47. Before a payment out of capital can be made one of the conditions that must be fulfilled is that the company must use all its distributable profits and proceeds of any new issue made for the purpose.

40.20 If a company redeems or purchases its shares out of 'capital' without having sufficient distributable profits or, as a private company, without following the statutory procedure, the acquisition will be void as it would be an unlawful reduction of capital. In such a situation, the shares will remain in issue and are deemed to be held by the shareholders who held them at the time of the attempted purchase or redemption was made. If a purchase is made in this way, the company will be liable to a fine and, in addition, the directors will be liable to a fine and/or imprisonment. [Sec 143(2)]. Such a payment out of capital may be an illegal distribution and the directors risk being in breach of their fiduciary duty to the company to act in its best interests.

Summary of basic funding rules

40.21 The basic rules mentioned above are represented in the following diagram. This shows how the purchase or redemption can be funded and is the basis of tables used in each of the examples in this chapter.

PLC		Private company	
Funding of purchase:		Funding of purchase:	
Out of the proceeds of a fresh issue of shares:		Out of the proceeds of a fresh issue of shares:	
1 Nominal value of shares purchased restricted to proceeds of fresh issue	X	1 Nominal value of shares purchased restricted to proceeds of fresh issue	Y
2 Where there is a premium on the shares being purchased and on their initial issue – the premium on purchase restricted to the lower of: (a) initial premium on issue of shares being purchased (b) balance on share premium account including any premium on fresh issue of shares	X	2 Where there is a premium on the shares being purchased and on their initial issue – the premium on purchase restricted to the lower of: (a) initial premium on issue of shares being purchased (b) balance on share premium account including any premium on fresh issue of shares	Y
Total not to exceed the proceeds of the fresh issue	X	Total not to exceed the proceeds of the fresh issue	Y
Balance out of distributable profits	X	Out of distributable profits	Y
Total cost of purchase	X		Y
		Balance out of capital	Y
		Total cost of purchase	Y

Capital maintenance

40.22 Unless it is a private company making an acquisition of its own shares out of capital (see para 40.19), all other companies are required to maintain their capital before and after the acquisition of shares. This generally means that a company has to make a transfer to a capital redemption reserve of an amount equal to the nominal value of the shares that it acquires. [Sec 170(1)]. But where the acquisition is funded wholly or partly by an issue of new shares (a 'fresh issue' of shares) the amount that is required to be transferred to the capital redemption reserve is the difference between the proceeds of the fresh issue and the nominal value of the shares being purchased. [Sec 170(2)]. In this situation, where the acquisition is funded by a fresh issue, the company's capital is still maintained, although some of the capital may now be represented partly by share premium and partly by an amount transferred to the capital redemption reserve.

Cancellation of shares

40.23 The company must treat any shares that it purchases or redeems as being cancelled immediately on acquisition and so the acquisition will reduce the issued (but not the authorised) share capital by the nominal amount of the shares purchased. [Sec 160(4)]. An acquisition will generally be complete when the executed stock transfer form and relevant share certificate are delivered to the company. The shares acquired must then be cancelled and cannot, therefore, be reissued.

Issue of further shares

40.24 Where a company is about to purchase or redeem its own shares, it has the power to issue shares up to the nominal value of the shares to be purchased or redeemed. [Sec 160(5)]. This is because the shares the company acquires have to be cancelled and, as a consequence after the acquisition, the company's shares in issue will remain within its authorised share capital limit (albeit that this limit could have been exceeded for a short period between the issue of the new shares and the cancellation of the shares acquired, but this is allowed under section 160).

Consent from shareholders having priority rights

40.25 Where the capital of the company includes shares that have priority on a return of capital over the shares that the company proposes to purchase, the company will need to obtain consent to a variation of their rights from the holders of the shares that have the priority right.

Effect of acquisition

40.26 Whenever any company wishes to purchase its own shares under the Act and this is not done in proportion to existing shareholdings, the effect of that purchase on the remaining shareholders needs to be considered carefully. For example, the cancellation of the shares purchased will, if no new issue is made, proportionately increase the holdings of the remaining shareholders. This may result in one shareholder or group of shareholders obtaining the power to pass ordinary or special resolutions.

Accounting for acquisitions of shares

Acquisition out of distributable profits

40.27 As explained above, section 160(1) requires that the acquisition of own shares (including any premium paid on the acquisition) must be made out of the company's distributable profits (or out of the proceeds of a fresh issue). An illustration of a company purchasing its own shares out of distributable profits and showing the effect on its balance sheet is given in the example below. The example also illustrates some of the steps a company needs to consider before making such a purchase. The legal procedures for purchasing or redeeming a company's shares are considered from paragraph 40.63 and the disclosure requirements that have to be made in the company's financial statements are dealt with in paragraph 40.41.

Example

Company Z (a private company) is a long established family manufacturing company. Mr Brown (a director of company Z) purchased for £10,000, many years ago, 10,000 of company Z's 100,000 issued ordinary £1 shares. He has now had a major disagreement with his fellow directors about the way in which company Z is run. The directors and the shareholders have agreed that it is in everyone's best interests for Mr Brown to sever his links with the company. He will resign as a director and the company will purchase his shares from him for £24,000 (which is the agreed market value). The company will make the payment out of distributable profits.

At present, company Z's articles of association do not permit it to purchase its own shares. Company Z cannot proceed with the purchase until it alters its articles of association and this will require a special resolution.

In addition, company Z can purchase Mr Brown's shares only under a contract with him. The terms of this contract will need to be authorised by a special resolution of the company before the contract is entered into. (Mr Brown cannot vote on this special resolution.) The company must send a copy of the special resolution to the Registrar of Companies within 15 days of its being passed. The terms of the contract will need to include, amongst other things, a description of, and the number of, the shares to be purchased, the amount of the payment, the date of the purchase and a statement that payment will be made at the time of the purchase. (The company can then purchase Mr Brown's shares at any time after the date of the special resolution to authorise the contract.)

If the special resolution is to be effective, company Z will need to make the contract available for inspection both at its registered office during the 15 days immediately preceding the meeting that will consider the special resolution and at the meeting itself. Within 28 days of the date on which Mr Brown's shares are delivered to company Z, the company will need to make a return to the Registrar of Companies together with any stamp duty payable. The return must be on the prescribed form and it must state the following:

- Class of shares.
- The number and the nominal value of the shares purchased.
- Aggregate amount paid for the shares.
- The date on which the shares were delivered to the company.
- The stamp duty payable.

Furthermore, company Z will need to keep the contract for the purchase at its registered office for ten years from the date of purchase. Throughout this time, the contract must be available during business hours for members to inspect.

In their report attached to the financial statements that relate to the year in which the purchase took place, the directors will have to state the following details in respect of the purchase:

- The number and the nominal value of the shares the company purchased and the percentage of the called-up capital of that description that these shares represent.
- The aggregate consideration the company paid and the reasons for the purchase.

Company Z must treat Mr Brown's shares as being cancelled on purchase and make the necessary entry in the Register of Members. Because the company made the payment out of distributable profits, company Z will need to transfer £10,000 (that is, the nominal value of the shares purchased) to the capital redemption reserve.

Using the table from paragraph 40.21 above, the purchase is made in the following way:

Funding of purchase:	£'000
Out of the proceeds of a fresh issue of shares	-
Balance out of distributable profits	24
Total cost of purchase	24

The effect on the balance sheet of company Z would be as follows, showing the position both before and after the purchase:

Balance sheet	Before purchase	Purchase of shares	Maintain capital	After purchase
	£'000	£'000	£'000	£'000
Share capital	100	(10)		90
Capital redemption reserve	-		10	10
Capital	100	(10)	10	100
Distributable reserves	50	(14)	(10)	26
	150	(24)	-	126
Net assets other than cash	125			125
Cash	25	(24)		1
	150	(24)	-	126

The double entry for this transaction is as follows:

	£'000	£'000
Dr Share capital	10	
Dr Distributable profits	14	
Cr Cash		24
To reflect the purchase of 10,000 £1 shares at a premium of £14,000		
Dr Distributable profits	10	
Cr Capital redemption reserve		10
To maintain the capital of the company		

40.28 It can be seen from the above example that the company's capital has been maintained at £100,000. The company is making the purchase out of distributable profits, as the total debited to distributable profits is £24,000 which equals the consideration for the purchase. Some might argue that the double entry should be to credit cash £24,000 and to debit distributable profits £24,000 and to debit share capital with £10,000 and credit the capital redemption reserve with £10,000, which is the way the Act expresses the purchase in sections 160 and 170. However for clarity, the double entry throughout this chapter shows each step in the process separately: namely the entries for any issue of fresh capital (there are none in the example above); then the entries for the acquisition of the old capital; followed by the entries needed to maintain the company's capital.

Where to charge the purchase cost

40.29 Where a company purchases some of its own shares out of distributable profits, the debit to distributable profits should be shown in the profit and loss account reserve note and, in accordance with FRS 3, in the reconciliation of movements on shareholders' funds (as opposed to the statement of total recognised gains and losses). This is because the charge represents the capital repaid to shareholders and, therefore, is not a recognised loss.

Expenses relating to the acquisition

40.30 The expenses directly relating to the acquisition should be treated as part of the overall cost of acquisition and like the purchase cost itself should be charged to distributable profits and shown in the profit and loss account reserve note (and shown in the reconciliation of movements on shareholders' funds) rather than on the face of the profit and loss account (see Table 40.2).

Table 40.2 – Taylor Woodrow plc – Annual Report – 31 December 1994

27 PROFIT AND LOSS ACCOUNT	Consolidated £m	Company £m
31 December 1993		
- as previously reported	168.9	80.3
- prior year adjustment (page 33)	(11.5)	-
- as restated	157.4	80.3
Exchange differences	(0.7)	-
Write back of dividend in respect of election for shares in lieu of dividend	0.2	0.2
Shares repurchased (including expenses)	(38.5)	(38.5)
Transfer to share premium account	0.3	0.3
Transfers from revaluation reserve	(9.1)	1.5
Balance for the year retained	23.6	11.0
31 December 1994	133.2	54.8

Treatment of irrecoverable ACT

40.31 In certain circumstances, where a company purchases its own shares it might result in the company having irrecoverable ACT that relates directly to that purchase. Under FRS 3, as mentioned above, companies will show the repurchase of shares as an item in the reconciliation of the movements on shareholders' funds. However, the write off of the irrecoverable ACT is a recognised loss rather than a repayment to shareholders and as such must either be reported in the profit and loss account or through the statement of total realised gains and losses (SORG). FRS 3 is silent on this issue, however, we prefer the write off of surplus ACT to be made in the profit and loss account.

Acquisition at a premium out of fresh share issue

40.32 The nominal value of the shares being acquired can, instead of being made out of distributable profits, be funded out of the proceeds of a fresh issue of shares made for the purpose of the acquisition. [Sec 160(1)(a)]. Generally, any premium paid on the shares that the company acquires has to be made out of distributable profits, but where the shares were initially issued at a premium, the company may fund the premium payable on their acquisition (or part of that premium) from the proceeds of a new issue of shares. The amount of premium that can be funded in this way is equal to the lower of the following two amounts:

- The aggregate of the premiums the company received when it first issued the shares it is now purchasing.

- The amount of the company's share premium account after crediting the premium, if any, on the new issue of shares it makes to fund the purchase or redemption.

[Sec 160(2)].

40.33 The example below illustrates a private company that uses the proceeds of a new issue as well as distributable profits to fund the purchase of its own shares and the resulting effect on its balance sheet.

Example

In January 1970, company Y issued 1,000,000 ordinary shares of £1 each, including 100,000 to Mr Green, at a premium of 10p per share. After the issue, the balance on company Y's share premium account was £100,000. In January 1972, company Y utilised the balance of £100,000 on its share premium account to make a bonus issue of shares to its shareholders.

In July 1994, company Y made an issue of 75,000 preference shares of £1 each at a premium of £1 per share for the purposes of purchasing, at a premium of £1.40 per share, Mr Green's 100,000 ordinary shares issued in January 1970. The balance of £90,000 of the purchase price of £240,000 was paid out of the cash resources of company Y.

Using the table in paragraph 40.21 company Y would make the purchase in the way shown below:

	£'000	£'000
Out of the proceeds of a fresh issue of shares:		
Nominal value shares purchased		100
Premium on purchase – the lower of:		
(a) Initial premium on issue of the shares being purchased (100,000 at 10p)	10	
(b) Balance on share premium account including premium on fresh issue of shares (see below)	75	
		10
Total not to exceed proceeds of fresh issue		110
Balance out of distributable profits		130
Total cost of purchase (nominal value plus premium = £2.40 × 100,000)		240

The effect on the balance sheet of company Y is as follows:

Balance sheet	Before purchase	Issue of shares	Purchase of shares	Maintain capital	After purchase
	£'000	£'000	£'000	£'000	£'000
Ordinary shares	1,100		(100)		1,000
Preference shares	-	75			75
Share premium	-	75	(10)		65
Capital redemption reserve *	-			-	-
Capital	1,100	150	(110)	-	1,140
Distributable profits	500		(130)		370
	1,600	150	(240)	-	1,510
Net assets other than cash	1,350				1,350
Cash	250	150	(240)		160
	1,600	150	(240)	-	1,510

The double entry for this purchase is as follows:

	£'000	£'000
Dr Cash	150	
Cr Share capital		75
Cr Share premium		75
To show the issue of 75,000 £1 shares at a premium of £1 per share.		
Dr Share capital	100	
Dr Share premium account	10	
Dr Distributable profits	130	
Cr Cash		240
To recognise the purchase of £100,000 £1 shares at a premium of £1.40 per share.		

* There is no transfer to capital redemption reserve because the nominal value of the shares purchased (that is, £100,000) is less than the aggregate proceeds of the new issue (that is £150,000 – see para 40.38) and, as a consequence, the company's capital has been maintained without the need to make such a transfer. The increase in capital is made up of the £50,000 additional capital arising from the fresh issue of shares and a reduction in capital of £10,000 which represents the amount by which the share premium account has been reduced. This is because of the effect of section 160(2) which allows the share

premium account to be reduced, in the example by £10,000, being the part premium payable on redemption which is allowed to be funded out of the proceeds of the fresh issue of shares as opposed to being made out of distributable profits.

40.34 Table 40.3 below shows the redemption by English China Clays plc of 500 preference shares having a nominal value of $0.5m (£0.3m). The purchase is made out of the proceeds of a rights issue and it can be seen from the reserves note that the payment has been made out of the share premium account and distributable reserves. There is no transfer to the capital redemption reserve, because the proceeds on the fresh issue of shares exceeds the nominal value of the shares redeemed.

Table 40.3 – English China Clays plc – Annual Report & Accounts – 31 December 1993

Notes to the Accounts (extract)

15 SHARE CAPITAL **(a) Ordinary shares** **(i) Authorised and issued**		**£M**
Authorised: 360,000,000 ordinary shares of 25p each		**90.0**
Allotted, called up and fully paid: At 31st December 1992 267,646,174 ordinary shares		66.9
Allotment of 35,243,638 ordinary shares		**8.8**
At 31st December 1993 302,889,812 ordinary shares		**75.7**
	1993	1992
Ordinary shares were issued as follows:		
Rights Issue	**33,497,162**	51,612,153
Scrip dividend elections	**457,457**	425,623
Exercise of share options	**417,055**	323,469
Conversion of 6½% Convertible Bonds Due 2003	**871,964**	241,991
	35,243,638	52,603,236

The shares issued under the Rights Issue, announced on 11th June 1993, were issued at 350p per share and raised approximately **£113.8M** net of expenses. Over 93% of the ordinary shares were taken up and those not taken up were sold on the market. The proceeds of the issue were used to repay US dollar bank borrowings and to redeem the remaining $50M of the US dollar preference shares.

(b) US dollar preference shares

	Authorised, allotted, called up and fully paid $M	£M
At 31st December 1992		
500 preference shares of US$1,000 each	0.5	0.3
Redemption of 500 preference shares	**(0.5)**	**(0.3)**
At 31st December 1993	-	-

The Company completed the redemption of the 500 preference shares on 30th July 1993

16 RESERVES (Extract)

	Group and Company	Group		Company
	Share Premium Account £M	**Revaluation Reserve £M**	**Profit and Loss Account £M**	**Profit and Loss Account £M**
At 31st December 1992 as previously reported	355.1	98.2	298.1	180.8
Prior year adjustment	-	-	(2.2)	
At 31st December 1992 as restated	**355.1**	**98.2**	**295.9**	**180.8**
Issue of ordinary shares	**113.9**	-	-	-
Costs in respect of the Rights Issue	**(3.5)**	-	-	-
Redemption of preference shares	**(32.4)**	-	**(1.1)**	**(1.1)**
Retained profit/(loss) for the year	-	-	**0.5**	**(66.3)**
Goodwill arising on acquisition	-	-	**(155.5)**	
Transfer	-	**(0.3)**	**0.3**	-
Exchange rate movements	**0.1**	**(0.1)**	**(3.4)**	**0.3**
At 31st December 1993	**433.2**	**97.8**	**136.7**	**113.7**

40.35 Table 40.4 also illustrates a purchase out of the proceeds of a rights issue made for the purpose of the acquisition, where the premium payable on redemption is less than or equal to the premium on the issue of the shares being redeemed, in which case the whole of the redemption can be made out of the share premium account. Again no transfer is made to the capital redemption reserve as the proceeds of the new issue exceed the nominal value of the shares being redeemed.

Table 40.4 – BET Public Limited Company – Annual Report – 27 March 1993

Notes to the consolidated accounts (extract)

Note 20 Called up share capital (extract)

ORDINARY SHARES	Considerati on £m	Number million	Aggregate nominal value £m
Beginning of year		747.3	186.8
Allotments under employee share schemes	0.1	0.1	0.1
Rights issue	200.8	186.8	46.7
Total allotments during year	200.9	186.9	46.8
End of year		934.2	233.6

Consideration in respect of the rights issue is shown after deducting costs of £4.7 million

NON-EQUITY US PREFERENCE SHARES	Number	Aggregate Nominal value £m
Beginning of year	5,000	2.9
Redemption during year	(3,800)	(2.0)
Exchange movement	-	(0.1)
End of year	1,200	0.8

US preference shares of US$1,000 were issued at a price of $100,000 per share. During the year the group made a 1 for 4 rights issue and redeemed 3,800 shares at the issue price of $100,000 per share; further details are provided in Note 21 below. On 14th April 1993 the remaining US preference shares were redeemed also at the issue price of $100,000 per share.

Dividends, which were cumulative, were determined every 28 days through auction procedures.

Note 21 Reserves (extract)

	Equity shareholders' reserves					Non-equity shareholders' reserves
	Ordinary share premium £m	Revaluation reserve £m	Other reserves £m	Profit and loss account £m	Associated undertakings £m	Preference share premium £m
Beginning of year	153.2	50.1	(323.4)	42.8	4.3	284.5
Currency adjustments	-	-	-	25.9	0.2	(6.1)
Retained loss	-	-	-	(71.0)	5.9	-
Rights issue (net of costs)	154.1	-	-	-	-	-
Redemption of US preference shares	-	-	-	-	-	(198.7)
Net premium arising on ordinary shares issued	0.1	-	-	-	-	-
Goodwill acquired during the year	-	-	(7.3)	-	-	-
Revaluation of land and buildings	-	(15.9)	-	-	-	-
Disposals of land and buildings	-	(10.5)	-	10.5	-	-
Transfers	-	(0.9)	(145.1)	144.1	1.9	-
End of year	307.4	22.8	(475.8)	152.3	12.3	79.7

As referred to in Note 20, during the year the group made a rights issue of ordinary share capital of £46.7 million with ordinary share premium of £154.1 million (net of costs). The proceeds of the issue amounted to £200.8 million and were used to redeem preference share capital and preference share premium of £2.0 million and £198.7 million respectively, as shown in Notes 20 and 21 above.

Capital maintenance

40.36 The Act requires both public and private companies when they purchase any of their own shares to transfer certain amounts to the capital redemption reserve to safeguard creditors by ensuring that the company's capital is maintained (except to the extent that a private company purchases its own shares out of capital). The capital redemption reserve carries the same restrictions on its use as share capital (so that the ordinary rules regarding the reduction of capital apply to it). One use to which the capital redemption reserve can be put is to pay up unissued shares allotted as fully paid bonus shares (see chapter 19). The Act also contains provisions that enable a private company to use its capital redemption reserve or share premium account or fully paid share capital to fund the purchase or redemption of shares in certain circumstances.

40.37 The provisions explained below relate to the maintenance of capital where a public or a private company purchases or redeems its own shares. These rules are, however extended further for private companies and these additional rules are explained from paragraph 40.55 onwards.

40.38 A transfer to the capital redemption reserve must be made by a company, whether public or private, in the following circumstances:

- Where the company has purchased or redeemed its shares wholly out of distributable profits (that is, where no fresh issue of shares is made and no payment is made out of capital), it must transfer to the capital redemption reserve an amount equivalent to the nominal value of the shares it purchased. [Sec 170(1)]. It also has to reduce the issued share capital by the nominal value of the shares purchased (see example in para 40.27).

- Where a company has purchased or redeemed its own shares wholly or partly out of the proceeds of a fresh issue (that is, where no payment out of capital is made) and the nominal value of the shares purchased (or redeemed) exceeds the amount of the proceeds, the company must transfer the difference to the capital redemption reserve. [Sec 170(2)]. This treatment is illustrated in the example that follows:

Example

Company H decides to redeem 100,000 £1 shares at a premium of £1 (the initial premium on the shares when they were issued was 10p). It also has a further 50,000 ordinary shares in issue which were issued for no premium. Company H makes the purchase partly out of the proceeds of a fresh issue of shares and partly out of its distributable profits. Company H issues 25,000 £1 preference shares at a premium of £1.40 (that is, proceeds of £60,000).

The amount that will need to be transferred to the capital redemption reserve is calculated as follows:

	£'000
Nominal value of shares redeemed	100
Proceeds of fresh issue	60
Amount to be transferred to the capital redemption reserve	40

Following the table in paragraph 40.21, company H makes the purchase in the way shown below:

		£'000	£'000
Out of the proceeds of the fresh issue:			
(a)	Nominal value of shares purchased restricted to proceeds of fresh issue	60	
(b)	Share premium account*	-	60
Balance out of distributable profits			140
Total cost of purchase (nominal value plus premium = £2 × 100,000)			200

* Some might argue that part of the purchase can be made out of the share premium account (£10,000 in the example, being the premium on the issue of the shares being purchased). However, if this argument is pursued, the effect is that the company's capital is reduced by £10,000 and, as a consequence, is not maintained, which is the intention of the Act. This approach can also be said to be wrong on the grounds that the proceeds of the fresh issue are £60,000 and this has all been used funding the purchase of the nominal value of the shares being purchased and as a consequence there is nothing else that can come out of the share premium account.

The effect on the balance sheet of company H is as follows:

Balance sheet	Before purchase	Issue of shares	Purchase of shares	Maintain capital	After purchase
	£'000	£'000	£'000	£'000	£'000
Ordinary shares	150		(100)		
Preference shares	-	25			50
Share premium	10				25
Capital		35			45
redemption	-				
reserve				40	40
Capital	160	60	(100)	40	160
Reserves	150		(100)		10
				(40)	
	310	60	(200)	-	170
Net assets other than cash	150				150
Cash	160	60	(200)		20
	310	60	(200)	-	170

The double entry for the purchase would be as follows:

	£'000	£'000
Dr Cash	60	
Cr Share capital		25
Cr Share premium		35
To show the issue of 25,000 £1 shares at a premium of £1.40 per share.		
Dr Share capital	100	
Dr Distributable profits	100	
Cr Cash		200
To recognise the purchase of £100,000 £1 shares at a premium of £1 per share.		
Dr Distributable profits	40	
Cr Capital redemption reserve		40
To maintain the capital of the company.		

40.39 Table 40.5 below illustrates a simple purchase out of distributable profits and maintenance of capital by the transfer of an amount equal to the nominal value of the shares redeemed to the capital redemption reserve.

Table 40.5 – Redrow Group plc – Annual Report & Accounts – 30 June 1994

Directors' Report (extract)

Repurchase of shares

In the process of flotation, Redrow Group Plc repurchased 2,147,000 of its own ordinary shares of 10p each, representing 1.0% of the post-flotation share capital, for an aggregate consideration of £2,862,000.

1,900,000 were purchased from the Redrow Staff Pension Scheme thereby bringing its level of self-investment within the limits set for listed companies.

247,000 were purchased from P L Pedley who wished to realise part of his investment.

Notes to the Financial Statements (extract)

Note 18. SHARE CAPITAL

	1994	1993 Redrow Holdings Limited
	£000	£000
Authorised:		
280,000,000 ordinary shares of 10p each (1993: 10,000,000)	**28,000**	1,000
Allotted, called up and fully paid	**22,117**	956

Movement in the period was as follows:	Ordinary shares of 10p each	Nominal value £000
The company was incorporated on 2 December 1993 with an authorised share capital of £100 divided into 100 ordinary shares of £1 each, such shares being subsequently divided into 10 ordinary shares of 10p each:	1,000	-
Capitalisation of £892,975 of reserves:	8,929,749	893
Shares issued to minority members of Redrow Holdings Limited:	657,370	66
18 for 1 issue by capitalisation of £17,258,614 of reserves:	172,586,142	17,259
Placing and public offer at 135p per share raising £55,362,219 gross:	41,009,051	4,101
Employee matching offer subscribed by trustees of the Redrow Group Employee Share Plan for a consideration of £177,127:	131,205	13
Cancellation of shares following repurchase for a consideration of £2,862,219 (see Directors' Report)	(2,147,000)	(215)
	221,167,517	22,117

Note 19. (extract) SHARE PREMIUM ACCOUNT AND RESERVES

(a) Group	Share premium account £000	Revaluation reserve £000	Special capital reserve £000	Capital redemption reserve £000	Consolidation reserve £000	Profit and loss account £000
At 1 July 1993	42	355	-	-	-	52,315
Prior year adjustment	-	-	-	-	-	(1,042)
Restated	42	355	-	-	-	51,273
Transfer to special reserve	-	-	4,405	-	-	(4,405)
Premium on shares issued	51,470	-	-	-	-	-
Purchase of own shares	-	-	-	215	-	(2,862)
Share issue costs	(2,290)	-	-	-	-	-
Gift	-	-	-	-	893	-
Profit retained	-	-	-	-	-	12,841
Goodwill	-	-	-	-	-	(420)
Transfer	-	(7)	-	-	-	7
Capitalisation	-	-	-	-	-	(18,152)
	49,222	348	4,405	215	893	38,282

Acquisition at a discount out of fresh share issue

40.40 In certain circumstances, it is possible to make acquisitions of shares at a discount. Where a fresh issue of shares has been made for the purpose of the acquisition, it will still be necessary to maintain the company's capital in accordance with the rules discussed above from paragraph 40.36, by transferring the difference between the amount raised on the fresh issue of shares and the nominal value of the shares being redeemed (if greater) to the capital redemption reserve. [Sec 170(2)].

Example

Company A decides to purchase 100,000 of its £1 shares for £90,000, a discount of 10% (the shares were initially issued at a premium of 10p per share). In addition, there are another 100,000 shares in issue which were issued at par. The purchase is made out of the proceeds of a fresh issue of 45,000 £1 preference shares issued at a premium of £1 (that is, proceeds of £90,000). The company has no distributable profits.

Following the table in paragraph 40.21, the company makes the purchase in the following way:

	£'000
Out of proceeds of fresh share issue:	
(a) Nominal value of shares purchased	90
(b) Share premium	-
	90
Out of distributable profits	-
Total cost of purchase	90

The amount to be transferred to the capital redemption reserve is then calculated as follows:

	£'000
Nominal value of shares purchased	100
Less: Proceeds of fresh issue (restricted)	90
Amount transferred to the capital redemption reserve	10

The balance sheets before and after are shown below:

Balance sheet	Before purchase	Issue of shares	Purchase of shares	Maintain capital	After purchase
	£'000	£'000	£'000	£'000	£'000
Ordinary shares	200		(100)		100
Preference shares	-	45			45
Share premium	10	45			55
Capital redemption reserve	-			10	10
Capital	210	90	(100)	10	210
Reserves	-		10	(10)	-
	210	90	(90)	-	210

Net assets other than cash	210				210
Cash	-	90	(90)		-
	210	90	(90)	-	210

The double entry for the purchase would be as follows:

	£'000	£'000
Dr Cash	90	
Cr Share capital		45
Cr Share premium		45
To show the issue of 45,000 £1 shares at a premium of £1 per share.		
Dr Share capital	100	
Cr Distributable reserves		10
Cr Cash		90
To recognise the purchase of £100,000 £1 shares at a discount of 10 per cent.		
Dr Distributable reserves	10	
Cr Capital redemption reserve		10
To maintain the capital of the company.		

It should be noted that no profit arises on this transaction, although it might appear at first sight that a profit of £10,000 arises on the purchase. This is because no profit is regarded as arising on a transaction with shareholders.

Disclosure requirements

40.41 The company's financial statements have to give various information concerning the shares it purchases during the year, the rights of redemption of any redeemable shares and the authority the company has to acquire any of its shares.

Directors' report

40.42 The directors' report in respect of the year in which the purchase of a company's own shares takes place must include the following details:

- The number and nominal value of the shares purchased or redeemed.
- The aggregate amount of the consideration paid on the purchase.
- The reasons for their purchase.

- The percentage of the called-up share capital that the shares purchased or redeemed represent. 'Called-up share capital' is defined in section 737. See further chapter 31.

[Sec 234, 7 Sch Part II].

40.43 For listed companies, the directors' report should, in addition to disclosing the details in respect of a purchase of own shares, give similar information in respect of any purchases or options or contracts to make such purchases it has entered into in respect of its own shares since the end of the year covered by the report. The company must also include in its financial statements:

- Particulars of any shareholders' authority for the purchase by the company of its own shares existing at the end of the period under review.

- In the case of purchases made off-market or otherwise than by tender or partial offer to all shareholders, particulars of the names of the sellers of the shares purchased or proposed to be purchased during the period under review.

[LR 12.43(n)].

These disclosure requirements also apply to contingent purchase contracts made by listed companies (see para 40.89).

40.44 The disclosure requirements required in the directors' report are illustrated in Table 40.6.

Table 40.6 – M&G Group P.L.C. – Annual Report and Accounts – 30 September 1992

REPORT OF THE DIRECTORS (extract)

Authority for Company to purchase its own shares

At the Annual General Meeting held on 15 January 1992, Members renewed the Company's authority under Section 166 of the Companies Act 1985 to make market purchases on the London Stock Exchange of up to 7,500,000 Ordinary Shares of 25p each of the Company (less the number of Ordinary Shares already purchased by the Company pursuant to previous authorities) at not more than 5% above their average middle market quotation in the London Stock Exchange Daily Official List on the ten dealing days prior to the date of purchase, nor less than 25p each.

Pursuant to this authority and the immediately preceding authority which it replaced, the Company has in the financial year of the Company ended 30th September 1992 purchased an aggregate of 650,000 Ordinary Shares of 25p each having a nominal value of £162,500 (representing 0.85% of the Company's issued share capital as at 30th September 1991) for an aggregate consideration of £3,236,000, an average cost of 498p per share. The

Company considers that these purchases were beneficial to Members as they have resulted in an increase in earnings per share. As a result of these purchases and the purchases of 2,535,000 Ordinary Shares made during previous financial years, the number of shares in respect of which the Company is now authorised to make market purchases has been reduced to 4,315,000 Ordinary Shares of 25p each (representing approximately 5.7% of the present issued share capital of the Company).

The renewed authority given by Members at the last Annual General Meeting for the Company to purchase its own shares expires on 14th July 1993 or (if earlier) at the next Annual General Meeting should a similar resolution be proposed. The Directors believe that it is in the best interests of the Company for the authority to be renewed at the forthcoming Annual General Meeting for a period which shall expire at the end of 18 months from the date of the Meeting or (if earlier) at the next Annual General Meeting if a renewal of this authority is proposed. Accordingly, it is intended to propose, as Special Business, at the forthcoming Annual General Meeting, a Special Resolution to renew the Directors' existing authority to purchase shares of the Company which shall again be limited to 7,500,000 Ordinary Shares of 25p each, less the number of Ordinary Shares pursuant to all previous authorities granted.

Notes to the financial statements

40.45 Where a company's allotted share capital consists of redeemable shares the following information is required, by paragraph 38(2) of Schedule 4 to the Act, to be given in the notes to the company's financial statements:

- The earliest and latest dates on which the company has power to redeem the shares.
- Whether the shares must be redeemed or are redeemable at the option of the company or the shareholder.
- The premium (if any) payable on redemption.

Paragraph 53(3) of Schedule 4 requires the notes to the accounts to contain a separate statement of any amount set aside for the redemption of share capital.

40.46 These disclosure requirements have been added to by the requirements of FRS 4. The standard requires the following information also to be given for redeemable shares which would be classified under FRS 4 as non-equity shares:

- The rights to dividends.
- Their priority and amounts receivable on winding up.
- Their voting rights.

The requirements of FRS 4 are considered further in chapter 18.

Acquisitions out of capital

40.47 The power to purchase or redeem shares out of 'capital' is available only to private companies as an exception to the rules safeguarding the maintenance of capital designed to protect creditors. Even then the company must be authorised by its articles of association and the further stringent provisions of sections 171 to 177 of the Act (referred to in paras 40.93 to 40.106) must be complied with before a payment out of 'capital' is made. These provisions apply equally to the redemption of redeemable shares. There are certain penalties that apply where the Act's provisions are not followed. Paragraphs 40.107 and 40.108 consider the situation where a liability can arise for directors and shareholders where a payment out of capital has been made and the company goes into liquidation within one year of the payment.

40.48 For the purposes of payments made out of capital, 'capital' is any payment by a company from a fund other than its distributable profits and the proceeds of a fresh issue. [Sec 171]. Therefore, a company makes a payment out of capital if it purchases or redeems its shares otherwise than out of distributable profits or the proceeds of a fresh issue of shares. Unrealised profits would be capital for this purpose. Before a payment can be made out of capital, a company must first exhaust its distributable profits and proceeds of any fresh issue.

Permissible capital payment

40.49 The payment that a company may make out of capital when purchasing its own shares is restricted to the permissible capital payment. The 'permissible capital payment' (PCP) is equal to the price of the shares being purchased or redeemed less the aggregate of any available profits and the proceeds of a fresh issue made to fund the purchase. [Sec 171(3)]. The effect of this rule is to require a private company to utilise its available profits and any proceeds arising from a new issue before it makes a payment out of capital. The calculation of the permissible capital payment is represented by the following formula:

PCP = acquisition price – (available profits + proceeds of fresh issue)

Available profits

40.50 The reference to available profits in the calculation of the permissible capital payment is to the company's profits that are available for distribution within the meaning of section 263 of the Act. Under section 263 a private company's profits available for distribution are its accumulated realised profits, so far as not previously utilised by distribution or capitalisation, less its accumulated realised losses, so far as not previously written off in a reduction or reorganisation of capital. However, the question as to whether the company has any profits to use for the purchase or redemption and for the purposes of calculating the permissible capital payment are restricted further by the provisions in section 172(2) to (6) of the Act.

40.51 Under those provisions the amount of the available profits is determined by reference to the items listed in paragraph 40.52 as they are stated in the relevant accounts. The relevant accounts for determining the permissible capital payment are those accounts drawn up as at any date within the period of three months ending on the date of the statutory declaration that the directors are required to make regarding the purchase out of capital (see further para 40.95).

40.52 The items that must be considered in determining whether the company has any distributable profits are as follows:

- Profits, losses, assets and liabilities.
- Provisions for depreciation, diminution in value of assets and retentions to meet liabilities or charges (that is, provisions of the kind mentioned in paragraphs 88 and 89 of Schedule 4 to the Act).
- Share capital and reserves (including undistributable reserves).

[Sec 172(2)].

40.53 The relevant accounts, which need not be audited, must enable a reasonable judgment to be made of the amount of any of the items mentioned above. In order to arrive at the permissible capital payment, any of the 'distributions' mentioned below where lawfully made after the date of the relevant accounts and before the date of the directors' declaration must be deducted from the amount of the company's available profits:

- Financial assistance made out of distributable profits for the purpose of acquiring the company's own shares or its parent company's shares where the assistance comes within sections 154 or 155 (see para 40.133).
- Any payment made out of distributable profits in respect of the purchase of any of the company's own shares.
- Any payment made out of distributable profits in respect of the company's acquisition of rights to purchase its own shares under a contingent purchase contract or the variation of an existing contract of purchase or the release from any obligation relating to such a purchase.

[Sec 172 (4)(5)].

40.54 The example below illustrates the calculation of the permissible payment.

Example

Company × purchases Mr Smith's shares partly out of the proceeds of a new issue of shares, partly out of distributable profits and partly out of capital. The rules can be illustrated as follows:

In January 1970, company × issued 100,000 ordinary shares of £1 each to Mr Smith at their nominal value. It had previously issued 100,000 at a premium of 50p per share. In July 1995 company × has distributable profits of £60,000 and it issues 50,000 ordinary shares of £1 each at a premium of £1 per share for the purposes of purchasing at a premium of £1 per share Mr Smith's 100,000 ordinary shares issued in January 1970.

In these circumstances, the permissible capital payment is calculated as follows:

	£'000	£'000
Price of purchase:		
100,000 £1 shares at a premium of £1 per share		200
Less: Proceeds of issue of 50,000 £1 shares at a premium of £1 per share	100	
Distributable profits	60	160
Permissible capital payment		40

Following the table in paragraph 40.21, the purchase would be made in the following way:

	£'000	£'000
Out of the proceeds of the fresh issue:		
(a) Nominal value of shares purchased	100	
(b) Share premium account*	-	100
Out of distributable profits		60
Balance out of capital		40
Total cost of purchase (nominal value plus premium = £2 × 100,000)		200

* No share premium arises on the issue of the shares being purchased.

The balance sheets would be as follows:

Balance sheet	Before purchase	Issue of shares	Purchase of shares	After purchase
	£'000	£'000	£'000	£'000
Share capital	200	50	(100)	150
Share premium	50	50	(40)*	60
Capital	250	100	(140)	210
Reserves	60	-	(60)	-
	310	100	(200)	210
Net assets other than cash	210			210
Cash	100	100	(200)	-
	310	100	(200)	210

The double entry for the purchase would be as follows:

	£'000	£'000
Dr Cash	100	
Cr Share capital		50
Cr Share premium		50
To show the issue of 50,000 £1 shares at a premium of £1 per share.		
Dr Share capital	100	
Dr Distributable profits	60	
Dr Capital reduction*	40	
Cr Cash		200
To recognise the purchase of £100,000 £1 shares at a premium of £1 per share.		

* The capital reduction should be deducted from a capital redemption reserve or a share premium account or the fully paid share capital or any unrealised profits of the company (see further para 40.59). In the example it has been deducted from the share premium account.

Capital maintenance

40.55 The general provisions concerning capital maintenance are explained from paragraph 40.36, but the rules differ for private companies purchasing or redeeming out of capital as explained in the paragraphs that follow.

Transfer to capital redemption reserve

40.56 Where a private company purchases or redeems its shares with a payment that includes a payment out of capital, the following transfers must be made to the company's capital redemption reserve (CRR):

- If the nominal value of the shares purchased or redeemed *exceeds* the permissible capital payment (where no fresh issue of shares is made), the company must transfer the difference to the capital redemption reserve. [Sec 171(4)].

- If the nominal value of the shares purchased or redeemed *exceeds* the aggregate of the permissible capital payment *and* the proceeds of a fresh issue, the difference must be transferred to the capital redemption reserve. [Sec 171(6)].

40.57 This rule can be represented in the following way:

Transfer to CRR =
nominal value of shares purchased – (PCP + proceeds of fresh issue)

The position where the permissible capital payment plus the proceeds of a fresh issue of shares exceeds the nominal value of the shares purchased or redeemed is considered in paragraph 40.59.

40.58 The example below illustrates the transfer that is required to be made to the capital redemption reserve.

Example

Companies A, B, C and D (all private companies) each purchase 10,000 of their own shares that were originally issued at their nominal value of £1 per share. In each case, a premium of £1.40 per share is payable on purchase. Company B is issuing 7,000 preference shares at par and company D is issuing 4,000 preference shares at par. The retained profits are company A £50,000, company B £30,000, company C £16,000 and company D £15,000. Following the table in paragraph 40.21, the purchases are thus to be made as follows:

	A	B	C	D
	£'000	£'000	£'000	£'000
Out of proceeds of new issue:				
(a) Nominal value of shares purchased restricted to proceeds of fresh issue	-	7	-	4
(b) Share premium	-	-	-	-
	-	7	-	4
Out of distributable profits	24	17	16	15
	24	24	16	19
Balance out of capital	-	-	8	5
	24	24	24	24

In these circumstances, the amount that each company must transfer to its capital redemption reserve is as follows:

	A	B	C	D
	£'000	£'000	£'000	£'000
Nominal value of shares purchased	10	10	10	10
Less: Proceeds of fresh issue	-	7	-	4
Permissible capital payment	-	-	8	5
	-	7	8	9
Transfer to the capital redemption reserve	10	3	2	1

The effect on the summarised balance sheets can be illustrated as follows:

Balance sheets	A	B	C	D
	£'000	£'000	£'000	£'000
Before purchase				
Share capital	100	100	100	100
Distributable reserves	50	30	16	15
	150	130	116	115

Net assets other than cash	125	105	90	80
Cash	25	25	26	35
	150	130	116	115
After purchase				
Ordinary shares	90	90	90	90
Preference shares	-	7	-	4
Capital redemption reserve	10	3	2	1
	100	100	92	95
Distributable reserves	26	13	–	–
	126	113	92	95
Net assets other than cash	125	105	90	80
Cash	1	8	2	15
	126	113	92	95

The double entry for the purchases is as follows:

Company A	£'000	£'000
Dr Share capital	10	
Dr Distributable reserves	14	
Cr Cash		24
To recognise the purchase of £10,000 £1 shares at a premium of £1.40 per share.		
Dr Distributable reserves	10	
Cr Capital redemption reserve		10
To maintain the capital of the company		
Company B		
Dr Cash	7	
Cr Share capital		7
To recognise 7,000 £1 shares issued at par.		
Dr Share capital	10	
Dr Distributable reserves	14	
Cr Cash		24
To recognise the purchase of £10,000 £1 shares at a premium of £1.40 per share.		

Dr Distributable reserves	3	
Cr Capital redemption reserve		3

To maintain the capital of the company

Company C

Dr Share capital	10	
Dr Distributable reserves	14	
Cr Cash		24

To recognise the purchase of £10,000 £1 shares at a premium of £1.40 per share.

Dr Distributable reserves	2	
Cr Capital redemption reserve		2

To maintain the capital of the company (£10,000 less the permissible capital payment of £8,000).

Company D

Dr Cash	4	
Cr Share capital		4

To recognise 4,000 £1 shares issued at par.

Dr Share capital	10	
Dr Distributable reserves	14	
Cr Cash		24

To recognise the purchase of £10,000 £1 shares at a premium of £1.40 per share.

Dr Distributable reserves	1	
Cr Capital redemption reserve		1

To maintain the capital of the company (£10,000 less the permissible capital payment of £9,000).

Nominal value less than PCP and proceeds of fresh issue

40.59 Where shares are purchased or redeemed with a payment that includes a payment out of capital (but not the proceeds of a new issue of shares) and the permissible capital payment exceeds the nominal value of the shares purchased or redeemed, the company may use the excess to reduce one of the following:

- The capital redemption reserve.
- The share premium account.
- Fully paid share capital.
- The revaluation reserve.

[Sec 171(5)].

40.60 Furthermore, even where shares are purchased or redeemed out of the proceeds of a new issue, if the nominal value of the shares being purchased or redeemed is *less* than the permissible capital payment *plus* the proceeds of the new issue, the company may use the excess to reduce the items listed in paragraph 40.59. [Sec 171(6)].

40.61 This rule is represented in the following way:

> Dr to reduce capital =
> PCP + proceeds of fresh issue – nominal value of shares purchased

The position where the permissible capital payment plus the proceeds of a fresh issue of shares is less than the nominal value of the shares purchased is considered in paragraph 40.56.

40.62 The following example illustrates the reduction of the capital redemption reserve and the share premium account to fund the excess.

Example

Companies E and F (both private companies) purchase 10,000 of their own shares that were originally issued at a premium of 10p per share. The nominal value of the shares in question is £1 per share and, in each case, a premium of £1.40 per share is payable. Company F issues 4,000 £1 preference shares at par to make the purchase. Before the purchase both companies have 100,000 £1 ordinary shares in issue and companies E and F have £11,000 and £9,000 distributable reserves respectively. Following the table in paragraph 40.21, the purchases are to be made as follows:

	E £'000	F £'000
Out of proceeds of fresh issue of shares:		
(a) Nominal value of shares purchased restricted to proceeds of fresh issue	-	4
(b) Share premium account	-	-
	-	4
Out of distributable profits	11	9
	11	13
Balance out of capital	13	11
Total cost of purchase (nominal value plus premium = £2.4 × 10,000)	24	24

Acquisition of own shares

In the above circumstances, the aggregate amount by which company E and company F may reduce their capital redemption reserve, the share premium account or the fully-paid share capital is as follows:

	E	F
	£'000	£'000
Permissible capital payment	13	11
Proceeds of new issue	-	4
	13	15
Nominal value of shares purchased	10	10
Excess available	3	5

If companies E and F use the available excess solely to reduce the share premium account, the effect on the summarised balance sheets can be illustrated as follows:

Balance sheet Company E	Before purchase	Issue of shares	Purchase of shares	After purchase
	£'000	£'000	£'000	£'000
Ordinary shares	100	-	(10)	90
Share premium	10		(3)	7
Capital	110	-	(13)	97
Distributable reserves	11	-	(11)	-
	121	-	(24)	97
Net assets other than cash	96	-		96
Cash	25	-	(24)	1
	121	-	(24)	97

Balance sheet Company F	Before purchase	Issue of shares	Purchase of shares	After purchase
	£'000	£'000	£'000	£'000
Ordinary shares	100	-	(10)	90
Preference shares	-	4	-	4
Share premium	10	-	(5)	5
Capital	110	4	(15)	99
Distributable reserves	9	-	(9)	-
	119	4	(24)	99

Net assets other than cash	83	-	-	83
Cash	36	4	(24)	16
	119	4	(24)	99

The total reduction in capital in both examples equals the permissible capital payment (that is, £13,000 for company E and £11,000 for company F).

The double entry for the purchases is as follows:

Company E	£'000	£'000
Dr Share capital	10	
Dr Distributable reserves	11	
Dr Capital (share premium account)	3	
Cr Cash		24
To recognise the purchase of £10,000 £1 shares at a premium of £1.40 per share.		
Company F		
Dr Cash	4	
Cr Share capital		4
To show the issue of 4,000 £1 preference shares at par.		
Dr Share capital	10	
Dr Distributable reserves	9	
Dr Capital (share premium account)	5	
Cr Cash		24
To recognise the purchase of £10,000 £1 shares at a premium of £1.40 per share.		

Legal procedures for purchase

40.63 The procedures that a company must follow if it wishes to purchase its own shares will depend on whether the purchase is to be an 'off-market' purchase or a 'market' purchase. Certain initial matters to consider are mentioned in paragraph 40.12.

Definition of 'off-market' and 'market'

40.64 A company's purchase of its own shares is an *off-market* purchase if either of the following apply:

- The shares are not purchased on a recognised investment exchange. The Stock Exchange is a recognised investment exchange for this purpose.

- The shares are purchased on a recognised investment exchange, but are not subject to a marketing arrangement on that investment exchange.

[Sec 163(1)].

Any other purchase is a *market* purchase.

40.65 Shares are subject to a marketing arrangement where either they are listed on the Stock Exchange or they can be dealt with on the Stock Exchange without prior permission for individual transactions from the authority governing the Stock Exchange and without time limit as to when those dealings can take place.

40.66 An off-market purchase will, therefore, *exclude* both a purchase of shares with a full listing on the Stock Exchange and a purchase of shares traded on the AIM.

40.67 A company can make an off-market purchase only where the terms of the proposed contract of purchase have received prior authorisation by the shareholders under section 164 (see para 40.73) or as a contingent purchase contract under section 165 (see para 40.89). The purchase by a private or an unquoted public company of its own shares will normally be an off-market purchase (see paras 40.79 and 40.73). A listed company will purchase its own shares either as an off-market purchase or a market purchase depending on the circumstances (see para 40.69).

Purchases by public companies

40.68 As discussed above, the statutory procedure that a public company should follow will depend on whether the purchase will be a market purchase or an off-market purchase.

Authority for market purchase

40.69 A market purchase by a listed public company of its own shares must first be authorised by ordinary resolution of the company in general meeting. The authority may be general or specific to a class or description of shares and unconditional or subject to conditions. The authority, however, must:

- Specify the maximum number of shares authorised to be acquired.

- Determine both the maximum and the minimum prices that may be paid for the shares. It may do this by specifying a particular sum or providing a basis or formula for calculating the amount of the price as long as the amount can be calculated without reference to any person's discretion or opinion.

- Specify a date not more than 18 months from the date of the resolution on which the authority is to expire. The terms of the authority may permit a purchase to be made after its expiry if the contract of purchase was concluded before the authority expired.

[Sec 166].

40.70 The authority may be varied, revoked or renewed at a company's general meeting by an ordinary resolution, but the company must comply with the conditions in paragraph 40.69 above. [Sec 166(4)]. A copy of any resolution giving, varying, revoking or renewing an authority to make a market purchase of a company's own shares must be sent to the Registrar of Companies within 15 days of the resolution being passed. [Secs 380, 166(7)].

40.71 Two important differences exist between the authority for a market purchase and the authority for an off-market purchase. With a market purchase, it is the purchase of the shares that requires approval in the form of the authority of the company in general meeting. With an off-market purchase, a specific purchase contract (rather than the shares to be purchased) must be approved and it must be approved by special resolution. The authority for a market purchase need not relate to any particular shares and it need be approved only by an ordinary resolution. However, this less stringent statutory requirement is supplemented for listed companies, first by the Stock Exchange's Listing Rules and secondly by the insider dealing provisions referred to in paragraph 40.81. Furthermore, the Investments Committee of the Association of British Insurers has also made recommendations regarding market purchases (see further para 40.131).

Authority for an off-market purchase

40.72 In the case of a public company, the special resolution giving the necessary authority mentioned in para 40.73 must specify a date not later than 18 months from the date of the resolution, on which the authority is to expire. [Sec 164].

40.73 A company may make an off-market purchase of its own shares only if it does so under a contract the terms of which have received prior authorisation by a special resolution at a general meeting of the company. [Sec 164]. Subsequently, this authority may be varied, revoked or renewed by a further special resolution. A similar authority must be obtained by a special resolution before a company can enter into a contingent purchase contract (see para 40.89). The special resolution giving the necessary authority must specify a date not later than 18 months from the date of the resolution on which the authority is to expire. [Sec 164].

40.74 The special resolution that confers the authority on the company to enter into a contract to purchase its own shares (or to authorise a contingent purchase contract) or to vary or to revoke or renew such authority will not be effective in the two situations described below.

40.75 First, the special resolution will not be effective where a shareholder to whom the resolution relates exercises his voting rights on the shares that are subject to the acquisition in voting on the resolution and the resolution would not have been passed if he had not voted. For this purpose the following will apply:

- a member who holds shares to which the resolution relates is regarded as exercising the voting rights carried by those shares not only if he votes in respect of them on a poll on the question whether the resolution shall be passed, but also if he votes on the resolution otherwise than on a poll;
- notwithstanding anything in the company's articles, any member of the company may demand a poll on that question; and
- a vote and a demand for a poll by a person or a proxy for a member are the same respectively on a vote and a demand by the member.

[Sec 164(5)].

40.76 Secondly, the resolution will not be effective unless a copy of the contract or, if it is not in writing, a written memorandum of its terms giving the names of the members whose shares are to be purchased, is available for inspection. The contract or memorandum must be available for inspection by members at the company's registered office for not less than 15 days ending on the day of the meeting of the company at which the resolution is to be passed and at the meeting itself. The memorandum must include the names of the members to which the contract relates and the contract must also have annexed to it a memorandum specifying any such names that do not appear on the contract itself. [Sec 164(6)]. In addition, the same procedure must be followed where there is a variation of any existing contract including a contingent purchase contract.

40.77 A copy of each special resolution passed by the company, including one passed as a written resolution, must be sent to the Registrar of Companies in the usual manner within 15 days of its being passed. [Sec 380].

Variation of existing contract

40.78 Where a company wishes to vary any of the terms of an existing contract to purchase its own shares, or the terms of a contingent purchase contract, there is a similar requirement for a special resolution and for the provisions described in paragraphs 40.73 to 40.77 to be complied with. [Sec 164(7)]. A payment in consideration of the variation of a contract approved under section 164 or section 165 must be made out of distributable profits. If this is not done, the purchase itself will be unlawful. [Sec 168(1)(b), (2)(b)].

Purchases by private companies

40.79 Paragraphs 40.73 to 40.78 set out the procedures to be followed for an off-market purchase when a public company proposes to purchase its own shares. However, unlike for public companies, a private company's special resolution giving the necessary authority does not have to specify a date on which the authority expires. In addition, where a private company makes a payment out of capital it must comply with the provisions referred to from paragraph 40.93.

40.80 Where a company uses a written resolution to authorise the purchase, or to vary such a contract or contingent purchase contract, the provisions of paragraph 5 of Schedule 15A apply. That is, a shareholder whose shares are the subject of the written resolution is not allowed to sign it and each relevant member must be supplied with a copy of the contract and the names of the vendors before signature. (Written resolutions are dealt with fully in chapter 38.)

Insider dealing

40.81 The provisions relating to the criminal offence of insider dealing are now contained in Part V of the Criminal Justice Act 1993 which has replaced the Company Securities (Insider Dealing) Act 1985. The provisions prohibit certain dealings in the shares and other securities (such as debt securities) of listed companies; and directors of such companies should be aware of the provisions of this Act that might affect a company's acquisition of its own shares. For example, if the directors are in possession of inside information and the company's shares are price-affected in relation to that information they may be guilty of insider dealing if they procure the company to buy, or to agree to buy, its shares. In addition, the directors and the company will be bound by the Stock Exchange Model Code (see para 40.121).

Returns and contracts

40.82 Following the completion of the purchase of its own shares a company must make certain returns under the Act. No later than 28 days after the delivery of shares to it, the company, whether public or private, must deliver a return in the prescribed form to the Registrar of Companies stating with respect to each class the number and nominal value of the shares purchased and the date they were delivered to the company. The form also requires the amount of stamp duty payable to be specified. Additionally, a public company must state the aggregate amount paid for the shares and the maximum and minimum prices paid in respect of shares of each class purchased. [Sec 169(2)]. Failure to file the form is a criminal offence and the directors in default are liable to a fine.

40.83 Both private and public companies must keep a copy of each contract for an off-market purchase or contingent purchase contract they enter into, together with any variations to any such contracts. These documents must be kept at the company's registered office from the date the contracts are concluded until the end of a period of ten years from the date of the purchase to which they relate. A private company must make a copy of such a contract available for inspection by any member without charge. A public company making an off-market purchase must similarly keep a copy of the contract available for inspection not only by any member, but also by any other person. [Sec 169(5)].

40.84 A public company that makes a market purchase must keep a copy of each contract for a purchase authorised by the company in general meeting, together with any variations to it. Again these must be kept at the company's registered office from the date the contract is concluded until the end of a period of ten years from the date of the purchase to which it relates. Similarly, a public company must make any such contract available for inspection not only by members, but also by any other person.

40.85 If any contract is not in writing, the company must keep a memorandum of its terms at its registered office and make that available instead of a copy of the contract. A company's obligations in relation to making the contracts and memoranda available for inspection by members and non-members are set out in the Companies (Inspection and Copying of Registered Indices and Documents) Regulations 1991 (SI 1991/1998).

40.86 For redeemable shares, within one month of redemption the company must give notice on the appropriate form, to the Registrar of Companies specifying the shares redeemed. [Sec 122 (1)(e)].

Prohibition on assignment of rights

40.87 The rights of a public or private company under a contract to make a market or an off-market purchase of its own shares or a contingent purchase contract cannot be assigned. This prohibition is designed to prevent a company from speculating against its own share price by buying or selling its rights to purchase its own shares. [Sec 167(1)].

40.88 An agreement by a company to release all or any of its rights under a contract to make an off-market purchase of its own shares or a contingent purchase contract is void unless the terms of the release are approved in advance by a special resolution of the company before the contract is entered into. The procedures referred to in paragraphs 40.72 to 40.77 and 40.79 apply to a company when seeking approval for the release as they apply to a proposed variation. [Sec 167(2)]. A payment made in consideration for the release of the company's obligations must be paid out of distributable profits or the release will be void. [Sec 168].

Contingent purchase contracts

40.89 A contingent purchase contract is defined in section 165 of the Act and is, briefly, a contract under which a company may (subject to any conditions) become either entitled or obliged to purchase its own shares. A contingent contract does not represent a contract to purchase those shares, but may give the company an option to purchase them or the shareholder the option to require their purchase by the company. Such a purchase contract might arise, for example, where a shareholder is prepared to maintain an investment in a company only if there are arrangements that ensure that he will be able to sell his shares back to the company at any time in the future. In this circumstance, the company may not wish to issue a new class of redeemable shares in order to satisfy the shareholder's wishes. Instead, it may prefer to make a contractual arrangement with the shareholder under which the company may purchase the shares at a later date at the shareholder's option. Similarly, a contingent purchase contract would include, for example, a contract under which a company may be obliged to purchase an employee's shares on his retirement.

40.90 The use of contingent purchase contracts to buy a company's own shares may be open to abuse unless they are accompanied by certain safeguards for other shareholders. The approach of the Act is to treat contingent purchase contracts as if they were off-market contracts of purchase, that is, to require the same full range of safeguards for shareholders that apply to off-market contracts (see para 40.72).

40.91 A company may only purchase its own shares under a contingent purchase contract if the terms of the contract have been approved in advance by a special resolution of the company before the contract is entered into. Such approval may be varied or revoked or renewed by a subsequent special resolution.

40.92 The prohibition on assignment by a company of its rights under a purchase contract referred to in paragraph 40.87 or the release of its rights under a purchase contract set out in paragraph 40.88, apply also to a contingent purchase contract. [Sec 167]. A payment in consideration of acquiring any right under a contingent purchase contract must be made out of distributable profits, or the purchase will be unlawful. [Sec 168].

Acquisitions out of capital

40.93 To make a payment out of capital, the company must be a private company and must be authorised to do so by its articles of association. (See Companies (Tables A to F) Regulations 1985 (SI 1985/805) Table A Regulation 35.)

40.94 The payment out of capital must be approved by a special resolution of the company in general meeting (see para 40.103). [Sec 173(2)]. Alternatively, the company may by written resolution obtain the unanimous agreement of all shareholders. However, in that situation, paragraph 6 of Schedule 15A to the Act will apply instead of paragraph 5 of that schedule. This means that a member holding shares to which the resolution relates is not entitled to sign the resolution.

Statutory declaration

40.95 The directors of a company proposing to make a payment out of capital must make a statutory declaration in the prescribed form. [Sec 173]. The form requires the directors to declare:

- Whether the company's business is that of an authorised institution, an authorised insurance company or some other business.

- That the company is proposing to make a payment out of capital.

- What the amount of the permissible capital payment for the shares in question will be.

40.96 The form also requires the directors to declare that they have made full enquiry into the affairs and prospects of the company and formed the opinion that both the following apply:

- As regards its initial situation immediately following the date the payment out of capital is proposed to be made, that there will be no grounds on which the company could then be found unable to pay its debts.

- As regards its prospects for the year immediately following that date, that, having regard to the directors' intentions for the management of the company's business during that year and to the amount and character of the financial resources that will in their view be available during that year, the company will be able to continue to carry on business as a going concern (and will accordingly be able to pay its debts as they fall due) throughout that year.

[Sec 173(3)].

40.97 In forming their opinion on the first point in the paragraph above, the Act states that directors must take into account the same liabilities (including prospective and contingent liabilities) that would be relevant under section 122 of the Insolvency Act 1986 to the question of whether a company is unable to pay its debts. A company will be deemed unable to pay its debts, for the purposes of section 122, if the value of the company's assets is less than the amount of its liabilities (taking into account its contingent and prospective liabilities). However, there is some doubt as to whether 'taking into account' means that the full value of all such liabilities should be included or only the amount of those liabilities that are likely to crystallise immediately and in the following 12 months. This is an area where a company's directors should take legal advice.

40.98 The overall policy of the legislation may be summarised as being to produce a situation where, at the end of the day creditors are not going to be prejudiced by the company continuing in business after making a payment out of capital. Consequently, if directors are in doubt as to whether their company would be able to pay all its debts if all the company's prospective and contingent liabilities were included in assessing its solvency, they should take legal advice before making the statutory declaration. If the company becomes insolvent the directors may incur certain penalties. For instance, under section 76 of the Insolvency Act 1986 a director has a liability to contribute to the company's assets if it is wound up within a year of the payment out of capital, unless he can show that he had reasonable grounds for forming the opinion set out in the declaration. See further paragraph 40.107.

40.99 It is a criminal offence (punishable by a fine and/or imprisonment) for a director to make a declaration without having reasonable grounds for the opinion expressed in the declaration. The directors should, therefore, arrange for financial statements to be prepared to enable the calculation of the permissible capital payment and arrange for properly worked out cash flow projections to support the opinion required to be expressed in the statutory declaration.

Auditors' report to the directors

40.100 The directors' statutory declaration must have attached to it a report by the company's auditors addressed to the directors stating that:

- The auditors have enquired into the company's state of affairs.

- The amount specified in the declaration as the permissible capital payment for the shares in question is, in the auditors' view, properly determined in accordance with sections 171 and 172.

- The auditors are not aware of anything to indicate that the opinion expressed by the directors in the declaration as to any of the matters mentioned in paragraph 40.96 is unreasonable in the circumstances.

[Sec 173(5)].

Procedure for acquisition

40.101 The special resolution for the payment out of capital mentioned in paragraph 40.94 must be passed by the company either on the same day as, or within one week after, the date on which the directors make the statutory declaration. The resolution will be ineffective in the following circumstances:

- If any member holding shares to which the resolution relates exercises the voting rights carried by any of those shares in voting on the resolution and the resolution would not have been passed if he had not done so.

  In considering whether a sufficient number of votes have been cast on a show of hands or a poll, sections 174(3) and 174(5) contain similar provisions to those described in paragraph 40.76 in relation to section 164(5).

- If the statutory declaration of solvency and the auditors' report attached to it are not available for inspection by members at the meeting at which the resolution is passed. This means that the directors must liaise with the company's auditors at an early stage, to ensure that they can obtain the auditors' report by the date on which the special resolution is to be passed.

[Sec 174].

40.102 The company must make the payment out of capital between five and seven weeks after the date of the resolution. This ensures that members and creditors who wish to object have time to apply to the court under section 176 (see para 40.103). This period cannot be shortened even if all members agree. The accounts required which are mentioned in the following diagram are discussed in paragraph 40.51.

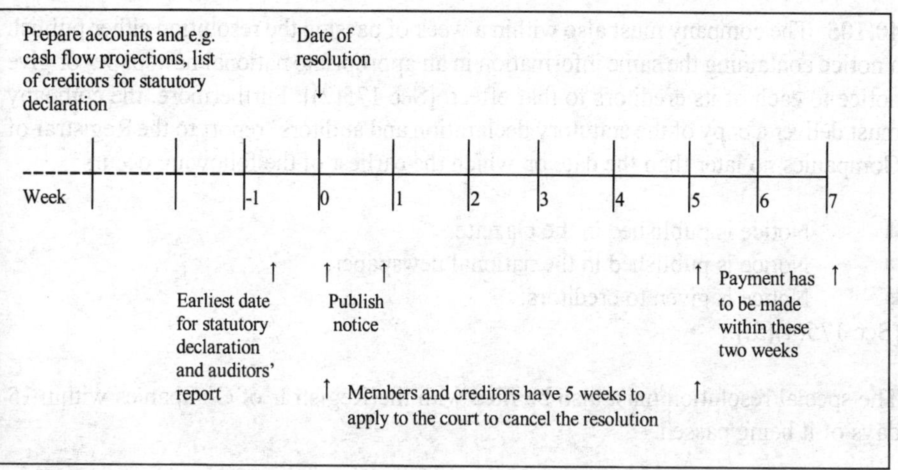

40.103 Where a resolution is passed approving a payment out of capital, any member (other than one who voted in favour of the resolution) and any creditor may within five weeks of the date on which the resolution is passed apply to the court to cancel the resolution. [Sec 176]. The court's powers are set out in section 177. The company is obliged to give notice to the Registrar of Companies if an application is made. [Sec 176(3)].

Publication of notice of acquisition

40.104 Within a week of passing the resolution for payment out of capital referred to in paragraph 40.94 the company must publish a notice in the London Gazette (for companies registered in England and Wales) or in the Edinburgh Gazette (for companies registered in Scotland) giving the following details:

- A statement that the company has approved a payment out of capital for the purpose of purchasing or redeeming its own shares.
- The amount of the permissible capital payment.
- The date of the resolution.
- A statement that the statutory declaration and the auditors' report are available for inspection at the company's registered office.
- A statement that any creditor of the company may, at any time within five weeks after the date of the resolution, apply to the court for an order that prohibits the payment (as discussed in para 40.103).

[Sec 175(1)].

40.105 The company must also within a week of passing the resolution either publish a notice containing the same information in an appropriate national newspaper or give notice to each of its creditors to that effect. [Sec 175(2)]. Furthermore, the company must deliver a copy of the statutory declaration and auditors' report to the Registrar of Companies no later than the date on which the earliest of the following occurs:

- Notice is published in the Gazette.
- Notice is published in the national newspaper.
- Notice is given to creditors.

[Sec 175(4)(5)].

The special resolution must also be filed with the Registrar of Companies within 15 days of it being passed.

40.106 The statutory declaration and auditors' report must be open to inspection by members and creditors without charge during business hours at the company's registered office for five weeks beginning with the date of the resolution for the payment out of capital. Failure to do so renders the company and every officer in default liable to a fine and the court can compel an immediate inspection. [Sec 175(6)-(8)]. (See also the Companies (Inspection & Copying of Registered Indices & Documents) Regulations 1991 (SI 1991/1998) for the obligations of companies in relation to inspection.)

Liability on winding up

40.107 Under section 76 of the Insolvency Act 1986, if a company is wound up within a year of making a payment out of capital in respect of a purchase or redemption of its shares and it proves to be insolvent, any shareholder whose shares were purchased or redeemed and the directors who signed the statutory declaration are liable to contribute to the assets of the company. However, a director will be exempt from such a liability if he can show that he had reasonable grounds for forming the opinion stated in the statutory declaration.

40.108 The liability of a person whose shares were redeemed or purchased to contribute to the assets of the company is limited to the amount of the payment out of capital he received when the company purchased his shares. Where this applies, the company's directors are jointly and severally liable with the past shareholder for that amount. A shareholder or director who has contributed to the assets of the company under section 76 of the Insolvency Act 1986 has certain rights to claim against any other person who is jointly and severally liable. A shareholder whose shares have been redeemed or purchased with a payment out of capital and who is, therefore, potentially liable to contribute to the assets under section 76, has the right, in order to limit his liability and prevent further loss to the assets, to petition for winding up. The grounds of the petition would be either that the company is unable to pay its debts or that it is just and equitable for the company to be wound up. [Sec 124(3) Insolvency Act 1986].

Failure to acquire shares

40.109 Where a company has agreed to purchase or redeem any of its shares and then fails to do so, the affected shareholder cannot sue the company for damages. However, this does not affect any other right that the shareholder has, except that a court will not order specific performance of the contract if the company shows that it cannot meet the costs of purchasing the shares in question out of distributable profits. [Sec 178(2)(3)].

40.110 If a company is liable to purchase or redeem shares, but has failed to do so at a time when it goes into liquidation, the terms of the purchase or redemption can be enforced against it. However, this will only apply if:

- Under their terms, the purchase or redemption was to take place before the winding up commenced.
- The company would have had distributable profits equal to the purchase or redemption price.

[Sec 178(5)].

40.111 Payments to creditors and to members who have preferred rights, however, will have priority in the winding up. [Sec 178(6)]. The shares purchased or redeemed must then be cancelled.

Requirements of regulators and other bodies

Stock Exchange

40.112 A listed company proposing to purchase its own shares must comply with the relevant conditions set out in chapter 15 of the Listing Rules Purchase of own securities. That chapter distinguishes between 'equity shares' (which include warrants or options to subscribe or purchase equity shares) and 'securities other than equity shares' (which include debt securities, preference shares or securities convertible into or exchangeable for equity shares). The latter securities are subject to more limited notification and other requirements. The relevant rules are described below.

Purchase of equity shares

40.113 The company must notify the Stock Exchange immediately the board decides to submit to the company's shareholders a proposal that the company should be authorised to purchase its own equity shares. The notification should indicate whether the proposal relates either to specific purchases (giving the names of the persons from whom the purchases are to be made) or to a general authorisation to make purchases. The company should immediately notify the Stock Exchange of the outcome of the shareholders' meeting and should as soon as possible forward to the Stock Exchange six copies of the relevant resolutions. [LR 15.1]. However, see paragraph 40.122 as to the timing of the purchase.

40.114 A circular seeking shareholders' authority need not be submitted for approval to the Stock Exchange (but any timetable included therein must be approved) unless it falls into one of the categories described in paragraph 40.115 and 40.116 below. The circular must include full details of proposals. In addition, where the authority the company seeks relates to specific proposals, the names of the shareholders who will be parties to the proposed contract should be stated in the circular. Where the board is seeking a general authority to purchase equity shares in the market, the board should state its intentions with regard to the authority. The board should notify shareholders of the method by which the company intends to acquire its equity shares and the number to be acquired in that way. [LR 15.2].

40.115 Where the purchase of equity shares is from a related party (for example, a director or a substantial shareholder or their associate) the circular to shareholders should be in accordance with the customary Stock Exchange procedure for such transactions and the company in general has to seek the shareholders' specific approval. [LR 15.3]. The circular must contain the information required by paragraph 11.10 of the Listing Rules as well as the information described in paragraph 40.114 above.

40.116 Where the company would purchase 15 per cent or more of its issued equity shares if it exercised fully the authority it seeks, the circular to shareholders must include:

- The company's name, registered office and if different the head office (as required by LR 6.C.1).
- The name of any person (excluding directors) who hold three per cent or more of the company's capital and their holding. If there are no such holdings this should be stated (as required by LR 6.C.16).
- A description of any significant change in the group's financial or trading position (as required by LR 6.E.8).

- A statement that the working capital available to the group is sufficient for the group's present requirements (as required by LR 6.E.18). This statement should assume that the authority sought to purchase the company's shares will be used in full at the maximum price allowed and this assumption must be stated.

- A note showing directors' interests (and interests of connected person of a director) in the company's shares (as required by LR 6.F.4,5).

- Information on the group's prospects for at least the current financial year (as required by LR 6.G.1(b)).

[LR 15.4].

40.117 Where there are in issue convertible securities or warrants or options to subscribe for equity shares of the class proposed to be purchased, the company must hold a separate class meeting of the holders. The purpose of the meeting is to obtain the shareholders' approval by extraordinary resolution before the company either enters into any contract to purchase its equity shares of any class or first exercises a general authority to make purchases in the market. However, the company does not require such approval where there are provisions in the relevant trust deed or terms of issue permitting the company to purchase its own equity shares. [LR 15.11].

40.118 The circular containing the notice of meeting required by the preceding paragraph must comply with the requirements for all circulars. In addition, it must set out clearly the apparent effect, in terms of attributable assets and earnings, on the expectations of the holders on conversion or subscription if the company were to exercise fully the authorisation that it seeks to purchase its own shares at a maximum price or a fixed price. In addition, any special adjustments that the company may propose should be set out and the information concerning the effect should be restated on the revised basis. [LR 15.12].

40.119 Where the company proposes to purchase 15 per cent or more of its equity shares within a period of 12 months, it must make these purchases by way of either a tender offer or a partial offer to all shareholders. [LR 15.7]. The company should make the tender offer on the Stock Exchange at a stated maximum price or at a fixed price. In addition, the company should give notice of the offer by means of a paid advertisement in two national newspapers at least seven days before the offer closes. [LR 15.8].

40.120 Where a company purchases less than 15 per cent of its equity shares within a 12 month period it may make the purchase through the market in the ordinary way, provided the price paid is not more than five per cent above the average of the market value of the shares for the ten business days before the purchase is made. [LR 15.6].

40.121 The Stock Exchange Model Code for securities transactions by directors of listed companies should be regarded as applying to a company's purchase of its equity shares. [LR 15.5]. Consequently, a listed company should not purchase its equity shares at any time when its directors would not be free to do so on their own account. One of the basic principles of the Code is that directors will always be thought to be in possession of more information than can be published and, therefore, should not deal at the times mentioned in the Code, even if they would not be prohibited from doing so by statute or common law. For instance, the Code says that dealings should not normally take place in the two months preceding the announcement of the annual and the half-yearly results (or, if shorter, the period from the relevant financial period end up to and including the time of announcement). The director should not sell shares during such periods, unless the circumstances are exceptional, (for example, where a pressing financial commitment has to be met). The statutory provisions relating to insider dealing relating to the purchase by a company of its own shares are briefly dealt with in paragraph 40.81.

40.122 The company should notify to the Stock Exchange all of its purchases of its equity shares as soon as possible and in any event by 8.30 am on the business day following the day of the purchase. The notification should include the date of purchase, the number of shares purchased and either the purchase price per share or the highest and the lowest prices paid. [LR 15.9]. Details of these notifications will appear in the Stock Exchange Weekly Official Intelligence. These provisions do not apply, however, to transactions entered into in the ordinary course of business by securities dealing businesses or transactions entered into by the company or other group member on behalf of third parties. [LR 15.10]. Consequently, this provision would allow the company not to notify the Stock Exchange where it purchases shares on behalf of (say) its employees for an employee share ownership plan (ESOP).

Purchase of non-equity shares

40.123 Where a listed company intends to make a proposal, which is to be open to all holders in respect of all or part of their holdings, to purchase any of its listed securities other than equity shares, it must:

- While the proposal is being actively considered, ensure that no dealings in the relevant securities are carried out by or on behalf of the company, until the proposal has either been notified to the Stock Exchange or abandoned.

- Notify the Stock Exchange of its decision to purchase, unless the purchases will consist of individual transactions in accordance with the terms of issue of the securities.

[LR 15.13].

40.124 Purchases and redemptions of the company's own listed securities (other than equity shares) by or on behalf of the company must be notified to the Stock Exchange when an aggregate of ten per cent of the initial nominal amount of the securities has been purchased or redeemed and for each five per cent in aggregate of the initial nominal amount acquired thereafter. Such notifications must be made as soon as possible and in any event no later than 8.30 am on the business day following the calendar day on which the dealing occurred to reach or exceed the relevant threshold. The notification must state the nominal amount of the securities acquired, redeemed or cancelled since the last such notification, the nominal amount of the securities remaining outstanding and whether or not the securities acquired are to be cancelled. [LR 15.14].

40.125 In circumstances where the purchase of own securities in not being made pursuant to a general offer and the purchase causes a relevant threshold to be reached or exceeded, no further purchases may be effected until after a notification to the Stock Exchange has been made as per the preceding paragraph. [LR 15.15].

40.126 In the case of securities which are convertible into, exchangeable for or carrying a right to subscribe for equity shares, unless a tender or partial offer is made to all holders of the class of securities on the same terms, purchases must not be made at a price more than five per cent above the average of the market values for the securities for the five business days immediately preceding the date of purchase. [LR 15.17].

Redemption of redeemable shares

40.127 Listed companies must additionally comply with the following Stock Exchange requirements where redemptions of securities are concerned:

- Any drawing or redemption of listed securities must be notified to the Stock Exchange immediately. Particulars to be given prior to any drawing should include the amount and date of drawing and, in the case of a registered security, the date of entitlement. After any drawing has been made particulars of the amount of the security outstanding should be supplied. Purchases to meet the sinking fund requirements of the current year need not be notified. [LR 9.10(d)(e)(f)]. (A company may set aside a predetermined sum annually by way of sinking fund to ensure that it has the amount required on the final redemption date. The terms of issue of the shares may permit the company to use the sinking fund to make partial redemptions by purchasing a part of the issue in the market at any time, normally at a price no greater than their nominal value. Furthermore, the provisions of FRS 4 have an impact on the accounting treatment of redeemable shares as these are classified as non-equity under that standard (see further chapter 18).

- Articles of Association. The articles of a company that is not subject to the Companies Act 1985 (such as a company incorporated outside the UK) must contain the provisions specified by paragraph 23(c) of appendix 1 to chapter 13 of the Listing Rules where power is reserved to purchase for redemption a redeemable share. This provides that purchases should be limited to a maximum price which, in the case of purchases through the market, is not to exceed five per cent above the average market value. The market value is defined as the middle market quotation for that security as derived from the Daily Official List for the relevant date. [LR definitions]. If purchases are made by tender, tenders should be available to all shareholders alike.

Trust deeds and listed debt securities

40.128 Trust deeds and similar documents must provide that during the existence of conversion rights no purchase by the company of its own shares shall take place, unless it has been sanctioned by an extraordinary resolution at a separate class meeting of the holders of the convertible securities. [LR 13 app 2 para 4(a), 15.11].

Panel on Takeovers and Mergers

40.129 Whenever any public company (and some private companies) wishes to redeem or purchase its own voting shares (or take authority from their shareholders to do so), it should consider the City Code and discuss the matter in advance with the Panel on Takeovers and Mergers. The City Code applies to all public companies as well as to private companies that have had some public involvement in the ten years before the purchase.

40.130 The rules governing Substantial Acquisition of Shares ('the SARs'), issued on the authority of the Panel on Takeovers and Mergers, regulate acquisitions that result in holdings of shares and rights over shares relating to 15 per cent or more, but less than 30 per cent of the voting rights in a company. 'Rights over shares' is defined to include any rights acquired by an agreement to purchase shares or an option to acquire shares. The SARs apply normally only to companies incorporated in the UK and listed on the Stock Exchange. A person is not required to notify the Stock Exchange under Rule 3 of the SAR if the change in his holding results only from the redemption or purchase by a company of its own shares. (However, a subsequent acquisition may trigger the operation of the rule.) In other circumstances, a person must notify the Stock Exchange by 12 noon on the next business day of the total holding he has acquired.

Institutional shareholders

40.131 The interests of large institutional shareholders are represented by investor protection committees that issue guidelines on matters of concern to shareholders. The Investments Committee of the Association of British Insurers has made certain recommendations on the subject of a purchase by a company of its own shares, but no formal guidelines have been published. They request that a special resolution is given for a market purchase, that the authority to purchase shares is renewed annually and that the effect on earnings per share, capital and dividend cover should be considered. They also request that companies undertake in the document that the authority to purchase its own shares will only be exercised if to do so would result in an increase in earnings per share and is in the best interests of shareholders generally.

40.132 The institutions are unlikely to object to small purchases (up to five per cent of the issued equity share capital in any one year). Hence it is common for such approval to be sought at each annual general meeting. Between five and ten per cent, enquiries may be raised as to any special features which might make the proposal undesirable. Above ten per cent, prior consultation should take place or support for the resolution will depend on the circumstance.

Financial assistance for acquisition of shares

General requirements

40.133 A company is not permitted by section 151 to give financial assistance for the acquisition of its shares. However, a purchase or redemption by a company of its own shares in accordance with the relevant provisions in sections 159 to 181 is stated by the exemption in section 153(3)(d) not to fall within the prohibition relating to financial assistance. However, in spite of this exemption, it is thought that the source of the monies out of which the purchase or redemption is made is important. Thus, if the company makes the payment with borrowed monies, there is a risk that it will not be covered by the exemption and the company may be giving financial assistance for the acquisition of its own shares. As a result, where a company is borrowing to fund the purchase and grants security for the borrowing, the giving of security or payment of interest may amount to financial assistance by the company. As there are criminal penalties for giving illegal financial assistance, it is, therefore, advisable for a company to consider the financial assistance provisions of sections 151 to 158 and to take legal advice.

40.134 Subject to the exemptions set out below the general rule is that companies cannot give, either directly or indirectly, financial assistance for the purpose of acquiring their own shares or the shares of their holding company. This applies to financial assistance given:

- Both before or at the same time as the acquisition.
- For the purpose of reducing or discharging after acquisition a liability incurred by any person for the purpose of the acquisition.

[Sec 151].

40.135 The above provisions do not prohibit the following transactions for a public company provided that it has net assets that are not thereby reduced or the reduction is provided out of distributable profits [Sec 153(4)]:

- Lending of money by a company in the ordinary course of its business.
  - Provision of financial assistance for an employees' share scheme.
  - Provision of financial assistance to enable or facilitate transactions in the company's shares by employees, former employees or their families.
- Loans to employees (who are not directors) to enable them to acquire beneficial ownership of fully paid shares in the company.

[Sec 154].

Giving financial assistance by these means would result in a reduction in the company's net assets if provision had to be made in the financial statements for the resultant debt. However, provided this reduction was made out of distributable profits, the financial assistance would be allowed.

40.136 The prohibition in section 151 does not apply if the company's principal purpose in giving financial assistance is not to give it for the purpose of acquiring shares, or the assistance given is an incidental part of some larger purpose of the company and the assistance is given in good faith and in the interests of the company. [Sec 153(1)(2)]. In the case of *Brady v Brady* [1989] AC 755 the House of Lords drew a distinction between the purpose of a transaction and the reason for which it was undertaken. It decided that a larger purpose was not the same as a more important reason and, therefore, even though the financial or commercial advantages of the transaction were possibly the most important reason for providing the assistance, they could not constitute part of the larger purpose. It is thought that the effect of this judgement is to severely reduce the usefulness of the exemptions in the sections.

40.137 The above provisions do not prohibit the following transactions, even though they may effectively represent financial assistance:

- Distributions made as a lawfully paid dividend or made in the course of winding up.
- Allotment of bonus shares.
- Reduction of capital confirmed by court order.
- Redemption or purchase of own shares made in accordance with sections 159-181 of the 1985 Act (see above).
- A scheme of arrangement between the company and its members or its creditors under section 425 or an arrangement under section 110 or Part I of the Insolvency Act 1986.

[Sec 153(3)].

Private companies

40.138 A private company may give financial assistance for the purchase of its own shares or, if its parent company and any intermediate parent companies are all private companies, its parent company's shares, provided that:

- The company's net assets are not thereby reduced or the reduction is provided out of distributable profits. [Sec 155(2)]. Section 154(2) applies for the interpretation of this section. It should be noted that for the purpose of calculating net assets, the company's assets and liabilities are to be taken at the amount at which they are stated in the company's accounting records immediately before the financial assistance is given.
- Before the financial assistance is given the company's directors make a statutory declaration in a presented form that immediately after the financial assistance has been given there will be no grounds on which the company, if it is intended to be wound up within 12 months, will be found unable to pay its debts within 12 months of the commencement of the winding up or, in any other case, the company will be able to pay its debts as they fall due during the next 12 months. Where the shares acquired or to be acquired are those of the company's parent the directors of that company and of any intermediate parent company must also make an equivalent statutory declaration. [Secs 155(6),156(1)-(3)].
- The statutory declaration has annexed to it a report by the auditors of the

company to the directors stating that they have enquired into the company's state of affairs and that they are not aware of anything to indicate that the directors' opinion is unreasonable in all the circumstances. [Sec 156(4)].

- The giving of financial assistance is approved by a special resolution passed in general meeting within one week of the statutory declaration. However, a special resolution is not required where the company is a wholly-owned subsidiary. Where the shares to be acquired are those of the parent company, approval by that company (and any partly owned intermediate parent company) by special resolution in general meeting is also required. [Secs 155(4)(5), 157(1)]. The statutory declaration and auditors' report thereon must be available for inspection at the meeting at which the resolution is passed. [Sec 157(4)].

- The financial assistance is not given before four weeks after the special resolution (if required) is passed or after eight weeks from the date of the statutory declaration. [Sec 158].

40.139 The statutory declaration, the auditors' report thereon and a copy of the special resolution passed (if applicable) must be delivered to the Registrar of Companies within 15 days after the passing of the resolution or, if no resolution is necessary, after the making of the statutory declaration. [Sec 156(5)].

Effect of contravention of section 151

40.140 The holders of not less than ten per cent of the company's issued shares or any class thereof who had either not consented to, or not voted in favour of, the special resolution may apply to the court for the resolution to give financial assistance to be cancelled. The court may make an order on such terms as it thinks fit either confirming or cancelling the resolution. [Sec 157(2)].

40.141 Where a company gives financial assistance in contravention of section 151, it is liable to a fine and every officer of it who is in default is liable to imprisonment and a fine. In addition, the transaction is void so that any property transferred is irrecoverable. The effect of a loan made in contravention of the prohibition in section 151 was considered in a recent case, *Coulthard v Neville Russell* (a firm) (New Law Digest 27 November 1997 No 2971117205).

40.142 The facts in the case were that the subsidiary had made a loan to its parent to enable the parent to repay loans which financed the purchase of the subsidiary's shares. The subsidiary subsequently went into insolvent liquidation and the Secretary of State brought proceedings seeking disqualification orders against the directors of the subsidiary. The directors in the meantime brought an action against the subsidiary's auditors alleging that the auditors owed them a duty of care to warn them that the loans were or might be in breach of section 151, and that, as a consequence of the loans' illegality, the financial statements would not give a true and fair view if they were included as assets. The auditors appealed that the proceedings disclosed no cause of action.

40.143 In the case the Court of Appeal considered the effect of a loan made in breach of the prohibition in section 151. A loan made for the purpose of giving financial assistance contrary to the prohibition in section 151 is illegal and unenforceable against the borrower. It follows that the loans made in contravention of the section cannot, properly, be treated as assets of the lending company and that a balance sheet in which such a loan is shown as the company's asset will fail to give a true and fair view of its financial affairs.

40.144 The Court of Appeal dismissed the appeal, without wishing to express any view that the directors' claim would succeed, on the basis that the directors had at least an arguable case against the auditors. The case highlights the importance of identifying potential financial assistance at an early stage by obtaining legal advice.

[The next page is 40059.]

Annex – Checklists for the acquisition of own shares

Checklist 1 – General requirements

For use where a public company or a private company purchases its own shares (excluding Stock Exchange and taxation considerations). The section references are references to the relevant sections of the Companies Act 1985.

Conditions to be satisfied

1. Do the company's articles of association authorise it to purchase its own shares? If not, is an article (including, in the case of a private company, authorisation to make a payment out of capital) being added by special resolution? [Secs 162(1), 171(1)].

2 Are there any rights under the Articles attached to classes of shares which would require the approval of the proposed purchase by the holders?

3 Are there any restrictions in shareholders' agreements or trust deeds which would restrict the proposed purchase?

4 Have the tax implications been considered?

5. After the purchase, will the company have at least two shares (one share in the case of a private company) in issue that are not redeemable? [Sec 162(3)].

6. After the purchase, will the company have at least two members (one member for a private company – see para 40.13)?

7. After the purchase, will a public company's allotted share capital be equal to or exceed the authorised minimum required by the Act? [Sec 11].

8. Are the shares to be purchased fully paid? [Secs 159(3), 162(2)].

9. Do the terms of purchase provide for payment in full to be made at the time that the shares are purchased? [Secs 159(3), 162(2)].

10. Is the payment by a *public* company either out of distributable profits or out of the proceeds of a new issue of shares the company has made for the purposes of the purchase? [Sec 160].

11. Is the payment by a *private* company made out of distributable profits or out of the proceeds of a new issue of shares the company has made for the

purposes of the purchase or out of capital? [Secs 160(1), 171]. (Note: Checklist 2 deals with payments out of capital.)

12. Is the premium, if any, that is payable on the purchase correctly treated (see para 40.32)? [Sec 160(1)(2)].

13. Have the shares been cancelled on purchase? [Sec 160(4)].

Procedures for market purchases (public companies)

14. Has the proposed purchase been authorised by an ordinary resolution of the company in general meeting (see para 40.69)?

15. Does the authority (see para 40.69):

- Specify the maximum number of shares that may be acquired?
- Determine both the maximum and the minimum prices that the company may pay for the shares?
- Specify the date on which it expires? Also, is this date within 18 months of the date of the resolution?

16. Has any variation to the authority been authorised by an ordinary resolution?

17. Has a copy of any resolution been sent to the Registrar of Companies within 15 days of its being passed (see para 40.70)?

Procedures for off-market purchases

18. Have the terms of the proposed contract been authorised by a special resolution (see paras 40.73 and 40.79)?

19. Has any proposed variation to an existing contract been authorised by a special resolution?

20. Does the authority given by a special resolution of a public company specify a date on which the authority expires and is that date no later than 18 months from the date of resolution?

21. For the special resolution to be effective, have certain documents been made available for inspection (see paras 40.76 and 40.79)?

22. Has a copy of the special resolution been filed within 15 days (see paras 40.77 and 40.79)?

Disclosure of a company's purchase of its own shares

23. Within 28 days of the date that shares purchased are delivered to the company, has the company sent a return in the prescribed form to the Registrar of Companies together with any stamp duty payable (see para 40.82)? [Sec 169(1)].

24. Is the company aware that it has to keep certain documents at its registered office for ten years? [Sec 169(4)].

25. Will the directors' report in respect of the year in which the purchases took place include details of the purchases (see para 40.42)? [Sch 7 Part II].

Maintenance of capital

25. Has the company made the appropriate transfer to the capital redemption reserve (see para 40.38)? (Alternatively, see para 40.56 where a payment out of capital has been made.) [Secs 170, 171].

Checklist 2 – Purchases made out of capital

For use where a private company purchases its own shares out of capital. The section references are references to the relevant sections of the Companies Act 1985.

1. Do the company's articles of association authorise it to make a payment out of capital? If not, is a suitable article to be added by special resolution (see para 40.94)? [Sec 171(1)].

2. Does the payment not exceed the permissible capital payment (see paras 40.49 to 40.54)? [Sec 171(3) to (6)].

3. Has the company prepared accounts as necessary to enable a reasonable judgement to be made for the purposes of the purchase (see paras 40.51-40.53)? [Sec 172(2),(3)].

4. Are these accounts prepared as at a date not more than three months before the date of the statutory declaration mention in 5 below (see para 40.51)? [Sec 172(6)].

5. Have the directors of the company made a statutory declaration within three months from the end of the period covered by the accounts in the prescribed form (see para 40.95)? [Sec 173(3)(4)].

6. Have the auditors made a report addressed to the directors (see para 40.100)? [Sec 173(5)].

7. Has the payment been approved at a general meeting by a special resolution passed on, or within one week after, the date on which the directors made the statutory declaration (see paras 40.94 and 40.101)? [Secs 173(2), 174(1)].

8. Were the statutory declaration and auditors' report available for inspection at the meeting (see para 40.101)? [Sec 174(4)].

9. Have copies of the statutory declaration, auditors report and special resolution been filed within the appropriate period (see para 40.105)? [Secs 175(5), 380(4)].

10. Is the payment to be made not earlier than five weeks, nor later than seven weeks, after the date of the resolution (see para 40.102)? [Sec 174(1)].

11. Has the company given the required publicity in respect of the payment (see paras 40.104 to 40.106)? [Sec 175].

Chapter 41

Financial instruments including derivatives

Page

Chapter 41

Financial instruments including derivatives

Introduction

41.1 Over the past ten years or so, the use of financial instruments by companies, and the complexity of those instruments, have increased remarkably. Many large companies now actively manage their risk using swaps, forward contracts and other such derivatives, but until recently the financial statements of such companies often gave only very limited disclosure of the use of these techniques.

41.2 There have been a number of examples of what were perceived to be conservatively-managed organisations incurring substantial losses because they failed to appreciate, monitor and control the risks created by the use of financial instruments. Such problems give financial instruments, and in particular derivatives, a reputation for increasing risk when in fact many are designed specifically to reduce or eliminate exposure to risk and achieve this when used properly.

41.3 At the heart of these well-publicised losses were internal control failures. One of the responses to this has been a call for tighter accounting rules to be set for financial instruments.

41.4 This is not exclusively an issue for the UK. In the US the FASB has developed over a number of years standards dealing with certain disclosure aspects of financial instruments. The IASC has also had a project on the subject and published its disclosure standard IAS 32 in June 1995. Both the FASB and IASC have been working concurrently on projects dealing with the measurement and recognition of financial instruments. The FASB published a standard on accounting for derivatives and hedging activities, FAS 133, in June 1998.

41.5 The IASC, slightly lagging behind, but trying to be more comprehensive, is developing a standard on recognition and measurement on all financial instruments, not just derivatives and hedging transactions. It issued a discussion paper 'Accounting for financial assets and financial liabilities' in March 1997. But following considerable debate on these proposals, it was clear that it would be almost impossible to secure agreement on a definitive standard by the end of 1998, being the target date for completion of its core standard programme. As a result it issued in June 1998 E62 'Financial instruments: recognition and measurement'. In respect of derivatives and hedging, E62 includes similar rules to FAS 133.

41.6 In the UK, in February 1996, the British Bankers' Association (BBA) and the Irish Bankers' Federation (IBF) jointly issued a SORP setting out recommendations for the accounting treatment and disclosure of derivatives in the financial statements of banks.

41.7 In June 1996 the ASB issued its discussion paper on derivatives and other financial instruments, which covered not only disclosure but also dealt with recognition, measurement and hedge accounting. This was followed by the publication in April 1997 of FRED 13, a draft financial reporting standard on the subject of disclosure of financial instruments. In July 1997 a supplement to FRED 13 was issued following consultation by the ASB with UK banks, which dealt with derivative and other financial instrument disclosure by banks and similar institutions. The ASB's standard on disclosure of derivatives and other financial instruments, FRS 13, was published on 24 September 1998 and applies primarily to listed companies and to all banks for accounting periods ending on or after 23 March 1999, but early adoption is encouraged.

41.8 FRS 13 requires entities within its scope to provide both narrative and numerical disclosures. The narrative disclosures describe the role that financial instruments (including derivatives and certain commodity contracts) have in creating or changing the risks faced by an entity, including its objectives and policies in using financial instruments to manage those risks. The numerical disclosures are intended to show how those objectives and policies were implemented in the period and provide supplementary information for evaluating significant or potentially significant exposures. Together these disclosures should provide a broad overview of the entity's financial instruments and of the risk positions created by them, focussing on the risks and instruments that are of greatest significance.

41.9 This chapter concentrates on the disclosure requirements set out in FRS 13. However, the other matters dealt with in the ASB's discussion paper on the recognition and measurement of financial instruments are summarised from paragraph 41.83.

Scope of FRS 13

41.10 FRS 13 applies to all entities that have any of their capital instruments (generally shares and debt) listed or publicly traded on a stock exchange or market (domestic or foreign). [FRS 13 paras 3, 119]. In addition, all banks and similar financial institutions (for example building societies), whether quoted or not, must make the required disclosures. [FRS 13 para 82].

41.11 The FRS sets different rules for non-financial entities, for banks and for other financial institutions that are not banks. The last category includes leasing companies, investment and unit trusts, money brokers and 'in-store' credit card companies. [FRS 13 para 119]. Although the required narrative disclosures are common to all entities the reporting entity's classification determines the type of numerical disclosures that should be given. Accordingly, the standard is split into three parts:

- Part A deals with disclosures for quoted reporting entities other than banks and other financial institutions.

- Part B deals with disclosures for all banks and similar institutions.

- Part C deals with disclosures for quoted non-bank financial institutions.

As the Manual of Accounting does not deal with banks and similar institutions or non-bank financial institutions, this chapter considers only the disclosures required for other reporting entities as set out in Part A of the standard.

41.12 The FRS does not apply to insurance companies or groups. However, the ASB is expected to add to its work programme a project on certain aspects of insurance accounting, which will include consideration of the disclosures that should be provided on derivatives and other financial instruments. [FRS 13 App VII para 19]. Entities to which the standard does not apply are encouraged, but not required, to comply with it. For example, compliance would be sensible for entities seeking a listing of their equity or debt.

41.13 Unquoted entities and subsidiaries, unless they are banks or similar institutions, need not comply. Moreover, a quoted parent company is not required to give the disclosures in its own financial statements if they are given on a group basis in its accompanying consolidated financial statements. [FRS 13 para 3(b)].

What is a financial instrument?

41.14 Although the media coverage of the losses to which reference is made above has directed public attention towards the use, and perhaps misuse, of derivatives, the accounting standard setters are working on projects applicable to all financial instruments. The ASB has defined a financial instrument as *"...any contract that gives rise to both a financial asset of one entity and a financial liability or equity instrument of another entity"*. [FRS 13 para 2]. This is almost identical to the definition given in IAS 32. Examples include:

- Cash, including foreign currency.
- Deposits, debtors, creditors, notes, loans, bonds and debentures.
- Finance lease obligations.
- Shares, options and warrants.
- Derivatives that are to be settled in cash or by another financial instrument (that is, commodity contracts are generally excluded, but see para 41.18).

- Contingent liabilities that arise from contracts and, if they crystallise, are to be settled in cash (for example, a financial guarantee).

41.15 A derivative is specifically defined as *"A financial instrument that derives its value from the price or rate of some underlying item"*. [FRS 13 para 2]. Such underlying items could include equities, bonds, commodities, interest rates, stock market and other indices. Hence, the term 'derivative' would apply to following instruments, although the range and complexity of other derivatives, which are effectively hybrids of these, are not only substantial but increasing:

- Forward contracts – contracts for the purchase or sale of a specified amount of a commodity or financial instrument (such as foreign currency) at a fixed price with delivery and settlement at a specified future date.

- Futures contracts – similar to forward contracts except that the purchase or sale is of standardised amounts that are traded on an exchange.

- Options and warrants – give the purchaser the right, but not the obligation, to purchase (call) or sell (put) a fixed amount of a commodity or financial instrument at a fixed price with delivery and settlement at either a specified future date or over a fixed future period.

- Swaps – parties to the contract exchange cash flows in order to access a particular market as if they had entered it directly. For example, interest paid at a fixed rate may be exchanged for interest paid at a floating rate (an interest rate swap) or borrowings denominated in different currencies may be exchanged (a currency swap).

- Caps – an interest rate cap is an agreement whereby the seller reimburses the purchaser with the excess of interest costs over and above a specified rate. Hence, interest costs for the purchaser are capped.

- Collars – an interest rate collar is a combination of a cap and its natural opposite, referred to as a floor. Hence, the purchaser locks into a specified range of interest rates.

41.16 The definition of a financial instrument is deliberately wide in order to capture newly devised instruments in the future without the need for continual updating of any accounting standard. However, the following items, which appear to satisfy the definition, are specifically excluded:

- Interests in subsidiaries, quasi-subsidiaries, associates, partnerships and joint ventures, other than those held exclusively with a view to resale.

- Equity minority interests.

- Employer's obligations under employee option and share schemes and any shares held in order to fulfil such obligations (for example, shares held in an ESOP trust).

- Pensions and other post-retirement benefits.

- Obligations under operating leases.

- Equity shares issued by the reporting entity and warrants or options on them, other than those held exclusively with a view to resale. But all non-equity shares (for example, preference shares) fall to be dealt with in the disclosures as a separate category of financial liabilities. [FRS 13 para 8].

- Financial assets, financial liabilities and cash-settled commodity contracts of an insurance company or group.

[FRS 13 para 5].

41.17 The FRS requires that although debtors and creditors fall within the definition of a financial instrument an entity can opt either to exclude all of its short-term debtors and creditors from all the disclosures (other than the currency disclosures) required by the standard or to include them. Whatever it does, the reporting entity must state how such items have been dealt with. [FRS 13 para 6].

41.18 Cash-settled commodity contracts are to be treated as if they are financial assets and liabilities for the purposes of: the narrative disclosures (see from para 41.24); the numerical disclosures on fair values (see from para 41.54); the disclosures of financial assets and liabilities issued for trading purposes (see from para 41.64); and disclosure of hedges (see from para 41.66). [FRS 13 para 64]. Cash and government securities should not be treated as commodities, but for this purpose commodity contracts do include hard commodities (such as metals including gold) and soft commodities (such as oils, grains, cocoa, cotton, soya beans and sugar). But contracts for the purchase of commodities for actual delivery and use by an entity in its business, such as raw materials in the manufacture of its products, are not cash-settled commodity contracts and so are outside the scope of the standard. [FRS 13 para 2].

41.19 A reporting entity might participate in an illiquid commodity market dominated by very few participants. Where this is the case, disclosure of some of the information on fair values and financial assets and liabilities held or issued for trading or hedging purposes required by the FRS in respect of its commodity positions could move the market significantly and prejudice the entity's interests. In order to avoid this happening, the standard allows disclosures that would be prejudicial in these circumstances to be omitted. [FRS 13 para 65]. The fact that the information has not been disclosed and the reasons for the omission must be stated.

41.20 References in this chapter to financial instruments include commodity contracts with similar characteristics as defined above, notwithstanding the commercial confidentiality exemption discussed in the previous paragraph.

Disclosure of financial instruments

41.21 For conventional instruments, such as shares and loans, other disclosure requirements give some indication of the risks to which a reporting entity is exposed. For example, the following must be disclosed in accordance with FRS 4 and the Companies Act:

- A summary of the rights of each class of share in issue. [FRS 4 para 56].
- Further details of redeemable shares including the period for redemption and whether any premium is payable. [4 Sch 38(2)].
- Details of any options to subscribe for shares in the company including the number in issue, the period during which they may be exercised and the price to be paid. [4 Sch 40].
- A maturity profile of debt. [FRS 4 para 33 as modified by FRS 13].
- Repayment terms and interest rates applicable to long-term liabilities. [4 Sch 48(2)].
- Details of conversion terms in respect of convertible debt. [FRS 4 para 62].
- Market values of listed investments if different to the book value. [4 Sch 45(2)].

41.22 Until FRS 13, neither company law nor accounting standards included detailed disclosure requirements in respect of derivatives. The Act does, however, require disclosure of financial commitments to the extent that they are relevant to a proper understanding of the company's state of affairs. [4 Sch 50(5)]. Therefore, where a company has outstanding forward contracts, the amounts outstanding under the forward contracts have had to be disclosed under this requirement. An example where a company has disclosed outstanding forward contracts, prior to the publication of FRS 13, is given in Table 41.1 below.

Table 41.1 – British Airways Plc – Report & Accounts – 31 March 1998

Notes to the accounts (extract)

36 Forward Transactions

The Group had outstanding forward transactions to hedge foreign currencies and fuel purchases as follows:

	in currency		Sterling equivalents	
	1998	*1997*	***1998***	*1997*
Maturing within one year:				
– to cover future capital commitments in US Dollars	***US$485m***	*US$590m*	***£289m***	*£362m*
– to hedge future currency revenues in US Dollars	***US$127m***	*US$39m*		
– to hedge future currency revenues against sterling			***£65m***	*£48m*
– to hedge future operating payments against US Dollars	***US$130m***	*US$31m*	***£78m***	*£19m*
– to hedge future fuel costs in US Dollars	***US$415m***	*US$165m*	***£247m***	*£101m*
– to hedge future operating payments against sterling			***£82m***	*£60m*
– to hedge debt in a foreign currency			***£90m***	
Maturing after one year:				
– to cover future capital commitments in US Dollars	***US$170m***	*US$140m*	***£101m***	*£86m*
– to hedge future currency revenues against sterling			***£1m***	*£1m*
– to hedge future operating payments against US Dollars			***£16m***	

41.23 FRS 13 requires a range of disclosures that are, in most areas, consistent with those required in the US and by the IASC. Broadly, these disclosures may be divided into descriptive and numerical information. The former is intended as an explanation of why the entity uses financial instruments and what it hopes to achieve. The latter aims to illustrate what actually happened during the reporting period. All of the required disclosures are outlined below, as are other disclosures which are made by certain companies, but are that not specifically required by the FRS.

Objectives, policies and strategies

41.24 FRS 13 requires that an entity should provide an explanation of the role that financial instruments have had during the period in creating or changing the risks it faces in its activities. This should include an explanation of the objectives and policies for holding or issuing financial instruments (including derivatives) and similar contracts, such as cash-settled commodity contracts, and the strategies that have been followed in the period for achieving those objectives as agreed by the directors. [FRS 13 para 13]. This will involve describing management's attitude to risk, in particular whether it is averse to cash flow risk or market price risk (steps taken to mitigate one often increases exposure to the other) and ensuring that its accounting (including hedging), treasury and risk management policies are clear and concise. For example, where an entity holds ten per cent gilts, changes in interest rates will cause their value to fluctuate (market price risk), but such changes do not alter future income (that is, no cash flow risk). If management acts to protect the gilts' value by, say, swapping the fixed rate interest for floating rate, it creates cash flow risk, because net income from the gilts and the swap will fluctuate with changes in interest rates.

41.25 The nature and extent of the discussion will vary depending on the circumstances of the organisation, but the ASB expects it to be at a high level and not commercially sensitive. Basically, it should set the scene for the numerical disclosures and should contain sufficient information to enable a reader to understand the reporting entity's objectives and policies and the strategies for achieving those objectives.

41.26 The discussion should focus only on the major financial risks faced by the reporting entity during the period and should cover the following matters:

- An explanation of the role that financial instruments have had during the period in creating or changing the risks faced by the company. This should include an explanation of the company's objectives and policies for holding or issuing financial instruments and similar contracts and its strategies for achieving those objectives. [FRS 13 para 13].

- A discussion of the nature of and purposes for which the main types of financial instruments and similar contracts are held or issued. This should cover separately instruments used for financing, risk management or hedging and for trading or speculation. [FRS 13 para 14].

- A discussion of the company's main risk management and treasury policies, quantified where appropriate, on:

  - The fixed/floating split, maturity profile and currency profile of financial liabilities (including borrowings) and financial assets.

  - The extent to which foreign currency financial assets and financial liabilities are hedged to the functional currency of the business unit concerned.

  - The extent to which foreign currency borrowings and other financial instruments (that is, derivatives) are used to hedge foreign currency net investments.

  - Any other hedging.

  [FRS 13 para 15].

- If the explanations given above reflect a significant change from the explanations given in the previous accounting period this should be explained and the reasons for the change given. [FRS 13 para 16].

- If the directors have agreed before the date of approval of the financial statements to change significantly the role that financial instruments will have in the next accounting period, this should be explained. [FRS 13 para 18].

- An explanation of how the period-end figures shown in the financial statements represent the objectives, policies and strategies of the entity, or, if the period-end position shown by the financial statements is considered to be materially unrepresentative of the entity's use of financial instruments and thus its exposure to risks, an explanation of the extent to which it is considered unrepresentative. [FRS 13 para 20].

- Where a company uses financial instruments as hedges is should describe:

  - The transactions and risks that are hedged, including the time until they are expected to occur.

  - The instruments used for hedging, disclosing those that have been accounted for using hedge accounting and those that have not.

  [FRS 13 para 21].

41.27 The disclosures referred to above should be included within the financial statements, the directors' report or the non-mandatory OFR. If the disclosures are included in the directors' report or the OFR they should be incorporated within the financial statements by a clear reference to the statement in which they are located. (It should also be remembered that these disclosures, as they form part of the financial statements, are required to be audited.) It seems logical that many companies will include the discussions within the OFR as the requirements do not represent a radical move away from the present recommended practice as specified in paragraphs 25 to 28, 'capital structure and treasury policy', of the current recommended OFR (see further chapter 33).

41.28 An example which includes some of the matters required by FRS 13 is shown in Table 41.2 below, although these financial statements were prepared prior to the publication of FRS 13.

Table 41.2 – Rolls Royce plc – Annual Report – 31 December 1997

Finance Director's review (extract)

Derivatives and other financial instruments

The Group uses various types of financial instruments to manage its exposure to market risks which arise from its business operations. The main risks, as in the past are from movements in foreign currency, interest rates and commodity prices.

The Board regularly reviews the Group's exposures and forward cover, which are also considered in detail by a specialist committee. All such exposures are managed by Group Treasury, which reports to the Finance Director and which operates within written policies approved by the Board.

Foreign exchange risk

The Group's most significant currency exposure is to the US dollar with the Deutschmark ranking next. US dollar income, net of dollar expenditure, represents about 32 per cent of Group turnover (excluding Allison). The Group has a less significant exposure to other foreign currencies.

The Group seeks to hedge its exposures using a variety of financial instruments, with the objective of minimising fluctuations in exchange rates on future transactions and cash flows.

All hedging is undertaken for commercial reasons and we continue to believe that the accounting treatment should reflect this position.

The level of cover taken is determined by the written policies set by the Board and the forward cover is managed within the parameters of these policies in order to achieve the Group's objectives.

The result has been to maintain a relatively stable achieved rate on foreign exchange. In converting transactions denominated in US dollars, 1997 results have suffered by about £5 million (0.7 cents on the achieved rate) by comparison with 1996.

Deutschmark cover extends for periods up to three years, whilst US dollar cover extends for up to ten years, though predominantly in the one to five year period. The majority of cover is in the form of standard foreign exchange contracts, although some cover, primarily of longer duration, includes instruments on which the exchange rates achieved may be dependent on future interest rates. Total US dollar cover approximates to two years net US dollar income. (unchanged from the end of 1996).

In the absence of hedging, the group is exposed to a gain/loss each year of at least £7 million per one cent movement in the US dollar/sterling relationship and up to £3.5 million for a 1 per cent movement in interest rates.

Interest rate risk

The Group has borrowed US$300 million through a subsidiary, Rolls-Royce Capital Inc., in order to provide a fixed rate loan for general Group purposes. This has been translated into sterling after taking account of future contracts and is managed by using interest rate swaps, which effectively change this fixed rate borrowing into a floating rate borrowing in order to match rates achieved on short-term deposits and cash at bank.

Additionally the Group has £150 million borrowing, with maturity in 1998, which is also managed by using interest rate swaps to convert the borrowing from a fixed rate into a floating rate.

Borrowings and interest rates

After taking into account the various currency and interest rate swaps entered into by the Group, the currency and interest rate structure of the gross borrowings of the Group as at December 31, 1997 was:

Currency	Total £m	Floating borrowings £m	Fixed borrowings £m
Sterling	428	402	28
US dollar	96	96	–
Other	27	18	9
	551	516	35

The analysis of fixed borrowings is as follows:

Currency	Total £m	Weighted average interest rate Per cent	Weighted average time for which rate is fixed Years
Sterling	26	5.5	4.4
Other	9	nil	10.2

The maturity of the Group's borrowings is as follows:

	1997 £m	1996 £m
Within 1 year	302	88
Between 1 and 2 years	8	158
Between 2 and 5 years	31	24
Over 5 years	210	221
	551	491

Commodity risk

The Group has an ongoing exposure to the price of jet fuel arising from business operations. The Group's policy is to minimise the impact of price fluctuations. The exposure is hedged in accordance with parameters set by the Board. Hedging is conducted using commodity swaps for periods up to four years.

Accounting policies

41.29 SSAP 2 requires financial statements to include a clear, fair and concise explanation of all material or critical accounting policies. Clearly, the disclosure of accounting policies for financial instruments and hedging will be necessary for all companies that are required to comply with FRS 13 as financial instruments and hedging practices are likely to be material for all listed companies. Furthermore, for other companies that use financial instruments, it will be necessary to explain material accounting policies to accord with SSAP 2. SSAP 2, reinforced by FRS 13, requires that such disclosure should include:

- The methods used to account for derivatives, the types of derivatives accounted for under each method and the criteria that determine the method used.
- The basis for recognising, measuring (both on initial recognition and subsequently) and ceasing to recognise financial instruments.

- How income and expenses (and other gains and losses) are recognised and measured.

- The treatment of financial instruments not recognised, including an explanation of how provisions for losses are recognised on financial instruments that have not been recognised.

- Policies on offsetting.

[FRS 13 para 74].

41.30 Where a company carries its financial instruments at historical cost, the accounting policies would typically cover the treatment of:

- Premiums and discounts on financial assets.

- Changes in the estimated amount of determinable future cash flows associated with a financial instrument, such as a debenture indexed to a commodity price.

- A fall in the fair value of a financial asset to below the asset's carrying value.

- Restructured financial liabilities.

[FRS 13 para 75].

41.31 Where a company accounts for its hedges using hedge accounting, the accounting policies should include a description of:

- The circumstances when a financial instrument is accounted for as a hedge.

- The recognition and measurement principles applied to a hedge instrument.

- The method used to account for an instrument that ceases to be accounted for as a hedge.

- The method used to account for a hedge when the underlying item or position matures, is sold, extinguished, or terminated.

- The method used to account for a hedge of a future transaction when that transaction is no longer likely to occur.

[FRS 13 para 76].

41.32 Examples of accounting policies from the financial statements of BP and BG are shown in Tables 41.3 and 41.4 below.

Table 41.3 – The British Petroleum Company p.l.c. – Annual Report and Accounts – 31 December 1997

Accounting policies (extract)

Derivative financial instruments

The group is a party to derivative financial instruments (derivatives) primarily to manage exposures to fluctuations in foreign currency exchange rates and interest rates, and to manage some of its margin exposure from changes in oil prices.

All derivatives which are held for trading purposes and all oil price derivatives held for risk management purposes are marked to market and all gains and losses recognised in the income statement.

Interest rate swap agreements, swaptions and futures contracts are used to manage interest rate exposures. Amounts payable or receivable in respect of these derivatives are recognised as adjustments to interest expense over the period of the contracts.

As part of exchange rate risk management, foreign currency swap agreements and forward contracts are used to convert non-US dollar borrowings into US dollars. Gains and losses on these derivatives are deferred and recognised on maturity of the underlying debt, together with the matching loss or gain on the debt. Foreign currency forward contracts and options are used to hedge significant non-US dollar firm commitments or anticipated transactions. Gains and losses on these contracts and option premia paid are also deferred and recognised in the income statement or as adjustments to carrying amounts, as appropriate, when the hedged transaction occurs.

Table 41.4 – BG plc – Annual Report and Accounts – 31 December 1997

Principal accounting policies (extract)

Financial instruments

Derivative instruments utilised by the Group are interest rate swaps, cross-currency swaps, forward rate agreements, interest rate swaptions and forward exchange contracts.

A derivative instrument is considered to be used for hedging purposes when it alters the risk profile of an existing underlying exposure of the Group in line with the Group's risk management policies.

Termination payments made or received in respect of derivatives are spread over the life of the underlying exposure in cases where the underlying exposure continues to exist. Where the underlying exposure ceases to exist, any termination payments are taken to the profit and loss account.

Interest differentials on derivative instruments are recognised by adjusting net interest payable. Premiums or discounts on derivative instruments are amortised over the shorter of the life of the instrument or the underlying exposure.

Currency swap agreements and forward exchange contracts are valued at closing rates of exchange. Resulting gains or losses are offset against foreign exchange gains or losses on the related borrowings or, where the instrument is used to hedge a committed future transaction, are deferred until the transaction occurs.

Detailed numerical disclosures

41.33 The aim of the numerical disclosures required in FRS 13 is to show how the entity's objectives and policies were implemented in the period. The disclosures include information relevant to an assessment of interest rate and currency risk together with an analysis of fair values and information on the impact of using hedge accounting.

41.34 The disclosures required by the FRS are intended to be highly summarised and the FRS prescribes in some detail the offsetting and aggregation to be used for particular disclosures. However, this does not mean that the offsetting permitted in the disclosures is appropriate for recognition and measurement purposes in the primary financial statements. [FRS 13 para 24]. One effect of the high degree of aggregation and offsetting required, or encouraged, by the FRS is that it may not be possible to trace components of the disclosures back to their respective balance sheet captions. Where this is the case, the FRS encourages additional detail to be provided to facilitate such a reconciliation, unless it would unduly complicate the disclosure. [FRS 13 para 25].

Interest rate risks

41.35 The standard requires extensive disclosure in respect of interest rate risks related to the company's financial liabilities. For this purpose, an entity's financial liabilities are its contractual obligations to deliver cash or other financial assets to another entity or to exchange financial instruments with another entity under conditions that are potentially unfavourable. [FRS 13 para 2]. A company may exclude from these disclosures those items that fall within the definition of short-term creditors. [FRS 13 para 6].

41.36 For each major currency, financial liabilities should be analysed to show those at fixed rates, those at floating rates and those on which no interest is paid. Financial liabilities on which no interest is paid do not include finance lease obligations, deep discounted bonds and other liabilities where the finance cost is allocated in accordance with FRS 4 or SSAP 21. [FRS 13 para 27]. Floating rate financial liabilities are defined as those that have their interest rate reset at least once a year. [FRS 13 para 2].

41.37 The standard requires the interest rate risk disclosures to be shown on a gross basis, that is without netting off cash, other liquid resources or similar items. [FRS 13 para 31]. Where a company wishes to show the interest rate risk disclosures on a net basis, for example where it manages its interest rate risk on a net basis, it can do so by giving additional information showing the net position as long as the gross position is also disclosed.

41.38 For each of the major currencies, the following details of interest rates should be disclosed:

- The weighted average interest rate for fixed rate financial liabilities.

- The weighted average period for which interest rates are fixed.

- The weighted average period until maturity of non-interest bearing financial liabilities.

- The benchmark rate for determining interest rate payments for floating rate financial instruments. This could, for example, result in disclosure that floating rate borrowings bear interest based on LIBOR. Although the standard has no requirement for disclosure of the interest differential this may well be caught by the disclosure requirement in company law (see para 41.21).

[FRS 13 para 30].

41.39 The analysis should take account of instruments such as swaps and other derivatives, the effect of which is to alter the interest basis or currency of the financial liability (described as 'non-optional derivatives'). For example, if the company has a floating rate borrowing and has taken out an interest rate swap to swap its interest obligation to fixed rate, the borrowing would be disclosed in the table as a fixed rate borrowing. Other instruments, such as caps and collars, that are associated with these financial liabilities and which convert those liabilities over only a limited range of interest rates (described as 'optional derivatives') and cannot be adequately reflected in the analysis should be excluded and explained separately, as should any financial liabilities and non-optional derivatives with unusual terms. [FRS 13 para 26]. Convertible debt is an example of a financial liability that may be more appropriately dealt with separately outside the analysis.

41.40 For those instruments excluded from the analysis, there should be disclosure of the main terms and conditions sufficient to enable the reader to understand their significance. This could include a summary of the following:

- Notional principal amounts involved.
- Rates of interest.
- Periods for which contracts are operative.
- Terms of any options contained within the instrument.

[FRS 13 para 29].

41.41 Examples that give many of the disclosures outlined above are shown in Tables 41.5 and 41.6 below, but these are given for borrowings only (as proposed by FRED 13) as opposed to the standard's requirements which covers all financial liabilities. Table 41.6 gives no information on floating rate borrowings, but does give a good summary of non-optional derivatives associated with the borrowings.

Table 41.5 – The British Petroleum Company p.l.c. – Annual Report and Accounts – 31 December 1997

Notes on accounts (extract)

24 Finance debt (extract)

	Fixed rate debt			Floating rate debt		1997	1996
	Weighted average interest rate	Weighted average time for which rate is fixed	Amount	Weighted average interest rate	Amount	Total	Total
Analysis of borrowings by currency	**%**	**Years**	**£ million**	**%**	**£ million**	**£ million**	**£ million**
Sterling	–	–	–	7	**33**	**33**	**137**
US dollars	9	12	**1,980**	6	**1,089**	**3,069**	**3,144**
French francs	–	–	–	–	–	–	**28**
South African rands	8	–	–	19	**38**	**38**	**51**
Other currencies	–	4	**16**	7	**107**	**123**	**150**
Trade loans			**1,996**		**1,267**	**3,263**	**3,510**

The group aims for a balance between floating and fixed interest rates. During 1997 the upper limit for the proportion of floating rate debt was set at 65% of total debt. Interest rates on floating rate debt denominated in US dollars are linked principaliy to LIBOR, with those on debt in other currencies based on equivalent in local markets. The group monitors interest rate risk using a process of sensitivity analysis. Assuming no changes to the borrowings and hedges described above, it is estimated that a change of 1% in the general level of interest rates on 1 January 1998 would change 1998 profit before tax by approximately £20 million.

Table 41.6 – Tate & Lyle Public Limited Company – Annual Report – 28 September 1998

Notes to the financial statements (extract)

32 Currency and Interest Rate Exposure of Borrowings

After taking into account the various interest rate and currency interest rate swaps entered into by the Group, the currency and interest rate exposure of the borrowings of the Group as at 27 September 1997, was:

	Total net borrowings £ million	Current assets investments and cash at bank £ million	Fixed rate net borrowings £ million	Fixed rate gross borrowings £ million	Average interest rate % of fixed rate gross borrowings	Average years to maturity of fixed rate gross borrowings
Sterling	169.1	22.4	166.1	166.1	11.0	3.3
United States Dollars	451.0	134.3	242.7	281.4	6.4	3.1
Canadian Dollars	34.7	3.3	–	–	–	–
Australian Dollars	18.9	2.5	–	–	–	–
EU currencies (excluding sterling)	242.3	84.5	2.5	7.6	4.3	3.7
Others	(7.2)	13.3	–	–	–	–
Total/average	908.8	260.3	411.3	453.1	8.0	3.2

The average sterling interest rate of 11% reduces to 8% if the amortisation of the premium on redemption of the 5.75% Guarantee Bonds is excluded. The floating rate borrowings, cash and current asset investments bear interest based on relevant national LIBOR equivalents or government bond rates.

The analysis of average interest rates and years to maturity is on fixed rate gross borrowings and after adjustments for interest rate swaps. The interest rate exposure is further protected by interest rate caps on £10 million at 10% until June 1998, £10 million at 8% until June 1999, US$50 million at 6.72% until July 1999, US$28.5 million at 6.65% until December 1999, US$200 million at 9.5% until October 2000 and US$150 million at 9.5% until November 2000. The Group also has a FFr400 million collar at 4.91% floor/6% cap expiring in January 1999 and a Bfr1,000 million collar at 6.03% floor/7% cap expiring in December 1999.

The Group has also entered into two flexible chooser caps which give the right to fix two six-month settings over a two-year period. The first is for FFr200 million at 6% and runs until October 1998 and the second is for FFr300 million at 6% and runs until January 1999. No fixings have yet been made in respect of either instrument.

Maturity analysis of financial liabilities

41.42 A maturity profile of the carrying amount of financial liabilities is also required. This would show the total amounts falling due:

- In one year or less, or on demand.
- In more than one year, but not more than two years.
- In more than two years, but not more than five years.
- In more than five years.

[FRS 13 para 38].

41.43 This profile, which is, to a large extent, an aggregation of the analyses of debt and finance leases already required by FRS 4 and SSAP 21, is based on the carrying amounts determined by reference to the earliest date on which payment can be required or on which the liability falls due. The standard requires the maturity analysis to include all financial liabilities, which include, for example, swaps and non-optional derivatives, if they are recognised on the balance sheet.

41.44 The maturity analysis bandings in FRS 4 have been changed to accord with the FRS 13 bandings given above. Where the FRS 4 analysis of debt and the SSAP 21 analysis of finance lease obligations is brought together in the maturity analysis, the analysis of debt and finance lease obligations will need to be based on the carrying amounts. They should not, for example, be based on the amounts to be paid on maturity or, in the case of finance lease obligations, on the gross obligations before deducting finance charges. In addition, an analysis of other financial liabilities should be given separately. One way of satisfying the requirements of FRS 4, SSAP 21 and FRS 13 would be to use a columnar approach with headings for debt, finance leases and other financial liabilities. Also the maturity analysis specified in SSAP 21 for finance leases requires disclosure of the amounts payable in the second to fifth years inclusive; this amount would have to be further analysed to satisfy FRS 13's requirements into amounts that are payable in more than one year but not more than two years and those that are payable in more than two years, but not more than five years. [FRS 13 para 39].

Maturity analysis of undrawn committed borrowing facilities

41.45 FRS 13 also requires an analysis to be given of the maturity of material undrawn committed borrowing facilities, showing separately amounts expiring:

- In one year or less.
- In more than one year, but not more than two years.
- In more than two years.

[FRS 13 para 40].

If there are conditions that attach to a particular facility, then it should only be included in the above analysis if all the conditions are satisfied at the balance sheet date.

41.46 The maturity analysis of financial instruments outlined in paragraph 41.42 above will include certain committed borrowing facilities. For example, a company might have an overdraft facility of £50 million, but at the year end its overdraft balance is £20 million, which would be included in the maturity analysis as an amount falling due for repayment 'in one year or less, or on demand'. To avoid double-counting, any amounts drawn down under such facilities should not also be disclosed in the maturity analysis of undrawn committed borrowing facilities. [FRS 13 para 41]. Consequently, in this example only £30 million, which is the undrawn element of the committed facilities, would be included in the undrawn committed facilities table. Furthermore, its inclusion in a particular banding in the table would depend on the date on which the facility expires. For example, if it were to expire in 18 months time, then it would appear in the line for amounts expiring 'in more than one year but not more than two years' even though the borrowing itself is categorised as 'in one year or less, or on demand'.

41.47 In order to enable the reader to assess the significance of these facilities, the FRS recommends that disclose be given of the purpose and the period for which these facilities are committed and the extent to which they are subject to annual review by the provider of finance. This additional information is not mandatory. [FRS 13 para 42]. In any case, for listed companies the OFR should already include a comment on liquidity and this may include details such as those suggested in the FRS (see further chapter 33).

Details of financial assets

41.48 If the reporting entity has significant holdings of financial assets, such as investments in interest-bearing assets (including finance lease receivables) or other debt instruments, analyses similar to those required for financial liabilities and described in paragraphs 41.26 to 41.40 above should be provided. [FRS 13 para 32]. A maturity profile similar to that described in paragraph 41.42 is not required, but may be presented if this would show the maturity analyses of financial liabilities and borrowing facilities in their proper context. [FRS 13 para 43].

41.49 Financial assets include investments in equity shares and other instruments that neither pay interest nor have a maturity date. For such instruments, the disclosures will typically be limited to information about any currency exposures involved. [FRS 13 para 33]. Financial assets on which no interest is earned do not include, for example, investments in deep discounted bonds for which an interest income can be imputed. [FRS 13 para 27].

Currency risk disclosures

41.50 The disclosure required by FRS 13 is an analysis of the net amount of monetary assets and monetary liabilities at the balance sheet date denominated in each currency, analysed by reference to the functional currencies of the operations involved. [FRS 13 para 34]. The term 'monetary assets and liabilities' refers to money held and amounts to be received or paid in money. [SSAP 20 para 44]. Consequently, short-term debtors and creditors fall within this definition and provided they fall due within 12 months of the balance sheet date they include: debtors; prepayments and accrued income; creditors falling due within one year (other than those items included under 'debenture loans' and 'bank loans and overdrafts'); provisions for liabilities and charges and accruals and deferred income. [FRS 13 paras 2, 6]. Whether or not short-term debtors and creditors have been included within the other disclosures required by FRS 13, they are required to be included in the table of currency risk exposures (see further para 41.17). [FRS 13 para 6]. The amounts disclosed should be after taking account of currency swaps, forward contracts and other derivatives. In addition, a summary of the main effect should be given of any such financial instruments that have not been taken into account.

41.51 Only the principal functional currencies and the principal currencies in which the monetary items are denominated need be given. Monetary assets and liabilities denominated in the same functional currency as the particular operation should be excluded from the analysis. Similarly, where a company has foreign currency borrowings that provide a hedge against foreign net investments, under SSAP 20 gains and losses arising on translation would be taken to the statement of total recognised gains and losses not to the profit and loss account; consequently, such borrowings are 'matched' and are excluded from the analysis. [FRS 13 para 34]. As mentioned above, the aim of the analysis is to show the reporting entity's currency exposures that give rise to gains and losses in the profit and loss account. This is best explained by reference to an example.

Illustration of the disclosure of currency exposures

Functional currency of group operation	Net foreign currency monetary assets/(liabilities)					
	Sterling £m	US dollar £m	Yen £m	F/franc £m	Other £m	Total £m
Sterling	–	20	10	–	–	30
US dollar	15	–	–	–	–	15
Yen	(30)	30	–	(90)	–	(90)
F/franc	25	(300)	40	–	–	(235)
Other	(10)	(30)	–	40	10	10
Total	–	(280)	50	(50)	10	(270)

The amounts in the table take into account the effect of currency swaps, forward contracts and other derivatives entered into to manage currency exposures.

41.52 In this example, the group has US dollar monetary assets of £20 million in the UK and £30 million in Japan and US dollar liabilities of £300 million in France and £30 million in other countries. Hence, the group has £280 million of aggregate US dollar net liabilities, which would result in gains or losses being recognised in the profit and loss account.

41.53 If the £300 million US dollar borrowing in France was treated as a hedge of US dollar assets on consolidation, the US dollar position would be reduced to an asset of only £20 million and the total net foreign currency exposure would be only £30 million. Hence, it is easy to see how the picture portrayed by this analysis can be changed significantly and, for companies with sophisticated treasury functions, it is likely that the preparation and interpretation of this disclosure will be complex.

Fair values

41.54 Disclosure is required of the fair values of all financial assets and liabilities (whether recognised or not) compared to their book value. [FRS 13 para 44]. For this purpose instruments should be grouped into appropriate categories (for example, showing separately instruments held for trading; instruments held to manage interest or currency profiles of assets or liabilities; borrowings; hedge instruments; and so on) and, for each category, there should be disclosure of the aggregate fair value together with the aggregate carrying amount.

41.55 When grouping financial instruments into categories, it is important to group like with like. Typically, the categories will follow the same structure, but be in more detail than that used in discussing the objectives, policies and strategies for holding or issuing financial instruments. Therefore, although financial assets and financial liabilities would not usually be included in the same category, an exception might be made to group together similar derivatives held or issued for the same purpose, regardless of whether their fair value was positive or negative. For example, interest rate and currency derivatives would usually be grouped separately. Furthermore, interest rate derivatives would usually be split between interest rate swaps and instruments such as caps and collars. [FRS 13 para 46].

41.56 The standard allows disclosure for a particular category of financial instrument of either the aggregate fair values (that is, a net figure) at the balance sheet date or the aggregate fair value of items with a positive fair value and the aggregate of items with a negative fair value. [FRS 13 para 44(a)(b)]. For example, some forward contracts will be in the money and have a positive fair value, whereas others will be out of the money and have a negative fair value. At any one time, an entity could have a portfolio of forward contracts, each issued for the same purposes, having both positive and negative fair values. A single forward contract could change from being a financial asset to a financial liability over time as it moves in and out of the money. Although the standard allows disclosure of either a single net fair value or the gross fair values (both negative and positive), it points out that for companies that may be developing systems to capture information for disclosure, a subsequent FRS might require that most or all financial assets and financial liabilities should be carried on the balance sheet at fair values. In this case, gross figures would be required.

41.57 For the purpose of the required disclosures, fair value is defined as *"...the amount at which an asset or liability could be exchanged in an arm's length transaction between informed and willing parties, other than in a forced or liquidation sale"*. [FRS 13 para 2]. Often, quoted market prices will provide the best evidence of fair value. However, where there is little or no activity in a particular market, or there is no market at all, the FRS requires that estimation techniques (such as prices of similar instruments, discounted cash flows or option-pricing models) will usually give a sufficiently reliable measure of fair value. If measurement of fair value proves particularly difficult, a range of values could be disclosed. [FRS 13 para 54(a); App IV paras 7-9]. In certain circumstances although a fair value might not be available for an individual financial instrument, it might be possible to value a portfolio of such instruments. Where this is so the standard requires the portfolio value to be used and disclosed. [FRS 13 para 54(b)]. The methods used and any significant assumptions used to determine fair value should be disclosed. [FRS 13 para 51]. Further guidance on fair valuing is given in appendix IV to the standard.

41.58 In extreme cases, where it is not practicable to estimate fair values with sufficient reliability, no fair value need be disclosed, but the following must be disclosed instead:

- A description of the financial asset or liability and its carrying amount.
- The reasons why it is not practicable to estimate fair value with sufficient reliability.
- Information about the principal characteristics of the instrument that are pertinent to estimating its fair value (for example, the factors that determine or affect the instrument's cash flows and the market for such instruments). But such information need not be disclosed if in the directors' opinion its disclosure at the level of aggregation and date of disclosure would be seriously prejudicial to the company's interests. The fact that such information has not been disclosed and the reason for non-disclosure should then be given.

[FRS 13 para 53].

41.59 The ASB expects that this exemption would be used only as a last resort, after all viable alternatives have been exhausted and it suggests that the following factors should generally be present if the exemption is to be invoked:

- The instrument is unique and no comparable instruments exist.
- The future cash flows associated with the instrument are difficult to predict with any degree of reliability.
- A reliable valuation model is not available.

[FRS 13 para 55].

41.60 It might only be possible for the fair value to be ascertained for some of the financial instruments included within a category. Where this is so, the standard requires the fair value of that sub-set to be disclosed and the disclosures set out in paragraph 41.58 above to be given for the rest of that category. [FRS 13 para 54(c)].

41.61 All financial instruments should be included in the table and their fair values given regardless of whether or not the instrument is used for hedging purposes. Whether or not the hedging instruments are included in the balance sheet at a value will depend on the company's accounting policy. Such instruments are, like other instruments, to be disclosed by category and the standard suggests that it might be useful to indicate the link between the hedging instrument and the item that it is hedging and explain whether the fair value of the hedged item is also disclosed. [FRS 13 para 47].

41.62 For some short-term financial instruments, such as cash, debtors and creditors (subject to normal trade credit terms), and in the case of floating rate debt, the difference between carrying amount and fair value will generally be immaterial. In such cases, the carrying amount may be used in place of fair value. However, both the carrying amount and fair value, which in this case will be the same figure, should still be disclosed, unless the company has decided to exclude all of its short-term debtors and creditors from this disclosure (see further para 41.17). [FRS 13 paras 6,48]. Clearly, certain longer-term debtors and creditors might have market values that differ from their carrying values. This will be the case for long-term fixed rate debt and also for long-term debtors where the delay in settlement might not be compensated by interest at current market rates.

41.63 Examples of the type of disclosure envisaged by the ASB are shown in Tables 41.7 and 41.8 below, which were issued prior to the publication of FRS 13. The former shows the fair values of derivative financial assets separately from fair values of derivative financial liabilities while the latter gives disclosure of a net figure.

Table 41.7 – Unilever PLC – Annual Accounts – 31 December 1997

Notes to the consolidated accounts (extract)

31 Financial instruments (extract)

The undernoted Table summarises the fair values and carrying amounts of the various classes of financial instruments as at 31 December:

£ million	Fair value		Carrying amount	
	1997	1996	**1996**	1996
Fixed investments	**940**	120	**85**	113
Current investments	**2 511**	375	**2 511**	375
Cash	**3 342**	1 313	**3 342**	1 313
Bonds and other loans	**(2 072)**	(2 580)	**(1 989)**	(2 502)
Bank loans and overdrafts	**(681)**	(879)	**(681)**	(879)
Interest rate swaps – assets	**81**	142	**13**	26
– liabilities	**(49**	(83)	–	–
Forward rate agreements	–	–	–	–
Foreign exchange contracts – assets	**38**	19	**(14)**	(34)
– liabilities	**(52**	(53)	–	–
Swaptions, caps, floors – liabilities	–	(6)	–	–

The fair values of fixed investments are based on their market value. The fair values of forward foreign exchange contracts represent the unrealised gain or loss on revaluation of the contracts to year end rates of exchange. The fair values of bonds and other loans, interest rate swaps, forward rate agreements, swaptions, caps and floors are estimated based on the net present value of the discounted anticipated future cash flows associated with these instruments.

Table 41.8 – British Telecommunications plc – Annual Report and Accounts – 31 March 1998

Notes to the Financial Statements (extract)

19. Financial instruments and risk management (extract)

(d) Fair value of financial instruments

The following table shows the carrying amounts and fair values of the group's financial instruments at 31 March 1998 and 1997. The carrying amounts are included in the group balance sheet under the indicated headings, with the exception of derivative amounts related to borrowings, which are included in debtors or other creditors as appropriate. The fair values of the financial instruments are the amount at which the instruments could be exchanged in a current transaction between willing parties, other than in a forced or liquidation sale.

	Carrying amount		Fair value	
	1998 £m	1997 £m	**1998 £m**	1997 £m
Non-derivatives:				
Assets				
Cash at bank and in hand	**62**	26	**62**	26
Short-term investments *(i)*	**731**	2,974	**731**	2,974
Liabilities				
Short-term borrowings *(ii)*	**550**	221	**550**	221
Long-term borrowings, excluding finance leases *(iii)*	**4,210**	2,953	**4,665**	3,168
Derivatives relating to borrowings (net) *(iv)*				
Assets	**48**	79	**–**	11
Liabilities	**–**	–	**114**	–

(i) The fair values of listed short-term investments were estimated based on quoted market prices for those investments. The carrying amount of the other short-term deposits and investments approximated to their fair values due to the short maturity of the instruments held.

(ii) The fair value of the short-term borrowings approximated to carrying value due to the short maturity of the instruments.

(iii) The fair value of the group's bonds, debentures, notes and other long-term borrowings has been estimated on the basis of quoted market prices for the same or similar issues with the same maturities where they existed, and on calculations of the present value of future cash flows using the appropriate discount rates in effect at the balance sheet dates, where market prices of similar issues did not exist.

(iv) The fair value of the group's outstanding foreign currency and interest rate swap agreements was estimated by calculating the present value, using appropriate discount rates in effect at the balance sheet dates, of affected future cash flows translated, where appropriate, into pounds sterling at the market rates at the balance sheet dates.

Financial assets and liabilities held for trading

41.64 If the reporting entity holds or issues financial assets or financial liabilities for trading the following disclosures have to be made:

- The net gain or loss from trading such instruments during the period included in the profit and loss account, analysed by type of financial instrument, business activity, risk or in such other way that is consistent with the entity's management of the activity.

- If the analysis above is given other than by type of financial instrument, a description for each line of that analysis of the types of financial instruments involved.

- The period-end fair values of financial assets and, separately, of financial liabilities held or issued for trading.

- If the period-end position is considered to be materially unrepresentative of the reporting entity's use of financial instruments for trading purposes during the period, the average fair value of instruments held in the period. The average should be calculated using daily figures, or where these are not available, the most frequent interval, generated for management, regulatory or other reasons, should be used. An example of this disclosure is given in Table 41.10 on page 41030.

[FRS 13 para 57].

41.65 If the ASB's proposals for the measurement of all financial instruments at fair value are adopted (see further para 41.83), the disclosure of such values will clearly be superfluous to requirements and will probably be dropped. However, as with revalued assets, disclosure of historical cost equivalents would presumably be required.

Disclosures concerning hedges

41.66 Companies use financial instruments for hedging purposes to reduce the risk associated with the hedged item. Depending on the accounting policy the company adopts, gains and losses on hedging instruments are often not recognised in the financial statements until the hedged transaction takes place. Companies that do recognise gains and losses carry them forward in their balance sheets to match the gains and losses on the hedged item in the next financial year.

41.67 Where financial assets and financial liabilities are used by a company for hedging purposes, the standard requires the following information about gains and losses to be disclosed:

- The cumulative aggregate gains and losses that are unrecognised at the balance sheet date. If the item's fair value has not been disclosed which is allowed for cash-settled commodity contracts in the situation described in paragraph 41.19, any gain or loss on that item need not be dealt with in this disclosure.

- The cumulative aggregate gains and losses carried forward in the balance sheet at the balance sheet date pending their recognition in the profit and loss account.

- The extent to which the gains and losses disclosed in the above two points are expected to be recognised in the profit and loss account in the next accounting period.

- The amount of gains and losses included in the reporting period's profit and loss account that arose in previous years and were either unrecognised or carried forward in the balance sheet at the start of the reporting period.

[FRS 13 para 59].

41.68 The standard includes an exemption from the disclosures required in the last three bullet points in paragraph 41.67 on pragmatic grounds, because of the problems that can arise in trying to keep records of gains and losses on hedges that have been included in the carrying amount of a fixed asset. Such amounts need not be included in the analysis; they are of course included in the carrying value of the fixed asset amortised to the profit and loss account. [FRS 13 paras 60,61].

41.69 In the rare circumstances where financial instruments that were previously designated as hedges are reclassified and no longer designated as hedges, there should be separate disclosure of any gains or losses recognised in the profit and loss account on reclassification. [FRS 13 para 62].

41.70 Reproduced below is an extract from appendix III to the standard which illustrates the disclosures set out above.

	Gains	**Losses**	**Total net gains/(losses)**
	£m	**£m**	**£m**
Unrecognised gains and losses on hedges at 1.1.X1	**53**	**28**	**25**
Gains and losses arising in previous years that were recognised in 19X1	22	21	1
Gains and losses arising before 1.1.X1 that were not recognised in 19X1	**31**	**7**	**24**
Gains and losses arising in 19X1 that were not recognised in 19X1	66	41	25
Unrecognised gains and losses on hedges at 31.12.X1	**97**	**48**	**49**
Of which:			
Gains and losses expected to be recognised in 19X2	71	40	31
Gains and losses expected to be recognised in 19X3 or later	26	8	18

41.71 Prior to the publication of FRS 13, Cadbury Schweppes presented much of the information required by the ASB in the form of a discussion (see Table 41.9).

Table 41.9 – Cadbury Schweppes plc – Annual Report – 3 January 1998

Notes to the accounts (extract)

21 Derivatives and other Financial Instruments (extract)

Treasury risk management

The Group has clearly defined policies for the management of foreign exchange risks. Transactions which create foreign currency cash flows are hedged with either forward contracts or currency options. The term of the currency derivatives is rarely more than one year. The Group has widespread overseas operations but does not hedge profit translation exposures as such hedges can only have a temporary effect.

In the normal course of business the Group enters into forward commitments for the purchase of certain raw materials. Depending on the contract terms, settlement by the counterparties may occur in cash or by physical delivery.

Such commitments are entered into only on the basis of forecast requirements.

Hedges of future transactions

At 3 January 1998 net unrecognised losses of £3m related primarily to hedges of future transactions which are expected to occur in 1998. Included in the 1997 profit and loss account are £1m of net losses on hedges arising in previous years for transactions which occurred during 1997.

41.72 As with the disclosure of fair values, these disclosures would probably not be required if the standard required all financial instruments to be measured at fair value in the balance sheet.

Market price risk

41.73 Disclosure of some measure of market price risk is an evolving area of financial reporting, both in the UK and internationally. Various techniques have been developed, but there is as yet no consensus as to which is the best method of providing adequate and meaningful information in a cost effective manner. Hence, the ASB encourages, rather than requires, entities other than banks to give some measure of the market price risk of all the financial instruments they hold or have issued (including cash settled commodity contracts and, if significant, all other items carrying market price risk.) [FRS 13 para 66]. Banks must give market price risk information in respect of their trading book. [FRS 13 para 104]. Market price risk is the risk of loss arising from changes in market prices, such as interest rates or exchange rates. It is necessary to appreciate that any disclosures concerning market price risk can only give an estimate of the risks to a company and can never be precise or accurate.

41.74 Entities providing market price risk information should include:

- A discussion of market price risk where necessary to set the numerical information in context and to assist in its interpretation.

- Additional numerical disclosures that facilitate an assessment of the magnitude of market price risk over the period. These disclosures should include:

  - An explanation of the method used and the key parameters and assumptions underlying the data provided.

  - An explanation of the objective of the method used and of the limitations that may cause the information not to reflect fully the overall market price risk of the assets and liabilities involved.

  - The reasons for material changes in the amount of reported risk compared to the previous accounting period.

[FRS 13 paras 67, 69].

41.75 The method chosen to measure market price risk should reflect how management manages the risk. If different approaches are used to manage market price risk in different parts of a business, separate disclosure for each part of the business is encouraged. [FRS 13 para 66]. In its simplest form, the information could be presented as a sensitivity analysis showing the impact on profit of, say, a one per cent change in interest rates. However, other methods such as 'value at risk' – that is, the expected loss from an adverse market movement with a specified probability over a specified period of time – may be more appropriate. Five possible approaches for reporting market price risk are discussed in paragraph 68 of the FRS, but it is acknowledged that this list is not exhaustive and other methods may be more appropriate.

41.76 Where material changes are made to the method or key assumptions and parameters used to calculate market price risk from one period to the next, the reasons for the change should be given and the previous period's information should be restated onto the new basis. [FRS 13 para 71].

41.77 An example of disclosure of market price risk based on the sensitivity of market values is shown in Table 41.10 below, which also includes disclosure of fair values, instruments held for trading and information on credit risk. Another example, giving the impact of changes in interest rates, is included in Tables 41.5 on page 41016. These financial statements were both issued before the publication of FRS 13.

Table 41.10 – The British Petroleum Company p.l.c. – Annual Report and Accounts – 31 December 1997

Notes on accounts (extract)

27 Derivative financial instruments (extract)

In the normal course of business the group is a party to derivative financial instruments (derivatives) with off-balance sheet risk, primarily to manage its exposure to fluctuations in foreign currency exchange rates and interest rates, and some movements in oil prices. The underlying economic currency of the group's cash flows is mainly US dollars. Accordingly, most of our borrowings are in US dollars or swapped into dollars where this achieves a lower cost of financing. Significant non-dollar cash flow exposures are hedged. Gains and losses arising on such hedges are deferred and recognised in the income statement or as adjustments to carrying amounts, as appropriate, only when the hedged item occurs. We also manage the balance between floating rate and fixed rate debt. In addition, we trade certain derivatives in conjunction with risk management activities.

These derivatives involve, to varying degrees, credit and market risk. With regard to credit risk, the group may be exposed to loss in the event of non-performance by a counterparty. The group controls credit risk by entering into derivative contracts only with highly credit rated counterparties and through credit approvals, limits and monitoring procedures and does not usually require collateral or other security. The group has not experienced material non-performance by any counterparty.

Market risk is the possibility that a change in interest rates, currency exchange rates or oil prices will cause the value of a financial instrument to decrease or its obligations to become more costly to settle. When derivatives are used for the purpose of risk management they do not expose the group to market risk because gains and losses on the derivatives offset losses and gains on the asset, liability or transaction being hedged. When derivatives are traded, the exposure of the group to market risk is limited to changes in their fair (market) values.

The measurement of market risk in trading activities is discussed further below.

The table shows the 'fair value' of the asset or liability created by derivatives. This represents the market value at the balance sheet date. Credit exposure at 31 December is represented by the column 'fair value asset'.

The table also shows the 'net carrying amount' of the asset or liability created by derivatives. This amount represents the net book value, i.e. market value when acquired or later marked to market.

£ million

	1997			1996		
	Fair value asset	Fair value (liability)	Net carrying amount asset (liability)	Fair value asset	Fair value (liability)	Net carrying amount asset(liability)
Risk management						
– interest rate contracts	**33**	**(144)**	**(32)**	34	129	(37)
– foreign exchange contracts	**80**	**(106)**	**75**	339	(59)	100
– oil price contracts	**12**	**(15)**	**(3)**	11	(39)	(28)
Trading						
– interest rate contracts	**1**	**(4)**	**(3)**	–	–	–
– foreign exchange contracts	**25**	**(24)**	**1**	24	(19)	5
– oil price contracts	**97**	**(69)**	**28**	70	(68)	2

Interest rate contracts include futures contracts, swap agreements, options and swaptions. Foreign exchange contracts include forward and futures contracts, swap agreements and options. Oil price contracts are those which require settlement in cash and include futures contracts, swap agreements and options.

The following table shows the average net fair value of derivatives and other financial instruments held for trading purposes during the year:

	£ million	
	1997	1996
	Average net fair value asset (liability)	Average net fair value asset (liability)
Interest rate contracts	**(2)**	–
Foreign exchange contracts	**1**	2
Oil price contracts	**15**	20
	14	22

The group measures its market risk exposure, i.e. potential gain or loss in fair values, on its trading activity using a value at risk technique. This technique is based on variance/covariance model and makes a statistical assessment of the market risk arising from possible future changes in market values over a 24-hour period. The calculation of the range of potential changes in fair value takes into account a snapshot of the end-of-day exposures, and the history of one day price movements over the previous twelve months, together with the correlation of these price movements. The potential movement in fair values is expressed to three standard deviations which is equivalent to a 99.7% confidence level. This means that, in broad terms, one would expect to see an increase or a decrease in fair values greater than the value at risk on only one occasion per year if the portfolio were left unchanged.

The group calculates value at risk on all instruments that are held for trading purposes and that therefore give an exposure to market risk. The value at risk model takes account of derivative financial instruments such as interest rate forward and future contracts, swap agreements, options and swaptions, foreign exchange forward and futures contracts, swap agreements and options and oil price futures, swap agreements and options. Financial assets and liabilities and physical crude oil and refined products that are treated as trading positions are also included in these calculations. The value at risk calculation for oil price exposure also includes derivative commodity instruments (commodity contracts that permit settlement either by delivery of the underlying commodity or in cash), such as forward contracts.

The following table shows values at risk for trading activities

					£ million	
	1997				1996	
	High	Low	Average	Year end	Average	Year end
Interest rate contracts	**5**	–	**2**	**1**	1	–
Foreign exchange contracts	**2**	–	**2**	**1**	2	–
Oil price contracts	**7**	**2**	**4**	**2**	4	2

In the light of evolving disclosure requirements in both the UK and the US, the presentation of trading results shown below now includes certain activities of the group's oil trading division which involve the use of derivative financial instruments in conjunction with physical and paper trading of oil. It is considered that a more comprehensive representation of the group's oil trading activities is given by the classification of the gains or losses on such derivatives along with the physical and paper trades to which they relate.

The following table shows the trading income arising from derivatives and other financial instruments. For oil price contract trading, this also includes income or losses arising on trading of derivative commodity instruments and physical oil trades, representing the net results of the oil-trading portfolio.

	£ million	
	1997	1996
	Net gain	Net gain
Interest rate contracts	**1**	1
Foreign exchange rate contracts	**14**	9
Oil price contracts	**88**	80
	103	90

For oil price contracts, a reconciliation from the presentation previously used to the current presentation is provided below.

	£ million	
	1997	1996
Trading income on derivative financial instruments under previous classification	**31**	5
Effect of linking to related derivative commodity instruments and physical oil positions	**57**	75
Net trading income on oil-trading portfolio	**88**	80

41.78 While the practice of disclosing a measure of market price risk is evolving, it should be recognised that this may not be the most significant risk faced by the reporting entity. For example, wage inflation or sales volumes may be far more significant. Clearly, therefore, any disclosed measure of market price risk should not be portrayed as comprehensive.

Other disclosures not required by FRS 13

41.79 Although not required by FRS 13, it is quite common for entities to disclose the principal amounts of financial instrument contracts – for example, the actual value of a debt subjected to a swap agreement. Indeed this disclosure is required in the US and, in certain circumstances, by IAS 32.

41.80 Disclosure of principal amounts not only gives an indication of the volumes of derivative activity, but also assists in an assessment of hedging performance. For example, in absolute terms, disclosure of an unrealised gain of £1 million on a forward contract means very little. It could have arisen on contracts to purchase $10 million or $1 billion.

41.81 Unilever is one of the companies that have disclosed principal amounts as shown in Table 41.11 below.

Table 41.11 – Unilever PLC – Annual Accounts – 31 December 1997

Notes to the consolidated accounts (extract)

31 Financial instruments (extract)

Under the interest rate management policy, interest rates are fixed on a proportion of debt and investments for periods up to 10 years. This is achieved by using fixed rate long-term debt issues together with a range of derivative financial instruments such as interest rate swaps, cross currency swaps, forward rate agreements, swaptions, and interest rate caps and floors.

At the end of the 1997 interest rates were fixed on approximately 80% of the projected debt for 1998, and 74% for 1999 (compared to 52% for 1997 and 47% for 1998 at the end of 1996). Similarly, interest receivable was fixed on approximately 48% of projected funds for 1998 and 35% for 1999 (compared to 61% for 1997 and 52% for 1998 at the end of 1996).This change in fixing levels resulted from the inflow of funds from the sale of speciality chemicals business. Fixing is expected to revert to previous levels during the next year. Nominal values of interest rate derivative instruments are shown in the table below. These nominal values are relatively high in relation to total debts and investments because certain financial instruments have consecutive strike and maturity dates on the same underlying debt in different periods. In addition, derivatives are used to swap fixed interest long-term debt into floating rate debt. Whilst the nominal amounts reflect the volume of activity, they do not therefore properly reflect the considerably lower amounts of credit and market risks to which the Group is exposed. The market value of these interest rate instruments at the end of 1997 represented an unrealised gain of £32 million (1996: £53 million).

£ million	Nominal amounts at 31 December	
	1997	1996
Interest rate swaps	**4 345**	5 580
Forward rate agreements	–	182
Swaptions, caps, floors	**101**	147
Total	**4 446**	5 909

Under the Group's foreign exchange policy, exposures with a maximum of one year maturity are generally hedged; this is achieved through the use of the forward foreign exchange contracts and, to a limited extend, foreign currency options. The market value of these instruments at the end of 1997 represented an unrealised loss of £14 million (1996: gain of £34 million).

£ million		Nominal amounts at 31 December	
		1997	1996
Foreign exchange contracts	– buy	**1 400**	1 487
	– sell	**2 575**	2 747
Total		**3 975**	4 234

41.82 Another disclosure required by IAS 32 and given by certain companies, but not required by FRS 13, is exposure to maximum credit risk and concentrations of such risk. It is argued in IAS 32 that information relating to credit risk enables users of the financial statements to assess the extent to which failures by counterparties to discharge their obligations could reduce the amounts of future cash flows from financial assets.

Although not required by FRS 13, this information is sometimes given in the UK as shown in Tables 41.12 and 41.13 below.

Table 41.12 – British Telecommunications plc – Annual Report and Accounts – 31 March 1998

Notes to the Financial Statements (extract)

19. Financial instruments and risk management (extract)

(c) Concentrations of credit risk and credit exposures of financial instruments
The group considers that it is not exposed to major concentrations of credit risk. The group, however, is exposed to credit-related losses in the event of non-performance by counterparties to financial instruments, but does not expect any counterparties to fail to meet their obligations. Based on interest and exchange rates in effect at 31 March 1998, the group had a maximum credit exposure of £118m (1997–£113m) to one counterparty under foreign currency and interest rate swap agreements. The group limits the amount of credit exposure to any one counterparty. The group does not normally see the need to seek collateral or other security.

Table 41.13 – Reuters Holdings PLC – Annual Report – 31 December 1997

Notes to the consolidated cash flow statement (extract)

14. CONCENTRATION OF CREDIT RISK
Reuters is exposed to concentrations of credit risk. Reuters invests in UK and US government securities and with high credit quality financial institutions. Reuters limits the amount of credit exposure to any one financial institution. Reuters is also exposed to credit risk from its trade debtors which are concentrated in the financial community. Reuters estimates that approximately 58% of its subscribers are financial institutions, 28% are corporations in other sectors of the business community, 5% are from the news media and 9% are government institutions and individuals worldwide (1996 – 57%, 28%, 6% and 9% respectively).

Instinet is exposed to the possibility of trades between its counterparties failing to settle. Due to the settlement mechanism employed the maximum exposure is generally limited to the market movement between the trade date and the settlement date. There are no material unprovided off balance sheet exposures or positions in respect of trades undertaken on or prior to 31 December 1997.

Measurement of financial instruments

41.83 At present, financial instruments are measured on a variety of different bases. Furthermore, certain instruments, because they involve little or no initial outlay, are not recognised in the financial statements at all. As noted in paragraph 41.7 above, FRS 13 does not deal, beyond disclosure, with the subjects of measurement and hedge accounting. These subjects were originally included in the ASB's discussion paper issued in July 1996 but, for the reasons given in paragraph 41.7, only the disclosure proposals have so far been progressed to an accounting standard. In the paragraphs that follow, the ASB's initial views on the subject of accounting for financial instruments, as set out in the discussion paper, are summarised.

41.84 In the discussion paper, the ASB considers several approaches to the measurement problem and it concludes that the only viable way forward is to measure all financial instruments at fair value. All gains and losses would then be recognised as they arose.

41.85 The ASB proposes that the gains or losses on the following instruments would be reported in the statement of total recognised gains and losses:

- Fixed rate borrowings (taken to include non-equity shares).
- Instruments that serve to convert a fixed rate borrowing to floating rate or *vice versa* (for example, an interest rate swap).
- Instruments that serve to mitigate the translation risk associated with a net investment in an overseas operation (for example, US dollar loan used to finance a US dollar investment).

All other gains and losses would be reported within the profit and loss account.

41.86 The proposals for measurement of all financial instruments at fair value are radical, especially in the context of long-term debt, and could have a significant effect on the balance sheets and performance measurement of many companies. Indeed, implementation of this proposal may require amendments to both UK company law and the EC 4th Directive. The taxation implications could also be significant.

Hedge accounting

41.87 By using hedge accounting, an entity may defer a gain or loss on an instrument, designated as a 'hedge', so that it may be recognised in the profit and loss account in the same period as the loss or gain on the 'hedged position' (see further chapter 29).

41.88 In its discussion paper, the ASB considers the problems associated with hedge accounting, but it does not propose a single solution. Instead it sets out three different approaches, each of which has support from certain members of the ASB. The three approaches are:

- No longer allow any form of hedge accounting (that is, all gains and losses on a hedge instrument would have to be recognised as they arise).
- Permit hedge accounting where it compensates for perceived accounting anomalies (for example, where the hedged position is carried at historical cost, but the hedge instrument is measured at current value).

- Allow hedge accounting in the above circumstances and also for hedges of some uncontracted future transactions (for example, where a company enters into a forward contract to protect itself from currency risk on future export sales).

41.89 The majority of the Board would allow some hedge accounting although with limitations. The following criteria are suggested as are detailed disclosures (see para 41.66):

- The hedge instrument must be designated as a hedge at the time that hedge accounting is first applied. It should not be designated in retrospect. In addition, a hedge instrument should cease to be designated as such only if the hedged position ceases to exist.

- At the time of designation, the significant characteristics and expected terms of the transaction being hedged must be documented, including dates and quantities.

- The terms of the hedge must be such that it is expected to be effective.

- In each subsequent period, the effectiveness of the hedge should be tested by comparing the gain or loss on the hedge instrument with changes in the expected future cash flows associated with the hedged transaction. To the extent that the hedge proves to be excessive, gains or losses should be reported in the profit and loss account.

- If the hedged position ceases to exist, hedge accounting should be discontinued and any previously deferred gain or loss recognised immediately in the profit and loss account.

[DP para 4.4.2].

41.90 A further question considered by the ASB is that of how hedge accounting should be achieved. If hedge accounting is to be permitted, the ASB tentatively proposes the following approaches:

- Measure the hedge instrument at current value in the balance sheet and record the resulting gain or loss within liabilities or assets respectively. Use of this method would result in losses being recorded as assets and gains as liabilities and this is not consistent with the draft Statement of principles.

- Alternatively, measure the hedge at current value in the balance sheet and report the resulting gain or loss in the statement of total recognised gains and losses. The gain or loss would then be 'recycled' to the profit and loss account in a later period when the hedged transaction occurs. This method has the disadvantage of being inconsistent with the ASB's stated aim of reporting gains and losses in either the profit and loss account or the statement of total recognised gains and losses only once.

41.91 Neither of the above approaches is conceptually preferable to the other, although the ASB has considered proposing a balance sheet treatment for hedges of assets and liabilities and firm contractual commitments and a 'recycling' approach for hedges of uncontracted future transactions.

41.92 It is recognised by the ASB that if the proposals for measurement of all financial instruments at current value were to be adopted the need for hedge accounting would be reduced substantially.

Comparison with IASs

41.93 The IASC issued IAS 32, 'Financial instruments: Disclosure and presentation', in March 1995. As regards disclosure, the requirements of this standard are similar in many ways to the ASB's proposals. A comparison is presented in the table below.

Comparison of ASB disclosure requirements with IAS 32

Subject	FRS 13	IAS 32
Narrative description	Major risks that arise from the use of financial instruments and how those risks are managed. Objectives, strategies and policies for using derivative financial instruments. Mandatory.	Extent of use of financial instruments, associated risks, purposes served and policies for controlling risks. Significant terms and conditions that may affect future cash flows. Non-mandatory.
Accounting policies	Policies and methods adopted.	Policies and methods adopted.
Financial liabilities	Financial liabilities analysed by currency and fixed/floating.	No equivalent.
	Details of interest rates and period of fix for fixed rates.	Earlier of contractual repricing or maturity dates and effective interest rates.
	Maturity profile of borrowings.	No equivalent.
	Analysis of borrowing facilities.	No equivalent.
Financial assets	Similar analyses to those for financial liabilities.	No equivalent.

Currency exposure	Analysis of net monetary assets and liabilities by currency analysed by reference to functional currency.	No equivalent.
Credit risk	No equivalent	Amount of maximum credit risk exposure and details of any significant concentrations of credit risk.
Fair values	All instruments by category. Exemption if not practicable only in extreme cases. No equivalent	All instruments by class. Exemption if not practicable. For financial assets carried at an amount in excess of fair value, both the carrying amount and the fair value together with reasons for the treatment.
Instruments held for trading	Separate disclosure of fair value. Net gains or losses in the year.	No equivalent.
Hedges	Description of all hedging activities and accounting used. Description of hedging instruments used. Details of gains and losses deferred or unrecognised at the year end and gains and losses recognised in the year.	Description of hedges of future transactions, including timing. Description of hedging instruments used. Details of gains and losses deferred or unrecognised at the year end in respect of hedges of future transactions.
Market price risk	Disclosure of market price risk encouraged.	No equivalent.

41.94 The IASC is also working on recognition and measurement. In March 1997 the IASC Financial Instruments Steering Committee published a discussion paper on accounting for financial instruments, addressing both on and off balance sheet items. Its proposals for fair valuing all financial assets and liabilities were not considered to be achievable in the short-term. Thus, in late 1997, the IASC announced that it would complete an interim international standard on the recognition and measurement of financial instruments in 1998. Its proposals were published in June 1998 as E62.

41.95 The main proposals of E62 are that all financial assets, including derivatives, would be carried in the balance sheet at fair value, except those that cannot be reliably measured and those fixed term securities that the enterprise has the intent and ability to hold to maturity. All financial liabilities would be measured at original cost less amortisation, except derivative and trading liabilities which will be measured at fair value.

41.96 E62 suggest two alternatives for dealing with gains and losses on non-hedged financial assets and liabilities measured at fair value. Either they are all reported in the income statement, or only those gains or losses arising on short-term trading would be reported in the income statement with all other gains and losses recorded in equity and 'recycled' to the income statement once the asset is sold or liability extinguished.

41.97 To qualify for hedge accounting treatment, E62 indicates that hedge relationships would need to meet certain qualifying criteria (for example, documentation requirements and hedge effectiveness). The exposure draft describes three main types of hedging relationships – fair value hedges, cash flow hedges and hedges of a net investment in a foreign entity. Hedging instruments would be carried at fair value. Gains and losses on fair value hedges of an existing asset or liability would be included in equity and recycled to the income statement when the hedged transaction affects net profit or loss, with the exception of forecasted asset acquisitions, where the gain or loss would either be left in equity when the asset is acquired and subsequently amortised, or included in the cost of the asset. Gains or losses on hedges of a net investment in a foreign entity would be included in equity within the foreign currency translation reserve and recycled to the income statement on disposal of the investment.

41.98 E62 proposes criteria for the derecognition of financial assets or liabilities, specifying that assets or liabilities should be removed from the balance sheet only when they are sold or transferred. The difference between carrying amount and sale proceeds should be included in net profit or loss for the period. If part of a financial asset or liability is sold or transferred, the carrying amount is split based on relative fair values. If fair values are not determinable then a cost recovery approach is used for recognising profit or loss.

41.99 At the same time as developing E62, the IASC is also working with major national standard setters on a project to develop an all-embracing long-term solution to the complex questions of recognition and measurement of financial instruments.

41.96 E62 suggests two alternatives for dealing with gains and losses on non-hedged financial assets and liabilities measured at fair value. Either they are all reported in the income statement, or only those gains or losses arising on short-term trading would be reported in the income statement with all other gains and losses recorded in equity and 'recycled' to the income statement once the asset is sold or liability extinguished.

41.97 To qualify for hedge-accounting treatment, E62 indicates that hedge relationships would need to meet certain qualifying criteria (for example, documentation requirements, and a high effectiveness test). The exposure draft describes three main types of hedging relationships – fair value hedges, cash flow hedges and hedges of a net investment in a foreign entity. Hedging instruments would be carried at fair value. Gains and losses on fair value hedges of an existing asset or liability would be included in equity and recycled to the income statement when the hedged transaction affects net profit or loss, with the exception of forecasted asset acquisitions, where the gain or loss would either be left in equity when the asset is acquired and subsequently amortised, or included in the cost of the asset. Gains or losses on hedges of a net investment in a foreign entity would be included in equity within the foreign currency translation reserve and recycled to the income statement on disposal of the investment.

41.98 E62 proposes criteria for the derecognition of financial assets or liabilities, specifying that assets or liabilities should be removed from the balance sheet only when they are sold or transferred. The difference between carrying amount and sale proceeds should be included in net profit or loss for the period. If part of a financial asset or liability is sold or transferred, the carrying amount is split based on relative fair values. If fair values are not determinable then a cost recovery approach is used for recognising profit or loss.

41.99 At the same time as developing E62, the IASC is also working with major national standard setters on a project to develop an all-embracing long-term solution to the complex questions of recognition and measurement of financial instruments.

Chapter 42

Accounting implications of the euro

Chapter 42

Accounting implications of the euro

Introduction

42.1 Although the UK is not participating in the first wave of countries adopting the euro, a number of large UK companies are planning to move to accounting in euro, from 1 January 1999. It is likely that this will force a number of smaller suppliers and customers to consider accounting and invoicing in euro. This chapter is also relevant for UK companies that either trade with participating Member States or have subsidiary undertakings in these states. It addresses issues from the point of view of the UK as an 'out' country and considers what would happen if the UK were to enter at a later date.

42.2 The DTI has stated that UK accounting principles are sufficiently robust to deal with the circumstances likely to arise from the introduction of the euro and as such no primary legislation will be introduced. However, there will be a range of practical issues, such as record keeping and legal status, to be resolved in respect of transactions recorded in national currencies that will either arise from the start of the introduction of the euro or take place within the transition phase. There will also be a significant number of issues relating to disclosure and presentation in financial statements.

42.3 Directorate General XV (DG XV) of the European Commission issued a paper (XV/D3/7002/97) in July 1997 setting out an authoritative guide on accounting for the introduction of the euro. The practical issues included in the paper and other issues identified to date are discussed in this chapter. Although the paper from the European Commission was intended to standardise accounting treatments across the EU, there will still be a number of different interpretations of particular issues. This chapter indicates where certain countries are proposing to diverge from the standard approach.

Realisation of foreign exchange differences

42.4 The bilateral exchange rates of currencies of participating countries to be effective on 31 December 1998, were fixed on 2/3 May 1998. Although these currencies will continue to fluctuate against each other in the intervening period, the bilateral rates to which they should converge by 31 December 1998 are now known. However, the bilateral exchange rate for the euro relative to other external currencies will not be fixed until midnight on 31 December 1998. As the economic event occurs in 1998 any exchange differences arising should be accounted for in the corresponding financial period.

42.5 In relation to exchange differences in the UK, the introduction of the euro should have little impact as at 31 December 1998 and the accounting treatment adopted in previous years should continue. There will be a considerable change in certain euro zone countries, in that the rates will be fixed and any differences are realised.

42.6 Under existing UK accounting practices, realised exchange differences are generally required to be recognised in the profit and loss account. However, it may be necessary to consider whether an exchange result relates to the current year or to some future period.

42.7 Deferred recognition of exchange results in the profit and loss account may be appropriate when this leads to a better matching of income and expenses, that is when they have a direct relationship with offsetting future income or expense items. Normally all realised exchange differences on monetary items are recognised in the profit and loss account. The exchange differences realised upon the introduction of the euro have, in all material respects, the same nature as other realised exchange differences and thus should be treated in the same way (see further chapter 29).

42.8 There is no reason for the changeover to the euro to change the accounting practices that are allowed under the Accounting Directives in the Member States. Therefore, while immediate recognition of negative differences is required, an application of the prudence principle in conformity with the Accounting Directives could allow the deferral of positive exchange differences until realised in cash (referred to as the 'imparity principle'). The DG XV paper considers, however, that the reason for not recognising such gains lies in the existence of credit risk, which has nothing to do with the question of recognition of exchange gains. It concludes that exchange gains on monetary assets must be taken into account and allowances for credit risks should be set up separately. This may mean that certain continental companies will have problems with regard to the payment of tax on these accumulated profits that now arise. In some countries profits will only be treated as realised when the cash flows occur. In certain other continental countries there is a proposal to pass these profits directly through reserves.

42.9 There are a number of ways in which the exchange differences may be classified in the profit and loss account. Normally gains and losses arising from trading transactions should be recognised within 'other operating income/charges', disclosed as exceptional items if warranted by virtue of their size and incidence. Gains and losses arising from financing transactions should be shown separately as part of 'other interest receivable and similar income' or as part of 'interest payable and similar charges'. Exchange gains and losses that arise from events that themselves fall to be disclosed as non-operating items under paragraph 20 of FRS 3, should be included as part of such items.

42.10 An issue arises when considering the treatment of cumulative foreign exchange translation differences that have been recognised in the statement of total recognised gains and losses (reserves) in periods prior to the introduction of the euro. The UITF in Abstract 21, 'Accounting issues arising from the proposed introduction of the euro', has stated that *"following the principle in FRS 3, cumulative foreign exchange translation differences recognised in the statement of total recognised gains and losses in accordance with SSAP 20, should remain in reserves after the introduction of the euro and should not be reported in the profit and loss account".*

Foreign exchange derivative contracts

42.11 It is common for companies in the EU to hedge their foreign exchange risks arising from positions in other national currencies using foreign exchange contracts. The risks arising from fluctuations in the national currencies of the participating Member States will be eliminated after the introduction of the euro. In the absence of exchange risks, the outcome of a foreign exchange contract can be calculated with certainty. A contract between two participating currencies will have a definite outcome and, as the hedge is no longer required, the exchange difference will be realised. This has certain consequences for entities in participating Member States, which will not arise for UK companies. These issues are considered below.

42.12 Whilst the legal framework for the use of the euro provides for the continuity of contracts, these foreign exchange contracts will no longer have any risk reducing effect. Consequently various options are available to the counterparties:

- allow the contract to continue with, in effect, agreed annuities to be paid on each payment date; or
- terminate the contract with a single payment to be made based on the present value of future cash flows.

42.13 The mechanics of each action will be determined by the relevant International Swap Dealers Association (ISDA) Master Agreement under which the transaction was effected, or by reference to ISDA's EMU Protocol. The purpose of each particular foreign exchange contract will decide whether or not the exchange differences should be recognised in the profit and loss account or in the statement of total recognised gains and losses.

42.14 Contracts may be categorised as follows:

- Speculative – differences arising on these contracts should be recognised immediately, since there is no offset of future income or expense.

- Hedges of balance sheet items – the combined exchange difference on the foreign exchange contract and the balance sheet item should be recognised in the profit and loss account immediately.

- Anticipatory hedges – there is currently no accounting standard dealing with anticipatory hedges. UITF Abstract 21 concludes that the introduction of the euro should have no impact on the accounting treatment adopted. Current practice is to defer gains and losses on anticipatory hedges and recognise them in the profit and loss account in the same period as the related income or expense or asset or liability being hedged.

The euro as a functional currency

42.15 It is possible for a UK company to produce its financial statements in euro for financial periods ending after 31 December 1998 if its 'local currency', as defined in SSAP 20, is the euro. SSAP 20 defines 'local currency' as the currency of the primary economic environment in which the entity operates and generates cash flows. In order to meet this definition, a company that adopts the euro as its local currency will be expected to have the majority of its income, expenses, assets and liabilities denominated in euro. In certain cases, however, it is likely that companies may invoice in euro and be invoiced by suppliers in euro, while most of their other expenses, particularly wages, salaries and rent, remain in sterling.

42.16 The national currencies of the participating Member States are replaced by the euro from 1 January 1999 and thereby cease to exist in a legal sense as currencies in their own right, but their units are maintained as sub-divisions of the euro. Consequently, a UK parent with extensive operations in the participating euro zone countries would be able to determine that the euro is the local currency. In such instances, a UK parent will be able to prepare and file its financial statements in euro only without the need to prepare financial statements in sterling.

42.17 In the US the term 'functional currency' is used rather than 'local currency', but the definition is very similar. However, the US guidance goes on to state that, where the facts in a given situation do not clearly identify the functional currency, the determination rests on the judgement of management. The FASB has developed guidelines, which indicate some factors to be considered when determining the functional currency. The following lists some of the indicators to consider in deciding whether or not the euro is the functional currency:

- Cash flow indicators – the currency of the company's principal cash flows.

- Sales price indicators – whether sales prices are determined principally by local competition or by exchange rate changes. For instance, if price changes are determined not by exchange differences between sterling and the euro, but by competition between companies pricing in euro, this might indicate that the functional currency is the euro.

- Sales market indicators – the entity may have a significant market in those countries where the euro is the principal currency, rather than having its principal market in a non-euro economy.
- Expense indicators – the denomination of the entity's costs of production (labour and materials etc).
- Financing indicators – whether financing is in euro or in domestic currency.

42.18 Application of the above indicators may mean that companies with extensive European operations will be able to determine that the euro is their functional currency. In some cases the determination may depend on the weighting given to one indicator relative to another. For instance, a company that makes most of its sales in euro, but incurs the majority of its costs in sterling, may give more weight to the sales price and sales market indicators in order to determine that the functional/local currency is euro.

Adoption of a reporting currency that is different from the functional/local currency

42.19 The term 'reporting currency' is not used in the UK or the US, as standards in those countries require the local/functional currency to be used for reporting purposes. However, in IAS 21, 'The effects of changes in foreign exchange rates', the term is used and defined simply as the currency used in presenting the financial statements. IAS 21 states that it does not specify the currency in which an entity presents its financial statements, but requires an entity to disclose the reasons for using any currency other than of the country in which it is domiciled. IAS 21, therefore, does not prevent a company using a reporting currency that is different from the local functional currency provided that the reason is given.

42.20 However, at the current time in the UK the use of a reporting currency that is different from the local/functional currency may be a departure from SSAP 20.

Filing of financial statements in euro

42.21 Although this matter is not specifically dealt with in the Companies Act, the Registrar of Companies accepts annual financial statements prepared in a foreign currency, provided that the currency exists legally and the exchange rate to sterling is disclosed in the notes to the financial statements.

42.22 Most national laws of euro zone countries do not permit a choice of reporting currency and, where this is the case, companies must continue to publish their financial statements in national currency. A number of countries are changing their local legislation. Companies in participating Member States will also have the option to prepare financial statements in either national currency or euro during the transition period from 1 January 1999 to 31 December 2001. Such companies may prepare their entity financial statements in national currency while publishing their consolidated financial statements in euro, or *vice versa.* From 1 January 2002 all companies in the participating euro zone must prepare their financial statements in euro.

42.23 UK companies will have a choice of filing financial statements in euro or in sterling once the euro becomes a legal currency (that is after 1 January 1999). As at present, the appropriate choice of reporting currency will depend on the functional currency. It will not be possible to publish financial statements in euro for periods ending before 1 January 1999, because the euro will not exist as a currency before that date.

Preparing financial statements when the euro has not existed for a full year

42.24 Where amounts in the profit and loss account are translated at the closing rate the introduction of the euro provides no complications. However, the issue is more complicated where an average rate is required when the euro has not existed for a full year.

42.25 An example is a UK company, with a 31 March 1999 year end, which decides to prepare its financial statements to that date in euro. There are three options to consider:

- Convert the sterling figures for the full year to euro at the year-end euro exchange rate (31 March 1999).
- Convert the sterling figures for the full year using an average exchange rate since the introduction of the euro (31 December 1998 to 31 March 1999).
- Convert the sterling figures for the nine months to 31 December 1998 using the 31 December 1998 fixing rate and convert the sterling figures for the three months to 31 March 1999 using an average exchange rate since the introduction of the euro (31 December 1998 to 31 March 1999).

42.26 The results of each method may vary according to exchange rate movements during the year. Sterling depreciated against the Deutschmark by six per cent between

1 April and 31 May 1998. We believe the third method to be preferable and the one that companies should use.

42.27 For following years, when the euro will have existed for the whole reporting period, the translation of transactions can be either on an actual exchange rate basis, on the average rate for the period, in accordance with current practice.

42.28 In another example, a UK company continuing to report in sterling has a Dutch subsidiary, with both companies having a 31 March 1999 year end. The results of the Dutch subsidiary will need to be converted into sterling in two stages: the nine months to 31 December 1998 from guilders to sterling and the three months to 31 March 1999 from euro to sterling. The alternative of using the euro results produced by the Dutch subsidiary for the year to 31 March 1999 may provide distorted figures.

Consolidation of foreign operations

42.29 The effects of the introduction of the euro on the methods of consolidation available are outlined below.

42.30 Translation differences arising on the consolidation of foreign operations, relating to both monetary and non-monetary assets and liabilities of the foreign operations, are recognised in reserves. Once the fixed conversion rates between the national currency units of the participating Member States are in effect, the translation differences on foreign operations denominated in one of the other participating currencies will become fixed amounts. Although these exchange differences are now realised, UITF Abstract 21 makes it clear that they should remain in reserves and not be taken to the profit and loss account. This provision has no impact in the UK until the UK becomes a participating Member State.

42.31 The Standing Interpretation Committee (SIC) of the IASC in Interpretation SIC-7 has also confirmed that it is not considered appropriate that the cumulative amount of these translation differences should be recognised immediately in the profit and loss account. Recognition should occur in the period in which the disposal of the foreign operation occurs.

Treatment of conversion and euro preparation costs

42.32 UITF Abstract 21 states that the costs of making the necessary modifications to assets to deal with the euro should be written off to the profit and loss account except:

- Where an entity already has an accounting policy to capitalise the assets of the relevant type.

- To the extent that the expenditure clearly results in an enhancement of an asset beyond that originally assessed rather than merely maintaining its service potential.

42.33 Other costs associated with the introduction of the euro should also be written off to the profit and loss account.

42.34 Expenditure incurred in preparing for the changeover to the euro and regarded as exceptional should be disclosed in accordance with FRS 3. Particulars of commitments at the balance sheet date in respect of costs to be incurred (whether to be treated as capital or revenue) should be disclosed where they are regarded as relevant to assessing the entity's state of affairs. Where the potential impact is likely to be significant to the entity, the UITF recommends that other information and discussion should be given, including an indication of the total costs likely to be incurred. This information may be more appropriately located in the directors' report or any operating and financial review or other statement included in the annual report published by the entity.

42.35 The ASB has recently published FRS 12 on provisions and contingencies which allows provision to be made only where *"an entity has a legal or constructive obligation to transfer economic benefits as a result of past events"*. This means that it is not appropriate to make provision for the costs of preparing for the introduction of the euro before they are incurred. However, if material, financial commitments to incur cash in future periods should be disclosed in accordance with the requirements of the Companies Act 1985. [4 Sch 50(5)].

Non-monetary assets

42.36 From 31 December 1998 the euro will provide a fixed exchange rate between participating currencies. A separate cross rate will then be established between sterling and those currencies. In financial statements to be prepared in euro, the issue arises of which rate of exchange to use for translation of non-monetary fixed assets. There are a number of possibilities, including:

- Translation of the sterling balance sheet carrying value, calculated using the historical exchange rate, at the sterling to euro exchange rate prevailing at the balance sheet date.

- Translation of the historical currency amount at the euro rate at 31 December 1998.

Example

A UK company preparing its accounts in euro with a German non-monetary fixed asset, purchased for DM70m, translates the asset at the historical rate of exchange of £1 = DM3.5 when recognising it on the UK balance sheet at £20m.

At 31 March 1999 assume €1 = DM2 and €1 = £0.8 giving a cross rate of £1 = DM2.5. Then:

- Translating the historical currency amount to sterling at the historical exchange rate, and then translating the £20m to euro, will give an asset cost of €25m.

- Translating the historical currency account of DM70m at the only historical euro rate available (that is, that on 31 December 1998) will give an asset cost of €35m.

42.37 For the example given, in economic terms the position at 31 March 1999 is that the asset cost of DM 70 million equates to €35 million, whilst in accounting terms £20 million is worth €25 million. If the DG XV paper is followed, no gain should be realised. We consider that it is more appropriate to state the historical cost in the legacy local currency and then convert to euro at the rate prevailing at the balance sheet date.

42.38 With the introduction of FRS 10, 'Goodwill and intangible assets', and FRS 11, 'Impairment of fixed assets and goodwill', it would seem an appropriate time for the assessment of the carrying value of all fixed assets. The introduction of the euro could significantly affect the estimated book value of certain fixed assets. Assets that deal with legal tender, such as cash registers and currency vending machines, may depreciate considerably in value as a result of the single currency. Any change in carrying value will also affect the future depreciation charges for those assets.

Accounting for unfair outturns

42.39 As described in the Euro Guide on Legal Issues, Article 3 of Regulation 1103/97 provides for the conversion of national currency units into euro and also states that *"the introduction of the euro shall not have the effect of altering any term of a legal instrument or of discharging or excusing performance under any legal instrument, nor give a party the right unilaterally to terminate such an instrument"*.

42.40 Therefore, a company in Germany may have a debenture with an interest rate of five per cent while a company in Italy may have a debenture paying 12 per cent, reflecting the historical weakness of the lira. When these debentures are converted into euro liabilities they will still have the same interest rates attaching. The issue of whether or not a company in these circumstances should be allowed to provide for the future interest differential payments on a net present value basis has been reviewed by the UITF. Although it did not publish an abstract, it concluded that it was appropriate to charge the interest on an ongoing basis and that an upfront provision was not appropriate.

Comparative information

42.41 Comparative figures are required for the preceding year in financial statements and, if published, also for five-year records for listed companies. The DG XV paper states that the preferred method for translating the comparative figures should be to translate them at the fixed conversion rate. Translation of the comparative figures using historical exchange rates is not possible, because the euro was not in existence before 1 January 1999. It is not appropriate to use the ecu as a surrogate for the euro, because the ecu exchange rate is determined by a basket of currencies, some of which will not be included in the euro. Nor is it considered appropriate to use a synthesised historical exchange rate based on the ecu. In addition, translating the comparative figures at the fixed euro exchange rate has the advantage of being very easy to apply. However, it sometimes presents a problem of interpretation of which the user of financial statements should be aware.

Example

Companies A and B both sell equal quantities of the same product for each of the years shown below. However, the sales of company A, denominated in currency X, increase as a result of the inflation in country X, whereas company B operates in an environment without inflation.

	1995	1996	1997	1998
Company A	X$100	X$104	X$109	X$112
Company B	Y$100	Y$100	Y$100	Y$100
Company A	€89	€93	€97	€100
Company B	€100	€100	€100	€100

When the sales figures of both companies are translated into euro using the fixed exchange rates, the sales for the year 1998 will be equal for both companies. However, for the period 1995-1997 company A will have a lower turnover in euro than company B, but company A will appear to be growing where company B is not. This may seem to be a strange side effect of the currency translation, but the same phenomenon exists in the financial statements in the original currencies. Nevertheless, it may confuse readers of financial statements who are not aware of the difference in inflation between country X and Y.

42.42 This may have a significant impact on understanding company and group financial statements for a number of years.

42.43 In the case of a consolidation, the UITF in the appendix to Abstract 21 has stated that it is not appropriate to rework the translations underlying the preparation of the original financial statements in the relevant national currency of the Member State. For example, a French subsidiary of an Irish company may have had level profits for two consecutive years when expressed in francs. However, when expressed in punts the figures will have reflected the change in the punt/franc exchange rate over the two years and the profits expressed in punts are unlikely to be level. Translation of the franc figures into euro should be carried out by first translating them into punts at the exchange rates ruling at the relevant dates and then translating those figures into euro.

Post-balance sheet events

42.44 For companies with a financial year not coinciding with the calendar year, the introduction of the euro should be accounted for in the period which contains 31 December 1998. However, it will not be possible to publish financial statements in euro units for financial periods ending before 1 January 1999, as the euro will only become the single currency of the participating Member States from that date.

42.45 For companies with accounting periods ending on or before 31 December 1998, but whose financial statements are not signed until after that date, the introduction of the euro is a post balance sheet event which can still have an impact on the financial statements for that financial year. Such companies should disclose the effects of the changeover to the euro in their financial statements for that period, if these effects are established after the announcement of fixed conversion rates.

No par value shares

42.46 UK companies will be able to issue new shares denominated in euro from 1 January 1999. However difficulties arise in relation to redenomination of existing shares. Redenomination of existing shares into euro is possible, but not easy under current UK law.

42.47 The cancellation of existing shares to enable the issuance of new shares requires both court and shareholder approval under English law. Redenomination of shares into euro would result in par values for those shares that would be restated to several decimal places. Renominalisation, the reorganisation of shares to achieve round par values, presents practical problems for companies whose shares have a relatively small par value.

42.48 One of the possible solutions under discussion is the introduction of 'no par value' shares. This concept is well established in the USA and Canada and would avoid altogether the need to renominalise shares. Under this method of accounting for share capital, the entire proceeds of any share issue would be classified as the share capital of the company and shares would be expressed as a percentage of the total shares issued rather than in terms of nominal values.

42.49 Such an approach would remove the share premium account from the balance sheet. An implication of this is that companies would lose the option to use this element of the share capital for paying fully paid bonus shares and for writing off preliminary expenses, expenses of share or debenture issues and the commission paid/discount allowed on any issue of shares or debentures.

42.50 It should be noted that UK law does not currently allow no par value shares and that amendments would be required to the Companies Act to change this. The DTI has issued a discussion paper to obtain views on this subject.

Small and medium-sized entities (SMEs)

42.51 Articles 11 and 27 of the 4th Directive define the thresholds for SMEs as follows:

	Small Entity ECU	Medium Entity ECU
Balance sheet total	1,000,000	4,000,000
Net turnover	2,000,000	8,000,000

42.52 These ecu amounts are presently translated into the national currency of Member States, subject to rounding restrictions which limit the increase in the ecu equivalent thresholds to ten per cent.

42.53 It is possible after the introduction of the euro that the euro amounts of the above thresholds may not be equal to the euro amounts in the national legislation of participating Member States. During the transition period it is expected that companies may continue to use the thresholds as determined in their national currency units in their national legislation, but the currency units of participating Member States may not be used from 1 January 2002. This would give rise to a position where participating Member States will use the euro denominated thresholds, as adjusted after the end of the transition period, while non-participating Member States could continue to use the ten per cent rounding rule.

42.54 In order to ensure consistency between Member States, it is expected that a review of the thresholds in 1999 will seek to introduce a Directive that guarantees equivalent treatment of SMEs across Member States, although it is not yet known how this is to be achieved.

Conversion, rounding and triangulation

42.55 The following section has been extracted from the Bank of England publication 'Practical issues arising from the introduction of the euro' (Issue No. 8) and provides details of issues relating to conversion, rounding and 'triangulation' under the Article 235 Regulation. These issues have very important implications for accounting and systems implementation.

42.56 It is important to note that all of the figures used below, and in particular the conversion rates and exchange rates, are purely illustrative. However, the implied bilateral conversion rates between EMU-participating currencies are consistent with the pre-announced bilateral rates that will be used to determine the irrevocable conversion rates between those currencies and the euro at the start of 1999. Throughout this section, the terms 'national currency unit' (NCU) and 'national denomination' are used interchangeably to refer to the currency units of those countries participating in EMU.

Conversion, rounding and triangulation between denominations of the euro

42.57 Following the start of EMU on 1 January 1999 there will be a need to convert monetary amounts between the euro and its 11 national denominations on a regular basis. The way in which these conversions should be carried out is governed by the provisions in the Article 235 Regulation, which applies in all 15 EU Member States (that is, including the UK).

42.58 It is only when converting between the euro and its 11 national denominations – whether converting from a national currency unit (NCU) to the euro, from the euro to a NCU, or from one NCU to another NCU – that the conversion and rounding rules of the Article 235 Regulation apply.

42.59 The rounding rules contained within the regulation apply solely in the context of a conversion between the euro and national denominations, or between national denominations. The rounding rules do not affect existing rounding practices in other contexts (for example, in the calculation of interest on a loan on a daily basis, where the amount of the loan, and the amounts of interest, are all expressed in the same denomination).

42.60 The EU communiqué issued on 3 May 1998 explained that the bilateral central ERM rates of participating countries' currencies would be used in determining the irrevocable conversion rates for each of these currencies against the euro at the start of 1999. But the bilateral rates will not be used for the purposes of conversion thereafter, as this will be prohibited by the Article 235 Regulation (since they would not produce the same results as the triangulation process, except for very small monetary amounts).

Conversion and rounding rules set out in the Article 235 Regulation

42.61 The rules for conversion, rounding and 'triangulation' contained in the regulation are summarised in the paragraphs that follow:

Conversion rates to six significant figures

42.62 The conversion rates must be adopted as one euro expressed in terms of each of the NCUs of the participating countries to six significant figures (note that the number of decimal places will vary from one NCU to another).

Example

One euro might be expressed as:

€1 = DM1.96804 €1 = FF6.60054 €1 = BF40.5918 etc...

Rounded and truncated conversion rates

42.63 These conversion rates must not be rounded or truncated when making conversions.

Example

When converting between the euro and Deutschmarks, it is only acceptable to use the rate of €1 = DM1.96804. Rounded rates of, say, €1 = DM2, €1 = DM1.97 or €1 = DM1.968 and truncated rates such as €1 = DM1.9 or €1 = DM1.96, are not acceptable.

42.64 When rounding monetary amounts to be paid or accounted for after a conversion, these must be rounded up or down to the nearest sub-unit (or in the absence of a sub-unit to the nearest unit) or according to national law or practice to a multiple or fraction of the sub-unit (or unit) of the NCU. If the result is exactly half-way, the result shall be rounded up.

Example

€2 would convert to DM3.93608, which would be rounded up to DM3.94. €10 would convert to DM19.6804, which would be rounded down to DM19.68. €125 would convert to DM246.005, which would be rounded up to DM246.01.

Converting from the euro to a NCU and vice versa

42.65 The conversion rates must be used for conversions in either direction between the euro and its national denominations.

Example 1

Converting from the euro to a NCU

100 euro converted into Deutschmarks would be €100 = DM100 × 1.96804 = DM196.804, which would be rounded to DM196.80.

Example 2

Converting from a NCU to the euro

100 Deutschmarks converted into euro would be DM100 = €100 ÷ 1.96804 = €50.811975…, which would be rounded to €50.81.

Inverse conversion rates

42.66 Inverse rates derived from the conversion rates must not be used.

Example

The inverse rate corresponding to the conversion rate of €1 = FF6.60054 would be FF1 = €0.151503. The number 0.151503 is an approximation to the reciprocal of 6.60054 (the true reciprocal is 0.1515027558…). This inverse rate must not be used.

Converting from one NCU to another via the euro (triangulation)

42.67 In practice, this means that when converting from the euro to a NCU, it is necessary to multiply the euro amount by the conversion factor. When converting from a NCU to the euro, it is necessary to divide the NCU amount by the conversion factor. Conversion between one NCU and another must be done via the euro (this procedure has become known as 'triangulation').

Example

10,000 French francs converted into Deutschmarks would first need to be converted into euro, before then being converted to Deutschmarks.

- Convert the French francs into euro.

  FF10,000 = €10,000 ÷ 6.60054 = €1,515.0275583…

- It is permissible to round the result of the first step (see below). In this example, the amount has been rounded to four decimal places, that is, €1,515.0276.

- Convert the intermediate euro amount into Deutschmarks.

€1,515.0276 = DM1,515.0276 × 1.96804 = DM2,981.634917…, which would be rounded to DM2,981.63.

Rounding to three or more decimal places

42.68 It is permissible, but not compulsory, to round the intermediate euro amount to no fewer than three decimal places.

Example

€1,515.0275583…rounded to 3 decimal places would be €1,515.028
€1,515.0275583…rounded to 4 decimal places would be €1,515.0276, etc.
It would not be permissible to round the intermediate amount to, say, €1,515.03.

42.69 It is not necessary to record in any way the intermediate euro amount.

Deriving different results depending on whether (and to what extent) the intermediate euro amount has been rounded

42.70 Different results may be derived from the triangulation process, depending on whether this intermediate euro amount is rounded (and, if so, to how many decimal places). If two different parties derive different results after triangulation, then they may wish to check whether they have rounded the intermediate euro amount, and, if they have, whether they have done so to the same number of decimal places.

Example

In the previous example, if the intermediate euro amount had been rounded to 3 decimal places (that is, €1,515.028), then converting this to Deutschmarks would have given DM2,981.635705…, which would be rounded to DM2,981.64.

By contrast, when the intermediate euro amount was rounded to 4 decimal places (that is, €1,515.0276), the subsequent conversion to Deutschmarks gave DM2,981.634917… which was rounded to DM2,981.63.

42.71 No alternative method of calculation may be adopted, unless it produces the same results. In practice, it is difficult to prove rigorously that alternative methods of calculation do produce the same results as the triangulation algorithm. The onus of proof, and the legal risk, rests with the person using an alternative method.

Conversions between the euro and other currencies

42.72 Foreign exchange transactions or conversions between the euro and other (EU or non-EU) currencies (such as £, $, or ¥) will take place in the same way that foreign exchange transactions are currently carried out. The conversion and rounding rules of the Article 235 Regulation do not apply to the calculations that are made after such operations. Indeed, there are currently no universally accepted rules about how amounts are converted and rounded after foreign exchange transactions or conversions and the introduction of the euro will not change this.

42.73 Likewise, the conversion and rounding rules of the Article 235 Regulation do not apply to any other types of conversion between the euro and other currencies such as £, $, or ¥.

Example

If at a point in time the exchange rate between the euro and the US dollar were €1 = $1.0838, a sum of €10 would convert to $10.838. There is no universally accepted convention about how this US dollar amount should be rounded (although in most instances, one would expect the amount to be rounded up to the nearest cent, that is, $10.84).

Conversions between the national denominations of the euro and other currencies

42.74 Some conversions may be required between the national denominations of the euro and other currencies such as £ or $. As with conversions between the euro and other currencies, these conversions could arise for a number of different reasons, including foreign exchange transactions and conversions of financial statements (although it is not expected that there will be significant amounts of trading between the national denominations of the euro and other currencies, such as sterling).

42.75 There are two methods for converting between the national denominations of the euro and other currencies. Both are equally valid, but do not necessarily produce the same result when applied to the same initial amount. If, therefore, parties derive different results, they may wish to check which method each has adopted.

Method 1: conversion via the euro

42.76 This method has two steps: conversion between the national denomination and the euro, and conversion between the euro and another currency. The conversion and rounding rules of the Article 235 Regulation do apply to this method, as follows. When converting from a national denomination of the euro to another currency, the conversion rules (but not the rounding rules) apply to the initial step. When converting from another currency to a national denomination of the euro, both the conversion and the rounding rules apply to the latter step. At no point do the conversion or rounding rules apply to the other step, that is, when converting between the euro and another currency.

Example 1

Converting from a NCU to a foreign currency via the euro

Using an exchange rate between sterling and the euro of €1 = £0.6778, and the conversion rate between the Deutschmark and the euro of €1 = DM1.96804, a sum of 1,000 Deutschmarks could be converted into sterling as follows:

- Convert the Deutschmarks into euro, following the Article 235 Regulation DM1,000 = €1,000 ÷ 1.96804 = €508.119753...

  Note that the conversion rules as set out in the Article 235 Regulation must be adhered to in this calculation. There is no need, however, to round this intermediate amount in accordance with the Article 235 Regulation, since it is not a *"sum to be paid or accounted for"*. (There are also no universally accepted conventions on how to round this intermediate result, if it is decided to do so.)

- Convert the intermediate euro amount into sterling. (NB for the purposes of this example, the intermediate euro amount has been rounded to the nearest euro cent, that is, €508.12.)

  €508.12 = £508.12 × 0.6778 = £344.403736

  There is no universally accepted convention on how to round the result of this latter conversion; in many instances, though, one might expect to round it to the nearest penny, that is, £344.40.

Example 2

Converting from a foreign currency to a NCU via the euro

When converting, say, a sum of £1,000 into Deutschmarks,

- Convert the sterling into euro.

  £1,000 = €1,000 ÷ 0.6778 = €1,475.361463...

  There is no universally accepted convention on whether (and if so how) to round after this first conversion. In this example, the amount has been rounded to the nearest euro cent, that is, €1,475.36.

- Convert the euro into Deutschmarks, following the Article 235 Regulation.

  €1,475.36 = DM1,475.36 × 1.96804 = DM2,903.567494... = DM2,903.57 (rounded to the nearest pfennig, in accordance with the Article 235 Regulation).

Method 2: conversion using a cross rate

42.77 It will be possible to derive cross rates between the national denominations of the euro and other currencies by using the fixed conversion rates and the exchange rates between the euro and other currencies quoted in the foreign exchange market. Although it is not expected that there will be much, if any, trading between the national denominations of the euro and other currencies, major banks in the UK are expected to quote such cross rates involving sterling for their customers' use. They may also be quoted in the foreign exchange markets themselves; or they may be derived and published by information service providers and by newspapers; or individuals may calculate these cross rates themselves.

42.78 Cross rates may be used to convert directly between the national denominations of the euro and other currencies. The conversion and rounding rules of the Article 235 Regulation do not apply to this method – neither when converting from a national denomination to a foreign currency, nor *vice versa.* There is no universally accepted convention on how many significant figures should be quoted in cross rates (though they are often quoted to four significant figures).

Example

Converting between a NCU and a foreign currency using cross rates

Using the same base figures as set out in method 1 the DM/£ cross rate might be 0.3444, which is an approximation to 1 ÷ (1.96804 ÷ 0.6778). Applying this cross rate to DM1,000 gives rise to the same result as for method 1, namely £344.40.

The £/DM cross rate might be 2.904, which is an approximation to 1.96804 ÷ 0.6778. Applying this cross rate to £1,000 gives rise to a *different* result, namely DM2,904.00, from the example set out under method 1.

Practical issues

42.79 The rounding requirements only apply when dealing with third parties. Internally a company or group is able to adopt its own procedures, for example with regard to consolidation procedures, stock valuations and fixed asset registers.

42.80 As described above, the application of an inverse or cross rate method of converting between participating national currency units rather than the triangulation method gives rise to rounding differences. While the economic effect of this rounding is negligible for a particular transaction, rounding can present problems when dealing with third parties and the system implications of such differences can result in significant problems. In order to clear a transaction on which a rounding error has occurred, another transaction must be raised that removes the remaining balance from the system. The problem is, therefore, not one of monetary value by transaction, but of matching in the financial information system in which the transaction is processed. Matching facilities may be compromised, leaving outstanding balances on ledgers where in fact they have been cleared.

42.81 Other practical issues relating to rounding are provided in the annex to this chapter.

Impact of the euro on financial information systems

42.82 The introduction of the euro will have a varying impact on accounting and operational systems, which will be required to cope with functioning in more than one currency. This section concentrates on the technical issues arising apart from rounding which has been covered above. However, it should be noted that there are also significant strategic and competitive implications to be considered.

42.83 The issues arise from the following key problems:

- Input functionality problem – enterprises will be receiving financial information in both euro and the NCU.
- Output functionality problem – enterprises may be required to produce financial information for external reporting purposes in either euro or the NCU, or both.
- Interface problem – it may not be possible to change all information systems to euro operation at the same time. This may result in the situation where information systems working in the NCU will have to communicate with systems working in euro.
- Conversion problem – when the stage is reached where all reporting is undertaken in euro, enterprises will face the problems associated with translation of historical information, as discussed above.

42.84 The extent to which input and output functionality problems are experienced by an organisation will depend to a large extent on the type of information systems that it uses. It is likely that these problems will be less important when a multi-currency input/output system or a system with multiple base currencies is in use.

Input functionality

42.85 An organisation may choose from a number of options when overcoming the input functionality issues:

- Manual translation of euro transactions may be an option if there are few such transactions. The importance of real time transaction processing (for example, at cash registers) should also be considered.

- Standard software solutions are available that involve the attachment of a foreign currency module to existing software packages. The resulting foreign currency functionality is restricted to areas such as invoicing, accounts receivable, accounts payable and cash or bank transactions.

- Modification of current systems to accept both the euro and the NCU as input incurs costs in the form of planning, testing, implementation and training. This option may increase the risk of error, whether in system design or in its use by unfamiliar users.

- Parallel systems could be utilised, with two versions of the existing financial information system running in parallel, one processing in NCUs and the other in euro. This may cause difficulties where transactions are related, but some are in the NCU and others are in euro. Furthermore, the output of one of the two systems will have to be translated at some point anyway.

- Sequential changeover between information systems may be appropriate in instances where the currency unit used depends on the type of transaction. Take for example the case where all purchases from corporate suppliers are in euro while all sales to individuals are in the NCU. The system processing the purchases could be in euro while the sales system continues in the NCU, with an interface between the two systems that converts the amounts from one currency to the other.

Output functionality

42.86 Many of the above solutions are equally applicable to output functionality problems. For instance, customers or government authorities may require financial information in the NCU while the enterprise has already changed over to euro. Where third parties wish to receive financial information in both euro and NCUs it is probable that only a manual solution or modification of information systems will be effective.

42.87 An organisation that switches to euro may wish to keep its historical data available in the NCU to maintain the existing audit trail. Indeed national law in most countries requires enterprises to keep their accounting records in their original form for five to ten years and they must be able to reproduce the accounting records in their original form. This problem could be addressed by printing hard copies of all financial information before changing over to euro, although this may result in a loss of audit trail. The more likely alternative for large organisations is to modify information systems.

Interface issues

42.88 Interface problems can be addressed using the following approaches:

- Interfaces may be designed that not only link two systems, but also convert the amounts from one currency unit to the other. This approach suffers from technical problems such as rounding.
- Simultaneous changeover of all information systems to the euro would eliminate interface problems altogether, but such an approach may not be practical when a large number of substantial systems are involved.
- The identification of autonomous groups of information systems with no, or few, links to other systems may allow simultaneous changeover to be performed on a group by group basis, making the process more manageable.

Conversion

42.89 Conversion of historical information is an issue relevant to most financial information systems, due to the need to multiply/divide historical balances by a fixed conversion rate. A one-off conversion utility, which automatically converts historical information, is relatively straightforward when the system is based on a standard database management system. The modification of information systems by building in a conversion utility is a more flexible option.

Base currency

42.90 The base currency is the currency unit in which a financial information system processes and stores financial information. Most enterprises use a single base currency system, which means that in order to process financial information originally expressed in another currency unit it must be translated manually into the base currency. Such a system presents substantial difficulties when changing over to the euro.

42.91 It is possible, however, to use a system with multi-currency input and/or output, or with multiple base currencies. The latter system will allow multiple currency input, output, processing and storage, with a high quality audit trail that makes it possible to trace a transaction from beginning to end in two base currencies. Such systems, while more expensive and difficult to properly create, do not have the rounding difficulties that would occur with a multi-currency input/output system, and allow an enterprise to start using the euro whenever it wants to do so.

Annex – Practical issues relating to rounding

1 Set out below are some examples and consequences arising from rounding.

Example of rounding difference

Assume the following conversion rates:
€1 = £0.704182 and €1 = FF6.73847

	£	€	FF
Triangulation method	467,167.35	663,418.48	4,470,425.50
Cross rate method (bilateral rate)	467,167.35		4,470,425.51

2 The rounding difference can be reduced by using greater accuracy, increasing the number of digits used in the cross rate. However, even a 15 digit cross rate has been found to produce occasional rounding differences.

Example

A French enterprise (A) sells goods to an English enterprise (B) in the amount of £467,167.35. Enterprise A uses the cross rate method and records the amount as FF4,470,425.51 in its information system. Enterprise A will receive FF4,470,425.50 when enterprise B (which uses the triangulation method) pays for the goods. When matching the sale of goods with the receipt of cash a difference of FF0.01 arises. The difference itself has no economic significance, but in order to clear it the user will need to enter an additional transaction that removes the balance from the system.

3 It is possible to reduce the frequency with which rounding errors arise under the cross rate and inverse rate methods by applying a very high level of accuracy, but the resulting software modification may be more difficult to implement than the triangulation method itself, particularly if one considers the cumulative cost of correcting differences over time.

Unavoidable rounding differences

4 Conversion and reconversion between currencies can result in unavoidable rounding differences. The so called granularity problem occurs in instances where one euro cent represents a greater or lesser value than one national currency 'cent'. In the example shown below, converting from € to £, then to € again, does not result in the original euro amount, because the smallest intermediate unit, the £ 'cent', is greater than a euro cent. The £-€-£ conversion does not result in rounding problems, because no accuracy is lost when converting from £ to €. For other NCUs rounding problems

occur when converting NCU-€-NCU, but not with €-NCU-€. This would be likely for a currency such as the Italian lira, which has a NCU unit equivalent to much less than a euro cent. Any rounding to a euro cent will result in a different lira amount when retranslated.

Example

Assume the, following conversion rate: £1 = €1.420087

Enterprise A decides to convert an invoice from € to £, but then finds it still needs the amount in € and decides to convert it back:

	€	£	€
Convert to £	250.00	176.05	
Convert back to €		176.05	250.01

The reconversion does not result in the original euro amount.

5 When converting financial information it is important to ensure that it is translated not more than once. Multi-currency input/output systems could produce such rounding problems, depending on the choice of base currency. Adoption of the currency unit with the smallest subdivision as the base currency is one possible method of addressing this issue.

Cumulative rounding differences when dealing with small amounts

6 It is possible for rounding to have a material effect on the outcome of calculations. In the situation where a small NCU amount converts to a euro amount which is rounded to the nearest cent, this rounding will represent a larger proportion of the euro value than would be the case for a larger euro amount. Put simply, the rounding by a euro cent will represent a greater proportion of a small euro amount than a large euro amount. In the example below, an enterprise which has a large number of low value items such as nuts and bolts, each valued at BEF3, could experience a rounding effect of six per cent on its inventory.

Example

Assume the following conversion rate: €1 = BF40.3555

Converting data from BF to €:

BF1 = €0.024780, to the nearest € cent = 0.02. Rounding as a percentage of rounded € = 24%

BF2 = €0.049560, to the nearest € cent = 0.05. Rounding as a percentage of rounded € = 1%

BF3 = €0.074339, to the nearest € cent = 0.07. Rounding as a percentage of rounded € = 6%

7 The problem of unavoidable rounding can be approached in a number of ways. Some rounding differences may have little impact on financial information systems. However, where a system uses a matching process to clear transactions it may be appropriate to build in a tolerance of a few euro cents, allowing the system to match amounts that equate to within say five euro cents.

8 An additional method of addressing the issue is to establish a simple automatic clearing procedure for small differences, which would transfer all rounding differences to a balancing account. This would reduce the effort required in dealing with rounding differences, but such a system would require periodic review to identify any irregularities and to reduce the risk of error.

9 Further details of information system implications and issues arising from the euro can be found in a report by the European Commission's Internal Market and Financial Services entitled 'Preparing financial information systems for the euro'.

Appendix 1

UK GAAP Limited
Example set of company financial statements

The example annual report that follows includes the financial statements of UK GAAP Limited a wholly-owned, large private subsidiary company. UK GAAP Limited is a fictitious company. The annual report has been prepared for illustrative purposes only and shows the disclosures and formats that might be expected for a company of its size that prepares its financial statements in accordance with Schedule 4 to the Companies Act 1985 as amended by the Companies Act 1989 and subsequent statutory instruments. The intention is not to show all conceivable disclosures and this annual report should not, therefore, to be used as a checklist. The suggested disclosures are not necessarily applicable for all private companies. These financial statements include many of the disclosure requirements contained in current Financial Reporting Standards, Statements of Standard Accounting Practice, Urgent Issues Task Force Abstracts and the Company Law. Proposals included in exposure drafts are not yet standard practice and have, therefore, not been reflected in these financial statements.

These illustrative financial statements do not cover (amongst other items):

- Discontinued activities.
- Exceptional items.
- ESOP and similar share schemes where the entity is a participant.
- Long-term contracts.
- Government grants.
- Investment properties.
- Sophisticated capital instruments.
- Impairment of fixed assets.
- Acquisition of a business.
- A cash flow statement.

An example of consolidated financial statements for a listed group of companies that includes many of these items is given in appendix 2.

Registered no: aabbcc

UK GAAP Limited
Example annual report
for the year ended 31 December 1998

UK GAAP Limited

Annual report
for the year ended 31 December 1998

UK GAAP Limited

1

Directors' report for the year ended 31 December 1998

The directors present their report and the audited financial statements of the company for the year ended 31 December 1998.

Principal activities

The company's principal activity during the year was the manufacture and sale of processed foods and bakery products.

All of the company's product areas continued to expand during the year but, because of difficult trading conditions, suffered a fall in profitability.

At the year end the company was in a strong position to take advantage of suitable expansion opportunities that may arise.

Review of business and future developments

The company expects to launch its new product 'Wonderloaf' early in the new year. This is a soft-grain, stay-fresh-longer bread packaged in a new resealable foil wrapper. It is expected that this product should increase significantly the company's share of this part of the bread market.

Results and dividends

The company's profit for the financial year is £361,000 (1997: £578,000). An interim dividend of 3.51p (1997: 2.57p) per ordinary share was paid on 1 September 1998. A final dividend of 5.0p (1997: 3.32p) per ordinary share amounting to £102,000 (1997: £67,000) is proposed and, if approved, will be paid on 6 April 1999. The company also paid a preference dividend amounting to £2,625 (1997: £2,625). The aggregate dividends on the ordinary and preference shares amount to £176,000 (1997: £122,000).

Directors and their interests

The directors who held office during the year are given below:

C D Jones (Chairman)
E F Logan (resigned 6 July 1998)
J F King (Company Secretary)
I D Davies (appointed 31 July 1998)

The interest of Mr C D Jones, who is also a director of the ultimate parent company, GAAP UK plc, is shown in the annual report of that company.

Mr I D Davies holds 161,875 (1997: 124,425) ordinary shares of 1p each in GAAP UK plc and had no interests in the shares or debentures of any other company within the GAAP UK plc group.

Mr J F King had no interests in the shares or debentures of the company or any other company within the GAAP UK plc group.

Notes:

(a) Disclosure of share options – the directors' report or the notes to the financial statements must state, with respect to each person who was a director of the company at the end of the financial year, whether, according to the register of directors' interests, any right to subscribe for shares(or debentures) of the company or another body corporate in the same group, was during the financial year, granted to or exercised by the director (Companies Act 1985 7 Sch 2B). In addition, the number of shares under option at the end of the year and the beginning of the year must be disclosed (Companies Act 1985 7 Sch 2A). See UITF Abstract 10 'Disclosure of directors' share options' for additional recommended disclosure for all companies that have granted share options to directors, however, note the Abstract is non-mandatory for unlisted companies.

(b) Exceptions from notifying interests – Statutory Instrument 1985/802 Companies (Disclosure of Directors' Interests) (Exceptions) Regulations 1985 introduced specific exceptions to the basic

UK GAAP Limited

obligation to notify (and hence disclose) interests (includes options) in the shares of the company or any other body corporate within the same group.

Year 2000

Many computer systems express dates using only the last two digits of the year. These systems require modification or replacement to accommodate the year 2000 and beyond in order to avoid malfunctions and resulting widespread commercial disruption. The operation of our business depends not only on our computer systems, but also to some degree on those of our suppliers and customers. There is, therefore, an exposure to further risk in the event that there is a failure by other parties to remedy their own year 2000 issues.

The company is participating in the GAAP UK plc group programme designed to address the impact of the year 2000 on all the group's businesses. The company has contributed a number of personnel to this group project and the board of directors is regularly updated on progress by the group's executive committee, which is controlling the exercise.

As part of the group exercise, an analysis of significant risks has been performed to determine the impact of the issue on our activities. From this, prioritised action plans have been developed that are designed to address the key risks in advance of critical dates and without disruption to the underlying business processes. Priority is being given to those systems that could cause a significant financial or legal impact on the company's business if they were to fail. The plan also includes a requirement for the testing of all critical systems.

The risk analysis also considers the impact on our business of year 2000 related failures by our significant suppliers and customers. In appropriate cases formal assurance is being sought from these other parties.

The total cost to complete modifications to our computer hardware and software is estimated at £130,000 of which some £40,000 is for new equipment and systems enhancements that will be capitalised and the remainder will be expensed as incurred. Of this £90,000 revenue cost, expenditure of £50,000 has been incurred during the year and the remaining £40,000 will be incurred in the first half of 1999.

Introduction of the euro

During the year we have appointed a full-time project manager and undertaken a high-level analysis of the introduction of the euro.

Although the company does not export any of its products, it does import certain ingredients and, on a less frequent basis, processing machinery from France and Germany. Consequently, the company will have to cope with handling invoices and making payments in euro to our suppliers from 1 January 1999. Therefore, the company as part of a group-wide initiative by its ultimate parent, GAAP UK plc, is in the process of upgrading its computer software to handle the euro and its implications. Training of the appropriate staff has also commenced. It is estimated that the total cost to the company will be £15,000 of which £5,000 has been incurred and expensed in 1998. The balance will be incurred in early 1999.

Research and development

The company is currently undertaking research and development into a new form of processed food based on soya beans.

Disabled persons

Applications for employment by disabled persons are always fully considered, bearing in mind the respective aptitudes and abilities of the applicant concerned. In the event of members of staff becoming disabled every effort is made to ensure that their employment with the company continues and the appropriate training is arranged. It is the policy of the company that the training, career development and promotion of a disabled person should, as far as possible, be identical to that of a person who does not suffer from a disability.

Note: This disclosure is required if the average number of employees during the year and working within the UK exceeds 250.

UK GAAP Limited

Employee involvement

Consultation with employees or their representatives has continued at all levels, with the aim of ensuring that views are taken into account when decisions are made that are likely to affect their interests and that all employees are aware of the financial and economic performance of their business units and of the company as a whole. Communication with all employees continues through the house newspaper and newsletters, briefing groups and the distribution of the annual report.

Note: This disclosure is required if the average number of employees during the year and working within the UK exceeds 250.

Policy and practice on payment of creditors

The company is a registered supporter of the CBI's Prompt Payers of Good Practice to which it subscribes when dealing with all of its suppliers. Copies of the CBI code are available from the Confederation of British Industry, Centre Point, 103 New Oxford Street, London, WC1A 1DU. Trade creditors at the year end represented 34 days (1997: 34 days) of purchases.

Note: This disclosure is required for any company that was at any time within the financial year a public company or a large private subsidiary of a plc. Large private companies are those which exceed the limits in section 247(3) of the Companies Act 1985.

Statement of directors' responsibilities

Company law requires the directors to prepare financial statements for each financial year that give a true and fair view of the state of affairs of the company and of the profit or loss of the company for that period. In preparing those financial statements, the directors are required to:

- Select suitable accounting policies and then apply them consistently.
- Make judgements and estimates that are reasonable and prudent.
- State whether applicable accounting standards have been followed, subject to any material departures disclosed and explained in the financial statements.
- Prepare the financial statements on the going concern basis, unless it is inappropriate to presume that the company will continue in business.

The directors are responsible for keeping proper accounting records that disclose with reasonable accuracy at any time the financial position of the company and enable them to ensure that the financial statements comply with the Companies Act 1985. They are also responsible for safeguarding the assets of the company and hence for taking reasonable steps for the prevention and detection of fraud and other irregularities.

Auditors

The auditors, PricewaterhouseCoopers, have indicated their willingness to continue in office, and a resolution concerning their reappointment will be proposed at the Annual General Meeting.

By order of the Board

A B Smith

Secretary 25 February 1999

Auditors' report to the members of UK GAAP Limited

We have audited the financial statements on pages 5 to 17 which have been prepared under the historical cost convention, as modified by the revaluation of certain fixed assets, and the accounting policies set out on page 8.

Respective responsibilities of directors and auditors

As described on page 3 the company's directors are responsible for the preparation of financial statements. It is our responsibility to form an independent opinion, based on our audit, on those statements and to report our opinion to you.

Basis of opinion

We conducted our audit in accordance with Auditing Standards issued by the Auditing Practices Board. An audit includes examination, on a test basis, of evidence relevant to the amounts and disclosures in the financial statements. It also includes an assessment of the significant estimates and judgements made by the directors in the preparation of the financial statements, and of whether the accounting policies are appropriate to the company's circumstances, consistently applied and adequately disclosed.

We planned and performed our audit so as to obtain all the information and explanations which we considered necessary in order to provide us with sufficient evidence to give reasonable assurance that the financial statements are free from material misstatement, whether caused by fraud or other irregularity or error. In forming our opinion we also evaluated the overall adequacy of the presentation of information in the financial statements.

Opinion

In our opinion the financial statements give a true and fair view of the state of the Company's affairs at 31 December 1998 and of its profit for the year then ended and have been properly prepared in accordance with the Companies Act 1985.

PricewaterhouseCoopers
Chartered Accountants and Registered Auditors
London 25 February 1999

UK GAAP Limited

Profit and loss account for the year ended 31 December 1998

	Note	£'000	1998 £'000	£'000	1997 £'000
Turnover - continuing operations			**11,275**		10,010
Change in stocks of finished goods and work in progress			**76**		74
Own work capitalised			**11**		9
Other operating income			**13**		11
			11,375		10,104
Raw materials and consumables		**(6,519)**		(5,537)	
Other external charges		**(293)**		(278)	
Staff costs	4	**(3,188)**		(2,831)	
Depreciation		**(202)**		(200)	
Other operating charges		**(500)**	**(10,702)**	(262)	(9,108)
Operating profit - continuing operations	4		**673**		996
Income from fixed asset investments			**17**		9
Profit on ordinary activities before interest and taxation			**690**		1,005
Interest receivable and similar income		**21**		13	
Interest payable and similar charges	7	**(163)**	**(142)**	(94)	(81)
Profit on ordinary activities before taxation			**548**		924
Tax on profit on ordinary activities	8		**(187)**		(346)
Profit for the financial year			**361**		578
Dividends – including non-equity	9		**(176)**		(122)
Retained profit for the financial year	20		**185**		456

The company has no recognised gains and losses other than the profit above and therefore no separate statement of total recognised gains and losses has been presented.

There is no difference between the profit on ordinary activities before taxation and the retained profit for the year stated above and their historical cost equivalents.

UK GAAP Limited 6

Balance sheet as at 31 December 1998

	Note		**1998**		1997
		£'000	**£'000**	£'000	£'000
Fixed assets					
Tangible assets	10	**2,385**		2,031	
Investments	11	**56**	**2,441**	76	2,107
Current assets					
Stock	12	**1,908**		1,779	
Debtors due within one year (including £205,000 (1997: £56,000) due after one year) *	13	**2,031**		1,509	
Investments	14	**50**		125	
Cash at bank and in hand		**146**	**4,135**	119	3,532
Creditors – Amounts falling due within one year	15		**(2,334)**		(2,026)
Net current assets			**1,801**		1,506
Total assets less current liabilities			**4,242**		3,613
Creditors – Amounts falling due after more than one year	16		**(719)**		(449)
Provisions for liabilities and charges	18		**(164)**		(17)
Net assets			**3,359**		3,147
Capital and reserves					
Called up share capital	19	**583**		580	
Share premium account	20	**144**		120	
Revaluation reserve	20	**177**		177	
Profit and loss account	20	**2,455**		2,270	
Total shareholders' funds	21		**3,359**		3,147
Analysis of shareholders' funds †					
Equity			**3,211**		2,999
Non-equity	24		**148**		148
			3,359		3,147

Notes:

* *Debtors due after one year must be disclosed separately if material compared to net current assets.*

† *The analysis of shareholders' funds between equity and non-equity elements may be given in the notes, if the non-equity element is not material.*

The financial statements on pages 5 to 17 were approved by the board of directors on 25 February 1999 and were signed on its behalf by:

C D Jones
Director

UK GAAP Limited 7

Notes to the financial statements for the year ended 31 December 1998

1 Accounting policies

These financial statements are prepared under the historical cost convention, as modified by the revaluation of certain tangible fixed assets, and in accordance with applicable accounting standards.

Note: The detailed accounting policies adopted should be disclosed here and include all of the following to the extent applicable.

- *Capital instruments.*
- *Deferred taxation.*
- *Depreciation and amortisation.*
- *Finance costs.*
- *Financial instruments.*
- *Fixed assets.*
- *Foreign currencies.*
- *Goodwill and intangible assets.*
- *Impairment and provisions.*
- *Government grants.*
- *Investment properties.*
- *Leases.*
- *Long-term contracts.*
- *Pensions.*
- *Post–retirement benefits.*
- *Research and development.*
- *Stocks and work in progress.*
- *Turnover.*

FRS 12 is effective for years ending after 23 March 1999, however, this standard has been adopted early in accordance with best practice.

2 Cash flow statement and related party disclosures

The company is a wholly-owned subsidiary of GAAP UK plc and is included in the consolidated financial statements of GAAP UK plc, which are publicly available. Consequently, the company has taken advantage of the exemption from preparing a cash flow statement under the terms of Financial Reporting Standard 1 (revised 1996). The company is also exempt under the terms of Financial Reporting Standard 8 from disclosing related party transactions with entities that are part of the GAAP UK plc group or investees of the GAAP UK plc group. (See note 27.)

3 Segmental reporting

The company's activities consist solely of the processing and sale of food in the United Kingdom.

Note: SSAP 25 disclosures are not required for a private company subsidiary where the disclosures are given in the financial statements of its parent. Neither are they required for a private company that is smaller than ten times the medium-sized thresholds as defined in section 247 of the Companies Act 1985, as amended from time to time by statutory instrument.

UK GAAP Limited 8

4 Operating profit

	1998 £'000	1997 £'000
Operating profit is stated after charging		
Wages and salaries	**2,572**	2,301
Social security costs	**515**	436
Other pension costs	**101**	94
Staff costs	**3,188**	2,831
Depreciation of tangible fixed assets	**159**	158
– owned assets	**43**	42
– leased assets		
Operating lease charges		
– plant and machinery	**42**	34
– other	**55**	48
Research and development – current year	**15**	18
Year 2000 modification costs	**50**	10
Costs incurred in preparation for the introduction of the euro	**5**	–
Auditors' remuneration:		
Audit services	**13**	13
Non-audit services	**5**	5

Notes:

(a) *Disclosure of research and development expenditure charged in the profit and loss account is not required for private companies that are smaller than ten times the medium-sized thresholds as defined in section 247 of the Companies Act 1985.*

(b) *Disclosure of auditors' remuneration for non-audit services is not required for companies that are small or medium-sized as defined in section 247 of the Companies Act 1985, as amended from time to time by statutory instrument.*

5 Directors' emoluments

	1998 £'000	1997 £'000
Aggregate emoluments	**210**	206
Aggregate amounts (excluding shares) receivable under long-term incentive schemes	**5**	7
Sums paid to third parties for directors' services	**2**	3

Retirement benefits are accruing to three (1997: two) directors under a defined benefit scheme. During the year two (1997: two) directors exercised options over 1p shares of GAAP UK plc.

Notes:

(a) *If the company has a defined contribution scheme, a separate figure is to be disclosed showing the aggregate value of any company contributions paid or treated as paid to a pension scheme in respect of money purchase benefits. The number of directors to whom retirement benefits are accruing under each of money purchase and defined benefit schemes must also be disclosed.*

(b) *For unlisted companies the net value of assets received or receivable under a long-term incentive scheme excludes shares and hence such companies must disclose the number of directors entitled to shares under a long-term incentive scheme, if applicable.*

Highest paid director

	1998 £'000	1997 £'000
Total amount of emoluments and amounts (excluding shares) receivable under long-term incentive schemes	**75**	70
Defined benefit pension scheme:		
Accrued pension at end of year	**38**	36

Note: Where the highest paid director exercised any share options, and where any shares under a long-term incentive scheme were receivable by him, these facts must be disclosed (Companies Act 1985 6 Sch 2(3))

6 Employee information

The average monthly number of persons (including executive directors) employed by the company during the year was:

By activity	**1998 £'000**	1997 £'000
Production	166	170
Selling and distribution	32	30
Administration	55	55
	253	255

7 Interest payable and similar charges

	1998 £'000	1997 £'000
Interest payable on overdrafts and bank loans	**109**	33
Interest payable on other loans	**18**	23
Finance leases	**36**	38
	163	94

8 Tax on profit on ordinary activities

	1998 £'000	1997 £'000
Taxation on the profit for the year		
UK corporation tax at 30.25% (1997: 31.5%)	**210**	359
Deferred tax	**(33)**	–
Prior year adjustment for under/(over) provision	**10**	(13)
	187	346

The charge for taxation on the profit for the year is higher by £4,000 (1997: lower by £44,000) due to the effect of timing differences on certain provisions partly offset by accelerated capital allowances on which, in accordance with the company's accounting policy, deferred taxation had not been provided.

UK GAAP Limited

9 Dividends

	1998 £'000	1997 £'000
Equity - Ordinary		
Interim paid: 3.51p (1997: 2.57p) per £0.25 share	**71**	52
Final proposed: 5.0p (1997: 3.32p) per £0.25 share	**102**	67
	173	119
Non-equity - Preference		
Paid: 3.5p (1997: 3.5p) per £1 share	**3**	3
	176	122

10 Tangible assets

	Land and buildings £'000	Plant and machinery £'000	Total £'000
Cost or valuation			
At 1 January 1998	1,291	1,561	2,852
Additions	246	426	672
Disposals	(24)	(106)	(130)
At 31 December 1998	**1,513**	**1,881**	**3,394**
Accumulated depreciation			
At 1 January 1998	211	610	821
Charge for the year	45	157	202
Disposals	(6)	(8)	(14)
At 31 December 1998	**250**	**759**	**1,009**
Net book amount			
At 31 December 1998	**1,263**	**1,122**	**2,385**
At 31 December 1997	1,080	951	2,031
Includes assets valued in 1992			
Gross amount at 31 December 1998 and 1997	280	85	365

	1998 £'000	1997 £'000
The net book amount of land and buildings comprises		
Freehold	**1,216**	1,031
Long leaseholds	**36**	37
Short leaseholds	**11**	12
	1,263	1,080

UK GAAP Limited

If land and buildings and plant and machinery had not been revalued, they would have been included at the following amounts:

	Land and Buildings		Plant and Machinery	
	1998	1997	**1998**	1997
	£'000	£'000	**£'000**	£'000
Cost	**173**	173	**71**	72
Aggregate depreciation	**(29)**	(20)	**(28)**	(22)
Net book amount	**144**	153	**44**	50

	1998	1997
	£'000	£'000
Assets held under finance leases and capitalised in plant and machinery		
Cost	**349**	396
Aggregate depreciation	**(116)**	(132)
Net book amount	**233**	264

11 Investments included in fixed assets

	£'000
At 1 January 1998	76
Disposals	(20)
At 31 December 1998	**56**

Investments principally comprise equity shares in a trade investment with a cost of £40,000 (1997: £40,000). These are listed on the London Stock Exchange and had a market value of £145,000 (1997: £170,000).

12 Stocks

	1998	1997
	£'000	£'000
Raw materials and consumables	**873**	820
Work in progress	**209**	182
Finished goods and goods for resale	**826**	777
	1,908	1,779

£200,000 (1997: £100,000) of finished goods are consignment stocks that are held on a sale or return basis from the manufacturer. Title to these stocks passes at the earlier of when they are sold or nine months from delivery date. On delivery a deposit of 30% is payable. The balance bears interest at LIBOR plus 1¾% and becomes payable when title passes is included in trade creditors.

The replacement cost of stocks exceeds balance sheet values as follows		
Raw materials and consumables	**40**	19

UK GAAP Limited

13 Debtors

	1998	1997
	£'000	£'000
Trade debtors	**1,533**	1,067
Amounts owed by group undertakings	**389**	367
Other debtors	**32**	21
Prepayments and accrued income	**77**	54
	2,031	1,509

Trade debtors include £205,000 (1997: £56,000) falling due after more than one year. Amounts owed by group undertakings are unsecured, interest free and have no fixed date of repayment.

Prepayments and accrued income includes a deferred tax asset of £16,000 (1997: nil).

14 Current asset investments

	1998	1997
	£'000	£'000
Government securities	**50**	125

The market value of the government securities is not materially different from their carrying amount

15 Creditors – Amounts falling due within one year

	1998	1997
	£'000	£'000
Debenture loans (Note 18)	**39**	12
Bank loans and overdrafts (Note 18)	**349**	307
Finance leases (Note 18)	**27**	31
Trade creditors	**1,016**	1,005
Amounts due to group undertakings	**300**	180
Other creditors	**15**	12
Taxation and social security	**343**	291
Accruals and deferred income	**143**	121
Proposed dividend	**102**	67
	2,334	2,026

Amounts due to group undertakings are unsecured, interest free and repayable on demand.

UK GAAP Limited 13

16 Creditors – Amounts falling due after more than one year

	1998	1997
	£'000	£'000
Debenture loans (Note 18)	**175**	207
Bank loans (Note 18)	**305**	43
Finance leases (Note 18)	**139**	149
Taxation and social security	**100**	50
	719	449

17 Loans and other borrowings

	1998	1997
	£'000	£'000
7% unsecured loan stock 1998/99	**39**	51
10% unsecured loan stock 2003/2004	**175**	168
Bank loans and overdrafts	**654**	350
Finance leases	**166**	180
	1,034	749
Maturity of debt		
In one year or less, or on demand	**388**	319
In more than one year, but not more than two years	**305**	82
In more than two years, but not more than five years	**–**	–
In more than five years	**175**	168
	868	569
Amount repayable otherwise than by instalments after more than five years	**175**	168

Note: The maturity time bandings in paragraph 33 of FRS 4 have been changed by paragraph 77 of FRS 13.

The 7% unsecured loan stock 1998/1999 is redeemable at par between 1 January 1998 and 31 December 1999. The 10% unsecured loan stock 2003/2004 is redeemable at par between 1 January 2003 and 31 December 2004.

Included in the bank loans is an amount of £450,000 which is payable in two annual instalments commencing 1 January 1999 and carries interest at 11% fixed. The balance of £80,000 carries interest at LIBOR plus 3% and is repayable in six quarterly instalments commencing 1 February 1999.

UK GAAP Limited

Finance leases

Future minimum payments under finance leases are as follows:

	1998	1997
	£'000	£'000
Within one year	**35**	40
In more than one year, but not more than five years	**111**	129
After five years	**68**	62
Total gross payments	**214**	231
Less finance charges included above	**(48)**	(51)
	166	180

The total value of leases repayable by instalments any part of which falls due after more than 5 years is £37,184 (1997: £35,875).

18 Provisions for liabilities and charges

	Pending litigation	**Reorganisation provision**	**Environmental provision**	**Deferred tax provision**	**Total**
	£'000	**£'000**	**£'000**	**£'000**	**£'000**
At 1 January 1998	–	–	–	17	17
Charged/(credited) to the profit and loss account	15	153	72	(33)	207
Transfer to deferred tax asset	–	–	–	16	16
Utilised during the year	–	(42)	(34)	–	(76)
At 31 December 1998	**15**	**111**	**38**	**–**	**164**

Pending litigation

The company is negotiating a series of legal claims. The directors, after taking appropriate legal advice, do not consider there is any material substance to the claims and are mounting a vigorous defence. The directors consider that disclosure of further details of these claims would seriously prejudice the company's negotiating position and, accordingly, further information on the nature of the obligations has not been provided.

Reorganisation

A rationalisation of product processes at the company's two factories in London and Bradford was announced on 11 December 1998. This rationalisation involving the introduction of new technology will result in the loss of 15 jobs in total over the next few months. Agreement had been reached at the end of November 1998 with the local union representatives that specified the number of staff involved and indicated the amounts payable to those made redundant.

Environmental

In April 1998 a spillage of cleaning chemicals contaminated land surrounding the Bradford factory. The company is committed to a policy of environmental protection and immediate action is being taken to deal with the contamination. A provision of £72,000 has been recognised for those clean-up costs, which are expected to be incurred over an eighteen-month period.

UK GAAP Limited

	1998	1997
	£'000	£'000
Deferred taxation provided in the accounts comprises		
Accelerated capital allowances	**13**	13
Other timing differences	**(29)**	4
Deferred tax (asset)/provision	**(16)**	17
The unprovided amounts of deferred taxation for timing differences are as follows		
Accelerated capital allowances	**23**	11
Other timing differences	**(13)**	2
	10	13

19 Called up share capital

	1998	1997
	£'000	£'000
Authorised		
2,640,000 ordinary shares of £0.25 each	660	660
Allotted and fully paid		
2,032,000 (1997: 2,020,000) ordinary shares of £0.25 each	**508**	505
75,000 3.5% cumulative preference shares of £1 each (issued at a premium of £1 each)	**75**	75
	583	580

During the year 12,000 ordinary shares were issued for cash. The nominal value of these shares was £3,000 and the consideration received was £27,000 after deducting expenses of £1,000.

The 3.5% cumulative preference shares carry a fixed cumulative preferential dividend at the rate of 3.5% per annum, payable half yearly in arrears on 31 December and 30 June. The shares have no redemption entitlement. On a winding up the holders have priority before all other classes of shares to receive repayment of capital plus any arrears of dividend. The holders have no voting rights unless the dividend is in arrears by six months or more.

20 Reserves

	Share premium account £'000	**Profit and loss account £'000**	**Revaluation reserve £'000**
At 1 January 1998	120	2,270	177
Premium on shares issued (net of £1,000 expenses)	24	–	–
Retained profit for the financial year	–	185	–
At 31 December 1998	**144**	**2,455**	**177**

The revaluation reserve arises from the revaluation of land and buildings and plant and machinery in 1992. No provision has been made for any tax liability that would arise if these assets were disposed of at their revalued amount, but if they were to disposed of, the potential amount of tax arising at the current rates would be £53,500 (1997: £55,700).

UK GAAP Limited 16

21 Reconciliation of movements in shareholders' funds

	1998	1997
	£'000	£'000
Profit for the year	**361**	578
Dividends	**(176)**	(122)
	185	456
Net proceeds of issue of ordinary share capital	**27**	50
Net addition to shareholders' funds	**212**	506
Shareholders' funds as at 1 January	**3,147**	2,641
Shareholders' funds as at 31 December	**3,359**	3,147

22 Contingent liabilities

The company has given a guarantee in respect of the bank borrowings of a fellow subsidiary, which amounted to £35,000 at 31 December 1998 (1997: £25,000).

The company is a participant in a Group banking arrangement under which all surplus cash balances are held as collateral for bank facilities advanced to group members. In addition, the company has issued an unlimited guarantee to the bank to support these group facilities.

23 Pension commitments

The company operates a defined benefit pension scheme operated by Coventry Life Pension Limited with assets held in a separately administered fund. In addition, some employees are members of the GAAP UK plc group scheme.

The total net pension cost of the company's scheme was £89,000 (1997: £90,000). The cost is assessed in accordance with the advice of Pensions Consulting Limited, consulting actuaries. The latest actuarial valuation of the scheme was performed as at 31 December 1997 using the attained age method. The principal assumptions adopted in the valuation were that, over the long term, the investment return would be 8.5% per annum, the rate of salary increase would be 6.5% per annum and the rate of pension increase would be 4% per annum. The assumed rate of dividend growth was 4.5%.

At the date of the latest actuarial valuation at 31 December 1997, the market value of the assets of the scheme was £7,860,000 and the actuarial value of the assets was sufficient to cover 102% of the benefits that had accrued to members, after allowing for expected future increases in earnings.

Details of the group scheme are given in the financial statements of GAAP UK plc. The cost of contributions to the group scheme amount to £12,000 (1997: £4,000) and are based on pension costs across the group as a whole.

The contributions of the company and employees will remain at 9.5% and 5% respectively. An amount of £3,200 (1997: nil) is included in creditors, which represents the excess of the accumulated pension cost over the payment of contributions to the pension fund.

24 Non-equity shareholders' funds

The non-equity shareholders' funds are as follows:

	1998 £'000	1997 £'000
Issue proceeds (including premium) of preference shares	150	150
Unamortised issue costs	(2)	(2)
	148	148

25 Capital and other commitments

	1998 £'000	1997 £'000
Contracts placed for future capital expenditure not provided in the financial statements	**145**	226
Contracts placed for future revenue expenditure not provided in the financial statements		
Year 2000 modifications	**40**	10
Introduction of the euro	**10**	-

26 Financial commitments

At 31 December 1998 the company had annual commitments under non-cancellable operating leases expiring as follows:

	1998 £'000	1997 £'000
Within one year	**12**	20
Within two to five years	**23**	12
After five years	**95**	65
	130	97

27 Other related party transactions

Note: Information concerning transactions with related parties should be disclosed here, if they are not disclosed elsewhere within the financial statements. Information concerning transactions with directors and loans, etc to officers should also normally be disclosed here.

28 Ultimate parent undertaking

The immediate parent undertaking is GAAP UK Intermediate Holdings Limited.

The ultimate parent undertaking and controlling party is GAAP UK plc, which is the parent undertaking of the smallest and largest group to consolidate these financial statements. Copies of GAAP UK plc consolidated financial statements can be obtained from the Company Secretary at GAAP Towers, 2 The Square, London EC4Y 2DE

Appendix 2

GAAP UK plc
Example set of consolidated financial statements

Example annual report under UK GAAP

The example annual report that follows includes the consolidated financial statements of the GAAP UK plc group of companies. The annual report has been prepared to show the disclosures and format that might be expected for a group of its size that prepares its financial statements in accordance with Schedule 4 and Schedule 4A to the Companies Act 1985 as amended by the Companies Act 1989 and subsequent Statutory Instruments.

GAAP UK plc is a fictitious listed UK company. It has a number of UK and overseas investments including subsidiaries and joint ventures.

The intention is not to show all conceivable disclosures in this annual report and it should not, therefore, be used as a checklist. Neither is it a substitute for exercising judgement as to the fairness of presentation. These financial statements include many of the disclosure requirements contained in current Financial Reporting Standards, Statements of Standard Accounting Practice, Urgent Issues Task Force Abstracts and Company Law. GAAP UK plc also includes the disclosures required by the London Stock Exchange Listing Rules (Yellow Book). These financial statements reflect the requirements of FRS 9 'Associates and joint ventures' (applicable from 23 June 1998), FRS 10 'Goodwill and intangible assets', FRS 11 'Impairment of fixed assets and goodwill' and FRS 14 'Earnings per share' (all of which are applicable from 23 December 1998). In addition, GAAP UK plc has adopted early FRS 12 'Provisions, contingent liabilities and contingent assets' and FRS 13 'Derivatives and other financial instruments: disclosures' (which are applicable from 23 March 1999). Proposals included in exposure drafts are not yet standard practice and have, therefore, not been reflected in these financial statements.

References to source material are given in the left hand margin.

The suggested disclosure throughout is intended for guidance only and would not necessarily be applicable to all groups or to all companies. The names of the undertakings included in the annual report are used for illustration only and any resemblance to any existing undertaking is not intended.

Abbreviations

APB 1996/1	=	Auditing Practices Board Bulletin, number
CC A.2.1	=	Combined Code, paragraph number
FRS 3 p14	=	Financial Reporting Standard [number], paragraph number.
GC 45	=	Going concern and financial reporting, paragraph number. (Provides guidance in complying with paragraph D.1.3 of the Combined Code.)
IC 8	=	Internal control and financial reporting, paragraph number. (Provides partial guidance in complying with paragraph D.2.1 of the Combined Code.)
LR 12.43(b)	=	The Listing Rules of the Stock Exchange, paragraph number.
OFR 38	=	Operating and Financial Review Statement, paragraph number.
s 706(2)(a)	=	Companies Act 1985, section number.
SAS 600 p20	=	Statement of Auditing Standards [number], paragraph number.
7 Sch 6	=	Schedule [number] to the Companies Act 1985, paragraph number.
SI 1996/189	=	Statutory Instrument [year/number].
SSAP 3 p14	=	Statement of Standard Accounting Practice [number], paragraph number.
100 Group	=	The Hundred Group of Financial Directors, Statement of Good Practice on Environment Reporting in Annual Accounts.
UITF 13 p8	=	Urgent Issues Task Force Abstract [number], paragraph number.

s 706(2)(a)

Registered no: xxyyzz

GAAP UK plc

Example annual report

for the year ended 31 December 1998

GAAP UK plc
Annual report
for the year ended 31 December 1998

i

Contents

Page

** Not illustrated in these financial statements*

CC C.2.4 Companies should arrange for the Notice of the AGM and related papers to be sent to shareholders at least 20 working days before the meeting.

GAAP UK Plc

1

OFR 2

Operating and financial review for the year ended 31 December 1998

CC D.1

The board should present a balanced and understandable assessment of the group's position and prospects.

OFR 38

Include a statement regarding the extent to which the ASB Statement 'Operating and financial review' has been followed. If it is stated or implied that the principles of the statement have been followed, fundamental departures from the principles of the Statement should be noted.

OFR 3

Operating review

Essential features

The essential features of an OFR are as follows:

- It should be written in a clear style and as succinctly as possible, to be readily understandable by the general reader of annual reports and should include only matters that are likely to be significant to investors.
- It should be balanced and objective, dealing even-handedly with both good and bad aspects.
- It should refer to comments made in previous statements where these have been borne out by events.
- It should contain analytical discussion rather than merely numerical analysis.
- It should follow a 'top-down' structure, discussing individual aspects of the business in the context of a discussion of the business as a whole.
- It should explain the reason for, and effect of, any changes in accounting policies.
- It should make it clear how any ratios or other numerical information given relate to the financial statements.
- It should include discussion of:
  - Trends and factors underlying the business that have affected the results, but are not expected to continue in the future.
  - Known events, trends and uncertainties that are expected to have an impact on the business in the future.

Significant features of operating performance

OFR 3,8,9,10,11

Cover all aspects of the profit and loss account to the level of profit on ordinary activities before taxation focusing on:

- The overall business – the main factors that underlie the business.
- Changes in the industry/environment in which the business operates.
- Any special factors that have affected the results.

GAAP UK Plc

Matters to be covered may include:

- – Changes in market conditions.
- – Changes in market share or position
- – Changes in exchange or interest rates.
- – Discontinued activities.
- – New products and services.
- – Changes in turnover or margins.
- – New activities.
- – Material acquisitions/disposals.

Dynamics of the business

OFR 9,12 The main factors and influences that may affect the business's future results whether or not they were material in the period under review, addressing:

- ■ Principal risks and uncertainties.
- ■ Management of those risks.
- ■ Potential impact of the risks.

Matters to be covered may include:

- – Scarcity of raw materials.
- – Patents, licences, franchises.
- – Product liability.
- – Environmental issues.
- – Exchange or interest rate fluctuations.
- – Skill shortages.
- – Dependence on suppliers/customers.
- – Health and safety.
- – Self-insurance.
- – Inflation.

Investment in the future

Discuss the activities/expenditure which should enhance future income and profit or mitigate risks:

OFR 14,15 ■ Capital expenditure (current and planned) and benefits of such expenditure.

OFR 16,17,18 ■ Other activities such as advertising, marketing, research, training, refurbishment and maintenance and the development of new products/services.

Year 2000

UITF 20 p11 ■ Risks and uncertainties associated with year 2000 problem and general plans to address the issues relating to its business and operations, and, if material, its relationship with customers, suppliers and other relevant parties.

■ Whether the total estimated cost of these plans (current and future) have been quantified and, where applicable, an indication of the total costs likely to be incurred, with an explanation of the basis on which the figures are calculated.

■ If no assessment of the problem has been made or its materiality not determined, this must be disclosed.

Note: The general expectation by those who have studied best practice in managing the Year 2000 problem is that even the best run projects will face some Year 2000 compliance failures. There can be no assurance that Year 2000 projects will be successful or that the date change from 1999 to 2000 will not adversely affect the group's operations and financial results. The group may be adversely affected by the inability of third parties to manage the Year 2000 problem.

Introduction of the euro

UITF 21 p18 ■ Potential impact of the introduction of the euro for the group (where significant) together with an estimate of the expenditure likely to be incurred.

GAAP UK Plc

OFR 19 **Overall return to shareholders**

This discussion should be on a group and by business unit basis and include comments on:

- Profit for the year.
- OFR 20 Other gains and losses in the Statement of total recognised gains and losses – cover unrealised gains and losses where significant, for example, for an investment company.
- OFR 21 Comparison between profit and dividends for the period – comment on the business's dividend policy.
- Explanation of additional EPS figures.

OFR 22 **Subjectivity**

OFR 3 Discussion of subjective judgements relating to the application of accounting policies to which the financial statements are sensitive, for example, change in accounting policy.

Financial review

OFR 23,24 Narrative commentary supported with figures covering:

- Capital structure of the business.
- Funding and treasury policy.
- Dynamics of the company's financial position – liquidity/financing requirements.

OFR 25 **Capital structure**

Comment on:

- Maturity profile of debt.
- Capital instruments used.
- Currency and interest rate structure (including ratios such as interest cover, debt to equity ratio).

OFR 26,27,28 **Funding and treasury policy**

Discussion of the business's funding and treasury policy including the objectives of, and results of implementing, policies in respect of:

- Foreign exchange and interest rate risk.
- Maturity profile of borrowings.
- Purpose and effect of major financing transactions undertaken.

FRS 13 p23 *Note: The narrative disclosure requirements of FRS 13 may be included in the financial review section of the OFR. If this option is chosen, the relevant notes to the financial statements should be cross-referred to the specific paragraphs in the OFR.*

OFR 30,31 **Cash**

Analyse the cash generated from operations and other cash inflows, commenting on:

- Special factors/influences during the period.
- Differences between segmental profit and segmental cash flows (for example, capital expenditure in a particular segment).

GAAP UK Plc

OFR 32,33 **Liquidity of business**

Comment on:

- Period and levels of borrowings.
- Seasonality of borrowings.
- Funding requirements for capital expenditure both committed and authorised.

OFR 34,35 **Restrictions on transfer of funds or credit facilities.**

Cover restrictions on the ability to transfer funds between group companies and restrictions on the use of other credit facilities due to covenants entered into.

Interest

OFR 28 Discuss the effect of interest rate costs and the potential impact of interest rate changes.

OFR 29 **Effective rate of taxation**

UITF 16 p6 Cover the main components of the reconciliation of the actual to standard tax charge.

Strengths and resources

OFR 37 Include the strengths and resources of the business not reflected in the balance sheet, such as brands and similar intangibles.

Directors' report
for the year ended 31 December 1998

s234(1) The directors present their report and the audited financial statements for the year ended 31 December 1998.

Note: Various matters listed below may be included in the Chairman's Report, the OFR or the notes to the financial statements provided there is a cross reference in the Directors' Report to where the matter may be found.

Principal activities

s 234(2)
7 Sch 6(d) The narrative should cover the principal activities of the company and its subsidiary undertakings and significant changes in the year. In addition, there should be an indication of the existence of branches outside the UK.

Review of business

s 234(1)(a)
LR 12.43(b) A fair review of the development of the group's business during the year and of its position at the year end. An explanation is required if the results for the period differ by 10% or more from any published forecast/estimate.

Future developments

7 Sch 6(b) An indication of the likely future developments in the company's/group's business.

Dividends

s 234(1)(b) Disclose details of the recommended dividend and of dividends paid in year.

Research and development

7 Sch 6(c)
s 234(3)
SSAP 13 p31

- An indication of the group's research and development activities.
- Comment on the profit and loss account charge for year (separately disclosed in notes to financial statements).

Donations

7 Sch 3, 4
s 234(4) Disclose political contributions over £200 listed by individual recipient and charitable donations in total.

Land and buildings

7 Sch 1(2)
s 234(4) If significant, indicate the difference between market value and book amount of land and buildings for the company or any of its subsidiary undertakings.

GAAP UK Plc

Post balance events

7 Sch 6(a)
s 234(4)
SSAP 17
p23,24

Particulars of any important events affecting the company or group since the year end.

Directors and their interests

s 234(2)

Names of all directors during any part of the period.

7 Sch 2,2A
7 Sch 2B
7 Sch 2A(4)
s 234(4)
s 234(2)

Disclose the directors' interests in shares (including share options) or debentures, of any member of the group at the beginning and end of the year for all directors at the end of the year. This information may be given in the notes to the financial statements, or in the Remuneration report, rather than in the Directors' report. Also, details of the shares or debentures options granted during the year to, or exercised by, a director (including immediate family) are required to be given, in respect of directors at the end of the year.

LR 12.43(k)

In addition, any changes must be disclosed in directors' interests (including immediate family), distinguishing between beneficial and non-beneficial interests, between the year end and a date not more than a month prior to the date of the notice of the general meeting at which the annual financial statements are laid before the company. If there is no change then a statement to that effect is required.

Further information is provided in the Remuneration report pages 12 and 13.

Non-executive directors

CC A.3.2

- Identity of independent non-executive directors, together with a short biographical note on each. The majority of non-executive directors should be independent of management and free from any business or other relationship that could materially interfere with the exercise of their independent judgement.

CC A.2.1

- Specify the chairman, chief executive and a senior independent director, other than the chairman, through whom concerns can be conveyed to the board in situations where it would not be appropriate to do so through the chairman or chief executive officer.

Re-election of directors

CC A.6.2

The names of directors submitted for election or re-election should be accompanied by sufficient biographical details to enable shareholders to make an informed decision on their election.

CC A.5.1
CC A.6.1
CC A.6.2

Note: Unless the board is small, a Nomination Committee should be established to make recommendations to the board on all new appointments. Non-executive directors should be appointed for specified terms subject to re-election and to Companies Act provisions relating to the removal of a director and reappointment should not be automatic. All directors should be subject to election by shareholders at the first opportunity and to re-election thereafter at intervals of no more than three years.

GAAP UK Plc

Committees

CC.A.5.1
CC B.2.3
CC.D.3.1

The names of the chairman and members of the Remuneration, Audit and Nomination Committees must be given.

Notes:

(a) These details may be provided in other suitable positions, such as the Remuneration report, the Corporate Governance report or the list of directors and advisers.

CC D.3.1
CC B.2.2
CC A.5.1

(b) The Audit Committee should comprise a minimum of three members, confined to non-executive directors with the majority being independent. The Remuneration Committee should consist exclusively of independent non-executives. The Nomination Committee should have a majority of non-executive directors and the chairman should be either the chairman of the board or a non-executive director.

CC C.2.3

(c) The chairman of the Audit, Remuneration and Nomination Committees should attend the AGM to answer questions.

Disabled persons

7 Sch 9

Include a statement as to the policy for employment, training, career development and promotion of disabled people and for the continuing employment of employees who have become disabled while employed by the company.

Employee involvement

7 Sch 11

Statement describing the action that has been taken during the period to introduce, maintain or develop arrangements aimed at involving UK employees in the company's affairs.

Policy and practice on payment of creditors

SI 1996/189
SI 1996/571
7 Sch 12

The company's policy and practice on payment of creditors should be disclosed, which should include a policy statement for the following financial year and the number of days (calculated in the prescribed manner) taken to pay bills in the current financial year. The statement must include whether:

- it is the company's policy to follow any code or standard on payment practice and, if so, give the name of the code or standard and the place where information about the code or standard can be obtained; and/or

- in respect of some, or all, of its suppliers, it is the company's policy to settle the terms of payment with those suppliers when agreeing the terms of each transaction and ensure that these suppliers are made aware of the terms of the payment and abide by the terms of payment.

Where the statement does not cover all suppliers, the policy for the other suppliers needs to be disclosed.

Note: An additional statement regarding the group's policy and practice and number of days for the company and its UK subsidiaries, whilst not mandatory, is considered best practice.

GAAP UK Plc

Purchase of own shares

7 Sch 7,8 Where a company purchases or places a charge on its own shares, there are specific disclosures to be made, for example the number and nominal value of the shares, aggregate consideration paid and the reasons for the purchase.

LR 12.43(n) Details of any shareholders' authority for the purchase by the company of its own shares still valid at the end of the period under review. Details of any such purchases made otherwise than through the market or by offer to all shareholders, including the information required by the Companies Act 1985 7 Sch Pt II.

Substantial shareholdings

LR 12.43(1) Particulars, as at a date not more than a month prior to the date of the notice of the general meeting at which the annual financial statements are laid before the company, of substantial shareholdings (three per cent or more) notified to the company, other than by directors, in any part of the company's share capital. Where there are no such shareholdings, this should be stated.

Placing of shares

LR 12.43(p) Where a listed company is a subsidiary, particulars should be given of the participation by its parent company in any placing made during the period under review.

Waiver of dividends

LR 12.43(e) Details of any arrangement under which a shareholder has waived or agreed to waive any dividends. Waivers of less than one per cent of the total value of any dividend may be disregarded provided that some payment has been made.

Contracts of significance

LR 12.43(r)(s)
LR 12.44 Particulars of any contract of significance (including contracts for the provision of services) between the company (including subsidiary undertakings) and controlling shareholder subsisting in the period. 'Significance' is defined as more than one per cent of the relevant transactions for the group.

LR 12.43(q)
6 Sch 15(c), 16(c) Particulars of any contract of significance in which a director is or was materially interested.

LR 12.43(t)
LR 11.8(c) Details of small related party transactions notified to the Stock Exchange.

Environment

100 Group Voluntary disclosure, covering areas such as:

- The group's environmental policy.
- Organisational responsibilities for environmental performance.
- Environmental impacts, risks and targets for segments.
- The group's commitment to its environmental policy.

GAAP UK Plc

Auditors

s 384(1) The auditors, PricewaterhouseCoopers, have indicated their willingness to continue in office, and a resolution that they be reappointed will be proposed at the annual general meeting.

s 234A(1) By order of the board

AB Smith

s 234A(2) **Company Secretary** 26 February 1999

s 234A(1),(3) *Notes:*

(a) The Directors' report has to be signed by the Company Secretary or a director after it has been approved by the Board of Directors.

(b) The copy of the Directors' Report which is delivered to the Registrar of Companies must be manually signed by the Company Secretary or a director.

GAAP UK Plc 10

LR12.43A(c)
CC B.3
CC B.3.1

Remuneration report for the year ended 31 December 1998

CC B.2.1 *To avoid potential conflicts of interest, boards of directors should set up remuneration committees of independent non-executive directors to make recommendations to the board, within agreed terms of reference, on the company's framework of executive remuneration and its cost, and to determine on their behalf specific remuneration packages for each of the executive directors, including pension rights and any compensation payments.*

CC B.2.6 *The chairman of the board should ensure that the company maintains contact as required with its principal shareholders about remuneration in the same way as for other matters.*

Compliance and policy

LR 12.43A(c)(i)
CC B.3.2
CC B.3.3

The board should report to the shareholders on the company's policy on executive directors' remuneration. The report should draw attention to factors specific to the company. The provisions in Schedule B of the Combined Code should be followed.

Notes:

(a) The details of compliance and policy will usually be set out as a Remuneration committee report. This must be adopted by the board as it is the board's responsibility to report to shareholders. Paragraph 12.43A(c) of the Listing Rules contains information to be included in the report.

CC B.3.5 *(b) The board should consider each year whether to put the remuneration report as a separate AGM item to seek shareholders' approval of the policy. The board's conclusions should be minuted.*

CC B.2.5 *(c) The Remuneration committee should consult the chairman and/or chief executive about their proposals and have access to professional advice inside and outside to the company.*

CC B.1
CC B.1.10

(d) Levels of remuneration should be sufficient to attract and retain the directors needed to run the company successfully, but companies should avoid paying more than is necessary for this purpose. A significant proportion of executive directors' remuneration should be structured so as to link rewards to corporate and individual performance. In designing schemes of performance-related remuneration, remuneration committees should follow the provisions of Schedule A to the Combined Code.

CC B.2.4 *(e) The remuneration of all non-executive directors should be determined by the board or a small sub-committee or, where required by the Articles of Association, the shareholders.*

Members of the Remuneration committee

CC B.2.3 The members of the Remuneration committee should be listed each year in the board's remuneration report to shareholders.

CC B.2.2 *Note: The Remuneration committee should consist exclusively of independent non-executive directors.*

Remuneration package

LR 12.43A(c)(ii)
6 Sch 1(1), 10(2), 12

Amounts of each element of the remuneration package for each director (executive and non-executive) by name from all sources, including but not restricted to:

GAAP UK Plc

- Basic salary and fees.
- Estimated money value of benefits in kind.
- Annual and deferred bonuses.
- 6 Sch 8 Compensation for loss of office/payments for breach of contract/other termination payments.
- Total remuneration for each director for current and corresponding accounting period.
- Significant payments to former directors made during the current accounting period.

LR 12.43(d) Such details are normally in tabular form and explanations are given as to what is included in each element of the remuneration package, which should include any arrangements to waive any emoluments.

LR 12.43A(c)(v)
CC Sch B There must be explanations and justifications given for any elements of remuneration except basic salary which are pensionable.

An example of the form of disclosure is given below.

LR12.43A(c)(ii) **Directors' detailed emoluments**

6 Sch 1(i),1(2),8

	1998					1997
Executive	**Salary & fees £000**	**Benefits £000**	**Annual bonus £000**	**Compensation for loss of office £000**	**Total £000**	Total £000
CD Jones	132	29	41	–	**202**	150
G Wallace	107	24	33	–	**164**	128
F James*	112	13	34	–	**159**	121
EF Logan	63	13	18	–	**94**	31
D Scott	31	3	10	103	**147**	93
J Rush	–	–	–	–	–	35
Non-executive						
R Graham (Chairman)	10	–	–	–	**10**	10
Lord Callender	10	–	–	–	**10**	10
N Jagger	10	–	–	–	**10**	10
A Cartwright	10	–	–	–	**10**	10
	485	82	136	103	**806**	598

Benefits in kind include the provision of a company car, fuel, driver financial counselling and medical and life insurance.

LR12.43A(c)(i)
6 Sch 9 * The above table includes an amount of £54,000 (1996: £62,000) paid to third parties in respect of making available the services of Mr F James to the company.

6 Sch 8
6 Sch 8(3)
best practice The compensation for loss of office payment to Mr D Scott who resigned on 29 March 1998 includes the monetary value of a car retained by the director and a contribution to his pension plan. For the year ended 31 December 1997, £87,000 was paid in respect of compensation for loss of office to Mr J Rush, former director.

LR12.43(d) No director waived emoluments in respect of the year ended 31 December 1998. In the year ended 31 December 1997 Mr CD Jones waived emoluments of £6,000.

LR12.43A(c)(ii)
6 Sch 7 An additional pension of £11,376 (1997: nil) was paid to Mr Rush in the year. The payment is in excess of Mr Rush's normal entitlement under the group's pension scheme arrangements.

GAAP UK Plc

Share schemes

UITF 10
LR 12.43A(c)(iii)
LR 12.43(k)
7 Sch 2A,2B

Information on share options including SAYE options should be given for each director, by name in accordance with UITF Abstract 10. Such details are normally in tabular form and explanations are given where necessary.

LR 12.43A(c)(viii)

A statement of the company's policy on the granting of options or awards under its employees' share schemes and other long-term incentive schemes, explaining and justifying any departure from that policy in the period and any change in policy from the preceding year.

UITF 10 A1(h)

A concise summary should be given of any performance criteria conditioned upon which the options are exercisable.

CC Sch B

Note: There should be an explanation and justification where share options are awarded in large blocks rather than phased.

An example of the form of disclosures relating to share options is given below.

LR12.43A(c)(iii)

Interests in share options

UITF10
7 Sch 2,2A,2B

Details of options held by directors are set out below:

Date of grant	Earliest exercise date	Expiry date	Exercise price (pence)	Number at 1 January 1998 (1p shares)	Granted in year	Exercised in year	Number at 31 December 1998 (1p shares)
CD Jones							
1.4.92	1.4.95	31.3.01	26.00	80,750	–	80,750	–
1.4.94	1.4.97	31.3.03	50.00	501,250	–	–	501,250
1.6.96	1.6.99	31.5.05	136.25	675,212	–	–	675,212
18.4.97	18.4.00	17.4.06	185.75	1,417,324	–	–	1,417,324
1.4.98	1.4.01	31.3.07	223.50	–	2,119,119	–	2,119,119
				2,674,536	**2,119,119**	**80,750**	**4,712,905**
F James							
1.4.92	1.4.95	31.3.01	26.00	49,025	–	49,025	–
1.4.94	1.4.97	31.3.03	50.00	451,327	–	–	451,327
1.6.96	1.6.99	31.5.05	136.25	511,111	–	–	511,111
18.4.97	18.4.00	17.4.06	185.75	989,517	–	–	989,517
1.4.98	1.4.01	31.3.07	223.50	–	1,750,175	–	1,750,175
				2,000,980	**1,750,175**	**49,025**	**3,702,130**
E F Logan							
28.9.97	28.9.00	27.9.06	185.75	675,212	–	–	675,212
1.4.98	1.4.01	31.3.07	222.50	–	1,750,175	–	1,750,175
LR 12.43A(c)(iv) 6 Sch1(1)(c)				**675,212**	**1,750,175**	–	**2,425,387**

UITF 10 A1

No options lapsed during the year. No other directors have been granted share options in the shares in the company or other group entities. The options are all performance related (details not illustrated).

UITF 10 A1

The market price of the company's shares at the end of the financial year was 219p and the range of market prices during the year was between 185p and 226p.

UITF 17 At the time that Mr E F Logan was granted his options in 1997, the option exercise price represented a 15% discount on the market price. In accordance with UITF 17 'Employee share schemes' the value of the discount of £223,000 is being charged on a straight-line basis over 3 years to the earliest exercise date being the period over which performance is assessed.

B.1.5 *Note: Executive share options should not be offered at a discount save as permitted by LR 13.30 and LR 13.31.*

Gains made by directors on share options

Best practice The table below shows gains made by individual directors from the exercise of share options during 1998. The gains are calculated as at the exercise date, although the shares may have been

UITF 10A1(g) retained. The market price of the company's shares at the date of exercise was £2.04.

		1998 £000	1997 £000
	C D Jones	**144**	99
	F James	**87**	58
6 Sch 1(1)(b)	**Total gains on share options**	**231**	157

s 243(4) **Interests in shares**

The interests of the directors in the shares of the company and other group members were:

7 Sch 2,2A,2B		1 January	**31 December**
	The company - ordinary shares 1p		
	R Graham	180,000	**180,000**
	CD Jones	5,625,420	**5,716,891**
	G Wallace	250,000	**272,549**
	F James	–	**51,470**
	EF Logan	–	**7,843**
	Lord Callender	50,000	**50,000**
	Austen Limited - ordinary shares £1		
	F James	10,000	**10,000**
	Trollope plc- preference shares 50p		
	A Cartwright	5,000	**5,000**

LR12.43(e) There has been no change in the interests set out above between 31 December 1998 and 25 February 1999.

Long-term incentive scheme

LR 12.43(c)(iv) Details of long-term incentive schemes, including the following, for each director, by name:

- Interests at the start and end of the period.
- Entitlements/awards granted and commitments made to each director during the period, showing which crystallised in the same period or later periods.
- 6 Sch 1(1)(c) Money value and number of shares, cash payments or other benefits received by each director under such schemes during the period.

GAAP UK Plc

Notes:

LR 12.43(u) *(a) Additional disclosures are required in the first annual report published following the date on which the relevant director becomes eligible to participate in an arrangement in which that director is the only participant and the arrangement is established specifically to facilitate, in unusual circumstances, the recruitment or retention of that director.*

CC Sch B *(b) There should be an explanation and justification where incentives are awarded in large blocks rather than phased.*

CC B.3.4 *(c) Shareholders should be invited specifically to approve all new long-term incentive schemes (including share option schemes) that potentially commit shareholders' funds over more than one year or dilute the equity, save as permitted by LR13.13A.*

An example of long-term incentive schemes' disclosures is given below.

LR12,43(c)(iv) **Directors' interests in the Long-Term Performance Plan**

Shares awarded to executive directors and former directors under the Long-Term Incentive Plan are as follows:

	Cycle ending	Award date	At 1.1.98 Number	Shares awarded Number	Shares vested Number	At 31.12.98 Number	Value vested £000	Vesting date
C D Jones	1998	7.2.95	59,310	–	**59,310**	–	**121**	7.2.98
	1999	8.2.96	65,525	–	–	65,525	–	8.2.99
	2000	22.3.97	43,210	–	–	43,210	–	22.3.00
	2001	27.3.98	–	41,140	–	41,140	–	27.3.01
G Wallace	1998	7.2.95	22,550	–	**22,550**	–	**46**	7.2.98
	1999	8.2.96	19,760	–	–	19,760	–	8.2.99
	2000	22.3.97	14,115	–	–	14,115	–	22.3.00
	2001	27.3.97	–	12,112	–	12,112	–	27.3.01
E F Logan	2001	27.3.98	–	41,140	–	41,140	–	27.3.01
D Scott	1998	7.2.95	45,098	–	**45,098**	–	**92**	7.2.98
	1999	8.2.96	39,520	–	–	39,520	–	8.2.99
	2000	22.3.97	28,230	–	–	28,230	–	22.3.00
	2001	27.3.98	–	12,112	–	12,112	–	27.3.01
F James	1998	7.2.95	51,470	–	**51,470**	–	**105**	7.2.98
	1999	8.2.96	65,525	–	–	65,525	–	8.2.99
	2000	22.3.97	43,210	–	–	43,210	–	22.3.00
	2001	27.3.98	–	41,140	–	41,140	–	27.3.01
Totals of awards vested in 1998					**178,428**		**364**	

The value of awards vested in 1998 is based on the average market price of GAAP UK plc shares on the date of vesting of £2.04.

The shares awarded in 1998 under the 1995 Plan have to be retained by the directors until at least 2001.

The performance of the company as measured against the target group described in Part 1 of the Remuneration report determines the percentage of the award that vests (not illustrated).

GAAP UK Plc

The shares awarded in February 1996 vested on 8th February 1999; based on the performance of the company over the three year period ended on that date the shares vested as to 100 per cent. The gain attributable to each director will be disclosed as remuneration in 1999.

The shares awarded in March 1997 and March 1998 vest in March 2000 and March 2001 respectively. At 31st December 1998 the performance percentage reflecting performance to date, was 80 per cent for the shares awarded in March 1997 and 100 per cent for the shares awarded in March 1998.

Pensions

LR 12.43A(c)(ix) CC Sch B

For defined benefit pension schemes there should be included in the report for each director, by name:

- Amount of the increase in accrued benefit during the year (excluding inflation).
- The accrued benefit as at the year end.
- The transfer value of the relevant increase in accrued benefit as at the year end or specific information to enable this value to be calculated.

Notes:

(a) Explain that the transfer value represents a liability of the company, but not a sum paid or due to the individual; and that it cannot meaningfully be added to annual remuneration.

(b) Where the group makes provisions in respect of unfunded pensions of a defined benefit type, it should take the related benefits provided to directors into account when determining the amounts to be disclosed in respect of directors' pension entitlements under defined benefit schemes.

(c) Voluntary contributions and benefits should not be disclosed.

LR 12.43A(c)(x) 6 Sch1(1)(d)

For money purchase schemes (for example, defined contribution) there should be disclosed for each director, by name the details of the contribution or allowance payable or made by the company. Disclosure includes provisions for unfunded money purchase benefits as well as actual contributions paid or payable to a scheme.

Note: If the numerical information required in respect of remuneration, share schemes, L-TIP's and pensions is disclosed in the notes to the financial statements, the Remuneration report can then cross refer to where the information can be found. This will simplify the audit report referencing.

An example of the form of disclosures relating to directors' pensions is given below.

GAAP UK Plc

LR12.43A(c)(ix) **Directors' pension entitlement**

Set out below are details of the pension benefits earned by each of the executive directors during the year ended 31 December 1998.

	Additional pension earned in the year £000	Accrued entitlement £000	Pension entitlement transfer value for the year £000
CD Jones	26	181	173
G Wallace	28	145	184
F James	16	158	113
E F Logan	25	94	164
D Scott*	7	128	148

*Mr D Scott retired from the company on 29 March 1998.

The accrued pension entitlement shown is the amount that would be paid each year on retirement based on service to the end of the current year.

The increase in the additional pension earned during the year excludes any increase for inflation.

The transfer value has been calculated on the basis of actuarial advice in accordance with Actuarial Guidance Note GN11, less directors' contributions. It does not represent a sum payable to individual directors and it, therefore, cannot be added meaningfully to annual remuneration.

Mr CD Jones and Mr G Wallace also participate in a US defined contribution pension arrangement. During the year their contributions amounted to £54,000 (1997: £nil) and £18,000 (1997: £nil) respectively

Note: The pension entitlement transfer value for the year need not be given if certain additional information is given concerning each director as set out in LR12.43A(c)(ix)(b)(ii).

Service contracts

CC B.1.7
CC B.1.8 *Note: The board should have the objective of setting notice or contract periods at one year or less. If it is necessary to offer longer notice or contract periods to new directors recruited from outside, such periods should reduce after the initial period.*

LR 12.43A(c)(vi) Details of any director's service contract with a notice periods greater than one year or with provisions for pre-determined compensation on termination which exceeds one year's salary and benefits in kind. Give the reasons for such notice periods or compensation provisions.

LR 12.43A(c)(vii) The unexpired term of any directors' service contract of a director proposed for re-election at the forthcoming annual general meeting and, if any director proposed for election does not have a directors' service contract, a statement to that effect.

Notes:

CC B.1.9 *(a) Remuneration committees should consider what compensation commitments (including pension contributions) their directors' contracts of service, if any, would entail in the event of early termination. They should in particular consider the advantages of providing explicitly in the initial contract for such compensation commitments except in the case of removal for misconduct.*

CC B.1.10 *(b) Where the initial contract does not explicitly provide for compensation commitments, remuneration committees should, within legal constraints, tailor their approach in individual early termination cases to the wide variety of circumstances. The broad aim should be to avoid rewarding poor performance while dealing fairly with cases where departure is not due to poor performance and to take a robust line on reducing compensation to reflect departing directors' obligations to mitigate loss.*

Waiver of emoluments

LR 12.43(d)

- Give details of any arrangement under which a director has waived or agreed to waive any emoluments from the company or any subsidiary.
- Where a director has agreed to waive future emoluments, give details of such waiver together with those relating to emoluments which were waived in the year.

On behalf of the board

N Jagger
Chairman of the Remuneration Committee 26 February 1998

Note: There is no requirement for the Remuneration report to be signed, but it would be best practice to do so.

GAAP UK Plc

Corporate governance

Compliance

LR 12.43 A(a) Statement of how the company has applied the principles in section 1 of the Combined Code, with explanation enabling shareholders to evaluate how principles have been applied.

LR 12.43A(b) Statement as to whether the company has complied with the Combined Code provisions set out in section 1. Where the company has complied with only some of the provisions, or for only part of the accounting period, then a statement to that effect needs to be made specifying the provisions and giving reasons for any non-compliance and (where relevant) specifying for what part of the period such non-compliance continued.

The board and committees of the board

CC A.1.1
- *The board should meet regularly, retain full and effective control over the group's activities and monitor the executive management.*

CC A.1.5
- *All directors should bring an independent judgement to bear on issues of strategy, performance, resources (including key appointments) and standards of conduct.*

CC A.3.1
CC A.3.2
- *The board should include non-executive directors (a minimum of three of which a majority should be independent) of sufficient calibre and number for their views to carry weight in the board's decisions. Non-executive directors are independent if they are free from management, business or other relationships which could materially interfere with the exercise of their judgement. Non-executive directors should comprise not less than one third of the board.*

CC A.2.1
- *The posts of chief executive and chairman should be held by different people. A decision to combine the posts of chairman and chief executive officer in one person should be publicly justified.*

CC A.1.4
- *All the directors should have access to the advice and services of the Company Secretary.*

CC A.1.6
- *All directors should receive appropriate training on first appointment.*

CC A.1.3
- *There should be an agreed procedure for directors to take, if necessary, independent professional advice at the company's expense.*

CC A.1.2
- *The board should have a formal schedule of matters specifically reserved to it for decision.*

CC B.2.1
CC D.3.1
- *All the committees should have written constitutions and terms of reference.*

CC A.4.1
- *The chairman should ensure all directors are properly briefed on issues arising at board meetings.*

Internal controls

CC D.2.1 The directors should at least annually conduct a review of the effectiveness of the group's system of internal control and should report to shareholders that they have done so.

The review should cover all controls, including financial, operational and compliance controls and risk management.

Note: Guidance for directors on the review of internal controls, and the reporting thereof, is under development by a committee of the Institute of Chartered Accountants in England and Wales. At the time of writing this guidance was not available.

For financial controls, the directors' statement on internal control should contain as a minimum:

IC 8

- Acknowledgement by the directors that they are responsible for the company's system of internal financial control.
- Explanation that such a system can provide only reasonable and not absolute assurance against material misstatement or loss.
- Description of the key procedures that the directors have established and which are designed to provide effective internal financial control.
- Confirmation that the directors (or a board committee) have reviewed the effectiveness of the system of internal financial control.

IC 9
IC 11 The directors' statement on internal control should cover the period of the financial statements and take into account any material developments between the balance sheet date and the date the financial statements are signed. The description of key procedures should address the specific high-level procedures used by the company/group and whether the directors have reviewed the effectiveness of the system of internal financial control.

Points that need to be considered when dealing with the statement on internal control are:

- IC 12 Whether any weaknesses in internal financial control have resulted in losses, contingencies or uncertainties which require disclosure.
- IC 13 Ensure the statement is not misleading.

CC D.2.2 The need for an internal audit function should be reviewed from time to time.

CC D.3.2 *The duties of an audit committee should include keeping under review the scope and results of the external audit and its cost effectiveness and the independence and objectivity of the external auditors. Where the external auditors also supply a substantial volume of non-audit services to the company, the committee should keep the nature and extent of such services under review, seeking to balance the maintenance of objectivity and value, for money.*

Going concern

LR 12.43(v)
CC D.1.3 Statement by the directors that the business is a going concern with supporting assumptions or qualifications as necessary. This statement should cover both the parent company and the group as a whole.

GAAP UK Plc

CC D.1.1 **Statement of directors' responsibilities**

SAS 600 p20 *Description of the directors' responsibilities for inclusion in a company's financial statements as set out in SAS 600 appendix 3.*

Company law requires the directors to prepare financial statements for each financial year that give a true and fair view of the state of affairs of the company and the group and of the profit or loss of the group for that period. In preparing those financial statements, the directors are required to:

- Select suitable accounting policies and then apply them consistently.
- Make judgements and estimates that are reasonable and prudent.
- State whether applicable accounting standards have been followed, subject to any material departures disclosed and explained in the financial statements.
- Prepare the financial statements on the going concern basis, unless it is inappropriate to presume that the company will continue in business.

The directors are responsible for keeping proper accounting records that disclose with reasonable accuracy at any time the financial position of the company and the group and to enable them to ensure that the financial statements comply with the Companies Act 1985. They are also responsible for safeguarding the assets of the company and the group and hence for taking reasonable steps for the prevention and detection of fraud and other irregularities.

By order of the Board

AB Smith
Company Secretary 26 February 1998

Note: There is no requirement for the corporate governance report to be signed. However, best practice is that it is signed by the company secretary or alternatively by the senior non-executive director.

LR 12.43A *The London Stock Exchange requires that the auditors should review the following aspects of the company's 'Statement of compliance' with the Combined Code of Best Practice:*

- *Formal schedule of matters specifically reserved for board decision.*
- *Procedure for directors to obtain independent professional advice.*
- *Period of appointment of non-executive directors.*
- *Process for appointment and election of directors.*
- *Directors' responsibility statement for preparing the financial statements and auditors' reporting responsibilities.*
- *Directors' report to shareholders on the company's system of internal controls.**
- *Composition and terms of reference of the audit committee.*

LR 12.43(v) *In addition, the London Stock Exchange requires that the auditors should review the director's statement on going concern.*

* *In relation to the requirement to review the system of internal control, guidance for directors is being developed by a committee of the Institute of Chartered Accountants in England and Wales.*

Note: In conjunction with its review of the form of reporting by auditors on Corporate Governance matters, the Auditing Practices Board is considering an amendment to the auditors' report on financial statements. In particular, an expanded section dealing with auditors' responsibilities. However, at the time of writing the changes are unknown.

s 235
SAS 600

Auditors' report on the financial statements to the members of GAAP UK plc

APB 1997/2
LR 12.43A
CC Sch B

We have audited the financial statements on pages 23 to 65, including the additional disclosures on pages 10 to 14 relating to the remuneration of the directors specified for our review by the London Stock Exchange, which have been prepared under the historical cost convention, as modified by the revaluation of certain fixed assets, and the accounting policies set out on pages 27 to 31.

CC D.1.1

Respective responsibilities of directors and auditors

As described on page 20 the company's directors are responsible for the preparation of financial statements. It is our responsibility to form an independent opinion, based on our audit, on those statements and to report our opinion to you.

Basis of opinion

We conducted our audit in accordance with Auditing Standards issued by the Auditing Practices Board. An audit includes examination, on a test basis, of evidence relevant to the amounts and disclosures in the financial statements. It also includes an assessment of the significant estimates and judgements made by the directors in the preparation of the accounts, and of whether the accounting policies are appropriate to the company's circumstances, consistently applied and adequately disclosed.

We planned and performed our audit so as to obtain all the information and explanations which we considered necessary in order to provide us with sufficient evidence to give reasonable assurance that the financial statements are free from material misstatement, whether caused by fraud or other irregularity or error. In forming our opinion we also evaluated the overall adequacy of the presentation of information in the financial statements.

s 235(1),(2)

Opinion

In our opinion the financial statements give a true and fair view of the state of affairs of the company and the group as at 31 December 1998 and of the profit and cash flows of the group for the year then ended and have been properly prepared in accordance with the Companies Act 1985.

s 236(1)-(3)

PricewaterhouseCoopers
Chartered Accountants and Registered Auditors
London 26 February 1999

Notes:

(a) Reference to modification of the historical cost convention is required where assets are stated at other than historical cost.

(b) The copy of the auditors' report on the financial statements delivered to the Registrar of Companies must be manually signed by the auditors.

GAAP UK Plc

Auditors' report on corporate governance matters to the directors of GAAP UK plc

Note: The form of reporting on Corporate Governance matters is under review by the Auditing Practices Board. It is likely to change from that used in previous years, but at the time of writing the changes are unknown.

GAAP UK Plc

Consolidated profit and loss account for the year ended 31 December 1998

Reference		Note	1998 £m	1998 £m	1997 (restated) £m	1997 (restated) £m
s 227(2)(b) 4 Sch Format 1						
	Turnover (including share of joint ventures)	1				
FRS 3 14,30	Continuing operations		**532.8**		450.5	
FRS 3 p64 FRS 3 p16 FRS 6 p28	Acquisitions		**741.4**	**1,274.2**	–	450.5
FRS 3 p17	Discontinued operations			**25.6**		35.3
		1		**1,299.8**		485.8
FRS 9 p21	Less: Share of turnover of joint ventures					
	Continuing operations		**(9.1)**		(9.9)	
	Acquisitions		**(29.8)**	**(38.9)**	–	(9.9)
	Turnover			**1,260.9**		475.9
4 Sch 8	Cost of Sales	2		**(1,070.9)**		(342.4)
4 Sch 8	Gross Profit			**190.0**		133.5
	Net operating expenses	2		**(46.3)**		(19.1)
FRS 3 p14,30	Continuing operations		**122.1**		107.3	
	Acquisitions (after £40.2m (1997: £nil) goodwill amortisation)		**21.6**	**141.5**	–	107.3
FRS 3 p17	Discontinued operations			**2.2**		7.0
4 Sch 8	**Group operating profit**			**143.7**		114.4
4A Sch 21 FRS 9 p21	Share of operating profit in joint ventures (after £0.9m (1997: £nil) goodwill amortisation)			**2.8**		1.2
	Total operating profit: group and share of joint ventures	1		**146.5**		115.6
FRS 3 p20	Profit on sale of subsidiary – discontinued operations	5		**6.3**		–
	Net interest (payable)/receivable					
	– Group	3	**(11.6)**		3.6	
FRS 9 p21	– Joint ventures		**0.7**	**(10.9)**	–	3.6
4 Sch 3(6)	**Profit on ordinary activities before taxation**	1&4		**141.9**		119.2
4 Sch 8	Tax on profit on ordinary activities	6		**(54.4)**		(41.7)
4 Sch 8	**Profit on ordinary activities after taxation**			**87.5**		77.5
4A Sch 17(3) FRS 2 p36 FRS 4 p60	Equity minority interests			**(0.5)**		(0.1)
	Profit attributable to shareholders			**87.0**		77.4
4 Sch 3(7)(b) FRS 4, p59,100	Dividends – including non-equity	8		**(35.2)**		(18.9)
4 Sch 3(7)(a)	**Retained profit for the financial year**	24		**51.8**		58.5
FRS 14 p69	**Earnings per 1p share**	9				
	– basic			**7.64p**		8.77p
	– diluted			**7.60p**		8.60p
FRS 14 p74	**Earnings per 1p share before goodwill amortisation**	9				
	– basic			**11.25p**		8.77p
	– diluted			**11.20p**		8.60p

GAAP UK Plc

FRS 3 p27

Statement of group total recognised gains and losses

	For the year ended 31 December 1998	1998 £m	1997 £m
FRS 3 p36	Profit attributable to shareholders	**87.0**	77.4
	Unrealised surplus on revaluation of properties	**5.4**	–
SSAP 20 p60(b)	Exchange adjustments offset in reserves	**(15.7)**	4.1
UITF 19 p9	Tax on exchange adjustments offset in reserves	**3.2**	(1.0)
FRS 3 p27	**Total recognised gains/(losses) for the year**	**79.9**	80.5

Notes:

FRS 3 p57 (a) *If the company or group has no recognised gains or losses other than its profit or loss for the period, a statement to this effect should be given immediately below the profit and loss account.*

FRS 9 p28 (b) *Where an associate or joint venture has gains and losses reported in its STRGL, or has such gains and losses when its accounts are restated on to the investor's GAAP, the investor's share of such gains and losses should be included in the investor's consolidated STRGL. The amounts should be shown separately under each heading, if material, either in the statement or in a note referred to in the statement.*

FRS 3 p26

Note of group historical cost profits and losses

For the year ended 31 December	1998 £m	1997 (restated) £m
Reported profit on ordinary activities before taxation	**141.9**	119.2
Realisation of property revaluation gains of previous years	**0.1**	0.1
Difference between historical cost depreciation charge and the actual depreciation charge of the year calculated on the revalued amount	**0.1**	–
Historical cost profit on ordinary activities before taxation	**142.1**	119.3
Historical cost profit for the year retained after taxation, minority interests and dividends	**52.0**	58.5

Reconciliation of movements in group shareholders' funds

	For the year ended 31 December	1998 £m	1997 £m
	Profit attributable to shareholders	**87.0**	77.4
	Dividends	**(35.2)**	(18.9)
		51.8	58.5
	Other recognised gains and losses relating to the year	**(7.1)**	3.1
FRS 4 p93	Proceeds of ordinary shares issued for cash (notes 21, 22)	**2.6**	4.7
FRS 4 p37	Nominal value of ordinary shares issued for the acquisition of Newsub plc (note 21)	**4.8**	–
	Premium (net of issue expenses) on ordinary shares issued for the acquisition of Newsub plc (note 25)	**913.6**	–
	Goodwill eliminated against reserves	**–**	(31.5)
	Goodwill resurrected on disposal of subsidiary	**3.9**	–
FRS 3 p47,52	**Net change in shareholders' funds**	**969.6**	34.8
	Shareholders' funds as at 1 January	**135.7**	100.9
	Shareholders' funds as at 31 December	**1,105.3**	135.7

Balance sheets at 31 December 1998

Reference		Note	Group 1998 £m	Group 1997 (restated) £m	Company 1998 £m	Company 1997 £m
s 225(3) s 227(2)(a) 4 Sch Format 1						
	Fixed assets					
4 Sch 8	Intangible assets	10	**1,140.9**	–	–	–
4 Sch 8	Tangible assets	11	**402.8**	87.3	**11.5**	9.7
4 Sch 8	Investments	12	**0.5**	–	**419.7**	98.5
FRS 9 p21	Interests in joint ventures:	12				
	Share of gross assets		**105.1**	7.2	–	–
	Share of gross liabilities		**(96.7)**	(5.4)	–	–
FRS 9 p29	Goodwill arising on acquisition		**8.1**	–	–	–
			16.5	1.8	–	–
			17.0	1.8	**419.7**	98.5
			1,560.7	89.1	**431.2**	108.2
4 Sch 8	**Current assets**					
	Stock	13	**33.8**	17.0	–	–
	Debtors	14	**290.6**	109.6	**68.3**	101.0
	Investments	11	**9.4**	55.3	–	48.7
	Cash at bank and in hand		**105.5**	46.6	**10.2**	6.6
			439.3	228.5	**78.5**	156.3
4 Sch 8	**Creditors – Amounts falling due within one year**	15	**(434.3)**	(165.8)	**(172.2)**	(100.9)
4 Sch 8	**Net current (liabilities)/assets**		**5.0**	62.7	**(93.7)**	55.4
4 Sch 8	**Total assets less current liabilities**		**1,565.7**	151.8	**337.5**	163.6
4 Sch 8	**Creditors – Amounts falling due after more than one year**	17	**(339.8)**	(4.5)	**(220.5)**	–
4 Sch 8	**Provisions for liabilities and charges**	20	**(119.1)**	(10.8)	–	(0.5)
			1,106.8	136.5	**117.0**	163.1
4 Sch 8	**Capital and reserves**					
4 Sch 8	Called up share capital	21	**15.8**	10.9	**15.8**	10.9
4 Sch 8	Share premium account	22	**11.8**	9.3	**11.8**	9.3
4 Sch 8	Revaluation reserve	23	**7.5**	2.5	**2.3**	0.8
4 Sch 8	Other reserves	25	**917.5**	5.8	–	–
4 Sch 8	Profit and loss account	24	**152.7**	107.2	**87.1**	142.1
FRS 4 p38	**Total shareholders' funds (including non-equity interests)**	26	**1,105.3**	135.7	**117.0**	163.1
FRS 2 p35 4A Sch 17	Equity minority interests		**1.4**	0.7	–	–
FRS 4 p40,50	Non-equity minority interests		**0.1**	0.1	–	–
			1.5	0.8	–	–
	Capital employed		**1,106.8**	136.5	**117.0**	163.1

SSAP 17 p26
s 233(1)-(4)

The financial statements on pages 23 to 65 were approved by the board on 26 February 1999 and was signed on its behalf by:

CD Jones
Director

GAAP UK Plc

26

Consolidated cash flow statement

FRS 1 p4,48 **for the year ended 31 December 1998**

		Note	1998 £m	1998 £m	1997 £m	1997 £m
FRS 1 p7	**Net cash inflow from operating activities**	27		**229.8**		130.0
FRS 1 p7*	**Dividends received from joint ventures**			**0.1**		0.2
FRS 1 p7	**Returns on investments and servicing of finance**					
FRS 1 p14(a)	Interest received		**12.2**		4.1	
FRS 1 p15(a)	Interest paid		**(21.6)**		(1.1)	
FRS 1 p15(b)	Issue costs of new bank loan		**(5.3)**		–	
FRS 1 p15(c)	Interest element of finance lease payments		**(1.0)**		–	
FRS 1 p15(e)	Dividends paid to minority interests		**(0.1)**		(0.1)	
FRS 1 p15(d)	Non-equity dividends paid to shareholders		**(0.1)**		(0.1)	
	Net cash (outflow)/inflow from returns on investments and servicing of finance			**(15.9)**		2.8
FRS 1 p7	**Taxation**			**(49.4)**		(37.2)
FRS 1 p7	**Capital expenditure and financial investment**					
FRS 1 p21(a)	Purchase of tangible fixed assets		**(106.1)**		(34.5)	
FRS 1 p20(a)	Sale of tangible fixed assets		**15.5**		6.7	
	Purchase of own shares	12	**(0.5)**		–	
	Net cash outflow for capital expenditure and financial investment			**(91.1)**		(27.8)
FRS 1 p7	**Acquisitions**					
FRS 6 p33	Purchase of subsidiary undertakings	28	**(320.6)**		(36.9)	
FRS 1 p24(a)	Net overdrafts acquired with subsidiary undertakings	28	**(15.1)**		–	
	Net cash outflow for acquisitions			**(335.7)**		(36.9)
FRS 1 p7	**Equity dividends paid to shareholders**			**(23.7)**		(15.8)
	Net cash (outflow)/inflow before use of liquid resources and financing			**(285.9)**		15.3
FRS 1 p7,26,52	**Management of liquid resources**					
	Reduction/(increase) in short-term deposits with banks	29		**91.7**		(21.9)
FRS 1 p7	**Financing**					
	Issue of ordinary share capital	21	**2.6**		4.7	
	Expenses of share issue to acquire Newsub plc		**(1.4)**		–	
	Capital element of finance lease payments	29	**(10.8)**		–	
	Increase in borrowings	29	**176.5**		21.1	
	Net cash inflow from financing			**166.9**		25.8
	(Decrease)/increase in net cash			**(27.3)**		19.2
FRS 1 p33	**Reconciliation to net (debt)/cash**					
	Net cash at 1 January			**59.3**		39.0
	(Decrease)/increase in net cash			**(27.3)**		19.2
	Borrowings net of short term deposits acquired with subsidiaries			**(57.1)**		–
	Movement in deposits			**(91.7)**		21.9
	Movement in borrowings			**(160.4)**		(21.1)
	Other non-cash changes			**(1.1)**		–
	Exchange adjustments			**4.5**		0.3
	Net (debt)/cash at 31 December	29		**(273.8)**		59.3

GAAP UK Plc

* As amended by FRS 9

Accounting policies

4 Sch 36A

These financial statements have been prepared under the historical cost convention, as modified by the revaluation of certain tangible fixed assets, and in accordance with applicable accounting standards. The directors consider that the accounting policies set out below are suitable, have been consistently applied and are supported by reasonable and prudent judgements and estimates.

s 256
SI 1990/1667

Note: Accounting standards means those issued by bodies prescribed by regulations. The Accounting Standards Board is the only body so prescribed. Hence UK statutory financial statements can only be drawn up in accordance with UK SSAPs and FRSs.

4 Sch 36
SSAP 2 p18

The accounting policies followed for dealing with items that are judged material or critical in determining the profit or loss for the year and in stating the financial position should be disclosed. The accounting policies, which should be as clear, fair and as brief as possible, should include the following to the extent applicable:

Consolidation

- Basis of consolidation.
- Inclusion of all subsidiaries.
- Equity accounting for associates and gross equity accounting for joint ventures.

SSAP 2
s 262

Turnover

- Basis of income recognition.

FRS 13 p74

Financial instruments

- Methods used to account for derivative financial instruments, the types of derivative financial instruments accounted for under each method and the criteria that determine the method used.
- The basis for recognising, measuring (both on initial recognition and subsequently), ceasing to recognise, financial assets and financial liabilities.
- How income and expenses (and other gains and losses) are recognised and measured.
- The treatment of financial assets and financial liabilities not recognised, including an explanation of how provisions for losses are recognised on financial assets and financial liabilities that have not been recognised.
- Policies on offsetting.

The disclosures should cover foreign currencies, interest rates and commodities and policies for finance leases, bank borrowings and fixed rate investments.

GAAP UK Plc

FRS 13 p75 Where financial instruments are carried on the historical cost basis, features covered by the description of accounting policies would typically include (where the choice of policy applied has had a material effect):

- Premiums and discounts on financial assets.
- Changes in the estimated account of determinable future cash flows associated with a financial instrument, such as a debenture indexed to commodity price.
- A fall in the fair value of a financial asset to below the asset's carrying amount.
- Restructured financial liabilities.

FRS 13 p76 Where financial instruments are used as hedges and accounted for using hedge accounting, the accounting policies should include (if the choice of policy has had a material effect) a description of:

- The circumstances in which a financial instrument is accounted for as a hedge.
- The recognition and measurement treatment applied to an instrument used as a hedge.
- The method used to account for an instrument that ceases to be accounted for as a hedge.
- The method used to account for the hedge when the underlying item or position matures, is sold, extinguished, or terminated.
- The method used to account for the hedge of a future transaction when that transaction is no longer likely to occur.

4 Sch 58(1)
SSAP 20 p59

Foreign currencies

- Basis of translating foreign currency assets and liabilities.
- Basis of translating results of foreign subsidiaries.
- Treatment of exchange differences arising on the retranslation of opening net investments in subsidiary companies and translation of results (if at average rate).
- Translation of all other exchange differences.
- UITF 9 Method adopted for dealing with results of foreign subsidiaries operating in hyperinflationary economies.

SSAP 21 p57, 60(a)

Leases

- Basis of recognition of fixed assets held under finance leases in the balance sheet.
- Depreciation policy for assets held under finance leases.
- Treatment of the interest element of finance lease rental obligations.
- Treatment of payments for operating leases.
- UITF 12 p8 Treatment of incentives to take on operating leases (for example, rent free periods).

Leases include hire purchase contracts which have characteristics similar to operating or finance leases.

FRS 12

Provisions

- Basis of provisioning for each class of provision.
- Extent of use of discounting.

GAAP UK Plc

FRS 4

Capitalisation of finance costs and interest

- Basis of capitalisation of interest and other finance costs.

SSAP 12 p25

Fixed assets

- Whether carried at cost or revalued amount.
- Basis and frequency of revaluations.
- What is included in cost.
- Policy on capitalisation of interest.
- Methods of depreciation (for example, straight line or reducing balance).
- Useful economic lives/depreciation rates.

FRS 10

Goodwill and intangible assets

FRS 10 p52
- The method used to value intangible assets.

FRS 10 p55
- The methods and periods of amortisation of goodwill and intangibles and the reasons for choosing those periods.
- Treatment of goodwill on disposal, including previously eliminated goodwill.

FRS 10 p56,57
- The reason for any change in the amortisation method or period, if the effect is material.

FRS 10 p58
- Where the period of amortisation exceeds 20 years, the grounds for rebutting the 20 year presumption.

FRS 10 p59
- Where goodwill is not amortised, particulars of the departure from the specific requirement of CA85 4 Sch p21, the reasons for it and the effect.

FRS 10 p64
- Where negative goodwill exceeds the fair values of the non-monetary assets, the source of the excess negative goodwill and the periods in which it is being written back.

Transitional arrangements under FRS 10:

- Treatment of goodwill previously eliminated against reserves (whether reinstated or not).
- If previous goodwill remains eliminated against reserves.

FRS 10 p71(a)(ii)
  - The accounting policy followed in respect of that goodwill.

FRS 10 p71(a)(iii)
  - The fact that this goodwill had been eliminated as a matter of accounting policy and would be charged or credited in the profit and loss account on subsequent disposal of the related business.

FRS 10 p71(b)
  - Treatment of any balance (debit or credit) on a separate goodwill write-off reserve.

FRS 11

Impairment of fixed assets and goodwill

- Basis for determining impairment write-down, by reference to higher of post-tax net realisable value and value-in-use.
- Use of discounting in determining value-in-use.
- Basis for using risk-free discount rate and method for adjusting cash flows for risk, where applicable.
- Treatment of impairment write down on revalued assets.

GAAP UK Plc

SSAP 4 p48

Government grants

- Treatment of capital grants.
- Treatment of revenue based grants.
- Period over which the grants are credited to the profit and loss account.

Investment properties

SSAP 19 p11
SSAP 19 p13

- Basis of inclusion in the balance sheet.
- Treatment of changes in value.

SSAP 24 p87,88

Pensions

- Type of scheme – defined contribution or defined benefit.
- For defined benefit schemes the funding policy (if different from the accounting policy).
- For defined benefit schemes – valuation frequency and method.
- Method of charging to profit and loss account.
- Treatment of variations from regular cost.
- How interest on provision is accounted for.

UITF 6 p10

Post retirement benefits

- Method of charging to the profit and loss account (in accordance with the principles of SSAP 24).

SSAP 13 p30

Research and development

- Classification of expenditure.
- Treatment of expenditure.

SSAP 9 p32

Stocks, work in progress and long-term contracts

- Basis of amount stated at in the balance sheet (for example, NRV, FIFO).
- Basis for inclusion of overheads.
- Basis of provision for obsolete, slow moving and defective stocks.
- Method of ascertaining turnover and attributable profit for long-term contracts.

Taxation including deferred tax

- Basis of charge for taxation.
- Policy adopted for providing for deferred taxation.
- Policy adopted in respect of the deferred taxation implications of pensions and other post retirement benefits. (SSAP 15 p32A)
- Treatment of recoverable advance corporation tax.

UITF 13 p8
UITF 17

Share schemes

- Basis of accounting.
- Employee share ownership plans (ESOP's).
- Low or nil cost schemes (UITF 17).

Changes in presentation of financial information

FRS 9

- FRS 9, 'Associates and joint ventures', has been adopted and, consequently, the group's profit and loss account, balance sheet and cash flow statement have been presented in accordance with the new requirements.

FRS 10 ■ FRS 10, 'Goodwill and intangible assets', has been adopted and, consequently, the balance on the goodwill reserve shown in the financial statements for 31 December 1997 has been eliminated against the profit and loss account reserve under the transitional arrangements in FRS 10.

FRS 11 ■ FRS 11, 'Impairment of fixed assets and goodwill', came into effect for these financial statements, but has not resulted in any changes in presentation.

FRS 12 ■ FRS 12, 'Provisions, contingent liabilities and contingent assets', has been adopted early. No restatement of prior year information has been necessary, but additional disclosures have been provided in accordance with the standard.

FRS 13 ■ FRS 13, 'Derivatives and other financial instruments: disclosures', has been adopted early. The group had previously presented information on financial instruments in accordance with the proposals in FRED 13, the predecessor to the standard. Consequently, this prior year information has been refined and disclosed on the same basis as that for the year ended 31 December 1998.

FRS 14 ■ FRS 14, 'Earnings per share', has been adopted and, consequently, basic and diluted earnings per share have been calculated in accordance with the new methodology. Comparative basic and diluted earnings per share for 1997 have been re-calculated on the same basis.

GAAP UK Plc

Notes to the financial statements for the year ended 31 December 1998

SSAP 25 p35-48

1 Segmental reporting

Reference		Turnover 1998 £m	Turnover 1997 £m	Profit before tax 1998 £m	Profit before tax 1997 £m	Net assets 1998 £m	Net assets 1997 £m
4 Sch 55(2)	**Geographical analysis**						
	United Kingdom	**576.9**	207.2	**90.8**	50.7	**153.4**	62.5
	Continental Europe						
FRS 9 p21	– Group	**243.1**	98.8	**39.8**	28.8	**67.1**	34.5
SSAP 25 p26	– Joint ventures	**38.9**	9.9	**2.8**	1.2	**16.5**	1.8
	North America	**344.7**	91.6	**27.8**	10.4	**92.0**	3.0
	Asia Pacific and Africa	**96.2**	78.3	**31.8**	24.5	**29.9**	20.7
	Central	**–**	–	**(40.2)**	–	**1,021.7**	(45.3)
		1,299.8	485.8	**152.8**	115.6	**1,380.6**	77.2
SSAP 25 p37	Interest (payable)/receivable	**–**	–	**(10.9)**	3.6	**–**	–
	Unallocated	**–**	–	**–**	–	**(273.8)**	59.3
	Total						
	– Group	**1,260.9**	475.9	**138.4**	118.0	**1,090.3**	134.7
FRS 9 p21	**– Joint ventures**	**38.9**	9.9	**3.5**	1.2	**16.5**	1.8
4 Sch 55(1)(a)	**Business analysis**						
	Food products	**404.4**	175.1	**78.3**	47.8	**160.4**	40.3
	Personnel services	**125.7**	3.3	**7.7**	0.3	**22.8**	0.1
	Retail services	**113.8**	113.3	**37.4**	37.0	**16.0**	28.4
	Distribution services						
FRS 9 p21	– Group	**259.3**	11.9	**33.2**	4.7	**135.8**	44.7
SSAP 25 p26	– Joint ventures	**38.9**	9.9	**2.8**	1.2	**16.5**	1.8
	Property services	**154.3**	84.9	**19.9**	18.0	**7.8**	10.1
	Health care	**203.4**	87.4	**13.7**	6.6	**(0.4)**	(2.9)
	Interest (payable)/receivable	**–**	–	**(10.9)**	3.6	**–**	–
	Central	**–**	–	**(40.2)**	–	**1,021.7**	(45.3)
	Unallocated	**–**	–	**–**	–	**(273.8)**	59.3
	Total						
	– Group	**1,260.9**	475.9	**138.4**	118.0	**1,090.3**	134.7
FRS 9 p21	**– Joint ventures**	**38.9**	9.9	**3.5**	1.2	**16.5**	1.8

SSAP 25 p34 Analyses by business are based on the group's management structure. Turnover between segments is immaterial. Geographical analysis is based on the country in which the order is received. It would not be materially different if based on the country in which the customer is located. Central net assets/(liabilities) comprise unamortised goodwill and investment in own
SSAP 24 p37 shares partially offset by dividend and taxation liabilities. Central loss before tax comprises the amortisation of goodwill relating to subsidiaries. Unallocated net (liabilities) / assets comprise the group's net (debt)/cash.

Notes:

SSAP 25 p36 *(a) The group's share of the profit before taxation and net assets of its joint ventures and associates, should be separately disclosed on a segmental basis if any exceed 20% of the relevant total.*

FRS 9 p21,27 *(b) Group turnover and operating profit should be clearly distinguished from that of joint ventures and associates.*

FRS 3 p15,53
FRS 6 p28

The above business analyses of turnover, profit before tax and net assets in 1998 includes contributions from Newsub plc:

	Turnover £m	Profit before tax £m	Net operating assets £m
Food products	214.7	20.9	31.1
Personnel services	121.7	6.8	18.1
Distribution services			
– Group	240.9	25.1	75.4
– Joint ventures	29.8	3.1	6.6
Property services	66.9	0.4	0.4
Health care	65.8	8.6	(1.2)
Goodwill amortisation (including £(0.9)m on joint ventures)	–	(41.1)	–
Net interest (including £0.7m in joint ventures)	–	(17.3)	–
	739.8	6.5	130.4

FRS 3 p53

The segmental analysis of turnover, profit before tax and net assets for the United Kingdom and Food Products includes £25.6m (1997: £35.3m), £1.4m (1997: £6.2m) and £5.5m (1997: £5.3m) in respect of Hathaway Limited which was sold during the year.

2 Cost of sales, gross profit, distribution costs and administrative expenses

FRS 3 p14

	1998 Continuing £m	1998 Discontinued £m	1998 Total £m	1997 Continuing £m	1997 Discontinued £m	1997 Total £m
Turnover	**1,235.3**	**25.6**	**1,260.9**	440.6	35.3	475.9
Cost of sales	**(1,008.9)**	**(18.3)**	**(1,027.2)**	(321.2)	(21.2)	(342.4)
Exceptional cost of sales	**(3.5)**	**–**	**(3.5)**	–	–	–
Goodwill amortisation (FRS 10 App 1 p16)	**(40.2)**	**–**	**(40.2)**	–	–	–
	(1,052.6)	**(18.3)**	**(1,070.9)**	(321.2)	(21.2)	(342.4)
Gross profit	**182.7**	**7.3**	**190.0**	119.4	14.1	133.5
Distribution costs (4 Sch 8)	**13.7**	**–**	**13.7**	–	–	–
Administrative expenses (4 Sch 8)	**30.0**	**5.1**	**35.1**	14.1	7.0	21.1
	43.7	**5.1**	**48.8**	14.1	7.0	21.1
Less: other operating income – royalties (4 Sch 8)	**(2.5)**	**–**	**(2.5)**	(2.0)	–	(2.0)
Net operating expenses	**41.2**	**5.1**	**46.3**	12.1	7.0	19.1
Group operating profit	**141.5**	**2.2**	**143.7**	107.3	7.1	114.4

FRS 3 p14

Cost of sales, gross profit, distribution costs and administrative expenses include, in respect of subsidiary undertakings acquired during 1998, £623.7m, £87.9m, £7.3m and £18.8m respectively.

GAAP UK Plc 34

3 Interest and similar items

		1998 £m	1997 £m
FRS 12 p48	Unwinding of discount in provisions	**(0.4)**	–
4 Sch 53(2)(a)	Interest payable on bank loans and overdrafts	**(16.4)**	(1.3)
FRS 4 p28	Amortisation of issue costs of bank loan	**(1.1)**	–
4 Sch 53(2)(b)	Interest payable on other loans	**(5.2)**	(0.1)
SSAP 21 p53	Interest payable on finance leases	**(1.2)**	–
FRS 4 p28	Total interest and similar charges payable	**(24.3)**	(1.4)
4 Sch 8	Interest receivable	**12.7**	5.0
	Net interest (payable)/receivable and similar items	**(11.6)**	3.6
FRS 3 p14	Continuing operations	**6.4**	3.6
	Acquisitions	**(18.0)**	–
		(11.6)	3.6

4 Sch 26(3)(b)
LR 12.43(c)
FRS 4 p76

Note: If the group capitalises interest or other finance cost into assets, the total finance cost for the year should be shown in the above table and the amount capitalised shown as a deduction in arriving at the net amount shown on the face of the profit and loss account.

4 Profit on ordinary activities before taxation

		1998 £m	1997 £m
	Profit before taxation is stated after charging/(crediting):		
4 Sch 8	Staff costs (note 32)	**617.4**	231.5
SSAP 12 p25(c)	Depreciation of tangible fixed assets		
	– owned assets	**64.6**	22.9
SSAP 21 p49	– under finance leases	**1.1**	–
	Amortisation of goodwill		
	– subsidiaries	**40.2**	–
	– associates	**0.9**	–
	Loss/(profit) on disposal of fixed assets – adjustment to depreciation	**1.6**	(1.3)
SSAP 21 p55	Hire of machinery and equipment	**12.2**	1.2
SSAP 21 p55	Other operating lease rentals	**5.2**	5.6
FRS 3 p19	Costs of product remediation (see below)	**3.5**	–
FRS 6 p31, 4 Sch 57(3), FRS 3 p19	Costs incurred in reorganising acquired businesses (see below)	**9.1**	–
SSAP 20 p60(a)	Net exchange differences on foreign currency borrowings less deposits	**5.4**	2.3
UITF 20 p10	Costs incurred in respect of work performed on year 2000 modifications	**9.0**	0.6
UITF 21 p18	Costs incurred in respect of preparation for the introduction of the euro	**0.7**	–
s 390A(3),(5)	Group audit fees and expenses of which the parent company was £0.2m (1997: £0.1m)	**1.4**	0.6

SI 1991/2128
SI 1995/1520

Fees paid to PricewaterhouseCoopers for non-audit services in the UK were £0.4m (1997: Price Waterhouse £0.1m).

Exceptional items

4 Sch 57(3) FRS 3 p19 During the year, a few batches of one of the group's food products were found to have been contaminated with small pieces of glass. As a precaution the group recalled all batches of this product made within 6 weeks of the contamination being discovered. The exceptional charge to cost of sales represents the cost of correcting the defective machinery, replacing the withdrawn product and meeting product liability claims to the extent they were not covered by the group's insurance.

FRS 3 p46 FRS 6 p31 The costs incurred in reorganising the businesses of Newsub plc arise from the integration and streamlining of the food products and health care divisions within the group's existing businesses. These costs relate to the project identified and controlled by management as part of the integration programme set up at the time of Newsub plc's acquisition.

5 Profit on sale of subsidiary

		1998	1997
	Discontinued operations	**£m**	£m
	Gain on disposal of subsidiary net tangible assets	**10.2**	–
FRS 10 p71(c)(ii)	Goodwill previously eliminated against reserves	**(3.9)**	–
FRS 3 p20	**Profit on sale of subsidiary**	**6.3**	–
4 Sch 54(3) FRS 3 p24	**Taxation**	**1.0**	–

4 Sch 57(2) On 1 December 1998, the group sold Hathaway Limited, a wholly-owned subsidiary, for £15.7m in cash. The consideration is due to be received in January 1999.

6 Tax on profit on ordinary activities

		1998 £m	1997 £m
4 Sch 54(3)	**United Kingdom**		
SSAP 8 p23	Corporation tax at 30.25% (1997: 31.5%)	**26.8**	30.2
SSAP 8 p22	Double tax relief	**(0.9)**	(13.1)
		25.9	17.1
	Overseas		
	Corporation taxes	**26.6**	23.8
FRS 9 p21	Share of joint ventures	**1.9**	0.8
		54.4	41.7
	Comprising		
	Current	**52.8**	40.6
SSAP 15 p33,36	Deferred (including prior year effect relating to rate change of £0.6m)	**1.6**	1.1
		54.4	41.7
	Tax on recognised gains and losses not included in the profit and loss account		
	United Kingdom corporation tax at 30.25% (1997: 31.5%)		
	Current tax credit/(charge)	**3.2**	**(1.0)**

SSAP 15 p35 The taxation charge for the year has been reduced by £5.5m (1997: £1.4m) in respect of the excess of tax allowances over depreciation and other timing differences on which, in accordance with the group's accounting policy, no deferred taxation has been provided.

4 Sch 54(2) FRS 7 p75 The overall tax charge is reduced from 1997 levels due to utilising losses brought forward which were acquired with Plants Direct Ltd in 1994, but which did not meet the criteria for recognition of deferred tax assets at the date of acquisition or in the period permitted for completing the fair value exercise.

GAAP UK Plc

7 Profits of holding company

s 230(1)(b),(4) Of the profit attributable to shareholders, a deficit of £16.6m (1997: profit of £51.1m) is dealt with in the accounts of GAAP UK plc. The directors have taken advantage of the exemption available under section 230 of the Companies Act 1985 and not presented a profit and loss account for the company alone.

4 Sch 3(7)(b)
FRS 4 p59

8 Dividends

	1998 £m	1997 £m
Equity – Ordinary		
Interim paid: 1.15p (1997: 0.60p) per 1p share	**10.3**	5.4
Final proposed: 1.79p (1997: 1.51p) per 1p share	**24.8**	13.4
	35.1	18.8
Non-equity – Preference		
Paid: 7p (1997: 7p) per £1 share	**0.1**	0.1
	35.2	18.9

UITF 13 p8(g)
FRS 14 p81(b) Dividends amounting to £4,523 (1997: nil) in respect of the company's shares held by an employee share trust (note 12) have been deducted in arriving at the aggregate of dividends paid and proposed.

FRS 4 p43,59 *Note: Where the finance costs for non-equity shares are not equal to the dividends the difference should be accounted for in the profit and loss account as an appropriation of profits. Such an appropriation should be disclosed separately.*

9 Earnings per share

FRS 14 p16 Basic earnings per share is calculated by dividing the earnings attributable to ordinary shareholders by the weighted average number of ordinary shares in issue during the year, excluding those held in the employee share trust (note 12) which are treated as cancelled.

For diluted earnings per share, the weighted average number of ordinary shares in issue is adjusted to assume conversion of all dilutive potential ordinary shares. The group has only one category of dilutive potential ordinary shares: those share options granted to employees where the exercise price is less than the average market price of the company's ordinary shares during the year.

FRS 14 p71 Reconciliations of the earnings and weighted average number of shares used in the calculations are set out below.

GAAP UK Plc

	1998			1997		
	Earnings £m	**Weighted average number of shares million**	**Per-share amount pence**	Earnings £m	Weighted average number of shares millions	Per-share amount pence
Profit attributable to shareholders	**87.0**			77.4		
Less: preference dividends	**(0.1)**			(0.1)		
Basic EPS						
Earnings attributable to ordinary shareholders	**86.9**	**1,137.8**	**7.64**	77.3	881.6	8.77
Effect of dilutive securities						
Options	**–**	**5.0**		–	17.2	
Diluted EPS						
Adjusted earnings	**86.9**	**1,142.8**	**7.60**	77.3	898.8	8.60

FRS 14 p73,74
FRS 3 p25

Supplementary earnings per share to exclude goodwill amortisation

Basic EPS	**86.9**	**1,137.8**	**7.64**	77.3	881.6	8.77
Effect of goodwill amortisation						
– subsidiaries	**40.2**		**3.53**	–		–
– joint ventures	**0.9**		**0.08**	–		–
Basic EPS excluding goodwill amortisation	**128.0**	**1,137.8**	**11.25**	77.3	881.6	8.77
Diluted EPS	**86.9**	**1,142.8**	**7.60**	77.3	898.8	8.60
Effect of goodwill amortisation						
– subsidiaries	**40.2**		**3.52**	–		–
– joint ventures	**0.9**		**0.08**	–		–
Diluted EPS excluding goodwill amortisation	**128.0**	**1,142.8**	**11.20**	77.3	898.8	8.60

FRS 14 p74
FRS 3 p25

Supplementary basic and diluted EPS have been calculated to exclude the effect of goodwill amortisation in respect of the subsidiaries and joint ventures acquired during 1998. The adjusted numbers provide a more meaningful comparison for the 1997 basic and diluted EPS which do not contain any goodwill amortisation as the group has adopted the transitional provisions of FRS 10 (note 24).

10 Intangible fixed assets

	Group	Goodwill £m
4 Sch 42(1)	**Cost**	
FRS 10 p53(a)	At 1 January 1998	–
FRS 10 p53(c)	Additions (note 28)	1,181.1
FRS 10 p53(a)	**At 31 December 1998**	**1,181.1**
4 Sch 42(3)	**Aggregate amortisation**	
FRS 10 p53(b)	At 1 January 1998	–
FRS 10 p53(c)	Charge for the year	40.2
FRS 10 p53(b)	**At 31 December 1998**	**40.2**
FRS 10 p53(d)	**Net book amount at 31 December 1998**	**1,140.9**
FRS 10 p53(d)	Net book amount at 31 December 1997	–

FRS 10 p55 The goodwill arising on the acquisition of Newsub plc is being amortised on a straight-line basis over 15 years and that in respect of the acquisitions of Potco Limited and Fransub SA on a straight-line basis over 5 years. These periods are the periods over which the directors estimate that the values of the underlying businesses acquired are expected to exceed the value of the underlying assets.

11 Tangible fixed assets

4 Sch 8	Group	Land and buildings £m	Plant and equipment £m	Vehicles and office equipment £m	Total £m
4 Sch 42(1)	**Cost or valuation**				
	At 1 January 1998	20.7	75.2	77.2	173.1
	Exchange adjustments	(3.2)	(14.7)	(9.3)	(27.2)
	Additions at cost	10.8	54.3	30.4	95.5
	Acquisitions	70.2	181.6	61.9	313.7
	Surplus on revaluation	3.1	–	–	3.1
	Disposals	(0.2)	(27.5)	(24.8)	(52.5)
SSAP 12 p25(d)	**At 31 December 1998**	**101.4**	**268.9**	**135.4**	**505.7**
4 Sch 42(3)	**Aggregate depreciation**				
	At 1January 1998	2.4	46.8	36.6	85.8
	Exchange adjustments	(0.3)	(5.5)	(4.2)	(10.0)
SSAP 12 p25(c)	Charge for year	6.4	39.5	25.2	71.1
	Revaluation	(2.3)	–	–	(2.3)
	Disposals	(0.2)	(24.6)	(16.9)	(41.7)
SSAP 12 p25(d)	**At 31 December 1998**	**6.0**	**56.2**	**40.7**	**102.9**
	Net book amount at 31 December 1998	**95.4**	**212.7**	**94.7**	**402.8**
	Net book amount at 31 December 1997	18.3	28.4	40.6	87.3

GAAP UK Plc

SSAP 21 p49,50 Assets held under finance leases, capitalised and included in plant and equipment and vehicles and office equipment:

	1998 £m	1997 £m
Cost	**13.1**	–
Aggregate depreciation	**(2.6)**	–
Net book amount	**10.5**	–

4 Sch 26(3)(b)
LR 12.43(c) *Note: If the group capitalises interest in tangible fixed assets the amount added in the year and the cumulative total of such interest included at the balance sheet date should be disclosed.*

		Land and buildings £m	Plant and equipment £m	Vehicles and office equipment £m	Total £m
4 Sch 8	**Company**				
4 Sch 42(1)	**Cost or valuation**				
	At 1 January 1998	9.5	0.3	1.1	10.9
	Additions at cost	0.4	–	0.3	0.7
	Surplus on revaluation	1.1	–	–	1.1
	Disposals	–	–	(0.3)	(0.3)
SSAP 12,25(d)	**At 31 December 1998**	**11.0**	**0.3**	**1.1**	**12.4**
4 Sch 42(3)	**Aggregate depreciation**				
	At 1 January1998	0.4	0.2	0.6	1.2
SSAP 12 p25(c)	Charge for year	0.1	–	0.2	0.3
	Revaluation	(0.4)	–	–	(0.4)
	Disposals	–	–	(0.2)	(0.2)
SSAP 12 p25(d)	**At 31 December 1998**	**0.1**	**0.2**	**0.6**	**0.9**
	Net book amount at 31 December 1998	**10.9**	**0.1**	**0.5**	**11.5**
	Net book amount at 31 December 1997	9.1	0.1	0.5	9.7

		Group 1998 £m	Group 1997 £m	Company 1998 £m	Company 1997 £m
4 Sch 43	**Analysis of land and buildings at cost or valuation**				
	At cost	**81.0**	8.4	–	3.1
	At valuation:				
	1998	**20.4**	–	–	–
	1993 or 1994	–	12.3	–	6.4
		101.4	20.7	**9.9**	9.5

4 Sch 33(2)
4 Sch 43(a) The group's freehold properties were revalued during 1993, and its long leasehold properties were revalued in 1994, on the basis of open market value for existing use by independent qualified valuers. The valuations were undertaken in accordance with the Appraisal and Valuation Manual of the Royal Institution of Chartered Surveyors in the United Kingdom by Castle & White, a firm of independent Chartered Surveyors, and overseas by valuers having equivalent professional qualifications. The book values of the properties were adjusted to the revaluations and the resultant net surplus was credited to the revaluation reserve. For the 1998 financial statements these valuations (thus excluding properties acquired during the year) have been updated on the same basis by Mr E F Logan, a director of the company and a Chartered Surveyor, in accordance with the Appraisal and Valuation Manual. No provision is made for
SSAP 15 p42 any tax on capital gains that might arise on the disposal of the group's properties at their balance sheet amounts (note 20).

GAAP UK Plc

Ref		Group 1998 £m	Group 1997 £m	Company 1998 £m	Company 1997 £m
4 Sch 44	**Analysis of net book value of land and buildings**				
4 Sch 83	Freehold	**87.1**	15.5	**8.1**	7.7
	Leasehold:				
	Over 50 years unexpired	**4.9**	1.2	**0.9**	0.9
	Under 50 years unexpired	**3.4**	1.6	**0.4**	0.5
		95.4	18.3	**9.4**	9.1

If the revalued assets were stated on the historical cost basis, the amounts would be:

Ref		Group 1998 £m	Group 1997 £m	Company 1998 £m	Company 1997 £m
	Freehold and long leasehold land and buildings				
	At cost	**8.2**	8.9	**4.3**	4.7
	Aggregate depreciation	**(1.3)**	(1.3)	**(0.6)**	(0.6)
4 Sch 33(3),(4)	Net book value based on historic cost	**6.9**	7.6	**3.7**	4.1

12 Investments

Ref			Group 1998 £m	Group 1997 £m	Company 1998 £m	Company 1997 £m
4 Sch 42(1)	**Fixed asset investments**					
	Shares in group undertakings					
	At 1 January		–	–	**98.5**	95.0
	Additions in year		–	–	**320.7**	3.5
	At 31 December		–	–	**419.2**	98.5
4A Sch 21(2)	**Interests in joint ventures**					
	At 1 January	– net assets	**1.8**	1.5	–	–
FRS 9 p29		– goodwill	–	–	–	–
			1.8	1.5		
	Exchange adjustments		**(0.9)**	(0.1)	–	–
	Additions	– net assets	**5.0**	–	–	–
		– goodwill	**9.0**	–	–	–
	Share of profits retained		**2.5**	0.4	–	–
	At 31 December – net assets		**8.4**	1.8	–	–
FRS 9 p29		**– goodwill**	**9.0**	–	–	–
			17.4	1.8	–	–
	Aggregate amortisation of goodwill					
	At 1 January		–	–	–	–
	Charge for the year		**(0.9)**	–	–	–
	At 31 December		**(0.9)**	–	–	–
	Net book amount at 31 December					
	– Net assets		**8.4**	1.8	–	–
FRS9 p29	**– Goodwill**		**8.1**	–	–	–
			16.5	1.8	–	–
UITF 13 p8	**Interests in own shares**		**0.5**	–	**0.5**	–
	Total fixed asset investments		**17.0**	1.8	**419.7**	98.5
	Current asset investments					
	Short-term deposits		**9.4**	55.3	–	48.7

FRS 9 p57,53 *Note: Further disclosures are required for associates if the 15% and/or 25% thresholds are exceeded.*

Investments in group undertakings are stated at cost. As permitted by section 133 of the Companies Act 1985, where the relief afforded under section 131 of the Companies Act 1985 applies, cost is the aggregate of the nominal value of the relevant number of the company's shares and the fair value of any other consideration given to acquire the share capital of the
s 231(5),(6) subsidiary undertakings. A list of principal subsidiary undertakings and joint ventures is given on page 64. A full list of subsidiary undertakings and joint ventures, at 31 December 1998, will be annexed to the company's next annual return.

FRS 10 p55 The goodwill arising on the joint ventures acquired with Newsub plc is being amortised on a straight-line basis over 5 years. This is the period over which the directors estimate that values of the underlying businesses are expected to exceed the values of the underlying assets.

UITF 13 p8,9 Interests in own shares represents the cost of 153,846 of the company's ordinary shares (nominal value of £1,538) purchased in April 1998. These shares were acquired by a trust in the open market using funds provided by GAAP UK plc to meet obligations under the senior executive share option scheme. The option scheme does not allow the executives to purchase shares at a
UITF 17 discount to the market value at the date of grant of the options, therefore, no charge to the profit and loss account arises. The costs of funding and administering the scheme are charged to the profit and loss account of the company in the period to which they relate. Dividend income from, and voting rights on, the shares held by the trust have been waived and the shares have been excluded from the earnings per share calculation. The market value of the shares at 31 December 1998 was £0.7m.

13 Stocks

		Group		Company	
		1998 **£m**	1997 £m	**1998** **£m**	1997 £m
	Stocks and work in progress				
	Raw materials	**6.1**	4.3	–	–
SSAP 9 p27	Work in progress	**3.0**	0.8	–	–
	Finished products	**24.7**	11.9	–	–
		33.8	17.0	–	–

4 Sch 27(3),(4) *Note: If there is a material difference between the balance sheet amount of stock and its replacement cost, the latter amount should be disclosed.*

GAAP UK Plc 42

14 Debtors

		Group		Company	
		1998	1997	**1998**	1997
		£m	£m	**£m**	£m
	Amounts falling due within one year:				
	Trade debtors	**211.4**	91.2	–	–
	Amounts owed by group undertakings	–	–	**58.0**	49.8
FRS 9 p55	Amounts owed by joint ventures *(all trading balances)*	**1.3**	1.5	–	–
	Amount due on sale of subsidiary	**15.7**	–	–	–
	Other debtors (see below)	**39.4**	5.8	**1.9**	1.8
4 Sch Note 6	Prepayments and accrued income	**12.0**	8.7	**7.2**	3.8
	Dividends due from group undertakings	–	–	**1.2**	45.6
		279.8	107.2	**68.3**	101.0
4 Sch Note 5	**Amounts falling due after one year:**				
	Pension prepayment	**10.8**	2.4	–	–
		290.6	109.6	**68.3**	101.0

UITF 4 p3 *Note: Debtors due after one year must be disclosed separately on the face of the balance sheet if material to net current assets.*

6 Sch 28,29(a) Other debtors at 31 December 1998 include £7,000 in respect of loans to two officers of the company.

6 Sch 15,22(b) Included in other debtors at 31 December 1998 is a bridging loan to Mr G Wallace, the marketing director. The loan was made prior to his appointment as a director and is unsecured, does not carry interest and is repayable on demand. The loan started and ended the year at
6 Sch 22(2)(d)(ii) £60,000. This was also the maximum amount during the year.

15 Creditors – Amounts falling due within one year

		Group		Company	
		1998	1997	**1998**	1997
		£m	£m	**£m**	£m
FRS 12 p11(a)	Trade creditors	**55.7**	15.3	–	–
	Amounts owed to group undertakings	–	–	**89.0**	35.4
FRS 9 p55	Amounts owed to joint ventures *(all trading balances)*	**2.4**	1.8	–	–
4 Sch 51(3)	Dividends payable	**24.8**	12.8	**24.8**	12.8
	Corporation tax	**65.2**	29.4	**2.4**	7.4
4 Sch Note 9	Other tax and social security payable	**43.7**	20.5	**0.1**	0.1
	Deferred consideration for acquisitions	**1.7**	1.6	–	–
	Other creditors	**39.0**	6.4	**1.3**	1.1
4 Sch Note 10 FRS 12 p11(b)	Accruals and deferred income	**109.6**	36.3	**1.2**	0.5
	Bank and other borrowings (note 16)	**92.2**	41.7	**53.4**	43.6
		434.3	165.8	**172.2**	100.9

FRS 9 p55 *Note: Amounts owed to (or owing from) an associate or joint venture should be analysed between loans and trading balances, if applicable.*

16 Bank and other borrowings due within one year

		Group		Company	
		1998 £m	1997 £m	**1998 £m**	1997 £m
	Bank loans and overdrafts due within one year or on demand:				
4 Sch 48(4)	Secured	**21.2**	–	–	–
	Unsecured	**66.4**	41.6	**53.4**	43.6
		87.6	41.6	**53.4**	43.6
	Unsecured debenture loans due within one year	**1.3**	0.1	–	–
SSAP 21 p51	Finance lease obligations	**3.3**	–	–	–
		92.2	41.7	**53.4**	43.6

4 Sch 48(2) Bank loans and other borrowings are denominated in a number of currencies and bear interest based on LIBOR or foreign equivalents or government bond rates appropriate to the country in which the borrowing is incurred.

17 Creditors – Amounts falling due after more than one year

	Group		Company	
	1998 £m	1997 £m	**1998 £m**	1997 £m
Deferred consideration for acquisitions	**0.8**	0.6	–	–
Other creditors	**42.5**	3.0	–	–
Bank and other borrowings (note 18)	**296.5**	0.9	**220.5**	–
	339.8	4.5	**220.5**	–

18 Bank and other borrowings due after more than one year

		Group		Company	
		1998 £m	1997 £m	**1998 £m**	1997 £m
	Bank loans:				
4 Sch 48(4)	Secured	**0.1**	–	–	–
	Unsecured	**221.6**	–	**220.5**	–
		221.7	–	**220.5**	–
	Debenture loans:				
	7⅞% US$110m bonds due 2002	**65.0**	–	–	–
	Other unsecured loans	–	0.9	–	–
SSAP 21 p51	Finance lease obligations	**9.8**	–	–	–
		296.5	0.9	**220.5**	–

GAAP UK Plc

4 Sch 48(2) Bank loans and the other unsecured debenture loans are denominated in a number of currencies and bear interest based on LIBOR or foreign equivalents or government bond rates appropriate to the country in which the borrowing is incurred. In June 1998, as part of the interest rate management strategy the company entered into one interest rate swap (1997: nil) for a notional principal amount of £100m maturing in 2002. Under this swap, the company receives interest on a variable basis and pays interest fixed at a rate of 8.8%.

4 Sch 48(4) Bank loans and overdrafts are secured by fixed charges over land and buildings and floating charges over stocks and debtors.

FRS 4 p27,28 Group and company unsecured bank loans are stated net of unamortised issue costs of £4.2m (1997: £nil). The company incurred total issue costs of £5.3m in respect of the 5 year committed multi-option facility entered into in June 1998 under which amounts have been drawn down to fund the acquisition of Newsub plc. These costs together with the interest expense are allocated to the profit and loss account over the five year term of the facility at a constant rate on the carrying amount.

The group's borrowing limit at 31 December 1998 calculated in accordance with the Articles of Association was £973m (1997: £331m).

19 Financial instruments

FRS 13 p3(b) *Note: The narrative and numerical disclosures are not required for a parent company when its financial statements are presented together with its consolidated financial statements.*

FRS 13 p13 *An explanation should be provided of the role that financial instruments have had during the period in creating or changing the risks the entity faces in its activities. This should include an explanation of the objectives and policies for holding or issuing financial instruments and similar contracts and the strategies for achieving the objectives – in both cases as agreed*
FRS 13 p23 *by the directors – that have been followed in the period. This narrative can be given in the OFR or other statement, provided that it is incorporated into the financial statements by a reference to the exact location of the disclosures.*

FRS 13 p16 *If there has been a significant change from the explanations provided for the previous accounting period this should be disclosed and the reasons for the change explained.*

FRS 13 p18 *If the directors agreed, before the date of approval of the financial statements, to make a significant change to the role that financial instruments will have in creating of changing the risks of the group, that change should be explained.*

FRS 3 p20 *An explanation should be provided of how the period-end numerical disclosures reflect the objectives, policies and strategies for holding or issuing financial instruments. If the period-end position is regarded as unrepresentative of the group's position during the period or its agreed objectives, policies and strategies, an explanation of the extent to which it is regarded as unrepresentative should be given.*

If the group uses financial instruments as hedges it should describe (a) the transactions and risks that have been hedged, including the period of time until they are expected to occur, and (b) the instruments used for hedging purposes, distinguishing between those that have been accounted for using hedge accounting and those that have not.

FRS 13 p21 **Short-term debtors and creditors**

Short-term debtors and creditors have been excluded from all the following disclosures, other than the currency risk disclosures.

FRS 13 p26,30 **Interest rate risk profile of financial liabilities**

The interest rate risk profile of the group's financial liabilities at 31 December 1998, after taking account of the interest rate and currency swaps used to manage the interest and currency profile, was:

Currency	Total £m	Floating rate financial liabilities £m	Fixed rate financial liabilities £m	Financial liabilities on which no interest is paid £m
Sterling				
– Financial liabilities	229.4	99.9	104.5	25.0
– Preference shares	2.0	–	2.0	–
US dollars	128.0	51.7	65.0	11.3
EU currencies (excluding Sterling)	70.9	21.1	42.8	7.0
Other currencies	3.7	3.7	–	–
At 31 December 1998	**434.0**	**176.4**	**214.3**	**43.3**
Sterling				
– Financial liabilities	30.8	8.1	19.6	3.1
– Preference shares	2.0	–	2.0	–
US dollars	11.2	–	10.7	0.5
EU currencies (excluding sterling)	2.9	–	2.9	–
Other currencies	1.3	1.3	–	–
At 31 December 1997	48.2	9.4	35.2	3.6

FRS 13 p25 All the group's creditors falling due within one year (other than bank and other borrowings) are excluded from the above tables either due to the exclusion of short-term items or because they do not meet the definition of a financial liability, such as tax balances.

FRS 13 p25 The effect of the group's interest rate swap is to classify £100m of Sterling borrowings in the above table as fixed rate. The group has two foreign currency/sterling swaps, which mature in June 1999, used to hedge its net investments in France and Holland. The swaps comprise French franc120m (£13.0m equivalent) and Dutch guilder 80m (£25.8m equivalent). The effect of the swaps in the above table was to reduce Sterling borrowings and increase EU currencies by £38.8m respectively.

In addition to the above, the group's provisions of £68.4m (1997: £6.3m) for vacant leasehold properties (note 19) meet the definition of financial liabilities. These financial liabilities are considered to be floating rate financial liabilities as, in establishing the provisions, the cash flows
FRS 12 p47 have been discounted and the discount rate is re-appraised at each half yearly reporting date to ensure that it reflects current market assessments of the time value of money and the risks specific to the liability.

FRS 13 p26,29 *Note: A summary should be provided of the main terms and conditions of any financial instruments not included in the above analysis, such as optional derivatives (for example, caps, collars, cylinders etc) and convertible debt.*

GAAP UK Plc

Currency	Fixed rate financial liabilities: Weighted average interest rate %	Fixed rate financial liabilities: Weighted average period for which rate is fixed Years	Financial liabilities on which no interest is paid: Weighted average period until maturity Years
Sterling			
– Financial liabilities	8.8	4.2	0.8
– Preference shares	7.0	7.0	–
US dollars	7.9	4.2	0.6
EU currencies (excluding Sterling)	3.3	2.3	0.3
At 31 December 1998	–	**3.9**	**0.7**
Sterling	8.0	2.3	0.8
– Financial liabilities	7.0	8.0	–
– Preference shares	6.2	5.2	0.6
US dollars	3.3	3.3	–
EU currencies (excluding Sterling)			
At 31 December 1997	–	3.5	0.8

Floating rate financial liabilities bear interest at rates, based on relevant national LIBOR equivalents, which are fixed in advance for periods of between one month and six months.

FRS 13 p32

Interest rate risk of financial assets

Currency	1998 Cash at bank and in hand £m	1998 Short-term deposits £m	1998 Total £m	1997 Cash at bank and in hand £m	1997 Short-term deposits £m	1997 Total £m
Sterling	**23.3**	**9.4**	**32.7**	10.7	48.8	59.5
US dollars	**27.8**	–	**27.8**	4.2	6.5	10.7
EU currencies (other than Sterling)	**42.2**	–	**42.2**	20.5	–	20.5
Other currencies	**12.2**	–	**12.2**	11.2	–	11.2
At 31 December	**105.5**	**9.4**	**114.9**	46.6	55.3	101.9
Floating rate	**74.9**	–	**74.9**	33.1	–	33.1
Fixed rate	**30.6**	**9.4**	**40.0**	13.5	55.3	68.8
At 31 December	**105.5**	**9.4**	**114.9**	46.6	55.3	101.9

The fixed rate cash and short-term deposits in Sterling and US dollars are placed with banks on a three-month rolling basis and earn interest at 7% and 5% per annum respectively. Floating rate cash earns interest based on relevant national LIBID equivalents or government bond rates.

FRS 13 p38

Maturity of financial liabilities

The maturity profile of the carrying amount of the group's financial liabilities, other than short-term creditors such as trade creditors and accruals, at 31 December was as follows:

FRS 4 p33
SSAP 21 p51,52

	Debt £m	Finance leases £m	Other financial liabilities £m	1998 Total £m	Debt £m	Other financial liabilities £m	1997 Total £m
Within 1 year, or on demand	**88.9**	**4.6**	**51.7**	**145.2**	41.7	4.1	45.8
Between 1 and 2 years	**0.5**	**4.5**	**16.8**	**21.8**	0.9	1.0	1.9
Between 2 and 5 years	**288.3**	**7.9**	**13.8**	**310.0**	–	1.0	1.0
Over 5 years	**4.1**	**–**	**29.4**	**33.5**	3.0	3.8	6.8
	381.8	**17.0**	**111.7**	**510.5**	45.6	9.9	55.5
Finance charges allocated to future periods	**–**	**(3.9)**	**–**	**(3.9)**	–	–	–
Unamortised issue costs	**(4.2)**	**–**	**–**	**(4.2)**	–	–	–
	377.6	**13.1**	**111.7**	**502.4**	45.6	9.9	55.5

FRS 13 p8
FRS 13 p25

Debt due after five years includes £2.0m (1997: £2.0m) in respect of the company's preference shares. Other financial liabilities includes the provisions for vacant leasehold properties £68.4m (1997: £6.3m).

FRS 4 p33,36

The company's £224.7m (gross of unamortised issue costs) bank loan is repayable within twelve months of the balance sheet date, but as the amount is drawn under a five year committed multi-option facility it is classified in the table above as repayable between two and five years on the basis of the expiry date of the facility in May 2002.

FRS 13 p40

Borrowing facilities

The Group has the following undrawn committed borrowing facilities available at 31 December in respect of which all conditions precedent had been met at that date:

	Floating rate £m	Fixed rate £m	1998 Total £m	1997 Total £m
Expiring within 1 year	**110.5**	**–**	**110.5**	50.0
Expiring between 1 and 2 years	**199.1**	**323.5**	**522.6**	100.0
Expiring in more than 2 years	**100.0**	**–**	**100.0**	–
	409.6	**323.5**	**733.1**	150.0

The facilities expiring within one year are annual facilities subject to review at various dates during 1999. The other facilities have been arranged to help finance the proposed expansion of the group's activities into continental Europe. All these facilities incur commitment fees at market rates.

FRS 13 p44

Fair values of financial assets and financial liabilities

The following table provides a comparison by category of the carrying amounts and the fair values of the group's financial assets and financial liabilities at 31 December 1998 and 1997. Fair value is the amount at which a financial instrument could be exchanged in an arm's length transaction between informed and willing parties, other than a forced or liquidation sale and

FRS 13 p51

excludes accrued interest. Where available, market values have been used to determine fair values. Where market values are not available, fair values have been calculated by discounting expected cash flows at prevailing interest and exchange rates. Set out below the table is a summary of the methods and assumptions used for each category of financial instrument.

GAAP UK Plc

	1998 Book value £m	**1998 Fair value £m**	1997 Book value £m	1997 Fair value £m
Primary financial instruments held or issued to finance the group's operations:				
Short-term borrowings	**(100.7)**	**(100.7)**	(41.7)	(41.7)
Long-term borrowings	**(296.5)**	**(304.1)**	(0.9)	(1.0)
Preference shares	**(2.0)**	**(1.9)**	(2.0)	(2.2)
Other financial liabilities	**(111.7)**	**(105.2)**	(9.9)	(9.5)
Short-term deposits	**9.4**	**9.4**	55.3	55.3
Cash at bank and in hand	**105.5**	**105.5**	46.6	46.6
Derivative financial instruments held to manage the interest rate and currency profile:				
Interest rate swaps	**–**	**(3.0)**	–	–
Currency swaps	**8.5**	**8.5**	–	–
Forward foreign currency contracts	**2.3**	**2.3**	2.5	2.5
Derivative financial instruments held or issued to hedge the currency exposure on expected future sales:				
Forward foreign currency contracts	**–**	**4.1**	–	3.2

Under the group's accounting policy, foreign currency assets and liabilities that are hedged using forward foreign currency contracts or currency swaps are translated at the forward rate inherent in the contracts. Consequently, the book value of the relevant asset or liability effectively includes the fair value of the hedging instrument. For the purpose of the above table, the book value of the relevant asset or liability is shown gross of the effect of the hedging instrument.

FRS 3 p51 **Summary of methods and assumptions**

Interest rate swap, currency swaps and forward foreign currency contracts	Fair value is based on market price of comparable instruments at the balance sheet date.
Short-term deposits and borrowings	The fair value of short-term deposits, loans and overdrafts approximates to the carrying amount because of the short maturity of these instruments.
Long-term borrowings	The fair value of the group's US $ bonds has been estimated using quoted market prices. In the case of bank loans and other loans, the fair value approximates to the carrying value reported in the balance sheet as the majority are floating rate where payments are reset to market rates at intervals of less than one year.
Preference shares	The company's preference shares are listed on the London Stock Exchange and their fair value is based on their quoted market price.

FRS 13 p66,67

Market price risk

Note: Entities are encouraged, but not required to provide:

(a) Additional numerical disclosures that show the magnitude of market price risk arising over the period for all financial instruments, cash-settled commodity contracts and, if significant, all other items carrying market price risk.

(b) Additional narrative about the group's approach to market price risk where necessary to set the numerical information in context and to assist in its interpretation.

Currency exposures

FRS 13 p20

As explained in paragraph [x] on page [y] of the operating and financial review, to mitigate the effect of the currency exposures arising from its net investments overseas the group either borrows in the local currencies of its main operating units or swaps other borrowings, using currency swaps, into such local currencies. Gains and losses arising on net investments overseas and the financial instruments used to hedge the currency exposures are recognised in the statement of total recognised gains and losses.

FRS 13 p34

The tables below show the extent to which group companies have monetary assets and liabilities in currencies other than their local currency. Foreign exchange differences on retranslation of these assets and liabilities are taken to the profit and loss account of the group companies and the group.

	Net foreign currency monetary assets/(liabilities)				
1998	**Sterling £m**	**US dollars £m**	**EU currencies £m**	**Other currencies £m**	**Total £m**
Functional currency of group operation:					
Sterling	–	(11.0)	11.6	–	0.6
US dollars	4.0	–	11.3	–	15.3
EU currencies (excluding Sterling)	(11.3)	–	–	9.6	(1.7)
Other currencies	–	–	(5.4)	–	(5.4)
Total	**(7.3)**	**(11.0)**	**17.5**	**9.6**	**8.8**

1997					
Functional currency of group operation:					
Sterling	–	2.6	10.5	–	13.1
US dollars	2.0	–	(13.4)	–	(11.4)
EU currencies (excluding Sterling)	–	–	–	4.6	4.6
Other currencies	–	–	–	(2.5)	(2.5)
Total	2.0	2.6	(2.9)	2.1	3.8

GAAP UK Plc

Hedges

FRS 13 p20 As explained in the operating and financial review in paragraph [z] on page [a], the group's policy is to hedge the following exposures:

- Interest rate risk – using interest and currency swaps.
- Currency risk – using currency swaps for net investments overseas and forward foreign currency contracts for foreign currency debtors. Forward foreign currency contracts are also used for currency exposures on next year's expected sales.

The table below shows the extent to which the group has off-balance sheet (unrecognised) and on-balance sheet (deferred) gains and losses in respect of financial instruments used as hedges at the beginning and end of the year. It also shows the amount of such gains and losses which have been included in the profit and loss account for the year and those gains and losses which are expected to be included in next year's or later profit and loss accounts.

All the gains and losses on the hedging instruments are expected to be matched by losses and gains on the hedged transactions or positions.

Under the group's accounting policy, foreign currency assets which are hedged using forward foreign currency contracts and borrowings swapped into other currencies are translated at the forward rate inherent in the contracts. Consequently, the carrying value of the relevant asset or borrowing effectively includes the gain or loss on the hedging instrument. Such gains and losses are treated as deferred for the purpose of the table below:

		Unrecognised			Deferred		
		Gains £m	Losses £m	Total net gains/ losses £m	Gains £m	Losses £m	Total net gains/ losses £m
	Gains and losses on hedges at 1 January 1998	3.2	–	3.2	2.5	–	2.5
FRS 13 p59(d)	Arising in previous years included in 1998 income	(3.2)	–	(3.2)	(2.5)	–	(2.5)
	Gains and losses not included in 1998 income						
	Arising before 1 January 1998	–	–	–	–	–	–
	Arising in 1998	4.1	(3.0)	1.1	2.3	–	2.3
FRS 13 p49(a),(b)	**Gains and losses on hedges at 31 December 1998**	**4.1**	**(3.0)**	**1.1**	**2.3**	–	**2.3**
	of which:						
FRS 13 p59(c)	Gains and losses expected to be included in 1999 income	4.1	(0.8)	3.3	2.3	–	2.3
	Gains and losses expected to be included in 2000 income or later	–	(2.2)	(2.2)	–	–	–

The £8.5m gain on the French franc and Dutch guilder currency swaps has been recognised in 1998 in the statement of total recognised gains and losses where it offsets the loss on retranslation of the net investments in the French and Dutch subsidiaries.

FRS 13 p57 **Financial instruments held for trading purposes**

The group does not trade in financial instruments.

20 Provisions for liabilities and charges

Reference		Group 1998 £m	Group 1997 £m	Company 1998 £m	Company 1997 £m
4 Sch 46(3)					
	Vacant properties				
4 Sch 46(1)	At 1 January	**6.3**	6.7	–	–
FRS 6 p32	On acquisition (note 28)	**68.1**	–	–	–
	Exchange adjustments	**(2.0)**	0.1	–	–
	Utilised in year:				
	– Existing properties	**(0.5)**	(0.5)	–	–
FRS 6 p32	– Acquired properties	**(3.8)**	–	–	–
FRS 12 p89(e)	Amortisation of discount	**0.3**	–	–	–
	At 31 December	**68.4**	6.3	–	–
	Restructuring provisions				
4 Sch 46(1)	At 1 January	**1.4**	2.3	–	–
FRS 6 p32	On acquisition (note 28)	**3.8**	–	–	–
	Exchange adjustments	**(0.4)**	–	–	–
	Charged to profit and loss account	**0.1**	–	–	–
	Utilised in year:				
	– Existing	**(1.4)**	(0.9)	–	–
FRS 6 p32	– Acquired	**(0.8)**	–	–	–
	At 31 December	**2.7**	1.4	–	–
	Environmental provisions				
4 Sch 46(1)	At 1 January	–	–	–	–
	On acquisition (note 28)	**18.3**	–	–	–
FRS 12 p89(e)	Amortisation of discount	**0.1**	–	–	–
	At 31 December	**18.4**	–	–	–
4 Sch 47	**Provision for deferred tax**				
4 Sch 46(1)	At 1 January	**3.1**	2.2	**0.5**	0.2
	On acquisition	**22.5**	–	–	–
	Exchange adjustments	**(0.3)**	0.1	–	–
SSAP 15 p38	Transfer from/to profit and loss account	**1.0**	1.1	**(0.3)**	0.3
SSAP 15 p 36	Prior year effect relating to tax rate change	**0.6**	–	–	–
	Other movements	**2.7**	(0.3)	**(0.2)**	–
	At 31 December	**29.6**	3.1	–	0.5
	Total provisions at 31 December	**119.1**	10.8	–	0.5

FRS12 p 89 *Note: Although comparative information has been provided, it is not required by FRS 12.*

GAAP UK Plc

Vacant properties

FRS 12 p90 Prior to the acquisition of Newsub plc, the group's vacant leasehold properties comprised the old Food Product's divisional head office in Swindon and a disused warehouse in Cleveland, Ohio. Full provision had been made for the residual lease commitments, together with other outgoings for the remaining period of the leases, which at 31 December 1998 is approximately 12 years. It is not expected that these premises will be sub-let.

With the acquisition of Newsub plc, the group has inherited a substantial number of vacant and partly sub-let leasehold properties arising from the significant downsizing and retrenchment undertaken by Newsub plc in the early part of the decade. The properties are primary located in London and Bradford in the UK and Los Angeles in the US. Provision has been made for the residual lease commitments, together with other outgoings, after taking into account existing sub-tenant arrangements. It is not assumed that the properties will be able to be sub-let beyond the periods in the present sub-lease agreements. This has resulted in increasing the provision already made by Newsub plc to bring its provisioning policy in line with the group's and has been reflected as a fair value adjustment. As indicated in note 28, investigations are still being made as to the extent that there might be other contractual arrangements separate from the sub-lease agreements that enable the sub-lessees to terminate their leases early. Should the investigations prove this to be the case, it may be necessary to increase the amount of the provision. In determining the provision for Newsub plc's properties, the cash flows have been discounted on a pre-tax basis using appropriate government bond rates.

FRS 12 p9(b)
FRS 13 p29

Maturity profile of provision	**1998 £m**	1997 £m
Within 1 year	**8.4**	0.5
Between 1 and 2 years	**16.8**	1.0
Between 2 and 5 years	**13.8**	1.0
Over 5 years	**29.4**	3.8
	68.4	6.3

Restructuring

FRS 12 p90 The restructuring of the Food Products division that commenced in November 1996 was completed in March 1998. The provision raised at the start of that restructuring has been fully utilised.

The new provision in 1998 arises in respect of a reorganisation commenced by Newsub plc in November 1997 of its health care activities. The restructuring of the health care activities involves the loss of 125 jobs at two factories and the closure of the site at Newark, New Jersey. Agreement had been reached in October 1997 with the local union representatives that specified the number of staff involved and quantified the amounts payable to those made redundant and customers and suppliers of the Newark site were informed in early November 1997. The associated impairment charge for the write-down of the property and other fixed assets at the Newark site was recognised in Newsub plc's financial statements for its year ended 31 March 1998, prior to the acquisition. As indicated in note 28, the level of provision at the date of Newsub plc's acquisition was reviewed and considered insufficient to cover the costs envisaged in the plans drawn up by Newsub plc's management. Consequently, an adjustment was made
FRS 12 p90(b) as part of the fair value exercise. The provision is expected to be fully utilised during the first half of 1999.

FRS 12 p90 A group company, UK GAAP Limited, announced on 11 December 1998 a rationalisation of product processes at two of its factories. A provision of £0.1m has been raised in respect of the redundancies that will occur over the next few months.

Environmental

FRS 12 p90 As part of the group's normal acquisition review procedures, Environmental Appraisers, Inc of San Francisco have been commissioned to ascertain the extent of land contamination of Newsub plc's operational sites in the US. The interim report received from the appraisers indicates that four sites require remediation to deal with chemical spills that have occurred over the last decade. A provisional estimate of the cost of the remediation has been made as part of the fair value exercise on the acquisition of Newsub plc (note 28). It is expected that the decontamination work will take three years to complete. In determining the provision, the cash

FRS 12 p90(b) flows have been discounted on a pre-tax basis using appropriate US Treasury bill rates.

	Deferred tax	Group		Company	
		1998	1997	**1998**	1997
		£m	£m	**£m**	£m
SSAP 15 p37	**Provision for deferred tax comprises:**				
	Accelerated capital allowances	**16.3**	1.6	**–**	0.2
	On dividends from overseas subsidiaries	**–**	0.3	**–**	0.3
	Other	**13.3**	1.2	**–**	–
		29.6	3.1	**–**	0.5

SSAP 15 p35,40 The unprovided amounts of deferred taxation for timing differences (excluding revaluation surpluses) are as follows:

	1998 £m	1997 £m	1998 £m	1997 £m
Accelerated capital allowances	**20.2**	1.2	**0.4**	0.4
Other	**13.9**	2.2	**–**	–
	34.1	3.4	**0.4**	0.4

FRS 2 p54 The unprovided amounts exclude any taxation which would arise if the accumulated reserves of subsidiary undertakings were to be remitted (note 24).

SSAP 15 p41 Furthermore, the unprovided amounts exclude tax on capital gains which might arise on the disposal of properties at their balance sheet amounts (including those valued at the date of acquisition of businesses and subsidiary undertakings) as any material liability is unlikely to crystallise due to the law relating to rollover relief. The amount, therefore, has not been quantified.

21 Called up share capital

		Group and Company	
		1998	1997
		£m	£m
	Ordinary shares of 1p each		
4 Sch 38(1)(a)	Authorised – 1,720,000,000 shares	**17.2**	11.7
4 Sch 38(1)(b)	Allotted and fully paid		
4 Sch Note 12	At 1 January – 887,125,690	**8.9**	8.8
4 Sch 39(b)(c)	Allotted under share option schemes (10,008,001 shares)	**0.1**	0.1
4 Sch 39(b)(c)	Allotted on acquisition of Newsub plc (486,586,318 shares)	**4.8**	–
	At 31 December – 1,383,720,009 shares	**13.8**	8.9

GAAP UK Plc

4 Sch 39(c) The value of the shares allotted on the acquisition of Newsub plc was £919.8m and the consideration received for the shares allotted under the share option schemes during 1998 was £2.6m. The shares allotted on the acquisition of Newsub plc did not rank for the interim dividend paid on 27 August 1998. Issue expenses of £1.4m arising on the allotment of the shares on the acquisition of Newsub plc have been charged to the merger reserve.

4 Sch 40(1) Certain senior executives hold options to subscribe for shares in the company at prices ranging from 26.0p to 223.5p under the share option schemes approved by shareholders in October 1992 and September 1997. Options on 10,008,001 shares were exercised in 1998 and 70,300 options lapsed. The number of shares subject to options, the periods in which they were granted and the periods in which they may be exercised are given below:

Year of grant	Exercise price (pence)	Exercise period	1998 Numbers	1997 Numbers
1992	26.00	1995 – 2001	**197,777**	10,205,778
1994	50.00	1997 – 2003	**1,152,500**	1,152,500
1996	136.25	1999 – 2005	**3,182,866**	3,182,866
1997	185.75	2000 – 2006	**7,451,486**	7,451,486
1998	223.50	2001 – 2007	**8,630,316**	–
			20,614,945	21,992,630

	Group and Company	1998 £m	1997 £m
	7% cumulative preference shares of £1 each		
4 Sch 38(1)(a)	Authorised – 3,000,000 shares	**3.0**	3.0
4 Sch 38(1)(b)	Allotted and fully paid		
	At 1 January and 31 December – 2,000,000 shares	**2.0**	2.0

The 7% cumulative preference shares, which do not carry any voting rights, were issued in 1995 at £1.50 per share and are redeemable at £1.50 at the option of the shareholders on 1 June 2004.
FRS 4 p56
4 Sch 38(2) Shareholders are entitled to receive dividends at 7% per annum on the par value of these shares on a cumulative basis; these dividends are payable on 22 December each year. On winding up, the preference shareholders rank above ordinary shareholders and are entitled to receive £1 per share and any dividends accrued but unpaid in respect of their shares. In the event that dividends on the preference share are in arrears for six months or more, holders of the preference become entitled to vote at general meetings of members.

22 Share premium account

	Group and Company	1998 £m
4 Sch 46	At 1 January 1998	**9.3**
	Premium on shares issued during the year under the share option schemes	**2.5**
	At 31 December 1998	**11.8**

23 Revaluation reserve

		Group £m	Company £m
4 Sch 46	At 1 January 1998	2.5	0.8
SSAP 20 p60(b)	Exchange adjustments	(0.2)	–
	Revaluation in year	5.4	1.5
4 Sch 46(2)	Transfer to profit and loss account	(0.2)	–
	At 31 December 1998	**7.5**	**2.3**

24 Profit and loss account

		Group £m	Company £m
4 Sch 46	At 1 January 1998		
FRS 3 p29	As previously reported	283.3	142.1
FRS 10 p71(b)	Elimination of goodwill reserve	(176.1)	–
	As restated	107.2	142.1
	Net exchange adjustments	(13.6)	(4.1)
UITF 19 p9	Tax on exchange adjustments	3.2	0.9
	Retained profit/(loss) for the year	51.8	(51.8)
	Goodwill resurrected on disposal of subsidiary	3.9	–
4 Sch 46(2)(b)	Transfer from revaluation reserve	0.2	–
	At 31 December 1998	**152.7**	**87.1**

Elimination of goodwill reserve

FRS 10 p71(b) / FRS 10 p69(c) — The profit and loss account reserve at 1 January has been restated to eliminate the balance on the goodwill reserve at 31 December 1997 and 1996 in accordance with the provisions of Financial Reporting Standard No 10, 'Goodwill and intangible assets'. This amount comprises all goodwill previously eliminated to reserves as the directors consider it would be impracticable to apply the provisions of FRS 10 retrospectively.

UITF 14 p3 — Had the group continued to apply its previous policy in respect of goodwill, £1,189.1m would have been included in the goodwill reserve, which would have then shown a balance of £1,361.3m. Retained profit for the year would have been £92.9m reflecting the lack of amortisation of goodwill in respect of subsidiaries and associates. The group's balance sheet would have shown net liabilities of £41.2m at 31 December 1998.

4A Sch 14 / FRS 10 p71(a)(ii) — Cumulative goodwill relating to acquisitions made prior to 1998, which has been eliminated against reserves, amounts to £172.2m (1997: £176.1m).

FRS 2 p53 — The reserves of subsidiary undertakings have generally been retained to finance their businesses. The ability to distribute £0.7m (1997: £1.2m) of consolidated retained profits of the group is restricted by exchange controls in certain countries.

SSAP 20 p60(b) — Included in net exchange adjustments are exchange gains of £16.9m (1997: £2.4m) arising on borrowings denominated in, or swapped into, foreign currencies designated as hedges of net investments overseas.

GAAP UK Plc

25 Other reserves

	Group	Merger reserve £m	Other reserves £m	Total £m
4 Sch 46	At 1 January 1998	–	5.8	5.8
	Premium on shares issued to former Newsub plc shareholders	915.0	–	915.0
	Issue expenses	(1.4)	–	(1.4)
SSAP 20 p60(b)	Exchange adjustments	–	(1.9)	(1.9)
	At 31 December 1998	**913.6**	**3.9**	**917.5**

Other reserves represent amounts set aside in compliance with local laws in certain countries where the group operates.

26 Shareholders' funds

		Group 1998 £m	Group 1997 £m	Company 1998 £m	Company 1997 £m
FRS 4 p40	Equity	**1,102.3**	132.7	**114.0**	160.1
	Non-equity	**3.0**	3.0	**3.0**	3.0
	At 31 December	**1,105.3**	135.7	**117.0**	163.1

FRS 4 p100 *Note: This analysis of shareholders' funds should be disclosed on the face of the balance sheet if the non-equity element is material.*

		Group 1998 £m	Group 1997 £m	Company 1998 £m	Company 1997 £m
FRS 4 p55	**Non-equity interests**				
	7% cumulative redeemable preference shares				
	Called up share capital	**2.0**	2.0	**2.0**	2.0
	Premium arising on the issue of these shares	**1.0**	1.0	**1.0**	1.0
	At 31 December	**3.0**	3.0	**3.0**	3.0

27 Cash flow from operating activities

FRS 1 p12 Reconciliation of operating profit to net cash inflow from operating activities:

	Group 1998 £m	Group 1997 £m
Continuing operations		
Operating profit	**141.5**	107.3
Depreciation charge (net of profit/loss on disposals)	**61.5**	15.5
Goodwill amortisation	**40.2**	–
Increase in stocks	**(2.7)**	(3.2)
Decrease/(increase) in debtors	**15.0**	(3.1)
(Decrease)/increase in creditors	**(33.2)**	(0.1)
Net cash inflow from continuing operations	**222.3**	116.4

FRS 1 example 2

Discontinued operations

Operating profit	**2.2**	7.0
Depreciation charge	**5.8**	6.1
Decrease in stock	**1.0**	2.0
(Increase) in debtors	**(3.8)**	(4.9)
Increase in creditors	**2.3**	3.4
Net cash inflow from discontinued operations	**7.5**	13.6
Total net cash inflow from operating activities	**229.8**	130.0

28 Acquisitions and disposals

(a) Acquisition of Newsub plc

4A Sch 13(2) FRS 6 p21

The group purchased three companies during the year for a total consideration of £1.239.0m of which £1,234.3m was in respect of the acquisition on 30 June 1998 of Newsub plc. The total adjustments required to the book values of the assets and liabilities of the companies acquired in order to present the net assets of those companies at fair values in accordance with group accounting principles were £136.2m, of which £135.5m related to Newsub plc, details of which are set out on pages 58 and 59, together with the resultant amount of goodwill arising. All of these purchases have been accounted for as acquisitions.

FRS 6 p35 FRS 1 p45 FRS 6 p34

From the dates of acquisition to 31 December 1998 the acquisitions contributed £741.4m to turnover (Newsub plc £739.8m), £64.9m to profit before interest (Newsub plc £64.4m) and £47.6m to profit after interest (Newsub plc £47.0m). Newsub plc contributed £77.0m to the group's net operating cash flows, paid £17.9m in respect of interest, £8.6m in respect of taxation and utilised £63.4m for capital expenditure.

4A Sch 13(4)

In its last financial year to 31 March 1998, Newsub plc made a profit after tax and minority interests of £56.6m. For the period since that date to the date of acquisition, Newsub plc management accounts show:

FRS 3 p38 FRS 6 p36,83

	£m
Turnover	94.3
Operating profit	4.0
Profit before taxation	2.9
Taxation and minority interests	(1.2)
Profit attributable to shareholders	1.7
Exchange adjustments	(0.3)
Total recognised gains for the period	1.4

GAAP UK Plc

	Newsub plc acquisition	Book value £m	Revaluations £m	Consistency of accounting policy £m	Other £m	Provisional fair value £m
4A Sch 13(5) FRS 6 p25	Intangible fixed assets	7.9	–	(7.9)	–	**–**
	Tangible fixed assets	330.5	(13.3)	(4.8)	–	**312.4**
	Investments in associates	17.5	(1.9)	(1.6)	–	**14.0**
	Stock	20.1	(1.7)	–	–	**18.4**
	Debtors	206.9	6.9	(0.3)	–	**213.5**
	Creditors	(244.2)	–	(3.4)	(30.9)	**(278.5)**
	Provisions					
	– Vacant property	(13.9)	–	(54.2)	–	**(68.1)**
	– Environmental	–	–	–	(18.3)	**(18.3)**
	– Pre-acquisition restructuring	(1.0)	–	–	(2.8)	**(3.8)**
	Taxation	(60.1)	–	–	1.8	**(58.3)**
	Cash	10.3	–	–	–	**10.3**
	Overdrafts	(25.7)	–	–	–	**(25.7)**
	Loans net of deposits	(54.0)	(3.1)	–	–	**(57.1)**
		194.3	(13.1)	(72.2)	(50.2)	**58.8**
	Minority interests	(0.8)	0.4	–	–	**(0.4)**
	Net assets acquired	193.5	(12.7)	(72.2)	(50.2)	**58.4**
	Goodwill					**1,175.9**
	Consideration					**1,234.3**
4A Sch 13(3)	**Consideration satisfied by:**					
FRS 6 p24	Shares issued (net of issue costs of £1.4m)					**918.4**
FRS 1 p45	Cash					**315.9**
						1,234.3

FRS 6 p25
4A Sch 13(5)
FRS 6 p27

The book value of the assets and liabilities have been taken from the management accounts of Newsub plc at 30 June 1998 (the date of acquisition) at actual exchange rates on that date. The fair value adjustments contain some provisional amounts, as indicated below, which will be finalised in the 1999 financial statements when the detailed acquisition investigation has been completed.

Revaluation adjustments in respect of tangible fixed assets comprise the provisional valuations of certain freehold properties and the write-off of obsolete plant and machinery. Professional property valuations of the freehold properties will be finalised in March 1999.

Revaluations of investments and stock reflects the write-down to estimated realisable value. The revaluation adjustment to debtors includes establishing an asset of £9.4m to reflect the pension fund surplus arising from provisional actuarial valuations, offset by various write-downs to reflect estimated realisable value of debtors. The actuarial valuation of the Newsub plc pension funds as at the date of acquisition will be completed in March 1999.

The revaluation of loans relates to an adjustment of £3.1m in order to reflect current market rate of interest on the Newsub plc US$ bond. Other adjustments to creditors of £30.9m relate to liabilities that were not fully reflected in the balance sheet of Newsub plc at the date of acquisition. These include adjustments to increase the creditor amounts for certain insurance and legal claims to reflect their final settlement shortly after 30 June 1998.

The provisional adjustment to taxation reflects a deferred tax asset of £5.9m for expected tax relief on fair value adjustments, which is partially offset by tax liabilities of £4.1m. The taxation liabilities had not been agreed with the appropriate tax authorities for many years and work is being carried out to agree computations, including some for companies which Newsub plc had sold, with indemnities relating to taxation liabilities, prior to the date of acquisition.

The fair value adjustment for alignment of accounting policies reflects the restatement of assets and liabilities in accordance with the group's policies including: the removal of capitalised in-store marketing costs (£7.9m); the write-off of capitalised container refurbishment costs in distribution companies (£4.8m); provision for the group's share of deferred consideration payable by an associated company for the acquisition of a business (£1.6m); establishing a creditor for outstanding holiday pay entitlement of employees and the alignment of general bad debt provisioning policy. A provisional additional amount (£54.2m) has also been added to the provision for vacant property costs relating to future net rental outgoings of the substantial number of vacant and partly sub-let properties leased by Newsub plc. However, work continues to establish the full extent to which there are contractual arrangements separate from sub-lease agreements which enable sub-lessees to terminate their leases.

A provisional adjustment (£18.3m) has been made for the remediation of Newsub plc operational sites in the US. The final report from Environment Appraisers, Inc. will not be available until April 1999 and further provision may be required.

The book values of the net assets acquired included provisions for reorganisation and restructuring costs amounting to £1.0m. These provisions were established by Newsub plc in November 1997 and relate to an irrevocable reorganisation commenced by Newsub plc management before the acquisition. However on review at the time of acquisition, the provisions were considered to be insufficient to cover the expected costs and have been increased by £2.8m.

(b) Other acquisitions	**£m**
Book value of net assets acquired (includes £0.3m cash)	**0.2**
Fair value adjustments	**(0.7)**
Goodwill	**5.2**
Consideration satisfied by cash	**4.7**

FRS 6 p21

Potco Limited and Fransub SA were acquired by GAAPsub Ltd on 6 May 1998 and 12 July 1998 respective. Fair value adjustments of £0.7m were made to align accounting policies in respect of fixed assets (£0.2m), stock (£0.2m) and creditors (£0.3m).

	(c) Disposal of Hathaway Limited	**£m**
4A Sch 15	Fixed tangible assets	**1.4**
	Stocks	**2.5**
FRS 2 p47	Debtors	**6.5**
	Creditors	**(4.9)**
FRS 10 p71(c)(ii)	Goodwill previously written off to reserves	**3.9**
		9.4
FRS 10 p54	Profit on disposal	**6.3**
FRS 1 p45	**Satisfied by cash**	**15.7**

FRS 1 p45 Hathaway Limited contributed £7.5m to the net operating cash flows, paid £0.8m in respect of net returns on investments and servicing of finance and £0.9m in respect of taxation

GAAP UK Plc

29 Reconciliation of movement in net debt

		At 1 Jan 1998 £m	Cash flow £m	Acquisition (excluding Cash and over-drafts) £m	Other non-cash changes £m	Exchange move-ments £m	At 31 Dec 1998 £m
FRS 1 p33	Cash in hand and at bank	46.6	64.7	–	–	(5.8)	**105.5**
	Overdrafts	–	(92.0)	–	–	5.0	**(87.0)**
			(27.3)				
	Debt due after 1 year	(0.9)	(228.3)	(65.8)	(1.1)	9.4	**(286.7)**
	Debt due within 1 year	(41.7)	57.1	(17.5)	–	0.2	**(1.9)**
	Finance leases due after 1 year	–	–	(17.8)	8.0	–	**(9.8)**
	Finance leases due within 1 year	–	10.8	(6.1)	(8.0)	–	**(3.3)**
			(160.4)				
	Liquid resources	55.3	(91.7)	50.1	–	(4.3)	**9.4**
		59.3	**(279.4)**	**(57.1)**	**(1.1)**	**4.5**	**(273.8)**

FRS 1 p26 Liquid resources comprise short-term deposits with banks which mature within 12 months of the date of inception.

Non-cash charges comprise amortisation of issue costs relating to debt issues and transfers between categories of finance leases.

Movement in borrowings	**£m**	**£m**
Debt due within 1 year:		
Repayment of part of bank loan		(57.1)
Debt due after 1 year:		
New secured bank loan	321.2	
Repayment of part of bank loan	(87.6)	233.6
Increase in borrowings		176.5
Issue costs of new bank loan		(5.3)
		171.2
Capital element of finance lease payment		(10.8)
Cash inflow		**160.4**

30 Cash flow relating to exceptional items

FRS 1 p37 Operating cash flows include under continuing operations an outflow of £8.5m which relates to the reorganisation costs of £9.1m incurred in integrating Newsub plc. The balance of £0.6m was paid in January 1999. In addition, operating cash flows from continuing operations includes an outflow of £3.5m in respect of the product remediation costs.

31 Major non-cash transactions

FRS 1 p46 Part of the consideration for the purchase of Newsub plc comprised shares. Further details of the acquisition are set out in note 28.

32 Employees and directors

		1998 £m	1997 £m
4 Sch 56(4)	**Staff costs for the group during the year**		
	Wages and salaries	**544.3**	203.7
	Social security costs	**62.2**	22.3
	Other pension costs (note 33)	**10.9**	5.5
		617.4	231.5

		1998	1997
4 Sch 56(1),(2) 4 Sch 56(3)	**Average monthly number of people (including executive directors) employed**		
	By business group		
	Food products	**18,630**	7,602
	Personnel services	**5,789**	138
	Retail services	**5,241**	4,758
	Distribution services	**13,735**	915
	Property services	**7,107**	3,565
	Health care	**9,368**	3,499
		59,870	20,477

		1998 £000	1997 £000
	Directors		
6 Sch 1(1)(a)	Aggregate emoluments	**703**	511
6 Sch 1(1)(b)	Aggregate gains made on the exercise of share options	**231**	157
6 Sch 1(1)(c)	Aggregate amounts receivable under long-term incentive schemes	**364**	239
6 Sch 1(1)(d)	Company contributions to money purchase pension schemes	**72**	–
6 Sch 7(1)	Additional pension paid to past director	**11**	–
6 Sch 8(1)	Compensation to past directors for loss of office	**103**	87
6 Sch 9(1)	Sums paid to third parties for directors' services	**54**	63
		1,538	1,057

6 Sch 1(1)(e) Two directors (1997: nil) have retirement benefits accruing under money purchase pension schemes. In addition, retirement benefits are accruing to five (1997: five) directors under the company's defined benefit pension scheme

6 Sch 1(6) *Note: The disclosures in respect of directors' emoluments and those of the highest paid director (below) do not take advantage of the permission in paragraph 1(6) of Schedule 6 to the Companies Act 1985 to omit any of the aggregate information that is capable of being ascertained from other information, such as that in the Remuneration report (pages 10 and 11). This permission does not apply to gains made by directors on exercise of share options.*

GAAP UK Plc

	Highest paid director	1998 £000	1997 £000
6 Sch 2(1)(a)	Aggregate emoluments, gains on share options and benefits under long-term incentive schemes	**646**	439
6 Sch 2(1)(b)	Company contributions to money purchase pension scheme	**54**	–
6 Sch 2(2)	Defined benefit pension scheme:		
	Accrued pension at end of year	**384**	295

The detailed numerical analysis of directors' remuneration are included in the report of the Remuneration Committee on pages 10 to 14 and form part of these financial statements.

6 Sch 2(2)(b) *Note: If the highest paid director is entitled to a lump sum payment on attaining normal pension age, the amount accrued at the balance sheet date should be disclosed.*

33 Pension commitments

	1998 £m	1997 £m
Regular cost	**17.2**	8.3
Variations from regular cost*	**(8.6)**	(4.2)
Notional interest	**(0.2)**	(0.2)
Pension cost in respect of the two principal UK plans	**8.4**	3.9
Other plans	**2.5**	1.6
Total	**10.9**	5.5

* Variations from regular cost arise from the surplus in the two principal UK plans being spread on a straight line basis over the average expected remaining service life of current employees.

SSAP 24 p87,88
4 Sch 50(4)

The group has established a number of pension schemes around the world covering many of its employees. The principal funds are those in the United Kingdom, the GAAP UK plc Staff Pension Plan and the Newsub plc Pension Plan. These are funded schemes of the defined benefit type with assets held in separate trustee administered funds. Outside of the United Kingdom, the schemes are predominantly of the money purchase type.

The most recent actuarial valuation of the GAAP UK plc Staff Pension Plan was at 1 April 1997 and the actuarial valuation (prior to the one now in progress) of the Newsub plc Pension Plan was at 1 April 1998. The valuations of both schemes used the projected unit method and were carried out by Ham & Timberlane, professionally qualified actuaries. The principal assumptions made by the actuaries were that investment returns would be 8.5% per annum, pensionable salaries would increase at 6.5% per annum and that pensions would increase at the rate of 4.5% per annum or at the rate provided in the Scheme Rules. The assumed rate of dividend growth was 4.5% per annum.

At the relevant dates of the most recent actuarial assessments, the market values of the principal UK pension schemes' assets totalled £235.5m and the actuarial value of those assets represented 110% of the benefits accrued to members after allowing for expected future increases in earnings. The increase in the annual cost was principally due to the acquisition of Newsub plc. At 31 December 1998, the pension prepayment held on the group's balance sheet is £10.8m (1997: £2.4m).

UITF 6 The group has no significant exposure to any other post-retirement benefits obligations.

34 Operating lease commitments

At 31 December 1998 the group has lease agreements in respect of properties, vehicles, plant and equipment, for which the payments extend over a number of years.

	Property £m	Vehicles, plant and equipment £m	1998 Total £m	1997 Total £m
SSAP 21 p56 **Annual commitments under non-cancellable operating leases expiring:**				
Within one year	**1.1**	**0.6**	**1.7**	0.6
Within two to five years	**6.1**	**3.5**	**9.6**	3.5
After five years	**6.9**	**0.5**	**7.4**	1.8
	14.1	**4.6**	**18.7**	5.9

35 Contingent liabilities

FRS 12 p91
4 Sch 59A
FRS 9 p58

The company has guaranteed bank and other borrowings of subsidiary undertakings and, jointly with its co-investors, of joint ventures amounting to £2.7m (1997: £0.4m) and £3.7m (1997: £0.7m) respectively.

4 Sch 50(2)
FRS 12 p91

Group companies are defendants in various legal actions. In the opinion of the directors, after taking appropriate legal advice, the outcome of such actions is unlikely to give rise to a material loss.

36 Capital and other financial commitments

FRS 9 p53

	Joint ventures		Group		Company	
	1998 £m	1997 £m	**1998 £m**	1997 £m	**1998 £m**	1997 £m
4 Sch 50(3) **Contracts placed for future capital expenditure not provided in the financial statements**	**2.1**	0.7	**12.9**	2.4	**0.1**	0.1
4 Sch 50(5) **Contracts placed for future expenditure not provided in the accounts in respect of**						
UITF 20 p10 Year 2000 modifications	**2.0**	0.2	**12.0**	9.0	**–**	–
UITF 21 p18 Introduction of the euro	**2.5**	–	**3.0**	–	**–**	–
SSAP 21 p54 **Commitments under finance leases entered into, but not yet provided for**	**1.0**	–	**6.7**	–	**–**	–

37 Other related party transactions

FRS 8 p6,19
FRS 9 p55
LR 12.43(q)

During the year the group purchased food products from two joint ventures, Lawrence AG and Michel Stuart AG to the value of £19.5m (1997: £16.7m). At 31 December 1998 £2.4m (1997: £1.8m) was payable in respect of these purchases. During the year the group sold health care products totalling £11.2m (1997: £13.4m) to Italia Health SpA, a joint venture. At 31 December 1998 the outstanding balances receivable from Italia Health SpA were £1.3m (1997: £1.5m).

GAAP UK Plc

s 346(5)
6 Sch PartII
FRS 8 p6

Mrs S James, wife of Mr F James, a main board director and Managing Director of the Healthcare Division, owns the entire share capital of CPS Inter Ltd. The nature of the business of the Healthcare Division necessitates the exporting of products to Saudi Arabia. CPS Inter Ltd acts as an export agency on behalf of a group subsidiary company. GAAPhealth Ltd. Throughout the year, CPS Inter Ltd has traded under the same terms as those available to other customers in the ordinary course of business. The value of export work performed during the year ended 31 December 1998 for GAAPhealth Ltd amounted to £9.7m (1997: £8.4m). The amount owed to CPS Inter Ltd at the year end amounted to £0.9m (1997: £0.8m).

38 Post balance sheet events

SSAP 17 p23-25
4 Sch 12(b)

On 15 February 1999, the company completed the purchase of Millennium Resources, Inc. for a total consideration of £75.1m. The company operates in North America providing health care services. At the date of acquisition it had estimated net assets of US$ 40m (£25m).

39 Principal subsidiaries, joint ventures and associates

LR 12.43(f)

Subsidiary undertakings

5 Sch 1,15

Particulars of subsidiary undertaking

(a) Name.
(b) Country of incorporation, if incorporated outside Great Britain.
(c) If unincorporated, address of principal place of business.
5 Sch 2,16
(d) Description and proportion of the nominal value of the shares of each class distinguishing between shares held by the parent undertaking and those held by the group.
(e) State whether or not included in the consolidation and explain if not.
5 Sch 15(4)
5 Sch 15(5)
(f) The specific definition of subsidiary undertaking which makes the undertaking a subsidiary – this need not be given if the reason is that the parent holds a majority of the voting rights and the proportion of shares and voting rights held are the same.
FRS 2 p34
(g) Where a subsidiary undertaking is consolidated on the basis of a participating interest with actual dominant influence, the basis of dominant influence should be disclosed.
(h) Proportion of voting rights held by group.
(i) Indication of nature of business.

LR 12.43(g)

Joint ventures and associates

For joint ventures and associates included in the group accounts, give:

5 Sch 22
FRS 9 p52

(a) Name.
(b) Country of incorporation, if incorporated outside Great Britain.
(c) If unincorporated, address of principal place of business.
FRS 9 p52(a)
(d) The identity and proportion of each class of shares held by the parent company and by the group, indicating any special rights or constraints attaching to them.
FRS 9 p52(c)
(e) Indication of nature of business.
FRS 9 p52(b)
(f) The accounting period or date of the financial statements used if they differ from the group's.

FRS 9 p56

Note; An explanation must be given to each case where the following presumptions are rebutted:

(a) An investor holding 20% or more of the voting rights.

(b) An investor holding 20% or more of the shares of another entity has a participating interest.

The financial statements of undertakings marked * have been audited by PricewaterhouseCoopers. Financial statements of undertakings audited by other firms contributed 21.2% of the 1998 group profit before tax.

Appendix 3

EC 4th Company Law Directive

Fourth Council Directive*

of 25 July 1978

based on Article 54(3)(g) of the Treaty on the annual accounts of certain types of companies

(78/660/EEC)

The Council of the European Communities,

Having regard to the Treaty establishing the European Economic Community, and in particular Article 54(3)(g) thereof,

Having regard to the proposal from the Commission,

Having regard to the opinion of the European Parliament,[1]

Having regard to the opinion of the Economic and Social Committee,[2]

Whereas the coordination of national provisions concerning the presentation and content of annual accounts and annual reports, the valuation methods used therein and their publication in respect of certain companies with limited liability is of special importance for the protection of members and third parties;

Whereas simultaneous coordination is necessary in these fields for these forms of company because, on the one hand, these companies' activities frequently extend beyond the frontiers of their national territories and, on the other, they offer no safeguards to third parties beyond the amounts of their net assets; whereas, moreover, the necessity for and the urgency of such coordination have been recognized and confirmed by Article 2(1)(f) of Directive 68/151/EEC;[3]

---

* OJ No. L 222, 14.8.1978, p. 11.

1 OJ No. C 129, 11.12.1972, p. 38.

2 OJ No. C 39, 7.6.1973, p. 31.

3 OJ No. L 65, 14.3.1968, p. 8.

Whereas it is necessary, moreover, to establish in the Community minimum equivalent legal requirements as regards the extent of the financial information that should be made available to the public by companies that are in competition with one another;

Whereas annual accounts must give a true and fair view of a company's assets and liabilities, financial position and profit or loss; whereas to this end a mandatory layout must be prescribed for the balance sheet and the profit and loss account and whereas the minimum content of the notes on the accounts and the annual report must be laid down; whereas, however, derogations may be granted for certain companies of minor economic or social importance;

Whereas the different methods for the valuation of assets and liabilities must be coordinated to the extent necessary to ensure that annual accounts disclose comparable and equivalent information;

Whereas the annual accounts of all companies to which this Directive applies must be published in accordance with Directive 68/151/EEC; whereas, however, certain derogations may likewise be granted in this area for small and medium-sized companies;

Whereas annual accounts must be audited by authorized persons whose minimum qualifications will be the subject of subsequent coordination; whereas only small companies may be relieved of this audit obligation;

Whereas, when a company belongs to a group, it is desirable that group accounts giving a true and fair view of the activities of the group as a whole be published; whereas, however, pending the entry into force of a Council Directive on consolidated accounts, derogations from certain provisions of this Directive are necessary;

Whereas, in order to meet the difficulties arising from the present position regarding legislation in certain Member States, the period allowed for the implementation of certain provisions of this Directive must be longer than the period generally laid down in such cases,

Has adopted this Directive:

Article 1

1. The coordination measures prescribed by this Directive shall apply to the laws, regulations and administrative provisions of the Member States relating to the following types of companies:

– in Germany:
die Aktiengesellschaft, die Kommanditgesellschaft auf Aktien, die Gesellschaft mit beschränkter Haftung;

– in Belgium:
la société anonyme / de naamloze vennootschap, la société en commandite par actions / de commanditaire vennootschap op aandelen, la société de personnes à responsabilité limitée / de personenvennootschap met beperkte aansprakelijkheid:

– in Denmark:
aktieselskaber, kommanditaktieselskaber, anpartsselskaber;

– in France:
la société anonyme, la société en commandite par actions, la société à responsabilité limitée;

– in Ireland:
public companies limited by shares or by guarantee, private companies limited by shares or by guarantee;

– in Italy:
la società per azioni, la società in accomandita per azioni, la società a responsabilità limitata;

– in Luxembourg:
la société anonyme, la société en commandite par actions, la société à responsabilité limitée;

– in the Netherlands:
de naamloze vennootschap, de besloten vennootschap met beperkte aansprakelijkheid;

– in the United Kingdom:
public companies limited by shares or by guarantee, private companies limited by shares or by guarantee.

2. Pending subsequent coordination, the Member States need not apply the provisions of this Directive to banks and other financial institutions or to insurance companies.

Section 1

General provisions

Article 2

1. The annual accounts shall comprise the balance sheet, the profit and loss account and the notes on the accounts. These documents shall constitute a composite whole.

2. They shall be drawn up clearly and in accordance with the provisions of this Directive.

3. The annual accounts shall give a true and fair view of the company's assets, liabilities, financial position and profit or loss.

4. Where the application of the provisions of this Directive would not be sufficient to give a true and fair view within the meaning of paragraph 3, additional information must be given.

5. Where in exceptional cases the application of a provision of this Directive is incompatible with the obligation laid down in paragraph 3, that provision must be departed from in order to give a true and fair view within the meaning of paragraph 3. Any such departure must be disclosed in the notes on the accounts together with an explanation of the reasons for it and a statement of its effect on the assets, liabilities, financial position and profit or loss. The Member States may define the exceptional cases in question and lay down the relevant special rules.

6. The Member States may authorize or require the disclosure in the annual accounts of other information as well as that which must be disclosed in accordance with this Directive.

Section 2

General provisions concerning the balance sheet and the profit and loss account

Article 3

The layout of the balance sheet and of the profit and loss account, particularly as regards the form adopted for their presentation, may not be changed from one financial year to the next. Departures from this principle shall be permitted in exceptional cases. Any such departure must be disclosed in the notes on the accounts together with an explanation of the reasons therefor.

Article 4

1. In the balance sheet and in the profit and loss account the items prescribed in Articles 9,10 and 23 to 26 must be shown separately in the order indicated. A more detailed subdivision of the items shall be authorized provided that the layouts are complied with. New items may be added provided that their contents are not covered by any of the items prescribed by the layouts. Such subdivision or new items may be required by the Member States.

2. The layout, nomenclature and terminology of items in the balance sheet and profit and loss account that are preceded by Arabic numerals must be adapted where the special nature of an undertaking so requires. Such adaptations may be required by the Member States of undertakings forming part of a particular economic sector.

3. The balance sheet and profit and loss account items that are preceded by Arabic numerals may be combined where:

(a) they are immaterial in amount for the purpose of Article 2(3); or

(b) such combination makes for greater clarity, provided that the items so combined are dealt with separately in the notes on the accounts. Such combination may be required by the Member States.

4. In respect of each balance sheet and profit and loss account item the figure relating to the corresponding item for the preceding financial year must be shown. The Member States may provide that, where these figures are not comparable, the figure for the preceding year must be adjusted. In any case, non-comparability and any adjustment of the figures must be disclosed in the notes on the accounts, with relevant comments.

5. Save where there is a corresponding item for the preceding financial year within the meaning of paragraph 4, a balance sheet or profit and loss account item for which there is no amount shall not be shown.

Article 5

1. By way of derogation from Article 4(1) and (2), the Member States may prescribe special layouts for the annual accounts of investment companies and of financial holding companies provided that these layouts give a view of these companies equivalent to that provided for in Article 2(3).

2. For the purposes of this Directive, 'investment companies' shall mean only:

(a) those companies the sole object of which is to invest their funds in various securities, real property and other assets with the sole aim of spreading investment risks and giving their shareholders the benefit of the results of the management of their assets;

(b) those companies associated with investment companies with fixed capital if the sole object of the companies so associated is to acquire fully paid shares issued by those investment companies without prejudice to the provisions of Article 20(1)(h) of Directive 77/91/EEC.[1]

3. For the purposes of this Directive, 'financial holding companies' shall mean only those companies the sole subject of which is to acquire holdings in other undertakings, and to manage such holdings and turn them to profit, without involving themselves directly or indirectly in the management of those undertakings, the aforegoing without prejudice to their rights as shareholders. The limitations imposed on the activities of these companies must be such that compliance with them can be supervised by an administrative or judicial authority.

Article 6

The Member States may authorize or require adaptation of the layout of the balance sheet and profit and loss account in order to include the appropriation of profit or the treatment of loss.

Article 7

Any set-off between asset and liability items, or between income and expenditure items, shall be prohibited.

Section 3

Layout of the balance sheet

Article 8

For the presentation of the balance sheet, the Member States shall prescribe one or both of the layouts prescribed by Articles 9 and 10. If a Member State prescribes both, it may allow companies to choose between them.

[1] OJ No. L 26, 31.1.1977, p.1.

Article 9

Assets

A. Subscribed capital unpaid

– of which there has been called
(unless national law provides that called-up capital be shown under 'Liabilities'. In that case, the part of the capital called but not yet paid must appear as an asset either under A or under D (II)(5)).

B. Formation expenses

– as defined by national law, and in so far as national law permits their being shown as an asset. National law may also provide for formation expenses to be shown as the first item under 'Intangible assets'.

C. Fixed assets

I. Intangible assets

1. Costs of research and development, in so far as national law permits their being shown as assets.
2. Concessions, patents, licences, trade marks and similar rights and assets, if they were:
   (a) acquired for valuable consideration and need not be shown under C (I) (3); or
   (b) created by the undertaking itself, in so far as national law permits their being shown as assets.
3. Goodwill, to the extent that it was acquired for valuable consideration.
4. Payments on account.

II. Tangible assets

1. Land and buildings.
2. Plant and machinery.
3. Other fixtures and fittings, tools and equipment.
4. Payments on account and tangible assets in course of construction.

III. Financial assets

1. Shares in affiliated undertakings.
2. Loans to affiliated undertakings.
3. Participating interests.
4. Loans to undertakings with which the company is linked by virtue of participating interests.
5. Investments held as fixed assets.

6. Other loans.
7. Own shares (with an indication of their nominal value or, in the absence of a nominal value, their accounting par value) to the extent that national law permits their being shown in the balance sheet.

D. Current assets

I. Stocks

1. Raw materials and consumables.
2. Work in progress.
3. Finished goods and goods for resale.
4. Payments on account.

II. Debtors

(Amounts becoming due and payable after more than one year must be shown separately for each item.)

1. Trade debtors.
2. Amounts owed by affiliated undertakings.
3. Amounts owed by undertakings with which the company is linked by virtue of participating interests.
4. Other debtors.
5. Subscribed capital called but not paid (unless national law provides that called-up capital be shown as an asset under A).
6. Prepayments and accrued income (unless national law provides for such items to be shown as an asset under E).

III. Investments

1. Shares in affiliated undertakings.
2. Own shares (with an indication of their nominal value or, in the absence of a nominal value, their accounting par value) to the extent that national law permits their being shown in the balance sheet.
3. Other investments.

IV. Cash at bank and in hand

E. Prepayments and accrued income

(unless national law provides for such items to be shown as an asset under D(II)(6)).

F. Loss for the financial year

(unless national law provides for it to be shown under A(VI) under 'Liabilities').

Liabilities

A. Capital and reserves

I. Subscribed capital
(unless national law provides for called-up capital to be shown under this item. In that case, the amounts of subscribed capital and paid-up capital must be shown separately.)

II. Share premium account

III. Revaluation reserve

IV. Reserves

1. Legal reserve, in so far as national law requires such a reserve.
2. Reserve for own shares, in so far as national law requires such a reserve, without prejudice to Article 22(1)(b) of Directive 77/91/EEC.
3. Reserves provided for by the articles of association.
4. Other reserves.

V. Profit or loss brought forward

VI. Profit or loss for the financial year
(unless national law requires that this item be shown under F under 'Assets' or under E under 'Liabilities'.)

B. Provisions for liabilities and charges

1. Provisions for pensions and similar obligations.
2. Provisions for taxation.
3. Other provisions.

C. Creditors

(Amounts becoming due and payable within one year and amounts becoming due and payable after more than one year must be shown separately for each item and for the aggregate of these items.)

1. Debenture loans, showing convertible loans separately.
2. Amounts owed to credit institutions.
3. Payments received on account of orders in so far as they are not shown separately as deductions from stocks.
4. Trade creditors.
5. Bills of exchange payable.
6. Amounts owed to affiliated undertakings.

7. Amounts owed to undertakings with which the company is linked by virtue of participating interests.
8. Other creditors including tax and social security.
9. Accruals and deferred income (unless national law provides for such items to be shown under D under 'Liabilities').

D. Accruals and deferred income

(unless national law provides for such items to be shown under C (9) under 'Liabilities'.)

E. Profit for the financial year

(unless national law provides for it to be shown under A(VI) under 'Liabilities'.)

Article 10

A. Subscribed capital unpaid

– of which there has been called

(unless national law provides that called-up capital be shown under L. In that case, the part of the capital called but not yet paid must appear either under A or under D(II)(5).)

B. Formation expenses

– as defined by national law, and in so far as national law permits their being shown as an asset. National law may also provide for formation expenses to be shown as the first item under 'Intangible assets'.

C. Fixed assets

I. Intangible assets

1. Costs of research and development, in so far as national law permits their being shown as assets.
2. Concessions, patents, licences, trade marks and similar rights and assets, if they were:
   (a) acquired for valuable consideration and need not be shown under C (I)(3); or
   (b) created by the undertaking itself, in so far as national law permits their being shown as assets.
3. Goodwill, to the extent that it was acquired for valuable consideration.
4. Payments on account.

II. Tangible assets

1. Land and buildings.
2. Plant and machinery.
3. Other fixtures and fittings, tools and equipment.
4. Payments on account and tangible assets in course of construction.

III. Financial assets

1. Shares in affiliated undertakings.
2. Loans to affiliated undertakings.
3. Participating interests.
4. Loans to undertakings with which the company is linked by virtue of participating interests.
5. Investments held as fixed assets.
6. Other loans.
7. Own shares (with an indication of their nominal value or, in the absence of a nominal value, their accounting par value) to the extent that national law permits their being shown in the balance sheet.

D. Current assets

I. Stocks

1. Raw materials and consumables.
2. Work in progress.
3. Finished goods and goods for resale.
4. Payments on account.

II. Debtors

(Amounts becoming due and payable after more than one year must be shown separately for each item.)

1. Trade debtors.
2. Amounts owed by affiliated undertakings.
3. Amounts owed by undertakings with which the company is linked by virtue of participating interests.
4. Other debtors.
5. Subscribed capital called but not paid (unless national law provides that called-up capital be shown under A).
6. Prepayments and accrued income (unless national law provides that such items be shown under E).

III. Investments

1. Shares in affiliated undertakings.
2. Own shares (with an indication of their nominal value or, in the absence of a nominal value, their accounting par value) to the extent that national law permits their being shown in the balance sheet.
3. Other investments.

IV. Cash at bank and in hand

E. Prepayments and accrued income

(unless national law provides for such items to be shown under D (II)(6).)

F. Creditors: amounts becoming due and payable within one year

1. Debenture loans, showing convertible loans separately.
2. Amounts owed to credit institutions.
3. Payments received on account of orders in so far as they are not shown separately as deductions from stocks.
4. Trade creditors.
5. Bills of exchange payable.
6. Amounts owed to affiliated undertakings.
7. Amounts owed to undertakings with which the company is linked by virtue of participating interests.
8. Other creditors including tax and social security.
9. Accruals and deferred income (unless national law provides for such items to be shown under K).

G. Net current assets / liabilities

(taking into account prepayments and accrued income when shown under E and accruals and deferred income when shown under K.)

H. Total assets less current liabilities

I. Creditors: amounts becoming due and payable after more than one year

1. Debenture loans, showing convertible loans separately.
2. Amounts owed to credit institutions.
3. Payments received on account of orders in so far as they are not shown separately as deductions from stocks.
4. Trade creditors.
5. Bills of exchange payable.
6. Amounts owed to affiliated undertakings.
7. Amounts owed to undertakings with which the company is linked by virtue of participating interests.
8. Other creditors including tax and social security.
9. Accruals and deferred income (unless national law provides for such items to be shown under K).

J. Provisions for liabilities and charges

1. Provisions for pensions and similar obligations.
2. Provisions for taxation.
3. Other provisions.

K. Accruals and deferred income

(unless national law provides for such items to be shown under F (9) or I (9) or both.)

L. Capital and reserves

I. Subscribed capital
(unless national law provides for called-up capital to be shown under this item. In that case, the amounts of subscribed capital and paid-up capital must be shown separately.)

II. Share premium account

III. Revaluation reserve

IV. Reserves
1. Legal reserves, in so far as national law requires such a reserve.
2. Reserve for own shares, in so far as national law requires such a reserve, without prejudice to Article 22 (l)(b) of Directive 77/91/EEC.
3. Reserves provided for by the articles of association.
4. Other reserves.

V. Profit or loss brought forward

VI. Profit or loss for the financial year

Article 11

The Member States may permit companies which on their balance sheet dates do not exceed the limits of two of the three following criteria:
– balance sheet total: 1,000,000 EUA,
– net turnover: 2,000,000 EUA,
– average number of employees during the financial year: 50, to draw up abridged balance sheets showing only those items preceded by letters and roman numerals in Articles 9 and 10, disclosing separately the information required in brackets in D (II) under 'Assets' and C under 'Liabilities' in Article 9 and in D (II) in Article 10, but in total for each.

Article 12

1. Where on its balance sheet date, a company exceeds or ceases to exceed the limits of two of the three criteria indicated in Article 11, that fact shall affect the application of the derogation provided for in that Article only if it occurs in two consecutive financial years.

2. For the purposes of translation into national currencies, the amounts in European units of account specified in Article 11 may be increased by not more than 10 percent.

3. The balance sheet total referred to in Article 11 shall consist of the assets in A to E under 'Assets' in the layout prescribed in Article 9 or those in A to E in the layout prescribed in Article 10.

Article 13

1. Where an asset or liability relates to more than one layout item, its relationship to other items must be disclosed either under the item where it appears or in the notes on the accounts, if such disclosure is essential to the comprehension of the annual accounts.

2. Own shares and shares in affiliated undertakings may be shown only under the items prescribed for that purpose.

Article 14

All commitments by way of guarantee of any kind must, if there is no obligation to show them as liabilities, be clearly set out at the foot of the balance sheet or in the notes on the accounts, and a distinction made between the various types of guarantee which national law recognizes; specific disclosure must be made of any valuable security which has been provided. Commitments of this kind existing in respect of affiliated undertakings must be shown separately.

Section 4

Special provisions relating to certain balance sheet items

Article 15

1. Whether particular assets are to be shown as fixed assets or current assets shall depend upon the purpose for which they are intended.

2. Fixed assets shall comprise those assets which are intended for use on a continuing basis for the purposes of the undertaking's activities.

3. (a) Movements in the various fixed asset items shall be shown in the balance sheet or in the notes on the accounts. To this end there shall be shown separately, starting with the purchase price or production cost, for each fixed asset item, on the one hand, the additions, disposals and transfers during the financial year and, on the other, the cumulative value adjustments at the balance sheet date and the rectifications made during the financial year to the value adjustment of previous financial years. Value adjustments shall be shown either in the balance sheet, as clear deductions from the relevant items, or in the notes on the accounts.

(b) If, when annual accounts are drawn up in accordance with this Directive for the first time, the purchase price or production cost of a fixed asset cannot be determined without undue expense or delay, the residual value at the beginning of the financial year may be treated as the purchase price or production cost. Any application of this provision must be disclosed in the notes on the accounts.

(c) Where Article 33 is applied, the movements in the various fixed asset items referred to in subparagraph (a) of this paragraph shall be shown starting with the purchase price or production cost resulting from revaluation.

4. Paragraph 3 (a) and (b) shall apply to the presentation of 'Formation expenses'.

Article 16

Rights to immovables and other similar rights as defined by national law must be shown under 'Land and buildings'.

Article 17

For the purposes of this Directive, 'participating interest' shall mean rights in the capital of other undertakings, whether or not represented by certificates, which, by creating a durable link with those undertakings, are intended to contribute to the company's activities. The holding of part of the capital of another company shall be presumed to constitute a participating interest where it exceeds a percentage fixed by the Member States which may not exceed 20 percent.

Article 18

Expenditure incurred during the financial year but relating to a subsequent financial year, together with any income which, though relating to the financial year in question, is not due until after its expiry must be shown under 'Prepayments and accrued income'. The Member States may, however, provide that such income shall be included in 'Debtors'. Where such income is material, it must be disclosed in the notes on the accounts.

Article 19

Value adjustments shall comprise all adjustments intended to take account of reductions in the values of individual assets established at the balance sheet date whether that reduction is final or not.

Article 20

1. Provisions for liabilities and charges are intended to cover losses or debts the nature of which is clearly defined and which at the date of the balance sheet are either likely to be incurred, or certain to be incurred but uncertain as to amount or as to the date on which they will arise.

2. The Member States may also authorize the creation of provisions intended to cover charges which have their origin in the financial year under review or in a previous financial year, the nature of which is clearly defined and which at the date of the balance sheet are either likely to be incurred, or certain to be incurred but uncertain as to amount or as to the date on which they will arise.

3. Provisions for liabilities and charges may not be used to adjust the values of assets.

Article 21

Income receivable before the balance sheet date but relating to a subsequent financial year, together with any charges which, though relating to the financial year in question, will be paid only in the course of a subsequent financial year, must be shown under 'Accruals and deferred income'. The Member States may, however, provide that such charges shall be included in 'Creditors'. Where such charges are material, they must be disclosed in the notes on the accounts.

Section 5

Layout of the profit and loss account

Article 22

For the presentation of the profit and loss account, the Member States shall prescribe one or more of the layouts provided for in Articles 23 to 26. If a Member State prescribes more than one layout, it may allow companies to choose from among them.

Article 23

1. Net turnover.
2. Variation in stocks of finished goods and in work in progress.
3. Work performed by the undertaking for its own purposes and capitalized.
4. Other operating income.
5.
1 Raw materials and consumables.
   (a) Other external charges.
6. Staff costs:
   (a) wages and salaries;
   (b) social security costs, with a separate indication of those relating to pensions.
7. (a) Value adjustments in respect of formation expenses and of tangible and intangible fixed assets.
   (b) Value adjustments in respect of current assets, to the extent that they exceed the amount of value adjustments which are normal in the undertaking concerned.
8. Other operating charges.
9. Income from participating interests, with a separate indication of that derived from affiliated undertakings.
10. Income from other investments and loans forming part of the fixed assets, with a separate indication of that derived from affiliated undertakings.
11. Other interests receivable and similar income, with a separate indication of that derived from affiliated undertakings.
12. Value adjustments in respect of financial assets and of investments held as current assets.
13. Interest payable and similar charges, with a separate indication of those concerning affiliated undertakings.
14. Tax on profit or loss on ordinary activities.
15. Profit or loss on ordinary activities after taxation.
16. Extraordinary income.
17. Extraordinary charges.

18. Extraordinary profit or loss.
19. Tax on extraordinary profit or loss.
20. Other taxes not shown under the above items.
21. Profit or loss for the financial year.

Article 24

A. Charges

1. Reduction in stocks of finished goods and in work in progress:
2. (a) raw materials and consumables;
   (b) other external charges.
3. Staff costs:
   (a) wages and salaries;
   (b) social security costs, with a separate indication of those relating to pensions.
4. (a) Value adjustments in respect of formation expenses and of tangible and intangible fixed assets.
   (b) Value adjustments in respect of current assets, to the extent that they exceed the amount of value adjustments which are normal in the undertaking concerned.
5. Other operating charges.
6. Value adjustments in respect of financial assets and of investments held as current assets.
7. Interest payable and similar charges, with a separate indication of those concerning affiliated undertakings.
8. Tax on profit or loss on ordinary activities.
9. Profit or loss on ordinary activities after taxation.
10. Extraordinary charges.
11. Tax on extraordinary profit or loss.
12. Other taxes not shown under the above items.
13. Profit or loss for the financial year.

B. Income

1. Net turnover.
2. Increase in stocks of finished goods and in work in progress.
3. Work performed by the undertaking for its own purposes and capitalized.
4. Other operating income.
5. Income from participating interests, with a separate indication of that derived from affiliated undertakings.
6. Income from other investments and loans forming part of the fixed assets, with a separate indication of that derived from affiliated undertakings.

7. Other interest receivable and similar income, with a separate indication of that derived from affiliated undertakings.
8. Profit or loss on ordinary activities after taxation.
9. Extraordinary income.
10. Profit or loss for the financial year.

Article 25

1. Net turnover.
2. Cost of sales (including value adjustments).
3. Gross profit or loss.
4. Distribution costs (including value adjustments).
5. Administrative expenses (including value adjustments).
6. Other operating income.
7. Income from participating interests, with a separate indication of that derived from affiliated undertakings.
8. Income from other investments and loans forming part of the fixed assets, with a separate indication of that derived from affiliated undertakings.
9. Other interest receivable and similar income, with a separate indication of that derived from affiliated undertakings.
10. Value adjustments in respect of financial assets and of investments held as current assets.
11. Interest payable and similar charges, with a separate indication of those concerning affiliated undertakings.
12. Tax on profit or loss on ordinary activities.
13. Profit or loss on ordinary activities after taxation.
14. Extraordinary income.
15. Extraordinary charges.
16. Extraordinary profit or loss.
17. Tax on extraordinary profit or loss.
18. Other taxes not shown under the above items.
19. Profit or loss for the financial year.

Article 26

A. Charges

1. Cost of sales (including value adjustments).
2. Distribution costs (including value adjustments).
3. Administrative expenses (including value adjustments).
4. Value adjustments in respect of financial assets and of investments held as current assets.
5. Interest payable and similar charges, with a separate indication of those concerning affiliated undertakings.

6. Tax on profit or loss on ordinary activities.
7. Profit of loss on ordinary activities after taxation.
8. Extraordinary charges.
9. Tax on extraordinary profit or loss.
10. Other taxes not shown under the above items.
11. Profit or loss for the financial year.

B. Income

1. Net turnover.
2. Other operating income.
3. Income from participating interests, with a separate indication of that derived from affiliated undertakings.
4. Income from other investments and loans forming part of the fixed assets, with a separate indication of that derived from affiliated undertakings.
5. Other interest receivable and similar income, with a separate indication of that derived from affiliated undertakings.
6. Profit or loss on ordinary activities after taxation.
7. Extraordinary income.
8. Profit or loss for the financial year.

Article 27

The Member States may permit companies which on their balance sheet dates do not exceed the limits of two of the three following criteria:

– balance sheet total: 4 million EUA,
– net turnover: 8 million EUA,
– average number of employees during the financial year: 250 to adopt layouts different from those prescribed in Articles 23 to 26 within the following limits:

(a) in Article 23: 1 to 5 inclusive may be combined under one item called 'Gross profit or loss';
(b) in Article 24: A(1), A(2) and B(1) to B(4) inclusive may be combined under one item called 'Gross profit or loss';
(c) in Article 25: (1), (2), (3) and (6) may be combined under one item called 'Gross profit or loss';
(d) in Article 26: A(1), B(1) and B(2) may be combined under one item called 'Gross profit or loss'.

Article 12 shall apply.

Section 6

Special provisions relating to certain items in the profit and loss account

Article 28

The net turnover shall comprise the amounts derived from the sale of products and the provision of services falling within the company's ordinary activities, after deduction of sales rebates and of value added tax and other taxes directly linked to the turnover.

Article 29

1. Income and charges that arise otherwise than in the course of the company's ordinary activities must be shown under 'Extraordinary income and extraordinary charges'.

2. Unless the income and charges referred to in paragraph 1 are immaterial for the assessment of the results, explanations of their amount and nature must be given in the notes on the accounts. The same shall apply to income and charges relating to another financial year.

Article 30

The Member States may permit taxes on the profit or loss on ordinary activities and taxes on the extraordinary profit or loss to be shown in total as one item in the profit and loss account before 'Other taxes not shown under the above items'. In that case, 'Profit or loss on ordinary activities after taxation' shall be omitted from the layouts prescribed in Articles 23 to 26.

Where this derogation is applied, companies must disclose in the notes on the accounts the extent to which the taxes on the profit or loss affect the profit or loss on ordinary activities and the 'Extraordinary profit or loss'.

Section 7

Valuation rules

Article 31

1. The Member States shall ensure that the items shown in the annual accounts are valued in accordance with the following general principles:

(a) the company must be presumed to be carrying on its business as a going concern;

(b) the methods of valuation must be applied consistently from one financial year to another;

(c) valuation must be made on a prudent basis, and in particular:

 (aa) only profits made at the balance sheet date may be included,

 (bb) account must be taken of all foreseeable liabilities and potential losses arising in the course of the financial year concerned or of a previous one, even if such liabilities or losses become apparent only between the date of the balance sheet and the date on which it is drawn up,

 (cc) account must be taken of all depreciation, whether the result of the financial year is a loss or a profit;

(d) account must be taken of income and charges relating to the financial year, irrespective of the date of receipt or payment of such income or charges;

(e) the components of asset and liability must be valued separately;

(f) the opening balance sheet for each financial year must correspond to the closing balance sheet for the preceding financial year.

2. Departures from these general principles shall be permitted in exceptional cases. Any such departures must be disclosed in the notes on the accounts and the reasons for them given together with an assessment of their effect on the assets, liabilities, financial position and profit or loss.

Article 32

The items shown in the annual accounts shall be valued in accordance with Articles 34 to 42, which are based on the principle of purchase price or production cost.

Article 33

1. The Member States may declare to the Commission that they reserve the power, by way of derogation from Article 32 and pending subsequent coordination, to permit or require in respect of all companies or any classes of companies:

(a) valuation by the replacement value method for tangible fixed assets with limited useful economic lives and for stocks;

(b) valuation by methods other than that provided for in (a) which are designed to take account of inflation for the items shown in annual accounts, including capital and reserves;

(c) revaluation of tangible fixed assets and financial fixed assets.

Where national law provides for valuation methods as indicated in (a), (b) and (c), it must define their content and limits and the rules for their application.

The application of any such method, the balance sheet and profit and loss account items concerned and the method by which the values shown are calculated shall be disclosed in the notes on the accounts.

2. (a) Where paragraph 1 is applied, the amount of the difference between valuation by the method used and valuation in accordance with the general rule laid down in Article 32 must be entered in the revaluation reserve under 'Liabilities'. The treatment of this item for taxation purposes must be explained either in the balance sheet or in the notes on the accounts.

For the purposes of the application of the last subparagraph of paragraph 1, companies shall, whenever the amount of the reserve has been changed in the course of the financial year, publish in the notes on the accounts *inter alia* a table showing:

– the amount of the revaluation reserve at the beginning of the financial year,
– the revaluation differences transferred to the revaluation reserve during the financial year,
– the amounts capitalized or otherwise transferred from the revaluation reserve during the financial year, the nature of any such transfer being disclosed,
– the amount of the revaluation reserve at the end of the financial year.

(b) The revaluation reserve may be capitalized in whole or in part at any time.

(c) The revaluation reserve must be reduced to the extent that the amounts transferred thereto are no longer necessary for the implementation of the valuation method used and the achievement of its purpose.

The Member States may lay down rules governing the application of the revaluation reserve, provided that transfers to the profit and loss account from the revaluation reserve may be made only to the extent that the amounts transferred have been entered as charges in the profit and loss account or reflect increases in value which have been actually realized. These amounts must be disclosed separately in the profit and loss account. No part of the revaluation reserve may be distributed, either directly or indirectly, unless it represents gains actually realized.

(d) Save as provided under (b) and (c) the revaluation reserve may not be reduced.

3. Value adjustments shall be calculated each year on the basis of the value adopted for the financial year in question, save that by way of derogation from Articles 4 and 22, the Member States may permit or require that only the amount of the value adjustments arising as a result of the application of the general rule laid down in Article 32 be shown under the relevant items in the layouts prescribed in Articles 23 to 26 and that the difference arising as a result of the valuation method adopted under this

Article be shown separately in the layouts. Furthermore, Articles 34 to 42 shall apply *mutatis mutandis*.

4. Where paragraph 1 is applied, the following must be disclosed either in the balance sheet or in the notes on the accounts, separately for each balance sheet item as provided for in the layouts prescribed in Article 9 and 10, except for stocks, either:

(a) the amount at the balance sheet date of the valuation made in accordance with the general rule laid down in Article 32 and the amount of the cumulative value adjustments; or

(b) the amount at the balance sheet date of the difference between the valuation made in accordance with this Article and that resulting from the application of Article 32 and, where appropriate, the cumulative amount of the additional value adjustments.

5. Without prejudice to Article 52 the Council shall, on a proposal from the Commission and within seven years of the notification of this Directive, examine and, where necessary, amend this article in the light of economic and monetary trends in the Community.

Article 34

1. (a) Where national law authorizes the inclusion of formation expenses under 'Assets', they must be written off within a maximum period of five years.

(b) In so far as formation expenses have not been completely written off, no distribution of profits shall take place unless the amount of the reserves available for distribution and profits brought forward is at least equal to that of the expenses not written off.

2. The amounts entered under 'Formation expenses' must be explained in the notes on the accounts.

Article 35

1. (a) Fixed assets must be valued at purchase price or production cost, without prejudice to (b) and (c) below.

(b) The purchase price or production cost of fixed assets with limited useful economic lives must be reduced by value adjustments calculated to write off the value of such assets systematically over their useful economic lives.

(c) (aa) Value adjustments may be made in respect of financial fixed assets, so that they are valued at the lower figure to be attributed to them at the balance sheet date.

(bb) Value adjustments must be made in respect of fixed assets, whether their useful economic lives are limited or not, so that they are valued at the lower figure to be attributed to them at the balance sheet date if it is expected that the reduction in their value will be permanent.

(cc) The value adjustments referred to in (aa) and (bb) must be charged to the profit and loss account and disclosed separately in the notes on the accounts if they have not been shown separately in the profit and loss account.

(dd) Valuation at the lower of the values provided for in (aa) and (bb) may not be continued if the reasons for which the value adjustments were made have ceased to apply.

(d) If fixed assets are the subject of exceptional value adjustments for taxation purposes alone, the amount of the adjustments and the reasons for making them shall be indicated in the notes on the accounts.

2. The purchase price shall be calculated by adding to the price paid the expenses incidental thereto.

3. (a) The production cost shall be calculated by adding to the purchasing price of the raw materials and consumables the costs directly attributable to the product in question.

(b) A reasonable proportion of the costs which are only indirectly attributable to the product in question may be added into the production costs to the extent that they relate to the period of production.

4. Interest on capital borrowed to finance the production of fixed assets may be included in the production costs to the extent that it relates to the period of production. In that event, the inclusion of such interest under 'Assets' must be disclosed in the notes on the accounts.

Article 36

By way of derogation from Article 35 (1)(c)(cc), the Member States may allow investment companies within the meaning of Article 5 (2) to set off value adjustments to investments directly against 'Capital and reserves'. The amounts in question must be shown separately under 'Liabilities' in the balance sheet.

Article 37

1. Article 34 shall apply to costs of research and development. In exceptional cases, however, the Member States may permit derogations from Article 34 (1)(a). In that case, they may also provide for derogations from Article 34 (1)(b), Such derogations and the reasons for them must be disclosed in the notes on the accounts.

2. Article 34 (1)(a) shall apply to goodwill. The Member States may, however, permit companies to write goodwill off systematically over a limited period exceeding five years provided that this period does not exceed the useful economic life of the asset and is disclosed in the notes on the accounts together with the supporting reasons therefore.

Article 38

Tangible fixed assets, raw materials and consumables which are constantly being replaced and the overall value of which is of secondary importance to the undertaking may be shown under 'Assets' at a fixed quantity and value, if the quantity, value and composition thereof do not vary materially.

Article 39

1. (a) Current assets must be valued at purchase price or production cost, without prejudice to (b) and (c) below.
   (b) Value adjustments shall be made in respect of current assets with a view to showing them at the lower market value or, in particular circumstances, another lower value to be attributed to them at the balance sheet date.
   (c) The Member States may permit exceptional value adjustments where, on the basis of a reasonable commercial assessment, these are necessary if the valuation of these items is not to be modified in the near future because of fluctuations in value. The amount of these value adjustments must be disclosed separately in the profit and loss account or in the notes on the accounts.
   (d) Valuation at the lower value provided for in (b) and (c) may not be continued if the reasons for which the value adjustments were made have ceased to apply.
   (e) If current assets are the subject of exceptional value adjustments for taxation purposes alone, the amount of the adjustments and the reasons for making them must be disclosed in the notes on the accounts.

2. The definitions of purchase price and of production cost given in Article 35 (2) and (3) shall apply. The Member States may also apply Article 35 (4). Distribution costs may not be included in production costs.

Article 40

1. The Member States may permit the purchase price or production cost of stocks of goods of the same category and all fungible items including investments to be calculated either on the basis of weighted average prices or by the 'first in, first out' (FIFO) method, the 'last in, first out' (LIFO) method, or some similar method.

2. Where the value shown in the balance sheet, following application of the methods of calculation specified in paragraph 1, differs materially, at the balance sheet date, from the value on the basis of the last known market value prior to the balance sheet date, the amount of that difference must be disclosed in total by category in the notes on the accounts.

Article 41

1. Where the amount repayable on account of any debt is greater than the amount received, the difference may be shown as an asset. It must be shown separately in the balance sheet or in the notes on the accounts.

2. The amount of this difference must be written off by a reasonable amount each year and completely written off no later than the time of repayment of the debt.

Article 42

Provisions for liabilities and charges may not exceed in amount the sums which are necessary.
The provisions shown in the balance sheet under 'Other provisions' must be disclosed in the notes on the accounts if they are material.

Section 8

Contents of the notes on the accounts

Article 43

1. In addition to the information required under other provisions of this Directive, the notes on the accounts must set out information in respect of the following matters at least:

(1) the valuation methods applied to the various items in the annual accounts, and the methods employed in calculating the value adjustments. For items included in the annual accounts which are or were originally expressed in foreign currency, the bases of conversion used to express them in local currency must be disclosed;

(2) the name and registered office of each of the undertakings in which the company, either itself or through a person acting in his own name but on the company's behalf, holds at least a percentage of the capital which the Member States cannot fix at more than 20 percent, showing the proportion of the capital held, the amount of capital and reserves, and the profit or loss for the latest financial year of the undertaking concerned for which accounts have been adopted. This information may be omitted where for the purposes of Article 2 (3) it is of

negligible importance only. The information concerning capital and reserves and the profit or loss may also be omitted where the undertaking concerned does not publish its balance sheet and less than 50 percent of its capital is held (directly or indirectly) by the company;

(3) the number and the nominal value or, in the absence of a nominal value, the accounting par value of the shares subscribed during the financial year within the limits of an authorized capital, without prejudice as far as the amount of this capital is concerned to Article 2 (1)(e) of Directive 68/151/EEC or to Article 2(c) of Directive 77/91/EEC;

(4) where there is more than one class of shares, the number and the nominal value of, in the absence of a nominal value, the accounting par value of each class;

(5) the existence of any participation certificates, convertible debentures or similar securities or rights, with an indication of their number and the rights they confer;

(6) amounts owed by the company becoming due and payable after more than five years as well as the company's entire debts covered by valuable security furnished by the company with an indication of the nature and form of the security. This information must be disclosed separately for each creditors item, as provided for in the layouts prescribed in Articles 9 and 10;

(7) the total amount of any financial commitments that are not included in the balance sheet, in so far as this information is of assistance in assessing the financial position. Any commitments concerning pensions and affiliated undertakings must be disclosed separately;

(8) the net turnover within the meaning of Article 28, broken down by categories of activity and into geographical markets in so far as, taking account of the manner in which the sale of products and the provision of services falling within the company's ordinary activities are organized, these categories and markets differ substantially from one another;

(9) the average number of persons employed during the financial year, broken down by categories and, if they are not disclosed separately in the profit and loss account, the staff costs relating to the financial year, broken down as provided for in Article 23 (6);

(10) the extent to which the calculation of the profit or loss for the financial year has been affected by a valuation of the items which, by way of derogation from the principles enunciated in Articles 31 and 34 to 42, was made in the financial year in question or in an earlier financial year with a view to obtaining tax relief. Where the influence of such a valuation on future tax charges is material, details must be disclosed;

(11) the difference between the tax charged for the financial year and for earlier financial years and the amount of tax payable in respect of those years, provided that this difference is material for the purposes of future taxation. This amount may also be disclosed in the balance sheet as a cumulative amount under a separate item with an appropriate heading;

(12) the amount of the emoluments granted in respect of the financial year to the members of the administrative, managerial and supervisory bodies by reason of

their responsibilities, and any commitments arising or entered into in respect of retirement pensions for former members of those bodies, with an indication of the total for each category;

(13) the amount of advances and credits granted to the members of the administrative, managerial and supervisory bodies, with indications of the interest rates, main conditions and any amounts repaid, as well as commitments entered into on their behalf by way of guarantees of any kind, with an indication of the total for each category.

2. Pending subsequent coordination, the Member States need not apply paragraph 1 (2) to financial holding companies within the meaning of Article 5 (3).

Article 44

The Member States may permit the companies referred to in Article 11 to draw up abridged notes on their accounts without the information required in Article 43 (1)(5) to (12). However, the notes must disclose the information specified in Article 43 (1)(6) in total for all the items concerned.
Article 12 shall apply.

Article 45

1. The Member States may allow the disclosures prescribed in Article 43 (1)(2):

(a) to take the form of a statement deposited in accordance with Article 3 (1) and (2) of Directive 68/151/EEC; this must be disclosed in the notes on the accounts

(b) to be omitted when their nature is such that they would be seriously prejudicial to any of the undertakings to which Article 43 (1)(2) relates. The Member States may make such omissions subject to prior administrative or judicial authorization. Any such omission must be disclosed in the notes on the accounts.

2. Paragraph 1 (b) shall also apply to the information prescribed by Article 43 (1)(8).

The Member States may permit the companies referred to in Article 27 to omit the disclosures prescribed by Article 43 (1)(8). Article 12 shall apply.

Section 9

Contents of the annual report

Article 46

1. The annual report must include at least a fair review of the development of the company's business and of its position.

2. The report shall also give an indication of:
(a) any important events that have occurred since the end of the financial year;
(b) the company's likely future development;
(c) activities in the field of research and development;
(d) the information concerning acquisitions of own shares prescribed by Article 22 (2) of Directive 77/91/EEC.

Section 10

Publication

Article 47

1. The annual accounts, duly approved, and the annual report, together with the opinion submitted by the person responsible for auditing the accounts, shall be published as laid down by the laws of each Member State in accordance with Article 3 of Directive 68/151/EEC.

The laws of a Member State may, however, permit the annual report not to be published as stipulated above. In that case, it shall be made available to the public at the company's registered office in the Member State concerned. It must be possible to obtain a copy of all or part of any such report free of charge upon request.

2. By way of derogation from paragraph 1, the Member States may permit the companies referred to in Article 11 to publish:
(a) abridged balance sheets showing only those items preceded by letters and roman numerals in Articles 9 and 10, disclosing separately the information required in brackets in D (II) under 'Assets' and C under 'Liabilities' in Article 9 and in D (II) in Article 10, but in total for all the items concerned; and
(b) abridged notes on their accounts without the explanations required in Article 43 (l) (5) to (12). However, the notes must disclose the information specified in Article 43 (1)(6) in total for all the items concerned.

Article 12 shall apply.

In addition, the Member States may relieve such companies from the obligation to publish their profit and loss accounts and annual reports and the opinions of the persons responsible for auditing the accounts.

3. The Member States may permit the companies mentioned in Article 27 to publish:
(a) abridged balance sheets showing only those items preceded by letters and roman numerals in articles 9 and 10 disclosing separately, either in the balance sheet or in the notes on the accounts:

- C(I)(3), C(II)(l), (2), (3) and (4), C(III)(1), (2), (3), (4) and (7), D(II)(2), (3) and (6) and D(III)(1) and (2) under 'Assets' and C(1), (2), (6), (7) and (9) under 'Liabilities' in Article 9, – C(I)(3), C(II)(1), (2), (3) and (4), C(III)(1), (2), (3), (4) and (7), D(II)(2), (3) and (6), D(III)(l) and (2), F(l), (2), (6), (7) and (9) and (I)(1), (2), (6), (7) and (9) in Article 10,
- the information required in brackets in D(II) under 'Assets' and C under 'Liabilities' in Article 9, in total for all the items concerned and separately for D(II)(2) and (3) under 'Assets' and C(1), (2), (6), (7) and (9) under 'Liabilities',
- the information required in brackets in D(II) in Article 10, in total for all the items concerned, and separately for D(II)(2) and (3);

(b) abridged notes on their accounts without the information required in Article 43 (1)(5), (6), (8), (10) and (11). However, the notes on the accounts must give the information specified in Article 43(1)(6) in total for all the items concerned.

This paragraph shall be without prejudice to paragraph 1 in so far as it relates to the profit and loss account, the annual report and the opinion of the person responsible for auditing the accounts.
Article 12 shall apply.

Article 48

Whenever the annual accounts and the annual report are published in full, they must be reproduced in the form and text on the basis of which the person responsible for auditing the accounts has drawn up his opinion. They must be accompanied by the full text of his report.

If the person responsible for auditing the accounts has made any qualifications or refused to report upon the accounts, that fact must be disclosed and the reasons given.

Article 49

If the annual accounts are not published in full, it must be indicated that the version published is abridged and reference must be made to the register in which the accounts have been filed in accordance with Article 47 (1). Where such filing has not yet been effected, the fact must be disclosed. The report issued by the person responsible for auditing the accounts may not accompany this publication, but it must be disclosed whether the report was issued with or without qualification, or was refused.

Article 50

The following must be published together with the annual accounts, and in like manner:

- the proposed appropriation of the profit or treatment of the loss,

– the appropriation of the profit or treatment of the loss, where these items do not appear in the annual accounts.

Section 11

Auditing

Article 51

1. (a) Companies must have their annual accounts audited by one or more persons authorized by national law to audit accounts.
   (b) The person or persons responsible for auditing the accounts must also verify that the annual report is consistent with the annual accounts for the same financial year.

2. The Member States may relieve the companies referred to in Article 11 from the obligation imposed by paragraph 1.
Article 12 shall apply.

3. Where the exemption provided for in paragraph 2 is granted the Member States shall introduce appropriate sanctions into their laws for cases in which the annual accounts or the annual reports of such companies are not drawn up in accordance with the requirements of this Directive.

Section 12

Final provisions

Article 52

1. A Contact Committee shall be set up under the auspices of the Commission. Its function shall be:
(a) to facilitate, without prejudice to the provisions of Articles 169 and 170 of the Treaty, harmonized application of this Directive through regular meetings dealing in particular with practical problems arising in connection with its application;
(b) to advise the Commission, if necessary, on additions or amendments to this Directive.

2. The Contact Committee shall be composed of representatives of the Member States and representatives of the Commission. The chairman shall be a representative of the Commission. The Commission shall provide the secretariat.

3. The Committee shall be convened by the chairman either on his own initiative or at the request of one of its members.

Article 53

1. For the purposes of this Directive, the European unit of account shall be that defined by Commission Decision No. 3289/75/ECSC of 18 December 1975.[1] The equivalent in national currency shall be calculated initially at the rate obtaining on the date of adoption of this Directive.

2. Every five years the Council, acting on a proposal from the Commission, shall examine and, if need be, revise the amounts expressed in European units of account in this Directive, in the light of economic and monetary trends in the Community.

Article 54

This Directive shall not affect laws in the Member States requiring that the annual accounts of companies not falling within their jurisdiction be filed in a register in which branches of such companies are listed.

Article 55

1. The Member States shall bring into force the laws, regulations and administrative provisions necessary for them to comply with this Directive within two years of its notification. They shall forthwith inform the Commission thereof.

2. The Member States may stipulate that the provisions referred to in paragraph 1 shall not apply until 18 months after the end of the period provided for in that paragraph.

That period of 18 months may, however, be five years:

(a) in the case of unregistered companies in the United Kingdom and Ireland;
(b) for purposes of the application of Articles 9 and 10 and Articles 23 to 26 concerning the layouts for the balance sheet and the profit and loss account, where a Member State has brought other layouts for these documents into force not more than three years before the notification of this Directive
(c) for purposes of the application of this Directive as regards the calculation and disclosure in balance sheets of depreciation relating to assets covered by the asset items mentioned in Article 9, C(II)(2) and (3), and Article 10, C(II)(2) and (3);

---

1 OJ No. L 327, 19.12.1975, p. 4.

(d) for purposes of the application of Article 47(1) of this Directive except as regards companies already under an obligation of publication under Article 2(1)(f) of Directive 68/151/EEC. In this case the second subparagraph of Article 47(1) of this Directive shall apply to the annual accounts and to the opinion drawn up by the person responsible for auditing the accounts;

(e) for purposes of the application of Article 51(1) of this Directive.

Furthermore, this period of 18 months may be extended to eight years for companies the principal object of which is shipping and which are already in existence on the entry into force of the provisions referred to in paragraph 1.

3. The Member States shall ensure that they communicate to the Commission the texts of the main provisions of national law which they adopt in the field covered by this Directive.

Article 56

The obligation to show in the annual accounts the items prescribed by Articles 9, 10 and 23 to 26 which relate to affiliated undertakings, and the obligation to provide information concerning these undertakings in accordance with Article 13(2), 14 or 43(1)(7), shall enter into force at the same time as a Council Directive on consolidated accounts.

Article 57

1. Until the entry into force of a Council Directive on consolidated accounts, and without prejudice to the provisions of directives 68/151/EEC and 77/91/EEC, the Member States need not apply to the dependent companies of any group governed by their national laws the provisions of this Directive concerning the content, auditing and publication of the annual accounts of such dependent companies where the following conditions are fulfilled:

(a) the dominant company must be subject to the laws of a Member State;

(b) all shareholders or members of the dependent company must have declared their agreement to the exemption from such obligation; this declaration must be made in respect of every financial year;

(c) the dominant company must have declared that it guarantees the commitments entered into by the dependent company;

(d) the declarations referred to in (b) and (c) must be published by the dependent company in accordance with the first subparagraph of Article 47(1);

(e) the annual accounts of the dependent company must be consolidated in the group's annual accounts;

(f) the exemption concerning the preparation, auditing and publication of the annual accounts of the dependent company must be disclosed in the notes on the group's annual accounts.

2. Articles 47 and 51 shall apply to the group's annual accounts.

3. Articles 2 to 46 shall apply as far as possible to the group's annual accounts.

Article 58

1. Until the entry into force of a Council Directive on consolidated accounts, and without prejudice to the provisions of Directive 77/91/EEC, the Member States need not apply to the dominant companies of groups governed by their national laws the provisions of this Directive concerning the auditing and publication of the profit and loss accounts of such dominant companies where the following conditions are fulfilled:

(a) this exemption must be published by the dominant company in accordance with Article 47(1);

(b) the annual accounts of the dominant company must be consolidated in the group's annual accounts;

(c) the exemption concerning the auditing and publication of the profit and loss account of the dominant company must be mentioned in the notes on the group's annual accounts;

(d) the profit or loss of the dominant company, determined in accordance with the principles of this Directive, must be shown in the balance sheet of the dominant company.

2. Articles 47 and 51 shall apply to the group's annual accounts.

3. Articles 2 to 46 shall apply as far as possible to the group's annual accounts.

Article 59

Pending subsequent coordination the Member States may permit the valuation of holdings in affiliated undertakings by the equity method provided the following conditions are fulfilled:

(a) the use of this method of valuation must be disclosed in the notes on the accounts of a company having such holdings;

(b) the amount of any differences existing when such holdings were acquired between their purchase price and the percentage of the capital which they represent, including the affiliated undertaking's reserves, profit and loss and profits and losses brought forward, must be shown separately in the balance sheet or in the notes on the accounts of a company having such holdings;

(c) the purchase price of these holdings shall be increased or reduced in the balance sheet of a company having such holdings by the profits or losses realized by the affiliated undertaking according to the percentage of capital held;

(d) the amounts specified in subparagraph (c) shall be shown each year in the profit and loss account of a company having such holdings as a separate item with an appropriate heading;

(e) when an affiliated undertaking distributes dividends to a company having such holdings, their book values shall be reduced accordingly;

(f) when the amounts shown in the profit and loss account in accordance with subparagraph (d) exceed the amounts of dividends already received or the payment of which can be claimed, the amount of the differences must be placed in a reserve which cannot be distributed to shareholders.

Article 60

Pending subsequent coordination, the Member States may prescribe that investments in which investment companies within the meaning of article 5(2) have invested their funds shall be valued on the basis of their market value.

In that case, the Member States may also waive the obligation on investment companies with valuable capital to show separately the value adjustments referred to in Article 36.

Article 61

Until the entry into force of a Council Directive on consolidated accounts, the Member States need not apply to the dominant companies of groups governed by their national laws the provisions of Article 43(1)(2) concerning the amount of capital and reserves and the profits and losses of the undertakings concerned if the national accounts of such undertakings are consolidated into the group's annual accounts or if the holdings in those undertakings are valued by the equity method.

Article 62

This Directive is addressed to the Member States.

Done at Brussels, 25 July 1978.

For the Council

The President

K. von DOHNANYI

Appendix 4

EC 7th Company Law Directive

Seventh Council Directive

of 13 June 1983

based on the Article 54(3)(g) of the Treaty on consolidated accounts

(83/349/EEC)

The Council of the European Communities,

Having regard to the Treaty establishing the European Economic Community, and in particular Article 54(3)(g) thereof,

Having regard to the proposal from the Commission,[1]

Having regard to the opinion of the European Parliament,[2]

Having regard to the opinion of the Economic and Social Committee,[3]

Whereas on 25 July 1978 the Council adopted Directive 78/660/EEC[4] on the coordination of national legislation governing the annual accounts of certain types of companies; whereas many companies are members of bodies of undertakings; whereas consolidated accounts must be drawn up so that financial information concerning such bodies of undertakings may be conveyed to members and third parties; whereas national legislation governing consolidated accounts must therefore be coordinated in order to achieve the objectives of comparability and equivalence in the information which companies must publish within the Community;

Whereas on 25 July 1978 the Council adopted Directive 78/660/EEC[4] on the coordination of national legislation which the power of control is based on a majority of voting rights but also those in which it is based on agreements, where these are permitted; whereas, furthermore Member States in which the possibility occurs must be permitted to cover cases in which in certain circumstances control

---

1. OJ No C121, 2.6.1976, p.2.
2. OJ No C 163, 10.7.1978, p.60.
3. OJ No C 75, 26.3.1977, p.5.
4. OJ No L222, 14.8.1978, p.11.

has been effectively exercised on the basis of a minority holding; whereas the Member States must be permitted to cover the case of bodies of undertakings in which the undertakings exist on an equal footing with each other;

Whereas the aim of coordinating the legislation governing consolidated accounts is to protect the interests subsisting in companies with share capital; whereas such protection implies the principle of the preparation of consolidated accounts where such a company is a member of a body of undertakings, and that such accounts must be drawn up at least where such a company is a parent undertaking; whereas, furthermore, the cause of full information also requires that a subsidiary undertaking which is itself a parent undertaking draw up consolidated accounts; whereas, nevertheless, such a parent undertaking may, and, in certain circumstances, must be exempted from the obligation to draw up such consolidated accounts provided that its members and third parties are sufficiently protected;

Whereas, for bodies of undertakings not exceeding a certain size, exemption from the obligation to prepare consolidated accounts may be justified; whereas, accordingly, maximum limits must be set for such exemptions; whereas it follows therefrom that the Member States may either provide that it is sufficient to exceed the limit of one only of the three criteria for the exemption not to apply or adopt limits lower than those prescribed in the Directive;

Whereas consolidated accounts must give a true and fair view of the assets and liabilities, the financial position and the profit and loss of all the undertakings consolidated taken as a whole; whereas, therefore, consolidation should in principle include all of those undertakings; whereas such consolidation requires the full incorporation of the assets and liabilities and of the income and expenditure of those undertakings and the separate disclosure of the interests of persons outwith such bodies; whereas, however, the necessary corrections must be made to eliminate the effects of the financial relations between the undertakings consolidated;

Whereas a number of principles relating to the preparation of consolidated accounts and valuation in the context of such accounts must be laid down in order to ensure that items are disclosed consistently, and may readily be compared not only as regards the methods used in their valuation but also as regards the periods covered by the accounts;

Whereas participating interests in the capital of undertakings over which undertakings included in a consolidation exercise significant influence must be included in consolidated accounts by means of the equity method; the undertakings to be consolidated;

Whereas certain derogations originally provided for on a transitional basis in Directive 78/660/EEC may be continued subject to review at a later date.

Has adopted this Directive

Section 1

Conditions for the preparation of consolidated accounts

Article 1

1. A Member State shall require any undertaking governed by its national law to draw up consolidated accounts and a consolidated annual report if that undertaking (a parent undertaking);

(a) has a majority of the shareholders' or members' voting rights in another undertaking (a subsidiary undertaking); or

(b) has the right to appoint or remove a majority of the members of the administrative, management or supervisory body of another undertaking (a subsidiary undertaking) and is at the same time a shareholder in or member of that undertaking; or

(c) has the right to exercise a dominant influence over an undertaking (a subsidiary undertaking) of which it is a shareholder or member, pursuant to a contract entered into with that undertaking or to a provision in its memorandum or articles of association, where the law governing that subsidiary undertaking permits its being subject to such contracts or provisions. A Member State need not prescribe that a parent undertaking must be a shareholder in or member of its subsidiary undertaking. Those Member States the laws of which do not provide for such contracts or clauses shall not be required to apply this provision; or

(d) is a shareholder in or member of an undertaking, and:

(aa) a majority of the members of the administrative, management or supervisory bodies of that undertaking (a subsidiary undertaking) who have held office during the financial year, during the preceding financial year and up to the time when the consolidated accounts are drawn up, have been appointed solely as a result of the exercise of its voting rights; or

(bb) controls alone, pursuant to an agreement with other shareholders in or members of that undertaking (a subsidiary undertaking), a majority of shareholders' or members' voting rights in that undertaking. The Member States may introduce more detailed provisions concerning the form and contents of such agreements.

The Member States shall prescribe at least the arrangements referred to in (bb) above.

They may make the application of (aa) above dependent upon the holdings representing 20% or more of the shareholders' or members' voting rights.

However, (aa) above shall not apply where another undertaking has the rights referred to in subparagraphs (a), (b) or (c) above with regard to that subsidiary undertaking.

2. Apart from the cases mentioned in paragraph 1 above and p~ending subsequent coordination, the Member States may require any undertaking governed by their national law to draw up consolidated accounts and a consolidated annual report if that undertaking (a parent undertaking) holds a participating interest as defined in Article 17 of Directive 78/660/EEC in another undertaking (a subsidiary undertaking), and:

(a) it actually exercises a dominant influence over it; or

(b) it and the subsidiary undertaking are managed on a unified basis by the parent undertaking.

Article 2

1. For the purposes of Article 1(1)(a), (b) and (d), the voting rights and the rights of appointment and removal of any other subsidiary undertaking as well as those of any person acting in his own name but on behalf of the parent undertaking or of another subsidiary undertaking must be added to those of the parent undertaking.

2. For the purposes of Article 1(1)(a), (b) and (d), the rights mentioned in paragraph 1 above must be reduced by the rights:

(a) attaching to shares held on behalf of a person who is neither the parent undertaking nor a subsidiary thereof; or

(b) attaching to shares held by way of security, provided that the rights in question are exercised in accordance with the instructions received, or held in connection with the granting of loans as part of normal business activities, provided that the voting rights are exercised in the interests of the person providing the security.

3. For the purposes of Article 1(a)(a) and (d), the total of the shareholders' or members' voting rights in the subsidiary undertaking must be reduced by the voting rights attaching to the shares held by that undertaking itself by a subsidiary undertaking

of that undertaking or by a person acting in his own name but on behalf of those undertakings.

Article 3

1. Without prejudice to Articles 13, 14 and 15, a parent undertaking and all of its subsidiary undertakings shall be undertakings to be consolidated regardless of where the registered offices of such subsidiary undertakings are situated.

2. For the purposes of paragraph 1 above, any subsidiary undertaking of a subsidiary undertaking shall be considered a subsidiary undertaking of the parent undertaking which is the parent of the undertakings to be consolidated.

Article 4

1. For the purposes of this Directive, a parent undertaking and all of its subsidiary undertakings shall be undertakings to be consolidated where either the parent undertaking or one or more subsidiary undertakings is established as one of the following types of company:

(a) *in Germany:*

die Aktiengesellschaft, die Kommanditgesellschaft auf Aktien, die Gesellschaft mit beschränkter Haftung;

(b) *in Belgium:*

la société anonyme / de naamloze vennootschap – la société en commandite par actions / de commanditaire vennootschap op aandelen – la société de personnes à responsabilité limitée / de personenvennootschap met beperkte aansprakelijkheid;

(c) *in Denmark:*

aktieselskaber, kommanditaktieselskaber, anpartsselskaber;

(d) *in France:*

la société anonyme, la société en commandite par actions, la société à responsabilité limitée;

(e) *in Greece:*

η ανώνυμη εταιρîα, η εταιρîα περιορισμĕνης ενθîνης, η ετερόρρυθμη κατά μετοχΰĕς εταιρîα;

(f) *in Ireland:*

public companies limited by shares or by guarantee, private companies limited by shares or by guarantee;

(g) *in Italy:*

la società per azioni, la società in accommandita per azioni, la società a responsabilità limitata;

(h) *in Luxembourg:*

la société anonyme, la société en commandite par actions, la société à responsabilité limitée;

(i) in the Netherlands:

de maamloze vennootschap, de besloten vennootschap met beperkte aansprakelijkheid;

(j) in the United Kingdom:

public companies limited by shares or by guarantee, private companies limited by shares or by guarantee.

2. A Member State may, however, grant exemption from the obligation imposed in Article 1(1) where the parent undertaking is not established as one of the types of company listed in paragraph 1 above.

Article 5

1. A Member State may grant exemption from the obligation imposed in Article 1(1) where the parent undertaking is a financial holding company as defined in Article 5(3) of Directive 78/660/EEC, and:

(a) it has not intervened during the financial year, directly or indirectly, in the management of a subsidiary undertaking;

(b) it has not exercised the voting rights attaching to its participating interest in respect of the appointment of a member of a subsidiary undertaking's administrative, management or supervisory bodies during the financial year or the five preceding financial years or, where the exercise of voting rights was necessary for the operation of the administrative, management or supervisory bodies of the subsidiary undertaking, no shareholder in or member of the parent undertaking with majority voting rights or member of the administrative, management or supervisory bodies of that undertaking or of a member thereof with majority voting rights is a member of the administrative, management or supervisory bodies of the subsidiary undertaking and the members of those bodies so appointed have fulfilled their functions without any interference or influence on the part of the parent undertaking or of any of its subsidiary undertakings;

(c) it has made loans only to undertakings in which it holds participating interests. Where such loans have been made to other parties, they must have been repaid by the end of the previous financial year; and

(d) the exemption is granted by an administrative authority after fulfilment of the above conditions has been checked.

2. (a) Where a financial holding company has been exempted, Article 43(2) of Directive 78/660/EEC shall not apply to its annual accounts with respect to any majority holdings in subsidiary undertakings as from the date provided for in Article 49(2).

(b) The disclosures in respect of such majority holdings provided for in point 2 of Article 43(1) of Directive 78/660/EEC may be omitted when their nature is such that they would be seriously prejudicial to the company, to its shareholders or members or to one of its subsidiaries. A Member State may make such omissions subject to prior administrative or judicial authorization. Any such omission must be disclosed in the notes on the accounts.

Article 6

1. Without prejudice to Articles 4(2) and 5, a Member State may provide for an exemption from the obligation imposed in Article 1(1) if as at the balance sheet date of a parent undertaking the undertakings to be consolidated do not together, on the basis of their latest annual accounts, exceed the limits of two of the three criteria laid down in Article 27 of Directive 78/660/EEC.

2. A Member State may require or permit that the set-off referred to in Article 19(1) and the elimination referred to in Article 26(1)(a) and (b) be not effected when the aforementioned limits are calculated. In that case, the limits for the balance sheet total and net turnover criteria shall be increased by 20%.

3. Article 12 of Directive 78/660/EEC shall apply to the above criteria.

4. This Article shall not apply where one of the undertakings to be consolidated is a company the securities of which have been admitted to official listing on a stock exchange established in a Member State.

5. For 10 years after the date referred to in Article 49(2), the Member States may multiply the criteria expressed in ECU by up to 2,5 and may increase the average number of persons employed during the financial year to a maximum of 500.

Article 7

1. Notwithstanding Articles 4(2), 5 and 6, a Member State shall exempt from the obligation imposed in Article 1(1) any parent undertaking governed by its national law which is also a subsidiary undertaking if its own parent undertaking is governed by the law of a Member State in the following two cases;

(a) where that parent undertaking holds all of the shares in the exempted undertaking. The shares in that undertaking held by members of its administrative, management or supervisory bodies pursuant to an obligation in law or in the memorandum or articles of association shall be ignored for this purpose; or

(b) where that parent undertaking holds 90% or more of the shares in the exempted undertaking and the remaining shareholders in or members of that undertaking have approved the exemption.

In so far as the laws of a Member State prescribe consolidation in this case at the time of the adoption of this Directive, that Member State need not apply this provision for 10 years after the date referred to in Article 49(2).

2. Exemption shall be conditional upon compliance with all of the following conditions;

(a) the exempted undertaking and, without prejudice to Articles 13; 14 and 15, all of its subsidiary undertakings must be consolidated in the accounts of a larger body of undertakings, the parent undertaking of which is governed by the law of a Member State;

(b) (aa) the consolidated accounts referred to in (a) above and the consolidated annual report of the larger body of undertakings must be drawn up by the parent undertaking of that body and audited, according to the law of the Member State by which the parent undertaking of that larger body of undertakings is governed, in accordance with this Directive;

(bb) the consolidated accounts referred to in (a) above and the consolidated annual report referred to in (aa) above, the report by the person responsible for auditing those accounts and, where appropriate, the appendix referred to in Article 9 must be published for the exempted undertaking in the manner prescribed by the law of the Member State governing that undertaking in accordance with Article 38. That Member State may require that those documents be published in its official language and that the translation be certified;

(c) the notes on the annual accounts of the exempted undertakings must disclose:

(aa) the name and registered office of the parent undertaking that draws up the consolidated accounts referred to in (a) above; and

(bb) the exemption from the obligation to draw up consolidated accounts and a consolidated annual report.

3 A Member State need not, however, apply this Article to companies the securities of which have been admitted to official listing on a stock exchange established in a Member State.

Article 8

1. In cases not covered by Article 7(1), a Member State may, without prejudice to Articles 4(2), 5 and 6, exempt from the obligation imposed in Article 1(1) any parent undertaking governed by its national law which is also a subsidiary undertaking, the parent undertaking of which is governed by the law of a Member State provided that all the conditions set out in Article 7(2) are fulfilled and that the shareholders in or members of the exempted undertaking who own a minimum proportion of the subscribed capital of that undertaking have not requested the preparation of consolidated accounts at least six months before the end of the financial year. The Member States may fix that proportion at not more than 10% for public limited liability companies and for limited partnerships with share capital, and at not more than 20% for undertakings of other types.

2. A Member State may not make it a condition for this exemption that the parent undertaking which prepared the consolidated accounts described in Article 7(2)(a) must also be governed by its national law.

3. A Member State may not make exemption subject to conditions concerning the preparation and auditing of the consolidated accounts referred to in Article 7(2)(a).

Article 9

1. A Member State may make the exemptions provided for in Articles 7 and 8 dependent upon the disclosure of additional information, in accordance with this Directive, in the consolidated accounts referred to in Article 7(2)(a), or in an appendix thereto, if that information is required of undertakings governed by the national law of that Member State which are obliged to prepare consolidated accounts and are in the same circumstances.

2. A Member State may also make exemption dependent upon the disclosure, in the notes on the consolidated accounts referred to in Article 7(2)(a), or in the annual accounts of the exempted undertakings, of all or some of the following information regarding the body of undertakings, the parent undertaking of which it is exempting from the obligation to draw up consolidated accounts:

- the amounts of the fixed assets,
- the net turnover,
- the profit or loss for the financial year and the amount of the capital and reserves,
- the average number of persons employed during the financial year.

Article 10

Articles 7 to 9 shall not affect any Member State's legislation on the drawing up of consolidated accounts or consolidated annual reports in so far as those documents are required:

- for the information of employees or their representatives, or
- by an administrative or judicial authority for its own purposes.

Article 11

1. Without prejudice to Articles 4(2), 5 and 6, a Member State may exempt from the obligation imposed in Article 1(1) any parent undertaking governed by its national law which is also a subsidiary undertaking of a parent undertaking not governed by the law of a Member State, if all of the following conditions are fulfilled:

(a) the exempted undertaking and, without prejudice to Articles 13, 14 and 15, all of its subsidiary undertakings must be consolidated in the accounts of a larger body of undertakings;

(b) the consolidated accounts referred to in (a) above and, where appropriate, the consolidated annual report must be drawn up in accordance with this Directive or in a manner equivalent to consolidated accounts and consolidated annual reports drawn up in accordance with this Directive;

(c) the consolidated accounts referred to m (a) above must have been audited by one or more persons authorized to audit accounts under the national law governing the undertaking which drew them up.

2. Articles 7(2)(b)(bb) and (c) and 8 to 10 shall apply.

3. A Member State may provide for exemptions under this Article only if it provides for the same exemptions under Articles 7 to 10.

Article 12

1. Without prejudice to Articles 1 to 10, a Member State may require any undertaking governed by its national law to draw up consolidated accounts and a consolidated annual report if:

(a) that undertaking and one or more other undertakings with which it is not connected, as described in Article 1(1) or (2), are managed on a unified basis pursuant to a contract concluded with that undertaking or provisions in the memorandum or articles of association of those undertakings; or

(b) the administrative, management or supervisory bodies of that undertaking and of one or more other undertakings with which it is not connected, as described in Article 1(1) or (2), consist for the major part of the same persons in office during the financial year and until the consolidated accounts are drawn up.

2. Where paragraph 1 above is applied, undertakings, related as defined in that paragraph together with all of their subsidiary undertakings shall be undertakings to be consolidated, as defined in this Directive, where one or more of those undertakings is established as one of the types of company listed in Article 4.

3. Articles 3, 4(2), 5, 6,13 to 28, 29(1), (3), (4) and (5), 30 to 38 and 39(2) shall apply to the consolidated accounts and the consolidated annual report covered by this Article, references to parent undertakings being understood to refer to all the undertakings specified in paragraph 1 above. Without prejudice to Article 19(2), however, the items 'capital', 'share premium account', 'revaluation reserve', 'reserves', 'profit or loss brought forward', and 'profit or loss for the financial year' to be included in the consolidated accounts shall be the aggregate amounts attributable to each of the undertakings specified in paragraph 1.

Article 13

1. An undertaking need not be included in consolidated accounts where it is not material for the purposes of Article 16(3).

2. Where two or more undertakings satisfy the requirement of paragraph 1 above, they must nevertheless be included in consolidated accounts if, as a whole, they are material for the purposes of Article 16(3)

3. In addition, an undertaking need not be included in consolidated accounts where:

(a) severe long-term restrictions substantially hinder:

(aa) the parent undertaking in the exercise of its rights over the assets or management of that undertaking; or

(bb) the exercise of unified management of that undertaking where it is in one of the relationships defined in Article 12(1); or

(b) the information necessary for the preparation of consolidated accounts in accordance with this Directive cannot be obtained without disproportionate expense or undue delay; or

(c) the shares of that undertaking are held exclusively with a view to their subsequent resale.

Article 14

1. Where the activities of one or more undertakings to be consolidated are so different that their inclusion in the consolidated accounts would be incompatible with the obligation imposed in Article 16(3), such undertakings must, without prejudice to Article 33 of this Directive, be excluded from the consolidation.

2. Paragraph 1 above shall not be applicable merely by virtue of the fact that the undertakings to be consolidated are partly industrial, partly commercial, and partly provide services, or because such undertakings carry on industrial or commercial activities involving different products or provide different services.

3. Any application of paragraph 1 above and the reasons therefor must be disclosed in the notes on the accounts. Where the annual or consolidated account of the undertakings thus excluded from the consolidation are not published in the same Member State in accordance with Directive 68/151/EEC[1], they must be attached to the case it must be possible to obtain a copy of such documents upon request. The price of such a copy must not exceed its administrative cost.

Article 15

1. A Member State may, for the purposes of Article 16(3), permit the omission from consolidated accounts of any parent undertaking not carrying on any industrial or commercial activity which holds shares in a subsidiary undertaking on the basis of a joint arrangement with one or more undertakings not included in the consolidated accounts.

2. The annual accounts of the parent undertaking shall be attached to the consolidated accounts.

3. Where use is made of this derogation, either Article 59 of Directive 78660/EEC shall apply to the parent undertaking's annual accounts or the information which would have resulted from its application must be given in the notes on those accounts.

Section 2

The preparation of consolidated accounts

Article 16

1. Consolidated accounts shall comprise the consolidated balance sheet, the consolidated profit-and-loss account and the notes on the accounts. These documents shall constitute a composite whole.

2. Consolidated accounts shall be drawn up clearly and in accordance with this Directive.

3. Consolidated accounts shall give a true and fair view of the assets, liabilities, financial position and profit or loss of the undertakings included therein taken as a whole.

---

1. OJ No L 65,14.3.1968, p. 8.

4. Where the application of the provisions of this Directive would not be sufficient to give a true and fair view within the meaning of paragraph 3 above, additional information must be given.

5. Where, in exceptional cases, the application of a provision of Articles 17 to 35 and 39 is incompatible with the obligation imposed in paragraph 3 above, that provision must be departed from in order to give a true and fair view within the meaning of paragraph 3. Any such departure must be disclosed in the notes on the accounts together with an explanation of the reasons for it and a statement of its effect on the assets, liabilities, financial position and profit or loss. The Member States may define the exceptional cases in question and lay down the relevant special rules.

6. A Member State may require or permit the disclosure in the consolidated accounts of other information as well as that which must be disclosed in accordance with this Directive.

Article 17

1. Articles 3 to 10, 13 to 26 and 28 to 30 of Directive 78/660/EEC shall apply in respect of the layout of consolidated accounts, without prejudice to the provisions of this Directive and taking account of the essential adjustments resulting from the particular characteristics of consolidated accounts as compared with annual accounts.

2. Where there are special circumstances which would entail undue expense a Member State may permit stocks to be combined in the consolidated accounts.

Article 18

The assets and liabilities of undertakings included in a consolidation shall be incorporated in full in the consolidated balance sheet.

Article 19

1. The book values of shares in the capital of undertakings included in a consolidation shall be set off against the proportion which they represent of the capital and reserves of those undertakings:

(a) That set-off shall be effected on the basis of book values as at the date as at which such undertakings are included in the consolidations for the first time. Differences arising from such set-offs shall as far as possible be entered directly against those items in the consolidated balance sheet which have values above or below their book values.

(b) A Member State may require or permit set-offs on the basis of the values of identifiable assets and liabilities as at the date of acquisition of the shares or, in the event of acquisition in two or more stages, as at the date on which the undertaking became a subsidiary.

(c) Any difference remaining after the application of (a) or resulting from the application of (b) shall be shown as a separate item in the consolidated balance sheet with an appropriate heading. That item, the methods used and any significant changes in relation to the preceding financial year must be explained in the notes on the accounts. Where the offsetting of positive and negative differences is authorized by a Member State, a breakdown of such differences must also be given in the notes on the account.

2. However, paragraph 1 above shall not apply to shares in the capital of the parent undertaking held either by that undertaking itself or by another undertaking included in the consolidation. In the consolidated accounts such shares shall be treated as own shares in accordance with Directive 78/660/EEC.

Article 20

1. A Member State may require or permit the book values of shares held in the capital of an undertaking included in the consolidation to be set off against the corresponding percentage of capital only, provided that:

(a) the shares held represent at least 90% of the nominal value or, in the absence of a nominal value, of the accounting par value of the shares of that undertaking other than shares of the kind described in Article 29(2)(a) of Directive 77/91/EEC[1];

(b) the proportion referred to in (a) above has been attained pursuant to an arrangement providing for the issue of shares by an undertaking included in the consolidation; and

(c) the arrangement referred to in (b) above did not include a cash payment exceeding 10% of the nominal value or, in the absence of a nominal value, of the accounting par value of the shares issued.

2. Any difference arising under paragraph 1 above shall be added to or deducted from consolidated reserves as appropriate.

---

[1] OJ No L26, 31.1.1977, p.1

3. The application of the method described in paragraph 1 above, the resulting movement in reserves and the names and registered offices of the undertakings included in the consolidation shall be shown in the consolidated balance sheet as a separate item with an appropriate heading.

Article 21

The amount attributable to shares in subsidiary undertakings included in the consolidation held by persons other than the undertakings included in the consolidation shall be shown in the consolidated balance sheet as a separate item with an appropriate heading.

Article 22

The income and expenditure of undertakings included in a consolidation shall be incorporated in full in the consolidated profit-and-loss account.

Article 23

The amount of any profit or loss attributable to shares in subsidiary undertakings included in the consolidation shall be shown in the consolidated profit-and-loss account as a separate item with an appropriate heading.

Article 24

Consolidated accounts shall be drawn up in accordance with the principles enunciated in Articles 25 to 28.

Article 25

1. The methods of consolidation must be applied consistently from one financial year to another.

2. Derogations from the provisions of paragraph 1 above shall be permitted in exceptional cases. Any such derogations must be disclosed in the notes on the accounts and the reasons for them given together with an assessment of their effect on the assets, liabilities, financial position and profit or loss of the undertakings included in the consolidation taken as a whole.

Article 26

1. Consolidated accounts shall show the assets, liabilities, financial positions and profits or losses of the undertakings included in a consolidation as if the latter were a single undertaking. In particular:

(a) debts and claims between the undertakings included in a consolidation shall be eliminated from the consolidated accounts;

(b) income and expenditure relating to transactions between the undertakings included in a consolidation shall be eliminated from the consolidated accounts;

(c) where profits and losses resulting from transactions between the undertakings included in a consolidation are included in the book values of assets, they shall be eliminated from the consolidated accounts. Pending subsequent coordination, however, a Member State may allow the eliminations mentioned above to be effected in proportion to the percentage of the capital held by the parent undertaking in each of the subsidiary undertakings included in the consolidation.

2. A Member State may permit derogations from the provisions of paragraph 1(c) above where a transaction has been concluded according to normal market conditions and where the elimination of the profit or loss would entail undue expense. Any such derogations must be disclosed and where the effect on the assets, liabilities, financial position and profit or loss of the undertakings, included in the consolidation, taken as a whole, is material, that fact must be disclosed in the notes on the consolidated accounts.

3. Derogations from the provisions of paragraph 1(a), (b) or (c) above shall be permitted where the amounts concerned are not material for the purposes of Article 16(3).

Article 27

1. Consolidated accounts must be drawn up as at the same date as the annual accounts of the parent undertaking.

2. A Member State may, however, require or permit consolidated accounts to be drawn up as at another date in order to take account of the balance sheet dates of the largest number or the most important of the undertakings included in the consolidation. Where use is made of this derogation that fact shall be disclosed in the notes on the consolidated accounts together with the reasons therefor. In addition, account must be taken or disclosure made of important events concerning the assets and liabilities, the financial position or the profit or loss of an undertaking included in a consolidation which have occurred between that undertaking's balance sheet date and the consolidated balance sheet date.

3. Where an undertaking's balance sheet date precedes the consolidated balance sheet date by more than three months, that undertaking shall be consolidated on the basis of interim accounts drawn up as at the consolidated balance sheet date.

Article 28

If the composition of the undertakings included in a consolidation has changed significantly in the course of a financial year, the consolidated accounts must include information which makes the comparison of successive sets of consolidated accounts meaningful. Where such a change is a major one, a Member State may require or permit this obligation to be fulfilled by the preparation of an adjusted opening balance sheet and an adjusted profit-and-loss account.

Article 29

1. Assets and liabilities to be included in consolidated accounts shall be valued according to uniform methods and in accordance with Articles 31 to 42 and 60 of Directive 78/660/EEC.

2. (a) an undertaking which draws up consolidated accounts must apply the same methods of valuation as in its annual accounts. However, a Member State may require or permit the use in consolidate!d accounts of other methods of valuation in accordance with the above mentioned Articles of Directive 78/660/EEC.

(b) Where use is made of this derogation that fact shall be disclosed in the notes on the consolidated accounts and the reasons therefor given.

3. Where assets and liabilities to be included in consolidated accounts have been valued by undertakings included in the consolidation by methods differing from those used for the consolidation, they must be revalued in accordance with the methods used for the consolidation, unless the results of such revaluation are not material for the purposes of Article 16(3). Departures from this principle shall be permitted in exceptional cases. Any such departure shall be disclosed in the notes on the consolidated accounts and the reasons for them given.

4. Account shall be taken in the consolidated balance sheet and in the consolidated profit-and-loss account of any difference arising on consolidation between the tax chargeable for the financial year and for preceding financial years and the amount of tax paid or payable in respect of those years, provided that it is probable that an actual charge to tax will arise within the foreseeable future for one of the undertakings included in the consolidation.

5. Where assets to be included in consolidated accounts have been the subject of exceptional value adjustments solely for tax purposes, they shall be incorporated in the consolidated accounts only after those adjustments have been eliminated. A Member State may, however, require or permit that such assets be incorporated in the consolidated accounts without the elimination of the adjustments, provided that their

amounts, together with the reasons for them, are disclosed in the notes on the consolidated accounts.

Article 30

1. A separate item as defined in Article 19(1)(c) which corresponds to a positive consolidation difference shall be dealt with in accordance with the rules laid down in Directive 78/660/EEC for the item 'goodwill'.

2. A Member State may permit a positive consolidation difference to be immediately and clearly deducted from reserves.

Article 31

An amount shown as a separate item, as defined in Article 19(1)(c), which corresponds to a negative consolidation difference may be transferred to the consolidated profit-and-loss account only:

(a) where that difference corresponds to the expectation at the date of acquisition of unfavourable future results in that undertaking, or to the expectation of costs which that undertaking would incur, in so far as such an expectation materializes; or

(b) in so far as such a difference corresponds to a realized gain.

Article 32

1. Where an undertaking included in a consolidation manages another undertaking jointly with one or more undertakings not included in that consolidation, a Member State may require or permit the inclusion of that other undertaking in the consolidated accounts in proportion to the rights in its capital held by the undertaking included in the consolidation.

2. Articles 13 to 31 shall apply *mutatis mutandis* to the proportional consolidation referred to in paragraph 1 above.

3. Where this Article is applied, Article 33 shall not apply if the undertaking proportionally consolidated is an associated undertaking as defined in Article 33.

Article 33

1. Where an undertaking included in a consolidation exercises a significant influence over the operating and financial policy of an undertaking not included in the consolidation (an associated undertaking) in which it holds a participating interest, as

defined in Article 17 of Directive 78660/EEC, that participating interest shall be shown in the consolidated balance sheet as a separate item with an appropriate heading. An undertaking shall be presumed to exercise a significant influence over another undertaking where it has 20% or more of the shareholders' or members' voting rights in that undertaking. Article 2 shall apply.

2. When this Article is applied for the first time to a participating interest covered by paragraph 1 above, that participating interest shall be shown in the consolidated balance sheet either:

(a) at its book value calculated in accordance with the valuation rules laid down in Directive 78/660/EEC. The difference between that value and the amount corresponding to the proportion of capital and reserves represented by that participating interest shall be disclosed separately in the consolidated balance sheet or in the notes on the accounts. That difference shall be calculated as at the date as at which that method is used for the first time; or

(b) at an amount corresponding to the proportion of the associated undertaking's capital and reserves represented by that participating interest. The difference between that amount and the book value calculated in accordance with the valuation rules laid down in Directive 78/660/EEC shall be disclosed separately in the consolidated balance sheet or in the notes on the accounts. That difference shall be calculated as at the date as at which that method is used for the first time.

(c) A Member State may prescribe the application of one or other of (a) and (b) above. The consolidated balance sheet or the notes on the accounts must indicate whether (a) or (b) has been used.

(d) In addition, for the purposes of (a) and (b) above, a Member State may require or permit the calculation of the difference as at the date of acquisition of the shares or, where they were acquired in two or more stages, as at the date on which the undertaking became an associated undertaking.

3. Where an associated undertaking's assets or liabilities have been valued by methods other than those used for consolidation in accordance with Article 29(2), they may, for the purpose of calculating the difference referred to in paragraph 2(a) or (b) above, be revalued by the methods used for consolidation. Where such revaluation has not been carried out that fact must be disclosed in the notes on the accounts. A Member State may require such revaluation.

4. The book value referred to in paragraph 2(a) above, or the amount corresponding to the proportion of the associated undertaking's capital and reserves referred to in paragraph 2(b) above, shall be increased or reduced by the amount of any

variation which has taken place during the financial year in the proportion of the associated undertaking's capital and reserves represented by that participating interest; it shall be reduced by the amount of the dividends relating to that participating interest.

5. In so far as the positive difference referred to in paragraph 2(a) or (b) above cannot be related to any category of assets or liabilities it shall be dealt with in accordance with Articles 30 and 39(3).

6. The proportion of the profit or loss of the associated undertakings attributable to such participating interests shall be shown in the consolidated profit-and-loss account as a separate item under an appropriate heading.

7. The eliminations referred to in Article 26(1)(c) shall be effected in so far as the facts are known or can be ascertained. Article 26(2) and (3) shall apply.

8. Where an associated undertaking draws up consolidated accounts, the foregoing provisions shall apply to the capital and reserves shown in such consolidated accounts.

9. This Article need not be applied where the participating interest in the capital of the associated undertaking is not material for the purposes of Article 16(3).

Article 34

In addition to the information required under other provisions of this Directive, the notes on the accounts must set out information in respect of the following matters at least:

1. The valuation methods applied to the various items in the consolidated accounts, and the methods employed in calculating the value adjustments. For items included in the consolidated accounts which are or were originally expressed in foreign currency the bases of conversion used to express them in the currency in which the consolidated accounts are drawn up must be disclosed.

2. (a) The names and registered offices of the undertakings included in the consolidation; the proportion of the capital held in undertakings included in the consolidation, other than the parent undertaking, by the undertakings included in the consolidation or by persons acting in their own names but on behalf of those undertakings; which of the conditions referred to in Articles 1 and 12(1) following application of Article 2 has formed the basis on which the consolidation has been carried out. The latter disclosure may, however, be omitted where consolidation has been carried out on the basis of Article 1(1)(a) and

where the proportion of the capital and the proportion of the voting rights held are the same.

(b) The same information must be given in respect of undertakings excluded from a consolidation pursuant to Articles 13 and 14 and, without prejudice to Article 14(3), an explanation must be given for the exclusion of the undertakings referred to in Article 13.

3. (a) The names and registered offices of undertakings associated with an undertaking included in the consolidation as described in Article 33(1) and the proportion of their capital held by undertakings included in the consolidation or by persons acting in their own names but on behalf of those undertakings.

(b) The same information must be given in respect of the associated undertakings referred to in Article 33(9), together with the reasons for applying that provision.

4. The names and registered offices of undertakings proportionally consolidated pursuant to Article 32, the factors on which joint management is based, and the proportion of their capital held by the undertakings included in the consolidation or by persons acting in their own names but on behalf of those undertakings.

5. The name and registered office of each of the undertakings, other than those referred to in paragraphs 2, 3 and 4 above, in which undertakings included in the consolidation and those excluded pursuant to Article 14, either themselves or through persons acting in their own names but on behalf of those undertakings, hold at least a percentage of the capital which the Member States cannot fix at more than 20%, showing the proportion of the capital held, the amount of the capital and reserves, and the profit or loss for the latest financial year of the undertaking concerned for which accounts have been adopted. This information may be omitted where, for the purposes of Article 16(3), it is of negligible importance only. The information concerning capital reserves and the profit or loss may also be omitted where the undertaking concerned does not publish its balance sheet and where less than 50% of its capital is held (directly or indirectly) by the above mentioned undertakings.

6. The total amount shown as owed in the consolidated balance sheet and becoming due and payable after more than five years, as well as the total amount shown as owed in the consolidated balance sheet and covered by valuable security furnished by undertakings included in the consolidation, with an indication of the nature and form of the security.

7. The total amount of any financial commitments that are not included in the consolidated balance sheet, in so far as this information is of assistance in assessing the financial position of the undertakings included in the consolidation taken as a whole. Any commitments concerning pensions and affiliated undertakings which are not included in the consolidation must be disclosed separately.

8. The consolidated net turnover as defined in Article 28 of Directive 78/660/EEC, broken down by categories of activity and into geographical markets in so far as, taking account of the manner in which the sale of products and the provision of services falling within the ordinary activities of the undertakings included in the consolidation taken as a whole are organized, these categories and markets differ substantially from one another.

9. (a) The average number of persons employed during the financial year by undertakings included in the consolidation broken down by categories and, if they are not disclosed separately in the consolidated profit-and-loss account the staff costs relating to the financial year.

(b) The average number of persons employed during the financial year by undertakings to which Article 32 has been applied shall be disclosed separately.

10. The extent to which the calculation of the consolidated profit or loss for the financial year has been affected by a valuation of the items which, by way of derogation from the principles enunciated in Articles 31 and 34 to 42 of Directive 78/660/EEC and in Article 29(5) of this Directive, was made in the financial year in question or in an earlier financial year with a view to obtaining tax relief. Where the influence of such a valuation on the future tax charges of the undertakings included in the consolidation taken as a whole is material, details must be disclosed.

11. The difference between the tax charged to the consolidated profit-and-loss account for the financial year and to those for earlier financial years and the amount of tax payable in respect of those years, provided that this difference is material for the purposes of future taxation. This amount may also be disclosed in the balance sheet as a cumulative amount under a separate item with an appropriate heading.

12. The amount of the emoluments granted in respect of the financial year to the members of the administrative, managerial and supervisory bodies of the parent undertaking by reason of their responsibilities in the parent undertaking and its subsidiary undertakings, and any commitments arising or entered into under the same conditions in respect of retirement pensions for former

members of those bodies, with an indication of the total for each category. A Member State may require that emoluments granted by reason of responsibilities assumed in undertakings linked as described in Article 32 or 33 shall also be included with the information specified in the first sentence.

13. The amounts of advances and credits granted to the members of the administrative, managerial and supervisory bodies of the parent undertaking by that undertaking or by one of its subsidiary undertakings, with indications of the interest rates, main conditions and any amounts repaid, as well as commitments entered into on their behalf by way of guarantee of any kind with an indication of the total for each category. A Member State may require that advances and credits granted by undertakings linked as described in Article 32 or 33 shall also be included with the information specified in the first sentence.

Article 35

1. A Member State may allow the disclosures prescribed in Article 34(2), (3), (4) and (5):

(a) to take the form of a statement deposited in accordance with Article 3(1) and (2) of Directive 68/151/EEC; this must be disclosed in the notes on the accounts;

(b) to be omitted when their nature is such that they would be seriously prejudicial to any of the undertakings affected by these provisions. A Member State may make such omissions subject to prior administrative or judicial authorization. Any such omission must be disclosed in the notes on the accounts.

2. Paragraph 1(b) shall also apply to the information prescribed in Article 34(8).

Section 3

The consolidated annual report

Article 36

1. The consolidated annual report must include at least a fair view of the development of business and the position of the undertakings included in the consolidation taken as a whole.

2. In respect of those undertakings, the report shall also give an indication of:

(a) any important events that have occurred since the end of the financial year;

(b) the likely future development of those undertakings taken as a whole;

(c) the activities of those undertakings taken as a whole in the field of research and development;

(d) the number and nominal value or, in the absence of a nominal value, the accounting par value of all of the parent undertaking's shares held by that undertaking itself, by subsidiary undertakings of that undertaking or by a person acting in his own name but on behalf of those undertakings. A Member State may require or permit the disclosure of these particulars in the notes on the accounts.

Section 4

The auditing of consolidated accounts

Article 37

1. An undertaking which draws up consolidated accounts must have them audited by one or more persons authorized to audit accounts under the laws of the Member State which govern that undertaking.

2. The person or persons responsible for auditing the consolidated accounts must also verify that the consolidated annual report is consistent with the consolidated accounts for the same financial year.

Section 5

The publication of consolidated accounts

Article 38

1. Consolidated accounts, duly approved, and the consolidated annual report, together with the opinion submitted by the person responsible for auditing the consolidated accounts, shall be published for the undertaking which drew up the consolidated accounts as laid down by the laws of the Member State which governs it in accordance with Article 3 of Directive 68/151/EEC.

2. The second subparagraph of Article 47(1) of Directive 78/660/EEC shall apply with respect to the consolidated annual report.

3. The following shall be substituted for the second subparagraph of Article 47(1) of Directive 78/660/EEC: 'It must be possible to obtain a copy of all or part of any

such report upon request. The price of such a copy must not exceed its administrative cost'.

4. However, where the undertaking which drew up the consolidated accounts is not established as one of the types of company listed in Article 4 and is not required by its national law to publish the documents referred to in paragraph 1 in the same manner as prescribed in Article 3 of Directive 68/151/EEC, it must at least make them available to the public at its head office. It must be possible to obtain a copy of such documents upon request. The price of such a copy must not exceed its administrative cost.

5. Articles 48 and 49 of Directive 78/660/EEC shall apply.

6. The Member States shall provide for appropriate sanctions for failure to comply with the publication obligations imposed in this Article.

Section 6

Transitional and final provisions

Article 39

1. When, for the first time, consolidated accounts are drawn up in accordance with this Directive for a body of undertakings which was already connected, as described in Article 1(1), before application of the provisions referred to in Article 49(1), a Member State may require or permit that, for the purposes of Article 19(1), account be taken of the book value of a holding and the proportion of the capital and reserves that it represents as at a date before or the same as that of the first consolidation.

2. Paragraph 1 above shall apply *mutatis mutandis* to the valuation for the purposes of Article 33(2) of a holding, or of the proportion of capital and reserves that it represents, in the capital of an undertaking associated with an undertaking included in the consolidation, and to the proportional consolidation referred to in Article 32.

3. Where the separate item defined in Article 19(1) corresponds to a positive consolidation difference which arose before the date of the first consolidated accounts drawn up in accordance with this Directive, a Member State may:

(a) for the purposes of Article 30(1), permit the calculation of the limited period of more than five years provided for in Article 37(2) of Directive 78/660/EEC as from the date of the first consolidated accounts drawn up in accordance with this Directive; and

(b) for the purposes of Article 30(2), permit the deduction to be made from reserves as at the date of the first consolidated accounts drawn up in accordance with this Directive.

Article 40

1. Until expiry of the deadline imposed for the application in national law of the Directives supplementing Directive 78/660/EEC as regards the harmonization of the rules governing the annual accounts of banks and other financial institutions and insurance undertakings, a Member State may derogate from the provisions of this Directive concerning the layout of consolidated accounts, the methods of valuing the items included in those accounts and the information to be given in the notes on the accounts:

(a) with regard to any undertaking to be consolidated which is a bank, another financial institution or an insurance undertaking;

(b) where the undertakings to be consolidated comprise principally banks, financial institutions or insurance undertakings.

They may also derogate from Article 6, but only in so far as the limits and criteria to be applied to the above undertakings are concerned.

2. In so far as a Member State has not required all undertakings which are banks, other financial institutions or insurance undertakings to draw up consolidated accounts before implementation of the provisions referred to in Article 49(1), it may, until its national law implements one of the Directives mentioned in paragraph 1 above, but not in respect of financial years ending after 1993:

(a) suspend the application of the obligation imposed in Article 1(1) with respect to any of the above undertakings which is a parent undertaking. That fact must be disclosed in the annual accounts of the parent undertaking and the information prescribed in point 2 of Article 43(1) of Directive 78/660/EEC must be given for all subsidiary undertakings;

(b) where consolidated accounts are drawn up and without prejudice to Article 33, permit the omission from the consolidation of any of the above undertakings which is a subsidiary undertaking. The information prescribed in Article 34(2) must be given in the notes on the accounts in respect of any such subsidiary undertaking.

3. In the cases referred to in paragraph 2(b) above, the annual or consolidated accounts of the subsidiary undertaking must, in so far as their publication is compulsory, be attached to the consolidated accounts or, in the absence of consolidated

accounts, to the annual accounts of the parent undertaking or be made available to the public. In the latter case it must be possible to obtain a copy of such documents upon request. The price of such a copy must not exceed its administrative cost.

Article 41

1. Undertakings which are connected as described in Article 1(1)(a), (b) and (d)(bb), and those other undertakings which are similarly connected with one of the aforementioned undertakings, shall be affiliated undertakings for the purposes of this Directive and of Directive 78/660/EEC.

2. Where a Member State prescribes the preparation of consolidated accounts pursuant to Article 1(1)(c), (d)(aa) or (2) or Article 12(1), the undertakings which are connected as described in those Articles and those other undertakings which are connected similarly, or are connected as described m paragraph 1 above to one of the aforementioned undertakings, shall be affiliated undertakings as defined in paragraph 1.

3. Even where a Member State does not prescribe the preparation of consolidated accounts pursuant to Article 1(1)(c), (d)(aa) or (2) or Article 12(1), it may apply paragraph 2 of this Article.

4. Articles 2 and 3(2) shall apply.

5. When a Member State applies Article 4(2), it may exclude from the application of paragraph 1 above affiliated undertakings which are parent undertakings and which by virtue of their legal form are not required by that Member State to draw up consolidated accounts in accordance with the provisions of this Directive, as well as parent undertakings with a similar legal form.

Article 42

The following shall be substituted for Article 56 of Directive 78/660/EEC:

'*Article 56*

1. The obligation to show in annual accounts the items prescribed by Articles 9, 10 and 23 to 26 which relate to affiliated undertakings, as defined by Article 41 of Directive 83/349/EEC, and the obligation to provide information concerning these undertakings in accordance with Articles 13(2), and 14 and point 7 of Article 43(1) shall enter into force on the date fixed in Article 49(2) of that Directive.

2. The notes on the accounts must also disclose:

(a) the name and registered office of the undertaking which draws up the consolidated accounts of the largest body of undertakings of which the company forms part as a subsidiary undertaking;

(b) the name and registered office of the undertaking which draws up the consolidated accounts of the smallest body of undertakings of which the company forms part as a subsidiary undertaking and which is also included in the body of undertakings referred to in (a) above;

(c) the place where copies of the consolidated accounts referred to in (a) and (b) above may be obtained provided that they are available.'

Article 43

The following shall be substituted for Article 57 of Directive 78/660/EEC:

'Article 57

Notwithstanding the provisions of Directives 68/151/EEC and 77/91/EEC, a Member State need not apply the provisions of this Directive concerning the content, auditing and publication of annual accounts to companies governed by their national laws which are subsidiary undertakings, as defined in Directive 83/349/EEC, where the following conditions are fulfilled:

(a) the parent undertaking must be subject to the laws of a Member State;

(b) all shareholders or members of the subsidiary undertaking must have declared their agreement to the exemption from such obligations; this declaration must be made in respect of every financial year;

(c) the parent undertaking must have declared that it guarantees the commitments entered into by the subsidiary undertaking;

(d) the declarations referred to in (b) and (c) must be published by the subsidiary undertaking as laid down by the laws of the Member State in accordance with Article 3 of Directive 68/151/EEC;

(e) the subsidiary undertaking must be included in the consolidated accounts drawn up by the parent undertaking in accordance with Directive 83/349/EEC;

(f) the above exemption must be disclosed in the notes on the consolidated accounts drawn up by the parent undertaking;

(g) the consolidated accounts referred to in (e), the consolidated annual report, and the report by the person responsible for auditing those accounts must be published for the subsidiary undertaking as laid down by the laws of the Member State in accordance with Article 3 of Directive 68/151/EEC.'

Article 44

The following shall be substituted for Article 58 of Directive 78/660/EEC:

'*Article* 58

A Member State need not apply the provisions of this Directive concerning the auditing and publication of the profit-and-loss account to companies governed by their national laws which are parent undertakings for the purposes of Directive 83/349/EEC where the following conditions are fulfilled:

(a) the parent undertaking must draw up consolidated accounts in accordance with Directive 83/349/EEC and be included in the consolidated accounts;

(b) the above exemption must be disclosed in the notes on the annual accounts of the parent undertaking;

(c) the above exemption must be disclosed in the notes on the consolidated accounts drawn up by the parent undertaking;

(d) the profit or loss of the parent company, determined in accordance with this Directive, must be shown in the balance sheet of the parent company.'

Article 45

The following shall be substituted for Article 59 of Directive 78/660/EEC:

'*Article 59*

1. A Member State may require or permit that participating interests, as defined in Article 17, in the capital of undertakings over the operating and financial policies of which significant influence is exercised, be shown in the balance sheet in accordance with paragraph 2 to 9 below, as subitems of the items "shares in affiliated undertakings" or "participating interests", as the case may be. An undertaking shall be presumed to exercise a significant influence over another undertaking where it has 20% or more of the shareholders' or members' voting rights in that undertaking. Article 2 of Directive 83/349/EEC shall apply.

2. When this Article is first applied to a participating interest covered by paragraph 1, it shall be shown in the balance sheet either:

(a) at its book value calculated in accordance with Articles 31 to 42. The difference between that value and the amount corresponding to the proportion of capital and reserves represented by the participating interest shall be disclosed separately in the balance sheet or in the notes on the accounts. That difference shall be calculated as at the date as at which the method is applied for the first time; or

(b) at the amount corresponding to the proportion of the capital and reserves represented by the participating interest. The difference between that amount and the book value calculated in accordance with Articles 31 to 42 shall be disclosed separately in the balance sheet or in the notes on the accounts. That difference shall be calculated as at the date as at which the method is applied for the first time.

(c) A Member State may prescribe the application of one or other of the above paragraphs. The balance sheet or the notes on the accounts must indicate whether (a) or (b) above has been used.

(d) In addition, when applying (a) and (b) above, a Member State may require or permit calculation of the difference as at the date of acquisition of the participating interest referred to in paragraph 1 or, where the acquisition took place in two or more stages, as at the date as at which the holding became a participating interest within the meaning, of paragraph 1 above.'

3. Where the assets or liabilities of an undertaking in which a participating interest within the meaning of paragraph I above is held have been valued by methods other than those used by the company drawing up the annual accounts, they may, for the purpose of calculating the difference referred to in paragraph 2 (a) or (b) above, be revalued by the methods used by the company drawing up the annual accounts. Disclosure must be made in the notes on the accounts where such revaluation has not been carried out. A Member State may require such revaluation.

4. The book value referred to in paragraph 2(a) above, or the amount corresponding to the proportion of capital and reserves referred to in paragraph 2(b) above, shall be increased or reduced by the amount of the variation which has taken place during the financial year in the proportion of capital reserves represented by that participating interest; it shall be reduced by the amount of the dividends relating to the participating interest.

5. In so far as a positive difference covered by paragraph 2(a) or (b) above cannot be related to any category of asset or liability, it shall be dealt with in accordance with the rules applicable to the item "goodwill".

6. (a) The proportion of the profit or loss attributable to participating interests within the meaning of paragraph 1 above shall be shown in the profit-and-loss account as a separate item with an appropriate heading.

(b) Where that amount exceeds the amount of dividends already received or the payment of which can be claimed, the amount of the difference must be placed in a reserve which cannot be distributed to shareholders.

(c) A Member State may require or permit that the proportion of the profit or loss attributable to the participating interests referred to in paragraph 1 above be shown in the profit-and-loss account only to the extent of the amount corresponding to dividends already received or the payment of which can be claimed.

7. The eliminations referred to in Article 26(l)(c) of Directive 83/349/EEC shall be effected in so far as the facts are known or can be ascertained. Article 26(2) and (3) of that Directive shall apply.

8. Where an undertaking in which a participating interest within the meaning of paragraph 1 above is held draws up consolidated accounts, the foregoing paragraphs shall apply to the capital and reserves shown in such consolidated accounts.

9. This Article need not be applied where a participating interest as defined in paragraph 1 is not material for the purposes of Article 2(3).'

Article 46

The following shall be substituted for Article 61 of Directive 78/660/EEC:

'*Article 61*

A Member State need not apply the provisions of point 2 of Article 43(1) of this Directive concerning the amount of capital and reserves and profits and losses of the undertakings concerned to companies governed by their national laws which are parent undertakings for the purposes of Directive 83/349/EEC:

(a) where the undertakings concerned are included in consolidated accounts drawn up by that parent undertaking, or in the consolidated accounts of a larger body of undertakings as referred to in Article 7(2) of Directive 83/349/EEC; or

(b) where the holdings in the undertakings concerned have been dealt with by the parent undertaking in its annual accounts in accordance with

Article 59, or in the consolidated accounts drawn up by that parent undertaking in accordance with Article 33 of Directive 83/349/EEC.'

Article 47

The Contact Committee set up pursuant to Article 52 of Directive 78/660/EEC shall also:

(a) facilitate, without prejudice to Articles 169 and 170 of the Treaty, harmonized application of this Directive through regular meetings dealing, in particular, with practical problems arising in connection with its application;

(b) advise the Commission, if necessary, on additions or amendments to this Directive.

Article 48

This Directive shall not affect laws in the Member States requiring that consolidated accounts in which undertakings not falling within their jurisdiction are included be filed in a register in which branches of such undertakings are listed.

Article 49

1. The Member States shall bring into force the laws, regulations and administrative provisions necessary for them to comply with this Directive before 1 January 1988. They shall forthwith inform the Commission thereof.

2. A Member State may provide that the provisions referred to in paragraph 1 above shall first apply to consolidated accounts for financial years beginning on 1 January 1990 or during the calendar year 1990.

3. The Member States shall ensure that they communicate to the Commission the texts of the main provisions of national law which they adopt in the field covered by this Directive.

Article 50

1. Five years after the date referred to in Article 49(2), the Council, acting on a proposal from the Commission, shall examine and if need be revise Articles 1(1)(d) (second subparagraph), 4(2), 5, 6, 7(1), 12, 43 and 44 in the light of the experience acquired in applying this Directive, the aims of this Directive and the economic and monetary situation at the time.

2. Paragraph 1 above shall not affect Article 53(2) of Directive 78/660/EEC.

Article 51

This Directive is addressed to the Member States.

Done at Luxembourg, 13 June 1983.

For the Council

The President

H. TIETMEYER

Appendix 5

Accounting standards, exposure drafts and discussion papers

Accounting standards

Statements of Standard Accounting Practice

SSAP 2	Disclosure of accounting policies
SSAP 3	Earnings per share
SSAP 4	Accounting for government grants
SSAP 5	Accounting for value added tax
SSAP 8	The treatment of taxation under the imputation system in the accounts of companies
SSAP 9	Stocks and long-term contracts
SSAP 12	Accounting for depreciation
SSAP 13	Accounting for research and development
SSAP 15	Accounting for deferred tax
SSAP 17	Accounting for post balance sheet events
SSAP 18	Accounting for contingencies
SSAP 19	Accounting for investment properties
SSAP 20	Foreign currency translation
SSAP 21	Accounting for leases and hire purchase contracts
SSAP 23	Accounting for acquisitions and mergers
SSAP 24	Accounting for pension costs
SSAP 25	Segmental reporting

Financial Reporting Standards

FRSSE	Financial reporting standard for smaller entities
FRS 1 (revised)	Cash flow statements
FRS 2	Accounting for subsidiary undertakings
FRS 3	Reporting financial performance
FRS 4	Capital instruments
FRS 5	Reporting the substance of transactions
Amendment to FRS 5	Reporting the substance of transactions – The Private Finance Initiative
FRS 6	Acquisitions and mergers
FRS 7	Fair values in acquisition accounting

FRS 8	Related party disclosures
FRS 9	Associates and joint ventures
FRS 10	Goodwill and intangible assets
FRS 11	Impairment of fixed assets and goodwill
FRS 12	Provisions, contingent liabilities and contingent assets
FRS 13	Derivatives and other financial instruments
FRS 14	Earnings per share

Statements by the ASB

Operating and financial review
The application of UITF abstracts
Interim reports
Preliminary announcements

UITF Abstracts

Foreword to UITF abstracts

UITF Abstract 3	Treatment of goodwill on disposal of a business
UITF Abstract 4	Presentation of long-term debtors in current assets
UITF Abstract 5	Transfers from current assets to fixed assets
UITF Abstract 6	Accounting for post-retirement benefits other than pensions
UITF Abstract 7	True and fair view override disclosures
UITF Abstract 9	Accounting for operations in hyper-inflationary economies
UITF Abstract 10	Disclosure of directors' share options
UITF Abstract 11	Capital instruments: issuer call options
UITF Abstract 12	Lessee accounting for reverse premiums and similar incentives
UITF Abstract 13	Accounting for ESOP Trusts
UITF Abstract 14	Disclosure of changes in accounting policy
UITF Abstract 15	Disclosure of substantial acquisitions
UITF Abstract 16	Income and expenses subject to non-standard rates of tax
UITF Abstract 17	Employee share schemes
UITF Abstract 18	Pension costs following the 1997 tax changes in respect of dividend income
UITF Abstract 19	Tax on gains and losses on foreign currency borrowings that hedge an investment in a foreign enterprise
UITF Abstract 20	Year 2000 issues: accounting and disclosures
UITF Abstract 21	Accounting issues arising from the proposed introduction of the euro
UITF Abstract 22	The acquisition of a Lloyd's business

Exposure drafts and discussion papers

Issued by the ASC

ED 55 Accounting for investments

Issued by the ASB

Exposure drafts:

Statement of principles for financial reporting
FRED 17 Measurement of tangible fixed assets
Amendment to SSAP 8 Presentation of dividend income
Amendment to Financial Reporting Standard for Smaller Entities

Discussion papers:

Accounting for tax
Accounting for pension costs
Segmental reporting

Appendix 6

FRRP Press notices

Issue number and date	Company Accounts date	Summary
PN01 27/06/91	N/A	*FRRPs working methods announced.*
PN02 25/07/91	N/A	*Requirement to state compliance with accounting standards.*
PN03 28/01/92	N/A	Disclosure of accounting policies - effect of 4 Sch para 36A.
PN04 28/01/92	Ultramar Plc 31/12/90	Irrecoverable ACT included in cost of dividend.
PN05 28/01/92	Williams Holdings plc 31/12/90	Exceptional items stated net of tax in P&L account; EPS stated net of exceptional items; names of acquired companies not disclosed.
PN06 31/01/92	The Shield Group plc 31/03/91	Diminution in property values treated as PYA.
PN07 04/02/92	Forte plc 31/01/91	Non-depreciation of properties.
PN08 11/06/92	N/A	*Statement of compliance with accounting standards - progress report.*
PN09 08/07/92	N/A	*FRRP progress report.*
PN10 10/08/92	Williamson Tea Holdings Plc 31/03/91	Disclosure of accounting policies; disclosure of reasons for a transfer to reserves; treatment of additional depreciation as a result of asset revaluation.
PN11 10/08/92	Associated Nursing Services plc 30/03/91	Policy for start up costs; explanation for change in accounting policy - should reiterate former policy.
PN12 07/10/92	GPG plc 30/09/91	Early adoption of FRED 1 resulting in non-compliance with SSAP 6 and SSAP 3.
PN13 15/10/92	Trafalgar House plc 30/09/91	Transfer from current fixed assets; ACT carried forward: statutory P&L formats.

Issue number and date	Company Accounts date	Summary
PN14 26/10/92	British Gas plc 31/12/91	P&L account presentation following change of year end.
PN15 26/10/92	S.E.P. Industrial Holdings plc 30/09/91	Non-depreciation of properties.
PN16 22/02/93	Eurotherm Plc 31/10/91	Extraordinary provision released as exceptional
PN17 17/03/93	Foreign & Colonial Investment Trust PLC 31/12/91	Disclosure of directors emoluments; non-consolidation of subsidiaries.
PN18 01/04/93	Warnford Investments PLC 25/12/91	Non-compliance with SSAP 19.
PN19 05/04/93	Penrith Farmers' and Kidds' PLC 31/03/92	Disclosure of particulars and reason for change in comparatives.
PN20 27/07/93	Breverleigh Investments 30/06/92	Non-consolidation of subsidiary; no cash flow statement; no 4 Sch (36A) note.
PN21 11/08/93	Royal Bank of Scotland Group plc 30/09/92	Change in policy not treated as PYA.
PN22 24/09/93	Control Techniques plc 30/09/92	Error in cash flow statement. Operating cash reconciliation did not exclude working capital of business sold.
PN23 27/09/93	N/A	*FRRP - revised working procedures.*
PN24 19/10/93	BM Group plc 30/06/92	Error in cash equivalents; incorrect description of profit on sale of shares in subsidiary.
PN25 25/10/93	Ptarmigan Holdings plc (now Graystone plc) 30/06/92	Disclosure of reasons for change in policy for goodwill.
PN26 29/11/93	Chrysalis Group plc 31/08/92	Associate carried at valuation in group accounts.
PN27 28/01/94	The Intercare Group plc 31/10/92	Errors in cash flow statement. Shares issued as consideration shown as cash flows.
PN28 11/02/94	Pentos Plc 31/12/92	Disclosure of treatment of reverse lease premiums.

Issue number and date	Company Accounts date	Summary
PN29 24/04/94	BET plc 27/03/93	Presentation of operating exceptional items under statutory categories.
PN30 02/11/94	Butte Mining Plc 30/06/93	Treatment of equity investment and loan as cash equivalents; classification of bank overdraft in balance sheet.
PN31 23/11/94	Clyde Blowers plc 31/08/93	Presentation and disclosure of provision for loss on disposal. Also, no disclosure of the cash flow effect of the partial disposal.
PN32 20/03/95	Alliance Trust plc 31/01/94	Non-consolidation of subsidiary on grounds of dissimilar activities and materiality - not accepted.
PN33 21/06/95	Courts PLC 31/03/94	Accounting treatment of long-term credit sales.
PN34 08/11/95	Caradon plc 31/12/94	Non-equity did not include reduced share premium.
PN35 13/12/95	Ferguson International Holdings PLC 28/02/95	Goodwill disclosed net of Sec 131 relief.
PN36 15/02/96	Securicor Group plc 30/09/94	Non-equity (participating preference shares) calculated on the basis of rights to profits.
PN37 08/03/96	Newarthill p.l.c. 31/10/94	Minority interest finance cost relating to premium not accrued.
PN38 28/03/96	Brammer plc 31/12/94	Assets held for rental classified as stock rather than fixed assets.
PN39 09/04/96	Foreign & Colonial Investment Trust plc 31/12/94	Inadequate explanation for departure from SSAP 1.
PN40 01/03/96	Alexon Group plc 28/01/95	Shareholders' funds not correctly analysed between equity and non-equity interests.
PN41 30/05/96	Ransomes Plc 30/09/95	Shareholders' funds not correctly analysed between equity and non-equity interests.
PN42 24/07/96	Sutton Harbour Holdings Plc 30/03/95	Disclosure of the use of the true and fair override did not meet the Act's requirements concerning the treatment of government grants and non-depreciation of investment properties.
PN43 02/10/96	Butte Mining Plc 30/06/95	Shares received in consideration of services cannot be regarded as giving rise to a realised profit where tradeability of the shares is subject to restrictions.

Issue number and date	Company Accounts date	Summary
PN044 17/02/97	Associated Nursing Services plc 31/03/95 and 31/03/96	Certain joint venture arrangements were required to be treated as quasi-subsidiaries rather than associates. Sale and leaseback arrangements should have been treated as financing.
PN45 15/04/97	Reckitt & Colman plc 30/12/95	Inadequate disclosure of hindsight adjustments to provisional fair values in the year after acquisition.
PN46 29/08/97	M & W Mack Limited 26/04/96	Non-compliance with UITF 13 for an employee share scheme.
PN47 02/10/97	Burn Stewart Distillers PLC 30/06/96	Inadequate disclosure of the commercial effect of a transaction excluded from the accounts under FRS 5.
PN48 10/11/97	Stratagem Group plc 31/08/96	FRS 6 disclosure – inadequate analysis of FRS 7 fair value adjustments.
PN49 25/02/98	Guardian Royal Exchange Plc 31/12/96	Treatment of insurance equalisation reserves in consolidated financial statements.
PN50 27/04/98	Stratagem Group Plc 31/08/97	FRS 3 presentation (description and position) of non-operating exceptional items.
PN51 12/05/98	RMC Group p.l.c. 31/12/95	Disclosure of fines required because of their nature and circumstance.
PN52 27/07/98	Reuters Holdings PLC 31/12/97	Amortisation of goodwill in profit and loss account required to be charged in arriving at operating profit.
PN53 07/08/98	H&C Furnishings plc 26/04/97	Fair value of shares issued as consideration for acquisition. Non-compliance with a number of detailed disclosure requirements
PN54 02/09/98	Photo-Me International Plc 30/04/97	Intra-group sales required to be excluded from group turnover in consolidated accounts
PN55 20/10/98	Concentric Plc 30/09/97	Insufficient disclosure (FRS 6 and FRS 1) in respect of acquisition.

Index

: index contains entries relating to topics, companies and cases featured in all parts of the manual, uding appendices and annexes.

:ators are:

ragraph numbers: 11.149, for Chapter 11, paragraph 149

apter numbers: **18**, for the whole of Chapter 18

pendix numbers: VI-A1, for Volume I, Appendix 1

nex numbers: 2Ann., for Chapter 2 Annex

dings for legal cases are in *italic* type: *Trevor* v *Whitworth.*

npany name headings are placed under the first part of the name: James Finlay P.L.C.

initions, examples and lists are indicated by subheadings in italic type: *definition; example; list.*

ries are in word-by-word alphabetical order, where a group of letters followed by a space is filed ore the same group of letters followed by a letter, eg 'capital structure and treasury policy' will ear before 'capitalisation'. In determining alphabetical arrangement, initial articles, conjunctions small prepositions are ignored.

D

E

G

Index

Q

R